AF183316

The Occupation of Iraq

The invasion and occupation of Iraq rank among the most controversial and complex issues in international law in recent history. This volume of documents covers the occupation of Iraq from the planning stages of the invasion of Iraq in early 2002 to the transfer of governing authority to the Iraqi Interim Government on 28 June 2004. The book presents 595 selected documents including the first complete set of all Regulations, Orders, Memoranda and Public Notices issued by the U.S.-led occupation administration of Iraq, the Coalition Provisional Authority (CPA), several of which were never published on the CPA's website or promulgated in *Alwaqai Aliraqiya*, the Official Gazette of Iraq. Some of these legal acts have shaped the economic and political system of present day Iraq and will be part of the country's legal order for years to come. The book also includes some 120 other CPA and CPA-related documents selected from more than 5000 unclassified CPA documents and received under freedom of information requests lodged in the United States, the United Kingdom, Australia and Switzerland. These documents include instructions and proclamations to the Iraqi people in the early stages of the occupation, organizational charts, internal legal opinions, diplomatic notes, international agreements concluded by the CPA with other States, and numerous internal memoranda for the head of the CPA, Ambassador Paul L. Bremer, on legal, diplomatic and political issues. The book also presents for the first time all 235 resolutions passed by the Iraqi Governing Council (IGC) between July 2003 and June 2004. The resolutions as well as many of the 25 other important IGC documents (including various political statements, press releases and decrees of the Council's Higher National De-Ba'athification Commission) have been translated from Arabic and are presented here for the first time in English. These documents are complemented by the relevant United Nations documents on the occupation of Iraq as well as some 50 policy documents of the United States, the United Kingdom and the Iraqi opposition movement as well as all relevant fatwās (religious rulings) of Grand Ayatollah Ali al-Sistani which shaped the internal Iraqi political process during the occupation.

This collection archives these important documents for future use and makes them easily accessible to researchers and professionals. Considering that the main source of information for the occupying powers in Iraq were the precedents set during the First and Second World Wars, the occupation of Iraq will serve as a modern precedent for future administrations of occupied territory. The documents are made easily accessible by a comprehensive table of documents, a list of abbreviations, more than 1100 explanatory notes and cross-references and a substantive subject index.

This volume is the second on *The Occupation of Iraq*. It is complemented by a monograph by the same author which, on the basis of the documents collection, presents a comprehensive analysis of The Governance of Occupied Territory in Contemporary International Law.

THE OCCUPATION OF IRAQ

Volume II

The Official Documents of
the Coalition Provisional Authority
and the Iraqi Governing Council

Stefan Talmon

•HART•
PUBLISHING

OXFORD AND PORTLAND, OREGON
2013

Published in the United Kingdom by Hart Publishing Ltd
16C Worcester Place, Oxford, OX1 2JW
Telephone: +44 (0)1865 517530
Fax: +44 (0)1865 510710
E-mail: mail@hartpub.co.uk
Website: http://www.hartpub.co.uk

Published in North America (US and Canada) by
Hart Publishing
c/o International Specialized Book Services
920 NE 58th Avenue, Suite 300
Portland, OR 97213-3786
USA
Tel: +1 503 287 3093 or toll-free: (1) 800 944 6190
Fax: +1 503 280 8832
E-mail: orders@isbs.com
Website: http://www.isbs.com

© Stefan Talmon 2013

Stefan Talmon has asserted his right under the Copyright, Designs and Patents Act 1988, to be identified as the author of this work.

All rights reserved. No part of this publication may be reproduced, stored in a retrieval system, or transmitted, in any form or by any means, without the prior permission of Hart Publishing, or as expressly permitted by law or under the terms agreed with the appropriate reprographic rights organisation. Enquiries concerning reproduction which may not be covered by the above should be addressed to Hart Publishing Ltd at the address above.

British Library Cataloguing in Publication Data
Data Available

ISBN: 978-1-84113-642-4

Typeset by Criteria International
Printed and bound in Great Britain by
TJ International Ltd, Padstow, Cornwall

FSC www.fsc.org MIX Paper from responsible sources FSC® C013056

Preface

The present collection of some 600 documents on the Occupation of Iraq is the result of ten years of research and hunting down documents in different parts of the world. It covers the occupation of Iraq from the planning stages of the invasion of the country in early 2002 to the transfer of governing authority by the occupying powers, the United States of America and the United Kingdom, to the Iraqi Interim Government on 28 June 2004. The book presents the first complete set of all Regulations, Orders, Memoranda and Public Notices issued by the U.S.-led occupation administration of Iraq, the Coalition Provisional Authority (CPA), several of which were never published on the CPA's website or promulgated in *Alwaqai Aliraqiya*, the Official Gazette of Iraq. These acts addressed everything from the de-Ba'athification of Iraqi society and reforming the criminal justice system to disbanding the Iraqi army and amending existing Iraqi laws. The CPA stood up new security organizations, including a new Iraqi army, the Iraq Civil Defence Corps, and the Facilities Protection Service. It created new departments and ministries for Iraq, including the Ministry of Electricity, the Department of Border Enforcement, the Ministry of Science and Technology, the Ministry of Environment, the Ministry of Human Rights, and the Ministry of Defence. To fight endemic corruption, the CPA established an Iraqi inspector general system, based on the U.S. model, and a Commission on Public Integrity. It appointed an independent electoral commission to ensure free and fair elections and promulgated regulations seeking to decentralize authority in Iraq by devolving power to regional and local government. The CPA also reformed trade and banking laws, the penal code, government salaries, and traffic regulations; opened the country to foreign investment; and established a modern stock exchange. Some of the CPA's legal acts have shaped the economic and political system of present day Iraq and will be part of the country's legal order for years to come. The book also includes some 120 other CPA and CPA-related documents selected from more than 5000 unclassified CPA documents and received under freedom of information requests lodged in the United States, the United Kingdom, Australia and Switzerland. These documents include instructions and proclamations to the Iraqi people in the early stages of the occupation, organizational charts, internal legal opinions, diplomatic notes, international agreements concluded by the CPA with other States, and numerous internal memoranda for the head of the CPA, Ambassador Paul L. Bremer, on legal, diplomatic and political issues. The book also presents for the first time all 235 resolutions passed by the Iraqi Governing Council (IGC) between July 2003 and June 2004. The resolutions as well as many of the 25 other important IGC documents (including various political statements, press releases and decrees of the Council's Higher National De-Ba'athification Commission) have been translated from Arabic and are presented here for the first time in English. These documents are complemented by the relevant United Nations documents on the occupation of Iraq[1] as well as some 50 policy documents of the United States, the United Kingdom and the Iraqi opposition movement as well as all relevant fatwās (religious rulings) of Grand Ayatollah Ali al-Sistani which were shaping the internal Iraqi political process during the occupation.

[1] UN documents are reproduced by kind permission of the United Nations Secretariat, Publications Board, New York.

Academic writings on the occupation of Iraq during and in the immediate aftermath of the occupation did not have the benefit of access to all the documents. Some of the findings on the creation of the CPA, the transition from the Office of Reconstruction and Humanitarian Assistance (ORHA) to the CPA, the relations and responsibilities of the occupying powers, the process of de-Ba'athification, the relationship between the CPA and the IGC, the privatization of State-owned enterprises, and the legislative powers of the IGC, to name but a few, might have to be reassessed in the light of the documents reproduced here.

The documents have been collected from a variety of sources, including *Alwaqai Aliraqiya*, the official CPA website and other internet sites as well as government publications and archives. The idea for the book was born in March 2003. From the first day of the occupation some 40 websites in English and Arabic were monitored on an almost daily basis.[2] Many of these websites, and the documents published there, are no longer available. Printouts were, however, taken at the time to preserve the record and are on file with the author. In June 2003, the CPA launched its own website at http://www.cpa-iraq.org which became one of the main sources of information on the occupation of Iraq. The website carried transcripts of speeches by CPA administrator L. Paul Bremer and other officials, fact sheets on Iraqi ministries, public-service announcements, press releases, and official documents such as regulations, memoranda and orders issued by the CPA. At the beginning of October 2003, the layout of the web page and its content was changed for the first time; a second change followed at the end of October. The ULR of the CPA's website was changed in November 2003 to http://www.iraqcoalition.org/. Subsequent changes to the layout occurred in mid-December 2003, at the end of March 2004 and at the end of May 2004. Each time, not only the layout but also the content of the website was changed. It was noted 'with regret that the Coalition Provisional Authority has impeded the scholarly and historical survey of the occupation by purging large portions of the material once available at the CPA website'.[3] Monitoring the CPA website throughout the occupation allowed the author to preserve most of the documents later dropped from the website such as public service announcements, newsletters produced by the CPA ministries, public notices, the original versions of CPA Orders and Memoranda, and the CPA Daily Updates published in the early days of the occupation. A list of all documents available on the CPA's website can be found in chapter X. At the time of writing, the latest version of the CPA's website is still available online. On 29 June 2004, one day after the end of the formal occupation, the CPA website carried the following notice: 'This site for the CPA-Iraq Coalition will no longer be updated. It will remain available for historical purposes until June 30, 2005.' The date was later changed to June 30, 2006, and finally dropped altogether for the notice to read: 'It will remain available for historical purposes, only.' However, there is no guarantee for this to continue indefinitely. The search function on the page has already been disabled.

[2] cpa-iraq.org/, cpa-ig.org/, iraqcoalition.org/, defendamerica.mil, vcorps.army.mil, usaid.gov/, state.gov/, rebuilding-iraq.net/, iraqdirectory.com/, export.gov/iraq/, iraq-today.com, centcom.mil/, tides.carebridge.org/, iamb.info/, iraqibusinesscenter.org/, countdowntosovereignty.org/, centaf.af.mil/ramcc/, cjtf7.com/, iraqmofa.net/, whitehouse.gov/, electroniciraq.net/, sistani.org/, dfid.gov.uk/, humanitarianinfo.org/, agoodplacetostart.org/, mod.uk/, reliefweb.int/, unjlc.org/, baghdadbulletin.com/, nciraq.org/, debaath.com/, iraqprocurement.com, iraq.pogar.org/, defenselink.mil/, un.int/, ukun.org/, motiraq.org/, kurdmedia.com/, kurdistanobserver.com/, krg.org/, irffi.org/, iwpr.net/, nahrain.com/, faylee.org/, 9neesan.com/, menalmuheetlelkaleej.com/, iraqipapers.com/, rumsfeld.com/, waranddecision.com/.

[3] Miller, Russell A., 'Before the Law: Military Investigations and Evidence at the Iraqi Special Tribunal' (2005) 13 *Michigan State Journal of International Law* 107-154 at 126, n. 73.

While most of the CPA legal and legislative acts (regulations, orders, memoranda and public notices) were made available on its website, only the version published in *Alwaqai Aliraqiya* is authoritative and has the force of law. A comparison of the online and print versions of the documents shows that their text and the date of their creation are not always identical.[4] The Official Gazette of Iraq has been published since 1921. On 17 June 2003, the CPA published the first post-war issue of *Alwaqai Aliraqiya* in both English and Arabic. It took the author some three years to acquire a full set of the relevant issues of *Alwaqai Aliraqiya*.[5] The author is greatly indebted to Mr Jason Majid, Attorney-at-law, then head of the Iraq law practice at the Doha head office of law firm Al Tamimi & Company, for providing him with copies of *Alwaqai Aliraqiya* through the firm's Baghdad office. The Official Gazette of Iraq is a good example of the volatility of the internet. While the relevant issues of the Gazette had been available for some time at http://iraqog.org/, they disappeared again with the expiry of the website in 2010. Not all the CPA's legal acts have been published in *Alwaqai Aliraqiya* as can be seen in the Comparative Table of CPA Legal Acts in chapter I, section 6. Those that are available in *Alwaqai Aliraqiya* are reproduced in the version printed there.

If it was difficult to get hold of copies of the relevant issues of *Alwaqai Aliraqiya*, it proved almost impossible to find the text of the resolutions adopted by the CPA selected 25-member Iraqi Governing Council. From 13 July 2003 to 1 June 2004, the IGC operated alongside the CPA, assisting the latter in the administration of occupied Iraq. During that time, the IGC adopted 235 resolutions dealing with everything from the de-Ba'athification of Iraqi society and the creation of special criminal tribunals to the privatization of Iraqi State-owned enterprises. In addition, it drafted laws, made political statements and issued numerous press releases. The large majority of these documents were available only in Arabic. For several years the author had tried to find the resolutions of the IGC with only limited success, when in 2007 he learnt of a collection in Arabic of the Resolutions of the Iraqi Governing Council.[6] Unfortunately, the collection could not be found in any library. It took several months and the invaluable help of Ms Tessa Gregory, a Solicitor with Public Interest Lawyers in Birmingham, to acquire a copy of the tiny 167-page booklet in Baghdad and to bring it via Jordan and Lebanon to the United Kingdom. It took a dedicated team of young Arabic speaking scholars another three years to translate the resolutions as well as other important IGC documents. I am most grateful to Ms Nisrine Jafaar, Mr Jordan Toone, Mr Muhammad Zubair Abbasi, Dr Marie Ghantous, Mr Ghaleb Mashni, Mr Joseph Leavitt, and Mr Marco Brandl for all their help with translating these documents.

Over the last couple of years numerous CPA and CPA-related documents have become available on the internet through freedom of information requests. The author himself has lodged more than 60 such requests. Many more documents could have been reproduced. It was thus inevitable to make a selection. By and large, internal CPA documents have been

[4] See e.g. CPA Order No 59 *[Doc 82]* published in *Alwaqai Aliraqiya* No 3982 (June 2004), 55, and the version available at http://www.iraqcoalition.org/.
[5] See *Alwaqai Aliraqiya*, vol. 44, no 3977 (17 June 2003) - vol. 45, no 3986 (September 2004). The first two issues were distributed 'Free of Charge'. Following issues cost ID 1000 and later ID 2000.
[6] Anbari, Sabah Sadiq (ed.), *Resolutions of the Governing Council 2003-2004* [in Arabic] (3rd edn., Baghdad: Encyclopedia of Arab Laws, 2006). Some of the resolutions could also be found in Arabic on the website of the Encyclopedia of Mesopotamia at http://www.nahrain.com/, as well as other Arabic language websites. Most of these websites are no longer available. Copies of the original resolutions are on file with the author.

included only if they shed light on the organization and functioning of the CPA or their content is of legal relevance.[7]

A project like this can only be undertaken with the help of many people. Besides those mentioned already, I am particularly grateful to Ms Fay Miller, Information Resource Centre, U.S. Embassy London; Ms Dawn Kral, United States Export-Import Bank; Mr Chanaka Wickremasinghe, Legal Advisers, Foreign and Commonwealth Office; Mr Doug Wilson, Legal Adviser, British Embassy Baghdad; Cdr Alan Cole, Royal Navy; Mr Aaron Renfro; Ms Kristina Schönfeldt; and the Secretariat of the Iraq Inquiry in the United Kingdom for providing me with documents and information. I also gratefully acknowledge the financial support provided by the Law Faculty of the University of Oxford and St Anne's College, Oxford, a member of which I had the privilege to be from 2003 to 2011. Finally, I am most indebted to Holly Wesener, JD for compiling the index and proofreading the whole text.

Institute for Public International Law
University of Bonn
December 2012

STEFAN TALMON

[7] Further, shorter documents can be found in the Chronology of Events section in volume I: *The Governance of Occupied Territory in Contemporary International Law.*

Contents

Abbreviations

AACO	Arab Air Carrier Organization
AA Guns	Anti-Aircraft Guns
AAPA	Association of Asia Pacific Airlines
ACSA	Acquisition and Cross-Servicing Agreement
ADM	Assyrian Democratic Movement
AEA	Association of European Airlines
AFP	Agence France Press
AFRAA	African Airlines Association
AFTN	Aeronautical Fixed Telecommunication System
AIRP	Accelerated Iraq Reconstruction Program
AML	Anti Money Laundering Law
ANS	Air Navigation Services
AOR	Area of Operational Responsibility
APOD	Air Port of Disembarkation
APU	Abuse Prevention Unit
AR	Average Rate
ARC	Accreditation Review Committee
ARRC	Allied Rapid Reaction Corps
ARDI	Agriculture Reconstruction and Development Program for Iraq
ASBCA	Armed Services Board of Contract Appeals
ASP	Archaeological Site Protection
ATA	Air Transport Association of America
ATC	Air Traffic Control
BBC	British Broadcasting Corporation
BBG	Broadcasting Board of Governors
BCC	Business Conduct Committee
BCT	Brigade Combat Team
BDE	Brigade
BIA	Basrah International Airport
BIAP	Baghdad International Airport
BIGC	Basrah Interim Governate Committee
BSS	Billing Support System
CAA	Civil Aviation Authority
CAP	Community Action Program
CBI	Central Bank of Iraq
CC	Constitutional Convention
CCC	Coalition Coordinating Council
CCCI	Central Criminal Court of Iraq
CD	Civil Defence
CDF	Commander's Discretionary Fund

CEDAW	Convention on the Elimination of all Forms of Discrimination against Women
CENTCOM	Central Command, USA
CEO	Chief Electoral Officer
CERP	Commander's Emergency Response Program
CFACC	Combined Forces Air Component Commander
CFLCC	Coalition Forces Land Component Command
CHF	Swiss Francs
CHRRP	Commanders Humanitarian Relief and Reconstruction Program
CIA	Central Intelligence Agency
CIC	Council for International Cooperation/Coordination
CID	Criminal Investigation Division, US Army
CIF	Cost, Insurance and Freight
CIMIC	Civil-Military Cooperation
CINCCENT	Commander in Chief, CENTCOM
CIO	Chief Information Officer
CIS	Communication and Information System
CJCS	Chairman, Joint Chiefs of Staff
CJTF-7	Combined Joint Task Force 7
CMATT	Coalition Military Assistance Training Teams
CMC	CIS Management Centre
CMM	Constitutional Monarch Movement
CMOC	Civil-Military Operations Center
Comd	Commander
COMM	Communications
COMPT	Comptroller
COO	Chief Operating Officer
COS	Chief of Staff
COTS	Commercial Off the Shelf
CPA	Coalition Provisional Authority
CPA (C-S)	Coalition Provisional Authority (Central-South)
CPA-IG	Office of Inspector General of the Coalition Provisional Authority
CPA(S)	Coalition Provisional Authority (South)
CPA-SC	Coalition Provisional Authority-South Central
CPATT	Coalition Police Advisory and Training Team
CPC	Constitutional Preparatory Committee, IGC
CPS	Cluster Pump Stations
CPIC	Coalition Press Information Center
CRM	Customer Relationship Management
CRS	Congressional Research Service
C-Staff	Coalition Support Staff
CSOs	Civil Society Organizations
CSW	Commission on the Status of Women
CTEG	Counter Terrorism Evaluation Group
D&F	Determination and Findings
DART	Disaster Assistance Response Team

DBE	Department of Border Enforcement
DBX	Destination Baghdad Expo
DC	Deputies Committee
DCMA	Defense Contract Management Agency/Administration
DDR	Disarmament, Demobilization, and Reintegration
DFI	Development Fund for Iraq
DFID	Department for International Development, UK
DG	Director-General
DISA	Defense Information Systems Agency
DO	Designated Official
DoD	Department of Defense
DOJ	Department of Justice
DOS	Department of State
DPS	Diplomatic Protection Service
DSA	Defense Support Agency
DSC	Direct Support Costs
ECA	Export Credit Agency, US DOS, Bureau of Educational and Cultural Affairs
ECGD	Export Credits Guarantee Department, UK
EIP	Emergency Infrastructure Programme
EMT	Emergency Medical Technician
EOD	Explosive Ordinance Disposal
EPID	Environment Protection and Improvement Directorate
ERG	Export Risk Guarantee Agency, Switzerland
ERP	Enterprise Resource Planning
ERW	Explosive Remnants of War
ESG	Executive Steering Group
ESL	English as Second Language
EXIM	Export-Import Bank, USA
FAA	Federal Aviation Administration
FAO	Food and Agricultural Organization of the United Nations
FCO	Foreign and Commonwealth Office
FDI	Foreign direct Investment
FFP	Food for Peace, USAID Office
FG	Financial Group
FIF	Free Iraqi Forces
FIR	Flight Information Region
FM	Frequency Modulation
FMO	Facilities Management Office
FOC	Full Operational Capability
FOO	Field Ordering Officer
FOT	Free On Truck
FPS	Facilities Protection Service
FR	Federal Register
FRAGO	Fragmentary Order

FRBNY	Federal Reserve Bank of New York
FRE	Former Regime Elements
FRN	First Responder Network
FSCO	Field Security Coordination Officer, UN
FTO	Field Training Officer
FY	Financial Year
G77	Group of 77
GATS	General Agreement on Trade in Services
GC	Governing Council, Governorate Coordinator
GCC	Gulf Cooperation Council
GCIV	Geneva Convention Relative to the Protection of Civilian Persons in Time of War of 12 August 1949
GCPP	Global Conflict Prevention Pool
GDP	Gross Domestic Product
GoI	Government of Iraq
GPA	Agreement on Government Procurement, WTO
GSE	Ground Support Equipment
GT	Governorate Team
GST	Governorate Support Team or Government Support Team
HACC-B	Humanitarian Assistance Coordination Center, Baghdad
HC	Humanitarian Coordinator
HC Debs	House of Commons Debates
HIC Iraq	Humanitarian Information Center Iraq
HJ Res	House Joint Resolution
HL Debs	House of Lords Debates
HOC	Humanitarian Operations Center
HQ	Headquarters
HVAC	Heating Ventilation and Air Conditioning
IA	Interim Administration
IAA	Iraqi Atomic Authority
IAC	Iraqi Assistance Center
I-ACC	Iraqi-American Chamber of Commerce and Industry
IAEA	International Atomic Energy Agency
IAF	Iraqi Armed Forces
IAMB	International Advisory and Monitoring Board
IAS	International Accounting Standards
IASA	International Aviation Safety Assessment
IASC	Inter-Agency Standing Committee
IASD	Iraqi Association of Securities Dealers
IATA	International Air Transport Association
IAW	in accordance with
IBRD	International Bank for Reconstruction and Development
ICAO	International Civil Aviation Organization
ICC	International Coordination Council

ICCPR	International Covenant on Civil and Political Rights
ICDC	Iraqi Civil Defense Corps
ICDF	Iraqi Coastal Defense Force
ICDRP	Iraqi Centre for Dialogue, Reconciliation and Peace
ICE	Iraqi Currency Exchange
ICAO	International Civil Aviation Organization
ICMC	National Communications and Media Commission of Iraq
ICRC	International Committee of the Red Cross
ICRP	Iraqi Committee for Reconciliation and Peace
ICS	Iraqi Corrections Service
ICTA	Interim Civilian Transitional Administrator
ICTAS	Iraqi Interim Committee to Administer Sport
ICTF	Iraqi Counter-Terrorism Force
ID	Iraqi Dinar, Identity Card
IDA	International Development Association
IDC	Iraqi De-Ba'athification Council
IDP	Internally Displaced Person
IECI	Independent Electoral Commission of Iraq
IEDs	Improvised Explosive Devices
IFAD	International Fund for Agricultural Development
IFB	Invitation for Bids
IFC	International Finance Corporation
IFF	Iraq Freedom Fund
IFIs	International Financial Institutions
IG	Inspector General
IGC	Iraqi Governing Council
IIA	Interim Iraqi Authority/Iraqi Interim Authority
IIG	Iraqi Interim Government/Interim Iraq Government
IJPs	International Judges and Prosecutors
IJU	International Judicial Unit
ILC	Iraqi Leadership Council
ILO	International Labour Organization
ILS	Instrument Landing System
IMAC	Iraqi International Medical Assistance Committee/Iraqi Mine Action Center
IMF	International Monetary Fund
IMN	Iraqi Media Network
IMO	International Maritime Organization
INA	Iraqi National Accord
INC	Iraqi National Congress
ING	Iraqi National Guard
INIS	Iraqi National Intelligence Service
INPF	Iraqi Non-proliferation Programs Foundation
INSS	Institute for National Strategic Studies
INTEL	Intelligence
INTERPOL	International Criminal Police Organization
IO	International Organization

IOM	International Organization for Migration
IP	Internet Protocol
IPA	Iraqi Port Authority
IPCC	Iraqi Property Claims Commission
IPRF	Iraqi Property Reconciliation Facility
IPS	Iraqi Police Service
IPU	Iraq Planning Unit, later Iraq Policy Unit
IRDC	Iraq Reconstruction and Development Council
IRP	Iraqi Railway Police
IRRF	Iraq Relief and Reconstruction Fund
IRFFI	International Reconstruction Fund Facility for Iraq
IRMO	Iraq Reconstruction Management Office
IRSRA	Iraqi Radioactive Source Regulatory Authority
ISC	International Service Center
ISFs	Iraqi Security Forces
ISG	Iraq Survey Group
ISX	Iraq Stock Exchange
IT	Information Technology
ITD	Interim Travel Document
ITF	Iraq Trust Fund, Iraqi Turkoman Front
ITI	International Transition Initiative
ITO	Iraq Theater of Operation
ITPC	Iraq Telecommunications & Postal Corporation
ITPT	Interagency Transition Planning Team
ITU	International Telecommunications Union
IVA	Iraqi Veterans Agency
IWN	Iraqi Women's Network
JCB	Joint Coordination Bureau
JCCs	Joint Coordination Centers
JDC	Joint Detention Committee
JHQ	Joint Headquarters
JRAT	Judicial Reconstruction Assistance Team
JRC	Judicial Review Committee
JTF	Joint Task Force
KAR	Kurdistan Autonomous Region
KBR	Kellogg Brown and Root, Inc.
KDP	Kurdistan Democratic Party
KMTB	Kirkush Military Training Base
KOICA	Korea International Cooperation Agency
KRG	Kurdistan Regional Government
KV	Kilovolt
LGP	Local Governance Program
LGT	Local Government Team
LNOs	Liaison Officers

LOA	Letter of Authority/Letter of Agreement
LOC	Lines of Communication
LOG	Logistics
LOGCAP	Logistics Civil Augmentation Program
LPG	Liquefied Petroleum Gas
LTG	Lieutenant General
MAG	Mines Advisory Group
MBPD	Million-Barrel Per Day
MCNS	Ministerial Committee for National Security
MCI	Multi-Command Instruction
MDM	Ministry of Displacement and Migration
MEM	Memorandum
METL	Missions Essential Task List
MHESR	Ministry of Higher Education & Scientific Research
MIC	Military Industry Commission Company
MIM	Ministry of Industry and Minerals
MNC-I	Multinational Corps-Iraq
MND	Multinational Division
MND(C-S)	Multinational Division (Central-South)
MND SE	Multinational Division South East
MNF	Multinational Force
MNF-I	Multinational Force-Iraq
MNLC	Multinational Logistics Centre
MoD	Ministry of Defense
MODM	Ministry of Displacement and Migration
MOEN	Ministry of Environment
MOF	Ministry of Finance
MOH	Ministry of Health
MOHE & SR	Ministry of Higher Education and Scientific Research
MOHC	Ministry of Housing and Construction
MOHR	Ministry of Human Rights
MOI	Ministry of Interior
MOLSA	Ministry of Labor and Social Affairs
MOO	Ministry of Oil
MoPDC	Ministry of Planning and Development Cooperation
MoT	Ministry of Trade
MOTC	Ministry of Transport and Communications
MOU	Memorandum of Understanding
MoWR	Ministry of Water Resources
MRA	Migration and Refugee Assistance
MSC	Major Subordinate Command
MW	Megawatt
NAC	Neighborhood Advisory Council
NACA	National Air Carrier Association of America
NARA	National Archives and Records Administration, USA

NATO	North Atlantic Treaty Organization
NCC	National Contingent Commander
NCCI	NGO Coordination Center in Iraq
NCCRL	National Center for Construction Research and Laboratories
NCO	Non-Commissioned Officer
NDC	National Dispatch Center
NDP	National Democratic Party
NCOHS	National Center for Occupational Health and Safety
NGL	Natural Gas Liquid(s)
NGO	Non-Governmental Organization
NHRC	National Human Rights Commission
NIA	New Iraqi Army
NID	New Iraqi Dinar
NLT	Not Later Than
NMAA	National Mine Action Authority
NNSA	National Nuclear Security Agency, USA
NOCI	National Olympic Committee of Iraq
NOTAM	Notice to Airmen
NPA	Norwegian People's Aid
NRRRF	Natural Resources Risk Remediation Fund
NSC	National Security Council, USA
NSE	National Support Element
NSPD	National Security Presidential Directive
OCHA	Office for the Coordination of Humanitarian Affairs
OCPA	Office of the Coalition Provisional Authority; Office of the Chief of Public Affairs
OFAC	Office of Foreign Assets Control, US Treasury Department
OFDA	Office for Foreign Disaster Assistance
OFF	Oil-for-Food
OFFP	Oil-for-Food Programme
OGC	Office of General Counsel
OHCHR	Office of the United Nations High Commissioner for Human Rights
OHDACA	Overseas Humanitarian, Disaster, and Civic Aid, US DoD
OHRTJ	Office of Human Rights and Transitional Justice, CPA
OIC	Organization of the Islamic Conference
OICC	Officer in Charge of Construction
OIF	Operation Iraqi Freedom
OIP	Office of the Iraq Programme, UN
OMA	Operations and Maintenance
OMB	Office of Management and Budget, US Government
OP	Occupying Power, Operative Paragraph, Operational Paragraph
OPC	Office of Program Coordination
OPCON	Operational Control
OPDAT	Overseas Prosecutorial Development, Assistance, and Training, US DOJ
OPEC	Organization of Petroleum Exporting Countries

OPIC	Overseas Private Investment Corporation, USA
OPO	Office of Provincial Outreach
OPORD	Operation Order
OPS	Operations
OPWP	Office of PostWar Planning
OR	Operating Room
ORD	Order
ORHA	Office for Reconstruction and Humanitarian Assistance
OSC	Office of Security Cooperation
OSD	Office of the Secretary of Defense
OSS	Operations Support System
OST	Office of Security Training
OUSD	Office of the Under Secretary of Defense
PC	Principals Committee
PCO	Project Contracting Officer, US Army Corps of Engineers; Project Coordination Office
PDS	Public Distribution System
PERS	Personnel
PID	Positive Identification
PJHQ	Permanent Joint Headquarters, UK
P.L.	Public Law
PM	Bureau of Political-Military Affairs, US DOS
PMO	Program Management Office, CPA
PN	Public Notice
POC	Point of Contact
POD	Port of Disembarkation
POTUS	President of the United States
PP	Preambular Paragraph
PPE	Personal Protective Equipment
PPOS	Project Purchasing Officers
PRB	Program Review Board, CPA
PRC	Program Review Committee, CPA
PRDC	Provincial Reconstruction Development Committee
PRM	Population, Refugees and Migration, US DOS Bureau of
PRT	Provincial Reconstruction Team
PSC	Private Security Company
PSD	Personal Security Detail; Public Security Directorate
PTAs	Parent-Teacher Associations
PTT	Postal, Telephone and Telegraph
PU	Première Urgence
PUK	Patriotic Union of Kurdistan
PVO	Private Voluntary Organization
PWPO	Post-War Planning Office
R3P	Rapid Regional Response Program
RAF	Royal Air Force

RAMCC	Regional Air Movement Coordination Center, US Air Force
RC	Regional Coordinator
RCC	Regional Control Center
RFI	Request for Information
RFP	Request for Proposal
RIE	Restore Iraqi Electricity
RIO	Restore Iraqi Oil
RMAC	Regional Mine Action Center
ROE	Rules of Engagement
RPG	Rocket Propelled Grenade
RSOM	Reception, Staging and Onward Movements
RTU	Remote Terminal Unit
SAC	Scientific Advisory Council
SCADA	Supervisory Control and Data Acquisition
SCBA	Self-Contained Breathing Apparatus
SCIRI	Supreme Council for the Islamic Revolution in Iraq
SCM	Supply Chain Management
SDR	Special Drawing Right
SECDEF	Secretary of Defense
SES	Senior Executive Service, US Government
SFIR	Stabilization Forces in Iraq
SIGIR	Special Inspector General for Iraq Reconstructions, USA
SJA	Staff Judge Advocate
SMA	Senior Military Advisor
SMEs	Small and Medium Size Enterprises
SNR	Senior National Representative
SOE	State Owned Entity/Enterprise
SOR	Statement of Requirement
SPOD	Sea Port of Disembarkation
SRSG	Special Representative of the UN Secretary-General
SSR	Security Sector Reform
TA	Technical Agreement
TAL	Law of Administration for the State of Iraq for the Transitional Period / Transitional Administrative Law
TBI	Trade Bank of Iraq
TCN	Troop Contributing Nation
telno	telegram number
TF	Task Force
TFA	Translation from Arabic
TFRIE	Task Force Restore Iraqi Electricity
TIP	Transition and Integration Program
TJWG	Transitional Justice Working Group, OHRTJ
TOA	Transfer of Authority
TOR	Terms of Reference
TR	Transition and Reintegration

TRIC	Transition and Reintegration Implementation Committee
TSPA	Treasury Special Purpose Account, USA
TWC	Temporary Weapons Authorization Card
UHF	Ultra High Frequency
UN	United Nations
UNAMI	United Nations Assistance Mission for Iraq
UNCITRAL	United Nations Commission on International Trade Law
UN CT	United Nations Country Team
UNCTAD	United Nations Conference on Trade and Development
UNDAC	United Nations Disaster Assessment and Coordination
UNDB	United Nations Development Business
UNDG	United Nations Development Group
UNDP	United Nations Development Program
UNDGITF	United Nations Development Group Iraq Trust Fund
UNESCO	United Nations Educational, Scientific and Cultural Organization
UNHAS	United Nations Humanitarian Air Service
UNHCR	United Nations High Commissioner for Refugees
UNIDO	United Nations Industrial Development Organization
UNIFEM	United Nations Development Fund for Women
UNIKOM	United Nations Iraq Kuwait Observation Mission
UNJLC	United Nations Joint Logistics Centre
UNMIR	United Nations Mission in Iraq
UNMOVIC	United Nations Monitoring, Verification and Inspection Commission
UNOHCI	United Nations Office of the Humanitarian Coordinator for Iraq
UNSCR	United Nations Security Council Resolution
UNSECOORD	Office of the United Nations Security Coordinator
UPU	Universal Postal Union
US	United States
USA	United States of America
USAID	United States Agency for International Development
USC	United States Code
USCENTCOM	United States Central Command
USD(P)	Under Secretary of Defence for Policy
USG	United States Government
USTDA	United States Trade and Development Agency
USTR	United States Trade Representative
USUN	United States Mission to the United Nations
UXO	Unexploded Ordnance
VAT	Value Added Tax
VFR	Visual Flight Rules
VHF	Very High Frequency
VRA	Voluntary Repatriation Agreement
VTC	Vocational Training Centre

WAFDI	Women's Alliance for Democratic Iraq
WEF	World Economic Forum
WFP	World Food Programme
WHO	World Health Organization
WiFi	Wireless Fidelity
WIPO	World Intellectual Property Organization
WMD	Weapons of Mass Destruction
WMO	World Meteorological Organization
WTO	World Trade Organization

Table of Documents

[Document numbers can be found in the top outside corner of each page]

I. Documents of the Coalition Provisional Authority [Doc No]

1. Regulations

2. Orders and Implementing Acts

3. Memoranda

4. Public Notices

2. Other Documents

III. United Nations Documents

V. United Kingdom Policy and Other Documents on Iraq

IX. Miscellaneous Documents

I

Documents of the Coalition Provisional Authority

1. Regulations

Document 1
Coalition Provisional Authority Regulation Number 1
CPA/REG/16 May 2003/01

[The Coalition Provisional Authority]

Pursuant to my authority as Administrator of the Coalition Provisional Authority (CPA), relevant U.N. Security Council resolutions, including Resolution 1483 (2003), and the laws and usages of war,
I hereby promulgate the following:

Section 1 The Coalition Provisional Authority

1) The CPA shall exercise powers of government temporarily in order to provide for the effective administration of Iraq during the period of transitional administration, to restore conditions of security and stability, to create conditions in which the Iraqi people can freely determine their own political future, including by advancing efforts to restore and establish national and local institutions for representative governance and facilitating economic recovery and sustainable reconstruction and development.

2) The CPA is vested with all executive, legislative and judicial authority necessary to achieve its objectives, to be exercised under relevant U.N. Security Council resolutions, including Resolution 1483 (2003), and the laws and usages of war. This authority shall be exercised by the CPA Administrator.

3) As the Commander of Coalition Forces, the Commander of U.S. Central Command shall directly support the CPA by deterring hostilities; maintaining Iraq's territorial integrity and security; searching for, securing and destroying weapons of mass destruction; and assisting in carrying out Coalition policy generally.

Section 2 The Applicable Law

Unless suspended or replaced by the CPA or superseded by legislation issued by democratic institutions of Iraq, laws in force in Iraq as of April 16, 2003 shall continue to apply in Iraq insofar as the laws do not prevent the CPA from exercising its rights and fulfilling its obligations, or conflict with the present or any other Regulation or Order issued by the CPA.

Section 3 Regulations and Orders issued by the CPA

1) In carrying out the authority and responsibility vested in the CPA, the Administrator will, as necessary, issue Regulations and Orders. Regulations shall be those instruments that define the institutions and authorities of the CPA. Orders are binding instructions issued by the CPA. Regulations and Orders will remain in force until repealed by the Administrator or superseded by legislation issued by democratic institutions of Iraq. Regulations and Orders issued by the Administrator shall take precedence over all other laws and publications to the extent such other laws and publications are inconsistent. The Administrator may also from time to time issue Public Notices.

2) The promulgation of any CPA Regulation or Order requires the approval or signature of the Administrator. The Regulation or Order shall enter into force as specified therein, shall be promulgated in the relevant languages and shall be disseminated as widely as possible. In the case of divergence, the English text shall prevail.

3) CPA Regulations and Orders shall bear the symbols CPA/REG/Date Month 2003/_ and CPA/ORD/Date Month 2003/_. A register of the Regulations and Orders shall indicate the date of entry into force, the subject matter and amendments or changes thereto, or the repeal or suspension thereof.

Section 4 Memoranda

1) The Administrator may issue Memoranda in relation to the interpretation and application of any Regulation or Order.

2) CPA Memoranda shall bear the symbols CPA/MEM/Date Month 2003/_. The provisions of Section 3 shall also apply to the promulgation of CPA Memoranda.

Section 5 Entry into Force

This Regulation shall enter into force on the date of signature [16 May 2003].[1]

Document 2

Coalition Provisional Authority Regulation Number 2

CPA/REG/10 June 2003/02

Development Fund for Iraq

Pursuant to my authority as Administrator of the Coalition Provisional Authority (CPA), and consistent with relevant U.N. Security Council resolutions, including Resolution 1483 (2003), and the laws and usages of war,

Noting the letter of May 8, 2003 from Permanent Representatives of the United States of America and the United Kingdom of Great Britain and Northern Ireland to the President of the United Nations Security Council (S/2003/538),[2]

Recognizing that ninety-five percent of the proceeds of all export sales of petroleum, petroleum products, and natural gas from Iraq, as well as funds from other sources, shall be deposited into the Development Fund for Iraq until an internationally recognized, representative government of Iraq is properly constituted, and that five percent of the proceeds referred to in paragraph 20 of Resolution 1483 shall be deposited into the Compensation Fund established in accordance with Resolution 687 (1991),

Reaffirming that a major CPA objective is to ensure that the newly established Development Fund for Iraq and other Iraqi resources, including Iraqi petroleum and petroleum products, are dedicated to the well-being of the Iraqi people,

Committed to ensuring, consistent with paragraph 14 of Resolution 1483, that the Development Fund for Iraq shall be used in a transparent manner to meet the humanitarian needs of the Iraqi people, for the economic reconstruction and repair of Iraq's infrastructure,

[1] CPA Regulation No 1 was rescinded by CPA Order No 100, sec 5(1) *[Doc 124]*.

[2] See *Doc 574*.

for the continued disarmament of Iraq, and for the costs of Iraqi civilian administration, and for other purposes benefiting the people of Iraq,

I hereby promulgate the following:

Section 1 Purpose

This Regulation applies to the administration, use, accounting and auditing of the Development Fund for Iraq (the 'Fund'). The Regulation is intended and shall be applied to ensure that the Fund is managed in a transparent manner for and on behalf of the Iraqi people, consistent with Resolution 1483, and that all disbursements from the Fund are for purposes benefiting the people of Iraq.

Section 2 Responsibilities

1) Administrator of the CPA (Administrator). Oversees and controls the establishment, administration and use of the Fund for and on behalf of the Iraqi people, and directs disbursements from the Fund for those purposes he determines to be for the benefit of the people of Iraq.

2) Director, Economic Policy, CPA, or other CPA official designated by the Administrator. Manages the Fund, in coordination with the Central Bank of Iraq, the U.S. Federal Reserve Bank of New York and, if the Administrator directs that accounts be opened in the Bank for International Settlements (Switzerland) and/or other financial institutions, in coordination with those institutions.

3) CPA Program Review Board (PRB). Reviews all competing requirements for the relief and recovery of Iraq, assesses all available resources, and, in consultation with the Iraqi interim administration, when established, develops for the approval of the Administrator spending plans, consistent with a comprehensive budgetary framework, that identify prioritized requirements for proposed disbursements from the Fund; considers in this process information provided by the CPA International Coordination Council, the International Advisory and Monitoring Board, and other entities, as appropriate.

4) CPA International Coordination Council. Advises the PRB on matters relating to international efforts to assist the people of Iraq in the relief, recovery and development of their economy, including proposing specific projects for funding consideration; supporting efforts to encourage the global donor community to participate in this effort; providing the PRB with information regarding the nature and scope of international assistance to Iraq; and, as requested, making recommendations to the PRB with regard to disbursements from the Fund.

5) International Advisory and Monitoring Board of the Development Fund for Iraq (the 'IAMB'). Including duly qualified representatives of the Secretary-General of the United Nations, the Managing Director of the International Monetary Fund, the Director-General of the Arab Fund for Social and Economic Development, and the President of the World Bank, and not to exceed three additional duly qualified members appointed by the IAMB with the approval of the Administrator. The IAMB shall approve independent public accountants responsible for auditing the Fund, the Oil Proceeds Receipts Account referred to in section 2(9), and auditing export sales of petroleum, petroleum products, and natural gas from Iraq. The Administrator, in consultation with the IAMB, may appoint up to five non-voting observers to the IAMB. Consistent with its terms of reference,[3] the IAMB shall perform functions similar to those of outside audit committees and may provide

[3] For the IAMB Terms of Reference, see *Doc 592*.

information and comments to the PRB and the Administrator as appropriate to serve the purposes of Resolution 1483 and this Regulation.

6) Central Bank of Iraq. Holds the Fund on its books and administers the Fund as directed by the Administrator or his delegee.

7) U.S. Federal Reserve Bank of New York (the 'Federal Reserve Bank') (and/or the Bank for International Settlements (Switzerland), and/or other financial institutions, if the Administrator directs that accounts in such institutions be opened). As agreed between such institution(s) and the Administrator, opens and maintains on its books the 'Central Bank of Iraq/Development Fund for Iraq' account, as requested by the Administrator. Pursuant to Resolution 1483 and this Regulation, it is understood that the Federal Reserve Bank will be requested to open and maintain on its books an Oil Proceeds Receipts Account (the 'Receipts Account') for the initial receipt of proceeds of all export sales of petroleum, petroleum products, and natural gas from Iraq and for the immediate transfer of ninety-five percent of such proceeds to the 'Central Bank of Iraq/Development Fund for Iraq' account and five percent of such proceeds to the appropriate United Nations Compensation Fund account.

8) Independent public accountants (auditors). Nominated by the Administrator, approved by the IAMB, and reporting to the IAMB and the Administrator, the independent public accountants audit the Fund and audit all export sales of petroleum, petroleum products, and natural gas from Iraq, supporting the objectives of ensuring that the Fund is used in a transparent manner and that such export sales are made consistent with prevailing international market best practices.

Section 3 Establishment of the Fund

The Fund shall be held on the books of the Central Bank of Iraq, and the corpus of the Fund shall be held in an account entitled 'Central Bank of Iraq/Development Fund for Iraq,' in the Federal Reserve Bank (and/or other financial institution(s), if the Administrator so directs), for the Central Bank of Iraq.[4]

Section 4 Control of the Fund

The Fund shall be controlled by the Administrator of the CPA, for and on behalf of the Iraqi people. The Central Bank of Iraq and the Federal Reserve Bank (and/or other financial institution(s), if the Administrator so directs), shall accept instructions, as agreed, concerning the Fund, including instructions to pay sums out of the Fund, only from the Administrator or his authorized delegee(s).

Section 5 Administration of the Fund

1) General. The Central Bank of Iraq/Development Fund for Iraq account in the Federal Reserve Bank shall be governed by the Federal Reserve Bank's standard terms and conditions regarding accounts of foreign central banks and governments, to the extent consistent with applicable law.[5]

2) Communications Protocol. The Fund will be controlled by the Administrator through a communications protocol to be agreed upon between the Administrator and the Federal Reserve Bank (and/or other financial institution(s), if the Administrator so directs). This protocol shall be documented in a funds transfer security procedures agreement.

[4] Sec 3 was amended by CPA Regulation No 11, sec 1(1) *[Doc 12]*.

[5] Sec 5(1) was amended by CPA Regulation No 11, sec 1(2) *[Doc 12]*.

3) Deposits into the Fund. One billion United States dollars from unencumbered funds in the accounts established pursuant to paragraphs 8(a) and 8(b) of United Nations Security Council Resolution 986 (1995) have been transferred to the Fund; and it is anticipated that certain restored and surplus funds, pursuant to paragraphs 17 and 23 of Resolution 1483, will be transferred to the Fund. In addition, ninety-five percent of the proceeds from all export sales of petroleum, petroleum products, and natural gas from Iraq shall be deposited into the Fund, pursuant to paragraph 20 of Resolution 1483, and five percent of such proceeds shall be deposited in the Compensation Fund established pursuant to Resolution 687 (1991), pursuant to paragraph 21 of Resolution 1483. There shall also be accepted for deposit into the Fund any gifts, contributions, donations or other funds, revenues or proceeds.

4) Internal Accounting. The CPA shall obtain the services of an independent, certified public accounting firm to support the objective of ensuring that the Fund is administered and used in a transparent manner for the benefit of the people of Iraq, and is operated consistent with Resolution 1483. The accountants performing this function shall be separate from those public accountants (auditors) approved by the International Advisory and Monitoring Board.

5) Privileges and Immunities. The Fund, including the accounts that comprise its corpus, and the Receipts Account, shall enjoy the privileges and immunities as set forth in paragraph 22 of Resolution 1483, as well as privileges and immunities to which the Fund may be entitled under any other law, regulation, order, or directive.[6]

Section 6 Disbursements from the Fund

1) Authority to Approve. Only the Administrator or his delegee may approve disbursements from the Fund.

2) Directions to Disburse. Sums shall be disbursed from the Fund, in accordance with this Regulation, only upon the express direction of the Administrator, or upon the express direction of individual(s) to whom the Administrator has delegated that authority.

3) Purposes. Sums may be disbursed from the Fund to meet the humanitarian needs of the Iraqi people and for the economic reconstruction and repair of Iraq's infrastructure; for the continued disarmament of Iraq; for the costs of Iraq's civilian administration; and for other purposes the Administrator determines to be for the benefit of the people of Iraq.

4) Proposals for Disbursements. Disbursements from the Fund generally shall be proposed through procedures prescribed in, or promulgated in implementation of the CPA Order [sic][7] establishing the PRB. These procedures shall ensure that proposed disbursements are set forth in a spending plan reflecting the cost, purpose and priority of the requirement, and that, prior to approval by the Administrator, all spending plans are developed in consultation with the Iraqi interim administration, once established.

Section 7 Auditing

The Fund and the export sales of petroleum, petroleum products, and natural gas from Iraq, shall be audited by independent public accountants nominated by the Administrator and approved by the IAMB. The expenses incurred in obtaining the services of the approved independent public accountants shall be charged against the Fund. The CPA shall cooperate fully with the IAMB and the approved independent public accountants in carrying out each party's respective responsibilities. In particular, the CPA shall provide the IAMB and

[6] Sec 5(5) was amended by CPA Regulation No 11, sec 1(3) *[Doc 12]*.
[7] The Program Review Board was established by CPA Regulation No 3 *[Doc 3]*.

such accountants with access to the Fund's financial records, with confidential materials protected in a manner agreed between the parties.

Section 8 Dissolution of the Fund
Until the Fund is dissolved by the Administrator in a manner consistent with Resolution 1483, the Central Bank of Iraq shall continue to hold on its books the Fund. Also, as agreed between the Administrator and the Federal Reserve Bank (and/or such other financial institution(s)), such institution(s) shall continue to maintain on its books the 'Central Bank of Iraq/Development Fund for Iraq' account, and shall continue to accept deposits into, make disbursements from, and otherwise operate the account, in accordance with applicable laws, regulations, policies and agreements.[8]

Section 9 Entry into Force
This regulation shall enter into force on the date of signature [15 June 2003].

Document 3
Coalition Provisional Authority Regulation Number 3

CPA/REG/18 June 2003/03

Program Review Board

Pursuant to my authority as Administrator of the Coalition Provisional Authority (CPA), and consistent with relevant U.N. Security Council resolutions, including Resolution 1483 (2003), and the laws and usages of war,

Noting the letter of May 8, 2003 from Permanent Representatives of the United States of America and the United Kingdom of Great Britain and Northern Ireland to the President of the United Nations Security Council (S/2003/538),[9]

Underscoring that the Development Fund for Iraq shall be used in a transparent manner to meet the humanitarian needs of the Iraqi people, for the economic reconstruction and repair of Iraq's infrastructure, for the continued disarmament of Iraq, and for the costs of Iraqi civilian administration, and for other purposes benefiting the people of Iraq,

Reaffirming that the CPA is committed to ensuring that all state- or regime-owned cash, funds or realizable securities that have been seized by Coalition Forces in Iraq consistent with the laws and usages of war, shall be used only to assist the Iraqi people and support the reconstruction of Iraq,

Noting that paragraph 8 of Resolution 1483 (2003) requests the Secretary General to appoint a Special Representative for Iraq whose responsibilities include, in coordination with the Authority, assisting the people of Iraq,

I hereby promulgate the following:

Section 1 Establishment
There is hereby established as a part of the CPA an entity to be known as the Program Review Board ('Board'). The Board shall report directly to the Administrator of the

[8] Sec 8 was amended by CPA Regulation No 11, sec 1(4) *[Doc 12]*.
[9] See *Doc 574*.

CPA ('Administrator'). The Board shall carry out its responsibilities, as defined in this Regulation, in a manner consistent with the CPA's obligation to ensure that funds available to the CPA for providing relief to, and the recovery of Iraq are managed in a transparent manner and consistent with applicable law, for and on behalf of the Iraqi people. In addition, the Board shall, when and to the extent appropriate, consult the Iraqi interim administration referred to in paragraph 9 of Resolution 1483 (2003), and shall seek every opportunity to further the CPA's objective of gradually transferring to the Iraqi interim administration the responsibility of budgeting Iraq's financial resources. This Regulation establishes the procedures applicable to the Board's operations.

Section 2 Responsibilities

1) Administrator of the CPA (Administrator). Acting on behalf of the CPA, oversees and controls the establishment and operations of the Board, for and on behalf of the Iraqi people, and takes final action on budgets proposed by the Board as he determines to be for the benefit of the people of Iraq, consistent with Resolution 1483 (2003) and applicable laws and regulations. Directly supervises the Chairman of the Board.

2) Council for International Coordination. Advises the Board on matters relating to international efforts to assist the people of Iraq in the relief, recovery and development of their economy, including proposing specific projects for funding consideration; coordinating technical assistance programs and other donor activities; encouraging the global donor community to participate in this effort by contributing to Iraq relief and recovery efforts; providing the Board with information regarding the nature and scope of international assistance to Iraq; and, as requested, making recommendations to the Board with regard to disbursements from resources available for the relief and recovery of Iraq.

3) International Advisory and Monitoring Board of the Development Fund for Iraq ['IAMB']. Advises the Board on matters relating to external audit processes, financial reporting and internal control systems of the Development Fund for Iraq.

Section 3 Chairman of the Board

The Administrator shall appoint a Chairman of the Board, who shall preside over all sessions of the Board, resolve all administrative matters relating to the execution of this Regulation, cast the deciding vote in any matter on which the votes of the Board's members are tied, forward to the Administrator all proposed actions on behalf of the Board, and represent the Board in communications with individuals and entities outside the CPA. The Chairman shall report directly to the Administrator.

Section 4 Membership of the Board

The Board shall consist of the Chairman and the following voting and nonvoting members, and such other voting or nonvoting members as the Administrator may appoint, consistent with the objective of furthering meaningful representation of the Iraqi people and the Iraqi interim administration in the process of developing budgets for the relief and recovery of Iraq.

1) Voting members. The following members, or their designees, shall attend formal sessions of the Board and vote on matters properly brought before the Board.

Chairman
Director, Economic Policy
Director, Civil Affairs Policy;
Director, Agency for International Development, Iraq mission;
Director, Operations;

Director, Security Affairs;
Authorized representatives of
Commander of Coalition Forces
Iraqi Ministry of Finance
United Kingdom
Australia
Chairman, Council for International Coordination

a. When taking action on any matter directly relating to the disposition of funds appropriated by the U.S. Congress, the voting membership of the Board also shall include authorized representatives of the U.S. Department of Defense, U.S. Department of Treasury and U.S. Department of State. With approval of the Administrator, a CPA Director who serves as a voting member may serve concurrently as an authorized representative of the U.S. Departments of Defense, Treasury or State.
b. The authorized representatives of the Iraqi Ministry of Finance, United Kingdom, Australia and Chairman, Council for International Coordination, who otherwise serve as voting members of the Board, shall serve as nonvoting members when the Board is taking actions as described in subsection 4 (l)(a), above.

2) Nonvoting members. The following members of the Board, or their designees, and such other members as the Administrator may designate, are authorized to attend all formal sessions of the Board:

CPA Comptroller
CPA General Counsel
Program Coordinator of the Board
Authorized representative of
U.S. Office of Management and Budget
U.S. Office of the Secretary of Defense
International Monetary Fund
World Bank
U.N. Special Representative of the Secretary General for Iraq
International Advisory and Monitoring Board

Section 5 Program Review Committee and Staff

The Chairman of the Board shall establish a Program Review Committee and a staff to assist the Board in carrying out its responsibilities under this Regulation. The Board's staff shall be headed by a Program Coordinator, who shall also serve as Chairman of the Program Review Committee and a nonvoting member of the Board.

1) Program Review Committee (PRC). The PRC shall be composed of individuals appointed by the Chairman of the Board, and should include representatives of the Coalition allies, the Council for International Coordination and the Iraqi Interim Administration (when established), and two nonvoting observers representing the International Auditing and Monitoring Board and the U.N. Special Representative of the Secretary General for Iraq. The PRC shall initially review all funding requests for which the PRB is responsible, categorize them, and make recommendations to the Board with respect to the priority, source of funding, and manner of executing the requirements. The PRC shall perform such other functions as the Chairman of the Board may direct.

2) Staff. Under the direction of the Program Coordinator, the Board's staff shall:

a. Distribute procedures to all CPA staff elements and other non-CPA entities regarding the process for submitting funding requests;

b. Create and maintain a database of all funding requests:
c. Monitor and account for balances of all available funds subject to budgeting by the Board under this Regulation;
d. Receive all funding requests and assist proponents as necessary to ensure that applications contain all necessary information;
e. Ensure that all spending requirements have undergone prior review at the regional or ministerial level prior to submission;
f. Ensure that spending requests are fully consistent with a comprehensive budgetary framework;
g. Distribute copies of all spending requirements and related information to all members of the Board for consideration;
h. Coordinate with proponents regarding any requests by the Board for additional information;
i. Organize and prepare materials for sessions of the Board;
j. Create, maintain and distribute, as appropriate, all official records of the Program Review Committee and the Board.

Section 6 Duties of the Board

1) General. The Board shall be responsible for recommending expenditures of resources from the Development Fund for Iraq and other resources identified in subsection 6 (3) of this Regulation, in a manner that meets the interests of the people of Iraq, furthers CPA's policy objectives, and comports fully with the CPA's stewardship and financial management duties under applicable laws and regulations, including United Nations Security Council Resolution 1483 (2003). The Board shall not be responsible for overseeing the manner in which approved spending requirements are executed.

2) Funding Plan. The Board shall be responsible for reviewing all identified requirements for the resources for which the Board is responsible; prioritizing these requirements; and integrating the prioritized requirements into a funding plan that forecasts available resources, recommends allocations of those resources, consistent with the purposes for which they are lawfully available and the relative priorities of all identified spending requirements; and sets forth the justification for the proposed expenditures and the recommended manner in which the expenditures should be executed (i.e., by contract or otherwise). In performing this function, the Board shall consider relevant information concerning relief and recovery efforts in Iraq and related budgeting documents, including the Iraqi Ministry of Finance budget of Iraqi resources.

3) Resources Subject to Funding Plan. In proposing funding plans for the relief and recovery of Iraq, the Board shall be responsible for recommending disbursements of:

a. Funds appropriated for such purposes by the U.S. Congress;
b. Iraqi property lawfully vested in the U.S. Treasury, to the extent that the Secretary of Defense is designated with authority to use such property to assist the Iraqi people and assist in the reconstruction of Iraq;
c. Iraqi state- or regime-owned cash, funds, realizable securities, or other state- or regime-owned movable property seized in Iraq consistent with the laws and usages of war;
d. The Development Fund for Iraq.

4) Preparation and Submission of Funding Plans.

a. Frequency. The Board shall submit funding plans at such times as the Chairman determines necessary to ensure the prompt and effective delivery of resources to Iraq, consistent with a comprehensive budgetary framework for Iraq.

b. Development. The Board shall, with the concurrence of a majority of voting members, prescribe such procedures as may be necessary to enable the timely preparation of funding plans, including instructions for identifying and submitting spending requirements to the Board for consideration, and procedures for advising the Board of current relief and recovery activities in Iraq.
c. Content and Format. Funding plans submitted by the Board shall include (i) a description of the amounts available within each source of funding subject to planning by the Board, as identified in Section 6 (3) of this Regulation; (ii) proposed funding requirements for each category of funding, prioritized to reflect the relative importance and urgency of the each such requirement; (iii) a recommendation as to the U.S. executive agency to which any funds appropriated by the U.S. government should be apportioned; and (iv) a recommendation as to the manner in which the prioritized spending requirements should be executed (i.e., by contract or otherwise). The Board shall submit proposed funding plans in a format to be approved by a majority of the Board's voting members.
d. Consultation with International Financial Institutions ('IFIs'). To ensure that proposed funding plans are developed in view of needs assessments being undertaken by the IFIs, the IFIs should be given an opportunity to consult with the Board and the PRC on projects of significant value.
e. Approval. All proposed funding plans shall be submitted to the Administrator for approval.
f. Publication. Approved funding plans shall be published in Arabic and broadly disseminated to the Iraqi people in a form to be prescribed by the Administrator.

5) Execution of Funding Plans. The Board shall propose principles and standards for expending funds for the relief and recovery of Iraq in a fair, consistent and transparent manner, through contracts or otherwise. In developing these proposed principles and standards, the Board shall consider prevailing international standards relating to procurement, including the codes and standards used by international financial institutions. Upon approval by a majority of the Board's voting members, the Chairman shall submit these principles and standards to the Administrator for final approval.

6) In carrying out these functions, the Board shall ensure appropriate coordination with the Special Representative of the Secretary General for Iraq, or his designee(s), in accordance with Resolution 1483 (2003) and, when and to the extent appropriate, shall consult the Iraqi interim administration referred to in paragraph 9 of Resolution 1483 (2003).

Section 7 Board Sessions

1) General. The Board shall meet at such times and in such locations as directed by the Chairman. The Board shall meet in formal session for the purpose of taking official action on any matter within the Board's responsibility, as set forth in this Regulation. At the Chairman's direction, the Board, or any part thereof, may meet in informal session, in order to plan or prepare for formal sessions of the Board, or carry out such other functions as the Chairman may prescribe, in furtherance of the Board's responsibilities.

2) Attendance. Formal sessions of the Board shall be attended by voting and nonvoting members and such other individuals as the Chairman may authorize. Informal sessions of the Board shall be attended by such members and other individuals as the Chairman may direct.

3) Quorum. The Board may take official actions only in formal sessions at which no fewer than seventy percent of the voting members of the Board are present.

4) Minutes. The Recorder of the Board shall prepare written minutes of each formal

session of the Board, summarizing the Board's consideration of, and action upon all matters brought before it. These minutes shall be made public.

5) Actions Relating to U.S. Government Appropriations. When taking action on any matter directly relating to the disposition of funds appropriated by the U.S. Congress, the voting and nonvoting membership of the Board shall be as prescribed in subsection 4(1) of this Regulation.

Section 8 U.S. Government Contracts and Grants
Nothing in this Regulation shall be construed to affect the validity of any contract or grant entered into by the U.S. Government with respect to relief or reconstruction in Iraq prior to the effective date of this Regulation.

Section 9 Dissolution of the Board
Until the Board is dissolved by the Administrator at the request of an internationally recognized, representative government of Iraq, the Board shall continue to operate in accordance with this Regulation and all other applicable laws, regulations, policies and agreements.

Section 10 Administrative Powers
The Board may prescribe such additional administrative procedures as may be necessary to carry out its responsibilities under this Regulation. Such procedures shall only be effective upon approval by a majority of the Board's voting members.[10]

Section 11 Entry into Force
This regulation shall enter into force upon the date of signature [19 June 2003].[11]

Document 4

Coalition Provisional Authority Regulation Number 4

CPA/REG/25 June 2003/04

Establishment of the Iraqi Property Reconciliation Facility

Pursuant to my authority as Administrator of the Coalition Provisional Authority (CPA) and the laws and usages of war, and consistent with relevant U.N. Security Council resolutions, including Resolution 1483 (2003),

Recognizing that large numbers of people from different ethnic and religious backgrounds in Iraq have been uprooted and forced to move from their properties to serve political objectives of the Ba'athist regime,

Recognizing that as a result of these Ba'athist policies, many individuals have conflicting claims to the same real property, resulting in instability and occasional violence,

Recognizing that pending the establishment of a means of finally resolving property related claims by a future Iraqi government, certain of these claims may be amenable to voluntary reconciliation immediately, thereby avoiding further instability and violence,

[10] Sec 10 was amended by CPA Regulation No 11, sec 1(5) *[Doc 12]*.

[11] Prior to its formal establishment, the PRB had held its first meeting on 6 June 2003. See Program Review Board Minutes of the meeting of 9 June 2003 (http://www.iraqcoalition.org/budget/PRB/archive/index.html).

I hereby promulgate the following:

Section 1 Establishment

1) There shall be established an Iraqi Property Reconciliation Facility (IPRF) that shall commence operation at a time to be fixed by the Administrator, for the purpose of collecting real property claims and promptly resolving such claims on a voluntary basis in a fair and judicious manner.

2) The IPRF shall operate under the authority of the Administrator and shall terminate operation at such time as the Administrator shall determine.

3) The Administrator may authorize the establishment of an IPRF Fund to be used in connection with the operations of the IPRF.

Section 2 Delegation of Authority

The Administrator may delegate any of the authorities hereunder, including by designating an international organization to implement IPRF.

Section 3 Composition

1) The IPRF central office shall be located in Baghdad, and it shall administer the IPRF and coordinate with other entities as necessary to accomplish the objectives of the IPRF.

2) The IPRF shall also have several regional offices located throughout Iraq. Each office will be staffed with one or more international staff and five or more Iraqis who are representative of the geographical area covered by that office.

3) The Administrator, or his delegee in consultation with the Administrator, will select the individuals who will serve in the regional offices and the Executive Secretariat.

Section 4 Powers and Functions

1) The head of the central office shall:
   a) provide advice to and coordinate with the regional offices to ensure consistent procedures and policies among the regional offices;
   b) report to the Administrator with respect to all aspects of the IPRF; and
   c) perform such other functions delegated by the Administrator.

2) The regional IPRF offices shall:
   a) provide information to the Iraqi public about the IPRF, its regional offices and the services provided by such offices;
   b) receive claims from individuals with property disputes;
   c) provide a voluntary dispute resolution and reconciliation facility that individuals may use to resolve their disputes; and
   d) perform such other functions delegated by the Administrator.

Section 5 Regulation

The IPRF shall be bound by and operate in accordance with any Regulations, Orders or Memoranda issued by the Administrator.

Section 6 Entry into Force

This Regulation shall enter into force on the date of signature [26 June 2003].[12]

[12] CPA Regulation No 4 was rescinded by CPA Regulation No 8, sec 3 *[Doc 9]*.

Document 5
Coalition Provisional Authority Regulation Number 5
CPA/REG/18 June 2003/05

Council for International Coordination

Pursuant to my authority as head of the Coalition Provisional Authority (CPA), and under the laws and usages of war, and consistent with relevant U.N. Security Council resolutions, including Resolution 1483 (2003),

Furthering paragraph 1 of Resolution 1483, appealing to Member States and concerned organizations to assist the people of Iraq in their efforts to reform their institutions and rebuild their country, and to contribute to conditions of stability and security in Iraq,

Furthering paragraph 2 of Resolution 1483 calling upon Member States in a position to do so to respond immediately to humanitarian appeals of the United Nations and other international organizations for Iraq and to help meet the humanitarian and other needs of the Iraqi people by providing food, medical supplies, and resources necessary for reconstruction and rehabilitation of Iraq's economic infrastructure,

Noting that paragraph 8 of Resolution 1483 requests the Secretary General to appoint a Special Representative for Iraq whose responsibilities include, in coordination with the CPA, assisting the people of Iraq,

Noting the letter of May 8, 2003 from the Permanent Representatives of the United States of America and the United Kingdom of Great Britain and Northern Ireland to the President of the Security Council (S/2003/538)[13] affirming that they and Coalition partners will work through the CPA to provide for security in and for the provisional administration of Iraq,

I hereby promulgate the following:

Section 1 Purpose

The Council for International Coordination (the 'Council') is hereby established as an organization that will work on behalf of the CPA, to support, encourage and facilitate participation of the international community in relief, recovery and development efforts with respect to Iraq. The Council's efforts will not include coordination of assistance with respect to establishing an Iraqi police capability, establishing a New Iraqi Army or other security matters.

Section 2 Membership

1) The Council shall be composed of representatives from Coalition members and other countries that:

a) support the territorial integrity of Iraq, and a representative government for the Iraqi people that does not possess weapons of mass destruction, does not support terrorism, and seeks peace with its neighbors;

b) possess expertise or other resources that will assist in furthering the purposes of the Council as set out in Section 1; and

c) offer to provide a representative in Iraq.

2) The Administrator of the CPA shall appoint the initial representatives to the Council from Coalition members. The Chairman, designated under Section 3 of this Order,

[13] See *Doc 574*.

shall after consultation with the existing members of the Council, nominate additional representatives for appointment by the Administrator.

3) Any remuneration or expenses of a representative to the Council will be the responsibility of the representatives' sending States.

4) The Council shall report to and work under the authority, direction and control of the Administrator.

Section 3 Chairman and Vice Chairman

1) The Administrator shall designate a Chairman and a Vice Chairman of the Council. The Chairman shall be from a country that is a member of the Coalition Forces, and the Vice Chairman shall be from Australia, the United Kingdom or the United States.[14]

2) The Chairman, and in his or her absence, the Vice Chairman, or other mutually agreed designee, will chair the meetings of the Council, and will participate in the CPA Program Review Committee and the CPA Program Review Board, both of which shall be established separately from this Order [sic].

3) The Chairman and the Vice Chairman shall nominate directors, as necessary, for appointment by the Administrator.

4) The Chairman and the Vice Chairman shall nominate a Senior Iraqi Advisor, for appointment by the Administrator.

Section 4 Functions and Powers of the Council

1) The Council shall have the following functions and responsibilities:

a) encourage the international community to provide funds and other forms of assistance to Iraq, consistent with Resolution 1483, and, in particular, paragraphs 1, 2 and 26 of Resolution 1483;

b) coordinate international assistance for Iraq from States, non-governmental organizations and international organizations, including receiving and analyzing project proposals from the international community, identifying priority needs for funding, and helping match international resources to prioritized needs;

c) report and make recommendations to the CPA Program Review Board on the international community's assistance efforts in Iraq;

d) inform the CPA Program Review Board of those priority assistance projects in Iraq for which international community funding has not been made available;

e) working through the Program Review Committee and the Program Review Board, make recommendations to the Administrator on project approvals;

f) provide briefings to, and work as a liaison with, the international community;

g) coordinate visits to CPA by international visitors;

h) identify available international expertise, and make recommendations to the Administrator, regarding possible use of this expertise within the CPA;

i) working through the Chairman and any appropriate subordinates, provide oversight to the facilities manager of the Iraq Forum;

j) recommend specific assistance projects for coordination and oversight by the Council, as directed by the Administrator; and

k) perform such other functions as the Administrator assigns to the Council.

2) In carrying out these functions, consistent with paragraph 8 of Resolution 1483, the Council shall ensure appropriate coordination with the Special Representative of the

[14] Sec 3(1) was amended by CPA Regulation No 5/AMENDMENT, sec 1 *[Doc 6]*.

Secretary General for Iraq, or his designee(s), and, consistent with paragraph 2 of Resolution 1483, with other organizations appealing for or providing humanitarian assistance for Iraq. The Council shall also coordinate its assistance efforts with the respective member State's assistance efforts, including groups such as the Senior Contribution Group.

Section 5 Meetings of the Council

1) Meetings of the Council shall be chaired by the Chairman, and, in his or her absence, by the Vice Chairman or a mutually agreed designee.

2) A quorum of half of the members of the Council, plus one, is required in order for the Council to meet and make its decisions. As necessary, the Chairman may permit participation pursuant to a written proxy.

3) Decisions of the Council shall be made by consensus whenever possible and otherwise by the majority vote of the Council. Each member shall have one vote. In the event of a tie, the chair for the meeting shall cast the deciding vote.

4) The Council may invite any persons to its meetings as may be necessary for the transaction of its business.

Section 6 Entry into Force

The Regulation shall enter into force on the date of its signature [17 June 2003].[15]

Document 6

Coalition Provisional Authority Regulation Number 5

CPA/REG/17 August 2003/05/AMENDMENT

Council for International Coordination (Amendment)

Pursuant to my authority as head of the Coalition Provisional Authority (CPA), and under the laws and usages of war, and consistent with relevant U.N. Security Council resolutions, including Resolution 1483 (2003),

[15] The Regulation was signed a day ahead of the official date given in the document number in the footer of the document. On 18 June 2003, the CPA issued the following statement 'Regarding the Council for International Coordination': 'The Administrator of the Coalition Provisional Authority (CPA) for Iraq has decided that the growing magnitude and importance of the contributions from the international community for the relief, recovery and development of Iraq calls for the establishment a Council for International Coordination, as part of the CPA. This Council will be chaired by Professor Marek Belka, former Deputy Prime Minister of Poland. Andrew Goledzinowski, a senior foreign affairs official from Australia, will be vice chair.

The Administrator will appoint additional representatives to the Council from those countries that want to contribute expertise or other resources to the relief, recovery and development of Iraq and that support the territorial integrity of Iraq and a representative government of the Iraqi people that does not possess weapons of mass destruction, does not support terrorism, and seeks peace with its neighbors.

The Council will be the CPA's focal point and coordinating body for international assistance in the relief, recovery and development of Iraq. The Council will encourage the international community to provide funds and other forms of assistance to Iraq and will coordinate international assistance provided by states, non-governmental organizations and international organisations. In carrying out its responsibilities, the Council will work closely with the UN Special Representative and his designees and other organizations involved in the relief, recovery and development efforts.'

CPA Regulation No 5 was rescinded by CPA Order No 100, sec 5(2) *[Doc 124]*.

Furthering the requirement to effectively manage CPA programs and activities through the assignment of responsibilities among CPA officials in a manner that responds to changes in personnel resources while preserving continuity of leadership,

I hereby promulgate the following:

Section 1 Amendment

Section 3, paragraph 1 of CPA Order [sic] No.5, Council for International Coordination (18 June 2003),[16] is hereby amended to read as follows: *'1) The Administrator shall designate a Chairman and a Vice Chairman of the Council.'*[17]

Section 2 Entry into Force

This Amendment shall enter into force on the date of signature [18 August 2003].[18]

Document 7

Coalition Provisional Authority Regulation Number 6

CPA/REG/13 July 2003/06

Governing Council of Iraq

Pursuant to my authority as Administrator of the Coalition Provisional Authority (CPA), relevant U.N. Security Council resolutions, including Resolution 1483 (2003), and the laws and usages of war,

Recognizing that, as stated in paragraph 9 of Resolution 1483, the Security Council supports the formation of an Iraqi interim administration as a transitional administration run by Iraqis, until the people of Iraq establish an internationally recognized, representative government that assumes the responsibilities of the CPA,

Noting that on July 13, 2003, the Governing Council met and announced its formation as the principal body of the Iraqi interim administration referred to in paragraph 9 of Resolution 1483,

Affirming that the CPA and the Special Representative of the U.N. Secretary General have worked together and will continue to work together in a cooperative and consultative process to support the formation and operation of the Governing Council and welcomed the formation of the Governing Council on July 13, 2003,

Acknowledging that, consistent with Resolution 1483, the Governing Council has certain authorities and responsibilities as representatives of the Iraqi people, including ensuring that the Iraqi people's interests are represented in both the interim administration and in determining the means of establishing an internationally recognized, representative government,

Emphasizing that, consistent with Resolution 1483, the Governing Council and the CPA, each in coordination with the Special Representative of the U.N. Secretary General,

[16] See *Doc 5.*

[17] The amendment meant that the chairman of the CIC no longer had to be from a country that is a member of the Coalition Forces other than Australia, the United Kingdom or the United States. On 22 August 2003, Ambassador Bremer announced that after the Madrid Donor Conference on 23-24 October 2003 the current CIC chairman, Ambassador Marek Belka of Poland, would be succeeded by the Australian diplomat Andrew Goledzinowski who had served as vice-chair of the CIC since June 2003.

[18] The amended CPA Regulation No 5 was rescinded by CPA Order No 100, sec 5(2) *[Doc 124].*

undertake to work together in a cooperative and consultative process for the benefit of the Iraqi people,

I hereby promulgate the following:

Section 1 Recognition of Governing Council

The CPA recognized the formation of the Governing Council as the principal body of the Iraqi interim administration, pending the establishment of an internationally recognized, representative government by the people of Iraq, consistent with Resolution 1483.[19]

Section 2 Relationship between Governing Council and the CPA

1) In accordance with Resolution 1483, the Governing Council and the CPA shall consult and coordinate on all matters involving the temporary governance of Iraq, including the authorities of the Governing Council.

2) All officials of the CPA are hereby instructed promptly to respond to all requests for experts, technical assistance or other support requested by the Governing Council.

Section 3 Entry into Force

The Regulation shall enter into force on the date of signature [13 July 2003].[20]

Document 8

Coalition Provisional Authority Regulation Number 7

CPA/REG/5 December 2003/07

International Donor Assistance

Pursuant to my authority as head of the Coalition Provisional Authority (CPA), and under the laws and usages of war, and consistent with relevant U.N. Security Council resolutions, including Resolutions 1483 and 1511 (2003),

Furthering paragraph 1 of Resolution 1483, appealing to Member States of the United Nations and concerned organizations to assist the people of Iraq in their efforts to reform their institutions and rebuild their country, and to contribute to conditions of stability and security in Iraq,

[19] The 25-member Governing Council was composed of 13 Shia Muslims, 5 Sunni Muslims, 5 Kurds, 1 Christian and1 Turkmen. The members were: Shia Muslims: Iyad Allawi, Ahmed al-Barak [Ahmad Shya'a al-Barak], Ahmed Chalabi [Ahmad Chalabi], Abdel-Aziz al-Hakim [Abd al-Aziz al-Hakim], Aqila al-Hashimi [Aqilah al-Hashimi] (assassinated, replaced by Salamah al-Khafaji), Ibrahim Jaafari [Ibrahim al-Ja'fari or Ebrahim Jafari Al Eshaiker], Raja Habib al-Khuzaai [Raja Habib al-Khaza'I], Wael Abdul Latif [Wa'il Abd al-Latif], Abdel-Karim Mahoud al-Mohammedawi [Abd-al Karim al-Mahmadawi], Hamid Majid Mousa [Hamid Majid Musa], Mouwafak al-Rabii [Muwaffaq al-Rubay'I], Ezzedine Salim [Izz al-Din Salim aka Abd al-Zahra Uthman Muhammad], Mohammed Bahr al-Ulloum [Muhammad Bahr al-Ulum]; Sunni Muslims: Naseer al-Chaderchi [Nasir Kamil Chadirchi], Mohsen Abdel Hamid [Muhsin Abd al-Hamid], Samir Shakir Mahmoud [Samir Shakir Mahmud], Adnan Pachachi, Ghazi Mashal Ajil al-Yawer [Ghazi Ajil al-Yawir]; Kurds: Massoud Barzani [Mas'ud Barzani], Salaheddine Bahaaeddin [Salah al-Din Muhammad Baha al-Din], Dara Noor Alzin [Dara Nur al-Din], Mahmoud Othman [Mahmud Uthman], Jalal Talabani; Christian: Younadem Kana [Yonadam Yousif Kanna]; Turkmen: Sondul Chapouk [Sungul Chabuk].

[20] CPA Regulation No 6 was rescinded by CPA Regulation No 9, sec 1(2) *[Doc 10]*. See also CPA Order No 100, sec 5(3) *[Doc 124]*.

Furthering paragraph 2 of Resolution 1483, calling upon Member States in a position to do so to respond immediately to humanitarian appeals of the United Nations and other international organizations for Iraq and to help meet the humanitarian and other needs of the Iraqi people by providing food, medical supplies, and resources necessary for reconstruction and rehabilitation of Iraq's economic infrastructure,

Furthering paragraph 15 of Resolution 1483, which calls upon the international financial institutions to assist the people of Iraq in the reconstruction and development of their economy and to facilitate assistance by the broader donor community,

Noting the statement of September 20, 2003, in Dubai, by the Ministers of Finance and Central Bank Governors of the Group of Seven Industrialized Nations, in which the participants affirmed their support for a multilateral effort to help rebuild and develop Iraq and for the International Monetary Fund (IMF) and the World Bank to provide financial and other assistance to Iraq rapidly, subject to their policies,[21]

Observing that the IMF and the World Bank already have provided significant technical assistance to Iraq, but that having these international financial institutions (IFIs) work closely with the Governing Council and Iraqi ministers now on arrangements necessary to enable the early commencement of IFI lending would further help the people of Iraq in the reconstruction and development of their country,

Recognizing that the Governing Council and its ministers, as provided in paragraph 4 of Resolution 1511, are the principal bodies of the Iraqi interim administration, which, without prejudice to its further evolution, embodies the sovereignty of the State of Iraq during the period of transition,

Recalling paragraph 20 of Resolution 1511, which urges the international financial institutions to take immediate steps to provide their full range of loans and other assistance to Iraq, working with the Governing Council and its ministers,

Noting the Conclusions by the Chair of the International Donors' Conference on Reconstruction in Iraq, held in Madrid October 23-24, 2003, which stated that the conference looks forward to the early creation of an Iraqi-led coordination mechanism to ensure that Iraqi priorities and needs guide the national development process and to prevent the emergence of gaps and duplication, and called upon all donors to work with this mechanism,[22]

I hereby promulgate the following:

Section 1 Iraqi Strategic Review Board

1) *Establishment.* The Iraqi Strategic Review Board (the 'Board') is hereby established as the Iraqi organization, operating under the authority of the Governing Council or its successor, that will work on behalf of the Iraqi people to forge a strong partnership among the interim Iraqi administration and contributing governments, international organizations and other entities that provide grants, loans, guarantees, or other financial or technical assistance in support of Iraq's relief, recovery and development efforts.

[21] The Statement of G7 Finance Ministers and Central Bank Governors said: 'We welcome both the Afghan donors meetings this month and the upcoming Iraq Donors' Conference. We reaffirm our support for a multilateral effort to help rebuild and develop Iraq, based on a needs assessment led by the World Bank at the Donors' Conference in Madrid, next month. We support the IMF and the World Bank rapidly providing, subject to their policies, financial and other assistance to Iraq and call upon regional financial institutions to do likewise. We call upon the Paris Club to make its best effort to complete the restructuring of Iraq's debt before the end of 2004. We urge all non-Paris creditors to cooperate.'

[22] See para 19 of the Conclusions by the Chair International Donors Conference for the Reconstruction of Iraq Madrid, 23–24 October 2003 *[Doc 593]*.

2) *Functions.*

a) The Board shall provide overall policy guidance with respect to multilateral and bilateral financial and economic development assistance for Iraq, setting and prioritizing needs in a transparent manner that does not unfairly discriminate among the Iraq's geographic regions and cultural and religious groups.

b) In addition, the Board shall take action on recommendations from the Ministry of Planning and Development Cooperation regarding the allocation of international financial and other assistance against Iraq's needs. In exercising this authority, the Board shall, within ten working days following the relevant Ministry's submission of a recommendation, either approve or disapprove the recommendation, or return it to the Ministry for reconsideration.

c) The Board shall work closely with the Ministry of Planning and Development Cooperation and the Ministry of Finance to ensure that international assistance for Iraq is actively fostered, properly allocated against Iraq's prioritized needs, effectively utilized and monitored, and integrated into the Iraqi national budget.

3) *Membership.* The Board shall consist of five individuals: two appointed by the Governing Council; the Minister of Planning and Development Cooperation, the Minister of Finance, and a representative of the CPA.[23]

4) *Chairmanships.*

a) The Board shall designate from amongst its membership a Chairman and a Vice Chairman.

b) The Chairman (or, in his or her absence, the Vice Chairman) shall participate in the International Reconstruction Fund Facility in such capacity as many be agreed with the IRFF Donor Committee.

5) *Board Meetings.*

a) Meetings of the Board shall be chaired by the Chairman, and, in his or her absence, by the Vice Chairman or a mutually agreed designee.

b) A quorum of four members is required in order for the Board to meet and make decisions. As necessary, the Chairman may permit participation pursuant to a written proxy.

c) Decisions of the Board shall be made by consensus whenever possible and otherwise by majority vote of the Board. Each member shall have one vote. In the event of a tie, the chair for the meeting shall cast the deciding vote.

d) The Board may invite any persons to its meetings as may be necessary for the transaction of its business.

Section 2 Ministry of Planning and Development Cooperation

1) *Renaming.* The Iraq Ministry of Planning is hereby renamed the Ministry of Planning and Development Cooperation. All references in previous orders, regulations, and memoranda or Iraqi laws and regulations to the Ministry of Planning shall be deemed to refer to the Ministry of Planning and Development Cooperation.[24]

2) *Support.* The CPA shall provide personnel support to the Ministry of Planning and Development Cooperation, in consultation with the Minister, in order to reinforce and develop local Iraqi capacity at all levels. In addition, the CPA and the Minister shall seek technical assistance for the Ministry from appropriate international sources.

[23] Sec 1(3) was rescinded and replaced by CPA Order No 100, sec 5(4)(a)-(b) *[Doc 124].*

[24] Sec 2(1) was amended by CPA Order No 100, sec 5(4)(c) *[Doc 124].*

3) *Functions.* The Ministry of Planning and Development Cooperation shall, consistent with the responsibilities of other Ministries specifically set forth in this Regulation and under the overall guidance of the Board:

a. Take such actions as it deems necessary to promote international assistance to Iraq, including liaising with existing and potential donors and following up on pledges of assistance;
b. Develop transparent procedures for allocating international assistance to geographic and/or functional sectors in Iraq; make recommendations, with the concurrence of the Ministry of Finance, to the Board regarding specific programs and/or the allocation of international assistance among these sectors; and authorize the disbursement of assistance for specific programs, projects and activities, within sector allocations approved by the Board;
c. With the concurrence of the Ministry of Finance, ensure that the recommendations presented to the Board reflect a single, comprehensive and integrated plan for matching all available revenues, regardless of source, against all known requirements in the manner that optimizes the use of those resources to meet Iraq's prioritized needs;
d. consistent with this Regulation, prescribe procedures for the Iraqi Ministries' performance of duties relating to international assistance to Iraq;
e. Serve, together with the Board, to represent the people of Iraq in connection with trust funds administered by the United Nations and World Bank, including reviewing and recommending for approval programs and projects to be financed by the Facility and participating in the Facility's Donor Committee and Coordinating Committee as may be agreed;
f. Work closely with the Ministry of Finance and the Central Bank of Iraq to ensure that assistance from the international financial institutions is allocated consistently with the national budget, and in a manner that supports the integration of capital improvements and operating requirements into a unified national budget as soon as practicable;
g. Work closely with the CPA's Program Management Office to ensure that pre-existing bilateral commitments and the U.S. Government's apportionment and obligation of funds that the U.S. Congress appropriates for Iraq relief and reconstruction are taken into account in their recommendations to the Board;
h. Monitor the implementation of international financial assistance to Iraq to ensure that resources are applied against Iraq's prioritized needs and equitably distributed among Iraq's geographic regions and cultural and religious groups;
i. Participate in the Council for International Coordination (CIC) through the assumption of the Chairmanship of the CIC by the Minister of Planning and Development Cooperation, as decided unanimously by the CIC on November 19, 2003.

Section 3 Roles and Responsibilities of the Iraqi Ministries

1) Iraqi Ministries shall submit program and plans for the expenditure of donor funds to the Ministry of Planning and Development Cooperation for the approval of the Board. In accordance with such approval, the Iraqi Ministries shall negotiate, execute and implement grant and technical assistance agreements with governments, non-governmental organizations, and other donors for projects and activities related to the particular Ministry's functional responsibilities.

2) Iraqi Ministers shall also ensure effective liaison and coordination, in their responsibility, with regional and local officials. The Ministry of Planning and Development Cooperation will work with Iraqi Ministries and regional and local officials to facilitate and assist in this regard.

Section 4 Bilateral Assistance

1) *Contracting Procedures.*

a) In negotiating and executing bilateral arrangements for financial and economic development assistance to Iraq, the Ministries may agree to terms that authorize contributing governments to designate project(s) or programs that will be funded by their assistance, and to direct all contracting activities necessary to carry out such project(s) or programs, including the selection of contractors and subcontractors. The Ministries shall encourage contributing governments to adopt contracting procedures that ensure competitive and open bidding and that are otherwise consistent with internationally accepted contracting principles; and to complement their bilateral assistance with assistance channeled through multi-donor trust fund(s) and other multilateral mechanisms.

b) To the extent that bilateral arrangements negotiated pursuant to this Regulation provide for the application of contracting procedures or the execution of contracting actions as specified by the contributing government, the CPA shall regard such procedures or actions as having the same legal force and effect as contracting procedures or actions adopted by the CPA. In addition, the CPA shall accord contractors and subcontractors selected by contributing governments pursuant to this subsection the same privileges, protection and support provided to contractors and subcontractors of Coalition partners.

2) *Additional Provisions.* In addition to the terms and conditions specified in subsection 4(1) of this Regulation, bilateral arrangements for assistance to Iraq may contain such other terms and conditions as the Board may determine necessary and appropriate, including provisions that:

a) Grant contributing governments direct access to communicate with Governing Council representatives or their successors and Iraqi Ministers regarding projects funded with their contributions;

b) Offer office facilities at the Iraqi Business Center in Baghdad for representative(s) of contributing governments;

c) Accord exporters of contributing governments access to the facilities of the Trade Bank of Iraq; and

Section 5 International Financial Institution Assistance

1) [sic] Subject to the overall guidance and final approval of the Board:

a) The Ministry of Finance shall be responsible for developing, negotiating and authorizing all IMF assistance to Iraq, as well as preparatory activities related thereto;

b) The Ministry of Planning and Development Cooperation shall be responsible for developing, negotiating and authorizing all World Bank and other IFI assistance to Iraq, as well as preparatory activities related thereto.

To ensure that grant, technical assistance, lending and other arrangements with the IFIs are made within the broader context of Iraq's economic infrastructure and social policies and are effectively coordinated with the national budgeting process, the Ministry of Finance, the Central Bank of Iraq, and the Ministry for Planning and Development Cooperation shall consult regularly on the development and negotiation of any such arrangements, as well as preparatory activities related thereto.

Section 6 Authority of the Governing Council and Iraqi Ministries
The CPA recognizes that, as stated in Resolution 1511, the Governing Council and its ministers are the principal bodies of the Iraqi interim administration, which, without prejudice to its further evolution, embodies the sovereignty of Iraq during the period of the transition, and that, consistent with Resolutions 1483 and 1511, these bodies have the authority to carry out the functions and responsibilities set forth in this Regulation. Any additional authority the CPA had with respect to such functions and responsibilities is hereby delegated to the Governing Council, for further delegation as it deems appropriate, consistent with this Regulation.[25]

Section 7 Effect on Other CPA Regulations
To the extent this Regulation is inconsistent with CPA regulations Nos. 1, 5, and 6, the provisions of this Regulation prevail.[26]

Section 8 Entry into Force
This Regulation shall enter into force on the date of signature [5 December 2003].

Document 9
Coalition Provisional Authority Regulation Number 8
CPA/REG/14 January 2004/08

Delegation of Authority Regarding an Iraq Property Claims Commission

Pursuant to my authority as Administrator of the Coalition Provisional Authority (CPA) and under the laws and usages of war, and consistent with relevant U.N. Security Council resolutions, including Resolutions 1483 and 1511 (2003),

Noting that large numbers of people from different ethnic and religious backgrounds in Iraq have been uprooted and forced to move from their properties to serve political objectives of the Ba'athist regime,

Recognizing that as a result of these Ba'athist policies, many individuals have conflicting claims to the same real property, resulting in instability and occasional violence,

Concluding that pending the establishment of a means of finally resolving property related claims by a future Iraqi government, certain of these claims may be amenable to voluntary reconciliation immediately, thereby avoiding further instability and violence,

I hereby promulgate the following:

Section 1 Delegation of Authority
The Governing Council is hereby authorized to establish the Iraq Property Claims Commission (IPCC) for the purpose of collecting and resolving real property claims and to

[25] Sec 6 was rescinded and replaced by CPA Order No 100, sec 5(4)(d) *[Doc 124]*.
[26] See *Docs 1, 5, 6, 7*.

promulgate procedures for promptly resolving such claims in a fair and judicious manner by promulgating a statute, the proposed provisions of which have been discussed between the Governing Council and the CPA and are set forth in Appendix A.[27]

Section 2 Terms and Conditions

The authority delegated under Section 1 of this Regulation shall be subject to the following terms and conditions:

a) The Governing Council shall ensure that all procedures established for the IPCC are consistent with orders, regulations, and memoranda promulgated by the CPA.

b) Representatives of the CPA shall be given the opportunity to advise and assist in the claims resolution process.

c) The CPA shall oversee the distribution of all funds for claims resolution provided by the Development Fund for Iraq or by Coalition or other donor States.

d) In the event of a conflict between any promulgation by the Governing Council and any promulgation of the CPA, the promulgation of the CPA shall prevail.

e) The Administrator reserves the authority to alter the Statute creating the Iraq Property Claims Commission or any procedures developed for the IPCC, or to otherwise intervene in the claims resolution process, if required in the interests of justice.

Section 3 Rescission

CPA Regulation Number 4, Establishment of the Iraqi Property Reconciliation Facility, (CPA/REG/25 June 2003/04)[28] is hereby rescinded.

Section 4 Effective Date

This Regulation shall enter into force on the date of signature [14 January 2004].

Annex A – Iraqi Property Claims Commission

SECTION ONE Establishment

Article One

This statute hereby establishes the Iraqi Property Claims Commission (the 'IPCC'), which shall resolve real property claims in a fair and judicious manner. The IPCC shall encourage the voluntary resolution of claims.

SECTION TWO Organization

Article Two

The IPCC shall consist of the following structures established by the Governing Council:

1. An Appellate Division, composed of judges and established as a separate chamber of the Iraqi Court of Cassation;

[27] The Statute of the Iraq Property Claims Commission was amended and restated in CPA Regulation No 12 *[Doc 13]* which also promulgated Instructions for the Operation of the Iraq Property Claims Commission.

In December 2003, the IGC had already approved a 19-article 'Law Establishing the Supreme Body to Resolve Disputes Involving Real Property'. The Law was to enter into force on 31 December 2003. The Law contained in Art 14 detailed legal principles for the solution of conflicts of ownership. The text of the IGC Law in Arabic may be found at http://nahrain.com/d/law/030.html.

[28] See *Doc 4*.

2. Regional commissions established in each governorate in Iraq. The Appellate Division may establish more than one regional commission in a governorate.

Article Three

A. The Appellate Division of the IPCC shall be composed of five judges who have experience in adjudicating property disputes, may be retired or serving judges, and are to be appointed by the Council of Judges.

B. Each Regional Commission (the 'Regional Commission') shall be comprised of (i) a judge, appointed by the Council of Judges, who shall preside, as chairman; (ii) the Director of the Office of Property Registration in the Governorate, or a representative; and (iii) the Director of State Property of such Governorate, or a representative. The Regional Commission may also request the assistance of persons who are experts on the subject of the claim.

Article Four

A. Each Regional Commission and the Appellate Division shall have a secretariat to assist in its administration.

B. The Governing Council shall ensure that the IPCC has the necessary funds to employ a secretariat and that the Regional Commissions find an appropriate place to operate in the capital of the relevant Governorate.

SECTION THREE Procedures

Article Five

A. The IPCC shall prepare a specialized claim form for purposes of filing claims.

B. The process of adjudicating claims filed with the IPC shall commence with the claimant(s), or his representative filing a claim form. The Parties shall submit the claim to the Regional Commission where the property is located.

Article Six

A. After receipt of a properly completed form, the secretariat of the relevant Regional Commission shall serve notice of the claim on interested parties, be that a natural or juridical person, in accordance with the Guidelines and Instructions issued by the Governing Council.

B. Following receipt of notice of a claim, the Regional Commission shall open a claim file and record the claim in the intake register in the order received.

C. The secretariat shall verify the claim and authenticate the identity of the parties, prior to submitting the file to the Regional commission.

D. The Regional Commission is entitled to request the assistance of other governmental and non-governmental parties for purposes of valuation of interests and related matters.

E. The Regional Commission shall issue its decision with respect to the claim and the secretariat shall be responsible for notifying the parties of the Commission's decision.

Article Seven

A. An appeal of a decision of the Regional Commission must be filed with the Appellate Division within 30 days.

B. Orders issued by the Regional Commission shall be final and conclusive and can be implemented immediately, unless appealed within 30 days.

C. A decision of the Regional Commission will be enforceable when (i) a final decision by the Appellate Division is rendered or (ii) the requisite period for filing an appeal has passed.

D. The final order shall be issued to all relevant parties and the appropriate Office of Property Registration for enforcement.

E. If the property in question is occupied, possessed or used by the non-prevailing party, and such party has no other property, then the non-prevailing party shall be granted a reasonable period of time to evacuate the premises. The secretariat shall also inform the displaced person(s) of the availability of any services for assistance.

SECTION FOUR General Principles of Adjudication

Article Eight

The IPCC shall comply with the following principles when resolving property claims. The Governing Council shall issue more detailed provisions regarding the process in the Guidelines and Instructions.

A. Any properties that were confiscated or seized, or on which liens were placed by the former government (not in the ordinary course of commercial business), but with title remaining in the name of the original owner, shall be returned to the original owner.

B. Any properties that were confiscated or seized, the titles of which were transferred to the Government of Iraq or an instrumentality thereof, and that were not sold to a third party, shall be returned to the original owner.

C. Any properties confiscated by the government that were used as mosques, other places of worship, religious schools, charities or were associated with such uses, shall be returned to the appropriate *waqfs* (religious endowments) connected to such uses or to the appropriate holders of title to such properties prior to their confiscation.

D. After ensuring appropriate due process of law, any property the title to which is in the name of senior members of the Iraqi Ba'athist Government shall be returned to the rightful owners, if it is established that such properties were improperly acquired.

E. If a property was confiscated and subsequently sold to a buyer (the 'First Buyer'), and (i) title remains in the name of the First Buyer and (ii) no improvements were made to the property, then title to the property will be transferred back to the original owner and the First Buyer would not be entitled to compensation from the original owner.

F. If the property was an unimproved property (that is, a property not built upon) when confiscated or otherwise seized, and then subsequently sold to the First Buyer, and the First Buyer has improved the property by building upon it, then the original owner would be entitled to either (i) having title transferred to him, provided that he pays the First Buyer the value of the improvements on the date such improvements were made or (ii) being paid appropriate compensation for the property (as an unimproved property) on the date of the passing of this statute.

G. If the property was sold to the First Buyer, who subsequently acquired an adjoining property from the state, then title to both the original property and the adjoining property shall be transferred to the original owner, provided that such original owner pays the First Buyer the amount that such First Buyer paid for the adjoining property.

H. If the property has a building on it and then was sold to the First Buyer, who subsequently demolished the original building and built a new building on it, then the original owner of the property may (i) request that title be transferred to him, after paying for the new building (valued on the day it was built) less the value of the old demolished building (valued on the date of the passing of this statute), or (ii) may request that the First Buyer acquire the property, including the demolished building, valued on the date of the passing of this statute (less any amounts paid by the First Buyer to the Government).

I. If the property was subsequently sold by the First Buyer to other buyers, then the original owner could either (i) request that title be transferred to him or (ii) request compensation for the value of the property valued at the date of the passing of this statute. If the original owner chooses option (i) above, then the final buyer would be entitled to compensation for the value of the property valued at the date of passing of this law.

J. If the property was granted as a security interest for a loan to the First Buyer and therefore had a lien on it, then title to the property would be transferred back to the original owner free and clear of any liens and the lender would have a claim against the First Buyer.

K. If the property was unimproved and a building was built on it by the First Buyer, and a lien was placed on the property by a lender, then any amounts due to the First Buyer by the original owner (pursuant to paragraph F above) would be paid by the original owner to the lender to fully or partially satisfy the loan.

L. If the property was confiscated and sold in a public auction and was purchased by either the original owner or his heirs, then they will be entitled to compensation from the state in an amount equivalent to the purchase price.

M. Any other relevant situation shall be addressed consistent with these provisions.

SECTION FIVE Other Matters

Article Nine

This statute applies to claims arising between July 17, 1968 and April 9, 2003 involving immovable property, assets affixed to immovable property, easements, or servitudes that were: (i) confiscated or seized for reasons other than land reform; or (ii) expropriated for reasons other than lawfully used eminent domain, or as a result of opposition to the Ba'athist Government of Iraq, or as a result of ethnicity, religion, sect of the owners, or for purposes of ethnic cleansing; or (iii) acquired for less than appropriate value by the Ba'athist Government of Iraq; or (iv) property otherwise affected.

Article Ten

A. Newly introduced inhabitants of residential property in areas that were subject to the policy of ethnic cleansing (i) can be resettled; (ii) can receive compensation from the state; (iii) can receive new land from the state near their residence in the governorate from which they came; and (iv) can receive cost of moving to such area.

B. The ministry of Displacement and Migration shall be responsible for administering this policy.

Article Eleven

A. Claims must be filed by December 31, 2004. Any claims filed with the IPCC after such date will not be accepted.

B. Any claims with respect to properties within the jurisdiction of this Statute but filed subsequently to December 31, 2004 can be referred to the Iraqi Court system, which shall apply the principles included in this Statute. This provision is not available to any claimant who has already filed a claim with respect to the same property with the IPCC.

Article Twelve

Any provisions in resolutions or orders or laws contradicting this statute are hereby suspended.

Article Thirteen

All ministers are required to implement this law.

Article Fourteen
The Governing Council shall issue Guidelines and Instructions that will regulate the procedures to be followed by the IPCC.

Article Fifteen
The Governing Council means the Iraqi Governing Council established on July 13, 2003. The authority of the Governing Council for purposes of this Statute will transfer to the Successor Government.

Article Sixteen
Transfers of real property pursuant to this statute shall not be subject to income tax, a tax on a transfer of real property, or any other tax or stamp duty.

Article Seventeen
This Statute will become effective on January 15, 2004.

Document 10
Coalition Provisional Authority Regulation Number 9

CPA/REG/9 June 2004/09

Governing Council's Dissolution

Pursuant to my authority as Administrator of the Coalition Provisional Authority, and under the laws and usages of war, and consistent with relevant U.N. Security Council resolutions, including Resolutions 1483 and 1511,

Noting that the Governing Council has approved the Law of Administration for the State of Iraq for the Transitional Period (TAL) and its Annex[29] and charted a course to elections and a democratic future for Iraq, and

Recognizing that the Governing Council has completed its work on behalf of the Iraqi people,

I hereby promulgate the following:

Section 1 Dissolution of the Governing Council

1) The CPA acknowledges the actions taken by the Governing Council to dissolve itself on June 1, 2004 as part of the ongoing evolution in the structures of the interim Iraqi administration, as contemplated by Resolutions 1483 and 1511.

2) CPA Regulation No. 6, Governing Council of Iraq (CPA/REG/13 July 2003/6)[30] and CPA Memorandum No. 6, Implementation of Regulation on the Governing Council (CPA/MEM/03 September 2003/6),[31] are hereby rescinded.

Section 2 Entry into Force
This Regulation shall enter into force on the date of signature [9 June 2004].

[29] See *Docs 511* and *516*.
[30] See *Doc 6*.
[31] See *Doc 131*.

Document 11
Coalition Provisional Authority Regulation Number 10

CPA/REG/9 June 2004/10

Members of Designated Iraqi Interim Government

Pursuant to my authority as Administrator of the Coalition Provisional Authority, and under the laws and usages of war, and consistent with relevant U.N. Security Council resolutions, including Resolutions 1483 and 1511,

Recognizing that the Special Advisor to the Secretary General of the United Nations has conducted extensive consultations with Iraqis of all regions and backgrounds in an effort to identify the principal members of the Iraqi Interim Government,

Noting that the members of the designated Iraqi Interim Government were announced on June 1, 2004,

I hereby promulgate the following:

Section 1 Support for Members of Designated Iraqi Interim Government

1) The CPA acknowledges that the individuals designated as members of the Iraqi Interim Government listed at Appendix A will exercise authorities in their respective ministries effective June 1, 2004 until such time as the Iraqi Interim Government assumes full governance authority for Iraq.

2) The CPA and the members of the designated Iraqi Interim Government will consult and coordinate on matters involving the temporary governance of Iraq until such time as the Iraqi Interim Government assumes full governance authority for Iraq.

Section 2 Entry into Force

The Regulation shall enter into force on the date of signature [9 June 2004].

Appendix A

President	Shaykh Ghazi M. Ajil al-Yawar
Deputy President	Dr. Ebrahim al-Jafari
Deputy President	Dr. Rowsch Shaways
Prime Minister	Dr. Ayad Allawi
Deputy PM, Nat'l Security Affairs	Dr. Barham Salih
Ministry of Agriculture	Dr. Sawsan Ali Magid al-Sharifi
Ministry of Communication	Dr. Mohamed Ali Alhakim
Ministry of Construction and Housing	Dr. Omar al-Farouq Salim al-Damluji
Ministry of Culture	Mr. Mufid Muhammad Jawad al-Jaza'iri
Ministry of Defense	Mr. Hazim al-Sha'lan
Ministry of Displacement and Migration	Ms. Pascale Sorya Isho
Ministry of Education	Dr. Sami al-Mudhaffar
Ministry of Electricity	Dr. Aiham Alsammarae
Ministry of Environment	Ms. Mishkat Moumin
Ministry of Finance	Dr. Adil Abdul Mahdi
Ministry of Foreign Affairs	Mr Hishiyar Mahmud Muhammad al-Zibari

Ministry of Health	Dr. Ala'din Adbul Sahid Alwan
Ministry of Higher Education	Dr. Taher Khalaf Jabur al-Bakaa
Ministry of Human Rights	Dr. Bakhtiar Amin
Ministry of Industry & Minerals	Dr. Hajim M. Al-Hasani
Ministry of Interior	Mr. Falah H. Al-Nakib
Ministry of Justice	Dr. Malik Dohan al-Hassan
Ministry of Labour & Social Affairs	Ms. Leyla Abdul Laif
Ministry of Municipalities and Public Works	Mrs. Nesreen M. Siddeek Berware
Ministry of Oil	Mr. Thamir Abbas Ghadban
Ministry of Planning	Dr. Medhu Hafedh
Ministry of Science and Technology	Dr. Rashad M. Omar
Ministry of Trade	Mr Mohammed al-Jibouri
Ministry of Transportation	Mr. Louay Hatem Sultan al-Erris
Ministry of Water Resources	Dr. Latif Rashid
Ministry of Youth & Sports	Mr. Ali Fa'if al-Ghabban
Minister of State, Provincial Affairs	Judge Wael Abdulatif
Minister of State, Women's Affairs	Ms. Narim Othman
Minister of State	Dr. Kassim Daoud
Minister of State	Dr. Mamu Farham Othman Pirali
Minister of State	Mr. Adnan al-Janabi

Document 12
Coalition Provisional Authority Regulation Number 11

CPA/REG/15 June 2004/11

Amendments to Coalition Provisional Authority Regulations No. 2 (CPA/REG/10 June 2003/02) and No. 3 (CPA/REG/18 June 2003/03)[32]

Pursuant to my authority as Administrator of the Coalition Provisional Authority (CPA), and under the laws and usages of war, and consistent with relevant U.N. Security Council resolutions, including Resolutions 1483 and 1511 (2003) and 1546 (2004),

Noting that the Coalition Provisional Authority will dissolve on June 30, 2004 and that full governance authority of Iraq will transfer to the Iraqi Interim Government on that date,

Recognizing that on June 30, 2004 the Iraqi Interim Government will assume control over all funds in the Development Fund for Iraq,

Acknowledging that the Coalitional [sic] Provisional Authority has entered into contracts on behalf of the people of Iraq and that many of these contracts require continued performance and payment from the Development Fund for Iraq after June 30, 2004,

Understanding that continued performance and payments due under these contracts after June 30, 2004 are critical to the redevelopment and reconstruction of Iraq,

[32] It should be noted that the dates in the document symbols of the two regulations are those used on the copies signed by Ambassador Bremer and published on the CPA's website. The date and document symbols used in the *Official Gazette* are 'CPA/REG/15 June 2003/02' and 'CPA/REG/15 June 2003/03'.

Desiring to amend Coalition Provisional Authority Regulation No. 2, Development Fund for Iraq, (CPA/REG/10 June 2003/02),[33] and Coalition Provisional Authority Regulation No. 3, Program Review Board, (CPA/REG/18 June 2003/03),[34] to provide for the orderly transition of authority over the Development Fund for Iraq from the Coalition Provisional Authority to the Iraqi Interim Government,

I hereby promulgate the following:

Section 1 Transition of Authority over Development Fund for Iraq

1) Section 3 of CPA Regulation No. 2, Development Fund for Iraq, (CPA/REG/10 June 2003/02), is amended to read as follows:

A sub-account of the account entitled 'Central Bank of Iraq/Development Fund for Iraq' shall be created. The sub-account shall be entitled 'Central Bank of Iraq/Development Fund for Iraq/Transition' and (when established) shall contain funds equal to or in excess of the total amount of outstanding contractual liability against the Development Fund for Iraq arising out of contracts or grants funded by the Development Fund for Iraq that:

a) were entered into on or before June 30, 2004 by the Coalition Provisional Authority or the Multi-National Force-Iraq in accordance with United Nations Security Council Resolution 1483 and implementing regulations;

b) require the continued performance and/or payment of money originating from the DFI past June 30, 2004; and

c) are not the subject of a fully-funded letter of credit intended to otherwise ensure performance under the contract or grant.

On June 30, 2004, all responsibilities, duties, powers, and authorities granted to the Administrator and the Coalition Provisional Authority under this Regulation shall transfer to the Prime Minister of the Iraqi Interim Government and the Iraqi Interim Government, respectively.

2) Paragraph 1 of Section 5 of CPA Regulation No. 2, Development Fund for Iraq, (CPA/REG/10 June 2003/02), is amended and restated as follows:

1) General. The Central Bank of Iraq/Development Fund for Iraq account and the Central Bank of Iraq/Development Fund for Iraq/Transition sub-account in the Federal Reserve Bank shall be governed by the Federal Reserve Bank's standard terms and conditions regarding accounts of central banks and governments, to the extent consistent with applicable law.

3) Paragraph 5 of Section 5 of CPA Regulation No. 2, Development Fund for Iraq, (CPA/REG/10 June 2003/02), is amended and restated as follows:

5) Privileges and Immunities. The Fund, including the accounts and sub-accounts that comprise its corpus, and the Receipts Account, shall enjoy the privileges and immunities as set forth in paragraph 22 of Resolution 1483 and continued in paragraph 27 of Resolution 1546, as well as privileges and immunities to which the Fund may be entitled under any other law, regulation, order, or directive.

4) Section 8 of CPA Regulation No. 2, Development Fund for Iraq, (CPA/REG/10 June 2003/02), is amended and restated as follows:

Until the Fund is dissolved by the Coalition Provisional Authority (or, after the transfer of governmental authority, by the Interim Iraqi Government) in a manner consistent with Resolutions 1483 and 1546, the Central Bank of Iraq shall continue

[33] See *Doc 2*.
[34] See *Doc 3*.

to hold on its books the Fund. Also, as agreed between the Administrator and the Federal Reserve Bank (and/or other financial institution(s)), such institution(s) shall continue to maintain on its books the 'Central Bank of Iraq/Development Fund for Iraq' account and all sub-accounts, including a sub-account entitled 'Central Bank of Iraq/Development Fund for Iraq/Transition,' and shall continue to accept deposits into, make disbursements from, and otherwise operate the account and sub-account, in accordance with applicable laws, regulations, policies and agreements.

5) Section 10 of CPA Regulation No. 3, Program Review Board, (CPA/REG/18 June 2003/03), is amended and restated as follows:

The Board may prescribe such additional procedures as may be necessary to carry out its responsibilities under this Regulation. Such procedures shall be effective only upon approval by a majority of the Board's voting members.

Notwithstanding any provisions to the contrary set forth in this Regulation, the Board shall take reasonable steps to ensure that funding initiatives that require payment or performance beyond June 30, 2004 are backed by fully-funded letters of credit from the Trade Bank of Iraq.

Section 2 Entry and Force

This Regulation shall enter into force on the date of signature [18 June 2004].

Document 13

Coalition Provisional Authority Regulation Number 12

CPA/REG/23 June 2004/12

Iraq Property Claims Commission

Pursuant to my authority as Administrator of the Coalition Provisional Authority (CPA), and under the laws and usages of war, and consistent with relevant U.N. Security Council resolutions, including Resolutions 1483 and 1511 (2003) and 1546 (2004),

Noting that the Statute of the Establishment of the Iraq Property Claims Commission, which was promulgated pursuant to Coalition Provisional Authority Regulation 8, Delegation of Authority Regarding an Iraq Property Claims Commission, (CPA/REG/14 January 2004/8),[35] did not provide adequate mechanisms for the appointment, management, and operation of the Iraq Property Claims Commission,

Recognizing that the Statute of the Establishment of the Iraq Property Claims Commission requires amendment to ensure that the Iraq Property Claims Commission can function properly,

Acknowledging that an initial set of Instructions for Operation are needed to implement the Statute of the Establishment of the Iraq Property Claims Commission so that claimants, court officials, and administrators can understand better the claims process of the Iraq Property Claims Commission, and

Desiring to amend the Statute of the Establishment of the Iraq Property Claims Commission and to promulgate the Instructions for Operation of the Iraq Property Claims Commission,

[35] See *Doc 9*.

I hereby promulgate the following:

Section 1 Amended Iraq Property Claims Commission Statute
The Statute of the Establishment of the Iraq Property Claims Commission, which became effective on January 15, 2004 pursuant to Coalition Provisional Authority Regulation 8, Delegation of Authority Regarding an Iraq Property Claims Commission, (CPA/REG/14 January 2004/8), is hereby amended and restated in full in the form attached hereto as Annex A.

Section 2 Promulgation of Instructions for Operation
The Instructions for Operation of the Iraq Property Claims Commission which are attached hereto as Annex B shall implement the Statute of the Establishment of the Iraq Property Claims Commission and shall apply to all claims filed before the Iraq Property Claims Commission.

Section 3 Entry and Force
This Regulation shall enter into force on the date of signature [24 June 2004].

ANNEX A Establishment of the Iraq Property Claims Commission (As Amended and Restated)

SECTION ONE Establishment

Article One
This Statute hereby establishes the Iraq Property Claims Commission (the 'IPCC'), which shall resolve real property claims in a fair and judicious manner. The IPCC shall encourage the voluntary resolution of claims.

SECTION TWO Organization

Article Two
The IPCC shall consist of the following structures established by the Iraqi Interim Government:

A. An Appellate Division, composed of judges and established as a separate chamber of the Iraqi Court of Cassation;

B. Regional Commissions established in each governorate in Iraq, and a maximum of three regional commissions in the Kurdistan Regional Government area. The Appellate Division may then establish more than one Regional Commission in a governorate; and

C. A National Secretariat which shall be responsible for overseeing all operational and management activities of the IPCC.

Article Three

A. The Appellate Division of the IPCC shall be composed of five judges, one of whom shall be nominated by the judicial authority in the Kurdistan Regional Government, who have experience in adjudicating property disputes. They may be retired or serving judges and are to be appointed by the Council of Judges.

B. Each Regional Commission shall be composed of (i) a judge, appointed by the Council of Judges, who shall preside as chairman, (ii) the Director of the Office of Real

Estate Registry in the Governorate, or his representative, and (iii) the Director of State Property of such Governorate, or his representative. The Regional Commission may also request the assistance of persons who are experts on the subject of any claim.

C. The National Secretariat shall be composed of (i) a Head of the National Secretariat who shall serve as the highest official of the National Secretariat, (ii) operational managers, auditors, data managers, legal advisers, public relations personnel, and any other staff necessary to ensure the orderly functioning of the National Secretariat, (iii) Regional Secretariats situated in each Governorate with all necessary staff to ensure the IPCC's orderly functioning, including Regional Commission Clerk's offices, which shall provide operational and legal support as necessary to each Regional Commission, and (iv) an Appellate Secretariat with the necessary staff to ensure the Appellate Division's orderly functioning, including an Appellate Division Clerk's office which shall provide operational and legal support as necessary to the Appellate Division.

Article Four

The Iraqi Interim Government shall ensure that the IPCC has the necessary funds to discharge its administrative duties and that the Regional Commissions and Regional Secretariats are provided with appropriate premises from which to operate in the capital of the relevant Governorate or Kurdistan Regional Government area or at any such locations as shall be deemed expedient by the IPCC.

SECTION THREE Procedures

Article Five

A. The IPCC shall designate the form of documents for submission of claims and for administrative purposes.

B. The process of adjudicating claims filed with the IPCC shall commence with the claimant(s), or his representative filing a claim in the proper form at any IPCC office, including any properly designated IPCC office outside Iraq.

Article Six

A. Following receipt of a properly completed claim form, the Regional Secretariat shall open a claim file and record the claim in the intake register in the order received.

B. After receipt of a properly completed claim form, the relevant Regional Secretariat shall serve notice of the claim on any interested parties, including natural or juridical persons, in accordance with the Guidelines issued by the National Secretariat and Instructions for Operation approved (if before June 30, 2004) by the Administrator or (if after June 30, 2004) the Iraqi Interim Government.

C. The Regional Secretariat shall serve notice of the claim on the General Directorate of Real Estate Registration, and the General Directorate of Real Estate Registration shall cause the official title record to be endorsed with the date and reference number of the claim.

D. The Regional Secretariat shall verify the claim administratively, and authenticate the identity of the parties.

E. The Regional Commission Clerk's Office shall then review each claim file, and, prior to submitting the file to the Regional Commission, prepare for the Regional Commission a case report which summarizes the factual background of the case, the legal issues involved, the parties' arguments, and the Clerk's Office's recommendation, made by a legal advisor, as to how the case should be decided.

F. The Regional Commission may request the assistance of other governmental and non-governmental parties for purposes of valuation of interests and other related matters.

G. The Regional Commission shall issue its decision with respect to the claim, but the Regional Secretariat shall be responsible for notifying the claimants and any known interested parties of the Regional Commission's decision.

Article Seven

A. Any appeal of a decision of the Regional Commission must be filed within sixty days from the date of the decision.

B. Orders issued by the Regional Commission shall be final and binding unless appealed within sixty days.

C. A decision of the Regional Commission will not be enforceable until the requisite period for filing an appeal has passed and no appeal has been lodged.

D. A decision made by the Appellate Division is final and binding in respect of any IPCC related matter.

E. The final order of the Regional Commission or Appellate Division, as appropriate, shall be issued to all relevant parties and the appropriate competent authorities for enforcement.

F. If the property in question is occupied, possessed or used by the non-prevailing party, and such party has no other property, then the non-prevailing party would be granted a prescribed period of time to surrender possession of the premises. The Regional Secretariat shall also inform the displaced person(s) of the availability of any services for assistance.

SECTION FOUR General Principles

Article Eight

The IPCC shall comply with, but not be limited to, the application of the following examples when resolving real property claims:

A. Any properties that were confiscated or seized, or on which liens or other encumbrances were placed by the former governments of Iraq (not in the ordinary course of commercial business), but with title remaining in the name of the original owner shall be returned to the original owner, freed and discharged from any such liens or other encumbrances.

B. Any properties that were confiscated or seized and whose title was transferred to the former governments of Iraq, or an agent thereof, and which were not sold to a third party, shall be returned to the original owner.

C. Any properties confiscated by the former governments of Iraq that were used as mosques, other places of worship, religious schools, charities or were associated with such uses shall be returned to the appropriate *waqfs* (religious endowments) connected to such uses or to the appropriate holders of title to such properties prior to their confiscation.

D. Any properties whose title is in the name of senior members of the former governments of Iraq shall be returned to the rightful owners, if it is established that such properties were improperly acquired.

E. If a property was confiscated and subsequently sold to a buyer (the 'First Buyer'), and (i) title remains in the name of the First Buyer and (ii) no improvements were made to the property, then title to the property will be transferred back to the original owner, and the First Buyer would not be entitled to compensation from the original owner.

F. If the property was an unimproved property (that is, a property not built upon) when confiscated or otherwise seized, and then subsequently sold to the First Buyer, and the First

Buyer has improved the property by building upon it, then the original owner would be entitled to either (i) having title transferred to him, provided that he pays the First Buyer the value of the improvements or (ii) being paid appropriate compensation for the property (as an unimproved property).

G. If the property was sold to the First Buyer, who subsequently acquired an adjoining property from the state, then title to both the original property and the adjoining property shall be transferred to the original owner, provided that such original owner pay the First Buyer the amount that such First Buyer paid for the adjoining property.

H. If the property has a building on it and then was sold to the First Buyer, who subsequently demolished the original building and built a new building on it, then the original owner of the property may (i) request that title be transferred to him, after paying for the new building, less the value of the old demolished building, or (ii) may request that the First Buyer acquire the property, including the demolished building (less any amounts paid by the First Buyer to the former governments of Iraq).

I. If the property was subsequently sold by the First Buyer to other buyers, then the original owner could either (i) request that title be transferred to him, or (ii) request compensation for the value of the property. If the original owner chooses option (i) above, then the final buyer would be entitled to compensation for the value of the property.

J. If the property was charged as security to a lender for a loan to the First Buyer, then title to the property would be freed and discharged from any such charge, and the lender would then have a right of action against the First Buyer to recover any outstanding balance due under the loan.

K. If the property was unimproved and a building was built on it by the First Buyer, and the property was charged to a lender as security for a loan, then any amounts due to the First Buyer by the original owner (pursuant to Paragraph F above) would be paid by the original owner direct to the lender to fully or partially satisfy the loan.

L. If the property was confiscated and sold in a public auction and was purchased by either the original owner or his heirs, then they will be entitled to compensation from the state in an amount equivalent to the purchase price.

M. If the property is currently being used for a public or charitable purpose, the property shall continue to be used for that purpose, and the Government or current owner, user or possessor shall provide the original owner, user or possessor with compensation.

N. Any other relevant situation in line with these provisions.

SECTION FIVE Other Matters

Article Nine

This Statute governs claims:

A. (1) Arising between July 17, 1968 and April 9, 2003, inclusive;

(2) Involving immovable property, assets affixed to immovable property, easements or servitudes ('real property'), or an interest in real property;

(3) That was confiscated, seized, expropriated, forcibly acquired for less than full value, or otherwise taken, by the former governments of Iraq for reasons other than land reform or lawfully used eminent domain. Any taking that was due to the owner's or possessor's opposition to the former governments of Iraq, or their ethnicity, religion, or sect, or for purposes of ethnic cleansing, shall meet this standard; or

B. (1) Arising between March 18, 2003 and June 30, 2005, inclusive;
(2) Involving real property, or an interest in real property;
(3) That was confiscated, seized, expropriated, forcibly taken for less than full value, or otherwise acquired and/or reacquired:
i. as a result of the owner's or possessor's ethnicity, religion, or sect, or for purposes of ethnic cleansing, or;
ii. by individuals who had been previously dispossessed of their property as a result of the former Ba'athist governments' policy of property confiscation.

Article Ten

A. Newly introduced inhabitants of residential property in areas that were subject to ethnic cleansing by the former governments of Iraq prior to April 9, 2003 may be (i) resettled, (ii) may receive compensation from the state, (iii) may receive new property from the state near their residence in the governorate or area from which they came, or (iv) may receive compensation for the cost of moving to such area.

B. The Ministry of Displacement and Migration shall be responsible for administering this policy.

Article Eleven

A. Claims must be filed in the proper form and properly completed by June 30, 2005. Any claims filed with the IPCC after such date will not be accepted.

B. Any claims with respect to properties within the jurisdiction of this Statute but filed subsequently to June 30, 2005 may be referred to the Iraqi Courts, which shall apply the principles included in this Statute. This provision is not available to any claimant who has already filed a claim with respect to the same property with the IPCC.

C. The IPCC is to have exclusive jurisdiction over all claims involving immovable property, assets affixed to immovable property, easements or servitudes on property or land or other interests in real property brought in accordance with Articles 9A and 9B. Any such cases pending must be transferred by the relevant court to the jurisdiction of the IPCC.

Article Twelve

The terms of this Statute shall take precedence over any provisions in resolutions or orders or laws that are inconsistent.

Article Thirteen

The National Secretariat shall issue Guidelines which will set forth the procedures to be followed by the IPCC.

The National Secretariat may issue interpretative memoranda which set forth the manner in which it shall construe the Instructions for Operation.

Article Fourteen

The Iraqi Interim Government means the Government appointed on June 1, 2004, and assuming sovereignty on July 1, 2004. The authority of the Iraqi Interim Government for the purposes of this Statute will transfer to the successor governments of Iraq.

Article Fifteen

Transfers of real property pursuant to this Statute shall not be subject to income tax, a tax on a transfer of real property, or any other tax or duty.

Article Sixteen
This Statute will become effective on 1 July 2004.

ANNEX B Iraq Property Claims Commission

INSTRUCTIONS FOR OPERATION

SECTION ONE General Provisions

Article 1
These Instructions implement the Statute of the Establishment of the Iraq Property Claims Commission (As Amended and Restated) (the 'Statute') and apply to all claims filed before the Iraq Property Claims Commission (IPCC). Unless otherwise stated, references to Articles are Articles in these Instructions.

Article 2
Together with the Statute, these Instructions govern:

a. The composition of the IPCC;
b. The submission of claims before the IPCC;
c. The reception of claims by the IPCC;
d. The process for deciding claims;
e. The legal effectiveness of IPCC decisions.

SECTION TWO Composition of the IPCC

Article 3
In accordance with Article 2 and Article 3 of the Statute, the IPCC shall consist of a National Secretariat, an Appellate Division and one or more Regional Commissions in each governorate or Kurdistan Regional Government area.

National Secretariat

Article 4
a. A National Secretariat for property claims shall be established. The initial Head of the National Secretariat shall be appointed by the Administrator after consultation with the Iraqi Interim Government for a term of two years which may be renewed once at the discretion of the Prime Minister of Iraq. The initial Head of the National Secretariat shall then take action to manage the work of the National Secretariat by setting up an office, including but not limited to, the following staff:

i. Operational managers to oversee IPCC operations, to coordinate among the different branches of the IPCC, and, where appropriate, to issue user manuals and operating guidelines to direct certain functions of the IPCC;
ii. Auditors to inspect IPCC operations for fraud, waste or mismanagement;
iii. Data managers to enter into the national database of claims the information on forms submitted to the IPCC, and to review the national database for cases with similar and recurrent factual patterns;

iv. Legal advisers to ensure consistent application of IPCC rules, to oversee orders of compensation, and, where appropriate, to request that the Appellate Division issue an advisory opinion addressing an unresolved issue of law or fact;
v. Public relations personnel to advertise the existence of the IPCC, the location of IPCC offices, the rules of procedure of the IPCC, and other issues it deems appropriate;
vi. Appellate Division Secretariat and Regional Secretariats in accordance with Article 3(C) of the Statute and Article 8, Article 9, Article 16, and Article 17; and
vii. Any other staff necessary to ensure an orderly functioning of the National Secretariat in accordance with the responsibilities outlined in these Instructions.

b. All subsequent appointments to the office of Head of the National Secretariat shall be for four years, without term limits, and made in accordance with the following procedure: The Council of Judges shall recommend three candidates to be considered for appointment as Head of the National Secretariat. The Iraqi Interim Government or successor Government of Iraq shall then appoint one of these candidates as Head of the National Secretariat.

Article 5

The National Secretariat shall:

a. Ensure consistent implementation of, and compliance with, the Statute, these Instructions, any legal determinations made by the Appellate Division, and any IPCC Guidelines issued by the National Secretariat;

b. Audit IPCC offices;

c. Establish a national database of claims, and enter into that database the information received from the Regional Secretariats, IPCC offices or from persons living outside Iraq.

d. Review the national database for cases with similar and recurrent factual patterns and common legal issues, and notify the Regional Commissions or Appellate Division, as necessary, of such cases for coordinated treatment.

e. Coordinate among the different branches of the IPCC, and between the IPCC and the Ministry of Housing, the Ministry of Justice, the Council of Judges, the Ministry of Displacement and Migration, and the Ministry of Finance, and any other resource as necessary;

f. Issue user manuals and operating guidelines;

g. Manage IPCC public relations and communications;

h. Oversee orders of compensation and the implementation of orders requiring persons to surrender possession of their property;

i. Support the Appellate Division and Regional Commissions; and

j. Accomplish other tasks assigned to it herein or in future IPCC Instructions.

Appellate Division

Article 6

The Appellate Division shall be an independent review body within the IPCC located in Baghdad and established as a separate chamber of the Iraqi Court of Cassation. It shall hear appeals of decisions made by the Regional Commissions.

Article 7

a. In accordance with Article 3(A) of the Statute, the Appellate Division shall be comprised of five retired or serving judges who have experience in adjudicating property disputes, to be appointed by the Council of Judges. The judges of the Appellate Division shall represent a cross section of the Iraqi population. Each Judge shall have a deputy who must be approved by the Council of Judges.

b. To the extent that the Council of Judges appoints to the Appellate Division any serving judges, such judges shall be transferred to the IPCC to serve on a full-time basis.

c. Each judge of the Appellate Division shall act as Chief Judge in turn, in an order of appointment to be determined by the Council of Judges. Each appointment shall have a maximum duration of two years.

Article 8

In accordance with Article 3(C) of the Statute, an Appellate Division Secretariat shall be established for the Appellate Division to assist in the IPCC's administration. The Appellate Division Secretariat shall report to, and take guidance and instructions from, the National Secretariat. To establish the Appellate Division Secretariat, the National Secretariat shall appoint a Head of the Appellate Division Secretariat, who shall then take action to establish a support service for the Appellate Division by setting up an office, including but not limited to, the following staff:

a. Receptionists to ensure the orderly flow of people through the office, and to answer basic questions relating to the IPCC.

b. Persons tasked with notifying the Regional Commissions and Regional Secretariats of Appellate Division decisions, as required by these Instructions.

c. Persons trained in: (i) distributing and receiving claim, response and appeal forms, and (ii) entering such forms into a computer and sending the electronic data to the National Secretariat for data processing.

d. Docket managers to oversee case files and issue final orders.

e. Any other staff necessary to ensure the orderly functioning of the Appellate Secretariat, in accordance with the responsibilities outlined in these Instructions

Article 9

In accordance with Article 3(C) of the Statute, an Appellate Division Clerk's Office shall be established in the Appellate Division Secretariat and provide operational and legal support as necessary to the Appellate Division. The Appellate Division Clerk's Office shall report to, and take guidance and instructions from the Appellate Division Secretariat and (as necessary) the National Secretariat.

To establish the Appellate Division Clerk's Office, the Head of the Appellate Division Secretariat (in consultation with the Head of the National Secretariat) shall provide the Chief Judge of the Appellate Division with a list of ten candidates qualified to serve as the Head of the Appellate Division Clerk's Office. The Chief Judge of the Appellate Division (in consultation with all other Appellate Division Judges) shall then appoint one candidate from the list of ten candidates provided by the Appellate Division Secretariat as the Head of the Appellate Division Clerk's Office. The Head of the Appellate Division Clerk's Office shall then set up an office in the Appellate Division Secretariat which shall be composed of legal advisors who shall review case files and prepare for the Appellate Division a case report which summarizes:

(i) the factual background of the case;
(ii) the legal issues involved;
(iii) the parties' arguments; and
(iv) the Clerk's Office's recommendation, made by a legal adviser, as to how the case should be decided.

Article 10
In accordance with Article 2(B) of the Statute, the Appellate Division may determine that a governorate or Kurdistan Regional Government area would benefit from more than one Regional Commission, and, if it does, shall establish the territorial boundaries of each Regional Commission within a governorate or government area. The Appellate Division also may determine that a Regional Commission should operate in more than one governorate.

Article 11
Upon request of the National Secretariat or a Regional Commission, the Appellate Division may issue an advisory opinion on any unresolved question of law or common issue of fact to establish the rule to be applied uniformly to subsequent similar cases.

Article 12
The term of office of the judges of the Appellate Division shall expire after five years and may be renewed upon decision by the Council of Judges, except that the term of office shall terminate upon completion of all claims before the Appellate Division.

Article 13
The standards under which a judge of the Appellate Division shall disqualify himself or herself from considering a claim are the same as the standards under which a Regional Commissioner shall disqualify himself or herself. Where a judge of the Appellate Division is not available to consider a claim, whether because they disqualify themselves or otherwise, their deputy may sit on the Appellate Division and act with the full powers of the unavailable judge.

Regional Commissions

Article 14
a. In accordance with Article 2(B) of the Statute, each Regional Commission shall serve a different governorate or Kurdistan Regional Government area and shall be located in the capital city of the governorate or Kurdistan Regional Government area in which it serves, unless the Appellate Division otherwise determines in accordance with Article 10.
b. Notwithstanding Paragraph (a) of this Article, a Regional Commission may sit in any part of the territory over which it has jurisdiction if the Chairman of the Regional Commission or the National Secretariat determines, in their discretion, that the circumstances so warrant.

Article 15
In accordance with Article 3(B) of the Statute, each Regional Commission shall be comprised of (i) a judge appointed by the Council of Judges, who shall serve as the

Chairperson; (ii) the Director of the Office of Real Estate Registry in the Governorate in which the Commission sits, or their representative; and (iii) the Director of State Property of such Governorate, or their representative.

Article 16

In accordance with Article 3(C) of the Statute, a Regional Secretariat shall be established for each Regional Commission to assist in the IPCC's administration. The Regional Secretariat shall report to, and take guidance and instruction from, the National Secretariat. To establish the Regional Secretariat, the National Secretariat shall appoint a Head of the Regional Secretariat, who shall then take action to establish a support service for the Regional Commission by setting up any necessary offices, including but not limited to, the following staff:

a. Receptionists to ensure the orderly flow of people through the office, and to answer basic questions relating to the IPCC.

b. Persons tasked with notifying interested parties, as required by these Instructions.

c. Persons trained in: (i) distributing and receiving claim, response and appeal forms, and (ii) entering such forms into a computer and sending the electronic data to the National Secretariat for data processing.

d. Docket managers to oversee case files and issue final orders.

e. Mediators and staff to assist in the voluntary resolution of claims.

f. Any other staff necessary to ensure the orderly functioning of the Regional Secretariat, in accordance with the responsibilities outlined in these Instructions.

Article 17

In accordance with Article 3(C) of the Statute, a Regional Commission Clerk's Office shall be established in each Regional Secretariat and provide operational and legal support as necessary to the Regional Commission. The Regional Commission's Clerk's Office shall report to, and take guidance and instructions from the Regional Secretariat and (as necessary) the National Secretariat.

To establish the Regional Commission Clerk's Office, the Head of the Regional Secretariat shall provide the Chairperson of the Regional Commission with a list of ten candidates qualified to serve as Head of the Regional Commission Clerk's Office. The Chairperson of the Regional Commission (in consultation with all other members of the Regional Commission) shall then appoint one candidate from the list of ten candidates provided by the Head of the Regional Secretariat as the Head of the Regional Commission Clerk's Office. The Head of the Regional Commission Clerk's Office shall then set up an office in the Regional Secretariat which shall be composed of legal advisers who shall (in accordance with Article 6(E) of the Statute) review case files and prepare for the Regional Commission a case report which summarizes:

(i) the factual background of the case;
(ii) the legal issues involved;
(iii) the parties' arguments; and
(iv) the Clerk's Office's recommendation, made by a legal adviser, as to how the case should be decided.

Article 18

Members of a Regional Secretariat may be required by these Instructions, by the Chairperson of the appropriate Regional Commission or by the National Secretariat to travel to any part of the territory over which the Regional Commission has jurisdiction in order to facilitate the intake or processing of claims.

Article 19
The commissioners' term of office shall expire after three years and may be renewed upon decision by the relevant appointing authority, except that the term of office shall terminate upon completion of the Regional Commission's consideration of the claims before it.

Article 20
a. A Regional Commissioner shall disqualify himself or herself from considering any claim in which their impartiality might reasonably be questioned.

b. The impartiality of a Commissioner might reasonably be questioned, *inter alia*, if:
   i. The Commissioner is a relative of one of the parties;
   ii. The Commissioner or their spouse, child, parent, son-in-law or daughter-in-law has an ongoing dispute with one of the parties;
   iii. The Commissioner has been a legal advisor for one of the parties, business partner of any kind, held an interest in a company, or been a board member of a company in which one of the parties has a controlling interest;
   iv. The Commissioner or their relative has given advice or an opinion on the particular case before it reached the Regional Commission; or
   v. The Commissioner has any other interest (financial or otherwise) in the claim.

c. For the purposes of these Instructions, 'relative' is defined as 'a relation through parentage, marriage or adoption up to the fourth degree'.

d. Where a Commissioner is not available to consider a claim, whether because they disqualify themselves or otherwise, their position shall be filled by an ad hoc appointment by the appointing authorities, so that the appointing authority which appointed the disqualified Commissioner shall appoint the ad hoc replacement.

Submission and Reception of Claims

A) Information on claim submission

Article 21
The National Secretariat shall carry out national and international information programs, and Regional Secretariats shall carry out such programs within the territories of their respective Regional Commissions, to ensure that potential claimants receive notice of, and instructions on submitting a claim to the IPCC. Such programs shall employ notices to be published widely (i.e., both inside and outside Iraq, as appropriate, and via a number of different media) and repeatedly in order to reach all potential claimants.

B) Submission of claims

Article 22
Any person, natural or juridical, or their heirs, may submit a claim to the IPCC so long as the claim:

A. (1) Arose between July 17, 1968 and April 9, 2003, inclusive;

(2) Involves immovable property, assets affixed to immovable property, easements or servitudes ('real property'), or an interest in real property;

(3) That was confiscated, seized, expropriated, forcibly acquired for less than full value, or otherwise taken, by the former governments of Iraq for reasons other than land reform or lawfully used eminent domain. Any taking that was due to the owner's or possessor's opposition to the former governments of Iraq, or their ethnicity, religion, or sect, or for purposes of ethnic cleansing, shall meet this standard; or

B. (1) Arose between March 18, 2003 and June 30, 2005, inclusive;

(2) Involves real property, or an interest in real property;

(3) That was confiscated, seized, expropriated, forcibly taken for less than full value, or otherwise acquired and/or reacquired:

i. as a result of the owner's or possessor's ethnicity, religion, or sect, or for purposes of ethnic cleansing, or;

ii. by individuals who had been previously dispossessed of their property as a result of the former Ba'athist governments' policy of property confiscation.

For purposes of the IPCC's jurisdiction, actions or inactions attributable to the former governments of Iraq include, but are not limited to:

1. The actions or inactions of any State organ in Iraq, whether of the central government or of a territorial unit of the State, and whether the organ exercised legislative, executive, judicial or any other functions within the former governments;
2. The actions or inactions of a Ba'ath party member, or of a relative of a senior official of the Government or party, operating with apparent authority, or under color of authority, or with the implicit or explicit license of the former governments.

Claims for damages only are not within the jurisdiction of the IPCC.

Article 23

A claimant who brings a claim in bad faith and with knowledge that such claim is fraudulent will be deemed to commit a criminal offence under the Iraqi Penal Code.

Article 24

A claimant who, after issuance of these Instructions, willfully returns to currently occupied property and takes measures to force the current occupiers to vacate that property will be deemed to commit a criminal offence under the Iraqi Penal Code.

Article 25

a. Claims shall be submitted in person, in the prescribed form, at any IPCC office as required under Article 5 of the Statute.

b. Claims submitted by persons located outside Iraq will be governed by a separate set of Instructions.

c. Claims will be deemed to be filed once the claim has been accepted by the Regional Secretariat acting through any IPCC office and the applicant has been issued an acknowledgment bearing the claim reference number.

Article 26

Where security conditions or geographical conditions so warrant, the Regional Secretariat may dispatch a mobile team, consisting of members of the Regional Secretariat, to an area with a concentrated population of potential claimants, to facilitate the intake and processing of claims.

Article 27

a. Where a representative acts on behalf of a claimant, the representative must prove their representation. The IPCC shall prescribe the form of evidence of representation, and the signature of the claimant authorizing representation on that form shall be considered sufficient evidence of representation unless there is reason to believe that such signature was wrongfully obtained.

b. Where property rights are communally held, and the person in whose name the property is registered cannot be found, other members of the community may file a claim on behalf of the entire community if such members offer proof of the registered person's absence and proof of membership in the community.

Article 28

The claimant, or their representative, shall attach to the claim form any available evidence, including any testimonial evidence, proving their rights to the claimed property.

a. Written testimony shall be sworn and notarized, in accordance with Iraqi law.

b. For documentary evidence, the claimant, or their representative, shall submit a certified copy. Wherever possible, the IPCC shall review and certify, as true and correct, any original documents pertaining to the claim, but the IPCC will not accept custody of any original documents.

Article 29

The claimant, or their representative, may withdraw the claim or part of the claim at any time until a decision is issued.

a. A withdrawal shall be explicit, in the prescribed form, signed by the claimant and filed in the manner specified for claims in Article 25.

b. Upon receipt of notification of a withdrawal, the Regional Commission may accept the withdrawal, with or without prejudice, and the Regional Secretariat shall record in the national database that the claim has been withdrawn.

C) Processing of Claims (in-country claimants)

Article 30

Upon receipt of a claim in the proper form, the Regional Secretariat shall review the form in the claimant's presence, or in the presence of their representative, to ensure that all obligatory information is provided. Where the claim form is missing obligatory information, the Regional Secretariat shall advise the claimant, or their representative, of what must be done to provide the missing information and shall return the claim form to the claimant, or to their representative, without processing it.

Article 31

Once the Regional Secretariat has reviewed the claim form and advised the claimant, or their representative, of any missing obligatory information, it is the responsibility of the claimant to complete the form within the filing period. The claim will not be accepted for processing by the Commission until all obligatory information is provided.

Article 32

Immediately upon receipt of a properly completed claim form, and, in the claimant's presence, or in the presence of their representative, the Regional Secretariat shall:

a. Assign the claim a unique claim number;

b. Affix a pre-printed label with the unique claim number to the claim form;

c. Provide the claimant with confirmation of receipt in the prescribed form showing the unique claim number for future reference.

Article 33

After assigning a unique claim number to the claim, the Regional Secretariat shall serve notice of the claim on all identifiable interested parties, in accordance with Article 6(B) of the Statute.

a. The Regional Secretariat shall serve notice of the claim on interested parties by:

   i. Physically posting notice for a minimum of one month on the subject property, at the office of the Regional Commission and in any local or electronic venues that may attract an interested party's attention; and

   ii. Communicating the notice in writing to any identifiable interested parties, unless impracticable.

b. Upon serving or posting notice (whichever is later), the Regional Secretariat shall record the date of notice.

c. The notice shall provide sufficient details to enable any interested party to file a response to the claim. Further information relating to the claim may be provided by the Regional Commission, if the Head of the Regional Secretariat determines that such information is necessary for the proper filing of a response.

Article 34

The Regional Secretariat shall identify interested parties by reviewing the national database for any other claims relating to the subject property, searching the appropriate property registry for current and previous owners, identifying any current users or occupiers of the property, and taking any other steps it deems appropriate.

Article 35

Absent good cause, interested parties shall have forty five days from the date on which notice is served or posted (whichever is later) to submit a response to the claim. A response shall be submitted in the prescribed form and shall be submitted in the manner specified for a claim form in Article 25.

Article 36

For any form received by the Regional Secretariat, the Regional Secretariat shall enter the data from the form into the computer, and transmit the electronic version of the form data to the National Secretariat for data processing. The Regional Secretariat shall also send the original version of the form to the National Secretariat for filing in the national repository.

Article 37

Upon receiving the data from the Regional Secretariat, the National Secretariat shall transfer that data into the national database. Upon receiving the original paper copy, the National Secretariat shall file it at a national repository.

D) Processing of Claims (of out-of-country claimants)

Article 38
The National Secretariat shall process the claims of out-of-country claimants in the same way that the Regional Secretariats process the claims of in-country claimants, except as provided herein or in future IPCC Instructions.

Article 39
The appropriate Regional Secretariat remains responsible for notifying all identifiable interested parties of a claim, and the Regional Commission with jurisdiction over the area in which the property is located shall decide the claim.

Process for Deciding Claims

Article 40
The Regional Secretariat or the National Secretariat may, at any time, consolidate claims that arise out of the same sequence of events or that are otherwise intertwined, in the interest of expediting the resolution of all claims.

A) Principles

Article 41
The IPCC shall comply with, but not be limited to, the application of principles set forth in Article 8 of the Statute.

B) Settlement

Article 42
The Regional Secretariat shall encourage the voluntary resolution of claims, and may arrange mediation or otherwise facilitate the amicable settlement of issues among the claimant(s) and any identifiable interested parties. The National Secretariat will provide guidance on the procedures to be followed.

Article 43
Where all parties resolve a claim voluntarily, the claim shall be removed from the Regional Commission's docket in one of the following ways:

a. The claimant may withdraw their claim, pursuant to Article 29; or

b. The parties may notify, in the prescribed form, the Regional Secretariat of the settlement.

c. Where the parties notify the Regional Secretariat of the settlement under Paragraph (b) above, the Regional Secretariat shall convey that form to the Regional Commission. The Regional Commission shall then approve or, in extraordinary circumstances, disapprove the terms of voluntary resolution.

Article 44
Where the Regional Commission approves the terms of voluntary resolution, such approval shall be final and binding between the parties to that resolution, not subject to appeal, and of the same force and effect as a Final Order.

a. If the settlement is not submitted to the Commission because the claim is withdrawn by the claimant, or the Commission disapproves the settlement, the voluntary resolution will have only the legal effect that it would have had under Iraqi law in the absence of the Statute and these Instructions.

b. Where the Commission disapproves the terms of settlement, the claim shall be adjudicated in accordance with these Instructions, unless the claimant chooses to withdraw the claim.

C) Adjudication

Article 45

Where the parties do not pursue amicable settlement or fail to resolve the claim voluntarily, the Regional Commission Clerk's Office shall review the case file and prepare for the Regional Commission a case report which summarizes:

(i) the factual background of the case;
(ii) the legal issues involved;
(iii) the parties' arguments; and
(iv) the Clerk's Office's recommendation, made by a legal adviser, as to how the case should be decided.

Article 46

If, in analyzing the evidence, the Regional Secretariat determines that the evidence submitted is insufficient or of doubtful reliability, the Regional Secretariat may initiate evidence collection and/or verification procedures.

Article 47

Upon receiving the case file and the case report from the Regional Secretariat, the Regional Commission may, in its discretion, hold a hearing to develop the factual record.

Article 48

a. In accordance with Article 6(F) of the Statute, the Regional Commission may request the assistance of other governmental and non-governmental parties for purposes of valuation of interests and other matters relating to the issues in dispute.

b. Where the Regional Commission requests the assistance of other governmental parties, such parties shall provide the requested assistance.

Article 49

The Regional Commission shall decide the claim and the appropriate remedy by majority vote with three members present.

Article 50

In making a decision, the Regional Commission shall look to the previous decisions of other regional commissions for guidance and shall accept the previous decisions of the Appellate Division as conclusive on any resolved issue of law or fact.

Article 51

The Regional Commission shall issue a decision that:

a. identifies the parties' names;
b. identifies the property at issue;
c. determines the parties' respective rights to the subject property, including ownership rights, rights of possession, and rights of use;
d. provides the legal basis for that determination;
e. sets forth such legal remedy as the Regional Commission deems appropriate; and
f. if applicable, identifies for the parties the availability of any governmental services or assistance.

Article 52
In accordance with Article 6(G) of the Statute, the Regional Secretariat shall notify the parties, or their representatives, of the Commission's decision by delivering to them a copy of that decision, if such delivery is practicable, and by posting notice of the decision both at the office of the Regional Commission and in any local or electronic venues that may attract the parties' attention.

Article 53
Decisions of the Regional Commissions shall be final and binding on the parties, unless appealed within sixty days from the date of decision, except that the Commissions may correct any clerical or technical errors in any earlier decisions.

D) Appeals

Article 54
Any party may appeal a decision of a Regional Commission on the grounds of new evidence or manifest error.

Article 55
To appeal a decision of the Regional Commission, a party shall file, within sixty days from the date of the Regional Commission's decision, an appeal in the prescribed form. Such form shall be filed in the manner specified for claims in Article 25.

Article 56
Upon receipt of an appeal, the Regional Secretariat shall:
a. Stay issuance of a Final Order; and
b. Enter the form into a computer and send the electronic version of it to the National Secretariat for data processing.
c. Forward the appeal form and the case file to the Appellate Division Secretariat.

Article 57
The Appellate Division Secretariat shall:
a. Notify the Regional Secretariat of its receipt of the Appeal;
b. Review the case file and the decision being appealed;
c. Transfer the case file and the decision being appealed to the Appellate Division Clerk's Office who shall prepare for the Appellate Division a case report setting forth:
(i) the decision below;
(ii) the ground for appeal;

(iii) a summary of the parties' arguments; and
(iv) the Appellate Division Clerk's Office's recommendation, made by a legal adviser, as to whether to consider the appeal and how to resolve it.

Article 58
All decisions by the Appellate Division shall be made by a majority vote and with five members present. In the event that a Judge is unavailable, their deputy may sit on the Appellate Division and act with the full powers of the unavailable judge.

Article 59
The Appellate Division may not reconsider its decision, but it may correct any clerical or technical errors of any earlier decision.

Article 60
The Appellate Division Secretariat shall notify the appropriate Regional Commission and Regional Secretariat of the Appellate Division's decision. The Regional Secretariats shall be responsible for notifying the parties, or their representatives, of the Appellate Division's decision in accordance with the provisions of Article 52.

Legal Effectiveness of IPCC Decisions

Article 61
Upon issuance of a decision by the Appellate Division, or, where no appeal is made, fifteen days after expiration of the sixty day period for appeal, the Regional Secretariat shall issue to the parties and to the appropriate Office of Property Registration a Final Order confirming that the decision is final and binding. The Final Order shall identify the name(s) of the rights holders, the subject property, and the remedy, if applicable. In addition, each Final Order shall have a unique serial number and shall be verified with an official stamp.

Article 62
In accordance with Article 7(E) of the Statute, Final Orders are directly enforceable by the competent authorities of the district where the subject property is located.

Article 63
Final Orders may be reopened only if a person:
a. Files a claim or response before the IPCC within the filing period;
b. Has a claim to the subject property under Article 22; and
c. Demonstrates that they did not know, and could not reasonably be expected to know, of the previous claim with respect to that property.

Article 64
In accordance with Article 7(F) of the Statute, Final Orders requiring the current occupants to surrender possession of the property may be enforced after sixty days if the occupants do not vacate the premises voluntarily. All other Final Orders may be implemented immediately.

Article 65
Where a Final Order results in a previous occupier, possessor or user of property surrendering possession of the premises, the Regional Secretariat shall inform that person of any services available for assistance, and of any policy of the Ministry of Displacement and Migration to resettle or compensate such persons, in accordance with Article 7(F) and Article 10(B) of the Statute.

Article 66
These Instructions may be revised or supplemented by the Iraqi Interim Government. Additional details regarding the claims process may also be found in Guidelines, interpretative memoranda, and literature prepared by the National Secretariat.

Article 67
The National Secretariat may issue interpretative memoranda which set forth the manner in which it shall construe the Instructions.

2. Orders and Implementing Acts

Document 14
Coalition Provisional Authority Order Number 1
CPA/ORD/16 May 2003/01

De-Ba'athification of Iraqi Society

Pursuant to my authority as Administrator of the Coalition Provisional Authority (CPA), relevant U.N. Security Council resolutions, and the laws and usages of war,

Recognizing that the Iraqi people have suffered large scale human rights abuses and deprivations over many years at the hands of the Ba'ath Party,

Noting the grave concern of Iraqi society regarding the threat posed by the continuation of Ba'ath Party networks and personnel in the administration of Iraq, and the intimidation of the people of Iraq by Ba'ath Party officials,

Concerned by the continuing threat to the security of the Coalition Forces posed by the Iraqi Ba'ath Party,

I hereby promulgate the following:

Section 1 Disestablishment of the Ba'ath Party

1) On April 16, 2003 the Coalition Provisional Authority disestablished the Ba'ath Party of Iraq. This order implements the declaration by eliminating the party's structures and removing its leadership from positions of authority and responsibility in Iraqi society. By this means, the Coalition Provisional Authority will ensure that representative government in Iraq is not threatened by Ba'athist elements returning to power ant that those in positions of authority in the future are acceptable to the people of Iraq.

2) Full members of the Ba'ath Party holding the ranks of 'Udw Qutriyya' (Regional Command Member), 'Udw Far' (Branch Member). 'Udw Shu'bah' (Section Member), and 'Udw Firqah' (Group Member) (together, 'Senior Party Members') are hereby removed from their positions and banned from future employment in the public sector. These Senior Party Members shall be evaluated for criminal conduct or threat to the security of the Coalition. Those suspected of criminal conduct shall be investigated and, if deemed a threat to security or a flight risk, detained or placed under house arrest.

3) Individuals holding positions in the top three layers of management in every national government ministry, affiliated corporations and other government institutions (e.g., universities and hospitals) shall be interviewed for possible affiliation with the Ba'ath Party, and subject to investigation for criminal conduct and risk to security. Any such persons detained [sic] to be full members of the Ba'ath Party shall be removed from their employment. This includes those holding the more junior ranks of 'Udw (Member) and 'Udw 'Amil (Active Member), as well as those determined to be Senior Party Members.

4) Displays in government buildings or public spaces of the image or likeness of Saddam Hussein or other readily identifiable members of the former regime or of symbols of the Baath Party or the former regime are hereby prohibited.

5) Rewards shall be made available for information leading to the capture of senior members of the Baath party and individuals complicit in the crimes of the former regime.

6) The Administrator of the Coalition Provisional Authority or his designees may grant exceptions to the above guidance on a case-by-case basis.[1]

Section 2 Entry into Force
This Order shall enter into force on the date of signature [16 May 2003].[2]

Document 15
Coalition Provisional Authority Order Number 2
CPA/ORD/23 May 2003/02[3]

Dissolution of Entities

Pursuant to my authority as Administrator of the Coalition Provisional Authority (CPA), relevant U.N. Security Council resolutions, including Resolution 1483 (2003), and the laws and usages of war,

Reconfirming all of the provisions of General Franks' Freedom Message to the Iraqi People of April 16, 2003,[4]

Recognizing that the prior Iraqi regime used certain government entities to oppress the Iraqi people and as instruments of torture, repression and corruption,

Reaffirming the Instructions to the Citizens of Iraq regarding Ministry of Youth and Sport of May 8, 2003,

I hereby promulgate the following:

[1] Sec 1(6) was rescinded by CPA Order No 100, sec 3(1) *[Doc 124]*.

[2] CPA Fact Sheet No. 5 on 'De-Ba'athification', issued on 29 April 2004:

'• The Ba'ath Party poisoned Iraqi political life and was one of the most brutal instruments of Saddam's tyranny. There is no room in the new Iraq for Ba'athist ideology nor for Ba'athist criminals.

• Banning the party and removing from public life those who used it to commit crimes was necessary and remains necessary if we are to build a democratic Iraq.

• De-Ba'athification was and remains the right policy for Iraq.

• But many Iraqis have complained that de-Ba'athification procedures have been applied unevenly and sometimes unfairly, particularly in the education sector where the requirement for teacher and professors to join the party was strongly enforced. The result was that many teachers who were Ba'ath Party members in name only were dismissed from their jobs.

• Therefore, in coordination with the Minister of Education, the Minister of Higher Education, and the Chairman of the Supreme National De-Ba'athification Commission, we are taking steps to ensure that the policy is implemented fairly and efficiently.

• De-Ba'athification Review Committees were established last year to review the thousands of appeals from former firqah-level Ba'athists who were dismissed from the jobs but, under the de-Ba'athification procedures, have a right to apply for reinstatement.

• The decisions made by local de-Ba'athification appeals committees of the Ministry of Education will be effective immediately.

• This will allow thousands of teachers to return to work.

• Thousands more will begin receiving pensions this week.

• Those primary and secondary school teachers formerly of the rank of firqah members whose appeals have not yet been heard will have their appeal adjudicated within 20 days.

• The National De-Ba'athification Commission will handle the cases of hundreds of university professors with the same urgency. Professors who did not use their posts to intimidate others or commit crimes should be allowed to return to work promptly.'

[3] For a draft of present Order, dated 20 May 2003, see Tab A of *Doc 182*.

[4] See *Doc 169*.

Section 1 Dissolved Entities
The entities (the 'Dissolved Entities') listed in the attached Annex are hereby dissolved. Additional entities may be added to this list in the future.

Section 2 Assets and Financial Obligations
1) All assets, including records and data, in whatever from maintained and wherever located, of the Dissolved Entities shall be held by the Administrator of the CPA ('the Administrator') on behalf of and for the benefit of the Iraqi people and shall be used to assist the Iraqi people and to support the recovery of Iraq.

2) All financial obligations of the Dissolved Entities are suspended. The Administrator of the CPA will establish procedures whereby persons claiming to be the beneficiaries of such obligations may apply for payment.

3) Persons in possession of assets of the Dissolved Entities shall preserve those assets, promptly inform local Coalition authorities, and immediately turn them over, as directed by those authorities. Continued possession, transfer, sale, use, conversion, or concealment of such assets following the date of this Order is prohibited and may be punished.[5]

Section 3 Employees and Service Members
1) Any military or other rank, title, or status granted to a former employee or functionary of a Dissolved Entity by the former Regime is hereby cancelled.

2) All conscripts are released from their service obligations. Conscriptions is suspended indefinitely, subject to decisions by future Iraq governments concerning whether a free Iraq should have conscription.

3) Any person employed by a Dissolved Entity in any form or capacity, is dismissed effective as of April 16, 2003. Any person employed by a Dissolved Entity, in any from or capacity remains accountable for acts committed during such employment.

4) A termination payment in an amount to be determined by the Administrator will be paid to employees so dismissed, except those who are Senior Party Members as defined in the Administrator's May 16, 2003 Order of the Coalition Provisional Authority De-Ba'athification of Iraqi Society, CPA/ORD/2003/01 ('Senior Party Members') (See Section 3.6).

5) Pensions being paid by, or on account of service to, a Dissolved Entity before April 16, 2003 will continue to be paid, including to war widows and disabled veterans, provided that no pension payments will be made to any person who is a Senior Party Member (see Section 3.6) and that the power is reserved to the Administrator and to future Iraqi governments to revoke or reduce pensions as a penalty for past or future illegal conduct or to modify pension arrangements to eliminate improper privileges granted by the Ba'athist regime or for similar reasons.

6) Notwithstanding any provision of this Order, or any other Order, law, or regulation, and consistent with the Administrator's May 16, 2003 Order of the Coalition Provisional Authority De-Ba'athification of Iraqi Society, CPA/ORD/2003/01, no payment, including a termination or pension payment, will be made to any person who is or was a Senior Party Member. Any person holding the rank under the former regime of Colonel or above, or its equivalent, will be deemed a Senior Party Member, provided that such persons may seek, under procedures to be prescribed, to establish to the satisfaction of the Administrator, that they were not a Senior Party Member.

[5] Sec 2(3) was amended by CPA Order No 100, sec 3(2)(a) and (b) *[Doc 124]*.

Section 4 Information
The Administrator shall prescribe procedures for offering rewards to persons who provide information leading to the recovery of assets of Dissolved Entities.

Section 5 New Iraqi Corps
The CPA plans to create in the near future a New Iraqi Corps, as the first step in forming a national self-defense capability for a free Iraq. Under civilian control, that Corps will be professional, non-political, militarily effective, and representative of all Iraqis. The CPA will promulgate procedures for participation in the New Iraqi Corps.[6]

Section 6 Other Matters
1) The Administrator may delegate his powers and responsibilities with respect to this Order as he determines appropriate. References to the Administrator herein include such delegates.
2) The Administrator may grant exceptions any limitations [sic] in this Order at his discretion.[7]

Section 7 Entry into Force
This Order shall enter into force on the date of signature [23 May 2003].

ANNEX

Institutions dissolved by the Order referenced (the 'Dissolved Entities') are:
- The Ministry of Defence
- The Ministry of Information
- The Ministry of State for Military Affairs
- The Iraqi Intelligence Service
- The National Security Bureau
- The Directorate of National Security (Amn al-'Am)
- The Special Security Organization

All entities affiliated with or comprising Saddam Hussein's bodyguards to include:
- Murafaqin (Companions)
- Himaya al Khasa (Special Guard)

The following military organizations:
- The Army, Air Force, Navy, the Air Defence Force, and other regular military services
- The Republican Guard
- The Special Republican Guard
- The Directorate of Military Intelligence[8]
- The Al Quds Force
- Emergency Forces (Quwat al Tawari)

[6] Sec 5 was rescinded by CPA Order No 100, sec 3(2)(c) *[Doc 124]*.
[7] Sec 6(2) was rescinded by CPA Order No 100, sec 3(2)(d) *[Doc 124]*.
[8] The Directorate of Military Intelligence had not been listed in the draft of the present Order, dated 20 May 2003; see Tab A of *Doc 182*.

The following paramilitaries:
- Saddam Fedayeen
- Ba'ath Party Militia
- Friends of Saddam
- Saddam's Lion Cubs (Ashbal Saddam)

Other Organizations:
- The Presidential Diwan
- The Presidential Secretariat
- The Revolutionary Command Council
- The National Assembly
- The Youth Organization (al-Futuwah)
- National Olympic Committee
- Revolutionary, Special and National Security Courts[9]

All organizations subordinate to the Dissolved Entities are also dissolved. Additional organizations may be added to this list in the future.[10]

[9] The last two organizations had not been listed in the draft of the present Order, dated 20 May 2003; see Tab A of *Doc 182*.

[10] A draft of this Order, dated 10 May 2003, reads as follows: 'By Order of the Administrator of the Coalition Provisional Authority:

The following institutions (the 'Dissolved Institutions') are hereby dissolved: The Ba'ath Party, The Ministry of Defence, The Ministry of Military Industrialization, The Ministry of Information, The Ministry of Interior, The Ministry of State for Military Affairs, The Iraqi Intelligence Service, The National Security Bureau, The Directorate of General Security (Amn al-Aam), The Directorate of Military Intelligence (Leti Khbarat), The Special Security Organization

All entitles affiliated with or comprising Saddam Hussein's bodyguards. To include: Muraeiqin (Companions), Himaya al Khasa (Special Guard), Himaya al Khasa (Special Guards)

The following military organizations: The Republican Guard, The Special Republican Guard, The Organization of Military Industrialization, The Al Quos Force, Emergency Forces (Quwal al Tawari)

The following paramilitaries: Saddam Fedayeen, Ba'ath Party Militia, Friends of Saddam, Saddam's Lion Cubs (Ashbal Saddam)

Other Organizations: The Presidential Diwan, The Presidential Secretariat, The Revolutionary Command Council, The National Assembly, The Youth Organization (at-Futuwwah)

And all entities and organizations subordinate to the Dissolved Institutions.

Additional entities and institutions may be added to this list in the future.

All assets, including records and data in whatever form maintained, wherever located, of the Dissolved Institutions are the property of the Administrator of the Coalition Provisional Authority as Receiver and Trustee. Those assets will be used for the benefit of the Iraqi people by the Administrator of the Coalition Provisional Authority and transitional interim authorities as they from time to time exist, pending the establishment of full representative self-government by Iraqis of Iraq. In appropriate cases such assets may be transferred to civilian agencies or privatized.

The Administrator of the Coalition Provisional Authority may delegate his powers and responsibilities as Receiver and Trustee to such person or persons, or entity or entities, as he determines appropriate.

All employees of the Dissolved Institutions are dismissed effective April 16,2003.

All persons employed, in any capacity or in any form, by the Dissolved Institutions remain subject to the penalties for acts committed during their tenure as such.

All military or other ranks granted to employees and functionaries of the Dissolved Institutions by the former Regime are hereby cancelled.

All obligations of the Dissolved Institutions, including those regarding pensions and other compensation for employees or former employees, including those who were in retired status on April 16, 2003, are suspended. Procedures will be established whereby persons claiming to be the beneficiaries of such obligations may apply for lifting the suspension.

Persons in possession of the assets of the Dissolved Institutions shall preserve those assets, promptly inform the Receiver and Trustee, through the local Coalition military or civilian authorities, of the assets in their possession, and immediately turn the assets over to the Receiver and Trustee, as directed by the local Coalition authorities.

Document 16
Coalition Provisional Authority Order Number 3
CPA/ORD/23 May 2003/03

Weapons Control

Pursuant to my authority as Administrator of the Coalition Provisional Authority (CPA), relevant U.N. Security Council resolutions, including Resolution 1483 (2003), and the laws and usages of war,

Recognizing that weapons control is necessary in order to ensure a secure environment for the people of Iraq and to promote public order and safety,

I hereby promulgate the following:

Section 1 Definitions

1) 'Heavy Weapons' are weapons firing ammunition larger than 7.62 MM, machine guns or crew-served weapons, anti-tank weapons (such as rocket-propelled grenades (RPGs)), anti-aircraft weapons (such as shoulder fired missiles and AA guns), indirect fire weapons (mortars and artillery pieces), armored vehicles or self-propelled weapons, high explosives and explosive devices (including mines and hand grenades).

2) 'Small Arms' includes rifles that fire up to 7.62 MM ammunition, shotguns, and pistols.

3) 'Weapons' includes Heavy Weapons and Small Weapons.

4) 'Coalition Forces' includes any and all personnel, including contractors, from Coalition Member States under the command or direction of the Coalition Provisional Authority or the Coalition Force Commander.

Section 2 Prohibition on Heavy Weapons

1) Other than as provided for in Section 2.2, no person shall possess, carry, conceal, hide, bury, trade, sell, barter, give or exchange heavy weapons.

2) Iraqi police, security and military forces in uniform under the supervision of Coalition Forces may possess heavy weapons, but only to the extent necessary to perform their duties and only those weapons that have been expressly permitted. Coalition Forces may possess weapons at any time.

Section 3 Control of Small Arms

1) Other than as provided for in Section 3.2, no person shall possess a small arm in a public place.

After the date of this Order, continued possession, or attempts to transfer or to conceal such assets of whatever character, will be subject to arrest and punishment.

Persons who provide information to the Coalition authorities relating to the Dissolved Institutions, or their assets or personnel, shall be suitably compensated as the Receiver and Trustee may determine.

The Administrator of the Coalition Provisional Authority plans to create in the near future a New Iraqi Corps, as the first step in the process of forming a national self-defense capability for a free Iraq. That Corps will be under civilian control, professional, non-political, militarily effective, and representative of all Iraqis. Former employees wishing to be considered tor employment by the Receiver and Trustee will be informed of procedures for application.

All provisions of General Franks' Freedom Message to the Iraqi People of 16 April 2003 are reconfirmed and remain in effect.'

2) Subject to Section 4.4, the following individuals are authorized to carry small arms openly in public places:

a) Coalition Forces,

b) Iraqi police and military forces on duty, in uniform and under the supervision of Coalition Forces, and

c) groups assisting the Coalition Forces who remain under the supervision of Coalition Forces, and individuals who have been authorized to carry weapons by the Coalition Forces.

3) Small arms may be possessed in a person's home or place of business. Small arms may not be possessed in a school, hospital or holy site except by individuals duly authorized by Coalition Forces.

Section 4 General Prohibitions

1) All weapons or arms markets are prohibited.

2) Other than for purposes of official duties or in self-defense, firing of weapons within city limits, to include celebratory firing, is prohibited.

3) No persons under the age of 18 are permitted to possess, carry, conceal, trade, sell, barter, give or exchange weapons.

4) Other than Coalition Forces and duly authorized police and security forces carrying weapons in the course of their duties, no person may carry a concealed weapon.

Section 5 Weapons Authorization Program

Individuals, not falling within Sections 2.2 and 3.2 of this Order, who can demonstrate a necessity to carry weapons, may apply for temporary weapons authorization cards (TWCs) in order to carry weapons.

Section 6 Collection Program

Any heavy weapons, except hand grenades or explosives, shall be turned into Coalition Forces at designated Weapons Control Points on specifically announced dates. Instructions will be issued by the relevant Coalition Forces authorities as to the procedures for handing-in such weapons. Any person handing in weapons during the designated time period will not be subject to the penalties set out in Section 7 of this Order.

Section 7 Penalty

1) Any unauthorized weapons or any weapons for sale in a public marked are subject to confiscation by Coalition Forces and other relevant authorities.

2) Any individual found in possession of an unauthorized weapon in violation of this Order may be detained, arrested, prosecuted and, if convicted, sentenced by relevant authorities to up to one year in prison and a US$ 1,000.00 fine.

Section 8 Entry into Force

This Order shall enter into force on the date of signature [23 May 2003].[11]

[11] The Order had initially been drafted as a CPA Directive. The draft Directive 'Weapons Prohibitions', dated 19 May 2003, stated:

'To ensure a secure environment for all the people of Iraq and to promote order and safety, the carrying and use of weapons must be limited. I direct, as head of the Coalition Provisional Authority, that the following measures are effective immediately. This Directive includes a limited amnesty period to provide every citizen the

Document 17
Coalition Provisional Authority Order Number 3 (Revised) (Amended)

CPA/ORD/31 December 2003/03

Weapons Control

Pursuant to my authority as Administrator of the Coalition Provisional Authority (CPA), and under the laws and usages of war, and consistent with relevant U.N. Security Council resolutions, including Resolution 1483 (2003),

Recognizing that weapons control is necessary in order to ensure a secure environment for the people of Iraq and to promote public order and safety,

I hereby promulgate the following:

Section 1 Definitions

1) 'Coalition Forces' includes any and all personnel, including contractors, from Coalition Member States under the command or direction of the Coalition Provisional Authority or the Coalition Force Commander.

2) 'Criminal Proceedings Law' means Criminal Proceedings Law No. 23 of 1971, as amended, including amendments contained in CPA Memorandum Number 3, Criminal Procedures, CPA/MEM/18 June 2003/03.[12]

3) 'Firearms' mean automatic (7.62mm (308 caliber) and under) and non-automatic rifles, shotguns and pistols for personal use, and associated ammunition. Such firearms are subject to licensing by the Ministry of Interior. Firearms do not include weapons rendered permanently inoperable, replicas, antiques or ceremonial weapons.

4) 'Iraqi security forces' include any and all Iraqi personnel from the Iraqi Police Service, Iraqi Civil Defense Corps, Facilities Protection Service, Iraqi Border and Customs Police or any organization whose mission includes physical security that may be established by the CPA or under Iraqi law subsequent to the signing of this Order.

5) 'Iraqi Weapons Code 1992' means the Law of Arms No. (13) of 1992, as amended by Law No. (15) of 2000.

6) 'Military Weapons' are any weapons systems, ammunition or explosives or explosive devices of any type designed for use by any military forces but not including 'Firearms' as defined in this Order. Military Weapons do not include weapons rendered permanently inoperable, replicas, antiques or ceremonial weapons. Military Weapons include 'Special Category Weapons.'

opportunity to turn in prohibited weapons. The possession of firearms and heavy weapons must be in accordance with the following rules: [...].'

CPA Order No 3 was rescinded by the revised and amended CPA Order No 3, sec 2(4) *[Doc 17]*. A Coalition Forces leaflet with the code number IZ G8569bab reads: 'Attention all Citizens of Al-Tashria Sector. CPA Order #3 outlaws the possession, distribution, sale, or use of explosives, improvised explosives or incendiary devices, grenades, rockets, shells or mines and any means of discharging such items (blasting cap, wires, remote detonators, timers). Crew-served weapons of a higher caliber than 7.62 mm and man-portable air defense systems of any kind are also prohibited. Violators of CPA Order #3 will face a mandatory prison sentence of 15 years to life in prison, and your family will be forced to move out of Al-Tashria.'

[12] See *Doc 127*.

7) 'Penal Code' means the Penal Code Law No. (111) of 1969, as amended, including Law (1) 2002 and CPA Order Number 7, Penal Code, CPA/ORD/9 June 2003/07.[13]

8) 'Public places' mean state-owned property, places of worship, holy sites, hospitals, schools, gathering places such as town squares and parks, streets and such other places that may be designated by the CPA.

9) 'Special Category Weapons' are any explosives, improvised explosives or incendiary devices, grenades, rockets, shells or mines and any means of discharging such items, crew-served weapons of any kind, and Man Portable Air Defense Systems of any kind.

Section 2 Relation to Existing Law

1) Article 6.2 of the Iraqi Weapons Code 1992 is hereby amended to suspend the exemption set out therein for employees of the governmental and social sector.

2) Article 8.2 of the Iraqi Weapons Code 1992, concerning licensing requirements, is amended to allow possession of no more than 50 rounds of ammunition for any licensed firearm.

3) In all other respects, including the penalties provisions (with the exception of the death penalty) the Iraqi Weapons Code 1992 remains in effect unless specifically inconsistent with this Order, in which event this order will take precedence.

4) CPA/ORD/23 May 2003/03 is superceded by this Order.

Section 3 Authorized Possession and Use of Firearms and Military Weapons

1) The following individuals are authorized to possess and use issued Firearms and Military Weapons, including Special Category Weapons:

a) Coalition Forces,
b) Iraqi security forces, and
c) Groups and individuals who have been authorized to carry weapons in the course of their duties by the CPA or Commander, Coalition Forces or their duly authorized delegates.

2) Private security firms may be licensed by the Ministry of the Interior to possess and use licensed Firearms and Military Weapons, excluding Special Category Weapons, in the course of their duties, including in public places.

3) Individuals may be authorized to possess Firearms for personal use by obtaining authorization from the Ministry of Interior, as described in Section 5 of this Order.

Section 4 General Prohibitions

1) Unauthorized possession, transport, distribution, or use of Firearms or Military Weapons, including Special Category Weapons, is prohibited.

2) Other than as provided for in Section 3, no person shall possess or use any Firearms or Military Weapons, including Special Category Weapons, in public places.

3) Other than by Coalition Forces and duly authorized Iraqi security forces whose duty position requires the carrying of concealed weapons in the course of their duties, the carrying of concealed weapons is prohibited.

4) All sales of Firearms and Military Weapons are prohibited, except as authorized by the CPA.

[13] See *Doc 21.*

Section 5 Weapons Authorization and Licensing
Individuals not otherwise authorized to possess or use Firearms or Military Weapons by this or any other CPA instrument may apply for weapons authorization. The licensing requirements for weapons set forth in the Iraqi Weapons Code 1992 and administered by the Ministry of Interior remain in effect. Firearms for personal use located in homes or places of business under rescinded Order Number 3 (CPA/ORD/23 May 2003/03) are subject to these licensing provisions. The Ministry of Interior shall issue procedures and establish timelines for licensing such Firearms. Possession of unlicensed Firearms in one's home or place of business for personal use, as permitted under rescinded Order Number 3, will continue to be authorized until the new procedures for licensing such Firearms become effective in accordance with a Public Notice to that effect.

Section 6 Penalties
1) Firearms or Military Weapons, including Special Category Weapons, possession or use of which is unauthorized, are subject to confiscation by Coalition Forces and other relevant authorities.

2) Any person in violation of this Order may be detained, arrested, and prosecuted. If convicted, all lawful punishments may be adjudged, and the following terms of imprisonment will apply:

a. For the conviction of unauthorized possession, transport, distribution, sale, or use of a Military Weapon, excluding Special Category Weapons, a minimum term of imprisonment of 6 months and maximum term of imprisonment of life imprisonment.

b. For the conviction of possession, transport, distribution, sale, or use of a Special Category Weapon, a minimum term of imprisonment of 30 years, unless the proviso at paragraph 3 applies, and maximum term of imprisonment of life imprisonment. Where a person may be convicted of another offense relating to the use of a Special Category Weapon, the mandatory minimum term of imprisonment of 30 years, unless the proviso at paragraph 3 applies, shall also be applied to that conviction.

3) The mandatory minimum term of imprisonment of 30 years is subject to the proviso that in exceptional circumstances relating to the offender or the offense, the punishment may be reduced. The transport, distribution, sale or use of a Special Category Weapon shall never constitute exceptional circumstances.

4) Except as provided in paragraphs 2 and 3 of this Section, sentences for convictions of offenses under this Order or the Iraqi Weapons Code 1992 and which involve Military Weapons, including Special Category Weapons, may not be reduced as a result of mitigating excuse pursuant to paragraph 130 of the Penal Code. Persons convicted of committing these offenses shall not be eligible for Conditional Discharge as set forth in paragraph 331 of the Criminal Proceedings Law.

5) For the purposes of this Order, sentences of life imprisonment shall mean the remaining natural life of the person.

6) Authorized officials of the CPA or Coalition Forces may grant a certificate of immunity from prosecution for offenses under this Order or the Iraqi Weapons Code 1992 to a person who provides information that leads to the apprehension and conviction of persons in relation to whom information is sought by the CPA and Coalition Forces, or that results in the prevention of a significant crime against public security, the CPA or Coalition Forces.

Section 7 Administrative Instructions
The interim Minister of the Interior, in consultation with the CPA Director of Interior Policy, may issue such Administrative Instructions as are necessary to carry out this Order.

Section 8 Entry into Force
This Order shall enter into force on the date of signature [31 December 2003].[14]

Document 18
Coalition Provisional Authority Order Number 4
CPA/ORD/25 May 2003/04

Management of Property and Assets of the Iraqi Baath Party

Pursuant to my authority as Administrator of the Coalition Provisional Authority (CPA), relevant U.N. Security Council resolutions, including Resolution 1483 (2003), and laws and usages of war,

Acting in accordance with the Administrator's Order Number 1 of May, 16 2003 on the De-Ba'athification of Iraqi Society (CPA/ORD 16 May 2003/01),[15]

Furthering CPA Order Number 2 on the Dissolution of Entities, (CPA/ORD/ 23 May 2003/02),[16]

Recognizing that the assets and property of the Iraqi Ba'ath Party constitute State assets, the Iraqi government having been a one party State under the rule of the Ba'athists from the years 1968 to 2003,

Acting on behalf, and for the benefit, of the Iraqi people,

I hereby promulgate the following:

Section 1 Definition
'*Property and assets*' includes all movable and immovable property, records and data, cash, funds, realizable assets and liquid capital, in whatever form maintained and wherever located, used, possessed, or controlled by the Ba'ath Party, its officials and members, and all members, and all residences occupied by officials or members assigned to them by the Party, a member of the Ba'ath Party or other State instrumentality and that were not purchased for full value by those officials or members.

Section 2 Register of Property and Assets
1) All persons shall, on request by the CPA, provide all information within their possession, control or knowledge concerning property and assets of the Iraqi Ba'ath Party, for the compilation of a Register of all such property and assets.

2) The Register will be maintained by the CPA.

[14] CPA Order No 3 (Revised) (Amended) was further amended by CPA Order No 100, sec 3(3)(a)–(j) *[Doc 124]*.

[15] See *Doc 14*.

[16] See *Doc 15*.

Section 3 Securing of Property and Assets

1) All property and assets of the Iraqi Ba'ath Party wherever existing and in whatever form, including property and assets that have been transferred or acquired by successor parties or institutions, are subject to seizure by the CPA on behalf, and for the benefit of the people of Iraq.

2) All financial obligations of the Iraqi Ba'ath Party are suspended. The Administrator of the CPA will establish procedures whereby persons claiming to be the beneficiaries of such obligations may apply for payment.

3) Persons in possession or control of property and assets of the Iraqi Ba'ath Party shall preserve those assets, promptly inform local coalition authorities, and immediately turn them over, as directed by those authorities. Continued possession, transfer, sale, use, conversion, or concealment of such assets following the date of this Order is prohibited and may be punished.

4) The CPA will hold in trust and for the use and benefit of the people of Iraq all the said property and assets of the Ba'ath Party that have seized in accordance with this Order.

5) Any expenditure or use of the seized property and assets by the CPA will be recorded and open to audit by outside auditors.

Section 4 Right of Appeal

1) A Confiscation Appeal Tribunal will establish to make determinations on disputes arising in relation to seizure action taken pursuant to this Order.

2) Any person adversely affected by actions taken pursuant to this order may appeal to the Confiscation Appeal Tribunal. The only grounds on which such as appeal may be based will be that the property or assets were purchased by the person for full value or that the property is not Ba'ath Party property or assets.

Section 5 Relationship to the Iraqi De-Baathification Council

The CPA may accept information provided to it by the Iraqi De-Baathification Council concerning the existence, location and possession of the property and assets of the Iraqi Baath Party including information obtained from the tracing of property and assets to successor parties or institutions within Iraq.

Section 6 Penalty

The penalty for failing to provide information, or failing to hand over property and assets to the Coalition Provisional Authority as required by this Order, will be imprisonment for up to 1 year or a fine of up to USD 1,000, to be determined by an appropriate authority.

Section 7 Entry into Force

This Order shall enter into force on the date of signature [25 May 2003].

Document 19
Coalition Provisional Authority Order Number 5
CPA/ORD/25 May 2003/05

Establishment of the Iraqi De-Baathification Council

Pursuant to my authority as Administrator of the Coalition Provisional Authority (CPA), relevant U.N. Security Council resolutions, including Resolution 1483 (2003), and the laws and usages of war,

Recognizing that the Iraqi people have suffered large scale human rights abuses and deprivations over many years at the hands of the Baath Party,

Noting the grave concern of Iraqi society regarding the threat posed by the continuation of Baath Party networks and personnel in the administration of Iraq, and the intimidation of the people of Iraq by Baath Party officials,

Concerned by the continuing threat to the security of the Coalition Forces posed by the Iraqi Baath Party,

Acting in accordance with the Administrator's Order Number 1 of May, 16 2003 on the De-Baathification of Iraqi Society (CPA/ORD 16 May 2003/01),[17]

Furthering CPA Order Number 2 on the Dissolution of Entities, (CPA/ORD/23 May 23/02)[18] and CPA Order Number 4 on the Management of Property and Assets of the Iraqi Baath Party (CPA/ORD/-May 2003/04),[19]

I hereby promulgate the following:

Section 1 Establishment of the Iraqi De-Baathification Council

1) There will be established an entity to be known as the Iraqi De-Baathification Council, 'the Council', which will commence operation at a time to be fixed by the Administrator.

2) The Council will operate at the discretion of the Administrator and will terminate operation at a time to be fixed by the Administrator or a subsequent Iraqi administration so authorised by the Administrator, or an Iraqi Government.

Section 2 Composition of the Council

1) The Council shall be composed entirely of Iraqi citizens who will be selected by and who shall serve at the discretion of the Administrator.

2) The number of members of the Council shall be determined by the Administrator but in any event shall not exceed twenty official members who may from time to time be supported by or supplemented in the performance of administration and investigations by technical personnel assigned by the Administrator.

3) Technical personnel supporting the Council will not be authorized to make official reports or findings directly to the Administrator; such reports or findings may only emanate from the Council.

Section 3 Powers and Functions

1) The Council will investigate, and gather information on the following matters:

[17] See *Doc 14*.
[18] See *Doc 15*.
[19] See *Doc 18*.

a) the extent, nature, location and current status of all Iraqi Baath Party property and assets including property and assets owned by Iraqi Baath Party officials and members and any methods of concealment or distribution adopted to avoid detection;
b) the identity and whereabouts of Iraqi Baath Party officials and members involved in human rights violations and exploitation of the Iraqi people;
c) details of any criminal allegations that may be made against Iraqi Baath Party officials and members; and
d) any other information relevant to the Order for the De-Baathification of Iraqi Society, issued by the Administrator of the Coalition Provisional Authority on May 16, 2003 (CPA/ORD/16 May 2003/01) and the Order on the Management of Property and Assets of the Iraqi Baath Party (CPA/ORD/– May 2003/04).

2) The Council will advise the Administrator of the following matters:
a) the most efficient and equitable means of eliminating the structure and means of intimidation and patronage of the Iraqi Baath Party;
b) a means of identifying and classifying Iraqi Baath Party officials and members;
c) the most efficient and equitable means of reclaiming Iraqi Baath Party property and assets; and
d) individuals who the Council considers should be exempt from the Order for the De- Baathification of Iraqi Society issued by the Administrator of the Coalition Provisional Authority on May 16, 2003 (CPA/ORD/16 May 2003/01).

3) The Council will report directly and solely to the Administrator and will not release information or material arising from its activities to any other person or organization unless authorized by the Administrator.

Section 4 Obligation to Provide Information

1) All persons shall, on request by the Council, provide all information within their possession, control or knowledge concerning any matter regarding which the Council is authorized to obtain information.

2) The penalty for failing to comply with a request by the Council for information, will be imprisonment for up to 1 year or a fine of up to USD$1,000 [sic] to be determined by an appropriate authority.

3) Any live testimony or written statements provided by individuals to the Council may not be tendered in evidence against them in any criminal proceedings.

4) Any individual affected adversely by reports, recommendations or findings by the Council will be entitled to a copy of the report and may make written representation to the Administrator for reversal of the report recommendation or finding.

Section 5 Authority of the Administrator

The Administrator will be the final authority with respect to all matters concerning the Council, including the release of any material or reports produced by the Council, any action to be taken arising from the work of the Council and the consequences for individuals reported on by the Council.

Section 5 [sic] Regulation of the Council

1) The Council shall be bound by and operate in accordance with any Regulations, Orders or Memoranda issued by the Administrator.

2) The remuneration of member of the Council will be fixed in accordance with regulations to be issued by the Administrator.

Section 6 Entry into Force
This Order shall enter into force on the date of signature [25 May 2003].[20]

Document 20
Coalition Provisional Authority Order Number 6
CPA/ORD/8 June 2003/06

Eviction of Persons Illegally Occupying Public Buildings

Pursuant to my authority as Administrator of the Coalition Provisional Authority (CPA), and the laws and usages of war, and consistent with relevant U.N. Security Council resolutions, including Resolution 1483 (2003),

Recognizing that the assets and property of the Iraqi Ba'ath Party constitute State assets,

Affirming the CPA's commitment to counter the threat to security and civil order posed by the illegal occupation of public property and improper disposition of that property,

Acting on behalf, and for the benefit, of the Iraqi people,

I hereby promulgate the following:

Section 1 Eviction

1) The CPA now exercises control over all public property and all property formerly owned by the Ba'ath Party within Iraq. Any individual or groups determined to be in illegal occupation of such public property shall be evicted.

2) The determination of illegal occupancy for purposes of this Order shall be made by the Commander of Coalition Forces or his designee.

Section 2 Inventory
The CPA Facility Manager shall prepare and maintain an inventory describing the location and contents of all public property and property formerly owned by the Ba'ath Party within Iraq.

Section 3 Right of Appeal
Individuals or groups who are evicted from public property, or property formerly owned by the Ba'ath Party within Iraq, may appeal their eviction by submitting, to the Administrator or his designee, written evidence showing a valid right of occupancy, such as evidence of purchase for full value, or that the property did not properly fall within Section 1 of this Order.

Section 4 Entry into Force
This Order shall enter into force on the date of signature [8 June 2003].[21]

[20] CPA Order No 5 was rescinded by CPA Memorandum No 7, sec 3 *[Doc 132]*. See also CPA Order No 100, sec 4(2) *[Doc 124]*.

[21] CPA Order No 6 was rescinded by CPA Order No 100, sec 4(3) *[Doc 124]*.

Document 21
Coalition Provisional Authority Order Number 7

CPA/ORD/9 June 2003/07

Penal Code

Pursuant to my authority as head of the Coalition Provisional Authority (CPA), relevant U.N. Security Council resolutions, including Resolution 1483 (2003), and the laws and usages of war,

Reconfirming the provisions of General Franks' Freedom Message to the Iraqi People of April 16, 2003,[22]

Recognizing that the former regime used certain provisions of the penal code as a tool of repression in violation of internationally recognized human rights standards,

Acting on behalf, and for the benefit, of the Iraqi people,

I hereby promulgate the following:

Section 1 Judges, Police and Prosecutors

All judges, police and prosecutors shall perform their duties in accordance with CPA Regulation No. 1 (CPA/REG/23 May 2003/01)[23] and in accordance with any other Regulations, Orders, Memoranda or instructions issued by the CPA.

Section 2 Suspension of Certain Provisions of Penal Code

1) Without prejudice to the continuing review of Iraqi laws, the Third Edition of the 1969 Iraqi Penal Code with amendments, registered in Baghdad on the fifth day of Jumada I 1389 or the nineteenth day of July 1969,[24] shall apply, with the exception that i) Part Two, Chapter Two, Paragraph 200,[25] and ii) Part Two, Chapter Three, Section One, Paragraph 225[26] are hereby suspended.

[22] See *Doc 169*.

[23] See *Doc 1*. The version of CPA Regulation No 1 posted on the CPA's website was apparently signed by Ambassador Bremer on 16 May 2003. The document symbol used for the website version is 'CPA/REG/16 May 2003/01'; however, the symbol used for the same regulation in the *Official Gazette* is 'CPA/REG/23 May 2003/01'.

[24] The Iraqi Penal Code with its 506 paragraphs is may be found at https://www.jagcnet.army.mil/.

[25] Paragraph 200 - (1) The following persons are punishable by death:

(a) Any person who is a member of the Arab Socialist Ba'ath Party and who willfully conceals any previous party or political membership or affiliation.

(b) Any person who is or has been a member of the Arab-Socialist Ba'ath Party and who is found to have links during his commitment to the Party with any other political or party organization or to be working for such organization or on its behalf.

(c) Any person who is or has been a member of the Arab Socialist Ba'ath Party and who is found to be, following the termination of his relationship with the Party, a member of any other political or party organization or to be working for such organization or on its behalf.

(d) Any person who recruits to a political or party organization another person who is affiliated to the Arab Socialist Ba'ath Party or recruits such person in any way to that organization following the termination of his affiliation with the Party while being aware of that affiliation.

(2) Any person who promotes or acclaims any movement that seeks to change the fundamental principles of the constitution or the basic laws of society or in order to raise one section of society over another or to oppress a particular section of society or to overthrow the basic social and economic laws of the State or the fundamental laws of society and the use of force, terror or any other illegal method is perceived in such action is punishable by a term of imprisonment not exceeding 7 years or by detention. The same penalty applies to any person who incites the overthrow of the appointed regime in Iraq or hatred of or scorn for such regime or acclaims or promotes

2) Legal proceedings may be brought with respect to the following offenses only with the written permission of the Administrator of the CPA:

a) Part One, Chapter Four, Paragraphs 81-84, publication offenses.
b) Part Two, Chapter One, Paragraphs 156-189, offenses against the external security of the state.
c) Part Two, Chapter Two, Paragraphs 190-195; 198-199; 201-219, offenses against the internal security of the state.
d) Part Two, Chapter Three, Section One, Paragraphs 223-224; 226-228, offenses against public authorities.
e) Part Two, Chapter Three, Section Two, Paragraph 229, offense of insulting a public official.

Section 3 Penalties

1) Capital punishment is suspended. In each case where the death penalty is the only available penalty prescribed for an offense, the court may substitute the lesser penalty of life imprisonment, or such other lesser penalty as provided for in the Penal Code.[27]

2) Torture and cruel, degrading or inhuman treatment or punishment is prohibited.

3) No person will be prosecuted for aiding, assisting, associating with, or working for Coalition Forces or the CPA.

Section 4 Nondiscrimination

In exercising their official functions, all persons undertaking public duties or holding public office, including all police, prosecutors, and judges, must apply the law impartially. No person will be discriminated against on the basis of sex, race, color, language, religion, political opinion, national, ethnic or social origin, or birth.

Section 5 Delegation of Authority

The Administrator of the CPA may delegate his authority under this Order.

Section 6 Entry into Force

This Order shall enter into force on the date of signature [10 June 2003].

anything that stirs up factional or sectarian chauvinism or encourages conflict between factions and classes or stirs up feelings of hatred and contempt among the population.

[26] Paragraph 225 - Any person who publicly insults the President or his representative is punishable by a term of imprisonment not exceeding 7 years or by detention.

[27] On 8 August 2004, the Iraqi Interim Government adopted Decree No 3 of 2004 reinstating capital punishment for murder, drug trafficking, kidnapping and threats to national security. See *Official Gazette*, vol 45, no 3987 (September 2004).

Document 22
Coalition Provisional Authority Order Number 8
CPA/ORD/7 June 2003/08

Traveling Abroad for Academic Purposes

Pursuant to my authority as head of the Coalition Provisional Authority (CPA), relevant U.N. Security Council resolutions, including Resolution 1483 (2003), and the laws and usages of war,

Reconfirming the provisions of General Franks' Freedom Message to the Iraqi People of April 16, 2003,[28]

Recognizing that the free exchange of ideas and the pursuit of academic excellence is necessary to the establishment of representative self-government in Iraq,

Acting on behalf, and for the benefit, of the Iraqi people,

I hereby promulgate the following:

Any statute, regulation, instruction or policy of the former Iraqi government that imposes restrictions or procedures on faculty, employees or students of public universities, colleges or other institutions of higher education who desire to travel abroad for educational purposes, is hereby rescinded. Effective immediately, the acting presidents of public universities, colleges or other institutions of higher education shall have exclusive authority to approve requests from faculty, employees and students of their institutions to travel abroad for any academic purpose, including teaching; pursuing programs of study; or attending or participating in sabbaticals, seminars, conferences, meetings or similar events.

[Signed 7 June 2003].

Document 23
Coalition Provisional Authority Order Number 9
CPA/ORD/8 June 2003/09

Management and Use of Iraqi Public Property

Pursuant to my authority as head of the Coalition Provisional Authority (CPA), and under the laws and usages of war, and consistent with relevant U.N. Security Council resolutions, including Resolution 1483 (2003),

Noting the needs of the Coalition Forces and the CPA with respect to the use of public property in order to meet their obligations and facilitate administrative functions,

Affirming the CPA's obligation to responsibly manage Iraqi public property on behalf of the Iraqi people,

Furthering CPA Order No. 4, Management of the Property and Assets of the Iraqi Ba'ath Party (CPA/ORD/25 May 2003/04),[29]

[28] See *Doc 169*.
[29] See *Doc 18*.

I hereby promulgate the following:

Section 1 Register of Public Property
The CPA Facility Manager shall maintain a Register of Property and Assets documenting relevant information concerning all public property occupied, used, managed and assigned by the CPA, including all information that must be recorded in accordance with CPA/ORD/25 May 2003/04.

Section 2 Categories of Public Property
This Order applies to the occupancy, use, management and assignment of two categories of public property:

a) **Category 1** – Property that is assigned to, occupied and used by the CPA, Coalition Forces, Iraqi Ministries, government offices of Coalition members, emerging Iraqi administrative or political organizations, and property that is necessary for the administration of social services to the people of Iraq; and

b) **Category 2** – Property that is temporarily made available to private individuals or organizations, including commercial or other enterprises that provide services to, or at the request of, the CPA.

Section 3 Category 1 Properties

1) Applications to occupy and use Category 1 properties shall be forwarded to the CPA Facility Manager for approval. Applications shall be in writing, and shall state the requirement for and proposed use(s) of the property, and specifically describe the property sought, including its condition and exact location.

2) Properties will be allocated at the discretion of the Facility Manager, in accordance with priorities and policies set by the Administrator.

3) Where a property is allocated, the Facility Manager shall issue a Letter of Authority that identifies the approved occupant, and the terms, conditions and duration of occupancy and use.

4) The maximum duration of any occupancy and use approved under this Order will be one year from the date of approval, or until the termination of the CPA, whichever occurs first.

5) The CPA's approval of an application to occupy and use a Category 1 property shall not give rise to any obligation or liability on the part of the CPA, or any State participating in the CPA, to any applicant, other than to be left in quiet possession for the duration of the approved term, subject only to the CPA's obligation to maintain security.

6) The CPA's approval of an application to occupy and use a Category 1 property shall not give rise to any obligation on the part of the Iraqi Government in any way.

Section 4 Category 2 Properties

1) Applications for Category 2 Properties shall be forwarded to the CPA Facility Manager for initial approval. Applications shall be in writing, and shall state the requirement for and proposed use(s) of the property, and specifically describe the property sought, including its condition and exact location.

2) Properties will be allocated at the discretion of the CPA Facility Manager, in accordance with priorities and policies set by the Administrator.

3) Following approval by the CPA Facility Manager, the application will be forwarded to the CPA Office of General Counsel, which will prepare a license governing terms,

conditions and duration of occupancy and use, and specify the required consideration for occupancy and use of the property.

4) The maximum duration of any license executed under this Order will be one year from the commencement date specified in the license, or until the termination of the CPA, whichever occurs first.

5) No license executed under this Order shall give rise to any obligation or liability on the part of the CPA or any State participating in the CPA to any licensee, other than to be left in quiet possession for the duration of the approved term, subject only to the CPA's obligation to maintain security.

6) No license executed under this Order shall give rise to any obligation on the part of the Iraqi Government in any way.

Section 5 Preservation of Current Arrangements

1) Coalition Forces, CPA offices, Coalition government offices, Iraqi Ministries and other Iraqi government entities already occupying public property shall follow the procedures set out in Section 3 herein for a Letter of Authority documenting their continuing occupancy and use of public property.

2) Any current occupations of Category 2 property shall follow the procedure set out in Section 4 herein for execution of a license governing continuing occupancy and use.

Section 6 Inspections

1) The CPA Facility Manager shall have the authority to enter properties covered under this Order, in order to inspect and inventory such properties and assets. The Facility Manager may remove furnishings, assets or other movable property from public buildings for storage, or transfer such property between or among public buildings, as he determines appropriate. No furnishings, assets or other movable property may be removed from or transferred between or among public buildings, without the written approval of the CPA Facilities Manager.

2) Interfering with the Facility Manager in the performance of his duties under this section, or removing furnishings, assets or other movable property from public buildings without the approval of the Facility Manager, shall constitute a violation of this Order, and may subject the violator to appropriate punishment.

Section 7 Assignment of Functions and Coordination

1) The CPA Facility Manager may assign duties to other elements of the CPA, and request the support of the Commander of Coalition Forces, as necessary to accomplish the public property management responsibility describes in this Order.

2) In carrying out his responsibilities under this Order, the Facility Manager shall coordinate closely with the Iraqi Ministry of Housing and Construction, in order to facilitate the transfer of public property management responsibilities to the future government of Iraq.

Section 8 Entry into Force

This Order shall enter into force on the date of signature [8 June 2003].

Document 24
Coalition Provisional Authority Order Number 9 (Revised)
CPA/ORD/27 June 2004/09

Management and Use of Iraqi Public Property

Pursuant to my authority as head of the Coalition Provisional Authority (CPA), and under the laws and usages of war, and consistent with relevant U.N. Security Council resolutions, including Resolutions 1483 (2003) and 1511 (2003),

Noting the needs of the Multinational Force and the CPA with respect to the use of public property in order to meet their obligations and facilitate administrative functions,

Affirming the CPA's obligation to responsibly manage Iraqi public property on behalf of the Iraqi people,

Furthering CPA Order No. 4, Management of the Property and Assets of the Iraqi Ba'ath Party (CPA/ORD/25 May 2003/04),[30]

Recalling that on 30 June 2004 responsibility for and authority over public property will pass to the Iraqi Government,

I hereby promulgate the following:

Section 1 Applicability

This Order applies to the assignment, occupancy, use and management of public property that is assigned to, occupied, used or managed by the CPA, Multinational Forces, Iraqi Ministries, government offices of Coalition members, emerging Iraqi administrative or political organizations; property that is necessary for the administration of social services to the people of Iraq; and public property that is temporarily made available to private individuals or organizations, including commercial or other enterprises that provide services to, or at the request of, the CPA.

Section 2 Register of Public Property

The CPA Facilities Manager shall compile and maintain a Register of Property and Assets documenting relevant information concerning all public property occupied, used, managed and assigned by the CPA, in accordance with CPA/ORD/25 May 2003/04.

Section 3 Procedures

1) Applications to occupy and use public properties shall be forwarded to the CPA Facilities Manager for approval. Applications shall be in writing, and shall state the requirement for and proposed use(s) of the property, and specifically describe the property sought, including its condition and exact location.

2) If an applicant seeks to occupy or use more than 10 properties, the applicant may request those properties collectively in one or more applications.

3) Properties will be allocated at the discretion of the CPA Facilities Manager, in accordance with priorities and policies set by the Administrator, until 30 June 2004.

4) When a property is allocated, the CPA Facilities Manager shall issue a Letter of Authority (LOA) that identifies the approved occupant, and the terms, conditions and

[30] See *Doc 18*.

duration of occupancy and use. The CPA Facilities Manager may issue one or more LOAs for applications that fall within Section 3(2) of this Order.

5) All LOAs in force as of 30 June 2004 shall continue in force until such time as a decision on use or occupancy of the subject property has been made by the Iraqi Interim Government, the Iraqi Transitional Government, or the Iraqi government elected under a permanent constitution as set forth in the Law of Administration for the State of Iraq for the Transitional Period (collectively 'the Iraqi Government').

6) The CPA's approval of an application to occupy and use public property shall not give rise to any obligation or liability on the part of the CPA, or any State participating in the CPA, to any applicant, other than to be left in quiet possession for the duration of the approved tenancy.

7) The CPA's approval of an application to occupy and use public property shall not give rise to any obligation on the part of the Iraqi Government in any way.

Section 4 Preservation of Current Arrangements

Multinational Forces, CPA offices, Coalition government offices, and Iraqi State entities already occupying public property but not yet in possession of a LOA shall, until 30 June 2004, follow the procedures set out in Section 3 herein for a LOA documenting their continuing occupancy and use of public property.

Section 5 Inspections

1) Until 30 June 2004, the CPA Facilities Manager shall have the authority to enter properties covered under this Order, in order to inspect and inventory such properties and assets. The Facilities Manager may remove furnishings, assets or other moveable property from public buildings for storage, or transfer such property between or among public buildings, as is deemed appropriate. No furnishings, assets or other movable property may be removed from or transferred between or among public buildings, without the written approval of the CPA Facilities Manager.

2) Interfering with the CPA Facilities Manager in the performance of his duties under this section, or removing furnishings, assets or other movable property from public buildings without the approval of the CPA Facilities Manager, shall constitute a violation of this Order, and may subject the violator to appropriate punishment.

Section 6 Assignment of Functions and Coordination

Until 30 June 2004, the CPA Facilities Manager may delegate authorities under this Order, and request the support of the Commander of the Multinational Forces, as necessary, to accomplish the public property management responsibility described in this Order.

Section 7 Entry into Force

This Order shall enter into force on the date of signature [27 June 2004].

Document 25
Coalition Provisional Authority Order Number 10
CPA/ORD/8 June 2003/10

Management of Detention and Prison Facilities

Pursuant to my authority as head of the Coalition Provisional Authority (CPA), and under the laws and usages of war, and consistent with relevant U.N. Security Council resolutions, including Resolution 1483 (2003),

Recognizing the urgent necessity to ensure safe and humane prisons in order to reestablish law and order and provide for the safety of the people of Iraq,

I hereby promulgate the following:

Section 1 Authority Over Detention and Prison Facilities
Full authority and control over all detention and prison facilities, currently exercised by the Ministry of Labor and Social Affairs and the Ministry of Interior, is hereby vested in the Ministry of Justice. The Directorate of Adult Prisons and the Directorate of Juvenile Prisons in the Ministry of Labor and Social Affairs, all facilities under their authority, and all employees thereof, are hereby transferred to the Ministry of Justice.

Section 2 Interagency Cooperation
The Ministry of Labor and Social Affairs, the Ministry of Interior, and the Ministry of Justice, and all other relevant elements of government, shall cooperate in this effort. The Ministry of Justice, under the authority, direction and control of the Administrator of the CPA, may prescribe any administrative procedures necessary to ensure a properly coordinated transfer of the detention and prison facilities in accordance with this Order.

Section 3 Prison and Detention Facility Standards
There shall be promulgated pursuant to this Order an Implementing Memorandum that will set out fundamental standards applicable to the operation of all prison and detention facilities under the authority of the Ministry of Justice.[31]

Section 4 Entry into Force
This Order shall enter into force on the date of signature [5 June 2003].

[31] See *Doc 126*.

Document 26
Coalition Provisional Authority Order 11
CPA/ORD/8 June 2003/11

Licensing Telecommunications Services and Equipment

Pursuant to my authority as Administrator of the Coalition Provisional Authority (CPA), and under the laws and usages of war, and consistent with relevant U.N. Security Council resolutions, including Resolution 1483 (2003),

Recognizing the need to restore essential telecommunications services throughout Iraq and to regulate licensing and frequency spectrum management on behalf of the people of Iraq,

I hereby promulgate the following:

Section 1 Definitions

1) '*Commercial telecommunications*' includes all telecommunications and radio services (and related equipment) that are offered for public use and for which a fee is charged;

2) '*frequency spectrum*' means the range of frequencies that are available for assignment to radio operators for the provision of commercial telecommunications, telecommunications, broadcasting and other such services;

3) '*telecommunication*' means the conveyance of speech, music and other sounds, visual images or signals by electric, magnetic, electro-magnetic, electro-chemical or electro-mechanical means.

Section 2 Authority to License

1) On behalf of the CPA, the Ministry of Transportation and Communications (the Ministry), shall resume responsibility for licensing all commercial telecommunications services in Iraq. Commercial telecommunications equipment may not be installed or operated without prior written authorization from the Ministry. Any equipment used for such commercial purposes without prior authorization will be subject to seizure without compensation.

2) This Order applies only to commercial telecommunications. Thus, services operated by government organizations, non-government organizations, international entities, and commercial enterprises for their own use, for which no fees are charged, can continue to operate without the prior authorization of the Ministry, unless the equipment requires use of the frequency spectrum.

3) The Ministry shall control, plan, administer, manage, and license the radio frequency spectrum. The Ministry shall honor Iraqi international commitments with respect to radio communication and telecommunication matters, unless prevented by security considerations or overriding international humanitarian law obligations. Accordingly, in exercising its responsibilities under this Order, the Ministry shall comply with applicable standards and requirements of the International Telecommunication Union and its Radio Regulations, as agreed to or adopted by Iraq, unless prevented by reason of security considerations or overriding international humanitarian law obligations.

4) Applications to provide commercial telecommunications services, or for civil use of the frequency spectrum, shall be made to the Ministry.

Section 3 Entry into Force
This Order shall enter into force on the date of signature [9 June 2003].[32]

Document 27
Iraq Radio Frequency Licensing Procedure for the Interim Period
2 October 2003

INTRODUCTION
The frequency spectrum is a limited natural resource and it should be used wisely.

There are many requirements for spectrum during this interim period, especially for services such as broadcasting and land mobile communications. This paper presents the applications procedures and requirements for a number of services.

The Iraqi government will eventually have full responsibility for radio frequency spectrum management including the licensing of all users of the radio spectrum. However, during this interim period, the Coalition Provisional Authority (CPA), under Order Number 11, is the licensing authority and radio frequency spectrum manager.

A draft joint table of frequency allocations had been developed by the CPA, the military, and the Iraqi spectrum manager. The joint table divides the frequency bands of the allocation table into coordinating responsibilities whereby each entity is the lead coordinator for specific bands, with a number of bands with shared coordinating responsibilities between the military and the Iraqi civilian spectrum manager.

The CPA retains the final licensing or authorization authority.

AUTHORITY
In accordance with Coalition Provisional Authority Order 11 effective 9 June 2003, under the laws and usages of war, and consistent with relevant United Nations Security Council resolutions, including Resolution 1483 (2003), the frequency spectrum licensing authority in Iraq is the Ministry of Transportation and Communications.

This paper provides guidance on the implementation of Order Number 11.

Interim Application and Licensing Procedures
The CPA, in coordination with the Iraqi spectrum management group, has developed a number of application and licensing procedures for the interim period.

More procedures may be developed in the future as the need arises.

The following services fall in the frequency bands that are being coordinated by the Iraqi Spectrum Manager. The completed application forms should be submitted to the ITPC Office of Spectrum Management.

RADIO, TELEVISION, AND SATELLITE BROADCASTING STATIONS
An application form has been developed for radio, television, and satellite broadcasting. All applications will be considered equally and fairly. Applicants must complete the form and be aware of and follow these procedures.

[32] CPA Order No 11 was rescinded by CPA Order No 100, sec 4(4) *[Doc 124]*.

Good Character Requirement

The applicants, the applicant's financial supporters, and the applicant's major stockholders are required to be of good character. Good character is defined as never being convicted of serious crimes.

Required Financial Disclosure Information

The applicant is required to provide evidence of financial resources sufficient to construct the broadcasting station or satellite broadcasting facility, and to operate it for three months without additional financial resources.

Broadcasting Content

Broadcasting content in violation of the orders and principles may result in violating principles of the Coalition Provisional Authority, taking special note of the latest edition of Coalition Provisional Authority Order Number 14, Prohibited Media Activity. Applicants must also become aware of and follow the latest edition of Coalition Public Notice 1, Regarding Public Incitement to Violence and Disorder. The applicant or applicants are required to sign a paper that states that they have read the order and public notice.

The licensee's broadcasting content must follow the pertinent orders and applicants are required to sign a paper that states that they have read the order and public notice.

Broadcasting content must conform to the Iraqi legal code unless superseded by orders or regulations.

Broadcasting content in violation of the orders and Iraqi code may result in revocation of the license and seizure of the equipment.

Broadcasting License New and Renewal Application Fees

The application fee for a new license of $500 is payable with the license application.
Renewal fees are $100.

Broadcasting License Terms

The length of the license shall be six months. The licensee may apply for renewal of a license no later than 14 days prior to its expiration date. If later than 14 days prior to the expiration date, the license will be renewed for not longer than six months.

Construction Time Requirements

The licensee has three months from the license issuance date to construct the station such that it is operating at its licensed technical performance level, or else the license is revoked.

LAND MOBILE COMMUNICATIONS (EXCEPT FOR CELLULAR)

Applicants are required to submit the application form.

New and Renewal Application Fees

The application fee for a new license of $100 is payable with the license application.
Renewal fees are $50.

License Terms

License terms are five years and may be renewed.

Construction Requirements

The licensee has three months from the license issuance date to construct the communications facility such that it is operating at its licensed technical performance level, or else the license is revoked.

COMMUNICATIONS SATELLITE EARTH STATIONS FIXED SERVICE STATIONS

Applicants must complete the appropriate application form.
All VSAT's (very small antenna terminals) must be licensed.

New and Renewal Application Fees
The application fee for a new license of $100 is payable with the license application. Renewal fees are $50.
License Terms
License terms are six months and may be renewed.
Construction Time Requirements
The licensee has three months from the license issuance date to construct the communications facility such that it is operating at its licensed technical performance level, or else the license is revoked.

AMATEUR SERVICE STATIONS
Iraqi amateur stations who held amateurs licenses in the past may obtain a new Iraqi amateur license by presenting evidence of having held such a license in the past and by completing the application form.

Amateurs holding foreign licenses may obtain an Iraqi license by showing evidence of holding such a license and completing the amateur license application form.

Document 28
Coalition Provisional Authority Order Number 12
CPA/ORD/7 June 2003/12

Trade Liberalization Policy

Pursuant to my authority as head of the Coalition Provisional Authority (CPA), relevant U.N. Security Council resolutions, including Resolution 1483 (2003), and the laws and usages of war,

Reconfirming the provisions of General Franks' Freedom Message to the Iraqi People of April 16, 2003,[33]

Recognizing the central role of international trade in Iraq's recovery and its development of a free market economy,

Acting on behalf, and for the benefit, of the Iraqi people,

I hereby promulgate the following:

Section 1 Suspension of Tariffs and Trade Restrictions
All tariffs, customs duties, import taxes, licensing fees and similar surcharges for good entering or leaving Iraq, and all other trade restrictions that may apply to such goods, are suspended until December 31, 2003. For the remainder of this year, the CPA will not collect any such fees for goods entering or leaving Iraq by land sea or air.

Section 2 Exceptions
The suspension directed under Section 1 of this order shall not apply to the goods described in the attached Annex to this Order.

[33] See *Doc 169*.

Section 3 Entry into Force
This Order shall enter into force on the date of signature [8 June 2003].[34]

ANNEX

PROHIBITED EXPORTS

Foodstuffs
- Sugar
- Tea
- Imported Rice
- Imported vegetable oils and fats
- Lentils and chickpeas
- Dried beans
- Milk powder and infant formula
- Yellow corn for animal feed

Animals
- Female camels, goats, cows, sheep, buffalo, donkeys and horses
- Deer and mules

Manufactured goods
- Cars, vehicles and other machinery
- Ferro-concrete, iron, iron reinforcing rods
- Galvanised iron plates, steel sheets and plates
- All kinds of wood
- Mineral water pipes and their fittings
- Ceramic and other bathroom furnishings including taps and sinks
- Plain and coloured window glass
- Copper and lead

Other articles
- Bar soap and detergents
- Date palm seedlings and shoots
- Historical artifacts

RESTRICTED AND PROHIBITED IMPORTS

Certain goods designated by the Ministry of Trade will still be subject to import requirements and fees, such as personal automobiles. Prohibitions remain on magazines and films contrary to public norms; on dual-use chemical materials in accordance with international obligations; and on the sale or supply to Iraq of arms and related material other than those required by the CPA, consistent with U.N. Security Council Resolution 1483.

[34] CPA Order No 12 was amended by CPA Memorandum No 8 *[Doc 133]*. Both instruments were rescinded by CPA Order No 54 *[Doc 76]*. See also CPA Order No 100, sec 4(5) *[Doc 124]*.

Document 29
Coalition Provisional Authority Order Number 13
CPA/ORD/18 June 2003/13

The Central Criminal Court of Iraq

Pursuant to my authority as head of the Coalition Provisional Authority (CPA) and the laws and usages of war, and consistent with relevant U.N. Security Council resolutions, including Resolution 1483 (2003),

Committed to promoting the development of a judicial system in Iraq that warrants the trust, respect and confidence of the Iraqi people,

Noting the continuing need for military support to maintain public order,

Furthering the CPA's duty to restore and maintain order and its right to ensure its security and fundamental standards of due process,

Recognizing the role that Iraqi jurists and legal systems must assume in addressing those serious crimes that most directly threaten public order and safety,

Acting on behalf, and for the benefit of the Iraqi people,

I hereby promulgate the following:

Section 1 Establishment of Central Criminal Court of Iraq

1) There shall be established a Central Criminal Court of Iraq (hereinafter 'the Central Court'), which shall sit in the city of Baghdad and in such circuit sessions in other locations in Iraq as provided for in this Order. The Central Court shall have national jurisdiction over matters referred to it in accordance with Section 21.

2) The Central Court shall consist of three chambers:

a) an Investigative Court;
b) a Trial Court; and
c) an Appellate Court.

Section 2 The Investigative Court

1) The Investigative Court shall consist of a single judge, and will operate in accordance with the requirements and procedure of Investigative Courts under the Iraqi Law on Criminal Proceedings of 1971, as amended, and as further modified by any CPA Orders, Implementing Memoranda and this Order.

2) The Investigative Court shall have jurisdiction over all criminal offenses assigned to it by the Administrator.

3) The Investigative Court shall not have jurisdiction over any civil matter or any matter not assigned to it by the Administrator.

Section 3 Trial Court

1) The Trial Court shall be constituted as a three member judicial panel, which will operate in accordance with the requirements and procedures of Felony Trial Courts under the Iraqi Law on Criminal Proceedings of 1971, as amended, and as further modified by any CPA Orders, Implementing Memoranda and this Order.

2) The Trial Court shall have jurisdiction only over matters referred to it by the Investigative Court of the Central Court.

Section 4 Appellate Court

1) The Appellate Court shall be constituted as a three member judicial panel, which will operate in accordance with the requirements and procedures of the Court of Cassation under the Iraqi Law on Criminal Proceedings of 1971, as amended, and as further modified by any CPA Orders, Implementing Memoranda and this Order.

2) The Appellate Court shall have jurisdiction only over matters arising on appeal from the Trial Court of the Central Court.

Section 5 Applicable Law

In exercising its jurisdiction, the Central Court shall apply the 1969 Penal Code of Iraq, as modified by CPA Order No 7 (CPA/ORD/9 June 2003/07)[35] and the 1971 Criminal Proceedings Code of Iraq as modified by CPA Implementing Memorandum No 3 (CPA/MEM/18 June 2003/03).[36] The Central Court shall have jurisdiction over crimes committed in Iraq since 19 March 2003.

Section 6 Judges of the Central Court

1) The Judges of the Central Court shall be appointed for a term of one year by the Administrator, following recommendations from the Judicial Review Committee. The term of appointment may be extended by agreement. Judges shall be appointed in accordance with the following criteria:

- a) be of high moral character and reputation;
- b) have a background of either opposition to the Ba'ath Party, non-membership of the Ba'ath Party or membership that does not fall within the leadership tiers described in CPA/ORD/16 May 2003/01[37] and entailed no involvement in Ba'ath Party activity;
- c) have no criminal record unless the record is a political or false charge made by the Ba'ath Party regime;
- d) have had no involvement in criminal activities;
- e) be an Iraqi national;
- f) have been a judge for at least five years and demonstrated a high level of judicial competence; and
- g) be prepared to sign an oath of office.

2) A judge of the Central Court may only be removed by the Administrator where there is clear evidence of unlawful or unethical conduct, breaches of the requirements of this Order, or incompetence on the part of the member.

3) The Administrator may appoint reserve judges of the Central Court in accordance with the criteria set out in this section. Reserve judges may act as judges of the Central Court when a panel member is for any reason unable to perform his or her duties, or otherwise provide additional support as necessary.

4) Judges of the Central Court shall not disclose any information or personal data related to or obtained in the discharge of their functions, except where authorized by the Administrator for public information or research purposes.

[35] See *Doc 21*.
[36] See *Doc 127*.
[37] See *Doc 14*.

Section 7 Independence of the Judiciary

1) Judges of the Central Court shall perform their duties independently and impartially, and in accordance with applicable laws in Iraq and the oath or solemn declaration pursuant to this Order.

2) Judges of the Central Court shall decide matters before them without discrimination on the grounds of race, nationality, ethnicity or religion and in accordance with their impartial assessment of the facts and their understanding of the law, without improper influence, direct or indirect, from any source.

3) Any hierarchical organization of the judges or any difference among judges in grade or rank shall in no way interfere with the duty of the judge, whether exercising jurisdiction individually or acting collectively on a panel, to deliberate and pronounce judgment in accordance with this Order.

4) While in office, judges and prosecutors of the Central Court shall be barred from accepting political or any other public office, or from accepting any employment, including for teaching law, participating in the drafting of law, or carrying out legal research on a part-time basis, unless for honorary unpaid purposes.

Section 8 Refusal of Justice

No judge of the Central Court may refuse to hear, try or decide a case that is brought before the court in accordance with the relevant procedural provisions.

Section 9 Disqualification of Judges

1) The Administrator may, at the request of a judge or a party to a proceeding, excuse that judge from the exercise of a function in any case in which the impartiality of the judge might reasonably be doubted on any ground.

2) A judge of the Central Court shall be disqualified from a case in accordance with this Order if that judge has previously been involved in any capacity in that case before the court.

3) A judge of the Central Court shall be obliged to request that the Administrator excuse him or her from the exercise of a function in any case in which a party to the proceedings is a spouse, relative of second degree or other close relationship of that judge.

4) Any question as to the disqualification of a judge shall be decided by the Administrator.

Section 10 Legal Cooperation

All Courts in Iraq shall cooperate with a request by the Central Court to:

a) question witnesses who are registered or permanently accommodated in the area of the requested court's jurisdiction;

b) carry out at-the-scene examinations or re-enactments of crimes in the area of the requested court's jurisdiction;

c) serve summonses of the Central Court on witnesses in the requested court's jurisdiction;

d) serve decisions of the Central Court on individuals in the requested court's jurisdiction;

e) execute the decisions of the Central Court if the subject of dispute is located in the requested court's jurisdiction;

f) access files of the requested court for information purposes or decision.

Section 11 Hearings

1) Hearings of the Central Court and deliberations, generally, shall take place at the seat of the court in Baghdad and in such circuit locations in any other part of Iraq as the Administrator determines.

2) The panel of judges or, where applicable, the individual judge may decide to hold hearings of the court in places other than at the seat of the court or circuit locations, if the interests of justice require. In making the decision, the panel of judges or the individual judge shall be guided by the particular circumstances of the case and their responsibility to facilitate equal access to justice.

3) Radio and television broadcasting within the courtroom is prohibited, except for the broadcast of a final judgment in appropriate cases.

4) The hearings of the court, including the pronouncement of the decision, shall be public, unless otherwise determined by the judge or judges in accordance with Iraqi law or due to security considerations.

5) The deliberations of a judge or judges shall remain confidential.

Section 12 Transcript of Proceedings

1) There shall be, in each hearing conducted by the Trial Court and the Appeal Court, a transcript of the proceedings. The transcript will be made available, on request, to all parties to the proceedings, including their legal counsel.

2) In the case of the Investigative Court, the judge shall take, as appropriate, notes of the proceedings and submit them to the files.

3) Upon request, the transcript or notes shall be made available to the public, unless a determination has been made under this Order that the hearing shall not be public.

Section 13 Translation Service

The Central Court shall provide translation and interpretation services in every case where a party to the proceedings, or a judge, or a witness, or expert witness does not sufficiently speak or understand the language spoken in that court.

Section 14 Penalties

The penalties imposed by the Central Court shall be as prescribed for their equivalent courts under Iraqi law, as modified by CPA/ORD/9 June 2003/07 or subsequent CPA Implementing Memoranda or Orders.

Section 15 Prosecution Service

1) The Public Prosecutor's Office shall have the authority to recommend proposed charges to the Investigative Judge, in matters that are to be brought before the Central Court.

2) The Public Prosecutor's office shall be represented at every stage of proceedings before any of the chambers of the Central Court and will appear as a full servant of the court to present witnesses, examine or cross examine all witnesses and adduce admissible evidence.

3) There shall be three Prosecutors appointed by the Administrator to the Central Court who shall serve for terms to be determined by the Administrator. Prosecutors shall not be eligible for selection to the Central Court unless they have at least five years experience. The Administrator shall have the authority to remove or dismiss a Prosecutor.

Section 16 Court Registry

1) There shall be a Registry for the Central Court. The Registry shall have responsibility for the receipt of documents to be filed in the court, for organizing court documents and ensuring security of court documents, and for such other functions as are permitted by Iraqi law and by CPA Order or Memorandum.

2) The staff of the Registry shall have legal and administrative skills, and shall be appointed by the Ministry of Justice.

Section 17 Court Staff

1) Each chamber of the Central Court shall have such qualified staff as may be required for the proper functioning of the chambers and the discharge of the responsibilities of its judges.

2) Each panel of judges or each individual judge shall be assisted during the trial sessions by a member of the court staff.

3) The court staff shall be selected by the Ministry of Justice.

Section 18 Investigative Support

1) The Investigative Court or Prosecutor shall be able to request the investigation of matters arising from material presented to the judge. Investigative support will be coordinated through the Senior Adviser of the Ministry of Justice.

2) The Prosecutor may draw on Iraqi and Coalition resources in order to meet the requests of the Investigative Court. Any material produced by Coalition resources will be admissible in evidence if it satisfies the requirements of Iraqi law as modified by any CPA Order or Memorandum.

3) The Central Court shall not be able to compel the production of Coalition documentary or other material or the attendance of Coalition personnel.

Section 19 Amicus Curiae

Any CPA or Coalition Forces personnel shall have the right to appear before any of the chambers of the Central Court as amicus curiae for the purpose of adducing or proving evidence and when so doing may exercise the same functions as a Prosecutor.

Section 20 Duration of Central Court

The Central Court shall remain in operation for a period to be determined by the Administrator or as provided by a future Iraqi Government. The functions, constitution and jurisdiction of the Central Court may be subject to adjustment by further Orders or Implementing Memoranda of the CPA.

Section 21 Selection of Matters

1) The Administrator, on the advice of the CPA General Counsel, shall determine the matters that are to be submitted to the Central Court. In making this determination the following criteria shall be applied:

- a) The accused is suspected of committing a felony that:
  - i) is intended to destabilize government institutions or processes, in Iraq;
  - ii) involves violence of a scale or organization that transcends provincial boundaries;
  - iii) involves race, nationality, interethnic or religious based violence;
  - iv) is related to the instigation of the removal by force of any government, the CPA or competent Iraqi authorities;

v) involves the illegal trafficking in weapons, drugs or persons across provincial boundaries or international borders; or
vi) involves the use of fraudulent practices across provincial boundaries and international borders.

b) The accused held a position of influence within the prior regime, and as a result of that position, may still be capable of influencing the decisions of the judiciary or other governmental institutions.
c) The accused is suspected of committing a crime of violence that involves multiple victims.
d) The accused, either acting alone or as part of a group, is engaged in criminal and or terrorist activities that are directed at the civilian population or members of the CPA or Coalition Forces operating legally within Iraq.
e) The accused is suspected of an offense that involves bribery, solicitation of a bribe or any form of public corruption or misconduct.

2) Requests for referrals of cases to the Central Court shall be forwarded by the Senior Adviser of the Ministry of Justice to the Administrator. The Senior Adviser may file such requests on his own initiative or in response to an application by:

a) accused persons under Iraqi law;
b) any Iraqi court;
c) the Commander Coalition Forces; and
d) the Senior Adviser of the Ministry of Interior.

3) This Order shall not apply to courts-martial, military commissions, provost courts and other military tribunals convened by member states of the Coalition. Nothing in this Order shall deprive courts-martial, military commissions, provost courts or other military tribunals of jurisdiction that exists under the law of a member state of the Coalition, or under the law of war or law of occupation. Coalition Forces shall not be permitted to retry any person dealt with by the Central Court for substantially the same offense.

4) No other Iraqi court shall be permitted to retry or punish any person already convicted or acquitted by the Central Court for substantially the same offense.

Section 22 Appeals

The accused and the Prosecutor shall have the right of appeal from the Appellate Court to the Court of Cassation.

Section 23 Representation of the Accused

1) All accused persons appearing before the Central Criminal Court of Iraq, shall have the right to representation by an attorney of their choice. Where an accused person is unable to afford the services of an attorney the Court will provide them with a suitably qualified attorney.

2) Any counsel provided for the accused in accordance with relevant Orders and Implementing Memoranda of the CPA shall have at least five years trial experience.

Section 24 Entry into Force

This Order shall enter into force on the date of signature [18 June 2003].

Document 30

Coalition Provisional Authority Order Number 13 (Revised)

CPA/ORD/11 July 2003/13

The Central Criminal Court of Iraq

Pursuant to my authority as head of the Coalition Provisional Authority (CPA) and the laws and usages of war, and consistent with relevant U.N. Security Council resolutions, including Resolution 1483 (2003),

Committed to promoting the development of a judicial system in Iraq that warrants the trust, respect and confidence of the Iraqi people,

Noting the continuing need for military support to maintain public order,

Furthering the CPA's duty to restore and maintain order and its right to ensure its security and fundamental standards of due process,

Recognizing the role that Iraqi jurists and legal systems must assume in addressing those serious crimes that most directly threaten public order and safety,

Acting on behalf, and for the benefit of the Iraqi people,

I hereby promulgate the following:

Section 1 Establishment of Central Criminal Court of Iraq

1) There shall be established a Central Criminal Court of Iraq (hereinafter 'the Central Court'), which shall sit in the city of Baghdad and in such circuit sessions in other locations in Iraq as provided for in this Order. The Central Court shall have national jurisdiction over matters referred to it in accordance with Section 20.

2) The Central Court shall consist of two chambers:

a) an Investigative Court; and

b) a Trial Court.

Section 2 The Investigative Court

1) The Investigative Court shall consist of a single judge, and will operate in accordance with the requirements and procedure of Investigative Courts under the Iraqi Law on Criminal Proceedings of 1971, as amended, and as further modified by any CPA Orders, Implementing Memoranda and this Order.

2) The Investigative Court shall have jurisdiction over all criminal offenses assigned to it by the Administrator.

3) The Investigative Court shall not have jurisdiction over any civil matter, other than victim compensation claims associated with a criminal matter before the court, or any matter not assigned to it by the Administrator.

Section 3 Trial Court

1) The Trial Court shall be constituted as a three member judicial panel, which will operate in accordance with the requirements and procedures of Felony Trial Courts under the Iraqi Law on Criminal Proceedings of 1971, as amended, and as further modified by any CPA Orders, Implementing Memoranda and this Order.

2) The Trial Court shall have jurisdiction only over matters referred to it by the Investigative Court of the Central Court.

Section 4 Applicable Law

In exercising its jurisdiction, the Central Court shall apply the 1969 Penal Code of Iraq, as modified by CPA Order No 7 (CPA/ORD/9 June 2003/07)[38] and the 1971 Criminal Proceedings Code of Iraq as modified by CPA Implementing Memorandum No 3 (CPA/MEM/18 June 2003/03).[39] The Central Court shall have jurisdiction over crimes committed in Iraq since 19 March 2003, such as are referred to it by the Administrator in accordance with Section 20.

Section 5 Judges of the Central Court

1) The judges of the Central Court shall be appointed for a term of one year by the Administrator, following recommendations from the Judicial Review Committee. The term of appointment may be extended by agreement. Judges shall be appointed in accordance with the following criteria:

a) be an Iraqi national;
b) be of high moral character and reputation;
c) have a background of either opposition to the Ba'ath Party, non-membership of the Ba'ath Party or membership that does not fall within the leadership tiers described in CPA/ORD/16 May 2003/01[40] and entailed no involvement in Ba'ath Party activity;
d) have no criminal record unless the record is a political or false charge made by the Ba'ath Party regime;
e) have had no involvement in criminal activities;
f) have demonstrated a high level of legal competence; and
g) be prepared to sign an oath of office.

2) A judge of the Central Court may only be removed by the Administrator where there is clear evidence of unlawful or unethical conduct, breaches of the requirements of this Order, or incompetence on the part of the member.

3) The Administrator may appoint reserve judges of the Central Court in accordance with the criteria set out in this section. Reserve judges may act as judges of the Central Court when a panel member is for any reason unable to perform his or her duties, or otherwise provide additional support as necessary.

4) Judges of the Central Court shall not disclose any information or personal data related to or obtained in the discharge of their functions, except where authorized by the Administrator for public information or research purposes.

Section 6 Independence of the Judiciary

1) Judges of the Central Court shall perform their duties independently and impartially, and in accordance with applicable laws in Iraq and the oath or solemn declaration given by them to the Administrator pursuant to this Order.

2) Judges of the Central Court shall decide matters before them without discrimination on the grounds of race, nationality, ethnicity or religion and in accordance with their impartial assessment of the facts and their understanding of the law, without improper influence, direct or indirect, from any source.

[38] See *Doc 21*.
[39] See *Doc 127*.
[40] See *Doc 14*.

3) Any hierarchical organization of the judges or any difference among judges in grade or rank shall in no way interfere with the duty of the judge, whether exercising jurisdiction individually or acting collectively on a panel, to pronounce judgment in accordance with this Order.

4) While in office, judges and prosecutors of the Central Court shall be barred from accepting political or any other public office, or from accepting any employment, including for teaching law, participating in the drafting of law, or carrying out legal research on a part-time basis, unless for honorary unpaid purposes.

Section 7 Refusal of Justice

No judge of the Central Court may refuse to hear, try or decide a case that is brought before the court in accordance with the relevant procedural provisions.

Section 8 Disqualification of Judges

1) The Administrator may, at the request of a judge or a party to a proceeding, excuse that judge from the exercise of a function in any case in which the impartiality of the judge might reasonably be doubted on any ground.

2) A judge of the Central Court shall be disqualified from a case in accordance with this Order if that judge has previously been involved in any capacity in that case before the court.

3) A judge of the Central Court shall be obliged to request that the Administrator excuse him or her from the exercise of a function in any case in which a party to the proceedings is a spouse, relative of second degree or other close relationship of that judge.

4) Any question as to the disqualification of a judge shall be decided by the Administrator.

Section 9 Legal Cooperation

All Courts in Iraq shall cooperate with a request by the Central Court to:

a) question witnesses who are registered or permanently accommodated in the area of the requested court's jurisdiction;
b) carry out at-the-scene examinations or re-enactments of crimes in the area of the requested court's jurisdiction;
c) serve summonses of the Central Court on witnesses in the requested court's jurisdiction;
d) serve decisions of the Central Court on individuals in the requested court's jurisdiction;
e) execute the decisions of the Central Court if the subject of dispute is located in the requested court's jurisdiction;
f) access files of the requested court for information purposes or decision.

Section 10 Hearings

1) Hearings of the Central Court and deliberations, generally, shall take place at the seat of the court in Baghdad and in such circuit locations in any other part of Iraq as the Administrator determines.

2) The panel of judges or, where applicable, the individual judge may decide to hold hearings of the court in places other than at the seat of the court or circuit locations, if the interests of justice require. In making the decision, the panel of judges or the individual judge shall be guided by the particular circumstances of the case and their responsibility to facilitate equal access to justice.

3) The hearings of the court, including the pronouncement of the decision, shall be public, unless otherwise determined by the Secretary or by Iraqi law.

4) Radio and television broadcasting within the courtroom is prohibited, except for the broadcast of a final judgment in appropriate cases.

5) The hearings of the Central Court, including the pronouncement of the decision, shall be public, unless otherwise determined by the judge or judges in accordance with Iraqi law or due to security considerations.

6) The deliberations of a judge or judges shall remain confidential.

Section 11 Transcript of Proceedings

1) The Secretary shall ensure that, in each hearing conducted by the Trial Court, a transcript of the proceedings. The transcript will be made available, on request, to all parties to the proceedings, including their legal counsel.

2) In the case of the Investigative Court the judge shall take, as appropriate, notes of the proceedings and submit them to the files.

3) Upon request, the transcript or notes shall be made available to the public, unless a determination has been made under this Order that the hearing shall not be public.

Section 12 Translation Service

The Central Court shall provide translation and interpretation services in every case where a party to the proceedings, or a judge, or a witness, or expert witness does not sufficiently speak or understand the language spoken in that court.

Section 13 Penalties

The penalties imposed by the Central Court shall be as prescribed for their equivalent courts under Iraqi law, as modified by CPA/ORD/9 June 2003/07 or subsequent CPA Implementing Memoranda or Orders.

Section 14 Prosecution Service

1) The Public Prosecutor's Office shall have the authority to recommend proposed charges to the Investigative Judge, in matters that are to be brought before the Central Court.

2) The Public Prosecutor's office shall be represented at every stage of proceedings before any of the chambers of the Central Court and will appear as a full servant of the court to present witnesses, examine or cross examine all witnesses and adduce admissible evidence.

3) There shall be three Prosecutors appointed by the Administrator to the Central Court who shall serve for terms to be determined by the Administrator. The Administrator shall have the authority to remove a Prosecutor.

Section 15 Court Registry

1) There shall be a Registry for the Central Court. The Registry shall have responsibility for the receipt of documents to be filed in the court, for organizing court documents and ensuring security of court documents, and for such other functions as are permitted by Iraqi law and by CPA Order or Memorandum.

2) The staff of the Registry shall have legal and administrative skills, and shall be appointed by the Ministry of Justice.

Section 16 Court Staff

1) Each chamber of the Central Court shall have such qualified staff as may be required for the proper functioning of the chambers and the discharge of the responsibilities of its judges.

2) Each panel of judges or each individual judge shall be assisted during the trial sessions by a member of the court staff.

3) The court staff shall be selected by the Ministry of Justice.

Section 17 Investigative Support

1) The Investigative Court or Prosecutor shall be able to request the investigation of matters arising from material presented to the judge. Investigative support will be coordinated through the Senior Adviser of the Ministry of Justice.

2) The Prosecutor may draw on Iraqi and Coalition resources in order to meet the requests of the Investigative Court. Any material produced by Coalition resources will be admissible in evidence if it satisfies the requirements of Iraqi law as modified by any CPA Order or Memorandum.

3) The Central Court shall not be able to compel the production of Coalition documentary or other material or the attendance of Coalition personnel.

Section 18 Amicus Curiae

Any CPA or Coalition Forces personnel shall have the right to appear before any of the chambers of the Central Court as amicus curiae for the purpose of adducing or proving evidence.

Section 19 Duration of Central Court

The Central Court shall remain in operation for a period to be determined by the Administrator or as provided by an internationally recognized, representative government established by the people of Iraq which assumes the responsibility of the CPA. The functions, constitution and jurisdiction of the Central Court may be subject to adjustment by further Orders or Implementing Memoranda of the CPA or as provided by an internationally recognized, representative government established by the people of Iraq which assumes the responsibility of the Authority.

Section 20 Selection of Matters

1) The Administrator, on the advice of the CPA General Counsel, shall determine the matters that are to be submitted to the Central Court. In making this determination the following criteria shall be applied:

a) The accused is suspected of committing a felony that:
   - i) is intended to destabilize government institutions or processes, in Iraq;
   - ii) involves violence of a scale or organization that transcends provincial boundaries;
   - iii) involves race, nationality, interethnic or religious based violence;
   - iv) is related to the instigation of the removal by force of any government, the CPA or competent Iraqi authorities;
   - v) involves the illegal trafficking in weapons, drugs or persons across provincial boundaries or international borders; or
   - vi) involves the use of fraudulent practices across provincial boundaries and international borders.

b) The accused held a position of influence within the prior regime, and as a result of that position, may still be capable of influencing the decisions of the judiciary or other governmental institutions.

c) The accused is suspected of committing a crime of violence that involves multiple victims.

d) The accused, either acting alone or as part of a group, is engaged in criminal and or terrorist activities that are directed at the civilian population or members of the CPA or Coalition Forces operating legally within Iraq.

e) The accused is suspected of an offense that involves bribery, solicitation of a bribe or any form of public corruption or misconduct.

2) Requests for referrals of cases to the Central Court shall be forwarded by the Senior Adviser of the Ministry of Justice to the Administrator. The Senior Adviser may file such requests on his own initiative or in response to an application [by]:

a) accused persons under Iraqi law;

b) any Iraqi court;

c) the Commander Coalition Forces; and

d) the Senior Adviser of the Ministry of Interior.

3) This Order shall not apply to courts-martial, military commissions, provost courts and other military tribunals convened by member states of the Coalition. Nothing in this Order shall deprive courts-martial, military commissions, provost courts or other military tribunals of jurisdiction that exists under the law of war or law of occupation. Coalition Forces shall not be permitted to retry any person dealt with by the Central Court for substantially the same offense.

4) No other Iraqi court shall be permitted to retry or punish any person already convicted or acquitted by the Central Court for substantially the same offense.

Section 21 Appeals

1) The accused, the plaintiff and the Prosecutor shall have the right of appeal from the decisions of the Investigative Court to the Trial Court.

2) The accused, the plaintiff, and the Prosecutor shall have the right of appeal from the decisions and judgments of the Trial Court to the Court of Cassation.

3) All appeals arising from Central Court proceedings shall be heard in accordance with the 1971 Criminal Proceedings Code of Iraq, as amended, and as modified by CPA Implementing Memorandum No 3 referred to herein.

Section 22 Representation of the Accused

1) All accused persons appearing before the Central Court, shall have the right to representation by an attorney of their choice. Where an accused person is unable to afford the services of an attorney the Central Court will provide them with a suitably qualified attorney.

2) Any counsel provided for the accused in accordance with relevant Orders and Implementing Memoranda of the CPA shall have at least five years trial experience.

Section 23 Entry into Force

This Order shall enter into force on the date of signature [11 July 2003].

Document 31
Coalition Provisional Authority Order Number 13 (Revised) (Amended)

CPA/ORD/22 April 2004/13

The Central Criminal Court of Iraq

Pursuant to my authority as head of the Coalition Provisional Authority (CPA) and the laws and usages of war, and consistent with relevant U.N. Security Council resolutions, including Resolutions 1483 and 1511 (2003),

Committed to promoting the development of a judicial system in Iraq that warrants the trust, respect and confidence of the Iraqi people,

Noting the continuing need for military support to maintain public order,

Furthering the CPA's duty to restore and maintain order and its right to ensure its security and fundamental standards of due process,

Recognizing the role that Iraqi jurists and legal systems must assume in addressing those serious crimes that most directly threaten public order and safety,

Acting on behalf, and for the benefit of the Iraqi people,

I hereby promulgate the following:

Section 1 Establishment of Central Criminal Court of Iraq

1) There shall be established a Central Criminal Court of Iraq (hereinafter 'the CCCI'), which shall sit in the city of Baghdad and in such sessions in other locations in Iraq as provided for in this Order. The CCCI shall have national jurisdiction over all matters set forth in Section 18.

2) The CCCI shall consist of two chambers:

a) an Investigative Court; and

b) a Felony Court.

Section 2 The Investigative Court

1) The Investigative Court shall operate in accordance with the requirements and procedure of Investigative Courts under the Iraqi Law on Criminal Proceedings of 1971, as amended, and as further modified by any CPA Orders, Implementing Memoranda and this Order.

2) The Investigative Court shall have jurisdiction over all matters that are set forth in Section 18.

3) The Investigative Court shall not have jurisdiction over any civil matter, other than victim compensation claims associated with a criminal matter.

Section 3 Felony Court

1) The Felony Court shall operate in accordance with applicable Iraqi Law.

2) The Felony Court shall have jurisdiction over matters as set forth in Section 18.

Section 4 Applicable Law

The CCCI shall apply Iraqi law as modified by applicable CPA Orders and this Order.

Section 5 Judges of the Central Court

1) Prior to the assumption of the functions of government on 1 July 2004, the judges of the CCCI shall be appointed by the Administrator and shall:

a) be an Iraqi national,
b) be of high moral character and reputation,
c) have a background of either opposition to the Ba'ath Party, nonmembership of the Ba'ath Party or membership that does not fall within the leadership tiers described in CPA/ORD/16 May 2003/01[41] and entailed no involvement in Ba'ath Party activity,
d) have no criminal record unless the record is a political or false charge made by the Ba'ath Party regime,
e) have had no involvement in criminal activities,
f) have demonstrated a high level of legal competence; and
g) be prepared to sign an oath or solemn declaration of office.

2) A judge of the CCCI may only be removed by the Administrator where there is clear evidence of unlawful or unethical conduct, breaches of the requirements of this Order, or incompetence on the part of the member.

3) The Administrator may appoint reserve judges of the CCCI in accordance with the criteria set out in this section. Reserve judges may act as judges of the CCCI when a panel member is for any reason unable to perform his or her duties, or otherwise provide additional support as necessary.

4) In light of the nationwide jurisdiction of the Court, the Chief Judges of both the Investigative and Trial Court shall automatically be promoted to Level I Judges, if not already at that level, and shall be compensated accordingly. Similarly, all other judges shall be automatically promoted to Level II, if not already at that level, and shall compensated accordingly and be eligible to advance to Level 1 in accordance with applicable procedures.

5) All judges appointed as of the date of this order or thereafter shall be permanent Iraqi judges and shall serve in accordance with Iraqi law.

6) After the effective date of the Transitional Administrative Law, the judges of the CCCI will be appointed, and removed from office in accordance with the procedures set forth in Iraqi law.[42]

Section 6 Independence of the Judiciary

1) Judges of the CCCI shall perform their duties independently and impartially, and in accordance with the applicable laws in Iraq and the oath or solemn declaration pursuant to this Order.

2) Judges of the CCCI shall decide matters before them without discrimination on the grounds of race, nationality, ethnicity or religion and in accordance with their impartial assessment of the facts and their understanding of the law, without improper influence, direct or indirect, from any source.

3) Any hierarchical organization of the judges or any difference among judges in grade or rank shall in no way interfere with the duty of the judge, whether exercising jurisdiction individually or acting collectively on a panel, to pronounce judgment in accordance with this Order.

[41] See *Doc 14*.
[42] Sec 5 was replaced by CPA Order No 100, sec 3(4)(a) *[Doc 124]*.

4) While in office, judges and prosecutors of the CCCI shall be barred from accepting political or any other public office, or from accepting any employment, including for teaching law, participating in the drafting of law, or carrying out legal research on a part-time basis, unless for honorary unpaid purposes.

Section 7 Refusal of Justice
No judge of the CCCI may refuse to hear, try or decide a case that is brought before the court in accordance with the relevant procedural provisions.

Section 8 Disqualification of Judges

1) The Administrator may, at the request of a judge or a party to a proceeding, excuse that judge from the exercise of a function in any case in which the impartiality of the judge might reasonably be doubted on any ground.

2) A judge of the CCCI shall be disqualified from a case in accordance with this Order if that judge has previously been involved in any capacity in that case before the court.

3) A judge of the Central Court shall be obliged to request that the Administrator excuse him or her from the exercise of a function in any case in which a party to the proceedings is a spouse, relative of second degree or other close relationship of that judge.

4) Prior to the assumption of the functions of government by Iraq, any question as to the disqualification of a judge shall be decided by the Administrator. After the assumption of the functions of government, the disqualification of a judge shall be decided in accordance with the applicable law.[43]

Section 9 Obligations of Local Courts

1) All local courts in Iraq shall comply with an order by the CCCI to:

a) question witnesses who are registered or permanently accommodated in the area of the requested court's jurisdiction,
b) carry out at-the-scene examinations or re-enactments of crimes in the area of the requested court's jurisdiction,
c) serve summonses of the CCCI on witnesses in the requested court's jurisdiction,
d) serve decisions of the CCCI on individuals in the requested court's jurisdiction,
e) execute the decisions of the CCCI if the subject of dispute is located in the requested court's jurisdiction,
f) provide files of the requested court for information purposes or decision,
g) refer cases to the CCCI.

2) All local criminal courts of first instance shall be required to follow the directives and orders of the CCCI. The CCCI shall at all times be subject to the jurisdiction of the Court of Cassation in accordance with the applicable law.

3) The failure of any local judge to follow the orders of the CCCI may be punished in accordance with Iraqi law.

Section 10 Hearings

1) Hearings of the CCCI and deliberations shall take place at the seat of the court in Baghdad and in such other locations in any other part of Iraq as the court determines is required.

[43] Sec 8 was partly rescinded and replaced by CPA Order No 100, sec 3(4)(b)–(d) *[Doc 124]*.

2) The panel of judges or, where applicable, the individual judge may decide to hold hearings of the court in places other than at the seat of the court if the interests of justice require. In making the decision, the panel of judges or the individual judge shall be guided by the particular circumstances of the case and their responsibility to facilitate equal access to justice.

3) Radio and television broadcasting within the courtroom shall be governed by the applicable law.

4) The testimony before the Felony Court shall be public, unless otherwise determined by the judge or judges in accordance with Iraqi law.

5) Verdicts of the Felony Court shall without exception be delivered in public.

6) The CCCI may receive testimony from witnesses who are not present in Iraq by Video Telephone Conference or similar communications technology.

7) The deliberations of a judge or judges shall remain confidential.

Section 11 Record of Proceedings

1) In each hearing conducted by the Felony Court, there shall be a record of the proceedings in accordance with Iraqi law. The record will be made available, on request, to all parties to the proceedings, including their legal counsel.

2) In the case of the Investigative Court the judge shall take, as appropriate, notes of the proceedings and submit them to the files in accordance with Iraqi law.

3) Upon request, the record or notes shall be made available to the public, unless a determination has been made under this Order that the hearing shall not be public.

Section 12 Translation Service

The CCCI shall provide translation and interpretation services in every case where a party to the proceedings, or a judge, or a witness, or expert witness does not sufficiently speak or understand the language spoken in that court.

Section 13 Penalties

1) The penalties imposed by the CCCI shall be as prescribed for their equivalent courts under Iraqi law, as modified by CPA orders.

2) Sentences may be reduced at the discretion of the CCCI where the accused has cooperated with investigative authorities. This discretion extends to the reduction of mandatory minimum sentences. The CCCI shall have the power to reduce sentences at any time, even after the defendant has been sentenced, if a defendant agrees to provide truthful testimony about criminal activity.

Section 14 Prosecution Service

The Prosecutors shall act in accordance with Iraqi law.

Section 15 Court Registry

1) There shall be a Registry for the CCCI. The Registry shall have responsibility for the receipt of documents to be filed in the court, for organizing court documents and ensuring security of court documents, and for such other functions as are permitted by Iraqi law and by CPA Orders or Memoranda.

2) The staff of the Registry shall have legal and administrative skills, and shall be appointed by the Judiciary in accordance with applicable procedures.

Section 16 Court Staff

1) Each chamber of the CCCI shall have such qualified staff as may be required for the proper functioning of the chambers and the discharge of the responsibilities of its judges.

2) Each panel of judges or each individual judge shall be assisted during the trial sessions by a member of the court staff.

3) The court staff shall be selected in accordance with Iraqi law.

Section 17 Investigative Support

1) The CCCI shall be able to request the support from the international community, any authorized foreign military forces in Iraq or diplomatic posts in Iraq for the investigation or trial of cases.

2) CCCI shall not compel the production of foreign military forces present in Iraq in support of operations sanctioned by a U.N. Security Council resolution or at the request of the Iraqi government, or diplomatic personnel or any documents under their control.

3) The Investigative Court and the Felony Court have the authority to direct any and all Iraqi government law enforcement and security agencies to assist the court in the performance of its duties.

Section 18 Jurisdiction

1) The CCCI shall have nationwide discretionary investigative and trial jurisdiction over any and all criminal violations, regardless of where those offenses occurred. Its jurisdiction shall extend to all matters that could be heard by any local felony, or misdemeanor court.

2) In exercising its discretionary jurisdiction, the CCCI should concentrate its resources on cases related to:

a) terrorism,
b) organized crime,
c) governmental corruption,
d) acts intended to destabilize democratic institutions or processes,
e) violence based on race, nationality, ethnicity or religion; and
f) instances in which a criminal defendant may not able to obtain a fair trial in a local court.

3) Any criminal defendant may request the CCCI to review his or her case if the defendant asserts that his case will not be fairly heard by a local criminal court.

4) Any felony, misdemeanor or investigative court in Iraq may refer a case to the court.

5) If the investigation of a case has been completed by a local investigative court, the CCCI may, if it chooses, conduct the trial of the case without conducting a further investigation. However, the court may order a new investigation, or supplement the prior investigation, if it believes it necessary in the interests of justice to do so.

6) The decision of the CCCI to take jurisdiction of a case will end any local courts jurisdiction over such case, and all local courts shall be required to immediately furnish all files to the CCCI and fully cooperate with the court as outlined in Section 9 above.

Section 19 Method of Selecting Cases

1) Prior to 1 July, 2004, the Administrator retains the authority to refer cases to the CCCI. The Court may also accept cases on its own authority, without the need for a referral from the Administrator, as of the date of this order, in accordance with provisions set forth herein. Cases referred by the Administrator will have priority.

2) Cases shall be selected by the Chief Investigative Judge, or in his absence the next most senior Investigative Judge. If a case is selected at the investigative stage, the court shall retain jurisdiction through both the investigation and the trial of the case, without the need to reconsider jurisdiction after the completion of the investigation.

3) The above method of selection includes those cases that may go directly to the Felony Court for trial in accordance with Section 18(5).

4) From 1 July 2004 the Court will receive matters in accordance with the provisions of this Order which do not relate to the authority of the Administrator.

5) After 1 July 2004, Diplomatic representatives may bring potential cases to the CCCI's attention so that it can determine whether to select them in accordance with this Section and Section 19. The CCCI, however, after 1 July 2004, is not required to hear cases brought to its attention in this matter.

Section 20 Issuing of Warrants and Ancillary Orders

1) Any judge on the court has the authority to issue an arrest warrant, a search warrant or order other investigative measures allowed under Iraqi law whether or not the case has been selected under Section 19 above.

2) A warrant or other order issued under this Section shall be valid in any proceedings notwithstanding any decision made under Section 19 above.

Section 21 Appeals

All appeals arising from CCCI proceedings shall be heard in accordance with applicable Iraqi law as modified by CPA orders but the Court of Cassation shall hear all appeals from the Felony Court.

Section 22 Representation of the Accused

All accused persons appearing before the CCCI, shall have the right to representation by an attorney of their choice. Where an accused person is unable to afford the services of an attorney the CCCI will provide them with a suitably qualified attorney free of charge.

Section 23 Entry into Force

This Order shall enter into force on the date of signature [22 April 2004].

Document 32

Coalition Provisional Authority Order Number 14

CPA/ORD/10 June 2003/14

Prohibited Media Activity

Pursuant to my authority as head of the Coalition Provisional Authority (CPA), and under the laws and usages of war, and consistent with relevant U.N. Security Council resolutions, including Resolution 1483 (2003),

Noting the extensive specific authority granted to the CPA under the laws and usages of war for the control of all appliances, whether on land, at sea, or in the air, adapted for the transmission of information, whether State or privately owned,

Recognizing the importance of the provision of accurate information to the Iraqi people,

Committed to creating an environment in which freedom of speech is cherished and information can be exchanged freely and openly,

Welcoming the emergence of a free and independent media in Iraq,

Determined to prevent the misuse of media to promote violence or undermine public security generally,

I hereby promulgate the following:

Section 1 Definition

'*Media organization*' includes individuals or groups, and private, corporate, or public entities, domestic or international, established for the purpose of transmitting information by any means.

Section 2 Prohibited Activities

Media organizations are prohibited from broadcasting or publishing original, re-broadcast, re-printed or syndicated material that:

a) incites violence against any individual or group, including racial, ethnic or religious groups and women;
b) incites civil disorder, rioting or damage to property;
c) incites violence against Coalition Forces or CPA personnel;
d) advocates alterations to Iraq's borders by violent means;
e) advocates the return to power of the Iraqi Ba'ath Party or makes statements that purport to be on behalf of the Iraqi Ba'ath Party.

Section 3 Detection of Prohibited Activities

1) The Administrator shall have the authority to use all the capabilities available to the CPA for the purpose of detecting prohibited activities under this Order,

2) The Administrator may authorize on-site inspections of Iraqi media organizations, without notice, in order to ascertain compliance with this Order and to seize any prohibited materials and production equipment and seal off any operating premises. No compensation will be allowed for any such material or equipment seized, or premises closed.[44]

Section 4 Emergency Security Response

1) Where any media activity poses an immediate threat to the security of Coalition Forces or CPA personnel, or a significant and immediate threat to public order, the Commander of Coalition Forces may take direct action to prevent or defeat the threat. Any action in accordance with this section will be immediately reported to the Administrator.

2) Nothing in this Order limits the authority of the Commander of Coalition Forces to execute military operations under applicable Rules of Engagement.[45]

Section 5 Penalties

1) Any media organization found to be broadcasting, publishing, or attempting to broadcast or publish prohibited material in violation of this Order may be detained, arrested, prosecuted and, if convicted, sentenced by relevant authorities to up to one year in prison or a fine of up to USD 1,000.00.

[44] Sec 3 was rescinded and replaced by CPA Order No 100, sec 3(5)(a) and (b) *[Doc 124]*.
[45] Sec 4 was rescinded by CPA Order No 100, sec 3(5)(c) *[Doc 124]*.

2) The Administrator may, in his discretion, withdraw the license, close the operation, confiscate the property, and seal the premises of any media organization found to be in breach of this Order.[46]

Section 6 Appeal by a Media Organization
Any media organization whose license, property, premises or operation has been withdrawn, seized, sealed or closed, may submit to the Administrator written evidence as to why the action should be reversed.[47]

Section 7 Entry into Force
This Order shall enter into force on the date of signature [signed without date].

Document 33
Coalition Provisional Authority Order Number 15
CPA/ORD/23 June 2003/15

Establishment of the Judicial Review Committee

Pursuant to my authority as Administrator of the Coalition Provisional Authority (CPA), and the laws and usages of war, and consistent with relevant U.N. Security Council resolutions, including Resolution 1483 (2003),

Noting the obligation on the CPA to restore and maintain order and the right of the CPA to take measures for its security, to ensure fundamental standards of due process and to promote the rule of law,

Noting that the Iraqi justice system has been subjected to political interference and corruption over the years of Iraqi Ba'ath Party rule,

Noting that it is inherent to the stability of any society that the judicial system is independent and impartial but is seen to be so,

Recognizing the role that the Judicial Review Committee will have in ensuring as far as possible the highest standard of judicial service in [sic],

Acting in accordance with the Administrator's Order Number 1 of May, 16 2003 on the De-Baathification of Iraqi Society (CPA/ORD/16 May 2003/01),[48]

I hereby promulgate the following:

Section 1 Establishment

1) There will be established an entity to be known as the Judicial Review Committee (hereinafter 'the Committee') which will commence operation at a time to be fixed by the Administrator.

2) The Committee will operate at the discretion of the Administrator and will terminate operation at a time to be fixed by the Administrator.

[46] Sec 5(2) was rescinded and replaced by CPA Order No 100, sec 3(5)(d) *[Doc 124]*.
[47] Sec 6 was rescinded and replaced by CPA Order No 100, sec 3(5)(e) *[Doc 124]*.
[48] See *Doc 14*.

Section 2 The Iraqi Judiciary Act
In accordance with Section Three of Coalition Provisional Authority Regulation Number One,[49] the Iraqi Organization of the Judiciary Act of 1979 ('Iraqi Judiciary Act') shall be suspended insofar as its provisions conflict with this Order, or any decision of the CPA, the Senior Advisor or the Judicial Review Committee. Nothing in the Iraqi Judiciary Act, or any other Iraqi law, shall impede the operation of the Committee as provided for in this Order and the Committee Terms of Reference.

Section 3 Composition of the Committee
1) The Committee shall be composed of three Iraqi members and three international members who shall be nominated by the Senior Advisor and appointed by the Administrator, and who shall serve at, the discretion of the Administrator.
2) The members of the Committee shall be qualified lawyers within their national jurisdictions and shall serve for a period of three months unless otherwise specified at the time of appointment.

Section 4 Powers and Functions
1) The Committee shall investigate and gather information on the suitability of Judges and Prosecutors to hold office. It shall have the power to remove judges and prosecutors from office, confirm their continued holding of office, appoint replacements for judges and prosecutors removed from office and resolve the claims of judges and prosecutors who assert that they were improperly removed from office.
2) The Committee will act in accordance with the Committee Terms of Reference.

Section 5 Obligation to Provide Information
1) [sic] All persons shall, on request by the Committee, and in accordance with the Terms of Reference, provide all authorized information within their possession, control or knowledge concerning any matter regarding which the Committee is authorized to obtain information.

Section 6 Regulation of the Council
1) The Council shall be bound by and operate in accordance with its Terms of Reference and any Regulations, Orders or Memoranda issued by the Administrator.
2) The Senior Adviser shall fix the remuneration of members of the Committee.
3) The Iraqi members of the committee shall retain any governmental positions that they hold. Any member of the Committee may continue to hold employment positions that they held prior to joining the Committee, if the Senior Advisor determines that they are able to do so without impeding their service on the Committee and that no conflict of interest or bias is created thereby.

Section 7 Entry into Force
This Order shall enter into force on the date of signature [23 June 2003].[50]

[49] See *Doc 1*.
[50] A new sec 8 was added by CPA Order No 100, sec 3(6) *[Doc 124]*.

Document 34
Coalition Provisional Authority Order Number 16
CPA/ORD/26 June 2003/16

Temporary Control of Iraqi Borders, Ports and Airports

Pursuant to my authority as Administrator of the Coalition Provisional Authority (CPA) and the laws and usages of war, and consistent with relevant U.N. Security Council Resolutions, including 1483 (2003),

Recognizing that it is desirable as soon as, possible to restore the normal transit and movement of people to and from Iraq,

Acknowledging that the Iraqi laws on immigration, customs and quarantine should remain in place unless exceptions prove necessary for security reasons or otherwise to accomplish the obligations of the CPA under the laws and usages of war,

Noting that the current security situation in Iraq does not permit the unrestricted resumption of normal transit and movement,

I hereby promulgate the following:

Section 1 Definitions

1) *'Authorized officer'* means any Coalition personnel or Iraqi officials designated by the CPA to perform border control, customs or quarantine services.

2) *'Coalition personnel'* means all non-Iraqi military and civilian personnel under the authority of the Coalition Forces Commander, as well as all non-Iraqi military and civilian personnel assigned to, or under the direction or control of, the Administrator of the CPA.

3) *'Goods'* means any substance, organism, article, or thing, whether manufactured or natural, which may be moved across the borders of Iraq and which is not a human body, a cadaver or human remains.

4) *'Member of a crew'* means a person, including a master, who is employed on a vehicle to perform duties during a voyage or trip related to the operation of the vehicle or the provision of services to passengers.

5) *'Terrorism'* means the use or threatened use of unlawful violence against civilians, noncombatants, or other innocents, calculated to cause fear or to coerce or intimidate governments or societies, and motivated by political, religious, or ideological goals.

6) *'Terrorist organization'* means an organization whose objective is to support or commit acts of terrorism, directly or indirectly, physically or financially.

7) *'Transportation company'* is any corporation, enterprise or other entity transporting persons to Iraq.

8) *'Travel documents'* means documents required by the CPA for entry into and exit from Iraq and may include a valid Iraqi passport or an internationally recognized document proving Iraqi citizenship, a valid entry or exit visa, and travel permits issued by an authorized travel permit issuing authority.

9) *'Vehicle'* means any conveyance that may be used for transportation by land, water or air.

Section 2 Preservation of Laws

1) All Iraqi laws regarding immigration, emigration, customs and quarantine shall remain in force unless specifically suspended by this Order.

2) Wherever a stipulation or provision of this Order or any other CPA Regulation, Order or Memorandum conflicts with a current provision of Iraqi immigration, emigration, customs and quarantine laws, the stipulation or provision contained in such Regulation, Order or Memorandum shall prevail.

3) The edict of the former President Saddam Hussein regarding the expiration of 'N' series passports issued during the years 1996 to 2002, fixing their expiration in the year 2003, is hereby suspended. All 'N' series passports will continue in effect for their statutory duration.

4) All Iraqi passports that have expired within the last four years will be deemed valid until December 31, 2003 for the exclusive purpose of direct return travel to Iraq, with such travel to be completed by December 31, 2003. Such a passport will not be considered valid for any other purpose.

5) All current Iraqi passports that have a four-year expiration period may be extended to eight years by any travel permit issuing authority. Any passport purporting to have been issued after March 19, 2003 that does not bear a CPA stamp is invalidated.

Section 3 Right to Exit

1) Subject to compliance with Iraqi law and with border control procedures established from time to time by the CPA, all persons may exit from Iraq, provided they are in possession of necessary travel documents and are not subject to any travel restrictions under applicable law including this Order.

2) The following persons shall require special clearance to exit Iraq and may be prevented from exiting at the discretion of the Senior Advisor of the Ministry of the Interior, in coordination with the Interim Minister of the Interior, when appointed [hereinafter Interim Minister of the Interior]:

a) Senior regime or military leadership and Senior Party Members or office holders of the Ba'ath Party, as described in CPA/ORD/16 May 2003/01;[51]

b) Persons suspected of having committed serious crimes;

c) Persons who are known or are suspected to have links to a terrorist organizations or who are suspected to have committed or to have provided financial, material, or technological support for acts of terrorism; and

d) Persons suspected of being involved with the manufacture, development, research, or transfer of technology or material related to weapons of mass destruction; or having knowledge of the location of weapons of mass destruction, or the identity of persons with such knowledge.

Section 4 Examinations for Entry

1) Subject to the present Order, a person seeking entry to Iraq shall appear before an authorized officer of the CPA (hereinafter 'officer') at a port of entry, border control station or at such other place as may be designated by the Senior Advisor of the Ministry of Interior, in coordination with the Interim Minister of the Interior, for examination to determine whether the person may be granted entry to Iraq.

[51] See *Doc 14*.

2) A person appearing for examination shall answer truthfully all questions put to that person and shall produce such documentation as may be required for the purpose of establishing whether the person may be granted entry.

Section 5 Permits to Enter Iraq

1) Persons seeking entry to Iraq are to be classified as either persons who require permits granting entry into Iraq (hereinafter 'permits') or persons who do not require such permits. Officers shall issue permits valid for up to 90 days, in accordance with this Order and with applicable law.

2) Persons not requiring permits to enter Iraq are all those persons not otherwise denied permits under this Order who are a) citizens of Iraq or persons who were born in Iraq, b) Coalition personnel, or c) United Nations officials or any official of any other U.N. organization. Persons requiring permits are all persons who are not listed in this Section 5.2.

3) Permits may be obtained and issued from any Iraqi embassies that have reopened, and from CPA offices established for this purpose within Iraq.

Section 6 Powers of an Officer

1) An officer who receives an application for a permit shall either approve or refuse the application, and shall notify the applicant of the decision. At any time after an application for a permit is approved, the officer may:

a) Alter or revoke any terms and conditions subject to which the person was granted entry;

b) Add terms and conditions as prescribed by the present Order and other CPA Regulations, Orders or Memoranda; and/or

c) Extend the permit.

2) Subject to the present Order, a visitor seeking an extension of a permit shall appear before an officer at such place as may be designated by the CPA Senior Advisor of the Ministry of the Interior, in coordination with the Interim Minister of the Interior, for examination to determine whether the visitor may be granted an extension of a permit.

3) A visitor appearing for examination shall answer truthfully all questions put to that visitor and shall produce such documentation as may be required for the purpose of establishing whether the visitor may be granted an extension of a permit.

Section 7 Persons Who May Be Denied Entry to Iraq

1) An officer who receives an application for a permit may refuse the application if the officer has reasonable grounds to believe that the applicant:

a) knowingly provided any false, misleading, or inaccurate information in the course of the application process;

b) is suffering from any serious communicable disease, or is suffering from any disorder, disability or other health impairment for which commercial health services are not readily available in Iraq;

c) will be unable or unwilling to support themselves, and those persons who are dependent on the applicant;

d) is or was a member of a criminal organization;

e) will commit offenses, or engage in criminal activity planned and organized by persons acting in concert with or in furtherance of the commission of any offense;

f) will engage in or has engaged in an act of terrorism, or is a member of a terrorist organization or an organization that there are reasonable grounds to believe will:

i) engage in acts which are offensive to the principles of democratic government, institutions or processes, in Iraq; or
ii) engage in or instigate the removal by force of any government;

g) will engage in acts of violence that may endanger the lives or safety of persons in Iraq, or who is a member of an organization that engages in such acts;
h) has committed acts or omissions that constituted a war crime or a crime against humanity; or
i) has previously been deported from, or denied entry to, Iraq by the CPA, or an international territory with border control formalities.

2) In exercising the discretion set out in this Order, an officer shall consider whether the entry of the person poses a substantial risk to the people or interests of Iraq or in the case of a person who has established that he or she is an Iraqi national, whether entry should be denied because of security or military necessity.

3) A person denied entry under this Order may appeal to the Senior Advisor of the Ministry of Interior and the Interim Minister of the Interior for a review of the case. The determination of the Senior Advisor of Ministry of the Interior, in coordination with the Interim Minister of the Interior, will be final.

Section 8 Notice to Depart

1) Where an officer, upon examination of a person, is of the opinion that it would be contrary to the present Order to grant entry to the person, or to extend the permit of a person, the officer may, as appropriate:

a) allow that person to leave Iraq immediately; and/or
b) serve that person with a Notice to Depart (hereinafter 'Notice') within a specified period.

2) A Notice must specify:

a) that the person must depart Iraq within a specified period;
b) the reasons why the Notice is being served;
c) that the person may object in writing to the Senior Advisor of the Ministry of Interior and the Interim Minister of the Interior within a specified time to this Notice, or give reasons why the Notice should not remain in force; and
d) that timely compliance will not have adverse consequences for the return of a person who otherwise complies with entry requirements.

3) Where the Senior Advisor of the Ministry of Interior or the Interim Minister of the Interior receives written objections from a person under this Order, the Senior Advisor of the Ministry of the Interior shall, in coordination with the Interim Minister of the Interior:

a) consider these promptly;
b) promptly determine the fair and lawful resolution of the matter; and
c) advise the person in writing of the decision.

Section 9 Revocation of a Permit

1) An officer may revoke a person's permit if:

a) the circumstances that formed the basis of the approval of the person's application for the permit no longer exist;
b) the person breaches a prescribed term of the permit, or another person required to comply with a condition of the permit has not met that condition;
c) the presence of the person in Iraq is, or would be, a risk to the health, safety or good order of the Iraqi community; or

d) the permit should not have been granted because the application for the permit was in contravention of the present Order or other applicable law.

Section 10 Identification and Seizure of Documents

1) Persons shall comply with the instructions of an officer regarding their identification if they a) seek entry into Iraq, b) make an application for the renewal of a permit, c) after being arrested or having been reported to a police officer, or other CPA or Coalition Force security personnel, or d) are subject to deportation under this Order.

2) For the purpose of identification, an officer may:

a) search persons or vehicles whom the officer believes have not revealed their identity or who have hidden on or about their person documents that are relevant to a decision as to whether they may be granted permission to enter Iraq, and may search any vehicle that conveyed the persons to Iraq and their luggage and personal effects;

b) search persons whom the officer reasonably believes have committed, or who are in possession of documents that may be used in the commission of an offense, and search any vehicle that conveyed the person to Iraq and their luggage and personal effects;

c) examine at a port of entry or any other place in Iraq, for the purpose of this Order or relevant directives, any travel document or any other document or object purporting to be any of those documents or objects that is, or is about to be, imported into or exported from Iraq.

3) An officer may seize and hold at a port of entry or any other place in Iraq any object or document if the officer reasonably deems this necessary for the discharge of the functions of the officer under this Order.

4) An officer may seize and hold any object or document if the officer reasonably believes that it has been fraudulently or improperly obtained or used, or that such action is necessary to prevent its fraudulent or improper use.

5) An officer shall provide a written receipt to any individual from whom he seizes an object or document under this Order.

Section 11 Search of a Person

1) An officer may, without a warrant, search a person who seeks entry to Iraq.

2) The search of a person must be made by an officer pursuant to the present Order and must be made on reasonable grounds.

3) No person shall be searched by a person who is not of the same sex, and if there is no officer of the same sex at the place at which the search is to take place, an officer may authorize any suitable person of the same sex to perform the search.

Section 12 Search and Seizure of Goods

1) An officer may, without a warrant, search the vehicle, luggage or personal effects of any person who seeks entry into Iraq.

2) Persons crossing the borders of Iraq must make declarations or manifests of all goods being carried by the person available to an officer on request.

3) An officer may confiscate any goods that may pose a threat to the peace, security, health, environment, or good order of Iraq or any antiquities or cultural items suspected of being illegally exported.

4) Goods that are not declared may be confiscated by an officer. Persons may also be ordered to return such goods, at their expense, to the jurisdiction from which they came.

5) Any goods confiscated must be immediately handed over to the Senior Advisor of the Ministry of Interior and the Interim Minister of the Interior, or to delegate(s) selected and agreed upon by the Senior Advisor and the Interim Minister, and a receipt must be issued to the person from whom the goods are confiscated.

Section 13 Offenses

The following shall constitute an offense under this Order:

a) failure to appear before an officer for examination as required by this Order;

b) failure to answer truthfully all questions put to that person by an officer during examination;

c) failure to produce documentation as may be required by the officer during examination;

d) failure to make a declaration or manifest of all goods being carried by the person on request by an officer;

e) failure to cooperate with a search of the person or search of the person's vehicle, luggage or personal effects pursuant to this Order;

f) knowingly making a false representation by reason of which a person is induced to seek entry to Iraq or is assisted in any attempt to seek entry or by reason of which that person's entry is procured;

g) entering Iraq or remaining in Iraq without a permit, where a person requires a permit;

h) entering Iraq or remaining in Iraq by use of a false or improperly obtained travel document or other document pertaining to the entry of that person or by reason of any fraudulent or improper means or misrepresentation of any material fact;

i) breaching a prescribed term of a permit;

j) escaping or attempting to escape from lawful custody or detention under the present Order and relevant directives; or

k) organizing or facilitating the entry or proposed entry into Iraq of a person, knowing the person would, upon entering Iraq, be guilty of an offense under this Section.

Section 14 Penalties

A person who commits an offense described in this Order is liable to have any goods in their possession confiscated and may be deported from Iraq. The person may also be liable to a penalty prescribed in an applicable Iraqi law or CPA Order, Regulation or other directive.

Section 15 Liability for Removal Costs

1) A transportation company shall ensure a) that the persons it conveys to Iraq are in possession of all travel documents required by applicable law, b) that upon arrival of each one of its vehicles in Iraq, present each person to an officer for examination at such place as may be designated by an officer and c) that no other person leaves the vehicle:

a) at any place other than that designated by an officer; or

b) until permission has been granted by an officer.

2) Where a person has been allowed or required to leave Iraq pursuant to this Order, a transportation company that has conveyed the person to Iraq may be required by an officer

to cause that person to be conveyed to the country from which that person came, or to such other country as the officer may approve at the request of the company.

3) Where a person has been required to leave Iraq because at the time of the arrival in Iraq the person was not in possession of a valid travel document required by applicable law, a transportation company that has conveyed the person to Iraq shall be liable to pay all costs of conveying that person to the country from which that person came, or to such other country as an officer may approve at the request of the company.

4) Where a person has been granted entry to Iraq, or where that person, at the time of arrival in Iraq, was in possession of a valid travel document, and where that person is required to leave Iraq pursuant to the present Order, a transportation company that has conveyed the person to Iraq and that is required to cause that person to be conveyed from Iraq is entitled to be reimbursed by the Senior Advisor of the Ministry of the Interior, in coordination with the Interim Minister of the Interior, for the costs of conveying that person from Iraq. However a transportation company shall not be reimbursed for the costs of conveying from Iraq a person who enters Iraq as, or to become, a member of a crew.

5) Where a person enters Iraq as, or to become, a member of a crew of a vehicle and ceases to be a visitor, the transportation company that operates that vehicle may be required to cause that person to be conveyed to the country from which that person came, or to such other country as the Senior Advisor of the Ministry of the Interior, in coordination with the Interim Minister of the Interior, may approve at the request of the company. The transportation company shall be liable to pay all costs of conveying that person from Iraq.

Section 16 Other Offenses

1) Where an officer has reasonable grounds to believe that a person who seeks entry to or exit from Iraq, or who seeks to remain in Iraq, is liable for an offense committed under applicable law in Iraq, other than an offense prescribed in this Order, the officer shall report the matter immediately to security forces, who may take such action as they deem appropriate.

2) Where the circumstances of the case require, an officer may arrest a person suspected of having committed an offense other than an offense prescribed in this Order. The arrest must be immediately reported to the Senior Advisor of the Ministry of Interior and the Interim Minister of the Interior, and the arrested person must, as soon as possible but no later than six hours after the arrest, be delivered into the custody of security forces.

Section 17 Review

A person against whom an adverse decision has been made by an officer under this Order may apply in writing to the Senior Advisor of the Ministry of the Interior and the Interim Minister of the Interior for a review of the decision. Within seven days of receipt of the application, the Senior Advisor of the Ministry of the Interior, in coordination with the Interim Minister of the Interior, shall review the decision and notify the applicant of the determination.

Section 18 Entry into Force

This Order shall enter into force on the date of signature [27 June 2003].

Document 35
Coalition Provisional Authority Order Number 16 (Revised)
CPA/ORD/1 December 2003/16

Temporary Control of Iraqi Borders, Ports and Airports

Pursuant to my authority as Administrator of the Coalition Provisional Authority (CPA) and under the laws and usages of war, and consistent with relevant U.N. Security Council Resolutions, including 1483 (2003) and Resolution 1511 (2003),

Recognizing that it is desirable as soon as, [sic] possible to restore the normal transit and movement of people to and from Iraq,

Acknowledging that the Iraqi laws on immigration, customs and quarantine should remain in place unless exceptions prove necessary for security reasons or otherwise to accomplish the obligations of the CPA under the laws and usages of war,

Recognizing that effective export and border controls are essential to prevent the proliferation of weapons of mass destruction, their delivery systems, advanced conventional weapons and related technologies,

Noting that the current security situation in Iraq does not permit the unrestricted resumption of normal transit and movement,

I hereby promulgate the following:

Section 1 Definitions

1) *'Authorized officer'* means any Coalition personnel or Iraqi officials designated by the CPA to perform border control, customs, immigration, consular or quarantine services.

2) *'Coalition personnel'* means all non-Iraqi military and civilian personnel under the authority of the Coalition Forces Commander, as well as all non-Iraqi military and civilian personnel assigned to, or under the direction or control of, the Administrator of the CPA.

3) *'Designated travel permit issuing authority'* means (a) Ministry of Interior offices and, if any, Ministry of Foreign Affairs offices designated by the Interim Minister of Interior or Deputy Interim Minister of Interior to issue interim travel documents and to extend Iraqi passports; (b) any Iraqi mission located outside Iraq designated by the Interim Minister of Foreign Affairs or the Director of Consular Affairs to issue interim travel documents and to extend Iraqi passports in addition to issuing diplomatic and official passports.

4) *'Goods'* means any commodity, substance, organism, article, document, data or thing, whether manufactured or natural, including any Controlled Item, that may be moved across the borders of Iraq. 'Goods' does not include human bodies, cadavers or human remains.

5) *'Member of a crew'* means a person, including a master, who is employed on a vehicle to perform duties during a voyage or trip related to the operation of the vehicle or the provision of services to passengers.

6) *'Controlled Item'* means any item contained in the control lists of the Missile Technology Control Regime, the Australia Group, the Nuclear Suppliers Group, the Zangger Committee or the Wassenaar Arrangement or any other documents, systems, components, materials, software or technology that may be intended to contribute to the acquisition, manufacture, development, research or transfer of Weapons of Mass Destruction, their delivery systems or advanced conventional military systems. 'Technology' includes

information necessary for the design, development, production, or use of a controlled commodity or software.

7) *'Terrorism'* means the use or threatened use of unlawful violence against civilians, noncombatants, or other innocents, calculated to cause fear or to coerce or intimidate governments or societies, and motivated by political, religious, or ideological goals.

8) *'Terrorist organization'* means an organization whose objective is to support or commit acts of terrorism, directly or indirectly, physically or financially.

9) *'Transportation company'* is any corporation, enterprise or other entity transporting persons to Iraq.

10) *'Travel documents'* means documents required by the CPA for entry into and exit from Iraq. These may include: a) an Iraqi passport valid on its face or which has had its validity extended consistent with this Order, b) a CPA Interim Travel Document (ITD), c) a document or documents proving Iraqi nationality (including an Iraqi Nationality Card) for return to Iraq, d) a travel permit issued by an authorized officer as defined by this Order, or e) a document issued by a foreign government or an international organization, such as the United Nations High Commissioner for Refugees or the International Committee of the Red Cross identifying the person as a refugee from Iraq.

11) *'Travel permit'* means a permit to enter Iraq issued pursuant to Section 5 of this Order.

12) *'Vehicle'* means any conveyance that may be used for transportation by land, water or air.

13) *'Weapons of Mass Destruction'* means nuclear, biological, or chemical weapons.

Section 2 Preservation of Laws

1) All Iraqi laws regarding immigration, emigration, customs and quarantine shall remain in force unless specifically suspended by this Order.

2) Wherever a stipulation or provision of this Order or any other CPA Regulation, Order or Memorandum conflicts with a current provision of Iraqi immigration, emigration, customs and quarantine laws, the stipulation or provision contained in such Regulation, Order or Memorandum shall prevail.

3) The edict of the former President Saddam Hussein regarding the expiration of 'N' series passports issued during the years 1996 to 2002, fixing their expiration in the year 2003, is hereby suspended. All 'N' and 'M' series passports will continue in effect for their statutory duration.

4) All Iraqi passports that have expired since June 27, 1999, or will expire before January 1, 2004, for the exclusive purpose of direct return travel to Iraq, will be deemed valid until December 31, 2003, with such travel to be completed by December 31, 2003. Such a passport will not be considered valid for any other purpose.

5) All Iraqi passports in the 'N' and 'M' series may be extended by any designated travel permit issuing authority. Passports presented to a designated travel permit issuing authority for extension on or before their original expiration date or within the two months immediately following their original expiration date may be extended for a period of 4 years. Passports presented to a designated travel permit issuing authority for extension after the two months following their original expiration date may be extended for a period of 2 years. Any passport purporting to have been issued after March 19, 2003 that does not bear a CPA/Ministry of Foreign Affairs stamp and/or a CPA/Ministry of Interior stamp, as appropriate, is invalid. Any Iraqi passport valid under this Order may be amended by any authorized officer at an Iraqi mission overseas to register a child born on or after January 1,

2001, on the passport of a parent, guardian, or legal trustee, in accordance with established Iraqi law and procedures.

6) Consistent with Section 2 of CPA Order No. 26 (CPA/ORD/24 August 2003/26),[52] the Ministry of Foreign Affairs has the authority to grant, issue, renew, extend or amend diplomatic and service passports in accordance with established procedures and for the purpose of facilitating official travel of Iraqi officials. As of January 1, 2004, all diplomatic and service passports that do not have a CPA/Ministry of Foreign Affairs stamp either to reflect issuance, renewal, extension or validation, are declared invalid for travel except for direct return travel to Iraq. Such passports may be confiscated by any authorized officer or any authorized representative of the Ministry of Foreign Affairs.

Section 3 Right to Exit

1) Subject to compliance with Iraqi law and with border control procedures established from time to time by the CPA, all persons may exit from Iraq, provided they are in possession of travel documents and are not subject to any travel restrictions under applicable law including this Order.

2) The following persons shall require special clearance to exit Iraq and may be prevented from exiting at the discretion of the Ministry of the Interior:

a) Senior regime or military leadership and Senior Party Members or office holders of the Ba'ath Party, as described in CPA/ORD/16 May 2003/01;[53]
b) Persons suspected of having committed serious crimes;
c) Persons who are known or are suspected to have links to a terrorist organizations or who are suspected to have committed or to have provided financial, material, or technological support for acts of terrorism; and
d) Persons suspected of being involved or attempting to be involved with the acquisition, manufacture, development, research, or transfer of technology or material related to Weapons of Mass Destruction or their delivery systems; or having knowledge of the location of Weapons of Mass Destruction or their delivery systems, or the identity of persons with such knowledge.

Section 4 Examinations for Entry

1) Subject to the present Order, a person seeking entry to Iraq shall appear before an authorized officer at a port of entry, border control station or at such other place as may be designated by the Ministry of the Interior for examination to determine whether the person may be granted entry to Iraq.

2) A person appearing for examination shall answer truthfully all questions put to that person and shall produce such documentation as may be required for the purpose of establishing whether the person may be granted entry.

3) A person may be detained for further examination upon entry and/or pending arrangements for his or her removal.

Section 5 Permits to Enter Iraq

1) Persons seeking entry to Iraq are to be classified as either persons who require permits granting entry into Iraq (hereinafter 'permits') or persons who do not require such permits. All persons who are not listed in Sections 5 (2) or 5 (3) of this Order require

[52] See *Doc 47*.
[53] See *Doc 14*.

permits. Authorized officers shall issue permits valid for up to 90 days, in accordance with this Order and with applicable law.

2) Persons not requiring permits to enter Iraq are all those persons not otherwise denied permits under this Order who are a) citizens of Iraq or persons who were born in Iraq, b) Coalition personnel, c) United Nations officials or any official of any other UN organization, and d) documented members of seagoing ships' companies during the stay of a ship in Iraqi waters, or e) documented members of airship companies during the stay of the aircraft in Iraqi territory. Persons requiring permits are all persons who are not listed in this Section 5.2.

3) Persons seeking entry into Iraq for tourism purposes require only those documents directed in writing by the CPA for such limited-duration visits.

4) Permits may be obtained and issued from any Iraqi missions or embassies that have reopened, and from CPA offices established for this purpose within Iraq and at authorized ports of entry.

Section 6 Powers of an Authorized Officer

1) An authorized officer who receives an application for a permit shall either approve or refuse the application, and shall notify the applicant of the decision. At any time after an application for a permit is approved, the authorized officer may:

a) Alter or revoke any terms and conditions subject to which the person was granted entry;

b) Add terms and conditions as prescribed by the present Order and other CPA Regulations, Orders or Memoranda; and/or

c) Extend the permit.

2) Subject to the present Order, a visitor seeking an extension of a permit shall appear before an authorized officer at such place as may be designated by the Ministry of the Interior for examination to determine whether the visitor may be granted an extension of a permit.

3) A visitor appearing for examination shall answer truthfully all questions put to that visitor and shall produce such documentation as may be required for the purpose of establishing whether the visitor may be granted an extension of a permit.

Section 7 Persons Who May Be Denied Entry to Iraq

1) An authorized officer who receives an application for a permit may refuse the application if the officer has reasonable grounds to believe that the applicant:

a) knowingly provided any false, misleading, or inaccurate information in the course of the application process;

b) is suffering from any serious communicable disease, or is suffering from any disorder, disability or other health impairment for which commercial health services are not readily available in Iraq;

c) will be unable or unwilling to support herself or himself, and those persons who are dependent on the applicant;

d) is or was a member of a criminal organization;

e) will commit offenses, or engage in criminal activity planned and organized by persons acting in concert with or in furtherance of the commission of any offense;

f) will engage in or has engaged in an act of terrorism, or is a member of a terrorist organization or an organization that there are reasonable grounds to believe will:

i) engage in acts which are offensive to the principles of democratic government, institutions or processes in Iraq; or

ii) engage in or instigate the removal by force of any government;

g) will engage in acts of violence that may endanger the lives or safety of persons in Iraq, or who is a member of an organization that engages in such acts;

h) has been involved or attempted to be involved with the acquisition, manufacture, development, research or transfer of technology or material related to Weapons of Mass Destruction, their delivery systems, or advanced conventional military systems, including dual use items;

i) has committed acts or omissions that constituted a war crime or a crime against humanity; or

j) has previously been deported from, or denied entry to, Iraq by the CPA, or an international territory with border control formalities.

2) In the case of a person is in [sic] possession of a valid travel document, or who can otherwise establish Iraqi nationality, his or her entry into Iraq shall not be denied; however, if security or military necessity requires, such a person may be detained upon entry into Iraq.

3) A person denied entry under this Order may appeal to the Ministry of the Interior for a review of the case. The determination of the Ministry of the Interior, will be final.

Section 8 Notice to Depart

1) Where an authorized officer, upon examination of a person, is of the opinion that it would be contrary to the present Order to grant entry to the person, or to extend the permit of a person, the authorized officer may, as appropriate:

a) allow that person to leave Iraq immediately; and/or

b) serve that person with a Notice to Depart (hereinafter 'Notice') within a specified period.

2) A Notice must specify:

a) that the person must depart Iraq within a specified period;

b) the reasons why the Notice is being served;

c) that the person may object in writing to the Ministry of the Interior within a specified time, or give reasons why the Notice should not remain in force; and

d) that timely compliance will not have adverse consequences for the return of a person who otherwise complies with entry requirements.

3) Where the Ministry of the Interior receives written objections from a person under this Order, the Ministry of the Interior shall:

a) consider such written objections promptly;

b) promptly determine the fair and lawful resolution of the matter; and

c) advise the person in writing of the decision.

Section 9 Revocation of a Permit

An authorized officer may revoke a person's permit if:

a) the circumstances that formed the basis of the approval of the person's application for the permit no longer exist;

b) the person breaches a prescribed term of the permit, or another person required to comply with a condition of the permit has not met that condition;

c) the presence of the person in Iraq is, or would be, a risk to the health, safety or good order of the Iraqi community; or

d) the permit should not have been granted because the application for the permit was in contravention of the present Order or other applicable law.

Section 10 Identification and Seizure of Documents

1) Persons shall comply with the instructions of an authorized officer regarding their identification a) if they seek entry into Iraq, b) if they make an application for the renewal of a permit, c) if they have been arrested, or d) if they are subject to deportation under this Order.

2) For the purpose of identification, an authorized officer may:

a) search persons who the authorized officer believes either have not revealed their identity or have hidden on or about their person documents that are relevant to a decision as to whether they may be granted permission to enter Iraq, and may search any vehicle that conveyed the persons to Iraq and their luggage and personal effects;

b) search persons who the authorized officer reasonably believes have committed an offense or are in possession of documents that may be used in the commission of an offense, and search any vehicle that conveyed the person to Iraq and their luggage and personal effects;

c) examine any travel document or any other document purporting to be a travel documents at a port of entry or any other place in Iraq, for the purpose of this Order or relevant directives, examine any object that is, or is about to be, imported into or exported from Iraq.

3) An authorized officer may seize and hold at a port of entry or any other place in Iraq any object or document if the authorized officer reasonably deems this necessary for the discharge of the functions of the officer under this Order.

4) An authorized officer may seize and hold any object or document if the officer reasonably believes that it has been fraudulently or improperly obtained or used, or that such action is necessary to prevent its fraudulent or improper use.

5) An authorized officer shall provide a written receipt to any individual from whom he seizes an object or document under this Order.

Section 11 Search of a Person

1) An officer may, without a warrant, search a person who seeks entry to Iraq.

2) The search of a person must be made by an authorized officer pursuant to the present Order and must be made on reasonable grounds.

3) No person shall be searched by a person who is not of the same sex, and if there is no officer of the same sex at the place at which the search is to take place, an authorized officer may request that another border control or customs employee of the same sex perform the search, when necessary to comply with this provision.

Section 12 Search and Seizure of Goods

1) An authorized officer may, without a warrant, search the vehicle, luggage or personal effects of any person who seeks entry into Iraq.

2) Persons crossing the borders of Iraq must make declarations or manifests of all goods being carried by the person available to an authorized officer on request.

3) An authorized officer shall confiscate any goods that may pose a threat to the peace, security, health, environment, or good order of Iraq, including Controlled Items. Authorized officers also shall confiscate any antiquities or cultural items suspected of being illegally exported.

4) The export or import of a Controlled Item shall require the prior written authorization of the Administrator, or his designee. Such prior written authorization requirement shall not apply to exports of Controlled Items by the CPA or Coalition personnel. Such prior

written authorization requirement shall also not apply to exports of Controlled Items by Coalition contractors, as defined in Section 1(5) of CPA Order No. 16 [sic];[54] provided, however, that the contractor must be exporting such Controlled Items in connection with the performance of its contract with the Coalition.

5) Goods that are not declared may be confiscated by an authorized officer. Persons may also be ordered to return such goods, at their expense, to the jurisdiction from which they came.

6) Any goods confiscated must be immediately handed over to the Ministry of the Interior or to his or her delegate(s), and a receipt must be issued to the person from whom the goods are confiscated.

Section 13 Offenses

1) Allegations of an offense shall be subject to review and action, if appropriate, by an investigative judge of a customs court of Iraq or a criminal court of Iraq, as appropriate to the alleged offense.

2) The following shall constitute an offense under this Order:

a) failing to appear before an authorized officer for examination as required by this Order;

b) failing to answer truthfully all questions by an authorized officer during examination;

c) knowingly concealing documentation as may be required by the authorized officer during examination;

d) failing to make a declaration or manifest of all goods being carried by the person on request by an authorized officer;

e) failing to cooperate with a search of the person or search of the person's vehicle, luggage or personal effects pursuant to this Order;

f) knowingly making a false representation, orally or in writing, to an authorized officer for the purposes of securing entry of a person into Iraq;

g) entering Iraq or remaining in Iraq without a permit, if one is required;

h) entering Iraq or remaining in Iraq by use of a false or improperly obtained travel document or other document pertaining to the entry of that person or by reason of any fraudulent or improper means or misrepresentation of any material fact;

i) failing to comply with a prescribed term of a permit;

j) escaping or attempting to escape from lawful custody or detention under the present Order and relevant directives;

k) organizing or facilitating the entry or proposed entry into Iraq of a person, knowing the person would, upon entering Iraq, be guilty of an offense under this Section; or

l) seeking to export or import, or exporting or importing Controlled Items without prior authorization issued pursuant to Section 12(4) of this Order.

Section 14 Penalties

A person who commits an offense described in this Order is liable to have any goods in his or her possession confiscated and may be deported from Iraq. The person may also be liable to a penalty prescribed in an applicable Iraqi law or CPA Order, Regulation or other directive.

[54] CPA Order No 16, sec 1(5) contains a definition of 'terrorism', see *Doc 34*.

Section 15 Liability for Removal Costs

1) A transportation company shall ensure that:

a) the persons it conveys to Iraq are in possession of all travel documents required by applicable law,

b) its presents each person to an authorized officer for examination at such place as may be designated by an authorized officer upon arrival of each one of its vehicles in Iraq, and

c) no other person leaves the vehicle i) at any place other than that designated by an authorized officer, or ii) until permission has been granted by an authorized officer.

2) Where a person has been allowed or required to leave Iraq pursuant to this Order, a transportation company that has conveyed the person to Iraq may be required by an authorized officer to cause that person to be conveyed to the country from which that person came, or to such other country as the authorized officer may approve at the request of the company.

3) Where a person has been required to leave Iraq because at the time of the arrival in Iraq the person was not in possession of a valid travel document required by applicable law, a transportation company that has conveyed the person to Iraq shall be liable to pay all costs of conveying that person to the country from which that person came, or to such other country as an authorized officer may approve at the request of the company.

4) Where a person has been granted entry to Iraq, or where that person, at the time of arrival in Iraq, was in possession of a valid travel document, and where that person is required to leave Iraq pursuant to the present Order, a transportation company that has conveyed the person to Iraq and that is required to cause that person to be conveyed from Iraq is entitled to be reimbursed by the Ministry of the Interior for the costs of conveying that person from Iraq. However a transportation company shall not be reimbursed for the costs of conveying from Iraq a person who enters Iraq as, or to become, a member of a crew.

5) Where a person enters Iraq as, or to become, a member of a crew of a vehicle and ceases to be a visitor, the transportation company that operates that vehicle may be required to cause that person to be conveyed to the country from which that person came, or to such other country as the Ministry of the Interior may approve at the request of the company. The transportation company shall be liable to pay all costs of conveying that person from Iraq.

Section 16 Other Offenses

1) Where an authorized officer has reasonable grounds to believe that a person who seeks entry to or exit from Iraq, or who seeks to remain in Iraq, is liable for an offense committed under applicable law in Iraq, other than an offense prescribed in this Order, the authorized officer shall report the matter immediately to security forces, who may take such action as they deem appropriate.

2) Where the circumstances of the case require, an authorized officer may arrest a person suspected of having committed an offense other than an offense prescribed in this Order. The arrest must be immediately reported to the Interim Minister of the Interior [sic], and the arrested person must, as soon as possible but no later than six hours after the arrest, be delivered into the custody of security forces.

Section 17 Review

1) A person against whom an adverse decision has been made by an authorized officer under this Order may apply in writing to the Ministry of the Interior for a review of the decision. Within seven days of receipt of the application, the Ministry of the Interior shall review the decision and notify the applicant of the determination.

2) A person whose goods have been confiscated may apply in writing, with a copy of the confiscation receipt attached, to the Ministry of Interior for a review of the decision. Within seven days of receipt of the application, the Ministry of Interior shall review the decision and notify the applicant of the determination.

3) The Ministry of Interior may issue Administrative Instructions in connection with such reviews.

Section 18 Entry into Force
This Order shall enter into force on the date of signature [1 December 2003].

Document 36
Coalition Provisional Authority Order Number 16 (Revised) (Amended)

CPA/ORD/4 June 2004/16

Temporary Control of Iraqi Borders, Ports and Airports

Pursuant to my authority as Administrator of the Coalition Provisional Authority (CPA) and under the laws and usages of war, and consistent with relevant U.N. Security Council Resolutions, including Resolution 1483 (2003) and Resolution 1511 (2003),

Recognizing that it is desirable as soon as possible to restore the normal transit and movement of people to and from Iraq,

Acknowledging that the Iraqi laws on immigration, customs and quarantine should remain in place unless exceptions prove necessary for security reasons or otherwise to accomplish the obligations of the CPA under the laws and usages of war,

Recognizing that effective export and border controls are essential to prevent terrorist activities and the proliferation of weapons of mass destruction, their delivery systems, advanced conventional weapons and related technologies,

Noting that the current security situation in Iraq does not permit the unrestricted resumption of normal transit and movement,

I hereby promulgate the following:

Section 1 Definitions

1) *'Authorized officer'* means any Coalition personnel or Iraqi official designated by the CPA, Ministry of Interior or Ministry of Foreign Affairs to perform border control, customs, immigration, consular or quarantine services. For purposes of issuance and revocation of travel documents (including permits) only, authorized officer means 'designated travel document issuing authority' as defined in Section 1.1 [sic].[55]

2) '*Coalition contractor*' and '*contractor*' has the same meaning as the definitions in Section 1 of CPA Order Number 17 as revised or amended.[56]

[55] Sec 1(1) was amended by CPA Order No 100, sec 3(7)(a) *[Doc 124]*.

[56] At the time of signature of the revised and amended CPA Order No 16 CPA Order No 17 had not yet been revised. The revised version of Order No 17 did no longer define 'coalition contractor'; see *Doc 38*. The definition of the term can be found in original CPA Order No 17, sec 1(5) *[Doc 37]*.

3) *'Coalition personnel'* means:
   a) all non-Iraqi military and civilian personnel under the authority of the Commander of Coalition Forces or the Commander Multi-national Force Iraq, as well as all non-Iraqi military and civilian personnel assigned to, or under the direction or control of, the Administrator of the CPA or its successor organization;
   b) citizens or nationals traveling to Iraq on official government business of the United States of America, United Kingdom, Australia, Italy, The Netherlands, Poland, Ukraine, Portugal; and
   c) citizens or nationals traveling to Iraq on official government business of any other designated state: such designations will be made by the CPA or the Ministry of Foreign Affairs.[57]

4) *'Designated travel document issuing authority'* means:
   a) [sic] with respect to issuance of regular passports, interim travel documents and extending Iraqi passports, the offices of the Ministries of Interior and Foreign Affairs so designated by the Minister or Deputy Minister of Interior, and any Iraqi mission located outside Iraq so designated by the Minister of Foreign Affairs or the Director of Consular Affairs;
   b) with respect to issuance of Iraqi diplomatic and official passports, the Ministry of Foreign Affairs;
   c) with respect to travel permits, the Ministry of Foreign Affairs and any Iraqi mission located outside Iraq so designated by the Minister of Foreign Affairs or the Director of Consular Services to do so, or Ministry of Interior offices so designated by the Minister or Deputy Minister of Interior; and
   d) with respect to special clearances the Ministry of Interior offices so designated by the Minister or Deputy Minister of Interior.

5) *'Goods'* means any commodity, substance, organism, article, document, data or thing, whether manufactured or natural, including any Controlled Item that may be moved across the borders of Iraq. 'Goods' does not include human bodies, cadavers or human remains.

6) *'Member of a crew'* means a person, including a master, who is employed on a vehicle to perform duties during a voyage or trip related to the operation of the vehicle or the provision of services to passengers.

7) *'Controlled Item'* means any item contained in the control lists of the Missile Technology Control Regime, the Australia Group, the Nuclear Suppliers Group, the Zangger Committee or the Wassenaar Arrangement or any other documents, systems, components, materials, software or technology that may be intended to contribute to the acquisition, manufacture, development, research or transfer of Weapons of Mass Destruction, their delivery systems or advanced conventional military systems. 'Technology' includes information necessary for the design, development, production, or use of a controlled commodity or software.

8) *'Terrorism'* means the use or threatened use of unlawful violence against civilians, noncombatants, or other innocents, calculated to cause fear or to coerce or intimidate governments or societies, and motivated by political, religious, or ideological goals.

9) *'Terrorist Organization'* means an organization whose objective is to support or commit acts of terrorism, directly or indirectly, physically or financially.

10) *'Transportation Company'* is any corporation, enterprise or other entity transporting persons and/or goods to and from Iraq.

[57] A new sec 1(3)(d) was added by CPA Order No 100, sec 3(7)(b). See also sec 3(7)(c) *[Doc 124]*.

11) *'Travel Documents'* means documents required by the CPA, Ministry of the Interior or Ministry of Foreign Affairs for entry into and exit from Iraq. These may include:

a) an Iraqi passport valid on its face or which has had its validity extended consistent with this Order;
b) a CPA Interim Travel Document (ITD);
c) a document or documents proving Iraqi nationality (including an Iraqi Nationality Card) issued for the purposes of return to Iraq;
d) a travel permit issued by an authorized officer as defined by this Order;
e) a document issued by a foreign government or an international organization, such as the United Nations High Commission for Refugees or *the International Committee of the Red Cross* identifying the person as a refugee from Iraq; and
f) passports of any country, government issued identification cards, military identification, government issued travel orders for military personnel, and U.N. issued travel documentations.

12) *'Travel permit'* means a permit to enter Iraq issued pursuant to Section 5 of this Order and includes visa, entry stamp or entry card.

13) *'Vehicle'* means any conveyance by land, water or air.

14) *'Weapons of Mass Destruction'* means nuclear, biological, or chemical weapons.

Section 2 Preservation of Laws

1) All Iraqi laws regarding immigration, emigration, customs and quarantine shall remain in force unless specifically suspended by this Order.

2) Wherever a stipulation, direction, instruction, guidance or provision of this Order or made pursuant to this Order or any other CPA Regulation, Order or Memorandum conflicts with a current provision of Iraqi immigration, emigration, customs and quarantine laws, the direction, instruction, guidance, or provision contained in or made pursuant to such Regulation, Order or Memorandum shall prevail.

3) The Ministry of Interior or Ministry of Foreign Affairs, in consultation with each other as appropriate, may issue directions, instructions or guidance to designated travel document issuance authorities consistent with this Order or any other CPA Regulation, Order or Memorandum.

4) The edict of the former President Saddam Hussein, fixing the expiration of 'N' series passports in the year 2003, issued during the years 1996 to 2002, is hereby suspended. All 'N' and 'M' series passports will continue in effect for their statutory duration.

5) All Iraqi passports in the 'N' and 'M' series may be extended by any designated travel document issuing authority. Passports presented to a designated travel document issuing authority for extension on or before their original expiration date or within the two months immediately following their original expiration date may be extended for a period of four (4) years. Passports presented to a designated travel document issuing authority for extension after the two months following their original expiration date may be extended for a period of two (2) years. Designated travel permit issuing authorities may validate Iraqi passports in any series. Any passport purporting to have been issued after March 19, 2003 that has not been validated with a stamp from either the CPA, the Ministry of Foreign Affairs or the Ministry of Interior, or with a combined CPA/Ministry of Interior/Ministry of Foreign Affairs stamp, is invalid. Any Iraqi passport valid under this Order may be amended by any authorized officer at an Iraqi mission overseas to register a child under the age of twelve (12) years, on the passport of a parent, guardian or legal trustee in accordance with established Iraqi law and procedures.

6) Consistent with Section 2 of CPA Order No. 26 (CPA/ORD/24 August 2003/26),[58] the Ministry of Foreign Affairs has the authority to grant, issue, renew, extend or amend diplomatic and official passports in accordance with established procedures and for the purpose of facilitating official travel of Iraqi officials. As of January 1, 2004, all diplomatic and official passports that do not have a CPA and/or Ministry of Foreign Affairs stamp either to reflect issuance, renewal, extension or validation are declared invalid for travel except for direct return travel to Iraq. Such passports may be confiscated by any authorized officer or any authorized representative of the Ministry of Foreign Affairs.

Section 3 Right to Exit

1) Subject to compliance with Iraqi law and with border control procedures established by the CPA or Ministry of Interior, all persons may exit from Iraq, provided they are in possession of travel documents and are not subject to any travel restrictions under applicable law, including this Order.

2) The following persons shall require special clearance from the Minister of Interior to exit Iraq and may be prevented from exiting at the discretion of the Minister of the Interior:

a) Senior regime or military leadership and Senior Party Members or office holders of the Ba'ath Party, as described in CPA/ORD/16 May 2003/01;

b) Persons suspected of having committed serious crimes;

c) Persons who are known or suspected to have links to a terrorist organization or who are suspected to have committed or to have provided financial, material, or technological support for acts of terrorism; and

d) Persons suspected of being involved or attempting to be involved with the acquisition, manufacture, development, research, or transfer of technology or material related to Weapons of Mass Destruction or their delivery systems; or having knowledge of the location of Weapons of Mass Destruction or their delivery systems, or the identity of persons with such knowledge.

Section 4 Examinations for Entry

1) A person seeking entry to Iraq shall appear before an authorized officer at a port of entry, border control station or at such other place as may be designated by the Ministry of the Interior for examination to determine whether the person may be granted entry to Iraq.

2) A person appearing for examination shall answer truthfully all questions and shall produce such documentation as may be required for the purpose of establishing whether the person may be granted entry.

3) A person may be detained for up to forty-eight hours for further examination upon entry and/or pending arrangements for his or her return based on established procedures, or his or her withdrawal of the request to enter Iraq.

Section 5 Permits to Enter Iraq

1) Persons seeking entry to Iraq are to be classified as either persons who require permits granting entry into Iraq (hereinafter 'permits') or persons who do not require such permits. All persons who are not listed in Sections 5(2) or 5(3) of this Order require permits. Authorized officers shall issue permits, in accordance with this Order, or in accordance with any direction from the Ministry of Interior, in consultation with the Ministry of Foreign Affairs, and in accordance with applicable law.

[58] See *Doc 47*.

2) Persons not requiring permits to enter Iraq are still those persons not otherwise denied permits under this Order who are:

a) citizens of Iraq or persons who were born in Iraq;
b) Coalition personnel;
c) United Nations officials or any official of any other U.N. organization;
d) documented members of seagoing ships' companies during the stay of a ship in Iraqi waters; and
e) documented members of airline companies during the stay of the aircraft in Iraqi territory.

3) The Ministry of Interior or Ministry of Foreign Affairs may issue permits for a variety of purposes, including but not limited to business, tourism, students, temporary visitors, residence and foreign liaison (diplomatic). The Ministry of Interior, in consultation with the Ministry of Foreign Affairs, shall issue directions relating to the number, duration and other conditions pertaining to the issuance of designated classes of permits.

4) Permits may be issued from CPA, any Iraqi mission or embassy that has reopened and has been authorized to do so by the Ministry of Foreign Affairs, and Ministry of Interior offices established or authorized for this purpose within Iraq and at authorized ports of entry.

Section 6 Powers of an Authorized Officer

1) A designated travel document issuing authority who receives an application for a permit shall either approve or refuse the application, and shall notify the applicant of the decision. At any time after an application for a permit is approved, the authorized officer may:

a) Alter or revoke any terms and conditions subject to which the person was granted entry;
b) Add terms and conditions as prescribed or authorized by the present Order and other CPA Regulations, Orders or Memoranda; and/or
c) Extend the permit.

2) Subject to the present Order, a visitor seeking an extension of a permit shall appear before an authorized officer for examination to determine whether the visitor may be granted an extension of a permit at such place as may be designated by the Ministry of the Interior.

3) A visitor appearing for examination shall answer truthfully all questions and shall produce such other documentation as may be required for the purpose of establishing whether the visitor may be granted an extension of a permit.

Section 7 Persons Who May Be Denied Entry to Iraq

1) An authorized officer who receives an application for a permit may refuse the application if the authorized officer has reasonable grounds to believe that the applicant:

a) knowingly provided any false, misleading, or inaccurate information in the course of the application process;
b) is suffering from any serious communicable disease, or is suffering from any disorder, disability or other health impairment for which commercial health services are not readily available in Iraq;
c) will be unable or unwilling to support herself or himself, and those persons who are dependent on the applicant;
d) is or was a member of a criminal organization;
e) will commit offenses, or engage in criminal activity planned and organized by persons acting in concert with or in furtherance of the commission of any offense;

f) will engage in or has engaged in an act of terrorism, or is a member of a terrorist organization or an organization that there are reasonable grounds to believe will:
 i) engage in acts which are offensive to the principles of democratic government, institutions or processes in Iraq; or
 ii) engage in or instigate the removal by force of any government;
g) will engage in acts of violence that may endanger the lives or safety of persons in Iraq, or who is a member of an organization that engages in such acts;
h) has been involved or attempted to be involved with the acquisition, manufacture, development, research or transfer of technology or material related to Weapons of Mass Destruction, their delivery systems, or advanced conventional military systems, including dual use items;
i) has committed acts or omissions that constituted a war crime or a crime against humanity; or
j) has previously been deported from Iraq by the CPA, or an international territory with formal border controls.

2) In the case of a person who is in possession of a valid travel document, or who can otherwise establish Iraqi nationality, his or her entry into Iraq shall not be denied. However, if security or military necessity requires, then such a person may be detained upon entry into Iraq.

3) A person denied entry under this Order may appeal to the Minister of Interior for a review of the case. The determination of the Minister of Interior will be final.

Section 8 Notice to Depart

1) Where an authorized officer, upon examination of a person, is of the opinion that it would be contrary to the present Order to grant entry to the person, or to extend the permit of a person, the authorized officer may:
 a) allow that person to leave Iraq immediately; or
 b) serve that person with a Notice to Depart (hereinafter 'Notice') within a specified period.

2) A Notice must specify:
 a) [sic] that the person must depart Iraq within a specified period;
 b) the reasons why the Notice is being served;
 c) that the person may object to the Notice in writing to the Ministry of the Interior within a specified time, or give reasons why the Notice should not remain in force; and
 d) that timely compliance will not have adverse consequences for the return of a person who otherwise complies with entry requirements.

3) Where the Minister of Interior receives written objections from a person under this Order, the Minister of Interior shall:
 a) [sic] consider such written objections promptly;
 b) promptly determine the fair and lawful resolution of the matter; and
 c) advise the person in writing of the decision.

Section 9 Revocation of a Permit

A designated travel document issuing authority may revoke a person's permit if:
 a) the circumstances that formed the basis of the approval of the person's application for the permit have substantially changed;

b) the person breaches a prescribed term of the permit, or another person required to comply with a condition of the permit has not met that condition;
c) the presence of the person in Iraq is, or would be, a risk to the health, safety or good order of the Iraqi community; or
d) the permit should not have been granted because the application for the permit was in contravention of the present Order or other applicable law.

Section 10 Identification and Seizure of Documents

1) Persons shall comply with the instructions of an authorized officer regarding their identification, if they:

a) seek entry into Iraq,
b) make an application for the renewal of a permit,
c) have been arrested, or
d) are subject to deportation under this Order.

2) For the purpose of identification, an authorized officer may in accordance with the provisions of Sections 11 and 12 below:

a) search persons who the authorized officer believes either have not revealed their identity or have hidden on or about their person documents that are relevant to a decision as to whether they may be granted permission to enter Iraq, and may search any vehicle that conveyed the persons to Iraq and their luggage and personal effects;
b) search persons who the authorized officer reasonably believes have committed an offense or are in possession of objects or documents that may be used in the commission of an offense, and may search any vehicle that conveyed the person to Iraq, their luggage and personal effects;
c) examine any travel document or any other document purporting to be a travel document at a port of entry or any other place in Iraq, for the purpose of this Order or relevant directives, examine any object that is, or is about to be, imported into or exported from Iraq.

3) An authorized officer may confiscate at a port of entry or any other place in Iraq any object or document if the authorized officer reasonably deems this necessary for the discharge of the functions of the officer under this Order.

4) An authorized officer may confiscate any object or document if the officer reasonably believes that it has been fraudulently or improperly obtained or used, or that such action is necessary to prevent its fraudulent or improper use.

5) An authorized officer shall provide a written receipt to any person from whom he or she confiscates an object or document under this Order, and shall provide the person with a written notice setting out the procedures for review pursuant to Section 17 below.

Section 11 Search of a Person

1) An authorized officer may, without a warrant, search a person who seeks entry to Iraq.

2) The search of a person must be made by an authorized officer pursuant to the present Order and must be made on reasonable grounds.

3) No person shall be searched by a person who is not of the same sex, and if there is no officer of the same sex at the place at which the search is to take place, an authorized officer may request that another border control or customs employee of the same sex perform the search, when necessary to comply with this provision.

Section 12 Search and Seizure of Goods

1) An authorized officer may, without a warrant, search the vehicle, luggage or personal effects of any person who seeks entry into Iraq.

2) Persons crossing the borders of Iraq must make declarations or manifests of all goods being transported by the person available to an authorized officer on request.

3) An authorized officer shall confiscate any goods that may pose a threat to the peace, security, health, environment, or good order of Iraq, including Controlled Items. Authorized officers also shall confiscate any antiquities or cultural items suspected of being illegally exported.

4) The export or import of a Controlled Item shall require the prior written authorization of the Administrator, his designee, or the Minister of Interior. Such prior written authorization requirement shall not apply to exports of Controlled Items by the CPA or Coalition personnel. Such prior written authorization requirement shall not apply to the export of Controlled Items by Coalition contractors, who are exporting such Controlled Items pursuant to the performance of its contract with the Coalition or Multi-national force.

5) Goods that are not declared may be confiscated by an authorized officer. Persons may also be ordered to return such goods, at their expense, to the jurisdiction from which they came.

6) Any goods confiscated must be immediately handed over to the Minister of the Interior or to his or her delegate(s). A receipt must be issued to the person from whom the goods are confiscated and the person must be provided with written notice setting forth the procedures for review pursuant to Section 17, below.

Section 13 Offenses

1) Allegations of an offense shall be subject to review and action, if appropriate, by either an investigative judge of a customs court or a criminal court of Iraq, depending on the alleged offense.

2) The following shall constitute an offense under this Order:

a) failing to appear before an authorized officer for examination as required by this Order;

b) failing to answer truthfully all questions by an authorized officer during examination;

c) knowingly concealing documentation as may be required by the authorized officer during examination;

d) failing to make a declaration or manifest of all goods being carried by the person on request by an authorized officer;

e) obstructing or interfering with a search of the person or search of the person's vehicle, luggage or personal effects pursuant to this Order;

f) knowingly making a false representation, orally or in writing, to an authorized officer for the purposes of securing entry of a person into Iraq;

g) entering Iraq or remaining in Iraq without a permit, if one is required;

h) entering Iraq or remaining in Iraq by use of a false or improperly obtained travel document or other document pertaining to the entry of that person or by reason of any fraudulent or improper means or misrepresentation of any material fact;

i) failing to comply with a prescribed term of a permit;

j) escaping or attempting to escape from lawful custody or detention under this Order and any other relevant instructions or directives;

k) organizing or facilitating the entry or proposed entry into Iraq of a person, knowing the person would, upon entering Iraq, be guilty of an offense under this Section; and

l) seeking to export or import, or exporting or importing Controlled Items without prior authorization issued pursuant to Section 12(4) of this Order.

Section 14 Penalties

A person who commits an offense described in this Order is liable to have any goods in his or her possession confiscated and may be deported from Iraq. The person may also be liable to a penalty prescribed in an applicable Iraqi law, CPA Order, Regulation or Memorandum, or other subordinate directive.

Section 15 Liability for Removal Costs

1) A transportation company shall ensure that:

a) the persons it conveys to Iraq are in possession of all travel documents required by applicable law,

b) it presents each person to an authorized officer for examination at such place as may be designated by an authorized officer upon arrival of each one of its vehicles in Iraq, and

c) no other person leaves the vehicle:

i) at any place other than that designated by an authorized officer, or

ii) until permission has been granted by an authorized officer.

2) Where a person has been allowed or required to leave Iraq pursuant to this Order, a transportation company that has conveyed the person to Iraq may be required by an authorized officer to cause that person to be conveyed to the country from which that person came, or to such other country as the authorized officer may approve at the request of the company.

3) Where a person has been required to leave Iraq because at the time of the arrival in Iraq the person was not in possession of a valid travel document required by applicable law, a transportation company that has conveyed the person to Iraq shall be liable to pay all costs of conveying that person to the country from which that person came, or to such other country as an authorized officer may approve at the request of the company.

4) Where a person has been granted entry to Iraq, or where that person, at the time of arrival in Iraq, was in possession of a valid travel document, and where that person is required to leave Iraq pursuant to the present Order, a transportation company that has conveyed the person to Iraq and that is required to cause that person to be conveyed from Iraq is entitled to be reimbursed by the Ministry of the Interior for the costs of conveying that person from Iraq. However a transportation company shall not be reimbursed for the costs of conveying from Iraq a person who enters Iraq as, or to become, a member of a crew.

5) Where a person enters Iraq as, or to become, a member of a crew of a vehicle and ceases to be a visitor, the transportation company that operates that vehicle may be required to cause that person to be conveyed to the country from which that person came, or to such other country as the Ministry of the Interior may approve at the request of the company. The transportation company shall be liable to pay all costs of conveying that person from Iraq.

Section 16 Other Offenses

1) Where an authorized officer has reasonable grounds to believe that a person who seeks entry into or exit from Iraq, or who seeks to remain in Iraq, is liable for an offense committed under applicable law in Iraq, other than an offense prescribed in this Order, the authorized officer shall report the matter immediately to law enforcement or other appropriate authorities.

2) Where the circumstances of the case require, an authorized officer may arrest a person suspected of having committed an offense other than an offense prescribed in this Order. The arrest must be immediately reported to the Interim Minister of the Interior, and the arrested person must, as soon as possible but no later than six hours after the arrest, be delivered into the custody of law enforcement or other appropriate authorities.

Section 17 Review

1) A person who is adversely affected by a decision of an authorized officer made pursuant this Order may apply in writing to the Minister of Interior or in person at the Ministry of Interior offices at border points of entry for a review of the decision by the Minister of Interior for decisions made in respect of applications for travel permits lodged within Iraq, or in writing to the Ministry of Foreign Affairs for review of any adverse decisions made in respect of applications for travel permits lodged outside of Iraq. Within seven (7) days of receipt of the application, the Minister of Interior or the Minister of Foreign Affairs, as appropriate, shall review the decision and notify the applicant of the determination in writing at the last provided address of the applicant.

2) A person whose goods have been confiscated may apply in writing, with a copy of the confiscation receipt attached, to the Minister of Interior for a review of the decision. Within seven days of receipt of the application, the Minister of Interior shall review the decision and notify the applicant of the determination in writing at the last provided address of the applicant.

3) The Minister of Interior and Minister of Foreign Affairs may issue Administrative Instructions in connection with such reviews.

Section 18 Collection of Fees

The Ministry of Interior, in coordination with the Ministry of Foreign Affairs, may establish fees for services provided under this Order. Under procedures established by the Ministry of Finance, the Ministries of Foreign Affairs and Interior may retain part or all of the fees to be utilized for the modernization of Iraq's border control system.

Section 19 Entry into Force

This Order shall enter into force on the date of signature [13 June 2004].

Document 37
Coalition Provisional Authority Order Number 17
CPA/ORD/26 June 2003/17

Status of the Coalition, Foreign Liaison Missions, their Personnel and Contractors

Pursuant to my authority as head of the Coalition Provisional Authority (CPA), and under the laws and usages of war, and consistent with relevant U.N. Security Council resolutions, including Resolution 1483 (2003),

Recalling that under international law occupying powers, including their forces, personnel, property and equipment, funds and assets, are not subject to the laws or jurisdiction of the occupied territory,

Conscious that states are contributing personnel, equipment and other resources to the Coalition in order to contribute to the security and stability that will enable the relief, recovery and development of Iraq,

Noting that states are sending Foreign Liaison Mission Personnel to Iraq,

Conscious of the need to establish and confirm the status of such Coalition and Foreign Liaison Mission Personnel in respect of the CPA and the local courts,

I hereby promulgate the following:

Section 1 Definitions

1) *'Coalition Personnel'* means all non-Iraqi military and civilian personnel assigned to or under the command of the Commander, Coalition Forces, or all forces employed by a Coalition State including attached civilians, as well as all non-Iraqi military and civilian personnel assigned to, or under the direction or control of the Administrator of the CPA.

2) *'Foreign Liaison Mission Personnel'* means those individuals who have been issued Foreign Liaison Mission personnel identification cards by the Iraqi Ministry of Foreign Affairs under the supervision of the CPA.

3) *'Legal Process'* means any arrest, detention or legal proceedings in the Iraqi courts or other Iraqi bodies, whether criminal, civil, administrative or other in nature.

4) *'Parent State'* means the state providing Coalition Personnel as part of the Coalition in Iraq or the state providing Foreign Liaison Mission Personnel.

5) *'Coalition contractors'* means non-Iraqi business entities or individuals not normally resident in Iraq supplying goods and/or services to or on behalf of the Coalition Forces or the CPA under contractual arrangements.

6) *'Coalition sub-contractors'* means non-Iraqi business entities or individuals not normally resident in Iraq supplying goods and/or services to or on behalf of Coalition contractors and in respect of Coalition or CPA activities under contractual arrangements.

Section 2 Coalition and Foreign Liaison Mission Personnel

1) CPA, Coalition Forces and Foreign Liaison Mission, their property, funds and assets of shall be immune from Iraqi Legal Process.

2) All Coalition personnel and Foreign Liaison Mission personnel shall respect the Iraqi laws applicable to those Coalition personnel and Foreign Liaison Mission personnel in the territory of Iraq and the Regulations, Orders, Memoranda and Public Notices issued by the Administrator of the CPA.

3) Foreign Liaison Mission personnel shall be immune from Legal Process.

4) All Coalition personnel shall be subject to the exclusive jurisdiction of their Parent States and, they shall be immune from local criminal, civil, and administrative jurisdiction and from any form of arrest or detention other than by persons acting on behalf of their Parent States, except that nothing in this provision shall prevent Coalition Forces personnel from preventing acts of serious misconduct by Coalition personnel, or otherwise temporarily detaining Coalition personnel who pose a risk of injury to themselves or others, pending expeditious turnover to the appropriate authorities of the Parent State. In all such circumstances the national contingent commander of the detained person shall be notified immediately.

5) In respect of those Coalition personnel who commit an act or acts in Iraq for which there are no criminal sanctions in the Parent State, the CPA may request from the Parent State waiver of jurisdiction to try such act or acts under Iraqi law. In such cases, no Legal Process shall be commenced without the written permission of the Administrator of the CPA.

Section 3 Contractors

1) Coalition contractors and their sub-contractors as well as their employees not normally resident in Iraq, shall not be subject to Iraqi laws or regulations in matters relating to the terms and conditions of their contracts in relation to the Coalition Forces or the CPA. Coalition contractors and sub-contractors other than contractors and sub-contractors normally resident in Iraq shall not be subject to Iraqi laws or regulations with respect to licensing and registration of employees, businesses and corporations in relation to such contracts.

2) Coalition contractors and their sub-contractors as well as their employees not normally resident in Iraq, shall be immune from Iraqi Legal Process with respect to acts performed by them within their official activities pursuant to the terms and conditions of a contract between a contractor and Coalition Forces or the CPA and any sub-contract thereto.

3) In respect of acts or omissions of Coalition contractors and sub-contractors as well as their employees not normally resident in Iraq, which are not performed by them in the course of their official activities pursuant to the terms and conditions of a contract between them and the Coalition or the CPA, no Iraqi or CPA Legal Process shall be commenced without the written permission of the Administrator of the CPA.

Section 4 Duration of Immunity From Legal Process

The immunity from Legal Process provided by the present Order to Coalition personnel and Foreign Liaison Mission personnel as well as Coalition contractors, sub-contractors and their employees not normally resident in Iraq operates only in respect to acts or omissions by them during the period of authority of the CPA.

Section 5 Waiver of Legal Immunity and Jurisdiction

1) The immunity from Legal Process of Coalition personnel, Foreign Liaison Mission personnel, Coalition contractors and their sub-contractors as well as their employees not normally resident in Iraq is not for the benefit of the individuals concerned and may be waived by the Parent State.

2) Requests to waive jurisdiction over Coalition personnel or Foreign Liaison Mission personnel shall be referred to the respective Parent State.

3) Requests to waive the immunities with respect to Coalition contractors and subcontractors and their employees not normally resident in Iraq as set forth in Section 3 of this Order shall be referred to the respective Parent State with which the contractor has contracted.

Section 6 Claims

1) Third party claims including those for property loss or damage and for personal injury, illness or death or in respect of any other matter arising from or attributed to Coalition personnel or any persons employed by them, whether normally resident in Iraq or not and that do not arise in connection with military combat operations, shall be submitted and dealt with by the Parent State whose Coalition personnel, property, activities or other assets are alleged to have caused the claimed damage, in a manner consistent with the national laws of the Parent State.

2) Third party claims for property loss or damage and for personal injury, illness or death or in respect of any other matter arising from or attributed to Foreign Liaison Mission personnel shall be submitted and dealt with by the Parent State whose Foreign Liaison Mission personnel, property, activities or other assets are alleged to have caused the claimed damage, in a manner consistent with the national laws of the Parent State.

Section 7 Entry Into Force

This Order shall enter into force on the date of signature [27 June 2003].

Document 38

Coalition Provisional Authority Order Number 17 (Revised)

CPA/ORD/27 June 2004/17[59]

Status of the Coalition Provisional Authority, MNF-Iraq, Certain Missions and Personnel in Iraq

Pursuant to my authority as head of the Coalition Provisional Authority (CPA), and under the laws and usages of war, and consistent with relevant U.N. Security Council resolutions, including Resolutions 1483 (2003), 1511 (2003) and 1546 (2004),

Noting the adoption of a process and a timetable for the drafting of an Iraqi constitution by elected representatives of the Iraqi people in the Law of Administration for the State of Iraq for the Transitional Period (TAL) on March 8, 2004,

Conscious that states are contributing personnel, equipment and other resources, both directly and by contract, to the Multinational Force (MNF) and to the reconstruction effort in order to contribute to the security and stability that will enable the relief, recovery and development of Iraq, as well as the completion of the political process set out in the TAL,

Noting that many Foreign Liaison Missions have been established in Iraq that after June 30, 2004 will become Diplomatic and Consular Missions, as defined in the Vienna Conventions on Diplomatic and Consular Relations of 1961 and 1963,

Recalling that there are fundamental arrangements that have customarily been adopted to govern the deployment of Multinational Forces in host nations,

[59] A draft Order entitled 'Status of the Coalition Provisional Authority, MNF-Iraq, Foreign Liaison Missions, Diplomatic and Consular Missions, Their Personnel, International Advisers and Contractors' had been sent to Washington on 15 June 2004 for Principals' approval. The draft contained a Section 2, Preservation of Authority, which reads: 'For the remainder of the occupation, the right to act in accordance with the laws and usages of war is preserved and may be exercised as necessary, notwithstanding this Order.' For the full text of the draft Order, see http://www.dod.gov/.

Conscious of the need to clarify the status of the CPA, the MNF, Foreign Liaison, Diplomatic and Consular Missions and their Personnel, certain International Consultants, and certain contractors in respect of the Government and the local courts,

Recognizing the need to provide for the circumstances that will pertain following June 30, 2004, and noting the consultations with the incoming Iraqi Interim Government in this regard and on this order,

I hereby promulgate the following:

Section 1 Definitions

1) 'Multinational Force' (MNF) means the force authorized under U.N. Security Council Resolutions 1511 and 1546, and any subsequent relevant U.N. Security Council resolutions.

2) 'MNF Personnel' means all non-Iraqi military and civilian personnel (a) assigned to or under the command of the Force Commander or MNF contingent commanders, (b) subject to other command authority to aid, protect, complement or sustain the Force Commander, or (c) employed by a Sending State in support of or accompanying the MNF.

3) 'Force Commander' means the Commander appointed to exercise unified command of the MNF, or his or her designee.

4) 'CPA Personnel' means all non-Iraqi civilian and military personnel assigned to, or under the direction or control of, the Administrator of the CPA.

5) 'Sending State' means a State providing personnel, International Consultants, services, equipment, provisions, supplies, material, other goods or construction work to: (a) the CPA, (b) the MNF, (c) international humanitarian or reconstruction efforts, (d) Diplomatic or Consular Missions, or (e) until July 1, 2004, Foreign Liaison Missions.

6) 'Foreign Liaison Missions' means representative missions operated by States until July 1, 2004.

7) 'Foreign Liaison Mission Personnel' means those individuals who are authorized by the Iraqi Ministry of Foreign Affairs to carry Foreign Liaison Mission personnel identification cards until July 1, 2004.

8) 'Diplomatic and Consular Missions' means those missions belonging to States with diplomatic or consular relations with Iraq that are in operation on or after June 30, 2004.

9) 'Premises of the Missions' means all premises, including the buildings or parts of buildings and the land ancillary thereto, irrespective of ownership, used for the purposes of Diplomatic and Consular Missions, including residences of the heads of missions on or after June 30, 2004.

10) 'Iraqi legal process' means any arrest, detention or legal proceedings in Iraqi courts or other Iraqi bodies, whether criminal, civil, or administrative.

11) 'Contractors' means non-Iraqi legal entities or individuals not normally resident in Iraq, including their non-Iraqi employees and Subcontractors not normally resident in Iraq, supplying goods or services in Iraq under a Contract.

12) 'Contract' means:

a) a contract or grant agreement with the CPA or any successor agreement thereto, or a contract or grant agreement with a Sending State, to supply goods or services in Iraq, where that supply is:
   i) to or on behalf of the MNF;
   ii) for humanitarian aid, reconstruction or development projects approved and organized by the CPA or a Sending State;
   iii) for the construction, reconstruction or operation of Diplomatic and Consular Missions; or

iv) until July 1, 2004, to or on behalf of Foreign Liaison Missions; or

b) a contract for security services provided by Private Security Companies to Foreign Liaison Missions and their Personnel, Diplomatic and Consular Missions and their personnel, the MNF and its Personnel, International Consultants, or Contractors.

13) 'Subcontractors' means non-Iraqi legal entities or individuals not normally resident in Iraq, including their non-Iraqi employees, performing under contract with a Contractor to supply goods or services in Iraq in furtherance of the Contractor's Contract.

14) 'Private Security Companies' means non-Iraqi legal entities or individuals not normally resident in Iraq, including their non-Iraqi employees and Subcontractors not normally resident in Iraq, that provide security services to Foreign Liaison Missions and their Personnel, Diplomatic and Consular Missions and their personnel, the MNF and its Personnel, International Consultants and other Contractors.[60]

15) 'Vehicles' means civilian and military vehicles operated by or in support of MNF, the CPA, Foreign Liaison Missions, International Consultants and, in the course of their official and contractual activities, Contractors.

16) 'Vessels' means civilian and military vessels operated by or in support of the MNF, the CPA, Foreign Liaison Missions, International Consultants and, in the course of their official and contractual activities, Contractors.

17) 'Aircraft' means civilian and military aircraft operated by or in support of the MNF, the CPA, Foreign Liaison Missions, International Consultants and, in the course of their official and contractual activities, Contractors.

18) 'The Government' means the Iraqi Interim Government from June 30, 2004, the Iraqi Transitional Government upon its formation, and any successor government for the duration of this Order, including instrumentalities, commissions, judicial, investigative or administrative authorities, and regional, provincial and local bodies.

19) 'International Consultants' means all non-Iraqi personnel who are not CPA personnel and, after June 30, 2004, are not accredited to a Diplomatic or Consular Mission, but are provided by Sending States as consultants to the Government and are officially accepted by the Government.

Section 2 Iraqi Legal Process

1) Unless provided otherwise herein, the MNF, the CPA, Foreign Liaison Missions, their Personnel, property, funds and assets, and all International Consultants shall be immune from Iraqi legal process.

2) All MNF, CPA and Foreign Liaison Mission Personnel and International Consultants shall respect the Iraqi laws relevant to those Personnel and Consultants in Iraq including the Regulations, Orders, Memoranda and Public Notices issued by the Administrator of the CPA.

3) All MNF, CPA and Foreign Liaison Mission Personnel, and International Consultants shall be subject to the exclusive jurisdiction of their Sending States. They shall be immune

[60] As of 20 January 2004 the following 14 'private security firms' were operating in Iraq: AD Consultancy (UK), ArmorGroup (UK), Control Risk Group (UK), Genric (UK), Global risk Strategies (UK), Group 4 Flack A/S (India), Hill and Associates (Hong Kong), ISI (Iraq), Meteoric Tactical Solutions (South Africa), Meyer & Associates (USA), Olive Security (UK) Limited (UK), Optimal Solutions Services (Australia), RamOPS Risk Management Group (USA), Wade-Boyd and Associates (USA). The list was provided by the US Consular Office in Baghdad, see US Department of Commerce, Iraq Investment and Reconstruction Task Force, *Doing Business in Iraq: Frequently Asked Questions (FAQs)*, 2-3.

from any form of arrest or detention other than by persons acting on behalf of their Sending States, except that nothing in this provision shall prohibit MNF Personnel from preventing acts of serious misconduct by the above-mentioned Personnel or Consultants, or otherwise temporarily detaining any such Personnel or Consultants who pose a risk of injury to themselves or others, pending expeditious turnover to the appropriate authorities of the Sending State. In all such circumstances, the appropriate senior representative of the detained person's Sending State in Iraq shall be notified immediately.

4) The Sending States of MNF Personnel shall have the right to exercise within Iraq any criminal and disciplinary jurisdiction conferred on them by the law of that Sending State over all persons subject to the military law of that Sending State.

5) The immunities set forth in this Section for Foreign Liaison Missions, their Personnel, property, funds and assets shall operate only with respect to acts or omissions by them during the period of authority of the CPA ending on June 30, 2004.

Section 3 Diplomatic and Consular Missions

All Premises of Diplomatic and Consular Missions will be utilized by Diplomatic and Consular Missions without hindrance and subject to the requirements of and receiving the protections provided for in the Vienna Convention on Diplomatic Relations of 1961 and the Vienna Convention on Consular Relations of 1963. This Order does not prevent the Government and any State from entering into other bilateral arrangements for existing or new premises.

Section 4 Contractors

1) Sending States may contract for any services, equipment, provisions, supplies, material, other goods, or construction work to be furnished or undertaken in Iraq without restriction as to choice of supplier or Contractor. Such contracts may be awarded in accordance with the Sending State's laws and regulations.

2) Contractors shall not be subject to Iraqi laws or regulations in matters relating to the terms and conditions of their Contracts, including licensing and registering employees, businesses and corporations; provided, however, that Contractors shall comply with such applicable licensing and registration laws and regulations if engaging in business or transactions in Iraq other than Contracts. Notwithstanding any provisions in this Order, Private Security Companies and their employees operating in Iraq must comply with all CPA Orders, Regulations, Memoranda, and any implementing instructions or regulations governing the existence and activities of Private Security Companies in Iraq, including registration and licensing of weapons and firearms.

3) Contractors shall be immune from Iraqi legal process with respect to acts performed by them pursuant to the terms and conditions of a Contract or any sub-contract thereto. Nothing in this provision shall prohibit MNF Personnel from preventing acts of serious misconduct by Contractors, or otherwise temporarily detaining any Contractors who pose a risk of injury to themselves or others, pending expeditious turnover to the appropriate authorities of the Sending State. In all such circumstances, the appropriate senior representative of the Contractor's Sending State in Iraq shall be notified.

4) Except as provided in this Order, all Contractors shall respect relevant Iraqi laws, including the Regulations, Orders, Memoranda and Public Notices issued by the Administrator of the CPA.

5) Certification by the Sending State that its Contractor acted pursuant to the terms and conditions of the Contract shall, in any Iraqi legal process, be conclusive evidence of the facts so certified.

6) With respect to a contract or grant agreement with or on behalf of the CPA and with respect to any successor agreement or agreements thereto, the Sending State shall be the state of nationality of the individual or entity concerned, notwithstanding Section 1(5) of this Order.

7) These provisions are without prejudice to the exercise of jurisdiction by the Sending State and the State of nationality of a Contractor in accordance with applicable laws.

Section 5 Waiver of Legal Immunity and Jurisdiction

1) Immunity from Iraqi legal process of MNF, CPA and Foreign Liaison Mission Personnel, International Consultants and Contractors is not for the benefit of the individuals concerned and may be waived pursuant to this Section.

2) Requests to waive immunity for MNF, CPA and Foreign Liaison Mission Personnel and International Consultants shall be referred to the respective Sending State. Such a waiver, if granted, must be express and in writing to be effective.

3) Requests to waive immunity for Contractors shall be referred to the relevant Sending State in relation to the act or acts for which waiver is sought. Such a waiver, if granted, must be express and in writing to be effective.

Section 6 Communications

1) The MNF shall engage in radiocommunications in accordance with the Annex hereto and is authorized, in coordination with the Government, to use such facilities as may be required for the performance of its tasks. Issues with respect to communications shall be resolved pursuant to this Order and the Annex hereto.

2) Subject to the provisions of paragraph (1) above:

a) The MNF, Diplomatic and Consular Missions and Contractors may, in consultation with the Government, install and operate radiocommunication stations (including terrestrial radio and television broadcasting stations and satellite stations) to disseminate information relating to their mandates. The MNF, Diplomatic and Consular Missions and Contractors also may install and operate radiocommunication transmitting and receiving stations, including satellite earth stations, and install and operate other telecommunications systems including by laying cable and land lines, to provide communications, navigation, radio-positioning and other services useful in fulfilling their respective mandates. The MNF, Diplomatic and Consular Missions and Contractors shall also have the right to exchange telephone, voice, facsimile and other electronic data with relevant global telecommunications networks. The MNF, Diplomatic and Consular Missions and Contractors may continue to operate after June 30, 2004 existing radiocommunication transmitting and receiving stations, including broadcasting stations and other telecommunications systems operated by them or their predecessors on or prior to June 30, 2004, in accordance with existing authorizations and assignments of radio frequency spectrum. Subject to the Annex hereto, the radio broadcasting stations, radio transmitting and receiving stations, and telecommunications systems operated pursuant to this Section by the MNF, Diplomatic and Consular Missions and Contractors shall be operated in accordance with the International Telecommunication Union Constitution, Convention and Radio Regulations, where applicable. The frequencies on which any new radiocommunication transmitting and receiving stations, including broadcasting stations, may be operated shall be decided upon in coordination with the Government to the extent required under and in accordance with the Annex hereto. Such use of the radio-frequency spectrum shall be free of charge for MNF and Diplomatic and Consular Missions.

b) The MNF, Diplomatic and Consular Missions and Contractors may connect with local telephone, facsimile and other electronic data systems. Existing connections to such local systems (made by them or their predecessor entities) shall remain in place following June 30, 2004. The MNF, Diplomatic and Consular Missions and Contractors may make new connections to such local systems after consultation and in accordance with arrangements with the Government. The use of such existing and new systems shall be charged at the most competitive rate to the MNF, Diplomatic and Consular Missions and Contractors.

3) The MNF may arrange through its own facilities for the processing and transport of private mail to or from MNF Personnel. The Government shall be informed of the nature of such arrangements and shall not interfere with or censor the mail of the MNF, or MNF Personnel.

4) The Code of Wireless Communications, Code No. 159 of 1980, to the extent not already superseded, is hereby repealed.

Section 7 Travel and Transport

1) All MNF, CPA and Foreign Liaison Mission Personnel, International Consultants and Contractors, to the extent necessary to perform their Contracts, shall enjoy, together with vehicles, vessels, aircraft and equipment, freedom of movement without delay throughout Iraq. That freedom shall, to the extent practicable with respect to large movements of personnel, stores, vehicles or aircraft through airports or on railways or roads used for general traffic within Iraq, be coordinated with the Government. The Government shall supply the MNF with, where available, maps and other information concerning the locations of mine fields and other dangers and impediments.

2) Vehicles, vessels and aircraft shall not be subject to registration, licensing or inspection by the Government, provided that Contractors' vehicles, vessels and aircraft shall carry appropriate third-party insurance.

3) All MNF, CPA and Foreign Liaison Mission Personnel, International Consultants and Contractors, to the extent necessary to perform their Contracts, together with their vehicles, vessels and aircraft, may use roads, bridges, canals and other waters, port facilities, airfields and airspace without the payment of dues, tolls or charges, including landing and parking fees, port, wharfage, pilotage, navigation and overflight charges, overland transit fees, and similar charges. Exemption will not be claimed from charges for services requested and rendered, and such charges shall be at rates most favourable to CPA, MNF and Foreign Liaison Mission Personnel, and International Consultants and Contractors.

4) The Force Commander shall coordinate with the appropriate institutions of the Government regarding the rules and procedures governing Iraqi civil airspace and will manage the air traffic system for all military and civilian air traffic. The Force Commander will control airspace required for military operations within Iraq for the purpose of deconflicting military and civil uses. The Force Commander shall implement the transfer to civilian control of the airspace over Iraq to the appropriate institutions of the Government in a manner consistent with ensuring the safe and efficient operation of an air traffic management system, with security requirements, and Iraqi national capability to resume control over Iraqi national airspace no later than the MNF departure from Iraq.

Section 8 Customs and Excise

1) The MNF may establish, maintain and operate commissaries, exchanges and morale and welfare facilities at its headquarters, camps and posts for the benefit of MNF Personnel, and, at the discretion of the Force Commander, other non-Iraqi persons who are the subject of this Order, but not of locally recruited personnel. Such commissaries, exchanges and morale and welfare facilities may provide consumable goods and other articles. The Force Commander shall take all reasonable measures to prevent abuse of such commissaries, exchanges and morale and welfare facilities and the sale or resale of such goods to persons other than MNF Personnel. The Force Commander shall give consideration to requests of the Government concerning the operation of the commissaries, exchanges and morale and welfare facilities.

2) MNF, CPA and Foreign Liaison Mission Personnel, International Consultants and Contractors may:

a) Import, free of duty or other restrictions, and clear without inspection, license, authorization, other restrictions, taxes, customs duties, or any other charges, equipment, provisions, supplies, fuel, technology, and other goods and services, including controlled substances, which are for their exclusive and official or contractual use and for the MNF for resale in the commissaries, exchanges and morale and welfare facilities provided for above;

b) Re-export unconsumed provisions, supplies, fuel, technology, and other goods and equipment, including controlled substances, without inspection, license, authorization, other restrictions, taxes, customs duties or any other charges, or otherwise dispose of such items on terms and conditions to be agreed upon with competent Government authorities.

3) An efficient procedure, including documentation, will be coordinated with the Government to expedite importation, clearances, transfer or exportation.

4) MNF, CPA and Foreign Liaison Mission Personnel, International Consultants and Contractors shall be subject to the laws and regulations of Iraq governing customs and foreign exchange with respect to personal property not required by them by reason of their official duties and presence in Iraq. A Sending State's certification that property of MNF, CPA and Foreign Liaison Mission Personnel, International Consultants and Contractors is required by them by reason of their official duties shall be conclusive evidence of the facts so certified.

5) Special facilities will be granted by the Government for the speedy processing of entry and exit formalities for MNF Personnel, including the civilian component, upon prior written notification from the Force Commander.

Section 9 Facilities for the MNF

1) The MNF may use without cost such areas for headquarters, camps or other premises as may be necessary for the conduct of the operational and administrative activities of the MNF. All premises currently used by the MNF shall continue to be used by it without hindrance for the duration of this Order, unless other mutually agreed arrangements are entered into between the MNF and the Government. While any areas on which such headquarters, camps or other premises are located remain Iraqi territory, they shall be inviolable and subject to the exclusive control and authority of the MNF, including with respect to entry and exit of all personnel. The MNF shall be guaranteed unimpeded access to such MNF premises. Where MNF Personnel are collocated with military personnel

of Iraq, permanent, direct and immediate access for the MNF to those premises shall be guaranteed.

2) The MNF may use water, electricity and other public utilities and facilities free of charge, or, where this is not practicable, at the most favorable rate, and in the case of interruption or threatened interruption of service, the MNF shall have, as far as possible, the same priority as essential government services. Where such utilities or facilities are not provided free of charge, payment shall be made by the MNF on terms and conditions to be agreed with the competent Government authority. The MNF shall be responsible for the maintenance and upkeep of facilities so provided.

3) The MNF may generate, within its premises, electricity for its use and may transmit and distribute such electricity.

4) There shall be an area within central Baghdad that shall be designated as the 'International Zone.' The International Zone shall have the boundaries that the MNF has established for this purpose. The MNF shall retain control of the perimeter of the International Zone and all rights of entry and exit, and all matters of security within the International Zone shall be subject to the control of the MNF. The activities and assignment of Iraqi security personnel within the International Zone shall be as mutually agreed upon between the MNF and the Government. Iraqi citizens living within the International Zone will remain subject to Iraqi law. Services, utilities and maintenance not otherwise performed or undertaken by the MNF within the International Zone shall be provided to the MNF by the Government free of charge or at the most favorable rate as agreed between the Force Commander and the Government.

Section 10 Taxation, Provisions, Supplies, Services and Sanitary Arrangements

1) The MNF, Sending States and Contractors shall be exempt from general sales taxes, Value Added Tax (VAT), and any similar taxes in respect of all local purchases for official use or for the performance of Contracts in Iraq. With respect to equipment, provisions, supplies, fuel, materials and other goods and services obtained locally by the MNF, Sending States or Contractors for the official and exclusive use of the MNF or Sending States or for the performance of Contracts in Iraq, appropriate administrative arrangements shall be made for the remission or return of any excise or tax paid as part of the price. In making purchases on the local market, the MNF, Sending States and Contractors shall, on the basis of observations made and information provided by the Government in that respect, avoid any adverse effect on the local economy.

2) Contractors shall be accorded exemption from taxes in Iraq on earnings from Contracts, including corporate, income, social security and other similar taxes arising directly from the performance of Contracts. MNF Personnel, CPA Personnel, Foreign Liaison Mission Personnel and International Consultants shall be accorded exemption from taxes in Iraq on earnings received by them in their capacity as such Personnel and Consultants.

3) The MNF and the Government shall cooperate with respect to sanitary services and shall extend to each other the fullest cooperation in matters concerning health, particularly with respect to the control of communicable diseases, consistent with relevant international law.

Section 11 Recruitment of Local Personnel

The MNF, Sending States and Contractors may recruit, hire and employ locally such personnel as they require. The terms and conditions of recruitment, hiring and employment by the MNF, Sending States and Contractors shall be determined by respectively the MNF, Sending States and the terms of the Contractor's Contract.

Section 12 Currency
The MNF shall be permitted to purchase from the Government in mutually acceptable currency, local currency required for the use of the MNF, including to pay MNF Personnel, at the rate of exchange most favorable to the MNF.

Section 13 Entry, Residence and Departure

1) MNF, CPA and Foreign Liaison Mission Personnel, and International Consultants shall have the right to enter into, remain in, and depart from Iraq.

2) The speedy entry into and departure from Iraq of MNF, CPA and Foreign Liaison Mission Personnel, Contractors and International Consultants shall be facilitated to the maximum extent practicable. For that purpose, MNF, CPA and Foreign Liaison Mission Personnel, and International Consultants shall be exempt from passport and visa regulations and immigration inspection and restrictions as well as payment of any fees or charges on entering into or departing from Iraq. They shall also be exempt from any regulations governing the residence of aliens in Iraq, including registration, but shall not be considered as acquiring any right to permanent residence or domicile in Iraq.

3) For the purpose of such entry or departure, MNF Personnel shall only be required to have: (a) an individual or collective movement order issued by or under the authority of the Force Commander or any appropriate authority of a Sending State providing personnel to the MNF; and (b) a national passport or personal identity card issued by the appropriate authorities of a Sending State providing personnel to the MNF.

4) For the proper performance of Contracts, Contractors shall be provided with facilities concerning their entry into and departure from Iraq as well as their repatriation in time of crisis. For this purpose, there shall promptly be issued to Contractors, free of charge and without any restrictions, all necessary visas, licenses or permits.

Section 14 Uniforms and Arms
While performing official duties, MNF Military Personnel shall wear the national military uniform of their respective Sending States unless otherwise authorized by the Force Commander for operational reasons. The wearing of civilian dress by MNF Military Personnel may be authorized by the Force Commander at other times. MNF Personnel and Private Security Companies may possess and carry arms while on official duty in accordance with their orders or under the terms and conditions of their Contracts. As authorized by the ambassador or the chargé d'affaires of a Sending State, Diplomatic and Consular personnel may possess and carry arms while on official duty.

Section 15 Identification
Upon request by the Government, a Sending State shall confirm that an individual falls into one of the categories covered by this Order.

Section 16 Permits and Licenses

1) A permit or license issued by the MNF, the CPA, Foreign Liaison Missions or Sending States for the operation by their Personnel, including non-Iraqi locally recruited personnel, of any vehicles and for the practice of any profession or occupation in connection with their functions, shall be accepted as valid, without tax or fee, provided that no permit to drive a

vehicle shall be issued to any person who is not already in possession of an appropriate and valid license issued by the appropriate authorities of the Sending State.

2) Licenses and certificates already issued by appropriate authorities in other States in respect of aircraft and vessels, including those operated by Contractors exclusively by or for the MNF, the CPA and Foreign Liaison, Diplomatic and Consular Missions shall be accepted as valid.

Section 17 Deceased Members

The Force Commander and Sending States may take charge of and transfer out of Iraq or otherwise dispose of the remains of any MNF, CPA and Foreign Liaison Mission Personnel, International Consultants and Contractors who die in Iraq, as well as their personal property located within Iraq.

Section 18 Claims

Except where immunity has been waived in accordance with Section 5 of this Order, third-party claims including those for property loss or damage and for personal injury, illness or death or in respect of any other matter arising from or attributed to acts or omissions of CPA, MNF and Foreign Liaison Mission Personnel, International Consultants, and Contractors or any persons employed by them for activities relating to performance of their Contracts, whether normally resident in Iraq or not and that do not arise in connection with military operations, shall be submitted and dealt with by the Sending State whose personnel (including the Contractors engaged by that State), property, activities or other assets are alleged to have caused the claimed damage, in a manner consistent with the Sending State's laws, regulations and procedures.

Section 19 Supplemental Arrangements

The Force Commander and the Government may conclude supplemental arrangements or Protocols to this Order and shall ensure close and reciprocal liaison at every appropriate level.

Section 20 Effective Period

This Order shall enter into force on the date of signature [27 June 2004]. It shall remain in force for the duration of the mandate authorizing the MNF under U.N. Security Council Resolutions 1511 and 1546 and any subsequent relevant resolutions and shall not terminate until the departure of the final element of the MNF from Iraq unless rescinded or amended by legislation duly enacted and having the force of law.

ANNEX

ARRANGEMENTS CONCERNING USE OF THE RADIO FREQUENCY SPECTRUM

Article I General Principles

1) The Government, including the Iraqi Communications and Media Commission and any successor or other entity with authority relating to radio frequency spectrum in Iraq (collectively referred to as the 'Commission'), shall render all decisions planning, managing, allocating and assigning radio frequency spectrum in a manner that recognizes and safeguards the radio frequency spectrum needs of the MNF.

2) Consistent with Sections 5(2)(i) and 5(2)(m) of CPA Order No. 65,[61] the Government, through the Commission, will coordinate with the Force Commander regarding any pending or proposed action or regulatory decision that may affect MNF's use of radio frequency spectrum, in order to ensure that no such actions or decisions will interfere with military requirements necessary in the interest of the national security of Iraq.

3) Nothing contained in this Annex shall be interpreted to abridge or deny the ability of the MNF to utilize existing and future frequency assignments to operate communications, navigation and other military facilities and networks required to facilitate internal operations and to safeguard the security and reconstruction of Iraq.

Article II Table of Allocations

1) The initial Table of Allocations, which designates bands as Civil, Military or Shared, is attached hereto as Appendix 1. Neither the Government nor the Force Commander may change the Table of Allocations except in accordance with the provisions set forth in this Annex.

2) No changes to the Table of Allocations that reallocate, reassign or otherwise affect the bands designated as Military, the MNF's use thereof, or the MNF's use of frequencies assigned to it in the bands designated as Civil or Shared Uses shall be effective unless agreed to by the Force Commander.

3) Subject to paragraph 2) of this Article II, the Commission may reallocate radio frequency spectrum and/or revise the Table of Allocations in the bands designated as Civil or Shared by providing thirty days' prior written notice to the Force Commander of such reallocation and/or revision.

Article III Assignment of Radio Frequencies

1) The Commission controls the assignment of frequencies in the bands designated as Civil or Shared Uses and serves as the approval authority for frequency assignments in these bands, and shall render its decisions in accordance with these regulations. Except as set forth in this Annex, no person may operate radio transmitting equipment in the bands designated as Civil or Shared without the authorization of the Commission.

2) The Force Commander controls assignment of frequencies in the bands designated as Military and serves as approval authority for these bands. Decisions by the Force Commander regarding assignments in the bands designated as Military are committed to his complete discretion and are not subject to review by the Government. No person may operate radio transmitting equipment in the bands designated as Military without the authorization of the Force Commander.

3) In addition to the use of any bands designated as Military Uses that have been authorized by the Force Commander, the Force Commander shall have the right to retain and request frequency assignments from the Commission whenever necessary, in the bands designated as Civil or Shared. Requests by the Force Commander for frequency assignments in the bands designated as Civil or Shared Uses shall be addressed and coordinated with the Commission in the following manner:

a) Following June 30, 2004, the military and civil defense forces (including the MNF) will retain the frequency assignments in the bands designated as Civil or Shared that were held immediately prior to that date, including those assignments held by the MNF, which shall retain the assignments previously

[61] See *Doc 89*.

held by Coalition Forces, and may transfer those assignments to any successor entity for the protection of Iraq's national security.

b) The Force Commander may submit written requests to the Commission for additional frequency assignments in the bands designated as Civil or Shared Uses. Upon receipt of a written request for frequency assignment(s) from the Force Commander, the Commission will render its written decision to grant or deny such request(s) in a manner that will not interfere with military requirements necessary in the interest of security;

c) The Commission shall respond in writing to requests for frequency assignments from the Force Commander within thirty days of receipt of such requests to either grant the requested authorization or provide a written explanation of its denial of the request;

d) If the MNF is not employing a frequency that is assigned to it in a band designated as Civil or Shared, the Commission may request that the unused assignment be returned for reassignment or reallocation, and such request shall be honored by the Force Commander, unless the Force Commander provides a written statement explaining that the MNF must continue to hold the assignment because of a security interest, such as civil defense or public safety. Such statement, if made by the Force Commander, shall be conclusive.

e) The MNF shall be exempt from any and all requirements to pay recurring or nonrecurring fees for use of radio frequency spectrum, or for requesting and obtaining existing or future frequency assignments, including any administrative, processing or other fees.

f) Requests for frequency assignments by the Force Commander shall be submitted to the Commission in a format agreed to between the Force Commander and the Commission.

g) The Commission will not release any information regarding the MNF's use of radio frequency spectrum to any person (including other Government agencies) without the explicit prior written consent of the Force Commander.

4) The Commission shall protect frequency assignments held by the MNF, Diplomatic and Consular Missions and Contractors from interference.

Article IV Changes to this Annex

1) The terms of this Annex may be changed only upon the written agreement of the Commission and the Force Commander.

2) The Commission and the Force Commander may agree on more detailed procedures, in writing, to carry out the intent of this Annex.

3) The Commission and the Force Commander may each delegate their responsibilities under this Annex to appropriate representatives.

Document 39
Coalition Provisional Authority Order Number 18
CPA/ORD/7 July 2003/18

Measures to Ensure the Independence of the Central Bank of Iraq

Pursuant to my authority as Administrator of the Coalition Provisional Authority (CPA), and under the laws and usages of war, and consistent with relevant U.N. Security Council resolutions, including Resolution 1483 (2003),

Noting the Central Bank of Iraq Law sets forth requirements for the involvement of the Ministry of Finance in setting monetary and credit policy,

Noting that the Central Bank of Iraq Law authorizes loans to government Ministries which undermines the ability of the Central Bank of Iraq (CBI) to control monetary growth,

Understanding that CBI's credit and monetary policy must be free from political or other governmental interference,

Determined to prevent the impoverishment of the Iraqi people and the breakdown of order by taking measures for the prevention of extreme inflation,

I hereby promulgate the following:

Section 1 Loans to Government Ministries
Articles 21 and 22 of the Central Bank of Iraq Law No. 64 of 1976 are hereby suspended to the extent that they authorize the CBI to loan funds to Iraqi Government Ministries.

Section 2 Central Bank Control of Monetary and Credit Policy
The CBI shall have the authority to determine and implement monetary and credit policy without the approval of the Ministry of Finance. The provisions of Article 14 of the Central Bank Law are suspended to the extent that they require Ministry of Finance approval of monetary and credit policy. Only members of the CBI Board who are CBI employees serving with the approval of the Administrator may decide matters determining or implementing monetary and credit policy.

Section 3 Entry into Force
This Order shall enter into force on the date of signature [7 July 2003].

Document 40
Coalition Provisional Authority Order Number 19
CPA/ORD/9 July 2003/19

Freedom of Assembly

Pursuant to my authority as Administrator of the Coalition Provisional Authority (CPA), and under the laws and usages of war and relevant U.N. Security Council resolutions, including Resolution 1483 (2003),

Noting the obligation of the CPA to restore and maintain order and the right of the CPA to take measures for its security and public order,

Concerned by the exploitation of demonstrations by persons intent on inciting violence against the Iraqi people, the CPA and Coalition Forces,

Noting that the provisions of the Third Edition of the 1969 Iraqi Penal Code, Part Two, Chapter Two, at paragraphs 220 to 222 unreasonably restrict the right to freedom of expression and the right of peaceful assembly,

Determined to remove the unacceptable restrictions on human rights of the former Iraqi Ba'ath Party regime, and to promote the freedom of the Iraqi people to demonstrate in a peaceful and orderly manner,

I hereby promulgate the following:

Section 1 Purpose

1) The prohibition on freedom of assembly contained in the Iraqi Penal Code is inconsistent with Iraq's human rights obligations and was an instrument of repression under the former Iraqi Ba'ath Party regime. It is the intention of the CPA to remove such prohibitions and advance towards normalization and the establishment of civil society as public security improves.

2) This Order is necessary to protect public health, welfare and safety. The maintenance of good order and safety in Iraq is a paramount responsibility of the CPA. The CPA is determined to prevent the exploitation of demonstrations by elements intent on causing death or injury.

a) The public health, welfare and safety of the community require that the movement of vehicular traffic on roadways be lawfully conducted with a minimum of disruption.

b) The practice of unhindered or unrestrained picketing or demonstrating on such roadways may cause disruption of police, emergency and relief services, and injury to participants and bystanders.

c) The practice of multiple demonstrations on the same day in different locations in municipalities may unreasonably deprive the citizens of police, emergency and relief services.

Section 2 Suspension of Laws

The provisions of the Third Edition of the 1969 Iraqi Penal Code, Part Two, Chapter Two, at paragraphs 220 to 222 which unreasonably restrict the right to freedom of expression and the right of peaceful assembly are hereby suspended.[62]

[62] Paragraph 220: 'If five or more people are assembled in a public place, thereby endangering the public security and the public authorities order them to disperse, any person who is given that order and refuses to comply with it is punishable by a period of detention not exceeding 1 year plus a fine not exceeding 100 dinars or by one of those penalties.'

Paragraph 221: 'Any person who calls for a gathering in a public place or who organizes such a gathering or participates in it while being aware of any ban on such gatherings by the public authorities is punishable by a period of detention not exceeding 1 year plus a fine not exceeding 100 dinars or by one of those penalties.

The same penalty applies to any person who publicly incites a gathering even though such incitement has no effect.'

Paragraph 222: '(1) If the intent of the gathering is to commit a felony or misdemeanor or to prevent the implementation of laws, regulations or decisions or to influence the affairs of the public authorities or to deprive another of his freedom of action with the use of force or menaces, then any person who calls for such a gathering or organizes it or who participates in it while being aware of its objective or any person who remains at it after

Section 3 Unlawful Demonstration

1) It is unlawful for any person, group or organization to conduct or participate in any march, assembly, meeting or gathering on roadways, public thoroughfares or public places in more than one specific area of or location in, any municipality on any given day, unless acting under authority of the Coalition Force Commander or a Divisional or Brigade Commander (hereinafter 'Approving Authorities').

2) It is unlawful for any group or organization or any individual acting with such group or organization, to conduct or participate in any march, assembly, meeting or gathering on roadways unless limited to such numbers as, upon the determination of an Approving Authority, will not unreasonably obstruct pedestrian or vehicular traffic. The Approving Authority shall, within 12 hours of receiving a notice of assembly under this Order, inform the group or organization as to the maximum number of authorized participants.

3) It is unlawful for any march, assembly, meeting or gathering held on roadways, public thoroughfares or public places, to continue for longer than four hours, or to be held within 500 meters of any CPA or Coalition Force facility.[63]

Section 4 Notice of Assemblage in Writing

It is unlawful for any group or organization to conduct or participate in any march, assembly, meeting or gathering on roadways, public thoroughfares or public places unless an Approving Authority has been given notice in writing of the location, the maximum number of persons participating, and the names and addresses of the organizers of any such march, assembly, meeting or gathering, its route, and its time of inception and duration at least 24 hours before such inception.

Section 5 Scheduling of Assembly

It is unlawful for any group, organization, or individual to conduct or participate in any march, assembly, meeting or gathering on roadways or public thoroughfares during peak traffic periods unless authorized by an Approving Authority for the area in which the march, assembly, meeting or gathering is to be held. Peak traffic periods, unless otherwise set by municipal or CPA authority, are for the purposes of this Order declared to be 0730 hours to 0900 hours, and from 1630 hours to 1800 hours in the afternoon, Saturday through Thursday except for national holidays.

Section 6 Prohibited Items

1) It is prohibited to bring to, or wear at, any march, assembly, meeting or gathering any:

a) firearm of any description;

having become aware of the objective is punishable by a period of detention not exceeding 2 years plus a fine not exceeding 200 dinars or by one of those penalties.

(2) If any of the participants in a gathering uses force or menaces or overtly carries a weapon or implement, the use of which may result in fatalities, the person who called for that gathering or organized it and any person who participated in it while being aware of its intended objective are punishable by detention plus a fine not exceeding 300 dinars or by one of those penalties.

(3) If any of the participants in the gathering commits an offence while pursuing the intended objective, every person who is present at the gathering at the time the offence is committed is punishable by the penalty prescribed by law if they were aware of the objective of the gathering. Any person who calls for the gathering or organizes it is punishable by the penalty prescribed by law for that offence even though he is not present at the gathering at the time the offence is committed.

(4) The provisions of this Paragraph do not prejudice any greater penalty prescribed by law.'

[63] Sec 3 was amended by CPA Order No 100, sec 3(9) *[Doc 124]*.

b) sharpened object of any kind;
c) projectiles intended to cause injury, including rocks;
d) poles, bats, sticks or any object that may be used as a club except for materials forming part of a sign; and
e) helmets, masks, balaclavas or other non-traditional facial covering.

2) Any such prohibited items brought to any march, assembly, meeting or gathering are liable to be confiscated immediately.

Section 7 Penalties
Any individual violating this Order may be detained, arrested, prosecuted and, if convicted, sentenced to up to one year in prison.[64]

Section 8 Entry into Force
This Order shall enter into force on the date of signature [10 July 2003].[65]

Document 41
Coalition Provisional Authority Order Number 20

CPA/ORD/17 July 2003/20[66]

Trade Bank of Iraq

Pursuant to my authority as Administrator of the Coalition Provisional Authority (CPA), and under the laws and usages of war, and consistent with relevant U.N. Security Council resolutions, including Resolution 1483 (2003),

Noting the letter of May 8, 2003, from Permanent Representatives of the United States of America and the United Kingdom of Great Britain and Northern Ireland to the President of the United Nations Security Council (S/2003/538),[67]

[64] The Explanatory Note [see n 65] issued by the CPA in addition prescribes 'a fine of up to USD 1,000.'

[65] Explanatory Note: CPA Order Providing for Freedom of Assembly (dated 11 July 2003): 'The CPA has promulgated an Order that will promote freedom of assembly in Iraq by removing the prohibitions in the Iraqi Penal Code that made demonstrations virtually impossible.

The Order introduces a regulated process for conducting demonstrations based on international standards as an interim measure until an internationally recognized, representative government established by the people of Iraq assumes the responsibility of the Authority.

The Order makes the Commander Coalition Forces, Divisional and Brigade Commanders 'Approving Authorities' for demonstrations. Persons wishing to hold demonstrations must provide 24 hours notice in writing to the Approving Authorities.

Demonstrations using roadways may not take place during peak hour traffic from 0730 to 0900 and 1630 to 1800. Demonstrations will not be permitted to last longer than four hours or come within 500 meters of a CPA or Coalition Force facility. It will not be permitted to hold demonstrations in more than one location in a municipality on the same day nor to unreasonably obstruct pedestrian or vehicular traffic.

The Order prohibits certain items to be brought to a demonstration including firearms, sharpened objects, projectiles including rocks, poles, bats or sticks other than as part of a sign, helmets, masks, balaclavas or non-traditional facial covering.

The penalty for violating these provisions will be up to one year in prison or a fine of up to USD 1,000.'

[66] The original document bears two different footers: on pp. 1 and 2 'CPA/ORD/14 July 2003/20' and on p. 3 'CPA/ORD/17 July 2003/20'.

[67] See *Doc 574*.

Underscoring the requirement that the Development Fund for Iraq (DFI) must be used in a transparent manner to meet the humanitarian needs of the Iraqi people, for the economic reconstruction and repair of Iraq's infrastructure, for the continued disarmament of Iraq, and for the costs of Iraqi civilian administration, and for other purposes benefiting the people of Iraq,

Reaffirming the commitment of the CPA to using effectively the resources of the DFI for the aforementioned purposes,

Noting that Iraq currently lacks financial institutions capable of facilitating imports and exports of goods and services to and from Iraq,

Noting the importance of economic trade to revitalizing the Iraqi economy, stimulating economic growth and providing employment for the Iraqi population in order to provide for sustainable development,

I hereby promulgate the following:

Section 1 Establishment

There is hereby established an institution to be known as the Trade Bank of Iraq (TBI). The TBI shall be an independent governmental entity, and is hereby authorized to perform such activities as are necessary to accomplish its purposes, consistent with the Charter of the TBI.

Section 2 Purpose

The TBI shall provide financial and related services to facilitate the importation and exportation of goods and services to and from Iraq in order to benefit the economy of Iraq. The Administrator may promulgate additional regulations, orders, memoranda or other documentation that further define the purpose of the DFI [sic].[68]

Section 3 President, Charter and Board of Directors

The Administrator shall appoint a President of the TBI. The President shall be the chief executive officer of the TBI. The President, with concurrence of the CPA Director, Economic Development, shall issue a Charter for the TBI, effective upon issuance, which will specify, among other things, the functions, powers, financial structure, governance, and reporting requirements of the TBI. The Charter for the TBI shall establish a Board of Directors for the purpose of governing the activities of the TBI.

Section 4 Initial Capitalization

The authorized capital of the TBI is $100,000,000. The Administrator may provide initial paid-in capital for the TBI from the DFI, in an amount not to exceed $5,000,000. The remaining $95,000,000 will exist as callable capital only in the event the TBI is unable to meet its current obligations. The Administrator may provide any required callable capital from the DFI.

Section 5 Contractual and Other Authorizations

In general, the President, on behalf of the TBI, is authorized to hire and pay the salaries of staff, procure goods and services, and enter into contracts and engage in such other acts as may be necessary or advisable to conduct the business of the TBI. In particular,

[68] It should probably have read TBI.

the President, on behalf of the TBI, is authorized to enter into a short-term contract with an Operating Consortium of financial institutions from various countries selected by the Administrator.[69] Under this contract, the members of the Operating Consortium shall provide, for a limited period of time, training, operational and technical support to the TBI and such other support as the President may deem advisable and necessary, including but not limited to, advising, issuing and confirming letters of credit on behalf of the TBI.

Section 6 Distribution of Profits
Profits generated by the operations of the TBI will be distributed to the DFI from time to time as determined by the President in consultation with the Administrator.

Section 7 Auditing and Review of Operations
To ensure that the TBI is managed transparently and for the benefit of the Iraqi people, the President may obtain the services of an independent certified public accounting firm for the purposes of auditing and publicly reporting on the TBI's operations.

Section 8 Transition
The TBI shall take appropriate steps to deal with issues relating to its operation that are associated with the assumption of government responsibilities by an internationally recognized representative government in Iraq in accordance with Resolution 1483.

Section 9 Entry into Force
This Order shall enter into force on the date of signature [17 July 2003].[70]

[69] On 1 September 2003, the CPA Administrator chose the bank J.P. Morgan Chase & Co. to lead the Operating Consortium of thirteen international banks.

[70] See also CPA Press Release No. 21 on Establishing a Trade Bank of Iraq, 21 July 2003: 'The CPA today announced measures for reviving the economy of Iraq. The Trade Bank of Iraq (TBI) has been established as a separate government entity, independent of the Central Bank of Iraq. It will provide financial and related services to facilitate the importation and exportation of goods and services to and from Iraq.

The TBI will provide expertise and a point of contact within Iraq to bolster confidence between trading partners that funds will be received in exchange for goods delivered. It is standard practice for specialist banking services to intermediate between the parties to provide such confidence. The TBI will work with commercial banks (the Operating Consortium), and other export-import banks, such as ExIm in the U.S. and ECGD in the UK.

Existing Iraqi banks are presently ill-equipped to support import-export trading activities. They lack sufficient expertise and international links. Moreover, existing financial institutions within Iraq are fully engaged in reestablishing basic banking services and have limited capacity for specialized trade services. The TBI will facilitate the transition from state owned enterprises to greater privatization.

The operations of the TBI will be directed by a President and Board of Directors. The new interim Minister of Finance, due to be selected by the Governing Council shortly, will act as the interim President, and will help select the Board of Directors.

The Coalition Provisional Authority has today, 21 July, issued a Request for Proposal, to encourage offers of assistance and partnership from international banks interested in helping establish the TBI.'

Document 42
Coalition Provisional Authority Order Number 21
CPA/ORD/5 August 2003/21

Interim Exercise of Baghdad Mayoral Authority

Pursuant to my authority as head of the Coalition Provisional Authority (CPA), and under the laws and usages of war, and consistent with relevant U.N. Security Council Resolutions, including Resolution 1483 (2003),

Noting that the position of Mayor in the City of Baghdad is currently vacant,

Recognizing that numerous laws and regulations governing the management of the City of Baghdad vest powers exclusively in the mayor; and that this thwarts the efficient and effective management of city business under current conditions,

Acting on behalf of the citizens of Baghdad and the people of Iraq,

I hereby promulgate the following:

Section 1 Temporary Authority of Deputy Mayors

1) All authority granted exclusively to the Mayor of Baghdad by any law, regulation, resolution or decree, is hereby vested in the three Deputy Mayors of Baghdad.

2) This authority may not be exercised absent the concurrence of at least two of the three Deputy Mayors.

3) The Deputy Mayors may develop and issue such internal administrative procedures or municipal ordinances as are necessary to implement this temporary authority.

Section 2 Duration of Authority

The authority extended to the Deputy Mayors by this Order shall remain in effect until such time as the position of Mayor of Baghdad is properly filled, or until this Order is amended or repealed.

Section 3 Entry into Force

This order shall enter into force on the date of signature [6 August 2003].[71]

Document 43
Coalition Provisional Authority Order Number 22
CPA/ORD/7 August 2003/22

Creation of a New Iraqi Army[72]

Pursuant to my authority as the head of the Coalition Provisional Authority (CPA), relevant U.N. Security Council resolutions including Resolution 1483 (2003), and the laws and usages of war,

[71] CPA Order No 21 was rescinded by CPA Order No 100, sec 4(6) *[Doc 124]*.

[72] The 'New Iraqi Army' was renamed the 'Iraqi Armed Forces' by CPA Order No 67, sec 1(1) *[Doc 91]*.

Noting that Resolution 1483 appeals to Member States *inter alia* to assist the people of Iraq to contribute to conditions of stability and security in Iraq,

Recalling that CPA Order Number 2 on the Dissolution of Entities[73] dissolved the Army, Air Force, Navy, Air Defense Force, and other regular military services, the Republican Guard, the Special Republican Guard, the Directorate of Military Intelligence, the Al Quds Force, the Quwat al Tawair, Saddam Fedayeen, Ba'ath Party Militia, Friends of Saddam and Saddam's Lions Cubs (Ashbal Saddam) and other entities,

Further recalling that Section 5 of CPA Order Number 2 looks forward to the creation of a New Iraqi Army as the first step in forming a national self-defense capability for a free Iraq,

Conscious of the need to start promptly to establish a military force for the national self-defense of free Iraq at the conclusion of the authority of the CPA,

Acknowledging the need to engage with Iraqi governmental institutions as they develop regarding the structure, institutions, and roles of the national armed forces of the new Iraq,

I hereby promulgate the following:

Section 1 Definitions

'Code of Military Discipline' is the Code of Military Discipline promulgated by the Administrator of the CPA under a separate CPA Order.[74]

'Commander in the New Iraqi Army' means an Iraqi officer appointed from time to time in accordance with this Order to command positions in the New Iraqi Army or the Iraqi armed forces generally.

'Defense Areas' are defined as any land, water, or super-adjacent air space contained within the territory of Iraq, or any building or part of a building or any other building that is reserved or set apart, used or otherwise controlled for defense purposes, by designation under section 10 of this Order.

'Extremist Organizations or Activities' are organizations or activities that advocate racial, gender or ethnic hatred or intolerance; advocate, create, or engage in illegal discrimination based on race, color, gender, religion, or regional or national origin; or use, or advocate the use of force or violence or other unlawful means for political purposes, whether internal or international.

'Heavy Weapons' are weapons firing ammunition larger than 7.62mm, machine guns, crew-served weapons, anti-tank weapons (such as rocket propelled grenades (RPGs)), anti-aircraft weapons (to include shoulder fired missiles and AA guns), indirect fire weapons (mortars and artillery pieces), armored vehicles or self-propelled weapons, high explosives and explosive devices (including mines and hand grenades).

'Member of the New Iraqi Army' or 'Army' means a person serving in the New Iraqi Army from the time of attestation until the date of termination of service.

'New Iraqi Army' means the military forces of Iraq organized for the purposes set forth in this Order including all components of the national armed forces of Iraq, specifically including the ground forces recruited, trained, and organized as the first step in the process of creating a military defense force for the new Iraq. Unless the context clearly requires otherwise, all references to the 'New Iraqi Army' are references to any element of the national defense forces of Iraq.

[73] See *Doc 15*.
[74] See *Doc 44*.

'Serious Offense' means a criminal offense under the criminal laws of Iraq or the Code of Military Discipline that authorizes, in the event of a conviction, confinement for a period in excess of three months as a punishment.

'Small Arms' includes shotguns, pistols, and rifles that fire ammunition up to and including 7.62mm.

Section 2 Existing Law

The Iraqi Military Law Code Number 13 of 1940, the Iraqi Military Procedures Code Number 44 of 1941, the Code of Legal Notification of Military Personnel Number 106 of 1960, Punishment of Military Deserters Law Number 28 of 1972, and the Penal Code of the Popular Army Number 32 of 1984 are hereby suspended.

Section 3 The Mission and Command Structure of the New Iraqi Army

1) There is hereby established the New Iraqi Army as the first step toward the creation of the national defense force of the new Iraq. The New Iraqi Army is an establishment intended to provide a capability in support of the security of Iraq during the period of the CPA's authority. The continued existence of the New Iraqi Army beyond the period of CPA's authority is subject to a decision by the future internationally recognized, representative government, established by the people of Iraq.

2) The mission of the New Iraqi Army and of the national defense forces generally is the military defense of the nation, including defense of the national territory and the military protection of the security of critical installations, facilities, infrastructure, lines of the communication and supply, and population. The tasks of the New Iraqi Army and of additional units of the national defense forces of Iraq include developing a military capability during the period of authority of the CPA in order to provide the basis for militarily effective, professional, and non-political armed forces for the military defense of the nation after the conclusion of the CPA's tenure. The New Iraqi Army shall not have, or exercise, domestic law enforcement functions, nor intervene in the domestic political affairs of the nation. Tasks of the New Iraqi Army will also include participation in domestic relief operations associated with natural or man-made disasters and humanitarian relief missions.[75]

3) Command positions in the New Iraqi Army and in other elements of the national defense force of Iraq will be held by Iraqi officers only. Supreme command, control and administrative authority over the New Iraqi Army and of additional units of the national defense forces of Iraq and all authority formerly vested in the Ministry of Defense will reside on an interim basis with the Administrator of the CPA as the civilian Commander-in-Chief pending transfer of such authority to an internationally recognized, representative government, established by the people of Iraq. The Administrator, or a civilian member of the CPA reporting directly to the Administrator and to whom authority has been specifically delegated in writing by the Administrator for this purpose, will commission officers in the New Iraqi Army and may designate Commanders of units of the New Iraqi Army, of the Army as a whole, or of the national defense force as a whole. The Administrator, or a civilian member of the CPA reporting directly to the Administrator and to whom authority has been specifically delegated in writing, will designate the officers to command the principal units of the New Iraqi Army, as they are created. The specific assignments of subordinate officers shall be made in accordance with procedures established by Administrative Instruction.[76]

[75] Sec 3(2) was rescinded and replaced by CPA Order No 100, sec 3(10)(a) *[Doc 124]*.

[76] Sec 3(3) was rescinded and replaced by CPA Order No 100, sec 3(10)(b) *[Doc 124]*.

4) Operational or tactical command of units of the New Iraqi Army operating with Coalition forces may be vested in an officer of Coalition forces of rank superior to that of the commander of such Iraqi units as shall be designated by the Administrator of the CPA or by a civilian member of the CPA reporting directly to the Administrator and to whom such authority is specifically delegated in writing.[77]

Section 4 Conduct

1) Members of the New Iraqi Army shall comply with the lawful orders of those superior in rank to them, according to regulations and the Code of Military Discipline.

2) Such members shall comply with the lawful orders of those persons who are not members of the Iraqi armed forces, whether military or civilian, who may be placed in operational command over them from time to time in conjunction with their duties, according to regulations and the Code of Military Discipline.

Section 5 Discipline

1) Members of the New Iraqi Army are subject to the jurisdiction of the civilian criminal courts pursuant to the Criminal Procedures Code No. 23 of 1977, as amended from time to time, for offenses under the Penal Code No. 111 of 1969, as amended from time to time, and to the jurisdiction for offenses established under a Code of Military Discipline promulgated under a separate CPA Order.[78] The jurisdiction over offenses under the Code of Military Discipline will be as determined by the Order creating the Code of Military Discipline.

2) In circumstances where both the civil and military authorities have jurisdiction over an offense, the civil authorities will have primary jurisdiction. In all cases, jurisdiction will be exercised, and allocated, as provided for in the Code of Military Discipline Order.

Section 6 Terms and Conditions of Service

1) Administrative Instructions with regard to Terms and Conditions of Service, as may be considered necessary to give effect to the terms of this Order, may be issued by the Administrator of the CPA or by a civilian member of the CPA reporting directly to the Administrator and to whom such authority is specifically delegated in writing.

ENLISTMENT

2) The minimum age for enlistment into the New Iraqi Army is 18 years of age.

3) Service in the New Iraqi Army will be voluntary and for a set term of enlistment which shall not be extended except in emergencies as officially declared by the Administrator.

4) Suitability for service in the New Iraqi Army will be determined on several criteria including, but not limited to:

a) demonstrated physical ability;
b) demonstrated minimum scholastic aptitude;
c) the absence of evidence of human rights violations or war crimes;
d) the absence of affiliation with the security and political control organs of the former regime;

[77] Sec 3 was amended by adding a new article 5 by CPA Order No 73, sec 2 *[Doc 97]*. All references in sec 3(4), 6(1), 6(10), 6(16)(b), 8(1), 10 and 11 to 'civilian member of the CPA reporting directly to the Administrator' were replaced with 'the Minister of Defence', see CPA Order No 100, sec 3(10(c) *[Doc 124]*. See also CPA Order No 67, sec 2(1)(b) *[Doc 91]*.

[78] See *Doc 44*.

e) the absence of association with Extremist Organizations or other groups that use or advocate the use of violence for political purposes whether internal or international;

f) provided, however, no qualified person will be denied the opportunity to serve on the basis of race, ethnic or regional origin, religion, creed or tribal affiliation;

5) Prior military service is not required, but persons with military experience will be eligible to join the New Iraqi Army, subject to meeting the applicable standards, including the criteria listed in paragraph 4 above. No person involved in Ba'ath Party activity within the leadership tiers described in CPA/ORD/16 May 2003/01[79] shall be eligible except with specific permission of the CPA.

RANK STRUCTURE

6) The New Iraqi Army will consist of commissioned officers and enlisted personnel with ranks that may include warrant officers and non-commissioned officers.

7) The ranks of officers will, in ascending order, be:

Tilmeez Daabet[80]	Officer Candidate
Mulaazem	2nd Lieutenant
Mulaazem Awwal	1st Lieutenant
Naqeeb	Captain
Raaed	Major
Muqaddam	Lt. Colonel
Aaaqeed	Colonel
Aameed	Brigadier General
Liwaa	Major General
Fareeq	Lt. General

8) The Administrator of the CPA, or a civilian member of the CPA reporting directly to the Administrator and to whom authority has been specifically delegated in writing by the Administrator under this Section, may, in accordance with Administrative Instructions, by instrument in writing, commission persons to be officers of the New Iraqi Army at a rank to be determined by the person conducting the commissioning. It shall be possible for personnel to be commissioned on entering the New Iraqi Army at a commissioned rank above Second Lieutenant.

9) The ranks of enlisted personnel, non-commissioned officers and warrant officers will, in ascending order, be:

Jundi[81]	Private
Jundi Awwal	Private 1st Class
Naeb Aareef	Corporal
Aareef	Sergeant
Aareef Awwal	Sergeant 1st Class
Wakeel	Master Sergeant
Wakeel Awwal	Sergeant Major
Muahhal	Warrant Officer
Muahhal Awwal	Chief Warrant Officer

10) The appointment of enlisted personnel and warrant officers will be made by the person authorized under Administrative Instructions issued by the Administrator of the

[79] See *Doc 14*.

[80] Arabic terms omitted.

[81] Arabic terms omitted.

CPA, or by a civilian member of the CPA reporting directly to the Administrator and to whom authority has been specifically delegated in writing, by the Administrator for this purpose. It shall be possible for personnel entering the service to be appointed to an enlisted rank above that of Private.

11) Promotion of officers and enlisted personnel will be made pursuant to procedures to be established by the Administrator of the Coalition Provisional Authority on the basis of merit established by reference to experience, demonstrated competence in the current rank and potential for exceptional performance in the next higher rank.

PAY AND ALLOWANCES

12) Pay and allowances for members of the New Iraqi Army will be determined by an Administrative Instruction.

13) A Member of the New Iraqi Army will automatically forfeit a day's pay and allowances for each full or partial calendar day that the Member absents himself from his place of duty or unit without the permission of a superior officer authorized to grant such permission, and shall in addition be subject to appropriate disciplinary action, including the commencement of Disciplinary Proceedings under the Code of Military Discipline.

LEAVE

14) Members of the New Iraqi Army may take leave subject to the needs of the service, upon receiving permission from a duly authorized officer. The period of leave and other relevant details are to be specified by Administrative Instructions.

TERM AND TERMINATION OF SERVICE

15) Volunteers for service in the New Iraqi Army obligate themselves to an initial term of service for a period not to exceed 26 months, subject to a decision by an internationally recognized, representative government, established by the people of Iraq, to continue its existence once such government assumes the responsibilities of the CPA and to the provisions of Section 6 (16)(b) and (c) below. At the end of any term of service, a member may extend service for a further term of 24 months, subject to agreement by the appropriate authorities and the interests of the service. No period of service shall be extended without the consent of the Member, except in national emergencies as officially declared according to law. Required minimum terms of service in special situations, e.g. advanced training, may be specified by Administrative Instruction.

16) Service in the New Iraqi Army may terminate on the occurrence of one of the following events:

a) Upon a determination that the Member's services are no longer required following the transfer of authority by the CPA to an internationally recognized, representative government, established by the people of Iraq, without prejudice to the right of an internationally recognized, representative government in Iraq, established by the people of Iraq, to assume the command and control of the New Iraqi Army and all on-going service obligations of its personnel;

b) Upon a determination by a commanding officer, based upon credible evidence, that a Member of the New Iraqi Army is unsuitable for further military service in the New Iraqi Army on the basis of one of the following:
   (i) commission of a Serious Offense
   (ii) a poor disciplinary record
   (iii) medical unsuitability
   (iv) consistently poor performance
   (v) failure to meet basic standards of performance

(vi) behavior which is discriminatory on the basis of gender, race, ethnic or regional origin, religion or tribal affiliation
(vii) unsuitability for military service
(viii) commission of a Military Offense
(ix) violations of Section 9 of this Order (relating to political activity)

Within seven days of notification of termination, Members who have completed initial entry training, may request that the decision to terminate their service be confirmed by the Administrator of the CPA or by a civilian member of the CPA reporting directly to the Administrator and to whom such authority is specifically delegated in writing in respect of this Section. A determination under this clause (b) shall be conclusive upon confirmation by Administrator of the CPA, or by a civilian member of the CPA reporting directly to the Administrator and to whom such authority is specifically delegated in writing with respect to this Section, or upon the elapse of seven days from the time of notification of termination, if no request for confirmation is made.

c) Service in the New Iraqi Army shall also terminate upon:
(i) the granting of an application from a Member of the New Iraqi Army for discharge based upon demonstrated need;
(ii) on the granting of an application to resign; or
(iii) a determination by the Administrator or his delegate that such termination is necessary for the good of the service.

Section 7 Weapons

The possession of Heavy Weapons and Small Arms by Members of the New Iraqi Army is regulated by CPA Order Number 3, Weapons Control Order (CPA/ORD/23 May 2003/03),[82] which Order may be supplemented by Administrative Instructions.

Section 8 Administrative Inquiries

1) The Administrator of the CPA, or a civilian member of the CPA reporting directly to the Administrator and to whom such authority is specifically delegated in writing, may, by Administrative Instruction, issue such rules made under this Section for the convening of an Administrative Inquiry to investigate any matter regarding the operation of any part of the New Iraqi Army. Reports of such inquiries shall establish the facts of the matter, draw conclusions, and make any recommendations as may be appropriate.

2) An Administrative Inquiry may be convened by an officer of the rank of Lieutenant Colonel or above who holds a command position with respect to any matter concerning a unit under his command and its operation or the Members of the New Iraqi Army under his command, except that an Administrative Inquiry may not be convened to investigate a matter already under investigation as a criminal matter until such time as the criminal investigation is completed. In circumstances in which an Administrative Inquiry has been commenced and it discovers evidence of a Military Offense then it may refer the matter to a Disciplinary Officer in accordance with the Code of Military Discipline. Following referral of the matter to a Disciplinary Officer, the Administrative Inquiry will be completed in accordance with the rules governing such Inquiries.

[82] See Sec 2(2) of CPA Order No 3 *[Doc 16]*.

Section 9 Political Activities

1) Members of the New Iraqi Army may not:
   a) be members of a political party, organization or association;
   b) participate in any activities of a political party, organization or association including the recruiting of members for political parties or organizations;
   c) publicly state or suggest any opinion of a political nature which includes efforts to indoctrinate members of the New Iraqi Army or any other person with a political ideology or otherwise convince any person to adhere to a particular political ideology; or
   d) participate in any manner in Extremist Organizations or Activities.

2) Nothing in this Section shall limit the right of a member of the New Iraqi Army to vote in elections for political office organized on a local, regional or national basis.

Section 10 Defense Areas

The administrator of the CPA, or a civilian member of the CPA reporting directly to the Administrator and to whom such authority is specifically delegated in writing, may prohibit or restrict access by any person to any Defense Area and may make all appropriate provisions for the control and security of any Defense Area. In the event such prohibitions or restrictions limit access to privately-owned property, reasonable compensation shall be promptly paid to the property owner during the period of limited access.

Section 11 Administrative Instructions

The Administrator of the CPA, or a civilian member of the CPA reporting directly to the Administrator and to whom such authority is specifically delegated in writing, may issue Administrative Instructions, not inconsistent with this Order, prescribing all matters that are necessary or convenient for giving effect to or carrying out the purposes of this Order.

Section 12 Entry into Force

This Order shall enter into force on the date of signature [18 August 2003].

Document 44

Coalition Provisional Authority Order Number 23

CPA/ORD/7 August 2003/23

Creation of a Code of Military Discipline for the New Iraqi Army

Pursuant to my authority as the head of the Coalition Provisional Authority (CPA), relevant U.N. Security Council resolutions including Resolution 1483 (2003), and the laws and usages of war,

Noting that Resolution 1483 appeals to Member States *inter alia* to assist the people of Iraq to contribute to conditions of stability and security in Iraq,

Recalling in this regard that CPA Order Number 22 created the New Iraqi Army,[83]

[83] See *Doc 43*.

Acknowledging the need to ensure that the New Iraqi Army has a system of discipline to maintain order,

Noting that CPA Order Number 22 provides for both military and civilian jurisdiction over members of the New Iraqi Army,

I hereby promulgate the following:

Section 1 Definitions

'Accused' means a Member of the New Iraqi Army subject to this Code of Military Discipline, against whom disciplinary proceedings are conducted in respect of an allegation of a Military Offense under this Code of Military Discipline,

'Charge' means a formal accusation in writing, prepared at the direction of the Disciplinary Officer and signed by a Disciplinary Officer, that a Member of the New Iraqi Army subject to this Code of Military Discipline has committed a Military Offense,

'Commander of the New Iraqi Army' means the Iraqi officer appointed by the Administrator of the CPA to command the New Iraqi Army,

'Disciplinary Proceedings' means the investigation into, hearing of and the decision reached, under this Code of Military Discipline in respect of an allegation of a Military Offense and includes any appeal of any such decision,

'Elements of Military Offenses' means the elements of the Offenses required to be proved to the required criminal standard before a member of the New Iraqi Army can be convicted of a Military Offense,

'Junior Disciplinary Officer' means either the officer of at least Captain in rank who at the time of any part of the Disciplinary Proceedings in respect of an allegation under this Code of Military Discipline commands the company or equivalent unit, or battalion or equivalent unit of which the Accused is a member, or the officer of at least the rank of Captain who is appointed, in accordance with the provisions of this Order, by an officer in command of a Brigade to be the Junior Disciplinary Officer of the Accused for the Disciplinary Proceedings,

'Member of the New Iraqi Army' means a person serving in the New Iraqi Army from the time of attestation until the date of termination of service,

'Military Court' means a civilian court with a civilian judge who has been appointed as a Military Judge pursuant to Section 5 of this Order,

'Military Judge' means a civilian judge with jurisdiction over Military Offenses in accordance with the provisions of this Order,

'Military Offense' means an act or omission described in Section 3 of this Code of Military Discipline,

'New Iraqi Army' means the military forces of Iraq organized for the purposes set forth in this Order including all components of the national armed forces of Iraq, specifically including the ground forces recruited, trained, and organized as the first step in the process of creating a military defense force for the new Iraq. Unless the context clearly requires otherwise, all references to the 'New Iraqi Army' are references to any element of the national defense forces of Iraq,

'Senior Disciplinary Officer' means either the officer of at least Lieutenant Colonel in rank who at the time of any part of the Disciplinary Proceedings in respect of an allegation under this Code of Military Discipline commands the Battalion of which the Accused is a member, or the officer of at least the rank of Lieutenant Colonel who is appointed, in accordance with the provisions of this Order, by the Commander of the New Iraqi Amy to be the Senior Disciplinary Officer of the Accused for the Disciplinary Proceedings.

Section 2 Military Jurisdiction

1) Members of the New Iraqi Army are subject to this Code of Military Discipline at all times from the date of their attestation until the date of termination of service.

2) A Member of the New Iraqi Army who is subsequently determined to have been ineligible for service in the New Iraqi Army remains subject to the Code of Military Discipline until discharged.

3) All Members of the New Iraqi Army will remain subject to the jurisdiction of the civilian courts while serving as Members of the New Iraqi Army; provided, Members of the New Iraqi Army enjoy immunity from civilian criminal prosecution or civil liability for acts or omissions arising within the scope of their duties and authorized operations to the same degree as other governmental officials.

Section 3 Military Offenses

1) Any Member of the New Iraqi Army subject to this Code of Military Discipline who commits any of the following shall commit a Military Offense and shall be liable on conviction to any punishment laid down in Sections 10 and 13 of this Order.

- a) mistreatment of Members of the New Iraqi Army of inferior rank;
- b) causing or engaging in a disturbance or behaving in a disorderly manner;
- c) behaving in an insubordinate manner;
- d) striking a Member of the New Iraqi Army or a member of another armed force of superior rank or civilian instructor placed in authority over the accused;
- e) while on sentry duty either
  - i) engaging in misconduct, or
  - ii) failing to do the Member's duty;
- f) disobeying a lawful order;
- g) drunkenness if, owing to the influence of alcohol or any drug, whether alone or in combination with any other circumstances, the Member is:
  - i) unfit to be entrusted with his duty,
  - ii) unfit to be entrusted with any duty which the Member was reasonably aware that he could be called upon to perform,
  - iii) behaving in a disorderly manner, or;
  - iv) behaving in any manner likely to bring discredit on the New Iraqi Army;
- h) absence without leave;
- i) avoiding the performance of a duty or negligently performing a duty;
- j) making a false statement concerning any official matter relating to the New Iraqi Army;
- k) fighting with another Member of the New Iraqi Army;
- l) willfully or by neglect damaging or causing damage to or the loss of any property of the New Iraqi Army;
- m) conduct to the prejudice of good order or military discipline;
- n) behaving in a manner likely to bring discredit on the New Iraqi Army.

2) The Elements of the Military Offenses are contained in Annex A to this Order.

3) Any Member of the New Iraqi Army subject to this Code of Military Discipline who commits a civilian criminal offense shall be guilty, by reason of so doing, of a Military Offense against this Section and liable to trial, and on conviction, to any punishment under the provisions of this Order.

4) Any Member of the New Iraqi Army subject to this Code of Military Discipline or any other person who by the law of war is subject to trial by a Military Court for any crime

or offense against the law of war who commits a violation of the law of war as adopted by Iraq or recognized as customary international law shall be guilty, by reason of so doing, of a Military Offense against this Section and liable to trial, and on conviction, to any punishment under the provisions of this Order. In the event the law of war convention or treaty was adopted without specifying the penalty for violations or otherwise fails to specify the criminal penalty, the maximum penalty shall be the maximum penalty specified for the most closely analogous offense under the civilian criminal code.

Section 4 Disciplinary Officers

1) Junior Disciplinary Officers have jurisdiction over all Military Offenses created under this Order, with the exception of the Military Offenses created under Sections 3(3) or 3(4), in respect of Members of the New Iraqi Army below the rank of Lieutenant.

2) An officer in the New Iraqi Army, not below the rank of Captain may be appointed in writing as a Junior Disciplinary Officer by an officer in command of a Brigade to be the Junior Disciplinary Officer of the accused in respect of the allegation of the commission of any Military Offense.

3) Senior Disciplinary Officers have jurisdiction over all Military Offenses created under this Order, with the exception of the Military Offenses created under Sections 3(3) or 3(4), in respect of members of the New Iraqi Army in the rank of Lieutenant and above, so long as the Senior Disciplinary Officer is at least one rank above the Accused. Senior Disciplinary Officers have jurisdiction over all appeals of decisions of Junior Disciplinary Officers.

4) An officer in the New Iraqi Army, not below the rank of Lieutenant Colonel may be appointed in writing as a Senior Disciplinary Officer by the Commander of the New Iraqi Army to be the Senior Disciplinary Officer of the accused in respect of the allegation of the commission of any Military Offense.

Section 5 Military Courts and Military Judges

1) Military Courts have jurisdiction over those Military Offenses created under Sections 3(3) and 3(4) of this Order.

2) Military Judges have jurisdiction over those Military Offenses created under Sections 3(3) and 3 (4) of this Order.

3) In circumstances in which allegations against an Accused involve Military Offenses under both Section 3(1) and Section 3(3) or 3(4), then the Military Court and Military Judge to which such matters are referred will have jurisdiction over Military Offenses under Section 3(1) in addition to those under Section 3(3) or 3(4).

4) Military Judges will be selected from sitting civil judges. The Senior Advisor, Ministry of Justice, in coordination with the Interim Minister of the Justice will appoint such civil judges, as he may deem appropriate, to be Military Judges on a standing basis who will sit as Military Judges when a Military Offense is referred to them in accordance with the provisions of this Order.

5) A civil court in which a Military Judge is conducting Disciplinary Proceedings in respect of a Military Offense will be deemed to be a Military Court for the duration of those Disciplinary Proceedings.

Section 6 Appellate Courts

In circumstances in which a Member of the New Iraqi Army has been convicted by a Military Court then the appellate court to which any appeal is made will have jurisdiction over any Military Offense referred. Appeals will be made to the appellate court with jurisdiction to hear appeals from the trial court.

Section 7 Arrest

1) Any Member of the New Iraqi Army subject to this Code of Military Discipline found committing a Military Offense, or reasonably suspected of committing a Military Offense, may be arrested in accordance with the provisions of this Section.

2) A Member of the New Iraqi Army subject to this Code of Military Discipline may be arrested by (a) a Member of the New Iraqi Army of superior rank, (b) by a civilian instructor placed in authority over the accused, (c) by a civilian police officer acting within the officer's authority, or a Member of the New Iraqi Army serving in a provost position.

3) As soon as possible, but in any event no later than 24 hours following arrest, the arrested Member of the New Iraqi Army must be informed of the reasons for his arrest.

4) Within 24 hours of arrest, unless the exigencies of operational circumstances prevent it, a Disciplinary Officer must be informed of the arrest and must consider the necessity of retaining the Member of the New Iraqi Army in arrest. The Disciplinary Officer shall order the release of the arrested Member of the New Iraqi Army unless he reasonably believes that if released:

a) the arrested Member of the New Iraqi Army will absent himself or flee disciplinary proceedings;

b) there is a risk that evidence will be lost, tainted or destroyed; or

c) the arrested Member of the New Iraqi Army will commit further Military Offenses if released.

5) If, in accordance with Section 7(5) [sic] of the present Order, the Disciplinary Officer shall have determined that the member of the New Iraqi Army under arrest shall be further retained, the period of such further retention shall not, unless the exigencies of operational circumstances prevent it, exceed 48 hours.

6) Except for the exigencies of operational circumstances or the referral of the matter to a Military Court, before the expiration of the period of 72 hours of arrest, the Disciplinary Officer must have either released the Member of the New Iraqi Army under arrest from arrest under this Section or dealt with the allegation of the Military Offense upon which the arrest is based through Disciplinary Officer action or referral to a Military Court.

7) In circumstances in which a suitable facility within a military location in which the Accused can be retained under arrest is unavailable, use may be made, with the agreement of the civilian police, of such civilian police or prison facilities as may be available.

8) Upon referral to a Military Court, that Military Court will determine whether an Accused shall remain in arrest on the basis of the civil procedures applicable in that court.

Section 8 Investigation of Allegations

1) An allegation that a Member of the New Iraqi Army has committed a Military Offense created under Section 3(1), Section 3(3), or Section 3(4) shall be reported to a Disciplinary Officer, who shall cause each such allegation to be investigated.

2) In circumstances involving an allegation of a Military Offense under Section 3(3) or Section 3(4), the Disciplinary Officer will act in accordance with Section 13 of this Order.

3) In circumstances in which allegations against an Accused involve Military Offenses under both Section 3(1) and Section 3(3) or Section 3(4), the Disciplinary Officer shall, if the Disciplinary Officer considers it is in the interests of justice for the matters to be tried together, refer all allegations to a Military Judge in accordance with Section 13 of this Order.

4) During the course of an investigation into an allegation of a Military Offense under section 3(1), if it becomes necessary to speak to the Accused, the Accused shall be offered the opportunity to have an officer of the member's choice, if reasonably available, and of at least the rank of the investigator present during the conversation to assist the Accused. It shall be explained that the Accused is not obliged to say anything unless the Accused wishes to do so. The answers of the Accused will be written down sequentially, together with the questions asked and the Accused shall have an opportunity to sign the record as accurate.

Section 9 Decision by Disciplinary Officers on Charging

1) In the case of an allegation against an Accused with respect to of a Military Offense under Section 3(1), the Disciplinary Officer will decide whether the evidence discovered during the investigation would support a Charge being preferred against the Accused.

2) If the Disciplinary Officer determines that a Charge should be preferred, the Charge shall be reduced to writing, signed by the Disciplinary Officer and a copy given to the Accused.

3) At the same time or as soon as reasonably practicable thereafter the Accused shall be provided a copy of all documentary evidence and access to all real evidence with respect to the charged Military Offense.

Section 10 Disciplinary Hearing

1) The Accused shall have at least 24 hours to prepare for the Disciplinary Hearing. The 24-hour period shall begin when the written Charge or copy of the evidence is provided to the Accused, whichever is later.

2) The Accused shall have the assistance of an Officer of his choice, subject to reasonable availability, in preparing for and during the Disciplinary Hearing.

3) Disciplinary Hearings will not be open to the Public.

4) Disciplinary Hearings will be conducted in accordance with the procedures set forth in Administrative Instructions issued by the Administrator of the CPA or by a civilian member of the CPA reporting directly to the Administrator and to whom authority to issue such Administrative Instructions is delegated.

5) Disciplinary Hearings shall be conducted in a manner that provides for the basic rights of an Accused, including but not limited to the following rights:

a) the Accused shall have the Charge explained by the Disciplinary Officer;

b) the Accused shall have the right to question witnesses called to give evidence against the Accused;

c) the Accused shall have the right to present evidence in support of his case, and if convicted, to present evidence or speak in mitigation of his punishment

d) the Accused shall have the right to remain silent and have no adverse consideration taken by the exercise of this right.

6) A Disciplinary Officer, having considered all the evidence presented to him, will only find an Accused guilty of the Military Offense charged if the Disciplinary Officer is satisfied that Accused committed the Offense in respect of each of the elements of the Military Offense listed in the Annex to this Order.

Section 11 Punishments by Disciplinary Officers

1) In adjudicating cases involving enlisted or non-commissioned personnel, a Disciplinary Officer may award the following punishments in respect of each Military Offense of which the member has been found guilty:

a) Detention for a period not longer than 7 days;
b) Fine not exceeding 14 days' pay;
c) A reprimand;
d) Extra duties to a maximum of 7 days;
e) In respect of a Private First Class, Corporal, or Sergeant, reduction by one rank;
f) Stoppages of pay in respect of damage or loss caused by the act or acts which formed the basis of the Offense charged, not exceeding 14 days' pay.

2) A Junior Disciplinary Officer may combine those punishments listed in Sections 11(1)(b) and 11(1)(f), except that no more than 28 days pay may be taken from the convicted member of the New Iraqi Army in respect of all the Offenses dealt with by the Junior Disciplinary Officer at one hearing.

3) Detention may only be awarded to a Private, Private First Class, or Corporal. It may not be combined with any other punishment except stoppages of pay.

4) Reduction in rank may not be combined with any other punishment.

5) A reprimand and extra duties may be combined with any other punishment not otherwise excepted under this Section.

6) In adjudicating cases involving officers, a Senior Disciplinary Officer may only award the following punishments in respect of each Military Offense of which the member has been found guilty:

a) Fine not exceeding 14 days' pay;
b) A reprimand;
c) Extra duties to a maximum of 7 days;
d) Stoppages of pay in respect of damage or loss caused by the act or acts which formed the basis of the Offense charged, not exceeding 14 days' pay.

7) A Senior Disciplinary Officer may combine those punishments listed in Sections 11(6)(a) and 11(6)(d), except that no more than 28 days pay may be taken from the convicted Member of the New Iraqi Army in respect of all the Offenses dealt with by the Senior Disciplinary Officer at one hearing.

8) A reprimand and extra duties may be combined with any other punishment not otherwise excepted under this Section.

Section 12 Appeal from Disciplinary Officers

1) An Accused who has been convicted by a Junior Disciplinary Officer of a Military Offense under Section 3(1) of this Code of Military Discipline shall be entitled to appeal to the Senior Disciplinary Officer. An Accused must submit the appeal and any supporting evidence in writing to the officer in command of the convicted member within 14 days of the Disciplinary Hearing.

2) An Accused who is an officer of the New Iraqi Army who is convicted by a Senior Disciplinary Officer of a Military Offense under Section 3 (1) of this Code of Military Discipline shall be entitled to appeal to the Commander of the New Iraqi Army or the senior Commander of the New Iraqi Army. An Accused must submit the appeal and any supporting evidence in writing to the officer in command of the convicted member within 14 days of the Disciplinary Hearing.

Section 13 Referral for Trial by Military Judge

1) In the case of an allegation of a Military Offense under Section 3(3) or Section 3(4) the Disciplinary Officer will refer the allegation, together with all available evidence relating to the allegation, to a Military Judge for consideration.

2) Where an investigation into an allegation of a Military Offense under Section 3(1) discovers evidence of additional Military Offenses under Section 3(3) or Section 3(4), the Disciplinary Officer shall terminate the investigation and refer the allegation, together with all available evidence, to a Military Judge for consideration.

3) In accordance with Section 8(3) of this Order, where there are allegations against an Accused involving Military Offenses under both Section 3(1) and Section 3(3) or Section 3(4) the Disciplinary Officer shall, if the Disciplinary Officer considers it in the interests of justice for the matters to be tried together, refer all allegations, together with all available evidence, to a Military Judge.

4) The Military Judge will investigate and otherwise deal with the allegation of the Military Offense referred in accordance with this Section in the manner applicable for civil Offenses laid down in the Iraqi Law of Criminal Procedure 1971 as amended by Iraqi law and by CPA Orders.[84]

Section 14 Punishments by Military Judge

The Military Judge will apply the sentences appropriate to the civil Offense charged under the provisions of Section 3(3) or Section 3(4), except that in determining the appropriate level of sentence within the sentencing range for the Offense, the Military Judge may consider the impact that the Military Offense had on good order and discipline within the New Iraqi Army.

Section 15 Appeal from Military Judge

1) An Accused who has been convicted by a Military Judge of a Military Offense shall be entitled to appeal in accordance with civil procedures.

2) The court hearing the appeal will consider the matter appealed in accordance with the applicable law and procedure for civil Offenses laid down in the Iraqi Law of Criminal Procedure 1971 with amendments and as amended by CPA Orders and the Third Edition of the Iraqi Penal Code 1969, with amendments and as amended by CPA Orders.[85]

Section 16 Suspension of Iraqi Laws

The Iraqi Military Law Code Number 13 of 1940, the Iraqi Military Procedures Code Number 44 of 1941, the Code of Legal Notification of Military Personnel Number 106 or 1960, Punishment of Military Deserters Law Number 28 of 1972, and the Penal Code of the Popular Army Number 32 of 1984 have been suspended under CPA Order Number 21 [sic][86] entitled Creation of a New Iraqi Army.

Section 17 Administrative Instructions

The Administrator of the CPA or a civilian member of the CPA reporting directly to the Administrator and to whom such authority is delegated may issue Administrative Instructions not inconsistent with this Order, prescribing all matters that are necessary or convenient for giving effect to or carrying out the purposes of this Order.

Section 18 Entry into Force

This Order shall enter into force on the date of signature [20 August 2003].

[84] See CPA Memorandum No 3 *[Doc 127]* and CPA Order No 31 *[Doc 52]*.
[85] See CPA Orders No 7 *[Doc 21]*, 16 *[Doc 34]*, 19 *[Doc 40]*, 31 *[Doc 52]*, 41 *[Doc 63]*.
[86] It should read CPA Order No 22; see *Doc 43*.

ANNEX

ELEMENTS OF MILITARY OFFENSES CREATED UNDER SECTION 3

(a) mistreating in any way of a Members [sic] of the New Iraqi Army of inferior rank;

Elements:

1. an act that amounted to mistreatment; and
2. the act was committed by a Member of the New Iraqi Army of superior rank (hereinafter in this subsection 'superior rank') on a Member of the New Iraqi Army or a member of another armed force acting with the New Iraqi Army of inferior rank; and
3. the superior rank (accused) knew the victim was inferior in rank; and
4. the superior rank (accused) deliberately carried out the act; and
5. the superior rank (accused) knew that the act amounted to mistreatment 'Mistreatment' means unwarranted, harmful, abusive, rough, or other unjustifiable treatment which, under all the circumstances:
   (a) results in physical or mental pain or suffering, and
   (b) is unwarranted, unjustified and unnecessary for any lawful purpose.

(b) causing or engaging in a disturbance or behaving in a disorderly manner;

Elements:

1. the accused EITHER
   (i) caused a disturbance, OR
   (ii) became involved in a disturbance, OR
   (iii) behaved in a disorderly manner; and

2) the accused acted in such a manner deliberately.

(c) behaving in an insubordinate manner;

Elements:

1. the actions OR words of the accused were insubordinate, insulting or disrespectful to a Member of the New Iraqi Army or a member of another armed force of superior rank (hereinafter in this subsection 'superior rank') or a civilian instructor placed in authority over the accused; and
2. the actions OR words of the accused were used in the presence of the superior or civilian instructor placed in authority over the accused; and
3. the accused knew that the superior or civilian instructor placed in authority over the accused was his or her superior or civilian instructor placed in authority over the accused; and
4. the accused deliberately spoke or acted in such insulting or disrespectful manner.

(d) striking a Member of the Iraqi Army, a member of another armed force acting with the New Iraqi Army of superior rank, or civilian instructor placed in authority over the accused (hereinafter in this subsection 'superior')

Elements:

1. the accused struck a Member of the New Iraqi Army, a member of another armed force acting with the New Iraqi Army, or civilian instructor placed in authority over the accused; and
2. the accused had no lawful excuse for striking the superior or civilian instructor placed in authority over the accused; and

3. the accused knew that the superior or civilian instructor placed in authority over the accused was his or her superior or civilian instructor placed in authority over the accused; and
4. the accused deliberately struck the superior or civilian instructor placed in authority over the accused

'Strike' means an intentional blow, and includes any offensive touching of the person of the superior, however slight.

(e) while on sentry duty either
(i) engaging in misconduct, or
(ii) failing to do the Member's duty;

Elements:

1. the accused was on sentry duty; and
2. the accused EITHER
   (i) deliberately engaged in misconduct, OR
   (ii) the accused failed to carry out a duty whether deliberately or by neglect.

(f) disobeying a lawful order;

Elements:

1. an order was given to the accused; and
2. the order was lawful; and
3. the accused was aware of the order having been given to him; and
4. the accused deliberately or by neglect did not obey the order.

(g) drunkenness if, owing to the influence of alcohol or any drug, whether alone or in combination with any other circumstances, the Member is:
(i) unfit to be entrusted with his duty,
(ii) unfit to be entrusted with any duty which the Member was reasonably aware that he could be called upon to perform;
(iii) behaving in a disorderly manner, or;
(iv) behaving in any manner likely to bring discredit on the New Iraqi Army;

Elements:

1. the accused knowingly took alcohol OR drugs; and
2. as a result thereof the accused EITHER
   (i) was unfit to be entrusted with his duties, OR
   (ii) was unfit to be entrusted with any duty that he was reasonably aware he could be called upon to perform, OR
   (iii) behaved in a disorderly manner, OR
   (iv) behaved in a manner likely to bring discredit on the Defence Force.

(h) absence without leave;

Elements:

1. the accused was required to be at his place of duty; and
2. the accused was not at his place of duty; and
3. the accused later returned to his place of duty; and
4. the accused did not have permission or a reasonable excuse for being away from his place of duty.

(i) avoiding the performance of a duty or negligently performing a duty;
Elements:
1. the accused had a duty to perform; and
2. the accused was aware of that duty; and, EITHER
   (i) the accused did not perform that duty; and
   (ii) the accused did not perform the duty either deliberately or by neglect, OR
   (iii) the accused performed the duty to a poor standard; and
   (iv) the accused performed the duty to a poor standard either deliberately or by neglect.

(j) making a false statement concerning any official matter relating to the New Iraqi Army;
Elements:
1. the accused made a statement about official New Iraqi Army matters; and
2. the statement was false in a significant way; and
3. the accused knew that the statement was false at the time he made it.

(k) without reasonable excuse, fighting with another Member of the New Iraqi Army;
Elements:
1. the accused was involved in a fight; and
2. the accused's involvement in the fight was deliberate; and
3. the fight was with another Member of the New Iraqi Army; and
4. the accused did not have a reasonable excuse for fighting.

(l) willfully or by neglect damaging or causing damage to or the loss of any property of the New Iraqi Army;
Elements:
1. the accused lost OR damaged property of the New Iraqi Army; and
2. that loss or damage resulted from EITHER
   (i) the deliberate acts of the accused, OR
   (ii) the neglect of the accused.

(m) conduct to the prejudice of good order or military discipline;
Elements:
1. an act or omission by the accused; and
2. such act or omission was likely to prejudice good order or military discipline
3. the accused was aware, at the time of such act or omission, that the same was likely to prejudice good order or military discipline.

(n) behaving in a manner likely to bring discredit on the New Iraqi Army;
Elements:
1. an act or omission by the accused; and
2. such act or omission caused discredit to the New Iraqi Army; and
3. the accused was aware, at the time of such act or omission, that the act or omission was likely to bring discredit on the New Iraqi Army.

Document 45
Coalition Provisional Authority Order Number 24

CPA/ORD/13 August 2003/24

Ministry of Science and Technology

Pursuant to my authority as Administrator of the Coalition Provisional Authority (CPA), and under the laws and usages of war, and consistent with relevant U.N. Security Council resolutions, including Resolution 1483 (2003),

Recognizing that Iraq possesses a large, well-trained engineering and technical work force fully capable of advancing scientific research and development initiatives to support the reconstruction and economic development of Iraq,

Recalling that Iraq's scientific expertise was employed in a manner inconsistent with accepted notions of scientific development and for purposes directed by the former regime,

Understanding that redirecting the efforts of Iraq's scientific and technical research efforts away from weapons development is necessary to transform and modernize Iraq's industrial base in support of the continued economic development of Iraq,

I hereby promulgate the following:

Section 1 Dissolution of the Ministry of Atomic Energy

In accordance with CPA Order No. 2, Dissolution of Entities (23 May 2003),[87] the Ministry of Atomic Energy is hereby dissolved. Employees and assets of the Ministry of Atomic Energy shall be transferred to the Ministry of Science and Technology established hereunder.

Section 2 Establishment of the Ministry of Science and Technology

There is hereby established the Ministry of Science and Technology as a ministerial level agency that shall identify, research and develop projects designed to restore and improve Iraq's infrastructure and industrial base.

Section 3 Purpose

The Ministry of Science and Technology will work with public and private industry, governmental agencies, and educational institutions to lead scientific and technological development for the purpose of fostering the restoration and improvement of Iraq's infrastructure and industrial base.

Section 4 Organization

The Ministry of Science and Technology shall be organized by centers of thought. These centers include:

1) Fossil Fuel/Solar Energy Research and Development Center. This Center will focus on the development of new technologies to maximize the potential of current fossil fuel production and to research alternative energy sources.

2) Environmental Protection Center. This Center will focus on standards and compliance measures to address radiation, air quality, hazardous materials, water management, and pollution prevention.

[87] See *Doc 15*.

3) Information and Electronics Technology Center. This Center will focus on research and technology to foster business productivity. The functional areas will include hardware and software, process engineering, and electronic devices.

4) Agriculture and Food Technology Center. This Center will focus on the redirection and refurbishment of the agriculture and food production capabilities of Iraq. The functional areas will include natural pesticides, improved seed stocks, processed foods, and hydroponics.

5) Materials and Chemistry Center. This Center will focus on supporting the emerging sectors by nurturing the development of material technologies. The functional areas will include plastics, ceramics and glass, metals, and building technology.

6) Industrial Development Center. This center will investigate potential solutions and processes that require the study of available raw materials and the commercial viability of supporting technologies. This includes the use of licensing agreements and outside experts and partners.

Section 5 Entry into Force

This Order shall enter into force on the date of signature [24 August 2003].

Document 46

Coalition Provisional Authority Order Number 25

CPA/ORD/31 August 2003/25

Confiscation of Property Used in or Resulting from Certain Crimes

Pursuant to my authority as Administrator of the Coalition Provisional Authority (CPA), under the laws and usages of war, and consistent with relevant U.N. Security Council resolutions, including Resolution 1483 (2003),

Recognizing that crimes involving the theft of natural resources or state property and crimes involving the damage of utility infrastructure including water and power facilities harm all Iraqi people,

Noting that one of the means of deterring such crimes is to deprive criminals of the proceeds of crime and of the property used or intended for use in the commission of crimes,

Understanding the need for a fair process to ensure that the rights of innocent persons are not infringed by unwarranted confiscation of property,

I hereby promulgate the following:

Section 1 Definitions

1) 'Confiscation Hearing' means the hearing in an Investigative Court conducted by an Investigative Judge for the purpose of determining whether seized property is Criminal Property as defined in this Order and subject to confiscation.

2) 'Criminal Property' means:

a) Property used or intended for use in the commission of a criminal offense involving Natural Resources or Utility Infrastructure including any means of transport or conveyances, such as aircraft, vehicles, or vessels that are used, or are intended for use, to transport, or in any manner facilitate the commission of such criminal offenses;

b) Property acquired through or as a result of the commission, or attempted commission of a criminal offense involving Natural Resources or Utility Infrastructure; and

c) All monies, negotiable instruments, securities, or other things of value furnished or intended to be furnished by any person in exchange for unlawfully acquired Natural Resources or parts of Utility Infrastructure, or to otherwise facilitate the commission of an offense within the scope of this order.

3) 'Natural Resources' means resources occurring in nature that can be used for the creation of raw materials or products as identified in Article 13 of the Interim Constitution of 1970[88] including products resulting from such resources such as refined petroleum, benzene, diesel fuel, or other petroleum products after refinement.

4) 'Utility Infrastructure' means:

a) any and all parts of public service facilities including power generation and supply equipment including wires and towers,

b) water treatment and delivery apparatus including irrigation systems and pipes, and

c) information technology components including telephone and computer cabling.

Section 2 Confiscation of Criminal Property

1) Criminal Property shall be subject to confiscation; confiscated property shall vest as provided in Section 6 below.

2) Criminal Property may be seized by Coalition Forces or Iraqi Police in the manner set forth below in Section 3.

3) Confiscation Hearing procedures described in this Order are in addition to other confiscation laws that require the conviction of the accused prior to the confiscation of the property.

4) A criminal conviction is not required under these procedures prior to the confiscation of Criminal Property.

5) The Confiscation Hearing procedures set forth in this Order are independent of criminal investigations or prosecutions and may be pursued irrespective of the disposition of criminal charges.

Section 3 Procedures for the Seizure and Confiscation of Criminal Property

1) When suspected Criminal Property is identified in connection with an investigation of or the apprehension of a person for the commission or attempted commission of a criminal offense involving Natural Resources or Utility Infrastructure, such suspected Criminal Property is subject to immediate seizure by Coalition Forces or Iraqi Police.

2) The authority seizing the suspected Criminal Property shall inform the person in possession or control of the property at the time of seizure that the property is being seized as suspected Criminal Property and will be subject to confiscation proceedings.

3) Within seven days of seizure pursuant to this Order, the authority that seized the suspected Criminal Property shall report the seizure of such property to a court of competent jurisdiction and to the Ministry of Finance. The following courts are courts of competent jurisdiction to conduct Confiscation Hearings:

[88] Art 13 [Public Property and Planning] of the 1970 Interim Constitution provides: 'National resources and basic means of production are owned by the People. They are directly invested by the Central Authority in the Iraqi Republic, according to exigencies of the general planning of the national.'

a) Except as provided in Section 3.3(b) below, the Investigative Court with jurisdiction over the geographic area in which the property was seized shall have jurisdiction to conduct Confiscation Hearings. For seizures within the territorial waters or airspace of Iraq, the Investigative Court nearest the port of entry or with jurisdiction over the geographic area of the storage location of the seized property shall have jurisdiction to conduct Confiscation Hearings.

b) The Investigative Court of the Central Criminal Court of Iraq shall have jurisdiction to conduct Confiscation Hearings involving seizures of suspected Criminal Property. Such cases shall be referred to the Central Criminal Court in accordance with the referral procedures set forth in CPA Order 13 (Revised), The Central Criminal Court of Iraq, CPA/ORD/11 July 2003/13.[89]

4) The report to the Investigative Court and the Ministry of Finance by the authority that seized the suspected Criminal Property shall describe the seized property with serial or identification numbers, if any, and state the time, date and place of seizure, the identity of the person possessing or in control of the property at the time of seizure, and any other available identifying information about the owner of the seized property.

5) Following the report of the seizure of suspected Criminal Property, the Investigating Judge shall make reasonable attempts to identify the owner and others with a documented interest in the suspected Criminal Property including the review of reasonably available property registration records.

6) Once identified, the owner of the seized property and others with a documented interest shall be notified within a reasonable time in writing of the Confiscation Hearing, which shall occur no earlier than seven days following notification.

7) In the event the Investigating Judge is unable to identify or notify the owner or others with a documented interest in the suspected Criminal Property, the Investigative Court shall publish a short description of the Criminal Property, the date and place of seizure, and the date and time of the Confiscation Hearing described in Section 4 below. This publication will be made in two general circulation newspapers in the vicinity of the location of the seizure for five consecutive issues if published in daily publications or two consecutive issues if published less than daily. Confiscation Hearings may not occur before the expiration of three days from the last date of publication.

Section 4 Confiscation Hearings

1) The circumstances surrounding the seizure of suspected Criminal Property shall be reviewed by the Investigating Judge in accordance with the procedures of Investigative Hearings set forth in Law (23) of 1971, the Law on Criminal Proceedings as modified by CPA Implementing Memorandum 3 (CPA/MEM/18 June 2003/03).[90]

2) Persons asserting lawful interests in suspected Criminal Property shall be provided an opportunity to be heard at the Confiscation Hearing.

3) The Investigating Judge shall review available evidence and information presented by persons with lawful interests in suspected Criminal Property at the Confiscation Hearing. The Investigating Judge shall determine whether the suspected Criminal Property is Criminal Property as defined in this Order.

4) In the event the Investigating Judge is satisfied that the property is Criminal Property and the owner knew or reasonably should have known that the property was used or was intended

[89] See *Doc 30.*
[90] See *Doc 127.*

to be used in a criminal offense involving Natural Resources or Utility Infrastructure, the Investigating Judge shall order that the property be confiscated. Following the Confiscation Hearing, the Investigating Judge shall promptly inform the Ministry of Finance of the description and location of the confiscated property. The owner of property ordered to be confiscated may appeal such order in accordance with Section 5 below.

5) In the event the Investigating Judge is not satisfied that the property is to be confiscated, the property shall be made available for release to the individual identified as the owner of the property, provided it is not necessary to retain the property for use in future criminal or other confiscation proceedings related to the suspected offense. The governmental authority may appeal such order in accordance with Section 5 below.

5) [sic] Courts conducting Confiscation Hearings shall report all such hearings to the Ministry of Justice and Ministry of Finance. Reports will include: the name of the suspected owner of the property, description of property, Investigative Court and Judge conducting the Confiscation Hearing, date of the Confiscation Hearing, and outcome. Reports will be made by the 15th day of the month and will report all Confiscation Hearings conducted in the prior month. Investigative Courts will also report to the Ministry of Justice any property not forwarded to the Ministry of Finance for disposition or returned to the owner within sixty days following the Confiscation Hearing.

Section 5 Appeal from Confiscation Hearings

1) Within thirty days of the decision regarding the confiscation of the Criminal Property, the decision of the Confiscation Hearing Investigative Judge may be appealed to the Felony Trial Court with jurisdiction over cases arising from the Investigative Court conducting the Confiscation Hearing or to the Felony Trial Court of The Central Criminal Court of Iraq.

2) The Felony Trial Court with jurisdiction to which the confiscation decision has been appealed shall review the evidence presented at the Confiscation Hearing and determine whether the decision of the Investigative Judge was warranted by the evidence. The owner or governmental authorities may present briefs accompanied by sworn affidavits to the Felony Trial Court for consideration. The appeal to the Felony Trial Court is not a new trial, but is limited to a review of the record of the Investigating Court and matters submitted by the persons with an interest in the confiscated property or governmental authorities.

3) In the event that the Felony Trial Court is satisfied that the property is Criminal Property subject to confiscation, the Felony Trial Court shall order that the property be confiscated and disposed of in accordance with Section 6 below. There shall be no further appeal from the determination of the Felony Trial Court.

4) In the event the Felony Trial Court is not satisfied that the property is Criminal Property, the Felony Trial Court shall order that the seized property be made available for release to the owner of the property, provided it is not necessary to retain the property for use in future criminal or other confiscation proceedings. The Felony Trial Court shall inform the Ministry of Finance that the property is to be released to the owner. In the event the property has been disposed of in accordance with Section 6 below prior to the decision of the Felony Trial Court granting the appeal, the Felony Trial Court shall inform the Ministry of Finance of the description of the property, owner, and appeal result. In the event the property cannot be returned, the Ministry of Finance shall pay (i) the amount of the assessed market value of the property at the time of seizure or (ii) the actual amount paid if sold at public auction, whichever is greater, to the owner within thirty days of the decision by the Felony Trial Court.

Section 6 Disposition of Criminal Property

1) Investigating Judges may not order the release of suspected Criminal Property prior to conducting a Confiscation Hearing.

2) Property determined to be Criminal Property by the Investigating Judge shall be disposed of by the Ministry of Finance. All monies, negotiable instruments, or securities will be accounted for by the Ministry of Finance and paid into the Central Bank of Iraq. For other property, the Ministry of Finance shall undertake an assessment of the fair market value at the time of seizure of the property confiscated under the Order.

3) Following a determination of the fair market value at the time of seizure of the Criminal Property, the Ministry of Finance, in its discretion, may retain such property for official governmental use and may deliver the property to ministries that have requirements for the use of such property or sell it in a public auction according to the Law of Selling and Leasing State Properties No. (32) of 1986. Proceeds of such sales shall be paid into the Central Bank of Iraq.

4) Appeals from the decision of the Investigative Court, shall not delay the disposition of such property.

5) In the event the Investigative Judge determines seized property is not Criminal Property subject to confiscation, the property shall be maintained for 60 days following the hearing so that it may be claimed by the owner. In the event the owner fails to claim such property within the 60-day period, the property shall be disposed of in accordance with this Section.

6) The Ministry of Finance shall deliver a Criminal Property report by the 15th day of each month to the CPA, Director of Management and Budget. The report will contain information regarding all Criminal Property disposed of during the prior month. The Criminal Property report will include the name of the suspected owner, Investigative Court conducting the Confiscation Hearing, date of the Confiscation Hearing, description of property, fair market value at the time of seizure, and amount paid if sold or the government agency in possession of the property if retained for government use.[91]

Section 7 Preservation of Other Confiscation Laws

This Order is in addition to other confiscation provisions of Iraqi law, and shall not preclude the enforcement of such provisions.

Section 8 Administration Instructions

The interim Minister of Justice, in coordination with CPA ministry advisors, may issue such Administrative Instructions as are necessary to carry out this Order. The interim Minister of Finance, in coordination with the CPA Director of Management and Budget, may issue such Administrative Instructions as are necessary to carry out the financial and property management aspects of this Order.

Section 9 Entry into Force

This Order shall enter into force on the date of signature [3 September 2003].

[91] Sec 6(6) was amended by CPA Order No 100, sec 3(11) *[Doc 124]*.

Document 47
Coalition Provisional Authority Order Number 26
CPA/ORD/24 August 2003/26

Creation of the Department of Border Enforcement

Pursuant to my authority as Administrator of the Coalition Provisional Authority (CPA), under the laws and usages of war, and consistent with relevant U.N. Security Council resolutions, including Resolution 1483 (2003),

Recognizing that border controls are essential to the establishment of a free and safe Iraq,

Recognizing that previous border functions were carried out by five different government entities within the former Iraqi regime, and that the former Iraqi regime often used these functions as tools to oppress the interests of the Iraqi public,

Recognizing that it is desirable as soon as possible to restore the normal transit and movement of people and commercial goods to and from Iraq,

Recognizing that such transit must be restored in a way that protects the security and safety of the Iraqi public people and others lawfully present in Iraq,

I hereby promulgate the following:

Section 1 Establishment of the Department of Border Enforcement

1) There shall be established the Department of Border Enforcement for Iraq as a department within the Ministry of the Interior.

2) The Department of Border Enforcement will monitor and control the movement of persons and goods to, from, and across the borders of Iraq.

3) The Department of Border Enforcement shall conduct its activities consistent with all applicable CPA Regulations, Orders, and Memoranda, including CPA Order 16 regarding the Temporary Control of the Iraqi Borders, Ports and Airports,[92] and all Iraqi laws regarding immigration, emigration, customs and quarantine, including the Customs Law of 1984, unless specifically suspended by the CPA.

Section 2 Responsibilities of the Department of Border Enforcement

1) Full authority, direction and control over all border-related functions formerly exercised by the Ministry of Foreign Affairs, the Ministry of Finance, the Ministry of Interior, the Ministry of Defense and the Presidential Office, including border police, customs police, customs inspections, immigration inspections, border port of entry facilities protection, detention and deportation, coastal patrol, airport immigrations and customs processing, passport issuance and inspections, and nationality and civil affairs functions, are hereby vested in the Department of Border Enforcement. The Ministry of Foreign Affairs retains the limited authority to issue diplomatic and official passports necessary for official travel.

2) All facilities, equipment, and vehicles engaged in border-related functions that were previously under the authority of the Ministry of Foreign Affairs, the Ministry of Finance, the Ministry of Interior, the Ministry of Defense, or the Presidential Office, all employees thereof, and all related funds for such functions or payroll, are hereby transferred to the Department of Border Enforcement. The Ministry of Foreign Affairs will retain such

[92] See *Doc 34*.

facilities and equipment as are necessary to accomplish the limited responsibility of issuing diplomatic and official passports.

Section 3 Cooperation Among Ministries and Governmental Offices
The Ministry of Foreign Affairs, the Ministry of Finance, the Ministry of Interior, national defense agencies, the Presidential Office and the Department of Border Enforcement, and all other relevant organs of government, shall cooperate in this effort, including prescribing, under the authority, direction and control of the CPA, any administrative procedures necessary to carry out this Order. The Ministry of Finance, under the authority, direction and control of the CPA, shall be responsible for developing policy regarding border-related revenue functions.

Section 4 Administrative Instructions
The interim Minister of the Interior, with the concurrence of the CPA Director of Interior Policy, may issue such Administrative Instructions as are necessary to carry out the purposes of this Order.

Section 5 Entry into Force
This Order shall enter into force on the date of signature [24 August 2003].

Document 48
Coalition Provisional Authority Order Number 27
CPA/ORD/4 September 2003/27

Establishment of the Facilities Protection Service

Pursuant to my authority as Administrator of the Coalition Provisional Authority (CPA), under the laws and usages of war, and consistent with relevant U.N. Security Council resolutions, including Resolution 1483 (2003),

Noting that Resolution 1483 appeals to Member States to assist the people of Iraq in their efforts to reform their institutions and rebuild their country and to contribute to conditions of stability and security in Iraq,

Understanding the need to preserve the facilities of the government ministries of Iraq,

Recognizing the need for a body of trained and appropriately equipped personnel that can contribute to efforts to protect the governmental installations of Iraq,

I hereby promulgate the following:

Section 1 Establishment of the Facilities Protection Service
This order establishes the Facilities Protection Service (FPS). The FPS is an organization of trained, armed, uniformed entities charged with providing security for ministry and governorate offices, government infrastructure, and fixed sites under the direction and control of governmental ministries and governorate administrations.

Section 2 Organization of the FPS
1) Governmental employees employed by the ministries or governorates are eligible to serve in the FPS. The FPS may also consist of employees of private security firms who are

engaged to perform services for the ministries or governorates through contracts, provided such private security firms and employees are licensed and authorized by the Ministry of Interior as provided in Section 7 herein. Persons who have participated in Ba'ath Party activity within the leadership tiers described in CPA Order Number 1, De-Ba'athification of Iraqi Society (CPA/ORD/16 May 2003/01)[93] may not serve in the FPS in any capacity except by the express grant of an exception by the Coalition Provisional Authority.

2) Ministers and heads of governorate administrations shall determine the need for FPS members at locations under their supervision. Each ministry or governorate administration is responsible for ensuring the FPS branch under its supervision is sufficient to protect key sites for which it is responsible, with the additional support of police or other forces in times of emergency.

3) Ministries and governorate administrations are responsible for the funding of FPS members assigned to their agency. Ministries and governorate administrations are responsible for the supervision and control of the FPS force assigned to their governmental agency, consistent with the standards and regulations established by the Ministry of Interior.

4) Governorates will establish Regional Operations Centers to coordinate the operations of FPS guards and to ensure their proper integration with police and other emergency services.

5) The Ministry of Interior will establish standards and training for the FPS including standards and training for private security firms performing FPS duties pursuant to contracts. Pursuant to this Order, the Ministry of Interior will issue FPS Administrative Instructions defining the standards for dress, training, certification, and deportment. All members of the FPS whether contracted or employed directly by the governmental agency are required to comply with the Administrative Instructions issued by the Ministry of Interior.

6) FPS organizations may be known by different names including, for example 'Electricity Police,' 'Diplomatic Protective Services,' or 'Oil Police' but each will have only the specific powers and authorities granted in this Order.

7) Members of the FPS may not participate in any manner in organizations or activities that advocate racial, gender or ethnic hatred or intolerance; advocate, create, or engage in illegal discrimination based on race, color, gender, religion, or regional origin; or use, or advocate the use of, force or violence or other unlawful means to achieve internal political goals. Violations may result in the removal of the member from employment in the FPS or the withdrawal of the authorization for the member to perform FPS responsibilities as a member of a private security firm.

Section 3 Authority of the FPS

1) Members of the FPS may, while performing their official duties, apprehend persons who (i) they witness committing or attempting to commit a criminal offense, (ii) have escaped after being lawfully arrested, or (iii) otherwise interfere with their lawful activities. Persons apprehended by the FPS must be turned over to the Iraqi police or Coalition Forces within twelve hours of apprehension or be released.

2) Members of the FPS may, while performing their official duties, conduct reasonable searches for weapons or other dangerous or prohibited items of persons entering or within the governmental property or offices they are securing, criminal suspects in their custody, or vehicles entering or within the governmental property or offices they are securing.

[93] See *Doc 14*.

3) Members of the FPS may, while performing official duties, use force against persons or things as is reasonable and necessary under the circumstances. However, the use of force that may be likely to cause death or serious bodily injury is not permitted unless the member reasonably believes that using such force is necessary to: (i) protect himself or others from the imminent use of deadly force or force likely to cause serious bodily injury, (ii) prevent the escape of a person suspected of committing murder or assault resulting in serious bodily injury, or (iii) defend ministry or governorate offices, government or state-owned infrastructure, and fixed sites under the direction and control of governmental ministries and governorate administrations, to prevent their destruction or incapacitation.

Section 4 Jurisdiction

1) Members of the FPS will be subject to Iraqi law at all times, and the courts of Iraq shall have jurisdiction over offenses alleged to have been committed by members of the FPS. The Administrator of the CPA may determine that offenses alleged to have been committed by members of the FPS while on duty may be submitted to the Central Criminal Court of Iraq in accordance with CPA Order Number 13 (Revised), The Central Criminal Court of Iraq (CPA/ORD/13 July 2003/13).[94]

2) Members of the FPS shall enjoy immunity from civil liability for acts or omissions arising within the scope of their duties and in the conduct of authorized operations to the same degree as other governmental officials under the law of Iraq.

Section 5 Weapons

The possession of weapons by members of the FPS is regulated by CPA Order Number 3, Weapons Control Order (CPA/ORD/23 May 2003/03).[95]

Section 6 Licensing Private Security Firms

Private Firms may provide contract FPS guards to ministries or governorates under license from the Ministry of Interior. Members of the FPS from private security firms will be integrated into Governorate coordination structures.

Section 7 Administration Instructions

The Administrator of the CPA or the Minister of the Ministry of Interior, in consultation with the CPA Director of Interior Policy, may issue Administrative Instructions consistent with this Order, prescribing all matters that are necessary or appropriate for giving effect to or carrying out the purposes of this Order.

Section 8 Entry into Force

This Order shall enter into force on the date of signature [4 September 2003].

[94] See *Doc 30*. There seems to be a typo in the date of the Revised Order No 13. The Order bears the symbol 'CPA/ORD/11 July 2003/13'.

[95] See *Doc 16*.

Document 49
Coalition Provisional Authority Order Number 28
CPA/ORD/3 September 2003/28

Establishment of the Iraqi Civil Defense Corps

Pursuant to my authority as head of the Coalition Provisional Authority (CPA), under the laws and usages of war, and consistent with relevant United Nations Security Council resolutions, including Resolution 1483 (2003),

Noting that Resolution 1483 appeals to Member States to assist the people of Iraq in their efforts to reform their institutions, rebuild their country, and to contribute to conditions of stability and security in Iraq,

Understanding the need to address promptly threats to public security and stability resulting from wrongful acts or disasters,

Recognizing that continued attacks and acts of sabotage by Ba'athist remnants and terrorists intent on undermining security in Iraq necessitate the temporary establishment of an Iraqi constabulary force to operate with Coalition Forces to counter the threat and maintain security in Iraq,

I hereby promulgate the following:

Section 1 Establishment of the Iraqi Civil Defense Corps

1) The Iraqi Civil Defense Corps is established as a temporary institution, subject to a decision by an internationally recognized, representative government, established by the people of Iraq, to continue or disband the Corps.

2) The Iraqi Civil Defense Corps is a security and emergency service agency for Iraq. The Iraqi Civil Defense Corps is composed of Iraqis who will complement operations conducted by Coalition military forces in Iraq to counter organized groups and individuals employing violence against the people of Iraq and their national infrastructure.

3) In support of Coalition operations to provide security and stability to the people of Iraq, the Iraqi Civil Defense Corps is authorized to perform constabulary duties, including the following tasks: patrolling urban and rural areas; conducting operations to search for and seize illegal weapons and other contraband; providing fixed site, check point, area, route and convoy security; providing crowd and riot control; disaster response services; search and rescue services; providing support to humanitarian missions and disaster recover operations including transportation services; conducting joint patrols with Coalition Forces; and, participating in other activities designed to build positive relationships between the Iraqi people and Coalition authorities including serving as community liaisons.

4) The Iraqi Civil Defense Corps is distinct from the Iraqi police force and the New Iraqi Army. The Iraqi Civil Defense Corps will complement the police force, but will be designed to perform operations that exceed the capacity of the police.[96]

a) While on duty and under the supervision of Coalition Forces, members of the Iraqi Civil Defense Corps will not be subject to the direction or control of the Iraqi Police. Except as provided herein, the Iraqi Civil Defense Corps will not have, or exercise, domestic law enforcement functions.

[96] Sec 1(4) was amended by CPA Order No 73, sec 3(1) *[Doc 97]*.

b) The Iraqi Civil Defense Corps is not a component of the New Iraqi Army established by CPA Order 22, Creation of a New Iraqi Army (CPA/ORD/9 August 2003/22)[97] and is not subject to the orders of the New Iraqi Army chain of command.

Section 2 Organization of the Iraqi Civil Defense Corps

1) The Iraqi Civil Defense Corps shall consist of active members in full-time employment, and may also include reserve members whose service will be governed by Administrative Instructions issued pursuant to this Order.

2) All Iraqis who meet the professional criteria established by applicable Administrative Instructions are eligible for selection to the Iraqi Civil Defense Corps, provided that no person involved in Ba'ath Party activity within the leadership tiers described in CPA Order Number 1, De-Ba'athification of Iraqi Society (CPA/ORD/16 May 2003/01)[98] shall be eligible except by express decision of the CPA to grant such an exception.

3) Service in the Iraqi Civil Defense Corps is voluntary. Volunteers for service in the Iraqi Civil Defense Corps will be required to serve for a period of 12 months subject to a decision either by the CPA or by an internationally recognized, representative government, established by the people of Iraq, to discontinue the Iraqi Civil Defense Corps. No term of service may be extended without the consent of the member of the Iraqi Civil Defense Corps except in the case of a national emergency proclaimed pursuant to law.

4) The Administrator of the CPA or a designee under the terms of Section 7 below shall have final authority over the selection and appointment of members of the Iraqi Civil Defense Corps and shall have the authority to dismiss such members on such grounds as he determines to be appropriate.

5) The terms and conditions of service and organization, including rank structure, of the Iraqi Civil Defense Corps may be further defined by Administrative Instructions, issued by the Administrator of the CPA or a designee, as may be considered necessary to give effect to the terms of this Order.

6) Members of the Iraqi Civil Defense Corps may not:

a) be members of a political party, organization or association;

b) participate in any activities of a political party, organization or association or recruit members for political parties or organizations;

c) publicly state any opinion of a political nature that constitutes an effort to indoctrinate members of the Iraqi Civil Defense Corps or any other person with a political ideology or otherwise convince any person to adhere to a particular political ideology;

d) advocate racial, gender or ethnic hatred or intolerance; advocate, create, or engage in illegal discrimination based on race, color, gender, religion, or regional origin; or use, or advocate the use of, force or violence or other unlawful means for political purposes, whether internal or international; or

e) participate in any manner in organizations or activities that involve, promote, or practice the conduct described in Section 2(6)(c) and (d).

[97] See *Doc 43*. There seems to be a typo in the date of the Order. The document symbol for Order No 22 on the signed version and the *Official Gazette* is 'CPA/ORD/7 August 2003/22' and 'CPA/ORD/8 Aug 2003/22', respectively. The Order was signed only on 18 August 2003.

[98] See *Doc 14*.

Nothing in this Section shall limit the right of a member of the Iraqi Civil Defense Corps to vote in elections for political office organized on a local, regional or national level. Violations may result in the removal of the member from employment in the Iraqi Civil Defense Corps.[99]

Section 3 Authority of the Iraqi Civil Defense Corps

1) Members of the Iraqi Civil Defense Corps may, while performing their official duties, apprehend persons who (i) they witness committing or attempting to commit a criminal offense, (ii) have escaped after being lawfully arrested, or (iii) otherwise interfere with their lawful activities. Persons apprehended by the Iraqi Civil Defense Corps must be turned over to the Iraqi police or Coalition Forces within twelve hours of apprehension or be released. Members of the Iraqi Civil Defense Corps may not interrogate, except under the direct supervision of Coalition Forces, or otherwise detain persons except as provided herein.

2) When acting under the supervision of Coalition Forces, the Iraqi Civil Defense Corps may limit access to certain areas as reasonably necessary to ensure the security of persons or property contained in or passing through such areas.

3) Members of the Iraqi Civil Defense Corps may, while performing their official duties, conduct reasonable searches for weapons or other dangerous or prohibited items (i) on persons or vehicles entering or in designated areas, (ii) on criminal suspects incident to apprehension, or (iii) when acting under the supervision of Coalition Forces, in areas or buildings where dangerous or prohibited items, including prohibited weapons, are reasonably believed to exist. Members of the Iraqi Civil Defense Corps may conduct reasonable searches at established checkpoints anywhere within Iraq and at other locations to prevent such items from being carried into, transported within, or out of designated areas.

4) Members of the Iraqi Civil Defense Corps may, while performing official duties, use force against persons or things as is reasonable and necessary under the circumstances. However, the use of force that may be likely to cause death or serious bodily injury is not permitted unless the member reasonably believes that using such force is necessary to: (i) protect himself or others from the imminent use of deadly force or force likely to cause serious bodily injury, (ii) prevent the escape of a person suspected of committing murder or assault resulting in serious bodily injury, or (iii) defend Coalition, ministry or governorate offices, government or state-owned infrastructure, and fixed sites under the direction and control of Coalition or governmental authorities, to prevent their destruction or incapacitation.[100]

Section 4 Functioning of the Iraqi Civil Defense Corps

1) The Iraqi Civil Defense Corps shall operate under the authority of the Administrator of the CPA and shall be subject to the supervision of Coalition Forces. The Administrator of the CPA may delegate to the senior military commander of Coalition Forces in Iraq responsibility and authority for the recruiting, training, organization, and control of the Iraqi Civil Defense Corps. This responsibility and authority may be redelegated pursuant to Section 7 below.

2) Operational or tactical command of units of the Iraqi Civil Defense Corps operating with Coalition Forces shall be vested in an officer of Coalition Forces designated by the senior military commander of Coalition Forces in Iraq pursuant to Section 7 below.

[99] Sec 2(4) and (6) were deleted in their entirety and sec 2(5) was re-designated as sec 2(4) by CPA Order No 73, sec 3(2) and (3) *[Doc 97]*.

[100] Sec 3 was amended by adding a new article 5 by CPA Order No 73, sec 3(4) *[Doc 97]*.

3) The Iraqi Civil Defense Corps will not be deployed outside the territory of Iraq, except for training or exchange programs.[101]

Section 5 Jurisdiction

1) Members of the Iraqi Civil Defense Corps will be subject to Iraqi law at all times and the civilian criminal courts of Iraq shall have jurisdiction over offenses alleged to have been committed by members of the Iraqi Civil Defense Corps. The Administrator of the CPA may determine that offenses alleged to have been committed by members of the Iraqi Civil Defense Corps while on duty may be submitted to the Central Criminal Court of Iraq in accordance with CPA Order Number 13 (Revised), The Central Criminal Court of Iraq (CPA/ORD/13 July 2003/13).[102]

2) Members of the Iraqi Civil Defense Corps shall enjoy immunity from civil liability for acts or omissions arising within the scope of their duties and in the conduct of authorized operations to the same degree as other governmental officials under the law of Iraq.[103]

Section 6 Weapons

The possession of weapons by members of the Iraqi Civil Defense Corps is regulated by CPA Order Number 3, Weapons Control Order (CPA/ORD/23 May 2003/03).[104]

Section 7 Delegation of Authority

The Administrator of the Coalition Provisional Authority may delegate responsibilities under this Order, as determined by the Administrator, to the senior military commander of Coalition Forces in Iraq. The senior military commander of Coalition Forces in Iraq may further delegate responsibilities under this Order to those under his command.

Section 8 Entry into Force

This Order shall enter into force on the date of signature [3 September 2003].

Document 50

Coalition Provisional Authority Order Number 29

CPA/ORD/7 September 2003/29

Amendment to Law of Estate Lease

Pursuant to my authority as Administrator of the Coalition Provisional Authority (CPA), under the laws and usages of war, and consistent with relevant U.N. Security Council resolutions, including Resolution 1483 (2003),

Noting that Law No. (56) of 2000 amended the Law of Estate Lease No. (87) of 1979 to give greater rights to residential landlords to terminate leases beginning in October of 2003,

[101] Sec 4 was amended by CPA Order No 73, sec 3(5)-(7) *[Doc 97]*.

[102] See *Doc 30*. There seems to be a typo in the date of the Revised Order No 13. The Order bears the symbol 'CPA/ORD/11 July 2003/13'.

[103] A new sec 5(3) was added by CPA Order No 73, sec 3(8) *[Doc 97]*.

[104] See *Doc 16*.

Understanding that the current economic conditions created by the former regime limit the ability of many Iraqi people to pay rent in a timely manner or incur significant increases in rental rates,

Concerned that widespread eviction of tenants will have a destabilizing effect on the security and well-being of Iraqi citizens,

Realizing that landlords can enforce rent collection through Iraqi courts,

Desiring to balance the rights and obligations between landlords and tenants in a fair manner,

I hereby promulgate the following:

Section 1 Extension of Current Leases

Article 15 of Law No. (56) of 2000, Amendment to the Law of Estate Lease No. (87) of 1979, is amended as follows:

a) Article 15, Paragraph 2 is amended to provide that the right specified in Article 4, Paragraph 5 of the Law of Estate Lease to request an assessment of the property for the purpose of adjusting the rental rate shall not be exercisable before 16 October 2004.

b) Article 15, Paragraph 3(A) (56) of 2000 is amended to provide that leases in existence for 12 or more years shall not be terminated, at the instance of the landlord, in the absence of other reasons authorized by law, before 16 October 2004.

Section 2 Limitation of Eviction Remedy

1) The remedy of eviction under Article 17, Paragraph 1 of the Law of Estate Lease, as amended by Article 10 of Law No. (56) of 2000, allowing landlords to evict tenants who fail to pay rent when due, is suspended for failures to pay the rent due for any period during the months of April to December 2003 inclusive.

2) Tenants remain obligated to pay rent as it becomes due. Tenants who fail to pay rent when due violate their contractual obligations. These obligations may be enforced by recourse to the courts for the collection of such debts.

Section 3 Entry into Force

This Order shall enter into force on the date of signature [7 September 2003].

Document 51

Coalition Provisional Authority Order Number 30

CPA/ORD/8 September 2003/30

Reform of Salaries and Employment Conditions of State Employees

Pursuant to my authority as Administrator of the Coalition Provisional Authority (CPA), under the laws and usages of war, and consistent with relevant U.N. Security Council resolutions, including Resolution 1483 (2003),

Understanding that the salaries of public workers under the former regime were paid through a complicated system largely composed of incentive pay that rewarded loyalty to the former regime over meritorious service,

Realizing that service in state agencies and state owned enterprises is important public service that requires appropriate compensation for efforts of workers to encourage the best qualified to choose public service,

Noting that salary and conditions of employment reform is essential to guarantee fairness within the public system to ensure that state employees receive appropriate compensation for their efforts, but also to provide incentives for meritorious service or sanctions for failure to perform appropriately,

Recognizing the need to establish a transparent system of compensation for those employed in public service,

I hereby promulgate the following:

Section 1 Definitions

1) 'Base Salary' means base compensation for public employment exclusive of any Special Pay.

2) 'Geographic Allowances' means any special payment made to a Public Service Employee as a result of the location the employee performs duties.

3) 'Grade' means the position level specified for any public service position set forth in the Salary Table attached as Annex A.

4) 'Public Service Employees' means all national government employees serving in any capacity in any national governmental agency or instrumentality including ministries, whether at the national, governorate or municipal level, and state-owned enterprises.

5) 'Public Service Employees' does not include municipal or local employees appointed by Coalition Forces.

6) 'Risk Allowances' means any special payment made to a Public Service Employee as result of the hazardous nature of their employment.

7) 'Special Pay' means any special payment or incentive payment including family allowances, staff bonuses, university service allowance, scientific status allowances, qualification allowances, position allowances, vocational allowances, transportation allowances, geographic allowances, risk allowances, or any other legal compensation other than Base salary paid in connection with public service.

8) 'Salary Table' means the table of payments of monthly salaries paid to Public Service Employees set forth in Annex A to this Order which shall be effective from 1 October 2003 until 30 September 2004.

Section 2 Purpose and Objectives

1) Salary reform for Public Service Employees is necessary to encourage the best qualified to choose careers in public service. A system of pay based upon complicated incentives lacks transparency and unfairly results in widely disparate levels of pay for the same work. The public sector salary system is reformed to foster transparency in payments and to regularize payments to ensure that individuals are compensated at comparable levels for comparable work across all areas of public service.

2) Reform of conditions of employment reform [sic] for Public Service Employees is also necessary to encourage the best qualified to choose careers in public service. The conditions of public service employment are reformed to enable the best qualified employees to rapidly advance to positions of greater responsibility, but also to allow for the removal of Public Service Employees who regularly fail to achieve the minimum standards expected of their Grade and position.

Section 3 Salary Reform

1) Effective 1 October 2003, all existing laws, regulations, orders, or other enactments establishing salaries, Special Pay, or other monetary incentives for Public Service Employees are hereby suspended. The CPA Director of Management and Budget, in coordination with the interim Minister of Finance, may grant limited exceptions to this suspension until 31 December 2003 for public agencies unable to implement this Order by the prescribed dates.

2) Effective 1 October 2003, all Public Service Employees shall be paid in accordance with the Salary Table except in cases where the CPA Director of Management and Budget has granted an exception to the implementation of this Order in accordance with Section 3(1) above or where the CPA Director of Management and Budget has authorized the public agency to implement the Salary Table prior to 1 October 2003.

3) As set forth in the Salary Table, the salary paid to an employee will be based upon the Grade of the employee as determined by the classification of the employee's position and the employee's employment Step as determined in part by the employee's length of service and in part by performance.

4) The CPA Director of Management and Budget may authorize the payment of Risk Allowances for particularly hazardous duties or Geographic Allowances. The only basis for approval of Geographic Allowances is a demonstrated history of an inability to fill the position at the authorized salary. Following the implementation of the salary reform provisions contained herein, all such Risk Allowances and Geographic Allowances must be approved by the CPA Director of Management and Budget.[105]

5) No Base Salary of Public Service Employees for the same position will be reduced by the implementation of the salary provision of this Order. In the event a Public Service Employee's prior Base Salary for the same position is more than the amount specified in the Salary Table, the pre-existing salary of the Public Service Employee will continue to be paid. The Base Salary of such employees will not be increased until the Public Service Employee is entitled to increased compensation as defined by the Salary Table. This provision does not affect the removal of Special Pay or other incentives as detailed elsewhere in this Order.

Section 4 Implementation of Salary Reform

1) All Ministers, state owned enterprise Directors, or other heads of public agencies shall establish salary Grade classifications for existing positions within their agency in accordance with the guidelines issued by the Ministry of Finance.

2) All such salary Grade classifications will be submitted to the Ministry of Finance for review and approval prior to implementation. The Ministry of Finance may reject or revise the salary Grade classifications presented by other agencies. The salary Grade classifications of the Ministry of Finance shall be consistent with the guidelines issued by the Ministry of Finance.

3) Based on the budget of the agency and the agreed upon salary Grade classifications, total annual salary budgets will be developed by each ministry, state owned enterprise, or other agency for approval by the Ministry of Finance. The Ministry of Finance may reject or revise the total annual salary budget presented by other agencies. The total annual salary budget of the Ministry of Finance shall be consistent with the guidelines issued by

[105] Sec 3(4) was amended by CPA Order No 100, sec 3(12)(a) *[Doc 124]*.

the Ministry of Finance. All ministries, state owned enterprises, or other agencies shall deliver the total annual salary budget to the Ministry of Finance no later than September 15 of each year.

Section 5 Impact of De-Ba'athification Removals
Public Service Employees who lost their civil service positions as a result of the implementation of CPA Order 1, De-Ba'athification of Iraqi Society,[106] are not entitled to retirement benefits.

Section 6 Reform of Conditions of Public Employment
HIRING AND PROMOTION PRACTICES

1) No ministry, governorate or municipal administration, state owned enterprise, or any other governmental agency is required to employ any person solely as a result of the person's training or qualifications. All employment decisions will be based upon the needs of the agency.

2) Persons formerly employed by a state agency have no special entitlement to resume their employment. All employment decisions will be based on the needs of the agency. Prior employment with the agency may be a factor in deciding to rehire a former employee to fill a vacancy.

3) Persons from outside the agency may be hired to fill vacancies. Hiring decisions will be based on an individual's qualifications without regard to race, religion, tribal membership, gender, or regional origin. The best-qualified person will be hired for the position.

4) Duty assignments within an agency are at the discretion of agency heads; provided, however, except as required by exigencies of the work requirements, the majority of the duties of Public Service Employees will be tasks appropriate for their employment Grade.

5) Promotions of Public Service Employees will be based upon the employee's potential for service, ability to assume more complex duties or responsibilities, and ability to perform at the higher Grade. Longevity of service, without the consideration of other qualifications, shall be an inappropriate basis for promotion.

6) Public Service Employees may only be promoted in the event there is a vacancy in the next higher Grade. Promotions in Grade prior to the occurrence of a vacancy in that Grade are not authorized.

EMPLOYMENT CONDITIONS

7) All Public Service Employees are expected to report to work in accordance with the reasonable instructions of their agency. Public Service Employees who fail to report to work without the authorization of their senior supervisor within the agency have no entitlement to be paid for days they do not work. The managers of Public Service Employees may withhold one day's pay for each day in which the employee failed to report to work for a substantial portion of the work day. One day's pay shall be calculated by dividing the total monthly pay specified in Salary Table for the employee by the number of scheduled work days in the month.

8) Public Service Employees who fail to report to work for five consecutive days or ten days in a month, except as authorized by their senior supervisor or as a result of verifiable medical incapacitation, may be dismissed from their employment. No public notice shall be required. Supervisors shall make reasonable attempts to notify employees in person. If the

[106] See *Doc 14.*

Supervisor cannot, through reasonable attempts, locate the employee after ten days, notice can be delivered to the employee's last known address and shall be sufficient to terminate the employment. No proof of actual notice shall be required. Public Service Employees may appeal such a dismissal in accordance with the procedures specified in Section 7.

9) Senior agency officials may withhold Step increases in salary in the event the performance of the employee does not meet reasonable expectations of performance for the position held. Public Service Employees whose Step increases are withheld under this provision may appeal this determination to the Ministry of Finance or in accordance with the procedures specified in Section 7.

10) Managers and agency heads will exercise oversight and control over the implementation of this Order to ensure fairness within the system. Employees who fail to adhere to the rules set forth herein may fail to meet the reasonable expectations of performance described above and may be subject to disciplinary measures.

Section 7 Procedure to Address Complaints

Public Service Employees may seek redress for adverse managerial actions inconsistent with this Order under the procedures described in Civil Service Law (13) of 1991.

Section 8 Administrative Instructions

The CPA Director of Management and Budget or interim Minster of the Finance, with the concurrence of the CPA Director of Management and Budget, may issue such Administrative Instructions[107] as are necessary to carry out the purposes of this Order.[108]

[107] Salary Implementation Instructions: 'The Iraqi Governing Council and the CPA Administrator have approved new salary scales to Iraqi civil servants and other Iraqi government employees. These instructions will explain the new structure and provide implementing instructions for the transition from the current four grade structure.

The new salary scale is the result of extensive study and interaction of a Salary Task Force composed of representatives of the Iraqi Ministries and government and out side pay experts brought in for the project. The Iraqi working group studied the issue for over a month and made valuable recommendations that form the basis for the plan.

The plan takes into consideration all those who are currently receiving salary payments under the four grade program. Their salaries will remain at their current levels unless their experience, productivity and performance will cause them to be slotted at a higher grade. Those grand-fathered under this save pay formula will remain at their pay level until promotions and longevity increases catch up to them. Thus all current Iraqi government employees will receive the same or greater pay under this system compared to the current system.

The new system is based on pay for work. No one will receive special bonuses or stipends. The workers pay will be based entirely on the base salary in the scale and not/not on other supplementary pays. The workers will be expected to work a normal Iraqi work week of at least 35 hours in order to be paid. Shift workers, those working overtime, and other similar issues will be compensated within salary scale limits by management decisions.

Transition to the new pay scale will take place over the next few months starting in most cases on 1 October 2003. The Iraqi task force is working on bench-mark job positions to aid managers in their decision about where an individual is placed on the scale. As Ministries and commissions and State owned industries complete their slate of employee assignments, the Ministry of Finance and Ministry of Planning will work together to ensure worker distribution conforms to the affordability percentage per grade. If they do not, then the situation will be considered by the Iraqi Salary Working group to resolve the distribution either by reclassification of some workers or a nation-wide cross-leveling. Once these classifications are finalized then the new salary scale will enter into effect the next month for that particular organization. No one can be paid under the new scale and job classification until the end of October pay dates, as the salaries will be paid in the new Iraqi dinar. All wages will be paid in Iraqi Dinars. Those payments taking place after October 15 will be paid with the new Iraqi dinar on a one-for-one basis.

Workers receiving their first month's pay under the new salary system will be required to provide recognizable photo identification. In subsequent payments, a bank account number where workers would like future wages to be deposited will be required.

Section 9 Inconsistent Legislation

Any portion of legislation inconsistent with any provisions of this Order is hereby suspended to the extent necessary to implement the provisions of this Order.

Section 10 Entry into Force

This Order shall enter into force on the date of signature [8 September 2003].[109]

Ministries will provide workers' names, identification numbers to both the Ministry of Planning and the Ministry of Finance, and a new grade/step classification for each employee. Once it is ascertained that the Ministry or Agency's list and grade structure is completed and approved by the Ministry of Finance, the salary funds will be included in the Ministry or Agency's operating budget for each remaining month in 2003 and will be the basis for a salary budget line in the 2004 budget.

TIMELINES

A. Wednesday 3 September. The Iraqi Salaries working group finalizes benchmark jobs.

B. Thursday 4 September. A CPA Administrator order will be issued making the salary scale official. These instructions, the Administrator's order, and the salary scale will be released to CPA Senior Advisors at the weekly CPA economic meeting.

C. Sunday 7 September. A press conference will take place at 1000 announcing the order and providing details on the new system. It will launch a broader strategic information plan that will disperse more information in coming weeks.

D. Saturday 6 September – 1 October. Ministries, Agencies, and commissions should be instructed to start the classification of employees into the new scale. Upon completion, they will provide copies to the Ministry of Planning and the Iraqi Salary working group for examination. This will ensure proper adherence to national-wide grade dispersion and affordability. Once approved, a copy will be provided to the Ministry of Finance for a final financial review.

E. 1 October – 1 January. Upon approval of the above ministries and working group, the employees may be informed of their new salary. Employees can appeal their salary assignment in writing through their management as outlined in the Administrator's order, but they will continue to be paid at their initial classification until their appeal is adjudicated. Those employees who do not continue/come to work at the new scale will be free to leave the civil service. Military, Police, firefighters, security guards and essential medical personnel will only be allowed to leave their duties with permission of their respective ministers. Employees of the CTF-7, such as security guards and municipal workers will be integrated into the new scale starting 1 October. Short term contract workers will continue to be paid according to their contracts by the contractor.

F. 1 October – 1 January. Salaries for approved Ministry/Commission salary classification plans will be implemented no later than the first day of the month following approval. Employees will be paid their new salary on the last work day of the month. Employees paid under the four grade pay system will be paid at that rate or the new scale whichever is higher. Employees who are paid under the four grade scale will remain at that rate until promotion or longevity/productivity allow for movement to a higher step or grade.

G. 30 October – 30 January. The first few payments will be in cash. Subsequent payments will be by direct deposit to an Iraqi bank account of the employees choosing. A full month's pay will be issued for a full month's work. Overtime may be paid by individual ministries or handled through compensatory time off. Their anticipated additional costs should be reflected in their 2004 budget proposals as a separate line under salaries and compensation.

G. [sic] 1 October – indefinite. New hires after the date of the CPA implementing order will be paid at the new salary rate as of 1 October. USAID (and their contractors) and CTF-7 will use the new scales for new hiring after 1 October. NGOs, independent contractors and international organizations will be encouraged to use the rates. Accordingly, some jobs will start at a lower rate than under the current four grade scale.'

[108] Sec 8 was amended by CPA Order No 100, sec 3(12)(a) *[Doc 124]*.

[109] A new sec 10 was included and the present sec 10 became sec 11 by CPA Order No 100, sec 3(12)(b) and (c) *[Doc 124]*.

ANNEX A

Salary Table
Monthly Salary Amounts in Thousands of Iraqi Dinars (000)

Grade	Step 1	Step 2	Step 3	Step 4	Step 5	Step 6	Step 7	Step 8	Step 9	Step 10
Super A	2250	2233	2316	2400	2483	2566	2650	2733	2817	3000
Super B	1500	1583	1666	1750	1833	1916	1999	2083	2166	2249
1	740	760	780	800	820	840	860	880	900	920
2	574	589	605	620	636	651	667	682	698	713
3	444	456	468	480	492	504	516	528	540	552
4	342	352	361	370	379	389	398	407	416	426
5	264	271	278	285	292	299	306	314	321	328
6	204	209	215	220	226	231	237	242	248	253
7	157	162	166	170	174	179	183	187	191	196
8	125	128	132	135	138	142	145	149	152	155
9	102	105	107	110	113	116	118	121	124	127
10	83	86	88	90	92	95	97	99	101	104
11	69	71	73	75	77	79	81	83	84	86

Document 52
Coalition Provisional Authority Order Number 31
CPA/ORD/10 September 2003/31

Modifications of Penal Code and Criminal Proceedings Law

Pursuant to my authority as Administrator of the Coalition Provisional Authority (CPA), under the laws and usages of war, and consistent with relevant U.N. Security Council resolutions, including Resolution 1483 (2003),

Recognizing that instances of kidnapping, rape, and forcible vehicle larceny represent a serious threat to the security and stability of the Iraqi population,

Understanding that attacks of looting or sabotage against critical electrical power and oil infrastructure facilities undermine efforts to improve the condition of the Iraqi people,

Noting that the denial of pretrial bail in certain cases and lengthy jail sentences represent deterrents to such conduct,

I hereby promulgate the following modifications of the Penal Code and Criminal Proceedings Law:

Section 1 Definitions

1) 'Means of Transportation' are motorized vehicles used for the movement of persons or goods including, automobiles, trucks, motorcycles, tractors, aircraft, ships, boats, or barges,

2) 'Penal Code' means the Penal Code Law No. (111) of 1969 as amended including Law (1) 2002 and CPA Order Number 7, Penal Code, CPA/ORD/9 June 2003/07,[110]

3) 'Criminal Proceedings Law' means Criminal Proceedings Law No. 23 of 1971 as amended including amendments contained in CPA Memorandum Number 3, Criminal Procedures, CPA/MEM/18 June 2003/03.[111]

Section 2 Modifications of Sentences for Kidnapping

1) The penalties for kidnapping offenses set forth in the Penal Code Paragraphs 421, 422, and 423 are hereby modified to provide a maximum punishment of life imprisonment for each offense. Sentences for the commission of kidnapping offenses may not be reduced as a result of mitigating circumstances pursuant to Paragraph 130 of the Penal Code. The maximum sentence limitation of Paragraph 87 of the Penal Code shall not apply to the specified kidnapping offenses. For the purposes of this modification, sentences of life imprisonment shall mean the remaining natural life of the person.

2) Penal Code Paragraphs 426 (1) and 426 (2) providing for the further mitigation of the sentence for kidnapping offenses is hereby suspended. Cooperation following the offense shall serve as a mitigating factor to be considered by the trial judge in determining the sentence.

3) Penal Code Paragraph 427 providing for the cessation of actions in the event the offender marries the victim is hereby suspended.

Section 3 Modifications of Sentences for Rape and Indecent Assault

1) The penalties for the offenses of rape and sexual assault set forth in Penal Code Paragraph 393 are hereby modified to provide a maximum punishment of life imprisonment. The maximum sentence limitation of Paragraph 87 of the Penal Code shall not apply to the offenses specified in Paragraph 393. For the purposes of this modification, sentences of life imprisonment shall mean the remaining natural life of the person.

2) The penalties for the offense of indecent assault set forth in Penal Code Paragraph 396 are hereby modified to provide a maximum punishment of fifteen years imprisonment.

Section 4 Modifications of Sentences for Offenses Involving Damage to Public Utilities or Oil Infrastructure

1) The penalties for wrecking, destroying or otherwise damaging water, electricity, or oil installations or other public utilities set forth in Penal Code Paragraph 353 (1), whether or not such damage could or does lead to the closure of an installation, are hereby modified to provide a maximum punishment of life imprisonment.

2) The maximum sentence limitation of Paragraph 87 of the Penal Code shall not apply to the offenses specified in Paragraph 353. For the purposes of this modification, life imprisonment shall mean the remaining natural life of the person. Persons convicted of committing these offenses shall not be eligible for Conditional Discharge as set forth in Paragraph 331 of the Criminal Proceedings Law.

Section 5 Modifications of Sentences for Theft Offenses Involving Means of Transportation

1) The penalties for theft under the aggravating factors specified in Paragraphs 440 through 443 of the Penal Code are hereby modified to provide a maximum punishment of

[110] See *Doc 21.*
[111] See *Doc 127.*

life imprisonment if the offense involves the use of force to commit the theft of a Means of Transportation.

2) The maximum sentence limitation of Paragraph 87 of the Penal Code shall not apply to offenses involving the use of force to commit the theft of a Means of Transportation. For the purposes of this modification, sentences of life imprisonment shall mean the remaining natural life of the person.

Section 6 Modifications to Bail Arrangements
Notwithstanding the bail provisions contained in Paragraph 109 of the Criminal Proceedings Law No. 23 of 1971 the reviewing judge may order a person suspected of committing an offense punishable by life imprisonment to be held without bail until trial.

Section 7 Entry into Force
This Order shall enter into force on the date of signature [10 September 2003].

Document 53
Coalition Provisional Authority Order Number 32
CPA/ORD/4 September 2003/32

Legal Department of the Ministry of Justice

Pursuant to my authority as Administrator of the Coalition Provisional Authority (CPA), and the laws and usages of war, and consistent with relevant U.N. Security Council resolutions, including Resolution 1483 (2003),

Recognizing that international litigation, claims and arbitrations involving the Government of Iraq and its agencies, instrumentalities and companies continue,

Noting that these cases; may result in significant adverse judgments, decisions or awards draining the resources of the people of Iraq, or in judgments or awards vindicating their claims or defenses,

Recalling that the Legal Department of the Office of the Council of Ministers managed these cases in the former regime,

Acknowledging that the Legal Department of the Office of the Council of Ministers can continue this task with the appropriate support from the Ministry of Justice,

I hereby promulgate the following:

Section 1 Purpose
This Order transfers the entity responsible for management of international litigation, claims and arbitrations involving the Government of Iraq and its governmental agencies, instrumentalities and companies from the previous regime's Office of the Council of Ministers to the Ministry of Justice. This action is necessary to, among other things, preserve rights and respond to judicial actions in foreign courts, international arbitrations, claims and other proceedings.

Section 2 Transfer of Responsibility

1) The Legal Department of the Office of the Council of Ministers, its personnel and all of its authorities and responsibilities shall be transferred to the Ministry of Justice. It shall be renamed the Legal Department of the Ministry of Justice and shall be headed by a Director General. Upon completion of the transfer, the Legal Department will begin the task of resuming the management of the international litigation, claims and arbitrations described in this Order.

2) The Ministry of Justice shall accept the Legal Department's current personnel and provide them with salaries and benefits commensurate with their positions and experience at the Office of the Council of Ministers, including any such salaries and benefits due since June 30, 2003.

3) The Legal Department, acting in coordination with the CPA, shall be responsible for managing international litigation, claims, and arbitrations, involving the Government of Iraq and its governmental agencies, instrumentalities and companies. The Minister of Justice may assign additional responsibilities to the Legal Department, provided that such responsibilities do not disrupt its principal task set forth herein.

Section 3 Entry into Force

This Order shall enter into force on the date of signature [4 September 2003].

Document 54

Coalition Provisional Authority Order Number 33

CPA/ORD/8 September 2003/33

Ministry of Municipalities and Public Works

Pursuant to my authority as Administrator of the Coalition Provisional Authority (CPA), and under the laws and usages of war, and consistent with relevant U.N. Security Council resolutions, including Resolution 1483 (2003),

Recognizing that in order to further the rehabilitation of Iraq, a ministerial-level organization is needed to coordinate activities surrounding the revitalization of the municipalities and the public works infrastructure of Iraq,

Understanding that to accurately reflect the importance of projects involving municipalities of Iraq, the present Ministry of Public Works should be renamed to accurately reflect its mission of coordinating programs involving municipalities in addition to general public works projects within Iraq,

I hereby promulgate the following:

Section 1 Renaming of the Ministry of Public Works

The Ministry of Public Works is hereby renamed the Ministry of Municipalities and Public Works.

Section 2 References in Previous Orders, Regulations and Memoranda

All references in previous orders, regulations, and memoranda to the Ministry of Public Works shall be deemed to refer to the Ministry of Municipalities and Public Works.

Section 3 Entry into Force

This Order shall enter into force on the date of signature [8 September 2003].

Document 55
Coalition Provisional Authority Order Number 34
CPA/ORD/13 September 2003/34

Amendment to Coalition Provisional Authority Order Number 2 (CPA/ORD/23 May 2003/02)

Pursuant to my authority as Administrator of the Coalition Provisional Authority (CPA), and under the law and usages of war, and consistent with relevant U.N. Security Council resolutions, including Resolution 1483 (2003),

Recognizing the previous functions of the Board of Supreme Audit, pursuant to the Board of Supreme Audit Law (Law No. 6 (1990)) in providing auditing services needed to monitor governmental financial transactions, and

Noting that internal audits are a critical component of a transparent financial management program,

I hereby promulgate the following:

Section 1 Continuance of Board of Supreme Audit
Notwithstanding any provision of CPA Order Number 2, Dissolution of Entities (CPA/ORD/23 May 2003/02)[112] to the contrary, the Board of Supreme Audit shall not be considered a 'Dissolved Entity', as defined in CPA Order Number 2, and shall continue to exist and perform the functions that it performed as of April 16, 2003.

Section 2 Entry into Force
This Order shall enter into force on the date of signature [13 September 2003].

Document 56
Coalition Provisional Authority Order Number 35
CPA/ORD/13 September 2003/35

Re-establishment of the Council of Judges

Pursuant to my authority as Administrator of the Coalition Provisional Authority (CPA), and consistent with relevant U.N. Security Council resolutions, including Resolution 1483 (2003), and the laws and usages of war,

Noting that, prior to the changes made by the former regime, Iraq had a functioning Council of Judges that administered the judicial and prosecutorial systems to insure that judges and public prosecutors were appointed from among persons enjoying the highest reputation for fairness and integrity and of recognized competence of law, and that the judicial system exercised its authority in accordance with the rule of law, and

Recognizing that a key to the establishment of the rule of law is a judicial system staffed by capable persons and free and independent from outside influences,

[112] See *Doc 15*.

I hereby promulgate the following:

Section 1 Purpose
This Order re-establishes the Council of Judges ('the Council'), which is charged with the supervision of the judicial and prosecutorial systems of Iraq. The Council shall perform its functions independently of the Ministry of Justice.[113]

Section 2 Membership

1) The following officials shall serve as members of the Council:
Chief Justice of the Supreme Court (President of the Council)
The Deputy Chief Justices of the Supreme Court
Director-General of the State Council Assembly
Director-General, Office of Public Prosecution
Director-General, Legal Supervision Office
Director-General, Administration, if such person is a Judge or Prosecutor
Presidents of the Appellate Courts

2) The Council shall also have a Secretary-General, who shall be selected by the President of the Council. The Secretary-General shall perform administrative functions for the Council, together with such additional employees as the Council and the Ministry of Finance may deem appropriate.

3) The President of the Council shall be the Chief Justice of the Supreme Court. The Vice President of the Council shall be selected by the Council from the Deputy Chief Justices of the Supreme Court.

Section 3 Duties

1) The Council shall have the following specific duties:
   a) To provide administrative oversight of all the judges and all public prosecutors, excluding, however, the members of the Supreme Court.
   b) To investigate allegations of professional misconduct and incompetence involving members of the judiciary or public prosecutors, and, when appropriate, to take appropriate disciplinary or administrative measures against members of the judiciary or public prosecutors, including but not limited to, removing a judge or prosecutor from office, including the members of the Supreme Court.
   c) To nominate capable persons as required to fill judicial vacancies or public prosecutor vacancies, and to recommend their appointment.
   d) To promote, advance, upgrade, and transfer judges and prosecutors.
   e) To assign or reassign judges and prosecutors to hold specific judicial and prosecutorial posts as provided for in the Law of Judicial Organization (Law No. 160 (1979)) and the Law of Public Prosecution (Law No. 159 (1979)).

2) The Council shall have such other duties as may be determined from time to time by law.

Section 4 Meetings

1) The Council shall conduct regular meetings at least monthly. The President of the Council may call special sessions of the Council when needed to conduct necessary business.

[113] The Council of Judges was replaced as of 30 June 2004 by the Higher Juridical Council; see CPA Order No 100, sec 3(13) *[Doc 124]*.

2) A quorum shall require at least three-fourths of the membership of the Council and the presence of either the President or the Vice-President of the Council. Decisions of the Council will be by majority vote of those members present.

Section 5 Disciplinary and Professional Standards Committee

1) The Council shall appoint a Disciplinary and Professional Standards Committee ('the Committee') of at least three (3) members from its own membership. The Committee shall investigate allegations of misconduct and incompetence by members of the judiciary and public prosecutors, and shall make appropriate decisions concerning disposition of those allegations, including but not limited to, the removal of that judge or prosecutor from office if the allegations are substantiated.

2) Any judge or prosecutor adversely affected by a decision of the Committee may appeal the decision to the Council within thirty (30) days from the date of the decision of the Committee. The decision of the Council on the appeal shall be final and conclusive, and no further appeal is authorized.

3) The Director General of Public Prosecutions shall also have the right to appeal any decision made by the Committee to the Council, within thirty (30) days from the date of the decision of the Committee.

Section 6 Independence of the Council

1) The Council shall perform its duties and responsibilities independently of any control, oversight, or supervision by the Ministry of Justice. To the extent that provisions of Iraqi law, specifically the Law of Judicial Organization (Law No. 160 (1979) and the Law of Public Prosecution (Law No. 159) (1979)) conflict with the provisions of this Order, those provisions of Iraqi law are suspended.

2) The Council of Judges shall take the place of the Council of Justice that was previously established by the Judicial Organization Law (Law No. 160) (1979) in so far as the Council of Justice exercised any authority over any judge or prosecutor. All administrative oversight of the judges and prosecutors shall now rest only with the Council of Judges. The Council of Justice shall continue in existence, but shall have no jurisdiction over any prosecutor or judge.

Section 7 Entry into Force

This Order shall enter into force on the date of signature [18 September 2003].

Document 57

Coalition Provisional Authority Order Number 36

CPA/ORD/3 October 2003/36

Regulation of Oil Distribution

Pursuant to my authority as Administrator of the Coalition Provisional Authority (CPA), under the laws and usages of war, and consistent with relevant U.N. Security Council resolutions, including Resolution 1483 (2003),

Recognizing that the theft and smuggling of the natural resources of Iraq are crimes that affect the wellbeing and future of all Iraqis,

Noting the complexity of the past regime's laws, regulatory provisions and instructions in the field of oil distribution, and the inconsistency and irregularity of their enforcement,

Determined to act decisively to tackle the theft and smuggling of natural resources pending the outcome of a full review of current Iraqi laws, provisions and instructions,

Resolved to provide the Coalition Forces with an easily accessible and ascertainable regulatory code with which to support the Iraqi authorities in the lawful distribution of oil into, out of and throughout Iraq,

I hereby promulgate the following:

Section 1 Definitions

1) *Authorization* means any written approval, authority, certificate, license, contract or other order issued by the Ministry of Oil, the Oil Products Distribution Company, the State Oil Marketing Organization, and the recognized representative regional organizations or companies of those bodies, the Coalition Provisional Authority, the Commander Coalition Forces, and in relation to fishing vessels the Iraqi Port Authority. Authorize and authority and all cognate and derivative words shall be construed accordingly.[114]

2) *Benzene* is also known as petrol and gasoline.

3) *Cargo Fuel* means fuel transported by any vehicle or vessel which is not being used or is not intended for use as fuel by that vehicle or vessel.

4) *Confiscation Order* means CPA Order Number 25, Confiscation of Property Used in or Resulting from Certain Crimes.[115]

5) *Criminal Proceedings Law* means Law of Criminal Proceedings Number 23 of 1971, as modified by CPA Orders and Memoranda.

6) *Customs Law* means Customs Law Number 23 of 1984, as amended.

7) *Diesel* see gasoil.

8) *Fuel* means crude oil, residue crude, oil products including for example diesel, kerosene, liquid petroleum gas, benzene.

9) *Gasoil* is also known as diesel.

10) *Gasoline* see benzene.

11) *Interdiction* means the stopping, search, arrest and the initial questioning of a suspect.

12) *Penal Code* means the Iraqi Penal Code Law Number 1 of 1969, as amended by CPA Orders and Memoranda.

13) *Petrol* see benzene.

14) *Port of Entry* means a designated land, sea or air point of entry or exit manned by Border Enforcement staff.

15) *Regulatory Offense* means a contravention of a Regulation under this Order.

16) *Territorial Jurisdiction* includes the territorial sea and all internal waters.

Section 2 Regulatory Code

1) There is hereby created the Regulatory Code for Oil Distribution. The Code is set out at the Annex.

2) The Regulatory Code may be amended from time to time by the Administrator of the Coalition Provisional Authority or his delegate.

3) It shall be a punishable offense to contravene a regulation in the Regulatory Code created under this Order.

[114] Sec 1(1) was amended by CPA Order No 100, sec 3(14)(a) *[Doc 124]*.
[115] See *Doc 46*.

4) The Regulatory Code is applicable to all vessels, vehicles and persons within the territorial jurisdiction of Iraq.

Section 3 Interdiction and Investigation

1) Interdiction of suspects may be carried out by Iraqi Police, Border Police, Customs Police, Customs officials, New Iraqi Army elements when duly authorized, Iraqi Civil Defense Corps and Coalition Forces.

2) The Iraqi Police, Border Police, Customs Police and Coalition Forces are competent authorities to investigate regulatory offenses and to refer cases to the customs courts or criminal courts for prosecution. Customs officials shall pass suspects to Police authorities for investigation.

Section 4 Jurisdiction

1) For a contravention of a regulation the offender may be tried either in the customs courts or in the criminal courts.

2) Where practicable an offender, in the first instance, should be brought before an Investigative Judge in the customs court.

3) Notwithstanding the primacy of jurisdiction accorded to customs courts at paragraph 2 above, an Investigative Judge in the criminal court may investigate a regulatory offense.

4) Where the description of the offense could lead to a charge either as:

a) A regulatory offense under this Order, triable in a criminal or customs court; or
b) A criminal offense under the Iraqi Penal Code, triable in a criminal court; or
c) A customs offense under the Customs Law, triable in a customs court, then it shall be open to an Investigative Judge to formulate the charge under the most appropriate Code or Law and to transfer the case to the appropriate court.

Section 5 Penalties

A person convicted of an offence under this Order is punishable with a term of detention not exceeding six months or a fine. The level of the fine shall not exceed five times the value of the cargo fuel. The penalties may be doubled for a second or subsequent offense. Following a conviction the court shall order the confiscation of any property used in the commission of the offense or obtained as a result of the offense, unless the rights of others who have acted in good faith, including a purchaser for value, would thereby be prejudiced. Confiscated property shall be dealt with in accordance with CPA Order Number 25. Fines shall be remitted to the Ministry of Finance.

Section 6 Application of Existing Law

1) The Regulatory Code introduced under this Order supplements the Penal Code and the Customs Law.

2) No description of, or penalty for, a regulatory offense described in this Order shall alter the offenses described in the Penal Code or Customs Law, or vary the sentencing guidelines in those laws for the offenses described therein.

3) This Order operates in conjunction with and does not supersede CPA Order Number 25. A confiscation hearing shall be convened in relation to property used or intended for use in the contravention of any regulation under this Order, and to property acquired through or as a result of the contravention of any regulation under this Order. For the purposes of applying the Confiscation Order to regulatory offenses, the words 'criminal offense' in that Order shall be deemed to include a regulatory offense in this Order.

4) For any proceedings in relation to a regulatory offense, the customs and criminal courts shall use the rules of evidence and procedure set out in the Criminal Proceedings Law and the criminal provisions set out in the Iraqi Penal Code as they would for any proceedings before them.

5) This Order operates in conjunction with and does not supersede CPA Order No. 17.[116]

Section 7 Expiration of Order

This Order will cease operation nine months from the date of entry into force unless otherwise extended by the Administrator.[117]

Section 8 Entry into Force

This Order shall enter into force on the date of signature [3 October 2003].

Annex A – Regulatory Code for Oil Distribution

Regulations for Road Tankers

1. It shall be prohibited for a road tanker driver to transport cargo fuel without a valid voucher or export/import manifest issued by a proper authority or the lawful owner of the cargo fuel.
2. It shall be prohibited for the road tanker to be loaded with cargo fuel at any place other than that listed in the valid voucher or manifest.
3. It shall be prohibited for the road tanker to be unloaded of its cargo fuel at any place other than an authorized delivery point. An authorized delivery point is the destination listed in the valid voucher or manifest, or an authorized depot or delivery point to which a road tanker may be diverted by the proper authorities.
4. It shall be prohibited for a person to distribute or download cargo fuel from a road tanker other than to the owner, operator or agent of the facility listed on the valid voucher or manifest.
5. It shall be the duty of the driver of a road tanker importing cargo fuel into Iraq to enter the country only at a designated Class A Port of Entry.
6. It shall be the duty of the driver of a road tanker exporting cargo fuel from Iraq to leave the country only at a designated Class A Port of Entry.
7. It shall be prohibited for a road tanker driver, without reasonable excuse, to deliver cargo fuel outside the following time limits:
   a) The same day if loading and delivery points are within the same governorate;
   b) 24 hours if the loading and delivery points are in adjacent governorates;
   c) 48 hours for all other deliveries within Iraq.

Regulations for All Vehicle Drivers

8. It shall be prohibited for the driver of any vehicle to cross the border from Iraq to a neighboring country with fuel for that vehicle's own consumption in excess of quantities prescribed by the Oil Products Distribution Company from time to time and published in local branches.

Regulations for Fishing Vessels

9. It shall be prohibited for a fishing vessel to receive fuel except for consumption by that vessel.

[116] See *Doc 37*.
[117] Sec 7 was rescinded by CPA Order No 100, sec 3(14)(b) *[Doc 124]*.

10. It shall be prohibited for a fishing vessel to receive fuel without authorization.

11. It shall be prohibited for a fishing vessel to receive fuel in excess of its authorized periodic allocation.

12. It shall be prohibited for a fishing vessel to sell, trade or in any way distribute or offload fuel from that vessel other than for reasons of safety or force majeure. Regulations for Vessels.

13. It shall be prohibited for the master or owner of any vessel, or any other person on board the vessel, to load or unload fuel other than at jetties or fuelling points designated by the proper authorities.

14. It shall be prohibited for the master or owner of any vessel, or the person having conduct of the vessel's navigation, to transport cargo fuel without authorization. Regulations for Service Station Owners and Managers.

15. It shall be the duty of a service station owner or manager to transfer the cargo fuel specified in the valid voucher or manifest from a road tanker into that service station's fuel storage tanks.

16. It shall be the duty of a service station owner or manager to keep an up-to-date, true and accurate record of each cargo fuel delivery, to sign for the delivery on the voucher or manifest, and to make periodic reports prescribed by the Oil Products Distribution Company.

17. It shall be prohibited for a service station owner or manager without specific authorization to transfer or cause to be transferred, under a sale transaction or otherwise, benzene or gas oil into any jerry can, container, canister, drum, barrel, bowser or any other receptacle.

Fuel Sales

18. It shall be prohibited for any person to sell any fuel within the territorial jurisdiction of Iraq without authorization.

Fuel Limits for Private Consumption

19. It shall be prohibited for a member of the public without reasonable excuse or authorization to transport, carry, hold, possess or control fuel for private consumption in excess of the following quantities:

- benzene 150 liters
- kerosene 1000 liters
- gasoil 1000 liters

Document 58

Coalition Provisional Authority Order Number 37

CPA/ORD/19 September 2003/37

Tax Strategy for 2003

Pursuant to my authority as Administrator of the Coalition Provisional Authority (CPA), and under the laws and usages of war, and consistent with relevant U.N. Security Council resolutions, including Resolution 1483 (2003),

Determined to create conditions suited to the economic reconstruction of Iraq,

Noting that the Tax Commission has not been operational,

Determined to complete a broad review of taxes in Iraq, in order to improve the operation and efficiency of the tax system,

Recognizing that these collections are for the benefit of the Iraqi people, and, as far as possible, are in accordance with the rules of assessment and incidence in effect under existing law,

Recognizing that until such a review is completed an interim tax strategy for the remainder of the year 2003 is required,

I hereby promulgate the following:

Section 1 Definition

For the purposes of this Order 'tax' means any tax or charge having the effect of a tax, including, without limitation, any income, value added, ad valorem, estate, occupational, professional, real property or municipal tax, and any levy, duty, withholding or fee.

Section 2 Suspension of Taxes

Subject to Section 6 of this Order, the following taxes are suspended from April 16, 2003 to the end of calendar year 2003:[118]

a) All income tax for assessed income resources detailed in Article 2 of Income Tax Law Number 113 of 1982;

b) Real property rent tax in accordance with Law Number 162 of 1959, as amended;

c) All other taxes not specifically identified in Section 3 below.

Section 3 Specified Taxes

1) The following specified taxes shall continue in force, and shall be levied for the remainder of the calendar year 2003:

a) Excellent and first class hotel and restaurant tax in accordance with Resolution Number 36 of 1997;

b) Tax upon the transfer of real property in accordance with Resolution Number 120 of 2002;

c) Car sale fee in accordance with Resolution Number 80 of 1998 and previous relevant laws in force;

d) Petrol excise duties including, but not limited to, those provided for in Law Number 9 of 1939, Resolution Number 82 of 1996 and the Order Number 66 of 1999 issued by the Economic Affairs Committee.

2) The taxes specified in paragraph 1 above shall not apply to the following persons or entities:

a) Coalition Provisional Authority;

b) Coalition Forces;

c) Forces of countries, their contractors and sub-contractors, acting in coordination with Coalition Forces;

d) Coalition contractors and sub-contractors, as defined in CPA Order Number 17,[119] who supply goods directly to or on behalf of the Coalition Provisional Authority and Coalition Forces;

[118] Sec 2 was amended by CPA Order No 84, sec 1(1) *[Doc 108]*.

[119] See *Doc 37*.

e) Departments and agencies of Coalition Forces' governments, and their contractors and sub-contractors that are providing technical, material, financial and human resource assistance to Iraq;
f) Governments, international organizations, and not-for-profit organizations providing technical, material, financial and human resource assistance to Iraq;
g) Members of the above categories to whom goods are consigned or by whom goods are imported for their personal use.

Section 4 Income Tax Rates in Future Years
The highest individual and corporate income tax rates for 2004 and subsequent years shall not exceed 15 percent.

Section 5 Tax Procedures
Notwithstanding any other provision in this Order, the tax laws as set out in existing Iraqi law, including those detailed in Tax Law Number 113 of 1982, with regard to the tax procedures, including tax rates, the system of collection, enforcement procedures, appeals, and the imposition and rate of penalties and interest for nonpayment or late payment of taxes, shall remain in force unless or until amended by the Administrator of the Coalition Provisional Authority or an internationally recognized, representative government of Iraq.[120]

Section 6 Retention of Collected Taxes
Taxes that have already been paid to the government or otherwise held by the government shall remain government property and are not liable to be returned to the taxed party.

Section 7 Relation to Existing Law
In order to give effect to this Order, all existing Iraqi law which is inconsistent with this Order is hereby suspended.

Section 8 Administrative Instructions
The Administrator of the Coalition Provisional Authority or his delegee may issue Administrative Instructions to give effect to this Order.

Section 9 Entry into Force
This Order shall enter into force on the date of signature [19 September 2003].

Document 59
Coalition Provisional Authority Order Number 38
CPA/ORD/19 September 2003/38

Reconstruction Levy

Pursuant to my authority as Administrator of the Coalition Provisional Authority (CPA), and under the laws and usages of war, and consistent with relevant U.N. Security Council resolutions, including Resolution 1483 (2003),

[120] Sec 5 was amended by CPA Order No 100, sec 3(15) *[Doc 124]*.

Determined to improve the standard of living for the Iraqi people,

Recognizing that the effective administration of Iraq requires funding for improvements to its infrastructure and capital public investment,

Recognizing the role of international trade in the development of a free market economy in Iraq,

Noting that tariffs and trade restrictions were suspended under CPA Order Number 12,[121]

I hereby promulgate the following:

Section 1 Imposition of Reconstruction Levy

1) Notwithstanding CPA Order Number 12 or any other CPA Order suspending a tax, levy, duty, charge, withholding, fee or tariff, there shall be created a levy known as the Reconstruction Levy.

2) For the purpose of calculating the Reconstruction Levy, the taxable value of goods shall consist of their total customs value assessed in accordance with international practice.[122]

3) The Reconstruction Levy shall be imposed at a rate of 5% of the taxable value of goods. The revenues from the Reconstruction Levy shall be used only to assist the Iraqi people and support the reconstruction of Iraq. It shall expire two years from the date that this Order enters into force.

4) Unless exempted under this Order, the Reconstruction Levy shall be imposed on all goods imported into Iraq from all countries beginning 1 January 2004.[123]

Section 2 Exemptions

1) The following goods shall be exempt from the Reconstruction Levy:

a) Food.

b) Medicines and medical equipment.

c) Clothing.

d) Books.

e) Goods imported to be delivered as humanitarian assistance to the people of Iraq or in support of reconstruction of Iraq.

f) Imports of the type exempted under the Vienna Conventions on Diplomatic Relations of 1961 and Consular Relations of 1963 and imports exempted under the Convention on the Privileges and Immunities of the United Nations.

g) Goods imported by the United Nations, other international organizations, not-for-profit organizations, or foreign governments to be used or distributed for the public benefit as defined in Administrative Instructions.[124]

2) The Reconstruction Levy shall not apply to the following persons or entities:

a) Coalition Provisional Authority;

b) Coalition Forces;

c) Forces of countries, their contractors and sub-contractors, acting in coordination with Coalition Forces;

[121] See *Doc 28*.

[122] 'International practice' is defined by CPA Order No 54, sec 4(1) *[Doc 76]*.

[123] Sec 1(4) was amended by CPA Order No 47, sec 1 *[Doc 69]*, CPA Order No 54, sec 7 *[Doc 76]* and CPA Order No 70, sec 1(1) *[Doc 94]*.

[124] The terms 'not-for-profit organization,' 'public benefit' and 'international organization' are defined by CPA Order No 54, sec 4(4)-(6) *[Doc 76]*.

d) Coalition contractors and sub-contractors, as defined in CPA Order Number 17,[125] who supply goods directly to the Coalition Provisional Authority and Coalition Forces;
e) Departments and agencies of Coalition Forces' governments, and their contractors and sub-contractors that are providing technical, material, financial, human resource assistance to Iraq;
f) Governments, international organizations and not-for-profit organizations providing technical, material, financial and human resource assistance;
g) Members of the above categories to whom goods are consigned or by whom goods are imported for their personal use.[126]

3) The Reconstruction Levy shall not apply to imports under the Oil for Food contracts.

4) Administrative Instructions may be issued under this Order further defining exempt goods in this Section and exempting defined persons and entities from payment of the Reconstruction Levy.

Section 3 Implementation of Order

1) The Administrator of the Coalition Provisional Authority or his delegee may issue Administrative Instructions to give effect to this Order.

2) All existing Iraqi law which is inconsistent with this Order is hereby suspended.

Section 4 Entry into Force

This Order shall enter into force on the date of signature [19 September 2003].

Document 60
Coalition Provisional Authority Order Number 39

CPA/ORD/19 September 2003/39

Foreign Investment

Pursuant to my authority as Administrator of the Coalition Provisional Authority (CPA) and the laws and usages of war, and consistent with relevant U.N. Security Council resolutions, including Resolution 1483 (2003),

Having worked closely with the Governing Council to ensure that economic change occurs in a manner acceptable to the people of Iraq,

Acknowledging the Governing Council's desire to bring about significant change to the Iraqi economic system,

Determined to improve the conditions of life, technical skills, and opportunities for all Iraqis and to fight unemployment with its associated deleterious effect on public security,

Noting that facilitating foreign investment will help to develop infrastructure, foster the growth of Iraqi business, create jobs, raise capital, result in the introduction of new technology into Iraq and promote the transfer of knowledge and skills to Iraqis,

Recognizing the problems arising from Iraq's legal framework regulating commercial activity and the way in which it was implemented by the former regime,

[125] See *Doc 37*.
[126] Sec 2(2) was rescinded and replaced by CPA Order No 100, sec 3(16) *[Doc 124]*.

Recognizing the CPA's obligation to provide for the effective administration of Iraq, to ensure the well being of the Iraqi people and to enable the social functions and normal transactions of every day life,

Acting in a manner consistent with the Report of the Secretary General to the Security Council of July 17, 2003, concerning the need for the development of Iraq and its transition from a non-transparent centrally planned economy to a market economy characterized by sustainable economic growth through the establishment of a dynamic private sector, and the need to enact institutional and legal reforms to give it effect,

Having coordinated with the international financial institutions, as referenced in paragraph 8(e) of the U.N. Security Council Resolution 1483, In close consultation with and acting in coordination with the Governing Council,

I hereby promulgate the following:

Section 1 Definitions

1) *'Administrator'* means the Administrator of the Coalition Provisional Authority.

2) *'Business entity'* means any entity constituted or organized by law of any country, including, but not limited to, any corporation, partnership, joint venture, firm, enterprise, State-owned enterprise, organization, or other similar entity.

3) *'Foreign investment'* means investment by a foreign investor in any kind of asset in Iraq, including tangible and intangible property, and related property rights, shares and other forms of participation in a business entity, and intellectual property rights and technical expertise, except as limited by Section 8 of this Order.

4) *'Foreign investor'* means (a) a business entity constituted or organized under the law of a country other than Iraq; (b) a natural person who is (i) a national of a country other than Iraq, (ii) a stateless person not residing permanently in Iraq, or (iii) a national of Iraq residing permanently outside of Iraq; or (c) a business entity constituted or organized by any of the above under the law of Iraq; that is making or has made an investment in Iraq.

5) *'Iraqi investor'* means (a) a business entity constituted or organized under the law of Iraq other than by a foreign investor; or a natural person who is (i) a national of Iraq residing permanently in Iraq, or (ii) a stateless person residing permanently in Iraq; that is making or has made an investment in Iraq.

Section 2 Purposes

This Order promotes and safeguards the general welfare and interests of the Iraqi people by promoting foreign investment through the protection of the rights and property of foreign investors in Iraq and the regulation through transparent processes of matters relating to foreign investment in Iraq. This Order specifies the terms and procedures for making foreign investments and is intended to attract new foreign investment to Iraq.

Section 3 Relation to Existing Iraqi Law

1) This Order replaces all existing foreign investment law.

2) This Order is subject to revision by the Administrator, or to adoption or replacement by an internationally recognized, representative government established by the people of Iraq.

3) Future Orders or other guidance will be issued concerning various sectors of the economy.

Section 4 Treatment of Foreign Investors

1) A foreign investor shall be entitled to make foreign investments in Iraq on terms no less favorable than those applicable to an Iraqi investor, unless otherwise provided herein.

2) The amount of foreign participation in newly formed or existing business entities in Iraq shall not be limited, unless otherwise expressly provided herein.

Section 5 Trade Offices & Branches

A foreign investor may open trade representation offices and branches in Iraq; such offices and branches shall be registered with the Iraqi Registrar of Companies.

Section 6 Areas of Foreign Investment

1) Foreign investment may take place with respect to all economic sectors in Iraq, except that foreign direct and indirect ownership of the natural resources sector involving primary extraction and initial processing remains prohibited. In addition, this Order does not apply to banks and insurance companies.

2) Foreign investment may take place in all parts of Iraq.

3) A foreign investor shall be prohibited from engaging in retail sales, unless at least 30 days prior to engaging in such retail sales such foreign investor deposits $100,000 in a non-interest-bearing account in a properly licensed Iraqi bank located in Iraq pursuant to procedures to be promulgated by the Ministry of Trade. Once a deposit is made pursuant to its procedures, the Ministry of Trade shall issue documentation to the foreign investor reflecting the authorization to engage in such retail sales. Such deposit must be maintained during the entire time that the foreign investor is engaged in retail sales; provided however, it shall be returned upon the request of the foreign investor at the completion of the retail sales activity.

Section 7 Implementing Foreign Investment

1) A foreign investor may implement foreign investment using, among other things, freely convertible currencies or Iraqi legal tender, in the following forms:

- a) establishing a wholly foreign-owned business entity in Iraq, including as a subsidiary of a foreign investor;
- b) establishing a business entity jointly with an Iraqi investor;
- c) establishing a branch office, as set forth in Section 5 herein; and
- d) directly acquiring an investment.

2) A foreign investor shall be authorized to:

- a) possess, use, and dispose of its investments;
- b) manage or participate in managing a business entity;
- c) transfer its rights and obligations to other persons in accordance with the law;
- d) transfer abroad without delay all funds associated with its foreign investment, including:
  - i) shares or profits and dividends;
  - ii) proceeds from the sale or other disposition of its foreign investment or a portion thereof;
  - iii) interest, royalty payments, management fees, other fees and payments made under a contract; and
  - iv) other transfers approved by the Ministry of Trade;
- e) exercise any other authority conferred upon it by law.

3) The Finance Minister and the Minister of Planning may jointly issue regulations to assist in the implementation of this Order.[127]

Section 8 Use of Real Property

1) After the date of this Order, unless otherwise permitted by law, a foreign investor or a business entity with any level of foreign investor participation may not under any circumstances purchase the rights of disposal and usufruct of private real property.

2) The duration of any license to use property shall be determined by the duration of operations related to the foreign investment. The initial term of a license shall not exceed 40 years, but may be renewed for further such periods. Licenses may be reviewed by the internationally recognized, representative government established by the people of Iraq upon its assumption of the responsibilities of the CPA.

3) If a business entity that is owned or controlled by a foreign investor or foreign investors is dissolved before the expiration of the license or lease, then the license or lease shall be terminated at the time of such dissolution.

Section 9 Insurance

A foreign investor shall be permitted to obtain insurance coverage for all aspects of its operation from any foreign or Iraqi source deemed appropriate by the foreign investor.

Section 10 Dispute Settlement

Disputes between a foreign investor and an Iraqi investor pertaining to investment in Iraq, or between a foreign investor and an Iraqi legal or natural person, shall be resolved in accordance with the dispute resolution provisions contained in any applicable written agreement governing the relationship between the parties. The parties may elect in any agreement to utilize the arbitration mechanisms outlined in Iraqi law.

Section 11 Dissolution of Entities

1) Within 14 days from the date of adopting a resolution or other instrument terminating the operations of a business entity that is owned or controlled by a foreign investor or foreign investors, the business entity with foreign investment shall submit the resolution or other instrument to the Iraqi Registrar of Companies.

2) Upon termination of operations and dissolution of the business entity with any level of foreign investment, any such foreign investor shall, consistent with Section 7 of this Order, have the right to transfer profits from the sale or liquidation to any foreign location, or as provided in a written agreement between the foreign investor and an Iraqi investor, provided that all amounts owed by such business entity to the government of Iraq and all Iraqi creditors have been paid in advance of the transfer.

Section 12 Tax Treatment

The Administrator may issue further orders to address the tax treatment of income derived from a foreign investment that is reinvested in a business entity in Iraq.

Section 13 Treatment of Investors

No legal text that impedes the operation of this Order shall hold and all investors, foreign

[127] Sec 7(3) was amended by CPA Order No 46, sec 1 *[Doc 68]*.

and Iraqi, shall be treated equally under the law, except as otherwise specifically provided in this Order.

Section 14 International Agreements
Where an international agreement to which Iraq is a party provides for more favorable terms with respect to foreign investors undertaking investment activities in Iraq, the more favorable terms under the international agreement shall apply.

Section 15 Evasion
Violations of Sections 6(3) and 8(1) of this Order may serve as a basis for suspension or cancellation of the rights of a foreign investor in Iraq that arise under this Order.

Section 16 Entry into Force
This Order shall enter into force on the date of signature [Signed without date].

Document 61
Ministerial Instruction No. 149

24 February 2004

Registration of Branches and Trade Representation Offices by Foreign Companies

Section I Introduction: Registration of Branches and Trade Representation Offices by Foreign Companies

1. Coalition Provisional Authority ('CPA') Order No. 39 on 'Foreign Investment', dated 19 September 2003, as amended by CPA Order No. 46, dated 20 December 2003,[128] establishes that foreign investors may do business in Iraq by, among other things, establishing branches or trade representation offices.

2. Pursuant to CPA Order No. 39, a branch or trade representation office may do business in the name of and for the account of a business entity organized under the laws of a foreign country. In no case shall the branch or trade representation office's foreign character disqualify it from registering to conduct business in Iraq, whether the business is in the nature of a commercial agency, distributorship, trading company or otherwise.

3. The present Ministry of Trade Ministerial Instruction implements CPA Order No. 39, and in particular Section 5 thereof, as to branches and trade representation offices of entities organized under the laws of foreign countries.

4. By virtue of CPA Order No. 39, Regulation No. 5 of 1989 on 'Branches and Offices of Foreign Companies and Economic Establishments' and any instructions thereunder contrary to this Instruction are nullified. Branches and offices currently registered under that Regulation are regarded as registered under this Instruction and shall provide updated information as of the time this Instruction requires.

5. By virtue of CPA Order 39, Law No. 51 of 2000 on 'Commercial Agency' and any instructions thereunder are nullified. Commercial agents on behalf of natural or juridical

[128] See *Doc 68*.

persons outside Iraq shall henceforth be regarded as subject to the same legislation as agents performing similar services on behalf of natural or juridical persons inside Iraq. Any other instruction, regulation or legislation conflicting with CPA Order No. 39 as implemented in this Instruction shall also be regarded as null and void.

Section II Business Entities Subject to this Instruction

1. Foreign business entities wishing to establish themselves to conduct business in Iraq are subject to registration by the Registrar of Companies, Ministry of Trade, in accordance with this Ministerial Instruction. Unless otherwise exempt under the laws and regulations of Iraq, including CPA Orders, foreign companies working under contract in Iraq are also subject to registration under this Ministerial Instruction.

2. Such foreign entities may conduct any business permissible under the laws and regulations of Iraq, including CPA Orders, without being required to post any advance financial bonds, guarantees or similar surety (except for a foreign investor engaging in retail sales).

Section III Application and Procedures for Registration

1. A foreign business entity wishing to register to do business in Iraq shall complete and file with the Registrar of Companies an Application in the form attached as Annex I to this Ministerial Instruction.[129] Two (2) copies of the completed form should be brought to the Registrar of Companies at the time of application (the Registrar of Companies will keep one and the other will be returned with a signed checklist to the applicant).

2. Each Application shall include the following information concerning the foreign business entity proposed to be registered by the Registrar of Companies:
   a. legal name;
   b. trade name;
   c. type of business activity;
   d. business address of its offices in Iraq;
   e. telephone, facsimile and electronic mail in Iraq, where available;
   f. name, address and telephone number of: (1) the chief management official in Iraq; (2) the agent for service of legal process in Iraq; and (3) the authorized representative for filings with the Registrar of Companies – (all of three must reside in Iraq);
   g. a yes/no question asking if the proposed entity in Iraq will be involved in: (1) land ownership; or (2) natural resource extraction or initial processing; or (3) retail sales;
   h. name, business address, telephone, facsimile and electronic mail of its agent for service of legal process and chief executive officer (or equivalent) in its home country of establishment or incorporation;
   i. to the extent applicable: (1) the amount of its charter or authorized capital (specifying currency); (2) net worth at close of most recent financial period (indicating date and specifying currency); and (3) the names and addresses of any owners holding ten percent (10%) or more of its equity; and
   j. perjury statement to be signed on behalf of the foreign business entity proposed to be registered by the Registrar of Companies.

[129] Annex I – a two page application form and one page of instructions for completion of the application form – has not been not reproduced.

3. The following documentation shall be submitted with each Application concerning the foreign business entity proposed to be registered by the Registrar of Companies:
   a. certificate of registration, as issued and authenticated by the competent authority in the home country of origin;
   b. a copy of the company's charter or equivalent, authenticated by the competent authority in the home country of origin;
   c. a letter on the stationery of the applicant company, signed by an officer or director of the company, authorizing the registration of the business entity in Iraq, consenting to service of process in Iraq, and identifying the chief management official in Iraq, the authorized agent for service of legal process in Iraq, and the representative for filings with the Registrar of Companies in Iraq (all three must reside in Iraq);
   d. the financial statements of the company for the last fiscal year;
   e. if the proposed entity is planning to operate in retail sales in Iraq, a bank statement showing that the sum of one hundred thousand United States dollars ($100,000.00) has been deposited in a non-interest bearing account (this can be furnished to the Registrar of Companies at a later date and the non-submission of it shall not be grounds for rejection of the Application; however, the bank statement will have to be furnished before actual sales activity may begin) in accordance with the Ministerial Instruction on retail trade;
   f. a copy of the passport (for a foreign citizen) or civilian identification card (for an Iraqi citizen) of the authorized representative for filings with the Registrar of Companies, as prescribed in the letter referred to in Item (c) in paragraph 3. above and as in Item (f) in paragraph 2. above (this is the person who is to actually submit the Application and he or she should also bring at the time of application, and in all future interactions with the Registrar of Companies, the original of his or her passport (for a foreign citizen) or civilian identification card (for an Iraqi citizen)).

4. An Application for the registration of a foreign business entity to do business in Iraq (including all required information and documents) may be filed in either the Arabic or English language. Translations shall be provided of home country documents not in the English or Arabic language.

5. Upon receiving an Application, the Registrar of Companies shall:
   a. review the Application for completeness;
   b. if the Application is incomplete, return it to the applicant company without collecting any fee;
   c. if the Application is complete, provide a signed checklist to the applicant company showing that all the required documentation has been received;
   d. log the accepted Application in the Registrar of Companies' official record as of the date of its receipt; and
   e. assign a temporary unique identification number to the Application.

6. The Registrar of Companies must approve or disapprove each Application within ten (10) business days from the day of its submission by the applicant company. The Registrar of Companies may only disapprove an Application for failure to comply with this Ministerial Instruction.

7. Upon approval of each Application, the Registrar of Companies shall promptly issue to the applicant company a registration license bearing the corresponding business entity's name and the Registrar of Companies' official seal, together with a permanent unique identification number.

8. The registered business entity shall acquire legal recognition as from the date of issuance of its registration license and permanent unique identification number by the Registrar of Companies. A registered entity is present in and subject to the jurisdiction of Iraq.

9. Upon issuance, the Registrar of Companies shall publish each registration in the 'Companies Bulletin' and in at least one (1) daily newspaper of wide circulation in Iraq.

10. The Registrar of Companies shall forward copies of each Application as approved, together with its respective permanent unique identification number as issued, to the Ministry of Finance (Tax Department), Ministry of Planning, Ministry of Labor and Social Affairs, and such other Iraqi Government departments and agencies as reasonably necessary.

11. The Registrar of Companies shall enter basic summary information on registered companies into a Ministry of Trade electronic database accessible to the public, including over the Internet. Implementation of this function shall not, however, be grounds for delay of registration.

Section IV Fees Payable

1. A single standard registration processing fee shall be due and payable, in the amount of two hundred thousand dinars (ID200,000.00), or equivalent, for each Application payable as follows:

(a) one-half (1/2) of the fee shall be paid upon submission and filing of the Application;

(b) the remaining one-half (1/2) of the fee shall be paid upon issuance of the registration and permanent unique identification number by the Registrar of Companies; and

(c) provided, however, that in the event of disapproval of an Application, the remaining one-half (1/2) of the fee referred to in Item (ii) above shall not be due or payable, and the one-half (1/2) of the fee referred to in Item (i) above shall be forfeited by the Registrar of Companies.

2. The Registrar of Companies shall collect said fees and issue the proper receipt evidencing payment directly to the Applicant or its representative.

3. The Registrar of Companies shall keep regular and accurate records and accounts to account for all registration fees collected.

Section V Appeal for Disapproval of Application

In the event the Registrar of Companies disapproves the Application for the registration of a foreign business entity, the Registrar of Companies must promptly notify the applicant company in writing stating the reasons for its disapproval. The applicant company has the right to contest the disapproval of the Registrar of Companies before the Minister of Trade within thirty (30) days from the date of notification. The Minister of Trade shall review the disapproval within thirty (30) days from the date of submission of the applicant company's appeal. If the Minister of Trade also disapproves the Application, the applicant company has the right to appeal the Minister's decision before the competent court of law within thirty (30) days of the date of the decision, which court shall have final disposition of the matter.

Section VI Update of Information at the Registrar of Companies

Information filed in connection with each registration must be correct as of the time of filing. Subsequent changes may be filed as they occur but at least by December 31 of each year, and address changes for the company's principal office in Iraq or its agent for service of legal process within seven (7) days of their occurrence. Companies will be held responsible for notifications and correspondence delivered to the address in the Registrar of Companies' files.

Section VII Entry into Force of this Instruction

1. This Ministerial Instruction shall enter into full force and effect upon its publication in the Companies Bulletin, as of the date of its signature.
2. The Registrar of Companies shall ensure that the section of the Companies Bulletin publishing this Ministerial Instruction is published in at least five (5) newspapers chosen to accomplish the broadest possible circulation in all regions of Iraq.

Signed: Dr. Ali Allawi
Name: Dr. Ali Allawi
Title: Minister of Trade, Republic of Iraq

Document 62
Coalition Provisional Authority Order Number 40

CPA/ORD/19 September 2003/40

Bank Law

Pursuant to my authority as Administrator of the Coalition Provisional Authority (CPA) and under the laws and usages of war, and consistent with relevant U.N. Security Council resolutions, including Resolution 1483 (2003),

Having worked closely with the Governing Council to ensure that economic change occurs in a manner acceptable to the people of Iraq,

Acknowledging the Governing Council's desire to bring about significant change to the Iraqi economic system,

Determined to improve the conditions of life, and opportunities for all Iraqis and to fight unemployment with its associated deleterious effect on public security through stable financial markets,

Recognizing the problems arising from Iraq's legal framework regulating banking activities and the way in which it was implemented by the former regime,

Further recognizing the CPA's obligation to provide for the effective administration of Iraq, to ensure the well being of the Iraqi people and to enable the social functions and normal transactions of every day life,

Recalling that U.N. Security Council Resolution 1483 (2003) called upon the CPA to promote economic reconstruction and the conditions for sustainable development,

Acting in a manner consistent with the Report of the Secretary General to the Security Council of July 17, 2003, concerning the need for the development of Iraq and its transition from a non-transparent centrally planned economy to a market economy characterized by sustainable economic growth through the establishment of a dynamic private sector, and the need to enact institutional and legal reforms to give it effect,

Having coordinated with the international financial institutions, as referenced in paragraph 8(e) of the U.N. Security Council Resolution 1483,

I hereby promulgate the following:

Section 1 Purpose
This Order establishes a safe, sound, competitive and accessible banking system for the purposes of providing a foundation for economic growth and the development of a stable Iraqi economy.

Section 2 Banking Law
The banking law attached to this Order in Annex A shall have the full force and effect of law.

Section 3 Inconsistent Legislation
Any provision of Iraqi law that is inconsistent with this Order or Annex A is hereby suspended to the extent of such inconsistency.

Section 4 Entry into Force
This Order shall enter into force on the day immediately following the date of signature [19 September 2003].[130]

Annex A – Iraq Banking Law

[The text of the Iraqi Banking Law has been omitted as it was rescinded only some ten months later by CPA Order No 94 (CPA/ORD/6 June 2004/94)[131] which promulgated the Banking Law of 2004. The revised Banking Law of 2004, which is reproduced in full as Annex to Order No 94, retained the structure and organization of the previous banking law. The substantive provisions of the two laws are largely identical; any differences have been noted in the footnotes to the Banking Law of 2004.]

Document 63

Coalition Provisional Authority Order Number 41

CPA/ORD/19 September 2003/41

Notification of Criminal Offenses

Pursuant to my authority as Administrator of the Coalition Provisional Authority (CPA), under the laws and usages of war, and consistent with relevant U.N. Security Council resolutions, including Resolution 1483 (2003),

Noting the requirement under Iraqi law to notify public authorities of information concerning an attempt to commit or the commission of certain offenses involving the use of explosives or firearms and the destruction or damage of public assets and infrastructure,

[130] CPA Order No 40 was rescinded by CPA Order No 94, sec 3 *[Doc 118]*.
[131] See *Doc 118*.

Recognizing the imperative that all persons in Iraq assist in and support the efforts of Iraqi public authorities, Coalition authorities, and the international community to improve the conditions and security of the people of Iraq,

Determined to act decisively to ensure public security and to prevent acts of sabotage and terror,

I hereby promulgate the following:

Section 1 Interpretation of Law

1) For the purposes of Paragraphs 190, 193-197, 216 (except with respect to Paragraphs 191 and 192) and 219 in the Penal Code Law No. (Ill) of 1969 as amended and modified by CPA Order Number 7, Penal Code, CPA/ORD/9 June 2003/07[132] ('the Code'), references to 'government' and the 'State' shall be interpreted to include the Governing Council, the interim Iraqi Ministers, those persons specifically authorized to draft the new Iraqi constitution, the CPA and Coalition Forces.[133]

2) For purposes of clarity, the notification requirement set forth in Paragraph 219 shall be applicable to, among other things, knowledge of offenses under Paragraph 197. This would include, for example, knowledge of offenses, committed with the intent to spread panic among the population or create anarchy, involving the destruction of or serious damage to public property of significant national economic importance (including an oil pipeline), public buildings (including a mosque), and government property (including a vehicle of the Governing Council, Coalition Forces or the CPA).

Section 2 Additional Penalties

1) At the discretion of the Administrator, foreign nationals convicted of an offense under Paragraph 219 of the Code may be deported consistent with applicable law.

2) Where individuals who are employees of organizations are convicted of an offense under Paragraph 219 of the Code for acts committed in the course of their employment duties, and the supervisors, management or executive officers of the organization aided, abetted, encouraged or acquiesced in the offense, then the organization shall be liable for a fine of up to US$5 million.

Section 3 Preservation of Discretion

Nothing in this Order shall in any way limit the right of the CPA and Coalition Forces to take direct action in accordance with international law, including Article 53 of the Hague Regulations of 1907.[134]

Section 4 Entry into Force

This Order shall enter into force on the date of signature [19 September 2003].

[132] See *Doc 21*.

[133] Sec 1(1) was amended by CPA Order No 100, sec 3(17)(a) *[Doc 124]*.

[134] Sec 3 was rescinded by CPA Order No 100, sec 3(17)(b) *[Doc 124]*.

Document 64
Coalition Provisional Authority Order Number 42
CPA/ORD/19 September 2003/42

Creation of the Defense Support Agency

Pursuant to my authority as Administrator of the Coalition Provisional Authority (CPA), and under the laws and usages of war, and consistent with relevant U.N. Security Council resolutions, including Resolution 1483 (2003),

Recalling that U.N. Resolution 1483 (2003) called upon the CPA to promote the welfare of the Iraqi people through the effective administration of the territory, including in particular working towards the restoration of conditions of security and stability,

Further Recalling that CPA Order Number 22[135] established a New Iraqi Army as the first step towards the creation of the national defense force which is essential to the security and stability of Iraq,

Acknowledging that effective, centralized administrative and logistical support are vital to the success of the New Iraqi Army,

I hereby promulgate the following:

Section 1 Establishment

1) This Order establishes the Defense Support Agency (DSA) as a civilian agency charged with the administrative and logistical support of the New Iraqi Army.

2) The DSA shall operate under the authority, direction and control of the CPA.

3) The DSA shall operate pursuant to this order unless or until it is dissolved by the Administrator of the CPA ('the Administrator') or the internationally recognized, representative government established by the people of Iraq.

Section 2 Duties

1) The DSA shall be responsible for the following functions in support of the New Iraqi Army:

a) Finance and accounting, including payroll, disbursements, and accounting for expenditures by the New Iraqi Army;
b) Personnel management;
c) Training support;
d) Recruitment;
e) Procurement;
f) Logistics support, including maintenance, supply, and transportation;
g) Medical support;
h) Legal affairs;
i) Real property management, including construction and repair of New Iraqi Army buildings and oversight of the management of military bases by their commanders; and
j) other duties in support of the New Iraqi Army as determined by the Administrator.

[135] See *Doc 43*.

2) The DSA shall not exercise any command authority or staff function over New Iraqi Army military units, or be responsible for setting security policy. Nor shall the DSA be responsible for determining the requirements of the New Iraqi Army.

3) The DSA shall submit a quarterly report to the Governing Council detailing its prior quarter activities and plans for the following quarter.

Section 3 Structure

1) The Administrator shall appoint a Director-General of the DSA. Until such appointment has been made, the CPA Director of Security Affairs (National Security and Defense) shall serve as interim Director-General. The Director-General shall report directly to the Administrator.

2) The DSA shall initially consist of six Departments:

a) Financial Management;
b) Personnel Management, Recruiting, and Training;
c) Procurement and Logistics Support;
d) Real Property Management;
e) Legal Affairs; and
f) Medical Support.

3) The Director-General, with the approval of the Administrator or his designee, shall appoint the Director of each Department.

4) The Director-General may establish, reorganize, or eliminate Departments by Administrative Instruction. Likewise, the Director-General may apportion, reapportion or remove Department responsibilities by Administrative Instruction. Any such Administrative Instructions shall require the approval of the Administrator or his designee.

5) Defense Support Agency personnel shall be civilians and may include former military personnel and civilian state employees. No person who was a full member of the Ba'ath Party holding the rank of 'Udw Qutriyya (Regional Command Member), 'Udw Far' (Branch Member), 'Udw Shu'bah (Section Member), or 'Udw Firqah (Group Member) shall be eligible for employment in the DSA except with specific permission of the Administrator.

6) Salaries of DSA personnel will conform to the salary structure applicable to Iraqi government employees.

Section 4 Administrative Instructions

The Director-General may issue Administrative Instructions, not inconsistent with Iraqi law or any CPA Order, Regulation, or Memorandum, as necessary to carry out the duties described under this Order.

Section 5 Entry into Force

This Order shall enter into force on the date of signature [19 September 2003].[136]

[136] CPA Order No 42 was rescinded by CPA Order No 67, sec 2(4) *[Doc 91]*. See also CPA Order No 100, sec 4(7) *[Doc 124]*.

Document 65

Coalition Provisional Authority Order Number 43

CPA/ORD/14 October 2003/43

New Iraqi Dinar Banknotes

Pursuant to my authority as Administrator of the Coalition Provisional Authority (CPA), and under the laws and usages of war, and consistent with relevant U.N. Security Council resolutions, including Resolution 1483 (2003),

Noting that different series of Iraqi dinar banknotes are currently circulating in Iraq,

Understanding that there is an urgent economic need for the issuance of banknotes that will instill public confidence and facilitate the use of money for its traditional purposes,

Recognizing the need to strengthen the monetary and financial systems of Iraq, in order to stabilize the economy and create monetary conditions for long-term growth,

Determined to provide a legal framework for the introduction of a new series of Iraqi dinar banknotes to be issued by the Central Bank of the Iraq to replace the currently circulating dinar banknotes,

I hereby promulgate the following:

Section 1 Definitions

'CBI' means the Central Bank of Iraq.

'Conversion Period' means the period of time from October 15, 2003, up to and including January 15, 2004.

'Legal instrument' means any legally binding legislative or statutory provision, act of administration or regulation, judicial decision, contract, unilateral legal act, payment instrument other than a banknote, and any other document or instrument with legal effect.

'Legal tender' means Iraqi dinar banknotes and coins issued by the CBI, that are valid and have not been repealed, which any debtor may legally use for payments of all public and private debts, public charges, taxes and dues of any amount denominated in Iraqi dinars and against which no creditor can legally refuse payment of any amount due to him or her denominated in Iraqi dinars.

'New Iraqi dinar' means the new series of Iraqi dinar banknotes that are issued by the CBI after the date that this Order enters into force.

'1990 dinar' means banknotes issued by the CBI from 1990 up to and including the date that this Order enters into force.

'Official Conversion Rates' means the rates of conversion set forth in Section 5.

'Swiss dinar' means banknotes and coins issued by the CBI from 1959 up to and including 1989.

Section 2 Currency Exchange

The CBI shall be responsible for the exchange of Iraqi dinar banknotes currently circulating in Iraq and may issue Administrative Instructions consistent with this Order, for the purpose of implementing and facilitating the issuance of the New Iraqi dinar and the currency exchange.

Section 3 Issue of New Iraqi Dinar Banknotes

1) The CBI is, pursuant to Article 34 of the Central Bank of Iraq Law No. 64 of 1976, as amended, the sole authority in the Republic of Iraq vested with the power to issue legal tender currency. The CBI, under the supervision of the CPA, shall issue New Iraqi dinar banknotes and determine the denominations, designs, technical specifications, and other characteristics of New Iraqi dinar banknotes.

2) The CBI shall ensure that the banknotes redeemed against New Iraqi dinar banknotes, as provided for by this Order, are safely, promptly and securely destroyed.

3) The CBI shall also decide on the volumes, costs and other particulars related to the production and distribution of the New Iraqi dinar banknotes and on the collection, transportation, and destruction of the banknotes and coins submitted in exchange for New Iraqi dinar banknotes.

4) New Iraqi dinars shall be legal tender within Iraq, effective on the first date of the Conversion Period.

Section 4 Conversion

1) The exchange of currently circulating 1990 dinar banknotes and Swiss dinar banknotes and coins against New Iraqi dinar banknotes shall take place during the Conversion Period by exchanges at the Official Conversion Rates, free of charge, at the offices of the CBI and banks and other institutions designated by the CBI.

2) Notwithstanding paragraph 1 of this Section, Swiss dinar banknotes with a face value of 25 dinars may not be exchanged during the Conversion Period. Such banknotes may only be exchanged pursuant to Administrative Instructions issued by the CBI pursuant to paragraph 3 of this Section.

3) Following the expiration of the Conversion Period, no 1990 dinar banknotes or Swiss dinar banknotes or coins shall be exchanged for New Iraqi dinar banknotes, except as permitted pursuant to Administrative Instructions issued by the CBI.

Section 5 Official Conversion Rates

The 1990 dinar banknotes and the Swiss dinar banknotes and coins shall be exchanged against New Iraqi dinar banknotes at the official conversion rates of one (1) 1990 dinar to one (1) New Iraqi dinar, and of one (1) Swiss dinar to one-hundred-and-fifty (150) New Iraqi dinars.

Section 6 Legal Tender Banknotes

1) During the conversion period, 1990 dinar banknotes, Swiss dinar banknotes and coins, and New Iraqi dinar banknotes shall all be legal tender banknotes in Iraq and each type of Iraqi dinar may be used as such in proportion to its Official Conversion Rate.

2) After January 15, 2004, only New Iraqi dinar banknotes issued by the CBI shall be legal tender banknotes.

Section 7 Freedom of Contract

Parties to a contract or to any other voluntary transaction may denominate the payment obligations arising from such a contract or transaction in Iraqi dinar that is legal tender or in any foreign currency they agree upon and payment in discharge of any such obligation may be made in any manner, as agreed upon, and as permitted by Iraqi law.

Section 8 Continuity of Contracts
The provisions of this Order shall not have the effect of altering any term of a legal instrument. The provisions of this Order shall not, unless otherwise mutually agreed by the parties to a contract, have the effect of discharging performance or excusing nonperformance under any legal instrument.

Section 9 Conversion of Monetary Obligations
Effective January 16, 2003, all references in legal instruments to the Swiss dinar shall be converted by operation of law to the New Iraqi dinar.

Section 10 Inconsistent Legislation
In the event of a conflict between this Order and any legislation, statute or regulation in force prior to the entry into force of this Order, this Order shall prevail.

Section 11 Entry into Force
This Order shall enter into force on the date of signature [14 October 2003].

Document 66
Coalition Provisional Authority Order Number 44
CPA/ORD/11 November 2003/44

Ministry of Environment

Pursuant to my authority as Administrator of the Coalition Provisional Authority (CPA), and under the laws and usages of war, and consistent with relevant U.N. Security Council resolutions, including Resolution 1483 (2003),

Recognizing that responsible management of the environment is essential to foster sustainable development,

Furthering the purposes of the Governing Council to create a ministry responsible for environmental issues,

Recalling CPA Memorandum Number 6,[137] publishing the appointment of the Interim Minister of Environment,

I hereby promulgate the following:

Section 1 Establishment

1) The Ministry of Environment (MOEN) is hereby established.

2) All acts and decisions of the interim Minister of Environment in connection with his office or the Ministry from his appointment by the Governing Council on 7 August 2003 to the formal establishment of the MOEN under this Order are hereby ratified. For the purposes of this ratification, the MOEN is deemed to have been established on 7 August 2003.[138]

[137] See *Doc 131*.

[138] According to a CPA Press Release of 26 May 2004, the 'Ministry of Environment was created by a resolution passed by the Iraqi Governing Council (IGC) and signed by CPA Administrator, Ambassador L. Paul Bremer on September 3, 2003.'

3) Subject to transitional provisions in this Order, the Environmental Protection and Improvement Directorate (EPID), established by paragraph 11 of Law Number 3 of 1997, Protection and Improvement of the Environment, is hereby transferred to the MOEN. From the date of transfer to the MOEN, the EPID shall cease to have its own separate legal personality, and Article 11(3) of Law Number 3 of 1997 is hereby suspended.

Section 2 Functions

1) The MOEN shall be responsible for the protection and conservation of Iraq's environment and for the protection of the residents of Iraq from environmental risks to human health and from environmental pollutants. The MOEN shall ensure that environmental protection is an integral factor in developing policies concerning natural resources, human health, economic growth, energy, transportation, agriculture, industry, and international trade.

2) The MOEN shall develop policies, run environmental programs and promulgate and enforce standards pursuant to Law Number 3 of 1997 and this Order.

3) The MOEN shall absorb the EPID into its structure, perform the EPID's functions under its authority, and exercise such powers accorded to the Minister of Health and the Council of Protection and Improvement of the Environment in Chapters III and IV of Law Number 3 of 1997. The MOEN may reorganize and reallocate the assets of the EPID.

Section 3 Structure

1) The interim Minister of the MOEN shall organize the MOEN into such divisions and departments as are necessary. The interim Minister shall ensure, as a minimum, that programs are organized to address environmental concerns in the following areas: radiation control; remediation; solid and hazardous waste management and control; control of toxic substances and hazardous chemicals; ground water; water quality and pollution; air quality and pollution; natural resource protection and land management; and biodiversity. The interim Minister shall ensure, as a minimum, that the following aspects of administration are addressed: media and press relations; security; facilities; personnel and finance; information and technology; legal; enforcement and compliance; international cooperation; a central analytical laboratory; and such regional and local programs as may be required.

2) The Council of Protection and Improvement of the Environment connected with the previous regime's Council of Ministers is hereby abolished. Paragraphs 3 to 6 inclusive of Law Number 3 of 1997 are hereby suspended. The interim Minister shall set up a consultative body composed of representatives of other Ministries to coordinate on policies and programs affecting the environment, and other Ministries shall co-operate with the MOEN.

Section 4 Personnel and Administration

1) The MOEN shall have the power to hire and employ personnel in accordance with Iraqi law, as amended by CPA Orders and Memoranda. Such hiring shall be consistent with CPA Order Number 1[139] and any authorized implementation thereof.

2) Salaries of MOEN personnel shall conform to the salary structure applicable to Iraqi government employees.

3) The staff of the EPID shall be transferred immediately to the MOEN, and the Minister of Environment shall assume full authority, direction and control over this staff.

[139] See *Doc 14*.

Section 5 Transitional Arrangements

1) The Ministry of Health (MOH) shall be responsible for the pay and personnel records of EPID staff until 1 January 2004, unless responsibility is transferred to the MOEN at an earlier date by mutual consent of the MOH and MOEN.

2) The MOH shall coordinate with the MOEN to transfer pay and personnel records as soon as practicable.

3) The MOEN and not the MOH shall administer the employees hired by the MOEN before January 1 2004.

4) The National Centre for Occupational Health and Safety (NCOHS) shall not be transferred with the EPID to the MOEN, but shall be transferred to the Ministry of Labor and Social Affairs.

Section 6 Property

All the movable and immovable property currently under the control of the EPID shall be transferred to the MOEN, with the exception of the movable and immovable property of the NCOHS which shall be transferred to the Ministry of Labor and Social Affairs.

Section 7 Budget

The MOEN shall coordinate with the Ministry of Finance to transfer to the MOEN the budget allocation of the EPID for the financial year 2004. The MOEN shall further coordinate with the Ministry of Finance on its own 2004 budget.

Section 8 Administrative Instructions

The interim Minister, in consultation with the CPA Senior Advisor for Environment, may issue Administrative Instructions, not inconsistent with Iraqi law or any CPA Order, Regulation or Memorandum, prescribing all matters necessary for carrying out the duties described under this Order.

Section 9 Entry into Force

This Order shall enter into force on the date of signature [24 November 2003].

Document 67

Coalition Provisional Authority Order Number 45

CPA/ORD/25 November 2003/45

Non-governmental Organizations

Pursuant to my authority as Administrator of the Coalition Provisional Authority (CPA) and under the laws and usages of war, and consistent with relevant U.N. Security Council resolution, including Resolutions 1483 and 1511 (2003),

Recognizing the CPA's obligation to provide for the effective administration of Iraq, and to ensure the well being of the Iraqi people,

Noting the need for a centralized method of registering non-governmental organizations, and the need to take measures to coordinate their activities,

Determined to ensure the security of the Iraqi people and prevent the misuse of non-governmental organizations or fraudulent or illegal purposes,

I hereby promulgate the following:

Section 1 Definition of Terms

1) *'Non-Governmental Organization'* (*'NGO'*) means any organization or foundation that is organized to undertake one or more of the following as its principal activities: humanitarian assistance and relief projects; human rights advocacy and awareness; community rehabilitation and resettlement; charitable works; educational, health and cultural activities; conservation; environmental protection; economic reconstruction and development; promotion of democratic practices; development of civil society; promotion of gender equality; or any other non-profit activity that serves the public interest. (Unless otherwise specified, the term 'NGO' in this Order refers to both Domestic and Foreign NGOs.)

2) *'Domestic NGO'* means an NGO that is established with its registered office or headquarters in Iraq.

3) *'Foreign NGO'* means an NGO that is established with its registered office or headquarters outside Iraq.

4) *'Minister'* means the Minister of Planning and Development Cooperation.

5) *'Ministry'* means the Ministry of Planning and Development Cooperation.[140]

6) *'The Office'* means the NGO Assistance Office within the Ministry of Planning and Development Cooperation.

7) *'Relevant Ministry'* means the ministry with which an NGO plans or implements part or all if its entire program in Iraq.

8) *'International Organization'* means an organization that (a) is created by an international agreement or other formal constitutive document, (b) established under international law, (c) has international legal identity, (d) performs functions of an genuinely international character, and (e) has an organ with independent decision-making. Such term includes, but is not limited to, the United Nations (including its agencies), the Arab League, and the International Monetary Fund, and the World Bank.

Section 2 Registration Requirements

1) NGOs wishing to operate in programs in Iraq must be registered.

2) International Organizations shall be accredited by the Minister of Foreign Affairs, or his or her designee, and are not required to register as NGOs.

3) NGOs that are not registered are not legally entitled to operate programs in Iraq.

4) An NGO registers by filing the following with the NGO Assistance Office, or with a regional registration representative designated by the Ministry:

- a) A Copy of its articles of association, constitution, or other document stating its aims, objectives, governing structure, and sources of funding.
- b) An application that shall include the following information:
  - i) Full name of the organization.
  - ii) Full address of the NGO's headquarters and contact person(s) outside of Iraq by name, title, phone number, and email address.
  - iii) Full address of the NGO in Iraq.

[140] On 24 October 2004, the Office of the Prime Minister issued a statement that the IIG had approved the transfer of the NGO Assistance Office from the Ministry of Planning and Development Cooperation to the Ministry for Civil Society Affairs.

iv) Date of arrival of the NGO's representative(s) in Iraq (if the application is made inside Iraq).
v) Complete list of any previous visits to or activities in Iraq.
vi) Complete statement of revenue and expenses and assets and liabilities for the current year and the previous 3 years (or the years the organization has existed, if less than 4).
vii) If the applicant has existed for less than one year, it must give financial data for the current year and projected budget for the next two years.
viii) List of any members of the governing body of the NGO who are also public officials or employees of any government or governmental entity.
ix) Domestic NGOs must provide the names and addresses of all members of the board of directors of the NGO, and Foreign NGOs must provide the name of the head of mission in Iraq and the name of the worldwide head of the NGO.
x) List of any organizations or individuals that effectively control, or any organizations that are effectively controlled by, the NGO. (For example, an NGO is effectively controlled by an organization to which it is required to report, or that provides the NGO with directives or policies that the NGO is required to follow. An organization or NGO is effectively controlled if more than 50% of the voting power (or percentage of ownership, if applicable) is controlled (directly or through another entity) by another organization or by another individual or group of individuals acting in concert.)
xi) List of names and addresses of any substantial contributors to the NGO (including, but not limited to, governments, governmental entities, and private foundations making grants to the NGO), amount of the substantial contribution, and relationship of the contributor to the organization. A contribution is substantial if it was received in the current year or any of the previous 3 years, and it is both valued at over 10,000,000 Iraqi dinar and is over 10% of the total revenue for the organization for the year in which it was received.
xii) List of loans to the NGO other than from banks or other lending institutions in excess of both 10,000,000 Iraqi and 10% of it total revenues. Identify the amount of the loan and the lender.

c) A notarized copy of registration or other proof that a Foreign NGO is a legal entity in a foreign country.
d) Certificate or other proof that the Foreign NGO is registered as a not-for-profit entity in its jurisdiction or organization.
e) Written statement by an authorized representative of the NGO's headquarters stating:
   i) Activities that the organization is planning to carry out in Iraq.
   ii) Name and address and other contact information of the individual or individuals in Iraq authorized to represent the organization and to receive official notices and inquiries.
   iii) That the organization is non-political, non-profit making, non-governmental and does not discriminate on the basis of race, religion, or national or ethnic origin.
   iv) Sources of its funding for the activities being undertaken within Iraq.
f) A report on its proposed program prepared with consultation with the Relevant Ministry and budget for the first year of its activities.

4) If an NGO is unable to provide the information required or needs additional time to provide the information required, it may request a waiver or extension of time, as appropriate. In filing a request for waiver or extension of time, the NGO shall provide as much of the required information as possible, and shall provide an explanation as to why it is unable to provide all the required information or why it needs additional time. The Office may, in its discretion, grant or deny the request for a waiver.

5) An NGO operating programs in Iraq shall:

a) Submit quarterly activity reports to the Office.

b) Submit all documents, to include those described in Section 2(3), above, in Arabic, Kurdish or English.

c) Observe and abide by the Orders, Regulations, and Memoranda promulgated by the Coalition Provisional Authority and the laws of Iraq.

Section 3 Processing Applications for Registration

1) If the application contains all required information, the Office shall issue to the NGO a registration certificate or written decision granting or denying registration within 45 business days of receiving an application to register. If the Office requests in writing further information or clarification in connection with the application, the 45-day period within which the Office must make a decision shall start from the date of receiving the requested information by the Office.[141]

2) The Office may deny a certificate if:

a) The registration documents do not comply with the requirements of this Order.

b) The NGO's constitution, conduct, or proposed activities would violate the laws of Iraq or otherwise constitute a threat to the public order, safety, stability or security of Iraq.

3) The NGO shall have temporary legal status in Iraq upon receipt of the application by the Office in accordance with this Order. This legal status shall be evidenced by (i) a copy of the application; and (ii) proof of filing of the application provided by the Office or proof of mailing provided by a national or international delivery service. Temporary legal status shall entitle the NGO to operate programs in Iraq pending approval of the application. Temporary legal status shall terminate upon the granting or denial of registration.

4) The NGO shall have legal status upon the granting of registration, which shall be evidenced by a registration certificate. Such legal status shall allow an NGO to operate programs in Iraq until such status lapses, or is suspended or revoked.

5) An NGO may in addition to its main office, open other local offices upon prior notification to the Office.

6) The Office may suspend or revoke a registration of an NGO if the NGO violates any provision of this Order.

7) If the NGO has its registration suspended, it may not operate in Iraq for the duration of the suspension.

8) If the NGO has its registration revoked, it may not operate in Iraq.

9) An NGO that has its registration suspended or revoked has sixty days to remedy the situation, and may apply for restoration of its registration with the Office.

10) The Office shall maintain a register of NGOs. The register shall state the name, address, organizational form, and purposes of each NGO. The register shall also include

[141] Sec 3(1) was amended by CPA Order No 100, sec 3(18)(a) *[Doc 124]*.

the name, address and other contact information of its authorized representative(s) in Iraq. The Office shall provide such information in the register to each Relevant Ministry and to Coalition Forces and to the CPA as necessary to carry out the laws of Iraq, including promulgations of the CPA, and to enable Coalition Forces and the CPA to carry out their responsibilities under international law.

Section 4 Dissolution and Cessation of Operations

1) The registration of an NGO shall lapse upon its dissolution or cessation of operations.

a) An NGO shall be deemed to have dissolved or to have decided to cease operations if a decision to this effect is issued by the NGO's governing body.

b) An NGO shall be deemed to have ceased operations if it does not commence operations in Iraq within one year of registration, unless a reasonable justification for the delay is provided to the Office. In such case, forty-five days prior to the expiration of one year from the date of registration, the Office shall send written, facsimile, or electronic notice to the NGO stating that its registration will lapse, and provide the NGO fourteen days from the date of the sending of the facsimile or electronic notice or forty-five days from the date of the mailing of the written notice, in which to respond. If after this time no response is received, the NGO's registration will lapse. If a response is received, the Office will make a determination within thirty days of receiving the response as to whether the delay is reasonably justified. If the delay is reasonably justified, the NGO shall have an additional year in which to commence operations. If it is not, the registration shall lapse.

2) In the event of a decision to dissolve or to cease operations, the NGO shall give a written, facsimile, or electronic notice to the Office thirty days prior to the date of decision to dissolve. If the NGO does not notify the Office within this time, the NGO will not be deemed to have taken the decision to dissolve until thirty days after the date of the electronic mail, facsimile, or the postmark or the envelope containing the notice.

3) An NGO that decides to dissolve or cease operations shall submit a report to the Office, stating:

a) The date of dissolution or cessation of operations.

b) The provisions made for terminating its affairs including arrangements for satisfactory completion of its ongoing projects in Iraq.

c) The amount of assets, if any, remaining after discharge of liabilities.

d) The disposition or intended disposition of those assets, if any.

e) How the determination to dispose of those assets, if any, was made.

4) The Office shall remove the NGO that has dissolved or ceased operations from the register of active NGOs in Iraq.

Section 5 Audit and Review

1) The Office may conduct audits and reviews of NGOs at such times and places in Iraq as it may determine to ensure that NGOs are in compliance with this Order.

2) The Office may request that an NGO supply such documentation to the Office as it determines necessary or appropriate to ensure that the NGO is in compliance with this Order. Such requests may be made electronically, by facsimile, or in writing mailed to the most recent e-mail address or postal address provided by the NGO to the Office. If, after 14 days from the date of the sending of the electronic request or the facsimile request or 45

days from the date of the mailing of the written request, the NGO has not responded, the Office may draw such conclusions as it deemed appropriate.

3) If the Office determines, as a result of an audit, review, or document request, that the NGO is not in compliance with this Order, it may (i) provide guidance to the NGO to assist it in complying with the provisions of this Order; (ii) or if the conduct is grossly negligent, fraudulent, criminal, or a threat to security (a) suspend the registration of the NGO for a defined period of time; or (b) revoke the registration of the NGO.

4) If the Office determines, as a result of an audit, review or document request, that the NGO is engaged in conduct that is grossly negligent, fraudulent, criminal, or a threat to public order, stability or security, it may (a) suspend the registration of the NGO for a defined period of time; or (b) revoke the registration of the NGO.

Section 6 Penalties

If an NGO is found to be operating programs after the suspension or revocation of its registration, the Administrator may, in his discretion, close the operation, confiscate the property, and seal the premises of the NGO.[142]

Section 7 Economic Activities

1) An NGO may engage in raising funds for sustaining its programs through income generation projects within Iraq.

2) An NGO may own property, or manage property without possessing it for the accomplishment of its purposes. Notwithstanding the foregoing, Foreign NGOs are not permitted to purchase or own real property, either directly or through an entity.

3) An NGO shall not distribute any net earnings or profits to any person. The assets, earnings, and profits of an NGO shall be used to support the not-for-profit purposes of the NGO and shall not be used to provide benefits, directly or indirectly, to any founder, director, officer, member, employee, or donor of the NGO or to any individual who is a spouse, child, grandchild, parent, grandparent, or sibling of any of the aforesaid, or majority owner of an entity that is a member of the NGO. This section does not preclude the payment of reasonable compensation and provision of reasonable employee benefits to such persons for work performed for the organization. The NGO may provide such individuals and entities with benefits that are generally available to the public.

4) No part of the income or property of an NGO may be paid to or for the benefit of any political party or for the benefit of any candidate or group of candidates for public office.

Section 8 Partnership Arrangements with Other Agencies and Local NGOs

1) An NGO shall inform the Office and the Relevant Ministry of its intention to enter into a joint venture or other contractual arrangement (an 'Arrangement') with one or more foreign entities or international organizations, if such an Arrangement is related to the NGO's operations in Iraq.

2) If an NGO intends to enter into an Arrangement with a local NGO, it is required to inform the Office of its proposed program, including budget, with the local NGO.

Section 9 General Provisions

1) The Minister may delegate to Ministry officials any authority conferred under this Order.

[142] Sec 6 was rescinded and replaced by CPA Order No 100, sec 3(18)(b) *[Doc 124]*.

2) The NGO shall submit to the Office an annual activity and financial report for the previous financial year.

3) Two or more NGOs may voluntarily merge in accordance with their constitutions and Iraqi law.

4) An NGO shall inform the Office within thirty business days of any material change with respect to documents submitted for registration.

5) The NGO shall submit a list of all foreign staff stating their qualifications and responsibilities within 90 days of approval of registration. The list shall be updated when the quarterly activity reports are submitted to the Office.[143]

6) This Order supersedes any inconsistent provision of Iraqi law, including statutes, rules, resolutions and judicial interpretations thereof, which relate to the registration and operation of Foreign NGOs in Iraq, including but not limited to, inconsistent provisions contained in Law Number 34 of 1962, and Law Number 13 of 2000.

7) All NGOs operating within Iraq prior to this Order shall comply with its provisions within 90 days of the date this Order entered into force.[144]

8) The Minister may issue Administrative Instructions as necessary to implement this Order.

9) An NGO should attend government coordination meetings as appropriate in order to ensure the effective delivery of assistance.

10) This Order shall terminate and be of no force or effect when the CPA transfers all governmental authority to the transitional Iraqi administration and recognizes the full sovereignty of that administration.[145]

Section 10 Entry into Force
This Order shall enter into force on the date of signature [27 November 2003].

Document 68

Coalition Provisional Authority Order Number 46

CPA/ORD/20 December 2003/46

Amendment to Coalition Provisional Authority Order Number 39 (CPA/ORD/19 September 2003/39)

Pursuant to my authority as Administrator of the Coalition Provisional Authority (CPA) and the laws and usages of war, and consistent with relevant U.N. Security Council resolutions, including Resolution 1483 (2003),

Recognizing the functions of the Ministry of Trade in providing registration services needed for the establishment of companies, domestic and foreign, wishing to do business in Iraq,

Noting that the registration of companies in accordance with simplified, uniform and transparent procedures is critical to the proper implementation of Coalition Provisional Authority Order Number 39 on Foreign Investment,[146]

[143] Sec 9(5) was amended by CPA Order No 61, sec 1(1) *[Doc 84]*.
[144] Sec 9(7) was amended by CPA Order No 61, sec 1(2) *[Doc 84]*.
[145] Sec 9(10) was rescinded by CPA Order No 100, sec 3(18)(c) *[Doc 124]*.
[146] See *Doc 60*.

I hereby promulgate the following:

Section 1 Amendment
Coalition Provisional Authority Order Number 39, Section 7, Article 3, on Foreign Investment is hereby amended in its entirety to read as: 'The Minister of Trade, in direct consultation with the CPA, shall promptly issue regulations to assist in the implementation of this Order, in coordination with the Minister of Finance and the Minister of Planning.'

Section 2 Entry into Force
This Order shall enter into force on the date of signature [20 December 2003].

Document 69

Coalition Provisional Authority Order Number 47

CPA/ORD/31 December 2003/47

Amendment to Coalition Provisional Authority Order Number 38 (CPA/ORD/19 September 2003/38)

Pursuant to my authority as Administrator of the Coalition Provisional Authority (CPA), and the laws and usages of war, and consistent with relevant U.N. Security Council resolutions, including Resolution 1483 (2003),

Recognizing that the effective administration of Iraq requires funding for improvements to its infrastructure and capital public investment,

Noting that the reconstruction levy was imposed under CPA Order Number 38,[147]

Determined that the collection of said levy be undertaken efficiently and effectively without impeding reconstruction efforts or import flow,

I hereby promulgate the following:

Section 1 Amendment
Coalition Provisional Authority Order Number 38, Section 7 [sic], Article 4,[148] on Reconstruction Levy is amended to read in it entirety as follows:

> '4) Unless exempted from this Order, the Reconstruction Levy shall be imposed on all goods imported into Iraq from all countries beginning March 1, 2004.'

Section 2 Entry into Force
This Order shall enter into force on the date of signature [31 December 2003].[149]

[147] See *Doc 59*.

[148] It should read Sec 1, Art 4. See CPA Order No 38 *[Doc 59]*.

[149] CPA Order No 47 was rescinded by CPA Order No 70, sec 2 *[Doc 94]*. See also CPA Order No 100, sec 4(8) *[Doc 124]*.

Document 70

Coalition Provisional Authority Order Number 48

CPA/ORD/9 December 2003/48

Delegation of Authority Regarding an Iraqi Special Tribunal

Pursuant to my authority as Administrator of the Coalition Provisional Authority (CPA), and under the laws and usages of war, and consistent with relevant U.N. Security Council resolutions, including Resolution 1483 (2003), Resolution 1500 (2003), and Resolution 1511 (2003),

Noting the call in U.N. Security Council Resolution 1483 for accountability for the crimes and atrocities committed by the previous Iraqi regime,

Acting on the appeal by the U.N. Security Council in Resolution 1483 to Member States to deny safe haven to those members of the previous Iraqi regime who are alleged to be responsible for crimes and atrocities and to support actions to bring them to justice,

Acknowledging that the Governing Council, reflecting the general concerns and interests of the Iraqi people, has expressed a desire to establish a Special Tribunal to try members of the Ba'athist regime accused of atrocities and war crimes,

Determined to prevent any threat to public order by revenge actions or vigilantism and to promote the rule of law in accordance with applicable international law,

I hereby promulgate the following:

Section 1 Delegation of Authority

1) The Governing Council is hereby authorized to establish an Iraqi Special Tribunal (the 'Tribunal') to try Iraqi nationals or residents of Iraq accused of genocide, crimes against humanity, war crimes or violations of certain Iraqi laws, by promulgating a statute, the proposed provisions of which have been discussed extensively between the Governing Council and the CPA and are set forth at Appendix A.

2) The statute shall establish the Tribunal, including its chambers, and set forth its jurisdiction, competence, and organization.

3) The statute shall provide rules for the appointment of qualified judges, prosecutors, and a director of administration.

4) The Governing Council shall be authorized to promulgate elements of crimes, the provisions of which shall be coordinated with the CPA.

5) The Governing Council may delegate to the judges of the Tribunal the power to promulgate rules of procedure, the provisions of which shall be coordinated with the Governing Council and the CPA.

6) The Administrator reserves the authority to alter the statute creating the Iraqi Special Tribunal, or any elements of crimes or rules of procedure developed for the Tribunal, if required in the interests of security.[150]

Section 2 Terms and Conditions

The authority delegated under Section 1 of this Order shall be subject to the following terms and conditions:

[150] Sec 1(6) was rescinded by CPA Order No 100, sec 3(19)(a) *[Doc 124]*.

1) The Governing Council will ensure that it promulgates a description of the elements that will apply to the crimes listed in the statute establishing the Tribunal, and that these elements are consistent with Iraqi law, as modified by CPA Orders, and international law.

2) The Governing Council will ensure that the Tribunal meets, at a minimum, international standards of justice.

3) In the event that, prior to the final transfer of governance authority to the transitional Iraqi administration, a conflict arises between any promulgation by the Governing Council or any ruling or judgment by the Tribunal and any promulgation of the CPA, the promulgation of the CPA shall prevail.

4) Non-Iraqi nationals may be appointed as judges of the Special Tribunal.

Section 3 Effective Date

This Order shall enter into force on the date of the signature [10 December 2003] and shall remain in force unless rescinded in writing by me or until the establishment of a representative, internationally recognized government of Iraq.[151]

Appendix A – The Statute of the Iraqi Special Tribunal

SECTION ONE The Establishment, Organization and Competence of the Tribunal

PART ONE Establishment and Competence of the Tribunal

Article 1.

a) A Tribunal is hereby established and shall be known as The Iraqi Special Tribunal (the 'Tribunal'). The jurisdiction and functioning of the Tribunal and its associated bodies as defined in Article 3 below shall be governed by the provisions of this Statute. The Tribunal shall be an independent entity and not associated with any Iraqi government departments.

b) The Tribunal shall have jurisdiction over any Iraqi national or resident of Iraq accused of the crimes listed in Articles 11 to 14 below, committed since July 17, 1968 and up until and including May 1, 2003, in the territory of the Republic of Iraq or elsewhere, including crimes committed in connection with Iraq's wars against the Islamic Republic of Iran and the State of Kuwait. This includes jurisdiction over crimes listed in Articles 12 and 13 committed against the people of Iraq (including its Arabs, Kurds, Turcomans, Assyrians and other ethnic groups, and its Shi'ites and Sunnis) whether or not committed in armed conflict.

c) The Tribunal shall only have jurisdiction over natural persons.

Article 2.

The Tribunal shall have its seat in the City of Baghdad, or, following a written proposal made by the President of the Tribunal, in any other Governorate in Iraq as determined by the Governing Council or the Successor Government.

PART TWO Organization of the Tribunal

Article 3.

a) The Tribunal's judiciary shall consist of the following:

1. one or more Trial Chambers;

[151] Sec 3 was rescinded and replaced by CPA Order No 100, sec 3(19)(b) *[Doc 124]*.

2. an Appeals Chamber, which shall have the power to review the decisions of the Trial Chambers referred to above; and
3. the Tribunal Investigative Judges.

b) The Tribunal will also have a Prosecutions Department.

c) The Tribunal will also have an Administration Department, which shall provide administrative services to the Tribunal's judiciary and the Prosecutions Department.

PART THREE The Trial Chambers and the Appeals Chamber

Article 4.

a) The Chambers shall be composed of permanent independent judges, and independent reserve judges.

b) Each Trial Chamber shall consist of five permanent judges.

c) (i) The Appeals Chamber shall be composed of nine members. Once appointed the Appeals Chamber shall select one of its members to fill the position of President of the Appeals Chamber. No member of any Trial Chamber can simultaneously be a member of the Appeals Chamber or a Tribunal Investigative Judge.

(ii) The President of the Appeals Chamber shall also be the President of the Tribunal and will overview [sic] the administrative and financial aspects of the Tribunal.

d) The Governing Council or the Successor Government, if it deems necessary, can appoint non-Iraqi judges who have experience in the crimes encompassed in this statute, and who shall be persons of high moral character, impartiality and integrity.

PART FOUR Qualification and Selection of the Judges

Article 5.

a) The permanent and reserve judges shall be persons of high moral character, impartiality and integrity who possess the qualifications required for appointment to the highest judicial offices. In the overall composition of the Chambers, due account shall be taken of the experience of the judges in criminal law and trial procedures.

b) Iraqi candidates for permanent and reserve judges in the Trial Chambers need not be serving judges, and could be lawyers and jurists (who should also have the necessary experience and qualifications). Judges in the Appeals Chamber must be serving or former judges.

c) Judges are to be nominated and appointed by the Governing Council or the Successor Government, after consultation with the Judicial Council.

d) The permanent judges of each Trial Chamber shall elect a Presiding Judge from amongst their number, who shall oversee the work of the Trial Chamber as a whole.

e) The permanent and reserve judges shall be appointed for a term of five years. The terms and conditions of service shall be those of the judges of the Iraqi judicial system as set out in the Law Number 160 of 1979 (Judicial Organization Law), save that matters of compensation shall be set by the Governing Council or the Successor Government in light of the increased risks associated with the position.

f) (1) A judge shall be disqualified for any of the following reasons:

i. He or she has a criminal record including a felony unless the felony is a political or false charge made by the Ba'ath Party regime;
ii. He or she has made a material misrepresentation; or
iii. He or she fails to carry out his or her duties without good reason.

(2) The decision to disqualify a judge shall be taken by the majority of permanent judges of the Tribunal after conducting appropriate investigations.

(3) The decision to disqualify the President shall be taken by the Governing Council or the Successor Government.

PART FIVE The Presidency of the Tribunal

Article 6.

a) The President shall:

(1) chair the proceedings of the Appeals Chamber.

(2) assign the judges to particular Trial Chambers;

(3) assign, from time to time, any reserve judges to a Trial Chamber; and

(4) have overall responsibility for the administration of the Tribunal.

b) The President of the Tribunal shall be required to appoint non-Iraqi nationals to act in advisory capacities or as observers to the Trial Chambers and to the Appeals Chamber. The role of the non-Iraqi nationals shall be to provide assistance to the judges with respect to international law and the experience of similar tribunals (whether international or otherwise), and to monitor the protection by the Tribunal of general due process of law standards. In appointing such non-Iraqi experts, the President of the Tribunal shall be entitled to request assistance from the international community, including the United Nations.

c) The non-Iraqi advisors and observers referred to in the above paragraph shall also be persons of high moral character, impartiality and integrity. In this regard, it would be preferable that such non-Iraqi advisor or observer shall have the following experience: (i) such person shall have acted in either a judicial or prosecutorial capacity in his or her respective country, or (ii) such person shall have experience in international war crimes trials or tribunals.

PART SIX Tribunal Investigative Judges

Article 7.

a) The Tribunal Investigative Judges shall be appointed in order to investigate individuals for the commission of crimes stipulated in Articles 11 to 14.

b) Tribunal Investigative Judges are to be nominated and appointed by the Governing Council or the Successor Government, after consultation with the Judicial Council.

c) There shall be up to twenty permanent Tribunal Investigative Judges, and up to ten reserve investigative judges.

d) The permanent and reserve investigative judges shall be persons of high moral character, impartiality and integrity who possess the qualifications required for appointment to the highest judicial offices. In the selection of investigative judges, due account shall be taken of the experience of the judges in criminal law and trial procedures.

e) The Tribunal Investigative Judges shall be headed by a Chief Tribunal Investigative Judge, who shall be chosen by the Tribunal Investigative Judges from among them.

f) The Chief Tribunal Investigative Judge shall assign cases to individual tribunal investigative judges.

g) Each Office of the Tribunal Investigative Judge shall be composed of the Tribunal Investigative Judge and such other qualified staff as may be required.

h) In accordance with Iraqi criminal procedure, each Tribunal Investigative Judge shall have the power to issue subpoenas, arrest warrants and indictments with respect to individuals that they are investigating.

i) Each Tribunal Investigative Judge may gather evidence from whatever source he considers suitable.

j) Each Tribunal Investigative Judge shall act independently as a separate organ of the Tribunal. He or she shall not seek or receive instructions from any Governmental Department, or from any other source, including the Governing Council or the Successor Government.

k) The decisions or orders of the Tribunal Investigative Judge can be appealed to the Appeals Chamber within fifteen days of the notification or deemed notification of the decision.

l) Each Tribunal Investigative Judge shall be appointed for a term of three years. The terms and conditions of service shall be those of the investigative judges of the Iraqi judicial system as set out in Law Number 160 of 1979 (Judicial Organization Law), save that matters of compensation shall be set by the Governing Council or the Successor Government in light of the increased risks associated with the position.

m) (1) Any Tribunal Investigative Judge shall be disqualified for any of the following reasons:

i) He or she has a criminal record including a felony unless the felony is a political or false charge made by the Ba'ath Party regime;

ii) He or she has made a material misrepresentation; or

iii) He or she fails to carry out his or her duties without good reason.

(2) The decision to disqualify a Tribunal Investigative Judge shall be taken by the majority of permanent judges of the Tribunal, after conducting appropriate investigations.

n) The Chief Tribunal Investigative Judge shall be required to appoint non-Iraqi nationals to act in advisory capacities or as observers to the Tribunal Investigative Judges. The role of the non-Iraqi nationals and observers shall be to provide assistance to the Tribunal Investigative Judges with respect to the investigations and prosecution of cases covered by the this Statute (whether in an international context or otherwise), and to monitor the protection by the Tribunal Investigative Judges of general due process of law standards. In appointing such advisors, the Chief Tribunal Investigative Judge shall be entitled to request assistance from the international community, including the United Nations.

o) The non-Iraqi advisors and observers referred to in this Article shall also be persons of high moral character, impartiality and integrity. In this regard, it would be preferable that such non-Iraqi advisor or observer shall have the following experience: (i) such person shall have acted in either a judicial or prosecutorial capacity in his or her respective country, or (ii) such person shall have experience in international war crimes trials or tribunals.

SECTION TWO Other Departments of the Tribunal

PART ONE The Prosecutions Department

Article 8.

a) The Prosecutions Department shall be responsible for the prosecution of persons responsible for crimes within the jurisdiction of the Tribunal.

b) Each Prosecutor shall act independently. He or she shall not seek or receive instructions from any Governmental Department or from any other source, including the Governing Council or the Successor Government.

c) The Prosecutions Department shall consist of up to twenty Prosecutors.

d) Prosecutors are to be nominated and appointed by the Governing Council or the Successor Government after consultation with the Judicial Council.

e) The Prosecution Department shall be headed by a Chief Prosecutor, who shall be selected from among the Prosecutors.

f) (1) A prosecutor shall be disqualified for any of the following reasons:

i) He or she has a criminal record including a felony unless the felony is a political or false charge made by the Ba'ath Party regime;

ii) He or she has made a material misrepresentation; or

iii) He or she fails to carry out his or her duties without good reason.

(2) The decision to disqualify a Prosecutor shall be taken by the Chief Prosecutor, after conducting appropriate investigations.

g) Each Office of the Prosecutor shall be composed of a Prosecutor and such other qualified staff as may be required.

h) The Chief Prosecutor shall assign individual cases to a Prosecutor. Such Prosecutor shall have the right to be involved in the investigative stages of a case and shall be the individual who prosecutes such case, consistent with the powers granted to prosecutors pursuant to Law Number 23 of 1971 (Iraqi Criminal Procedure Law).

i) Each Prosecutor shall be appointed for a term of three years. The terms and conditions of service shall be those of prosecutors of the Iraqi judicial system as set out in Law Number 159 of 1979 (The Law of Prosecutors), save that matters of compensation shall be set by the Governing Council or the Successor Government.

j) The Chief Prosecutor shall be required to appoint non-Iraqi nationals to act in advisory capacities or as observers to the prosecutors. The role of the non-Iraqi nationals and observers shall be to provide assistance to the prosecutors of the Tribunal with respect to the investigations and prosecution of cases covered by this Statute (whether in an international context or otherwise), and to monitor the performance of the Prosecutor. In appointing such advisors, the Chief Prosecutor shall be entitled to request assistance from the international community, including the United Nations.

k) The non-Iraqi advisors and observers referred to in this Article shall also be persons of high moral character, impartiality and integrity. In this regard, it would be preferable that such non-Iraqi advisor or observer shall have the following experience: (i) such person shall have acted in a prosecutorial capacity in his or her respective country, or (ii) such person shall have experience in international war crimes trials or tribunals.

PART TWO The Administration Department

Article 9.

a) The Administration Department shall consist of a Director of the Administration Department and such other staff as may be required.

b) The Administration Department shall be responsible for the administration and servicing of the Tribunal and the Prosecutions Department.

c) The Director of the Administration Department shall initially be appointed by the Governing Council or the Successor Government. He or she shall serve for a three year term and be eligible for reappointment. The terms and conditions of service of the Director of the Administration Department shall be those of a General Director in an Iraqi government department.

d) The staff of the Administration Department shall be appointed by the Director of the Administration Department.

e) The Director of the Administration Department shall appoint a public relations expert to the position of spokesman of the Tribunal. Such spokesman shall give regular briefings to the press and the public at large with respect to the developments relating to the Tribunal.

SECTION THREE Jurisdiction and Crimes

PART ONE Jurisdiction of the Tribunal

Article 10.

The Tribunal shall have jurisdiction over any Iraqi national or resident of Iraq accused of the crimes listed in Articles 11-14, committed since July 17, 1968 and up and until May 1, 2003, in the territory of Iraq or elsewhere, namely:

a) The crime of genocide;
b) Crimes against humanity;
c) War crimes; or
d) Violations of certain Iraqi laws listed in Article 14 below.

PART TWO The Crime of Genocide

Article 11.

a) For the purposes of this Statute and in accordance with the Convention on the Prevention and Punishment of the Crime of Genocide, dated December 9, 1948, as ratified by Iraq on January 20, 1959, 'genocide' means any of the following acts committed with intent to destroy, in whole or in part, a national, ethnical, racial or religious group, as such:

1. killing members of the group;
2. causing serious bodily or mental harm to members of the group;
3. deliberately inflicting on the group conditions of life calculated to bring about its physical destruction in whole or in part;
4. imposing measures intended to prevent births within the group; and
5. forcibly transferring children of the group to another group.

b) The following acts shall be punishable:

1. genocide;
2. conspiracy to commit genocide;
3. direct and public incitement to commit genocide;
4. attempt to commit genocide; and
5. complicity in genocide.

PART THREE Crimes Against Humanity

Article 12.

a) For the purposes of this Statute, 'crimes against humanity' means any of the following acts when committed as part of a widespread or systematic attack directed against any civilian population, with knowledge of the attack:

1. Murder;
2. Extermination;
3. Enslavement;
4. Deportation or forcible transfer of population;
5. Imprisonment or other severe deprivation of physical liberty in violation of fundamental norms of international law;
6. Torture;
7. Rape, sexual slavery, enforced prostitution, forced pregnancy, or any other form of sexual violence of comparable gravity;
8. Persecution against any identifiable group or collectivity on political, racial, national, ethnic, cultural, religious, gender or other grounds that are universally recognized as impermissible under international law, in connection with any act referred to in this paragraph or any crime within the jurisdiction of the Tribunal;
9. Enforced disappearance of persons; and
10. Other inhumane acts of a similar character intentionally causing great suffering, or serious injury to body or to mental or physical health.

b) For the purposes of paragraph a):

1. 'Attack directed against any civilian population' means a course of conduct involving the multiple commission of acts referred to in the above paragraph against any civilian population, pursuant to or in furtherance of a state or organizational policy to commit such attack;
2. 'Extermination' includes the intentional infliction of conditions of life, such as the deprivation of access to food and medicine, calculated to bring about the destruction of part of a population;
3. 'Enslavement' means the exercise of any or all of the powers attaching to the right of ownership over a person and includes the exercise of such power in the course of trafficking in persons, in particular women and children;
4. 'Deportation or forcible transfer of population' means forced displacement of the persons concerned by expulsion or other coercive acts from the area in which they are lawfully present, without grounds permitted under international law;
5. 'Torture' means the intentional infliction of severe pain or suffering, whether physical or mental, upon a person in the custody or under the control of the accused; except that torture shall not include pain or suffering arising only from, inherent in, or incidental to lawful sanctions;
6. 'Persecution' means the intentional and severe deprivation of fundamental rights contrary to international law by reason of the identity of the group or collectivity; and
7. 'Enforced disappearance of persons' means the arrest, detention or abduction of persons by, or with the authorization, support or acquiescence of, the State or a political organization, followed by a refusal to acknowledge that deprivation of freedom or to give information on the fate or whereabouts of those persons, with the intention of removing them from the protection of the law for a prolonged period of time.

PART FOUR War Crimes

Article 13.

For the purposes of this Statute, 'war crimes' means:

a) Grave breaches of the Geneva Conventions of 12 August 1949, namely, any of the following acts against persons or property protected under the provisions of the relevant Geneva Convention:

1. Willful killing;
2. Torture or inhuman treatment, including biological experiments;
3. Willfully causing great suffering, or serious injury to body or health;
4. Extensive destruction and appropriation of property, not justified by military necessity and carried out unlawfully and wantonly;
5. Willfully denying the right of a fair trial to a prisoner of war or other protected person;
6. Compelling a prisoner of war or other protected person to serve in the forces of a hostile power;
7. Unlawful confinement;
8. Unlawful deportation or transfer; and
9. Taking of hostages.

b) Other serious violations of the laws and customs applicable in international armed conflict, within the established framework of international law, namely, any of the following acts:

1. Intentionally directing attacks against the civilian population as such or against individual civilians not taking direct part in hostilities;
2. Intentionally directing attacks against civilians objects, that is, objects which are not military objectives;
3. Intentionally directing attacks against personnel, installations, material, units or vehicles involved in a peacekeeping mission in accordance with the Charter of the United Nations or in a humanitarian assistance mission, as long as they are entitled to the protection given to civilians or civilian objects under the international law of armed conflict;
4. Intentionally launching an attack in the knowledge that such attack will cause incidental loss of life or injury to civilians or damage to civilian objects which would be clearly excessive in relation to the concrete and direct overall military advantage anticipated;
5. Intentionally launching an attack in the knowledge that such attack will cause widespread, long-term and severe damage to the natural environment which would be clearly excessive in relation to the concrete and direct overall military advantage anticipated;
6. Attacking or bombarding, by whatever means, towns, villages, dwellings or buildings which are undefended and which are not military objectives;
7. Killing or wounding a combatant who, having laid down his arms or having no longer means of defense, has surrendered at discretion;
8. Making improper use of a flag of truce, of the flag or of the military insignia and uniform of the enemy or of the United Nations, as well as of the distinctive emblems of the Geneva Conventions, resulting in death or serious personal injury;
9. The transfer, directly or indirectly, by the Government of Iraq or any of its instrumentalities (including by an instrumentality of the Arab Socialist Ba'ath Party), of parts of its own civilian population into any territory it occupies, or the deportation or transfer of all or parts of the population of the occupied territory within or outside this territory;

10. Intentionally directing attacks against buildings that are dedicated to religion, education, art, science or charitable purposes, historic monuments, hospitals and places where the sick and wounded are collected, provided they are not military objectives;
11. Subjecting persons of another nation to physical mutilation or to medical or scientific experiments of any kind that are neither justified by the medical, dental or hospital treatment of the person concerned nor carried out in his or her interest, and which cause death to or seriously endanger the health of such person or persons;
12. Killing or wounding treacherously individuals belonging to the hostile nation or army;
13. Declaring that no quarter will be given;
14. Destroying or seizing the property of an adverse party unless such destruction or seizure be imperatively demanded by the necessities of war;
15. Declaring abolished, suspended or inadmissible in a court of law, or otherwise depriving, the rights and actions of the nationals of the adverse party;
16. Compelling the nationals of the hostile party to take part in the operations of war directed against their own country, even if they were in the belligerent's service before the commencement of the war;
17. Pillaging a town or place, even when taken by assault;
18. Employing poison or poisoned weapons;
19. Employing asphyxiating, poisonous or other gases, and all analogous liquids, materials or devices;
20. Employing bullets which expand or flatten easily in the human body, such as bullets with a hard envelope which does not entirely cover the core or is pierced with incisions;
21. Committing outrages upon personal dignity, in particular humiliating and degrading treatment;
22. Committing rape, sexual slavery, enforced prostitution, forced pregnancy, or any other form of sexual violence of comparable gravity;
23. Utilizing the presence of a civilian or other protected person to render certain points, areas or military forces immune from military operations;
24. Intentionally directing attacks against buildings, material, medical units and transport, and personnel using the distinctive emblems of the Geneva Conventions in conformity with international law;
25. Intentionally using starvation of civilians as a method of warfare by depriving them of objects indispensable to their survival, including willfully impeding relief supplies as provided for under international law; and
26. Conscripting or enlisting children under the age of fifteen years into the national armed forces or using them to participate actively in hostilities.

c) In the case of an armed conflict, any of the following acts committed against persons taking no active part in the hostilities, including members of armed forces who have laid down their arms and those placed *hors de combat* by sickness, wounds, detention or any other cause:

1. Violence to life and person, in particular murder of all kinds, mutilation, cruel treatment and torture;
2. Committing outrages upon personal dignity, in particular humiliating and degrading treatment;

3. Taking of hostages; and
4. The passing of sentences and the carrying out of executions without previous judgment pronounced by a regularly constituted court, affording all judicial guarantees which are generally recognized as indispensable.

d) Serious violations of the laws and customs of war applicable in armed conflict not of an international character, within the established framework of international law, namely, any of the following acts:

1. Intentionally directing attacks against the civilian population as such or against individual civilians not taking direct part in hostilities;
2. Intentionally directing attacks against buildings, material, medical units and transport, and personnel using the distinctive emblems of the Geneva Conventions in conformity with international law;
3. Intentionally directing attacks against personnel, installations, material, units, or vehicles involved in a peacekeeping mission in accordance with the Charter of the United Nations or in a humanitarian assistance mission, as long as they are entitled to the protection given to civilians or civilian objects under the international law of armed conflict;
4. Intentionally directing attacks against buildings that are dedicated to religion, education, art, science, or charitable purposes, historic monuments, hospitals and places where the sick and wounded are collected, provided they are not military objectives;
5. Pillaging a town or place, even when taken by assault;
6. Committing rape, sexual slavery, enforced prostitution, forced pregnancy, or any other form of sexual violence of comparable gravity;
7. Conscripting or enlisting children under the age of fifteen years into armed forces or groups or using them to participate actively in hostilities;
8. Ordering the displacement of the civilian population for reasons related to the conflict, unless the security of the civilians involved or imperative military reasons so demand;
9. Killing or wounding treacherously a combatant adversary;
10. Declaring that no quarter will be given;
11. Subjecting persons who are in the power of another party to the conflict to physical mutilation or to medical or scientific experiments of any kind that are neither justified by the medical, dental or hospital treatment of the person concerned nor carried out in his or her interest, and which cause death to or seriously endanger the health of such person or persons; and
12. Destroying or seizing the property of an adversary, unless such destruction or seizure be imperatively demanded by the necessities of the conflict.

PART FIVE Violations of Stipulated Iraqi Laws

Article 14.

The Tribunal shall have the power to prosecute persons who have committed the following crimes under Iraqi law:

a) For those outside the judiciary, the attempt to manipulate the judiciary or involvement in the functions of the judiciary, in violation, *inter alia*, of the Iraqi interim constitution of 1970, as amended;

b) The wastage of national resources and the squandering of public assets and funds, pursuant to, *inter alia*, Article 2(g) of Law Number 7 of 1958, as amended; and
c) The abuse of position and the pursuit of policies that may lead to the threat of war or the use of the armed forces of Iraq against an Arab country, in accordance with Article 1 of Law Number 7 of 1958, as amended.

SECTION FOUR Individual Criminal Responsibility

Article 15.

a) A person who commits a crime within the jurisdiction of this Tribunal shall be individually responsible and liable for punishment in accordance with this Statute.

b) In accordance with this Statute, and the provisions of Iraqi criminal law, a person shall be criminally responsible and liable for punishment for a crime within the jurisdiction of the Tribunal if that person:

1. Commits such a crime, whether as an individual, jointly with another or through another person, regardless of whether that other person is criminally responsible;
2. Orders, solicits or induces the commission of such a crime which in fact occurs or is attempted;
3. For the purpose of facilitating the commission of such a crime, aids, abets or otherwise assists in its commission or its attempted commission, including providing the means for its commission;
4. In any other way contributes to the commission or attempted commission of such a crime by a group of persons acting with a common purpose. Such contribution shall be intentional and shall either:
   i. Be made with the aim of furthering the criminal activity or criminal purpose of the group, where such activity or purpose involves the commission of a crime within the jurisdiction of the Tribunal; or
   ii. Be made in the knowledge of the intention of the group to commit the crime;
5. In respect of the crime of genocide, directly and publicly incites others to commit genocide;
6. Attempts to commit such a crime by taking action that commences its execution by means of a substantial step, but the crime does not occur because of circumstances independent of the person's intentions. However, a person who abandons the effort to commit the crime or otherwise prevents the completion of the crime shall not be liable for punishment under this Statute for the attempt to commit that crime if that person completely and voluntarily gave up the criminal purpose.

c) The official position of any accused person, whether as president, prime minister, member of the cabinet, chairman or a member of the Revolutionary Command Council, a member of the Arab Socialist Ba'ath Party Regional Command or Government (or an instrumentality of either) or as a responsible Iraqi Government official or member of the Ba'ath Party or in any other capacity, shall not relieve such person of criminal responsibility nor mitigate punishment. No person is entitled to any immunity with respect to any of the crimes stipulated in Articles 11 to 14.

d) The fact that any of the acts referred to in Articles 11 to 14 of the present Statute was committed by a subordinate does not relieve his superior of criminal responsibility if he knew or had reason to know that the subordinate was about to commit such acts or had done so and the superior failed to take the necessary and reasonable measures to prevent such acts or to submit the matter to the competent authorities for investigation and prosecution.

e) The fact that an accused person acted pursuant to an order of a Government or of a superior shall not relieve him of criminal responsibility, but may be considered in mitigation of punishment if the Tribunal determines that justice so requires.

SECTION FIVE Rules of Procedure and Evidence

Article 16.
The President of the Tribunal shall draft rules of procedure and evidence for the conduct of the pre-trial phase of the proceedings, trials and appeals, the admission of evidence, the protection of victims and witnesses and other appropriate matters (including regulations with respect to the disqualification of judges or prosecutors), where the applicable law, including this Statute does not, or does not adequately provide for a specific situation. He shall be guided by the Iraqi Criminal Procedure Law. Such rules shall be adopted by a majority of the permanent judges of the Tribunal.

SECTION SIX General Principles of Criminal Law

Article 17.
a) Subject to the provisions of this Statute and the rules made thereunder, the general principles of criminal law applicable in connection with the prosecution and trial of any accused person shall be those contained: (i) in Iraqi criminal law as at July 17, 1968 (as embodied in The Baghdadi Criminal Code of 1919) for those offenses committed between July 17, 1968 and December 14, 1969; (ii) in Law Number 111 of 1969 (the Iraqi Criminal Code), as it was as of December 15, 1969, without regard to any amendments made thereafter, for those offenses committed between December 15, 1969 and May 1, 2003; and (iii) and in Law Number 23 of 1971 (the Iraqi Criminal Procedure Law).

b) In interpreting Articles 11 to 13, the Trial Chambers and the Appellate Chamber may resort to the relevant decisions of international courts or tribunals as persuasive authority for their decisions.

c) Grounds for exclusion of criminal responsibility under the said Iraqi Criminal Code shall be interpreted in a manner consistent with the Statute and with international legal obligations concerning the crimes within the jurisdiction of the Tribunal.

d) The crimes stipulated in Articles 11 to 14 shall not be subject to any statute of limitations.

SECTION SEVEN Investigations and Indictment

Article 18.
a) The Tribunal Investigative Judge shall initiate investigations *ex-officio* or on the basis of information obtained from any source, particularly from the police, and governmental and non-governmental organizations. The Tribunal Investigative Judge shall assess the information received or obtained and decide whether there is sufficient basis to proceed.

b) The Tribunal Investigative Judge shall have the power to question suspects, victims and witnesses, to collect evidence and to conduct on-site investigations. In carrying out these tasks, the Tribunal Investigative Judge may, as appropriate, request the assistance of the relevant governmental authorities concerned, who shall be required to provide full co-operation with the request.

c) If questioned by a Tribunal Investigative Judge, the suspect shall be entitled to be assisted by counsel of his or her own choice, including the right to have legal assistance assigned to him or her without payment by him or her in any such case if he or she does not have sufficient means to pay for it. The suspect is entitled to have non-Iraqi legal representation, so long as the principal lawyer of such suspect is Iraqi.

d) Upon a determination that a *prima facie* case exists, the Tribunal Investigative Judge shall prepare an indictment containing a concise statement of the facts and the crime or crimes with which the accused is charged under the Statute.

PART ONE Review of Indictment

Article 19.

a) If the Chief Tribunal Investigative Judge is satisfied that a *prima facie* case has been established by the Tribunal Investigative Judge, then he/she shall confirm the indictment. If not so satisfied, the indictment shall be dismissed without prejudice.

b) Upon confirmation of an indictment, the Tribunal Investigative Judge may, at the request of the Chief Tribunal Investigative Judge, issue such orders and warrants for the arrest, detention, surrender or transfer of persons, and any other orders as may be required for the conduct of the trial.

PART TWO Rights of the Accused

Article 20.

a) All persons shall be equal before the Tribunal.

b) Everyone shall be presumed innocent until proven guilty before the Tribunal in accordance with the law.

c) In the determination of any charge, the accused shall be entitled to a public hearing, having regard to the provisions of the Statute and the rules of procedure made hereunder.

d) In the determination of any charge against the accused pursuant to the present Statute, the accused shall be entitled to a fair hearing conducted impartially and to the following minimum guarantees:

1. to be informed promptly and in detail of the nature, cause and content of the charge against him;
2. to have adequate time and facilities for the preparation of his defense and to communicate freely with counsel of his own choosing in confidence. The accused is entitled to have non-Iraqi legal representation, so long as the principal lawyer of such accused is Iraqi;
3. to be tried without undue delay;
4. to be tried in his presence, and to defend himself in person or through legal assistance of his own choosing; to be informed, if he does not have legal assistance, of this right; and to have legal assistance assigned to him, in any case where the interests of justice so require, and without payment by him in any such case if he does not have sufficient means to pay for it;
5. to examine, or have examined, the witnesses against him and to obtain the attendance and examination of witnesses on his behalf under the same conditions as witnesses against him. The accused shall also be entitled to raise defences and to present other evidence admissible under this Statute and Iraqi law; and

6. not to be compelled to testify against himself or to confess guilt, and to remain silent, without such silence being a consideration in the determination of guilt or innocence.

SECTION EIGHT Trial Proceedings

Article 21.

a) A person against whom an indictment has been issued shall, pursuant to an order or an arrest warrant of the Tribunal Investigative Judge, be taken into custody, immediately informed of the charges against him and transferred to the Tribunal.

b) The Trial Chambers shall ensure that a trial is fair and expeditious and that proceedings are conducted in accordance with this Statute and the rules of procedure and evidence, with full respect for the rights of the accused and due regard for the protection of victims and witnesses.

c) The Trial Chamber shall read the indictment, satisfy itself that the rights of the accused are respected, confirm that the accused understands the indictment, and instruct the accused to enter a plea.

d) The hearings shall be public unless the Trial Chamber decides to close the proceedings in accordance with its rules of procedure and evidence. The decision to close the proceedings shall be exercised on a very limited basis.

Article 22.

The Tribunal shall, in its rules of procedure and evidence, provide for the protection of victims and witnesses. Such protection measures shall take into account the rights of the accused and shall include, but shall not be limited to, the conduct of *in camera* proceedings and the protection of the identity of the victim or witness.

Article 23.

a) The Trial Chambers shall pronounce judgments and impose sentences and penalties on persons convicted of crimes within the jurisdiction of the Tribunal.

b) The judgment shall be rendered by a simple majority of the judges of the Trial Chamber, and shall be delivered by the Trial Chamber in public. It shall be accompanied by a reasoned opinion in writing, to which separate or dissenting opinions may be appended.

Article 24.

a) The penalties that shall be imposed by the Tribunal shall be those prescribed by Iraqi law (especially Law Number 111 of 1969 of the Iraqi Criminal Code), save that for the purposes of this Tribunal, sentences of life imprisonment shall mean the remaining natural life of the person.

b) Subject to paragraph a) above, the penalties for crimes under Article 14 shall be those prescribed under the relevant provisions of Iraqi law.

c) The penalty for crimes under Articles 11 to 13 shall be determined by the Trial Chambers, taking into account the factors contained in paragraph d) and e) below.

d) A person convicted of:

1. An offence involving murder or rape as defined under Iraqi law; or
2. An offence ancillary to such offence of murder or rape, shall be dealt with as for an offence of, as the case may be, murder or rape or the corresponding ancillary offences in relation to murder or rape.

e) The penalty for any crimes under Articles 11 to 13 which do not have a counterpart under Iraqi law shall be determined by the Trial Chambers taking into account such factors as the gravity of the crime, the individual circumstances of the convicted person and relevant international precedents.

f) The Trial Chambers may order the forfeiture of proceeds, property or assets derived directly or indirectly from that crime, without prejudice to the rights of the *bona fide* third parties.

g) In accordance with Article 307 of the Iraqi Criminal Procedure Code, the Tribunal has authority to confiscate any goods prohibited by law regardless of whether the case has been discharged for any lawful reason.

SECTION NINE Review and Appeals Proceedings

PART ONE Appellate Proceedings

Article 25.

a) The Appeals Chamber shall hear appeals from persons convicted by the Trial Chambers or from the Prosecutor on the following grounds:

1. an error on a question of law invalidating any decision;
2. an error of procedure; or
3. an error of material fact which has occasioned a miscarriage of justice.

b) The Appeals Chamber may affirm, reverse or revise the decisions taken by the Trial Chambers.

c) Where a verdict of acquittal is reversed by the Appeals Chamber, the case shall be referred back to a Trial Chamber for retrial.

PART TWO Review Proceedings

Article 26.

a) Where a new fact has been discovered which was not known at the time of the proceedings before the Trial Chambers or the Appeals Chamber and which could have been a decisive factor in reaching the decision, the convicted person or the Prosecutor may submit to the Tribunal an application for review of the judgment.

b) The Appeals Chamber shall reject the application if it considers it to be unfounded. If it determines that the application has merit, it may, as appropriate:

1. Reconvene the original Trial Chamber;
2. Constitute a new Trial Chamber; or
3. Retain jurisdiction over the matter, with a view to, after hearing the parties, arriving at a determination on whether the judgment should be revised.

SECTION TEN Enforcement of Sentences

Article 27.

Sentences shall be carried out by the legal system of Iraq in accordance with its laws.

SECTION ELEVEN General Principles and Other Matters

Article 28.

The judges, investigative judges, prosecutors and the Director of the Administration Department shall be Iraqi nationals, except as provided for in Article 4(d).

Article 29.

a) The Tribunal and the national courts of Iraq shall have concurrent jurisdiction to prosecute persons for those offences prescribed in Article 14 that fall within the jurisdiction of the Tribunal.

b) The Tribunal shall have primacy over all other Iraqi courts with respect to the crimes stipulated in Articles 11 to 13.

c) At any stage of the procedure, the Tribunal may demand of any other Iraqi court to transfer any case being tried by it involving any crimes stipulated in Articles 11 to 14 to the Tribunal, and such court shall be required to transfer such case.

Article 30.

a) No person shall be tried before any other Iraqi court for acts for which he or she has already been tried by the Tribunal, in accordance with Articles 300 and 301 of the Iraqi Criminal Procedure Code.

b) A person who has been tried by any Iraqi court for acts constituting crimes within the jurisdiction of the Tribunal may be subsequently tried by the Tribunal only if the Tribunal determines that the previous court proceedings were not impartial or independent, were designed to shield the accused from international or Iraqi criminal responsibility, or the case was not diligently prosecuted, provided that the requirements of Article 303 of the Iraqi Criminal Procedure Code are met or one of the conditions contained in Article 196 of the Iraqi Civil Procedure Code apply.

c) In considering the penalty to be imposed on a person convicted of a crime under the present Statute, the Tribunal shall take into account the extent to which any penalty imposed by an Iraqi court on the same person for the same act has already been served.

Article 31.

a) The Tribunal, the judges, the Tribunal Investigative Judges, the Prosecutors, the Director of the Administration Department and their staffs shall have immunity from civil suits for their official acts.

b) Other persons, including the accused, required at the seat of the Tribunal shall be accorded such treatment as is necessary for the proper functioning of the Tribunal.

Article 32.

For purposes of this statute, the 'Governing Council' shall mean the Governing Council of Iraq established on July 13, 2003. The powers conferred on the Governing Council in this Statute shall be transferred to the executive authority in any future government (the 'Successor Government') established following the disbanding of the Governing Council.

Article 33.

No officer, prosecutor, investigative judge, judge or other personnel of the Tribunal shall have been a member of the Ba'ath Party.

Article 34.
Arabic shall be the official language of the Tribunal.

Article 35.
The expenses of the Tribunal shall be borne by the regular budget of the Government of Iraq.

Article 36.
The President of the Tribunal shall submit an annual report of the Tribunal to the Governing Council or the Successor Government.

Article 37.
The Governing Council or the Successor Government has the powers to establish other rules and procedures in order to implement this Statute.

Article 38.
This law shall become effective on the 10th day of December, 2003 and shall be published in the Official Gazette.[152]

Document 71
Coalition Provisional Authority Order Number 49
CPA/ORD/19 February 2004/49

Tax Strategy of 2004

Pursuant to my authority as Administrator of the Coalition Provisional Authority (CPA), and under the laws and usages of war, and consistent with relevant U.N. Security Council resolutions, including Resolutions 1483 and 1511 (2003),

Noting the suspension by CPA Order Number 37[153] of all income tax for assessed income resources detailed in Article 2 of Income Tax Law Number 113 of 1982 and the real property rent tax of Law Number 162 of 1959 as amended, and all other taxes not specifically identified in Order 37 as continuing in force from April 16, 2003, to the end of calendar year 2003 and the reinstatement of these taxes on April 1, 2004, including the reinstatement of the income tax at the lower maximum rate of 15 percent,

Noting the desire of the Governing Council to subject both private and public sector employees to tax in order to ensure that the tax burden is shared by all sectors of Iraqi society,

[152] Iraqi Governing Council Law No. 1 of 10 December 2003 ('The Statute of the Iraqi Special Tribunal') was revoked by Law No. 10 of 9 October 2005 ('Law of The Iraqi Higher Criminal Court' or 'Law of the Iraqi High Tribunal'), *Al-Waqai Al-Iraqiya*, vol. 47, no. 4006 (18 October 2005). The Special Tribunal was replaced by a Higher Criminal Court which was to be incorporated in the regular federal court system. The new law does not address a number of human rights concerns that existed with regard to the previous Tribunal, such as the lack of transparency in proceedings, application of the death penalty, and the rights of the accused. On the legality of the Iraqi High Tribunal, see the judgment of the nine-member Iraqi High Tribunal Appellate Chamber in the *Dujail Trial* (Case No 29/c/2006), 26 December 2006, pp. 8-9 (unofficial English translation).

[153] See *Doc 58*.

Recognizing that these revenues are for the benefit of the Iraqi people, and

Determined to create conditions suited to the economic reconstruction of Iraq, including an efficient and modern income tax system,

I hereby promulgate the following:

Section 1 Purpose

The purpose of this Order is to revise the tax rates and tax exemptions of Income Tax Law Number 113 of 1982, and the Real Estate Rent Tax Law Number 162 of 1959, to provide certain additional exemptions from tax, to suspend certain taxes, and to provide rules for applying unused losses against income from the same source earned in future years ('carrying forward losses') in light of the suspension of income taxes for financial year 2003 and for the first three months of financial year 2004.

Section 2 Increase in Allowances

1) Item (1) of Article 12 of Income Tax Law Number 113 of 1982 is amended to read as follows:

'(1) A resident person shall be granted the following allowances per each year of assessment on the basis of his or her status in the year in which the income has arisen:

a) ID 2,500,000 for the taxpayer himself (or herself, if she is unmarried (other than a widow or divorcee) or if her income is not added to her husband's income), and ID 2,000,000 for his wife, or wives, if she is a housewife and has no income or if her income is added to his income.

b) ID 200,000 for each of his children irrespective of their number.

c) ID 3,200,000 for the widow or divorcee herself and ID 200,000 for every child lawfully maintained by her, regardless of the number.'

2) Item (5) of Article 12 of Income Tax Law Number 113 of 1982 is amended to read as follows:

'(5) The taxpayer shall be granted an additional allowance of ID 300,000 if his age is more than 63 years of age, in addition to allowances granted to him in other sections of this Article.'

3) The allowances as set forth in paragraphs (1) and (2) of this section shall be reduced by one-fourth during financial year 2004.[154]

Section 3 Reduction in Income Tax Rates

1) Item (1) of Article 13 of Income Tax Law Number 113 of 1982 is amended to read as follows:

'(1) Tax shall be imposed on the taxpayer in respect of each year of assessment at the following rates:

(A) Income of resident individual after granting the allowance(s) provided for in Article 12 as modified by this Order:

At the rate of 3% on amounts up to ID 250,000.

At the rate of 5% on amounts over ID 250,000 and up to ID 500,000.

At the rate of 10% on amounts over ID 500,000 and up to ID 1,000,000.

At the rate of 15% on amounts over ID 1,000,000.

[154] Sec 2(3) was amended by CPA Order No 84, sec 3(1) *[Doc 108]*. A new sec 2(4) was added by CPA Order No 84, sec 3(2) *[Doc 108]*.

(B) Income of non-resident individual (other than the income provided for in Article 19 of this Law).
At the rate of 3% on amounts up to ID 250,000.
At the rate of 5% on amounts over ID 250,000 and up to ID 500,000.
At the rate of 10% on amounts over ID 500,000 and up to ID 1,000,000.
At the rate of 15% on amounts over ID 1,000,000.
(C) Income of limited liability companies, at a fixed rate of 15%.
(D) Income of private joint-stock companies, at a fixed rate of 15%.
(E) Income of mixed joint-stock companies, at a fixed rate of 15%.
(F) The amounts delineating the tax brackets as set forth in paragraphs (A) and (B) shall be reduced by one-fourth for financial year 2004.'[155]

2) Item (2) of Article 13 of Income Tax Law Number 113 of 1982 is amended to read as follows:

'(2) Iraqi nonresident individuals shall be subject to tax at the rates for Iraqi residents set forth in Section 3(1) of this Order on their income from Iraqi sources.'

3) Foreign companies that are registered in Iraq or otherwise have a permanent establishment in Iraq will be subject to tax at a fixed rate of 15% on their income in Iraq.[156]

Section 4 Exemptions

1) The CPA, Coalition Forces, forces of countries acting in coordination with Coalition Forces, and departments and agencies of Coalition Forces' governments, are not liable for any tax or similar charge within the territory of Iraq.

2) Governments and international organizations are not liable for any tax or similar charge within the territory of Iraq.

3) Foreign (non-Iraqi) employees and foreign (non-Iraqi) contractors and subcontractors of the CPA, Coalition Forces, forces of countries acting in coordination with Coalition Forces, and departments and agencies of Coalition Forces' governments, that are providing technical, financial, logistical, administrative or other assistance to Iraq, and foreign employees of such contractors and subcontractors, shall not be liable to pay any tax on income or similar charge within the territory of Iraq on income from foreign sources or on income from or paid on behalf of the CPA, Coalition Forces, forces of countries acting in coordination with Coalition Forces, or departments or agencies of the governments of Coalition Forces.

4) Foreign (non-Iraqi) employees and foreign (non-Iraqi) contractors and subcontractors of foreign (non-Iraqi) governments, international organizations, and non-governmental organizations registered pursuant to CPA Order Number 45, that are providing technical, financial, logistical, administrative or other assistance to Iraq, and foreign employees of such contractors and subcontractors, shall not be liable to pay any tax on income or similar charge within the territory of Iraq on income from foreign sources or on income from or paid on behalf of such governments, international organizations, and non-governmental organizations.

5) In addition to the foregoing, the following persons shall be exempt from payment of income tax:

a) members of foreign diplomatic missions to Iraq, as well as members of their households, if they are not citizens of Iraq;
b) members of consular offices, as well as members of their households, if they are not citizens of Iraq;

[155] Sec 3(1) was amended by CPA Order No 84, sec 3(3) *[Doc 108]*.
[156] A new sec 3(4) was added by CPA Order No 84, sec 3(4) *[Doc 108]*.

c) honorary consuls of foreign countries, but only for income received from the country that has appointed them honorary consul.

6) In accordance with administrative guidance to be issued by the Ministry of Finance, non-governmental organizations registered pursuant to CPA Order Number 45 and nonprofit organizations that are not required to register as non-governmental organizations that are not engaged in political activities are not liable for tax on income or similar charge within the territory of Iraq.

Section 5 Losses

Article 11 of Income Tax Number 113 of 1982 is amended by adding new Items (3), (4) and (5) to read as follows:

'(3) Income from financial year 2003 and for the first three months of financial year 2004 shall not be taken into consideration in determining the income against which losses from preceding financial years may be deducted under this article.

(4) Financial year 2003 shall not be taken into account in determining the 5 consecutive years to which losses may be carried under this article.

(5) Losses incurred in financial year 2003 and in the first three months of financial year 2004 may not be carried forward under this article.'

Section 6 Reduction in Real Estate Rental Rates

The Law of the Real Estate Tax Number 162 for the year 1959 and its modifications ('the Law of Real Estate Tax') is amended as follows:

(1) Item (1) of Article 2 of the Law of Real Estate Taxis amended to read as follows:

'(1) A tax is assessed and collected that is 10% of the annual revenue from all real estate including the subject's living share from the real estate (other than income from sales of real estate).'

(2) Item (2) of Article 2 of the Law is deleted and Item (3) of the Law of Real Estate Tax is renumbered to Item (2).

(3) Item 1 of Article Twenty-One of the Law of Real Estate Tax is amended to read as follows:

'The tax is to be collected in two equal parts; the first is due the first of January of the financial year and the second is due the first of July of the financial year. For financial year 2004, the tax will be paid in one part and is due on 1 July 2004. The subject has the right to pay this tax at the location of his residence, his work location or in the governorate where the majority of his real estate is located. All revenue shall be combined. A memo setting forth the calculation and form should be submitted with the payment.'

(4) Item 2 of Article Twenty-One of the Law of Real Estate Tax is deleted.

(5) Item 1(b) of Article Twenty-Two of the Law of Real Estate Tax is deleted and item 1(c) is renumbered item 1(b).

(6) Article Twenty-three of the Law of Real Estate Tax is amended to read as follows:

'The tax is collected according to the Law of Governmental Secured Debt Collection and is considered a secured debt on the subject real estate.'

Section 7 Suspension of 25% Levy on Company Profits

1) Law No. 101 of 1964 Regulating the Disposal of Company Profits is hereby suspended.

2) Law No. 9 of 1998 Amending Law No. 101 of 1964 is hereby suspended.

Section 8 Suspension of Certain Taxes Until March 31, 2004

The following taxes are suspended from January 1, 2004, until March 31, 2004:

1) All income tax for assessed income resources detailed in Article 2 of Income Tax Law Number 113 of 1982, as amended; and[157]

2) Real Property rent tax in accordance with Law Number 162 of 1959, as amended.

3) Other taxes not specifically identified, but that were suspended by CPA Order Number 37 (Tax Strategy for 2003).

4) The following specified taxes are not suspended and shall continue in force:

a) Excellent and first class hotel and restaurant tax in accordance with Resolution Number 36 of 1997;

b) Tax upon the transfer of real property in accordance with Resolution Number 120 of 2002;

c) Car sale fee in accordance with Resolution Number 80 of 1998 and previous relevant laws in force;

d) Petrol excise duties including, but not limited to, those provided for in Law Number 9 of 1939, Resolution Number 82 of 1996 and the Order Number 66 of 1999 issued by the Economic Affairs Committee.

5) The persons and entities listed in Order 37, paragraph 3(2), shall continue to be exempt from the taxes specified in paragraph 8(4), above after March 31, 2004.

Section 9 Depreciation

The System of Depreciation and Elimination for Private, Mixed and Cooperative Sectors Regulation No. 9 of 1994 is modified as follows:

1) Item (3) of Article 3 is modified by adding the following sentence at the end thereof: 'No part of book value shall be considered to have been cancelled during financial year 2003 and for the first three months of financial year 2004.'

2) New Item (5) is added to Article 3 to read as follows: '(5) A taxpayer that used the decreased installment method listed in Item 1(b) of Article 6 during financial year 2002 will compute the depreciation deduction for financial year 2004 by reconfiguring the opening balance of each asset account as of April 1, 2004. The opening balance of each asset account as of April 1, 2004, is equal to the balance of the asset account at the end of 2002, increased by the cost of assets purchased in the asset account and decreased by the fair market value of assets sold from the asset account in financial year 2003 and during the first three months of financial year 2004.'

Section 10 2002 Taxes

1) The suspension of income taxes for financial year 2003 by CPA Order Number 37 does not affect income taxes for financial year 2002 and previous years, which remain payable by taxpayers and collectible by the Tax Commission.

2) In case of late payment of taxes owed for financial year 2002, a taxpayer may file a written request with the Tax Commission requesting waiver of interest and penalties. The Tax Commission may, in its discretion, upon making a good faith determination that there was reasonable cause for the late payment, waive such interest and/or penalties.

[157] Sec 8(1) was amended by CPA Order No 84, sec 3(5) *[Doc 108]*.

Section 11 Government and State-Owned Enterprise Employees

1) To ensure that the tax burden is shared by all sectors of Iraqi society, salaries, wages and allowances received by employees of the Government Offices, public and mixed sectors are subject to tax, beginning April 1, 2004. Accordingly:

a) The phrase in paragraph (5) of Article 2 of the Income Tax Law No. 113 of 1982 'other than those working for government offices, socialist and mixed sector companies' is deleted.

b) Paragraph (5) of Article 7 of the Income Tax Law No. 113 of 1982 is deleted.

2) To ensure that the Ministry of Finance has sufficient capability to accurately and comprehensively assess and collect taxes on both public and private sector employees in a transparent manner:

a) For financial year 2004, employees of the government offices, public and mixed sectors shall be entitled to an allowance of ID 5,300,000 for themselves, spouse, and children collectively under Item (1) of Article 12 of the Income Tax Law No. 113 of 1982. If an employee of the public sector has more than 4 children, he or she shall be entitled to an additional exemption of ID 200,000 per child.[158]

b) The allowances as set forth in paragraph (2)(a) of this section shall be reduced by one-fourth during financial year 2004.

c) Beginning January 1, 2005, employees of the Government Offices, public and mixed sectors shall be entitled to the same allowances as employees of the private sector, as set forth in Section 2 of this Order.

Section 12 Foreign Tax Credit

Article 5 of the Income Tax Law No. 113 of 1982 is revised by adding new paragraph (4) to read as follows:

'(4) Income tax paid to a foreign country on income earned in that country may be credited against tax paid to Iraq. The amount of the credit may not exceed the amount of tax assessed in Iraq on the income earned in the foreign country at the rate in effect in Iraq. If taxes paid to a foreign country exceed the amount of this limitation then the excess taxes may be carried forward to credit in 5 consecutive years subject to the limitation in those years. The taxes paid in the carried forward year will be credited first. If, during a taxation period, income is earned in more than one country, the credit allowed by this paragraph will be applied on an individual basis to the income earned in each foreign country. To be credited, the amount of foreign tax paid to the foreign country must be confirmed by either a copy of the tax paid receipt or a confirmation of the amount of tax paid from the tax collection agency of the foreign country.'

Section 13 Implementation

The Minister of Finance, in consultation with the CPA Office of Management and Budget, may issue Administrative Instructions to implement this Order.

Section 14 Applicability

The provisions of this Order shall apply beginning with financial year 2004, which commences January 1, 2004.

[158] Sec 11(2)(a) was amended by CPA Order No 84, sec 3(6) *[Doc 108]*.

Section 15 Entry into Force
This Order shall enter into force on the date of signature [20 February 2004].

EXPLANATORY NOTE
CPA ORDER NUMBER 49, TAX STRATEGY OF 2004

I. Introduction
This note explains how CPA Order Number 49 resumes income taxes that were suspended for the 2003 financial year by CPA Order Number 37 (Tax Strategy for 2003). Taxes suspended in that Order included the corporate and personal income taxes that were imposed on employees in the private sector, the self-employed, professionals and small enterprises. Under CPA Order Number 49 corporate and personal income taxes will be reintroduced on April 1, 2004, at significantly reduced rates of no more than 15 percent as compared to the maximum rate of 40 percent under the previous income tax system. In addition, the existing allowances have been substantially increased.

As a result of these changes, the income tax burden on the average Iraqi family will be eliminated or substantially reduced. For example, beginning in 2005, the first full calendar year in which the tax will be in effect, a one-earner family with four children will not pay tax on the first ID 5,300,000 of income compared to ID 1,400,000 under existing law. If that family's income is ID 9,000,000, the tax will be reduced from ID 2,715,000 to ID 475,000, a savings of ID 2,240,000. Annex I describes the impact of the new tax rate structure in 2005 for families and single taxpayers. Similar reductions in tax will occur in 2004 for the nine months the income tax is in effect.

Reducing the income tax rates, increasing the allowances, and retaining the rules in effect under existing law are important steps in supporting current reconstruction and stabilization efforts in Iraq. At the same time, the Ministry of Finance is committed to modernizing the current tax system to improve compliance and reduce the administrative burden on taxpayers. Resuming the existing income tax system, therefore, is an interim measure pending the completion of the tax reform process and restoration of the tax administration capabilities of the Tax Commission.

II. Individual Income Tax

1. Increased Allowances
To lower the tax burden on individuals, the allowances for individuals described in Article 12 of Income Tax Number 113 of 1982 are increased by CPA Order Number 49. The full increase of exemptions will not occur until 2005, the first full year to which the order applies. Beginning in 2005, for each taxpayer, the allowance will increase from ID 600,000 to ID 2,500,000, with the allowance for a nonworking wife increasing from ID 400,000 to ID 2,000,000. The allowance for each child will double from ID 100,000 to ID 200,000, while the allowance for a widow will increase from ID 1,000,000 to ID 3,200,000. These exemptions will be decreased by one-fourth for the year starting April 1, 2004, to reflect the fact that the income tax will not be reinstated for the first quarter of 2004.

2. Top Rate Lowered to 15 Percent
The personal income tax imposed on employees of private sector companies and collected through withholding by their employers will recommence on April 1, 2004, with a maximum rate of 15 percent as shown in the table below.

Rate	Annual Income (after allowances)
3%	Up to ID 250,000
5%	Over ID 250,000 and up to ID 500,000
10%	Over ID 500,000 and up to 1,000,000
15%	Over ID 1,000,000

The amount delineating the tax bracket amounts will be decreased by one-fourth for the year starting April 1, 2004, to reflect the fact that the income tax will not be reinstated for the first quarter of 2004.

Many workers will be exempt from the tax because of the increased allowances provided for in CPA Order Number 49. For those workers subject to the tax, the lower rates of 3-15 percent, compared to the former top rates of 40 percent for Iraqi residents and 45 percent for non-residents (Article 13 of Income Tax Law No.113), will reward work, encourage savings and investment by workers, and increase compliance with tax laws.

3. Compliance Measures

The wage withholding system will be improved in 2004 to better assist employers to meet their obligations under the law. The Tax Commission will create a new comprehensive taxpayer identification number system that will facilitate tracking of and improved control over tax payments. The Tax Commission will issue a new guide for employers that contains withholding tables reflecting the new rate structure. In addition, the Tax Commission will simplify information returns and payment forms. These new processes and forms will be distributed to employers well in advance of the deadline for remitting the tax on wages earned in 2004.

4. Public and Mixed Sector Employees

Beginning April 1st, public and mixed sector employees will have to share the tax burden along with the rest of Iraqi society. This is necessary to ensure that sufficient tax revenues can be collected while not overburdening any segment of society with high tax rates. To ensure that the tax on public and mixed sector employees is collected accurately and transparently, tax collection systems for those employees need to be developed. This will take time. Therefore, to ensure that the tax is accurately and transparently collected in 2004, higher allowances will apply to public and mixed sector workers. These higher allowances will effectively exempt many public and mixed sector workers from taxation, and with fewer such workers to tax initially, the capacity of the tax collection system can be properly developed over time. Beginning January 1, 2005, however, public, mixed, and private sector workers will be subject to taxation at the same rates.

Example:

Financial year 2004. Assume a public sector employee with a wife and two children is paid wages of ID 430,000 by the public sector employer during each month of financial year 2004. The employee will not be subject to tax in financial year 2004 since the monthly allowance allowed the employee during financial year 2004 is ID 441,667 (i.e., one-ninth of the presumed annual allowance of ID 3,975,000. The presumed annual allowance for financial year 2004 is ID 3, 975,000 or ID 5,300,000 reduced by one-quarter to take into account that the income tax is reinstituted on April 1, 2004).

Financial year 2005. Beginning on January 1, 2005, the employee is paid ID 450,000 per month. Under the order, the employee for financial year 2005 is entitled to a total allowance of ID 4,900,000 (i.e., personal allowance of ID 2,500,000, a spousal allowance of ID 2,000,000 and an allowance of ID 200,000 for each child) or a monthly allowance of ID 408,334. Accordingly, the employee will be subject to tax on ID 41,666 of wages. The taxpayer's public sector employer will be required to withhold tax from that amount.

III. Corporate Income Tax

1. Lower 15 Percent Tax Rate

The tax rate for income earned by corporations from April 1, 2004 will be a flat 15 percent. As provided for in the current Income Tax Law Number 113 of 1982, the rate will be levied on the income of private sector companies, including income of foreign companies operating in Iraq. This lower rate, compared to the prior rate of up to 40 percent, will encourage reinvestment of company profits. This in turn will encourage increased capital investment and job creation in Iraq by private sector firms. The lower flat rate also will lead to increased revenue collection as companies respond to Iraq's transition to a free market-based economy.

2. Transition Rules

CPA Order Number 49 includes two transition rules to clarify the application of certain tax provisions to compute net income properly beginning on April 1, 2004.

a. Treatment of Losses under Article 11 of Income Tax Law Number 113 of 1982

Under Article 11 of Income Tax Law Number 113, taxpayers can apply losses in excess of income against income earned from the same source in future years ('carry-forward' the unused loss) for up to five years. CPA Order Number 49 includes three modifications to Article 11 of Law Number 113. First, CPA Order Number 49 provides that income from financial year 2003 and the first three months of financial year 2004 shall not be considered in determining the income against which losses may be deducted. Second, CPA Order Number 49 provides that any unused losses as of 31 December 2002 may be carried forward for an additional year. Third, CPA Order Number 49 provides that losses incurred in financial year 2003 and in the first three months of financial year 2004 may not be carried forward under Article 11.

Examples:

- Modification 1: In 2002, Company A incurred a loss of 10 million dinars. In 2003, Company A had profits of 8 million dinars. Because the income tax was suspended for 2003, the carryforward loss of 10 million dinars cannot be used to offset the profits of 8 million dinars. Instead, the 10 million dinar loss is carried forward for up to five years beginning with the financial year beginning on April 1, 2004.
- Modification 2: In 2003, Company B incurred a loss of 5 million dinars. Because the income tax was suspended for 2003, the 5 million dinar loss cannot be carried forward and is extinguished for tax purposes.
- Modification 3: Company C in 2000 had a net operating loss of 10 million dinars. Under prior law, the loss could be used to offset profits earned in 2001-2005. In 2001 and 2002, the company had profits of 2 and 4 million dinars, respectively, and it offset these profits with the 10 million dinar loss. At the end of 2002, its net operating loss was 4 million dinars. Under the transition rule announced in CPA Order Number 49, the 4 million dinar loss can be used to offset cumulative profits earned up to that amount in 2004, 2005 and 2006.

b. Depreciation Deductions

Under Article 8 of Income Tax Law Number 113 of 1982 and the 'System of Depreciation and Elimination for Private, Mixed and Cooperative Sectors Number. 9 of 1994,' taxpayers are entitled to take deductions for depreciation of buildings and other tangible assets and for amortization of intangible assets. CPA Order Number 49 modifies Regulation Number 9 on depreciation rules regarding computation of depreciation deductions in 2004. The Order contains 3 modifications to Regulation Number 9. First, no part of book value shall be considered to have been cancelled during financial year 2003 and the first three months of 2004. Second, if the taxpayer used the straight line method of depreciation in 2002, the depreciation deduction in 2004 is computed by extending the useful life of depreciable property by one year and three months. With respect to depreciable property purchased in 2003, the useful life of such property will commence in 2004.

If the taxpayer used the declining balance method of depreciation in 2002, the depreciation deduction for 2004 is computed by reconfiguring the opening balance of each group as of April 1, 2004. The opening balance of each group for 2004 is equal to the balance of the group at the end of 2002 increased by the cost of property purchased in the group and decreased by the fair market value of property sold from the group in 2003 and the first three months of 2004.

Examples:

- Straight-line: Company A purchased depreciable property with a useful life of five years for 1.2 million dinars in 2000. It took depreciation deductions using the straight line method of depreciation of 240,000 dinars each year, 20,000 per month, from 2000-2002. To compute depreciation deductions beginning April 1, 2004 the useful life of the property is extended by one year and three months to March 31, 2006. As a result, Company A can claim a depreciation deduction for such property in 2004 of 180,000, another depreciation deduction of 240,000 in 2005, and 60,000 in 2006.
- Straight-line: Company B purchased depreciable property with a useful life of 10 years for 4 million dinars in 2003. Company B can depreciate the property over 10 years beginning on April 1, 2004.
- Declining Balance: Company C uses the declining balance method of depreciation. At the end of 2002, the balance of Group 3 property was 10 million dinars. No purchases or sales were made in 2003 or during the first three months of 2004. Company C can claim a depreciation deduction beginning April 1, 2004 for Group 3 property equal to 15 percent (the yearly full rate is 20% for this group of property) of 10 million or 1.5 million dinars for Group 3 property.
- Declining Balance: Company D uses the declining balance method of depreciation. In 2003, it purchased Group 2 property for 5 million dinars. At the end of 2002, the balance of Group 2 property was 15 million dinars. Assuming no purchases or sales of property in Group 2 in 2003 and the first three months of 2004, Company D can claim a depreciation deduction in 2004 for Group 2 property equal to 15% of 20 million dinars (the yearly rate for Group 2 property is 20%) or 3 million dinars.

3. Revision of Company Tax Return

In order to ease the compliance burden on companies and improve tax collection, the Tax Commission will redesign the company tax return, simplifying the computation of tax liability. The new form will clearly explain how each element of the return should be computed and will require more detail on the income and deductions of the company so that its tax liability may be more easily determined. At the same time, the new form will eliminate the requirement to furnish significant commercial information unrelated to the tax liability computation. The new form will reconcile financial statement information with the tax return and will facilitate the transcription of the information to a computerized tax database. A draft form will be prepared by mid-2004 and will be made available for public comment.

4. Compliance Measures

In tandem with the changes outlined above, the Ministry of Finance will introduce in 2004 several measures to boost compliance and ease the administrative burden on taxpayers and the Tax Commission. One of the most significant initiatives will be the introduction of taxpayer identification numbers for the largest companies. This in turn will enable the Tax Commission to track payments made by each company to ensure greater accountability and control. The Tax Commission will phasein computerization of the existing interim tax system during 2004 to facilitate processing of tax returns and payments. In addition, the Tax Commission will launch a comprehensive tax training program for tax officials, along with a program to educate companies and their accountants on the revised company tax return.

IV. Foreign Tax Credit

The Order modifies Article 5 of the Income Tax Law Number 113 of 1982 to provide for a foreign tax credit for taxes paid to foreign countries. Because the foreign tax credit is intended to alleviate double taxation, and not to reduce Iraqi tax liabilities on profits earned within Iraq, the foreign tax credit is limited to Iraqi tax liability on income earned in the foreign country. For example, an Iraqi company (or individual) with ID 20,000,000 of income earned in Jordan that faces an Iraqi tax rate of 15 percent has a foreign tax credit limit of ID 3,000,000 (15 percent of ID 20,000,000). If the company (or individual) pays Jordanian income taxes of less than ID 3,000,000, then the company (or individual) would be entitled to claim a foreign tax credit for all of its Jordanian income taxes paid. If, however, the company (or individual) firm pays ID 4,000,000 of Jordanian taxes, then it would be permitted to claim no more than ID 3,000,000 of foreign tax credits. The excess Jordanian taxes in the amount of ID 1,000,000 may be carried forward to the next 5 years and claimed as a credit subject to the limitation in those 5 years. The foreign taxes paid in the carried forward year will be credited first.

The order provides that the limitation on the amount of foreign taxes that will be creditable is to be determined separately for each country to which the company (or individual) paid tax. In addition, the Order provides that the foreign tax will not be creditable unless the taxpayer substantiates the amount of tax paid by either supplying a copy of the payment receipt or a statement from the tax authority of the foreign country verifying the amount of tax paid.

V. Real Estate Rents Tax

In order to simplify the administration of the real estate rents tax (Real Estate Tax Law Number 162 of 1959), the Order provides that rents from real estate will be taxed at a flat rate of 10% of the combined rental income from all real estate rented by the taxpayer. This replaces the two-tier system of current law.

VI. Conclusion

This note summarizes measures necessary to resume income taxation in Iraq in 2004 and improve compliance on an interim basis. The tax system must be reformed to support a market economy. Towards that end, the Ministry of Finance will comprehensively assess the tax system to identify means of (i) eliminating distortions that interfere with market activity; (ii) improving fairness by removing exemptions; and (iii) simplifying rules to improve compliance and ease administrative burdens on individual and corporate taxpayers. The Tax Commission will also be modernized by: (i) adopting a functional structure; (ii) computerizing processes and systems; and (iii) improving the training of tax officials. A formal consultation process with the taxpaying public will ensure that these reforms will serve the needs of the Iraqi people.

ANNEX I
Impact of New Tax Rate Structure in 2005

One-earner Family with 4 Children

Annual Income	Current Tax	New Tax	Changes in Tax
I.D.	I.D.	I.D.	I.D.
1,000,000	0	0	0
1,500,000	10,000	0	-10,000
2,000,000	95,000	0	-95,000
3,000,000	355,000	0	-355,000
5,000,000	1,115,000	0	-1,115,000
6,000,000	1,515,000	40,000	-1,475,000
9,000,000	2,715,000	475,000	-2,240,000

One-earner Family with 2 Children

Annual Income	Current Tax	New Tax	Changes in Tax
I.D.	I.D.	I.D.	I.D.
1,000,000	0	0	0
1,500,000	35,000	0	-35,000
2,000,000	135,000	0	-135,000
3,000,000	415,000	0	-415,000
5,000,000	1,195,000	3,000	-1,192,000
6,000,000	1,595,000	85,000	-1,510,000
9,000,000	2,795,000	535,000	-2,260,000

Single Taxpayer with no Dependents

Annual Income	Current Tax	New Tax	Changes in Tax
I.D.	I.D.	I.D.	I.D.
600,000	0	0	0
700,000	10,000	0	-10,000
750,000	15,000	0	-15,000
800,000	20,000	0	-20,000
1,000,000	55,000	0	-55,000
1,500,000	155,000	0	-155,000
2,000,000	295,000	0	-295,000
3,000,000	635,000	20,000	-615,000
5,000,000	1,435,000	295,000	-1,140,000

Document 72
Coalition Provisional Authority Order Number 50

CPA/ORD/10 January 2004/50

The Ministry of Displacement and Migration

Pursuant to my authority as Administrator of the Coalition Provisional Authority (CPA), and under the laws and usages of war, and consistent with relevant U.N. Security Council resolutions, including Resolution 1483 (2003),

Recognizing that the return, relocation and reintegration of refugees and internally displaced persons (IDPs) is vital to Iraq's social and political stability,

Furthering the purposes of the Governing Council to create a ministry responsible for refugees and displaced persons,

Recalling CPA Memorandum Number 6,[159] publishing the appointment of the Interim Minister for Displacement and Migration,

I hereby promulgate the following:

Section 1 Establishment

1) The Ministry of Displacement and Migration (MODM) is hereby established.

2) All acts and decisions of the Interim Minster of Displacement and Migration in connection with his office or the Ministry from his appointment by the Governing Council on 31 August 2003 to the formal establishment of the MODM under GC Resolution Number 30[160] and this Order are hereby ratified. For the purposes of this ratification, the MODM is deemed to have been established on 30 August 2003.

3) The Palestinian Affairs Office of the Ministry of Labor and Social Affairs (MOLSA) shall be transferred to the MODM, which will perform that office's functions.

Section 2 Functions

1) The MODM shall be responsible for all matters pertaining to Iraqi refugees and displaced persons, including but not limited to matters associated with their repatriation, relocation, resettlement, and reintegration. The MODM shall also be responsible for policies and programs relating to all non-Iraqi refugees residing within Iraq.

2) The MODM shall develop policies and implement repatriation, relocation, resettlement and reintegration programs as are needed to give effect to this Order.

3) The MODM, in consultation with the CPA Senior Advisor for Displacement and Migration, may issue Administrative Instructions to enure and maintain compliance with promulgated standards for the repatriation, relocation, resettlement, and reintegration of refugees and internally displaced persons.

4) The MODM shall be the focal point in the interim national government for relations with the United Nations High Commissioner for Refugees, the International Organization for Migration, and other organizations dealing with refugees and internally displaced persons.

[159] See *Doc 131*.

[160] For IGC Resolution no 30 of 2003, see *Doc 293*.

Section 3 Structure

1) The interim Minister shall organize the MODM into such divisions and departments as are necessary. The interim Minister shall ensure, as a minimum, that policies are developed and implemented to address the repatriation, relocation, resettlement, and reintegration of Iraqi refugees and displaced persons and the provision of protection for and assistance to, as necessary or appropriate, non-Iraqi refugees residing within Iraq. The interim Minister shall ensure, as a minimum, that the following aspects of administration are addressed: legal; inspector general; personnel and finance; facilities; information and technology; international co-operation; security; media and press relations; and such regional and local programs as may be required.

2) The interim Minister may set up a consultative body comprising representatives of other Ministries to coordinate on policies and programs affecting refugees and displaced persons.

3) The interim Minister may set up such regional offices as are needed to facilitate, implement, and coordinate the work of the MODM at the local level.

Section 4 Personnel and Administration

1) The MODM shall have the power to hire and employ personnel in accordance with Iraqi law, as amended by CPA Orders and Memoranda. Such hiring shall be consistent with CPA Order Number 1[161] and any authorized implementation thereof.

2) Salaries of MODM personnel shall conform to the salary structure applicable to Iraqi government employees.

3) The staff of the Palestinian Affairs Office of the MOLSA shall be transferred immediately to the MODM within their existing pay grades and status, and the Minister of Displacement and Migration shall assume full authority, direction and control over his staff.

Section 5 Transitional Arrangements

1) The MOLSA shall be responsible for the salaries, benefits and personnel records of the Palestinian Affairs Office staff from January 1, 2004.

2) The MOLSA shall co-ordinate with the MODM to achieve the smooth and timely transfer of salaries, benefits and personnel records.

Section 6 Property

All the moveable and immovable property under the control of the Palestinian Affairs Office of MOLSA and the records and data pertinent to that Office shall be transferred to the MODM.

Section 7 Budget

The MODM shall co-ordinate with the Ministry of Finance on its 2004 budget. The MODM shall further co-ordinate with the Ministry of Finance to transfer to the MODM the budget allocation of the Palestinian Affairs Office for 2004.

Section 8 Administrative Instructions

The interim Minister, in consultation with the CPA Senior Advisor for Displacement and Migration, may issue Administrative Instructions, not inconsistent with Iraqi law or any

[161] See *Doc 14*.

other CPA Order, Regulation, or Memorandum, prescribing all matters necessary for carrying out the duties described under this Order.

Section 9 Entry into Force
This Order shall enter into force on the date of signature [11 January 2003].

Document 73
Coalition Provisional Authority Order Number 51
CPA/ORD/14 January 2004/51

Suspension of Exclusive Agency Status of Iraqi State Company for Water Transportation

Pursuant to my authority as Administrator of the Coalition Provisional Authority (CPA), and under the laws and usages of war, and consistent with relevant U.N. Security Council resolutions, including Resolutions 1483 and 1511 (2003),

Noting that the Iraqi State Company for Water Transportation (hereafter 'the Company') is the successor in interest to the Iraqi State Organization for Water Transportation (hereafter 'the Organization'),

Noting further that the Company has performed exclusively as the maritime agent in Iraqi ports, a role previously performed by the Iraqi State Enterprise for Iraqi Maritime Agencies, a body of the Organization,

Understanding that the rights and obligations of the Organization have devolved upon the Company,

Determined to create conditions for the development of a free market economy by encouraging trade and open competition,

I hereby promulgate the following:

Section 1 Suspension of Exclusive Agency Status

1) The right of the Company to act as the exclusive maritime agent in Iraqi ports is hereby suspended. The Company shall, however, be permitted to provide maritime agency services in competition with other companies.

2) To the extent that Article 1 of Law Number 56 of 1985 (Maritime Agencies) or any other provision of Iraqi law is inconsistent with this Order, those inconsistent provisions are suspended.

Section 2 Entry into Force
This Order shall enter into force on the date of signature [Signed without date].[162]

[162] This Order was not signed by Ambassador Bremer but bears the signature of [Ambassador] 'Richard H. Jones, Acting'. Ambassador Jones was Chief Policy Officer and Deputy Administrator of the CPA.

Document 74
Coalition Provisional Authority Order Number 52

CPA/ORD/6 January 2004/52

Payment of Pensions for Judges and Prosecutors Who Die While Holding Office

Pursuant to my authority as Administrator of the Coalition Provisional Authority (CPA), and under the laws and usages of war, and consistent with relevant U.N. Security Council resolutions, including Resolutions 1483 and 1511 (2003),

Recognizing that the administration of justice depends upon an independent and impartial judiciary and prosecution composed of persons of the highest quality and integrity, free of all outside influence,

Noting that according to the decision of the Revolutionary Command Council of 13 September 1983 issued pursuant to Article 42 of the Interim Iraqi Constitution of 1970, no provision is made for a pension for the family of Judges and Prosecutors who die or are killed in office, until the date when such Judge or Prosecutor would have reached the age of retirement,

Determined to make special provision for the families of Judges and Prosecutors who are killed while holding office,

I hereby promulgate the following:

Section 1 Payment of Pensions for Judges and Prosecutors who Die in Office

In the event of death of a Judge or Prosecutors who was holding office at the time of death, the surviving relatives of the Judge or Prosecutor shall be paid a pension in accordance with this Order.

Section 2 Rate of Pension for Judges or Prosecutors who Die Other than as Result of Homicide While Serving in Office

1) The amount of the pension to be paid to the surviving relatives of a Judge or Prosecutor who dies other than as a result of homicide while serving in office shall be the equivalent of 80% of the salary paid to a Judge or Prosecutor of the same grade as the deceased Judge or Prosecutor.

2) The pension paid under paragraph 1 above shall be paid from the date of the deceased person's death until the date when the Judge or Prosecutor would have reached retirement age, after which the pension to be paid to the surviving relatives shall be at the same rate as the normal retirement pension for Judges and Prosecutors.

Section 3 Rate of Pension for Judges or Prosecutors who are Killed while Serving in Office

1) The amount of the pension to be paid to the surviving relatives of a Judge or Prosecutor who is killed while serving in office shall be the equivalent to the full salary paid to a Judge or Prosecutor of the same grade as the deceased Judge or Prosecutor.

2) The pension paid under paragraph 1 above shall be paid from the date of the deceased person's death until the date when the Judge or Prosecutor would have reached retirement age, after which the pension to be paid to the surviving relatives shall be at the same rate as the normal retirement pension for Judges and Prosecutors.

Section 3 [sic.] Administration and Payment of Pensions

1) The pensions authorized under this Order shall be administered and paid by the Ministry of Justice.

2) Such pensions shall be paid to those surviving relatives of the deceased Judge or Prosecutor whom the Judge or Prosecutor was supporting at the time of his or her death and whom the Minister of Justice determines to be qualified for such pensions under regulations to be promulgated by the Ministry of Justice. Pensions shall be paid to qualified surviving relatives in such proportions as the Minister of Justice determines to be equitable.

Section 4 Entry into Force

This Order shall enter into force on the date of signature [8 January 2004], but shall apply retroactively to all deceased judges or prosecutors who died after 1 June 2003 while serving in office.

Document 75

Coalition Provisional Authority Order Number 53

CPA/ORD/16 January 2004/53

Public Defender Fees

Pursuant to my authority as Administrator of the Coalition Provisional Authority (CPA), and under the laws and usages of war, and consistent with relevant U.N. Security Council resolutions, including Resolutions 1483 and 1511 (2003),

Recognizing the fundamental human right and indispensability to justice of representation at court by competent criminal defense counsel, as reflected in CPA Memorandum No. 3,[163]

Recognizing further the necessity of adequate compensation to procure such counsel,

I hereby promulgate the following:

Section 1 Determination of Public Defender Fees

Notwithstanding any other provision of law, the schedule of fees to be paid to attorneys appointed under Article 144 of the Criminal Procedure Code of Iraq of 1971, as modified by CPA Memorandum No. 3, shall be established by the Council of Judges. The prior schedule of fees established by Article 144 and Article 63(c) of the Law on Advocacy, No. 173 of 1965, or any other law, is hereby suspended.

Section 2 Scope of Right to Counsel

The right to court appointed counsel shall not extent to infractions as defined by Iraqi law, but shall apply only to misdemeanors and felonies.

Section 3 Retroactive Payments

The Council of Judges may authorize retroactive payments for legal defense services rendered to indigent criminal defendants since March 18, 2003.

[163] See *Doc 127*.

Section 5 Entry into Force
This Order shall enter into force on the date of signature [18 January 2004].[164]

Document 76
Coalition Provisional Authority Order Number 54
CPA/ORD/24 February 2004/54

Trade Liberalization Policy 2004

Pursuant to my authority as Administrator of the Coalition Provisional Authority (CPA), and the laws and usages of war, and consistent with relevant U.N. Security Council resolutions, including Resolutions 1483 and 1511 (2003),

Noting the responsibility of the Department of Border Enforcement, in CPA Order Number 26, to monitor and control the movement of persons and goods into and out of Iraq, *Further* implementing the Reconstruction Levy imposed by CPA Order Number 38 (CPA/ORD/19 September 2003/38),[165]

Having worked closely with the Governing Council, international organizations and relevant Ministries in developing policies that will foster international trade and a free market economy in Iraq,

I hereby promulgate the following:

Section 1 Suspension of Customs Charges
All customs tariffs, duties, import taxes (not including the Reconstruction Levy imposed by CPA Order Number 38), and similar surcharges for goods entering or leaving Iraq are suspended until the sovereign transitional Iraqi administration imposes such charges following the CPA's transfer of full governance authority to that administration.

Section 2 Contraband
1) Prohibited imports and exports ('Contraband') and restricted exports and restricted imports are listed in Annex A to this Order.

2) Except with respect to the Contraband and restricted exports and restricted imports listed in Annex A, there shall be no restriction as to the kind, origin or source of goods that may be imported into or exported from Iraq.

Section 3 Application to Existing Law
1) Notwithstanding any provision in this Order, the following laws shall remain in force:
   a) CPA Order Number 38, Reconstruction Levy (CPA/ORD/19 September 2003/38); and
   b) Drugs Law Number 68 of 1965.

2) This Order shall not apply to the importation or exportation of crude oil, residue crude and all other oil products, which may only be imported or exported by, or with the

[164] This Order was not signed by Ambassador Bremer but bears the signature of [Ambassador] 'Richard H. Jones, Acting Administrator'. Ambassador Jones was Chief Policy Officer and Deputy Administrator of the CPA.

[165] See *Doc 59*.

authorization of, the State Oil Marketing Organization. However, importation of petroleum products intended for use by the Coalition Provisional Authority, Coalition Forces, and forces of nations working in coordination with Coalition Forces shall not require authorization of the State Oil Marketing Organization.

3) Customs Law Number 23 of 1984, as amended, ('Customs Law') shall remain in force except as amended by this or any other CPA Order, including in particular CPA Order Number 16, Temporary Control of Iraqi Borders, Ports and Airports (CPA/ORD/26 June 2003/16)[166] and CPA Order Number 26, Creation of the Department of Border Enforcement (CPA/ORD/24 August 2003/26).[167]

4) CPA Order Number 12, Trade Liberalization Policy (CPA/ORD/7 June 2003/12)[168] and CPA Memorandum Number 8, Exportation of Scrap Metal Under Order Number 12, Trade Liberalization Policy (CPA/MEM/25 January 2004/8)[169] are hereby rescinded. Notwithstanding the foregoing, any licensing regime established under CPA Memorandum Number 8 shall continue to be effective to the extent that it is not inconsistent with the terms of this Order.

Section 4 Reconstruction Levy

1) The Minister of Finance, in consultation with the Director of the CPA Office of Management and Budget, may issue policy guidance as necessary to implement the reconstruction levy pursuant to Section 3 of CPA Order Number 38. Consistent with such policies, the Minister of Interior, in consultation with the Senior Advisor for Interior, may issue administrative instructions and procedures for implementing the reconstruction levy.

2) For the purpose of Section 1(2) of CPA Order Number 38, 'international practice' means the customs valuation as set forth in the Agreement on Implementation of Article VII of the General Agreement on Tariffs and Trade 1994. The customs value shall be determined by the transaction value of the imported goods, which shall be the price actually paid or payable for the goods when sold for export to the country of importation plus certain adjustments as provided for in the Agreement on Implementation. If the customs value cannot be determined on the basis of the transaction value, it will be determined using one of the following methods, as provided for in the Agreement on Implementation, in hierarchical order:

a) The transaction value of identical goods;
b) The transaction value of similar goods;
c) The deductive value method;
d) The computed value method; and
e) The fall-back method.

Notwithstanding the definition of value as set forth in Article 34 of the Customs Law Number 23 of 1984 as amended ('Customs Law'), the principles of this Section 4(3) shall apply in determining customs value.

3) The reconstruction levy exemption for goods listed at Section 2(1) of CPA Order Number 38 shall also apply to goods that are imported for the personal use of the traveler when those goods are not intended for sale.

[166] See *Doc 43*. CPA Order No 16 had been revised on 1 December 2003, i.e. prior to this Order, but the revised Order No 16 was not referenced.

[167] See *Doc 47*.

[168] See *Doc 28*.

[169] See *Doc 133*.

a) With respect to an individual who is a resident of Iraq, this exemption will apply only where the total value of the goods entering Iraq with this individual is less than ID 500,000 for any 72 hour period. In no event will personal use exceed the following:

Cigarettes—200
Cigars—10
Cigarillos—25
Smoking tobacco—250 grams
Beer—8 liters
Wine—2 liters
Spirits—1 liter
Fortified wine (e.g. port/sherry)—2 liters

b) With respect to an individual who is not a resident of Iraq, the exemption in Section 4(4)(a) of this Order will apply to goods entering Iraq with this individual for personal use irrespective of value of the goods, provided that the goods are not intended for sale. Procedures for administering this exemption will be issued by the Ministry of Finance in consultation with the Director of the CPA Office of Management and Budget.

4) For purposes of section 2(1)(g) and (2)(f) of CPA Order Number 38, and subject to Section 4(8) of this Order, a 'not-for-profit organization' is an organization that is not organized for commercial purposes and no part of the income or surplus of which is at any time payable to, or otherwise available for the personal benefit of, any proprietor, member, shareholder, or any individual who is a spouse, child, grandchild, parent, grandparent, or sibling of any of the aforesaid, or majority owner of an entity that is a member or shareholder of the organization. The organization may provide such a proprietor, member, shareholder or any individual who is a spouse, child, grandchild, parent, grandparent, or sibling of any of the aforesaid, or majority owner of an entity that is a member or shareholder of the organization with benefits that are generally available to the general public.

5) For purposes of section 2(1)(g) of CPA Order Number 38, the term 'public benefit' means activities aimed at achieving a universal or common good for the general public through the advancement, protection, maintenance, support, improvement or enhancement of:

a) Health, which includes without limitation, the prevention and relief of sickness, disease or of human suffering;
b) Education;
c) Social and community welfare, which without limitation includes:
   i. The prevention and relief of poverty;
   ii. The care, support and protection of the aged, minors, vulnerable persons and populations, and people with a disability;
   iii. The care and support of members or former members of the armed services;
d) Religion;
e) Culture;
f) The natural environment; and
g) Other purposes beneficial to Iraq.

6) For purposes of Sections 2(1)(g) and (2)(f) of CPA Order Number 38, an 'international organization' is an organization with an international legal personality and an independent decision-making organ that is established under international law by an international agreement or other formal constitutive document, and performs functions of

a genuinely international character. Such term includes, but is not limited to, the United Nations (including its agencies), the Arab League, the International Monetary Fund, the World Bank, the Organization for the Prohibition of Chemical Weapons, the International Atomic Energy Agency, and the World Trade Organization.

7) Organizations that meet the definitions of not-for-profit organizations and international organizations set forth in Section 4, paragraphs (4) and (6), respectively, of this Order will be considered a not-for-profit organization or international organization for purposes of Section 2(1)(g) and (2)(f) of CPA Order Number 38 only after the organization has registered with the Customs Department, including, where applicable, registration as a non-governmental organization pursuant to CPA Order Number 45.[170] An organization that has not registered with the Customs Department prior to importation of goods will be required to pay the reconstruction levy at the time of importation. The levy will be refunded if the organization meets the applicable definition and registers with the Customs Department within 60 days of the date of importation.

8) The reconstruction levy exemption for the persons and entities listed at Section 2(2) of CPA Order Number 38 shall apply as follows:

a) Section 2(2)(c) of CPA Order Number 38 covers forces of countries and their contractors and sub-contractors acting in coordination with Coalition Forces only to the extent of activities that are in coordination with Coalition Forces and with respect to goods imported for such activities;

b) Section 2(2)(d) of CPA Order Number 38 covers Coalition contractors and subcontractors only with respect to imported goods supplied to the Coalition Provisional Authority and Coalition Forces; and

c) Sections 2(2)(e) and 2(2)(f) of CPA Order Number 38 cover contractors and sub-contractors of Coalition Forces' departments and agencies, governments, international organizations, and not-for-profit organizations, only with respect to goods that those persons or entities import for the provision of technical, material, financial and human resource assistance.

Section 5 Revision of Customs Law

For purposes of implementing the reconstruction levy, the Customs Law shall be applied with the following revisions:

1) Article 55 of the Customs Law is revised by adding the following sentences at the end of that article to read as follows:

> The Director General of Customs shall determine the type of Reconstruction Levy Computation Form, number of copies, information that must be included on the form, documents to be attached and any exceptions to the stated requirements. Reference to 'Customs Declaration' or 'Declaration' in this law shall refer to the 'Reconstruction Levy Computation Form' whenever applicable.

2) Claims for repayment of overpayments of the reconstruction levy resulting from disputes of valuation may be submitted to the Opposition Body pursuant to Articles 74 to 77 of the Customs Law, regardless of whether the goods remain in the custody of the Customs Department.

3) Article 77(2) of Customs Law is hereby suspended for purposes of this Order.

4) The exemption provided by free zones legislation will not apply to the reconstruction levy.

[170] See *Doc 67*.

5) The reconstruction levy will not be imposed on the value of goods that entered Iraq under an exemption set forth in section 2 of CPA Order Number 38 if the property is destroyed or is otherwise no longer usable. Article 149(2)(c) of the Customs Law is hereby suspended for purposes of this Order.

6) The reconstruction levy shall not be refunded as a drawback when goods are re/exported abroad. Articles 151 and 152 of Customs Law are hereby suspended for purposes of this Order.

7) The reconstruction levy shall not be imposed on goods in transit, as defined in Part 8 of the Customs Law.

8) Section 2 of CPA Order Number 38 provides the exclusive list of exemptions (both exempt goods and exempt persons and entities) for purposes of the reconstruction levy. Part 10 of the Customs Law is hereby suspended for purposes of this Order.

9) Fines imposed for offenses under Part 15, Chapters 4, 5, and 7 of the Customs Law (as amended by Decision 103 of 2001) shall apply to the reconstruction levy. To account for inflation, the amount of fines listed in dinars in those chapters will be multiplied by 10.

Section 6 Excise Tax on Alcohol and Tobacco

Notwithstanding Section 1 of this Order, the Administrator or his delegee may reinstate the Excise Tax on Alcohol and Tobacco products.

Section 7 Effective Date of Reconstruction Levy

The reconstruction levy shall be imposed on goods imported Iraq beginning April 1, 2004.

CPA Order Number 38, Section 7 [sic], paragraph (4)[171] on the Reconstruction Levy is therefore amended to read in its entirety as follows:

> '4) Unless exempted under this Order, the Reconstruction Levy shall be imposed on all goods imported into Iraq from all countries beginning April 1, 2004.'[172]

Section 8 Entry into Force

This Order shall enter into force upon signature [26 February 2004].

ANNEX A

Restricted Imports

The following items cannot be imported in any quantity unless the Ministry of Trade issues a license authorizing the import:

- Non-military explosives imported for industrial and commercial uses;
- Industrial materials that may be used in the manufacture of explosives, but that have a primary use unconnected to the manufacture of explosives, such as fertilizer; and
- Fowl or poultry products from countries known or suspected to have had outbreaks of pathogenic bird flu (avian influenza virus). As of the date of signing of CPA Order Number 54, these countries are Cambodia, Japan, the Republic of Korea, Viet Nam, Indonesia, Laos, China and Thailand.

[171] It should read Sec 1, Art 4. See CPA Order No 38 *[Doc 59]*.

[172] Sec 7 was deleted in its entirety and sec 8 was re-designated as sec 7 by CPA Order No 70, sec 1(2) *[Doc 94]*.

Items and technologies listed in the following international nonproliferation regimes (that are not otherwise prohibited under United Nations Security Council Resolutions or CPA Orders) cannot be imported in any quantity unless the Ministry of Trade issues a license authorizing the import:

- Australia Group
- Missile Technology Control Regime
- Nuclear Suppliers Group
- Wassenaar Arrangement

PROHIBITED IMPORTS

- Magazines, films, videotapes and CDs contrary to public norms;
- Arms, ammunition, all explosives other than industrial and commercial explosives, and materials used in the manufacture of explosives that do not have a primary use unconnected to the manufacture of explosives (other than any such items required by, or for purposes of, the CPA (including contractor security personnel), Coalition Forces, and foreign liaison mission security personnel;
- Non-medical narcotics (heroin, cocaine, cannabis etc.);
- Nuclear, chemical, biological materials or weapons; components of such systems; technologies and equipment for the development, manufacture, use or storage of such materials or systems; delivery systems for such weapons; components of delivery systems for such weapons; technologies and equipment for the development, manufacture, use or storage of such delivery systems; and
- Nuclear materials, except for radioisotopes for legitimate industrial, agricultural or medical purposes.

RESTRICTED EXPORTS

The following items cannot be exported in any quantity unless a license is issued by the Ministry of Trade authorizing the export:

- Non-military explosives imported for industrial or commercial use
- Industrial materials that may be used in the manufacture of explosives, but that have a primary use unconnected to the manufacture of explosives, such as fertilizer

Items and technologies listed in the following international nonproliferation regimes (that are not otherwise prohibited under United Nations Security Council Resolutions or CPA Orders) cannot be exported in any quantity unless the Ministry of Trade issues a license authorizing the export:

- Australia Group
- Missile Technology Control Regime
- Nuclear Suppliers Group
- Wassenaar Arrangement

The following items in quantities in excess of personal use cannot be exported unless the Ministry of Trade issues a license authorizing the export:

Foodstuffs

- Sugar

- Tea
- Imported Rice
- Wheat and Wheat Flour
- Imported Vegetable Oils and Fats
- Lentils and Chickpeas
- Dried Beans
- Milk Powder and Infant Formula
- Yellow Corn for Animal Feed

Animals
- All animals (including fowl), excluding household pets

Manufactured Goods
- Ferro-concrete, Iron, Iron Reinforcing Rods
- Galvanized Iron Plates, Steel Sheets and Plates
- Wood of all kinds
- Mineral Water Pipes and their Fittings
- Ceramic and other Bathroom Furnishings including Taps and Sinks
- Plain and Colored Window Glass
- Metals of all kinds, including scrap

Other Articles
- Bar soap and detergents (in quantities that exceed personal use)
- Date palm seedlings and shoots

PROHIBITED EXPORTS

- Historical artifacts (excluding modern military artifacts and items not prohibited from export under existing Iraqi law)
- Magazines, films, videotapes, and CDs contrary to public norms
- Arms, ammunition, and all explosives other than industrial and commercial explosives and materials used in the manufacture of explosives that do not have a primary use unconnected to the manufacture of explosives (other than such items originally imported by, or required for historical or other purposes of, the CPA (including contractor security personnel), Coalition Forces, and foreign liaison mission security personnel)
- Non-medical narcotics (heroin, cocaine, cannabis, etc.)
- Nuclear, chemical, biological materials or weapons; components of such systems; technologies and equipment for the development, manufacture, use or storage of such materials or systems; delivery systems for such weapons; components of delivery systems for such weapons; technologies and equipment for the development, manufacture, use or storage of such delivery systems. Except that such materials, components, systems may be delivered to Coalition authorities for disposition and elimination.
- Nuclear materials, except for radioisotopes for legitimate industrial, agricultural or medical purposes, and nuclear materials delivered to Coalition authorities for disposition and elimination.

Document 77
Ministerial Instruction
9 April 2004

General License to Export Scrap Metal

1. In accordance with the Coalition Provisional Authority ('CPA') Order No. 54 on 'Trade Liberalization Policy 2004', dated 26 February 2004 , metals of all kinds cannot be exported unless the Ministry of Trade issues a license authorizing their export. Exclusive competence in the area of customs has also been vested in the Iraqi Transitional Government pursuant to the Transitional Administrative Law, dated 8 March 2004.
2. This Ministerial Instruction implements an export control licensing policy by publishing this 'General License to Export Scrap Metal.' Pursuant to this General License, exporters have the right to export scrap metal from Iraq provided they comply with the requirements in this instruction.
3. The General Licensing procedures are provided as an attachment.

Signed: ____________
Name: Dr. Ali Allawi
Title: Minister of Trade, Republic of Iraq

Procedures for the General License for the Export of Scrap Metal

Article (1)
This Ministerial Instruction establishes a policy for licensing the export of scrap metal and assigns responsibility within the Ministry for collecting data and receipts on the utilization of these General Licenses. Metals of all kind, including scrap, may not be exported without compliance with the terms of this instruction.

Article (2)
The policy of the Ministry is to allow the export of scrap metals that have been lawfully acquired, and comply with the terms of this instruction.

Article (3)
For purposes of this instruction the following terms are defined:
1. 'Exporter' – the person or company primarily responsible for exporting the scrap metal out of Iraq , or their agent such as the driver of the truck moving the scrap metal.
2. 'Scrap Metal' – is metal material that has been finished and put to use as a product or part of a product, but has lost its intended usefulness as a result of obsolescence, damage or destruction, excluding copper and lead. The Minister of Trade may further define what metals are permitted or prohibited from exportation through an announcement referencing this instruction and published in the Official Gazette.
3. 'General License to Export Scrap Metal': includes this Ministerial Instruction and the attached procedures only, no other payments, approvals, documents, photographs or certificates are required.
4. 'General License to Export Scrap Metal Fee' the only administrative fee required to comply with the terms of this General License is specified in this instruction.

5. 'General License Fee to Export Scrap Metal Receipt': An original receipt issued by a designated branch of a bank licensed in Iraq, that proves the administrative license fee was paid. Minister of Trade may define what banks and branches are designated through an announcement referencing this instruction and published in the Official Gazette.

Article (4)
Any exporter that complies with the procedures of this instruction is hereby granted a General License to Export Scrap Metal.

Article (5)
An administrative handling fee entitled General License to Export Scrap Metal Fee is hereby imposed at the rate of ID 50,000 per metric tonne. This fee must be paid at least three days in advance of the export via a designated bank branch. The Minister will issue separately a list of designated bank branches. The exporter must specify the point of exit at the time of paying the fee. The original receipt provided by the bank will be accepted by all government agents as the official 'General License Fee to Export Scrap Metal Receipt'.

Article (6)
Enforcement of the General License to Export Scrap at Iraq's international borders:

1. The exporter must present the original version of the 'General License to Export Scrap Metal Receipt' to an official of the Ministry of Interior, Customs Service at the international border prior to exportation.
2. The government official will examine this receipt to ensure its validity for every truckload of scrap, prior to its exportation.
3. No export shall be permitted unless accompanied by the original version of this receipt.

Article (7)
The Exporter shall provide an original or a photocopy of commercial documents that contain the following information:

1. Name, address and contact details of the Exporter
2. Name of buyer
3. Destination
4. Total tonnage
5. Type of material
6. Declaration that the material has been lawfully acquired

Article (8)
Valid receipts and documents described in articles (3) and (7) will be collected at the border by the Customs Service and returned to the Baghdad office of the Ministry of Trade, Department of Rationing and Planning, Import / Export section. This office will be responsible for coordinating the enforcement of this instruction with the Ministry of Interior, Customs Service; and for answering public inquires on the operation of this General License.

Article (9)
Presentation of a forged receipt is a crime, and will be punished to the extent provided by the relevant provision of the Iraqi Penal Law. Any exporter who is found to have presented false receipts may have his vehicle and its contents confiscated. The exporter shall be denied the privilege of exporting for five years.

Article (10)
The Minister of Trade may vary these instructions or issue additional instructions to facilitate the execution of these provisions. These instructions should be enforced from the date of their publication in the Official Gazette.

Signed: ____________
Name: Dr. Ali Allawi
Title: Minister of Trade, Republic of Iraq

Document 78
Coalition Provisional Authority Order Number 55
CPA/ORD/27 January 2004/55

Delegation of Authority Regarding the Iraq Commission on Public Integrity

Pursuant to my authority as Administrator of the Coalition Provisional Authority (CPA), and under the laws and usages of war, and consistent with relevant U.N. Security Council resolutions, including Resolution 1483 (2003), Resolution 1500 (2003), and Resolution 1511 (2003),

Avowing that corruption is the bane of good governance and prosperity,

Recognizing that the Iraqi people deserve leaders who are honest and dedicated to the transparent governance of Iraq,

Emphasizing that effective governance depends on the confidence that Iraqi people have in their leaders and corruption erodes that confidence,

Underscoring that honest and transparent governance will promote lasting prosperity of the Iraqi people by assuring them and the world community of the integrity of the Iraqi leaders,

Noting that Iraq has long prohibited corruption in government, but that enforcement has been arbitrary and intermittent and that corruption has proliferated under the Baath regime,

Acknowledging that the battle against corruption is a long-term struggle that requires lasting commitment to change behavior at all levels of government,

Recognizing that the CPA is committed to the effective administration of Iraq and that building the Iraqi capacity to fight corruption contributes to civilian administration,

Noting that the Governing Council is leading the development of an anti-corruption strategy for Iraq,

I hereby promulgate the following:

Section 1 Delegation of Authority

The Governing Council is hereby authorized to establish the Iraq Commission on Public Integrity (Commission) as an independent body responsible for enforcing anti-corruption laws and public service standards; proposing additional legislation as necessary; and heightening the Iraqi people's demand for honest, transparent and accountable leadership through public awareness and education initiatives. Proposed provisions establishing the Commission have been discussed between the Governing Council and the CPA are set forth in Appendix A.

Section 2 Terms and Conditions

The authority delegated under Section 1 of this Regulation [sic] shall be subject to the following terms and conditions:

a) The Governing Council shall ensure that the Commission is established and acts in a manner consistent with orders, regulations, and memoranda promulgated by the CPA.
b) The Governing Council shall ensure that the Commission acts as the principal enforcement arm of Iraq's anti-corruption laws and performs its duties in conjunction with the Board of Supreme Audit ('Board') and the Inspectors General of Iraqi ministries.
c) The Governing Council understands and acknowledges that the Commission, the Board and the Inspectors General have expressly defined powers and areas of responsibility. Accordingly, the Governing Council shall ensure (i) that the Board serves as Iraqi's supreme audit institution and remains responsible for detecting fraud, waste and abuse in Iraqi ministries and other government organizations; (ii) that the Board retains no prosecutorial or enforcement powers and must refer all evidence of fraud, waste, and abuse to the Inspector General of the relevant ministry; (iii) that the Inspectors General, in turn, and in addition to policing their own ministries, must investigate all referred matters and report their findings and recommendations to the relevant minister and to the Commission for final review and appropriate action; and (iv) that only the Commission is empowered to dispose of cases involving misconduct through criminal proceedings.
d) The Governing Council acknowledges that this system is expressly designed to facilitate transparent governance and combat corruption at all levels by enabling oversight agencies to operate independently and by ensuring that investigative and enforcement functions are performed separately and discretely. The Governing Council shall therefore ensure that the system is implemented as designed.
e) As part of the delegation in Section 1, the Governing Council is authorized to modify existing Iraqi law as set forth in Appendix A and to permit the Commission to promulgate a revision of the Code of State Employees and Social Sector Discipline.
f) In the event of a conflict between any promulgation by the Governing Council and any promulgation of the CPA, the promulgation of the CPA shall prevail.
g) The Administrator reserves the authority to alter the statute creating the Commission or any rules and regulations promulgated by the Commission, or to otherwise intervene to prevent and uproot government corruption in Iraq, if required in the interests of justice.[173]

[173] Sec 2(g) was rescinded by CPA Order No 100, sec 3(20) *[Doc 124]*.

Section 3 Effective Date
This Regulation [sic] shall enter into force on the date of signature [28 January 2004].

APPENDIX A
THE COMMISSION ON PUBLIC INTEGRITY

Avowing that corruption is the bane of good governance and prosperity,

Recognizing that the Iraqi people deserve leaders who are honest and dedicated to the transparent governance of Iraq,

Underscoring that honest and transparent governance will promote lasting prosperity of the Iraqi people by assuring them and the world community of the integrity of the Iraqi leaders,

Noting that Iraq has long prohibited corruption in government, but that enforcement has been arbitrary and intermittent and that corruption has proliferated in Iraq since July 17, 1968,

Acknowledging that the battle against corruption is a long-term struggle that requires lasting commitment to change behavior at all levels of government,

Be it approved by the Governing Council:

Section 1 Purpose
This statute encourages honest and transparent governance by establishing a truly independent body capable of effectively enforcing anti-corruption laws and public service standards, proposing additional legislation as necessary, and heightening the Iraqi people's demand for honest, transparent and accountable leadership though public awareness and education initiatives; by requiring Iraq's leaders to demonstrate their commitment to ethical public services through oaths of office and public disclosure of personal financial interests; and by strengthening and clarifying Iraq's standards of ethical public service and its criminal laws prohibiting public corruption.

Section 2 Definitions
For purposes of this law, the following definitions shall apply. Words importing the singular include and apply to several persons, parties, or things; words importing the plural include the singular; and words importing the masculine gender include the feminine:

1) 'Person' means any natural person, corporation, company, association, firm, partnership, society, union, institution or organization.

2) 'Penal Code' means the Iraqi Penal Code of 1969, as amended.

3) 'Code of Conduct' means the Code for State Employees and Social Sector Discipline, Resolution No. 144.

4) 'Corruption Case' means a criminal case that involves a suspected violation of:
   a) Paragraphs 233, 234, 271, 272, 275, 276, 290, 293, or 296 of the Penal Code,
   b) Paragraphs 307 though 342 (Chapter Six) of the Penal Code,
   c) Any provision of the Penal Code to which Paragraph 135(5), (6) or (7), added by Section 6 of this measure, applies, or
   d) Any other provision of the Penal Code, where the suspected violation arises from the same operative facts as a suspected violation of a provision listed in subsections (a) through (d), above.

5) 'Covered persons' means:
   a) Governing Council members and their deputies;
   b) Ministers and deputy ministers;

c) Governors;
d) Judges;
e) The Commissioner, Deputy Commissioner, and all Directors and investigators of the Commission;
f) Members of the National Legislature after the Transition; and
g) The chief executive of Iraq on and after the Transition.

6) 'Transition' means the moment at which the sovereign transitional Iraqi administration assumes full governance authority in Iraq.

7) Before the Transition, 'National Legislature' means the Governing Council. After the Transition, 'National Legislature' means the body that is vested with the national legislative authorities and duties.

Section 3 Commission on Public Integrity

The Commission on Public Integrity (Commission) is hereby established as a separate and independent government office that will implement and enforce this statute, by investigating and referring cases to courts for criminal proceedings; promoting the people's trust in the government of Iraq through financial disclosure and other programs; and fostering a culture in government and in the public of personal integrity, ethical public service, and accountability, though public awareness and education programs. The Commission may develop and propose for enactment additional legislation, promulgate regulations as authorized herein, and take such other actions as it deems necessary and appropriate to achieve its objectives.

Section 4 Powers and Duties

1) The Commission shall have the authority to investigate, and through an investigator of the first class, present to an investigative judge a Corruption Case involving actions dating as far back as July 17, 1968. Upon presentation of the case to the investigative judge, the Commission shall become a party to the case.

2) The Commission may refer information regarding the possible violations of the Code of Conduct to the head of the government agency that employs the suspected violator or that agency's Inspector General, with or without a recommendation for disciplinary action.

3) The Commission shall establish procedures to receive, through the office of an Ombudsman, and investigate allegations of corruption, including anonymous allegations. The Commission shall take all necessary and appropriate steps to protect the identity of informants to the maximum extent permitted by law, unless the informant waives such protection.

4) The Commission shall employ, among others, financial auditors, investigators, and investigators of the first class. An investigator of the first class is hereby empowered to exercise the powers of a court investigator under Iraqi law in any part of Iraq, and a request, motion, information, application, or supplication of whatever form submitted to a judge by an investigator of the first class shall be received and entertained in the same manner as such submissions from a court investigator.

5) An investigating judge shall notify the Director for Legal Affairs of the Commission upon commencing an investigation into a Corruption Case. At the Commission's request, the investigating judge shall update the Commission about the investigation as it progresses. The Commission may elect at any time to assume responsibility for such an investigation. If the Commission elects to assume responsibility, the investigating judge shall transfer

the entire case file to the Commission immediately, cooperate with and fully inform the Commission about the case, and cease his investigation.

6) The Commission shall promulgate mandatory financial disclosure regulations in accordance with Section 7. The regulations shall be designed to gain public trust and confidence in the honesty and transparency of government service. The regulations shall have the force and effect of law, and may be amended from time to time as the Commission deems necessary to achieve their purpose. The regulations shall require, at a minimum, disclosure of the information called for by the form annexed hereto as Appendix A.

7) The Commission shall promulgate a revision to the Code of Conduct, to clarify and strengthen the standards of ethical conduct to which Iraq's government employees must adhere. In revising the Code of Conduct the Commission will consult with the National Center for Consultation and Development of Government Administration and with the inspectors general of the Iraq Ministries. The Code of Conduct shall address the duty of government employees:

a) to report corruption to an appropriate authority;
b) to act impartially and not to give unfair and unlawful preferential treatment to any organization or individual;
c) not to engage directly or indirectly in financial transactions using official, nonpublic information;
d) not knowingly to provide false, misleading, or incomplete information to the Commission;
e) not to accept gifts of more than a nominal value to be specified by the Commission, except for bona fide gifts from bona fide friends of long standing;
f) not to participate personally and substantially in official matters that have a direct and predictable effect upon the financial interests of themselves, their spouses or their family relations to the second degree, except where expressly authorized by law.

Every government employee must sign a written pledge of adherence to the Code of Conduct as a condition of employment. Heads of government agencies will take appropriate actions to ensure that employees sign such pledges.

8) The Commission may propose to the National Legislature legislation designed to eradicate corruption and foster a culture of integrity, honesty, transparency, accountability, submission to questioning, and fair dealing in government.

9) The Commission shall make available to government employees and the Iraqi public such education and public awareness programs as the Commission deems appropriate to foster a culture of integrity, honesty, transparency, accountability, and fair dealing in public service. It should enforce submission to questioning and impartial dealing in public service. In performing this responsibility, the Commission shall work with education officials to develop a national school curriculum to promote public integrity.

10) In performing its duties, the Commission and its officials shall not discriminate on the basis of, and shall act without regard to, religion, confession, race, ethnicity, gender, political affiliation or ideology, or familial affiliation or tribe. Any act of the Commission based on or motivated by such a distinction is invalid and null. The subject of such an act may sue to have it so declared in a court of law.

11) The Commission shall, in all of its operations, fastidiously observe and ensure the protection of due process under the law.

Section 5 Organization and Functions

1) The Commission shall be chaired by a Commissioner, who shall serve a term of five years. A Commissioner shall be nominated by the Governing Council and appointed to his initial term by the Administrator. Commissioners after the initial Commissioner shall be appointed by the chief executive of Iraq from a pool of three nominees of the Council of Judges, subject to confirmation by a majority vote of the National Legislature. The nominees of the Council of Judges shall have the highest standards of ethical behavior and a reputation for integrity and honesty. The Commissioner may be removed from office by a two-thirds vote of the National Legislature for incapacity, serious misconduct in or out of office, dereliction of duty, or abuse of office.

2) The Commissioner shall:

a) authorize, direct and control all operations of the Commission and ensure that it fulfils its duties under law;

b) propose a budget for and approve expenditures by the Commission;

c) hire, fire and discipline Commission personnel in accordance with the Code of Conduct except as otherwise provided by law, and prescribe their training and qualifications;

d) promulgate and ensure compliance with financial disclosure regulations as directed in this statute, and the procedural rules described in Section 4(3) of this statute; and

e) promulgate amendments to and help ensure compliance with the Code of Conduct as set forth in Section 4(7) of this statute.

The Commissioner may delegate his duties to his subordinates in the Commission.

3) The Commission shall have a Deputy Commissioner, a Director for Investigations, a Director for Legal Affairs, a Director for Prevention, a Director for Education and Public Relations, a Director for Relations with Non-Governmental Agencies, and a Director for Administration, each of whom shall be appointed by the Commissioner and shall serve under his authority, direction and control.

4) The Deputy Commissioner shall be the chief assistant to the Commissioner. The Deputy Commissioner shall act as the Commissioner, with all appurtenant authorities, powers, rights, responsibilities and duties, during the Commissioner's incapacity.

5) The Director of Investigations shall be primarily responsible for the detection and investigation of corruption in the government of Iraq, and for establishing procedures for receiving and investigating allegations of corruption, including anonymous allegations.

6) The Director for Legal Affairs shall insist and advise the Commissioner in ensuring compliance with the law of Iraq, and in suggesting legislation to the Commissioner for submission to the national legislature.

7) The Director of Prevention shall be primarily responsible for assisting the Commissioner in fulfilling his duties under subsections 4(6)-(7) of this statute.

8) The Director of Education and Public Relations shall assist the Commissioner in fulfilling the duty imposed on the Commission by subsection 4(9) of this statute. He shall educate public officials, government employees and the public as to the principles of ethical public service, the Code of Conduct, and the financial disclosure regulations applicable to government employees. He shall develop with the Ministry of Education and other education officials and organizations a national school curriculum to promote ethics in public service, and may carry out such training, studies, media campaigns, conferences, seminars and similar events, and hire consultants in furtherance of these activities.

9) The Director of Relations with Non-Governmental Organizations shall work with non-governmental organizations to promote a culture of ethics in both the public and private sectors, by developing and disseminating materials, conducting training programs and media outreach efforts, and other actions in furtherance of these activities.

10) The Director for Administration shall be responsible for office administration and personnel and human resources.

Section 6 Penal Code Amendments

The Penal Code is amended:

1) By appending to the end of Paragraph 135 the following:

'(5) The abuse of public or trusted office for private gain or the offering, granting or acceptance of some advantage in violation of the person's trusted or public official duties and the official abuse of the rights of others, or attempting to induce such abuse or violation.

'(6) The commission of an offense in connection with, in furtherance of, or to impede detection of any of the offenses described in Sections 2(4)(a) through (d) of the organic law establishing the Commission o Public Integrity.

'(7) Violation of financial disclosure regulations promulgated by the Commission on Public Integrity.'

2) By appending to the end of Paragraph 136 the following:

'(4) If the offense involves a provision described in Sections 2(4)(a) through (d) of the organic law establishing the Commission on Public Integrity, then the offending person shall be immediately and permanently disqualified from government employment or from contracting to provide goods or services to the government and, unless a more harsh sentence is prescribed by another provision of law, the sentence may be imprisonment of up to 10 years, and a fine of up to $10 million or its equivalent in Iraqi Dinars, and the forfeiture and restitution of any and all amounts, objects, and tangible assets of unjust enrichment resulting from the offense or related activities.'

Section 7 Financial Disclosure

1) Within 30 days of the date of assuming office, the initial Commissioner shall promulgate regulations requiring, at a minimum, that Covered Persons annually disclose the information called for by the form annexed hereto as Appendix A.

2) Timely compliance with Commission regulations promulgated pursuant to this statute shall be a condition of employment.

3) The Commission shall make available to the public for inspection and copying the information and forms filed pursuant to the financial disclosure regulations promulgated pursuant to this statute.

4) The Commission shall review, audit, and investigate as appropriate Covered Persons' financial disclosures ensure honest compliance.

Section 8 Reporting Requirements

After the Transition, the Commissioner shall provide the chief executive of Iraq and the National Legislature with a report on the activities of the Commission, at least annually. Such reports shall include statistics on cases reported, investigated, referred, dropped, and prosecuted as well as information on the Commission's public outreach activities. The Commissioner shall make these reports available to the public.

Appendix A
Annual Iraqi Financial Statement

ALL QUESTIONS REFER TO CALENDER YEAR (JANUARY 1 THROUGH DECEMBER 31) UNLESS OTHERWISE SPECIFIED.

Please answer all questions and where your answer is 'none' or 'not applicable' so state. **ANSWERS SHOULD BE PRINTED OR TYPED**, and additional sheets may be used if more space is needed. For clarification of any question, read instruction sheet.

Note: The failure to file a Yearly Financial Statement by a Covered Person, as defined in the law establishing the Commission on Public Integrity, is a violation of the law and may subject the official to penalties, including fines and suspension from office.

1. ______________________________
NAME OF OFFICIAL (First) (Middle) (Surname)

2. ______________________________
HOME ADDRESS (Street) (City/Town)

3. List Public Office(s) you hold and governmental unit:

____
(Public Office) (Municipality, Governorate, or National)

____
(Public Office) (Municipality, Governorate, or National)

4. List the names of any non-governmental employer from which you, your spouse, or dependent child received [$1000 or equivalent dinars] or more gross income during the calendar year, or in which you, your spouse, or dependent child held a position as a director, officer, partner, trustee, or management position. If self-employed, list any occupation from which [$1000 or equivalent dinars] or more gross income was received. If employed by a governorate or municipal Ministry or agency, or if self-employed and services were rendered to a state of municipal agency for an amount of income in excess of [$250.00 or equivalent dinars], list the date and nature of services rendered. If the public office or employment listed in #3, above, provides you with an amount of gross income in excess of [$250.00 or equivalent dinars] it must be listed here (**Do Not List Amounts**.)

NAME OF FAMILY MEMBER EMPLOYED	NAME AND ADDRESS OF EMPLOYER OR OCCUPATION	DATE AND NATURE OF SERVICES RENDERED

5. List the address or legal description of any real estate, other than your principal residence, in which you, your spouse, or dependent child has a financial interest

NAMES	NATURE OF INTEREST	ADDRESS OR DESCRIPTION

6. List name of any trust, name and address of the trustee of any trust, from which you, your spouse, or dependent child or children have a beneficial interest of [$1000 or equivalent dinars] or more. List assets if known. (**Do Not List Amounts**)

NAME OF TRUST: ______________________________

NAME OF TRUSTEE AND ADDRESS: ______________________________

NAME OF FAMILY MEMBER RECEIVING TRUST INCOME: ____________________

ASSETS: ____________________

7. List the name and address of any person, business entity, or other organization which had made total gifts or total contributions of [$100 or equivalent dinars] or more in cash or property during the calendar year to you, your spouse or dependent child. Certain gifts from relatives and certain campaign contributions are excluded. (See instructions)

NAME OF PERSON RECEIVING GIFT OR CONTRIBUTION	NAME AND ADDRESS OF PERSON OR ENTITY MAKING GIFT OR CONTRIBUTION, AND RELATIONSHIP TO RECIPIENT

8. If you, your spouse, or dependent children were indebted in an amount in excess of [$1,000 or equivalent dinars] to any person, business entity or other organization other than (i) any person related to you, your spouse, or dependent children at any time within the third degree of consanguinity (see instructions), or (ii) a financial institution regulated by the Iraqi Government where such indebtedness is secured solely by an mortgage of record on real property used exclusively as your principal residence, or (ii) [sic.] any indebtedness arising from transactions involving credit, please list the following:

NAME AND ADDRESS OF DEBTOR	NAME AND ADDRESS OF LENDER

I certify under penalty of perjury, that this Financial Statement is a complete and accurate response to the questions presented.

____

SIGNATURE

Document 79

Coalition Provisional Authority Order Number 56

CPA/ORD/1 March 2004/56

Central Bank Law

Pursuant to my authority as Administrator of the Coalition Provisional Authority (CPA) and under the laws and usages of war, and consistent with relevant U.N. Security Council resolutions, including Resolution 1483 (2003),

Having worked closely with the Governing Council to ensure that economic change occurs in a manner acceptable to the people of Iraq,

Acknowledging the Governing Council's desire to bring about significant change to the Iraqi economic system,

Determined to stabilize domestic prices and to foster an economic climate conducive to the establishment of a stable and competitive market economy,

Recognizing the problems arising from the former regime's policies regarding governance of the Central Bank of Iraq,

Further recognizing the CPA's obligation to provide for the effective administration of Iraq, to ensure the well being of the Iraqi people and to enable the social functions and normal transactions of every day life,

Recalling that U.N. Security Council Resolution 1483 (2003) called upon the CPA to promote economic reconstruction and the conditions for sustainable development,

Acting in a manner consistent with the Report of the Secretary General to the Security Council of July 17, 2003, concerning the need for the development of Iraq and its transition from a non-transparent centrally planned economy to a market economy characterized by sustainable economic growth through the establishment of a dynamic private sector, and the need to enact institutional and legal reforms to give it effect,

Having coordinated with the international financial institutions, as referenced in paragraph 8(e) of the U.N. Security Council Resolution 1483,

I hereby promulgate the following:

Section 1 Purpose

This Order establishes a safe, sound, and independent Central Bank for the purposes of achieving and maintaining domestic price stability, fostering and maintaining a stable and competitive market-based financial system, and promoting sustainable growth, employment, and prosperity in Iraq.

Section 2 Central Bank Law

The Central Bank of Iraq Law attached to this Order in Annex A shall have the full force and effect of law.

Section 3 General Provisions

The term 'Appointing Authority' shall mean the Administrator in consultation with the Governing Council, during the period prior to the transfer of full governmental authority to the transitional Iraqi administration and the recognition of the sovereignty of that administration by the CPA.

Those actions to be taken by 'upon the recommendation of the Appointing Authority and confirmation by the Legislature' under the Central Bank of Iraq Law in Annex A shall be undertaken upon the recommendation of the Governing Council and confirmation by the Administrator, during the period prior to the transfer of full governmental authority to the transitional Iraqi administration and the recognition of the sovereignty of that administration by the CPA. Likewise, during the that period, those actions requiring nomination by the Appointing Authority and confirmation by the Legislature shall be undertaken by way of nomination by the Governing Council and confirmation by the Administrator.

Those actions to be taken by the Legislature by itself shall be undertaken by the Governing Council with the approval of Administrator during the period prior to the transfer of full governmental authority to the transitional Iraqi administration and the recognition of the sovereignty of that administration by the CPA.

Section 4 Nominations

The Governing Council shall forward nominees for the Governor, the Deputy Governors and the other members of the Board of the Central Bank to the Administrator for his approval within one month of the date of the signing of this Order. Should the Governing Council fail to forward such a list of nominees to the Administrator within this time period, the Administrator shall nominate and appoint the Governor, the Deputy Governors, and other members of the Board of the Central Bank.

Section 5 Inconsistent Legislation
Any provision of Iraqi law that is inconsistent with this Order or Annex A is hereby suspended to the extent of such inconsistency.

Section 6 Entry into Force
This Order shall enter into force on the day of signature [6 March 2004].

ANNEX A
CENTRAL BANK OF IRAQ LAW OF 2004

Section 1 – Definitions, Autonomy, Objectives and Functions

Article 1 Definitions

The following terms shall have the meanings set forth below:

'*Appointing Authority*' means the head of the Government;

'*bank*' means a person holding a license or permit under the Banking Law to engage in banking business and other banking activities;

'*banking business*' means the business of receiving deposits of money or other repayable funds from the public for the purpose of making credits or investments for its own account;

'*Board*' means the Board of Directors of the CBI;

'*CBI*' means the Central Bank of Iraq;

'*credit*' means any disbursement or commitment to make a disbursement of a sum of money in exchange for the right to repayment of the amount disbursed and outstanding and to payment of interest or other charges on such amount, whether secured or unsecured, any extension of the due date of a debt, any guarantee issued, and any purchase of a debt security or other right to payment of a sum of money that may provide for the payment of interest either directly or by a discounted purchase price;

'*currency*' means the monetary unit of a country;

'*deposit*' means a certain sum of money paid to a person, whether or not evidenced by any entry in a record of the person receiving the sum, on terms under which the deposit will be repaid or transferred to another account, with or without interest or a premium, either on demand or at a time or in circumstances agreed to by or on behalf of the depositor and that person;

'*Deputy Governor*' means a Deputy Governor of the CBI;

'*dinar*' means the Iraqi dinar;

'*fit and proper person*' means a person who is regarded as honest and trustworthy and whose professional qualifications, background and experience, financial position, or business interests do not disqualify that person in the judgment of the Appointing Authority or, with respect to Article 64, the Minister of Justice, provided, however, that no person shall be regarded as a fit and proper person if the person:

- (i) has been convicted by a criminal court of an offense for which the person was or could have been sentenced to imprisonment for a term of one year or more without the option of a fine unless such sentence, in the judgment of the Appointing Authority, or, with respect to Article 64, the Minister of Justice, was or would have been motivated by his religious or political views or activities;
- (ii) has been declared bankrupt by a court of law within the past seven years;
- (iii) has been disqualified or suspended by a competent authority from practicing a profession on grounds of personal misconduct unrelated to his religious or political views or activities; or
- (iv) has been declared unfit to manage a company by a court of law or under an order issued by a competent agency;

'*foreign exchange*' means any bank note or coin, cheque, draft, promissory note, bill of exchange, payment order, credit, balance of account or any other means of effecting payments in any currency other than the Iraqi currency;

'*Government*' means the entity exercising temporary governmental authority in Iraq on the date this law enters into force and then the transitional Iraqi administration upon the transfer to it of full governmental authority and the recognition of the sovereignty of that administration by the CPA, and then the internationally recognized representative government of Iraq once it assumes the responsibilities of such authority;

'*Governor*' means the Governor of the CBI;

'*legal tender*' means banknotes and coins which any creditor is obligated to accept in payment for a debt denominated in Iraqi *dinars*;

'*Legislature*' means the principal legislative body of Iraq, or a component or subordinate body thereof empowered for purposes of oversight of the CBI pursuant to this Law;

'*Official Publication*' means the *Official Gazette* or such other general publication of wide circulation as specified by the Appointing Authority;

'*State*' means the Republic of Iraq;

'*Tribunal*' means the Financial Services Tribunal as described in Articles 63 through 70 of this Law.

Article 2 Legal capacity and autonomy

1. The CBI, established under the Central Bank of Iraq Law, Law No. 64 of 1976, as amended from time to time, is a legal entity with the full capacity to enter into contracts, to sue and be sued, and to carry out its functions under this and any other law. In carrying out its functions, the CBI may: (i) administer and hold property, (ii) hire staff, define their duties, and determine their compensation; and (iii) determine and fund its own budget. Nothing in this Law shall be construed to interfere with the continuation of the existence of the CBI as a legal entity under prior law, or with any of the authority, rights, duties or obligations of the CBI under prior law, except as otherwise provided for under this Law.

2. In the pursuit of its objectives and the performance of its tasks, the CBI shall be autonomous and accountable as provided for in this Law. Except as otherwise specified in this Law, the CBI shall not take instructions from any other person or entity, including government entities. The autonomy of the CBI shall be respected and no person or entity shall seek improperly to influence any member of a decision-making body of the CBI in the discharge of his duties towards the CBI or to interfere in the activities of the CBI.

3. The CBI's head office shall be located in the City of Baghdad and, in order to discharge its functions within Iraq and abroad, it may open such branches, agencies and bureaus, and appoint such correspondents as it may require.

Article 3 Objectives

The primary objectives of the CBI shall be to achieve and maintain domestic price stability and to foster and maintain a stable and competitive market-based financial system. Subject to these objectives, the CBI shall also promote sustainable growth, employment, and prosperity in Iraq.

Article 4 Functions

1. The functions of the CBI in achieving the objectives set forth in Article 3 and as further described in this Law, shall be to:

a. formulate and implement monetary policy, including exchange rate policy, for Iraq in accordance with Section 6;
b. hold and manage all official foreign reserves of Iraq, other than working balances of the government, in accordance with Article 27;
c. hold gold and manage the State reserves of gold;
d. provide services as advisor and fiscal agent to the Government in accordance with Section 4;
e. provide liquidity services to banks in accordance with Articles 28 and 30;
f. issue and manage Iraqi currency in accordance with Section 7;
g. compile and publish data on the banking and financial system and the economy in accordance with Article 41;
h. establish, oversee and promote sound and efficient payment systems in accordance with Article 39;
i. issue licenses or permits to banks and to regulate and supervise banks as further specified in this Law and in the Banking Law;
j. open and maintain accounts on the books of foreign central banks and international financial organizations;
k. open and maintain on its own books accounts for foreign central banks, foreign governments and international organizations; and
l. carry out any ancillary tasks or transactions incidental to the exercise of its functions under this Law.

2. In addition, the CBI may take whatever action it deems necessary to: (i) counter money laundering and terrorist financing, and (ii) regulate and supervise lending companies, microfinance companies, and any other non-bank financial institutions not otherwise regulated under Iraqi law.

3. The CBI shall have the power to issue regulations for the purpose of implementing this Law and carrying out its functions under this Law. Regulations issued under this Law, and any subsequent amendments thereto, shall be published in the Official Publication.

4. If the CBI proposes to issue a regulation pursuant to this Law, it shall publish a draft of the proposed text of the regulation in a form and in a manner determined by it to be best calculated to bring the proposed regulation to the attention of the domestic financial sector and the general public. The draft shall be accompanied by an explanation of the purpose of the proposed regulation and a request for comments within a specified time of not less than one month after the date of publication of the draft. The CBI shall have regard to any comment received and issue the final text of the regulation accompanied by an account in general terms of the comments. The procedure set out in this paragraph shall not apply if the CBI determines that the delay involved would be a serious threat to the interests of the financial system or hinder the effective conduct of monetary policy, provided that such decision by the CBI shall be explained in the preamble to the regulation.

5. In carrying out its functions in accordance with the provisions of this Law, the CBI shall have the power to issue legally-binding orders addressed to specified individuals or entities and directing such persons or entities to undertake specific actions which are in accordance with this Law.

6. The CBI shall have the power to issue internal rules or guidelines on the organization and administration of the CBI.

Section 2 – Capital, Reserves and Net Profits

Article 5 Capital and reserves

1. The authorized capital of the CBI shall be 100 billion *dinars* and shall be fully paid in by the State in exchange for one hundred percent of the CBI's capital stock.

2. The authorized capital stock of the CBI shall [be] held solely by the State, shall not pay a dividend, and shall not be transferable or subject to encumbrance.

3. The authorized capital may be increased by such amounts as the Minister of Finance may approve upon the recommendation and approval of the Board.

4. The CBI shall hold a general reserve account, an unrealized profits reserve account and such other reserve accounts as may be appropriate under international accounting standards.

Article 6 Computation of profits and losses; allocation of net operating loss

1. Within three months after the end of each financial year, the CBI shall determine in accordance with the rules set out in Articles 7 and 45 its net profits available for distribution or its net losses.

2. If the CBI incurs a net operating loss for any financial year, that loss shall first be charged to the general reserve and subsequently to capital.

Article 7 Treatment of unrealized gains

1. Where unrealized gains for a financial year on assets or liabilities of the CBI that are recorded at fair value or are denominated in foreign currency are included in the net income of the CBI for that year, the net profits of the CBI available for distribution under Article 8 shall be determined as follows:

   a. by deducting from the net income the total amount of any unrealized gains included in the net income, and by allocating an equivalent amount to the unrealized profits reserve account; and

   b. by deducting from the unrealized profits reserve account and adding to the net profits available for distribution as determined in sub-paragraph (a) the amount of any unrealized gain that was deducted from the net income for one or more previous years and was realized during the financial year.

2. No other deductions shall be made from the unrealized profits reserve except those permitted under this Article.

Article 8 Distribution of net profits

1. Within three months after the end of each financial year, the Board shall distribute the net profits available for distribution as follows:

   a. 80 percent of any net profits available for distribution shall be transferred to the general reserve account until such time as the general reserve account of the CBI reaches a sum equal to 10 percent of the total assets of the CBI;

   b. any remaining net profits available for distribution shall be transferred to any other reserve account that may be established by the CBI pursuant to paragraph (4) of Article 5.

2. No distribution shall be made out of retained or current income of the CBI, except as permitted by paragraph (1). No distribution of net profits shall include any portion of unrealized gains.

3. No distribution shall be made under paragraph (1) if, as a result thereof, the assets of the CBI would be less than the sum of its liabilities and unimpaired capital and reserves.

Article 9 Coverage of shortfalls in capital

In the event that the audited annual balance sheet of the CBI prepared in accordance with paragraph (3) of Article 45 shows that the value of its assets falls below the sum of its liabilities and unimpaired authorized capital, the Board shall, with the advice of the external auditor of the CBI, assess the situation and prepare a report on the causes and extent of the shortfall. If the Board determines that a capital contribution is required, the Board shall consult with the Minister of Finance and request a capital contribution be made on behalf of the State. Upon the receipt of this request, the Minister of Finance shall, within a period of no more than two months, make a request to the Legislature for the approval of the capital contribution for the CBI over such period and in such amount as is necessary to remedy the shortfall.

Section 3 – Management

Article 10 Board of Directors and committees

1. The Board shall be responsible for conducting the business, and carrying out the responsibilities of the CBI, as further described in this section.
2. The Board may, as it deems necessary, establish committees composed of members of the Board to consider particular issues and to make recommendations to the Board, and to grant such committees executive authority to take decisions, within guidelines established by the Board.

Article 11 Composition of the Board

The Board shall consist of nine members as follows:

a. the Governor as chairman of the Board;
b. two Deputy Governors;
c. three Senior Managers of the CBI, including Branch Managers on a rotating basis; and
d. three other individuals with suitable monetary, banking or legal expertise and who have not been employed by the CBI in any capacity within one year of the date of their nomination to the Board.

Article 12 Eligibility for appointment and service

1. The Governor, the Deputy Governors and other members of the Board shall be persons of recognized integrity who hold a university degree or who have extensive professional experience in a field related to banking, economics, finance, commerce, or law.
2. A person shall be ineligible for appointment to serve on the Board if, in the judgment of the Appointing Authority:
   a. the person is not a citizen of Iraq;
   b. the person is not a fit and proper person; or
   c. the person, or any person who is related to the person by marriage, blood or kinship, including adopted children or foster children of the person, and any other person residing in such person's household, holds direct or indirect business interests that would make it necessary for that person to refrain, to an unacceptable extent, from taking part in the decision-making of the Board.

3. The Governor, the Deputy Governors and other members of the Board shall not, during their tenure:

a. hold any employment other than with the CBI, whether remunerated or not, except that they may engage in a limited amount of lecturing and other academic activity so long as such activity is not remunerated and does not interfere with the performance of the individual's duties and responsibilities at the CBI;
b. hold any position, other than with the CBI, in public service, except as nominee of the CBI;
c. be a member of the Legislature;
d. be an employee or official of the Government; or
e. be a director, officer, employee or shareholder of any bank or other entity subject to the supervision of the CBI.

Article 13 Appointment and terms of service of Board members

1. The Governor, the Deputy Governors and the other members of the Board shall be nominated by the Appointing Authority and confirmed by the Legislature. The Appointing Authority shall consult with the Governor and his two Deputies with respect to the nomination of Senior Managers as Board Members. All members of the Board shall have a five-year term of office and may be re-appointed upon the recommendation of the Appointing Authority and confirmation by the Legislature, provided that, in order to achieve staggered terms of office, the initial terms of office shall be: (i) for the Governor, five years; (ii) for one Deputy Governor, four years and, for the other Deputy Governor, three years; (iii) for one Senior Manager five years, for another Senior Manager, four years, and for the third Senior Manager, three years; and (iv) for two of the Board Members appointed pursuant to Article 11, paragraph (d), three years, and for the other Board Member appointed pursuant to Article 11, paragraph (d), two years.

2. Any vacancy on the Board shall be filled by the appointment of a new member of the Board to serve the remaining term of the Board member replaced.

3. The Governor shall determine in advance the order in which the Deputy Governors shall succeed the Governor during any period of the Governor's absence or disability.

4. The Appointing Authority shall establish the terms and conditions of service of the members of the Board. When establishing the remuneration for the members of the Board, the Appointing Authority shall be guided by need to attract and retain highly qualified individuals to serve as members of the Board.

5. The remuneration and other terms and conditions of service of a Board member shall not be rendered less favorable during the term of office for which the Board member has been appointed.

Article 14 Resignation and removal of Board members

1. The Governor, a Deputy Governor or any other member of the Board may resign his office after giving at least one month written notice to the Appointing Authority, if such resignation is accepted. If the Appointing Authority does not accept such resignation, the relevant member of the Board may be required by the Appointing Authority to serve not more than three additional months from the date of the member's original resignation notice.

2. The Governor, a Deputy Governor or any other member of the Board shall be removed from office by the Appointing Authority only if the person:

a. has been convicted by a criminal court of an offense for which the person was or could have been sentenced to imprisonment without the option of a fine unless, in the judgment of the Appointing Authority, such sentence was motivated by his religious or political views or activities;

b. has been declared bankrupt by a court of law;

c. has been found guilty by a court of law of conduct involving a lack of probity in financial matters or other serious misconduct;

d. has been disqualified or suspended by a competent authority from practicing a profession on grounds of personal misconduct unrelated to his religious or political views or activities;

e. has been declared unfit to manage a company by a court of law or under an order issued by a competent agency;

f. has taken up any office, position or employment in violation of paragraph (3) of Article 12 or paragraph (3) of Article 21;

g. is suffering from such mental or physical infirmity which, in the opinion of the Appointing Authority, renders him unfit to discharge his duties under this Law;

h. has been found by the Appointing Authority to have violated the provisions of paragraphs (1) or (2) of Article 15; or

i. has been absent from meetings of the Board for a consecutive period or [sic] more than three months without approval of the Board.

3. No member of the Board shall be removed from office on any ground specified in paragraph (2) without first being given the opportunity of hearing before the Appointing Authority.

4. Any decision on removal from office under paragraph (2):

a. shall be made public along with a statement of the reasons for removal, and any written response received from the Board member concerned; and

b. may be appealed to the Court of Cassation within two months of service of the decision.

5. Any member of the Board having been removed from office shall continue to receive remuneration and other benefits applicable under the terms and conditions to a member of the Board until such time that any hearing or appeal in the matter, whichever is later, has been decided.

Article 15 Disclosure of interests

1. Each member of the Board shall, upon his appointment and annually thereafter, declare in writing to the Board, in compliance with any instructions that may be issued by the Board, the direct and indirect business interests that he or any person who is related to the Board member by marriage, blood or kinship, to the extent provided by regulation, may hold, and the Board shall submit such declarations for information to the Appointing Authority, the Minister of Finance and to the external auditor.

2. Before a matter concerning a declared interest as mentioned in paragraph (1) is raised for discussion by the Board, the Board member concerned shall again disclose his interest and shall not thereafter participate in any discussion or decision on that matter.

3. For a period of one year immediately following his or her departure from the CBI, no former Governor, Deputy Governor or chief internal auditor shall serve or represent another bank or other entity subject to the supervision of the CBI or deal with the CBI in any way in connection with any matter or issue the former Governor, Deputy Governor, or chief internal auditor worked on or was otherwise involved in while employed by the CBI, without the prior written consent of the Board. The Board may establish the remuneration to be paid to

such former Governor, Deputy Governor or chief internal auditor together with any other terms and conditions that shall be applicable during this period. In the event the Board does elect to provide such remuneration, this remuneration shall be automatically reduced by an amount equal to any income the former Governor, Deputy Governor or chief internal auditor may receive from any employment while he or she is receiving the remuneration.

Article 16 Powers and functions of the Board

While observing the primary objective and other objectives set out in Article 3, the Board shall, within the limits set out in this Law:

a. develop and define the primary monetary policy objective;
b. formulate policies to attain the primary monetary policy objective, including the exchange rate policy, limits on open market operations to be conducted by the CBI, policies regarding interest rates for other provisions of funds to the banking sector, and the types and levels of reserves that banks will be required to maintain; except that the Board shall not have the power to enter into a fixed exchange rate regime, such as a monetary union or currency board.
c. decide on the issuance of Iraqi banknotes and coins in accordance with Article 32;
d. issue licenses or permits and adopt procedures to regulate the safety and soundness of banks as further specified in the Banking Law;
e. determine the terms for the provision of services as banker, advisor and fiscal agent to the Government in accordance with Section 4;
f. adopt the rules for payment systems in accordance with Article 39;
g. approve all reports and recommendations that the CBI is to make to the Government or the Legislature;
h. decide on the participation of the CBI in international organizations whose membership is open to central banks;
i. decide whether the CBI will open and maintain an account on its books for a foreign central bank, foreign government or international organization, and also whether the CBI will open and maintain an account in its name on the books of a foreign central bank or international financial organization;
j. decide whether debt securities should be issued by the CBI, and if so, the terms and conditions thereof;
k. determine the categories of assets that shall be suitable for the investment of the foreign exchange reserves and other financial resources of the CBI;
l. determine the terms pursuant to which discount operations may be engaged in by the CBI in accordance with Article 28;
m. approve, with the consent of at least three-fifths of the members of the Board present, each loan or guarantee to be extended to a bank under Article 30;
n. adopt by-laws, internal guidelines and rules applicable to the administration and operation of the CBI, and determine the organizational structure of the CBI, including the locations of any CBI branches;
o. approve procedures to be followed in the CBI's internal decision-making process;
p. approve systems of internal controls within the CBI;
q. determine the annual budget and the personnel plan of the CBI;
r. approve, issue and publish the annual report and the annual financial statements;
s. adopt all regulations and guidelines of general application to be issued by the CBI; and

t. take action upon any other matter, within the competence of the CBI, responsibility for which is not specifically assigned in this Law to any other person or group.

Article 17 Meetings
The Board shall convene upon the initiative of its chairman or upon the initiative of at least one-third of its members but in any event at least once a month.

Article 18 Quorum
A quorum shall exist for the Board's meetings when at least a majority of its members, including the Governor or, in his absence, a Deputy Governor acting as chairman, are present.

Article 19 Decisions of the Board

1. Board decisions shall be adopted by majority vote of the members present. If the vote is evenly divided, the chairman's vote shall be the deciding vote.
2. Board decisions shall take effect in whatever way and at whatever time as may be directed by the Board as recorded in the minutes of the meeting or, absent such direction, immediately. Any abstentions or dissenting opinions shall be recorded in those minutes.

Article 20 Governor as chief executive

1. The Governor shall, as chief executive of the CBI, be responsible for the implementation of the decisions of the Board. The Governor shall conduct the day-to-day operations of the CBI and may exercise any powers delegated to the Governor by the Board.
2. The Deputy Governors shall assist the Governor in conducting the day-to-day operations of the CBI.
3. The Board may establish provisions regulating the extent to which the Governor may delegate any of his powers to other members of the Board or to senior staff of the CBI, including whether delegation may be made to a single person, or to two persons jointly.
4. The Governor shall appoint and terminate the appointment of the employees, agents and correspondents of the CBI, within the general terms and conditions of the personnel plan and other guidelines, if any, adopted by the Board.

Article 21 Conflicts of interests

1. During their service or employment by the CBI, the Governor, Deputy Governors, other members of the Board, and employees of the CBI shall not receive credit from any bank or other entity subject to the supervision of the CBI, except with the prior approval of the Board. The person to receive such credit shall not participate in any decision by the Board concerning such credit. The Board shall authorize routine borrowings made on market terms from such institutions to enable the borrowers to finance the purchase of a residence for the borrower's own use, to pay for educational or medical expenses, and for other family purposes. The Board may establish internal guidelines specifying relevant criteria for such credits.
2. The Board may establish a facility to provide credits on market terms to the Governor, Deputy Governors, other members of the Board, and employees of the CBI for the purchase of a residence for the borrower's personal use, to pay for educational or medical expenses, and for other family related purposes. The Board shall establish and publish internal guidelines specifying relevant criteria for such credits.

3. While holding office, the Governor, the Deputy Governors, and other members of the Board shall devote the whole of their professional services to the CBI, and none of them shall occupy any other office or employment, whether remunerated or not, except (i) as nominee of the CBI or (ii) a limited amount of lecturing and other academic activity so long as such activity is not remunerated and does not interfere with the performance of the individual's duties and responsibilities at the CBI.

4. No employee of the CBI shall simultaneously have any other employment, whether gainful or not, provided, however, that the Board may establish internal guidelines exempting certain categories of staff positions or certain categories of other employment, such as teaching, from this requirement if the Board is satisfied that no conflict of interest will arise.

5. No Governor, Deputy Governor, other member of the Board, or employee of the CBI shall accept any gift or credit for himself, or on behalf of any person with whom he has family, business or financial connections, if the acceptance thereof would result, or give the appearance of resulting, in diminishing his impartial devotion to his duties to the CBI.

Article 22 Confidentiality and exchange of information

1. No person who serves as Governor, Deputy Governor, other member of the Board, or employee, agent or correspondent of the CBI, shall:

   a. permit access to, disclose or publicize nonpublic information which was obtained in the performance of official duties except when required to do so pursuant to paragraph (2) of this Article, as necessary for the fulfillment of any duty or responsibility imposed by this Law, the Banking Law, or any other relevant legislation; or
   b. use such information, or allow such information to be used, for personal gain.

2. The CBI may exchange information on supervisory matters, preferably based on a memorandum of understanding, with central banks and with financial supervisory authorities. The exchange of such information may include confidential information, provided that the CBI has satisfied itself that reasonable steps have been taken to ensure the confidentiality of any such information submitted.

3. The CBI may enter into memoranda of understanding with central banks or with financial supervisory authorities setting out the scope, procedures and further details for the exchange of information.

Article 23 Immunity from legal action

1. No member of the Board, employee or agent of the CBI shall be personally liable in damages for any act or omission taken in the discharge or purported discharge of official functions within the scope of his employment or engagement under this Law.

2. The CBI shall indemnify a member of the Board, employee or agent of the CBI against any legal costs incurred in the defense against legal action brought against such person in connection with the discharge or purported discharge of official functions within the scope of his employment or engagement under this Law, provided that no such indemnification shall apply if such person has been convicted of a crime arising out of the activities that are covered by such legal action.

Section 4 – Relations with the Government

Article 24 Consultation with the Government

1. The Governor and other representatives of the CBI and officials of the Government shall hold regular meetings to exchange information and opinions on the extent to

which monetary and fiscal policies can, each within their own areas of responsibility, be coordinated, and on other matters of mutual interest and responsibility.

2. The Governor and the Deputy Governors may, upon invitation by an official of the Government, attend meetings with the Government at which they may provide, on behalf of the CBI, advice and information within the CBI's area of competence.

Article 25 Actions on behalf of Government

1. The Government may entrust the CBI with the following:
   a. hold the Government's accounts;
   b. engage in and manage, as fiscal agent, domestic and foreign borrowings by the Government;
   c. participate with other representatives of the Government or, with the Government's permission, represent the Government in negotiations with foreign countries as well as with international institutions on monetary and financial issues;
   d. perform financial operations, at market rates, in relation to deposits, foreign exchange operations or other operations based on payment, clearing or economic agreements arising out of international financial arrangements concluded by the Government with foreign parties, provided that (i) the Government shall bear all financial obligations and liabilities incurred by the CBI with respect to such performance and (ii) the CBI shall not perform any financial operation which involves bearing financial obligations or liabilities (direct or indirect) on behalf of the Government; and
   e. perform, to the extent the Government determines, tasks derived from the State's membership in international, financial and monetary institutions.

2. The CBI shall be remunerated by the Government on a cost recovery basis for carrying out the functions under this Article.

Article 26 Prohibition on lending to the Government

1. The CBI shall not grant any direct or indirect credits to the Government or any other public agency or State-owned entity, except that the CBI may provide liquidity assistance under Article 30 to government-owned commercial banks that are subject to the supervision of the CBI, provided that such assistance is granted on the same terms and conditions as would be extended for the benefit of privately-owned commercial banks.

2. The CBI may purchase government securities provided that such purchases are only made in the secondary market and are only made in connection with market operations.

3. Nothing in this Article 26 shall be construed to prohibit the use of government securities in connection with any aspect of open market operations or as collateral for standing facilities.

Section 5 – Official Foreign Reserves

Article 27 Management of official foreign reserves

The CBI shall conduct transactions in foreign assets and manage all official foreign reserves of the State consistent with international best practices and subject to the objectives of monetary policy. The Board may invest such reserves in any or all of the following assets:

a. monetary gold held in the vaults of the CBI;
b. banknotes and coins in foreign currencies normally used in the making of international payments held by or for the account of the CBI;

c. credit balances that are payable on demand or within a short term in foreign currencies normally used in the making of international payments and that are maintained in accounts of the CBI, or otherwise invested through repurchase agreements, with foreign central banks, international financial organizations or major international banks designated by the Board;
d. special drawing rights held in the account of Iraq in the International Monetary Fund;
e. the reserve position of Iraq in the International Monetary Fund; and
f. any readily-marketable debt securities issued by, or bearing the full faith and credit of, foreign governments, central banks, or international financial institutions, that are paid in foreign currencies normally used in the making of international payments and that are held by or for the account of the CBI.

Section 6 – Monetary Functions

Article 28 Open market operations and standing facilities

The CBI may, for the achievement of its objectives, (i) perform open market operations with commercial banks that are licensed or hold permits issued by the CBI under the Banking Law or, at the discretion of the CBI and subject to regulations set forth by the CBI, other appropriately licensed financial intermediaries; and (ii) provide standing facilities to commercial banks that are licensed or hold permits issued by the CBI under the Banking Law and subject to regulations set forth by the CBI by:

a. purchasing or selling outright (spot and forward), or under repurchase agreements or other similar financial instruments, debt securities issued by the CBI or by the Government, bearing market yields provided that purchases of debt securities issued by the Government through open market operations shall only be made in the secondary market.
b. purchasing or selling outright (spot and forward) foreign exchange;
c. discounting bills of exchange or promissory notes;
d. making loans fully secured by pledges of collateral; and
e. accepting interest-bearing deposits from banks.

Article 29 Reserve requirements

1. In order to implement the monetary policy of Iraq, the CBI shall, by regulation, require that banks maintain reserves in the form of cash holdings or deposits with the CBI. Such reserves shall be kept at prescribed minimum levels, calculated as the average of end-of-day reserve levels over such time periods as determined by the CBI and which relate to the size, type or maturity of the banks' deposits, borrowed funds and such other liabilities as the CBI may designate. Banks shall not be permitted to operate overdrafts on reserve accounts at any time. These required reserve levels shall be the same for all banks for each category of liabilities and may be remunerated.

2. The CBI may impose on and collect from any bank that fails to maintain required reserves at the minimum levels prescribed in accordance with paragraph (1) a penal interest rate on the shortfall in such bank's required reserves, until the shortfall is corrected.

Article 30 Lender of last resort

In exceptional circumstances, the CBI may, on such terms and conditions as it determines, act as lender of last resort for a bank that is licensed or holds a permit issued by the CBI under the Banking Law. Such support may be provided by granting financial assistance to the bank, or for the bank's benefit, for periods not exceeding three months that may be renewed by the CBI on the basis of a program specifying the measures that the bank concerned will be taking, provided, however, that no such commitment shall be made by the CBI unless:

a. the bank, in the opinion of the CBI, is solvent and provides adequate collateral, and the request for financial assistance is based on the need to improve liquidity; or
b. such assistance is necessary to preserve the stability of the financial system and the Minister of Finance has issued to the CBI a guarantee in writing on behalf of the Government securing the repayment of the loan.

Section 7 – Currency

Article 31 Unit of currency
The national monetary unit in Iraq shall be the *dinar*.

Article 32 Issuance of currency

1. The CBI shall have the exclusive right to issue banknotes and coins intended for circulation in Iraq. Banknotes issued under this Article shall be a first charge on the assets of the CBI. The CBI shall make appropriate arrangements for the issue of its banknotes and coins as required for circulation in Iraq. Banknotes and coins issued by the CBI and intended for circulation in Iraq are not promissory notes, bills of exchange, or any other type of commercial document under the applicable commercial law, and the CBI is obligated to honor them only as provided for in this Law.
2. Only banknotes and coins issued by the CBI that have not been demonetized shall be legal tender in Iraq.
3. The CBI may, by regulation, limit the amounts of banknotes and coins that must be accepted as a legal tender in payment for an obligation and restrict the denominations of such banknotes and coins in which payment may be made to specified amounts or a range of amounts.
4. The CBI shall be responsible for the supply of Iraq's banknotes and coins and shall endeavor to maintain the availability of an adequate number of banknotes and coins in all regions at all times.

Article 33 Printing of banknotes and minting of coins; accounting treatment of currency issued

1. The CBI shall determine by regulation the denominations, measures, form, material, content, weights, designs, and other features of banknotes and coins. The plates necessary to print or mint the currency and the intellectual property rights to the designs of the currency shall be the property of the CBI.
2. The CBI shall arrange for the printing of banknotes and the minting of coins, and for the security and safekeeping of banknotes and coins that have not yet been issued.
3. The CBI shall be exclusively responsible for the safe and secure destruction of banknotes and coins and for the custody and destruction, as may be necessary, of plates, dies, and retired banknotes and coins. The CBI shall have the exclusive right to melt coins and to sell the metals derived thereby.
4. Upon request by any individual or entity, the CBI shall exchange, free of charge or commission, banknotes and coins with other banknotes or coins in equivalent amounts.

5. The aggregate amount of circulating banknotes and coins issued by the CBI shall be noted in the financial statements of the CBI as a liability; such liability shall not include banknotes and coins in the currency reserve inventory.

Article 34 Withdrawal of unfit banknotes and coins

1. Banknotes and coins in circulation that are unfit for circulation shall cease to be legal tender. Subject to paragraph (2) of this Article, the CBI shall withdraw, destroy, and replace, with banknotes or coins of an equivalent amount, any banknotes or coins presented to it that are unfit for circulation.

2. The CBI may decline to replace an unfit banknote or coin if its designs are illegible, misshaped or perforated, or if more than fifty percent of its surface has been lost; such a banknote or coin shall be withdrawn and destroyed without indemnity to the owner, unless there is evidence satisfactory to the CBI that the missing portions have been totally destroyed, in which case the CBI may, in its sole and absolute discretion, grant compensation in whole or in part.

3. The CBI shall not be required to provide any compensation for banknotes or coins that were lost, stolen or destroyed; it may confiscate without compensation any banknotes that have been altered in their external appearance, including in particular banknotes that have been written on, painted on, overprinted, stamped or perforated, or to which adhesive matter has been applied.

Article 35 Disposition of Counterfeit Currency

Every person who comes into possession of counterfeit banknotes or coins shall forward to the CBI all such counterfeit banknotes or coins.

Article 36 Redemption of currency

1. The CBI may decide to redeem banknotes or coins by issuing, free of charge, other banknotes or coins in equivalent amounts. A decision to redeem banknotes or coins shall be issued in the form of a regulation of the CBI specifying the period during which the exchange shall take place and the locations and times at which withdrawn banknotes or coins shall be presented for redemption.

2. At the end of the exchange period, or at any other time specified by the CBI, redeemed banknotes and coins shall be demonetized and cease to be legal tender.

3. The CBI shall notify the public, by publication in the Official Publication, of the banknotes and coins that are legal tender.

Article 37 Freedom of currency

Parties to a contract or any other voluntary undertaking or transaction, including a bill, note or instrument or security for money, may denominate a payment obligation in any currency agreed upon. Payment in discharge of any debt or liability arising from a contract or any other voluntary undertaking or transaction, including on a bill, note, instrument or security for money, may be made in any currency agreed upon as the currency of payment. An agreement under this Article may be express or implied from surrounding circumstances including course of dealing, usage of trade, or course of performance.

Article 38 Enforcement of foreign currency obligations

A foreign currency obligation may be enforced according to its terms. When a person obtains an order to enforce an obligation in a foreign currency, the order shall require payment of an amount in the currency of Iraq sufficient to purchase the amount of the obligation in the foreign currency at a bank in Iraq at the close of business on the first day on which the bank quotes a *dinar* rate for purchase of the foreign currency before the day payment of the obligation is due to be received by the creditor, provided, however, that if the court determines that such method would, under the circumstances, be inequitable, it shall select a method of conversion that is equitable.

Section 8 – Other Functions

Article 39 Payment systems

1. The CBI shall establish and maintain or promote the establishment and maintenance of sound and efficient systems for the clearing and settlement of payment transactions in accordance with international standards and best practices.
2. The CBI shall be exclusively responsible for the regulation, registration, licensing, and supervision of payment systems operated by parties other than the CBI.
3. In connection with its supervision of payment systems and payment system operators, the CBI may by regulation:
    a. require the registration or licensing of any payment system or payment system operator; and
    b. require any payment system or payment system operator to observe such safe and sound conditions and requirements as may be established by the CBI, including those designed to facilitate supervision of such operators by the CBI and to preserve the safety of the assets entrusted by the public to their care.
4. The CBI shall be authorized to take such action as it deems necessary to carry out the tasks described in paragraph (1), including promoting, organizing, participating in and operating payment systems and establishing the applicable charges.
5. The CBI may make arrangements to facilitate:
    a. the integration of its payment system and related arrangements with other payment systems;
    b. the development of new methods and technologies for payments in domestic or foreign currencies; and
    c. the design and periodic modification of a plan for the evolution of the national payment system of Iraq.

Article 40 Supervision of Banks

The CBI shall have the exclusive authority to take all such actions as may be necessary: to license, regulate and supervise banks and their subsidiaries to obtain compliance with this Law and in the Banking Law, including the authority to conduct off-site surveillance and onsite examinations of licensees and their subsidiaries in the manner and at the times chosen by the CBI; to require banks and their subsidiaries to provide all such information as the CBI may request regarding the affairs of a bank, its subsidiaries, and their customers; and to take remedial action, as provided in this Law and in the Banking Law, to enforce compliance by licensees and their subsidiaries with such laws and with any regulations, prudential standards, guidelines or directives issued by the CBI in connection with its implementation of such laws. Actions by an entity of the Government other than the CBI to regulate the lending and credit activities of banks are without legal force.

Article 41 Compilation and publication of financial statistics

1. At the request of the CBI, banks and any other entities supervised by the CBI according to this Law or the Banking Law shall provide the CBI with such information or data as the CBI determines necessary to:

a. follow developments in foreign exchange, credit, deposit, money and capital markets;
b. establish and publish monetary statistics;
c. establish and publish balance of payments statistics;
d. collect and compile financial data that reflect the risk positions of banks or any other entities supervised by the CBI; and
e. compile and, provided that no confidential business relationship is thereby disclosed, publish any other financial statistics.

2. In carrying out its responsibilities as specified in this Law and other legislation, the CBI shall endeavor to develop and implement policies consistent with international standards and best practices for central banks.

Article 42 Unlicensed persons

1. The CBI shall be empowered, upon obtaining a warrant from the appropriate authorities, to enter the offices and to examine the accounts, books, documents and other records of any person if the CBI determines that there are reasonable grounds to suspect that such person engages in an activity that is subject to the jurisdiction of the CBI without the appropriate license, permit or registration from the CBI even though such license, permit or registration is required by law or is an activity otherwise contrary to this Law; upon request of the CBI, law enforcement officials shall, if necessary by force, assist the CBI to gain access to the premises of such persons and to examine the accounts, books and other records of such person.

2. If the CBI determines that a person engages in an activity without the appropriate license, permit or registration issued by the CBI when such license, permit or registration issued by the CBI is required by law, the CBI shall serve an order directing that person promptly to cease such activity. The order shall be accompanied by a statement describing the facts and law supporting the existence of a violation, and shall request such person to provide a written response within three days after the date of service of such order. If, after a review of any such response and, in any event, within one calendar week from the date of service of its order, the CBI determines that the activity has not ceased, the CBI may impose administrative penalties on such person, the amount of which shall be established pursuant to paragraphs (2) and (3) of Article 62.

Section 9 – Miscellaneous

Article 43 Ownership of property

1. CBI may acquire such movable and immovable properties and equipment as may be required to carry out its functions.

2. Notwithstanding the limitations of paragraph (1), the CBI may, in order to protect, secure or collect a claim, acquire all types of property. Such property shall be sold as soon as possible, consistent with the CBI's interest in minimizing losses and, in any case, not later than at a date at which such disposition may occur without incurring a loss.

Article 44 Exemption from certain taxes

1. The CBI shall be exempted from the following taxes and duties:
   a. taxes on income or profits of the CBI;
   b. personal property taxes on assets of the CBI;
   c. taxes on transfers of funds and other financial transactions;
   d. taxes in the form of stamp duties on issuance of the CBI's securities and banknotes;
   e. customs duties, import duties, sales taxes, value added taxes on imports of gold, banknotes, and coins to be delivered to the CBI; and
   f. sales tax on domestic supplies of gold, banknotes, and coins to the CBI.
2. The CBI shall be liable for property taxes on immovable property only if, as a general rule, Government ministries are liable for such taxes and duties on the immovable property in their ownership or use.
3. The CBI shall be liable for any other taxes or duties, except as otherwise stipulated in the specific laws regulating such taxes or duties.

Section 10 – Financial Statements and Audit

Article 45 Books and records; financial statements and reports

1. The Board shall at all times ensure that the books and records of the CBI, including its financial statements, are prepared and maintained in conformity with internationally-accepted accounting standards.
2. The CBI shall, as soon as possible after the end of each month, prepare and publish in the Official Publication and on its official Internet website balance sheets showing the condition of the CBI as of the close of business on the last business day of the month that has just ended.
3. The CBI shall, within three months after the end of each financial year, prepare annual financial statements that shall ensure a correct and complete reporting in a transparent manner of the CBI's financial status.
4. The Board shall, within three months after the end of each financial year, submit to the Appointing Authority, with copies to the Minister of Finance and to the Legislature:
   a. the annual financial statements of the CBI, approved by the Board, signed by the Governor and certified by the external auditor, together with any reports or remarks that the external auditor may wish to make; and
   b. a report on the CBI's operations during the financial year that has just ended, in particular in relation to its monetary policy objectives and events that affected the economy of Iraq. This report should also include a statement regarding the CBI's outlook for the economy for the coming year with emphasis on monetary policy issues. In its review of policy developments, the report shall include:
      (i) a review of the policies and measures adopted by the Board during the year and an analysis of the economic and financial circumstances which prompted those policies and measures;
      (ii) a discussion of the condition of the financial system of Iraq with special emphasis on the banking and payment systems; and
      (iii) the texts of the major legal enactments and administrative measures adopted by the Government and the CBI during the year which relate to the functions or operations of the CBI and of banks and other financial institutions operating in Iraq.

5. The CBI shall publish the audited annual financial statements in the Official Publication and on its website. The reports referred to in paragraph (4) shall be published.

6. The CBI shall, on a quarterly basis, publish reports on monetary policy and financial stability that provide information on developments in the current year, including events that affect the economy of Iraq as described in paragraph (4), sub-paragraph (b).

7. The Governor shall report on the CBI's operations and its monetary policy objectives, including events that affect the economy of Iraq as described in paragraph (4), subparagraph (b), to the Legislature no less than once a year.

Article 46 Internal audit

The CBI's internal audit department, headed by the chief internal auditor, shall perform internal audit functions which shall include the following:

a. the review and recommendation to the Board of procedures and practices for proper risk management and, thereafter, the supervision of their implementation on a continuing basis;
b. the performance of periodic audits of the administration and operations of the CBI to ensure proper observance of laws applicable to the CBI and of decisions of the Board;
c. the review of the periodic financial statements referred to in Article 44, paragraphs (2) and (3), and related documents of the CBI;
d. the preparation and delivery to the Board, whenever deemed appropriate by the Board and at least once every quarter, of reports and recommendations regarding the financial statements and records, the budgetary and accounting procedures, the risk management and other controls within the CBI, the efficiency and cost effectiveness at which the CBI operates, and any other matter within its competence and area of responsibilities on which a report may be requested by the Board; and
e. any other assignment that may be given to the internal audit department by the Board, provided that such assignments do not disrupt its principal task set forth herein.

Article 47 Chief internal auditor

1. The chief internal auditor shall be appointed by the Board for a term of five years, and shall be selected from among that pool of distinguished candidates comprised of persons with extensive professional experience in the field of accounting or audit appropriate to prepare them for the responsibilities of the position. The chief internal auditor may be reappointed.

2. The chief internal auditor, as head of the internal audit department, shall be responsible to the Board for the proper discharge of the functions of the internal audit department.

3. The salary and other employment benefits of the chief internal auditor shall be commensurate with those received by persons in equivalent positions in commercial banks and other financial institutions and shall be determined by the Board.

4. The chief internal auditor may resign from office after giving not less than three months' written notice to the Board and shall be subject to the provisions of Article 15(3).

Article 48 External audit

1. The financial statements of the CBI shall be audited in accordance with international standards on auditing at least once a year by a reputable external audit firm with recognized experience in the auditing of central banks and major international financial institutions.

2. The external audit firm shall be appointed annually by the Minister of Finance. No external audit firm shall be appointed consecutively for a cumulative period exceeding five years.

3. The CBI shall provide the external auditor with such assistance as the external auditor may require and the external auditor shall have access, upon request, to all accounts, books, minutes, records, and other documents or written or oral information or data.

4. The Minister of Finance shall determine the compensation to be paid to the external auditor, taking into consideration the size and nature of the task normally to be performed. Such compensation shall be included as expenses in the budget of the CBI and borne by the CBI.

5. The CBI shall be subject to audit by the Board of Supreme Audit.

Section 11 – Criminal Offenses

Article 49 Interpretation

In this section:

'*banknote*' includes any instrument intended to be used as money or as the equivalent of money, immediately on issue or at some time subsequent thereto, issued under lawful authority in Iraq or elsewhere;

'*counterfeit money*' includes:

a. false coin or false paper money that resembles or is apparently intended to resemble or pass for a current coin or current paper money,
b. a forged banknote or forged blank banknote, whether complete or incomplete,
c. a genuine coin or genuine paper money that is prepared or altered to resemble or pass for a current coin or current paper money of a higher denomination, including an instrument prepared by placing or connecting together different parts of two or more banknotes or other genuine instruments,
d. a current coin from which the milling is removed by filing or cutting the edges and on which new milling is made to restore its appearance,
e. a coin cased with gold, silver or nickel, as the case may be, that is intended to resemble or pass for a current gold, silver or nickel coin, and
f. a coin or a piece of metal or mixed metals that is washed or colored by any means with a wash or material capable of producing the appearance of gold, silver or nickel and that is intended to resemble or pass for a current gold, silver or nickel coin;

'*counterfeit token of value*' means a counterfeit excise stamp, postage stamp or other evidence of value, by whatever technical, trivial or deceptive designation it may be described, and includes genuine coin or paper money that has no value as money;

'*current*' means lawfully in use in Iraq or elsewhere by virtue of a law in force in Iraq or elsewhere as the case may be;

'*utter*' includes sell, pay, tender and put off.

Article 50 Making

Each person who makes or begins to make counterfeit money is guilty of an indictable offense and liable to a fine not exceeding fifty million *dinars* or to imprisonment for a term not exceeding five years or to both.

Article 51 Possession

Each person who, knowingly and with intent to defraud

a. buys, receives or offers to buy or receive,

b. has in his custody or possession, or

c. introduces into Iraq, counterfeit money is guilty of an indictable offense and liable to a fine not exceeding fifty million *dinars* or to imprisonment for a term not exceeding five years or to both.

Article 52 Uttering

1. Each person who, knowingly and with intent to defraud

   a. utters or offers to utter counterfeit money or uses counterfeit money as if it were genuine, or

   b. exports, sends or takes counterfeit money out of Iraq, is guilty of an indictable offense and liable to a fine not exceeding one hundred million *dinars* or to imprisonment for a term not exceeding ten years or to both.

2. Each person who, with intent to defraud, knowingly utters

   a. a coin that is not current, or

   b. a piece of metal or mixed metals that resembles in size, figure or color a current coin for which it is uttered, is guilty of an indictable offense and liable to a fine not exceeding fifty million *dinars* or to imprisonment for a term not exceeding five years or to both.

Article 53 Slugs and tokens

Each person who, knowingly and with intent to defraud

a. manufactures, produces or sells, or

b. has in his possession

anything that is intended to be fraudulently used in substitution for a coin or token of value that any coin or token-operated device is designed to receive is guilty of an offense and liable to a fine not exceeding twenty-five million *dinars* or to imprisonment for a term not exceeding two years or to both.

Article 54 Defacing

Each person who

a. defaces a current coin,

b. utters a current coin that has been defaced,

c. without the authority of the CBI defaces any banknote by printing, stamping or by any like means impressing on it any words, letters or figures, or

d. utters a current banknote that has been defaced contrary to sub-paragraph (c), is guilty of an offense punishable on summary conviction and liable to a fine not exceeding one million *dinars* or to imprisonment for a term not exceeding six months or to both.

Article 55 Likeness of banknotes

1. No person shall make, publish, print, execute, issue, distribute or circulate, including by electronic or computer-assisted means, anything in the likeness of

   a. a current banknote, or

   b. an obligation or a security of a government or bank.

2. Paragraph (1) does not apply to:
   a. the CBI or its employees when they are carrying out their duties under Section 7 of this Law;
   b. the police or its members or employees when they are carrying out their duties to prevent and investigate any violation of this Law; or
   c. any person acting under a contract or license from the CBI or the police in connection with the duties described in (a) and (b) of this paragraph 2.
3. A person who contravenes paragraph (1) is guilty of an offense punishable on summary conviction and liable to a fine not exceeding one million *dinars* or to imprisonment for a term not exceeding six months or to both.
4. No person shall be convicted of an offense under paragraph (3) in relation to the printed likeness of a banknote issued by the CBI if it is established that the length or width of the likeness is less than three-fourths or greater than one-and-one-half times the length or width, as the case may be, of the banknote and
   a. the likeness is in black-and-white only, or
   b. the likeness of the banknote appears on only one side of the likeness.

Article 56 Instruments or materials

Each person who knowingly

a. makes or repairs,
b. begins or proceeds to make or repair,
c. buys or sells, or
d. has in his custody or possession,

any machine, engine, tool, instrument, material or thing that he knows has been used or that he knows is adapted and intended for use in making counterfeit money or counterfeit tokens of value is guilty of an indictable offense and liable to a fine not exceeding fifty million *dinars* or to imprisonment for a term not exceeding five years or to both.

Article 57 Conveying instruments for coining out of mint

Each person who, without lawful justification or excuse, the proof of which lies on him, conveys out of any mint licensed or authorized to mint coins in Iraq,

a. any machine, engine, tool, instrument, material or thing used or employed in connection with the manufacture of coins,
b. a useful part of anything mentioned in sub-paragraph (a), or
c. coin, bullion, metal or a mixture of metals, is guilty of an indictable offense and liable to a fine not exceeding fifty million *dinars* or to imprisonment for a term not exceeding five years or to both.

Article 58 Advertising and trafficking

1. Each person who knowingly
   a. by an advertisement or any other writing, offers to sell, procure or dispose of counterfeit money or counterfeit tokens of value or to give information with respect to the manner in which or the means by which counterfeit money or counterfeit tokens of value may be sold, procured or disposed of, or
   b. purchases, obtains, negotiates or otherwise deals with counterfeit tokens of value, or offers to negotiate with a view to purchasing or obtaining them, is guilty of an indictable offense and liable to a fine not exceeding fifty million *dinars* or to imprisonment for a term not exceeding five years or to both.

2. No person shall be convicted of an offense under paragraph (1) in respect of genuine coin or genuine paper money that has no value as money unless, at the time when the offense is alleged to have been committed, the person knew that the coin or paper money had no value as money and the person had a fraudulent intent in his dealings with or with respect to the coin or paper money.

Article 59 Special provisions as to proof

1. Every offense relating to counterfeit money or counterfeit tokens of value shall be deemed to be complete notwithstanding that the money or tokens of value in respect of which the proceedings are taken are not finished or perfected or do not copy exactly the money or tokens of value that they are apparently intended to resemble or for which they are apparently intended to pass.
2. In any proceedings under this section, a certificate signed by a person designated as an examiner of counterfeit by the CBI, stating that any coin, paper money or banknote described therein is counterfeit money or that any coin, paper money or banknote described therein is genuine and is or is not, as the case may be, current in Iraq or elsewhere, is evidence of the statements contained in the certificate without proof of the signature or official character of the person appearing to have signed the certificate.
3. A party against whom a certificate described in paragraph (2) is produced may, with leave of the court, require the attendance of the examiner of counterfeit designated by the CBI, for the purposes of cross-examination. No certificate shall be received in evidence pursuant to paragraph (2) unless the party intending to produce it has, before the trial, given to the other party reasonable notice of his intention and a copy of the certificate.

Article 60 Unauthorized issue of banknotes, coins, instruments, tokens

Each person who issues

a. a banknote or coin in violation of paragraph (1) of Article 32, or
b. any other instrument or token intended for circulation in Iraq as money other than as authorized by this section, is guilty of an indictable offense and liable to imprisonment for a term not exceeding ten years.

Article 61 Forfeiture

1. Counterfeit money, counterfeit tokens of value and anything that is used or is intended to be used to make counterfeit money or counterfeit tokens of value belong to the Government.
2. A police officer may seize and detain:
   a. counterfeit money;
   b. counterfeit tokens of value; and
   c. machines, engines, tools, instruments, materials or things that have been used or that have been adapted and are intended for use in making counterfeit money or counterfeit tokens of value, and anything seized shall be sent to the CBI to be disposed of or dealt with as he may direct, but anything that is required as evidence in any proceedings shall not be sent to the CBI until it is no longer required in those proceedings.
3. For the purpose of this Article, a banknote or coin issued in violation of Article 32(1), or any other instrument or token intended for circulation in Iraq as money other than as authorized by this section, is to be treated as counterfeit money or token for value.

Article 62 Administrative penalties

1. The CBI shall be authorized to enforce compliance with this Law, the Banking Law, and with all regulations and orders issued by the CBI under those laws, through the imposition of administrative penalties upon licensees, officers, directors and agents of licensees; and upon persons who, though not licensees, or officers, directors or agents of licensees, are required to take action, or to refrain from taking action, by this Law, the Banking Law, or by regulations or orders issued by the CBI under those laws.

2. Penalties as described in this Article are civil, not criminal, in nature, and may be imposed directly by the CBI. Administrative penalties may be imposed, at the discretion of the CBI, in amounts that range up to ten million *dinars* per violation; and, at the discretion of the CBI, they may be imposed on a daily basis for each day that the violation continues until the CBI determines that compliance is achieved. The CBI shall, before imposing administrative penalties, provide a detailed statement to the person against whom the penalty is to be imposed describing the facts and law supporting the existence of a violation, and shall give such person a full opportunity to provide facts and arguments as to why the penalty should not be imposed. The CBI shall issue regulations setting forth the procedures it will use in connection with its imposition of administrative penalties.

3. In determining whether to impose administrative penalties, and in determining the amount of such penalties, the CBI shall take into consideration: the severity of the violation; whether it was recurring; whether depositors or other persons were injured thereby; whether the person against whom the penalty is to be imposed profited from the conduct at issue; the financial resources of such person; any mitigating factors; and such other factors as, in its discretion, it believes to be relevant.

4. The imposition by the CBI of administrative penalties stipulated in this Article shall not bar any civil or criminal accountability under the provisions of any law.

Section 12 – Financial Services Tribunal

Article 63 Establishment and jurisdiction of Tribunal

1. There is hereby established a tribunal to be known as the Financial Services Tribunal which shall have jurisdiction to review the following decisions and orders of the CBI:
   a. rejecting an application for a banking license or permit, attaching a condition or restriction to a license or permit, or revoking a license or permit under the Banking Law or this Law;
   b. imposing enforcement measures or administrative penalties under the Banking Law or this Law;
   c. enjoining a person engaged in an activity requiring a license or permit from engaging in such activity without such a license or permit issued by the CBI pursuant to paragraph (2) of Article 42 of this Law;
   d. extending the term of a conservator;
   e. taking any action provided for in Sections 11 through 14 of the Banking Law with respect to which an appeal to the Tribunal is provided therein; and
   f. regarding any other matter as specified by the law.

2. The Tribunal shall also have jurisdiction to review actions taken by a conservator or receiver under Sections 11 through 14 of the Banking Law. Such review shall be limited to a determination as to whether the action of the conservator or receiver was taken in a manner that exceeded the authority granted to such conservator or receiver under the Banking Law.

3. The Tribunal shall also have jurisdiction to adjudicate any dispute between banks and between financial institutions that is referred to the Tribunal pursuant to a written agreement between the parties to the dispute, which agreement may provide either that an appeal of the Tribunal's decision may be taken to the Court of Appeal or that no appeal shall be permitted.

4. The Tribunal shall not have jurisdiction to review the CBI's decisions or actions with respect to developing and implementing monetary policy, including exchange rate policy.

5. The jurisdiction of the Tribunal shall be exclusive of the jurisdiction of any other tribunal or court of law.

6. Unless otherwise determined by the Tribunal, decisions and orders by the CBI shall, notwithstanding the filing of an appeal, remain in full force and effect until a final decision on review by the Tribunal annuls the decision or order, or until the decision or order is modified by the CBI, or until the decision or order terminates pursuant to its terms, or pursuant to a decision of the CBI, or pursuant to a provision of law.

7. The Tribunal shall not have jurisdiction over any violation of law which is punishable by imprisonment. The Tribunal shall refer any such matter to the Minister of Justice.

Article 64 Composition of Tribunal

1. The Tribunal shall be composed of one or more panels of three to five judges and shall be headed by a chief judge. The Minister of Justice shall appoint a judge of the Tribunal to serve as the chief judge of the Tribunal. The chief judge shall form one or more panels of judges, as the caseload of the Tribunal may require, by selecting judges from the pool of judges to be formed as described in paragraph (2) of this Article.

2. The pool of judges shall initially be comprised of five judges, three of whom shall be appointed by the Minister of Justice and shall be lawyers with professional experience as judges, practicing attorneys or professors of administrative, civil or commercial law. The other two judges in the pool of judges shall be appointed by the Minister of Finance; one of these shall be an experienced accountant by profession, while the other shall have extensive professional experience in financial transactions.

3. In selecting judges for a panel, the chief judge shall attempt to harmonize the qualifications of the members of particular panels to the needs of the specific cases to be resolved by those panels. On each panel, the chief judge shall designate a judge with legal training to serve as its presiding judge to preside over the discharge of the functions of the panel.

4. Judges in the pool of judges may serve on a full-time or part-time basis, as, in the judgment of the chief judge, the caseload of the Tribunal requires. If the chief judge determines that the pool of judges must be expanded in order to resolve the Tribunal's caseload within a reasonable period of time, the chief judge shall submit a request to the Ministers of Justice and of Finance to increase the pool of judges through the appointment of additional judges.

5. No person shall be eligible to serve as a judge on the Tribunal and, if appointed, the person shall be removed from the Tribunal by a decision of the Minister of Justice, if the person, in the judgment of the Minister of Justice:

   a. is not a citizen of Iraq;
   b. is not a fit and proper person;
   c. is also serving as an officer or a full-time or part-time employee or consultant, with or without remuneration, of a bank or other entity subject to the supervision of the CBI;

d. is also serving as a member of the Board or full-time or part-time employee or consultant of the CBI;
e. is also a member of the Legislature;
f. is also serving as a Minister, Deputy Minister or other high ranking official of the State;
g. has been or is declared bankrupt or unable to pay his debts as they fall due by a court decision;
h. is, or would be, unable to perform the functions of this office because of an infirmity of body or mind that has lasted for more than six months;
i. has been engaged in a significant violation of the law or in serious misconduct in office, or has actively participated in political activities, diminishing or giving the appearance of diminishing the reputation of the Tribunal as an independent and impartial judicial institution; or
j. the person, or any person who is related by marriage, blood or kinship, including adopted children or foster children of the person, and any other person residing in such person's household, hold direct or indirect business interests that would make it necessary for that person to refrain, to an unacceptable extent, from taking part in the decision-making of the Tribunal.

6. Judges of the Tribunal shall be appointed for a ten-year term of office and may be reappointed; however, upon giving written notice to the Minister of Justice, a judge may resign at any time. The Minister of Justice shall specify by regulation the remuneration and other benefits of the judges of the Tribunal.

7. No judge shall be removed from the Tribunal on any ground other than as stated in paragraph (5) and no judge shall be removed from the Tribunal before a hearing has been held by the Minister of Justice at which such judge or his legal representative has been afforded a reasonable opportunity to present his views.

Article 65 Administration of Tribunal

1. The Minister of Justice shall be responsible for the organization of the Tribunal and for the supervision of its administration.

2. The chief judge of the Tribunal shall be directly responsible for the administration of the Tribunal. He shall be assisted by a staff including a clerk of the Tribunal, an administrator of the Tribunal, and an accountant of the Tribunal. The staff of the Tribunal shall be appointed by the Minister of Justice, and shall have such duties and serve on such terms and conditions as may be specified by the Minister of Justice.

3. No person shall be liable in damages for an act done as chief judge or judge of the Tribunal, except that, if such person shall be convicted of a crime on account of such act, the person may be held liable in a civil proceeding for damages caused by that criminal act.

4. Each judge shall, upon first becoming a judge of the Tribunal and annually thereafter, disclose in full to the Minister of Justice the significant commercial interests which he or members of his household have, directly or indirectly. Whenever any case before a panel of the Tribunal is related to a significant commercial interest held by a judge or members of his household, directly or indirectly, the judge shall disclose his interest to the panel, recuse himself, and be replaced by another judge. Any failure to do so shall be deemed to be a significant violation of law constituting grounds for removal under, and following the procedures provided by paragraph (5) of Article 64.

5. No judge of the Tribunal and no member of its staff shall accept any gift or credit for himself, or on behalf of any person with whom he has family, business or financial

connections, if the acceptance thereof would diminish, or give the appearance of diminishing, the reputation of the Tribunal as an independent and impartial judicial institution.

6. No person who serves as a judge or as a member of the staff of the Tribunal shall:
   a. permit access to, disclose or publicize nonpublic information which was obtained in the performance of official duties, except when required to do so by any court of law or as necessary for the fulfillment of any duty or responsibility imposed by this Law, the Banking Law, or any other relevant legislation; or
   b. use such information, or allow such information to be used, for personal gain.

7. Failure to observe the provisions of paragraph (6) shall be considered a significant violation of law for purposes of paragraph (5), sub-paragraph (i) of Article 64.

Article 66 Authority of Minister of Justice

The Minister of Justice shall, by regulation: (i) make rules governing the place or places where the Tribunal shall sit; (ii) make rules governing the proceedings of the Tribunal; (iii) make rules governing directions the chief judge of the Tribunal may give to panels of the Tribunal concerning procedures to be followed in individual cases; and (iv) specify the circumstances under which hearings of the Tribunal, for exceptional reasons, shall not be open to the public.

Article 67 Evidence

1. The Tribunal may, by summons, require any person to attend, at such time and place as is specified in the summons, to give testimony or to produce documents in his custody or control which the Tribunal considers it necessary to examine.

2. Each person who, without lawful justification or excuse,
   a. refuses or fails to attend a session of the Tribunal following the issue of a summons by the Tribunal, or to give evidence, or
   b. alters, suppresses, conceals or destroys, or refuses to produce, a document which he may be required to produce for the purposes of proceedings before the Tribunal,

   is guilty of an indictable offense and liable to a fine not exceeding twenty-five million *dinars* or imprisonment for a term not exceeding two years or to both.

3. A person accused of violating Paragraph 2 of this Article bears the burden of proving lawful justification or excuse.

Article 68 Decisions of the Tribunal

1. Decisions of the Tribunal shall be taken by a majority of the judges on a panel. Decisions must be recorded in a document which states the reasons for the decision and is signed by the presiding judge of the panel dealing with the case addressed by the decision. The Tribunal must, as soon as is reasonably practicable, notify each party of the decision by sending each party a copy of the decision.

2. Decisions of the Tribunal may award expenses, damages and interest. Decisions shall take effect on the day specified in the decision or, if no effective date is specified, it shall take effect one week from the date of notification of the parties.

3. Decisions of the Tribunal shall be enforced as other court decisions.

Article 69 Procedure for review by Tribunal

1. An application for review of a decision or order of the CBI or an act of a conservator or receiver must be made by a written request submitted to the Tribunal by one or more

parties aggrieved by the decision, order or act. The request must be filed within thirty days following the date of the decision, order or act or within such shorter period of time as is specified by law. Upon receipt of the request, the clerk of the Tribunal shall send a copy of the request to the CBI and other interested parties and shall notify the parties to attend every hearing of the panel dealing with the request.

2. Decisions and orders of the CBI shall remain in full force and effect until: (i) a final decision on review by the Tribunal annuls the order or decision; (ii) the decision or order is modified by the CBI acting on remand from the Tribunal; or (iii) the decision or order terminates pursuant to its terms; provided, however, that the Tribunal may suspend such order or decision of the CBI prior to reaching a final decision either on the basis of a finding that there is a substantial likelihood that the aggrieved party will prevail in the case before it, or in exceptional circumstances where the immediate application of the decision or order would cause undue hardship or irreparable harm.

3. Notwithstanding any other provision in this section, in any case brought with respect to a decision, order or action adopted or taken by a conservator, receiver, the CBI, the Minister of Finance or the State under Sections 11 through 14 of the Banking Law, the Tribunal, or other appropriate court, may only award monetary damages, expenses and interest and shall not annul, remand, suspend, enjoin, terminate or bar such decision, order or action, except with respect to a decision by the Tribunal regarding the removal of a conservator under Article 63 of the Banking Law.

4. The Tribunal may annul or remand to the CBI for further consideration an order or decision of the CBI, or award of monetary damages, expenses and interest with respect to a decision or order of the CBI only on one or more of the following grounds:

   a. in taking the decision or issuing the order, the CBI exceeded or abused its authority;
   b. the procedures followed by the CBI in reaching its decision or order were materially inconsistent with the procedures prescribed by law in a manner which resulted in substantially prejudicing the rights, obligations or interests of an aggrieved party; or
   c. the decision was adopted in an arbitrary and capricious manner.

5. The Tribunal shall give great weight to the evidence presented to the CBI and to the CBI's resolution of issues arising under any laws it is charged with the responsibility to administer.

6. Decisions and orders of the CBI that were remanded by the Tribunal to the CBI for further consideration and that are not modified or terminated by the final date specified by the Tribunal in its order of remand shall terminate on that date.

Article 70 Appeals

1. Final orders and decisions of the Tribunal shall be subject to appeal to the Court of Appeal.

2. A party to a decision rendered by the Tribunal pursuant to Articles 63 and 68 may appeal to the Court of Appeal; unless otherwise determined by the Court of Appeal, the decision, pending the conclusion of the appeal, shall remain in full force and effect.

3. The Court of Appeal may, upon appeal, remand or annul a decision of the Tribunal on one or more of the following grounds:

   a. the Tribunal lacks jurisdiction;
   b. the decision of the Tribunal is not supported by substantial evidence, or is predicated on false evidence, including false testimony and documents that are false, falsified or materially tampered with;

c. in cases involving paragraph (3) of Article 63, where the agreement referred to therein permits appeal, the decision of the Tribunal exceeds the scope of the agreement on which the jurisdiction of the Tribunal is based, or fails to address all or part of a dispute referred to the Tribunal; or
d. is otherwise contrary to law.

4. The appeal must be instituted within 30 days from the date of notification of the decision, except that, for the grounds described in paragraph (3), sub-paragraph (b) this period shall begin not earlier than the day of discovery of documents offering *prima facie* proof of false evidence, fraud or deception.

Section 14 [sic] – Final Provisions

Article 71 Precedence over inconsistent laws
Any provision of law that was enacted prior to the effective date of this Law and which is inconsistent with this Law shall be superceded by this Law.

Article 72 Immunity from prejudgment attachment
No attachment or execution shall be issued against the CBI or its property, including gold, special drawing rights, currency, credits, deposits or securities, and any proceeds thereof, before the issuance of final judgment in any legal action brought before the Tribunal or in the courts of Iraq.

Article 73 Repeal
The Central Bank of Iraq Law No. 64 of 1976, as amended, shall be repealed when this Law comes into effect.

Article 74 Entry into force
This Law shall enter into force on March 1, 2004.

Document 80

Coalition Provisional Authority Order Number 57

CPA/ORD/5 February 2004/57

Iraqi Inspectors General

Pursuant to my authority as Administrator of the Coalition Provisional Authority, and under the laws and usages of war, and consistent with relevant U.N. Security Council resolutions, including Resolutions 1483 and 1511,

Noting that the former regime fostered inefficiency and corruption in Iraqi governmental institutions, and that a concerted effort is needed to restore public trusts and confidence in these institutions,

Acknowledging that ministers need a corps of qualified, objective professionals dedicated to improving ministry performance and eliminating fraud, waste and specified authorities and powers,

Emphasizing that to be effective, the corps of professionals referred to above requires strong leadership, significant independence, adequate resources, and specified authorities and powers,

Determined to improve the efficiency, effectiveness and integrity of the Iraqi ministries, and to restore public trust and confidence in government,

I hereby promulgate the following:

Section 1 Purpose

This Order establishes an effective program of audit, investigation and performance review to provide increased accountability, integrity and oversight of the ministries and to prevent, deter, and identify waste, fraud, abuse of authority and illegal acts. It establishes independent Offices of Inspectors General to conduct investigations, audits, evaluations, inspections and other reviews in accordance with generally accepted professional standards.

Section 2 Establishment

1) There is hereby established within each Iraqi ministry an Office of Inspector General to be headed by an Inspector General.

2) The initial Inspector General in each ministry shall be appointed to a 5-year term by the Administrator. Any Inspector General vacancy that occurs before the sovereign transitional Iraqi administration's assumption of full governance authority shall be filled pursuant to the same procedure.

3) After the assumption of full governance authority by the sovereign transitional Iraq administration, Inspectors General shall be appointed to vacant positions by the chief executive of the transitional Iraqi administration, subject to confirmation by majority vote of the body vested with national legislative powers.[174]

4) Inspectors General shall be selected without regard to political affiliation (consistent with applicable de-Baathification policy) and on the basis of integrity, capability for strong leadership, and demonstrated ability in accounting, auditing, financial analysis, public administration, investigation, criminal justice administration, or other closely related fields. In addition, the Inspector General should possess demonstrated knowledge, skills, abilities and experience in conducting audits and investigations.

5) Inspectors General shall be appointed for a term of five years, which term may be renewed for additional 5-year period(s) at the discretion of the chief executive of the transitional Iraqi administration, subject to confirmation by majority vote of the body vested with national legislative powers.

Section 3 Reporting and Independence

1) Inspectors General shall report directly to the relevant minister and shall respond to requests or inquiries submitted by the Coalition Provisional Authority (or the body of the Iraqi administration vested with national legislative powers). In cases involving allegations of misconduct by the relevant minister, an Inspector General shall report to the administrator (or to the Commissioner on Public Integrity, upon the transitional Iraqi administration's assumption of full governance authority in Iraq).

2) No individual or organization shall attempt to prevent, impair or deter an Inspector General from taking authorized actions necessary to initiate, carry out, or complete any

[174] Sec 2(3) was amended by CPA Order No 100, sec 3(21)(a) *[Doc 124]*.

audit, investigation or review or from obtaining documents relevant to any pending audit or investigation. Individuals who violate this subsection shall be subject to investigation and prosecution by the Commission on Public Integrity, in accordance with applicable law.

Section 4 Removal from Office

1) An Inspector General may be removed by the relevant minister only for cause. 'Cause' shall include, but shall not be limited to, malfeasance, abuse of office, and bribery.

2) In the case of a removal, the relevant minister shall report the removal and the grounds for removal to the Administrator, until the transitional Iraqi administration assumes full governance authority in Iraq. Thereafter, such reports, including the basis for the removal, shall be submitted to the body of the transitional Iraqi administration vested with national legislative powers. The Administrator or national legislative body may request additional information from the relevant minister regarding the removal, which may be overturned by the Administrator or by a majority vote of the national legislative body.

Section 5 Functions

Each Office of Inspector General shall:

1) Audit all records and activities of the ministry, for purposes of ensuring the integrity, transparency and efficiency of ministry operations, and provide information for decision-making and recommend improvements to ministry programs, policies and procedures as appropriate;

2) Conduct administration investigations consistent with the powers defined in Section 6, below;

3) Audit the economy, efficiency, and effectiveness of the ministry's operations and functions and review any ministry systems for measuring performance;

4) Receive, assess, and process complaints of fraud, waste, abuse of authority and mismanagement affecting ministry interests; forward complaints to appropriate investigative authority; and provide quality control, to include timeliness, independence, and thoroughness, for responses;

5) Conduct follow-up to ensure adequacy of corrective actions in response to Inspector General findings and recommendations;

6) Provide information and evidence regarding potentially criminal acts to appropriate law enforcement officials;

7) Receive and investigate complaints from any source or upon its own initiative concerning alleged fraud, waste and abuse and inefficiencies, including deficiencies in the operation and maintenance of facilities;

8) Engage in activities designed to prevent fraud, waste and abuse and inefficiencies, including but not limited to review of legislation, rules, regulations, policies, procedures, and transactions; and presentation of training and education programs;

9) Refer matters for further civil, criminal and administrative action to appropriate administrative and prosecutorial agencies;

10) Recommend non-binding remedial actions to be taken by the ministry to overcome or correct operating or maintenance deficiencies and inefficiencies that were identified by the Office;

11) Issue public reports as set forth in section 9, below;

12) Monitor implementation of recommendations made by the Office and other audit agencies;

13) Promulgate written policies and procedures to guide functions and processes conducted by the Office;

14) Train employees of the ministry in the prevention and identification of waste, fraud and abuse, and establish programs for fostering a culture of accountability and integrity;

15) Maintain information regarding the cost of investigations and cooperate with appropriate administrative and prosecutorial agencies in recouping such costs from nongovernmental entities that are determined to have engaged in willful misconduct;

16) Cooperate fully in assisting the work of law enforcement agencies, investigators and courts, including the Iraq Commission on Public Integrity;

17) Take such actions as may be necessary to ensure the efficient performance of Inspector General functions at every level of the Ministry's operations; and

18) Perform such other duties within the scope of their powers, as defined in Section 6, below as may be necessary to carry out their responsibilities under this Order.

Section 6 Powers

1) To accomplish the functions set forth in Section 6 of this Order, each Office of Inspector General is hereby granted:

a) Full and unrestricted access to all offices, limited access or restricted areas, employees, records, information data, reports, plans, projections, matters, contracts, memoranda, correspondence and any other materials, including electronic data of the ministry;

b) Authority to subpoena witnesses, administer oaths or affirmations, to take testimony and to compel the production of such books, records and documents, including the electronic data as is deemed to be relevant to any inquiry or investigation undertaken;

c) Reasonable access to the head of any governmental entity (including without limitations ministries, departments, agencies, and state owned entities), when necessary for purposes related to the work of the Office; and

d) Authority to require employees of the ministry to report to the Office of Inspector General information regarding fraud, waste, abuse, corruption, and illegal acts.

2) Each Office of the Inspector General shall adhere to Section 9 with respect to any information derived from exercising the powers set forth in Section 6(1).

Section 7 Resources

1) Each ministry shall fund its Office of Inspector General from its annual budget received from the national budget. Each ministry must allocate and deliver funds that are adequate to meet the mission of its Office of Inspector General.[175]

2) The Inspectors General shall establish the organizational structure appropriate to carrying out the responsibilities and functions of his or her office, and may appoint, employ, promote, and remove such assistants, employees, and personnel as deemed necessary for the efficient and effective administration of the office.

3) Within budget limitations, the Inspector General may obtain the services of Chartered Accountants, qualified management consultants, or other professional experts necessary to perform independently the functions of the office.

[175] Sec 7(1) was rescinded and replaced by CPA Order No 100, sec 3(21)(b) *[Doc 124]*.

Section 8 Record Keeping

1) During the course of audit and investigation activities, records produced by an Office of Inspector General shall not be made public.

2) Each Office of Inspector General shall take all steps necessary to prevent unauthorized public disclosure of audit and investigative reports, including any such disclosure that would jeopardize the national security of Iraq.

3) Names and identities of complainants will not be disclosed to the public without the complainant's written consent, unless required by Iraqi law or judicial process.

4) Each Office of Inspector General shall maintain the confidentiality of any classified information obtained by the Office, and shall be subject to the same penalties as the custodian of those records for violating statutes governing the handling of classified information.

5) Each Office of Inspector General shall take all steps appropriate to protect the privacy of individuals to the extent possible in the context of the judicial or administrative processes initiated to protect the public.

Section 9 Reporting

1) Each Inspector General will report the findings and recommendations of the Office's work to the respective minister, to appropriate elected and appointed leadership, and, except for law enforcement sensitive or confidential information, to the public.

  a) Each Inspector General shall report potentially criminal investigative matters to the appropriate law enforcement and prosecutorial agencies.

  b) Each Inspector General shall immediately report to the head of the relevant ministry significant problems, abuses, or deficiencies relating to the administration of programs and operations of the ministry or interference with Inspector General operations.

2) Within 60 days of the end of each fiscal year, each Inspector General shall issue an annual report that separately lists audit and review reports and other investigative or assistance efforts completed during the fiscal year.

  a) The report shall describe the activities of the Office of Inspector General. Copies of the report shall be provided to the minister as well as any legislative bodies with oversight authority with respect to the ministry or the Office of Inspector General.

  b) Upon issuance, members of the media and the public shall be promptly advised of the issuance of the report. Such reports will be provided to their representatives upon request.

Section 10 Professional Standards

Audits, investigations, inspections, and reviews conducted by the Office of Inspector General will conform to generally accepted professional standards promulgated by independent professional auditing, evaluation and investigative organizations that promote the functions of audit, inspection/evaluation and investigative activities within government.

Section 11 Quality Review

Audits, investigations, inspections and reviews shall be subject to quality assurance review by the Board of Supreme Audit of Iraq at least every three years. A copy of the written report resulting from this review shall be furnished to the minister and any legislative bodies with oversight authority with respect to the Office of Inspector General. This report shall also be made available to the public, when requested.

Section 12 Entry into Force
This Order shall enter into force on the date of signature [10 February 2004], and shall remain in force unless the transitional Iraqi administration enacts superseding legislation.

Document 81
Coalition Provisional Authority Order Number 58
CPA/ORD/5 February 2004/58

Maysan And Muthanna Courts of Appeal

Pursuant to my authority as Administrator of the Coalition Provisional Authority, and under the laws and usages of war, and consistent with relevant U.N. Security Council resolutions, including Resolutions 1483 and 1511 (2003),

Recognizing the importance of the proper and efficient administration of the court system,

Recognizing further that the former regime manipulated the court system against disfavored regions and peoples of Iraq by denying them access to local justice,

I hereby promulgate the following:

Section 1 Establishment of Courts of Appeal in Mayson and Muthanna Governorates
Pursuant to Article 16(3) of the Judicial Organization Code, Law No. 160 of 1979, there are hereby established Court of Appeal districts in the Maysan and Muthanna governorates.

Section 2 Entry into Force
This Order shall enter into force on the date of signature [10 February 2004].

Document 82
Coalition Provisional Authority Order Number 59
CPA/ORD/1 June 2004/59

Protection and Fair Incentives for Government Whistleblowers

Pursuant to my authority as Administrator of the Coalition Provisional Authority, under the laws and usages of war, and consistent with relevant U.N. Security Council resolutions, including Resolutions 1483 and 1511 (2003),

Reconfirming the principles set forth in CPA Order Nos. 55, 57, and 77,[176] which established, respectively, the Iraqi Commission on Public Integrity, the Inspectors General for individual ministries, and the Iraqi Board of Supreme Audit,

Avowing to protect the rights of every Iraqi to expose government corruption and wrongdoing by contacting and cooperating with these institutions,

Committed to providing meaningful avenues for the Iraqi people, individually and collectively, to hold government leaders and institutions accountable without fear of repercussion or retribution,

[176] See *Docs 78, 80* and *101*, respectively.

Determined to restore trust and confidence in the honesty and integrity of public officials at all levels of government, and to ensure that public offices in Iraq are truly public trusts of the Iraqi people,

Recognizing that the CPA is committed to the effective administration of Iraq, and that building the Iraqi capacity to fight corruption contributes to civilian administration,

I hereby promulgate the following:

Section 1 Purpose

This Order promotes active enforcement of anti-corruption laws by encouraging eyewitnesses to illegal activity, such as corruption or misuse of public resources, to contact and communicate with appropriate institutions in order to hold accountable those who abuse the public trust. The Order rests on the established principle that secrecy is the breeding ground for corruption and thus protects the right of every Iraqi to vigorously expose official wrongdoing at all levels of government in Iraq.

Section 2 Prohibitions on Retaliation

1) No government employee or government contractor shall be discharged, demoted, transferred, threatened, intimidated, discriminated against, harassed, and/or otherwise retaliated against in any way ('Adverse Action') for reporting what he or she reasonably believes to be a violation of any law, rule, regulation, the Code for State Employees and Social Sector Discipline, Resolution No. 144, gross mismanagement, a gross waste of funds, an abuse of authority, a substantial and specific danger to health or safety, or any other 'Corruption Case' as defined in Section 2.4 of Annex A to CPA Order No. 55 (CPA/ORD/27 January 2004/55),[177] establishing the Commission on Public Integrity (collectively 'Government Wrongdoing').

2) No Adverse Action shall be taken against any government employee or government contractor who cooperates with an investigation of or provides information to the Commission on Public Integrity, the Inspectors General of individual Ministries, the Board of Supreme Audit, or any other government entity charged with investigating and exposing evidence of illegal activity, public corruption, or official wrongdoing.

3) Sections 2.1 and 2.2 of this Order shall apply to Adverse Actions taken after the date this Order enters into force.

4) The provisions of Sections 2.1 and 2.2 shall not apply if the government can demonstrate that the decision to take the Adverse Action was not influenced in any way by the government employee's or government contractor's decision to report any Government Wrongdoing or to cooperate with or report information to any government entity charged with investigating and exposing evidence of illegal activity, public corruption, or official wrongdoing.

5) The provisions of Sections 2.1 and 2.2 shall not apply to persons who knowingly disclose false information or make false reports, make reports or disclose information that (from an objective viewpoint) is clearly untrue, or who make reports or disclose information about matters which by law cannot be reported or disclosed.

6) It shall be the government's burden to demonstrate that a person is not entitled to the protections of Sections 2.1 and 2.2 of this Order.

[177] See *Doc 78*.

Section 3 Remedies and Procedures

1) Persons who violate Section 2 of this Order by taking an Adverse Action against government employees or government contractors who report Government Wrongdoing or cooperate with, or report to, institutions charged with investigating and exposing corruption and official wrongdoing in Iraq shall:

a) be liable to the aggrieved government employee or government contractor for money damages and any other relief deemed necessary by a court of competent jurisdiction to make an aggrieved government employee or government contractor whole, including reinstatement of employment with back pay; and/or

b) be liable for criminal sanction in accordance with all applicable laws, regulations, and standards of procedural due process.

2) Government employees or government contractors alleging a violation of Section 2 of this Order must, within 90 days of the Adverse Action, file an Initial Complaint with the Inspector General appointed to their relevant ministry unless the Complaint relates to actions taken by a minister or the Inspector General. The Commission on Public Integrity shall promulgate procedures and regulations which permit Inspectors General to receive and investigate such Complaints. These procedures and regulations shall require Inspectors General to issue a Final Report that analyzes the merits of any Complaint within 60 days of filing and recommends whether: (i) to dismiss the Complaint, (ii) to pursue civil and/or criminal charges in a court of competent jurisdiction consistent with Section 3.1(b) of this Order, or (iii) to take any other action deemed necessary under the particular facts and circumstances so long as such action is consistent with the law and due process.

3) Upon issuance of a Final Report, the Inspector General must forward it (and all accompanying records and files generated to create the Final Report) to the Commission on Public Integrity. The Commission on Public Integrity shall independently review the Final Report, records, and file and determine whether to adopt the Final Report in full, modify, wholly or partly reject, or resubmit the Final Report to the Inspector General with instructions. In the event the Complaint is dismissed, the aggrieved government employee or government contractor may bring a civil action in a court of competent jurisdiction seeking appropriate judicial relief. The court in such a case may consider the findings and analysis contained in the Final Report, as well as any additional findings and analysis rendered by the Commission on Public Integrity.

4) If the Inspector General fails to issue a Final Report within 60 days after the Complaint's filing, or the Commission on Public Integrity fails to make any determination about whether to adopt, modify, reject, or resubmit the Final Report within 30 days after its receipt, and there is no showing that such delays are due to the bad faith of the claimant, the claimant may (within 30 days after the passage of either deadline) bring a civil action in a court of competent jurisdiction seeking appropriate judicial relief. The institution of any such civil action under this paragraph shall not prejudice the Inspector General from continuing its investigation and submitting its Final Report to the Commission on Public Integrity. The institution of any civil action under this paragraph shall not prejudice the Commission on Public Integrity from dismissing the Complaint, pursuing criminal penalties (as permitted under Sections 3 and 4 of this Order and Section 4 of Annex A to Order No. 55) against persons who violate Section 2 of this Order, or taking any other action deemed necessary under the particular facts.

5) The Commission on Public Integrity shall also promulgate procedures and regulations for receiving and investigating Complaints that relate to actions taken by ministers or

Inspectors General. The regulations promulgated shall require the Commission on Public Integrity to analyze the merits of such Complaints and to issue a Final Report within 60 days of filing. Upon issuance of the Final Report, the Commission on Public Integrity shall: (i) dismiss the Complaint, (ii) pursue civil and/or criminal charges in a court of competent jurisdiction consistent with Section 3.1(b) of this Order, or (iii) take any other action (not including criminal or civil relief available in a court of competent jurisdiction) deemed necessary under the particular facts and circumstances so long as such action is consistent with law and due process. In the event the Complaint is dismissed, the aggrieved government employee or government contractor may bring a civil action in a court of competent jurisdiction seeking appropriate judicial relief. The court in such a case may consider the findings and analysis contained in the Final Report.

6) If the Commission on Public Integrity has not issued a Final Report within 60 days after the filing of a Complaint that relates to actions taken by a minister or an Inspector General and there is no showing that such delays are due to the bad faith of the aggrieved government employee or government contractor, then the aggrieved government employee or government contractor may bring a civil action in a court of competent jurisdiction seeking appropriate judicial relief. The institution of any such civil action under this paragraph shall not prejudice the Commission on Public Integrity from pursuing criminal penalties (as permitted under Sections 3 and 4 of this Order and Section 4 of Annex A to Order No. 55) against ministers or Inspectors General who violate Section 2 of this Order.

7) To further encourage individuals to come forward with evidence of corruption and official misconduct and widely publicize procedures that permit the Government of Iraq to transfer to a person (or persons) who first reports particular actionable misconduct up to 25 per cent of any recovery (regardless of whether such recovery is awarded to the government from a court of competent jurisdiction, received by settlement, or received by other means) by the government from a wrongdoer. The regulations promulgated shall not permit any person (or persons) to receive any portion of a recovery unless the recovery was in substantial part received because the person (or persons) reported the particular actionable conduct at issue.

Section 4 Penal Code Amendment

The Penal Code is amended by appending to the end of Paragraph 329 the following:

> '(3) The same penalty apples to any public official or agent who discharges, demotes, transfers, intimidates, discriminates against, harasses, and/or otherwise retaliates against in any way any person reporting to, or otherwise cooperating with, the Iraqi Commission on Public Intergrity, Inspectors General of the Ministries, the Board of Supreme Audit, or any other government body charged with investigating and exposing corruption and misconduct by those charged with the public trust.'

Section 5 Entry into Force

This Order shall enter into force on the date of signature [1 June 2004], and shall remain in force unless the transitional Iraqi administration enacts superseding legislation. In case of conflict between the Arabic and English versions of the text, the English version shall govern.

Document 83
Coalition Provisional Authority Order Number 60

CPA/ORD/19 February 2004/60

Ministry of Human Rights

Pursuant to my authority as Administrator of the Coalition Provisional Authority (CPA), and under the laws and usages of war, and consistent with relevant U.N. Security Council resolutions, including Resolutions 1483 and 1511 (2003),

Recognizing that the Iraqi people have long suffered from terrible abuses of their fundamental human rights and fundamental freedom; and that the implementation of the rule of law and a system of protections for human rights and fundamental freedoms, as well as the adoption of international standards of human rights and the revival of traditional Iraqi standards of humane treatment are vital to Iraq's social and political stability,

Furthering the purposes of the Governing Council to create a ministry responsible for addressing past human rights atrocities and safeguarding the human rights and fundamental freedoms of all persons within the territory of Iraq in the future,

Recalling CPA Memorandum Number 6,[178] publishing the appointment of the Interim Minister of Human Rights, and

Recognizing the obligations assumed by Iraq under international human rights treaties to which it is party, including the International Covenant on Civil and Political Rights, the Convention on the Elimination of All Forms of Racial Discrimination, the Convention on the Elimination of All Forms of Discrimination Against Woman [sic], and the Convention on the Rights of the Child,

I hereby promulgate the following:

Section 1 Establishment

1) The Ministry of Human Rights (MOHR) is hereby established.

2) All acts and decisions by the interim Minister of Human Rights (hereinafter 'interim Minister') in connection with this office and within his authority, together with all acts and decisions by the Ministry made within its authority from its appointment by the Governing Council on September 3, 2003, are hereby ratified. For the purpose of this ratification, the Ministry of Human Rights is deemed to have been established on September 3, 2003.

Section 2 Functions

1) The MOHR shall work to establish, through appropriate programs, services, initiatives, and studies, conditions conducive to the protection of human rights and fundamental freedoms in Iraq, and the prevention of human rights violations in Iraq.

2) The MOHR shall make formal recommendations regarding the establishment of new institutions, or the effective operation and reform of present institutions, as deemed necessary to prevent human rights violations in Iraq.

3) The MOHR shall establish programs to assist all the people of Iraq and Iraqi society in general in healing from the atrocities committed by the Ba'athist regime to include appropriate cooperation with the Iraqi Special tribunal or other judicial institutions. This

[178] See *Doc 131*.

shall include requesting and coordinating appropriate support from the CPA, Coalition Forces and non-governmental agencies.[179]

4) The MOHR shall develop policies and implement programs as may be necessary to give effect to this Order.

5) The MOHR shall be the focal point in the transitional Iraqi administration for relations with the United Nations High Commissioner for Human Rights, the United Nations Commission on the Status of Women and other international, national, and nongovernmental organizations promoting human rights.

6) The MOHR shall provide advice to lawmakers on whether proposed legislation is consistent with international human rights law, including the obligations Iraq has assumed pursuant to international human rights treaties it has ratified.

Section 3 Organization

1) The interim Minister shall organize the MOHR into such divisions and departments as he deems necessary and appropriate. The interim Minister shall ensure, at a minimum, that programs and policies are developed and implemented to address the atrocities committed by the Ba'athist regime; that institutions are in place and operating to protect the fundamental rights of all the people of Iraq, including women and children; that these institutions receive the support required to achieve their goals; that the Iraqi people are educated and knowledgeable on fundamental human rights, including the standards and norms of international human rights law; and that Iraq takes an active role in initiating a regional and international dialogue on human rights issues.

2) The interim Minister shall ensure, at a minimum, that the following administrative needs of the new MOHR are accomplished: hiring and training qualified personnel; developing a finance department; nominating an Inspector General and a senior Ministry legal advisor; establishing at least one Ministry facility; and creating an information and technology management office and a press relations office.

3) The interim Minister may establish a consultative body comprised of representatives from other Ministries to coordinate on policies and programs relating to human rights and fundamental freedoms of all person in Iraq and to ensure that new legislation is adopted taking into account the obligations that Iraq has assumed pursuant to the international human rights treaties it has ratified.

4) The interim Minister may set up such regional offices as he deems necessary and appropriate to facilitate, implement, and coordinate the work of the MOHR at the local level.

Section 4 Personnel and Administration

1) The MOHR may hire and employ personnel in accordance with Iraqi law, as amended by CPA Orders and Memoranda, and subject to established budget constraints. Such hiring shall be consistent with CPA Order Number 1[180] and any authorized implementation thereof.

2) Salaries of MOHR personnel shall conform to the salary structure applicable to Iraqi government employees.

Section 5 Property

In accordance with CPA Order No. 9, Management and Use of Iraqi Public Property (June 8, 2003),[181] the MOHR shall be granted the use of properties needed to accomplish its missions.

[179] Sec 2(3) was rescinded and replaced by CPA Order No 100, sec 3(22) *[Doc 124]*.
[180] See *Doc 14*.
[181] See *Doc 23*.

Section 6 Budget
The MOHR shall coordinate with the Ministry of Finance regarding its budget.

Section 7 Administrative Instructions
The interim Minister, in consultation with the CPA Senior Advisor for Human Rights, may issue administrative instructions prescribing all matters necessary for carrying out the duties described under this Order. These instructions must not be inconsistent with any CPA Order, Regulation or Memorandum, or any Iraqi law or obligation assumed by Iraq under international human rights instruments to which it is party.

Section 8 Durability and Precedence
This order will remain in force unless repealed by the Administrator or superseded by legislation issued by an internationally recognized Iraq government. This order shall take precedence over all other laws and publications to the extent such other laws and publications are inconsistent.

Section 9 Entry into Force
This Order shall enter into force on the date of signature [22 February 2004].

Document 84

Coalition Provisional Authority Order Number 61

CPA/ORD/22 February 2004/61

Amendment to Coalition Provisional Authority Order Number 45 (CPA/ORD/25 November 2003/45)

Pursuant to my authority as Administrator of the Coalition Provisional Authority (CPA) and under the laws and usages of war, and consistent with relevant U.N. Security Council resolutions, including Resolutions 1483 and 1511 (2003),

Noting that the requirement to register NGOs was imposed under CPA Order Number 45,[182]

Recognizing the CPA's obligation to provide for the effective administration of Iraq, and to ensure the well being of the Iraqi people,

Noting the need for a centralized method of registering non-governmental organizations, and the need to take measures to coordinate their activities,

Determined to ensure the security of the Iraqi people and prevent the misuse of non-governmental organizations for fraudulent or illegal purposes,

Recognizing that additional time is needed to build the capacity of the NGO Assistance Office,

I hereby promulgate the following:

Section 1 Amendment

1) Coalition Provisional Authority Order Number 45, Section 9, Article 5, on Registering of Nongovernmental Entities is amended to read in its entirety as follows:

[182] See *Doc 67*.

'The NGO shall submit a lost of all foreign staff stating their qualifications and responsibilities by May 1, 2004. The list shall be updated when the quarterly activity reports are submitted to the Office. Quarterly activity reports shall be due on the first of the month every three months following May 1, 2004.'

2) Coalition Provisional Authority Order Number 45, Section 9, Article 7, on Registering of Nongovernmental Entities is amended to read in its entirety as follows:

'All NGOs operating within Iraq prior to this Order shall comply with its provisions by May 1, 2004.'

Section 2 Entry into Force

This Order shall enter into force on the date of signature [23 February 2004].[183]

Document 85

Coalition Provisional Authority Order Number 62

CPA/ORD/26 February 2004/62

Disqualification from Public Office

Pursuant to my authority as Administrator of the Coalition Provisional Authority (CPA), and under the laws and usages of war, and consistent with relevant U.N. Security Council resolutions, including Resolutions 1483 and 1511 (2003),

Noting the obligation of the CPA to restore and maintain order and the right of the CPA to take measures for its security and public order,

Concerned that groups and individuals are attempting to undermine Coalition efforts, as called for in U.N. Security Council Resolution 1483 (2003), to create conditions in which the Iraqi people can freely determine their own political future,

Determined to assist the Iraqi people in establishing an internationally recognized, representative government by creating an environment in which democratic institutions can be formed, personal liberties can be safeguarded, and the rule of law is respected and can be enforced,

I hereby promulgate the following:

Section 1 Authority to Disqualify

1) When determined necessary for security and public order within Iraq, the Administrator of the CPA may disqualify an individual from participating in an election as a candidate for, accepting a nomination to, or holding public office, at any level, if that individual:

a) Had engaged in, ordered, or publicly incited violence against Coalition Forces or CPA personnel;
b) Was a full member of the Ba'ath Party holding the rank of 'Udw Qutriyya (regional Command Member), 'Udw Far' (Branch Member), 'Udw Shu'bah (Section Member), or 'Udw Firwah (Group Member), as determined by the Higher National De-Baathification Commission;
c) Is an agent of a foreign government;

[183] CPA Order No 61 was rescinded by CPA Order No 100, sec 4(9) *[Doc 124]*.

d) Has been convicted of a serious offense;
e) Is reasonably suspected of having committed, participated in, ordered, or permitted war crimes, genocide, crimes against humanity, atrocities, or gross violations of human rights; or
f) Has publicly espoused political philosophies or legal doctrines contrary to the democratic order and rule of law established in Iraq.

2) The Administrator may take such actions as he deems necessary to notify the individual concerned of a disqualified action under this section and to ensure a disqualified individual is prevented from assuming or continuing to hold public office. To the extent practicable, consistent with the CPA's responsibilities and authorities, the Administrator should inform the public of his determinations and the bases for them.

Section 2 Existing Law
Any laws or regulations inconsistent with the provisions of this Order are hereby suspended to the extent they are inconsistent with the provisions of this Order.

Section 3 Entry into Force and Duration
This Order shall enter into force on the date of signature [1 March 2004] and shall remain in effect only until the CPA is dissolved.[184]

Document 86
Coalition Provisional Authority Order Number 63
CPA/ORD/6 March 2004/63

Public Security Sector Death and Disability Benefits

Pursuant to my authority as Administrator of the Coalition Provisional Authority (CPA), and under the laws and usages of war, and consistent with relevant U.N. Security Council resolutions, including Resolutions 1483 and 1511 (2003),

Recognizing the dangers faced and the sacrifices made by the brave and patriotic Iraqi citizens who choose to serve in the public security sector,

Determined to provide for the families of employees of public sector security organizations killed because of their services,

I hereby promulgate the following:

Section 1 Definitions
1) '*Public Security Sector Organizations*' means the Iraqi Police Service; Iraqi Department of Border Enforcement established pursuant to CPA Order Number 26;[185] Iraqi Facilities Protection Service established pursuant to CPA Order Number 27;[186] Iraqi Civil Defense (Fire and Emergency Services); Iraqi Corrections Service; New Iraqi Army (to include all element of the Iraqi Armed Forces) established pursuant to CPA Order Number

[184] CPA Order No 62 was rescinded by CPA Order No 100, sec 4(10) *[Doc 124]*.
[185] See *Doc 47*.
[186] See *Doc 48*.

22;[187] Defense Support Agency established pursuant to CPA Order Number 28;[188] and any future Ministry of Defense and elements thereof that may be established by the CPA.

2) '*Eligible Employee*' means an employee of a public security sector organization who is injured or killed Due to His Service. An individual who has entered into an employment contract directly with a public security organization in anticipation of being hired as an employee of that or a successor security sector organization shall be deemed to be an employee of that organization for purposes of this Order.

3) '*Due to His Service*' means the employee is injured or killed as a direct and proximate result of an action or accident while on duty and faithfully executing his responsibilities or the member is injured or killed as a result of his official position while off duty. Such term does not include injury or death as a result of a previous medical condition or the employee's own misconduct.

Section 2 Benefits Payable to Public Security Sector Personnel

1) The disability, pension, and death gratuity provisions contained in Articles 49 through 52 of Law Number 1 of 1978, Law for the Service and Retirement of the Interior Security Forces, as amended, shall apply to Eligible Employees of the Iraqi Police Service, Iraqi Department of Border Enforcement, Iraqi Facilities Protection Service, Iraqi Civil Defense (Fire and Emergency Services), and the Iraqi Corrections Service.

2) The disability, pension and death gratuity provisions contained in Articles 58 through 61 of Law Number 1 of 1975, Law for the Military Service and Retirement, as amended, shall apply to Eligible Employees of the New Iraqi Army (to include all elements of the Iraqi Armed Forces), Defense Support Agency, Iraqi Civil Defense Crops, and any future Ministry of Defense and elements thereof.

3) The benefits authorized herein shall be calculated and paid in accordance with the provisions of the applicable law and shall be in lieu of any other disability, pension, or death gratuity authorized by Iraqi law.

Section 3 Administration and Payment of Pensions

1) An Eligible Employee's Ministry shall be responsible for determining eligibility for disability, retirement, and other benefits in accordance with the relevant Iraqi law under this Order and for administering the payment of such disability, retirement, and other benefits.

2) The interim Ministers of the affected Ministries may issue Administrative Instructions, not inconsistent with Iraqi law or any CPA Order, Regulation, or Memorandum, as they deem necessary to carry out the duties for their respective Ministries described in this Order.

Section 4 Existing Law

1) Ministry of Finance policy, Public Security Survivor Benefits, dated October 28, 2003, is hereby superseded. Retirement benefits currently being paid to individuals under that policy shall be adjusted to reflect the entitlements set forth in this Order; provided that the amount of any benefits paid to such individuals under this Order shall not be less than what would have been paid to such individuals under the superseded Ministry of Finance policy.

2) Nothing in CPA Order Number 30[189] or any other CPA Order, Regulation, or Memorandum shall be deemed to suspend existing Iraqi law relating to disability, retirement, or other benefits payable under this Order.

[187] See *Doc 43*.
[188] See *Doc 49*.
[189] See *Doc 51*.

3) Any portion of legislation inconsistent with any of the provisions of this Order is hereby suspended to the extent necessary to implement the provisions of this Order.

Section 5 Entry into Force
This Order shall enter into force on the date of signature [6 March 2004].

Document 87
Coalition Provisional Authority Order Number 64
CPA/ORD/29 February 2004/64

Amendment to the Company Law No. 21 of 1997

Pursuant to my authority as Administrator of the Coalition Provisional Authority (CPA) and under the laws and usages of war, and consistent with relevant U.N. Security Council resolutions, including Resolutions 1483 and 1511 (2003),

Having worked closely with the Governing Council to ensure that economic change as necessary to benefit the people of Iraq occurs in a manner acceptable to the people of Iraq,

Acknowledging the Governing Council's desire to bring about significant change to the Iraqi economic system as necessary to improve the condition of the people of Iraq,

Determined to improve the conditions of life, technical skills, and opportunities for all Iraqis and to fight unemployment with its associated deleterious effect on public security,

Recognizing that some of the rules concerning company formation and investment under the prior regime no longer serve a relevant social or economic purpose, and that such rules hinder economic growth,

Noting that Iraqi entrepreneurs and businesses will benefit from more streamlined requirements for forming companies and investing in them,

Recognizing the CPA's obligation to provide for the effective administration of Iraq, to ensure the well-being of the Iraqi people and to enable the social and economic functions and normal transactions of every day life,

Acting in a manner consistent with the Report of the Secretary General to the Security Council of July 17, 2003, concerning the need for the development of Iraq and its transition from a non-transparent centrally planned economy to a free market economy characterized by sustainable economic growth through the establishment of a dynamic private sector, and the need to enact institutional and legal reforms to give it effect,

Having worked closely with the Governing Council, international organizations and relevant Ministries in developing policies that will organize and facilitate the infusion of capital into Iraqi businesses, private sector investment, and transferability of interests,

I hereby promulgate the following:

Section 1 Amendments to the Company Law
1) Article 1 of the Company Law No. 21 of 1997 ('the Law') is amended to read as follows:

'The objectives of this law are to:

1. organize companies;
2. protect creditors from fraud;

3. protect owners from conflicts of interest and related abuses by company officials, majority owners, and others with practical control over the affairs of the company; and
4. promote the provision of full information to owners in connection with decisions affecting their investment and their company.'

2) Article 2 of the Law is suspended.

3) Article 3 of the Law is amended to read as follows: 'This law applies to mixed and private companies and to all investors. Its provisions shall apply to banks to the extent they do not conflict with Coalition Provisional Authority (CPA) Orders, including but not limited to CPA Order No. 40, promulgating the Banking Law,[190] and CPA Order No. 18, prescribing Measures to Ensure the Independence of the Central Bank of Iraq,[191] and regulations issued under such CPA Orders. This law shall apply to securities transactions, financial investment companies and insurance and re-insurance companies to the extent it does not conflict with the legislation applicable to these transaction [sic] and entities or the jurisdiction of the competent state authorities for those sectors. Decisions of the Registrar of Companies (hereinafter 'Registrar') hereunder shall be based upon this law and not upon considerations of economic planning or development policy. Decisions by the Registrar shall not in general foreclose a claim for compensation arising from violation of the law by an injured third party against those responsible for the violation.'

4) The heading of Sub-Section One of Section 2 of the Law is amended to read as follows: 'The Company's Contract and Owners' Mutual Obligations'.

5) Article 4, paragraph Second of the Law is amended to read as follows: 'With the exception of the provisions of paragraph First of this article:

1. A company may be established by one natural person in accordance with the provisions of this law. Such a company will henceforth be referred to as a 'sole owner enterprise'.
2. A limited liability company may be formed with one owner in accordance with the provisions of this law.

6) Article 4 of the Law is supplemented with the following paragraph Third, which shall read as follows: 'Owners of capital in a company may not exercise their voting or other authority in the company to cause it to do or consent to acts that:

1. harm or disadvantage the company to benefit themselves or those associated with them at the expense of other owners of the company; or
2. jeopardize the rights of creditors by causing withdrawal of capital or transfer of assets when insolvency is imminent or when prohibited by law.'

7) Article 6, paragraph Second of the Law is amended to read as follows: 'The mixed or private limited liability company shall be formed by no more than 25 natural or juridical persons, who will subscribe to its shares and will be responsible for the company's debts insofar as the nominal value of the shares to which they subscribed.'

8) Article 6, paragraph Third of the Law is amended to read as follows: 'The joint liability company shall be formed by not less than two and not more than 25 persons, each owning a quota of its capital. They shall jointly assume personal and unlimited responsibility for all of its obligations.'

9) Article 7, paragraph First of the Law is amended to read as follows: 'The mixed company shall be formed by the agreement between one or more persons from the state sector and one or more persons from outside this sector. The state sector's share in the

[190] See *Doc 62*.
[191] See *Doc 39*.

mixed company's capital must not initially be less than 25 percent. A mixed company may also be formed by two or more persons from the mixed sector. When the state sector's share falls below 25%, the company shall be treated as a private company, as permitted in article 8, paragraph Second, point 2.'

10) Article 8, paragraph Second, subparagraph 1 of the Law is amended to read as follows: 'Form a sole owner enterprise of one natural person or a sole owner limited liability company of one juridical or natural person.'

11) Article 9, paragraph First of the Law is amended to read as follows: 'The Financial Investment Company is a company organized in Iraq whose main activity is to direct savings toward investment in Iraqi financial securities, including shares, bonds, treasury bills and fixed deposits.'

12) Article 10, paragraph First of the Law is suspended.

13) Article 10, paragraph Second of the Law is amended to read as follows: 'Companies engaging in any of the following activities must become joint-stock companies:

1. Insurance and re-insurance.
2. Financial investment.'

14) Article 12, paragraph First of the Law is amended to read as follows: 'A juridical or natural person foreign or domestic has the right to acquire membership in the companies stipulated in this law as founder, shareholder, or partner, unless such person is banned from such membership under the law, or due to a decision issued by a competent court or authorized governmental body.'

15) Article 12, paragraphs Second and Third of the Law are suspended.

16) The chapeau paragraph of Article 13 of the Law, and paragraphs First through Third thereof are amended to read as follows:

> 'Article 13: The founders shall prepare a contract for the company, which is signed by them or their legal representative. The contract shall contain at a minimum:
>
> First: The company's name, and corporate form, with the word 'mixed' added if it is a mixed sector company, and any other acceptable elements.
>
> Second: The company's head office, which must be in Iraq.
>
> Third: The purposes for which the company is established and the general nature of the business to be transacted.'

17) Article 13, paragraph Fourth of the Law is suspended.

18) Article 14 of the Law is amended to read as follows: 'The founder of a limited liability company when there are no other founders, or the founder of a sole owner enterprise shall prepare a statement, which shall serve the purpose of a company contract and shall be subject to the provisions that are applicable to the contract whenever they occur in this law.'

19) Article 15 of the Law is amended to read as follows: 'The founders of the company shall subscribe to the company's capital in accordance with their agreed to contributions.'

20) Article 16, paragraph First of the Law is amended to read as follows: 'The founders shall deposit the company's capital specified in Article 28, paragraph First, of this law with one or more banks authorized to operate in Iraq. It is permissible for the company capital also to include contributions in kind as stipulated in Article 29 of this law.'

21) Article 16, paragraph Second of the Law is suspended.

22) Article 16, paragraph Third, subparagraph 1, items (b), (d) and (f) of the Law are amended to read as follows:

> 'b. Follow up on the procedures for establishing the company and submit the contract of association and the subscription document to the Registrar of Companies

– including the names, signatures, addresses and nationalities of the founders as well as other requirements.'

'd. Open a joint account in the name of the committee with one or more banks authorized to operate in Iraq.'

'f. Obtain a license, if necessary, for the project and conclude the necessary contracts for its establishment, following the issuance of the decision approving its establishment.'

23) Article 17, paragraph Third of the Law is amended to read as follows: 'A statement from the bank or banks proving that the capital required in Article 28 has been deposited.'

24) Article 18 of the Law is suspended.

25) Article 19 of the Law is amended to read as follows: 'The Registrar shall approve the application unless it finds it contrary to a specific provision of this law and shall issue the approval or disapproval of the establishment application within 10 days from the date of receiving it. Except for joint stock companies, the certificate shall be issued at the time of the approval and shall be the evidence of the company's establishment. If the Registrar disapproves an application, it shall issue a written decision stating the reasons for the disapproval. In the case of a joint-stock company, the Registrar shall publish a written notice of his or her decision at the time of the approval or disapproval. No certificate shall be issued without payment of the applicable fee.'

26) Article 20 of the Law is suspended.

27) Article 21, paragraph First, subparagraph 1 of the Law is amended to read as follows: 'The Registrar shall publish the decision approving the establishment of the company in the special bulletin published under the provisions of Article 206 of this law, which henceforth will be referred to as "the Bulletin."'

28) Article 21, paragraph Second of the Law is suspended.

29) Article 22 of the Law is amended to read as follows: 'The company acquires corporate status from the date of the issuance of its establishment certificate. This certificate is considered proof of this status.'

30) Article 24 of the Law is amended to read as follows: 'If the Registrar rejects the application for the establishment of the company, it must state in writing the legal provisions violated and the facts underlying each violation. The applicant for the establishment has the right to contest the Registrar's rejection before the Minister of Trade within 30 days from the date of notification. The Minister of Trade must consider the rejection within 30 days from the date of its submission. If the Minister also rejects the application, the applicant has the right to appeal the Minister's decision before the competent court within 30 days.'

31) Article 28 of the Law is amended to read as follows: 'First: The capital of a joint stock company shall not be less than two million (2,000,000) dinars. The capital of a limited liability company shall not be less than one million (1,000,000) dinars. The capital of all other companies shall not be less than fifty thousand (50,000) dinars. Second: A joint stock company's liabilities may not exceed 300 percent of its total capital and other equity rights.'

32) Article 29, chapeau of paragraph Second of the Law is amended to read as follows: 'In the joint-stock company and the limited liability company, the capital may include shares that are offered in exchange for tangible or intangible in-kind property contributions by one or more of the founders.'

33) Article 29, paragraph Second, subparagraph 1 of the Law is amended to read as follows: 'In the case of a joint-stock company, property-in-kind shares shall be evaluated by a committee approved by the Registrar as to expertise and objectivity, and including experts in law, accounting and the company's line of business.'

34) Article 29, paragraph Second, subparagraph 2 of the Law is amended to read as follows: 'In the case of the mixed joint-stock company, the committee established pursuant to subparagraph 1 in this paragraph shall submit its report to the Registrar within 60 days from the date of its formation. The Registrar shall submit its report to the Financial Control Bureau for endorsement within 30 days from the date of its submission. In the case of non-approval, the Registrar shall return the report to the committee for further consideration.'

35) Article 29, paragraph Second, subparagraph 3 of the Law is amended to read as follows: 'In the case of the private joint-stock company, all founders shall agree on the value of property-in-kind shares as assessed in the manner stipulated in subparagraph 1 of this paragraph. A joint stock company's or limited liability company's contract must state the type of property-in-kind share and its value as approved by the rest of the founders, the name of the founder who offered the share, and the percentage of his contribution to the capital through this share. The founder offering the property in- kind shall be accountable to any person for its assessed and accepted value. If it is proven that the assessed value is less than the actual value, he or she must pay the difference in cash to the company. The other founders may be asked to cooperate in paying the difference.'

36) Article 30 of the Law is amended to read as follows: 'The nominal value of the share shall be one dinar. It should not be issued higher or lower than that except as provided in Articles 54 through 56.'

37) Article 31 of the Law is suspended.

38) Article 32, paragraphs First and Second of the Law are suspended.

39) Article 37, paragraph Second of the Law is amended to read as follows: 'The creditors of a sole owner enterprise may take legal action against it or the owner of the quota in it. His or her funds shall be considered as a guarantee for debts on the enterprise. It is permissible to seize his or her funds without warning the enterprise and in accordance with applicable legal procedures.'

40) Article 39, paragraph First of the Law is amended to read as follows: 'The founders in the mixed joint-stock company shall subscribe by not less than 30 percent and not more than 55 percent of its nominal capital, and this should include the minimum 25 percent fixed for the state sector.'

41) Article 39, paragraph Second of the Law is amended to read as follows: 'At the establishment of the company, the founders in the private joint-stock company shall subscribe by not less than 20 percent in its nominal capital.'

42) Article 39, the chapeau portion of paragraph Third of the Law is amended to read as follows: 'The remaining shares shall be offered for public subscription within 30 days from the date of the approval of the establishment of the company in a statement issued by the founders and published in the bulletin and at least two daily papers, after obtaining the approval of the Registrar, which shall be granted within that time unless the Registrar finds the registration materials submitted would be materially misleading to investors. In the latter case, it shall refer a matter within its jurisdiction to the competent state authority for the securities markets. The statement shall include the following:'

43) Article 39, paragraph Fourth of the Law is amended to read as follows: 'Founders shall not subscribe to the shares while they are being offered for public subscription, except after the end of 30 days from the beginning of the subscription or during the extended period stipulated in Article 42 of this law.'

44) Article 41, paragraph First of the Law is amended to read as follows: 'The subscription shall take place in a bank authorized to operate in Iraq in a form bearing the name of the company and containing the following:

1. The request to subscribe to a specific number of shares.
2. The subscriber's approval of the company's contract.
3. The subscriber's name, address, profession, and nationality.
4. Any other information which the founders may want to add.'

45) Article 41, paragraph Second of the Law is amended to read as follows: 'The form shall be submitted to the party handling the subscription signed by the subscriber or his legal representative. The required payment shall be made against a receipt.'

46) Article 41, paragraph Third of the Law is amended to read as follows: 'The subscriber shall be given a copy of the company's contract and its technical and economic feasibility study, subject to Article 47, paragraph Third of this law.'

47) Article 42 is amended to read as follows: 'The subscription period shall not be less than 30 days or more than 60 days. If the subscription period expires without the subscribed shares reaching 75 percent of the nominal capital, including the shares owned by the founders, it is permissible to extend it for a further period of not more than 60 days. The founders shall again publish the subscription statement and make the extension announcement.'

48) Article 43, paragraph First of the Law is amended to read as follows: 'If the subscription does not reach 75 percent of the nominal capital at the end of the extension period, the founders must decrease the company's capital, so that the value of the subscribed shares will be equal to 75 percent of the decreased nominal capital, unless the founders cancel the establishment of the company. The founders shall inform the Registrar of such a decision.'

49) Article 43, paragraph Second of the Law is suspended.

50) Article 43, paragraph Third of the Law is amended to read as follows: 'If it is decided to cancel the establishment of the company under the provisions of Paragraph First of this article, the founders shall notify the bank and jointly bear the expenses for establishing the company. The bank handling the subscription shall return the money paid by all subscribers in full upon notification and within a period of not more than 30 days.'

51) Article 44, paragraph Second of the Law is amended to read as follows: 'If it transpires after the closure of the subscription that the shares offered have been over-subscribed, the shares must be distributed among the subscribers according to the percentage of subscription allotted for each subscriber.'

52) Article 45, paragraph First of the Law is amended to read as follows: 'Any person whose lawful rights would be infringed by violations of the subscription rules, the Registrar and the competent state authority for the securities market has the right to contest the soundness of the subscription process before the competent court and ask for its cancellation within 15 days from the closure of the subscription. The court must examine such cases urgently. The court's decision can be contested before the court of appeal, which shall sit as a court of cassation, and its decision in this capacity shall be final.'

53) Article 45, paragraph Second of the Law is amended to read as follows: 'If the subscription is ruled to be in violation of the law, the founders must carry it out anew.'

54) Article 47, paragraph First of the Law is amended to read as follows: 'Once the company has been established and some shares are still not subscribed for, the board of directors may, after six months from the date of the issuance of the establishment certificate, pursue one of two courses:

1. sell the shares on the Baghdad Stock Exchange market; or
2. place the shares for public subscription in accordance with the procedures followed during the constituent subscription.'

55) Article 47, paragraph Second of the Law is amended to read as follows: 'If the shares are not sold in the market or subscribed by the public, the company's nominal capital shall be decreased by the value of the unsold shares. The company shall be liable for materially misleading assertions or omissions in sales or subscriptions as shall be its responsible directors, employees and agents.'

56) Article 48, paragraph First of the Law is amended to read as follows: 'In the joint-stock company, the subscription shall require payment in full for issued shares. Unpaid shares already outstanding under previous law shall be governed by this Article.'

57) Article 48, paragraph Second of the Law is suspended.

58) Article 51 of the Law is amended to read as follows: 'Every shareholder in a limited liability company and every subscriber who has fully paid the value of his shares in a joint-stock company shall be given a permanent certificate including the data contained in the temporary certificate, plus a declaration that the shares have been paid. Any temporary certificate should be cancelled.'

59) Article 54, paragraph Second of the Law is amended to read as follows: 'In the joint-stock company and the limited liability company, the increase of capital must be in accordance with a general assembly decision to amend the contract and issue new shares.'

60) Article 54, paragraph Third of the Law is suspended.

61) Article 54, paragraph Fourth of the Law is amended to read as follows: 'The Registrar shall within fifteen days of a lawful request approve the increase. The Registrar shall be deemed to approve the increase, and to give notice of the approval, unless it rejects the request, giving the legal and factual basis for the determination in writing.'

62) Article 55, paragraph Second of the Law is amended to read as follows: 'Transferring funds from the accumulated surplus or the issuance allowance reserve into shares to be distributed among the shareholders in the ratio of their subscription to the capital.'

63) Article 55 is supplemented by a paragraph Fourth, to read as follows: 'In cases where the shares will be offered in exchange for cash, such decision must specify the number of shares to be issued and the price at which they will be offered for sale or the means of establishing that price. Shares may be offered at a price equal to or greater than their nominal value in accordance with the general assembly's decision and priced in light of the company's performance and, where applicable, the prices of its shares in the Baghdad Stock Exchange market. The proceeds reflecting the difference between the issue price and nominal price, which is considered issuance allowance, shall be recorded in the account of the issuance allowance reserve, after deducting all issuance expenses. This reserve may not be distributed as profits. In the case of the joint-stock company, the company shall submit to the Registrar a decision by its general assembly to increase the capital, backed by an economic study giving the justifications for this increase and the fields in which it will be expended, as well as any other essential data. It shall be furnished to purchasers, subject to the liability in the second paragraph of article 47 of this law, unless the Registrar finds it materially misleading. In this case, it shall refer a matter within its jurisdiction to the competent state authority for the securities market.'

64) Article 56, paragraph First of the Law is amended to read as follows: 'In the joint-stock company, the new shares must be placed for public subscription within 30 days from the date on which the company is notified of the Registrar's approval of the increase in the capital. The subscription shall remain open for a period of not less than 30 days and not more than 60 days, which may be renewable once for a similar period, provided the value of the shares is paid during subscription. The increase in the capital is achieved by

the number of shares subscribed and paid up on the closure of the subscription. Otherwise, and insofar as it does not conflict with the nature of the increase in the capital, the original provisions on subscription shall be applied on the new shares, including the provisions of Articles 44 and 47 of this law.'

65) Article 56, paragraph Third of the Law is amended to read as follows: 'Every shareholder has the priority right to buy shares at the subscription price proportional to the number of the shares he owns. Shareholders shall be allowed to exercise this right within a period of 15 days from the date they are invited to do so. The invitation must state the beginning and end of the subscription period and the nominal value of the shares. If some shares are not subscribed after the period stipulated in paragraph First of this Article, the board of directors may place the shares for sale in the Baghdad Stock Exchange market in the manner it deems suitable.'

66) Article 56 is supplemented by a paragraph Fourth as follows: 'Fourth. In the case of banks increasing capital by a sale of shares for cash, the company may issue shares without public subscription and/or without offering existing shareholders the right to participate, provided the following conditions are met:

1. The issuance is approved by a majority of the votes of the subscribed shares whose due installments have been paid; and
2. The Central Bank of Iraq concurs that the sale is for fair value, in view of all the circumstances, and is fair to shareholders not entitled to participate, in view of the benefit to the company as a whole.'

67) Article 58 of the Law is amended to read as follows: 'A company may decrease its capital if it exceeds its needs or incurs losses. A decrease in capital that is part of an arrangement to achieve a net increase in capital through additional investments shall not be subject to the requirements in Article 59, paragraph Third, and Articles 60-63.'

68) Article 59, paragraph Third, subparagraph 2 of the Law is suspended.

69) Article 59, paragraph Third, subparagraph 3 of the Law is amended to read as follows: 'If the Registrar finds the decrease lawful, it shall announce the decrease in the bulletin and two daily papers. It shall also give every creditor to or claimant on the company the right to object to the decision on the decrease within 30 days from the date of the publication of the announcement.'

70) Article 63 of the Law is amended to read as follows: 'In the case of the joint liability company and the sole owner enterprise, any decrease of the capital must take place through a decision by the general assembly to amend the contract.'

71) Article 64, paragraph First of the Law is amended to read as follows: 'Founders of joint-stock companies may not transfer ownership of their shares except in the following situations:

1. The lapse of at least one year since the establishment of the company.
2. The distribution of dividends that are not less than five percent of the paid up nominal capital.'

72) Article 64, paragraph Second of the Law is suspended.

73) Article 65, paragraph Third of the Law is amended to read as follows: 'If several shareholders want to buy the shares at the same price, the shares shall be divided among them in the ratio of their subscription, to the nearest correct share.'

74) The chapeau paragraph of Article 67 of the Law is amended to read as follows: 'If an Iraqi shareholder in a joint-stock company or a limited liability company dies, the ownership of the shares shall revert to his or her heirs in accordance with the ratios specified

by the Shari'a law. In cases in which the shareholder is a citizen of another country, the shares shall revert to the shareholder's heirs in accordance with the applicable law of that country. In each case, the following shall be taken into consideration:'

75) Article 67, paragraph Second of the Law is amended to read as follows: 'If the distribution of shares among the heirs will result in an increase in the number of partners in the limited liability company over the number set by the law, the shares shall be considered a joint ownership by the heirs in accordance with the ratios specified under the applicable inheritance law and considered as one person. In such a case, one of the heirs will represent the rest before the company. They shall be asked to choose this representative within 60 days from the date of the registration of the shares in the company's ledger.'

76) Article 74 of the Law is amended to read as follows: 'First: The reserve shall be used for the purposes of expanding and developing the company's business, and improving the conditions of its workers, participating in projects relevant to the company's activity, and contributing to the protection of the environment and social welfare programs. Dividends shall not be distributed from the reserve. Second: The reserve shall be used to meet the company's debts, provided they do not exceed 50 percent of the reserve. Any increase over that limit shall be subject to the approval of the Registrar.'

77) Article 76 of the Law is amended to read as follows: 'First: If the company's losses amount to 50 percent of its capital or more, it must notify the Registrar within 60 days from the day the losses are established in the balance sheet. Second: If the losses amount to 75 percent of the capital or more, the company must take one of the following steps:

1. decrease or increase the capital of the company; or
2. recommend liquidation of the company.'

78) Article 78, paragraph Second of the Law is amended to read as follows: 'The total amount of the bond issue must not exceed the company's capital.'

79) Article 79 of the Law is amended to read as follows: 'The company shall submit to the Registrar the general assembly's decision on the issuance of the credit bonds backed by an economic study stating the reasons for the issue, the fields in which the credit will be expended, and any other essential data. It shall be furnished to purchasers, subject to the liability in the second paragraph of Article 47 of this Law, unless the Registrar finds it materially misleading. In the latter case, it shall refer a matter within its jurisdiction to the competent state authority for the securities markets.'

80) Article 80, paragraph Third of the Law is amended to read as follows: 'Information on the company's financial condition and results of operations, including earnings.'

81) Article 86 of the Law is amended to read as follows: 'The general assembly in the joint-stock company shall meet at least once a year. In the other companies, it shall meet at least once every six months.'

82) Article 87, paragraph Third of the Law is amended to read as follows: 'The Registrar on its own initiative or at the request of the accounts controller.'

83) Article 88, paragraph Second of the Law is amended to read as follows: 'If the founders or the chairman of the board of directors in the joint-stock company or the managing director in the other companies fail to address the invitation to a meeting of the general assembly at the legally scheduled date, the Registrar shall address them directly to the members – in the case of the joint-stock companies – by announcing that in the bulletin, two daily papers, and the Baghdad Stock Exchange Market and fixing the place and date of the meeting.'

84) Article 88 of the Law shall be supplemented by a paragraph Third, to read as follows: 'It shall be unlawful to manipulate notice of a meeting or dissemination of information concerning it in order to bias the outcome of its decisions.'

85) Article 90 of the Law shall be amended to read as follows: 'The meetings may be held at the company's head office or any other place in Iraq if necessary, provided inconvenience to the owners is minimized.'

86) Article 91, paragraph Third, subparagraph 1 of the Law is suspended.

87) Article 92 of the Law is amended to read as follows: 'First: The meeting of the general assembly shall be held with the attendance of the members owning the majority of subscribed shares whose installments have been paid, in the case of the joint-stock company; the majority of paid-up shares in the limited liability company; and the majority of quotas in the joint liability company. If a quorum is not reached, the meeting shall be postponed to the same day on the following week and in the same place. A quorum is considered attained in the second meeting if 25% of the number of such shares or quotas is represented. The company may apply to the Registrar for waiver of the 25% minimum if, in view of the agenda and other circumstances, the minimum requirement would disserve the interests of the owners generally. The company's contract may require more stringent conditions for a quorum.

Second: If the agenda calls for amending the company's contract, increasing or decreasing its capital, dismissing the chairman or a member of its board of directors; or deciding on its merger, transformation, sale of more than half its assets in a transaction outside its ordinary business, a transaction under paragraph Fourth of Article 56 or liquidation, the quorum required for the first meeting must be attained.'

88) Article 93 of the Law is amended to read as follows: 'In the case of the joint-stock company, the meeting of the general assembly must be attended by the representatives of the Registrar. It must also be attended by most members of the board. If representatives of the Registrar or board members fail to attend after being notified, the meeting can be held in their absence within half an hour after the scheduled time of the meeting. The representative of the Registrar will withdraw after confirming that a quorum is present unless his or her continued presence is requested by a shareholder.'

89) Article 94, paragraph First of the Law is amended to read as follows: 'Prior to the beginning of the meeting, the name of the participant in the meeting shall be recorded along with the number of the shares he or she owns or represents, provided he or she produces the certificate of the shares or the power of attorney if he or she represents a shareholder in the company. Share certificates submitted to a depository for book-entry transfer need not be presented, provided adequate evidence of ownership is furnished under the rules of the depository approved by the competent state authority for the securities market. The participant shall put his or her signature against the name of the shareholder he or she represents.'

90) Article 98, paragraph Second of the Law is amended to read as follows: 'Unless the company's contract requires a higher proportion, decisions on amending the contract of the company, increasing or decreasing its capital, selling more than half its assets in a transaction outside its ordinary business, approving a transaction under paragraph Fourth of Article 56, merging the company, transforming it, or liquidating it must be based on: the majority of the votes of the subscribed shares whose due installments have been paid, in the case of the joint-stock company; the majority of the votes of the paid-up shares at the time of calling the meeting, in the case of the limited liability company; and the unanimous vote of the quotas, in the case of the joint liability company. In the case of a tie vote in the limited liability company, and the impossibility of obtaining a unanimous vote in the joint liability company, it is permissible to resort to the competent court to settle the matter. Decisions on other matters shall be made on the basis of the majority of the votes

of shares or quotas represented in the meeting, unless the company's contract requires a higher proportion.'

91) Article 101 of the Law is amended to read as follows: 'In the sole owner enterprise, or a limited liability company having one owner, the owner replaces the general assembly and the provisions stipulated in this law, other than those pertaining to meetings, apply to him, her or it.'

92) Article 102, paragraph Second is amended to read as follows: 'Decide on the election of the representatives of shareholders from outside the state sector in the board of directors of the mixed company, and the representatives of all shareholders in the board of directors of the private joint stock company, as well as on their dismissal.'

93) Article 102, paragraph Fourth is amended to read as follows: 'Discuss the company's final accounts and approve them.'

94) Article 102, paragraph Tenth is amended to read as follows: 'Approve employment rules in the mixed joint-stock company as worked out by the board of directors.'

95) Article 102, paragraph Tenth of the Law is amended to read as follows: 'Approve employment rules in the mixed joint-stock company as worked out by the board of directors.'

96) Article 103 of the Law is amended to read as follows: 'First: The board of directors in the mixed joint stock company shall consist of seven original members who are chosen as follows:

1. Two members representing the state sector who are appointed under a decision by the competent minister or his deputy in the sector to which the company belongs, unless at the time of the selection, the state sector's share in the mixed company's capital exceeds 50%. In such a case, the competent minister or his deputy in the sector to which the company belongs shall appoint three members representing the state sector.
2. Five members representing shareholders from outside the state sector elected by the company's general assembly, unless at the time of the selection, the state sector's share in the mixed company's capital exceeds 50%. In such a case, the company's general assembly shall elect four members representing shareholders from outside the state sector.

Second: The board of directors in the mixed joint stock company shall have seven reserve members, who will be selected in the manner and ratio used in the case of the original members.'

97) Article 104, paragraph First of the Law is amended to read as follows: 'The board of directors in the private joint-stock company shall consist of not less than five and not more than nine original members to be elected by the company's general assembly.'

98) Article 105 of the Law is suspended.

99) Article 108, paragraph First of the Law is amended to read as follows: 'If a vacancy occurs in the membership representing the state sector in the board of directors, the council shall invite a reserve member – in the order of the reserve list in the sector – to fill the vacancy and attend the board meeting.'

100) Article 110, paragraph First of the Law is amended to read as follows: 'A person cannot be a member in the boards of directors of more than six companies at the same time. But, he can also assume the chairmanship of one or two other boards at the same time.'

101) Article 113 of the Law is amended to read as follows: 'The quorum shall be counted 30 minutes after the board has convened. It shall meet with the attendance of the majority of its members.'

102) Article 114, paragraph Second of the Law is suspended.

103) Article 117, paragraph Fourth (chapeau portion) of the Law is hereby amended to read as follows: 'Discuss and approve an annual plan for the company's activity in the following year. This plan must be prepared by the managing director during the last six months of the year in light of the company's aim. The plan shall include a full report on the company's activity and a draft budget outlining:'

104) Article 117 is supplemented by a new paragraph Eighth to read as follows: 'The board of directors shall establish committees of its members to make recommendations as to (a) selection of the company's external, independent auditors (audit committee); and (b) compensation form and amount for the board and the managing director (compensation committee). Members of these committees shall not be officers or employees of the company nor holders of 10% or more of the company's shares, nor related to any of these by blood, marriage or personal or economic interest in a degree likely to materially bias their judgment. Any departure from the recommendation of such a committee, and the reasons for it, shall be announced at the general assembly and recorded in its minutes. The audit committee shall meet privately with the company's external auditors and have special responsibility for ensuring the accuracy and reliability of their work. It shall ensure that a record is kept in the course of the year of all material related-party transactions, within the meaning of international accounting standards, for discussion with the company's external auditors.'

105) Article 119 of the Law is amended to read as follows: 'First. It is impermissible for the chairman or a member of the board to have direct or indirect interests in deals that are concluded with the company, except after obtaining the permission of the general assembly with full disclosure of the nature and extent of such interests. The chairman or board member shall be liable to the company for any damage to it arising from violation of this Article. Compliance with this Article shall not exclude liability under Article 4, paragraph Third.

Second. It is impermissible for the chairman or a member of the board to vote upon or participate in a matter in which he or she has direct or indirect interests without disclosing the nature and extent thereof to disinterested members and receiving the permission of a majority of them. If no members are disinterested, all may act. In either case, however, the details of the matter shall be recorded in the minutes of the board and made available to the general assembly and the company's external auditors.'

106) Article 124 of the Law is amended to read as follows: 'In the exercise of his jurisdictions and powers, the managing director is subject to the provisions of Articles 119 and 120 of this Law. In addition, the compensation of the five most highly compensated employees of the company, in whatever form received, shall be disclosed in writing to the general assembly.'

107) Article 125 of the Law is amended to read as follows: 'Control is aimed at guaranteeing that the company is applying the provisions of its contract and the law.'

108) Article 127 of the Law is amended to read as follows: 'First: A copy of the invitation to the general assembly meeting held to discuss the final accounts shall be sent to the Registrar. The following shall be attached to the invitation:

1. the annual list;
2. the final accounts for the previous year and the accounts controller's report on them; and
3. the managing director's report on the company's progress in implementing its plan for the previous year.

Second: In the case of the joint-stock company, the invitation shall be sent to the Registrar, along with the statements and reports mentioned in subparagraphs 1 and 2 of paragraph First in this Article as well as the board of directors' report on the company's progress in implementing its plan for the previous year. As for members, they have the right to obtain copies of the annual report and other statements and reports.'

109) Article 128 of the Law is amended to read as follows: 'The Registrar has the right to obtain any statements, clarifications or documents from the company in order to implement its duties under the law.'

110) Article 133, paragraph First of the Law is amended to read as follows: 'The accounts of the mixed company shall be subject to control and audit by the Financial Control Bureau. As for the accounts of the private company, they shall be subject to control and audit by auditors appointed by the company's general assembly. Accounts should be consolidated with those of related companies in accordance with international accounting standards unless specifically modified by standards in force in Iraq.'

111) Article 134, paragraphs First and Second of the Law are amended to read as follows: 'First: The significant contracts concluded by the company during the previous year and the businesses in which owners of 10% or more of the company's shares, the members of the board or the managing director had interests, including interests of their families, entities under their control and any other interest that would render the transaction a related-party transaction under international accounting standards insofar as permissible to apply these in Iraq.

Second: The results of operations (including earnings) and distribution of net profit.'

112) Article 139 of the Law is amended to read as follows: 'Copies of the final accounts, the annual plan, and the reports on them as well as the general assembly's decisions on them shall be sent to the Registrar.'

113) Article 140, paragraph First of the Law is suspended.

114) Article 141 is amended to read as follows: 'The Registrar has the right to appoint an inspector when necessary without asking the permission of any quarter. If the company believes that the Registrar has exercised its powers under this section for improper purposes, it may apply to the competent court to prove this and obtain an order restraining any improper action.'

115) Article 142, paragraph Second of the Law is amended to read as follows: 'The appointed inspector shall submit his or her report on the inspection to the Registrar, who shall send copies of the report to the company and the person making the claim referred to in Article 140.'

116) Article 149, paragraphs First and Fourth of the Law are suspended.

117) Article 150, paragraph Third of the Law is amended to read as follows: 'If, within 15 days of receiving them, the Registrar has not found that the decisions are inconsistent with the law, it will promptly issue its permission and inform the companies concerned of this decision; the companies will then cause it to be published in the Bulletin and one daily paper.'

118) Article 150, paragraphs Fourth and Fifth of the Law are suspended.

119) Article 150, paragraph Sixth of the Law is amended to read as follows: 'The companies receiving the Registrar's permission for their merger will call their general assemblies to a joint meeting within 60 days from the date of the publication of the merger decision in order to amend the contracts of the existing companies or draw up a new contract for the merger company, depending on the circumstances. The contract shall be sent to the Registrar within 10 days for endorsement and publication in the bulletin and one daily paper.'

120) Article 155, paragraph First of the Law is amended to read as follows: 'If, within 15 days of receiving them, the Registrar does not find that the transformation decision and the amended contract are inconsistent with the law, it shall promptly endorse the transformation decision and the amended contract. It shall also notify the company of the permission; the company shall publish the permission in the Bulletin and a daily paper.'

121) Article 155, paragraphs Second and Third of the Law are suspended.

122) Article 158, paragraph First, subparagraph 1 of the Law is amended to read as follows: 'If the general assembly decides to liquidate the company, or if any of the reasons stipulated in paragraphs First, Second, Third, and Fifth of Article 147 of this Law materialize and the general assembly recommends liquidation of the company, the company must appoint one or more liquidator, specify his or her jurisdictions and remuneration, and send the decision or recommendation to the Registrar.'

123) Article 158, paragraph Second of the Law is suspended.

124) Article 159 of the Law is amended to read as follows: 'The liquidation decision or recommendation shall be backed by reasons and sent to the Registrar within 14 days of its adoption. The latter has the right to request additional information or discuss matters with the company's general assembly to ascertain the reasons.'

125) Article 160 of the Law is amended to read as follows: 'If the Registrar has verified that the reasons for the liquidation are not fraudulent or unlawful, it shall issue the company's liquidation decision and appoint a liquidator within ten days of the verification. The Registrar shall communicate this information to the company; the company shall then cause the information to be published in the Bulletin and one daily newspaper.'

126) Articles 161,162 and 169 of the Law are suspended.

127) Article 175, paragraph Fourth, shall be amended to read as follows: 'Any sequestration of company funds after the initiation of the liquidation process shall not be valid except under a decision by the competent court, except for sequestrations that are carried in the interest of the state, the state sector or employees in order to pay their wages.'

128) Article 178 of the Law shall be designated as Article 178, paragraph First, and the following paragraph Second shall be added: 'Second. Distributions to foreign investors in the company shall conform to CPA Order Number 39, section 12(2).'

129) Article 203 of the Law is amended to read as follows: 'The company's contract is not considered valid until it has been endorsed by the Registrar in accordance with Article 19.'

130) Article 204 of the Law is amended to read as follows: 'It is permissible to object to the decisions of the Registrar before the Minister of Trade within 30 days from the date of notification. The Minister's decision may be appealed as provided in article 24 of this law.'

131) Article 208 of the Law shall be designated as Article 208, paragraph First, and the following paragraph Second shall be added: 'Second. The Agency Registration Law No. 4 of 1999 shall be inapplicable to the registration of a company, and a company is not required to retain a commercial agent to register, though it may choose to do so. Furthermore, no certification of tax compliance or of the absence of tax delinquency shall be required for the registration of a company. The Minister of Trade is hereby authorized to issue instructions to coordinate the activities of the Registrar of Companies and the Chamber of Commerce regarding the registration and approval of commercial trade names, notwithstanding anything to the contrary in The Law on Establishment of Chambers of Commerce No. 43 of 1989.'

132) Article 209 is amended to read as follows: 'The fees for the paperwork pertaining to this law shall be charged in accordance with the chart attached to this law. The Ministry of

Trade may amend the chart in accordance with changes in costs and to align the fees with processing costs.'

133) Article 211, paragraph First of the Law is amended to read as follows: 'The branches and offices of foreign companies and establishments shall be subject to the provisions of CPA Order No.39 and regulations and administrative instructions issued thereunder.'

134) Article 213, paragraph Second of the Law is amended to read as follows: 'The punishment stipulated in paragraph First of this Article shall apply to every company branch or office that must be re-registered or liquidated, for every day of delay after the periods stipulated in regulations and administrative instructions issued under CPA Order No. 39.'

135) Article 215 of the Law is amended to read as follows: 'First: Anyone carrying out a business in the name of a joint-stock company, limited liability company, joint liability company, or sole owner enterprise without obtaining registration of its establishment shall be subject to a fine of not more than 3,000,000 dinars, while taking into consideration the severity of the violations and the provisions of paragraph First of Article 21 of this law.

Second: Anyone carrying out a business in the name of a branch or an office for a foreign company or economic establishment without obtaining the registration required shall be subject to the penalties provided in paragraph First of this Article unless otherwise provided in applicable legislation.'

136) Article 216 of the Law is amended to read as follows: 'Any company that does not prepare the records stipulated under this law shall be subject to a fine of not more than 10,000,000 dinars, depending on the severity of the violation.'

137) Article 217 of the Law is amended to read as follows: 'Any company failing to submit the required statements and information to a competent official quarter at the times fixed under the provisions of this law shall be subject to punishment of a fine of not more than 300,000 dinars for every day of delay, depending on the severity of the violation.'

138) Article 218 of the Law is amended to read as follows: 'Any company official who purposely gives inaccurate statements or information to an official quarter on the company's business, results of operations, financial condition, member shares and quotas, or distribution of dividends shall be subject to punishment of imprisonment for a period of not more than one year, or a fine of not more than 12,000,000 dinars, or both, depending on the severity of the violation.'

139) Article 219 of the Law is amended to read as follows: 'Any company official who bars a competent quarter from seeing the company's records and documents shall be subject to punishment of imprisonment for a period of not more than six months or a fine of not more than 12,000,000 dinars, or both, depending on the severity of the violation.'

Section 2 General Provisions

1) All references in the Law to 'him,' 'he' or 'his' not specifically amended in this Order shall hereby refer to both male and female genders, and things, where appropriate.

2) All references to an 'Iraqi Bank' not specifically amended in this Order are hereby amended to read: 'bank authorized to operate in Iraq'.

3) All references in the Law to the 'socialist sector' not specifically amended in this Order are hereby amended to read 'state sector'.

4) The increase of penalties in Section Three of Chapter VIII of the Law shall take effect 90 days from the date this Order enters into force.

5) The provisions of this Order requiring action by the general assembly or board of directors of a company shall be implemented within the later of (a) 90 days from the date this Order enters into force; or (b) the next meeting of the body concerned or the time of its next legally required meeting if it should fail to convene one. The reduction in state sector board members effected in Section 1, paragraph 91, of this Order shall occur at the end of the current terms of the members affected, as shall the elimination of members under paragraphs 91 and 92 of Section 1. The additional member allowed under Section 1, paragraph 91, to shareholders outside the state sector may, however, be elected at the next general assembly, without regard to the possibility that this may increase the total number of directors above seven when allowing for an incumbent state sector member to finish his or her term.

6) Subject to such further rules as the competent state authority for the securities markets may adopt, references in the Law to the Baghdad Stock Exchange shall be deemed to mean a stock exchange authorized by law, and if there is more than one, the one most appropriate for obtaining the prices, effecting the sales or providing the notifications required. The provisions of article 66, paragraph Second of the Law shall apply with respect to any exchange authorized by law, subject to such further rules as may be adopted by the competent state authority for the securities markets.

Section 3 Entry into Force

This Order shall enter into force on the date of signature [3 March 2004].

ANNEX A

LAW No. 21 of 1997 (as amended in 2004)

In the name of God the merciful, the compassionate
The Republic of Iraq
In the name of the people

Company Law No. 21 of 1997

Chapter I: Main Rules

Section One: The Aims, Bases, and Validity Scope of the Law

Article 1: The objectives of this law are to

1. organize companies;
2. protect creditors from fraud;
3. protect shareholders from conflicts of interest and related abuses by company officials, majority owners, and others with practical control over the affairs of the company; and
4. promote the provision of full information to owners in connection with decisions affecting their investment and their company.

Article 2: Suspended.

Article 3: This law applies to mixed and private companies and to all investors. Its provisions shall apply to banks to the extent they do not conflict with Coalition Provisional Authority (CPA) Orders including CPA Order No. 40 promulgating the Banking Law, CPA

Order No. 18 prescribing Measures to Ensure the Independence of the Central Bank of Iraq, the Central Bank of Iraq Law No. 64 of 1976, as amended, and regulations issued under the foregoing orders. This law shall apply to securities transactions, financial investment companies and insurance and re-insurance companies to the extent it does not conflict with legislation applicable to these transactions and entities or the jurisdiction of the competent state authorities for those sectors. Decisions of the Registrar of Companies (hereinafter 'Registrar') hereunder shall be based upon this law and not upon considerations of economic planning or development policy. Decisions by the Registrar shall not in general foreclose a claim for compensation arising from violation of the law by an injured third party against those responsible for the violation.

Section Two: The Company in General

Sub-Section One: The Company's Contract and Owners' Mutual Obligations

Article 4: First: The company is a contract binding two or more persons. Each person shall subscribe to the economic project by a quota of the capital or service in order to share the resulting profit or loss.

Second: With the exception of the provisions of Paragraph First of this article:

1. A company may be established by one natural person in accordance with the provisions of this law. Such a company will henceforth be referred to as a 'sole owner enterprise.'
2. A limited liability company may be formed with one owner in accordance with the provisions of this law.

Third: Owners of capital in a company may not exercise their voting or other authority in the company to cause it to do or consent to acts that:

1. harm or disadvantage the company to benefit themselves or those associated with them at the expense of other owners of the company; or
2. jeopardize the rights of creditors by causing withdrawal of capital or transfer of assets when insolvency is imminent or when prohibited by law.

Article 5: The company shall acquire the corporate status in accordance with the provisions of this law.

Sub-Section Two: Types of Companies

Article 6: First: The mixed or private joint-stock company shall be formed by not less than five persons, who will participate in it by owning shares through public subscription and will be responsible for the company's debts in so far as the nominal value of the shares to which they subscribed.

Second: The mixed or private limited liability company shall be formed by no more than 25 natural or juridical persons, who will subscribe to its shares and will be responsible for the company's debts in so far as the nominal value of the shares to which they subscribed.

Third: The joint liability company shall be formed by not less than two and not more than 25 persons, each owning a quota of its capital. They shall jointly assume personal and unlimited responsibility for all of its obligations.

Fourth: The sole owner enterprise is a company formed by one person, who owns the one quota in it and assumes personal and unlimited responsibility for all of its obligations.

Article 7: First: The mixed company shall be formed by the agreement between one or more persons from the state sector and one or more persons from outside this sector. The state sector's share in the mixed company's capital must not initially be less than 25 percent. A mixed company may also be formed by two or more persons from the mixed sector. When the state sector's share falls below 25%, the company shall be treated as a private company, as permitted in article 8, paragraph Second, point 2.

Second: The mixed sector company can be a joint-stock company or a limited liability company.

Article 8: First: The private sector company shall be formed by the agreement between two or more persons from outside the state sector with private capital.

Second: With the exception of the provisions of Paragraph First of this article, it is permissible to:

1. Form a sole owner enterprise of one natural person or a sole owner limited liability company of one juridical or natural person.
2. Include the state sector in the private joint-stock company or limited liability company with a share of less than 25 percent of the capital. Those excluded from this percentage are: Government insurance and reinsurance companies, the Labor and Social Security Department, and any other investment quarter which the cabinet may add under this sub-paragraph.

Third: The private sector company can be a joint-stock company, a limited liability company, a joint liability company, a sole owner enterprise, or a simple company.

Article 9: First: The Financial Investment Company is a company organized in Iraq whose main activity is to direct savings toward investment in Iraqi financial securities, including shares, bonds, treasury bills and fixed deposits.

Second: The Financial Investment Company is considered one of the intermediary financial establishments for the purposes of Iraqi Central Bank Law No. 64 of 1976. The bank is the sectoral quarter, which will be concerned with its activity and exercise the authority of its supervision and control, in accordance with an ordinance which will be issued for this purpose within 180 days from the date of the publication of this law in the Official Gazette.

Article 10: First: Suspended.
Second: Companies engaging in any of the following activities must become joint-stock companies:

1. Insurance and re-insurance.
2. Financial investment.

Article 11: Any economic project, which is not covered under the provisions of Article 10 of this law can take the form of one of the companies stipulated in this law.

Section Three: Membership in the Company

Article 12: First: A juridical or natural person, foreign or domestic, has the right to acquire membership in the companies stipulated in this law as founder, shareholder, or partner, unless such person is banned from such membership under the law, or due to a decision issued by a competent court or authorized governmental body.

Second: Suspended.

Third: Suspended.

Chapter II: Establishment of the Company

Section One: Requirements of Establishment

Article 13: The founders shall prepare a contract for the company which is signed by them or their legal representative. The contract shall contain at a minimum:

First: The company's name and corporate form, with the word 'mixed' added if it is a mixed sector company, and any other acceptable elements.

Second: The company's head office, which must be in Iraq.

Third: The purposes for which the company is established and the general nature of the business to be transacted.

Fourth: Suspended.

Fifth: The company's capital divided in quotas and shares.

Sixth: The method of distributing profits and losses in the joint liability company.

Seventh: The number of elected members in the board of directors of the private joint-stock company.

Eighth: The names of the founders and their nationalities, professions, permanent addresses, and the number of shares they own as well as their percentage of the capital.

Article 14: The founder of a limited liability company when there are no other founders, or the founder of a sole owner enterprise shall prepare a statement, which shall serve the purpose of a company contract and shall be subject to the provisions that are applicable to the contract whenever they occur in this law.

Article 15: The founders of the company shall subscribe to the company's capital in accordance with their agreed to contributions.

Article 16: First: The founders shall deposit the amounts of the company's capital specified in Article 28, paragraph First of this law with one or more banks authorized to operate in Iraq. It is permissible for the company capital to include contributions in kind as stipulated in Article 29 of this law.

Second: Suspended.

Third:

1. The joint-stock company's members, who must not be more than 100, shall elect from among themselves a committee which shall be called the 'Founders Committee.' The committee, which will consist of not less than three and not more than seven members, will undertake the following duties and tasks:
   a. Conclude a contract with specialized and experience for the purpose of conducting an economic and technical feasibility study of the business to be carried out by the company.
   b. Follow up on the procedures for establishing the company and submit the contract of association and the subscription document to the Registrar of Companies including the names, signatures, addresses, and nationalities of the founders as well as other requirements.
   c. Disburse expenditures until the procedures for the establishment of the company are completed.
   d. Open a joint account in the name of the committee with one or more banks authorized to operate in Iraq.

e. Keep the records, including the decisions that have been made and the duties and tasks that have been fulfilled.
f. Obtain a license, if necessary, for the project and conclude the necessary contracts for its establishment, following the issuance of the decision approving its establishment.
g. Prepare the founders' report, specify the establishment expenditures, and call a meeting of the General Assembly.

2. The Founders Committee's duties shall end with the election of the board of directors.
3. The members of the Founders Committee shall be jointly answerable to the founders.

Section Two: Establishment Procedures

Article 17: The application for establishment shall be submitted to the Registrar with the following attachments:

First: The company's contract.

Second: The subscription document of the joint-stock company signed by the founders.

Third: A statement from the bank or banks proving that the capital required in Article 28 has been deposited.

Fourth: The technical and economic feasibility study on the joint-stock company.

Article 18: Suspended.

Article 19: The Registrar shall approve the application unless it finds it contrary to a specific provision of this law and shall issue the approval or disapproval of the establishment application within 10 days from the date of receiving it. Except for joint stock companies, the certificate shall be issued at the time of the approval and shall be the evidence of the company's establishment. If the Registrar disapproves an application, it shall issue a written decision stating the reasons for its disapproval. In the case of a joint stock company, the Registrar shall issue a written notice of its decision at the time of approval or disapproval. No certificate shall be issued without payment of the applicable fee.

Article 20: Suspended.

Article 21: First:

1. The Registrar shall publish the decision approving the establishment of the company in the special bulletin published under the provisions of Article 206 of this law, which henceforth will be referred to as 'the Bulletin.'.
2. In the case of the joint-stock company, the certificate of establishment shall be issued after the public subscription to its shares and within 15 days from the date on which the founders submit the data stipulated in Article 46 of this law.

Second: Suspended.

Article 22: The company acquires corporate status from the date of the issuance of its establishment certificate. This certificate is considered proof of this status.

Article 23: A company which is established in Iraq in accordance with the provisions of this law is considered an Iraqi company.

Article 24: If the Registrar rejects the application for the establishment of the company, it must state in writing the legal provisions violated and the facts underlying each violation. The applicant for the establishment has the right to contest the Registrar's rejection before the Minister of Trade within 30 days from the date of notification. The Minister of Trade must consider the rejection within 30 days from the date of its submission. If the Minister also rejects the application, the applicant has the right to appeal the Minister's decision before the competent court within 30 days.

Article 25: The founders may submit a new application for the establishment of the company once the reason for its rejection has been eliminated.

Chapter III: The Company's Funds

Section One: The Capital

Article 26: The company's capital shall be specified in Iraqi dinars.

Article 27: The capital shall be allocated to carry out the business specified in the company's contract and to fulfill its obligations. It is impermissible to dispose of the capital in any other way.

Article 28: First: The capital of a joint stock company shall not be less than two million (2,000,000) dinars. The capital of a limited liability company shall not be less than one million (1,000,000) dinars. The capital of all other companies shall not be less than fifty thousand (50,000) dinars.

Second: A joint stock company's, liabilities may not exceed 300 percent of its total capital and other equity rights.

Section Two: Division of Capital

Sub-Section One: Division of Capital in the Joint-Stock Company and the Limited Liability Companies

Article 29: First: The capital of the joint-stock company and the limited liability company shall be divided into shares of equal cash value. The shares shall be indivisible.

Second: In the joint-stock company and the limited liability company, the capital may include shares that are offered in exchange for tangible or intangible in-kind property contributions by one or more of the founders.

1. In the case of a joint stock company, property-in-kind shares shall be evaluated by a committee approved by the Registrar as to expertise and objectivity, and including experts in law, accounting and the company's line of business.
2. In the case of the mixed joint-stock company, the committee established pursuant to sub-paragraph 1 of this paragraph shall submit its report to the Registrar within 60 days from the date of its formation. The Registrar shall submit its report to the Financial Control Bureau for endorsement within 30 days from the date of its submission. In the case of non-approval, the Registrar shall return the report to the committee established pursuant to subparagraph 1 for further consideration.
3. In the case of the private joint-stock company, all founders shall agree on the value of property-in-kind shares as assessed in the manner stipulated in sub-paragraph 1 of this

paragraph. A joint-stock company's or limited liability company's contract must state the type of property-in-kind share and its value as approved by the rest of the founders, the name of the founder who offered the share, and the percentage of his contribution to the capital through this share. The founder offering the property-in-kind shall be accountable to any person for its assessed and accepted value. If it is proven that the assessed value is less than the actual value, he or she must pay the difference in cash to the company. The other founders may also be asked to cooperate in paying the difference.

4. In the case of the joint-stock company, the committee's report must be submitted to the constituent meeting of its general assembly, provided the founders deposit the aforementioned report with the quarter conducting the subscription so the subscribers can read it. And, if the assessment is higher, the subscriber of the property-in-kind share must pay the difference in cash. The other founders may also be asked to cooperate in paying this difference. Article 30: The nominal value of the share shall be one dinar. It should not be issued higher or lower than that except as provided in Articles 54 through 56.

Article 31: Suspended.

Article 32: First: Suspended.

Second: Suspended.

Third: It is impermissible for the Investment Company to invest more than 5 percent of its capital in the shares of any company. It is also impermissible for it to own more than 10 percent of the capital of any company, while taking the previous percentage into consideration. Its cash liquidity must not, at any time, be less than 10 percent of the paid-up capital.

Article 33: The shareholder is answerable to the company's debts to the extent of the nominal value of the shares he owns.

Sub-section Two: Division of capital in the Joint Liability Company and the Sole Owner Enterprise

Article 34: The capital of the joint liability company is divided into quotas among the partners according to the company's contract. The sole owner enterprise consists of one quota.

Article 35: Whoever has a share in the joint liability company or the sole owner enterprise assumes personal and unlimited responsibility for the debts of the company. His responsibility is collective in the joint liability company.

Article 36: If the company becomes insolvent, every partner in it becomes insolvent.

Article 37: First: The creditors of a joint liability company may take legal action against the company or any partners who were members when the obligation occurred. The partners are obligated to honor the joint liability. It is impermissible to sequester the partner's funds before warning the company.

Second: The creditors of a sole owner enterprise may take legal action against it or the owner of the quota in it. His or her funds shall be considered as a guarantee for debts on the enterprise. It is permissible to seize his or her funds without warning the enterprise and in accordance with applicable legal procedures.

Section Three: Public Subscription in the Capital

Article 38: Public subscription shall take place in the capital of a jointstock company only.

Article 39: First: The founders in the mixed joint-stock company shall subscribe by not less than 30 percent and not more than 55 percent of its nominal capital, and this should include the minimum 25 percent fixed for the state sector.

Second: At the establishment of the company, the founders in the private joint-stock company shall subscribe by not less than 20 percent in its nominal capital.

Third: The remaining shares shall be offered for public subscription within 30 days from the date of the approval of the establishment of the company in a statement issued by the founders and published in the bulletin and at least two daily papers, after obtaining the approval of the Registrar, which shall be granted within that time unless the Registrar finds the registration materials submitted would be materially misleading to investors. In the latter case, it shall refer a matter within its jurisdiction to the competent state authority for the securities markets. The statement shall include the following:

1. The text of the company's contract.
2. The number of shares offered for subscription, the value of each share, and the sum which must be paid toward each share.
3. The minimum and maximum number of shares one can subscribe for.
4. The place and period of subscription.
5. The expenses of the establishment of the company.
6. The contracts and agreements which the founders have undertaken in the interest of the company.
7. Any other information which the founders may want to add.
8. The report of the committee formed under Paragraph Second of Article 29 of this law in the case of the existence of a property-in-kind share.

Fourth: Founders shall not subscribe to the shares while they are being offered for public subscription, except after the end of 30 days from the beginning of the subscription or during the extended period stipulated in Article 42 of this law.

Article 40: The founders are jointly responsible for any damages caused to any subscriber due to an error or shortcoming in the subscription statement.

Article 41: First: The subscription shall take place in a bank authorized to operate in Iraq in a form bearing the name of the company and containing the following:

1. The request to subscribe to a specific number of shares.
2. The subscriber's approval of the company's contract.
3. The subscriber's name, address, profession, and nationality.
4. Any other information which the founders may want to add.

Second: The form shall be submitted to the party handling the subscription signed by the subscriber or his legal representative. The required payment shall be paid against a receipt.

Third: The subscriber shall be given a copy of the company's contract and its technical and economic feasibility study, subject to Section 47, paragraph Third of this law.

Article 42: The subscription period shall not be less than 30 days or more than 60 days. If the subscription period expires without the subscribed shares reaching 75 percent of the nominal capital, including the shares owned by the founders, it is permissible to extend it for a further period of not more than 60 days. The founders shall again publish the subscription statement and make the extension announcement.

Article 43: First: If the subscription does not reach 75 percent of the nominal capital at the end of the extension period, the founders must decrease the company's capital, so that the value of the subscribed shares will be equal to 75 percent of the decreased nominal capital, unless the founders cancel the establishment of the company. The founders shall inform the Registrar of such a decision.

Second: Suspended. Third: If it is decided to cancel the establishment of the company under the provisions of Paragraph First of this article, the founders shall notify the bank and jointly bear the expenses for establishing the company. The bank handling the subscription shall return the money paid by all subscribers in full upon notification and within a period of not more than 30 days.

Article 44: First: The bank shall be responsible for the soundness of the subscription process and undertake the following:

1. Close the subscription at the end of its period, announcing the closure in two daily papers, and also notify the Founders Committee.
2. Keep all the money received from the subscribers and not give any to the founders.
3. Return any surplus funds to the subscribers within 15 days from the distribution of the shares among the subscribers in accordance with Paragraph Second of this article.

Second: If it transpires after the closure of the subscription that the shares offered have been over-subscribed, the shares must be distributed among the subscribers according to the percentage of subscription allotted for each subscriber.

Article 45: First: Any person whose lawful rights would be infringed by violations of the subscription rules, the Registrar and the competent state authority for the securities market has the right to contest the soundness of the subscription process before the competent court and ask for its cancellation within 15 days from the closure of the subscription. The court must examine such cases urgently. The court's decision can be contested before the court of appeal, which shall sit as a court of cassation, and its decision in this capacity shall be final.

Second: If the subscription is ruled to be in violation of the law, the founders must carry it out anew.

Article 46: The founders shall, within 30 days from the end of the period for contesting the subscription, provide the Registrar with all data on the subscription process, including the names of subscribers, the number of shares subscribed by each one of them, their addresses, professions, nationalities, and the sums they paid against the value of the shares.

Article 47: First: Once the company has been established and some shares are still not subscribed for, the board of directors may, after six months from the date of the issuance of the establishment certificate, pursue one of two courses:

1. Sell those shares in the Baghdad Stock Exchange market; or
2. place the shares for public subscription in accordance with the procedures followed during the constituent subscription.

Second: If the shares are not sold in the market or subscribed by the public, the company's nominal capital shall be decreased by the value of the unsold shares.

Third: The company shall be liable for materially misleading assertions or omissions in sales or subscriptions as shall be its responsible directors, employees and agents.

Section Four: Payment of Capital

Article 48: First: In the joint-stock company, the subscription shall require payment in full for issued shares. Unpaid shares already outstanding under previous law shall be governed by this Article.

Second: Suspended.

Third: The outstanding installments are considered a privileged debt which must be paid to the company. A deferment interest of not less than 5 and not more than 7 percent shall be charged on the debt annually for any delay in paying the installment on the date set by the board of directors. No dividends shall be paid on the debt.

Fourth: The company shall continue to withhold the dividends due to the shareholder in order to cover the value of the overdue installments and the interest on them until all installments and their interest have been paid.

Article 49: If the shareholder does not pay the installment on his shares on the set date without a legitimate reason, the board of directors may take steps to sell those shares as follows:

First: The company shall notify the shareholder in two daily papers, the bulletin, and the Baghdad Stock Exchange Market, to pay the overdue installment within 30 days from the date of publication. The notification shall state the number of shares he owns and the amount of the installment which must be paid and its due date.

Second: If the shareholder does not pay the installment within the above respite, the company shall offer his shares for sale by public auction in the Baghdad Stock Exchange Market.

Third: The company shall announce the sale in the bulletin, one daily paper, and the Baghdad Stock Exchange Market, its date and place, and the number of shares offered for auction, provided the period between the announcement and the sale is not more than 15 days.

Fourth: The shareholder whose shares have been announced for sale can pay the debt up to one day before the auction date. In such a case the sale will be canceled and the shareholder will bear all the company's expenses on the sale procedures.

Fifth: The shares shall be sold at the highest price reached at the auction. The company shall deduct from this price its debts, including the installments, the interest, and the expenses, and return the remainder to the shareholder. But, if the price of the sold shares does not cover the debt, the company shall obtain the difference from the shareholder.

Sixth: The company's records on the sale shall be considered correct unless they are proven otherwise.

Article 50: The subscriber to the joint- stock company shall be given – after paying all due installments and producing the receipts as proof – a temporary certificate with a serial number signed by an authorized person in the company. The certificate shall state the name of the shareholder, the number of shares he owns, the amount paid toward their value, and the remaining installments and their due dates. The installments paid shall be ticked in this certificate.

Article 51: Every shareholder in a limited liability company and every subscriber who has fully paid the value of his shares in a joint-stock company shall be given a permanent certificate including the data contained in the temporary certificate, plus a declaration that the shares have been paid. Any temporary certificate should be cancelled.

Article 52: The shareholder may pay one or more installments toward the value of his shares before their due date. In such a case, they will be considered as still due even if the same installments have not yet been paid by the other shareholders. No dividends will be paid for installments which are paid before their due date.

Article 53: In the case of the limited liability company, the joint liability company, and sole owner enterprise, the capital must be paid up before the issuance of the certificate of establishment.

Section Five: Increase and Decrease of Capital

Sub-Section One: Increase of Capital

Article 54: First: A company may increase its paid-up capital.

Second: In the joint-stock company and the limited liability company, the increase of capital must be in accordance with a general assembly decision to amend the contract and issue new shares.

Third: Suspended.

Fourth: The Registrar shall within fifteen days of a lawful request approve the increase. The Registrar shall be deemed to approve the increase, and to give notice of the approval, unless it rejects the request, giving the legal and factual basis for the determination in writing.

Article 55: The general assembly of the joint-stock company and the limited liability company may cover the increase in the capital by any of the following methods:

First: Issuing new shares whose value is paid in cash.

Second: Transferring funds from the accumulated surplus or the issuance allowance reserve into shares to be distributed among the shareholders in the ratio of their subscription to the capital.

Third: Withholding part of the company's profits as a reserve for expanding and developing the enterprise instead of distributing them as dividends. When this reserve is added to the capital and new shares equivalent to it are issued, the shares shall be distributed among shareholders in the ratio of their subscription to the capital.

Fourth: In cases where the shares will be offered in exchange for cash, such decision must specify the number of shares to be issued and the price at which they will be offered for sale or the means of establishing that price. Shares may be offered at a price equal to or greater than their nominal value in accordance with the general assembly's decision and priced in light of the company's performance and, where applicable, the prices of its shares in the Baghdad Stock Exchange market. The proceed reflecting the difference between the issue price and nominal price, which is considered issuance allowance, shall be recorded in the account of the issuance allowance reserve, after deducting all issuance expenses.

This reserve may not be distributed as profits. In the case of the joint-stock company, the company shall submit to the Registrar a decision by its general assembly to increase the capital, backed by an economic study giving the justifications for this increase and the fields in which it will be expended, as well as any other essential data. It shall be furnished to purchasers, subject to the liability in the second paragraph of article 47 of this law, unless the Registrar finds it materially misleading. In this case, it shall refer a matter within its jurisdiction to the competent state authority for the securities market.

Article 56: First: In the joint-stock company, the new shares must be placed for public subscription within 30 days from the date on which the company is notified of the Registrar's approval of the increase in the capital. The subscription shall remain open for a period of not less than 30 days and not more than 60 days, which may be renewable once for a similar period, provided the value of the shares is paid during subscription. The increase in the capital is achieved by the number of shares subscribed and paid up on the closure of the subscription. Otherwise, and in so far as it does not conflict with the nature of the increase in the capital, the original provisions on subscription shall be applied on the new shares, including the provisions of Articles 44 and 47 of this law.

Second: In the limited liability company, the value of the new shares must be paid within 30 days from the issuance of the general assembly's decision to increase the capital. The increase is achieved by the number of shares whose value is paid up at the end of the period.

Third: Every shareholder has the priority to buy shares at the subscription price proportional to the number of the shares he owns. Shareholders shall be allowed to exercise this right within a period of 15 days from the date they are invited to do so. The invitation must state the beginning and end of the subscription period and the nominal value of the shares. If some shares are not subscribed after the period stipulated in paragraph First of this Article, the board of directors may place the shares for sale in the Baghdad Stock Exchange market in the manner it deems suitable.

Fourth: In the case of banks increasing capital by a sale of shares for cash, the company may issue shares without public subscription and/or without offering existing shareholders the right to participate, provided the following conditions are met:

1. The issuance is approved by a majority of the votes of the subscribed shares whose due installments have been paid; and
2. The Central Bank of Iraq concurs that the sale is for fair value, in view of all the circumstances, and is fair to shareholders not entitled to participate, in view of the benefit to the company as whole.

Article 57: In the case of the joint liability company and sole owner enterprise, the increase of the capital occurs in accordance with a decision by the general assembly to amend the contract, provided the increase is paid within 30 days from the date of the issuance of the decision.

Sub-section Two: Decrease of Capital

Article 58: A company may decrease its capital if it exceeds its needs or incurs losses. A decrease in capital that is part of an arrangement to achieve a net increase in capital through additional investments shall not be subject to the requirements in Article 59, paragraph Third, and Articles 60-63.

Article 59: First: In the case of the joint stock company and the limited liability company, the capital is decreased by canceling shares which are equivalent in value to the sum to be deducted from the capital. The cancellation shall be in the ratio of each member's subscription in the company, to the nearest correct share.

Second: The decision to decrease the capital shall be made by the company's general assembly which shall state the reasons for the decrease.

Third: After making the decision on the decrease, the following steps shall be taken:

1. The chairman of the board of directors in the joint-stock company and the managing director in the limited liability company shall refer the decision on the decrease to the Registrar coupled with a certified statement by the chief accountant including the company's debts and the names and addresses of the creditors, as well as an economic and technical study on the reasons for the decrease.
2. Suspended.
3. If the Registrar finds the decrease lawful, it shall announce the approval in the bulletin and two daily papers. It shall also give every creditor to or claimant on the company the right to object to the decision on the decrease within 30 days from the date of the publication of the announcement.

Article 60: First: If an objection is made during the legal respite by a creditor to or a claimant on the company, the Registrar must seek an amicable settlement of the objection in the manner he deems suitable within 30 days from the end of the objection period.

Second: If the Registrar is unable to settle the objection, he must refer it with all the pertinent documents and papers to the competent court within 15 days from the end of the amicable settlement period. The examination of such objections is an urgent matter.

Article 61: First: If the court reaches a settlement on the objections, or if it is satisfied that the assurances given by the company are adequate, it shall issue its decision supporting the decision on the decrease. But, if a settlement is not reached on the objections and the assurances given by the company are not adequate, the court shall decide on canceling the decrease or approving only a partial decrease that does not adversely affect the rights of the objectors. Its decision shall be final.

Second: Irrespective of the decision made by the court, the company must deposit a copy of the decision with the Registrar within 15 days of its issuance.

Article 62: If there is no objection to the decision on the decrease, or the decision has been signed and settled before the Registrar or the court, the company's contract shall be considered amended by law. A copy of the amendment shall be sent to the Registrar for registration and publication in the bulletin and one daily paper.

Article 63: In the case of the joint liability company and the sole owner enterprise, any decrease of the capital must take place through a decision by the general assembly to amend the contract.

Section Six: Disposal of Shares and Quotas

Sub-section One: Transfer of Ownership

Article 64: In the case of the joint-stock company and the limited liability company, the shareholder may transfer ownership of his shares to another shareholder or outsiders, while bearing in mind the following considerations:

First: Founders of joint-stock companies may not transfer ownership of their shares except in the following situations:

1. The lapse of at least one year since the establishment of the company.
2. The distribution of dividends that are not less than five percent of the paid up nominal capital.

Second: Suspended.

Third: The shareholder from the private sector cannot transfer ownership of his or her shares:

1. If they are mortgaged, seized, or sequestered under a court decision.
2. If their certificate is lost and a replacement has not been issued.
3. If the shares to be transferred owe debts to the company.
4. If the transferee is prohibited to own shares in the company under a law or a decision issued by a competent quarter.

Article 65: Shareholders in a limited liability company prefer to sell their shares to outsiders. If a shareholder wishes to sell his or her shares, he or she must follow the following steps:

First: The seller must notify the other shareholders through the managing director of his desire to sell his or her shares. He or she must mention the number of shares, the number of their certificate, and the price he wants or that has been offered by a buyer supported by evidence.

Second: If after 30 days of notification, none of the other shareholders have come forth to buy the shares, or have offered a price lower than the required one, the buyer shall be free to sell his or her shares to others at a price higher than the one offered by the shareholders. If he sells the shares at the lower price offered by the shareholders, the sale shall be considered null and void.

Third: If several shareholders want to buy the shares at the same price, the shares shall be divided among them in the ratio of their subscription, to the nearest correct share.

Article 66: First: The sale of shares in a joint-stock company or a limited liability company shall take place at a meeting between the seller and the buyer, or their legal representatives, in the presence of the representative of the managing director. A contract shall be made mentioning the names of the seller and the buyer and their addresses, the number of the certificate of the shares, the date of the transaction, the price, a statement from the seller that he received the price, and a pledge by the buyer that he approves of the company's contract. The transaction contract shall be recorded in the company's special register for transferred shares along with the signatures of the contractors and the representative of the company. Any transaction that is concluded outside the board shall be considered null and void and shall not be recorded in the company's register.

Second: Ownership of shares in the joint-stock companies trading in the Baghdad Stock Exchange market shall be transferred in accordance with the market's by-laws and the guidelines issued on its basis.

Article 67: If an Iraqi shareholder in a joint-stock company or a limited liability company dies, the ownership of the shares shall revert to his or her heirs in accordance with the ratios specified by the Shari'a law. In cases in which the shareholder is a citizen of another country, the shares shall revert to the shareholder's heirs in accordance with the applicable law of that country. In each case, the following shall be taken into consideration:

First: If the heir is prohibited to own shares in the companies or has received more than the maximum limit of shares allowable under the law, he or she must take steps to transfer their ownership within 90 days from the date they become transferable. If he or she fails, the board of directors in the joint-stock company and managing director in the limited liability company shall announce their sale through public auction.

Second: If the distribution of shares among the heirs will result in an increase in the number of partners in the limited liability company over the number set by the law, the shares shall be considered a joint ownership by the heirs in accordance with the ratios specified under applicable inheritance law and considered as one person. In such a case, one of the heirs will represent the rest before the company. They shall be asked to choose this representative within 60 days from the date of the registration of the shares in the company's ledger.

Article 68: Any transfer of ownership of shares other than through the sale method must be recorded in the company's register on the basis of a decision issued by the competent court.

Article 69: First: In the joint liability company, the partner may transfer ownership of his share of the capital to another partner. It is impermissible to transfer ownership to outsiders without the unanimous approval of the general assembly. In all cases, this is done by amending the company's contract.

Second: In the sole owner enterprise, the owner can transfer ownership to another person by amending the company's statement. If it is to be transferred to more than one person, or if only a part of the ownership is to be transferred, this can be done only by changing the enterprise into another type of company, such as those stipulated in this law.

Article 70: First: If a partner in a joint liability company dies, the partnership shall continue through his heirs. But, if the heir, or his legal representative if he is underage, or the other partners in the company object to that; or if that is prevented by any legal obstacle, the company shall continue among the remaining partners. The heir shall get only the share of his inheritor. This share shall be determined on the basis of its value on the day of the death and shall be paid in cash. The heir shall not have any rights on the company afterward except those resulting from operations prior to the death. In all cases, the company's contract must be changed to a sole owner enterprise, if only one partner remains.

Second: If the owner of the single quota in the sole owner enterprise dies and he has several heirs wishing to join the enterprise and there is no legal objection to that, the enterprise must be changed to any of the types of companies stipulated in this law.

Third: If a partner becomes insolvent or if his assets in the joint liability company are sequestered, the company shall continue among the remaining partners and the share of the insolvent and sequestered partner shall be liquidated. His share shall be assessed on the basis of its value on the day the insolvency or sequestration ruling is issued. He shall not have any rights on the company, other than those resulting from operations prior to the insolvency or sequestration. In all cases, the company's contract must be changed in accordance with its new condition or transformed into a sole owner enterprise, if there is one owner left.

Sub-Section Two: Mortgage and Sequestration of Shares and Quotas

Article 71: First: It is permissible to mortgage shares owned by the private sector in a joint-stock company or a limited liability company, provided the mortgage contract is recorded in the company's special register. The mortgage will only be deleted from the register after the mortgagee acknowledges its release, or after the competent court has issued its decision on it.

Second: It is impermissible to mortgage quotas in the capital of a joint liability company, sole owner enterprise, or a simple company.

Article 72: First: It is permissible to sequester the shares owned by the private sector in a joint-stock company or limited liability company as a security against a debt on their owner, provided the sequestration decision issued by a competent quarter is recorded in the company's special register. The sequestration will only be deleted from the register after a decision by a competent quarter.

Second: It is impermissible to seize the quotas in the capital of a joint liability company, simple company or a sole owner enterprise except against a privileged debt. It is permissible to seize its dividends.

Section Seven: Profits and Losses

Article 73: The company's net profit shall be distributed after making all the legal deductions as follows:

First: At least five percent as compulsory reserve until it reaches 50 percent of the paid-up capital. It is permissible under a decision by the general assembly to continue deducting for the compulsory reserves even if it exceeds 100 percent of the paid-up capital.

Second: The remainder of the profit or part of it shall be distributed among the members according to their quotas or shares.

Article 74: First: The reserve shall be used for the purposes of expanding and developing the company's business, and improving the conditions of its workers, participating in projects relevant to the company's activity, and contributing to the protection of the environment and social welfare programs. Dividends shall not be distributed from the reserve.

Second: The reserve shall be used to meet the company's debts, provided they do not exceed 50 percent of the reserve. Any increase over that limit shall be subject to the approval of the Registrar.

Article 75: The losses of the joint liability company shall be divided according to the ratios stipulated in its contract which are similar to the ratios for the distribution of profits.

Article 76: First: If the company's losses amount to 50 percent of its capital or more, it must notify the Registrar within 60 days from the day the losses are established in the balance sheet.

Second: If the losses amount to 75 percent of the capital or more, the company must take one of the following steps:

1. decrease or increase the capital of the company or
2. recommend liquidation of the company.

Section Eight: Credit Bonds

Article 77: The joint-stock company can seek a loan by issuing nominal bonds in accordance with the provisions of this law and inviting the public to buy these bonds. The subscriber shall be issued bonds against the sums of money he loans to the company. He has the right to charge an interest, which shall be paid to him at fixed periods. The value of the bonds shall be re-paid from the company's funds. These bonds will be of one nominal value. They will also be exchangeable, but not divisible. Each bond issue will have separate serial numbers and shall be stamped with the company's seal.

Article 78: It is impermissible to issue credit bonds before meeting the following conditions:

First: The company's capital must be fully paid.

Second: The total amount of the bond issue must not exceed the company's capital.

Third: The general assembly's approval of the issuance on the recommendation of the board of directors must be obtained in advance.

Article 79: The company shall submit to the Registrar the general assembly's decision on the issuance of the credit bonds backed by an economic study stating the reasons for the issue, the fields in which the credit will be expended, and any other essential data. It shall be furnished to purchasers, subject to the liability in the second paragraph of Article 47 of this Law, unless the Registrar finds it materially misleading. In the latter case, it shall refer a matter within its jurisdiction to the competent state authority for the securities markets.

Article 80: The invitation to subscription to the credit bonds shall be published in the bulletin and two daily papers and shall include the following details, which shall also be noted in the credit bond upon its issuance:

First: The company's name and capital.

Second: The date of the general assembly's decision approving the issuance of the credit bonds.

Third: Information on the company's financial condition and results of operations, including earnings.

Fourth: The rate of interest and its due dates.

Fifth: The value of the issue, its maturity date, and nominal value of each bond.

Sixth: Method and duration of subscription and method of payment.

Seventh: Maturity dates of the nominal bonds.

Eighth: Purpose of the loan.

Ninth: Guarantees of re-payment.

Tenth: Credit bonds previously issued by the company.

Eleventh: Any other details and information.

Article 81: The bank undertaking the subscription process for the credit bonds must close the subscription at the end of its period, or once all bonds have been subscribed and announced in two daily papers. It shall then immediately provide the Registrar with the full information on the subscription process, including the names of subscribers; the number of bonds subscribed by each of them; their addresses, professions, and nationalities; the sums paid; and the value of the bonds.

Article 82: First: The subscriber to the credit bonds has the right to contest before the competent court the soundness of the subscription process and ask for cancellation of the payment if the company did not comply with the procedures for the issuance of bonds or the subscription to them, or if it invited subscription seven days before the closing date. The court must consider the appeal urgently. Its decision can be appealed before the court of appeal, which shall sit as a court of cassation, and its decision in this capacity shall be final.

Second: If the court decision is to cancel the subscription to the credit bonds, the bank must, as soon as it is notified of the cancellation, return the money to the subscribers in full within a period of not more than 30 days.

Article 83: The company shall sell the outstanding bonds in the Baghdad Stock Exchange Market at less than the nominal value.

Article 84: The debtor company must re-pay the value of the credit bonds in accordance with the conditions set during or before the issuance. It is impermissible to delay the maturity date.

Chapter IV: The Company's Management

Section One: The General Assembly

Sub-Section One: The Formation of the General Assembly and its Meetings

Article 85: The general assembly shall consist of all the members of the company.

Article 86: The general assembly in the joint-stock company shall meet at least once a year. In the other companies, it shall meet at least once every six months.

Article 87: The invitation to a meeting of the general assembly shall be issued by one of the following bodies or persons:

First: The founder of the company for the purpose of holding the constituent meeting within 30 days from issuance of the company's certificate of establishment.

Second: The chairman of the board of directors of the joint- stock company under a decision by the board, and the managing director in other companies; or at the request of company members who own not less than 10 percent of its paid-up capital.

Third: The Registrar on its own initiative or at the request of the accounts controller.

Article 88: First: In the case of the joint-stock company, the invitation to attend a meeting of the general assembly must be announced in the bulletin, two daily papers, and the Baghdad Stock Exchange Market. The invitation in the case of the other companies shall be sent out in registered letters through the members' postal addresses or by informing them through the company's administrative office. The invitation shall fix the place and date of the meeting. The period between the date of the invitation and the day of the meeting must not be less than 15 days.

Second: If the founders or the chairman of the board of directors in the joint-stock company or the managing director in the other companies fail to address the invitation to a meeting of the general assembly at the legally scheduled date, the Registrar shall address them directly to the members – in the case of the joint-stock companies – by announcing that in the bulletin, two daily papers, and the Baghdad Stock Exchange Market and fixing the place and date of the meeting.

Third: It shall be unlawful to manipulate notice of a meeting or dissemination of information concerning it in order to bias the outcome of its decisions.

Article 89: Every invitation to a meeting of the general assembly must include the agenda of the meeting. It is impermissible to overlook the agenda during the meeting unless it is proposed by the representatives of at least 10 percent of the company's capital and approved by the majority of the voices represented in the meeting and the unanimity of all the members in the joint liability company. The provisions stipulated in Paragraph Second of Article 92 of this law are excepted.

Article 90: The meetings may be held at the company's head office or any other place in Iraq if necessary, provided inconvenience to the owners is minimized.

Article 91: First: The member may, under a certified power of attorney, appoint a proxy to attend, speak, and vote on his behalf in the meetings of the general assembly. He can also appoint another member for this purpose.

Second: The Registrar shall issue guidelines specifying the form to be used for the power of attorney, its contents, and the method of its preparation.

Third: In the case of the joint-stock company:

1. Suspended.
2. The representational power of attorney must be deposited at the company's administrative office at least three days before the meeting. The company's administrative office shall check them to make sure that they are correct. The power of attorney will remain valid for any other meeting to which the first is adjourned.

Article 92: First: The meeting of the general assembly shall be held with the attendance of the members owning the majority of subscribed shares whose installments have been paid, in the case of the joint-stock company; the majority of paid-up shares in the limited liability company; and the majority of quotas in the joint liability company. If a quorum is not reached, the meeting shall be postponed to the same day on the following week and in the same place. A quorum is considered attained in the second meeting if 25% of the number of such shares or quotas is represented. The company may apply to the Registrar for waiver of the 25% minimum if, in view of the agenda and other circumstances, the minimum requirement would disserve the interests of the owners generally. The company's contract may require more stringent conditions for a quorum.

Second: If the agenda calls for amending the company's contract, increasing or decreasing its capital, dismissing the chairman or a member of its board of directors; or deciding on its merger, transformation, sale of more than half its assets in a transaction outside its ordinary business, a transaction under paragraph Fourth of Article 56, or liquidation, the quorum required for the first meeting must be attained.

Article 93: In the case of the joint-stock company, the meeting of the general assembly must be attended by the representative of the Registrar. It must also be attended by most members of the board. If representatives of the Registrar or board members fail to attend after being notified, the meeting can be held in their absence within half an hour after the scheduled time of the meeting. The representative of the Registrar will withdraw after confirming that a quorum is present unless his or her continued presence is requested by a shareholder.

Article 94: First: Prior to the beginning of the meeting, the name of the participant in the meeting shall be recorded along with the number of the shares he or she owns or represents, provided he or she produces the certificate of the shares or the power of attorney if he or she represents a shareholder in the company. Share certificates submitted to a depository for book-entry transfer need not be presented, provided adequate evidence of ownership is furnished under the rules of the depository approved by the competent sectoral quarter for the securities market. The participant shall put his or her signature against the name of the shareholder he or she represents.

Second: A member of the board of directors shall be entrusted with recording the names of the participants in the meeting. The board shall be responsible for what is recorded in the minutes.

Third: The participant shall be given a card to enable him to join the meeting. The card shall state number of votes he is allowed to cast.

Article 95: First: The meeting shall be headed by the chairman of the board of directors or the chairman of the Founding Committee in the case of the joint-stock companies – and the managing director in the other companies – until the president of the general assembly is elected.

Second: The chairman of the meeting shall choose from among the participants a reporter to record the minutes and a controller to establish the quorum and collect the votes.

Third: The quorum must be established within 30 minutes from the start of the meeting. If the chairman of the meeting finds that the quorum has been attained, he shall declare the meeting open and call for electing the president of the general assembly.

Fourth: The elected president shall assume his responsibilities immediately after being elected. He will immediately call for a discussion of items in the order in which they are listed in the agenda.

Article 96: First: The meeting's discussions, proposals, and decisions, including the conflicting opinions shall be recorded in the special minutes book. The minutes shall be signed by the president of the general assembly, the reporter, the controller, and the representative of the Registrar if present. It shall be stamped with the company's stamp and a copy shall be sent to the Registrar.

Second: The general assembly's decisions shall be recorded in a special record book, stamped with the company's seal, and signed by the president of the general assembly.

Third: Any member of the general assembly has the right to contest the soundness of the meeting's procedures-from the date of the issuance of the invitations to the meeting to the date of the issuance of the decisions before the Registrar within three days after the end of the meeting. The Registrar must consider the context within seven days from the date of its submission. He has the power to cancel those procedures, if they conflict with the law, and compel the company to repeat the procedures. His decision in this respect is final.

Article 97: First: In the joint-stock company and the limited liability company, every shareholder shall have a number of votes equal to the number of shares he owns.

Second: In the joint liability company, the votes are calculated on the basis of each partner's quota in the capital.

Article 98: First: The voting shall be open except on matters relating to the election or dismissal of the chairman or a member of board of directors, in the case of the joint-stock company, and the dismissal of the managing director in the case of other companies; or when requested by several members who own not less than 10 percent of the shares or quotas and are represented in the meeting, regardless of the subject to be voted on. In such a case the voting will be secret.

Second: Unless the company's contract requires a higher proportion, decisions on amending the contract of the company, increasing or decreasing its capital, selling more than half its assets in a transaction outside its ordinary business, approving a transaction under paragraph Fourth of Article 56, merging the company, transforming it, or liquidating it must be based on: The majority of the votes of the subscribed shares whose due installments have been paid, in the case of the joint-stock company; the majority of the votes of the paid-up shares at the time of calling the meeting, in the case of the limited liability company; and the unanimous vote of the quotas, in the case of the joint liability company. In the case of a tie vote in the limited liability company, and the impossibility of obtaining a unanimous vote in the joint liability company, it is permissible to resort to the competent court to settle the matter. Decisions on other matters, shall be made on the basis of the majority of the votes of shares or quotas represented in the meeting, unless the company's contract requires a higher proportion.

Article 99: The general assembly's decisions shall be sent to the Registrar within four days from their adoption. The certified copy issued by the Registrar shall be an acceptable document to any quarter.

Article 100: Holders of five percent of the shares of the company can object to the general assembly's decisions before the Registrar within seven days from their adoption. The Registrar shall issue his decision 15 days from the submission of the objection. His decision can be contested before the competent district court within seven days from the date of notification. The court must examine such objections urgently, and its decision on them shall be final.

Article 101: In the sole owner enterprise, or a limited liability company having one owner, the owner replaces the general assembly and the provisions stipulated in this law, other than those pertaining to meetings, apply to him, her or it.

Sub-Section Two: The Jurisdictions and Powers of the General Assembly

Article 102: The general assembly is the highest authority in the company. It decides on all matters that serve its interest; and, it is empowered to do the following:

First: Discuss and approve the founders' report on procedures pertaining to the establishment of the company at the constituent meeting.

Second: Decide on the election of the representatives of shareholders from outside the state sector –in the board of directors of the mixed company, and the representatives of all shareholders in the board of directors of the private joint stock company, as well as on their dismissal.

Third: Discuss the reports of the board of directors of the joint-stock company, the managing director of the other companies, and the accounts controller, as well as any other reports reaching it from competent quarters and make the necessary decisions on them.

Fourth: Discuss the company's final accounts and approve them.

Fifth: Discuss and approve the proposed annual plan and the budget for the following year in other than joint-stock companies.

Sixth: Appoint the accounts controller and specify his remuneration in the case of private companies.

Seventh: Discuss proposals pertaining to loans, mortgage, and securities and make decisions on them in the case of the limited liability company and joint liability company.

Eighth: Approve the percentage of profit to be distributed among the members and specify the percentage of compulsory reserve and any other reserves it deems appropriate.

Ninth: Fix the remuneration of the chairman and members of the board of directors in the mixed and private joint-stock companies commensurate with their efforts in fulfilling their tasks and achieving company plans and profits.

Tenth: Approve employment rules in the mixed joint-stock company as worked out by the board of directors.

Section Two: The Board of Directors in the Joint-Stock Company

Sub-Section One: Formation of the Board of Directors

Article 103: First: The board of directors in the mixed joint- stock company shall consist of seven original members who are chosen as follows:

1. Two members representing the state sector who are appointed under a decision by the competent minister or his deputy in the sector to which the company belongs, unless at the time of the selection, the state sector's share in the mixed company's capital exceeds 50%. In such a case, the competent minister or his deputy in the sector to which the company belongs shall appoint three members representing the state sector.
2. Five members representing shareholders from outside the state sector elected by the company's general assembly, unless at the time of the selection, the state sector's share in the mixed company's capital exceeds 50%. In such a case, the company's general assembly shall elect four members representing shareholders from outside the state sector.
3. Suspended.

Second: The board of directors in the mixed joint-stock company shall have seven reserve members, who will be selected in the manner and ratio used in the case of the original members.

Article 104: First: The board of directors in the private joint-stock company shall consist of not less than five and not more than nine original members to be elected by the company's general assembly.

Second: The board of directors in the private joint-stock company shall have reserve members, who will be chosen in the manner and ratios used in the case of the original members.

Article 105: Suspended.

Article 106: First: The member of the board of directors must:

1. Enjoy legal qualification.
2. Not be banned from managing companies under the law or any decision issued by a legal quarter.
3. Be owner of not less than 1,000 shares, if he represents the private sector. If his shares drop below this level, he must make up the difference within 30 days from the date of becoming member of the board of directors. Otherwise, he will be deemed as having lost the board membership at the end of the above respite.

Second: If a member of the board of directors loses any of the conditions stipulated in Paragraph First of this article, he shall lose his membership in the board as of the date of losing that condition. Any decision made during his attendance shall be considered null and void, if his vote has influenced the decision.

Third: The period of membership in the board of directors is three years from the date of the first board meeting. This period is renewable.

Article 107: First: If the elected shareholder declines to accept membership in the board of directors, he should inform the board within seven days from his election to the board, if he was present during the election meeting; and, from the date of being notified, if he was absent.

Second: If a member of the board of directors resigns, his resignation must be in writing. The resignation will be considered valid only from the date of its acceptance by the board.

Article 108: First: If a vacancy occurs in the membership representing the state sector in the board of directors, the council shall invite a reserve member – in the order of the reserve list in the sector – to fill the vacancy and attend the board meeting.

Second: If a vacancy occurs in the membership representing the private sector in the board of directors, the chairman shall invite the reserve member with the majority of votes to attend. And, if several reserve members have an equal number of shares, the chairman shall choose one of them.

Third: If several vacancies occur in the membership representing the private sector in the board of directors and the reserve members are not enough to fill all the vacancies, the chairman of the board shall call a meeting of the general assembly in order to elect original members to fill any vacancies in the board of directors, after including the reserve members; and, to also elect reserve members in their place within 60 days from the occurrence of the vacancies.

Fourth: If the board of directors in a private joint-stock company loses half of its members at once, it shall be considered as dissolved. In such a case, a meeting of the general assembly shall be convened within 30 days from this loss to elect a new board.

Article 109: If a member of the board of directors fails to attend meetings, the steps outlined in Paragraphs First and Second in Article 108 of this law shall be applied, depending on the circumstances. A reserve member shall replace the original member during his absence.

Article 110: First: A person cannot be a member in the boards of directors of more than six companies at the same time. But, he can also assume the chairmanship of one or two other boards at the same time.

Second: The chairman or member of a board of directors of a company cannot become a chairman or member in the board of directors of another company that engages in similar business, unless he has been authorized by the general assembly of his company.

Sub-Section Two: The Meeting of the Board of Directors

Article 111: The board of directors shall meet within seven days of its formation. It shall elect from among its members by secret ballot its chairman and his deputy, who will replace him in his absence, for a one-year term, which is renewable.

Article 112: First: The board of directors shall meet at least once every two months at the invitation of its chairman or at the request of any of its other members.

Second: The board meetings shall be held at the company's head office or any other place in Iraq that is chosen by the chairman, if it is not possible to hold the meeting at the head office.

Article 113: The quorum shall be counted 30 minutes after the board has convened. It shall meet with the attendance of the majority of its members.

Article 114: First: Board decisions shall be made on the basis of the absolute majority of the members present. In the case of a tie, the side supported by the board chairman shall prevail.

Second: Suspended.

Article 115: If the chairman of the board or his deputy fails to attend three consecutive meetings without a legitimate reason, or if he fails to attend successive meetings for a period of more than six months without a legitimate reason, he shall be considered as having resigned.

Article 116: First: The minutes of the board meeting shall sum up the subjects discussed, the proposals made, and the opposite opinions expressed. The minutes shall be signed by the members.

Second: The board's decisions shall be entered in the records book and signed by the chairman.

Third: Certified copies of the board's decisions from the records book are valid documents to present to any quarter, provided the Registrar keeps his copies of these decisions.

Sub-Section Three: The Jurisdictions and Powers of the Board of Directors

Article 117: The board of directors shall handle the necessary administrative, financial, planning, organizational, and technical duties for running the company's business, other than those that fall within the jurisdiction of the general assembly. It shall, in particular, assume the following jurisdictions:

First: Appoint the managing director, specify his wages, remunerations, jurisdictions, and powers, supervise and guide his work, and also decide on his dismissal.

Second: Carry out the general assembly's decisions and follow up on their implementation.

Third: Prepare the final accounts of the previous year within the first six months of each year, write up a report on them and on the results of implementing the annual plan, and submit them all to the general assembly for discussion and approval. These shall include:

1. The general budget.
2. The profit and loss account.
3. Any other statements requested by the competent quarters.

Fourth: Discuss and approve an annual plan for the company's activity in the following year. This plan must be prepared by the managing director during the last six months of the year in light of the company's aim. The plan shall include a full report on the company's activity and a draft budget outlining:

1. Cash reserves.
2. Sales.
3. Purchases.
4. Manpower.
5. Capital investments.
6. Production.

Fifth: Follow up on the implementation of the annual plan and submit periodic reports to the accounts controller and an annual report to the general assembly on the results of the implementation.

Sixth: Prepare statistical studies with the view to developing the company's business.

Seventh: Make the decisions on loans, mortgages, and securities.

Eighth: The board of directors shall establish committees of its members to make recommendations as to (a) selection of the company's external, independent auditors (audit committee); and (b) compensation form and amount for the board and the managing director (compensation committee). Members of these committees shall not be officers or employees of the company nor holders of 10% or more of the company's shares, nor related to any of these by blood, marriage or personal or economic interest in a degree likely to materially bias their judgment. Any departure from the recommendation of such a committee, and the reasons for it, shall be announced at the shareholders meeting and recorded in its minutes. The audit committee shall meet privately with the company's external auditors and have special responsibility for ensuring the accuracy and reliability of their work. It shall ensure that a record is kept in the course of the year of all material related-party transactions, within the meaning of international accounting standards, for discussion with the company's external auditors.

Article 118: First: Any decision made by the board of directors must be signed by its chairman and stamped with the company's seal.

Second: The decisions of the board of directors must be carried out as soon as they are issued in accordance with the provisions of the law.

Third: The majority members of the board of directors in a mixed joint-stock company have the right to object to the cabinet against any measures or guidelines that are not consistent or harmonious with the provisions of the law.

Fourth: The chairman of the board of directors is responsible for following up on the implementation of the board's decisions.

Article 119: First. It is impermissible for the chairman or a member of the board to have direct or indirect interests in deals that are concluded with the company, except after obtaining the permission of the general assembly with full disclosure of the nature and extent of such interests. The chairman or board member shall be liable to the company for any damage to it arising from violation of this article. Compliance with this Article shall not exclude liability under Article 4, paragraph Third.

Second: It is impermissible for the chairman or a member of the board to vote upon or participate in a matter in which he or she has direct or indirect interests without disclosing the nature and extent thereof to disinterested members and receiving the permission of a majority of them. If no members are disinterested, all may act. In either case, however, the details of the matter shall be recorded in the minutes of the board and made available to the general assembly and the company's external auditors.

Article 120: The chairman and members of the board of directors shall do their best to serve the interests of the company as they would serve their own personal interests, and run the company in a sound and legal manner. They are responsible before the general assembly for any work they undertake in this capacity.

Section Three: The Managing Director

Sub-Section One: The Appointment and Dismissal of the Managing Director

Article 121: First: Each company shall have a managing director, who can be from within the company or an outsider who is specialized and experienced in the company's activity. The managing director shall be appointed and his jurisdictions, powers, wage, and remunerations shall be fixed by the board of directors in the joint- stock company, and the general assembly in the other companies.

Second: It is impermissible to combine the post of chairman or deputy chairman of the board of directors of a joint-stock company with the post of managing director in it. It is also impermissible for a person to serve as managing director in more than one joint-stock company.

Article 122: The managing director is dismissed under a decision by the quarter that appointed him, while citing the reasons for the dismissal.

Article 123: First: The managing director shall undertake all the necessary tasks for the management of the company and its activity within the jurisdictions and powers assigned to him by the quarter that appointed him and according to its directives.

Second: Taking into consideration the provisions of Paragraph First in this article, the managing director in the limited liability company, the joint liability company, or the sole owner enterprise shall enjoy the jurisdictions of the board of directors in the joint-stock company, as stipulated in Paragraphs Second, Third, Fourth, Fifth, and Sixth of Article 117 of this law.

Article 124: In the exercise of his jurisdictions and powers, the managing director is subject to the provisions of Articles 119 and 120 of this Law. In addition, the compensation of the five most highly compensated employees of the company, in whatever form received, shall be disclosed in writing to the general assembly.

Chapter V: Control of Companies

Section One: The Aim of Control and its Requirements

Article 125: Control is aimed at guaranteeing that the company is applying the provisions of its contract and the law.

Article 126: The board of directors in the joint-stock company, and the managing director in the other companies, shall prepare in the first month of each year a list containing the following data:

First: The name of the company; the address of its head office; and the addresses of its branches, if they exit.

Second: The amount of capital and the quotas and shares making up this capital.

Third: The installments which were paid from the value of the shares in the joint stock company; the shares which were paid during the year; and the shares which were not paid, but are due for payment.

Fourth: The total number of shares whose owners have no right to hold.

Fifth: The names, nationalities, professions, and shares or quotas held by the following:

1. The members of the company and the members who have gained membership or whose membership has expired since the preparation of the last annual list, or since the registration of the company, when preparing the first annual list.
2. The chairman and members of the board of directors and the managing director in the joint-stock company, and the managing director in the other companies.

Article 127: First: A copy of the invitation to the general assembly meeting held to discuss the final accounts shall be sent to the Registrar. The following shall be attached to the invitation:

1. The annual list;
2. The final accounts for the previous year and the accounts controller's report on them; and
3. The managing director's report on the company's progress in implementing its plan for the previous year.

Second: In the case of the joint-stock company, the invitation shall be sent to the Registrar, along with the statements and reports mentioned in sub-paragraphs 1 and 2 of paragraph First in this Article as well as the board of directors' report on the company's progress in implementing its plan for the previous year. As for members, they have the right to obtain copies of the annual report and the other statements and reports.

Article 128: The Registrar has the right to obtain any statements, clarifications or documents from the company in order to implement its duties under the law.

Article 129: The joint-stock company, the limited liability company, and the joint liability company shall each prepare a register for its members, which shall be kept in its head office. The register shall contain the following information:

First: The names, nationalities, professions, and addresses of the members, the number of quotes or shares they own, and the dates of their ownership.

Second:The shares owned by each member, the sum paid for each share in the joint-stock company or limited liability company.

Third: The expiration of membership and the reasons.

Article 130: If a person's name has been erroneously entered in or deleted from the members' register, or if there has been an undue failure or delay in entering those who qualify for membership or deleting those whose membership has expired, that person or member has the right to demand the rectification of the records. And, if the company declines, he has the right to ask the Registrar to oblige the company to make the rectification, without also prejudicing his right to demand compensation from the company for any damages.

Article 131: All that is included in the members' register is considered correct unless proved otherwise.

Article 132: First: A company member has the right of access to the members' register. If he is prevented from doing so, he has the right to ask the Registrar to oblige the company to permit him to have such access.

Second: In the joint-stock company, the limited liability company, and joint liability company, records must be made accessible to members for 10 days prior to the meeting of the general assembly and also while the assembly in session.

Section Two: Financial Control

Article 133: First: The accounts of the mixed company shall be subject to control and audit by the Financial Control Bureau. As for the accounts of the private company, they shall be subject to control and audit by auditors appointed by the company's general assembly. Accounts should be consolidated with those of related companies in accordance with international accounting standards unless specifically modified by standards in force in Iraq.

Second: The accounts controller shall submit a report to the company on the accounts within 30 days from the accomplishment of these accounts.

Article 134: The board of directors' report on the final accounts in the case of the joint-stock company, and managing director's report in the case of the other companies shall include detailed statements on the company's activities, especially on the following:

First: The significant contracts concluded by the company during the previous year and the businesses in which owners of 10% or more of the company's shares, the members of the board or the managing director had interests, including interests of their families, entities under their control and any other interest that would render the transaction a related party transaction under international accounting standards insofar as permissible to apply these in Iraq.

Second: The results of operations (including earnings) and distribution of net profit.

Third: The reserve balance and its uses.

Fourth: The sums received by current and previous members of the board of directors and the managing director in the form of wages or awards in cash or in kind, which they enjoy.

Fifth: The sums which have been spent on publicity, travel, entertainment, and donations.

Article 135: The general assembly shall hold a meeting to discuss and approve the final accounts within 60 days from the date the audit is complete.

Article 136: The accounts controller shall give his opinion on the final accounts of the joint-stock company before its general assembly. The same can be done in the other companies. In all cases, the controller must give his opinion on the following:

First: The soundness of the company's accounts, the correctness of the statements in the final accounts, the access allowed to the data on the company's activity, and the board of directors' report.

Second: The extent of the company's application of modern accounting procedures, especially those dealing with book-keeping, accountancy, and stocktaking of company assets and liabilities.

Third: The extent to which the final accounts express the true financial status of the company and the results of its business at the end of the year.

Fourth: The extent to which the accounts comply with the provisions of this law and the company's contract.

Fifth: Violations of the provisions of this law or the company's contract which have adversely affected the company's business and financial status, including a statement indicating if the violations still existed at the time of auditing the final accounts.

Article 137: The accounts controller shall be questioned about the truth of the statements contained in his report in his capacity as the company's agent for controlling and auditing its accounts.

Article 138: The final accounts shall be signed by the chairman of the board of directors and the managing director in the case of the joint-stock companies and by the managing director in the case of the other companies. Each signatory shall be responsible for the truth of the statements contained in these accounts.

Article 139: Copies of the final accounts, the annual plan, and the reports on them as well as the general assembly's decisions on them shall be sent to the Registrar.

Section Three: Inspection

Article 140: The company shall be subject to inspection by one or several professional inspectors, who will be chosen by the Registrar, in the case of a justifiable claim made by any of the following quarters that the company has violated the provisions of this law, its contract, or the decisions of its general assembly:

First: Suspended.

Second: Members of the company who hold at least 10 percent of the value of subscribed quotas or shares.

Third: A member of the board of directors in the joint-stock company and the managing director in the other companies.

Article 141: The Registrar has the right to appoint an inspector when necessary without asking the permission of any quarter. If the company believes that the Registrar has exercised its powers under this section for improper purposes, it may apply to the competent court to prove this and obtain an order restraining any improper action.

Article 142: First: The Registrar shall specify the inspector's task and scope of work in detail and the kind of report to be prepared on the subject.

Second: The appointed inspector shall submit his or her report on the inspection to the Registrar, who shall send copies of the report to the company and the person making the claim referred to in Article 140.

Article 143: The company's general assembly can appoint its own inspector to inspect the company's work. It shall also specify his task, the scope of his work, and the type of report he must submit, provided a copy of the report is sent to the Registrar.

Article 144: Company employees must allow the inspector to have access to all of their books, documents, and records. The inspector may also interview the employees and those connected with the company on the case which is being investigated.

Article 145: If the inspector's report shows that a member of the board of directors, the managing director, or any other company official is questionable on something, now or in the past, the Registrar must inform the responsible authorities so that appropriate action can be taken.

Article 146: The Registrar shall carry out the appropriate steps to steer and guide the company in light of the proposals contained in the inspector's report.

Chapter VI: Termination of the Company

Section One: Reasons for Termination

Article 147: A company is terminated in accordance with the provisions of this law for the following reasons:

First: Failure to start its activity without any legitimate reason despite the lapse of one year since its establishment.

Second: Suspension of its activity for more than one year without any legitimate reason.

Third: Completion of the project for which it was established or the impossibility of completing it.

Fourth: Merger with another company or transformation into another type of company under the provisions of this law.

Fifth: Loss of 75 percent of its nominal capital and its failure to take the steps stipulated in sub-paragraph 1 of Paragraph Second of Article 76 of this law within 60 days from the time the loss is established in the budget.

Sixth: The general assembly's decision to liquidate it.

Section Two: Merger of Companies

Article 148: It is permissible to merge one company into another company or several companies in order to form one company.

Article 149: For the merger to be valid:

First: Suspended.

Second: It should not lead to:

1. The joint-stock company losing its corporate status in favor of a limited liability company or joint liability company.
2. The limited liability company losing its corporate status to a joint liability company.
3. The joint-stock company, the limited liability company, the joint liability company, or the sole owner enterprise losing its corporate status in favor of a simple company.

Third: It should not increase the members of the merged company above the limits set under the law for different types of companies.

Fourth: Suspended.

Article 150: For the purposes of the merger, the following measures shall be taken:

First: An economic and technical study shall be made of the joint-stock companies to be merged, including the aims, reasons, conditions of the merger, and any other studies. The studies shall be submitted to the general assembly of each company.

Second: The merge decision shall be made by the general assembly of each company separately. The decision shall specify the name and type of the merger company as well as its capital, members, and activity. The decisions and the studies shall be sent to the Registrar within 10 days from their adoption.

Third: If, within 15 days of receiving them, the Registrar has not found that the decisions are inconsistent with the law, it will promptly issue its permission and inform the companies concerned of this decision; the companies will then cause it to be published in the Bulletin and one daily paper.

Fourth: Suspended.

Fifth: Suspended.

Sixth: The companies receiving the Registrar's permission for their merger will call their general assemblies to a joint meeting within 60 days from the date of the publication of the merger decision in order to amend the contracts of the existing companies or draw up a new contract for the merger company, depending on the circumstances. The contract shall be sent to the Registrar within 10 days for endorsement and publication in the bulletin and one daily paper.

Article 151: The merger shall be considered effective as of the last publication date of the amended or new contract, depending on the circumstances. On this date, the corporate status of the companies merging into the new company shall be terminated. The Registrar's endorsement of the contract is tantamount to a license of establishment.

Article 152: All the rights and commitments of the merger shall be transferred to the company with which it was merged, or the company resulting from the merger.

Section Three: Transformation of a Company

Article 153: A company can be transformed to any of the types stipulated in this law, with the following exceptions:

First: It is impermissible to transform a joint-stock company into a limited liability company, a joint liability company, or sole owner enterprise; or the limited liability company into a joint liability company.

Second: It is impermissible to transform the limited liability company or the joint liability company into a sole owner enterprise, except when they are short of one member.

Third: It is impermissible to transform the joint-stock company, the limited liability company, the joint liability company, or the sole owner enterprise into a simple company.

Article 154: First: The company shall prepare an economic and technical study containing the aims and reasons for the transformation and submit them to the general assembly.

Second: The transformation shall take place under a decision to be issued by the company's general assembly which will also amend the contract consistent with the new status. The decision, coupled with the study and the amended contract, shall be sent to the Registrar within 10 days of its issuance.

Third: The transformation to a joint stock company can take place by including new members, issuing new shares for public subscription, and applying the original subscription provisions to the new shares, including the provisions of Articles 44 and 47 of this law.

Article 155: First: If, within 15 days of receiving them, the Registrar does not find that the transformation decision and the amended contract are inconsistent with the law, it shall promptly endorse the transformation decision and the amended contract. It shall also notify the company of the permission; the company shall publish the permission in the Bulletin and a daily paper.

Second: Suspended.

Third: Suspended.

Article 156: The transformation shall be considered valid as of the last date of publication of the transformation decision and the amended contract.

Article 157: In the case of the transformation of a joint liability company or a sole owner enterprise into a joint stock company or a limited liability company, the responsibility of the members for its obligations before the transformation shall be an unlimited personal responsibility. The obligations shall be a joint liability responsibility in the case of the members of the joint liability company.

Article 158: First:

1. If the general assembly decides to liquidate the company, or if any of the reasons stipulated in paragraphs First, Second, Third, and Fifth of Article 147 of this Law materialize and the general assembly recommends liquidation of the company, the company must appoint one liquidator – or more – and specify his jurisdictions and remuneration and send the decision or recommendation to the Registrar.
2. The liquidator shall be considered the representative of the company within the limits of his jurisdictions during the liquidation period.

Second: Suspended.

Article 159: The liquidation decision or recommendation shall be backed by reasons and sent to the Registrar within 14 days of its adoption. The latter has the right to request additional information or discuss matters with the company's general assembly to ascertain the reasons.

Article 160: If the Registrar has verified that the reasons for the liquidation are not fraudulent or unlawful, it shall issue the company's liquidation decision and appoint a liquidator within 10 days of the verification. The Registrar shall communicate this information to the company; the company shall then cause the information to be published in the Bulletin and one daily newspaper.

Article 161: Suspended.

Article 162: Suspended.

Article 163: Once notified of the liquidation decision, the company must stop making any changes in its membership or assuming any new obligations. But, it will continue to operate in so far as fulfilling its obligations under the liquidation process.

Article 164: First: The company shall retain its corporate status during the liquidation period, provided it states that it is under liquidation whenever its name is mentioned.

Second: The company's general assembly shall continue to function throughout the liquidation period, its board of directors, if it still exists, shall be considered dissolved, and the managing director's duty shall stop from the date of receiving the liquidation decision.

Article 165: The liquidation does not acquit the company founders, members, or management staff of any responsibility resulting from the exercise of their functions in the company.

Article 166: Any interested party has the right to confirm before a competent court any financial obligation that the company has taken upon itself within the last six months prior to the issuance of the liquidation decision.

Article 167: If the company's general assembly does not appoint a liquidator within 30 days from its notification of the liquidation decision, or if the liquidation decision has been issued by the Registrar in accordance with Paragraph Second of Article 158 of this law, the Registrar has the right to appoint the liquidator and specify his jurisdictions and remunerations, which must be borne by the company.

Article 168: As soon as he is appointed, the liquidator shall seize all the company's assets, including records, documents, and papers, make an inventory, and write a full report on the company's condition including its debts and rights as well as other parties' rights on it, and send a copy to the Registrar.

Article 169: Suspended.

Article 170: The liquidator shall, within 10 days of his appointment, call the company's creditors and whoever has claims on it through an advertisement in two local papers to meet with him at a fixed date and place in order to settle the debts and claims on the company, without impinging on the right of any party to take legal proceedings.

Article 171: The liquidator shall submit a report to the Registrar on the progress of the liquidation process every three months at least. The Registrar may call the liquidator for deliberations on any legal matter relating to the liquidation process.

Article 172: If the quarter which appointed the liquidator finds that he is failing in his assignment, it has the right to dismiss him and appoint another one. It also has the right to appoint another liquidator or more at any stage of the liquidation process, if it thinks that the liquidation process demands that, provided the dismissal or appointment decision is published in the bulletin and one daily newspaper.

Article 173: The liquidator shall call the company's general assembly to meet during the first two months of each fiscal year in order to discuss and approve the previous year's annual budget and accounts, the accounts controller's report, the annual report on the progress of work, and the appointment of an accounts controller for the new year. He may also call the assembly at any time, if the liquidation process demands that.

Article 174: The liquidator shall settle the company's debts in the following order, after deducting the liquidation expenses:

First: The sums that are due to the company employees.

Second: The sum that is due to the state.

Third: Any other sums that are due under existing laws, in the order of priority.

Article 175: First: Submission of the request for liquidation, and the liquidation decision itself, are considered a declaration of the debtor's insolvency with regard to safeguarding the rights of creditors.

Second: Any transfer, concession, or disposal of the funds of the company, which is under liquidation, shall be considered null and void, if it is an attempt to favor some creditors at the expense of others by way of fraud.

Third: All mortgage contracts or contracts which constitute a lien on the company's property and assets that have been concluded only three months prior to the beginning of the liquidation process, shall be considered null and void, unless it is proven that the company will again be solvent after the liquidation process. In such a case, the provision on the nullity of those contracts shall only apply to anything extra to the sums paid to the company for the said contracts during its establishment or afterward, and the legal interest on them.

Fourth: Any sequestration of company funds after the initiation of the liquidation process shall not be valid except under a decision by the competent court, except for sequestrations that are carried in the interest of the state, the state sector, or employees in order to pay their wages.

Article 176: As soon as the liquidation process is accomplished, the liquidator shall prepare the final report and final accounts backed by the report of the accounts controller. He shall then call a meeting of the general assembly to discuss and approve them. He shall send a copy of the meeting's minutes and decisions, coupled with the final report, the final accounts, and the accounts controller's report to the Registrar.

Article 177: First: The Registrar shall issue his decision to delete the company's name from his records and publish the decision in the bulletin and one daily newspaper within 10 days, under one of these two conditions:

1. If it has been established that the liquidation has been completed in accordance with the law.
2. If the liquidation process has continued for more than five years after the issuance of the liquidation decision and that the Registrar has become certain that it will be impossible to finalize it.

Second: The company's corporate status shall be considered expired as of the issuance of the decision to delete its name.

Article 178: First. The liquidator shall distribute the rest of the company's funds among its members in accordance with their shares and quotas within 30 days from being notified of the decision on the deletion of the company's name. But, he may disburse some of these to the members even during the liquidation phase, provided that this will not affect the company's obligations.

Second. Distributions to foreign investors in the company shall conform to CPA Order Number 39, section 12(2).

Article 179: It is impermissible to claim a debt or right on the company after the issuance of the decision on the deletion of its name. If a creditor shows up with a claim and the liquidator has no knowledge of it, the creditor may ask the company members to honor it according to the ratio of their quotas and shares in the capital within three years from the date of the deletion. Any claim after this period shall not be considered.

Article 180: The liquidator shall keep the company's records for five years from the date of the deletion of its name.

Chapter VII: The Simple Company

Article: 181: The simple company shall consist of several partners, who are not less than two and not more than five and who have contributed shares to the capital. In such a company, one or more may contribute services, and others funds.

Article 182: The simple company's contract must be notarized by the public notary. A copy of the contract must be deposited with the Registrar, otherwise the contract will be considered null and void.

Article 183: The simple company shall acquire a corporate status as of the date of the deposition of a copy of its contract with the Registrar.

Article 184: The contract shall specify the share of each partner in the simple company's capital. Otherwise, the shares shall be considered equal. If the share is service, then its nature must be stated in the contract.

Article 185: First: If the contract specifies the partners' share in the profit only, then this shall be considered as their share in the loss also. And, if it specifies it in the loss only, this shall be considered as their share in the profit also. But, if the contract does not specify the share in the profit or loss, the share of each partner shall be in the ratio of his subscribed share in the company's capital.

Second: If the contract does not specify the share of the partner who contributes with service, his share in the profit or loss shall be assessed on the basis of the company's profit in that service. If, in addition the service, he contributed funds, he will have a share of profit for the service and a share for the funds.

Article 186: First: If it is agreed that one of the partners will not have a share in the profit or loss, the company's contract shall be considered null and void.

Second: It is possible to agree on excluding the partner, who has contributed with service only, from the loss, provided it has not been agreed to pay him a wage for his service.

Article 187: The company's contract shall specify the method of management and the appointment of the managing partner. It shall also specify his powers, otherwise the contract shall be considered null and void.

Article 188: The managing partner shall assume the management of the company within these powers under the guidance of the quarter that appointed him.

Article 189: The managing partner will do his best to take care of the company's interests the way he takes care of his own interests.

Article 190: The simple company can be terminated for any of the reasons stipulated in Paragraphs First, Second, Third, or Fourth of Article 147 of this law. It can also be terminated for any of the following reasons:

First: A unanimous decision by the partners to dissolve it.

Second: The withdrawal of either partner from a company consisting of two partners.

Third: The issuance of a final decision by a competent court.

Article 191: The partners may ask for a court decision to exclude a partner, whose behavior could be a cause for dissolving the company, provided the company can continue to exist with the remaining partners.

Article 192: If a partner withdraws, he has the right to transfer his share of the capital to another person with the approval of the remaining partners. If they do not approve, they must accept the value of the withdrawing partner's share as decided by the court.

Article 193: In the case of the death, insolvency, or interdiction of a partner, the provisions stipulated in Article 70 of this law shall be applied, depending on the circumstances.

Article 194: The simple company shall be liquidated in accordance with the provisions of its contract. If there are no such provisions, it shall be liquidated in the manner agreed upon unanimously by the partners. Otherwise, it shall be liquidated in accordance with a decision by the court.

Article 195: The powers of the managing partner are terminated with the dissolution of the company. However, the corporate status of the company shall remain as long as necessary and until the liquidation is accomplished.

Article 196: First: When necessary, the liquidation will be carried out by all the partners or by one or more liquidators appointed by the majority of the partners. If they cannot agree on appointing a liquidator, the court shall undertake his appointment.

Second: In the cases where the company is considered null and avoid, the court shall automatically, or at the request of the interested party, appoint a liquidator and specify the method of liquidation.

Third: The managing partner shall be considered the liquidator before others until a liquidator is appointed.

Article 197: First: The liquidator has no right to initiate any new work in the company except what is essential to complete previous work.

Second: The liquidator may sell the company's movable and immovable property directly or through an auction, unless he is restricted by his appointment order. He has no right to sell the company's property except to the extent that it is necessary to honor its debts, with the approval of the partners.

Article 198: First: After paying the creditors and deducting the sums needed to honor other undisputed debts or cover expenses and loans, which any partner may have undertaken in the name of the company, the remaining funds shall be divided among the partners.

Second: Each partner shall get a share equivalent to the value of the quota he contributed to the capital as stated in the contract, or equivalent to the value of this quota at the time of its payment if it is not stated in the contract, unless the partner has contributed services only. The remainder shall be divided among the partners according to each one's share in the profit. If the company's net funds are not sufficient to cover the shares of the partners, the loss shall be divided among them.

Article 199: The division of the simple company's funds shall be in accordance with the procedures that are followed in dividing common property.

Chapter VIII: Miscellaneous Rules

Section One: General Rules

Article 200: The company's registered address shall be deemed the official address for correspondence and notification. The company must notify the Registrar about any change in the address within seven days of the change.

Article 201: The company must state its full name and capital, with all its descriptions, in the head office, the branches if there are any, and the other businesses. These must also be printed on the letterheads, certificates, documents, and any statements that are issued by it. All these should be in Arabic. However, it is permissible to use a foreign language as an addition.

Article 202: The company shall have a special seal with which to stamp its, businesses, correspondence, documents, certificates, and any other statements it issues. The stamp can only be used by an authorized person.

Article 203: The company's contract is not considered valid until it has been endorsed by the Registrar in accordance with Article 19, except as otherwise provided in this law.

Article 204: It is permissible to object to the decisions of the Registrar before the Minister of Trade within 30 days from the date of notification. The Minister's decision may be appealed as provided in article 24 of this law.

Article 205: If the company members are less than what is stipulated in the law for its type, the number must be completed within 60 days from the occurrence of the shortage. If this period expires and the Registrar does not grant a respite, the company must be transformed into a type that is permitted by the law.

Article 206: The Registrar shall issue a special bulletin for the companies in which he will publish, at their expense, everything that pertains to their affairs in accordance with the provisions of this law.

Article 207: The Ministry of Trade, in cooperation with the Ministry of Finance, the Financial Control Bureau, and the Planning Board, shall issue guidelines for the accounting system to be adopted by the companies and everything that pertains to their final accounts.

Article 208: First. The minister of trade shall issue guidelines to facilitating the implementation of this law.

Second. The Agency Registration Law No. 4 of 1999 shall be inapplicable to the registration of a company, and a company is not required to retain a commercial agent to register, though it may choose to do so. Furthermore, no certification of tax compliance or of the absence of tax delinquency shall be required for the registration of a company. The Minister of Trade is hereby authorized to issue instructions to coordinate the activities of the Registrar of Companies and the Chamber of Commerce regarding the registration and approval of commercial trade names, notwithstanding anything to the contrary in The Law on Establishment of Chambers of Commerce No. 43 of 1989.

Article 209: The fees for the paperwork pertaining to this law shall be charged in accordance with the chart attached to this law. The Ministry of Trade may amend the chart in accordance with changes in costs and to align the fees with processing costs.

Section Two: Temporary Rules

Article 210: Within 90 days from the enforcement of this law, the economic projects stipulated in Article 10 of this law must take the form of a company. The competent sectoral quarters shall supply the Registrar with their lists of the registered economic projects that are subject to this law in the period between the publication of the law and its enforcement.

Article 211: First: The branches and offices of foreign companies and establishments shall be subject to the provisions of CPA Order No. 39 and regulations and administrative instructions issued thereunder.

Second: The penalties stipulated in Articles 216, 217, 218, and 219 shall apply to these branches, offices, and their officials for any proven offense.

Article 212: The provisions on bankruptcy due to insolvency wherever they occur in this law shall apply until the promulgation of the law on insolvency.

Section Three: Penal Rules

Article 213: First: Any economic project that does not take the form of a company shall be punishable by a fine of 1,000 dinars for every day of delay after the grace period stipulated in Article 210 of this law.

Second: The punishment stipulated in paragraph First of this Article shall apply to every company branch or office that must be re-registered or liquidated, for every day of delay after the periods stipulated in regulations and administrative instructions issued under CPA

Order No. 39 Article 214: If three months of daily fines elapse without the parties mentioned in Article 210 of this law taking the necessary steps to change or rectify their conditions, the Registrar shall approach the competent sectoral quarter in order to take the appropriate measures against the defaulting party, while continuing to levy the daily fine on it.

Article 215: First: Anyone carrying out a business in the name of a joint-stock company, limited liability company, joint liability company, or sole owner enterprise without obtaining registration of its establishment shall be subject to a fine of not more than 3,000,000 dinars, while taking into consideration the severity of the violations and the provisions of paragraph First of Article 210 of this law.

Second: Anyone carrying out a business in the name of a branch or an office for a foreign company or economic establishment without obtaining the registration required shall be subject to the penalties provided in paragraph First of this Article unless otherwise provided in applicable legislation.

Article 216: Any company that does not prepare the records stipulated under this law shall be subject to a fine of not more than 10,000,000 dinars, depending on the severity of the violation.

Article 217: Any company failing to submit the required statements and information to a competent official quarter at the times fixed under the provisions of this law shall be subject to punishment of a fine of not more than 300,000 dinars for every day of delay, depending on the severity of the violation.

Article 218: Any company official who purposely gives inaccurate statements or information to an official quarter on the company's business, results of operations, financial condition, member shares and quotas, and distribution of dividends shall be subject to punishment of imprisonment for a period of not more than one year, or a fine of not more than 12,000,000 dinars, or both, depending on the severity of the violation.

Article 219: Any company official who bars a competent quarter from seeing the company's records and documents shall be subject to punishment of imprisonment for a period of not more than six months or a fine of not more than 12,000,000 dinars, or both, depending on the severity of the violation.

Section Four: Final Rules

Article 220: First: Company Law No. 36 of 1983 is hereby canceled. The regulations and guidelines issued under that law that do not conflict with the provisions of this law shall remain valid until they are replaced or canceled.
Second: Any provision contrary to the provisions of this law is invalid.

Article 221: This law shall be enforced within 90 days from the date of its publication in the Official Gazette.

Annex – Fee Chart

First: As provided in regulations to be issued by the Minister of Trade, the Registrar of Companies shall charge a fee of 200,000 dinars for the registration of a joint stock company, and a fee of 20,000 dinars shall be payable for all other forms of company.

Second: As provided in regulations to be issued by the Minister of Trade, the Registrar shall charge a fixed fee of 200,000 dinars for the registration of branch for a foreign company or economic establishment.

Third: The Minister or Trade shall publish regulations or schedules of such other fees as he or she may deem appropriate for other services provided by the Registrar of Companies.

Document 88
Ministerial Instruction No. 196

15 March 2004

The Registration of Companies

Section I Introduction: The Right to Register a Business Entity

1. Pursuant to Coalition Provisional Authority (CPA) Order 64, dated March 3, 2004, certain amendments have been effected to Company Law No. 21 of 1997. This Instruction implements these changes pursuant to Article 208 of that Law and, consistent with CPA Order 39,[192] provides for equal treatment of foreign and domestic investors in most respects. In no case shall the nationality of a founder disqualify a company from being established, whether its business shall be in the nature of commercial agency, distributorship, trading company or otherwise.
2. This Instruction implements the new law. Any other instruction conflicting with this Instruction shall be considered inoperative.

Section II Persons Subject to this Instruction

Persons (natural or juridical) establishing mixed or private Iraqi companies pursuant to Company Law No. 21 of 1997, as amended, or any successor law, are subject to the provisions of this Instruction.

Section III Application and Procedures for Registration

1. Persons wishing to found a company under the laws of Iraq shall complete and file with the Registrar of Companies an Application in the form attached as Annex I to this Instruction.[193] Two (2) copies of the completed form should be brought to the Registrar of Companies at the time of application (the Registrar of Companies will keep one and the other will be returned with a signed checklist to the applicant).
2. Each Application shall include the following information concerning the business entity proposed to be registered by the Registrar of Companies:

[192] See *Doc 61*.

[193] Annex I – a three page application form and one page of instructions for completion of the application form – has not been reproduced.

a. name;
b. type of business activity;
c. business address, phone number, facsimile number, and e-mail address of its offices in Iraq;
d. corporate form (joint-stock, limited liability, joint liability, sole owner enterprise, or simple company);
e. ownership structure (wholly Iraqi owned, wholly or partially foreign owned);
f. a yes/no question asking if the proposed entity will be involved in: (a) land ownership; (b) natural resource extraction or initial processing; (c) retail sales; or (d) acting as a commercial agent.
g. name, address, telephone number, fax number and e-mail address of (a) the agent for service of legal process in Iraq (must reside in Iraq); (b) the authorized representative for filings with the Registrar of Companies (must reside in Iraq; pursuant Article 208, Paragraph 2 of the Company Law of 1997, as revised by CPA Order 64, The Agency Registration Law No. 4 of 1999 shall be inapplicable to the registration of a company, and a company is not required to retain a registration agent to register, though it may choose to do so); and (c) each founder (as well as of its managing director or equivalent officer in the case of founders who are juridical persons) (founders do not need to live in Iraq or be Iraqi citizens);
h. perjury statement signed by the authorized representative for filings with the Registrar of Companies.

3. The following documentation shall be submitted with each Application:
   a. the contract of the company, signed by the founders or their legal representatives, covering:
      (a) the points required in article 13 or 14, whichever is applicable, of Company Law No. 21 of 1997, as amended, and
      (b) the information regarding shares issued for property-in-kind required by article 29, paragraph Third of that Law;
   b. a bank statement from a bank authorized to operate in Iraq evidencing that the founders of the proposed company have deposited, for the proposed company pending registration by the Registrar of Companies:
      (a) capital for a joint stock company of not less than two million dinars (ID2,000,000),
      (b) capital for a limited liability company of not less than one million dinars (ID1,000,000), and
      (c) capital for all other business entities of not less than fifty thousand dinars (ID50,000);
   c. if the Application is for foundation of a joint stock company, additionally, the subscription document signed by the founders and the technical and economic feasibility study;
   d. if the proposed entity has a foreign ownership component and is planning to operate in retail sales in Iraq, a bank statement showing that the sum of one hundred thousand United States dollars ($100,000.00) has been deposited in a non-interest bearing account (this can be furnished to the Registrar of Companies at a later date and the non-submission of it shall not be grounds for rejection of the Application; however, the bank statement will have to be furnished before actual sales activity may begin) in accordance with the Ministerial Instruction on retail trade;

e. if the proposed entity is to be a commercial agent, then additional documentation must be submitted to the registrar pursuant to the Ministerial Instruction on commercial agencies (this can be furnished to the Registrar of Companies at a later date and the non-submission of it shall not be grounds for rejection of the Application; however, the materials will have to be furnished to the Registrar before commercial agency activity may begin);

f. a copy of the passport (for a foreign citizen) or civilian identification card (for an Iraqi citizen) of the authorized representative for filings with the Registrar of Companies, as prescribed in Item g.(b) in paragraph 2. above (this is the person who is to actually submit the Application and he or she should also bring at the time of application, and in all future interactions with the Registrar of Companies, the original of his or her passport (for a foreign citizen) or civilian identification card (for an Iraqi citizen)).

4. An Application for the registration of a company (including all required information and documents) may be filed in either the Arabic or English language.

5. Upon receiving an Application, the Registrar of Companies shall:

a. review the Application for completeness;

b. if the Application is incomplete, return it to the applicant without collecting any fee;

c. if the Application is complete, provide a signed checklist to the applicant showing that all the required information and documentation has been received;

d. log the accepted Application in the Registrar of Companies' official record as of the date of its receipt; and

e. assign a temporary unique identification number to the Application.

6. The Registrar of Companies shall conduct (through other agencies if necessary until this capacity has been established within the Registrar's office; pursuant to Article 208, Paragraph 2 of the Company Law of 1997, as revised by CPA Order 64, the Minister of Trade is authorized to issue instructions to coordinate the activities of the Registrar of Companies and the Chamber of Commerce regarding the registration and approval of commercial trade names) or verify that a search has been conducted to determine whether the company's business name has already been registered in Iraq by a person other than the founders. In the event the company's business name has already been registered in Iraq, the Registrar of Companies shall afford the founders the opportunity to select a name (also subject to search) under which the company might do business without confusion as to its true identity and without implying an association with the person (natural or judicial) who already has registered the name. If this is not possible, the application will be rejected with the advice that the applicant may challenge the prior claim on the name under separate regulations and law.

7. The Registrar of Companies must approve or disapprove each Application within ten (10) business days from the day of its submission. The Registrar of Companies may only disapprove an Application for failure to comply with this Ministerial Instruction.

8. Upon approval of each Application, the Registrar of Companies shall promptly issue to the applicant a certificate of establishment bearing the corresponding business entity's name and the Registrar of Companies' official seal, together with a permanent unique identification number, except that for a joint stock company these shall be issued only after its public subscription is completed, in accordance with article 21, paragraph First, point 2, of Company Law No. 21 of 1997, as amended.

9. The registered business entity shall acquire legal personality as from the date of issuance of its certificate of establishment and permanent unique identification number by the Registrar of Companies.

10. Upon issuance, each registration shall be published in the 'Companies Bulletin' and in at least one (1) daily newspaper of wide circulation in Iraq.

11. The Registrar of Companies shall forward copies of each Application as approved, together with its respective permanent unique identification number as issued, to the Ministry of Finance (Tax Department), Ministry of Planning, Ministry of Labor and Social Affairs, and such other Iraqi Government departments and agencies, as reasonably necessary.

12. The Registrar of Companies shall enter basic summary information on registered companies into a Ministry of Trade electronic database accessible to the public, including over the Internet. Implementation of this function shall not, however, be grounds for delay of registration.

Section IV Fees Payable

1. A fee of 200,000 dinars shall be payable for the registration of a joint stock company, and a fee of 20,000 dinars shall be payable for all other corporate forms. The fee is payable as follows:
    a. one-half (1/2) of the fee shall be paid upon submission and filing of the Application;
    b. the remaining one-half (1/2) of the fee shall be paid upon issuance of the registration and permanent unique identification number by the Registrar of Companies; and
    c. provided, however, that in the event of disapproval of an Application, the remaining one-half (1/2) of the fee referred to in Subsection b. directly above shall not be due or payable, and the one-half of the fee referred to in Subsection a. directly above shall be returned to the applicant by the Registrar of Companies.
2. The Registrar of Companies shall collect said fees and issue the proper receipt evidencing payment directly to the Applicant or its representative.
3. The Registrar of Companies shall keep regular and accurate records and accounts to account for all registration fees collected.

Section V Appeal for Disapproval of Application

In the event the Registrar of Companies disapproves the Application for the registration of a business entity, the Registrar must promptly notify the applicant in writing stating the reasons for its disapproval. The applicant has the right to contest the disapproval of the Registrar of Companies before the Minister of Trade within thirty (30) days from the date of receipt of notification. The Minister of Trade shall review the disapproval within thirty (30) days from the date of submission of the applicant's appeal. If the Minister of Trade also disapproves the Application, the applicant has the right to appeal the Minister's decision before the competent court of law within thirty (30) days, which court shall have final disposition of the matter.

Section VI Update of Information at the Registrar of Companies

Information filed in connection with each registration must be correct as of the time of filing. Subsequent changes may be filed as they occur but at least by December 31 of each year, and address changes for the company's principal office in Iraq or its agent for service of legal process within seven (7) days of their occurrence. Companies will be held responsible for notifications and correspondence delivered to the address in the Registrar of Companies' files.

Section VII Entry into Force of this Instruction

1. This Ministerial Instruction shall enter into full force and effect upon its publication in the Companies Bulletin, as of the date of its signature.
2. The Registrar of Companies shall ensure that these instructions are published in one newspaper of wide circulation in Iraq.

Signed: ___________
Name: Dr. Ali Allawi
Title: Minister of Trade

Document 89

Coalition Provisional Authority Order Number 65

CPA/ORD/20 March 2004/65

Iraqi Communications and Media Commission

Pursuant to my authority of the Coalition Provisional Authority (CPA) and under the laws and usages of war, and consistent with relevant U.N. Security Council resolutions, including Resolutions 1483 and 1511 (2003), and having consulted with the Iraqi Governing Council,

Recalling that U.N. Resolution 1483 (2003) called upon the CPA to promote the welfare of the people of Iraq through the effective administration of the territory and to contribute to conditions of stability and security,

Recognizing that open and rigorous debate based upon the free exchange of information is essential to the development of a modern democracy and the holding of free and fair elections in Iraq, and that key to this is unfettered and universal access to a vigorous, professional, free and diverse media,

Further Recognizing that telecommunications plays a major role in the economic development of nation and that creating legal certainty for market entrants will enhance economic growth and stability,

Noting the need to develop effective self-regulatory mechanisms for the media, especially the press, while assuring orderly structuring of a communications infrastructure,

Underscoring that the role of a regulator is to protect public safety and consumer welfare, and that establishing an independent and appropriately staffed regulatory mechanism will be a bulwark in protecting emerging freedoms,

Observing that independence is the key to effectiveness in regulating and promoting a competitive market that benefits consumer and market participants and that independence in this context means freedom from control or undue influence by any regulated entity or market participant; undue partisan political interference or pressure; and influence or conflict of interest by personal incentives such as share ownership in market participants,

Endorsing the commitment to international principles of freedom of speech and of the press as articulated in the International Covenant of Civil and Political Rights and other documents,

Noting that the worldwide trend towards convergence of technology and transmission methods in the communications industry requires clear and comprehensive regulation and that a single regulator for communications will allow for swift and efficient reactions to economic and industry conditions, a necessity in this dynamic and economically crucial sector,

Further Noting that modern and efficient telecommunications and telecommunications-related information services infrastructures are essential to the economic growth and prosperity of Iraq and to the social and economic well-being of its citizens and that:

1) The development of such infrastructure requires a predictable and sound regulatory regime that is conducive to attracting investments to these sectors,
2) An open and transparent regulatory organization that reflects international best practices will attract private sector investment and promote public confidence and accountability,
3) A critical necessity for achieving a modern telecommunications infrastructure is a forward-looking regulatory authority that develops policies that encourage the provision of new technologies and services to the public, and
4) A major objective of national telecommunications policy is to make available to all Iraqi citizens modern services at reasonable costs,

Further noting that in order for there to be informed public debate in Iraq it is vital to maximize the availability, quality and professionalism of news and information and that:

1) A vibrant broadcasting environment is essential to economic development and a functioning civil society by providing quality public education, current affairs and entertainment programming,
2) It is important to facilitate maximum diversity by balancing vigorous commercial and public sectors that provide services at the national, regional and local levels,
3) This must be encouraged through clear policy aimed at providing diverse services that benefit all of Iraq's citizens and that ensure conformity with generally accepted standards,
4) Regulation in this context should provide for the fullest exercise of freedom of expression as defined by International Convention, must encourage pluralism and diverse political debate and must empower rather than restrain independent and impartial commentary, and,

Acknowledging the vital importance of the transfer of authority to Iraqi governing institutions,

I hereby promulgate the following:

Section 1 Purpose

This Order is designed to:

1) Foster pluralism of and competition among Iraq's communications and media services, thereby promoting an informed and culturally diverse citizenship that derives maximum benefit in terms of choice, price and quality;

2) Protect the interests of the citizens of Iraq as consumers of communications services;

3) Establish the framework for full and fair competition among all providers;

4) Encourage the evolution of electronic media and communications networks to the greater benefit of all who live in Iraq;

5) Ensure that Iraqi telecommunications, broadcast and information services are operated in a manner consistent with public safety;

6) Promote and defend freedom of the media and assist the media community in Iraq to develop, strengthen and maintain professional working practices that support the media's role as a public watchdog; and

7) Establish an open and transparent regulatory organization that reflects international best practices and will attract private sector investment and promote public confidence and accountability.

Section 2 Definitions

1) 'Broadcasting' means any point-to-multipoint transmission or emission of signals, text, images, audio or video content, or data by wire, optical fiber, radio or any other electromagnetic means, intended for general reception by all or a portion of the public, *provided* that the definition of Broadcasting is not intended to include Information Services or Telecommunications.

2) 'Code(s) of Ethics' means one or more sets of ethical standards governing journalistic behavior and press responsibility.

3) 'Code(s) of Practice' means one or more legally binding sets of regulations, rules or standards governing the actions of entities licensed to provide communications services regulated by the Commission.

4) 'Communications' includes telecommunications, broadcasting (including cable television), and information services delivered via telecommunications and broadcasting facilities.

5) 'Information Services' means the offering of a capability to generate, acquire, store, transform, process, retrieve, utilize or make available information, including voice, data and audio or video content, via telecommunications, including the provision of access to the Internet, *provided*, that the definition of Information Services is not intended to include Broadcasting or Telecommunications.

6) 'Media' means entities that provide news, information or entertainment to the general public, or on a subscription basis, using means including printed material, film, video, recordings or communications services.

7) 'Radio-frequency spectrum' means the range of electromagnetic frequencies that are available for the provision of telecommunications, broadcasting and information services.

8) 'Telecommunications' means the transmission by wire, optical fiber, radio, or any other electromagnetic means, including but not limited to satellite networks as well as fixed and mobile terrestrial networks, of information of the user's choosing, between or among points of the user's choosing, without change in the content of information sent and received, provided, that the definition of Telecommunications is not intended to include Broadcasting or Information Services.[194]

Section 3 Establishment

1) There is hereby established the Iraqi Communications and Media Commission ('the Commission') as an independent and non-profit-making administrative institution. The Commission shall be solely responsible for licensing and regulating Telecommunications, Broadcasting, Information Services and other Media in Iraq, and shall be committed to the principles of objectivity, transparency, non-discrimination, proportionality and due process in carrying out its duties.

2) The Commission shall be guided by the International Covenant on Civil and Political Rights, Article 19, regarding freedom of expression and attendant duties and responsibilities, and by the relevant Regulations and Recommendations of the International Telecommunication Union and shall adhere to the General Agreement on Trade in Services (GATS).

Section 4 Organization

The Commission shall be comprised of a Board of Commissioners, one member of which shall be appointed as Chair; a Director General; a Hearings Panel; an Appeals Board; an

[194] Sec 2 was amended by CPA Order No 100, sec 3(23)(b) *[Doc 124]*.

Inspector General; and such advisory boards as the Board of Commissioner or the Director General deems necessary. The Director General may establish any departments or other internal units or subdivisions he/she deems necessary, and staff those departments in a manner that will most efficiently fulfill the Commission's mandate. The Director General shall designate one such department, internal unit or subdivision to act as a point of liaison with the Coalition Forces and Iraq military. Following consultation with the Iraq Governing Council (IGC) and the Ministry of Communications, the Administrator of the Coalition Provisional Authority (the 'Administrator') shall appoint the initial Chair, two Commissioners, the Director General and the Inspector General, who shall immediately begin operating the Commission. The Administrator shall appoint the remaining Commissioners by 30 June 2004.

1) The Board of Commissioners.
   a) The Board of Commissioner shall have nine (9) members, one of which shall be appointed by the Board as the Chair.
   b) The Board shall oversee and receive reports from the Director General, provide strategic and budgetary guidance to the Commission, adopt codes of practice, rules and regulations for broadcasting and telecommunications, finally approve the Commission's budget and define rules of procedure for its operations and those of the Hearings Panel.
   c) The Board shall meet at least once a month and all decisions of the Board of Commissioners shall be made by majority vote, provided that at least six (6) of the members are present and vote. The Chair shall cast the deciding vote in case of [a] tie vote by the Board members on any matter before the Board.
   d) Commissioners shall have senior-level experience in legal affairs, management, business, regulation, engineering, telecommunications, broadcasting, or journalism and shall be individuals of impeccable character.
   e) The Chair shall have an initial term of office of two (2) years, and Commissioners shall be appointed, on an alternating basis, to initial terms of office to two (2), three (3) or four (4) years, in order to ensure staggered terms of office that will promote continuity of experience on the Board. The Chair and Commissioners may be reappointed only once. Subsequent Chairs and Commissioners shall be appointed or reappointed to four (4) year terms of office by the Prime Minister, subject to approval by majority vote of the body vested with national legislative authority.
   f) Commissioners may not hold any executive, legislative or judicial position, whether appointed or elected, at any level of government, nor be an appointed, elected or voluntary official of any political party while serving on the Board.
   g) While serving with the Commission, no Commissioner shall have any financial or business relationship with a telecommunications operator, broadcaster, information services provider or media interest or, with any group or association that represents the interest of telecommunications operators, broadcasters, information service providers or media interests.
   h) Commissioners shall be paid a stipend and reimbursed for authorized expenses from the budget of the Commission.
2) Director General
   a) The Director General shall be the Commission's chief executive officer responsible for all functions of the Commission, including the preparation and submission

of the Commission's budget, except those functions reserved to the Board of Commissioners under this Order. The Director General shall have a term of four (4) years and may be re-appointed only once. The Board of Commissioners shall appoint a successor to the initial Director General following the completion of his/her 4-year term or upon his/her earlier dismissal for cause.

b) The Director General shall have senior-level experience in legal affairs, management, business, regulation, engineering, telecommunications, broadcasting, or journalism and shall be an individual of impeccable character.

c) The Director General may not hold any executive, legislative or judicial position, whether appointed or elected, at any level government, nor be an appointed, elected or voluntary official of any political party while serving as Director General.

d) While serving with the Commission, the Director General shall not have any financial or business relationship with a telecommunications operator, broadcaster, information services provider or media interest, or with any group, organization or association that represents the interests of telecommunications operators, broadcasters, information services providers or media interests.

3) Hearings Panel.

a) The Hearings Panel shall consider and determine grave and serious breaches of codes and licenses and shall consist of five (5) members, who shall have backgrounds in the legal profession or in relevant fields.

b) The Board of Commissioners shall appoint the members of the Hearings Panel, in consultation with the IGC and the Administrator.

c) Unless the Director General determines otherwise, evidentiary sessions of the Hearings Panel shall be public and its decision shall made public.[195]

4) Appeals Board.

a) A three (3) person independent Appeals Board shall hear appeals of decisions by the Commission, whether rendered by the Director General or by the Hearings Panel.

b) The Appeals Board shall consist of a Judge, an attorney with communications regulatory experience and a member with professional or business experience in the legal profession or the relevant fields. The Appeals Board shall elect one of its members as Chair.

c) Members of the initial Appeals Board shall be appointed by the Administrator in consultation with the IGC; two (2) for a period of four (4) years and the third for a period of two (2) years. Subsequent appointments to the Appeals Board shall be made by the Minister of Justice or the head of its successor body. Members of the Appeals Board may be reappointed only once.

d) Unless determined otherwise by the Chair of the Appeals Board, evidentiary sessions of the Appeals Board shall be made public. All decisions by the Appeals Board shall be made public.

e) To ensure independence from the Commission, members of the Appeals Board shall be remunerated by the Ministry of Justice or its successor body.

5) Inspector General. There is hereby established within the Commission an Office of Inspector General, which shall be appointed and operate in accordance with CPA Order No. 57, Inspectors General.[196]

[195] Sec 4(3) was amended by CPA Order No 100, sec 3(23)(a) *[Doc 124]*.

[196] See *Doc 80*.

Section 5 Functions

1) The Commission shall manage communications and media licensing processes in Iraq, and shall ensure that the radio frequency spectrum is used in a manner that recognizes the value and scarcity of this resource.

2) The Commission shall establish a regulatory regime for telecommunications, broadcasting and information services, by:

a) Promulgating a comprehensive statement of Iraqi communications policy as its first order of business, in consultation with internationally recognized experts in the fields of telecommunications, broadcasting and information services;

b) Drafting and promulgating rules and regulations that are necessary and appropriate for the competitive provision of telecommunications, broadcasting and information services in Iraq;

c) Commencing work on a comprehensive draft law for the regulation of communications in Iraq, within thirty 30 days following commencement of Commission operations;

d) Establishing a regime to license telecommunications network operators, broadcasters and providers of telecommunications, broadcasting and information services, in consultation with the industry;

e) Establishing license conditions required to ensure compliance with the rules, regulations and mandates established by the Commission pursuant to this order, and monitoring licensees' compliance with said licensing conditions;

f) Establishing procedures and requirements for the registration of those enterprises that provide information services as deemed necessary by the Commission;

g) Creating effective and mandatory Codes of Practice governing the actions of licensed entities, with the participation of the industry. At a minimum, the Commission shall draft and implement standards and rules for the following:

(1) Interconnection rates, terms and conditions;

(2) Competitive provision of telecommunications, broadcasting and information services, including the tariffing of telecommunications services not subject to effective competition;

(3) Access to inputs required for deployment of networks and services, including rights of way and pole attachments;

(4) Access to numbering resources;

(5) Quality of service offered by licensed entities;

(6) Fraud and misleading business practices;

(7) Broadcasting responsibility;

(8) Advertising and sponsorship;

(9) Media activities during election periods;

(10) Protection of copyrights;

(11) Negotiation of network termination charges among carriers, and international settlement rates, pursuant to recommendations of the International Telecommunications Union (ITU); administration of such charges and rate through Network Operations and Billing Support Systems (OSS/BSS);

(12) International charging agreements for telecommunications services; and

(13) Development and promotion of policies for Universal Access to basic telephone services as deemed necessary by the Commission.

h) Encouraging freedom of expression and professionalism of the press by working with the Iraqi press community to develop a Code of Ethics for the press and, in consultation with the industry and relevant professional journalists' associations, developing a system to implement the Code through self-regulation. The written press shall not require a license to operate within Iraq;

i) Planning, managing, allocating and assigned radio-frequency spectrum, subject to the needs of the military, and publishing a radio-frequency usage plan for Iraq;
j) Establishing and maintaining a license fee system for both broadcasting and telecommunications;
k) Requiring the disclosure and provision of such information as is necessary for the due performance of its regulatory obligations.
l) Administering the requirements of all related Orders issued by the Administrator and following the transfer of governance authority to the transitional Iraqi administration, implementing the stated communications policy thereof; and
m) Coordinating with each of the CPA (or the U.S. Embassy, Baghdad, following the transfer of full governance authority to the Iraqi Interim Government), the Iraqi Ministry of Communications, Ministry of Defense and the Commander of Coalition Forces (or Commander, Multinational Force, following the transfer of full governance authority to the Iraq Interim Government) regarding any actions that may affect their use of telecommunication, broadcasting and information services or networks and radio-frequency spectrum, to ensure that no such actions interfere with military requirements necessary in the interest of national security.

Section 6 Dismissal Authority

From the transfer of full governance authority to the Iraq Interim Government until the formation of an Iraqi government pursuant to a permanent constitution, the body vested with national legislative authority may terminate the appointment of the Director General or a member of the Board of Communications only upon two-thirds vote. Until such transfer of full governance authority, the Administrator shall have sole authority to terminate the appointment of the Director General or a member of the Board of Commissioners. Such terminations by the Administrator or the body vested with national legislative authority may occur for only the following reasons:

1) Incapacity caused by illness;
2) Conviction of a crime punishable by imprisonment;
3) Conflict of interest, as defined in the Commission's Code of Ethics, including when a member of the household of the person to be removed is an owner, shareholder, or member of the board, supervisory board or other relevant governing body, or director, president or other manager of any licensee or associate undertaking of any licensee and such conflict of interest is not remedied in accordance with the Commission's Code of Ethics;
4) Failure to perform duties pursuant to relevant legislation, internal Commission rules or Contracts of Employment, including, in the case of members of the Board of Commissioners, failure to participate in three (3) or more successive meetings; or
5) Violation of the Commission's Code of Ethics or other applicable law.

Section 7 Conflicts of Interest

Neither the Director General, nor any member of the Board of Commissioners, the Hearings Panel or the Appeals Board may work on any matter that will affect (i) his or her personal financial interests, (ii) the financial interest of his or her spouse or minor child (iii) the financial interests of his or her business partner, (iv) the financial interest of any organization in which he or she serves as an officer, director, general partner, employee, or trustee or (v) the financial interest of any entity with whom he or she has an arrangement for employment or is negotiating for employment. In such situations, he or she may either divest the interest causing the conflict or recuse him or herself from any involvement in the matter. The Director General shall apply this section to the Commission staff, as appropriate.

Section 8 Adverse Actions

1) The Board of Commissioners shall develop criteria for determining whether the terms of a media license or other rule or regulation of the Commission have been violated. Such criteria shall provide that either the Director General or Hearings Panel may determine whether a violation occurred, and that the Hearings Panel shall address more serious allegations.

2) In cases under the jurisdiction of the Director General, the Director General shall review the facts of the case and if necessary, request additional information from the broadcaster, telecommunications operator or information services provider affected. The Director General shall base his or her decision on this evidence, and shall include in the analysis, whether or not a breach or violation exists and, where appropriate, the level of damage accrued, the seriousness of the offense, and whether mitigating or aggravating circumstances are present.

3) In such other cases or in cases of persistent or repetitious violation, the Hearings Panel shall determine whether a violation occurred, in the following manner:

a) The Director General shall present the complaint to the Hearing Panel. The broadcaster, telecommunications operator or information services provider affected shall have a full and adequate opportunity to reply;

b) Upon the evidence and arguments presented, the Hearings Panel shall adjudicate and issue a decision that shall be forwarded to the Director General for implementation. The Hearings Panel's decision must be presented in writing and must conclude whether or not a breach or violation exist; assess, where appropriate, the level of damage accrued and the seriousness of the offense; and address whether mitigating or aggravating circumstances are present.

4) If the Director General has reason to believe that an operation poses an imminent threat to the public safety or order, he or she may immediately suspend operations thereof, pending an accelerated review by the Hearings Panel.

5) Decisions of the Commission, whether rendered by the Director General or the Hearings Panel, may be appealed to the Appeals Board. The appellant shall have thirty (30) days within which to appeal a decision of the Commission, whether rendered by the Director General or the Hearings Panel. Any party to the case that wishes to oppose or comment on the appeal must do so within fifteen (15) days of the filing of the appeal. Once this fifteen (15)-day period ends, the Appeals Board may hold a hearing or require the submission of written testimony. The Appeals Board must then render its decision on the Appeal within thirty (30) days after the initial Appeal hearing or submission of testimony.

6) Decisions of the Director General and of the Hearings Panel remain binding and in force, pending the resolution of any appeal by the Appeals Board. The Appeals Board, upon hearing timely arguments from the parties, may uphold, overturn or remand decisions or orders before it to the Director General or the Hearings Panel. Once upheld by the Appeals Board, decisions are final.

7) All decisions, whether made by the Director General, Hearings Panel, or Appeals Board shall be in writing and shall be made available to the public.

8) Any person aggrieved by a rule, regulation, Code of Practice or decision adopted by the Commission may appeal that rules, regulation, Code of Practice or decision to the Appeals Board in accordance with the provisions of this Section.[197]

Section 9 Enforcement

1) Except as otherwise specifically provided in this order, the Commission may secure compliance with license terms and conditions, Codes of Practice, and other rules and regulations, by applying and enforcing appropriate and proportionate sanctions including:

a) Issuing warnings;
b) Requiring publication of an apology;
c) Requiring mitigation or repair of harm to consumers;
d) Imposing financial penalties and placing liens on relevant bank accounts, if the penalties are not paid on time;
e) Suspending licenses;
f) Seizing equipment for which access into the licensee's premises is granted hereby;
g) Suspending operations;
h) Closing operations; and
i) Terminating or withdrawing licenses.

2) The Commission may enlist the support and assistance of Iraq law enforcement authorities, which authorities shall assist in a timely, professional and responsible manner. In addition, the Commission may, consistent with military operational requirements, request the support of Coalition Forces in enforcement efforts, if Iraqi police support is unavailable.

Section 10 Public Accountability

1) The Commission shall produce and publish an annual report of its activities and expenditures, and shall provide to the legislature an annual financial audit prepared in accordance with international accounting standards.

2) The Chair, the Board of Commissioners and /or the Director General shall appear before appropriate legislative or executive committees upon request, to defend or explain the Commission's activities and reports, and shall otherwise cooperate fully with legislative and executive entities in explaining Commission activities.

3) The Chair, Board of Commissioners, Director General, Hearings Panel and Appeals Board shall make available to the public, in full written form, all Commission decisions, rules guidelines and codes, in an appropriate and timely manner.

4) The Commission shall adopt a public consultation process through which the views of government, the regulated industries, citizens and citizen organizations can be solicited with respect to proposed rules, guidelines, codes and policies.

5) All decisions of the Board of Commissioners shall be made public.

6) The Commission shall develop and adopt a Code of Ethics governing the Commission and its staff. Violations of this Code shall constitute grounds for appropriate disciplinary action.

Section 11 Funding and Compensation

1) The Commission shall be funded from the following sources:

a) Recurring and non-recurring fees collected from licensees;

[197] Sec 8 was amended by CPA Order No 100, sec 3(23)(c) *[Doc 124]*.

b) Grants or donations received by the Commission from any source, insofar as they are in conformity with applicable law; and

c) Funds appropriated by the U.S. Congress for the relief and reconstruction of Iraq.[198]

2) The Director General shall prepare the Commission's annual budget, which shall be submitted to the Board of Commissioners for final approval.

3) Funds received by the Commission shall be used in accordance with the Commission's budget as directed by the Board of Commissioners.

4) Fines collected by the Commission in the performance of its right to apply enforcement measures shall be remitted to the Iraqi treasury.

5) The Commission's budget and use of funds shall be subject to review by both an independent domestic audit institution and an international audit institution annually.

6) All mobile cellular licenses issued on or after 22 December 2003 and the operations of the licensees shall be regulated and enforced by the Commission, and the Commission shall collect all license fees associated with the issuance of such licenses. License fees already collected by the Ministry of Communications shall be transferred to the Commission.

7) Notwithstanding CPA Order No. 30, Reform of Salaries and Employment Conditions of State Employees, 8 September 2003,[199] employees of the Commission shall be compensated at rates prescribed by the Administrator or, following the transfer of full governance authority to the new Iraqi government, the Prime Minister.

Section 12 Effect on Previous Orders

1) Within thirty (30) days following establishment of the Commission, the licensing responsibilities set forth in CPA Order Number 11, Licensing Telecommunications Services and Equipment,[200] shall be transferred from the Ministry of Communications to the Commission. CPA Order Number 11 shall be rescinded thirty (30) days following the effective date of this Order, or upon the Administrator's determination that the licensing responsibilities have been effectively transferred in full, whichever is earlier.

2) CPA Order Number 14 regarding Prohibited Media Activity,[201] shall remain in force until the Commission promulgates rules and regulations applicable thereto and the Administrator rescinds that Order, or until the transitional Iraq administration enacts superseding legislation.

Section 12 Entry into Force

This Order shall enter into force on the date of signature [20 March 2004] and shall continue in effect until such time as the transitional Iraqi administration enacts superseding legislation.

[198] Sec 11(1) was rescinded and replaced by CPA Order No 100, sec 3(23)(d) *[Doc 124]*.

[199] See *Doc 51.*

[200] See *Doc 26.*

[201] See *Doc 32.*

Document 90
Coalition Provisional Authority Order Number 66
CPA/ORD/20 March 2004/66

Iraq Public Service Broadcasting

Pursuant to my authority as Administrator of the Coalition Provisional Authority (CPA), and under the laws and usages of war, and consistent with relevant U.N. Security Council resolutions, including Resolutions 1483 and 1511 (2003),

Recalling that U.N. Resolution 1483 (2003) called upon the CPA to promote the welfare of the people of Iraq through the effective administration of the territory and to contribute to conditions of stability and security,

Underscoring the significance of the media in building a democratic society and the need to encourage a professional, impartial and independent broadcasting sector,

Emphasizing that open and rigorous debate is essential to development of the democratic process in Iraq, and the vital role of public service broadcasting in facilitating such debate,

Recognizing the right of freedom of expression, including freedom of the press and the right to hold opinions without interference as articulated in the International Covenant of Civil and Political Rights to which Iraq is a party, and as guaranteed in the Transitional Administrative Law approved unanimously and without reservation by the Iraq Governing Council,

Further recognizing the corresponding duty of governments not to interfere with the independence of the media, and emphasizing that independence in this context means freedom from control, undue influence, interference, or pressure from political or other external forces,

Noting that CPA Order Number 65[202] regarding the establishment of the Iraq Communications and Media Commission grants authority thereto to regulate broadcasting,

Desiring to create an impartial and independent tool for public debate, which acts as an agent of pluralism and diversity, and as an instrument for building a constructive national identity accessible to the entire population of Iraq,

Further noting the unique capabilities of public service broadcasting to serve, on a non-discriminatory basis, the viewing needs of a diverse public, including underrepresented national minorities and other niche segments of society,

I hereby promulgate the following:

Section 1 Purpose

This Order is designed to:

1) Establish an institutional framework that will educate, entertain and inform the people of Iraq, but will not be a tool of political or other inappropriate outside interests;

2) Create an open forum that respects and promotes human rights and freedoms, notably the right to freedom of expression, in which views can be debated and where information, opinions and criticism circulate without interference;

3) Create a platform to reflect and foster the varied values of Iraqi society, which facilitates access by the public to information vital to participating in a rapidly globalizing world and which contributes to an unbiased representation of Iraq society to the world;

[202] See *Doc 89*.

4) Create a forum within which minority languages and culture are allowed to develop in a non-divisive manner and in a way that contributes to reconciliation, tolerance and unity;

5) Create an organization mandated to encourage and promote innovation and experimentation in broadcasting; and

6) Foster indigenous creative capacity through the development, commissioning and/or purchase of domestic productions;

7) Incorporate the Iraqi Media Network, including its newspaper and publishing activities, as the Iraq Public Service Broadcaster.

Section 2 Definitions

1) 'Broadcasting' means any point-to-multipoint transmission or emission of signals, text, images, audio or video or data by wire, optical fiber, radio, or any other electromagnetic means intended for reception by all or a portion of the public.

2) 'Charter' means the document that serves as the moral contract between the public broadcaster and the people of Iraq and lays out what is expected of the public broadcaster in return for the public funds used to finance its operations.

3) 'Distinctiveness' describes the sustained effort by the public service broadcaster to distinguish itself in programming and aspiration from other broadcasting services including state and commercial broadcasting.

4) 'Diversity' describes a sustained effort to meet the multiple needs and interests of society through different genres and by responding to the otherwise unmet needs of a variety of segments within the viewing public.

5) 'Independence' means the ability to operate financially, editorially and managerially free from influence or control by the government, or by inappropriate external interests.

6) 'Public Service Broadcasting' means broadcasting pursuant to a legal obligation to entertain, educate and inform all segments of Iraq society on a wide variety of issues, developments, events and phenomena in the country and abroad. Other obligations include, but are not limited to, ensuring open and free discussion of issues of public interest, fostering civil society, encouraging indigenous creative capacity and representing the needs of the general public.

7) 'Universality' means ensuring that as much of the population of the country as possible should have access to public broadcasting services.

Section 3 Establishment

1) This Order hereby establishes the Iraqi Media Network ('IMN') as the public service broadcaster for Iraq, which shall broadcast across the territory of Iraq. The public service broadcaster shall be an independent institution charged with disseminating information in accordance with this Order and with the terms and conditions of its operating license. It shall have the status of a legal person with all rights attendant thereto.

2) The public service broadcaster shall act in accordance with the principles of independence, universality, diversity and distinctiveness. The public service broadcaster shall reflect the democratic, social and cultural values of Iraqi society and at all times shall strive to reflect fairly and equally the regional, cultural and political diversity of Iraq and its people.

3) The public service broadcaster shall be license by the Iraq Communications and Media Commission in accordance with this Order and other applicable law and shall be subject to the Commission's regulatory authority.

Section 4 Organization

The public service broadcaster shall have a Board of Governors; a Financial Committee; a Director General; and such advisory boards and other committees as the Board of Governors deems necessary. The Director General may establish any departments or other internal units or subdivisions he or she deems necessary, and staff those departments in a manner that will most efficiently fulfill the public service broadcaster's mandate. Following consultation with the Iraqi Governing Council ('IGC') and the Ministry of Communications, and as soon as practicable, the Administrator shall appoint the initial Chair, two Governors, the three members of the Financial Committee, at least one of whom shall be a representative of a donor nation(s), who collectively, shall immediately begin operating the public service broadcaster. The Administrator shall appoint the remaining Governors and the Director General by 30 May 2004, following the same consultative process. The Board of Governors shall appoint successor Directors General. The Chair and members shall have a term of office of four (4) years and may be reappointed only once. Vacancies shall be filled by the Administrator and, after the transfer of full governance authority to the Iraqi Interim Government, the Prime Minister, subject to approval by a two-thirds vote of the body vested with national legislative authority.

1) Board of Governors.
   a) The Board of Governors shall have nine (9) members, including a Chair. Eight (8) of the members shall be Iraqi citizens, and the remaining shall be an non-Iraqi with international experience in broadcasting.
   b) The Board of Governors shall serve as the guardian of the public interest and as such, shall ensure that the obligations of the public service broadcaster operating license are met; comply with the provisions of the public service broadcaster Charter; represent the public with regard to programming, serve as a buffer between the public service broadcaster and the government and other external pressures and oversee and receive reports from the Director General, as required.
   c) The Board of Governors shall be the sole body authorized to dismiss the Director General, pursuant to the conditions set forth in Section 5(2), below.
   d) Within thirty (30) days following commencement of public service broadcaster's operations, the Board of Governors shall commence work on a comprehensive Charter for public service broadcaster that shall convey to the people of Iraq what is expected of the public service broadcaster in return for the public funds used to finance its operations. A thirty (30) day period of public notice and consultation shall be provided prior to the adoption of the Charter by the Board of Governors. The Board of Governors shall adopt a Code of Ethics for their operations and other internal rules, as appropriate.
   e) Additionally, the Board of Governors shall, by the deadline specified in subsection (d), above, begin consultations with the Iraqi Communications & Media Commission, or appropriate legislative committees, to draft as law that comprehensively addresses public service broadcasting in Iraq and fully respects the principles set forth in Section 3(2) of this Order.
   f) The Board shall meet at least once a month and all decisions of the Board of Governors shall be made by majority vote, providing that at least six (6) of the members are present and vote. The Chair shall cast the deciding vote in case of tie vote by the Board members on any matter before the Board.
   g) The Board of Governors shall produce and publish an annual report of its activities and expenditures, and shall provide to the legislature an annual financial audit prepared in accordance with international standards.

h) Except as provided elsewhere in this Order, members of the Board of Governors should be drawn from Iraqi civil society and shall represent a cross-section of the viewing public. Governors shall be individuals of impeccable character and reputation.
i) Members of the Board of Governors may neither hold any executive, legislative or judicial position, whether appointed or elected, at any level of government, nor be an appointed, elected or voluntary official of any political party while serving on the Board.

2) Financial Committee
a) The Financial Committee shall have three (3) members, all of whom shall be experts in finance or business administration.
b) The Financial Committee shall act as a supervisory body to ensure that public funds and donated funds and/or equipment are utilized efficiently and transparently. The Financial Committee shall examine expenditures and prepare reports and/or issue recommendations on financial matters for the Board of Governors. In preparing these reports, the Financial Committee may compel the Director General to submit relevant information and respond to questions regarding such information.
c) The Financial Committee shall examine and authorize the budget submitted to it by the Director General and shall authorize expenditures in excess of 150,000,000 Iraqi Dinars. The Financial Committee may raise this amount at their discretion.
d) The Financial Committee shall meet at least monthly and when requested by the Director General to authorize expenditures above 150,000,000 Iraqi Dinars. Decisions shall be made by majority vote.
e) The Financial Committee shall not have any authority with regard to programming or editing nor shall it have executive authority over any employee of the public service broadcaster.
f) The Financial Committee shall, within thirty (30) days of their appointment:
   i) Inventory all technical assets of IMN, including transmitter sites, perform a valuation of said assets and create a standard operating procedure for monitoring control thereof;
   ii) Review for submission to the Board of Governors all potential funding sources for the public service broadcaster, with the goal of eliminating/reducing the risk of political interference;
   iii) Create a 5-year Financial plan for the public service broadcaster based upon the review conducted under subsection (f)(ii), above, and recommend the amount of a one-time start-up payment from the Iraq government, if any.
g) Members of the Financial Committee may neither hold any executive, legislative or judicial position, whether appointed or elected, at any level of government, nor be an appointed, elected or voluntary official of any political party, while serving on the Committee.

3) Director General
a) The Director General shall be the public service broadcaster's chief executive officer, responsible for all functions of the public service broadcaster, including the preparation and submission of the public service broadcaster's budget. The Director-General shall also be [the] public service broadcaster's editor-in-chief and shall have final authority over all programming matters.

b) The Director General should have senior-level experience in broadcasting, journalism, business management, finance, and/or broadcast engineering.

c) The Director General shall report to the Board of Governors. The specific duties and responsibilities of the Director General shall be set forth in the Charter.

d) The Director General shall represent the public service broadcaster in all legal matters.

e) The Director General shall appoint a Deputy for a term of service not exceeding the length of the Director General's mandate.

f) The Director General shall serve a term of office of four (4) years and may be reappointed only once. The Director General may not hold any executive, legislative or judicial position, whether appointed or elected, at any level of government, nor be an appointed, elected or voluntary official of any political party while serving on the Board.

4) Conflicts of Interest.

a) The Director General, members of the Board of Governors and members of the Financial Committee, with the exception of the international member(s), whose task is to represent donor nation(s) and safeguard their interests, are prohibited from working on any matter that will affect:

i) His or her personal financial interests;

ii) The financial interests of his or her spouse or child;

iii) The financial interests of his or her business partner;

iv) The financial interest of any organization in which he or she serves as an officer, director, general partner, employee or trustee; or

v) The financial interest of any entity with whom he or she has an arrangement for employment or is negotiating for employment. In such situations, he or she may either divest the interest causing conflict or recuse him or herself from any involvement in the matter.

b) The Director General shall apply this subsection to the public service broadcaster staff, as appropriate.

Section 5 Termination Authority

1) Until such time as full governance authority is transferred to the Iraqi Interim Government, the Administrator shall have sole authority to terminate the appointment of any of the members of the Board of Governors before completion of their terms. After such transfer of governance authority, members of the Board of Governors may be dismissed only upon a two-thirds vote of the body vested with national legislative authority.

2) The Board of Governors shall have sole authority to terminate the appointment of the Director General.

3) Such terminations of the Director General or members of the Board of Governors may occur only in the limited circumstances defined as follows:

a) Illness rendering the Director General or any members [sic] of the Board of Governors incapable of performing his or her duties;

b) Conviction of a crime punishable by imprisonment;

c) A conflict of interest by the Director General, or a member of the Board of Governors, which includes situations where a household member thereof is an owner, shareholder, or member of the supervisory board or other relevant governing body, director, president or other manager of any licensee or associate undertaking of any licensee;

d) Non-performance of duties for members of the Board of Governors, as reflected by failure to participate in three (3) or more successive meetings; or
e) Failure of the Director General or member of the Board of Governors to perform his/her duties pursuant to relevant legislation, internal rules, Charter or his/her contract of employment;
f) Violation of the public service broadcaster's Code of Ethics.

Section 6 Public Accountability

In furtherance of its mandate to serve the public interest and conduct its operations in an efficient and transparent manner, the public service broadcaster shall:

1) Publish in advance broad frameworks for its schedules with commitments as appropriate for the individual channels;

2) Report, at the end of the year, on its performance against established goals, these reports being subject to independent review;

3) Provide details in its annual report of the cost and revenues associated with each of its services, including its commercial operations, if any:

4) Keep detailed financial records in a manner that will enable independent auditors, including the Board of Supreme Audit, to evaluate its performance in fulfilling its statutory remit;

5) Recognize, encourage and welcome the public's expression of views on its performance, and establish and develop means of enhanced communications with its audience, as well as ensure that all complaints are logged, acknowledged and investigated;

6) Adopt a code of fair trading to clarify how its activities will operate in a broadcasting landscape that has competing interest;

7) Pledge to deliver to its audience the highest level of programming in return for the public investment; and

8) Provide details of non-Arabic language programming and other non-Arabic language services in its Annual Report.

Section 7 Editorial and Programming Matters

1) The mandate of the public service broadcaster is to serve the public interest through the provision of diverse and distinct programming in the variety of languages spoken in Iraq, including Arabic, Kurdish, Assyrian and Turkmen, and shall include, among other things, the following:

a) Programs that entertain, inform and educate;
b) Programs of news and current affairs;
c) Coverage of sporting, religious and cultural activities;
d) Children's programming;
e) Coverage of national government activities, as determined by the responsible editor;
f) Indigenous Iraqi production;
g) Programming that facilitates and encourages citizen participation in democratic processes, including programming that relates to political campaigns;
h) Programming and a programming structure that reflects the diversity of Iraq society;
i) Programming that encourages understanding of issues of gender, age, disability, race, religion, membership in a political group or membership of a minority community in Iraqi society,

2) The Public Service Broadcaster shall:
   a) Inform the public on all political, economic, social, health, cultural, educational, scientific, religious, ecological, sporting and other developments, events and phenomena in the country and abroad, as well as ensure open and free discussion on all issues of public interest;
   b) Foster, encourage, and develop all forms of domestic audio-visual creativity that contribute to the development of Iraqi culture, art and entertainment, and to the international representation of the Iraqi cultural identity;
   c) Broadcast programs intended for members of the Iraqi community outside Iraq;
   d) Inform and educate the citizens in all aspects of the preservation of cultural heritage;
   e) Inform and educate the citizens in all aspects of the protection of the environment, as well as promote the right of all to a healthy environment;
   f) Foster and encourage the development of civil society and the rule of law.

3) The public service broadcaster shall encourage respect for and promote fundamental human rights and freedoms, including freedom of expression, democratic values and institutions, and the culture of public dialogue.

4) The public service broadcaster shall respect and encourage public understanding of political and religious pluralism.

5) This public service broadcaster shall treat impartially all political, economic, social, health, cultural, educational, scientific, ecological and other issues, and not advocate the positions or interests of any particular political, religious, commercial or other party. In doing so, the public service broadcaster shall ensure the public is aware of different points of view in order to create informed public opinion.

Section 8 Financing and Compensation

1) The Board of Governors, in conjunction with the Financial Committee, shall analyze various methods and create a plan for reliable funding of the public service broadcaster. Possible funding sources shall include, but shall not be limited to:
   a) Tax on receiver purchase;
   b) Subscription fee;
   c) Advertising and sponsorship;
   d) Revenues from technical services;
   e) Donations and fund-raising through pledge drives or other means; and
   f) Direct government grant.

2) Notwithstanding CPA Order No. 30, Reform of Salaries and Employment Conditions of State Employees, 8 September 2003,[203] employees of the public service broadcaster shall be compensated at rates prescribed by the Administrator or, following the transfer of full governance authority to the new Iraqi government, the Prime Minister.

Section 9 Entry into Force

This Order shall enter into force on the date of signature [20 March 2004] and shall continue in effect until such time as the new Broadcasting, Telecommunications and Media laws are adopted.

[203] See *Doc 51*.

Document 91
Coalition Provisional Authority Order Number 67
CPA/ORD/21 March 2004/67

Ministry of Defence

Pursuant to my authority as Administrator of the Coalition Provisional Authority (CPA), and under the laws and usages of war, and consistent with relevant U.N. Security Council resolutions, including Resolutions 1483 and 1511 (2003),

Recalling that U.N. Security Council Resolution 1483 (2003) calls upon the CPA to promote the welfare of the Iraqi people through the effective administration of the territory, including in particular working towards the restoration of conditions of security and stability,

Noting that CPA Order Number 2, Dissolution of Entities, May 23, 2003, as amended,[204] dissolved the Ministry of Defence, the Ministry of State for Military Affairs, and other military organizations,

Noting that CPA Order Number 22, Creation of a New Iraqi Army, August 7, 2003,[205] established a military force for the national self-defense of a future free Iraq,

Noting that CPA Order Number 23, Creation of a Code of Military Discipline for the New Iraqi Army, August 7, 2003,[206] established a system of discipline to maintain order in the New Iraqi Army,

Noting that CPA Order Number 28, Establishment of the Iraqi Civil Defense Corps, September 3, 2003,[207] established a temporary security and emergency service agency for Iraq to complement operations conducted by Coalition military forces in Iraq,

Noting that CPA Order Number 42, Creation of the Defense Support Agency, September 19, 2003,[208] established a civilian agency charged with the administrative and logistical support of the New Iraqi Army,

Further noting the adoption of the Law of Administration for the State of Iraq for the Transitional Period on March 8, 2004,

Acknowledging the need to take measures to provide for the security of the Iraqi people and their inherent right to form a national self-defense capability for a free Iraq,

Recognizing the need to establish a new national ministry to provide proper civilian control of the Iraqi Armed Forces and supporting organizations,

I hereby promulgate the following:

Section 1 Establishment

1) A new Ministry of Defence (MoD) is hereby established. The new MoD is a wholly distinct and separate entity from the organization with the same name that previously existed in Iraq and was dissolved by CPA Order Number 2.

2) The MoD will operate under the authority, direction, and control of the Administrator of the CPA pending transfer of full governance authority to the Iraqi Interim Government established in accordance with the Law of Administration for the State of Iraq for the Transitional Period. The Administrator, after consultation with the Governing Council, will

[204] See *Doc 15*.
[205] See *Doc 43*.
[206] See *Doc 44*.
[207] See *Doc 49*.
[208] See *Doc 64*.

appoint an interim Minister of Defence. The interim Minister shall report directly to the Administrator.[209]

3) The MoD will consist of the Ministry proper (including organizations for policy oversight, financial management and administration and logistics of the Iraqi Armed Forces), the Iraqi Armed Forces (IAF), and those members of the Facilities Protection Service (FPS) employed by the MoD for the defense of its installations.

Section 2 Transfer of Responsibility

1) The New Iraqi Army (including all associated personnel, facilities, and equipment) established pursuant to CPA Order Number 22 is hereby renamed the 'Iraqi Armed Forces' and transferred to the MoD. All references to the 'New Iraqi Army' in CPA Orders, Regulations, and Memoranda shall be deemed to refer to the 'Iraqi Armed Forces.'

(a) The IAF will consist of the Army, Air Force, Coastal Defense Force, reserve components (when established), Iraqi Civil Defense Corps (ICDC) when transferred to the IAF, Iraqi Counter-Terrorism Force (ICTF), and associated headquarters.[210]

(b) All references in CPA Order Number 22 to 'a civilian member of the CPA reporting directly to the Administrator and to whom authority has been specifically delegated in writing' shall be deemed to refer to the interim Minister of Defence.

2) On June 1, 2004, unless sooner directed by the Administrator of the CPA, the ICDC (including all associated personnel, facilities, and equipment) established pursuant to CPA Order Number 28 shall be transferred to the MoD as a component of the IAF.

3) The Code of Military Discipline established by CPA Order Number 23 shall apply to all elements of the IAF, including reserve components and the ICDC (when transferred to the IAF).

4) The Defense Support Agency (DSA), established by CPA Order Number 42, is hereby subsumed into the new MoD. The staff of the DSA shall be transferred immediately to the MoD, and the interim Minister shall assume full authority, direction and control over this staff. CPA Order Number 42 is hereby cancelled.

Section 3 Existing Law

Any laws or regulations inconsistent with the provisions of this Order are hereby suspended to the extent they are inconsistent with the provisions of this Order.

Section 4 Mission and Organization

1) Subject to the authority of the Administrator of the CPA, the interim Minister shall be responsible for management and employment of the IAF, to include the ICDC when transferred to the IAF, and shall exercise direction and control (including commissioning and appointments) over the IAF, to include the ICDC when transferred to the IAF, and its organizational structure in accordance with CPA Orders Number 22 and 28, respectively.

2) In light of the current emergency situation within Iraq, and consistent with Iraq's stated desire to join other nations in helping to maintain peace and security and fight terrorism

[209] Sec 1(2) was amended by CPA Order No 100, sec 3(24)(a) *[Doc 124]*.
[210] Sec 2(1)(a) was rescinded and replaced by CPA Order No 100, sec 3(24)(b) *[Doc 124]*.

during the transitional period pursuant to the provisions of United Nations Security Council Resolution 1511, all trained elements of the IAF, to include the ICDC when transferred to the IAF, shall at all times be under the operational control of the Commander of Coalition Forces for the purpose of conducting combined operations and providing other support in accordance with CPA Orders Number 22 and 28, respectively, and any future relevant CPA Orders. The interim Minister shall exercise administrative control over elements of the IAF that are under the operational control of the Commander of Coalition Forces.[211]

3) The mission of the MoD is to secure, protect, and guarantee the security of Iraq's borders and to defend Iraq. In fulfilling this mission, the MoD shall:

(a) serve all Iraqis regardless of religious, sectarian, tribal, ethnic or political affiliations; and

(b) be accountable for the efficiency and effectiveness with which it carries out its mission.

4) The interim Minister shall organize the MoD into such groups, divisions and branches as are necessary to accomplish its mission, consistent with the positions and structures specified herein and the principles upon which the Ministry is established.

5) The interim Minister shall ensure that the organization is structured to provide civilian oversight of the following MoD functions:

(a) all aspects of defense, including military policy;
(b) budget and financial matters;
(c) human resources (civilian and military), including recruitment and training;
(d) acquisition, sustainment and logistics;
(e) infrastructure (including overseeing construction and facility management); and
(f) defense intelligence analysis and requirements.

6) The interim Minister, with the Administrator's support and approval, shall appoint personnel to serve in the following positions for a set term of three years:

(a) A Secretary General to act in the capacity of the senior civil servant and to serve as acting interim Minister of Defence during any temporary disability of the interim Minister of Defence or any vacancy in that position, to include any period of vacancy prior to the appointment of the initial interim Minister of Defence. If an interim Minister of Defence has not been appointed upon the establishment of the Ministry of Defence, the Administrator (or a civilian member of the CPA reporting to the Administrator and to whom authority has been specifically delegated in writing) shall appoint a Secretary General to perform the functions and exercise the authorities specified herein for the interim Minister of Defence, pending the appointment of an interim Minister of Defence.

(b) A Senior Military Advisor to the interim Minister and other senior government officials, to provide them with independent advice on operational and other military issues;

(c) A Chief of Staff of the IAF responsible for operational command and control of all Iraqi military forces;

(d) Directors General, as needed, to oversee and manage groups within the MoD. Directors General may be either civil servants or, selectively, uniformed officers.

(e) A General Counsel to provide legal analysis and advice on matters affecting the MoD and employment of the IAF. The General Counsel shall report directly to the interim Minister.

[211] Sec 4(2) was amended by CPA Order No 100, sec 3(24)(c) *[Doc 124]*.

7) The Administrator of the CPA shall appoint an Inspector General for the MoD, to serve for a term of five years, and to operate and perform functions in accordance with CPA Order Number 57.[212]

Section 5 Principles

The interim Minister shall ensure that the MoD adheres to the following key principles:

(a) Service: The MoD serves the Iraqi people. The IAF and MoD staff perform their duty selflessly, in a spirit of service.

(b) Loyalty: The IAF and MoD employees are loyal to their legally constituted superiors and to their subordinates.

(c) Civilian Control: The IAF and all those who work in the MoD are responsible to lawfully elected civilian authority.

(d) Professionalism: The culture and character of the MoD will reflect professionalism, technical competence, non-interference in domestic affairs, merit, patriotism, respect for individual rights, and the rule of law. The MoD will understand and respect Iraqi society.

(e) Unity: The MoD will play its full part in reinforcing national unity, and will not be used to foster or institutionalize disunity.

(f) Representative: Though based on merit, the MoD broadly represents Iraqi society. No person will be selected for or denied advancement in the MoD on grounds of race, color, gender, religion, sect, tribal or regional origin.

(g) Integrity: Corruption is unacceptable. Rules and regulations will be established to eliminate waste, fraud, and abuse, and avoid conflicts of interest.

(h) Stewardship: The MoD will earn the respect and confidence of the Iraqi people by responsibly accounting for resources, acting in the country's interest, being effective in assigned missions, abiding by laws, and telling the truth.

(i) Transparency: The Iraqi people and their elected representatives have the right to know about MoD policies, organizations, financial matters, and operations. The MoD will be transparent in its international affairs, including active participation in international security institutions and the development of cooperative security relations.

(j) Security: The IAF and MoD employees will keep secret the national security information entrusted to them by lawful authority.

(k) Affordability: The MoD will keep the scale, capabilities, and costs of defense efforts in line with the needs of the country and within the budget provided by elected authority.

Section 6 Personnel Administration and Pay

1) The MoD shall accept the current personnel of the IAF, the Defense Support Agency, and the ICDC (when transferred to the IAF) and provide them with salaries and benefits commensurate with their positions and experience in those organizations. Such civilian and military personnel shall become employees of the MoD.

2) Employees of the dissolved former Ministry of Defence have no right or entitlement to be employed by the new MoD. However, nothing herein precludes such former employees from being employed by the new MoD, nor does it affect such former employees' entitlements to pensions, if any.

[212] See *Doc 69*. Sec 4(7) was amended by CPA Order No 100, sec 3(24)(d) *[Doc 124]*.

3) The MoD shall have the power to hire and employ personnel in accordance with Iraqi law, as amended by CPA Orders, Regulations, and Memoranda. Such hiring and employment shall be consistent with CPA Order Number 1[213] and any authorized implementation thereof.

4) Salaries of MoD employees shall conform to the salary structure applicable to Iraqi government employees.

5) Death and disability benefits for Eligible Employees of the MoD shall be paid and administered in accordance with CPA Order Number 63.[214]

Section 7 Property

1) All movable and immovable property, including real estate, belonging to, used, possessed, or occupied by or under the control of the DSA, IAF, and ICDC (when transferred to the IAF) shall be transferred to the MoD.

2) All assets and facilities, including real estate, belonging to, used, possessed, or occupied by the dissolved former Ministry of Defence still held by the Administrator on behalf of and for the benefit of the Iraqi people shall be transferred as needed to the new MoD.

Section 8 Budget

1) The MoD shall coordinate with the Ministry of Finance and the CPA Office of Management and Budget to effect the transfer of the budget allocation for the DSA and IAF for the financial year 2004 to the MoD. The MoD shall further coordinate with the Ministry of Finance on the development of its own budgets.

2) The new MoD shall not be liable for any financial obligations of the dissolved former Ministry of Defence.

Section 9 Political Activities

1) Employees of the MoD shall not:

(a) publicly state or suggest any opinion of a political nature that constitutes an effort to indoctrinate members of the MoD, IAF (to include the ICDC when transferred to the IAF), or any other person with a political ideology,

(b) advocate racial, gender or ethnic hatred or intolerance; advocate, create, or engage in discrimination based on race, color, gender, religion, sect, tribal or regional origin; or use, or advocate the use of, force or violence or other unlawful means for political purposes, whether internal or international; or

(c) participate in any manner in organizations or activities that involve, promote, or practice the conduct described in b) above.

2) Members of the IAF, to include the ICDC when transferred to the IAF, may not hold or stand for election to political office or campaign for candidates.

3) A former member of the IAF may not hold political office unless the individual has resigned his commission or rank or retired from duty at least eighteen months prior to serving.

4) Nothing in this Section shall limit the right of an employee of the MoD to vote in elections for political office organized on a local, regional or national level.

Section 10 Conflicts of Interest

Employees of the MoD and their immediate family members shall not, directly or indirectly:

[213] See *Doc 14.*

[214] See *Doc 86.*

1) Hold financial interests that conflict with the employee's conscientious performance of duty.

2) Engage in private financial transactions using nonpublic Government information or allow the improper use of such information to further any private interest.

3) Solicit or accept any gift or other item of monetary value from any person or entity seeking official action from, doing business with, or conducting activities regulated by the MoD, or whose interests may be substantially affected by the performance or nonperformance of the employee's duties.

4) Use public office for private gain.

5) Conduct any private activity that might give rise to the appearance of a conflict with official status or responsibilities.

Section 11 Administrative Instructions

The interim Minister may issue Administrative Instructions, not inconsistent with Iraqi law or any CPA Order, Regulation, or Memorandum, as the interim Minister deems necessary to carry out the duties described in this Order.

Section 12 Entry into Force

This Order shall enter into force on the date of signature [21 March 2004].

Document 92

Coalition Provisional Authority Order Number 68

CPA/ORD/4 April 2004/68

Ministerial Committee for National Security

Pursuant to my authority as Administrator of the Coalition Provisional Authority (CPA), and under the laws and usages of war, and consistent with relevant U.N. Security Council resolutions, including Resolutions 1483 and 1511 (2003),

Recalling that U.N. Security Council Resolution 1483 (2003) calls upon the CPA to promote the welfare of the Iraqi people through the effective administration of the territory, including in particular working towards the restoration of conditions of security and stability and the creation of conditions in which the Iraqi people can freely determine their own political future,

Noting the adoption of the Law of Administration for the State of Iraq for the Transition Period on March 8, 2004,[215]

Acknowledging the need to have consistent access to high quality, impartial assessments of Iraqi national security interests from an Iraqi perspective,

Recognizing the immediate need for structures to coordinate the work of the various agencies and Ministries charged with protecting and advancing the national security interests of Iraq particularly in defining policies to counter the threat of terrorism,

I hereby promulgate the following:

[215] See *Doc 511*.

Section 1 Establishment

1) The Ministerial Committee for National Security (MCNS) is hereby established. The role of the MCNS is to facilitate and coordinate national security policy among the Ministries and agencies of the Iraqi government tasked with national security issues. It is the primary forum for Ministerial-level decision making on these issues.

2) The MCNS shall operate under the authority, direction, and control of the Administrator of the CPA, and shall be chaired by the Administrator pending transfer of full governance authority to the Iraqi Interim Government. Upon transfer of authority to such a government, the MCNS will be chaired by the head of the Iraqi Interim Government (which, for the purposes of this Order, shall be the senior civilian head of the Iraqi Interim Government with national command authority as set forth in the Annex to the Law of Administration for the State of Iraq for the Transitional Period). Upon the formation of the Iraqi Transitional Government and dissolution of the Iraqi Interim Government, the MCNS will be chaired by the Prime Minister in accordance with Article 39 of the Law of Administration for the State of Iraq for the Transitional Period.

Section 2 Membership of the Ministerial Committee for National Security

1) The permanent members of the MCNS shall be the Administrator of the CPA (until such time as full governance authority is transferred to the Iraqi Interim Government, after which time it shall be the individual serving as Chair in accordance with Section 1.2), the Minister of Defence, the Minister of Interior, the Minister of Foreign Affairs, the Minister of Justice, and the Minister of Finance. Other Ministries may also participate in specific meetings at the request of the Chair. In the event a Minister is unable to participate due to travel or disability, a deputy or other designated senior ministry official may represent him or her. Until such time as all relevant Ministers are named, the senior representative of the relevant ministry may serve on the MCNS.

2) The MCNS shall also include, as permanent advisory members, the Senior Military Advisor, the Director General of the Iraqi National Intelligence Service, and the National Security Advisor.

3) The Commander of the Multinational Force operating in Iraq pursuant to United Nations Security Council Resolution 1511, and any relevant subsequent resolutions, maybe invited to attend and participate in meetings of the MCNS.

Section 3 The National Security Advisor

1) There is hereby established the position of National Security Advisor. The National Security Advisor is the primary advisor to the Administrator and the MCNS on national security matters, and shall manage and supervise the National Advisory Staff.

2) The National Security Advisor will be appointed by the Administrator, after consultation with the Governing Council. Upon formation of the elected Iraqi Transitional Government, the Prime Minister may chose either to retain the interim National Security Advisor or to name a new one.

3) The National Security Advisor appointed or retained by the Prime Minister of the Iraqi Transitional Government, and each of such National Security Advisor's successors, shall be appointed for a set term of five years. The National Security Advisor may be removed from office only for cause. 'Cause' shall include, but shall not be limited to, malfeasance, abuse of office, and bribery.

Section 4 The National Security Advisory Staff

1) The MCNS shall be supported by a staff of civil servants and military personnel detailed from Ministries and agencies (to include the INIS) represented on the MCNS, as well as up to five additional civil service staff hired specifically for this purpose. The total staff shall not comprise more than 20 personnel at any given time.

2) Civil service employees hired specifically to work on the National Security Advisory Staff shall be hired and employed in accordance with Iraqi law, as amended by CPA Orders, Regulations, and Memoranda. Such hiring and employment shall be consistent with CPA Order Number 1[216] and any authorized implementation thereof.

3) Salaries of civil service employees hired specifically to work on the National Security Advisory Staff shall conform to the salary structure applicable to Iraqi government employees.

4) The National Security Advisory Staff shall be considered a 'Public Security Sector Organization' for purposes of CPA Order Number 63.[217]

a) A civil service employee detailed or specifically hired to work on the National Security Advisory Staff who meets the definition of 'Eligible Employee' shall be entitled to death and disability benefits in accordance with Section 2.2 of CPA Order Number 63. For purposes of application of the Section 4.4(a), a civil service staff member detailed to work on the National Security Advisory Staff shall deemed to be employed by that office.

b) If by virtue of being an employee of the detailing Ministry or agency a detailed civil service member would be entitled to a greater death or disability benefit than that specified in Section 4.4(a) above, then the employee shall be entitled to the greater benefit.

c) Military personnel detailed to the National Security Advisory Staff shall continue to qualify for death and disability benefits as employees of the Ministry of Defence.

Section 5 Entry into Force

This Order shall enter into force on the date of signature [4 April 2004].

Document 93

Coalition Provisional Authority Order Number 69

CPA/ORD/1 April 2004/69

Delegation of Authority to Establish the Iraqi National Intelligence Service

Pursuant to my authority as Administrator of the Coalition Provisional Authority (CPA), and under the laws and usages of war, and consistent with relevant U.N. Security Council resolutions, including Resolutions 1483 and 1511 (2003),

Recalling that U.N. Security Council Resolution 1483 (2003) calls upon the CPA to promote the welfare of the Iraqi people through the effective administration of the territory,

[216] See *Doc 14*.
[217] See *Doc 86*.

including in particular working towards the restoration of conditions of security and stability,

Noting that CPA Order Number 2, Dissolution of Entities, May 23, 2003, as amended,[218] dissolved the Iraqi Intelligence Service,

Further noting the adoption of the Law of Administration for the State of Iraq for the Transitional Period on March 8, 2004,

Acknowledging that timely and accurate information about terrorism, domestic insurgency, espionage, narcotics production and trafficking, weapons of mass destruction, serious organized crime and other issues related to the national defense or threats to Iraqi democracy is essential to the security of Iraq,

Recognizing the need to establish a new national intelligence service to collect, analyze, and disseminate accurate and timely information related to the national defense and other threats to the security of Iraq,

I hereby promulgate the following:

Section 1 Delegation of Authority

1) The Governing Council is hereby authorized to establish a new Iraqi National Intelligence Service (INIS) by promulgating a statute on or before April 3, 2004, adopting the Charter for the INIS, the substance of which has been discussed between the Governing Council and the CPA and the proposed provisions of which are set forth in Appendix A. The INIS will be a wholly distinct and separate entity from any intelligence services that have previously existed in Iraq, to include the Iraqi Intelligence Service that was dissolved by CPA Order Number 2.

2) All references in the Charter to actions, authorities, and responsibilities to be exercised or performed by any organ of the Iraqi Government under the Law of Administration for the State of Iraq for the Transitional Period shall be deemed to refer to the Administrator of the CPA, pending transfer of full governance authority to the Iraqi Interim Government.

3) Upon promulgation of a statute adopting the Charter, the Administrator of the CPA, in consultation with the Governing Council, shall appoint an interim Director General of the INIS. The interim Director General shall report directly to the Administrator until such time as full governance authority is transferred to the Iraqi Interim Government, after which time the Director General shall report directly to the head of government.

a) Upon formation of the elected Iraqi Transitional Government, the Prime Minister may choose either to retain the interim Director General or to name a new one.
b) The Director General appointed or retained by the Prime Minister of the Iraqi Transitional Government, and each of such Director General's successors, shall be appointed for a set term of five years in accordance with the Charter.

Section 2 Terms and Conditions

The authority delegated under Section 1.1 of this Order shall be subject to the following terms and conditions:

1) In the event of a conflict between any promulgation by the Governing Council and any promulgation of the CPA, the promulgation of the CPA shall prevail.

2) The INIS shall work with the Ministry of Finance to develop its budget and, notwithstanding any existing salary scales applicable to Iraqi government employees, to establish a salary scale for INIS employees.

[218] See *Doc 15.*

3) The INIS shall be considered a 'Public Security Sector Organization' for purposes of CPA Order Number 63.[219] Unless otherwise specified in the Charter, an INIS employee who meets the definition of 'Eligible Employee,' as defined in CPA Order Number 63, shall be entitled to death and disability benefits equivalent to those afforded to members of the Iraqi Armed Forces in accordance with Section 2.2 of that Order.

4) The Administrator reserves the authority to alter the statute establishing the INIS and adopting the INIS Charter or any rules or regulations promulgated by the INIS, if required to provide for the safety and security of Coalition Forces or the Iraqi people.[220]

5) The Charter for the INIS shall provide that the Administrator shall appoint an Inspector General to the INIS, who shall possess the authorities and perform the responsibilities of Inspectors General as set forth in CPA Order No. 57, Iraqi Inspectors General, 10 February 2004,[221] consistent with significant national security interests.[222]

Section 3 Entry into Force

This Order shall enter into force on the date of signature [Signed without date].

APPENDIX A:
CHARTER FOR THE IRAQI NATIONAL INTELLIGENCE SERVICE
Chapter One – Preamble

Article 1.

This charter establishes the Iraqi National Intelligence Service (INIS or the Service).

Article 2.

All activities of the Iraqi National Intelligence Service will be conducted in accordance with the Law of Administration for the State of Iraq for the Transitional Period, signed March 8, 2004, and other laws of Iraq. At such time as the permanent Constitution of Iraq is adopted, the activities of the Service will be conducted in accordance with that constitution.

Article 3.

Timely and accurate information about terrorism, domestic insurgency, espionage, narcotics production and trafficking, weapons of mass destruction, serious organized crime and other issues related to the national defense or threats to Iraqi democracy is essential to the security of Iraq. All reasonable and lawful means must be used to ensure that Iraq will receive the best intelligence available. For that purpose, the INIS will collect, analyze and disseminate this intelligence in a vigorous and responsible manner. The principles set forth in this Charter are designed to achieve the proper balance between the work of the INIS and protection of individual rights and liberties.

Chapter Two – Authorities and Responsibilities

Article 4.

The Iraqi National Intelligence Service has the authority to collect intelligence and conduct related intelligence activities regarding:

[219] See *Doc 86*.
[220] Sec 2(4) was rescinded by CPA Order No 100, sec 3(25)(a) *[Doc 124]*.
[221] See *Doc 80*.
[222] Sec 2(5) was amended by CPA Order No 100, sec 3(25)(b) *[Doc 124]*.

- Threats to the national security of Iraq.
- Terrorism and insurgency.
- Proliferation of weapons of mass destruction, narcotics production and trafficking, and serious organized crime.
- Espionage and other acts threatening to Iraqi democracy.

Intelligence collected under this article may be disseminated to appropriate government entities both within and outside of Iraq. Any other dissemination of intelligence will be strictly limited to what is essential to the national security of Iraq. All intelligence activities will be strictly required to further national security, and will be subject to the oversight provisions of this Charter.

Article 5.
The INIS will take no action to further or undermine the interests of any legal Iraqi political party or of any official within the Iraqi government.

Article 6.
The INIS will take no action to further or undermine the interests of any Iraqi citizen or group based on race, religion, sect, gender, language, origin or tribal affiliation.

Article 7.
The Service will conduct its activities in accordance with the fundamental freedoms and human rights contained in and protected by the Law of Administration for the State of Iraq for the Transitional Period, and in the permanent Constitution when adopted.

Article 8.
The Service will provide objective, accurate and timely information to relevant government entities and policy makers.

Article 9.
The Service will protect the security of its activities, information, members and property by appropriate means, including investigations of applicants, employees and contractors as necessary.

Article 10.
The Service may conduct administrative support activities needed to perform its functions.

Article 11.
The Service shall provide intelligence support and coordination to Iraqi military forces in furtherance of national security.

Chapter Three – Relations with Law Enforcement

Article 12.
The INIS shall have no power to arrest or detain persons. The Service may provide intelligence support and coordination to Iraqi law enforcement authorities not precluded by other law.

Article 13.
When a member of the Service becomes aware of a possible serious violation of Iraqi criminal law, it will be reported by the Service to the appropriately authorized government authority. The report shall be made in a manner consistent with the protection of classified information. The handling of this information by a law enforcement authority will also be done in a manner, approved by the Director General of the Service, which protects classified information. Upon receipt of this report, the Governorate authority will refer the matter, as appropriate, for prosecution in the court having jurisdiction over the offense. Prior to the passage of legislation governing the protection of classified information in any court, this information will be protected pursuant to procedures adopted by the Higher Juridical Council and approved by the Director General of the INIS.

Chapter Four – Director General of the INIS

Article 14.
The head of government shall appoint the Director General of the INIS, subject to confirmation by the body vested with national legislative authority. This appointment shall be made on the basis of integrity, compliance with the security standards of the Service, and demonstrated ability in government administration and national security issues. The Director General will serve for a period of five years.

Article 15.
The Director General of the Service shall:

- Act as the principal adviser to the head of government and the Council of Ministers for intelligence matters related to the national security. This will include serving in an advisory role on all ministerial level executive branch structures relating to national security policy, intelligence policy, and other issues as might be deemed relevant by the Government of Iraq.
- Have responsibility for the collection, analysis, production and dissemination of intelligence, which should be objective and independent of political, racial, religious, gender, language or origin or tribal considerations, and is otherwise subject to Articles 5, 6 and 7 above.
- Coordinate all intelligence activities of the Iraqi Government institutions.
- Ensure that no information is obtained by the Service except so far as necessary for the proper discharge of its responsibilities as set out in Article 4 above, and that no information is disclosed by it except for the purposes set out in Articles 4, 8, 11, and 12 above.
- Protect intelligence sources and methods and other classified information from disclosure without lawful authority.
- Make an annual report on the work of the Service to the Council of Ministers and may at any time report to the head of government on any matter relating to its work.
- Promulgate such rules and regulations, consistent with the Charter, as are necessary to carry out the functions of the INIS. The application of such rules and regulations to specific citizens is subject to judicial review by courts of competent jurisdiction.

Article 16.
The Director General will have:

- Authority to appoint members to the Service.

- Authority, notwithstanding the provision of any other law, in his discretion to terminate the employment of any member of the Service whenever he deems it necessary or advisable in the interest of national security. This authority may not be exercised in violation of the Law of Administration for the State of Iraq for the Transitional Period or the permanent Constitution, when adopted.
- Authority to enter into relationships and intelligence activities with intelligence and security agencies of foreign governments in furtherance of the authorities specified in Article 4 of this charter.

Article 17.
To assist the Director General in carrying out the Director General's responsibilities under this charter, there shall be a Deputy Director General of the INIS, who shall be appointed in the same manner and who shall act for, and exercise the powers of, the Director General during his absence or disability.

Chapter Five – Protection for INIS Information

Article 18.
In the interests of the national security of Iraq and in furtherance of the Director General's responsibility to protect classified information from disclosure without lawful authority, the INIS will be exempt from any Iraqi laws requiring public disclosure of the organization, functions, names, titles, salaries or numbers of personnel employed by the Service. Service members (for purposes of this charter, service members include employees and contractors) must protect official secrets, and will sign a secrecy agreement as a condition of employment.

This secrecy agreement will include the requirement for pre-approval by the Service of any writing or electronic dissemination outside officially sanctioned channels that may contain classified information. This obligation does not cease when the member is no longer employed by or under contract with the Service.

Article 19.
A person who is or has been a member of the INIS, or who otherwise has been given access to classified information, and who communicates any such information to a person to whom he knows that the information ought not to be communicated, shall be punished in accordance with the Iraqi penal code. In addition, a member of INIS who commits such an offense will be subject to appropriate disciplinary action by the Service, including dismissal from INIS.

Chapter Six – Inspector General

Article 20.
The head of government shall appoint an Inspector General for the INIS whose responsibility it is to conduct inspections of Service activities. The appointment of the Inspector General shall be made without regard to political affiliation (consistent with applicable de-Ba'athification policy) and on the basis of integrity, capability for strong leadership, compliance with the security standards of the Service, expertise in national security issues, and demonstrated ability in accounting, auditing, financial analysis, law, management

analysis, public administration, investigation, criminal justice administration, or other closely related fields. In addition, the Inspector General should possess demonstrated knowledge, skills, abilities and experience in conducting audits and investigations.

Article 21.
It is the responsibility of the Inspector General to:

- Establish an effective program of audit, investigation and performance review to provide increased accountability, integrity and oversight of the INIS and to prevent, deter and identify waste, fraud, abuse of authority and illegal acts.
- Conduct investigations, audits, evaluations, inspections and other reviews in accordance with generally accepted professional standards.
- Report findings and recommend corrective actions directly to the Director General, except in cases involving allegations of misconduct by the Director General, in which case he shall report his findings and recommendations directly to the head of government.
- Monitor the progress of any corrective actions ordered by the Director General.
- Protect classified information in any report or recommendation that he makes.
- Subject to the policies of the Director General, select other employees of the Service to assist him in carrying out his functions.

Article 22.
The Inspector General will have access to Service members and records which relate to the activities being inspected. The Director General may prohibit the Inspector General from initiating, carrying out or completing any inspection or financial audit, except in cases involving allegations of misconduct by the Director General, if the Director General believes it is necessary to protect significant national security interests. The Director General must report this action to the head of government within one week.

Chapter Seven – Legislative Oversight

Article 23.
During the transitional period (which shall be defined to mean the period described in Article 2(A) of the Law of Administration for the State of Iraq for the Transitional Period), legislative oversight of the INIS will be carried out by a committee of the body vested with national legislative authority. Following the adoption of a permanent constitution, this oversight will be carried out by one committee of the body vested with national legislative authority.

Article 24.
The Committee will consist of a suitable number of members appointed by the body vested with national legislative authority from among its members. Its function is to examine the expenditures, administration and policy of the Service. The Committee may request information regarding specific activities of the INIS. To the maximum extent practicable, and consistent with national security interests, the Director General of the INIS, with the approval of the head of government, shall provide information to the Committee on such activities.

Article 25.
The Committee shall make an annual report on the discharge of its functions to the head of government and may at any time report to him on any matter relating to the discharge

of those functions. The head of government will present to the body vested with national legislative authority a copy of each annual report made by the Committee. If it appears to the head of government, after consultation with the Committee, that the publication of any matter in a report would be prejudicial to the continued discharge of the functions of the Service, the head of government may exclude that matter from the copy of the report presented to the body vested with national legislative authority. The report will contain a statement as to whether any matter has been excluded from the report.

Article 26.
The Committee will establish written procedures to protect all classified information that is furnished to the Committee from disclosure without lawful authority. These procedures shall be approved by the Director General of the INIS. No staff officer of the Committee may be given access to any classified information unless the officer has (1) agreed in writing and under oath to be bound by the security rules of the Committee both during and after his employment with the Committee, and (2) received a security clearance as determined by the Committee and approved by the Director General of the Service.

Chapter Eight – Collection of Information

Article 27.
The Service is authorized to collect, retain and disseminate to other government entities and for other lawful governmental purposes information concerning citizens of Iraq only in accordance with written regulations established by the Director General and approved by the Minister of Justice. These procedures shall permit collection, retention and dissemination of the following types of information:

- Information that is publicly available or collected with the consent of the person concerned.
- Information for the purposes of a lawful counter-terrorist, counterinsurgency, counter-proliferation, counter-narcotics, counterintelligence or other activity to protect against threats to Iraqi democracy.
- Information needed to protect intelligence sources and methods from disclosure without lawful authority.
- Information concerning persons who are reasonably believed to be potential sources or contacts of the Service for the purpose of determining their suitability or credibility.
- Information arising out of a lawful personnel, physical or communications security investigation.
- Information obtained that may indicate involvement in activities that may violate Iraqi or foreign laws.
- Information necessary for administrative purposes.

Article 28.
Entry on or interference with property or interception of communications by the Service will be done only in accordance with minimization standards that are designed to minimize the unintentional acquisition, retention and dissemination of information about citizens of Iraq that is not of value in its work on national security, including serious organized crime issues. The INIS will use these techniques upon approval of the Director General or Acting Director General. In addition, for Service activities, the advance authorization of a judge,

who is approved by the Higher Juridical Council, will be obtained in the form of a warrant to conduct the technique. This warrant will be valid for a period of no longer than ninety days, at which time it may be renewed by the judge, if sufficient cause continues to exist. If the action authorized is no longer necessary before the end of the period authorized by the warrant, the Service will end the use of the technique immediately. A warrant will be issued only where the judge finds that the warrant is likely to provide information relating to national security, including serious organized crime, and where the information cannot reasonably be obtained by other means.

Chapter Nine – Organization and Administration

Article 29.
The Service will have the necessary number of offices within the Governorates, in addition to its central office in Baghdad. The number and structure of offices will be determined upon proposal by the Director General, and approved by the head of government. All offices will follow the directives of the Director General.

Article 30.
The Director General will issue regulations for the administration of the Service. These will include security, training, disciplinary proceedings and other personnel matters, logistics, and other issues of importance within the Service.

Article 31.
The Service shall enjoy a juridical personality legally represented by the Director General of the INIS, or the acting Director General, or other Service member authorized by the Director General.

Article 32.
The Service may contract with other persons and institutions to perform tasks related to the authorized functions of the Service, in accordance with appropriate security standards established by the Director General.

Chapter Ten – Coordination with Government Entities

Article 33.
Other ministries and government entities shall cooperate with and assist the Service in performing its duties regarding national security, including serious organized crime, unless otherwise prohibited by law.

Article 34.
The Service will disseminate, as appropriate, to other ministries and government entities the results of its analysis. This will be done on a timely basis and consistent with the protection of classified information. The service may also provide expert assistance unless otherwise precluded by law.

Chapter Eleven – Duties and Rights of Service Members

Article 35.
Laws and other regulations regarding employment, medical care, pension, disability insurance and other issues involving civil servants shall apply to the INIS unless otherwise regulated by this charter.

Article 36.
In addition to general conditions for employment that apply to civil servants, the Director General of the Service may establish conditions for service members regarding expertise, health, work assignments, and security requirements that are consistent with the interests of the national security of Iraq. The terms and conditions will be issued after consultation with the head of government.

Article 37.
The Director General, or those to whom he has delegated this responsibility, may issue a disciplinary order against a member who is found to have violated service terms and conditions or orders. Disciplinary proceedings will be conducted in accordance with written terms and conditions issued by the Director General.

Article 38.
The Director General will issue a code of conduct for Service members.

Article 39.
A Service member cannot be a member of the body vested with national legislative authority or hold other political office, run for political office, or publicly campaign on behalf of political candidates.

Article 40.
A Service member who is disabled due to illness or injury received in the line of duty and not due to misconduct will continue to receive his salary during the period of disability or until otherwise eligible for retirement, whichever occurs first.

Article 41.
If a Service member is acting within the scope of his duties and does not misuse his governmental position, the Service member will not be subject to legal liability for the performance of his governmental actions. If brought before a court for actions performed in the line of duty, the Service member will be provided legal counsel by the Service, unless the member was acting outside the scope of his duties or otherwise misused his governmental position. This article applies during the member's employment by the Service and continues even after that employment has ended.

Article 42.
Pursuant to written regulations issued by the Director General, in consultation with the Minister of Interior, and after appropriate training, the Director General may authorize service members to carry a weapon in the performance of their duties, and use reasonable force to protect the service member or others against death or serious physical injury.

Chapter Twelve – Charter Approval

Article 43.
This charter for the Iraqi National Intelligence Service will take effect upon adoption by the Iraqi Governing Council in accordance with the authority delegated to it by the Administrator of the Coalition Provisional Authority.

Article 44.
This Charter can be amended by the majority vote of the body vested with national legislative authority.

Document 94
Coalition Provisional Authority Order Number 70
CPA/ORD/3 April 2004/70

Amendments to Reconstruction Levy

Pursuant to my authority as Administrator of the Coalition Provisional Authority (CPA), and under the laws and usages of war, and consistent with relevant U.N. Security Council resolutions, including Resolutions 1483 and 1511 (2003),

Recognizing that the effective administration of Iraq requires funding for improvements to its infrastructure and capital public investment,

Noting that the reconstruction levy was imposed under CPA Order Number 38,[223]

Noting that the effective date for imposition of the reconstruction levy was delayed until March 1, 2004, pursuant to CPA Order Number 47,[224]

Noting further that the effective date for imposition of the reconstruction levy was again delayed until April 1, 2004, pursuant to CPA Order Number 54, Section 7,[225]

Determined that the collection of said levy be undertaken efficiently and effectively without disrupting trade relations or impeding reconstruction efforts or import flow,

I hereby promulgate the following:

Section 1 Amendments

1) Coalition Provisional Authority Order Number 38 (CPA/ORD/19 September 2003/38), Reconstruction Levy, Section 1, Article 4, is amended to read in its entirety as follows:

> '4) Unless exempted under this Order, the Reconstruction Levy shall be imposed on all goods imported into Iraq from all countries beginning April 15, 2004.'

2) Coalition Provisional Authority Order Number 54 (CPA/ORD/24 February 2004/54), Trade Liberalization Policy 2004, is hereby amended by deleting Section 7 in its entirety and redesignating existing Section 8 as Section 7.

Section 2 Rescission
CPA Order Number 47 (CPA/ORD/31 December 2003/47), Amendment to Coalition Provisional Authority Order Number 38, is hereby rescinded.

[223] See *Doc 59*.
[224] See *Doc 69*.
[225] See *Doc* 76.

Section 3 Entry into Force
This Order shall enter into force on the date of signature [9 April 2004].

Document 95
Coalition Provisional Authority Order Number 71
CPA/ORD/6 April 2004/71

Local Governmental Powers

Pursuant to my authority as Administrator of the Coalition Provisional Authority (CPA), and under the laws and usages of war, and consistent with relevant U.N. Security Council resolutions, including Resolutions 1483 and 1511 (2003),

Recalling that the CPA has recognized the Governing Council as the principal body of the Iraqi interim administration, pending the establishment of an internationally recognized, representative government by the people of Iraq, consistent with Resolutions 1483 and 1511, and that the Governing Council, in performing its functions on behalf of the people of Iraq, has appointed Interim Ministers to exercise responsibility for the daily administration of the Iraqi Ministries,

Recalling the adoption of the Transitional Administrative Law (TAL) on 8 March 2004 to govern the affairs of Iraq during the transitional period from 30 June 2004 until a duly elected government, operating under a permanent and legitimate constitution achieving full democracy shall come into being,

Noting that the system of government in Iraq shall be republican, federal, democratic, and pluralistic, and powers shall be shared between the federal government and the regional governments, governorates (also known as provinces), municipalities, and local administrations and that each Governorate shall have the right to form a Governorate Council, name a Governor and form municipal and local councils and that regions and governorates shall be organized on the basis of the principle of de-centralization and the devolution of authorities to municipal and local governments,

Recognizing the Kurdistan Regional Government as the official government of the territories that were administered by that government on 19 March 2003 in the governorates of Dohuk, Arbil, Sulaimaniya, Kirkuk, Diyala and Ninevah, and its right to continue its current functions throughout the transitional period, except with regard to those issues which fall within the exclusive competence of the federal government,

Emphasizing that, consistent with Resolution 1483, the Governing Council and the CPA, each in coordination with the United Nations, are dedicated to working together in a cooperative and consultative process for the benefit of the Iraqi people,

I hereby promulgate the following:

Section 1 Purpose
This Order describes the authorities and responsibilities of the governorate, municipal and local levels of government. It implements the principle of decentralization of governing power embodied in the TAL. By appropriately empowering government bodies at the governorate, municipal and local levels, the Order is designed to improve the delivery of public services to the Iraqi people and make the Iraqi government more responsive to their

needs. This Order encourages the exercise of local authority by local officials in every region and governorate; recognizes the Kurdistan Regional Government; and shall have no effect on the administration of the territories under that government's jurisdiction on 19 March 2003 in the governorates of Dohuk, Arbil, Sulaimaniya, Kirkuk, Diyala and Ninevah.

Section 2 Governorate Councils

1) Each Governorate may form a Governorate Council, which shall be funded from national budget allocations that are separate from the budgets of the ministries and other national institutions.

2) The Governorate Councils may set priorities for the provinces; amend, by two-thirds vote, a specific local project described in an annual ministry budget plan, provided that no such amendment shall increase the spending limits set forth in the ministry plans, or interfere with the efficient and uniform execution of national objectives as implemented by specific programs; monitor and recommend improvements in the delivery of public services; represent the concerns of constituents; independently generate and collect revenues by imposing taxes and fees; organize the operations of the provincial administration; initiate and implement provincial projects alone or in partnership with international and non-governmental organizations; and conduct other activities, consistent with applicable laws.

3) Governorate Councils shall perform their responsibilities independently from the control or supervision of any ministry. Governorate Councils may, by majority vote, and within two weeks following the appointment, approve or veto the appointment by the ministries of Directors General and local ministerial officials for positions designated as 'senior positions' by the Administrator (which designations shall be set forth in an appendix to this Order);[226] establish subcommittees and convene meetings of, or request reports and testimony from, the Directors General; and remove Directors General and officials occupying designated 'senior positions' for cause as defined in this Order, by a two thirds vote for removal, provided that Directors General whose official responsibilities directly affect more than one province may be removed only if each of the Governorate Councils responsible for the provinces so affected votes for removal as specified herein. As used in this Order, the term 'Director General' shall not apply to the Presidents of Universities in Iraq.[227]

4) The members of each Governorate Council shall be selected in accordance with criteria agreed upon by the Governing Council and CPA. All individuals who hold office as Governorate Council members on the effective date of this Order shall continue to hold such office. Should vacancies occur Governorate Councils may add new members who meet the eligibility requirements set forth in Article 31 of the TAL, through a fair, open and competitive selection process agreed to by two thirds majority of the Governorate Council. Elections for Governorate Councils will take place at the same time as elections for the National Assembly, no later than 31 January 2005.[228]

5) The Governorate Councils are hereby authorized to select and appoint Governors and Deputy Governors. Governors and Deputy Governors selected by Governorate Councils prior to the date of this Order are hereby appointed. The Governorate Councils may remove Governors and Deputy Governors for cause as specified in this Order, upon a two-thirds vote. Should vacancies in the positions of Governor or Deputy Governor occur, Governorate Councils may elect a new Governor or Deputy Governor through majority vote of the Council.

[226] The Appendix is not available.
[227] Sec 2(3) was amended by CPA Order No 100, sec 3(26)(a) *[Doc 124]*.
[228] Sec 2(4) was rescinded by CPA Order No 100, sec 3(26)(b) *[Doc 124]*.

Section 3 Governors and Deputy Governors

1) The Governor is the head civil official of a Governorate and is accountable to the Governorate Council. The Governor shall direct, coordinate and oversee actions in implementation of the Governorate Council's decisions. The Governor shall be selected, dismissed and replaced in accordance with subsection 2(5) of this Order.

2) The Deputy Governors report to the Governor and the most senior Deputy Governor (based on length of public service) shall assume the role of the Governor in the latter's absence.

3) Governors and Deputy Governors may attend the regular meetings of the Governorate Councils as non-voting members.

4) Governors shall appoint governorate officials, provided that their appointments of Directors General serving directly on the governorate staff and other senior positions, as defined by the Administrator, shall be subject to the approval by majority vote of the Governorate Councils within two weeks following the appointment, except for Directors General, who shall be appointed and removed as specified in Section 2(3) of this Order. Governors shall exercise final authority to remove those officials who they are authorized to appoint, subject to the concurrence, by majority vote, of the Governorate Council.

5) To encourage consistent development and application of policies regarding regional matters, Governors shall regularly coordinate with each other on matters of common interest.[229]

Section 4 Local Councils

1) Each Governorate may, by majority vote, form sub-provincial regional councils, municipal councils and other relevant local councils organized geographically, such as *Qada'* and *Nahiya*, City Councils, Beladiya Councils and Hayy Councils, as necessary to achieve greater efficiency and economies of scale in coordinating the provision of public services, and to facilitate unified and coordinated administration of cities. Local councils are responsible for representing their constituents; ensuring that public services respond to local needs; organizing the operations of the local administration; reviewing local ministry plans; collecting and retaining local revenues, taxes and fees; identifying local budgetary requirements through the national budgeting process; and recommending appropriate action to Governorate Councils with respect to government officials, on the basis of misconduct, inefficiency or Ba'athist Party affiliation. They shall assist in initiating and implementing local projects alone or in conjunction with international and non-governmental organizations; and conducting other activities as are granted to them by Governorate Councils, consistent with applicable law.

2) The members of each local council, including the Chair, shall be selected in accordance with regulations approved by majority vote of the Governorate Council. All local councils in existence on the date of this Order, and all individuals who hold office as members of such councils of the date of this Order, shall continue to exist and hold office unless removed in accordance with this Order.

3) Local councils shall, by majority vote, elect Mayors and Deputy Mayors. Mayors and Deputy Mayors selected by local councils prior to the date of this Order shall continue to hold office, unless removed in accordance with this Order. Local councils may remove Mayors and Deputy Mayors upon a two-thirds vote. Should vacancies occur in the

[229] Sec 3 was amended by CPA Order No 100, sec 3(26)(c)–(e) *[Doc 124]*.

positions of Mayor or Deputy Mayor, local councils may elect a new Mayor or Deputy Mayor through majority vote of the council.

Section 5 Mayors and Deputy Mayors

1) Mayors (in Arabic 'Mudeer al-Nahia,' 'Qa'im Maqam,' and 'Ameen') are the senior administrators of local councils and are accountable to the local council. Mayors shall direct, coordinate and oversee actions in implementation of decisions of the local councils, and shall serve as the primary liaison between the local councils and the Governors.

2) Mayors shall be elected and removed pursuant to section 4(3) of this Order.

3) The Deputy Mayors report to the Mayor and the most senior Deputy Mayor (based on length of public service) shall assume the role of the Mayor in the absence of the latter official.

4) Mayors and Deputy Mayors may attend the regular meetings of the local councils as nonvoting members.

5) Mayors shall appoint local government officials, provided that their appointments of Directors General serving directly on the local government staff and other senior positions, as defined by the Administrator, shall be subject to the approval, by majority vote, of the local council, within two weeks following the appointment. Mayors may, for cause as defined under this Order, remove those officials whom they are authorized to appoint, subject to the concurrence, by majority vote, of the local council.

6) Mayors shall meet regularly with all Directors General within their geographic areas of responsibility to monitor, and where authorized by applicable laws and regulations to direct, the delivery of public services.

7) Mayors shall meet regularly with other Mayors to ensure that services are being provided equitably and efficiently.

Section 6 Chiefs of Police

1) Within each Governorate, there shall be a Chief of Police, responsible for overseeing all civil law enforcement activities within the Governorate.

2) Chief of Police vacancies will be advertised nationally by the Ministry of Interior and the Governorate Council shall be notified of such vacancies. Applications for Chief of Police positions shall be sent to the Ministry of Interior, which shall identify fully qualified applicants and provide the names of those applicants to the Governorate Council in a timely manner. The Governorate Council shall, upon a majority vote within two weeks following its receipt of the names of fully qualified applicants from the Ministry of Interior, select the most suitable candidate from these nominees. Chiefs of Police shall be appointed to a 3-year term, which may be renewed.

3) Chiefs of Police may be removed by the Minister of Interior, or by the Governorate Council upon two-thirds majority vote, for cause as defined in this Order.

4) Under the supervision of the Minister of Interior, the Chief of Police shall prepare an annual policing plan that will take into account local and national priorities. The Governorate Council and Governor will ensure that the Chief of Police is responsive to local policing requirements. Annual policing plans shall become effective upon approval, by two-thirds majority, of the Governorate Council, which shall monitor the implementation of this plan by the Chief of Police. Chiefs of Police shall consult regularly with the relevant Governor and Governorate Council and shall meet weekly with the Governorate Council, or otherwise as agreed.

5) Local police chief vacancies will be advertised by the Ministry of Interior at least within the relevant Province, and the Governorate Council shall be notified of such vacancies. Applications for local police chief positions shall be sent to the Ministry of Interior, which shall identify fully qualified applicants and provide the names of those applicants to the Governorate Council in a timely manner. The Governorate Council shall, upon a majority vote, select the most suitable candidate from these nominees. Local police chiefs shall be appointed to a 3-year term, which may be renewed.

6) Local police chiefs may be removed by a two-thirds majority vote of the relevant Governorate Council for cause, as defined in this Order.

Section 7 Grounds for Removal

1) Members of Governorate Councils, Governors and Deputy Governors, members of Local Councils, Mayors and Deputy Mayors, Chiefs of Police and local police chiefs may be removed only for cause, in accordance with the procedures specified in this Order.

2) For purposes of this Order, 'cause' shall mean incapacity, serious misconduct in or out of office, dereliction of duty, or abuse of office.

3) Officials listed in section 7(1) of this order who are removed for cause as defined herein, and the subordinates of such officials who are removed in accordance with existing Iraqi law on similar grounds, shall be barred from holding any position in the Iraqi government for a period of five years following the removal.

4) Individuals who are removed from public office and barred from public service under section 7(2), above, shall have the right to bring suit in Iraqi courts and obtain redress in the form of reinstatement to public office, upon the court's determination that the removal was wrongful.

Section 8 Effect on Other Laws

1) Any provision of Iraqi law, including but not limited to Law No. 159 of 1969, that is inconsistent with this Order is hereby suspended to the extent of such inconsistency, provided, however, that nothing in this Order shall be construed to eliminate or reduce the authority of provincial or local government entities under existing Iraqi laws and regulations to generate, assess, collect, retain, administer or expend taxes, fees, assessments or similar revenues under existing Iraqi law, including Income of Municipalities Law, No. 130 of 1963, as amended. Notwithstanding existing Iraqi law, Governorates are hereby authorized to impose althma'am of no greater than 5 percent of the relevant taxes.

2) Except as otherwise specified in this Order, local government officials shall be hired and dismissed in accordance with applicable Iraqi law.

Section 9 Entry into Force

This Order shall enter into force on the date of signature [6 April 2004].[230]

[230] Sec 9 was re-designated sec 10 by CPA Order No 100, sec 3(26)(f) *[Doc 124]*, but no new sec 9 was added.

Document 96
Coalition Provisional Authority Order Number 72

CPA/ORD/10 June 2004/72

Iraqi Radioactive Source Regulatory Authority

Pursuant to my authority as Administrator of the Coalition Provisional Authority (CPA), and under the laws and usages of war, and consistent with relevant United Nations Security Council resolutions, including Resolutions 1483 and 1511 (2003),

Furthering paragraph 1 of Resolution 1483, appealing to member states and concerned organizations to assist the people of Iraq in their efforts to reform their institutions and rebuild their country, and to contribute to conditions of stability and security in Iraq,

Noting that United Nations Security Council Resolution 687 (1991) decides that Iraq shall unconditionally agree not to acquire or develop nuclear weapons or nuclear-weapons-usable material or any subsystems or components or any research, development, support or manufacturing facility related to the above,

Noting that United Nations Security Council Resolution 707 (1991) permits Iraq to use (radioactive) isotopes for medical, agricultural or industrial purposes,

Noting further the adoption of the Law of Administration for the State of Iraq for the Transitional Period on March 8, 2004,

Recalling that on September 8, 2003, the Board of Governors of the International Atomic Energy Agency approved a revised Code of Conduct on the Safety and Security of Radioactive Sources, IAEA/CODEOC/2004.

Recognizing that uses of ionizing radiation introduce important benefits in medicine, industry, agriculture, and related research, but that radiation exposure carries with it the potential to produce harmful effects in people and the environment, and

Determining to establish a national organization to regulate the use of radioactive sources and other radioactive materials in order to protect the health, security, and safety of human beings while permitting the beneficial uses of ionizing radiation,

I hereby promulgate the following:

Section 1 Establishment

1) The Iraqi Radioactive Source Regulatory Authority (hereinafter 'the IRSRA') is hereby established. The IRSRA shall be an independent agency.

2) The IRSRA shall have authority to regulate radioactive sources and all activities associated with exposure or the potential exposure to ionizing radiation from radioactive sources and radioactive waste, except those radioactive source activities and radioactive sources which are expressly excluded herein.

3) The IRSRA shall not have responsibility for radiological environmental monitoring or for regulating cleanup and remediation of the environment.

4) In carrying out its responsibilities, the IRSRA shall follow, to the extent practicable, the guidance in the International Atomic Energy Agency's Code of Conduct on the Safety and Security of Radioactive Sources and any revisions thereto.

5) All references herein to the Administrator of the CPA shall refer to the head of the Iraqi government following transfer of full governance authority to the Iraqi Interim Government.

Section 2 Purpose
The IRSRA shall promulgate and enforce regulations to allow for beneficial uses of radioactive sources, to provide for adequate protection of human beings against the harmful effects of ionizing radiation, and to ensure the safety and security of radioactive sources. The IRSRA shall also investigate technical issues associated with low level radioactive waste disposal.

Section 3 Definition of Radioactive Source
A radioactive source is radioactive material that is either permanently sealed in a capsule or closely bonded and in a solid form. For purposes of this Order, the term radioactive source will also be considered to include commercial radioisotopes in liquid form. The term will also include any radioactive material released if a sealed radioactive source is leaking or is broken or if a spill occurs in the case of liquid radioisotopes. For purposes of this Order, radioactive sources do not include nuclear material encapsulated for disposal, or nuclear material within the nuclear fuel cycles of research and power reactors.

Section 4 Chairman and Management Staff
1) The Chairman of the IRSRA shall initially be appointed by the Administrator of the CPA, after consultation with the Iraqi Interim Government, for a fixed term of two years. Thereafter, Chairmen of the IRSRA shall be appointed by the head of government for fixed terms of five years. The Chairman of the IRSRA shall be responsible for the overall management and operation of the IRSRA and shall report directly to the Administrator of the CPA.

2) The IRSRA shall be organized into such Divisions as necessary and appropriate to carry out its functions. Each Division shall be headed by a Division Manager reporting directly to the Chairman. Prior to transfer of full governance authority to the Iraqi Interim Government, Division Managers will be appointed by the Administrator of the CPA. Following transfer of full governance authority to the Iraqi Interim Government, Division Managers will be appointed by and serve at the pleasure of the Chairman.

Section 5 Budget and Funding
1) The IRSRA shall coordinate with the Ministry of Finance regarding its budget.

2) Following transfer of full governance authority to the Iraqi Interim Government, resources for staffing and staff training, acquisition and maintenance of facilities and equipment, and inspection costs for IRSRA shall be provided through the national fiscal process and reviewed annually.

Section 6 Salary and Employment Conditions
1) The IRSRA shall have the power to hire, employ and discharge personnel in accordance with Iraqi law, as amended by CPA Orders, Regulations, and Memoranda. Such hiring and employment shall be consistent with CPA Order Number 1[231] and any authorized implementation thereof.

2) Salaries of IRSRA personnel shall conform to the salary structure applicable to Iraqi national government employees.

[231] See *Doc 14*.

Section 7 Authority and Functions

1) The IRSRA is empowered to:

a) prepare laws and orders for approval by the Administrator of the CPA governing radioactive sources and activities associated therewith, and radioactive waste disposal. This shall include establishing radiation protection and radiation safety requirements in all areas except those involving long-term radiological environmental monitoring and cleanup or remediation of the environment;

b) issue regulations that govern the life cycle management of radioactive sources, as required to provide for public health, safety or security;

c) define radioactive sources that are excluded from regulatory requirements on the basis of their being not amenable to regulatory control;

d) establish and promulgate an application procedure and issue licenses (authorizations) for the possession and use of radioactive sources; grant exemptions and maintain appropriate records relating to applications, licenses and exemptions;

e) define in the regulations and authorizations the specific obligations to be placed on those who possess radioactive sources including, but not limited to the following:

i) financial conditions;

ii) inventory controls;

iii) appropriate radioactive source container markings;

iv) appropriate radiological work practices and work area controls;

v) use of traceable radioactive source identification markings;

f) conduct announced and unannounced inspections to assess radiation safety conditions and to assess compliance with applicable regulations and other requirements specified in authorizations to use radioactive sources,

g) take such action as necessary to enforce compliance with regulatory requirements and authorizations, and to protect the health and safety of workers and the public and to impose sanctions for non-compliance with IRSRA requirements subject to the maximum specified by the Administrator of the CPA or, following transfer of full governance authority, the government of Iraq;

h) levy fees for authorizations and inspections; all proceeds from fees shall be deposited in the general operating account of the IRSRA;

i) levy fines for non-compliance with applicable regulations and authorizations; all proceeds from fines shall be deposited in the general operating account of the Ministry of Finance;

j) respond to reports of orphan sources and assist in radiological emergencies;

k) advise other governmental authorities and organizations on matters within the competence of the IRSRA;

l) promote and carry out research on radiation safety issues of regulatory concern;

m) maintain contact for information exchange and cooperation with regulatory bodies of other countries and relevant international organizations, most importantly the IAEA; and

n) establish appropriate mechanisms to insure substantive public participation in the regulatory process, and to inform the public about the radiation safety aspects of regulated practices.

2) Duly authorized officials of the IRSRA and Ministry of the Environment are permitted access to premises and facilities in which radioactive sources are located in order to obtain information about the status of radiation safety and to verify compliance with regulatory requirements.

3) The IRSRA is authorized to engage consultants to serve as individual expert advisers or as members of its advisory committees as may be useful and appropriate for the IRSRA to discharge its responsibilities.

4) The IRSRA is authorized to communicate directly with CPA authorities, or following transfer of full governance authority, Iraqi government officials, in all cases in which this is considered necessary to exercise effectively the functions of the IRSRA.

Section 8 Prohibitions

Following transfer of full governance authority to the Iraqi Interim Government, no radioactive source activity shall be adopted or introduced, continued or discontinued or ceased, and no radioactive source shall, as applicable, be designed, manufactured, constructed or assembled, acquired, imported or exported, distributed, sold, loaned or hired, possessed, located, commissioned, used and operated, maintained or repaired, transferred or decommissioned, disassembled or transported, stored or disposed of, except in accordance with the requirements established by the IRSRA, unless the exposure from such activity is excluded from such requirements, or the activity or the source is exempted by the IRSRA from the requirements of the Regulations, including the requirements of notification and authorization.

Section 9 Relation to Other Laws and Organizations

1) In the event that other laws governing occupational, public, medical, or environmental protection and safety under the control of other regulatory bodies also address the use of ionizing radiation, the IRSRA and other such regulatory bodies are encouraged to enter into agreements for cooperation and coordination to avoid gaps or overlap in regulatory control while discharging respective responsibilities. If appropriate agreements cannot be developed to the mutual satisfaction of the agencies involved, the issues will be directed to the Administrator of the CPA for resolution.

2) A permanent mechanism for information exchange and cooperation shall be established between the IRSRA and Ministry of the Interior, Department of Border Enforcement, to ensure adequate control over radioactive sources entering and leaving the country and proper identification and authorization of the persons importing or receiving and exporting or sending the radioactive sources.

3) A permanent mechanism for information exchange, reporting and cooperation shall be established between the IRSRA and appropriate authorities within the Ministry of the Environment to ensure clear delineation of authority and responsibility in accordance with this order and to ensure free flows of information and effective regulation and application of standards for sources of radiation. Such a mechanism shall be established through written agreement signed between the Chairman of IRSRA and the Minister of the Environment.

Section 10 Regulatory Authority

The IRSRA shall adopt such Regulations, not inconsistent with Iraqi law or any CPA Order, Regulation, or Memorandum, as are necessary to carry out the purposes of the IRSRA.

Section 11 Entry into Force

This Order shall enter into force on the date of signature [15 June 2004].

Document 97
Coalition Provisional Authority Order Number 73
CPA/ORD/22 April 2004/73

Transfer of the Iraqi Civil Defense Corps to the Ministry of Defence

Pursuant to my authority as Administrator of the Coalition Provisional Authority (CPA), under the laws and usages of war, and consistent with relevant United Nations Security Council resolutions, including Resolutions 1483 and 1511 (2003),

Noting that CPA Order Number 22, Creation of a New Iraqi Army, August 7, 2003,[232] established a military force for the national self-defense of a future free Iraq,

Noting that CPA Order Number 23, Creation of a Code of Military Discipline for the New Iraqi Army, August 7, 2003,[233] established a system of discipline to maintain order in the New Iraqi Army,

Noting that CPA Order Number 28, Establishment of the Iraqi Civil Defense Corps, September 3, 2003,[234] established a temporary security and emergency service agency for Iraq to complement operations conducted by Coalition military forces in Iraq,

Noting the adoption on March 8, 2004 of the Law of Administration for the State of Iraq for the Transitional Period,[235]

Further noting that CPA Order Number 67, Ministry of Defence, promulgated on March 21, 2004,[236] redesignated the New Iraqi Army as the Iraqi Armed Forces, established a new national ministry to provide civilian control of the Iraqi Armed Forces and supporting organizations, and provided for the eventual transfer of the Iraqi Civil Defense Corps to the Ministry of Defence as a component of the Iraqi Armed Forces,

Recognizing, in light of current circumstances within Iraq, the need to transfer the Iraqi Civil Defense Corps to the Ministry of Defence as a component of the Iraqi Armed Forces and to provide additional clarification with respect to the status and authority of the Iraqi Civil Defense Corps and its members,

I hereby promulgate the following:

Section 1 Transfer

1) The Iraqi Civil Defense Corps, to include all associated personnel, facilities, and equipment, established pursuant to CPA Order Number 28 is hereby transferred to the Ministry of Defence as a component of the Iraqi Armed Forces.

2) As a component of the Iraqi Armed Forces, the Iraqi Civil Defense Corps shall be subject to the terms of CPA Order Number 22, as amended; provided that in the event of a conflict between the terms of CPA Order Number 22, as amended, and CPA Order Number 28, as amended, the terms of CPA Order Number 28, as amended, shall govern.

3) The transfer of administrative functions for the Iraqi Civil Defense Corps shall be accomplished in a manner and on a timeline agreed to by the interim Minister of Defence and the senior military commander of Coalition Forces in Iraq consistent with the Ministry of Defence's capability to administer such responsibilities.

[232] See *Doc 43*.
[233] See *Doc 44*.
[234] See *Doc 49*.
[235] See *Doc 511*.
[236] See *Doc 91*.

Section 2 Amendment to CPA Order Number 22

Coalition Provisional Authority Order Number 22, Section 3, is hereby amended by adding a new Section 3, Article 5, as follows:

> '5) The Iraqi Civil Defense Corps shall operate as a component of the Iraqi Armed Forces in accordance with the terms of this Order, CPA Order Number 28, as amended, CPA Order Number 67, and CPA Order Number 73; provided that in the event of a conflict between the terms of this Order and CPA Order Number 28, as amended, the terms of CPA Order Number 28, as amended, shall govern.'

Section 3 Amendments to CPA Order Number 28

1) Coalition Provisional Authority Order Number 28, Section 1, Article 4, is hereby amended to read in its entirety as follows:

> '4) The Iraqi Civil Defense Corps is a component of the Iraqi Armed Forces. The Iraqi Civil Defense Corps shall operate in accordance with the terms of this Order, as amended, CPA Order Number 22, as amended, CPA Order Number 67, and CPA Order Number 73; provided that in the event of a conflict between the terms of this Order, as amended, and CPA Order Number 22, as amended, the terms of this Order, as amended, shall govern.'

2) Coalition Provisional Authority Order Number 28, Section 2, Article 4, is hereby deleted in its entirety and the existing Section 2, Article 5, is hereby redesignated as Section 2, Article 4.

3) Coalition Provisional Authority Order Number 28, Section 2, Article 6, is hereby deleted in its entirety.

4) Coalition Provisional Authority Order Number 28, Section 3, is hereby amended by adding a new Section 3, Article 5, as follows:

> '5) Notwithstanding Section 3, Article 4 above, members of the Iraqi Civil Defense Corps under the operational control of a Coalition Forces officer may use force consistent with rules of engagement or rules for the use of force applicable to Coalition Forces to execute their assigned missions and taskings.'

5) Coalition Provisional Authority Order Number 28, Section 4, Article 1, is hereby amended to read in its entirety as follows:

> '1) The Iraqi Civil Defense Corps shall operate under the authority of the Administrator of the CPA. Subject to the authority of the Administrator of the CPA, the interim Minister of Defence shall be responsible for management and employment of the Iraqi Civil Defense Corps and shall exercise direction and control (including commissioning and appointments) over the Iraqi Civil Defense Corps and its organizational structure. During the period in which the Iraqi Civil Defense Corps is under the operational control of a commander of Coalition Forces for the purpose of conducting combined operations and providing other support, as provided for in CPA Order Number 67, the Administrator of the CPA may delegate to the senior military commander of Coalition Forces in Iraq responsibility and authority for the recruiting, training, organization, and control of the Iraqi Civil Defense Corps. This responsibility and authority may be re-delegated pursuant to Section 7 below.'

6) Coalition Provisional Authority Order Number 28, Section 4, is hereby amended by adding a new Section 4, Article 2, as follows:

> '2) While the Iraqi Civil Defense Corps is under the operational control of Coalition Forces, the senior military commander of Coalition Forces in Iraq may set the standards

for manning, training, and equipping Iraqi Civil Defense Corps forces, as well as establishing their mission essential task list (METL) and operational employment.'

7) Coalition Provisional Authority Order Number 28 existing Section 4, Articles 2 and 3 are hereby redesignated as Section 4, Articles 3 and 4, respectively.

8) Coalition Provisional Authority Order Number 28, Section 5, is hereby amended by adding a new Section 5, Article 3, as follows:

'3) Notwithstanding any other provision in this or any other CPA Order, Regulation, or Memorandum or any provision in Iraqi law, Iraqi Civil Defense Corps members acting within the scope of their mission or tasking and consistent with applicable Coalition rules of engagement or rules for the use of force are immune from Iraqi criminal, civil, and administrative jurisdiction and from any form of arrest or detention. The Administrator of the CPA shall have the exclusive authority to determine when a particular act was performed in an official capacity and consistent with the rules of engagement or rules for the use of force applicable to Coalition Forces, and such determination is binding on all governmental, judicial and administrative entities within Iraq.'[237]

Section 4 Entry into Force

This Order shall enter into force on the date of signature [25 April 2004].

Document 98

Coalition Provisional Authority Order Number 74

CPA/ORD/18 April 2004/74

Interim Law on Securities Markets

Pursuant to my authority as Administrator of the Coalition Provisional Authority (CPA), and under the laws and usages of war, and consistent with relevant U.N. Security Council resolutions, including Resolutions 1483 and 1511 (2003),

Having worked closely with the Governing Council to ensure that economic change as necessary to benefit the people of Iraq occurs in a manner acceptable to the people of Iraq,

Acknowledging the Governing Council's desire to bring about significant change to the Iraqi economic system as necessary to improve the condition of the people of Iraq,

Determined to improve the conditions of life, technical skills, and opportunities for all Iraqis and to fight unemployment with its associated deleterious effect on public security,

Recognizing that some of the regulations concerning securities markets under the prior regime are not well-suited to a modern, efficient, transparent and independently regulated securities market,

Noting that Iraqi entrepreneurs and businesses will benefit from the revival of Iraq's capital markets,

Recognizing the CPA's obligation to provide for the effective administration of Iraq, to ensure the well being of the Iraqi people and to enable the social and economic functions and normal transactions of every day life,

[237] Sec 3(8) was rescinded by CPA Order No 100, sec 3(27) *[Doc 124]*.

Acting in a manner consistent with the Report of the Secretary General to the Security Council of July 17, 2003, concerning the need for the development of Iraq and its transition from a non-transparent centrally planned economy to a free market economy characterized by sustainable economic growth through the establishment of a dynamic private sector, and the need to enact institutional and legal reforms to give it effect,

Having worked closely with the Governing Council, international organizations, relevant Ministries and Iraqi business people in developing policies that will organize and facilitate fair, efficient, and orderly securities transactions in Iraq,

I hereby promulgate the following:

Section 1 Definitions

For the purposes of this law, the following terms shall be defined as follows:

1) 'Commission' means the interim Iraq Securities and Exchange Commission.

2) 'Commissioners' mean the members of the Iraq Securities and Exchange Commission.

3) 'Exchange' means the Iraq Stock Exchange ('ISX') or such other exchange as the Commission, pursuant to its rules, may license under this Law.

4) 'General Assembly' means the body consisting of all Exchange members and companies listed on the Exchange.

5) 'Board of Governors' or 'Board' or 'Governors' means the Board of Governors of the Exchange or the Governors who sit on the Board.

6) 'Governing Council' means the Governing Council of Iraq and, following the transfer of full governance authority to the Interim Iraqi Government, the body vested with national executive authority.[238]

7) 'Chair' means the Chair of the Exchange's Board of Governors of the Exchange; or Chair of the Securities and Exchange Commission, as the context indicates.

8) 'CEO' means the Chief Executive Officer of the Exchange.

9) 'Member' of the Exchange means a licensed Broker of the Exchange

10) 'Broker' means a natural person licensed by the Board of Governors under Section 5(1) (a) of this Law to engage in securities transactions on the Exchange or a legal person so licensed under Section 5(1) (b). A bank may be accepted as a Broker if authorized to act in that capacity under the Banking Law.

11) 'Bank' means an entity authorized by the Central Bank of Iraq to conduct banking operations in Iraq.

12) 'Company' means a joint stock Company that is an issuer of securities subject to the provisions of this Law or a Company referred to in Section 5(1) (b) (ii) of this Law.

13) 'Depository' means the Iraq Depository which will serve as the central clearing and settlement facility for all securities transactions.

14) 'Licensed Securities Market' shall mean any securities market that is granted a license by the Iraq Securities Commission to conduct securities transactions.

15) 'Securities' mean tradable interests representing financial value, including shares of corporate stock or mutual funds, bonds issued by corporations or the government, stock options, warrants and other derivative securities, limited partnership units and various other form 'investment instruments'.

16) 'Government Securities' means Securities backed by the full faith and credit of, or guaranteed by, the Government of Iraq.

[238] Sec 1(6) was amended by CPA Order No 100, sec 3(28)(a) *[Doc 124]*.

17) 'Listed Companies' shall mean all companies that are listed for trading on a Licensed Securities Market.

18) 'IASD' means the Iraqi Association of Securities Dealers, a trade organization for all brokers wishing to become participants in Licensed Securities Markets.

19) 'Law' or 'Interim Law' means this Interim Law on Securities Markets.

20) 'Permanent Securities Law' means the successor law to this law, which will establish the comprehensive legal and regulatory framework for securities trading, oversight and securities markets in Iraq.

Section 2 Organization and Objectives

1) The Baghdad Stock Exchange shall cease operations. A new Exchange known as the 'Iraq Stock Exchange' is hereby established under this Law.

a) The Exchange's headquarters shall be in Baghdad, with no prohibition against opening branch offices in other Iraqi cities.
b) Its corporate existence, including limitation of liability to its own assets and not those of its members, commences immediately.
c) The Exchange shall have no responsibility for any obligations of the Baghdad Stock Exchange.
d) The Registrar of Companies in the Ministry of Trade shall have no oversight authority over the Exchange and it need not register with the Ministry of Trade.
e) References in the Company Law of 1997, No. 21, its amendments or other laws to the Baghdad Stock Exchange shall, subject to amendment of such laws, henceforth be read to mean licensed stock exchanges; or arrangements insofar as specified by Commission rules.
f) Upon liquidation of the Baghdad Stock Exchange, any monies remaining after discharge of its obligations shall go to the public budget.

2) The Exchange shall be a legal entity with financial and administrative independence, the right to submit claims before courts, judicial authorities or any other authority, and shall be represented by the Chair of the Board of Governors or a person authorized by the Chair.

3) The Exchange shall be a not-for-profit, member-owned and self-regulatory organization. It shall be independent of the Iraqi Government and the Ministry of Finance. Its business with third parties is commercial in a manner not contradictory to this Law. Its internal governance and the disposition of its assets upon liquidation after payment of lawful claims shall be according to the terms of this Law and the Exchange's rules as authorized and approved hereunder.

4) No stock exchange or other organized securities market may operate without a license from the Commission. The Exchange is hereby licensed and authorized by virtue of this Law to commence operations immediately, subject to regulatory oversight of the Commission. At such time as a new securities law is adopted, the Exchange shall be required to exist and operate in accordance with the terms and conditions of such law. No other interim exchange licenses shall be granted before the first anniversary of the effective date of this Law unless the Commission specifically finds that the interests of investors could not be well-served otherwise.

5) Contracts for the purchase and sale of securities concluded on the Exchange shall be exempt from stamp fees. Companies whose securities are admitted to trading on the Exchange shall have no right to collect any fees with respect to the issuance or transfer of their securities except in such limited circumstances as the Commission may by rule define to promote the convenience or lower the expenses of investors.

6) The Exchange aims to achieve the following:
   a) To operate and regulate its members and listed companies in a manner that is consistent with the goal of protecting investors and promoting investor confidence in the market.
   b) To promote the interests of investors in efficient, reliable, competitive, transparent and honest markets.
   c) To organize and facilitate fair, efficient and orderly transactions in securities, including the clearance and settlement of such transactions.
   d) To regulate its members' dealings in securities-related services and transactions and define the rights and obligations of parties concerned and the means to protect their legal interests.
   e) To assist in capital-raising for companies which either are listed, or which desire to list on the Exchange.
   f) To engage, as appropriate, in investor education programs to educate potential investors about opportunities for investments at the Exchange.
   g) To collect, analyze and publish statistics and information necessary to achieve the goals stipulated in this Law.
   h) To establish and support contacts with the stock exchanges of Arab and international markets that may be beneficial to the development of the Exchange.
   i) To undertake other services and activities necessary to support its objectives.

Section 3 Transactions on the Exchange

1) No securities transactions shall take place on the Exchange unless the Company has listed that class of securities for trading on the Exchange and the transactions are conducted in accordance with the Exchange's rules.

2) The Exchange's rules regarding transactions in securities and other matters shall be adopted by the Exchange's Board of Governors and shall be subject to approval by the Commission.

3) Securities transactions shall be restricted as follows:
   a) All transactions on the Exchange shall be restricted to those conducted by the Brokers authorized by the Exchange to engage in such transactions.
   b) No Broker or person in the business of effecting transactions in securities for proprietary or client accounts shall engage in any such securities brokerage services off the Exchange, regardless of whether the securities involved in such transaction are admitted to trading on the Exchange, unless those securities are subject to other relevant regulation by the Commission.
   c) The restriction in subparagraph (b) of this paragraph 3 of Section 3 shall not apply to:
      i) Public subscription for securities at issuance, provided there is compliance with the provisions of Company Law No. 21 of 1997, as amended, any successor laws or amendments and the rules of the Commission.
      ii) Transfer by gift to relatives of the second degree (parents, parents-in-law, siblings, siblings-in-law, children, children-in-law) or transfer by inheritance or court order
      iii) The restrictions in subparagraph (b) of this paragraph 3 of Section 3 shall not apply to the issuance of Government Securities, provided there is compliance with the rules of the Central Bank of Iraq and Ministry of Finance.
   d) The restrictions in subparagraph (b) of this paragraph 3 of Section 3 shall not apply in other circumstances that the Commission may by rule define regarding:

i) Transparent and competitive pricing and trading arrangements;
ii) Investor cost and convenience;
iii) Optimal interaction of supply of and demand for the security;
iv) Disclosure of issuer financial condition, ownership and control;
v) Reliable settlement arrangements; and
vi) Competent and reliable providers of investment services.

4) The Exchange shall have authority to invalidate any transaction in securities on the Exchange that is in violation of this Law, the rules of the Exchange, or the rules of the Commission.

5) The Exchange shall admit an Iraqi Company's securities for trading on the Exchange provided that the Iraqi Company complies with the Exchange's listing standards, which shall, at a minimum, require that:

a) The Company has held its most recent annual general assembly required by law;
b) The Company has submitted to the Exchange and made publicly available financial statements of the Company current as of a date not more than six months prior to the opening day of trading prepared in accordance with such requirements as to form, content and applicable accounting standards and accompanied by such assurances and explanations as the Exchange may require;
c) The Depository has certified to the Exchange that the Company's securities proposed to be admitted for trading on the Exchange are eligible for the Depository based upon such assurances that the Depository may require from the Company or the Company's registrar regarding the completeness and accuracy of information concerning the amount of the securities outstanding and the ownership of such securities;
d) The securities offered for trading are not subject to any legal restriction on transfer;
e) The Company has agreed to make timely public disclosure of any information that might have a significant effect on the price of its securities to be admitted for trading, and has agreed to comply with such other requirements as the Exchange may impose as a condition for admitting the Company's securities for trading on the Exchange; and
f) The Exchange may (either pursuant to a Commission order or based upon its own determination) remove an Iraqi Company's securities from trading on the Exchange when the issuer fails to comply with Exchange rules or the securities law, or if its securities no longer meet the Exchange's listing requirements.

6) A Company with a class of securities admitted to trading on the Exchange pursuant to Section 3(5) shall be required to comply with the following requirements in order for such securities to continue to be admitted to trading from the opening of the Exchange onward.

a) The Company shall file with the Exchange and the Commission and make publicly available not later than 60 days after the close of each of the first three quarters of the Company's fiscal year unaudited, quarterly financial reports that include summary balance sheets as of the close of the quarter and the most recent fiscal year and comparative quarterly and year-to-date summary statements of income and cash flow through the close of the quarter and for the comparable prior year periods. The quarterly reports shall be prepared in accordance with such requirements as to form, content and applicable accounting standards, and accompanied by such management assurances and explanations, as the Exchange and the Commission may require by rule. For the purposes of this Law, the first unaudited quarterly financial report will be due 60 days following the close of the second quarter of 2004 (on or before August 31, 2004).

b) The Company shall file with the Exchange and the Commission and make publicly available not later than 150 days after the close of the Company's fiscal year, financial statements that shall include a balance sheet as of the close of the fiscal year and statements of income, cash flow and changes in ownership equity for the fiscal year.

c) Commencing with the annual report for the Company's 2004 fiscal year, the financial statements shall be presented on a comparative basis with financial statements for the preceding fiscal year pursuant to the following guidelines

i) The financial statements included in the annual report shall be audited in accordance with international auditing standards by an independent auditor duly licensed in Iraq and shall be presented in accordance with international accounting standards to the extent permissible under the standards in force in Iraq.

ii) The financial statements shall be accompanied by a signed copy of the independent auditor's audit report indicating that they have been audited in accordance with international auditing standards to the extent permissible under the standards in force in Iraq and that they represent a true and fair view of the Company's financial results.

iii) The financial statements shall also be accompanied by such management assurances and explanations as the Exchange and the Commission may require by rule;

iv) The Commission may by rule allow additional time for the audit and audit report if conditions in Iraq indicate that this is necessary.

d) The Company shall hold its annual general assembly not later than 60 days after the date that its audited financial statements are publicly available or such earlier date as may be prescribed by law; and

e) The Company shall comply with such other requirements as the Exchange may impose as a condition for the continued trading of such securities on the Exchange. All information submitted by the Company shall be accurate and objective.

7) The Board of Governors may adopt separate rules regarding the listing, second market and third market trading of Securities.

8) Any joint stock company whose securities are not admitted to trading on the Exchange shall notify the Exchange or such other authority as the Commission may designate as to the dates, quantities, prices or other terms and parties to any transactions in its securities, according to such rules as the Commission may prescribe. By rule or order, the Commission may prescribe a requirement for joint stock companies to apply for admission to trading on the Exchange in order to conduct securities transactions.

Paragraphs 9 and 10 relate to transactions that were conducted after March 19, 2003 (after the closure of the Baghdad Stock Exchange and the opening of the Iraq Stock Exchange). Any transactions that fall under paragraphs 9 or 10 will be subject to specific Exchange regulation and stringent oversight to ensure that such transactions were not fraudulent or manipulative in nature.

9) Any transactions conducted outside of the Baghdad Stock Exchange following its closure on March 19, 2003 until the opening of the Iraq Stock Exchange, other than those

transactions specified in paragraph 9 below, shall not be recognized by the Exchange and/or Commission as valid transactions, unless such transactions are executed at the Iraq Stock Exchange by a licensed Broker following the opening of the Iraq Stock Exchange.

10) Transactions resulting from transfer by gift to relatives of the second degree (parents, parents-in-law, siblings, siblings-in-law, children, children-in-law), transfer by inheritance or transfer by court order shall not be subject to the restrictions in paragraph 9 above.

Section 4 General Assembly

1) The General Assembly shall consist of the Brokers authorized to engage in securities transactions on the Exchange.

2) The General Assembly shall have authority to elect the members of the Exchange Board of Governors as further provided in the Exchange's rules, and to exercise such other powers as may be assigned under the Exchange's rules.

3) The Exchange's rules shall determine a date for meetings of the General Assembly and the procedures for holding such meetings.

Section 5 Brokers

1) A Broker authorized to do business on the Exchange shall be one of the following:
   a) A bank authorized under the Banking Law, including foreign banks, subsidiaries and branches, to engage in securities operations in Iraq;
   b) A Company established according to Company Law No. 21 of 1997, as amended, or its successor laws and amendments, that has a specialty in securities brokerage activities, investment management or investment advisory work and whose authorized director satisfies the conditions set forth in Section 5(2), below; or
   c) A Partnership, established according to relevant law, that has a specialty in securities brokerage activities, investment management or investment advisory work and whose authorized director satisfies the conditions set forth in Section 5(2) below.

2) A director or representative of a Broker who is authorized to conduct securities transactions on the Exchange ('Representative') shall be a natural person who:
   a) is no less than 21 years old and is a legal resident of Iraq as defined by Iraqi law;
   b) is of legal capacity;
   c) is not an undischarged bankrupt;
   d) has not been convicted of a felony in a court of competent jurisdiction;
   e) has not been convicted of a misdemeanor related to financial fraud in a court of competent jurisdiction;
   f) is a holder of a university diploma or its equivalent;
   g) has at least five years experience in financial and commercial affairs as deemed acceptable by the Exchange;
   h) shall conduct brokerage activities within Iraq or at other locations as authorized by the Exchange and approved by the Commission.

3) An associated person of a Broker ('Associated Person') who is authorized to assist in the brokerage business either on the Exchange or at a Broker's place of business shall be a natural person who:
   a) is no less than 18 years and is a legal resident of Iraq as defined by Iraqi law;
   b) is of legal capacity;
   c) is not an undischarged bankrupt;
   d) has not committed a felony;

e) has not committed a misdemeanor related to financial fraud or honor;
f) is a holder of a secondary school certificate or equivalent;
g) has appropriate references as deemed acceptable by the Exchange;
h) shall conduct brokerage activities within Iraq or at other locations as authorized by the Exchange and approved by the Commission.

4) A Broker shall be required to adopt and conduct business under a commercial name.

5) A Broker shall not be permitted to engage in securities transactions on the Exchange unless the Broker satisfies the following conditions:

a) The Broker has been admitted to membership on the Exchange;
b) The Broker has been accepted as a participant in the Depository either directly or indirectly through another participant, including through a correspondent clearing participant of the Depository;
c) The daily trading limits for the Broker shall be determined pursuant to Exchange regulation based upon the Broker's net capital adequacy. The Broker's net capital adequacy shall be determined based upon the Depository's assessment of the Broker's ability to meet its trading obligations, as well as the advice from the settlement bank to the Depository; and

6) A Broker that was authorized to engage in securities transactions on the Baghdad Stock Exchange immediately prior to the closure of such exchange March 19, 2003, is hereby granted interim authority and an interim license to engage in securities transactions on the Exchange in accordance with this Law, provided that:

a) Such Broker shall be required to comply with such additional rules applicable to the Broker under this Law as well as subject to such additional rules as may be prescribed by the Exchange, the Depository, the Board of Governors or the Commission.
b) Brokers holding interim or other authority to conduct securities transactions on the Exchange shall comply continuously with any licensing or other requirements necessary to conduct securities transactions in accordance with any revised terms and conditions.

7) A Broker must be represented at the Exchange by one or more of its Representatives who satisfy the conditions set forth in Section 5(2) above and whom the Broker authorizes to conduct the Broker's business on the Exchange, or a person under the supervision and control of the Broker, and for whom the Broker assumes responsibility in accordance with such rules as may be prescribed by the Exchange.

8) The Board of Governors shall adopt rules regulating the circumstances under which a Broker may engage in securities transactions for the Broker's own account or related accounts.

9) A Broker shall act on behalf of the seller or purchaser of securities in a manner that complies with the rules adopted by the Board of Governors. Such rules will include, but not be limited to a requirement that each client provide a signed authorization of the brokerage relationship on appropriate account opening documents. Brokers may not engage in securities transactions for a client or request disbursement of client funds or securities without appropriate client authorization.

10) A Broker shall be required to:

a) Pay all fees related to the Broker's authorization to conduct business on the Exchange according to the Exchange's rules;
b) Keep and maintain books, registers and documents as specified by rules adopted by the Board of Governors of the Exchange or by the Commission.

11) A Broker shall not engage in a sale of securities on behalf of a customer unless the Broker has determined, in accordance with such rules as may be prescribed by the

Exchange or the Depository, that the securities are in the custody of the Depository and that the customer has an appropriate ownership interest in the securities.

12) A Broker shall not engage in a purchase of securities on behalf of a customer unless the Broker has determined, in accordance with such rules as may be prescribed by the Exchange or the Depository that the customer has sufficient funds to pay for the securities.

13) A Broker shall be bound to do the following:

a) Protect confidential information regarding investors except where legally obligated to reveal such information;
b) Act with honesty, integrity and adherence to the rules of the Exchange and commercial norms;
c) Act in the best interest of clients at all times, including placing the interests of clients ahead of the Broker's interests, protecting clients' rights and informing clients of all relevant information relating to clients' securities transactions;
d) Abstain from engaging in false or sham transactions, other forms of market manipulation and acts and practices that have the effect of misleading or deceiving investors or creating false or misleading impressions.
e) To act as a fiduciary for client funds and as such, to not co-mingle client funds or accounts with broker funds or accounts.

14) The Commission and the Exchange shall have the authority to gain access to any information relevant to enforcement of this Law or the rules of the Exchange or Commission from Brokers or their agents, employees or owners, without any need for notice or approval by that Broker, their Representatives or Associated Persons.

15) The Broker shall maintain a required level of cash or collateral in its account, as determined by the Board of Governors according to Exchange rules, which is to be held at the Depository or Depository settlement bank. If the required amount is deficient for any reason, the Broker shall complete it within a period specified by rules of the Exchange, the Depository or the Depository settlement bank, as applicable. The failure of the Broker to do so shall be grounds for prohibiting the Broker from engaging in further securities transactions until complete financial assurance is provided.

16) A Broker shall be required to disclose all fees, commissions and mark-ups charged to its clients prior to entering into any agreements or understandings with a customer. The Exchange may prescribe rules relating to maximum commission, mark-up and fee levels, as well as disclosure requirements, as approved by the Commission.

Section 6 Board of Governors

1) The Exchange shall be governed and operated under the direction of a nine-member Board of Governors whose members, during the period governed by this law, shall serve for the shorter of a one-year term or until the Permanent Securities Law is promulgated. Members of the Board of Governors are eligible but not guaranteed for re-appointment under the Permanent Securities Law.

2) The composition of the Board of Governors shall be as follows:

a) The Chair of the Board of Governors. One or more nominees shall be proposed by the Board of Governors or a Nominating Committee of the Board of Governors.
b) The Chief Executive Officer of the Exchange, whose appointment shall be approved by the Administrator in consultation with the Board of Governors.[239]

[239] Sec 6(2)(b) was rescinded and replaced by CPA Order No 100, sec 3(28)(b) *[Doc 124]*.

c) A member representing the companies whose securities are listed or admitted to trading on the Exchange, for which one or more nominees shall be proposed by the Board of Governors or its Nominating Committee.
d) A member who shall be a senior officer of the Iraqi Association of Securities Dealers (IASD) or a senior member of an IASD member firm, for which the IASD shall propose one or more nominees.
e) A member representing Brokers that are authorized to engage in securities transactions on the Exchange, for which the Board of Governors shall propose one or more nominees.
f) Four qualified public governors who are, and must remain, independent of the Exchange or any of its constituencies shall be proposed by the Board of Governors. One of these candidates shall have expertise in information technology matters, for which the independent members of the Board of Governors shall propose three or more nominees.

3) Except for the Chief Executive Officer, all members of the interim Board of Governors shall be appointed by the Administrator following consultation with the Governing Council. The interim term of these members shall commence on the effective date of this Law and shall expire at the sooner of the enactment of the Permanent Securities Law or one year after this law is promulgated. The members of the interim Board of Governors are eligible, but not guaranteed for reappointment.[240]

4) Members of the Board of Governors will also be appointed under the Permanent Securities Law. Thereafter, the Board of Governors shall be elected by the General Assembly in accordance with the rules of the Exchange.

5) For the purposes of this law and for the expedient purpose of opening the Iraq Stock Exchange, Sections 6.1 and 6.2 above notwithstanding, for the initial term, the Board of Governors should, but is not required to be comprised of persons who meet the criteria specified in this Law.

6) The Board of Governors shall perform or may authorize directors, officers or managers of the Exchange to:

a) Establish the general policy and organizational framework of the Exchange.
b) Create the Exchange's rules and submit them to the Commission for approval, including rules to prevent conflicts of interest from influencing the work of the Board and the Exchange and providing for the withdrawal of Governors from voting when a conflict of interest arises.
c) Establish other rules related to transactions in securities, to be filed with the Commission.
d) Implement financial, administrative and accounting rules necessary to regulate the Exchange's operations, subject to Commission approval.
e) Review and approve, approve subject to conditions, or disapprove, applications for admission of securities to trading on the Exchange, including procedures for removing securities from admission to trading.
f) Review and approve, approve subject to conditions or disapprove, applications of persons who seek to become Brokers authorized to engage in securities transactions on the Exchange.
g) Verify and approve the budget and final accounts of the Exchange, enclosed with a report of an independent auditor, and submit them to the Commission and the General Assembly.

[240] Sec 6(3) was amended by CPA Order No 100, sec 3(28)(c) *[Doc 124]*.

h) Take necessary measures with regard to suspicious operations according to the Exchange rules, this Law, and the rules of the Commission.
i) Conduct oversight of all activity at the Exchange, stop the Exchange activity if necessary for the protection of investors and ban trading in securities for a period not exceeding five business days and, with the Commission's approval, for any additional period.
j) Stop trading in securities of a particular Company for the protection of investors for a period not exceeding ten business days and, with the Commission's approval, for any additional period.
k) Check and inspect Brokers' registers, records, books, and business, and require members to furnish documents or witnesses under their control for the investigation or adjudication of disciplinary or arbitration matters.
l) Engage in internal discipline of a formal or informal nature including imposing fines and suspensions pursuant to rules of the Exchange and this interim Law.

7) The Board of Governors shall authorize the CEO to have the authorities mentioned in Section 6(5) (i) through (l), above, according to the limits it decides.

8) The Board of Governors may delegate other authority of the Board and the Chair to the CEO, other officers of the Exchange or a Committee of the Board as deemed appropriate, provided that such delegations shall be reflected in rules of the Exchange. The Board, its delegates, and all Exchange officers shall act diligently in the best interests of the Exchange, its members and the investing public and shall strive to effectuate the purposes and provisions of this Law.

9) The Administrator, in consultation with the Commission and notification to the Governing Council, may remove a Governor prior to the expiration of his or her term only for cause, which shall be defined to mean conviction of a violation of this Law or another law, other than minor infractions, physical inability to perform his or her duties, or gross incompetence.[241]

Section 7 Exchange Finance

1) The Exchange's finances shall consist of the following:
a) Fees paid by companies for admission of their securities to trading and for continued trading on the Exchange.
b) Fees paid by Exchange members related to authorization of the members and their employees and agents to engage in securities transactions on the Exchange, including but not limited to, an entry fee and annual dues.
c) Commissions or fees based upon the volume of trading taking place on the Exchange.
d) Fines imposed by the Exchange on those persons subject to the Exchange's jurisdiction who violate this Law or the rules or regulations of the Exchange or the Commission.
e) Revenues from the sale of Exchange transaction data, statistics and publications, subject to rules of the Commission assuring the dissemination of basic information.
f) Donations and loans to the Exchange, which shall be subject to Exchange and Commission rules.
g) Revenues from investment of Exchange funds.

[241] Sec 6(9) was rescinded and replaced by CPA Order No 100, sec 3(28)(d) *[Doc 124]*.

h) Other revenue sources authorized by the Board of Governors, subject to Commission approval and consistent with relevant laws, including Orders of the Coalition Provisional Authority.

2) The Board of Governors shall establish the above-mentioned fees, commissions and charges for services offered by the Exchange, subject to Commission approval, recognizing that the continued operating and development needs of the Exchange shall be taken into consideration, but that accumulation of unnecessary surplus funds is to be avoided.

3) The Exchange's final accounts and annual report shall be subject to approval by the Board of Governors and then shall be filed with the Commission as soon as practicable, regardless of whether or not they have been presented to the General Assembly. Any amendments to the final accounts and annual report shall be timely filed with the Commission. The final accounts and annual report shall be presented to the General Assembly at its annual meeting, which shall be scheduled in accordance with the Exchange's rules.

4) The Exchange's financial year shall commence on the first of January of each year and end on the last day of December, provided, however, that the initial financial year shall begin upon the commencement of Exchange operations and shall concluded December 31, 2004.

Section 8 Exchange Operations and Oversight

1) The Government of Iraq shall have no ownership interest in the Exchange or any revenues or assets of the Exchange, provided, however, that nothing contained in this Law shall prevent an otherwise qualified legal entity owned in whole or in part by the Government of Iraq from being a member of the Exchange or Depository and participating in the General Assembly.

2) All governing instruments and rules of the Exchange shall be subject to approval, supplementation and abrogation by the Commission, which shall have authority to inspect all operations of the Exchange and impose appropriate disciplinary sanctions in the event that the Exchange fails to enforce any provision of this Law for which it is responsible or any rule or regulation of the Exchange.

3) The Board of Governors may form committees to address the needs of the Exchange. The Exchange's rules shall specify the work of these committees. Such committees may include, but not be limited to the following:

a) Executive Committee
b) Compliance Committee
c) Business Conduct Committee and a Sub-Committee of Member Officials (on-floor rulings)
d) Finance Committee
e) Membership Committee
f) Marketing/Public Relations Committee
g) Arbitration Committee

4) All Exchange Governors, officers and employees shall be required to agree to and sign a Code of Conduct which will include but not be limited to, full disclosure of all financial dealings of those individuals, potential conflicts of interest and such additional components according to the rules of the Exchange.

Section 9 Depository – Clearance and Settlement

1) There is hereby established a securities depository known as the Iraq Depository. Subject to the further provisions of this Section, the Depository shall be a division of

the ISX open to participation by any member of the Exchange subject to such terms and conditions as the Director of the Depository shall specify by rule, subject to the approval of the Board of Governors and the Commission. The Depository aims to:

a) Promote the timely, safe and efficient settlement of securities transactions in accordance with the terms of those transactions;

b) Promote open and non-discriminatory access to clearance and settlement services.

The Commission may by rule require fair access to the Depository by persons who are not members of the Exchange but whose securities holdings or activities are such as to make their direct participation beneficial to the efficient functioning of the market or who should be able have access through a member.

2) The Depository shall be governed and operated under the terms and conditions of its rules, as approved by the Board of Governors and the Commission.

3) All securities transactions taking place on the Exchange shall be required to be cleared and settled through the facilities of the Depository on a book-entry basis. Once securities have been deposited in the Depository, they may not be withdrawn or subsequently transferred in physical form. Depository rules shall provide for evidence of ownership of securities. The Commission may adopt rules regarding the necessity of depositing at the Depository for book-entry transfer other securities not admitted to trading on the Exchange but that have been or shall be offered for public subscription.

4) Securities transactions on the Exchange or as otherwise provided by Commission rules that are cleared and settled through the facilities of the Depository shall be entitled to a presumption of finality. This section shall supersede Article 66, first paragraph, of Company Law No. 21 of 1997. Lawful transfers on the books of the Depository of deposited securities shall supersede the provisions of Article 68 of the Company Law.

5) Securities registered at the Depository in the names of others for holding and transfer in book-entry form shall not be regarded as property of the Depository or the Exchange or be subject to the claims of their creditors.

6) Liabilities or assets acquired by the Depository as central counterparty, maintainer of a settlement guarantee fund or otherwise purely in the course of settling trades and transfers shall not be subject to third-party claims disruptive of the settlement process.

7) The Depository or Exchange may establish a guarantee fund for the settlement of trades or transfers. This fund shall not be available for any other use by the Depository or Exchange or be subject to claims of their creditors, except claims arising from the rules of participation in such fund or the settlement provisions of those rules. This section shall supercede bankruptcy law.

8) The Depository is hereby authorized to commence operations at the same time that the Exchange commences operations. All governing instruments and rules of the Depository shall be subject to the approval of the Exchange and the Commission.

Section 10 Principal Holders of Securities and Control Transactions

1) 'Affiliated Persons' for purposes of this Section 10 shall mean two or more persons working together for the purpose of holding or exercising practical control over the affairs of a company, but shall in all cases include at least persons with the following relationships if one is aware of the holdings of another in a subject company:

a) Spouse, minor children or other persons living in the same household or any other relatives to the fourth degree (parents, parents-in-law, siblings or siblings-in-law, children and/or paternal and maternal cousins);

b) When one is a legal person and the other is its officer, director or employee or an owner of 10% or more of the votes from shares or quotas in it.

2) Any Person or Affiliated Persons who, at the time this Law comes into effect or thereafter own or have a right to own 10% or more of the shares entitled to vote in a joint stock company:

a) Shall inform the Exchange and the Commission in writing;
b) Shall inform the Exchange and the Commission about any dealing or conduct that leads to an increase in this percentage as soon as such dealing occurs;
c) Shall report any decrease in such ownership to below 8%.

All of the above disclosures shall be made public by the Exchange and the Commission.

3) It shall be unlawful for a Person or Affiliated Persons to acquire or seek to acquire a right to more than 30% of the shares entitled to vote of any joint stock company unless the person or persons, whether natural or legal, identify themselves and disclose their holdings to the Exchange and the Commission and comply with such rules as the Commission may prescribe with respect to such transactions and the protection of minority owners. Such reports shall be made public by the Exchange and the Commission. This provision shall apply also to persons holding such positions at the time this Law comes into effect.

4) Each joint stock company's registrar and the Depository shall report to the Commission the holdings of any owner in its records having more than 10% of a joint stock company's shares entitled to vote.

Section 11 Disciplinary Matters

1) The Exchange shall have a Business Conduct Committee ('BCC') that, pursuant to Exchange rules, will have authority to make decisions binding upon members and listed companies with respect to violations of this Law, Exchange rules and Commission rules applicable to the Brokers' activities on the Exchange or a Company's compliance with obligations for admission to trading.

2) The BCC shall be appointed by the Board of Governors and its by-laws shall be set forth in Exchange rules. The BCC shall be comprised of public and industry members; with the Chair of the BCC being the Chief Regulatory Officer of the Exchange, or the CRO's delegate.

3) Pursuant to Exchange rules, the BCC may delegate to officers or members of the Exchange the authority to resolve disputes arising at the Exchange in the normal course of business, provided that the delegate comply with the Exchange's rules in resolving such disputes.

4) The procedures of the BCC shall provide any member, member organization or associated person it may discipline with notice of the charges against the person and reasonable opportunity to present evidence and arguments in the person's favor. Further procedures relating to the disciplinary process will be set forth in the rules of the Exchange. Temporary action may be taken in advance of full hearing but only in exigent circumstances according to the rules of the Exchange.

5) The BCC may make findings with respect to matters it considers, which may include but not be limited to a dismissal of the charges, or a finding that the charges are substantiated, along with a finding of appropriate penalties.

6) Imposition of penalties by the BCC will be set forth in Exchange rules, including:

a) A Letter of Warning;
b) Letter of Consent with Compliance Undertakings;
c) Financial fine, restitution or disgorgement of profits;

d) Suspension of a Broker, a Broker's Representative or Associated Person from work for a period of time;
e) Suspension or halt of trading in securities of a Company for a period of time;
f) Revocation of a Broker's authorization to trade securities on the Exchange;
g) Removal of a Company's securities from admission to trading on the Exchange.

7) BCC disciplinary decisions may be appealed in accordance with the rules of the Exchange. In general the appellate process shall be to the:

a) Board of Governors, and if the appellant is not satisfied, to the Commission.
b) Decisions of the Commission are final when issued unless appealed in accordance with Section 13(2), below.

Section 12 Interim Iraq Securities Commission

1) There is hereby established an interim Iraq Securities Commission comprised of five Commissioners including a Chair, whose members shall be appointed by the Administrator following consultation with the Governing Council. The Chair may, from time to time, designate a Vice Chair to assume the Chair's responsibility in the event that the Chair is unable or unavailable to perform the required duties.

2) The positions of Chair and one other Commissioner shall be full-time positions, whereas the other three Commissioners may hold other employment.

a) No Commissioner shall, however, participate, directly or indirectly, in any brokerage business, or transactions of a character subject to regulation by the Commission pursuant to this Law, nor accept anything of value from any person involved in the trading or distribution of securities, their auditors or the affiliates of any of them, except in the ordinary course of business on terms available to the general public and in conformity with the code referred to in Section 12(7) below.
b) No Commissioner shall participate in the consideration of a matter in which he or she has a direct or indirect personal financial interest, subject to the provisions of the code referred to in Section 12(7), below.

3) The term of the Commission and the Commissioners shall expire on the first to occur of:

a) The effective date of a Permanent Securities Law that provides for the establishment of a permanent Securities and Exchange Commission or equivalent regulatory body; or
b) The second anniversary of the effective date of this Law.

The Administrator in consultation with the Governing Council may remove a Commissioner prior to the expiration of his or her term only for cause, which shall be defined to mean conviction of a violation of this Law or another law, other than minor infractions, physical inability to perform his or her duties, or gross incompetence.

4) The Commission shall have a legal personality and shall have the right to sue and be sued, and may be represented in legal proceedings by the Government of Iraq or any attorney the Commission appoints for such purpose.

5) The Commission shall be accountable to and shall submit an annual report of its activities to the executive branch of the Government of Iraq not later than ninety days after the close of the Commission's fiscal year. The Commission's books, records and accounts shall be subject to inspection and its financial statements shall be subject to audit in the same manner as provided for other agencies or authorities of the Government of Iraq.

6) The salaries, benefits, and all financial entitlements of the Commissioners shall be presented to the Administrator for his approval in consultation with the Governing

Council. The Commission is authorized to fix the compensation of such officers, attorneys, accountants, examiners, economists and other experts or employees as may be necessary for carrying out its functions under this Law.[242]

7) The Commission shall adopt and publish a written code of conduct applicable to the Commissioners and all employees of and consultants to the Commission, which shall address conflicts of interest and potential misuse of nonpublic information that may arise in connection with such persons' duties with the Commission and define related restrictions on such persons holdings of or trading in securities.

8) Notwithstanding the fact that any nonpublic information in the possession or within the knowledge of Commissioners, officers and employees of the Commission shall be deemed confidential and that any unauthorized disclosure of such information may be subject to punishment by the Commission or under other laws and regulations, the Commission shall be authorized to use and make public disclosure of such information as it deems necessary for enforcement of the provisions of this Law and consistent with the public interest and the protection of investors.

9) No Commissioner, employee or agent of the Commission, or any person appointed by the Commission under this Law to carry out any function under this Law shall be personally liable in damages for any act or omission taken in the discharge or purported discharge of official functions within the scope of his or her authority, employment or engagement under this Law, absent a finding of malice and intentional abuse of office. The Commission shall indemnify any person referred to in the preceding sentence against any legal costs incurred in the defense against a legal action brought against such person in connection with the discharge or purported discharge of official functions within the scope of the person's employment or engagement under this Law, provided that no such indemnification shall apply if the person has been convicted of a crime arising out of the activities that are covered by such legal action.

10) The Commission's budget shall be determined annually as part of the overall budget process of the Government of Iraq. Any fines or monetary penalties that may be imposed by the Commission in enforcing the provisions of this Law shall not be retained by the Commission, but shall be paid into the general treasury of the Government of Iraq.

11) The Commission may issue, amend or repeal rules, regulations and orders only as authorized by specific provisions of this Law. The Commission's rules, regulations and orders may classify persons, securities, transactions or filings, and prescribe different requirements for different classes. The Commission may issue a declaratory ruling as to the applicability of this Law or any rule or order under this Law to any person, security or transaction.

For purposes of Section 12, paragraph 12 et al., below, any references to the 'Exchange' shall also be deemed to apply to any other Licensed Securities Markets approved by the Commission

12) The Commission is authorized to:

a) Review the actions of and approve, disapprove or, where necessary and upon notice and opportunity for comment, supplement or abrogate the governing instruments and other rules of the Exchange and the Depository under this Law;
b) Require the Exchange, the Depository, and Brokers authorized to engage in securities transactions on the Exchange to maintain such records and make such

[242] Sec 12(6) was rescinded and replaced by CPA Order No 100, sec 3(28)(e) *[Doc 124]*.

reports on their financial condition and business related to securities transactions as the Commission deems necessary to implement the provisions of this Law;

c) Inspect the operations of the Exchange, the Depository and any Broker or other person authorized to effect securities transactions directly on the Exchange or to participate directly in the Depository.

d) Notwithstanding any provisions of the Banking Law, inspect Brokers who are banks including their securities operations and related personnel and records;

e) Issue subpoenas for the production of documents or witnesses;

d) [sic] Inspect the operations of Companies who have any class of securities listed for trading on the Exchange.

e) Promulgate rules for disclosure of information and reports required to be made publicly available by companies whose securities are or have been offered for public subscription or distribution or admitted to trading on the Exchange; review such information and reports, and require revision of such information and reports where the information provided is materially incomplete, false or misleading, notwithstanding any provision of the Law on Companies of 1997, No. 21 as amended, or any successor law to the contrary;

f) Promulgate rules related to the disclosure of major holdings and for acquisition of control-affecting blocks of securities in joint stock companies;

g) Promulgate rules relating to investment management and investment advisory activities for Brokers, Banks or other Companies or Partnerships.

h) Enforce this Law, any rules adopted under this Law and any rules of the Exchange or the Depository; and take appropriate disciplinary action against any person who violates such Law or any such rules ; and

i) Exercise all of the other duties and rights given the Commission by this Law.

13) The Commission shall act in a timely manner upon rule filings and other relevant requests from the Exchange or any other Licensed Securities Market. In the event that the Commission does not respond to any such rule filing or request no later than 120 days from the date of receipt of such request; the request or filing shall be deemed to be approved.

14) The Commission shall have the powers to bring civil and criminal actions relating to this Law and the rules hereunder, including Exchange and Depository rules. Any person from whom the Commission requests information or documents, on the basis of its reasonable belief that such information or document is relevant to a possible such violation, shall provide such information or documents. If any person refuses to provide such document or information, the Commission may seek relief in a court of competent jurisdiction.

15) If the Commission finds, after notice and opportunity for hearing, that any person has violated, is violating or is about to violate any provision of this Law or any rule hereunder, the Commission may:

a) Enter an order requiring such person to cease and desist from committing the violation and any future violation of the same provision or rule. Such an order also may require such person to comply with the provisions or rules upon the terms and within the time that the Commission may specify in such order.

b) Impose an administrative penalty upon such person, payable to the Treasury of the Government of Iraq, of up to 50 million dinars for any violation involving fraud, deceit or willful or reckless disregard of a regulatory requirement, or of up to 25 million dinars for any other violation.

c) In exigent circumstances, the Commission may, upon such notice as is practical in the circumstances, provisionally order a person to cease and desist where the evidence indicates that awaiting resolution by a full hearing of the matter carries a more serious risk of harm than issuing a provisional order. No provisional order may remain in force more than ten business days without further opportunity for hearing and presentation of evidence by the persons subject to the order.

16) Appeal and enforcement of the orders and decisions of the Commission shall follow the procedures applicable to appeal of orders of a court of first instance. Orders that are not appealed in such manner may not be challenged in proceedings to enforce them. An appeal of an order or decision of the Commission shall not stay or suspend the imposition of any sanction or penalty levied by the Commission unless the Commission or the court of appeals takes affirmative action to stay or suspend such sanction or penalty.

17) If in its opinion the public interest and the protection of investors so require, the Commission is authorized by order to:

a) Summarily suspend trading in any security admitted to trading on the Exchange or that has been offered for public subscription for a period not exceeding ten business days; and,

b) Suspend or revoke the Exchange's listing or authorization of trading of a security, if the Commission finds, on the record and after notice and opportunity for hearing, that the issuer of such security has failed to comply with any provision of this Law or the rules hereunder.

Section 13 General

1) The Commission shall ensure that rules of the Exchange and the Depository provide fair and open access to membership, facilities and services and impose no burdens on competition except insofar as required to promote transparency, efficiency and financial responsibility in the trading of securities, and that such rules provide for fair and reasonable procedures for the denial, revocation or restriction of access to such membership, facilities or services.

2) Commission decisions regarding appeal of a Board of Governors decision to impose a sanction or penalty specified in Section 11(5) of this Law may be appealed to a court of appeals within 30 days of the final Commission decision. An appeal of such a decision of the Commission shall not stay or suspend the imposition of any sanction or penalty levied by the Commission unless the Commission or the court of appeal takes affirmative action to stay or suspend such sanction or penalty.

3) During the course of any investigation by the Exchange, or disciplinary proceeding by the BCC, the Board of Governors or the Commission, if the evidence indicates that a crime may have been committed, the appropriate body, as applicable, shall transmit the evidence of the crime to a public prosecutor or court that would have jurisdiction to prosecute or adjudicate the crime. Such criminal reference, however, shall not constitute grounds for a stay or suspension of any investigation or proceeding undertaken by the Exchange, the BCC, Board of Governors or Commission, as applicable.

4) The rules of the Baghdad Stock Exchange shall be applicable to the Iraq Stock Exchange, but only to the extent consistent with this interim Law and the rules hereunder.

5) Persons authorized to engage in securities transactions according to this Law shall not, unless they are banks, be required to be licensed under the Banking Law as to securities-related dealing or brokerage, investment advisory or investment management activities.

6) Following the transfer of full governmental authority to the Iraqi Interim Government, the duties of the Administrator and the Governing Council under this Order shall be assumed by the body vested with national executive authority unless otherwise provided in this Law.[243]

Section 14 Arbitration

1) The Exchange may adopt rules providing for arbitration of disputes between members and between members and such of their customers who shall consent to arbitration. The Exchange may delegate the authority for arbitration to another organization approved by the Commission, provided that all arbitration rules shall be subject to approval, supplementation and abrogation by the Commission.

a) The Commission shall monitor, and obtain reports, from time to time, from the Exchange's arbitration committee.

b) The arbitration committee's mandate, as set forth in Exchange rules, shall be to arbitrate disputes that may arise between two or more Brokers; or between Brokers and customers that are:

i) Related to securities transactions effected on the Exchange;

ii) Subject to clearance and settlement through the Depository Conducting transactions in securities on the Exchange shall be considered an acknowledgement by a Broker to subject any disputes to arbitration.

2) The Exchange arbitration procedures shall be set forth in Exchange rules and approved by the Board of Governors, then submitted to the Commission for approval.

a) With respect to disputes between Brokers, the arbitration committee decisions shall be binding on all parties, subject to such provision for appeal as the Commission, for the protection of investors, may see fit to adopt by rule.

b) With respect to disputes between Brokers and clients, either party may appeal the decision to the Board of Governors of the Exchange; and, if still dissatisfied, to the Commission. The Commission's decision shall be binding and not subject to further appeal.

Section 15 Penalties

Persons who willfully violate the provisions of this Law or a lawful order of the Commission or who fail to comply with the Commission's lawful demand for information or documents under this Law, as well as persons who knowingly and substantially assist such conduct, shall be subject to fines and penalties as specified by law, which may include imprisonment upon a conviction by a court of competent jurisdiction.

Section 16 Entry into Force

This Order shall enter into force upon signature [19 April 2004].[244]

[243] Sec 13(6) was rescinded by CPA Order No 100, sec 3(28)(f) *[Doc 124]*.

[244] A list of nominees for initial members of the Iraq Stock Exchange Board of Governors and the Interim Securities and Exchange Commission may be found in *Al-Waqai Al-Iraqiya*, vol 44, no 3983 (June 2003), 84.

Document 99
Coalition Provisional Authority Order Number 75
CPA/ORD/15 April 2004/75

Realignment of Military Industrial Companies

Pursuant to my authority as Administrator of the Coalition Provisional Authority (CPA), and under the laws and usages of war, and consistent with relevant U.N. Security Council resolutions, including Resolutions 1483 and 1511 (2003),

Furthering commitments to promote public order and safety and restore the conditions of security and stability for the Iraqi people,

Having worked closely with the Governing Council to ensure that economic change occurs in a manner acceptable to the people of Iraq,

Recognizing that many state-owned enterprises previously engaged in military industrial production (heretofore 'military industrial companies') sit idle and largely abandoned throughout Iraq,

Concerned that buildings and factories of companies formerly assigned to the military industrial commission (or 'military industrial companies') often contain stockpiles of hardware and materials that remain deployable for violent uses against Coalition Forces and the people of Iraq, and that employees of these companies remain needlessly underemployed and unable to utilize their skills to promote the welfare of Iraq,

Determined to secure and dispose of these stockpiles and to assign responsibility for reconstituting military industrial companies and reassigning their employees as necessary for the promotion of peace, security, and stability in Iraq,

I hereby promulgate the following:

Section 1 Purposes and Objectives

This Order promotes public order and safety for the Iraqi people by providing for the security and destruction of materials abandoned after the closure of military industrial companies throughout Iraq. This order also restores conditions of stability in Iraq by assigning responsibility for the personnel and assets of military industrial companies to appropriate ministries and facilitating the reconstitution of such companies for peaceful and resourceful uses.

Section 2 Military Industrial Companies

1) Military industrial companies subject to this Order include those state-owned enterprises listed in Annex A. The absence of appropriate responsibility for the facilities and assets of these enterprises has been determined by the Administrator to constitute a continuing threat against Coalition Forces and the people of Iraq if not appropriately secured.

2) State-owned enterprises formerly assigned to institutions dissolved under CPA Order No. 2 (CPA/ORD/23 May 2003/02), Dissolution of Entities,[245] and those enterprises formerly assigned to the military industrial commission are generally subject to inclusion in Annex A.

3) The military industrial commission is an entity dissolved under CPA Order No. 2 (CPA/ORD/23 May 2003/02).

[245] See *Doc 15*.

4) The Administrator retains authority to add state-owned enterprises to Annex A if it is determined that such enterprises previously engaged in military industrial production and either (a) threaten public order and safety on account of stockpiles and/or abandoned materials that may be used for violent purposes against Coalition Forces and the people of Iraq, or (b) have real property or other tangible assets that the enterprise as presently constituted cannot adequately safeguard and thus stand in danger of being looted, severely damaged, or destroyed.[246]

5) The Minister of Industry shall be notified of any additions or deletions to Annex A within ten days of such action being taken by the Administrator. The Minister of Industry shall also inform the Administrator of any state-owned enterprise known to have been engaged in military industrial production, but not listed in Annex A.

Section 3 Disposition of Military Industrial Assets and Employees

1) The Administrator retains authority to secure facilities and dispose of the material assets of enterprises listed in Annex A so long as the Administrator finds that such facilities or assets or the lack of control over such facilities and assets constitute a continuing threat to Coalition Forces and the people of Iraq.

2) The Administrator also retains authority to reclassify and/or reorganize the enterprises listed in Annex A, so long as the Administrator finds such reclassification and/or reorganization essential to the safety of Coalition Forces and the people of Iraq, the preservation of assets and property for the people of Iraq, or the restoration of societal conditions necessary to the self determination of the Iraqi people. Where an enterprise listed in Annex A is not reassigned to another Iraqi ministry, the liabilities of such enterprise shall be assumed by the Ministry of Finance.

3) The Administrator further retains authority to reassign otherwise unemployed workers of the enterprises listed in Annex A to other Iraqi ministries, governmental agencies, governmental instrumentalities, or state-owned enterprises, so long as the Administrator finds such reassignment furthers the security and safety of Coalition Forces and the people of Iraq or furthers the restoration of societal conditions necessary to the self determination of a free people.

4) To ensure continuity in the economy of Iraq and the salaries of workers reassigned under this Section, the Minister of Finance will assure that the budget of any enterprise reassigned and/or reclassified under this Section, and the associated payroll information for any employee reassigned under this Section, shall follow that enterprise or employee to their new ministry or place of employment. Employees reassigned under this Section shall be guaranteed a salary commensurate with the salary paid by their former employer.

5) The Minister of Industry must be notified in writing of any action taken under this Section, and within 14 days of such notice may issue an opinion as to whether such action serves the interests of the Iraqi people. The Minister of Industry may make specific recommendations for alternative courses of action, keeping in mind that the Administrator retains full authorization under the laws and usage of war to ensure and restore public order and security in Iraq.[247]

[246] All references in sec 2(4), 3(1), 3(2) and 3(3) to 'the Administrator' were replaced with 'the Prime Minister in consultation with the Council of Ministers' by CPA Order No 100, sec 3(29)(a) *[Doc 124]*.

[247] Sec 3(5) was rescinded and replaced by CPA Order No 100, sec 3(29)(b) *[Doc 124]*.

Section 4 Assignment and Consolidation

1) Responsibility for military industrial companies and the assets and personnel thereof not listed in Annex A shall be assigned to the Ministry of Industry and Minerals or such other ministry as the Administrator deems appropriate. These companies shall include all state-owned enterprises formerly supervised or owned by institutions dissolved under CPA Order No. 2 (CPA/ORD/23 May 2003/02), or formerly assigned to the military industrial commission.

2) Military industrial companies assigned to the Minister of Industry and Minerals under this Section may be subject to consolidation pursuant to the procedures set forth in other CPA Orders.

Section 5 Administrative Instructions

The Administrator may delegate authority to issue Administrative Instructions to clarify and implement this Order.

Section 6 Inconsistent Legislation

Any provision of Iraqi law that is inconsistent with this Order or Annex A is hereby suspended to the extent of such inconsistency.

Section 7 Entry into Force

This Order shall enter into force on the date of signature [20 April 2004].

ANNEX A

Military Industry Commission Companies (MIC's) to Ministry of Industry and Minerals (MIM):

Enterprise Name	Area of Activity	Total Amount of Workers	Buildings Level of Destruction (%)	Machines Destruction and Looting (%)	Assign Employees and Assets to:
1. Al Saheed	Copper production	1,300	11.9%	45%	MIM
2. Tareq	Pesticides, chemicals	896	30.6%	25%	Ministry of Finance
3. Hammurabi	Pistols, small arms	636	2.8%	15%	Ministry of Finance
4. Al Tahady	Electromecanichal	399	10.4%	35%	MIM
5. Ibn Waleed	Heavy armored veh. Rep	926	10.5%	60%	Ministry of Finance
6. Al Ikhaa	Mechanical, optics	2,382	1.7%	20%	MIM
7. Al Rasheed	Co2 producer, mechanical	2,290	43.2 %	50%	Ministry of Finance
8. Asahf al Kabir	Concrete additives	86	26.1%	35%	Ministry of Finance
9. Al Noaman	Plastic injection, irrigation	643	6.0%	10%	MIM
10. Al Uboor	Mechanical machining	1,217	70.4%	100%	Ministry of Finance
11. Al Mansour	Solar cells, IC, gases	670	0.2%	5%	MIM
12. Radhwan	Machining	760	34.0%	60%	Ministry of Finance
13. Al Nidaa	Dies, molds, gears	1,281	41.8%	80%	Ministry of Finance
14. Al Salam	Construction Equip.	752	7.7%	100%	Ministry of Housing
15. Ibn Majed	Eng. Mfg. Marine et al.	1,648	21.6%	30%	MIM

MIC's to Ministry of Labor and Social Affairs (MOLSA):

Enterprise Name	Area of Activity	Total Amount of Workers	Buildings Level of Destruction(%)	Machines Destruction and Looting(%)	Assign Employees and Assets to:
1. [sic] Training Center	All defense SOE's specialties	N/A	N/A	N/A	Ministry of Labor

MIC's That Will Have Surviving Assets and Employees Transferred to Other Iraqi Government Agencies:

Enterprise Name	Area of Activity	Total Amount of Workers	Buildings Level of Destruction (%)	Machines Destruction and Looting (%)	Assign Employees and Assets to:
1. Jaber ben Hayan	Plastic, rubber, filters	904	25.7%	95%	Ministry of Finance
2. Yarmuk	Ammunitions, barbed wire	2,708	65.8%	100%	Ministry of Finance
3. Al ezz	Electronic switching	1,046	23.7%	100%	Ministry of Finance
4. Al Kadissiya	Guns, grenades, mortars	3,035	69.9%	100%	Ministry of Finance
5. Al Fidaa	Hydraulic, pneumatic systems	1,285	50.2%	100%	Ministry of Finance
6. Al Karama	Missiles, mechanical	2,287	51.4%	40%	Ministry of Finance
7. Al Qaqa	Explosives, powder, TNT	5,365	36.6%	85%	Ministry of Finance
8. Bader	Tools, dies	1,631	82.8%	100%	Ministry of Finance
9. Tabook	Powder for cartridges	532	0.3%	20%	Ministry of Finance
10. Al Hadhar	Chemical products	572	70.6%	100%	Ministry of Finance
11. 7 Nissan	Fuses, military shells	2,652	94.2%	100%	Ministry of Finance
12. Al Hareth	Radars, welding equipment	1,387	0.0%	60%	Ministry of Finance
13. Al Kindi	R & D radars	976	38.0%	90%	Ministry of Finance
14. Sanahareeb	Irrigation systems	675	22.3%	100%	Ministry of Finance
15. Salahuddeen	Communication, radars	2,900	34.2%	75%	Ministry of Finance
16.Ibn Rushd	Qa, testing, inspection	448	50.0%	100%	Ministry of Finance
17. Hutten	Ammunition, guns, mortars	5,473	25.9%	70%	Ministry of Finance

Document 100
Coalition Provisional Authority Order Number 76

CPA/ORD/20 May 2004/76

Consolidations of State-Owned Enterprises

Pursuant to my authority as Administrator of the Coalition Provisional Authority (CPA) and under the laws and usages of war, and consistent with relevant U.N. Security Council resolutions, including Resolutions 1483 and 1511 (2003),

Having worked closely with the Governing Council to ensure that economic change occurs in a manner acceptable to the people of Iraq,

Acknowledging the Governing Council's desire to bring about significant change to the Iraqi economic system by promoting economic reconstruction and the conditions for sustainable development in a competitive global marketplace,

Determined to encourage more efficient Iraqi governance by consolidating government functions carried out by certain state-owned enterprises into government agencies,

Further committed to improve the production and economic performance of some Iraqi state-owned enterprises by merging them together,

I hereby promulgate the following:

Section 1 Purpose

This Order provides for the consolidation and reorganization of certain state-owned enterprises into government ministries or agencies. This Order also clarifies the operation of existing procedures with respect to the merger of state-owned enterprises.

Section 2 Consolidation

1) The state-owned enterprises listed in Column 1 of Annex A shall be consolidated into the Iraqi ministries listed opposite those companies in Column 2 and may be reorganized or reclassified as appropriate under the particular economic facts and circumstances, so long as such reorganization remains consistent with this Order. The Administrator may add to and remove state-owned enterprises from Annex A. A minister may propose to the Administrator a state-owned enterprise for consolidation. Following the transfer of governmental authority to the Interim Iraqi Government, a minister shall make proposals for consolidation of state-owned enterprises to the Council of Ministers or its successor. Generally, state-owned enterprises selected for consolidation will be those that are not a complete business, but that provide a needed and valuable service, the operations and assets of which can be successfully transferred to a ministry. State-owned enterprises that include any private ownership shall not be consolidated pursuant to this Order.

2) Such consolidation shall be effected on approval of the Administrator and executed under the direction of the minister of the ministry into which the state-owned enterprise will be consolidated (the 'gaining ministry'). Following the transfer of authority to the Interim Iraqi Government, a consolidation shall be effected on approval of the Council of Ministers or its successor. The minister shall have the authority to reorganize the state-owned enterprise or components thereof in a manner that effectively integrates the enterprise into the respective ministry.

3) The gaining minister may, with the written approval of the Minister of Planning (or his delegee), and as provided by law, sell or otherwise dispose of any surplus assets, except real property and cultural property (as defined in the Convention for the Protection of Cultural Property in the Event of Armed Conflict of 1954), of the state-owned enterprise or the ministry that are no longer necessary to the continued functioning of such enterprise or ministry as a result of the consolidation; provided, however, that such sale or disposition is accomplished through a transparent and market-based transaction between two parties with independent interests, operating in good faith and at arms-length, resulting in fair market value compensation to the ministry. The proceeds of any sale or disposition under this Section shall be paid to the Ministry of Finance, which may, in its discretion and with a view toward encouraging the sale of unnecessary surplus assets, pay up to 50% of such proceeds to the gaining ministry, so long as the proceeds are paid through the gaining ministry's existing accounts and reported in line with usual budget and accounting procedures.

4) Once the consolidation of a state-owned enterprise is complete, the gaining minister shall submit a completion certificate to the Ministry of Finance, the Governing Council and the Administrator. Following the transfer of governmental authority to the Interim Iraqi

Government, the gaining Ministry shall submit a completion certificate to the Ministry of Finance and to the Council of Ministers or its successor.

5) The completion certificate shall contain, at a minimum, the following:
   a) the name of the consolidated state-owned enterprise;
   b) the name of the relevant ministry;
   c) any assets disposed of as part of the consolidation and the amounts received as a result of that disposal;
   d) the date on which the consolidation was completed;
   e) the budget for the consolidated state-owned enterprise within the ministry, including a sheet of spent, committed, and remaining budget allocations for the current year; and
   f) a list of employees consolidated into the relevant ministry.

6) After submission of the completion certificate and approval of budget allocations for the current year by the Ministry of Finance, paragraph (3) above shall no longer be applicable and Iraqi law shall prevail. The Ministry of Finance shall expedite procedures for reviewing submitted completion certificates, and current year budget allocations shall be deemed approved if not acted upon within two weeks of submission.

7) In cases where the state-owned enterprise is consolidated into a ministry that did not supervise the state-owned enterprise, the gaining ministry shall agree in writing with the releasing ministry on the terms of the consolidation, including, with respect to the payment and identification of any and all outstanding obligations, disposition of assets and employee-related matters. Such an agreement is not required where the former ministry of the state-owned enterprise has itself been dissolved prior to the consolidation, including all ministries dissolved pursuant to CPA Order No. 2 (CPA/ORD/23 May 2003/2).[248]

Section 3 Contracts, Property and Budgets

1) By operation of this Order, the ministry into which the state-owned enterprise is consolidated shall be substituted for the state-owned enterprise as a party in each contract to which the state-owned enterprise is a party. Upon consolidation, the substituting ministry shall be entitled to exercise all of the rights and receive all of the benefits of the enterprise.

2) Notwithstanding paragraph (1) above, the substitution of the relevant ministry for the state-owned enterprise in a contract shall not constitute an explicit or implicit waiver of any immunity, including sovereign immunity, to which the relevant ministry is entitled. Nor shall the relevant ministry retain benefits and entitlements concerning revenue generation, such as raising funds by issuing debt, making loans from a bank other than the Central Bank of Iraq, or holding a bank account outside the Central Bank of Iraq.

3) Except as set forth in Section 2(3), title to all property owned by the state-owned enterprise being consolidated – whether movable or real, tangible or intangible – shall be transferred to the gaining ministry. The gaining ministry shall accomplish such transfer of property through the means or procedures prescribed by Iraqi law.

4) After a completion certificate is delivered to the Governing Council and the Administrator, (or the Council of Ministers or its successor, as appropriate) the Ministry of Finance shall transfer to the gaining ministry the allocation of the national budget associated with the state-owned enterprise being consolidated.

[248] See *Doc 15*.

Section 4 Legal Identity

1) Upon the date that the completion certificate is submitted to the Governing Council and the Administrator, (or the Council of Ministers or its successor, as appropriate) the state-owned enterprise shall no longer have a separate legal identity and shall cease to exist.

2) Notwithstanding paragraph (1), the authorities granted by law, regulation or rule to the state-owned enterprise being consolidated shall be transferred to the gaining ministry and may be exercised by the gaining ministry as part of its own authorities.

Section 5 Modifications to the State Companies Law

To effectuate the terms of this Order, the State Companies Law shall be modified as follows:

1) Article 31, Paragraph First of the State Companies Law, No. 22 of 1997 (the 'State Companies Law') shall be amended to read in full: 'It is permissible to merge two or more wholly state-owned enterprises into a single state-owned enterprise, provided they engage in a similar or integrated activity. If all of the state-owned enterprises involved are overseen by a single ministry, the relevant minister may propose the merger. If each of the state-owned enterprises involved is overseen by a different ministry, ministers of all involved ministries must agree in writing to the merger, including with respect to which ministry will ultimately oversee the state-owned enterprise resulting from the merger (for the purposes of Article 31, 32, 33 and 34, the 'new enterprise').'

2) Article 31, Paragraph Second of the State Companies law shall be amended to read in full: 'The involved minister or ministries shall prepare a proposal describing the merger and submit it for final approval to the Administrator in consultation with the Governing Council. Following the transfer of governmental authority to the Interim Iraqi Government, the proposal shall be submitted to the Council of Ministers or its successor for approval.'

3) Article 32 of the State Companies Law shall be amended to read in full: 'Once the Administrator in consultation with the Governing Council (or the Council of Ministers or its successor, as appropriate) has approved the merger pursuant to Article 31, Paragraph Second, the ministry that will ultimately supervise the new enterprise shall amend the original contract or draw up a new contract. The board of directors shall amend the basic law or draft a new basic law.'

4) Article 33 of the State Companies Law shall be amended to read in full: 'The ministry that will ultimately oversee the new enterprise shall inform the Registrar of the amended contract or provide the Registrar with the new contract. The merger shall be considered valid as of the date of the Administrator's (or Council of Ministers' or its successors', as appropriate) approval, unless otherwise specified by the Administrator in consultation with the Governing Council (or the Council of Ministers or its successor, as appropriate). On the date the merger becomes valid, the corporate status of the enterprise or enterprises being merged into the new enterprise shall expire. The Registrar shall issue a new certification of establishment.'

5) Article 34, Paragraph First of the State Companies Law shall be amended to read in full: 'The Governing Council, and subsequent to the transfer of authority to the Interim Iraqi Administration, the Council of Ministers or its successor, shall publish notice of its merger decision in the Official Gazette of Iraq and, if available, the bulletin issued by the Registrar.'

6) Article 34, Paragraph Second of the State Companies Law shall be amended to read in full: 'The rights and obligations of the enterprise or enterprises being merged shall revert to the new enterprise.'

7) Following the transfer of full governmental authority to the Iraqi Interim Government, the duties of the Administrator and the Governing Council under this Order shall be assumed by the body vested with national executive authority.[249]

Section 6 Administrative Instructions
The Administrator may delegate authority to issue Administrative Instructions to clarify and implement this Order.

Section 7 Inconsistent Legislation
Any provision of Iraqi law that is inconsistent with this Order or Annex A is hereby suspended to the extent of such inconsistency.

Section 8 Entry into Force
This Order shall enter into force on the date of signature [28 May 2004].

ANNEX A

SOEs to be Merged:

1. The Industrial Bank into Rafidain Bank, with Rafidain Bank surviving
2. The Real Estate Bank into Rafidain Bank, with Rafidain Bank surviving
3. The Agricultural Bank into Rasheed Bank, with Rasheed Bank surviving
4. The Socialist Bank into Rasheed Bank, with Rasheed Bank surviving.

Document 101
Coalition Provisional Authority Order Number 77
CPA/ORD/18 April 2004/77

Board of Supreme Audit

Pursuant to my authority as Administrator of the Coalition Provisional Authority (CPA), and under the laws and usages of war, and consistent with relevant U.N. Security Council resolutions, including Resolutions 1483 and 1511 (2003),

Noting that the Board of Supreme Audit Law, No. 6 of 1990, (the 'Board of Supreme Audit Law' or the 'Law') names the Board of Supreme Audit as the supreme audit institution of Iraq,

Understanding that an effective supreme audit institution is needed to (1) provide the public and government with objective, accurate information about government operations and financial conditions, and (2) promote economy and efficiency by carrying out a broad range of financial and performance audits and program evaluations,

Understanding that an effective supreme audit institution can serve as a public guardian by identifying fraud, waste, and abuse, and by promoting anti-corruption and integrity in government,

Determined to ensure the independence and effectiveness of the Board of Supreme Audit of Iraq, while preserving the Board's basic structure,

[249] Sec 5(7) was amended by CPA Order No 100, sec 3(30) *[Doc 124]*.

Having consulted with the Iraqi Governing Council and the Board of Supreme Audit, I hereby promulgate the following:

Section 1 Purpose

This Order reestablishes the Board of Supreme Audit as an independent public institution empowered to enhance the economy, efficiency, effectiveness and credibility of the Iraqi government. It provides that the Board shall work in conjunction with the Commission on Public Integrity and Inspectors General of individual ministries to ensure that the Iraqi government remains honest, transparent and accountable to the people of Iraq.

Section 2 Board of Supreme Audit

The Board of Supreme Audit Law shall remain in effect except to the extent amended by this Order:

1) All powers and authorities granted by the Board of Supreme Audit Law to the now-dissolved Office of the President, Revolutionary Command Council and its Council Chairman are hereby revoked.

2) Article 1 of the Board of Supreme Audit Law is amended to read as follows:

'First: The Board of Supreme Audit is hereby established as a separate and independent government institution with juridical personality empowered to enhance the economy, efficiency, effectiveness, and credibility of the Iraqi government. The Board shall work in conjunction with the Commission on Public Integrity and the Inspectors General of individual ministries to ensure that the Iraqi government remains honest, transparent and accountable to the people of Iraq.

Second: The head of the Board shall be the Board President who shall be supported by two Deputy Presidents. The Administrator shall appoint the initial Board President and Deputy Presidents after consultation with the Governing Council. The terms of these appointments shall end after five years, or one year after the adoption of a permanent constitution pursuant to the Transitional Administrative Law, whichever is sooner. The Prime Minister shall appoint successor Board Presidents and Deputy Presidents for terms of five years, from a pool of three nominees for each appointment to be submitted by the Higher Juridical Council. In submitting its nominees, the Higher Juridical Council shall take account of any views expressed by the Board. A Board President or Deputy President shall serve no more than two terms, whether or not successive.

Third: The Board President and Deputy Presidents shall be selected without regard to political affiliation (consistent with applicable de-Baathification policy) and on the basis of integrity, proven leadership, and training and experience in accounting, auditing, financial analysis, management analysis, public administration, or related fields. In addition, the Board President and Deputy Presidents shall possess demonstrated knowledge, skills, abilities and experience in conducting audits and performance evaluations.

Fourth: The Board President is at the level of minister and enjoys all the rights and privileges of a minister, with authority over Board affairs, personnel, establishment, and budget. The Board President is independent and may not serve in the cabinet in any capacity.

Fifth: The Board President and Deputy Presidents can be removed from office only for cause, as determined by the Administrator in consultation with the Iraqi Governing

Council. After the Iraqi Interim Government assumes full governance authority in Iraq, the Board President or a Deputy President may be removed from office only by a two-thirds vote in the body vested with national legislative authority, for incapacity, serious misconduct in or out of office, dereliction of duty, or gross abuse of office.'

3) Article 2 of the Board of Supreme Audit Law, paragraph Fourth, is amended to read as follows: 'Promulgate auditing and accounting regulations, based on internationally accepted auditing and accounting standards and best practices, and cooperate with the Commission on Public Integrity to continually improve the rules, practices, and standards applicable to the management, accounting and auditing of public funds in Iraq.'

4) Article 2 of the Board of Supreme Audit Law is amended to add at the end the following paragraphs:

'Fifth: Detect through audits and performance evaluations evidence of corruption, fraud, waste, abuse and inefficiency in matters related to the receipt, disbursement, and use of public money.

Sixth: Investigate and report on matters relating to the efficient disbursement and use of public funds as formally requested by the Coalition Provisional Authority, the Iraqi Governing Council or any successor body vested with national legislative authority.

Seventh: Refer all allegations or evidence of corruption, fraud, waste, abuse or inefficiency in the disbursement and use of public funds to the Inspector General of the relevant ministry or, where appropriate, directly to the Commission on Public Integrity.

Eighth: Prescribe regulations and procedures for carrying out its duties as the supreme audit institution of Iraq.'[250]

5) Article 3 of the Board of Supreme Audit Law is amended to read as follows:

'First: The Board shall annually prepare and publish a plan (the 'Annual Plan') for fulfilling its mission as the supreme audit institution of Iraq. The Annual Plan shall describe and comment on (a) all anticipated audits and performance evaluations to be undertaken in the coming year; (b) anticipated areas of cooperation with the Commission on Public Integrity and Inspectors General of individual ministries; and (c) any other matter deemed by the Board to be necessary to the achievement of transparent, accountable, and efficient government in Iraq.

Second: The Board shall annually prepare and publish a report (the 'Annual Report') that discusses in detail the audits and performance evaluations undertaken over the previous twelve months. The Annual Report shall include a statement of audits, evaluations, and related work initiated by the Board. It shall also include a statement of audits, evaluations, and related work initiated upon formal request by the Commission on Public Integrity, the Coalition Provisional Authority, the Iraqi Governing Council, or the body vested with the national legislative authority. The Annual Report shall further assess the overall adequacy and effectiveness of government measures taken to ensure efficiency and transparency in the use and disbursement of public funds in Iraq, and include any legislative or other proposals determined by the Board to be necessary to the fulfillment of its duties as a supreme audit institution.

Third: The Board shall publish and widely disseminate the final results of its work product, including all audits and performance evaluations, plans and reports. At least quarterly, the Board shall publish a list of its recent audit reports and distribute the list as widely as possible, using the Internet if available. All reports shall be made available

[250] Sec 2(4) was amended by CPA Order No 100, sec 3(31) *[Doc 124]*.

to the press and any interested person upon written request. This Section does not apply to information classified for national security purposes by authorized agencies.
Fourth: The Board shall establish procedures for preparing and submitting to the body vested with national legislative authority the Annual Plan and the Annual Report within 90 days of the end of each fiscal year.'

6) Article 7 of the Board of Supreme Audit Law is amended to add at the end the following paragraphs:

'Fourth: When records necessary to conducting a Board audit or performance evaluation are not made available to the Board within a reasonable time, the Board shall make a written request to the Inspector General of the ministry under review. The request shall state the authority for inspecting the records and the reason for the inspection. The relevant ministry has 20 days to make the records available to the Board or describe the basis on which the records are being withheld. If the Board is not satisfied that reasonable ground exist for withholding the records, the Board may refer the matter to the Commission on Public Integrity for further investigation and, if necessary, enforcement of relevant disclosure obligations.

Fifth: The Board shall have the authority to audit classified programs and issue classified reports, so long as the auditors have the proper security clearance and protect the classified information pursuant to all applicable laws and regulations.'

7) Article 8 of the Board of Supreme Audit Law is suspended.

8) Article 9 of the Board of Supreme Audit Law is amended to read as follows:
'The Board shall have authority to perform financial evaluations of public contracts and to ensure that government grants, loans, facilities and privileges are employed for the purposes for which they were offered or loaned.'

9) Article 10 of the Board of Supreme Audit Law is amended to read as follows:
'First: Upon discovering a financial infringement, or reasonable suspicion of a financial infringement, or other financial irregularity, the Board shall instruct the Inspector General of the relevant ministry to investigate and correct the infringement or irregularity. The Board shall immediately notify the Commission on Public Integrity whenever a matter is referred to an Inspector General pursuant to this Section.

Second: If a disagreement occurs between the Board and a ministry or other government entity, and the Board determines that referral to the ministry or other government entity would be futile, the Board may refer a matter directly to the Commission on Public Integrity for further investigation or enforcement of relevant laws and regulations.'

10) Article 11, paragraph First, subparagraph c, of the Law is amended to read as follows: 'd- Violations of the Code for State Employees and Social Sector Discipline or other regulations promulgated by the Commission on Public Integrity.'

11) Article 12 of the Board of Supreme Audit Law is suspended.

12) Article 13 of the Board of Supreme Audit Law is suspended.

13) Article 15 of the Board of Supreme Audit Law is suspended.

14) Article 17 of the Board of Supreme Audit Law is amended to read as follows: 'When necessary, the Board's President may and in the manner that he decides, enlist outside experts to assist the Board. Such experts shall be compensated in a manner to be determined by the Board, so long as such compensation is consistent with law and fully disclosed in the Annual Report.'

15) Article 19 of the Board of Supreme Audit Law is suspended.

16) Article 22, Second, of the Supreme Board of Audit Law [sic] is suspended.

Section 3 Entry into Force
This Order shall enter into force on the date of signature [25 April 2004].

Document 102
Coalition Provisional Authority Order Number 78
CPA/ORD/19 April 2004/78

Facilitation of Court-Supervised Debt Resolution Procedures

Pursuant to my authority as Administrator of the Coalition Provisional Authority (CPA) and under the laws and usages of war, and consistent with relevant U.N. Security Council resolutions, including Resolutions 1483 and 1511 (2003),

Having worked closely with the Governing Council to ensure that economic change as necessary to benefit the people of Iraq occurs in a manner acceptable to the people of Iraq,

Acknowledging the Governing Council's desire to bring about significant change to the Iraqi economic system as necessary to improve the condition of the people of Iraq,

Determined to improve the conditions of life, technical skills, and opportunities for all Iraqis and to fight unemployment with its associated deleterious effect on public security,

Recognizing that companies, lenders and entrepreneurs require a fair, efficient, and predictable mechanism for resolving burdensome indebtedness when incurred by businesses,

Noting that several provisions within Iraqi legislation call for unduly harsh punishments for financially distressed entrepreneurs,

Further noting that resolving the indebtedness of large corporations through in-court procedures is a challenging task requiring training and experience,

Recognizing the CPA's obligation to provide for the effective administration of Iraq, to ensure the well being of the Iraqi people and to enable the social and economic functions and normal transactions of every day life,

Acting in a manner consistent with the Report of the Secretary General to the Security Council of July 17, 2003, concerning the need for the development of Iraq and its transition from a non-transparent centrally planned economy to a free market economy characterized by sustainable economic growth through the establishment of a dynamic private sector, and the need to enact institutional and legal reforms to give it effect,

Having coordinated with the international financial institutions, as referenced in paragraph 8(e) of U.N. Security Council Resolution 1483,

In close consultation with and acting in coordination with the Governing Council, I hereby promulgate the following:

Section 1 Definitions

1) 'Bankruptcy Law' means Part V of Law No. 149 of 1970 on the Code of Commerce, as amended.

2) 'Penal Code' means the Law No. 111 of 1969 on the Penal Code, as amended.

3) 'Enforcement Law' means Law No. 45 of 1980 on Enforcement of Judgments (Law on Execution).

4) 'Civil Code' means Law No. 40 of 1953 on the Civil Law.

5) Gender specific language in this Order shall apply equally to male and female, and where appropriate, to entities (juridical persons) and things.

Section 2 Designation of Judges to Hear Petitions for Bankruptcy and Schemes of Arrangement

1) One or more first instance court judges in each governate [sic] shall be designated to hear cases arising from petitions for bankruptcy or a scheme of arrangement.

2) A judge described in paragraph 1 of this Section shall also hear petitions for relief filed by foreign companies with a head branch office in his designated region.

3) The Council of Judges shall designate the judges described in paragraph 1 of this Section within 45 days from the date this Order enters into force. Such judges shall have demonstrated a high level of expertise and/or potential ability with respect to disputes concerning companies, entrepreneurs, and banks.

4) The designated judges shall hear petitions for bankruptcy or a scheme of arrangement as a portion of their regular caseloads.

Section 3 Licensing of Bankruptcy Trustees

1) The Ministry of Justice ('Ministry') shall be authorized to license individuals to serve as bankruptcy trustees under the Bankruptcy Law. The Ministry shall issue licensing procedures to govern this activity.

2) The Ministry's licensing procedures shall ensure that license holders have a clear understanding of the procedures under the bankruptcy law as well as particular expertise in at least one of the following areas:

a) commercial law and civil procedures;
b) accounting and business finance;
c) business management.

The procedures shall further ensure that license holders have a general knowledge in the areas described item (a) through (c) where they lack particular expertise.

3) The Ministry shall ensure that license holders perform their duties in conformity with the Bankruptcy Law and its goals. A license holder failing to perform his duties may be subject to fine, or suspension or cancellation of his license in accordance with procedures to be established by the Ministry.

4) The Ministry shall establish and promote a licensing program sufficient to provide bankruptcy judges and creditors a reasonable number of choices of qualified candidates to serve as bankruptcy trustees by no later six months after the date this Order enters into force.

Section 4 Amendments to the Bankruptcy Law

1) A new, unnumbered heading entitled 'Preliminary Provisions' shall be added to the Bankruptcy Law ('Law') prior to Chapter One.

2) Four new articles shall be added to the Law under Preliminary Provisions and prior to Chapter One. The articles shall read as follows:

Article 562. In this Part of the Commercial Code, the terms below shall be defined as follows:

(1) A 'general privileged creditor' is a creditor that has a preference in payment to the debtor's property that is not subject to a mortgage or special privilege. The general privileged creditors include those described in sub-paragraphs (a) - (c) of paragraph 2 of Article 708.

(2) An 'ordinary creditor' is a creditor whose claim is neither secured by mortgage nor otherwise privileged.

(3) The 'body of creditors' consists of the general privileged and ordinary creditors.

(4) The 'state of union of creditors' is the stage of the bankruptcy proceedings where the property of the bankrupt is disposed of, with the proceeds used to repay the creditors to the extent possible.

Article 563. The purpose of this Part of the Commercial Code is to establish judicial proceedings by which a trader and his creditors may resolve the trader's indebtedness in a collective, transparent, and realistic manner, when the trader no longer can pay debts when they come due. Such resolution may result in a judicially approved agreement between the trader and his creditors or may result in the sale of the trader's property for the repayment of the trader's debts. In either case, the proceedings shall respect the pre-existing contractual and property rights of the trader's creditors to the extent possible.

Article 564. A trader holding a permit or license to engage in banking business and other banking activities may not be subject as a debtor to the proceedings described in this Part.

Article 565. During the proceedings established in this Part, Articles 1361-1380 of the Civil Code shall apply to the extent they do not conflict with the provisions contained herein.

3) Article 569 (chapeau paragraph) is amended to read as follows:

(1) A trader must present a bankruptcy petition against himself within fifteen days of the date of suspension of payments. This period may be extended up to an additional forty-five days if the trader has informed substantially all his creditors of his financial difficulties and is attempting in good faith to renegotiate the terms of his obligations. The bankruptcy petition shall be in the form of a report, giving the grounds for the suspension of payments, and must be presented to the court with the following documents:

4) Article 570, paragraph 1 of the Law is amended to read as follows: 'A creditor or group of creditors with undisputed commercial debts worth more than five hundred thousand dinars, the scheduled payments for which have been missed for more than thirty days, may present a bankruptcy petition against the debtor.

5) Article 570 of the Law is supplemented with paragraphs 3, 4 and 5, which shall read as follows:

(3) Five or more employees of a trader with undisputed claims for wage arrears exceeding one month may jointly present a bankruptcy petition against the debtor.

(4) The government body or bodies authorized to enforce obligations to pay taxes and other mandatory payments to the state treasury may present a bankruptcy petition against the debtor. The bases for presentment shall be the same as those for bringing a forced execution of obligations for payment of taxes and other mandatory payments to the state under applicable law.

(5) A debt described in this Article shall be presumed to be undisputed if it is reflected in a judgment or an executive document.

6) Article 571 of the Law is suspended.

7) Article 573 of the Law is amended to read as follows:

'(1) The court of first instance designated to hear cases arising from petitions for bankruptcy or schemes of arrangement in the governate [sic] or subsection thereof wherein lies the head office of the debtor shall have jurisdiction to adjudicate his bankruptcy.

(2) A trader that is under bankruptcy proceedings in a foreign state and that has a branch in Iraq may seek the following relief in the court designated to hear bankruptcy petitions:

(a) an order suspending all individual suits brought against the trader in any court in Iraq by ordinary creditors or those having general privileged rights;

(b) an order prohibiting the seizure of assets of the trader wherever located in Iraq unless such assets are subject to a mortgage or privileged right under Iraqi law;

(c) an order requiring third parties holding the trader's property to surrender such property to the representative of the trader;

(d) an order providing other necessary relief.

(3) In determining whether to grant the relief described in the preceding paragraph, the court shall consider:

(a) the protection of creditors in Iraq and the inconvenience in pursuing their claims in a foreign proceeding;

(b) the just treatment of all creditors through resort to a unified bankruptcy proceeding;

(c) whether other jurisdictions have given recognition to the foreign proceeding;

(d) the extent that the foreign proceeding recognizes the rights of creditors and other interested parties in a manner substantially in accordance with the bankruptcy proceedings in Iraq;

(e) the extent that the foreign proceeding has recognized and shown deference to Iraqi bankruptcy proceedings.'

8) Article 574, paragraph 2 of the Law is suspended.

9) Article 576 of the Law is amended to read as follows: 'The judge who adjudicates the bankruptcy shall be the judge in charge of the bankruptcy (Judge Commissaire); the court of appeal may at anytime order his replacement by another judge designated to hear bankruptcy cases if it determines that such replacement will serve the general interests of the creditors and the debtor.'

10) Article 578 of the Law is supplemented with a new paragraph 2, which shall read as follows: 'The date of payment suspension will be the date on which the debtor could no longer make payments on his debts as they fell due regardless of whether he paid such debts in part.' Paragraph 2 of Article 578 shall be renumbered as paragraph 3.

11) Article 580, paragraph 2 of the Law is amended to read as follows: 'On the day following the adjudication, the court shall cause the applicable order to be posted on the Bulletin Board of the court for thirty days. Within five days from the adjudication date, the trustee in bankruptcy shall submit copies thereof to every court within the jurisdiction of which lies a head office, branch, agency or office of the debtor for having the same posted on the Bulletin Board of such court for thirty days.'

12) Article 585, paragraph 1 of the Law is amended as follows: 'twenty' is replaced with 'one hundred thousand' and 'two hundred' is replaced with 'one million.'

13) Article 586 of the Law is amended to read as follows:

(1) The court may in the bankruptcy adjudication appoint a paid agent to manage the bankruptcy, who shall be called the 'bankruptcy trustee.'

(2) The court shall choose the bankruptcy trustee from a roster of individuals licensed by the Ministry of Justice to perform such duties. Where the number of licensed bankruptcy trustees in the court's jurisdiction willing to serve is less than

three, the court may designate a lawyer to serve as the bankruptcy trustee, even if such lawyer lacks a bankruptcy trustee's license.

14) Article 587, paragraph 1 of the Law is amended to read as follows: 'A person may not be appointed as a bankruptcy trustee if he is a creditor, debtor, or competitor of the bankrupt, the spouse of the bankrupt, or has a relation to the bankrupt of the fourth degree or closer. He may not be appointed if he has been a partner, employee, accountant, or agent (attorney) of the bankrupt during the two years preceding the declaration of bankruptcy.'

15) Article 587 is supplemented with articles 3 and 4, which shall read as follows:

(3) A bankruptcy trustee shall immediately disclose to the Judge Commissaire and the controller (auditor) any of the circumstances in paragraphs 1 or 2, should they arise during the course of the proceedings.

(4) The Judge Commissaire shall dismiss the bankruptcy trustee unless the latter can demonstrate that the circumstances will not undermine his ability to serve the best interests of the creditors and the confidence that the creditors have in him.

16) Article 589 of the Law is amended to read as follows:

(1) The bankruptcy trustee may delegate the performance of tasks to others where such delegation is likely to more efficiently and effectively safeguard the assets of the bankrupt, benefit the creditors, or otherwise facilitate the progress of the bankruptcy proceedings.

(2) The bankruptcy trustee shall be jointly liable with his deputies for the latter's actions.

(3) No delegation may occur without the prior approval of the Judge Commissaire, save for instances in which actions by deputies are necessary to safeguard the assets of the bankrupt or otherwise protect the interests of the creditors. In such cases the bankruptcy trustee shall apply for post-delegation approval as soon as reasonably possible, explaining in his application the basis for the delegation.

17) Article 591 of the Law is amended to read as follows: 'The bankruptcy judge may of his own accord, or upon application being made by the bankrupt or the controller, decide to dismiss the trustee; the Judge Commissaire shall give a ruling in regard to such application within ten days of its submission, which is subject to appeal.'

18) Article 593, paragraph 2 of the Law is amended to read as follows: 'The Judge Commissaire shall summon the creditors to a meeting in the cases stipulated in the law and shall chair such meetings or delegate such duties to the bankruptcy trustee.'

19) Article 594 of the Law is supplemented with a paragraph 3, which shall read as follows: 'The Judge Commissaire may name the bankruptcy trustee as the official agent to receive service of decisions and summonses on behalf of interested parties or a group thereof if such appointment would expedite proceedings and facilitate distribution of information. In such cases, the bankruptcy trustee shall subsequently serve notices on interested parties in accordance with procedures approved by the Council of Judges.'

20) Article 595, paragraphs 2 and 3 of the Law are amended as follows: In paragraph 2, 'three' is replaced with 'ten'. In paragraph 3, 'ten' is replaced with 'twenty'.

21) Article 596, paragraph 1 of the Law is amended to read as follows: 'The Judge Commissaire shall appoint a controller from among the creditors who nominate themselves for the post, or, with consent of a majority of the seven largest creditors from the private sector, shall appoint an independent auditor chosen by such group. In the latter case, the independent auditor shall serve as a controller but shall be compensated in accordance with procedures for compensating the bankruptcy trustee. He shall also be subject to the restrictions in Article 587.

22) Article 599, paragraph 1 of the Law is amended to read as follows: 'The controller shall not receive fees in consideration of his work, except in cases provided for in Article 596.'

23) Article 602, paragraphs 1 and 2 of the Law are amended to read as follows:

(1) A person who is adjudicated bankrupt shall disclose such information upon request, and, regardless of request, shall disclose such information to any person relying on the bankrupt's integrity and competence.

(2) An adjudication of bankruptcy may be the basis for a justified termination of any arrangement in which the bankrupt's integrity and competence is relied upon by the counterparty.

24) Article 604 of the Law is amended to read as follows: 'Having been adjudicated bankrupt, a bankrupt may not pay or receive debts owing to him. Negotiable instruments reflecting an obligation of the bankrupt shall be deemed opposed.'

25) Article 614 of the Law is amended to read as follows: 'All acts of disposal by the bankrupt occurring 90 days prior to suspending payments other than those set down and within the time limits stipulated in the preceding Article shall be adjudged ineffectual against the body of creditors and shall result in the return of the asset for the benefit of the creditors, if the act of disposal is detrimental to their interests and the counterparty in the disposal was aware at the time of the disposal that the bankrupt had suspended payments.'

26) Article 622 of the Law is amended to read as follows: 'The adjudication of bankruptcy bars the running of interest on ordinary debts and debts that are subject to a general privilege in regard to the body of creditors only; interest on secured debts may only be claimed on amounts resulting from the sale of the mortgaged or charged property; the principal amount of the debt is collected in the first place, then the interest which accrues prior to the bankruptcy adjudication, and then interest which accrues thereafter.

27) The title of Section III of Chapter III is amended to read as follows: 'Creditors whose Debts are Secured by a Mortgage or Special Privileged Right over Movable Property and Creditors with General Privileged Rights'.

28) Article 631, paragraph 1 of the Law is amended to read as follows: 'After seeking the leave of the Judge Commissaire, the trustee may within the ten days following the adjudication of bankruptcy pay out of the funds available to him, and notwithstanding the existence of any other debt, the wages and salaries accruing to the workers and employees before the adjudication of bankruptcy for thirty days; where the trustee does not have at his disposal sufficient funds to pay the foregoing debts, payment thereof must be made from funds of the bankrupt or the first lot of funds coming to the bankruptcy that have resulted from the sale of property not subject to mortgage or special privilege, or from excess proceeds from the sale of such property, even though there are other debts having a priority of order.'

29) Article 633 of the Law is amended to read as follows: 'The general privileged right accorded to the Government on grounds of various kinds of taxes shall cover only the principal portion of the debt of the tax due from the bankrupt for the two years which preceded the adjudication of bankruptcy; other taxes due shall be considered ordinary debts.'

30) Article 634 of the Law is amended to read as follows: 'Where a distribution of the properties to which the right of the body of creditors relate is to occur prior to the sale of movable property secured by mortgage or special privilege, such creditors may participate in such distributions as ordinary creditors to the extent they have abandoned their claim to such security. Mortgagees or creditors having priorities who have not received all or part of their debts from the price of the movable property may participate in regard to the balance remaining for them with the ordinary creditors in the distribution of the properties to which the right of the body of creditors relate, provided their debts have been proved.'

31) An article, to be enumerated as Article 637-A and to be inserted after Article 637 shall read as follows: 'The bankruptcy trustee may, at any time after obtaining leave from the Judge Commissaire, pay the debt secured by a mortgage and or special privilege on immovable property and recover it for the account of the body of creditors.'

32) Article 646 of the Law is amended to read as follows:

(1) Where a purchaser is adjudged bankrupt before he pays the price of goods which have entered into his possession or that of his agent, the vendor may not claim rescission of the sale nor the recovery of the goods and he loses his right of priority, except as provided in paragraph 2 of this Article.

(2) A stipulation enabling the vendor to recover or retain his right of priority over the goods may not be adduced against the body of creditors, unless there is a stipulation which retains ownership of the property in the seller, which has been registered according to the applicable law.

(3) A vendor who has made the stipulation in paragraph (2) and has registered it according to the applicable law shall have the same rights over the goods that a mortgagee has over the mortgaged property.

33) Article 661, paragraph 2 of the Law is amended as follows: 'five hundred' is replaced with 'two million, five hundred thousand'.

34) Article 666 paragraph 1 of the Law shall have appended to it the following sentence: 'If the bankruptcy trustee is effecting service in accordance with paragraph 3 of Article 594, the statement shall also include the preferred method by which the creditor shall receive notices with regard to the proceedings.'

35) Article 667 of the Law is amended as follows: In paragraph 1, 'ten' is replaced with 'thirty'. In paragraph 2, 'ten' is replaced with 'thirty' and 'twenty' is replaced with 'sixty'.

36) Article 668, paragraph 3 of the Law is suspended.

37) Article 669, paragraph 2 of the Law is amended as follows: 'sixty' is replaced with 'one-hundred'.

38) Article 670 of the Law is amended as follows: 'ten' is replaced with 'thirty'

39) Article 678, paragraph 1 of the Law is amended to read as follows: 'The debtor, or creditors representing 25% of the amount of the ordinary debt, may request that a composition offer be considered. The right to submit such request shall expire on the tenth day after the filing of the list of debts prepared in accordance with Article 671. In such cases, the Judge Commissaire shall summon the creditors whose debts have been accepted finally or provisionally to be present at the deliberations of the composition.

40) Article 678, paragraph 3 of the Law is amended to read as follows: 'The bankruptcy trustee shall within the time limit stipulated in the preceding paragraph have the notice to the meeting to be present at the composition deliberations published in one or more daily newspapers determined by the Judge Commissaire.'

41) Article 679, paragraph 1 of the Law is amended to read as follows: 'The composition meeting shall be held at the place and time determined by the Judge Commissaire who shall preside over the meeting. Such meeting shall occur within thirty to forty-five days after the last newspaper publication of the notice stipulated in Article 678.'

42) Article 681 of the law is amended to read as follows: 'The composition shall not be concluded except with the consent of a majority of the creditors with the right to vote whose debts have been accepted finally or provisionally provided they hold two thirds of such debts; creditors who did not participate in the voting shall not be counted for the purposes of the foregoing two majorities and their debts shall not be considered.'

43) Article 682, paragraph 2 of the Law is suspended.

44) Article 683 of the Law is amended to read as follows:

(1) Creditors holding a mortgage or special privilege over particular property of the bankrupt or having the status of a general privileged creditor may not take part in the voting on composition for their debts secured or privileged as aforesaid unless they abandon such securities or privileges in advance; the abandonment may be confined to part of the security or privilege; the abandonment shall be mentioned in the minutes of the meeting.

(2) Any one of the creditors mentioned in the preceding paragraph who takes part in the voting on the composition but fails to declare abandonment of all or part of his security or privilege shall be deemed to have abandoned the entire security or privilege.

(3) In all cases, the abandonment shall be final regardless of whether the composition is concluded.

(4) The security or privilege covered by the abandonment shall regain its validity if the composition is annulled.

45) Article 684, paragraph 2 of the Law shall be amended to read as follows: 'Where the consent stipulated in Article 681 is not attained, the deliberations shall be adjourned for ten days, after which no adjournment shall be made.'

46) Article 687 of the Law is supplemented with new paragraphs 4 and 5, which shall read as follows:

'(4) A composition shall provide for equal treatment of ordinary creditors. An ordinary creditor may nevertheless agree to less favorable treatment under the composition.

(5) A composition shall not be concluded unless all of the arrears on obligations corresponding to claims secured by mortgage or that are otherwise privileged are paid, unless individual creditors with such claims agree to less favorable treatment.'

47) Article 689 of the Law is amended to read as follows:

'(1) A composition shall be valid in regard to the ordinary creditors even when they have not participated in the proceedings or did not approve the composition.

(2) A composition shall have no effect with respect to claims secured with a mortgage or that are otherwise privileged, except where the creditors with such claims agree on an individual basis to be subject to the composition.'

48) Article 691, paragraph 1 of the Law is amended to read as follows: 'All the effects of bankruptcy shall cease by the issue of the order of the Judge Commissaire approving the composition, except for the consequences mentioned in Article 602.'

49) Article 699 of the Law is supplemented with new paragraphs 4 and 5, which shall read as follows:

'(4) So long as general privileged creditors are paid in full, such composition may stipulate the full forgiveness of debts in exchange for the abandonment of the debtor's property.

(5) When the debtor is a limited liability company or joint stock company, the composition may allow for the cancellation of all outstanding shares of the debtor and the issuance of new shares. In lieu of selling the debtor's property, such shares may be sold with the price thereof distributed to the creditors.'

50) Article 701, sub-paragraph (a) of the Law is amended to read as follows: 'if the debtor fails to apply for a composition within the time limits established in Article 678;'.

51) Article 705 of the Law is supplemented with a new paragraph 1, which shall read as follows:

'(1) The property of the debtor available for the benefit of the body of creditors shall include:

(a) property not subject to mortgage or special privilege;
(b) property not subject to recovery under Articles 641- 646;
(c) property not exempted from execution;
(d) the excess proceeds described in Articles 630 and 635.'

The remaining paragraphs in Article 702 are renumbered accordingly.

52) Article 708 of the Law is amended to read as follows:

'(1) The fees, expenses of the administration of the bankruptcy, the aids determined for the bankrupt and his dependents and sums due to creditors enjoying priorities shall be deducted from the proceeds of the sale of the bankrupt's property and the balance distributed to the creditors in accordance with this Article.

(2) The balance described in the preceding paragraph shall be distributed among the body of creditors according to the following order:

(a) the claims described in paragraph 1 of Article 1372 of the Civil Code;
(b) claims for unpaid taxes, duties, and other obligatory payments to the government that arose within the two year period prior to the adjudication of bankruptcy and during its administration;
(c) all claims not having a general privilege, and claims of creditors who have fully or partially abandoned secured or privileged claims.

(3) No category of creditor in the preceding paragraph shall receive distributions until the prior category has been paid in full. Where a distribution is not sufficient to pay a category of creditors in full, creditors in such category shall be paid in proportion to the amount of their claims.

(4) The dividends of the contested debts shall be set aside and kept until a decision is made in regard to said debts.'

53) Article 714 of the Law (chapeau paragraph) is amended as follows: 'one thousand' is replaced with 'five million'.

54) Article 717, paragraph 2 of the Law is amended to read as follows: 'The report provided for in Article 569 shall be submitted to the court designated to hear bankruptcy cases within the jurisdiction of which lies the head office of the company.'

55) Article 719 of the Law is suspended.

56) Article 722, paragraph 1 of the Law is amended to read as follows: 'The Judge Commissaire may of his own initiative or pursuant to an application by the trustee, controller or a creditor order that the consequences stipulated in Article 602 be suffered by directors or managers of a company who would have committed gross faults which led to the disruption of the business or the suspension of payments of the company.'

57) Article 730 of the Law is amended to read as follows: 'Except for the case of fraudulent bankruptcy, the consequences described in Article 602 shall cease to have legal effect after the lapse of one year from the date on which the bankruptcy terminated (was concluded).'

58) Article 743, paragraphs 1 and 3 of the Law are amended to read as follows:

'(1) A trader may present an application for a scheme of arrangement if his financial operations suffered a disruption which may result in a suspension of payments.

***

(3) A scheme of arrangement may be granted to a company which satisfies the terms laid down in the preceding two paragraphs; nevertheless a scheme of arrangement may not be granted to a company in liquidation.'

59) Article 744, paragraph 1 of the Law is amended as follows: 'two years' is replaced with 'one year'.

60) Article 749, paragraph 1, sub-paragraph (c) of the Law is amended by replacing 'the two years' with 'the year'.

61) Article 753 of the Law is amended as follows: 'twenty' is replaced with 'one hundred thousand' and 'two hundred' is replaced with 'one million'.

62) Article 754, paragraph 1 of the Law is amended to read as follows: 'Where the court decides to accept the petition for a scheme of arrangement, it shall order the opening of proceedings, establish a preliminary date of the suspension of payments, and appoint in the order a trustee to carry on and follow up the proceedings of the scheme.'

63) Article 760 of the Law is supplemented with the following paragraphs 3 and 4:

> '(3) The stay of proceedings of execution with respect to claims secured by mortgage or special privilege shall expire as a matter of law either as of the date the order approving the scheme of arrangement or 120 days from the date of the order opening the proceedings, which ever comes first.
>
> (4) A creditor described in paragraph 3 of this Article shall be entitled to a level of security equal to the extent to which his claim was secured as of the date of the order opening the proceedings. The judge in charge shall have the authority and duty to take all steps necessary to ensure the level of security is maintained for such a creditor.'

64) Article 761 of the Law is amended to read as follows:

> '(1) The making of the order of opening the proceedings of the scheme shall not cause the debts owing by the debtor to mature nor shall it stop the running of interest thereon; any stipulation to the contrary shall be void.
>
> (2) The effects on the debtor's contracts stipulated in paragraphs 2 and 3 of Article 638 and paragraphs 2, 3, and 4 of Article 639 shall apply to proceedings for a scheme of arrangement.
>
> (3) The debtor may continue to retain possession of property of others so long as he is performing the obligations on which his right of possession is based. Any stipulation otherwise is null and void.
>
> (4) The trustee may initiate suits resulting from the application of the provisions of Articles 613, 614, 615, 616 and 618.'

65) Article 763, paragraphs 1 and 2 of the Law are amended as follows: In paragraph 1, 'ten' is replaced with 'thirty'. In paragraph 2, 'twenty' is replaced with 'sixty'.

66) Article 765, paragraph 1 of the Law is amended as follows: 'thirty' is replaced with 'seventy'.

67) Article 774, paragraph 1 of the Law is amended to read as follows: 'The scheme shall not be concluded except with the consent of the creditors who hold more than half of the ordinary debts which have been accepted finally or provisionally.'

68) Article 776, paragraph 2 of the Law is amended to read as follows: 'Where the consent stipulated in Article 774(1) is not attained, the stipulations of Article 684 shall be applied.'

69) Article 776 shall be supplemented with a paragraph 3, which shall read as follows: 'A proposal for a scheme of arrangement that is not approved in the second meeting shall be deemed rejected. Creditors shall be free to pursue their claims, pending any judgment of bankruptcy against the debtor.'

70) Article 778 of the Law is supplemented with paragraphs 4 and 5, which shall read as follows:

> '(4) A scheme of arrangement shall provide for equal treatment of ordinary creditors. An ordinary creditor may nevertheless agree to less favorable treatment under the scheme of arrangement.
>
> (5) A scheme of arrangement shall not be concluded unless all of the arrears on obligations corresponding to claims secured by mortgage or that are otherwise privileged are paid, unless individual creditors with such claims agree to less favorable treatment.'

71) Article 780, paragraph 1 of the Law is amended to read as follows: 'A scheme of arrangement shall be valid in regard to the ordinary creditors even when they have not participated in the proceedings or did not approve the scheme of arrangement. It shall have no effect, however, with respect to claims secured with mortgage or that are otherwise privileged, except where the creditors with such claims agree on an individual basis to be subject to the scheme of arrangement.'

Section 5 Amendments to the Penal Code

1) Article 470 of the Penal Code (chapeau paragraph) is amended as follows: '100 dinars' is replaced with '500,000 dinars.'

2) Article 470, paragraph 4 of the Penal Code is amended to read as follows: 'If he fails to make application to the bankruptcy trustee or the judge in charge of the proceedings in person when required to do so without a reasonable excuse or if he fails to provide statements required by such persons or if such statements are false.'

3) Article 470 of the Penal Code is supplemented by a paragraph (6), which reads as follows: 'If, after adjudication of bankruptcy, he fails to disclose such fact to persons when required to do so by law.'

4) Article 474 of the Penal Code (chapeau paragraph) is amended as follows: '200 dinars' is replaced with '1,000,000 dinars.'

Section 6 Amendments to the Enforcement Law

Article 108, paragraph 2 of the Enforcement Law is suspended.

Section 7 Amendments to the Civil Code

Article 1370, paragraph 2 of the Civil Code is suspended.

Section 8 Clarifying and Implementing Instructions

1) The Council of Judges is authorized to issue instructions to judges that implement, clarify, and/or supplement procedures and practices under the Bankruptcy Law. Unless stated otherwise and where applicable, such instructions shall be binding upon judges, bankruptcy trustees, their deputies, controllers, and parties to the bankruptcy proceeding.

2) Where such instructions conflict with the Bankruptcy Law, the latter shall govern. Where the Bankruptcy Law conflicts with Law No. 83 of 1969 on Civil Actions, the former shall govern.

Section 9 Entry into Force

Section 4 of this Order shall enter into force on the sixtieth day after the date of signature [26 April 2004]. All other sections shall enter into force on the date of signature.

Document 103
Coalition Provisional Authority Order Number 79
CPA/ORD/19 June 2004/79

The Iraqi Nonproliferation Programs Foundation

Pursuant to my authority as Administrator of the Coalition Provisional Authority (CPA), and under the laws and usages of war, and consistent with relevant United Nations Security Council resolutions, including Resolutions 1483 (2003), 1511 (2003), and 1546 (2004),

Furthering paragraph 1 of Resolution 1483, appealing to member states and concerned organizations to assist the people of Iraq in their efforts to reform their institutions and rebuild their country, and to contribute to conditions of stability and security in Iraq,

Further noting the provisions of the preamble and subsection 27(E) of the Law of Administration for the State of Iraq for the Transitional Period[251] calling on the government to respect and implement Iraq's international obligations regarding the non-proliferation, non-development, non-production, and non-use of nuclear, chemical, and biological weapons, and associated equipment, materiel, technologies, and delivery systems for use in the development, manufacture, production, and use of such weapons,

Recognizing that United Nations Security Council Resolution 1540 (2004) affirms that proliferation of nuclear, chemical, and biological weapons and their means of delivery constitutes a threat to international peace and security and requires that all States take effective measures to prevent the proliferation of such weapons, including by establishing appropriate controls over materials, equipment and technology which could be used for the design, development, production or use of such weapons,

Reaffirming the need to prevent the proliferation of technologies and expertise related to weapons of mass destruction (WMD) – nuclear, chemical, and biological weapons – their delivery systems, and other advanced military technologies,

Determining to establish a national foundation to support and assist former WMD scientists, technicians, engineers, and technical personnel involved in the design of delivery systems for WMD in Iraq to transition into activities for peaceful civilian purposes so as to minimize the risk of WMD and delivery system proliferation,

Realizing that the success of this foundation will require strong support from the Iraqi government, other foundations, academic and scientific institutions, intergovernmental, and non-governmental organizations,

I hereby promulgate the following:

Section 1 Establishment and Purpose

1) The Iraqi Non-proliferation Programs Foundation (hereinafter 'the INPF') is hereby established. The INPF shall be a not-for-profit, tax-exempt, juridical entity with full legal personality and shall be independent of any Iraqi Ministry.

2) The INPF shall have authority to develop, approve, and finance science, technology, and commercialization projects and related activities carried out at institutions and facilities, public and private, located principally but not solely in Iraq in order to provide individuals employed by the former regime in the development, creation, or production of WMD, particularly those who possess knowledge and skills related to nuclear, chemical,

[251] See *Doc 511*.

and biological weapons, or delivery systems (collectively 'WMD and delivery system personnel'), opportunities to redirect their expertise to transparent peaceful civilian activities that further the scientific, technological, nonproliferation, and economic development of Iraq. In accordance with Section 6(2), the INPF shall also have the authority to audit and monitor any and all projects that it sponsors.

3) After transfer of full governance authority to the Iraqis on June 30, 2004, all responsibilities herein ascribed to the Administrator of the CPA shall be assumed by the head of the Iraqi government.

4) The INPF shall operate under its Statute ('INPF Statute'). The INPF Statute shall include all elements needed to organize, manage, and maintain the INPF, including provisions which specify: general principles of operation, terms of reference of the Scientific Advisory Committee, description of financial management, contracting, grant-making, and acquisition practices, project oversight guidelines, and audit requirements. The INPF Statute is annexed hereto but may be amended by the Board of Directors in accordance with the procedures set forth in Section 2, paragraph 3.

5) The Administrator shall have the right to audit the INPF's activities and the INPF shall submit to the Administrator an annual report on its activities that will include a statement of accounts.

Section 2 Board of Directors, Executive Officer, and Management of Staff

1) The Ministers of Science and Technology, Higher Education and Scientific Research, Agriculture, Industry and Minerals, Health, and Environment, and the President of Iraqi National Academy of Science shall constitute the founding Board of Directors for the INPF. Board members (whether founding or otherwise) may be represented by designees (who shall have all the rights, privileges, and powers of a Board member) provided that the designee has experience in both management and technology. The Board of Directors shall be responsible for:

a. Determining the INPF's policy and its own rules of procedure;
b. Providing overall guidance and direction to the INPF staff;
c. Approving the INPF's budget for submission to funding authorities;
d. Governing the financial and other affairs of the INPF;
e. Approving general criteria and priorities proposed by the Scientific Advisory Council for the approval of projects;
f. Funding projects recommended by the Scientific Advisory Council;
g. Amending the INPF Statute and other implementing documents as necessary; and
h. Other functions necessary for the implementation of this Order.

2) Each Director will a serve two-year term. The terms of the founding Board members will be staggered, so that initially the Ministers of Agriculture, Industry and Minerals, and Health will be appointed to one-year terms and the remaining Directors will be appointed to two-year terms. When a founding Board member's term expires, his or her successor shall be appointed by the head of the Iraqi government after consultation with Iraqi ministries, civil society, and, as appropriate, relevant international experts.

3) Decisions of the Board shall be by simple majority of all the members of the Board for procedural decisions. Full consensus of the Board is required to amend the INPF Statute and in other special cases as defined in the INPF Statute.

4) The Board of Directors will select a Chairman and Vice Chairman from among its members.

5) In the event of a vacancy on the founding Board of Directors, the Administrator will appoint a new director, as appropriate, in accordance with Section 2(1) of this Order. In all other circumstances, the Administrator shall fill a vacancy on the Board by appointing a new director, as appropriate, in accordance with Section 2(2) of this Order.

6) The Board of Directors shall appoint an Executive Officer who will report directly to the Board of Directors. The Executive Officer will lead the daily operation of the INPF. The Executive Officer will serve a three-year term, which may be renewed once.

7) The Executive Officer will organize the INPF's personnel in a way that he/she deems necessary and appropriate to carry out the functions of the INPF. The Board of Directors will approve the organization plan of the INPF.

8) The Board of Directors may remove a director or the Executive Officer for malfeasance, misuse of public funds, failure to fulfill INPF duties or because of permanent incapacitation.

9) The INPF shall consult with relevant Iraqi governmental ministries not already represented on the founding Board of Directors, including, but not limited to Oil, Interior, Communications, Foreign Affairs, and Electricity to ensure that proposed projects are not duplicative and that they support Iraq's reconstruction efforts.

Section 3 Scientific Advisory Council

1) The Board of Directors shall establish a Scientific Advisory Council ('SAC'), made up of 16 members at least half of whom will have WMD or delivery system backgrounds. The SAC shall have a balanced membership that reflects the diversity of Iraq.

2) The SAC shall be composed of qualified Iraqi scientists, technicians, engineers, or managers from a range of disciplines. They will provide the INPF with expert scientific and other necessary professional advice in furtherance of the INPF's goals, including the review of grants, proposals and other funding initiatives of the INPF.

3) The terms of reference and method and duration of appointment will be specified in the INPF Statute.

Section 4 Budget, Funding, and Taxes

1) Within 7 days of the Administrator's approval of this Order, $37.5 million ('Initial Funding') shall be transferred from the Development Fund for Iraq to the INPF. The Initial Funding shall be used to effectuate the responsibilities given to the INPF under Section 6 of this Order. In addition, such funding shall also be used to finance the operating and programmatic expenses of the INPF for its first two years of operation.

2) Following transfer of full governance authority, resources for staffing and staff training, headquarters and equipment acquisition and maintenance, and operational costs necessary for the INPF to discharge its responsibilities (including all duties set forth in Section 6) shall be provided through the national fiscal process and reviewed annually.

3) In financial transactions, the INPF shall not pay in the Republic of Iraq taxes of any kind, including profit tax, value added tax, personal income tax, local taxes as well as any other tariffs, dues, custom duties, import taxes, fees, or any other similar imposed taxes or charges.

Section 5 Salary and Employment Conditions

1) The Executive Officer shall have the power to hire, employ and discharge personnel in accordance with Iraqi law, as amended by CPA Orders, Regulations, and Memoranda.

CPA Order Number 1, De-Ba'athification of Iraqi Society (CPA/ORD/16 May 2003/1),[252] shall not apply to WMD or delivery system personnel hired by the INPF and shall not be construed to prohibit WMD or delivery system personnel from participating in any of the programs set forth in Section 6 of this Order.

2) Salaries of INPF staff shall conform to the salary structure applicable to Iraqi government employees.

Section 6 Authority and Functions

1) The INPF is empowered to:

a) issue grants and contracts to individuals, foundations, universities, consortia, and other organizations to employ former Iraqi WMD and delivery system scientists, technicians and engineers to undertake peaceful, civilian activities;

b) establish training programs to retrain and redirect former WMD and delivery system scientists, technicians and engineers toward peaceful, civilian employment;

c) fund travel and other expenses related to participation by former Iraqi WMD and delivery system scientists, technicians and engineers in conferences, national and international research collaborations, and training activities;

d) issue grants and contracts to renovate, construct, and equip facilities in which WMD and delivery system scientists, technicians and engineers will undertake peaceful, civilian activities;

e) allocate funds to support commercial development of products and technologies that support the transition of former Iraqi WMD and delivery system scientists, engineers, and technicians to civilian employment, including establishing a venture capital fund;

f) engage in outreach and information activities to promote the goals of the INPF;

g) participate in multilateral efforts to reduce the proliferation of WMD and missile/delivery system expertise;

h) support initiatives that the Iraqi government takes to comply with its obligations under United Nations Security Council Resolution 1540 (2004); and

i) develop a voluntary code of conduct which Iraqi scientists, engineers, and technicians can utilize to ensure that their endeavors, activities, and expertise are utilized for transparent peaceful civilian activities that further the scientific, technological, and economic development of Iraq.

2) All funding initiatives described in Section 6, paragraph 1 must comply with the purposes set forth in Section 1, paragraph 2.

3) The INPF shall have the right to access, monitor, and audit funds used in support of all projects and activities funded through the INPF and monitor scientific and technical progress, including:

a) To examine on-site INPF project activities, materials, supplies, project-related services and use of funds, upon its notification;

b) To inspect or audit, upon its request, any records or other documentation in connection with INPF activities and use of funds, wherever such records or documentation are located, for a period as determined in a grant or contract; and

c) To have access to project staff, their laboratories, laboratory or project notebooks, logs, or other records, and to request outside evaluation of projects as determined necessary.

[252] See *Doc 14*.

If it is determined that the terms and conditions of a project have not been requested, the INPF may terminate the project and take appropriate steps in accordance with the terms of th grant or contract.

Section 7 Relation to Other Laws and Organizations
A permanent mechanism for information exchange, reporting and cooperation shall be established between the INPF and appropriate Iraqi authorities to ensure clear delineation of authority and responsibility in accordance with this Order and to ensure the free flow of information and effective implementation of non-proliferation programs.

Section 8 Entry info Force
This Order shall enter into force on the date of signature [19 June 2004].

ANNEX Iraq Nonproliferation Programs Foundation

Statute
This Statute is adopted and promulgated pursuant to Section 1, paragraph 4 of Coalition Provisional Authority Order 79, The Iraqi Non Proliferation Programs Foundation, (CPA/ORD/19 June 2004/79) (the 'Order'). In the event of a discrepancy between this Statute and the Order, the latter shall prevail.

Article I Name and Location

A. The Iraqi Nonproliferation Programs Foundation (hereinafter referred to as 'the INPF') is established pursuant to Section 1 of the Order.

B. The Headquarters of the INPF shall be located at Baghdad, in the Republic of Iraq.

Article II Powers

A. Section 1, paragraph 2 of the Order provides as follows:
The INPF shall have authority to develop, approve, and finance science, technology, and commercialization projects and related activities carried out at institutions and facilities, public and private, located principally but not solely in Iraq in order to provide individuals employed by the former regime in the development, creation, or production of WMD, particularly those who possess knowledge and skills related to nuclear, chemical, and biological weapons, or delivery systems (collectively 'WMD and delivery system personnel'), opportunities to redirect their expertise to transparent peaceful civilian activities that further the scientific, technological, and economic development of Iraq. In accordance with Section 6(3), the INPF shall also have the authority to audit and monitor any and all projects that it sponsors.

B. The INPF is authorized to carry out the activities enumerated in Section 6 of the Order and shall use its resources solely for the accomplishment of its objectives.

Article III Board Purpose, Membership, Procedures

A. The Board has the responsibilities set forth in Section 2 of the Order.

B. The Board's membership is fixed at seven members. Founding Board members shall be the Ministers of Science and Technology, Higher Education and Scientific Research, Agriculture, Industry and Minerals, Health, and Environment, and the President of Iraqi National Academy of Science. Succeeding Board members shall be appointed by the head of the Iraqi government after consultation with Iraqi ministries, civil society, and, as appropriate, relevant international experts.

C. The Board shall select from its membership a Chair and Vice Chair who shall serve for one year.

D. The Board shall meet as needed, but not less than four times annually, upon fifteen (15) days prior notice from the Chair, except whenever a shorter period of notice is agreed to by all members. At a request from four or more members of the Board to the Chair, an extraordinary meeting of the Board shall be held upon fifteen (15) days prior notice except whenever a shorter period of notice is agreed to by all the Parties.

E. The Board may meet physically, through written procedure, or by teleconference. All actions taken at such meetings shall be confirmed in writing to the INPF Executive Officer within 5 days following such meetings.

F. A simple majority of the Board is necessary to approve any procedural matters, including, but not limited to, determining the INPF's policy; approving the INPF budget; general financial issues; approving the INPF's internal documents, such as financial regulations; and approving recommendations and proposals from the Scientific Advisory Council. Full consensus of the Board is required to amend the INPF Statute, appoint or remove the Executive Officer, and make recommendations to the Iraqi Head of government on changes to the Order establishing the INPF.

G. The Board may establish any committees and task forces it believes are necessary to carry out the objectives of the INPF.

H. The Board shall decide its own rules of procedure, which shall address, inter alia, the method by which representatives to the Board shall cast their votes and the participation of non-Board members, including other governments, inter-governmental organizations, non-governmental organizations, in Board meetings, and the establishment of any committees and task forces.

Article IV Staff

A. The Executive Staff of the INPF consists of the Executive Officer and other staff as necessary to carry out the work of the INPF.

B. The Executive Officer supervises the INPF's daily administration and is responsible for implementing the Board's policies and decisions. All members of the Staff report to the Executive Officer. The Executive Officer is appointed for a three-year term, which may be renewed once.

C. The Executive Officer, consistent with decisions of the Board, shall develop an organizational plan for the INPF staff and will submit the plan to the Board for approval. In making staff appointments, the Executive Officer shall consider the paramount importance of employing staff members who possess the highest standards of efficiency, technical competence, integrity, and commitment to nonproliferation principles. The Executive Officer shall limit appointments of staff to only those necessary to carry out the work of the INPF and shall seek to limit the administrative costs of the INPF.

D. Under the guidance of the Executive Officer, the Staff shall be responsible for, inter alia:

[i] Disseminating information about the INPF, including its objectives and functions;

[ii] Receiving project proposals and information required in accordance with this Statute and preparing proposals for transmission to the Board;

[iii] Responding to statements of interest from institutions and individuals;
[iv] Assisting the participants in the development of project proposals and communicating with those who submit project proposals;
[v] Collating the advice on the scientific and technical merit of project proposals given pursuant to Article VII of this Statute;
[vi] Bringing together specialists in Iraq with other specialists with similar interests;
[vii] Proposing the INPF's activity plan and a budget for each year;
[viii] Preparing Annual Reports of the INPF's activities, with the first Report to be submitted to the Board at the end of calendar year 2004; and
[ix] Making the necessary arrangements for handling business confidential information, as defined in Article XI.A. The INPF personnel shall conclude confidentiality agreements with the INPF for the period of their work at the INPF and two years thereafter. Upon a complaint or on his or her own initiative, the Executive Officer shall take appropriate administrative actions, up to and including dismissal, against an INPF employee who has disclosed business confidential information.
[x] Other functions assigned to the Staff by the Order, this Statute, the Board, or the Executive Officer.

Article V Scientific Advisory Council

A. Within sixty (60) days of the Order's signature, the Board will appoint 16 individuals to serve on the INPF Scientific Advisory Council (SAC), which is established pursuant to Section 3 (1) of the Order. The persons appointed shall be prominent members of Iraq's scientific, technical, or engineering communities relevant to the INPF's objectives and shall have fulfill the duties set forth in this Article and Article VII.

B. The SAC members shall serve for two-year terms and shall receive an honorarium for their service to the INPF. The level of the honorarium will be set annually by the Board.

C. The SAC shall meet at least once a quarter to advise the Board on fields of research and applications to be encouraged, discuss and establish proposal application processes, develop project selection criteria, and monitor the progress of grants. Its first meeting shall occur within thirty (30) days after all members of the SAC are appointed. SAC members are not prohibited from submitting proposals to the INPF but shall recuse themselves from meetings where their presence may result in a conflict of interest.

D. The members of the SAC may also represent the INPF at international meetings and engage in general outreach activities to promote the INPF's nonproliferation, scientific, and reconstruction objectives.

E. In addition to meetings described in paragraph C. of this Article, the SAC shall meet upon request of the Board, to provide advice on questions referred to it by the Board. The Chairman of the SAC may also request that the Board call a meeting of the SAC.

Article VI Proposal Submissions

A. Proposals may be accepted from individuals, qualified governmental and private institutions and organizations provided that a clear link can be established to the nonproliferation goals of INPF. Standards of qualification will be set by the SAC with INPF Board approval.

B. Proposals shall be made through the Executive Officer.

C. Each acceptable proposal shall comply with the instructions issued by the INPF, which shall set forth requirements concerning information to be contained in proposals and the format for proposals. These instructions are prepared by the Executive Officer and approved by the Board. At a minimum, the instructions shall require for each proposal:

[i] A summary of the project, including names and resumes for the project manager and principal investigator(s); a short narrative description of the project's purpose, activities, anticipated results, materials and methods, contribution to science, location, and participants; a clear statement of the relationship of the project to INPF nonproliferation goals and the reconstruction of Iraq; and the project's duration and budgeted costs, identified by element of expense to include at least: salaries, equipment, materials, travel, and institutional overhead of up to 10% of direct costs, excluding equipment and travel;

[ii] A description of all program and financial aspects of the project, including anticipated commercial results and intellectual property rights, if any;

[iii] A statement certifying that all participants concur with the work being proposed; and

[iv] Technical monitoring and financial auditing assurances from the institution, individuals, entities, or organizations submitting the proposal sufficient for implementing the obligations of Section 6(3) of the Order.

These instructions will help ensure that each proposal contains information sufficient for the Executive Officer, Scientific Advisory Council, and Board to fulfill their responsibilities under this Statute and the Order.

D. The INPF will give due regard to preventing:

[i] the transfer of information prohibited under relevant international rules and practices for the nonproliferation of weapons and other sensitive technologies,

[ii] unauthorized disclosures of proprietary and business confidential information.

Applicants are responsible for ensuring that their proposals comply with applicable laws and regulations regarding sensitive information and with all laws governing export controls.

E. Proposals are regarded as submitted when the Executive Officer determines that the information required in paragraph C. of this Article is complete.

Article VII Scientific and other Professional Advice

A. Within five (5) days of a proposal's submission, the Executive Officer shall send it to at least two SAC members with relevant competencies in the field of the proposal. The Executive Officer shall include at least the information required in Article VI.C. and other information he or she deems relevant, and a form on which the review shall be completed. The Executive Officer shall prepare that form after consultation with the SAC.

B. SAC members may solicit the opinions of up to three (3) experts scientific or other appropriate professional when reviewing a proposal. Reviewers may be Iraqi and/or international experts and may (if the Board so approves) receive compensation for their work.

C. Not more than sixty (60) days after receiving a proposal from the Executive Officer, SAC members shall provide the Executive Officer with a single completed form which synthesizes the reviews obtained in accordance with paragraph B. of this Article, together with copies of those reviews and his or her own recommendation as appropriate; or confirmation that no review has been undertaken.

D. A completed review shall contain:

[i] The reviewers' names and qualifications, including any qualifications related to the specific proposal;

[ii] An analysis of the scientific, technical, and commercial merit of the proposals and how the proposed work supports nonproliferation goals and Iraq's reconstruction;

[iii] An opinion as to whether the project's objective can be accomplished within the framework proposed and time allowed;

[iv] An analysis, to the extent possible, of the qualifications of the proposed participants and of the skills necessary to meet the project's objectives; and

[v] Recommendations for the proposal's improvement, approval, and/or rejection.

Article VIII Project Approval

A. The Executive Officer shall transmit, the proposal, the completed review, and an assessment (which the Executive Officer shall prepare) as to whether the project is in accordance with the objectives of the INPF, as described in Section 1, paragraph 2 of the Order.

B. Approval of projects by the Board:

[i] Unless the Board decides otherwise with regard to a specific proposal, it shall have at least thirty (30) days to consider a proposal after the proposal has been transmitted to it by the Executive Officer. It shall consider the proposal no later than its first meeting after the thirty (30) day period ends.

[ii] The Executive Officer shall communicate the Board's decision to approve or reject the proposal to the institution, individual, entity, or organization that submitted the proposal.

C. In deciding whether to approve a project, the Board will be guided by criteria and priorities established according to Section 1, paragraph 2 of the Order and shall consider whether the financing requested is adequate to accomplish the proposal's goals.

D. The Board shall effectuate the approval of a proposal by issuing a grant to or entering into a written contract (collectively 'project agreement') with the institution, individual, entity, or organization that submitted the proposal.

Article IX Project Agreements

A. For each proposal approved and financed through the INPF, the INPF, acting through the Executive Officer or his or her designee, shall enter into a project agreement with the recipient organization, individual, entity, or institution. The project agreement shall expressly provide that it is subject to the provisions of the Order and the Statute, both of which shall prevail in the case of conflict with the project agreement.

B. At a minimum, a project agreement shall contain provisions that:

[i] Specify conditions under which costs shall be eligible for reimbursement and ensuring that they are allowable under the terms of the project or activity, reasonable as to amount and properly allocated to the project or activity;

[ii] Designate responsibility for performance of technical and financial tasks under the project or activity and delineate procedures to be followed in the resolution of disputes;

[iii] Establish a schedule for performance and conditions to be met in order to obtain payment;

[iv] Provide for the INPF the right of full INPF access pursuant to the Order, after notice of not less than 10 days or as specified in the agreement, to carry out on-site scientific or technical monitoring and financial audit of all activities of the project

or activity; specify the portions of the facilities, equipment, documentation, information, data systems, materials, supplies, personnel, and services which will concern the project and so will be accessible for the monitoring and audit;

[v] Require the recipient entity to account for resources used, to identify the types of records required to support expenditures for the project, and to return unspent funds within a stated period of time;

[vi] Require regular technical and financial reports detailing the progress of the project or activity and of expenditures made against the agreement by the same elements of expense identified in the approved proposal, including accounting for any interest earned by the recipient on funds accepted from the INPF;

[vii] Require that allowable costs not include, inter alia, any element of profit;

[viii] Set a standard contribution for overhead costs up to 20% of direct costs, excluding equipment and travel;

[ix] Require that allowable costs not include amounts imposed for taxes of any kind, including profit tax, value added tax, personal income tax, local taxes as well as any other tariffs, dues, custom duties, import taxes, fees, or any other similar taxes or charges;

[x] Prohibit the transfer of sensitive information that is prohibited under relevant international rules and practices for the nonproliferation of weapons, delivery systems, and other sensitive technologies, and unauthorized disclosures of proprietary and business confidential information; and

[xi] Provide for the termination of the project as follows:

(a) When the agreement is terminated other than pursuant to paragraph (b) below, costs shall be limited to the allowable costs incurred by the recipient entity prior to the termination and such other costs as the INPF considers to be fair and reasonable, having regard to commitments reasonably entered into and which cannot be cancelled or avoided. The recipient entity shall comply with any directions of the INPF in the termination notice to reduce or mitigate these costs.

(b) When the INPF determines that the recipient entity has not complied with the terms and conditions of the project agreement, the recipient entity shall, upon demand, promptly return all payments and equipment contributions previously made.

(c) Any disputes on the above matter shall be settled by a procedure involving, in case of appeal, a final decision of the Board.

Article X Contributions to the INPF

A. Without prejudice to Articles XI and XII, foreign governments, international organizations, nongovernmental organizations, foundations and scientific organizations, private concerns, or individuals may contribute funds in any currency to the INPF for operating costs, projects, and all other expenses in accordance with its laws and regulations into an account in the name of the INPF or directly into the INPF project and administrative accounts. Private concerns or individuals who contribute funds to the INPF may require (by written contract) that the funds be utilized for a specific project.

B. Funds that are deposited in the INPF's bank accounts pursuant to paragraph A. of this Article shall be disbursed from the bank account by the Executive Officer or his designee in accordance with procedures approved by the Board.

C. Contributions made to the INPF may be maintained in an INPF account established by the Executive Officer, with the approval of the Board. Disbursement procedures for these funds shall be established by the Board.

D. Disbursements of funds for projects may be made to the appropriate organizations and individuals in hard currency or local currency.

Article XI Intellectual Property Rights

A. For the purposes of the Order and this Statute:

'Intellectual Property' shall have the meaning defined in Article 2 of the Convention Establishing the World Intellectual Property Organization, done at Stockholm on July 14, 1967.

'Business confidential information' means information containing know-how, trade secrets, or technical, commercial or financial information, which either:

[i] Has been held in confidence by its owner;

[ii] Is not generally known or available from other sources;

[iii] Has not been made available by its owner to other parties without an obligation concerning its confidentiality; or

[iv] Is not available to the receiving party without obligations concerning confidentiality.

B. Each project agreement shall provide for the adequate protection of intellectual property and business confidential information exchanged or provided in the course of an INPF project or activity.

C. The INPF shall use its best endeavors to ensure that rights acquired are exercised in such a way as to encourage, consistent with the Statute:

[i] The dissemination and use of non-confidential information created, provided, or exchanged in the course of a project;

[ii] The adoption and implementation of international technical standards; and

[iii] Fair competition in areas affected by the Order. Entities having rights should make adequate efforts to exploit their intellectual property rights consistent with the objectives of the Agreement. To that end, the INPF (or its designee) and the recipient entity (or its designee) shall agree to protect, allocate, and manage intellectual property arising under the project agreement, consistent with the principles of the Order and relevant laws and regulations.

Article XII Financing of Administrative Expenses

A. The fiscal year of the INPF shall be the same as that of the Iraqi national fiscal year.

B. Beginning in 2005, the Executive Officer shall submit (by May 1) to the Board the annual budget estimates for the operating and program expenses of the INPF for the following fiscal year. The Board shall approve the INPF's budget requirements and submit it to the Ministry of Finance by June 1 of each fiscal year. The Ministry of Finance shall consider the budgetary request and will determine the appropriate amount of funding for the forthcoming fiscal year according to the budget preparation process set forth in CPA Order 95, Financial Management Law and Public Debt Law, (CPA/ORD/2 June 2004/95).[253]

C. Relevant government Ministries and agencies will be encouraged to second staff and provide other support to the INPF at no cost to the INPF's budget. The INPF may, as necessary, enter into agreements concerning seconded staff and support.

[253] See *Doc 119*.

Article XIII Financial Procedures

A. Quarterly financial reports shall be provided to the Board on the INPF's administrative costs, project awards, grants, contracts and other expenditures in a format consistent with Iraqi law and standard international accounting practices.

B. An annual audit by an auditor approved by the Board shall be conducted of the INPF's expenditures and related financial activities. Results of the audit shall be reported to the Board within 30 days after completion and will be included in the INPF's annual report to the Iraqi head of government.

Article XIV Auditing and Monitoring

A. All funds contributed for a project or activity through the INPF shall be subject to audit and technical monitoring by the INPF and the Board of Supreme Audit in accordance Iraqi law and the following principles:

[i] Audit of costs shall assure that costs reimbursed are allowable under the terms of the project agreement;

[ii] The INPF or audit organizations as specified by the Board may perform such audits, or engage others to do so.

[iii] Accounting systems used by project recipients must be acceptable to the INPF in regard to projects and activities it finances and shall be subject to review and audit;

[iv] Audit reports pertaining to a project shall be available to the entities audited, to the INPF, the Board.

[v] Allowable costs based on the result of an audit shall be determined by the entity performing the audit or engaging others to do so. Any disputes shall be settled in accordance with resolution of dispute procedures contained in the project agreement.

[vi] The INPF or its designees shall have access to facilities, personnel and records for technical monitoring of scientific, technical, engineering, or other work conducted under the project to ensure that work is being performed in a manner and according to timelines provided in the project agreement.

[vii] Provisions for an entity that wholly or partly finances a project or activity and for the INPF to have the right of full INPF Order access, after notice of not less than 10 days or as specified in the project agreement, to carry out on-site monitoring and audit of all activities of the project; specifications of the portions of the facilities, equipment, documentation, information, data systems, materials, supplies, personnel, and services which will concern the project and so will be accessible for the monitoring and audit; such specification shall permit the recipient entity the right to protect those portions of facilities that are not related to the project. After completion or termination of an INPF project or activity the recipient entity may utilize the facility or portion of the facility previously used for the INPF project for other work; however, all documentation and records including those associated with equipment, data systems, materials, supplies and services utilized on the INPF project or activity must be maintained for up to two years following such completion or termination and such documents and records and personnel must be available to the auditor for up to two years following such completion or termination.

B. Approved projects and activities funded other than through the INPF shall be subject to audit by the funding entity and/or their representatives taking into account the principles set forth in paragraph A of this Article.

Article XV Amendment of Statute
This Statute may be amended by unanimous consent of the Board.

Article XVI Effective Date
This Statute is effective as of the date the Order is signed.

Document 104
Coalition Provisional Authority Order Number 80
CPA/ORD/26 April 2004/80

Amendment to the Trademarks and Descriptions Law No. 21 of 1957

Pursuant to my authority as Administrator of the Coalition Provisional Authority (CPA) and under the laws and usages of war, and consistent with relevant U.N. Security Council resolutions, including Resolution 1483 and 1511 (2003),

Having worked closely with the Governing Council to ensure that economic change as necessary to benefit the people of Iraq occurs in a manner acceptable to the people of Iraq,

Acknowledging the Governing Council's desire to bring about significant change to the Iraqi intellectual property system as necessary to improve the economic condition of the people of Iraq,

Determined to improve the conditions of life, technical skills, and opportunities for all Iraqis and to fight unemployment with its associated deleterious effect on public security,

Recognizing that companies, lenders and entrepreneurs require a fair, efficient, and predictable environment for protection of their intellectual property,

Noting that several provisions of the current Iraqi trademark legislation do not meet current internationally-recognized standards of protection, and that current Iraqi legislation does not extend protection to geographical indications,

Recognizing the demonstrated interest of the Iraqi Governing Council for Iraq to become a full member in the international trading system, known as the World Trade Organization, and the desirability of adopting modern intellectual property standards,

Acting in a manner consistent with the Report of the Secretary General to the Security Council of July 17, 2003, concerning the need for the development of Iraq and its transition from a non-transparent centrally planned economy to a free market economy characterized by sustainable economic growth through the establishment of a dynamic private sector, and the need to enact institutional and legal reforms to give it effect,

In close consultation with and acting in coordination with the Governing Council, I hereby promulgate the following:

Section 1 Amendments to the Trademarks and Descriptions Law No. 21 of 1957

1) The Trademark and Descriptions Law No. 21 of 1957 is hereby renamed the 'Trademark and Geographical Indications Law'.

2) Article 1, definition for 'Mark' is amended to read as follows: 'Mark' – Shall include trademarks, service marks, collective marks and certification marks.

3) Following the definition for 'Mark', a definition for 'Trademark' is added to read as follows: 'Trademark' – Any sign, or any combination of signs, capable of distinguishing the

goods of one undertaking from those of other undertakings, shall be capable of constituting a trademark. Such signs, in particular words including personal names, letters, numerals, figurative elements and colors as well as any combination of such signs, shall be eligible for registration as trademarks. Where signs are not inherently capable of distinguishing the relevant goods or services, registrability will depend on distinctiveness acquired through use. Signs need not be visually perceptible in order to be eligible for protection as trademarks.

4) Following the definition for 'Trademark', a definition for 'Service Mark' is added to read as follows: 'Service Mark' – Any sign, or any combination of signs, used by a person to identify and distinguish the services of one person, including a unique service, from the services of others and to indicate the source of the services, even if that source is unknown. Titles, character names, and other distinctive features of radio or television programs may be registered as service marks notwithstanding that they, or the programs, may advertise the goods of the sponsor. Marks used in connection with retail services, whether associated with the selling of the goods of the service provider or those of others, or both, are eligible for protection as service marks.

5) Following the definition for 'Service Mark' a definition for 'Certification Mark' is added to read as follows: 'Certification Mark' – Any sign, or any combination of signs, used by a person other than its owner to certify regional or other origin, material, mode of manufacture, quality, accuracy, or other characteristics of such person's goods or services or that the work or labor on the goods or services was performed by members of a union or other organization. Certification marks shall include geographical indications.

6) Following the definition for 'Certification Mark' a definition for 'Geographical Indications' is added to read as follows: 'Geographical Indications' – Indications which identify a good as originating in the territory of a country, or a region or locality in that territory, where a given quality, reputation or other characteristic of the good is essentially attributable to its geographical origin.

7) Following the definition for 'Geographical Indications' a definition for 'Collective Mark' is added to read as follows: 'Collective Mark' – A trademark or service mark used by the members of a cooperative, an association, or other collective group or organization, and includes marks indicating membership in a union, an association, or other organization.

8) Following the definition for 'Collective Mark' a definition for 'Nice Classification' is added to read as follows: 'Nice Classification means the classification established by the Nice Agreement Concerning the International Classification of Goods and Services for the Purposes of the Registration of Marks, signed at Nice on June 15, 1957, as revised and amended.'

9) Article 2.1 is amended to read as follows: '1. There shall be kept at the Ministry of Industry a Register in the custody of the Registrar, wherein shall be recorded all the marks, the names and addresses of their owners, and descriptions of their goods. The public shall be entitled to inspect the Register. The public shall also be entitled to receive certified copies thereof on payment of the prescribed fees.'

10) Article 2.2 is suspended.

11) Article 3 is amended to read as follows: 'A mark shall be deemed to be the property of the person who registered it. The ownership of the mark may not be contested if the owner used it for five consecutive years from the date of completion of registration, except as provided in Article 21.'

12) Article 4 is amended to read as follows: 'Any natural person or legal entity shall have the right to apply for the registration of a trademark with all attendant rights in accordance with the provisions of this Law.'

13) Article 4*bis* is added following Article 4 to read as follows:

'1) The owner of a registered trademark shall have the exclusive right to prevent all third parties not having the owner's consent from using in the course of trade identical or similar signs for goods or services which are identical or similar to those in respect of which the trademark is registered where such use would result in a likelihood of confusion. In case of the use of an identical sign for identical goods or services, a likelihood of confusion shall be presumed.

2) The owner of a well-known trademark shall have the right to enjoy the protection conferred by this Law even if such a mark is not registered in Iraq.

3) The preceding provision shall apply to marks intended for use in connection with goods or services which are not identical with those of the well-known mark, where the use of the marks in relation to those non-identical goods or services would indicate a connection between the owner of the well-known mark and those products, and that such a use may be prejudicial to the interests of the owner of the well-known mark.'

14) Article 4*quater* is added following Article 4*ter* to read as follows: 'Collective and certification marks, including geographical indications, shall be registrable in the same manner and with the same effect as trademarks by any natural persons or legal entities, including nations, states, municipalities, and other regional authorities, exercising legitimate control over the use of the marks sought to be registered. When registered, they shall be entitled to the protection provided in this chapter in the case of trademarks.'

15) Article 5.1 is amended to read as follows: '1. Marks devoid of any distinctive character or which are used in trade to describe the kind, nature, quantity or place of production of the goods, or marks which in the ordinary language of Iraq indicate any of such matters. Where signs are not inherently capable of distinguishing the relevant goods or services, registrability will depend on distinctiveness acquired through use.'

16) Article 5.2 is amended to read as follows: '2. Marks, expressions, or designs which are contrary to public order or morality.'

17) Article 5.3 is amended to read as follows: 'Marks which are identical with, or similar to armorial bearings, flags or other State emblems of Iraq or other countries of the Paris Union or international intergovernmental organizations, official signs or hallmarks, indicating control and warranty adopted by them, and any imitation from a heraldic point of view.'

18) Article 5.4 is amended to read as follows: '4. Marks which are identical with, or similar to, the insignia of the Red Cross, Red Crescent, or Geneva Cross.'

19) Article 5.5 is amended to read as follows: '5. The name, title, portrait, or armorial bearing of a person except with that person's written consent.'

20) Article 5.6 is amended to read as follows: '6. Designations of honorary degrees to which the applicant is unable to prove a right.'

21) Article 5.7 is amended to read as follows: '7. Marks which are likely to mislead or confuse the public, or which contain false descriptions as to the origin of products, whether goods or services, or their other qualities, as well as the signs that contain an indication of a fictitious, imitated or forged trade name.'

22) Article 5.8 is amended to read as follows: '8. Marks that are identical or similar to a well-known mark, or marks that are identical or similar to a previously registered trademark if registration of that mark will result in confusing the consumer public as to the goods distinguished by the mark or other similar goods.'

23) Articles 5.9-5.12 are suspended.

24) Article 6*bis* is added following Article 6 to read as follows: 'Where an application for registration of a mark is filed:

a) by any person whose country of origin is a member in the Paris Union, the WTO, or party to any convention or treaty relating to trademarks, trade or commercial names, or the repression of unfair competition, to which Iraq is a party, or a country which extends reciprocity to Iraq;
b) in a country described in subsection (a) the applicant, or rightful successor, may, within six months from the date of filing the application, file with the Registrar a similar application for the same mark covering the same products included in the previous application in accordance with the terms and conditions prescribed by this Law and its Regulations. In such a case the priority date shall be that of the first application filed in the foreign country.'

25) Article 7 is amended to read as follows:

'1. A mark shall be permitted to be registered in respect of one or more articles or in one or more classes. The application shall indicate the goods or services by their names, grouped according to the classes of the Nice Classification.
2. Goods or services may not be considered as being similar to each other solely on the ground that, in any registration or publication, they appear in the same class of the Nice Classification. Conversely, goods or services may not be considered as being dissimilar from each other solely on the ground that, in any registration or publication, they appear in different classes of the Nice Classification.
3. In a single application, an applicant may apply to register the same mark in multiple classes for all of the goods and/or services on or in connection with the mark that is sought to be protected. The applicant must specifically identify the goods or services in each class. A single certificate of registration shall issue for such mark.'

26) Article 8 is amended to read as follows: 'Where before any publication is made two or more persons apply simultaneously for the registration of the same mark or of identical or similar marks in respect of goods or articles of the same class of products, the Registrar may suspend all such applications until the renunciation by one of the disputants is duly attested to or a final decision is made in favor of one of them.'

27) Article 8*bis* is added following Article 8 to read as follows:

'1. The Registrar may require the applicant to disclaim an unregistrable component of a mark otherwise registrable. An applicant may voluntarily disclaim a component of a mark sought to be registered.
2. No disclaimer shall prejudice or affect the applicant's or registrant's rights then existing or thereafter arising in the disclaimed matter, or his right of registration on another application if the disclaimed matter be or shall have become distinctive of his goods or services.'

28) Article 9 is suspended.

29) Articles 12.2 and 12.3 are suspended.

30) Article 15 is amended to read as follows:

'1. The owner of a mark shall, on completion of registration thereof, be given a certificate containing the particulars published in the aforementioned bulletin.
2. The registration of a trademark shall in all legal proceedings constitute *prima facie* evidence of the validity and ownership of the trademark.'

31) Article 17 is amended to read as follows: 'The ownership of a mark shall be transferable and the mark shall be pledged or seized together with the business dealing in

the goods carrying that mark, or with that part of the business connected with the use of and symbolized by the mark.'

32) Article 18*bis* is added following Article 18 to read as follows:

'1. The owner of a mark may license one or more natural persons or legal entities to use the owner's mark on all or some of the products for which the mark was registered. Such license to a third party shall not prevent the owner from using the mark, unless otherwise agreed.

2. Recordal of an assignment or a license for the mark shall not be required for the assignee or licensee to establish the validity of the mark or to assert rights in the mark against third parties.'

33) Article 19 is suspended.

34) Article 20 is amended to read as follows:

'1. The duration of protection of a mark shall be for ten years, renewable for like periods upon application made during the last year in the manner prescribed in the regulation and payment of the prescribed fee.

2. The owner of the mark may request a renewal within six months after the date of its expiry against payment of the prescribed fees and a supplemental fee prescribed by the regulations, failing which the Registrar shall proceed to cancel the said mark from the register.'

35) Article 21 is amended to read as follows:

'1. Any interested person shall be entitled to apply to the Court within five years of the registration of any mark for its cancellation, stating the grounds relied upon.

2. Notwithstanding paragraph 1 of this Article, a petition to cancel a registration of a mark may be filed at any time if the registered mark:

a) becomes the generic name for the goods or services, or a portion thereof, for which it is registered;

b) is functional;

c) was obtained fraudulently or contrary to the provisions of registrability;

d) has gone unused for an uninterrupted period of three years, unless such nonuse may be proved to be due to uncontrollable cause or lawful excuse; or

e) is being used by, or with the permission of, the registrant so as to misrepresent the source of the goods or services on or in connection with which the mark is used.'

36) Article 24.1 is suspended.

37) Article 24.2 is suspended.

38) Article 24.3 is amended to read as follows: '3. Decisions issued by the Registrar in accordance with paragraph 2 of Article 5, and Article 21 of this Law are subject to appeal to the Minister within 30 days from the date of notification of the decision, and those concerned may object to the Minister's decision, subject to appeal to the court within 30 days from the date of notification of the Minister's decision.'

39) Article 25 is suspended.

40) Article 26 is amended to read as follows: 'The Registrar may, whenever there is justification, make any alteration in the Register if this alteration is designed to correct a mistake or to complete a technical deficiency.'

41) Article 27 is suspended.

42) Article 32 is amended to read as follows: 'Trade indications may not be misleading to the public, whether they are placed on the goods themselves, on the premises or stores or in their firm names, or on packages, invoices, letters, advertising materials and the like, which are used in offering the goods to the public.'

43) Article 33.1 is suspended.

44) Article 35 is amended to read as follows: 'Any person who commits any of the following acts shall be punished by imprisonment for a period of not less than one year and not more than five years and by a fine of not less than 50,000,000 Dinars and not more than 100,000,000 Dinars, or by one of those penalties:

1) Whoever counterfeits a trademark, which is lawfully registered or imitates it in such a manner as to mislead the public, or uses in *mala fide* a counterfeited or an imitated trademark;
2) Whoever unlawfully uses a registered trademark owned by another party;
3) Whoever puts, in *mala fide*, a registered trademark owned by another party on that person's products;
4) Whoever knowingly sells or offers for sale or circulation or possesses for the purpose of sale, products bearing a counterfeited or an imitated trademark, or a trademark which is unlawfully affixed; or
5) Whoever intentionally offers rendering services under a forged, imitated or unlawfully used mark.

In all cases, the court shall order the confiscation of the infringing products, goods, firm name, wrapping materials, papers, hang tags, stickers, etc., which bear the mark of the subject matter of the offence, the revenue and the returns of such products as well as the implements used in the infringement.'

45) Article 36 is suspended.

46) Article 36*bis* is added following Article 36 to read as follows: 'Any person who commits for the second time one of the offenses mentioned in Articles 35 and 36 of this Law, shall be punished by imprisonment for a period of not less than 5 years and not more than 10 years and by a fine of not less than 100,000,000 Dinars and not more than 200,000,000 Dinars in addition to the closure of the commercial store or enterprise for a period of not less than fifteen days and not exceeding six months, together with the publication of the judgment at the expense of the infringer.'

47) Article 37 is amended to read as follows:

'1. The owner of a mark may, at any time even before the institution of any civil or criminal action, obtain, upon application supported by evidence establishing the registration of the mark, an order from the examining magistrate or from the court which has the jurisdiction to hear and determine the offence or damages to take provisional measures, more particularly to seize the instruments and tools used in the commission of the offence as well as the products, goods, firm name, wrapping materials, papers, hang tags, stickers, etc., which bear the mark of the subject matter of the offence. This includes seizure of products, goods, firm name, wrapping materials, papers, hang tags, stickers, etc., that are imported from abroad.

2. The judicial authorities shall have the authority to adopt provisional measures inaudita altera parte where appropriate, in particular where any delay is likely to cause irreparable harm to the right holder, or where there is a demonstrable risk of evidence being destroyed.

3. Provisional measures taken on the basis of paragraphs 1 and 2 shall, upon request by the defendant, be revoked or otherwise cease to have effect, if proceedings leading to a decision on the merits of the case are not initiated within 20 working days or 31 calendar days, whichever is the longer.

4. Where the provisional measures are revoked or where they lapse due to any act or omission by the applicant, or where it is subsequently found that there has

been no infringement or threat of infringement, the judicial authorities shall have the authority to order the applicant, upon request of the defendant, to provide the defendant appropriate compensation for any injury caused by these measures.'

48) Article 38 is amended to read as follows:

'A. The court competent to hear any civil action shall be permitted to order:

i) damages adequate to compensate for the injury the right holder has suffered as a result of the infringement;

ii) profits of the infringer that are attributable to the infringement and are not taken into account in computing the amount of the actual damages referred to in clause (i) of this Article; and

iii) seizure and destruction of the infringing articles, as well as materials and implements that have been used in the manufacture or creation of such counterfeit goods. The charitable donation of counterfeit trademark goods shall not be ordered by the competent court without the authorization of the right holder. In no case shall the simple removal of the trademark unlawfully affixed be sufficient to permit the release of goods into the channels of commerce.'

49) Article 38*bis* is added following Article 38 to read as follows: 'The court shall provide final judicial decisions in writing and shall state any relevant findings of fact and the reasoning or the legal basis upon which the decisions are based. The court shall publish such decisions or, where such publication is not practicable, otherwise make publicly available.'

50) Article 39*bis* is added following Article 39 to read as follows: 'Any person whose country or origin is a party to any convention or treaty relating to trademarks, trade or commercial names, or the repression of unfair competition, to which Iraq is also a party, or extends reciprocal rights to nationals of Iraq by law, shall be entitled to the benefits of this section under the conditions expressed herein to the extent necessary to give effect to any provision of such convention, treaty or reciprocal law, in addition to the rights to which any owner of a mark is otherwise entitled by this chapter.'

Section 2 Entry into Force

This Order shall enter into force on the date of signature [26 April 2004].

Document 105

Coalition Provisional Authority Order Number 81

CPA/ORD/26 April 2004/81

Patent, Industrial Design, Undisclosed Information, Integrated Circuits and Plant Variety Law

Pursuant to my authority as Administrator of the Coalition Provisional Authority (CPA) and under the laws and usages of war, and consistent with relevant U.N. Security Council resolutions, including Resolution 1483 and 1511 (2003),

Having worked closely with the Governing Council to ensure that economic change as necessary to benefit the people of Iraq occurs in a manner acceptable to the people of Iraq,

Acknowledging the Governing Council's desire to bring about significant change to the Iraqi intellectual property system as necessary to improve the economic condition of the people of Iraq,

Determined to improve the conditions of life, technical skills, and opportunities for all Iraqis and to fight unemployment with its associated deleterious effect on public security,

Recognizing that companies, lenders and entrepreneurs require a fair, efficient, and predictable environment for protection of their intellectual property,

Noting that several provisions of the current Iraqi Patent and Industrial Design Law and related legislation does not meet current internationally-recognized standards of protection,

Recognizing the demonstrated interest of the Iraqi Governing Council for Iraq to become a full member in the international trading system, known as the World Trade Organization, and the desirability of adopting modern intellectual property standards,

Acting in a manner consistent with the Report of the Secretary General to the Security Council of July 17, 2003, concerning the need for the development of Iraq and its transition from a non-transparent centrally planned economy to a free market economy characterized by sustainable economic growth through the establishment of a dynamic private sector, and the need to enact institutional and legal reforms to give it effect,

In close consultation with and acting in coordination with the Governing Council, I hereby promulgate the following:

Section 1 Amendments to the Patents, Industrial Design, Undisclosed Information, Integrated Circuits and Plant Variety Law

1) The Patent and Industrial Designs Laws and Regulations (No. 65 of 1970) is hereby renamed the Patents, Industrial Design, Undisclosed Information, Integrated Circuits and Plant Variety Law (the 'Law').

2) Article 1.1 is amended to read as follows: 'Minister—Minister of Industry.'

3) Article 1.4 is amended to read as follows: 'Invention—Any innovative idea, in any of the fields of technology, which relates to a product or a manufacturing process, or both, and practically solves a specific problem in any of those fields.'

4) Article 1.6 is amended to read as follows: 'Patentee—The natural or legal person to whom the patent is granted.'

5) Article 2 is amended to read as follows: 'Patents of invention shall be granted pursuant to the provisions of this Law for each invention that is industrially applicable, novel and involves an inventive step, either concerning new industrial products, new industrial methods, or new application of known industrial methods.'

6) Article 3.2 is suspended.

7) Article 4 is amended to read as follows: 'An invention shall not be considered as new in the following three cases:

a) If, the invention has been publicly worked out in or outside Iraq, or if the description or drawing of the invention has been publicized in periodicals within Iraq or outside it in such a clear way that enables experts to exploit;

b) If, letters patent had been granted to the invention or part thereof to a person other than the inventor or to whom the rights of the invention have been assigned, or that others had already applied for the same patent, or part thereof; or

c) Notwithstanding subparagraphs (a) and (b), the disclosure of the invention to the public shall not be taken into account if it occurred twelve months before the filing date of the application or its priority date, if any, and it occurred by actions taken by the applicant or applicant's predecessor or due to an abuse by third parties against the applicant or predecessor.'

8) Article 5 is amended to read as follows: 'Notwithstanding the grant of the patent, a person who, in good faith, manufactures, uses an industrial manufacturing process of a

product, or makes serious preparations therefore, before the filing date of an application by another person, or before the priority date of the application pertaining to the same product or process, shall have the right to continue such use or to use the invention as envisioned in such preparations. Assignment or transfer of the said right is only permitted together with the establishment or with that part of the establishment in which the use or preparations for use have been made.'

9) Article 7.3 is amended to read as follows: 'Nationals of States Party to a relevant international agreement to which Iraq is a member.'

10) Article 7.5 is amended to read as follows: 'Companies, societies and establishments formed in Iraq or in countries that are members of a relevant international agreement to which Iraq is a member, and enjoying juridical personality, industrialists, manufacturers, merchants or laborers, provided that the invention shall be primarily registered in the name of the inventor, unless when the invention had already been patented outside Iraq, in which case such invention may be registered in the name of the company, establishment or society that owns it.'

11) Article 12 is amended to read as follows: 'A patent shall grant its owner the following rights:

a) Where the subject of the patent is a product, the right to prevent any person who has not obtained the owner's authorization from making, exploiting, using, offering for sale, selling or importing that product.
b) Where the subject of the patent is an industrial process, the rights to prevent any person who has not obtained the owner's authorization from using the process or the product directly made by the process, offering for sale, selling or importing the product.'

12) Article 13.1 is amended to read as follows: 'The term of duration of the patent shall not end before the expiration of a period of twenty years for registration under the provisions of this Law as from the date of the filing of the application for registration under the provisions of this Law.'

13) Article 13.2 is suspended.

14) Article 16.2 is amended to read as follows:

'(2) An applicant for a patent shall disclose the invention in a manner sufficiently clear and complete for the invention to be carried out by a person skilled in the art.

(2)*bis* An applicant for a patent shall provide information concerning the applicant's corresponding foreign applications and grants.'

15) Article 17 is suspended.

16) Article 18(2) is amended to read as follows: 'That the specification and drawing disclose the invention in a manner sufficiently clear and complete for the invention to be carried out by a person skilled in the art.'

17) Article 27 is amended to read as follows:

'The Registrar may grant a license to use a patent to third parties without obtaining the patentee's consent in any of the following cases exclusively:

A. If the use of the patent by the state authorities or licensed third parties is a necessity for national defense or emergency or for noncommercial public good provided that the patentee is notified as soon as it becomes possible.

B. 1. If the patentee does not exploit it or exploits it insufficiently before the elapse of four years as of the application date or three years as of the granting date, the period to be applied is the one that elapses later. However, the Registrar may grant the patentee an additional grace period if it is deemed that reasons beyond the control of the patentee have prevented exploitation.

2. For the purposes of item (1) of this paragraph, and without prejudice to the provisions of the relevant International Conventions, the importation of the subject goods of the patent to Iraq shall be deemed utilization of the patent.

C. If rights are exercised by the patentee in such a way as to prevent others from competing fairly.'

18) Article 28 is amended to read as follows: 'The following shall be taken into consideration when compulsory licenses are granted:

A. Each application for a license shall be decided separately for its specific conditions and circumstances.

B. The applicant shall have tried to obtain a license from the patentee under reasonable remuneration and conditions but did not reach an agreement during a reasonable period of time in the case provided for in paragraph (B) of Article 27 of this Law.

C. The scope and duration of the license shall be limited to the purpose for which it is granted. If the license application relates to semiconductor technology, then it shall only be granted for noncommercial public good or to rectify practices deemed by the competent judicial or administrative authority to be anticompetitive.

D. The license to exploit shall not be exclusive.

E. The license shall not be assignable to third parties.

F. The license shall only be granted for meeting the demand in the local market except in cases where practices have been deemed by the competent judicial or administrative authority to be anticompetitive.

G. The patentee shall receive an equitable remuneration which takes into account the economic value of the patent.'

19) Article 29 is amended to read as follows: 'The Registrar may cancel the compulsory license *sua sponte* or on the strength of an application from the patentee if the reasons for its grant lapsed. This license cancellation shall, however, preserve the rights of those involved in the compulsory license.'

20) Article 30 is amended to read as follows: 'The provisions and procedures related to licensing of patent utilization shall be prescribed pursuant to regulations to be issued to this aim.'

21) Article *30bis* is added following Article 30 to read as follows: 'The Registrar's compulsory license decision shall be appealable to the Minister within 60 days of its notification.'

22) Article 34 is amended to read as follows: 'Patentee's rights shall not be affected by the exploitation of the invention in land, sea or air means of transport belonging to any of the countries that are members of the Paris Convention for the Protection of Industrial Property or the World Trade Organization or that treat Iraq on a reciprocal basis, during their temporary or accidental existence in Iraq.'

23) Article 36.2*bis* is added following Article 36.2 to read as follows: 'The application for registration of industrial designs or models shall be granted where the industrial design or model is new or original.'

24) Article 36.2*ter* is added following Article 36.2*bis* to read as follows: 'The industrial design or model applied for is not considered novel if:

(1) It has been displayed, described or its uses were described to the public prior to the date of deposit of the application for registration.

However, the industrial design or model shall still be considered novel, if its description or display had been made after the application for the registration in a country that treats Iraq on reciprocal basis, or if such is displayed in national or international exhibitions, or the industrial design or model has been made public in a conference or in scientific journals within a period not exceeding six months prior to the date of the application for the registration in Iraq.

(2) It includes non-basic differences in respect of a prior industrial design or model, or is dedicated to another type of product other than to which the previously registered industrial design or model was designed for.'

25) Article 36.2*quater* is added following Article 36.2*ter* to read as follows: 'Application for registration of industrial designs that are dictated essentially by technical or functional considerations shall not be granted.'

26) Article 37*bis* is added following Article 37 to read as follows:

'1. The owner of a protected industrial design shall have the right to prevent a third party not having the owner's consent from making, selling or importing articles bearing or embodying a design which is a copy, or substantially a copy, of the protected design, when such acts are undertaken for commercial purposes.

2. The Minister may, by regulation, provide limited exceptions to the protection of industrial designs, provided that such exceptions do not unreasonably conflict with the normal exploitation of protected industrial designs and do not unreasonably prejudice the legitimate interests of the owner of the protected design, taking account of the legitimate interests of third parties.'

27) Article 41 is amended to read as follows: 'The term of protection of industrial designs shall be ten years as from the date of issue of the certificate, provided payment of the prescribed renewal annual fees is carried out.'

28) Article 44 is amended to read as follows:

'A. The owner of a patent or industrial design registered in Iraq, upon bringing suit to prevent the infringement of rights in the patent or design, may file a complaint with the competent court, with a bond, which the court shall accept for the following provisional measures:

1. Cease the infringement;
2. Seize the products subject of the infringement wherever it occurs; or
3. Preserve evidence related to the infringement.

B. 1. The patent or design owner, before bringing a claim of infringement, may, with a bond, request the court to order any of the procedures provided in paragraph (A) of this Article without notifying the defendant. The court may grant the owner's request if the owner proves any of the following:

– the patent or design is being infringed;
– the infringement is imminent and may cause irreparable harm; or
– the risk that the evidence will disappear or be damaged is great.

2. If the patent or design owner does not file the lawsuit within eight days from the date of the court's order for precautionary procedures, the ordered procedures shall be deemed canceled.

3. The defendant may appeal the court's decision of precautionary procedures to the Court of Appeals within eight days from the date the defendant was notified of the decision. The decision of the Court of Appeals is final.

C. The defendant may file a request, with a bond, to ask the court to discontinue the precautionary measures including the closure of the enterprise, factory, or other related businesses. This decision shall be appeal able within eight days as of the date of its notification. The decision of the Court of Appeals shall be final.

D. The defendant may seek equitable compensation for damages suffered if the court concludes that the plaintiff's lawsuit is without merit or was not filed within the prescribed period.

E. The court may, in all cases, seek the help of experts and specialists.

F. The court may order the confiscation of the infringing products, as well as the materials and tools substantially used in the infringement of the patent. The court may order them destroyed or disposed of for noncommercial purposes.'

29) Chapter Three*bis* is added following Article 54 for protection of Undisclosed Information.

30) Article 1 is added as the first article in Chapter Three*bis* to read as follows: 'Natural and legal persons shall have the possibility of preventing information lawfully within their control from being disclosed to, acquired by, or used by others without their consent in a manner contrary to honest commercial practices so long as such information:

a) is secret in the sense that it is not, as a body or in the precise configuration and assembly of its components, generally known among or readily accessible to persons within the circles that normally deal with the kind of information in question;
b) has commercial value because it is secret; and
c) has been subject to reasonable steps under the circumstances by the person lawfully in control of the information to keep it secret.'

31) Chapter Three*bis,* Article 2 is added to read as follows: 'If the Minister requires the submission of data pertaining to secret tests, or any data which has been derived as a result of considerable efforts in order to approve the marketing of pharmaceuticals or chemical agricultural products which contain new chemical substances, then the Minister shall comply with the following:

a) Protection of such data from unclassified commercial use through prohibiting any other person who did not obtain the consent of the submitter to rely on it for marketing that other person's pharmaceuticals and products except after the lapse of five years as of the date of obtaining the submitter of such data the approval to market those products; and
b) The protection of this data from disclosure with the exception of the following:
   i) Should disclosure be necessary for the protection of the public; or
   ii) Should the Minister realize the necessary precautions to guarantee unclassified commercial use of such data.'

32) Chapter Three*ter* is added following Chapter Three*bis* for protection of Integrated Circuits.

33) Chapter Three*ter,* Article 1 is added to read as follows: 'The following words and phrases shall have the following meanings wherever mentioned in this Chapter, unless otherwise indicated:

o **The Ministry**: The Ministry of Industry.
o **The Minister**: The Minister of Industry.
o **Integrated Circuit/IC**: A product, in its final form or an intermediate form, in which the elements, at least one of which is an active element, and some or all

of the interconnections are integrally formed in and/or on a piece of material and which is intended to perform an electronic function.

- o **Design**: Three-dimensional array of the elements constituting the circuit forming the integrated circuit or specifically prepared for manufacturing the integrated circuit.
- o **Protected Design**: A design in respect of which the conditions of protection referred to in this Chapter are fulfilled.
- o **Registrar**: The Registrar of Integrated Circuit Designs in the Ministry as appointed by the Minister.
- o **Register**: The register of Integrated Circuit Designs.
- o **Rights holder**: The creator of the protected design or legal successors.'

34) Chapter Three*ter*, Article 2 is added to read as follows:

'A. A Register shall be established under the supervision of the Registrar and shall be entitled "Register of Integrated Circuit Designs." In such Register, all information related to designs, rights holders, their addresses and certificates issued on their behalf shall be handwritten and registered together with the measures and legal procedures taken to include:

B. [sic] Any transfer, acquisition, assignment or licensing from rights holder to third party/parties; and

1. [sic] Any mortgage, lien, seizure, levy or any constraint in utilizing such design.

C. The public may access the Register pursuant to regulations issued by the Minister as published in the Official Gazette.

D. Computers may be used to register designs and related information. Information and documents certified by the Registrar are presumed evidence of registration, unless otherwise proven.'

35) Chapter Three*ter*, Article 3 is added to read as follows: 'The design is registrable, if:

A. The design is original in the sense that it is the result of its creator's own intellectual effort and is not commonplace among creators of integrated circuit designs and manufacturers of integrated circuits at the time of its creation; and

B. The application for registration is presented within two years of its first commercial exploitation anywhere worldwide.'

36) Chapter Three*ter*, Article 4 is added to read as follows: 'The beneficiaries for design protection shall be as follows:

A. The creator or to whomever the design rights are accrued;

B. All participants in the design if the design is a result of a combined effort. Registration shall be equally owned unless otherwise agreed;

C. If the design was designed by more than one independent individual, the right is to the creator prior in applying for registration; or

D. The employer, if designed by an employee in fulfillment of an employment agreement, or commission, unless employment agreement otherwise stipulates.'

37) Chapter Three*ter*, Article 5 is added to read as follows: 'The design is registered by filing the application for registration to the Registrar on the designated form, with requested information, samples and drawings attached. The application for registration is valid for only one registration.'

38) Chapter Three*ter*, Article 6 is added to read as follows:

'A. The date the Registrar receives the application for registration of the design is considered the date of filing provided it fulfills all legal requirements and the information identifying the applicant and the design diagrams is attached.

A. [sic] If the Registrar determines that the application is incomplete as mandated by paragraph (A) of this Article, applicant may be given a period determined by regulation to complete the application, or make necessary amendments provided that such amendments exceed what was previously stated in the original application. The date of completion or amendment shall be the date of filing the application. Alternatively, the Registrar may determine that the applicant abandoned the application. Such decision may be appealed in the Court of Appeals within sixty days of the date of notification.'

39) Chapter Three*ter*, Article 7 is added to read as follows:

'A. If the application fulfills all conditions and legal requirements, the Registrar shall accept the registration and assess the fees.

B. If the Registrar announces such registration in the Official Gazette, any third party may file an objection within ninety days from the date of the published announcement. The appellate procedures shall be based on the regulations stipulated by this Chapter.

C. If no objection is filed against the acceptance of the registration of the design, the Registrar shall approve its registration and issue a certificate after assessing the determined registration fees.'

40) Chapter Three*ter*, Article 8 is added to read as follows:

'A. The rights holder of the registered design is entitled to authorize or prohibit the following acts:

1. Reproduction of the protected design, in whole or in part, whether incorporated in an integrated circuit or by any other means, except reproduction of any part that does not comply with the requirement of originality; or
2. Importation, sale or other distribution for commercial purposes of the protected design or an integrated circuit in which a protected design is incorporated.

B. It shall be an infringement of the rights of the owner of the protected design if any of the acts provided for in paragraph (A) of this Article are committed by third parties without consent of the rights holder and shall be liable to punishment.

C. A design comprising a combination of elements and interconnections that are commonplace shall be protected only if the combination, taken as a whole fulfills the conditions of originality as stipulated in this Chapter.'

41) Chapter Three*ter*, Article 9 is added to read as follows: 'Notwithstanding the provisions of Article 8 of this Chapter, the performance without the authorization of the right holder, of the following:

A. Reproduction of the design in the following cases:

1. If reproduction is performed by a third party for private purposes or for the sole purpose of evaluation, analysis, research or teaching; or
2. If reproduction is of a non-original part of the design.

B. Incorporation of the protected design in an integrated circuit if, on the basis of evaluation or analysis of the protected design, creates a design complying with the requirement of originality referred to in Article 3 (A);

C. Any of the acts as stipulated in subparagraph 2 of paragraph (A) of Article 8 of this Chapter with respect to:

1. a similar design that is original and which was independently created;
2. a design or an integrated circuit incorporated in which is a design offered on the market by the rights holder or the rights holder approved offering of such; or

3. an integrated circuit that incorporates an illegally reproduced design or a product that incorporates such circuit and alleged infringer when acquiring such circuit or product was unaware and could not have been aware that such circuit or product contains a design that was illegally reproduced, in compliance with Article 10 of this Chapter.'

42) Chapter Three*ter*, Article 10 is added to read as follows: 'If a person commits an act stipulated in subparagraph 3 of paragraph (C) of Article 9 of this Chapter and the right holder had legally notified such person, then that person is entitled to dispose of the stocked products before being held liable provided that such person compensates the rights holder with a sum equivalent to reasonable revenues had such act been based upon a license between the parties.'

43) Chapter Three*ter*, Article 11 is added to read as follows:

'A. Protection of the design shall be effective from the date the application for registration is filed in Iraq.

B. The period of the design protection is ten years from the date of first commercial exploitation anywhere worldwide, such period shall, however, not exceed fifteen years from the date of creation of the design.'

44) Chapter Three*ter*, Article 12 is added to read as follows:

'A. Any third party is entitled to request the cancellation of the design in the following cases:

1. the design is unregistrable due to lack of any of the conditions stipulated in Article 3 of this Chapter; or
2. the application for registration does not include all the required information, or if such information or attached documents are contrary to the facts or in violation of the provisions of this Chapter.

B. The Registrar's decision to cancel the registration of the design in accordance with paragraph (A) of this Article may be appealed to the Court of Appeal within sixty days of notification.'

45) Chapter Three*ter*, Article 13 is added to read as follows:

'A. 1. Design ownership may be transferred in whole or in part, with or without compensation. The design may have a lien against it or be levied, which shall be published in the Official Gazette.

2. Transfer of design ownership, liens or levies to a third party is effective only as of the date of registration in the Register.

B. Ownership of the design may be transferred by inheritance.'

46) Chapter Three*ter*, Article 14 is added to read as follows: 'Procedures for design ownership transfer, liens and levies on ownership and all legal procedures shall be stipulated by regulation issued by the Minister and published in the Official Gazette.'

47) Chapter Three*ter*, Article 15 is added to read as follows: 'The owner may license a third party to exploit the protected design according to a written agreement to be registered with the Registrar. The Registrar shall keep the agreement of the contract confidential.'

48) Chapter Three*ter*, Article 16 is added to read as follows:

'A. The rights holder upon bringing suit to prevent infringement of the design or in anticipation of such a suit, may file a complaint with the competent court, with a bond, which the court shall accept for the following provisional measures:

1. Cease the infringement;
2. Seize goods subject of the infringement wherever it occurs; or
3. Preserve evidence related to the infringement.

B. 1. Before bringing a claim of infringement, the rights holder may, with a bond, request the court to order any the procedures provided for in paragraph (A) of this Chapter, without notifying the defendant. The court may grant the rights holder's request if any of the following is proven:

– the design was infringed;
– infringement is imminent, and may cause irreparable harm; or
– the risk that the evidence will disappear or be damaged is great.

1.[sic] If the right holder does not file the lawsuit within eight days from the date of the court's order for precautionary procedures, the ordered procedures shall be deemed canceled.

2.[sic] The defendant may appeal the court's decision to order precautionary procedures to the Court of Appeals within eight days from the date of the defendant's notification of the decision. The Court of Appeals' decision shall be final.

3.[sic] The defendant may claim compensation for damages if it is proved that the plaintiff was unjustified in his claim for precautionary procedures or the plaintiff did not bring the lawsuit within the period prescribed in item 2 of this paragraph.

C. The defendant may seek compensation for the damages suffered, if the court concludes that the plaintiff's lawsuit is without merit.

D. The court may, in all cases, seek the opinions of experts and specialists.

E. The court may order the confiscation of the infringing products and the material and tools mainly used in infringement upon the design of these products. The court may also order destruction of these products, material and tools or dispose of them for any noncommercial purpose.'

49) Chapter Three*ter*, Article 17 is added to read as follows: 'The Minister shall issue the necessary regulations for implementing the provisions of this Law including fixing the fees to be assessed.'

50) Chapter Three*ter*, Article 18 is added to read as follows: 'The protection of layout designs of integrated circuits provided under this Law shall be extended to foreigners, whether natural or juridical persons, on a basis no less favorable than that accorded to Iraqi nationals with regard to the protection and enjoyment of such rights and any benefits derived from such rights.'

51) Chapter Three*quater* is added following Chapter Three*ter* for the protection of new varieties of plants.

52) Chapter Three*quater*, Article 1 is added to read as follows: 'The following words and phrases shall have the following meanings wherever mentioned in this Chapter, unless otherwise indicated:

o **The Ministry**: The Ministry of Agriculture.
o **The Minister**: The Minister of Agriculture.
o **The Plant taxonomy**: Plants gradation in the plant kingdom is from the group to the class to the family to the sort to the varieties.
o **The variety**: Any plant grouping within a single botanical taxon of the lowest known rank, which grouping, irrespective of whether the conditions for the grant of a breeder's right are fully met, can be defined by the expression of the characteristics resulting from a given genotype or combination of genotypes, distinguished from any other plant grouping by the expression of at least one of the said characteristics and considered as a unit with regard to its suitability for being propagated unchanged.
o **The protected variety**: The variety registered according to the provisions of this Chapter.

- o **The education**: Breeding a new plant variety or discovering and developing such.
- o **The breeder**: The person who bred, discovered or developed a new variety, or the legal successor to such person.
- o **The Registrar**: The Registrar of the new plant varieties nominated by the Minister.
- o **The Register**: The Register of the new plant varieties.'

53) Chapter Three*quater*, Article 2 is added to read as follows: 'The provisions of this Chapter shall become effective with respect to the varieties listed under the various plant denomination determined by the regulation issued in accordance with the provisions of this Chapter.'

54) Chapter Three*quater*, Article 3 is added to read as follows:

'A. A Register shall be regulated in the Ministry under the supervision of the Registrar and shall be called the "Register of New Plant Varieties" in which all the data related to the new plant varieties shall be maintained. The name, the names and addresses of breeders, the registration certifications and the resulting procedures and dispositions shall be registered, including:

1. Any transfer, assignment or transfer of title, or licensing from its owner to third parties for use while taking into consideration the confidentiality included in the license contract; and

2. The mortgage or lien on the protected variety or any limitation for usage of such.

B. 1. The public shall have the right to view the Register and the documents related to the rights granted to the breeder and to view the growth tests or any other necessary tests as stipulated in this Chapter according to the instructions issued by the Minister and published in the Official Gazette; and

2. The data and other documents that are reproduced and maintained by the Registrar shall be considered to be the same as originals unless otherwise determined.'

55) Chapter Three*quater*, Article 4 is added to read as follows:

'The variety may be registered according to the following criteria:

A. If the variety is novel such that at the date of filing the registration application or at the date of the priority provided in paragraph (A) of Article 8 of this Chapter and according to what may be required, then plant propagating and harvesting materials of the variety have not been sold or otherwise transferred to others by or with consent of the breeder for purposes of exploitation of the variety:

1. For more than one year inside Iraq and for more than four years outside Iraq; or
2. For more than six years outside Iraq if related to trees or vines;

B. If such materials are distinctive so that the variety differs clearly from any other variety whose existence is a matter of common knowledge at the time of filing the application, considering that any filing of an application for the granting of plant variety protection or for the entering of another variety in an official register of varieties, in any country, shall be deemed to render that other variety a matter of common knowledge from the date of the application, provided that the application leads to the granting of the right or to the entering of the said other variety in the Register, as the case may be;

C. If it is uniform subject to the variation that may be expected from the particular features of its propagation; or

D. If it is stable such that its relevant characteristics remain unchanged after repeated propagation or, in the case of a particular cycle of propagation, at the end of each such cycle.'

56) Chapter Three*quater*, Article 5 is added to read as follows: 'The right in registering the variety shall be as follows:

A. To the breeder or to whom the variety rights shall be transferred to;

B. To all persons participating in its education if it is an outcome of their joint effort provided that it is registered in equal shares among them, unless they otherwise agree;

C. To the breeder prior in filing the variety's registration application if such is educed by more than one person and if each person is independent from the other; or

D. To the employer if the variety is educed by the employee in accordance with an employment agreement in which the employee is obliged to undertake such education unless the agreement may provide otherwise.'

57) Chapter Three*quater*, Article 6 is added to read as follows: 'The variety shall be registered as follows:

A. The registration application shall be filed with the Registrar on the designated form indicating the plant taxonomy of the variety, the proposed denomination, and any other matters or data defined by the issued regulation pursuant to the provisions of this Chapter;

B. Registration shall not be permissible if the application contains more than one variety, and one fee is paid; and

C. If the applicant is not a citizen or resident of Iraq, then the applicant shall appoint an authorized agent in Iraq.'

58) Chapter Three*quater*, Article 7 is added to read as follows:

'A. The date at which the Registrar received the application for registration shall be deemed as its filing date provided that it fulfills all the legal requirements and includes the applicant's identification information and a sample of the variety intended for registration.

B. If the Registrar discovers that the application does not fulfill the requirements determined in paragraph (A) of this Article, the applicant may either complete the application or make the necessary modifications within thirty days from the date of notification by the Registrar. The date the application is completed shall be considered the filing date. Where the application is not completed as requested, the Registrar shall have the right to consider the application abandoned, with an opportunity for appeal to the Court of Appeals within sixty days from the date of notifying the applicant.'

59) Chapter Three*quater*, Article 8 is added to read as follows:

'A. 1. The applicant for plant variety registration shall include with the application, a claim for the right of priority based on a previous application filed in a country member of the World Trade Organization or other relevant international agreement to which Iraq is also a member provided that the application is filed in Iraq within a period not to exceed twelve months as calculated from the date following the first filing date.

2. If the application includes a priority claim pursuant to item (1) of this Article, the Registrar may ask the applicant, within three months from the filing date, to provide an exact copy of the documentation related to the first application approved from the office in which it was filed. The Registrar may ask the applicant within such period to provide any samples or other evidence which affirms that the variety subject of the first application is the same variety of the application related to the priority right. In such case, the filing date of the application shall be deemed as the same date on which the application was filed in the other country.

B. If the applicant is unable to demonstrate the claimed priority right in accordance with paragraph (A) of this Article, the application shall be registered on the date filed with the Registrar.

C. The applicant may ask for a grace period of two years after the expiration of the priority period to provide the Registrar with the necessary information, documentation and required materials in accordance with this Chapter for the purposes of examination pursuant to Article 9 of the Chapter. If the filed application in the other country was not accepted or was withdrawn, the applicant shall be given a grace period of six months from the date of rejection or withdrawal of the application to provide the necessary information and documentation for the examination.'

60) Chapter Three*quater*, Article 9 is added to read as follows:

'A. The variety may be subjected to a technical examination to verify the following:

1. It is listed under the plant taxonomy determined in its application; and

2. It fulfills the conditions of distinctiveness, uniformity and stability provided in paragraphs (B), (C) and (D) of Article 4 of this Chapter.

B. The examination provided in item (2) of paragraph (A) of this Article shall be carried out under the supervision of the Ministry by one of the following methods:

1. Pursuant to the growth and germination examinations and any other necessary tests carried out by a technical authority inside or outside Iraq if such examinations or tests have been done in environmental conditions comparable to those of Iraq; or

2. The Ministry shall carry out the examinations and tests cited in subparagraph (1), or at the expense of the breeder, designate an authority to perform the examinations or tests on its behalf.

C. A technical committee of those experienced and skilled in the art shall be established in accordance with instructions issued by the Minister and shall be asked to evaluate the results of the examinations and tests provided in paragraph (B) of this Article to comply with the procedures of registering the variety provided that such instructions shall include defining the other tasks of this Committee; how it shall work, make decisions and all related matters.'

61) Chapter Three*quater*, Article 10 is added to read as follows:

'A. The Registrar shall ask the applicant to provide all the necessary information and documentation for undertaking the technical examination provided in Article 9 of this Chapter within the period defined in a regulation issued in accordance with this Chapter. If the applicant does not provide the requested information, the Registrar shall consider the application as abandoned; this decision may be appealed to the Court of Appeals within sixty days from the date of notification.

B. The standards provided in Article 9 of this Chapter shall be met in approving the application. Additional tests and examinations may be undertaken after registration to ensure the maintenance of the variety's uniformity and stability.'

62) Chapter Three*quater*, Article 11 is added to read as follows:

'A. If the application fulfills all the conditions and requirements defined in this Chapter, the Registrar shall accept the application and grant the applicant preliminary approval that shall be published in the Official Gazette after collecting the established fees. The publication shall include the name of the variety and its plant class.

B. Any person shall have the right to object to the registration of any new variety within ninety days from the date of announcement of the preliminary approval in the Official Gazette.

C. Regulations shall be issued to determine the periods within which the publication shall be completed, data shall be published, procedures, and extensions of time for objecting to provisional approval, and other related issues.'

63) Chapter Three*quater*, Article 12 is added to read as follows: 'The applicant shall be given provisional protection during the period between the date of publication of the application in the Official Gazette and the date of registration of the variety. The applicant shall have the right during such period to use and make the variety, and be entitled to equitable remuneration from any person who, during this period, has carried out acts which, once the registration is granted, require the authorization of the breeder as provided for in Article 14.'

64) Chapter Three*quater*, Article 13 is added to read as follows: 'Unless an objection is made against the registration of the variety, or the objection against the registration is rejected, the Registrar shall register the variety and shall provide the breeder with a certificate after collecting the established fees.'

65) Chapter Three*quater*, Article 14 is added to read as follows: 'Taking into consideration the provisions of Articles 15 and 16 of this Chapter:

A. After registration of the variety, the following acts with respect to the propagating material of the protected variety shall require the authorization of the breeder:

1. production or reproduction (multiplication);
2. conditioning for the purpose of propagation;
3. offering for sale;
4. selling or otherwise marketing;
5. exporting;
6. importing; or
7. stocking for any of the purposes mentioned cited in this paragraph.

B. The authorization of the breeder shall be required to carry out the acts cited in paragraph (A) of this Article in respect of the harvested material, including the entire plants and parts of plants obtained through the unauthorized use of propagating material of the protected variety, unless the breeder has had reasonable opportunity to exercise the breeder's right in relation to the said propagating materials.

C. The provisions of paragraphs (A) and (B) of this Chapter shall be also applicable to the following varieties:

1. The varieties which are essentially derived from the protected variety where the protected variety is not itself an essentially derived variety. The variety is considered essentially derived from another variety according to the following criteria;

a) it is predominantly derived from the initial variety, or from a variety that is itself predominantly derived from the initial variety while retaining the expression of the essential characteristics that result from the genotype or combination of genotypes of the initial variety;

b) it is clearly distinguishable from the initial variety; and

c) except for the differences which result from the act of derivation, it conforms to the initial variety in the expression of the essential characteristics that result from the genotype or combination of genotypes of the initial variety. If it is similar to the original variety as for its main properties resulting from the hereditary composite or a group of the hereditary composites for the original variety, except what is related to the differences resulting from the derivation;

2. The varieties which are not clearly distinguishable from the protected variety in accordance with paragraph (B) of Article 4 of this Chapter; and

3. The varieties whose production requires the repeated use of the protected variety.

D. It shall be permissible to obtain the essentially derived varieties as a result of the selection of a natural or induced mutant, or of a somaclonal variant, the selection of a variant individual from plants of the initial variety, backcrossing, or transformation by genetic engineering.

E. The third party's performance of the acts provided in paragraphs (A) and (B) of this Article shall be deemed as an infringement of the rights of the breeder and shall be subject to penalties if the defendant knew, or had reason to know, that the defendant infringed the rights of the breeder.'

66) Chapter Three*quater*, Article 15 is added to read as follows:

'A. Notwithstanding Article 14 of this Chapter, the breeder's right shall not include the following acts of third parties for personal non-commercial purposes, for purposes of experimentation or education of new varieties.

B. Farmers shall be prohibited from re-using seeds of protected varieties or any variety mentioned in items 1 and 2 of paragraph (C) of Article 14 of this Chapter.'

67) Chapter Three*quater*, Article 16 is added to read as follows:

'A. The breeder's right shall not include acts related to the materials of the protected variety, or to the materials of the protected variety, or to the materials of any variety covered under paragraph (C) of Article 14 of this Chapter, or to materials derived from these materials, and which the breeder has sold or marketed in any other form directly or with the consent of the breeder in Iraq, unless these acts include the following:

1. Further propagation of the relevant variety; or

2. Exporting of material of the variety, which enables the propagation of the variety, into a country which does not protect varieties of the plant genus or species to which the variety belongs, except where the exported material is for final consumption.

B. The word "material" wherever mentioned in paragraph (A) of this Article shall mean the propagation material of any kind, harvested material, including entire plants and parts of plants, and any product made directly from the harvested material.'

68) Chapter Three*quater*, Article 17 is added to read as follows: 'The term of protection for the protected variety shall be twenty years from the date of filing the application. With respect to trees and vines, the term of protection shall be twenty five years.'

69) Chapter Three*quater*, Article 18 is added to read as follows:

'A. It shall be permitted to transfer, mortgage or lien all or some of the breeder's rights with or without compensation.

B. The right in the protected variety shall be transferred to the heirs by inheritance.

C. The procedure for transferring, mortgaging and placing a lien on the title of the protected variety and all relevant legal practices, including licensing for its use in accordance with instructions issued for such purpose by the Minister and published in the Official Gazette, shall be determined.

D. The transfer of title of the variety shall be considered as evidence against a third party only as of the date of registration of the transfer in the Register and its publication in the Official Gazette.'

70) Chapter Three*quater*, Article 19 is added to read as follows: 'It shall be permissible for the breeder to grant a license to a third party for use of the protected variety in accordance with a written contract that shall be registered with the Registrar.'

71) Chapter Three*quater*, Article 20 is added to read as follows: 'The variety's registration shall be nullified only according to the following criteria:

A. If it is proven that the conditions in Article 4 were not complied with at the time of the grant of the breeder's right;

B. If it is proven that where the grant of the breeder's right has been essentially based upon information and documentation furnished by the breeder, the variety is not uniform or stable at the time of the grant of the breeder's right; or

C. That the breeder's right has been granted to a person who is not entitled to it, unless it is transferred to the person who is so entitled.'

72) Chapter Three*quater*, Article 21 is added to read as follows:

'A. The Registrar may cancel the variety's registration only according to the following criteria:

1. If it is demonstrated as a result of the technical examination provided in Article 9 of this Chapter, that the variety's uniformity and stability are no longer fulfilled;
2. If the breeder does not provide the Registrar with the information, documentation or materials deemed necessary for verifying the maintenance of the variety;
3. If the breeder fails to pay the annual fixed fees; or
4. If the breeder does not propose, where the denomination of the variety is cancelled after the grant of the right, another suitable denomination.

B. For the purposes of applying subparagraphs 2, 3 and 4 of paragraph (A) of this Article, the Registrar shall notify the breeder of the cancellation; the cancellation shall not be done except after the expiration of the period fixed by the issued regulation governing this Chapter.'

73) Chapter Three*quater*, Article 22 is added to read as follows: 'The Registrar shall register the decision of the registration nullity or its cancellation, which shall be published in the Official Gazette.'

74) Chapter Three*quater*, Article 23 is added to read as follows: 'Decisions shall be subject to appellate review to the Court of Appeals within sixty days from the date of the notification of the decision.'

75) Chapter Three*quater*, Article 24 is added to read as follows:

'A. Each variety shall be registered with a denomination which will be its generic designation. The denomination may be composed of a word, a combination of words and numbers or a combination of letters and numbers, which may or may not have a meaning. The denomination shall not be composed of numbers except where this is an established practice for designating varieties.

B. A variety must be submitted to the Registrar under the same denomination used in other countries unless the denomination is considered unsuitable in Iraq.

C. It shall be prohibited to use or register a denomination that otherwise identifies another variety as it may cause confusion with the earlier-registered variety from the same plant genus or one closely resembling it. The denomination of the earlier-registered variety may be registered or known either in Iraq or in any other country. This prohibition shall remain in effect even after the expiration of rights in the variety as the denomination may have acquired a certain meaning related to the variety.

D. Taking into consideration paragraph (E) of this Article, anyone who, within Iraq, offers for sale or markets propagating material of a variety protected within Iraq shall be obliged to use the denomination of that variety, even after the expiration of the breeder's right in that variety.

E. Prior rights of third persons shall not be affected. If, by reason of a prior right, the use of the denomination of a variety is forbidden to a person who, in accordance with the provisions of paragraph (D), is obligated to use it, the Registrar shall require the breeder to submit another denomination for the variety.

F. It shall be permissible to associate a trademark, trade name or any similar indication with the registered variety denomination. If marketing a variety or offering a variety for sale, such denomination must be easily recognizable.'

76) Chapter Three*quater*, Article 25 is added to read as follows: 'It shall not be permissible to register the denomination of the variety if the denomination is:

A. In conflict with the provisions of this Chapter;

B. In conflict with the public order and morals; or

C. Misleads or causes confusion regarding the variety's characteristics, value or identity of the variety or the identity of the breeder.'

77) Chapter Three*quater*, Article 26 is added to read as follows: 'The proposed denomination for the variety shall be determined in the application and the procedures of registering the denomination, its publication and the periods related to such shall be determined by regulation issued according to the provisions of this Chapter.'

78) Chapter Three*quater*, Article 27 is added to read as follows:

'A. The breeder of the protected variety, upon bringing suit to prevent the infringement of rights in the protected variety or in anticipation of such suit, may file a complaint with the competent court, with by a bond, which the court shall accept for the following provisional measures:

1. Cease the infringement;
2. Seize goods subject of the infringement wherever it occurs; or
3. Preserve evidence related to the infringement

B. 1. The breeder of the protected variety, before bringing a claim of infringement, may, with by a bond, request the court to order any of the procedures provided in paragraph (A) of this Article, without notifying the defendant. The court may grant the breeder's request if the owner proves any of following:

– the breeder's rights have been infringed;
– the infringement is imminent and may cause irreparable harm; or
– the risk that the evidence will disappear or be damaged is great.

2. If the breeder of the protected variety does not file the lawsuit within eight days from the date of the court's order for precautionary procedures, the ordered procedures shall be deemed canceled.

3. The defendant may appeal the court's decision of precautionary procedures to the Court of Appeals within eight days from the date of the defendant's notification of the decision. The Court of Appeals' decision shall be final.

C. The defendant may seek compensation for the damages suffered if the court concludes that the plaintiff's lawsuit is without merit.

D. The court may, in all cases, seek the help of experts and specialists.

E. The court may order the confiscation of the infringing variety as well as the materials and tools substantially used in the infringement of the protected variety. The court may also decide to destroy the infringing variety as well as the materials and tools or to dispose of them in any noncommercial purpose.'

79) Chapter Three*quater*, Article 28 is added to read as follows:

'A. The Minister shall issue the necessary regulations for implementing the provisions of this Chapter including determining the annual fees for renewing the registration, and other fees in accordance with the provisions of this Chapter.

B. The instructions referred to in this Chapter shall be published in the Official Gazette.'

Section 2 Entry into Force
This Order shall enter into force on the date of signature [26 April 2004].

Document 106
Coalition Provisional Authority Order Number 82
CPA/ORD/28 April 2004/82

Iraqi National Foundation for Remembrance

Pursuant to my authority as Administrator of the Coalition Provisional Authority (CPA), and under the laws and usages of war, and consistent with relevant U.N. Security Council resolutions, including Resolutions 1483 and 1511 (2003),

Recognizing that the Iraqi people have long suffered from terrible abuses of their fundamental freedoms and human rights,

Acknowledging that the Iraqi people are still uncovering long-hidden evidence of the brutality inflicted on them by the previous regime,

Noting that accounting publicly for the past atrocities and educating the Iraqi people about them will serve as a crucial safeguard against future abuses of fundamental freedoms and human rights,

Desiring that the establishment of monuments, memorials and other historical and artistic exhibitions will create a lasting record of the crimes committed against the Iraqi people, a tribute to Iraqi resilience and a caution to future generations,

I hereby promulgate the following:

Section 1 Purpose
The Iraqi National Foundation for Remembrance (the 'Foundation') will take steps to ensure that the atrocities of the previous regime are memorialized so that current and future generations of Iraqis will understand and remember this dark period of Iraqi history and take those steps necessary to preserve an open and democratic government which protects human rights, fundamental freedoms and dignity.

Section 2 Establishment

1) The Iraqi National Foundation for Remembrance is hereby established.

2) The Foundation will consider proposals from across the nation on how best to memorialize the victims of these brutal atrocities and the sacrifices made by Iraqi individuals and the communities of Iraq. The Foundation will seek proposals to memorialize and commemorate, among others, those who suffered or lost their lives during the 1991 Intifada, the 1988 Anfal campaign and other massacres, the 1986-1988 chemical attacks, the 'Arabization' and other forced relocation campaigns, the draining of the Marshlands, the 1999 Student Uprising in Najaf, as well as the many other atrocities committed by the previous regime against members of the political opposition in all ethnic and religious groups. The Foundation may obligate funds for selected proposals by grant or direct contracting.

3) The Foundation will publish and distribute widely requests for proposals for monuments, memorials, historical and artistic exhibitions (both permanent and traveling) and other programs to educate and inform the public. The selection criteria will be

transparent and non-discriminatory and be included in all requests for proposals. The Foundation, by a majority vote of its Board of Directors, will choose the proposals to be funded from its budget after fairly and objectively evaluating each proposal submitted.

4) The Foundation will seek to raise private funds for establishing a national memorial museum in Baghdad. This museum will document, study and present publicly the history of atrocities suffered under the previous regime. The Foundation, by a majority vote of its Board of Directors, will decide on the acceptance of each private donation for the museum. The Foundation will adopt procedures providing for any solicitation and acceptance of funds for the museum, including procedures to ensure that no funds are accepted from donors who are seeking special benefits from or access to the Governments of Iraq through such donations, to ensure that no person or entity is advantaged or disadvantaged because of a donation or a failure to donate, and to ensure that any solicitation and acceptance of funds will be separate from any of the funding decisions authorized in Section 2(3) of this Order. The Foundation will ensure that funding for the establishment of this museum will not affect or influence in any way decisions made pursuant to Section 2(3) of this Order.

5) The Foundation will develop policies and implement programs as may be necessary to give effect to this Order.

6) The Foundation will seek the enactment of such legislation as necessary to protect and preserve memorials, monuments, other historical and artistic exhibitions and the museum.

Section 3 Organization

1) A Board of Directors, comprised of seven Directors, will guide the Foundation. The Administrator will appoint the Board of Directors after consultations with the Iraqi Governing Council, other public figures, civil society and, as appropriate, relevant international experts.

2) Each Director will serve two-year terms. The terms of the Directors will be staggered, so that initially three directors will be appointed to one-year terms and four directors will be appointed to two-year terms.

3) The Board of Directors will select a Chairman and Vice Chairman from among its members. The Chairman will manage the activities and discussions of the Foundation and schedule, convene and chair all meetings of the Foundation. When the Chairman is unavailable, the Vice Chairman will assume these duties.

4) The Administrator will appoint an Executive Director after consultations with the Iraqi Governing Council. The Executive Director will report directly to the Board of Directors. The Executive Director will lead the daily operation of the Foundation. The Executive Director will serve a five-year term, which may be renewed once.[254]

5) In the event of a vacancy on the Board of Directors or in the Executive Director position prior to June 30, 2004, by reason of death, resignation, or removal, then the Administrator will appoint a new director or Executive Director, as appropriate, in accordance with Section 3(1) or Section 3(4) of this Order. In the event of a vacancy after June 30, 2004 on the Board of Directors or in the Executive Director position by reason of the expiration of a term in office, death, resignation, or removal, a new director or Executive Director, as appropriate, will be appointed by the Iraqi head of government with the ratification of the body vested with national legislative authority. The Board, by a vote of six directors, may remove a director or the Executive Director for malfeasance, misuse of public funds, failure to fulfill Foundation duties or because of permanent incapacitation.

6) The Executive Director will organize the Foundation's personnel into such departments as is deemed necessary and appropriate.

[254] Sec 3(4) was amended by CPA Order No 100, sec 3(32)(a) *[Doc 124]*.

7) The Executive Director may set up such regional offices as is deemed necessary, appropriate and cost-efficient to facilitate, implement, and coordinate the work of the Foundation at the local level.

8) The Foundation will have an Inspector General who will be appointed and will serve consistent with CPA Order No. 57 (CPA/ORD/5 February 2004/57).[255] The Inspector General will report directly to the Executive Director except as provided for in Section 3(1) of the CPA Order No. 57 (CPA/ORD/5 February 2004/57).

9) The Board of Directors and the Executive Director may establish an advisory committee which could include, for example, the Minister of Culture, the Minister of Human Rights, the Director of the National Museum, and other experts who could provide expertise to the Foundation.

10) The Foundation should consult with relevant Iraqi governmental institutions, including the Ministry of Human Rights, the Ministry of Displacement and Migration, and the Ministry of Culture, to ensure that proposed programs are not duplicative and instead complement their efforts.

Section 4 Personnel and Administration

1) The Executive Director, in the name of the Foundation, may hire and employ personnel in accordance with Iraqi law, as amended by CPA Orders and Memoranda, and subject to established budget constraints. Such hiring will be consistent with CPA Order Number 1 (CPA/ORD/16 May 2003/01)[256] and any authorized implementation thereof.

2) The salaries of Foundation personnel will conform to the salary structure applicable to Iraqi government employees.

3) All contracting by the Foundation, including project selection, will be conducted to the maximum extent practicable consistent with CPA Memorandum No. 4 (CPA/MEM/19 August 2003/04),[257] including applicable conflict-of-interest rules, and any successor law on government procurement.

Section 5 Budget

The Executive Director will be responsible for developing and implementing the budget of the Foundation, while the Board of Directors will be responsible for approving the budget. The Foundation will coordinate with the Ministry of Finance regarding its budget.

Section 6 Durability and Precedence

This order will remain in force unless repealed by the Administrator or superseded by legislation duly enacted and having the force of law. This order will take precedence over all other laws and publications to the extent such other laws and publications are inconsistent.[258]

Section 7 Entry into Force

This Order shall enter into force on the date of signature [28 April 2004].

[255] See *Doc 80*.
[256] See *Doc 14*.
[257] See *Doc 129*.
[258] Sec 6 was rescinded by CPA Order No 100, sec 3(32)(b) *[Doc 124]*.

Document 107
Coalition Provisional Authority Order Number 83
CPA/ORD/29 April 2004/83

Amendment to the Copyright Law

Pursuant to my authority as Administrator of the Coalition Provisional Authority (CPA) and under the laws and usages of war, and consistent with relevant U.N. Security Council resolutions, including Resolution 1483 and 1511 (2003),

Having worked closely with the Governing Council to ensure that economic change as necessary to benefit the people of Iraq occurs in a manner acceptable to the people of Iraq,

Acknowledging the Governing Council's desire to bring about significant change to the Iraqi intellectual property system as necessary to improve the economic condition of the people of Iraq,

Determined to improve the conditions of life, technical skills, and opportunities for all Iraqis and to fight unemployment with its associated deleterious effect on public security,

Recognizing that companies, lenders and entrepreneurs require a fair, efficient, and predictable environment for protection of their intellectual property,

Noting that several provisions of the current Iraqi copyright legislation does not meet current internationally-recognized standards of protection,

Recognizing the demonstrated interest of the Iraqi Governing Council for Iraq to become a full member in the international trading system, known as the World Trade Organization, and the desirability of adopting modern intellectual property standards,

Acting in a manner consistent with the Report of the Secretary General to the Security Council of July 17, 2003, concerning the need for the development of Iraq and its transition from a non-transparent centrally planned economy to a free market economy characterized by sustainable economic growth through the establishment of a dynamic private sector, and the need to enact institutional and legal reforms to give it effect,

Having coordinated with the international financial institutions, as referenced in paragraph 8(e) of the U.N. Security Council Resolution 1483,

In close consultation with and acting in coordination with the Governing Council, I hereby promulgate the following:

Section 1 Purpose

The purpose of this Order is to amend Copyright Law No. 3 of 1971 to ensure that Iraqi copyright law meets current internationally-recognized standards of protection, and to incorporate the modern standards of the World Trade Organization into Iraqi law.

Section 2 Amendments to Copyright Law

1) Article 1 of the Copyright Law No. 3 of 1971 ('the Law') is amended to read as follows:

> '1. This law protects the authors of original literary, artistic and scientific works, whatever their type, method of expression, importance and purpose.
>
> 2. The person in whose name the work is published, whether by mentioning his name on the work or by any other means, shall be considered the author, unless there is evidence to the contrary. This provision shall apply to pseudonyms, provided there is not the least doubt as to the identify of the author.'

2) Article 2 is amended to read as follows:
'The protection shall include the works whose method of expression is in writing, sound, drawing, painting or movement, and in particular the following:
1. Written works of all types
2. Computer programs, whether in source or object code, which shall be protected as literary works
3. Works conveyed verbally such as lectures, lessons, speeches, sermons and the like
4. Works entered under the arts of drawing and painting with lines and colors, engraving, sculpture and architecture
5. Dramatic works and musical plays
6. Works performed by artistic movements or steps and are materially prepared for production
7. Musical works, whether accompanied by words or not
8. Photographic and cinematographic works
9. Works prepared for radio and television
10. Charts, drawings and scientific three-dimensional figures
11. Public recitals of the Holy Koran
12. Sound recordings
13. Compilations of data'

3) Article 3 is amended to read as follows: 'Protection shall include the title of the work, if it is characterized by originality and not indicative of the work's subject matter.'

4) Article 6 is amended to read as follows:
'Protection shall include the following where characterized by originality, arrangement or any other personal effort which deserves protection:
1. Collections which comprise various works of verse, prose, music and other collections, without affecting the copyrights of the author of each of these works
2. Collections of works which have fallen into the public domain
3. Collections of official documents, such as texts of international laws, regulations and agreements, judicial judgments and various official documents'

5) Article 8 is amended to read as follows:
'The author holds the exclusive right to exercise the rights in his/her works. Without the written permission of the author or his/her successors, no person shall do any of the following acts:
1. Reproduce a work in any manner or form, whether transitory or permanent, including onto photographic (including cinematographic) film or onto a digital or electronic storage medium.
2. Translate, adapt, musically arrange or otherwise transform a pre-existing work.
3. Authorize commercial rental to the public of the original and copies of the work.
4. Distribute the original and copies of a work through sale or other transfer of ownership.
5. Import any copies of a work. This includes copies that were prepared with the permission of the copyright owner.
6. Transmit or otherwise communicate a work to the public by means of a recital, speech, lecture, display, acting performance, radio or television broadcast, cinema or any other wire or wireless means, including the making available to the public of

works in a way that the members of the public may access the work from a place and at a time individually chosen by them.'

6) Article 9 is suspended.

7) A new provision is supplemented between Articles 10 and 11 to read as follows:
'1. If the work was created on behalf of another person, the rights in the work shall revert to the author unless there is a written agreement stipulating otherwise.

2. Notwithstanding subparagraph (a), and in any other Law, if an employee created during his employment a work related to the activities or business of the employer, or uses the experiences, information, instruments or articles of the employer under the employee's own disposal in his attempt to create such work, the rights in the work shall be to the benefit of the employer, unless otherwise agreed upon in writing.

3. The rights in the work shall be to the benefit of the employee if the rights created by the same are not related to the business of the employer, and the employee does not use the experiences, information, instruments or raw materials of the employer in his attempt to create the work, unless otherwise agreed upon in writing.'

8) Article 11 is suspended.

9) Article 15 is amended to read as follows: 'Copying may not be made of serialized novels, short stories or other literary, artistic or scientific works published by their authors in the newspapers or periodicals, except with their permission.'

10) A new provision is supplemented between Article 15 and Article 16 to read as follows: 'Exceptions to exclusive rights of the author shall be confined to certain special cases which do not conflict with a normal exploitation of the work and do not unreasonably prejudice the legitimate interests of the right holder.'

11) Article 20 is amended to read as follows:
'1. The author's economic rights provided for in this Law shall be protected throughout the lifetime of the author and for 50 years from the date of his death.

2. The economic rights relating to works of joint authorship shall be protected throughout the lives of all co-authors and for 50 years from the death of the last survivor.

3. Where the copyright holder is a legal entity, the economic rights relating to the authors of collective works, other than authors of works of applied art, shall be protected for 50 years from the date on which the work was published or made available to the public for the first time, whichever comes first. Where the copyright holder is a natural person, the protection period shall be calculated according to the rule stipulated in sub-paragraph (a) and (b). The economic rights relating to a work published for the first time after the death of the author shall expire after 50 years from the date on which the work was published or made available to the public for the first time, whichever comes first.

4. The economic rights relating to a work published anonymously or under pseudonym shall be protected for a period of 50 years, from the date on which the work was published or made available to the public for the first time, whichever comes first, unless the identity of the author is known and established or revealed by the author, in which case the term of protection shall be calculated according to the rule stipulated in subparagraph (a).

5. The economic rights of the author of a work of applied art shall expire after a period of 50 years from the date on which the work was published or made available to the public for the first time, whichever comes first.

6. In cases where the term of protection is calculated from the date on which the work was published or made available to the public for the first time, the term shall be calculated taking into consideration the date that comes first, regardless of any re-publication or making available to the public, unless substantial changes were made by the author in the work so that it may be considered as a new work. Where the work consists of several parts or volumes published separately and at intervals, each part or volume shall be considered as an independent work for the purpose of calculating the term of protection.'

12) Article 21 is suspended.

13) Article 23 is suspended.

14) A new provision is supplemented between Article 34 and Article 35 to read as follows:

'1. Performers shall have the following exclusive rights:

(a) broadcasting and communication to the public of their unfixed performances except where the performance is already a broadcast performance and the fixation of their unfixed performances;

(b) authorizing the direct or indirect reproduction of their performances fixed in phonograms in any manner or form whether transitory or permanent, including digital electronic format;

(c) distributing to the public the original and copies of their phonograms containing the fixations of their performance through sale or other transfer of ownership;

(d) importing copies of their phonograms whether or not the phonogram was made with the performer's authorization;

(e) making available to the public, by wire or wireless means, any performance fixed in a phonogram, in such a way that members of the public may access the fixed performance from a place and at a time individually chosen by them.

2. Independently of a performer's economic rights, and even after the transfer of those rights, the performer shall, as regards his/her live aural performances or performances fixed in phonograms, have the right to claim to be identified as the performer of his/her performances, except where omission is dictated by the manner of the use of the performance, and to object to any distortion, mutilation or other modification of his/her performances that would be prejudicial to his/her reputation.

3. Performers shall enjoy an exclusive economic right for the exploitation of their performances for a period of 50 years calculated from the date on which the performance or the recording took place, as may be the case.

4. The producer of phonograms shall have the following exclusive rights:

(a) broadcasting and communication to the public of their unfixed performances except where the performance is already a broadcast performance and the fixation of their unfixed performances;

(b) authorizing the direct or indirect reproduction of their performances fixed in phonograms in any manner or form whether transitory or permanent, including digital electronic format;

(c) distributing to the public the original and copies of their phonograms containing the fixations of their performance through sale or other transfer of ownership;

(d) importing copies of their phonograms whether or not the phonogram was made with the performer's authorization;

(e) making available to the public, by wire or wireless means, any performance fixed in a phonogram, in such a way that members of the public may access the fixed performance from a place and at a time individually chosen by them.

5. Producers of sound recordings shall enjoy an exclusive economic right to exploit their recordings for a period of 50 years calculated from the date on which the recording was made or made public, whichever comes first.

6. Broadcasting organizations shall have the following exclusive rights:

(a) fix and record their broadcasts and to authorize direct or indirect reproduction of the fixations of their broadcasts

(b) rebroadcast their programs by wireless means and transmit them to the public.

7. Broadcasting organizations shall enjoy an exclusive right to exploit their programs for a period of 50 years calculated from the date on which the program was broadcast for the first time.'

15) A new provision is supplemented between Article 34*bis* and Article 35 to read as follows: 'In order to ensure that no hierarchy is established between rights of authors, on the one hand, and rights of at least performers and producers of phonograms, on the other hand, each Party shall establish that in cases where authorization is needed from both the author of a work embodied in a phonogram and a performer or producer owning rights in the phonogram, the need for the authorization of the author does not cease to exist because the authorization of the performer or producer is also required. Likewise, each Party shall establish that in cases where authorization is needed from both the author of a work embodied in a phonogram and at least of a performer or producer owning rights in the phonogram, the need for the authorization of the performer or producer does not cease to exist because the authorization of the author is also required.'

16) Article 35 is suspended.

17) Article 36 is suspended.

18) Article 44 is amended to read as follows: 'Each author whose rights in his work provided in accordance with the provisions of this law are infringed upon, shall be entitled to appropriate compensation. In deciding compensation, the cultural standing of the author, the literary, scientific or artistic value of the work and the extent the infringer benefited by exploiting the work shall be taken into consideration.'

19) Article 45 is amended to read as follows: 'Any act committed by any of the following shall be considered an act of piracy punishable by a fine of not less than 5,000,000 dinars and not exceeding 10,000,000 dinars.'

20) Article 45(2) is amended to read as follows: '2. Whoever offers for sale, distribution or rental of an infringing work, transmits an infringing work to the public in any manner, uses an infringing work for material gain, brings an infringing work into or out of Iraq, knowing or having adequate reason to believe that the work is unauthorized.'

21) The final paragraph of Article 45 is amended to read as follows: 'In case of subsequent conviction, the offender shall be sentenced to imprisonment for a period not less than five years and not more than ten years and to a fine not less than 100,000,000 dinars and not more than 200,000,000 dinars or to any one of these penalties. The Court may also, in the case of subsequent conviction, order the closure, for a certain period or for good, of the establishment which has been used by the counterfeiters or their partners to commit the offense.'

22) An additional paragraph of Article 45 is added to read as follows: 'The Court may also order the forfeiture and destruction of all infringing copies or sound recordings and all implements, devices or equipment used in the manufacture of such infringing copies or sound recordings.'

23) Article 46 is amended to read as follows:

'1. The Court may upon proper application by the copyright owner or any of his/her heirs or successors issue injunctive relief in relation to any infringement of the rights set forth in Articles 5, 7, 8, 10 and 34*bis* of this Law provided that the application contain a detailed and complete description of the work, performance, phonogram, or program against which the infringement occurred. The Court may decide to:

(a) Order the infringer to cease infringing activities;

(b) Confiscate the infringing copies and any materials and devices used in the commission of the infringement; and

(c) Confiscate the proceeds of the infringement.

2. The request may be presented before, during or after filing the lawsuit.

3. Upon verification that the petitioner is the owner of the right and that his rights have been violated or that a violation is imminent, the Court may apply any of the procedures provided for in subparagraph (a) of this Article on a provisional basis to prevent the occurrence of the infringement or to preserve some evidence related to the act of infringement.

4. In cases where delay may cause damage to the right holder which is difficult to calculate, or in cases where there is a proven risk that delay may lead to the loss of evidence related to the infringement, the Court may adopt any of the procedures stipulated in subparagraph (a) of this Article on a provisional basis without notifying the defendant and in his absence. The defendant shall be notified of the procedures adopted by the Court as soon as the procedure is implemented. The defendant may request a hearing within a reasonable period after his notification of the procedure. The Court shall decide to confirm, amend or nullify the provisional measure at the time of the hearing.

5. The request for application of provisional measures provided for in subparagraphs (c) and (d) of this Article must be accompanied by an adequate monetary guarantee to prevent abuse and to guarantee any damages which may occur to the defendant if the plaintiff is not justified in his claim.

6. Upon request of the defendant, the provisional measures applied prior to the filing of a lawsuit under subparagraphs (c) and (d) of this Article shall be nullified if the lawsuit is not filed within eight days from the date on which the Court issued the decision to apply the provisional measures.

7. In cases where the provisional measures applied in accordance with subparagraphs (c) and (d) of this Article are nullified due to a lapse of the filing period of the lawsuit, the default of the claimant, or based on evidence that there is no infringement or threat of infringement, the court may, upon the request of the defendant, order adequate compensation for the damages resulting from these procedures.

8. The Court may order the claimant who acted abusively in requesting any of the procedures listed in this article to adequately compensate the party against whom the procedures were taken for damages incurred as a result [of] this abuse.'

24) Article 47 is amended to read follows: 'In no case shall buildings and what they have in or on them of engravings, drawings, ornamentations or geometrical shapes be subject to seizure. Furthermore, no ruling shall order their destruction, the change of their features, or their confiscation for the purpose of safeguarding the copyrights of the architect whose designs were used for the building and whose drawings were put in them illegally. This shall not violate his right in obtaining fair compensation for the foregoing.'

25) Article 48 is suspended.

26) Article 49 is amended to read as follows: 'The provisions of this law shall apply to the works of Iraqi and foreign authors which are published, acted or presented for the first time in the Republic of Iraq, as well as to the works of Iraqi authors which are published, acted or presented for the first time in a foreign country. The protection of copyright and related rights provided under this Law shall be extended to foreigners, whether natural persons or legal entities, on a basis no less favorable than that accorded to Iraqi nationals with regard to the protection and enjoyment of such intellectual property rights and any benefits derived from such rights.'

27) A new provision is supplemented between Article 49 and Article 50 to read as follows: 'The provision of this Law shall apply to works existing at the time it takes effect, provided the term of protection for those works have not yet fallen into the public domain in their country of origin.'

Section 3 Entry into Force
This Order shall enter into force on the date of signature [1 May 2004].

Document 108
Coalition Provisional Authority Order Number 84
CPA/ORD/30 April 2004/84

Amendments to Coalition Provisional Authority Order Number 37 (CPA/ORD/19 September 2003/37) and Coalition Provisional Authority Order Number 49 (CPA/ORD/19 February 2004/49)

Pursuant to my authority as Administrator of the Coalition Provisional Authority (CPA), and under the laws and usages of war, and consistent with relevant U.N. Security Council resolutions, including Resolutions 1483 and 1511 (2003),

Determined to create conditions suited to the economic reconstruction of Iraq,

Determined to complete a broad review of taxes in Iraq, in order to improve the operation and efficiency of the tax system,

Recognizing that until such a review is completed an interim tax strategy is required,

Recognizing that these collections are for the benefit of the Iraqi people, and, as far as possible, are in accordance with the rules of assessment and incidence in effect under existing law,

Noting that CPA Order Number 37[259] established a new Tax Strategy for 2003 and that CPA Order Number 49[260] established a new Tax Strategy for 2004,

Emphasizing that effective administration of the Tax Strategy requires increased capacity of the Tax Commission,

Recognizing that additional time is needed to develop the infrastructure for effective tax collection,

I hereby promulgate the following:

[259] See *Doc 58*.
[260] See *Doc 71*.

Section 1 Purpose
The purpose of this Order is to revise the interim tax strategy to suspend the collection of taxes on income until the appropriate infrastructure can be established.

Section 2 Amendment to CPA Order Number 37
1) The introductory language of CPA Order Number 37, Tax Strategy for 2003 (CPA/ORD/19 September 2003/37),[261] is amended to read as follows:

'Subject to Section 6 of this Order, the following taxes are suspended for calendar year 2003:'

Section 3 Amendment to CPA Order Number 49
The following amendments are made to CPA Order Number 49, Tax Strategy of 2004 (CPA/ORD/19 February 2004):

1) Section 2, Item 3 is amended to read as follows:

'The allowances as set forth in paragraphs (1) and (2) of this section shall be reduced by one-third during financial year 2004.'

2) A new Item 4 is added to Section 2 to read as follows:

'Item (6) of Article 12 of Income Tax Law Number 113 of 1982 is amended to read as follows:

(6) Allowances shall not be granted for children who have completed the age of 18 years and have an independent income exceeding ID 200,000 per year, even if they are continuing their studies.'

3) Section 3, Item 1 is amended by revising Article 13(1)(F) of Income Tax Law Number 113 of 1982 to read as follows:

'(F) The amounts delineating the tax brackets as set forth in paragraphs (A) and (B) shall be reduced by one-third for financial year 2004.'

4) A new Item 4 is added to Section 3 to read as follows:

'4) Article 19(1) of Income Tax Law Number 113 of 1982 is amended by changing "20%" to "15%".'

5) Section 8, Item 1, is revised to read as follows:

'All income tax for assessed income resources detailed in Article 2 of Income Tax Law Number 113 of 1982, as amended. Income tax for assessed income resources with regard to individuals detailed in Article 2 on Income Tax Law Number 113 of 1982, as amended, are suspended from January 1, 2004, until April 30, 2004;'

6) Section 11, Item 2(a), is amended by deleting the last sentence, which reads 'If an employee of the public sector has more than 4 children, he or she shall be entitled to an additional exemption of ID 200,000 per child.'

Section 4 Amendment to the Civil Pension Law
Article 5(1)(a)-(d) of Law Number 33 of 1966 on Civil Pensions is amended to read as follows:

'There shall be deducted from the pay of an official the contribution towards the pension for the period of his pensionable service according to the following rates, provided that no deduction shall be made for any period in which his service was not a pensionable one nor for periods of leave enjoyed without pay, nor for periods

[261] It should read 'the introductory language of section 2 of CPA Order Number 37'; see CPA Order No 37, *Doc 58*.

of leave at half pay. These rates shall be applied on the period of service that started after the date of the coming into force of this Law.

(a) 1% of the salary, if the official's gross salary was 69,000 dinars or more, but less than 204,000 dinars.
(b) 4% of the salary, if the official's gross salary was 204,000 dinars or more, but less than 574,000 dinars.
(c) 7% of the salary, if the official's gross salary was 574,000 dinars or more, but less than 1,500,000 dinars.
(d) 10% of the salary, if the official's gross salary was 1,500,000 or more.'

Section 5 Relation to Existing Law
Any provision of Iraqi law that is inconsistent with this Order is suspended to the extent of such inconsistency.

Section 6 Administrative Instructions
The Administrator of the Coalition Provisional Authority or his delegate may issue Administrative Instructions to give effect to this Order.

Section 7 Entry into Force
This Order shall enter into force on the date of signature [30 April 2004].

Document 109
Coalition Provisional Authority Order Number 85

CPA Order 85 has not been used and is empty.[262]

Document 110
Coalition Provisional Authority Order Number 86

CPA/ORD/19 May 2004/86

Traffic Code

Pursuant to my authority as the Administrator of the Coalition Provisional Authority (CPA), under the laws and usages of war, and consistent with relevant UN Security Council resolutions including Resolutions 1483 and 1511 (2003),

Having worked closely with the Baghdad General Directorate of Traffic to ensure that an updated traffic code addresses the motor vehicle related issues of Iraq,

Noting the substantial increase in traffic since the end of the war, in particular in Baghdad, and the absence of an enforceable traffic code since the fall of the regime of Saddam Hussein,

[262] See *Official Gazette*, vol 45, no 3984 (June 2004), 15. CPA Order No 85 was never approved. A draft was sent to Ambassador Bremer in early June 2004. He did not sign because of outstanding questions, and these questions were not resolved prior to CPA dissolution.

Recognizing the CPA's obligation to maintain law and order, and to provide for the effective administration of the laws of Iraq,

Determined to provide traffic officials with the tools necessary to deal with traffic problems, motor vehicle registration and motor vehicle licensing, and

Determined further to eliminate corruption engrained in the traffic law enforcement system under the previous regime, and protect the rights of all motor vehicle owners and operators,

I hereby promulgate the following:

Section 1 Definitions

1) 'Motor Vehicle' or 'Vehicle' means a form of transportation which has wheels and is powered by a mechanical engine or physical power or is dragged by any means. For the purposes of this order the term vehicle does not include trains or any vehicles that operate on a railway. The term vehicle shall include the following:

a) 'Car' means a vehicle used for transportation powered by a mechanical engine;
b) 'Private car' means a vehicle used for transporting persons without charge or fees;
c) 'Public car' means a vehicle used for transporting persons in return for a charge or fees;
d) 'Truck' means a vehicle used for transporting people along with cargo and goods, including pick-up trucks;
e) 'Agricultural vehicle' means a vehicle used for agricultural purposes and powered by a mechanical engine, such as tractors, harvest machines, etc;
f) 'Construction vehicle' means a vehicle used for construction purposes and powered by a mechanical engine such as a road paver, crane, etc;
g) 'Motorcycle' means a two or three wheeled vehicle powered by a mechanical engine of 125 cc or more not designed in the form of a car;
h) 'Bicycle' means a vehicle with two or three wheels designed to be operated by human power and not by a mechanical engine; not to include children's bicycle. Any vehicle powered by a mechanical engine of less than 125 cc but with the size, design and form of a bicycle shall be considered a bicycle for the purpose of this section;
i) 'Wagon' means a vehicle used for transporting persons or goods which is dragged by a human or an animal; and
j) 'Trailer' means a dragged vehicle with no mechanical engine designed for loading or carrying cargo, goods, or anything else. It may be separated from or attached to a vehicle powered by a mechanical engine and dragged.

2) 'Driver' means any person who drives a vehicle and possesses a driver's license.

3) 'Driver's license' means a certificate for driving a vehicle which is issued by a registration officer.

4) 'Database for driver's licenses' means the system which is used to record all proceeding [sic] concerning driver's licenses.

5) 'Registration Officer' means the Director General of Traffic or his/her agents and/or designees.

6) 'Registration Database' means the system used to record all matters concerning the registration of vehicles.

7) 'Registration Certificate' means the certificate which is issued by the registration officer to the vehicle owner and which shall contain, at a minimum, the following information:

a) motor vehicle registration number and type of the vehicle;
b) name and address of the owner of the vehicle;
c) chassis number;
d) engine number;
e) color;
f) date of issuance;
g) expiration date;
h) number of passengers and cargo;
i) model.

8) 'Registration Plate' means a metal plate carrying information that distinguishes a vehicle from other vehicles.

9) 'Traffic police officer' means an internal security policeman who carries the rank of lieutenant or higher authorized by the Minister of Interior or his/her designee to enforce the provisions of this code.

10) 'Road' means any area, paved or unpaved that is designed or ordinarily used for vehicular and pedestrian travel as further defined in Section 14 of this Code. May be divided into multiple lanes for traffic to travel in the same direction or in the opposite direction.

11) 'Shoulder' means that area immediately next to the side of a road.

12) 'Emergence lane' or 'Breakdown lane' means a part of the road on both sides that may be paved or unpaved. It is not more than 2.5 meters wide to permit vehicles to stop or park to allow passengers to enter or exit the vehicle. It the road is paved, it shall be separated from the road by a straight line to indicate the edge of the road. It is used ordinarily on highways.

13) 'Lane' means one section of a road that is divided into two or more lanes permitting travel in opposite directions. Lanes are designated by either broken or unbroken lines.

14) 'Passage' means a part of a lane designed to permit vehicles to proceed in one column. The lane usually has three passages. In some conditions these passages increase and decrease according to the kind of road. These passages are:

a) Left passage: Designed for traffic traveling at the maximum speed allowed by law, turning, or passing to the left side by emergency vehicles;
b) Middle passage: Designed for traffic traveling between the minimum and maximum speeds allowed by law; and
c) Right passage: Designed for traffic traveling at minimum speed allowed by law, right turns, where authorized, and parking.
d) Emergence passage or Breakdown lane: Farthest most left or right passage of the highway separated from traffic movement by connected lines designed for emergency parking. (Based on #12 definition.)

15) 'U-turn lane' means the part of the road designed and authorized for turning through the median to the opposite side.

16) 'Intersections of roads' means where two or more roads intersect.

17) 'Parking' means stopping a vehicle for a limited period of time due to traffic conditions or for purposes of allowing passengers to enter, exit, or load or unload cargo as permitted by traffic signs, markings or signals.

18) 'Maneuver' means the movement required to drive the car and choose the appropriate lane.

19) 'Traffic priority' or right of way means vehicles must yield to the vehicle assigned priority as stated in Section 17.

Section 2 Production and Classification of Driver's Licenses

1) Any individual who is driving will carry the driver's license issued to that person. Upon demand of a traffic police officer, a person who is driving a vehicle shall produce the driver's license to that person.

2) Driver's licenses will be classified according to the type of vehicle to be driven. Those classifications will be established by the Minister of Interior. A driver is permitted to drive only those vehicles covered by his/her license classification.

Section 3 Driver's License Eligibility Criteria

1) A driver's license shall be granted to any person who meets all of the following criteria:

a) The person must have completed his/her sixteenth year of age to drive a motorcycle, eighteenth year of age for all private vehicles, and twenty first year of age to drive public cars and trucks;
b) The person must not be prohibited legally from driving a vehicle;
c) The person must be of good physical fitness. The person's fitness for driving must be approved by a medical committee according to regulations issued by the Ministry of Health, Baghdad; and
d) The person must pass a test on vehicle driving and traffic rules according to the type of driver's license for which the person has applied.

2) A traffic police shall revoke a driver's license from a driver who does not meet the conditions stipulated in paragraphs 1b) and c) of this section.

3) When renewing a license, the conditions mentioned in paragraphs 1b) and c) of this article must be taken in consideration.

4) A person who is not a citizen of Iraq may be granted a private driver's license according to the provisions of paragraph 1 of this article on the condition that he/she is residing legally in Iraq in compliance with his/her residence documents.

5) A driver's license issued and valid in any other country shall be considered valid in Iraq according to the principle of reciprocity.

6) The period of validity for a driver's license is five years.

Section 4 Exemptions

1) Accredited diplomatic and consular staff, upon presentation of an international driver's license or a valid driver's license issued by his/her country or origin to the Ministry of Foreign Affairs, will receive authorization to drive in Iraq.

2) Members of the Multinational Force, their contractors and employees carrying a valid operator's license from another nation will not be required to acquire an Iraqi operator's license or present their operator's license to the Minister of the Interior.

Section 5 Vehicle Registration

1) All vehicles must be registered with the registration office except wagons and bicycles, or those exempted by special law.

2) No vehicle will be issued a registration certificate unless an inspection document is presented indicating that the vehicle was inspected at an authorized inspection facility and it meets safety qualifications.

3) When transferring the ownership of a vehicle to another person, the previous owner and the new owner or their legal representative must appear before the registration officer

to inform him/her of the transfer. The previous owner and the new owner must pay transfer fees. The registration officer shall record the transfer in the registration record.

4) The Minister of Interior or his/her designee may authorize the transfer of a vehicle registration for humanitarian reasons in order to certify the transfer of the vehicle ownership.

5) The registration record (computerized or other) shall be presumptive evidence of the ownership of a vehicle.

6) The judiciary shall be competent to settle disputes concerning the ownership of vehicles.

7) A vehicle sale shall not be valid unless the vehicle is registered at the competent registration office in accordance with paragraph 3) of this section or unless otherwise exempted by law.

8) The period of validity of the vehicle registration is five years.

Section 6 Driver's License and Registration Fees

The Ministry of Interior Directorate of Traffic will establish fees for issuing and renewing driver's licenses and vehicle registrations. These fees are set out in Annex A to this Traffic Code.

Section 7 Exemptions from Vehicle Registration Fees

1) The following vehicles owners are exempt from paying vehicle registration fees:

a) Vehicles that belong to the Government, or official or semi-official departments;

b) Vehicles owned by accredited diplomatic and consular staff according to the principle of reciprocity;

c) Vehicles owned by charitable organizations and organizations which are considered to be a public interest as determined by the Minister of Interior of his/her designee;

d) Vehicles owned by international organizations with an exemption certificate issued by the Ministry of Foreign Affairs;

e) Vehicles that enter Iraq by Trip Ticket or pass note issued in accordance with customs laws permitting the person and vehicle to stay in Iraq for a designated period of time. Vehicles permitted to enter Iraq under this section must obtain a permission document from a registration officer; and

f) Vehicles operated by Multinational Forces, their contractors and employees.

Section 8 Changing Color or Classification of Vehicle Registration

1) A vehicle owner must obtain approval from the registration officer if he/she intends to change the vehicle's color.

2) A vehicle owner may request a change in the classification of a vehicle from private to public or from public to private by presenting a request to the registration officer and obtaining an amended registration certificate.

3) The Minister of Interior or his/her designee may establish additional rules and regulations to facilitate vehicle registration.

Section 9 De-Registration

1) If a person elects not to renew a driver's license or if the vehicle owner elects not to renew the registration certificate, the person must inform the registration officer and return the driver's license or registration certificate so that it may be cancelled and recorded. A driver's license or registration certificate so that it may be cancelled and recorded. [sic] A

driver's license or registration that has been cancelled cannot be renewed. Operation of an unregistered vehicle is prohibited.

2) In the event of the death of a person who was issued a driver's license, his/her heirs must notify a registration officer of the person's death and return the driver's license.

Section 10 Discretion of the Minister of Interior to Alter Fees
The Minister of Interior in coordination with the Minister of Finance may increase or decrease fees and fines as reasonable and necessary, and according to economic conditions.

Section 11 Use of Proceeds from Fees
Half of the revenue from license fees, registration fees, and fines stipulated in this law shall be allocated to the budget of the Ministry of Interior to be used for expenditures related to traffic safety. The remaining fifty percent of the revenue shall be allocated to the general revenues of the Ministry of Finance.

Section 12 Unregistered Vehicles
Unregistered vehicles shall not be driven, except those exempted under this Code or other law, treaty or this order. If a vehicle is unregistered, the traffic police officer shall seize the vehicle until it is registered and the owner shall pay all expenses. If the owner is not able to prove the date of entrance into Iraq the vehicle shall be referred to customs.

Section 13 Safety Standards

1) Traffic police officers shall stop and inspect a vehicle, in accordance with applicable laws and regulations, when the vehicle does not meet safety standards.

2) Vehicles – The following equipment on vehicles must meet or exceed minimum safety standards:

a) Engine;
b) Steering – must be located on the vehicle's left side, unless exempted;
c) Lights – front, rear, reverse, hazard, and turn signals;
d) Horn – shall be factory installed or equivalent;
e) Exhaust system;
f) Brakes;
g) Mirrors – side and rearview;
h) Windshield;
i) Registration plate illumination or reflective plates; and
j) Shatterproof glass on windows and windshield.

3) Motorcycles – the following equipment on motorcycles must meet or exceed minimum safety standards:

a) Engine;
b) Brakes;
c) Horn shall be factory installed or equivalent;
d) Lights: front, rear, reverse, hazard, and turn signals;
e) Exhaust system; and
f) Mirrors.

4) Agriculture, construction vehicles, and trailers – the following equipment on agriculture and construction vehicles must meet or exceed minimum safety standards:

a) Engine;

b) Brakes;
c) Steering; and
d) Lights: front, rear, reverse, hazard, and turn signals.

Section 14 Road Types
Iraq has the following road types:

a) Expressway – Limited access highway composed of two or more traffic lanes traveling in two directions designed to eliminate the principal traffic hazards.
b) Divided highway – Road composed of two paved lanes separated by a protective fence or other divider. Points of entrance and exit are not designed for turn around except for emergency vehicles;
c) Secondary – Not designed for pedestrians, bicycles or any transport vehicle traveling at less than the minimum speed limit.
d) Outside roads – Roads that link governorates.
e) Internal roads – Roads used inside a city, divided into major and minor. Major roads are wider to allow for heavy traffic.
f) Service roads – Roads that serve the surrounding areas and are separated from major roads.

Section 15 Driving Regulations
All road users shall comply with the regulations set out in Annex A of this Traffic Code.

Section 16 Regulations Pertaining to Different Road Users
Road users are divided into three categories - Pedestrians, Passengers and Drivers. Regulations pertaining to these road users are contained in Annex A.

Section 17 Right of Way
1) Traffic priorities shall be as follows unless otherwise directed by a traffic police officer or traffic signs:

a) Obey the signs given by traffic police officers, the traffic lights and traffic signs on the road;
b) Moving vehicles have priority over stopped vehicles;
c) Vehicles operating on a major road have priority over vehicles operating on a minor street;
d) Vehicles operating on the straight portion of a road has [sic] priority over vehicles operating on a curved portion of the road;
e) Vehicles operating in front have priority over vehicles behind it;
f) Vehicles in the intersection or crossroad have priority over vehicles approaching the intersection of the crossroad, unless turning left;
g) At an intersection or crossroad, vehicles coming from the right have priority;
h) Vehicles going up a gradiant have priority over vehicles descending a gradiant;
i) Vehicles traveling in the lane or passage have priority over vehicles that intend to move into the lane; and
j) Trains or other means moving on a railway have priority over other vehicles.

2) Emergency vehicles have priority over all other vehicles when they are on duty. The following are emergency vehicles:

a) ambulances;

b) fire and rescue vehicles;
c) police vehicles;
d) vehicles of the Directorate of Traffic;
e) vehicles involved in official ceremonies;
f) vehicles of members of Multinational Forces operating in accordance with United Nations Security Council Resolutions; and
g) any vehicle being used for emergency purposes.

3) Pedestrians in a crossing zone have priority over vehicles.
4) A vehicle is not allowed to occupy two lanes of a road in which priority is for others.

Section 18 International Traffic Signs
The international traffic signs, including traffic signs, markings and signals as stated in international treaties are observed by Iraq.

Section 19 Fines for Motor Vehicle Violations
The Ministry of Interior Directorate of Traffic will establish fines for motor vehicle violations. These are contained in Annex A.

Section 20 Traffic Police Powers and Right of Appeal
1) No police officer, including traffic police officers, shall ask for or accept money or any form of payment for any type of traffic violations. All amounts and fines shall be paid directly to the accounts officer at the police sector headquarters within 30 days of the date of violation.

2) Traffic police officers, as defined in section 1, paragraph 9 of this Code shall have the authority of a misdemeanor judge in imposing punishments for the violations that occur before him and which are stipulated in paragraph 27 of Annex A of this Code. All other offenses, including any for which the punishment is jail, will be referred to the appropriate court (not the Appeal Committee).

3) In the case of a person not paying the fine within the period stipulated in paragraph 1 of this section the fine shall be doubled for one time and entered in the computer record of the vehicle.

4) The violating driver, upon payment of the administrative fee of five thousand (5,000) ID, shall have the right to appeal to the Appeal Committee formed for this purpose in the competent Traffic Department. The rules of this Appeal Committee are to be established by the Minister of Interior. Members of the Appeal Committee are to be appointed by the Minister of Interior or his/her designee and shall include the following: an officer from the Internal Affairs Division, a representative from the City Council, a representative from the community. Appeals shall be filed within two weeks from the date of offense. The Appeals Committee shall have the right to adjust, to cancel or to approve the fine.

5) If the driver appears before the Appeals Committee, he/she shall be informed by the Appeals Committee of the decision. The driver must acknowledge receipt of the decision. If the driver does not appear before the Appeals Committee, then he/she shall be considered informed of the decision by mailing to the decision to the address recorded on the driver's license.

6) If the driver who commits a violation according to paragraph 21 d of Annex A of this Code drives a car that belongs to a Government office, official, or semi-official office and fails to pay the fine within the fixed period, then a traffic police officer shall inform his/

her office to pay the fine from his/her salary. And the amount is to be sent to the competent Traffic Directorate.

7) If the driver who commits a violation according to paragraph 21 d of Annex A of this Code drives a car with the customs entry registration plates and did not pay the fine during the fixed period, then the traffic police officer shall inform the customs department in order to send the sum to the competent Traffic Directorate.

Section 21 Unlicensed Drivers

1) A driver who drives a vehicle without having a driver license or whose driver's license has been cancelled, or suspended or who has a license different from the type of vehicle he/she is driving, will be punished by a period of incarceration of no less than one month and not to exceed six months.

2) A person who owns a vehicle and who knows or should have known that another person does not possess a driving license shall not permit that person to drive his/her vehicle. A driver who violates this section will be punished by a period of incarceration for not less than one month and not to exceed six months or a fine of not less than one hundred thousand (100,000) ID and not to exceed one hundred and fifty thousand (150,000) ID or both.

Section 22 Impaired Driving

1) A driver who drives while under the influence of alcohol or drugs will be punished by a period of incarceration of not less than three months and not to exceed one year or a fine of not less than three hundred thousand (300,000) ID and not to exceed five hundred thousand (500,000) ID, or both, and seizure of the vehicle for one year. The driver's license will be revoked for not less than two months and not to exceed one year.

2) A driver who within one year from the date of sentence on a first violation under this section commits a second violation of the provisions of paragraph 1) of this section will be punished by a period of incarceration not less than six months and not to exceed one year, or a fine of not less than five hundred thousand (500,000) ID and not more than one million (1,000,000) ID, or both, and his/her driver's license will be revoked for a period of time not less than six months and not to exceed one year.

Section 23 Careless/Reckless Driving

1) A driver is guilty of negligent driving by operating a vehicle in a careless or imprudent manner that endangers any person or property by causing serious property damage, personal injury, or permanent disability or defect. A driver who violates this section will be punished by a period of incarceration not less than six months and not to exceed two years, or a fine not less than four hundred thousand (400,000) ID and not to exceed one million (1,000,000) ID, or both.

2) If the offense is due to reckless driving, or under the influence of alcohol or drugs, and if the driver does not request help for any person injured as a result of his/her actions, then the driver will be incarcerated for not less than one year and not to exceed 3 years, or a fine not less than five hundred (500) ID and not to exceed one million (1,000,000) ID, or both.

Section 24 Causing Death by Dangerous Driving

1) A driver who causes the death of another by driving his/her vehicle in a careless and imprudent manner will be punished by a period of incarceration of not less than five years and not to exceed seven years, or a fine of not less than one million (1,000,000) ID and not to exceed one million, five hundred thousand (1,500,000) ID, or both.

2) If a driver commits the crimes stipulated in section 22, paragraph 1 and causes the death of one or more persons, or causes the death of a person and causes physical illness, damage, or permanent defect to more than one person, then the driver will be punished by a period of incarceration of not less than seven years and not to exceed 10 years, or a fine of not less than one million, five hundred thousand (1,500,000) ID and not to exceed three million (3,000,000) ID, or both.

3) A driver who causes the death of another person by driving a vehicle in a reckless and negligent manner and was under influence of alcohol, or who flees the scene of the accident and does not notify the competent authorities of the accident will be punished for a period of incarceration of not less than seven years and not to exceed 10 years, or a fine of not less than three million (3,000,000) ID and not to exceed five million (5,000,000) ID, or both.

4) If the offense indicated in paragraph 3 of this section caused the death of one or more persons, or the death of one person and caused physical damage, illness, or permanent defect to more than one person, then the driver will be incarcerated for not less than 10 years and not to exceed 20 years, or a fine of not less than five million (5,000,000) ID and not to exceed seven million (7,000,000) ID, or both.

Section 25 Pedestrian Crossings

1) It shall be considered an aggravating circumstance for the punishments stipulated in sections 23 and 24 of this Code if the accident takes place in the area of a pedestrian crossing where there are signs for crossing pedestrians, if the driver doesn't help the injured person by transferring him to hospital, or if the driver leaves the scene of the accident without permission from the traffic police officer.

2) It shall be considered [an] extenuating circumstance for the punishments stipulated in sections 23 and 24 of this Code if the accident takes place outside of a pedestrian crossing area, if the driver transfers the injured person as soon as practicable to a hospital, or if he/she informs the police station of the accident.

Section 26 Interfering With or Assaulting Traffic Officials

1) Anyone who interferes with or threatens a traffic police officer while he/she is performing his/her duties shall be punished by a period of incarceration not to exceed two years.

2) Anyone who assaults a traffic police officer while he/she is performing his/her duties shall be punished by a period of incarceration not to exceed three years.

3) Anyone who assaults a traffic police officer while he/she is performing his/her duties and causes a wound or injury shall be incarcerated for a term not to exceed five years. The punishment shall not violate any other more severe punishment stipulated in any other law.

Section 27 Suspension of Driver's Licenses

When the court issues a conviction judgment in accordance with the provisions of this Code, it may suspend the driving license of the convicted person for a period of not less than one year and not to exceed three years. If the driver is unlicensed, then the court may prevent him/her from getting a driver's license for three years starting from the date of judgment or the date of the fine.

Section 28 Application of Severest Available Punishment

If any other law stipulates a more severe punishment for an act stipulated in this law, then the more severe punishment may be applied.

Section 29 Admissible Evidence

The following evidence is admissible at trial for an offense under the Traffic Code if the court finds it is relevant: pictures, statements and decisions taken by means of checking and measuring the degree of intoxication, a plan for the accident that is organized by a traffic police officer whose rank shall be Sergeant, forensics reports, video/surveillance camera tape, sketches, and recorded statements.

Section 30 Issuance of Receipt Sufficient for Court Notification

Issuance of a Receipt for Seized Driver's License by the traffic police officer shall be considered notification to appear before the designated court.

Section 31 Maximum Period of Seizure of Vehicle

When a driver commits a violation of the provisions of paragraph 21 of Annex A, section 21, section 22 or section 24 of this Code, the traffic police officer shall have the authority to seize the vehicle for no more than 10 days subject to a valid third party claim.

Section 32 Impounding of Vehicles

1) When ordered by a judge, the traffic police must tow away any vehicle to be seized and deposit it with a third person, who is authorized to perform this type of duty, at the expense of the vehicle's owner until the legal procedures are completed in accordance with a judicial or executive decision.

2) If a vehicle is illegally parked, creating a hazard or otherwise impeding the movement of traffic, the traffic police officer has the authority to tow such vehicle at the expense of the vehicle's owner.

3) Traffic patrols are not responsible for any damages caused to the vehicle during the tow or seizure.

Section 33 Promotion of Traffic Safety

The Minister of Interior or his/her designee may appoint such committees as necessary to facilitate and promote traffic safety.

Section 34 Implementation of the Traffic Code

1) The Minister of Interior or his/her designee may issue such statements, rules, and instructions as necessary to implement the provisions of this law.

2) The Director General of Traffic may issue a statement according to the Code in the following matters:

a) Assigning the direction of traffic on the public roads;
b) Fixing the shape and dimensions of the registration plate, driver's license, and the vehicle registration along with the color and contents;
c) Implementing the provisions of the international treaties to which Iraq is a signatory related to the Traffic Code; and
d) Testing procedures and information used to approve an application for a driver's license.

Section 35 Road Safety Training

1) The Traffic Division in each Governorate shall reserve a week every year to try to focus the public's attention on traffic safety, which reduces accidents.

2) In cooperation with other related offices, the Traffic Division in each Governorate shall prepare appreciation certificates for drivers who do not commit any traffic violations in 20 years.

Section 36 Issuance of Regulations by Minister of Interior
Regulations regarding the following matters shall be issued by the Minister of Interior:

a) Teaching the vocation of driving cars;
b) Inspecting and checking vehicles by private garages; and
c) Dimensions for color and the placement of the registration plate on the vehicle, and who will manufacture such registration plates.

Section 37 Revocation of Previous Traffic Laws
This Traffic Code revokes and replaces the following previous traffic laws:

a) Traffic Law number 48 of 1971 and all amendments from whatever source, including but not limited to: the Revolutionary Command Council, the Ministry of Interior, and the Office of Traffic Directorate.

Section 38 Entry into Force
This Law shall enter into force on the date of signature [20 May 2004].

ANNEX A
Driving and Vehicle Regulations, Vehicle Registration Fees and Fines for Motor Vehicle Violations

Regulations Pertaining to Different Road Users

1. Pedestrian road users are to abide by the following regulations when walking along the road:

a) Pedestrians must walk on the sidewalk of a road;
b) If no sidewalk is available, pedestrians must walk safely, close to the left edge facing traffic. If pedestrians are walking in a group, they should walk in single file;
c) Pedestrians walking during darkness or cloudy weather shall wear light or reflective clothing.

2. Pedestrians crossing roads and passing to the opposite side of the road shall be conducted according to following conditions:

a) Pedestrians shall cross roads from designated areas such as marked cross walks, bridges, tunnels and traffic light controlled pedestrian cross places. If these are not available, pedestrians shall cross according to the following: stop at the sidewalk of the road, look left, then right, then left and pass smoothly and quickly. If the road contains a median divider, the crossing procedure shall be repeated as looking right and left then right;
b) Pedestrians shall not cross from between parked vehicles for it is not easy for drivers to observe pedestrians;
c) Pedestrians crossing one way roads or lanes shall make sure of traffic direction;
d) Pedestrians crossing roads shall attempt to cross in illuminated areas.

3. Passengers – The following regulations should be observed when entering and exiting vehicles:

a) Passengers shall enter and exit only from fully stopped vehicles in designated or otherwise safe locations;

b) Passengers seeking to cross after exiting a bus, shall wait until the bus has moved and the driver is able to observe the road;

c) Passengers seeking to exit a bus or hire vehicle must inform the driver at adequate distance to permit a safe stop.

4. Drivers – The following regulations should be observed when driving:

a) The driver must be capable of driving with complete control of the vehicle and with a clear view of the road and traffic movement;

b) The driver shall hold the steering wheel with both hands;

c) The driver shall obey the speed limits as set by law;

d) The driver shall obey traffic signs and signals and directions from traffic police;

e) The driver shall check the front lights and back lights while driving at night;

f) Use of high beams is prohibited when approaching oncoming traffic;

g) Proper use of horn to warn and in emergency conditions only;

h) Safety belts must be worn especially on outside roads or highways;

i) Adequate space must be left between vehicles. This distance shall increase according to vehicle speed and if the road is wet;

j) Traffic priority (Right of way) must be given for pedestrians crossings at unmanned or unmarked areas;

k) Emergency vehicles shall be given the right of way in the left lane;

l) Long distance driving may cause drowsiness or fatigue. To avoid this, rest should be taken for 5 minutes to every one hour driving;

m) Drivers shall slow down and not use the horn when driving close to animals.

5. Start conditions – Before starting vehicles, drivers should check for any obstacle behind them, check the conditions of the tires, then start the engine and tighten safety belt before observing the following conditions:

a) Mirror: check to make sure of passing vehicles by inside and outside mirror and look left. If there are any approaching vehicles, the driver must wait;

b) Turn signals: Left turn signal must be used to warn other road users of movement.

6. Passing: Passing another vehicle from the left side shall be conducted according to the following conditions:

a) Where passing is allowed;

b) After making sure the road is clear for adequate distance;

c) Using side mirrors to make sure road is clear of vehicles;

d) Using signals; and

e) Start acceleration and pass then go back to normal lane.

7. Illegal Passing – Passing is prohibited in the following conditions:

a) Near pedestrian crossings;

b) Near crossroads, curves, bridges, tunnels, hill, on slippery roads, narrow roads and at railway cross roads;

c) Where posted 'No Passing' or where obstructed by a barrier;

d) When passing would force another driver to change his speed or direction;

e) If the vehicle ahead is passing another car;

f) If the vehicle behind is passing another car;

g) If an oncoming vehicle is passing on a roadway with no separation, median or connected lines;

h) If the vehicle to be passed is traveling at the maximum speed limit; and

i) If visibility is bad.

8. In the case of passing a column of vehicles, passage must be done in stages.
9. Left turn must be conducted as follows:
   a) Move to left lane at a safe distance;
   b) Use the mirrors to check traffic movement behind;
   c) Use left turn signal;
   d) Turn left safely.
10. Right turn must be conducted as follows:
   a) Move to right lane at a safe distance;
   b) Use the mirror to check traffic movement behind;
   c) Use right turn signal;
   d) Turn right safely.
11. Changing lanes must be conducted as follows:
   a) Look in mirror to make sure that the lane you intend to move into is clear of traffic;
   b) Use turn signal to warn road users;
   c) Change lanes safely.

12. Parking – When parking for more than five minutes with the engine off, drivers shall park vehicles parallel to and not more than thirty centimeters from the sidewalk with the doors closed. Parking shall be conducted as follows:
   a) Slowdown [sic];
   b) Use rearview mirror to observe traffic;
   c) Use turn signal to indicate direction of travel;
   d) Pull over to far most right side of the road before opening vehicle doors;
   e) Make sure lane is clear of pedestrians before opening vehicles doors;
   f) Exit from vehicles [sic] right side close to side walk.

13. Parking is prohibited as follows:
   a) Where traffic signs indicate parking prohibited;
   b) When parking will obstruct visibility at or near to:
      i. Crossroads;
      ii. Curves;
      iii. Railway crossroads;
      iv. Cliff edge;
      v. Arched bridge;
      vi. Bus stop;
      vii. Pedestrians crossing area;
      viii. School and office main gates;
      ix. Parking on left side of roadway;
      x. Double parking;
      xi. When parking will obstruct movement of traffic;
      xii. On narrow roads;
      xiii. In tunnels;
      xiv. On bridges;
      xv. At entrances of garages (private and public);
      xvi. Near road works and construction sites;
      xvii. If parking obstructs visibility of a traffic light or sign.

14. Lights – The following conditions should be observed in using lights:
   a) Make sure front and back lights of vehicle are according to its design;

b) Use high beams on roads with no electric lights and dim lights when a vehicle approaches from the opposite direction;
c) Use full lights in case of fog or bad visibility;
d) Flash headlights to give warning, same as with horn, especially during hours of darkness;
e) Use of high beams is prohibited when stopped, parking and waiting;
f) Use emergency flashers when vehicle is disabled.

15. Other general driving and vehicle regulations are as follows:
a) Vehicles are not permitted to enter or exit roads except from special points which are acceleration and slow down lanes;
b) Backing, turning and parking except as designated by traffic control signs or for emergency reasons is prohibited;
c) Vehicle travel at more than the maximum and less than the minimum speed limit provided for by law is prohibited;
d) Vehicle tires must be properly checked before travel and petrol, water and oil quantities must be sufficient;
e) Drivers of defective or disabled vehicles must exploit continuation of the vehicle's movement to exit to emergency lane and use emergency flashers or a reflective triangle at a distance not less than 50 meters on highways and at an appropriate distance on internal roads continuation of the vehicle's movement to exit to emergency lane and use emergency flashers or a reflective triangle at a distance not less than 50 meters on highways and at an appropriate distance on internal roads [sic];
f) It is unlawful to use a vehicle not designed for towing to tow a vehicle. When towing a disabled or defective vehicle, the vehicle's emergency flashers shall be activated;
g) Vehicles more than 2.5 meters wide are prohibited from operating on highways unless escorted by a traffic vehicle to direct and warn other drivers;
h) Parking, stopping or waiting inside a vehicle at locations other than those designated is not permitted except in case of emergency.

16. Public vehicle regulations:
a) Smoking is not allowed inside public vehicles;
b) Passengers must keep their body fully inside public vehicles;
c) Passengers on public vehicles shall not distract the driver;
d) Public vehicles must be kept clean;
e) Visibility shall not be obstructed by materials or baggage;
f) Passengers shall not give traffic signs instead of the driver;
g) Children shall be seated in the back seat;
h) Standing inside transport buses is prohibited for it obstructs driver's rear view vision.

Vehicle Registration Fees

17. The following fee schedule is in effect until amended or replaced pursuant to section 32 of this Code.

18. The following are the fees for issuing and renewing driver licenses:
a) Motorcycles – five thousand ID;
b) All other vehicles – ten thousand ID.

19. The following are fees for vehicle registration certificates, first time and renewals:

a) Motorcycles – five thousand ID;
b) All types of cars – ten thousand ID;
c) Trailers carrying over 12 tons and vehicles carrying more than 25 passengers – fifty thousand ID.

20. Transfer of ownership fees must be paid fifty percent by the previous owner and fifty percent by the new owner. The following are fees for transfer of ownership of vehicles:

a) Private cars – fifty thousand ID;
b) Public cars and buses – fifty thousand ID;
c) Trucks and trailers – one hundred thousand ID;
d) Agriculture vehicles, construction vehicles, trailers (dragged vehicles) and tourist caravan vehicles – fifty thousand ID;
e) Motorcycles – five thousand ID.

21. The following are fees for reissuing a driver license or registration certificate when it is lost, stolen or destroyed:

a) The first time – ten thousand ID;
b) The second time – twenty thousand ID;
c) More than two times – forty thousand ID.

22. The following fees are for losing or destroying the vehicle registration plate:

a) The first time – twenty thousand ID;
b) The second time – forty thousand ID;
c) More than two times – sixty thousand ID.

23. If the loss or destruction of the registration plate is accidental or unintentional the fee is two thousand ID.

24. There is no fee for the loss or destruction of the registrations plate caused by the burning of, robbery and/or collision of the vehicle when certified by documents.

25. Transactions related to vehicles and driver licenses shall be exempted from the provisions of the law of stamp fees number 16 of 1974.

Fines for Motor Vehicle Violations

26. The following fines will be in effect until changed or amended pursuant to section 32 of this Code.

27. Anyone who commits the following violations shall be fined thirty thousand ID:

a) Failure to obey traffic control device or traffic police signal;
b) Driving against traffic;
c) Driving without front or rear lights at night;
d) Driving a vehicle without registration plate;
e) Reckless or negligent driving;
f) Driving at a speed greater than reasonable or in excess of speed limit;
g) Failure to register vehicle within 30 days of purchase;
h) Violating the rules of traffic on highways;
i) Violating instructions or statements issued by the Directorate General of Traffic.

28. Anyone who commits the following violations shall be fined twenty thousand ID:

a) Failure to cover the cargo securely to prevent cargo from falling during driving or shaking;
b) Parking in no-parking area;
c) The use of tinted windows or textile or metal curtains on rear or side windows;
d) Turning in the places where it is not allowed to turn;

e) Failure to stop when exiting from side road to main road;
f) Failure to yield the right of way to pedestrians.

29. Anyone who commits the following violations shall be fined fifteen thousand ID:
 a) Stopping large trucks, buses, construction or agricultural vehicles in travel lanes, on internal streets or in residential regions, except when loading or unloading;
 b) Carrying cargo in trucks in excess of height requirements;
 c) Driving a vehicle with damaged or unclear registration plate;
 d) Failure to use safety belts in moving vehicle;
 e) Improper use of horn, including use of horns other than factory installed or equivalent;
 f) Passing a vehicle on the right side on roadways.
30. Anyone who commits the following violations shall be fined ten thousand ID:
 a) Improper use of high beam lights;
 b) Driving a vehicle that doesn't meet the minimum safety standards for equipment (as stipulated in section 13 of this law);
 c) Putting stickers, decorations or notices on the front windshield or rear window;
 d) Violating the rules of safe driving;
 e) Failure to renew driving license or vehicle registration;
 f) Failure to observe clear traffic signs, signals or markings;
 g) Transporting passengers on the side, decks, hood roof or tail of a vehicle;
 h) Opening a vehicle door and causing traffic obstruction.
31. Anyone who commits one of the following violations shall be fined five thousand ID:
 a) Failure to signal intention prior to turning;
 b) Moving the vehicle before being sure that the traffic side is empty;
 c) Failure to produce a driver license on demand.

Document 111

Coalition Provisional Authority Order Number 87

CPA/ORD/14 May 2004/87

Public Contracts

Pursuant to my authority as Administrator of the Coalition Provisional Authority (CPA), and under the laws and usages of war, and consistent with relevant U.N. Security Council resolutions, including Resolutions 1483 and 1511 (2003),

Recognizing that public contracts laws should conform to international standards of transparency, predictability, fairness of treatment; provide for dispute resolution mechanisms; be free from corruption and undue influence; and create a system to procure goods and services at the best possible value for the government,

Noting that the concept of full, fair and open competition is of critical importance to the economy of Iraq and the goal of free trade among nations,

Building on the existing Iraqi laws in the field, including administrative instructions, and modernizing them in accordance with best international practice,

I hereby promulgate the following:

Section 1 Principles of Government Public Procurement

1) This Order applies to all procurements of goods, services, and construction services by the State of Iraq acting through Ministries or other federal agencies (collectively 'agencies'); or governmental units including Regions; Governorates; and all other subdivisions of the State of Iraq (collectively 'governmental units') that may commit public funds. Procurement is the acquiring by contract with public funds of goods, services or construction services by and for the use of the government through purchase or lease. The State of Iraq through Ministries or other federal agencies; Regions; Governorates; and all other subdivisions of the State of Iraq shall commit public funds in accordance with the following basic principles:

a) To the maximum extent practicable, full, fair and open competitive public bidding procedures, including, but not limited to: effective tender publication; objective bid evaluation criteria; public bid opening; and, the use of electronic commerce methods.
b) International standards of transparency, predictability, fairness and equality of treatment;
c) Procurement process integrity, minimum ethical standards and non-conflict of interest;
d) Offeror's right to file tender protests and related appeals;
e) Tender dispute resolution mechanisms and the timely resolution of such disputes.

Section 2 Office of Government Public Contract Policy

1) Establishment and Responsibilities
   a) There shall be established, within the Ministry of Planning and Development Cooperation, an Office of Government Public Contract Policy. The head of this Office shall report directly to the Minister of Planning.
   b) The Office of Government Public Contract Policy shall have responsibility for:
      i) Coordination of government public contract policy for all ministries and public entities of the government, including, but not limited to, the issuance, after appropriate provision for notice to and comment by interested parties, of implementing regulations and administrative instructions in the Arabic and Kurdish languages, and such other languages as appropriate, in furtherance of this Order;
      ii) Establishment and adoption of rules for an independent Administrative Tribunal to have jurisdiction over complaints and disputes arising under or relating to the award of public contracts by the government;
      iii) Recommendations for amendments to this Order and related Iraqi laws, regulations and administrative instructions;
      iv) Development and adoption of standard government public contract provisions; and
      v) Training of government public contracting personnel for the proper application of this Order and its implementing regulations and administrative instructions.
2) Application
   a) Every governmental unit or agency described in Section 1.1 'government' shall designate a contracting office that shall be responsible for the contracting activities of the governmental unit or agency. For reasons of administrative convenience, a

governmental unit or agency may agree with another governmental unit or agency that the latter will be responsible for the contracting activities of the former.

b) In addition to the standard contract provisions adopted for all governmental units or agencies, each individual governmental unit or agency, after concurrence by the Office of Government Public Contract Policy, may include standard contract provisions that are necessary for the particular objectives of said governmental unit or agency.

c) This Order applies to Iraqi state-owned enterprises when awarding public contracts for the procurement of goods, services or construction services that are directly financed by government funds.

Section 3 Contracting Authority

1) The authority to obligate government funds, award and sign government public contracts, enter into and authorize material modifications to such contracts, and authorize the payment of invoices and claims, shall rest solely with a qualified government agency or a committee within each governmental unit or agency, duly appointed under the authority of this Order.

a) Agency and committee members shall not be political appointees or members of the office within the governmental unit or agency that requires or benefits from the contractor's performance under the contract to be awarded. Political appointees are Governing Council members and their deputies; ministers and deputy ministers; governors; judges; members of national commissions, deputy commissioners of such commissions, directors and equivalent officials within Iraqi commissions, boards or similar organizations; all elected members of the Iraqi Interim Government or Iraqi Transitional Government, including the national executive; and those individuals appointed by the public officials listed in this Section to advise them.

b) The individuals vested with the authority described in this Section shall not directly report to the official or office requiring or benefiting from the contractor's performance under the contract.

2) In all public contracts, there shall be a standard provision advising contractors of the public agency or committee that shall have this authority and the full scope of that authority. Included in that provision, there shall be reference to the fact that direction from the government to the contractor that affects the rights and liabilities of the parties to the contract from anyone other than the designated responsible public official shall not be authorized and shall not have any effect.

Section 4 Full and Open Competition

To the maximum extent practicable, government public contracts shall be awarded on a competitive basis. Prior to the competitive award of public contracts, the Contracting Authority, vested with the authority pursuant to Section 3 of this Order, shall state in writing the awarded contract price to be fair and reasonable under the prevailing facts and circumstances.

1) Exceptions – Public contracts may be awarded using other than full and open competitive public contracting procedures under the following conditions:

a) When, for technical or artistic reasons, or for reasons connected with the protection of exclusive rights, the goods or services to be purchased under the contract may only be manufactured or supplied by a particular entity or otherwise is available from a very limited number of entities.

b) When for reasons of extreme urgency brought about by events not attributable to the Contracting Authority, the public interest does not permit award on a fully competitive basis.
c) When the goods to be purchased are:
    i) Required as a partial replacement for or addition to goods purchased under an existing or previous contract; or
    ii) Required to be compatible or interchangeable with existing goods purchased from the original source who supplied the existing goods.
d) When the use of other than full and open competitive public contracting procedures is necessary to promote economic or institutional development among certain population sectors or geographic regions of the State of Iraq or of Iraqi state-owned enterprises. These regulations shall also indicate the circumstances where the use of other than full and open competitive public contracting procedures may be used to promote economic or institutional development among certain population sectors or geographic regions of the State of Iraq or of Iraqi state-owned enterprises.
e) When international agreements (bilateral, plurilateral, or multilateral) or treaties to which the State of Iraq is a party require the use of other than full and open competitive public contracting procedures, either by their explicit terms or by implication.
f) If the anticipated value of the public contract is below certain monetary thresholds, as determined by regulations issued in accordance with Section 2, a streamlined procedure for the procurement of lower priced goods and services shall be used.
g) The Office of Government Public Contract Policy shall issue implementing regulations indicating, among other matters, those circumstances permitting other than full and open competition and specifying the streamlined procedures for awarding public contracts using other than full and open competitive public contracting procedures. These regulations shall require documentation previous to every occasion where other than full and open competitive public contracting procedures are used.

2) <u>Prequalification</u> – Prequalification of offerors, including required deposits or bonds, shall be implemented in such a manner that does not unreasonably limit competition.

If a deposit is required as a condition for participating in a competitive tender, such deposit shall be reasonable in amount, based upon the value of the contract, and returned to an unsuccessful offeror. The use of bonds, as opposed to deposits, is encouraged.

3) <u>Notice of Tenders</u> – The Office of Government Public Contract Policy shall issue implementing regulations that address, but are not limited to, the following:

a) The notice of tenders shall provide the maximum possible exposure of the proposed public procurement action. Notices shall be published at a minimum in the Arabic and Kurdish languages, as well as such other language as may be appropriate where it is anticipated that offers will be made from entities or individuals outside the State of Iraq.
b) The notice shall provide potential offerors with sufficient information, including but not limited to, standard terms and conditions, the statement of work and a delivery schedule, to reasonably respond to the tender. In this regard, all tenders shall also contain the factors upon which offerors shall be evaluated, and the failure of the government to evaluate an offer against the stated evaluation factors in the notice shall be a basis for filing a tender protest pursuant to this Order.

c) The notice shall provide potential offerors with sufficient time to reasonably respond.
d) The notice shall provide potential offerors the opportunity to request clarifications about the tender and for extensions of time to respond to the tender, if necessary.
e) The notice shall provide a date by which responses to tenders shall be due, and provide those specific instances where late offers can be accepted.
f) The implementing regulations to this Order shall provide for exceptional circumstances when the notice is not required.

Section 5 Negotiated Contracts

1) Authorization – Although competitive bidding is preferred in general, competitive negotiated contracts that comply with this Order are hereby specifically authorized and should be employed whenever the interests of the governmental unit or agency concerned will best be served by awarding the contract on a basis other than the lowest price.

2) Process

a) Tender notices for negotiated contracts shall specifically indicate that the contract shall be awarded on a basis other than the lowest price.
b) The notice shall state those factors, in addition to price, that will be evaluated and the relative importance of each of these factors (this is not an exhaustive list, and all of these factors, except price or cost, may not necessarily be required on all procurements):
   i) The merit of the technical solution proposed to meet the government's requirements;
   ii) The risk associated with the offeror's proposed approach as it relates to accomplishing the requirements of the tender;
   iii) Past performance on recent and relevant government and commercial efforts;
   iv) Experience of key personnel; and/or
   v) Management structure.
c) The notice shall state the relationship between the price and the non-price factors in making an award (e.g., are the non-price factors more important, less important, or of equal importance to price).
d) The government shall have the right to enter into direct negotiations with offerors after their written response to the tender has been received by the government. The purpose of entering into direct negotiations is to clarify offers, respond to questions, and negotiate price. At no time during the negotiation process (and after award) shall information, including price, about proposals from other offerors be discussed or made public. The price of the awarded contract shall be made public.
e) If requested, offerors shall have the right to amend their offers after negotiations and prior to final evaluations.
f) All members of procurement evaluation teams shall be bound by the principles stated in Section 8 of this Order on 'Procurement Integrity and Conflicts of Interest'.

Section 6 Standard Public Contract Provisions

1) The Office of Government Public Contract Policy shall issue and publish implementing regulations that include standard public contract provisions. These provisions may include additional conditions not specifically required by, but otherwise consistent with this Order.

These regulations may provide that certain conditions apply or do not apply depending on the value or type of the public contract.

2) The Office shall, in preparing the implementing regulations required by this Order, be guided by recognized and accepted international standards and best practices, such as those contained in the United Nations Commission on International Trade Law (UNCITRAL), 'Model Law for Procurement of Goods, Construction, and Services', Directives of the European Union, and the World Trade Organization Agreement on Government Procurement. Where appropriate, these regulations shall also apply generally accepted international commercial practices.

Section 7 Statements of Work, Contract Specifications, and Contract Types

1) Statements of Work and contract specifications must accurately reflect the government's needs and must be written in such a way that they do not unduly restrict competition.

2) Proprietary features or brand names shall be avoided. If a brand name or proprietary feature is included in a specification, offerors must be notified of the features of the brand name and be advised that they may offer an equivalent or equal product.

3) The contract type has a direct effect on risk allocation in public contracts. Fixed-priced contracts are generally preferred over cost contracts, especially where a reasonable price estimate can be made by the government and the contract anticipates a specific deliverable.

a) A fixed-price contract provides for a price that is not subject to adjustment on the basis of the contractor's costs incurred in performing the contract. A fixed-price contract places upon the contractor maximum risk and full responsibility for all costs and resulting profit or loss.

b) A Cost-reimbursement contract provides for payment of allowable incurred costs, to the extent prescribed in the contract. These contracts establish an estimate of total cost for the purpose of committing funds and establishing a ceiling that the contractor may not exceed (except at its own risk) without the approval of the contracting officer.

Section 8 Procurement Integrity and Conflicts of Interest

1) The Office of Government Public Contract Policy shall issue and publish implementing regulations that implement, at a minimum, the following ethical standards:

2) [sic] No minister, official or consultant under contract to support the governmental unit or agency involved in any tender shall have a financial interest in the outcome of the tender.

a) All proprietary or competition sensitive information received by ministers, officials, or contractors during the tender process shall remain confidential.

b) The post-government employment of ministers and officials substantially involved in the government procurement process shall be restricted for a reasonable period of time in accordance with this Section. Those ministers and officials substantially involved in the following activities shall not seek nor accept employment with the offeror awarded the contract:

i) A particular tender;

ii) The administration of the contract awarded subsequent to a particular tender; or

iii) The surveillance of the work performed under a particular contract.

c) No offer or shall have a business interest that is in conflict with its ability to use its best efforts to satisfy the requirements of the contract.

Section 9 Exclusions from Participation

1) To ensure the integrity of the procurement process, entities and individuals may be excluded from competing for government public contracts in accordance with the following provisions.

a) As defined in the implementing regulations issued under the authority of this Order, misconduct, including but not limited to the following, shall be the basis for exclusion:
   - i) Willful violations of this Order or the implementing regulations issued under the authority of this Order;
   - ii) Willful failure to perform in accordance with one or more material terms of a public contract;
   - iii) Conviction of a criminal offense; or
   - iv) Other misconduct indicating a lack of business integrity or business honesty that seriously and directly affects the ability of the contractor to perform.

b) Responsibilities for ensuring the integrity of the procurement process shall be carried out by the Office of Government Public Contract Policy which shall issue implementing regulations that shall, at a minimum:
   - i) Provide standards for exclusion;
   - ii) Provide a fair, equitable and expeditious process with an opportunity to be heard before a determination for exclusion is made;
   - iii) Provide a method by which an excluded entity may apply for re-instatement; and
   - iv) Provide that a public record be maintained and published of all excluded individuals and entities.

Section 10 Financial Requirements

1) No tender notice shall be published, nor any tender commenced, prior to a certification by the senior financial officer, or his official designee, of the governmental unit or agency offering the tender that there are funds available sufficient to satisfy the government's estimated cost of any resulting contract.

2) No contract shall be awarded without a certification that sufficient funds are available and dedicated (i.e., may not be used for any other purpose) to the contract in an amount equal to the full contract price.

3) Regulations shall be issued and published providing for the right of any governmental unit or agency awarding a public contract to have access to and have the authority to audit a contractor's financial records related to the public contract that was awarded. This right to audit, together with any additional oversight responsibilities, shall be exercised by an office that is not responsible for tender issuance. The Office of Government Public Contract Policy may establish a central agency for public procurement audit services.

Section 11 Termination for the Convenience of the Government

1) The right of the government, acting through the Contracting Authority vested with the authority described in Section 3 of this Order, to terminate public contracts entered into under the authority of this Order, in whole or in part, when it is in the government's best interest, may be included in contracts awarded by the government.

2) If a contract is terminated for the convenience of the government, the rights, duties, and obligations of the parties, including compensation to the contractor, shall be in accordance with the procedures set forth in Section 12 of this Order on 'Dispute Resolution'.

3) The Office of Government Public Contract Policy shall issue implementing regulations describing the circumstances under which the government can terminate public contracts pursuant to the authority of this Order.

Section 12 Dispute Resolution

All interested parties, as defined below, to a government public contract tender process and those entities and individuals that have been awarded government public contracts have certain rights against the government that may include the ability to seek and obtain monetary relief against the government.

1) Tender Protests

a) Right to File - Any offeror deemed to be an interested party, that believes it has not received fair treatment in the award of a government public contract, or believes that the provisions of a tender unfairly restrict full and open competition in a manner that inappropriately excludes it from competing, may file a tender protest with the Administrative Tribunal established pursuant to the authority of this Order.

i) An interested party is an actual or prospective bidder or offeror that has a reasonable chance for award and whose direct economic interest would be affected by the award of a public contract or by the failure to award such a contract.

ii) The Tribunal shall rule on the protest within the shortest period of time practicable and may, among other reasonable remedies, direct the contracting authority to take corrective action, including but not limited to, terminating the awarded contract, resoliciting tenders, reevaluating tenders received for consideration, award reasonable tender preparation costs, or take other actions necessary to comply with this Order and the implementing regulations promulgated under the authority of this Order.

b) Results of Filing – Upon the filing of a tender protest after award, the governmental unit or agency that awarded the public contract shall immediately order the awarded contractor to cease working on the contract.

i) If a minister or the senior official responsible for contracting within [the] governmental unit or agency awarding the contract determines the requirement being satisfied by the contract is of such importance to the public interest that ceasing work will unduly harm the public interest, such minister or official may, by written determination of such undue harm, and after notice to the Tribunal, order the governmental unit or agency to notify the contractor to proceed with the contract.

ii) The minister or official, in making this determination, shall also consider the likelihood of success of the protest.

c) Effect of Grant of Protest – If the Tribunal sustains the tender protest and either directs the contracting authority to award the contract to the protestor or directs the contracting agency to take corrective action consistent with this Order or the regulations promulgated under the authority of this Order, the governmental unit or agency shall immediately terminate the contract with the originally awarded contractor, if that contractor is not selected for award following the corrective action ordered by the Tribunal. Such contractor may have certain rights against the government as discussed in Subsection 2 below.

d) Additional Rights of Unsuccessful Offerors – There shall be notices published of all public contract awards. All unsuccessful offerors in a government public contract competition shall be notified by the authority offering the tender, and such unsuccessful offerors shall be entitled to receive a written explanation of the factors upon which it was not successful. Such explanations shall be provided promptly and with full consideration to the proprietary nature of the information provided to the government by the other offerors, including the awardee, of the tender. Decisions of the Tribunal may be appealed by either party to the appropriate Court with jurisdiction over the procurement.

e) Implementing Regulations – The Office of Government Public Contract Policy shall issue implementing regulations published in conjunction with this provision that address, but are not limited to, the following:
   i) The establishment of the independent Administrative Tribunal referred to in Section 2.1(b)(ii) of this Order;
   ii) The rules of the Tribunal, including time and place requirements for filing protests, both before and after public contract award (including the effect on such time requirements if a request for explanation is made), and for issuing decisions;
   iii) The time requirements for an unsuccessful offeror to request an explanation of the governmental unit or agency decision and for the governmental unit or agency to respond to that request;
   iv) The nature of the relief that may be granted by the Tribunal; and
   v) The legal bases upon which a tender protest may be filed.

2) <u>Claims</u>

a) Right to File – A contractor has a right to make a claim to the authority awarding the public contract that a condition of the contract has not been followed or that it has otherwise been treated in an unfair way. This right to make a claim shall also apply to a contractor whose contract has been terminated as a result of a decision by the Tribunal hearing a tender protest to terminate its contract where it believes it is entitled to additional compensation for work under its terminated contract, but not yet paid.

b) Process – A contractor seeking to exercise its rights under this Subsection must first seek a final written decision on the merits of its claim from the governmental unit or agency that awarded the contract by submitting a written request to the contracting authority for that governmental unit or agency. This request shall specify that amount that the contractor believes it is owed and the basis for the request. This final decision must be prepared by the contracting authority and it must be issued within a reasonable period of time. If after a reasonable period of time, the contractor does not receive a final written decision from the appropriate authority, the contractor may deem this lack of a response as a denial of its claim.

c) Appeal – If the contractor is dissatisfied with the final written decision of the governmental unit or agency, it shall have the right to file an appeal with the court having jurisdiction over disputes between the government and private parties (or such other Court granted jurisdiction to hear such cases), which shall render its decision within a reasonable period of time.

d) Regulations – The Office of Government Public Contract Policy shall issue regulations in coordination with the Ministry of Justice implementing the claims process described in this subsection. The regulations shall include the following subjects and may include other subjects:

i) The office within the governmental unit or agency where claims may be filed;
ii) The time for filing claims with the governmental unit or agency and for its decision;
iii) The time for filing appeals and for decisions on such appeals;
iv) The scope of review, including but not limited to, whether to completely review all of the facts and circumstances of the claim or to review a narrow point of law, or whether a rational basis exists to support the contracting authority's decision;
v) The responsibility of the contractor to continue prosecuting the work under the contract while a claim or appeal is pending;
vi) The legal bases upon which claims may be filed including, but not limited to, claims concerning contract modifications and terminations; and
vii) Such additional rules and procedures consistent with the responsibilities and jurisdiction granted by this Order.

e) The State of Iraq, acting through the Contracting Authority vested with the authority described in Section 3 of this Order, shall be able to make a claim in a court of proper jurisdiction against the contractor to enforce the government's rights under the contract. The State of Iraq shall be represented in the court of proper jurisdiction by a representative designated by the Ministry of Justice.

f) Alternative Dispute Resolution – In resolving all such disputes (i.e., whether they are tender protests or claims during administration of a public contract), principles of alternative dispute resolution shall be used to the maximum extent possible, so long as both parties agree.

Section 13 Effect on Present Iraqi Law

1) Tenders instructions (Outfitting and Buying) for State Agencies and the Social Sector, issued by the Legal Department/Planning Organization/Council of Ministers/Republic of Iraq, 2001 (Tender Instructions) are hereby suspended.

2) Instructions for Implementation and Follow up of Projects and Works of National Development Plan. Issued by the Legal Department/Ministry of Planning/Republic of Iraq, 1988 (Implementation Instructions) are hereby suspended.

3) Any provision of Iraqi law, including but not limited to, statutes, decrees, regulations, and instructions, that is inconsistent with this Order is hereby suspended to the extent of such inconsistency.

Section 14 Implementation

1) The Minister of Planning, through the Office of Government Public Contract Policy shall issue Administrative Instructions and regulations to implement this Order.

2) Until such time as regulations are promulgated by the Ministry of Planning and Development Cooperation under the authority of this Order, Coalition Provisional Authority Memorandum Number Four and its appendices, dated 19 August 2003 (CPA/MEM/19 August 2003/04) ('Memorandum Four'),[263] shall serve as the implementing regulation for this Order.

3) In the event of an inconsistency between Memorandum Four and this Order, Memorandum Four shall be interpreted in a manner that is consistent with this Order.

[263] See *Doc 129*.

4) Except as otherwise specifically provided by Coalition Provisional Authority Order Number 71, Local Governmental Powers, dated 6 April 2004 (CPA/ORD/6 April 2004/71),[264] or other law or regulation, including other Coalition Provisional Authority orders, this Order shall apply to the federal and regional governments, Governorates, and municipal and local governments.

Section 15 Entry into Force
This Order shall enter into force upon signature [16 May 2004].

Document 112
Coalition Provisional Authority Order Number 88
CPA/ORD/12 May 2004/88

Rights of Judicial Officials to Return to the Judiciary after certain Government Service

Pursuant to my authority as Administrator of the Coalition Provisional Authority (CPA), under the laws and usages of war, and consistent with relevant U.N. Security Council resolutions, including Resolutions 1483 and 1511 (2003),

Noting that the Law of Administration for the State of Iraq for the Transitional Period (TAL)[265] carefully guards against persons serving simultaneously in several governmental roles in order to prevent conflicts of interest,

Recognizing that the Iraqi judiciary, having been vetted by the Judicial Review Committee, offers a number of talented and fair individuals who could assume important and meaningful senior roles within the Iraqi government,

Acknowledging the importance of the safeguard in the TAL against conflicts of interest and the value of having all persons, including judges, leave their employment before assuming a senior governmental position,

Recognizing that the return of Iraqi judges after serving in another governmental capacity to service in the judiciary is vital to the long-term interests of Iraq's judicial system,

Understanding that current Iraqi practice would require each such judge to seek and receive approval for reappointment,

Concluding that establishing a means for members of the Iraqi judiciary to be reinstated immediately after their service in other governmental capacities would honor and preserve the safeguards of the TAL,

I hereby promulgate the following:

Section 1 Right to Return to Judicial Service
1) Any federal judge or prosecutor ('Judicial Official') who leaves the Iraqi judiciary to serve on a Commission established by the federal government (a 'Commission'), consistent with Article 51 of the TAL, or to serve as a member of the National Assembly, the Presidency Council, or the Council of Ministers, consistent with Article 28 of the TAL, shall have the right to be reinstated as a member of the Iraqi judiciary after leaving

[264] See *Doc 95*.
[265] See *Doc 511*.

such Commission or such service as a member of the National Assembly, the Presidency Council, or the Council of Ministers.

2) A Judicial Officer must exercise this right to return to the Iraqi judiciary within 90 days after leaving a Commission or service in the National Assembly, the Presidency Council, or the Council of Ministers. If a Judicial Official exercises this right to return to the Iraqi judiciary, that Judicial Official shall be reinstated immediately at the same level as he or she held before joining a Commission or serving as a member of the National Assembly, the Presidency Council, or the Council of Ministers.

Section 2 Disqualification for Matters Arising out of Prior Service

No Judicial Official who served on a Commission or as a member of the National Assembly, the Presidency Council, or the Council of Ministers, and subsequently returns to the Iraqi Judiciary, shall participate in any case arising out of such service.

Section 3 Use of Judicial Title While Serving Outside the Judiciary

In recognition of a Judicial Official's right to return to the Iraqi judiciary, a Judicial Official shall have the right to use the relevant honorary title of 'Judge' or 'Prosecutor' while serving on a Commission or in the National Assembly, the Presidency Council, or the Council of Ministers.

Section 4 Entry into Force

This Order shall enter into force on the date of signature [12 May 2004].

Document 113

Coalition Provisional Authority Order Number 89

CPA/ORD/30 May 2004/89

Amendments to the Labor Code—Law No. 71 of 1987

Pursuant to my authority as Administrator of the Coalition Provisional Authority (CPA) and under the laws and usages of war, and consistent with relevant U.N. Security Council resolutions, including Resolutions 1483 and 1511 (2003),

Having worked closely with the Governing Council to ensure that social and economic change as necessary to benefit the people of Iraq occurs in a manner acceptable to the people of Iraq,

Acknowledging the Governing Council's desire to bring about significant change to the Iraqi labor law as necessary to improve the condition of the people of Iraq,

Determined to improve the conditions of work, life, technical skills, and opportunities for all Iraqis and to fight unemployment and underemployment with its associated deleterious effect on public security,

Noting that labor by young persons is endemic in Iraq and is deleterious to the health, safety and morals of children,

Further noting that Iraq has ratified International Labour Convention 182 and 138, which requires signatory nations to take affirmative steps towards eliminating child labor,

Recognizing the CPA's obligation to provide for the effective administration of Iraq, to ensure the well being of the children and workers of Iraq and to enable the social and economic functions of everyday life,

Acting in a manner consistent with the Report of the Secretary General to the Security Council of July 17, 2003, concerning the need for the development of Iraq and its transition from a non-transparent centrally planned economy to a free market economy characterized by sustainable economic growth through the establishment of a dynamic private sector, and the need to enact institutional and legal reforms to give it effect,

Having coordinated with the International Labour Organization, as referenced in paragraph 8(a) of U.N. Security Council Resolution 1483,

In close consultation with and acting in coordination with the Governing Council, I hereby promulgate the following:

Section 1 Amendments to the Labor Code

The Chapter of the Labor Code, Law No. 71 of 1987 (the 'Labor Code') entitled 'Part VI—Chapter II' is amended to read as follows:

Chapter II – Protection of young persons

Article 90. Prohibition of Child Labor and Definition

90.1 The minimum age for admission to any kind of employment or work within the territory of Iraq and on means of transport registered in the territory of Iraq shall be fifteen years.

90.2 Unless otherwise indicated, in the present chapter the term 'young person' means any person who has not reached eighteen (18) years of age.

90.3 Unless otherwise indicated, in the present chapter the term 'youth' means any person that has not reached sixteen (16) years of age.

Article 91. Work that young persons are prohibited to perform

91.1 Young persons may not be employed to perform work which, by its nature or the circumstances in which it is carried out, is likely to harm their health, safety or morals.

91.2 The list of the types of work to which the above provision applies shall be periodically examined and revised as necessary by the Ministry, in consultation with the organizations of employers and workers concerned, and it shall include but not be limited to the following:

(a) work underground, under water, at dangerous heights or in confined spaces;

(b) work with dangerous machinery, equipment and tools, or that involves the manual handling or transport of heavy loads;

(c) work in an unhealthy environment that may, for example, expose young persons to hazardous substances, agents or processes, or to temperatures, noise levels, or vibrations damaging to their health;

(d) work under particularly difficult conditions such as work for long hours or in certain circumstances during the night or work where the young person is unreasonably confined to the premises of the employer.

91.3 The following shall be considered worst forms of child labor and shall be prohibited:

(a) all forms of slavery or practices similar to slavery, such as the sale and trafficking of children, debt bondage and serfdom and forced or compulsory labor, including forced or compulsory recruitment of children for use in armed conflict;

(b) the use, procuring or offering of a child for prostitution, for the production of pornography or for pornographic performances;
(c) the use, procuring or offering of a child for illicit activities, in particular for the production and trafficking of drugs as defined in the relevant international treaties;
(d) work which, by its nature or the circumstances in which it is carried out, is likely to harm the health, safety or morals of children. The list of the types of work to which this clause applies shall be periodically examined and revised as necessary by the competent Ministry, in consultation with the organizations of employers and workers concerned.

91.4 Whoever promotes, aids or benefits from acts destined to use child labor under its worst forms shall be guilty of an offense and on conviction shall be liable to prosecution under the Penal Code.

91.5 The Government of Iraq shall design and implement programs of action to eliminate as a priority the worst forms of child labor. To this end it will take specific measures:
(a) to prevent the engagement of children in the worst forms of child labor;
(b) to provide the necessary and appropriate direct assistance for the removal of children from the worst forms of child labor and for their rehabilitation and social integration;
(c) to ensure access to free basic education, and, wherever possible and appropriate, vocational training, for all children removed from the worst forms of child labor;
(d) to identify and reach out to children at special risk; and
(e) to take account of the special situation of girls who, because of their gender, may be more vulnerable to some of the worst forms of child labor.

91.6 For the purposes of Article 91, the term 'child' shall apply to all persons under the age of 18.

Article 92. Medical examination and supervision of young persons in employment

92.1 Young persons shall not be admitted to employment or work unless they have been found fit for the work in question by a thorough medical examination.

92.2 The medical examination for fitness for employment shall be carried out by a qualified physician approved by the competent authority and shall be certified either by a medical certificate or by an endorsement on the work permit or in the workbook.

92.3 The document certifying fitness for employment may be issued–
(a) subject to specified conditions of employment;
(b) for a specified job or for a group of jobs or occupations involving similar health risks that have been classified as a group by the competent authority.

92.4 The fitness of a young person for the employment in which he or she is engaged shall be subject to medical supervision until he or she has reached the age of eighteen years.

92.5 The continued employment of a young person shall be subject to the repetition of medical examinations at intervals of not more than one year.

92.6 The medical examinations required by the preceding articles shall not involve the young person, or his or her family, in any expense.

92.7 The term 'the competent authority' means the Ministry in charge of labor or the Ministry in charge of health or both.

Article 93. Hours of work and annual leave of young person

93.1 A young person who has not reached eighteen (18) years of age may not work for more than seven (7) hours per day.

93.2 Daily hours of work shall include one or more rest periods totaling at least one (1) hour in order to allow the young person to rest; the rest periods shall be arranged so that no period of work lasts more than four (4) consecutive hours.

93.3 Young persons who have been admitted to work shall have the right to thirty (30) days paid annual leave per year.

Article 94. Creation and posting of provisions and maintenance of register of young persons

94.1 An employer who employs young persons who have been permitted to work in accordance with the law shall post at the workplace a copy of the provisions regarding the protection of young persons at work.

94.2 The employer shall also maintain a register specifying their names, ages and the work to which they have been assigned.

94.3 The employer shall be required to file and keep available to labor inspectors the medical certificate for fitness for employment that is specified under article 92, or to provide the labor inspector with the reference of the register where the certificate is filed.

Article 95. Liability in the Event of Unlawful Employment

When an employment relationship exists between an employer and a young person who, under the provisions of this law, is not permitted to work yet is working unlawfully, the employer shall, upon discovery of the working young person, be obligated to:

a.) pay the young person the agreed wage for work of a similar quality and kind as if completed by an adult, and

b.) compensate him or her if he or she has an accident during or as a result of work, regardless of who was at fault, and

c.) immediately cease employing all young persons working unlawfully.

The provisions of Article 95 shall not affect the application of any other criminal or civil recovery in regards to this chapter.

Article 96. Exclusion of young persons in family enterprises

Other than the provisions set forth in Sections 91.1 through 91.4, which shall apply with respect to all young persons irrespective of the circumstances of their employment, the provisions of this law do not apply to youths that have reached the age of 15 and are engaged in a family enterprise under the authority or supervision of the youth's spouse, father, mother, brother or sister.

Article 97. Penalties

Any person infringing the provisions on the protection of young persons as provided in chapter II of this Part shall be guilty of an offense and on conviction shall be liable to imprisonment for a period of ten (10) days to three (3) months, or to a fine from twelve (12) times the daily minimum wage to twelve (12) times the monthly minimum wage.

The Part of the Labor Code entitled 'Part IX' in the 1987 is amended to read as follows:

PART IX – TRANSITIONAL AND MISCELLANEOUS PROVISIONS

Article 170. Non-retroactive effect

The rights to which workers are entitled by virtue of prior laws and that involve a period prior to the entry into force of this law as amended shall be dealt with in accordance with the provisions of those laws.

Article 171. Records maintained by the employer

171.1 The employer shall maintain the following records:

(a) a register of workers' names
(b) a register of workers' wages
(c) a register of workers' hours of work
(d) a leave register
(e) a register of young persons employed
(f) a register of inspection visits

171.2 The Ministry shall draw up and maintain models for the registers referred to in section 171.1, above.

Article 172. Ministry to issue regulations and instructions

The Ministry shall issue instructions, regulations and orders to facilitate the implementation of this law, no later than three (3) months from the date of coming into force of the present law. The Ministry shall continue to issue instructions, regulations and orders from time to time as may be needed to effectively implement, clarify or augment this law.

Article 173. Repeal of laws

Any law (to include any statute, ministerial instruction, order, or Revolutionary Command Council resolution) that is inconsistent with this law as amended is hereby suspended to the extent of such inconsistency.

Section 2 Amendments to Fines and Penalties

The Chapter of the Labor Code, entitled 'Part II—Chapter I Employment' is amended as follows:

Article 24. Penalties

24.1 Any person or entity violating the provisions of this chapter relative to the employment of workers shall be guilty of an offense and on conviction shall be subject to a fine in an amount between three (3) times the daily minimum wage and three (3) times the monthly minimum wage per violation.

24.2 Any person or entity violating the provisions of this chapter relative to the employment of foreigners, shall be guilty of an offense and on conviction shall be subject to a fine in an amount between three (3) times the daily minimum wage and three (3) times the monthly minimum wage per violation.

The Chapter of the Labor Code, entitled 'Part III—Chapter II Protection and Determination of the Wages' is amended as follows:

Article 53. Penalties

Any person or entity violating the provisions of this chapter, relative to wages, shall be guilty of an offense and on conviction shall be subject to a fine in an amount between six (6) times the daily minimum wage and six (6) times the monthly minimum wage per violation. If the violation concerns paying a wage that is lower than the minimum wage for an unskilled worker, the party shall be subject, in addition to paying the fine imposed, to pay the worker compensation in an amount that is two (2) times the difference between the wage paid and the minimum wage.

The Chapter of the Labor Code, entitled 'Part IV—Chapter II, Section (ii) Sick Leave' is amended as follows:

Article 79. Penalties

Any person or entity violating the provisions of this chapter, relative to hours of work, shall be guilty of an offense and on conviction shall be subject to a fine in an amount between three (3) times the daily minimum wage and three (3) times the monthly minimum wage per violation.

The Chapter of the Labor Code, entitled 'Part VI Chapter IV Work Precautions' is amended as follows:

Article 113. Penalties

Any person who infringes the provisions regarding occupational safety measures contained in this chapter shall be liable to a fine of from twelve (12) times the daily to twelve (12) times the monthly minimum wage, or to imprisonment ranging from one (1) to six (6) months.

The Chapter of the Labor Code, entitled 'Part VI Chapter V Work Inspection' is amended as follows:

Article 118. Penalties

(2) Any person who impedes the labor inspector or the inspection committee in entering the work premises for purposes of inspection or who interferes in any way with the fulfillment of the committee's activities shall be liable to a fine of from twelve (12) times the daily to twelve (12) times the monthly minimum wage, or to imprisonment ranging from one (1) month to six (6) months.

Section 3 Transitional Minimum Wage Benchmark

1) For the purpose of the fines established in this Order, the minimum wage shall be defined as the hourly equivalent of the wage of a Grade 11, Step 1 public employee as established in CPA Order Number 30 (CPA/ORD/1 September 2003/30)[266] until such time as the official minimum wage is established by the appropriate authority.

2) For the purpose of calculating the fines in this Order, the workday shall be deemed eight (8) hours long.

[266] See *Doc 51*. There seems to be a typo in the date of the document symbol. The symbol on the signed version and in the *Official Gazette* is 'CPA/ORD/8 September 2003/30' and 'CPA/ORD/8 Sep 2003/30', respectively.

Section 4 Entry into Force
This Order shall enter into force on the date of signature [30 May 2004].

Document 114
Coalition Provisional Authority Order Number 90
CPA/ORD/28 May 2004/90

Special Task Force for Compensating Victims of the Previous Regime

Pursuant to my authority as Administrator of the Coalition Provisional Authority (CPA), and under the laws and usages of war, and consistent with relevant U.N. Security Council resolutions, including Resolutions 1483 and 1511 (2003),

Understanding that justice for the crimes of the past regime demands proper compensation for the victims and their families,

Acknowledging that under the former regime, many lost their jobs, their property and their lives because they opposed the regime, refused to join the Ba'ath party or simply were related to someone considered by the previous regime as an opponent,

Noting that compensating victims of past crimes is a complex undertaking involving many thousands of people,

Recognizing that ultimately the offenses committed by the past Iraqi regime against Iraqi citizens should be compensated by Iraqis in accordance with Iraqi standards of justice and through Iraqi means,

Desiring to help the process of correcting these injustices of the past to begin quickly,

I hereby promulgate the following:

Section 1 Establishment

1) The Special Task Force on Compensating Victims of the Previous Regime ('Special Task Force') is hereby established.

2) The Special Task Force shall be composed of a Chairman and two Assistant Chairmen. The Chairman shall be appointed by the Administrator of the CPA and shall head the Special Task Force. The Assistant Chairmen shall be selected by the Chairman and shall assist in the work of the Special Task Force.[267]

Section 2 Responsibilities

1) The Special Task Force shall work with victims and Ministries to define the types of injustice for which compensation should be provided, other than wrongs already being addressed through other processes. The Special Task Force shall:

a) Define the categories of victims to be compensated;
b) Devise a means of estimating the numbers of victims in each category;
c) Estimate what would constitute fair compensation for each category of victim;
d) Recommend a system by which victims may make claims for compensation as well as a system to fairly adjudicate those claims.

[267] Sec 1(2) was amended by CPA Order No 100, sec 3(33) *[Doc 124]*.

2) By August 1, 2004, the Special Task Force shall provide the Iraqi Interim Government with a report containing the Special Task Force's findings and recommendations.

Section 3 Endowment
To carry out the Special Task Force's recommendations, twenty-five million dollars from the Development Fund for Iraq shall be set aside to be used in the future effort to compensate victims and their families.

Section 4 Entry into Force
This Order shall enter into force on the date of signature [29 May 2004].

Document 115
Coalition Provisional Authority Order Number 91
CPA/ORD/2 June 2004/91

Regulation of Armed Forces and Militias Within Iraq

Pursuant to my authority as Administrator of the Coalition Provisional Authority (CPA), and under the laws and usages of war, and consistent with relevant U.N. Security Council resolutions, including Resolutions 1483 and 1511 (2003),

Recalling that U.N. Security Council Resolution 1483 (2003) calls upon the CPA to promote the welfare of the Iraqi people through the effective administration of the territory, including in particular working towards the restoration of conditions of security and stability,

Noting that the former oppressive regime of Saddam Hussein has been removed,

Further noting the adoption of the Law of Administration for the State of Iraq for the Transitional Period on March 8, 2004,[268]

Further noting that Article 27(B) of the Law of Administration for the State of Iraq for the Transitional Period provides that 'Armed forces and militias not under the command structure of the Iraqi Transitional Government are prohibited, except as provided by federal law,'

Acknowledging that those who fought against the Ba'athist regime in resistance forces should receive recognition and benefits as military veterans for their service to their people,

Intending to give such individuals the chance to further themselves, support their families, and serve their peoples by pursuing civilian lives and jobs,

Considering that the Iraqi Armed Forces and other Iraqi security forces are in need of trained and experienced professionals,

Desiring to establish a mechanism that will ensure armed forces and militias come into compliance with the Law of Administration for the State of Iraq for the Transitional Period,

I hereby promulgate the following:

Section 1 Definitions
1) 'Administrator' means the Administrator of the Coalition Provisional Authority and, following transfer of full governance authority to the Iraqi Interim Government, the

[268] See *Doc 511*.

civilian head of the Iraqi government exercising national command authority, or his or her designee, unless otherwise designated.

2) 'Armed Force' means an organized group of individuals bearing firearms or weapons. The term 'Armed Force' includes government forces and Militias.

3) 'Militia' means a military or paramilitary force that is not part of the Iraqi Armed Forces or other Iraqi security forces established pursuant to CPA Orders, Regulations and Memoranda, or pursuant to Iraqi federal law and the Law of Administration for the State of Iraq for the Transitional Period.

4) 'Private Security Company' means a private business, properly registered with the Ministry of Interior and Ministry of Trade that seeks to gain commercial benefits and financial profit by providing security services to individuals, businesses and organizations, governmental or otherwise. Private Security Companies are subject to, and must comply with all applicable criminal, administrative, commercial and civil laws and regulations unless exempted by CPA Order Number 17, 'Status of Coalition, Foreign Liaison Missions, their Personnel and Contractors.'[269]

5) 'Illegal Armed Force or Militia' means an Armed Force or Militia existing in violation of the prohibition contained in Section 2 of this Order.

6) 'Residual Element' means the parts of a former Armed Force or Militia under an approved Transition and Reintegration Plan that are still extant and drawing down during the period of transition and reintegration and that are regulated by the relevant governmental authorities in accordance with this Order and the Transition and Reintegration Plan for that Armed Force or Militia.

7) 'Qualified Member' means a member of a Residual Element who:

a) is specifically identified by an Armed Force or Militia, at the time the Armed Force or Militia's command becomes subject to a Transition and Reintegration Plan, as having been a member of the Armed Force or Militia on or before May 1, 2003;
b) has not engaged in terrorist activities or violated the laws of war or Iraq's recognized principles of human rights;
c) has not been convicted of a felony offense under the criminal laws of Iraq after May 1, 2003;
d) is not acting as an agent of a foreign government; and
e) continues at all times to meet the criteria for qualification set forth herein.

8) 'Transition and Reintegration Plan' means a documented and recorded plan that sets forth milestones and processes for the complete transition and reintegration of a Residual Element of an Armed Force or Militia.

Section 2 Prohibitions

Armed Forces and Militias, and membership therein, are prohibited within Iraq, except as provided for herein.

Section 3 Exceptions

1) The prohibition contained in Section 2 shall not apply to:

a) Armed Forces and members thereof under the control of the CPA (or, following transfer of full governance authority, the Iraqi Interim Government and any future Government of Iraq) including, but not limited to, all security forces

[269] See *Doc 37*.

under the control of the Ministry of Interior and the Iraqi Armed Forces under the control of the Ministry of Defence;

b) Armed Forces specifically permitted under the Law of Administration for the State of Iraq for the Transitional Period;

c) Armed Forces and members thereof under the operational control of the Commander of the Multinational Force operating in Iraq pursuant to United Nations Security Council Resolution 1511, and any relevant subsequent resolutions;

d) A Residual Element currently and continuously meeting the criteria set forth in Section 4.5, to include members thereof. Those Residual Elements currently meeting the criteria for an exception under this Section 3.1(d) are listed in Annexes A, Armed Forces, and B, Militias; and

e) A Private Security Company or the officers and employees of such Private Security Company, provided the Private Security Company meets all of the following criteria:

   i. the Private Security Company is properly licensed and regulated by the Ministry of Interior and Ministry of Trade;

   ii. all firearms and weapons used by the Private Security Company are licensed in accordance with applicable CPA Orders, Regulations, and Memoranda, and Iraqi laws and regulations; and

   iii. all company officers, armed members, and supervisors exercising control of armed members of the Private Security Company have undergone background checks conducted by the Ministry of Interior and possess the requisite weapons authorizations issued by the Ministry of Interior.[270]

f) Those contractors covered by CPA Order Number 17.

Section 4 Transition and Reintegration of Residual Elements of Armed Forces and Militias

1) Only Armed Forces and Militias that are identified by the Administrator or after the transfer of full governance authority the Transition and Reintegration Implementation Committee as participating in the political process leading to a peaceful, prosperous, and progressive Iraq will be considered eligible for Residual Element status and for transition and reintegration in accordance with this Order.

2) In order to attain the status of a Residual Element, a Transition and Reintegration Plan must be accepted by the commander, head or leader of an Armed Force or Militia, and the Administrator or after the transfer of full governance authority the Transition and Reintegration Implementation Committee. The plan must include:

a) a complete list of Qualified Members, including all members of the Residual Element, and such list must be provided to the Iraqi Veterans Agency;

b) the processes by which all of its Qualified Members will be transitioned or reintegrated; and

c) clearly defined milestones for completion of the transition and reintegration of the Residual Element.

3) Only the Administrator or after the transfer of full governance authority the Transition and Reintegration Implementation Committee may decide to confer Residual Element status to an Armed Force or Militia. Upon approval of the Transition and Reintegration Plan, the Armed Force or Militia shall become a Residual Element.

[270] Sec 3(1)(e) was rescinded and replaced by CPA Order No 100, sec 3(34)(a) *[Doc 124]*.

4) Once a Transition and Reintegration Plan has been approved by the Administrator or after the transfer of full governance authority the Transition and Reintegration Implementation Committee, processes and milestones may be revised only with the consent of the Transition and Reintegration Implementation Committee.

5) Residual Elements of an Armed Force or Militia qualify for the exception in Section 3.1(d) once there is an approved Transition and Reintegration Plan. Continued qualification for the exception in Section 3.1(d) is dependent upon meeting all of the terms of the applicable Transition and Reintegration Plan, and complying with the following conditions:

a) All Qualified Members of the former Armed Force or Militia registered with the Iraqi Veterans Agency as members of the Residual Element. The Iraqi Veterans Agency shall provide this information to the Ministry of Interior immediately upon registering a new Residual Element.

b) The Residual Element shall not recruit or otherwise add members, either to its active forces or to its reserve or stand-by forces.

c) The Residual Element shall not conduct operations or activities of any type, whether armed or unarmed, without express advance authorization from the Ministry of Interior and the Commander of the Multinational Forces operating in Iraq pursuant to United Nations Security Council Resolution 1511, and any relevant subsequent resolutions.

d) The Residual Element shall not organize, support, or participate in criminal activity, undertake any effort designed to destabilize any portion of Iraq, promote violence, or otherwise threaten the safety and security of the Iraqi people.

e) The Residual Element and all of its members must promptly register all firearms and weapons with the Ministry of Interior in accordance with CPA Order Number 3 (Revised/Amended), Weapons Control, dated December 31, 2003,[271] and any other applicable Iraqi laws.

f) The Residual Element shall not manufacture, purchase, or otherwise acquire additional firearms, weapons, or ammunition; nor shall the Residual Element's members acquire firearms, weapons, or ammunition for use in Militia activities; nor shall the Residual Element or its members import firearms, weapons, or ammunition into Iraq from a foreign country, or hire others to do so on their behalf.

g) The Residual Element and its members shall not endorse, finance, or campaign for candidates for political office at any level.

h) The Residual Element shall be subject to and fully cooperate with such actions as the CPA or government of Iraq following transfer of full governance authority deems necessary to verify compliance with the accepted process and ensure transparency and accountability of the Residual Element's members, functions and operations during the period of transition and reintegration.[272]

6) During the period of transition, the Transition and Reintegration Implementation Committee is responsible for determining if a Residual Element fails to comply with any of the milestones, processes or conditions set out in the agreement required by Section 4.5. A determination that a Residual Element has failed to comply with its Transition and Reintegration Plan disqualifies the Residual Element and all of its members from the exception in Section 3.1(d) and results in re-designating the Residual Element as an

[271] See *Doc 17*.

[272] Sec 4(5)(h) was amended by CPA Order No 100, sec 3(34)(b) *[Doc 124]*.

Illegal Armed Force or Militia, pursuant to Article 7 of this Order. However, if a Transition and Reintegration Plan is rendered unachievable due to changes in the availability of positions for Residual Element members in any component program, then the Transition and Reintegration Implementation Committee may adjust the Transition and Reintegration Plan, and the Residual Element will not be deemed to have failed to comply with it. Such adjustments will be limited to changes in transition and reintegration schedules, and in particular will not permit an increase in the number of Qualified Members of a residual element.

7) Qualified Members of Residual Elements may be transitioned and reintegrated into Iraqi society using the following processes:

a) Entry of individuals into the Iraqi Armed Forces or other Iraqi security forces. In accordance with administrative instructions to be promulgated by the Ministry of Defence or the Ministry of Interior, as the case may be, and subject to the manning needs of the respective forces, individuals with the appropriate training and experience may enter into the Iraqi Armed Forces or other Iraqi security forces, to include security forces under ministries and agencies other than the Ministry of Interior. In accordance with administrative instructions to be promulgated by the employing ministry or agency, individuals whose service in a former Armed Force or Militia can be characterized and quantified shall be given credit for their time in service.

b) Retirement. In accordance with administrative instructions to be promulgated by the Ministry of Defence, individuals whose service in a former Armed Force or Militia can be characterized and quantified, and who would qualify for retirement had they served in the Iraqi Armed Forces shall be provided the opportunity to retire with the same pension they would have received had they served in the Iraqi Armed Forces.

c) Reintegration. In accordance with administrative instructions to be promulgated by Iraqi Ministries, agencies and the Transition and Reintegration Implementation Committee, individuals who do not qualify for retirement and who do not enter into the Iraqi Armed Forces or other Iraqi security forces shall be offered a reintegration program designed to help assimilate them into Iraqi civil society and economy. Elements that may be included in a reintegration program include skills screening, education benefits, job training and placement, and a limited stipend program. All relevant CPA offices and Ministries will cooperate in supporting established reintegration programs.

Such Qualified Members shall be deemed to be military veterans for purposes of determining eligibility for benefits, preferences and programs, and time in service if they transition into one of the Iraqi Security Forces.

8) In accordance with administrative instructions to be promulgated by the Ministry of Defence, widows and orphans of deceased members of Armed Forces and Militias that are subject to a Transition and Reintegration Plan shall be entitled to benefits based upon the service of the deceased member in accordance with any applicable statutes, regulations and rules determining such benefits for which current members of the Iraqi Armed Forces qualify; provided that the deceased member must have died on or before May 1, 2003, and such deceased member's service can be characterized and quantified.

9) In accordance with administrative instructions to be promulgated by the Ministry of Defence, disabled members of Armed Forces and Militias that are subject to a Transition and Reintegration Plan shall be entitled to benefits based upon their service in accordance

with any applicable statutes, regulations and rules determining such benefits for which current members of the Iraqi Armed Forces qualify; provided that the member was disabled on or before May 1, 2003, and the member's service can be characterized and quantified.

10) Any individual receiving benefits or status under this Order shall forfeit the right to such benefits or status should they thereafter participate in an Illegal Armed Force or Militia.

11) In view of the recognition given to Qualified Members in deeming them to have been former soldiers, and consistent with Article 28(B) of the Law of Administration for the State of Iraq for the Transitional Period, in no event may a member of a Residual Element be a member of the National Assembly, Minister, Prime Minister, or member of the Presidency Council unless the individual has resigned his or her commission or rank, or retired from duty in the Residual Element, at least eighteen months prior to serving. Nothing herein shall affect limitations on political activity that will be applicable to Qualified Members who choose to join the Iraqi Armed Forces.

12) Residual Elements and their members shall enjoy no special privileges or immunities and shall be subject to all applicable Iraqi civil, administrative, and criminal laws.

13) Nothing in this Order shall be interpreted as exonerating individuals belonging to Armed Forces, Militias, or Residual Elements from responsibility for criminal acts or war crimes conducted individually or as part of such Armed Forces, Militias, or Residual Elements.

Section 5 Transition and Reintegration Implementation Committee

1) The Transition and Reintegration Implementation Committee ('Committee') is hereby established to exercise oversight of the transition and reintegration process and to take such disciplinary or other action as may be necessary upon a determination that a Residual Element of an Armed Force or Militia no longer qualifies for an exception. The Committee shall be chaired by the Minister of Interior and shall report to the Ministerial Committee for National Security.

- a) In addition to the Minister of Interior, the Committee shall include permanent representatives from the Ministry of Defence, Ministry of Justice, Ministry of Foreign Affairs, Ministry of Finance, Ministry of Labor and Social Affairs, Ministry of Education, Iraqi Veterans Agency (separate from the representative from the Ministry of Defence), and such other ministries, agencies, and governorates as the Ministerial Committee for National Security may determine.
- b) The Chair may invite representatives from other ministries, agencies, and organizations, both governmental and non-governmental, to attend Committee meetings or participate in Committee activities as needed.
- c) The Commander or other representative of the Multinational Force operating in Iraq pursuant to United Nations Security Council Resolution 1511, and any relevant subsequent resolutions, may be invited to attend and participate in Committee meetings.

2) The functions of the Committee are to:

- a) Oversee the status of the various transition and reintegration programs;
- b) Revise individual Transition and Reintegration Plans when programs to absorb Residual Element members are not available as planned or for other reasons as agreed to by the Committee and the Residual Element of the Armed Force or Militia involved;
- c) Coordinate Iraqi government transition and reintegration policy and implementation with various governmental and non-governmental agencies and Ministries;

d) Regularly inform the Ministerial Committee for National Security, and through it the Administrator or after the transfer of full governance authority the Prime Minister, of the status of transition and reintegration related programs and any issues that affect Iraqi security arising from these programs;
e) Coordinate with the CPA, and subsequently consult with coalition diplomatic missions which are directly supporting Transition and Reintegration Plans, on programs and policy related to transition and reintegration;
f) Coordinate with the Commander of the Multinational Force on Iraqi policy, decisions, and determinations that have security implications; and
g) Perform other functions related to transition and reintegration as determined by the National Security Advisor.

3) The Committee will meet regularly with the leaders of the various Residual Elements, and the political parties that support them, as well as relevant governmental and non-governmental agencies and Ministries to coordinate transition and reintegration efforts and share information.

Section 6 Disciplinary Measures and Penalties

1) An Armed Force or Militia that does not qualify for an exception as set forth in Section 3, or a Residual Element that having previously qualified for an exception under Section 3.1(d) has ceased to so qualify by virtue of failing to continue to meet the criteria for such exception, shall be considered an Illegal Armed Force or Militia. All weapons and other property, whether movable or immovable, held by an Illegal Armed Force or Militia, shall be subject to immediate confiscation through such measures as may be determined by the Transition and Reintegration Implementation Committee in coordination with the Ministry of Interior and the Commander of the Multinational Force. An Illegal Armed Force or Militia shall be subject to any actions as the Administrator or following the transfer of full governance authority the Transition and Reintegration Implementation Committee decides is necessary for the safety and security of the Iraqi people.

2) All members of an Illegal Armed Force or Militia shall be subject to criminal prosecution in accordance with the laws of Iraq. The Transition and Reintegration Implementation Committee shall notify the Ministries of Justice, Interior and Defense immediately upon a determination that a Residual Element has become an Illegal Armed Force or Militia. Paragraph 135 of the Iraqi Penal Code, Law No. 111 of 1969, as amended, is hereby modified to add the following aggravating circumstance:

> '(5) The commission of an offense while acting as a member of an Illegal Armed Force or Militia or while a member of a Residual Element.'

3) A person who fills a leadership position or otherwise participates in an Illegal Armed Force or Militia in violation of the prohibition contained in Section 2, or who is a principal, accessory, or conspirator in such violation, shall be subject to judicial action in accordance with the Iraqi Penal Code, Law No. 111 of 1969, as amended, to include possible prosecution under paragraphs 194 and 195 of the Penal Code, and to such other civil and administrative actions as may be provided for in CPA, Orders, Regulations and Memoranda, and in Iraqi laws and regulations.

4) A member of an Illegal Armed Force or Militia may not hold political office at any level. An individual determined to have been a member of an Illegal Armed Force or Militia shall be barred from holding political office at any level for a period of three years from the date such individual ceased to be a member of an Illegal Armed Force or Militia.

5) The penalties specified herein, to include the amendment to the Penal Code, shall apply only to Illegal Armed Forces and Militias and to those who commit criminal offenses after the date this Order is published in the Official Gazette.

6) Any political party, and the leaders of any political party, that controls, supports or is associated with an Illegal Armed Force or Militia shall be subject to penalties in accordance with Iraqi electoral law.

Section 7 Existing Law

Any laws or regulations inconsistent with the provisions of this Order are hereby suspended to the extent they are inconsistent with the provisions of this Order. Nothing in this Order shall affect the rights or obligations of the Multinational Force under United Nations Security Council Resolution 1511, including the right to take measures in relation to Residual Elements or Illegal Armed Forces or Militias necessary to contribute to the maintenance of security and stability in Iraq.

Section 8 Administrative Instructions

Ministers and head of agencies may issue administrative instructions, not inconsistent with Iraqi law or any CPA Order, Regulation, or Memorandum, as they deem necessary to carry out the duties for their respective ministries and agencies described in this Order.

Section 9 Entry into Force and Effective Dates

This Order shall enter into force on the date of signature [7 June 2004].[273]

[273] On 5 June 2004, the CPA issued a press release headed 'Armed Forces and Militia Agreement Announced' which reads: 'The Coalition Provisional Authority announced today the successful completion of negotiations on the nationwide transition and reintegration of militias and other armed forces previously outside of state control. As a result of this achievement, the vast majority of such forces in Iraq – about 100,000 armed individuals – will enter either civilian life or one of the state security services, such as the Iraqi Armed Forces, the Iraqi Police Service, or the Internal Security Services of the Kurdish Regional Government.

This agreement includes all individuals that have borne arms on behalf of nine major political parties – Kurdistan Democratic Party (KDP), Patriotic Union of Kurdistan (PUK), Iraqi Islamic Party, Supreme Counsel of the Islamic Revolution in Iraqi/Badr Organization, Iraqi National Accord (INA), Iraqi National Congress (INC), Iraqi Hezbollah, Iraqi Communist Party, and Da'wa. All of these parties have accepted detailed plans, timetables and terms for the complete transition and reintegration of the armed groups under their authority.

While recent news has associated the term 'militia' with the sort of violence orchestrated by Muqtada Al Sadr, in fact most of these groups and individuals were part of the resistance against Saddam Hussein's regime. To reward these former resistance fighters for their service, opportunities have been created for them to join state security services or lay down their arms and enter civilian life. Those who choose to enter official security forces will be able to safeguard their communities and their country, and good use will be made of their skill in building Iraqi security forces and meeting Iraq's new security challenges. Those who choose to return to civilian life will receive valuable job training and other benefits.

With these negotiations done, CPA is releasing Order 91, which activates the Transitional Administrative Law's ban on militias and other armed forces outside of state authority except as provided by federal law. CPA Order 91 provides for the orderly, timely, and complete transition and reintegration of the armed groups controlled by the participating parties. According to agreed plans, about 90-percent of the 100,000 individuals affected will have joined state security forces or entered civilian life by the time of Iraq's first elections, and the remainder will do so within a few months thereafter.

The forces of the parties that accept this process will begin transition and reintegration promptly; indeed some have already done so. Those awaiting transition or reintegration will be designated 'Residual Elements,' to be registered, monitored, and regulated by the state. A small percentage will be transformed into Private Security Companies under strict regulation of the Ministry of Interior. As of now, all armed forces outside of state control, as provided by Order 91, are illegal. Those that have chosen violence and lawlessness over transition and reintegration will be dealt with harshly.

The completion of these negotiations and the issuance of Order 91 mark a watershed in establishing the rule of law, placing all armed forces under state control, and strengthening the security of Iraq. The CPA applauds those

Annex A: Armed Forces in Compliance
The Armed Forces of the following parties are in compliance with this order.

- Kurdistan Democratic Party
- Patriotic Union of Kurdistan.

Annex B: Militias in Compliance
The following Militias, or Militias of the following parties, are in compliance with this order.

- Badr Organization
- Da'awa
- Iraqi Communist Party
- Iraqi Hezballah
- Iraqi Islamic Party
- Iraqi National Accord
- Iraqi National Congress

Document 116
Coalition Provisional Authority Order Number 92
CPA/ORD/31 May 2004/92

The Independent Electoral Commission of Iraq

Pursuant to my authority as Administrator of the Coalition Provisional Authority (CPA), and under the laws and usages of war, and consistent with relevant U.N. Security Council resolutions, including Resolution 1483 (2003), and Resolution 1511 (2003),

Reaffirming the right of the Iraqi people, as recognized in Resolutions 1483 and 1511, to freely determine their own political future,

Noting that the Law of Administration for the State of Iraq for the Transitional Period (the 'TAL')[274] provides for the Iraqi people to choose their government through genuine and credible elections to be held no later than 31 January 2005,

Determined to achieve the transitional goals of the TAL, including the drafting and ratification of a permanent constitution, and the establishment of an elected government under that constitution,

Underscoring the need for international cooperation to achieve these goals and the essential role to be played by the United Nations and other internationally recognized experts in electoral administration,

Committed to establishing an impartial and internationally recognized body of Iraqi professionals and expert advisors to coordinate and oversee genuine and credible elections in Iraq,

parties that have worked so openly and closely to get Iraq to this important point and calls on them to continue this cooperation during implementation. The coalition is pleased that this result has been achieved at the very moment the Iraqi Interim Government is formed, thus giving that government and the Iraqi people a clearer path to a secure future.' The CPA also published a fact sheet 'Armed Forces and Militia Transition and Reintegration'.

[274] See *Doc 511*.

Having consulted extensively with the Iraqi Governing Council and representatives of the United Nations,

I hereby promulgate the following:

Section 1 Purpose

This Order establishes the Independent Electoral Commission of Iraq (the 'Commission') and empowers the Commission to organize, oversee, conduct, and implement all elections set forth in the TAL. The Commission is structured to ensure complete independence from political influence and to benefit from close consultation with international entities, such as the United Nations, that have impartially and effectively administered genuine and credible elections in nations emerging from periods of tyranny, conflict, and violent strife.

Section 2 Definitions

For purposes of this Order, the following definitions shall apply. Words importing the singular include and apply to several persons, parties, or things; words importing the plural include the singular; and words importing the masculine gender include the feminine:

1) 'Transfer of Authority' means the formal transfer of governmental authority from the Coalition Provisional Authority to the Iraqi Interim Government.

2) 'Transitional Period' means the period commencing with the Transfer of Authority and lasting until the formation of an elected Iraqi government pursuant to a permanent constitution.

3) 'Iraqi Interim Government' means the government that will assume governmental authority on 30 June 2004 and retain such authority until the formation of the Iraqi Transitional Government.

4) 'Iraqi Transitional Government' means the government that is to be established after nationwide elections occurring no later than 31 January 2005.

5) 'Elections Law' means the law that will govern elections during the transitional period.

6) 'Political Parties Law' means the law that will govern the recognition of political entities in Iraq during the Transitional Period.

7) 'Council of Judges' means the independent body of judges and other impartial officers that was re-established in CPA Order No. 35.[275]

8) 'Higher Juridical Council' means the independent body that will assume the role of the Council of Judges upon the Transfer of Authority, as set forth in Article 45 of the TAL.

9) 'Disqualifying Crime' means a crime committed with intent to cause bodily harm to an individual or group of individuals.

Section 3 Establishment of the Commission

1) The Independent Electoral Commission of Iraq is hereby established as an independent and autonomous, non-partisan, neutral and professional government office that shall have authority to promulgate, implement, and enforce regulations, rules and procedures with the full force of law in connection with elections during the Transitional Period. It is independent of the executive, legislative and judicial branches of government, and it shall be the exclusive electoral authority throughout Iraq during the Transitional Period. The Commission shall be made up of the Board of Commissioners (the 'Board') and the Electoral Administration.

[275] See *Doc 56*.

2) The principal duty of the Commission is to ensure the successful administration of elections in accordance with the TAL. To that end, the Commission is empowered to take all necessary measures consistent with Chapter Two of the TAL to oversee and administer genuine and credible elections throughout Iraq. The Commission will benefit from the experience of international electoral experts, including, especially, the United Nations.

3) The Commission shall have the following principal functions, in addition to any other function the Board finds appropriate for carrying out the Commission's electoral functions:

a) Determine, establish, develop, certify, subdivide, and maintain the voter roll;
b) Help build societal support for and confidence in the electoral process throughout Iraq;
c) Regulate and conduct the registration and certification of political parties;
d) Regulate and conduct the registration and certification of candidates for office;
e) Accredit election observers and other officers engaged in monitoring and/or observing elections in Iraq;
f) Manage the polling and ballot tabulation activities;
g) Adjudicate electoral grievances and disputes; and
h) Certify election results.

Section 4 The Board of Commissioners

A Board of Commissioners ('Board') shall head the Commission. The Board shall have the exclusive authority to promulgate, implement, and enforce regulations, rules, procedures and decisions, and take any other action consistent with Chapter Two of the TAL to ensure the successful organization, planning, implementation and oversight of nationwide and local elections throughout Iraq. The Board shall act strictly within its mandate under this Order and shall not attempt to regulate or exert influence over activities that are not fairly related to the administration of elections during the Transitional Period.

Section 5 Board of Commissioners Organization

1) The Board shall consist of nine members, including seven voting members who shall be Iraqi citizens, and two non-voting members. The two non-voting members shall be the Chief Electoral Officer ('CEO') as described in Section 6(2) of this Order and an international electoral expert to be chosen by the United Nations. The Board's seven voting members shall serve until a new Commission is formed after the end of the Transitional Period, or until three months after the certification of the first election conducted under a permanent constitution, whichever is shorter. Board decisions shall, wherever possible, be taken on consensus. Where consensus cannot be reached, a simple majority of the voting members present – provided that a quorum is present – shall prevail unless this Order stipulates otherwise.

2) Iraqi nationals and Iraqi organizations may propose nominees for the Board's seven voting members to the United Nations. Drawing from these nominations, the United Nations will create a list of qualified candidates and present it to the Governing Council, which will rank candidates from the list for appointment by the Administrator. Thereafter, the Administrator shall appoint the Board's seven voting members. The Secretary General of the United Nations shall appoint the international electoral expert to serve as a non-voting member of the Board.

3) All voting members of the Board shall be Iraqi citizens and shall be chosen based on their reputation for impartiality, integrity, rectitude, professionalism and good judgment and

must meet the criteria in Article 31(B) of the TAL. Persons who will be deemed an Iraqi citizen pursuant to Article 11 of the TAL, or who will be entitled to reclaim Iraqi citizenship pursuant to Article 11 of the TAL, shall fulfill the citizenship requirement for Board membership. Preferred qualifications for Board membership include demonstrated skills in administration, justice, education, commerce, social advocacy, and other forms of civil leadership.

4) The seven voting Board members and the CEO shall receive compensation equivalent to the Head of a Ministry and no Board member shall hold paid employment while serving out his or her term, except as permitted by regulations to be promulgated by the Board. In addition, no Board member may hold or run for public office in any capacity with any government agency at any government level while serving out his or her term.

5) Each Board member shall take an oath of office pledging to perform the duties of the office in an independent, non-partisan, neutral and professional manner. The actions of Board members shall be governed by this oath, as well as by rules of ethics to be developed by the Board shortly after its formation. If a Board member is convicted of a Disqualifying Crime, that member can be removed from office by a two-thirds majority vote of the Board. If a Board member knowingly violates the Board's rules of ethics, or suffers permanent incapacitation, that member can be removed from office by a two-thirds majority vote of the disinterested members of the Board, provided that this vote is accompanied by the assent of the Board's international electoral expert.

6) In the event of a vacancy before the Transfer of Authority by reason of death, resignation, or removal of any Board member, a new Board member will be appointed pursuant to the procedure in Section 5(2) above. Should such a vacancy arise after the Transfer of Authority but before the election of a National Assembly pursuant to the TAL, the United Nations will present a list of not less than three qualified candidates to the Iraqi head of government, who will appoint a new Board member. Should such a vacancy arise upon or after the election of a National Assembly pursuant to the TAL, the United Nations will present a list of not less than three qualified candidates to the President of the National Assembly, who will appoint a new Board member.

7) As the first point of order at the Board's inaugural meeting, the Board shall select a President and Vice President from among its voting members. The President shall manage the Board's regulatory activities and policy discussions; regularly schedule, convene and chair all Board meetings, including any meeting requested by at least four members of the Board; and report on electoral progress to other branches of the Iraqi government, the Iraqi people, and the international community. When the President is unavailable, the Vice President shall assume these duties.

8) The Board shall begin hiring staff to service its responsibilities immediately after selection of the President and Vice President. Staffing needs shall be evaluated and completed with the assistance of the United Nations and other appropriate organizations. The Board shall appoint a Secretariat to provide such services as recordkeeping, legal research, secretarial services, and other responsibilities specific to the business of the Board.

9) The Iraqi government shall ensure that the Commission receives all of the resources necessary for administering elections throughout the Transitional Period. Notwithstanding the foregoing, the Commission may seek to enlist the international community for appropriate assistance in this regard, including the direct provision of additional funds or resources. All Commission resources shall be solely managed and obligated by the Commission. The CEO shall be responsible for the accounting of these resources.

Section 6 Electoral Administration

1) The Commission shall have an Electoral Administration headed by the CEO and made up of the National Office and Electoral Offices, which shall be established in the governorates and the regions. The Electoral Administration shall answer to the Board and shall be in charge of administering the Board's regulations, rules, procedures, and decisions at the local and regional level throughout Iraq. The structure and precise role of the National Office and the Electoral Offices shall be defined by the Board pursuant to regulations that shall issue promptly after the selection of the Board President and Vice President.

2) The CEO, under direction of and subject to oversight by the Board, shall organize the Electoral Administration, including the National Office and the Electoral Offices throughout the country.

a) Iraqi nationals and Iraqi organizations may propose nominees for the CEO to the United Nations. Drawing from these nominations, the United Nations will create a list of qualified candidates and present it to the Governing Council, which will rank the candidates prior to submission to the Administrator, who shall appoint one of the qualified candidates as the CEO.

b) The CEO shall be an ex-officio non-voting member of the Board and shall serve as the Commission's principal administration and operations officer. The CEO shall provide the link between the Board and the Electoral Administration at the local and regional level throughout Iraq.

c) If the CEO is found to have violated the rules of ethics developed by the Board, is convicted of a Disqualifying Crime, suffers permanent incapacitation or is determined to be unfit to serve, the CEO may be removed from the position by a two-thirds majority vote of the Board.

d) In the event of a vacancy by reason of death, resignation, or removal of the CEO before the Transitional Period, a new CEO will be appointed pursuant to the procedure in paragraph (a) above. In the event of a vacancy by reason of death, resignation, or removal of the CEO during or after the Transitional Period, the United Nations will present a list of qualified candidates to the Board, which shall select one candidate by a majority vote for appointment as the new CEO.

3) The Electoral Administration is wholly subordinate to the Board but separate from the Board's staff and Secretariat established in Section 5(8) of this Order. Accordingly, the CEO shall ensure that the Electoral Administration is staffed with all appropriate resources and personnel at the local and regional levels as soon as practicable after the selection of the President and Vice President.

Section 7 Dispute Resolution

1) The Board has exclusive jurisdiction with respect to the civil enforcement of its own procedures and regulations. The Board may refer a criminal case to appropriate authorities if it finds evidence of criminal misconduct relating to the integrity of the electoral process.

2) Except as provided herein, and in Section 7(3) of this Order, the Board has exclusive jurisdiction to resolve disputes arising out of the preparation for and execution of national, regional and governorate elections throughout the Transitional Period. The Board shall promulgate necessary procedures for resolving such disputes, including procedures for filing a claim and conducting expedited factual inquiries, and may delegate jurisdiction to resolve disputes in the first instance to the Electoral Administration.

3) Decisions of the Board may be appealed only to a Transitional Electoral Panel (the 'Panel') composed of three judges appointed by the Higher Juridical Council. Panel judges are not members of the Commission for the purpose of Article 51 of the TAL and are not required to sit exclusively on the Panel. Any work associated with the panel, however, must take priority over all other matters.

4) Appellate review shall only be permissible for final decisions of the Board, and no Board decision may be overturned unless the Panel determines that the decision was arbitrary, capricious, in excess of jurisdiction, or rendered in bad faith. Administrative and interlocutory decisions may not be appealed. Decisions by the Board are binding until overturned by the Panel. An appeal of any final decision must be submitted by an individual or entity directly implicated in the decision within two days of the publication of the decision. Such appeals may be submitted to the National Office or any Electoral Office.

5) Within two days of submission of any appeal, the Panel must determine if the appeal satisfies the jurisdiction and standing requirements set forth in this Section 7(4).

6) If the Panel determines that the appeal has adequate jurisdiction and standing, such appeal must be decided within ten days of that determination. All decisions of the Panel shall be final and not subject to review by any other authority, including a judicial authority. If an appeal is not decided by that deadline, the decision of the Board will continue in force and may not be overturned.

7) Upon its formation, the Panel shall establish general procedures consistent with this Order for resolving appeals. Such procedures must be submitted to the Board for review and approval.

Section 8 Effective Date
This Regulation [sic] shall enter into force on the date of signature [31 May 2004].

Document 117
Coalition Provisional Authority Order Number 93
CPA/ORD/2 June 2004/93

Anti-Money Laundering Act of 2004

Pursuant to my authority as Administrator of the Coalition Provisional Authority (CPA), and under the laws and usages of war, and consistent with relevant U.N. Security Council resolutions, including Resolution 1483 and 1511 (2003),

Having worked closely with the Governing Council to ensure that economic change occurs in a manner acceptable to the people of Iraq,

Acknowledging the Governing Council's desire to bring about significant change to the Iraqi economic system,

Determined to improve the conditions of life for the Iraqi people by combating terrorism, financial crime, and fraud,

Realizing that effective deterrence and policing of terrorism, financial crime and fraud requires rigorous controls aimed at the heard of these illegal activities,

Recognizing the need for an effective legal framework regulating financial transactions,

Further recognizing the need to ensure the well-being of the Iraqi people and to enable the social functions and normal transactions of everyday life,

I hereby promulgate the following:

Section 1 Purpose

The purpose of the Anti-Money Laundering Law is to secure financial institutions and combat instability by criminalizing the acts of laundering money, financing crime, financing terrorism, and structuring certain transactions.

Section 2 Anti-Money Laundering Law

The Anti-Money Laundering Law attached to this Order as Annex A shall have the full force and effect of law.

Section 3 Inconsistent Legislation

Any provision of Iraqi law issued prior to the date of this Order that is inconsistent with this Order or Annex A is hereby suspended to the extent of such inconsistency.

Section 4 Entry into Force

This Order shall enter into force on the date of signature [3 June 2004].

ANNEX A

Iraq
Anti-Money Laundering Law of 2004

Section 1: General Provisions

Article 1: Declaration of Purpose
This Anti-Money Laundering Law of 2004 (the 'Law') governs financial institutions in connection with: money laundering; financing crime, financing terrorism; and the vigilance required of financial institutions in regard to financial transactions. The Law also makes it a crime to launder money, finance crime, finance terrorism, and structure transactions.

Article 2: Definitions
As used in this Act, unless otherwise indicated:
1. 'Money laundering' refers to the acts described in Article 3.
2. 'Financing of crime' refers to the acts described in Article 4.1.
3. 'Terrorist financing' refers to the acts described in Article 4.2.
4. 'Structure a transaction' means to conduct or attempt to conduct a financial transaction with the intent to avoid a reporting requirement under this law or established pursuant to the provisions of Article 20 or 21.
5. 'Financial institution' shall include the following:
    a. banks;
    b. the managers of investment funds;
    c. insurance institutions, if they carry on direct life assurance business or offer or distribute shares in investment funds;
    d. persons who trade in securities;
    e. money transmitters, direct and indirect, and formal and informal, including persons who provide services related to payments, including but not limited to electronic transfers on behalf of third parties, and persons who issue or manage means of payment, such as credit cards and travelers checks, or persons who undertake hawala transactions;
    f. foreign currency exchange houses, or any other entity that effects foreign exchange transactions on a regular basis above 15 million Iraqi dinar per week.
6. 'Financial institution' shall also refer to persons who, on a professional basis, accept, keep on deposit, invest or transfer, or assist in the investment or transfer, of financial assets belonging to others. Such persons shall include, but not be limited to, those who:
    a. undertake credit transactions (including consumer credit or mortgages, factoring, financing of commercial transactions or financial leasing);
    b. trade, on their own account or for others, in bank notes or cash, money market instruments, currency, precious metals, raw materials for use in production of

c. [sic] other items, commodities, or securities (bearer or other), and derivatives of any such tradable items;
d. offer or distribute shares in funds, in the capacity of distributor of a domestic or foreign investment fund, or in the capacity of representative of a foreign investment fund;
e. undertake asset management;
f. make investments as investment adviser;
g. keep or manage securities; and
h. deal in precious metals, stones, or jewels.

The CBI may, by regulation, determine that the definition of financial institution applies only to entities above a specified size and designate other persons who shall also be considered financial institutions for purposes of this Act.

7. 'Person' means a natural person or a juridical person.
8. 'Customer' means a person to whom a financial institution provides a product or service, and includes a person who either holds or opens an account, as well as a person who receives a product or service from a financial institution that does not involve an account, such as cashing a check, sending a wire transfer, or selling a check or money order.
9. 'Suspicious transaction' refers to a transaction, including but not limited to the opening of an account, if the financial institution knows, suspects, or has reason to suspect that:
   a. the transaction involves funds derived from illegal activities or money laundering or the transaction is intended or conducted in order to evade any law or regulation or to avoid any transaction reporting requirement under any law or regulation, including but not limited to the requirements of Article 20 of this Act;
   b. the transaction involves funds intended for financing of crime, including, but not limited to, terrorism;
   c. the transaction involves funds or assets over which a criminal organization has power of disposal;
   d. the transaction is designed to evade any requirements of this Law or any regulations or orders issued under the authority of this Act; or
   e. the transaction has no apparent business or other lawful purpose or is not the sort in which the particular customer would normally be expected to engage, and the bank knows of no reasonable explanation for the transaction after examining the available facts, including the background and possible purpose of the transaction.
10. 'Insurance institution' refers to an institution that underwrites or brokers insurance, or otherwise participates in the provision of insurance policies to any person.
11. 'Insurance' refers to an agreement that requires one party to indemnify another against loss in return for premiums paid, whether or not the agreement also regards an investment by the insured related to but in addition to the indemnification specified.
12. 'CBI' refers to the Central Bank of Iraq.
13. 'Reporting Office' and 'MLRO' refer to the Money Laundering Reporting Office.
14. 'Beneficial owner' means a person, whether or not named as the owner, who can effectively manage or direct the use of the funds in an account.
15. 'Non-public', for the purpose of Article 14, means information or documents disclosed to or gathered by a body of the Government of Iraq, which information or documents is or are not commonly available or widely known in the public.
16. 'Monetary instrument' means both Iraqi and foreign currency, bank notes, checks, promissory notes or other evidence of indebtedness, loans, traveler's checks, wire transfers, all negotiable instruments in such form that title passes upon delivery, all

incomplete instruments signed but with the payee's name omitted, and securities or stock in bearer form or otherwise in such form that title passes upon delivery and any other items that the CBI may deem appropriate.

17. '1267 Committee' means the United Nations Security Council Committee established pursuant to paragraph 6 of United Nations Security Council Resolution 1267 (1999), which oversees the implementation by States of the sanctions imposed by the Security Council on individuals and entities belonging or related to the Taliban, Usama Bin Laden and the Al-Qaida organization and maintains a list of individuals and entities for this purpose.
18. 'Former Iraqi Regime' means the Saddam Hussein regime that governed Iraq until on or about April 9, 2003.
19. 'Development Fund for Iraq' means the fund established on or about May 21, 2003 on the books of the Central Bank of Iraq and all accounts held for the fund or for the Central Bank of Iraq in the name of the fund.
20. 'Iraqi person' means any Iraqi citizen or any juridical person organized under the laws of Iraq.
21. 'Foreign person' means a natural or juridical person that is not an Iraqi person.
22. 'Other senior official' means an individual who had a position in a ministry, armed forces, governmental entity or semi-governmental entity during the time that the former regime was in power at the minister level or director general of a ministry level or the rank of at least brigadier general, or equivalent civilian or military position, and who was a full member of the Ba'ath Party holding the rank of 'Udw Qutriyya (Regional Command Member), 'Udw Far' (Branch Member), 'Udw Shu'bah (Section Member), or 'Udw Firqah (Group Member).
23. 'Immediate family member' means spouse, father, mother, brother, sister, son, or daughter

Section 2: Penalties

Article 3: Money Laundering

Whoever conducts or attempts to conduct a financial transaction that involves the proceeds of some form of unlawful activity knowing that the property involved is the proceeds of some form of unlawful activity, or

Whoever transports, transmits, or transfers a monetary instrument or funds that represent the proceeds of some form of unlawful activity knowing that the monetary instrument or funds represent the proceeds of some form of unlawful activity–

(a) With the intent to promote the carrying on of unlawful activity, to benefit from unlawful activity, or to protect from prosecution those who have engaged in unlawful activity; and

(b) Knowing that the transaction is designed in whole or in part–

(i) to conceal or disguise the nature, location, source, ownership, or control of the proceeds of unlawful activity; or

(ii) to avoid a transaction or other reporting requirement,

Shall be sentenced to a fine of not more than 40 million Iraqi dinar, or twice the value of the property involved in the transaction, whichever is greater, or imprisonment for not more than 4 years, or both.

Article 4: Financing of Crime and Terrorist Financing

1. **Financing of Crime** Whoever provides property, or conceals or disguises the nature, location, source, or ownership of property, knowing or intending that such property is to be used in preparation for, or in carrying out, a violation of law, or in preparation for, or in carrying out, the concealment of an escape from the commission of any such violation, or attempts or conspires to do such an act, shall be fined not more than 20 million Iraqi dinar, or imprisoned for not more than 2 years, or both.
2. **Terrorist Financing** Whoever provides, or invites another person to provide, property, support, or financial or other related services intending that it be used, or knowing that it will likely be used, in whole or in part, to carry out
   a. An act or omission that provides a benefit to a terrorist group, or
   b. Any other act or omission intended to cause death or serious bodily harm to a civilian or any other person not taking an active part in the hostilities in a situation of armed conflict, if the purpose of the act or omission is to intimidate the public or to compel a government or an international organization to do or refrain from doing any act, shall be fined not more than 20 million Iraqi dinar, or imprisoned for not more than 2 years, or both.
3. 'Property' for purposes of this Article includes but is not limited to currency, monetary instruments, and financial securities.

Article 5: Structuring transactions

Whoever–

a. causes or attempts to cause a financial institution, as that term is used for purposes of that Act, to fail to file a report required under Article 20; or
b. structures or assists in structuring, or attempts to structure or assist in structuring, any transaction with one or more financial institutions,

shall be fined not more than 10 million Iraqi dinar or imprisoned for not more than 1 year, or both.

Article 6: Property forfeiture

1. **Criminal Finance** Any court, in imposing sentence on a person convicted of an offense in violation of Articles 3, 4, 5, Article 19.4, or Article 20.5 of this Act, if the violation was committed intending to, or knowing that the likely result would be to, aid another person in the commission of a crime, or aid another person in the evasion of prosecution for a crime already committed, shall order the person to be sentenced to forfeit to the Government of Iraq any property, real or personal, including but not limited to funds, involved in the offense, or any property traceable to the property, or any property gained as a result of the offense, without prejudicing the rights of bona fide third parties.
2. **Blocked Property**
   a. Funds or other financial assets or economic resources (excluding real property, a claim for which falls within the jurisdiction of the Iraqi Property Claims Commission pursuant to CPA Regulation Number 8)[276] that have been either removed from Iraq, or acquired, by Saddam Hussein or other senior officials of the former Iraqi regime and their immediate family members, including entities owned or controlled, directly

[276] See *Doc 8*.

or indirectly, by them or by persons acting on their behalf ('Ba'ath Party persons') or at their direction that are within or hereafter come within Iraq, are blocked. Property that is blocked may not be transferred, paid, exported, withdrawn, or otherwise dealt in. The Minister of Finance, with the approval of the Council of Ministers, is authorized to confiscate property that is blocked pursuant to this Article 6.2 subject to a prior judicial, administrative, or arbitral lien or judgment issued by a court of competent jurisdiction, and subject to such rights of appeal as may be provided by law. All right, title, and interest in such confiscated blocked property shall promptly be transferred to the Development Fund for Iraq (DFI) or the successor to the DFI, if any. Should there be no successor to the DFI, such confiscated blocked property shall be transferred to the Ministry of Finance. Upon transfer to the DFI, its successor, or the Ministry of Finance (as appropriate), such confiscated blocked property shall be unblocked. Any transaction by an Iraqi or foreign person within Iraq that evades or avoids, has the purpose of evading or avoiding, or attempts to violate any of the prohibitions of this Article 6.2 is prohibited and shall constitute a money laundering violation under Article 3 of this Law. A person whose property is blocked pursuant to this Article 6.2 may appeal the action taken to the Financial Services Tribunal under Section 12 of the Central Bank of Iraq law.

b. For purposes of this Article, a person is considered to be 'acting on behalf of' another to the extent that the person is authorized by formal or informal contract to take significant actions for the other or, whether there is an agreement or not, the person takes significant actions for the benefit of the other as if they were the agent of the other. This Article 6.2 applies to funds, financial assets, or other economic resources that between July 17, 1968 and April 16, 2003 were: (i) confiscated, seized, or expropriated by the Ba'athist Government of Iraq or Ba'ath Party persons for reasons other than legitimate governmental purposes such as taxation, customs, anti-narcotics activities or enforcement of criminal penalties; or (ii) expropriated as a result of opposition to the Ba'athist Government of Iraq, or as a result of ethnicity, religion, sect of the owners, or for purposes of ethnic cleansing. Property owned by the Government of Iraq and/or occupied by acting government ministers or other acting government officials pursuant to a transaction that is lawful and has a legitimate governmental purpose (including reasonable compensation of governmental officials) shall not be subject to this Article 6.2.

Section 3: Supervision

Article 7: Duties

1. With respect to this Act, the Central Bank of Iraq (the 'CBI') shall perform the following duties:
   a. The CBI shall supervise compliance of financial institutions with their obligations under Section 5.
   b. The CBI shall inform the financial institutions it supervises of their obligations under Section 5, and may issue regulations directing how they must comply The regulations shall require all financial institutions to establish internal policies, procedures, and controls adequate for the institutions' businesses, and adequate employee training programs, and shall require banks and those other financial institutions that the CBI designates, to designate a compliance officer and an independent audit function to test the institution's AML program.

c. The CBI shall issue and periodically update a list of financial activities which may constitute 'suspicious transactions' for the purposes of this Act, including money laundering, financing crime, financing terrorism, transactions involving funds over which a criminal organization has a right of disposal, or transactions designed to evade reporting, recording, or other legal requirements. The CBI shall publish the list for the benefit of financial institutions.
d. The CBI shall have the authority to delegate its supervisory powers to other supervisory authorities set up by other Acts, in which case the CBI shall supervise the activities of those authorities, while retaining the authority, in the CBI's sole discretion, to act regarding any financial institution's obligations under Section 5. Any such authorities shall ensure that regulatory provisions applicable in their respective fields are substantively equivalent.
e. The CBI shall either perform on-site examinations of financial institutions for which it has direct responsibility, or, in the alternative, instruct an auditing body that the CBI designates to perform examinations and forward any reports of such examinations directly to the CBI.
f. The CBI shall compile and provide to financial institutions a list of individuals and institutions whose transactions the financial institutions are to report to the relevant body of the Government of Iraq upon discovery. The list shall include, but not be limited to, the New Consolidated List of Individuals and Entities Belonging to or Associated with the Taliban and Al-Qaida Organization as Established and Maintained by the 1267 Committee.

2. The CBI is authorized to create offices to execute any of its responsibilities as designated in this Act, and to promulgate regulations governing the manner in which those responsibilities are executed.

Article 8: Right to Information

The CBI is authorized to require financial institutions it supervises and the institutions' auditing bodies to provide to the CBI all information and documents needed for the performance of the CBI's duties.

Article 9: Regulatory Enforcement

1. If the CBI determines that a financial institution it supervises has violated this Law it may take appropriate enforcement measures. In particular, the CBI may:
   a. issue an order to cease the activity resulting in the violation;
   b. assess a monetary penalty under the provisions of the Central Bank of Iraq Law to the violating institution, or any person engaged in or participating in activity violating this Act;
   c. publish the results of any enforcement action, including the name(s) of any persons involved;
   d. issue an order that a person found to have violated this Law or participated in a violation of this Law shall not be permitted to be involved in the affairs of a financial institution either permanently or temporarily;
   e. withdraw authorization to act as financial institutions, if the institutions themselves or persons responsible for administering or managing their business are found to have seriously or repeatedly violated their obligations under this Act.

2. A person subject to an enforcement measure described in Article 9.1 may appeal the action taken to the Financial Services Tribunal under Section 12 of the Central Bank of Iraq law.

Article 10: Other powers
The CBI shall retain all other powers granted it under other Acts.

Article 11: Funding
The CBI may require payment or reimbursement from a financial institution it supervises for the cost of the CBI's supervisory activity under this Law (including the cost of legal, accounting, and auditing fees).

Article 12: Money Laundering Reporting Office

1. The CBI shall establish the Money Laundering Reporting Office, which shall be administratively subordinate to the CBI but shall retain operational independence. The Reporting Office shall:
    a. collect, process, analyze, and disseminate information on financial transactions subject to financial monitoring and reporting;
    b. participate in implementing Iraqi policy on preventing money laundering, financing of crime, and financing of terrorism;
    c. cooperate and interact with and exchange information with Iraqi state authorities, competent bodies of other countries and international organizations on money laundering, financing of crime, and financing of terrorism;
    d. represent Iraq, according to the established procedure, in international organizations dealing with preventing money laundering, financing of crime, and financing of terrorism.
2. The Reporting Office shall be staffed and funded separately from the CBI, but shall be administratively subordinate to the Governor of the CBI.
3. The Reporting Office shall verify information reported to it, and shall take such steps, and shall have the authority to take such steps, including but not limited to the promulgation of regulations by the CBI as are necessary in order to fulfill its duties under this Act.
4. If the MLRO reasonably suspects that a transaction, conducted or attempted, involves funds derived from illegal activities, money laundering, funds to be used in the financing of crime, funds that a criminal organization has a right of disposal over, terrorist financing, or that the transaction is otherwise in furtherance of an illegal purpose, it shall immediately notify the competent prosecuting and investigative authority.
5. The Reporting Office shall respond to any inquiry by a financial institution under Article 18 paragraph 2, within one week of the inquiry, by providing guidance to that institution as to how that institution should proceed. Guidance may include: informing the competent prosecutor's office, performing further research on the issues causing the financial institution's concern, filing a formal report of a suspicious transaction with the MLRO, or taking no action other than completing the transaction as requested by the customer. The guidance shall be binding upon the financial institution and all other affected parties.
6. No officer or employee of the CBI who learns of a suspicious transaction that has been reported may disclose to any person involved in the transaction that the transaction has been reported, other than as necessary to fulfill the official duties of the officer or employee.

Section 4: Mutual Administrative Assistance

Article 13: In General

1. The CBI and the Money Laundering Reporting Office may, in the CBI's discretion, provide information and documents to Iraqi governmental ministries, authorities, and agencies concerning matters governed by this Law and may request from Iraqi governmental ministries, authorities and agencies any information and documents the CBI believes may be useful or necessary to carry out the CBI's and MLRO's responsibilities under this Act.
2. The prosecuting authorities shall notify the Reporting Office of all pending procedures relevant to this Law and of judgments and cases dismissed.
3. The Reporting Office shall inform the CBI of decisions by prosecuting authorities.

Article 14: Central Bank of Iraq and Money Laundering Reporting Office

The CBI and the Reporting Office may request foreign authorities responsible for supervision of financial institutions or markets, foreign financial intelligence units, or criminal or judicial prosecution authorities, to provide them with information and documents required for the performance of their duties. The CBI and the Reporting Office may share with such foreign authorities as are prepared to provide reciprocal services to the CBI and Reporting Office, information and documents, including nonpublic information and documents, within their discretion, related to or gathered pursuant to this Act, for the purpose of preventing money laundering or the commission of crime, including but not limited to terrorist financing.

Section 5: Obligations of Financial Institutions

Article 15: Verification of the Identity of the Customer

1. Upon opening an account for a customer for any amount, or performing a transaction or series of potentially related transactions whose value is equal to or greater than 5 million Iraqi dinars for a non account holder, whether an individual or legal person, the financial institution involved should obtain and record the customer's: legal name and any other names used; correct permanent address including the full street address; telephone number, fax number, and e-mail address; date and place of birth; for a legal person, charter or other establishing document; nationality; occupation, public position held and/or name of employer; an official personal identification number or other unique identifier contained in an unexpired official document (e.g. passport, identification card, residence permit, driving license) that bears a photograph of the individual customer; type of account and nature of the banking relationship; and signature. The financial institution may determine the extent it uses these measures on a risk sensitive basis depending on the type of customer, business relationship or transaction, but shall verify all information collected.
2. Where a financial institution is performing a transaction for a non account holder and the total value of the transaction or series of possibly related transactions is less than 5 million Iraqi dinars, the financial institution need only collect and verify the customer's name and address.
3. A financial institution that has reason to know of a suspicious transaction must collect the information described in paragraph 1 even if the amount involved does not exceed the threshold amount.

4. The institution shall check the name of the customer against the list compiled by the CBI under Article 7.1.b of this law of individuals and institutions designated by the CBI for reporting to the Government of Iraq, and shall immediately report any matches to the relevant government body.
5. A financial institution shall take the action required by this article in retrospect, regarding any account established prior to the effective date of this Act, unless the financial institution reasonably believes that it knows the true identity of the customer.

Article 16: Identification of the Beneficial Owner of Funds

1. The financial institution shall require the customer to provide a written declaration of the owner of funds, if:
   a. the customer is clearly not the owner or, in the opinion of the financial institution and at its discretion, the ownership of funds is subject to doubt; or
   b. a cash transaction is effected for a sum greater than 10 million Iraqi dinars.
2. The financial institution shall verify the identification information provided under this Article.

Article 17: Further Verification of Identity

1. When, in the course of conducting business, the financial institution has reason to doubt the identity of the customer or the beneficial owner of the funds, the financial institution shall take steps to further verify identity. The financial institution shall undertake such verification as is necessary in order to form a reasonable belief that it knows the true identity of its customer and/or any beneficial owner of the funds involved. The financial institution must have in place procedures, including escalation protocols, to resolve discrepancies and to decline or cease to do business with a customer when it cannot form a reasonable belief as to the customer or beneficial owner's true identity, and shall report any suspicious transactions to the Money Laundering Reporting Office.
2. If an insurance company refunds a premium or distributes or transfers a benefit, the insurance company shall verify the identification of the beneficial owner if the beneficial owner is not the person designated as beneficial owner when the contract was entered into.

Article 18: Further Verification of Purpose and Nature of Transactions

1. The financial institution shall immediately verify the source of funds, and the purpose and intended nature of a transaction or business relationship, when there is reason to suspect that assets are the proceeds of a crime, that they may be intended for the financing of crime or terrorist financing, or that a criminal organization has power of disposal over them.
2. A financial institution that has reason to know that a proposed transaction or series of transactions is/are suspicious transactions shall immediately report to and seek guidance and direction from the Money Laundering Reporting Office. Any financial institution or other person making such a report shall be entitled to the protection of Article 22 paragraph 1 of this Act.
3. If the financial institution makes full disclosure of the facts and circumstances to the Reporting Office, and follows the guidance of the Reporting Office, neither the institution nor any director, officer, employee, or agent of the financial institution, shall be liable to any person under any law or regulation of Iraq, any constitution, law, or regulation of any political subdivision of Iraq, or under any contract or other legally enforceable agreement,

including any arbitration agreement, for acting in accordance with the direction of the MLRO, or for any failure to provide notice of such action to any person involved or affected.

4. A financial institution seeking verification under paragraph 1 or making a report to the Money Laundering Reporting Office under paragraph 2 shall immediately freeze the relevant assets until the financial institution receives any necessary verification and/or any necessary guidance from the Money Laundering Reporting Office.
5. An institution acting under this Article shall not reveal to the customer, or a third party other than the Money Laundering Reporting Office or an Iraqi government office, that verification is being or has been sought for the purpose of ascertaining an illegal purpose or connection to a transaction, that guidance is being or has been sought, or that assets are or have been blocked, except that the institution shall, in response to a request by the customer to use blocked assets, explain that the assets have been blocked and refer the customer to the Reporting Office.

Article 19: Reporting Obligation

1. A financial institution that has reason to know that a suspicious transaction has occurred, whether effected by a customer or other person, where the total value of the transaction or series of potentially related transactions is equal to or greater than 4 million Iraqi dinars or, in the case of suspected structuring transactions to evade reporting requirements, regardless of the amount, shall notify the Money Laundering Reporting Office of the transaction, including all facts and circumstances. Such a report shall be made as soon as is reasonably possible, but in no case later than 14 days after the occurrence of the event causing suspicion or giving reason for suspicion. An institution making a report under this paragraph shall not reveal that fact to a customer or other third party.
2. A financial institution may report a transaction or transactions to the Money Laundering Reporting Office under this Article, if the financial institution believes that the transaction or transactions are relevant to a possible violation of any law or regulation, even if the report is not required under this Act.
3. Financial institutions shall keep separate files containing all documents related to reporting pursuant to this Article. Financial institutions shall only transmit data in such files to the CBI, the Money Laundering Reporting Office and the prosecuting authorities. Such records must be retained for at least five years after the reporting of information to the Money Laundering Reporting Office. In the event that the financial institution is thus notified by the CBI or MLRO, such records must be maintained indefinitely until otherwise directed by the CBI or MLRO.
4. A person who willfully violates the provisions of paragraph 1 shall be fined not more than 10 million Iraqi dinars, or imprisoned for not more than 1 year, or both.

Article 20: Cash Transaction Reports

1. The CBI may by regulation require each financial institution to file a report with the MLRO of each deposit, withdrawal, exchange of currency or other payment or transfer, by, through, or to such financial institution which involves a transaction in currency or other monetary instrument of more than 15 million Iraqi dinars, except as otherwise provided in this Article. In the case of suspected structuring transactions to evade reporting requirements, the financial institution shall file a report of the transaction or transactions regardless of amount involved.

2. 'Financial institution' for purposes of this Article, includes all of its domestic branch offices, and any recordkeeping facility, wherever located, that contains records relating to the transactions of the institution's domestic offices.
3. For purposes of this Article, multiple currency transactions shall be treated as a single transaction if the financial institution has knowledge that they are by or on behalf of any person and result in either cash in or cash out totaling more than 15 million Iraqi dinars during any one business day. Deposits made at night or over a weekend or holiday shall be treated as if received on the next business day following the deposit.
4. No bank is required to file a report under this Article with respect to any transaction in currency between the bank and:
   a. Another bank to the extent of the bank's domestic operations;
   b. A department or agency of the Government of Iraq, or any political subdivision of Iraq;
   c. Any entity established under the laws of Iraq or a political subdivision thereof, that exercises governmental authority on behalf of the Government of Iraq or such political subdivision; or
   d. Any other person so designated by the CBI, in the CBI's sole discretion.
5. A person who willfully violates any reporting requirement under paragraph 1 shall be fined not more than 10 million Iraqi dinars or imprisoned for not more than 1 year, or both.

Article 21: Cross-Border Currency Reporting Requirement

1. The Central Bank of Iraq is authorized to require all persons to submit a report of currency and monetary instruments with the Money Laundering Reporting Office and/or the Iraq Customs Service when transporting currency or other monetary instruments greater than 15 million Iraqi dinar from a place within Iraq to a place outside Iraq, or from a place outside Iraq to a place within Iraq.
2. A report under this article shall be filed at the time and place the MLRO prescribes. The report shall contain the following information to the extent the MLRO prescribes:
   a. the legal capacity in which the person filing the report is acting;
   b. the origin, destination, and route of the currency and/or monetary instruments;
   c. the amount and kind of monetary instruments and/or currency transported;
   d. other additional information as required.

Article 22: Obligation to Make and Retain Records

1. A financial institution shall keep the records required to be made in this Act, and shall make and retain a record of each verification exercise or inquiry to the Money Laundering Reporting Office, for five years after the closing of an account or termination of a customer relationship; information collected only for the purpose of a transaction or series of transactions shall be kept for at least five years after the last such transaction.
2. Records shall be made of all transactions above 500,000 Iraqi dinars and retained for five years after the transactions involved.
3. A wire transfer (funds transfer) shall include the name and address of the originator and beneficiary. Originator and beneficiary name and address information shall remain with the wire from origination of the wire transfer until disbursement of the proceeds to the beneficiary. Records of wire transfers shall be made and retained for five years by all financial institutions involved in the wire transfer.
4. Persons that provide a service for the transmission of money or value including through an informal money or value transfer system or network including a hawala shall retain

records of all transactions above 500,000 Iraqi dinars including, but not necessarily limited to, originator and any originator's agent, ultimate beneficiary, all intermediaries, and dates, amounts, and forms of all transactions.

5. Records required to be made and retained under this Law shall be maintained in such a manner that knowledgeable third parties are able to assess transactions and business relationships and the institution's compliance with the provisions of this Act, and that subpoenas for such records by governmental authorities may be fulfilled within a reasonable period of time, not to exceed ten business days.

Article 23: Exclusion of Liability and 'Whistleblower' Protection

1. A financial institution, or director, officer, employee, or agent of a financial institution, that reports a possible violation of law or regulation or a suspicious transaction, or information potentially relevant to such a violation, to the MLRO, or otherwise under the authority of this Act, shall not be liable under any law or regulation of Iraq, any constitution, law, or regulation of any political subdivision of Iraq, or under any contract or other legally enforceable agreement, including any arbitration agreement, for the disclosure or for any failure to provide notice of the disclosure to the person who is the subject of the disclosure or any other person identified in the disclosure.
2. No financial institution, supervisory authority, or government body may discriminate against any employee with respect to compensation, terms, conditions, or privileges of employment because the employee or any person acting pursuant to the request of the employee provided information to any supervisory authority, or government body regarding a possible violation of any provision of this Act, or any regulation promulgated thereunder, by the financial institution, supervisory authority, or government body. An aggrieved past or present employee may bring suit within 2 years of the alleged discrimination. A court may order any person who committed a violation to reinstate the employee to their former position, pay compensatory damages, or take other appropriate actions to remedy past discrimination. The protections of this paragraph shall not apply to any employee who deliberately causes or participates in the alleged violation of law or regulation, or knowingly or recklessly provides substantially false information to a supervisory authority, or government body.

Section 6: Final Provisions

Article 24: Execution

The CBI shall issue regulations as necessary for the implementation of this Law. The Law shall take effect on the date indicated in Article 26, but with a deferred implementation date of September 30, 2004, or such later date as may be specified in the regulations issued by the CBI.

Article 25: Relationship to other laws of Iraq

In case of inconsistency with a provision of any other law of Iraq, this Law shall prevail.

Article 26: Entry into Force

Subject to the provisions of Article 24, this Law shall enter into force on the same date that the Order authorizing this Law enters into force.

Document 118
Coalition Provisional Authority Order Number 94

CPA/ORD/6 June 2004/94

Banking Law of 2004

Pursuant to my authority as Administrator of the Coalition Provisional Authority (CPA), and under the laws and usages of war, and consistent with relevant U.N. Security Council resolutions, including Resolutions 1483 and 1511 (2003),

Having worked closely with the Governing Council to ensure that economic change occurs in a manner acceptable to the people of Iraq,

Acknowledging the Governing Council's desire to bring about significant change to the Iraqi economic system,

Determined to improve the conditions of life, and opportunities for all Iraqis and to fight unemployment with its associated deleterious effect on public security through stable financial markets,

Recognizing the problems arising from Iraq's legal framework regulating banking activities and the way in which it was implemented by the former regime,

Further recognizing the CPA's obligation to provide for the effective administration of Iraq, to ensure the well being of Iraqi people and to enable the social functions and normal transactions of every day life,

Further recognizing the need to revise the Bank Law promulgated by CPA Order No. 40 of 19 September 2003 (CPA/ORD/19 September 2003/40)[277] to comprehensively address issues identified since its promulgation,

Recalling that U.N. Security Council Resolution 1483 (2003) called upon the CPA to promote economic reconstruction and the conditions for sustainable development,

Acting in a manner consistent with the Report of the Secretary General to the Security Council of July 17, 2003, concerning the need for the development of Iraq and its transition from a non-transparent centrally planned economy to a market economy characterized by sustainable economic growth through the establishment of a dynamic private sector, and the need to enact institutional and legal reforms to give it effect,

Having coordinated with the international financial institutions, as referenced in paragraph 8(e) of the U.N. Security Council Resolution 1483,

I hereby promulgate the following:

Section 1 Purpose

This Order builds upon the reforms to the banking system provided by CPA Order No. 40 and Annex A thereto, and comprehensively establishes a safe, sound, competitive and accessible banking system for the purposes of providing a foundation for economic growth and the development of a stable Iraqi economy.

Section 2 Banking Law

The Banking Law of 2004 attached to this Order as Annex A shall have the full force and effect of law.

[277] See *Doc 62*.

Section 3 Inconsistent Legislation

1) CPA Order No. 40 and Annex A thereto, Bank Law (CPA/ORD/19 September 2003/40) are rescinded.

2) Any provision of Iraqi law that is inconsistent with this Order or the Banking Law of 2004 attached hereto as Annex A is hereby suspended to the extent of such inconsistency.

Section 4 Entry into Force

This Order shall enter into force on the date of signature [7 June 2004].

ANNEX A Banking Law of 2004

Section 1 – General Provisions

Article 1 Definitions

For the purposes of this Law, the following terms shall have the meanings indicated below:

'*administrator*' means, with respect to a domestic bank, any person who is a member of the board of directors, authorized manager or member of the audit committee of the bank, and, with respect to a foreign bank, a designated branch manager;[278]

'*affiliate*' means a company that controls a bank, any other company that is controlled by the company that controls the bank, and any other company as determined pursuant to criteria specified in regulation by the CBI;

'*authorized manager*' means a person responsible for the management of the day-to-day operations of the bank;

'*bank*' means a person engaged in the banking business including a state company organized under Law No. 22 of 1997 on State Companies as amended;[279]

'*bank holding company*' means a company that owns or controls a bank;

'*banking activities*' means the activities that are listed in Article 27;

'*banking business*' means the business of receiving deposits of money or other repayable funds from the public for the purpose of making credits or investments for its own account;

'*branch*' means a place of business forming a legally dependent part of a bank where all or some banking activities are conducted; for the purposes of this Law all domestic branch offices of a foreign bank shall be treated as a single branch office and all communications from the CBI to any such branch office may be validly made to the branch office designated by the foreign bank to the CBI for this purpose, or failing such notification, to a branch office selected by the CBI;

'*bridge bank*' means a bank referred to in Article 67A;[280]

'*CBI*' means the Central Bank of Iraq;

'*control*' is deemed to exist over another company if a person:

(i) directly or indirectly, or acting through one or more persons owns, controls or has the power to vote 25 percent or more of the voting shares of the company;

(ii) has the power to elect a majority of the directors of the company; or

(iii) exercises a controlling influence as the CBI may determine.

'*credit*' means any disbursement or commitment to make a disbursement of a sum of money in exchange for the right to repayment of the amount disbursed and outstanding and to payment of interest or other charges on such amount, whether secured or unsecured, any extension of the due date of a debt, any guarantee issued, and any purchase of a debt security or other right to payment of a sum of money that may provide for the payment of interest either directly or by a discounted purchase price;

'*debt security*' means any negotiable instrument of indebtedness and any other instrument equivalent to such instrument of indebtedness, and any negotiable instrument giving the right to acquire another negotiable debt security by subscription or exchange; negotiable debt securities may be in certificated or in book-entry form;

'*deposit*' means a certain sum of money paid to a person, whether or not evidenced by any entry in a record of the person receiving the sum, on terms under which the deposit will be repaid or transferred to another account, with or without interest or a premium, either on demand or at a time or in circumstances agreed to by or on behalf of the depositor and that person;

[278] The words 'with respect to a domestic bank' and 'with respect to a foreign bank' were added in 2004.

[279] The Iraqi Banking Law of 2003 had read: '"*bank*" means a person holding a license or permit under this Law to engage in banking business and other banking activities'.

[280] The Iraqi Banking Law of 2003 had read: '"*bridge bank*" means a bank organized under paragraph (6) of Article 61'.

'*designated branch manager*' means a person notified to the CBI pursuant to paragraph (1), sub-paragraph (d) of Article 6 as being responsible for the operations in Iraq of a foreign bank;

'*dinar*' means the Iraqi dinar;

'*domestic*', when applied to a juridical person, means a juridical person whose head office is located in Iraq, and when applied to an office, means an office located in Iraq;

'*dormant account*' has the meaning given in Article 37;

'*fit and proper person*' means a person who is regarded as honest and trustworthy and whose professional qualifications, background and experience, financial position, or business interests do not disqualify that person in the judgment of the CBI to be an owner, administrator, senior bank official, conservator, or receiver of a bank, provided, however, that no person shall be regarded as a fit and proper person if the person:[281]

(i) has been convicted by a criminal court of an offense for which the person was or could have been sentenced to imprisonment for a term of one year or more without the option of a fine unless such sentence was or would have been motivated by his or her religious or political views or activities;

(ii) has been declared bankrupt by a court of law within the past seven years;

(iii) has been disqualified or suspended by a competent authority from practicing a profession on grounds of personal misconduct unrelated to his or her religious or political views or activities; or

(iv) has been declared unfit to manage a company by a court of law or under an order issued by a competent agency;

'*list*' means the list of the names of banks in the register of banks published by the CBI;

'*foreign*', when applied to a juridical person or office, means a juridical person or office that is not a domestic juridical person or office;

'*person*' means a natural person or a juridical person, or both;

'*qualifying holding*' means a direct or indirect holding by a person acting alone or through or in concert with one or more other persons in an undertaking which represents ten percent or more of the capital or the voting rights or which makes it possible to exercise significant influence over the management of the undertaking in which the holding exists, as the CBI may determine;

'*related person*', in relation to a bank, means:

(i) any administrator of the bank;

(ii) any person who is related to an administrator by marriage, blood or kinship up to the second degree, including adopted children or foster children of the administrator, and any other person residing in the administrator's household;

(iii) any person who has a qualifying holding in the bank, and any undertaking in which any such person or any administrator of the bank has a qualifying holding, and any administrator of such person or undertaking; and

(iv) any undertaking, not subject to consolidation in the preparation of financial statements of the bank, in which the bank holds a qualifying holding, and any administrator of such undertaking;

'*representative office*' means a place of business forming a legally dependent part of a bank where activities are limited to the provision of information and liaison functions, and where no banking business is conducted and no deposits or other repayable funds may be received from the public;

[281] The words 'senior bank official' and 'or receiver' were added in 2004.

'*senior bank official*' means a person (other than an administrator) who holds the title or, without regard to title, performs the functions of one or more of the following positions at a domestic bank or, in the case of a foreign bank, a branch in Iraq: chairman, director general, general manager, president, chief executive officer, chief operating officer, chief financial officer, chief lending officer, or chief investment officer. 'Senior bank official' also includes any other person who is required by the CBI to comply with the requirements of paragraph (4) of Article 18 of this Law.[282]

'*subsidiary*' means any juridical person in which another person or group of persons acting in concert holds the equivalent of fifty percent or more of the voting shares of such juridical person; or a qualifying holding that permits such other person or group of persons to exercise effective control over the management or policies of the juridical person in which the holding exists;

'*Tribunal*' or '*Financial Services Tribunal*' means the Financial Services Tribunal established in the Central Bank of Iraq Law.

Article 2 Regulatory objectives

1. The primary regulatory objective of this Law is to maintain confidence in the banking system. Other regulatory objectives include those of promoting public understanding of the banking system by providing appropriate information, maintaining an appropriate degree of protection for depositors, and helping to reduce financial crime, including fraud, money laundering and terrorist financing.

2. The CBI shall discharge its functions in a way which is compatible with the regulatory objectives and which the CBI considers most appropriate for the purpose of meeting those objectives. Actions by an entity of the government other than the CBI that affects a matter subject to the jurisdiction of the CBI shall be without legal force.[283]

Article 3 Prohibitions

1. No person in Iraq shall engage in the banking business without a banking license or permit issued by the CBI, other than a person exempted by the CBI pursuant to paragraph (3) or paragraph (6). Except as otherwise provided by law, no person in Iraq shall engage in the business of receiving deposits or other repayable funds from the public without a banking license or permit issued by the CBI.[284]

2. The following persons do not fall under the scope of this Law:
   a. persons who fund the credits they make exclusively from non-repayable capital subscriptions, proceeds of credits received from financial institutions or debt securities issued in the capital markets; or
   b. persons who, in exchange for the issuance of corporate debentures or corporate bonds, receive repayable funds from the public and use such funds solely for the purpose of making investments for their own account.

3. Persons who, by virtue of the cooperative nature and size of their operations, do not carry on banking business on a scale which requires a commercially organized business undertaking may be exempted by the CBI from the requirements of this Law, provided that exemptions so granted by the CBI may be conditional or limited in time, or may be partial and list certain provisions of this Law that shall apply to such person.

[282] The sub-paragraph on 'senior bank officials' was added in 2004.
[283] The second sentence was added in 2004.
[284] The second sentence was added in 2004.

4. No one shall use the word 'bank' or derivatives of the word 'bank' in any language in respect of a business, product, or service without a banking license or permit issued by the CBI, unless such usage is established or recognized by law or international agreement, or unless it shall be clear from the context in which the word 'bank' is used that it does not concern banking activities. Representative offices shall not use the word 'bank' in their name, except in cases where the word 'bank' forms an integral part of the name of the foreign bank to which they belong, provided that, in such cases, the words 'representative office' shall be added.

5. The CBI shall be empowered to enter the offices and to examine the accounts, books, documents and other records of any person if the CBI determines that there are reasonable grounds to suspect that such person engages in activities that are incompatible with the preceding provisions of this article; immediately upon the request of the CBI, law enforcement officials shall, if necessary by the use of force, assist the CBI to gain access to the premises of such person and to examine the accounts, books and other records of such person.

6. Activities performed pursuant to micro and small business credit access or similar grant programs by entities other than banks shall be permitted as authorized by entities exercising governmental authority. Such activities shall be exempt from the application of this law. Such entities exercising governmental authority shall provide notice and periodic reports to the CBI concerning their exempted credit access and grant programs.

Section 2 – Licensing

Article 4 Licenses and permits

1. Establishing a bank in Iraq, including as a majority or wholly-owned subsidiary of a foreign bank or bank holding company, shall require the prior issuance of a banking license by the CBI. Establishing a branch or representative office of a foreign bank in Iraq shall require the prior issuance of a permit by the CBI. The subsidiary of foreign owned banks shall be required to have 50 billion dinars of capital. There is no restriction on where that capital is invested.

2. A license or permit granted under this Law shall be granted in writing for an indefinite period of time and shall not be transferable. The license or permit, or its attachments, shall specify the terms and conditions under which it has been issued. Compliance with all conditions relating to the issuance of a license or permit shall be a continuing requirement applicable to all licenses or permit holders, unless later modified by the CBI.

3. Licenses may be issued only to companies established in the form of juridical persons pursuant to the laws of Iraq and appropriately registered. Such companies may be wholly or majority-owned subsidiaries of a foreign bank or bank holding company. In the case of a subsidiary, a license may be issued only if the parent bank is subject to comprehensive consolidated supervision by a supervising authority in the country in which the parent bank's head office is located.[285]

4. Permits for branches may be issued only to foreign banks that are subject to comprehensive consolidated supervision by a supervisory authority in the country in which the foreign bank's head office is located.[286]

[285] The word 'comprehensive' was added in 2004.

[286] The Banking Law of 2003 read: '[...] are subject to comprehensive supervision or regulation on a consolidated basis by a supervisory authority [...]'.

5. Except as otherwise provided in this Law, subsidiaries and branches of banks in part or totally owned by foreign persons are to be treated under the laws of Iraq no less favorably than domestic banks.

6. A foreign person may hold shares in an existing or new domestic bank subject to any specific requirements of this Law and its implementing regulations.

7. A foreign person may not acquire a qualifying holding or control in a domestic bank unless that person is a foreign bank subject to comprehensive consolidated supervision by a supervisory authority in the country in which the foreign bank's head office is located or a multilateral development bank.[287]

Article 5 License application

1. Licenses shall be applied for in writing to the CBI. Applications shall be in such form and detail, and shall be accompanied by such documents, as shall be prescribed by regulation of the CBI.

2. For a company established in the form of a juridical person pursuant to the laws of Iraq the application shall include the following documents and information:

a. an authenticated copy of the instrument under which the applicant is formed, together with the memorandum of association or bylaws, if any, and the address of its head office;
b. the amounts of the authorized and subscribed capital of the applicant, including the amounts that have been paid in;
c. the name, nationality, permanent place of residence, and business or profession of every administrator, together with a statement detailing the qualifications and professional experience and at least three references for each administrator;
d. the name, nationality, permanent place of residence, and business or profession of every owner of a qualifying holding, including the ultimate beneficial owner of such qualifying holding, together with at least two references verifying good financial standing, and, in case the owner of a qualifying holding is a body corporate, copies of the latest three audited annual financial statements, including balance sheets and profit and loss accounts, if applicable;
e. a list of shareholders and ultimate beneficial owners of shares stating the name, address and respective shareholding, and, for registered shares, a copy of the shareholder register;
f. for each administrator and owner of a qualifying holding, including the ultimate beneficial owner of such qualifying holding, an affidavit duly signed by the individual disclosing any convictions for offenses by a criminal court, personal bankruptcy filings, disqualifications from practicing a profession, or past or present involvement in a managerial function in a body corporate or other undertaking subject to insolvency proceedings, if any (the standard text for such affidavit to be determined by the CBI);
g. a business plan setting out the business objectives and types of activities envisaged for the proposed bank, including a description of its organizational structure

[287] The Banking Law of 2003 read: 5. Subsidiaries and branches of banks in part or totally owned by foreign persons are to be treated under the laws of Iraq in the same way is as [sic] domestic banks. 6. The total number of licenses for banks controlled by foreign persons is limited to six banks through December 31, 2008. Thereafter there is no limit to the number. 7. A foreign person can own 50% or less in an existing or new domestic bank without that license counting toward the limitation of article 4.6. 8. Foreigners can own banks or stock of banks only if they are a bank subject to consolidated supervision by a supervisory authority in another country.

and internal control systems (including adequate measures to counter money-laundering and terrorist financing as defined in the Anti-Money Laundering Law of 2004 (AML)) together with projected balance sheets, profit and loss accounts and cash flow statements for the next three full financial years;[288]

h. a statement by an auditor indicating the auditor's undertaking to take on the external auditing function pursuant to Article 46;

i. for the applicant and for each owner of a qualifying holding, including the ultimate beneficial owner, as defined in the AML, of such qualifying holding, a list of undertakings in which participations exist, specifying the size of such participations and the registered addresses of those undertakings;

j. the location of the principal place of business and any other place in or outside Iraq where it proposes to conduct banking business;[289]

k. proof of payment of the application fee;

l. such other information as the CBI may require for the purpose of the application; and

m. in any case where the applicant is a subsidiary of a foreign bank or bank holding company, a statement that the foreign supervisory authority responsible for the prudential supervision of the applicant in the country of formation of the foreign bank or bank holding company has no objection to the proposed establishment of operations in Iraq, and exercises comprehensive consolidated supervision over the applicant.[290]

3. For companies that are not yet established pursuant to the laws of Iraq, the procedure for a banking license consists of two stages, namely, a first stage beginning with the submission of a preliminary application for a banking license by the founders of the company, and a second stage beginning with the submission of a final application for a banking license by the company after it has been established and appropriately registered in the commercial register. The preliminary application shall be accompanied by the supporting information and documents set out in paragraph (2), provided that, with the approval of the CBI, certain documents may be submitted in draft form. When, after having received a preliminary application for a banking license and having met with the founders and the proposed administrators of the bank, the CBI determines that the preliminary application and supporting documents are satisfactory, the CBI shall notify the applicants that their preliminary application is complete and request that the second stage be initiated by the submission of a final application for a banking license.

Article 6 Permit application for a branch

1. The CBI may permit the opening in Iraq of a branch of a foreign bank authorized to conduct banking business in the country of its formation. Branches of foreign banks shall be permitted to engage in any of the activities that are authorized for domestic banks, subject to the terms and conditions of their banking permits. Permits shall be applied for in writing to the CBI. Applications shall be in such form and detail, and shall be accompanied by such documents, as shall be prescribed by regulation of the CBI, and shall include:

[288] In 2004, the words 'as defined in the Anti-Money Laundering Law of 2004 (AML)' were added. The original sub-paragraph g. which read 'copies of the latest three audited annual financial statements, including balance sheets and profit and loss accounts of the applicant, if applicable' was deleted and the sub-paragraphs were renumbered.

[289] In 2004, the words 'as defined in the AML' were added.

[290] In 2004, the word 'comprehensive' was added.

a. the information and documents as set out in Article 5, paragraph (2), subparagraphs (a) through (g), (j) and (l), for the foreign bank as applicant, except that paragraph (2), sub-paragraphs (c) and (f) shall only apply to the senior administrator of the head office of the foreign bank;
b. the information and documents as set out in paragraph (2), sub-paragraphs (h), (i) and (k) of Article 5 concerning the proposed branch operation;
c. a certificate of designation specifying the name, nationality, permanent place of residence and business or profession of its designated branch manager, being the senior bank officer in Iraq responsible for carrying out the functions of the bank, together with a statement detailing such person's qualifications and professional experience and including at least three references.
d. for each administrator of the branch, an affidavit pursuant to paragraph (2), subparagraph (f) of Article 5;
e. a statement that the foreign supervisory authority responsible for the prudential supervision of the foreign bank in the country of its formation has no objection to the proposed establishment of a branch in Iraq, and exercises comprehensive consolidated supervision over the applicant; and
f. such other information as the CBI may require for the purpose of the application, including an undertaking by the applicant issued by the head office through its principal officer, supported by an appropriate resolution of its board of directors, that it will, on demand of the CBI, make available, in the currency and at such place as may be specified by the CBI, funds necessary to cover all obligations and liabilities incurred in the conduct of banking business authorized under the permit.

2. Following prior notification to and approval by the CBI, the main branch may open additional branch offices in Iraq, provided that one branch is designated a main branch of the foreign bank in Iraq where any process may be served.

Article 7 Permit application for a representative office

1. The CBI may permit the opening in Iraq of one or more representative offices of a foreign bank, provided such foreign bank is authorized to conduct banking business in the country of its formation. Representative offices shall limit their activities to the provision of information and liaison functions, and shall not engage in banking business or other similar activities or receive deposits or other repayable funds from the public in Iraq.

2. Permits for representative offices shall be applied for in writing to the CBI. Applications shall be in such form and detail, and shall be accompanied by such documents necessary for purposes of the permit application, as shall be prescribed by regulation of the CBI.

Article 8 Granting of license or permit

1. Within two months from the date of the submission of an application or preliminary application for a banking license or permit, the CBI shall notify the applicant whether the application is deemed complete. Within six months from the date of a notification by the CBI that the application is deemed complete, the CBI shall approve or reject the application and shall send the applicant a copy of its decision.

2. For final applications submitted pursuant to paragraph (3) of Article 5 the CBI shall render its decision within two months after the submission of such final application.

3. In exceptional circumstances, the CBI may extend the deadlines set out in paragraphs (1) and (2), provided it notifies the applicant of the reasons for the delay prior to reaching the deadline.

4. Before it approves an application for a banking license or permit, the CBI shall carry out financial, criminal, personal and professional background checks of owners of qualifying holdings in the proposed bank and administrators of the proposed bank for which the application is pending. To that end, banks and other financial institutions subject to the CBI's oversight and the national and local tax collection and law enforcement authorities shall provide such information to the CBI as the CBI shall request. The CBI may contact any state or local agency or ministry including any government state ministry, or enforcement agency to request information that may be useful or relevant for any bank license, permit or application.[291] The CBI shall establish direct contact with the relevant foreign supervisory authority in order to verify statements provided pursuant to paragraph (2), sub-paragraph (m) of Article 5[292] or paragraph (1), sub-paragraph (e) of Article 6.

5. Applications for a banking license or permit shall be rejected if the CBI is not satisfied that the conditions specified by or pursuant to this Law for issuing such license or permit are fulfilled. The CBI shall publish by regulation standards that it will apply in evaluating applications for a banking license or permit.

6. The CBI shall grant a license or permit on being satisfied regarding:
   a. the validity of the documents submitted pursuant to Article 5 or Article 6, as applicable;
   b. the financial status and history of the applicant;
   c. the character and professional experience of the administrators as fit and proper persons;
   d. the identity and character of the owners as fit and proper persons, in particular persons with qualifying holdings;
   e. the adequacy of the staffing, operational and financial resources and capital structure of the proposed bank to cover all obligations and liabilities incurred in the conduct of the proposed banking activities to be authorized under the license or permit;
   f. the soundness of the proposed operations;
   g. the viability of the business plan;
   h. the applicant's intention to maintain a physical presence at a fixed address in Iraq; and
   i. in any case where the applicant is a subsidiary or a foreign bank or bank holding company or concerning the permit for a branch of a foreign bank, that comprehensive consolidated supervision is exercised by the relevant foreign supervisory authority.[293]

7. A decision by the CBI to grant a license or permit shall be notified to the applicant and published in the *Official Gazette* or if the *Official Gazette* is not available for such use on a frequent basis, then published in a widely circulated general publication(s) (here after the 'Official Publication.') Upon issuance of the license or permit, the bank shall be added to the list in the register of banks.

8. If a license or permit is denied, the CBI shall serve notice of the denial decision accompanied by a description of the reasons for the denial. If an application remains incomplete or fails to meet the requirements within three months following receipt of a

[291] This sentence was added in 2004.

[292] The Banking Law of 2003 read: 'sub-paragraph (n)'.

[293] The Banking Law of 2003 read: 'an adequate level of prudential supervision is exercised on a consolidated basis by the relevant foreign supervisory authority.'

notification by the CBI pursuant to paragraph (1) above, the applicant shall be regarded as having abandoned the application. In all cases, the applicant shall not be entitled to a refund of the application fees paid.

9. Banks must notify the CBI of any changes in circumstances that affect the statements they made in the license or permit application. A domestic bank shall obtain the CBI's prior approval for any proposed amendment to its instrument of formation or bylaws. Such amendment or change shall not enter into force until after the CBI has granted approval and such amendment or change has been recorded in the register of banks. A foreign bank holding a permit shall notify the CBI of any material changes to the bank's instrument of formation without undue delay.[294]

Article 9 Additional offices

No bank shall open a branch or representative office or establish a subsidiary in Iraq without first notifying and obtaining the prior approval of the CBI. No domestic bank shall open a branch or representative office or establish a subsidiary outside Iraq without first obtaining the CBI's prior approval. Banks shall notify the CBI of any change in location or closure of any branch, representative office or subsidiary.

Article 10 Register of banks

1. The CBI shall prepare and maintain a central register of banks for inspection by the public. The register shall record for each licensed bank and for each branch and representative office of a foreign bank holding a permit: the name, address and registration number, the date on which the license or permit was issued or revoked by the CBI, the instrument of formation and other statutory documents of the bank concerned, information concerning the administrators of the bank, including the scope of their authority to commit the bank, and the addresses of any domestic branch or representative offices and offices abroad, if any. Additionally, for branch offices and representative offices of foreign banks, the name and address of the head office of the foreign bank to which they belong shall be recorded. The entire list of license and permit holders, showing only the names, head office addresses, and type of license or permit held, shall be published by the CBI in the Official Publication during the month of January of each year. Any changes to the list that occur during the course of the year shall also be published in the Official Publication at regular intervals.

2. Banks must indicate their assigned registration number and include the head office address on all documents, authorizations, and papers used in their transactions.

Article 11 Fees

1. In order to cover part of its expenses associated with bank licensing and supervision, the CBI shall charge and collect an application fee on account of each application for a banking license or permit as well as a maintenance fee for each year that a banking license or permit is in effect.

2. The fee structure shall be specified by the CBI in regulation and shall reflect the size, volume and nature of business accounted for by banks. The CBI may take into account special supervision costs, if any, attributable to particular banking activities.

[294] The Banking Law of 2003 read: 'Banks holding a permit shall notify the CBI of any changes to the bank's instrument of formation or bylaws without undue delay.'

Article 12 Voluntary termination of operations

1. No bank may terminate its operations without first obtaining the CBI's prior approval to do so. A bank may be liquidated at the decision of its owners after the voluntary termination of its operations has been approved by the CBI and a written request for the revocation of the license or permit has been submitted to the CBI.

2. The revocation shall not be granted unless the CBI determines that the bank has fulfilled, or settled in a manner acceptable to the CBI, all of the bank's obligations to its depositors and other creditors, customers, and employees.

3. Upon determination by the CBI that the bank has met the requirements under paragraph (2), the CBI shall revoke the license or permit.

Article 13 Revocation of banking license or permit

1. A license or permit may be revoked only by decision of the CBI on one or more of the following grounds:
   a. the license or permit has been obtained on the ground of fraudulent statements or other material irregularities that occurred in connection with the application;
   b. the bank has not made use of the license or permit within twelve months after the date of its effectiveness, or the bank has ceased for more than six months to engage in the business of receiving money deposits or other repayable funds from the public or making credits or investments for its own account;
   c. the bank conducts its administration or operations in an unsafe or unsound manner;
   d. the bank violates an order of the CBI;
   e. the bank, in a manner which materially affects the financial soundness of the bank, violates a law, a regulation of the CBI, or any condition or restriction attached to a license or permit issued by the CBI;
   f. the bank, or the foreign bank or bank holding company of which the bank is a subsidiary, or a subsidiary of the bank, has engaged in criminal activities constituting fraud, money-laundering or terrorist financing;
   g. the foreign bank or bank holding company of which the bank is a subsidiary has lost its operating license;
   h. the CBI is hindered in supervising the bank because the bank has moved all or part of its administration, operations, books or records outside Iraq without the prior written approval of the CBI;
   i. the CBI is hindered in supervising the bank because the bank is a member of a group of companies, or because the bank is a subsidiary of a foreign bank or a bank holding company that is not adequately supervised; or
   j. the foreign supervisory authority responsible for the supervision of the bank or the foreign bank or bank holding company of which the bank is a subsidiary has appointed a conservator or receiver for the bank, foreign bank or bank holding company.
2. The CBI shall revoke a license or permit:
   a. at the time that bankruptcy proceedings are opened against the bank by decision of the Financial Services Tribunal pursuant to Article 78; or
   b. pursuant to paragraph (3) of Article 12.

3. Decisions to revoke a license or permit pursuant to this article shall be in writing and include the grounds on which they are taken. Each such decision shall be promptly served on the bank concerned, registered in the register of banks and published in the Official

Publication by the CBI. A decision taken pursuant to this article shall take effect at the time that it is served on the bank concerned, unless the decision specified another date for its entry into force not later than 30 days after the decision is served. The requirement of service of such decision on a foreign bank may be met by serving the decision on its designated branch office or representative office addressed by the decision.

4. Decisions by the CBI to revoke a license or permit pursuant to paragraph (1) shall include the appointment of a conservator in accordance with Article 69 to liquidate the bank.

Section 3 – Capital

Article 14 Minimum capital of domestic banks

1. The capital of a domestic bank shall be specified in *dinars*. A bank shall at all times maintain minimum paid-up capital that is not less than 10 billion *dinars* or such higher amount as may be established by the CBI. Existing banks must reach this capital within 18 months of the effective date of this order.

2. No bank may declare, record in an account or pay to shareholders any portion of profits, or make any transfer of profits, if such transfer or payment results in a reduction of its capital or reserves below the minimum levels required under this Law or as required by regulation or order of the CBI.

3. No bank may distribute profits to shareholders before extinguishing all expenses related to the establishment and initial organization of the bank.

4. There is no limit to the amount of capital that can be placed in the bank in any given calendar period.

Article 15 [Reserved][295]

Article 16 Other capital requirements

1. Each bank shall at all times maintain capital, including its unimpaired capital and reserves, in Iraq of not less than the equivalent of 12 percent of the total value of its assets determined on a risk-adjusted basis, or such higher percentage as specified by regulation of the CBI, whereby not less than one-half of such capital shall consist of core capital. For the purposes of the application of this provision, the CBI shall define the meaning of capital, core capital, reserves and categories of risk assets in regulations, and the definition and determination of capital, core capital, reserves and assets shall be consistent with international standards.

2. The amount of any holding of capital in another bank or financial institution shall be deducted from the bank's capital for purposes of calculating the ratio pursuant to paragraph (1).

3. The CBI shall specify by regulation principles for establishing and holding a bank's paidup minimum capital.

[295] Art 15 [Net domestic assets required for branches of foreign banks] of the Banking Law of 2003 read: 'Each branch of a foreign bank, if so directed by the CBI, shall maintain in Iraq an excess of assets over its liabilities to residents of Iraq in such amount, if any, as the CBI may stipulate.'

Section 4 – Management of a Bank

Article 17 Board of directors of a domestic bank

1. The board of directors of a bank shall be responsible for conducting the business and establishing the policies of the bank. In particular, the board of directors shall establish the risk-management standards, investment policies, minimum prudential ratios, accounting standards and internal control systems of the bank.

2. The board of directors shall have not less than five members. The members of the board of directors shall be appointed at the general meeting of shareholders for a period of not more than four years; they may be reappointed for subsequent periods of equal length. At the general meeting of shareholders, the bank's shareholders may establish the remuneration for members of the board of directors. The board of directors shall select a chairman from among its members.

3. The chairman and all members of the board of directors must:
   a. possess legal capacity and be fit and proper persons; and
   b. be at least 30 years old.

4. The majority of the members of the board of directors must have significant banking experience and shall not work full time for the bank.

5. A member of the board of directors may not be:
   a. an administrator or employee of another bank, unless the bank is a subsidiary of such other bank or both banks are under common control, provided that, in that case, such members may not constitute a majority of the members of the bank's board of directors; or
   b. a government official who heads a ministry or holds a cabinet position.

6. The members of the board of directors shall act honestly and in good faith with a view to the best interests of the bank. In carrying out their functions, they shall exercise the care, diligence and skill that a reasonably prudent person would exercise in comparable circumstances.

7. The decisions of the board of directors shall be adopted by majority vote of the members present. If the vote is evenly divided, the chairman's vote shall be the deciding vote.

Article 18 Management

1. Subject to the provisions of paragraph (4) of this article, the board of directors of a domestic bank shall appoint one of its members as the authorized manager of the bank. The authorized manager is responsible for the implementation of the decisions of the board of directors and for the management of the day-to-day operations of the bank.

2. The board of directors of a domestic bank shall appoint a chief internal auditor who shall be a qualified member of a recognized professional association with extensive professional experience in the field of accounting or audit.

3. The board of directors of a domestic bank shall designate the compliance officer of the bank.[296]

4. A person to be appointed to serve as authorized manager of a bank, designated branch manager, or other senior bank official as specified by the CBI, must:
   a. possess legal capacity and be a fit and proper person;

[296] In 2004, the words 'of a domestic bank' were added to paras 1 to 3.

b. possess the banking competence and expertise required for the conduct of banking operations;
c. not be an administrator or employee of another bank; and
d. reside in Iraq and engage full time in the management of the bank's operations.

5. The CBI may specify other senior bank positions, including chief internal auditor and compliance officer, to which the provisions of paragraph (4) above are applicable.

Article 19 Changes of administrators

1. Banks shall obtain the prior written approval of the CBI, subject to a determination by the CBI of the person's professional experience and qualifications as a fit and proper person pursuant to Article 17, paragraphs (3) through (5) or Article 18, paragraph (4), as applicable, before appointing or electing an administrator or senior bank official.

2. An administrator or senior bank official of a bank shall cease the administrator's or senior bank official's functions at the bank if the board of directors finds that the individual no longer meets one or more of the legal requirements for the position as specified in Article 17, paragraphs (3) through (5) or Article 18, paragraph (4), as applicable. The board of directors shall inform the shareholders of the bank of such finding.[297]

3. Banks shall notify the CBI of the dismissal or the acceptance of the resignation of an administrator, as well as the reasons for said dismissal or resignation, within a period of three days of such event.

Article 20 Removal of administrators

1. An administrator who is removed by the CBI from office pursuant to paragraph (2), subparagraphs (h) through (j) of Article 56 may not be a member of the board of directors, the authorized manager or designated branch manager, or work in a senior bank position in any other bank.

2. A person who has been an administrator of a bank whose license has been revoked or whose involuntary liquidation has been decided during the administrator's term of office may not be an administrator or work in a senior bank position in another bank.

3. In exceptional circumstances, having been satisfied as to the qualifications, professional experience and conduct of a person, the CBI may exempt an administrator from the provisions of paragraph (2) after the expiration of an appropriate period following the relevant event, and from the provisions of paragraph (1) after the expiration of ten years following the relevant event.

Article 21 Disclosure of personal interest

1. Each administrator or senior bank official shall disclose in full to the board of directors any significant personal financial interests, directly or indirectly, that the administrator or senior bank official may have. Each also must disclose the same information for other individuals in the administrator's or senior bank official's household. Subject to paragraph (2) of this article, such written disclosures shall be made by the administrator or senior bank official upon appointment or election, and annually thereafter, in accordance with guidelines adopted by the bank and pursuant to any regulations issued by the CBI.

2. Whenever any matter related to such significant personal financial interest comes up for discussion by the board of directors or in any other committee or working group of the

[297] The words 'or senior bank official' were added in 2004 to paras 1 and 2.

bank with decision-making authority, the administrator or senior bank official concerned shall disclose the interest at the beginning of the discussion and shall not thereafter participate in the discussion, shall withdraw himself from the meeting while discussions on the matter are ongoing, and shall take no part in the decision on such matter; and the administrator's or senior bank official's presence shall not be counted for the purpose of constituting a quorum.[298]

Article 22 Changes in ownership and acquisition of qualifying holding

1. Any person, acting directly or indirectly or through or in concert with other persons, who proposes to acquire a qualifying holding in a bank, shall obtain prior approval of the CBI and shall give at least 90 days prior notice to the CBI.
2. The notice of proposed acquisition of a qualifying holding shall include:
    a. the name, nationality, permanent place of residence, and business or profession of every proposed owner of a qualifying holding, including the ultimate beneficial owner of such qualifying holding, together with at least two references verifying good financial standing;
    b. for each proposed owner of a qualifying holding, including the ultimate beneficial owner of such qualifying holding, an affidavit pursuant to paragraph (2), subparagraph (f) of Article 5;
    c. in case a proposed owner of a qualifying holding or its ultimate beneficial owner is a body corporate, copies of the latest three audited annual balance sheets and profit and loss accounts, if applicable;
    d. a list of undertakings in which the proposed owner of a qualifying holding, including the ultimate beneficial owner of such qualifying holding, holds participations, specifying the size of such participations and the registered addresses of those undertakings;
    e. the terms and conditions of the proposed acquisition and the manner in which the acquisition is to be made;
    f. the identity, source and amount of the funds to be used in making the acquisition;
    g. any plans or proposals regarding a major change in the bank's business, corporate structure or management; and
    h. such other information as the CBI may require.
3. The CBI shall assess the expected effects on the financial soundness of the bank and satisfy itself as to the identity and character of the proposed owners, in particular owners of a qualifying holding. The CBI shall not approve a proposed acquisition referred to in paragraph (1) if it would substantially lessen competition, jeopardize the financial soundness of the bank or endanger the interests of the bank's depositors.
4. Any person, acting directly or indirectly or through or in concert with other persons, who proposes to increase an existing qualifying holding in a bank in a manner that would reach or exceed a threshold of 20 percent, 33 percent or 50 percent of the bank's capital or the voting rights, respectively, shall give at least 30 days prior notice to the CBI.
5. Any bank becoming aware of a proposed acquisition of a qualifying holding in the bank or of a proposed increase in an existing qualifying holding in the bank pursuant to paragraph (4) shall give at least 30 days prior notice to the CBI, or once it becomes aware of such proposal, whichever is earlier.

[298] The words 'or senior bank official' were added in 2004 to paras 1 and 2.

6. Any bank becoming aware of circumstances that indicate that any of its owners and, in particular, owners of a qualifying holding, are no longer fit and proper persons, shall notify the CBI.

Article 23 Merger

1. No bank shall merge or consolidate with any other bank or acquire, either directly or indirectly, substantially all of the assets of, or assume liability to pay any deposits made in, any other bank except with the prior approval of the CBI.

2. Any bank which intends to engage in any merger, consolidation, acquisition or assumption of liability under paragraph (1) shall give at least 90 days prior notice to the CBI, and provide the CBI with such information as the CBI may require.

3. The CBI shall assess the financial and managerial resources and future prospects of the existing and proposed bank, and shall not approve the proposal unless the bank to result from the transaction would satisfy all criteria were it seeking to be licensed as a new bank. The CBI shall not approve a proposed transaction referred to in paragraph (2) which would substantially lessen competition unless any anti-competitive effects are clearly outweighed by the transactions' expected positive effects.

Article 24 Audit Committee

1. Each bank shall establish an audit committee. The audit committee shall be a committee of the board of directors and shall have the following duties and powers:
   a. to review and recommend the approval of the accounting procedures, annual audit plan and accounting and risk management controls for the bank;
   b. to recommend and approve an auditor for appointment pursuant to Article 46 as the bank's external auditor;
   c. to review the external auditor's report on the bank's financial statements and to report any findings to the board of directors before the approval of the financial statements by the board of directors;
   d. to request reports from the bank's chief internal auditor;
   e. to monitor compliance with the laws and regulations applicable to the bank and report to the board of directors thereon;
   f. to review reports to be submitted by the bank to the CBI;
   g. to report on any matters submitted to it by the board of directors;
   h. to review operations and transactions of the bank on the basis of plans adopted by the audit committee, at the request of the board of directors, at the request of shareholders together holding more than 10 percent of total voting rights, or as specified by the instrument of formation of the bank; and
   i. to report at least annually to the bank's shareholders at the general meeting of shareholders on its activities.

2. The audit committee of a domestic bank shall have not less than three members. The members are appointed by the shareholders at the general meeting of shareholders of the bank from among the members of the board of directors for periods of not more than four years; they may be reappointed for subsequent terms of equal length. The chairman of the board of directors, the authorized manager, and any other officer or employee of the bank shall not be members of the audit committee. The shareholders at the general meeting of shareholders shall designate a member of the audit committee to be chairman of the audit committee.

3. The decisions of the audit committee shall be adopted by majority vote of the members present. If the vote is evenly divided, the chairman's vote shall be the deciding vote.[299]

Article 25 Application of certain provisions

1. In the absence of specific provisions to the contrary set out in this Law, the provisions of the Company Law No. 21 of 1997, as amended, shall be observed regarding matters pertaining to the board of directors, authorized manager and general meeting of shareholders of a bank.[300]

2. For banks that are solely owned by the State, the Minister of Finance shall, on behalf of the State, exercise any powers granted to shareholders at the general meeting of shareholders under this Law. In the absence of specific provisions to the contrary set out in this Law, for banks that are solely owned by the State the provisions of Law No. 22 on State Companies[301] shall be observed regarding matters pertaining to the internal organization and management of a bank.

Section 5 – Rules for the Conduct of Banking Activity

Article 26 General banking principles

1. Banks shall conduct their administration and operations in a sound and prudent manner and in accordance with the requirements of the law, any conditions and restrictions attached to their banking licenses or permits issued by the CBI, and the regulations, guidelines and orders issued by the CBI.

2. Banks shall: maintain adequate capital and liquidity; make adequate provision for depreciation of assets, for discharge of liabilities, and for losses; maintain adequate accounting and other records of business; observe sufficient and effective risk controls; and ensure that their assets are diversified as to risk of loss.

3. The CBI shall, by regulation, prescribe detailed standards of conduct for banks which the CBI shall apply in its prudential supervision in accordance with international standards and best practices.

4. The CBI shall issue regulations specifying how the operational requirements specified for banks by the provisions of this section, and in regulations issued by the CBI thereunder, apply to banks and their subsidiaries on a worldwide consolidated basis.

5. Banks shall not establish group structures that hinder the exercise of effective supervision. The CBI may issue regulations specifying rules regarding affiliates of a bank, in particular, concerning the requirements for transactions between banks and any affiliates that are not subject to consolidation in the preparation of financial statements.

[299] Para 2 in the Banking Law of 2003 read: 'The audit committee shall have not less than three members. The members are appointed by the shareholders at the general meeting of shareholders of the bank from among the members of the board of directors for periods of not more than four years; they may be reappointed for subsequent terms of equal length. The chairman of the board of directors and the authorized manager of a bank shall not be members of the audit committee. The majority of the members of the audit committee shall not work full time for the bank. The shareholders at the general meeting of shareholders shall designate a member of the audit committee, who is not an employee of the bank, to be chairman of the audit committee. For a branch of a foreign bank, the members of the audit committee shall be appointed by the head office, provided that the designated branch manager shall not be a member of the audit committee.'

[300] The Banking Law of 2003 spoke of 'the Private Companies Law'.

[301] The Banking Law of 2003 read: 'provisions of the Public Companies'.

6. The CBI shall issue regulations specifying how the operational requirements specified for banks by the provisions of this section, and in regulations issued by the CBI thereunder, shall apply to domestic branch offices of foreign banks.

7. Whenever an administrator of a bank discovers that the capital of the bank is less than the capital required by law or by regulation of the CBI, the administrator must promptly notify the CBI thereof.

8. The CBI may provide guidance, including by means of establishing rules for good business conduct, or specify by regulation rules to ensure the banks' good relations with their depositors and customers.

Article 27 Banking activities

1. A bank may engage in the following activities subject to the terms and conditions of its banking license or permit:

a. receiving money deposits (in the form of demand deposits, time deposits or other types of deposit) or other repayable funds, bearing interest or not;
b. extending credits (whether secured or not by collateral or liens), including without limitation: consumer and mortgage credit; factoring, with or without recourse; financing of commercial transactions, including forfeiting (purchasing negotiable instruments at discount without recourse); and financial leasing services; subject to regulation of the CBI, a bank may charge interest on interest, and the total amount of interest it may receive shall not be limited by the principal amount of a credit;[302]
c. buying and selling for its own account or for the account of customers (including underwriting and brokerage services) of any of the following: money market instruments (including checks, bills of exchange, promissory notes and certificates of deposit); foreign currencies and precious metals; exchange and interest rate instruments; stocks and other transferable securities; and forward contracts, swap agreements, futures, options, and other derivatives relating to currencies, stocks, bonds, precious metals or interest rates;
d. entering into contingent commitments, including guarantees and letters of credit, for its own account and for the account of customers;
e. providing clearing, settlement and transfer services for money, securities, payment orders and payment instruments (including checks, credit, debit and other payment cards, travelers' checks; and bank drafts, wire transfers, and pre-authorized debits and credits);
f. money brokering;
g. safekeeping and administration of valuables, including securities;
h. providing trust services;
i. providing services as portfolio manager of securities or as financial adviser, agent or consultant;
j. providing financial information and credit reference services; and
k. anything that shall be incidental to the foregoing and such other activities, not prohibited by Article 28, as the CBI may by regulation authorize as banking activities.

2. The CBI may, in its discretion, and subject to such conditions as it may stipulate, require banks to conduct certain banking activities through separately capitalized subsidiaries that are wholly or majority-owned by the relevant bank.

[302] The last sub-sentence was added in 2004.

Article 28 Prohibited activities

No bank shall engage in or participate as an agent, partner or co-owner in wholesale or retail trade, manufacturing, transportation, agriculture or fisheries, mining, building, re-insurance, insurance underwriting or other business activities except for activities that are authorized by Article 27. Notwithstanding the foregoing, and with the prior written approval of the CBI, a bank may temporarily carry on or participate in the carrying on of such activities to the extent necessary to obtain satisfaction of claims, provided that the CBI may require the bank to cease such activities by a date specified in the license or permit.

Article 29 Prudential requirements

1. Each bank shall develop and maintain internal policies in the form of maximum and minimum ratios, exposure limits, risk-management standards, investment policies and other prudential ratios to be maintained by the bank concerning its assets, off-balance sheet items and various categories of capital and reserves. Such internal policies shall be consistent with regulations on prudential requirements issued by the CBI pursuant to paragraph (3) of this article.

2. In particular, banks shall establish and apply internal policies on prudential ratios governing:

   a. their liquid resources in relation to the value or change in value of their assets (including guarantees and collateral received), or in relation to their liabilities, provided that banks shall be permitted to meet the requirements concerning liquid resources by maintaining with the CBI money deposits of an equivalent value;
   b. the maximum aggregate amount of all or certain categories of their credits and investments;
   c. the classification and evaluation of assets, and provisions to be made on the basis of such classification and evaluation, and the time when earnings on non-performing loans may no longer be accounted for as income except as received in cash; and
   d. prohibitions, restrictions or conditions concerning: (i) the types or forms of credits and investments made, and liabilities assumed (contingent or otherwise); (ii) matching as to maturity and interest in respect of assets and liabilities (contingent or otherwise); and (iii) unhedged positions, exceeding a specified ratio, in foreign currencies or precious metals; exchange and interest rate instruments; stocks and other transferable securities; and forward contracts, swap agreements, futures, options, and other derivatives relating to currencies, stocks, bonds, precious metals or interest rates.

3. The CBI shall by regulation prescribe prudential requirements as well as the common procedures and methods of calculation to be followed by banks in their application. The CBI may specify requirements, prescribed in response to exceptional circumstances, concerning the rate of interest, maturity and other conditions applicable to any type or form of financing extended or received (including deposits) or applicable to contingent liabilities.

Article 29A Net domestic assets required for branches of foreign banks

Each branch of a foreign bank, if so directed by the CBI, shall maintain in Iraq an excess of assets over its liabilities to third parties other than any other office, or any affiliate, or any subsidiary of the foreign bank in such amount, if any, as the CBI may direct.[303]

[303] Art 29A was added in 2004.

Article 30 Large exposures

1. No bank shall grant credit to a person if as a result thereof:
    a. the aggregate outstanding principal amount of all of the bank's credits to that person would exceed the equivalent of fifteen percent, or such lower percentage as specified by regulations issued by the CBI, of the bank's unimpaired capital and reserves (large credit exposure), without obtaining prior approval of the CBI;
    b. the aggregate outstanding principal amount of all of the bank's credits to that person would exceed the equivalent of 25 percent, or such lower percentage as specified by regulations issued by the CBI, of the bank's unimpaired capital and reserves; or
    c. the aggregate outstanding principal amount of all large credit exposures of the bank pursuant to sub-paragraphs (a) and (b) would exceed the equivalent of 400 percent, or such lower percentage as specified by regulations issued by the CBI, of the bank's unimpaired capital and reserves.

2. The limitations specified in paragraph (1) shall not apply to any principal amount of credit that is fully secured by readily marketable collateral in accordance with the standards prescribed for that purpose by regulation of the CBI, provided, however, that no bank shall grant such secured credit if, as a result thereof, the aggregate outstanding principal amount of all its secured credits to the person receiving such credit would exceed the equivalent of 20 percent of the bank's unimpaired capital and reserves, or such lower percentage as specified by regulations issued by the CBI.

3. The provisions of paragraphs (1) and (2) shall not apply to:
    a. transactions with, or guaranteed by, the government;
    b. transactions secured by obligations of, or fully guaranteed as to principal and interest by, the Government of Iraq or any agency or instrumentality of the Government of Iraq specified by the CBI by regulation;
    c. transactions denominated in Iraqi dinars that are fully secured by deposits in a segregated account at the bank denominated in Iraqi dinars; and,
    d. amounts paid against uncollected funds in the ordinary process of collection.[304]

4. For the purposes of applying this article or any regulations issued pursuant thereto, a person shall be deemed to include any other person with whom such person is connected, directly or indirectly, in such a way that the financial soundness of any of them may affect the financial soundness of the other or others, or the same factors may affect the financial soundness of some or all of them, or if as a result of the structure of their relationship the other person is in fact ultimately responsible for the credit outstanding.

5. For purposes of this article and any regulations issued pursuant thereto, the term 'bank' means, with respect to a domestic bank, the bank together with its subsidiaries and, with respect to a foreign bank with a permit to operate a branch in Iraq, its Iraqi branch or branches.[305]

Article 31 Transactions with related persons and senior bank officials

1. No bank may extend credit to a related person or senior bank official:
    a. if, in the case of a domestic bank, the credit and its financial terms and conditions have not been approved by the board of directors;[306]

[304] Sub-paras b. to d. were added in 2004. The original sub-para b. read: 'transactions between banks with a maturity of one year or less.'

[305] Para 5 was added in 2004.

[306] Art 1, para a., of the Banking Law of 2003 read: 'if the credit and its financial terms and conditions have not been approved by the board of directors or, in the case of a branch of a foreign bank, the designated branch manager'.

b. if the credit is granted to an administrator or senior bank official of the bank and the credit would cause the aggregate amount of credit disbursed by the bank to that person and outstanding, including any credit granted by one or more of the bank's subsidiaries, to exceed the equivalent of 50 percent of the annual remuneration of that person, or if the credit would cause the aggregate amount of credits disbursed to all related persons and senior bank officials and outstanding to exceed ten percent of the unimpaired capital and reserves of the bank, or such lower percentage as specified by regulation issued by the CBI, provided, however, that the foregoing percentage limits shall not apply to any credit that is secured by a mortgage on property for a local primary residence whose appraised value, in the opinion of the CBI, at the time that that credit is granted exceeds the principal amount of the credit by not less than one third of that principal amount;[307]

c. if the credit is granted on terms and conditions that are less favorable to the bank than the terms and conditions that are offered by the bank to the public in the ordinary course of business at the time when the credit is granted; or

d. if the credit is not fully secured in the amount and manner specified by regulation issued by the CBI.[308]

2. No bank may purchase assets from or sell assets to a related person that is a natural person, or any officer or employee of the bank or a related person.

3. No bank may purchase assets from a related person that is a juridical person:

a. if, in the case of domestic bank, the asset purchase and its financial terms and conditions have not been approved by the board of directors; or

b. if the asset purchase is on terms and conditions that are less favorable to the bank than the terms and conditions that are offered by the bank to the public in the ordinary course of business at the time when the asset purchase occurs.

4. In the case of a domestic bank, every credit provided by a bank to, or asset purchased from, a related person or senior bank official shall be promptly reported to the audit committee of the bank. If credit has been provided by a bank to, or an asset purchased from, a related person or senior bank official in violation of the provisions of paragraph (1), the credit must be immediately repaid, and the members of the board of directors or the designated branch manager, as the case may be, shall be personally liable, jointly and severally, for payment of principal of, and interest and other charges on, credit granted in violation of paragraph (1) with their knowledge and without their objection.

5. The CBI may instruct a bank to deduct any lending to a related person or senior bank official from capital for purposes of calculating the ratio pursuant to paragraph (1) of Article 16.

6. The limitations contained in sub-paragraph (b) of paragraph (1) shall not apply to the portions of credits denominated in Iraqi dinars fully secured in the manner specified by the CBI by regulation, by deposits in a segregated account at the bank denominated in Iraqi dinars, or the portions of credits fully secured by, or fully guaranteed as to principal and interest by, the Government of Iraq or any agency or instrumentality of the Government of Iraq specified by the CBI by regulation.

7. Definitions. For the purposes of this article and any regulations issued pursuant thereto:

a. 'Bank' means, (i) with respect to a domestic bank, the bank together with its subsidiaries and (ii) with respect to a foreign bank with a permit to operate a branch in Iraq, its Iraqi branch or branches.

[307] The words 'or senior bank official' were added in 2004.

[308] Sub-para d. was added in 2004.

b. 'Related person' means a related person as that term is defined in Article 1 of this Law and, in addition, any spouses and children of persons related in the first or second degree to an administrator of the bank.
c. 'Senior bank official' means a senior bank official as that term is defined in Article 1 of this Law and, in addition, any person related to a senior bank official in the first or second degree, and any spouses and children of such persons.[309]

Article 32 Foreign currency exposure
The CBI may issue regulations to set the maximum foreign currency exposure which banks may incur in foreign currency generally or in any specified currency or currencies.

Article 33 Investment restrictions
1. It shall be prohibited for any bank without the CBI's prior approval to invest in the stocks, shares, or equity-linked bonds of any undertaking in an amount that exceeds 20 percent of the bank's unimpaired capital and reserves. To the extent that any stocks, shares, or equity-linked bonds transferred to the bank in the course of its banking operations would cause the bank's holdings to exceed such limit, the bank shall dispose of such stocks, shares, or equity-linked bonds as soon as practicable and not later than at a date at which such disposition may occur without incurring a loss, and, in any case, within two years of their acquisition at the latest. Upon request by the bank, this period may be extended for a period of up to one year by decision of the CBI.
2. Except in connection with the granting of mortgage loans in the conduct of its banking operations, it shall be prohibited for any bank to possess real estate other than real estate essential to the conduct of its operations and for the housing of its employees and workers. This provision shall not bar the bank from leasing any excess portion of real estate held for the conduct of its operations, provided it obtains the CBI's prior approval. A bank shall dispose of any real estate transferred to it in the course of its banking operations other than mortgage lending as soon as practicable and not later than at a date at which such disposition may occur without incurring a loss and, in any case, within two years of acquiring it at the latest. Upon request by the bank, this period may be extended for two periods of up to two years each by decision of the CBI.
3. It shall be prohibited for any bank to acquire a participation in another bank or financial institution without first obtaining the CBI's prior written approval and without meeting the requirements stipulated by the CBI.
4. It shall be prohibited for any bank to possess shares in other banks or financial institutions without the CBI's prior approval unless such shares were transferred to the bank in the course of its banking operations. In this case, the bank shall sell the shares as soon as practicable and not later than at a date at which such disposition may occur without incurring a loss and in any case, within two years of acquiring them at the latest, unless the CBI grants approval to retain the shares.

[309] The Banking Law of 2003 only had three paragraphs which provided: '2. Every credit provided by a bank to a related person shall be promptly reported to the audit committee of the bank. If credit has been provided by a bank to a related person in violation of the provisions of paragraph (1), such credit must be immediately repaid, and the members of the board of directors or the designated branch manager, as the case may be, shall be personally liable, jointly and severally, for payment of principal of, and interest and other charges on, credit granted in violation of paragraph (1) with their knowledge and without their objection. 3. The CBI may instruct a bank to deduct any lending to a related person from capital for purposes of calculating the ratio pursuant to paragraph (1) of Article 16.'

5. It shall be prohibited for any bank without first obtaining the CBI's prior written approval to acquire stock or shares in a company established outside Iraq, except when such stock or shares are transferred to it in the course of its banking operations.

Article 34 Bank holidays
All banks must open their doors for business with the public on all days and during all office hours approved by the CBI, excluding Fridays and bank holidays. The CBI shall, by regulation, announce the holidays to be observed by banks. No bank may open its doors to the public during these bank holidays, be they official or unofficial holidays. In the event that circumstances require the suspension of banking operations, the CBI may order banks to close their doors temporarily, cease their operations, and resume them only by order of the CBI.

Article 35 Suspicious transactions
1. If a bank or any of its administrators, officers or employees learns that the execution of any banking transaction or the receipt or payment of any sum of money pertains or may pertain to any crime or illegal act, the bank shall immediately notify the appropriate official or judicial authority to this effect. The bank shall inform the CBI on a monthly basis about suspicious transaction reports submitted, if any, and concerning any need for additional action regarding this matter.
2. A bank's disclosure of any information in good faith under this article shall not be considered a breach of banking confidentiality. In addition, neither the CBI nor the bank shall bear any liability as a result thereof.

Article 36 Restriction on bank shares
No bank may grant any credit, including loans and advances, or provide a guarantee or security to a customer that uses the customers' shares in the bank as collateral to secure the loan. A bank may not purchase its own shares without prior approval of the CBI.

Article 37 Dormant accounts
1. Amounts on deposit in an account at a bank, and any other property held by a bank are subject to special rules if the accounts are considered dormant accounts or the property held by a bank is considered abandoned. The requirements of this article apply only to dormant accounts maintained at an office in Iraq or abandoned property located in Iraq.[310]
2. If a customer has not evidenced any interest in the amounts on deposit or other property by recorded transaction or written correspondence with the bank for seven years beginning no earlier than the date that this Law entered into effect, on the first business day of the following calendar year, the bank shall dispatch by registered post a notice to the customer at the customer's last known address containing particulars of the dormant account or other abandoned property, and publish in at least two newspapers of general circulation and the Official Publication the name of the customer. Not less than 30 days after such notice and publication, if the customer cannot be located, the bank shall make a detailed report to the CBI, which report the CBI shall maintain in its records for at least 20 years from the date the property is turned over to it, and shall turn over the amount on deposit or other property to the CBI, to be held in a special account at the CBI. In the case

[310] Art 37, para 1, of the Banking Law of 2003 read: 'Amounts on deposit in an account at a bank are subject to special rules if the accounts are considered dormant accounts.'

of property other than funds on deposit, the CBI shall sell the property in a public auction or other appropriate method designed to generate the maximum value for the property.[311]

3. The CBI shall hold the funds in a special account to be invested in Iraqi government securities, or other securities if Iraqi government securities are not available, provided that, for a period of twenty years from the date the property was turned over to the CBI, any owner who, to the satisfaction of the CBI furnishes proof of ownership, shall be entitled to repayment of the amounts by the CBI. After the expiration of such period, any remaining unclaimed amounts shall be transferred to the Ministry of Finance for deposit in the State Treasury.[312]

Article 38 Records

1. Banks shall keep on file in Iraq for at least seven years the pertinent documents for each one of their transactions, namely:
   a. customer identification records;
   b. application and all contract documents pertaining to the transaction (including credit, guarantee and collateral agreements) and a signed written record of the decision of the bank approving the transaction;
   c. financial records concerning counterparties (including borrowers and guarantors), and any other documentary evidence on which the bank relied in approving the transaction;
   d. the account agreements with its customers; and
   e. such other documents as the CBI may specify by regulation.

2. Records shall be kept in written form. A bank may retain books, records, statements, documents, correspondence, cables, notices, and other documents relating to its financial activities in reduced form (microfilm, electronic data storage or other current technological devices) instead of the original for the period established in the law, to the extent that adequate data recovery systems and procedures are in place. Such reduced copies shall have the probative effect of the original. The CBI may issue regulations setting out detailed systems requirements.

Article 39 Payment system

1. Banks may establish cooperative systems and clearing houses for the transfer of funds and for the settlement of accounts and payment instruments among themselves and among other financial institutions. The CBI may establish rules and procedures to govern the conduct of these activities.

2. Banks may establish credit reporting agencies or credit bureaus to collect and to disseminate to other banks such information concerning the financial affairs of existing and prospective customers as the banks may need in order to make prudent banking decisions. Such information shall be furnished only to banks having an actual or prospective banking relationship with the person concerning whom the information is provided. Such information

[311] Art 37, para. 2, of the Banking Law of 2003 read: 'If an account holder has not evidenced any interest in the amounts on deposit by recorded transaction or written correspondence with the bank for ten years, on the first business day of the following calendar year, the bank shall dispatch by registered post a notice to the account holder at the holder's last known address containing particulars of the dormant account, and publish in at least two newspapers of general circulation and the Official Publication the name of the account holder. Not less than 30 days after such notice and publication, if the account holder cannot be located, the bank shall make a detailed report to the CBI and shall turn over the amount on deposit to the CBI, to be held in a special account at the CBI.'

[312] In 2004, the words 'from the date the property was turned over to the CBI' were added.

shall be furnished subject to such restrictions, including rules and procedures that may be adopted by the CBI under paragraph (e) of Article 51, as shall be necessary to protect the confidentiality of banking information and to prevent the unauthorized dissemination of such information.

Section 6 – Accounts and Financial Statements

Article 40 Financial year

The financial year of domestic banks shall begin on January 1 and end on December 31 of the same year. For a branch of a foreign bank, the financial year may differ.

Article 41 Periodic reporting

1. Each bank shall furnish the CBI at the relevant intervals specified by regulation with:
   a. statements showing its assets and liabilities;
   b. statements on the foreign currency exposures, capital adequacy ratio, reserve position, liquid assets, large exposures and credits to related persons;
   c. information or statistics concerning its various accounts and activities, including information on deposits, banking facilities, credit plans, or credit and contingent liabilities granted to the bank's customers;
   d. information, statements, tables, or budgets concerning its various accounts and activities, either in a consolidated form or for each of its branches separately, at the times and according to the format and method stipulated by the CBI by regulation; and
   e. such other statements or information as requested by the CBI.

2. The CBI may request reports from any of the bank's subsidiaries or affiliates if deemed necessary for the exercise of consolidated supervision of the bank's activities.

3. The expenses incurred in complying with reporting obligations or requests by the CBI to provide information shall be borne by the relevant bank.

Article 42 Principles for accounting and preparation of financial statements

1. Banks shall:
   a. maintain proper books and records required for orderly operations in accordance with the provisions set out in Article 38;
   b. apply accountancy rules and systems in conformity with international accounting standards (IAS), including the use of full accrual accounting on a daily basis, and in compliance with any special requirements stipulated by the CBI in this regard; and
   c. prepare its financial statements comprising the balance sheet, profit and loss account, cash flow statement and statement of changes in the bank's capital account in an adequate manner that reflects the reality of the financial positions of the bank and its branches. The financial statements shall be prepared in accordance with international accounting standards (IAS) and in compliance with any special requirements stipulated by the CBI in this regard. The financial statements shall give a true and fair view of the state of affairs of the bank and shall include a statement on the bank's internal control systems.

2. Banks shall comply with any regulations or orders issued by the CBI with respect to the rules set out in paragraph (1). The CBI shall issue, by regulation, provisions on the accounting system and rules applicable to banks.

Article 43 Financial statements

1. Each bank shall prepare financial statements. Each bank that has one or more subsidiaries shall also prepare consolidated financial statements.

2. The CBI may specify other affiliates of a bank, in particular a company that controls a bank and any other company that is controlled by the company that controls the bank, for which consolidated financial statements shall be submitted.

3. Each foreign bank with one or more branch offices in Iraq shall prepare accounts and financial statements for its operations in Iraq as if such offices together were to constitute a single entity.

4. A copy of each bank's audited financial statements, including audited consolidated financial statements, if applicable, shall be submitted by the bank to the CBI when they become available and within four months after the end of the financial year at the latest. Each foreign bank with one or more branch offices in Iraq shall also submit a copy of the foreign bank's audited consolidated financial statements to the CBI when they become available.

5. The audited financial statements of a bank shall be made available to its shareholders not less than 30 days prior to the general meeting of shareholders at which the financial statements are to be presented for approval.

Article 44 Publication of financial statements

1. A bank shall publish, in two newspapers of general circulation, its audited financial statements, including audited consolidated financial statements, if applicable, not later than four months after the end of the financial year.

2. Each bank shall display in a prominent location at its head office and its branches its most recent audited financial statements, including audited consolidated financial statements, if applicable, and a list of the names of the members of its board of directors.

Article 45 Annual report

1. Each bank shall send copies of the annual report to the CBI not later than 30 days after it becomes available, and within six months after the end of the bank's financial year at the latest.

2. The annual report shall contain such information as prescribed by regulation of the CBI, including a report by the board of directors on the bank's business during the preceding year and the business projections for the coming year.

Section 7 – Audit

Article 46 Audit

1. Each bank shall appoint an independent external auditor with qualifications and experience in the audit of banks acceptable to the CBI. The external auditor shall be appointed by the bank's shareholders at the general meeting of shareholders, provided that if the bank fails to appoint an auditor satisfactory to the CBI, the CBI shall appoint such auditor.

2. The auditor, or any member of the audit firm, shall not be an administrator, owner, affiliate, employee, agent or representative of the bank for which the auditor is to be appointed and shall not have an interest in the bank, with the exception of holding a deposit in the bank. Should the auditor acquire any such interest in the bank during the course of the appointment, the services of the auditor shall be terminated and a temporary alternate auditor be appointed by the CBI until the bank appoints a new auditor.

3. The auditor shall not provide services to the bank that are connected with the internal audit function of the bank, except for occasional training purposes.

4. No bank shall appoint the same auditor continuously for a period of more than 5 years without an exemption granted by the CBI.

5. In accordance with internationally-recognized auditing standards and any standards issued by regulation of the CBI, the auditor shall audit the bank's operations on a consolidated basis and:

a. issue a statement to the bank indicating whether the auditor or any member of the audit firm: (i) holds an ownership interest in the bank; and (ii) complies with the provision of paragraph (3);
b. assist the bank in maintaining proper accounting systems and procedures;
c. assist the bank in maintaining proper financial control and risk management systems and procedures;
d. upon request by the audit committee, attend meetings of the audit committee;
e. within three months after the end of the financial year, prepare for the board of directors of the bank an audit report together with an audit opinion as to whether the financial statements are complete, fair and properly drawn up and present a full and fair view of the financial condition of the bank in accordance with the provisions of this Law; in particular, the audit report shall state:
   (i) whether any explanation or information requested from the administrators, employees or agents of the bank in the course of the audit was satisfactory;
   (ii) the degree of adequacy of, and the bank's adherence to, internal control measures and accounting systems in effect;
   (iii) the method for keeping documents, records, and books, and the latter's orderliness and inclusion of operations needed to enable monitoring, auditing, and internal and external audit;
   (iv) the adequacy and performance of the bank's management regarding protection of the funds of the bank and depositors;
   (v) deficiencies in the bank's activities, the auditor's recommendations for the management regarding the deficiencies, and the extent to which management applied the auditor's recommendations and remarks made in connection to operations in previous years; and
   (vi) the degree of accuracy of periodic statements sent to the CBI; and the correspondence of the statements with the content of records, books, accounting systems and practices in effect at the bank and with the CBI's orders in this regard;
f. provide the board of directors and the CBI with a report stating the auditor's opinion on the bank's system of loan classification and concerning the provisioning for doubtful claims indicating any deficiency in the provisioning needed for the bank's assets according to the CBI's orders;
g. inform each member of the board of directors and the CBI about any act by an administrator, officer, employee or agent of the bank of which the external auditor has become aware that constitutes a material violation of a provision of this Law or any regulation or order issued by the CBI; and
h. inform each member of the board of directors and the CBI about any irregularity or deficiency in the bank's administration or operations of which the external auditor has become aware and which could be expected to result in a material loss for the bank.

6. Each bank shall send copies of the audit report to the CBI not later than 30 days after it becomes available. Where the CBI is not satisfied with the auditor's report, it may require the appointment of another auditor to prepare a new audit report within a specified time.

Article 47 Additional duties

1. The CBI may impose on an auditor, in addition to any duty specified in Article 46, a duty to:
   a. submit to the CBI such additional information in relation to the audit as the CBI considers necessary;
   b. submit a report, carry out an inspection or establish any procedure as specified by the CBI;
   c. submit to the CBI a report on the financial and accounting systems and internal controls of the bank; or
   d. certify whether or not adequate measures to prevent money-laundering or terrorist financing have been adopted by the bank and are being implemented in accordance with such regulations, orders and guidelines issued by the CBI.
2. The auditor's costs for performing any such additional duties requested by the CBI shall be borne by the bank.

Article 48 Application of certain provisions

1. The provisions of the Private Companies Law shall apply to bank auditors unless stipulated otherwise in this Law.
2. Auditors shall observe professional and banking confidentiality requirements, provided that the auditor shall not incur legal liability for the disclosure of confidential information concerning a bank or a bank customer that the auditor provides in good faith to the CBI under this Law. In particular, a report by the auditor to the CBI pursuant to paragraph (5), sub-paragraphs (g) and (h) of Article 46 shall not be construed as a breach of professional or banking confidentiality obligations.

Section 8 – Confidentiality

Article 49 Banking confidentiality

A bank shall maintain confidentiality regarding all accounts, deposits, trusts, and safe deposit boxes of customers. It shall be prohibited to provide information on the aforesaid, directly or indirectly, without the written approval of the relevant customer; or, in the event that the customer is deceased, without the consent of the customer's legal representative, or one of the customer's heirs or legatees; or without the decision of a court of law or the public prosecutor in an existing judicial dispute or the existence of one of the cases permitted under this Law. This prohibition shall remain in effect even if the relationship between the customer and the bank ends for any reason.

Article 50 Individual confidentiality

It shall be prohibited for any current or former administrator, officer, employee or agent of a bank to provide information or statements on customers or their accounts, deposits, trusts, or safe deposit boxes, or transactions or to disclose or enable a third party to examine such information and statements in other than those cases permitted under this Law. This prohibition shall also apply to any person, including auditors and employees and agents of the CBI, and any person appointed by the CBI to carry out an examination pursuant to Article 53, who examines such statements and information directly or indirectly by virtue of their profession, position, or work.

Article 51 Exceptions
The provisions of Articles 49 and 50 of this Law shall not apply to disclosure of information in the following cases:

a. the performance of duties legally assigned to auditors appointed by the bank or by the CBI according to this Law;
b. information and documents requested by the CBI in connection with its duties under this Law or the Central Bank of Iraq Law;
c. actions taken in good faith in the course of the performance of duties or responsibilities imposed by this Law or in the implementation of measures countering money-laundering and terrorist financing pursuant to regulations of the CBI;
d. the issuance of a certificate or statement of the reasons for refusing to pay a check based on the request of a rightful holder;
e. the provision of information on: (i) customers' indebtedness to provide the necessary data for determining the soundness of granting credit; (ii) bad checks; or (iii) any other transaction deemed necessary by the CBI because of its pertinence to the soundness of the banking sector to banks, the CBI or any other agencies approved by the CBI to facilitate the exchange of such information pursuant to rules and procedures specified in regulation of the CBI;
f. a bank's disclosure of all or some information on a customer's transactions to prove its claim in a judicial dispute between it and its customer regarding these transactions; and
g. information provided by the CBI to supervisory authorities under Article 54 of this Law.

Article 52 Information provided by banks

1. Any information collected from a bank revealing its individual customers, customer transactions or other particulars pertinent to its relations with its individual customers shall be considered confidential and may be disclosed only with the consent of the bank or as authorized by this Law. The CBI shall restrict access to such individual customer information within the CBI to authorized employees.
2. The CBI may publish, in its entirety or in part, information provided to it by banks, provided such publication does not disclose confidential information. Unless the CBI first obtains the consent of the bank, the CBI shall not disclose particulars of the bank's operations other than as may be contained in the financial statements approved by the bank's board of directors, or information already in the public domain.

Section 9 – Supervision and Examinations

Article 53 Examinations
The CBI shall supervise banks on a consolidated basis in the following manner:

1. The CBI shall review the statements, documents, information, clarifications, and proof submitted by banks in the application of this Law.

2. The CBI may request that banks, or any of its subsidiaries or affiliates, provide, and corroborate in writing when it deems necessary, any additional information, reports, documents, clarifications, or proof.

3. The CBI may at any time cause an on-site examination of a bank, its subsidiaries or affiliates, to be made by one or more employees of the CBI, or by any other person or persons appointed by the CBI for this purpose. The examination shall review the operations of a bank to ascertain its financial position and the extent to which the bank complies with the provisions of laws and regulations regarding the management of its activities and adheres to internal policies. The CBI shall examine all banks on a regular basis, and at least once every year, except that representative offices shall be examined at least once every two years.

4. Any person authorized to carry out an examination under this article shall be subject to confidentiality requirements and may require any administrator, officer, employee or agent of a bank, or its subsidiaries or affiliates, to provide access to all necessary books, accounts, documents, and records. Any information deemed necessary and requested by the examiner shall be furnished in a timely manner during the course of the examination.

5. Examiners shall submit to the CBI a report on the results of the examination. The CBI shall notify the board of directors of the relevant bank of the examination results.

Article 54 Exchange of information

1. The CBI may exchange information on supervisory matters, preferably based on a Memorandum of Understanding, with financial supervisory authorities in Iraq and with banking supervisory authorities in other countries. The exchange of such information may include confidential information, provided that the CBI has satisfied itself that reasonable steps have been taken to ensure the confidentiality of any such information submitted.

2. The CBI may enter into Memoranda of Understanding with financial supervisory authorities in Iraq or with banking supervisory authorities in other countries setting out the scope, procedures and further details for the exchange of information.

Article 55 Immunity from legal action

1. No member of the board of directors of the CBI, employee of the CBI, agent of the CBI, any person appointed pursuant to the provisions of this Law (i) to carry out an examination pursuant to Article 53, (ii) as conservator, or (iii) as receiver, or any person engaged by a conservator or receiver pursuant to paragraph (3) of Article 62 or paragraph (4) of Article 80 shall be personally liable in damages for any act or omission taken in the discharge or purported discharge of official functions within the scope of their employment or engagement under this Law.

2. The CBI shall indemnify a member of the board of directors of the CBI, employee of the CBI, an agent of the CBI, any person appointed pursuant to the provisions of this Law (i) to carry out an examination pursuant to Article 53, (ii) as conservator or (iii) as receiver, or any person engaged by a conservator or receiver pursuant to paragraph (3) of Article 62 or paragraph (4) of Article 80 against any legal costs incurred in the defense against legal action brought against such person in connection with the discharge or purported discharge of official functions within the scope of their employment or engagement under this Law, provided that no such indemnification shall apply if such person has been convicted of a crime arising out of the activities that are covered by such legal action.

Section 10 – Enforcement Measures and Penalties

Article 56 Prompt corrective action and administrative penalties

1. The CBI may take any measure or impose any administrative penalty stipulated in paragraph (2) of this article in cases where it is evident that a bank, an administrator of a bank or any other person:
   a. violated the provisions of law or any regulation or order issued by the CBI;
   b. conducted unsafe or unsound banking operations.
2. If any of the violations stipulated in paragraph (1) above occur, the CBI may take one or more of the following measures or administrative penalties:
   a. send a written warning to the bank;
   b. give orders to the bank;
   c. order that the bank submit a program of measures it intends to take or a detailed description of measures it has taken to eliminate the violation and correct the situation;
   d. order that the bank cease some of its operations, or bar it from distributing profits or dividends;
   e. impose any restriction on the granting of credit deemed appropriate;
   f. in addition to any minimum balance stipulated in the Central Bank of Iraq Law and other legally required deposits, require the bank to deposit and maintain balances with the CBI without interest for a period deemed appropriate by the CBI;
   g. order that the chairman of the board of directors convene the board of directors to review and examine the violations attributed to the bank and to take the necessary measures to eliminate the violations; in this case, one or more representatives of the CBI shall attend the board of directors' meeting;
   h. order that the bank temporarily or finally suspend from office any authorized manager or designated branch manager, depending on the seriousness of the violation;
   i. order that the bank remove the chairman or any of the members of the bank's board of directors;
   j. dissolve the bank's board of directors and appoint a conservator in accordance with paragraph (2) of Article 59; or
   k. impose an administrative penalty on the bank, provided that at the discretion of the CBI, administrative penalties may be imposed on a daily basis until the violation has eased or compliance is obtained, and such administrative penalties shall not exceed five percent of the bank's paid-up capital overall.[313]
3. The CBI may impose an administrative penalty on a bank of up to 5 million *dinars* per day until the violation has eased or compliance is obtained, and not to exceed five percent of its paid-up capital overall in the following cases:
   a. if the bank intentionally submitted to the CBI statements, statistics, or information that are deficient or false; or
   b. if the bank does not provide the CBI with information on a customer, certain risks of particular customers, or any other information as requested by the CBI. The imposition of the administrative penalty stipulated in this paragraph shall

[313] In sub-paras c., d., g., h. and i. the word 'order' replaced the word 'request' in the banking Law of 2003. Sub-para l. which read 'revoke the bank's license or permit pursuant to the provisions of Article 1' was deleted.

not bar the CBI or other aggrieved bank from demanding compensation from the bank in violation for damages arising from actions referred to in sub-paragraphs (a) and (b) of this paragraph.

4. Other than in an emergency situation requiring urgent action, the CBI shall, before deciding whether an order shall be given to a bank pursuant to this article, serve the bank with a notice of charges, including a statement of the facts constituting the alleged violation or threat of violation, describing the order that the CBI proposes to issue, requesting a written response from the bank by a date not earlier than 30 days nor later than 60 days after the date of service of such notice. If requested by the bank in its written response, the CBI shall schedule a hearing to determine whether an order should be issued. Any order shall be accompanied by the reasons for issuing such an order. The CBI may issue such regulations as it may deem necessary prescribing the procedures for the conduct of hearings.[314]

5. The imposition by the CBI of measures or administrative penalties stipulated in this article shall not bar any civil or criminal accountability under the provisions of any other law.

Article 57 Illegal banking business

1. Each person who engages in banking activities as a business without a banking license or permit issued by the CBI is guilty of an indictable offense and liable to the penalty for fraud contained in the Penal Code.

2. The penal courts shall be responsible for hearing actions initiated by the public prosecutor based on the request of the CBI or any concerned party.

Article 58 Collection of administrative penalties

The CBI shall collect the administrative penalties imposed on a bank under this Law. Any administrative penalties collected shall be paid to the State Treasury.

Section 11 – Conservatorship

Article 59 Grounds for appointment of a conservator

1. The CBI shall appoint a conservator for a bank when the CBI determines that:
   a. the bank fails to pay its financial obligations, including but not limited to deposit liabilities, as they fall due;
   b. the capital of the bank is less than 50 percent of the minimum capital required by law or by regulation of the CBI pursuant to paragraph (1) of Article 16;
   c. a petition has been submitted for opening bankruptcy proceedings against the bank, as set forth in Article 72; or
   d. The Governor of the CBI has determined that the appointment of a conservator for the bank is necessary to ensure the stability and soundness of the banking system as a whole.[315]

[314] In the Banking Law of 2003 the text read: '[...] requesting a written response from the bank within two weeks after the date of service of such notice. If requested by the bank in its written response, the CBI shall schedule a hearing for a date not later than two weeks after the date of receipt of such request. Within two weeks after receiving a written response, or in the case of a hearing, the conclusion of such hearing, the CBI shall decide whether or not to issue an order. Any order shall be accompanied by the reasons for issuing such an order.'

[315] Sub-para d. was added in 2004.

2. The CBI may appoint a conservator for a bank when the CBI determines that:
   a. the bank fails to carry out an order given to the bank by the CBI;
   b. the capital of the bank is less than 75 percent of the minimum capital required by law or by regulation of the CBI pursuant to paragraph (1) of Article 16; or
   c. there is evidence that the bank or any of its administrators have engaged in criminal activities punishable by imprisonment of one year or more or there is reasonable cause to believe that the bank or any of its administrators are engaging in such criminal activities.
   d. the bank's license or permit has been obtained on the ground of fraudulent statements or other material irregularities that occurred in connection with the application;
   e. the bank has not made use of its license or permit within twelve months after the date of its effectiveness, or the bank has ceased for more than six months to engage in the business of receiving money deposits or other repayable funds from the public or making credits or investments for its own account;
   f. the bank conducts its administration or operations in an unsafe or unsound manner;
   g. the bank, in a manner which materially affects the financial soundness of the bank, violates a law, a regulation of the CBI, or any condition or restriction attached to a license or permit issued by the CBI;
   h. the bank, or the foreign bank or bank holding company of which the bank is a subsidiary, or a subsidiary of the bank, has engaged in criminal activities constituting fraud, money-laundering or terrorist financing as defined in the Anti-Money Laundering Act of 2004;
   i. the foreign bank or bank holding company of which the bank is a subsidiary has lost its operating license;
   j. the CBI is hindered in supervising the bank because the bank has moved all or part of its administration, operations, books or records outside Iraq without the prior written approval of the CBI;
   k. the CBI is hindered in supervising the bank because the bank is a member of a group of companies, or because the bank is a subsidiary of a foreign bank or bank holding company that is not adequately supervised;
   l. the foreign supervisory authority responsible for the supervision of the bank or the foreign bank holding company of which the bank is a subsidiary has appointed a conservator or receiver for the bank, foreign bank or bank holding company; or
   m. The Governor of the CBI has determined that the appointment of a conservator for the bank is necessary to ensure the stability and soundness of the banking system as a whole.[316]

3. The provisions of this section shall apply to the domestic branch offices and domestic representative offices of a foreign bank as if all these offices together were to form a single legal entity. All assets, liabilities, acts and omissions of the foreign bank resulting from or otherwise relating to the business of any such office shall be attributed to that single entity in applying the provisions of this section. The conservator shall be authorized to take all actions with respect to such single entity as could be taken, were it to be a domestic bank, by the authorized manager or by shareholders at the general meeting of shareholders.

[316] Sub-paras d. to m. were added in 2004.

Article 60 Appointment of a conservator

1. A conservator shall be appointed by decision of the CBI. A conservator may be an individual or, in the discretion of the CBI, a group of individuals that is organized as specified by the CBI. Only a fit and proper person is eligible to serve as conservator for a bank.[317]

2. If at any time a conservator becomes ineligible to serve, the conservator shall be replaced by the CBI.

3. Conservators shall be appointed for a term, not exceeding eighteen months, specified in the decision on their appointment. The term of appointment may be extended by the CBI once for another period not exceeding eighteen months. The conservator shall be employed by the CBI and receive remuneration from the CBI. All costs incurred by the CBI on account of the conservatorship shall be borne by and charged to the bank for which the conservator is appointed.

4. The decision by the CBI appointing a conservator or extending the term of appointment of a conservator shall be in writing, shall specify the grounds on which it is given and shall list the principal duties of the conservator. The CBI shall ensure that promptly after the decision is given each such decision is served on the bank for which the conservator is appointed, is recorded in the register of banks and is published in the Official Publication.

Article 61 Effects of the appointment of a conservator

1. The decision of the CBI appointing a conservator for a bank shall take effect immediately, unless the decision provides otherwise.

2. The decision of the CBI appointing a conservator for a bank shall suspend the powers of the shareholders to take action at the general meeting of shareholders of the bank. Thereafter, the conservator shall have the power to take all of the actions in the ordinary course of business including those that could be taken at the general meeting of shareholders of the bank, such as the sale and disposition of assets and such other actions as may be necessary to place the bank in a safe and solvent condition, except that a transaction involving the participation of the bank in the capital stock of other financial institutions or any of the transactions referred to in Article 84 may be entered into only in circumstances and on terms and conditions that have been approved by the Financial Services Tribunal at the request of the CBI.

3. The decision of the CBI appointing a conservator for a bank shall suspend the powers of the administrators of the bank and shall have the effect of transferring all the powers of the administrators of the bank to the conservator. The conservator may delegate to other persons, including administrators and employees of the bank, such powers as the conservator deems necessary or appropriate, unless the CBI determines otherwise in a written notice to the conservator. In the absence or inability of the conservator to act, the CBI may exercise the powers of the conservator.

4. Actions taken by or on behalf of a bank after the decision appointing a conservator for that bank takes effect shall be null and void, unless they are taken by or by the authority of the CBI or the conservator, or unless they are money or securities transfer orders covered by Article 83.

5. A conservator shall be accountable only to the CBI for the performance of duties and for the exercise of the powers as conservator. The conservator shall only be subject to the duties, rules and instructions given to the conservator by the CBI.

[317] The second sentence was added in 2004. Sentence 3 originally read: 'Only fit and proper persons are eligible to serve as conservator for a bank.'

6. Notwithstanding any requirements set forth in Article 14, the CBI, in its sole discretion, may organize and license a bridge bank which will be owned and controlled by the CBI, to receive any assets and liabilities of one or more banks as to which a conservator under section 11 or receiver under section 14 has been appointed. A bridge bank (i) may be placed under the control of a conservator or receiver under this section 11; and (ii) shall terminate its operations at the end of a two-year period following the issuance of a license, except that the CBI, in its discretion, may extend its status for three additional one-year terms.

7. In the performance of its duties, the conservator shall conduct the operations of the conservatorship in a manner which maximizes the return from the sale or disposition of the bank's assets, minimizes the amount of any losses, and provides for the fair and equitable treatment of creditors.[318]

Article 62 Taking control of the bank

1. Immediately upon appointment, the conservator shall take control of the bank for which he has been appointed and secure the assets, books and records of the bank, and thereafter manage the bank during the period of conservatorship in order to prevent the dissipation of such assets, including but not limited to theft or other improper action.

2. The conservator shall have unrestricted access to and control over the assets, the offices, and the books of account and other records, of the bank for which he has been appointed. Immediately upon the request of a conservator, law enforcement officials shall, if necessary by use of force, assist the conservator to gain access to the premises of the bank for which the conservator has been appointed and to gain control over and to secure the assets, books and records of the bank. The decision of the CBI appointing the conservator shall have the legal force and effect of an enforceable court order requiring law enforcement authorities to provide such assistance.

3. A conservator may employ at the expense of the bank for which the conservator has been appointed, such independent attorneys, accountants and consultants on such terms as the CBI shall approve.

4. All legal acts of the bank that are taken within 60 business days before the date of the CBI's decision appointing the conservator shall upon application of the conservator be declared null and void by the CBI if the bank and its counterparty in the act knew or should have known at the time of the act that the act would damage the interests of creditors of the bank. Such knowledge shall be presumed whenever the act consists of any act described in Article 82.8.a. through f. of the Banking Law.

5. The conservator may unilaterally terminate all current contracts or portions of contracts of the bank within a reasonable time not to exceed 60 business days from the date of its appointment, provided, however, that any party or beneficiary to such contract may file a claim for compensation for breach of contract, which compensation shall be limited to actual direct compensatory damages up to the date of termination of such contract by the conservator, with interest to the date of payment, but which shall not include any punitive damages, damages for pain and suffering, or any damages for lost profits or lost opportunities.

6. Subject to Article 88 of this Law, the conservator may enforce any contract of the bank notwithstanding any provision of the contract providing for termination, default, acceleration, or exercise of rights upon, or solely by reason of, insolvency or the appointment of a conservator or receiver.

[318] Para 7 was added in 2004.

7. No provision of this article shall be construed as permitting the avoidance of any legally enforceable or perfected security interest in any of the assets of a bank except where such an interest is taken in contemplation of the bank's insolvency or with the intent to hinder, delay, or defraud the institution or the creditors of the bank.[319]

Article 63 Review of appointment

1. Within five business days from the date of service of the decision appointing the conservator for a bank, the board of directors of the bank may make written representations on behalf of the bank to the CBI challenging the appointment of the conservator. In the event that no such challenge is made within the five-day time period referred to above, the bank shall be deemed to have consented to the decision appointing the conservator. The members of the board of directors of the bank shall not be liable to the bank's shareholders, depositors, or creditors for a good faith decision not to challenge the appointment of a conservator.[320]

2. Upon the timely receipt of such a challenge, the CBI shall review the appointment of the conservator in light of the arguments made against it and decide either to affirm the appointment or to terminate the appointment, giving the grounds for its decision in writing. The decision shall be served promptly upon the chairman of the board of directors of the bank.

3. If the appointment of the conservator is terminated, the conservator shall immediately return control of the bank and its assets, books and records to the authorized manager of the bank.

4. Any decision of the CBI appointing a conservator that is not a decision to which the bank has consented, and any decision of the CBI affirming the appointment of a conservator under paragraph (2) above, may be submitted by the bank, any administrator of the bank, creditor, depositor or shareholder to the Financial Services Tribunal for review within 20 business days from the date of service of the decision. The appointment and powers of the conservator shall remain in full force and effect until a final decision is taken by the Tribunal.

Article 64 Report of the conservator and plan of action

1. Not later than ten business days after the appointment, the conservator shall prepare and present to the CBI a report on the financial condition and future prospects of the bank for which the conservator has been appointed. The CBI may extend the date the report is due for up to 30 calendar days after the appointment if supported by a request from the conservator.[321] The conservator shall include in the report an assessment of the amount of assets likely to be realized in a liquidation of the bank. The report may be prepared with the assistance of such independent experts as the conservator may determine in accordance with paragraph (3) of Article 62.

2. The report shall be accompanied by a proposed plan of action, where relevant, that shall discuss the relative costs and benefits associated with:

a. returning the bank to compliance with the law by carrying out a plan of corrective action;
b. rehabilitation of the bank under the procedure set forth in Article 67; and
c. opening of bankruptcy proceedings against the bank.[322]

[319] Paras 4 to 7 were added in 2004.
[320] Sentence 3 was added in 2004.
[321] This sentence was added in 2004.
[322] The Banking Law of 2003 had included a sub-para c. which read: 'a voluntary liquidation under Article 68, or a revocation of the banking license and liquidation of the bank in accordance with the provisions of Article 69; and'.

Article 65 Moratorium

1. If required to protect the financial condition of a bank for which a conservator has been appointed, the CBI may at any time declare deposits and investments by the public in the bank, other than deposits and investments in segregated fiduciary accounts, to be totally or partially blocked for a maximum period of 30 calendar days,[323] provided that measures are taken which, in the opinion of the CBI, will preserve the approximate value of these deposits and investments together with interest accrued before and during the moratorium. In extraordinary cases, the conservator, with the approval of the CBI, may at any time permit the withdrawal of some or all of the deposits held in the name of a natural person not to exceed 5 million *dinars* for each such case.

2. Upon the appointment of a conservator, all court proceedings against the bank shall be stayed for 12 business days. Any applicable statute of limitations will be tolled for the duration of this stay.[324]

Article 66 Termination of conservatorship

1. The appointment of a conservator shall terminate upon the earlier of:
   a. completion of the term specified in the decision appointing the conservator or in the decision last extending the term of the conservator;
   b. a decision by the CBI or the Financial Services Tribunal to that effect; or
   c. appointment of a receiver pursuant to Article 78.

2. Upon termination of the appointment of a conservator as described in sub-paragraphs (a) or (b) of paragraph (1), the conservator shall immediately return control of the bank and its assets, books and records to the authorized manager of the bank.

3. Within 20 business days of the termination of the appointment, the conservator shall prepare and submit to the CBI a final report and accounting of the conservatorship.

Section 12 – Rehabilitation of Banks

Article 67 Rehabilitation procedures

1. A bank shall be rehabilitated by the conservator appointed for the bank under supervision of the CBI if the Minister of Finance has decided, based upon the written recommendation of the CBI, that the stability of the banking system of Iraq requires the rehabilitation of the bank. Once the Minister of Finance has taken a decision regarding the rehabilitation of a bank, the Minister of Finance may in the Minister's discretion authorize or make available financing in connection with the transactions, costs and expenses referred to in paragraphs (3), (4), and (5) of this article.[325]

2. The recommendation of the CBI to rehabilitate a bank shall be accompanied by a rehabilitation plan prepared by the CBI in consultation with the conservator. The plan shall identify the existing weaknesses in the administration or operations of the bank, determine the corrective measures required to remedy such weaknesses, and provide a timetable and financing plan for the proposed rehabilitation. The plan shall also review and evaluate strategies for transferring the core business of the bank to another bank, including but not limited to a bridge bank, through one or more of the transactions authorized by Article 84 and shall to the extent practicable preclude the enrichment of bank owners at the expense

[323] In the Banking Law of 2003 it had said: 'a maximum period of three months'.

[324] Para 2 was added in 2004.

[325] In the Banking Law of 2003 it had read: 'paragraphs (4) and (5) of this article.'

of the State. At any time during the execution of the plan, the Minister of Finance, after having consulted the CBI, may (i) terminate the rehabilitation plan or (ii) request that the CBI submit a petition to the Financial Services Tribunal for the institution of bankruptcy proceedings under Article 72.[326]

3. For the purpose of conserving the assets, protecting deposits and managing the business of a bank under rehabilitation on a going concern basis, the CBI may direct the conservator to transfer all or part of the assets and liabilities of the bank to a bridge bank capitalized by the State, which transfer shall become effective immediately. If some obligations of the bank to creditors would be excluded from such a transfer, the conservator shall take the interests of such creditors into account. Such a transfer shall not require the consent of the bank or any of its governing bodies. The transfer of liabilities shall be published by notice in the Official Publication and in two or more newspapers of general circulation designated by the CBI.

4. In addition to the powers granted under Article 61 and 62 of this Law, the CBI may:
   a. authorize the conservator for the bank under rehabilitation to carry out one or more of the transactions referred to in Article 84, which may include financing provided by the State in the form of capital, loan, deposits, grants, or guarantees; or,
   b. order the bank under rehabilitation to increase the authorized capital of the bank and to issue shares of capital stock of the bank on such terms and conditions as the CBI may determine.[327]

5. The costs incurred on account of rehabilitation of a bank shall be charged to the bank, and, in the event that the assets of the bank shall prove insufficient, to the State.

Article 67A Bridge banks

1. The CBI, in its sole discretion, may organize and license a bridge bank pursuant to Article 61(6) which will be owned and controlled by the CBI, to receive any assets and liabilities of one or more banks as to which a conservator under section 11 or receiver under section 14 has been appointed.

2. The CBI may organize and license a bridge bank pursuant to Article 67(3), which will be capitalized by the State, to acquire all or part of the assets and liabilities of a bank under rehabilitation.

3. The CBI shall appoint the members of the board of directors of a bridge bank who shall each be a fit and proper person. The board of directors of a bridge bank shall execute the memorandum of association of the bridge bank as approved by the CBI and shall adopt such bylaws as may be approved by the CBI.

4. A bridge bank shall have all corporate powers granted to banks by, and be subject to the requirements of, this Law, except that:

[326] In 2003, the last sentence read: 'At any time during the execution of the plan, the Minister of Finance, after having consulted the CBI, (i) may terminate the rehabilitation plan, (ii) request the CBI to revoke the license or permit of the bank if grounds exist under Article 13, or (iii) request that CBI submit a petition to the Financial Services Tribunal for the institution of bankruptcy proceedings under Article 72.'

[327] In the Banking Law of 2003, para 4 read: 'With respect to the bank, including but not limited to a bridge bank, in accordance with the rehabilitation plan, the CBI may: a. authorize the conservator for the bank to carry out one or more of the transactions referred to in Article 84, which may include financing provided by the State in the form of capital, loans, deposits, grants, or guarantees; b. order an increase in the authorized capital of the bank and the issue of shares of capital stock of the bank on such terms and conditions as the CBI may determine; or c. authorize the conservator to terminate all or some current contracts of the bank for the delivery of goods or services by analogous application of the provisions of Article 89.'

a. the bridge bank shall be exempt from the requirements of Article 14 and Article 16 of the Banking Law;
b. the CBI may exempt the bridge bank from or modify the requirements of Articles 30, 31, and 33 of this Law and the regulations issued thereunder; and
c. the CBI may appoint or remove any of the bridge bank's administrators and senior bank officials.

5. Any judicial action to which a bridge bank becomes a party by virtue of its acquisition of any assets or assumption of any liabilities of a bank in default shall be stayed from further proceedings for a period of up to 45 days at the request of the bridge bank.

6. Except with the prior approval of the CBI, a bridge bank may not, in any transaction or series of transactions, issue capital stock or be a party to any merger, consolidation, disposition of assets or liabilities, sale or exchange of capital stock, or similar transaction, or change its charter.

7. A bridge bank (i) may be placed under the control of a conservator or receiver under this section 11; and (ii) shall terminate its operations at the end of a two-year period following the issuance of a license, except that the CBI, in its discretion, may extend its status for three additional one-year terms.[328]

Section 13 – Liquidation of Banks

Article 68 Voluntary liquidation

1. A bank may be liquidated at the decision of its owners after the voluntary termination of operations has been approved by the CBI, at their request, pursuant to Article 12, and the license has been revoked. The liquidation shall be carried out by the bank, in compliance with the procedures to be issued by the CBI and under supervision of the CBI.

2. The bank shall provide the CBI with such documents and information as the CBI shall request and shall grant the employees of the CBI, or any other person or persons appointed by the CBI for this purpose, access to the buildings, books and records of the bank whenever the CBI decides that such access is required to discharge its supervisory responsibilities.

3. If the CBI determines that the bank does not ensure an orderly liquidation or if the bank fails to comply with the provisions of paragraph (2), the CBI shall appoint a conservator under paragraph (1) of Article 69 who shall carry out or complete the liquidation of the bank.

Article 69 [Reserved][329]

[328] Art 67A was added in 2004.

[329] Art 69 [Forced liquidation] of the Banking Law of 2003 read: '1. The decision of the CBI to revoke a banking license or permit pursuant to paragraph (1) of Article 13 must provide for the liquidation of the bank in accordance with the procedures prescribed by this article by a conservator appointed for the bank by the CBI under Article 60, provided, however, that only Articles 61, 62 and 65 of section 11 shall govern the CBI and conservator. The CBI shall arrange for the prompt publication of the decision by notice in The Official Publication and in at least two newspapers of general circulation.

2. From the time of the decision of the CBI to revoke the banking license of a bank and to liquidate a bank:

a. acts performed by or on behalf of the bank are legally void and unenforceable, except for acts performed by or by authority of the conservator for the bank, acts deemed beneficial to the estate of the bank by the conservator and ratified by the conservator, and money and securities transfer orders covered by Article 83;

b. all attachments and liens in aid of execution in favor of the bank's creditors or other restraints on the bank's assets shall be deemed removed by operation of law;

Section 14 – Receivership of Banks

Article 70 General insolvency law does not apply to banks
Neither the Bankruptcy Law nor any other provisions amending or replacing the Bankruptcy Law in whole or part shall apply to banks.

Article 71 Grounds for opening bankruptcy proceedings
Upon receipt of a satisfactory petition under Article 72 and the appointment of a conservator under Article 73 by the CBI, the Financial Services Tribunal shall grant the petition and open bankruptcy proceedings against a bank on one or more of the following grounds:[330]

a. the bank is not paying its financial obligations, including deposit liabilities, as they fall due;
b. the CBI determines that the capital of the bank is less than 25 percent of the capital required pursuant to paragraph (1) of Article 16;
c. the CBI determines that the value of the assets of the bank is less than the value of the liabilities of the bank; or
d. the CBI determines that any of the grounds for the appointment of a conservator identified in Article 59 exist.[331]

Article 72 Petition for opening bankruptcy proceedings
1. Petitions for opening bankruptcy proceedings against a bank shall be submitted in writing to the Financial Services Tribunal.
2. No petition for opening bankruptcy proceedings against a bank may be granted by the Tribunal unless:

a. the petition is presented by the CBI, together with financial statements of the bank certified by the CBI, showing the basis on which one or more applicable grounds under Article 71 for opening bankruptcy proceedings applies; or
b. the petition has been filed with the Tribunal and served on the CBI by three or more creditors of the bank with obligations aggregating more than 4 billion *dinars* that are due and unpaid, together with documentary evidence showing that the bank is not paying its financial obligations as they fall due under paragraph (a) of Article 71.

c. the assets of the bank shall be immune from attachment and execution, except for assets encumbered by a mortgage or lien to the extent of the debt secured by such encumbrance; and
d. no bankruptcy proceeding may be opened against the bank.
3. The liquidation shall be carried out by the conservator in accordance with procedures to be issued by the CBI that are consistent with those set forth in Article 85 up to and including Article 98, provided, however, that any such procedures shall not incorporate Articles 89 and 96.
4. Upon the written request of the CBI, the conservator for a bank whose banking license has been revoked shall apply to the Financial Services Tribunal for approval to carry out one or more of the transactions authorized by Article 84, and, upon the receipt of such approval, the CBI may direct the conservator to carry out one or more of such transactions.
5. The provisions of this article shall apply to the domestic branch offices and domestic representative offices of a foreign bank as if all these offices together were to form a single legal entity. All assets, liabilities, acts and omissions of the foreign bank resulting from or otherwise relating to the business of any such office shall be attributed to that single entity in applying the provisions of this article. The conservator shall be authorized to take all actions with respect to such single entity as could be taken, were it to be a domestic bank, by the authorized manager or by shareholders at the general meeting of shareholders.'

[330] In 2004, the words 'grant the petition and' were added.
[331] Sub-para d. was added in 2004.

Article 73 Appointment of conservator

1. As soon as a petition for opening bankruptcy proceedings against a bank has been served on the CBI by creditors of the bank under paragraph (2), sub-paragraph (b) of Article 72, or the CBI has presented a petition to the Tribunal under paragraph (2), sub-paragraph (a) of Article 72, a conservator shall be appointed by the CBI pursuant to paragraph (1), subparagraph (a) of Article 59. The provisions of Article 63 shall not apply and decisions of the CBI appointing a conservator pursuant to this article shall not be subject to review by the Financial Services Tribunal.

2. In the event that the Tribunal rejects the petition for opening bankruptcy proceedings under Article 75, the appointment of the conservator hereunder shall terminate.

Article 74 Tribunal hearing

1. Upon filing of a petition for opening bankruptcy proceedings against a bank, the Financial Services Tribunal shall summon the CBI and any other petitioner, the conservator appointed for the bank, and one or more administrators of the bank to attend a public hearing to consider the petition. In exceptional situations the Financial Services Tribunal may decide to conduct a non-public hearing. The hearing shall begin not later than two business days from the time of filing of the petition.

2. If the petition is filed by the CBI under paragraph (2), sub-paragraph (a) of Article 72, the hearing shall be concluded within one week. If the petition is filed by creditors of the bank under paragraph (2), sub-paragraph (b) of Article 72, the hearing shall be concluded within two weeks. At the conclusion of the hearing, the Tribunal shall either reject the petition or grant the petition.

Article 75 Grounds for rejecting the petition

1. A petition for opening bankruptcy proceedings against a bank shall be rejected by the Tribunal if:
   a. the petition is not accompanied by the documents required by paragraph (2) of Article 72 or otherwise does not meet the requirements of the law; or
   b. the CBI opposed the petition under paragraph (2) of this article.
2. If the petition is made by creditors of the bank, the CBI may oppose the petition only if:
   a. the CBI has determined that none of the statutory grounds identified in paragraphs (a), (b), or (c) of Article 71 for opening bankruptcy proceedings against the bank applies; the Tribunal may require the CBI to produce evidence supporting its determination including financial statements of the bank certified by the CBI; or
   b. the CBI submits to the Tribunal a decision of the Minister of Finance in accordance with Article 67 that the stability of the banking system of Iraq requires the rehabilitation of the bank. At its request, the CBI shall be granted two weeks in which to submit such evidence or decision, before the Tribunal rules on the petition.[332]

[332] In the Banking Law of 2003, para 2 read: 'If the petition is made by creditors of the bank, the CBI may oppose the petition only if: a. the CBI has determined that no statutory ground for opening bankruptcy proceedings against the bank applies; the Tribunal may require the CBI to produce evidence supporting its determination, including financial statements of the bank certified by the CBI; b. the CBI provides evidence to the Tribunal demonstrating that, before the application for opening bankruptcy proceedings against the bank was served upon the CBI, the banking license of the bank had been revoked and a conservator had been appointed to liquidate the bank; or c. the CBI submits to the Tribunal a decision of the Minister of Finance in accordance with Article 67 that the stability of the banking system of Iraq requires the rehabilitation of the bank. At its request, the CBI shall be granted two weeks in which to submit such evidence or decision, before the Tribunal rules on the petition.'

Article 76 Rejection of frivolous petitions filed by bank creditors

1. At any time after the filing of a petition for opening bankruptcy proceedings against a bank by creditors of the bank, the Tribunal may reject the petition in writing, with or without a hearing, on the ground that the petition is frivolous, in which case the petitioners may be held liable for monetary damages, including costs and expenses resulting from the filing of the petition, which the Tribunal may award to the bank and to the CBI.

2. In exceptional circumstance the filing of a frivolous petition for opening bankruptcy proceedings against a bank may constitute an offense that, upon conviction in a penal court, may be punished by imprisonment for a period not exceeding 6 months or by the payment of a fine not exceeding 1 billion *dinars* or both.

3. Anyone who is determined by the Tribunal to have filed a frivolous petition for opening bankruptcy proceedings against a bank may be subject to prosecution in the penal courts in a proceeding initiated by the public prosecutor based on the request of the Tribunal.

Article 77 [Reserved][333]

Article 78 Bankruptcy decision

By the decision of the Tribunal to grant a petition for opening bankruptcy proceedings against a bank, the bank shall be declared bankrupt, bankruptcy proceedings opened against the bank and a receiver appointed by the Tribunal under Article 80. Upon such a decision, the CBI shall revoke the bank's license or permit pursuant to Article 13(2).[334]

Article 79 Service and publication of bankruptcy decision

Immediately after the Tribunal has issued a decision opening, or rejecting a petition for opening, bankruptcy proceedings against a bank, the decision shall be served by the Tribunal on the CBI, the creditors filing such petition, and on the bank and the Tribunal shall arrange for publication of the decision in the Official Publication and in at least two newspapers of general circulation.

Article 80 Receiver

1. The receiver appointed by a decision of the Tribunal opening bankruptcy proceedings against a bank, or under paragraph (5) of this article with respect to any replacement receiver, shall be selected by the Tribunal from a list of candidates submitted to the Tribunal by the CBI. Only fit and proper persons are eligible to serve as receiver or replacement receiver for a bank. The bankruptcy decision shall specify the remuneration and the other terms and

The Law of 2003 also included a para 3 which read: 'Otherwise, the Tribunal may reject a petition for opening bankruptcy proceedings against a bank only if: a. any document or other evidence submitted to the Tribunal in support of the petition is manifestly false or inaccurate and without such document or other evidence the petition does not meet the requirements of the law; or b. the bank shows to the satisfaction of both the Tribunal and the CBI that payments of supplemental subscriptions to the capital of the bank have been received by the bank in immediately available funds sufficient to eliminate the grounds for opening bankruptcy proceedings against the bank under Article 71.'

[333] Art 77 [Forced liquidation if bankruptcy petition is rejected] of the Banking Law of 2003 read: 'If a petition presented by the CBI for opening bankruptcy proceedings against a bank is rejected by the Tribunal on grounds other than those specified in Articles 75 or 76, or the Tribunal fails to observe the time periods set forth under this Law or to render a decision in a timely manner under Article 74 or paragraph (2) of Article 84, the CBI shall revoke the banking license of the bank and liquidate the bank in accordance with the procedures prescribed by Article 69.'

[334] Sentence 2 was added in 2004.

conditions of employment of the receiver. The remuneration and other costs and expenses incurred on account of the receiver shall be paid from the assets of the bank for which the receiver is appointed.

2. The CBI shall indemnify the receiver of a bank for all liabilities and all costs and expenses incurred by the receiver on account of the receivership to the extent that such liabilities, costs or expenses exceed the assets of the bank available to meet them.

3. Receivers shall carry out their activities under the direction and supervision of the CBI, which on the appointment of the receiver, shall provide the receiver with written directions including a list of activities which the receiver may undertake without the need for involvement of the CBI. Such directions shall include a delegation of authority to the receiver to enter into individual transactions not to exceed a stated amount for each such transaction, including, but not limited to, sales of assets, individually or by bulk sale. Although the receiver may at any time apply to the CBI for directions, the receiver shall be obligated to apply to the CBI for directions only where specifically required to do so by a provision of this Law.

4. A receiver may employ at the expense of the bank for which the receiver has been appointed such independent attorneys, accountants and consultants, on such terms and conditions, as the CBI shall approve.

5. The Tribunal shall replace the receiver immediately upon the request of the CBI:

a. upon the resignation, death or incapacity to act of the receiver;
b. in the event that the receiver does not diligently perform the receiver's tasks;
c. in the event that the receiver no longer is a fit and proper person; or
d. if for any other reason, the receiver becomes ineligible to serve in that capacity.

6. Whenever a receiver is replaced, the person replacing the receiver shall succeed to the powers of the receiver being replaced, and the books, records and remaining assets of the bank in the custody of the receiver being replaced as well as the books and records of the receivership shall be promptly transferred into the custody of that person.

7. In the performance of its duties, the receiver shall conduct the operations of the receivership in a manner which maximizes the return from the sale or disposition of the bank's assets, minimizes the amount of any losses, and provides for the fair and consistent treatment of claimants in accordance with Article 92.[335]

Article 81 Powers of the receiver

1. Upon appointment the receiver shall become the sole legal representative of the bank, and shall succeed to all rights and powers of the shareholders of the bank relating to their shares of capital stock of the bank, the board of directors of the bank, and the authorized manager of the bank. Such rights and powers shall include holding title to the books, records, and assets of the bank; operating the bank; marshalling assets and claims; transferring or disposing of assets; and taking any other action necessary to the effective liquidation of the bank.

2. Claims against the bank shall be served on the receiver for the bank.

Article 82 Effect of bankruptcy decision

1. The decision of the Tribunal opening bankruptcy proceedings against a bank shall take effect at the time that the decision is taken.

[335] Para. 7 was added in 2004.

2. Immediately upon the decision referred to in paragraph (1) above taking effect, the bank shall cease to take deposits from the public.

3. Acts performed by or on behalf of the bank after the bankruptcy decision takes effect shall be legally void and unenforceable, except for acts performed by or under authority of the receiver for the bank and acts deemed beneficial to the estate of the bank by the receiver and ratified by the receiver.

4. As a result of the bankruptcy decision, all current court proceedings against the bank are stayed and no court proceeding against the bank shall commence after the bankruptcy decision takes effect.[336]

5. As a result of the bankruptcy decision, all attachments or liens in aid of execution in favor of the bank's creditors or other restraints on the bank's assets shall be deemed removed by operation of law. Attachments placed and acts of execution performed after the bankruptcy decision takes effect shall be void, except for execution in accordance with the provisions of Article 91 of assets encumbered by a mortgage or lien to the extent of the debt secured by such encumbrance.

6. Neither interest nor any other charge shall accrue on liabilities of a bankrupt bank after the bankruptcy decision takes effect.

7. Transfers of shares of a bankrupt bank made after the bankruptcy decision takes effect, except for transfers made with the prior consent of the CBI, shall be void.

8. All legal acts of the bank that are taken within 60 business days before the date of the CBI's decision appointing a conservator for the bank shall upon application of the receiver be declared null and void by the CBI if the bank and its counterparty in the act knew or should have known at the time of the act that the act would damage the interests of creditors of the bank. Such knowledge shall be presumed whenever the act consists of:[337]

a. a gift or other transfer without consideration to any person;
b. a payment or transfer to an owner, administrator or employee of the bank, unless such owner, administrator or employee shows to the satisfaction of the Tribunal that the payment or transfer concerned his or her employment by the bank or concerned an account maintained with the bank, or that he did not know that the payment or transfer would damage interests of creditors of the bank;
c. a payment or transfer before its due date or the transfer of collateral for a debt before the due date of the debt;
d. the conclusion or performance of a contract imposing obligations on the bank that are significantly more onerous than the obligations imposed on the other party or parties to the contract;
e. an arrangement between the bank and one or more others, other than an eligible financial contract defined in Article 88, permitting an offset between rights and obligations of the bank that without such arrangement would not have been permissible before the time of the bankruptcy decision; or
f. interbank transfers between a domestic branch of a foreign bank and such foreign bank or its branches or subsidiaries abroad.

[336] The Banking Law of 2003 included the proviso 'except with the leave of the Tribunal and subject to such terms as the Tribunal imposes.'

[337] The phrase 'before the date of the CBI's decision appointing a conservator for the bank' replaced the formulation 'before the time of the decision whereby bankruptcy proceedings are opened against the bank' in the Banking Law of 2003.

Article 83 Finality in payment and securities settlement systems

1. Irrevocable money and securities transfer orders entered by a bank into a payment or securities settlement system recognized as such by the CBI shall be legally enforceable and binding on third parties, even in the event of a decision of the Financial Services Tribunal opening bankruptcy proceedings against the bank, but only if the transfer orders become irrevocable before the bankruptcy decision takes effect.

2. Where a bank enters irrevocable money or securities transfer orders into a payment or securities settlement system recognized as such by the CBI after the Tribunal's decision opening bankruptcy proceedings against the bank takes effect and the transfer orders are carried out on the date of the Tribunal decision, the transfer orders shall be legally enforceable and binding on third parties, unless the receiver proves that the system operator was ware [sic] of the bankruptcy decision before the transfer orders became irrevocable.

3. Netting agreements of a payment or securities settlement system recognized as such by the CBI shall be enforceable notwithstanding the Tribunal's decision opening bankruptcy proceedings against its participant.

4. For the purposes of this article:
   a. a transfer order entered into a money or securities settlement system becomes irrevocable at the time defined by the rules of that system; and
   b. 'netting' means the conversion into one net claim or one net obligation of claims and obligations resulting from transfer orders which a participant or participants in a settlement system either issue to, or receive from, one or more other participants in that system with the result that only a net claim or a net obligation remains.

5. Nothing in this article limits the receiver's powers under paragraph (8) of Article 82 of this Law.[338]

Article 84 Transfers of bank shares, bank assets and liabilities

1. In the interests of preserving the soundness of the banking system and to maximize the value of a bank for its creditors, in the event that the receiver, with the concurrence of the CBI, determines that engaging in a transaction or series of transactions set forth in subparagraphs (a) or (b) of this paragraph is necessary, the receiver shall apply to the Tribunal for approval to:
   a. transfer all or substantially all of the shares in capital stock of the bank; or
   b. transfer all or substantially all of the assets of the bank or all or substantially all of the liabilities of the bank, or both; provided, however, that the approval of the Tribunal shall not be necessary for transactions other than those referred to in sub-paragraphs (a) and (b) above.

[338] Art 83 of the Banking Law of 2003 read: '1. Notwithstanding the provisions of paragraph (4) of Article 61, paragraph (2), subparagraph (a) of Article 69, and paragraph (2) and paragraph (7), sub-paragraphs (b) and (c) of Article 82: a. irrevocable money and securities transfer orders entered by a bank into a payment or securities settlement system recognized as such by the CBI shall be legally enforceable and binding on third parties, even in the event of a decision of the Financial Services Tribunal opening bankruptcy proceedings against the bank, but only if the transfer orders become irrevocable before the bankruptcy decision takes effect; or b. where a bank enters irrevocable money or securities transfer orders into a payment or securities settlement system after a court decision opening bankruptcy proceedings against the bank takes effect and the transfer orders are carried out on the day of the Tribunal decision, the transfer orders shall be legally enforceable and binding on third parties, unless the receiver proves that the system operator was aware of the bankruptcy decision before the transfer orders became irrevocable. 2. No law, regulation, rule or practice on the setting aside of contracts and transactions issued or adopted before the Tribunal decision opening bankruptcy proceedings against a bank takes effect shall lead to the unwinding of a netting by a payment or securities settlement system recognized as such by the CBI because of that decision.' Para 3 of the 2003 Law is identical with para 4 of the 2004 Law.

2. The Tribunal shall render a decision approving or disapproving the application of the receiver referred to in paragraph (1) above within three business days of receipt of such application.

3. A transaction pursuant to paragraph (1) may be requested and authorized at any time after the filing of a petition for opening bankruptcy proceedings against the bank until the bank has been liquidated.

4. A transfer of liabilities under paragraph (1), sub-paragraph (b) shall become effective for all interested parties at the beginning of the day following the day of publication of a notice of the transfer in the Official Publication.

Article 85 Property report

1. Within two weeks from the date of the Tribunal decision opening bankruptcy proceedings against a bank, the receiver shall submit to the CBI a property report listing:

   a. the assets of the bank, including claims of the bank on account of unpaid subscriptions of capital stock of the bank, loan and guarantee agreements, and agreements of purchase or sale, as well as the book values and estimated liquidation values of the assets;
   b. the contracts pursuant to which property of the bank is held by other parties, including rental, lease and collateral agreements;
   c. the contracts pursuant to which the bank receives services; and
   d. the significant transactions entered into by the bank during the period of 60 business days immediately preceding the date of the bankruptcy decision.

2. The report shall be updated quarterly and shall be made available at the CBI for inspection by the creditors of the bank whose claims are included on the list of approved claims prepared pursuant to Article 87.

Article 86 Registration of claims

1. Except as provided in paragraphs (1) and (2) of Article 87, claims on a bankrupt bank shall be registered with the receiver in writing within 60 business days from the date that the Tribunal decision opening bankruptcy proceedings against the bank is published in the *Official Gazette*; at the request of three or more creditors submitted to the Tribunal at least ten days prior to the expiration of the period referred to in this paragraph, the Tribunal may once extend this term for all creditors by 20 business days on grounds of equity.

2. Claims shall be registered together with documentary evidence of the claim and the following information:

   a. the name and address of the creditor;
   b. the amounts of interest and other charges, penalties and taxes included in the principal amount of the claim; and
   c. details concerning any mortgage, lien or guarantee securing the claim, including the name and address of any guarantor.

3. The decision of the Tribunal opening bankruptcy proceedings against a bank suspends the authority of depositors to access their deposits recorded in the books or records of the bank.

4. Creditors shall be given a registration receipt by the receiver on the registering of a claim, which receipt shall be conclusive evidence of registration.

Article 87 Admission of claims

1. Only claims that are registered in accordance with Article 86 may be admitted by the receiver, except that claims on account of deposits recorded in the books or records of the bank shall be admitted for the amounts so recorded without requiring registration.

2. Registered claims recorded in the books or records of the bank shall be admitted by the receiver as recorded without further proof, except that claims registered for an amount that is less than the amount recorded by the bank shall be admitted only for the lesser amount.

3. Creditors of the bank with claims secured by a mortgage or lien resting on assets of the bank may register their claims for the amount by which the amount of the claim exceeds the expected sales value of the asset in a public auction or the market value as determined by an independent appraiser. Any claim so registered shall not be admitted until the auction has taken place or title to the asset has been otherwise transferred pursuant to Article 91.

4. Claims whose value is uncertain may be admitted for a value estimated by the receiver.

5. After examining the registered claims, the receiver shall record the claims admitted by the receiver on a list of admitted claims and the claims contested by the receiver on a list of contested claims specifying the reasons for the opposition. Registered claims contested in part shall be recorded on both lists for the admitted part and the contested part respectively. Both lists shall for each claimant specify name and address, the amounts of the claims, and whether the claims are secured by collateral; claims of equal ranking shall be listed together, in the order of their priority of payment.

6. Both lists shall be completed and submitted to the Tribunal for approval within 30 business days from the deadline for registration of claims. Thereafter, the receiver shall submit quarterly updated lists to the Tribunal for approval. Before approving the lists, the Tribunal may move claims from one list to the other in consultation with the receiver. The Tribunal may specify the evidence required for the approval of contested claims.

7. The Tribunal shall set dates for hearings where creditors whose claims are contested may submit evidence to prove their claims to the receiver and the Tribunal, provided that such hearings shall be held not later than 40 business days after the date on which the list of contested claims is submitted to the Tribunal. Creditors shall be notified of the date of each hearing by mail and by notice placed by the receiver in the Official Publication. No creditor need be notified of a hearing by mail more than once for the same claim. Following the hearing, the Tribunal shall decide whether the contested claims shall be approved or rejected. Claims for which the creditor fails to appear at the hearing of which the creditor has been notified by mail shall be regarded as rejected. Creditors whose claims have been rejected shall be notified by the receiver in writing.

8. The approval by the Tribunal of claims shall be final. Claims approved by the Tribunal shall be removed from the list of admitted claims or the list of contested claims and be recorded on a list of approved claims kept by the Tribunal and the receiver. Creditors whose claims have been approved by the Tribunal shall be notified by the receiver in writing.

9. No payment shall be made by the receiver on account of claims that are rejected by the Tribunal. The creditor whose claim has been rejected by the Tribunal may appeal the decision of the Tribunal to the appropriate appellate court within two weeks after the date of receipt of notice of the decision.

Article 88 Set off and netting

1. Except as otherwise stated in this article, nothing in this Law and no decision made under this Law shall prevent or prohibit the set off by operation of law of obligations between a bankrupt bank and its contractual counterparties.

2. In determining the rights and obligations between a bankrupt bank and its contractual counterparties, effect shall be given to the termination provisions of eligible financial contracts between them. The net termination value determined in accordance with an eligible financial contract between them shall be a claim of the bank on the counterparty or shall be admitted after its registration as a claim of the counterparty on the bank. In this paragraph (2), 'eligible financial contract' means any of the following agreements:

a. a currency or interest rate swap agreement;
b. a basis swap agreement;
c. a spot, future, forward or other foreign exchange agreement;
d. an agreement providing for a cap, collar or floor transaction;
e. a commodity swap agreement;
f. a forward rate agreement;
g. a repurchase or reverse repurchase agreement;
h. a spot, future, forward or other commodity agreement;
i. an agreement to buy, sell, borrow or lend securities, to clear or settle securities transactions or to act as a depository for securities;
j. any derivative, combination or option in respect of, or agreement similar to, an agreement referred to in sub-paragraphs (a) to (i);
k. any master agreement in respect to an agreement referred to in sub-paragraphs (a) to (j);
l. any master agreement in respect of a master agreement referred to in subparagraph (k);
m. a guarantee of the liabilities under an agreement referred to in sub-paragraphs (a) to (l); and
n. any agreement of a kind prescribed by regulation of the CBI; and 'net termination value' means the net amount obtained after setting off the mutual obligations between the parties to an eligible financial contract in accordance with its provisions.

3. Except as provided by Article 83, no set off shall be allowed with respect to claims acquired and debts assumed with respect to a bank after the Tribunal decision opening bankruptcy proceedings against the bank takes effect or with respect to claims acquired and debt assumed in bad faith before that decision takes effect.

Article 89 Termination of current contracts

1. All current contracts or portions of contracts of a bankrupt bank may be terminated unilaterally by the receiver within a reasonable time after the petition for opening bankruptcy proceedings has been granted not to exceed 60 business days . . . [sic][339]

2. Subject to Article 88 of this Law, the receiver may enforce any contract of the bank notwithstanding any provision of the contract providing for termination, default,

[339] The single paragraph of Art 89 of the Banking Law of 2003 had read: 'All current contracts or portions of contracts of a bankrupt bank for the delivery of goods or services, including contracts of sale, rental and lease contracts, hire purchase contracts and employment contracts, may be terminated unilaterally by the receiver within a reasonable time after the petition for opening bankruptcy proceedings has been granted not to exceed 60 business days, provided, however, that any party or beneficiary to such contract may register a claim for compensation for breach of contract, which compensation shall be limited to direct compensatory damages up to the date of termination of such contract by the receiver, with interest to the date of payment, but which shall not include any punitive damages, damages for pain and suffering, or any damages for lost profits or lost opportunities.'

acceleration, or exercise of rights upon, or solely by reason of, insolvency or the appointment of a conservator or receiver.

Article 90 Negotiated settlements

With the prior approval of the CBI, the receiver for a bank may enter into and carry out negotiated settlements of claims with any creditor and debtor of the bank. No such settlement shall be subject to opposition, review or appeal.

Article 91 Secured claims

1. Assets securing an approved claim of a creditor against the bank shall be sold in a commercially reasonable manner and the secured creditor shall be deemed repaid in full to the extent that proceeds of the sale provide sufficient funds to cover the approved claim. If proceeds of the sale exceed the approved value of a claim, any such excess funds shall be remitted to the receiver for inclusion in the assets of the bank available for distribution to other creditors as provided in paragraph (1) of Article 92. If the proceeds of the sale are insufficient to satisfy the approved value of a claim in full, the balance shall be treated as an unsecured claim of the creditor against the bank pursuant to paragraph (1), sub-paragraph (f) of Article 92.
2. In the case of secured claims of the bank against other persons, if the claim is due on demand or is mature, or if the maturity of the claim can be accelerated, the assets securing the bank's claim shall be placed at the disposal of the receiver promptly upon the receiver's request. The assets shall be sold in a commercially reasonable manner and the bank shall be deemed repaid in full to the extent that the proceeds of the sale generate sufficient funds to cover the claim. If proceeds of the sale exceed the value of the bank's claim, any such excess funds shall be remitted to the owner of the assets. If the proceeds of the sale are insufficient to satisfy the value of the bank's claim in full, the receiver may proceed against the obligor to recover the deficiency. Secured claims of the bank against other persons that are not yet mature where the maturity cannot be accelerated under the terms of any applicable agreement may be sold by the receiver without the consent of such other persons.
3. Assets shall be deemed to have been sold in a commercially reasonable manner when they are disposed of as follows:
   a. securities, foreign currencies and other assets that can be readily sold at market sold in the markets where they are traded; and
   b. sold at public auction, provided that if the receiver determines that no reasonable price can be obtained for assets in a public auction, the CBI may authorize the receiver to sell the assets privately at a price approved by the CBI.
4. Any dispute between the receiver and a secured creditor as to the value of an asset securing a claim shall be resolved by the CBI unless the asset is sold at market or at public auction, in which event the sales price at market or at public auction shall be conclusive as to the value of the asset.
5. Notwithstanding paragraph (1) above, with respect to assets other than those set forth in paragraph 3, sub-paragraph (a), the receiver may satisfy the claim of any secured creditor by payment to such creditor without the need for a public auction. In such event, the receiver may rely on an appraisal of an independent third party of the assets in question.

Article 92 Priority of payments

1. The assets of a bankrupt bank shall be distributed among its creditors in the following order of priority:
   a. claims with regard to deposits that are not in the form of debt securities up to a maximum amount of 5 million *dinars* per depositor;
   b. all costs and expenses on account of the administration of the bankruptcy or the conservatorship including the costs of additional or new financing, goods or services provided after the bank is placed under the control of the conservator or receiver;[340]
   c. liabilities of the bank on account of conservatorship and rehabilitation;
   d. state and local taxes and state social security premiums due over a period of not more than one year preceding the date of the bankruptcy decision;
   e. salary payments to employees of the bank, excluding any remuneration of members of the board of directors, as accrued to the date of the decision to open bankruptcy proceedings;
   f. any claims of depositors not paid under sub-paragraph (a) together with claims of unsecured creditors; and
   g. any claims relating to subordinated debt.
2. Remaining assets shall be transferred to the owners of the bank pro rata to their respective ownership shares.

Article 93 Liquidation plan

1. Within 60 business days from the date of the decision of the Tribunal opening bankruptcy proceedings against a bank, the receiver shall prepare and submit to the CBI for its approval a detailed liquidation plan for the bank. The plan shall include:
   a. a current pro forma balance sheet showing the assets and liabilities of the bank valued at their estimated liquidation value and a pro forma balance sheet of the expected assets and liabilities of the bank at a date about three months later; the balance sheets shall show liabilities as admitted claims of creditors as well as approved claims and contested claims of creditors;
   b. quarterly statements of past and projected income and expenses of the bank;
   c. a progress report on the sale and on plans for the sale of major assets or groups of assets of the bank;
   d. a report on the judicial or extrajudicial pursuit of claims of the bank, including court action to obtain annulment of fraudulent agreements and the transfers made and rights created by them;
   e. a report on illegal activities of administrators of the bank and actions to obtain compensation for the bank;
   f. a report on the continuation or termination of ongoing contracts, such as insurance, employment and service contracts of the bank, including a detailed analysis of financial provisions for bank employees;
   g. a report on the liabilities of the bank and a schedule of expected payments to creditors of the bank during the next quarter; and
   h. a report on the costs and expenses of the receivership as of the date of the liquidation plan, and an estimate of future costs and expenses.

[340] The part of the sentence starting with 'including [...]' was added in 2004.

2. The liquidation plan shall be updated quarterly. After its approval by the CBI, the liquidation plan shall be available for inspection by the creditors of the bank whose claims are included on the list of approved claims prepared pursuant to Article 87.

Article 94 [Reserved][341]

Article 95 No compromise with creditors
Subject to the provisions of Article 90, there shall be no compromise or other arrangement with groups of creditors concerning a bankrupt bank.

Article 96 General meeting and committee of creditors
1. There shall be no general meeting of creditors concerning the liquidation of a bankrupt bank unless, at the request of the receiver, the CBI decides that such meeting is desirable to achieve an efficient liquidation of the bank.
2. There shall be no committee of creditors concerning the liquidation of a bankrupt bank unless, at the request of the receiver, the CBI decides that such committee is desirable to represent and protect significant interests of one or more classes or groups of creditors.
3. The CBI decisions authorizing a general meeting of creditors or a committee of creditors shall specify the tasks of the meeting or the committee and the scope of its activities.

Article 97 Immediate advances to depositors
Claims on account of demand deposits with a bankrupt bank that are not in the form of debt securities may be paid in advance of any other distribution to unsecured creditors up to a maximum amount of 5 million *dinars* per depositor.

Article 98 Distribution of payments
1. Subject to Article 92, approved claims shall be ranked and combined according to their priority of payment and recorded in a distribution schedule. Except for the provisions of Article 97, the amounts to be paid on claims of the same class shall be determined on the basis of the same percentage applied to the amount of available funds.
2. At any time, and consistent with Article 92, the receiver may propose and the CBI may approve a distribution schedule of payments to be made to creditors of the bank with approved claims.
3. Immediately after the approval of a distribution schedule by the CBI, the receiver shall make the payments listed in that distribution schedule. Amounts included in a distribution schedule that cannot be paid because the creditors cannot be identified or contacted shall be deposited in an account with the CBI. The receiver shall publish a notice in the Official Publication and two newspapers of general circulation inviting these creditors by name to come forward. The amounts so deposited shall remain available for payment to the creditors or their successors until the statute of limitations for the claims has run out, in which case the unpaid amounts shall be transferred to the State Treasury.

Article 99 Bankruptcy proceedings concerning branch or representative office
1. Bankruptcy proceedings may be opened against a domestic branch office or a domestic representative office of a foreign bank:

[341] Art 94 [Rehabilitation of bankrupt banks] of the Banking Law of 2003 had read: 'No bankrupt bank shall be rehabilitated in whole or in part except as provided by Article 67.'

a. if any of the grounds listed in Article 71 applies to such office as if it were a separate legal entity; or
b. at the petition of the CBI, if bankruptcy proceedings have been opened against the foreign bank in the country where its head office is located or where it principally carries on business.

2. The provisions of this section shall apply to the domestic branch offices and domestic representative offices of a foreign bank as if all these offices together were to form a single legal entity. All assets, liabilities, acts and omissions of the foreign bank resulting from or otherwise relating to the business of any such office shall be attributed to that single entity in applying the provisions of this article. The receiver shall be authorized to take all actions with respect to such single entity as could be taken, were it to be a domestic bank, by the authorized manager or shareholders at the general meeting of shareholders.

3. At the time that the decision of the Tribunal opening bankruptcy proceedings against a domestic branch office or a domestic representative office of a foreign bank is served on that office, the foreign bank shall cease all banking activities in Iraq, except for banking activities carried out by or with the prior written authorization of the receiver appointed for that office.

4. In its application in bankruptcy proceedings opened against an office of a foreign bank, Article 88 only applies to the set off and netting of obligations resulting from or otherwise relating to the business of the foreign bank in Iraq.

5. Bankruptcy proceedings in Iraq opened against an office of a foreign bank shall not limit the rights of creditors of the foreign bank to pursue foreign assets of that bank in satisfaction of their claims.

Article 100 Cross border bank insolvency

1. In order to promote equal access of domestic and foreign creditors to a universal pool of assets of a bankrupt bank with cross border activities:
a. if a bankrupt domestic bank has branch offices or representative offices in a foreign country, the CBI shall cooperate as much as possible with the authorities of that country;
b. if a creditor of a bankrupt domestic bank has received partial payment on its claims in a foreign country, the balance of its claims may be presented for payment together with costs incurred in the proceeding in Iraq;
c. the Financial Services Tribunal shall decide to what extent foreign bankruptcy decisions, conservation measures and bank rehabilitation measures concerning foreign banks should be recognized with respect to their domestic branch offices and representative offices; and
d. if a foreign bank is in liquidation in the country in which its head office is located or where it principally carries on business, the Tribunal may at the request of the CBI authorize the transfer to the liquidator in that country of such assets of the foreign bank as the CBI shall deem advisable and in the interest of the creditors of that bank.

2. A receiver or conservator for any bank shall be the sole representative of such bank, its branches, offices, and subsidiaries, wherever situated, and may take such action in the courts of Iraq or other jurisdictions, as may be necessary or appropriate to carry out the provisions of this Law.

Article 101 Consultations between the Financial Services Tribunal and CBI
Before taking any decision affecting a bank declared bankrupt, the Tribunal shall inform the CBI of its proposed decision and afford the CBI a reasonable opportunity to give its advice to the Tribunal concerning the proposed decision. In making its decision, the Tribunal shall take account of the advice of the CBI. In the event that the Tribunal rejects all or part of the advice of the CBI, the decision shall describe the advice so rejected and give the grounds for the rejection.

Article 102 Termination of bankruptcy proceedings
1. Upon termination of the receiver's tasks, the receiver shall be discharged by decision of the Tribunal, but not before the receiver has prepared and submitted to the Tribunal a report of the receivership. The decision of discharge by the Tribunal shall direct where the books and records of the bank and the receivership shall be deposited.
2. The bankruptcy proceedings against a bank shall be terminated by decision of the Tribunal when all assets of the bank have been liquidated and the proceeds paid to the creditors of the bank or deposited with the CBI to remain available for payment to creditors of the bank pursuant to paragraph (3) of Article 98.
3. The decision of the Tribunal terminating bankruptcy proceedings against a bank shall be published by the Tribunal in the Official Publication.

Section 15 – Final Provisions

Article 103 Applicability of certain laws
The provisions of the Public Companies Law or any other law that may replace either of the aforesaid two laws shall apply to banks to the extent that these provisions do not conflict with the provisions of this Law and the Central Bank of Iraq Law and regulations and orders issued there under.

Article 104 Regulations
1. The CBI shall have the power to issue regulations, orders, guidance, and information to facilitate the implementation of this Law. Regulations, and any subsequent amendments thereof, shall be published in the Official Publication.
2. If the CBI proposes to issue a regulation pursuant to this Law, it shall publish a draft of the proposed text of the regulation in a form and in a manner determined by it to be best calculated to bring the proposed regulation to the attention of the domestic banking industry and the general public. The draft shall be accompanied by an explanation of the purpose of the proposed regulation and a request for comments within a specified time of not less than one month after the date of publication of the draft. The CBI shall have regard to any comment received and issue the final text of the regulation accompanied by an account in general terms of the comments. This procedure shall not apply if the delay involved would be a serious threat to the interests of the banking system, provided that such decision by the CBI shall be explained in the preamble to the regulation.

Article 105 Judicial review
1. Final orders and decisions of the CBI under this Law shall be subject to review in a court of law only as stipulated in this Law.

2. Any aggrieved party may, within 30 days following the date of receipt of the order or decision, or within such shorter period of time as is specified in this Law, appeal any final order or decision of the CBI:

a. rejecting the application for a license or permit under paragraph (8) of Article 8;
b. revoking the license or permit under Article 13; or
c. imposing any measure or administrative penalty pursuant to paragraph (2) of Article 56 to the Tribunal, which must decide the appeal pursuant to the Central Bank of Iraq Law, provided that the filing of an appeal does not automatically result in a suspension of the revocation or any measures or administrative penalties imposed by the CBI.

3. Tribunal decisions may be appealed for judicial review only as provided for in the Central Bank of Iraq Law.

4. Notwithstanding paragraph (2) above, in any case brought under Articles 59 through 102 of this Law, the Tribunal, or other appropriate court may award monetary damages, but shall not suspend, enjoin, terminate or bar any act of a conservator, receiver, the CBI or the State, except with respect to a decision by the Tribunal regarding the removal of a conservator under Article 63.

Article 106 Transitional provisions

1. The Post Office shall be exempted from the application of this Law through December 31, 2005.

2. Every bank that, on the date that this Law enters into effect, carries a banking license or permit issued by the CBI may continue to operate as a bank and shall be subject to the provisions of this Law.

3. Every bank that, on the date that this Law enters into effect, carries a banking license or permit shall provide the CBI with a list of shareholders as described in paragraph (2), subparagraph (e) of Article 5, and for each owner of a qualifying holding, including the ultimate beneficial owner of such qualifying holding, the information and an affidavit as described in paragraph (2), sub-paragraphs (d), (f) and (j) of Article 5, and such other information on their owners, in particular owners of a qualifying holding, as requested by the CBI, within one year of the law's entry into force.

4. The capital requirements set out in paragraph (1) of Article 14 and paragraph (1) of Article 16 shall not apply through December 31, 2005 for every bank that, on the date that this Law enters into effect, carries a banking license or permit issued by the CBI and which has obtained the CBI's approval of a plan and timetable detailing the proposed increase of its capital by December 31, 2005.

5. The prohibition established in paragraph (1), sub-paragraph (b) of Article 30 shall not apply through December 31, 2005, provided that banks may not increase the aggregate outstanding principal amount of any such single large credit exposure to exceed the limit of 25 percent of the bank's unimpaired capital and reserves over that time period.[342]

6. Through December 31, 2004, banks are prohibited from engaging in active trading in equities for their own account and shall not acquire stocks, shares, or equity-linked bonds by means of purchase without the CBI's prior approval.

7. Notwithstanding the limit established in paragraph (3) of Article 60, through December 31, 2005, the term of appointment of a conservator may be extended for two

[342] In the Banking Law of 2003 it had read: 'such single large credit exposure exceeding the limit of 25 percent during that time.'

further periods of up to 18 months each, provided that such appointment shall extend through June 30, 2007 at the latest.

8. Through December 31, 2004, the provisions of section 7 shall not apply to banks that are solely owned by the State, provided they are subject to a government audit by the Board of Supreme Audit.

Article 107 Relationships to other provisions of the laws of Iraq

1. Provisions in the Law of Companies that limit the percent of participation in companies is not applicable to shareholdings in banks.

2. In case of inconsistency with a provision of any other law of Iraq, this Law shall prevail.

Article 108 Entry into force

This law shall enter into force on the same date that the Order authorizing this law enters into force. Thereafter, this law shall be published in the Official Publication.

Document 119

Coalition Provisional Authority Order Number 95

CPA/ORD/2 June 2004/95

Financial Management Law and Public Debt Law

Pursuant to my authority as Administrator of the Coalition Provisional Authority (CPA) and under the laws and usages of war, and consistent with relevant U.N. Security Council resolutions, including Resolutions 1483 and 1511 (2003),

Having worked closely with the Governing Council to ensure that economic change occurs in a manner acceptable to the people of Iraq,

Acknowledging the Governing Council's desire to bring about significant change to the Iraqi economic system,

Determined to improve the conditions of life, and opportunities for all Iraqis and to fight unemployment with its associated deleterious effect on public security through stable financial markets,

Recognizing that Iraq needs laws concerning the issuance and payment of public debt to assist in financing the Government and to promote confidence in the country's economic system,

Further recognizing the CPA's obligation to provide for the effective administration of Iraq,

Recalling that U.N. Security Council Resolution 1483 (2003) called upon the CPA to promote economic reconstruction and the conditions for sustainable development,

Acting in a manner consistent with the Report of the Secretary General to the Security Council of July 17, 2003, concerning the need for the development of Iraq and the need to enact institutional and legal reforms to give it effect,

I hereby promulgate the following:

Section 1 Purpose

1) This Order promulgates the Financial Management Law, which establishes a comprehensive framework for the conduct of fiscal and budgetary policy in line with international best practices, by setting a structured process for the formulation of the federal budget and a number of reporting requirements aimed at increasing the accountability and transparency of the budgeting process.

2) This Order promulgates the Public Debt Law, which authorizes the Ministry of Finance to issue and pay debt securities guaranteed by the Government, and establishes certain related authorities and duties, for the purposes of financing Government operations and promoting a stable Iraqi economy.

Section 2 Financial Management Law

The Financial Management Law attached to this Order as Annex A shall have the full force and effect of law.

Section 3 Public Debt Law

The Public Debt Law attached to this Order as Annex B shall have the full force and effect of law.

Section 4 General Provisions

1) Prior to the transfer of governance authority to the Iraqi Interim Government in accordance with Article (2)(B)(1) of the Law of the Administration for the State of Iraq for the Transitional Period, the powers and responsibilities assigned to the Prime Minister and Council of Ministers by the Financial Management Law and the Public Debt Law shall be exercised by the Administrator.

2) Until such time as the Iraqi Interim Government assumes full governance authority in accordance with Article (2)(B)(1) of the Law of the Administration for the State of Iraq for the Transitional Period, the Ministry of Finance is prohibited from issuing new debt securities if the issuance of such securities would increase the total level of Iraq's public debt, including obligations to the Central Bank, beyond the current level of such debt.

3) Notwithstanding any provision of the Financial Management Law to the contrary, spending units shall submit requests for allocation of funds for the budget for fiscal year 2005 to the Ministry of Finance not later than 15 June 2004.

Section 5 Inconsistent Legislation

Any provision of Iraqi law that was enacted prior to the effective date of this Order, Annex A, or Annex B is hereby suspended to the extent of such inconsistency.

Section 6 Entry into Force

This Order shall enter into force on the date of signature [4 June 2004].

ANNEX A[343]

Iraq
Financial Management Law of 2004

Section 1 Purpose

This Law shall regulate the arrangements governing the preparation, adoption, recording, management, execution, and reporting of the federal budget of Iraq and related issues including public borrowing and guarantees, internal control, accounting, and auditing. The principles of transparency, comprehensiveness, and unity shall be of fundamental importance in the preparation and execution of the federal budget of Iraq, and in related issues.

The principle of transparency requires that budget information be classified according to accepted international standards and presented in a way that facilitates policy analysis and promotes accountability.

The principle of comprehensiveness requires that the budget cover all government agencies and institutions undertaking government operations, so that the budget presents a consolidated and complete view of these operations and is voted on, as a whole, by the body vested with national legislative authority.

The principle of unity requires that all government resources be directed to a common pool to be allocated and used for public expenditure according to the priorities of the government.

Section 2 Definitions for the Purposes of this Law

1) '*Budget appropriation*' is the legal authorization given to the government to spend public money over the fiscal year for specified purposes.

2) '*Authorized person*' is a person delegated authority in writing by the Minister of Finance to manage public money.

3) '*Borrowings*' are funds received in return for a legally binding agreement to repay.

4) '*Budget*' is a financial program based on annual estimates of government cash receipts and payments, transfers, and transactions in kind.

5) '*Budget executor*' is an authorized person, or person delegated authority by the budget executor, responsible for the execution of the budget.

6) '*Capital expenditures*' are the use of funds to acquire or upgrade capital assets, such as buildings, structures, machinery, and equipment, and financial assets.

7) '*Cash payments*' are any monetary transactions resulting in a reduction in the balance of a bank account or cash balance.

8) '*Chart of accounts*' is a structured list of accounting codes used to classify and record budget revenue and expenditure transactions.

9) '*Commitment*' is an undertaking to make an expenditure following the conclusion of a binding agreement that will result in a payment.

10) '*Contingency reserves*' are funds allocated to the Ministry of Finance in the annual budget law or supplementary budget laws for the purpose of making expenditures that are urgent and unforeseen at the time of passage of the annual budget law.

[343] The phrase 'the body vested with the national legislative authority,' which appears at Annex A, Sections 1, 4(2), 6(8), 7(1), 7(3), 7(4), 7(5), 9(6), 9(8), 10(7), 11(5), 11(6), 11(8), and 15(7) of the Financial Management Law of 2004, was defined by CPA Order No 100, sec 3(35) *[Doc 124]*.

11) '*Council of Ministers*' is the Council of Ministers described in the Law of Administration for the State of Iraq for the Transitional Period (the 'Transitional Administration Law' or 'TAL').

12) '*Current expenditures*' are expenditures which are not capital expenditures, such as salaries, supplies, services, and fuel.

13) '*Economic classification*' is a systematic arrangement of budget revenue and expenditure items by type for the purposes of financial statistical reporting and analysis.

14) '*Financial assets*' include foreign or domestic cash, deposits, loans, bonds, financial derivatives, accounts receivable, other types of claims, monetary gold, special drawing rights (SDRs), treasury bills, and shares.

15) '*Fiscal year*' is the general government's accounting period, which begins on January 1st and ends on December 31st.

16) '*Federal budget*' is the estimate of the total annual receipts and payments as approved by the Federal Government.

17) '*Federal government*' is the Iraqi Interim Government, the Iraqi Transitional Government, or the Government to be elected pursuant to a permanent constitution, as set forth in Article 61 of the Law of Administration for the State of Iraq for the Transitional Period (the 'Transitional Administration Law' or 'TAL').

18) '*Federal government bank account*' is a bank account for the receipt, payment, or transfer of public money belonging to the federal government.

19) '*Functional classification system*' means the array of budget authority, expenditures, and other budget data according to the major purpose served – for example, agriculture, national defense, and transportation.

20) '*General government*' comprises all government units primarily engaged in non-market operations, including the federal government, regional governments, governorates, municipal and local governments.

21) '*Government debt securities*' are debt securities issued by the Ministry of Finance, including debt securities lawfully issued prior to the effective date of the Public Debt Law promulgated in 2004.

22) '*Governorates' budgets*' are the estimates of annual receipts and payments of the governorates.

23) '*Governorate Councils*' are the Governorate Councils described in Section 2 of CPA Order Number 71, Local Governmental Powers (the 'Local Governmental Powers Law').[344]

24) '*Line items*' are the payments specifically itemized in the budget law.

25) '*In kind*' means a transfer or exchange in which payment takes the form of tangible property, intangible property, or services rather than cash.

26) '*Liability*' is a present obligation arising from past events, the settlement of which is expected to result in a future payment in cash or in kind.

27) '*Outlay*' means a payment to liquidate an obligation other than borrowing.

28) '*Payment arrears*' arise when a payment is not made by its due-for-payment date.

29) '*Petroleum*' means hydrocarbons, including, but not limited to, crude oil, natural gas, and natural gas liquids and refined petroleum products.

30) '*Petroleum revenue account*' means the Development Fund for Iraq (DFI) account as described in United Nations Security Council Resolution 1483 (2003) or any successor account to the DFI.

[344] See *Doc 95*.

31) '*Public money*' means cash and bank deposits within the custody and control of the federal government.

32) '*Public corporations*' are –

(1) State companies, as defined in Law Number 22 of 1997 on State Companies; and

(2) any other juridical person or unit that is owned or controlled by the federal government, and produces goods or services for the market and, in the case of a unit which is not a juridical person, functions independently and is capable of maintaining separate accounting.

33) '*Special budgetary funds*' are special funds whose sources, uses, and purposes are established by law.

34) '*Spending units*' are the ministries of the federal government and the administrative bodies of the federal and regional governments, governorates, and municipal and local governments, to which funding is allocated in the annual budget law.

35) '*Reallocate,*' in relation to a budget appropriation, means to move budgetary resources from one budget account, unit, or line item to another.

36) '*Transfers*' are the provision of goods and services, assets (including financial assets), or labor that do not require the recipient to provide a good, service, payment, or payment-in-kind in return.

37) '*Treasury Consolidated Account*' is a system managed by the Ministry of Finance for consolidating the balances of the cash accounts of the federal government for the purpose of efficient cash management.

38) '*Treasury general ledger*' is a system, based on double entry principles, of accounting for, executing, and reporting the budget.

39) '*Treasury Single Account*' is a bank account, or a set of linked bank accounts, of the government through which all government receipts and payments are channeled. It is controlled by the Ministry of Finance and is maintained at the Central Bank.

40) '*Government*' is the public authorities and agencies of Iraq, which are entities established through political processes, and that exercise legislative, judicial or executive authority within the territory of Iraq. Government does not include public corporations.

41) '*Government debt*' consists of all liabilities of the government that require payment or payments of interest and/or principal by the borrower to the lender at a date or dates in the future.

42) '*Petroleum revenue*' is petroleum export revenue, non-tax revenue earned from the sale of petroleum to domestic buyers (collectively, petroleum non-tax revenue), and tax revenue levied on petroleum (petroleum tax revenue).

43) '*Petroleum export revenue*' is non-tax revenue earned from the sale of petroleum to foreign buyers.

44) '*Publicly available*' means that information is available for ready access by any member of the public. This includes, but is not limited to, publication in the *Official Gazette*, on an unrestricted website, or in widely available public newspapers.

Section 3 Exercise and Delegation of Authority

1) The Minister of Finance may issue regulations, instructions, guidelines or directions as necessary to give effect to and implement this Law.

2) The Minister of Finance may delegate to officials within the Ministry of Finance who are authorized persons those authorities that are conferred upon him under this Order,

except the authority to waive the right of the federal government to collect amounts owing, to submit the draft annual federal budget to the Council of Ministers, and to sign borrowing and guarantee contracts of the federal government.

Section 4 General Provisions

1) The budget is adopted for the fiscal year and shall be valid during the year for which it is passed. Unspent appropriations will lapse at the end of the fiscal year for which they have been approved, except to the extent that goods and services have been validly ordered and received.

2) The draft annual budget law will be determined by the Council of Ministers and will be submitted by the Minister of Finance by October 10th to the body vested with national legislative authority for approval or adjustment pursuant to Article 33(C) of the TAL.

3) Pursuant to Article 25 of the TAL, the federal government has exclusive competence in drawing up the federal budget of Iraq. The Governorate Council, pursuant to Section 2 of the Local Governmental Powers Law, possesses the limited amendment authority to amend the budget plan of a ministry with regard to a specific project. Individual governorates' budgets for the fiscal year shall be passed by the Governorate Councils. Individual regions' budgets for the fiscal year shall be passed by the regional governments.

4) The annual federal budget shall comprise:

a) the receipts and payments in cash or in kind of all government ministries, organizations, and agencies of the federal government; and

b) transfers, including to regional governments, governorates, and municipal and local governments, including special budgetary funds.

5) The source of all receipts shall be specifically identified in the budget. All payments for the budget year and commitments for future years shall be disclosed in the budget, and the nature and duration of these commitments shall be limited as specified in the annual budget laws.

6) The difference between receipts (excluding borrowings) and payments (excluding repayments of debt principal) is the budget surplus (if positive) or the budget deficit (if negative).

7) Receipts consist of:

a) Tax revenues:
   1. Petroleum tax revenues;
   2. Non-petroleum tax revenues;

b) Non-tax revenues:
   1. Petroleum non-tax revenues;
   2. Non-petroleum non-tax revenues;
      1) Social security contributions;
      2) External grants;
      3) Others;

c) Domestic and external borrowing;

d) Repayment of government lending;

e) Proceeds from asset transfers;

f) Transfers of surplus profits from the Central Bank of Iraq in accordance with the relevant provisions of the Central Bank Law;

g) Transfers from public corporations;

h) Transfers from regional governments, governorates, and municipal and local governments, including special budgetary funds.

8) Payments consist of:
   a) Current expenditures, including for salaries and other allowances, outlays for goods and services, current transfers, including pensions and social security payments, that are paid in cash or have been issued in kind, interest payments and transfers in kind;
   b) Capital expenditures for purchase of fixed assets, inventories, intangible assets, financial assets, capital transfers that are paid in cash or have been issued in kind, and grants;
   c) Gross lending;
   d) Repayment of external and domestic debt;
   e) Other payments in accordance with the laws of the federal government;
   f) Transfers to the Central Bank of Iraq in accordance with the relevant provisions of the Central Bank Law;
   g) Transfers to public corporations;
   h) Transfers to regional governments, governorates, and municipal and local governments, including special budgetary funds.

9) A Treasury Consolidated Account shall be established and maintained within the Ministry of Finance. Subject to the transition provisions in Section 15, all receipts shall be credited to the Treasury Consolidated Account and paid into the Treasury Single Account, and all payments shall be debited to the Treasury Consolidated Account and withdrawn from the Treasury Single Account. All federal budget receipts, commitments, expenditures, and other payment transactions shall be entered into the Treasury's General Ledger.

10) The Minister of Finance shall issue orders to open bank accounts and such accounts must have a title that includes the words 'federal government.' An authorized person may dispose of federal government money only in accordance with this law and with regulations properly promulgated by the Minister of Finance. An authorized person must not misapply, improperly dispose of, or improperly use federal government money in contravention of this Law. Violations of this Law are subject to applicable administrative and criminal penalties under the legislation of Iraq, including Article 2(g) of Law Number 7 of 1958, Wastage of Natural Resources and Squandering of Public Assets and Funds, and applicable provisions of Law Number 111 of 1969, as amended, including provisions relating to bribery by public officials, embezzlement by public officials, and officials who overstep the bounds of their duty.

11) Subject to the monetary limits established by the Council of Ministers, the Minister of Finance may waive the right of the federal government to collect an amount owing, postpone the time of payment, or allow payment by installment only under the conditions and procedures provided by law.

12) The Minister of Finance shall report each and every such written-off sum or postponement to the Council of Ministers with the explanation for the write-off. This report shall be submitted quarterly with a final summary report to be submitted with the annual final accounts of the federal budget. These reports will be made publicly available.

13) The annual federal budget shall stipulate the use of the budget surplus or the means of financing the budget deficit.

14) The budget deficit shall be financed by cash balances of the federal government, short-term borrowings, domestic and external loans, or by the issuance of government debt securities. Short-term borrowings may be used for the purpose of ensuring liquidity during a period no longer than six months.

15) The annual federal budget shall be accompanied by documents that shall state the objectives and operating rules for fiscal policy, including constraints on borrowing and federal government debt, in accordance with the principles stated in Section 1 and with the provisions in Section 6(1) of this law and following Section 7(1), and will report on progress against these objectives.

Section 5 Management of Petroleum Revenues

1) All proceeds from the sale of petroleum or otherwise derived from current and prospective petroleum extraction, including from the federal government's production shares and royalties, and from the amount paid in respect of a right to explore for petroleum resources, and any amount derived from the investment of amounts in the petroleum revenue account, shall accrue to the budget. Except as provided in paragraph 2 of this section, below, or as may otherwise be required by applicable United Nations Security Council Resolutions (UNSCRs), the receipts from the export of petroleum shall be deposited into the Development Fund for Iraq (DFI) account to be held in the name of the Central Bank of Iraq, or a successor account to the DFI, hereafter generically referred to as the petroleum revenue account, and reflected accordingly as receipts and transfers to and from the budget.

2) Pursuant to United Nations Security Council Resolution 1483 (2003), and subsequent related UNSCRs, five percent (or such other percentage as may be determined by the United Nations Security Council or jointly by the internationally recognized, representative government of Iraq and the Governing Council of the United Nations Compensation Commission in accordance with UNSCR 1483) of the receipts from the export of petroleum shall be transferred to the Compensation Fund established in accordance with UNSCR 687 (1991) and subsequent relevant UNSCRs and the balance of receipts from the export of petroleum shall be deposited into the petroleum revenue account. These transfers to the Compensation Fund will be shown in the budget.

3) Disbursements from the petroleum revenue account shall be restricted to disbursements necessary to finance the budget, which shall include adequate provision for the government's obligations under any relevant UNSCRs or international law.

4) In the event that a successor account to the original DFI is established or the original DFI is continued beyond the date of the transfer of governance authority to the Iraqi Interim Government, the following will apply:

a) Operational responsibility for the petroleum revenue account will be with the Minister of Finance, reporting to the Council of Ministers, which shall take advice from the Governor of the Central Bank and such other individuals as the Council may deem appropriate. The Council, in its discretion, may delegate responsibility for oversight of the operation of the petroleum revenue account to a committee, which shall be composed of such individuals as the Council may determine, and shall include, as a minimum, the Minister of Finance, the Minister of Oil and the Governor of the Central Bank in an advisory capacity.

b) Disbursements from the petroleum revenue account require the authorizing signature of at least two authorized persons, one of whom is an official in the offices supporting the Prime Minister or Council of Ministers and reporting to the Prime Minister and the other a permanent employee of the Ministry of Finance, designated by the Prime Minister and the Minister of Finance, respectively. The persons to whom authority has been delegated may not delegate to another person.

c) Any positive balance in the petroleum revenue account may be invested by the Minister of Finance with the written consent of the Council of Ministers or the committee mentioned in section 5(4)(a) of this law. Any amount so invested shall at all times remain the property of the Government of Iraq. No contract or agreement that purports to encumber the assets of the petroleum revenue account shall be enforceable, and the assets shall continue to enjoy all privileges and immunities to the extent provided by UNSCR 1483, or as otherwise decided by the UN Security Council.

d) The activities of the petroleum revenue account shall be subject to external audit conducted under the oversight of the Board of Supreme Audit, which shall act in accordance with Law Number 6 of 1990 as amended by CPA Order Number 77 (CPA/ORD/18 April 2004/77),[345] except as otherwise provided by relevant UN Security Council Resolution.

5) The Minister of Finance shall make publicly available details of the petroleum revenue account; including opening and closing balance, underlying assets, and summary of movements, within three weeks of the end of each month. The Minister of Finance will authorize a quarterly review of the investment position, and by the end of the month following the end of each quarter submit a report on the results of the review to the Council of Ministers or the committee mentioned in section 5(4)(a) of this law. The final report for each year will detail each investment and enumerate the changes in the portfolio over the year and will be made publicly available.

Section 6 Budget Preparation

1) The preparation of the federal budget shall be based on the projections of economic development, the pursuit of macroeconomic stability, economic policy, and applicable laws and regulations, and shall be prepared with due regard to the desirability of ensuring the sustainability of Iraq's fiscal position, minimizing fluctuations in government spending, and achieving efficient revenue collection. In particular, the preparation of the federal budget will be based upon prudent and conservative forecasts for petroleum prices, petroleum production, and tax and customs revenue. The projections shall be prepared by the Ministry of Finance in consultation with the Central Bank and other Ministries in their respective areas of expertise.

2) During the month of May of each year, the Minister of Finance, shall issue a report on the priorities for fiscal policy for the next fiscal year, including the proposed total limit on spending and the limits for each individual spending unit, and submit it to the Council of Ministers for approval, together with the Final Accounts of the Federal Budget as submitted to the Board of Supreme Audit according to section 11(6) of this law, and an update on progress in execution of the budget in the current fiscal year. The Minister of Finance shall consult with the Minister of Planning and Development Cooperation on priorities, estimates of total funding, and procedures for preparing the capital spending plan and current budgetary implications of capital expenditures, including those to be implemented or financed by external sources.

3) In the month of June of each year, the Minister of Finance, in consultation with the Minister of Planning and Development Cooperation, and based on the priorities for fiscal policy established by the Council of Ministers, shall issue a circular setting guidelines

[345] See *Doc 101*.

and objectives of fiscal policy for spending units for the preparation of their budgets. The circular shall include key economic parameters, based on the macroeconomic framework referred to in Section 7(1), the procedures and timetable for budget preparation, as well as total levels of expenditure for each spending unit. This will serve as the basis for the spending unit to prepare its budget request.

4) In the month of July of each year, spending units will submit requests, including the information prescribed below, to the Minister of Finance for the allocation of funds. Copies of requests for the capital portion of the budget will also be submitted to the Ministry of Planning and Development Cooperation. Each request shall include:

a) The expenditure estimates for the budget year as prescribed in the economic and functional classification systems determined by the Minister of Finance in accordance with international accounting standards, including the value of outstanding commitments for the current or prior year;
b) Consistent with the guidelines issued by the Minister of Finance, the expenditure estimates for the year following the budget year (the 'upcoming fiscal year') and to the extent permissible given conditions prevailing in Iraq, for the two fiscal years following the upcoming fiscal year as prescribed in the economic and functional classification system determined by the Minister of Finance, in accordance with international accounting standards;
c) Estimates of personnel requirements for which budgetary funds are required;
d) Estimates of the requirements for other operating costs;
e) Multi-year commitments or multi-year payments, along with separately prepared capital expenditures; and
f) Estimates of receipts from the core activities of spending units.
g) Estimates of the proportion of expenditures that would be due in foreign currency.

5) The Minister of Finance may determine more specific requirements for the content and format of the request.

6) The Minister of Finance, in consultation with the Minister of Planning and Development Cooperation shall, on the basis of the estimates of revenue and submitted budget proposals for the allocation of budget funds, and in the light of discussions with proposing Ministers, determine estimated payments for spending units for the budget, as well as any amounts to be included in the contingency reserve.

7) In the event of an irreconcilable disagreement during discussions on the draft annual federal budget between the Minister of Finance and the Ministers responsible for spending units, the Minister of Finance will note the disagreement and explain his proposed solution in his submission of the draft annual federal budget. In determining the proposed solution, the Ministry of Finance may consult with the Ministry of Planning and Development Cooperation regarding the prioritization of capital expenditures. The Council of Ministers may, within the agreed aggregate limit, adjust appropriations in accordance with their collective priorities. Any increase in the aggregate spending limit must be based on a proposal submitted by the Minister of Finance and approved by the Council of Ministers.

8) In the month of September of each year, the Minister of Finance shall prepare the draft annual federal budget and submit it to the Council of Ministers for approval. The Minister of Finance shall submit the budget by October 10th to the body vested with the national legislative authority for approval.

Section 7 Budget Law

1) In preparing the draft annual budget law the following shall be taken into account, disclosed to the body vested with national legislative authority, and made publicly available in the documents accompanying the budget law:

a) A statement of the objectives and operating rules for fiscal policy in accordance with the principles stated in this law, and an explanation of how these objectives relate to provisions in the annual budget law;

b) A comprehensive and consistent quantitative macroeconomic framework, and the main assumptions underlying the budget, including the assumptions for oil prices and oil production. To the extent permissible given conditions prevailing in Iraq, the macroeconomic framework shall cover the budget year and the subsequent three years;

c) New policies being introduced in the annual budget and their quantified fiscal impact;

d) Major fiscal risks, quantified where possible, including variations in economic assumptions and the uncertain costs of specific expenditure commitments, including financial restructuring;

2) The draft annual budget law shall include:

a) The estimation of receipts in cash and in kind in accordance with economic classification;

b) The estimation of payments in cash and in kind in accordance with economic, organizational, and functional classifications;

c) The use of any surplus, and the financing of any deficit;

d) The contingency reserve, which shall be no greater than 5% of the non-interest expenditures of the federal budget;

e) Clear specification of the rules for authorization of expenditure and limits to expenditure. Limits on borrowing, issuance of government debt securities, change in stocks of government debt securities, and guarantees consistent with the Public Debt Law, and the authority granted to the Minister of Finance to buy, redeem, or refund outstanding government debt securities; and the draft budget law shall be accompanied by a report on the economic and financial situation, including the assumptions, methods, and outcomes of the economic projections on the basis of which the draft annual Federal budget law is established, including actual revenues, expenditures, balance and total debt of the general government for the past two years.

3) The body having national legislative authority has the right to reallocate proposed spending and to reduce the total amounts in the federal budget. It also has the right to propose an increase in the overall amount of expenditures to the Council of Ministers if necessary, and provide notice of this proposal to the Minister of Finance. The Minister of Finance will make a nonbinding recommendation to the Council of Ministers with respect to this proposal.

4) If the federal budget is not approved by the body vested with national legislative authority by December 31st, the Minister of Finance will, on a monthly basis, approve funds for spending units up to 1/12 (one twelfth) of appropriations of the previous fiscal year until a budget is approved. The funds so provided for can be used only for liquidation of existing commitments, salaries, pensions, social security payments, and debt service.

5) The annual federal budget may be amended through a supplementary budget only on the basis of a significant and unexpected change in economic circumstances or national

priorities. The supplementary budget must be determined by the Council of Ministers on recommendation of the Minister of Finance and approved by the body vested with national legislative authority. Should the Minister of Finance conclude that a supplementary budget is required, he shall make appropriate recommendations, including on proposed total receipts and payments, to the Council of Ministers. The Minister of Finance shall, within eight weeks after recommending that the Council of Ministers adopt a supplementary budget, submit details of the draft supplementary budget to the Council of Ministers for approval. The Council of Ministers shall approve such recommendations, with any appropriate modifications, within two weeks of receiving them. The draft supplementary budget, as approved by the Council of Ministers, shall be submitted to the body vested with national legislative authority within one week of such approval. The Minister of Finance shall issue regulations and guidelines for the procedures to be followed in preparing the supplementary budget.

6) The revenues and expenditures of special budgetary funds are to be reflected in the annual budget law.

7) The approved federal annual and supplementary budgets shall be published in the *Official Gazette* and made publicly available in other media, as appropriate.

Section 8 Public Corporations

1) Each public corporation shall prepare its budget proposal, and after approval by its directors and the competent minister, submit it to the Minister of Finance for review and final approval. The budget should, among other things, show budgeted revenues, expenses, profits or loss, capital expenditure, cash flows, borrowings, grants, transfers, contingent liabilities including guarantees, and balance sheet. Any amendments to the budget shall also be submitted to the Minister for Finance for review and approval. The Minister of Finance shall respect the operational independence of public corporations.

2) The budgets of public corporations are not incorporated into the federal government budget and are not incorporated into the budgets of any other level of government.

3) Public corporations shall submit by August 31st estimates of total loans and short-term borrowings to be raised in the forthcoming fiscal year for approval by the Minister of Finance. Public corporations will report monthly to the Minister of Finance on the amount of loans and short term borrowings raised. Guarantees given by the federal government in respect of public corporations borrowings shall be in accordance with law, and shall be disclosed in the final accounts of the federal government.

4) All public corporations shall submit their monthly accounts to the competent ministry 10 days following the end of each month. All public corporations shall submit semi-annual accounts to the Minister of Finance no later than July 15th. Each public company shall submit its audited final accounts to the Minister of Finance no later than March 31st of the year following the fiscal year ended. The final accounts shall include balance sheet, profit and loss statement, cash flow statement, and notes to the final accounts covering, among other things, accounting policies, revenues and expenses, assets and liabilities including borrowings, commitments, and contingent liabilities. The final accounts shall be prepared in accordance with international standards and shall be audited by an independent auditor.

Section 9 Budget Execution

1) The Minister of Finance is responsible for the execution of the federal budget.

2) No payments will be made from the Treasury Consolidated Account except under an appropriation made in the annual budget or supplementary budget law, under a standing

appropriation of another Law, or to make an investment in terms of Section 5(4)(c) of this Law.

3) Spending units will use the funds determined in the federal budget in accordance with a spending plan that has been approved by the Minister of Finance.

4) Spending units may not commit to making expenditures that exceed the amounts allocated to them, unless otherwise provided by the budget law.

5) Budget executors are responsible for ensuring that allocated funds within their spending units are used for lawful purposes.

6) Appropriations for contingency reserve funds may be used for payments that are urgent and that were unforeseen at the time the annual budget law was passed, if approved by the Council of Ministers and the Minister of Finance. The Minister of Finance shall propose the criteria for using reserve funds for approval by the Council of Ministers. All expenditures from the reserve will be reported to the body vested with national legislative authority.

7) In accordance with regulations prescribed by the Minister of Finance, the spending units, governorates, and special budgetary funds shall submit reports on realized receipts and executed payments to the Minister of Finance within 30 days following the end of each month. By the 15th of the subsequent month, the Ministry of Finance shall compile a consolidated report on realized receipts and executed payments on the basis of the reports submitted, and make it publicly available in the *Official Gazette* and other media, as appropriate.

8) The Ministry of Finance can authorize the responsible Minister or Ministers, subject to the provision below, to reallocate the approved budget appropriations from one spending unit to another up to a limit of five per cent of the amount approved by the annual or supplementary budget law for the spending unit that is to have its appropriation reduced. The following restrictions apply:

a) No funds can be reallocated between a current expenditure of one spending unit and the capital expenditures of another or between transfer payments of one spending unit and other items, including salaries, goods, and services or capital expenditures, of another.

b) Spending units may, with the approval of the Minister of Finance, reallocate their approved funds between line items by up to 5% of the total amount of funds approved provided that no funds can be reallocated from capital to current expenditures or between transfer payments and other current expenditures, including salaries, goods and services. Virement from salaries or current spending to capital spending of up to 5% may be permitted with the approval of the Minster of Finance.

c) A report of these transfers shall be prepared by Ministry of Finance and submitted on a quarterly basis to the body vested with national legislative authority. A copy of such report will be forwarded to the Minister of Planning and Development Cooperation.

9) Funds approved for spending units may be used only until the December 31st of the fiscal year, except to the extent that goods and services have been validly ordered and received. Receipts received after the end of a fiscal year will be recorded as receipts of the next fiscal year budget.

Section 10 Borrowings and Guarantees

1) Federal government debt may be in the form of domestic and foreign loans, short-term borrowings, and securities issues. The issue and redemption of securities shall

be managed by the Central Bank of Iraq as the agent for the federal government. The Ministry of Finance and the Central Bank shall share information on government cash and borrowing needs and current monetary conditions in order to ensure effective coordination of monetary and budgetary policy.

2) Governorates and regional governments may, upon notification to the Minister of Finance, raise funds through borrowings, and issue loan guarantees subject to the debt limit set in the annual budget law, and to the specific debt limit set for each entity under the apportionment approved by the Council of Ministers on a recommendation of the Minister of Finance. Regional governments and governorates shall submit by August 31st estimates of total outstanding borrowings, and borrowings to be raised in the forthcoming fiscal year for review and for approval by the Minister of Finance. Regional governments and governorates will report to the Minister of Finance monthly on the amount of outstanding borrowings raised and loan guarantees issued.

3) The Ministry of Finance shall submit to the Council of Ministers for approval with the draft annual budget law, the financial plan on loans, short-term borrowing, and the issuing of guarantees by the federal government, governorates regional governments. In addition, the Ministry will submit to the Council of Ministers a report any time that the plan must be changed. Such changes must remain within the limits set by the budget. The Ministry of Finance shall have the right, upon notification to the affected governorate or regional government, to adjust the timing of the issuance of governorate or regional government debt approved in the plan on the basis of macroeconomic and debt policy considerations.

4) The annual budget law shall determine the terms, conditions, and the limit on the annual increase in the total existing federal government, regional government and governorate and public corporation debt, and shall establish the total amount of guarantees to be issued by the federal government, regional governments, governorates, and public corporations.

5) The federal government shall set limits for guarantees issued by regional governments and governorates, but shall not guarantee them, unless explicitly provided in law.

6) The Minister of Finance shall sign the borrowing and guarantee contracts of the federal government, and shall enter into a contract with the Central Bank for services required in implementing all decisions on issues of securities.

7) The Minister of Finance shall maintain a record of all federal government debt. The authorized body within the regional governments and governorates shall maintain a record of existing regional government and governorate debt, loans granted, short-term borrowings, and issued guarantees, and shall provide the Ministry of Finance with an updated record of this information within 30 days of the end of each month.

8) The Minister of Finance shall prepare a consolidated report on all government debt within 90 days of the end of each fiscal year and shall make this report available to the public.

Section 11 Internal Control and Accounting

1) Budget executors shall be responsible for the accounting and internal control of transactions related to receipts, commitments, and payments of spending units and sub-units falling within their jurisdiction.

2) The Minister of Finance shall, on behalf of the federal government, have responsibility for the accounting, internal control, borrowing, and debt transactions associated with the budget.

3) The Minister of Finance shall prescribe internal control arrangements, accounting procedures and standards, submission of reports on the usage of budget funds, and the manner of recording receipts, payments, and commitments.

4) The Minister of Finance may issue special orders to spending units, governorates, municipal and local governments, and other budget entities for their submission of financial reports and shall prescribe the submission of the Final Accounts of spending units, including regional governments, governorates, municipal and local governments, and other budget entities.

5) The Minister of Finance shall submit to the body vested with national legislative authority by May 31st and November 30th, quarterly reports on the execution of budget revenue, expenditures, and financing for the quarters ending March 31st and September 30th, respectively. This report will include the execution of budget revenue, expenditures and financing of the federal budget. The Minister of Finance shall also submit to the body vested with national legislative authority by August 31st of each year a mid-year report on execution of budget revenue, expenditures, and financing for the half year ending June 30th. This report will include detailed information on the execution of budget revenue, expenditures and financing of the budget.

6) The Minister of Finance shall, by April 15th of the succeeding year, prepare the annual final accounts of the federal budget, including special budgetary funds, and submit it to the Board of Supreme Audit. The Board of Supreme Audit will provide an audit report on the final accounts by June 15th. The Council of Ministers will submit final accounts and the related audit report to the body vested with national legislative authority by June 30th.

7) The final accounts of the federal budget must be in accordance with the content and classifications of the budget and international accounting standards, and shall include the following:

a) An external audit report from the Board of Supreme Audit in accordance with the Board of Supreme Audit Law, as amended, and its established procedures;
b) The initial and final balance of the Treasury Consolidated Account and a summary of movements for the year;
c) A report on differences between budgeted and executed receipts and payments and on the financing of any deficit or the use of any surplus;
d) A report of all federal government borrowings for the year, and the total debt outstanding, including any payment arrears;
e) A report of spending from the budget contingency reserves;
f) A report on federal government guarantees issued during the fiscal year;
g) The Minister of Finance shall prepare a report of all borrowings by regional governments and governorates;
h) Outstanding amounts on capital contracts;
i) Retentions due on contracts;
j) Letters of credit entered into for which funds have been placed but for which goods have not been received;
k) The Minister of Finance shall prepare a report on all guarantees by regional governments and governorates.

8) Following approval of the final accounts of the annual federal budget by the body vested with national legislative authority, the final account shall be published in the *Official Gazette* and made publicly available.

Section 12 Ministry of Finance Functions

1) The Ministry of Finance shall be responsible for, but is not limited to, conducting the following treasury functions:

a) Executing all cash and non-cash payments on the basis of documentation and data supplied manually or electronically by spending units, in accordance with this Law;
b) Maintaining the Treasury general ledger and subsidiary accounts;
c) Processing budget allocations to spending units;
d) Preparing the federal government's final accounts;
e) Ensuring that no budget executor can exceed his annual appropriation;
f) Developing and managing the federal government's accounting and financial information system;
g) Providing regular financial reports as required;
h) Supporting analysis and improvements to the federal government's financial systems;
i) Making payments from the current and permanent reserves;
i) [sic] Managing the cash balances of the Treasury Consolidated Account and the investment of the federal government's surplus cash balances;
j) Managing the recording of domestic and external debt;
k) Managing the recording of international grants, assistance, and loans;
l) Preparing government accounting and financial management standards, regulations, and related legislation;
m) Managing the opening, recording, and reconciliation of government bank accounts; and
n) Managing the operations of the Regional Treasury Offices.

2) The Ministry of Finance shall be responsible for, but is not limited to, the following budget formulation functions:

a) Managing the process of budget preparation, planning and development, including the preparation of macroeconomic and other economic advice;
b) Proposing guidelines for the preparation, planning, execution, revision, and evaluation of budgets;
c) Preparing the annual budget law, any supplementary budget laws, and making them publicly available;
d) Monitoring receipts and execution of payments, including petroleum revenues;
e) Preparing cash flow forecasts;
f) Providing advice to the Council of Ministers on requests by spending units for the reallocation of appropriations and implementing decisions on reallocations;
g) Making payments from the current and permanent reserves.
h) Providing advisory support on budgetary issues to all spending units; and
i) Preparing reports on budget preparation and budget execution for international economic organizations.
j) Preparing regulations, instructions, guidelines and directions under this Law and on amendments to this Law.

Section 13 Internal Audit

1) The Minister of Finance shall prescribe the manner and procedures by which Ministries, spending units, and public corporations will undertake internal audits, and is responsible for ensuring that the internal audit process is conducted in accordance with these rules and procedures.

2) Internal Audit performance consists of the following:

a) Providing regular assessments of the adequacy and effectiveness of the Ministries' decision-making processes, minimization of risk, and internal control;
b) Reporting significant internal control issues and improving the control processes and information system in order to minimize risk in the decisionmaking process;
c) Reviewing the efficiency and effectiveness of the use of existing services, and proposing more efficient ways of providing these services;
d) Liaising with the external audit agency; and
e) Providing periodically information on the status of the execution of the annual audit plan.

Section 14 External Audit

1) The federal budget and any supplementary budget shall be subject to annual audits by the Board of Supreme Audit, according to the law.

2) In order to facilitate this audit, the Minister of Finance shall make available to the Board of Supreme Audit:

a) The approved federal budget and any supplementary budgets, and any accompanying documents;
b) The reported results of all internal audits;
c) The quarterly and annual reports on loans, borrowings, guarantees, and debt;
d) Final accounts of public corporations and the results of all audits;
e) Documents discussed by the Council of Ministers its role of oversight of operations for any successor to the DFI, or by any committee delegated with this role according to section 5(4) of this Law, as well as the results of any internal audits; and
f) Any other documents, information and explanation requested by the Board of Supreme Audit in connection with the performance of its audit functions.

Section 15 Transitional Arrangements

1) To the extent that this Law is inconsistent with existing laws, the provisions of this Law shall prevail.

2) Regulations implementing this Law shall be approved within 12 months from the day of enactment of this Law. Until these regulations are approved, existing regulations shall continue to apply, to the extent consistent with this Law.

3) In transitioning to the Treasury Single Account, the Minister of Finance is hereby authorized to close the accounts of the federal government Budget Accounts opened at the Central Bank or in any other banks. Resources remaining in Federal Budget user accounts are to be transferred to the Treasury Single Account and reflected in the Treasury Consolidated Account. Until the closure of the existing bank accounts is completed and the Treasury Single Account is fully established, the Minister of Finance is authorized to operate the existing bank accounts on a zero-balance basis under which balances of these accounts will be transferred to the Treasury Single Account on a daily basis. Should circumstances make daily transfers impracticable, the Minister of Finance shall institute transfers as frequently as practicable.

4) Law Number 107 of 1985 on Consolidated Government Budget (as amended by Law Number 48 of 1990), and Law Number 20 of 1940 on General Accounting Principles shall not have effect for the fiscal year 2005 and subsequent years.

5) The Minister of Finance is authorized to promulgate rules that will facilitate accurate financial reporting during the period in which Iraq is undergoing the transition to international

accounting standards ('interim standards'). These interim standards shall apply only for the fiscal year with respect to which they are promulgated. Reports prepared for these periods that are otherwise required to comply with international accounting standards may comply with either the interim standards or international accounting standards.

6) Unless otherwise provided by relevant UNSCR and the Transitional Administration Law, including its Annex, prior to the establishment of a national legislature, the Council of Ministers shall serve as the final approval authority for the federal budget, subject to the approval of the Presidency. During such period, if the federal budget is not approved by the Presidency and the Council of Ministers, the Minister of Finance will, on a monthly basis, approve funds for spending units up to 1/12th one twelfth of appropriations of the previous fiscal year until the budget is approved.

7) To the extent that the relevant UNSCR and the Transitional Administration Law, including its Annex, attributes executive power to a body or person different than the Council of Ministers, powers and responsibilities delegated to the Council of Ministers by this Law shall be delegated instead to the executive body or person so identified in the relevant UNSCR or the Transitional Administration Law.

8) Upon the transfer of governmental authority to the Iraqi Interim Government, the Program Review Board established pursuant to Coalition Provisional Authority Regulation Number 3 (CPA/REG/18 June 2003/3)[346] shall cease to perform budgetary functions for Iraq and shall dissolve.

Section 16 Entry into Force

This Law shall enter into force on the same date that the Order authorizing this law enters into force. It shall apply to the budget of the fiscal year 2005 and subsequent years, and additionally, following the transfer of governance authority to the Iraqi Interim Government, shall apply to any supplementary budgets for fiscal year 2004.

ANNEX B

Iraq
Public Debt Law

Section I Definitions

For the purposes of this law, the terms below are defined as follows:

'*Bank*' means a bank as defined under the Banking Law.

'*Government*' means the entity exercising temporary governmental authority in Iraq on the date this law enters into force and then the transitional Iraqi administration upon the transfer to it of full governmental authority and the recognition of the sovereignty of that administration by the CPA, and then the internationally recognized representative government of Iraq once it assumes the responsibilities of such authority.

'*Government Debt Security*' means a debt security issued by the Ministry of Finance, including debt securities lawfully issued prior to the effective date of this Law. The term 'debt security' shall have the same meaning assigned to it in the Banking Law.

'*Minister*' means the Minister of Finance acting in an official capacity.

'*Official Publication*' means the *Official Gazette* or such other general publication of wide circulation as specified by the Council of Ministers or its delegee.

[346] See *Doc 3*.

'*Owner*' means the person registered as the owner of a Government Debt Security on the books of the government securities registrar.

Section II Authorities and Duties Pertaining to the Issuance of Government Debt Securities

1. The Minister shall have authority to issue Government Debt Securities as an obligation guaranteed by the Government only in amounts reasonably necessary for expenditures authorized by law and in amounts necessary to buy, redeem, or refund outstanding Government Debt Securities.
2. The issue and redemption of Government Debt Securities shall be managed by the Central Bank of Iraq as the agent for the Government.
3. The Minister shall have authority to set the terms and conditions for Government Debt Securities before they are issued, such as:
   (a) the date of maturity;
   (b) the offering price and interest rate;
   (c) the method of computing the interest rate;
   (d) the dates for paying principal and interest;
   (e) whether a debt security is to be issued on an interest-bearing basis, a discount basis, or an interest-bearing and discount basis;
   (f) the form of the security;
   (g) the currency in which the debt is issued; and
   (h) any other condition not prohibited by law.
4. The Minister shall have authority to determine how it will offer Government Debt Securities for sale, such as by competitive auction and by subscription.
5. The Minister shall have authority to offer Government Debt Securities for sale to any person.
6. The Minister shall deposit without delay all proceeds from the sale of Government Debt Securities into the public treasury or an authorized depositary.

Section III Authorities and Duties Pertaining to Outstanding Debt Securities

1. The Minister shall have authority to buy, redeem, or refund Government Debt Securities in accordance with their terms and conditions using public funds.
2. The Minister shall have authority to give relief to owners of lost, defaced, or destroyed Government Debt Securities in accordance with regulations issued by the Minister.
3. The Minister shall pay principal and interest in legal tender when due, or earlier in his discretion, in accordance with the terms and conditions of the Government Debt Security.
4. The Minister shall have a permanent and indefinite appropriation of public funds for the purpose of buying, redeeming, or refunding Government Debt Securities and for the purpose of paying interest on those securities.

Section IV Authorities Pertaining to Fiscal Agents and Depositaries

1. The Minister shall have authority to engage the Central Bank of Iraq, and any other Bank, as a fiscal agent for the purpose of carrying out any function authorized by this Law.
2. The Minister shall have authority to designate Banks that are eligible to act as depositaries for any part of the proceeds from the issuance of Government Debt Securities. The Minister shall have authority to prescribe conditions for the deposit of public money, including the interest rate on amounts deposited.

3. The Minister shall have authority to transfer public money in a depositary's possession to the public treasury, and to transfer public money between depositaries.

4. The Minister shall have the authority to require his fiscal agent and depositaries to provide him with any information about their activities under this Law.

Section V Administrative Authorities and Duties

1. The Minister shall have authority to issue regulations, prescribe policies, and issue announcements for the purpose of implementing this Law and carrying out the Minister's functions under this Law.

2. The Minister shall have authority to delegate his duties and functions under this Law, except the power to delegate, to any person within the Ministry of Finance.

3. The Minister shall publish all regulations issued under this Law in the Official Publication.

4. Prior to any sale, the Minister shall list the terms and conditions applying to a Government Debt Security in a regulation or an offering announcement. An offering announcement shall be publicized in a manner that ensures wide circulation among potential buyers.

5. If the Minister proposes to issue a regulation pursuant to this Law, he shall publish a draft of the proposed regulation in the Official Publication. Along with the proposed regulation, the Minister shall publish an explanation of the regulation and provide at least thirty days after publication for the public to submit comments. The Minister shall consider all comments received. If the Minister determines that a final regulation is appropriate, the Minister shall issue the regulation accompanied by a general description of the comments and his response to those comments. The Minister may issue a final regulation without publishing a draft or considering public comment if the Minister determines that the delay involved would be a serious threat to the interests of the financial system or hinder the effective conduct of monetary policy. In such an event, the Minister shall publish an explanation of his decision to depart from the procedures in this paragraph in the Official Publication.

6. The Minister shall maintain a system of books and records
   (a) describing all issued Government Debt Securities;
   (b) identifying the dates when outstanding obligations come due; and
   (c) stating all amounts of principal and interest paid on Government debt securities.

7. The Minister shall make all its books and records pertaining to Government Debt Securities available for inspection upon request by the Prime Minister and Council of Ministers or its delegee.

8. On or before the end of the fiscal year, the Minister shall submit a report to the Prime Minister and Council of Ministers on the public debt activities of the Ministry of Finance. The report shall include, at a minimum:
   (a) A table showing the public debt from all outstanding Government Debt Securities as of the date of the report, the interest cost for that debt in the current year, and the projected interest cost for government debt over the next five fiscal years, taking into account projections for the budget.
   (b) A table showing the maturity distribution of the public debt from all Government Debt Securities outstanding as of the date of the report.
   (c) An explanation of the overall financing strategy used in determining the distribution of maturities and interest rates for Government Debt Securities issued during the current fiscal year.

Section VI Final Provisions

1. Any provision of Iraqi law that was enacted prior to the effective date of this Law and that is inconsistent with this Law is hereby superseded.
2. This Law shall enter into force on the same date that the Order authorizing this Law enters into force.

Document 120
Coalition Provisional Authority Order Number 96

CPA/ORD/7 June 2004/96

The Electoral Law

Pursuant to my authority as Administrator of the Coalition Provisional Authority (CPA), and under the laws and usages of war, and consistent with relevant U.N. Security Council resolutions, including Resolution 1483 (2003), and Resolution 1511 (2003),

Reaffirming the right of the Iraqi people, as recognized in Resolutions 1483 and 1511, to freely determine their own political future,

Noting that the Law of Administration for the State of Iraq for the Transitional Period (the 'TAL')[347] provides for the Iraqi people to choose their government through genuine and credible elections to be held by the end of December 2004 if possible and, in any event, no later than 31 January 2005,

Determined to achieve the transitional goals of the TAL, including the drafting and ratification of a permanent constitution, and the establishment of an elected government under that constitution,

Committed to electing the drafters of the Iraqi constitution by a direct, universal and secret ballot of the Iraqi people,

Noting the Iraqi Governing Council's adoption of Resolution 87 of 2004[348] endorsing use of a single electoral district and proportional representation in the election of the National Assembly of the Iraqi Transitional Government,

Having consulted extensively with representatives of the United Nations and benefited from their consultations with the Governing Council and a broad cross-section of Iraqis,

I hereby promulgate the following:

Section 1 Purpose

This Order forms part of the legal framework for genuine and credible elections to determine the membership of the National Assembly of the Iraqi Transitional Government.

Section 2 Definitions

For purposes of this Order, the following definitions shall apply. Words importing the singular include and apply to several persons, parties, or things; words importing the plural include the singular; and words importing the masculine gender include the feminine:

[347] See *Doc 511*.
[348] See *Doc 489*.

1) 'Commission' means the Independent Electoral Commission of Iraq, as established by CPA Order No. 92 (CPA/ORD/31 May 2004/92).[349]

2) 'Iraqi Interim Government' means the government that will assume full governmental authority on 30 June 2004 and retain such authority until the formation of the Iraqi Transitional Government.

3) 'Iraqi Transitional Government' means the government that is to be established after nationwide elections occurring no later than 31 January 2005.

4) 'National Assembly' means the National Assembly of the Iraqi Transitional Government, as described in the TAL.

5) 'Political Parties and Entities Law' means the law that will govern the recognition of Political Entities in Iraq during the Transitional Period.

6) 'Political Entity' means a political entity as defined in the Political Parties and Entities Law.

7) 'Threshold' means the minimum number of valid votes necessary to obtain a seat in the National Assembly.

Section 3 System of Representation

1) The election for the National Assembly shall be by direct, universal and secret ballot.

2) Consistent with Article 31 of the TAL, elections for the National Assembly will choose 275 members. Consistent with Article 31(A) of the TAL, a separate law enacted after such elections will govern the replacement of members of the National Assembly in the event of resignation, removal or death.

3) Iraq will be a single electoral constituency. All seats in the National Assembly will be allocated among Political Entities through a system of proportional representation.

4) The formula for the allocation of seats in the National Assembly will be based on a first calculation employing a simple quota (Hare quota) and subsequent calculations employing the largest remainders. The Threshold shall be the natural threshold, which is calculated by dividing the total number of valid votes by 275. The procedure for use of this formula shall be set forth in such regulations promulgated pursuant to Section 6.

Section 4 Electoral Candidates

1) Any Political Entity may present a list of candidates for election to the National Assembly to the Commission so long as the candidates on the list meet the applicable legal criteria.

2) The lists presented to the Commission must have the candidates in a ranked order. Seats in the National Assembly shall be allocated to candidates according to the ranked order on the list. The candidates on the lists may not be reordered or otherwise changed after a date to be established by the Commission.

3) No fewer than one out of the first three candidates on the list must be woman [sic]; no fewer than two out of the first six candidates on the list must be woman [sic]; and so forth until the end of the list.

4) No list shall contain fewer than twelve or more than 275 candidates, except that individual persons certified as Political Entities by the Commission may present themselves on a list as a single candidate. The requirement of Section 4(3) does not apply where a list contains an individual person certified as a Political Entity.

[349] See *Doc 116*.

5) Seats shall be allocated to candidates, not Political Entities. At no time may a Political Entity withdraw a seat in the National Assembly from the candidate to whom it was allocated.

Section 5 Entitlement to Vote

1) To be eligible to vote in the election of the National Assembly, a person must:
   a) According to Article 11 of the TAL, be deemed an Iraqi citizen, be entitled to reclaim Iraqi citizenship or be eligible for Iraqi citizenship;
   b) Have been born on or before 31 December 1986; and,
   c) Be registered to vote according to procedures issues by the Commission.

2) The Commission shall interpret Article 11 of the TAL in an inclusive manner. The Commission shall not be dependent on the conclusion of any administrative or legal processes undertaken by the Iraqi Interim Government in order to implement Article 11 of the TAL.

3) The decisions of the Commission shall not prejudice future administrative or legal processes undertaken by the Iraqi Transitional Government in order to implement Article 11 of the TAL.

Section 6 Implementation

The Commission may issue regulations, rules, procedures and decisions to implement this Order.

Section 7 Inconsistent Legislation

Any provision of Iraqi law that is inconsistent with this Order is hereby suspended to the extent of such inconsistency.

Section 8 Effective Date

This Order shall enter into force on the date of signature [15 June 2004].

Document 121

Coalition Provisional Authority Order Number 97

CPA/ORD/7 June 2004/97

Political Parties and Entities Law

Pursuant to my authority as Administrator of the Coalition Provisional Authority (CPA), and under the laws and usages of war, and consistent with relevant U.N. Security Council resolutions, including Resolution 1483 (2003), and Resolution 1511 (2003),

Reaffirming the right of the Iraqi people, as recognized in Resolutions 1483 and 1511, to freely determine their own political future,

Noting that the Law of Administration for the State of Iraq for the Transitional Period (the 'TAL') provides for the Iraqi people to choose their government through genuine and credible elections to be held by the end of December 2004 if possible and, in any event, no later than 31 January 2005,

Determined to achieve the transitional goals of the TAL, including the drafting and ratification of a permanent constitution, and the establishment of an elected government under that constitution,

Underscoring the need for international cooperation to achieve these goals and the essential role to be played by the United Nations and other internationally recognized experts in electoral administration,

Committed to establishing an impartial and internationally recognized body of Iraqi professionals and expert advisors to coordinate and oversee genuine and credible elections in Iraq,

Having consulted extensively with the representatives of the United Nations and benefited from their consultations with the Governing Council and a broad cross-section of Iraqis, I hereby promulgate the following:

Section 1 Purpose

This Order forms part of the legal framework for genuine and credible elections that fairly reflects Iraq's rich diversity of political thought by encouraging and impartially regulating the development of vibrant political entities across Iraq.

Section 2 Recognition of Political Entities

1) A 'political entity' means an organization, including a political party, of eligible voters who voluntarily associate on the basis of common ideas, interests or views, for the purpose of articulating interests, obtaining influence and having their representatives elected to public office, so long as that organization of eligible voters is officially certified as a political entity by the Independent Electoral Commission of Iraq ('Commission'). A 'political entity' also means an individual person who intends to stand for election to public office, so long as the individual person is officially certified as a political entity by the Commission.

2) The Commission shall establish regulations that govern the certification and decertification of political entities. Such regulations shall include the total number of eligible voters – as measured by signatures, personal marks, or other identifiable means – required for certification as a political entity, provided that the total number of eligible voters required for certification of organizations or individual persons shall not exceed 500.

Section 3 Status and Treatment of Political Entities

1) Each political entity, except certified individuals, shall become, upon certification, a distinct legal entity in Iraq, unless it already had such status.

2) As distinct legal entities, political entities shall be capable of owning, leasing or having legal tenure of property, entering into contracts, and conducting transactions. Political entities shall enjoy any additional legal entitlement or protection provided by the Commission through regulations, rules, procedures, and decisions.

3) All political entities, including certified individual persons, are equal before the law, and shall be treated equally at all times by all levels of government in Iraq.

4) No organization or group of individuals may offer candidates for elections in Iraq unless certified as a political entity by the Commission. No individual person may stand for election in Iraq unless certified as a political entity by the Commission.

Section 4 Recognition of Common Principles

1) Political entities will be bound by regulations, rules, procedures, and decisions promulgated by the Commission.

2) The Commission will duly establish actions and omissions that are electoral offenses and subject to sanction. Sanction for electoral offenses may include, without limitation, injunction, financial penalty, public notice, certification suspension and decertification. Such offenses and sanctions shall be in addition to criminal offenses set forth in Iraqi law.

3) The following principles shall apply to all political entities in Iraq and shall be incorporated into and implemented by the Commission's regulations governing political entities:

a) No political entity may have or be associated with an armed force, militia or residual element as defined in CPA Order No. 91, Regulation of Armed Forces and Militias within Iraq (CPA/ORD/June 2004/91);[350]

b) No political entity may be directly or indirectly financed by any armed force, militia, or residual element;

c) No political entity may put forth any candidate who fails to meet the applicable legal criteria;

d) Political entities must abide by all laws and regulations in Iraq, including public meeting ordinances, prohibitions on incitement to violence, hate speech, intimidation, and support for, the practice of and the use of terrorism;

e) Political entities must operate pursuant to the code of conduct that will be promulgated by the Commission – such code must include, among other things, the requirements in Section 4(3)(d) of this Order;

f) Political entities other than individuals certified as political entities must promulgate a statute to govern their organization and operation, including the method or process for selecting leaders and candidates, and this statute must be available to any member of the public upon request;

g) Political entities, to compete freely and openly in an election, are free to form coalitions to aggregate interests, and to build a campaign for candidates around coalitions of such interests; and

h) Political entities must strive, to the extent possible, to achieve full transparency in all financial dealings. In this regards, the Commission may issue regulations with respect to financial disclosure.

4) The Commission retains full discretion to define mechanisms for enforcing its regulations against political entity.

Section 5 Modification and Further Regulation

All further matters regarding the regulation and certification of political entities lie with the Commission exclusively.

Section 6 Inconsistent Legislation

Any provision of Iraqi law that is inconsistent with this Order is hereby suspended to the extent of such inconsistency.

Section 7 Effective Date

The present Order shall enter into force upon the date of signature [15 June 2004].

[350] See *Doc 115*.

Document 122
Coalition Provisional Authority Order Number 98
CPA/ORD/27 June 2004/98

Iraqi Ombudsman for Penal and Detention Matters

Pursuant to my authority as Administrator of the Coalition Provisional Authority (CPA) and under the laws and usages of war, and consistent with relevant U.N. Security Council resolutions, including Resolutions 1483 and 1511 (2003),

Recognizing the need to promote the development of an effective framework for officials of the Iraqi Government to participate in the oversight of the detention of individuals in Iraq,

Determining the necessity of an independent means of investigating complaints of abuse and acting in accordance with UNSCR 1483 to promote the protection of human rights,

Acting in accordance with the consultations between the Coalition Provisional Authority and the Iraqi Interim Government,

I hereby promulgate the following:

Section 1 Definitions

1) 'Detaining authority' means any Iraqi, Multinational Force or contracted personnel employed, engaged in, supervising or commanding, criminal or security custody in Iraq with respect to persons held in such custody for any period. This does not include Multinational Force detention of its own personnel.

2) 'The Government' means the Iraqi Interim Government and the Iraqi Transitional Government.

3) 'Complainant' means a person complaining of adverse treatment by a detaining authority.

4) 'Conduct' means any action or inaction relating to the behavior or administrative functions of a detaining authority.

5) 'Head of Government' means, before June 30, 2004, the CPA Administrator, and thereafter means the Prime Minister of the Iraqi Interim Government or the Iraqi Transitional Government.

Section 2 Office of the Ombudsman

1) The Head of Government may, on the recommendation of the Minister of Justice, appoint an Ombudsman on such terms and conditions, consistent with and subject to this Order, as are specified in the instrument of appointment.

2) For administrative purposes, and without prejudice to the powers and responsibilities vested in the Ombudsman under this Order, the Ombudsman shall be considered an officer of the Ministry of Justice and shall be entitled to a salary at a level commensurate with the duties and responsibilities of the office, as determined by the Minister of Justice, which salary shall not be reduced during the Ombudsman's tenure.

3) Subject to this Order, the Ombudsman holds office for such period, not exceeding seven years, as is specified in the instrument of his or her appointment and is eligible for re-appointment.

4) To be eligible for appointment as Ombudsman the person must:

a) be an Iraqi national,
b) be of high moral character and reputation for impartiality and integrity,
c) have a background of opposition to the Ba'ath Party, non-membership in the Ba'ath Party or membership that does not fall within the leadership tiers described in CPA Order 1, dated May 16, 2003[351] and entailed no involvement in Ba'ath Party activity, and
d) have no criminal record unless the record consists only of a political or false charge made by the Ba'ath Party regime.

5) The Head of Government may replace an Ombudsman from office of Ombudsman, if the Head of Government considers that one or more of the following grounds have been established, but such grounds shall be presented in writing and shall be subject to appeal to the Courts of Iraq:

a) acceptance of any gainful employment outside the duties of the office, unless with the permission of the Minister of Justice;
b) decision to stand for election as a member of the National Assembly or of the any [sic] provincial governate [sic] or council,
c) resignation of the office by instrument in writing addressed to the Head of Government;
d) physical or mental disability affecting his or her capacity to perform his or her functions, or failure in the execution of his or her functions; or
e) conviction for a criminal offense punishable by a term of imprisonment.

6) The Ombudsman has and may exercise the functions conferred or imposed on the Ombudsman by or under this or any other law.

Section 3 Deputy and Assistant Ombudsmen

1) The Ombudsman may appoint one or more Deputy Ombudsmen and Assistant Ombudsmen. Deputy or Assistant Ombudsmen shall exercise such authority and perform such duties as the Ombudsman delegates, without limitation.

2) The Ombudsman may employ such assistance as he or she deems proper for the carrying out of any inquiry or investigation, and may, in writing, authorize any person so employed to inspect and report upon documents or other items, or (without affecting the generality of the foregoing) accounts, he/she considers relevant to the subject matter of the inquiry.

Section 4 Right to Complain

1) Subject to this section, any person (including a public authority) may complain in writing to the Ombudsman about the conduct of a detaining authority unless the conduct took place before the date of entry into force of this Order.

2) A member of the Government may complain to the Ombudsman on behalf of a complainant.

3) A detaining authority must permit and facilitate the confidential transmission of a complaint to the Ombudsman, including transmitting immediately and unopened any written matter addressed to the Ombudsman.

4) The Ombudsman may accept a complaint that is not in writing, in which case he or she shall reduce the complaint to writing within three days of receiving the complaint.

[351] See *Doc 14*.

Section 5 Investigations

1) Notwithstanding any provision of law existing at the time of the signing of this Order, the Ombudsman may investigate conduct referred to in Section 16, regardless of whether a complaint has been filed, however nothing herein authorizes the Ombudsman to investigate any matter that occurred prior to the date of this Order.

2) In deciding whether to investigate or discontinue the investigation of a complaint, the Ombudsman may consider such matters as he or she thinks fit, including but not limited to whether:

a) the complaint is frivolous, vexatious or not in good faith,
b) the subject matter of the complaint is trivial,
c) the conduct complained of occurred at too remote a time to justify investigation, or
d) internal remedies have previously been exhausted.

3) Where the Ombudsman declines to investigate a complaint, or discontinues the investigation of such complaint, the Ombudsman shall inform the complainant in writing of his or her decision and the reasons for the decision.

4) The Ombudsman, upon deciding to investigate the conduct of a detaining authority, shall give notice of the decision:

a) to the complainant, and
b) to the head of the detaining authority and, if practicable, to the detaining authority.
c) A notice under this section must be in writing, must describe the conduct under investigation, and must, so far as practicable, identify the detaining authority and may request that the alleged perpetrator of the conduct be removed from direct control, supervision of, or contact with the complainant.

Section 6 Public Disclosure

An investigation under this Order shall not be disclosed to, and shall be made in the absence of, the public until completion. The names of individuals shall be withheld until the completion of any civil, criminal or administrative proceedings that may involve those individuals. The name of a complainant shall not be publicly disclosed without that person's consent.

Section 7 Detaining Authority to Give Information

1) For the purposes of an investigation under this Order, and subject to Subsection (3) of this Section, the Ombudsman may require a detaining authority:

a) to give the Ombudsman a statement of information,
b) to produce to the Ombudsman any document or other thing, or
c) to give the Ombudsman a copy of any document.

2) A request under this section must be in writing, must specify or describe the information, document or thing required, and must fix a time and specify a place for compliance.

3) The Ombudsman may request the Multinational Force Commander or his delegate to produce documents, copies of documents or real evidence. The Multinational Force Commander or his delegate may deny such requests if concurrence would result in an unacceptable breach of operational security or if otherwise prevented or denied pursuant to law.

4) The Multinational Force Commander or his delegate may submit, and the Ombudsman shall consider, the results or report of any Multinational Force investigation concerning the subject of an investigation.

5) The Ombudsman shall maintain the confidentiality of all confidential or classified information and date obtained, with special attention being given to the safety of complainants and witnesses.

Section 8 Inquiries

1) In an investigation under this Order, the Ombudsman may make or hold inquiries.

2) Where it is shown to the satisfaction of the Ombudsman that any person is substantially and directly interested in any subject-matter of the inquiry, or that the person's conduct in relation to any such matter has been challenged to the person's detriment, the Ombudsman may authorize such person to appear at the inquiry. Persons involved in such an inquiry have the right to be represented by legal counsel.

3) Any legal counsel so appointed and any person so authorized or the person's legal counsel may, with the leave of the Ombudsman, examine or cross-examine any witness on any matter which the Ombudsman deems relevant to the inquiry.

4) The Ombudsman may by notice in writing summon any person who is not a member of the Multinational Force to attend an inquiry at a time and place named in the summons, and then and there to give evidence and to produce any documents or other things in the person's custody or control which the person is required by the summons to produce.

5) The Ombudsman may request the Multinational Force Commander or his delegate to permit the attendance of Multinational Force personnel as witnesses at an inquiry. The Multinational Force Commander or his delegate may deny such requests if he or his delegate determines that compliance would result in an unacceptable breach of operational security, provision of the personnel would prejudice the conduct of operations, such witnesses are not reasonably available or their attendance is otherwise prevented by law.

6) The Ombudsman may administer an oath to any person appearing as a witness at the inquiry, whether the witness has been summoned or appears without being summoned, and may examine the witness upon oath or affirmation.

7) Every witness who has been summoned to attend the commission shall appear and report from day to day unless the witness is excused from attendance or until the witness is released from further attendance by the Ombudsman.

8) A witness summoned, in accordance with Subsection (4) of this Section, to attend before the Ombudsman shall not be entitled to refuse to:

- a) be sworn or to make an affirmation,
- b) answer any question relevant to the inquiry put to the witness by the Ombudsman, or
- c) produce any document or other thing in the witness's custody or control which the witness is required by the summons to produce.

9) Nothing in this Order shall make it compulsory for any witness:

- a) to answer any question or produce any document or other thing if the witness has a reasonable excuse for refusing, or
- b) to disclose any operationally classified information or material.

Section 9 Inspection and Copies of Documents

1) The Ombudsman may retain documents or other material for such reasonable period as required to complete an inquiry.

2) When the retention of a document or other material ceases to be reasonably necessary for the purposes of the inquiry to which it relates, the Ombudsman is required, if a person

who appears to the Ombudsman to be entitled to the document or other thing so requests, to cause it to be returned to that person.

3) The requirement under Subsection (2) does not apply if the Ombudsman has furnished the document or other thing or proposes to furnish it to a person or body referred to in section 12 or the Ombudsman deals with it or proposes to deal with it otherwise according to law.

Section 10 Communication of Information

The Ombudsman may communicate any information or furnish any material (including evidence) that it obtains in the course of the inquiry conducted by it to a law enforcement agency, if the information or material relates or may relate to a breach of a law of Iraq in relation to Iraqi detaining authorities.

Section 11 Entry to Premises

In an investigation under this Order, the Ombudsman may, at any time:

a) enter and inspect any premises occupied or used by a detaining authority to deprive persons of their liberty, and
b) inspect any document or thing in or on the premises, subject only to the limitation that the Multinational Force Commander or his delegate may deny access for reasons of imperative military necessity as an exceptional and temporary measure, or prevent the inspection of operationally classified documents.

Section 12 Persons to be Heard

1) In an investigation under this Order, the Ombudsman shall give an opportunity to the subject of the investigation to make submissions.

2) Where, in an investigation under this Order, the Ombudsman considers that there are grounds for adverse comment in respect of any person, the Ombudsman, before making any such comment in any report, shall, so far as practicable:

a) inform that person of the substance of the grounds of the adverse comment, and
b) give the person an opportunity to make submissions.

Section 13 Consultation with the Minister of Justice

1) In an investigation under this Order, the Ombudsman shall, on request by the Minister of Justice, consult the Minister on the conduct of the investigation.

2) Before publishing a report under this Order the Ombudsman:

a) shall inform the Minister of Justice that he or she proposes to publish such a report, and
b) shall, on request by that Minister, consult that Minister.

Section 14 Report of Investigation

1) Where, in an investigation under this Order, the Ombudsman finds that the conduct the subject of the investigation, or any part of the conduct, is of any one or more of the following kinds:

a) contrary to law,
b) unreasonable, unjust, oppressive or improperly discriminatory,
c) in accordance with any law or established practice but the law or practice is, unreasonable, unjust, oppressive or improperly discriminatory,

d) based wholly or partly on improper motives, irrelevant grounds or irrelevant consideration,
e) based wholly or partly on a mistake of law or fact, or
f) otherwise wrong, the Ombudsman shall make a report accordingly, giving his or her reasons.

2) In preparing his or her report, the Ombudsman will consider any report of an investigation concerning the same or a similar subject that the Multinational Force has made available for his or her review.

3) In a report under this section, the Ombudsman may recommend that:
a) action be taken to rectify, mitigate or change the conduct or its consequences,
b) reasons be given for the conduct,
c) any law or practice relating to the conduct be changed,
d) compensation be paid to any person, or
e) any other appropriate actions be taken.

4) The Ombudsman shall give a report under this Section to the:
a) Head of Government and the Minister of Justice, and
b) the head of the detaining authority whose conduct is the subject of the report.

5) The Ombudsman may give a copy of a report or summary of the factual findings and recommendations under this Section:
a) where the investigation arises out of a complaint to the Ombudsman, to the complainant, and
b) to the detaining authority to whose conduct the report relates.

6) The person to whom a report is given under Subsection (3) (b) may, and on request by the Ombudsman shall, notify the Ombudsman of any action taken or proposed in consequence of a report under this section.

Section 15 Serious Misconduct

Where the Ombudsman is of the opinion that a detaining authority is or may be guilty of misconduct in the course of performing his or her functions to such an extent as, in the opinion of the Ombudsman, may warrant dismissal, removal or punishment, the Ombudsman shall report the opinion to the Head of Government, the Minister of Justice and to the head of the detaining authority, giving reasons for the opinion.

Section 16 Incriminatory Statement

1) Where a person is required under this Order to give a statement that tends to incriminate that person, neither the requirement nor the statement may be used in any proceedings against that person.

2) Subsection (1) applies whether the person required to give a statement objects to giving it or not.

Section 17 Disclosure by Ombudsman or Officer

The Ombudsman shall not, nor shall an officer of the Ombudsman, disclose any information obtained by the Ombudsman or officer in the course of the Ombudsman's or officer's inquiry or investigation, unless the disclosure is made:
a) where the information is obtained from a detaining authority, with the consent of the head of that authority or of the Minister of Justice,
b) where the information is obtained from any other person with the consent of that person, or

c) the disclosure is pursuant to section 12 or 16 herein.

Section 18 Offenses

1) A person shall not:

a) without lawful excuse, willfully obstruct, hinder or resist the Ombudsman or an officer of the Ombudsman in the exercise of the Ombudsman's or officer's powers under this or any other Order, law or regulation,

b) without lawful excuse, refuse or willfully fail to comply with any lawful requirement of the Ombudsman or an officer of the Ombudsman under this or any other Order, law or regulation, or

c) willfully make any false statement to or mislead, or attempt to mislead, the Ombudsman or an officer of the Ombudsman in the exercise of the Ombudsman's or officer's powers under this or any other Order, law or regulation.

The maximum penalty for these offences shall be USD$100.

2) A person who uses, causes, inflicts or procures any violence, punishment, damage, loss or disadvantage to any person for or on account of:

a) complaining to the Ombudsman,

b) assisting the Ombudsman, or

c) providing evidence to the Ombudsman,

is guilty of a felony offense. The maximum penalty for these offenses shall be USD$1,000 or imprisonment for 5 years, or both.

3) This Order is subject to the provisions of any United Nations Security Council Resolution, treaty, agreement or law dealing with the status of non-Iraqi citizens in Iraq.

Section 19 Entry into Force

This Order shall enter into force on the date of signature [27 June 2004].

Document 123

Coalition Provisional Authority Order Number 99

CPA/ORD/27 June 2004/99

Joint Detainee Committee

Pursuant to my authority as Administrator of the Coalition Provisional Authority (CPA) and under the laws and usages of war, and consistent with relevant U.N. Security Council resolutions, including Resolutions 1483 (2003), 1511 (2003) and 1546 (2004),

Noting that prison facilities across Iraq were largely destroyed as a result of the acts of the former regime and are not currently capable of providing a safe and secure environment for the pre-trial confinement of many detainees,

Noting further that, as an interim measure, the Multinational Force maintains safe and secure facilities for the custody of certain numbers of security internees and criminal detainees,

Affirming the importance of properly implementing the authority of the Multinational Force under U.N. Security Council Resolution 1546 (2004) to take all necessary measures to contribute to the maintenance of security and stability in Iraq in accordance with the letters annexed to that resolution,

Acting in accordance with the consultations between the Coalition Provisional Authority and the Iraqi Interim Government,

I hereby promulgate the following:

Section 1 Purpose

This Order provides a mechanism for facilitating the partnership between the Multinational Force-Iraq (MNF-I) and the Iraqi Interim Government (IIG) on all matters relating to the management of, and the formulation of policy regarding, security internees and criminal detainees in the custody of the MNF-I. It is designed to ensure that detention operations comport with applicable law and human rights standards.

Section 2 Joint Detainee Committee

1) There shall hereby be established a Joint Detainee Committee ('Committee'), which shall be composed of representatives of the MNF, the IIG and the States exercising custody over detainees. The Committee shall be co-chaired by the Prime Minster and the MNF-I Commander or their authorized delegates.

2) There shall be up to twenty-one official members of the Committee, representing the following entities in the manner indicated:

a) The IIG shall be represented by the Prime Minister, the Ministers of Defence, Interior, Justice, Finance, and the Director General of the Iraqi National Intelligence Service.

b) The MNF shall be represented by the Commander MNF-I, his Chief of Staff, the Deputy Chiefs of Staff for Operations, Intelligence and Logistics, the Staff Judge Advocate and the senior Theatre Commanders for the Military Police and the United States Corps of Engineers.

c) The United States as a detaining State shall be represented by the Chief of Mission.

d) The United Kingdom as a detaining State shall be represented by its Ambassador to Iraq.

3) Other official members of the Committee may be agreed by the co-chairs.

4) From time to time, and at the discretion of the co-chairs, other persons may be permitted to attend as observers, to present reports to the Committee, or for other purposes determined by the co-chairs. Such persons may include representatives of the Iraqi Ombudsman on Detention and Penal Matters and delegates of the International Committee of the Red Cross (ICRC).

Section 3 Functions

The Committee shall be responsible for:

1) Establishing criteria for the detention of individuals, including the basis for release or transfer to Iraqi jurisdiction or custody.

2) Monitoring and if necessary proposing standards and safeguards for the conditions and rights of detainees, including processes for determining initial detention decisions and reviewing such decisions.

3) Considering issues relating to the prosecution of criminal detainees and proposing investigative, evidentiary or other measures that will enhance successful prosecution.

4) Evaluating infrastructure imperatives, deficiencies or maintenance requirements and proposing project or budgetary action to address these.

5) Making recommendations concerning improvements to the command, control and liaison aspects of detainee management; the effective recording of information for individual detainees; the tracking of the location, movement or transfer of detainees and the proper communication of detainee information to their families; and any other matter related to detention operations and policies.

6) Advise on legal issues associated with the status and management of persons held in detention or otherwise constrained by the MNF, and propose remedial legislation as appropriate.

Section 4 Evaluation Standards

In making its deliberations and recommendations, the Committee shall have due regard to the provisions of Iraqi law as supplemented by CPA Memoranda Nos. 2 and 3, the Memorandum of Understanding between the MNF and the IIG concerning the handling of High Value Detainees, reports of the Iraqi Ombudsman on Detention and Penal Matters and reports of the ICRC.

Section 5 Reporting Requirements

1) The Committee shall issue reports of its deliberations and recommendations not later than two months after its initial meeting, and thereafter on a bi-monthly basis. The reports shall be delivered to the Prime Minister of the IIG, the Commander, MNF-I, and the U.S. and UK Ambassadors to Iraq.

2) With the agreement of the report recipients identified in subsection 5(1) above, reports of the Committee may be made public, with the exception of:

a) Confidential reports of the ICRC.
b) Material that is related to or part of criminal proceedings before an Iraqi Court or MNF tribunal, until the conclusion of those proceedings.
c) Material that is protected by confidentiality or privacy provisions of the law governing the Iraqi Ombudsman on Detention and Penal Matters.
d) Material that is the property of or has been generated by one of the Committee members, and that is not available for release to the public under law or policy.

Section 6 Entry into Force

This Order shall enter into force on the date of signature [27 June 2004].

Document 124

Coalition Provisional Authority Order Number 100

CPA/ORD/28 June 2004/100

Transition of Laws, Regulations, Orders, and Directives Issued by the Coalition Provisional Authority

Pursuant to my authority as Administrator of the Coalition Provisional Authority (CPA), and under the laws and usages of war, and consistent with relevant U.N. Security Council resolutions, including Resolution 1483 (2003), Resolution 1511 (2003), and Resolution 1546 (2004),

Reaffirming that the laws, regulations, orders, memoranda, instructions and directives of the CPA remain in force unless and until rescinded or amended by legislation duly enacted and having the force of law, as set forth in Article 26(C) of the Law of Administration for the State of Iraq for the Transitional Period ('TAL'),[352]

Recognizing that the Government of Iraq will be responsible for interpreting and implementing these laws, regulations, orders, memoranda, instructions and directives following the transfer of full governing authority on 30 June 2004,

Noting that many of these laws, regulations, orders, memoranda, instructions and directives require technical amendment and/or rescission to properly reflect the transfer of full governing authority and the dissolution of the Coalition Provisional Authority on 30 June 2004,

Further noting that many of these laws, regulations, orders, memoranda, instructions and directives require technical amendment and/or rescission to reflect the structure of the Iraqi Interim Government and to allow for proper delegation of responsibilities within that Government and subsequent Iraqi Governments,

Determined to facilitate the continuity of Iraqi law and to ensure a smooth transfer of full governing authority to the Iraqi Interim Government on 30 June 2004,

Having consulted with the Iraqi Interim Government, including the Prime Minister,

I hereby promulgate the following:

Section 1 Purpose

This Order makes appropriate revisions to laws, regulations, orders, memoranda, instructions and directives issued by the CPA to facilitate an orderly transfer of full governing authority to the Iraqi Interim Government on 30 June 2004. The Order seeks to ensure that the Iraqi Interim Government and all subsequent Iraqi governments inherit full responsibility for these laws, regulations, orders, memoranda, instructions and directives so that their implementation after the transfer of full governing authority may reflect the expectations of the Iraqi people, as determined by a fully empowered and sovereign Iraqi Government. This is the final Order of the CPA, which will dissolve on 30 June 2004, after the transfer of full governing authority to the Iraqi Interim Government.

Section 2 General Rules

Except where otherwise noted in this Order, the following General Rules shall apply to every law, regulation, order, memorandum, instruction and directive issued by the CPA:

1) All powers, authorities, and responsibilities granted to the Administrator under any law, regulation, order, memorandum, instruction or directive of the CPA transfer to the Prime Minister and shall be exercised pursuant to law, including the TAL and its Annex. As the official with day-to-day responsibility for management of the federal government, the Prime Minister may delegate such powers and responsibilities to an appropriate minister or ministry.

2) All powers, authorities, and responsibilities granted to the CPA under any law, regulation, order, memorandum, instruction or directive of the CPA transfer to the Federal Government and shall be exercised pursuant to law, including the TAL and its Annex. The Federal Government means the Iraqi Interim Government, the Iraqi Transitional Government, and the Iraqi Government to be elected under a permanent Iraqi constitution as set forth in Chapter 9 of the TAL.

[352] See *Doc 511*.

3) All references to 'consultation' or 'coordination' with the CPA, or CPA 'direction,' 'supervision,' or 'control' of an Iraqi Ministry or other Iraqi government entity or official, or any related reference, are hereby rescinded.

4) All references to the Iraqi federal government in any form, including references to 'an internationally recognized, representative government' or 'a transitional Iraqi administration,' shall apply equally to the Iraqi Interim Government, and all subsequent Iraqi governments, including the Iraqi Transitional Government and the Iraqi Government to be elected under a permanent constitution as set forth in Chapter 9 of the TAL. This rule does not implicate references to regional, governorate, local, or municipal government entities in Iraq.

5) All provisions that contemplate present or future orders, regulations, and/or memoranda issued by the Administrator or the CPA shall be read to contemplate present or future orders or regulations of the Iraqi Interim Government as well as duly enacted legislation or duly promulgated regulations of any subsequent Iraqi Government.

6) The word 'interim' when immediately preceding 'minister' or 'ministers' shall be deleted. All references to a minister or ministers shall refer equally to a minister or ministers serving in the Iraqi Interim Government, the Iraqi Transitional Government, or the Iraqi Government to be elected under a permanent Iraqi constitution as set forth in Chapter 9 of the TAL.

7) References to 'CPA or Coalition personnel' or 'Coalition Authorities' or 'Coalition personnel' shall be read to cover all foreign national personnel performing services for, or on behalf of, a foreign embassy, including foreign contractors and subcontractors, whether hired by the Federal Government or hired by a foreign government and operating legally in Iraq.

8) All references to 'Coalition Forces' and related references shall apply equally to Multinational Forces operating in Iraq pursuant to United Nations Security Council Resolutions 1511 and 1546.

9) All references to 'the Iraqi Governing Council' are hereby rescinded and shall refer instead to the Federal Government generally, including the Iraqi Interim Government, the Iraqi Transitional Government, and the Iraqi Government to be elected under a permanent Iraqi constitution as set forth in Chapter 9 of the TAL.

10) The phrase 'body vested with national legislative powers' shall refer to the Council of Ministers in the Iraqi Interim Government and the National Assembly in the Iraqi Transitional Government. The same phrase shall apply to the body having legislative powers in the Iraqi Government to be elected under a permanent Iraqi constitution as set forth in Chapter 9 of the TAL.

11) The terms 'chief executive,' 'head of the Iraqi Government,' and 'head of the Iraqi Government exercising national command authority' shall refer to the Prime Minister in the Iraqi Interim Government and Transitional Government and the equivalent office in the Iraqi Government to be elected under a permanent Iraqi constitution as set forth in Chapter 9 of the TAL. All Iraqi governments subsequent to the transfer of full governing authority from the CPA, however, enjoy the authority inherent in sovereignty to divide authorities and responsibilities among the Presidency Council, the Prime Minister, and any other office, in a manner consistent with law.

12) All references to 'foreign liaison mission' shall apply equally after 30 June 2004 to diplomatic and consular missions.

Section 3 Revisions of Specific CPA Order Provisions

Notwithstanding the General Rules set forth in Section 2 of this Order, the following specific provisions of CPA Orders shall be amended, rescinded, or otherwise changed as follows:

1) CPA Order Number 1, De-Ba'athification of Iraqi Society[353] Section 1(6) shall be rescinded in its entirety.

2) CPA Order Number 2, Dissolution of Entities[354]
   a) In Section 2(3), the term 'local Coalition authorities' shall be rescinded and replaced with the following: 'federal government authorities.'
   b) The following shall be appended to the end of the final sentence of Section 2(3): 'in accordance with law.'
   c) Section 5 shall be rescinded in its entirety.
   d) Section 6(2) shall be rescinded in its entirety.

3) CPA Order Number 3 (Revised) (Amended), Weapons Control[355]
   a) CPA Order Number 3 shall not apply to personnel or Member States of the Multinational Force operating in Iraq pursuant to United Nations Security Council Resolutions 1511 and 1546. Accordingly, all references to 'Coalition Forces,' 'Coalition Member States,' 'Coalition Force Commander,' and/or 'Commander, Coalition Forces,' shall be rescinded.
   b) In Section 1(4), the definition of 'Iraqi security forces' shall be amended to include 'the Iraqi Armed Forces.'
   c) In Section 1, a new subsection (10) shall be inserted as follows: '10) 'Private Security Company' means a private business, properly registered with the Ministry of Interior and Ministry of Trade that seeks to gain commercial benefits and financial profit by providing security services to individuals, businesses and organizations, governmental or otherwise.'
   d) Section 3(1)(c) shall be rescinded in its entirety and replaced with the following: 'Groups and individuals who have been authorized by the Minister of the Interior to carry weapons in the course of their duties.'
   e) Section 3(2) shall be rescinded and replaced with the following: 'Private security companies may be licensed by the Minister of the Interior to possess and use licensed Firearms and Military Weapons, including Special Category Weapons, in the course of their duties, including in public places.'
   f) Section 4(3) shall be rescinded and replaced with the following: 'The carrying of concealed weapons is prohibited, other than by (a) Iraqi security forces; (b) Private Security Companies; (c) security officers from diplomatic missions; and (d) any other group or individual so authorized by the Minister of the Interior.'
   g) The first sentence of Section 5 shall be rescinded and replaced with the following: 'Individuals not otherwise authorized to possess or use Firearms or Military Weapons by this, any other CPA instrument, or any other provision of Iraqi law, may apply for weapons authorization.'
   h) In Section 6(1), the phrase 'are subject to confiscation by Coalition Forces and other relevant authorities' shall be rescinded and replaced with the following: 'are subject to confiscation by the Iraqi Security Forces.'
   i) Section 6(6) shall be rescinded in its entirety and replaced with the following: 'An investigative judge of competent jurisdiction may grant a certificate of immunity from prosecution for offenses under this Order or the Iraqi Weapons Code of 1992, but only upon written findings that the person to be granted such

[353] See *Doc 14*.
[354] See *Doc 15*.
[355] See *Doc 17*.

immunity provided information that (a) led to the apprehension and conviction of persons in relation to whom information was sought by the Federal Government or (b) resulted in the prevention of a violent crime against public security, including a violent crime against the Federal Government and its personnel, or the Multinational Force operating in Iraq pursuant to United Nations Security Council Resolutions 1511 and 1546 and its personnel.'

j) The following sentence shall be appended to the end of Section 7: 'This Order and all regulations promulgated hereunder shall be interpreted in a manner consistent with CPA Order Number 17 (Revised), (CPA/ORD/27 June 2004/17).'

4) CPA Order Number 13 (Revised) (Amended), The Central Criminal Court of Iraq[356]
   a) Section 5 shall be rescinded in its entirety and replaced with the following: 'All judges of the Central Criminal Court of Iraq shall be appointed pursuant to Article 46(A) of the TAL and subject to removal only pursuant to Article 47 of the TAL.'
   b) Sections 8(1) shall be rescinded in its entirety.
   c) Section 8(3) shall be rescinded in its entirety and replaced with the following: 'A judge of the CCCI shall remove himself or herself from any case in which a party to the proceeding is a spouse, relative of second degree or other close relationship of that judge.'
   d) The first sentence of 8(4) shall be rescinded.
5) CPA Order Number 14, Prohibited Media Activity[357]
   a) Section 3 shall be rescinded in its entirety and replaced with the following: 'The Prime Minister shall have the authority to enforce Section 2 of this Order, consistent with Chapter 2 of the TAL and Iraq's obligations under international law.'
   b) Section 3 shall be retitled 'Enforcement.'
   c) Sections 4(1) and 4(2) shall be rescinded in their entirety.
   d) Section 5(2) shall be rescinded in its entirety and replaced with the following: Additionally, media organizations penalized in accordance with Section 5(1) shall be referred to the Iraqi Communications and Media Commission for consideration of other appropriate sanction, including withdrawal of duly issued licenses.'
   e) Section 6 shall be rescinded in its entirety and replaced with the following: 'Any media organization sanctioned under Section 5(1) of this Order may appeal to a court of competent jurisdiction for a determination of whether the sanction complies with applicable law, including Chapter 2 of the TAL and the International Covenant on Civil and Political Rights.'
6) CPA Order Number 15, Establishment of the Judicial Review Committee[358]
   A new Section 8 shall be added, entitled 'Expiration,' which shall provide as follows: 'This Order shall expire and the Judicial Review Committee shall be abolished upon the transfer of governing authority to the Iraqi Interim Government on 30 June 2004; provided, however, that (1) all of the Committee's decisions prior to 30 June 2004 shall remain in full force and effect and (2) the Iraqi Judiciary Act, to the extent consistent with the TAL and relevant CPA Orders, shall remain in full force and effect. All judicial appointments to, and removals from, the federal courts after 30 June 2004 shall be conducted pursuant to Chapter 6 of the TAL.'

[356] See *Doc 31*.
[357] See *Doc 32*.
[358] See *Doc 33*.

7) CPA Order Number 16 (Revised) (Amended), Temporary Control of Iraq Borders, Ports, and Airports[359]

a) In Section 1(1), 'Coalition Personnel' shall be rescinded and replaced with 'Multinational Force Personnel.'

b) A new Section 1(3)(d) shall be added as follows: 'citizens and nationals traveling to Iraq on official government business of any state which contributes more than 500 military personnel to the Multinational Force operating in Iraq pursuant to United Nations Security Council Resolutions 1511 and 1546.'

c) The remainder of Section 1(3) shall be read and interpreted according to its express terms, notwithstanding Section 2(7) of this Order.

8) CPA Order Number 17 (Revised), Status of Coalition Provisional Authority, MNF-Iraq, Certain Missions and Personnel in Iraq[360]

This Order shall not apply to Order Number 17.

9) CPA Order Number 19, Freedom of Assembly[361]

a) In Section 3(1), the phrase 'unless acting under authority of the Coalition Force Commander or a Divisional or Brigade Commander (hereinafter 'Approving Authorities')' shall be rescinded and replaced with the following: 'unless acting under authority of the Ministry of Interior (the 'Approving Authority') pursuant to a regularized procedure for issuing permits for such marches, assemblies, meetings, or gatherings. The Ministry of Interior shall promulgate regulations to establish this regularized procedure as soon as possible after 30 June 2004. All such regulations shall be consistent with the TAL and Iraq's obligations under international law.'

b) In Section 3(3), the phrase 'or to be held within 500 meters of any CPA or Coalition Force facility' shall be rescinded and replaced with the following: 'or to be held within 500 meters of any foreign embassy, including foreign embassy regional offices and consulates, facility of the Multinational Force operating in Iraq pursuant to United Nations Security Council Resolutions 1511 and 1546, or public building actively used by the Iraqi government.'

c) At the end of Section 3, the following shall be inserted as a new subsection: '4) Any party denied an opportunity to march, assemble, meet, or gather pursuant to this Order shall have recourse to a federal court for review of whether such denial should be reversed on account of being arbitrary, capricious, or otherwise contrary to law.'

10) CPA Order Number 22, Creation of an Iraqi Armed Forces[362]

a) Section 3(2) shall be rescinded in its entirety and replaced with the following: 'The mission of the Iraqi Armed Forces is the military defense of the nation, including defense of the national territory and the military protection of the security of critical installations, facilities, infrastructure, lines of communication and supply, and population. The tasks of the Iraqi Armed Forces include developing a military capability in order to provide the basis for militarily effective, professional, and non-political armed forces for the military defense of the nation. Except as authorized by orders or regulations of the Iraqi Interim Government as well as duly promulgated legislation or regulations of any

[359] See *Doc 36*.
[360] See *Doc 38*.
[361] See *Doc 40*.
[362] See *Doc 43*.

subsequent Iraqi government, the Iraqi Armed Forces shall not have, or exercise, domestic law enforcement functions. Nor shall the Iraqi Armed Forces intervene in the domestic political affairs of the nation. Tasks of the Iraqi Armed Forces will also include, when so ordered, participation in domestic relief operations associated with natural or man-made disasters and humanitarian relief missions.'

b) Section 3(3) shall be rescinded in its entirety and replaced with the following: 'The President of the State will commission officers in the Iraqi Armed Forces who have been approved for commissioning by the Prime Minister. The Prime Minister or the Minister of Defence will designate Commanders of units of the Iraqi Armed Forces, including officers to command the principal units of the Iraqi Armed Forces, as they are created.'

c) In Sections 3(4), 6(1), 6(8), 6(10), 6(16)(b), 8(1), 10 and 11, all references and associated references to 'a civilian member of the CPA reporting directly to the Administrator and to whom such authority is specifically delegated in writing' shall be rescinded and replaced with the following: 'the Minister of Defence.'

11) CPA Order Number 25, Confiscation of Property Used in or Resulting From Certain Crimes[363]

In Section 6(6), the reference to 'the CPA, Director of Management and Budget' shall be rescinded and replaced with the following: 'the Prime Minister or any official the Prime Minister deems most appropriate to receive the Criminal Property report.'

12) CPA Order Number 30, Reform of Salaries and Employment Conditions of State Employees[364]

a) In Section 3(4) and 8, all references to the 'CPA Director of Management and Budget' shall be rescinded and replaced with the following: 'the Iraqi Minister of Finance.'

b) Section 10 shall become Section 11.

c) A new Section 10 entitled 'Other Matters' shall provide as follows: 'The Office of the Council of Ministers, which served under the previous regime, shall be dissolved immediately prior to the transfer of full governing authority to the Iraqi Interim Government. Each employee, if he or she chooses, shall be transferred at that time with his or her rank to the Office of Surplus Personnel in the Ministry of Finance for reassignment to other civil service employment within the federal government. In the alternative, each employee may choose to retire and, in such a case, the employee shall receive his or her pension pursuant to Iraqi law.'

13) CPA Order Number 35, Re-Establishment of the Council of Judges[365]

Pursuant to Article 45 of the TAL, the Higher Juridical Council shall assume the role of the Council of Judges as of 30 June 2004. The membership of the Higher Juridical Council is set forth in Article 45 of the TAL. To the extent Order 35 is inconsistent with Article 45 or any other provision of the TAL, the TAL provision shall control.

14) CPA Order Number 36, Regulation of Oil Distribution[366]

a) In Section 1(1), the references to 'the Coalition Provisional Authority' and 'Commander Coalition Forces' shall be rescinded.

b) Section 7 shall be rescinded in its entirety.

[363] See *Doc 46*.
[364] See *Doc 51*.
[365] See *Doc 56*.
[366] See *Doc 57*.

15) CPA Order Number 37, Tax Strategy for 2003[367]
In Section 5, the reference to 'the Administrator of the Coalition Provisional Authority or' shall be rescinded.

16) CPA Order Number 38, Reconstruction Levy[368]
Section 2(2) shall be rescinded in its entirety and replaced with the following: 'The Reconstruction Levy shall not apply to (a) Multinational Forces and departments and agencies of Multinational Force Governments and (b) Foreign (non-Iraqi) employees and foreign (non-Iraqi) contractors and subcontractors of Multinational Force Governments as specifically defined in CPA Order Number 17 (Revised), (CPA/ORD/27 June 2004/17).'

17) CPA Order Number 41, Notification of Criminal Offenses[369]
   a) In Section 1(1), the phrase 'the Governing Council, the interim Iraqi Ministers, those persons specifically authorized to draft the new Iraqi constitution, the CPA and Coalition Forces' shall be rescinded and replaced with the following: 'the Iraqi Interim Government and the Iraqi Transitional Government and any subsequent Iraqi Government elected under a permanent constitution as set forth in Chapter 9 of the TAL.'
   b) Section 3 shall be rescinded in its entirety.

18) CPA Order Number 45, Non-Governmental Organizations[370]
   a) The following shall be appended to the end of Section 3(1): 'The Office shall issue a registration certificate or a written decision within 60 business days of receiving an application to register from a non-profit organization. If neither a registration certificate nor a written decision is issued within 60 business days, an application shall be considered provisionally approved until receipt of subsequent communication from the Office confirming approval or denial of the application.'
   b) Section 6 shall be rescinded and replaced with the following: 'If an NGO is found to be operating programs after the suspension or revocation of its registration, or is engaged in conduct that is a direct threat to security or public safety while operating programs regardless of whether registered or not, the Minister of Planning may recommend that the Prime Minister direct closure of the NGO. The Prime Minister may then direct the appropriate minister to effect such closure. In cases of an immediate and substantial threat to security or public safety, as determined by the Prime Minister in consultation with the Presidency Council, the Prime Minister may direct that the assets of an NGO which has had its operations closed in accordance with this paragraph be confiscated and its premises sealed. The NGO may appeal the decision to close its operations and/or confiscate its assets and/or close its premises to a court of competent jurisdiction.'
   c) Section 9(10) shall be rescinded in its entirety.

19) CPA Order Number 48, Delegation of Authority Regarding an Iraqi Special Tribunal[371]
   a) Sections 1(6) of the Delegation of Authority shall be rescinded in its entirety.
   b) Section 3 of the Delegation of Authority shall read in its entirety 'This Order shall enter into force on the date of signature.' The remainder of Section 3 shall be rescinded.

[367] See *Doc 58*.
[368] See *Doc 59*.
[369] See *Doc 63*.
[370] See *Doc 67*.
[371] See *Doc 70*.

20) CPA Order Number 55, Delegation of Authority Regarding the Iraqi Commission on Public Integrity[372]

Section 2(g) of the Delegation of Authority shall be rescinded in its entirety.

21) CPA Order Number 57, Iraqi Inspectors General[373]

a) The following sentence shall be appended to the end of Section 2(3): 'In the event a vacancy arises in the position of Inspector General for the Amanat Baghdad, a position created by CPA Memorandum Number 13 (CPA/MEM/2 June 2004/13), the Mayor of Baghdad shall fill the vacancy by appointment.'

b) Section 7(1) shall be rescinded in its entirety and replaced with the following: 'To enhance their independence, all ministerial Offices of Inspectors General (which shall include the Inspector General for the Amanat Baghdad) shall be centrally funded from an allocation within the annual national budget. Any such allocation shall be prepared by the relevant Inspector General in consultation with the Commissioner for Public Integrity and the President of the Board of Supreme Audit, be limited only to those functions and duties required of Inspectors General under this Order, and submitted to the Ministry of Finance. The Ministry of Finance shall consider the budgetary request and determine the appropriate amount of funding for the forthcoming fiscal year in accordance with the budget preparation process set forth in CPA Order Number 95, Financial Management Law and Public Debt Law, (CPA/ORD/2 June 2004/95).'

22) CPA Order Number 60, Ministry of Human Rights[374]

Section 2(3) shall be rescinded in its entirety and replaced with the following: 'This shall include requesting and coordinating appropriate support from external sources, including non-governmental and other international organizations, the United Nations, and the Multinational Force operating in Iraq pursuant to United Nations Security Council Resolutions 1511 and 1546.'

23) CPA Order Number 65, Iraqi Communications and Media Commission[375]

a) In Section 4(3), the phrase 'in consultation with the IGC and the Administrator' shall be rescinded.

b) The following definition shall be added to Section 2: '"Media organization" includes individuals or groups, and private, corporate, or public entities, domestic or international, established for the purpose of transmitting information by any means.'

c) All references in Section 8 to 'broadcaster, telecommunications operator or information services provider' shall be replaced with 'broadcaster, telecommunications operator, information services provider, or any other media organization.'

d) Section 11(1) shall be rescinded in its entirety and replaced with the following: 'The Commission shall be funded from the following sources: (a) Recurring and non-recurring fees collected from licensees and registrations; and (b) Grants, donations or other amounts received by the Commission from any source, insofar as they are in conformity with applicable law.'

24) CPA Order Number 67, Ministry of Defence[376]

a) The following sentence shall be appended to the end of Section 1(2): 'If the position of Minister of Defence becomes vacant for any reason after the transfer

[372] See *Doc 78*.
[373] See *Doc 80*.
[374] See *Doc 83*.
[375] See *Doc 89*.
[376] See *Doc 91*.

of full governmental authority to the Iraqi Interim Government, a new Minister of Defence shall be appointed in accordance with Article 38(A) of the TAL.'

b) Section 2(1)(a) shall be rescinded and replaced with the following: 'The IAF will consist of the Army, Air Force, Coastal Defence Force, and reserve components (when established), and associated headquarters.'

c) In Section 4(2), the reference to 'the provisions of United Nations Security Council Resolution 1511' shall be rescinded and replaced with the following: 'the provisions of United Nations Security Council Resolutions 1511 and 1546.'

d) The following sentence shall be appended to the end of Section 4(7): 'All subsequent Inspectors General for the MoD shall be appointed pursuant to the process set forth in Section 2 of CPA Order Number 57, (CPA/ORD/10 Feb. 2004/57).'

25) CPA Order Number 69, Delegation of Authority to Establish the Iraqi National Intelligence Service[377]

a) In the Delegation of Authority, Section 2(4) shall be rescinded in its entirety.

b) In the Delegation of Authority, the following sentence shall be appended to the end of Section 2(5): 'All subsequent Inspectors General for the INIS shall be appointed pursuant to the process set forth in Section 2 of CPA Order Number 57, (CPA/ORD/10 Feb. 2004/57).'

26) CPA Order Number 71, Local Government Powers[378]

a) The following sentence shall be appended to the end of Section 2(3): 'After the transfer of authority on 30 June 2004, additional positions may be designated as 'senior positions' by the Prime Minister with approval of the Presidency Council.'

b) Section 2(4) shall be rescinded in its entirety.

c) The current Section 3(5) shall become Section 3(7).

d) A new Section 3(5) shall provide as follows: 'At least two weeks prior to any Governorate Council vote on whether to remove a Director General pursuant to Section 3(4) of this Order, the Governorate Council shall notify in writing the relevant Ministry that such a vote will be held. The Ministry may avail itself of this two week period to hold consultations with the Governor and Governorate Council regarding the proposed removal of the Director General. Only at the conclusion of this two week period may the Governorate Council bring the proposed removal to a vote.'

e) A new Section 3(6) shall provide as follows: 'Notwithstanding any provision of this Order or any other law, the removal of a Director General or an official in a designated senior position may be suspended for 6 months upon the Prime Minister's certification in writing that such removal will cause significant damage to national security and upon the unanimous approval of that certification by the Presidency. To continue the suspension of a removal vote for another 6 months, the Prime Minister must recertify in writing that the removal will cause significant damage to national security and the Presidency must unanimously approve that certification.'

f) The current Section 9 shall become Section 10.

27) CPA Order Number 73, Transfer of the Iraqi Civil Defense Corps to the Ministry of Defense[379]

Section 3(8) is rescinded in its entirety.

[377] See *Doc 93*.
[378] See *Doc 95*.
[379] See *Doc 97*.

28) CPA Order Number 74, Interim Law on Securities Markets[380]

a) The following sentence shall be appended to the end of Section 1(6): 'For purposes of this Order, the body vested with national executive authority in both the Iraqi Interim and Transitional Governments shall be the Council of Ministers.'

b) Section 6(2)(b) shall be rescinded in its entirety and replaced with the following: 'The Exchange's Board of Governors shall appoint the Chief Executive Officer of the Exchange.'

c) The following sentence shall be appended to the end of Section 6(3): 'Subsequent selections of members of the Board of Governors shall be made by a vote taken by the General Assembly of the Exchange, in conformance with the Exchange's bylaws and/or relevant rules.'

d) Section 6(9) shall be rescinded in its entirety, and replaced with the following: 'A Governor may be removed prior to the expiration of his or her term only for cause and by a super majority (seventy five percent) vote of the Commission.'

e) Section 12(6) shall be rescinded in its entirety and replaced with the following: 'The Commission may set its own salaries, benefits and financial entitlements in conformance with the Ministry of Finance's requirements for budgetary management of Iraq's public money.'

f) Section 13(6) shall be rescinded in its entirety.

29) CPA Order Number 75, Realignment of Military Industrial Companies[381]

a) In Sections 2(4), 3(1), 3(2), and 3(3), all references to 'the Administrator' shall be rescinded and replaced with the following: 'the Prime Minister in consultation with the Council of Ministers.'

b) Section 3(5) shall be rescinded in its entirety and replaced with the following: 'The Minister of Industry may make specific recommendations to the Prime Minister for alternative courses of action.'

30) CPA Order Number 76, Consolidation of State Owned Enterprises[382]

The following sentence shall be appended to the end of Section 5(7): 'Following the transfer of full governmental authority to the Iraqi Interim Government, the duties of the Administrator under this Order shall transfer to the Prime Minister and the duties of the Governing Council under this Order shall transfer to the Council of Ministers.'

31) CPA Order Number 77, Board of Supreme Audit[383]

In Section 2(4), references to 'the Coalition Provisional Authority' and 'the Iraqi Governing Council' shall be rescinded.

32) CPA Order Number 82, Iraqi National Remembrance Foundation[384]

a) In Section 3(4), references to 'the Iraqi Governing Council' shall be replaced with 'the Council of Ministers.'

b) Section 6 shall be rescinded in its entirety.

33) CPA Order Number 90, Special Taskforce for Compensating Victims of the Previous Regime[385]

The following sentence shall be appended to the end of Section 1(2): 'Should a vacancy in the Chairmanship arise at any time, the Prime Minister shall appoint a new Chairman after consultation with the Presidency Council.'

[380] See *Doc 98*.
[381] See *Doc 99*.
[382] See *Doc 100*.
[383] See *Doc 101*.
[384] See *Doc 106*.
[385] See *Doc 114*.

34) CPA Order Number 91, Regulation of Armed Forces and Militias in Iraq[386]
   a) Section 3(1)(e) shall be rescinded in its entirety and replaced with the following: 'A Private Security Company and officers and employees of a Private Security Company, provided the Private Security Company meets all of the licensing and regulation requirements of Iraqi law, including the Memorandum regulating Private Security Companies.'
   b) In Section 4(5)(h), the reference to 'the CPA or government of Iraq following transfer of full Governance authority' shall be rescinded and replaced with the following: 'the Transition and Reintegration Implementation Committee.'

35) CPA Order Number 95, Financial Management Law and Public Debt Law[387]
The phrase 'the body vested with national legislative authority,' which appears at Annex A, Sections 1, 4(2), 6(8), 7(1), 7(3), 7(4), 7(5), 9(6), 9(8), 10(7), 11(5), 11(6), 11(8) and 15(7) of the Financial Management Law of 2004, shall mean the Interim National Council of the Iraqi Interim Government; the elected National Assembly of the Iraqi Transitional Government; and the elected assembly in whatever form of the Iraqi Government to be elected under a permanent constitution.'

Section 4 Rescission of CPA Orders
The following CPA orders are hereby, or have been, rescinded in their entirety and shall have no force and effect whatsoever after the transfer of full governing authority to the Iraqi Interim Government on 30 June 2004:

1) CPA Order Number 4, Management of Property and Assets of the Ba'ath Party[388]
2) CPA Order Number 5, Establishment of the Iraqi De-Ba'athification Council[389]
3) CPA Order Number 6, Eviction of Persons Illegally Occupying Public Buildings[390]
4) CPA Order Number 11, Licensing Telecommunications Service and Equipment[391]
5) CPA Order Number 12, Trade Liberalization Policy[392]
6) CPA Order Number 21, Interim Exercise of Baghdad Mayoral Authority[393]
7) CPA Order Number 42, Creation of Defense Support Agency[394]
8) CPA Order Number 47, Amendment of CPA Order 38 on Reconstruction Levy[395]
9) CPA Order Number 61, Amendment to CPA Order Number 45[396]
10) CPA Order Number 62, Disqualification from Public Service[397]

Section 5 Revisions of CPA Regulations
Notwithstanding the General Rules set forth in Section 2 of this Order, the following specific provisions of CPA Regulations shall be amended, rescinded, or otherwise changed as follows:

[386] See *Doc 115*.
[387] See *Doc 119*.
[388] See *Doc 18*.
[389] See *Doc 19*.
[390] See *Doc 20*.
[391] See *Doc 26*.
[392] See *Doc 28*.
[393] See *Doc 42*.
[394] See *Doc 64*.
[395] See *Doc 69*.
[396] See *Doc 84*.
[397] See *Doc 85*.

1) CPA Regulation Number 1, Coalition Provisional Authority[398]
A new Section 7 entitled 'Dissolution' shall provide as follows: 'Upon dissolution of the CPA, this Regulation shall have no force and effect.'
2) CPA Regulation Number 5 (Amended), Council for International Coordination[399]
This Regulation shall be rescinded in its entirety.
3) CPA Regulation Number 6, Governing Council of Iraq[400]
This Regulation shall be rescinded in its entirety.
4) CPA Regulation Number 7, International Donor Assistance[401]
    a) Section 1(3) shall be rescinded in its entirety and replaced with the following: '*Membership*. The Board shall consist of the following individuals: two appointed by the Governing Council; the Minister of Planning and Development Cooperation; the Minister of Finance; and one or two individuals appointed by the Prime Minister upon recommendation of the Minister of Planning and Development Cooperation in his capacity as Chairman of the Board.'
    b) The following sentence shall be added to the end of Section 1(3): 'The occupants of the first two positions listed above as of 30 June 2004 will continue for a period of two years. The Minister of Planning and Development Cooperation will recommend a replacement or reappointment to the Prime Minister after the elapse of one year or in the event that the position(s) become vacant.'
    c) The following shall be appended to the end of Section 2(1): 'The Council for International Coordination ('Council') will continue to be the in-country coordinating body for international assistance in the relief, recovery and development of Iraq. The Council will encourage the international community to provide funds and other forms of assistance to Iraq and will assist in coordinating international assistance provided by contributing States, non-governmental organizations, and international organizations.'
    d) Section 6 shall be rescinded in its entirety and replaced with the following: 'The Federal Government alone has the authority to carry out the functions and responsibilities set forth in this Regulation.' Section 6 shall be retitled as follows: 'Exclusive Authority of the Federal Government.'

Section 6 Revisions of CPA Memoranda Provisions

Notwithstanding the General Rules set forth in Section 2 of this Order, the following specific provisions of CPA Memoranda shall be amended, rescinded, or otherwise changed as follows:

1) CPA Memorandum Number 1, Implementation of De-Ba'athification Order No. 1[402]
This Memorandum shall be rescinded in its entirety.
2) CPA Memorandum Number 2, Management of Detention and Prison Facilities[403]
    a) Section 2(3) shall be rescinded in its entirety and replaced with the following: 'To ensure these standards are met, the Minister of Justice shall remain in full control of the Iraqi prison system and shall report periodically to the Prime

[398] See *Doc 1*.
[399] See *Doc 6*.
[400] See *Doc 7*.
[401] See *Doc 8*.
[402] See *Doc 125*.
[403] See *Doc 126*.

Minister regarding the status of the Iraqi prison system and any changes in Iraqi law that may be necessary to comply with this Memorandum and the Federal Government's obligations under international law and the TAL.'

b) Section 2(4) shall be rescinded in its entirety.

3) CPA Memorandum Number 3, Criminal Procedure[404]
In Section 2, references to 'the Coalition or any of its member States' and 'a Coalition member State' shall be rescinded and replaced with the following: 'the Multinational Force operating in Iraq pursuant to United Nations Security Council Resolutions 1511 and 1546 and all States contributing forces to that Multinational Force.'

4) CPA Memorandum Number 4, Contract and Grant Procedures with Appendices[405]

a) All references to the Program Review Board shall apply to its successor board in the Iraqi Government.
b) In Section 1, all but the first sentence shall be deleted.
c) All references to the term 'Iraqi Funds' shall be replaced by 'Public Funds.'
d) Section 2(5) shall be rescinded in its entirety and replaced with the following: 'Others delegated such authority by the Prime Minister.'
e) Section 3(8) shall be rescinded in its entirety and replaced with the following: "Public Funds': Funds owned and controlled by the Federal Government.'
f) Section 4(1) and 4(2) shall be rescinded in entirety and replaced with the following: 'The Ministry of Finance shall determine which officials are authorized to appoint Contracting Officers who may enter into Contracts or Grants within their directorates, commands, or organizations.'
g) In Section 4(3), the phrase 'the officials listed in paragraph 2 above' shall be rescinded and replaced with the following: 'officials.'
h) Section 6(1) shall be rescinded in its entirety and replaced with the following: 'Identification of Parties. Contracts and Grants must prominently identify the parties.
i) In Section 10(1), the following phrase shall be deleted: 'The CPA Office of Management and Budget will allocate funds to the Iraqi Ministry of Finance for further distribution to the Iraqi Ministries, in accordance with the national Budget.'
j) In Section 12, the final sentence shall be deleted.
k) In Appendix B(12) 'United States currency' shall be replaced with 'Iraqi currency.'
l) Appendix (B)(16) shall be rescinded in its entirety and replaced with the following: 'Disputes. Failure of the parties to this contract to reach agreement on any request for equitable adjustment, claim, appeal, or action arising under or relating to this contract shall be a dispute to be resolved in accordance with the laws of Iraq. The contractor shall proceed diligently with performance of this contract, pending final resolution of any dispute arising under the contract.'
m) Appendix B(35), Appendix B(36), and Appendix B(40) shall be rescinded their entirety.
n) Appendix D shall be rescinded in its entirety.

5) CPA Memorandum Number 5, Implementation of Weapons Control Order Number 3 with Annex.[406]

[404] See *Doc 127.*
[405] See *Doc 129.*
[406] See *Doc 130.*

a) All references to 'foreign liaison mission[s]' shall be replaced with 'diplomatic or consular missions.'
b) In Section 1(iii), the reference 'authorized by the CPA' shall be rescinded and replaced with the following: 'authorized by the Iraqi government and/or the Multinational Force operating in Iraq pursuant to United Nations Security Council Resolutions 1511 and 1546.'
c) In Section 4, the two references to 'the CPA office advising the' shall be rescinded.
d) In Annex A, the text and the chart preceding, but not including, the phrase 'United Nations Specialized and Related Agencies are' shall be rescinded. The remainder of Annex A shall remain unchanged.

6) CPA Memorandum Number 6, Implementation of Regulation on the Governing Council[407]

This Memorandum shall be rescinded in its entirety.

7) CPA Memorandum Number 7, Delegation of Authority Under De-Ba'athification Order Number 1[408]

All authority delegated under this Memorandum shall be withdrawn and the Higher National De-Ba'athification Council,[409] established pursuant to that authority, shall be abolished at such time as the Iraqi Interim Government issues an order establishing the Independent Iraqi De-Ba'athification Council.

8) CPA Memorandum Number 9, Appointment of Deputy Ministers[410]

This Memorandum shall be rescinded in its entirety.

9) CPA Memorandum Number 10, Rewards Program for Information Leading to the Recovery of Iraqi State and Former Regime Assets[411]

Section 2 shall be rescinded in its entirety and replaced with the following: 'The Prime Minister in coordination with the Minister of Finance may authorize the payment of financial rewards to eligible individuals who provide the Iraqi government or the Multinational Force operating in Iraq pursuant to United Nations Security Council Resolutions 1511 and 1546 with information that leads to the recovery of state assests or former regime-owned assets.'

Section 7 Effective Date

This Order shall enter into force immediately prior to the transfer of governing authority from the CPA to the Iraqi Interim Government [28 June 2004].

[407] See *Doc 131*.

[408] See *Doc 132*.

[409] The terminology used in CPA and IGC documents is not uniform. Sometimes the term 'Higher National De-Ba'athification Council' is used, sometimes the term 'Higher National De-Ba'athification Commission' is employed.

[410] See *Doc 134*.

[411] See *Doc 135*.

3. Memoranda

Document 125
Coalition Provisional Authority Memorandum Number 1
CPA/MEM/3 June 2003/01

Implementation of De-Ba'athification Order No. 1 (CPA/ORD/16 May 2003/01)

Pursuant to my authority as Administrator of the Coalition Provisional Authority (CPA), relevant U.N. Security Council resolutions, including Resolution 1483 (2003), and the laws and usages of war,

Recognizing that the Iraqi people have suffered large scale human rights abuses and deprivations over many years at the hands of the Ba'ath Party,

Noting the grave concern of Iraqi society regarding the threat posed by the continuation of Ba'ath Party networks and personnel in the administration of Iraq, and the intimidation of the people of Iraq by Ba'ath Party officials,

Implementing CPA Order No. 1, De-Ba'athification of Iraqi Society (CPA/ORD/16 May 2003/01),[1] and CPA Order No. 5, Establishment of the Iraqi De-Ba'athification Council (CPA/ORD/25 May 2003/05),[2]

I hereby promulgate the following:

Section 1 Objective

1) This Memorandum prescribes a two-staged process for carrying out the de-Ba'athification of Iraqi society. To expedite the identification of Ba'ath Party members at the outset of the CPA's restoration of Iraq, the Commander of Coalition Forces, through Accreditation Review Committees (ARCs), will initially perform the investigative function, relying upon military investigative resources with training and experience in performing analogous fact-finding duties.

2) Later, as higher levels of the former Iraqi government undergo a reliable and rigorous de-Ba'athification process and the Iraqi De-Ba'athification Council demonstrates sufficient capability, the Administrator will task the IDC to assume increasing and ultimately full responsibility for the process, subject to the authority, direction and control of the Administrator. The ARCs shall remain in operation until the people of Iraq adopt a representative from of self-government.

Section 2 Interim Process for Identifying Ba'ath Party Members

1) The commander of Coalition Forces shall provide military investigative resources sufficient to receive and compile information concerning possible Ba'ath Party affiliations of employees at all ministries. These resources may be augmented or replaced by U.S. civilian investigators as necessary, and should include professional Iraqis whenever possible.

[1] See *Doc 14*.
[2] See *Doc 19*.

2) These investigators will:
   a) *Conduct Investigations.* Investigators will be posted to the ministries to receive and compile information concerning the possible Ba'ath Party affiliations of their employees. These investigators will draw from available and relevant information, such as:
      [i] Interviews with the individual (conducted by the investigators using the standardized form already developed);
      [ii] Public records and announcements documenting the ascension or promotion of party members;
      [iii] Judgments of CPA senior ministry advisors;
      [iv] Testimony of Iraqis who have worked with the person in question;
      [v] Findings of the Iraqi De-Ba'athification Council described below (passed to the investigators through the Administrator);
      [vi] Assessments of leading Iraqi political figures; and
      [vii] Government records revealing bonuses or other privileges associated with being a party member.
   b) *Make Determinations of Ba'ath Party Membership.* The investigator will make a factual finding about the person's affiliation with the Ba'ath Party. The investigator will advise the employee that he or she has the right to appeal this factual finding (whether he or she was a Ba'ath Party member). Based upon the investigator's finding, the Senior Ministry Advisor will take action in accordance with the criteria for removal set forth in CPA Order No. 1 (CPA/ORD/16 May 2003/01), unless an exception is granted.
   c) *Prepare the Case for Exceptions Where Appropriate.* When the ministry team requests an exception for an individual, the investigator will determine whether the person in question is eligible. The investigator will subsequently prepare the case for an exception.

Section 3 Phased Process for Identifying Ba'ath Party Members

1) As the Administrator determines that the responsibility for identifying Ba'ath Party members effectively can be transferred to Iraqi citizens, the Administrator shall direct the Iraqi De-Ba'athification Council to assume an increasingly significant role in carrying out the De-Ba'athification process.

2) Initially, the Council will advise the Coalition on De-Ba'athification policies and procedures (including the appropriateness of granting exceptions to CPA Order No. 1 (CPA/ORD/16 May 2003/01)) and meaningfully involve the Iraqis in the De-Ba'athification effort.

3) The Council will provide information to the investigators (through the Administrator) and nominate Iraqi legal professionals to participate in the ARCs described in Section 4 herein, and in the investigatory process. When appropriate, it is anticipated that the Council will assume the investigative responsibility entirely.

Section 4 Accreditation Review Committee

1) [sic] The Commander of Coalition Forces is authorized to establish and administer one or more ARCs. These bodies will be comprised of one military and two civilian members (one of whom will be an Iraqi). The ARCs shall remain in operation until the people of Iraq adopt a representative form of self-government. The ARCs will:
   a) *Hear Appeals of Fact.* The ARCs will hear the appeals of Iraqis who believe they were wrongly found to be ba'atheists. These appeals will be conducted in a

manner that comports as nearly as practicable to tribunals convened by Coalition Forces under Article 5 of the 1949 Geneva Convention.

b) *Grant or Deny Requests for Exception.* The ARC will review applications for exceptions prepared by the investigators, and grant or deny them. All ARC decisions will be immediately reported to the Administrator, who retains the authority to overturn any decision to grant or deny an exception. The ARC will take into account all available and relevant information, including whether the individual:
   [i] Is willing to denounce the Ba'ath Party and his past association with it;
   [ii] Was a senior Ba'ath Party member or simply a 'full' party member;
   [iii] Has exceptional educational qualities;
   [iv] Left the Ba'ath Party before April 16, 2003;
   [v] Continues to command the support of his colleagues and respect of their subordinates;
   [vi] Is judged to be indispensable to achieving important Coalition interests, at least in the immediate term;
   [vii] Can demonstrate that he joined the party to hold his job or support his family.

c) The information listed above in Section 4.1(b) shall be considered in deciding whether to grant an exception, but shall not in itself ensure that an exception will be granted.

Section 5 Entry into Force
This Memorandum shall enter into force on the day of signature [3 June 2003].[3]

Document 126
Coalition Provisional Authority Memorandum Number 2
CPA/MEM/8 June 2003/02

Management of Detention and Prison Facilities

Pursuant to my authority as Administrator of the Coalition Provisional Authority (CPA), and under the laws and usages of war, and consistent with relevant U.N. Security Council resolutions, including Resolution 1483 (2003),

Recognizing the urgent necessity to ensure secure and humane prisons in order to re-establish law and order and provide for the safety of the people of Iraq,

Noting the obligation of the CPA to restore public order and safety and to maintain and ensure fundamental standards for persons detained,

I hereby promulgate the following:

Section 1 Purpose

1) This Memorandum prescribes standards to be applied in the Iraqi prison system, under the authority of the Ministry of Justice.

[3] CPA Memorandum No 1 was rescinded by CPA Order No 100, sec 6(1) *[Doc 124]*.

2) All prisons within Iraq shall, to the greatest extent practicable, operate in accordance with the following standards until otherwise directed. Any and all existing Iraqi prison regulations are hereby suspended.

Section 2 Basic Principles and Control

1) The following standards shall be applied impartially. There shall be no discrimination on the grounds of race, color, sex, language, religion, political or other opinion, national or social origin, property, birth or other status.

2) It shall nevertheless be a requirement, consistent with the need to maintain prison security, to respect the religious beliefs and moral precepts of the group to which a prisoner belongs.

3) To ensure these standards are met, the Administrator will remain in full control of the Iraqi prison system and may at any time amend this Memorandum as necessary, or direct other action with respect to the prison system.[4]

4) In addition, CPA officials of the Justice Ministry and Coalition Forces operating under their oversight shall have the right to enter and inspect any Iraqi prison system, and give directions regarding the operation of that system, consistent with the terms of this Memorandum.[5]

Section 3 Register

1) In every place where persons are imprisoned there shall be kept a bound registration book with numbered pages in which shall be entered in respect of each prisoner received:

a) information concerning his identity;
b) the reasons for his commitment and the authority therefor; and
c) the day and hour of his admission and release.

2) No person shall be received in an institution without a valid commitment order, the details of which shall have been entered in the register.

Section 4 Separation of Categories

Different categories of prisoners shall be kept in separate institutions or parts of institutions, taking account of their sex, age, criminal record, the legal reason for their detention and the necessities of their treatment, so that:

a) men and women shall be detained in separate institutions;
b) untried prisoners shall be kept separate from convicted prisoners;
c) persons imprisoned for debt and other civil prisoners shall be kept separate from persons imprisoned by reason of a criminal offense; and
d) prisoners under 18 years of age shall be kept separate from adults.

Section 5 Accommodation

1) Where sleeping accommodation is in individual cells or rooms, each prisoner should occupy by night a cell or room by himself. The central prison administration may make an exception to this rule for special reasons, such as temporary overcrowding.

2) Where dormitories are used, they shall be occupied by prisoners carefully selected as being suitable to associate with one another in those conditions. There shall be regular supervision by night, in keeping with the nature of the institution.

[4] Sec 2(3) was rescinded and replaced by CPA Order No 100, sec 6(2)(a) *[Doc 124]*.
[5] Sec 2(4) was rescinded by CPA Order No 100, sec 6(2)(b) *[Doc 124]*.

3) All accommodation provided for the use of prisoners, and in particular all sleeping accommodations, shall, to the extent practicable, meet all requirements of health, due regard being paid to climatic conditions and particularly to cubic content of air, minimum floor space, lighting, heating and ventilation.

4) In all places where prisoners are required to live or work:

a) the windows shall be large enough to enable the prisoners to read or work by natural light, and shall be so constructed that they can allow the entrance of fresh air whether or not there is artificial ventilation; and

b) artificial light shall be provided sufficient for the prisoners to read or work without injury to eyesight.

5) The sanitary installations shall be adequate to enable every prisoner to comply with the needs of nature when necessary and in a clean and decent manner.

6) Adequate bathing and shower installations shall be provided so that every prisoner may be enabled and required to have a bath or shower, at a temperature suitable to the climate, as frequently as necessary for general hygiene according to season and geographical region, but at least once a week.

7) All bed pans or ablution facilities of an institution regularly used by prisoners shall be properly maintained and kept scrupulously clean at all times.

Section 6 Personal Hygiene

1) Prisoners shall be required to keep their persons clean, and to this end they shall be provided with water and with such toilet articles as are necessary for health and cleanliness.

2) In order that prisoners may maintain a good appearance compatible with their self-respect, facilities shall be provided for the proper care of the hair and beard, and men shall be enabled to shave regularly.

Section 7 Clothing and Bedding

1) Every prisoner who is not allowed to wear his or her own clothing shall be provided with an outfit of clothing suitable for the climate and adequate to keep him in good health. Such clothing shall in no manner be degrading or humiliating.

2) All clothing shall be clean and kept in proper condition. Underclothing shall be changed and washed as often as necessary for the maintenance of hygiene.

3) If prisoners are allowed to wear their own clothing, arrangements shall be made on their admission to the institution to ensure that it shall be clean and fit for use.

4) Every prisoner shall be provided with a separate bed, and with separate and sufficient bedding that shall be clean when issued, kept in good order and changed often enough to ensure its cleanliness.

Section 8 Food

1) Every prisoner shall be provided by the administration at regular hours with food of nutritional value adequate for health and strength, and of wholesome quality.

2) Drinking water shall be available to every prisoner whenever he needs it.

Section 9 Exercise and Sport

Every prisoner who is not employed in outdoor work shall have at least one hour of suitable exercise in the open air daily if the weather permits.

Section 10 Medical Services

1) At every institution there shall be available the services of at least one qualified medical officer who should have some knowledge of psychiatry.

2) Sick prisoners who require specialist treatment shall be transferred to specialized institutions or to civil hospitals. Where hospital facilities are provided in an institution, their equipment, furnishings and pharmaceutical supplies shall be proper for the medical care and treatment of sick prisoners, and there shall be a staff of suitably trained officers.

3) The services of a qualified dental officer shall be available to every prisoner.

4) In women's institutions there shall be special accommodation for all necessary prenatal and postnatal care and treatment. Arrangements shall be made wherever practicable for children to be born in a hospital outside the institution. If a child is born in prison, this fact shall not be mentioned in the birth certificate.

5) Where nursing infants are allowed to remain in the institution with their mothers, provision shall be made for a nursery staffed by qualified persons, where the infants shall be placed when they are not in the care of their mothers.

6) The medical officer shall see and examine every prisoner as soon as possible after his admission and thereafter as necessary, with a view particularly to the discovery of physical or mental illness and the taking of all necessary health measures; the segregation of prisoners suspected of infectious or contagious conditions; the noting of physical or mental defects that might hamper rehabilitation, and the determination of the physical capacity of every prisoner for work.

7) The medical officer shall have responsibility for the care of the physical and mental health of the prisoners and should daily see all sick prisoners, all who complain of illness, and any prisoner to whom his attention is specially directed.

8) The medical officer shall report to the prison master whenever he considers that a prisoner's physical or mental health has been or will be injuriously affected by continued imprisonment or by any condition of imprisonment.

9) The medical officer shall regularly inspect and advise the prison master upon the:
   a) quantity, quality, preparation and service of food;
   b) hygiene and cleanliness of the institution and the prisoners;
   c) sanitation, heating, lighting and ventilation of the institution;
   d) suitability and cleanliness of the prisoners' clothing and bedding; and the
   e) observance of the provision concerning physical education and sports, in cases where there is no technical personnel in charge of these activities.

10) The prison master shall take into consideration the reports and advice that the medical officer submits in accordance with this regulation and, in case he concurs with the recommendations made, shall take immediate steps to give effect to those recommendations; if they are not within his or her competence or if he or her [sic] does not concur with them, he shall immediately submit his or her own report and the advice of the medical officer to higher authority.

Section 11 Discipline and Punishment

1) Discipline and order shall be maintained with firmness, but with no more restriction than is necessary for safe custody and well-ordered community life.

2) No prisoner shall be employed, in the service of the institution, in any disciplinary capacity.

3) This standard shall not, however, impede the proper functioning of systems based on self-government, under which specified social, educational or sports activities or

responsibilities are entrusted, under supervision, to prisoners who are formed into groups for the purposes of treatment.

4) The following shall always be determined by the law or by the regulation of the competent administrative authority:

a) conduct constituting a disciplinary offense;
b) the types and duration of punishment that may be inflicted; and
c) the authority competent to impose such punishment.

5) No prisoner shall be punished except in accordance with the terms of such law or regulation, and never twice for the same offense.

6) No prisoner shall be punished unless he has been informed of the offense alleged against him and is given a proper opportunity to present his defense. The competent authority shall conduct a thorough examination of the case.

7) Where necessary and practicable, the prisoner shall be allowed to make his or her defense through an interpreter.

8) Corporal punishment, punishment by placing in a dark cell, and all cruel, inhuman or degrading punishments shall be completely prohibited as punishments for disciplinary offenses.

9) Punishment by close confinement or reduction of diet shall never be inflicted unless the medical officer has examined the prisoner and certified in writing that he is fit to sustain it.

10) The same shall apply to any other punishment that may be prejudicial to the physical or mental health or a prisoner.

11) The medical officer shall daily visit prisoners undergoing such punishments and shall advise the prison master if he considers the termination or alteration of the punishment necessary on grounds of physical or mental health.

Section 12 Instruments of Restraint

1) Instruments of restraint, such as handcuffs, chains, irons and strait-jacket [sic], shall never be applied as a punishment. Furthermore, chains or irons shall not be used as restraints. Other instruments of restraint shall not be used except in the following circumstances:

a) as a precaution against escape during a transfer, provided that they shall be removed when the prisoner appears before a judicial or administrative authority;
b) on medical grounds by direction of the medical officer; and
c) by order of the prison master, if other methods of control fail, in order to prevent a prisoner from injuring himself or others or from damaging property; in such instances the prison master shall at once consult the medical officer and report to the higher administrative authority.

2) The patterns and manner of use of instruments of restraint shall be decided by the central prison administration. Such instruments must not be applied any longer than is strictly necessary.

Section 13 Information to and Complaints by Prisoners

1) Every prisoner on admission shall be provided with written information about the regulations governing the treatment of prisoners of his category, the disciplinary requirements of the institution, the authorized methods of seeking information and making complaints, and all such other matters as are necessary to enable him to understand both his rights and his obligations and to adapt himself to the life of the institution.

2) If a prisoner is illiterate, the aforesaid information shall be conveyed to him or her orally.

3) Every prisoner shall have the opportunity each week day of making requests or complaints to the prison master of the institution or the officer authorized to represent him or her.

4) It shall be possible to make requests or complaints to the inspector of prisons during his or her inspection. The prisoner shall have the opportunity to talk to the inspector or to any other inspecting officer without the prison master or other members of the staff being present.

5) Every prisoner shall be allowed to make a request or complaint, without censorship as to substance but in proper form, to the central prison administration, the judicial authority or other proper authorities through approved channels.

6) Unless it is patently frivolous or groundless, every request or complaint shall be promptly dealt with and replied to without undue delay.

Section 14 Communications and Contacts with Others

1) Prisoners shall be allowed under necessary supervision to communicate with their family and reputable friends at regular intervals, both by correspondence and by receiving visits.

2) Prisoners who are foreign nationals shall be allowed reasonable facilities to communicate with the diplomatic and consular representatives of the State to which they belong.

3) Prisoners who are nationals of States without diplomatic or consular representation in Iraq and refugees or stateless persons shall be allowed similar facilities to communicate with the diplomatic representative of the State that takes charge of their interests or any national or international authority whose task it is to protect such persons.

4) Prisoners shall be permitted to read publications that do not pose a threat to security, and to hear wireless or television transmissions as authorized or controlled by the prison administration.

5) Access shall be granted to official delegates of the International Committee of the Red Cross (ICRC) whenever sought, to be conducted at mutually arranged times. ICRC delegates shall be permitted to inspect health, sanitation and living arrangements and to interview all detainees in private. They shall also be permitted to record information regarding the detainee and to pass messages to and from the family of the detainee subject to reasonable censorship by the prison authorities.

Section 15 Books

Every institution shall have a library for the use of all categories of prisoners, adequately stocked with both recreational and instructional books, and prisoners shall be encouraged to make full use of it.

Section 16 Religion

1) If the institution contains a sufficient number of prisoners of the same religion, a qualified representative of that religion shall be appointed or approved. If the number of prisoners justifies it and conditions permit, the arrangement should be on a full-time basis.

2) A qualified representative appointed or approved under paragraph (1) shall be allowed to hold regular services and to pay pastoral visits in private to prisoners of his religion at proper times.

3) Access to a qualified representative of any religion shall not be refused to any prisoner. On the other hand, any prisoner may refuse to receive a visit of any religious representative, his attitude shall be fully respected.

4) So far as practicable, every prisoner shall be allowed to satisfy the needs of his religious life by attending the services provided in the institution and having in his or her possession the books of religious observance and instruction of his denomination.

Section 17 Retention of Prisoners' Property

1) All money, valuables, clothing and other effects belonging to a prisoner which under the regulations of the institution he is not allowed to retain shall on his admission to the institution be placed in safe custody. An inventory thereof shall be signed by the prisoner. Steps shall be taken to keep them in good condition.

2) On the release of the prisoner all such items shall be returned to him except in so far as he or her [sic] has been authorized to spend money or send any such property out of the institution or it has been found necessary on hygienic grounds to destroy any article of clothing. The prisoner shall sign a receipt for the articles and money returned to him.

3) Any money or effects received for a prisoner from outside shall be treated in the same way.

4) If a prisoner brings in any drugs or medicine, the medical officer shall decide what use shall be made of them.

Section 18 Notification of Death, Illness, Transfer, etc.

1) Upon the death or serious illness of, or serious injury to a prisoner, or his or her removal to an institution for the treatment of mental afflictions, the prison master shall at once inform the spouse, if the prisoner is married or the nearest relative and shall in any event inform any other person previously designated by the prisoner.

2) A prisoner shall be informed at once of the death or serious illness of any near relative. In case of the critical illness of a near relative, the prisoner should be authorized, whenever circumstances allow, to visit the relative either under escort or alone.

3) Every prisoner shall have the right immediately to inform his or her family of his or her imprisonment or his transfer to another institution.

Section 19 Removal of Prisoners

1) When prisoners are being removed to or from an institution, they shall be exposed to public view as little as possible and proper safeguards shall be adopted to protect them from insult, curiosity and publicity in any form.

2) The transport of prisoners in conveyances with inadequate ventilation or light, or in any way that would subject them to unnecessary physical hardship, shall be prohibited.

3) The transport of prisoners shall be carried out at the expense of the administration, and equal conditions shall obtain [sic] for all of them.

Section 20 Institutional Personnel

1) The prison administration shall provide for the careful selection of every grade of the prison personnel, since it is on their integrity, humanity, professional capacity and personal suitability for the work that the proper administration of the institutions depends.

2) The prison administration shall constantly seek to awaken and maintain in the minds both of the prison personnel and of the public the conviction that this work is a social service of great importance, and to this end all appropriate means of informing the public should be used.

3) To secure the foregoing ends, prison personnel shall be appointed on a full-time basis as professional prison officers and have civil service status with security of tenure subject only to good conduct, efficiency and physical fitness.

4) The personnel shall possess an adequate standard of education and intelligence.

5) Before entering on duty, the personnel shall be given a course of training in their general and specific duties.

6) All members of the personnel shall at all times so conduct themselves and perform their duties as to influence the prisoners for good by their example and to command their respect.

7) The prison master of an institution should be adequately qualified for his task by character, administrative ability, suitable training and experience.

8) He shall devote his entire time to his official duties and shall not be appointed on a part-time basis.

9) When two or more institutions are under the authority of one prison master, he shall visit each of them at frequent intervals. A responsible resident official shall be in charge of each of these institutions.

10) The prison master, his or her deputy, and the majority of the other personnel of the institution shall be able to speak the language of the greatest number of prisoners, or a language understood by the greatest number of them.

11) Whenever necessary, the services of an interpreter shall be used.

12) In institutions that are large enough to require the services of one or more full- time medical officers, at least one of them shall reside on the premises of the institution or in its immediate vicinity.

13) In other institutions the medical officer shall visit daily and shall reside near enough to be able to attend without delay in cases of urgency.

14) In an institution for both men and women, the part of the institution set aside for women shall be under the authority of a responsible woman officer who shall have the custody of the keys of all that part of the institution.

15) No male member of the staff shall enter the part of the institution set aside for women unless accompanied by a woman officer.

16) Women prisoners shall be attended and supervised only by women officers. This does not, however, preclude male members of the staff, particularly doctors and teachers, from carrying out their professional duties in institutions or parts of institutions set aside for women.

17) Officers of the institutions shall not, in their relations with the prisoners, use force except in self-defense or in cases of attempted escape, or active or passive physical resistance to an order based on law or regulations. Officers who have recourse to force must use no more than is strictly necessary and must report the incident immediately to the prison master of the institution.

18) Prison officers shall be given special physical training to enable them to restrain aggressive prisoners.

19) Except in special circumstances, staff performing duties that bring them into direct contact with prisoners should not be armed. Furthermore, staff should in no circumstances be provided with arms unless they have been trained in their use.

Section 21 Inspection

There shall be a regular inspection of penal institutions and services by qualified and experienced inspectors appointed by a competent authority. Their task shall be in particular to ensure that these institutions are administered in accordance with existing laws and regulations and with a view to bringing about the objectives of penal and correctional services.

STANDARDS APPLICABLE TO SPECIAL CATEGORIES

A. Prisoners under Sentence

Section 22 Classification of Prisoners

1) The medical services of the institution shall seek to detect and shall treat any physical or mental illnesses or defects that may hamper a prisoner's rehabilitation. All necessary medical, surgical and psychiatric services shall be provided to that end.

2) The these principles require individualization of treatment and for this purpose a flexible system of classifying prisoners in groups; it is therefore desirable that such groups should be distributed in separate institutions suitable for the treatment of each group.

Section 23 Treatment

1) The treatment of persons sentenced to imprisonment or a similar measure shall have as its purpose, so far as the length of the sentence permits, to establish in them the will to lead law-abiding and self-supporting lives after their release and to prepare them to do so. The treatment shall be such as will encourage their self respect and develop their sense of responsibility.

2) To these ends, all appropriate means shall be used to the extent possible, including religious care, education, vocational guidance, training and employment counseling, in accordance with the individual needs of each prisoner, taking account of his or her social and criminal history, his or her physical and mental capacities and aptitudes, his or her personal temperament, the length of his sentence and his or her prospects after release.

3) For every prisoner with a sentence of suitable length, the prison master shall receive, as soon as possible after his or her admission, full reports on all the matters referred to in the foregoing paragraph. Such reports shall always include a report by a medical officer, wherever possible qualified in psychiatry, on the physical and mental condition of the prisoner.

4) The reports and other relevant documents shall be placed in an individual file. This file shall be kept up to date and classified in such a way that it can be consulted by the responsible personnel whenever the need arises.

Section 24 Classification and Individualization

1) The purposes of classification shall be:

   a) To separate from others those prisoners who, by reason of their criminal records or bad characters, are likely to exercise a bad influence, or pose a danger to themselves or others;

   b) To divide the prisoners into classes in order to facilitate their treatment with a view to their social rehabilitation.

2) So far as possible separate institutions or separate sections of an institution shall be used for the treatment of the different classes of prisoners.

Section 25 Privileges

Systems of privileges appropriate for the different classes of prisoners and the different methods of treatment shall be established at every institution, in order to encourage good conduct, develop a sense of responsibility and secure the interest and cooperation of the prisoners in their treatment.

Section 26 Work

1) Prison labor must not be of an afflictive nature.

2) All prisoners under sentence may be required to work, subject to their physical and mental fitness as determined by the medical officer.

3) Sufficient work of a useful nature shall be provided to keep prisoners actively employed for a normal working day.

4) So far as possible the work provided shall be such as will maintain or increase the prisoners' ability to earn an honest living after release.

5) Where prisoners are employed in work not controlled by the administration, they shall always be under the supervision of the institution's personnel. Unless the work is for other departments of the government the full normal wages for such work shall be paid to the administration by the persons to whom the labor is supplied, account being taken of the output of the prisoners.

6) The precautions specified in Iraqi law governing labor and working conditions to protect the safety and health of workers shall be equally observed in institutions.

7) The maximum daily and weekly working hours of the prisoners shall be fixed in accordance with Iraqi law governing labor and working conditions.

8) The hours so fixed shall leave one rest day a week and sufficient time for education and other activities required as part of the treatment and rehabilitation of the prisoners.

9) There shall be a system of equitable remuneration of the work of prisoners.

10) Under the system prisoners shall be allowed to spend at least a part of their earnings on approved articles for their own use and to send a part of their earnings to their family.

11) The system should also provide that a part of the earnings should be set aside by the administration so as to constitute a savings fund to be handed over to the prisoner on his release.

Section 27 Education and Recreation

1) Provision shall be made for the further education of all prisoners capable of profiting thereby, including religious instruction. The education of illiterates and young prisoners shall be compulsory and special attention shall be paid to it by the administration.

2) So far as practicable, the education of prisoners shall be integrated with the educational system so that after their release they may continue their education without difficulty.

3) Recreational and cultural activities shall be provided in all institutions for the benefit of the mental and physical health of prisoners.

Section 28 Social Relations and After-Care

1) Special attention shall be paid to the maintenance and improvement of such relations between a prisoner and his family as are desirable in the best interests of both.

2) From the beginning of a prisoner's sentence consideration shall be given to his future after release and he shall be encouraged and assisted to maintain or establish such relations with persons or agencies outside the institution as may promote the best interests of his or her family and his own social rehabilitation.

3) Services and agencies, governmental or otherwise, that assist released prisoners to re-establish themselves in society shall ensure, so far as is possible and necessary, that released prisoners are provided with appropriate documents and identification papers, have suitable homes and work to go to, are suitably and adequately clothed having regard to the climate and season, and have sufficient means to reach their destination and maintain themselves in the period immediately following their release.

4) The approved representatives of such agencies shall have all necessary access to the institution and to prisoners and shall be taken into consultation as to the future of a prisoner from the beginning of his sentence.

5) It is desirable that the activities of such agencies shall be centralized or coordinated as far as possible in order to secure the best use of their efforts.

B. Insane and Mentally Abnormal Prisoners

Section 29 Psychiatric Care

1) Persons who are found to be insane shall not be detained in prisons and arrangements shall be made to remove them to mental institutions as soon as possible.

2) Prisoners who suffer from other mental diseases or abnormalities shall be observed and treated in specialized institutions under medical management.

3) During their stay in a prison, such prisoners shall be placed under the special supervision of a medical officer.

4) The medical or psychiatric service of the penal institutions shall provide for the psychiatric treatment of all prisoners who are in need of such treatment.

C. Prisoners under Arrest or Awaiting Trial

Section 30 Untried prisoners

1) Persons arrested or imprisoned by reason of a criminal charge against them, who are detained either in police custody or in prison custody but have not yet been tried and sentenced, will be referred to as 'untried prisoners', hereinafter in these rules.

2) Prisoners who have not been convicted are presumed to be innocent and shall be treated as such.

3) Without prejudice to legal rules for the protection of individual liberty or prescribing the procedure to be observed in respect of untried prisoners, these prisoners shall benefit by a special regime that is described in the following rules in its essential requirements only.

4) Untried prisoners shall be kept separate from convicted prisoners.

5) Young untried prisoners shall be kept separate from adults and shall where possible be detained in separate institutions.

6) Untried prisoners shall sleep singly in separate rooms.

7) Within the limits compatible with the good order of the institution, untried prisoners may, if they so desire, have their food procured at their own expense from the outside, either through the administration or through their family or friends. Otherwise, the administration shall provide their food.

8) An untried prisoner shall be allowed to wear his own clothing if it is clean and suitable.

9) If he wears prison dress, it shall be different from that supplied to convicted prisoners.

10) An untried prisoner shall always be offered an opportunity to work, but shall not be required to work. If he chooses to work, he shall be paid for it.

11) An untried prisoner shall be allowed to procure at his own expense or at the expense of a third party such books, newspapers, writing materials and other means of occupation as are compatible with the interests of the administration of justice and the security and good order of the institution.

12) An untried prisoner shall be allowed to be visited and treated by his or her own doctor or dentist if there is reasonable ground for his application and he or her [sic] is able to pay any expenses incurred.

13) An untried prisoner shall be allowed to inform immediately his or her family of his or her detention and shall be given all reasonable facilities for communicating with his or her family and friends, and for receiving visits from them, subject only to restrictions and supervision as are necessary in the interests of the administration of justice and of the security and good order of the institution.

14) For the purpose of his defense, an untried prisoner shall be allowed to apply for free legal aid where such aid is available, and to receive visits from his or her legal adviser with a view to his defense and to prepare and hand to him confidential instructions. For these purposes, he shall if he so desires be supplied with writing material. Interviews between the prisoner and his or her legal adviser may be within sight but not within the hearing of a police or institution official.

D. Civil Prisoners

Section 31 Debtor Prisoners
Person imprisoned for debt shall not be subjected to any greater restriction or severity than is necessary to ensure safe custody and good order. Their treatment shall be not less favorable than that of untried prisoners, with the reservation, however, that they may possibly be required to work.

Section 32 Entry into Force
This Memorandum shall enter into force on the date of signature [8 June 2003].

Document 127

Coalition Provisional Authority Memorandum Number 3

CPA/MEM/18 June 2003/03

Criminal Procedures

Pursuant to my authority as Administrator of the Coalition Provisional Authority (CPA) and the laws and usages of war, and consistent with relevant U.N. Security Council resolutions, including Resolution 1483 (2003),

Recognizing the CPA's obligation to restore law and order, provide for the safety of the people of Iraq, and ensure fundamental standards for persons detained,

Acting, in particular, consistent with the Fourth Geneva Convention of 1949 Relative to the Treatment of Civilians in Time of War (hereinafter 'the Fourth Geneva Convention'),

Noting the deficiencies of the Iraqi Criminal Procedure Code with regard to fundamental standards of human rights,

I hereby promulgate the following:

Section 1 Purpose

1) This Memorandum implements CPA Order No.7[6] by establishing procedures for applying criminal law in Iraq, recognizing that the effective administration of justice must consider:

a) the rehabilitation of the Iraqi investigative and trial capability;

[6] See *Doc 21*.

b) the continuing involvement of Coalition forces in providing critical support to many functional aspects of the administration of justice;
c) the need to transition from this dependency on military support;
d) the need to modify aspects of Iraqi law that violate fundamental standards of human rights;
e) the ongoing process of security internee management as provided for by the Fourth Geneva Convention; and
f) the possibility of the exercise of jurisdiction by Coalition authorities regarding the commission of war crimes against Coalition forces.

2) The procedures set out in this Memorandum will be subject to review and amendment as circumstances warrant, to continue to improve the rights of Iraqis and the administration of justice in Iraq. The provisions set out herein give effect to the requirements of international humanitarian law.

Section 2 Relation of Jurisdictions

1) The provisions of this Memorandum do not apply to, bind, or in any manner affect any military courts, commissions or tribunals or any associated process, established by the Coalition or any of its member States.

2) Nothing in this Memorandum shall deprive courts martial, military commissions or military tribunals of their jurisdiction as provided for under the laws of a Coalition member State or in accordance with the laws and usages of war.

3) No Iraqi court, including the Central Criminal Court of Iraq as established by CPA/ORD/18 Jun 2003/13,[7] shall have jurisdiction over any personnel of a Coalition member state in any matter, whether civil or criminal.[8]

Section 3 Preservation of Laws

All provisions of the Iraqi Law on Criminal Proceedings of 1971, as amended (hereinafter 'the Procedure Code'), shall continue in force unless expressly modified by this Memorandum.

Section 4 Suspension and Amendment of Provisions

The following provisions of the Procedure Code shall be suspended and or amended:

a) In paragraph 61 (c) delete the word 'may' and insert the word 'must'.
b) In paragraph 70 delete the words 'As far as possible'.
c) In paragraph 123 add the following; '(b) Before questioning the accused the examining magistrate must inform the accused that:
   i. he or she has the right to remain silent and no adverse inference may be drawn from accused's decision to exercise that right;
   ii. he or she has the right to be represented by an attorney, and if he or she is not able to afford representation, the Court will provide an attorney at no expense to the accused;

[7] See *Doc 29*.

[8] All references in sec 2 to 'the Coalition or any of its member States' and 'a Coalition member State' were replaced with 'the Multinational Force operating in Iraq pursuant to United Nations Security Council Resolutions 1511 and 1546 and all States contributing forces to that Multinational Force', see CPA Order No 100, sec 6(3) *[Doc 124]*.

(c) The examining magistrate or investigator must determine if the accused desires to be represented by an attorney before questioning the accused. If the accused desires an attorney the examining magistrate or investigator shall not question the accused until he or she has retained an attorney or an attorney has been appointed by the Court.'

d) Paragraph 136 is hereby suspended.[9]
e) In paragraph 144 (a) delete the words 'at a rate of no less that 10 dinars and no more than 50 dinars, with the cost borne by the state treasury.', and in 144 (b) delete the words 'of no more than 50 dinars'.
f) In paragraph 168 (b) delete the words 'via the court'.
g) In paragraph 179 delete the words 'A refusal to answer will be considered as evidence against the defendant.'[10]
h) In paragraph 184 (a) delete the word 'must' and insert the word 'may'.
i) In paragraph 199 (a) delete the words 'based on permission from the Minister of Justice'.
j) In paragraph 213 (c) delete the words 'and if there is no other evidence which proves it to be a lie.'
k) In paragraph 218 delete everything in the paragraph after the word 'coercion' where occurring for the first time.
l) Paragraph 221 is hereby suspended.
m) Paragraphs 285-293 are hereby suspended.[11]
n) In paragraph 298 delete the words 'by one half of one dinar' wherever occurring.
o) In paragraph 299 (b) delete the words 'one day for each one half of one dinar outstanding' and insert in place the words 'reduced proportionally to the amount outstanding'.
p) Paragraph 306 is hereby suspended.
q) In paragraph 320 delete the words 'and with the payment, within a specified period, of surety of not less than 20 dinars and not more than 200 dinars'.
r) In paragraph 324 delete the words 'of no less than 50 dinars and not exceeding 500 dinars'.
s) Paragraph 371 (b) is hereby suspended.

Section 5 Advice of Rights

At the time an Iraqi law enforcement officer arrests any person, the officer shall inform that person of his or her right to remain silent and to consult an attorney.

Section 6 Criminal Detentions

1) Consistent with the Fourth Geneva Convention, the following standards will apply to all persons who are detained by Coalition Forces solely in relation to allegations of criminal acts and who are not security internees (hereinafter 'criminal detainees'):

a) Upon the initial induction into a Coalition Force detention centre a criminal detainee shall be apprised of his rights to remain silent and to consult an attorney.

[9] Art 136(b) was restored by Interim Government Order 14 of 2005, Official Gazette, no 3995 (3 March 2005).

[10] Art 179 is not mentioned in revised CPA Memorandum No 3 of 27 June 2004 *[Doc 128]*. This may be explained by the fact that the Art 179 of the Criminal Procedure Code had the opposite meaning ('A refusal to answer will *not* be considered as evidence against the Defendant' [emphasis added]) and therefore did not need amendment.

[11] Arts 285-293 [operation of the death penalty] were restored with retrospective effect by Law No 13 of 2007.

b) A criminal detainee suspected of a felony offence may consult an attorney 72 hours after induction into a Coalition Force detention centre.
c) A criminal detainee shall be promptly informed, in writing, in a language which they understand, of the particulars of the charges preferred against them.
d) A criminal detainee shall be brought before a judicial officer as rapidly as possible and in no instance later than 90 days from the date of induction into a Coalition Force detention centre.
e) Access to detainees shall be granted to official delegates of the International Committee of the Red Cross (ICRC). Access will only be denied delegates for reasons of imperative military necessity as an exceptional and temporary measure. ICRC delegates shall be permitted to inspect health, sanitation and living conditions and to interview all detainees in private. They shall also be permitted to record information regarding a detainee and to pass messages to and from the family of a detainee subject to reasonable censorship by the facility authorities.

2) Where any criminal detainee held by Coalition Forces is subsequently transferred to an Iraqi Court, a failure to comply with these procedures shall not constitute grounds for any legal remedy, but any period spent in detention awaiting trial or punishment shall be deducted from any period of imprisonment imposed.

Section 7 Coalition Forces Security Internee Process

1) Consistent with the Fourth Geneva Convention, the following standards will apply to all persons who are detained by Coalition Forces when necessary for imperative reasons of security (hereinafter 'security internees'):

a) In accordance with Article 78 of the Fourth Geneva Convention, Coalition Forces shall, with the least possible delay, afford persons held as security internees the right of appeal against the decision to intern them.
b) The decision to intern a person shall be reviewed not later than six months from the date of induction into an internment facility by a competent body established for the purpose by Coalition Forces.
c) The operation, condition and standards of any internment facility established by Coalition Forces shall be in accordance with Section IV of the Fourth Geneva Convention.
d) Access to internees shall be granted to official delegates of the ICRC. Access will only be denied delegates for reasons of imperative military necessity as an exceptional and temporary measure. ICRC delegates shall be permitted to inspect health, sanitation and living conditions and to interview all internees in private. They shall also be permitted to record information regarding an internee and to pass messages to and from the family of an internee subject to reasonable censorship by the facility authorities.
e) If a person is subsequently determined to be a criminal detainee following tribunal proceedings concerning his or her status, or following the commission of a crime while in internment, the period that person has spent in internment will not count with respect to the period set out in Section 6 (1) (d) herein.
f) Where any security internee held by Coalition Forces is subsequently transferred to an Iraqi Court, a failure to comply with these procedures shall not constitute grounds for any legal remedy, but may be considered in mitigation of sentence.

Section 8 Legal Consultation and Representation

1) With the exception of the circumstances set out in Section 6 (1) (b) all criminal detainees suspected of a felony offense shall have the right to consult with an attorney while in detention.

2) All accused persons appearing before any Iraqi court, including the Central Criminal Court of Iraq, shall have the right to representation by any attorney of their choice. Where an accused person is unable to afford the services of an attorney the Court will provide them with a suitably qualified attorney at no expense to the accused person.

Section 9 Entry into Force

This Memorandum shall enter into force on the date of signature [18 June 2003].

Document 128

Coalition Provisional Authority Memorandum Number 3 (Revised)

CPA/MEM/27 June 2004/03

Criminal Procedures

Pursuant to my authority as Administrator of the Coalition Provisional Authority (CPA), and under the laws and usages of war, and consistent with relevant U.N. Security Council resolutions, including Resolutions 1483 (2003), 1511 (2003) and 1546 (2004),

Recognizing the CPA's obligation to restore law and order, provide for the safety of the people of Iraq, and ensure fundamental standards for persons detained,

Acting pursuant to the mandate for the Multinational Force set out in UN Security Council Resolutions 1511 (2003) and 1546 (2004) to take all necessary measures to provide security in Iraq,

Determining, that the relevant and appropriate provisions of the Fourth Geneva Convention of 1949 Relative to the Treatment of Civilians in Time of War (hereinafter 'the Fourth Geneva Convention') constitute an appropriate framework consistent with its mandate in continuance of measures previously adopted,

Noting the deficiencies of the Iraqi Criminal Procedure Code with regard to fundamental standards of human rights,

I hereby promulgate the following:

Section 1 Purpose

1) This Memorandum implements CPA Order No. 7[12] by establishing procedures for applying criminal law in Iraq, recognizing that the effective administration of justice must consider:

a) the continuing involvement of the Multinational Force (MNF) in providing critical support to some aspects of the administration of justice;
b) the need to transition from this support;
c) the need to modify aspects of Iraqi law that violate fundamental standards of human rights;

[12] See *Doc 21*.

d) the ongoing process of security internee management in accordance with the relevant and appropriate standards set out in the Fourth Geneva Convention which shall be applied by the MNF as a matter of policy in accordance with its mandate.

Section 2 Preservation of Laws
All provisions of the Iraqi Law on Criminal Proceedings of 1971, as amended (hereinafter 'the Procedure Code'), shall continue in force unless expressly modified by this Memorandum.

Section 3 Suspension and Amendment of Provisions
The following provisions of the Procedure Code shall be suspended and or amended:

a) In paragraph 61 (c) delete the word 'may' and insert the word 'must'. In paragraph 70 delete the words 'As far as possible'.
b) In paragraph 123 add the following; '(b) Before questioning the accused the examining magistrate must inform the accused that:
    i) he or she has the right to remain silent and no adverse inference may be drawn from accused's decision to exercise that right;
    ii) he or she has the right to be represented by an attorney, and if he or she is not able to afford representation, the Court will provide an attorney at no expense to the accused;
c) [sic][13] The examining magistrate or investigator must determine if the accused desires to be represented by an attorney before questioning the accused. If the accused desires an attorney the examining magistrate or investigator shall not question the accused until he or she has retained an attorney or an attorney has been appointed by the Court.'
d) [sic][14] The Criminal Procedure Code is hereby amended as follows:
    i) Paragraph 136 is hereby suspended.
    ii) In paragraph 144 (a) delete the words 'at a rate of no less than 10 dinars and no more than 50 dinars, with the cost borne by the state treasury.', and in 144 (b) delete the words 'of no more than 50 dinars'.
    iii) In paragraph 168 (b) delete the words 'via the court'.
    iv) In paragraph 184 (a) delete the word 'must' and insert the word 'may'.
    v) In paragraph 199 (a) delete the words 'based on permission from the Minister of Justice'.
    vi) In paragraph 213 (c) delete the words 'and if there is no other evidence which proves it to be a lie.'
    vii) In paragraph 218 delete everything in the paragraph after the word 'coercion' where occurring for the first time.
    viii) Paragraph 221 is hereby suspended.
    ix) Paragraphs 285-293 are hereby suspended.
    x) In paragraph 298 delete the words 'by one half of one dinar' wherever occurring.
    xi) In paragraph 299 (b) delete the words 'one day for each one half of one dinar outstanding' and insert in place the words 'reduced proportionally to the amount outstanding'.

[13] This paragraph is part of the amendment to paragraph 123 and should be numbered (c).
[14] This sub-paragraph should correctly be numbered 'c)'.

xii) Paragraph 306 is hereby suspended.
xiii) In paragraph 320 delete the words 'and with the payment, within a specified period, of surety of not less than 20 dinars and not more than 200 dinars'.
xiv) In paragraph 324 delete the words 'of no less than 50 dinars and not exceeding 500 dinars'.
xv) Paragraph 371 (b) is hereby suspended.

Section 4 Advice of Rights
At the time an Iraqi law enforcement officer arrests any person, the officer shall inform that person of his or her right to remain silent and to consult an attorney.

Section 5 Criminal Detentions
1) A national contingent of the MNF shall have the right to apprehend persons who are suspected of having committed criminal acts and are not considered security internees (hereinafter 'criminal detainees') who shall be handed over to Iraqi authorities as soon as reasonably practicable. A national contingent of the MNF may retain criminal detainees in facilities that it maintains at the request of appropriate Iraqi authorities based on security or capacity considerations. Where such criminal detainees are retained in the detention facilities of a national contingent of the MNF the following standards will apply:

a) Upon the initial induction into the detention centre a criminal detainee shall be apprised of his rights to remain silent and to consult an attorney by the authority serving an arrest warrant.
b) A criminal detainee suspected of a felony offence may consult an attorney 72 hours after induction into the detention centre.
c) A criminal detainee shall be promptly informed, in writing, in a language which they understand, of the particulars of the charges preferred against them by the authority serving an arrest warrant.
d) A criminal detainee shall be brought before a judicial officer as rapidly as possible and in no instance later than 90 days from the date of induction into the detention centre.
e) Access to detainees shall be granted to the Iraqi Prisons and Detainee Ombudsman (hereinafter 'the Ombudsman'). Access will only be denied the Ombudsman for reasons of imperative military necessity as an exceptional and temporary measure. The Ombudsman shall be permitted to inspect health, sanitation and living conditions and to interview all detainees in private and to record information regarding a detainee.
f) Access to detainees shall be granted to official delegates of the International Committee of the Red Cross (ICRC). Access will only be denied the delegates for reasons of imperative military necessity as an exceptional and temporary measure. The ICRC delegates shall be permitted to inspect health, sanitation and living conditions and to interview all detainees in private. They shall also be permitted to record information regarding a detainee and may pass messages to and from the family of a detainee subject to reasonable censorship by the facility authorities.

2) Where any criminal detainee held by a national contingent of the MNF is subsequently transferred to an Iraqi Court, a failure to comply with these procedures shall not constitute grounds for any legal remedy or negation of process, but any period spent in detention awaiting trial or punishment shall be deducted from any period of imprisonment imposed.

Section 6 MNF Security Internee Process

1) Any person who is detained by a national contingent of the MNF for imperative reasons of security in accordance with the mandate set out in UNSCR 1546 (hereinafter 'security internee') shall, if he is held for a period longer than 72 hours, be entitled to have a review of the decision to intern him.

2) The review must take place with the least possible delay and in any case must be held no later than 7 days after the date of induction into an internment facility.

3) Further reviews of the continued detention of any security internee shall be conducted on a regular basis but in any case not later than six months from the date of induction into an internment facility.

4) The operation, condition and standards of any internment facility established by the MNF shall be in accordance with Section IV of the Fourth Geneva Convention.

5) Security internees who are placed in internment after 30 June 2004, must in all cases only be held for so long as the imperative reasons of security in relation to that internee exist and in any case must be either released from internment or transferred to the Iraqi criminal jurisdiction not later than 18 months from the date of induction into an MNF internment facility. Any person under the age of 18 interned at any time shall in all cases be released not later than 12 months after the initial date of internment.

6) Where it is considered that, for continuing imperative reasons of security, a security internee placed in internment after 30 June 2004 who is over the age of 18 should be retained in internment for longer than 18 months; an application shall be made to the Joint Detention Committee (JDC)[15] for approval to continue internment for an additional period. In dealing with the application the members of the JDC will present recommendations to the co-chairs who must jointly agree that the internment may continue and shall specify the additional period of internment. While the application is being processed the security internee may continue to be held in internment but in any case the application must be finalized not later than two months from the expiration of the initial 18 month internment period.

7) Access to internees shall be granted to the Ombudsman. Access will only be denied the Ombudsman for reasons of imperative military necessity as an exceptional and temporary measure. The Ombudsman shall be permitted to inspect health, sanitation and living conditions and to interview all internees in private and to record information regarding an internee.

8) Access to internees shall be granted to official delegates of the ICRC. Access will only be denied the delegates for reasons of imperative military necessity as an exceptional and temporary measure. The ICRC delegates shall be permitted to inspect health, sanitation and living conditions and to interview all internees in private. They shall also be permitted to record information regarding an internee and may pass messages to and from the family of an internee subject to reasonable censorship by the facility authorities.

9) If a person is subsequently determined to be a criminal detainee following a review of his or her status, or following the commission of a crime while in internment, the period that person has spent in internment will not count with respect to the period set out in Section 5 (2) herein.

10) Where any security internee held by a national contingent of the MNF is subsequently transferred to an Iraqi Court, a failure to comply with these procedures shall not constitute grounds for any legal remedy or negation of process, but may be considered in mitigation of sentence.

[15] The JDC was established by CPA Order No 99 *[Doc 123]* which, however, names it the 'Joint Detainee Committee'.

Section 7 Legal Consultation and Representation

1) With the exception of the circumstances set out in Section 5 (1) (b) all criminal detainees suspected of a felony offense shall have the right to consult with an attorney while in detention.

2) All accused persons appearing before any Iraqi court, including the Central Criminal Court of Iraq, shall have the right to representation by an attorney of their choice. Where an accused person is unable to afford the services of an attorney the Court will provide them with a suitably qualified attorney at no expense to the accused person.

Section 8 Entry into Force

This Memorandum shall enter into force on the date of signature [27 June 2004].

Document 129

Coalition Provisional Authority Memorandum Number 4

CPA/MEM/19 August 2003/04

Contract and Grant Procedures Applicable to Vested and Seized Iraqi Property and the Development Fund for Iraq

Implementation of Regulation Number 3, Program Review Board

Pursuant to my authority as Administrator of the Coalition Authority (CPA) and the laws and usages of war, and consistent with relevant U.N. Security Council resolutions, including Resolution 1483 (2003),

Underscoring that the Development Fund for Iraq (DFI) shall be used in a transparent manner to meet the humanitarian needs of the Iraqi people, for the economic reconstruction and repair of Iraq's infrastructure, for the continued disarmament of Iraq, and for the costs of Iraqi civilian administration, and for other purposes benefiting the people of Iraq, and that the Program Review Board[16] as authorized by CPA Regulation Number 3 (18 June 2003)[17] is responsible for recommending expenditures of resources from the DFI.

Noting that Resolution 1483 (2003) states that independent public accountants approved by and reporting to the International Advisory and Monetary Board (IAMB) shall audit the DFI to ensure that the DFI is used exclusively for the purposes stated in Resolution 1483 (2003),

Reaffirming that the CPA is committed to ensuring that all state- or regime-owned cash, funds or realizable securities that have been seized by Coalition Forces in Iraq consistent with the laws and usages of war, shall be used only to assist the Iraqi people and support the reconstruction of Iraq,

Implementing CPA Regulation Number 3, Program Review Board (CPA/REG/18 June 2003/03),

I hereby promulgate the following:

[16] All references to the 'Program Review Board' are to apply to its successor board in the Iraqi Government, see CPA Order No 100, sec 6(4)(c) *[Doc 124]*.

[17] See *Doc 3*.

Section 1 Purpose

This memorandum establishes procedures applicable to the execution of contracts and grants for the benefit of the Iraqi people using Iraqi Funds,[18] as defined herein. As steward for the Iraqi people, the CPA will manage and spend Iraqi Funds, which belong to the Iraqi people, for their benefit. Although Iraqi Funds are not subject to the same laws and regulations that apply to funds provided to the CPA directly from coalitions governments, they shall be managed in a transparent manner that fully comports with the CPA's obligations under international law, including Resolution 1483.[19]

Section 2 Applicability

This Memorandum applies to contracts and grants executed by or on behalf of the CPA, when those instruments obligate and expend Iraqi Funds. It covers contracts and grants executed by:

1) CPA Regional Directors carrying out the Regional Directors' Emergency Response Program;
2) CPA Regional Directors carrying out the Construction Initiative for Iraq Program;
3) Interim Ministry Officials, working in conjunction with Senior Ministry Advisors, when carrying out requirements that are not funded through the national Ministry budget process;
4) CPA's Head of Contracting Activity, or designee(s), and
5) Others delegated such authority by the Administrator.[20]

This Memorandum does not apply to:

1) Iraqi Ministries and governmental agencies executing contracts or grants to fulfill requirements approved through the national budget process if the Administrator, or his designee, determines that the contracting procedure of the Ministry or agency is adequate to ensure the transparent use and management of Iraqi funds. However, if the contracting procedures of the particular Ministry or agency are not determined to be adequate, this Memorandum shall apply, and
2) Coalition Forces commanders carrying out the Commanders' Emergency Response Program. The Commanders' Emergency Response Program will use the procedures contained in FRAGO 89 (Appendix E) or any subsequent amended guidance to FRAGO 89.

Section 3 Definitions

1) 'Competitive Range': A group of proposals that are eligible for award of a particular contract or grant, as determined by a Contracting Officer on the basis of cost and other factors stated in the solicitation.

2) 'Contract': A written agreement whereby the CPA or Coalition Forces acquire goods, services or construction from a person or entity under prescribed terms and conditions, for the purpose of assisting the Iraqi people or assisting in the recovery of Iraq.

[18] All references to 'Iraqi Funds' were replaced with 'Public Funds', see CPA Order No 100, sec 6(4)(c) *[Doc 124]*.

[19] Sec 1 was amended by CPA Order No 100, sec 6(4)(b) *[Doc 124]*.

[20] Sec 2(5) was rescinded and replaced by CPA Order No 100, sec 6(4)(d) *[Doc 124]*. As of 4 April 2004, the CPA Contracting Activity, Iraq Project and Contracting Office had awarded 1,988 contracts, grants, and purchase delivery orders valued at approximately US$ 1.04 billion. Of this total, 1,928 contracts valued at approximately US$ 847 million were awarded with DFI funds (CPA, Inspector General, *Coalition Provisional Authority's Contracting Processes Leading Up To and Including Contract Award*, Report No 04-013, 27 July 2004, 1).

3) 'Contract Award Committee': As used in this Memorandum, a group of three or more officials selected by the Contracting Officer appointing authority responsible for reviewing preliminary award decisions of Large Purchases for compliance with this Memorandum and sound business judgment. The Contract Award Committee need not convene as a group; however, except as provided in Section 7 below, a majority of the members must concur in the award decision prior to award.

4) 'Contracting Officer': As used in this Memorandum, an individual who has been authorized by the Administrator, CPA, in accordance with Section 4 below, to enter into Contracts or Grants using Iraqi Funds.

5) 'Grant': A written instrument that transfers Iraqi Funds from the CPA or Coalition Forces to a recipient grantee, in order to carry out a program or project that directly benefits the Iraqi people or assists in the recovery of Iraq.

6) 'Invitation for Bids': An invitation to prospective contractors to submit proposals to meet CPA requirements. An invitation for bids describes a requirement for a prospective contract by explaining the nature of the opportunity, including the goods or services to be provided, required performance, the time for performance, requirements to demonstrate the responsibility of the potential source, unique requirements, the closing date for bids, and other information necessary for a potential source to submit a bid. With an IFB, the award is determined solely on the basis of price or price-related factors.

7) 'Iraqi-based': A company (including a subsidiary company) whose principal place of business is located within Iraq.

8) 'Iraqi Funds': Funds under the control of the Authority consisting of (a) proceeds from Iraqi state-owned property that has been vested or seized in accordance with applicable law and made available to the CPA to assist the Iraqi people and assist in the reconstruction of Iraq; and (b) funds in the Development Fund for Iraq, the establishment of which is noted in Resolution 1483 (2003). As used in this Memorandum, 'Iraqi Funds' do not include funds provided through the appropriations process of Coalition member governments (for example, funds provided directly to the CPA by the governments of the United States or the United Kingdom).[21]

9) 'Large Purchase': A contract with a value of greater than US$500,000.

10) 'Micro Purchase': A contract with a value of US$5,000 or less.

11) 'Request for Proposal': An invitation to prospective contractors or grant recipients to submit proposals to meet CPA requirements. A request for proposal usually includes a description of a requirement for a prospective Contract or Grant that explains the nature of the opportunity including the goods or services to be provided, required performance, the time for performance, the evaluation criteria for Contract award, requirements to demonstrate the responsibility of the potential source, unique requirements to demonstrate the responsibility of the potential source, unique requirements, the closing date for proposals, and other information necessary for a potential source to submit a proposal.

12) 'Small Purchase': A contract with a value greater than US$5,000 and less than or equal to US$500,000.

13) 'Solicitation': A request to submit offers or quotations to fulfill a requirement for goods or services that can be met through a Contract. 'Request for Proposal' and 'Invitation for Bids' are types of solicitation.

[21] Sec 3(8) was rescinded and replaced by CPA Order No 100, sec 6(4)(e) *[Doc 124]*.

Section 4 Appointment of Contracting Offices[22]

1) General. For the purpose of carrying out programs to assist the Iraqi people and assist in the recovery of Iraq using Iraqi Funds, the officials identified in paragraph 2 may appoint Contracting Officers who may enter in to Contracts or Grants on behalf of the CPA. Unless otherwise terminated by the Administrator, this delegation shall remain in effect until the establishment of an internationally recognized, representative government by the people of Iraq.

2) The following officials are authorized to appoint Contracting Officers within their directorates, commands or organizations, in writing and in a form prescribed by the Head of Contracting Activity, CPA, in consultation with the CPA General Counsel:

a) Head of Contracting Activity, CPA, or the Principal Assistant Responsible for Contracting, CPA;
b) CPA Directors of Oil Policy; Civil Affairs; Economic Development; AID; Operations and Infrastructure; Interior Affairs; Private Sector Development; and Security Affairs;
c) Senior Iraqi Ministry Advisors, in coordination with the interim Iraqi Ministers, for contracting officers within the ministry concerned, and
d) Other persons specifically authorized by the Administrator.

3) In exercising their authority to appoint Contracting Officers, the officials listed in paragraph 2 above shall consider the training and experience of prospective appointees and shall, to the extent practicable, confer Contracting Officer authority on those officers already holding Coalition government contracting warrants and/or experience as contingency contracting officers or field ordering officers. The Head of Contracting Activity, COA, with the approval of the Administrator, may prescribe additional requirements (such as completion of prescribed training requirements) that persons must hold prior to receiving Contracting Officer appointments.

4) Contracting Officers responsible for carrying out programs must actively coordinate proposed funding initiatives with all other Contracting and Grant-making officials in their geographic areas, in order to ensure against duplication of effort.

Section 5 Technical Supervision of Contracting Officers

The Head of Contracting Activity, CPA, shall be responsible for providing technical supervision over Contracting Officers appointed pursuant to Section 4, above. This technical supervision may include prescribing training requirements and prescribing appropriate forms for use in solicitations, contract awards, and grant awards. For contracting officers assigned to the CPA Contracting Activity, the Head of Contracting Activity, CPA, shall provide administrative oversight as well as technical supervision.

Section 6 Principles Applicable to Instruments

1) <u>Identification of Parties.</u> Contracts and Grants must prominently contain the following language to identify the parties:

> 'This contract/grant is entered into under the authority of the Administrator as head of the Coalition Provisional Authority (CPA), which is temporarily exercising governmental authority in Iraq pursuant to the law and usages of war and relevant United Nations Security Council Resolutions, including Resolution 1483 (2003) ("Coalition") and by ______________________ ("Contractor").'[23]

[22] Sec 4 was amended by CPA Memorandum No 15, sec 1 *[Doc 140]* and CPA Order No 100, sec 6(4)(f)-(g) *[Doc 124]*.

[23] Sec 6(1) was rescinded and replaced by CPA Order No 100, sec 6(4)(h) *[Doc 124]*.

2) Competition.

a) Contracts. Unless otherwise exempted under this Memorandum, competition is mandatory for all Contracts. Reasonable efforts will be made to obtain competitive offers by publicizing a solicitation through bulletin boards, the CPA World Wide Web page, the UNDB, vendor databases developed by the Head of Contracting Activity, and other means. If circumstances required award of a contract without competition, a written justification describing the exigencies requiring contracting without competition will be documented in the Contract file. Contracts will be awarded to the offer providing the greatest value to the CPA or Coalition Forces, based on price and all other evaluation factors contained in the solicitation.

b) Grants. Reasonable efforts will be made to identify all organizations capable of performing the Grant. Grants in excess of $500,000 will be tendered for proposals by capable organizations, except as authorized for good cause, in writing, by the official that appointed the Contracting Officer involved.

3) Preference for Iraqi Vendors. Iraqi-based vendors who are capable of performing a Contract or Grant in a responsible and responsive manner will be afforded the following preferences when competing with foreign firms. If the Contracting Officer determines that at least two Iraqi-based vendors are available, the Contracting Officer may limit the competition to Iraqi-based vendors only. It the Contracting Officer determines that limiting competition to Iraqi-based vendors is not appropriate, the Contracting Officer may use the amount of Iraqi participation in the contract (as a subcontractor or otherwise) as an evaluation criterion for purposes of determining who is entitled to the award of the contract.

4) Fair and Reasonable Price. The Contracting Officer must determine that the price of a contract is fair and reasonable. Prices for goods and services will not exceed their fair market value–as determined by the Contracting Officer–after considering the time for delivery or urgency of the service, and other relevant factors.

5) Conflicts of Interests. Contracts or Grants administered under this Memorandum will not directly or indirectly benefit any Ministry, CPA or Coalition Forces official or employee involved in the contracting or grant-making process, or the family members of such officials or employees. Persons involved in the contracting process, from the development of the requirement through the completion of performance, shall not:

a) Hold financial interests that conflict with the conscientious performance of duty.

b) Engage in financial transactions using nonpublic Government information or allow the improper use of such information to further any private interest.

c) Solicit or accept any gift or other item of monetary value from any person or entity seeking official action from, doing business with, or conducting activities regulated by the CPA, or whose interests may be substantially affected by the performance or nonperformance of the employee's duties.

d) Knowingly make unauthorized commitments or promises of any kind purporting to bind the CPA.

e) Use public office for private gain.

An official or employee of the CPA or Coalition Forces involved in the contracting process shall:

a) Act impartially and not give preferential treatment to any private organization or individual.

b) Disclose waste, fraud, abuse, and corruption to appropriate authorities.

c) Endeavor to avoid any actions creating the appearance that they are violating the law or ethical standards.

6) Combining and Dividing Awards. To the extent practicable, requirements for a project or related projects may be consolidated into one contract, in order to reduce the administrative burden of contracting. Requirements may not be split to avoid the application of these rules.

7) Responsibility. Contracting officers must determine that a contractor who receives a contract award must be responsible. This means that the contractor must:

a) Have adequate financial resources to perform the contract, or the ability to obtain them;
b) Be able to comply with the required or proposed delivery or performance schedule, taking into consideration all existing commercial and governmental business commitments;
c) Have a satisfactory performance record, if the contractor has performed contracts in the past;
d) Have a satisfactory record of integrity and business ethics;
e) Have the necessary organization, experience, accounting and operational controls, and technical skills, or the ability to obtain them;
f) Have the necessary production, construction, and technical equipment and facilities, or the ability to obtain them; and
g) Be otherwise qualified and eligible to receive an award under applicable laws and regulations.

Section 7 Contracts

1) Micro-Purchases. Micro-Purchase Contracts may be awarded without competition if the Contracting Officer determines that the offered price and terms are fair and reasonable. However, Contracting Officers are encouraged to obtain competition when possible. Oral solicitations may be used. Micro-Purchases will be documented in summary files demonstrating competition (if any), basis for award (if other than lowest price), and material terms. The documentation will be tailored to the size and nature of the acquisition.

2) Small Purchases. Contracting Officers, when possible, will obtain at least three competitive offers for Small Purchases. For Small Purchases from $5,000.01 to $25,000, oral solicitations may be used; however, Contracting Officers must maintain documentation of sources solicited. For Small Purchases greater than $25,000, written solicitations will be used. Sufficient information will be included in the contract file to enable a review of the transaction, including evidence of competition or the basis for contracting without competition, price quotations, and the basis for the contract award if price is not the determining factor. Written justifications detailing the unique qualifications of the contractor or other exigent circumstances requiring an award without competition will be prepared for Small Purchases. Requirements for justifications are contained in Appendix A.

a) Blanket Purchase Agreements. Contracting Officers are encouraged to use blanket purchase agreements for repetitive requirements to reduce administrative burdens and to obtain favorable pricing.
b) All Small Purchase contracts will contain payment terms including an agreed upon payment schedule (preferably with milestones tied to performance) for service contracts, and performance requirements clearly defining the responsibilities and time for performance. Additionally, the Contracting Officer will use appropriate contract provisions listed in Appendix B to this Memorandum for the particular solicitation or contract involved.

c) Requirements in excess of $10,000 should be posted at a public location and disseminated in a manner that will foster competition, including advertising in local media when appropriate, through bulletin boards, the CPA World Wide Web page, vendor databases developed by the Head of Contracting Activity, and other means.

3) Large Purchases.

a) Large Purchase Contracts will be competed [sic], except as authorized below. All Large Purchase contract opportunities will be posted and advertised to the maximum extent practicable, with a goal of obtaining at least three competitive offers.

b) The Head of Contracting Activity, CPA, will ensure that experienced contracting officials are assigned to execute contracts underneath the HCA and provide technical assistance to all other appointed Contracting Officers or Iraqi Ministry Contracting Activities with respect to all Large Purchase solicitations.

c) Acquisitions generally will be made through negotiation. The contracting agency will develop a Request for Proposal (RFP) for submission to prospective contractors. The RFP will set forth the essential information necessary to fully describe the contracting opportunity. Contracting Officers may hold a pre-proposal conference to answer questions and to clarify the RFP, provided all prospective contractors are informed of the conference. Award evaluation factors will be tailored to the acquisition, but must include price as a factor. Others factors may include technical expertise, financial stability of the contractor based upon a review of financial statements, and prior contract performance. The Contracting Officer may request final proposals from contractors in the competitive range. Based upon the review of the proposals, a preliminary award decision will be made.

d) If a contracting officer determines that (1) time permits the solicitation, submission and evaluation of sealed bids; (2) award will be made only on the basis of price or price-related factors; (3) discussions with prospective bidders will not be necessary, and (4) there is a reasonable expectation of receiving more than one sealed bid, the contractor may, instead of an RFP, use an Invitation for Bids (IFB) to compete the acquisition. The IFB will set forth the essential information necessary to fully describe the contracting opportunity. Contracting Officers may hold a pre-bid conference to answer questions and to clarify the IFB provided all prospective contractors are informed of the conference. Because an IFB requires that the requirement be clearly stated prior to issuing the solicitation, IFBs will only be used by contracting officers under the direct control of the Head of the Contracting Activity, CPA.

e) Written justifications detailing the unique qualifications of the contractor or other exigent circumstances requiring an award without competition will be prepared for all Large Purchases awarded without competition. Requirements for justifications are contained in Appendix A. All Large Purchase justifications will be reviewed and approved in writing by either the Contracting Officer's appointing authority or the Head of Contracting Activity, CPA, or his designee.

f) Except for awards by Contracting Officers appointed by the Head of Contracting Activity or the Principal Assistant Responsible for Contracting, CPA, Large Purchase preliminary award decisions will be reviewed by a Contract Award Committee of at least three officials, designated by the official who appointed the Contracting Officer for the particular project, prior to award. The Committee will review the proposals and Contract file to ensure compliance with procedural and competition requirements, that the contract represents sound business judgment, that the process used was fair and impartial, and that the proposed award represents the best value based upon the evaluation factors. Large Purchase preliminary award decisions by Contracting Officers appointed by the Head of the Contracting Activity, CPA will be coordinated with the Head of Contracting Activity, CPA, or his designee, prior to award.

g) Notwithstanding paragraph 3(e) above, Large Purchase Contracts may be executed in the absence of a Contract Award Committee, provided the Head of Contracting Activity, CPA, determines that there are sufficient alternative means to ensure that the particular solicitation action has been appropriately managed.

h) Contracting officers are encouraged to establish payment schedules that provide for payments as the vendor accomplishes specified performance milestones.

4) Contract Modifications and Amendments. Contract modifications and amendments are subject to the same documentation provisions as original contracts. Contracting Officers must ensure the cost of the contract modification or amendment is fair and reasonable. Amendments or modifications that are outside the scope of the contract or that constitute new requirements should be addressed through new contracts.

Section 8 Monitoring Contract Performance

Consistent with their programmatic responsibility to ensure that contractors and grantees properly perform their duties, Contracting Officers shall be responsible for regularly monitoring the post-award execution of all Contracts they approve. This monitoring process includes ensuring that the contractor provides the agreed upon goods, services or construction in accordance with the provisions, and that payments are made in a timely manner.

Contracting Officers shall include in the Contract file a written report describing post-award performance by contractors or grantees, including a final assessment upon completion of the Contract. Contracting officers shall rely upon locally available military engineering resources in assessing all repair and construction projects. All documents related to the establishment and execution of Contracts will be maintained in a Contract file that includes the materials described in Appendix A to this Memorandum.

Section 9 Grants

Consistent with Program Review Board requirements, Grants may be made available to support important public initiatives.

1) Applications for Grants must describe the initiative, anticipated costs and the desired results. The applications should also set forth objective standards for measuring the success of the Grant.

2) In reviewing grant applications, consideration shall be given to the number of people affected by the grant and the impact on community development. Grants should be reviewed during implementation and where appropriate funds should be made available on a schedule tied to the accomplishment of specific milestones specified by the CPA or Coalition Forces, and related to the objective measures of success.

3) Although there generally is little substantial involvement between the CPA or Coalition Forces and the grantee following the award of the Grant, a grant agreement will be conducted according to a form prescribed by the Head of Contracting Activity, CPA, in coordination with

the Office of the General Counsel, CPA, and the grantee's performance must be monitored to ensure that the granted funds are expended for appropriate purposes consistent with the Grant, and to assess the grantee's suitability for future Grants. Contracting Officers responsible for Grants shall include in the Grant file a written report describing post-award performance by or [sic] grantees, including a final assessment upon completion of the Grant.

Section 10 Funds Allocated through the National Budget Process

1) Funds allocated through the National Budget Process will be made available to the interim Iraqi Ministries in accordance with the National Budget. The CPA Office of Management and Budget will allocate funds to the Iraqi Ministry of Finance for further distribution to the Iraqi Ministries, in accordance with the national Budget and in a manner that will ensure appropriate transparency. The interim Iraqi Ministries may draw on allocated funds by submitting a request for funds to the Iraqi Ministry of Finance.[24]

2) Contracts or grants executed by interim Iraqi Ministries may be carried out in accordance with applicable Iraqi laws and Ministry contracting procedures only if the Administrator or his designee determines that the Ministry's application of these controls will ensure transparency. However, in the event that a protest is filed against the proposed award of a contract or grant, the provisions of the Protests clause in Appendix B of this Memorandum shall apply. If the Administrator or his designee does not determine that applicable Iraqi laws and Ministry contracting procedures can ensure transparency in the use of Iraqi funds, the rules of this Memorandum shall apply.

3) As part of the CPA's responsibility to ensure that CPA Funds are used for their intended purpose, the CPA Comptroller, in coordination with the Head of Contracting Activity, CPA, may, in his discretion, review contracting actions of interim Iraqi Ministries.

Section 11 Appendices

The Appendices provide supplemental instructions on preparing and executing Contracts and Grants pursuant to this Memorandum. The Program Review Board is hereby authorized to modify existing Appendices to this Memorandum, and issue additional Appendices, as may be required to ensure the effective execution of funding for the benefit of the Iraqi people. Any such modification or issuance shall be deemed to satisfy the requirements of CPA Regulation No. 3, section 6 (5).

Section 12 Protection of Confidential Acquisition Information

Contracting officers, or other persons involved in the contracting process, are specifically prohibited from releasing information contained in a proposal to any person not involved with the contracting process. For purposes of this section, 'proposal' means any proposal, including a technical, management, or cost proposal, submitted by a contractor in response to the requirements of a solicitation for a competitive proposal. Any other disclosure of confidential acquisition information, including information concerning a successful proposal that is incorporated by reference into a contract, shall be protected in a manner consistent with 5 U.S.C. Section 552 and Parts 3 and 24 of the U.S. Federal Acquisition Regulation.[25]

Section 13 Entry into Force

This Memorandum shall enter into force on the date of signature [20 August 2003].

[24] Sec 10(1) was amended by CPA Order No 100, sec 6(4)(i) *[Doc 124]*.

[25] Sec 12 was amended by CPA Order No 100, sec 6(4)(j) *[Doc 124]*.

APPENDIX A

Contract File Requirements

Micro Purchases ($5,000 or less)

Contract file must include:

- Notes or documentation reflecting competition efforts, if any, including a written summary of oral solicitations if award is based on an oral solicitation.
- The basis for the award decision if other than lowest price.
- Material Contract terms (Who is to do What, When, and for How much?)
- Information demonstrating the outcome (such as receipts, delivery notices, notes of the contracting officer regarding contractor performance for services).
- Micro Purchase files will be maintained for 1 year following final contract payment.

Small Purchases ($5,000.01 - $500,000)

Contract file must include:

- Documentation of oral solicitations made for contracts less than $25,000, written solicitations for contracts from $25,000.01 to $500,000.
- Evidence of competition, such as posted notices (including the location and length of time posted), direct solicitations, advertisements, posting on web pages.
- For solicitations in which only one source is solicited (i.e., sole-source contract awards), a written justification prepared in accordance with this Appendix.
- Evaluation Criteria, if applicable.
- Significant correspondence with vendors.
- Notification to successful vendor.
- Written contract containing required terms for agreements exceeding $10,000 or a summary of material terms for agreements less than $10,000.
- Invoices for progress payments and verification of performance including notes of inspections or monitoring where appropriate.
- Small Purchase Files will be maintained for 1 year following final contract payment.

Large Purchases (more than $500,000)

Documentation will be sufficient to enable review by the Contract Award Committee prior to award and then by auditors during the period of contract performance and thereafter. Files will include:

- A statement of need for the requirement to be addressed. This may be a request for services from the agency requesting the contract.
- Evidence of Competition, such as posted notices (including the location and length of time posted), direct solicitations, advertisements, posting on web pages, or other means used to publicize the opportunity to bid.
- All fully eligible responses from vendors to allow the Contract Award Committee to review the contracting options to ensure the proposed contract award is based upon sound business judgment.
- For contracts in which only one source is solicited, a written justification prepared in accordance with this Appendix.
- Contract award Evaluation Criteria. Price must be one of the contract evaluation criteria. Other criteria may include experience, prior contract performance, technical expertise, and delivery terms.

- Memorandum for record memorializing the action by the Contract Award Committee acting to select the successful vendor. The MFR should identify board members, the bids considered, the criteria used, and the selected vendor.
- Significant correspondence with vendors.
- Notification to successful vendor.
- Written contract containing required terms.
- Contract Modifications and Amendments.
- Contract performance and outcome information including notes of inspections or monitoring where appropriate.
- Large Purchase Contract files will be maintained for a period of 3 years following final contract payment.

Sole-Source Contracting Justification and Approval Requirements

- Contracting Officers must document compelling reasons justifying sole source contracting in all contracts. Compelling reasons that may be considered when justifying sole-source contracting:
    - There is only one responsible source and no other supplies or service will satisfy requirements. This may include unacceptable delays in delivery or other unique circumstances, such as intellectual property rights or compatibility with existing systems.
    - Unusual or compelling urgency to satisfy requirements. This justification will only be used in cases where competition would represent a serious risk to agency objectives. Failure to accurately forecast agency needs is a not a sufficient justification.
- The justification must demonstrate the circumstances for forgoing adequate competition. If the circumstance is urgent and compelling, specifically explain the time constraints. Identify unique capabilities that are possessed by only one contractor.
- Justifications will include a description of efforts to obtain competition.
- Justifications will include facts supporting the Contracting Officer's determination that a fair and reasonable price was obtained.
- Justifications for sole-source awards in excess of $500,000 must be approved by the Contracting Officer's Appointing Authority or the Head of Contracting Authority, CPA.

Grants

Files will contain a statement of the community need to be addressed and intended purposes of the grant. Generally, the grant application is sufficient. The file will also contain outcome information including as assessment of the community impact of the grant.

Special Requirements for Construction Projects

- Maintain engineering drawings and approvals of plans until contract performance is complete.
- Cost Estimates by independent engineers should be obtained for Large Purchase projects to assist in the assessment of fair and reasonable value.
- Fixed-priced arrangements are preferred for construction contracts.
- Certificates of Completion.
- Change Orders and Amendments will be fully documented.

APPENDIX B

Standard Terms and Conditions for Solicitations and Contracts in Excess of $5,000

Solicitation Terms and Conditions

1. **Submission of Offers.** The contractor will submit signed and dated offers to the office specified in this solicitation at or before the exact time specified in the solicitation. Offers may be submitted on letterhead stationery or as otherwise specified in the solicitation. At a minimum, offers must show:
   a. The solicitation number.
   b. The time specified in the solicitation for receipt of offers.
   c. The name, address, and telephone number of the offeror.
   d. A technical description of the items being offered in sufficient detail to evaluate compliance with the requirements in the solicitation. This may include product literature, or other documents, if necessary.
   e. Terms of any express warranty.
   f. Price and any discount terms.
   g. Payment address (if different from mailing address).
   h. Acknowledgment of solicitation amendments (if any).
   i. Past performance information, when included as an evaluation factor, to include recent and relevant contracts for the same or similar items and other references (including contract numbers, points of contact with telephone numbers, and other relevant information).
   j. A statement specifying the extent of agreement with all terms, conditions, and provisions included in the solicitation. Offers that fail to furnish required representations or information, or reject the terms and conditions of the solicitation may be excluded from consideration.
2. **Period for Acceptance of Offers.** The offeror agrees to hold the prices in its offer firm for 30 calendar days from the date specified for receipt of offers, unless another time period is specified in an addendum to the solicitation.
3. **Product Samples.** When required by the solicitation, product samples shall be submitted at or prior to the time specified for receipt of offers. Unless otherwise specified in this solicitation, these samples shall be submitted at no expense, and returned at the sender's request and expense, unless they are destroyed by pre-award testing.
4. **Multiple Offers.** Offerors are encouraged to submit multiple offers presenting alternative terms and conditions or items for satisfying the requirements of this solicitation. Each offer submitted will be evaluated separately.
5. **Late Submissions, Modifications, Revisions, and Withdrawals of Offers.**
   a. Offerors are responsible for submitting offers, and any modifications, revisions, or withdrawals, so as to reach the Contracting Officer designated in the solicitation by the time specified in the solicitation. If no time is specified in the solicitation, the time for receipt is 1630 hours, local time, for the designated contracting office on the date that offers or revisions are due.
   b. Any offer, modification, revision, or withdrawal of an offer received at the contracting office designated in the solicitation after the exact time specified for receipt of offers is 'late' and will not be considered unless it is received before award is made, the Contracting Officer determines that accepting the late offer would not unduly delay the acquisition, and

1) if it was transmitted through an electronic commerce method authorized by the solicitation, it was received at the initial point of entry to the contracting office not later than 1700 hours one working day prior to the date specified for receipt of offers, or
2) there is acceptable evidence to establish it was received at the location designated for the receipt of offers and was under government control prior to the time set for receipt of offers, or
3) if the solicitation was a request for proposals, it was the only proposal received.

c. However, a late modification of an otherwise successful offer that makes the offer's terms more favorable to the contracting organization issuing the solicitation will be considered at any time it is received and may be accepted.

d. Acceptable evidence to establish the time of receipt at the contracting office includes the time/date stamp of that installation on the offer wrapper, other documentary evidence of receipt maintained by the installation, or oral testimony or statements of contracting office personnel.

e. If an emergency or unanticipated event interrupts normal processes so that offers cannot be received at the contracting office designated for receipt of offers by the exact time specified in the solicitation, and urgent requirements preclude amendment of the solicitation or other notice of the extension of the closing date, the time specified for receipt of offers will be deemed to be extended to the same time of day specified in the solicitation on the first work day on which normal processes resume.

f. Offers may be withdrawn by written notice received at any time before the exact time set for receipt of offers. Oral offers in response to oral solicitations may be withdrawn orally. If the solicitation authorizes facsimile offers, offers may be withdrawn via facsimile received at any time before the exact time set for receipt of offers, subject to the conditions specified in the solicitation concerning facsimile offers. An offer may be withdrawn in person by an offeror or its authorized representative if, before the exact time set for receipt of offers, the identity of the person requesting withdrawal is established and the person signs a receipt for the offer.

6. **Contract Award.** The Contracting Officer intends to evaluate offers and award a contract without discussions with offerors. Therefore, the offeror's initial offer should contain the offeror's best terms from a price and technical standpoint. However, the Contracting Officer reserves the right to conduct discussions if later determined by the Contracting Officer to be necessary. The Contracting Officer may reject any or all offers if such action is in the public interest; accept other than the lowest-priced offer; and waive informalities and minor irregularities in offers received.

7. **Multiple Awards.** The Contracting Officer may accept any item or group of items of an offer, unless the offeror qualifies the offer by specific limitations. Unless otherwise provided in the schedule, offers may not be submitted for quantities less than those specified. The Contracting Officer reserves the right to make an award on any item for a quantity less than the quantity offered, at the unit prices offered, unless the offeror specifies otherwise in the offer.

8. **Evaluation.** The Contracting Office will award a contract resulting from this solicitation to the responsible offeror whose offer conforming to the solicitation will be most advantageous to the contracting activity, price and other factors considered. The following factor shall be used to evaluate offers.

(Contracting Officer lists factors here, in order of importance)

9. **Options.** The Contracting Office will evaluate offers for award purposes by adding the total price for all options to the total price for the basic requirement. The Contracting Officer may determine that an offer is unacceptable if the option prices are significantly unbalanced. Evaluation of options shall not obligate the Contracting Officer to exercise the option(s).

10. **Notice of Award.** A written notice of award or acceptance of an offer, mailed or otherwise furnished to the successful offeror within the time for acceptance of the offer, shall result in a binding contract without further action by either party. Before the offer's scheduled expiration time, the Contracting Officer may accept an offer (or part of an offer) whether or not there are negotiations after its receipt, unless a written notice of withdrawal is received before award.

11. **Protests.** A contractor wishing to object to the terms of a solicitation, the termination of a solicitation, the award of a contract, or the termination of the award of a contract, shall present the matter to the Contracting Officer for an initial decision. The contractor shall state to the Contracting Office the basis for the protest. If the contractor does not agree with the Contracting Officer's initial decision, the Contractor may appeal the initial decision to the Head of Contracting Activity, CPA, for resolution. The decision of the Head of Contracting Activity, CPA, shall be the final decision in the matter.

12. **Evaluation of Foreign Currency Offers.** If the Contracting Officer receives offers in more than one currency, the Contracting Officer will evaluate offers by converting the foreign currency to United States currency using _______________ rate in effect on the date specified for receipt of offers, if award is based on initial offers, or, if award is based on revised offers, on the date specified for receipt of proposal revisions.[26]

Contract Terms and Conditions

13. **Inspection/Acceptance.** The Contractor shall only tender for acceptance those items that conform to the requirements of this contract. The Contracting Officer reserves the right to inspect or test any supplies or services that have been tendered for acceptance. The Contracting Officer may require repair or replacement of nonconforming supplies or reperformance of nonconforming services at no increase in contract price. The Contracting Officer must exercise the post-acceptance rights:

   a. Within a reasonable time after the defect was discovered or should have been discovered, and
   b. Before any substantial change occurs in the condition of the item, unless the change is due to the defect in the item.

14. **Assignment.** The Contractor shall not assign, transfer, or make any other disposition of this Contract, or any part thereof, without the prior written consent of the Contracting Officer.

15. **Changes.** Changes in the terms and conditions of this contract may be made only by written agreement of the parties.

16. **Disputes.** This contract is not subject to the Contract Disputes Act of 1978, as amended (41 U.S. Code, Sections 601-613). Failure of the parties to this contract to reach agreement on any request for equitable adjustment, claim, appeal, or action arising under or relating to this contract shall be a dispute to be resolved in accordance with the United States Federal Acquisition Regulation Clause 52.233-1, Disputes, which is incorporated herein

[26] Appendix B(12) was amended by CPA Order No 100, sec 6(4)(k) *[Doc 124]*.

by reference except that appeals from final decisions of a Contracting Officer may only be appealed to the U.S. Armed Services Board of Contract Appeals (ASBCA). The decision of the ASBCA shall be final. The contractor shall proceed diligently with performance of this contract, pending final resolution of any dispute arising under the contract.[27]

17. **Excusable Delays.** The Contractor shall be liable for default unless nonperformance is caused by an occurrence beyond the reasonable control of the Contractor and without its fault or negligence such as, acts of God or the public enemy, acts of the Governmental activity in either its sovereign or contractual capacity, fires, floods, epidemics, quarantine restrictions, strikes, unusually severe weather, and delays of common carriers. The Contractor shall notify the Contracting Officer in writing as soon as it is reasonably possible after the commencement of any excusable delay, setting forth the full particulars in connection therewith, shall remedy such occurrence with all reasonable dispatch, and shall promptly give written notice to the Contracting Officer of the cessation of such occurrence.

18. **Invoice.** The Contractor shall submit an original invoice and three copies (or electronic invoice if authorized) to the address designated in the contract to receive invoices. The invoice must include:

a. Name and address of the Contractor.
b. Invoice date and number.
c. Contract number, contract line item number, and, if applicable, the order number.
d. Description, quantity, unit of measure, unit price, and extended price of the items delivered.
e. Shipping number and date of shipment, including the bill of lading number and weight of shipment if shipped on a bill of lading.
f. Terms of any discount for prompt payment offered.
g. Name, title, and phone number of person to notify in event of defective notice.

19. **Patent Indemnity.** The Contractor shall indemnify the Government agency involved in this contract and its officers, employees, and agents against liability, including costs, for actual or alleged direct or indirect contributory infringement of, or inducement to infringe, any patent, trademark, or copyright, arising out of the performance of this contract, provided the Contractor is reasonably notified of such claims and proceedings.

20. **Payment.** Payment shall be made for items accepted by the Contracting Officer that have been delivered to the delivery destinations set forth in this contract. In connection with any discount offered for early payment, time shall be computed from the date of the invoice. For the purpose of computing the discount earned, payment shall be considered to have been made on the date which appears on the payment check or the specified payment date if an electronics fund transfer payment is made.

21. **Risk of Loss.** Unless the contract specifically provides otherwise, risk of loss or damage to the supplies provided under this contract shall remain with the Contractor until, and shall pay to the Contracting Officer:

a. Delivery of the supplies to a carrier, if transportation is f.o.b. origin.
b. Delivery of the supplies to the Contracting Officer or a representative at a destination specified in the contract, if transportation is f.o.b. destination.

22. **Taxes.** The contract price includes all applicable taxes and duties.

23. **Termination for Convenience.** The Contracting Officer reserves the right to terminate this contract, or any part hereof, for the sole convenience of the Government

[27] Appendix B(16) was rescinded and replaced by CPA Order No 100, sec 6(4)(l) *[Doc 124]*.

activity. In the event of such termination, the Contractor shall immediately stop all work hereunder and shall immediately cause any and all of its suppliers and subcontractors to cease work. Subject to the terms of this contract, the Contractor shall be paid a percentage of the contract price reflecting the percentage of the work performed prior to the notice of termination, plus reasonable charges the Contractor can demonstrate to the satisfaction of the Contracting Officer using its standard record keeping system, have resulted from the termination. The Contracting Officer, upon reasonable advanced notice, may inspect the financial records relating to this Contract including the amounts paid to subcontractors and the locations where any portion of the Contractor's performance occurs. The Contracting Officer may review the Contractor's financial statements upon request.

24. **Termination for Cause.** The Contracting Officer may terminate this contract, or any part hereof, for cause in the event of any default by the Contractor, or if the Contractor fails to comply with any contract terms and conditions, or fails to provide the Contracting Officer, upon request, with adequate assurances of future performance. In the event of termination for cause, the Government agency shall not be liable to the Contractor for any amount of supplies or services not accepted, and the Contractor shall be liable for any and all rights and remedies provided by law. If it is determined that the Contracting Officer improperly terminated this contract for cause, such termination shall be deemed a termination for convenience.

25. **Title.** Unless specified elsewhere in this contract, title to items furnished under this contract shall pass to the Government agency upon acceptance, regardless of when or where the Government agency takes physical possession.

26. **Warranty.** The Contractor warrants and implies that the items delivered hereunder are merchantable and fit for use for the particular purpose described in this contract.

27. **Immunities.** Except as provided in this contract, the Government of Iraq or its agents, including the CPA or other governmental agencies, have not waived any of their privileges or immunities.

28. **Legal Status.** The Contractor is an independent contractor. The Contractor's employees will not be considered government employees for any purpose. The Contractor is solely responsible for compensation agreements with employees.

29. **Contractor's Responsibility for Employees.** The Contractor is responsible for the professional and technical competence of its employees and will select reliable individuals who will perform effectively in the implementation of this Contract, respect the local customs, and conform to a high standard of moral and ethical conduct. The Contracting Officer may require that the Contractor remove from the job employees who endanger persons or property, or whose continued employment under this contract is inconsistent with the interest of military security.

30. **Subcontracting.** Except as authorized in this contract, the Contractor may not subcontract any portion of the performance of this Contract to another without the prior written consent of the Contracting Officer. The terms of any subcontract will be subject to and conform with the provisions of this Contract.

31. **Indemnification.** The Contractor shall defend, indemnify, and hold harmless all government entities involved in this contract, together with the entities' officers, agents, and employees from and against all suits, claims, or liabilities of any kind arising out of acts or omissions of the Contractor, its employees, or the Contractor's subcontractors.

32. **Insurance.** The Contractor represents and warrants that it shall maintain appropriate insurance including general commercial liability and workers compensation coverage in

an adequate amount to cover third parties claims arising from or in connection with this Contract. Upon request, the Contractor will provide satisfactory evidence of the insurance required under this article.

33. **Use of Names and Symbols.** Except as required by this Contract, the Contractor will not advertise or otherwise makes [sic] public the fact that it is a contractor to the governmental entity in this Contract, nor will the Contractor use the name or emblem of the governmental entity for commercial purposes.

34. **Limitation of Liability.** Except as otherwise provided by an express warranty, the Contractor will not be liable to the governmental entity for consequential damages resulting from any defect or deficiencies in accepted items.

35. **Inconsistency between English Version and Translation of Contract.** In the event of inconsistency between any terms of this contract and any transaction into another language, the English language meaning shall control.[28]

36. **Correspondence in English.** The Contractor shall ensure that all contract correspondence that is addressed to the governmental entity awarding this contract is submitted in English or with an English translation.[29]

37. **Conflicts of Interest.** The Contractor warrants that no governmental official has received or will be offered by the Contractor any direct or indirect benefit in connection with or arising from the award of this contract. The Contractor agrees that any breach of this provision is a breach of an essential term of this Contract.

38. **Order of Precedence (except for Construction Contracts).** Any inconsistencies in this solicitation or contract shall be resolved by giving precedence in the following order:

a. The schedule of supplies/services.
b. The Assignments, Disputes, Payments, Invoice, Other Compliances clauses of this contract.
c. Addenda to this solicitation or contract, including any license agreements for computer software.
d. Solicitation provisions (if this is a solicitation).
e. The other standard clauses in this contract.
f. Other documents, exhibits, and attachments.
g. The specification (the narrative description of the work).

39. **Other Compliances.** The Contractor shall comply with all applicable laws, rules, and regulations applicable to its performance under this contract.

40. **Source of Funds.** The obligation under this contract is made with Iraqi Funds, as defined in CPA Memorandum Number 4, dated 19 August 2003. No funds, appropriated or other, of any Coalition country are or will be obligated under this contract.[30]

41. **Option to Extend the Term of the Contract.**

a. The governmental entity awarding this contract may extend the term of this contract by written notice to the Contractor within _______ days (insert number of days) prior to the end of the term of the contract, or the end of any option period previously exercised under the contract; provided that the Government entity gives the Contractor a preliminary written notice of its intent to extend at least _______ (insert number of days) before the contract period (including option periods exercised) expires. The preliminary notice does not commit the

[28] Appendix B(35) was rescinded by CPA Order No 100, sec 6(4)(m) *[Doc 124]*.
[29] Appendix B(36) was rescinded by CPA Order No 100, sec 6(4)(m) *[Doc 124]*.
[30] Appendix B(40) was rescinded by CPA Order No 100, sec 6(4)(m) *[Doc 124]*.

governmental entity to an extension. If the Government exercises this option, the extended contract shall be considered to include this clause.

b. At the end of the contract period, or at the end of the final option period under this contract, whichever is later, if the governmental entity requires continued performance of services within the limits and at the rates specified in the contract for an additional period not to exceed six months, by giving written notice to the Contractor at least _____ days before the end of the contract period or the end of the final option period exercised, whichever is later.

42. **Liquidated Damages.**

a. If the Contractor fails to perform within the time specified in this contract, the Contractor shall, in place of actual damages, pay to the governmental entity liquidated damages of $_________________ per calendar day of delay.

b. If the governmental entity terminates this contract in whole or in part under the Termination for Cause clause, the Contractor is liable for liquidated damages accruing until the governmental entity reasonably obtains similar delivery or performance. These liquidated damages are in addition to excess costs of repurchase under the Termination for Cause clause.

c. The Contractor will not be charged with liquidated damages when the delay in delivery or performance is beyond the control and without the fault or negligence of the Contractor as defined in the Excusable Delay clause.

Construction Contract Terms and Conditions (For Construction Contracts Only)

43. **Performance of Work by the Contractor.** The Contractor shall perform on the site, and with its own organization, work equivalent to at least _____ percent of the total amount of work to be performed under the contract. This percentage may be reduced by a supplemental agreement to this contract if, during performing the work, the Contractor requests a reduction and the Contracting Officer determines that the reduction would be to the advantage of the Government.

44. **Differing Site Conditions.**

a. The Contractor shall promptly, and before the conditions are disturbed, give a written notice to the Contracting Officer of:

(1) Subsurface or latent physical conditions at the site which differ materially from those indicated in the Contract, or

(2) Unknown physical conditions at the site, of an unusual nature, which differ materially from those ordinarily encountered and generally recognized as inhering in work of the character provided for in the contract.

b. The Contracting Officer shall investigate the site conditions promptly after receiving the notice. If the conditions do materially so differ and cause an increase or decrease in the Contractor's cost of, or the time required for, performing any part of the work under this contract, whether or not changed as a result of the conditions, an equitable adjustment shall be made under this clause and the contract modified in writing accordingly.

c. No request by the Contractor for an equitable adjustment to the contract shall be allowed, unless the Contractor has given the written notice required; provided, that the time prescribed in paragraph (a) of this clause for giving written notice may be extended by the Contracting Officer.

d. No request by the Contractor for an equitable adjustment to the contract for differing site conditions shall be allowed if made after final payment under this contract.

45. **Site Investigation and Conditions Affecting the Work.**

a. The Contractor acknowledges that it has taken steps reasonably necessary to ascertain the nature and location of the work, and that it has investigated and satisfied itself as to the general and local conditions which can affect the work or its cost, including but not limited to (1) conditions bearing upon transportation, disposal, handling, and storage of materials; (2) the availability of labor, water, electric power, and roads; (3) uncertainties of weather, river stages, tides, or similar physical conditions at the site; (4) the conformation and conditions of the ground; (5) the character of equipment and facilities needed preliminary to and during work performance. The Contractor also acknowledges that it has satisfied itself as to the character, quality, and quantity of surface and subsurface materials or obstacles to be encountered insofar as the information is reasonably ascertainable from an inspection of the site, including all exploratory work done by the governmental agency involved, as well as from the drawing and specifications made a part of this contract. Any failure of the Contractor to take the action described and acknowledged in this paragraph will not relieve the Contractor from responsibility for estimating properly the difficulty and cost of successfully performing the work, or for proceeding to successfully perform the work without additional expense to the governmental agency involved.

b. The governmental agency involved in this contract assumes no responsibility for any conclusions or interpretations made by the Contractor based on the information made available by the Government, nor does the governmental agency assume responsibility for any understanding reached or representation made concerning conditions which can affect the work by any of its officers or agents before the execution of this contract, unless that understanding or representation is expressly stated in this contract.

46. **Material and Workmanship.**

a. All equipment, material, and articles incorporated into the work covered by this contract shall be new and of the most suitable grade for the purpose intended, unless otherwise specifically provided in this contract. References in the specifications to equipment, material, articles, or patented processes by trade name, make, or catalog number, shall be regarded as establishing a standard of quality and shall not be construed as limited competition. The Contractor may, at its option, use any equipment, material, article, or process that, in the judgment of the Contracting Officer, is equal to that named in the specifications, unless otherwise specifically provided in this contract.

b. The Contractor shall obtain the Contracting Officer's approval of the machinery and mechanical and other equipment to be incorporated into the work. When requesting approval, the Contractor shall furnish to the Contracting Officer the name of the manufacturer, the model number, and other information concerning the performance, capacity, nature, and rating of the machinery and mechanical and other equipment. When required by this contract or by the Contracting Officer, the Contractor shall also obtain the Contracting Officer's approval of the material or articles which the Contractor contemplates incorporating into the work. When requesting approval, the Contractor shall provide full information concerning the material or articles. When directed to do so, the Contractor shall submit samples for approval at the Contractor's expense, with all shipping charges prepaid. Machinery, equipment, material, and articles that do not have the required approval shall be installed or used at the risk of subsequent rejection.

c. All work under this contract shall be performed in a skillful and workmanlike manner. The Contracting Officer may require, in writing, that the Contractor remove from the work any employee the Contracting Officer deems incompetent, careless, or otherwise objectionable.

47. **Superintendence by the Contractor.** At all times during performance of this contract and until the work is completed and accepted, the Contractor shall directly superintend the work or assign and have on the worksite a competent superintendent who is satisfactory to the Contracting Officer and has authority to act for the Contractor.

48. **Permits and Responsibilities.** The Contractor shall, without additional expense to the governmental entity awarding this contract, be responsible for obtaining any necessary licenses and permits, and for complying with any laws, codes, or regulations applicable to the performance of the work. The Contractor shall also be responsible for all damages to persons or property that occurs as a result of the Contractor's fault or negligence. The Contractor shall also be responsible for all materials delivered and work performed until completion and acceptance of the entire work, except for any completed unit of work which may have been accepted under the contract.

49. **Protection of Existing Vegetation, Structures, Equipment, Utilities, and Improvements.**

a. The Contractor shall preserve and protect all structures, equipment, and vegetation (such as trees, shrubs, and grass) on or adjacent to the work site, which are not to be removed and which do not unreasonably interfere with the work required under this contract. The Contractor shall only remove trees when specifically authorized to do so, and shall avoid damaging vegetation that will remain in place. If any limbs or branches of trees are broken during contract performance, or by the careless operation of equipment, or by workmen, the Contractor shall trim those limbs or branches with a clean cut and take such other action as the Contracting officer may direct.

b. The Contractor shall protect from damage all existing improvements and utilities (1) at or near the work site, and (2) on adjacent property of a third party, the locations of which are made known to or should be known by the Contractor. The Contractor shall repair any damage to those facilities, including those that are the property of a third party, resulting from failure to comply with the requirements of this contract or failure to exercise reasonable care in performing the work. If the Contractor fails or refuses to repair the damage promptly, the Contracting Officer may have the necessary work performed and charge the cost to the Contractor.

50. **Operations and Storage Areas.**

a. The Contractor shall confine all operations (including storage of materials) to areas authorized or approved by the Contracting Officer. The Contractor shall hold and save the government entity awarding this contract, its officers and agents, free and harmless from liability of any nature occasioned by the Contractor's performance.

b. Temporary buildings (such as storage sheds, shops, offices) and utilities may be erected by the Contractor only with the approval of the Contracting Officer and shall be built with labor and materials furnished by the Contractor without expense to the governmental entity awarding this contract. The temporary buildings and utilities shall remain the property of the Contractor and shall be removed by the Contractor at its expense upon completion of the work. With the written consent of the Contracting Officer, the buildings and utilities may be abandoned and need not be removed.

c. The Contractor shall, under rules established by the Contracting Officer, use only established roadways, or use temporary roadways constructed by the Contractor when and as authorized by the Contracting Officer. When materials are transported in prosecuting the work, vehicles shall not be loaded beyond the loading capacity recommended by the manufacturer of the vehicle or prescribed by law or regulation. When it is necessary to cross curbs and sidewalks, the Contractor shall protect them from damage. The Contractor shall repair or pay for the repair of any damaged curbs, sidewalks, or roads.

51. **Cleaning Up.** The Contractor shall at all times keep the work area, including storage areas, free from accumulations of waste materials. Before completing the work, the Contractor shall remove from the work and premises any rubbish, tools, scaffolding, equipment, and materials that are not the property of the Government. Upon completing the work, the Contractor shall leave the work area in a clean, neat, and orderly condition satisfactory to the Contracting Officer.

52. **Accident Prevention.**

a. The Contractor shall provide and maintain work environments and procedures which will:
   (1) Safeguard the public and governmental entity personnel, property, materials, supplies, and equipment exposed to Contractor operations and activities,
   (2) Avoid interruptions of governmental entity operations and delays in project completion dates, and
   (3) Control costs in the performance of this contract.

b. For these purposes on contracts for construction or dismantling, demolition, or removal of improvements, the Contractor shall:
   (1) Provide appropriate safety barricades, signs, and signal lights.
   (2) Ensure that any additional measures the Contracting Officer determines to be reasonably necessary for the purposes are taken.

c. Whenever the Contracting Officer becomes aware of any noncompliance with these requirements or any condition which poses a serious or imminent danger to the health and safety of the public or governmental entity personnel, the Contracting Officer shall notify the Contractor orally, with written confirmation, and request immediate initiation of corrective action. This notice, when delivered to the Contractor or the Contractor's representative at the work site, shall be deemed sufficient notice of the noncompliance and that corrective action is required. After receiving the notice, the Contractor shall immediately take corrective action. If the Contractor fails or refuses to promptly take corrective action, the Contracting Officer may issue an order stopping all or part of the work until satisfactory corrective action has been taken. The Contractor shall not be entitled to any equitable adjustment of the contract price or extension of the performance schedule on any stop work order issued under this clause.

d. The Contractor shall insert this clause, including this paragraph (d), with appropriate changes in the designation of the parties, in subcontracts.

53. **Schedules for Construction Contracts.**

a. The Contractor shall, within five days after the work commences on the contract or another period of time determined by the Contracting Officer, prepare and submit to the Contracting Officer for approval three copies of a practicable schedule showing the order in which the Contractor contemplates starting and completing the several salient features of the work (including acquiring materials and equipment). The schedule shall be in the form of a progress chart of suitable scale to indicate approximately the percentage of work scheduled for completion by any given date during the period. If the Contractor fails to submit a schedule within the time prescribed, the Contracting Officer may withhold approval of progress payments until the Contractor submits the required schedule.

b. The Contractor shall report progress under the schedule to the Contracting Officer as directed by the Contracting Officer. If, in the opinion of the Contracting Officer, the Contractor falls behind the approved schedule, the Contractor shall take steps necessary to improve its progress, including those that may be required by the Contracting Officer, without additional cost to the governmental entity awarding this contract. In this circumstance, the Contracting Officer may require the Contractor to increase the number of shifts, overtime operations, days of work, and other efforts, and to submit for approval any supplementary schedule or schedules as the Contracting Officer deems necessary to demonstrate how the approved rate of progress will be regained.

c. Failure of the Contractor to comply with the requirements of the Contracting Officer under this clause shall be grounds for a determination by the Contracting Officer that the Contractor is not prosecuting the work with sufficient diligence to ensure completion within the time specified in the contract. Upon making this determination, the Contracting Officer may terminate the Contractor's right to proceed with the work, or any separable part of it, in accordance with the default terms of the contract.

54. **Specifications and Drawings for Construction.** The Contractor shall keep on the work site a copy of the drawings and specifications (the written description of the work) and shall at all times give the Contracting Officer access thereto. Anything mentioned in the specifications and not in the drawings, or shown on the drawings and not mentioned in the specifications, shall be of like effect as if shown or mentioned in both. In case of difference between drawings and specifications, the specifications shall govern. If case of difference in the figures between the drawings or in the specifications, the matter shall be promptly submitted to the Contracting Officer, who shall promptly make a determination in writing. Any adjustment by the Contractor without such a determination shall be at its own risk and expense. The Contracting Officer shall furnish from time to time such detailed drawings and other information as considered necessary, unless otherwise provided.

APPENDIX C
Guidance for Issuing Grants

Considerations for Drafting Grant Agreements of Solicitations for Grant Proposals

- Identify the objectives of the grant and need for assistance. Pinpoint any relevant physical, economic, social, financial, institutional, or other problems to be addressed by the grant.
- Consider the anticipated results or benefits expected. Identify costs and benefits to be derived. For example, show how problem will be improved as a result of the grant. Explain how the project will benefit the public.
- Examine the execution approach. List the activities in chronological order to show that schedule of accomplishments and expected completion dates. Identify the kinds of data to

be collected and maintained, and discuss the criteria to be used to evaluate the results and success of the project. Explain the methodology that will be used to determine if the needs identified and discussed are being met and if the results and benefits identified are being achieved. List each organization, cooperator, consultant, or other key individuals who will work on the project along with a short description of the nature of their effort or contribution.

- Develop assessment and control measures. Establish criteria for judging the effectiveness and value of the grant. For larger grants, progress payments or other control measures should be included to ensure the grant is used effectively.

Executing Grants

- Grants may be made to government entities or other organizations for purposes benefiting the public good. Small reconstruction and public works projects, as well as projects that positively impact education and health care, may be appropriate for grants.
- Grant agreements will be recorded on forms prescribed by the Head of Contracting Activity, CPA, in consultation with the Office of the General Counsel, CPA.
- When executing grants ensure the granted understands the purpose of the grant and the need to exercise fiscal responsibility including obtaining receipts for significant payments and for documenting the use of funds.
- Conduct periodic inspections of the grant activity to ensure the grant is being used appropriately.

APPENDIX D

Frequently Asked Questions

What projects are appropriate for the expenditure of DFI Funds?

UN Security Council Resolution 1483 (2003) provides the following:

> *14. Underlines that the Development fund for Iraq shall be used in a transparent manner to meet the humanitarian needs of the Iraqi people, for the economic reconstruction and repair of Iraq's infrastructure, for the continued disarmament of Iraq, and for the costs of Iraqi civilian administration, and for other purposes benefiting the people of Iraq;*

This is the standard for use of DFI funds. If the contracting requirement does not fit squarely within these categories, other funding sources must be used. Requirements for the support of Coalition Forces may not be satisfied with DFI funds.

What special rules apply for contracts with Iraqi Funds?

Obligations under contracts with Iraqi Funds will be satisfied only with Iraqi Funds. A special clause is included in the contract to put all parties on notice of this important issue.

Military Units: Military units should not execute contracts in their names or in the name of their government for projects using Iraqi Funds. These contracts must contain the following language:

> 'This contract/grant is entered into under the authority of the Administrator as head of the Coalition Provisional Authority (CPA), which is temporarily exercising governmental authority in Iraq pursuant to the law and usages of war and relevant United Nations Security Council Resolutions, including Resolution 1483 (2003) ("Coalition") and by________________________("Contractor")'

Coalition Provisional Authority: In order to clearly state the authority upon which the contract is being entered into, the clause set forth above must be included in each contract.

The CPA's authority is of limited duration and will terminate upon the establishment of an internationally recognized, representative government of Iraq. Therefore, it is important to ensure there is a 'termination for convenience' clause in each contract.

Ministries of the Iraqi Government: Ministries of the Iraqi government should use Iraqi government contracting procedures when using CPA Funds, if the Administrator determines that the contracting procedures are adequate. If those procedures are inadequate, these procedures will be used.

When should I use a grant and when should I use a contract?

When the primary purpose is to support or stimulate the efforts of the recipient rather that to acquire a product or service, grants may be made to community agencies in support of community development or outreach programs. Grants have more limited oversight and are intended to allow the applicant greater flexibility. While the effectiveness of the grant should be assessed, the requirement need not be filled by another source if the intended aims are not achieved. Grants are generally awarded to government entities and non-profit organizations. Contracts are used to acquire goods or services.

What factors should be used when evaluating potential contractors?

The requirements for each contract should be tailored to the acquisition. However all decisions to award contracts should involve consideration of the following factors:

- Value. While price is very important in determining a contract award, it [sic] ensuring the performance of the contract in [a] responsible manner is also important.
- Financial Stability of Contractor. The financial stability of the contractor must be evaluated in all Large Purchase contracts or contracts involving a substantial percentage payment of the full contract award in advance. This review should include an analysis of its financial statements; audits where possible; credit reports; and other data assessing the fitness of the company.
- Past Performance. Past performance should be considered if the entity has performed previous services.[31]

APPENDIX E

Frago 98

HQ, CJTF-7
Camp Victory, Iraq
192346JUNE03

(U) FRAGO 98 [Commander's Emergency Response Program (CERP) formerly the Brigade Commanders' Discretionary Fund] to CJTF-7 OPORD 03-036

(U) This FRAGO has been reviewed and approved for release by Col. Radcliffe, CJTF-7 C3 CHOPS

Subj: Commander's Emergency Response Program (CERP)

(U) References: [...]

(U) Maps: [no change]

[31] Appendix D was rescinded by CPA Order No 100, sec 6(4)(n) *[Doc 124]*.

(U) Time zone used throughout this order: Delta
(U) Task Organization: [no change]
1. (U) Situation. [no change]
2. (U) Mission. [no change]
3. (U) Execution. [no change]
(U) Commander's intent [no change]

3.B. (U) Concept of the operation. Coalition Provisional Authority (CPA) has expanded and increased the funds available to brigade and division commanders. This program has been renamed the Commanders Emergency Response Program (CERP). Brigade commanders will be given $200,000 with an individual project limit of $50,000.00. This authority remains limited to brigade/o-6 and governorate level commanders. Additionally, division commanders will be given a fund of $500,000 with an individual project limit of $100,000.00. The intent is to provide MSC with a greater capability and flexibility to take immediate action to make positive impacts in their area of responsibility.

3.B.1 Brigade/O-6 and governorate level commanders, utilizing OPCON civil affairs assets, will aggressively execute their spending plan in order to benefit the people of Iraq. Brigade/o-6 and governorate level commanders will have the authority to use initial cash funding, at their own discretion, to purchase goods and services related to reconstruction efforts for the Iraqi people. At the brigade/group level individual projects are not to exceed $50,000.

3.B.2. Division commanders have the authority to approve projects up to $100,000. Projects exceeding $100,000 will be submitted through C8/comptroller channels to OCPA IAW procedures that will be published by separate FRAGO.

3.B.3. As funds are exhausted, brigades/divisions will coordinate through their organization G8/comptrollers to gain additional funding authority. These funds are monies derived from seized Iraqi assets.

3.B.4. The Commander's Emergency Response Program (CERP) is a CPA funded authority provided for reconstruction assistance to the Iraqi people. Reconstruction assistance is the building, repair, reconstruction, and reestablishment of the social and material infrastructure in Iraq. This includes, but is not limited to: water and sanitation infrastructure, food production and distribution, agriculture, electrical power generation and distribution, healthcare, education, telecommunications, projects in furtherance of economic, financial, management improvements, transportation, and initiatives which further restore of the rule of law and effective governance, irrigation systems installation or restoration, day laborers to perform civic cleaning, purchase or repair of civic support vehicles, and repairs to civic or cultural facilities.

3.B.5. Expenditures can include goods and services (i.e. can purchase parts to fix something or pay an Iraqi contractor to fix it).

3.B.6. CJTF-7 will issue resource distribution documents to subordinate units C8/ comptrollers to fund brigade/division commanders.

3.B.7. The new limits are effective immediately for funds already distributed to units.

3.C. Tasks to subordinate units

3.C.1. Tasks to MSCs

3.C.1.B. Project purchasing officers (PPOS) must be appointed, in writing by their commander, have been certified as a field ordering officer (FOO), and must maintain a copy of the FRAGO authorizing the CERP program.

3.C.1.C. Coordinate for finance support with local finance elements to provide currency support and pay agent training.

3.C.1.D. Provide security for funds as necessary

3.C.1.E. Provide transportation and security to pay agents as required

3.C.1.F. Coordinate with organic finance elements for required pay agent documentation necessary to draw cash.

3.D. Coordinating Instructions

3.D.1. Coordinate all projects with regional OCPA offices, GST and civil affairs elements to prevent duplication of effort and to ensure synchronization.

3.D.2. Iraqi seized assets used for this program are not unlimited. Work to ensure reasonable prices are paid for goods/services received, and projects are constructed to a modest, functional standard.

3.D.3. Limitations on fund expenditures:

3.D.3.A. Funds will not be used for either the direct or indirect benefit of CJTF-7 forces, to include coalition forces.

3.D.3.B. Funds will not be used for entertainment of local Iraqi population.

3.D.3.C. Funds will not be used to fund any type of weapons buy back programs or rewards programs.

3.D.3.D. Funds will not be used to buy firearms, ammunition, or the removal of unexploded ordnance (UXO) for any purpose.

3.D.3.E. Funds will not be used for duplication services available through municipal governments.

3.D.3.F. Units cannot mix CERP funds and unit operations and maintenance (OMA) funds. PPOS must use separate SF44's [sic] and document register for these funds.

3.D.3.G. Funds will not be used to provide support to individuals or private businesses (exceptions possible, i.e. repair damage caused by coalition forces.)

3.D.3.H. Units will not pay salaries to the civil work force, pensions, or fund emergency civil service worker payments. Salaries and emergency payments are handled directly by OCPA via Iraqi ministries and local GST. See COMCFLCC FRAGO 366/416 for these procedures.

3.D.3.I. Violations of these restrictions will result in termination of CERP funds for that unit.

3.D.4. All project purchasing officers will reconcile their accounts with finance, resource management, and their brigade/division commander. Commanders must clear PPO with memo validating all projects and submit PRB-1 (provided separately to comptrollers) through comptroller channels to CJTF-7 C8.

3.D.5. Pay agents are encouraged to draw funds as needed rather than large bulk sums.

3.D.6. Record all payments on SF44 to document purchases made under this program. Project purchasing officers are authorized to make purchases and to pay for projects up to $50,000 and $100,000 with the SF44 for this program only.

3.D.7. Commanders are not authorized to deliberately over pay. Extra precaution should be taken for expenses over $10,000.00 For projects over $10,000, brigade commanders must inform division commanders in advance, obtain three bids for the project, and identify an individual to manage the project. Document your efforts to verify costs are reasonable. For larger projects (over $10,000) progress payments should be made as opposed to a lump sum payment up front.

3.D.8. Commanders will consult with their servicing staff judge advocates and finance officers/resource managers for guidance on the implementation of this program within their command.

3.D.9. Units are encouraged to only request the funds they reasonably expect to execute.

3.D.10. Reports

3.D.10.A. Units must provide weekly commanders discretionary fund feeder reports on Saturday of each week through unit comptrollers to V CORPS/CJTF-7 G8/Comptroller. Include unit, date of project, location, amount spent, and project description. This report should be prepared reflecting all projects performed under the bulk fund. Unit comptrollers will consolidate and forward these reports NLT 1200 on Saturday.

Unit	Date of Project	Location	Amount Spent	Brief Description of Project

3.D.10.B. Prior to receiving an additional increment of funds, units will submit an OCPA PRB-1 forms for all projects.

3.D.10.C. Submit both reports above to the CJTF-7 Deputy C8, LTC Dave Goddard.

3.D.11. Project purchasing officer/pay agent teams will clear outstanding SF44s prior to obtaining additional funding approval.

3.D.12. DFAS annex E and OSD directives authorize project purchasing officers to continue their duties under their current certification and training by contracting officers.

3.D.13. POC for this FRAGO is CJTF-7 C8, LTC Dave Goddard DNVT 302-550-2650, SIPRNET Goddard@C5MAIN.HQ.C5.ARMY.SMIL.MIL, NIPRNET ACSRMXO@HQ.C5.ARMY.MIL

4. (U) Service Support. [no change]

5. (U) Command and signal. [no change]

Acknowledge
Sanchez
LTG

Document 130

Coalition Provisional Authority Memorandum Number 5

CPA/MEM/22 August 2003/05

Implementation of Weapons Control Order No. 3 (CPA/ORD/23 May 2003/03)[32]

Acknowledging that the CPA, relying upon Coalition Forces, is obligated to take all measures in its power to restore and ensure, insofar as possible, public order and safety in Iraq,

Recognizing that while the Coalition Provisional Authority generally seeks to protect diplomatic premises insofar as the current security environment permits, it is not required to protect diplomatic facilities beyond the general obligation to restore, and ensure as far as possible, public order and safety,

Noting that foreign liaison officials may bring into Iraq and/or maintain their own security forces only in full coordination with and with the agreement of Coalition Forces, including compliance with the procedures established pursuant to CPA Order Number 3 on Weapons Control, dated 23 May 2003,

Implementing CPA Order No. 3, section 5, which establishes a Weapons Authorization Program whereby individuals who can demonstrate a necessity to carry weapons may

[32] See *Doc 16.*

apply for temporary weapons authorization cards (TWCs) in order to carry weapons,

I hereby promulgate the following:

Section 1 Definitions

'Foreign Mission Security Personnel' means (i) security personnel who are nationals of the country represented by a foreign liaison mission[33] who are accompanying the mission and providing security services to such missions, (ii) employees of the United Nations or United Nations Specialized and Related Agencies designated in Annex A who are providing security services to the United Nations or the United Nations Specialized and Related Agencies, and (iii) security firms authorized by the CPA to provide security services to foreign liaison missions, the United Nations or the United Nations Specialized and Related Agencies.[34]

'Small Arms and Defensive Weapons' means Small Arms as defined in CPA Order 3 including pistols, shotguns, and rifles firing ammunition up to an including 7.62mm and Defensive Weapons including crew-served machine guns, non-lethal weapons and riot control agents.

Section 2 Purpose

This Memorandum specifically authorizes foreign liaison missions, the United Nations, and the United Nations Specialized and Related Agencies to enter into and execute contracts for security services, and expressly permits the providers of such services to perform those actions that are necessary to ensure proper security of foreign mission personnel and facilities, including the carrying of weapons.

Section 3 Authorization of Security Contracts

Foreign liaison missions in Iraq are hereby authorized to carry out any actions necessary to enter into and execute contracts with private security firms for the purpose of providing appropriate security of foreign liaison mission facilities, personnel, and operations.

Section 4 Weapons Authorization

Subject to the regulations of the Ministry of Interior, Foreign Mission Security Personnel, so long as they remain authorized to provide such services within Iraq, are hereby authorized to carry Small Arms and Defensive Weapons, when providing security services to foreign liaison missions, the United Nations and the United Nations Specialized and Related Agencies, their facilities, their personnel and their operations. Such missions are directed to provide the locations of their facilities with armed personnel to the CPA office advising the Ministry of Foreign Affairs and the CPA office advising the Ministry of Interior.[35]

Section 5 Suspension of Laws

Any extant Iraqi law or regulation inconsistent with this Memorandum is hereby suspended.

Section 6 Entry into Force

This Memorandum shall enter into force on the date of signature [22 August 2003].

[33] All references to 'foreign liaison misson[s]' were replaced with 'diplomatic or consular missions', see CPA Order No 100, sec 6(5)(a) *[Doc 124]*.

[34] Sec 1(iii) was amended by CPA Order No 100, sec 6(5)(b) *[Doc 124]*.

[35] Sec 4 was amended by CPA Order No 100, sec 6(5)(c) *[Doc 124]*.

ANNEX A[36]

Security personnel authorized by the CPA may possess Small Arms and Defensive Weapons to provide security for the following foreign liaison missions, the United Nations, and the United Nations Specialized and Related Agencies, their facilities, their personnel and their operations:

Algeria	Italy	Sri Lanka
Australia	Iran	Spain
Bahrain	Japan	Sudan
Bangladesh	Jordan	Switzerland
Bulgaria	Korea	Tunis [sic]
China	Morocco	Turkey
Czech Republic	Netherlands	UAE
Denmark	Palestine	United Kingdom
Egypt	Philippines	United States
France	Poland	
Germany	Romania	
Greece	Russia	United Nations
India	Serbia/Montenegro	United Nations Specialized and Related Agencies

Security personnel of additional missions may be authorized to possess Small Arms and Defensive Weapons by the CPA office advising the Ministry of Interior from time to time.

United Nations Specialized and Related Agencies are:

1. Food and Agricultural Organization of the United Nations (FAO)
2. The International Bank for Reconstruction and Development (IBRD) and its affiliates, the International Development Association (IDA) and the International Finance Corporation (IFC)
3. International Civil Aviation Organization (ICAO)
4. International Fund for Agricultural Development (IF AD)
5. International Labour Organization (ILO)
6. International Maritime Organization (IMO)
7. International Monetary Fund (IMF)
8. International Organization for Migration (IOM)
9. International Telecommunication Union (ITU)
10. United Nations Educational, Scientific and Cultural Organization (UNESCO)
11. United Nations Industrial Development Organization (UNIDO)
12. Universal Postal Union (UPU)
13. World Health Organization (WHO)
14. World Intellectual Property Organization (WIPO)
15. World Food Program (WFP)
16. World Meteorological Organization (WMO)

[36] Annex A was not published in the Official Gazette. See vol 44, no 3979, 108. Annex A was amended by CPA Order No 100, sec 6(5)(d) *[Doc 124]*.

Document 131
Coalition Provisional Authority Memorandum Number 6
CPA/MEM/2 September 2003/06

Implementation of Regulation on the Governing Council (CPA/REG/13 Jul 2006/06)

Pursuant to my authority as Administrator of the Coalition Provisional Authority (CPA), the laws and usages of war and consistent with relevant U.N. Security Council resolutions, including Resolution 1483 (2003),

Recognizing that the Governing Council of Iraq in performing its functions on behalf of the people of Iraq has nominated Interim Ministers to assume responsibility of the daily administration of the Iraqi Ministries,[37]

Implementing CPA Regulation Number 6, Governing Council of Iraq (CPA/REG/13 Jul 2003/06),[38]

I hereby promulgate the following:

Section 1 Recognition of Interim Ministers

The CPA recognizes the appointment by the Governing Council of Interim Ministers as set out at Annex A to be responsible for the daily operations of the Iraqi Ministries they have been appointed to.

Section 2 Entry into Force

This Memorandum shall enter into force on the date of signature [3 September 2003].[39]

ANNEX A

List of Approved Interim Ministers Selected by the Governing Council of Iraq

1 – Ministry of Agriculture:	Abdul Amir al-Abood
2 – Ministry of Communication:	Dr. Haydar al-Abadi
3 – Ministry of Construction & Housing:	Bayan Baqir Solagh (Bayan Jabur)
4 – Ministry of Culture:	Mufid Muhammad Juwad al-Jaza'iri
5 – Ministry of Education:	Dr. Ala'din Abdul Sahib Alwan
6 – Ministry of Electricity:	Dr. Aiham Alsammarae
7 – Ministry of Environment:	Abdel Rahman Sadiq Karim
8 – Ministry of Expatriates & Immigrants:	Muhammad Jasim Khdeir
9 – Ministry of Finance:	Kamel al-Keilani
10 – Ministry of Foreign Affairs:	Hoshiyar Mahmud Muhammad al-Zibari
11 – Ministry of Health:	Dr. Khidr Abbas
12 – Ministry of Higher Education:	Ziad Adbel Razzaq Muhammad Aswad
13 – Human Rights:	Abdel Basit Turki
14 – Ministry of Industry & Minerals:	Eng. Muhammad Tawfiq Rahim
15 – Ministry of Interior:	Nori Badran

[37] See the IGC's Resolution No 28 of 31 August 2003 *[Doc 291]*.

[38] See *Doc 7*.

[39] CPA Memorandum No 6 was rescinded by CPA Regulation No 9, sec 1(2) *[Doc 10]*. See also CPA Order No 100, sec 6(6) *[Doc 124]*.

16 – Ministry of Irrigation:	Dr. Latif Rashid
17 – Ministry of Justice:	Hashim Abdel Rahman al-Shibli
18 – Ministry of Labour & Social Affairs:	Sami Azara al-Ma'jun
19 – Ministry of Oil:	Dr. Ibrahim Bahr al-Uloum
20 – Ministry of Planning:	Dr. Medhi al-Hafidh
21 – Ministry of Public Works:	Mrs. Nasreen Mustafa Sadiq Barwari
22 – Ministry of Science & Technology:	Rashas Omar Mindan
23 – Ministry of Trade:	Dr. Ali Allawi
24 – Ministry of Transport:	Bahnam Ziya Boulous
25 – Ministry of Youth and Sports:	Ali Fa'iq al-Ghabban

Document 132
Coalition Provisional Authority Memorandum Number 7

CPA/MEM/4 November 2003/07

Delegation of Authority under De-Baathification Order No. 1 (CPA/ORD/16 May 2003/01)[40]

Pursuant to my authority as Administrator of the Coalition Provisional Authority (CPA), and under the laws and usages of war, and consistent with relevant U.N. Security Council resolutions, including Resolution 1483 (2003),

Recognizing that the Iraqi people have suffered large scale human rights abuses and deprivations over many years at the hands of the Baath Party,

Noting the grave concern of Iraqi society regarding the threat posed by the continuation of Baath Party participation in the public sector, including in particular the education system,

Observing that under the prior regime some Iraqis may have become affiliated with the Ba'ath Party for reasons not primarily related to their ideological beliefs,

Recognizing that organizing and expediting de-Baathification is an urgent task that is necessary to put Iraq on the path towards reconstruction and renewal,

Acknowledging that the Governing Council has created a Higher National De-Ba'athification Commission in order to contribute to a secure, stable environment that will sustain freedom and democracy for the Iraqi people,

Recalling the steps already taken in CPA Order Number 1, De-Baathification of Iraqi Society (CPA/ORD/16 May 2003/01),

I hereby promulgate the following:

Section 1 Delegation of Authority

1) The Governing Council is hereby empowered to carry out the de-Baathification of Iraqi society consistent with CPA Order No. 1, De-Baathification of Iraqi Society (CPA/ORD/16 May 2003/01). To the extent consistent with CPA Order No. 1 (CPA/ORD/16 May 2003/01), Decisions 1 and 2 of the Higher National De-Baathification Commission, made on September 14, 2003, are hereby ratified.[41] Notwithstanding such ratification, any action taken by the Administrator pursuant to Section 1(6) of CPA Order No. 1 (CPA/ORD/16

[40] See *Doc 14*.
[41] For Decisions 1 and 2 of the Iraqi Higher National De-Baathification Commission, see *Docs 498, 499*.

May 2003/01) shall remain in effect unless and until terminated on a case-by-case basis by the Higher National De-Baathification Commission.

2) The Governing Council is further authorized to seize and manage property and assets of the Baath Party, consistent with CPA Order No. 4, Management of Property and Assets of the Iraqi Baath Party, May 25, 2003.[42] The Governing Council shall consult with the CPA in developing procedures to ensure that such property is seized and managed fairly and judiciously.

Section 2 Terms and Conditions

The authority delegated under Section 1 of this Memorandum shall be subject to the following terms and conditions:

1) The Governing Council may further delegate the authority conferred under Section 1 of this Memorandum to the Higher National De-Baathification Commission or other organization established by the Governing Council.

2) To the extent practicable, factual determinations regarding an Iraqi citizen's affiliation with the Baath Party, or involvement with the Special Security, National Security, Special Protection for the Presidency, Military Intelligence, Feda'iyeen Saddam, General Security or Mukhabarat, should be made at the governorate (or equivalent) level of government or below, by individuals selected on the basis of their ability to analyze information objectively and render fair and judicious determinations. These factual determinations shall be made in accordance with policies and procedures to be established by the Governing Council for uniform application throughout Iraq.

3) The Governing Council, in coordination with the concerned Minister or equivalent official, may establish special de-Baathification procedures for application to particular professions or groups of individuals. Such procedures may concern the process of making factual determinations and the consequences of such determinations. Consistent with this paragraph, the Governing Council shall authorize the continued employment of current or recently discharged Iraqi civil servants who were:

a) held as a POW by Iran during the period September 4, 1980 through June 1, 2003;
b) released and repatriated to Iraq by Iran after being held in that status; and
c) granted 'Udw Firqah' status following his or her release and repatriation to Iraq and because of his or her status as a former POW.

An Iraqi civil servant's eligibility for an exception to the de-Baathification policy under this provision may be established through official documentation issued by the International Committee of the Red Cross, or other independent organization or government organization. If the Higher National De-Baathification Commission determines that credible information establishes that an Iraqi civil servant who seeks or has been granted an exception under this delegation of authority was promoted to the rank of 'Udw Firqah' for reasons other than his or her status as a former POW, or that his or her involvement in the Baath Party was incompatible with continued service as a civil servant, the Higher National De-Baathification Commission may deny or at any time rescind an exception for that individual.

4) Any Iraqi citizen who is dismissed from his or her position of employment as a result of the exercise of the authority conferred herein shall be entitled to:

a) advance written notification explaining the grounds for dismissal and the procedures for appealing that dismissal;

[42] See *Doc 18*.

b) a reasonable opportunity to respond to the notification in writing or in person and present evidence; and
c) a reasonable opportunity to appeal immediately any adverse decision, in writing or in person, to a fair and impartial entity independent of the individual or organization that rendered the adverse decision, which shall promptly render a written decision in the case.

5) In any case in which a dismissed employee's appeal is denied, the dismissed employee shall have the right to request further review of the matter by the Higher National De-Baathification Commission or a national committee established by the Higher National De-Baathification Commission for this purpose.

6) If an appeal results in an employee's reinstatement, the employee shall be paid back pay from the date of dismissal to the date of reinstatement.

7) Following consultation with the Governing Council, the Administrator may reinstate an employee if he concludes that it is in the interests of the Iraqi people or that failing to reinstate the employee would be fundamentally unfair.

8) The Governing Council shall coordinate with the Minister of Finance before exercising the authority conferred under this Memorandum in a manner that will significantly affect the national budget of Iraq.

9) The Governing Council shall consult with the Administrator, or his designee, with respect to the use of the de-Baathification procedures in any area identified by the Administrator where the number and/or concentration of Iraqi citizens affected by the procedures may raise security concerns.

10) The Higher National De-Ba'athification Commission shall provide monthly reports to the Administrator of the CPA and the Governing Council describing the manner in which the authority delegated herein has been exercised. Such reports shall include the names and positions of any Iraqi citizen dismissed from a position of employment as a result of this delegation, and the names of any Iraqi citizens hired to replace a dismissed employee.

Section 3 Transition Provisions

CPA Order Number 5, Establishment of the Iraqi De-Ba'athification Council (CPA/ORD/25 May 2003/05)[43] is hereby rescinded.

Section 4 Effective Date

This Memorandum shall enter into force on the date of signature [4 November 2003].[44]

[43] See *Doc 19*.

[44] Authority delegated under CPA Memorandum No 7 was withdrawn by CPA Order No 100, sec 6(7) *[Doc 124]*. However, the Higher National De-Ba'athification Commission was to remain in place until the Iraqi Interim Government would establish the Independent Iraqi De-Ba'athification Council, see CPA Order No 100, sec 6(7) *[Doc 124]*. See also the Memorandum on 'De-Ba'athification: An Iraqi Process' from the Administrator to CPA Senior Advisors, CPA Governance Teams and CJTF-7, dated 8 December 2003 *[Doc 239]*.

Document 133
Coalition Provisional Authority Memorandum Number 8
CPA/MEM/25 January 2004/08

Exportation of Scrap Metal under Order Number 12, Trade Liberalization Policy (CPA/ORD/7 June 2003/12)

Pursuant to my authority as Administrator of the Coalition Provisional Authority (CPA), and under the laws and usages of war, and consistent with relevant U.N. Security Council Resolutions, including Resolutions 1483 and 1511 (2003),

Acknowledging the central role of international trade in Iraq's recovery and its development of a free market economy,

Noting that the export of certain items, including certain metal products, is currently prohibited,

Recognizing that the legitimate export of scrap metal is a potentially important source of income for Iraqi businesses,

Emphasizing the need to control black-market activities while promoting opportunities for legitimate businesses,

I hereby promulgate the following:

Section 1 Purpose and Definition

1) This Memorandum provides rules for the export of scrap under CPA Order Number 12.[45]

2) 'Scrap' is defined to mean material that has been finished and put to use as a product or part of a product, but has lost its intended usefulness as a result of obsolescence, damage or destruction.

Section 2 Exclusion of Scrap as Prohibited Export

The manufactured goods that are prohibited from export under the Annex to CPA Order Number 12 (CPA/ORDANNEX/7 June 2003/12) shall not include scrap ceramics or scrap metal, excluding copper and lead. Scrap copper and lead are prohibited exports.

Section 3 Licenses

Effective February 1, 2004, metal, including scrap metal, shall not be exported without authorization from the Ministry of Trade. Prior to February 1, 2004, scrap metal, excluding copper and lead, may be exported without a license.

Section 4 Entry into Force

This Memorandum shall enter into force on the date of signature [25 January 2004].[46]

[45] See *Doc 28*.

[46] CPA Memorandum No 8, which amended CPA Order No 12 *[Doc 28]*, was rescinded by CPA Order No 54, sec 3(4) *[Doc 76]*. However, any licensing regime established under CPA Memorandum No 8 continued to be effective to the extent that it was not inconsistent with the terms of CPA Order No 54.

Document 134
Coalition Provisional Authority Memorandum Number 9
CPA/MEM/25 February 2004/09

Appointment of Deputy Ministers

Pursuant to my authority as Administrator of the Coalition Provisional Authority (CPA), and under the laws and usages of war, and consistent with relevant U.N. Security Council resolutions, including Resolutions 1483 and 1511 (2003),

Noting that appointments of interim deputy Iraqi ministers provide key opportunities to advance the CPA's efforts to restore and establish representative government institutions in Iraq, including national ministry staffs that reflect the ethnic, religious and cultural diversity of the Iraqi people and the crucial role that Iraqi women must assume in achieving an internationally recognized, representative government of Iraq;

Recognizing that the Governing Council of Iraq in performing its functions on behalf of the people of Iraq has nominated Deputy Ministers to assume responsibility of the daily administration of the Iraqi Ministries,

Implementing CPA Regulation Number 6, Governing Council of Iraq (CPA/REG/13 Jul 2003/06),[47]

I hereby promulgate the following:

Section 1 Appointment of Interim Deputy Ministers
The Administrator shall have the exclusive authority to appoint Deputy Ministers. Unless specifically appointed in writing by the Administrator, no individual may assume the position of Deputy Minister or exercise the authority or enjoy the privileges of such office.

Section 2 Exception for Currently Serving Deputy Ministers
Notwithstanding Section 1 of this Memorandum, individuals who are serving as Acting Deputy Ministers on the effective date of this Memorandum may continue to hold the position of Acting Deputy Minister, and exercise the authority and enjoy the privileges of such office, until removed by the Administrator.

Section 3 Entry into Force
This Memorandum shall enter into force on the date of signature [24 February 2004].[48]

[47] See *Doc 7*.
[48] CPA Memorandum No 9 was rescinded by CPA Order No 100, sec 6(8) *[Doc 124]*.

Document 135
Coalition Provisional Authority Memorandum Number 10
CPA/MEM/4 April 2004/10

Rewards Program for Information Leading to the Recovery of Iraqi State and Former Regime Assets

Pursuant to my authority as Administrator of the Coalition Provisional Authority (CPA), and under the laws and usages of war, and consistent with relevant U.N. Security Council resolutions, including Resolutions 1483 and 1511 (2003),

Recognizing that Saddam Hussein and his family and other members of the former regime engaged in the systematic looting, theft and illegal transfer of Iraqi assets for the purpose of enriching themselves at the expense of the people of Iraq,

Emphasizing that financial assets of the former Government of Iraq and former regime members that are located abroad must be repatriated back to Iraq,

Noting the obligation of the CPA to recover the maximum amount of these assets so they can be used for the benefit of the Iraqi people,

I hereby promulgate the following:

Section 1 Purpose and Definitions

1) This Memorandum provides conditions for the payment of rewards for information leading to the recovery of Iraqi state or regime-owned assets.

2) 'Iraqi state assets' is defined to mean funds or other financial assets or economic resources of the previous Government of Iraq or its state bodies, corporations, or agencies located outside Iraq as of May 22, 2003.

3) 'Former regime-owned assets' is defined to mean funds or other financial assets or economic resources of Saddam Hussein or other senior officials of the former Iraqi regime and their immediate family members, including entities owned or controlled, directly or indirectly, by them or by persons acting on their behalf or at their direction.

Section 2 Authority

1) The Administrator or his designee, in coordination with the Ministry of Finance, may authorize the payment of financial rewards to eligible individuals who provide the Coalition with information that leads to the recovery of Iraqi state assets or former regime-owned assets.

2) Reward payments shall be paid in advance in an amount determined by the Administrator or his designee, provided that no payment shall exceed 3% of the amount of assets recovered, or $10 million, whichever is less. The terms of each reward payment will be based on the totality of the circumstances, subject to the conditions stated herein.

3) Payments will be issued only after the assets recovered as a result of the information provided have been deposited into the Development Fund for Iraq, or other account properly established to receive Iraqi state assets or former regime-owned assets.

4) Governmental officials and immediate family members, including current officials in Iraqi Ministries, and members of the Coalition, are not eligible for a reward under this program.

5) Receipt of a reward under this program does not immunize the recipient from prosecution for offenses unrelated to the possession or concealment of the Iraqi state or former regime-owned assets for which a reward was paid.[49]

Section 3 Reporting
The Administrator or his designee will report all reward payments issued pursuant to this program to the Program Review Board.

Section 4 Entry into Force
This Memorandum shall enter into force on the date of signature [5 April 2004].

Document 136
Coalition Provisional Authority Memorandum Number 11

Memorandum Number 11 was never approved. A draft was sent to Ambassador Bremer in April 2004. He did not sign because of outstanding questions, and apparently these questions were not resolved prior to CPA dissolution.

Document 137
Coalition Provisional Authority Memorandum Number 12

CPA/MEM/8 May 2004/12

Administration of Independent Judiciary

Pursuant to my authority as Administrator of the Coalition Provisional Authority (CPA), and under the laws and usages of war, and consistent with relevant U.N. Security Council resolutions, including Resolutions 1483 and 1511 (2003),

Recognizing that an independent judiciary as provided for in CPA Order No. 35[50] and the Law of Administration for the State of Iraq for the Transitional Period[51] requires an independent judicial administration,

Recognizing further that Iraqi law still reflects the lack of an independent judiciary which was one fundamentally malign feature of the former regime that undermined the rule of law,

I hereby promulgate the following:

Section 1 Purpose
This Memorandum implements CPA Order No. 35 and Chapter six of the Law of Administration for the State of Iraq for the Transitional period.

[49] Sec 2 was rescinded and replaced by CPA Order No 100, sec 6(9) *[Doc 124]*.
[50] See *Doc 56*.
[51] See *Doc 511*.

Section 2 Definition
For purposes of this regulation, 'Council of Judges' means the Council of Judges reestablished by CPA Order 35, or its successor organization as provided by the Law of Administration for the State of Iraq for the Transitional Period.

Section 3 Budget
The Council of Judges and the Court of Cassation shall each have its own, separate budget by no later than June 1, 2004. The Ministry of Finance shall cooperate fully to create, fund, and support each such budget, including reallocating money from the budget of the Ministry of Justice as appropriate. For the year 2004, the Ministry of Finance shall determine, in consultation with the Ministry of Justice, the Council of Judges, and the Court of Cassation, the amount of the budget of the Ministry of Justice for 2004 that shall be reallocated to the latter two entities, and shall attempt to minimize any additional 2004 budget expenditures concerning these two entities.

Section 4 Personnel
All employees who work for or are primarily associated with the courts, including but not limited to all judges, prosecutors, court investigators, court clerks, personnel on the Committee of Judicial Supervision, security personnel, and support and administrative staff, and are currently employed by the Ministry of Justice, shall, no later than June 1, 2004, become employees of the Council of Judges or of the Court of Cassation, as appropriate.

Section 5 Property
All interests in property, real, tangible, or otherwise, including but not limited to furniture, motor vehicles, office equipment, libraries, and housing for judges and prosecutors, that is primarily used for or associated with courts and the judiciary and that is assigned to the Ministry of Justice, shall, no later than June 1, 2004, be assigned to the Council of Judges or to the Court of Cassation, as appropriate.

Section 6 State Consultative Council
The State Consultative Council shall remain a part of the Ministry of Justice.

Section 7 References in Law
References in Iraqi law to the Ministry of Justice or the Minister of Justice shall, where necessary and proper in light of CPA Order 35 or the Law of Administration for the State of Iraq for the Transitional Period, or where otherwise necessary and proper to maintain the independence of the judiciary, be construed to refer to the Council of Judges or its President, or to the Court of Cassation or its Chief Judge, or to the Supreme Federal Court or its Presiding Judge, as appropriate. The courts shall have sole jurisdiction to adjudicated disputes in this connection.

Section 8 Cooperation
The Ministry of Justice, the Council of Judges, the Court of Cassation, the Ministry of Finance, and all other concerned government institutions shall cooperate to the greatest possible extent in effectuating this regulation and CPA Order 35.

Section 9 Entry into Force
This Order [sic] shall enter into force on the date of signature [8 May 2004].

Document 138
Coalition Provisional Authority Memorandum Number 13
CPA/MEM/30 May 2004/13

Appointment of Inspector General to the Baghdad City Council

Pursuant to my authority as Administrator of the Coalition Provisional Authority (CPA), and under the laws and usages of war, and consistent with relevant U.N. Security Council resolutions, including Resolutions 1483 and 1511 (2003),

Noting that CPA Order Number 57, Iraqi Inspector General (CPA/ORD/5 February 2004/57),[52] is unclear as to whether it permits the CPA to appoint an inspector general to the Baghdad City Council (the 'Amanat Baghdad'),

Understanding that the Amanat Baghdad is a public body on a scale and complexity comparable with many Ministries,

Recognizing that creating an Office of Inspector General is an important step in improving the efficiency and effectiveness of the Amanat Baghdad, which carries out vital governmental functions, similar to government ministries,

Implementing CPA Order Number 57, Iraqi Inspectors General (CPA/ORD/5 February 2004/57),

I hereby promulgate the following:

Section 1 Appointment of an Inspector General to the Amanat Baghdad
There is hereby established an Office of Inspector General for the Amanat Baghdad. The Inspector General shall be appointed by the Administrator, report directly to the Ameen of Baghdad and exercise the roles and responsibilities of ministry inspectors general, as set forth in CPA Order No. 57, and serve for the same term. All references to 'minister' in that Order shall be interpreted as applying equally to the Ameen of Baghdad.

Section 2 Entry into Force
This Memorandum shall enter into force on the date of signature [2 June 2004].

[52] See *Doc 80*.

Document 139
Coalition Provisional Authority Memorandum Number 14
CPA/MEM/1 June 2004/14

Establishment of Office of Chief Advisor to the National Assembly

Pursuant to my authority as Administrator of the Coalition Provisional Authority (CPA), and under the laws and usages of war, and consistent with relevant U.N. Security Council resolutions, including Resolutions 1483 and 1511 (2003),

Noting that the Law of Administration for the State of Iraq for the Transitional Period[53] establishes a National Assembly of Iraq, which shall be composed of 275 members who will be elected, in accordance with an electoral law and a political parties law, on or about December 31, 2004,

Recognizing that much preparatory work needs to be accomplished between now and the time that the National Assembly of Iraq becomes operational,

Acknowledging that an Office responsible for coordinating, administrating and conducting the procedural duties of the National Assembly must be formed and commence operations immediately so that the National Assembly is able to function effectively once it is formed,

Expanding upon Law of Administration for the State of Iraq for the Transitional Period,

I hereby promulgate the following:

Section 1 Establishment of an Office of the Chief Advisor to the National Assembly of Iraq

There is hereby established an Office of the Chief Advisor to the National Assembly of Iraq. The Chief Advisor shall be appointed by the Administrator and be the highest ranking permanent official of the National Assembly [of] Iraq. The Chief Advisor shall report directly to the Administrator or (when formed) the head of the Iraqi Interim Government. The Chief Advisor shall exercise all necessary duties to manage the administrative affairs of the National Assembly of Iraq, including but not limited to, having oversight responsibility for all administrative offices, legislative committees, and professional departments within the National Assembly, recruiting, hiring, and the management of staff, and coordination with other government entities.

Section 2 Entry and Force

This Memorandum shall enter into force on the date of signature [1 June 2004].

[53] See *Doc 511*.

Document 140
Coalition Provisional Authority Memorandum Number 15
CPA/MEM/15 June 2004/15

Amendment to Coalition Provisional Authority Memorandum 4 (CPA/MEM/19 August 2003/04)[54]

Pursuant to my authority as Administrator of the Coalition Provisional Authority (CPA), and under the laws and usages of war, and consistent with relevant U.N. Security Council resolutions, including Resolutions 1483 and 1511 (2003) and 1546 (2004),

Noting that the Coalition Provisional Authority will dissolve on June 30, 2004 and that full governance authority of Iraq will transfer to the Iraqi Interim Government on that date,

Recognizing that on June 30, 2004 the Iraqi Interim Government will assume control over all funds placed into the Development Fund for Iraq,

Acknowledging that the Coalitional [sic] Provisional Authority has entered into contracts on behalf of the people of Iraq and that many of these contracts require continued performance and payment from the Development Fund for Iraq after June 30, 2004,

Understanding that continued performance and payment of sums due under these contracts after June 30, 2004 are critical to the redevelopment and reconstruction of Iraq,

Desiring to amend Coalition Provisional Authority Memorandum 4, Contracts and Grant Procedures, (CPA/MEM/19 August 2003/04), to provide for the orderly transition of authority over the Development Fund for Iraq from the Coalition Provisional Authority to the Iraqi Interim Government,

I hereby promulgate the following:

Section 1 Powers of Iraqi Interim Government

Section 4 of Coalition Provisional Authority Memorandum 4, Contracts and Grant Procedures, (CPA/MEM/19 August 2003/04) is amended to read as follows:

(5) The Minister of Finance may designate the Director, Program Management Office of the Coalition Provisional Authority, or, following the transfer of full governance authority to the Iraqi Interim Government of Iraq, the Chief of Mission of the United States Embassy, Baghdad and/or the Commander of the Multi-National Force-I, with responsibility to monitor and confirm performance, certify and/or make payments, and otherwise administer contracts or grants funded with monies from the Development Fund for Iraq that:

(a) were entered into on or before June 30, 2004 by the Coalition Provisional Authority or the Multi-National Force-Iraq in accordance with United Nations Security Council Resolution 1483 and implementing regulations;

(b) require the continued performance and/or payment of money from the DFI past June 30, 2004; and

(c) Are not the subject of a fully funded letter of credit intended to otherwise ensure performance under the contract or grant.

(6) Designees appointed under paragraph 5 shall be required to coordinate their activities with relevant officials from the Iraqi Interim Government and, consistent with U.N. Security Council Resolution 1546 (2004), to satisfy

[54] See *Doc 129*.

outstanding obligations against the Development Fund for Iraq. Designees appointed under paragraph 5 also shall be required to assist in the termination, amendment, or novation of contracts or grants at the discretion of the Iraqi Interim Government.

(7) Designees appointed under paragraph 5 above shall account for all disbursements made on behalf of the Iraqi Interim Government on the books of the sub-account entitled 'Central Bank of Iraq/Development Fund for Iraq/Transition,' established pursuant to CPA Regulation 11, Amendments to Coalition Provisional Authority Regulation 2 (CPA/REG/10 June 2003/02)[55] and No. 3 (CPA/REG/18 June 2003/03), (CPA/REG/12 June 2004/10 [sic][56]),[57] or otherwise, in accordance with internationally recognized auditing and accounting standards.

(8) Designees appointed under paragraph 5 shall maintain records of all disbursements made on behalf of the Iraqi Interim Government and shall submit reports of all expenditures, payments and outflows as directed by the Ministry of Finance.

(9) To facilitate the ability of Designees to carry out their responsibilities under this Memorandum, an account in the Central Bank of Iraq, Rafidain Bank, and/or Rasheed Bank shall be established. Designees appointed under paragraph 5 shall have the authority to disburse funds from this account in order to carry out their duties so long as the procedures set forth in paragraphs 6, 7, and 8 are followed. The Minister of Finance may (at his discretion) transfer funds from the Development Fund for Iraq into this account from time to time.

(10) Designees appointed under paragraph 5 above may (if expressly authorized in writing by the Iraqi Interim Government) further delegate all powers, privileges, rights, and authorities provided herein.

Section 2 Entry and Force

This Memorandum shall enter into force on the date of signature [18 June 2004].

Document 141

Coalition Provisional Authority Memorandum Number 16

No record of Memorandum Number 16 or any record of deliberations toward a document to be named Memorandum Number 16 could be found. There is also no indication of why the subsequently promulgated Memorandum Number 17 was given that designation rather than 16.

[55] See *Doc 12*.

[56] It must correctly read '(CPA/REG/15 June 2004/11)'.

[57] See *Doc 3*.

Document 142
Coalition Provisional Authority Memorandum Number 17
CPA/MEM/26 June 2004/17

Registration Requirements for Private Security Companies (PSC)[58]

Pursuant to my authority as Administrator of the Coalition Provisional Authority (CPA), and under the laws and usages of war, and consistent with relevant U.N. Security Council resolutions, including Resolutions 1483, 1511 (2003) and 1546 (2004),

Recognizing that all Private Security Companies (PSC) need to be registered with the Ministry of Trade and regulated by the Ministry of Interior, and that various CPA orders and memoranda, and Iraqi law provide guidance for PSC operations (see Annex C),

Noting that a number of PSC and their employees are already operating in Iraq without the benefit of appropriate registration and authorization of the Ministry of Interior and Trade,

Desiring to establish a mechanism whereby all PSC will be registered, regulated and vetted and to update Iraqi law as it relates to PSC,

I hereby promulgate the following:

Section 1 Purpose and Definitions

1) This Memorandum provides guidance for PSC that intend to operate within Iraq. Annex A provides binding Rules for the Use of Force that must be adhered to by all PSC, their officers and employees. Annex B is a Code of Conduct that all PSC must follow.

a) 'Private Security Company' means a private business, properly registered with the Ministry of Interior (MOI) and Ministry of Trade (MOT) that seeks to gain commercial benefits and financial profit by providing security services to individuals, businesses and organizations, governmental or otherwise.

b) 'Weapons Card' means a card issued by the MOI under Section 6 of this Memorandum.

c) 'Business License' means a document issued by the MOT under Company Law No. 21 of 1997, as amended by CPA Order 64[59] that proves that the PSC has been validly registered to carry on business in Iraq.

d) 'Operating License' means a license issued by the MOI under this Memorandum, which permits PSC to operate in Iraq.

Section 2 Registration, Vetting and Licensing

1) PSC may not operate in Iraq without a:

a) Business License and an Operating License, or

b) Temporary Operating License.

Any PSC operating without the necessary Licenses will be in breach of Iraqi law and subject to prosecution.

2) In order to obtain a Business License PSC shall apply to the MOT for registration under the Company Law, No. 21 of 1997, as amended by CPA Order 64.

[58] The version of CPA Memorandum No 17 published in the *Official Gazette*, vol 45, no 3985 (July 2004), at 100, differs considerably from the signed version published on the CPA website. The text reproduced here is that of the more comprehensive version published on the website.

[59] See *Doc 87*.

3) PSC that have been granted or applied for a Business License may apply to the PSC Registration and Vetting Office of the Ministry of Interior for an Operating License.

4) An application for an Operating License must include the following information:

a) a copy of the PSC Business License or proof that an application for a Business License has been lodged;

b) the full names of all employees, company officers and directors, and proof of registration of the company, and if the PSC is registered in a State other than Iraq proof of registration of the company in its home State;

c) details of the work PSC will be carrying out in Iraq, including any relevant documentation (e.g. a copy of any contracts for services or statement of intent to hire the PSC, including details of number of employees and customers); and

d) details and serial numbers of all weapons that may be used by the PSC.

5) PSC, their officers and employees will be vetted by the MOI according to the criteria below to ensure that any criminal or hostile elements are identified and to prevent attempts by illegal organizations (e.g. criminal organizations, illegal militias) to legitimize their activities.

6) In order to comply with MOI vetting standards, employees of PSC must:

a) Be older than 20 years;

b) Be mentally and physically fit for duties;

c) Be willing to respect the law and all human rights and freedoms of all citizens of the country;

d) Pass a security/background check, that confirms:

i. compliance with the amended CPA Order Number 1 (De-Ba'athification of Iraqi Society);

ii. no prior felony convictions; and

iii. no history of involvement in terrorist activity; and

e) Receive operations and weapons training to the minimum standard set for the Facilities Protection Service.

7) For non-Iraqi employees, the MOI may accept a copy of a comparable certification from a foreign Governmental authority issued pursuant to its official rules and procedures to meet some or all of the requirements in Section 2(6), above.

8) Other reasonable vetting procedures and requirements may be added by the MOI to ensure necessary standards are met. In such case, new procedures and requirements shall be published no less than 60 days before they are to take effect.

Section 3 Bonds and Insurance

1) PSC must submit a minimum refundable bond of US$25,000 or the equivalent sum in Iraqi Dinars, to the MOI before commencing operations in Iraq and being granted an Operating License or Temporary Operating License. Additional bonds, to be determined by the MOI, may be required depending on the number of employees of the PSC. The amount of the bond will increase as the number of employees increases, in accordance with an internationally recognized pro-rata industry-wide scale to be determined by the MOI. This scale shall be published 30 days before any additional bond requirement [sic] are to take effect. Any changes in bonding requirements will be approved by the Minister of Interior, and published in writing no less than 60 days before institution.

2) Failure to provide information to the MOI as required by Section 7 may result in forfeiture of the bond lodged in accordance with Section 3(1) or part thereof. MOI shall

provide the PSC with written notice of any breaches and allow a one week grace period to come into compliance before any forfeiture of the bond or part thereof takes effect.

3) While the standards laid out in this Memorandum provide the minimum requirements, any breaches of Iraq or other applicable law by employees or companies may result in forfeiture of the bond by the MOI lodged in accordance with Section 3(1) or part thereof and may result in a review and revocation of the Operating License of the PSC. Where a PSC, or an employee of that PSC, breaches this Memorandum or any other law in force in Iraq, the MOI may declare the bond or any part thereof forfeit. Any such decision to declare the bond forfeit must be based on reasonable grounds and be proportional to the breach of the law initiating such action. The MOI will take into account actions taken by the PSC with respect to individual violations (e.g. termination, prompt and open coordination with law enforcement) in determining whether a PSC should forfeit its bond or any part thereof.

4) PSC must submit evidence that they have sufficient public liability insurance to cover possible claims against them for a reasonable amount to be advised and published by the MOI. If securing such insurance is not practicable the PSC will inform the MOI in writing and seek an exemption from this requirement.

5) Bonds will be refunded within 30 days if PSC ceases operation in Iraq unless there are reasonable grounds to believe that PSC have failed to comply with this Memorandum.

Section 4 Refusal, Suspension or Revocation of Licenses, and Provisional Licenses

1) The MOI will grant Temporary Operating Licenses pending completion of the licensing processes of the MOT and MOI. The minimum requirements for the grant of a Temporary license are:

a) Submission to MOI of proof that an application for a Business License has been lodged with the MOT; and
b) Submission to the MOI of an application for an Operating License, including any other requirements that the MOI may notify.

2) Operating Licenses may be suspended, revoked or refused in accordance with the following provisions:

a) The MOI may, at their sole reasonable discretion, refuse to grant an Operating License if the conditions of this Memorandum are not met. The reason for the decision shall be communicated to the applicant in writing. The applicant may reapply for an Operating License after taking remedial action with respect to the breaches identified by the MOI.
b) Where a PSC, or an employee of that PSC, breaches this Memorandum or any other law in force in Iraq, the MOI may suspend or revoke the Operating License. Any such decision to revoke or suspend an operating license must be based on reasonable grounds and be proportional to the breach of the law initiating such action. If the Operating License is revoked, the bond, or part thereof, lodged in accordance with Section 3(1) will be forfeited. The MOI will take into account actions taken by the PSC with respect to individual violations (e.g. termination, prompt and open coordination with law enforcement) in determining whether a PSC should forfeit its license as the result of such violations.
c) Where a PSC application for an Operating License is deficient in any way, the MOI may grant a Provisional Operating License for a specified period of time. The grant of an Operating License will be subject to the applicant demonstrating that they have remedied the deficiency (e.g., providing complete information to

allow background checks on all employees, or giving appropriate training to all employees).

3) Any Provisional or Temporary Operating License will be cancelled if:
   a) either of the applications for the Business and Operating License is denied or withdrawn; or
   b) on the grant by the MOI of a full Operating License.

4) Unless it has been affirmatively denied a Business License or Operating License, notwithstanding the provisions of this Memorandum, PSC may operate without a Business License, Operating License or Temporary Operating License until 31 August 2004 or such later date as determined by MOI, pending completion of the requirements of this Memorandum.

Section 5 Audit

PSC are liable to periodic audits by the MOI regarding their operations in Iraq. All audits will be carried out by an independent auditing firm engaged for this purpose by MOI. The purpose of MOI audits is to ensure that the standards set out in Section 2(6) above are being maintained. Financial audits may also be carried out by MOT.

Section 6 Weapons

1) Where an Operating License is granted, or the Minister of Interior accepts the certification or guarantee of a Diplomatic or Consular Mission under Section 10(5), the MOI shall issue Weapons Cards to those PSC employees who will bear arms as part of their duties. Such Weapons Card shall constitute a license to possess and use firearms. PSC must instruct employees to carry their Weapons Cards whenever carrying a weapon. All PSC employees must carry the relevant Weapons Cards when in possession of any PSC weapon. If a PSC's Temporary, Provisional or full Operating License, certification, or guarantee is revoked, all Weapons Cards issued to the employee of that PSC shall be returned to the MOI.

2) Where a Temporary License is granted, the MOI shall also issue Temporary Weapons Cards to those PSC employees who will bear arms as part of their duties. Such Temporary Weapons Cards shall constitute a license to possess and use firearms. PSC must instruct employees to carry their Temporary Weapons Cards whenever carrying a weapon. All PSC employees must carry the relevant Temporary Weapons Cards when in possession of any PSC weapon.

3) A PSC intending to import weapons into Iraq must obtain from the MOI a weapons import certificate. The PSC must provide details of all weapons and their serial numbers to MOI immediately upon importation.

4) The use of weapons by PSC shall be regulated as follows:
   a) PSC shall notify the MOI of details and serial numbers of all weapons in its possession.
   b) PSC will notify the MOI of any changes in the PSC's weapons inventory within one (1) month of such changes.
   c) PSC shall store all weapons and ammunition in a secure armory or other secure facility.
   d) PSC shall ensure that only employees carrying Weapons Cards may carry weapons and only when such employees are on official duty. PSC shall also ensure that its employees return all PSC weapons to the armory or other secure facility, as the case may be, when no longer on duty. This provision does not

restrict the right of PSC employees to carry weapons while not on duty under the provisions of other Iraqi laws.

e) PSC may only own and its employees may only use categories of weapons allowed by CPA Order Number 3 (Revised) (Amended) Weapons Control,[60] other [sic] applicable Iraqi law.

f) Under no circumstance may privately owned weapons be used for PSC duties.

Section 7 Provision of Further Information

On request, PSC must provide the following information to the MOI every six (6) months: financial and employment records, contract status, weapons data, and any other data the MOI may advise they require. Failure to comply may result in revocation of the PSC Operating License. MOI shall provide the PSC with a written notice of any failure to comply with this provision and a one week grace period to comply before any revocation of an Operating License.

Section 8 Oversight Committee

MOI will establish an independent PSC Oversight Committee that will have general inspection and auditing responsibility (consistent with the provisions of CPA Order 57, Iraqi Inspectors General[61]) over the implementation of this Memorandum. Such oversight shall include assessing enforcement of the standards set forth in this Memorandum as well as equitable and non-discriminatory treatment of PSC. The Minister will appoint the members of the Committee, which shall include the Inspector General of MOI, who shall be the only MOI representative on the committee, a member of the Judiciary and a representative of the MOT. The PSC Oversight Committee will report annually to the Minister on the implementation of this Memorandum.

Section 9 Limitations and Responsibilities of Private Security Companies

1) The primary role of PSC is deterrence. No PSC or PSC employee may conduct any law enforcement functions.

2) A licensed PSC shall be responsible for the actions of its employees. PSC officers and employees may be held liable under applicable criminal and civil legal codes, including the Iraqi Penal Code Law Number 111 of 1969 as amended, the Iraqi Weapons Code of 1992 as amended, and the CPA Order Number 3 Weapons Control, except as otherwise provided by law.

3) PSC are subject to, and must comply with all applicable criminal, administrative, commercial and civil laws and regulations, except as otherwise provided by law.

4) PSC must conduct operations in accordance with the provisions of the Rules for the Use of Force in Annex A and the MOI PSC Code of Conduct in Annex B.

Section 10 Implementation and Review

1) Nothing in this Memorandum is intended to prevent PSC from conducting operations consistent with and as permitted by the Iraqi Law, including those laws in Annex C.

2) Nothing in this Memorandum is intended to limit or abridge relevant privileges or immunities provided by Iraqi law or applicable international agreements.

[60] See *Doc 17*.
[61] See *Doc 80*.

3) The MOI may issue administrative directions in connection with the implementation of this Memorandum and amend the Annexes to this Memorandum.

4) A person who is adversely affected by a decision of the MOI made pursuant to this Order may apply in writing to the Minister of Interior for a review of the decision by the Minister of Interior. Within seven (7) days of receipt of the application, the Minister of Interior shall review the decision and notify the applicant of the determination in writing at the last provided address of the applicant.

5) With respect to non-Iraqi legal entities or individuals not normally resident in Iraq that provide security services to Diplomatic and Consular Missions and their personnel, or to the official humanitarian, reconstruction or development projects in Iraq funded by such missions, the Diplomatic and Consular Missions may intervene on behalf of the PSC applying for registration and any other requirements and matters under this Order. Where approved by the Minister of Interior, the certification or guarantee of the relevant Mission may be accepted in satisfaction of the requirements of this Order in lieu of a direct submission by the PSC, save that Section 6(1) shall apply. The Minister of Interior may revoke its acceptance of such certification or guarantee where the PSC in question breaches this memorandum or any other law in force in Iraq. Any decision to revoke must be based on reasonable grounds and be proportional to the breach of the law initiating such action. The Minister will take into account actions taken by the PSC with respect to individual violations (e.g. termination, prompt and open coordination with law enforcement) in determining whether its acceptance should be revoked as a result of such violations.

Section 11 Entry into Force

This Memorandum shall enter into force on date of signature [26 June 2004].

ANNEX A: USE OF FORCE

RULES FOR THE USE OF FORCE BY CONTRACTORS IN IRAQ

NOTHING IN THESE RULES LIMITS YOUR INHERENT RIGHT TO TAKE ACTION NECESSARY TO DEFEND YOURSELF.

1. **CONTRACTED SECURITY FORCES:** Cooperate with Coalition, Multi-national and Iraqi Security Forces and comply with theater force protection policies. Do not avoid or run Coalition, Multi-national or Iraqi Security Force checkpoints. If authorized to carry weapons, do not aim them at Coalition, Multi-national or Iraqi Security Forces.
2. **USE OF DEADLY FORCE:** Deadly force is that force which one reasonably believes will cause death or serious bodily harm. You may use NECESSARY FORCE, up to and including deadly force, against persons in the following circumstances:
   a. In self-defense.
   b. In defense of persons as specified in your contract.
   c. To prevent life threatening offenses against civilians.
3. **GRADUATED FORCE:** You should use graduated force where possible. The following are some techniques you can use if their use will not unnecessarily endanger you or others.
   a. SHOUT; verbal warnings to HALT.
   b. SHOVE; physically restrain, block access, or detain.

c. SHOW; your weapon and demonstrate intent to use it.
d. SHOOT; to remove the threat only where necessary.

4. **IF YOU MUST FIRE YOUR WEAPON:**
(1) Fire only aimed shots.
(2) Fire with due regard for the safety of innocent bystanders.
(3) Immediately report incident and request assistance.

5. **CIVILIANS:** Treat Civilians with Dignity and Respect.
a. Make every effort to avoid civilian casualties.
b. You may stop, detain, search, and disarm civilian persons if required for your safety or if specified in your contract.
c. Civilians will be treated humanely.
d. Detained civilians will be turned over to the Iraqi Police or Coalition or Multinational Forces as soon as possible.

6. **WEAPONS POSSESSION AND USE:** Possession and use of weapons must be authorized by the Ministry of Interior and must be specified in your contract.
a. You must carry proof of weapons authorization.
b. You will maintain a current weapons training record.
c. You may not join Coalition or Multi-national Forces in combat operations except in self-defense or in defense of persons as specified in your contracts.
d. You must follow Coalition or Multi-national Force weapons condition rules for loading and clearing.

ANNEX B: CODE OF CONDUCT FOR PRIVATE SECURITY COMPANIES OPERATING IN IRAQ

Private Security Company Code of Conduct for Operations in Iraq

As a duly registered and vetted Private Security Company, the following pledge is made:

To conduct operations professionally with honesty, sincerity, integrity, fidelity, morality and good conscience in all dealings with clients.

To preserve forever clients' confidence under any and all circumstances consistent with law and deal justly, and impartially with each situation with each individual, irrespective of social, political, racial, ethnic, or religious considerations, economic status, or physical characteristics.

To conduct all operations within the bounds of legality, morality, and professional ethics.

To counsel clients against any illegal or unethical course of action.

To explain to the full satisfaction of clients all applicable fees and charges and to render accurate, factual and timely reports.

To support to the best of ability the professionalism of Private Security Companies operating in Iraq; to contribute to better community relations; through work and deed to elevate the status of the Private Security Company profession.

To ensure that all employees adhere to this code of conduct.

ANNEX C: REFERENCES

- Coalition Provisional Authority Order 3 (Revised) (Amended), Weapons Control

- Coalition Provisional Authority Memorandum 5, Implementation of Weapons Control Order No. 3[62]
- Coalition Provisional Authority Memorandum 5A, Memo 5 Annex A[63]
- Coalition Provisional Authority Order 27, Establishment of the Facilities Protection Service[64]
- Coalition Provisional Authority Order 54, Trade Liberalization Policy with Annex A[65]
- Coalition Provisional Authority Order 64, Amendment to the Company Law Number 21 of 1997
- Coalition Provisional Authority Order 91, Regulation of Armed Forces and Militias within Iraq[66]

[62] See *Doc 130.*
[63] See *Doc 130.*
[64] See *Doc 48.*
[65] See *Docs 76, 77.*
[66] See *Doc 115.*

4. Public Notices

Document 143
Creation of Iraqi Central Bank Development Fund for Iraq
19 May 2003

Pursuant to the authority vested in me by the President of the United States, and as Administrator of the Coalition Provisional Authority responsible for the temporary governance of Iraq, I am establishing, in the Central Bank of Iraq, a Development Fund for Iraq.

The Coalition Provisional Authority administers the Development Fund for Iraq for and on behalf of the Iraqi people. The Development Fund for Iraq will be managed and used openly and publicly, will include an international advisory and monitoring board, and will be audited by independent public accountants approved by such board.

All proceeds from the sale for export, barter, and trade of State- or regime-owned oil and petroleum products from Iraq; assets of Iraq that may be returned from other nations; and other assets of Iraq will be deposited into the Development Fund for Iraq. Sums in the Development Fund for Iraq shall be disbursed at the direction of the Coalition Provisional Authority, in consultation with the Iraqi interim administration, once it is formed, and used only for purposes benefiting the people of Iraq, as determined by the Coalition Provisional Authority.

Document 144
Public Incitement to Violence and Disorder
5 June 2003

The Administrator of the Coalition Provisional Authority (CPA) hereby advises all citizens, residents of, and visitors to Iraq of the following security measure.

Any person making a prohibited pronouncement in a public place or distributing or attempting to distribute any prohibited material in whatever form, will be subject to immediate detention by CPA security forces and held as a security internee under the Fourth Geneva Convention of 1949.

Prohibited pronouncements and material are pronouncements and material that:

a) incite violence against any individual or group, including racial, ethnic or religious groups and women;
b) incite civil disorder, rioting or damage to property;
c) incite violence against Coalition Forces or CPA personnel;
d) advocate alterations to Iraq's borders by violent means;
e) advocate the return to power of the Iraqi Ba'ath Party or make statements that purport to be on behalf of the Iraqi Ba'ath Party.

These prohibitions are not designed to exclude legitimate debate and criticism, and in particular are not meant to prohibit expression of dissatisfaction with political processes as they emerge. Rather, they are designed to discourage public pronouncements and the distribution of materials that could incite violence or destabilize the sensitive environment that currently exists in Iraq.[1]

Document 145
Organization in the Workplace

6 June 2003

The Administrator of the Coalition Provisional Authority (CPA) hereby advises all citizens, residents of, and temporary workers in Iraq of the following information concerning organizations in the workplace.

To the extent consistent with its obligation to maintain security and civil order, the Coalition Provisional Authority respects Iraqi laws. This extends to Iraqi labor laws prescribing the conditions under which employees of government instrumentalities and enterprises continue to work under the CPA on behalf of the people of Iraq. Although Iraqi labor [sic] permits these employees to elect their representatives, the law does not authorize employee elections of Directors or Directing Staff of government instrumentalities and enterprises.

Therefore, the CPA will not recognize the election of Directors, or otherwise allow interference with managerial prerogatives of the Directing Staff of government instrumentalities and enterprises. The CPA will authorize appropriate changes in government Directing Staffs when warranted by reason of poor performance, corruption, security requirements, or as part of the De-Baathification process.

The form of industrial and labor relations ultimately will be a matter for the Iraqi people and the future Iraqi government to decide.

[1] The Notice was attached to a 'Memorandum for Commander, Coalition Forces' concerning the 'Implementation of Public Notice Regarding Incitement to Violence' which was signed by Ambassador Bremer and dated 5 June 2003. The Memorandum reads: 'Operation Iraqi Freedom was fought to liberate the Iraqi people from the brutal regime of Saddam Hussein. Since the collapse of the regime, Iraqis across the country are expressing their freedom in numerous ways. Freedoms of speech and expression were among the freedoms most repressively suppressed under Saddam Hussein's dictatorship, and it is a central Coalition goal to ensure that the Iraqi people are free to think, speak, and worship as they please.

The enclosed 'Notice Regarding Public Incitement to Violence and Disorder' is clearly authorized by the law of occupation, which gives the occupying power significant discretion to control the media, maintain public order, and ensure the security of the occupying power and the people in occupied territories. It is also consistent with relevant provisions of United Nations Security Council Resolution 1483 (2003). The law of occupation recognizes the central role that the media and public pronouncements play in the context of military operations and the effective administration of occupied territory, and accords occupying powers broad authority in this area as a result.

Notwithstanding this wide-ranging authority, the Notice is not intended to preclude legitimate debate and criticism. One of the objectives of the CPA is to promote a free and responsible Iraqi media, and our actions must reflect this, insofar as current circumstances permit. Accordingly, I request that the Notice be implemented consistent with the following guidelines:

- Speech that promotes violence or public disturbance undermines the public law and order that are required for the responsible exercise of freedom. Public comments inciting riots, attacks, or other violence therefore warrant appropriate action. This extends to organized campaigns to interfere with Coalition efforts to maintain order and security for the Iraqi people.
- For this reason, consistent Resolution 1483 and its responsibilities as an occupying power, the CPA has issued a public notice regarding public incitement to violence and disorder.
- The intention of the order is to discourage public pronouncements and the distribution of materials that incite violence and thereby threaten the safety and well-being of Iraqi citizens or Coalition personnel. It is especially intended to [page missing].'

Document 146
Trade Liberalization Policy
7 June 2003

The Administrator of the Coalition Provisional Authority (CPA) hereby advises all citizens, residents of, and visitors to Iraq of the following.

United Nations Security Council Resolution 1483 ended nearly 13 years of sanctions on Iraq. International trade now can play a central role in Iraq's economic recovery and its development of a free market economy. As a first step, the CPA and the Ministry of Trade declare a suspension of tariffs and other trade restrictions in Iraq through the end of this year. During this time, the CPA will not collect any customs duties, import taxes, licensing fees or other surcharges for goods entering and leaving Iraqi ports of entry – including all eleven land border points, two airports and two sea ports – except with respect to goods listed in the annex to this Notice.[2] The goods that are exempt from this suspension make up less than five percent of Iraq's trade; the exemption is needed to protect food supplies and control the possible export of looted items.

The CPA continues to work with Iraqi officials from all concerned Iraqi institutions as well as the private sector to 1) create the conditions required for the Iraqi people to rebuild their country expeditiously; 2) promote the legal and regulatory environment needed to support a transparent, market-oriented economy; 3) facilitate foreign direct investment and services in Iraq; and 4) enhance Iraq's stature in the global trading community through participation in international commercial organizations, conventions and agreements.

Document 147
Administrative Procedures for Establishing Trading Agencies
9 June 2003

The Administrator of the Coalition Provisional Authority (CPA) hereby advises all citizens, residents of, and visitors to Iraq of the following administrative measure.

The Iraqi Companies Code allows Iraqis to establish direct trading agencies with international trading companies. However, the former Iraqi regime made it difficult for honest Iraqi business people to use this authority. The former regime established extensive administrative procedures, and applied these procedures in a manner that extorted and exploited Iraqi business people who did not support the regime.

The CPA recognizes and supports the law permitting Iraqis to establish direct trading agencies with international trading companies.[3] However, the CPA has suspended the former Iraqi regime's administrative procedures regarding this law.

Iraqi business people are now free to negotiate directing [sic] trade relationships with international trading companies, without the administrative constraints imposed by the former regime.

[2] The Annex has been omitted. See the Annex to CPA Order No 12 *[Doc 28]*.
[3] The Law in question was Law No. 51 of 2000.

Document 148
Towards a Responsible Iraqi Media
10 June 2003

The Administrator of the Coalition Provisional Authority (CPA) hereby advises all citizens, residents of, and temporary workers in Iraq that he has today signed a CPA order concerning media activity in Iraq.[4]

The CPA recognizes the importance of providing accurate information to the Iraqi people, and is committed to establishing an environment in which responsible media organizations will flourish. The free exchange of information is essential to the emergence of democracy in Iraq. Disseminating material that incites violence, however, poses a direct threat to personal freedoms, and is therefore banned under the terms of this order, as it is in any civilized society. Equally, advocating the return to power of the repressive and criminal Ba'athist regime would undermine civil order and the freedom from fear of political repression, both of which are necessary for the development of a free and democratic Iraq. Thus, the CPA is issuing an Order that prohibits Iraqi media organizations from broadcasting or publishing material that would seriously undermine security and civil order in Iraq. The types of material to which the Order applies are identical to the prohibited pronouncements and materials described in the CPA's recent Public Notice regarding Public Incitement to Violence and Disorder.

If a media organization is found to have violated the Order, the Administrator may withdraw the license, close the operation, confiscate the property and seal the premises of any Iraqi media organization that violates the Order. Violators of the Order also face up to one year in confinement and a USD 1,000 fine. Finally, the Order establishes a means by which media organizations may appeal to the administrator and seek reversal of actions taken against them under the Order.

Document 149
The Council for International Coordination
18 June 2003

The Administrator of the Coalition Provisional Authority (CPA) for Iraq has decided that the growing magnitude and importance of contributions from the international community for the relief, recovery and development of Iraq calls for the establishment [of] a Council for International Coordination, as part of the CPA. This Council will be chaired by professor Marek Belka, former Deputy Prime Minister of Poland. Andrew Goledzinowski, a senior foreign affairs official from Australia, will be vice chair.

The Administrator will appoint additional representatives to the Council from those countries that want to contribute expertise or other resources to the relief, recovery and development of Iraq and that support the territorial integrity of Iraq and a representative government for the Iraqi people that does not possess weapons of mass destruction, does not support terrorism, and seeks peace with its neighbors.

[4] See CPA Order No 14 *[Doc 32]*.

The Council will be the CPA's focal point and coordinating body for international assistance in the relief, recovery and development of Iraq. The Council will encourage the international community to provide funds and other forms of assistance to Iraq and will coordinate international assistance provided by States, non-governmental organizations and international organizations. In carrying out its responsibilities, the Council will work closely with the UN Special Representative and his designees and other organizations involved in the relief, recovery and development efforts.

Document 150
The Creation of a Central Criminal Court of Iraq and Adjustments to the Criminal Procedure Code

18 June 2003

The Administrator of the Coalition Provisional Authority (CPA) hereby advises all citizens, residents of, and visitors to Iraq of the following security measure.

The CPA has taken steps to meet the urgent security needs of the people of Iraq and Coalition Forces by creating a Central Criminal Court of Iraq. This court will apply and operate under Iraqi law, as amended to ensure fundamental fairness and due process for accused persons, and will be modeled on the current Iraqi court system. The Central Criminal Court will consist of an Investigative Court, a Trial Court and an Appeal Court, with the right of further appeal to the Iraqi Court of Cassation. The judges and prosecutors will be locally selected Iraqis.

The Court will deal with serious offenses that most directly threaten the security and civil order in Iraq. This interim measure will address the immediate need for a reliable and fair system of justice. The CPA will continue to assist in restoring the capability of the Iraqi court system, as it recovers from years of Iraqi Ba'ath Party abuse and perversion.

In tandem with this measure, the CPA has modified the Criminal Procedure Code to accord the people of Iraq fundamental due process protections and shield them from human rights violations. The CPA has also introduced provisions ensuring that persons detained by Coalition Forces are treated in accordance with international law and receive prompt justice before Iraqi courts.

Document 151
Managing Financial Resources for Iraq

18 June 2003

The Administrator of the Coalition Provisional Authority (CPA) hereby advises all citizens, residents of, and visitors to Iraq that the CPA has promulgated a regulation designed to ensure that financial resources available for relief and recovery activities in Iraq are managed transparently on behalf of, and for the benefit of the Iraqi people. The regulation establishes the CPA Program Review Board, which will identify, integrate, and prioritize funding requirements for relief and recovery operations in Iraq, and develop funding plans that propose allocations of resources available to meet those requirements. The PRB will promote the CPA's objective of actively involving Iraqis in the financial planning process, and transferring to the Iraqi interim administration the responsibility for budgeting Iraq's financial resources.

Composed of members representing Iraq's Ministry of Finance, the International Monetary Fund, the World Bank, the U.N. Special Representative of the Secretary General for Iraq, and the International Advisory and Monitoring Board, as well as officials of the CPA, Coalition Forces, the United Kingdom and Australia, the PRB is committed to stewarding available resources in a manner that will ensure the most effective use of funds appropriated by the U.S. Congress, vested and seized Iraqi property, and the Development Fund for Iraq. The regulation prescribes procedures whereby the Development Fund for Iraq and other resources shall be used in a transparent manner to meet the humanitarian needs of the Iraqi people and to further the recovery of Iraq, in accordance with all applicable laws and regulations, as well as the CPA's financial management responsibilities under U.N. Security Council Resolution 1483 (2003).

Document 152
Safeguarding of Iraq's Borders

26 June 2003

The Administrator of the Coalition Provisional Authority (CPA) hereby advises all citizens, residents of, and visitors to Iraq that the CPA has issued an Order establishing border policies that control entry into and departures from Iraq.[5] The policies normalize travel to and from Iraq, consistent with the CPA's obligation to ensure security and civil order throughout the country.

Under the Order, individuals must have a valid Iraqi passport or obtain a travel permit before entering Iraq, unless they are citizens of Iraq, were born in Iraq, or are part of the CPA, Coalition Forces, Coalition governments or CPA contractors. Any passport that has expired within the last four years will be considered valid until December 31, 2003. The Order suspends the former regime's attempt to cancel 'N' series passports in 2003, and invalidates any passport issued after March 19, 2003 that does not bear a CPA stamp. The 'H' series passports remain valid according to their stated terms. Certain individuals may be denied entry into Iraq in order to preserve public security and safety, including persons who are suffering from serious communicable disease, cannot support themselves, or are associated with criminal activity, including terrorism.

All persons have the right to exit from Iraq if they possess necessary travel documents, unless they are senior members of the Ba'ath Party; are suspected of serious crimes; are linked to terrorist organizations or acts, or are suspected of involvement with weapons of mass destruction.

[5] See CPA Order No 16 *[Doc 34]*.

Document 153
The Status of Coalition, Foreign Liaison and Contractor Personnel
26 June 2003

The Administrator of the Coalition Provisional Authority (CPA) hereby advises all citizens, residents of, and visitors to Iraq of the status of Coalition, Foreign Liaison and contractor personnel.

In accordance with international law, the CPA, Coalition Forces and the military and civilian personnel accompanying them, are not subject to local law or the jurisdiction of local courts. With regard to criminal, civil, administrative or other legal process, they will remain subject to the exclusive jurisdiction of the State contributing them to the Coalition. A mechanism exists for this immunity and jurisdiction to be waived by the State contributing the personnel to the Coalition at their discretion.

Foreign Liaison Missions and their personnel enjoy immunity from Iraqi legal proceedings, but are subject to the CPA's jurisdiction. Coalition contractors who are not normally resident in Iraq may be subject to the CPA's or Iraq's jurisdiction, as authorized by the Administrator. Additionally, some of the administrative regulations regarding contractors will not apply to their contracts with the Coalition.

The immunities provided will not prevent legal proceedings against Coalition personnel for unlawful acts they may commit. It simply ensures that such proceedings will be undertaken in accordance with the laws of the State that contributed the personnel to the Coalition. Furthermore, the immunity will only apply to acts or omissions during the authority of the CPA within Iraq.

Document 154
The Prohibition under Iraqi Law of Vehicles with Tinted Windows
27 June 2003

The Administrator of the Coalition Provisional Authority (CPA) hereby advises all citizens, residents of, and visitors to Iraq of the following security measure.

Iraqi law prohibits the use of tinted windows and curtains in vehicles. The CPA has not suspended this law and intends to enforce it, due to security threats that have emerged in relation to persons attempting to conceal criminal activity and weapons in vehicles with tinted windows.

All vehicles with tinted windows must have the tinting removed or tinted windows replaced by 20 July 2003. No vehicle is permitted to have window curtains and these should be removed immediately. Any vehicle found on the road after 20 July 2003 with tinted windows will be impounded. Owners of vehicles impounded will be issued receipts and will be permitted to reclaim their vehicle upon production of a signed quotation indicating arrangements for the removal of the tinted windows.

Details of vehicles and owners of released vehicles will be recorded and if vehicles are impounded a second time they will be held for the duration of the CPA administration.

This prohibition does not apply to Coalition vehicles and other official vehicles authorized by the Coalition to have tinted windows.[6]

Document 155
Internal Administrative Borders
4 December 2003[7]

The Administrator of the Coalition Provisional Authority (CPA) hereby advises all citizens, residents of, and visitors to Iraq of the following.

No person or body, including the CPA, Coalition Forces, the Governing Council, the Ministers, Directors General, Governors, or Provincial or Local Councils, may alter the internal borders, boundaries, or similar administrative geographical divisions of Iraq, and any attempt to do so, including but not limited to, by way of decree, order, proclamation, or public statement, is null and void and of no legal effect. Such adjustments may only be made by the future internationally recognized, representative government of Iraq.

Any attempt by any person, group or organization to exercise authority over any geographical area of Iraq pursuant to any such decree, order, proclamation, or public statement will not be permitted.

L. Paul Bremer III
Administrator

Document 156
Increased Sentences for Persons Convicted of Crimes after Receiving Amnesty
19 December 2003

The Administrator of the Coalition Provisional Authority (CPA) hereby advises all citizens, residents of, and visitors to Iraq of the following.

Under Iraqi law, any person who was released from prison pursuant to Revolutionary Command Council Resolution No. 225, dated October 20, 2002,[8] and is thereafter convicted of another crime may be sentenced using rules that allow stiffer punishments based on aggravating circumstances. These rules permit judges to impose significantly longer sentences than are otherwise authorized for the particular offense. For example, if

[6] The Public Notice bears the signature of 'L. Paul Bremer, Administrator, Coalition Provisional Authority' and is dated 25 June 2003. In the Official Gazette, vol 44, no 3978 (17 August 2003), at 93, the Public Notice is listed as 'CPA/PUB NOT/27 June 2003/03'.

[7] This Public Notice was prepared by the CPA Office of the General Counsel in response to the Iraqi Minister of the Interior's Statement No 441 of 12 October 2003 which purported to remove the Al Nakheib area from Al Anbar province and attach it to Karbala province. The Public Notice was never published on the CPA's website and it is unclear whether it was ever formally approved by Ambassador Bremer.

[8] Revolutionary Command Council Resolution No 225 concerned the 'general, comprehensive and final amnesty for Iraqi prisoners (civilian and military) inside and outside Iraq'.

the penalty for a crime is imprisonment for a term of years, a judge may impose a sentence that is greater than the maximum limit, provided that the increase in the sentence does not exceed half the maximum limit (up to 25 years total).

This law allowing harsher punishments continues in force and judges should consider it when sentencing persons who were granted amnesty under Resolution No. 225. Persons who were released under that Resolution should be aware that they will be subject to the severest sentences authorized by law if they commit further crimes.[9]

Document 157

Increased Sentences for Persons Convicted of Weapons Violations under Amended Revised CPA Order 3 after Having Been Conditionally Released from Internment

31 December 2003

The Administrator of the Coalition Provisional Authority (CPA) hereby advises all citizens, residents of, and visitors to Iraq of the following:

Any person who was conditionally released from internment by Coalition Forces and is thereafter convicted of any violation of Revised Amended CPA Order 3,[10] shall be sentenced using rules that allow greater punishment based on aggravating circumstances. These rules permit judges to impose significantly longer sentences than otherwise authorized for the particular offense.

Persons conditionally released from internment should be aware that they will be subject to the severest sentences allowed by law if they commit crimes subsequent to their conditional release.[11]

[9] The Public Notice bears the signature of 'L. Paul Bremer III, Administrator' but no date.
[10] See *Doc 17*.
[11] The Public Notice bears the signature of 'L. Paul Bremer III, Administrator' but no date.

5. Other CPA and CPA-Related Documents

Document 158
Organizational Chart of the Post-War Planning for Iraq
15 October 2002

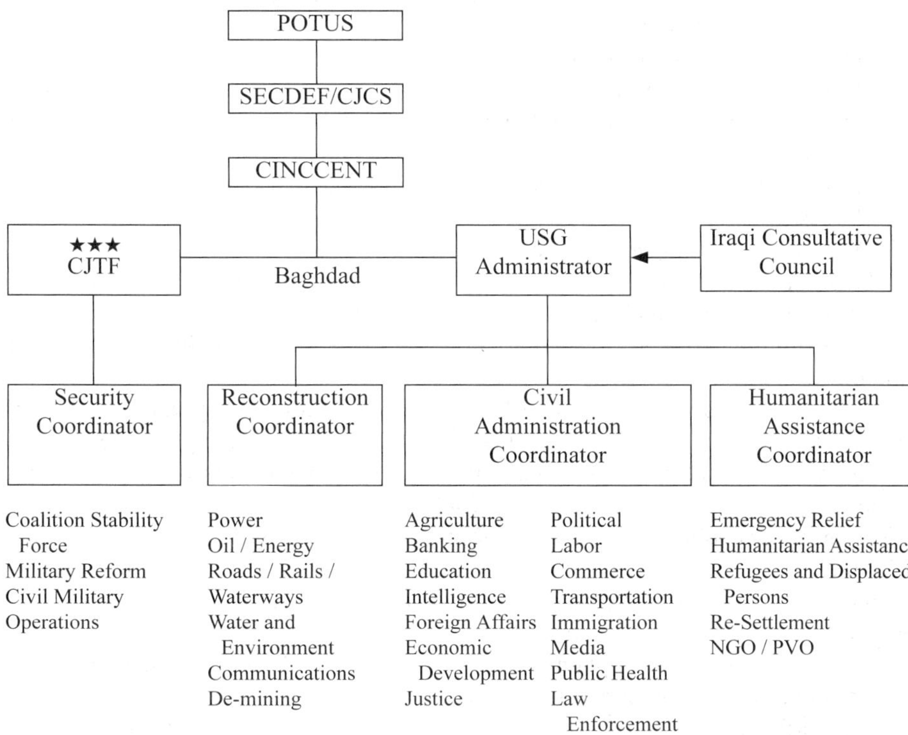

Document 159
Draft NSPD on Post-War Planning Office
7 January 2003[1]

If U.S. armed forces occupy Iraq, we will become responsible in the immediate aftermath of the occupation, for the governance of the country and the welfare of its population. The

[1] The Draft NSPD on Post-war Planning Office was sent on 9 January 2003 from the Under Secretary of Defense for Policy, Douglas J. Feith, to Secretary of Defense Rumsfeld. The cover note, dated 8 January 2003, reads as follows: 'Steve Hadly [Deputy National Security Adviser] and I think that the best way to ensure interagency cooperation on the DoD postwar planning office might be to have an NSPD directing the other agencies to provide detailees. We have provided the attached draft NSPD to the NSC staff, where it is now being reworked.'

The Draft NSPD seems to be largely identical with NSPD 24 which was signed by President Bush on 20 January 2003. NSPD 24 remains classified but has been summarized and paraphrased as follows:

'• If the United States liberates Iraq, it will want to meet the humanitarian, reconstruction, and administration challenges. Immediate responsibility will fall on CENTCOM, but overall success will require a national effort.

immediate responsibility will fall on U.S. Central Command – overall success, however, will require a national effort.

To support this effort, the Department of Defense will establish a Post-war Planning Office. The planning office will be responsible for conducting execution-level planning across the spectrum of issues that the USG would face with respect to the post-war governance of Iraq, including:

– Maintaining the internal security and territorial integrity of Iraq.
– Assisting with humanitarian relief.
– Dismantling weapons of mass destruction.
– Defeating and exploiting terrorist networks.
– Protecting energy supplies and infrastructure.
– Facilitating the country's economic reconstruction.
– Reshaping the Iraqi military by establishing non-aggressive, civilian controlled armed forces.
– Supporting the transition to Iraqi-led authority over time.

The office will draw on the interagency work that has already been accomplished in this regard, and will maintain close liaison with the groups already active. It will receive policy guidance from the Executive Steering Group, the Deputies Committee and the Principals Committee.

The office will build links to the Free Iraqi opposition, the specialized UN agencies and non-governmental organizations that can play a role in meeting the needs of the Iraqi people, and to counterpart planning offices in the governments of coalition countries. Under the policy guidance of the ESG, DC and PC, it will invite representatives of the governments of coalition countries to participate in its efforts.

In the event of a U.S. occupation of Iraq, the planning office would deploy to Iraq to form the nucleus of the administrative apparatus that would assist the authorities installed by the USG to exercise power in Iraq.

To make full use of all the planning that has occurred and is continuing to be done within the USG and to draw on expertise located throughout the government for any additional planning efforts, the planning office will require the full-time services of detailees from across the interagency.

- The Defense Department shall establish a Postwar Planning Office to conduct detailed planning on such issues as:
  - Humanitarian relief
  - Dismantling WMD
  - Defeating and exploiting terrorist networks
  - Protecting natural resources
  - Reconstruction
  - Key civilian services, such as food, water, electricity, and health care
  - Reshaping the Iraqi military and other security institutions
  - Supporting the transition to Iraqi-led authority over time
- The Planning Office will draw on the existing interagency work. It will receive policy guidance and direction from the Executive Steering Group, the Deputies Committee, and the Principals Committee, as appropriate.
- The Planning Office will build links to United Nations, nongovernmental organizations, and Free Iraqi forces. It will invite coalition partners to participate in its efforts.
- The Planning Office shall be deployed to Iraq to form the nucleus of the administrative apparatus that will assist in administering Iraq for a limited period of time.
- The Planning Office will require the full-time services of employees of a number of federal departments and agencies. The relevant agencies shall provide such employees as detailees to the Planning Office' (Feith, *War and Decision: Inside the Pentagon at the Dawn of the War on Terrorism* (2008), at 616-617).

The following departments and agencies should respond immediately to requests by the Department of Defense to supply one or more detailees to work full time with the planning cell:

- State (including AID)
- Treasury and Commerce
- Energy
- CIA (and other intelligence agencies)
- Agriculture
- Education
- Justice
- OMB

The detailees will provide substantive expertise and should be sufficiently senior (SES level – senior O-6 to O-7 in case of military) to coordinate issues throughout their agencies when required.

This effort is of the highest priority and time-sensitivity, and will require the wholehearted support of your department or agency.

Document 160
Organizational Chart, US Department of Defense, Office of Reconstruction and Humanitarian Assistance

February 2003[2]

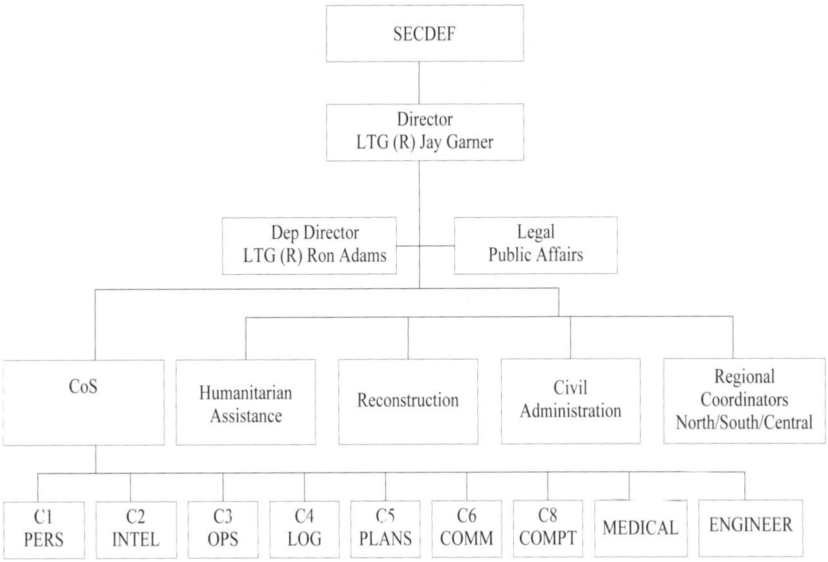

[2] The three pillars Humanitarian Assistance, Reconstruction and Civil Administration were mainly staffed with civilian personnel from the US State Department, USAID and the US Treasury. The Chief of Staff and the Coalition support staff (C-Staff) were made up of mostly active military personnel with colonels heading up each cell. See Gary Minor, Financing the Fight – From The Front (2004) 38/1 *The Air Force Comptroller* 4-8 at 4.

Document 161
Background Briefing on Reconstruction and Humanitarian Assistance in Post-War Iraq
11 March 2003

Staff: This is going to be a background briefing on the Office of Reconstruction and Humanitarian Assistance. [...]

Senior Defense Official:[3] [...] On the – about the 20th of January, the president signed a directive that established our office, and it was to deal with the post-Saddam conditions in Iraq. And we began putting a group together from the interagencies. DOD was given the responsibility for putting the office together, and that's why the organization ended up here in this building. We started out very slowly. The first week we only had three or four people. And as these things occur, it began building, and now we have close to 200 people from the military and from the interagency process. [...].

Our goal from day one has been to put together as solid set of plans that we could implement with a goal of going into country, implementing those plans, staying as long as necessary to be able to stand up a government in Iraq and get out as fast as we can. And our goal is to turn Iraq over to the Iraqi people, but with a government that expresses the free will of the people of Iraq. We intend to immediately start turning some things over, and every day, we'll turn over more things. I believe that's our plan. [...].

[Hands out the ORHA Organizational Chart reproduced below, *Doc 162*].

Let me walk you through the three boxes.

The first one is a reconstruction coordinator. And what you see listed under there are the functions that he's going to be most involved with. And the reconstruction coordinator is a very experienced U.S.AID official who, after he gets in country, he will initially stand up all the U.S.AID functions in country – done a lot of this; very experienced.

The civil administrator – under him you see all the functions that he's responsible for. He is a DOD official – has a great deal of experience also. [...].

The humanitarian assistance coordinator is a former ambassador. Excellent, excellent man. [...].

So what you see in those three boxes are the functions that have to be accomplished in country. Now each one of those is almost a vertical stovepipe, and what we needed was something that horizontally allowed these vertical stovepipes to work. So my friend here put together an operations group, and that operations group is responsible for the logistical functions, the operational functions, the staffing, transportation, all the things it takes to make an organization move.

Now below that you see three other boxes, and those are three coordinators. Because Iraq is so large, what we're going to have to do is have coordinators in the country, and so we have a coordinator for the northern part, and you have under him a core staff of about 12 people. And then we'll have the same thing in the South. And in the central [sic], we'll have a coordinator who – about 80 percent of their time will be spent on just the city of Baghdad.

[3] The Senior Defence Official, it is assumed, was the ORHA Director, Lt Gen (Ret) Jay M. Garner. The Other Senior Defence Official was the ORHA's Chief of Staff, Lt Gen (Ret) Jerry [Jared L.] Bates. See Jay Garner, Iraq Revisited, in: Brian M. De Toy (ed.), *Turning Victory Into Success: Military Operations After the Campaign* (2004), 253-273 at 263.

Each one of them will have a small staff, and what we're trying to do is we're working now to hire and enlist free Iraqis, from the United States, from Britain, from democratic European countries, that represent the provinces, each of the 17 provinces and Baghdad, that we can use to go down to the provinces and form groups from the people of each one of those provinces that begin to nominate to us things that they – that need to be done in terms of reconstruction, in terms of humanitarian aid.

Now that process – I had great hopes for that process, but that's not going to – it'll happen, but it's not going as fast as I wanted. We've hired several free Iraqis, but we need to hire over a hundred, and we haven't approached that number yet.

We're putting them under contract, and they are for a short period of time, somewhere between 90 and, at the most, 180 days.

What we're doing is we're – the reason we're bringing them in is because they have lived in a democratic country now. They understand the democratic process. And as we use them to facilitate what's going on, we think that that's a good recipe – to have people that were born and raised in those provinces but now have lived in a democracy. And they can explain things to the people there, who have been oppressed for the last 30 or so years. These coordinators will then set up committees in each of the provinces. Like I said before, those provinces will nominate to us work that they want to see done.

Now, as you know, this is a very labor-intensive business when you get into this type thing. So one of our goals is to take a good portion of the Iraqi regular army – I'm not talking about the Republican Guards, the special Republican Guards, but I'm talking about the regular army – and the regular army has the skill sets to match the work that needs to be done in construction. So our thought is to take them and they can help rebuild their own country. We'd continue to pay them. And these committees will nominate work for them to do, do things like engineering, road construction, work on bridges, remove rubble, demine, pick up unexploded ordnance, construction work, et cetera, et cetera.

That also allows us – and using army allows us not to demobilize it immediately and put a lot of unemployed people on the street. So it works a pretty good process. They're working to rebuild their country. It's reestablishing some of the prestige that the regular army has lost over the years, and it allows us to get a lot of good things done for the country.

The other thing we're trying to do with free Iraqis is bring in two to three with the right skill sets for each of the 21 or 22 ministries; say, from public health, bring in a free Iraqi that's an expert in public health.

Now in the ministries, the Iraqis are going to continue to run the ministries, as – they run it now. And we're going to have them keep running it and we're going to pay them, pay them their salaries. But what we want to do is bring in a free Iraqi who understands the democratic process to help us facilitate making that ministry more efficient.

The time frame right now is to be ready to go when called or when directed. Our time frame in country is to get in there as soon as we can and begin this work, and end it as fast as possible, but at the same returning to the Iraqi people a set of things that weren't as good when we got them and are better now and begin the democratic process and to have, like I said, a government that represents the free will of the people. [...].

[Other] Senior Defense Official: [...] Just one statement of the obvious, and that is this all assumes a decision by the president of the United States to execute military operations.

Q: Is the United States willing to accept anything other than a Western style democracy and a capitalistic economy for Iraq?

Senior Defense Official: I think what the United States is willing to accept – this [sic] me talking now – is any government that expresses the – any elected government that expresses the will of the people. [...].

Q: One, security is not laid out in much detail here. This horizontal line to General Franks, what exactly is the chain of command between your organization and CentCom?

Senior Defense Official: [...] right now my organization coordinates with CentCom. But as soon as we come into country, we'll work with CentCom. General Franks will be my boss.

[...].

Q: How much of this plan here, how many of these players are actually in place now with you, ready to move? And two, how much of this plan is drawn from lessons learned based on experiences in Afghanistan?

Senior Defense Official: Well, I think the plans are based on experiences learned all throughout the '90s, since we've been involved in this. I've got about 180 people with me now, but we have a lot of people in country. The DART team is already in place. The coordinator that runs reconstruction is deployed; he deployed a little over a week ago with portions of his team. He's deployed an advance party that left last Friday, that we speak to daily. So when you get in – when we get in there, it will not only be all these people that I just talked about, but it will also be the mechanisms they set up to do the work, such as contracting.

Q: But they're already staging in the region, so they're ready to move immediately?

Senior Defense Official: Large bulks are already stationed in the region, you're right.

Q: [...] And have you established the coordinators? Are they going to be U.S. military or are they going to be –

Senior Defense Official: They're all civilian. They're all U.S. and they're all civilian. [...].

Q: Could you explain – is your office going to be in charge of the immediate humanitarian relief that the military supposedly is going to provide? Or how are you planning on interfacing, if you are, with –

Senior Defense Official: Well, what we have – as you know, the military has Civil Affair brigades that get involved in them. We have embedded DART teams that really are part of the humanitarian assistant coordinator.

Q: DART teams. [...]

Senior Defense Official: They're the teams from U.S.AID; they're the Disaster Response Teams. They're already in place. They're in place in Kuwait now. [...]

Q: Well, you've got people embedded with the military –

Senior Defense Official: Right.

Q: – from U.S.AID.

Senior Defense Official: Right.

Q: Their responsibility is humanitarian assistance.

Senior Defense Official: That's right.

Q: I'm just trying to get a sense of how you're planning – how that's going to coordinate and what the resource levels are at this point for that aid.

Senior Defense Official: If I could – that coordination will go on between our organization and the organization; if hostilities break out, that we'll prosecute those hostilities – that – what's called the CFLCC (ph). And all of that Civil Affairs structure is embedded in that military organization. We will be coordinating on our level with the commander of CFLCC (ph) and providing him every – all the information we have with regard to those kinds of issues that you suggest will generate early in the process. The resources to support those will flow from the U.N., from ICRC, from all the NGOs and IOs and use the assessment capability extent in the DART teams, the Civil Affairs brigades and all of those other agencies that are out there looking at what the requirements are. [...].

Q: Thank you. Can you talk generally about how you plan to manage oil – in particular, what the plan is for – what you do with revenues, that income, and how you manage how much of that goes to reconstruction and how much not?

Senior Defense Official: Okay. Number one, the oil belongs to the Iraqi people. I see my involvement in oil to be to repair – begin the repairs of anything that's damaged, to ensure that the refineries are capable of doing what they need to do, to look at the pipeline, begin the initial repairs on the pipeline. But I don't intend to be the guy that sells Iraqi oil. That's – I think the oil belongs to the Iraqi people. Whatever the U.N. does in resolutions to allow more use of revenues, I think that ought to be very transparent, widely audited, and it ought to go to work for the Iraqi people. So I'm not getting into the sale of oil business.

Q: Having said that, do you anticipate the U.S. having to pay for everything that you're about to undertake on its own, or do you anticipate some of that revenue, because it's Iraqi, being used for Iraqi reconstruction?

Senior Defense Official: I would think, as we go down this road – this is my thought – that over time, some of that revenue will go for the reconstruction of Iraq, to build schools, to build hospitals, to put in better power grids, improve roads. [...].

Q: On the issue of budget, I know that you said that it's part of the supplemental, but do you have any working estimates of how much it's going to cost to pay all the people in the ministries and the Iraqi military, et cetera, et cetera?

Q: What are you asking for?

Senior Defense Official: The – we've had a number that's been dancing on the – what we need to do up front is pay the people in the ministries, be able to pay the army and be able to pay the law enforcement agencies and the court system. We spent a lot of time trying to establish what that pay scale is, what are they getting now and how much should they get. And when you do that, you have to factor in the fact that over 60 percent of them are receiving food, and so if they receive less food in the future, the wage scale has to be higher. So we about completed that. That's still in the works. And there are several that – they're looking at several places for those revenues. One of them is frozen Iraqi assets, and I think that's being discussed this week. [...] But I don't have an answer for you right now. I'd just tell you it's a work in progress. [...].

Q: As you look at the ministries, I mean, some of them are benign, health ministries, and some of them are not so benign.

Senior Defense Official: Some of them go away.

Q: Interior ministries, the ministry of prisons and stuff like that, some of which you actually need to continue to have function. So are you going to go in and gut some of the less benign ministries? How do you –

Senior Defense Official: Let me throw them into a couple categories, okay? I think to begin with, you have to have a face, a U.S. face, a government, interagency face for every ministry. Then the ministries begin to fall in categories. One of them is those that you're probably not going to keep and don't want to keep, but you still have to have some oversight ability because you have to have a way of dismantling it.

The second category would be those that you can turn over pretty quick, hand back to the Iraqi people. The third category are those that will take a while longer to turn over but you're going to work on turning them over as fast as you can.

The last category would be the ones that are difficult to turn over. An example of that might be defense. And that may end up over time being turned over to an international agency or somebody else. But our intent is to keep the ministry people in place, have them continue to function in ministries until we either, A, disestablish that ministry or, B, turn it back over to the Iraqis.

Q: You have now described several different parts of the government that you are going to pay salaries for – army, court system –

Senior Defense Official: Right. Somebody is going to pay salaries.

Q: – and some of the ministries. There are other chunks of the government that – if you can help us out – do you plan on keeping schools and hospitals? Do you plan on paying teachers? I mean, how deep are you going to go with this largesse of pretending to have revenue flowing in – not pretending, having revenue flow in? What other institutions will you support with revenue, with money?

Senior Defense Official: I think [...] when I say ministries, and you take education, yes, I think that flows all the way down the school system. You take public health, yes, that flows all the way down into the medical system.

Q: So it's not the ministries you're trying to (keep afloat?), you're trying to keep the whole school system.

Senior Defense Official: When you talk about ministries, we're talking about probably in the neighborhood of 2 million or more people.

Q: You're describing a vastly more invasive and widespread operation than even is remotely going on in Afghanistan. And we've been told that in Afghanistan there is no time set when the troops might come out; they'll be there for a long, long time. I know the answer is 'as long as it takes,' but are we talking months, years, decades?

Senior Defense Official: I'm talking – I'll probably come back to hate this answer, but I'm talking months. But in Iraq you do have a somewhat more sophisticated country and a somewhat more structured country than you do in Afghanistan. And that – and I think also, that – even though it's been an oppressed country, it has the structure and the mechanisms in there to run that country and run it fairly efficiently. At one time, it was probably one of the most efficient countries in that part of the world, and a lot of that talent's still there. So I think it's hard to try to put an Afghan template over Iraq. I don't think you'll be able to do that.

[Other] Senior Defense Official: There's a – my view is that there's a couple of branches that could occur here. First of all, remember that this organization we would call the interim transitional civil administrator. And so the branches that could come off of that could be that one could have an international flavor. I think someone here raised the question of, will there be an international figure? That is one branch. This could, hopefully sooner rather than later, be internationalized to deal with this issue.

And the other branch is one that had a more U.S. face, but that was a civilian face, and interagency face so that you have more people from the other very capable departments of the U.S. government involved.

But if you look at this from our standpoint, it's a short term effort to get this started, just put the wheels in motion, and then to hand that off to one of those two branches. I think probably everybody would agree that a larger international face would be better than a smaller international face. It would deal with some of – (name omitted) – issues that he talked about in terms of, okay, who's going to pay the bills over time.

And I think the other thing is, everyone's focused on, you start with the oil program. Okay, the oil program feeds the food issue in the country, and you need to make sure it continues to feed that process. As he said, you got 60 percent of the people getting a large amount of their food out of that process. You can't shut it down and turn that revenue in some other direction, even if it's all for the Iraqi people. So you got to deal with that. But as you go forward, then, you know, the natural resources of the country begin to kick in. [...].

Q: On the issue – on the issue of free Iraqis, you said you're trying to hire a number of them to go to different provinces; you're hoping to have some of the (ministers ?). Could you talk a little bit more about who these people will be and what exactly – how you're choosing them?

Q: And did you say they wouldn't be INC? You weren't seeking to hire them? [...]

Senior Defense Official: We haven't gone out to hire people from the INC, okay. [Clarification: DoD is not hiring or contracting with the Iraqi National Congress (INC) members as such, but some of the Iraqi expatriates working with DoD may be INC members. The INC has played an important role over the years in getting various Iraqi opposition groups to cooperate with one another. The U.S. government admires the INC's success in organizing the endorsement by those groups of principles that the USG favors for the creation of a new democratic government for Iraq.[4]] [...].

Senior Defense Official: [...] And we've been contacted by Iraqis in Switzerland and Iraqis in Sweden, some in Germany.

First thing we do is we give them a fairly quick security check, to the degree that we can, for whatever knowledge we have on them.

The second thing we do is we don't bring them on for a very long period of time, because we don't want them in Iraq as competitors to indigenous Iraqis.

And the third thing is, the ones we talk to – their kids were born – a lot of their kids were born here. Their jobs are here. They want to come back here when it's over. They just want to go – they want go back home. They want to help their country for a couple of months. And so what we've done is we've written a letter to their bosses, saying, 'If this is a – we need this person's skill set, talents, and we'd like for you to give them a leave of absence for a specified period of time,' up to, I think, 120 days. But the boss picks out that period of time, or the Iraqi themselves.

Q: Are some of them from the State Department's Freedom of Iraq – Future of Iraq Project? Do you know?

Senior Defense Official: Yes, we have Future of Iraq people.

Q: May I follow up on the month – you said it would take a month to complete. Just exactly what are you envisioning in that month period? Is it – and is it going to set the government on track in that month period? And who exactly is going to guide them on what sort of government to set up? Just U.S.?

Senior Defense Official: No. It'll be greater than that. We're – the reason I kind of danced from you a little bit – we're still coming up with the governance process. It's being worked right now in the interagency mechanism, with the deputies and principals. [Clarification: U.S. policy is for the Iraqis to mange their own constitutional commission to devise their own governmental institutions. The U.S. government envisions a post-Saddam Hussein Iraq as being governed by broad-based, representative institutions that will put Iraq on a democratic path toward safeguarding the rights of all Iraqis.]

Q: So you're trying to come up with a sort of government for them?

[4] The reference is to a four-page joint statement adopted by Iraqi opposition groups on 1 March 2003 after a three-day meeting in Kurdish controlled northern Iraq.

Senior Defense Official: The deputies and principals will come with that, and we'll execute that –

Q: Sorry. My second question, on international – yesterday there were bids – companies, U.S. companies, were mentioned for reconstruction. Would you be then open to other countries or – in the second phase? Or how do you envisage that? [...].

Senior Defense Official: Our – the one thing I want to try to do with that is, as you come contract for work in Iraq, it'll be our goal to make sure that you must first try to find a Iraqi subcontractor to do that. And the reason for that is to – number one, is to begin to jump-start the economy; begin a process of economic development; and number three, to broaden the employee base for people to – for more jobs.

Q: What are you going to do if you get in a region that already is fairly well-organized, like the Kurdish area? They come up after a war and they say, 'Okay, these are the guys we want to have in charge. We've got' – (off mike). You bring in your guy, and they say, 'Uh-uh. Don't want him. We've got ourselves organized. We don't need you' –

Senior Defense Official: What guy are you talking about?

Q: Your free Iraqi person –

Senior Defense Official: We're not – I should – we're not doing that up north. We're not doing that in the Kurdish – in the three Kurdish provinces.

[Other] Senior Defense Official: We're not bringing a free Iraqi person in there to run things. We're bringing him in as an advisor, a technical advisor, a technocrat; someone who can assist what's already there –

Senior Defense Official: A hometown boy or girl –

[Other] Senior Defense Official: – help us shape what it ought to look like in the future. But not to be in charge.

Q: Will they maintain their autonomy, though, in the north?

Senior Defense Official: Well, there will be one unified Iraq when this is all over. Now, I would think that in the governance process, the differences between the three Kurdish provinces and the remaining 14 would be worked out as part of the new Iraqi government.

Q: But your people are not going in there – you're not going in there at all?

Senior Defense Official: Sure we are. We'll be up there doing reconstruction and whatever humanitarian. But we're – hey, but we're not going to tell the – we're not going to try to re-design the ministry system and the governmental system that the Kurds have put in. We'll let the Kurds and Iraqis do that as they work out their own government. [...].

Document 162
Organizational Diagram, US Department of Defense, Office of Reconstruction and Humanitarian Assistance
11 March 2003[5]

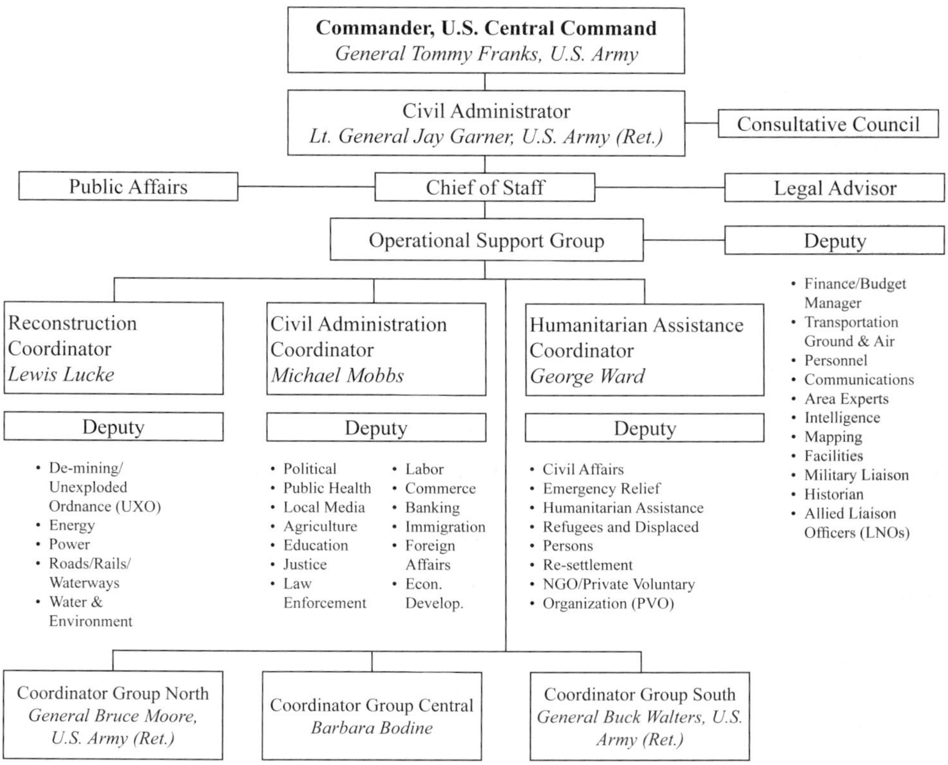

Document 163
Civilian Administration Team Ministry Guidance for CFLCC
25 March 2003[6]

TO: **Jay Garner**
FROM: **Mike Mobbs**[7]
DATE: **25 March 2003**
SUBJECT: **Civilian Administration Team Ministry Guidance for CFLCC**

[5] This Chart was created by the US Department of Defense and was made available on the internet; it is no longer available.

[6] The document pages are headed 'Working draft'. It seems that the document was passed on as such to CFLCC on 26 March 2003 with a one-page document headed 'Guidance for CFLCC's Priorities for Securing Key Baghdad Institutions' which provided:

'In addition to obtaining basic access to all ministries, coalition forces should secure the facilities and prevent the destruction or removal of equipment and sensitive records (including paper and electronic media) in key

Attached is the guidance prepared by the Civilian Administration Team to assist the CFLCC planners:

- Generic Guidance for CFLCC Use Regarding the Ministries (applicable to all ministries)
- Ministry Specific Guidance:
  - Culture
  - Finance & Central Bank
  - Foreign Affairs
  - Higher Education & Scientific Research
  - Industry and Military Industrialization
  - Information
  - Interior
  - Justice
  - Oil
  - Planning
  - Religious Affairs
  - Trade
- Guidance re. border integrity issues

We have also provided the Reconstruction Team with copies of this material to assist them in the preparation of their guidance to CFLCC.

Generic Guidance for CFLCC's Use Regarding the Ministries

MINISTRY

Initial Contact

- Secure ministries and related facilities (see 'Guidance for CFLCCs Priorities for Securing Key Iraqi Institutions').
- Determine damage, if any, to ministry facilities. If main ministry building is significantly damaged or destroyed, establish temporary ministry facility to ensure continuity of essential operations and communicate new location to public and employees.
- Identify and make contact with top officials in ministry. Present Proclamation No. 1 in Arabic and English, formally setting out the powers of the Military Government, and take control of ministry.[8]
- Remove immediately all designated ministry officials. Call ministry's senior employees together (roughly equivalent to office director and above; ~50-100) and

Iraqi institutions in Baghdad. All the following institutions are critical and merit securing by coalition forces as soon as possible to prevent further damage, destruction, and/or pilferage of records and assets: 1) Central Bank, key commercial banks & vaults 2) The Iraqi Museum and the Abbasid Palace 3) Ministry of Foreign Affairs 4) Ministry of Defense 5) Ministry of Interior 6) Ministry of Industrialization 7) Ministry of Higher Education & Scientific Research 8) Ministry of Justice 9) Ministry of Trade (for Oil-for-Food database) 10) National Control Center (electric grid) 11) Ministry of Planning 12) Ministry of Finance 13) Ministry of Information & key media outlets 14) Ministry of Industry & Minerals 15) Ministry of Transportation & Communication 16) Ministry of Oil.'

[7] ORHA Civil Administration Coordinator.

[8] The text of Proclamation No. 1 has not been available.

announce the provisions of Proclamation No. 1 and removal of top few employees associated with previous regime.
- Explain that the Office of Reconstruction and Humanitarian Assistance will soon place a senior civilian advisor to the ministry.
- Reassure that ORHA will provide for emergency payments to civil servants pending restoration of salary benefits systems.

Immediate Actions
- Secure ministry's records in priority order. List of employees and payroll is a top priority for all ministries.
- Direct that offices of removed officials remain empty.
- Distribute Proclamation No. 1 throughout ministry's internal and national structure. Ensure that no instructions should be issued from ministry to subordinate organizations without written ORHA clearance.
- Refer all who arrive and purport to be or wish to become 'advisors to the ministry and the transitional military or civilian authority' to military command headquarters for appropriate action.
- Establish *no* Military Government offices in ministry, except as needed to secure records.
- Assess attitudes of Iraqi employees.
- Determine the nature of ministry's ongoing functions. Report functions inconsistent with Proclamation No. 1 to military command headquarters for appropriate action.
- Determine ministry's organizational structure, including formal and informal reporting arrangements.
- Identify reliable, experienced civil servants, as well as any that may require replacement.
- Assess quality of ministry infrastructure.
- Identify pay structure.
- Determine nature of ministry's termination of employment process, if any.

OPERATIONS LEVEL
- Identify ministry's key subordinate operating organizations that require military command civil affairs advisory units.
- Employ all available ministry-specific guidance.

Specific Guidance for CFLCC Use With Respect to the Ministry of Culture

FUNCTIONS: The Ministry of Culture is responsible for running a large network of cultural institutions in Iraq. Among other assets, it controls Iraq's museums and archeological sites, which contain many priceless art treasures and antiquities of world importance, which should be protected from all forms of looting in the post-war period.

OPERATIONS LEVEL: Iraq contains an enormous number of cultural sites and treasures. Since it will be impossible to protect everything, here is a list of the most valuable sites, which should be safeguarded by the stationing of US forces.

Baghdad:

Baghdad contains one of the largest archeological museums in the world, the **Iraqi Museum**, located in Central Baghdad. It contains literally thousands of priceless historical objects, many of them of gold, silver, and precious stones, as well as priceless works of art. Its collections cover over 5000 years of recorded history and represent the fruits of 200 years of scientific investigation by both Western and Iraqi archeologists. It will be a prime target for looters. Central Baghdad in the vicinity of the Defense Ministry also contains the **Abbasid Palace**, another museum containing very valuable collections. In the outskirts of Baghdad stands an ancient ziggurat temple at **Abu Ghrayb**. Finally, the Ministry of Culture is located in Baghdad as well.

The North:

- Nineveh: the northern city of Mosul contains a similarly valuable archeological museum, which will also be a magnet for looters. The ruins of the ancient city of **Nineveh** are located in eastern Mosul.
- The important ruins of **Nimrud** and **'Ashur** are also located in the vicinity of Mosul.

The South:

- **Babylon**: ruined city located south of Baghdad near the city of al-Hilla.
- **Ur**: major archeological site east of Nasiriyya.
- **Akkad**: important archeological site east of Nasiriyya.
- **Ctesiphon**: large ruined city east of Baghdad.

All of these archeological sites of world importance and could be subject to looting.

LIMITS OF OPERATIONS: Coalition forces must secure these facilities in order to prevent looting and the resulting irreparable loss of cultural treasures of enormous importance to all of humanity. The necessary guidance and procedures established by CFLCC for field commanders should include provisions for arresting and detaining looters and turning them over to the custody of the Ministry of Justice for detention and trial. Museums and archeological sites should be closed to the public initially.

RECORDS: Locate and secure the following records as soon as possible after arrival at the Ministry of Culture, to avoid their destruction or alteration:

1. Personnel files, including address, payroll, training and proficiency records;
2. Financial records;
3. Records relating to archeological sites and local museums and their contents.
4. If possible, preserve or document any evidence of sabotage by Saddam regime designed to blame damage of cultural sites on coalition operations.

For each category of records, identify the location and principal custodian.

IDENTIFYING PERSONNEL: Obtain the title, full name (personal name, father's name, place of origin name, and tribal name), address, and telephone number of senior members of the Ministry, including the field directors of major archeological sites.

ASSESSMENT: Perform preliminary assessments of the Ministry assets listed above in Baghdad and the North and South. In doing so, report on:

1. Records availability, with particular emphasis upon those listed above under the 'Records' section.
2. Ranks and titles of senior of Ministry personnel.
3. Location of museums and archeological sites and inventories of their contents, including an estimate of loss due to looting, if looting has already occurred.

4. Initial assessment of damage done to these facilities as a result of coalition military activity, in order to facilitate possible reconstruction.

For ease of evaluation and presentation, these elements may be rated as either 1-Good; 2-Fair/acceptable; 3-Fair/unacccptable; or 4-Poor.

[...][9]

Specific Guidance for CFLCC Use With Respect to the Ministry of Foreign Affairs

FUNCTIONS: The Ministry of Foreign Affairs is responsible for traditional diplomatic duties in Baghdad and the direction of Iraqi posts abroad. It is also deeply implicated in the planning and conduct of espionage and terrorist activities and, therefore, presents an immediate security threat.

The USG has demarched host governments to withdraw recognition [of] Iraq's current diplomatic missions as well as halt their communications through diplomatic channels.

OPERATIONS LEVELS: The main Ministry of Foreign Affairs facilities are located in Baghdad, with over a hundred foreign missions.

LIMITS ON OPERATIONS: Apply and enforce the limits on the operations of the Ministry of Foreign Affairs contained in Coalition Provisional Authority Law No. 1.[10] Secure all remaining international communications equipment in ministry facilities and suspend all communication between the Ministry and Iraqi diplomatic missions abroad. If possible, prepare to instruct highest ranking remaining Iraqi ministry official [to] transmit in his/her name cable to all missions instructing them to lower flag at all facilities, stop issuing visas and passports, make no representations to host governments and other organizations, and suspend all but humanitarian services until instructed otherwise. If communications with foreign missions is not possible, please pass this information immediately to ORHA POC: [...].[11] (The initial draft of this cable is now being drafted by ORHA staff and, when complete, will be sent to through ORHA front office, through DOD, to the Department of State for final development.)

RECORDS: Locate and secure the following records as soon as practicable after arrival at the Ministry of Foreign Affairs to avoid their destruction or alteration:

1) Personnel files including address, payroll, training, and proficiency and disciplinary records;
2) Classified and unclassified correspondence and cable traffic to/from posts abroad, as well as all equipment related to communication with posts abroad;
3) Records related to diplomatic pouch and passports;
4) Internal ministry records and those related to intra-ministry communications (especially those potentially related to security or espionage); and
5) Training materials.

For each category, identify the location and principal custodian.

[9] Specific Guidance of CFLCC with Respect to the Ministry of Finance and with Respect to the Central Bank omitted.

[10] CPA Law No. 1 has not been available.

[11] Name deleted.

IDENTIFYING PERSONNEL: Obtain the full name (personal name, father's name, place of origin name, and tribal name), address, and contact information of senior members of Ministry and of those who are found to be reliable or who may need replacing.

ASSESSMENT: Perform preliminary assessments of the components of the Ministry of Foreign Affairs. In so doing, report on:

1. Records availability with particular emphasis upon those listed above under the 'Records' section;
2. Current tables of organization;
3. Rank/Status structure;
4. Operational performance and capability deficiencies with particular emphasis on systemic human rights abuses or other inappropriate activities;
5. Nature and quality of all personnel development/training programs;
6. Adequacy of management structure and controls, i.e. policies, procedures, etc.;
7. Number, location, and quality of all facilities;
8. Immediate equipment requirements; and
9. Other relevant conditions, deficiencies and/or problems and competencies.

For ease of evaluation and presentation, where appropriate, these elements may be rated as either, 1- Good; 2- Fair/acceptable; 3- Fair/unacceptable; or 4- Poor.

Specific Guidance for Ministry of Higher Education and Scientific Research

FUNCTIONS: The Ministry of Higher Education and Scientific research oversees the legitimate administration of the Iraqi University system. It has also served as a cover organization for the Iraqi Biological Warfare program. The program was initiated in 1974 at the Al Hazan Ibn Al Hathem Institute, a subordinate of the MOHE & SR.

ORHA's involvement in re-orientation of the Ministry is vital from both international security and economic perspectives. Central to this endeavor is clarifying the relationship between the Ministry and the Iraqi weapons of mass destruction WMD program. Achieving clarity on this relationship is critical to successful implementation and execution of CFLCC's Iraqi Reconstruction Plan for stabilization, recovery and transition to a fully functional Iraqi government. As of this writing, 25 March 2003, the MOHE & SR had not been damaged by coalition bombing and can be expected to be intact. It is co-located with the Ministry of Education on Al Nidal Street, Baghdad. Both have a unique cubed shaped architecture.

The overarching goal for ORHA is two-fold: to normalize the Ministry so that legitimate educational administration may resume, and to identify and terminate illegitimate practices in support of WMD development and acquisition. The preservation of all evidence within this Ministry will be essential in conducting the post-mortem investigation of the Iraqi WMD program. A suspension of Ministry activities may temporarily cause administrative problems with Iraq's Universities, but will not endanger or welfare of the Iraqi people.

Several assumptions are key to this objective:

- The Ministry has played a key role in developing Iraq's military program including by [sic] not necessarily limited to Biological research and weapons development and the training of WMD scientists.
- Compartmentalization of information and activity has occurred so that very few people have an understanding of the complete program.

- The Ministry used a series of state-owned entities SOEs to buy and build the military power Saddam desired for Iraq.
- The complexities of the MOHE & SR are such that it will require a specialized investigative team to unmask the breath [sic] of involvement of this ministry in WMD.

<u>OPERATIONAL LEVELS</u>: Upon the re-entry of the UN Inspection regime, scientists affiliated with the Iraqi WMD program were parceled out to various universities. Here, in the guise of regular staff professors, they were hidden from Inspectors and their identities protected.

<u>LIMITS ON OPERATIONS</u>: Given the gravity of the WMD program and the necessity to fully uncover the details of the research, development, and possible human testing of Biological agents, it is recommended that the MOHE & SR be completely secured from entry by anyone other than coalition personnel.

<u>RECORDS</u>: CFLCC must identify and secure records (immediately to avoid the destruction or alteration of those materials) for all factories producing both chemicals and other industrial products for military and WMD uses. Rank these firms into four categories:

a) those that can be easily converted to civilian use;
b) those that will require minimal capital investment;
c) those that will require major capital investment and retooling;
d) and those that need to be destroyed.

CFLCC should also locate and secure the following records:

a) Suppliers for dual use products and parts.
b) Facility and property records.
c) Financial statements.

<u>IDENTIFYING PERSONNEL</u>: Obtain the full name (personal name, father's name, place of origin name, and tribal name), address and telephone number of senior members of the Ministry.

<u>ASSESSMENT</u>: CFLCC shall perform preliminary assessments of the Ministry in all locations, including SOEs. In doing so, CFLCC will focus upon:

1. Records availability with particular emphasis upon those listed above under the 'Records' section;
2. Nature, extent and types of corrupt practices.
3. Current organization structure.
4. Functions assigned to the ministry.
5. Rank structure.
6. Identification of competent management, engineers and technicians.
7. Operational performance and capability deficiencies with particular emphasis on systemic human rights abuses or other inappropriate activities;
8. Nature and quality of all personnel development/training programs;
9. Adequacy of management controls, i.e. policies, procedures, etc.
10. Number, location, and quality of all facilities;
11. Immediate equipment requirements;
12. Competitive ability of SOEs.
13. Other relevant conditions, deficiencies and/or problems and competencies.

Fore [sic] ease of evaluation and presentation, these elements may be rated as either, 1-Good; 2-Fair/acceptable; 3-Fair/unacceptable; or 4-Poor.

OTHER ADVISORS: CFLCC shall consult with ORHA regarding questions of concern relating to the MOHE & SR. Other persons or organizations offering assistance to CFLCC with respect to the MOHE & SR or SOEs shall be referred to ORHA.

[...][12]

Border Integrity: Customs, Borders. Immigration:
Guidance for CFLCC at Points of Entry to Iraq

Introduction

This is a one-off paper to provide guidance (until further notice) to CFLCC (the Coalition Forces Land Component Commander) at points of entry into Iraq.

I. Central Ministries

There is no single Central Ministry responsible for 'border integrity'. We believe that the subject matter falls within the remits of the following Ministries:

- Interior (nationality / passports),
- Defense (presumably import / export of components for WMD and other weaponry),
- Health (human health),
- Finance (collection of customs duties, taxation),
- Trade (determining customs duties), and
- Agriculture (plant and animal health).

Guidance for securing records etc within each Central Ministry is provided within the papers for those Ministries.

II. Border control in the First Few Days

Assumption: Coalition forces have taken / will take control of all key border crossings. Coalition forces will therefore need to know:

- who to let in and out of the country
- what to let in and out of the country (how to identify goods authorised by the UN Sanctions Committee)
- what to look for in consignments entering the country
- what, if any, tariff to apply on import / export
- what to do with oil exports.

Coalition forces will be unable to achieve full security of Iraq's borders. I understand that they currently intend to tell the border guards at the main border crossings to 'carry on as usual', though will watch out for bribe-taking. This will be insufficient. The border guards are presumably not currently enforcing sanctions (which continue), nor are they preventing smuggling. They will be enforcing nationality (and presumably residence) rules we consider unacceptable.

[12] The Specific Guidance for CFLCC Use With Respect to the Ministry of Industry and Military Industrialization, Ministry of Information, Ministry of Interior, Ministry of Justice, Oil Ministry, Ministry of Planning, Ministry of Religious Affairs and Awqaf (Religious Foundations) and Ministry of Trade are largely identical with the Specific Guidance reproduced and thus have been omitted.

General

Coalition forces should seek to prevent bribe taking, and ensure accounting for all payments.

People

Categories / passports

Large numbers of refugees may seek to return shortly. Many have had their nationality revoked, or would for other reasons not be permitted to enter under the Nationalities Law.

In the absence of other guidance, border guards should:

- seek identification;
- allow entry to those able to provide some credible indication in writing of previous Iraqi residence or nationality, and their accompanying children (even if over the age of 18); CFLCC have discretion to permit entry in exceptional circumstances on oral evidence of previous Iraqi residence or nationality
- allow entry to foreign nationals with a current visa issued under Saddam Hussein's regime; allow also entry of those who they assess to be bona fides humanitarian assistance workers (CFLCC discretion: they should seek identification of some sort);
- allow exit of Iraqi and foreign nationals not on the black / grey lists (careful search for records / computers / discs needed).

If refugees return in such numbers that massive queues form, the priority must be to avoid humanitarian suffering. If there is suitable provision of humanitarian assistance near the crossing, the entry requirements should be enforced. If necessary, however, refugees should be permitted to enter to obtain humanitarian relief.

CFLCC need:

– a list of people who should not be allowed to enter the country

– a list of people who should not be allowed to leave the country

– a list of people who should be detained

I know that lists have been worked on. I understand that they are with CFLCC. Is this correct?

Counter-terrorism: is any Agency able to provide additional identification equipment?

Money

In the absence of further guidance:

- subject to the rule on re-export below, no-one should be allowed to leave Iraq with more than $200 cash (or the equivalent in dinars or foreign currency);
- re-export should be permitted with a valid currency declaration issued by border controls under Coalition control (but not with currency declarations issued under Saddam Hussein);
- there should be no limit on bringing money into Iraq (eg by returning refugees); a currency declaration should be made for amounts over $200 if re-export is intended.

Goods, including food

Background: under continuing UN sanctions, a certificate is a requirement for all imports.

Border posts should ask to see UN certificates for all imports other than personal effects. Personal effects should be interpreted liberally for used goods (eg returning refugees should be able to return with their household goods).

Border posts should exercise discretion over the import of humanitarian assistance: if food, medicines, or other humanitarian assistance are being imported by an apparently bona fides importer, they should be permitted entry.

Tariffs should continue to be levied in accordance with the current schedule. (*This is not currently available to us. Border posts will presumably have a current list of accounts.*)

Oil

Oil smuggling is big business, on which many livelihoods (and the recipients – eg Jordan) depend. In theory, all oil distribution points in Iraq should be in state control. We shall therefore address oil smuggling at point of distribution, not at borders.

Border posts should ensure that tankers carrying oil are indeed carrying oil (and nothing else), but should otherwise permit exports.

Goods to search for

No import of weapons permitted. Suggested maximum knife blade length: 8 inches (CFLCC discretion).

No computers, floppy disks or CD roms to be exported. (Danger of export of records.)

Question: Anything else, the import or export of which should be prohibited?

III. The Future of the Sanctions Regime

The above reflects our current understanding of the sanctions regime. However, the sanctions regime and its strict import controls will seem absurd once the coalition has secured all points of entry to Iraq.

It would be helpful to know when UN sanctions will be lifted or suspended.

IV. Longer term

The first stage will be to conduct an assessment of Iraq's current border integrity. Plans for this will follow.

Any offer of assistance (urgently required) would be greatly appreciated.

Document 164

Coalition Forces Leaflet: The Citizens of Iraq

April 2003

Coalition forces in Iraq have come as liberators of the Iraqi people, not as their oppressors. The purpose of our presence here is to eliminate from your nation a regime that has oppressed its citizens and threatened its neighbors for years. Our stay in Iraq will be temporary, and will end when a government that is representative and peaceful, and reflects the will and interests of all Iraqi people is created and fully functioning. The Coalition forces will respect your religion and culture and impose the minimum disruption to your daily lives. To that end:

All local government services will continue to function.

All mosques and other places of worship will remain open. Religious freedom will be observed.

All schools will reopen as quickly as possible. Teachers and students should report to school.

Police and law enforcement agencies, fire departments, ambulance services, and other public safety and health agencies will continue to function unless otherwise suspended by Coalition forces.

Hospitals will operate as normal and, when possible, be supported by Coalition forces and international civilian agencies.

Shops, markets, and other businesses will be allowed to operate as normal.

Persons incarcerated in prisons and other government facilities will be treated humanely, and all corporal/capital punishment is suspended. All confined persons will remain incarcerated pending additional orders of the Coalition forces.

Current rationing cards for food, medicine, and clothing will continue in use.

In order to ensure the safety, security, and public order of the Iraqi people and the Coalition forces the Iraqi people are hereby prohibited from:

- Making threats against the Coalition forces.
- Carrying out any acts of violence against your neighbors, other Iraqi people, and Coalition forces. This includes theft and looting of public and private property.
- Carrying out any acts of terrorism, or sabotage against Coalition forces.
- Carrying or possessing weapons or ammunition in public, and possessing explosives.[13]

Document 165
Outline Brief for Potential International Partners

April 2003[14]

Organizational Objective:
The Office of Reconstruction and Humanitarian Assistance (ORHA) will oversee the immediate post-conflict ('Phase IV') humanitarian and reconstruction effort in Iraq and restore normal functioning of Iraqi ministries and provinces. The ultimate objective is to restore full control of the instruments of government to the Iraqis themselves.

Structure:
ORHA is a multi-agency unit with US people from the Departments of Defense, State, Treasury, Justice, Agriculture, Commerce, Energy, the US Agency for International Development and the International Board of Broadcasters. International support from the UK and Australia is already embedded. The Office is led by Jay Garner, who was previously involved in humanitarian relief activities in northern Iraq. He has three deputies. Ron Adams is the deputy for operations in charge of relief and reconstruction activities in Iraq. Tim Cross is the deputy for international support. Ryan Henry is the deputy for Policy. Jerry Bates is the ORHA Chief of Staff.

[13] The statement was distributed by Coalition Forces as leaflet bearing code number IZ G2505.

[14] The document was probably created on 16 April 2003. ORHA staff had relocated to Kuwait on 16 April 2003. The telephone number given at the end of the document starts with +965, the country code for Kuwait.

There are three Functional Pillars:

- Humanitarian Assistance headed by George Ward, former US Ambassador to Namibia. In cooperation with international agencies and NGOs, his team will identify and address immediate humanitarian needs (food, water, shelter)
- Reconstruction headed by Lew Lucke, a career USAID officer and Middle East expert. Restore Iraqi infrastructure (i.e. power grid, ports, roads, bridges, telecommunications) and functions (i.e. banking, agriculture, education, health care). This may include both war-damaged infrastructure and infrastructure already in disrepair. Local governance is included within this pillar
- Civil Administration headed by Mike Mobbs, an international attorney and former senior policy official in the Reagan administration. Work with existing Iraqi ministries and institutions to ensure that critical services continue to be delivered. ORHA will be aided in this effort by international technical advisors who will work closely with the leadership of each ministry.

Regional Development:
In each of three regions, North, Central and South, ORHA will establish 'regional offices' staffed with representatives from each of the three functional pillars. These officials will be charged with liaising with leaders and officials in provincial and local governments. They will work to ensure that critical services are provided and that US and international assistance is directed to where the needs are greatest.

Needs:
ORHA will work to identify the most critical needs, both immediate and near-term, through a variety of means:

- Disaster Assistance Response Teams (DARTs) from USAID will enter the country as soon as possible to conduct assessment of the most pressing humanitarian requirements in liberated areas
- Core ORHA staff members will work closely with the UN, NGOs, and international partners to identify immediate humanitarian needs and direct assistance to these areas
- ORHA staff members will work with USAID headquarters in Washington to develop plans for near-term to long-term relief and reconstruction projects.

Food, water, sanitation and shelter will be immediate requirements under any scenario. The most effective way for international partners to contribute will be to provide cash and resources to UN agencies or NGOs already positioned on the ground.

It is difficult to identify longer-term requirements until a wide range of needs assessments have been conducted. Such requirements are, however, likely to include agriculture, irrigation, education, health care, ports, roads, railroads, democratization, local political development and human rights, among many other areas. Obviously, a substantial effort will be required to assist the Iraqis with both reconstruction and transformation of its governance. It will be at least one month before a recovery program has been instituted and initial assessments completed, but estimates of the requirements in general terms are shown below and more detailed requirements will be developed as planning matures.

Estimated Functional Requirements:
Health Care professionals, e.g. doctors, nurses, systems managers

Environmental Experts – especially Land Reclamation and Irrigation
Water/Sanitation specialists
Telecommunications expertise
Air traffic controllers
Highway Systems Administration
Bank Managers
Museum curators/Archaeological Preservation Experts
Defense Training Experts
Border Security and passport surety/Customs & Immigration
Experienced City/Municipal Services Managers
Administration of Provinces
Civil Law Jurists/Court Administrators/Judicial Educators/Public Prosecutors
Justice Sector Information Specialists
Law Society Administrators
  Police Advisors and Internal Security
  Managers/Supervisors
  Trainers
  Technical Advisors
    All comporting with UNCIVPOL standards
Prisons

Skill Sets:
International debt restructuring
International trade expertise
Management Information Systems specialists (and equipment)
Civil Aviation
Technical training expertise
Management trainers
Training of trainers expertise
English Language Training
Human Resources planners
Small Business advisors

Contributing International Partners:
ORHA would welcome the secondment of international experts who can make a contribution to the totality of this relief and reconstruction effort. Rather than send generalists who can report on the full range of ongoing developments, it would be best if partners could send functional experts, who could serve on the ORHA staff as 'desk officers' working on particular issues. Much experience has been gained in previous post-conflict assistance programs. Donors are welcome to propose highly qualified and experienced experts and to offer programs which complement existing programs. These proposals will receive rapid responses. Partners considering the contribution of experts should initially contact the International Deputy through the ORHA Secretariat in order to enable mutual agreement on the modalities and timings of assignment. Our current telephone numbers are: +965 372 4112/4117.

Document 166
Support for the Office of Reconstruction and Humanitarian Assistance
2 April 2003

THE SECRETARY OF DEFENSE

MEMORANDUM FOR Secretaries of Military Departments
Chairman of the Joint Chiefs of Staff
Under Secretary of Defense for Policy
Under Secretary of Defense (Comptroller)
Commander, U.S. Central Command
General Counsel, Department of Defense
Directors of the Defense Agencies
Directors of the DoD Field Activities

SUBJECT: Support for the Office of Reconstruction and Humanitarian Assistance

The President directed the Department of Defense to form a post-war planning group for Iraq. This group has been designated the Office of Reconstruction and Humanitarian Assistance (ORHA) and is directed by Mr. Jay Garner. This office deployed in early March to the Central Command area of responsibility.

The office is under the operational control of Commander, U.S. Central Command. ORHA's mission is critical to help create the conditions for transition to Iraqi self-rule and withdrawal of coalition forces upon completion of their military objectives. The Secretaries of the Military Departments, the Office of the Secretary of Defense, commanders of combatant commands, and defense agencies and field activities shall provide support to ORHA, as required.

[Signed] *Donald Rumsfeld*

Document 167
A Unified Mission Plan for Post-hostilities Iraq (Draft – Version 3)
16 April 2003[15]

INTRODUCTION

> *'The object in war is a better state of peace – even if only from your own point of view. Hence it is essential to conduct war with constant regard to the peace you desire.'*
> Liddell Hart

1. History will judge the war against Iraq not by the brilliance of its military execution, but by the effectiveness of the post hostilities activities. Therefore, at the heart of our thinking has been the imperative to avoid a strategically barren victory: that is military

[15] This document is a draft. Parts of the sections below are incomplete. The document was published by FRONTLINE at http://www.pbs.org/wgbh/pages/frontline/yeariniraq/documents/orha.html.

achievements that, however impressive in their own right, nonetheless fail to alter the political context in which they occur.

2. This Unified Mission Plan describes the way in which the Office of Reconstruction and Humanitarian Affairs (ORHA) intends to set about empowering the Iraqi people to shape their own destiny, once they are free from the persecution by Saddam Hussein and his brutal and corrupt regime. It is a Civil-Military Plan for an environment which will see an evolving transition from military to civil primacy, throughout which civil and military actors must be viewed as equal partners. Using classical strategy terms, it seeks to marry the Ends and the Means by setting out the manner in which the latter is applied to the former, in other words by describing the Ways.

3. In this challenging endeavor, there are a number of fundamental principles which will guide our efforts and must remain uppermost in our thoughts.

- Unity of effort, civil and military.
- Commitment to stay and commitment to go.
- Iraq's oil and other resources belong to the Iraqi people.
- Iraq is maintained as a unified state with its territorial unity intact.
- Effective representative government by and for the Iraqi people.

4. There is no doubt in my mind that ORHA is a pioneering organization and a potential model for the future. The internal design may change but the creation of an organization to fuse the efforts of the many agencies and actors involved in a post conflict situation is the fundamental idea that lies at the heart of the National Presidential Security Directive which created ORHA.

5. This Unified Mission Plan is in two parts; Part 1 sets out the overall strategy, principal goals and themes for Post Hostilities Iraq, and is designed to be enduring in nature. Part 2 explains the way in which ORHA, as it is currently configured, intends to deliver the ideas laid out in Part 1. It is designed primarily to serve as a focus for the efforts of all ORHA staff, but is also of clear relevance to a wide range of other military and civil organizations operating within Iraq, and externally to other governments and international organizations.

J M Garner,
Director OHRA/Interim Civil Administrator?? [sic]

PART 1 – A CONCEPTUAL FRAMEWORK

SECTION 1 – PLANNING SCENARIO

Geopolitical Overview.

1.1 While Iraq has not been a popular neighbor or responsible international actor, Western military action against Iraq is equally unpopular. Additionally, the Muslim and Arab world accuse the West of hypocrisy over its approach to Israel, which is in stark contrast to the hard line adopted towards Iraq. Indeed, the Israeli 'occupation' of Palestine is of much greater concern to Arabs than Saddam Hussein's atrocities. Consequently, any perception that coalition forces have invaded Iraq to seize oil reserves, or because Iraq is a Muslim-state, will have an adverse impact on the US and coalition partners in terms of international political support for the mission and its wider political objectives. Therefore longer term occupation or heavy-handed post conflict activities will exacerbate anti-US feelings, across the Middle East in particular. This may in turn erode support for the global war on terrorism.

1.2 Short description of Iraq: tribal family; religious; ethnic; historical; political aspects.

The Operating Environment.

1.3 An intervention operation such as this entails simultaneous humanitarian, peace support and combat operations. Within this doctrinal construct certain considerations prevail – all of which are variables not absolutes – which will determine the size, shape, capabilities and focus for a military force, and impact on the conduct of civil activities:

a. The level of threat, both to the mission and to the individual.
b. The extent to which high intensity combat operations are required, an issue which has individual and force connotations.
c. The varying number of civil and military actors and their importance at different levels.
d. And who is compliant and who is actively resisting.

1.4 Such operations do not develop in a linear way, with neat transition phases, all carefully controlled by some detailed and rigid master campaign plan. They evolve and fluctuate at different levels, in different ways and in different places. In this, a clear visualization of time, timing and consequences is important in order to allow civil and military decision-makers to shape their environment; i.e. when to do something, how long to do it for and what are the desired resultant effects? The complex post hostilities operating environment in which both military forces and civilian organizations will operate requires a truly integrated civil/military approach and structural and intellectual agility, at every level.

Prevailing Security Conditions.

1.5 In broad terms the military role is to create a secure and stable environment in order to assist the civil authorities to empower existing legitimate organizations and dismantle separate or parallel power structures. This has both internal and external aspects, the former primarily related to civil disorder, the latter to border control. This may require military forces to 'police the security gap' and to support counter terrorism activities, but the transfer to a credible and legitimate law enforcement organization must be urgently pursued. In such a security environment, the establishment of a secure environment is the highest priority military task.

1.6 The potential for instability, likely to exist for some time after the war is over. The most probable threat will come from residual pockets of fanatics, secessionist groups, terrorists and those would seek to exploit ethnic, religious, and tribal fault lines for personal gain. The threat from these groups would manifest itself in high impact tactics such as car or suicide bombings, sniping, and 'hit and run' raids. A high level of such attacks will have an adverse impact on the creation of stability, a prerequisite for self-sustaining peace.

SECTION 2 - ASSUMPTIONS

Assumptions.

(*Be ruthless. Ensure they are relevant to the planning; if they do not allow the planning to continue, they are irrelevant. The final list becomes the issues we must track or do something to mitigate against.*)

2.1 Initially USG/Coalition operation. UN role uncertain at this stage but unlikely to be authoritative in the early stages.

2.2 Infrastructure damaged but not completely destroyed. Sufficient infrastructure exists at the end of hostilities – buildings, roads, transportation, communications – to support initial reconstruction and humanitarian activities.

2.3 Essential government functions will have to be carried out immediately. Iraqi governance at all levels will be ineffective and will require both oversight and assistance. Civil Affairs officers will provide the initial presence and represent the initial governance authority until ORHA personnel arrive. Some Iraqi officials [are] so tainted as to be unusable, but others can be retained. Technocrats will be essential to start governance. Free Iraqis/expats can identify reliable Iraqis with relevant expertise who can be entrusted with positions of responsibility.

2.4 The political parties established by the expatriate Iraqi community will become active in-country. A strategy to interact effectively with this community will be developed based on the conditions. Opportunities to work with various Iraqi groups will present themselves. These opportunities must be carefully handled both to avoid pitfalls and to take advantage of genuine prospects of hastening progress toward meeting ORHA's objectives.

2.5 No major environmental dangers will exist that impair the progress of the mission.

2.6 Justice sector institutions will be maintained and used to extent possible. Must remove unacceptable individuals from office, disband units and organizations, and eliminate law and processes that impede development. Saddam's political appointees will remain with police, judiciary and prison systems at lower ranks. Legitimate demands upon justice system in the immediate post-conflict period will likely exceed Iraqi capabilities which are likely to be in disarray.

2.7 Maintaining law and order will be necessary from Day 1. Existing police/security forces lack any legitimacy with Iraqi people and are seen as oppressors. Extent of public voluntary compliance with law will be low. 200,000 security personnel in three ministries require vetting, supervision and reform.

2.8 A security environment sufficiently stable for the provision of relief and humanitarian assistance will be established, using military resources as necessary. Real potential for conflicts arising from vigilante/retribution activities, property disputes, and civil disturbances which may limit the ability of ORHA civilians to perform their operations and require daily prioritization of tasks and allocation of security forces.

2.9 IDPs and Refugees:

- Anticipated return of approximately 3 million internally displaced persons (IDPs) and up to 1 million refugees now in neighboring countries.
- Displacement of 1.3 million civilians toward borders in addition to 700,000 current refugees. Near Baghdad: an additional 900,000 displaced persons, adding to current 800,000 IDP total.
- Rapid conclusion of conflict would limit additional IDP and refugee movements.
- U.S. military distribution of humanitarian relief in immediate post-conflict period will be available on an emergency basis.

2.10 Interruption of Oil for Food (OFF) due to UN evacuation, security environment, availability and increased cost of shipping insurance.

- 60% of Iraqis are completely dependent on OFF. Iraqi civilians will stockpile four to six weeks of food prior to conflict.
- OFF humanitarian goods and distribution will be necessary for at least six months post conflict.
- Initial absence of NGO and 10 implementing partners will inhibit humanitarian operations.
- Retail distribution system has ceased to function WFP standby arrangements with neighboring countries and pre-positioned food could help bridge food gap until OFF restart.

- Fundamental changes in OFF will be difficult to pass through UNSC.

2.11 Education. Schools open as soon as possible in secure areas. Sufficient resources to pay teachers will exist.

2.12 Housing.

- Returning exiles, IDPs, refugees will place additional strains on existing housing stock.
- The creation of an affordable housing program for the nation is finance-based rather than commodity-based.
- Damage to housing stock will not be severe and there will be room to integrate housing finance in the banking sector.
- DART will assume immediate shelter requirements.

2.13 Availability of Iraqi records and data will be sufficient to enable at least basic functioning of civil ministries. Military forces will be able to secure key administration buildings (bank vaults, personnel records systems, financial records, etc) and maintain that protection until ORHA civilian advisors have determined their disposition.

2.14 Health?

2.15 Economy. Oil sector dominates economy, however, oil revenue insufficient to cover reconstruction costs. Costs of rebuilding economy directly impacted by extent of damage to key economic structures. Full restoration would be an inappropriate objective. Returning economy to pre-Gulf War levels (or any other artificial benchmark) is cost prohibitive and could take many years. Target is to place the economy on the path of sustainable growth.

- Short-term US Engagement (12-18 months): U.S. post-conflict reconstruction establishes foundation for broad-based economic reform and growth.
- Long-term International Engagement: Iraq aided by international financial institutions (World Bank, IMF, etc.), builds upon this economic foundation.

SECTION 3 - POLICY PLANNING

Campaign Legitimacy.

3.1 What will provide post hostilities campaign authority? What do we need and what is the impact if we don't get it? Key to internationalizing this issue and therefore reducing the chance of a backlash/intifada is removing/reducing the levels of the US-led coalition 'invading forces' as quickly as possible. Western, and particularly US-basing, is a 'burning thorn' in Arab terms and the sooner that multinational force of minimum numbers is in place the better. It is unlikely that countries, not in the original coalition, will be willing to joining CJTF(I) without a recognized form of legitimacy such as a UN mandate (or UNSCR).

United Nations Security Council Resolutions

3.2 Initial

3.3 (UNSCR) 1441. (adopted at security Council meeting 4644, 8 November 2002)

3.4 Subsequent - OFF and beyond

National Security Presidential Directive-24

3.3 Narrative????

3.4 The specific tasks contained in NSPD-24 are listed below:

- Assisting with humanitarian relief

- Dismantling WMD
- Defeating and exploiting terrorist networks
- Protecting natural resources and infrastructure
- Facilitating reconstruction; protecting infrastructure and economy
- Assisting re-establishment of key civilian services (food supply, water, power, and health care)
- Reshaping and reforming Iraqi military with civilian control
- Reshaping internal security institutions
- Supporting transition to Iraqi authority
- Build links to specialized UN agencies and NGO's [sic]
- Build links to planning counterparts in coalition governments

Her Majesty's Government Policy Objectives.

3.4 ??

Australian Government Policy Objectives.

3.5 ??

Other Coalition?

3.6 ??

SECTION 4 - THE ROAD TO TRANSFORMATION

The Ultimate Goal - Towards the Strategic End-state.

4.1 The universally agreed end-state for a post-Saddam Iraq is defined as:

> *A stable Iraq, with its territorial integrity intact, and a broad-based government that renounces WMD development and use and no longer supports terrorism or threatens its neighbors.*

4.2 This goal was reaffirmed at the Azores Summit of March 2003 at which Coalition leaders declared:

> *We envisage a unified Iraq with its territorial integrity respected. All the Iraqi people – its rich mix of Sunni and Shiite Arabs, Kurds, Turkomen, Assyrians, Chaldeans, and all others – should enjoy freedom, prosperity, and equality in a united country.*[16]

Measurable Benchmarks.

4.3 Having identified the ultimate goal, it is important to derive a set of measurable benchmarks which, when achieved in combination, indicate that the End-state has been achieved.

a. A national identity that unites all Iraqis while preserving individual tribal, ethnic and religious heritages. Education
b. A broad-based, freely elected government in-place that:
    - Is a responsible member of the international community
    - Respects and protects the basic human rights of all Iraqis (Rule of Law??)
    - Maintains territorial integrity
    - Does not own or pursue a WMD capability

[16] For the full text of the 'Azores Summit Declaration', see *Doc 572*.

c. A self supporting economy with a rejuvenated oil industry, but not solely dependent on oil revenue. Agriculture/rations tourism?
d. An Iraqi 'National Defense Force' in place that is representative of Iraqi society, properly balanced and capable of defending its territorial integrity using only conventional means, which is subordinate to and supports the national civil authority, and with systems in place to complete the transformation to a professional military organization.

Identifying the Greatest Impediments to Success.

4.4 *Self Determination*. Iraq has the natural resources plus the national characteristics to be a potential role model within the Middle East, exerting a positive influence on its immediate neighbors and providing a wider incentive internationally. This latent capacity will only be realized by a bottom-up drive from the Iraqi population to embrace new ways and to modernize, without losing the strength of their cultural basis. Thus, the 'thing' on which the achievement of the strategic End-state bears is assessed to be the resolve of the Iraqi people to build a better future; in other words self determination. This hinges on two key factors; the posture and conduct of the military force, and the speed with which control of key resources and institution is returned to Iraqi nationals. Success will depend on the quality of the process ORHA and the international community jointly establish with the Iraq [sic]. To achieve this requires tangible and culturally sensitive commitment on behalf of the international community, and careful perception management to prevent runaway expectations. It is highly desirable that this is achieved wholly by consent, but in extremis, coercion should be used, where necessary and carefully, to ensure compliance.

4.5 *Countering Erroneous Perceptions*. The greatest threat to the post hostilities mission has two interconnected strands to it. The first is the perception, internally within Iraq and internationally, that the war was all about gaining control of Iraq's natural resources. The second is apprehension over an ostensible increase in US hegemony. To counter such a perception it will be important to widen the contribution from the international community, to ensure that the Campaign Authority (i.e. the legal underpinning of operations) is regionally accepted (especially in Iraq), and that tangible economic and social improvements in the life of the Iraqi people, funded by Iraqi oil and other natural resources, are evident.

4.6 *Impartiality*. Under Saddam's dictatorship the Iraqi people have been isolated from the international community; politically, militarily, economically and technologically. The people are war weary, their spirit has been tested to breaking point and they are deeply suspicious of any administration. No matter how impartial international civil or military actors strive to be, virtually every action that is taken will be more to the advantage or disadvantage of one party or another. Accusations of partiality will undoubtedly occur, but their impact can be minimized if actions are transparent to all. The significance of impartiality is that if it is discarded, and the international mission is perceived as being partial, it will have a negative effect upon the level of consent for the operation and thus make the conduct through effective communications will be [sic] key in achieving the End-state.

a. Civil actors
b. Coalition Forces must be seen as a liberating force – a force for good – whose prime purpose is to empower the Iraqi people to shape their own future. There must be no perception of an occupying force, no talk of defeat or claims of victory. The military must act in line with the highest standards of professional conduct and their posture must be one that projects an image of a credible and robust force, firm but fair in their actions.

Drawing the Roadmap.

4.7 Having determined the End-state and the ways in which it can be measured, the key 'milestones' (each of which is a particular condition to be achieved) are set out along the appropriate Lines of activity, and sequenced in time and space, dividing it into phases or stages if appropriate. Finally, the critical path can then be set out. A schematic depiction of this is shown below[17] and in more detail at Annex?

4.8 (Describe the road map.) Stages, phases, passages: stabilize, meet essential needs, decon/recon, improve their material conditions, empower, set on the path, ensure irreversibility of processes. Confidence, mutual understanding, gaining trust over time. Transparency.

Lines of Activity - Vision Statements.

4.9 *Rule of Law.* A system of laws and institutions (police, prosecution, courts and corrections) which operates impartially, without regard for ethnicity, religion, sex, race, political affiliation or other natural characteristic, and provides sufficient public order, levels of human and property rights and objective dispute resolution so as to enable the people of Iraq to enjoy personal freedoms, economic prosperity, representative government and domestic tranquility.

4.9 [sic] *Social/Cultural.*

a. Tradition versus modernity and the youth figures. Exposure of youth to global influences and Middle East problem of liberalizing religious basis of politics. Youth must have say. Downstream challenge.
b. Religion??
c. Cultural/historical??

4.10 *Economic Reconstruction.* Build a foundation to put the Iraqi people on the path to self-managed economic prosperity as part of the global community, with economic opportunities in a market-based economy and privately owned enterprises. Construct a functioning market-driven agricultural system. Private sector forces will be optimized by limiting governmental agricultural assistance to inherently governmental functions (e.g. extension, water planning-delivery, re-establishing marketing links).

4.11 *Governance/Diplomatic.*

a. Ensure that each Iraqi can be an active member of the social and political aspects of nationhood through the re-development of provincial and community level governance structures.
b. Help to rebuild regional and international relations??

4.12 *Education/Health.*

a. Rebuild the health and education systems of Iraq to ensure that these services are available to all Iraqis through the provision of technical assistance.
b. Levels of education and what each people at each level have known (influence of memory)

4.13 *Humanitarian Assistance.*

a. Relieve human suffering by establishing a responsive humanitarian assistance organization that coordinates and facilitates the delivery of relief and humanitarian assistance to those in need, including:
    - Essential, basic health care needs

[17] Schematic depiction omitted.

- Minimally adequate levels of potable water and waste disposal
- Adequate nutrition
- Emergency shelter

b. Restore and protect the human rights and dignity of the Iraqi people.

c. Prevent loss of civilian lives by initiating humanitarian mine and unexploded ordonance action programs.

4.14 *Information.*

a. Indigenous Media: Within 12 months, reconstitute indigenous Iraqi media as a model for free media in the Arab world.

b.

4.15 *Military.* Given the historical role of the Army in Iraqi society, the reformation of the military is a key aspect of achieving the End-state. The military must embrace change, principally a recognition that its role is to support, not dominate, the civil authority; it must become apolitical. Organizational change restructuring and re-equipping will be a relatively straightforward process, but it must be underpinned, from the outset, by a significant adjustment in Iraqi military ethos. Of critical importance to the generation of a new ethos is the creation of a professional and representative military leadership that recognizes and accepts its role in safeguarding civil society. Minimizing the psychological and physical gap between the surrender of the Iraqi Armed Forces and the beginning of reformation process is of central importance.

WMD??????? Elimination is defined as a capability which has been rendered operationally ineffective and would take considerable time and effort to reconstitute. Disabling WMD will be a significant task requiring substantial support from military resources.

SECTION 5 - CONCEPT FOR IMPLEMENTATION

ORHA Mission Statement.

5.1 The role of ORHA is to: help alleviate dependence on Humanitarian Assistance; assist in the rejuvenation of a broad-based Iraqi economy by supporting the recovery and repair of critical infrastructure; underpin the creation of effective Governance based on Iraq's rich and diverse cultural, ethnic and religious heritage; so as to assist the Iraqi people to build their own future.

Overall concept of Operations.

5.2 *The Concept of Transition and Transformation.* Transition and transformation are two post-conflict concepts which can be described as having a complex, symbiotic relationship. Transition speaks to the activities, role and posture of the civil and military actors in a post conflict environment. A rapid and orderly transfer of authority from the international mission to the host nation is of the essence. The process of transformation is driven by the indigenous people and is fuelled by their desire to build a self sustaining peace. An important role for the military is to assist the civil authorities in empowering existing legitimate organizations and dismantling separate or parallel power structures in order to create the basis for Iraqi self-government. Parallel, not sequential, deconstruction and reconstruction underpins transition and transformation. The goal is to set the conditions to enable the rapid transfer of government to the Iraqi people.

5.3 *The Process as the Path – Engaging the Ministries.* The pressure to achieve products, measures of effectiveness, and results is immense. The focus of attention on milestones toward the End-state is important, yet it risks not giving the attention needed on establishing an effective process. In one past crisis response, the term 'the process is equally important to the product' was extensively used, for good reason. The Iraqis will want to institute and receive assistance to facilitate processes which make them full partners in the path/route of achieving our mutual goals. This will need to be done by the ministries as well as at the regional and local levels. Examples of essential processes which will effectively engage and depend on Iraqi participation are the following:

- Constitution development.
- Ministry management development strategies developed with ministry personnel.
- Creating a new institution (e.g. ministry) for personnel management, procedures and training.
- Develop Iraqi consultation processes to address national issues and specific needs (e.g. reconstruction committees) necessary to create a participative democracy.
- Find effective ways to criminalize the practices of the old regime and enforce those laws to counter the destructive forces.
- Create an Iraqi capacity to manage and resolve potential conflict situations through non-violent means.
- Establish the principle of accountability of the government to the population through developing transparent practices of budgeting and staffing; strengthen civil society to hold the government accountable.
- Develop an effective process for Iraqis to address cross-cutting issues such as using a Marketing Economics Simulation (SENSE) around specific issues.
- Strengthening local governance.

5.4 *Deployment.* ORHA will move forward into Iraq in stages, and as the environment becomes more permissive. The outline concept sees a near simultaneous deployment of Regional Coordinator North and South followed by, at later point, again near simultaneous deployment of Regional Coordinator Central and Headquarters ORHA, but not any three elements together. Locations and timings are subject to the conditions which exist in each region.

5.5 *Organization and Operation.*

- Evolutionary Path from military to military-civil to civil-military. Avoid rigid phases. Describe the kind of evolving environment. In such an operating environment, this concept relies on a clear understanding of Commander's Intent and decentralized decision-making and execution of operations.
- Acting in close cooperation with the military. Importance of holistic view and coordinated progress in post conflict stabilization activities.
- Empowerment through the Ministries.
- Regional Coordinators.
- How to do central control and coordination i.e. HQ operation.

Resources.

5.6

RESOURCES

Reprogramming of FY 2003 Funds and Supplemental FY 2003 funding for relief and reconstruction:

- USAID/OFDA (DART, FFP)

- Dept of State (PRM, PM)
- DOD (OHDACA)

Personnel

- DART, Civil Affairs Personnel

Document 168
Cable from General Franks to Secretary of Defense Rumsfeld

16 April 2003

SUBJ: OPERATION IRAQI FREEDOM

PERSONAL FOR SECDEF

1. Mr Secretary, we have achieved decisive military victory in Iraq. Coalition armed forces have defeated Iraq's elite and fielded military forces, captured the main population centers, protected Iraq's oil wealth, and destroyed the regime's capacity to threaten the Iraqi people and regional neighbors.
2. Believe now is the time to officially acknowledge the end of decisive combat operations (Phase III) and the beginning of stability operations (Phase IV). I believe such a move will have significant impact upon international participation in Iraq's post-war stability. The arrival of additional international combat and police/paramilitary forces will allow us to accelerate the withdrawal of our troops.
3. With the beginning of Phase IV, I will designate the CFLCC (LTG McKiernan), Commander, CJTF-Iraq. While this is primarily a name change, it also indicates to all a new beginning. Jay Garner will sit at the side of Dave McKiernan and orchestrate the initialization of Iraqi institutions. We will replace McKiernan within 90 days with another three-star headquarters – either us or international (e.g. the Allied Rapid Reaction Corps – ARRC). As this moves forward, we will further reduce our combat forces.
4. In accordance with your vision, our military action must now be matched by an equally decisive campaign to achieve stability and to return Iraq to full Iraqi control. The challenges ahead require more political and financial muscle than military muscle and will demand the full application of our nation's resources and those of the international community. Jay Garner is moving to Baghdad now, and within 90 days his actions will begin to take precedence over that [sic] of our military commander. My sense is that the speed with which we are able to reduce the US military footprint is directly tied to the speed with which we are able to fund reconstruction and build the future Iraqi Government. Very respectfully, Tom Franks.

Document 169
Freedom Message to the Iraqi People
16 April 2003[18]

Peace be upon you.

Coalition Forces in Iraq have come as liberators, not as conquerors. We have come to eliminate an oppressive and aggressive regime that refused to comply with UN Security Council resolutions requiring the destruction of weapons of mass destruction. The Coalition is committed to helping the people of Iraq heal their wounds, build their own representative government, become a free and independent people and regain a respected place in the world. We will ensure that Iraq's oil is protected as a national asset of and for the Iraqi people. Iraq and its property belong to the Iraqi people and the Coalition makes no claim of ownership by force of arms. Coalition forces respect the Iraqi people, their religious practices, history and culture, and will safeguard Iraq's unity and territorial integrity.

We are working with the international community to ensure the delivery of humanitarian assistance and to promote law and order so that Iraqis can live in security, free from fear. We are establishing the stability that will allow early progress toward political freedom and economic prosperity. Our stay in Iraq will be temporary, no longer than it takes to eliminate the threat posed by Saddam Hussein's weapons of mass destruction, and to establish stability and help Iraqis form a functioning government that respects the rule of law and reflects the will, interests, and rights of the people of Iraq. Meanwhile, it is essential that Iraq have an authority to protect lives and property, and expedite the delivery of humanitarian assistance to those who need it. Therefore, I am creating the Coalition Provisional Authority to exercise powers of government temporarily, and as necessary, especially to provide security, to allow the delivery of humanitarian aid and to eliminate weapons of mass destruction. To facilitate these objectives, I proclaim the following:

Members of the armed forces and security organizations shall lay down their arms, stay away from their weapons, and remain in place. They shall obey the orders of the nearest Coalition military commander. All other Iraqis should continue their normal daily activities; officials should report to their places of work until told otherwise. All those engaged in the delivery of essential services should return to their jobs. The Arab Socialist Renaissance Party of Iraq (Hizb al-Ba'th al-Arabi al-Ishtiraki al-Iraqi) is hereby disestablished. Property of the Ba'th Party should be turned over to the Coalition Provisional Authority. The records of the Ba'th Party are an important part of the records of the Government of Iraq and should be preserved. All those with custody of the records of the Ba'th Party or the Government of Iraq should preserve and protect those records, and turn them over to the Coalition Provisional Authority. Saddam Hussein's intelligence and security apparatus, the Al-Mukhabarat al-Iraqiyya, is hereby deprived of all powers and authority. All Iraqis are now free to express their views without fear of retribution. At an appropriate time, free elections will make Iraqis self-governing in local, regional, and soon, national affairs. All parties and political groups may participate in Iraq's political life, except those who advocate or practice violence. Iraqis must not seek revenge. There will be a just legal process that will safeguard the honor and dignity of the Iraqi people. The Coalition Provisional Authority will seek a fair and prompt solution to the problem of displaced persons and refugees.

[18] The Freedom Message was made public by Coalition Forces as a leaflet beading code number IZ C 148.

There will be a legal, organized process to address restitution of homes that have been seized by the former regime. The Coalition will work with Iraqis to set up a commission to deal with such claims. I call upon Iraqis to inform Coalition Forces regarding the location of weapons of mass destruction or related materials, facilities where such weapons are made, and individuals connected to weapons of mass destruction. All records concerning these activities should be preserved. Iraqis should not pass weapons of mass destruction to terrorists or terrorist organizations. I call upon Iraqis to inform Coalition Forces regarding the location of: foreign fighters and terrorists; members of the regime's security apparatus; and individuals who have perpetrated crimes against humanity or war crimes. All records concerning these activities should be preserved. Rewards may be provided for especially important information on these matters.

All barriers to free movement of people and goods, including illegal roadblocks and checkpoints, must come down. We will work with regional leaders, entities and governments that are committed to peace and democracy to integrate them into the Coalition's activities. Coalition Forces are here to ensure safety and security, and to help the people of Iraq create a better future for their country. We pledge our support to all Iraqis who seek Iraq's freedom and prosperity, and the blessings of peace and security.

16 April 2003
General Tommy R. Franks
Commander of Coalition Forces

Document 170
Instructions to the Citizens of Iraq

16 April 2003[19]

Coalition Provisional Authority Directive

To Ensure the safety, security, and public order of the people of Iraq and Coalition Forces,

1. All persons in Iraq are directed to:
   a. Lay down arms, cease resistance, and obey all orders of the Coalition Forces;
   b. Not make threats against the Coalition Forces;
   c. Not carry out acts of reprisal or violence against other Iraqi people, the Coalition Forces, or neighboring peoples. This includes theft and looting of public and private property;
   d. Not carry or possess weapons or ammunition in public, and not possess explosives. Do not fire weapons in celebration – may be mistaken for hostile fire.
2. Iraqi government employees (civilian and military) should provide any requested assistance to Coalition Forces and the Coalition Provisional Authority at all levels and

[19] This Directive was also made public by Coalition Forces as a leaflet beading code number IZ C 149. The text of the latter differs however slightly from the Directive published as a CPA document. The draft text of the 'Coalition Provisional Authority Directive: Instructions to the Citizens of Iraq' had already been finalized on 18 March 2003. The text of the 18 March 2003 draft is almost identical with the final Directive.

without hesitation. They are instructed to prepare for surrender to Coalition Forces all equipment including weapons, equipment, codes and other information, including but not limited to maps of minefields and locations of areas used for weapons research, testing, or storage, as well as any other dangerous or sensitive sites.

3. Additionally, I call upon all persons in Iraq to:[20]
   a. Report all suspected terrorists and criminal activity to the Coalition Provisional Authority or Coalition Forces.[21]
   b. Cease all work immediately on any programs for the acquisition of nuclear, chemical, and biological weapons, missiles, and other advanced military technologies; report in a full and factual manner information on such programs; and preserve all records;
   c. Report in a full and factual manner information pertaining to prisoners and missing persons from the conflicts with Iran and Kuwait; and preserve all records;[22]
   d. Report in a full and factual manner information pertaining to property and documents seized by Iraqi nationals during the conflicts with Iran and Kuwait, whether the seizures were made pursuant to military commands or orders, or for personal gain; and preserve all records;[23]
   e. Report in a full and factual manner information pertaining to all military and civilian regime leaders, their subordinates, and anyone who may have committed crimes and atrocities against the people of Iraq, Iran, or Kuwait; or against the economic patrimony of Iraq, such as energy facilities; and preserve all records;
   g. Safeguard public property and protect it from damage or destruction. This includes all public infrastructure, energy facilities, and official records of any kind in any form (paper, electronic, magnetic tape, compact disc, or any other form of storage). Report any suspected destruction or the threat of destruction to Coalition Forces immediately.[24]
4. The following temporary conditions concerning public order and safety are in effect:
   a. A curfew may be declared by the local Coalition Force commander.[25] The following persons are exempted: police, law enforcement, fire, ambulance, hospital, and other public safety and health agency personnel while performing official duties during curfew hours or transiting to or from their places of work; persons requiring emergency medical care; and officials and employees of public services, utilities, and other authorized essential work;
   b. Unless otherwise suspended by direction of the Coalition Provisional Authority, all local government services should continue to function: All government

[20] The draft of 18 March 2003 read: 'Additionally, all persons in Iraq are hereby ordered to:'.

[21] The text in leaflet IZ C 149 reads: 'a. Report all suspected terrorists, IIAS members, Fedayeen Saddam, SSO and SRG to the Coalition Provisional Authority or Coalition Forces.' The words 'and criminal activity' do not appear in the draft of 18 March 2003.

[22] The text in leaflet IZ C 149 reads: 'c. Report in a full and factual manner information pertaining to prisoners and missing persons from Operation Iraqi Freedom, as well as the conflicts with Iran and Kuwait; and preserve all records'.

[23] The text in leaflet IZ C 149 included an additional paragraph which reads: 'e. Report in a full and factual manner information pertaining to wealth accumulation and maintenance by the regime, both inside and outside of Iraq; and preserve all records.'

[24] The text in leaflet IZ C 149 included an additional paragraph which reads: 'h. Report in a full and factual manner information concerning the outflow from Iraq of WMD and contraband and preserve all records.'

[25] The 18 March 2003-draft read: 'A curfew is declared – all persons shall remain in their homes and other places of residence from [7 PM until 6 AM] [one hour after evening prayers until dawn] daily.'

employees should report to their places of work and perform their normal duties as usual, unless otherwise directed;[26]

c. Private shops, markets, and other businesses may[27] operate during non-curfew hours at the discretion of their proprietors;
d. All mosques and other places of worship may remain open;
e. After the Coalition Provisional Authority determines it is safe, all schools may reopen and remain open during non-curfew hours. When that happens, teachers and students should report to school;
f. Unless otherwise suspended by direction of the Coalition Provisional Authority, police and law enforcement agencies, courts, fire departments, ambulance services, banks, postal services, media and other public safety and health agencies should continue to function under the oversight, direction, and orders of the Coalition Provisional Authority and will operate during curfew and non-curfew hours;
g. Hospitals should operate 24 hours/day, during curfew and non-curfew hours;
h. Persons incarcerated in prisons and other government facilities shall be treated humanely, and all corporal/capital punishment is suspended. All confined persons shall remain incarcerated pending additional orders of the Coalition Provisional Authority;
i. Current rationing cards for food, medicine, and clothing shall continue in use.

5. Full members of the Arab Socialist Renaissance party of Iraq (Hizb al-Ba'th al-Arabi al-Ishtiraki al-Iraqi) and Officers of the Iraqi security forces are called upon to identify themselves at once to Coalition Forces Authorities, and await instructions from them.

6. Any person violating any of the mandatory provisions (paragraphs 1, 4a, and 4h) of this directive shall,[28] upon conviction by a Coalition Provisional Authority Court be liable to lawful punishment as such court may determine.

7. This directive shall become effective on the date of its promulgation.

General Tommy R. Franks
Commander of Coalition Forces

Document 171

Instructions to Iraqi Armed Forces

16 April 2003[29]

Coalition Provisional Authority Directive

You are now a surrendered force under the control and authority of the Commander of Coalition Forces that are conducting military operations within Iraq. All Iraqi military

[26] The draft of 18 March 2003 said: 'are to report'.

[27] The draft of 18 March 2003 said: 'shall operate'. Similarly, in sub-paragraphs d, e and f, the word 'may' initially read 'shall' or 'will', respectively.

[28] The draft of 18 March 2003 read: 'Any person violating any of the provisions of this directive shall [...].'

[29] The draft text of the 'Coalition Provisional Authority Directive: Instructions to Iraqi Armed Forces' was finalized on 18 March 2003 at the same time as the 'Instructions to the Citizens of Iraq'. It is assumed that both Directives were issued on the same day, although no independent confirmation for this or, indeed, a copy of the finally issued directive, was available.

personnel will be treated humanely and in accordance with the Geneva Conventions and the Law of War. Our fight was with the regime of Saddam Hussein that oppressed the people of Iraq. The people of Iraq are not our enemy.

At this moment in Iraq's history, I ask that each one of you in the Iraqi armed forces carefully consider your personal conduct and how future generations will remember your actions. The eyes of all Iraqis are now upon you, as are the world's. Much depends on the events of the next few days. There are some in Iraq who hope to profit from the turmoil. These people will attempt to incite violence and cause chaos. You, as members of the military, swore to defend the nation – and its people – and you must not allow this to happen. You will serve your country best by contributing to an orderly and peaceful transition to the Coalition Provisional Authority.

The soldiers of the Coalition are the best trained and equipped in the world. They will not hesitate to intervene to stop criminal acts.

There are several guidelines you must abide by. You must comply with all orders and instructions issued by Coalition Forces. To help in these important efforts, you must do the following:

- Cease all combat operations against Coalition Forces immediately. Prominently display a large white flag in front of your headquarters, and place large white flags on all equipment, vehicles, and facilities. These markings must be clearly visible from the air.
- If you are currently located at a garrison, barracks, or cantonment, remain there to await orders and instructions from Coalition Forces. If you are not located in a garrison, barracks, or cantonment, remain at your current position. Do not move more than one kilometer from your vehicle or your position. Do not convoy or march to any other location unless directed and escorted by Coalition Forces.
- If your Commanding Officer is not present, the senior ranking Officer or Non-Commissioned Officer shall take charge, see to the safety and welfare of his troops, secure all weapons, maintain order and unit integrity, conduct an inventory of all personnel and weapons, and remain in place pending instructions from a Coalition Forces Officer.
- Do not threaten Coalition Forces or interfere with any operations.
- Immediately obey all orders and instructions issued by Coalition Forces.
- Do not contact other Iraqi military or paramilitary forces or other internal security units, or personnel. Within 72 hours, a Coalition Forces representative will contact you and give you additional instructions.
- Turn off all radars, computers, and communications systems immediately, and leave them off. *[CENTCOM should be authorized to determine any exceptions to this general rule]*.
- Immediately park all military aircraft away from runways. Do not block, damage, or destroy any roads or runways.
- Immediately park all vehicles. Place all heavy and/or crew served weapons systems in formations. Rotate all weapons tubes over the back deck. Clear all weapons. Park all vehicles in squares no larger than a battalion size.
- Unload ammunition from every vehicle and weapon. Store all ammunition separately and safely away from all weapons systems.
- Secure all personal weapons in unit arms rooms or locked within tactical vehicles. Do not damage or destroy these weapons. Officers may retain their side arms to

defend their subordinates against persons attempting or committing acts likely to cause serious bodily injury or death. Prepare written inventories of all weapons for presentation to Coalition Forces representatives. Be prepared to surrender these weapons if ordered by Coalition Forces representatives.

- Do not destroy or disable any military weapons, equipment, official or personal records, or facilities. Do not destroy or disable any communications equipment, computer or cryptological devices of any kind.
- Do not attempt to leave your unit. Remain in uniform at all times. Maintain unit integrity and good order and discipline your units. Obey the orders of your commanders that are consistent with the terms of surrender. Commanders must treat subordinates fairly and humanely. Corporal punishment of subordinates is prohibited.
- Immediately notify Coalition Forces of any storage or production facility related to nuclear, chemical, or biological weapons or missiles.
- Immediately notify Coalition Forces of the location of all mines, minefields, man-portable air-defense systems, and anti-aircraft systems.
- You will receive food, water, and medical care if required. Should your soldiers require immediate medical treatment or food or water, display a large crescent of any color that is visible from the air. Do not attempt to make contact with Coalition Forces by firing flares or any other method. Coalition Forces will contact you.
- Do not damage or destroy transportation systems, public utilities, factories, or natural resources and facilities associated with their extraction, processing, and storage.

REMEMBER: If you pick up arms, resume combat operations, or threaten any Coalition Forces after surrendering, you will be attacked. If you survive, you may be subject to prosecution.

General Tommy R. Franks
Commander of Coalition Forces

Document 172

Proclamation to the People of Iraq

23 April 2003

I, Lieutenant General David McKiernan, Commander of all Coalition Ground Forces in Iraq, affirm to the citizens of Iraq the Coalition's commitment to restoring security, stability and rapidly repairing Iraq's damaged infrastructure. As the head authority in Iraq, I call for the immediate cessation of all criminal activity to include acts of reprisal, looting, and attacks on Coalition forces. Those who commit criminal acts will be apprehended and be subjected to criminal punishment. I expect the support and assistance of the proud people of Iraq to restore stability to Iraq. To this end, I charge the citizens of Iraq to immediately return to work. Citizens who have served in leadership positions must identify themselves to Coalition forces to assist in the building of a new Iraqi government.

The Coalition, and the Coalition alone, retains absolute authority within Iraq. The Coalition will remain in control until it transfers its authority to a new firmly established and internationally recognized Iraqi Government. Individuals or organizations may not claim control of property, civil institutions or represent themselves as civil or military authorities without the explicit endorsement of the Coalition. Furthermore, the wearing of any distinguishing uniforms denoting a position of civil or military authority, specific group or organization is not authorized unless sanctioned by the Coalition. Likewise no one is authorized to speak as my representative or for Coalition forces. Those choosing to represent themselves in this manner will be considered a disruption to the stability of Iraq and treated as criminals. Additionally, all checkpoints and traffic control points, both established and planned, are not authorized unless directed and supervised by Coalition forces.

Together the noble people of Iraq and the Coalition will endeavor to reestablish a viable nation state and a model of success in the international community.

[Signed] *David D. McKiernan*
Lieutenant General, United States

Document 173
Forms Disavowing or Denouncing the Ba'ath Party

23 April 2003

Declaration to Disavow the Ba'ath Party

I, __________________(name), hereby disavow and renounce my membership in the Arab Socialist Renaissance Party of Iraq (Ba'ath Party). I understand that the Ba'ath Party is disestablished and abolished. I expressly reject and denounce the Ba'ath Party and Saddam Hussein and his regime, as well as my previous association with it.

I acknowledge that any continued association with, or involvement in, the Ba'ath Party or its activities constitutes a violation of an order by the Coalition Provisional Authority. I pledge to cooperate fully with the Coalition Provisional Authority in serving the people of Iraq and building a new Iraqi government. I will obey the laws of Iraq and all proclamations, orders and instructions of the Coalition Provisional Authority. As God is my witness:

Date:_______________, 2003

____________________________	____________________________
(name of signatory)	(signature)
____________________________	____________________________
(name of witness)	(signature)
____________________________	____________________________
(name of witness)	(signature)

Declaration to Denounce the Ba'ath Party

I, __________________(name), am not, nor have I ever been, a member of the Arab Socialist Renaissance Party of Iraq (Ba'ath Party). I understand that the Ba'ath Party is disestablished and abolished. I expressly reject and renounce the Ba'ath Party and Saddam Hussein and his regime, as well as my previous association with it.

Date_____________, 2003

_________________________ _________________________

(name of signatory) (signature)

_________________________ _________________________

(name of witness) (signature)

_________________________ _________________________

(name of witness) (signature)

Document 174

Radio Address to the Iraqi People by ORHA Director Lt. General (Ret.) Jay Garner and his British Deputy Major General Tim Cross

27 April 2003

Hello I'm Jay Garner and I'm here to help you rebuild your country, and turn your government into one that serves you. Across Iraq, my staff is already hard at work. Most of you now have the electricity back on, and many of you have clean water again in their homes. The hospitals are starting to get supplies and the service that they need to operate. Over the next few days, over the next few weeks you will all see these services restored and along with the military we're working to keep your streets safe. As security continues to be improved, this security job will be done more and more by Iraqis, but by Iraqis who work with you and not against you. I'll be here for a short time, just to help get things going. But this is your country and your future. Your new government will be an open government and an honest government. That is your dream, it is my dream and it's the dream of the world. You must return to work – in government institutions and in the town services, so that you can help shape the government and you can help shape your future. It's your skills and it's your pride that will rebuild the country. And I promise you, you will be paid for your work. My colleague, General McKiernan made a short announcement last night about security and you will hear that announcement now,[30] followed by a few words by my deputy Major General Tim Cross. Thank you.

My name is Tim Cross, I'm Jay Garner's British deputy. Amongst my tasks, is to ensure that this organisation, the office for reconstruction and humanitarian assistance, is a truly international force. Among our staff we have already had Americans and British, Australians, Danes, Spanish and Romanians, and staff from many other countries all over the world are already on their way to assist. And of course we have many Iraqis too, and we will be employing and working with many more. Now that you have been freed of the tyranny of Saddam Hussein, the world as a whole wants to see Iraq succeed as a free and great country, This international effort is a reflection of that will. And most important is that determination, which I have already witnessed in the short time that I have been here. It is that determination that will make Iraq a great success. Personally, like Jay, who helped Iraqis in northern Iraq after the last Gulf War, I have experience of helping a people rebuilding their country after oppression and war and working with Muslims in the Balkans, was a particular honour for me. Now I am greatly honoured to be working with you to help rebuild this great country.

[30] Lt-Gen McKiernan's statement was not available.

Document 175
Delegation of Authority to the Director, Office of Reconstruction and Humanitarian Assistance
28 April 2003

United States Central Command
Office of the Commander in Chief
7115 South Boundary Boulevard
MacDill Airforce Base, Florida 33621-5101

MEMORANDUM FOR Director, Office of Reconstruction and Humanitarian Assistance
SUBJECT: Delegation of Authority

As the Coalition Provisional Authority responsible for the temporary governance and civil administration of the State of Iraq, I authorize you, on my behalf, to reestablish, reorganize, provide oversight, and reform the Iraqi central government ministries and infrastructure for the benefit of the people of the State of Iraq.
[Signed] *Tommy R. Franks*
General, USA

Document 176
Coalition Postwar Government in Iraq
May 2003[31]

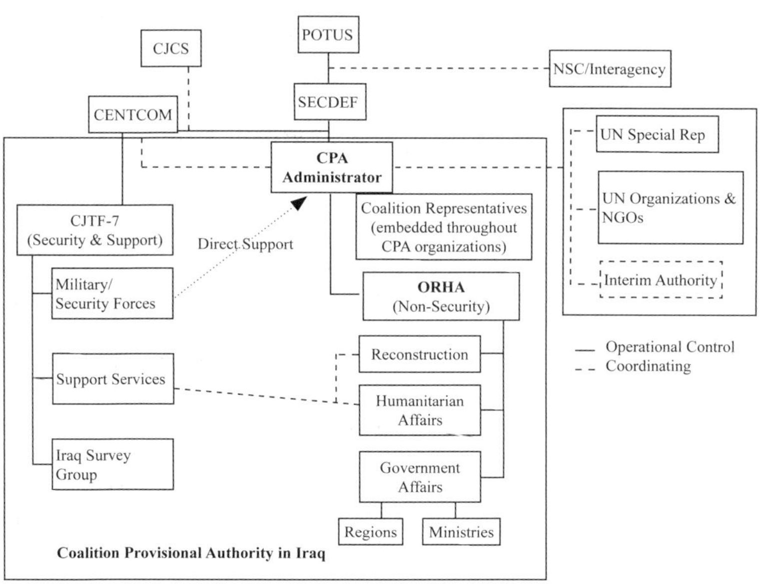

[31] This Chart was created by the US Department of Defense and was made available on the internet; it is no longer available. The Chart was not dated but the legend below the Chart mentions Lt.-Gen. David D. McKiernan as Commander of CJTF-7 and Sergio Vieira de Mello as UN Special Representative. This indicates that the Chart reflects the situation after the latter's appointment on 27 May 2003.

Document 177
Appointment of Senior Ministry Advisor
2 May 2003

U.S. Department of Defense
Office of Reconstruction and Humanitarian Assistance
CFLCC-ORHA
APO AE 09304

To: Ministry of Youth
From: Director, Office of Reconstruction and Humanitarian Assistance
Subj: Appointment

On behalf of the Coalition Provisional Authority, I am authorized to oversee the reestablishment of Iraqi central government ministries and infrastructure.

I hereby appoint Don Eberly as the Senior Ministry Advisor from the Office of Reconstruction and Humanitarian Assistance to the Ministry of Youth to act on my behalf in matters related to that Ministry. In that capacity, he will supervise the activities of this Ministry on behalf of the Coalition Provisional Authority.

As public servants, you have a responsibility to Iraq and to the Iraqi people. I expect your full cooperation and adherence to Mr. Eberly's supervision.

[Signed] *Jay Garner*
Director
Office of Reconstruction and Humanitarian Assistance

Document 178
Draft Policy Guidance: De-Baathification of Iraq
7 May 2003

The Problem:

- Under Saddam Hussein, the Baath Party played a key role in enforcing the writ of the regime, monitoring the population, mobilizing popular support, and socializing Iraqi youth.
  - The Party included approximately 70,000-100,000 full members, and 700,000-1 million affiliates.
  - The Baath Party maintained a pervasive presence in every institution and every city, town, and village in Iraq.
- Former regime Baath Party networks are believed to have organized violence against Coalition forces, and may subvert the Iraqi Interim Authority (IIA), intimidate Iraqis working with the Coalition, and engage in criminal activities.
- Baathist practices and ideology could hinder the transition to democracy in Iraq.
- Failure to implement de-Baathification with urgency and to sever contact with former regime figures trying to reestablish themselves could turn popular Iraqi opinion against the Coalition.

Overall Objectives:

- Break the barrier of fear created by the Baath that continues to hold many Iraqis in thrall, hinders cooperation with the Coalition, and precludes effective de-Baathification.
- De-Baathification of Iraqi government and society, by dismantling the Baath Party and its popular and youth organizations, eliminating the party's influence, and breaking up surviving party networks.

Policy Guidance:

- The following section consists of two parts:
  - The first part provides guidance regarding breaking the barrier of fear – the first step toward de-Baathification.
  - The second provides guidance regarding de-Baathification of Iraqi government and society.

Policy Guidance – Breaking the Barrier of Fear:

- ***Seek Information:*** Actively seek information from Iraqis concerning the identity of Baath Party members, and the crimes and abuses of th Baathist regime, to demonstrate Coalition commitment and obtain information critical to the de-Baathification effort.
  - Devote special effort to obtaining Baath Party membership rolls.
- [...].[32]
- ***Actively Pursue de-Baathification and De-Saddamization of the Government and Society:*** Identify and vet party members, senior ministry officials, government and party minders, and former members of the intelligence and security services, IAW guidance set forth below.
- ***Publicize De-Baathification Measures:*** Publicize the surrender and detention of senior members of the Baath Party, through press releases to the local media and Commando Solo broadcasts.[33]
- ***Initiate Rewards Programs:*** Offer public rewards for information leading to the capture of senior members of the Baath Party, and individuals complicit in the crimes of the former regime.
- ***Ban Symbols of the Old Order:*** Ban the display of the image or likeness of Saddam Hussein or other readily identifiable members of the former regime, or symbols of the Baath or the former regime, in government buildings or public spaces.
- ***Reinforce Coalition Presence:*** Increase the overall Coalition presence in Iraq – to permit a rapid reaction capability for all cities and larger towns – while minimizing the fixed force footprint in heavily populated areas.
  - The augmented presence will reassure Iraqis inclined to work with the Coalition and IIA, and provide a capability to deal with a likely backlash against de-Baathification in some areas.
  - Whenever possible, routes taken by fixed and rotary wing aviation assets should pass close to population centers to multiply the effect of the Coalition presence, and provide comfort to those Iraqis friendly to the Coalition.

[32] The document was declassified only in part.

[33] Commando Solo is an US airborne broadcast station that started broadcasting over Iraq on 12 December 2002.

- ***Shut Down Arms Bazaars:*** Crack down on public arms bazaars, which may provide income for Baathist networks, and which contribute to an ongoing sense of insecurity and lawlessness in Iraq.

Policy Guidance – De-Baathification of Iraqi Government and Society:

- ***Baath Party Hierarchy:*** All full members of the Baath Party (i.e. those holding the rank of *'udw*, *'udw 'amil*, *'udw firqah*, *'udw shu 'bag*, or *'udw far'*) will be banned from employment in the public sector or as teachers. They should be removed from any public sector or teaching job they hold, and interviewed;
  - Those who cooperate with the Coalition will be free to return home. Those who are uncooperative, may be detained and held IAW international law, including Geneva Convention III and IV, as appropriate.
  - Exceptions to the ban on employment in the public sector or in teaching jobs will be considered (e.g., for individuals who clandestinely worked for the opposition or the Coalition, who acted to prevent atrocities, or who are deemed acceptable by non-Baathi colleagues and neighbors).
  - More junior party associates may be banned from public sector employment upon acquisition of sufficiently adverse information.
  - In considering the impact of such actions, de-Baathification will take precedence over administrative efficiency or convenience.
  - Those banned from public sector employment may be re-employed in the private sector. Some will require retraining, and assistance in finding gainful employment.
  - The efficacy and impact of these steps should be re-evaluated within two years.
- ***Government Ministries:*** Individuals holding positions in the top three layers of management at every government ministry (down to the level of Assistant Secretary – or the equivalent US government rank) should be interviewed regarding their relationship to the Party.
  - Full Baath Party members (i.e., those holding the Baath Party rank of *'udw*, *'udw 'amil*, *'udw firqah*, *'udw shu 'bag*, or *'udw far'*), will be removed from their jobs.
  - Those in the top three layers of management who are not full party members should be eligible for reinstatement.
  - Character references should be sought from workplace colleagues and neighbors.
  - Adverse information should lead to the banning of such individuals from public sector employment and, if appropriate, criminal prosecution.
  - Absent adverse information, those who cooperate with the Coalition should be reinstated, or remain eligible for public sector employment elsewhere.
  - Those who are uncooperative, may be detained and held IAW international law, including Geneva Convention III and IV, as appropriate.
  - More junior ministry members may be banned from public sector employment upon acquisition of sufficiently adverse information.
- ***Minders:*** Government or party 'minders' are to be identified and removed from their jobs, effective immediately.
  - Exceptions will be considered (e.g., for individuals who clandestinely worked for the opposition or the Coalition, who acted to prevent atrocities, or who are deemed acceptable by non-Baathi colleagues and neighbors).

– Members of the Iraq Reconstruction and Development Council (IRDC), assisting the Office for Reconstruction and Humanitarian Assistance (ORHA), will assist with all aspects of the vetting process for Baath Party members, government ministry officials, and government or party minders.

- ***Expunging Baathist Ideology:*** Text books reflecting Baathist views used by civil and military schools and institutions will be replaced by proper texts.
- ***Dismantling Saddamist Institutions:*** De-Baathification should also entail 'De-Saddamization' – the dismantling of Saddam-era intelligence and security services, including the Special Security Organization, the Iraqi Intelligence Service, General Directorate for Military Intelligence, and Feda'iyyi-Saddam, and the vetting of personnel from these organizations.
  – [...].
  – Those banned from public sector employment may be re-employed in the private sector. Some will require retraining, and assistance in finding gainful employment.
  – De-Saddamization will result in the banning of large numbers of individuals from particular tribal groups from Tikrit and nearby towns and villages.
  – Special efforts must be made to cultivate individuals and tribes from these areas who were at odds with the former regime, to discredit potential efforts to case de-Saddamization as a cover for a vendetta directed against these tribal groups, or the Sunni Arab community at large.
  – Members of the Iraq Reconstruction and Development Council (IRDC), that are assisting the Office for Reconstruction and Humanitarian Assistance (ORHA), will assist with all aspects of this vetting process for members of the former regime's intelligence and security services.
- ***Vetting New Appointees:*** Before appointing an Iraqi to any 'significant position' of responsibility as defined in 'Implementing Guidance for Appointing Iraqis to Positions of Responsibility,' the individual's name, along with as much biographical information as can be obtained (IAW standard biographic reports), should be forwarded to OSD Policy, via USCENTCOM, for vetting and approval.
  – ORHA, in consultation with local IIA officials, will be responsible for vetting all other applicants (lower- to mid-level positions).
  – Should incriminating evidence subsequently be found, the individual should be removed from his job, and tried, if appropriate.
- ***Complementary Supporting Actions:*** To succeed, de-Baathification shall be coupled with:
  – [...].[34]

[34] The document was declassified only in part. The document was prepared by the US Department of Defense and was shared with the British Embassy in Washington DC which in TelNo 655 of 14 May 2003 reported the content of it to London.

Document 179
Letter from US President George W. Bush to Ambassador L. Paul Bremer

9 May 2003

The Honorable L. Paul Bremer
Presidential Envoy to Iraq
Department of Defense
Washington, D.C. 20301

Dear Jerry:

Exercising my constitutional authority as Commander in Chief, and consistent with pertinent statutes, I hereby appoint you to serve as my Presidential Envoy to Iraq, reporting through the Secretary of Defense. Subject to the authority, direction, and control of the Secretary of Defense, you are authorized to oversee, direct, and coordinate all United States Government (USG) programs and activities in Iraq, except those under the command of the Commander, U.S. Central Command. This authority includes the responsibility to oversee the use of USG appropriations in Iraq, as well as Iraqi state- or regime-owned property that is properly under U.S. possession and made available for use in Iraq to assist the Iraqi people and support the recovery of Iraq. You and the Commander, U.S. Central Command, will communicate fully and continually, and cooperate in carrying out your respective responsibilities.

All USG elements in Iraq, other than those under the command of the Commander, U.S. Central Command, will keep you fully informed, at all times, of their current and planned activities. You will regularly review the resources of these elements (other than those under the command of the Commander, U.S. Central Command) and exercise final authority with respect to their personnel composition, staff levels, and funding. Every USG agency under your authority must obtain your approval before changing the composition or mandate of its staff, regardless of the employment category. You have the authority to see all communications to or from all USG elements in Iraq, however transmitted, except as determined by the Secretary of Defense, or as specifically exempted by law or Presidential decision. All USG personnel other than those in Iraq under the command of the Commander, U.S. Central Command, must obtain country clearance before entering Iraq on official business. You may refuse country clearance, or place conditions or restrictions on such personnel, as you deem necessary.

As Presidential Envoy to Iraq, you are not only my personal representative in Iraq, but also that of our country. America remains engaged in the world by history and by choice. We will protect the American people and support freedom throughout the world.

As you begin your work, I know your own sense of patriotism, selflessness, and desire for excellence will serve America well. Please be assured of my warmest regards and the best wishes of a grateful Nation.

Sincerely,

[Signed] *George W. Bush*

Document 180
Designation as Administrator of the Coalition Provisional Authority
13 May 2003

MEMORANDUM FOR PRESIDENTIAL ENVOY TO IRAQ
SUBJECT: Designation as Administrator of the Coalition Provisional Authority

Pursuant to the President's letter of May 9, 2003, appointing you as Presidential Envoy to Iraq, and my authority under applicable law, I hereby designate you as the head of the Coalition Provisional Authority, with the title of Administrator. You shall be responsible for the temporary governance of Iraq, and shall oversee, direct and coordinate all executive, legislative and judicial functions necessary to carry out this responsibility, including humanitarian relief and reconstruction and assisting in the formation of an Iraqi interim authority.

As the Commander of Coalition Forces, the Commander of U.S. Central Command shall directly support the Coalition Provisional Authority by deterring hostilities; maintaining Iraq's territorial integrity and security; searching for, securing and destroying weapons of mass destruction; and assisting in carrying out U.S. policy generally.

[Signed] *Donald Rumsfeld*
cc:
Chairman of the Joint Chiefs of Staff
Commander of U.S. Central Command

Document 181
Ambassador Bremer's Opening Statement at his First Press Conference in Baghdad
15 May 2003[35]

I'm delighted to be in Iraq. President Bush sent me to help the Iraqi people retake and rebuild their own country. In the short time that I have been here, I have seen many symbols and examples of the depth of depravity and evil of the former president, Saddam Hussein.

I've seen dozens and dozens of buildings, built purely for his own self-aggrandizement and I've seen the poverty which he forced his people to live in. In the past few days, I've seen the shocking and haunting pictures of mass graves which contain some of the thousands and thousands of Iraqis which Saddam murdered. And I have heard from dozens of Iraqis about their gratitude that the coalition has relieved them, finally, of this horror.

Saddam Hussein was a truly evil man. He repressed, tortured and murdered his own people, and he didn't go a day too soon. And now the Iraqi people are free from his terror, and they are rightly looking forward to a new beginning.

[35] There is a slight discrepancy between the transcript of the press conference and the press release issued by the US Department of Defense on that press conference. The text reproduced here is that of the transcript; for the text of the US DoD press release, see Opening statement from Ambassador Bremer's press conference in Baghdad, Iraq, 16 May 2003, http://www.defenselink.mil/transcripts/2003/tr20030515-0186.html.

It is my responsibility, as the administrator of the coalition provisional authority, to help the Iraqi people turn Iraq into a stable, safe, peaceful and prosperous country. I take that responsibility seriously, and I'm going to make sure that we can help them – we and the coalition partners can help them in every way possible.

Across most of Iraq, life is already getting better.

- The regime of fear and oppression is gone.
- The Shi'a of Iraq have been able to honor their religious traditions for the first time in decades.
- Town councils and local politicians are already starting to meet and openly and freely select their leaders.
- Water quality today is better in Basra than it was – has been for years.
- More Iraqis today have access to electricity than ever before.

But there are a number of problems – in particular, the problem of law and order here in Baghdad. Since I arrived on Monday [12 May], I've traveled around Baghdad every day, and I've seen shops open and people going about their lives. But there is a serious law-and-order problem. We will continue to address it.

We recall that Saddam released some 100,000 prisoners onto the streets last October. Many of these people were political prisoners, but some of them were criminals, violent criminals. It's time these people were put back in jail, and that's where we will put them. In the past 48 hours, we've arrested about 300 of them.

Police are now coming back to work, and we're starting to train them. In the old days, they received their orders from on high in Saddam's regime. In the new Iraq, they will be answerable to the Iraqi people. And those who were on high before – in particular, the Ba'athists – who used their power to repress the Iraqi people, will be removed from office. The Coalition Provisional Authority disestablished the Ba'athist Party on April 16th. Shortly, I will issue an order on measures to extirpate Ba'athists and Ba'athism from Iraq forever.

- We have and will aggressively move to seek to identify these people and remove them from office.
- We have hunted down and will continue to deal with those members of the old regime who are sabotaging the country and the coalition's efforts.
- We will ensure that representations of Saddam Hussein and other Ba'athist symbols are removed systematically from public display.
- And we will work with the Iraqis to set up a process of bringing Ba'athist officials to justice for their past crimes.

But we must do more than just deal with the past. We have an obligation to Iraq's future. The coalition will work to provide the conditions for Iraqis to govern themselves in the future. And to that end, the Coalition Provisional Authority will work with responsible Iraqis to begin the process of establishing a government representative of all Iraqi people.

Finally, let me just say how delighted I am to confirm that the United Nations mission here has agreed that the U.N. will use oil-for-food funds to purchase the Iraqi cereal crop, which is already being harvested. This will be a first, because under Saddam Hussein, he preferred to manipulate the cereal harvest for political ends. And he often used oil-for-food funds to build projects like his Olympic stadium.

When I met with the U.N. representative here yesterday, Mr. da Silva, we both agreed on the importance of securing a new United Nations resolution to allow the Iraqi people quickly to make use of their money now held by the United Nations. And I certainly hope that the Security Council will work swiftly on the draft resolution before them lifting those sanctions.

Document 182
Memorandum from Ambassador Bremer for Secretary of Defense Rumsfeld, Dissolution of the Ministry of Defense and Related Entities

19 May 2003

In the coming days I propose to issue the attached order (Tab A) carrying forward the de-Ba'athification effort by dissolving Saddam's key security ministries. I could also implement the policies in Tab B on payments related to the dissolved entities. I believe it is desirable to issue these orders as soon as possible to maintain the momentum of our de-Ba'athification campaign.

The entities to be dissolved were the core of the Saddam system. The property of these entities will vest in the CPA and their employees will be dismissed. The order also makes clear we will begin the process of establishing new armed forces for the new Iraq to provide for legitimate self-defense needs.

The generally positive reaction to the earlier de-Ba'athification order of 16 May 03 leads me to believe this order will generate a good deal of public support, despite its impacting many more people. In any event, it is a critical step in our effort to destroy the underpinnings of the Saddam regime, to demonstrate to the Iraqi people that we have done so, and that neither Saddam nor his gang is coming back.

Some organizations that were undoubtedly in large part also part of the system are left in existence for now. For example, I do not at this time propose to dissolve the Ministry of Interior because it oversees the police, which we are using to help restore order, as well as customs and, incredibly, the sewer system; the Ministry (or commission) of Military Industrialization, because it runs state-owned enterprises with significant civil functions; and the Ministry of Higher Education and Science because it administers universities that we are working to re-open. Elements of those entities will likely be dissolved after further review.

The order will affect large numbers of people. There were some 400,000 employees of the MOD alone. Therefore it is necessary to establish a policy on payments to employees and retirees of the dissolved entities. I intend to adopt the payment policy outlined in Tab B.

That policy continues pension payments for people who were drawing a pension from dissolved entities before the war ended, provides for a termination payment to employees of dissolved entities, and authorizes employment of such persons as individuals in civilian jobs by other Iraqi and Coalition agencies. All this is subject to the overriding principle that no payments will be made to 'disqualified persons,' i.e., people barred from government employment by the de-Ba'athification order (notably those in the top three ranks of the party). All military officers with the rank of Colonel and above will be presumed to be Disqualified Persons, unless they can establish otherwise. Moreover, the policy reserves our right to revoke pensions as a penalty for past or future illegal conduct, and to modify pension arrangements to eliminate special privileges granted by the old regime.

There is obviously something that catches in the craw about paying anything to people who worked at the heart of Saddam's regime. Against this, however, we must balance the risks of serious discontent, increased terrorism, and much higher crime rates that may result if we cut of [sic] all military and security sector pensioners in a heavily militarized society. For this reason, I recommend that we pay most pensions – to include military retirees who retired before 16 April – the date of Gen Franks Freedom Message dissolving the

Ba'ath Party.[36] I also recommend severance payments to employees of dissolved entities. Disqualified persons, of course, would receive neither type of payment. If you concur with this policy in principal, the next step is development of payment plans.

There will be some delay in making these payments, because, in contrast to the situation for most civilian agencies, we do not have employee rosters, or contacts with administrative officials of the dissolved entities. In conjunction with the intelligence community, we are starting to assemble the necessary dates and make the necessary data and make the necessary mechanical preparations for the payments. When we have those data, at least in approximate form, we will estimate the likely costs and request, pursuant to the procedures for civilian agency payments, an allocation of Iraqi funds needed for payment. The mechanics of payments will follow, in so far as possible, the process that has worked fairly well in the case of the 'emergency' and salary payments to civil servants in civilian agencies.

In short, I believe these policies, taken together, are necessary to show both our determination to root out Saddamism, at the same time mitigating the risks to our broad objectives for security which these measures might otherwise cause.[37]

[Tab A]
Order of the Administrator of the Coalition Provisional Authority
Dissolution of Entities
May 20, 2003[38]

The following Entities (the 'Dissolved Entities') are hereby dissolved:

The Ministry of Defence
The Ministry of Information
The Ministry of State for Military Affairs
The Iraqi Intelligence Service
The National Security Bureau
The Directorate of National Security (Amn al-'Am)
The Special Security Organization

All Entities affiliated with or comprising Saddam Hussein's bodyguards to include:

- Murafaqin (Companions)
- Himaya al Khasa (Special Guard)

The following military organizations:

- The Army, Air Force, Navy, the Air Defence Force, and other regular military services
- The Republican Guard
- The Special Republican Guard
- The Al Quds Force
- Emergency Forces (Quwat al Tawari)

The following paramilitaries:

- Saddam Fedayeen
- Ba'ath Party Militia
- Friends of Saddam
- Saddam's Lion Cubs (Ashbal Saddam)

[36] For the text of the Freedom Message, see *Doc 169*.
[37] The Memorandum was cc'ed to Paul Wolfowitz, Doug Feith, Jim Haynes.
[38] For the text of CPA Order No 2, Dissolution of Entities, see *Doc 15*.

Other Organizations:

- The Presidential Diwan
- The Presidential Secretariat
- The Revolutionary Command Council
- The National Assembly
- The Youth Organization (al-Futuwah)

All organizations subordinate to the Dissolved Entities are also dissolved.

Additional Entities may be added to this list in the future.

All assets, including records and data in whatever form maintained, wherever located, of the Dissolved Entities are the property of the Administrator of the Coalition Provisional Authority as Receiver and Trustee. Those assets will be used for the benefit of the Iraqi people by the Administrator of the Coalition Provisional Authority and transitional interim authorities as they from time to time exist, pending the establishment of full representative self-government by Iraqis of Iraq. In appropriate cases such assets may be transferred to civilian agencies or privatized.

The Coalition Provisional Authority may delegate his powers and responsibilities as Receiver and Trustee to such person or persons, or entity or entities, as he determines appropriate.

All employees of the Dissolved Entities are dismissed effective April 16, 2003.

All persons employed, in any capacity or in any form, by the Dissolved Entities remain subject to the penalties for acts committed during their tenure as such.

All military or other ranks granted to employees and functionaries of the Dissolved Entities by the former Regime are hereby cancelled.

All financial obligations of the Dissolved Entities are suspended. Procedures will be established whereby persons claiming to be the beneficiaries of such obligations may apply for lifting the suspension. Pensions being paid before 16 April 2003 will continue to be paid, including to war widows, provided that the power is reserved to the CPA and to the future Iraqi government to revoke or reduce pensions as a penalty for past or future illegal conduct or to modify pension arrangements to eliminate improper privileges granted to the Baathist regime.

Persons in possession of the assets of the Dissolved Entities shall preserve those assets, promptly inform the Receiver and Trustee, through the local Coalition military or civilian authorities, of the assets in their possession, and immediately turn the assets over to the Receiver and Trustee, as directed by the local Coalition authorities.

After the date of this Order, continued possession, or attempts to transfer or to conceal such assets of whatever character, will be subject to arrest and punishment.

Persons who provide information to the Coalition authorities relating to the Dissolved Entities, or their assets or personnel, shall be suitably compensated as the Receiver and Trustee may determine.

The Coalition Provisional Authority plans to create in the near future a New Iraqi Corps, as the first step in the process of forming a national self-defense capability for a free Iraq. That Corps will be under civilian control, professional, non-political, militarily effective, and representative of all Iraqis. Former employees wishing to be considered for employment by the Receiver and Trustee will be informed of procedures for application.

All provisions of General Frank's Freedom Message to the Iraqi People of 16 April 2003 and all prior orders of the Coalition Provisional Authority are reconfirmed and remain in effect.

[Tab B]

Outline of Policy Re Payments to Former Military/MOD and related persons

- No further payments will be made to persons disqualified for government service under the de-Baathification policy announced on 16 May 03 ('Disqualified Persons' or 'DPs'). Officers COL and above will be rebuttably presumed to be DPs, and will not be paid until they establish that they are not DPs.
- Employees of Dissolved Entities, i.e., those entities dissolved by CPA Order of May —, [the order dissolving the MOD, intelligence agencies, armed forces, etc.] will be terminated effective the date of that order.
- Those terminated employees will not be eligible to claim a pension, regardless of retirement rules that may be alleged to entitle them to retire on pension rather than be terminated. Unless they are Disqualified Persons, they will, however, be paid a one-time 'transition payment' (equivalent to a month's pay at new scales). Disqualified Persons will not be paid a termination payment.
- Pensions of former employees of the Dissolved Entities, including military pensions and pensions of survivors (including war widows), that were being paid prior to 16 Apr 03 will be continued. Purported retirements after that date are ineffective, and do not entitle a person to a pension. CPA reserves the power for itself and the future Iraqi government to end or modify a person's pension as a penalty for illegal conduct, before or after 16 April 03, and to modify pension arrangements to eliminate improper privileges granted by the Baathist regime.
- Former employees of dissolved entities (other than Disqualified Persons) are eligible for employment by other Iraqi government agencies. For example, military medical personnel can be employed by civilian health agencies and paid as such. Former employees of Dissolved Entities do not, however, have any special eligibility or other privileges for such employment by reason of their service for Dissolved Entities.
- Similarly, former employees of dissolved entities (other than Disqualified Persons) can be hired as individuals by Coalition military or civil authorities, for example as security guards. They are not hired as reconstituted old units, as soldiers, or as part of the future Iraqi military.
- A New Iraqi Corps will be established as the first stage of creating a self-defense capability for the new Iraq. Former military personnel, below the rank of COL and not otherwise disqualified, will be eligible for the NIC. However, recognize that numbers will be limited, especially for officers.
- Note: Payments to police and other employees of entities other than the Dissolved Entities will continue as announced and being implemented already.

Document 183

Designation of the Secretary of the Army as Department of Defense Executive Agent for the Office of Reconstruction and Humanitarian Assistance

21 May 2003

MEMORANDUM FOR SECRETARY OF THE MILITARY DEPARTMENTS
CHAIRMAN OF THE JOINT CHIEFS OF STAFF UNDER SECRETARIES OF DEFENSE
COMBATANT COMMANDERS
GENERAL COUNSEL, DEPARTMENT OF DEFENSE
ASSISTANTS TO THE SECRETARY OF DEFENSE
DIRECTOR, ADMINISTRATION AND MANAGEMENTS
DIRECTORS OF THE DOD FIELD ACTIVITIES

SUBJECT: Designation of the Secretary of the Army as Department of Defense Executive Agent for the Office of Reconstruction and Humanitarian Assistance

Pursuant to Title 10 U.S.C. §113 and consistent with DoD Directive 5100.88 and my memorandum of April 2, 2003 on support for the Office of Reconstruction and Humanitarian Assistance,[39] I hereby designate the Secretary of the Army as the DoD Executive Agent for Support of the Office of Reconstruction and Humanitarian Assistance (ORHA), with responsibility to provide such administrative, logistics, and contracting support as ORHA requires for humanitarian relief and reconstruction for the people of Iraq.

The Secretary of the Army, in coordination with the Director, ORHA, shall coordinate the financial requirement for support to ORHA with the Under Secretary of Defense (Comptroller) and Director, Administration and Management who shall identify funding for these requirements and provide appropriate management oversight for all funding provided to support this mission. In addition, the DoD Executive Agent, in coordination with the Under Secretary of Defense (Acquisition, Technology, and Logistics) and Director, Administration and Management, will establish appropriate management oversight for the acquisition and contracting support provided to ORHA.

The Director, Administration and Management shall issue the DoD directive establishing the DoD Executive Agent for ORHA ensuring appropriate responsibilities and reporting relationships are defined and, in coordination with the DoD Executive Agent, shall provide appropriate management oversight for the accession process by which DoD civilians, military personnel, and contractors are hired, assigned, or detailed to ORHA.

[Signed] *Paul Wolfowitz*

[39] See *Doc 166*.

Document 184
CPA Legal Instruments

22 May 2003

TO: L. Paul Bremer, III
FROM: Office of General Counsel
SUBJECT: CPA Legal Instruments

Objective

Your appointment as Presidential Envoy to Iraq, and your designation as head of the Coalition Provisional Authority (CPA) with the title as Administrator necessitates publication of a regulation prescribing the means by which you will exercise your authority.

Recommendation

Issue a Regulation No. 1[40] clearly stating the authority and responsibilities of the Administrator of the CPA. The Regulation should clearly set out the law-making powers of the Administrator and clarify the applicable law in Iraq. The Regulation would also affirm that the CPA Administrator is the sole authority responsible for the promulgation of national legislation at this time.

Background

Various instruments define and impact upon the authority and structure of the CPA.

ORHA

On January 20, 2003, NSPD-24 created the Office of Reconstruction and Humanitarian Assistance (ORHA) as a planning office within the Department of Defense. ORHA's mandate includes '[assisting] in administering Iraq for a limited period of time.'

This document does not address ORHA's role within the CPA.

Proclamations and Delegations issued by Military Commanders.

The Franks Freedom Message: On April 16, 2003, General Franks issued the Freedom Message to the Iraqi People in which he specifically created 'the Coalition Provisional Authority to exercise powers of government temporarily, and as necessary, especially to provide security, to allow the delivery of humanitarian aid and to eliminate weapons of mass destruction.'[41] Attached to the Freedom Message were two sets of instructions: Instructions to the Iraqi Armed Forces and Instructions to the Citizens of Iraq.[42] The Instructions to the Citizens of Iraq, which were issued as a Directive at the time the Freedom Message was issued, provided that certain mandatory provisions of the Directive would be punishable by a Coalition Provisional Authority Court. This Court has not been established.

[40] See *Doc 1*.
[41] For the full text of General Franks' Freedom Message, see *Doc 169*.
[42] These Instructions are reproduced as *Doc 170* and *Doc 171*.

The Freedom Message does not define the structure or institutions that form the CPA or allocate responsibilities within the CPA.

The McKiernan Proclamation: On or around 24 April 2003, Lieutenant General McKiernan, as the Commander of all Coalition Ground Forces in Iraq, issued a Proclamation to the People of Iraq designed to prevent individuals from representing themselves as having control over civil institutions.[43] This document was issued by McKiernan as 'the head authority in Iraq.'

Franks Delegation of Authority to ORHA: On 28 April 2003, General Franks issued a memorandum stating that General Garner, as director of ORHA, had the authority, on behalf of the CPA, 'to reestablish, reorganize, provide oversight, and reform the Iraqi central government ministries and infrastructure for the benefit of the people of the State of Iraq.'[44]

Designation of the Presidential Envoy to Iraq: On May 9, 2003, the President appointed you as the Presidential Envoy to Iraq. The President's letter states that, subject to the Secretary of Defense's authority, direction and control, you are authorized to oversee, direct and coordinate all USG programs and activities in Iraq, except those under the command of the Commander, U.S. Central Command.[45] The appointment states that the Presidential Envoy and the Commander, U.S. Central Command will communicate fully and continually, and cooperate in carrying out their respective mandates.

Designation of the CPA Administrator: On May 13, 2003, the Secretary of Defense designated you as the head of the CPA, with the title of Administrator, and directed you to 'oversee, direct and coordinate all executive, legislative and judicial functions necessary' to temporarily govern Iraq, including 'humanitarian relief and reconstruction and assisting in the formation of an Iraqi interim authority.'[46] The memorandum also specified that 'the Commander of the U.S. Central Command shall directly support the CPA by deterring hostilities; maintaining Iraq's territorial integrity and security; searching for, securing and destroying weapons of mass destruction; and assisting in carrying out U.S. policy generally.'

This document reaffirms your broad authority to govern Iraq temporarily, specifies that this authority includes the responsibility for Iraq relief and reconstruction activities and assisting Iraq's political transformation, and clarifies the Commander, U.S. Central Command's supportive role as Commander of the Coalition Forces.

Conclusion

Pursuant to the President's appointment letter of May 9, 2003, and consistent with the Secretary of Defense designation of May 3, 2003, you possess lawmaking authority in Iraq as head of the CPA. The Commander of the Coalition Forces military supports you in the

[43] For the full text of the Proclamation to the People of Iraq, see *Doc 172*.

[44] For the full text of the Delegation of Authority to the Director, Office of Reconstruction and Humanitarian Assistance, see *Doc 175*.

[45] The Letter from US President George W. Bush to Ambassador L. Paul Bremer is reproduced as *Doc 179*.

[46] For the Secretary of Defense's Memorandum, see *Doc 180*.

performance of your responsibilities. The Presidential appointment letter of May 9, 2003 emphasizes that the CPA Administrator and the Commander, US Central Command 'will communicate fully and continually and cooperate in carrying out [their] responsibilities.'

A Regulation No. 1 should be issued clearly setting out your authorities and responsibilities and identifying you as the source of binding legal authority for the Coalition Provisional Authority and the Iraqi population and institutions.

Document 185
Letter from the Administrator to President George W. Bush

22 May 2003[47]

Mr. President:

After a week on the ground, I thought it might be useful to give you my first impressions of the situation here. We have two important goals in this immediate period. We must make it clear to everyone that we mean business: that Saddam and the Baathists are finished. And we must show the average Iraqi that his life will be better.

I have now visited cities in the North and South and have traveled around Baghdad every day, speaking often to Iraqis on the streets or in stores. As I have moved around, there has been an almost universal expression of thanks to the US and to you in particular for freeing Iraq from Saddam's tyranny. In the northern town of Mosul yesterday, an old man, under the impression that I was President Bush (he apparently has poor TV reception), rushed up and planted two very wet and hairy kisses on my cheeks. (Such events confirm the wisdom of the ancient custom of sending emissaries to far away lands).

No doubt you have seen reports of demonstrations criticizing America. But these relate almost entirely to the continued lack of order (which is largely a Baghdad phenomenon) and basic services. No one publicly supports Saddam.

The dissolution of his chosen instrument of political domination, the Baath Party, has been very well received. Several Iraqis have told me, literally with tears in their eyes, that they have waited 30 years for this moment. While the resulting dismissal of public servants has caused some inefficiencies and griping, in most cases younger civil servants have expressed pleasure, even joy, at the measure. (At a minimum they are attracted to the prospect of promotion opportunities.) I will parallel this step with an even more robust measure dissolving Saddam's military and intelligence structures to emphasize that we mean business. We are seeing signs that the outlawed organizations are behind some of the street violence here.

We will combine these declaratory policies with vigorous steps to impose law and order on the streets of Baghdad. This, far more than the much-discussed evolution of political structures, is what dominates the life of the average urban resident. General McKiernan and I are cooperating closely to increase the visible presence of police and armed forces on the streets. People must no longer fear to send their children to school or their wives to work.

Restoring law and order is a necessary but insufficient condition for success. We face a series of urgent issues involving the restoration of basic services. We have made great progress under Jay Garner's leadership. Iraqis in the north and south have more electricity, and residents

[47] The letter was drafted on 20 May 2003 and sent to President Bush on 22 May through Secretary of Defense Donald H. Rumsfeld. The letter was first published on the New York Times website on 4 September 2007.

of Basra have more water, than they had before the war. In Baghdad our priority remains getting electricity back to prewar levels, for on it also depend the water and sewer systems.

I have relaunched the political dialogue with Iraqi leaders. My message is that full sovereignty under an Iraqi government can come after democratic elections, which themselves must be based on a constitution agreed by all the people. This process will take time. Patience will be a virtue (though evidence of it is thus far lacking). At the same time, I am stressing that we are prepared to move that process as quickly as the Iraqis provided it is one that leads to a representative government at peace with its neighbors.

Our immediate goal will be to arrange a National Conference this summer which will set in motion the writing of a constitution, and reform of the judicial, legal and economic systems. As the Iraqis are progressively more prepared to assume responsibility, we would be prepared to give it to them. But we must be firm and clear: a legitimate sovereign Iraqi government must be built on a well-prepared base.

Respectfully,
Jerry Bremer
Baghdad
May 20, 2003[48]

Document 186
Guidance for the Implementation of De-Ba'athification Policy

23 May 2003

1. Who qualifies for an exception?

The Administrator of the Coalition Provisional Authority has the discretion to grant exceptions to the de-ba'athification policy. Although he may choose to delegate this authority, he retains the ability to reverse any decision to grant or refuse an exception.

In considering whether to grant an exception, the CPA will take a number of factors into account, including whether the individual:

- Is willing to denounce the Ba'ath Party and his past association with it;
- Was a senior Ba'ath Party member or simply a 'full' party member;
- Has exceptional educational qualifications;
- Left the Ba'ath Party before April 16, 2003;
- Continues to command the support of his colleagues and respect of their subordinates;
- Is judged to be indispensable to achieving important Coalition interests at least in the immediate term;
- Can demonstrate that he joined the party to hold his job or support his family.

[48] President Bush replied in a letter, dated 23 May 2003, which reads:
'Dear Jerry:
Thank you for your May 22nd letter. Your leadership is apparent. You have quickly made a positive and significant impact. You have my full support and confidence. You also have the backing of our Administration that knows our work will take time. We will fend off the impatient as you and your team steadily improve the lives of the Iraqi people.
I am told living conditions for ORHA are terrible. Improve them quickly so decisions are sound and life is bearable.
All my best.
Sincerely,
George W. Bush.

As soon as can be arranged, a professional investigator or an administrative law judge attached to the Coalition Provisional Authority will determine whether a person meets the above criteria. Meanwhile, exceptions will be determined by the Administrator. Exceptions may either allow the individual to stay on in his current position or specify that he can only continue employment at the ministry in a lower position. The Administrator reserves the right to overturn an exception if new evidence comes to light that is grounds for altering the original decision.

2. Will members of the top three tiers of management be allowed to maintain their current positions pending the start of the exception process?
No. All employees who were 1) in the top four layers of the Ba'ath Party or 2) full Ba'ath Party members in the top three tiers of ministry management (including Dgs) must leave their jobs immediately. In unusual circumstances, a temporary exception may be granted if the senior advisor can make the case that removing an individual immediately will seriously harm important U.S. or Coalition interests (such as restoration of law and order in Iraq, the reestablishment of a judicial system, and the repair of power and water systems). Exceptions will not be granted simply to preserve the convenience or efficient running of institutions. If a senior advisor wishes to request a temporary exception, he or she will use the attached form addressed to the CPA Administrator.[49]

3. Will we pay pensions to those who lose their jobs due to their Ba'ath Party involvement?
No. Senior advisors and other ORHA staff may respond to pension queries by saying 1) that the Coalition has no plans to pay the pensions of people who lose their job under the de-ba'athification policy and 2) our unwillingness to do so does not prejudice the ability of a future Iraqi government to decide otherwise. We reserve the right to revisit this issue if we find the consequences of this approach to be contrary to Coalition interests.

4. Should DGs be included in the top three tiers of management?
Yes. The de-ba'athification policy will be applied down to and including the DG level, regardless of how many tiers of management sit above DGs.

5. How many ministry employees will we investigate for senior Ba'ath Party membership?
We will investigate 1) all employees in the top three tiers of ministry management (to include DGs as stated above) and 2) all individuals for whom we receive at least two independent allegations that they were senior ba'athists.

6. Will people have the right to appeal?
Yes. An appeal mechanism will be created for those who wish to contest the facts of their case (i.e. that they were members of the Ba'ath Party). We will not consider appeals over the denial of an exception.

7. Will ex-members of the Ba'ath party be exempt from the de-ba'athification policy?
Having left the Ba'ath Party before 16 April 2003 will not in itself be sufficient for an individual to avoid the consequences of the de-ba'athification policy. It may weigh in a person's favor when an exception is being considered.

[49] The form is not available.

8. Are those removed from positions of management on account of Ba'ath Party full membership (opposed to being a senior party official) allowed to stay on as ministry employees at lower levels?
As a rule, no. Those removed from positions of management should assume that they must leave employment in their ministry altogether. Willingness to serve in a lower position in the ministry could weigh in favor of an exception should one be sought. But all such requests for an exception must be based on the factors listed in paragraph #1 above. Persons requesting such an exception would have to sign the denunciation form.[50]

9. Will we continue to issue letters of authority to ministry members before the investigative process is complete?
No. There is a moratorium on issuing letters of authority signed by the Administrator of the CPA until we understand the full ramifications of de-ba'athification. Until then, senior advisors may sign specific authorities (i.e. for the payment of salaries) and continue verbally to designate people as having interim authorities to make decisions and implement policies.

10. Will we screen individuals replacing those we fire for Ba'ath Party affiliation?
We will adopt hiring procedures to ensure that the new ministry employees are not ba'athists. Applicants will be required to fill out a questionnaire regarding their past party involvement; it shall be clear that falsification of answers is grounds for termination of their position. New hires will need to sign a form either disavowing or denouncing the Ba'ath Party (depending on whether they were ever affiliated with it).[51] We will also conduct a character reference check that includes questions about the individual's past party affiliation.

11. Should we reclaim property and privileges that Ba'ath Party members gained as a perk of membership?
Yes. Officials who are to be removed from office should first be asked to return ministry property such as cars, computers, cell phones, etc. We should inform these people that a failure to return ministry property could have prosecutable consequences. Such efforts must be complemented by the search for records detailing the ministry property distributed to employees.

12. What sort of support should we provide to advisors seeking to remove the worst ba'athists (i.e. potentially dangerous criminals)?
We will alert CJTF7 that some senior advisors might need the help of MPs to remove and arrest allegedly serious criminals from their ministries. CJTF7 will require appropriate documentation and timely notice.

[50] See *Doc 173*.
[51] See *Doc 173*.

Document 187
The Future of Governance in Basrah Province
25 May 2003

I wish to identify a suitable representative from each public department and utility within Basrah Province to sit on the Basrah Interim Governorate Committee (BIGC), which will meet for the first time on Sunday, 1st June 2003. It is essential that responsible individuals participate in this process and those identified to represent their respective department must attend this meeting.

The Coalition Force and ORHA plan for the development of governance in Basrah Province is now complete. There will be two components to the governance plan. The first will be a non-political body, which focuses on the workings of public utilities and departments. This will be known as the Basrah Interim Governorate Committee (BIGC). Secondly, a Civic Forum will be established which will concentrate on the political development within Basrah Province. Details of the Civic Forum will be given later.

The BIGC will comprise of the Heads (Directors) of public utilities and departments based in Basrah Province. This will reflect the important Baghdad Ministries and therefore some 22 sectors should be represented. There will also be a representative from each of the Town Councils within Basrah Province, selected by their respective council. Basrah City will have 4 representatives. These representatives will only provide a liaison function, not a political one. Their task will be to communicate pertinent technical or public utility issues, from their areas, to the BIGC. They will then update their own council on the decisions and subsequent actions that occur at the provincial level. In addition 7-8 people, selected from a spectrum of society, will advise the BIGC but will have no executive authority.

The BIGC will have the executive authority to make strategic decisions under the direction of the Chairman. The Committee will initially be chaired by the Coalition Force Commander for Basrah Province, a role that will devolve to ORHA. The UN will also be closely involved. The decisions and actions of the BIGC will be posted outside the committee building and publicised through the media. The BIGC will be located in the old Radio and TV complex building on Government Street. The first meeting will take place on Sunday 01 June 2003 at 1000 at the BIGC building.

Brigadier Bradshaw[52]

Document 188
Certain State- or Regime-Owned Property in Iraq
29 May 2003

MEMORANDUM FOR	ADMINISTRATOR OF THE COALITION PROVISIONAL AUTHORITY
SUBJECT:	Certain State- or Regime-Owned Property in Iraq

[52] Brigadier Bradshaw, Commander 7th Armoured Brigade, Commander Coalition Forces, Basrah Province.

I hereby delegate to you the authority confirmed in the attached memorandum from the President, subject as above, dated April 30, 2003, regarding the seizure, sale, administration, or use of state or regime-owned property in Iraq.

Property taken under U.S. control under this delegation shall be held on behalf of and for the benefit of the Iraqi people, and shall be used only to assist the Iraqi people and support the reconstruction of Iraq. You may redelegate this authority in writing, and assign such duties and responsibilities in writing to other Department of Defense (DoD) officials as you deem necessary, and shall consider the feasibility of contracting out administrative functions related to your exercise of this authority, as appropriate and authorized by law.

The authority delegated herein shall be exercised in accordance with DoD procedures developed in consultation with the Department of the Treasury, the Department of State, and the Office of Management and Budget. These procedures shall ensure that all property subject to this delegation is appropriately accounted for, audited, and used only for the purposes specified herein. Under these procedures, DoD officials remain responsible for property under their control until the property is disbursed to recipients or to a non-DoD entity for distribution to recipients in accordance with safeguards that ensure the property will be (1) secured at al times; (2) used only for purposes authorized by law; (3) provided only to recipient who are entitled to such payments; and (4) subjected to appropriate accounting and auditing controls.

This delegation of authority shall expire 1 year following the date of this memorandum.

[Signed] *Paul Wolfowitz*
Attachment:
As stated[53]
cc: Chairman, Joint Chiefs of Staff

Document 189
Appointment of Interim Town Councils
31 May 2003

MEMORANDUM FOR COMMANDER OF COALITION FORCES
SUBJECT: Appointment of Interim Town Councils

Free, democratic, representative government is not simply a function of elections. It is rooted in constitutional principles that assure, among other things:

- limits on governmental power,
- accountability for governmental actions,
- guarantees of individual and minority rights,
- religious tolerance,
- property rights, and
- rights of free speech, assembly, and political and social organization.

Freedom depends on the health of private institutions as well as of local and regional institutions of government.

[53] The attachment is reproduced as *Doc 551*.

In Iraq, many of these public and private institutions need to be built, and many of these practices need to be established, after decades of totalitarian repression. This process should begin now. As it unfolds, the Iraqi people will gain valuable experience in fostering their unity and building a new Iraqi society under liberty and law.

To begin the process of establishing local government structures run by Iraqis, the Coalition Provisional Authority (CPA) and Joint Task Force (JTF)-7 commanders will apply the following procedures. These procedures should help to ensure consistency across Iraq and transparency in the selection process.

Interim Town Councils

The CPA will designate a local representative to assume responsibility over the procedures outlined below. If circumstances warrant, the CPA may designate the local military commander to assume this responsibility in coordination with a local civilian CPA representative. (This designated person is hereinafter referred to as the 'Coalition representative.')

Caucus Method: If the Coalition representative deems it practicable or desirable, the following procedures will be followed.

- The Coalition representative will appoint delegates to an interim town council caucus. There should be wide consultations in the community to identify a sufficient number of delegates to ensure broad geographic and demographic representation. Mathematical formulae that could lead to quotas, however, should be avoided. The number of delegates will vary according to local population and should exceed the number of town councilor positions.
  - Delegates may be chosen for a variety of reasons, including their competence, standing and respect in the community, their suitability to represent a specific demographic profile (religious, ethnic or tribal) or their professional background (doctors, lawyers, engineers, business sector representatives, educators, artisans, academics, workers, etc.). Women will be included.
- The following should not be appointed as delegates:
  - Members of the four highest levels of the Ba'ath Party or former members of any of the intelligence services, consistent with CPA Order No 1.[54]
  - Anyone who supports opposition to the CPA or advocates the removal of the CPA by force.
- Once the delegates have been identified, the Coalition representative should announce when the local selection caucus will meet; the meeting should occur within two weeks of the announcement.
- The caucus of delegates should convene at the appointed time and determine who among their number are willing to serve as interim town councilors. The size of the interim town council will vary according to local population or other considerations.
- The delegates will select the interim town councilors. They may nominate individuals, or vote on competing slates of names, or adopt other processes of selection that are transparent to the local populace. The Coalition representative will retain the authority to disapprove candidates or procedures.
- Once the selection is made and the results are verified, the Coalition representative will appoint the newly selected interim town council.

[54] See *Doc 14*.

- Points on procedure:
  - The above-described process should not be subject to an arbitrary time deadline. The caucus should select a full interim town council prior to adjourning.
  - If voting takes place, the Coalition representative will provide ballot boxes and ballots.
  - The Coalition representative will oversee the process but encourage the delegates to count and tally the results.
- The Commander of Coalition Forces is requested to support the CPA by providing an appropriate level of security. There should be no weapons in the caucus hall.

Direct appointment method: If the Coalition representative deems that circumstances do not permit the caucus method of selection, he/she may appoint the members of an interim town council directly, after wide consultation in the community.

Whether appointed directly by the Coalition representative or selected by caucus, the resulting body should be referred to as the 'Interim Town Council.'

Conclusion

Iraq has left behind the regime of Saddam Hussein and is on the path toward democratic government. The CPA recognizes and pays tribute to:

- the patriotism of those Iraqis who are continuing to consult with CPA advisors in the various ministries;
- the spirit and initiative of those Iraqi communities that have already chosen their new leadership; and
- the willingness of those selected to serve their communities and their country.

However, because the key constitutional and legal underpinnings for a fully democratic electoral process are not yet in place, all such positions of authority and responsibility are necessarily provisional.

- Accordingly, any titles held by Iraqis who are filling government positions, or who have been selected by their fellow Iraqis, regardless of position, should be preceded by the word 'Interim' (e.g. 'interim mayor' or 'interim governor').

The CPA retains authority over all appointments, including the power of removal, until Iraqi governance is established and is fully functional on a constitutional democratic basis. The CPA is committed to hastening the day when that will occur. It is also committed to assisting the Iraqi people in ensuring the fairness, representativeness, and inclusiveness of this emerging political process until that time.

L. Paul Bremer, Administrator
Coalition Provisional Authority

Document 190
Organization Chart
1 June 2003[55]

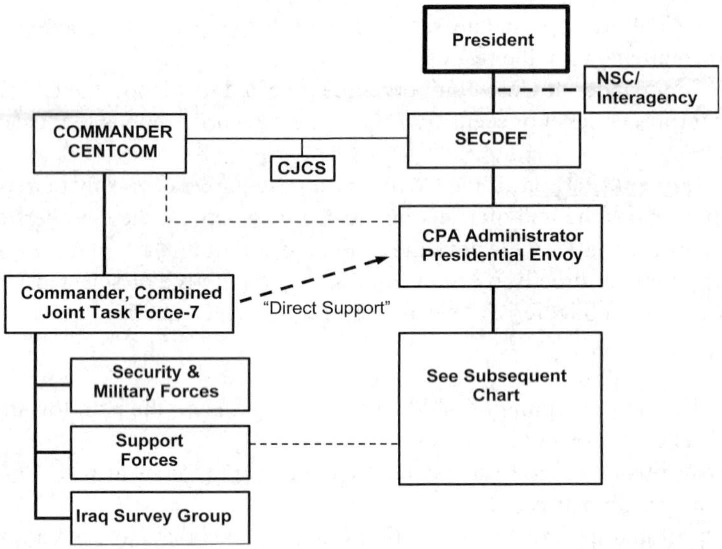

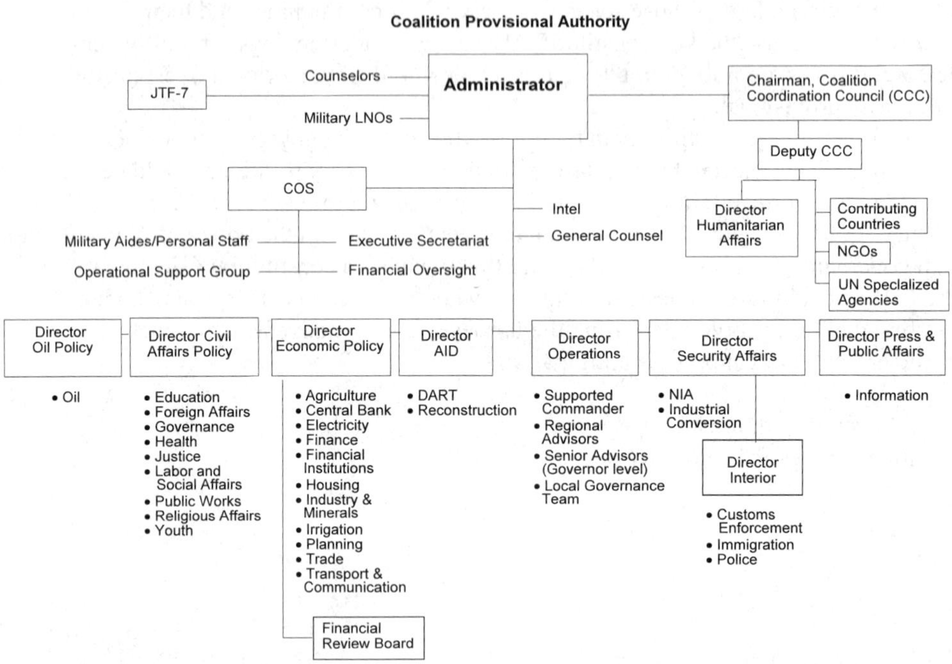

[55] The Chart may be found in United States President, *Report to Congress Pursuant to Section 1506 of the Emergency Wartime Supplemental Appropriations Act, 2003 (Public Law 108-11)*, 2 June 2003, 11.

Document 191
Memorandum by Ambassador Bremer on his Meeting with Iraqi Political Leaders

2 June 2003

TO: Secretary Rumsfeld
FROM: Paul Bremer
SUBJECT: Meeting with Iraqi Political Leaders

I held my second meeting with the Leadership Council Sunday [1 June] night. I began by stressing the commitment of President Bush and Prime Minster Blair to the economic and political reconstruction of Iraq. The coalition shares with Iraqis a vision of Iraq that is democratic, free, and prosperous. I then laid out our vision for establishing an interim administration (IA) in the next five to six weeks. Stressing my desire to consult broadly with all Iraqis to reach this goal, I reiterated the coalition's commitment to an IA that was representative of all strands of Iraqi society. I then outlined our concept of the IA by specifying it would have two main bodies: the Political Council and the Constitutional Convention. I said we would welcome their advice on these plans.

The Political Council

The Political Council (25-30 Iraqis) would be the 'public face' of the IA and Iraq's main interlocutor with the coalition and the world at large. Membership on the Political Council would be personal, meaning that an individual, while perhaps affiliated to a party, could not endorse another person to take his seat on the council in his absence. Being a member of the Political Council would be a paid full-time commitment, one that the coalition hoped would be assumed by the most senior representatives of Iraqi political parties and the country's most-respected figures. All members of the Political Council would be permitted to stand for office in Iraq's first election. Consultation between Coalition Provisional Authority (CPA) and the council would be close. I noted that I would plan to meet with the council often, perhaps weekly.

The Political Council would have two major responsibilities. First, this body would play a role in getting the government ministries back up and running. The council would nominate to the CPA a candidate to be a Chief Advisor to each ministry. (A person could not simultaneously be a Chief Advisor and sit on the council.) This Chief Advisor would have increasing responsibilities within the ministry, working with the CPA Senior Advisor, having full access to all the ministry's staff and files, and being party to all ministry decision-making. The Chief Advisor would be available to brief the Political Council as it wished on the progress of the ministry. When both the Political Council and the CPA determined that a ministry was ready to assume greater responsibility, the CPA would ask the IA to nominate a candidate for the position of Interim Minister.

The Political Council would also be responsible for addressing long-term issues that will ultimately determine the shape of Iraqi society. Education, economics, de-ba'athification, and electoral laws were just some of the topics about which Iraqis will want to develop recommendations and strategies. I suggested that the Political Council might set up committees on these issues to serve as a focal point for a broad dialogue with Iraqi people on such subjects. The CPA would welcome advice on these issues.

The Constitutional Convention

Turning to the second body in the IA, I stated that in my private consultations with Iraqis, including the groups present, I had found unanimous agreement that a new constitution must precede a national election. A Constitutional Convention, therefore, was essential. The selection of this group must be done carefully through a nationwide process to ensure a representative body. Although I stressed that I was open to ideas about how the Constitutional Convention might function and on its size, I expected that, after convening, the convention would establish a 12-15 person drafting committee. Once the committee completed its work, the constitution would be submitted back to the Convention for approval and then to the Iraqi people for their endorsement in a referendum. I stated that the timeline for completion of the constitution was for the Iraqi people to determine.

I concluded my opening comments by stressing the coalition's desire to move ahead. The next step was broadening the consultative process to ensure that both bodies of the IA would ultimately be more representative. I underscored how the creation of the IA would be 'an agreed process' between the CPA and Iraqis. I did, however, note that legally, I would be the one to appoint the body. I reminded each of the leaders that we had asked them to bring to this meeting the names of people to add into the consultative process. We hoped they would give us these suggestions now. We also sought their recommendations on people who could play an important role in the Constitutional Convention and on the Iraqi De-Ba'athification Council announced last week.[56] I stated that we expected to accelerate the pace and breadth of our consultations and would meet again on Friday in an expanded forum that included additional Iraqis.

The British Envoy then made clear that his government agreed entirely with the approach outlined and, like us, stood ready to receive the advice and views of the Iraqis present.

Reaction of the Leadership Council

The Iraqis asked several points of clarification after our presentations. These queries related to: the selection of people for the Constitutional Convention (we noted that we believed the convention should be broadly representative and that we would welcome their views on how best to achieve this), the role of a possible national conference (we said we held open the possibility of convening one sometime later in the process if it seemed useful), and the authorities of the Political Council. In response to a question about qualifications for membership on that council, I noted that members would have to endorse our broad vision for Iraq as captured in the Nasiriyah declaration of principles.[57] No one present offered explicit criticism of our plans while at the table.

During informal discussions with attendees at a reception after the meeting, it was apparent that the Iraqis differed in their reception to CPA plans. The INC itself gave contradictory signals, saying to some CPA representatives they were pleased with our approach and telling others they were unhappy with the indirect Iraqi role in governing. The INA, by contrast, thought the approach was sound. The PUK and KDP seemed generally on board, but clearly wished to consider further the implications of the proposal for their own situation. SCIRI, which had been antagonistic to the ideas before, seemed to take a pragmatic approach, asking clarifying questions, but avoiding antagonism. The Dawa Party cautioned that the Group of Seven was not representative and the US should not project the impression that it was treating

[56] See above *Doc 19*.

[57] For the Nasiriyah Declaration of Principles, see below *Doc 580*.

them as any kind of collective leadership. The NDP was focused on the need to start the Constitutional Convention process as soon as possible.

Next Steps

We will move out smartly this week. Our goal is to subsume the G-7 into a broader and more representative 'consultative committee.' We will quickly identify another six to ten people to invite to our consultative meeting Friday night (which will include the original G-7 as well). We will present our ideas again to then and seek ways to broaden our reach even further. I plan to set a rapid pace over the next month, meeting with our expanding circle of Iraqis in formals sessions at least weekly while our folks actively canvass the country for fresh candidates – for the Political Council, its likely specialized committees, and the Constitutional Convention.

Document 192
Status of Foreign Missions in Iraq
4 June 2003

TO: L. Paul Bremer, Administrator
Coalition Provisional Authority
FROM: Office of General Counsel
SUBJECT: Status of Foreign Missions in Iraq

There are a number of foreign embassies and diplomatic premises in Iraq, and diplomatic personnel have started to return. This memorandum clarifies the status of these premises and persons.

BACKGROUND:

• Status of Diplomatic Premises in Iraq

The CPA does not have the power to confer diplomatic status upon individuals and premises. However, the CPA is bound by the Geneva Convention IV (1949) and the 1907 Hague Regulations, and generally must respect the laws in force in Iraq on April 16, 2003 (*see* CPA/REG/2003/1).[58] Thus, the CPA, relying upon Coalition Forces, is obliged to take all measures in its power to restore and ensure, insofar as possible, public order and safety in Iraq. As such, the Coalition Provisional Authority is generally obligated to protect diplomatic premises, insofar as the current security environment permits. There is, however, no obligation to protect diplomatic facilities beyond the general obligation to restore, and ensure as far as possible, public order and safety. Where necessary, the CPA or Coalition Forces may enter diplomatic premises to restore law and order or for other security reasons.

Previous U.S. Central Command guidance provided that CENTCOM is obligated to respect the inviolability of diplomatic facilities. Given the political implications of any entry into current or former diplomatic premises, the CPA should advise CFLCC of premises formerly or currently used by the diplomatic community, and request that, to the extent

[58] See *Doc 1.*

practicable, local commanders notify the CPA Administrator of any intention to enter such premises prior to entry or immediately thereafter in the case of exigent circumstances.

• Status of Neutral Diplomats in Iraq

Under traditional U.S. military policy, 'diplomatic agents of neutral States must be treated with all courtesy and must be permitted such freedom of action as it is possible to allow, with due regard to the necessities of war;' the same treatment is accorded to 'consular personnel of neutral States, except those who are enemy nationals.' Dep't of the Army, FM 27-10, The Law of Land Warfare par. 549, at 192 (1956). Diplomats seeking to enter Iraq would need to present exequaturs or credentials to a future legitimate sovereign in order to have diplomatic privileges and immunities. Thus, diplomats who enter Iraq now do so without diplomatic privileges and immunities.

To the extent that any neutral diplomats remained in country throughout the armed conflict, or are returning to the country after having been accredited and being temporarily absent, the status of their diplomatic privileges and immunities is unclear. Consistent with Department of Defense policy guidance issued on May 8, 2003,[59] the CPA has no absolute obligation to honor diplomatic immunities of any diplomatic or consular officials who may have remained in Iraq during, or entered subsequent to, hostilities. The privileges of these neutral diplomats could be limited to the extent dictated by the occupant's military necessities, and the occupying power may ask them to leave.

Consistent with Department of Defense Policy guidance issued on May 8, 2003, the CPA cannot provide normal diplomatic services, nor will normal diplomatic activities in Iraq be supported at this time. Pursuant to the law of military occupation, the CPA reserves the right to expel any foreign government official, regardless of diplomatic privilege afforded by the former regime, should that person's presence in Iraq be considered detrimental to the public order and safety.

Given the political implications of detaining, arresting or expelling members of the diplomatic community, local commanders should notify the CPA Administrator prior to any such action or immediately thereafter in the case of exigent circumstances.

RECOMMENDATION: That the Administrator:

- Issue the attached notice to foreign government offices, advising the members of those offices that we cannot ensure their security or extend privileges and immunities.
- Request the relevant CPA and Coalition Forces elements (Director, Civil Affairs Policy; Director, Security Affairs; International Coordination Council; C-1, C-2 and C-4) work together to establish an appropriate badging system for members of foreign government officials [sic] and a register of current and former diplomatic premises.
- Issue the enclosed Memorandum, requesting that the Commander of Coalition Forces instruct local commanders to notify the CPA Administrator, insofar as practicable, of any intention to a) enter current or former diplomatic premises; or b) detain, arrest or expel any person who claims diplomatic status, or is connected to a foreign government office. In the case of exigent circumstances, such notification may take place immediately after the action.

Coordinated: Director, Civil Affairs Policy
Director, Security Affairs

[59] The DoD Policy Guidance, dated 8 May 2003, has not been available.

Document 193
Memorandum for Commander of Coalition Forces, Foreign Missions
5 June 2003

MEMORANDUM FOR COMMANDER OF COALITION FORCES

SUBJECT: Foreign Missions

With the return of diplomatic personnel to Iraq, it is appropriate to review the obligations and authorities of Coalition Forces pertaining to diplomatic premises and personnel.

- Insofar as the current security environment permits, Coalition Forces are requested to pay special attention to the protection of diplomatic premises, in keeping with their general obligation to restore and ensure public order and safety.
- Coalition Forces may enter diplomatic premises: (1) with the consent of an appropriate official of the foreign government involved; or (2) without consent, under extraordinary circumstances when necessary to restore law and order or for other security reasons. Attached is a list of former and current diplomatic premises.[60] Commanders are requested to notify the Administrator of the CPA in advance of an intention to enter such premises, or immediately thereafter in the case of exigent circumstances.
- Diplomats now in Iraq have no absolute right to diplomatic privileges and immunities. Because of the sensitivities of detaining, arresting or expelling members of the diplomatic community, however, request that local commanders notify the CPA Administrator prior to any such act on, or immediately thereafter in the case of truly exigent circumstances.

The Ministry of Foreign Affairs will be issuing a memorandum to foreign government offices,[61] advising them they do not currently have an entitlement to diplomatic privileges and immunities here, and that the Coalition cannot guarantee the safety or security of foreign government facilities or personnel.

[Signed] *L. Paul Bremer*
L. Paul Bremer, Administrator
Coalition Provisional Authority

Document 194
Circular Notice to All Foreign Government Offices in Iraq
5 June 2003

Ministry of Foreign Affairs, Baghdad, Iraq

Circular notice to all Foreign Government Offices in Iraq

We wish to inform foreign government offices in Iraq that you enter and remain in Iraq at your own risk. The Coalition Provisional Authority is not in a position to extend the

[60] The list is not available.
[61] See *Doc 194*.

privileges and immunities normally provided to diplomatic missions and their personnel, nor is there presently an Iraqi government in place to extend such privileges and immunities.

Coalition forces generally undertake to protect the property of foreign governments in Iraq consistent with security, military necessity, and the overall need to restore, and ensure as far as possible, public order and safety. The Coalition Provisional Authority cannot, however, guarantee the safety or security of foreign government property or personnel. Foreign government officials may bring into Iraq and/or maintain their own security forces only in full coordination with, and with the agreement of, Coalition forces, including compliance with the procedures established pursuant to Coalition Provisional Authority Order Number 2 [sic],[62] on Weapons Control (CPA/ORD/23 May 2003/03).[63]

The Ministry of Foreign Affairs, under the supervision of the Coalition Provisional Authority, will compile a list of foreign government personnel and issue identification badges to them. Representatives of foreign liaison offices should contact the Protocol Office of the Ministry of Foreign Affairs in the morning between the hours of 9:00 a.m. and 12:00 p.m. Sunday through Thursday. The issuance of these identification badges does not afford privileges and immunities.

Document 195

Transporting Humanitarian Aid Personnel and Cargo into Iraq

11 June 2003

TO: All Humanitarian Aid Organizations
FROM: Office of the Coalition Provisional Authority
SUBJECT: Transporting Humanitarian Aid Personnel and Cargo into Iraq

Effective immediately all Humanitarian Aid International Organizations and Non-Governmental Organizations will follow procedures set forth by the Iraqi Assistance Center (IAC) to obtain approval for movement of personnel and cargo into Iraq. All ministries will ensure proper coordination with the IAC is completed for ministry related movement of personnel and goods.

The IAC will coordinate air operations with the Regional Air Movement Coordination Center (RAMCC) for flight slot times. Existing flight procedures posted on the RAMCC web site and by Notices to Airmen (NOTAM) remain in effect; however, no flights will be authorized without IAC approval. Coalition military units will provide security, customs and immigration control in accordance with OCPA directives. No personnel or cargo will be allowed to exit Iraq without the written permission from an OCPA Senior Advisor or above.

These procedures are necessary to ensure the health, safety and security of the Iraqi people. Your assistance in complying with this policy is greatly appreciated.
Office of the Coalition Provisional Authority

[62] This is a typo in the original. It should read Order Number 3.
[63] See *Doc 16*.

Document 196
Authority of the Administrator of the Coalition Provisional Authority and Support Relationships
16 June 2003

MEMORANDUM FOR SECRETARIES OF THE MILITARY DEPARTMENTS
CHAIRMAN OF THE JOINT CHIEFS OF STAFF UNDER
SECRETARIES OF DEFENSE
COMBATANT COMMANDERS
ASSISTANT SECRETARIES OF DEFENSE
GENERAL COUNSEL OF THE DEPARTMENT OF DEFENSE
INSPECTOR GENERAL OF THE DEPARTMENT OF DEFENSE
ASSISTANTS TO THE SECRETARY OF DEFENSE
DIRECTOR, ADMINISTRATION AND MANAGEMENT
ADMINISTRATOR, COALITION PROVISIONAL AUTHORITY
DIRECTORS OF THE DEFENSE AGENCIES
DIRECTORS OF THE DOD FIELD ACTIVITIES

SUBJECT: Authority of the Administrator of the Coalition Provisional Authority and Support Relationships

In light of the President's May 9, 2003 letter appointing L. Paul Bremer as his Presidential Envoy to Iraq,[64] and pursuant to the Secretary's May 13, 2003 memo designating Mr. Bremer as Administrator of the Coalition Provisional Authority (CPA),[65] the Office of Reconstruction and Humanitarian Assistance (ORHA) is dissolved and its functions, responsibilities and legal obligations assumed by the CPA.

Administrative support previously provided to ORHA pursuant to the Secretary's memo of April 2, 2003 shall now be provided to the same extent to the CPA.[66] In addition, the responsibilities of the Secretary of the Army with regard to providing administrative support to ORHA under my May 21, 2003 memo[67] designation as the Department of Defense executive agent for ORHA shall be exercised in support of the CPA.
[Signed] *Paul Wolfowitz*

[64] See *Doc 179*.
[65] See *Doc 180*.
[66] See *Doc 166*.
[67] See *Doc 183*.

Document 197
L. Paul Bremer, Address to the World Economic Forum
22 June 2003

After thirty years of totalitarian rule, the people of Iraq are free. In the last few months, they have begun to enjoy life on their own terms, and also started to embrace the responsibilities that freedom entails. Iraqi citizens have joined neighborhood watch groups, helping the Coalition make Baghdad's streets safer. They have joined district advisory councils, making the first steps towards a vibrant civil society. Along with Coalition combat forces, more than 30,000 Iraqi police officers, an increase of over 200 percent in the past 30 days, are working to establish the rule of law throughout the country. [...]

Let me say a word about the President's vision for Iraq and about our Coalition's plan to realize it. President Bush and Prime Minster Blair have clearly stated their vision. It is of a free Iraq, at peace with its neighbors and governed by a representative government chosen by democratic elections.

How then do we intend to achieve this goal? We are working on three important areas.

The first job of any government is to provide security and to maintain law and order. With the help of the Iraqis, we have confronted looting and sabotage, secured critical sites, and called police officers back to work. Last night two thousand Iraqi police officers patrolled Baghdad streets alongside Coalition soldiers. Within two weeks we will start introducing soldiers into a New Iraqi Army, which in time will secure Iraq's borders. Today Iraqis feel safer leaving their homes, Baghdad traffic jams are back, and there is exuberant retail activity on the streets.

Iraq will continue to face difficult challenges in the area of security, as remnants of the regime engage in continued acts of violence and political sabotage – acting with the same cruelty and disregard for the welfare of Iraq in their last days as they did in their first. But let me be clear. The Coalition will not let the last vestiges of Saddam's regime turn the clock back for the Iraqi people, whose best days are yet to come.

As we provide for Iraq's security we have begun its political transformation. In the next month, we will announce the establishment of a Political Council to assist in the management of the Iraqi government. The Political Council will be representative of the major strands of Iraqi society. It will have real authority from its first day. It will nominate ministry heads and form commissions to recommend policies concerning issues significant to Iraq's future from reform of the educational curriculum, to plans for a telecommunications infrastructure, to proposals for stimulating the private sector.

We will also convene a broader Constitutional Conference, run entirely by Iraqis to draft a new constitution. That document will be the subject of intense public debate and once adopted, it will provide the foundation for national elections for a free and sovereign Iraqi government.

Let me turn to our third and most immediate priority: Ensuring that political freedom is accompanied by economic freedom. The nations' liberation would be incomplete if Iraqis were secure in their persons, but not their property; if Iraqis looked foreword to rising political representation, but stagnant living standards.

Just as forming a vibrant political climate in Iraq will entail many challenges, so too creating a vibrant economy in Iraq will not be easy. I mentioned the political sabotage during [the] past several weeks, which must be stopped.

Less obvious to the outside world but more damaging to Iraq's economy is the legacy of decades of economic mismanagement of the Ba'athist regime. Put simply, Saddam

Hussein's regime devastated Iraq's economy from the inside out. Even before the war over 50 percent of Iraqis were unemployed. And the former regime expanded [sic] at least one third of GDP in the military. Still today over 60% depend of government food rations. Between militarization, misguided central planning and outright theft, for decades Iraq has experienced pervasive misallocation of capital.

The precious nature of this devastation is common to regimes that enjoy neither political or economic freedom. In modern economies, firms supply what consumers want. In Iraq, state owned enterprises were forced to produce what central planners demanded.

Without the discipline of the market, state-owned enterprises not only failed to create value, they destroyed it. To keep these firms afloat, the former regime fed them with costly subsidies in the form of cheap energy, tax breaks, and uncollected debt arrears. The Central Bank of Iraq was forced to print money, and predictably, inflation raged and the domestic currency weakened.

In the past 15 years, other countries have attempted to break this cycle. The experience of these economies shows that there is no substitute for a vibrant private sector. Markets allocate resources much more efficiently than politicians. So our strategic goal in the months ahead is to set in motion policies which will have the effect of reallocating people and resources from state enterprises to the more-productive private firms. A fundamental component of this process will be to force state enterprises to face hard budget constraints by reducing subsidies and special deals.

Lower subsidies will allow us to reduce Iraq's taxes while maintaining a level playing field for its private firms to compete. Reducing subsidies will also reduce the temptation to print money with the attendant risks to inflation and interest rates. Following these policies will help accomplish many of our goals for Iraq's macroeconomy: vigorous competition, fiscal discipline, and low inflation and interest rates. But we recognize that these policies will exacerbate political and social strains unless they are accompanied by the establishment of a humane social safety net.

For economies in transition, as in the United States, small and medium-sized private enterprises play a vital role in providing employment. In Iraq's case, small firms have the best chance of creating jobs quickly and fuelling the economic recovery. But for this to happen, Iraq's private sector needs a clear commercial code, honest courts, low barriers to entry, and transparent corporate governance arrangements. Countries around the world are rediscovering these prerequisites to growth, and a burgeoning academic literature confirms their importance in empirical data. We will need to learn from and apply best practices in these areas too.

By improving domestic economic policy, Iraq will be able to participate fully in the global marketplace. Today, Iraq's workers, factories and consumers rely on equipment and technologies from the 1950s and 1960s. Free trade and investment will allow Iraq to benefit from the ideas and technologies that have lifted living standards around the world. It is not just a question of buying better machines or obtaining better blueprints. By limiting foreign investment, Iraq has been denied the chance to benefit from the world's best know-how that also raises economic growth.

Like other countries, Iraq will no doubt find that opening its borders to trade and investment will increase competitive pressure on its domestic firms and thereby raise productivity.

Iraq starts this process with many advantages: potentially fertile farmland, an educated population eager to join the international community, and oil wealth. In fact, just this weekend the first Iraqi oil tanker will be departing Turkey. Iraqi's oil industry is back in business, only this time for the Iraqi people, not Saddam Hussein.

In my brief time in Iraq, I have been repeatedly impressed with the extraordinary technical capabilities of Iraqis working in government and industry. They just need the opportunity to put these skills to productive work. We will give them that chance. To take full advantage of these assets, Iraq's resources cannot be restricted to a lucky or powerful few. Iraq's natural resources should be shared by all Iraqis, and every Iraqi should have the opportunity to participate fully in the country's economic life.

One way to share Iraq's blessings among its people would be with a special program funded with oil revenues. Some profits from oil sales could be distributed to Iraq's citizens as 'dividends', along the lines of the system used by the State of Alaska. Alternatively, oil revenues could be deposited in a national 'trust fund' used to finance public pensions or other elements of a social safety net needed to ease the transition from a state-dominated to a private sector economy.

In either case, every individual Iraqi would come to understand his or her stake in the country's economic success. I believe this type of proposal could be profitably debated when an interim Iraqi authority is convened in the months ahead.

Let me summarize for you our immediate priorities in this demanding, but exciting economic transformation. It is to:

- Start a thoroughgoing reform of Iraq's financial sector in order to provide liquidity and credit for the Iraqi economy.
- Simplify the regulatory regime so as to lower barriers to entry for new firms, domestic and foreign.
- Review Iraq's body of commercial law to determine which changes are needed to encourage private investment.
- Lift unreasonable restrictions on property rights.
- Develop anti-trust and competition laws.
- Develop an open market trade policy providing for a level playing field with regional trade partners.
- Encourage the adoption of laws and regulations to assure that Iraq has high standards of corporate governance.
- Develop accelerated training programs for business managers in best practices and business ethics.

For the past 14 years, I have been a businessman. I know many of the businessmen and women in the audience today. And I want to say to them that I am optimistic and that the Coalition will succeed in transforming the Iraqi economy from a closed, dead-end system to an open vibrant place to do business. Opportunities for productive investment abound, and we aim to be sure they are realized.

I spoke earlier about President Bush's vision for Iraq. Just yesterday in his weekly radio address, he spoke to that vision again when said, 'we are working to improve the lives of the Iraqi people after three decades of tyranny and oppression.'[68] The President is committed to this mission. This means providing political freedom in a secure environment. But it is also a historical axiom that political and economic freedom go hand in hand. The transition to a free-market economy will take time, but there are many people ready to help. Working together, we can bring about an Iraq that is both free and economically prosperous, and

[68] For the full text of US President Bush's Radio Address, 21 June 2003, see http://www.whitehouse.gov/news/releases/2003/06/20030621.html.

only then will we meet the President's goal of truly improving the lives of the Iraqi people. Thank you.

Document 198
Letter to UNESCO, Inscription of Ashur on the World Heritage List

25 June 2003

COALITION PROVISIONAL AUTHORITY
Ministry of Culture
From: Ambassador Pietro Cordone – Senior Advisor

World Heritage Committee
UNESCO
Paris

25 June 2003

ASHUR

As you will be aware, in the absence of an Iraqi Government, the Coalition Provisional Authority (CPA) is the interim administration for Iraq. Matters pertaining to my Ministry are discussed by a Cultural Cabinet that comprises designated Iraqi advisors and advisors from the coalition. The Cabinet is consequently the ultimate decision making body for issues relating to culture and heritage in Iraq today.

This letter confirms a decision taken by the Cabinet that at the Paris meeting of the World Heritage Committee at the end of June the Committee should proceed with inscribing Ashur onto the World Heritage List. The Cabinet has also agreed that simultaneously Ashur should be entered on the 'in danger' list.

The immediate threat to Ashur from dam construction no longer exists under CPA administration but we cannot vouch for decisions that might be taken by our successors. Listing Ashur as 'in danger' is a strong signal to a future Iraqi administration of the importance of preserving this wonderful site for the world.

I will pass a signed copy of this letter to the UNESCO delegation I am to meet here in Baghdad on Saturday 28 June.

Pietro Cordone
Ambassador
Senior Advisor – Culture

Document 199
Ministry of Justice National Policy Guidance
26 June 2003

TO: All Coalition Provisional Authority officials with responsibility for matters relating to the Ministry of Justice
FROM: Judge Donald F. Campbell, CPA Senior Advisor to the Ministry of Justice
DATE: 26 June 2003
SUBJECT: Ministry of Justice National Policy Guidance

This memorandum sets forth national policy and guidance regarding matters in the purview of the Ministry of Justice. It is intended to guide all levels of the Coalition Provisional Authority (CPA) and Coalition military commanders, with whose assistance it will be implemented. Some of the policies contained herein are new. Others have already been promulgated, but inadequately communicated. Due to difficulties with communication and coordination, consistency has heretofore been impossible to achieve; due to different circumstances, it has not necessarily been appropriate. As communications and infrastructure improve, however, and as Iraq progresses back to civilian rule, a uniform nationwide approach to justice is desirable.

This memorandum seeks to move the Ministry of Justice in that direction. In addition to providing guidance as to how Ministry of Justice activities should currently be operating, it seeks to open channels for information to flow in as well as out. It summarizes what we know so far, and requests you to correct errors and fill in gaps.

The policies and practices of the past regime left much to be desired, but also much with which we can work. We have made strides undoing the bad and identifying the good, and will continue to do so.

Please note that a synopsis of all information requested by this memorandum is attached as appendix 1. Please provide this information as best you are able within 10 days.

1. Mission Statement

The principal mission of the CPA Ministry of Justice office is to institute the rule of law in Iraq to the maximum possible extent. All CPA Ministry of Justice activities aim towards that end.

The rudiments of a rule of law include:

- equal protection of the laws without regard to race, creed, ethnicity, or gender
- judicial independence
- objective, impartial enforcement and application of laws
- general right to notice and hearing before deprivation of liberty or property
- likes are treated alike
- decisions based on law, not on nepotism, cronyism, bribery, or personal characteristics
- public trials
- the right to court-appointed counsel in criminal cases, and the right to be informed of this right
- the right against self-incrimination, and the right to be informed of this right

- the right to compulsory process
- the right to cross-examine adverse witnesses
- no *ex post facto* laws
- swift and certain punishment of the guilty and acquittal of the innocent
- public confidence that the above conditions prevail

The CPA Ministry of Justice office will attempt to realize these elements through funding, supervision, training, and operational involvement in the judicial system. Ultimately, however, any changes are provisional and subject to eventual reversal or adoption by the duly constituted Iraqi sovereign.

The Ministry of Justice also now is responsible for all prisons throughout Iraq. Our primary goals in that department are to establish or reconstruct facilities adequately to hold humanely the criminals that are being apprehended, and to operate those facilities up to the standards established by CPA Memorandum No. 2,[69] attached as appendix 2. A corollary goal is successful coordination between prisons and courts, as well as police.

The Ministry of Justice also has responsibility for notaries public, deeds and records, and judicial training. The CPA will attempt to restore these functions.

2. Communication and chain-of-command

Communication is indispensable to consistency and coordination. The lack of information coming into this office from areas outside Baghdad, and our inability to communicate effectively to the governorates, has delayed issuance of this nationwide guidance directive. With the information provided recently by the justice assessment teams and the reports coming in through military channels (pursuant to FRAGO 154),[70] we are now in a position to provide some informed guidance. In order to build on this, however, and to craft a more comprehensive policy, we must establish regular lines of communication for upward and downward information flow.

There are a variety of ways in which to contact the central CPA Ministry of Justice office:

- E-mail one of the Ministry's Executive Assistants:
  CPT Earl Matthews, earl.g.matthews@us.army.mil
  1LT Bruce Fein, bruce.ellis.fein@us.army.mil
- Telephone:
- DSN: 318-239-5802 or -5804
- Commercial: 781-280-5802 or -5804
- MCI cellular:
  914-360-6546 (Judge Donald F. Campbell, Senior Advisor)
  914-360-6547 (Michael Dittoe, Ministry Coordinator)
  914-360-3581 (William Irvine, Chief of Prisons)
  914-360-6556 (MAJ Anthony Ricci, Chief of Staff)
  914-360-6550 (Pamela Murphy, Policy Analyst)
  914-360-6549 (CPT Matthews, Assistant Operations Officer)
  914-360-6548 (1LT Bruce Fein, Executive Assistant to the Senior Advisor)

Clarity as to who is responsible for Ministry of Justice affairs in each governorate is important to establish. Accordingly, each local Coalition official, whether military or civilian, with responsibility for Ministry of Justice affairs should please e-mail all staff

[69] See *Doc 126*.

[70] FRAGO 154 established procedures for administrative personnel reporting at the Forward Operating Base (FOB).

names, area of responsibility, and all available methods of communication, to 1LT Fein (bruce.ellis.fein@us.army.mil).

Judge Donald F. Campbell is currently the Senior Advisor to the Ministry of Justice.[71] Judge Campbell succeeded Clint Williamson on 21 June. The Senior Advisor, or his delegate, acting under the authority of the Administrator, CPA, is responsible for Ministry of Justice policy.

Local CPA and military officials may take decisions or actions that they deem necessary and proper to implement the national Ministry of Justice policy, subject to the review and approval of the Senior Advisor or his delegate. Local CPA and military officials should keep the central Ministry apprised of all activities in their areas of responsibility, in greater or lesser detail as the significance of the matter and common sense dictate.

In addition to case-by-case reporting, we may develop regular weekly, monthly, or other reporting forms. We also welcome your comments, questions, or suggestions. This information will enable us to develop policies to address these issues.

Within the Ministry itself, a Management Committee has been appointed, with responsibility for Ministry operations, subject to the direction and control of the Administrator, CPA. The Committee comprises all Directors General, and is to be chaired by Medhat Mahmood. Mr. Mahmood, who will serve in this capacity on appointment by the CPA Administrator, is also the President of the State Advisory Council, has been a justice on the Court of Cassation (Supreme Court) since 1997, and was never a member of the Ba'ath party.

In addition to the Senior Advisor and his staff, we have formulated a plan for involvement of other Coalition personnel in operating and reforming the Ministry of Justice, attached as appendix 3. While [the] plan has not been formally approved by the Administrator, it reflects our current direction.

3. Court operations

All courts should be operating to the maximum extent permitted by the available facilities and personnel. The Senior Advisor has issued an instruction to that effect, attached as appendix 4. With certain exceptions, Coalition authorities should take all steps necessary to reestablish regular court proceedings, including transporting suspects or defendants between detention center or prison and court. Crimes against Coalition forces will be addressed in accordance with existing arrangements that preserve the jurisdiction of Coalition Forces. Persons suspected of crimes that are particularly disruptive to public safety or of crimes with potentially national ramifications, and prominent defendants, will be considered for trial by the Central Criminal Court of Iraq described below.

In some cases, court personnel have been reluctant to return to work without a direct order. Local commanders may direct such employees to return to work. Employees who continue to refuse to return to work should be replaced. Otherwise, judges, prosecutors, and other court personnel who were employed prior to the war should resume their duties.

If local commanders or CPA officials believe that circumstances warrant the removal of any judicial official, these matters should be referred to the Judicial Review Committee (JRC) which is described in more detail below. Likewise, if local officials have already removed judges or prosecutors or have appointed replacements, these cases should also

[71] Judge Campbell, a judge on the Superior Court of New Jersey, is also a Major General in the United States Army Reserves. He was mobilized for Operation Iraqi Freedom. He was succeeded in the post of Senior Adviser by Judge Daniel L. Rubini on 3 September 2003 (who served until 4 February 2004).

be referred to the JRC. It should be clear that all such dismissals and appointments are considered provisional until ratified by the JRC.

Where court facilities have been so badly damaged as to foreclose current use, it may be prudent to move or consolidate cases into other facilities nearby. In Baghdad, for example, the Senior Advisor issued an instruction consolidating all criminal trials into two courthouses. Local authorities wishing to issue a similar order in the future should first submit the order to the Senior Advisor for review and approval. Local authorities who have already implemented a similar order or arrangement may continue the order in effect, but should report to the Senior Advisor. Alternative facilities need not be other courts. Funding may be available to lease or construct facilities, as well.

One of the greatest difficulties encountered in Baghdad has been transportation of prisoners to and from court. This requires close logistical coordination between Coalition forces, the Iraqi police, and court personnel. For a variety of reasons, however, this coordination has been lacking and transports of prisoners to Iraqi courts have been inconsistent. The Administrator, CPA has stressed that resolution of this issue is a high priority as re-establishment of the courts is a key component of the CPA's strategy to create a secure and stable environment. To address this problem in Baghdad, a comprehensive plan has been drawn up by V Corps SJA and is currently being implemented. If logistical problems in your area of responsibility hinder processing prisoners into the Iraqi court system, please notify this office immediately.

4. Facilities repair, rehabilitation, construction, and security

Many courthouses and other Ministry facilities nationwide have been looted, damaged, or destroyed. Our judicial assessment teams have reported regarding several such facilities, but we lack a comprehensive list. We have access to funds, public and private, for refurbishing and refurnishing courthouses, and possibly for acquiring or constructing new buildings, if needs be. Only with a comprehensive list can we prioritize and allocate funding for these projects.

Security, without which repair and refurbishment are pointless, is a natural concomitant of renovation.

Accordingly, we must compile data on nationwide facilities and security needs. A spreadsheet of all Ministry facilities of which we are aware, organized by governorate, is attached as appendix 5. We request that the local Coalition or military authority with responsibility for Ministry of Justice affairs in each governorate identify the needs, if any, for the facilities in its area of responsibility by completing, editing, or adding to the spreadsheet. At your request, we can also e-mail the spreadsheet to be filled in electronically. The spreadsheet will enable you to tell us whether we have an accurate assessment of the state of facilities in your area, an estimate of repair and refurbishment expenses, and to prioritize your area's needs. We will then work to form a funding plan in coordination with the CPA Program Review Board. The Program Review Board was established by CPA Regulation No. 3[72] to identify, integrate and prioritize funding requirements.

A facilities protection force has been established by the Coalition to secure important government locations. The force comprises mainly former members of the Iraqi armed forces. If Ministry facilities in your area of responsibility require security, you may forward a prioritized list including facility name and type, location, and an explanation of the need for security. We will then try to accommodate that need through the CPA and the Program Review Board.

[72] See *Doc 3*.

5. Court structure

By now, local officials are likely familiar with the structure of the Iraqi court system. Still, the organizational charts attached as appendix 6 may be helpful. The law is generally secular, except for the law of family relations, in which Sharia (Islamic) law is applied as to Muslims. Several special security courts, designed to punish enemies of the previous regime without due process, have been eliminated by CPA Order No. 2,[73] attached as appendix 7.

In addition to the courts depicted in appendix 6, a new Central Criminal Court of Iraq (CCCI) is being established as a model of procedural fairness and judicial integrity and to hear especially serious cases. CPA Order No. 13, establishing the CCCI,[74] is attached as appendix 8, along with a public notice regarding the same, and is discussed below.

The CPA Administrator has identified the CCCI as a top justice priority. It will commence hearing cases as soon as possible, hopefully by 15 July.

Also as noted above, the military retains the right to try any person accused of crimes against Coalition forces, including war crimes.

6. Applicable substantive and procedural law

The applicable criminal law in Iraq is the Iraqi Penal Code of 1969, as modified by CPA Order No. 7,[75] attached as appendix 9. Local Coalition authorities should ensure that judges are applying this law and that the bench and bar are aware of Order No. 7.

The applicable criminal procedure is that of the Iraqi Criminal Procedure Code of 1971, as modified by CPA Memorandum No. 3,[76] attached as appendix 10 together with a public notice regarding the same. Memorandum No. 3 implements certain fundamental legal rights, including:

- in criminal cases, the defendant will enjoy a right to appointed counsel beginning with the first appearance before a magistrate, rather than at trial only, and must be informed of this right
- confessions extracted by torture will be inadmissible as inculpatory evidence under any circumstances; before, such confessions were admissible if corroborated by other evidence, even if that other evidence was obtained through torture
- no person shall be forced to testify against himself, and he must be advised of this right before custodial questioning

Memorandum No. 3 also requires that Coalition forces afford to criminal detainees the following:

- upon arrival in a detention center, immediate notice of the right to remain silent and to consult an attorney
- in felony cases only, the right to consult with an attorney after 72 hours have elapsed since such arrival (persons held for offenses not rising to the level of a felony enjoy no right to counsel)
- a prompt written explanation of the charges
- appearance before a judicial officer 'as rapidly as possible' and no later than 90 days after detention
- access to the International Committee of the Red Cross, unless contrary to imperative military necessity

[73] See *Doc 15*.
[74] See *Doc 29*.
[75] See *Doc 21*.
[76] See *Doc 127*.

Requirements for persons detained to protect security are also imposed by Memorandum No. 3.

Local Coalition authorities should carefully read and ensure that Iraqi judges and police, as well as Coalition forces, rigorously obey and enforce these new rules.

Other changes to the law, and all Coalition Orders, Regulations, and Proclamations, will be reflected in the official Iraqi Legal Gazette. The Legal Gazette has been the official publication for Iraqi laws since the 1920s. Publication was recently resumed after a halt during the war. The first post-war edition, attached as appendix 11, should have been distributed to the chief Court of Appeals judge and all law libraries in each governorate. Please inform us whether such distribution occurred in your governorate or area of responsibility. Coalition authorities should read each edition of the Gazette to apprise themselves of all recent orders and to ensure that Coalition directives are being carried out properly.

In the future, other laws of Iraq will be reviewed, and changes are possible. Any such changes will appear in the Gazette.

We can provide the Iraqi Penal Code and the Iraqi Penal Procedure Code by e-mail, at your request. If you are in possession of English translations of any other Iraqi laws, please provide them to us. We are aware of and are trying to fill the deficiency of English-language Iraqi codes.

7. Reforms

A number of legal reform initiatives are underway, and more may follow:

New criminal suspect rights

Significant new legal rights have been established for criminal defendants, as described in the preceding section and CPA Memorandum No. 3 and the accompanying public notice, attached as appendix 10.

Judicial Review Committee

The Judicial Review Committee (JRC) has been formed to review each of the roughly 850 judges and prosecutors in the country for significant Ba'ath party links, complicity in crimes of the former regime, malfeasance and corruption. CPA Order No. 15,[77] establishing the JRC, is attached as appendix 12. It is designed quickly to establish a measure of public trust in the legal system by removing bad actors whom the public distrusts and endowing the others with a measure of enhanced credibility. The JRC will depend heavily on local Coalition authorities to provide information and evidence.

In many cases, public outcry has compelled local Coalition authorities to remove and replace judges or prosecutors. Each removed and replacement judge or prosecutor must be reviewed by the JRC. The JRC will have the option of reinstating removed judges or of rejecting a replacement judge. It will, of course, strongly consider the commander's reasons for removal and replacement in the first place. Please provide us with a list of every removed or replacement judge or prosecutor.

The JRC is scheduled to begin its work in the next week, and should finish within three or four months. Especially because the JRC will lack the resources to conduct an extensive background check of every judge and prosecutor, all Coalition authorities are requested to provide the JRC with relevant information regarding judges and prosecutors, including

[77] See *Doc 33*.

actively collecting such information if possible. This would include protests or accusations from the bar or from the public about particular lawyers or prosecutors, documentation of past bad acts or significant Ba'ath party involvement, or otherwise. Evidence of good reputation or character would also be helpful. Please forward all such information to the central CPA Ministry office as soon as possible, using G-2 channels for classified information.

The decisions of the JRC will be supplemental to, and not a replacement for, determinations by the Iraqi De-Ba'athification Council, described below. That Council may override a JRC decision based on Ba'ath party ties.

Judicial Inspection Unit

A Judicial Inspection Unit (JIU) is to be established as a follow-on to the JRC and as a more permanent oversight mechanism. The JIU will investigate malfeasance based on accusations or on its own initiative, and will recommend disciplinary action (reprimand, suspension, or removal from office) in cases where wrongdoing is proven. The JIU will likely not begin its work until after the work of the JRC is complete.

Central Criminal Court of Iraq

As described in appendix 8, the CCCI is designed to be a model of procedural fairness and judicial integrity that will hear charges of especially serious crimes that may have national ramifications (i.e., crimes of inter-ethnic or religious violence, mass crimes), crimes with security implications (i.e., crimes committed in retaliation for cooperation with Coalition authorities), and other serious crimes with the potential to undermine public confidence in overall safety. The judges and prosecutors participating in the CCCI will be drawn from the most highly regarded in the country.

Cases will be recommended for CCCI hearing by the Senior Advisor, who will consider cases brought to his attention by judges, prosecutors, defense counsel, or Coalition authorities. The Administrator, CPA will then decide whether to transfer the case. We anticipate that the CCCI will hear dozens, but not hundreds, of cases.

The judges and prosecutors of the CCCI will be the first vetted by the JRC. The CCCI should begin work by 15 July.

Iraqi De-Ba'athification Council

Accreditation Review Committees and an Iraqi De-Ba'athification Council have been established to vet all Iraqi government employees for Ba'ath party involvement pursuant to the de-Ba'athification policy set forth in CPA Order No. 1,[78] attached as appendix 13. The Accreditation Review Committees were established by CPA Memorandum No. 1,[79] attached as appendix 14, and the Council was established by CPA Order No. 5,[80] attached as appendix 15. The Council will vet all personnel as required by Order No. 5. Local Coalition authorities may be called upon to assist or cooperate with the Council.

8. Property claims

Property claims may arise against the Coalition, between Iraqis, or between Iraqis and the government of Iraq.

Claims against the Coalition for maneuver damage, post-conflict damage, expropriation, or seized property should, at least for now, be processed through regular military channels.

[78] See *Doc 14.*
[79] See *Doc 125.*
[80] See *Doc 19.*

Claims between Iraqis or between Iraqis and the Iraqi government may arise in a variety of circumstances: expropriation without compensation, ethnic cleansing or 'Arabization,' unjust enrichment of Ba'athist henchmen, or otherwise. Coalition policy on how to resolve these disputes is still in development, including which claims will be recognized, who may bring them, statute of limitations, whether a special facility will be established to adjudicate the claims, rules for resolution, and establishing effective repositories for claims. A special Coalition office is being established to deal with these issues, headed by David Hodgkinson. His MCI cellular phone number is 914-360-6831, and his e-mail address is hodgkinsond@orha.centcom.mil.

9. Transitional justice: crimes against humanity, war crimes, and mass graves

Coalition policy on how most efficaciously to redress crimes against humanity and war crimes, and how to handle mass graves, is still being formulated by a special office. Points of contact are David Hodgkinson (hodgkinsond@orha.centcom.mil, MCI cellular phone number 914-360-6831) and Sandra Hodgkinson (hodgkinsons@orha.centcom.mil or MCI cellular phone number 914-360-6596). You should direct all questions and information in this regard to them.

10. Prisons and detention centers

Under the previous regime, responsibility for prisons and detention centers fell under the Ministry of Labor and Social Affairs and the Ministry of Interior, respectively. Generally, prisoners were held at police detention centers from the time of arrest until they completed their initial court proceedings. Thereafter, they were transferred to prisons. By CPA Order No. 10,[81] attached as appendix 16, responsibility for prisons and detention centers was transferred to the Ministry of Justice.

CPA Memorandum No. 2, attached as appendix 2, establishes the standards with which every prison and detention facility nationwide must comply. Local authorities should commence immediate action to bring all facilities up to the standard of Memorandum No. 2.

Where Coalition forces are operating prisons or detention centers – either in the form of pre-existing or temporary facilities – it is a high priority to facilitate the re-opening of civilian-controlled facilities as soon as possible. In many cases this is currently impossible due to the damage or total destruction of such facilities. It is important, though, that all information on pre-existing prisons and detention centers be communicated to the CPA Ministry of Justice office. This information is vital as a comprehensive prison reconstruction plan is developed for the entire country.

William Irvine is the head of the new Prisons Department in the Ministry of Justice, and all queries and information regarding prisons should be directed to him. Mr. Irvine may be reached by MCI cell phone at 914-360-3581 or by e-mail at irvine@un.org.

11. Other programs and the road ahead

A number of additional special programs have been or will be established:

Pro bono program

The recent hostilities effectively shut down the legal system, leaving lawyers unemployed. To induce them to apply their skills for the public good, we introduced a pro bono program,

[81] See *Doc 25*.

under which lawyers perform legal services to needy clients and receive $2 per hour, up to 125 hours. We have secured $100,000 in funding, and have disbursed about 150 payments.

Thus far, the pro bono program has been implemented primarily in and around Baghdad, where it has been so popular that we have been obliged to stop enrolling new participants, lest the fund be depleted. If we are able to secure additional funding, we will re-open participation, in which case we will ask local authorities to inform attorneys through announcements or postings. In the meantime, queries about the program should be answered by saying that enrollment is closed.

Most attorneys in Baghdad recorded implausibly high quantities of hours worked, i.e., the maximum permitted 16 hours per day, every day of every week. To stanch cheating, we required the attorneys to sign a form certifying the veracity of hours claimed. If the program is re-opened, each attorney submitting a claim will be required to sign the same or a similar form. Payment for work so certified will be arranged through the central CPA Ministry office.

Criminal defense program

The new right to defense counsel at all stages of criminal proceedings will require an expanded criminal defense program. Details are still being sorted out, but all investigative judges must now appoint defense counsel to serve beginning at the investigative stage for all criminal investigations. For the present, the investigative judges should use the same procedure that was formerly used for appointment of counsel in felony trials. The appointed lawyer has a right to fair compensation. The method of providing that compensation is one of the undecided details under active and urgent consideration. We have requested $5 million for this program, based on an estimated $400 for a felony investigation and trial, $100 for a misdemeanor.

Salary payment system

The current system for paying salaries to the regions and governorates should have been transmitted through other channels. We understand that local Coalition authorities have proceeded in a variety of ways to disburse the $20 and $30 emergency payments, and regular salaries. A new plan for salary payment is being evolved, and the CPA four-tier salary structure will likely be refined. For the time being, attempt to pay salaries according to the extant system, and coordinate with the central CPA Ministry office. Pamela Murphy (murphyp@orha.centcom.mil or MCI cellular phone no. 914-360-6550) is the salaries point-of-contact.

National assessment

A comprehensive national assessment of the entire Iraqi legal system has been prepared by judicial assessment teams sent by the United States Department of Justice.[82] It contains much useful information and benchmarks against which to measure our performance. It is too long to include with this memorandum, but we will provide it electronically at your request.

12. Other functions

The Ministry of Justice, in addition to operating the legal system, has a number of directorates dedicated to related areas, including deeds and records, notaries public, and judicial training.

[82] In May 2003, the United States Department of Justice (DOJ), with the assistance of Canadian, British and Danish delegates, undertook a country-wide legal needs assessment. This assessment was organized by the CPA. The Report included reference to the following areas: infrastructure, court organizational structure, personnel, the applicable law, law enforcement, judicial appointments and qualifications, legal education, training and bar associations.

Regarding judicial training, CPA Administrator Bremer re-opened the Iraqi Judicial College (formerly called the Judicial Training Institute) in Baghdad on 17 June, marking completion of the first major rebuilding project since the fall of Saddam Hussein. The curriculum of the College is now under review, to eliminate vestiges of the former regime and to emphasize the importance of a rule of law. Admission standards are also being examined.

Our goal with respect to the other directorates is to ensure that they resume operations with maximum possible efficiency and efficacy. Guidance regarding these areas may follow as we acquire the resources necessary to enable us to turn our attention to them. Any information you have relating to their facilities and operations would be appreciated. Further guidance may follow.

13. Conclusion

This document contains directions aimed at facilitating national consistency and implementation of CPA policy in instituting the rule of law in Iraq and restoring Ministry of Justice functions. The Iraqi judicial system was assumed to be corrupt, complicit in Saddam's bidding, and inefficient – and also possessed of some very capable and courageous individuals. We have been and will continue to work to eradicate the undesirable vestiges of the former regime and enable the people of rectitude to improve the legal system for the people of Iraq. Improving communications and coordination should facilitate that task. Feel free to contact us anytime about anything relating to the Ministry of Justice.

A summary of all information requested herein can be found in appendix 1. Please provide us with this information as best you are able within 10 days.

APPENDIX I – INFORMATION REQUESTS

Please supply the following information within 10 days of the date of this memorandum (NLT July 5, 2003), by e-mail to 1LT Fein (bruce.ellis.fein@us.army.mil) or by other method of communication:

- All staff names with responsibility for matters within the purview of the Ministry of Justice, geographical area of responsibility, and all available methods of communication
- Any order or arrangement, whether or not written, of which you are aware that transfers court functions to different facilities from where they are normally conducted
- Whether prisoners are being adequately transported between detention facilities, courts, and prisons
- Confirm, edit, or add to appendix 5 (all known Ministry facilities)
- Whether the Legal Gazette was distributed in your area of responsibility
- Whether you possess English translations of any Iraqi laws
- A list of every judge or prosecutor that you have removed or installed
- Any information about any judge or prosecutor
- Any information about the deeds and registries or notaries public Ministry functions
- General information regarding all activities in your area of responsibility, in greater or lesser detail as the significance of the matter and common sense dictate.

APPENDIX 2 –CPA MEMORANDUM NO. 2: MANAGEMENT OF DETENTION AND PRISON FACILITIES
[omitted, see *Doc 126*]

APPENDIX 3 – MINISTRY OF JUSTICE PERSONNEL PLAN

ACTION MEMORANDUM

To: Presidential Envoy Ambassador L. Paul Bremer
From: Clint Williamson; Senior Advisor, Ministry of Justice
Subject: CPA Justice Presence
Date: 16 June 2003

SUMMARY AND PURPOSE

Pursuant to our discussion on 6 June, and in line with the parameters you suggested, I have drawn up a revised plan for an international justice presence in Iraq. Recognizing that the Iraqis themselves are to staff the courts and the central ministry and are to have responsibility for most operations, it will nevertheless be necessary to place international advisors in key positions to steer the reform process and to exercise oversight of the Iraqi justice system as it transitions to a democratic model. The first part of this proposal addresses those needs and provides for staffing of a number of posts in the key functional areas of the ministry. The second part of the proposal allows for the introduction of international judges and prosecutors – working in an operational capacity – if it is determined that conditions warrant their use. The third and final part of the proposal relates to prisons and detention facilities, a functional area which has recently been transferred from the Ministry of Labor and Social Affairs to the Ministry of Justice.

DISCUSSION

This proposal addresses only the international component of the justice presence and the functional areas where I believe attention should be directed. In addition to the international posts I describe, a large number of Iraqis will be required to support the international staff in roles such as interpreters, secretaries, and even legal officers. Beyond that, the CPA will be able to draw on the considerable resources of the Ministry of Justice, an organization of some 12,000 employees.

Relying on personnel that have already been deployed in justice-sector assessment teams, some of the core posts I have proposed below can be filled in relatively short order. Other posts are currently occupied by military judge advocates on assignment to the CPA, and most of them will remain in place for the next two to three months. Some of the positions can be staffed with attorneys provided by the US Department of Justice (DOJ) Office of Overseas Prosecutorial Development, Assistance, and Training (OPDAT). Additional lawyers can be provided through DOD recruitment or by Coalition partners. In regard to the latter, the United Kingdom, Spain, South Korea, and Denmark have already expressed interest in providing personnel to work in the justice sector. Undoubtedly, other countries will be in a position to contribute lawyers as well.

My suggestion is to put in place a staff to carry out core functions as soon as possible – ideally by late-July 2003. This group, consisting of approximately 21 international staff members, would be assigned to key posts in the central ministry, the proposed Central Criminal Court, and to four regional monitoring centers. If necessary, four additional regional monitors and an operations officer would be deployed in October 2003. At that same time, if it is determined that international judges and prosecutors are to be used, they will begin deploying in a staged process, reaching their full complement by February 2004.

In relation to corrections, the majority of personnel discussed in this proposal will be required in the near future. While the core justice staff required at the beginning will primarily be in advisory roles, the prison personnel will be deployed in an operational capacity from the outset. This is necessary because the prison setting is much more conducive to abuse of persons under government control than are courts, or even police. This factor has led to the adoption of well-developed international standards on the rights of prisoners, and as the occupying powers, the US and the UK will bear ultimate responsibility for prison conditions – even if facilities are managed by Iraqis – for the entire period of occupation. Accordingly, while operational involvement in courts is optional, the Coalition will have little choice but to be actively involved in the running of the prisons.

Core Justice Presence

Senior Advisor/Management Element (7 posts)

Senior Advisor to the Ministry of Justice (1 international post)
The senior post within the CPA justice presence will be the Senior Advisor to the Ministry. This individual will oversee the work of all of the other international justice personnel and he or she will have primary responsibility for development and implementation of policy. The Senior Advisor, acting either as the *de facto* minister, as is the case now, or working closely with an Iraqi minister once one is put in place will ensure that the Ministry as a whole operates in accordance with CPA policy.

Chief Operational Advisor (1 international post)
As justice operations expand – particularly if an international judge and prosecutor program is established – there will be a need to coordinate operations. The Ministry of Justice operates 156 courthouses and employs approximately 12,000 personnel throughout Iraq. For the foreseeable future, the CPA will shoulder much of the responsibility for operational effectiveness, therefore, an individual dedicated to oversight of this matter is required. Additionally, with international justice personnel distributed nationwide, extensive coordination will be required in respect to them as well.

Administrative/Finance Officer (1 international post)
Thus far, much of the work of the Senior Advisor and his staff has been related to administrative, financial, and budgetary matters within the Ministry of Justice. As the ministry becomes fully functional again, these issues will only loom larger. As a result, I would recommend that an administrative officer be included within the Senior Advisor's immediate office. This individual will have responsibility for all contacts with the ministry administrative staff and will also oversee all of the administrative issues related to the international justice presence.

Facilities Officer/Engineer (1 international post)
Currently, around 75% of Ministry facilities are damaged and are non-functional. Although emergency repairs are being implemented to get courts and other buildings operational, it will be necessary to engage in a reconstruction and renovation program for several months to come. The scale of this program and the extent to which it will be reliant on international assistance requires that an individual with expertise in this field be dedicated to this issue. I would suggest, however, that this post only be staffed for a period of six months, to coincide with the most intense period of physical reconstruction work. If it is determined that ongoing projects require continuing someone in this post, a decision can be taken at the end of 2003 to extend the individual's contract.

Support Element (3 international posts)
To support the work of the Senior Advisor and the justice presence generally, I would recommend placing three internationals in the immediate office of the Senior Advisor: a secretary, a legal officer, and an operations officer. A capable secretary will be required from the outset as will a legal officer. The number of legal matters coming to the Senior Advisor on a daily basis will require that he or she have someone available to research issues, draft documents, and provide advice on a range of subjects. The third post – that of an operations officer – will be filled only if an international judge and prosecutor program is established. If this occurs, an additional individual will be needed to assist the Chief Operational Advisor with internal international justice presence operations.

Ministry Advisors (10 posts)

Judicial Inspection Unit (3 international posts)
This office will be the most crucial one in the ministry for ensuring that meaningful reform takes place and that corruption and other problems are adequately addressed. With the mandate to investigate judges and prosecutors for acts of impropriety, malfeasance, or professional incompetence, this office will have significant power. Acting either on complaints or on its own initiative, it will conduct investigations and then offer recommendations for disciplinary action (reprimand, suspension, or removal from office). Where evidence of criminal conduct is found, it can refer cases for prosecution. If it does its job properly, it will weed out a number of bad judges and prosecutors and have a strong deterrent effect on those who remain. While this office should be led by the three internationals, it should be staffed by a number of Iraqi lawyers who have been thoroughly vetted.

Office of the Director of Prosecutions (1 international post)
This office supervises all of the prosecutors throughout Iraq, and thus can have considerable influence over the administration of justice. Currently, prosecutors have a more limited role than in common law jurisdictions, but it is expected that their responsibilities will expand significantly in coming months. It will be necessary to closely monitor the prosecution service as this transformation takes place and prosecutors take on a much more substantive role than they had under Saddam. Accordingly, an international advisor can assist with this process and can affect development of policy in a positive way. He or she can also identify training requirements for prosecutors and feed this information back to capitals so that programs can be set up to address these needs.

Judicial Training Institute (2 international posts)
All judges are required to complete a two-year course at the Judicial Training Institute before being sworn in as judges and assigned to courts. The director of the Institute exercises considerable power in that he determines who will be admitted to the Institute and thus who will become judges. He also sets the curriculum, thereby fashioning the education and training potential judges receive. For these reasons, it is crucial that we have a strong presence in the Institute. One international would serve as principal advisor to the director of the Institute, where he or she could closely monitor admission practices and also ensure development of a suitable curriculum. The other international would coordinate training programs for sitting jurists, which will be required to upgrade the skills of retained judges and prosecutors. This individual will also be responsible for liaising with OPDAT to arrange deployments of lawyers to conduct specialized training programs.

Judicial Advisory Council (1 international post)
The Council, which has in the past had a key role in creating judicial policy, was sidelined under Saddam. Formerly headed by the President of the Court of Cassation, leadership of the Council was vested with the Minister of Justice under the last regime. Whether the Council is again established as an independent body (the recommendation of the Iraqi Jurists Association) or remains as a component part of the Ministry, it will play an important role in judicial reform. Thus, it is extremely important that we have an advisor in place working on a full-time basis with the Council and with the Court of Cassation. Whenever significant projects are undertaken, the advisor can draw upon additional experts who can be deployed to work on specific issues.

Office of Court Administration (2 international posts)
Early indications are that the court system in Iraq is plagued by inefficiency. In large part, this is due to deprivation of resources under the last regime, but it is also due to the use of outmoded practices and procedures. Administrative reform will significantly affect the functioning of the system and will be absolutely crucial as the legitimate courts (i.e., those in the Ministry of Justice) take on increased responsibilities. To address this problem, I would suggest placing two court administration experts in this office.

Juvenile Directorate (1 international post)
A directorate for juvenile affairs oversees the work of the juvenile courts and the offices dealing with juvenile rehabilitation, education, and re-location. Although this directorate is arguably in better shape than some other aspects of the central ministry, the treatment of juveniles is still at a level significantly lower than in the developed world. Accordingly, I would suggest placing an advisor, experienced in juvenile issues, in this directorate. This advisor will also work with the juvenile prisons directorate, which is being transferred from the Ministry of Labor and Social Affairs.

Central Criminal Court of Iraq (1 post)

A decision has recently been taken to establish the specialized Central Criminal Court of Iraq (CCCI) which will handle cases from all over the country involving the most serious criminal offenses. The CCCI will be comprised of selected Iraqi judges and prosecutors who have been thoroughly vetted. They will prosecute and hear cases referred to the court by the Administrator, on the recommendation of the Senior Advisor. Thus, it is expected that most high-profile matters such as those involving terrorism, organized crime, and inter-ethnic crimes will be addressed in this court, at least for the near term. It is also possible that this court could evolve over time into the forum where crimes of the Saddam regime are addressed, either with or without international participation. In light of the very serious responsibilities attached to this organ, it is extremely important that an international advisor be placed at the CCCI. This individual will assist in the set-up of the court, in enhancing its operational capabilities, and will additionally serve as the principal liaison from the CPA to the court.

Judicial Monitors/Advisors (8 posts)

Regional Offices (4 international posts initially; 4 additional optional posts)
In order to monitor courts and prosecutors' offices throughout the country, I would suggest placing lawyers in four regional offices situated in Mosul, Baghdad, Al Hillah, and Basra. They will be in a position to ensure that policies are implemented at the local level and also that problems are reported back to the central ministry and the CPA. Four of these lawyers would be deployed in July 2003 and an additional four could be deployed in October 2003, if it is determined that a need exists to supplement the original group.

Training Component

In addition to these twenty-five Iraq-based lawyers and support staff, other attorneys could be brought in, as suggested above, for short or medium-term missions to provide training or advice on selected issues. In terms of training, OPDAT can draw upon all areas of expertise in the US justice system and arrange for prosecutors or judges to deploy for one or two-week stints to conduct training in their respective areas of specialization. Likewise, as legal reform issues come under consideration, US DOJ, the Department of State, and others can contribute advisors to assist the Iraqis in revising and drafting laws. If a specialized legal reform committee is established, as is being discussed now, OPDAT can provide lawyers to assist in the process for the lifetime of the committee. The American Bar Association and other NGO's [sic], working under the auspices of USAID, can be called upon to provide training to the defense bar and attorneys engaged in civil practice.

International Judges and Prosecutors

In the next two to three months, a final decision should be taken on whether it is necessary to use international judges and prosecutors (IJPs) in Iraq. This decision will largely be contingent on two factors: the extent to which international police are to engage in investigative and operational functions; and, the capability of Iraqi courts to handle sensitive cases (e.g., inter-ethnic cases, terrorism, organized crime, etc.). In relation to the first issue, the use of IJPs may be warranted if international police officers are given primary responsibility for the conduct of most investigations, or if specialized units of internationals are set up to exclusively handle the more sophisticated investigations. In either case, the substantial resources invested by the international community in investigating these cases may justify the use of IJP's [sic] to ensure that the cases are competently handled when they reach court. Iraqi judges and prosecutors may be able to do this, but if they prove incapable, mishandling of these matters in court will effectively negate the work done by the police.

In terms of the capabilities of Iraqi courts to handle sensitive cases, it is probably premature to make conclusions on this issue. Unlike the situation in the Balkans where courts were re-established after violent inter-ethnic wars, there is nothing to suggest that Iraq will devolve into an ethnic battleground where courts are incapable of objectively handling inter-ethnic matters. Although this is a possibility, it certainly should not be taken as a given at this point that this will occur. So, the primary justification for using IJPs in Kosovo – to protect the rights of ethnic minorities – is not a readily apparent factor in Iraq. Of greater concern is the ability of Iraqi courts to effectively handle sensitive matters such as organized crime or terrorism cases, and to do this in the face of threats and/or corruption. Although this is a concern in all immature judicial systems, a determination must be made if the problem is so widespread and so pervasive that it will significantly undermine the rule of law and thus justify the replacement of local judges and prosecutors by internationals.

Finally, it should be recognized that the use of IJPs is a much more intrusive measure than the use of international police. Although international policemen may engage in policing activities alongside their Iraqi counterparts, and may even have the leading role, it is easier to present their work as a partnership effort where responsibilities and decision making are shared. When international prosecutors and judges are used, however, they completely supplant the locals and take on decision making roles in a very public setting. While this may be justified under certain circumstances, such as those I have described above, a decision to introduce IJPs should be taken only after all other alternatives for delivery of justice by local personnel have been exhausted. One such alternative may be the establishment of the Central Criminal Court, comprised of selected Iraqi judges and prosecutors, to handle serious cases. If the CCCI operates successfully for some time, it may negate the need for international intervention in this sphere. If, on the other hand, it is determined that the CCCI does not adequately address all of the security needs of the CPA, it would nevertheless be a convenient venue for placement of IJPs as it would be a consolidated court along the lines suggested above.

Should a decision be taken to introduce international judges and prosecutors (IJPs) into Iraq, it will be necessary to create a specialized unit which will include them and their support element. The proposal I set out in this memorandum provides for the creation of this unit through a staged deployment beginning in October 2003. Well in advance of that time, the size of the international police contingent, and the nature of the work in which they will be engaged, should be much clearer. Also, by that time, we should have a much better appreciation of the capabilities and shortcomings of the Iraqi judicial system and thus be in a position to decide if there is a sufficient basis for introducing IJPs.

International Judicial Unit (41 posts)

<u>Legal Issues and Procedures</u>

In order to set up an IJP program, a sufficient legal foundation will have to be laid. This would involve the promulgation of a regulation by the CPA establishing the jurisdiction of IJPs and the procedure whereby cases could be removed from the normal Iraqi system and diverted to chambers in which IJPs constituted a majority of the membership. These chambers could either be in the already established Iraqi courts, or alternatively in separate courts set up for the purpose of IJP interventions. In light of the large number and widespread geographical distribution of Iraqi criminal courts, the latter option is probably preferable. I have adopted this model for the purposes of this proposal.

The criteria for diverting cases to IJPs will have to be very clear-cut and must be stated in the enabling regulation. I would recommend giving them jurisdiction solely in criminal matters. IJP participation would be limited to serious cases (e.g., with potential penalties of 5 years or more) in which significant doubts exist about the objectivity or capabilities of Iraqi judges and/or prosecutors. These might include inter-ethnic crimes, war crimes/crimes against humanity cases, terrorism cases, organized crime cases, and public integrity matters, among others. Determining the types of cases that warrant the use of IJPs goes back to the initial analysis of whether such a program should be established in the first place. If Iraqi judges or prosecutors prove incapable of rendering justice in certain kinds of cases, then those obviously should be included in the jurisdictional ambit of IJPs. Within the broad categories of cases, though, additional specific criteria will have to be satisfied in relation to each case that is diverted to IJPs. These criteria would relate to specific disqualifying factors for Iraqi jurists which call into question their abilities to adjudicate any specific case (e.g., evidence of a judge receiving threats related to a pending case; local prominence of a defendant which might interfere with the judge making a decision, etc.).

In order to divert a case to IJPs, the Senior Advisor should file a request with the Administrator of the CPA. This request would contain a brief description of the facts of the case and would lay out the reasons why diversion is required. If the Administrator agrees, the case would then be assigned to an international prosecutor and/or an international judge or a panel of international judges, depending on the stage of the proceedings. I would suggest that three regional courts be established in Baghdad, Basra, and Mosul respectively. Each of these courts would have jurisdiction over the criminal and investigative court districts within their geographical areas of responsibility.

At any stage of the proceedings, an international prosecutor could be appointed. If it is determined that the use of international judges is warranted in any given case, this could occur prior to the initiation of any specific stage of the proceedings. If a case is diverted during the investigative stage, the case would be sent to the regional court for hearing by a single international judge, sitting alone. During the trial stage, a case would be heard in the regional court location by a panel of three judges, two of whom would be internationals and one of whom would be an Iraqi judge from the court district which would have been the appropriate venue for the case but for the diversion.

Should a matter be appealed from the regional IJP court, an appeals panel would be composed of two international judges from the other regional courts and one Iraqi judge from the Court of Appeals district which would have had jurisdiction over the matter had it not been diverted. Finally, should a case be appealed to the Court of Cassation, the case would be heard by a panel of five judges, three of whom would be internationals (two assigned to the Supreme Court and one drawn from one of the regional courts) and two Iraqi members of the Court of Cassations criminal panel.

Since judges would be barred from sitting on more than one stage of any given case, the number of judges must be sufficient to accommodate investigative proceedings, trials, intermediate appeals, and appeals at the level of the Court of Cassation. With this essential constraint, it is possible that eight judges could be utilized in one case if international judges were included in proceedings at all levels. Although this may seem like a high number, I would suggest that it is probably the most efficient mechanism for use of IJPs that still roughly tracks the Iraqi system and procedures. Any other option which would utilize fewer judges and prosecutors would either require significant modification of Iraqi procedures (e.g., elimination of the appellate stage) or consolidation of all IJPs into one central court in Baghdad – a move that would result in considerable logistical burdens on all of the other participants in the judicial process (police, local judges and prosecutors, prisons). Even under this option, extensive coordination will be required as IJPs, local judges and prosecutors, police, and prisoners are shifted from court to court. Accordingly, a coordination cell is built into the proposal for the IJP program.

Staffing and Operations

The International Judicial Unit (IJU) will fall under the overall supervision of the Senior Advisor, but will be headed by its own coordinator, assisted by a small management and support element. This management cell will coordinate the operations of the judges and prosecutors, will track cases, and will provide a centralized legal pool responsible for drafting diversion requests and for legal analysis.

In order to cover all stages of the criminal process, international judges must be assigned to the trial courts and to the Court of Cassation. Investigative proceedings and intermediate appellate proceedings would be handled by international judges assigned to the trial courts, but shifted to the other functions as needs require. As stated above, the IJPs would be assigned to three regional courts, sitting in Baghdad, Basra, and Mosul respectively. Assuming that a decision is taken to introduce IJPs by September 2003, the IJP Coordinator and the other members of the management cell would deploy in October 2003. The first IJPs, assigned to the Court of Cassation and the Baghdad regional court, would be deployed with their support staffs in December 2003. They would be followed in January 2004 by the IJPs going to Mosul and then in February by those going to Basra. If a decision on the use of IJPs is delayed beyond September, this staged deployment schedule could be implemented over a similar period of time, but commencing at a later date.

Each IJP will require a three person staff, consisting of a legal officer, a secretary, and an interpreter (of which two or possibly all three may be Iraqis). In Mosul, each IJP will probably require two interpreters – one for Arabic and one for Kurdish. In any event, these support personnel are absolutely essential for IJPs to be operational. Thus, their deployments must coincide with those of the IJPs. Likewise, should a decision be taken at a later date to increase the number of IJPs, each judge and prosecutor brought on would have to have the three-person support staff. Under the proposed structure, it would be relatively easy to do this within the operational framework suggested.

One other issue should be considered in relation to the deployment of IJPs and that is the security requirements that will attach to them. Due to the fact that they would be handling very high-profile cases, would be doing so in an extremely visible manner, and would be the ones determining the outcome of any matter (as opposed to police), the threat levels attributed to each of them will usually be very high. In Kosovo, almost all of the close protection resources of the UN mission were dedicated to security for IJPs. As it was necessary to provide secure accommodations, an armored vehicle, a chase vehicle, and at least four bodyguards for each one, this became a very burdensome obligation which had carry-over effects to other areas of the mission. Since close protection resources are generally in high demand, but are often in short supply, the resource implications connected to IJP's in this regard should not be underestimated.

Handling of War Crimes/Crimes Against Humanity Cases

In the 'Legal Issues and Procedures' section above, I included war crimes and crimes against humanity cases among the matters that could potentially be handled by IJPs. I am not suggesting, however, that all cases of this type be diverted to IJPs. The number and scale of crimes committed by the last regime are such that if prosecutions were launched in even a small portion of those cases, this would completely overwhelm the IJP resources I have proposed. Rather, I am suggesting here that if there are lower-level cases not addressed by a special tribunal, and those are relatively few in number, they could be possibly be included within the jurisdiction of IJPs.

Conversely, should a decision be taken that the best method for dealing with prosecutions of atrocities committed by the last regime is a mixed Iraqi/international process, the IJP program I have proposed in this memorandum could serve as the foundation for an expanded operation of this nature. Obviously, significant modifications would have to be made and the numbers of IJP's [sic] and support staff would have to be increased significantly. It might also be preferable to consolidate trials of this type into one special court, probably situated in Baghdad.

Prisons

One of the most sensitive issues that the CPA will have to address is the management of prisons. As I stated at the beginning of this memorandum, the Coalition will have ultimate responsibility for prison conditions and for the treatment of prisoners, even if correctional facilities are staffed with Iraqi officers. As the occupying powers, the US and the UK will have an obligation to maintain these facilities at a level of internationally acceptable standards. The CPA, therefore, will have little choice but to be actively involved in operations of prisons to a degree that may not be true of courts or police. Furthermore, considering that the entire management structure of the Iraqi prison system has been removed and that most lower-level personnel were poorly trained or not trained at all, and the vulnerability of persons in prison custody to abuse, the extent to which Iraqi capabilities in this area must be raised is significantly higher than for either courts or police. Accordingly, I am proposing a very pro-active approach in regard to prisons in which the CPA exercises overall management and operational responsibilities for the near-term, combined with an extensive training program.

Central Management (15 posts)

Office of the Director (2 international posts)
In order to oversee and manage the prisons system effectively, an experienced and senior corrections expert should be installed as the Director of the Prison Service. Although he or she will report to the Senior Advisor to the Ministry of Justice, the Director will head a largely self-contained unit which need not rely on other resources within the Ministry of Justice. I would also suggest that an international secretary be provided for the Director to ensure that his or her immediate office functions efficiently.

Administration, Finance, and Legal Support (3 international posts)
As the prison system is effectively an independent element within the Ministry, it should be as self-sufficient as possible. Furthermore, since the administrative and financial issues relating to prisons are distinct from those relating to other justice functions, it will be beneficial to have two administrative/finance officers dedicated to prison issues. Likewise, a number of specialized legal matters will undoubtedly arise in connection with

the operation of prisons and with the prisoners themselves. Accordingly, a legal officer responsible solely for these issues should be included in the international prison staff.

Operations (3 international posts)
A Chief of Operations would effectively serve as the deputy to the Director and would have responsibility for day-to-day operational control of the prison system. He or she would be assisted by two deputies, one with responsibility for adult male prison facilities and the other responsible for adult women and juvenile facilities. This arrangement would be consistent, to some extent, with the previous structure under which two separate directorates existed within the Ministry of Labor and Social Affairs for adult and juvenile prisons respectively. While I do not believe that it is necessary to maintain two separate directorates – with duplication of functions – it is essential that some division between operations of the two be preserved.

Security Office (2 international posts)
To effectively operate a prison system it is necessary to have a coordinated security approach common to all facilities. In order to do this, there has to be management from a central point wherein the security policies are created and monitored. Additionally, the security office should be the repository for criminal intelligence information on individuals held in custody. To carry out these functions, I am suggesting that two international experts be placed in charge of the office. One would serve as Chief of Security and the other as his or her deputy.

Medical Unit (2 international posts)
The physical and mental health of prisoners is always an area of great concern. Although Iraqi physicians will primarily be used to provide health care to prisoners, it will be necessary to exercise oversight of this very sensitive issue and to ensure that certain standards are maintained. Accordingly, I am proposing that an international medical doctor and an international psychiatrist be included among the international prison staff.

Engineering Unit (3 international posts)
At the present time, there are no prison facilities in Iraq that are completely functional. All of the facilities have been destroyed or damaged to the point that they are currently unusable. Although efforts are underway to quickly repair and renovate several prisons, these are temporary measures which will not meet long-term needs. As a result, numerous facilities around the country must be reconstructed or renovated in the coming months. To coordinate this work, I am suggesting that an architect, a civil engineer, and an electrical engineer be included among the international presence.

Field Facilities Management (54 posts)

Each prison and detention facility should be managed by an international prison officer until Iraqi capabilities are developed to the point that the CPA is comfortable that local operation of the facilities is feasible. To do this effectively, each facility must have assigned to it a director and at least two deputy directors, depending on the size of the institution. One of the deputies would serve additionally as the primary training tutor for Iraqi correctional officers working within their facility. With at least three international officers assigned to each facility, it should be possible to ensure that at least one international is present at any facility at all times. Based on preliminary estimates that five major prisons and twelve smaller detention facilities will become operational in coming months, fifty-five international prison officers would be needed to cover these requirements.

Training Element (8 posts)

As I stated above, the level of training among Iraqi correctional officers is very low or in many cases, simply non-existent. It will be necessary, therefore, to basically start from scratch in terms of training any officers that we would wish to retain. Likewise, all newly hired officers would have to receive basic training as well. To conduct the training programs, I am proposing that eight international training officers be deployed as soon as possible. Ideally, the training program for correctional officers could be co-located with the new police training program, so that common areas of instruction (e.g., human rights training) could be combined. The specialized instruction required for corrections personnel would be offered by these eight training officers. They would start immediately with two-week short courses designed to educate prison guards in the most basic skills and practices of prison operations. All current and newly-hired officers would receive this training. Subsequently, these personnel would be rotated back through the training facility for a more intensive course which would largely track the training program that will eventually be offered to new recruits.

Conclusion

This revised proposal for the justice presence is based on an appreciation of needs as of the first week of June 2003. It has been prepared at a time when communications with areas outside Baghdad are still extremely problematic and when most central ministry functions and courts are operating at only the basic levels, if at all. With that in mind, I have tried to build in as much flexibility as possible while anticipating problems that are likely to be encountered in coming weeks and months. I strongly believe that the core presence of justice personnel, as described in the first part of this proposal, will be necessary under any circumstances. The option to use international judges and prosecutors, as set out in the second part of the proposal, remains available should circumstances warrant it. I would reiterate that I do not believe that we are in a position to make this decision yet, and such a serious decision should be taken only when sufficient information is developed. The final part of the proposal, pertaining to prisons, addresses a pressing need and should, I believe, be implemented as soon as possible. Finally, I would add that effective implementation of all parts of this proposal is contingent upon a permissive security environment, adequate communications, and sufficient logistical support.

RECOMMENDED ACTION

I, therefore, request and recommend that you approve this medium-term plan for assignment of international legal advisors in key positions in the Ministry of Justice.

____ Approve ____Disapprove ____ Approve with Modification

Appendix A
Staffing Chart
[omitted]

APPENDIX 4 – INSTRUCTION THAT ALL COURTS SHOULD BE UP AND RUNNING TO THE EXTENT POSSIBLE

In my capacity as Senior Adviser to the Ministry of Justice and acting pursuant to the powers vested in me by the Coalition Provisional Authority, I hereby reiterate and request that, if they have not done so already, all Ministry of Justice employees should return to their workplaces and resume performance of their duties to the fullest extent possible. This instruction applies to all judges, prosecutors, court investigators, and other employees, subject however to decisions of local military commanders and/or Coalition Provisional Authority officials that circumstances warrant the provisional exclusion of any specific individual whose presence would disrupt the functioning of the local court system. I also hereby reiterate and request that, if they have not done so already, all Ministry of Justice employees shall work expeditiously to organize and perform repair, clean-up, and restoration of their respective courthouses and other Ministry buildings wherever necessary.

Clint Williamson
Senior Adviser
Ministry of Justice
31 May 2003

APPENDIX 5-16
[omitted][83]

Document 200
Baghdad Commercial Air Service: Notice Inviting Applications
1 July 2003

Summary: By this Notice, the Office of the Coalition Provisional Authority (OCPA) invites all airlines interested in providing scheduled passenger commercial air transportation to and from Baghdad, Iraq, to file applications in order to allow OCPA to allocate the limited available capacity among interested airlines at Baghdad International Airport.

[83] Appendix 5–Ministry of Justice Facilities, Appendix 6–Ministry of Justice Organizational Chart and Court Organizational Chart, Appendix 7–CPA Order No 2: Dissolution of Entities *[Doc 15]*, Appendix 8–CPA Order No 13: The Central Criminal Court of Iraq *[Doc 29]*, Appendix 9–CPA Order No 7: Penal Code *[Doc 21]*, Appendix 10–CPA Memorandum No 3: Criminal Procedure *[Doc 127]*, Appendix 11–First Postwar Issue of Legal Gazette, Appendix 12–CPA Order No 15: Judicial Review Committee *[Doc 33]*, Appendix 13–CPA Order No 1: De-Ba'athification *[Doc 14]*, Appendix 14–CPA Memorandum No 1: Implementation of De-Ba'athification Order No 1 *[Doc 125]*, Appendix 15–CPA Order No 5: Iraqi De-Ba'athification Council *[Doc 19]*, Appendix 16–CPA Order No 10: Ministry of Justice Responsibility for Prisons *[Doc 25]*.

Background: This Notice is being issued in anticipation of the reopening of Baghdad International Airport.[84] Capacity at the airport will initially be limited to three (3) roundtrip flights per day, seven days per week. In light of these circumstances, OCPA has decided to invite applications for Iraq service that will allow OCPA to allocate the available capacity at the airport among those airlines that are interested in providing service. Grants of authority will be for an initial period of three months. They may be renewed or revoked in the discretion of the OCPA.

Iraq Air Service Needs

Currently, OCPA has made the following threshold determinations in order to best serve ongoing efforts to reconstruct and develop the economy of Iraq and restore its civil aviation services:

- Two round trips per day will be made available for conducting Middle East regional services; one round trip per day will be made available for worldwide operations, including global code-share arrangements;
- Each airline chosen must be prepared to conduct at least two flights per week;
- Each airline chosen must be prepared for a maximum 2-hour ground turnaround without fueling, catering, or other ground services being provided;
- Each airline chosen must be prepared to operate without the carriage of cargo into or out of Baghdad; and
- Other factors which may be relevant in the current circumstances.

Minimum Eligibility Requirements

To be eligible for consideration, airline applicants must submit valid evidence with their applications that they meet each of the following criteria:

- Each airline must be duly licensed by its home government to conduct international air transportation to and from Iraq;
- Each airline must hold the appropriate level of passenger and third-party liability insurance as required by its home government;
- Each airline must be a signatory to the International Air Transport Association (IATA) Intercarrier Agreement on Passenger Liability, opened for signature on 31 October 1995; and the IATA Agreement on Measures to Implement the IATA Intercarrier Agreement, opened for signature in May 1996;
- Each airline must meet certain safety standards (see attachment to this Notice).

Application Procedures, Selection Decision, and Timetable: CPA invites all interested airlines, which meet the eligibility requirements indicated above, to submit applications with CPA by noon, 8 July (Baghdad time) 2003. OCPA intends to make its selection(s) based on which airline(s) proposal(s) will best serve ongoing efforts to reconstruct and develop the economy of Iraq. Therefore, each airline's application should describe in detail how its proposed operations would best meet the air service needs identified above.

At a minimum, applications from eligible airlines should include the following: a complete description of the proposed operations, including complete routings and flight

[84] More than 20 airlines – including British Airways, Lufthansa, KLM, SAS, and Air France – applied to fly into and out of Baghdad International Airport (BIA). BIA, however, was not reopened to scheduled commercial air services until August 2004. Throughout the period of occupation BIA was used only for receiving humanitarian goods, mail delivery and other emergency services.

schedules; frequency of service; illustrative fares; start-up date; equipment type; and whether services will be operated directly or by code share. If applying to serve the market by using tickets issued through a code share, in addition to the foregoing, provide the identity of the operating airline and the code share partners.

Applications must be submitted electronically, in English, through the following OCPA electronic mail account: biap@orha.centcom.mil. This Notice will be made available on the OCPA website at the following address http://www.cpa-iraq.org and will be distributed through the International Air Transport Association (IATA), Air Transport Association of America (ATA), the National Air Carrier Association of America (NACA), the Association of European Airlines (AEA), the Arab Air Carrier Organization (AACO), the Association of Asia Pacific Airlines (AAPA), and the African Airlines Association (AFRAA). The applications and OCPA's selection decision will also be available on the OCPA website.

ATTACHMENT

Safety Criteria

1) Airlines from countries that are currently listed as Category 1 under the U.S. Federal Aviation Administration's (FAA) International Aviation Safety Assessment (IASA) program are acceptable.

2) Airlines from a country that is IASA Category 2 or that is not currently categorized by the FAA may be acceptable.

- a) An airline's acceptability depends on whether it is capable of conducting its operations in accordance with minimum international standards.
- b) Determinations of acceptability will be made on a case-by-case basis considering all relevant information that may be available, including:
  - ICAO USOAP reports
  - FAA IASA reports
  - Reports of audits of the airline by code share or alliance partners
  - Reports of FAA surveillance of the airline's U.S. operations, if applicable
  - Information from other Civil Aviation Authorities on the airline's operations
- c) Other considerations on whether an airline is acceptable include
  - Whether special emphasis ramp inspections or other direct monitoring should be performed to ensure safety.
  - Whether additional conditions or limitations should be required to ensure safety (e.g., whether operations must be under visual flight rules (VFR) only).

Note that U.S. airlines need to be appropriately approved by their respective FAA certificate management offices in order to fly into Iraq.[85]

[85] A similar Notice Inviting Applications for Basrah Commercial Air Services was issued on 25 July 2003. However, Basrah International Airport, the second largest airport in Iraq, was also not reopened to scheduled commercial air services until 4 June 2005. On 28 August 2003, the London-based newspaper 'Al-Quds al-Arabi' published a statement of the Iraqi Ba'ath party which reads: 'Through their occupation of the Basra Governorate and their deployment at Basra International Airport, which they have made their headquarters, the British occupation forces are trying to impose an illegal administrative and political situation. They have decided to commercially operate the airport by allowing civilian planes of various nationalities to land at and take off from Basra International Airport, in accordance with a program that starts end of August 2003. The various media have reported that some Arab and foreign airlines companies have positively responded and have decided to use the airport for regular and irregular flights. We appeal to the Arab and foreign airlines, which have expressed their readiness and intention to operate civilian flights by submitting a request to the occupation forces in this regard, to halt their programs and to refrain from cooperating with the illegal British occupation forces. We look forward

Document 201
A Vision to Empower Iraqis (Draft)
4 July 2003

Introduction

Now that Saddam Hussein's regime has been removed, the opportunity exists for the Iraqi people to create the conditions for a stable, prosperous and democratic Iraq. The Coalition Provisional Authority (CPA), in close partnership with the Iraqi Interim Administration, the United Nations, and the international community, has a key role to play in the next stage of rebuilding Iraq so that it is once again able to take its rightful place as a proud nation of the international community.

The aim of this document is to describe the CPA's role in this historic process. It also seeks to outline both the way ahead and also the approach I wish to take so that everyone in the organization is clear on their part in the process. While initially, the CPA has and will have a dominant role in the first stages of establishing the transformation of Iraq, we should all be clear that shortly we will have a significant partner in the Governing Council (GC) of the Interim Administration that will represent the voice of the Iraqi people to the CPA. Together the CPA and the GC will forge a strong partnership that will guide the nation forward in its transformation. The GC and the CPA will expand its partnership not only to the Iraqi people but also to the region and the rest of the world.

This document is designed therefore to direct the work of the CPA, and the JTF in a flexible manner that recognizes the critical need to retain the support of the Iraqi people in all that we do, knowing that without their support we will fail. In so doing it is also aimed at the international community whose political and financial backing will be essential if the overall objectives that the Iraqis set for themselves are to be achieved. Furthermore the intention of this plan is to provide a guide for the direction for the Coalition. In addition, since time is pressing and Iraqi expectations are high, I envisage this plan as laying down the principal components which will form a basis for further planning in coordination with the GC as the process of rebuilding Iraq evolves. Finally, while full economic recovery will take years, the economic reform program provides a hope for a future of freedom and prosperity that we will work diligently with the GC to implement in the very short term.

At the heart of the plan, I have articulated my vision, and my views of our mission and end-state which I request every member of CPA to be familiar with and to work towards. The plan then describes the six core elements that will need to be weaved together to rebuild Iraq. From these core elements flow a series of key tasks, milestones and targets.

to a declared decision in this regard by the Jordanian, Qatari, Yemeni, Egyptian, and other airlines. The valiant Iraqi resistance has foiled the US occupation forces' plans to commercially operate Saddam International Airport by directing fire at the airport, which it considers a legitimate military target, and at the planes using the airport. Our statement issued on 16 July 2003 warned Arab and foreign airlines companies against sending their planes to Saddam International Airport or using its air corridors. We thus foiled the US occupation forces' plans. Also as we mentioned in our statement issued on 10 August 2003, the Al-Habbaniyah military airport was and still is a military target for the valiant resistance, as well as other airports and airbases, such as the Al-Bakr Airbase, the Al-Faris airport, and the Al-Basil airport. After this appeal, we warn that Basra airport will be considered a legitimate military target. The valiant resistance will consider the planes using the airport legitimate targets. The resistance's air defense means, which are prepared for this task, will open fire at these planes. This warning will not be repeated.'

None the less, we should consider this plan as a dynamic document, suitable to a dynamic reality that will require flexibility and innovation.

The plan should describe a critical path within the various core elements that should direct the CPA's priorities in the short, medium and long-term. From this, we should be in a position to review what we have achieved and where we need to readjust as necessary. Finally the plan will assist us and the Governing Council not only to allocate our resources and those of Iraq but also to attract critical resources and capabilities from the international community.

L. Paul Bremer, Administrator
Coalition Provisional Authority

Background

Operating Environment

Ultimately the Coalition's achievements in Iraq will be judged not by the success of the military campaign to remove Saddam Hussein's regime but rather by the foundations that it lays together with the Iraqi people in the post-conflict phase.

The environment in which the Coalition finds itself is complex. It entails the combination of military combat and security operations to establish the peace alongside expanding political, reconstruction and economic activities which will set the conditions for rebuilding Iraq. This requires a truly integrated civil-military approach that will have an additional nexus in the Governing Council. In addition, an inherent flexibility of approach, based upon a firm understanding of the overall mission and end-state, is critical to attack whatever challenges the prevailing circumstances might pose.

Opportunities and Challenges/Critical Paths

There is wide approval, both within Iraq and also the region, for the removal of Saddam Hussein's regime. This provides a unique opportunity for the Iraqi people to create the conditions for a stable, prosperous and democratic Iraq with our help. The vast majority of Iraqis want us to succeed, knowing that our success is their success. At the same time, expectations are high and this window of opportunity will not be indefinite. Hence a careful balance is being struck between the measured consideration of a wide range of options in consultation with the Iraqi people against a requirement to make continual and tangible progress. This process will be facilitated once the Interim Administration is established.

Central to this ability to demonstrate evidence of lasting progress in the short-term is the early creation of a *secure and safe environment* in order to allow the civil authorities fully to take the lead in all aspects of the CPA mission. The potential for instability is likely to exist for some time following the end of the warfighting. At the extremes, the threat is manifested in residual pockets of fanatics, terrorists and externally-supported elements seeking to undermine the CPA's authority. At the same time, reprisal killings, and organized crime is present in the immediate post-conflict period. These factors will constrain the early development of Iraq's capacity to manage and maintain a safe and secure environment for itself. They also require a holistic approach to security sector reform, including the integration of the military, police, judicial, penal systems and border control elements of future Iraqi society.

The most fragile countries are those in the early phases of *democratization.* Only mature democracies and totally authoritarian regimes are stable. Iraq, then, is vulnerable to internal strife as the country transitions from an institutionalized dictatorship to an open society and ultimately to democratic elections for a representative government. This is why I have made it a high priority to establish the Interim Administration, to give voice to the Iraqi people and the real sense that they have authority over their future.

Nurturing the environment for a *responsible civil society* has a significant role in the path to transforming Iraq from an authoritarian regime to a democracy. This is why I made de-Ba'athification my highest priority. Without eradicating the structures of the Ba'ath Party and its instruments of terror, true civil society could not emerge. The next stage in de-Ba'athification will need to be done in close partnership with the Iraqi Interim Administration, as will a lot of the remaining work to establish the conditions for a vibrant civil society including the desirability of some process of reconciliation.

The creation of *transparent government financial management institutions* requires a significant effort in a country where secrecy, use of public resources for private use and indiscriminate punishment were the standard practices. This includes working with Iraqis and Iraqi institutions to build new budgeting, banking and accounting practices. The new practices need to be pervasive, not only at the national government, ministry and municipal levels but also in civil society organizations and even in the private sector, where appropriate. Modern information systems technology can be an important part of this institution-building process.

Finally *economic regeneration* is the key driver in the overall process of rebuilding Iraq and will provide the most tangible evidence of progress being made by both the CPA and the Interim Administration. Iraq's enormous assets, both in terms of its physical resources and its skilled, energetic people, creates significant opportunities for Iraq as a nation. Clearly, the potential benefits to the Iraqi people are huge. Attracting the emerging Iraqi leadership to partner with the CPA to put in place the economic governance mechanisms which can result in the maximum gains is a high priority. The benefit to the international community of a responsible, democratic Iraq in the region is also significant.

As a result, *Iraqi political-economic leadership, the achievement of prosperity and growth, and the management of a free market economy* will require significant attention and accelerated training programs. The conventional practice of learning on-the-job takes years, but time may be a luxury in the Iraq recovery program. Success will require governance transformation practices different in important ways from conventional practices. Responsible Iraqi leadership will be achieved by a careful selection process, highly innovative training, and a commitment by these leaders to rapidly learn new behavior.

The Path to Transformation; End State or Next State

Expectations are a serious matter. Iraqis, legislators, press, taxpayers, home offices, think tanks and international citizens all develop expectations of the future. Perhaps the most important function that planning documents and processes can do is to satiate the need for information on plans, increase the cooperative efficiency of the many entities that contribute directly or indirectly to planning, encourage contributions in critical areas from those who wish to invest, and improve the productivity of all operational entities in Iraq. The value of setting realistic, interim targets toward an end state is that expectations can be more effectively managed. If a post-conflict reconstruction program will indeed take years to achieve, then the 'Next State' which can be achieved over a shorter time period en route to an End State may be important to define. A planning process can focus on achieving certain important milestones along the way to an End State.

Political transformation will naturally take the leading role. Stages of this transformation, some of which have already been alluded to are as follows:

- Establishing a Governance Council to begin to take management responsibility in the ministries and a process leading to a new constitution;
- National consensus on a constitution; and
- National elections to elect a national government.

A matrix of corresponding measures of progress in each 'core element' will be created for each stage. The objectives listed for each 'core element' will be used as a guide to develop the priority measures in each. Special attention will be paid to the 'transformation' objectives, as the most critical path is likely to be centered in this area.

The CPA Vision

After decades of a ruthless dictatorship, the Iraqi people can at last control their destiny and establish the conditions for a free and stable future. The CPA with the international community will help the Iraqi people to achieve the President's and Prime Minister's vision for Iraq.[86] Our foundation of authority is firmly embedded in international law and in accord with United Nations Resolution 1483.[87] This recognizes legitimacy by granting a mandate to the 'Authority' [CPA] to 'assist the people of Iraq in their efforts to reform their institutions and rebuild their country [...] and to establish an Interim Administration'. At the core of this new Iraq will be the development of a democratic, accountable, and self-governing civil society respectful of human rights and freedom of expression. So the CPA succeeds when Iraq succeeds. The future prosperity of its citizens depends on the use of Iraqi resources to foster the development and establishment of a market-based economy for and by them. Furthermore our goal is an Iraq at peace with itself and its neighbors, once again able to play a responsible role in the international community. The Coalition is firmly committed to the future of Iraq. Hence we will stay as long as necessary, and not a day longer. But we will not leave until we have succeeded in carrying out the President's and Prime Minister's vision of a free Iraq governed by a representative government chosen through a democratic election on the basis of a new constitution.

The Mission

The CPA will work with the Iraqi people and the Iraqi Interim Administration to establish the conditions for the creation of a free, sovereign, democratically-elected representative government in an Iraq that is stable, united, prosperous, at peace with its neighbors and able to take its rightful place as a responsible member of the region and the international community that uses its resources for the benefit of its people.

The End State

The ultimate goal is a durable peace for a unified and stable, democratic Iraq that: provides effective and representative government for and by the Iraqi people; is underpinned by new and protected freedoms and a growing market economy; and no longer poses a threat to its neighbors or international security and is able to defend itself.

[86] See *Doc 572*.
[87] For the full text of resolution 1483 (2003), see *Doc 523*.

CPA Planning Assumptions

General:

- International law and UNSCR 1483 provide the necessary mandate for CPA to achieve its mission.
- The International Community and the UN will be positively engaged in helping the CPA achieve its mission. Their relationships with the CPA may change over time.
- The Coalition will stay as long as necessary and leave as soon as its job is done.
- The Coalition will work closely with the Interim Iraqi Administration to establish the process for success for a future Iraq and will do so cooperatively in each of the following areas.

Security:

- An atmosphere of security is the 'sine qua non' of all Coalition and Iraqi efforts to rebuild Iraq.
- The Coalition and International Community will provide sufficient forces for the appropriate duration to establish and maintain a safe and secure and environment.
- The International Community will assist in building the Iraqi capacity to manage their own security sector, but the major burden will fall on American and British forces for the foreseeable future.
- Real, continuing and well-organized security threats (crime, extremists, terrorists) as well as the potential of external aggression and subversion will undermine Coalition progress.
- The transformation of the economy from a highly protected and controlled command economy to a market system will be very painful for many and even if successful in economic terms will produce fresh security problems.
- Resources of money, people and integrity needed for the new military, police and security services will be limited. Yet meeting the security challenges will require a substantial Coalition commitment of resources and political will.
- Iraqi police will be trained rapidly and soon begin to contribute importantly to establishing security and law and order. A full police force trained in community policing methods necessary to gain community support in law enforcement will take considerably longer.
- Selected Iraqi military will participate constructively in the security sector.
- The effects of this effort will allow Iraq to provide adequate protection for its citizens both internally and externally without posing a threat to its neighbors. Timely accomplishment of this will require a conscious, planned effort.
- Oversight mechanisms to maintain accountability of the security, police, justice, and custodial sectors will be a long-term requirement which must be built into the Iraqi democratic institutions.

Essential Services and Civil Society:

- Reconstruction efforts to restore essential public services will proceed aggressively to improve the quality of life and to enable progress in other sectors.
- An Iraqi capacity to manage any new humanitarian emergencies, with some international assistance, will evolve.
- Free market economic transition will increase unemployment in the short run which will need to be mitigated by a social safety net.

– Encourage Iraqi people to support and remain engaged in the process of reform and promote an active role for women in society.
– The policy of Deba'athification and the evolving guidelines for its implementation will remain a priority for achieving the CPA mission.

Economy:

– Full transition to open market economy is beyond the scope of the Coalition mission. But we can set the Iraqi economy on the path for sustainable growth and establish strong momentum toward a full open market economy.
– There will be continued economic and financial resources from both Iraq and the international community including the United States to accomplish the mission.
– The early provision of employment opportunities will be a critical requirement if the Iraqi people are to remain engaged.
– The CPA will engage the private sector, both domestic and international, in reconstruction and support the return of talent.

Preparing for Democracy:

– Little Iraqi experience exists among Iraqi leaders and the population for managing and supporting a participative democracy (the same was argued in Japan, South Korea, Taiwan, Indonesia, Mongolia, most of Latin America.).
– Equally, little Iraqi experience exists to manage a free market economy.
– Democratic institutions, e.g., responsible political parties, independent representative organizations, public interest groups or electoral bodies or systems have little pre- existing traditions or roots upon which to build, thus will require substantial assistance to develop.
– Efforts to instill an understanding of democratic principles, what they do and do not mean, and a grasp of the responsibilities that go with freedom will be a critical requirement.
– Educational institutions at all levels will require extensive curriculum reform to support a democratic system and a free market economy.
– Nurturing the growth of vigorous and responsible civil society organizations to hold governments accountable at all levels is essential.
– Extensive and accelerated education, training, and focused experience activities will be essential to support a rapid transformation in politics and economics.

Governance and Sovereignty:

– Iraqi people will accept legitimacy of the Interim Administration.
– The election of an accountable and representative government will be based upon a Constitution borne of a popular participative process.
– The Iraqi people will embrace and remain committed to electoral reform.
– The Iraqi people will support a united national government structure.
– The neighboring states will ultimately:
  • Accept the CPA as a legitimate authority and;
  • Recognize the new Iraq as a legitimate sovereign state;
  • Support the emerging Iraqi governance structure as a legitimate part of the regional community, and;
– Efforts by some neighbors to disrupt the CPA mission will not succeed.

Information:

- A coherent and coordinated information campaign will be an essential pre-requisite for integrating the various strands of the CPA and ultimately achieving its mission.
- CPA will successfully overcome the perception, internally within Iraq and externally within much of the international community that the Coalition prosecuted the war for Western gain of Iraq's natural resources.
- CPA will establish an accepted, effective and transparent information exchange with the Iraqi people.

Core Foundations and Sub-Objectives

- *Security ... addresses all aspects of the establishment of a safe and secure environment. The objective is to create an Iraqi capacity to manage and resolve any and all potential conflict situations in both the civil and military sectors.*
  - Creation of a safe and secure environment by CPA/CJTF-7.
  - Create Iraqi capacity to maintain structural stability.
  - Develop Iraqi security forces which are effective in protecting the society and the constitutional order as well as respect for human rights.
  - Iraqi military formation/training; with full oversight mechanisms to ensure civilian control of the military.
  - Assist Iraq develop a constructive security relationship with its friends in the region and with the Coalition.
  - Transforming the police/guards as accountable to the community.
  - Reform of the criminal justice system, penal code, prisons.
  - Reform of the intelligence service and oversight mechanisms.
  - Anti-corruption measures in all security organizations.
  - Elimination of the threat of violence as a means to secure political goals.

- *Essential Services and Civil Society ... restore essential services to acceptable standards, reconstruct infrastructure necessary to return to normal, and begin to create a vigorous and responsible civil society which participates in improving social and physical infrastructure for the benefit of the population.*
  - Restore physical and social infrastructure and public utilities including:
    - Water, power and health infrastructure.
    - Management of continued outbreaks of water-borne and other diseases.
    - Health education.
    - Vaccination of children.
    - Local resources to support the communities.
    - Reform and restore education, including school infrastructure repairs, curriculum reform, and training of teachers.
  - Provide knowledgeable contribution to public expenditure management and civil service reform.
  - Encourage participation of responsible NGOs.
  - Develop effective women's organizations.
  - Develop and implement trade unions.
  - Develop an independent judiciary.
  - Develop and regulate a free and professional print and broadcast media.

- Develop professional associations.
- Help create law enforcement and corrections system respectful of human rights.
- Encourage impartial, open and accountable governmental institutions.
- Contribute as requested by the Iraqis to a fair constitution and body of law.
- Help establish mechanisms for monitoring human rights.

• *Economy ... initiate processes leading to robust economic policy reform and effective free market economy management, including a focus on regulatory change, training and routing out corruption.*
  - Generate the growth of small and medium-sized private enterprises.
  - Effectively manage the transition, as quickly as possible, from value-destroying public enterprises to value-creating private ones.
  - Encourage foreign and domestic investment as essential to fundamental economic transformation.
  - Reform the management of agriculture and other resources for the benefit of the Iraqi people.
  - Insure that the legal system facilitates property ownership by domestic and foreign investors, privatization, contract management, taxation, trade, and other measures essential to the creation of a free market.
  - Restructure the banking system and find ways to introduce competition, technology, service and quality that will move towards the international standard.
  - Strengthen the Central Bank; make it independent, and assure that Iraq has sound and stable currency to sustain growth.
  - Put in place a national budget system to allow Iraq to muster its resources effectively for economic growth.
  - Encourage initiatives to diversify the economy.
  - Develop open market trade policy priorities for level playing field with regional trade partners.
  - Encourage the private sector to lead in reconstruction.
  - Develop accelerated training programs for business managers, management best practices, and business ethics.

• *The Path to Transformation … the empowerment of the Iraqi people to learn and manage a free market democracy requires an intensive, cross-sectoral, multidisciplinary approach.*
  - Design and conduct innovative and accelerated training and education programs in the complexities of democratic government and a free market economy.
  - Engage the Iraqi managers selected to be leaders as early, as often and as substantively as possible in educational programs on the workings of democratic institutions, organizing political parties and the fundamental principles of democratic society.
  - Engage the Iraqi managers selected to be leaders as early, as often and as substantively as possible in working with CPA advisers and experts to address and resolve reconstruction problems and restoring the Iraqi economy.
  - Identify specific policy reform requirements, project implementation problems, assessment needs, and management issues which can serve as experience-based, on-the-job training vehicles to facilitate learning new behaviors and techniques in functioning effectively in a democratic society and in managing a free market economy.

  - Introduce and provide training in the use of information systems technology which facilitates the learning process and increases the efficiency of the transformation. Use simulations as appropriate.

- *Governance and Sovereignty ... transform governance to a participative democratic system which balances local and national governance, builds a new constitutional process, and transfers responsibility for governance to the population.*
  - Transfer responsibility for De-Ba'ahthification to an Iraqi De-Ba'ahthification Council.
  - Encourage the Iraqis to write as quickly as possible a modern constitution embodying democratic and individual rights and the rule of law. Seek immediate ratification of the constitution immediately thereafter. Hold election for a sovereign Iraqi government, at which point the coalition relinquishes sovereignty.
  - Immediately establish a Governing Council to give Iraqis substantial responsibility for running the government.
  - Encourage a process of reconciliation among the Iraqi people.
  - Nurture civil society actors to progressively marginalize spoilers.
  - Build effective administration and political bodies at the local, governorate and national levels.
  - Strengthen the rule of law and respect for human rights.
  - Create a government system responsive to a healthy and responsible civil society.
  - Develop transparency and accountability in all governmental institutions.
  - Set conditions for an Iraq 'deserving' of economic assistance.
  - Develop beneficial regional economic relationship.

- *Information ... provides a disciplined application of coordinated themes and messages to inform local, regional and other international audiences of CPA actions and intentions on behalf of the Iraqi people. It installs for Iraqis the mechanisms to share thoughts and ideas necessary to reach decisions based on a common understanding.*
  - Develop a coherent and coordinated Information Campaign to the principal Iraqi, regional, and international audiences, in order to:
    - Communicate the CPA's intent and program of action.
    - Explain the increasing role of the Iraqi people to be players in setting the conditions for a new Iraq.
  - Establish and maintain the support of the significant majority of the Iraqi people for a new Iraq.

Document 202

Interim Budget for the Period July to December 2003

7 July 2003

This interim budget provides authority for the commitment and expenditure of money by the Interim Government of Iraq for the period July to December 2003. It sets the groundwork for the preparation and authorization of the budget for 2004.

It was prepared using the existing systems, forms and formats that have traditionally been used in Iraqi budgets. Each Iraqi Ministry and Kurd region prepared a budget with their Coalition Senior Advisor. That budget was discussed with the Coalition Finance Advisor. The proposed Budget was then reviewed by appropriate officials from the Iraqi Finance and Planning Ministries, briefed to AID and UN representatives and approved by the CPA Program Review Board.

The Budget balance for July to December 2003 shows a deficit of around $US2.2 billion. This will be funded from committed financial assets, without the need for borrowing.

Budget Summary	**($USm)**
Expenditures	
Operating	2,002.1
Capital	352.7
Reconstruction	256.8
Other Expenditures	3,488.0
Total	**6,099.6**
Revenues	
Oil revenues	3,455.0
Fees, charges and taxes	59.1
Returns from State Owned Enterprises	373.6
Total	**3,887.7**
BUDGET BALANCE (Deficit)	**-2,211.9**

The Budget ensures fiscal discipline in the use of budgetary resources in order to rebuild the confidence necessary for the international donor and investment community to support the country's efforts.

Oil revenues totaling around $3.4 billion are fully committed to programs that benefit the Iraqi people.

Major priorities addressed include the reconstruction and restoration of essential facilities and services such as water, electricity, education and health care to meet the basic needs of the Iraqi people; restoring and revitalizing the banking system, productive enterprises, agriculture and trade to reintegrate Iraq into the world economy.

Key initiatives of this budget include (in $US millions):

• Electrical improvements	$294
• Subsidies to state owned enterprises reduced by:	$269
• Reconstruction	$257
• Security and Justice improvements	$233
• Defense funding	$225
• Public Health improvements	$211
• Communications improvements	$150
• Water and Sewerage improvement	$73

In addition, $900m/year has been redirected from army and special Baathist programs to needs of the Iraqi budget.

Table 1: Net Budget Position

	($USm)
Revenues	3,887.7
Expenditures	6,099.6
Budget Balance (Deficit)	**-2,211.9**

Table 2: Budget Financing

	($USm)
Vested Assets	1,700.0
Seized Assets	795.0
Development Fund for Iraq	1,192.0
Iraq Relief (appropriated)	2,475.0
Natural Resource Risk Remediation Fund	489.0
less spending before 1 July 2003	1,248.0
NET Position as at 1 July 2003	**5,403.0**
less:	
Budget Deficit	2,211.9
Central bank currency support	2,100.0
NET POSITION as at 31 December 2003	**1,091.1**

Table 3: Expenditures by Organization

Organization	**Operational Expenditure ($USm)**	**Capital Expenditure ($USm)**	**Total ($USm)**
Ministry of Agriculture	9.4	10.0	19.4
Baghdad Mayoralty	12.1	4.3	16.4
Board of Supreme Audit	0.4	0.0	0.4
Central Organization of Standards	0.0	0.0	0.0
Ministry of Culture	1.2	61.6	62.8
Ministry of Defense	45.0	120.0	165.0
Ministry of Education	9.7	0.0	9.7
Electricity Commission	24.0	77.6	101.6
Ministry of Foreign Affairs	23.5	0.0	23.5
Ministry of Finance	199.4	1.2	200.6
Ministry of Health	210.6	1.0	211.6
Ministry of Higher Education and Scientific Research	32.8	4.0	36.8
Ministry of Housing and Construction	6.0	32.6	38.6
Ministry of Industry & Minerals	209.1	0.3	209.4
Ministry of the Interior	2.4	20.5	22.9
Ministry of Irrigation	2.7	30.5	33.2
Ministry of Labor and Social Affairs	6.4	0.0	6.4
Ministry of Justice (excluding Prisons)	5.8	25.7	31.5
Ministry of Justice (Prisons)	6.3	21.9	28.1
Ministry of Oil*	*	*	*
Ministry of Planning	4.6	0.0	4.6
Ministry of Municipalities and Utilities/ Public Works	20.8	52	72.8
Ministry of Religious Affairs	0.7	3.2	3.9
Iraq Science and Technology Commission	11.8	1.6	13.4
Ministry of Trade	4.0	0.0	4.0
Ministry of Transport and Communication	10.8	138.7	149.6
Youth Commission	2.6	2.8	5.4

Total Organization Expenditures (excl Salaries)	**862.1**	**609.5**	**1,471.6**
Total salaries and pensions			1,140.0
Total Organization Expenditures			**2,611.6**

*Operational and capital expenditure to be funded through extra realized revenues. Over $ 1 billion of capital expenditure to be funded off-budget

Table 4: Operating Expenses by Input

	($USm)
Service Requirements	133.9
Goods Requirements	221.9
Assets Maintenance	46.5
Operating capital	48.2
Transferred Expenditures (plus SOE support)	234.5
Foreign Obligations (Kuwait war reparations)	177.0
Special Programs	0.1
Total Operating Expenses by Input	**862.1**

Table 5: Other Proposed Expenditure

	($USm)
Social Safety Net	1350.0
Electricity restructuring	192.0
Police	150.0
LPG and Gas	135.0
Currency Reprinting	100.0
Construction Fund	100.0
Military De-Mobilization	60.0
Regional Commanders	6.0
US Government Department and Agency Support	35.0
Program Review Board	35.0
Various Expenditures	925.0
USAID programs Bechtel	400.0
Total Additional Expenditures	**3488.0**
TOTAL EXPENDITURES	**6,099.6**

Table 6: Revenues

	($USm)
Oil revenues	3455.0
Transfers from State Enterprises	373.6
Taxes, Fees and Charges	59.1
TOTAL REVENUES	**3,887.7**

Document 203
Passport Update
10 July 2003

Currently, Iraq has no capacity to issue passports or other internationally recognized travel document. In order to assist Iraqi nationals to travel, the Coalition Provisional Authority (CPA) has taken several actions.

On 27 June 2003 CPA Order 16[88] was signed by Amb. Bremer which, in part, cancelled the edit of former President Saddam Hussein that limited the period of validity of the 'N' series passports. This action restored the statutory limitation of each passport, making them valid until the expiration date originally printed on the document. Also, under Order 16 any Iraqi passport that has expired within the last four years is deemed valid for the exclusive purpose of a one-time return trip to Iraq if travel is completed before 31 December 2003.

Additionally, a CPA issued Interim Travel Document that can be used in lieu of a passport is under review, and procedures for issuing such a document are being developed. It is anticipated that an Interim Travel Document will be available by late July or early August, and further information concerning how a person may obtain one will be released as soon as it is available.

Until then, Iraqi nationals are free to travel, and international travel is possible without a passport. To accomplish this, persons wishing to travel to another country should contact the nearest consular representative of the country they wish to visit to determine what requirements they must meet in order to enter that country. This applies to all persons whether they have a passport or not.

Document 204

Statement Agreed between the Coalition Provisional Authority and the Iraqi Governing Council Establishing the Authorities of the Governing Council

13 July 2003

The Governing Council is the principal body of the interim administration of Iraq called for in Security Council Resolution 1483. The Governing Council will exercise specific powers immediately, in addition to representing the interests of the Iraqi people to the Coalition Provisional Authority (CPA) and the international community during Iraq's transition to a sovereign, democratic, and representative government. This paper is an agreed document of initial Governing Council authorities, which are expected to evolve over time.

Ministerial Authorities

The Governing Council shall name an Interim Minister for each ministry. Ministers shall be selected on the basis of their skills, experience, and vision for each ministry.

The Interim Ministers shall be responsible to the Governing Council, reporting back to it regularly. The Governing Council shall oversee the Interim Ministers, and may require that they testify before the Council. The Governing Council shall have the authority to dismiss ministers should they lose the Council's confidence.

Policy Authorities

The CPA will be required to consult the Governing Council on all major decisions and questions of policy.

The Governing Council shall have the right to set policies and take policy decisions in cooperation with the CPA. Such initiatives may be in any area of national policy, including

[88] See *Doc 34*.

financial and economic reform, the education curriculum, electoral law, health care, de-Baathification, and so on.

The Governing Council shall decide how it wishes to organize itself for the purpose of preparing new policies. It may choose to form specialist commissions to generate detailed proposals for submission to the Governing Council. The Governing Council could also include on such commissions international experts from the United Nations, the Coalition Provisional Authority or other bodies.

Foreign Affairs

In addition to naming Iraq's Interim Minister of Foreign Affairs and overseeing his or her work, the Governing Council will arrange for international representation during the interim period. Together with the Coalition, the Council shall name Iraqi nationals to serve as representatives to international organisations and conferences. The Council will also have the authority to appoint heads of Iraq's bilateral missions abroad and to receive representatives from other countries. The Governing Council may choose to appoint a Foreign Affairs Commission to advise on matters of foreign policy.

Finance

The Governing Council will name an Interim Finance Minister and oversee his or her activities. Additionally, the Council, with the CPA, and with the involvement of representatives of the IMF, World Bank and UNDP, will play a full part in drawing up the 2004 National Budget. The 2004 Budget will be subject to the approval of the Council. The Council will additionally have the right to consider substantial amendments to the 2003 Emergency Budget. The Governing Council shall have the right to develop policies regarding monetary and fiscal matters.

Security

In addition to naming Interim Ministers of the relevant ministries and overseeing their work, the Governing Council shall have the right to prepare policies on matters concerning Iraq's national security, including the rebuilding and/or reform of Iraq's armed forces, police, and justice sector. The Governing Council will be responsible for ensuring that Iraq's police and military are depoliticized, and that the principle of civilian oversight and supervision of the military is established. Operational security matters will remain the responsibility of the Coalition during the period of the transition.

Constitutional Process

The Governing Council shall consider appointing a Preparatory Constitutional Commission to recommend a process by which a new constitution for Iraq will be prepared and approved. The Preparatory Constitutional Commission would report to the Governing Council. The recommended procedure would need to be legitimate in the eyes of the Iraqi people. It should lead to a new constitution, based on the principles adopted at the Salahuddin[89] and Nasariya[90] conferences. Once adopted, the constitution would pave the way for national elections leading to a new, fully sovereign Iraqi government which will immediately take over the powers and responsibilities of the Coalition.

[89] For the Final Statement of the Salah-al-Din conference, see *Doc 578*.
[90] For the results of the Nasiriyah conference, see *Doc 580*.

Document 205
Reorganization of CPA
16 July 2003[91]

TO: ALL HANDS
FROM: THE CHIEF OF STAFF
SUBJECT: REORGANIZATION OF CPA

Ambassador Bremer has decided that we need to reorganize the CPA. The reorganization set forth here builds on lessons learned since the first, preliminary organization was established. Clearly, we will continue to learn in the future, but this reorganization is needed now.

The changes in organization affect for the most part the Directorates of Economic Affairs, Civil Affairs, Operations and Governance. Other changes to the organization chart announce decisions made earlier but not yet reflected in the organization chart. These decisions named former NYC Police Commissioner Bernie Kerik as Director of Interior Affairs, and established the Office of Strategic Communications and the Office of Policy Planning.

David Oliver will head up a new Office of Management and Budget. This will place budgeting and resource allocation under one manager. A Directorate for Private Sector Development will provide a focus on this important sector that it does not have. Reuben Jeffery will be its Director. All State Owned Enterprises (SOEs) will be grouped within the Directorate for Private Sector Development regardless of which Iraqi Ministry they belong to.

It is apparent that critical infrastructure sectors need special management attention. The Electricity Commission, Public Works and Transport and Communications will be moved to a renamed Directorate of Operations and Infrastructure under Andy Bearpark.

Oil will continue to stand alone. Its importance and breadth of activities, from exploration to production and distribution to marketing and sales continue to justify a separate Directorate. Phil Carroll will remain Director.

The Economic Affairs Directorate will be renamed Economic Development. Agriculture and Irrigation will be moved there. Finance, the Central Bank, debt restructuring, economic policy and financial institutions will remain under Peter McPherson as Director of Economic Development.

The Governance Team will stand alone from the Directorate for Civil Affairs and will report directly to the Administrator. It will be headed by Ryan Crocker. This will better position the Governance Team for the work that will follow the standing up of the Governing Council. This will also provide the opportunity for more attention to the Ministries now in Civil Affairs, where Judge Campbell will be in charge.

[91] The reorganization of the CPA was prepared by a Memorandum for Ambassador Bremer, dated 11 July 2003 and entitled 'The Need to Reorganize', which reads in part: 'We believe that we need to reorganize the CPA. We need to do this for internal management reasons. We also believe that with the changes we propose we will be better positioned to handle real world developments that are corning. These developments include the standing up of the Governance [sic] Council, the prospect of joint planning with CJTF, the issuance of the CPA vision paper and the beginning of strategic planning, the creation of a new management structure designed to coordinate more closely CPA operations as well as planning with those of CJTF (the new Steering Group), the arrival soon of a number of World Bank/IMF teams, the prospect of the World Bank assessment and the need to respond to it, the need to support a supplemental request of the US Congress, the UN phase out, and the UN sponsored donor conference. Although we recommend other adjustments the greatest need for change is with the Directorates of Economic Affairs and Civil Affairs, and the latter's relationship to the work of the Governance Team. [...].'

One important policy consideration regarding the responsibilities of the Governance Team and the Director of Operations and Infrastructure at headquarters and the Regional Coordinators and the Senior Advisor at the Governorate level bears elaboration. The Governance Team is responsible to the Administrator for policy and political guidance to the Regional Coordinators and the Senior Advisors. The Director of Operations and Infrastructure is responsible to the Administrator for guiding and assisting the Coordinators and Senior Advisors with local development activities, and for operations and civil/military coordination. The Director of the Governance Team will keep the Office of the Director of Operations and Infrastructure closely informed of instructions and guidance sent by his Office to the Regional and Governorate level.

Ambassador Bremer considers the Regional Coordinators and the Senior Advisors an extension of his office and the official representatives of the CPA at their levels. They report to him through the Governance Team on political and policy matters and through the Director of Operations and Infrastructure for all other matters.

The new 'Steering Group,' is a management tool set up to improve coordination and to provide direction to the organization based on our overall strategy. The membership of this group is: Major General Viggers, Ambassador Kennedy, Brigadier General Hahn, and Ambassador McManaway. The Chairman is Andy Bearpark.

With regard to the Ministries in general, one important activity is the daily coordination meeting that Ambassador Raphel has continued to oversee. Upon her departure, the Chief of Staff will chair these meetings twice weekly.

This is a hefty reorganization. The cooperation of everyone affected will be important and appreciated. [...][92] will manage the reorganization to completion. Once completed, she will assume the responsibilities of Executive Assistant to the Administrator and Executive Secretary of CPA.

These changes are reflected in the attached organization charts.[93]

[92] The document was released in part only.

[93] Not all organization charts have been released. For one of the charts, see *Doc 206*.

Document 206
Organization Chart
16 July 2003

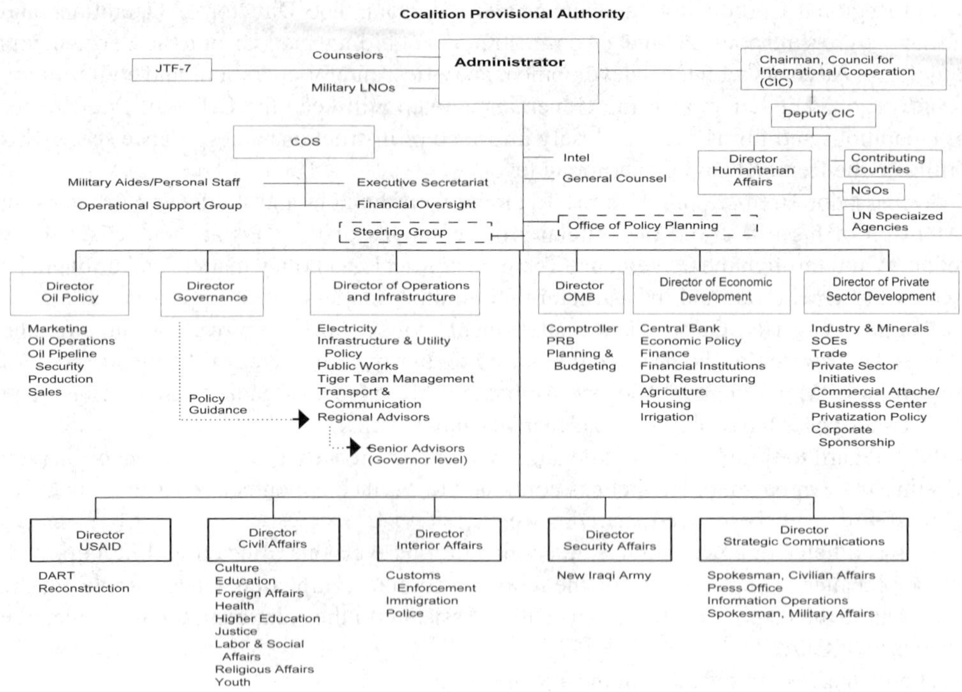

Document 207
Declaration to the United States District Court for the District of Columbia
23 July 2003

I, L. Paul Bremer, III, Administrator of the Coalition Provisional Authority ('CPA') in Iraq, hereby declare pursuant to 28 U.S.C. § 1746 that to the best of my knowledge, information, and belief, and under penalty of perjury, the following is true and correct.

Summary

1. I submit this Declaration for the Court's consideration in the matter of *Acree v. Federal Reserve Bank of New York, et al.,* Civil Action No. 03-1549, pending in the United States District Court for the District of Columbia. This Declaration addresses the following topics:

- My qualifications as Administrator of the CPA;
- The role and mission of the CPA;
- The funding used by the CPA;

- The harm that will result if the entire $721.7 million in vested Iraqi assets held in the U.S. Treasury Special Purpose Account is not made available for use by the CPA as soon as possible.

2. Based upon information provided to me in the course of my official duties, I am familiar with each of the topics addressed in this Declaration.

3. The CPA requires large amounts of resources to continue the efforts to restore conditions of security and stability, to meet the humanitarian needs of the Iraqi people, to create conditions in which the Iraqi people can freely determine their own political future, and to assist in the rebuilding of the Iraqi economic infrastructure. My assessment is that the asset availability that is hindered by the relief requested in this lawsuit will materially degrade these vitally important efforts.

Qualifications as Administrator of the CPA

4. On May 9, 2003, President Bush, exercising his constitutional authority as Commander in Chief and consistent with pertinent statutes, appointed me as Presidential Envoy to Iraq. Subject to the authority, direction, and control of the Secretary of Defense, I have been authorized by the President to 'oversee the use of [United States Government] appropriations in Iraq, as well as Iraqi state- or regime-owned property that is properly under U.S. possession and made available for use in Iraq to assist the Iraqi people and support the recovery of Iraq.' *See* Presidential Memorandum dated May 9, 2003 (attached as Exhibit A).[94]

5. On May 13, 2003, the Secretary of Defense designated me as Administrator of the CPA. In this role I am responsible for temporary governance of Iraq. This includes overseeing, directing, and coordinating all executive, legislative, and judicial functions necessary to carry out this responsibility, including the provision of humanitarian relief and reconstruction assistance in the formation of an Iraqi interim authority. *See* Memorandum from the Secretary of Defense dated May 13, 2003 (attached as Exhibit B).[95]

Role and Mission of the CPA

6. The United States is committed to creating conditions that support a secure state in which the Iraqi people can live in freedom, peace, and prosperity. One of the United States' primary goals in assisting the Iraqi people is to ensure that sufficient resources are devoted to economic reconstruction and repairs of Iraq's infrastructure. Only through supporting efforts of the Iraqi people to rebuild their country and live in safety, with liberty and with economic prosperity, can the United States Government help create the conditions in Iraq in which the Iraqi people can finally determine their own political future, which is in the security interests of the United States.

7. The President is relying upon the CPA to ensure that U.S. goals in Iraq are achieved. The CPA is responsible for exercising powers of government temporarily to provide for the effective administration of Iraq during the period of transitional administration, to restore conditions of security and stability, to create conditions in which the Iraqi people can freely determine their own political future, and to facilitate economic recovery.

8. Furthermore, as stated in U.N. Security Council Resolution 1483, adopted May 22, 2003, the CPA has been called upon to promote the welfare of the Iraqi people through the

[94] See *Doc 179*.
[95] See *Doc 180*.

effective administration of Iraq, including in particular working towards the restoration of conditions of security and stability and the creation of conditions in which the Iraqi people can freely determine their own political future.

Funding of the CPA

9. The requirements of the CPA already vastly exceed the available funds. As just one example of this, the budget balance for the Interim Government of Iraq for July to December 2003 shows a deficit of approximately $2.2 billion.

10. Although certain funds appropriated by Congress have been authorized for use for humanitarian and reconstruction efforts in Iraq, most of these funds have been committed or obligated. For example, $1,236 billion of the $2.475 billion appropriated by Congress in the Iraq Relief and Reconstruction Fund, which is used for humanitarian assistance in and around Iraq and for rehabilitation and reconstruction in Iraq, has been committed, and the remainder will be committed against further stability and reconstruction requirements such as law enforcement, telecommunications, and transportation. Likewise, the Natural Resources Risk Remediation Fund (NRRRF) ($489.3 million), to be used for fire fighting, repair of oil facilities, and preservation of an oil distribution capability, is entirely committed or programmed.

11. The Development Fund for Iraq (DFI) account presently contains only approximately $1,314 billion. U.N. Security Council Resolution 1483 calls for the transfer of assets of the former Iraqi regime that have been removed from Iraq, and for their deposit into the DFI. Although foreign governments have frozen certain assets, none of these funds has been transferred to the CPA for deposit into the DFI, and it is uncertain whether any such funds will be transferred in the near term. Approximately $415 million is committed against identified relief and reconstruction requirements, and the balance of current funds and projected revenues from oil sales is committed against the Iraqi ministries' operating and capital budget requirements over the next six months.

12. The CPA also has the authority to use state- or regime-owned cash, funds, or realizable securities found in Iraq to assist the Iraqi people and support the reconstruction of Iraq, but the assets seized to date have been completely obligated or expended.

13. Iraqi assets that have been vested pursuant to the International Emergency Economic Powers Act are a source of funding that has been invaluable in providing a flexible mechanism for assisting the Iraqi people generally, and particularly for assisting in the reconstruction of Iraq. To date, approximately $1 billion in vested funds has been used or will be used to make a number of essential payments that have been instrumental in improving security and stability in Iraq. Although some of the funds have been used to finance such items as emergency repairs to critical infrastructure, severance payments to Iraqi civil servants, payments for security forces, and payments to pensioners, the majority of the funding, approximately $954 million, has been allocated to pay government workers' salaries.

Potential Harm of Failing to Make the Remaining Vested Iraqi Funds Immediately Available for Use in Iraq

14. In Executive Order 13290, dated March 20, 2003, the President ordered that approximately $1.7 billion in certain Iraqi public property be vested in the Department of the Treasury and that such property be used to assist the Iraqi people and assist in the reconstruction of Iraq. These funds are critical to maintaining peace and stability in Iraq, thereby directly supporting the U.S. mission in Iraq, including contributing to the safety and protection of U.S. forces and furthering the national security interests of the United States.

15. The Department of Defense relies on these funds to pay certain humanitarian assistance and reconstruction costs. If we are unable to expend the remaining vested assets, we must rely on other rapidly dwindling sources of funding that are already overextended. This would render the CPA unable to carry out the tasks to which other funds are committed. At this stage of our economic reconstruction and humanitarian assistance initiatives, virtually all of our activities in these areas are critical to creating conditions of security and stability in which the broader objectives to benefit the Iraqi people can be realized. If we are forced to refrain from expending funds for any such activities, or if funding for such activities is unduly delayed, our ability to achieve these important goals in Iraq will be seriously undermined.

16. Current media reports do not fully and accurately convey the extent to which the CPA's expenditures of vested funds continue to ameliorate security threats to Coalition Forces and Iraqi citizens. During major combat operations, salaries were not paid to over 70 percent of Iraq's civil servants. When President Bush declared that major combat activities in Iraq were concluded, these civil servants had gone without pay for almost two months. Continuing salary payments with vested funds ensures that this sizeable portion of the Iraqi population can purchase food, medicine, and other supplies necessary to sustain daily living. The payments also enable the CPA to return civil servants to their jobs and to restore essential government services to the Iraqi population.

17. Coalition Forces could very well be subject to increased hostilities if vested funds are not available to be expended for these purposes, as evidenced by violent demonstrations by former Iraqi military members protesting the fact that they were excluded from the initial stage of the payment program. Additionally, such hostilities could significantly undermine the Coalition's ability to engage in reconstruction activities in Iraq. The resulting delays in restoring basic services unquestionably could undermine civil order and security throughout Iraq.

18. In summary, the United States has an urgent and critical national security need to make use of vested Iraqi funds as soon as possible for humanitarian assistance and reconstruction efforts in Iraq. Restricting these funds as a result of this litigation would affect adversely the ability of the United States to achieve security and stability in the region, would compromise the safety of U.S. forces and Iraqi civilians, and would be harmful to U.S. national security interests.

[Signed] *L. Paul Bremer, III*
Administrator, Coalition Provisional Authority
Executed on 23 July 2003

Document 208

Summary of Changes to Ministry Budgets Arising from 30 Day Review

26 July 2003

Overview

CPA Ministry of Finance and Iraqi Ministry of Finance undertook a 30-day review of the 2003 Budget, to identify expenditures that had not been budgeted for, and correct errors or omissions.

Following Finance Ministry review, the CPA Budget Office met with Finance on 26 July to discuss proposed Finance Ministry changes to Budget allocations for the remainder of 2003. This followed discussions between the Finance Ministry and their Iraqi counterparts in each Ministry.

Significant Changes affecting Ministry Budget allocations are outlined below:

Increases:
- **Oil** – significant additional spending ($300m) granted to accelerate Oil reconstruction process.
- **Interior** – additional $120m allocated for Iraqi police force.
- **Electricity** – additional $20.2m capital allocated to improve electricity supply.
- **Agriculture** – reduction in returns expected from largest State Company, offset by reduction in operating expenditures.
- **Baghdad Mayorality** – additional spending approved for water and sewerage improvements.

Decreases:
- **Culture** – capital allocation reduced to address likely under-spend in 2003.
- **Justice (including Prisons)** – capital allocation reduced to match identified requirements.
- **Trade** – revenues expected from State Companies increased.

[Table Revisions to Ministry Budgets omitted]

MAJOR CHANGES TO MINISTRY BUDGETS FOR 2003

Agriculture
- Dividends from State Owned Enterprises (SOEs) estimate reduced to $100m (150b ID) to reflect pessimism in likely amount to be collected.
- Operating expenditures reduced by $5.9m (8.9b ID) following negotiations between Finance and Agriculture Ministries.

Baghdad Mayorality
- An additional $12m (18b ID) capital expenses added for sewerage and water programs.
- Additional funding of $5.3m (8b ID).
- Revenues reduced by $1m (1.5b ID) reflecting pessimism on amount likely to be collected.

Board of Supreme Audit
- $0.2m (300m ID) reallocated from operating expenditures to capital.

Central Organization of Standards
- Allocated modest budget of $0.2m (225m ID) to allow Organization to perform limited operations.

Culture
- Capital expenditures reduced by $37.2m (55.8b ID), reflecting risk of underspend in 2003.
- $4m (6b ID) new revenue identified from hotels (eg Al Rashid) that will be paid to the Ministry of Finance.

Security Affairs
- To remain as per 7 July.

Education
- $0.33m (500m ID) transferred within operating, from goods to services. Reduced funding for lecturers is offset by the amounts paid to exam proctors.

Electricity

- Additional $20.2m allocated to capital expenditures.

Foreign Affairs

- Operating expenditures reduced by $6m (9.1b ID) due to closed embassies – will refer allowances for foreign staff issue to Governing Council.

Finance

- $3.8m of ILO fees transferred from Labor and Social Affairs (5.7b ID), and will be paid by Finance.
- $1.56m (1.9bn ID) increase for Governorate Treasury offices.
- $2.6m (3.9b ID) increase for capital expenditures.

Health

- To remain as per 7 July.

Higher Education

- To remain as per 7 July, but conditional on H.Ed collecting the course fees provisioned for in the published Budget.

Housing and Construction

- Capital expenditures reduced by $15m (22.5 ID) ('long lead items' reduced to zero) to reflect expenditure that would occur through SOEs. $15m (22.5b) ID reallocated to 'support to SOEs'.
- Finance and the CPA OMB noted that projects funded in 2003 should generate revenues in 2004.

Industry and Minerals

- To remain as per 7 July, but $150m (225b ID) of revenue now netted off support to SOEs.

Interior

- Capital expenditures ('Headquarters reconstruction') reduced by $4m (6b ID) to reflect revised estimates of the amount required for reconstruction.
- An additional 120m (180b ID) allocated to establish Iraqi police force.

Irrigation

- Operating expenditures increased by $1.2m (1.8b ID) to reflect increased costs.

Labor and Social Affairs

- Operating expenditures reduced by 3.8m (5.7b ID) reflecting ILO fees to be paid by Finance.

Justice

- Operating expenditures reduced by $2.1m (3.1b ID). Reconstruction amounts (capital expenditure) reduced by $12.5m (23.6b ID) reflecting likely underspend in 2003.

Justice – Prisons

- Capital reduced by $11.9m (17.8b ID) to reflect likely underspend.

Oil

- Grossed up $1.27m (1.9b ID) in revenues, with this amount also added to operating expenditures to ensure Ministry able to spend according to Iraqi budget processes.
- An additional $300m (450b ID) added to accelerate oil infrastructure restoration-$256m (384b ID) added to capital spending, and $44m (66b ID) added to operating expenditures for electricity generators for oil fields.

Planning

- 1.6m (2.4b ID) of additional spending afforded for Ministry to conduct labor force survey.

Public Works/Municipalities and Local Authorities
- Ministry to retain $6.6m (9.9b ID) revenues, which Finance will net off its outlays.

Endowments and Religious Affairs
- To remain as per 7 July, noting name correction.

Science and Technology Commission
- Operating expenses decreased by $1.47m (2.2b ID) to reflect revision to pollution clean up estimates.

Trade
- Expected revenues increased by $16.6m (24.9b ID).

Transport and Comm
- To remain as per 7 July.

Youth
- To remain as per 7 July.

Document 209
Statement of Objectives for Iraq Mobile License Offer
27 July 2003

INTRODUCTION

1. This document states the objectives for the Iraq mobile license offer. Bidders are required as a minimum to meet the general requirements listed herein and this document shall form the basis of the license agreement. [...]

LEGAL AUTHORITY

48. The Coalition Provisional Authority is exercising governmental authority in Iraq temporarily until such time as the Iraqi people can establish a permanent government. The Coalition Provisional Authority (CPA), has been recognized by the United Nations as the temporary government in Iraq pursuant to United Nations Security Council Resolution (UNSCR) 1483 (2003).[96] CPA Regulation 1[97] states that Iraqi law that was in effect as of 16 April 2003 remains in effect unless suspended. CPA Order 11[98] authorises the Ministry of Transportation and Communications to license and regulate all commercial telecommunications services within Iraq.

49. CPA has not been enforcing former Iraqi law concerning the foreign ownership registration provisions and the provisions of Iraqi law concerning restrictions on foreign ownership. The CPA is at this time conducting a review to determine what Iraqi laws, if any, should be suspended during the transition time in order to assist the economic recovery of Iraq. It is anticipated that the Administrator of the CPA will, in fact, suspend the operation of certain Iraqi commercial laws pending a more thorough review. However, the exact laws involved have not been determined at this time.

50. With this background information, firms wishing to submit offers in response to this solicitation should be aware of the following:

[96] See *Doc 523*.
[97] See *Doc 1*.
[98] See *Doc 26*.

51. The licenses to be awarded under the terms of this solicitation will be issued for a period not to exceed 24 months. This is to facilitate the transfer of authority to a permanent Iraqi government when such government is established.

52. At the present time, the restrictions of Iraqi commercial law concerning business activities by non-Iraqi firms, although not formally suspended, are not being enforced. As stated above, it is expected that the CPA will formally suspend certain laws in the near future to aid Iraq's economic recovery. When that occurs, to the extent practicable, prospective offerors will be notified.

53. Firms wishing to submit offers in response to this solicitation, and firms, who ultimately receive licenses from the Ministry as a result of this solicitation, are strongly encouraged to keep abreast of the current state of Iraqi commercial law to ensure compliance with local laws, which will be a condition of the licenses to be awarded under this solicitation.

54. Firms who ultimately receive licenses from the Ministry as a result of the solicitation are reminded that the governmental authority of the CPA and the Ministry expires upon the establishment of a permanent government in Iraq. Although it is likely that the licenses awarded under this solicitation will be continued by the new permanent Iraqi government, neither the CPA nor the Ministry makes any representation that the permanent government will continue the current licenses on the same terms and conditions as the Ministry.

55. Bid submissions made to this request, once accepted become part of the license and compliance to the submitted bid is contractually one with the license award. If the license holder does not comply with their submissions, the license may be revoked or transferred to a CPA designated holder.[99]

Document 210
Letter from Ambassador Bremer to the President of the Security Council

30 July 2003

The Coalition Provisional Authority hereby requests your assistance in transmitting the attached letter from the Acting Governor of the Central Bank of Iraq, Mr. Faleh Salman, to the United Nations Security Council and United Nations Member States. The identification of foreign Iraqi assets, and the transfer of these assets to the Development Fund for Iraq in accordance with resolution 1483 (2003), is a critical part of Iraq's economic reconstruction and the Coalition Provisional Authority's efforts to assist the Iraqi people at this time. On behalf of the Coalition Provisional Authority, I would greatly appreciate your cooperation.

[*Signed*] L Paul Bremer III
Administrator

[99] On 3 August 2003, Issue 2.0 of the Statement of Objectives for Iraq Mobile License Offer was published. The text of Issue 2.0, in the relevant parts, is identical with Issue 1.0 of 27 July 2003 with the exception of para. 55 where the second sentence was deleted. The Statement of Objectives was further amended on 8 August 2003 but none of the amendments is of relevance here.

Attachment

On behalf of the Central Bank of Iraq, I have the honour to refer to Security Council resolution 1483 (2003) and to express appreciation for actions taken by the United Nations in adopting this resolution and seeking to enforce it. As you are aware, resolution 1483 (2003) creates an obligation for all Member States to identify, freeze, and immediately transfer to the Development Fund for Iraq, all funds, financial assets, or economic resources in their jurisdictions that were established or held by the previous Government of Iraq. These funds, assets, and resources include not only those of the previous Government of Iraq but also its state bodies, corporations, agencies, such entities that have been removed from Iraq, or acquired by Saddam Hussein or other senior officials of the former Iraqi regime and their immediate family members. It also includes entities owned or controlled by them, directly or indirectly, and persons acting on their behalf or at their direction.

I am sure you understand the vital importance of ensuring the prompt transfer of these funds to the Development Fund for Iraq. These funds are urgently needed for humanitarian, reconstruction, civilian administration, and other purposes benefiting the people of Iraq.

As you know, an account for the Development Fund for Iraq, named 'Central Bank of Iraq/Development Fund for Iraq', has been established at the United States Federal Reserve Bank of New York to allow Member States to fulfil their obligations under resolution 1483 (2003). I respectfully ask that you urge all Member States to transfer Iraqi assets in their jurisdictions to this account without delay. I further ask that you encourage all Member States to do everything possible to identify, freeze, and transfer Iraqi assets that may be in their respective jurisdictions, but that have not yet been identified, even if the account holders have not been specifically listed under resolution 1483 (2003).

Thank you for your assistance in helping to locate and recover Iraqi assets, so that they can be used for the benefit of the Iraqi people.

[*Signed*] Faleh Dawod Salman
Acting Governor
Central Bank of Iraq[100]

Document 211

Procedures Applicable to Vested and Seized Iraqi Property

31 July 2003

MEMORANDUM FOR UNDER SECRETARY OF DEFENSE (POLICY)
DIRECTORS OF THE DEFENSE AGENCIES
ADMINISTRATOR, COALITION PROVISIONAL AUTHORITY
DIRECTOR, JOINT STAFF
ASSISTANT SECRETARY OF THE ARMY (FINANCIAL MANAGEMENT & COMPTROLLER)

[100] UN Doc. S/2003/782, 31 July 2003, Annex. Ambassador Bremer's letter was transmitted in a letter by the US Permanent Representative to the United Nations to the President of the Security Council requesting that the letter and its attachment be circulated as a document of the Security Council to both Council members and States Members of the United Nations.

ASSISTANT SECRETARY OF THE NAVY (FINANCIAL MANAGEMENT & COMPTROLLER)
ASSISTANT SECRETARY OF THE AIR FORCE (FINANCIAL MANAGEMENT & COMPTROLLER)

SUBJECT: Appendices for Procedures Applicable to Vested and Seized Iraqi Property

I have approved the attached appendices , as required by the 'Procedures for Administering, Using and Accounting for Vested and Seized Iraqi Property' that the Secretary approved. You are directed to use these appendices in your management and accounting of vested and seized Iraqi property.

[Signed] *Dov S. Zakheim*

Attachments:
As stated
cc: Under Secretary of Defense (AT & L)
General Counsel of the Department of Defense

APPENDIX D[101]
DEVELOPMENT OF FUNDING REQUIREMENTS FOR VESTED AND SEIZED IRAQI PROPERTY

A. Applicability. This appendix addresses the duties, responsibilities, and procedures to be followed by the Coalition Provisional Authority (CPA) when working with the Iraqi Ministries to identify and develop requirements for spending plans in restoring and rebuilding the country of Iraq for its people. There are multiple funding sources available for the purpose of stabilization, reconstruction and humanitarian assistance for the benefit of the Iraqi people.

B. Responsibilities. It is the responsibility of the ministry officials and coalition commanders to explain the requirements for obtaining Vested and Seized Iraqi property for projects that achieve the mission of the CPA.

1. Ministry officials and coalition commanders are responsible for requesting funding from Vested and Seized Assets to accomplish CPA projects and ministry requirements by submitting the PRB 01 Funding Request Form to the Program Review Board (PRB). The electronic version of the PRB 01 Funding Request Form, along with instructions, is available on the CPA intranet website and upon request to the Program Review Board staff (krahams@orha.centcom.mil).
2. The majority of funding requirements for ministries are expected to be included in ministry budgets. However, unanticipated and emergency requests by ministries will be accepted by the PRB for consideration. CPA ministries and offices shall prepare complete PRB 01 forms to request funding for requirements not addressed in budget submissions, according to the attached instructions.

[101] Appendix A: Shipment and Distribution of Vested Funds for Humanitarian Assistance and Reconstruction Efforts in Iraq; Appendix B: Duties on Assuming Possession of Seized Property; Appendix E: Allocation and Disbursement of Vested and Seized Iraqi Property; Appendix F: Monthly Inventory Report of Vested and Seized Property; Appendix G: Monthly Disbursement Report; and Appendix H: Reporting on Vested and Seized Assets on DoD Financial Statements are not reproduced. Appendix C was reserved for future use. The text of all appendices can be found at http://comptroller.defense.gov/.

C. Procedures.

1. The PRB 01 will be reviewed in accordance with the CPA Process for the Allocation of Funds. The Program Review Committee (PRC) will conduct the initial review of all program funding requests and project submissions, categorize them, and make recommendations to the PRB for the allocation of vested and seized funds. The PRB is responsible for preparing and submitting allocation requests to the Administrator for approval. The requests will identify, integrate and prioritize requirements for the relief and recovery activities in Iraq. The PRB allocation requests will include proposed allocations of available resources. The specific roles, responsibilities, and membership of the CPA Program Review Board are set forth in CPA Regulation No. 3.[102] For approved projects using Seized and Vested Assets , CPA is the final authority. After CPA approval, the CPA Comptroller will provide the PRB 01 and related decision documents to OUSD (Comptroller) and Army Headquarters Budget Office.
2. Once Funding Requests are approved by the Administrator, the requestor must submit a completed Form 5000, Iraqi Asset Disbursement Record, along with a Spending Plan to the CPA Comptroller for the disbursement of funds.

Document 212

Relationship between the GC, CPA, and the Ministries

2 August 2003

FOR: THE GOVERNING COUNCIL
FROM: THE ADMINISTRATOR, Coalition Provisional Authority
SUBJECT: Relationship between the GC, CPA, and the Ministries

This paper lays out the relationship between the Governing Council, the Coalition Provisional Authority, and the ministries. It explains how policy is initiated, how it is implemented, and who is accountable to whom during this interim period before elections are held under a new constitution. The relationship between the GC, CPA, and ministries has two distinct phases: that before interim ministers are appointed and that after interim ministers are appointed.

Before the GC Names Ministers

In the period before interim ministers are appointed, the senior-most individual in each ministry is the coalition advisor. Ministry staffs are directly accountable to this person, who in turn is accountable to the Administrator of the CPA.

During this time, policy can be initiated in a number of ways:

1) *By the CPA*. The coalition has committed not to make any major policy initiatives without consulting the GC. It therefore will present the GC with briefings and policy papers and either request GC endorsement of the proposal or identify key areas for decision by the GC. Where appropriate, the CPA and GC will discuss – through subcommittees or designated individuals – the joint announcement of policy initiatives.

[102] See *Doc 3*.

2) *By the GC*. The GC may also initiate policy during this time. It can:
   - Propose its own policy initiatives in papers addressed to the Administrator;
   - Request CPA to work with established GC committees to develop joint policies to meet objectives identified by the GC;
   - Ask CPA to provide it with a briefing or strategic plan for dealing with any challenge facing Iraq.
3) *From within the Ministries*. Routine ministry business will continue to be handled at the ministerial level. New policies that change the course of a ministry's work in a substantive way will be handled through one of the above channels.

All policy during this period is implemented by the ministries under the supervision of the CPA, in consultation with the GC. In addition to consulting with the GC on major policy issues, the CPA will be responsive to other requests from the GC. The GC has the right to initiate a review of policy or to propose alternative policies at any time.

Once GC-Identified Interim Ministers are in Place

Once interim ministers are appointed, the balance in the ministry will shift. These interim ministers will be the most senior officials in the ministries; coalition advisors will provide counsel to the interim ministers. Interim minister and coalition advisors will be required to consult closely on all major policy or budgetary initiatives.

The interim ministers will be held directly accountable to the GC, which will serve as a collective executive body for these purposes. The GC may choose to hold the interim ministers accountable in either or both of the following ways:

- Calling for periodic testimony (in writing or in person) of the interim minister to the entire GC body;
- Requiring regular interaction between ministry officials and relevant GC-appointed committees or commissions.

During this time, policies can be initiated by either the CPA or the GC. Close coordination between the GC and CPA – and between interim ministers and coalition advisors – will be required before any major initiatives can be launched.

Policy initiatives will be implemented by the ministries under the supervision of the GC, to which they are accountable. The CPA will also monitor the implementation of the policies by the ministries through its coalition advisors, who report to the CPA Administrator. The CPA will be responsive to requests from the GC or interim ministers for assistance in implementing policy.

Document 213
Establishing and Implementing Governing Policies
8 August 2003

MEMORANDUM[103]

FOR: Commander, CJTF-7
Coalition Provisional Authority (CPA) Officials
Iraqi Ministry, Governorate and Municipal Officials
FROM: Administrator, CPA
SUBJECT: Establishing and Implementing Governing Policies

The purpose of this memorandum is to ensure that governors, mayors and municipal councils who have come to power since the collapse of the previous regime clearly understand the authorities of national government offices. It outlines the national government's power, explains the significant authorities and responsibilities of local officials, and describes the role the CPA and CJTF-7 play in encouraging them to exercise those authorities.

With respect to national policy making, CPA Regulation Number 1 affirms that 'CPA is vested with all executive, legislative and judicial authority necessary to achieve its objectives, to be exercised under relevant U.N. Security Council resolutions, including Resolution 1483 (2003), and the laws and usages of war.'[104] Further, as clarified in a May 13, 2003 Memorandum from the Secretary of Defense, the Commander of Coalition Forces shall directly support the CPA by deterring hostilities, maintaining Iraq's territorial integrity and security, searching for, securing and destroying weapons of mass destruction, and assisting in carrying out Coalition policy generally.[105]

In accordance with Regulation 1, the central ministries and CPA exercise authority by working together with respect to national government policies. In particular, the following key functions are exclusive prerogatives of the central ministries and CPA, and may not be performed by governors and mayors:

a. Creating or eliminating positions, and hiring and firing of ministry officials posted in governorate branch offices or facilities such as food warehouses, silos, public utility plants;
b. Debathification policies and procedures, including the granting of any exceptions in accordance with the Debathification Order Number 1 (CPA/ORD/16 May 2003/01);[106]
c. Establishing salaries and other benefits for present or retired ministry workers;
d. Designating ministry individual(s) specifically authorized to have access to bank accounts;
e. Planning distribution of national assets such as electricity, water, or food ration items, including for example, the electrical power allocation policy;

[103] The Memorandum was prepared by the CPA Office of General Counsel. The Action Memo which recommends that the Administrator sign the Memorandum does not bear Ambassador Bremer's signature or initials. It is thus not clear whether it was ever sent to the addressees.

[104] For CPA Regulation No 1, see *Doc 1*.

[105] The Secretary of Defense's Memorandum is reproduced as *Doc 180*.

[106] See *Doc 14*.

f. Establishing tariffs or fees for nationally provided items such as electricity, water, telephone or food ration baskets;
g. Setting national government procurement policies or prices;
h. Establishing tariff structures for international border points;
i. Designating specific uses for public buildings; and
j. Controlling financial or material assets of state-owned enterprises.

Although the constitutional and legislative framework for a fully democratic electoral process is not yet in place, CPA has empowered citizen participation in the governing of their country through the establishment of sub-national advisory councils.

Governorate, regional and local authorities provide a critical link to the population, as they represent the will of the people and are best positioned to inform CPA policies. Local authorities carry out their responsibilities to address local concerns in part by engaging the CPA and central ministries on those policy issues that affect their respective constituents.

These councils have been empowered to assist the military, the CPA and the central ministries in prioritizing local infrastructure projects, and, in these efforts, they have relied almost entirely on their own abilities, with the support of regional military commanders, to get essential services up and running. Various donor activities related to health, education and other services are also assisting these efforts. To date, the central ministries have played little role in supporting these efforts.

Iraq's law of governorates, enacted in 1969, authorized sub-national governments to address citizen concerns through both the central ministries and their own independent structures. Although the former regime used this law to control rather than empower, it identifies significant responsibilities that are best performed by sub-national entities. In part, the law of governorates permitted local governing councils to exercise the following responsibilities, which continue to be properly performed at the local level:

a. Oversee central ministry operations in their administrative regions, except the army, courts and university system. This oversight includes consulting on ministerial regional appointments, evaluating ministry performance, and coordinating on major policy and program decisions;
b. Develop industry and eliminate unemployment;
c. Promote sanitation and public health;
d. Preserve historic sites;
e. Develop general public works projects including housing;
f. Estimate and collect taxes and fees;
g. Prepare budgets for their administrative region, and submitting these budgets to the next higher authority for review and incorporation into the overall national budget;
h. Oversee the Ministry of Finance operations in their region to ensure compliance with budgets and programs; and
i. Address other issues of concern.

Central ministries keep chief executives and councils informed of activities in their regions. The CPA encourages this symbiotic relationship between national and sub-national government, and will empower sub-national government units to carry out these activities in accordance with existing Iraqi law, where possible and appropriate.

Coalition Forces also play a significant role in this process, by assisting policy implementation at the local level, and by informing the development of these policies through the military chain of command. Military commanders should provide guidance and assistance to advisory councils to help the councils meet their constituents' concerns. This support is especially vital while these sub-national governing structures develop the capacity to operate independently.

Our temporary governance role requires that we make every effort to maintain and improve the level of public services for the Iraqi people. This job is too great to be handled by the central ministries alone. Harnessing the commitment and energy of the advisory councils can help us achieve our goal.

Document 214
Memorandum from US Secretary of Defense to Coalition Provisional Authority and Commander, US Central Command, Operational Relationships and Guidance

11 August 2003

This memorandum serves to clarify the intent for US Central Command's (USCENTCOM's) direct support relationship with the Coalition Provisional Authority (CPA), delineate policy development responsibilities and designate near-term priorities in assisting the CPA.

Direct Support Relationship with CPA. Commander, USCENTCOM (CDRUSCENTCOM) will support the CPA and is authorized to respond directly to CPA requests for assistance. While security in Iraq remains the key to all stability operations, assisting the CPA in the near term is just as critical. CDRUSCENTCOM should be responsive, within means, to CPA direct support requests including but not limited to communications, intelligence, logistics, transportation, engineering and civil military operations. CPA requests that exceed USCENTCOM's current means will be identified to the Chairman of the Joint Chiefs of Staff. Every effort should be made to transition non-military tasks performed by military units as rapidly as possible.

Requirements beyond current means and conflicting priorities between CPA requests for direct support and existing USCENTCOM stability operations that cannot be resolved should be referred for resolution by the Secretary of Defense, if necessary.

Policy Development Responsibilities. Because of your unique relationship, the following guidance for policy, manning and funding is provided to clarify key responsibilities and procedures.

a. Policy Development. Requests for policy guidance may come from the CPA, CDRUSCENTCOM and others, including the Joint Staff, OSD and other US Government (USG) agencies. The Under Secretary of Defense for Policy (USD(P)) will be responsible for drafting and coordinating policy in Washington and may assign a lead organization for particular policy guidance. USD(P) will coordinate this draft policy with the CPA and the Joint Staff and with Coalition allies and other USG agencies, as appropriate. Joint Staff will coordinate with USCENTCOM, other combatant commanders and Services as appropriate. Draft policy generated by the CPA will be coordinated with OSD as appropriate. The CPA Representative, with responsibility for representing the Administrator of the CPA in Washington, will play an important role in this process. Approved policy guidance applicable to CPA and CDRUSCENTCOM will be distributed via memorandum. Of course, it is important that you coordinate with each other on details of policy implementation.

b. Manning. CPA will submit requests for civilian and military manning through the CPA Representative as requirements are identified. The CPA Representative will coordinate military requests through the Joint Staff for my approval. Requests for forces will be submitted by USCENTCOM through existing channels.

c. Funding and Resource Allocation. The President has authorized CPA to oversee, direct and coordinate all USO activities in Iraq, including the use of all USO appropriations, except those under the command of the combatant commander. USD(P) and the Under Secretary of Defense (Comptroller) will continue to work with the Joint Staff and other USG agencies to make the necessary resources available.

Request CDRUSCENTCOM assess the most pressing direct assistance issues with particular emphasis on additional military support required, if any. Because success in Iraq depends upon effective and timely CPA operations, every effort must be made to make those supporting organizations as effective as possible during this critical phase.

[Signed] *Donald Rumsfeld*
cc: Chairman of the Joint Chiefs of Staff

Document 215
The Iraqi Flag
17 August 2003

FOR: THE GOVERNING COUNCIL
FROM: THE ADMINISTRATOR, Ambassador Paul Bremer III
SUBJECT: The Iraqi Flag

The design of an Iraqi flag is for the people of Iraq to decide. I understand that the adoption of a new Iraqi flag is a sensitive issue that ideally would wait until after the referendum on a new constitution. However, the Governing Council may wish either address the issue directly or search for an interim solution, as there are several pending events where it would be very beneficial for Iraq to display its new colors:

- The opening of diplomatic liaison offices in Washington and London will likely take place in late August or early September. Iraq is moving to re-establish diplomatic ties with its Arab neighbors as well;
- The next Arab League Ministerial will take place on September 9;
- The United Nations General Assembly will meet in September, providing the opportunity for a delegation to represent Iraq's interests;
- The first 850-man battalion of the New Iraqi Army will graduate in October and begin preparations to join Coalition Forces in securing Iraq.

Iraqis are likely to want to display a flag at each of these events. Your diplomatic representatives will need to distinguish themselves in international fora; your soldiers and officers will need colors to salute and display on their uniforms.

There are at least two approaches the GC could adopt to address the issue of the flag:

1) The GC could appoint a commission as soon as possible to propose a design for a new Iraqi flag. This commission would make a recommendation that the GC could adopt.

2) The GC could endorse an interim measure – such as the current flag without the Arabic writing or the current flag with the Arabic in a standard calligraphy – to serve as Iraq's flag until a new, sovereign Iraqi government can adopt a new flag.

I suggest that the GC take action to ensure that in the coming months an accepted flag is flown behind Iraqi diplomats and soldiers.

Document 216

Agreement between the Coalition Provisional Authority and the National Archives and Records Administration

19 August 2003

Whereas, in early May 2003, the Coalition Provisional Authority (CPA) discovered in the flooded basement of the Mukhabahrat headquarters in Baghdad certain historic and modern books, documents and parchment scrolls, including rare and modern printed and manuscript materials in Hebrew, Arabic, Judeo-Arabic and English most of which pertain to the Jewish community of Iraq (hereinafter, the 'Archive');

Whereas, the Archive will likely deteriorate rapidly and be destroyed unless certain conservation steps are taken immediately;

Whereas, the appropriate personnel, technical and infrastructure resources do not exist in Iraq, and an unacceptable amount of time would be needed to acquire the necessary resources;

Whereas, such a delay would likely result in the destruction of the Archive;

Whereas, the CPA, as the custodian of the Archive, intends to take the most necessary measures of preservation with respect to the Archive;[107]

Whereas, the National Archives and Records Administration (NARA) is well-positioned to oversee and supervise the steps needed to preserve, conserve and restore the Archive, provided that NARA receives complete funding in accordance with section V herein;

Whereas, the U.S. Department of State possesses the authority to accept gifts to support the preservation, conservation, restoration and exhibition of the Archive, or otherwise expend public funds to have said work done;

Whereas, on behalf of the CPA and upon the completion of the preservation, conservation and restoration activities described in Section II herein, NARA intends to exhibit the Archive to the general public, to the extent practicable, in order to facilitate additional education, scholarship and research; and

Therefore, the CPA and NARA hereby agree to the following:

[107] On 17 August 2003, Dr Jaber Khalil Ibrahim, Chairman of the Iraqi State Board of Antiquities and Heritage at the Iraqi Ministry of Culture, wrote to Ambassador Bremer, Coalition Provisional Authority, Baghdad, Iraq, and Ambassador Cordony, Ministry of Culture:

'Dear Sir,

With reference to the e-mail we received from Mr Kristen on August 05, about the Jewish archive discovered in the flooded basement of the Mukhabarat, we have viewed them, and we support your effort to protect these documents from further damage, and agree with your staff that we do not, at this time, have the resources to undertake this lengthy process.

According to paragraph [sic] No 21 of the Iraqi Antiquities Law No 55 for the year 2002, we agree with your plan to send the documents to the United States temporarily for the restoration by National Archives and Records Administration (NARA) on the condition that, following the restoration, the documents are returned to Iraq, in a period not exceeding two years from the day of this approval, and according to the attached list.'

I. Temporary Physical Custody

1. On a temporary basis and consistent with its desire to protect and preserve the Archive to the extent security conditions permit, the CPA will allow NARA to take physical custody of the Archive, for limited purposes of its preservation, conservation, restoration and exhibition, as described in Sections II and III. The CPA and NARA agree that NARA, in accepting temporary physical custody for the purposes described in Sections II and III, will at no time acquire or hold any ownership interest in the Archive or, except with respect to the activities described in Sections I, II and III, have any role or responsibility in determining access to the Archive or in addressing any other legal issues relating to the Archive.

2. NARA will take temporary physical custody of the Archive from the CPA at a location and time to be agreed upon by both parties and will accept and acknowledge such custody of the Archive pursuant to the receipt attached hereto as Attachment A.

3. Thereafter, NARA may relocate the Archive, as necessary, to the appropriate NARA and/or contractor facilities to undertake the activities described in Section II and III. NARA agrees to remain responsible for ensuring the safety and security of the items of the Archive if a NARA contractor facility or any other party takes physical custody of any item of the Archive.

4. NARA agrees to return physical custody of the Archive to the CPA, or its designee,[108] when the activities described in Sections II and III are completed. NARA also agrees to return physical custody of the Archive to the CPA, or its designee, at any time prior to the completion of the activities described in Sections II and III, if the Administrator of the CPA ('Administrator'), or a designee thereof, requests such return in writing twenty business days in advance. NARA will take any and all necessary steps, as requested by the CPA, to effect such return of the Archive, including such steps as are necessary to prevent additional or further harm to the Archive.

II. The Project

1. NARA will oversee and/or supervise the taking of all steps that are necessary to stabilize the Archive and halt further damage to it, including the following: (a) the freeze-drying of the Archive, and (b) the remediation of the Archive for mold such that personnel will be able to handle the Archive without causing further damage to it. NARA will catalog or arrange for cataloging of each item of the Archive at the first opportunity that will not result in further damage to the Archive.

2. In consultation with any representatives appointed by the Administrator, and utilizing such experts as are appropriate or necessary, NARA will (a) assess the contents

[108] On 28 June 2004, CPA Deputy Administrator, Ambassador Richard H Jones, sent the following 'Letter of Designation' to Lewis J Bellardo, Deputy Archivist of the United States: ' The CPA has been briefed on the current status of the Archive, as that term is used in the Agreement between the Coalition Provisional Authority (CPA) and the National Archives and Records Administration (NARA), effective as of August 20, 2003 (the "Agreement").

We understand that the NARA, upon the receipt of adequate funds, must continue its work with the Archive pursuant to Sections II and III of the Agreement, including mold remediation; an assessment of the Archive's contents and its historical, archival and curatorial importance; a determination of the conservation and reformatting needs of the items within the collection, based on a curatorial/archival and preservation assessment; and, to the extent practicable, temporary exhibition within the United States.

The CPA invites NARA to draw on such experts as are appropriate or necessary during this process. The CPA also requests that the NARA develop and implement that protocol described in Section II(4) for controlling access to the Archive for the purposes of carrying out the preservation, conservation, and restoration activities.

For the purpose of Sections I(4) and VIII, the CPA hereby designates the Ministry of Culture. As you know, when the Iraqi Interim Government (IIG) assumes full governing responsibility and authority for Iraq, the IIG will have the authority to modify this Designation pursuant to the Agreement.'

of the Archive and its historical, archival and curatorial importance, and (b) determine the conservation and reformatting needs of the items within the collection, based on a curatorial/archival and preservation assessment.

3. NARA will take all actions necessary to (a) conserve individual items of the Archive deemed to have artifactual importance, (b) conserve to the degree necessary to permit handling and/or duplication items in the Archive deemed to have research but not artifactual significance, (c) document the conservation measures taken with respect to the Archive, (d) house the Archive so it can be stored properly and used in the future, (e) provide interim storage of the Archive in appropriate facilities as the Archive is preserved, conserved and restored by NARA, (f) microfilm materials as appropriate, and (g) provide training in paper, book and parchment preservation to Iraqi professionals, as appropriate, and to the extent that the CPA can make all arrangements to bring such professionals into the United States.

4. NARA agrees to take every appropriate measure to ensure the safety and security of the Archive. NARA and the CPA will jointly establish a protocol to control access to the Archive for the purposes of carrying out the activities under this section. Except with respect to the exhibition pursuant to Section III, the CPA will be solely responsible for authorizing access to the Archive for any purpose outside those authorized in the protocol. Except with respect to the general public that views an exhibition of the Archive, NARA also agrees to maintain a daily record, including dates and times, of the personnel who work on or view items in the Archive.

5. NARA's ability and obligation to perform its responsibilities under this Section is subject to the receipt of complete funding pursuant to Section V of this Agreement, except that NARA agrees to undertake reasonable measures to prevent additional or further harm to the Archive, using available funding pursuant to Section V, so long as such funds exist.

III. The Exhibition

1. After the completion of the preservation, conservation and restoration activities described in Section II, NARA will, in consultation with the CPA and to the extent practicable with due regard for the preservation, conservation and restoration of the Archive, exhibit the Archive in the United States in order to facilitate education, scholarship and research regarding the Jewish community of Iraq. Such exhibition will be held at a cultural exhibition, assembly, or activity and administered, operated or sponsored by NARA or another educational or cultural institution, provided that the exhibition is open to the general public, held in a way that is respectful of the Archive's cultural significance, and not operated for a profit. Such exhibition shall last for such period as is proposed by NARA and approved by the CPA, but no longer than six months, unless both parties agree to a longer duration due to overriding circumstances. NARA and the CPA agree that all funding for any such exhibition will be provided and used in accordance with Section V of this Agreement.

2. NARA will take all necessary steps to ensure that the exhibition of the Archive will not jeopardize the preservation, conservation and restoration of the items in the Archive. The exhibition site and display technique/mounting should meet NARA's standard preservation and security requirements for comparable items.

IV. Immunity

1. The CPA understands that, pursuant to 22 U.S.C. § 2459(a),[109] the U.S. Department of State has determined that (a) the items in the Archive are of cultural significance and (b) that their temporary exhibition or display in the United States is in the national interest. The CPA understands that the U.S. Department of State has taken the appropriate steps to cause these determinations to be published in the Federal Register prior to importation of the Archive into the United States.[110]

2. NARA agrees that it will take all appropriate measures in order for the Archive to enjoy the protections available under 22 U.S.C. § 2459(b),[111] including contacting the U.S. Department of Justice (DoJ) to request that DoJ act pursuant to the aforementioned statute.

V. Funding Sources

1. The CPA understands that the U.S. Department of State has the authority, pursuant to Section 25 of the State Department Basic Authorities Act, 22 U.S.C. 2697, to accept on behalf of the United States gifts for the carrying out of any of the Department's functions. Expenditure of funds by the U.S. Department of State for the purpose of restoration of damaged foreign cultural property, including in support of cultural and educational research, is consistent with the Department of State's authorities under Section 102(b) of the Fulbright-Hays Act, 22 U.S.C. 2452. The CPA understands that such monies will be used by NARA through arrangements made pursuant to 31 U.S.C. § 1535, or other available means. NARA agrees that it will use such monies to fund all of the activities in this Agreement. If this Agreement terminates pursuant to Section VIII, all unused monies shall be returned pursuant to the appropriate procedures.

[109] 22 U.S.C. § 2459 (a), Agreements; Presidential determination; publication in Federal Register, provides: 'Whenever any work of art or other object of cultural significance is imported into the United States from any foreign country, pursuant to an agreement entered into between the foreign owner or custodian thereof and the United States or one or more cultural or educational institutions within the United States providing for the temporary exhibition or display thereof within the United States at any cultural exhibition, assembly, activity, or festival administered, operated, or sponsored, without profit, by any such cultural or educational institution, no court of the United States, any State, the District of Columbia, or any territory or possession of the United States may issue or enforce any judicial process, or enter any judgment, decree, or order, for the purpose or having the effect of depriving such institution, or any carrier engaged in transporting such work or object within the United States, of custody or control of such object if before the importation of such object the President or his designee has determined that such object is of cultural significance and that the temporary exhibition or display thereof within the United States is in the national interest, and a notice to that effect has been published in the Federal Register.'

[110] See Department of State, Public Notice 4454 – Culturally Significant Objects Imported for Exhibition Determinations: Cultural Artifacts from Iraq:

'SUMMARY: Notice is hereby given of the following determinations: Pursuant to the authority vested in me [...] I hereby determine that the historic and modern books, documents, parchment scrolls, and other items discovered in early May 2003 in the basement of the Mukhabahrat in Baghdad, most of which pertain to the Jewish community, imported from abroad for temporary exhibition in the United States, including restoration necessary thereto, are of cultural significance. The objects are imported pursuant to an agreement with the foreign owner or custodian. I also determine that their temporary exhibition or display by the National Archives and Records Administration, or another educational or cultural institution, is in the national interest. Public Notice of these Determinations is ordered to be published in the Federal Register. [...]

Dated: August 18, 2003

Patricia S. Harrison, Assistant Secretary for Educational and Cultural Affairs, Department of State' (FR, vol 68, no 162 (21 August 2003), 50570). See also FR, vol 68, no 205 (23 October 2003), 60625-60626.

[111] 22 U.S.C. § 2459(b), Intervention of United States attorney in pending judicial proceedings, provides: 'If in any judicial proceeding in any such court any such process, judgment, decree, or order is sought, issued, or entered, the United States attorney for the judicial district within which such proceeding is pending shall be entitled as of right to intervene as a party to that proceeding, and upon request made by either the institution adversely affected, or upon direction by the Attorney General if the United States is adversely affected, shall apply to such court for the denial, quashing, or vacating thereof.'

2. Any donor providing funding to preserve or protect the Archive will gain no rights whatsoever in exchange for providing such funding.

VI. Contacts

The Administrator will designate one or more CPA persons who will assist NARA in connection with its activities hereunder. NARA will designate one or more NARA persons who will be responsible for coordinating NARA's activities hereunder.

VII. Additions to the Archive

At any time prior to the exhibition described in Section III, the CPA may add to the Archive items pertaining to the Jewish community of Iraq recovered in Iraq, provided that NARA agrees that such items will be covered under this Agreement at the time of the proposed transfer of temporary physical custody. The CPA understands that the U.S. Department of State would need to take the steps described in Section IV(1) with respect to these additional items. Completion by NARA and the CPA of a receipt similar to that attached hereto as Attachment A with respect to the additional items described in this Section shall establish that this Agreement applies to such items.

VIII. Termination

This Agreement will be terminated and physical custody of the Archive will be returned to the CPA, or its designee, if: (1) the CPA, or its designee, requests return of the Archive pursuant to Section I(4); (2) NARA provides the CPA with 45 days prior written notice; (3) the U.S. Department of State does not cause a public notice to be published in the Federal Register under Section IV(1); (4) complete funding cannot be provided in a reasonable timeframe to NARA in accordance with Section V; or (5) there is, at any time, mutual agreement of the parties to terminate the Agreement.

IX. Execution in Counterparts

This Agreement may be executed in several counterparts, each of which shall be deemed an original, and all of which together shall constitute one and the same instrument.

X. Effective Date

This Agreement is effective as of August 20, 2003.

This Agreement has been duly authorized and executed by the undersigned.

THE NATIONAL ARCHIVES AND RECORDS ADMINISTRATION
[signed] *Lewis J. Bellardo [19 August 2003]*
Lewis J. Bellardo, Deputy Archivist of the United States

THE COALITION PROVISIONAL AUTHORITY
[signed] *Patrick F. Kennedy*
Patrick F. Kennedy, Chief of Staff

ATTACHMENT A
[FORM OF RECEIPT]
ACCEPTANCE OF PHYSICAL CUSTODY OF THE ARCHIVE

The National Archives and Records Administration (NARA) hereby accepts and acknowledges receipt of physical custody of certain rare, historic and modern books, documents and parchment scrolls, including rare and modern printed and manuscript materials in Hebrew, Arabic, Judeo-Arabic and English pertaining to the Jewish community of Iraq as described below (collectively, hereinafter the 'Archive') pursuant to the terms and conditions of the Agreement between the Coalition Provisional Authority (CPA) and NARA, dated August ___ , 2003. Based on an on-site assessment made by NARA conservators on June 20-22, 2003 in Baghdad and additional information provided by CPA staff, the Archive presently includes the following:

Trunk 1

Partially full. Tikim.

Trunk 2

Full. Mix of materials: paper files, bound volumes, loose sheets, pamphlets, Hebrew language training pamphlet (multiple copies), newspaper. Paper files contained in mechanical compression storage units ('Elba Rado' [brand or tradename] – 'Mathematical Magic') with lightweight front and back covers and rusted metal components. Mix of alphabets (Hebrew and Arabic scripts).

Trunk 3

Full trunk. Appears largely to be loose files in mechanical binders.

Trunk 4

Full. Mix of loose sheets and bound volumes (some appear historical); also some paperback bindings. Materials intermingled and distorted; mold visible. 10 volumes relatively intact but exhibit mold. 9 bindings/units are more severely damaged and exhibit mold, distorted covers and text pages, as well as fragments and random covers. Some evidence of older binding structures (volumes sewn on leather cords), though this could also be an artifact of the bookbinding tradition of the geographic location(s) from which the bindings originated. Numerous bound volumes, some of which had been placed in sealed plastic bags but later removed; a text fragment remains in one bag. In addition, a pamphlet was noted that related to the constitution and rules of the Jewish community in Baghdad, published in 1942 by the Iraq Ministry of Justice.

Trunk 5

Full trunk. Documents, some loose but most appear to be secured in mechanical binders.

Trunk 6

Full trunk. Documents, some loose but most secured in mechanical binders. Printed and manuscript materials.

Trunk 7

Full trunk. Primarily bound materials, though some few loose sheets in mechanical binders. Evidence of possible early binding structures. Several small format volumes and some with limp covers.

Trunk 8

Full trunk. Papers in disarray but appear to be in relatively good condition. Materials include loose sheets (correspondence) in rigid binders, newspaper clippings, color photograph.

Trunk 9

Approximately 3/4 full trunk. Mix of materials, including volumes sewn on leather thongs, modern printed books, paperbacks, and loose sheets. Also some large format volumes without boards (i.e., covers).

Trunk 10

Full trunk. Appears to be primarily bindings – large and small formats, some old (sewn on leather things), some without boards. Evidence that volumes were originally covered in leather, some boards still retain marbled paper. Some loose sheets.

Trunk 11

Approximately one quarter full trunk. Appear to be printed texts. A mixture of text blocks, detached sheets, and partial text blocks with no boards.

Trunk 12

Full trunk. A mixture of loose and bound materials (primarily modern), both printed and typescript.

Trunk 13

Full trunk. Primarily loose sheets in mechanical binders, though some sheets are detached. Appears to be printed material with possibly some manuscript text.

Trunk 14

Full trunk. Primarily bindings, with leather detached from boards. A few volumes have intact text blocks, but most a distorted with detached boards. Some damaged text blocks with detached and crumpled sheets. Many volumes appear old.

Trunk 15

Full trunk. Handle missing from left side of trunk. Small to medium format bindings; age likely varies. Some volumes sewn on cloth tapes, boards detached. Appear to be printed texts.

Trunk 16

Full trunk. Appears to be primarily volumes with printed texts, bindings sewn on cloth tapes. One volume exhibits previous insect feeding (wormholes). Partial imprint visible: Jarowth Dewasch, Lemberg 1863, Druck-von B.Leib Necheles und Abr. Nissen.

Trunk 17

Full trunk. Some sheets attached (frozen) to inner trunk lid. Appears to be primarily loose sheets, some in mechanical binders and others stitched with green string or cord into paper wrappers. Appears to be correspondence: a mixture of printed text, typescript, and manuscript annotations.

Trunk 18

Full trunk. A jumble of loose sheets, in disarray but in good condition; appear to be modern. Printed documents with manuscript notations, some documents in green paper folders. One modern postcard visible.

Trunk 19

Full trunk. Primarily volumes but some loose files. Hebrew and Arabic texts, one pertaining to Israel and Zionism.

Trunk 20

Three quarters full trunk. A mixture of volumes, pamphlets, files, text leaves and fragments. Boards missing from volumes.

Trunk 21

Almost full trunk. Contents include bound volumes and fragments, possibly some older book structures present (volumes sewn on leather thongs and leather core headbands).

Trunk 22

Full trunk. Materials in disarray. Includes many small format volumes as well as fragments and crumbled detached text leaves. Age appears to vary. Printed texts. Contents include a textile fragment.

Trunk 23

Almost full trunk. Contents frozen solid. Files in mechanical binders that exhibit dust and distortion but not much evidence of mold. Text fragment visible: 'University of London, General Certificate of Education...'.

Trunk 24

Approximately half full trunk. A mixture of files in mechanical binders, volumes (some small format with leather spines and decorative paper boards), and paper fragments and crumbled sheets.

Trunk 25

Approximately half full hunk. Contents appear to be primarily volumes, pamphlets, and fragments of text with perhaps some paper files. Evidence of mold, distortion, and detached boards.

Trunk 26

Three quarters full trunk. Mixture of volumes, pamphlets, and files. Many volumes sewn on leather thongs and covered in half or quarter leather. Appears to include some modern materials. The title on the cover of one volume is an Arabic translation of Turkish or Persian text.

Trunk 27

Half full trunk. Contents include approximately 5 bundles containing scrolls and/or fragments of scrolls. The scrolls were wrapped in cotton sheeting and taped closed, though one bundle has an outer wrapping of plastic. To provide minimal disruption, only one package containing scrolls was opened. It contained several folded or rolled units that appeared to be fragments or incomplete scrolls; one retained its wooden dowel or stave.

I have been duly authorized by NARA to accept the Archive on behalf of NARA. I also acknowledge that NARA will at no time acquire or hold any ownership interest in the Archive. I have received the Archive, as described above, in [________ ,_____] on August __, 2003.

THE NATIONAL ARCHIVES AND RECORDS ADMINISTRATION
By: ________________________
Title: ________________________

Document 217
Clarifying the De-Ba'athification Policy

24 August 2003

ACTION MEMO

TO: CPA Directors and Local Military Commanders
FROM: L. Paul Bremer, Administrator, Coalition Provisional Authority
SUBJECT: Clarifying the De-Ba'athification Policy

Objectives of the Policy

Rooting out and destroying the last vestiges of the Ba'ath Party continues to be a key CPA priority. The long-term health of Iraqi society can only be accomplished through the rigorous removal of senior Ba'ath Party officials who benefited from Saddam's regime and the prosecution of those guilty of crimes. This objective is shared by virtually the entire Iraqi population, which is why the first order I issued upon my arrival in Baghdad was the one to de-ba'athify Iraqi society. The order, issued May 16th,[112] outlines a process that makes clear that Ba'athist organizations and individuals who fail to renounce Saddam's Ba'ath Party have no place in a liberated Iraq. The purpose of this memo is to outline the scope of the policy and to reinforce among coalition representatives the critical nature of its implementation.

The de-ba'athification policy seeks to 1) eliminate from positions of power and responsibility high level Ba'athists who supported Saddam, 2) open those same positions to those who suffered under the regime, and 3) leave the door ajar for people who were essentially a-political, lower-level Ba'athists to contribute to Iraq's future.

The policy is not a one-size fits all policy. It does not paint everyone with the same brush, but instead recognizes the different levels of involvement in the party and the former

[112] See *Doc 14*.

regime. Even at its most expansive, the policy targets around 30,000 people, only a tiny fraction of the estimated 1.5 million associated in some manner with the Ba'ath Party.

This policy has, and will continue to be, in the interest of the coalition and the Iraqi people. But, like any policy, it is not without unintended consequences. Where possible, the coalition has sought to mitigate these consequences, by granting a limited number of exceptions to individuals and to categories of people, such as former prisoners of war who were automatically granted high-level party status upon their return from Iran. The soon-to-be-established Governing Council [sic][113] and all future Iraqi governments will have the authority to alter the de-ba'athification policy as they deem it appropriate and in the interest of the Iraqi people. The decisions of these bodies will be retroactive if they so choose.

After nearly two months of de-ba'athification efforts, we have found that fewer people have been affected by the policy than we originally anticipated. As de-ba'athification proceeds in Baghdad and in the governorates, these numbers will grow and there will be further destabilizing effects. Nonetheless, a negligible percentage of the entire Iraqi society will be affected by the policy.

<u>Parameters of the Policy</u>

The policy, as laid out in the May 16th order, has several basic components:

1. *Senior Ba'ath Party Members*. All civil servants who are senior Ba'ath Party members are to be removed from their jobs, regardless of the level of their position in the ministry or municipality. A senior Ba'ath Party member is defined to be anyone who is in the top four tiers of the Ba'ath party: Regional Command (Qutriyya), Branch (Far), Section (Shu'bah), Group (Firqah).
2. *Top Levels of Management in the Ministries*. Those in the top levels of management of the ministries or municipalities are subject to even greater scrutiny because of their positions of leadership. Anyone of the level of Director General or above in any ministry or municipality must be removed if he or she was in the top five tiers of the Ba'ath Party – the four tiers listed above plus the Full Party Member status (Udw). Senior ministry or municipal managers can keep their jobs if they were never a member of the Ba'ath Party or if their affiliation was at a level below the Full Party (Udw) level.
3. *Junior Ba'ath Party Members*. Any Iraqi who was associated with the Ba'ath Party at a level below Full Party member (Udw) retains his job in the public sector.
4. *Mid-Level and Junior Civil Servants*. Any Iraqi who was a Full Party member (Udw) and held a job below the DG level retains his position.
5. *Exceptions*. The administrator of the Coalition Provisional Authority has the ability to make exceptions to any element of this policy. No one else has the authority to make such exceptions unless explicitly delegated by the Administrator and to date no one has been delegated that authority anywhere in Iraq.

<u>Implementation of the Policy</u>

The following questions and answers provide guidance on the actual implementation of the policy. Any questions regarding the implementation of the policy not answered below

[113] The IGC was established on 13 July 2003. The document reproduced here is dated 24 August 2003 which suggests that it was drafted much earlier, i.e. in early July 2003. See also the next paragraph which speaks of 'nearly two months of de-ba'athification efforts'. De-Ba'athification started with CPA Order No 1 of 16 May 2003.

should be referred to either CPA headquarters in Baghdad (POC) or CPA regional offices in Basra, Hilla, or Mosul.

1. Who qualifies for an exception?

The Administrator of the Coalition Provisional Authority has the discretion to grant exceptions to the de-ba'athification policy. Although he may choose to delegate this authority, he retains the ability to reverse any decision to grant or refuse an exception.

In considering whether to grant an exception, the CPA will take a number of factors into account, including whether the individual:

- Is willing to denounce the Ba'ath Party and his past association with it;
- Was a senior Ba'ath Party member or simply a 'full' party member;
- Has exceptional educational qualifications;
- Left the Ba'ath Party before April 16, 2003;
- Continues to command the support of his colleagues and respect of their subordinates;
- Is judged to be indispensable to achieving important Coalition interests at least in the immediate term;
- Can demonstrate that he joined the party to hold his job or support his family.

As soon as can be arranged, a professional investigator or an administrative law judge empowered by the Coalition Authority will determine whether a person meets the above criteria. Meanwhile, exceptions will be determined by the Administrator. Exceptions may either allow the individual to stay on in his current position or specify that he can only continue employment at the ministry in a lower position. The Administrator reserves the right to overturn an exception if new evidence comes to light that is grounds for altering the original decision.

2. Will members of the top three tiers of management be allowed to maintain their current positions pending the start of the exception process?

No. All employees who were 1) in the top four layers of the Ba'ath Party or 2) full Ba'ath Party members in the top three tiers of ministry management (including DGs) must leave their jobs immediately. A temporary exception may be granted in unusual circumstances if the senior advisor can make the case that removing an individual immediately will seriously harm important U.S. or Coalition interests (such as restoration of law and order in Iraq, the reestablishment of a judicial system, and the repair of power and water systems). So far, only around 100 temporary exceptions have been granted country-wide. It is important to remember that exceptions will not be granted simply to preserve the convenience or efficient running of institutions. If a senior advisor or coalition representative wishes to request a temporary exception, he or she will use the attached form addressed to the CPA Administrator.[114]

3. Will we pay pensions to those who lose their jobs due to their Ba'ath Party involvement?

No. Senior advisors and other CPA staff may respond to pension queries by saying 1) that the Coalition has no plans to pay the pensions of people who lose their jobs under the de-ba'athification policy and 2) our unwillingness to do so does not prejudice the ability of a future Iraqi government to decide otherwise. We reserve the right to revisit this issue if we find the consequences of this approach to be contrary to Coalition interests.

[114] The form is not available.

4. Should DGs be included in the top three tiers of management?
Yes. The de-ba'athification policy will be applied down to and including the DG level, regardless of how many tiers of management sit above DGs.

5. How many ministry employees will we investigate for senior Ba'ath Party membership?
We will investigate 1) all employees in the top three tiers of ministry management (to include DGs as stated above) and 2) all individuals for whom we receive at least two independent allegations that they were senior ba'athists.

6. Will people have the right to appeal?
Yes. An appeal mechanism will be created for those who wish to contest the facts of their case (i.e. that they were members of the Ba'ath Party). We will not consider appeals over the denial of an exception.

7. Will ex-members of the Ba'ath Party be exempt from the de-ba'athification policy?
Having left the Ba'ath Party before 16 April 2003 will not in itself be sufficient for an individual to avoid the consequences of the de-ba'athification policy. It may weigh in a person's favor when an exception is being considered.

8. Are those removed from positions of management on account of Ba'ath Party full membership (opposed to being a senior party official) allowed to stay on as ministry employees at lower levels?
As a rule, no. Those removed from positions of management should assume that they must leave employment in their ministry altogether. Willingness to serve in a lower position in the ministry could weigh in favor of an exception should one be sought. But all such requests for an exception must be based on the factors listed in paragraph #1 above. Persons requesting such an exception would have to sign the denunciation form.[115]

9. Will we continue to issue letters of authority to ministry members before the investigative process is complete?
No. There is a moratorium on issuing letters of authority signed by the Administrator of the CPA until we understand the full ramification of de-ba'athifiction. Until then, senior advisors may sign specific authorities (i.e. for the payment of salaries) and continue verbally to designate people as having interim authorities to make decisions and implement policies.

10. Will we screen individuals replacing those we fire for Ba'ath Party affiliation?
We will adopt hiring procedures to ensure that the new ministry employees are not ba'athists. Applicants will be required to fill out a questionnaire regarding their past party involvement; it shall be clear that falsification of answers is grounds for termination of their position. New hires will need to sign a form either disavowing or denouncing the Ba'ath Party (depending on whether they were ever affiliated with it).[116] We will also conduct a character reference check that includes questions about the individual's past party affiliation.

[115] For the form, see *Doc 173*.
[116] For the forms, see *Doc 173*.

11. Should we retain property and privileges that Ba'ath Party members gained as a perk of membership?
Yes. Officials who are to be removed from office should first be asked to return ministry property such as cars, computers, cell phones, etc. We should inform these people that a failure to return ministry property could have prosecutable consequences. Such efforts must be complemented by the search for records detailing the ministry property distributed to employees.

12. Is there a policy in regard to the POWs who were automatically granted firqah level status upon their return from Iran?
POWs who were automatically granted firqah level status in the Ba'ath Party on account of their captivity in Iran – and are able to demonstrate this – will not be removed from their positions.

Document 218
Iraqi Oil Trust
24 August 2003

INFO MEMO

FOR: THE GOVERNING COUNCIL
FROM: THE ADMINISTRATOR, Coalition Provisional Authority
SUBJECT: IRAQI OIL TRUST

The natural wealth of Iraq has for far too long been abused and squandered by its leaders. It is high time that the riches of Iraq were used solely for the benefit of the Iraqi people. In order to achieve this, the new Iraqi Oil Minister could announce the creation of an Oil Trust. The establishment of an Iraqi Oil Trust, into which a portion of oil revenues would be paid, would have a number of advantages:

– It would enable oil revenues to be saved and used directly for the benefit of the Iraqi people. This can be done through direct payments to citizens in the form of dividends, or by managing long term needs of the state, such as by paying for pensions.
– It would protect the state against volatility in the global oil market. Saving a portion of oil revenues would mean that the state could draw upon financial reserves to meet fiscal deficits caused by a drop in oil prices.
– It would create a transparent and accountable means of managing oil revenues and would be designed and managed according to international 'best practice'.
– It would enable the state to plan and implement economic goals for the near-term, medium-term, and long-term thereby allowing it to address the diverse economic needs of the country.
– It would cultivate broad popular and social support among Iraq's population, through the provision of much needed social benefits.

In the near term, due to the massive demands for reconstruction expenditure not much oil revenue will be routed through the Trust. The only feasible payments to the trust will be pension's [sic] payments. But sourcing oil revenue into the Trust, which will produce clear benefits to Iraqis in terms of direct payments, will be a good means of demonstrating to the people that their livelihood is directly linked to oil production. Damaging oil production will harm their future prospects.

Document 219

L. Paul Bremer, Address to the Iraqi People: 'Path to Sovereignty'

5 September 2003

Masaa al Khair.

I am Paul Bremer, administrator of the Coalition Provisional Authority.

The Coalition came to Iraq as liberators. We came to rid Iraq of Saddam Hussein's cruel and evil regime and we have done that. We came to restore Iraq's government and resources to you, the Iraqi people. That restoration is in progress.

You have freedoms now that you have never had before – the freedom to print and read what you like, the freedom to travel, the freedom to speak your mind. You have the freedom to criticize anyone you please, including me, the Coalition or the Governing Council.

I do not like, and the United States does not like, being an occupying power. Like you, we have wives and husbands and mothers and fathers and children with whom we would prefer to be. We want to go home as soon as possible.

I know you would rather not see foreign troops and tanks on your streets. Some say we should leave today, this moment. They say that you are capable of running your own government.

To those people I say, 'Of course Iraqis can run their own government. Iraqis are intelligent, resourceful and adaptive.' You can govern yourselves, but you need a framework for your government. The problem is that when Saddam and the Baathists had you by the throat, they destroyed the essential framework of government. All the laws, resources and powers of government belonged to one man. If Saddam desired one thing and the law required another, Saddam simply changed the law to suit his desires. Then, the Coalition approached Baghdad and Saddam filled two huge trucks with money and ran away.

Thus, when the Coalition arrived in Baghdad there was no government. There was only the vacuum Saddam left behind when he fled.

Now you must have a government. You must have a government which governs for your benefit and which derives from your will. That means you must have elections for your own government.

But to elect a government without a permanent constitution is to elect a Pharaoh, someone who, once elected, would have no limits on his power. And unlimited power, one-man absolutism placed tens of thousands of your fathers, mothers, brothers and daughters in the mass graves where Saddam dumped them, unidentified, unhonored and unsung.

You must have a new, permanent constitution. It would be irresponsible for us to topple Saddam, but then leave before you have a chance to establish a government to replace him. To do so would encourage terrorism and civil violence and invite the return of Saddam or some other tyrant.

The Coalition wants you to have:

A government whose acts are authorized, defined and limited by a permanent constitution, a government that represents your interests, a government that represents you, the free

Iraqi people before all the nations of the world, a government that can protect you from criminals, saboteurs and terrorists. That is what the Coalition wants. That is what you want. That is what you are going to have.

The process to make that happen has already started. You are on the path to full sovereignty. There are seven steps on that path and three of them have already been taken.

Step one: Establishing a Temporary Iraqi Government

That step was taken two months ago when the Governing Council was created.

Step two: Deciding How to Write a Constitution

That step was taken last month when the Governing Council named a Preparatory Committee to determine how you, the people of Iraq, should write your constitution.

Step Three: Iraqis Begin to Run the Country

This crucial step was taken on Tuesday when 25 ministers appointed by the Governing Council took office.

Now each ministry is run by an Iraqi appointed by Iraqis.

These newly appointed ministers, who serve at the pleasure of Council, have important responsibilities:

- They run the ministries, conducting the day-to-day business of your government.
- They are preparing the 2004 budget. They must operate their ministries according to those budgets.
- These are important responsibilities, but the Coalition believes ministers must have authorities equal their responsibilities.
- Therefore, as the ministers settle into their positions the Coalition will thrust authority at the ministers.

Step four: Iraqis Write a New Constitution

On September 15 the Preparatory Committee appointed by the Governing Council will present the Council with recommendations on a process for writing the Constitution. Thereafter, presumably something like a constitutional convention will be convened and Iraqis will begin writing a new constitution.

I do not know how long this will take. No doubt the drafters will have to deal with complex and sensitive issues.

But I believe that the Iraqis drafting your constitution will recognize that they must act as Iraqis and not solely as advocates for their community.

They will recognize that compromises must be made, that no individual can have everything he or she wants, that no group can have everything it wants.

I am confident that these Iraqis will produce the permanent constitution for which all their countrymen are waiting.

Step five: Ratifying the Constitution

Once written, the constitution will be widely circulated among the Iraqi people. Then all adult Iraqis will have the opportunity to vote for or against it.

For the first time in your history, you will have a permanent constitution which you have approved.

Step Six: Electing a Government

Shortly after the constitution is ratified by your vote there will be an election to fill the elective offices specified in the constitution. Officials in charge of that government will be chosen by you in an open and honest election.

When that government is elected, Iraq will have a government designed and approved by Iraqis.

Step Seven: The Coalition Authority Ends

Once Iraq has a freely elected government the Coalition will happily yield the remainder of its authority to that sovereign Iraqi government.

How long will these seven steps take?

I cannot say, but the process I have described is in your hands. Iraqis run the Governing Council. Iraqis run all the ministries. Iraqis are deciding on the mechanism for writing a constitution. Iraqis will write the constitution. Iraqis will convoke and operate the elections to ratify the constitution and elect a government.

While I cannot say how long the process will take, I have suggested that the Governing Council establish and publish a timetable so that you can clearly see the steps on the path to full sovereignty.

There is something each of you can do to bring closer the day when you have your own sovereign government.

Help the Governing Council, the Iraqi police and the Coalition identify and arrest the saboteurs and terrorists who are trying to disrupt this process.

These criminals will not succeed, but their campaigns of murder, sabotage and destruction can slow this process.

Report them to the Iraqi police or to the Coalition forces. They will be arrested or, if they fight, killed.

Let us cooperate to bring about a freely elected, wholly sovereign Iraqi government at the earliest possible date.

Document 220

FY04 Supplemental Request to Rehabilitate and Reconstruct Iraq

17 September 2003[117]

Introduction

Prior to the war, the President outlined an ambitious vision for post-war Iraq that could serve as a model to the Arab world. He described a secure and stable country, governed by a democratically-elected government and served by a robust and open economy. Whether Iraq embraces this future is, ultimately, up to the Iraqis. The Coalition, however, has an obligation to lay the groundwork for the new Iraq, and to leave the country with a real chance of fulfilling the President's vision. In order to support this commitment the Coalition Provisional Authority requires an additional $20.3 billion in fiscal year (FY) 2004 and is requesting the Congress to provide these resources as emergency non-offset supplemental appropriations. Expeditious approval of this emergency supplemental requires is [sic] critical for the Coalition to lay the groundwork for an Iraq governed by and for the people of Iraq, to serve as the model for democracy in the mideast and to help fight the global war on terrorism by providing an alternative framework for governance.

[117] There are several (slightly) different versions of this document in circulation. The present version was submitted on 17 September 2003 to the Congress Armed Services Committee and is reproduced in U.S. Military Commitments and Ongoing Military Operations Abroad, Hearing before the Committee on Armed Services, United States Senate, 108th Congress, 1st Session, 9 September 2003 (Washington: GPO, 2004), pp. 62-115. Table of Contents omitted.

This additional $20.3 billion will finance the most critical needs for security and infrastructure that cannot be met with anticipated revenues from oil sales until the entire oil infrastructure becomes more robust. These needs are immediate and urgent. We are ready to begin execution of these funds before the end of 2003.

Highlights of this $20.3 billion FY 2004 emergency supplemental request include

- $2.1B to fund public safety including border enforcement, police, fire and customs and enhanced security communications
- $2.1B to establish national security forces and the Iraq Civil Defense Corps
- $0.9B to provide justice and civil society development
- $5.7B to rehabilitate the electric power infrastructure
- $2.1B to rehabilitate oil infrastructure and secure domestic consumption
- $3.7B to fund repairs and improvements to water and sewerage services
- $0.9B to fund repairs to facilitate and conserve water resources
- $0.8B to repair transportation facilities and telecommunications infrastructure
- $0.5B to upgrade housing, public buildings, roads and bridges
- 40.9B to fund construct, repair, and equip hospitals and primary clinics
- $0.3B to invest into private sector business initiatives and jobs training programs
- $0.3B to assist refugees, provide for human rights and develop civil society

In each instance, our Supplemental request is designed to ensure adequate resources to put Iraq on the path to a secure, economically hopeful future. The programs in this supplemental are thus all based upon Coalition evaluations and estimates. They are all fiscally conservative numbers.

The Coalition Provisional Authority is requesting non-offset emergency supplemental funding to directly support the rehabilitation and construction of Iraq, and in particular, to invest in essential security and stabilization initiatives and urgent infrastructure repairs and requirements. Further, the coalition requests urgent passage of the supplemental to announce the United States commitment to provide one-for-one matching funds at the Madrid Donor Conference scheduled for 23-24 Oct 2003 and for donations which will follow later.

Detailed Overview of Requirements
(Dollars in Millions)

Security		
Public Safety Requirements:		
Border Enforcement	$150	
National Police Service	$150	
International Police Training Mission	$800	
Traffic Police	$ 50	
Fire and Civil Defense	$500	
Facility Protective Services	$ 67	
Public Safety Training	$274	
Nat'l Security Communications Network	$150	
Subtotal Public Safety		$2,141
National Security:		
New Iraqi Army	$2,000	
Iraqi Civil Defense Corps	$ 76	
Subtotal National Security		$2,076

Justice:			
Technical assistance for investigations into crimes against humanity	$100		
Security for Judges and Prosecutors	$200		
Witness Protection Program	$100		
Other technical investigative methods	$ 10		
Prison system technical assistance	$ 10		
Reconstruction & modernization of 26 detention and prison facilities	$ 99		
Two new 4,000 bed maximum security prisons	$400		
Subtotal Justice		$ 919	
Subtotal Security			$5,136
Infrastructure			
Electricity			
Generation	$2,900		
Transmission networks	$1,550		
Distribution networks	$1,000		
Communications and control	$ 150		
Institutional strengthening	$ 25		
Security	$ 50		
Subtotal Electricity		$5,675	
Oil Infrastructure/Production			
Oil Investment	$1,200		
Oil products purchase	$ 900		
Subtotal Oil Infrastructure		$2,100	
Public Works			
Improve access to potable water	$2,830		
Reducing water losses	$ 30		
Improve sewer services	$ 69		
Improving solid waste management	$ 153		
Subtotal Public Works		$3,710	
Water Resources			
Pumping Stations	$ 75		
Standby Generators	$ 75		
Irrigation/Drainage Systems	$ 130		
Complete Projects Halted by War	$ 130		
Rural Water Supply Dams	$ 25		
Dam Safety Repairs	$ 100		
Water Pipeline and Treatment Plant	$ 200		
Environmental Restoration	$ 100		
Tidal Channel Flushing	$ 40		
Subtotal Water Resources		$ 875	
Transportation & Telecommunication			
Civil Aviation	$ 165		
Ports	$ 45		
Railroads	$ 303		
IPTC network systems	$ 124		

Iraqi communications systems	$ 109		
Iraqi communications operations	$ 89		
Subtotal Trans/Telecomm.		$ 835	
<u>Housing and Construction</u>			
Housing	$ 100		
Public Buildings	$ 130		
Roads and Bridges	$ 240		
Subtotal Housing & Construction		$ 470	
<u>Health</u>			
Construct Pediatric Hospital in Basrah	$ 150		
Refurbish Health System	$ 393		
Repair/Replace Equipment	$ 300		
Partnership for Health	$ 7		
Subtotal Health		$ 850	
<u>Private Sector Development</u>			
American-Iraqi Enterprise Fund	$ 200		
Expand Network of Employment Centers	$ 8		
On The Job Training	$ 35		
Market Oriented Specialized Training	$ 110		
Subtotal Private Sector Development		$ 353	
Subtotal Infrastructure			$14,868
<u>Refugees, Human Rights and Civil Society</u>			
Migration and Refugee Assistance	$ 105		
Local Governance & Municipalities	$ 90		
Property Claims Tribunal	$ 30		
Update antiquated banking system	$ 30		
Catch up business training	$ 20		
Human Rights	$ 15		
Civic Programs	$ 10		
Subtotal Refugees, Human Rights and Civil Society		$ 300	
Grand Total			**$20,304 M**

Overview of Appropriation Request

Iraq Relief and Reconstruction Fund	$20,069M
American-Iraqi Enterprise Fund	$ 235M
Grand Total	**$20,304M**

PUBLIC SAFETY

Although the coalition has made great strides to stabilize Iraq and enhance security, the Iraqi citizenship faces three levels of threats: the hardened criminals the previous regime let loose into the streets; the remnants of the old regime who have nowhere to flee; and foreign terrorists. Dealing with these security threats is our highest priority.

Border Enforcement

Bureau of Border and Customs Police: Divided into three Sections of Patrol, Investigations and Detention & Deportation. Border and Customs Police enforce the immigration and customs laws and regulations along the border between the ports of entry and the interior of Iraq. Currently, facilities include a headquarters office, three regional offices and 264 border police stations. Each border police station accommodates 10-30 policemen. Our goal is to leverage technology to greatly reduce the number of border police stations, possibly by as much as 75 per cent. However, that effort will require that at least 50 new border police stations be constructed. The headquarters and three regional offices will require complete renovation, due to war damages, post-war looting and years of neglect. Further, because the previous border police used conscripts, almost all of whom deserted, a massive recruitment/ training program must be implemented to develop a professional, reliable police service. The Investigation Section and the Detention & Deportation Section are elements new to the Border/Customs Police and will, consequently, have a massive impact on infrastructure and training. The current number of personnel is estimated to be about 4,000. An additional 2,000 should be immediately recruited. Total required personnel are 6,000.

Bureau of Border Inspections: Also divided into three Sections of Immigration Inspections, Customs Inspections and a Border Guard Section. Personnel will be assigned to 14 land ports of entry, three airport ports of entries, and two seaport ports of entries. Besides the ports of entry, are a headquarters and three regional offices. Consideration is being given to the establishment of secondary ports of entry. There are currently about 2,500 Customs Inspectors who inspect imported and exported products and about 350 Border Guards who perform perimeter and internal security of the respective port of entry compounds. Duties of Immigration Inspectors were previously conducted by elements of Saddam's security police, so the entire Section of Immigration Inspections requires basic law enforcement and specific immigration and nationality law training. We estimate that at least 2,500 Immigration Inspectors will be recruited and trained. Facilities at virtually each port of entry were damaged and/or looted and will require a significant amount of refurbishment. Total required personnel are about 5,350.

Bureau of Nationality & Civil Affairs: Like the previous two bureaus, it is divided into three Sections of Passport, Nationality & Civil Affairs (includes vital statistics), and Immigration. The Passport Section is responsible for the issuance of passports to Iraqi citizens and secure control of unassigned documents. The previous passport facility was completely destroyed and must be replaced. Because all previous employees were members of the security police, an entirely new workforce of an estimated 350 personnel must be recruited and trained. The Nationality & Civil Affairs Section is responsible for determining citizenship, issuance of national identification cards, and for vital statistics functions, such as the recording of births, deaths, marriages, divorces, etc. and will perform these tasks with about 1,400 civilian personnel working from 26 separate field offices in Baghdad, three regional offices and a headquarters facility. A proposal has been made to consolidate the 26 field offices into just two Baghdad facilities and all buildings require significant repairs due to neglect, vandalism and looting. The Immigration Section, consisting of an estimated 500 personnel will adjudicate petitions pertaining to both immigrant and non-immigrant visas and will forward decisions to respective foreign posts operated by the Ministry of Foreign Affairs. Total required personnel are approximately 2,250.

Summary of Border Enforcement: When rebuilt, the Department of Border Enforcement will employ approximately 13,600 personnel. Of those, approximately 4,500 recruits for police type positions must be identified and trained as soon as possible. Beyond basic academy and refresher training, 75 long term advisors are required to ensure successful transition of border related enforcement into a single ministry. At least 53 Border Police facilities, 19 port of entry facilities, and 5 Nationality and Civil Affairs facilities will require refurbishment or complete construction. The total incremental cost to improve border and customs enforcement is estimated at $150M. Without this investment, the nation continues to be at tremendous risk of penetration by members of terrorist cells and other subversive organizations; smuggling will continue to bleed the revenues necessary for the Iraqi economy to stand on its own and Iraq will not be able to control its borders.

Police, Traffic Police and Motor Vehicles

General Police Forces. An estimated $150M is urgently required to recruit, train, equip and operate viable, sustainable policing services in Iraq, capable of dealing in a professional manner with all issues falling within their mandate. There are significant immediate costs to restoring competent, trustworthy police forces due to significant damage if not outright destruction Iraq-wide of facilities and looting of property, the training and equipping of a new police force, as well as associated operations and maintenance costs.

International Police Training. The coalition requires an estimated $800M to immediately begin building an international police training force of 1500 to provide the level of professionalism and assistance upon which the Iraqi native police force will achieve. This force will support training and development of the Iraqi police with field training officers (FTO), and advisors to enable the new police to effectively apply the skills learned in classroom training. In addition, such a mission would provide 'hands on' guidance to all levels of the Iraqi police forces to help them understand modern, democratically based principles of civilian policing.

Traffic Police. The Iraq Traffic Police has 5,200 officers and 27 office buildings countrywide. They are responsible for the control of traffic, enforcement of traffic laws, and accident investigation. Their buildings, fleet, and equipment have been almost completely destroyed or looted, and will require funding priority near term to stand up operational capability to at least pre-war capacity. Estimated cost: $50M

Fire and Civil Defense

Summary of Request: $500M is required to provide adequate fire service, civil defense needs, mine action requirements and to repair public safety facilities for the safety of the Iraqi people.

Fire Service: The Fire Service is the principal agency responsible to serve the security and safety needs of the populace by controlling the destructive force of fire, natural, and human-made hazards in an effort to diminish the loss of life and property. Firefighters are also the principal emergency responders for the entire country and serve the needs of over 26.2 million Iraqis. Firefighters also serve as the EOD experts for the country, responding to and mitigating the effects of all unexploded ordnance which litters the entire country. The department needs at least 20 fully trained and capable EOD units in order to minimize the paralyzing and destructive effects of misplaced ordnance.

The Fire Service currently stands at over 5200 full-time trained professionals that provide fire suppression and mitigation services for structure fires, petroleum industry incidents, and fire in nature (e.g. sulfur mines and agricultural fires). The country needs an additional 5000 firefighters in order to support its mission. There is a need for a national academy to train these men. Fire fighting and suppression services are delivered through the employment of equipment and personnel. The war and subsequent looting destroyed over 165 firehouses throughout the country. There are no tools or equipment in any firehouse. There is a need for major communication overhaul. There are no phones or portable radios to coordinate and communicate with. Major end items and support required near term include personal protective equipment, operational, maintenance, and training needs.

The greatest cost associated with the fire service comes from the need to purchase equipment to replace those items either destroyed by the looters during hostilities, or from ten years of minimal attention being paid to the operational maintenance of fire suppression equipment. Second, the lack of personal protective equipment (PPE) commonly referred to as 'bunker gear' or 'turn out gear' is non-existent. At over $2,500 per complete set of protective gear (helmet, PPE, gloves, haligan tools, self- contained breathing apparatus (SCBA), footwear, pioneer tools, and high-angle personal rescue gear) the cost for outfitting the current fire personnel throughout Iraq is significant. Besides purchasing SCBA, money will also need to be spent on the operation and maintenance of the equipment to include fitting, sealing, seal repair, and recharging of the air tanks. Estimated cost: $290M.

Civil Defense: Civil Defense is the main Iraqi agency responsible for all civil support during all emergencies. Civil Defense personnel must quickly respond to incidents emanating from the discovery of unexploded ordinance (UXO); improvised explosive devices (IED); and explosive remnants of war (ERW). They must possess the capability to respond to all natural and man made hazards and threats to include earthquakes, floods, epidemics, disease and WMD events. And they must provide emergency support to all aspects of an emergency to include command and control, operations, personnel and logistical support. To meet these requirements the Ministry needs a robust communications package of UHF, VHF, digital, mobile and FM capabilities. Logistics support include trucks, cots, tents, generators, lighting, stocked CD centers, medical equipment, blankets, food, hygiene material, wood, water, specialized engineering equipment, and a vast assortment of equipment to support the operation. Personnel need specialized training in Incident Command, size up, WMD, first responder, train the trainer, interagency workshops, UN request for Aid procedures, and other emergency management and disaster mitigation courses. Staff needs to be assembled from within governorates and across all ministries to work together, conduct coordination, and practice tactics and procedures. Estimated minimum cost: $57M.

Mine Action: The national mine action authority in the Ministry of Planning is responsible for coordination of removal of all explosive remnants of war. This involves several organizations, both local and international. Our omnibus State Department partner is RONCO, but we also fund numerous NGOs such as Mines Advisory Group (MAG) and Norwegian People's Aid (NPA). $61M is required to sustain 12-15 more local and or international organizations already part of the Oil for Food Program (OFF) in the north or working contracts in the central and south. This will include the governance piece of the National Mine Action Authority (NMAA), Iraqi Mine Action Center (IMAC) and three Regional Mine Action Centers (RMAC) already formed or paid for in the 03 budget through State. Iraq is the most heavily mined and UXO contaminated country in the world with 100s of casualties per month. The other telling problem is that they block or impede almost all other sector's [sic] development from transportation, reconstruction, electricity, education, agriculture etc. Estimated minimum cost: $61M.

Public Safety Facilities: Public Safety Facilities Repair, Remodel, and Refit in the post-conflict period following cessation of major combat operations, significant looting, vandalism, burning, and wanton destruction of public safety facilities occurred. Work must continue on the refurbishing of facilities to include glazing, painting, electrical, plumbing, and HVAC work. Office furniture, equipment, computers, and telephone systems will also need to be brought into the facilities. Significant cost will be required near term for repair, remodeling, refurbishing, refitting, operations, maintenance, and training needs. Estimated minimum cost: $92M.

Facilities Protection Service (FPS)

FPS. Facilities protection is critical to the reconstruction of Iraq and therefore a high priority to the CPA. Without a safe working environment, workers will be reluctant to return to the workplace. Facilities cannot be refurbished until there is protection against continuing vandalism and theft. If these issues are left unresolved, reconstruction will stall. To achieve adequate facilities protection would require $66.7M for two separately managed programs.

(1)The Facility Protection Program: FPS is currently a federated program under which Ministries and Governates [sic] each form their own fixed site security forces that operate under Ministry control in accordance with standards established by the Ministry of Interior. Ministries are currently working FPS costs into their individual budgets. Approximately 20K FPS guards are required to deploy countrywide by Jan 2004 to protect structures, contents and assigned personnel. With the current decentralized model for FPS funding, security issues are in competition with other important aspects of Ministerial budgets.

By centrally funding FPS requirements, the CPA ensures critical security needs are properly resourced. Under this scheme, Ministry of Interior is funded to administer the FPS account, disburse FPS funds to other Ministries, run a training program for FPS guards, and provide administrative and operational oversight of the FPS program, to include certifying guards and private security firms and inspecting FPS operations countrywide. Ministries will hire guards and administer their FPS programs IAW Ministry of Interior guidance.

Basis of estimate: Centralized funding for salaries ($24M – $100/man/month ave), uniforms ($1.2M – $60/person), MoI training program and FPS administration ($15M for both), vehicles for selected Ministries ($2.64M – 80 pickup trucks), communications ($3.63M for 400 handheld radios and 200 Thurayas), badging ($2.0M – 18 sites) and tribal pay for tribes along power lines and oil pipelines ($1.056M), mandated Regional Operations Center in each Governate [sic] ($7.2M – 18 sites). Estimated minimum cost: $56.7M.

(2) The FPS Professional Standards and Training Program: The FPS Professional Standards and Training Program. This program regulates FPS activities of each of the ministries, other public agencies and the activities of private guard companies. Facilities protection was originally provided by a unit within the police department. To many, this unit was perceived as a corrupt and unprofessional organization that was part of a larger scheme to misappropriate public resources. If facilities protection is to have the trust and confidence of the Iraqi people, a separate office is necessary with oversight authority and to establish, regulate and inspect the standards and training of the guards of the public facilities. $10M is required to develop a program office with a staff of 48 to provide administrative and operational oversight, to train and certify guards, and to inspect guard operations for all of Iraq.

Public Safety Training

Training. $274M is required to provide initial training to ensure the success of the overall reform of all departments within the MOI: Department of Border Enforcement, Iraq Police Service, Traffic Police, Facilities Protection Service and Fire & Emergency Services. The CPA seeks to reconstitute these departments while increasing the professional standards of law enforcement officers and emergency service personnel within its ministry. All MOI training programs (for existing personnel and as well as all new personnel) will be developed and presented in a manner consistent with the principles of democratic policing (service in a free society) through an educational philosophy that is based on international human rights standards.

The CPA seeks to use a Public Safety construct to achieve the training goals for all MOI departments throughout Iraq. This concept has two primary benefits. First, the basic training programs for most of these departments are similar, and many in-service and/or advanced training courses will require multi-disciplinary participation. All of these departments must work together in order to provide the best possible protection and service to the citizens of Iraq, and therefore it will be important for them to train in a cooperative environment. Second, the utilization of Public Safety Academies, as opposed to numerous specialized academies, will provide for economies of scale reducing training costs significantly while ultimately increasing the effectiveness of the law enforcement/emergency services functions.

The requested training is for the following organizations in the MOI: IPS, Traffic Police, Customs and Border Police, Customs and Border Investigators, Customs Inspectors, Immigration Inspectors, Detention and Deportation Officers, Border Guards, Passport Officers, Nationality and Civil Affairs personnel, Facilities Protection Service guards, and Fire and Emergency Services personnel. This request docs not duplicate training provided by the International Police Training requirement.

To support this effort, at least three Public Safety Academies must be built/refurbished (Baghdad, Mosul and Basrah), outfitted (furniture, operational equipment and supplies, training equipment and supplies), staffed and maintained. Reform courses will be conducted for all existing MOI police, traffic police, DBE personnel, fire and emergency service personnel country wide as well the delivery of in-service and advanced/specialized courses – approximately 60,000 existing MOI police and emergency personnel. The CPA as a part of its exit strategy will begin to develop the indigenous training capacity (Iraqi trainers) in all departments through the creation and delivery of comprehensive Instructor Development Programs (train-the-trainers). Further, it is possible that new basic recruit training will be conducted outside the country for approximately 34,000 police/traffic personnel in the next two years. Also, approximately 8,000 new DBE personnel will need to be trained, along with 5,000 new Fire and Emergency Services personnel.

Iraq National Security Communications Network

National security and first responder (police, ambulance, border and customs, key facilities protection, fire and civil defense) communications network with 911 dispatch capability for Iraq. Given Iraq's vulnerable security position, and complete lack of communications capabilities locally and nationally, a security and first responder operational communications network is imperative in the near term. Network would include a dispatch '911' capability so citizens could call one number in the event of an emergency instead of the current Iraqi system of separate numbers for each of the first responder assets, police, fire, or ambulance.

This dispatch capability would be operated regionally. The master site based at the national command center in Baghdad would receive and oversee all of the information and data relating '911' and other regional as well as national contingencies.

This network concept spans all the major population centers connected via a fiber backbone. This effort will be directly by the [sic] managed by the Ministry of Transport and Communications (MOTC), as well as the CPA communications support office. The MOTC has affirmed that it is able to support this network and provide the fiber that is required to link all of the centers and bring them back to Baghdad. The majority of the fiber is already in place and currently being reworked to be stood up over the next two months. Time is of the essence because of the complete lack of interoperable communications throughout Iraq.

Regionally, security forces are suffering due to the lack of communication in the hands of the Iraqi police, who are supposed to be performing patrolling duties but are reluctant to do so as they have no means to call for assistance. Fire and ambulance service, while not a matter of national security, is a matter of public health and safety and also dependent on an effective communications network for its ability to respond quickly. This in turn would instill confidence in the general security and services, and in turn the government providing them. $150M is needed to implement this network. Costs include installation of communications infrastructure and equipment, to include (but not limited to) hand-held radios, base stations, repeaters, communications towers, with associated installation, training, operations and maintenance costs. Separate network costs to support the first responder requirement are addressed in the Transportation & Communications section of this supplemental request.

NATIONAL SECURITY FORCES

Summary of Request. Iraq's military forces were decimated in the war and the surviving leadership was too closely tied to the Baath Party. An entirely new military structure is necessary to help stabilize the country and to demonstrate to the people that a professional military is part of the foundation of a constitutional democracy. $2,076M is required to fund the equipment acquisition needs of the New Iraqi Army, Support Agency/HQ, and Civil Defense Forces. This force is quickly growing from 4,000 toward a goal of 40,000 (3 divisions, 9 brigades and 27 battalions, including 3 heavy). Our goal is to have this force operational by August 2004.

New Iraqi Army (NIA)		
NIA Facilities	$745.4M	
NIA Equipment	$879.3M	
NIA Operations	$205.3M	
US Contract Training	$164.0M	
Purchased International Training	$ 6.0M	
Subtotal		$2,000.0M
Iraqi Civil Defense Corps (ICDC)		
Operations	$ 39.5M	
Salaries	$ 18.9M	
Vehicles & minor procurement	$ 17.2M	
Subtotal ICDC		$ 75.6M
Grand Total		**$2,075.6M**

New Iraqi Army (NIA). After the transfer of full sovereignty to an elected government, Iraq will need to have a militarily effective force for the defense of its territory that is non-political, representative of the country as a whole, and committed to protection of the country, not the perpetuation in power of a particular regime. Further, from the point of view of developing a working constitutional government in Iraq, it is important that such a force be under law-based civilian control and subject to public and parliamentary oversight. To form the foundation for such a force, the US and its coalition allies have begun to establish a New Iraqi Army that embodies these principles. The first battalions are already in training. As the units of this army become operational, they will participate directly in military operations in Iraq, led by Iraqi officers, and, like other coalition forces, under overall Coalition operational command. They will perform critical military tasks, including protecting the borders, route and convoy security, and control of territory, thereby reducing the burden on US and other coalition military units and speeding the day when those units can be relieved of security tasks in Iraq.

$2,000M is required to have 9 brigades (27 battalions) of the NIA fully operational by 2005. This program provides funds for US support for the costs of training, facilities, and equipment for a basic Iraqi ground force of 9 motorized infantry brigades, plus costs for setting up the necessary administrative support structures, reopening the military academy to provide a source of young officers, purchasing advanced training for military and civilian leaders, and standing up a new ministry of defense in consultation with the emerging Iraqi governmental authorities. Iraqi funds would be used to pay costs of salaries and subsistence. The initial equipment will make maximum use of commercially available military and civilian items. An initial armored and mechanized force (armored brigade) is also to be set up and will consist of one armor battalion, one mechanized battalion, and one mobile artillery battalion. Our intent is to use recovered and refurbished equipment to fill the equipment needs where possible. This also includes the re-establishment of depot repair and refurbishment of facilities within Iraq. Rolling Stock, engineer equipment, combat support and combat service support resources, crew-served weapons systems, and individual soldier equipment is also to be acquired. Also included is $137.2M for an Army Aviation Element. These prices are based on provision of a small number of helicopters (generally second hand) and procurement/refurbishment of a small medium lift capability, i.e., C130 equivalent. Together this will provide mobility through an Army Aviation element. Includes costs associated with purchase of necessary support equipment, e.g., GSE.

Overall strong attention and focus will be applied to using existing Iraqi resources to provide and maintain the equipment sets desired. Without this equipment, graduated battalions from the New Iraqi Army Training Center in Kirkush will have no equipment and will be meaningless units, incapable of offering assistance to Coalition Forces to provide stability. Other significant components of the NIA include:

NIA-Contract Training. An existing contract is in place to provide trainers to the New Iraqi Army training base at Kirkush, Iraq. $164M additional contract funding is required (included in the $2B) for further refinement and additional curriculum for the training mission. Continued funding support of the New Iraqi Army is critical to establishing a military capable of defending the post-regime nation of Iraq from emerging threats. The trained light infantry division plus armored brigade would free up US Army and Marine Corps units and their support elements.

Coast Guard. Included in the $2B requirement is $81.9M for a small coast guard force. Piracy, slave trading, terrorism and smuggling on the rivers and costal waterways of Iraqi are of great concern to the coalition. For this reason a modest funding requirement has been raised to combat these activities and protect vital Iraqi assets. Funding is based on refurbishment of existing vessels and the procurement of a small number of support craft, plus the equipping of a Naval Infantry Battalion to support critical port and on load/off load facilities. The requirement includes $41M for facilities, $37M for equipment and $3.9M for operations.

NIA- Iraqi Manned Defense Support Agency. Included in the $2B requirement for the NIA is $22M to set up the Iraqi Manned Defense Support Agency (DSA) in order to provide executive and support services to the New Iraqi Army and to lay the groundwork for the eventual establishment of a new Iraqi Ministry of Defense. Funding includes necessary equipment purchases ($3.5M) such as vehicles and automated command and control information technology systems. Also included is $2.5M for one year of operating costs.

Without this funding, the Coalition Provisional Authority will have to increase the Coalition staffing of the OSA office to administer the NIA. As the Iraqi Ruling Council grows in strength and ability to assume responsibility for post-regime Iraq, a functional Ministry of Defense, built on this foundation, will be critical to develop capability to deal with internal and external threats.

NIA- Professional Military Education Military Academies. The New Iraqi Army will need a professional Officer and NCO Corps and thus education facilities and equipment to train them. This $51.4M (included within the $2B) requirement will allow vehicles, training equipment, and training systems to help develop this professional Officer and NCO Corps. The requirement includes $46.2M for facility refurbishment, $4.4M for equipment and $0.8M for operating costs. Without these resources, the newly trained Iraqi armed forces will not have professional leadership trained in the ways and understanding of the role of the armed forces in a functional society. Coalition Forces will be forced to provide force structure to lead these leaderless units. Those Iraqi's [sic] who are appointed or promoted into leadership positions will not have a new professional paradigm to draw from and will naturally revert to the behavior and traditions derived from the former regime.

NIA- Military Education and Training. A crucial part of developing the nucleus of a professional Officer and NCO Corps is giving them the opportunity to attend overseas training in the professional development institutions of the different Coalition Partners. Embedding core values essential to a post-regime Iraq will take place during this overseas training of key Iraqi military personnel. $6M is required (included within the $2B) to send the best and brightest to professional military schools to better learn principles of civilian control of military, and the role of the military in a democratic society.

Iraqi Civil Defense Corps. The Coalition Provisional Authority urgently requires $75.6M to develop a military support organization in each Iraqi Governate [sic]. Each of the 18 governates [sic] will be assigned one battalion (approximately 600 strong) of a new paramilitary force called the Civil Defense Corps. These battalions will assist Coalition Forces in bringing stability to Iraq. They will be lightly armed and will be trained to act as guides, interpreters, conduct searches, and man checkpoints. They will require minimal training and will be trained and operate predominantly in their home areas.

Costs for these forces are mainly salary ($18.9M for 18 battalions at $70k/month plus special allowances) and subsistence, fuel, and other costs ($39.5M annual cost). An additional $17.2M is required to properly equip this force. The major procurement requirements are for 2 'jeeps' and 12 cargo trucks per battalion at $244K per bn) [sic] , communications gear (99 platoon net and 25 company and battalion net radios per battalion at a cost of $132.5K per bn), basic 'tented' infrastructure (overhead cover, ablutions, plastic furniture, and secure storage containers for each battalion at a cost of $15.1K per bn) and personal protective gear (cold weather gear, helmet and body armor for each member at $.5K per person). Vehicles are needed to speed ICDC response, particularly in rural sectors, ensure public perception of ICDC cooperation with Coalition Forces, and reduce ICDC reliance on Coalition transport. Radios are required to increase the flexibility and responsiveness of ICDC units and to reduce ICDC reliance on Coalition communications equipment. Basic Barracks Infrastructure is required to provide ICDC with suitable locations at which units can muster, train, secure stores, and, equally importantly, develop their identity. Finally, helmets and body armor are prudent personal protection items given an ICDC mission set that includes crowd and Riot Control, Route and Convoy Security, and Fixed Site Security.

Once trained and operating, these battalions will be a significant force multiplier, increasing the effectiveness and potentially freeing Coalition Battalions in their area of operations. Without these elements, Coalition maneuver [sic] battalions must continue their deployment to provide stability.

JUSTICE AND CIVIL SOCIETY DEVELOPMENT

Summary of Request. Reforming the Iraqi justice system, including prison system and courts, is prerequisite to improving confidence in justice outcomes for the country and laying the foundation for a constitutional democracy. After decades of corrupt Baathist party rule, the following investments are critical to reforming the system and establishing the rule of law.

Technical assistance for investigations into crimes against humanity		$100M
Security for Judges and Prosecutors		$200M
Witness Protection Program		$100M
Other technical investigative methods		$ 10M
Prison system technical assistance		$ 10M
Reconstruction & modernization of 26 detention and prison facilities		$ 99M
Two new 4,000 bed maximum security prisons		$400M
	TOTAL	$919M

Technical Assistance for Crimes Against Humanities* [sic] *Investigations. The Iraqi Justice system lacks the technical expertise needed to conduct investigations related to the systematic commission of crimes against humanity by the former regime. Specifically, assistance is needed in forensic analysis, document analysis and financial analysis. In the prosecution of crimes against humanities [sic] it is critical to have expert testimony to establish the commission of the crime and command responsibility of higher officials. This expert testimony is dependent upon an accurate and complete investigation. Thus, forensic analysis is needed to corroborate testimony concerning the manner in which killings were conducted. This expert evidence is critical in corroborating the testimony of persons having knowledge of the crime in order to establish the witness's credibility. Similarly, the analysis of documents showing the command structure of the regime is needed in order to prove knowledge and criminal responsibility by members of that command structure. Finally, financial analysis is needed in order to demonstrate the squandering of state assets for the personal benefit of governmental officials. These resources are not available in Iraq, and the investigation of these crimes is a massive undertaking. The technical assistance for humanitarian investigation was based on a cost of $200,000 per expert for a minimum 500 experts and investigators. This cost includes an estimated salary of $100,000 for each expert and a logistics cost of $100,000 for each expert for a total of $100M for 500 experts. **Estimated Minimum Cost: $100M**

Security for Judges and Prosecutors. Iraq is facing regular attacks by foreign terrorists and members of the former regime. As a government is formed, these matters need to be addressed in the criminal justice system. To the extent possible democratic societies use the criminal justice system to prosecute terrorists located within their borders. When this occurs, the Justice system then becomes a source of attack. Under the prior regime, the Justice Ministry was marginalized and controlled by the state. Thus the Ministry of Justice now has insufficient resources to address the security requirements faced by a Justice system that is the target of terrorists precisely because it is being used to combat terrorism. Consequently, judges and prosecutors need to be supplied with personal security details and the physical structures of the courts need to be hardened against terrorist attack. None of these items are currently in place and the judges and prosecutors in Iraq present an inviting target to the terrorists. Consequently, a massive undertaking is needed to strengthen the Iraqi court system so that it can fairly adjudicate these cases. This task requires a massive undertaking.

The Security Program cost estimate was made based on a pilot security program that was established on an emergency basis for the central criminal court of Iraq. That program, which provides security for 15 judges, costs $10 million on an annualized basis. In order for the security program to be effective, it needs to be extended to more than 15 judges as well as making modifications to the infrastructure of the courts. This amount comes to approximately 50,000 per judge and includes vehicles, security details, weapons and communications capability. Thus, funds in the amount of $20 million would provide security for approximately 400 judges and prosecutors. There are currently 860 judges and prosecutors in Iraq. The courts in Iraq need to be hardened with a variety of physical and technical security measures, including X-Ray devices, bomb detection devices, protective blast walls and other physical and [sic] improvements. There are 130 court buildings in Iraq, and this proposal would allocate approximately 1.3 Million per courthouse. This security package is thus reasonable and would enable the judiciary to function free of fear and intimidation. **Estimated minimum cost: $200M**

Witness Protection Program. Not only is Iraq facing daily attacks from terrorists, organized crime is flourishing in the disorder created in the aftermath of the war. Organized crime members and terrorists function in a similar manner even though their motivations are different. Indeed, terrorist organizations often fund their activities through organized crime. In order to effectively prosecute these offenses, witnesses to the commission of these offenses are required. These witnesses can not be developed unless there is a mechanism in place to protect them. Consequently, a witness protection program is needed in order to allow victims as well as criminals who become government witnesses to testify without fear of being killed by the reaming [sic] members of the organization against whom they are testifying. Without an effective witness protection program, it is simply not possible to prosecute these cases.

Protecting witnesses is one of the single most expensive components of criminal prosecutions in that it involves short term and long term protection. The witness must be relocated far outside the danger area, which may involve international relocation for terrorism and organized crime cases. This estimate is based on $200,000 per person per year. This would allow for 100 families with an average of five persons each to be relocated for a total cost of $100M. **Estimated minimum cost: $100M**

Other Technical Investigative Methods. Although the prior regime used technical means to gather information, this was not done for the purpose of securing admissible evidence for a criminal prosecution. Long and bitter experience with terrorism and organized crime has demonstrated that technical evidence gathering is critical in the investigation and prosecution of these activities. Because in a democratic society these crimes should be addressed through the due process system of the Courts, the ability to gather such evidence is required in order to prove criminal responsibility. Iraq has become a focus for terrorist activity, and the use of unclassified technical means of gathering evidence is critical to the successful prosecution of these cases. An initial allocation of l0M for this purpose will enable the Iraqi government, under coalition supervision, to start using this unclassified technical evidence gathering means. This cost estimate is based on an extrapolation from a similar $1M dollar package that was used in Kosovo, which has one tenth of the population of Iraq. **Estimated minimum cost: $10M**

Prison System Technical Assistance. This request is for 100 international prison experts for six months, to identify suitable establishments for reconstruction, training and monitoring of prison operations in accordance with international requirements. The technical assistance requirement is based on a six-month cost of $100,000 per expert for a minimum 100 experts and investigators. This cost includes an estimated salary of $50,000 for each expert and a logistics cost of $50,000 for each expert for a total of $10M. **Estimated minimum cost: $10M**

26 Detention and Prison Facilities for Juveniles and Adults. Prison facilities are a vital component to the credibility of the criminal justice system and essential in establishing the security of Iraq. This expenditure provides for the new build, reconstruction and modernization of 26 adult and juvenile detention and prison facilities. This expenditure would provide a wider geographical coverage than under the previous regimes. It would ensure that the establishments conform to international accepted standards. They would increase prison capacity by 10,000 (i.e., from 11,200 under current plans to 21,200) and free military resources currently tasked to operate detention facilities. At least local 4,800 jobs would be created in the prison service. The estimated average cost per facility is approximately $2.3 million, $0.5 million in start up costs and $1 million in initial operating costs. **Estimated minimum cost: $99M**

2 New 4,000 Bed Maximum Security Prisons. This spending would allow two new maximum security prisons to be constructed in accordance with international standards, with inbuilt security features that reduce staffing costs and achieve economies of scale. These facilities would house 4,000 prisoners each (8,000 additional prison beds) and would take four years to construct.[118] Funding is needed immediately for engineering and design and to start construction. **Estimated minimum cost: $400M**

ELECTRICITY

Summary of Request. The electrical power infrastructure in Iraq is in a perilous state. Without significant investment in the immediate future, the situation will actually deteriorate further. The CPA has been managing the sector since the war and fully understands the problems. The UN, which has been active in the sector since 1996 and working with the World Bank, has recently completed a needs assessment of the electrical power infrastructure. We are fortunate to have the results of this assessment which match

[118] In another version of the document the following sentence was added: 'The addition of these two prisons would bring the total prison capacity to 27,700 beds.'

our own findings. To make significant progress in a short period of time, the following investments must be made immediately into the electric power infrastructure.

Generation	$2,900M
Transmission networks	$1,550M
Distribution networks	$1,000M
Communications and control	$ 150M
Institutional strengthening	$ 25M
Security	$ 50M
TOTAL	$5,675M

Generation. The level of generating capacity in Iraq, at present, varies between 3000 MW and 3300 MW. The estimated demand is 6500 MW and is expected to increase significantly as the economy grows, industry is restarted and oil production increases. It is hard to overstate the problems caused by the shortfall between generating capacity and demand of approximately 50%. It is the major cause of discontentment of the Iraqi population and, quite apart from the physical discomfort, is preventing industries, factories and oil refineries from operating. This exacerbates the problems inherent in having large numbers of people without employment or an income.

The lack of generating capacity and the geographic location of that capacity has created major differences in the power distributed to people in different parts of Iraq. In particular, the citizens of Baghdad have suffered disproportionately, as generating capacity is concentrated in the South and North, These imbalances have led to political divisions between the areas that are net generators of power and those that are net recipients.

As a means of sharing power between consumers, deliberate load-shedding is being used where local lines serving a neighborhood are switched off, so that other lines may be switched on. Although there is no alternative at this time, this practice causes much greater wear on the components of the already decrepit electrical power infrastructure.

Generation levels are low because the power stations were targeted during the Gulf War of 1991. In addition, the sanctions that followed meant that it was very difficult to procure materials to maintain power stations properly. Management practices also deteriorated, including acting under political pressure to maintain generation levels rather than to undertake long overdue maintenance work. Although some improvements were made under the UN Oil for Food Program, the timescales, costs and the level of verification required under this scheme made progress slow.

The result is that almost all power stations in Iraq are in very poor condition, generating well below their rated level and are extremely unreliable. Unplanned outages are daily events. Without urgent remedial action, the situation could get much worse. An intensive program is now underway to increase generation levels to pre-war levels, stated as 4400 MW, by undertaking repairs to power stations and through other actions to put into production units not currently in production for various reasons. There are three main means of increasing generation within Iraq:

- Rehabilitation of existing power stations and providing adequate spare parts
- Installation of new gas turbine power stations
- Construction of new thermal power stations

The most cost-effective means of increasing generation is to rehabilitate existing power plants – both gas and thermal units. Rehabilitation results in the generating units being restored to a condition close to that when they were first commissioned. Because there is no requirement to perform either engineering design or civil construction work, the costs and timescales are very much less than building new plant [sic]. We intend to rehabilitate a significant proportion of the total generation capacity, prioritizing those that are not in service at present.

Gas turbine units can be installed within a 3 to 7 month timescale. We intend to install and commission at least eleven 40 MW gas turbine units in a number of strategic sites before the end of 2003. In addition, we plan to build some larger gas turbine power stations, of 150 MW capacity, to meet short to medium-term demands. Gas turbine units may also be run on several types of fuel and we shall ensure that we are not overly dependent on the availability of certain fuels.

Thermal power stations are more expensive and typically take up to three years to build. However, they are capable of providing high levels of generation, using fuels such as crude oil or heavy fuel oil (some of which are waste products). They are also comparatively cheaper to maintain. As such, thermal power stations will form a vital component of Iraq's electrical power generation capabilities. Several thermal power stations have been under construction for many years, with progress interrupted by wars and by delays in the UN MoU program. We shall review the status of each thermal power station construction project and, where continuation makes financial and technical sense, propose to complete the work under an accelerated timetable. In other cases, we need to commence construction of new thermal power stations and ensure that sufficient funding is in place to enable completion. The costs associated with each area of increased generation are:

Rehabilitation of existing power stations	$1,000M
New gas turbine generation	$ 800M
New thermal power stations	$1,000M
Maintenance	$ 100M
Total	**$2,900M**

Transmission networks. Transmission networks perform the task of transporting power from where it is generated to the area which [sic] it is consumed. In Iraq, the transmission networks are comprised of the 400 KV network, with its 22 substations, and the 132 KV network with approximately 200 substations. Before the recent war, the transmission networks were in a degraded but operable state. Inadequate maintenance and poor operational procedures had resulted in corroded power lines, damaged towers, switchgear with frequent faults, damaged transformers, and a multitude of other faults which degrade network performance and that risked the safety of Electricity Commission staff.

Since the recent war, continuing acts of looting and deliberate sabotage on a vast scale have reduced the capabilities of the transmission networks to a point where the national grid barely functions. The network, as it currently stands, is highly unstable resulting in frequent blackouts, and is incapable of delivering sufficient power from power stations to population centers, most notably Baghdad.

Some 400 KV power lines have been almost completely destroyed. For example, the Coalition Forces recently surveyed 1175 km of lines and found 623 downed towers out of a total of 2554. However, in total, it is hard to provide accurate figures of the number of towers and miles of power lines that it will be necessary to replace. Although all Iraqi line repair crews are fully deployed to repair power lines, it is evident that the scale of the task is far beyond their capacities. Therefore, we urgently need to bring in international engineering firms specializing in this type of work, to repair the lines and substations.

As generation capacity increases over 2004 and beyond, the transmission networks will also have to be increased in capacity. This shall necessitate the implementation of new lines and new substations. We intend to use the services of specialist consultants to analyze the electrical power infrastructure so as to design changes to the transmission network, especially the addition of new infrastructure. Our estimates for work urgently required to restore the transmission networks with adequate spare parts, and to add capacity to support additional generation are based on our surveys and those of the UN/World Bank assessments.

Repair of 400 KV lines	$200M
Repair of 132 KV lines	$300M
Expansion of 400 KV lines	$250M
Expansion of 132 KV lines	$250M
Rehabilitation of substations	$300M
Additional substations	$250M
Total	**$1,550M**

Distribution networks. Distribution networks deliver power carried over the transmission networks to local areas. The distribution networks were relatively unaffected by the recent war but were in a highly deteriorated condition beforehand. Equipment is operating without adequate electrical protection and is generally overloaded. The majority of 33/11 KV substations suffer from the effects of being switched too frequently (due to load shedding), a lack of maintenance and insufficient augmentation to cater for new loads. There has also been, and continues to be, damage to distribution networks caused by acts of looting and vandalism.

We intend to commence a program of rehabilitation and replacement of distribution network infrastructure. However, it must be recognized that the scale of the problem is such that this program will have to take place over several years. Based on the information supplied by the UN/World Bank assessment, we anticipate the costs of the work we need to undertake until the end of 2004 as being:

33/11KV substation rehabilitation and development	$150M
33KV network rehabilitation and development	$ 56M
11KV network rehabilitation and development	$185M
Distribution transformer rehabilitation and development	$125M
0.4KV network rehabilitation and development	$204M
O&M material and equipment	$180M
Vehicles, machinery, training, studies and review, etc	$100M
Total	**$1,000M**

Communications & Control. The lack of an automated monitoring and control system means that it is not possible to effectively monitor power distribution or enforce load shedding plans. This lack of monitoring capability has impeded CPA's efforts to reestablish an effective and efficient electrical sector in Iraq. The Electricity Commission requires a Supervisory Control And Data Acquisition (SCADA) system to provide this monitoring and control capability. SCADA is a distributed system that collects data from individual power substations, and delivers it to a central monitoring and control centre. It consists of several components, including:

1. A National Dispatch Center (NDC) to provide national oversight of the electricity network;
2. One or more Regional Control Centers (RCC's [sic]);
3. Multiple Remote Terminal Units (RTU's [sic]) located at the 400 kilovolt (KV) substations and the 33KV substations. These RTU's [sic] capture critical data from the substation equipment;
4. Communications equipment to deliver data from the RTU's [sic] to the RCC's [sic] and NDC. Communications between the substations and the NDC will be provided via a fibre optic network, a radio network, or microwave network, or a combination thereof, in order to minimize costs. Several communication networks already exist in varying states of repair and capability in Iraq, and these will be utilized if possible.

The SCADA system will be implemented extremely rapidly in order to gain management control of the distribution of electricity in Iraq. Such an implementation depends upon the timely provision of funds in order to procure the equipment, personnel and other resources required to perform this task.

This SCADA system will provide critical improvements to the management of the electricity grid in Iraq. It will permit the accurate monitoring of the electricity grid of Iraq on a national basis. In addition, it will assist in the assessment of equipment failures by providing remote alarms and warnings. Finally, it will assist in the fair and equitable distribution of electricity to the Iraqi population. The cost of the full SCADA system implementation and associated communications infrastructure is estimated at $150m.

Institutional strengthening. The Electricity Commission is institutionally very weak. In order to build an effective organization capable of managing the continued operation and development of the electrical power infrastructure in Iraq, we wish to invest in strengthening the institution. This shall be done by rehabilitating the buildings, providing consultants embedded within the organization, developing a Master Plan for continued development, and investing in extensive staff training. The estimated cost of providing this program is $25m.

Security. There is little point in investing in transmission line repairs if they cannot be secured. The Coalition Forces are overstretched and cannot provide adequate security to electrical power infrastructure. Moreover, they will not be in Iraq indefinitely. Therefore, other arrangements must be made. It is our intention to strengthen the existing Electricity Commission Power Police and to augment their capabilities with contracted helicopter surveillance. The estimated cost of providing an improved service is $50m.

OIL PRODUCTION

Summary of Request. The coalition has assisted the Iraq Ministry of Oil in making progress towards reestablishing pre-war production levels. However, we must do more to lay the foundation for the national economic recovery, and to ensure that Iraq has the revenue for a self-sustaining government. Factors that must be addressed include continued repair of war damage and repair of looting damage. At the same time, continued terrorist sabotage activity is hampering progress. The funds requested will be used to repair the infrastructure, counter the terrorist threat to protect the current investments, and to compensate for the losses that are a direct result of previous successful terrorist attacks. Once production has stabilized, funds will then be used to continue to improve the Iraqi petroleum production systems with the ultimate goal of restoring pre-war production levels.

Detailed Overview of Requirements
(Dollars in Millions)

Oil Investment			
Requirements:			
Rapid Pipeline Repair Capability	$ 55		
Topping Plant Acquisitions	$ 125		
Port Facilities Upgrades	$ 9		
Petroleum Distribution	$ 68		
Infrastructure Security	$ 60		
Personnel Security	$ 8		
Qarmat Ali Water Plant	$ 125		
Qarmat Ali Water Study	$ 5		
Retain Subject Matter Experts	$ 5		
Oil Reservoir Management	$ 40		
Pump Station and Pipeline for North Rumalia	$ 40		
Repairs to NGL Plant	$ 15		
Repairs to LPG Plant	$ 50		
Repairs to Bulk Storage	$ 20		
Infrastructure Repair	$ 575		
Subtotal Oil Investment		$ 1,200	
Oil Products Purchase			
Requirements:			
Petroleum Product Imports	$ 900		
Subtotal Oil Products Purchase		$ 900	
Grand Total			**$ 2,100**

Oil Investment

Rapid Pipeline Repair Team Contract. Multiple acts of sabotage and looting, and mechanical failure due to historically poor maintenance have resulted in extended downtime on main pipelines. There is a need to extinguish any associated fire and effect repairs to the pipeline without allowing the remainder of the line to drain. The pipelines range in diameter from 8 to 46 inches and are used to carry either crude or refined products. Failure to repair these pipelines results in significant lost revenues to the Iraqi people...as much as $7 million per day in the case of the Iraq-Turkey crude oil pipeline. Funds will be used to provide a quick reaction pipeline repair team in order to return pipelines to operational condition within 96 hours of notification that the area is secure. **Estimated minimum cost: $55M**

Topping Plant Acquisitions. Import of refined petroleum products is currently costing $3-4 million per day. Acquiring additional Topping Plants will have a direct effect on reducing this outlay, and thereby reducing the future need to appropriate funds for these imports. Topping plants are the first step in the process of converting crude oil to refined petroleum products, and can provide diesel, LPG and kerosene directly from crude in remote locations. In several cases, there is a need for refined products closer to the oilfields than to the established refineries. Acquisition of 4 'Topping Plants' to be placed strategically throughout Iraq will ensure quicker, cheaper, and more efficient delivery of refined products to the end users. This will have the direct effect of reducing the need for imports, and reducing the need for additional funds for imports. **Estimated minimum cost: $125M**

Port Facilities Upgrades. As stated previously, there is an urgent need for additional imports of petroleum fuels. A large part of the task will involve the use of port facilities. While some of the port infrastructure currently exits, there is a need to ensure safe operations for the downloading of hazardous materials – gasoline, diesel and kerosene. Funds will be used to upgrade these facilities to meet the targets for imports. $6 million will be used to dredge the Khawr Az Zubayr waterway. $2 million will be used to remove sunken vessels impeding traffic. $1 million will be used to hire a barge to unload confiscated smuggling vessels. **Estimated minimum cost: $9M**

Petroleum Distribution Requirements. The vulnerability of the pipelines has created the need to establish redundancy in the petroleum distribution system; namely, enough trucks to meet distribution requirements when interruptions in pipeline flow occur. Funds will be used to purchase 200 fuel tankers and 250 Liquefied Petroleum Gas (LPG) trucks to meet this need. **Estimated minimum cost: $68M**

Oil Infrastructure Security Requirements. As stated before, security of the oil infrastructure is a key concern. Even with quick repair of damaged facilities, losses due to terrorist activity can easily total in the tens of millions of dollars. Investments made to thwart these attacks will certainly pay for themselves. Funds will be used to train and equip an oil infrastructure security force. The purpose of this force is solely to protect the oil infrastructure, and will not duplicate other security efforts being undertaken. Current security is provided by coalition forces and an inefficient assortment of local security services. **Estimated minimum cost: $60M**

Personnel Security Requirements. Funds will be used to provide continuous personal security for the Minister of Oil and his Director-Generals, as requested by General Abizaid in his 28 August memo to the Secretary of Defense. The life of one of the Director-Generals was threatened as recently as late August, so this is a critical requirement. **Estimated minimum cost: $8M**

Qarmat Ali Water Plant. Repair of the Qarmat Ali Water Plant and associated Cluster Pump Stations (CPS) is required to provide water injection for the Southern Rumaylah oil fields, a process critical to maintaining current production rates and preventing damage to the reservoir during production. Funds will be used to provide the necessary equipment, materials, and personnel to complete emergency repairs to restore oil production to pre-hostility levels. Failure to complete this work will adversely impact oil production rates, and will drastically affect long-term production of this oilfield. **Estimated minimum cost: $125M**

Qarmat Ali Water Study. In order to make the most efficient use of the Qarmat Ali Water Plant, and decrease the likelihood of causing costly, permanent damage to the oilfield, an extensive geologic study is required to determine the appropriate locations for the injector wells. Funding this study will result in a significant return on investment in terms of both higher production rates and lower lift costs. Failure to fund will result in continuation of current inefficient practices and potential damage to the oilfield. **Estimated minimum cost: $5M**

Retain Subject Matter Experts. Bringing Iraq from zero production using antiquated systems to full production using modern technology requires the assistance of those with specialized training and considerable experience in the oil industry. Like many of the other requests, this funding will directly impact the speed with which production and exports reach pre-war levels. **Estimated minimum cost: $5M**

Oil Reservoir Management. Modern techniques and technologies are available to improve the location and management of oil reservoirs. Making use of the assets available will maximize production from existing reservoirs, find new reservoirs, and ensure optimum production from all petroleum sources. This investment will improve efficiency and ultimately increase the total available supply of oil. **Estimated minimum cost: $40M**

Pump Station and Pipeline for North Rumalia. Process water is essential to the operation of the Degassing Stations and the NGL plant in the North Rumalia Oil fields. Current source of process water for these facilities is the Qarmat Ali Water Treatment Plant, which is under reconstruction. When reconstruction is complete, water from Qarmet Ali will primarily meet the demands of water injection and process water will still be inadequate. Due to the poor condition of the water treatment plant and the deteriorated state of the existing pipeline network, the current system will not be able to meet peak demands for process water in North Rumalia. The new pump station and associated pipeline will meet process water needs in North Rumalia. This new network will be isolated to allow Qarmet AH to meet the demands for water injection more efficiently. With a new pump station and pipeline, production from the North Rumalia fields will be more reliable. **Estimated minimum cost: $40M**

Repairs to NGL Plant. The Natural Gas Liquification plant is currently receiving repairs that will make the plant operable, however, it will still be in extremely poor condition. The poor condition of this plant will result in unstable production of feedstock to send to the LPG plant. Rebuilding a gas turbine compressor, repairing the water system, replacing excessively worn fin fans and replacing electrical cables will make the NGL plant more stable and slightly increase production. This work will increase the reliability of LPG production from the LPG plant. **Estimated minimum cost: $15M**

Repairs to LPG Plant. Current repairs to the LPG plant will make the plant operable to produce OCT 03 LPG goals. In order to make pre-war production of LPG, another LPG unit must be brought online. This requires replacing missing motors and installing new cable that was looted after the war, rebuilding the burnt control room, and replacing looted electrical switchgear. These repairs will make it possible to achieve prewar LPG production. **Estimated minimum cost: $50M**

Repairs to Bulk Storage. Repairs are needed at the Bulk Storage facility. Work includes replacing damaged chillers, refurbishing utilities and reworking the control room. **Estimated minimum cost: $20M**

Infrastructure Repair. The restoration of the Iraqi oil infrastructure is critical to the overall success of the Coalition Provisional Authorities [sic] mission. The oil infrastructure provides for the generation of significant revenue for the Iraqi national budget and delivers refined products to fuel the economy and the quality of life for the Iraqi people.

In June 2003 Task Force Restore Iraqi Oil (RIO) and the Ministry of Oil (MOO) completed a Rough Order of Magnitude for the restoration of the Iraq Oil Infrastructure and initiated a funding request. A workshop was conducted in July with RIO and the MOO with the end product being the Restoration of Iraqi Oil Infrastructure Work Plan. This plan included the project management plan, scope of work as defined by the list of 220 projects and a rough order of magnitude budget estimate for each project.

This work plan is an integrated plan that was carefully developed and coordinated with every MOO operating company and TF RIO. The plan was developed with the focus being to restore the Oil Infrastructure to pre-war production levels. Each project in the work plan has an impact on the restoration of the infrastructure and an impact on production levels.

The Work Plan has been sub-divided into three phases. Phase One projects are to be complete by October 2003, Phase 2 by December 2003, and Phase 3 by March 2004.

Phase 2 and 3 combined represent eighty projects. These projects will provide for a 20% increase in production of crude which represents conservatively $12 million per day of revenue for the Iraqi people.

Several other critical projects need to be completed, but are longer-term projects that were not included in the aforementioned Work Plan. Funds could be used to complete improvements to the Upstream (ground to refinery) and Downstream (refinery and beyond) sectors of the oil industry as well as complete long delayed repair of 1991 war damage. Projects proposed include the following:

Upstream Sector. Improvements in the upstream sector include enhancements to the export system that will increase the flow capability, thereby, increasing export capacity. The funding will also initiate the development of new oil and gas fields. New oil fields in both the north and south regions are planned to produce no less than 250K barrels per day. Development of two new gas fields, both north and south, will provide natural gas to meet power generation requirements, lessening the use of diesel and residual oil. The fields will provide liquefied petroleum gas (LPG) for the domestic market in the amount of 200 million standard cubic feet per day.

Downstream Sector. Funding will allow the commencement of the planned new refinery that will increase domestic refinery capacity by 70K barrels per day to meet the increasing demand of the local market and to reduce import requirements. Improvements will be made at current refineries to add new reforming units. These units improve the quality of domestically produced gasoline, thereby reducing the need for environmentally damaging tetra-ethyl lead additives. Hydrodesulfurization units will also be added to lessen the content of sulfur in diesel to reduce sulfur dioxide emissions to the atmosphere. Expansions to the northern gas processing plant by the addition of a new processing train will increase the capability to meet the needs of the newly developed fields in the upstream sector. Increased storage capability for products and LPG will be initiated to stabilize operation of the refineries and gas plants to meet seasonal demand and improve distribution efficiency. Distribution will also be enhanced by an improved product pipeline network that will reduce road transport with its inherent inefficiencies and hazards.

Repair of 1991 war damage. The supplemental funding will allow the rebuilding of the lubricating oils plant in the Baiji refinery to meet the increasing market demand for these products. Additionally, rebuilding of product storage tanks at the Basrah refinery and at some of the product distribution storage depots will allow a more stabilized refinery production operation as well as avoiding seasonal shortages as product demand fluctuates.

These investments will accelerate the growth in Iraqi export dollars, and thereby shorten the period during which the Iraqi government will be reliant on international aid. **Estimated minimum cost: $575M**

Oil Products Purchase

Petroleum Product Imports. Interruptions to the flow of crude to the refineries, difficulties at the refineries themselves, and interruptions to the flow of refined product to the cities have created the need to import more petroleum products than originally projected. Funds will be used to cover the difference between Iraqi demand and refinery production, and to establish and maintain a 30-day reserve in all major products to ensure no interruptions in basic services due to future terrorist activity. The main products required are Liquefied Petroleum Gas (LPG), used for cooking; kerosene, used for heating in the winter months; benzene, for auto fuel; and diesel, to fuel larger equipment and power generation. Failure to provide any of these will directly affect the quality of life of the average Iraqi. $600 million will be needed in the first quarter to compensate for the large difference between demand and production, and to build the 30-day reserve. $300 million will be required for the remainder of the fiscal year to compensate for continued production shortfalls while maintaining the reserve. **Estimated minimum cost: $900M**

PUBLIC WORKS

Summary of Request. $3,7l0M is required to meet critical water and sanitation requirements. Our overall priorities in implementing the various public works programs are:

1. Providing potable water.
2. Improving efficiency of the distribution system.
3. Improving sewerage facilities and solid waste management.

Although our immediate thrust concentrates on the restoration of conditions to pre-war conditions, we also intend to emphasize improving and expanding services and coverage in all governorates. Our initial requirements to help the Iraqi people improve their public works include

Raising potable water access across Iraq	$2,830M
Reducing water loss from 60% to 40%	$ 30M
Increasing sewerage service in cities to 15%	$ 697M
Improving solid waste management	$ 153M
TOTAL	$3,710M

Different assessment studies by International organizations have all agreed that the above public work programs are the best way to improve the performance of the sector and the living conditions of Iraqis. This work should commence as soon as possible and be completed by the end of 2004.

Currently, the responsibility for the delivery of basic municipal services is centrally controlled in terms of budget allocation and priority setting. Over time the responsibility for basic services will be devolved to the governorate and the municipality level. These programs will also help develop the capacity of governing authorities, and demonstrate to local authorities and the central agencies (such Ministry of Finance and Public Works) on proper administrative procedures for major public works.

Raising potable water access across Iraq 90%. $2,300M is required to provide potable water access to most of Iraq. Our plan to reach that level involves first working up to 75% access, then working further improvements to reach 90% access for cities, towns, rural areas and villages.

The coverage figure in urban areas at this time is approximately 60% however the supply is not 100% of the time and the quality is suspect. The existing supply system is stretched to its limit and system strengthening/master planning is required before coverage can be increased by any significant percentage. Master plans have to be completed before accurate figures on the incremental costs of service coverage can be given. Infrastructure required will include larger feeder water mains, service reservoirs to balance daily and hourly flows and the provision of dividing and control valves to allow the creation of supply zones and mains to be shut down for repairs and maintenance. The estimated cost to increase urban coverage to 75% is $1,000M and is based on extending coverage to 2.7M people at a per capita cost of $370/capita for water treatment and network. This per capita cost estimate is based on theoretical analysis using a hypothetical residential area.

To raise coverage levels across the country to 75%, supplies to rural areas and villages will have to be improved. Many small towns and villages are served by tankers coming many miles to provide potable water on a frequency of once a day, once every 2 days and in some cases once every 10 days. To improve coverage will require the installation of treatment plants capable of treating saline water (reverse osmosis), reticulation systems and additional tankers. To achieve the coverage target approximately 2.2M additional people in rural areas will have to be served. Four techniques have been identified for serving the additional people. Details and costs are:

Extension of existing urban systems	$370/capita
The use of compact units plus local reticulation	$186/capita
Tankering potable water to them	$373/capita
Using well to supply water	$267/capita

Estimates have been made of the population to be served by the different supply methods and the total cost of the program has been estimated to be $530M.

To raise supply levels across the country to 90% will require improvements in supplies to cities, towns, rural areas and villages. To improve coverage across the nation, we intend to install treatment plants capable of treating saline water (reverse osmosis), reticulation systems and additional tankers. The increased populations served by this program are:

- Urban 2.7M people
- Rural 1.3M people

Using the per capita construction costs quoted above the cost of raising universal coverage of potable water to 90% is $1300M.

Reducing water loss from 60% to 40%. Reducing water losses in an arid environment is a national priority. Water losses are currently estimated at 60% of the potable water produced from the water treatment plants. $30M is required to repair the water distribution networks to ensure that safe water (free of pathogens and other harmful chemicals) actually reach [sic] families is a priority. This will also require a full inspection and mapping of the networks. Reducing water losses has a three fold effect of:

- increasing coverage because there is more water available;
- reducing operational costs because less water is required; and
- reducing the risk of illness because leaks into the system are repaired preventing the contamination of potable water.

An initial reduction to 40% ($30M) involves the rectification of visible leaks. There are approx. 15,000km of water main in Iraq and using consultants' studies the cost per kilometer for the rectification of visible leaks has been estimated to be $500/km. The cost of the program is estimated to be approximately $30m allowing for the variables in the network and the scale of the leaks likely to be encountered.

Increasing sewerage service in cities to 11%. The current coverage across Iraq is estimated at 6%. This situation is unsatisfactory in that wastewater can come in contact with children causing illness and death. As water supply increases the situation will become more critical as more water becomes available adding to the amount of wastewater with the potential to spread disease. CPA requests $697M as initial seed funding to increase sewerage service to 11% in urban areas which will involve extending treatment facilities and collection systems within cities. This will require innovation in treatment techniques such as aquaculture and alternative collection system such as low pressure systems. The funding will be used to test treatment and construction techniques so that larger sewerage programmes will be more effective.

To increase the coverage to the target of 11% translates to an additional 0.9M people being served. The cost per capita for providing sewerage services has been estimated to be $775 of which $570 is for the collection system and $205 for treatment. The estimated cost of the program is $697M.

Improving Solid Waste Management. There is no overall solid waste management strategy for Iraq. $153M is required to finalize a strategy which must include the construction of correctly designed landfill sites, equipment to operate the landfill site, regular collection of solid waste requiring vehicles, education campaigns to sort rubbish at source and demonstration/startup recycling plants. Recycling can help to protect the environment, generate employment, and reuse valuable nutrients from food-waste and sewage for safe utilization in horticulture, aquaculture, forestry and food production. More needs to be done to ensure the safe management of medical and industrial waste as these pose a serious health hazard to those who work with waste and to children who play in unprotected landfills. These more hazardous wastes need to be treated at source.

The capital cost of such a program has been estimated based on 50 landfill sites at $0.5M/site, $0.5M/site for operating equipment, 40 collection vehicles for each site at $50,000/vehicle and six demonstration plants at $0.5M each. The total cost of the program is estimated to be $153M.

WATER RESOURCES

Summary of Request. The water resources infrastructure in Iraq suffered some damage after the war due to looting and vandalism, however, the overall functionality of the system was not significantly affected. Still, investment in this sector is strategically important to the Coalition both immediately and over the long term. To meet our immediate objectives, CPA requires $935 M to repair and improve water and sewerage services.

Agriculture and irrigation sustain the lives of a large sector of the population and water supply is essential to prosperity. Although many of these initiatives increase the condition or service beyond prewar conditions, investment in the projects included below will clearly demonstrate a commitment to the people of Iraq in important and visible ways.

Pumping Stations. $75M is required to replace pumps and electrical control appurtenances for 125 priority pumping stations (of 270 stations). Each pumping station has, on average 4-6 pumps for the purpose of reliability, maintenance and operational flexibility. Pumps vary in size, capacity and lift, but average cost is $125K per unit (includes pump, motor, starter and control box) [600x$125K=$75M]. Approximately half of the inventory (600 pumps) require immediate replacement with western standards equipment. Maintenance, refurbishment, and replacement of irrigation pumps have been largely neglected since 1980. New equipment delivered and installed under FFO contracts is of low quality and reliability.

Replacement of irrigation pumps on a large scale will demonstrate to the people of rural Iraq that the Coalition is dedicated to improving their lives and livelihood. This project is needed immediately as farmers throughout the country are negatively affected by the current situation. This project would improve the current system beyond the prewar condition.

Replace Standby Generators. $75M is needed to replace standby generators for key pumping stations, barrages, and dam sites. There are about 100 key points (of ~ 300) in the vast system of reservoirs, barrages and pumping stations that require backup generators to assure electricity for running the pumps, providing municipal water, irrigation, lifting the gates on barrages, and operating other essential emergency equipment. The standard 750Kw generator costs ~$750K [100 units x $750K = $75M]. Minor site work (construction) will be required.

Generators are necessary to return the operation and reliability of pump stations to prewar standards throughout the country. The current state of the national power grid does not allow pump stations to function adequately. Pump stations require continuous power to operate and the grid currently provides three hours on and three hours off, at best. Lack of reliable, continuous electricity from the grid has caused a significant reduction in irrigation pump service and benefit to farmers.

The installation of this equipment will demonstrate the Coalition's commitment to the rural areas of Iraq. There is a common belief that many people are worse off now with respect to public services, than prior to the war. This would reverse that trend.

Rehabilitate irrigation and drainage systems. $130M is needed to rehabilitate old operating irrigation and drainage systems for improving water use efficiency and water quality. Every existing system needs major rehabilitation, consisting of cleaning irrigation and drainage canals; replacing regulators and sluice gates and lining irrigation canals with concrete to reduce water losses through infiltration. There are 20 projects which serve approximately 500,000 hectares which, when rehabilitated, would result in water savings of 25-35%.

Maintenance and refurbishment of the irrigation infrastructure has been neglected since 1980. This requirement would increase the efficiency of water delivery and use throughout the country to higher than prewar levels. Projects would be concentrated in the southern Governorates and can be started immediately.

This effort would directly benefit the agricultural community by improving the efficiency and reliability of water use. As a nation, Iraq could determine how best to allocate the water conserved, either to additional irrigation, municipal and industrial uses, or ecological/ environmental restoration. This project would signal strong support for hundreds of thousands of rural Iraqis whose support is critical to the success of the coalition. The many village and tribal leaders need clear examples of improvement to gain the confidence and backing of their members.

Completion of 10 major irrigation/drainage projects. $130M is required to complete construction of 10 major ongoing irrigation and drainage projects. Numerous worthy projects were initiated during the past few years which need completion. Five major irrigation projects will have concrete lined canals for water savings, and will be connected to 5 drainage canals to ensure that saline water flows to the main outfall drain (MOD) and the sea, reducing the salinity loads to the Tigris and Euphrates Rivers. The total new irrigated area is approximately 400,000 ha.

Projects would open new, more productive areas to agriculture, allowing less productive land to be retired. This would result in a net savings of water and increased production. Projects would also have a positive environmental impact, by reducing high salinity return flows into the Tigris and Euphrates Rivers.

Construct 11 rural water supply dams. $25M is required to initiate construction of 11 rural water supply dams in Western Al-Anbar governorate desert (roughly $2.3M per dam). There are many semi-nomadic desert dwellers, with villages and livestock dependent on the sporadic flows of ephemeral streams during a short rainy season. There is a need for small dams at 11 sites to provide water for villages and livestock. Engineering and design can begin now with construction following immediately thereafter.

These projects would more than double the prewar amount of water available to the villages and herdsmen of western Iraq, who suffer from water shortages. This project would demonstrate to the people of the western desert that resources are distributed fairly. Building trust and allegiance in this vast, remote region is strategically important because this area borders Syria, Jordan, and Saudi Arabia.

Rural Groundwater Supply Projects. $60M is required to initiate rural groundwater supply projects in [the] Kurdish region (~100 villages, average cost $2M x 30 clusters = $60M). Many villages in the north, particularly in the Kurdish areas, depend on groundwater for village and livestock water supply. Groundwater availability varies, and the villages that are clustered together can maximize their supply reliability and availability by interconnecting the systems and building a common storage tank and distribution system. There are numerous such clusters of 3-5 villages that can be interconnected. Engineering and design can begin now with construction following immediately thereafter.

Connecting water supply systems would provide a measure of insurance against mechanical failure or groundwater availability in any single village. The project would improve water supply to greater than prewar levels. Investment in the north of Iraq is important to demonstrate the commitment and fairness of the coalition.

Dam safety repair and major structural rehabilitation. $ 100M is required to make repairs identified by a Corps of Engineers Dam safety team which completed an assessment of 16 dams and barrages. The critical repairs are currently underway to return structures to prewar levels. Dams and barrages requiring repair are distributed throughout the country with the large dams in the north, and other structures along the Tigris and Euphrates Rivers. Many shortcomings are readily repairable with little design or lead time required. For more significant work, engineering and design can begin now with construction following immediately thereafter.

Completion of this work would ensure the overall safety and reliable operation of the water control infrastructure in Iraq above prewar levels. Investigation of questionable practices and repair of structures would put to rest numerous recurring concerns that coalition forces have discovered. For example, constructed over layers of soluble gypsum, Mosul Dam is particularly import to address.

Basra/Umm Qasr water supply pipeline and water treatment plant. Currently, water to Basra only flows through an open, 260km long canal, only half of which is concrete lined. There are large evaporation losses along the way, and saline water infiltrates into the water supply. A pipeline would effectively reduce water losses by 33%, ensuring reliability and quality of supply. The savings in water would be sufficient to supply Umm Qasr as well. Engineering and design is ongoing, but $200M is required to initiate first stage construction (an additional $800M is required to complete the plant).

This project would provide higher quality raw water to Basra, the second largest city in Iraq. Umm Qasr, historically receiving poor quality, highly saline water, would also benefit. This project would purchase the necessary pipe from the factory in Basra, employing several hundred workers.

Environmental Restoration (Euphrates). $50M is required to reconnect the Euphrates River, which is contained within a 200km dike system, to villages via regulators and culverts. A major flood control levee system was built along much of the lower Euphrates River. The effect was to cut off access for the numerous villages and farms to flood waters and floodplains for their livestock and irrigation of palm trees. Box culverts and regulators would be installed at regular intervals to serve the villages, and provide easy access to the Euphrates waters. Only limited engineering and design is required and sites are independent, so this project is ready for immediate execution.

This effort will benefit the lives of tens of thousands of citizens who will regain access to the Euphrates River and floodplain for farming and livestock. This access will rectify the actions of the former regime and improve the lives of the people along the lower Euphrates well beyond their prewar condition.

Environmental Restoration (Hawizeh Marsh). $50M is required to construct regulators on Kasara Escape and Al Sweeb River to establish control of outflow from the Hawizeh Marsh (2 regulators at approximately $25M each). Kasara Escape and the Al Sweeb River carry the discharge from the Hawizeh Marsh to the Euphrates River near Qurna. Installation of control structures (regulators) would allow management of the outflow and hence the water level within the marsh. This increase in control will greatly assist the effort to expand the Hawizeh Marsh by improving the efficiency of water use. While the marshes will likely never cover the same vast areas that they once did, water conserved can be used to maintain optimum water levels in the existing marsh and/or allocated to former marsh areas for restoration purposes. Engineering and design can begin now with construction following immediately thereafter.

Completion of the regulators would be a significant first step in the investment to restore the marshes of southern Iraq. This project would be seen as a positive move by the Coalition to rectify some [of] the environmental and socioeconomic tragedies of the past 25 years. These regulators, as part of a larger effort, will improve the environment and the lives of Marsh Arabs beyond prewar conditions.

Basra Channel Regulators – Tidal Channel Flushing. $40M is required to flush out canals in Basra. A network of canals extends throughout the city of Basra. All of these canals contain stagnant water and debris and present a health hazard to a large number of people. This project would allow the natural rise and fall of the tidal cycle to flush out the canals at frequent intervals. A series of six gates are needed where each canal joins the Shatt Al-Arab. Because the canals can be separated as individual loops, a pair of gates, one at each end of a loop, can be alternately opened and closed when the tide rises and falls, thus creating a current to flush the canal. This project is ready for execution pending the availability of funds.

This project would improve the health and environment of tens of thousands of citizens in Basra, a long neglected city. This end state would be an improvement over the prewar condition.

TRANSPORTATION AND TELECOMMUNICATIONS

Summary of Requirements. The Coalition requires $835M to restore transportation and telecommunications to basic levels of service. $513M is needed for transportation (civil aviation – $165M; ports – $45M; and railroads – $303M) and $322M for telecommunications (IPTC[119] & CPA Network Systems Architecture Planning & Analyses – $124M; Iraqi communications systems – $109M; and Iraqi communications operations – $89M).

[119] This should probably read ITPC.

Civil Aviation. $165M is required to complete airspace and airport opening: Funds will be used to complete the reopening of Baghdad and Basra airports. In addition, there are approximately 120 airports in the country of Iraq including the major airport, Mosul, to the north. No funds have been made available in the current year budget for any airport with the exception of Baghdad and Basra. Funds will be used to repair the infrastructure, obtain avionic equipment, and train aviation personnel to international standards and to provide safety and security systems. A more detailed listing for each of these categories follows.

Infrastructure: Funds will be used to repair control towers, repair sewage and electrical systems, water system repair, refurbishment of runways and taxiways, fuel system repairs and basic cosmetics (parking lots, escalators, glass/glazing, etc). Estimated minimum cost – $95M.

Avionic Equipment: Funds will be used to purchase, control tower console/ radio replacement, install precision approach path indicators, install and provide maintenance for radar systems at Basrah and Mosul, to repair/replace ILS landing systems at various airports, install fiber optic cables for communication equipment, to repair/install airfield substations and lighting vaults, and install AFTN communications systems. Estimated minimum cost – $40M.

Training: Iraqi aviation personnel require training to meet the minimum international (ICAO) standards. Personnel include air traffic controllers, flight standards, equipment technicians, mechanics, ramp personnel, aircraft safety inspectors, etc. Estimated minimum cost – $10M.

Safety/Security systems: Funds will be used to conduct security assessments, install internal and external security systems meeting ICAO standards, purchase ground support equipment, purchase crash, fire and rescue equipment, install airport surface detection equipment, repair/replace airport. Estimated minimum cost – $20M.

Ports. $45M is required to fix serious shortcomings at the port of Umm Qasr which is a vital transportation node in the Iraqi economy. The port of Umm Qasr is without electric power from the grid. It lacks water for vessel servicing, habitability and fire protection. It lacks perimeter fencing and security lighting. While some aspects of this are being addressed by specific Bechtel taskings, the port requires additional equipment for handling cargo both container and break bulk. The current level of port activity is not sufficient to fund these urgently required needs.

Railroad. $303M is required to restore the railroad to a functioning system. Funds would be spent to repair, rehabilitate the following areas of rail infrastructure:

Rehabilitation/Restoration of Buildings and Other Facilities: Serious looting and vandalism in the immediate aftermath of the active fighting, and extending to the present time, has left the railroad virtually devoid of the tools, machinery and spare parts necessary to maintain their plant and equipment. Fewer than half of the fifty mainline locomotives received in 2002 are still in operating condition and the number shrinks almost daily. Hundreds of older, but still potentially useful, locomotives sit out of service. Passenger cars have had air conditioning and other equipment removed and interiors vandalized, all with no means to repair. Freight cars sit out of service for lack of parts as simple as air hoses. Buildings have been looted to the extent that roofing has been torn off and door and window frames removed. Estimated minimum cost – $70M.

Repair/Renewal of Track Structure: The track structure has suffered from a combination of severe neglect ever since the first Gulf War, coupled with what money there was being largely wasted on ill-advised new construction schemes. Virtually the entire railroad is in a state of deferred maintenance, some so severe as to present a serious risk of derailment. In addition, mechanized track machinery has mostly all been looted and vandalized so as to make it unusable. Two bridges remain out due to war damage. What little emergency funding has been made available is being spent on the very worst section, but overall the condition of the track structure continues to deteriorate. Estimated minimum cost – $125M.

Replacement of Signal and Communications Systems: The mainline is being operated using a jury-rigged radio network set up by the Army. There has already been one collision, resulting in a fatality that would have been avoided had the signal system, which used to exist, been in service. In addition to the obvious safety issues, the lack of signals and communications put severe limitations on the capacity of the line. At present, the line between Umm Qasr/Basrah and Baghdad only has the capacity for one additional pair of trains though there is the potential for significant new business on the line. Estimated minimum cost – $65M.

Repair/Acquisition of Locomotives and Cars: The rolling stock situation is alarming due to the lack of repair facilities and spare parts. There are twenty new locomotives of the 2002 order still at the manufacturer's plant waiting for payment. Prompt acquisition of these locomotives would help avert a short-term crisis. A critical commodity in winter is LP Gas and additional specialized cars to transport this product are sorely needed. Passenger equipment is in a deplorable state and presents a seriously negative public image. Estimated minimum cost – $ 25M.

Development/Acquisition of Intermodal Facilities and Equipment: A major source of possible new business is the handling of intermodal containers. The port of Umm Qasr has the potential capacity for handling a significant increase in container traffic, and international container traffic could develop to and through Turkey to continental Europe. At present, Baghdad is the only inland point capable of loading and off-loading containers, and even there it is done very inefficiently using a 50ton crane. Inland container terminals must be built at selected locations and equipped with suitable handling equipment, and additional container cars acquired, if the railroad is to be successful in developing this important business. Estimated minimum cost – 15M.

Bridges: The Ministry of Transportation and Communication's initial assessments of the Railroad bridge network in Iraq has revealed that only 2 bridges (the Akashat and the Al-Fattah) will need to be funded for repair. Estimated minimum cost – $3M.

IPTC[120] & CPA Network Systems Architecture Planning & Analyses ($124M).

CPA Enterprise Systems – LAN/WAN/PSTN. The CPA Communications intends to launch comprehensive technical and business process studies of CPA and ITPC operations. The objective is to provide a detailed systems study that will lead to needed systems architectures prior to undertaking network design and construction. The output of these studies will feed directly into capital upgrades of the Iraqi public telephone network. Many current and planned systems upgrades, such as increasing fiber optic trunking, linking into international gateways, standing up packet switched data networks (for high volume transactional data and Internet traffic), and wireless cellular networks require immediate expansions to the Iraqi switching and transmission systems infrastructure. In addition to supporting planned increases in network traffic, yet additional infrastructure is required to support background networks for

[120] This should probably read ITPC.

managing these networks. These new systems include operations support systems and billing support systems. The CPA requires a parallel, yet modest, investment to stand up Enterprise Systems for supporting the management of the Iraqi PTT (ITPC) and what will be its newly established regulatory agency. Estimated minimum cost: $54M.

CPA Enterprise Systems – Applications. This increment of investment capital and direct expense is aimed at bringing modern business automation into the business infrastructure of the Iraqi telecommunications environment. These investments include reengineering Iraqi PTT business practice around COTS Enterprise Software systems. These systems go by a variety of names such as Enterprise Resource Planning (ERF), Supply Chain Management (SCM), and Customer Relationship Management (CRM). These names all connote the automation of business processes. The amounts requested include computer equipment, intrapremises networking gear, and enterprise level software licenses for both network-based, and premises-based software applications. The CPA will engineer links between its governmental operations to the ITPC and Postal Commissions, with links to regulated commercial telephony service providers. Estimated minimum cost: $27M.

Postal IT Architecture and Systems. The Postal system of Iraq remains antediluvian. Seed investments of Information Technology will allow the Iraqi Postal authority to reengineer its business practices and to support them with automated systems such as letter and package bar coding, establishment of ZIP codes, letter and package tracking systems, and linkages into financial accounting systems. Estimated minimum cost: $9M.

WiFi Capabilities for ITPC. These investments will allow the ITPC to build wireless Internet Protocol (IP) networks to support its internal business operations. The IP network will link into its public network and to Wireless Fidelity (WiFi) networks for mobile users. The WiFi network will, in turn, promote capabilities provided by unregulated service providers, but with provisions for security and network management unavailable in the former domain. Portions of these monies will be used to build prototype capabilities at CPA headquarters and field locations for supporting intra-ministerial communications. Estimated minimum cost: $19M.

CIO Function – Operations. The CPA MoTC Communications organization is being increasingly seen as the organization to manage intra-ministerial and intra-agencies communications and information management. As such, this Chief Information Officer function requires bringing standardized business processes and office automations systems to harness the information stovepipes now being built in the rush of post-war action. The CIO will manage all standard IT functions including those currently being provisioned by DoD and its Defense Agency (DIS A) and support contractors. The CIO will manage all voice and data services at the Tiers 2 and 3 levels, and, upon request, build interfaces to those Tier 1 systems managed by Joint Coalition Forces. Estimated minimum cost: $15M.

Iraqi Communications Systems (IPTC[121] and Other Ministries) @ $109M.

Public Safety Information Services Network IOC. The Ministry of Interior has requested the development and stand-up of an enhanced services, wireless network. The network will be used by 'Security and First Responders', including police, fire, and EMT teams. Little or no capabilities exist within the Iraqi infrastructure either for centrally-dispatched communications, nor point-to-point communications. The Iraqi Self-Defense Forces are also prospective clients of the Public Safety Network as they stand up and eventually relieve Coalition Forces. The funds for this program will focus upon validating systems

[121] This should probably read ITPC.

concepts being developed jointly among OSD, CJTF-7, CPA (MoTC) and other CPA ministries. Upon systems validation, CPA will oversee the rapid build out of an operational network using either publicly available wireless networks, or special purpose government funded networks. Estimated minimum cost: $73M.

Commercial TV and Radio: Management and Licensing. Under the purview of CPA resides the commercial broadcast network over open airwaves and what will be an emergent rebroadcast (cable) network over fixed wired media. The funds will be used to restart and expand commercial broadcast operations, including installing modern broadcast transmitters. Behind the camera, funds will be used to modernize the business practices of the regulated television and radio industry. Funds will also be used for spectrum enforcement. Rogue broadcasters will be licensed, have their spectra moved, or altogether shutdown. Estimated minimum cost: $10M.

Numbering Schema and 911 Initiative for IPTC[122] and Independent Wireless Service Providers. Funds will be used to develop a nationwide numbering scheme for Iraq, and a '911' emergency response system. (Note: Outside of the USA, the 911 name goes by '112'.) The Iraqi ITPC will be first to implement the nationwide numbering scheme that will stand up country, area, and city codes. Concurrently, the commercial wireless service providers will build 911 response features into their systems, at their own cost. Estimated minimum cost: $4M.

Replacement of Back-up Generators for Outside Telecom Plant. Site surveys have revealed that significant numbers of emergency diesel generators have either been looted or remain inoperative due to lack of maintenance and spare parts. Preliminary economic analyses suggest scrapping the remaining inventory of ITPC owned assets. Funds will be used to buy computer automated generators for providing immediate power needs and for anticipated growth requirements in central offices and local loop plants. Estimated minimum cost: $22M.

Iraqi Communications Operations (Miscellaneous @ $89M).

Iraqi-FAA Operations. Upgrade Baghdad airport facilities to modern aviation standards. Conduct Engineering studies at other major Iraqi airfields. Build and modernize departure and in-route air traffic control (ATC) center communications. Funds will form a pool to support the communications need of industrial ministries which depend upon the publicly switched network. Estimated minimum cost: $14M.

Technical and Management Training for ITPC. Train personnel on vendor-specific equipment for wired network upgrades, and for reprogramd [sic] Iraqi workers to the newly licensed wireless service providers.[123] This training will fall outside of programs instituted by the Ministry of Education. Estimated minimum cost: $5M.

Emergency Repairs and Payment to ITPC Network – Not Elsewhere Specified. As the ITPC continues site surveys to battle-destroyed switching centers and sabotaged trunk lines, the bill to repair or replace this equipment continues to rise. Funds request are for a CPA- managed reserve that will be used to restore essential services and network upgrades required to support interfaces into privately owned networks and into international gateways. Estimated minimum cost: $70M.

[122] This should probably read ITPC.

[123] Another version of the document reads: 'Fund will be used to train personnel on vendor-specific equipment for wired network upgrades and to train Iraqi workers to work for the newly licensed wireless service providers.'

HOUSING AND CONSTRUCTION

Housing. There has been virtually no housing activity across Iraq over the past 20 years. There is a need for dramatic increase in the scope of Government funded housing projects. $100M is required to dramatically increase the amount of housing activity underway and to give a strong initial push to the Housing sector. Our intent is to initiate work leading to the initiation of construction on at least 3,528 new houses over the next year. This construction will be a significant challenge in that it will require the development of a housing infrastructure to supply local water, sanitation, and electrical capacity that does not currently exist.

We expect that this initial effort will be augmented with a greatly increased rate of construction activity in the year following, as the construction infrastructure becomes more robust and able to accomplish an increased rate of home production, despite dramatic increases in the cost of construction materials.

$100 million dollars will create 7 housing communities, totaling 3,528 housing units, as well as the supporting infrastructure such as basic services, roads, a primary school, two secondary schools, a clinic, a place of worship, and a market in each community. This amount will address 0.35% or a tiny fraction of the total housing need in Iraq; however, this may be enough to start an effective housing program, which will require an approximate $2 billion annual budget. This amount will also enable the Ministry of Housing and Construction to develop and implement a short term housing program that will lead to long term success and stability. This short term housing program would hire architects and engineers to begin the master planning and design for each major city in Iraq, begin construction of several affordable housing communities throughout the country, provide the ministry with the resources to invest in home financing and mortgage insurance programs that will encourage investments from the private sector, and invest in developing the resources and capabilities of the housing construction industry in Iraq.

Iraq faces a housing crisis and has a current need for more than a million housing units; although, this need will not be met in the short term, construction of new housing projects will show the Iraqi people that both the Coalition forces and the new Iraq government are taking immediate steps to address their housing issues. The policies implemented by the former government resulted in a society dependent on the government. Also, Iraq has experienced three wars within the last 20 years. Over these 20 years, Iraq has been ruled by an oppressive regime and has lacked a social housing program to address the issues of the urban poor, normal population growth, and internally displaced families evicted from their homes due to ethnic strife. The housing shortage continues to be exacerbated by the return of large numbers of refugees and ex-patriots [sic] to Iraq. If these housing issues are not addressed quickly and effectively, the homeless population in Iraq will continue to grow and threaten the security and stability of Iraq. More and more families will become desperate for shelter and lose faith in the new Iraqi government. The Ministry of Housing and Construction (MOHC) has already started the construction of 1,008 housing units in Iraq and has coordinated with the United Nations (UN) to begin construction of 7 housing projects that would create 504 housing units each or 3,528 total housing units. These UN housing projects will be funded under the UN Oil-for-Food program. The $1.6 million housing budget for 2003 is well short of what the new Iraqi government will need to develop an effective and successful housing program. The supplemental budget would fund the construction of 7 additional housing communities in cities throughout Iraq making a positive impact in each of those areas. With the additional supplemental funding, the current housing program would begin construction of 8,064 total housing units throughout Iraq. These new housing construction projects will illustrate to the people that the new Iraqi government is making progress and cares enough to address their housing concerns and issues. In addition, this supplemental funding would create additional housing construction projects employing approximately 14,815 laborers over a 20 month period and infuse money back into the Iraqi construction industry. The new Iraqi government must continue to address these housing issues effectively by showing concrete results in the form of new housing communities since it is both a social and economic problem. Failure to do so will result in political and economic instability throughout Iraq, as the people will continue to feel that their government does not legitimately care about their problems.

The $100 million supplemental budget will support the current housing program and start construction of approximately 7 communities or 3,528 housing units throughout Iraq. The housing program will incorporate proper urban planning and design so that housing areas and zones can be identified and existing urban areas can support continued expansion and growth. This program will accommodate anticipated increases in the population over time and avoid overcrowding that leads to high levels of unemployment in cities. This program will also fund the Ministry of Housing and Construction's ability to design new projects, contract funded projects, and provide construction oversight and program management for next year's anticipated housing construction effort. Over time, the private sector's role in the housing industry will grow while reducing the government's role in directly building these complexes. Until then, there is an immediate requirement to support designing, contracting, providing oversight, and program management for next year's anticipated housing construction effort in order to develop a successful and effective long term housing program that will contribute to Iraq's economic and social stability.

Public Buildings. There are many requirements for Public Buildings across Iraq. This has been an active area which can be further accelerated. $130M is required to dramatically accelerate our schedule to define contracts, which are currently undefined as a result of direction to Iraqis to re-start previously ongoing contract work early in the construction efforts within Iraq. The supplemental will also allow the Ministry to continue ongoing work or initiate new work at an even faster rate as a result of increased infrastructure capability and equipment purchases. There are also requirements for improvements to Ministry of Housing and Construction facilities across the Governates [sic] and Regions of Iraq. These improvements, new equipment, and new facilities, will provide significant new capabilities to the Ministry to support improved construction rates. The facilities will also provide appropriate protection for new equipment and construction infrastructure necessary to support resurgence within the construction industry in Iraq, protecting an investment necessary to jump start the Construction Industry.

If this additional $130 million is not funded it will prolong the disruption to the government operations and thousands of governmental employees of Iraq, have an adverse ripple effect on the overall economy and slow down the transition to the new Iraqi government. This effort really only is a stopgap measure and does not fully provide for the full needs of the reconstruction of the Iraqi building infrastructure. The economic consequence of not funding this supplemental budget request will have immeasurable indirect costs in the continued degradation of the employee's work places and family life's [sic].

This $130 million will fund the following types of projects:

1) 1,325 basic repair projects at $40,000 each for $53 million. This basic repair work will put a building back in operation after years of neglect and deferred maintenance.

2) 140 refurbishment projects at $250,000 each for $35 million. This refurbishment work will allow for the upgrade of currently obsolete building components and limited construction.
3) 6 major reconstruction projects at $7 million dollars for $42 million. These major reconstruction projects will replace all of the buildings comments[124] to current international safety and building standards.

These projects will allow these public buildings to successfully meet the overall operational and serviceability needs of the building occupants. The various building components that will be maintained, repaired or replaced in these projects will be: general cleaning, doors/frames/hardware, windows/glazing, walls, floors/walkways, stairwells, plumbing, plumbing fixtures, painting, electrical power, light fixtures, electric fans/HVAC systems and other construction incidentals.

Roads and Bridges. Investments in the amount of $240 Million must be made on Iraq's Road and Bridge infrastructure as a prerequisite to begin the economic redevelopment of the nation. A robust transportation network is imperative for efficient movement of essential products such as fuel, wheat, water, construction materials and equipment, and other supplies which fuel the economic foundations of Iraq. The current disrepair caused by lack of maintenance over an extended period of time affects over 74,000 KM of major highways and local road systems. In addition, a total of 32 bridges are currently damaged and will not adequately support the high volume of transportation required to support national recovery. We have determined the necessary repairs and system improvements for recovery from the 15 years of neglect and minimal improvements will cost $12 Billion. The proposed $240 Million for the Supplemental Budget for FY03[125] will provide enough money to fund the remaining War-damaged Bridges on the Priority Projects list and invest a significant amount of funds into Expressway 1 for critical equipment and paving of gaps in the project that are deteriorating due to military convoys. The $240 Million is only 2% of the total Road and Bridge repair, maintenance, and system upgrades required, but this amount will nonetheless make a significant down payment on beginning the required recovery effort.

Expressway 1, the major north-south route in Iraq (an absolutely vital asset) is a 146 KM stretch of road that has never been completed. Many portions have deteriorated such that they will require significant repair and rehabilitation in order to support any sustained amount of traffic. This same highway is also in need of major rehabilitation and maintenance north of the capital city. Similarly, local roads and bridges are the essential lifeline for farmers to bring goods to market yet they have not received adequate maintenance or construction for decades.

There are many bridges throughout Iraq that have not been properly maintained or repaired. It is estimated that 160 bridges may, because of war damage or poor maintenance, become unusable within the next year unless immediate maintenance and repair is accomplished. Funding should be focused on repairing and maintaining safe and sound bridges and roads that will support the long-term growth and development of Iraq. This will be accomplished through a two part program. Part one, the Main Artery Road and Bridge repair Program, will begin repairs and maintenance on roads and bridges which traverse the most highly traveled corridors across Iraq. Composed of 700 major bridges and 42,000 KM of the largest highways, these form the backbone of the Iraqi transportation system. Part two, the

[124] Another version of the document reads: 'building components'.
[125] This should probably read 'FY04'.

Governate [sic] Road and Bridge Repair Program, composed of approximately 600 bridges and 32,000 KM of secondary and rural roads, will address the road network which supports the manufacturing areas and rural communities which play such an important part in Iraqi commercial activities. With the proposed Supplemental Budget for the FY03, we will be focused on Priority Bridge Projects and Expressway 1 and spend $20 Million dollars to start emergency repairs on some of the 160 critical bridges in Iraq.

The Iraqi Ministry of Housing and Construction, working with their counterparts from the Coalition Provisional Alliance [sic] and the Governates [sic], have determined that the following funding areas will be required for repairs and maintenance as discussed previously but also will provide for badly needed new roads, highways and expressways. While the total funds for the proposed Supplemental Budget Request in FY04 is $240 million which is only 2% of the total amount required, it will make a dramatic initial impact to support of the recovery of the Iraqi road and bridge system.

- In order for Iraq to complete projects started before the war, it will cost $174 million dollars to make emergency maintenance repairs and return the transportation system to prewar capacity. This includes $100 million for Express Way #1, $16 million for emergency maintenance, $28 million to complete ongoing projects started in FY03 and $30 million to complete war damaged projects started in FY03.
- Concurrently with these projects, work will begin on an additional $66 million in rehabilitation, maintenance, and new roads and bridges to address 15 years of neglect and poor planning. This will be distributed as follows: $20 million to conduct additional maintenance for structures and roadways to a minimal level of service; $10 million to rehabilitate intercity and rural roads in the governorates; $10 million for new intercity and rural roads in the governorates; $10 million for rehabilitation of highway and expressway systems including roads and bridges; and $16 million for the addition of 20 km of new roads that connect towns, hamlets and market centers among each other.

A comprehensive review of the Iraqi Highways, Roads and Bridges infrastructure, that combines the efforts of the Ministry of Housing and Construction with the Governates [sic], will help set a new direction on how Capital improvement in the National Highway System and local Roads and Bridges are allocated and disbursed. The CPA Ministry of Housing and Construction has projected a required $1.253 billion of funding for the Roads and Bridges program in 2004. The $240 Million Supplemental Budget Request for FY03 will provide an immediate boost to this effort and provide the trail blazing through the projected difficulty of implementing such a massive and critical program in Roads and Bridges. While these funds are only a fraction (2%) of the funds required, they will reverse a trend of marginal spending and bring roads and bridges back to a safe operational condition where economic growth is not deterred by poorly maintained highways or neglected local road systems.

HEALTH

Summary of Request. $850M is required to bring health care in Iraq up to pre-sanction standards, but updated to current technologies. The pre-war standard is untenable due to the abysmal erosion of health care over the past 14 years (only an average of 4% of facilities saw any rehabilitation or reconstruction in the past 14 years). Health care vital statistics and purchasing power adjusted health care expenditures in Iraq trail many countries in the region. For example, while Turkey has an estimated infant death rate of 46 per 1000 live births, this statistic for Iraq has been reported to be as high as 108 per 1000. In addition, as many as 13% of all Iraqi children die before they reach the age of 5. Without the requested funds, the Iraqi people will continue to suffer from substandard health care. The three main areas of emphasis are:

Major new children's hospital		$150M
Refurbishing pediatric hospitals, primary health care services and outreach		$393M
Repair/replacement of equipment		$300M
Partnership for Healthcare		$ 7M
	TOTAL	$850M

Major New Children's Hospital. $150M is required to start basic construction on a tertiary pediatric treatment facility in Basrah. Other than the low life expectancy, no other Iraqi negative health statistic stands out like those related to infant, maternal and child health. With over 41% of the total population being 14 years old or younger, there is not only a need now for specialty services for this population, but the population distribution indicates that there will be a significant 'baby boom' in Iraq within the next 7 to 10 years. This request is for funds to build a state-of-the-art tertiary care children's hospital in Southern Iraq. The hospital will be designed to handle top level care for pediatric oncology, plastic surgery, burn treatment, specialized surgeries and high risk pregnancies with the latest technologies in radiology, ultrasound, physical therapy and other procedures. This facility will be the base for cutting edge research and postgraduate development for Iraqi physicians. This effort will create a pediatric hospital that will be a visible sign of the transformation of the health care system in Iraq. Total cost of this facility is estimated between $500M to $700M depending on the final number of tertiary specialties offered. Capital and benchtop equipment, general medical supplies and equipment, general logistics supplies and equipment, salaries for consultants, salaries for support staff and other requirements will come from donors or other sources of funding.

Hospital Refurbishment. $393M is needed to reduce infant and childhood deaths by 50% through the provision of services that can address the underlying causes of these dismal statistics. New efforts to be undertaken throughout the country to provide those necessary public health efforts that can have definitive impacts on early mortality and morbidity (immunization, nutrition counseling, clean water and appropriate sewage disposal activities). Major shortfalls of all pediatric and primary health care facilities tend to be with major structural subsystems. The medical gas system is largely nonexistent or need [sic] extensive repairs. This supplemental aims to refurbish and reequip every one of the 1200 primary care clinics in Iraq and 5 regional maternal and pediatric referral centers in Basra, Al Najaf, Erbil, Baghdad and Mosul. The result will be a network of clinics that will have the capability to provide those basic maternal and infant support services so critical to positive birth outcomes. In addition, when they identify high risk cases, they will finally have the ability to transfer the case to one of the 5 regional centers of excellence for maternal, infant and pediatric care. Our strategy is to rehabilitate 200 of the 240 hospitals and 900 of 1200+ Primary Health Care Clinics. Major structure subsystems are all in dire need of repair, rehabilitation or expansion (water/sewage, electrical, HVAC and med gas especially). Cost of construction is 1/10th of US standard per sqft in general construction, 1/5th in specialized medical construction and 8/10th in specialty construction. Materials for health care are not indigenous and will have to be imported which will raise the low cost of construction in this country to European construction cost levels (up to 80% of US health care construction costs in specialized areas such as OR, radiology, laboratory etc).

Equipment Replacement. $300M is required to repair the deplorable state of the nation's 240 hospitals. Early studies indicate that as much as 50% of the equipment in these facilities is in desperate need of repair or replacement. All equipment is poorly maintained. This includes everything from; incinerators to dispose of medical waste, x-ray machines, in hospital lab equipment and especially generators. While a nearly emergency effort is underway to supply generators, the initial effort will only cover 30 to 35 hospitals, then quickly expand to 150 hospitals. Training staff to use this equipment is equally important. Iraq lacks credentialed, skilled bio-medical engineers and technicians and has a significant shortfall of technically up to date engineers and technicians (skill sets run to pre-sanction levels). We estimate that 100% of current staff will require retraining. An additional 25% staff increase is required to properly man these hospitals. This equipment and associated training effort should provide a much needed upgrade to the remaining facilities and if basic infrastructure services such as sewage and potable water can occur at the same time, the hospitals in Iraq may more closely come to resemble 'hospitals' in many parts of the rest of the world.

Partnership for Healthcare. $7M is required to facilitate the establishment of partnerships between American health care organizations/leaders and selected Iraqi healthcare centers. We envision a consortia of health care institutions in the U.S., international donors, and U.S. government agencies for the purpose of providing professional education, technical advice and support, equipment, supplies, pharmaceuticals, and managerial expertise to selected Iraqi healthcare centers. This modest investment will bring immediate returns in the form of improved public health, accelerated modernization of Iraq's medical schools, community hospitals and clinics, and establish long term relationships between elements of the American health care system and those in Iraq who will lead it to a democratic future.

PRIVATE SECTOR DEVELOPMENT

Establish an American-Iraqi Enterprise Fund. $200M is required to capitalize an Iraqi-American Enterprise Fund. This fund would operate independently from the US Government under the guidance of a Board of Directors. The primary purpose of this fund would be to promote the private sector development of Iraq. To accomplish this, the Fund would invest in a wide array of private enterprises, disseminate western business know-how, and assist business to play an appropriate role in shaping public policy. Estimated minimum cost: $200M.

Expand network of Employment Centers. Iraq has 27 cities with a population exceeding 100,000. Funding was approved in 2003 for 5 centers. Each Employment Center would serve the unemployed by offering aptitude and ability testing, job counseling, job search assistance, and referrals to employment and training opportunities. Funds would cover 22 new Employment Centers at a cost of $350,000 each. Estimated minimum cost: S8M.

On-the-job Training for Private Sector Employment. CPA requests $35M to offer private sector employers a subsidy to cover the on-the-job costs of training newly hired workers. De facto a wage subsidy, this should provide a major incentive to private employers to increase their employment. These funds are to be executed through the American-Iraqi Enterprise Fund.

Program design elements: Private employers would be eligible to receive a subsidy, averaging $25/month, for wages paid to newly hired (through local Ministry of Labor offices) workers. Subsidies would range from 25,000 Iraqi dinars to 50,000 ID per month per worker, depending upon the wage, occupation and intensity of training. Subsidies would last four to six months. Employers who do not retain the workers after the subsidy ends would not be eligible for future participation.

Cost calculation: $25/worker x 100,000 enrolled = $2.5 million/month wage costs (=$30 million/year). Four to six month enrollment duration implies 2.5 yearly turnover =250,000 newly hired workers. Plus $5 million for program administration, intake, referral, and monitoring of wages/worksites. Estimated minimum cost for a one year program: $35 million.

Market-Oriented Specialized Training. $110M is required to fund four separate employment training programs.

1) *Basic Computer Literacy Training*. $40M is needed to increase productivity of the Iraqi workforce and facilitate a qualified labor force for emerging private sector jobs. At 250 locations throughout Iraq, each with approximately 20 desktops, provide currently employed (first priority) or unemployed (second priority) workers introductory computer skills; program is envisioned as half- day training for one month, allowing two shifts per day at each location = 10,000/month.

   Cost calculation for a one-month course for 120,000 trainees: Capital costs, including 5,000 computers, = $15 million; instructional salaries = $20 million; operating expenses = $5 million. (Providing each student a $25/month stipend would add $3 million, plus admin costs). Estimated minimum cost: $40M.

2) *Specialized Computer Training*. Funds to drive up productivity of the workforce by developing market oriented skills. At approximately 50 locations in Iraq, each with 20 places, provide public and private sector employees with enhanced computer skills relevant to their jobs.

   Cost calculation for three-month, afternoon/evening courses for 9,000 trainees: Capital costs = $4 million; instructional salaries = $9 million; operating expenses = $2 million. Estimated minimum cost: $15M.

3) *English as a Second Language (ESL)*. $30M is required to increase productivity of Iraqi workforce, and ease Iraq's integration into the world economy. At 250 training locations, each with 20 spaces, provide half-day ESL instruction for six months to each participant.

   Cost calculation to provide intensive (4 hours/day) ESL to 20,000 Iraqis for six months: Capital costs = $5 million; instructional salaries = $20 million; operating expenses = $5 million. (As above, providing a stipend adds $3 million). Estimated minimum cost: $30M.

4) *Modernize Vocational Training Institutes*. The Ministry of Labor has six vocational training centers (Arbil, Mosul, Kerkuk, Baghdad, Najaf, and Basrah) which are well located, but with antiquated equipment and curriculum unsuited to a new Iraqi economy. Updated at a cost of $25M, they would serve both employer needs and as train-the-trainer locations for staff of the 265 Ministry of Education vocational education facilities.

   Cost calculation of new curriculum development, equipment, materials, and train-the-trainers activities for six existing vocational training centers: $3 million per location for curriculum, equipment, training materials, supplies; $1 million per institute for staff development; = $4 million per institute plus $1 million for central planning/coordination. Estimated minimum cost: $25M.

REFUGEES, HUMAN RIGHTS & CIVIL SOCIETY

Migration and Refugee Assistance (MRA). CPA must respond to the immediate protection and assistance needs of Iraqis and support the eventual return of over 500,000 Iraqis from neighboring countries and over one million internally displaced persons (IDPs) through international and non-governmental partners.

Current and Planned Activities: To date, the State Department Bureau of Population, Refugees and Migration (PRM) has allocated nearly $40 million to International Organization (IO) and Non-Governmental Organization (NGO) partners. An additional $26 million to be provided to UNHCR, IOM, WFP, UNSECOORD, and a number of NGOs is pending Congressional Notification, but has been approved by CPA and OMB to support humanitarian assistance activities. Anticipated large-scale returns have not yet begun, but are expected in 2004. CPA is working on a national strategy, which includes a significant refugee and internally displaced persons (IDP) return component. Even if conditions are not ripe for significant refugee returns early in 2004, we expect that over one million Iraqi IDPs will require immediate support and hopefully integration to new communities and that refugee returns will commence in large numbers when security conditions dictate. Ambassador Bremer and CPA will rely heavily on UN and NGO partners to implement an orderly and voluntary repatriation operation; these partners will rely on support from State and USAID. Insecurity and access remain challenges for the international relief community and some UN/NGO staffs have drawn down. However, by 2004, we expect security to improve and staff levels to be restored, if not increased, in order to implement programs as the repatriation operation gets underway. We will be launching a major effort to secure international funding for reconstruction activities in Iraq. That effort will only be successful if adequate security assurances are offered. Those same assurances will describe the conditions necessary to support significant refugee and IDP returns.

ICRC has been present and active in Iraq without interruption since 1980. Although major hostilities have ended in Iraq, ICRC's work is far from over. In recent months ICRC had been building up a large-scale operation to ensure protection and assistance for Iraqis. The murder of one of its delegates in July led to tightened security for the organization and temporarily reduced staff in country, but work has resumed to visit detainees, trace family members, and implement major water and sanitation activities. We expect ICRC's program to remain at current levels in 2004, if not expand in order to implement its mandate under the Geneva Conventions.

Partners:

United Nations High Commission for Refugees (UNHCR) – coordinates and facilitates CPA-led refugee and IDP returns. Refugee returns will come primarily from Iran, Jordan, and Saudi Arabia. IDP returns will be coordinated closely with IOM in the north. Assistance includes registration, non-food items, construction materials, quick impact reintegration programs, seeds and tools (for rural dwellers), and other assistance. FY 2003 USG response – $31M. FY 2004 – $50M.

International Committee of the Red Cross (ICRC) – implements major protection and assistance activities, including tracing, prison visits, missing, family reunification, water and sanitation, and some health activities. FY 2003 USG response – $10 million. FY 2004 – $26M.

International Organization for Migration (IOM) – transports refugee and IDP returnees in the region in addition to facilitating overall IDP returns in southern Iraq. Will continue to assist with the return of Third Country Nationals. FY 2003 PRM response – $6.63M. FY 2004 – $6.5M.

Other International Organizations (IOs) – provide key complimentary assistance (health, education, water and sanitation, security, coordination) to returning refugees and IDPs as well as the coordination and security functions necessary for the implementing agencies. FY 2003 PRM response – $3.6M. FY 2004 – $10M.

Non-Governmental Organizations (NGOs) – assume key roles in health, shelter, food distribution, water and sanitation, and reintegration activities connected with expected large- scale returns. As in other repatriation operations, we expect to support those NGO activities filling gaps in the provision of UN assistance. Projected FY 2003 response from PRM – $1.5M. FY 2004 current funding – $10M. Additional FY 2004 – $12M.

Partner	Est. Add'l '04 Needs		PRM Contribution
UNHCR	$200M		$50M
ICRC	$100M		$26M
IOM	$25M		$6.5M
Other Ios	N/A		$10M
NGOs	N/A		$12M
PRM Admin	$0.5M		$0.5M
		TOTAL	**$105M**

Local Governance and Municipalities. The innovative decentralization processes initiated in each of the Governorates in Iraq since April 2003 has [sic] brought a new sense of local ownership and prioritization for the delivery of services. The primary challenge facing the Ministry of Municipalities and Public Works now is to coordinate these new local political structures – the Governorate and Municipal Councils – with the existing decentralized Ministry administrative network so that development proposals and investments can reflect local priorities, and payments can flow to pay for the local administration, together with the coordination of essential maintenance and capital projects that are required to restore especially the water and sewerage services (funded elsewhere) and the municipal services of garbage collection, cleaning and road repairs. These works also need to be also seen in the context of longer term planning of urban development and the forecasting of capital investment required for a workable and efficiently built environment in all the towns and cities in Iraq, and belonging to the people of Iraq.

In order to provide the decentralized service delivery functions of the Ministry of Municipalities and Public Works more effectively there is a need to invest in both people and facilities. There is a need to develop better public access to information locally through Public Information Centers that can provide electronic communication for all local services – planning, municipal services, water and sanitation administrative systems that gives the public the ability to participate in the affairs of service delivery, local government and its oversight. These Centers will require restructured physical space and equipment, including reference libraries and general information in each of the 266 Municipalities across the country. In addition the Ministry and the local government staff will require computer links to back up this service, and training to be leaders in local service delivery. **Estimated minimum cost: $90M.**

Property Claims Tribunal. The fabric of Iraqi society is torn by on going land disputes linked to the actions of the prior regime. These disputes center around land taken by Ba'th party members and then sold to potentially innocent bona fide purchasers, with the result that two innocent persons may claim the same property, i.e., the person from whom the land was originally taken and the person who purchased the land not knowing that the seller obtained it through the despotic action of the prior regime. The former regime forced thousands of Iraqi citizens from all ethnic backgrounds from their homes, land, and other property without adequate compensation, including in some cases, demolition of entire villages. Iraqis currently face complex legal problems that have emerged from disputed ownership suits resulting from the former regime forcing legal owners to give up their homes, land, and other property and the subsequent sale and expropriation by the regime of these assets. Resolving property claims, legally and peacefully, will be complex and expensive, but will also play a critical role in addressing some of the most egregious actions of the former regime. Spending on land title regularization will ensure uniform standards across Iraq, and ensure that land claims are resolved in a fair and equitable manner. A tribunal is required to work on resolving those claims and to provide funding to partially compensate the innocent person who will no longer have possession of the property. This process would help right a wrong and also generate considerable good will toward the coalition. Estimates are based on the ongoing adjudication costs in Iraq. **Estimated minimum cost: $30M.**

Update antiquated banking system. The Iraqi banking system was nearly destroyed during post war looting. Numerous banks were stripped, vaults looted, and some burned. To support national payment systems, electronic movements of funds, and to create trust in checking accounts which are little used, the coalition seeks to develop and implement a modern system that features networks, integrated databases, and file servers that allows accountability of transactions, monitoring of all aspects of the budget, accurate and timely reporting of data from field offices and collated to date. This will allow for greater efficiencies of manpower where currently thousands of workers do manual reporting by pen and paper. The system would not only integrate the entire banking system but would also allow foreign capitalists greater insight into bank records thereby taking their concerns into consideration for greater accessibility and improved infrastructure, which allow them to invest capital in Iraq. Purchases include equipment, training, transference of old records to new databases and infrastructure development. **Estimated minimum cost: $30M.**

Catch-up Business Training. Develop and train cadre of business and entrepreneurs in business fundamentals and concepts that were missing in the former Iraqi regime. Classes would include management, budgeting, capitalization, cost accounting, leadership, ethics training and leadership. Mid level managers throughout the country have a general lack of knowledge on what is considered western business practices. As Iraq opens its doors to direct foreign capital investment it will need managers and leaders who understand those concepts. Average cost of 4 week course is $10,000 per pupil. Program depends upon a preponderance of foreign teachers who have experience in this area. **Estimated minimum cost: $20M.**

Human Rights (Office of Human Rights and Transitional Justice Projects). Iraq has undergone decades of trauma due to [the] brutal regime of Saddam Hussein. We require $15M to support Iraqis to begin the reconciliation and healing process through programs already identified and being developed.

Research into Past Atrocities: Although Ministry of Justice funding will focus on the investigation of key Ba'ath officials for criminal accountability, the vast majority of all research and documentation of past atrocities will take place outside of the justice system, for healing, truth and reconciliation, and historical record. To accomplish this, it is essential to fund testimony-taking projects, the establishment of a physical document archive, training for Iraqis to take testimony and scan documents for information on past atrocities, and local initiatives to establish memorials and museums. To begin the process of researching and documenting past atrocities, the Office of Human Rights and Transitional Justice, through the newly created Ministry of Human Rights, seeks to fund the following specifically defined.

- Documentation and Memorial Workshop: to bring in 8-10 leading experts and past grantees for two days on the establishment of a National Archive of Documents for Past Atrocities, and Memorials and Museums to document past atrocities. Each expert would bring 2 local Iraqi to the table as well to discuss who will take [a] leading role in particular projects. (September) Anticipated cost: $.04M.
- Abu Gharaib Memorial: We are working to establish a memorial and museum at Abu Gharaib with local Iraqi NGO participation. Desire to put out an RFP 9/03. Anticipated cost of memorial: $0.5M.
- Memory Foundation: Fund Documentation portion of Kanan Makiya's proposal to create a national information center and museum as CPA's contribution to the creation of a National Archive for Documents of Past Atrocities. Anticipated cost: $1M.
- Athletes Committee: Memorial or Conference to document and tell the world about past atrocities committed against Iraqi athletes. Anticipated cost: $.05M.
- Witness Database: This database will provide information on atrocities committed in the past, and witness contact information. Anticipated cost: $0.96M.
- Document Database: This database will provide information on atrocities committed in the past that is contained in documents. Anticipated cost: $0.96M.

Mass Graves/Missing Persons: To strengthen local capacity on exhumations and to assist families in the reconciliation process, we anticipate the following:

- Forensic Anthropology Training Programs to train local communities in forensic exhumation. Anticipated Cost: $0.94M.
- Equipment for Iraqis to use in Forensic and Local Digging which strengthens the local-capacity to perform exhumations. Anticipated Cost: $1M.
- Family advocacy (for families with victims) programs to ensure that families who have lost loved ones advocate for legislation which provides them with needs and closure; and psychological counseling programs to train local trainers in community-based counseling. Anticipated Cost: $0.7M.
- Assist Iraqis in Development of Iraqi National Bureau for Missing Persons. Anticipated cost: $1.5M.
- Fund for investigative/documentary purposes. Funds to purchase videos, and photos of past atrocities currently being sold in Baghdad. Anticipated cost: $0.5M.

Human Rights Ministry: To foster a culture of respect for human rights and dignity in Iraq, and to assist the Iraqi reconcile with atrocities committed by the former regime.

- Establishment of a Human Rights Commission. Establish an independent human rights commission which will question the government. Anticipated cost: $1M.
- Develop a Human Rights Civic Education Program. To train Iraqis, in schools and at the community level, in fundamental human rights. To increase public awareness through brochures, publications and news releases. Anticipated cost: $2.1M.
- Truth and Reconciliation Commission. Assist Iraqis in developing regional truth and reconciliation commissions. Anticipated cost: $2.5M.
- NGO Coordination and Development. Start-up funds for local NGOs. Anticipated cost: $1.25M.

Civic Programs. One of the hallmarks of a democratic society is a vibrant civil society that holds government accountable, organizes citizen participation in government, and empowers traditionally underrepresented groups to participate in governance. $10M is required for the following programs.

Women's programming – $5M. To give women the skills necessary to participate in public life, to include civic education campaigns, women's resource centers throughout Iraq, leadership training and exchange programs.

Youth programming – $2M. To expose youth to new models of civic participation through exchange programs, youth groups and University programming.

Civic education – $3M. Programs to promote new ideas and concepts, such as democracy, civil society, rights and responsibilities of citizenship. Building consensus on these ideals is the first step in transformation to democratic society. Programs to include book distribution, posters, pamphlets, speakers tours, fora, etc.

Document 221

Cable from Ambassador Bremer to Secretary Rumsfeld, Path to Sovereignty

19 September 2003

1. Summary: The Path to Iraq's sovereignty should run through the constitutional process. Any proposal to restore Iraq's sovereignty by vesting it in the Governing Council (GC) or in an 'Alternative Provisional Government' would entail a number of serious disadvantages. End Summary.

2. I want to review with you my concerns about the arguments for 'early sovereignty.' One major problem would be the lack of any formal constitutional structure to specify the powers of the national government. Restoring Iraq's sovereignty without a new constitution would essentially grant the Governing Council (GC) or some other non-elected body authority unconstrained by any constitution. There would be no guarantee of checks and balances, or of the separation of powers. Politically, it would be near-impossible for the Coalition to intervene to affect its desired end-state if sovereignty were restored to Iraq before these preconditions were established.

3. Another concern is that the balance of power in Iraqi national politics does not currently favor U.S. interests, or the interests of a liberal, national and democratic Iraqi political order. Currently, the Coalition possesses a great deal of leverage in Iraqi politics. We are able to influence the discussions and decision-making processes, ensuring that separatist Kurds, pro-Ba'athist elements of the GC, and extreme Islamists from getting [sic] their way. Whether they admit it or not, our pro-democratic friends in Iraqi politics are currently not strong enough to overcome these extremist elements without our help. The danger of handing over political authority too early is that we will forfeit our place at the bargaining table. Compromises will be made among the Iraqis that will negatively impact our interests. Consider the following:

- The Committee of 65 from the London Conference, chosen almost exclusively by the current leaders of the GC (Chalabi, Hakim, Alawi, Barzani, Talabani) was disproportionately dominated by SCIRI-backed Islamists.

- The GC recently appointed Ayad Alawi as chairman of its Security Committee, and Nuri Badran as Minister of the Interior. Both have strong Ba'ath Party connections, and have recently floated plans to rehire former members of the Republican Guard.
- The Constitutional Preparatory Committee has apparently endorsed an election scheme which, in order to placate the Kurds, requires that Iraqis cast votes in their places of origin as of 1957.
- [...][126]

4. An additional problem is that, were sovereignty restored to Iraq immediately, there would be no guarantee the Iraqi Government would want U.S. troops to remain for any necessary period of time. From the Iraqi point of view, the 'occupation' of their country is not a result of the language of UNSCR 1483,[127] or the GC's lack of sovereign power. The perception of 'occupation' stems, rather, from the fact that there are 150,000 Coalition troops across the country and that they have the authority to tell Iraqis what to do. Giving the GC nominal sovereignty will not alleviate the discomfort Iraqis feel under Coalition authority. Once the GC is granted sovereign power including, presumably, the power to require that Coalition troops leave Iraq, political pressure will build inside the country for the GC to do just that. SCIRI and other Islamists have already begun to call for us to leave – probably confident in the fact that, since we retain authority as the 'occupying power,' we can safely ignore them. If the GC is given sovereignty, the Islamists will be under tremendous pressure to follow through on their rhetoric. While we of course want to keep the occupation short, we would be derelict to our interest in a stable Iraq to leave before a responsible Iraqi Government capable of providing for the country's security is established.

5. Furthermore, restoring Iraq's sovereignty would give up any guarantee we now have that a constitutional process will take place and be carried through to completion. Restoring Iraq's sovereignty immediately would cede any influence the Coalition might otherwise have in building a constitutional process that preserves Iraq's territorial integrity, ensures democratic structures, and guarantees religious freedom. Iraq's history of working under 'interim' constitutions that last far longer than originally intended is not heartening. The latest 'interim' constitution was put in place by Saddam in 1970. If the Coalition relinquishes its authority before an Iraqi constitution is written and ratified, it will be difficult to intervene if powerful constituencies – a power-hungry GC, for example, or independence-minded Kurds – later decide that completing such a process is no longer in their interest.

6. Another problem is the lack of a formal, agreed-upon definition of the relationships between the central government and the many local councils which we have established in governorates and cities across Iraq. Currently, the Coalition presence has allowed real political power to devolve to the local authorities. Local Iraqi councils have been formed in each of the 18 governorates, working under the supervision of local Coalition commanders. The GC is on record as strongly opposing the makeup of these local councils. In their view, local governors should be appointed by and responsible to the GC. Ceding full political authority in Iraq to the GC would therefore severely upset the relationship between the central government and the provinces. And, it would work against our broader objective of devolving power away from Baghdad as a check on future tyranny. Recent consultations with Iraq's governors confirm that the provinces would most likely actively disobey the GC.

7. Finally, another disadvantage of restoring sovereignty to Iraq before a constitution has been written for U.S. policy in Iraq and ratified [sic] is that it would signal yet another

[126] The document was declassified only in part.
[127] See *Doc 523*.

fundamental change of course. Already, the switch from 'ORHA' to 'CPA' and the return to the UN for a second resolution have signaled weakness to Iraqis and the Arab world. President Bush and Secretary Powell have now been absolutely clear and on the record concerning Iraq's path to sovereignty. A sudden change in this position would suggest that we are on the run, lacking confidence and resolution in our current course of action.

8. Overall, most members of the GC have come to understand that sovereignty is divisible and that it can accrete. As we have said, the GC was the first step in this process, and the establishment of ministers was the second.[128] Seating an Iraqi behind the placard at the UN will move further in this direction. The fact is that a piece of paper will not afford legitimacy (or sovereignty) – otherwise we could have solved the Israeli-Palestinian conflict years ago at the UN. Only the actions of the GC and its cabinet with patient, steady, and where necessary, firm Coalition guidance, can do that. Only when average Iraqis see the GC and its ministers addressing their concerns will they give both institutions legitimacy. Ultimately, this legitimacy may translate into full sovereignty in legal terms. Simply assigning sovereignty now, however, will risk greater political destabilization in Iraq as many who remain outside the unrepresentative GC will feel as though they have been betrayed by the Coalition.

9. In short, it is abundantly clear that we must retain our leverage and authority until we have in place a respectable political order which maximizes the chances of our achieving the President's vision of a stable, democratic Iraq.

Document 222
Request to Rehabilitate and Reconstruct Iraq
Summary of the Request

22 September 2003[129]

<u>SECURITY</u>

Objective: Ensure a secure environment for people and property that enables citizens to participate fully in political and economic life. Create conditions and provide means for Iraqis to assume responsibility for their own security. ***Request: $5.136 billion***

Accomplishments:

- Security remains top priority. Major focus of CPA security efforts has been to increase Iraqi participation and responsibility for a safe and secure Iraq
- Security situation is complex
  - 80% of Iraq is permissive environment – people returning to normal pace of life
  - Remaining 20% are less permissive, with entrenched Saddam loyalists, international terrorists and general lawlessness hindering recovery efforts
- Nearly 60,000 Iraqis now under arms assisting in security
  - 46,000 Iraqi police nationwide
  - 8,700 facility protection officers augmenting the Iraqi police at 243 locations

[128] See Ambassador Bremer's speech to the Iraqi people 'Path to Sovereignty', above *Doc 219*.

[129] The Summary of the Request is reproduced here because its section on 'Governance' goes beyond the FY04 Supplemental Request to Rehabilitate and Reconstruct Iraq, reproduced as *Doc 220*.

- 4,000 border and customs police helping to enforce immigration and customs laws along the borders and stem the tide of foreign fighters entering Iraq
- Civil Defense Corps is in the process of being developed
• Beginning to train New Iraqi Army; first battalion graduates in October
• In September, the Iraqi Ministry of Justice established an independent judiciary

Plan for requested funds:
I. Public Safety Projects ($2.141 billion):
• Reinforcement and training of police forces
  - Recruiting police officers, continuing operations and maintenance ($150 million)
  - New police training force of 1,500 focusing on democratic principles ($800 million)
  - Recruiting and training of 5,200 traffic officers ($50 million)
• Establishment of a Department of Border Enforcement ($150 million)
  - 13,600 new personnel
  - Rehabilitation of infrastructure
• Facilities protection, mine removal, fire service, and public safety facility and equipment repairs ($500 million)
• Establish Facility Protection Services ($67 million)
• Conduct Public Safety Training to increase professional standards ($274 million)
• Develop a National Security Communications Network ($150 million)

II. National Security Forces Projects ($2.076 billion):
• Establishment of New Iraqi Army (NIA) ($2 billion)
  - Full manning by September, 2004
  - Training 9 brigades, including 1 armored brigade and army aviation
  - Small coast guard
  - Military academies and military training facilities
• Establishment of Iraqi Civil Defense Corps (CDC) ($76 million)
  - Military support corps for the 18 Iraqi governates [sic]
  - One battalion for each governate [sic]

III. Justice and Civil Society Development Projects ($919 million):
• Technical assistance for investigations of crimes against humanity ($100 million)
  - Establish a working system of criminal investigations and trials
• Security for judges and prosecutors, renovate and harden courthouses ($200 million)
• Witness Protection Program ($100 million)
• Other technical investigative methods ($10 million)
• Prison system rehabilitation
  - Prison system technical assistance ($10 million)
  - Reconstruction and modernization of 26 detention facilities ($99 million)
  - 2 new 4,000 bed facilities ($400 million)

ESSENTIAL SERVICES AND INFRASTRUCTURE

Objective: Restore essential services to acceptable standards and to begin to create a civil society which participates in improving social and physical infrastructure. Provide foundation from which Iraqis can rebuild Iraq. ***Request: $14.868 billion***

Accomplishments:

- Under difficult conditions, there has been no food or health crisis
  - Sufficient food stockpiles and distribution system; total distribution since the beginning of operations has exceeded 1.8 million MT
  - All hospitals and primary care clinics are open, have power 24 hours a day, and are being supplied with adequate medical supplies for the first time in many years
  - All schools and universities are open
- Coalition and Iraqi engineers are working to restore electric power production to pre-war levels – generation has improved from virtually nothing following major combat operations to 3,200 MW in July and 3,734 MW in August
- Water and sanitation – By July, much of Iraq at pre-war conditions; CPA has shifted focus to specific rehabilitation projects; Baghdad had first ever city-wide garbage clean up in August
- Restoration of the oil industry is helping to rehabilitate the economy
  - Iraqi/CPA oil management team is highly respected internationally
  - Crude oil production is averaging about 1.7mil barrels per day which is 160% higher than June average and 70% of prewar output
  - Oil exports are averaging 860k barrels per day which represents approximately $21 million and is 165% higher than July average and 45% of prewar level
  - Sabotage remains an issue

Plan for requested funds:

I. Electrical Projects ($5.675 billion):

- Electricity generation ($2.9 billion)
  - Rehabilitate existing power stations and spare parts
  - New gas turbine generation
  - New thermal power stations
- Repair, expansion, and rehabilitation of transmission ($1.55 billion)
  - Repair, expansion of 400 KV and 132 KV lines
  - Rehabilitation and construction of substations
- Rehabilitation and replacement of network infrastructure over several years ($1 billion)
  - 33 KV and 11 KV substation and network rehabilitation and development
- Development of an automated monitoring and control system ($150 million)
- Institutional strengthening ($25 million)
- Security of stations and transmission lines ($50 million)

II. Oil Projects ($2.1 billion):

- Investment in oil infrastructure ($1.2 billion)
  - Rapid repair caused by sabotage and looting
  - Convert to topping plants to reduce importation of refined petroleum
  - Establishment of transport redundancy due to sabotage
  - Development of oil infrastructure and personnel security
  - Increased efficiency of water plant for the Ramayllah reservoir
  - Other repairs to rehabilitate upstream and downstream sectors
- Importation of refined petroleum products to overcome shortfalls due to sabotage and looting ($900 million)

***III. Public Works Projects ($3.710 billion)*:**
- Raising potable water access to 90% from 60%
  - Costs are estimated at $500/km for 15,000 km of water main line ($2.83 billion)
  - Includes efforts to reduce water loss ($30 million)
- Increasing sewerage service from 6% to 15% ($697 million)
- Improving solid waste management ($153 million)

IV. Water Resources Projects ($875 million):
- Replace pumping station standby generators, pumps, electrical control devices ($150 million)
- Rehabilitation of irrigation and drainage systems ($130 million)
- 10 major irrigation projects, reducing salinity loads to Tigris and Euphrates ($130 million)
- Dam repair, rehabilitation, and new construction ($125 million)
- Umm Qasr to Basra water pipeline and treatment plant ($200 million)
- Environmental restoration of Euphrates, Hawizeh Marsh, and Basra Channel Regulators to benefit millions of people ($140 million)

V. Transportation and Communications Projects ($835 million):
- Airspace and airport opening in Baghdad and Basra, and 120 smaller airports ($165 million)
  - Repair infrastructure, purchase avionic equipment, training to meet ICAO standards
- Umm Qasr Port rehabilitation ($45 million)
- Railroad rehabilitation and restoration ($303 million)
- Restoration of Iraqi Telecom and Postal Corporation ($124 million)
- Iraqi Communications systems, including Iraqi media ($109 million)
- Iraqi communications operations ($89 million)

VI. Housing and Construction Projects ($470 million):
- Housing ($100 million)
  - Construction of 3,500 new housing units including 7 housing communities
  - Pilot program for Ministry of Housing and Construction, 1 million housing units needed
- Public buildings ($130 million)
  - 1,325 basic repairs and 140 refurbishment projects
  - 6 major reconstruction projects at $7 million each
- Roads and bridges ($240 million)
  - 2% of need for total road and bridge repair
  - Repair to Expressway 1

VII. Health Projects ($850 million):
- Major new children's hospital ($150 million)
  - 41% of total population is under age 14
  - Demographics point to baby boom within next ten years
- Hospital refurbishment ($393 million)
  - Reduce infant and childhood deaths by 50%
  - Refurbish 1,200 primary care clinics and 5 regional maternal/pediatric referral centers
  - Construction cost in Iraq is one-tenth that of US

- Equipment replacement ($300 million)
  - Early studies estimate that 50% of all equipment needs replacement
  - Equipment and training of technicians
- Partner with American health care organizations, intern. donors, and schools ($7 million)

VIII. Private Sector Development Projects ($353 million):
- An American-Iraqi Enterprise Fund ($200 million)
  - Promote private sector of Iraq
  - Independent fund would invest in private enterprises, and disseminate Western business know-how
- Expand network of Employment Centers ($8 million)
- On-the-job training ($35 million)
- Market-oriented specialized training ($110 million)

GOVERNANCE

Objective: Enable the transition to a legitimate constitutional government. Help Iraqis on the path to a democratic society and full sovereignty. ***Request: $300 million***

Accomplishments:
- Iraqi Governing Council, comprised of 25 men and women representing Iraq's religious and ethnic diversity, was established on July 13th and has had several accomplishments
  - Welcomed by UN Security Council as step toward a sovereign, democratic Iraq
  - Appointed constitutional preparatory committee
  - Appointed 25 member Cabinet, responsible for the day to day management of Iraqi government ministries
  - Iraqi Foreign Minister has been seated by the League of Arab States in early September
  - Growing international recognition that GC is the political voice of Iraq
  - GC prepared to open embassies in U.S., U.K. and 5 Arab nations
- 90% of the Iraqi people live under local representative governing councils
- Iraq has 3 pillars required for achieving a democratic society: free press and speech, freedom of religion and an independent judiciary

Plan for requested funds:
I. Refugees, Human Rights, and Civic Society ($300 million):
- Migration and Refugee Assistance ($105 million)
- Local Governance & Municipalities ($90 million)
- Property Claims Tribunal ($30 million)
- Update antiquated banking system ($30 million)
- Catch up business training ($20 million)
- Human Rights ($15 million)
- Civic Programs ($10 million)

Document 223
Letter of Authorization for the Governorate Coordinator for the Governorate of Al Qadisiyah

25 September 2003

FOR: Henry Ensher
FROM: Ambassador L. Paul Bremer III, Administrator of the Coalition Provisional Authority
SUBJECT: Governorate Coordinator Appointment – Al Qadisiyah[130]

I am pleased to confirm your appointment as the Coalition Provisional Authority (CPA) Governorate Coordinator (GC) for the Governorate of Al Qadisiyah. You are the CPA's principal representative to the local governments in Al Qadisiyah. You will lead a Governorate Team (GT) comprised of a CPA staff element, a military Governorate Support Team, a contracted Local Governance Team, and Iraqi advisors.

The GT will provide local governance; identify, train, and mentor local Iraqi leaders for roles within future Iraqi government; monitor local contracts and provide program management; coordinate with coalition military and non-governmental organizations; and advise local government ministry officials in Al Qadisiyah,

You will report to me through the Director of Operations and Infrastructure for operational matters and through the Director of Governance for political issues. You may draw on the Regional Coordinator's and CPA staffs as needed for technical and program support.

Your team's actions in support of the CPA objectives, goals and vision will fundamentally support the first steps toward a truly self-governing and independent Iraqi nation.

[Signed] L. Paul Bremer III, Administrator
Coalition Provisional Authority

ATTACHMENTS: None

Document 224
Guidelines for the Relocation of Displaced Persons

October 2003

The Problem

Based on estimates compiled by the UN, NGOs, Iraqi officials and U.S. Army Civil Affairs, there may be as many as 70,000 internally displaced persons (IDPs), refugees and urban poor 'squatting' in various municipal or government buildings around Baghdad. Many have taken up residence in facilities that are needed by CPA in its efforts to restore government functions and ensure the continuity of essential public

[130] Similar letters of appointment were issued on 25 September for the governorates of Al Muthana, Babil, Najaf, Al Anbar, Maysan, Salh al-Din.

services. Some are living under extremely difficult conditions and are in need of relocation on humanitarian grounds. The UN is prepared to assist CPA in beginning to address the needs of these populations, but will only do so within the framework of a clear set of guidelines.

Objective

The immediate objective is to temporarily relocate and assist only those IDPs, refugees or urban poor squatters who are presently occupying facilities needed by CPA. Alternative housing may not, at this time, [be] available for the entire caseload. Candidates for relocation will be determined on an as needed, space available basis by CPA and the Iraqi authorities in coordination with the U.N. Office of the Humanitarian Coordinator for Iraq.

Guiding Principles

The following principles will be applied to the relocation of all individuals in the caseload referred to in this document:

- The displaced people will be **disaggregated and treated as distinct groups**: IDPs; refugees; urban poor. This disaggregation will facilitate the provision of assistance and protection, for those who need it, by the U.N. and other relief agencies.
- The immediate objective is **temporary relocation** of the highest priority caseloads while more durable solutions are identified. However, long-term solutions are not easy or obvious, given Iraq's 1.4 million unit housing shortfall. Some solutions may have to wait for broader urban revitalization and resumption of construction activities.
- Relocations will be brought about by **negotiation and persuasion**, not by force. It is understood that CPA Order No. 9[131] authorizes clearance of buildings by force if necessary; use of force, however, should only be considered as a last resort.
- As the occupying power in Iraq, CPA, in cooperation with the Iraqi Government, will have responsibility for **maintaining a secure environment** in the areas to which beneficiary populations have been relocated, as it does throughout all of Iraq.

Plan of Action

The HACC-B working group on displace populations has been focusing its attention on this issue for some weeks now. The group's membership includes:

- 1st Armored Division Governorate Support Team (GST)
- CPA Refugee/IDP Office
- Facilities Management
- Ministry of Housing
- Ministry of Labor and Social Welfare
- Baghdad Area Coordination Office of the UN Office of the Humanitarian Coordinator for Iraq (UNOHCI)
- UNCHS (Habitat)
- International Organization for Migration (IOM)
- Premiere Urgence (PU)

[131] See *Doc 23*.

- United Iraqi Medical Society (UIMS)
- Hellenic Rescue Society

The group, under the chairmanship of the GST, has developed a plan of action for the orderly relocation of IDPs, refugees and other urban poor squatters and the provision of appropriate assistance to those in need. It includes the following steps:

1. **Caseload identification and assessment** – Information on IDPs, refugees and urban poor squatters is shared with 1AD by UN agencies, NGOs, Ministries, Brigade Combat Teams (BCTs) or other means. PU, IOM's designated IDP focal point Baghdad Governorate, conducts assessments for the identification and categorisation of populations as IDPs or other. The GST works with the relevant ministry to determine future plans for the facility occupied by the individuals and places it on a prioritized list for relocation. All of this information is stored in a public access database maintained by 1AD.
2. **Identification and evaluation of alternative site locations** – CPA is responsible for the determining and approving the appropriateness of locations and facilities for relocation to meet the current needs of the targeted populations. GST works with the CPA Facilities Manager to develop a list of possible alternative site locations. The specialised agencies of the UN, IOM and NGOs carry out initial assessments of sites that could be potentially selected for relocation. This information is shared with CPA for their final approval of the site as a relocation site for the targeted population.
3. **Notification/eviction** – The District Director General and the Iraqi police are responsible for delivering the eviction notification, with the support of Civil Affairs and Military Police personnel. The notification is given 2-4 weeks in advance of the date which they must be out of the facility. Those with an alternative means of housing will be encouraged to take advantage of it.
4. **Site preparation and relocation** – Within the framework of the UN Humanitarian Programme in Iraq, UN specialised agencies, other international organizations and NGOs will carry out specific interventions to prepare and rehabilitate relocation sites. Just prior to the date of eviction, a visit by community leaders to the renovated relocation site will be facilitated. Once the leaders have had a chance to report to the community members, CPA (GST) in cooperation with Iraqi officials will arrange and fund non-military transportation of the population to the new location.
5. **Provision of assistance** – The provision of general care for the relocated population is the responsibility of the CPA as the occupying power in Iraq. Also within the framework of the UN Humanitarian Programme in Iraq, UN specialised agencies, other international organizations and NGOs will carry out specific interventions to assist these populations.

Document 225
Achieving the Vision to Restore Full Sovereignty to the Iraqi People (Strategic Plan)

1 October 2003[132]

Introduction

This progressive plan is an overview of the strategy necessary for early restoration of full sovereignty to the Iraqi people. The strategy is driven by more detailed action plans (e.g., plans for the New Iraqi Army, the police, restoring electrical power, etc.).

Our strategy has four principle objectives or 'core foundations':

- **Security** – establishing a secure and safe environment
- **Essential services** – restoring basic services to levels which promote stability in Iraq
- **Economy** – creating the conditions for economic growth
- **Governance** – enabling the transition to transparent and inclusive democratic governance

These objectives are intertwined: none can be pursued in isolation. Political and economic progress depends in part on security, but should itself help to create a safer environment.

L. Paul Bremer, Administrator
Coalition Provisional Authority

Summary

Now that Saddam Hussein's regime has been removed, the Iraqi people have the opportunity to realize the vision of a stable, prosperous and democratic Iraq. The Coalition Provisional Authority (CPA), in close cooperation with the Iraqi Interim Administration (the Governing Council and Interim Ministers), the United Nations, and the international community, has a key role to play in the next stage of rebuilding Iraq.

This document describes the CPA's strategy for carrying out its role in this historic process. While the CPA remains the legally sovereign power in Iraq, we now have a significant partner in the Interim Administration. The Governing Council now represents the voice of the Iraqi people to the CPA, and to the world. Interim Ministers are now running Iraq's ministries. Together, Iraqis and the CPA are forging a partnership to guide the nation forward in its transformation.[133]

This document is designed to direct the work of the CPA and the coalition militaries in a flexible manner. It recognizes the need to retain the support of the Iraqi people in all that we do, knowing that their support is vital to our success. It is also aimed at the international community whose political and financial backing will be essential if our overall objectives are to be achieved. The plan recognizes the need for further planning in coordination with the Interim Administration as the process of rebuilding Iraq evolves. While full economic recovery will take years, the economic reform program provides a

[132] This was a Working Document as of 1 October 2003. An earlier version of this document entitled 'Achieving the Vision to Restore Full Sovereignty to the Iraqi People (An Overview)', which on 23 July 2003 was sent to the United States Senate Committee of Armed Serviced, may be found in Ongoing Military Operations and Reconstruction Efforts in Iraq, Hearing before the Committee on Armed Services, United States Senate, 108th Congress, 1st Session, 25 September 2003 (2004), 44-71.

[133] The 23 July version reads: 'we now have a significant partner in the Governing Council (GC) of the Interim Administration.' While the October document regularly speaks of the 'Interim Administration' the July version spoke of the 'Governing Council'.

vision of a future of freedom and prosperity towards which we and the Iraqis will work in the short term.

The plan describes key action steps within the various core elements that determine the CPA's priorities in the short, medium and long-term. From this, we can review what we have achieved and where we need to adjust. Finally, the plan will assist us and the Iraqis to allocate our resources and those of Iraq. It will also assist in attracting critical resources and capabilities from the international community.

The CPA Vision

After decades of a ruthless dictatorship, the Iraqi people can at last control their destiny and establish the conditions for a free and stable future. With the international community, the CPA will help the Iraqi people achieve the President's and Prime Minister's vision for Iraq – a free Iraq governed by a representative government chosen through democratic elections.[134] At the core of this new Iraq is the development of a democratic, accountable, and self-governing civil society respectful of human rights and freedom of expression. The future prosperity of Iraq's citizens depends on the use of Iraqi resources to foster the development of a market-based economy. This needs to be done in a manner that is economically, socially and environmentally sustainable for the long term benefit of all Iraqi people. Furthermore, our goal is an Iraq free of terrorists and weapons of mass destruction,[135] at peace with itself and its neighbors and once again able to play a responsible role in the international community. The Coalition is firmly committed to the future of Iraq. The CPA succeeds when Iraq succeeds. Hence we will stay as long necessary, and not a day longer. But we will not leave until we have succeeded in carrying out the President's and the Prime Minister's vision. Our foundation of authority is firmly embedded in international law and in accord with United Nations Security Council Resolution 1483.

The Mission

The CPA will work with the Iraqi people and the Iraqi Interim Administration to establish the conditions for a free, sovereign, democratically-elected representative government. We want to work with Iraqis to establish an Iraq that uses its resources for the benefit of its people. It should be an Iraq that is stable, united, prosperous, at peace with its neighbors and able to take its rightful place as a responsible member of the region and the international community. This Iraq must be free of weapons of mass destruction and terrorists.

The End-State

The ultimate goal is a unified and stable, democratic Iraq that: provides effective and representative government for the Iraqi people; is underpinned by new and protected freedoms for all Iraqis and a growing market economy; is able to defend itself but no longer poses a threat to its neighbors or international security.

ACHIEVING THE VISION
Taking Forward the CPA Strategic Plan for Iraq

Goal

The primary goal of the Coalition Provisional Authority (CPA) is the early restoration of full sovereignty to the Iraqi people. We seek:

[134] For the US President's and the British Prime Minister's vision for Iraq, see *Doc 572*.

[135] The phrase 'free of terrorists and weapons of mass destruction' does not appear in the July version.

'a unified and stable, democratic Iraq that provides effective and representative government for the Iraqi people; is underpinned by new and protected freedoms and a growing market economy; is able to defend itself but no longer poses a threat to its neighbors or international security.'

A major step towards that goal was taken on July 13, with the establishment of a Governing Council of 25 Iraqis representing all major strands of Iraqi society. The Council has substantial powers. On August 15 [sic][136] the Council appointed a committee to recommend a process for writing a new Iraqi constitution. On September 1 the Council appointed 25 interim ministers. The ministers are now running Iraq's government on a day to day basis. Iraq's Interim Administration will be consulted on all major policy issues and on our planning for the transfer of power to a sovereign government.

Strategy

Our strategy has four principal objectives or 'core foundations':

- **Security** – establishing a secure and safe environment
- **Essential services** – restoring basic services to help stabilize Iraq
- **Economy** – creating the conditions for economic growth
- **Governance** – enabling the transition to transparent and inclusive democratic governance

These objectives are intertwined: none can be pursued in isolation. Political and economic progress depends in part on security, but should itself help to create a safer environment.

Security

Coalition forces will help Iraqis to eliminate the threats to their security and will remain in country for as long as they are needed. **Over time the transfer of security responsibilities to local military and police forces will determine the speed with which we can advance reconstruction and build up institutions of good governance.**

The Iraqi people are already contributing to that effort but must acquire the ability to assume full responsibility for meeting the country's security needs as soon as practicable – thus enabling the draw-down of coalition forces. Our priorities therefore include:

- Development and training of Iraqi security forces, including a new Iraqi army, new civil defense corps and an effective police force
- Development of national security and civilian oversight mechanisms
- Measures to ensure border security
- Measures to build the justice system and improve the penal system
- Ensuring that Iraq is free of weapons of mass destruction.

Essential Services

Effective delivery of basic services is a major priority for the Iraqi people and the CPA. Our Program involves:

- Reconstituting the power infrastructure
- Improving water resource management
- Ensuring food security
- Improving health care – quality and access
- Rehabilitating key transport infrastructure

[136] The IGC formed the 25-member Constitutional Preparatory Committee (CPC) on 11 August 2003.

- Improving education and housing – quality and access
- Reconstructing the telecommunications system.

The Economy

To realize the country's full potential for economic growth, Iraq will need initially to:

- Build financial market structures
- Promote private business
- Determine the future of state-owned enterprises

Policy work is also in progress on:

- Monetizing and phasing out subsidies, while building a social safety net
- Designing an oil trust fund
- Reform of the tax and tariff system.

Governance

Iraq has suffered from decades of tyranny. **Effective representative government, sustained by democratic elections, requires the rapid development of new frameworks and capacities**, including:

- A constitution drafted by Iraqis and approved by Iraqis
- Institutions and processes to conduct free and fair elections
- Open and transparent political processes
- Measures to improve the effectiveness of elected officials, including strengthened local government systems
- Effective and fair justice systems
- Respect for the rule of law and human rights
- Creation of a vibrant civil society.

Information

Strengthening the media is essential for the development of healthy democracy in Iraq. This will require legislation to protect free speech as well as to regulate broadcasting and promote responsible journalism. Professional bodies have a role to play in setting journalistic standards.

We must ensure that our policies are communicated accurately and effectively at all times to the Iraqi people.[137] **The CPA's communications strategy is designed to get our message out in an honest, clear and timely way** – and then to take account of the responses of the Iraqi people, including their expression through the media.

Resources

It is difficult at this point fully to quantify the external assistance needed to support Iraq's transition to representative government and a market economy. Eastern European experience suggests that a substantial international commitment will be needed. But Iraq starts the process at a lower level of economic and political development. Its energy resources have been badly mismanaged for decades, leaving the country unable from its own resources at present to provide an acceptable living standard for its people. All infrastructure sectors suffer from chronic underinvestment.

Clearly, the United States and the international community and institutions must take the lead. **Only a co-ordinated international effort can bring prosperity and stability to the**

[137] The July version reads: 'The transitional administration in Iraq must ensure [...].'

Iraqi people, discourage terrorists from using Iraq as a safe haven and contribute to a lasting peace in the Middle East.[138]

Planning

Our planing, which is a dynamic and iterative process, involves:

- An unprecedented joint civilian and military CPA/CJTF7 planning process to produce a joint strategic plan – the military contribute vitally to all key objects
- A comprehensive and evolving plan for the short, medium and longer term, but
- Necessary flexibility to change, and to learn from experience.

The attached charts give further details, in their latest available iteration, of the sectoral plans being taken forward in military and Ministerial plans.[139] The charts identify progress to date and establish targets and planning goals for the next 90 and 360 days. We shall monitor progress against our strategic objectives and continue to refine the detailed plans set out here, in consultation with the Interim Administration and as the changing situation in Iraq may require.

Document 226
Interim Travel Document

7 October 2003[140]

COALITION PROVISIONAL AUTHORITY IN IRAQ
INTERIM TRAVEL DOCUMENT

NOTICE TO ALL IMMIGRATION AND BORDER CONTROL OFFICIALS:

The bearer of this document (identified below) is a citizen of or born in Iraq and does not possess a valid Iraqi passport, but has identified him/herself to the undersigned issuing authority. Presently, Iraq does not have the capacity to issue traditional travel documents such as a passport, and the Coalition Provisional Authority (CPA) requests that this Interim Travel Document, supported by other legal identification as may be required to substantiate the bearer's identity, be honored for the same purposes. This document does not itself constitute proof of Iraqi nationality, but sufficient identification for exiting and entering Iraq consistent with CPA Order 16.[141]

Further, all competent authorities are requested to allow passage of the bearer of this Interim Travel Document and to afford all lawful aid and assistance in case of need.

[138] The phrase 'discourage terrorists from using Iraq as a safe haven' was added to the October version.

[139] The 19-page charts are reprinted in Ongoing Military Operations and Reconstruction Efforts in Iraq, Hearing before the Committee on Armed Services, United States Senate, 108th Congress, 1st Session, 25 September 2003 (2004), 53-71.

[140] The CPA Interim Travel Document (ITD) was first issued on 7 October 2003. The ITD was a three-colour letter-size sheet of paper which was endorsed with a serial number and the stamp of the CPA Ministry of Interior, Iraq. Sample on file with author. Typos corrected.

[141] See *Doc 34*.

BEARER/TRAVELER:

Name: ______________________

Gender: ______________________

Residence: ______________________

Occupation: ______________________

Place of Birth: ______________________

Date of Birth: ______________________

National Identity Card or Other Identification Number: _________

Photo

____

Signature of Bearer

BELOW INFORMATION TO BE PROVIDED BY ISSUING AUTHORITY ONLY

____

Date and Location of Issue

______________________	______________________
Date of Expiration	Issuing Official
______________________	______________________
Date of Exit from Iraq	Date of Entry to Iraq

This document remains the property of the Coalition Provisional Authority (CPA) and shall be returned to the CPA or designated Iraqi authority upon demand. If this document is found, please return it to the CPA Ministry of Interior, Baghdad, Iraq.

Document 227
2004 Budget
13 October 2003

Budget Overview[142]

This Budget provides authority for the commitment and expenditure of money by the Interim Government of Iraq for 2004 and sets the fiscal framework for 2005 and 2006.

As a consequence of over two decades of neglect by the former regime, Iraq has immediate reconstruction and redevelopment needs well in excess of available revenues.

The Budget meets, to the extent possible with available revenues, the recurrent costs of the Iraqi government, some of the most pressing capital projects and around NID 940 billion ($US 625 million) in urgent nation building programs.

Iraq will run a deficit in 2004 of NID 886.3 billion ($US 590.9 million), financed by refunds of unspent Oil-for-Food funds. In 2005 and 2006, the budget is in balance (see Table 1).

[142] (a) The following definitions are used in this Budget Paper: • Budget year refers to 2004, while the forward years refer to 2005 and 2006, and the Budget period is 2004-6; and • one billion is equal to one thousand million.

(b) Figures in tables and generally in the text have been rounded. Discrepancies in tables between totals and sums of components are due to rounding: • estimates are in New Iraqi Dinar (NID); • estimates are generally rounded to the nearest 100 million New Iraqi Dinar; and • estimates midway between rounding points are rounded up.

(c) For the budget balance, a negative sign indicates a deficit while no sign indicates a surplus.

(d) The following notations are used: NID = New Iraqi Dinar; - = Nil; na = not available; bn = billion; $m = $ million.

Table 1: Budget Aggregates for 2003 to 2006

	2003(a) bn NID	2004 bn NID	2005 bn NID	2006 bn NID
Revenues				
Oil	4,096.5	18,000.0	27,750.0	28,950.0
Customs Duty	-	450.0	525.0	-
Income Tax	-	45.0	120.0	240.0
Returns from State Owned Entities	337.5	562.5	142.5	150.0
User pays fees and charges	85.5	96.3	132.5	185.1
Other taxes and income	76.5	105.0	105.0	120.0
Total Revenues	**4,596**	**19,258.8**	**28,775**	**29,645.1**
Expenditures				
Operating Expenditure	7,362.3	19,026.7	21,119.2	21,463.8
Capital Projects	1,869.9	1,118.4	7,636.5	8,154.0
Total Expenditures	**9,232.2**	**20,145.1**	**28,755.7**	**29,617.8**
Budget Balance (Deficit)	**4,636.2-**	**886.3-**	**19.3**	**27.3**

(a) The 2003 Budget only covers July to December 2003

In 2005 and 2006, revenue growth will permit Iraq to commit increased expenditures to much needed investment projects. These investment projects will grow to around NID 8 trillion ($US 5.3 billion) in 2005 and 2006.

The Budget process identified very substantial reconstruction and redevelopment needs, nearly all of which are not able to be funded in the 2004 Budget. The Iraqi Governing Council, in conjunction with the Coalition Provisional Authority, is seeking the support of the international donor and investment community to meet these unmet needs.

BUDGET FINANCING

Consistent with responsible fiscal policy this Budget does not rely on increased borrowing or printing money. Rather, the Budget deficit of NID 886.3 billion ($US 590.9 million) for 2004 will be financed from the return of unspent Oil-for-Food program funds.

Table 2 outlines the financing of Iraq's budgets for the coming years.

Table 2: Budget Financing for 2003 to 2006

	2003 bn NID	2004 bn NID	2005 bn NID	2006 bn NID
Opening Financial Capital				
Development Fund for Iraq	1,500.0	1,513.8	177.4	166.7
Vested Assets	1,350.0	-	-	-
Seized Assets	825.0	-	-	-
Total Opening Financial Capital	**3,675.0**	**1,513.8**	**177.4**	**166.7**
Plus: Capital Inflow				
Oil-for-Food Program Refunds	2,025.0	900.0	420.0	-
Transfer of Iraqi Assets from abroad	450.0	-	-	-
Less: Capital Outflow				
Transfer to Central Bank Reserves	-	1350.0	450.0	-
plus/less: Budget Surplus/deficit	4,636.2-	886.3-	19.3	27.3

Closing Financial Capital				
Development Fund for Iraq	1,513.8	177.4	166.7	194.0
Vested Assets	-	-	-	-
Seized Assets	-	-	-	-
Total Closing Financial Capital	**1,513.8**	**177.4**	**166.7**	**194.0**
Memorandum Item				
Cumulative Central Bank Reserves	450.0	1800.0	2,250.0	2,250.0

The **Development Fund for Iraq** (DFI) was established by the United Nations Security Council Resolution 1483 to be administered by the CPA, in consultation with the interim Iraqi authority. Contributions to the DFI have included a $US1 billion (NID 1.5 trillion) transfer from Iraq's Oil-for-Food program account, proceeds from oil export sales, and funds in other countries that belonged to the previous regime. These funds may only be used for humanitarian assistance, economic reconstruction, Iraqi civil administration and other purposes benefiting the Iraqi people.

Vested assets consisted of approximately $1.7 billion (NID 2.55 trillion) in Iraqi funds that previously belonged to the former regime in Iraq were frozen in US bank accounts and vested by the President of the United States in a special account of the United States Department of Treasury. These funds will be fully disbursed in paying salaries and pensions to Iraqi civil service workers and to fund other Iraq relief and reconstruction projects in 2003.

Seized Assets These funds consist of state owned or regime owned cash that was captured and safeguarded by Coalition Forces in Iraq. The authority for use of these funds was delegated to the CPA Administrator to use only to assist the Iraqi people and to support reconstruction of Iraq. All of these funds will be disbursed in 2003.

In addition to these funds, US Government appropriated funds are also being used to assist in the reconstruction of Iraq.

Relative to the 2003 Budget that was published in July, the 2004 Budget has reclassified US Government appropriated funds to being 'off budget' sources of finance. These appropriated funds however are noted below.

Iraq Relief and Reconstruction Fund (IRRF):	$US 2.475 billion (NID 3.71 trillion)
Natural Resources Risk Remediation Fund (NRRRF):	$US 0.502 billion (NID 753 billion)
Army Operations and Maintenance Funds for the New Iraqi Army transferred from the Iraq Freedom Fund:	$US 0.101 billion (NID 151.5 billion)

These funds will be fully committed against 2003 requirements.

ECONOMIC AND FISCAL POLICY OVERVIEW

This section provides an overview of the fiscal and economic policy issues and challenges confronting Iraq. It starts with an analysis of Iraq's economy over the past three decades. An assessment of the current state of Iraq's economy and the challenges confronting it follows. This is followed by an outline of the fiscal and economic policy framework proposed to re-develop Iraq's economy to improve the living standards of the population, drawing on the lessons from other transition economies.

The decline of Iraq's economy

It is very difficult to get reliable economic and fiscal data for Iraq over the past two decades.

Since 1979 the Iraqi national Budget was prepared in secret, and very closely held by the highest levels of the regime. Similarly, releasing core economic information about Iraq (Gross Domestic Product, unemployment and inflation rates) to the wrong hands carried the death penalty.

Nevertheless, the devastating economic effect of the previous regime's policies is undeniable. Saddam Hussein and his Ba'ath party presided over a very significant fall in living standards in Iraq, both in absolute and relative terms.

Chart 1: Iraqi per capita GDP: 1968-2001 ($US 2002) [omitted].

Thirty years ago, Iraq was an economic leader in the Arab world. Iraq had a strong workforce, modern infrastructure, and an effective public administration.

Today, while incomes of the rest of the world have gone forwards, per capita income in Iraq is a fraction of what it was 20 years ago (Chart 1).

The scale of this economic tragedy is difficult to overstate. The result is that Iraq today is an impoverished country, having once been a middle income country.

This decline in income co-incided with a collapse in infrastructure investment (Chart 2). This long term neglect of Iraq's vital infrastructure has left a legacy of a decrepit and fragile public infrastructure, and a capital stock a fraction of what it was two decades ago.

Chart 2: Gross Capital Formation in Iraq: 1980-2001 [omitted].

The economic legacy of Saddam Hussein

The source of Iraq's current problems stems from decades of economic mismanagement and corruption at the hands of Saddam Hussein and Iraq's Ba'ath party.

War, Opulence and Isolation

To some extent, this mismanagement is well known and broadly accepted. For example, the former regime:

- Started wars of aggression that cost untold Iraqi lives and tens of billions of dollars;
- Squandered Iraq's oil wealth on an opulent lifestyle for favoured officials of the previous regime, while ordinary Iraqis suffered a sustained decline in living standards; and
- Chose to isolate Iraq from the international community rather than dismantle its capacity for further military aggression against its neighbours and demonstrate that it had done so.

Some of the consequences of these policies are obvious.

The previous regime's wars and opulence diverted scarce resources away from social infrastructure and economic development. Its self-imposed isolation from the international business community has seen two decades of technological development pass it by, making state-owned enterprises increasingly inefficient. This is particularly evident in the crippled state of the banking and payments system.

Other consequences are less obvious.

The population policy of the previous regime was based on actively encouraging rapid growth in population to provide additional soldiers for its wars. However investment in education and housing declined, rather than increase in line with demand – in part reflecting the increased number of people seeking their share of Iraq's oil wealth.

In the first part of the 1990s, the previous regime's response to the international isolation it chose was to finance its spending by printing additional currency. The inevitable resultant hyperinflation created massive distortions throughout the economy, including the destruction of the real value of households saving deposits in the banks.

In the second part of the 1990s, the previous regime systematically and corruptly manipulated the humanitarian Oil-for-Food program instituted by Security Council resolution 986 and monitored by the United Nations.

The previous regime required that 10 per cent of the face value of contracts they submitted under the Oil-for-Food program be paid directly to the regime. These bribes were a key part in financing the palaces of the previous regime and maintaining and developing its military capability. In return, companies received inflated prices more than covering this additional cost.

In addition, a significant proportion of the goods imported under the Oil-for-Food program were on-sold by the State-owned enterprises at very significant discounts (over 50 per cent) in either local markets or smuggled out of the country to be sold in regional markets. The proceeds – much less than the oil exports used to purchase the goods – were then shared by the employees of the State-owned enterprises as 'profit' bonuses and the Iraqi budget (which in turn mainly funded the presidency and the military).

The result of this manipulation and corruption was that the humanitarian object of the Oil-for-Food program was undermined to a very significant degree. The extent of corruption under this program warrants further investigation.

State-Run Economy

Perhaps less obvious was the damage that the previous regime inflicted on Iraq through centralised command style economic policies.

The previous regime nationalised by force many industries from the 1970s. The consequence was a sustained reduction in the private sector's share of an already declining economy, as the private sector lost its incentive to save, invest and innovate.

The model of the State, rather than capital and product markets, determining the allocation of scarce financial capital has proven a failure across the world, as demonstrated by the collapse of the former Soviet Union. The experience of Iraq over the past two decades is yet another example, albeit among the most extreme, to add to this list.

Leaving aside the manner in which they were acquired, the enterprises run by the State have, almost without exception, been destroyers not creators of value, surviving only with subsidies from oil production.

Iraq's Economic Challenge

Iraq is a country with enormous economic potential. With sound policies, significant investments and assistance from international donors over the next several years, Iraq has the human and natural resources to return to the position of economic leadership it once held.

Fiscal and Economic Policy Approach

Iraq has significant reserves of natural resources. However ultimately, Iraq's economic future will depend on the adoption of sound fiscal and economic policies.

The objective of Iraq's fiscal and economic policy is to raise the living standards of all Iraqis as rapidly as possible through sustained economic growth.

Responsible fiscal policy is a key component of Iraq's economic strategy. The 2004 Budget was prepared on the basis that Iraq needs to demonstrate that it can operate with the resources available to it. The 2004 Budget does not rely on increased borrowing or printing money.

More generally, there are five core principles guiding Iraq's economic policy agenda:

1. Economic openness
2. Private sector development
3. International integration
4. Public sector transparency
5. A safety net for the poor.

Economic Openness

Economic openness is essential for markets to function properly, for business and job creation to occur, for ideas and entrepreneurship to flourish, and for Iraq to realise its full potential. The public sector has an important, but limited, role to play in everyday economic life.

Private Sector Development

The private sector, especially small and medium-sized companies that are often the most flexible and growth-oriented sector, will be strongly encouraged.

International Integration

Iraq is eager to fully rejoin the community of nations – practically and economically. Iraq will seek new and open trade relationships, financial links and other ties to the outside world to facilitate economic growth.

Public Sector Transparency

Iraq's institutions will be open to public scrutiny. Iraq's institutions will operate by clearly defined rules and will be held strictly accountable for their performance. This will help to reduce room for corruption and strengthen the confidence of investors and the Iraqi people alike.

A Safety Net for the Poor

Iraq must also help those suffering hardship now during this difficult economic transition. All Iraqis must share in Iraq's economic wealth. This will be done in a way that leaves people free to make their own choices but will also build a strong foundation for a market economy.

Lessons From Transition Economies

From the experience of other countries, we know that economic transitions are not easy and take time. The three decades of economic destruction wrought by the previous regime will not be undone overnight.

The history and stark facts of the twenty-odd transition economies during the last twenty years is that all of them suffered severe depressions and none of them started to grow in less than two years from the date they made the decision to change.

Iraq is in a much more difficult situation than other transitional economies since, unlike the transitional economies in the former Soviet Union, there is a significant security problem and a grossly inadequate infrastructure.

Given the years of neglect and war, the economy can't get into full gear unless the security problem is solved and the basic infrastructure which will facilitate economic development is repaired – electricity, water, sewage, transportation, communications and health.

The 2004 Iraqi Budget is the bare minimum necessary to keep Iraq going. It is nowhere near enough to kick-start the economy and create an enabling environment for future growth and prosperity.

Iraq will need international assistance to help it through this transition period, and enable it to take large strides back on the path to economic prosperity.

If started now, the security situation could be improved significantly within a year, the communications and electrical situation well on its way to being workable, and the water, sewage, health and transportation problems demonstrably on their way to success, completely changing the environment for investment.

These projects will of course significantly improve the employment situation and provide positive feedback on the security side.

Without this crucial investment there is little chance that the depressed private sector will recover in the short to medium term.

IRAQ'S BUDGET PROCESS AND FRAMEWORK

Budget Process

The 2004 Budget process began in July 2003. Officials from the Ministries of Finance and Planning, in conjunction with the Coalition Provisional Authority (CPA), prepared and circulated guidance to Ministries, including 'top line' provisional budget figures against which they needed to bid.

It included guidance on key assumptions to be used in the preparation of submissions, including a single exchange rate – 1500 NID to the US dollar.

In keeping with the principle of public sector transparency, this guidance was published on the internet at the same time it was provided to Ministries.

Ministries' budget submissions were received by the end of August. The Ministries of Finance and Planning conducted joint hearings in the first week of September in which each Ministry had the opportunity to explain and expound on the expenditure priorities they identified. These hearings were chaired by the Ministry of Finance and conducted in Arabic, with technical assistance provided by CPA officials.

The outcome of these hearings was then consolidated, and presented to the Governing Council and the CPA Administrator for approval.

Budget Coverage

Geographically, Iraq's budget was previously only for the Center and South of the country. This Budget covers all 18 governorates of Iraq, including the northern regions of Dohuk, Erbil and Suleymaniah. In the 2004 Budget, the northern regions of Iraq are treated as regional governments, with revenues flowing into the central Treasury consolidated revenue account and expenditures centrally funded by tied grants.

Budget Framework

Iraq's budget framework is characterized by a dichotomy between public entities that are 'on-budget' (all Ministries and their agencies that perform a public function) and 'off-budget' entities (also known as 'self-financing' entities).

All revenues of 'on-budget' entities are required to be put into consolidated revenue, controlled by the Ministry of Finance. Expenses of 'on-budget' entities are made against Budget appropriation lines.

Support for 'off-budget' entities is regarded as a transferred expenditure. Revenues of 'off-budget' entities are not required to be paid directly into consolidated revenue. Profits of State-owned enterprises are generally required to be transferred to the Ministry of Finance.

To avoid confusion, residual receipt of goods under the Oil-for-Food program are not recognised in the 2004 Budget.

The Budget Challenge

A key challenge in preparing the 2004 Budget was the lack of a clear base on where funds were spent by the previous regime.

Of the appropriations 'on-budget', a variety of exchange rates were used, as a means of providing subsidies, and little detail exists on how or where military or Presidency appropriations were spent.

Further, the vast bulk of public expenditure under the previous regime was 'off-budget', reflecting goods received under the Oil-for-Food program. The manipulation of this program by the former regime presented a significant challenge in preparing the 2004 Budget.

Chart 3: Iraq's budget challenge [omitted].

RISKS SURROUNDING THE ESTIMATES

The estimates of revenue and expenditure in this Budget incorporate the best information available at the time of publication. A range of factors may influence the actual budget outcome in future years.

The disclosure of these factors in this statement increases the transparency of the fiscal projections and ensures they remain 'on-balance' estimates.

Events that could affect fiscal outcomes include changes in economic and other parameters and matters not included in the fiscal forecasts because of uncertainty about their timing, magnitude and/or likelihood.

In particular, there are upside and downside risks to the oil price and export volume forecasts. Similarly, there is a possibility that tax revenues will be higher or lower than expected.

Should anticipated revenues be lower than expected, either expenditures would need to be reduced, or other revenue sources identified.

REVENUES

An important element of the Budget fiscal strategy is the resumption of existing, and the creation of new, revenue sources. This is balanced against the impact on the development of the private sector. While the oil sector will provide the substantial majority of revenues in the near term, in 2004 Iraq will begin to diversify its revenue sources.

Total revenue for 2004 is forecast at NID 19.3 trillion ($US 12.8 billion), increasing to NID 28.8 trillion ($US 19.2 billion) in 2005 and nearly NID 30 trillion ($US 19.8 billion) in 2006 as oil production increases (see Table 3).

Table 3: Revenues

	2003 bn NID	2004 bn NID	2005 bn NID	2006 bn NID
Oil Revenue	4,096.5	18,000.0	27,750.0	28,950.0
Reconstruction Levy	-	450.0	525.0	-
Personal Income Tax	-	15.0	45.0	90.0
Corporate income Tax	-	30.0	75.0	150.0
Interest Income	76.5	15.0	-	-
Transfers from SOEs	337.5	562.5	142.5	150.0
User Pay Charges	85.5	96.3	132.5	185.1
Other Taxes and Charges	-	90.0	105.0	120.0
Total	**4,596.0**	**19,258.8**	**28,775.0**	**29,645.1**

Oil Revenue

The Budget assumes that the level of oil exports will rise over the forecast period to reach pre-war level of 2.5 million barrels per day in 2005 – rather than the production target of the end of 2004. It also assumes a decline in the oil price from current levels to $US 21 per barrel over the Budget period. These assumptions reflect the need for Budget revenues to prudently balance risks.

	2004	2005	2006
Oil Revenue (NID bn)	18,000	27,750	28,950
Oil Exports (mb/d)	1.6	2.4	2.5
Oil Price ($US)	21	21	21

Reconstruction Levy

A 5 per cent reconstruction levy will be levied on all goods, except humanitarian goods, imported into Iraq from 1 January 2004. The revenues from the Reconstruction levy shall be used only to assist the Iraqi people and support the reconstruction of Iraq. It shall expire on 1 January 2006.

NID billion	2004	2005	2006
Reconstruction Levy	450	525	-

Personal Income Tax

From 1 January 2004, personal income tax will recommence, with a maximum rate of 15 per cent. It will be levied on the income of individuals, as defined under existing Iraqi income tax law. This lower rate, compared to the 75 per cent top rate that existed previously, will encourage compliance and reward effort.

NID billion	2004	2005	2006
Personal Income Tax	15	45	90

Company Income Tax

From 1 January 2004, company income tax will recommence at a flat rate of 15 per cent. It will be levied on the income of companies, including on the profits of foreign companies operating in Iraq.

NID billion	2004	2005	2006
Company Income Tax	30	75	150

Interest Income

The funds invested in the Development Fund for Iraq earn interest income.

NID billion	2004	2005	2006
Interest Income	15	-	-

Transfers from State Owned Enterprises (SOEs)

The following transfers are expected from SOEs in the forward estimates period.

Table 4: Revenue from State Owned Enterprises

	2003 bn NID	2004 bn NID	2005 bn NID	2006 bn NID
Central Bank of Iraq	-	75.0	90.0	105.0
Shopping Centers Company	-	75.0	7.5	-
Automobiles Company	-	150.0	7.5	-
Construction Material Company	-	150.0	7.5	-
Agriculture Supplies Company	135.0	105.0	7.5	-
Al Rasheed Hotels	7.5	7.5	22.5	45.0
Other enterprises	195.0	-	-	-
Total	**337.5**	**562.5**	**142.5**	**150.0**

Transfers are only expected from several of the nearly two hundred State Owned Enterprises (SOEs) in 2004. The bulk of the transfers anticipated in 2004 reflect the proceeds from the resale of goods imported under the Oil-for-Food program by companies overseen by the Ministries of Trade and Agriculture. The transfer from the Central Bank of Iraq reflects interest earned on Treasury notes less operating expenses, approved capital projects and some retained earnings.

User Pay Charges

One of the general principles underpinning this Budget is that Iraqis must contribute to the recovery of their economy. This includes paying for services used – at least to the extent this was done under the previous regime. By 2004 user pay arrangements will be re-implemented for:

- Vehicle registration;
- Other fees from emergency services;
- Passport Fees;
- Higher Education Course Fees;
- Court Fees; and
- Social Security Rental Income.

The revenue expected from these charges is displayed in the table below.

Table 5: Revenues from User Charges

	2003 bn NID	2004 bn NID	2005 bn NID	2006 bn NID
Passport Fees	-	0.8	0.8	0.8
Pharmaceutical scrip charge	15.00	30.0	37.5	45.0
Entry Fees to Cultural Institutions	0.15	0.8	0.8	0.8
Consultancy Charges	-	0.2	0.3	0.5
Sale of Statistical Publications	-	0.2	0.2	0.2
Court Fees	3.00	7.5	7.5	7.5
Social Security Rental income	1.50	3.0	3.0	3.0
Vehicle Registration	-	30.0	45.0	60.0
Higher Education Course Fees	1.50	1.5	7.5	30.0
Other fees from Emergency Services	-	7.5	15.0	22.5
Flight overpass fees	7.50	15.0	15.0	15.0
Other fees and charges	56.85	-	-	-
Total	**85.50**	**96.3**	**132.5**	**185.1**

The structure of each of these fee arrangements will be reviewed by the responsible Minister, in consultation with the Minister of Finance, to assess its adequacy relative to the service provided. The details of this review for each of these fees and charges will be published no later than 31 December 2003.

In addition, there are several new fees and charges applicable in 2004:

- Flight overpass fees
- Pharmaceutical scrip charge (for non-exempt)
- Entry Fees to Cultural Institutions
- Consultancy Charges
- Sale of Statistical Publications

Flight overpass fees are charges for the use of Iraqi airspace by commercial airlines. A pharmaceutical scrip charge of NID 1500 per scrip will apply to help defray the large cost of pharmaceuticals. Exemptions will apply to this charge where its application would result in significant hardship. Entry fees will be charged at cultural institutions such as Baghdad Museum. The Ministry of Planning will charge for consultancy services and statistical publications provided to commercial interests (domestic and foreign) investigating investing in Iraq.

There are also some significant examples of other user pay arrangements in place that do not appear as budget revenue. For example, electricity charges are paid to State Owned Enterprises monitored by the Electricity Commission, rather than directly into consolidated revenue. Similarly, municipal water rates and charges are paid to the municipality directly.

Other Taxes

Several other taxes will be raised in 2004. These are outlined in the table below.

Table 6: Other Taxes

	2003 bn NID	2004 bn NID	2005 bn NID	2006 bn NID
Excise Tax	-	15.0	15.0	15.0
Hotel and Restaurant Service Tax	-	7.5	7.5	7.5
Land Tax	-	15.0	30.0	45.0
Other	-	52.5	52.5	52.5
Total	**-**	**90.0**	**105.0**	**120.0**

A 15 per cent excise tax will apply to alcohol and tobacco products and other items to be determined. Collection of the 10 per cent tax on 4 and 5 star hotel accommodation and restaurants and the real estate transfer tax resumed on 19 September 2003. A range of other smaller existing taxes will continue to be collected. It includes taxes collected by regional governments.

In order to fund an indigenous effort to search for and recover funds stolen from Iraq under the previous regime, a luxury tax of ten per cent will be placed on the profits of businesses delivering remote television access.

BUDGET EXPENDITURES

This Budget provides authority for around NID 20 trillion ($US 13.4 billion) in expenditure in 2004, increasing to NID 28.8 trillion ($US 19.2 billion) in 2005 and NID 29.6 trillion ($US 19.7 billion) in 2006, in line with increased revenues.

Table 7: Expenditure Aggregates

	2003 bn NID	2004 bn NID	2005 bn NID	2006 bn NID
Expenditures				
Operating Expenditure	7,362.3	19,026.7	21,119.2	21,463.8
Capital Projects	1,869.9	1,118.4	7,636.5	8,154.0
Total Expenditures	**9,232.2**	**20,145.1**	**28,755.7**	**29,617.8**

Expenditure information is presented in several different forms. First, operating expenditure and capital projects are presented for each Ministry and Statutory Authority, along with employment levels and staffing costs.

Operating expenditures are then broken down into the eight headings of the existing Iraqi budget system: staffing expenditures, service requirements, goods requirements, asset maintenance, capital expenditures, transferred expenditures, foreign obligations and staff and retirement rewards.

However, this presentation does not provide satisfactory guidance on what is being achieved by this spending. To correct for this gap, operating expenditures are also broken down into major initiatives in the Budget, along with normal ministry operating expenses.

Capital projects funded by the budget are listed, along with their estimated cost in 2004 and total project cost.

Finally, for each Ministry and statutory authority a summary of all expenditure items is presented.

Expenditure Summary by Ministry

Table 8 provides a summary of operating expenditure, capital projects and total expenditure approved in the 2004 Budget by Ministry and Statutory Authority.

Table 8	2004			2005			2006		
	Operating bn NID	Capital bn NID	**Total bn NID**	Operating bn NID	Capital bn NID	**Total bn NID**	Operating bn NID	Capital bn NID	**Total bn NID**
Agriculture	35.4	17.7	**53.2**	42.2	75.0	**117.2**	45.5	75.0	**120.5**
Communications	1.8	7.5	**9.3**	6.3	225.0	**231.3**	6.3	225.0	**231.3**
Culture	12.3	1.5	**13.8**	9.3	22.5	**31.8**	9.3	22.5	**31.8**
Displacement and Migration	0.9	1.5	**2.4**	0.9	7.5	**8.4**	0.9	15.0	**15.9**
Education	805.9	10.0	**815.9**	806.2	30.0	**836.2**	806.2	30.0	**836.2**
Electricity Commission	2.2	-	**2.2**	2.2	2,250.0	**2,252.2**	2.2	2,475.0	**2,477.2**
Environment	0.9	1.5	**2.4**	0.9	30.0	**30.9**	0.9	60.0	**60.9**
Finance	15,683.8	132.9	**15,816.7**	17,441.4	240.0	**17,681.4**	17,545.4	240.0	**17,785.4**
Foreign Affairs	57.6	9.0	**66.6**	56.9	15.0	**71.9**	56.9	15.0	**71.9**
Governing Council	9.6	-	**9.6**	12.0	-	**12.0**	15.0	-	**15.0**
Health	1,345.5	75.0	**1,420.5**	1,592.9	150.0	**1,742.9**	1,790.5	150.0	**1,940.5**
Higher Education	171.1	12.0	**183.1**	171.1	7.5	**178.6**	171.1	7.5	**178.6**
Housing	55.2	200.1	**255.3**	46.7	450.0	**496.7**	46.7	450.0	**496.7**
Human Rights	0.9	1.5	**2.4**	0.9	7.5	**8.4**	0.9	15.0	**15.9**
Industry and Minerals	12.0	-	**12.0**	9.0	1.5	**10.5**	9.0	1.5	**10.5**
Interior	187.3	-	**187.3**	200.0	150.0	**350.0**	215.0	150.0	**365.0**
Justice	144.6	63.3	**207.9**	134.4	150.0	**284.4**	134.4	150.0	**284.4**
Labour and Social Affairs	49.2	3.1	**52.3**	52.2	7.5	**59.7**	67.2	7.5	**74.7**
Municipalities and Public Works	60.0	249.0	**309.0**	84.5	727.5	**812.0**	84.5	975.0	**1,059.5**
Oil	2.7	-	**2.7**	1.9	1,500.0	**1,501.9**	1.9	1,500.0	**1,501.9**
Planning	45.0	22.5	**67.5**	54.9	-	**54.9**	61.6	-	**61.6**
Science and Technology	28.6	7.7	**36.4**	31.0	15.0	**46.0**	31.0	15.0	**46.0**
Trade	10.8	4.5	**15.3**	6.3	-	**6.3**	6.3	-	**6.3**
Transport	34.2	93.0	**127.2**	8.1	750.0	**758.1**	8.1	750.0	**758.1**
Water Resources	25.2	192.3	**217.5**	29.3	750.0	**779.3**	29.3	750.0	**779.3**
Youth and Sport	18.2	4.2	**22.4**	18.2	75.0	**93.2**	18.2	75.0	**93.2**
Statutory Authorities									
Board of Supreme Audit	4.1	0.5	**4.5**	3.8	-	**3.8**	3.8	-	**3.8**
Central Organisation for Standards	2.7	-	**2.7**	1.7	-	**1.7**	1.7	-	**1.7**
Awqaf (Religious Endowments)	2.1	8.1	**10.2**	2.3	-	**2.3**	2.3	-	**2.3**
Iraqi Media Network	2.2	-	**2.2**	2.2	-	**2.2**	2.2	-	**2.2**
New Iraqi Army	34.8	-	**34.8**	109.8	-	**109.8**	109.8	-	**109.8**
Unallocated	180.0	-	**180.0**	180.0	-	**180.0**	180.0	-	**180.0**
Total	**19,026.7**	**1,118.4**	**20,145.1**	**21,119.2**	**7,636.5**	**28,755.7**	**21,463.8**	**8,154.0**	**29,617.8**

Staffing Levels and Expenditure Summary by Ministry

This table provides a summary of the number of employees on the direct Government payroll by Ministry. An allocation of salaries has been provided to each Ministry to meet salary costs for these employees, using the interim four tier salary scale. The new 13 tier salary scale will increase the overall public sector wage bill. The budget allocation to fund this increase is only transferred to a Ministry when the proposed aggregate plan for allocating all of the Ministry's staff into the new tiers has been approved.

Table 9: Ministry Staffing Levels

	2004 Employees	2004 bn NID
Agriculture	8,166	19.7
Communications	174	0.3
Culture	3,213	5.1
Displacement and Migration	34	0.1
Education	324,532	655.9
Electricity Commission	846	1.4
Environment	34	0.1
Finance	6,633	14.4
Foreign Affairs	1,410	2.7
Health	105,481	220.5
Higher Education	50,055	107.3
Housing	16,409	30.2
Human Rights	34	0.1
Industry and Minerals	584	1.3
Interior	65,105	155.0
Justice	21,433	44.1
Labour and Social Affairs	5,413	11.7
Municipalities and Public Works	22,874	39.5
Oil	770	1.9
Planning	1,050	2.4
Science and Technology	10,041	16.0
Trade	1,419	3.0
Transport	1,888	4.1
Water Resources	6,958	14.3
Youth and Sport	2,427	3.2
Statutory Authorities		
Board of Supreme Audit	1,216	3.0
Central Organisation for Standards	500	1.0
New Iraqi Army	26,500	34.8
Iraqi Media Network	1,322	2.2
Governing Council	125	1.2
Centrally Funded Employees	353,578	1,762.5
Total	**1,047,718**	**3,159.0**

Operating Expenditure Summary by Input

This table provides a summary of operating expenditure broken down into the eight headings of the existing Iraqi budget system.

Table 10: Operating Expenditure Summary by Input

	2003 bn NID	2004 bn NID	2005 bn NID	2006 bn NID
Staff Expenditures	1,467.6	3159.0	3,153.0	3,148.5
Service Requirements	277.2	544.8	544.2	584.0
Goods Requirements	419.7	1,101.1	1,354.0	1,528.9
Assets Maintenance	99.4	154.4	193.0	204.1
Capital Expenditures	154.1	159.4	179.3	192.8
Transferred Expenditures	4,173.1	11,182.8	12,406.2	12,223.7
Foreign Obligations	205.7	925.2	1,414.3	1,631.8
Salaries & Retirement rewards	565.5	1,800.0	1,875.0	1,950.0
Total Budget Inputs	**7,362.3**	**19,026.7**	**21,119.2**	**21,463.8**

Capital expenditures are regarded as operating expenditures if they represent the regular purchase of capital items necessary for the operation of a ministry, rather than representing a capital project or investment. New vehicle expenditures, for example, are recorded under this expenditure line.

Transferred expenditures include, amongst other things, the cost of the public distribution system and support for State Owned Enterprises.

The **Foreign obligations** category includes the war reparations to Kuwait required under Security Council resolution 1483 (discussed further below).

Operating Expenditure Summary by Output

Table 11 below provides a summary of operating expenditure by program initiatives. A brief description of each item follows.

Table 11: Operating Expenditure Summary by Output

	2003 bn NID	2004 bn NID	2005 bn NID	2006 bn NID
Public Distribution System	-	5,250.0	7,350.0	7,350.0
Oil product imports	2,287.5	-	-	-
Normal Ministry Operating Expenditure	869.2	2,192.7	2,353.4	2,430.5
Contingency Reserve	-	1,125.0	1,500.0	1,500.0
Local/Regional Government Grants	294.0	1,117.5	1,117.5	1,117.5
Reserve for New Salary Scale	-	1,065.0	1,065.0	1,065.0
Regional Development Projects	340.5	1,116.0	450.0	450.0
Nation Building Projects	466.5	937.5	75.0	75.0
Pharmaceuticals	-	930.0	1,125.0	1,275.0
Kuwait War Reparations	205.5	900.0	1,380.0	1,447.5
Support for SOEs	558.0	750.0	675.0	600.0
Economic Restructuring Programs	160.5	750.0	750.0	750.0
Centrally funded salaries	1,467.0	697.5	697.5	697.5
Pensions and other Transfer Payments	225.0	675.0	750.0	825.0
Stipends to Demobilised Military	180.0	375.0	375.0	375.0
Agricultural Subsidies	-	300.0	300.0	300.0
Interest on Foreign Debt	-	-	300.0	300.0
Interest on Treasury Notes	-	210.0	210.0	210.0
Payment System Fees	-	135.0	135.0	135.0
Oil Export Production Fee	-	109.5	146.0	182.5
Consultancies	-	75.0	75.0	75.0
Haj subsidies	-	56.3	56.3	56.3
New Office for Landmine Removal	-	30.0	37.5	45.0

On the job training initiative	-	7.5	9.0	15.0
Recovery of Iraqi Assets from Abroad	-	5.4	-	-
Office of Foreign Litigation	-	5.3	-	-
Iba Agricultural Research Institute	-	3.0	3.0	3.0
Privatisation Consultants	-	3.0	-	-
Economic Policy Consultancy	-	3.0	3.0	3.0
Transition Management Assistance	-	3.0	-	-
Other Measures	308.5	199.6	181.0	181.0
Total Operating Expenditures	**7,362.3**	**19,026.7**	**21,119.2**	**21,463.8**

Public Distribution System

A central element of the Oil-for-Food program under Security Council Resolution 986 was the monthly provision of a ration of food to each Iraqi citizen in return for a nominal fee. This ration represents the principal income of many Iraqi households. The estimated full year total cost of this program is NID 7.4 trillion. A reduced level of funding is necessary in 2004, reflecting the residual provision of food items under the Oil-for-Food program.

This amount is included under transferred expenditures.

Estimated cost (bn NID)	2003	2004	2005	2006
Public Distribution System	-	5,250	7,350	7,350

Normal Ministry Operating Expenses

Ministries require a level of funding to meet the normal (or base case) operating expenses (including salaries – except in 2003, where they were centrally financed).

Estimated cost (bn NID)	2003	2004	2005	2006
Normal Ministry Operating Expenses	869.2	2,192.7	2,353.4	2,430.5

Contingency Reserve

Given the uncertainty surrounding Iraq's situation, it is prudent to set aside a contingency reserve to cover the level of currently unidentified needs likely expected to arise over the Budget period. This amount is included under transferred expenditures.

Estimated cost (bn NID)	2003	2004	2005	2006
Contingency Reserve	-	1,125	1,500	1,500

Local and Regional Government Grants

Local and Regional governments provide services direct to their communities. Grants will be provided to these governments to supplement, not replace, their traditional financing sources – fees and charges for the services provided. This amount is included under transferred expenditures.

Estimated cost (bn NID)	2003	2004	2005	2006
Local/Regional Government Grants	294	1,117.5	1,117.5	1,117.5

Reserve for New Salary Scale

A new thirteen tier salary scale takes effect in October 2003. This reserve reflects the estimated additional cost of the new salary scale. The amount allocated to Ministries for salary expenses in this Budget reflect the previous four tier scale. As each Ministry has its allocations across the thirteen tiers approved, the additional cost will be transferred from this reserve to the Ministry's budget appropriation. This amount is included under salary expenditures.

Estimated cost (bn NID)	2003	2004	2005	2006
Reserve for New Salary Scale	-	1,065	1,065	1,065

Nation Building Projects

With the fall of the previous regime, Iraq is in the transition to becoming a free and democratic society. This transition process requires many of the traditional democratic institutions and structures to be built, or at least significantly reconstructed. This measure provides funding of around NID 938 billion in 2004 and NID 75 billion in 2005 and 2006 for nation and institution building projects.

The projects that are expected to be funded under this measure are listed below. The Ministers of Finance and Planning have joint responsibility for assessing these proposals for submission to the Governing Council. This amount is included under transferred expenditures.

Table 12: Nation Building Projects

	2003 bn NID	2004 bn NID	2005 bn NID	2006 bn NID
National Census	-	150.0	-	-
Elections Assistance	-	75.0	-	-
Constitutional Development	-	45.0	-	-
Civil Society and Community Dvmt	-	30.0	-	-
WMD Scientist Retention	-	90.0	30.0	30.0
Legal claims/debt negotiation	-	15.0	-	-
Modernize banking system	-	30.0	15.0	15.0
Tax administration modernization	-	15.0	15.0	15.0
Stock Exchange modernization	-	7.5	-	-
Economic indices development	-	22.5	-	-
Labour force survey development	-	22.5	-	-
Other projects	466.5	435.0	15.0	15.0
Total Nation Building Projects	**466.5**	**937.5**	**75.0**	**75.0**

Kuwait War Reparations

United Nations Security Council resolution 1483 requires Iraq to pay 5 per cent of gross oil export revenues to meet reparation claims from the first Gulf war. This amount is included under foreign obligations.

Estimated cost (bn NID)	2003	2004	2005	2006
Kuwait War Reparations	205.5	900.0	1,380.0	1,447.5

Support for State Owned Enterprises (SOEs)

Iraq's State Owned Enterprises (SOEs) employ nearly 500,000 people. From 1 January 2004, salaries of SOEs employees will no longer be centrally funded directly from the Budget, but will need to [be] paid from SOEs revenues. With the greater consumer choice and lower prices associated with open borders many of these enterprises will be unprofitable as currently structured.

This budget provides NID 750 billion in 2004 in support for SOEs to enable them to resume and maintain operations as options for their future are assessed – it does not allow for significant reconstruction of destroyed facilities or significant new investment. Lesser amounts are set aside for 2005 and 2006 reflecting both an expected improvement in the profitability of these enterprises and the expectation that some less profitable enterprises would be closed.

This support has yet to be allocated to each SOE, as sufficient information is not yet available. Through their responsible monitoring Ministry, SOEs will apply to the Ministry of Finance for access to this support on a case by case basis as information on their needs becomes clearer. Updated lists of allocations to individual SOEs will be published at regular intervals.

This amount is included under transferred expenditures.

Estimated cost (bn NID)	2003	2004	2005	2006
Support for SOEs	-	750	675	600

Economic Restructuring Programs

The transition of Iraq's economy from centrally managed to one driven by market forces will involve significant restructuring of the economy. Economic restructuring programs are necessary to assist this transition process. Payments to workers made redundant through the closure or restructuring of State Owned Enterprises will reduce the hardship associated with this necessary but difficult process. Similarly training programs will assist in providing a closer match of the skills of the workforce with the changing demands of the labour market. This amount is included under transferred expenditures.

Estimated cost (bn NID)	2003	2004	2005	2006
Economic Restructuring Programs	160.5	750	750	750

Pensions and Other Transfer Payments

There is a range of pension and transfer payments in Iraq, including: pensions to retired public servants, military and their dependents; 'private' pension arrangements previously financed through the social security fund, and the 'family social bonus' paid to those in greatest need. The number of beneficiaries is expected in increase over the Budget period, as previous restrictions (eg, caps) are lifted. This amount is included under salaries and retirement rewards.

Estimated cost (bn NID)	2003	2004	2005	2006
Pensions and Other Transfer Payments	225	675	750	825

Stipends to Demobilised Military

With the dissolution of the old Iraqi Army, the Coalition Provisional Authority decided to pay, for an indefinite period, stipends to the demobilised military. A future Iraqi government will need to decide whether or not to continue paying these stipends. This amount is included under salaries and retirement rewards.

Estimated cost (bn NID)	2003	2004	2005	2006
Stipends to Demobilized Military	180	375	375	375

Agricultural Subsidies

Iraq's agricultural sector has a long history of state support and control. On the one hand this has involved the subsidized provision of agricultural inputs, while on the other hand price controls discouraged and distorted the pattern of agricultural production. The strategy in this Budget has two pillars – increasing agricultural output prices to market prices and delivering subsidies in a more efficient manner. This amount is included under transferred expenditures.

Estimated cost (bn NID)	2003	2004	2005	2006
Agricultural Subsidies	-	300	300	300

Interest on Treasury Notes

Iraq has around NID 3.5 trillion in Treasury notes on issue, with a coupon of 6 per cent per annum. The vast majority of these notes are held by the Central Bank of Iraq and the State owned commercial banks. Meeting the interest obligations on these notes will cost NID 210 billion per annum. This amount is included under transferred expenditures.

Estimated cost (bn NID)	2003	2004	2005	2006
Interest on Treasury notes	-	210	210	210

Interest on Foreign Debt

Iraq has very substantial levels of foreign debt. Security Council resolution 1483 provides a moratorium on interest and principal repayments until the end of 2004. The level of interest and principal payments on foreign debt beyond 2004 is a matter for future negotiations. In this budget, NID 300 billion is set aside for interest payments in 2005 and 2006. This amount is included under transferred expenditures.

Estimated cost (bn NID)	2003	2004	2005	2006
Interest on Foreign debt	-	-	300	300

Payment System Fees

The execution of this budget requires the movement and payment of significant amounts of currency. In 2003 many of these services have been provided by Coalition forces. In 2004, these services will need to be purchased by the Government of Iraq – usually, but not necessarily by SOEs (in particular the banks). The budget sets aside NID 135 billion per annum for fees and charges associated with payment system services provided to the Government. The amount paid for particular services is a matter for competitive commercial negotiations. This amount is included under service expenditures.

Estimated cost (bn NID)	2003	2004	2005	2006
Payment System Fees	-	135	135	135

Oil Export Production Fee

Gross oil export revenue is recognized directly on the budget, in accordance with Security Council resolution 1483. It follows that expenses associated with the production of oil exports also need to be funded through the budget. This budget provides for NID 200 per barrel of oil exported to be paid to companies monitored by the Ministry of Oil. This amount is included under transferred expenditures.

Estimated cost (bn NID)	2003	2004	2005	2006
Oil Export Prod'n Fee	-	109.5	146	182.5

Consultancies

Iraq's Ministries will be confronted with a range of new issues and challenges over the period ahead, outside their recent institutional experience and expertise. To meet this challenge, Ministries will need to engage independent external consultants to advise on these issues and more generally to assist in building institutional capacity.

The range and type of these issues is not yet known with certainty, so it is not yet possible to allocate these amounts by Ministry and/or project. Rather, this funding provides a capped general allocation of NID 75 billion per annum that Ministries can apply to the Minister of Finance for access on a case by case basis as needs emerge. The Minister of Finance will publish details on consultancies approved at regular intervals. This amount is included under service requirements.

Estimated cost (bn NID)	2003	2004	2005	2006
Consultancies	-	75	75	75

Economic Policy Consultancy

The Minister of Finance will engage independent consultants to advise him on a range of economic policy issues. This amount is included under service requirements.

Estimated cost (bn NID)	2003	2004	2005	2006
Economic Policy Consultancy	-	3	3	3

Document 228

Revisions to 2004 Budget

March 2004[143]

1. REVISIONS TO BUDGET 2004[144]

This document sets out the revisions to the Iraqi national budget for 2004, updating the fiscal framework to take into account changes that have occurred since the original 2004 budget was published in October 2003.

Increased resources and their use

The fiscal circumstances for Iraq have changed significantly since the publication of the original 2004 Budget in October of 2003. Greater than expected capital inflows resulted in a higher than expected opening financial capital at the beginning of 2004. A lower-than expected need for central bank reserves and some transfers of assets from abroad have increased net capital inflows.

[143] The document is produced out of chronological sequence immediately after the document it modifies.

[144] (a) The following definitions are used in this Budget Revisions paper: 'Budget year' refers to 2004. 'One billion' is equal to one thousand million.

(b) Figures in tables and generally in the text have been rounded. Discrepancies in tables between totals and sums of components are due to rounding.

(c) Estimates are in billions of new Iraqi Dinar (ID).

Buoyant prices and greater output have greatly increased oil revenues over expectations, more than compensating for a reduction in expected tax revenues. These combined increases in resources have all been allocated to increased expenditures and to a prudent increase in the forecast closing financial capital.

Table 1. Use of increased resources	Change
Increased resources	
Increased opening financial capital (1 Jan 2004)	+6,602.4
Increased revenues	+2,470.3
Increased capital inflows	+750.0
Sub-total	*+9,822.7*
less Increased use of resources	
Increase in expenditure	+9,744.7
Change in closing financial capital (31 Dec 2004)	+78.0
Sub-total	*+9,822.7*
UNALLOCATED RESOURCES (Difference)	**0**

The remainder of this document sets out the specific changes in resources and expenditures. Annex A shows the changes in Budget forecasts for 2003 and 2004, tracking the changes by date of publication.

2. INCREASED RESOURCES

Projected resources available for 2004 are expected to be ID 9822.7 bn greater than was projected in October last year. This increase consists of changes in opening financial capital, net capital inflows plus increased revenues (primarily oil).

Table 2.1 Total expenditures (ID bn)	Original	Revised	*Change*
Opening financial capital (1 Jan 2004)	1,513.8	8,116.2	*+6,602.4*
plus Net Capital Inflows	-450.0	300.0	*+750.0*
plus Revenues	19,258.8	21,729.1	*+2,470.3*
TOTAL RESOURCES	**20,322.6**	**30,145.31**	***+9,822.7***

This increase has been incorporated into the revised Budget 2004 as the baseline and has therefore already been allocated. These allocations are reflected in the expenditures listed in the revised Budget.

Opening Balance

On December 31st 2003 there was ID 8116.2 bn remaining of uncommitted funds in the DFI account. Uncommitted funds are those that have not been earmarked to pay for money released under Budget 2003 or to pay for outstanding bills. Compared to the projection made in October 2003 this reflects an increase of ID 6602.4 bn. This reflects greater than expected capital inflows in 2003.

Increase in projected net capital inflows for 2004

Projected net capital inflows have increased by ID 750 bn over the projections made in October. These increases come from a lower than expected need for central bank reserves, which has substantial reserves of over ID 2,250 bn and given the appreciation of the Iraqi Dinar no requirement is foreseen. There has also been an ID 300 bn transfer of Iraqi assets from Jordan. However, the projected refunds from the Oil-for-Food programme (OFF) materialised in 2003.

Table 2.2 Capital inflows (ID bn)	Original	Revised	*Change*
Capital Flows in			
Transfer of Iraqi assets from abroad	0.0	300.0	*+300.0*
Oil for Food Programme Refunds	900.0	0.0	*-900.0*
Less Capital Outflows			
Transfer to Central Bank	1,350.0	0.0	*-1,350.0*
TOTAL NET CAPITAL INFLOWS	**-450.0**	**300.0**	***+750.0***

**Columns will not add because only changed lines are shown above.*

Increase in projected revenues in 2004

Projected revenues for 2004 have increased by ID 2470.3 bn over the projection made in October. These projections come from increases in oil revenues and a proposed Civil Service Pension Contribution. However, expected revenues from state-owned enterprises (SOEs) are not expected to materialise in 2004.

Oil revenues are estimated using a prudent assumption of a gradual fall in net oil price received to US$ 21 per barrel (ID 31,500) in June. Oil exports are assumed to reach 1.9 million barrels per day by the end of the year. If oil prices rise significantly or exports are greater than expected then there could be a very notable increase in net revenues -but for budgeting purposes a more cautious approach is needed.

Tax revenues are expected to fall. The late implementation of the Reconstruction Levy will reduce the expected revenue from this tax and revenues for other taxes have also been revised downwards.

Table 2.3: Revenues (ID bn)	Original	Revised	*Change*
Oil Revenues	18,000.0	21,262.9	*+3,262.9*
Reconstruction Levy	450.0	172.5	*-277.5*
Personal Income Tax	15.0	7.5	*-7.5*
Civil Service Pension Contribution	0.0	101.4	*+101.4*
Corporate Income Tax	30.0	0.0	*-30.0*
Transfers from State Owned Enterprises	562.5	0.0	*-562.5*
Excise Tax	15.0	3.0	*-12.0*
Land Tax	15.0	10.5	*-4.5*
TOTAL REVENUES*	**19,258.8**	**21,729.1**	***+2,470.3***

**Columns will not add because only changed lines are shown above.*

3. INCREASED EXPENDITURES

Expenditures in 2004 are projected to rise by ID 9756.3 bn.

Table 3.1 Total expenditures (ID bn)	Original	Revised	*Change*
Total Staff Expenditure	3,159.0	3,879.5	*+720.5*
Total Operating Expenditure	1,959.7	2,961.7	*+1,002.1*
Total Ministry Capital Projects	1,118.4	3,797.5	*+2,679.1*
Total Transferred Expenditures	11,921.3	15,882.7	*+3,961.4*
Total Foreign Obligations	925.2	2,172.8	*+1,247.7*
Total Salaries and Retirement Rewards	1,050.0	1,195.5	*+145.5*
TOTAL EXPENDITURES	**20,133.5**	**29,889.8**	***+9,756.3***

Increase in Staff Expenditures in 2004

The move from the 4-tier to the 11-tier scale plus the Facility Protection Service and the introduction of Hazardous Duty Pay has increased projected staff expenditures by ID 720.5 bn.

Table 3.2 Staff expenditures (ID bn)	Original	Revised	*Change*
Ministry Salaries (including reserve for new salary scale)	2,461.5	2,800.7	*+339.2*
Hazardous Duty Pay	0.0	225.0	*+225.0*
Facility Protection Service Guards	0.0	90.6	*+90.6*
Iraqi Civil Defence Force Pay	0.0	65.7	*+65.7*
TOTAL STAFF EXPENDITURES*	**3,159.0**	**3,879.5**	***+720.5***

** Columns will not add because only changed lines are shown above.*

Increase in non-staff Operating Expenditures in 2004

Projected spending on non-staff operating expenses in 2004 has risen by ID 1002.1 bn. Most of the change results from increases in Ministry operating costs, including ID 129 bn for increased Ministry of Interior security operations. Funding for consultancies was removed from the Budget. Spending on pharmaceuticals has dropped by ID 63 bn, but this simply reflects a shift in resources from pharmaceuticals towards other health spending, under normal ministry operating expenditure.

Table 3.3 Operating costs (ID bn)	Original	Revised	*Change*
Normal Ministry Operating Expenditure	1,384.6	1,850.0	*465.5*
Pharmaceuticals	930.0	867.0	*-63.0*
Oil for Food Audit	0.0	4.5	*+4.5*
IMN Operating Contract	0.0	144.0	*+144.0*
Consultancies	75.0	0.0	*-75.0*
TOTAL OPERATING COSTS*	**1,959.7**	**2,961.74**	***+1,002.1***

** Columns will not add because only changed lines are shown above.*

Increase in Ministry Capital Projects in 2004

Spending on capital projects by ministries is now projected to be almost three times larger than was originally projected – an increase of ID 2679.1 bn.

Table 3.4 Ministry capital projects	Original	Revised	*Change*
Ministry capital projects	1,118.4	3,797.5	*+2,679.1*

Increase in Transferred Expenditures in 2004

Projected transferred expenditures are ID 5202.7 bn higher than estimated in October 2003.

Expenditures that were previously allocated to service Ministry of Finance domestic debt obligations underestimated these costs. At present, the Ministry of Finance has ID 4,600 bn in outstanding Treasury bills. The revised figure of ID 75 bn reflects expected debt servicing costs in 2004, including a need to convert a Ministry of Finance overdraft with the Central Bank to domestic securities that will also result in additional interest costs.

Table 3.5 Transferred expenditures	Original	Revised	*Change*
Debt Negotiations Costs	0.0	75.0	*+50.0*
Reconciliation of External Debt	0.0	6.0	*+4.0*
Fuel Imports	0.0	3,150.0	*+3,150.0*
Interest on Treasury Notes	210.0	319.5	*+109.5*
Public Distribution System	5,250.0	3,600.0	*-1,650.0*
Transfer Payments (was Contingency Fund)	1,125.0	2,506.1	*+1,381.1*
Transfer Capital	0.0	300.0	*+300.0*
Salary Reserve	0.0	19.2	*+19.2*

Local/Regional Government Grants	1,117.5	1,246.2	*+128.7*
KRG Normal Operating Costs	0.0	1,200.0	*+1,200.0*
KRG Ongoing Projects	0.0	900.0	*+900.0*
Municipal Services Directorate Support	0.0	46.5	*+46.5*
Water Directorate Support	0.0	44.7	*+44.7*
Sewerage Directorate Support	0.0	12.5	*+12.5*
Baghdad Amanat Salaries	0.0	27.3	*+27.3*
Baghdad Amanat Support	0.0	57.3	*+57.3*
Baghdad Amanat Capital Projects	0.0	30.0	*+30.0*
Dewan support	0.0	9.4	*+9.4*
Regional Development Projects	1,116.0	0.0	*-1,116.0*
Commanders Emergency Response Programme (CERP)	0.0	105.0	*+105.0*
Rapid Regional Response Programme Funds	0.0	337.6	*+337.6*
State-Owned-Enterprise Support	750.0	1,330.2	*+580.2*
Economic Restructuring Programs	750.0	0.0	*-750.0*
125,000 Jobs Programme	0.0	187.5	*+187.5*
Employment Centers	0.0	13.5	*+13.5*
Additional Security Spending	0.0	750.0	*+750.0*
Oil Export Production Fee	109.5	127.8	*+18.3*
Oil for Food Contracts	0.0	404.3	*+404.3*
Iraqi Property Claims Commission	0.0	52.5	*+52.5*
Commission on Public Integrity	0.0	30.0	*+30.0*
Militia Reintegration	0.0	3.6	*+3.6*
Nation Building	937.5	856.8	*-80.7*
TOTAL TRANSFERRED EXP.*	**11,921.3**	**17,124.0**	***+5,202.7***

** Columns will not add because only changed lines are shown above.*

Nation building measures are broken down in more detail in Annex B.

Increase in Foreign Obligations in 2004

Higher than projected oil revenues mean that Kuwaiti War Reparations are higher, as these are 5% of gross revenues. Oil for Food Contracts have risen also, combining to increase projected spending for 2004 by ID 843.1 bn.

Table 3.6 Foreign obligations (ID bn)	Original	Revised	*Change*
Kuwaiti War Reparations	900.0	1,063.1	*+163.1*
International Monetary Fund and World Bank Arrears	0.0	680.0	*+680.0*
TOTAL FOREIGN OBLIGATIONS*	**925.2**	**1,768.3**	***+843.1***

** Columns will not add because only changed lines are shown above.*

Increase in Salaries and Retirement Rewards in 2004

Quarterly public sector pensions have been increased for every pensioner by ID 25,000 from 1st April, increasing costs by ID 145.5 billion in 2004. This will be financed by the new Civil Service Pension Contributions of ID 101.4 bn, the remainder of which will go to financing existing pension obligations.

Table 3.7 Salary & retirement awards	Original	Revised	*Change*
Pensions and other transfer payments	675.0	820.5	*+145.5*
TOTAL SALARIES & RETIREMENT*	**1,050.0**	**1,195.5**	***+145.5***

** Columns will not add because only changed lines are shown above.*

Annex A. CHANGES IN BUDGET ESTIMATES

This annex sets out the different estimates that have been made for budget financing for financial years 2003 and 2004. There are three publications that have set out budget estimates:

1. (May 2003) Budget Revenues and Expenses 2003. Sets out initial estimates for financial year 2003 only.
2. (Oct 2003) *2004 Budget*. Sets out revised estimates for 2003 and initial estimates for 2004.
3. (March 2004) Revisions to 2004 Budget. This document, with estimated out-turn for 2003 and revised estimates for 2004.

Table A. Published budget estimates (ID bn)	**Date of Publication of Estimate**		
	May 2003	**October 2003**	**March 2004**
Financial year 2003	*(estimate)*	*(estimate)*	*(provisional)*
Opening financial capital (1 July)	8,104.5	3,675.0	3,675.0
plus Net Capital Inflows	-3,150.5	2,475.0	7,886.8
plus Revenues	5,831.6	4,596.0	5,589.4
less Expenditures	9,149.4	9,232.2	9,035.0
Closing balance 31 Dec 04	**1,636.7**	**1,513.8**	**8,116.2**
Financial year 2004		*(estimate)*	*(estimate)*
Opening financial capital (1 July)		1,513.8	8,116.2
plus Net Capital Inflows		-450.0	300.0
plus Revenues		19,258.8	21,729.1
less Expenditures		20,145.1	29,890.9
Closing balance 31 Dec 04		**177.5**	**254.4**

Annex B. NATION BUILDING AND OTHER PROJECTS

The tables below break down the totals given in table 3.5 for Nation Building Projects and R3P projects (Rapid Regional Response Programmes).

Table 3.1 Nation Building (ID bn)	**Original**	**Revised**	***Change***
Mortgage Bank	0.0	45.0	*+45.0*
Elections Assistance	75.0	390.0	*+315.0*
Elite Athlete / Olympic Team Support	0.0	15.0	*+15.0*
Olympic Stadium Refurbishment	0.0	4.5	*+4.5*
Armoured Cars (Money Movement)	0.0	15.0	*+15.0*
New Commissions and Organization	0.0	15.0	*+15.0*
National Assembly Building Renovation	0.0	19.8	*+19.8*
Constitutional Development	45.0	0.0	*-45.0*
Civil Society and Community Development	30.0	0.0	*-30.0*
Other Projects	435.0	0.0	*-435.0*
TOTAL NATION BUILDING*	**937.5**	**856.8**	***-80.7***

**Columns will not add because only changed lines are shown above.*

Table 3.2 R3P Funds (ID bn)	**Original**	**Revised**	***Change***
Rapid Regional Response Programme	0.0	256.5	*+256.5*
Local Governance Funds	0.0	72.0	*+72.0*
Samarra	0.0	6.0	*+6.0*
Nasiriyah	0.0	3.0	*+3.0*
TOTAL R3P Funds	**0.0**	**337.6**	***+337.6***

Document 229
Side Letter between the Coalition Provisional Authority in Iraq and the Government of the Hashemite Kingdom of Jordan Concerning Reimbursement for Logistical Support Concerning Access to and Use of Facilities in Jordan for International Police Training

17 October 2003

This Side Letter ('Letter') is entered into between the Coalition Provisional Authority, which is exercising temporary governmental authority in Iraq pursuant to the laws and usages of war, and consistent with United Nations Security Council resolutions, including Resolution 1483, (hereinafter 'the CPA') and the Government of the Hashemite Kingdom of Jordan (hereinafter, 'Jordan'), represented by the Public Security Directorate (hereinafter referred to as 'the PSD').

WHEREAS, the CPA and the PSD (hereinafter 'the Parties') have entered into a contractual agreement concerning access to and use of facilities in Jordan for Iraqi police training (hereinafter 'the Basic Agreement')[145] and,

WHEREAS, Article IV of the Basic Agreement provides that the CPA and the PSD will negotiate terms and conditions for the PSD to provide logistics support for the purpose of supporting Iraqi police training under the terms of the Basic Agreement.

NOW THEREFORE, in order to more fully implement the foregoing article of the Basic Agreement, the Parties agree as follows:

ARTICLE I AMOUNT OF LOGISTICAL SUPPORT

The Parties agree that the CPA, in accordance with Article IV of the Basic Agreement, will enter into a contract or similar instrument with the PSD containing a mutually agreed scope of work and mutually agreed terms and conditions to provide logistical and base operations support as described in Article IV. The Parties agree that the cost for the support described above will be in an amount not to exceed Eighty-Nine Million Dollars ($89,000,000) for the first year, except as mutually agreed upon between the Parties.

ARTICLE II OBLIGATION OF FUNDS

The Parties agree that the obligation by the CPA to pay the PSD under the provisions of this Letter is specifically subject to the availability of proper funds.

IN WITNESS WHEREOF, the respective representatives, duly authorized for the purpose, have signed the present Side Letter.

Done in Amman Jordan on the 17th day of October, 2003, in the English language.[146]

[145] The Contractual Agreement between the Coalition Provisional Authority in Iraq and the Government of the Hashemite Kingdom of Jordan Concerning Access to and Use of the Facilities in Jordan for Iraq Police Training was concluded on 13 October 2003. The existence of the agreement was confirmed under FOIA request no 10-F-1446 but the text was not released.

[146] On the same day, the two parties also signed a Side Letter Concerning Partial Reimbursement of Security Arrangements Concerning Access to and Use of Facilities in Jordan for International Police Training.

Document 230

Draft Agreement Governing the Operation of the Iraqi Mission to the United States under the Auspices of the Protecting Power Agreement between the Government of Bahrain and the Governing Council of the Republic of Iraq

31 October 2003[147]

Role of the Protecting Power: Whereas the United States of America and the Republic of Iraq do not currently have diplomatic relations, the Government of Bahrain has agreed to act as Iraq's Protecting Power to facilitate the provision of consular services to Iraqi citizens and official communication between the United States and Iraq.

Entry in Force: The provisions contained in this agreement will enter in force upon the exchange of diplomatic notes between the Department of State and the Embassy of Bahrain confirming both parties' mutual desire to enter into the arrangement described herein. Simultaneous delivery of a diplomatic note to the Embassy of the Republic of Algeria shall confirm the termination of the protecting power agreement that previously governed official relations between the United States and Iraq.

Iraqi Mission to the United States: The Iraqi entity operating under the Protecting Power agreement will be known as the 'Iraqi Mission to the United States' (hereafter referred to as the 'Iraqi Mission'). Consistent with standard practice governing such arrangements, the Iraqi Mission will operate as a part of the Embassy of Bahrain. It will be physically located in the former Iraqi chancery building at 1801 P St. NW.

The Iraqi mission will be entitled to fly the Iraqi flag; send and receive official correspondence to and from Baghdad or other Iraqi diplomatic missions via diplomatic pouch under its seal; and send encrypted communications to and from Baghdad.

Activities of the Iraqi Mission: The activities of the Iraqi Mission will be confined to:

- Providing consular services consistent with those enumerated in the Vienna Convention on Consular Relations to Iraqi nationals legally present in the United States.
- Providing travel information and, if necessary, travel documentation to citizens of the United States planning to travel to Iraq.
- Receiving and delivering official communications between the United States and Iraq.
- Publicly representing, under the authority of the Iraqi Ministry of Foreign Affairs, the official positions of the Governing Council of Iraq, or any successor entity that reflects the evolution of political institutions in Iraq toward a legitimate, internationally recognized government as contemplated by UN Security Council Resolution 1511.[148]

[147] In October 2003, the CPA got concerned that the IGC would proceed without CPA input with an Agreement with Bahrain on the latter acting as the protecting power of Iraq in the United States. The reproduced draft agreement was submitted to Ambassador Bremer on 31 October 2003. The Memorandum of Understanding, whereby Bahrain took care of the interests of Iraq in the United States, was signed in Manama on 8 December 2003 on behalf of Bahrain by the Deputy Prime Minister and Minister of Foreign Affairs, Sheikh Mohammed bin Mubarak Al Khalifa, and on behalf of Iraq by the Iraqi Foreign Minister, Hushiar Zebari.

[148] For UN Security Council resolution 1511 (2003), see *Doc 531*.

- The Iraqi Mission shall undertake no activities beyond those cited above without written authorization of the Department of State. Any request for such authorization should be directed to the State Department's Office of Northern Gulf Affairs.

Iraqi Official Staff: The Iraqi Ministry of Foreign Affairs will be permitted to staff the Iraqi Mission with Iraqi officials who shall be notified to the Department of State as members of the Diplomatic Mission of Bahrain.

There will be no numerical limitation on the number of Iraqi staff assigned to the Iraqi Mission.

Credentials for official staff, including ID cards, tax exemption cards, and vehicle license plates shall be provided by the State Department's Office of Protocol and Office of Foreign Missions through the Embassy of Bahrain.

New staff will be notified to the State Department by the Embassy of Bahrain.

Individuals proposed for duty at the Iraqi Mission must be acceptable to the Government of the United States.

Official staff members will enjoy appropriate privileges and immunities, and be subject to obligations in accordance with applicable provisions of international law.

Officials on temporary, short-term assignment to the Iraqi Mission may be accorded diplomatic privileges and immunities at the discretion of the Department of State. Under the auspices of this agreement, the Department of State may also accord diplomatic privileges and immunities, including diplomatic visas, to visiting Iraqi officials of sufficient rank and stature.

Principal Officer: The official title of the principal officer of the Iraq Mission will be 'Iraqi Representative to the United States'. He or she may be referred to as 'Ambassador' if the Iraqi Ministry of Foreign Affairs has conferred that rank on him or her. For protocol purposes, he or she will be equivalent to a Chargé d'Affairs.

Support Staff: The Iraqi Mission may employ as support staff (hereafter referred to as local employees) United States Citizens or other individuals whose immigration status permits both extended residence and employment in the United States.

All local employees must be notified in writing to the State Department Office of Protocol in accordance with established procedure. Hiring or discharge of local staff must be notified to the Department of State within 48 hours of effective date.

There are no numerical limitations on the number of local employees that may be employed by the Iraqi Mission.

Property: The former chancery of Iraq, located at 1801 P St. NW, together with the property and archives located therein, will be under the custody of the Government of Bahrain.

Vehicles and other property under the custody of the former protecting power, the Government of Algeria, will pass into the custody of the Government of Bahrain. Any additional vehicles acquired for use by the Iraqi Mission will similarly pass into the custody of the Government of Bahrain. The disposition of such vehicles, including arrangements for the registration and operation thereof, will be the responsibility of the Embassy of Bahrain. The State Department Office of Foreign Missions will cooperate with the Embassy of Bahrain regarding such arrangements.

Any communication regarding Iraqi Mission property, including maintenance of building and grounds and all matters pertaining to vehicles, should be conducted between the Embassy of Bahrain and the State Department Office of Foreign Missions in consultation with appropriate administrative officials at the Iraqi Mission.

The former residence of the Iraqi Ambassador will pass from the custody of the State

Department Office of Foreign Missions to the Embassy of Bahrain for use by the Iraqi Representative at such time that all parties agree that the Iraqi Mission has the intention and capability to bring the property into compliance with relevant District of Columbia housing codes.

Financial Operations: There shall be no restrictions or otherwise non-standard controls placed on the financial activities of the Iraqi Mission.

Official Travel: There shall be no restrictions placed on travel by official staff of the Iraqi Mission or their families.

Document 231

Memorandum from Ambassador Bremer for Secretary Rumsfeld, Strategy for Iraq's Political Transition

10 November 2003

Based on my meeting with the Governing Council's presidential group of nine last Thursday [6 November 2003], and on subsequent conversations with [...][149] and other GC members, I have concluded that the time has come to readjust our planned program for Iraq's political transition. Although 20 of 24 GC members support our proposal to choose delegates to a constitutional convention through the use of indirect 'local elections,' it is now clear that they are unwilling to force that option on the religious Shi'a members of the Council. My discussions with these Shi'a members persuade me that it would be a mistake to encourage such a move.

At the Thursday meeting, Talabani talked about generating a consensus in advance on basic principles for eventual inclusion in the permanent constitution. In discussions with him and others, we have been working to synthesize this notion into an overall political plan that is compatible with our objective. What has evolved is an alternative way forward that would include the drafting of a transitional constitution or 'basic law' by the GC (in coordination with CPA), the conduct of direct elections to fill the legislative and/or executive bodies created by that transitional constitution in late summer or early fall of 2004, and the recognition of a fully-sovereign Iraqi Transitional Government shortly thereafter. The transitional constitution would be unamendable, and would include a sunset provision and a clear timetable for the drafting of a permanent constitution.

In accordance with the provisions of the transitional constitution, the new government would initiate a process for the drafting of a permanent constitution by a separate body to be directly elected by the Iraqi people. This would be followed by popular ratification, national elections, and the first Iraqi government under its permanent constitution.

This alternative would meet many of the concerns about the political timetable raised by members of the GC over the past few months, and would be consistent with our own interests as well. [...] It would meet the requirement of the religious Shi'a that Iraq's permanent constitution be drafted by a directly-elected body. Finally, [...].

While ideally we would wait until a permanent constitutional process were complete before ending the occupation, this proposal is the best alternative course of action available to us. The transitional constitution option would ensure an honorable end to the occupation under the desired timeframe. We would recognize a fully sovereign Iraqi government only

[149] Declassified in part only.

after establishing a transitional constitution respecting democracy and human rights, and after holding the first free and fair elections in Iraq's history. While there is a risk involved with holding national elections this early, we could mitigate the dangers by making certain that the transitional constitution protects individual liberties, establishes the separation of powers, and presents a clear timetable for the drafting and adoption of a permanent constitution. During this period we would use the time to identify and nurture potential national leaders.

In parallel to this process, we would need to negotiate a series of bilateral agreements with the GC. These would grant authority to the Coalition to continue to station forces in Iraq to conduct stabilization operations, and would govern the management and expenditure of U.S. taxpayer funds for Iraqi reconstruction. We would try to include these agreements in the transitional constitution.

Once the transitional constitution is complete, we would also consider returning to the United Nations Security Council to obtain a third UNSCR. This resolution could endorse the transitional plan, and could make explicit reference to the timelines specified in the transitional constitution for establishing a process by which Iraq would write and ratify a permanent constitution.

We must more rapidly if we are to secure this compromise before Talabani travels later this month and well before the 15 December UNSCR deadline. I would like your guidance as soon as possible.[150]

Document 232

Agreement on Political Process between the Coalition Provisional Authority and the Governing Council of Iraq

15 November 2003

1. The 'Fundamental Law'

- To be drafted by the Governing Council, in close consultation with the CPA. Will be approved by both the GC and CPA, and will formally set forth the scope and structure of the sovereign Iraqi transitional administration.
- Elements of the 'Fundamental Law':
  - Bill of rights, to include freedom of speech, legislature, religion; statement of equal rights of all Iraqis, regardless of gender, sect, and ethnicity; and guarantees of due process.
  - Federal arrangement for Iraq, to include governorates and the separation and specification of powers to be exercised by central and local entities.
  - Statement of the independence of the judiciary, and a mechanism for judicial review.
  - Statement of civilian political control over Iraqi armed and security forces.
  - Statement that Fundamental Law cannot be amended.
  - An expiration date for Fundamental Law.
  - Timetable for drafting of Iraq's permanent constitution by a body directly elected by the Iraqi people; for ratifying the permanent constitution; and for holding elections under the new constitution.
- Drafting and approval of 'Fundamental Law' to be complete by February 28, 2004.

[150] The Memorandum was cc'ed to Secretary Powell and Dr. Rice.

2. Agreements with Coalition on Security
- To be agreed between the CPA and the GC.
- Security agreements to cover status of Coalition forces in Iraq, giving wide latitude to provide for the safety and security of the Iraqi people.
- Approval of bilateral agreements complete by the end of March 2004.

3. Selection of Transitional National Assembly
- Fundamental Law will specify the bodies of the national structure, and will ultimately spell out the process by which individuals will be selected for these bodies. However, certain guidelines must be agreed in advance.
- The transitional assembly will not be an expansion of the GC. The GC will have no formal role in selecting members of the assembly, and will dissolve upon the establishment and recognition of the transitional administration. Individual members of the GC will, however, be eligible to serve in the transitional assembly, if elected according to the process below.
- Election of members of the Transitional National Assembly will be conducted through a transparent, participatory, democratic process of caucuses in each of Iraq's 18 governorates.
  - In each governorate, the CPA will supervise a process by which an 'Organizing Committee' of Iraqis will be formed. This Organizing Committee will include 5 individuals appointed by the Governing Council, 5 individuals appointed by the Provincial Council, and 1 individual appointed by the local council of the five largest cities within the governorate.
  - The purpose of the Organizing Committee will be to convene a 'Governorate Selection Caucus' of notables from around the governorate. To do so, it will solicit nominations from political parties, provincial/local councils, professional and civic associations, university faculties, tribal and religious groups. Nominees must meet the criteria set out for candidates in the Fundamental Law. To be selected as a member of the Governorate Selection Caucus, any nominee will need to be approved by an 11/15 majority of the Organizing Committee.
  - Each Governorate Selection Caucus will elect representatives to represent the governorate in the new transitional assembly based on the governorate's percentage of Iraq's population.
- The Transitional National Assembly will be elected no later than May 31, 2004.

4. Restoration of Iraq's Sovereignty
- Following the selection of members of the transitional assembly, it will meet to elect an executive branch, and to appoint ministers.
- By June 30, 2004 the new transitional administration will be recognized by the Coalition, and will assume full sovereign powers for governing Iraq. The CPA will dissolve.

5. Process for Adoption of Permanent Constitution
- The constitutional process and timeline will ultimately be included in the Fundamental Law, but need to be agreed in advance, as detailed below.
- A permanent constitution for Iraq will be prepared by a constitutional convention directly elected by the Iraqi people.
- Elections for the convention will be held no later than March 15, 2005.

- A draft of the constitution will be circulated for public comment and debate.
- A final draft of the constitution will be presented to the public, and a popular referendum will be held to ratify the constitution.
- Elections for a new Iraqi government will be held by December 31, 2005, at which point the Fundamental Law will expire and a new government will take power.

For the Governing Council: [*Signed*] Jalal **Talabani**
For the Coalition Provisional Authority: [*Signed*] L. Paul **Bremer**, David **Richmond**.[151]

Document 233
Information Leaflet on the 15 November 2003 Agreement

November 2003

The November 15 Agreement: Timeline to a Sovereign, Democratic and Secure Iraq

The Iraqi Governing Council and the Coalition Provisional Authority agreed November 15 to a timetable for the restoration of full Iraqi sovereignty, the creation of a permanent constitution, and the holding of free, national elections. Key dates of the agreement:

The Transitional Administrative Law: A Guarantee of Basic Rights

By February 28, 2004, the Iraqi Governing Council will approve a Transitional Administrative Law that defines the structures of a transitional government and the procedures for electing delegates to a constitutional convention. This Transitional Administrative Law will guarantee certain basic rights for all Iraqis during this transition, including freedom of speech and the press. It will also respect the Islamic identity of the majority of the Iraqi people, while providing guarantees of religious freedom for all Iraqis. The Transitional Administrative Law will expire by the end of 2005, after a permanent constitution has been approved and elections have been held.

By May 31, 2004, local caucuses will be convened in each of Iraq's 18 governorates to elect delegates from among their number for an Iraqi Transitional National Assembly.

Full Sovereignty: End to Occupation

By June 30, 2004, the Iraqi Transitional National Assembly will elect it's [sic] leaders and assume full sovereignty for Iraq.

The Governing Council and the Coalition Provisional Authority will be dissolved. This will end the responsibilities of the Coalition as an occupying power as specified in the United Nations resolutions.

Democracy: Constitution and Elections

By March 15, 2005, direct one-man, one-vote elections will be held for a constitutional convention. This convention will meet to write a permanent constitution, to be approved by the Iraqi people in a referendum.

[151] On 1 December 2003, Administrator of the Coalition Provisional Authority Paul Bremer and President of the Iraqi Governing Council Jalal Talibani issued 'A Statement to the Iraqi People'. The text is reproduced in *Doc 233*.

By December 31, 2005, national elections for a new Iraqi government will be held based on the new constitution. The elected government will assume power. The transitional government will be dissolved.

Security
Throughout this process, Coalition Forces will continue to work side-by-side with new Iraqi police and security institutions to ensure a peaceful transition to a sovereign, democratic, secure Iraq. The Coalition will work with the Iraqi Governing Council and the new Transitional National Assembly to define these security arrangements.

A Statement To the Iraqi People

The November 15 Agreement signed by the Iraqi Governing Council and the Coalition Provisional Authority is an historic step.

It provides for Iraqis to choose a new Iraqi Government, chosen through direct, national elections by the end of 2005, on the basis of a permanent constitution.

It provides for a new constitution drafted by Iraqis who will be chosen by full direct elections by March 2005.

It restores Iraqi sovereignty and ends the occupation by June 30, 2004.

It allows a Transitional Iraqi Government, chosen by caucuses in each governorate, to assume sovereignty and administer elections to draft a constitution.

It ensures that the Transitional Government will operate under a law, drafted by Iraqis, which will provide basic guarantees of freedom for the Iraqi people.

It provides the Iraqi people an opportunity to participate at every stage of the process that restores sovereignty and guarantees your freedom.

[Signed] *L. Paul Bremer*, Administrator
Coalition Provisional Authority

[Signed] *Jalal Talabani*, President
Iraqi Governing Council

Document 234
Organization Chart
November 2003

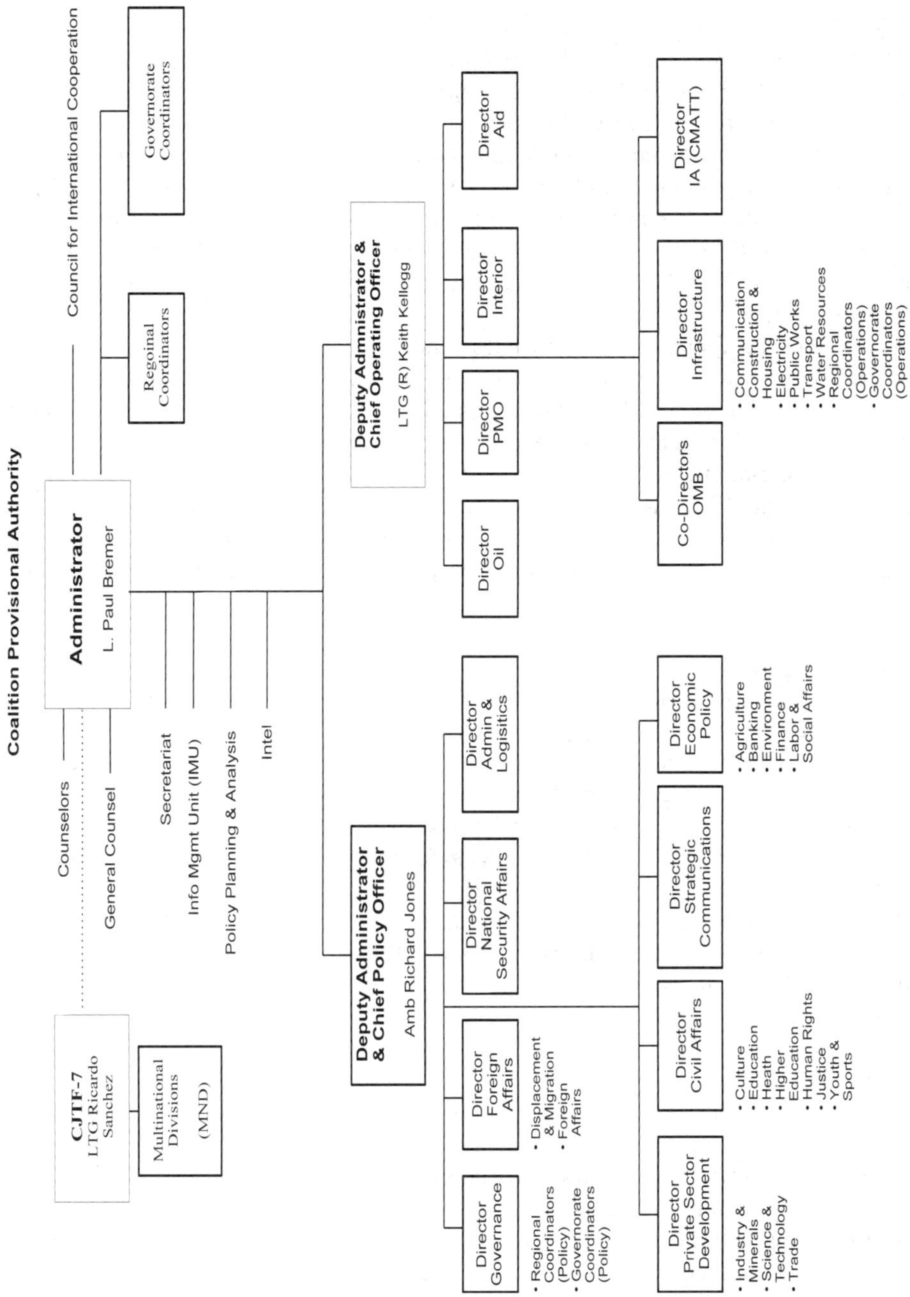

Document 235
Oil-for-Food Programme Transition Briefing Document Provided to the Security Council's 661 Committee

17 November 2003

OVERVIEW

NOTE: This document is provided to 661 Committee members in order to help clarify questions raised in prior discussions. Ambassador Steven Mann will present a comprehensive briefing to the Committee on 17 November. This informal document is intended to help frame the upcoming, detailed briefing by Ambassador Mann.

The Coalition Provisional Authority (CPA) continues to put in place the necessary processes and controls to manage effectively the transfer of operational responsibility for the Oil for Food (OFF) programme on 21 November per UNSCR 1483 (2003). Significant effort and resources have been devoted to the transition by Iraqi officials, UN agencies and Coalition members.

The top priorities for smooth logistical flow include: food, medicine, and essential spare parts. Food constitutes the most important issue. We take seriously the need to ensure an uninterrupted food pipeline. The CPA has established a coordination center to track and facilitate the flow of these and other goods throughout the country. Finally, the CPA intends to purchase a one-month buffer stock of food.

In the North, the CPA has prepared a transition process that will shift 99 projects worth nearly USD 750 million from UN administration to Iraqi hands. This transfer will result in real responsibility for administration and project management to be driven primarily by Iraqis.

MAJOR ISSUES

WFP follow-on role: The World Food Programme (WFP) has previously worked successfully to maintain the long chain between foreign suppliers and Iraqi distributors; we have asked WFP to continue their work in this area. Between November 2-4, CPA and Ministry of Trade (MoT) representatives met with the WFP in Amman to discuss arrangements for a smooth transition for the food distribution after 21 November. Specific details are being negotiated for a timely agreement on a tripartite memorandum of understanding (MOU).

CPA believes WFP can play a vital role regarding arrangements for transport of some of the goods to be delivered under renegotiated OFF contracts (the expected total is 3.1 million MT). WFP will also be asked to procure a one-month buffer stock to help ensure a sufficient back-up reserve in the food pipeline.

Ministry of Trade functions:

- **Distribution**: continue to manage the distribution of commodities at a national, Governorate and regional level;
- **Procurement**: review and revise procurement procedures in preparation for future procurement of commodities and;
- **Coordination**: coordinate closely with WFP and CPA, both in Amman and Baghdad, to ensure close coordination for what will be a major logistical operation.

In a related area, CPA has been working with the MoT and WFP to ensure that the commodities contained in the Public Distribution System (PDS) food pipeline are sufficiently stocked with supplies through mid-2004 with an additional three-month commodity reserve. The Iraqis, through the tripartite process, sent forward more than 500 OFF contracts to accomplish this goal. The MoT has also been involved in contacting suppliers and requesting delivery dates of goods be moved forward as much as possible. The urgent starting point for this reserve is to procure a one-month buffer stock immediately. The CPA is identifying budget resources that will ensure that this vitally important element of addressing the needs of the Iraqi people is set in motion.

SHIPMENT ISSUES

To ally suppliers' concerns regarding the flow of OFF-contracted goods, we have created a **Coordination Center** in Baghdad to provide oversight of the movement of OFF goods both inside and outside Iraq. The comprehensive center will contain Iraqi and CPA experts in transportation/logistics, communication, and security. It will correspond on a daily basis with border authentication points, foreign trans-shipment and staging locations. Staff will also be trained to help 'trouble-shoot' potential problems and be equipped with equipment (computers, internet access, phone/fax communication, etc). Iraqi ministries receiving OFF goods will be represented in the center, as well as have staff located at each designated OFF border point. Approximately 40 personnel, including key Iraqi Ministry employees, will work in the center – which will, in effect, act as a centralized hub for all OFF-related issues post-21 November. Coordination with relevant Iraqi Ministries will be conducted via the Coordination Center.

Security: It is of paramount importance to the Iraqis, the CPA, the UN and suppliers that OFF goods arrive safely at their destinations in order to meet the urgent humanitarian needs of the Iraqi people. To address security concerns, the CPA has approved funding for a security contractor whose personnel will integrate with currently existing Iraqi and CPA security assets. Their main task will be to provide additional security coverage along the convoy routes and to liaise with relevant Coalition military officials.

UN FOLLOW-ON

On 21 November, UN agencies are due to cease their activities under the OFF program. Most continued UN involvement in Iraq would come under UNAMI or as part of an individual country program, as circumstances permit. Under current circumstances, the CPA envisions UN agencies playing a follow-on role in three focused areas: *food, medicine* and *logistics*.

- WFP will manage transport of goods and procurement.
- The World Health Organisation (WHO) will manage the facility in Amman, where OFF medicines are stored, and transport them into Iraq.
- The UN and CPA are reviewing a possible role for the UNJLC to assist with non-food humanitarian goods.

IRAQI PARTICIPATION

The former Government of Iraq coordinated OFF goods shipments for seven years; the CPA's goal is to utilize those proper, established supplier relationships and expertise – while augmenting Iraqi capacity. In many cases, this means improving some operational aspects and providing broad management and planning assistance at key points. The CPA's objective will be to ensure that Iraq can utilize these methods and apply them to a period following the termination of the OFF programme, when 'normal' commercial practices will apply.

The OFF programme in the three Northern Governorates consisted of programmes and projects executed by the UN. Following the transfer of assets (fixed and non-fixed) by the UN and its various agencies to the CPA, authority for these programmes and assets will in turn be transferred to the Iraqis on 21 November.

In some instances, it has been identified that local capacities do not exist to a sufficient degree for local authorities to accept full responsibility for the ongoing management and planning of particular projects. Where a modest capacity exists, the CPA will provide sectoral and technical advisors within the Iraqi ministries, as well as within the administrative unit that will manage the projects (the Office of Program Coordination – OPC). These advisors will help ensure a smooth continuation of key infrastructure projects and public services.

The OPC will be based in Erbil and be empowered by the Governing Council to administer programmes and projects that are transferred by the United Nations to the CPA before 21 November. The CPA is disappointed that we still require project dossier information from the WHO and UNESCO. This will have significant bearing on the CPA's ability to accept responsibility for projects in these sectors.

Also in the North, the CPA has catalogued, verified, and begun the transfer of tangible assets contracts under the 13% account. Transfer of contracts is well underway in Iraq and in Amman (for international contracts). We have had extensive discussions with the authorities on the structures of the transfer and subsequent management. The CPA will insist on a robust audit capability in administering the projects.

There are more than 2600 Iraqi UN employees whose expertise will greatly support the future administration of the programs. An Iraqi-CPA-UN working group has identified these employees and made plans for the transfer of most to local government or retention on personal services contract. The role currently performed by WFP in the three northern Governorates will continue but in an advisory role, providing assistance in warehouse and food distribution management to local authorities.

CONTRACTS UPDATE/PRIORITIZATION

At this time 99.6% of the approved and funded contracts have been reviewed for relative utility. Of the contracts sent for re-negotiation, UN agencies have completed 89% of their processing task. The CPA expects UN agencies to continue the re-negotiation process until 21 November.

In the event that a small number of contracts still require re-negotiation, the Coalition will direct contracting and legal officers to work on them. As CPA representatives said in the Security Council on 28 October, *the CPA will continue to honor the fulfillment of all prioritized contracts that are not re-negotiated by the UN agencies by 21 November*. The financing of these contracts will come from funds held in the UN escrow account and the Letters of Credit (L/Cs) currently/previously assigned to those contracts.

Contract prioritization resulted from detailed exchanges among the parties involved in the tripartite review process – Iraqi Ministries, UN agencies and the CPA. Iraqis were at the centre of decision made in the tripartite review process. Meeting urgent Iraqi reconstruction needs – as advanced by them – served as the sole criterion throughout the process. The CPA believes that attempts to establish prioritization 'criteria' is clearly beyond the scope of UNSCR 1483; such an effort would also inevitably lead to unnecessary controversy among suppliers. While some delegations have expressed a desire for determining prioritization criteria – on, in effect, a set of formal tripartite justifications – there remains no common Committee position on the matter. It is worth noting, in this regard, that roughly 80% of the contracts considered for prioritization were included in the final prioritized lists that went forward to UN agencies for amendment.

ADDRESSING SUPPLIER CONCERNS WHILE MEETING IRAQI NEEDS

- **Payment**: We recognize that some suppliers remain unsure of the procedures that will guarantee payment and have thus voiced reluctance to ship. CPA will provide continuity in payment mechanism by employing the same system and process used prior to the conflict.
- **Security**: We recognize that the security situation in Iraq represents a concern. The CPA will provide convoy security through a privately contracted firm. The Ministry of the Interior will provide security at Iraq's borders with warehouse security to be handled by individual Ministry Facility Protection Service. Route security will include a 'Command and Control' team located in the Coordination Center. Additional teams will be located at the four OFF supply entry points. The new security arrangements will enable armed security patrols to monitor up to 12 convoys per day; additional satellite tracking will be available for 30 more convoys per day.
- **Port capacity**: Backlogs at Umm Qasr cause unwanted demurrage fees. The Coordination Center will address these issues in conjunction with strategic shipping resources from WFP for food shipments. We expect the flow of goods from the port to become smoother as improved communication links are established and Iraqi and CPA staff are supplemented. (NOTE: Ambassador Martin and Major-General Figgures, Deputy Commander of Coalition forces, will travel to Umm Qasr to ensure that the measures in place are sufficient for the task at hand.)
- **Communication with recipients**: Suppliers currently have been communicating directly with the UN agencies. The CPA will provide information to suppliers, through its web site, on how suppliers can re-establish the system whereby they contacted the Iraqi recipient directly. This will clarify lines of communication and facilitate goods delivery. Information on this will be communicated to Sanctions Committee members in due course.

To maintain the flow of goods to Iraq by ensuring that suppliers will receive payment, CPA continues discussions with Cotecna representatives. We anticipate that a final agreement will be reached soon. Continuity and re-assurance for suppliers of OFF goods remains a top CPA priority. Once negotiations are concluded, we will be in a position to inform all interested parties about the follow-on Cotecna contract. CPA will cover the costs until 31 December 2003. After that date, a new contract would be offered that would likely include some modifications to the scope of work. The CPA will share with the Committee all relevant information that will flow from the discussion with Cotecna once ongoing discussions are concluded.

AUTHENTICATION OF OFF-RELATED SERVICES CONDUCTED PRIOR TO THE CONFLICT

The CPA, in conjunction with relevant Iraqi Ministries, has attempted to ascertain whether services notified to the Office of the Iraq Programme as having been completed have indeed been performed. In some instances it became clear, following investigations by Iraqi Ministry officials, that the services had not been performed. Therefore confirmation/ authentication could not take place as requested. The CPA and Iraqi Ministry officials continue to investigate the remaining cases notified by OIP. This time consuming process will continue up to 21 November and beyond.

Where it is possible to authenticate services, the CPA will, as stated earlier, honor its commitment to fulfill contracts. Payment for outstanding services related to contracts will be processed by the UN Treasury, which in turn will notify BNP-Paribas to allow payment to be made. This process, however, would only occur after the CPA and Iraqi

Ministry officials are satisfied that services have been performed and can be verified to meet contract requirements. It would be improper, and indeed inconsistent with Security Council resolution 1483 and its demand for proper financial controls, simply to authorize payments from the UN escrow account without proper authentication.

PAYMENT MECHANISM POST 21 NOVEMBER

As stated above, the CPA is in contractual discussions with Cotecna to extend their authentication services up to 31 December and possibly beyond. Linked to this will be the question of how suppliers will be able to receive payment for the delivery of their goods. The CPA's overriding principle throughout this process has been to minimize disruptions to suppliers. A key element is maintaining, to the extent possible, the current authentication system. But the reality on 22 November will be that the Office of the Iraq Programme (OIP) will not exist and therefore unable to perform its current role in the authentication process. Any new procedure will need to acknowledge the absence of OIP in the post 21 November payment arrangements.

In this instance, the CPA envisages a process whereby once Cotecna have successfully authenticated the arrival of OFF supplies, the UN Treasury would be notified as such by Cotecna. Upon receipt from Cotecna that the goods have arrived, as per the Letter of Credit and Terms and Conditions of the contract, the UN Treasury would notify BNP Paribas accordingly. This would allow payment to be made to the supplier.

The summary process set out above will mirror existing procedure with the exception of the involvement of OIP. To the greatest extent possible, both Cotecna and the UN Treasury would use existing procedures for authentication and payment to suppliers.

Document 236

Reorganization of the Coalition Provisional Authority

15 November 2003

MEMO FOR: Deputy Administrator & Chief Policy Officer, CPA
Counselor to the Administrator, CPA
Chief Operating Officer, CPA
Commander, CJTF-7
Directors, CPA
General Counsel, CPA
FROM: Administrator
SUBJECT: Reorganization of the Coalition Provisional Authority (CPA)

1. Purpose. This memorandum documents my decision to reorganize the CPA in a manner that will enhance the organization's ability to manage relief and reconstruction funding promptly, transparently and wisely, while guiding Iraq's establishment of an internationally recognized, representative government and its development of a free market economy.

2. Responsibilities.

a. Deputy Administrator and Chief Policy Officer. The Deputy Administrator and Chief Policy Officer shall perform the functions of the Administrator in the Administrator's absence; oversee CPA's development of policy (including plans for returning governing responsibilities and authorities to the people of Iraq as soon as practicable, and promoting economic reconstruction and development); and carry out such other functions as the Administrator may prescribe. The Chief Policy Officer shall oversee and coordinate the following Directors:

(1) Director, Governance;
(2) Director, Private Sector Development;
(3) Director, Civil Affairs;
(4) Director, Foreign Affairs;
(5) Director, National Security Affairs;
(6) Director, Strategic Communications;
(7) Director, Economic Policy.

b. Chief Operating Officer. The Chief Operating Officer (COO) shall oversee CPA's day-to-day operations, including the reconstruction of Iraq's infrastructure and the training and deployment of Iraqi police and security forces, and shall perform such other duties as the Administrator may prescribe. The COO shall oversee and coordinate the following Directors:

(1) Director, AID
(2) Director, Oil
(3) Director, Office of Management and Budget
(4) Director, Program Management Office
(5) Director, New Iraqi Army
(6) Director, Interior
(7) Director, Infrastructure
(8) Director, Administration and Logistics

c. Director, Administration and Logistics. The Director of Administration and Logistics shall oversee the performance of administrative and logistical services in support of the CPA, including personnel support services; coordinate with CJTF-7, security contractors and other entities as necessary to ensure proper application of safety and security measures within CPA; and perform such other duties as the Administrator or the Chief Operating Officer may direct.

3. CPA Executive Board

a. Purpose. The Executive Board will develop comprehensive, integrated policies and implementation plans with respect to the most complex and sensitive issues that the CPA faces. These issues include those that implicate interests of multiple CPA Directorates or otherwise pose policy-making or management challenges that are best addressed by transcending the decision-making process of any single Directorate. In addition, the Board shall serve as a forum for resolving issues that arise from the interrelationship between the military and civilian elements of the Coalition. The Board's advice and recommendations shall be informed by its capability to conduct objective, independent analyses through the CPA's Policy Planning and Analysis office.

b. Composition. The Executive Board shall be chaired by the Deputy Administrator/Chief Policy Officer, and shall include the Chief Operating Officer, who shall serve as Vice Chairman; the Director, National Security Affairs; the Deputy Commander, CJTF-7; the Chief of Staff, CJTF-7; a Senior Counselor; and the Head of CPA Executive Secretariat (as a nonvoting member). To facilitate development of proactive strategies for carrying out the Board's recommendations in compliance with applicable laws and regulations, the General Counsel shall attend all meetings of the Board.

c. Authorities and Duties.

(1) The Board will act under the Administrator's authority, direction and control, and shall report directly to the Administrator with respect to all matters referred to the Board.

(2) The Board may direct the CPA Directors to perform such actions as the Board determines to be necessary to carry out its responsibilities. The Board may oversee implementation of the Administrator's decisions and may act on behalf of the Administrator to ensure that implementation plans reflect the Coalition's various interests and requirements, and the Administrator's intent.

(3) The Board will manage reviews and revisions of CPA's Strategic Plan.

(4) To ensure that key CPA policies are closely coordinated with the Coalition Forces and support the preservation of security in Iraq, the Board shall encourage CJTF-7's active and timely involvement in formulating policies and plans that harmonize the perspectives of the Coalition's civilian and military elements.

(5) On behalf of the Administrator, the Board will invite CPA officials to participate in its review of issues through briefings, presentations or reports to the Board, or otherwise, as necessary to explain or justify their positions on matters before the Board for action.

(6) The Policy Planning and Analysis office shall, at the Board's direction, conduct independent and objective analyses of issues presented to the Board for action.

(7) The CPA Executive Secretariat will serve as the Board's secretariat, and shall ensure that the Board is informed of all CPA activities relevant to the Board's responsibilities and receives full and timely administrative support, including record keeping and assistance in coordinating matters with concerned CPA elements.

4. Questions regarding the implementation of this reorganization should be addressed to the Deputy Administrator and Chief Policy Officer.

Document 237
Letter from Ambassador Bremer to Grand Ayatollah Sistani

2 December 2003

His Eminence Grand Ayatollah
Al-Sayyid Ali Al-Sistani
Najaf, Iraq

Your Eminence,

Thank you for meeting recently with my colleague, Mr. Dhia, to discuss your views on the political and constitutional process in Iraq. I appreciate your warm welcome of Mr. Dhia and would like to continue to use him as my confidential channel to you.

I recognize your concerns regarding the implementation of the November 15 agreement. I believe that the November 15 Agreement addresses our overriding mutual objective that the permanent constitution be written for Iraqis, by Iraqis. The best way to ensure this is through the direct elections to the constitutional convention provided for in the Agreement. I also assure you that the Law of Administration will respect the Islamic identity of the majority of the Iraqi people, while providing for full freedom of worship.

I have asked Mr. Dhia to make himself available to meet with you at any time in order to continue our confidential dialogue.

Respectfully,

L. Paul Bremer III
Administrator

Document 238
Framework Agreement between the Coalition Provisional Authority, the Trade Bank Of Iraq and the [Swiss] Export Risk Guarantee Agency

5 December 2003[152]

This FRAMEWORK AGREEMENT (this 'Agreement') is entered into as of December 5, 2003 by and between the Coalition Provisional Authority ('CPA'), which exercises temporary governmental authority in Iraq pursuant to the laws and usages of war, and consistent with relevant United Nations Security Council Resolutions, including Resolution 1483 (2003), the Trade Bank of Iraq ('TBI'), established under CPA Order No 20, and the Export Risk Guarantee Agency ('ERG') acting on behalf of the Swiss Confederation.

WITNESSETH

Whereas, the CPA and TBI desire to facilitate the import of goods and services to Iraq by public and private sector purchasers;

Whereas, ERG wishes to support the financing of the export of certain Swiss goods and services to Iraq by issuing short-term, export credit insurance policies in connection with letters of credit issued by or on behalf of TBI;

Whereas, the CPA wishes to support the repayment of certain obligations to Swiss exporters or banks enjoying ERG's cover in connection with such letters of credit; and

Whereas, the Development Fund for Iraq (the 'DFI') was established pursuant to United Nations Security Council Resolution 1483 (2003) by the proceeds from the export sale of Iraqi oil and other petroleum products and is to be disbursed at the direction of the CPA, in consultation with the Iraqi interim administration, for the financing needs of Iraq's reconstruction and development;

Now therefore, in the spirit of mutual cooperation and in the furtherance of common economic interests, the parties hereto agree as follows.

1. Export Credit Insurance

(a) ERG may from time to time issue short-term, export credit insurance policies (each a 'Policy') with respect to (i) one or more irrevocable letters of credit (each a 'Letter of Credit') issued by TBI and confirmed by an eligible bank (a 'Confirming Bank'), or (ii) one or more payment undertakings (each a 'Payment Undertaking') issued by TBI in connection with a Letter of Credit issued by an eligible bank (an 'Issuing Bank') on behalf of TBI.

(b) In accordance with ERG law and practice, an application for a Policy shall be submitted by the Swiss exporter to ERG. Upon his respective instruction and the subsequent approval of the ERG Board the Policy may be assigned to the Confirming or Issuing Bank. ERG decides on providing cover in its sole discretion.

ERG shall insure payment to the Confirming Bank or Issuing Bank of up to ninety five percent (95%) of the principal amount of each Letter of Credit or Payment Undertaking, as the case may be, plus documented interest from the date of default to the date of claim

[152] Largely identical Framework Agreements were concluded with 17 export credit agencies from 16 different countries, including the Export-Import Bank of the United States (U.S. Ex-Im Bank), an independent agency of the United States of America. The Agreement with ERG was provided by the Swiss Government. A copy provided by U.S. Ex-Im Bank Agreement is on file with the author.

payment (but in any event, no longer than 180 days) (such principal and interest, the 'Covered Amount'), all in accordance with the terms and conditions of the applicable Policy.

2. Authorization Process

The CPA and TBI shall issue a purchase authorization in the form of Annex A hereto (a 'Purchase Authorization') to evidence their approval of each purchase to be financed under the Agreement, and the delivery of such Purchase Authorization shall be a drawing condition under the Letters of Credit issued by or on behalf of TBI.

3. Adequacy of Funds

(a) The CPA agrees to (i) ensure that Obligations do not exceed the Base Amount for each of the succeeding 180-day and 360-day periods; (ii) calculate the Obligations and Base Amount no less than once per month; and (iii) report to ERG and TBI such calculations no later than the fifth (5th) calendar day of each month (including (x) reasonable detail as to expected oil export volume per month and as to the futures index utilized to calculate oil prices, and (y) a certification as to compliance with the covenant set forth in clause (i) above). For the purposes of this Agreement, 'Obligations' shall mean, as of any date of determination, an amount equal to the sum of all obligations or liabilities of any entity (including, without limitation, TBI) that have been incurred and are or may become due and payable using funds in the DFI over the succeeding 180-day and 360-day periods (including, without limitation, contingent liabilities and all amounts covered by outstanding Purchase Authorizations). 'Base Amount' shall mean, as of any date of determination, an amount equal to the sum of (a) ninety percent (90%) of the collected balances in the DFI, (b) seventy-five percent (75%) of all amounts reasonably expected to be deposited into the DFI over the succeeding 180-day period, and (c) in the case of calculations with respect to the succeeding 360-day period, fifty percent (50%) of all amounts reasonably expected to be deposited into the DFI during the succeeding 181-day to 360-day period.

(b) The CPA shall establish and maintain a sub-account in the DFI for the purpose of allocating and accruing amounts due under any Letter of Credit or Payment Undertaking issued or entered into, as the case may be, by TBI. The CPA shall transfer into such sub-account the Required Amount with respect to each outstanding Letter of Credit or Payment Undertaking no later than the fifth (5th) calendar day of each month. For the purposes of this Agreement, 'Required Amount' shall mean an amount equal to (i) the principal amount of the relevant Letter of Credit or Payment Undertaking, *divided by* (ii) the original tenor of such Letter of Credit or Payment Undertaking (expressed as a number of months).

4. Eligibility Requirements

- The Policy may only be granted to enterprises which are domiciled in Switzerland and registered in the Swiss commercial register.
- The deliveries must be of Swiss origin or contain an adequate Swiss portion in an individual transaction.
- Legal provisions of the ERG Act and the related Ordinance as well as the common business principles of the ERG have to be respected.

5. Repayment Terms

The repayment terms of each Letter of Credit or Payment Undertaking, as the case may be, shall be no more than one hundred and eighty (180) days; except for purchases of bulk agricultural commodities, fertilizers and capital equipment, which may be eligible for terms up to three hundred and sixty (360) days.

6. CPA Reimbursement Obligation

(a) In the event (i) an Exporter is not able to perform an export contract covered by a Policy before the shipment due to the cancellation of the export contract attributable to a public buyer under the export contract or the CPA, or (ii) TBI fails to reimburse or otherwise make payment to a Confirming Bank or Issuing Bank, as the case may be, in accordance with the terms and conditions of any Letter of Credit or Payment Undertaking covered by a Policy and ERG pays a claim with respect thereto, the CPA shall cause ERG to be reimbursed for the Covered Amount paid with respect to such claim by utilizing funds in the DFI. In the case of (a)(i) above, the parties agree that the maximum indemnity to be paid by the CPA from DFI funds for pre-shipment claims shall be calculated in accordance with Annex B hereto.[153] The parties acknowledge and agree that (i) due and outstanding claims for payment (including payments to be made under the Agreement or any similar agreements with other institutions) against the DFI shall be satisfied on a pro rata, pari passu and (ii) the CPA's reimbursement obligation hereunder shall be limited to the funds available in the DFI collected in accordance with the United Nations Security Council Resolution 1483 (2003), from time to time, and, ERG shall not have recourse to other assets of the CPA for any deficiency in the DFI.

(b) Upon ERG's payment of any claim under a Policy, ERG shall notify the CPA with a copy to TBI in writing of such claim payment and request reimbursement therefore. The reimbursement request shall include (i) the Letter of Credit number; (ii) the Covered Amount paid with respect to the claim; (iii) the identity of the purchaser and description of the goods and/or services financed; (iv) a copy of the relevant drawing documents (including Purchase Authorization); and (v) any other information reasonably requested by the CPA. Upon receipt of the completed request for reimbursement, the CPA shall pay to ERG within 30 calendar days in immediately available funds such Covered Amount, without set-off or counterclaim.

(c) All payments to ERG under this Agreement shall be made in the original currency of the Letter of Credit or Swiss Francs (CHF) to

Swiss National Bank, Bern (Clearing no. 110)
account no. 001158-1530-5-030
in favour of F+RW/ERG
sub-account no. 11129.963.001

7. Transition Undertaking

The CPA shall notify ERG no later than 90 days prior to the CPA's relinquishment of the authority to direct disbursement of the DFI in accordance with paragraph 13 of United Nations Security Council Resolution 1483 (2003) and transference of such authority to the government of Iraq. If the CPA shall not retain such authority, the CPA shall (a) ensure that prior to the expiry of such ninety-day period, funds from the DFI are allocated to TBI in an amount sufficient to satisfy all amounts with respect to outstanding Letters of Credit or Payment Undertakings and (b) take such other actions as may be reasonably requested by ERG to secure TBI's repayment obligations under Letters of Credit or Payment Undertakings.

[153] Annex B not reproduced; on file with author.

8. Consultation

The CPA, TBI and ERG shall review the activity under the Agreement on a periodic basis and consult with each other regarding utilization and performance hereunder.

9. Notices

All notices and other communications in connection with this Agreement shall be made in writing, in the English language, sent to the attention of the person indicated below and shall be effective upon receipt:

(a) TBI:
Trade Bank of Iraq
Central Bank of Iraq Building
al-Rasheed Street
Baghdad, Iraq
Attention: Hussein al-Uzri, President

(b) CPA:
OCPA HQ
Ministry of Finance
APO AE 09335
Attention: Marek Belka, Director of Economic Policy

(c) ERG:
Export Risk Guarantee Agency
Kirchenweg 8
8032 Zurich
Switzerland
email: office@swiss-erg.com
fax: +41 1 384 47 87

10. Due Authorization

Each of the CPA and TBI represents that (a) it has the necessary authority to execute and deliver this Agreement and to perform its obligations hereunder, and (b) this Agreement has been duly authorized, executed and delivered by it and constitutes a legal, valid and binding agreement of the CPA and TBI, respectively.

11. Amendment, Waiver

This Agreement may not be amended or modified without the written consent of the parties hereto, and no provision hereof may be waived without the written consent of the party to be bound thereby. No failure or delay by any party in enforcing any right hereunder shall operate as a waiver or impair any such right.

12. Termination

This Agreement may be terminated at any time by any party upon (30) days written notice to the other parties hereto; provided that, the termination of this Agreement shall not affect the validity of any rights or obligations of any of the parties hereto, including without limitation, any payment obligations of the CPA to ERG with respect to any Letter of Credit or Payment Undertaking insured by ERG prior to the date of termination.

In witness thereof, each of the parties hereto has caused this agreement to be duly executed and delivered as of the date first above written,

COALITION PROVISIONAL AUTHORITY
By: ______________________________
Name: Marek Belka
Title: Director of Economic Policy, CPA

TRADE BANK OF IRAQ
By: ______________________________
Name: Hussein al-Uzri
Title: President, Trade Bank of Iraq

Export Risk Guarantee Agency ERG
By: ____________________________
Name: Peter W. Silberschmidt
Title: Managing Director, ERG

Annex A

________, 200_

Purchase Authorization

[Name of Exporter]
[Address of Exporter]
Re: Framework Agreement regarding Short Term Export Credit Insurance

Pursuant to the terms and conditions of the Framework Agreement, dated as of December 5, 2003, among the Coalition Provisional Authority, Trade Bank of Iraq, and ERG (the 'Framework Agreement'), we hereby confirm that the financing of the transaction described below has been authorized for coverage under the Framework Agreement. Capitalized terms used but not defined herein shall have the meanings set forth in the Framework Agreement.

We hereby certify that as of the date of the Purchase Authorization, Obligations (including the payment obligations incurred in connection herewith) do not exceed the Base Amount for each of the succeeding 180-day and 360-day periods.

Exporter:
Buyer:
Amount:
Repayment Term:
Goods/services:
[Purchase Order/Invoice Number]
Issuing Bank:[154]
Confirming Bank:[155]

Sincerely yours,

[Coalition Provisional Authority] [Trade Bank of Iraq]
By: ____________________ By: __________________

[154] Include this item only if an eligible bank is issuing a Letter of Credit on behalf of TBI.
[155] Include this item if TBI is issuing a Letter of Credit to be confirmed by an eligible bank.

Document 239
De-Ba'athification: An Iraqi Process
8 December 2003

FOR: CPA Senior Advisors
CPA Governance Teams
CJTF-7
FROM: THE ADMINISTRATOR
SUBJECT: De-Ba'athification: An Iraqi Process

Attached is CPA Memorandum Number 7,[156] which delegates authority to the Iraqi Governing Council and any entity it designates to establish and implement de-Ba'athification for all Iraqi government employees, consistent with CPA Order Number One.[157] Order Number One removed from their positions and banned from future employment in the public sector full members of the Ba'ath Party holding ranks of Firqah and above; it also prohibited anyone holding the lesser position of full (amil) party member in the Ba'ath Party from holding a job in the top three tiers of any ministry.

De-ba'athification is now an Iraqi process. CPA civilians and Coalition Military personnel are no longer responsible for de-ba'athification. You should therefore immediately cease any involvement in de-Ba'athification.

The Governing Council is in the process of developing procedures necessary to fully implement its authority. In this interim period before such procedures are formulated and publicized, you should refer questioners to the relevant ministry where the individual worked or to the Governing Council.

Memorandum No. 7 ratifies the Governing Council's decision of September 14,[158] to the extent that it is consistent with CPA Legal Order No.1, which called for all Firqah and above government employees to be immediately dismissed with an option to appeal at a later time.

Consultations: The Governing Council shall coordinate with the Ministry of Finance before taking actions on matters with fiscal consequences, and with the CPA on actions where the number and/or concentration of Iraqi citizens affected may raise security concerns.

Appeals: All dismissed employees will have basic due process rights of written dismissal notification, an opportunity to respond to the factual allegations upon which the dismissal is based, and a two-step process of appeals. At the local level, ministers will form local de-ba'athification committees. Those denied reinstatement can then appeal to the Governing Council's Higher National De-Ba'athification Commission.

Reinstatement: Reinstated employees will receive back pay, retroactive to the date they were dismissed.

Exemptions: Exemptions previously granted by CPA Administrator Bremer, and only those granted by CPA Administrator Bremer, will remain in effect unless and until termination on a case-by-case basis by the Governing Council's Higher National de-Ba'athification Commission. After consultations with the Governing Council, Ambassador Bremer reserves the right to reinstate employees removed under de-Ba'athification; he will only exercise this right in unusual circumstances.

[156] See *Doc 132.*
[157] See *Doc 14.*
[158] See *Docs 498, 499.*

Special Cases: Allows the Governing Council to establish procedures for exempting groups, such as POWs from the Iran-Iraq War, who acquired high-level Ba'ath Party status by default.

Property and Assets: Allows the Governing Council to seize and manage Ba'ath Party assets. (To date, the GC has issued no instructions on how this process will be implemented.)

Effective date: November 5, 2003.

FAQs:

Pensions: To date, decisions on whether to award pensions have been unevenly implemented in the ministries. The Governing Council has not yet decided if/how they will award pensions to employees who have lost their jobs through de-Ba'athification.

Reinstatement Order: On September 29, the Governing Council issued Decision No. 51,[159] which called for the immediate reinstatement of all those government employees who had lost their jobs for political reasons under Saddam. The GC has not yet developed procedures to implement this order. The order was put on hold in a GC press statement, which said that ministries should make a list of petitioners and the issue would be reconsidered at a later time.

Who is in charge: This is a national policy, and Governing Council decisions on de-Ba'athification take precedence over the wishes of mayors. governors or other local officials. The relevant ministers, through their directorates general, are leading this process. The GC, however, is required to operate in accordance with the procedures laid out in the legal order, including those to provide due process and those to ensure adequate consultation with the CPA before decisions having financial or security implications are taken.

Document 240
De-Ba'athification

14 December 2003

FOR:	THE GOVERNING COUNCIL DE-BA'ATHIFICATION COMMITTEE
FROM:	THE ADMINISTRATOR, Ambassador L. Paul Bremer
SUBJECT:	De-Ba'athification

Many thanks for the briefing you provided me with on Wednesday December 11[160] during your most recent de-Ba'athification committee meeting. I was pleased to hear of your plans to move forward in formulating and implementing de-Ba'athification policy. The Coalition recognizes the importance of a process which continues de-Ba'athification, with reconciliation enabling Iraq to untangle itself from its past and in paving the way for a stable and prosperous future.

The CPA is committed to de-Ba'athification as a policy and is supportive of the Governing Council's efforts to implement it. However, as mentioned in my letter of December 7, the GC must consult with me when de-Ba'athification is likely to have

[159] See *Doc 314*.

[160] The meeting was on Wednesday 10 December 2003.

financial or security implications. De-Ba'athification should also proceed subject to the transparent and non-political procedures the GC has committed itself to formulating. CPA remains willing to help the GC, the committee, and the Higher De-Ba'athification Council achieve what many members have identified to me and my staff as the stated goal: bringing to justice Ba'ath Party members who have committed criminal acts and intimidation and finding a way to reconcile more nominal party members with plans for Iraq's future.

Several recent developments will help ensure that Ba'athists who committed crimes will be held accountable. The establishment of the Iraqi Special Tribunal will be an important vehicle for punishing the worst violators of the human rights of Iraqis. Moreover, the Ministry of Justice and CPA are in the midst of an ambitious review of the records and conduct of Iraqi judges; those found to be corrupt or having close affiliation with the previous regime will be relieved of their duties. Already, more than 100 judges have been dismissed. Such efforts will restore faith in Iraq's judicial system and give the people confidence that Ba'athists guilty of lesser crimes will also be held responsible for their actions.

In contrast to these steps forward, as I mentioned Wednesday, there have not yet been comparable efforts to promote reconciliation. Some GC members and ordinary Iraqis have acknowledged to me that many Iraqis who joined the Ba'ath Party – and even rose to quite high levels – were guilty of no crimes, except to gain favor with the party in order to maintain their jobs, gain entrance to universities, or protect family members from intimidation. Your exemption of those firqah-level Ba'athists who were POWs in Iran from the overall de-Ba'athification implicitly acknowledges this distinction.

I encourage the GC De-Ba'athification Committee and the Higher Council on De-Ba'athification to consider additional ways to make these distinctions both in word and deed and thereby promote the needed process of reconciliation. While we all agree that those guilty of serious crimes must be held to account, the interests of Iraq are not served by alienating large numbers of nominal Ba'athists from Iraq's political and economic future. As Iraq moves away from its dark past and becomes a democratic and free nation, it must find a way of reintegrating people who are willing and eager to contribute to the new Iraq.

As I mentioned to the committee on Wednesday, I am prepared to transfer the de-Ba'athification files that CPA has compiled, both on individuals to whom we granted temporary exceptions and on broader investigations conducted on those accused of being high-level Ba'athists. At the recommendation of CPA's Legal Counsel, I will pass these files to the Governing Council as soon as the implementation procedures for de-Ba'athification are finalized and publicized. These procedures must specify how the GC wishes de-Ba'athification to proceed in each ministry, the mechanisms created to govern any exception process, and the systems developed to ensure due process. CPA stands ready to assist or advise in the formulation of these procedures if the GC Committee desires.

Again, thank you for your time on Wednesday and good luck in your efforts.

Document 241
Proposed Agenda for the December 31 Meeting [with the Governing Council]

29 December 2003

INFO MEMO

FOR: THE GOVERNING COUNCIL
FROM: THE ADMINISTRATOR, L. Paul Bremer
SUBJECT: Proposed Agenda for the December 31 Meeting

On Wednesday, I will come to the Governing Council to continue our weekly discussion. I welcome advance notice of any topics the Council wishes to raise with me during our session.

In addition, I would like to provide a brief update on my recent trip to Washington. I am also interested in sharing with the Council the feedback I have received on the Town Hall meeting on the November 15 Agreement that was held in Basra on Monday, as well as the preliminary results of the focus groups being conducted nationwide.

I am interested in the GC providing me with an update on recent developments in the drafting of the Transitional Administrative Law. Moreover, I would like to know how the Council has progressed in the nomination of Deputy Ministers.

I look forward to a good discussion.[161]

Document 242
Memorandum of Understanding between the United Nations World Food Programme, the Ministry of Trade of Iraq, and the Coalition Provisional Authority

8 January 2004

The United Nations World Food Programme, hereinafter referred to as 'WFP',
the Ministry of Trade of Iraq, hereinafter referred to as 'MOT',
and the Coalition Provisional Authority, hereinafter referred to as 'CPA',

Noting that under the provisions of Article 55 of the Fourth Geneva Convention, to the fullest extent of the means available to it, the CPA as the Occupying Power has the duty of ensuring the food supplies of the population and that it should, in particular, bring in the necessary foodstuffs if the resources of the occupied territory are inadequate, as recalled by Security Council Resolution 1472 (2003),

Recognizing that regular and uninterrupted food supply to the Public Distribution System (PDS) is critical to ensuring the food supplies of the Iraqi population, and that this could be

[161] This is just one example of a 'Proposed Agenda' sent to the Governing Council by CPA Administrator Bremer or by his deputy, Ambassador Richard H. Jones, in preparation for CPA's (weekly) meetings with the IGC.

facilitated by the temporary continuation of WFP's emergency assistance to Iraq, including thorough capacity building activities,

Noting that CPA has made a specific request for assistance to WFP, for the purpose of providing support to the PDS from 22 November 2003 through June 2004,

Noting that the Minister of Trade of Iraq has made a specific request to WFP for the same purpose,

Noting that the Security Council resolved in its Resolution 1511 (2003) that the United Nations should strengthen its vital role in Iraq, including by providing humanitarian relief,

Recalling United Nations General Assembly Resolutions 43/131 and 45/100 on humanitarian assistance to victims of natural disasters and similar emergency situations,

Recognizing the importance and full force of the Operations Agreement signed by CPA and WFP on [date] which extends to WFP all privileges, immunities and safeguards to which it is normally entitled,

Agree to carry out the following activities:

1. PROCUREMENT OF BUFFER STOCKS AND SHORTFALL COMMODITIES

1.1 For the purpose of commodity procurement, MOT shall provide WFP with detailed commodity specifications for each commodity contained in the PDS food basket within one week of the signing of this MOU.

1.2 WFP shall procure, in accordance with its rules and regulations, commodities as requested by CPA, initially in the amount of $110 million worth of wheat, rice, vegetable oil, infant formula, and tea, as per table in annex 1.[162] Additional procurement may follow as agreed by all parties until March 31, 2004. Procurement thereafter shall be the responsibility of MOT.

1.3 WFP shall contract in accordance with its rules and regulations with suppliers to ensure procurement of commodities under this Agreement.

2. SHIPPING AND OVERLAND TRANSPORT

2.1 WFP shall deliver to Iraq in accordance with the provisions of Articles 2.3 to 2.14 all those commodities procured under Article 1.2.

2.2 WFP shall have no operational responsibility in the delivery of commodities resulting from CIF contracts renegotiated under SCR 1483.[163]

2.3 WFP shall arrange ocean and overland transport and final delivery of commodities described in Article 1.2. to three designated hubs in Iraq, namely Baghdad, Mosul and the port of Umm Qasr (warehouse and silo).

2.4 WFP shall deliver commodities to the port of Umm Qasr on truck alongside vessel or landed in port sheds, at WFP's sole discretion. MOT shall receive the commodities as fast as the vessel(s) can discharge.

2.5 WFP shall use up to four land corridors for the transport of commodities into Iraq, including but not limited to corridors via Jordan, Turkey and Syria. WFP will maintain offices in each of these countries. In addition, WFP will maintain offices in Kuwait to monitor deliveries into Umm Qasr.

2.6 MOT shall accept as proof of conformity to specifications certificates of origin and other internationally accepted shipping/transport/quality control documents provided by WFP and suppliers.

[162] Annex 1 on 'Quantities to be procured' is not reproduced.

[163] See *Doc 523*.

2.7 WPP shall undertake quality testing at load point for commodities in accordance with MOT specifications referred to in Article 1.1. Any further quality testing, if required, by MOT shall take place subsequent to passage of title.

2.8 WFP shall place a representative of an independent surveyor in each of the hubs named in Article 2.3, including the silo complex in Umm Qasr, with the responsibility of certifying on behalf of WFP and jointly with MOT quantities of delivered goods.

2.9 WFP's responsibility for ensuring transport and delivery of the said commodities shall end F.O.T. upon delivery at the three hubs defined in Article 2.3 and certification by the independent surveyor, after which point title shall pass to MOT.

2.10 MOT and CPA acknowledge that the independent surveyor appointed by WFP under this clause shall be freely allowed to inspect commodities and take samples for analysis at his discretion at the three hubs named in Article 2.3, including the silo complex at Umm Qasr, without restriction or interference.

2.11 WFP shall contract in accordance with its rules and regulations with transporters to ensure delivery of commodities under this Agreement.

2.12 MOT shall ensure that no trucks carrying WFP waybills will be diverted to locations other than the one stated on the waybill.

2.13 MOT shall ensure that truck off-loading time at hubs does not exceed 48 hours upon arrival. Any demurrage thereafter shall be the sole responsibility of MOT.

2.14 WFP shall provide the MOT and CPA with a daily dispatch report for each corridor.

2.15 Pursuant to Article V of the Operations Agreement[164] and for the avoidance of doubt, WFP is not liable to pay the reconstruction levy coming into force on 1 January 2004 in respect of goods imported into Iraq.[165]

3. PIPELINE DATA

3.1 Taking into account needs and current stock levels MOT, endorsed by CPA, shall provide WFP on a monthly basis for the duration of this MOU with an updated monthly allocation plan by commodity for each hub defined in Article 2.3, supported by a monthly distribution plan by governorate.

3.2 MOT shall provide WFP with a weekly countrywide stock report per commodity, and with a monthly stock report within five days of the end of the month for each hub defined in Article 2.3 and for PDS stocks in each governorate.

3.3 MOT and CPA shall provide WFP with all relevant information on expected arrivals of food and non-food cargo likely to impact port or storage availability for PDS commodities.

3.4 On the basis of information provided under Articles 3.1 to 3.3, WFP shall prepare a pipeline document for PDS commodities showing expected arrival time per commodity to the hubs defined in Article 2.3, and implement a delivery plan accordingly.

3.5 WFP shall share the updated pipeline document with MOT and CPA on a weekly basis.

4. OTHER PDS MANAGEMENT, COORDINATION AND CAPACITY ISSUES

4.1 MOT responsibilities:

- to commit appropriate resources to efficiently manage the PDS;
- to provide appropriate staff to work in the Coordination Centre in Baghdad, as requested by CPA;

[164] Operations Agreement not reproduced.

[165] The Reconstruction Levy was introduced by CPA Order No 38; see *Doc 59*.

- to manage distribution system from hubs defined in Article 2,3 to food agents, including continued operation of the ration registration centres;
- in consultation with CPA to set and announce the food ration for each month according to schedule;
- to provide accurate local and national inventory monitoring and recording systems for the storage of food products;
- to provide audit inventory stocks at storage points upon request of CPA;
- to develop improved quality testing arrangements with CPA;
- to ensure adequate storage space and handling capacity in warehouses and silos for the receipt and dispatch of food commodities; and
- to ensure security of storage space and warehouses and silos as well as the commodities located therein;
- to permit WFP to retain its existing office space within the MOT compounds;
- to ensure competent and fair distribution of commodities to PDS beneficiaries.

4.2 CPA responsibilities:

- to establish and manage a coordination centre in Baghdad and satellite cells to support and facilitate logistics operations, and assign points of contact within the centre for PDS operations as necessary;
- to assign liaison staff at key points of operation to provide support to WFP and MOT at their request;
- to provide MOT with communications capability in key locations;
- to ensure authentication facilities are established and operating at all entry points;
- to provide appropriate voice and data connectivity at the three hubs defined in Article 2.3 in order to facilitate communications with the representatives of the WFP independent surveyor;
- to guarantee sufficient resources to MOT so that the three hubs defined in Article 2.3 should be able to receive the food quantities delivered by WFP in accordance with the pipeline document defined in Article 3.4.

5. FINANCING

5.1 The goods and services to be provided by WFP under the present MOU have been costed in the estimated budget available in annex 2.[166] They include:

- Cost of the commodities procured under Article 1.2;
- Cost of external and overland transport, as defined in Article 2;
- Direct support costs (DSC), being costs of WFP services, including staff costs, relating to procurement, external and overland transport and pipeline management and any other WFP activity directly related to the implementation of the present MOU;
- Indirect support costs established at 4.5 per cent of direct costs.

5.2 WFP costs do not include the cost of obligations established between CPA and MOT under the present MOU.

5.3 CPA shall fund:

- The cost of commodities procured under Article 1.2;
- The cost of external and overland transport for commodities defined in Article 2.1;
- Direct support costs (DSC) up to the level budgeted in annex 2, excluding DSC funded directly by WFP in accordance with the provisions of Article 5.4;
- Indirect support costs established at 4.5 per cent of the above direct costs.

[166] Annex 2 on the 'Budget' is not reproduced.

5.4 WFP shall determine which fund balances, if any, resulting from OIP indemnities paid pursuant to Security Council Resolutions 1472 (2003)[167] and 1483 (2003)[168] can be appropriately used against DSC requirements expressed in annex 2 and shall use them to this effect.

5.5 CPA shall transfer in advance to WFP funds sufficient to cover costs referred to in Article 5.3. CPA payments shall be made in tranches, according to a schedule mutually agreed upon by WFP and CPA, based on projected disbursements. The first tranche shall be paid within two weeks of the signing of this MOU and shall be sufficient to cover the cost of procurement of commodities referred to in Article 1.2.

5.6 WFP shall communicate to CPA on a monthly basis, a detailed report of its disbursements against direct costs defined under Article 5.1 and shall return all unspent funds received from CPA against these costs upon termination of this MOU.

6. IMPLEMENTATION PERIOD

The present MOU shall be effective once the Operations Agreement between CPA and WFP has been signed by both parties. Once the Operations Agreement has been signed, this MOU will then take effect from the date of signature, and remain in effect until 30 June 2004 or until such time as all commodities referred to in this MOU have been delivered in accordance wife the provisions in Article 2.

7. DISPUTE RESOLUTION

Any dispute between the Parties arising out of or relating to this Memorandum of Understanding that cannot be settled by negotiation or other agreed mode of settlement shall be submitted to arbitration at the request of any of the Parties. For the purposes of the implementation of this Section, each Party shall appoint one arbitrator and advise the other Party of the name of its arbitrator. Should the arbitrators fail to agree upon an award they shall immediately appoint an umpire. In the event that within thirty (30) days of the request for arbitration either Party has not appointed an arbitrator, or that the arbitrators appointed fail to agree on an award and/or on the appointment of an umpire, either Patty may request the President of the International Court of Justice to appoint an arbitrator or an umpire, as the case may be. A majority vote of the arbitrators shall be sufficient to reach a decision, including decisions on procedural matters, which shall be final and binding. The expenses of arbitration shall be borne by the Parties as laid down in the arbitral award.

8. AMENDMENTS

No changes or amendments to this MOU can be made unless agreed in writing by all the parties.

9. INDEMNITY

The CPA shall indemnify, hold and save harmless, and defend, at its own expense, WFP, its personnel and agents and sub-contractors from and against all suits, claims, demands, and liability of any nature or kind, including their costs and expenses, arising out of activities in relation to any contract negotiated by WFP prior to or subsequent to 21 November 2003, and undertaken pursuant to this Memorandum of Understanding. For the avoidance of doubt, the CPA shall be responsible for dealing with claims by third parties, where loss of or damage to

[167] See *Doc 519*.
[168] See *Doc 523*.

property, personal injury or death occurred during or in connection with activities undertaken by the Parties, and shall include any claim by any third party as a result of any contract cancellation arising from activities by the parties undertaken pursuant to this Memorandum of Understanding. The CPA will directly indemnify WFP up to 200 million dollars, with any indemnities beyond this amount being covered from the Development Fund of Iraq.

10. PRIVILEGES AND IMMUNITIES
The CPA shall extend to WFP and its officials the privileges and immunities contained in the Convention on the Privileges and Immunities of the United Nations, adopted by the United Nations General Assembly on 13 February 1946[169] and the Convention on the Privileges and Immunities of the Specialized Agencies and its Annex II, concerning the Food and Agriculture Organization of the United Nations, adopted by the United Nations General Assembly on 21 November 1947.[170]

11. PUBLIC STATEMENTS
Neither CPA nor MOT shall issue any written statement concerning this agreement, or concerning any work done by WFP in conjunction with CPA or MOT at any time, without prior written approval of WFP.

Document 243
Delegation of Authority to Sign Operational Letters of Agreement
11 January 2004

Pursuant to my authority as Administrator of the Coalition Provisional Authority (CPA), relevant U.N. Security Council resolutions, including Resolution 1483 (2003), and the laws and usages of war and in accordance with CPA Regulation No. 1, dated 23 May 2003, I hereby delegate to the Minister of Transportation or Director General of the Civil Aviation Authority the authority to sign operational letter agreements providing the terms under which the respective civilian aviation authorities in Iraq and the countries bordering Iraq intend to operate air traffic control service in their respective areas of responsibility and such other agreements the Iraqi Civilian Aviation Authority must enter into to open commercial air traffic into Iraq. The Minister of Transportation or Director General of the Civil Aviation shall exercise this authority in coordination with the CPA Senior Advisor for the Iraqi Civilian Aviation Authority, concerned Iraqi ministry officials, including the Interim Minister of Civilian Aviation Authority, if appointed. Such agreements shall be in form approved by the CPA General Counsel's Office.

This delegation of authority may be revoked at any time by the CPA Administrator.

L. Paul Bremer III
Administrator
Coalition Provisional Authority[171]

[169] For the text of the Convention, see 1 UNTS 15 and 90 UNTS327.
[170] For the text of the Convention, see 33 UNTS 261.
[171] The document does not bear the signature of Ambassador Bremer. The document was accompanied by an Action Memo for the Administrator from Ambassador Darrell Trent on the subject of 'Signature Authority

Document 244
Implementing Decisions of the Governing Council
14 January 2004

FOR: THE IRAQI CABINET
FROM: L. Paul Bremer III, Administrator
SUBJECT: Implementing Decisions of the Governing Council

It has come to my attention that the Governing Council has been advising you of the decisions that they issue and requesting that you implement them. This has created some confusion and some instances of ministers implementing actions that do not yet have the force of law.

As you are aware, no decision by the Governing Council has the effect of law unless it has been made pursuant to a specific delegation of authority from the CPA, or until it is ratified by a CPA Order which I sign. Particularly with respect to issues that concern changes in law or policy and any financial matters, please consult with your CPA Senior Advisor before implementing any decisions by the Governing Council.

We continue to work with the Governing Council in an effort to ensure close cooperation on policy formulation and implementation, and I would appreciate your assistance in this endeavor.

Document 245
Delegation of Authority to Sign a Voluntary Repatriation Agreement with the Government of Turkey and the United Nations Commissioner for Refugees
10 February 2004

MEMORANDUM FOR: Mr. Mohammed Jassim Khudayir, Interim Minister of Displacement And Migration

Delegation of Authority

Pursuant to my authority as Administrator of the Coalition Provisional Authority (CPA) and under the laws and usages of war, and consistent with relevant United Nations Security Council Resolutions, including Resolutions 1483 and 1511 (2003), I hereby delegate to you the authority to sign, execute and oversee the implementation of a Voluntary Repatriation Agreement with the Government of Turkey and the United Nations High Commissioner for Refugees, which shall address, in a manner consistent in all

for Minister of Transportation or Director General of Civil Aviation Authority to Sign Operational Letters of Agreements', dated 8 January 2004. The Action Memo provides in part:

'BACKGROUND: We feel this authority to approve operational letters of agreement concerning the conduct of air traffic control service with the countries bordering Iraq is the necessary first step in reestablishing Iraq within the international aviation community. This authority will be needed as the drawdown of the military ATC begins and eventual control of the airspace is returned to Iraq. Governance supports our request as consistent with your objective to build authority in the new Iraqi government institutions.'

material respects with the draft agreement appended hereto,[172] the voluntary repatriation and reintegration of refugees from Turkey who currently reside in Iraq. The authority conferred under this agreement shall be exercised in coordination with the concerned Ministries, the Governing Council and the Commander, CJTF-7, as appropriate.

The authority conferred hereunder may not be further delegated, shall be effective on this date, and shall remain in effect until rescinded by me or at the direction of a fully sovereign transitional Iraqi administration, following the CPA's final transfer of governance authority to that administration.

[Signed] *L. Paul Bremer III*
Administrator

Document 246
Note on the Role of Senior Advisors to the Iraqi Ministries
21 February 2004

There are no written guidelines delineating the senior advisors' role, responsibilities and authorities. The Administrator expects the interim Iraqi Ministers to assume responsibility for and exercise authority over all recurring day-to-day functions of their Ministries. We are increasingly empowering the interim Ministers, consistent with their capacities. The senior advisors serve as the primary liaison between the Administrator and the Ministers. They provide advice and assistance to the Ministers, but do not exercise decision making authority over routine ministry matters. The advisors are expected to keep the Administrator fully informed of activities within their Ministries, and ensure proper development, coordination, promulgation and implementation of any ministry policy initiatives that extend beyond routine ministry functions.[173]

Document 247
Letter from Ambassador Bremer to Grand Ayatollah Sistani
1 March 2004

Your Eminence

Please accept my best wishes for a safe and holy Ashura. In my religion, too, this is a time of prayer and reflection and I want you to know that I am thinking and praying for you. The martyrdom of Imam Hussein reminds all believers of the power men can have when they believe in principles.

[172] The draft agreement itself was not made available under a FOIA request. An earlier draft of the Voluntary Repatriation Agreement (VRA) between 'the Government of Turkey, the Authorities in Iraq and the United Nations High Commissioner for Refugees (UNHCR)' which had been negotiated in Ankara on 20-22 January 2004 is available at http://wikileaks.ch/cable/2004/01/04ANKARA 509.html. The agreement was never signed. See also the Interoffice Memorandum to the Chief, Legal Affairs Section, Executive Office, Office of the UNHCR, Regarding the Voluntary Repatriation (Tripartite) Agreement, 19 February 2004, reproduced as *Doc 537*, which deals with the question of whether UNHCR may conclude such a VRA with the occupying power.

[173] Note by the CPA Office of General Counsel.

Thank you for receiving our friend last week. I find our consultations extremely valuable and appreciate the time and effort you have put into them. You may be sure that I will continue to welcome and respect your views on matters of Iraq's future. I have asked our friend to speak to you about how we might assist with your security.

As you know, the Governing Council reached agreement earlier today on the text of the Transitional Administrative Law, a copy of which I hope to get to you as soon as the English and Arabic texts are conformed. This historic document recognizes the important role of Islam for the majority of Iraqi people, while guaranteeing the freedom of each individual to practice their own religion. And after thirty four years of ruthless dictatorship, the law sets Iraq on the path to a full democracy by means of direct popular elections, perhaps by the end of this year but in any case no later than January 31, 2005. I am grateful for your support of this process.

I welcome continued contact with you in the days and months ahead.

Respectfully,

[Signed] *L. Paul Bremer*
L. Paul Bremer III
Administrator

Document 248
Revised Guidance on Accepting Donations from Private Entities

4 March 2004[174]

Pursuant to my authority as Administrator of the Coalition Provisional Authority (CPA) and under the laws and usages of war, and consistent with relevant U.N. Security Council Resolutions, including Resolution 1483 (2003), I hereby prescribe the following guidance concerning the processing of offers from private entities to provide assistance in furtherance of the relief and reconstruction of Iraq, or to otherwise benefit the people of Iraq:

Section 1 Purpose

This Memorandum delegates authority to coordinate and authorize donations from Private Entities (as defined herein) to the Executive Director, CPA-Washington. This Memorandum further clarifies procedures to be used by CPA personnel in coordinating with Private Entities wishing to provide assistance to further the reconstruction of Iraq or otherwise benefit the people of Iraq. In particular, all donations from Private Entity [sic] must heretofore be authorized and approved by CPA-Washington. This revised guidance will better ensure compliance with all existing laws, regulations, and procedures, and greatly facilitate the efficient delivery of donations within Iraq to areas in need.

[174] The Revised Guidance on Accepting Donations from Private Entities was included in a Memorandum from the Administrator for Iraqi Interim Ministers, Senior Ministry Advisors, and the Executive Director, CPA-Washington. It was accompanied by a Memorandum from the Administrator for Senior Ministry Advisors, dated 3 March 2003 (initialed 5 March 2003), which reads: 'The attached Memorandum delegates to Mr. Reuben Jeffery, Executive Director, CPA-Washington the authority to accept private donations in support of Iraqi relief and reconstruction efforts. The centralized approval process established in the memorandum will ensure that all donations comply with existing laws, regulations, and procedures, and greatly facilitate the receipt and distribution of donations within Iraq. Senior Ministry Advisors shall understand and comply with the policies set forth in the attached Memorandum and ensure that all donations – whether cash or in-kind – are submitted for approval by CPA-Washington. Accepting or coordinating the receipt of private assistance without such approval is prohibited.'

Section 2 Definitions

1) 'Assistance' means personal property (other than funds) or services that will be used primarily to further reconstruction of Iraq or to otherwise benefit the people of Iraq. It does not include property or services to be used primarily for the benefit of the CPA or Coalition Forces.

2) 'Donation' is a contribution of Assistance by a Private Entity to Iraq with no expectation of public recognition or other action by the CPA in return. However, nothing in the Memorandum prohibits Private Entities from advertising or making known to the public the existence of the Donation.

3) 'Endorsement' is an act by the CPA, or any personnel associated with the CPA, indicating or implying that the CPA approves of or supports the products, services, business, or activities of a Private Entity other than through a memorandum of appreciation or a Private Assistance Agreement.

4) 'Preferential Treatment' is an act by the CPA, or any personnel associated with CPA, giving or suggesting favorable treatment, other than as provided in a Private Assistance Agreement, or, conversely, giving unfavorable treatment for failing or refusing to provide assistance.

5) 'Private Entity' means a for-profit or non-profit business or charitable entity, including but not limited to sole proprietorships, partnerships, corporations, limited liability companies, joint ventures, trusts, private foundations, charities, and other similar organizations.

6) 'Private Assistance Agreement' is an agreement with a Private Entity to provide Assistance to Iraq for a limited period of time in return for public recognition, permission to advertise or conduct other promotions, or other non-monetary consideration, as provided under this Memorandum.

Section 3 Assistance

There shall be established, within CPA-Washington, a section responsible for taking the following actions to coordinate the provision of Assistance:

1) Publicizing, by all reasonable means, present and projected needs that can be met in whole or in part by Assistance from Private Entities.

2) Responding to queries from Private Entities concerning present and projected needs for Assistance that can be met in whole or in part by assistance from Private Entities.

3) Approving proposed provision of Assistance prior to delivery. Prior to approval of the Assistance, the Private Entity is required to provide the following information:

a) Name of the Private Entity providing the Assistance;
b) Description of the proposed Assistance, including any proposed limitations or conditions on the use of the Assistance. Limitations or conditions on Assistance are discouraged.
c) Value of the proposed Assistance;
d) Purpose of the proposed Assistance (how the proposed Assistance would further the reconstruction of Iraq or otherwise benefit the Iraqi people);
e) Proposed destination of Assistance;
f) Proposed entity within Iraq, in coordination with CPA, that will receive Assistance; and
g) Proposed logistics arrangements, in coordination with CPA, necessary to deliver the Assistance to its destination within Iraq.

4) Coordinating with Private Entities providing assistance concerning terms of delivery of Assistance to CPA or its designee for further distribution as appropriate.

5) Coordinating with appropriate CPA or other organizations to ensure appropriate and prompt disposition of the Assistance to the people of Iraq.

6) Coordinating with donation programs of the United Nations, the European Union, the Council for International Coordination, and other similar organizations to avoid duplicating effort.

7) Advising the Program Review Board, on a regular basis, of Assistance received or proposed to be received in order to avoid duplication.

8) Ensuring that Private Entities providing Assistance receive appropriate recognition through memoranda of acknowledgment or otherwise.

9) Solicit through an open process and by all reasonable public means Private Entities capable of providing Assistance. In situations where only one Private Entity is required to provide Assistance and multiple Private Entities desire to do so, then the solicitation will be made on a competitive basis.

10) Decide whether to accept appropriate offers for a Private Assistance Agreement from Private Entities that offer Assistance on their own volition. The acceptance of an unsolicited offer does not require solicitation of other sources of similar Assistance.

11) Maintain a database containing information of all Private Entities participating and all Assistance received under the terms of this Memorandum for purposes of obtaining information for public dissemination concerning the objectives of this Memorandum.

12) Maintain appropriate delivery records, including a written receipt from the ultimate recipient of the Assistance provided.

13) Maintain an effective and reliable system for receiving in-kind donations and distributing such donations within Iraq. Private entities making in-kind donations may be required to assume the costs of shipping until an effective and reliable system for distributing such donations is established and operating. Cash donations shall be preferred.

14) Establish and maintain a comprehensive one-stop shopping website.[175] This website shall include facts and information on essential needs for the reconstruction of Iraq, explain how Private Entities can receive assistance in ensuring that their donations are received and effectively utilized in Iraq, and generally facilitate the actions set forth in this Section.

Mr. Jefferies shall delegate responsibilities within CPA-Washington to carry out and oversee the responsibilities of this Section.

Section 4 Prohibitions

CPA personnel shall not accept or coordinate Assistance through Donations or Private Assistance without prior authorization and approval from CPA-Washington. Senior Ministry Advisors shall provide for immediate notification of CPA-Washington whenever such Assistance is planned, offered, or received.

Additionally, CPA personnel accepting Assistance through Donations or through Private Assistance shall not:

1) Provide an Endorsement to a Private Entity. For United States military and civilian personnel, Endorsements may constitute a violation of the Standards of Ethical Conduct for Employees of the Executive Branch, 5 C.F.R. 2635 et seq. (Standards of Ethical Conduct). Improper endorsement may also violate the ethics laws and regulations that apply to

[175] See http://www.cpa-iraq.org/Donations/.

personnel of coalition countries. The following provision, or words to that effect, will be inserted in all Private Assistance Agreements and in all written materials concerning the Assistance:

> This does not constitute endorsement by the Coalition Provisional Authority of the Provider or of the products or services provided.

2) Provide Preferential Treatment to Private Entities entering into Private Assistance Agreements (except as provided under terms of the agreement itself) or making Donations. For United States military and civilian personnel, improper Preferential Treatment may constitute a violation of the Standards of Ethical Conduct. Similarly, improper preferential treatment may violate the ethics laws and regulations that apply to personnel of coalition countries.

Section 5 Entry into Force

This Memorandum shall enter into force on the date of signature [5 March 2004] and shall supersede prior guidance with respect to CPA donations policy.

ANNEX A – SAMPLE DONATION INVITATION LETTER

President
XYZ Corporation
Anytown, USA 12345

As you are aware, the United States, the United Kingdom, Australia, and other nations are working together to exercise governmental authority in Iraq temporarily until such time as the Iraqi people can establish for themselves a permanent government. This temporary governmental authority, known as the Coalition Provisional Authority (CPA), has been recognized by the United Nations as the temporary government in Iraq pursuant to United Nations Security Council Resolution (UNSCR) 1483 (2003).

One of the major CPA objectives, as recognized by UNSCR 1483, is to promote the reconstruction of Iraq by developing programs to encourage Iraq's economic recovery. This is accomplished by assisting concerned organizations who desire to help meet the humanitarian and other needs of the Iraqi people by providing food, medical supplies, and other goods and services necessary for the reconstruction and rehabilitation of Iraq's economic infrastructure.

To further this objective, the CPA has established a liaison office in the Pentagon to coordinate with concerned organizations that express an interest in donating goods and/or services to the Iraqi people. This office will provide specific information concerning needs of the Iraqi people, and also technical assistance concerning the transportation and other issues to interested organizations that desire to assist us.

If your company wants to consider making a donation of goods and services to assist us in our efforts to build a revitalized and democratic Iraq, and wishes further information, please contact the Executive Director, CPA-WAshington, Mr. Reuben Jeffery, at ___________ .

Sincerely,

ANNEX B – SAMPLE PRIVATE ASSISTANCE INVITATION LETTER

President
XYZ Corporation
Anytown, USA 12345

As you are aware, the United States, the United Kingdom, Australia, and other nations are working together to exercise governmental authority in Iraq temporarily until such time as the Iraqi people can establish for themselves a permanent government. This temporary governmental authority, known as the Coalition Provisional Authority (CPA), has been recognized by the United Nations as the temporary government in Iraq pursuant to United Nations Security Council Resolution (UNSCR) 1483 (2003).

One of the major CPA objectives, as recognized by UNSCR 1483, is to promote the reconstruction of Iraq by developing programs to encourage Iraq's economic recovery. This is accomplished by assisting concerned organizations who desire to help meet the humanitarian and other needs of the Iraqi people by providing food, medical supplies, and other goods and services necessary for the reconstruction and rehabilitation of Iraq's economic infrastructure.

To further this objective, the CPA has established a liaison office in the Pentagon to coordinate with concerned organizations that would like to transfer goods and/or services to the Iraqi people in return for an agreed-upon consideration (usually some form of advertising or other promotional consideration). This office will provide specific information concerning needs of the Iraqi people, and also technical assistance concerning the specific terms of any sponsorship agreement (including transportation of goods and the specific nature of the promotional consideration).

I strongly urge your company to consider participating in our Private Assistance Program to assist us in our efforts to build a revitalized and democratic Iraq. If you wish further information, please contact the Executive Director, CPA-WAshington, Mr. Reuben Jeffery, at _________ .

Sincerely,

ANNEX C – SAMPLE DONATION ACKNOWLEDGMENT LETTER

President
XYZ Corporation
Anytown, USA 12345

Dear Sir:

On behalf of the Coalition Provisional Authority, this letter constitutes acceptance of your donation on the terms and conditions below:

NAME OF DONATING ORGANIZATION:
DESCRIPTION OF GOODS/SERVICES BEING DONATED:
APPROXIMATE VALUE OF THE GOODS/SERVICES BEING DONATED:
PURPOSE OF THE DONATION:
FINAL DESTINATION OF GOODS/SERVICES BEING DONATED:
FINAL RECIPIENT OF GOODS/SERVICES BEING DONATED:
LOGISTICS ARRANGEMENTS: (TERMS OF SHIPMENT, DELIVERY DATE, ETC.)

As has been explained previously, this letter does not constitute endorsement by the Coalition Provisional Authority of your company or of the products or services provided.

Thank you for your generous efforts in rebuilding the economic system of Iraq and in providing assistance to the Iraqi people. If you have questions, please contact ___________.

Sincerely,

Executive Director
CPA-Washington

ANNEX D – SAMPLE PRIVATE ASSISTANCE AGREEMENT

This Private Assistance Agreement is entered into under the authority of the Administrator of the Coalition Provisional Authority (CPA) on behalf of the Coalition temporarily exercising governmental authority in Iraq pursuant to the law and usages of war and relevant United Nations Security Council Resolutions, including 1483 (2003) ('Coalition') and by ______('Contractor').

WHEREAS, the Coalition has established the Private Assistance Program to further its objective, as recognized by United Nations Security Council Resolution 1483 (2003), to assist concerned organizations that wish to help meet the needs of the Iraqi people by providing food, medical supplies, and other resources necessary for reconstruction and rehabilitation of Iraq's economic infrastructure, and

WHEREAS, the Contractor wishes to provide goods and services to help meet the needs of the Iraqi people, in return for consideration as described below.

NOW, THEREFORE, THE PARTIES AGREE AS FOLLOWS:

1. The Contractor agrees to provide the following goods and services for the benefit of the Iraqi people: (Describe the goods and services) on the following conditions and terms: (Describe any special conditions or limitations concerning the use of the goods/services) for the following purpose: (Describe the purpose for which the foods/services will be used).

2. The approximate value of the goods/services that the Contractor intends to provide under this Private Assistance Agreement in $_____ .

3. The final destination of the goods/services that the Contractor will provide under this Private Assistance Agreement will be __________ (destination) and the entity within Iraq that will be the ultimate recipient of the goods/services will be _________ (recipient).

4. The parties agree to the following terms and conditions concerning the transportation of goods/delivery of services from the Contractor to the final recipient within Iraq. (Describe here arrangements concerning the transportation of goods from the Customer [sic][176] to the final destination, method of transport within Iraq, etc.).

5. In return for the Contractor's [sic] providing the goods and services described above, the Coalition agrees to provide the following promotional consideration: (Describe the agreed-upon promotional consideration).

6. The parties agree to the following standard terms and conditions:

   a. In the event that the Contractor fails to comply with the terms and conditions described above, the Coalition, at its discretion, may terminate this contract upon giving notice to the Contractor of said termination. Additionally, in its discretion, the Coalition may disqualify the Contractor from further participation in the Private Assistance Program.

[176] It should read 'Contractor'.

b. In the event that the Contractor is prohibited from performing under this contract due to natural disaster, act of God, security situation, or other cause beyond the Contractor's control, the parties shall agree, if possible, to reschedule the times for performance under this contract. In the event that the parties are unable to reschedule the performance under the contract, the contract shall be terminated without penalty to either party.
c. The Contractor shall not assign any of its rights or responsibilities under this Agreement to another person or entity without the consent of the Coalition.
d. Except as permitted under the terms of this Private Assistance Agreement, no employee or representative of the Coalition may provide any form of endorsement or other promotional consideration to the Contractor. The mere existence of this Private Assistance Agreement does not constitute endorsement by the Coalition Provisional Authority of the Contractor or of the products or services provided.
e. Except as permitted under the terms of this Private Assistance Agreement, no employee or representative of the Coalition may provide any form of favorable or otherwise preferential treatment to the Contractor as a reward or consideration for the Contractor's performance under this Private Assistance Agreement.

This Agreement is entered into on the later of the signatures described below.

FOR THE COALITION:	FOR THE CONTRACTOR:
____________________	____________________
DATE_______________	DATE_______________

Document 249
Letter of Approval of the Transitional Administrative Law

8 March 2004

Dear Mr. President:

The Coalition Provisional Authority congratulates you and the Governing Council on the signing today of the transitional administrative law for the state of Iraq. The law joins the best traditions of the Iraqi people with a commitment to democratic ideals under the rule of law.

The Coalition Provisional Authority approves the transitional administrative law. Its adoption inspires all who share our common goal of forging a free, democratic and unified Iraq.

This day begins the formal process recognized by the November 15th agreement,[177] by which the Iraqi people will reclaim their sovereign authority after more than 30 years of tyranny and murderous oppression. As established in the transitional administrative law, the Iraqi people soon will have their own representative government dedicated to the rule of law, built on a separation of powers, and committed to honoring and protecting the liberties of all Iraqis irrespective of religion, ethnicity or gender.

The institutions of this new government are products of debate and compromise by individuals representing the rich diversity of political and religious thought in Iraq.

[177] See *Doc 232*.

The adoption of the transitional administrative law therefore demonstrates a triumph of cooperation over division, and sets Iraq firmly on course for a future of peace, stability, freedom and hope.

As the state of Iraq enters the final stages of reclaiming its rightful place within the community of peaceful and law-abiding nations, we will continue to work with the Iraqi people to guarantee full, free and fair elections and the final transition to self-rule under a permanent constitution.

L. Paul Bremer III, Administrator, the Coalition Provisional Authority.[178]

Document 250
Promulgation of Coalition Provisional Authority (CPA) Orders During Remainder of Occupation

14 March 2004

1. Summary. To date, I have issued 64 orders in my capacity as Administrator of the Coalition Provisional Authority (CPA). Under the laws and usages of war, and consistent with relevant U.N. Security Council Resolutions, including UNSCRs 1483[179] and 1511 (2003),[180] these orders have the force and effect of law. The Transitional Administrative Law (TAL) recognizes these orders and continues their force and effect until rescinded or amended by duly enacted legislation.[181] We have now completed a comprehensive review of all orders and regulations that CPA intends to promulgate during the remainder of the occupation. These initiatives will lay a proper legal foundation for a stable and free Iraq.

2. The CPA Office of General Counsel (OGC) oversees the drafting and coordination of all orders, regulations and other legal instruments promulgated by CPA.

   a. Before any order is drafted, OGC carefully reviews extant Iraqi law to determine whether any revision is necessary and ensure that amendments are as narrowly drafted as possible, consistent with the CPA's obligations under occupation law.
   b. Draft orders generally are prepared by subject matter experts either within or in coordination with OGC, although the drafting of certain highly technical orders is accomplished by experts with U.S. executive agencies or other specialized organizations such as the N.Y. Federal Reserve. We are especially appreciative of consistently superb and timely support from the Offices of General Counsel in the Departments of Defense, Treasury and Commerce and the Office of the Legal Adviser, Department, of State.
   c. The drafting process entails close coordination with the relevant interim Iraqi ministers and their ministry staffs, and often includes sessions with Iraqi academic and business leaders.
   d. Once drafted, proposed orders are staffed through an interagency process involving the Departments of Defense, State, Justice, Treasury and Commerce. The Coalition capitals in the United Kingdom and Australia also are provided

[178] The letter from Ambassador Bremer to the President of the IGC, Dr. Bahr Uloum, was signed on 8 March 2004 and transmitted on 9 March 2004.

[179] See *Doc 523*.

[180] See *Doc 531*.

[181] See TAL, Art 26(C). The TAL is reproduced as *Doc 511*.

copies for review and comment, and all commercial law reforms are staffed with the international financial institutions as well. Finally, most draft orders (including all economic and governmental reform orders) are coordinated with the Iraqi Governing Council.

e. Following the U.N.'s withdrawal from Iraq in August 2003, it has proven difficult to consult and coordinate with the U.N. on proposed CPA orders, where required under U.N. Security Council Resolution 1483. Accordingly, we request the assistance of the Department of State and the USUN in establishing a practice that will appropriately include the U.N. in the coordination process, consistent with U.N. Security Council Resolution 1483 and CPA's need to adhere to a firm schedule. In our view, such a practice cannot rely solely upon informal coordination in Iraq with the U.N. Secretary-General's Special Representative, due to the irregularity of his travel to Iraq. Another solution must be developed to ensure the strongest possible legal basis for CPA' s commercial and government reform initiatives.

3. We have applied the following principles in prioritizing our efforts:
   a. The highest priority is given to orders that create commissions, organizations or offices that will require time to establish, staff and begin functioning;
   b. The next priority is accorded to those orders that contribute to transparency, honesty and accountability of the Iraqi government;
   c. The third priority includes those orders that contribute to a stable, free market economy and that promote economic reconstruction and the conditions for sustainable development.

4. Consistent with these principles, the pending orders and regulations have been grouped into three categories: mission critical, very important and important.

a. There are 14 mission critical orders currently pending promulgation. Failure to enact these orders during the occupation could jeopardize our efforts to stabilize, reconstruct, and transform Iraq.

(1) CPA will soon begin drafting an Election Commission Order[182] and a Political Parties Order.[183] It is important that the Commission be established and that it promulgate election regulations by May 31, to ensure integrity and transparency during the campaign as well as fair and free elections that will be recognized as such by the Iraqis and the international community.

(2) In view of the uncertainty regarding a status of forces agreement or a U.N. Security Council resolution, an order that provides adequate legal protection for military, diplomatic and contractor personnel after the occupation must be in place.[184] In the same vein, a 'housekeeping' order is also needed to provide for the transition on 30 June and bring all extant orders and regulations into conformity with the TAL.[185]

(3) In the national security arena, four orders will be needed. An order establishing the new Ministry of Defence is complete and in final coordination with the Governing Council now.[186] Orders establishing a new

[182] See CPA Order No 92 of 31 May 2004 establishing the Independent Electoral Commission of Iraq, *Doc 116*.

[183] See CPA Order No 97 of 7 June 2004, Political Parties and Entities Law, *Doc 121*.

[184] See CPA Order No 17 (Revised) of 27 June 2004, Status of the Coalition Provisional Authority, MNF-Iraq, Certain Missions and Personnel in Iraq, *Doc 38*.

[185] See CPA Order No 100 of 28 June 2004, Transition of Laws, Regulations, Orders, and Directives Issued by the Coalition Provisional Authority, *Doc 124*.

[186] See CPA Order No 67 of 21 March 2004 establishing the Iraqi Ministry of Defence, *Doc 91*.

Iraqi National intelligence service[187] and regulations governing the armed forces, including militias, are being drafted.[188]

(4) In the general governance arena we will reconstitute the Board of Supreme Audit as an independent public agency empowered to enhance the economy, efficiency, effectiveness and credibility of the Iraqi government.[189] A completed draft is in coordination. We will also put in place an Organic Budget Order[190] and Public Procurement Order.[191] They are being designed to install budgeting and procurement mechanisms that are transparent, credible and embrace competition. Drafting is underway on both orders.

(5) An Interim Governmental Powers Order has been drafted and coordinated, and will be signed this week. This order will clearly articulate the respective roles, authorities and responsibilities of interim Ministers, Governors and other local governing authorities.[192]

(6) An order is also needed to establish a new visa system as part of a broader border control program.[193] This order is being drafted now by CPA.

(7) Finally, a regulation is necessary to formally establish the Program Management Office (PMO) and prescribe its composition, authorities and program management and acquisition functions during the occupation (and facilitate its proposed transition to the Department of Defense). The PMO is currently operating without a specific and comprehensive enabling regulation. This regulation has been drafted and is in coordination.[194]

b. Fifteen pending orders have been identified as 'very important'. These orders will enable Iraq to maintain momentum in its progress toward an open and stable society. Many focus upon economic and commercial reform, while others deal with communications, general governance and judicial reform.

(1) Drafting is underway on a revision to an earlier Banking Law that will facilitate commercial banking operations and support true market reforms.[195] Banking Regulations are also being written that set forth detailed guidance to implement the Banking Law.[196]

(2) Administrative Retail Registration instructions have been completed and are being coordinated with the Iraqi Ministry of Trade.[197] These regulations will provide the procedures for foreign investors to register to do retail business in Iraq pursuant to CPA Order No. 39.[198]

[187] See CPA Order No 69 of 1 April 2004 authorizing the IGC to establish the Iraqi National Intelligence Service, *Doc 93*. See also IGC Resolution No 51 of 2004, *Doc 454*.

[188] See CPA Order No 91 of 2 June 2004, Regulation of Armed Forces and Militias Within Iraq, *Doc* 115.

[189] See CPA Order No 77 of 18 April 2004, Board of Supreme Audit, *Doc 101*.

[190] See CPA Order No 95 of 2 June 2004, Financial Management Law and Public Debt Law, *Doc 119*.

[191] See CPA Order No 87 of 14 May 2004, Public Contracts, *Doc 11*.

[192] See CPA Order No 71 of 6 April 2004, Local Governmental Powers, *Doc 95*.

[193] See CPA Order No 16 (Revised) (Amended) of 4 June 2004, Temporary Control of Iraqi Borders, Ports and Airports, *Doc 36*.

[194] No such regulation was adopted.

[195] For this earlier Bank Law, see CPA Order No 40 of 19 September 2003, *Doc 62*. The revised Banking Law of 2004 was issued as CPA Order No 94 of 6 June 2004, *Doc 118*.

[196] These regulations were to be issued by the Central Bank of Iraq; see Art 104 of the Banking Law of 2004 annexed to CPA Order No 94. No such regulations were issued before the formal end of the occupation.

[197] These Instructions were first published by the Iraqi Ministry of Trade on 29 February 2004; see *Doc 61*.

[198] See *Doc 60*.

(3) A Labor Law Order has been drafted and is being coordinated. This will provide greater flexibility for job creation, labor mobility and equal treatment for Iraqis and non-Iraqis.[199]

(4) A Bankruptcy Law modernizing Iraqi dissolution, liquidation and bankruptcy proceedings has been drafted. Coordination is ongoing.[200]

(5) A Secured Transactions Order has been drafted and is under coordination. This order will provide for a registry and specific protections for property rights.[201]

(6) Orders dealing with intellectual property matters including patents, trademarks, trade names and copyrights are being drafted and will soon be coordinated with Iraqi government officials prior to interagency coordination.[202]

(7) An order dealing with Competition Policy setting forth anti-monopoly rules will be drafted.[203]

(8) A Pension Reform Order will be drafted to permit private pension funds and update extant pension policies.[304]

(9) A Central Government Functions Order will create an infrastructure to support the Prime Minister and Council of Ministers. It will include the Iraqi Security Council, the senior governmental body that will establish national security policies and priorities. This order has not been drafted.[205]

(10) An order establishing an independent commission for licensing and regulating telecommunications, broadcasting and other media has been drafted and coordinated, and is expected to be signed this week.[206]

(11) An order establishing the Iraqi Broadcasting Network as Iraq's public services broadcaster also has been drafted and coordinated, and is expected to be signed this week.[207]

(12) A 'Whistle Blower' Protection order has been drafted to protect those who come forward with evidence of corruption and official wrongdoing. Coordination is underway.[208]

(13) A draft revision of the order creating the Iraqi Civil Defense Corps (ICDC) has been completed; the revision would provide for the ICDC's participation in counterinsurgency operations. Coordination is underway.[209]

(14) An Omnibus Judiciary Order is needed to create the administrative structures to transfer the judicial support functions from the Ministry of Justice to the Judicial Council. This order has not been drafted.[210]

c. Another 28 orders would significantly contribute to establishing a basic legal framework in Iraq. Again, most focus on commercial and economic reforms.

[199] See CPA Order No 89 of 30 May 2004, Amendments to the Labor Code—Law No. 71 of 1987, *Doc 113*.

[200] For the amendments to the Iraqi Bankruptcy Law, see sec 4 of CPA Order No 78 of 19 April 2004, Facilitation of Court-Supervised Debt Resolution Procedures, *Doc 102*.

[201] No such order was promulgated.

[202] See CPA Orders Nos 80 [*Doc 104*], 81 [*Doc 105*], 83 [*Doc 107*].

[203] No such order was promulgated.

[204] No such order was promulgated.

[205] Only parts of the envisaged Order were realized during the CPA's tenure. See CPA Order No 68 of 4 April 2004, Ministerial Committee for National Security, *Doc 92*.

[206] See CPA Order No 65 of 20 March 2004, Iraqi Communications and Media Commission, *Doc 89*.

[207] See CPA Order No 66 of 20 March 2004, Iraqi Public Service Broadcasting, *Doc 90*.

[208] See CPA Order No 59 of 1 June 2004, Protection and Fair Incentives for Government Whistleblowers, *Doc 82*.

[209] See CPA Order No 73 of 22 April 2004, Transfer of the Iraqi Civil Defense Corps to the Ministry of Defence, *Doc 97*.

[210] No such order was promulgated.

(1) Four commercial reform initiatives have been drafted and received interagency and international input: Reconstruction Levy Instructions,[211] Consolidation of State Owned Enterprises,[212] Disposition of Military Industrial Company Assets and Personnel,[213] and Iraqi Interim Securities Law.[214] All are being coordinated.

(2) Five commercial reform initiatives are currently being drafted: an anti-money laundering law,[215] a comprehensive revision of Securities Law,[216] Commercial Agency Regulations,[217] Public Debt Law,[218] Consumer Protection and a comprehensive revision of Iraq's Company Law.[219]

(3) We have plans to prepare additional orders in the commercial reform arena dealing with Insurance Law, Social Security Law, Transportation Customer Funds, a National Oil Company Law, a Commercial Leasing Law, comprehensive revision of the Tax Law, a Funds Transfer Law and an International Trade Negotiation Law.[220]

(4) In the national security arena, we have completed a draft revision of the New Iraqi Army Order that authorizes Coalition Forces to exercise command and control of the IAF and permits its use in counterinsurgency operations. Coordination is underway.[221]

(5) An order establishing the Iraqi Radioactive Source Authority, a regulatory agency to monitor and enforce regulations governing ionizing radiation usage, has been completed. Coordination has not begun.[222]

(6) Drafting is underway for the Iraqi International Center for Science and Industry, an organization designed to employ Iraqi scientists, technicians and engineers who were employed in WMD programs.[223]

(7) A weapons registration order has been drafted to register and regulate the importation and possession of weapons by security companies and contractors.[224]

(8) An order decentralizing the power to appoint and remove academic officials will be drafted.[225]

(9) A Civil Service Order will be drafted including merit management and an oversight commission.[226]

(10) An order authorizing covert investigations with judicial oversight is being considered for drafting.[227]

[211] See CPA Order No 70 of 3 April 2004, Amendments to Reconstruction Levy, *Doc 94*.
[212] See CPA Order No 76 of 20 May 2004, Consolidations of State-Owned Enterprises, *Doc 100*.
[213] See CPA Order No 75 of 15 April 2004, Realignment of Military Industrial Companies, *Doc 99*.
[214] See CPA Order No 74 of 18 April 2004, Interim Law on Securities Markets, *Doc 98*.
[215] See CPA Order No 93 of 2 June 2004, Anti-Money Laundering Act of 2004, *Doc 117*.
[216] No order was promulgated.
[217] No order was promulgated.
[218] See CPA Order No 95 of 2 June 2004, Financial Management Law and Public Debt Law, *Doc 119*.
[219] No order was promulgated.
[220] None of these orders were promulgated during the CPA's tenure.
[221] No order was promulgated.
[222] See CPA Order No 72 of 10 June 2004, Iraqi Radioactive Source Regulatory Authority, *Doc 96*.
[223] See CPA Order No 79 of 19 June 2004, The Iraqi Nonproliferation Programs Foundation, *Doc 103*.
[224] No such order was promulgated, but see sec 6 of CPA Memorandum No 17 of 26 June 2004, Registration Requirements for Private Security Companies (PSC), *Doc 142*.
[225] No such order was promulgated.
[226] No such order was promulgated.
[227] No such order was promulgated. A draft order ordering wiretaps and undercover investigations was submitted to Ambassador Bremer on 21 June 2004.

(11) A traffic code is currently being drafted to ensure that regulation of motor vehicle operations is not a source of graft and corruption for lower level authorities.[228]

5. Although this is a very ambitious plan, I am convinced we will be able to have all of these orders and regulations completed by 30 June. An area of particular concern is the Iraqi Governing Council's ability to absorb this extraordinary legislative agenda. Nonetheless, we recognize that coordination with the Governing Council is necessary to ensure the legal sufficiency and long-term viability of CPA's orders. We will carefully monitor this process and continue to accord the Governing Council an opportunity meaningfully to review and respond to the orders in a prioritized sequence, and at a rate that does not exceed its capacity.

Document 251

Letter from the Administrator of the Coalition Provisional Authority Addressed to the Secretary-General of the United Nations

17 March 2004

Thank you for sending the fact-finding mission led by Mr. Brahimi to Iraq last month. The Coalition Provisional Authority is deeply grateful for the willingness of the United Nations to respond so quickly to the Iraqi Governing Council's request for assistance.

The Governing Council took an important step towards the establishment of an independent, democratic state with the adoption of the Transitional Administrative Law on 8 March 2004. In a letter dated 17 March addressed to you, it has now invited the United Nations to return to Iraq urgently to assist with both the formation of the interim government and in the preparations for national direct elections. The Coalition Provisional Authority also believes that the United Nations has a significant role to play in assisting Iraq as it continues with this process.

We hope that Mr. Brahimi and his team will be able to return to Iraq as soon as possible to help build consensus among Iraqis on the powers, structure and composition of the interim government and the process for its establishment. We also welcome the advice and assistance of the United Nations in the creation of the electoral infrastructure and hope that the United Nations elections experts will arrive in Iraq early in the week of 21 March.

Let me assure you that we will cooperate closely with the United Nations and the Governing Council to provide the security required for the United Nations to carry out these missions.

We greatly value the commitment of the United Nations to assisting the Iraqi people. I look forward to the return of the United Nations to Iraq as soon as possible.

[*Signed*] L. Paul Bremer III
Administrator, Coalition Provisional Authority[229]

[228] See CPA Order No 86 of 19 May 2004, Traffic Code, *Doc 110*.

[229] The Secretary-General replied to the CPA Administrator in a letter dated 18 March 2004: 'I would like to thank you for your letter dated 17 March 2004, which I received today. I have taken note that the Coalition Provisional Authority is fully supportive of the Governing Council's request for the United Nations to lend advice and assistance in the formation of an interim Iraqi government, to which sovereignty will be transferred on 30

Document 252
Discussion Paper: Private Security Companies Operating in Iraq

April 2004[230]

SUMMARY

Private Security Companies (PSCs) operating in Iraq provide only defensive services. In the execution of these services, PSC divide into two broad categories. The first category includes PSCs with which the Coalition Provisional Authority (CPA) contracts directly. The second category includes PSCs to which companies doing work for the CPA have awarded subcontracts. The overwhelming majority of PSCs are subcontractors. Because such information is proprietary and may have privacy implications, subcontracted PSCs and their parent companies generally do not make available details concerning the prices of their contracts, salaries, or number of employees.

The Ministry of Interior (MOI) is drafting regulations for the registration and vetting of PSCs. The regulations will comply with and complement existing and proposed Iraqi law and CPA orders, such as Iraq's new business law (CPA Order 64,[231] which replaced the Iraqi new Company Law 21 of 1997). We anticipate completion of the PSC regulations sometime in May.

The Department of Defense (DOD) is coordinating with affected agencies to issue uniform guidance regarding PSCs employed in Iraq under contracts using U.S. appropriations.

DISCUSSION

CPA's Program Management Office (PMO), CPA Contracting, and the CPA-MOI have records of 60 PSCs in Iraq (Enclosure). Of those 60, the CPA has direct contacts with only 8, for obligations currently totaling about $147 million: 81.3 million appropriated dollars and 65.5 million in dollars in funds from the Development Fund for Iraq (DFI). It is important to note that more subcontracted PSCs will arrive in Iraq in support of the post-transition PMO reconstruction effort.

Approximately 20,000 personnel are employed by PSCs in Iraq. These employees are U.S. citizens, third country nationals, and Iraqis.

PSCs provide three distinct security services: personal security details for senior civilian officials, non-military site security (buildings and infrastructure), and non-military convoy security. These services are defensive in nature.

PSCs work for the agency that contracts for their services. A PSC works for CPA if it has a contract with the CPA. If a PSC has a subcontract with a prime contractor to the CPA, then the PSC reports to the prime contractor.

June 2004, as well as in the preparations for direct elections to be held before the end of January 2005. The United Nations remains committed to doing everything within its capacity to assist the people of Iraq, when and as they request. I have therefore asked my Special Adviser, Mr. Lakhdar Brahimi, and his team, as well as an electoral assistance team, to return to Iraq as soon as possible, in order to lend the advice and assistance that has been requested. They will be in contact with you in the coming days to discuss the details of their arrival. I would like to take this opportunity to extend my thanks to the Coalition Provisional Authority, in advance, for providing for their security and other logistics support. I am concurrently informing the members of the United Nations Security Council of my intention and am copying this exchange of letters to its President. [*Signed*] Kofi A. Annan.' The two letters are reproduced in UN Doc. S/2004/225, 19 March 2004, annexes III and IV.

[230] The Discussion Paper by the CPA was produced in response to a letter, dated 2 April 2004, from Representative Ike Skelton to Secretary of Defense Donald Rumsfeld. It was posted on Rep Skelton's website under 'Press Releases'.

[231] See *Doc 87*.

Disciplining contractor personnel is the contractor's responsibility, not the CPA's. Normally, an individual who requires discipline is immediately removed from the country by the contractor. In the event that criminal accusations are made against contractor personnel, such accusations would be handled through a complaint made to the local Iraqi Police. In such a case, if the PSC employee was acting within the scope of his or her official employment under the terms and conditions of a contract with the Coalition Forces or CPA, and if the employee was not an Iraqi, then he or she would be immune from Iraqi legal process under the terms of CPA Order 17.[232] The parent country of the contractor maintains a right to waive the immunity. If, however, the PSC employee acted outside the scope of his or her official employment, the employee would be subject to Iraqi law. At this time, the approval of the CPA Administrator would still be required in order to proceed with legal action against a PSC employee.

Enclosure
List of Private Security Companies Operating in Iraq

1. AD Consultancy	21. Erinys	41. Omega Risk Solutions
2. AKE Limited	22. Excalibre	42. Optimal Solution Services
3. Al Hamza	23. GE International Inc.	43. Orion Management
4. Armor Group	24. Genric	44. Overseas Security & Strategic Information, Inc/ Safenet – Iraq
5. Babylon	25. Global	45. Parsons
6. Bechtel	26. Group 4 Flack A/S	46. RamOPS Risk Management Group
7. BH Defense	27. Hart Group	47. Reed
8. BHD	28. Henderson Risk Ltd	48. RONCO
9. Blackwater International LLC	29. Hill & Associates	49. Rubicon
10. Blackwater	30. ICP Group Ltd	50. SAS/SASI
11. BritAm Defense	31. IRC	51. Sentinel
12. Castleforce Consultancy	32. ISI	52. SGS
13. Control Risks Group	33. KBR	53. Smith Brandon Int
14. CTU ASIA	34. Kroll Associates	54. SOC-SMG
15. Custer Battles	35. Meteoric Tactical Solutions	55. Sumer International Security
16. D.S. Vance	36. Meyer & Associates	56. Tarik
17. Diligence Middle East	37. MVN	57. Triple Canopy
18. DTS Security	38. NAF Security	58. Unity Resources
19. Dyncorp Intl	39. Neareast Security	59. USA Environmental
20. EODT	40. Olive	60. Wade-Boyd and Associates LLC

[232] See *Doc 37*.

Document 253
Written Submission from the Coalition Provisional Authority to the United Nations High Commissioner for Human Rights

28 May 2004

POLITICAL BACKGROUND

After the end of the former Ba'athist regime, the US and UK accepted the responsibilities of occupying powers and the Coalition Provisional Authority (CPA) was established as the executive body, evolving from the Office of Reconstruction and Humanitarian Assistance. In UN Security Council Resolution 1483 (2003),[233] the Security Council supported the formation of an Iraqi interim administration as a transitional administration run by Iraqis, until the people of Iraq establish an internationally recognized, representative government that assumes the responsibilities of the CPA. On 13 July 2003 the Iraqi Governing Council (IGC) met and announced its formation as the principal body of the Iraqi interim administration referred to in UNSCR 1483. By CPA Regulation No. 6,[234] the CPA recognized the formation of the IGC as the principal body of the Iraqi interim administration, pending the establishment of an internationally recognized, representative government by the people of Iraq, consistent with UNSCR 1483. In UNSCR 1511 (2003),[235] the Security Council determined that the IGC and its ministers are the principal bodies of the Iraqi interim administration, which, without prejudice to its further evolution, embodies the sovereignty of the State of Iraq during the transitional period until an internationally recognized, representative government is established and assumes the responsibilities of the CPA. The IGC represents the majority of the different ethnicities, religions and political sectors of Iraqi society. The November 15 Agreement[236] set out a timeline and program for the transfer of governmental authority to Iraqis, the drafting of a permanent constitution, the establishment of democratic processes and institutions and provided for the assumption by Iraqis of full sovereign powers. On March 8, 2004, the IGC members signed the Transitional Administrative Law (TAL)[237] which will serve as the Supreme Law of Iraq from 30 June 2004 until a democratically elected National Assembly drafts a Constitution to be ratified via a referendum scheduled for 2005. By June 30 of this year, the CPA and IGC will be dissolved and replaced with a sovereign Iraqi Interim Government to be selected by the United Nations after a wide-ranging consultative process.

In addition, the CPA has supported a transparent process to ensure that city and provincial councils reflect the composition and character of the localities which they represent. Through caucuses, consultations and elections, Iraqis have chosen those who will represent them at the local level. In addition, with CPA's support, Iraqis have held numerous, well- attended town meetings to discuss their country's transition to democracy. The Administrator has also promulgated an order (CPA Order No. 71, Local Governmental Powers Order[238]) that further devolved certain powers to the provincial and municipal councils, consistent with the TAL's call for decentralizing government powers.

[233] See *Doc 523.*
[234] See *Doc 7.*
[235] See *Doc 531.*
[236] See *Doc 232.*
[237] See *Doc 511.*
[238] See *Doc 95.*

SECURITY SITUATION IN IRAQ

UNSCR 1511 (2003) authorizes a multinational force (MNF) under a unified command to take all necessary measures to contribute to the maintenance of security and stability in Iraq. This includes ensuring the necessary conditions for the implementation of the timetable and program as well as contributing to the security of the United Nations Assistance Mission for Iraq, the IGC and other institutions of the Iraqi interim administration, and key humanitarian and economic infrastructure. The current security situation in Iraq is difficult and complex. Anti-MNF Force elements are attempting to thwart the efforts of the MNF to create a safe and secure environment within Iraq. They are attacking MNF directly. They are using intimidation and direct attacks on Iraqi Security Force personnel, to disrupt and prevent the creation of an effective and capable Iraqi Security Force. They are also attacking the infrastructure of the country. The level of such activity has increased significantly over recent months and is likely to remain at a high level in the run-up to the transition to Iraqi sovereignty within the next few weeks, as Anti-MNF Forces try to disrupt and discredit this process and mobilize popular support against continued MNF presence within Iraq. The Coalition is making strenuous efforts to ensure that the citizens of Iraq are able to go about their daily lives free from intimidation from Former Regime Elements (FRE), foreign fighters and other extremist elements in Iraq and to protect them from the dangers posed by these elements.

PROTECTION OF CIVILIANS

Prior to the conflict, the U.S. Government established the Disaster Assistance Response Team (DART) to coordinate humanitarian assistance for the civilian population. The DART created the Abuse Prevention Unit (APU) which focused on protection of vulnerable groups and mitigating post-conflict violence and human rights abuses. The APU provided outreach and training for NGOs, CPA officials, military personnel and some UN personnel.

To compensate for injuries and deaths of Iraqis during military operations, the CPA created a $10 million Civilian Casualty Assistance Fund. This includes such matters as funding for medical treatment, micro-credit lending and materials for rebuilding homes. This is in addition to compensation paid out by individual States' military forces for property damage during the conflict.

The rules of engagement currently being taught to the new Iraqi Army allow the use of force in self-defense when threatened or attacked. Positive Identification (PID) is required, which is defined as 'reasonable certainty' that the object of attack is a legitimate military target. PID is based on reasonable military judgment in the circumstances at the time. Troops must comply with the Laws of War concerning discrimination of targets. Troops are taught that they may use aimed shots to engage enemy combatants, but should take care to avoid injury to civilians in the area. They may not engage individuals until they have PID, that they are demonstrating hostile intent, or they are committing a hostile act. Positive Identification of hostile intent/hostile act requires more than just weapon possession.

It is imperative that, in order to promote respect for the forces of law and order, those forces are seen to abide by the relevant provisions of international humanitarian and human rights law.

The Inspector of the Coalition's Office of Security Cooperation (OSC) is educating its Coalition Military Assistance Training Teams (CMATT) and Coalition Police Assistance Training Teams (CPATT) on issues of human rights in order to ensure the protection of civilians in Iraq.

CMATT and CPATT will then provide training with special focus on protection of civilians during military/police security situations for the instructors, Iraqi Army trainees and military leaders down to platoon level within the military academy, in addition to trainers and trainees in the police training academy.

The academy will use publications of the Office of the High Commissioner for Human Rights and human rights and humanitarian law treaties will form the backbone of its syllabus. It is expected that this syllabus will be a two hour time block of instruction. The syllabus will be written and reviewed in cooperation with the Ministry of Defense and the Ministry of Human Rights. A directive is in progress ordering that the issue of human rights is to be discussed in a classroom setting prior to the formal syllabus being completed. The Inspector of OSC will complete the draft syllabus by 1 June and complete implementation by 15 June.

Basic methods for arrest and detention currently being taught to Iraqi Army recruits are based on Search, Silence, Segregate, Safeguard and Speed. Restraint techniques include the use of blindfolds, zip tying hands and feet and gagging (as long as the prisoner can breathe). Prisoners are segregated as soon as possible by rank, status, gender. Recruits are obliged to then protect individuals against further harm from other detainees, friendly forces or enemy forces. Army recruits must respect the human rights of detained persons and not deny them basic necessities (food, water and safety). Detainees must be treated with dignity and protected. They must not be subjected to unreasonable punishment. They are to be treated in accordance with the Geneva Conventions, so that they are provided with food, clothing and shelter. They are to receive sanitary living conditions with facilities for proper hygiene, medical care and an opportunity to practice religion. They are also entitled to receive a translated copy of their rights, to keep personal property and can send and receive mail.

Regarding the Iraqi Police Service (IPS), human rights training is interwoven throughout both the eight week basic course for new recruits and the three week-long Transition Integration Programme (TIP course). Through the TIP course for serving police and the basic course for new recruits, it is intended that all police in Iraq will be trained in human rights and democratic policing principles. At least 30 hours of human rights related topics are included in both courses. This covers the principles of human rights and deals with them in a practical way. The syllabus for the TIP course is attached as an example. The same subjects are taught to new recruits.

The subject matter covered during the basic and TIP courses include the following:

- Democratic policing principles
- Human rights
- International law basics
- Community policing
- Police ethics and code of conduct
- Police use of force standards

To reinforce the message that the IPS is a civilian police service for and answerable to the people, a code of conduct has recently been published that all Iraqi police must sign. This sets out basic standards of behavior, breach of which may lead to disciplinary action being taken against them. A public signing ceremony involving senior Iraqi police is planned to inform the public of the new standards.

A new discipline code now being drafted will specify the breaches of discipline for which punishments can be awarded.

The Minister of the Interior has asked for a letter to be sent to all Iraqi police that specifically addresses the issue of torture by police. It makes it clear that any Iraqi police officer found to be engaged in any torture or abuse of prisoners will be dismissed and will face criminal charges. The letter is with the Minister and ready for promulgation.

The Minister and his police chiefs take allegations of torture and abuse of prisoners very seriously. A recent case in Baghdad investigated allegations of torture and sexual abuse by IPS staff against women detainees. Following the IPS investigation the Inspector General instructed the Chief of Baghdad Police to dismiss five officers and report them with a view to prosecution for their alleged crimes. It is worth noting that the IPS investigators on this case did a very efficient job and substantiated the allegations made. This is an example of good IPS officers working hard to improve their service.

Much work is being done to improve the IPS, often by the IPS itself. The pre-conflict police viewed torture as an effective interrogation technique that was permitted by law. Many of the IPS were police before the conflict and may have engaged in such acts of brutality. They are changing, but it takes time and firm action by their leaders when instances of torture are alleged.

TREATMENT OF SECURITY DETAINEES

In accordance with Article 29 of the Fourth Geneva Convention and Article 12 of the Third Geneva Convention, and in line with the view of the ICRC, US and UK military forces retain legal responsibility for those prisoners of war and detainees in US and UK custody respectively. The US and UK will therefore respond separately on the issue of treatment of detainees within their custody.

JUSTICE & THE RULE OF LAW

When the CPA assumed its responsibilities, the prison system in Iraq had effectively been destroyed and the total criminal population of 38,000 inmates had been released onto the streets. Most courts were not functioning, and most court facilities were destroyed or damaged. The judiciary included corrupt individuals, human rights violators and technically incompetent Ba'ath Party functionaries. The practices of a police state that had been responsible for mass killings and systematic, State-sanctioned torture supported by an extensive policing and intelligence apparatus had to be substantially remodeled.

The CPA's legislative response to this situation included revising the Iraqi Penal Code to excise draconian political crimes and liberalize restrictions on the freedom of the media and the right to demonstrate. The Iraqi Criminal Procedure Code was amended to prohibit torture, to ensure accused persons were advised of their rights, to provide defense counsel at every level of proceedings and to ensure representation to the indigent. The CPA removed prison management responsibilities from repressive agencies and inappropriate organizations, consolidated that responsibility in the Ministry of Justice, and enacted a comprehensive reform of penal administration laws and regulations that meet UN standards. A new Central Criminal Court was established as a court capable of dealing with the most serious national crimes under reformed criminal procedures. The CPA also ensured the independence of the judiciary, freeing it from the politicization of the Ba'ath regime.

The criminal justice system is the responsibility of the Iraqi Ministry of Justice, assisted by the CPA. In the move toward the transition to complete Iraqi control of the government by July, the CPA is working to ensure that more and more government functions are in the hands of Iraqis. The Iraqi courts are now run almost entirely by Iraqis, as are many detention facilities for individuals accused or convicted of crimes. The Iraqi juvenile courts are in Iraqi hands, and are among the best managed in the system.

The judiciary has been re-established as a separate branch of government under the supervision of a Council of Judges. It was previously under the control of the executive branch as part of the Ministry of Justice. The judiciary now has its own budget, payroll and property, endowing it with the requisite independence to adjudicate criminal cases and enforce rights without political pressure or interference from the executive. A Judicial Review Committee, comprising equal numbers of Iraqi and Coalition members, vetted all 860 judges and prosecutors nationwide for past corruption, ties to the Ba'ath party or former regime, or complicity in atrocities. This was done through CPA Orders 15 & 35 and CPA Memorandum 12.[239] Approximately 180 judges were removed and replaced with new appointments or reappointments of persons improperly removed by the former regime. Judicial salaries have also been increased to reduce the temptation to accept bribes.

Regular training for judges is in progress to inculcate a culture of respect for human rights, due process, and basic tenets of the rule of law. This has included a training course in The Hague in early May 2004 attended by US Supreme Court Justices Kennedy and O'Connor, and Lord Justice Woolf from the British House of Lords.

Criminal defendants are now also guaranteed their rights with regard to due legal process, including the inadmissibility of evidence extracted by torture, an inviolable right against self-incrimination, a right to legal counsel at all stages of criminal proceedings, at government expense if necessary. The right to counsel had previously been available only at the actual trial, after most evidence had already been gathered and entered into the record. Defendants have the right to be informed of these rights. The Council of Judges has been empowered to increase the untenably low legal fees for government-appointed defense counsel.

A Central Criminal Court (CPA Order 13[240]) has been established to investigate and try cases of national importance and in line with the new rights described above.

All of the measures above have been enshrined in the Transitional Administrative Law, which will take effect on July 1, 2004.

CPA advisors have worked with the Ministry of Interior and the Iraqi Corrections Service to ensure that criminal suspects receive the initial judicial hearing to which they are entitled within 24 hours of detention, and if detained afterwards, are not returned to police custody but are transferred to pre-trial detention centers under the control of the Ministry of Justice. Efforts are being made to enforce the 24-hour rule and to forbid return of suspects to police custody in order to forestall opportunities for police corruption and abuse which prevailed under the former regime.

Control of pre-trial detention centers and prisons has been consolidated in the Ministry of Justice. Such facilities are required to be governed according to internationally accepted standards as provided in CPA Memorandum 2.[241] Coalition advisors are training Iraqi Corrections Service guards in those regulations, with an emphasis on human rights standards, and assisting in civilian prison operations.

The CPA has promulgated several laws directly related to prison management. These include CPA Order No. 10, Management of Detention and Prison Facilities (5 June 2003);[242] CPA Memorandum No. 2, Management of Detention and Prison Facilities (8 June 2003); and CPA Memorandum No. 3, Criminal Procedures (18 June 2003).[243] Section 7 of CPA

[239] See *Docs 33, 56*, and *137*.
[240] See *Doc 31*.
[241] See *Doc 126*.
[242] See *Doc 25*.
[243] See *Doc 127*.

Memorandum No. 3 prescribes specific standards applicable to the treatment of all persons who are detained by Coalition Forces as Security Internees. Subsection 7(1)(c) states that the 'operation, condition and standards of any internment facility established by Coalition Forces shall be in accordance with Section IV of the Fourth Geneva Convention.' These legal reforms have been coupled with substantial improvements of physical facilities, including court houses, prisons, training facilities for prison guards and police, and the Judicial College.

Other parts of the criminal justice system are currently administered jointly by the CPA and Iraqis, and some are still primarily administered by US and UK MNF troops. For example, should an investigation by US or UK military police determine that an individual is criminally culpable in an attack on MNF, he is transferred to an Iraqi criminal detention facility, where his case will be investigated by an Iraqi Investigating Judge and his trial will be before the Central Criminal Court of Iraq. In addition, MNF troops currently assist in the administration of Iraq's principal criminal detention facilities, and frequently provide transportation for defendants to and from court. However, criminal detainees are dealt with by the Iraqi criminal justice system.

Criminal detainees are allowed family visits: Sundays for female visitors, Mondays for male visitors. Both parents are authorized to visit together with the juveniles on Sundays and Mondays. Visits in Abu Ghraib have been temporarily suspended following some disturbances while cells are being restored. Visits should resume there shortly.

IRAQI SPECIAL TRIBUNAL

The CPA recognized from the outset the importance of addressing past human rights abuses through legal process. The Office of Human Rights & Transitional Justice (OHRTJ) was established to create mechanisms for the Iraqi people to begin to deal with the enormous suffering caused by Saddam Hussein's regime. OHRTJ has assisted with the establishment of the Iraqi Special Tribunal (IST) which will try former members of the regime of Saddam Hussein for genocide, crimes against humanity and war crimes.

The Statute for the IST was adopted by the IGC in December 2003, following lengthy consultation with CPA officials and the IGC's Legal Committee. It provides for the establishment of a court to try members of the former Iraqi regime for war crimes, crimes against humanity and genocide. It allows for international assistance for the judges, prosecutors and investigators and to this effect a Regime Crimes Liaison Office has been created to provide international assistance and necessary expertise to the IST. Defendants will have full legal rights. US Institute of Peace sponsored a seminar in The Hague in March to bring international experts together with Iraqi judges to discuss the mechanics of the IST.

A total of $75 million has been allocated for this in addition to $14.4 million from Iraqi funds. An international team is being recruited to staff the Regime Crimes Liaison Office, which will provide the Iraqi judges, prosecutors and particularly investigators with the necessary expertise in the field of investigations under international humanitarian law and work to ensure that all aspects of the investigation and trial process meet international standards.

OHRTJ forensic staff have also been assessing over 250 suspected mass grave sites to determine which may yield evidence for the Tribunal and which may be exhumed for humanitarian purposes such as return of remains and identification of the fate of missing persons. OHRTJ staff have been training Iraqi professionals in this latter task to ensure a sustainable effort is created.

OHRTJ has built an evidence storage facility and regime document processing facility which will use the latest computer software to analyze millions of government documents to assist the work of the IST and for other human rights purposes.

DISPLACED PERSONS

The pre-conflict estimate is that as many as 800,000 persons were internally displaced throughout northern Iraq and an additional 100,000 to 300,000 persons were displaced in the center and south. However these are estimates and obtaining reliable figures has not been possible in the post-conflict climate. An estimated 900,000 Iraqis are considered to be refugees or in a refugee- like situation in countries neighboring Iraq and beyond. An estimated 50,000 to 100,000 Iraqi refugees have returned since May 2003, either spontaneously or with assistance from Iraqi institutions, the CPA, regional authorities and international organizations. There are also about 70,000 non-Iraqi refugees in Iraq. This includes: 40,000 Palestinians living primarily in the Baghdad area; 13,000 Iranian Kurdish refugees living west of Baghdad, in northern Iraq and in the no-man's land along the Jordan- Iraq border; 14,000 Turkish Kurds in northern Iraq and another 1,200 – 1,400 Syrians and Iranian refugees of Arab decent (Ahwazi refugees) in the south.

Living Conditions

Although living conditions for internally displaced persons (IDPs) are very poor throughout the country and there are limited outbreaks of communicable disease, overall crude mortality rates do not indicate a humanitarian emergency. Assistance, however, is essential to ensure that in the parts of Iraq where the situation is fragile, it does not deteriorate into crisis.

Living conditions of IDPs vary considerably according to area and length of displacement. Some IDPs have generally integrated in their areas of displacement, although some percentage would return to their original area, if given assistance to do so. Other IDPs live in less stable conditions, e.g., public buildings, tents and other makeshift shelter with difficult access to basic services, e.g., water, health, education facilities. Priority assistance needs include access to water (a perennial problem in the region), housing, and access to education and health facilities, especially in rural areas.

A large number of the refugees who are returning from Iran come spontaneously and are not registered, and often find their homes destroyed or occupied, and their former means of livelihood no longer viable (such as the Marsh Arabs). These persons often migrate to urban areas, seeking housing and jobs. In the south, displacement has increased the population density in communities without adequate public services, like sewerage, creating the potential for outbreaks of disease. Many returnees in the south have struggled with access to public services, such as the public distribution system, but this has now improved.

Living conditions for the refugees in Iraq vary according to location and situation, but predominately their situation is more settled and they have access to public services. Most receive assistance and protection from Iraqi institutions and the United Nations High Commissioner for Refugees (UNHCR).

Protection Concerns

Protection concerns of displaced people in the north include threat of eviction of those living in public buildings by the authorities reclaiming the public building or by individuals returning to their homes. Non-Kurdish populations sometimes report intimidation and harassment from returning Kurdish populations. National and municipal authorities are responsible for the care and protection of IDPs, but their capacity to provide the necessary protection and assistance is severely limited by security constraints, funding and inadequate staffing and training in care and protection of displaced populations.

While Iraq is not a party to the 1951 Convention Relating to the Status of Refugees or its Protocol, laws have been adopted concerning refugees, most specifically the 1971 Political Refugee Act, which grants refugee status on political and military grounds. Many of the refugee populations in Iraq received preferential treatment from the former regime and after its fall, some faced legitimate protection concerns. UNHCR and the authorities in Iraq are implementing programs to ensure the continued protection of these populations. Access to some populations is limited at this time due to security concerns.

Durable Solutions

CPA first implemented a 'stay put' policy for IDPs throughout Iraq and encouraged countries hosting Iraqi populations to discourage immediate refugee returns, in an effort to stem population movements in an often non-permissive environment. However, a return strategy has been developed in the north to provide more assistance to people returning to 'noncontentious areas,' i.e., areas where returns will not fuel political or ethnic tension and areas where there are unlikely to be property disputes.

The IGC established the Iraq Property Claims Commission (IPCC) as the entity responsible for resolving disputes arising from violation of property rights by the former regime (since 1968). There is a mechanism in place to initiate a legal, peaceful resolution to property claims by IDPs. This is a key step for finding durable solutions for much of Iraq's displaced populations, particularly in the north. After a claimant files a claim for property they believe to be theirs, the Commission will inform the respondent (the current occupant of the property), who will in turn have the chance to present a written case stating the basis for his claim to the property. A panel of three senior officials, chaired by an Iraqi judge, will then make a determination. There is a right of appeal. It is expected that on average cases will take about six months from initial filing to settlement (although some may take considerably longer). $30 million has been allocated for the administration of this from the supplemental. $180m for compensation has just been released from the Oil for Food funds.

UNHCR and the authorities in Iraq are seeking durable solutions for the refugees in Iraq, including return, local integration, and third-country resettlement, based on the unique situation of each population and the options available.

SITUATION OF WOMEN

Women's rights

Newly formed Iraqi women's groups have taken an active role in advocating fair representation in their government bodies and calling attention to the rights of women in all spheres of Iraq's democratic development. The TAL enshrines fundamental human rights for both men and women and states that the electoral law 'shall aim to achieve the goal of having women constitute no less than one-quarter of the members of the National Assembly', a positive step in ensuring that Iraqi women are given the opportunity to assume national leadership roles.

Over the last year, Iraqi women have organized conferences in Baghdad and in the regions to discuss women's political participation and human rights issues. In addition, since June 2003, many Iraqi women have attended international meetings and conferences that offered them the chance to bring attention to their needs and hopes for the future.

Eighteen women's centers have been established throughout the country. These centers offer opportunities for women to acquire skills that will open up employment or other economic opportunities, and take part in programs that will lead them to a better understanding of their rights and how to be active participants in the decisions that affect their lives. Small grants have been provided to women's organizations to assist them in a variety of efforts, as well as coordination with organizations that wish to expand the prospects for women in isolated, rural areas, addressing concerns such as health care, child development, women's rights, education and economic development.

Domestic violence, rape

Article 12 of the TAL is clear that discrimination against an Iraqi citizen on the basis of gender is prohibited. Reliable statistics are still not available, but domestic violence, kidnapping and rape are cited by Iraqi women as major areas of concern. Culturally these issues are not publicly discussed but various women's groups that have emerged in the post-conflict period having begun working to address the problem by seeking ways to establish safe houses, or transitional protection services, where women can receive medical attention and counseling. Through a combined effort between CPA, Iraqis and non-governmental organizations (NGOs), steps are being taken to establish a Transitional Protective Service program for women who have been kidnapped, raped, and/or abused and to establish facilities to provide a temporary safe place for women or girls who face physical or sexual abuse by their families.

Traditional Iraqi culture and the right to privacy often mask abuses of women, largely domestic violence. Addressing such abuse, especially because of the cultural traditions concerning women's status inside the families, should therefore not be passed over by state institutions and NGOs. Shelters for women and their children, in case of domestic violence, are administered by the Ministry of Labor & Social Affairs (MOLSA) and we hope this responsibility will be increasingly taken on by local NGOs. Orphanages and child care institutions deal with the immediate intervention of the state on behalf of the superior interest of the child.

SITUATION OF CHILDREN

Child labor

The draft revised Labor Code, in accordance with the ILO conventions ratified previously by Iraq (Abolition of Forced Labor Convention no. 105/1957 – ratified in 1959, ILO Convention no. 138 on the minimum age – ratified in 1985 and the Convention 182 from 1999 on the worst forms of child labor – ratified in 2001) forbids any forced labor and establishes the age of 15 as the minimum working age. Despite the fact that Iraq has assumed international obligations relevant to prohibiting many forms of child labor, child labor was and still is prevalent in Iraq. An estimated two million school-age children have dropped out of school over the past few years and turned to labor in attempts to help provide family subsistence. Children are often found working as street vendors and beggars and street children. Many fall into hazardous occupations on the 'black' labor market which make them vulnerable to various types of exploitation, including physical abuse, sexual exploitation and recruitment by resistance and/or terrorist forces.

The Department of Labor of MOLSA established a Child Labor Unit in January 2004. Staff are preparing for training later in May 2004 in Dohuk. The responsibilities of this Unit are:

1) serving as a body to coordinate efforts (of NGOs, as well as governmental and international agencies) in the country to eliminate the worst forms of child labor
2) overseeing a number of child labor inspectors across the country
3) increasing awareness and advocacy to eliminate the worst forms of child labor and abuse.

PROTECTION OF HUMAN RIGHTS AND FUNDAMENTAL FREEDOMS

Article 23 of the TAL states that 'The enumeration of [specific human rights in the TAL] must not be interpreted to mean that they are the only rights enjoyed by the Iraqi people. They enjoy all the rights that befit a free people possessed of their human dignity, including the rights stipulated in international treaties and agreements, other instruments of international law that Iraq has signed to and to which it has acceded, and others that are deemed binding upon it, and the law of nations. Non-Iraqis within Iraq shall enjoy all human rights not inconsistent with their status as non-citizens.'

Freedom of Religion

Article 7 of the TAL states 'Islam is the official religion of the State and is to be considered a source of legislation. No law that contradicts the universally agreed tenets of Islam, the principles of democracy, or the rights cited in Chapter Two of this Law may be enacted during the transitional period. This Law respects the Islamic identity of the majority of the Iraqi people and guarantees the full religious rights of all individuals to freedom of religious belief and practice.'

The Iraq Committee for Reconciliation and Peace (ICRP) brought together several religious leaders for the signing of a ten-point document, known as 'The Baghdad Religious Accord'.[244] It calls for an end to violence, and pledges that Iraqi religious leaders will work together to help Iraq become a democracy. The ICRP is holding a formal conference to create a robust, actionable agenda of inter-religious reconciliation initiatives.

[244] The Baghdad Religious Accord was signed on 24 February 2004; it reads: 'In the name of God who is Almighty, Merciful and Compassionate: We who have gathered as clerics, intellectuals and political leaders representing all religions and doctrines, pray and appeal for the peace of Iraq and declare our commitment to doing all in our power to ensure the ending all acts of violence and bloodshed that deny the right to life, freedom and dignity. "We have dignified man" (a verse from the Holy Quran).

According to our faith traditions killing innocents in the name of God is a desecration of the laws of heaven and defames religion not only in Iraq but in the world.

We also declare to the world at large that:

1. The acts of corruption, violence and destruction are the work of the devil that must be opposed by all as we seek together to rebuild our nation.

2. We as Iraqis from different traditions have decided to endeavour to live together as one family respecting the moral and religious integrity of every individual and we call upon all to condemn and renounce the culture of incitement, hatred and the demonization of the other.

3. The land of Iraq is holy in all scriptures. Therefore it is a duty for the followers of all divine religions to respect the sanctity of our land whose good soil must not be desecrated by bloodshed.

4. The sanctity of all our places of worship and religious sites must be protected and preserved by all. The freedom of religious worship and expression must be guaranteed for all. "No coercion in religion" (a verse from the Holy Quran).

5. We call on the political leaders in Iraq to work for a just, fair and peaceful transfer to democracy, inspired by the divinely inspired commandments of messengers and prophets.

6. We call on and urge the international community in the name of religion to assist us in the reconstruction of Iraq away from violence and chaos.

7. We shall endeavour to the establishment of a process of truth, openness and reconciliation which will enable the spiritual, political and physical reconstruction of Iraq.

8. We shall devote ourselves to continue our joint efforts for the unity of the people of Iraq and for the creation of a climate of togetherness in which our present and future generations may live with mutual trust and respect. We shall also educate our present the future generations accordingly to maintain this commitment.

9. We as clerics and intellectuals recommend that those involved in politics and government do not to slide down the slippery slope of sectarian politics, which has resulted in our present situation; the absence of nationhood and the importation of alternative culture. Rule should be based on good citizenship and competence governed by a system of rights and obligations irrespective of national, religious or racial affiliation.

10. We hereby announce the founding of the Iraqi Centre for Dialogue, Reconciliation and Peace (ICDRP), whose membership will be from the people of Iraq and which will take a lead to ensure that the tenets of this accord are continually implemented.'

Formerly, permission to make the Haj pilgrimage to Mecca was heavily restricted for political reasons. Restrictions now are based purely on logistical, not political, factors (in terms of the numbers accepted by Saudi Arabia). Many religious rituals, such as those associated with the commemoration of Ashura, were banned by the former regime. The people of Iraq are now free to practise them openly.

Other civil and political rights

A good indicator of democratic development is the number of voluntary organizations that emerge in a post-conflict setting. In April 2003, newly formed NGOs began to attend meetings at the CPA Convention Center, in the Green Zone, and at Civil Military Operations Centers (CMOCs) all over Iraq. The CPA began holding weekly meetings at the Convention Center and bi-weekly training courses on how to establish an NGO, were well-attended. On 1 May 2004, the deadline passed for NGO registration with the Iraqi government. Within the Ministry of Planning and Development Cooperation (MOPDC), the NGO Assistance Office is tasked with managing the registration process for both Iraqi and foreign NGOs. CPA has been working closely with the MOPDC to develop its institutional capacity to manage this process and to understand its role in supporting NGOs. Over 1,000 NGOs have submitted applications to the Office. These include women's centers, human rights organizations, social service and civic education, youth, media, and many others representing a wide range of NGO work. This in large part is made possible by the CPA commitment to promote democratic development as the fundamental basis for long-term stability.

CPA South Central, in particular has led the way in promoting the infrastructure for civil society development in the region. Covering six provinces, CPA-South-Central has set up 18 democracy centers (six women, six human rights, six tribal) through which budding associations can find resources and a safe environment for civic action. Throughout Iraq, foreign NGOs, in coordination with CPA, are training, mentoring, and financially supporting NGOs and community-based organizations.

Several CPA-initiated civic education projects are training Iraqis to educate tens of thousands of Iraqis directly on basic concepts about democracy and the interim institutions that are governing Iraq until a new constitution comes into force, for example, training Iraqis as discussion facilitators using Democracy Toolkits. Currently, there are 600 Iraqi facilitators reaching as many as 5000 Iraqis each week around the country. A similar program, Ambassadors of Democracy, focuses on university campuses.

Programs are in place to identify and support civil society organizations throughout Iraq, at the grass roots level and at the national level. Civil society organizations (CSOs) have been provided with grants and training on organizational strategies, fundraising, and computers. Workshops on democracy and democratic values, conflict management and tolerance have also been held. An increasing number of independent CSOs are being formed or consolidated, and are more effectively representing the interests of their members.

Political Parties and Elections

Article 13 of the TAL states that the right to form and join political parties freely, in accordance with the law, shall be guaranteed.

Article 30 of the TAL states that elections for the National Assembly shall take place by 31 December 2004 if possible, and in any case no later than by 31 January 2005.

Article 20 of the TAL states that every Iraqi who fulfills the conditions stipulated in the electoral law has the right to stand for election and cast his ballot secretly in free, open, fair, competitive, and periodic elections. No Iraqi may be discriminated against for purposes of voting in elections on the basis of gender, religion, sect, race, belief, ethnic origin, language, wealth, or literacy.

Article 30 of the TAL states that the National Assembly shall be elected in accordance with an electoral law and a political parties' law. The electoral law shall aim to achieve the goal of having women constitute no less than one-quarter of the members of the National Assembly and of having fair representation for all communities in Iraq, including the Turcomen, ChaldoAssyrians, and others. Article 31 of the TAL states that a nominee to the National Assembly must fulfill the following eight conditions: He shall be an Iraqi no less than 30 years of age. He shall not have been a member of the dissolved Ba'ath Party with the rank of Division Member or higher, unless exempted pursuant to the applicable legal rules. If he was once a member of the dissolved Ba'ath Party with the rank of Full Member, he shall be required to sign a document renouncing the Ba'ath Party and disavowing all of his past links with it before becoming eligible to be a candidate, as well as to swear that he no longer has any dealings or connection with Ba'ath Party organizations. If it is established in court that he lied or fabricated on this score, he shall lose his seat in the National Assembly. He shall not have been a member of the former agencies of repression and shall not have contributed to or participated in the persecution of citizens. He shall not have enriched himself in an illegitimate manner at the expense of the homeland and public finance. He shall not have been convicted of a crime involving moral turpitude and shall have a good reputation. He shall have at least a secondary school diploma, or equivalent. He shall not be a member of the armed forces at the time of his nomination.

CPA has supported various conferences that engage political parties in creating common agendas and promote alliances that will strengthen the ability of these parties to participate in the forthcoming political process. The assistance encourages political parties to develop strategies to achieve their goals through the political transition, and to work for the establishment of a government respectful of civil liberties, free economic systems, equal opportunity for women, protection of minorities, and civilian control of the military. At least 200 political parties now exist in Iraq.

<u>Freedom of Movement and Freedom of Assembly</u>

Article 13(d) of the TAL states that each Iraqi has the right of free movement in all parts of Iraq and the right to travel abroad and return freely.

Article 13(c) of the TAL also states that the right of free peaceable assembly and the right to join associations freely, as well as the right to form and join unions and political parties freely, in accordance with the law shall be guaranteed.

<u>Freedom of Speech and the Media</u>

Article 13(b) of the TAL states that public and private freedoms shall be protected; the right of free expression shall be protected.

Since April 2003, Iraqis have been able to purchase satellite dishes and access regional and international news and entertainment sources. Over 200 newspapers and magazines have sprung up throughout Iraq, as well as local radio and television stations. However, the vast majority of print publications are affiliated with political and regional interests, and reporting is often based on rumor and innuendo. Production values tend to be low, pictures and programs are pirated from international sources, and there are reports of news organizations and journalists asking for bribes to report news.

Over $170 million has been allocated since January 2003 to support the start-up of broadcast and print media in post-Saddam Iraq, including the transformation of the former Ministry of Information to the Iraqi Media Network (IMN). IMN encompasses the al-Iraqiyah television station, Radio Baghdad and al-Sabah newspaper. Work has been ongoing to establish three news bureaus, a satellite TV network, a national newspaper and a training program for journalists. IMN will be expanded into two television channels, two radio stations, and the one national newspaper. US, Lebanese and Kuwaiti-based companies will provide technical infrastructure, programming content, and training to IMN. Small grants have been provided to support the start-up of regional IMN broadcast affiliates and grants for training, technical assistance and equipment for civic education activities. IMN is currently transitioning into an independent public service broadcaster. The Board of Governors and Director-General were appointed on 13 May 2004.

To ensure a credible legal framework within which a free media can operate, and to provide accountability and improve professional standards, an Independent Communications and Media Commission has been established under CPA Order 65. Together with a self-regulatory body for the print media, this will obviate the need for future government legislation to further regulate the media in Iraq, thus supporting the nascent free press.

However, journalists continue to be killed in Iraq, with 27 killed since March 2003 (gunfire from Coalition Forces being responsible for seven of those deaths). On 28 March 2004 the CPA ordered the offices of the Baghdad weekly *Al-Hawza*, which is affiliated with radical Shiite cleric Moqtada al-Sadr, to be closed for 60 days as the publication had violated a CPA decree promulgated last June that prohibits 'incitement' in the media. Specifically, the letter said the paper had published 'many articles' containing false information and intended to 'disturb public order and incite violence against the coalition forces and the employees of the CPA'. In January 2004, the IGC barred the Qatar-based satellite broadcaster Al-Jazeera from covering official IGC activities. The action came in response to an Al-Jazeera talk show in which a guest leveled allegations that some IGC members have had relations with Israel or visited the country. In November 2003, the IGC banned United Arab Emirates-based satellite channel Al-Arabiyya from broadcasting in Iraq, accusing the station of incitement after it aired an audiotape purportedly of Saddam Hussein urging Iraqis to resist the U.S.-led occupation of Iraq. The station was allowed to resume broadcasting in late January. In September 2003, the IGC barred reporters from both Al-Arabiyya and Al-Jazeera from covering official press conferences and from entering official buildings for two weeks because the IGC said that the channels incite 'sectarian differences in Iraq,' 'political violence,' and the murders of Council and U.S. coalition members. Last July, the CPA closed the publication *Al-Mustaqillah*, which had cited the calls of Islamic clerics for the death of 'spies' who cooperate with U.S. troops. The clerics said killing spies was a religious duty.

Economic, Social and Cultural Rights

Social and cultural rights

Citizens may freely organize, form and join trade unions. Trade unions are encouraged to organize and to defend workers' rights. Iraqis have the right to demonstrate and strike peaceably in accordance with the law.

Employment opportunities

According to Article 12 of the TAL, discrimination against any Iraqi citizen on the basis of gender, nationality, religion or origin is prohibited. Additionally, it is anticipated that the Iraqi Labor Code, currently being drafted, will provide sanctions against employers promoting discrimination on the basis of gender, nationality, religion or origin.

According to Article 14 of the TAL, the Iraqi state and its governmental units, including the federal government, the regions, governorates, municipalities, local administrations, within the limits of their resources and with due regard to other vital needs, shall strive to provide prosperity and employment opportunities to the people.

For those in poverty, the current social welfare law regulates social benefits for families with children, but the amount of benefits is not means driven nor does it take account of family size. Social benefits for handicapped people only address those who are blind or paralyzed, and there are no comprehensive and effective institutional instruments for training such individuals for employment. Real employment opportunities for the disabled are also currently quite limited. The CPA MOLSA team is outlining for consideration by the future government draft principles for a new Iraqi social welfare system, based on means testing. The 'means tested' social welfare system will provide Iraqi families in need with social benefits and services.

- **Employment Service Centers**

  The primary goal established by MOLSA in August 2003 was to open 28 Employment Services Centers by July 1, 2004. The Ministry currently has 18 centers open (by early May 2004). The goal of the Centers is to match job seekers with employment and training opportunities. Former militia and military, disenfranchised youth, women, and other unemployed Iraqis are target groups. Currently, there are limited training classes in certain of the centers for teaching basic computer skills and English as a second language. Fundamental to the economic recovery of Iraq will be the rapid emergence of employment opportunities in both the private and public sectors. The Employment Service Centers currently register job seekers and have established outreach to the employer community. As demand for workers increases, especially with the investment of foreign aid in the construction and reconstruction of infrastructure and other needed or desired services or goods, the Centers will provide the workers to fill those jobs.
- **Vocational training**

  The CPA MOLSA team and the Iraqi Ministry are focused on vocational training centers and programs for Iraqis looking for employment.

  The primary goal established by MOLSA in August 2003 was to open 17 vocational training centers to provide training facilities for those workers needing training or upgraded training for employment opportunities.

  The six traditional Vocational Training Centers (VTC) across Iraq are Baghdad, Irbil, Mosul, Najaf, Kirkuk and Basra. Baghdad-Central will be the largest and will serve as a hub for the coordination of efforts in the other governorates. KOIKA (a South Korean governmental organization) has approved a four-year $7 million project to construct, equip and provide international technical assistance and training for the Baghdad Vocational Training Center (VTC). This Center will train five vocations in Baghdad and serve as a center for training the trainers across the country. In addition to the Baghdad VTC, the training program will offer courses in English as a Foreign Language, computer skills and construction skills, among other courses. 11 further centers will be opened across the country. Currently, six centers are functioning.

The percentage of women employed is still low, primarily for cultural reasons. Single parents (mainly women) caring for numerous children are poorly equipped to survive without relying on child labor.

Social Security

Article 14 of the TAL guarantees the right of the individual to social security, although a definition of that right is not spelled out. According to the current legislation, any individual working in the state sector (either directly in government or in state-owned enterprises), or in private companies on the basis of an employment contract, has the right to have social insurance. Currently, two distinctive public pensions systems co-exist: a Social Security system covering private employers that have three or more employees and a pension plan covering those workers who are employed by either the government or a state-owned enterprise. Private sector employers having less than three workers currently do not have to join or pay into the Social Security system. This exemption substantially exempts many workers from coverage because the economy is dominated by government employment and a far smaller private sector base of small employers.

In order to universalize social security insurance and to prevent workers from future poverty in the event they lose their job because of sickness, maternity or old age, the CPA MOLSA team is working to design alternative strategies for consideration by the new government. Those strategies envision a strong unified public social security system in Iraq covering all workers, both those employed by the public and private sectors. The social security reform unfolding in Iraq is part of the World Bank interest area for future involvement in the Iraqi reconstruction process. The main principles of the new social security system are:

- universal contribution
- unification of the existing public pensions systems
- fair recompense of pensioners for the contributions they paid (proportional redistribution of the pension fund on an earning-related benefit formula)
- reasonable qualifying conditions (age of retirement and length of service), in accordance with the life expectancy at birth and at the age of retirement and with traditional, cultural issues in Iraq
- replacing income during maternity and child care leave
- replacing income during sick leave and work injury or occupational disease recovery period
- disability pensions for long term working incapacity
- survivors' pensions.

NATIONAL/RACIAL/ETHNIC MINORITIES

Article 9 of the TAL states that the Arabic language and the Kurdish language are the two official languages of Iraq. Article 9 also states that the right of Iraqis to educate their children in their mother tongue, such as Turcoman, Syriac, or Armenian, in government educational institutions in accordance with educational guidelines, or in any other language in private educational institutions, shall be guaranteed.

OVERSIGHT AND ACCOUNTABILITY

UNSCR 1511 (2003) authorized a multinational force under unified command to take all necessary measures to contribute to the maintenance of security and stability in Iraq. A fundamental principle of a unified command is that the commander of such a force is responsible for the conduct of military operations. This includes responsibility for ensuring that such operations comply with all applicable humanitarian and human rights laws. Thus, the Multi-National Force (MNF) Commander is responsible for oversight of and accountability for MNF operations.

Discipline of individual members of the MNF is the responsibility of the individual States contributing to the Force. This accords with well established principles of coalition forces operating under a Chapter VII mandate. This concept is incorporated into CPA Order Number 17:

> All Coalition personnel shall be subject to the exclusive jurisdiction of their Parent States and, they shall be immune from local criminal, civil, and administrative jurisdiction and from any form of arrest or detention other than by persons acting on behalf of their Parent States, except that nothing in this provision shall prevent Coalition Forces personnel from preventing acts of serious misconduct by Coalition personnel, or otherwise temporarily detaining Coalition personnel who pose a risk of injury to themselves or others, pending expeditious turnover to the appropriate authorities of the Parent State.

In the governance arena, CPA has also taken a series of complementary steps to institutionalize principles of public integrity. The Commission on Public Integrity (established by CPA Order 55, 28 January 2004)[245] is an independent commission vested with broad authority to investigate and initiate criminal cases involving corruption, imposes an annual financial disclosure requirement on senior Iraqi leaders, and requires the Commission to establish anti-corruption education programs. The CPA Inspector General Order (Order 57, 10 February 2004)[246] ensures that each Ministry includes an independent Office of Inspector General capable of conducting investigations, audits, evaluations, and other reviews in accordance with generally accepted professional standards. Inspectors General have extensive authority to access records, subpoena witnesses, and compel the reporting of fraud, waste, abuse or criminal acts. Finally, CPA Order 77 (25 April 2004)[247] revitalized the Iraqi Board of Supreme Audit by confirming that the Board works in conjunction with the newly established Inspectors General and the Commission on Public Integrity to facilitate honest and transparent government in Iraq. The Board is granted broad enforcement powers to compel production of records necessary to audit effectively the disbursement of public funds and may propose new legislative initiatives to further accountability and efficiency at all levels of government in Iraq.

The TAL provides for both a National Human Rights Commission and an Ombudsman which will exercise oversight and accountability of government bodies. These are discussed below. In addition, the Ministry of Human Rights has an oversight function with regard to legislation and a Ministry lawyer sits on the IGC's Legal Committee.

HUMAN RIGHTS INSTITUTIONS

Plans to create a sustainable culture of respect for human rights and an effective system of control and supervision to identify and remedy breaches of human rights in the future Iraq rest on four independent, yet complementary platforms: an effective Ministry of Human Rights; an Ombudsman; an independent National Human Rights Commission; and viable, active and independent human rights NGOs.

[245] See *Doc 78*.
[246] See *Doc 80*.
[247] See *Doc 101*.

Ministry of Human Rights

The first Ministry of Human Rights in the history of Iraq was formally established in September, 2003. It was given the mandate of addressing past human rights atrocities and safeguarding the human rights and fundamental freedoms of all persons within the territory of Iraq in the future. Specifically, the Ministry of Human Rights is [(1)] to help establish conditions conducive to the protection of human rights and fundamental freedoms in Iraq and prevent human rights violations in Iraq; [(2)] to make formal recommendations for measures to prevent human rights violations; (3) assist all people in society in healing from the atrocities committed by the Ba'athist regime to include appropriate cooperation with the Iraqi Special Tribunal (IST) or other judicial institutions; (4) serve as focal point for relations with the UN High Commissioner for Human Rights, the UN Commission on the Status of Women, and other international human rights organizations; and (5) provide advice to lawmakers on whether proposed legislation comports with international human rights law, including the legal obligations Iraq has assumed through ratification of international treaties.

CPA secured funds for the refurbishment of a substantial building which was opened by the Minister for Human Rights, Abdul Basit Turki, and Ambassador Bremer on 14 February 2004. In April 2004, Ambassador Bremer and the IGC approved the appointment of Bakhtiar Amin, a well-known human rights activist, as Deputy Minister of Human Rights. The Minister attended meetings of the Human Rights Committee of the Arab league in Egypt in December 2003 and the UNCHCR in Geneva earlier this year. Following the Minister's resignation in April 2004, Mr Amin has taken over his duties as Acting Minister. The Ministry has been supported and assisted throughout by the CPA Office of Human Rights and Transitional Justice.

There are approximately 150 employees at the Ministry and now that the infrastructure and management are in place, their substantive work will begin. Not all of these individuals are appropriately qualified as yet, but there is considerable enthusiasm and a substantial degree of expertise amongst the Iraqi technocrats which should ensure competence. An Inspector-General has been appointed. A two-week training course in Amman will be held in June for officials from the Ministry of Human Rights with the support of the UN Office of the High Commissioner for Human Rights and UNICEF. CPA officials have been advising the Acting Minister on a restructuring program to ensure the effectiveness of ministry departments and create specific achievable objectives.

Ministry Activities

International human rights experts and secondees from other governments have sometimes been reluctant to travel to Iraq or have returned home early, and providing secure space for training inside Iraq is not always a simple matter. However, efforts to provide training in secure locations outside Iraq are ongoing. A conference for Iraqi human rights and humanitarian NGOs was held in Beirut in March 2004. The Swiss government is sending a Missing Persons Expert to assist in developing the Ministry's Missing Persons Bureau, which has created an ante- mortem data form for distribution throughout Iraq. This expert will build on the work of a team from the Department of Defense's Missing in Action/Prisoner of War team which visited earlier this year. MoHR staff have compiled a CD-ROM containing reports and descriptions of mass grave locations throughout Iraq.

Negotiations are ongoing with the Canadian government to host training for NGOs there. At the suggestion of the CPA, the Ministry has plans to host a conference in Suleimaniyah in conjunction with the Ministers of Human Rights from the two Kurdish regions. The objective is to partner nascent NGOs from the rest of Iraq with more established NGOs from the north which have had the benefit of some international assistance and funding and have had an opportunity to thrive in a post-conflict environment. The two Kurdish ministers have recently agreed to work more closely with the national ministry. The Ministry of Human Rights has begun to host weekly workshops on women's issues including CSW, CEDAW and UNIFEM, in partnership with the Ministry of Foreign Affairs and Ministry of Labor & Social Affairs. The Ministry is planning to develop links with women's groups in the UK with a view to establishing a National Commission for Women. The Ministry has recently signaled its intention that Iraq should become a signatory to the UN Convention Against Torture & Other Cruel, Inhuman or Degrading Treatment or Punishment, 1984 and will be holding workshops with other government departments.

Minister Turki met with the UN Special Rapporteur on the Situation of Human Rights in Iraq, Andreas Mavrommatis, and bilaterally with officials from many nations at the Madrid Conference in October, 2003, as well as making visits to other Middle Eastern countries to ask for assistance with ministry programs. Both Minister Turki and Acting Minister Amin have developed contacts with the OCHCR and Acting Minister Amin is strengthening the Ministry's contacts with European partners and the EU, as well as the UNDP. The Ministry will work with the Ministry of Foreign Affairs to reestablish a Committee on War Victims to assist Iraqis in proper repatriation of remains from the international wars with Iran and Kuwait.

These programs will run in tandem with widespread efforts to introduce human rights training in schools and universities and to raise awareness of human rights nationwide.

With the full support of CPA, the Ministry has also designated two of its lawyers to act as onsite monitors in the criminal detainee section of Abu Ghraib prison and act as liaison for the families. Following recent positive meetings with Major-General Miller (Deputy Commanding General of Detention Operations carried out by US forces), the Ministry's mandate at Abu Ghraib has been extended to security internees also and Ministry staff will meet with representatives of the security detainees and be given full access to the women's, juvenile and medical sections.

In addition the Ministry will oversee an oral history project designed to interview thousands of Iraqis about human rights abuses under the former regime and store this information in a searchable secure database for use in locating missing persons, preparing for a possible future Truth commission or simply building a historical record of the past to help Iraqis come to terms with the abuses and assist in preventing them reoccurring.

<u>National Human Rights Commission</u>

Article 50 of the TAL provides for the establishment of a National Human Rights Commission (NHRC). CPA has recruited an expert in National Human Rights Commissions from Canada to come to Iraq at the end of May to advise on establishing the Iraqi NHRC. It will be an independent body. One of its powers will be to accept complaints from individuals and organizations concerning alleged government violations of human rights. It will also be able to conduct public inquiries on its own initiative to address effectively the violations of the rights of the most vulnerable and disadvantaged.

<u>Ombudsman</u>

The establishment of this office was also specifically provided for in Article 50 of the TAL. The office will act as a further check on action by the government that is arbitrary or contrary to law and look into maladministration.

Funding for Human Rights

The initial budget for 2004 is 10.7 billion New Iraqi Dinars (approximately US$7.1 million) rising to 21.4 billion New Iraqi Dinars (approximately US$14.3 million) by 2006. This is to cover capital building projects to create human rights training centers, human rights training courses and materials, Ministry staff salaries and operating costs. In addition, $15 million has been allocated to human rights under the Supplemental Budget from the U.S. Congress. Some of this is aimed at recording the past abuses of the previous regime and assisting the Iraqi people in coming to terms with them; a considerable portion is dedicated to supporting the efforts of the Ministry and creating a strong human rights culture in Iraq. $1.5 million has been attached to USAID's already substantial civic education programs specifically to concentrate on human rights education. An additional $600,000 is available for direct grants to organizations to assist in this. $1.25 million has been allocated specifically to assisting in the coordination and development of human rights NGOs in Iraq. Requests for proposals were issued by the U.S. State Department in April 2004. The Department is currently reviewing proposals and intends to expedite these programs as quickly as possible. The UK government has provided further funding for mass grave forensic assessments. In addition the UK has provided grants to initiate projects to analyze regime documentation and gather oral histories relating to regime crimes, as well as providing NGO funding under its Global Conflict Prevention Pool (GCPP), with more to come under this fund.[248]

Document 254

Letter of Approval of the Annex to the Transitional Administrative Law

1 June 2004

Sheikh Ghazi Ajil Al-Yawar
President
Iraqi Governing Council
Baghdad

Dear Mr. President:

The Coalition Provisional Authority congratulates you and the Governing Council on the approval today of the Annex to the Law of Administration for the State of Iraq for the Transitional Period.[249] The Annex establishes the legal framework for the Iraqi Interim Government, which will govern Iraq from June 30th until the formation of an elected government.

The Annex completes the task first undertaken by the Governing Council in the November 15th Agreement[250] and greatly advanced in its drafting and adoption of the Law of Administration for the State of Iraq for the Transitional Period.[251] It puts Iraq firmly on the path to elections and a democratic future. The Coalition Provisional Authority approves the Annex completed on May 31, 2004.

[248] UN Doc. E/CN.4/2005/4, 9 June 2004, Annex I.
[249] See *Doc 517*.
[250] See *Doc 232*.
[251] For the text of the TAL, see *Doc 511*.

We will continue to work with the Iraqi people to bring about a transition to a democratic, stable and secure Iraq.

[Signed] *L. Paul Bremer III*
Administrator

Document 255
Directive on the Cessation of Certain Contracting Activities at Camp Alpha, Iraq

9 June 2004

MEMORANDUM FOR	COMMANDER, MNF-I HEAD OF CONTRACTING ACTIVITY, CPA DIRECTOR, PROGRAM MANAGEMENT OFFICE
SUBJECT:	Cessation of Certain Contracting Activities at Camp Alpha, Iraq

Pursuant to my authority as Administrator of the Coalition Provisional Authority (CPA) and under the laws and usages of war, and consistent with relevant U.N. Security Council Resolutions, including Resolutions 1483 and 1511 (2004), and the obligations of the CPA under applicable international law, including Article 56 of the Hague Regulations[252] and Article 5 of the Cultural Property Convention,[253] I hereby direct all contractors operating in Iraq to immediately stop all construction, excavation or other activities at or adjacent to Camp Alpha that are likely to cause archaeological damage.

This directive shall not apply to activities that the MNF-I Commander or his designee determines are absolutely essential requirements for force protection.

Violations of this directive may result in appropriate administrative and/or disciplinary action.

This directive shall be effectively [sic] immediately, and shall remain in effect until rescinded, in writing, by me or until June 30, 2004, whichever occurs first.

L. Paul Bremer III
Administrator

[252] Regulations Respecting the Laws and Customs of War on Land, Art 56 provides in the relevant part: 'All seizure of, destruction or wilful damage done to institutions of this character [i.e. institutions dedicated to religion, charity and education, the arts and sciences], historic monuments, works of art and science, is forbidden, and should be made the subject of legal proceedings.'

[253] The Hague Convention of 14 May 1954 for the Protection of Cultural Property in the Event of Armed Conflict, Art 5 provides in the relevant paragraph: '1. Any High Contracting Party in occupation of the whole or part of the territory of another High Contracting Party shall as far as possible support the competent national authorities of the occupied territory in safeguarding and preserving its cultural property.'

Document 256
Disclaimer on Contracting
11 June 2004

Transfer of Authority. The contractor hereby recognizes that a transfer of authority (TOA) from the Coalition Provisional Authority (CPA) to the interim Iraqi Governing Council is scheduled to take place June 30, 2004. Furthermore, the contractor recognizes that upon the TOA on June 30, 2004, or upon any later TOA date if delayed, the CPA is dissolved. The CPA, U.S. Government or Coalition Government will not be liable to the contractor for any performance undertaken after the TOA. The contractor hereby waives any claims and rights it now has or may have in the future against the CPA, U.S. Government or Coalition Governments in connection with the contract. The interim Iraqi Governing Council may but is not obligated to be bound to the obligations of the CPA before the TOA with respect to performance undertaken after the TOA. The interim Iraqi Governing Council may but is not obligated to ratify all previous actions taken by the CPA and agree to be bound with the same force and effect as if the action had been undertaken by the interim Iraqi Government. If the interim Iraqi Governing Council undertakes any obligations under this contract, the CPA recognizes the interim Iraqi Government as its successor in interest with respect to any such obligations. All payments and reimbursements previously made by the CPA to the contractor and all other previous actions taken by the CPA under this contract shall be considered to have discharged those parts of the CPA's obligations under this contract. The contractor agrees that the CPA, the U.S. Government, or any Coalition Government is not obligated to pay or reimburse the contractor, or otherwise give effect to, any costs, taxes, or other expenses, or any related increases, directly or indirectly arising from the TOA. Nothing herein shall be construed as a waiver of any rights the CPA, U.S. Government or a Coalition Government may have against the contractor.

Document 257
Joint Statement Issued by Ambassador L. Paul Bremer III and Lt. Gen. Ricardo Sanchez
11 June 2004

Recently, the Coalition dispatched a team of archaeologists and Iraqi cultural antiquities experts to the city of Babylon (Babil) to assess the current condition of the archaeological site located at Camp Alpha, a Coalition base originally established to protect and defend the ancient city of Babylon during military operations in 2003.

Based on the experts' findings, Ambassador L. Paul Bremer III and Lt. Gen. Ricardo Sanchez have collectively taken the following action: 1) Issued a directive calling for all contractors working in or around the vicinity of the Babylon site to halt any activities that are or may be likely to cause archaeological damage, 2) Directed an official investigation into the construction and expansion of Camp Alpha to ensure that the Coalition is respecting the surrounding archaeological site, 3) Instructed that planning begin for the relocation of all Coalition troops in the immediate area of Babylon, and 4) Consider remediation for any damage determined through the investigation.

The Coalition is committed to continue working with the citizens of Iraq and the Ministry of Culture to preserve Iraq's cultural heritage. Any future construction, excavation, or expansion of facilities in the vicinity of Babylon will be done in close consultation with the Iraqi State Board of Antiquities. Iraq's treasures are not only of great importance to Iraq, but to the entire international community and civilization as a whole.

Document 258
Iraqi Funds under Coalition Provisional Authority Control
26 June 2004

Deposits (rounded to thousands)		
	Development Fund for Iraq:	$20,706,395,000
	Treasury Special Purpose Account:	$ 1,916,496,000
	Seized Iraqi Cash	$ 926,700,000
	(Transfer from TSPA to DFI)	*($ 208,564,000)*
	Total Iraqi deposits under U.S. control:	$23,341,027,000
Withdrawals		
	Disbursements from DFI:	$14,058,659,000
	Cash shipped to Iraq from TSPA:	$ 1,707,931,000
	Seized Cash disbursed or obligated:	$ 774,400,000
	Commitments from DFI:	$ 3,104,909,000
	Total amount disbursed or obligated by U.S.:	$19,645,899,000
Balance		
	Transfer from CPA to interim Iraqi govt:	$ 3,695,128,000

Document 259
Development Fund for Iraq Disbursements by Agency
26 June 2004

Disbursements by Agency since Inception:[254]

Baghdad Central	$3,294,750.00
Central Bank of Iraq	$19,674,105.44
CJTF 7	$9,606,184.18
Coalition Military Assistance Training Team	$16,248,317.94
Commanders Emergency Response Program	$360,554,507.03
Communication Support Office	$1,659,897.06
Comptrollers Office	$3,565,200.00
CPA Front Office	$2,774,978.44
Governance	$10,000.00
Ministry of Agriculture	$31,250,385.00
Ministry of Communications	$2,080,000.00
Ministry of Culture	$20,000.00

[254] Reformatted from <http://www.iraqcoalition.org/budget/DFI_26jun2004.xls>.

Ministry of Defense	$562,711.50
Ministry of Education	$1,100,000.00
Ministry of Electricity	$639,205,316.51
Ministry of Finance	$7,711,940,159.57
Ministry of Health	$55,033,103.15
Ministry of Housing and Construction	$405,031.66
Ministry of Industry and Minerals	$18,950.00
Ministry of Interior	$47,852,851.64
Ministry of Justice	$1,000,219.50
Ministry of National Security & Defense	$3,130,506.39
Ministry of Oil	$2,012,397,915.48
Ministry of Planning	$5,558,698.00
Ministry of Public Works	$26,116.00
Ministry of Trade	$444,076,620.36
Ministry of Transportation	$1,706,687.00
Office of Security Cooperation	$40,419,321.46
Private Sector Development	$13,665.00
Program Management Office	$76,720,000.00
Rapid Regional Response Program	$244,216,497.75
Regional Projects – CPA South	$46,783,087.16
State Oil Marketing Organization	$76,620,172.65
Strategic Communications	$361,000.00
World Food Programme	$143,376,100.00
Grand Total	**$11,893,196,850.37**

Document 260

Development Fund for Iraq – Financial Reporting Matrix

26 June 2004

Development Fund for Iraq (DFI) – Financial Reporting Matrix

Reporting Date: **June 26, 2004**
As of Date: **June 24, 2004**
Inception Date: **May 28, 2003**

Bank Accounts and Investments	**US Dollars**
Central Bank of Iraq – Oil Proceeds Receipt Account, FRB, NY	616,499.19
DFI Account – Federal Reserve Bank, New York	151,544.75
DFI Account – Central Bank of Iraq, Baghdad	1,050,527,283.09
DFI Account – Treasury Bills at Purchase Price	4,768,665,359.51
DFI Account – Overnight Deposits, FRB, New York	1,673,300,000.00
DFI Account – Vested Assets, Federal Reserve Bank, New York	21,716.63
DFI Account – Temporary Cash Holding	70,971,490.00
Total – DFI Assets	**7,564,253,893.17**

Cash Inflow (Since Inception)	
Oil For Food	8,100,000,000.00
Proceeds from Oil Exports	11,111,692,362.73
UNSCR 1483	1,014,805,645.22
Interest Income – Treasury Bills	33,874,372.53
Interest Income – Overnight Deposits, Repurchase Agreements	7,636,464.80
Returned Letter of Credit Funding	3,686,295.39

Other Deposits	542,455.97
Donations	20,000.00
United Nations World Food Program	145,878,779.00
Vested Assets (Including Interest)	16,291,014.19
Transactional Deposits from Public Sector Entities	162,954,456.80
Total Cash Inflow	**20,597,381,846.63**
Cash Outflow (Since Inception)	
Ministry Budgets	(8,825,926,528.27)
Payments for Projects	(3,348,865,439.20)
Transactional Withdrawals – Public Sector Entities	(886,846, 675.18)
Miscellaneous Transactions	(32,105,810.00)
Total Cash Outflow	**(13,093,744,452.65)**
Net Cash Position	7,503,637,393.98
Outstanding Contractual Commitments	
Total PRB Approved Commitments (Since Inception)	19,697,863,666.63
Commitments Returned / Cancelled	(3,185,642,810.08)
Commitments Paid	(11,892,642,550.37)
Outstanding Commitments	**4,619,578,306.18**
DFI Assets On Hand Committed to Remaining 2004 Budget	**2,884,059,087.80**

Document 261
Coalition Provisional Authority Accomplishments
28 June 2004

Introduction
On June 30, 2004 Iraq will again become a fully sovereign nation. When this occurs, the Coalition Provisional Authority (CPA), the international body that has governed Iraq since April, 2003, will have achieved its primary goal, and will cease to exist.

Over the course of the last fourteen months the Coalition Provisional Authority has focused on helping Iraqis build four foundational pillars for their sovereignty: Security, Essential Services, Economy, and Governance.

Security
• CPA assisted the Iraqi government in constructing the means to assume responsibility for external and internal security, including its own defense and police forces, and in establishing relationships with regional states and with the international community. CPA also assisted Iraq to clearly define within a legal framework, the roles and accountabilities of organizations providing security.

• Three Iraqi ministries play a primary role in Security: Defense, Interior and Justice.

Essential Services
• CPA helped the Iraqi government to reconstitute Iraq's infrastructure, maintain a high level of oil production, ensure food security, improve water and sanitation infrastructure, improve health care quality and access, rehabilitate key infrastructures such as transportation and communications, improve education, and improve housing-quality and access.

• Eleven Iraqi ministries play a primary role in Essential Services: Education, Higher Education, Health, Displacement and Migration, Communications, Municipalities and Public Works, Electricity, Housing and Construction, Water Resources, Transportation, Environment.

Governance

• CPA worked with Iraqis to ensure the early restoration of full sovereignty to the Iraqi people. The July 13, 2003 establishment of a Governing Council (GC), and the June 1, 2004 establishment of the Interim Iraqi government were major steps toward that goal. The establishment of effective representative government, ultimately sustained by democratic elections, has required the rapid development of new frameworks and capacities.

- o An interim Constitution
- o Respect for the rule of law and human rights
- o Effective and fair justice systems
- o Open and transparent political institutions and processes
- o Creation of a vibrant civil society
- o Measures to improve the effectiveness of elected officials, including strengthened local government systems

• Six Iraqi ministries play a primary role in Governance: Foreign Affairs, Women's Issues, Human Rights, Culture, Youth and Sport, and Planning and Development Cooperation.

Economy

• CPA helped the Iraqi government to build financial market structures by:

- o modernizing the Central Bank, strengthening the commercial banking sector and re-establishing the Stock Exchange and securities market
- o developing transparent budgeting and accounting arrangements, and a framework for sound public sector finances and resource allocation
- o laying the foundation for an open economy by drafting company, labor and intellectual property laws and streamlining existing commercial codes and regulations
- o promoting private business and SMEs through building up the domestic banking sector and credit arrangements
- o and establishing the structure of the oil industry

• Seven Iraqi ministries play a leading role in Economy: Oil, Labor and Social Activity, Agriculture, Trade, Science and Technology, Industry and Minerals, and Finance.

SECURITY

Overall National Security Structure

Strategic Goals and Objectives

• The ultimate goal for Iraq is a durable peace for a unified and stable, democratic Iraq that is underpinned by new and protected freedoms and a growing market economy.

• A key long-range strategic objective is a secure environment for people and property that enables citizens to participate fully in political and economic life.

• This means that the Iraqi government must have the means, including its own defense and police forces, to assume its responsibility for external and internal security, including policing of its borders and that relationships with regional states and with the international community have been established.

• Moreover it requires that the roles and accountabilities of organizations providing security are clearly defined within a legal framework.
• A key task required to achieve these objectives is the development of Iraq's defense capabilities and security oversight mechanisms.
Security Requirements and Strategic Needs
• Internal security will be Iraq's greatest challenge in coming years.
• This will include the fight against insurgency, terrorism, ethnic conflict, and violent extremism of all sorts.
• External security will be provided by a combination of capable defense forces, growing regional security ties, ties with 'Western' states, and involvement in global and regional multilateral organizations and groups.
• An ever-changing threat from groups using terrorist tactics will be an increasingly critical security challenge.
• Radical Sunni Islamists will be a significant and growing component of this.
• Iraq must develop capacity to prevent and preclude acts of extreme violence and counter the groups that seek to perpetrate them.
• This requires integration of a variety of forces and organizations at the policy, operational, and tactical levels.
• Iraq will face the challenge of ensuring that it is compliant with the broad range of nonproliferation agreements and arrangements it is appropriate for it to comply with. With U.S. and other assistance, Iraq will also work to establish effective export control mechanisms for WMD and related materials. Former WMD research personnel will be engaged and, as possible, employed in peaceful research efforts through the WMD Personnel Redirection Program and the Iraqi International Center for Science and Industry.

In the face of these security challenges, CPA has made remarkable progress toward reaching its security goals and objectives as noted below:

Overview
• On July 1, 2004, the Iraqi Ministry of Defense (MoD) assumes sovereign responsibility for the Iraqi Armed Forces (IAF).
• National Command Authority will flow from the Prime Minister to the MOD to the Chief of Staff (COS), Iraqi Armed Forces, to the operational commander.
• The Minister of Defense is a member of the Ministerial Committee on National Security (MCNS), with the responsibility of representing the interests of the Ministry within the Government.
• The Senior Military Advisor (SMA) is a permanent advisor to the MCNS.
• MOD will be responsible, among other functions, for formulating Iraqi defense policy, determining capabilities, budgeting, providing communications, analyzing intelligence, building military infrastructure, and sustaining the forces.
• The Joint Headquarters (JHQ) of the MOD, co-located in the same building with the civilian MOD staff, will organize, train, and equip the IAF to ensure they are prepared and available for operations.

National Security Institutions Formed
• The MOD was created March 22, 2004. The MOD is completely accountable, transparent, and non-discriminatory, and it's operating as a modern, democratic, professional and

civilian-controlled system. It's overseeing the Iraqi Armed Forces so that they will be an effective guarantee of the security of all Iraqis. These forces include a new army, air force, and coastal defense force among others.
• An Iraqi National Intelligence Agency (INIS) has also been established to provide information about terrorism, domestic insurgency, narcotics production and trafficking, espionage, weapons of mass destruction, serious organized crime, and other issues related to the national defense or threats to Iraqi democracy. The INIS cannot arrest or detain anyone.
• The MCNS facilitates and coordinates national security policy among the Ministries and agencies of the Iraqi government with responsibility for national security. It does not interfere in or manage the work of individual ministries, but rather ensures that the work of individual ministries and agencies is part of a coherent security strategy.

Then and Now
• The old MOD was controlled by a military system that wasn't accountable to the people it defended. In fact, it was used against the very people it was meant to protect. The new MOD serves all Iraqi people.
• The former Ministry of Defense [was] completely disestablished. The new MOD, starting with no personnel and no headquarters building, now has more than 250 employees including almost 100 new civil servants, operating out of a newly renovated building far from the old MOD facility.
• Almost 1400 Iraqi MOD candidates from all regions of Iraq were interviewed for these 100 positions. It is expected that the number of MOD civil servants will grow to about 2000 personnel including the JHQ.
• The Minister of Defense is a member of the Iraqi Interim Government; he reports directly to the Prime Minister.
• There are two Iraqi four-star generals – the Senior Military Advisor and Chief of Staff of the Iraqi Armed Forces.
• The senior career civil servant is the Secretary General of the MOD. Five Directors General report to him – Policy and Requirements, Programs and Budget, Acquisition and Logistics, Personnel, and Communications, Intelligence, and Security.
• Over 90% of the civil servants were sent to the United States for training in the basics of building a democratic institution in the new Iraq.
• A new Joint Headquarters for the IAF, co-located with the MOD, was just established.
• The intelligence service was used as a political tool by the former regime – not to protect the Iraqis, but to protect Saddam Hussein alone. The new INIS is forbidden from reporting on domestic political issues or involving itself in the political process.

Command Authority
• Command authority for the IAF flows from the head of government (Prime Minister) to the Defense Minister to the IAF Chief of Staff to the operating commander.
• (Internal Security national command authority issues from the head of government to the Minister of Interior to police or other internal security force commander(s).)

Ministry of Defense
• Established by CPA Order 67, March 22, 2004.
• Provides policy oversight of the Iraqi Armed Forces (The IAF, consisting of the Army, Costal Defense, Air Force, ICTF, ICDC) and formulates overall defense policy.

• Civilian controlled, transparent, professional, merit-based, and broadly representative of the Iraqi people.
• Former military may serve in civilian roles. On an exceptional basis, uniformed officers may occupy official positions, reporting to civilians.
• Secretary General (the number-two MOD position) and Senior Military Advisor roles insulated from political change.
• The civilian MOD staff, which will grow gradually, is working in the areas of personnel, acquisition, budgeting, contracting, and intelligence analysis.

Veteran's Agency
• Established by a Ministry of Defense regulation April 1, 2004.
• The Iraqi Veterans Agency (IVA) is an independent agency under the Ministry of Defense.
• The role of the IVA is to represent veterans' issues across Government and to be a single reference point for veterans to contact regarding their concerns.
• Key component of strategy to address militia transition and reintegration process.

Iraqi National Intelligence Service
• Established by CPA Order 69, April 1, 2004.
• From the TAL: The Iraqi Intelligence Service shall collect information, assess threats to national security, and advise the Iraqi government.
• INIS shall be under civilian control, shall be subject to legislative oversight, and shall operate pursuant to law and in accordance with recognized principles of human rights.
• Internal intelligence focus (CT and counterinsurgency), not foreign collection.
• Answers to an independent judiciary and reports to the Prime Minister.
• No authority to arrest or detain – works with other security services, primarily MoI to ensure that information leading to arrest or detention is appropriately utilized.
• 'First among equals' of Iraqi intelligence services (MoD, MoI will have small intelligence arms).

Multinational Force, Iraq (MNF-I)
• The Multinational Force, Iraq (MNF-I) will operate in support of Iraqi MoI forces, which retain primary responsibility for Iraqi internal security beginning on July 1, 2004.
• IAF will also assist MNF-I after transition under strict rules of engagement.
• MNF-I will coordinate with Iraqi internal security services at the provincial level through Joint Coordination Centers (JCCs).
• MNF-I will transfer responsibility for security to appropriate civil authorities as conditions permit.

Ministerial Committee for National Security (MCNS)
• MCNS Established by CPA Order 68, April 1, 2004.
• The MCNS facilitates and coordinates national security policy among the Ministries and agencies of the Iraqi government tasked with national security issues.
• This is the primary forum for Ministerial-level decision making on these issues.
• Core of developing effective interministerial coordination, risk assessment capacity and intelligence fusion to respond to the full range of national security priorities.
• Consists of the head of government (chair), the Minister of Defense, the Minister of Interior, the Minister of Foreign Affairs, the Minister of Justice, and the Minister of Finance.

Other Ministers may also participate in specific meetings at the request of the Chair. The Senior Military Advisor, the Director General of the Iraqi National Intelligence Service, and the National Security Advisor also participate as permanent advisory members.

Militias

• Addressed in CPA Order 91, June 7, 2004.
• The TAL states that there can be no armed forces in Iraq other than those specifically provided for by federal law; thus, all armed forces aligned with political parties or individuals must be eliminated.
• Militias that agree to the transition and reintegration process will be treated as in compliance with federal law while they undergo this process.
• It will support the retirement and work-force reentry of former militia members.
• Some of them will be melded into Iraqi security services as individuals.

Ministry of Defense

The Ministry of Defense will be responsible, among other functions, for formulating Iraqi defense policy, determining capabilities, budgeting, providing communications, analyzing intelligence, building military infrastructure, and sustaining the forces.

Iraq Armed Forces

• The Iraqi Armed forces will consist of six main elements:
  o Iraqi Army (2 Divisions motorized infantry) to total about 27,000
  o Iraqi National Guard (45 battalions and 6 Brigade Headquarters) to total about 41,088
  o Iraqi Intervention Force to total about 6,665
  o Iraqi Special Operations Forces – Iraqi Counter Terrorist Force to total about 764 plus a Commando Battalion to total about 828
  o Iraqi Coastal Defense Force (6 Patrol Boats) to total about 405
  o Iraqi Air Force (operating 6 Hercules and 16 UHIH) to total about 500
• Interoperable with allies and friends.
• Defining mission of the IAF is the defense of Iraq.
• Domestic use of the IAF is a last resort and under tight control.
• International deployment for multilateral peacekeeping and humanitarian operations possible in the future.
• Interior lines of communications and mobility, no force projection, limited logistics.
• The IAF will be heavily reliant on civil infrastructure and support services.
• Manning, training, equipping of Armed Forces provided by OST (Office of Security Training).
• Merit-based assignment and promotion, competitive pay.
• The military justice system relies heavily on the civilian justice system for serious offenses, with civilian judges acting as courts-martial.

The Iraqi Army

• Iraqi Army formally dissolved May 23, 2003.
• First 1,000 recruits began training Aug. 2 [2003].
• Four Battalions graduated; First Battalion (554), Second Battalion (507), Third Battalion (582) and Fourth Battalion (637) from KMTB.

• 549 Officers Graduated from Military Academy on 19 March 2004.
• 1,132 Senior NCOs have graduated from the Senior NCO course; 384 on 25 March, 393 on April 22 and 355 on 20 May. Next Class is scheduled to graduate on 17 June.
• The Senior NCO Course is currently taught by Vinnell Co. personnel and Coalition soldiers, to include Iraqi soldiers.
• 1,060 Soldiers have graduated from the Squad Leader Course, 450 on 17 April, 616 on 20 May. Next class is scheduled to graduate on 3 July.
• The Squad Leaders Course is currently taught by Coalition soldiers, to include Iraqi soldiers.
• Training takes place at Kirkush Military Training Base in Kirkush, Iraq. KMTB is also the training site for the NCOs, while the officer candidates train in Jordan.
• 20 Officers will graduate from BDE/BN Commander's Course on 17 JUN 04 and 16 graduated from the BDE/BN Staff Officer's Course 2 April 2004.
• 19 Iraqi Air Force Officers completed helicopter flight training in Jordan on 27 May.

Iraqi Armed Forces Strength
TOTAL STRENGTH: 10,173
(Breakdown Below)

Iraqi Army:

All Personnel (Including 944 Iraqi National Task Force Soldiers)	9,659
Soldiers Fielded	5,296
In Training	4,363
Goal Strength	32,557
Shortfall	22,898
Completion Date	February 2005

Iraqi Air Force:

All Personnel	217
Servicemen Fielded	162
In Training	55
Goal Strength	500
Shortfall	283
Completion Date	December 2004

Iraqi Coastal Defense Force:

All Personnel	297
Servicemen Fielded	187
In Training	110
Goal Strength	409
Shortfall	112
Completion Date	September 2004

Note: Force strength information from OSC J-1 Personnel and CMATT as of 19 JUN 04.

Recruiting
• Major recruiting centers are located in Baghdad, Mosul and Basrah.
• Mobile recruiting teams in Irbil and Sulaymanah will become permanent by the end of April 2004.

• About 60 percent of the privates in the Iraqi Army, and virtually all the officers and NCOs, have previous military experience.
• Coalition Military Assistance Training Team Goal for Iraqi Army is 27 Battalions (27,000 light infantry troops and some military police units).
• Coalition goal is 35,000 troops total, to include the JHQ, IAxF and ICDF.
• Currently recruiting Officer Candidates for Military Academy in Rastamiah, scheduled to start first class Sept 2004. Goal: graduate 270 by Sept 2005.

Recruit Training

• Nine-week training period (eight weeks of training).
• Pay:
  o A progressive pay scale starting at 150,000 Iraqi Dinars ($100 American) a month for recruits.
  o 120,000 Iraqi Dinars ($80 American) a month for hazardous duty pay.
• Rank upon graduation is merit based.
• Training POI consists of the following:

First aid	Convoy operations
Formation and drill	Guard duty
Map reading, land navigation	Search and security
Physical training	IED response
Code of conduct	Minefield operations
Law of warfare	Individual movement
Marksmanship	Movement under fire
EPW handling	Combat orders

Officer and NCO Training

• Iraqi officer candidates have been sent to Jordan for initial training
  o 400 Senior NCOs will be trained per month thru June.
  o 1,500 officers will be trained as of June 2004.
  o 2,500 NCOs will be trained as of August 2004.
  o Jordanians created the training program of instruction based off CMATT requirements.
  o Three groups of Officer Candidates Training Programs:
    ▪ platoon and company commanders
    ▪ brigade / battalion staff
    ▪ brigade / battalion commanders[255]
• Non commissioned officers currently trained by Coalition personnel under CMATT control in Kirkush Military Base (east of Baghdad)
  o Two month course
  o Two groups: basic NCO (Squad Leader Course) and Platoon Sergeant/ SGM (Sr. NCO Course)
  o Sr. NCOs graduated:
    ▪ Class #1 384 on 25 March 2004
    ▪ Class #2 393 on 22 April 2004
    ▪ Class #3 355 on 20 May 2004
    ▪ Class # 4 runs from 8 May to 17 June

[255] NOTE: After graduation from the different courses key officer positions will be filled with the organizations based on merit and experience.

- o Squad leaders graduated
  - ▪ Class #1 450 on 17 April 2004
  - ▪ Class #2 611 on 20 May 2004
  - ▪ Class #3 runs from 23 May to 3 July
  - ▪ Class #4 runs from 4 July to 7 August

• Once Iraqi officers and NCOs have been trained, they will be responsible for training their own recruits

• Rank upon graduation is merit based

General Information

• The Coalition is focused on training the professional soldier with core values, positive leadership, self-confidence, determination to succeed and the skills to defend this country against its enemies. Though limited in its capability for the next year or two, the Iraqi Army will be able to provide fixed site security, protect the borders, and provide route security around the county. The future of this army, in terms of its capabilities and armaments depends on the governing council and ultimately on the Iraqi people.

• Those who complete training and become members of the Iraqi Army will immediately assist the Coalition with the mission of bringing security to the country. Specifically, their mission will be to defend the territorial sovereignty of Iraq.

• One of the important characteristics of the Iraqi Armed Forces is that it is a diverse group of men from all over the country who generally reflect the ethnic picture of the Iraqi population. There are challenges in bringing different groups of people together in a training environment and the recruits are learning every day about each other and how to work together in order to accomplish the mission.

Ministry of Interior

The Iraqi Ministry of Interior's mission involves preserving order in Iraq, defending the territorial integrity of Iraq's borders, and protecting critical infrastructure throughout the country. The agencies within the Ministry of Interior responsible for these tasks include the Iraqi Police Service (IPS), the Department of Border Enforcement (DBE), Facilities Protection Service (FPS) and civil defense.

The Iraqi Police Service

• Retrained thousands of former Iraqi police in a three-week Transition and Integration Program (TIP) training course during which they were instructed in international standards for human rights, modern police patrol procedures and techniques, and Iraqi criminal law and procedures;

• Ramped up the IPS to over 78,000 police who are protecting Iraqi citizens each and every day throughout the country;

• Renovated and updated the Baghdad Policy Academy to adequately train Iraqi Police recruits;

• Partnered with neighboring Jordan to train 1,500 police recruits per month;

• Developed a high-end law enforcement capability in the form of an Iraqi SWAT team;

• Introduced a Police Code of Conduct;

• Developed institutional structures and organizations that will support a modern policing approach;

• Worked with the Office of the Inspector General and other Iraqi accountability mechanisms to build accountability into the IPS;
• Near completion on specialized training facility at Adnon Palace;
• Completed formalization of institutional structures for command and control of specialized and national units.

Department of Border Enforcement Officials
• Increased deployments of border police to over 10,000 officers with more to come;
• Installed the PISCES identification equipment at Baghdad International and Muntheria, with more sites to come, to track visitors and workers coming into Iraq. Two suspected terrorists were caught at Ar Ar during the Hajj as a result of this equipment;
• Began to maintain the integrity of 605 kilometers of border with Syria, 181 kilometers of border with Jordan, 1,458 kilometers of border with Iran, 240 kilometers of border with Kuwait, 814 kilometers of border with Saudi Arabia, and 352 kilometers of border with Turkey;
• Instituted the five-percent Reconstruction Levy at various Iraqi points of entry to help collect revenue for the rebuilding of Iraq. Millions of dollars were collected for reconstruction efforts in the just the first [sic] two weeks of collection;
• Began to rebuild dozens of points of entry on the borders of Iraq;
• Closed suspected illegal crossing points from Iran;
• Completed work at Baghdad Int'l Airport which is now fully functioning and operational;
• Instituted Riverine patrols in southern Iraq to combat smuggling and to defend the integrity of Iraq's water borders.

Facilities Protection Service
• Nearly 75,000 members of the Facilities Protection Service (FPS) have been protecting nearly 3,000 sites of critical infrastructure throughout Iraq;
• Transferred authority of FPS to the Ministries on March 1, 2004;
• Has Diplomatic Protection Service protecting over 30 Embassies, soon to be 48;
• Established 14 Regional Commanders who are providing support to regional FPS operations;
• Increased basic certification training for recruit FPS guards from 3 to 5 days;
• Plans underway to provide certification and verification for all Tier 1 (high-security) sites throughout Iraq;
• Established FPS Strength Transfer Office within MOI to relocate displaced FPS guards in other ministries. Over 500 fully trained and certified FPS guards rehired by other Ministries;
• Established Ministry of Finance / FPS approval criteria for increases of FPS guards within Ministries needing additional guards;
• Conducted site and security assessments at the direction of Ambassador Bremer;
• Distributed 18,000 weapons for a distribution of 1 weapon for every 3 guards.

The Iraqi Civil Defense Directorate
• Held the first ever 'National Leaders Forum' for Iraqi Civil Defense Directorate in Baghdad on 15 – 16 May 2004 to develop a strategic vision as the Transfer of Authority approaches on 30 June 2004;

• Had 125 Fire Stations renovated across the country with 27 new fire stations under construction;
• Built force of firefighters to 8,000 nationwide;
• Has recruited and begun to train 4,000 new firefighters over the next two years;
• Signed a contract to begin construction of a new Civil Defense Directorate Headquarters and Training Academy.

Other Accomplishments
• Police Working Group established on February 16, 2004
• Police Plan presented to CJTF-7 commanding general March 7, 2004
• Baghdad Police Academy established
• Training partnership with Jordan Police Academy instituted
• Specialized training programs at Adnan Training Facility in Baghdad established
• Mosul Police Academy facility identified
• Specialized IPS Military Operations in Urban Terrain training began at Kurkush Military Training Base, May 2004
• Public Order Training plan to run 1,200 IPS officers through riot control training began, with end date of July 2004
• Infrastructure plan to establish 18 Provincial Police HQs, 8 Class A commercial border stations, 425 police stations, 9 training facilities and 84 border facilities constituted

Iraqi Civil Security Forces Strength
TOTAL APPROXIMATE STRENGTH: 175,964 OFFICERS
(Breakdown Below)

Iraqi Police Service:

Iraqi Police Service Goal	89,369
Iraqi Police on Duty	83,789
Trained and Deployed*	26,876
Untrained and Deployed*	56,913
In Training (Not Deployed)	1,670
Total Assigned	85,459
Shortfall	3,910
Manning Goal Date	January 2005

* Included in 'Iraqi Police on Hand' number.

Iraqi Border Police:

Iraqi Border Police Goal	12,376
Border Police on Duty	11,839
In Training	25
Total Assigned	11,864
Shortfall	512
Manning Goal Date	September 2004

Iraqi Customs Police:

Iraqi Customs Police Goal	2,900
Customs Police on Duty	1,800
In Training	0
Total Assigned	1,800

Shortfall	1,100
Manning Goal Date	September 2004

Iraqi Immigration Police:

Iraqi Immigration Police Goal	1,000
Immigration Police on Duty	400
In Training	0
Total Assigned	400
Shortfall	600
Manning Goal Date	September 2004

Iraqi National Security Police:

Iraqi National Security Police Goal	4,144
National Security Police on Duty	4,144
In Training	0
Total Assigned	4,144
Shortfall	0
Manning Goal Date	September 2004

Iraqi Facilities Protection Service:

Iraqi Facilities Protection Service Goal	N/A
Facilities Protection Servicemen on Duty	71,992*
In Training	77
Total Assigned	72,069*
Shortfall	N/A
Manning Goal Date	July 2004

* Approximate Figure

Iraqi Diplomatic Protection Service:

Iraqi Diplomatic Protection Service Officers Goal	N/A
Diplomatic Protection Service Officers on Duty	2,000*
In Training	33
Total Assigned	2,033
Shortfall	N/A
Manning Goal Date	July 2004

*Approximate Figure

Note: The strength numbers above are provided by CPATT 19 JUN 04.

General Information

• Despite the fact that for so many years police were feared as political weapons of the former regime, public trust in Iraqi police is on the rise. A recent survey conducted by the US State Department Office of Research, shows that nearly 80 percent of Iraqis feel that, in general, local Iraqi police are trusted by most members of their communities. A percentage almost as large – 70 percent – believe that local Iraqi police are accessible to help resolve problems.

• Iraq's newly hired and trained police officers are trained in human rights, the rule of law and the values of service and justice. The Iraqi Police Service has recently developed the capacity to conduct internal investigations. In addition, an independent inspector general (IG) to the Ministry of Interior has been appointed; the IG will work to eliminate fraud, waste and abuse of authority.

• Iraqi's have a sense of patriotism and national pride that can now be felt on the streets. As the number of police officers continues to increase, Iraqis take a larger role in the protection and building up of the future of their country.
• Many brave Iraqis are serious about protecting their country and its people. Despite the fact that attacks on police stations began last fall, Iraqis are continuing to come forward in large numbers to sign up to protect their country.
• Iraqi Police have made their presence known as the crime rate continues to decrease. As Iraqi Police assume their duties, they become a more powerful team that can help alleviate the security challenges that Coalition Forces face such as friction and resentment, caused from conducting searches, manning checkpoints and guarding installations.

Ministry of Justice (MOJ) and Iraq's Judiciary

Under the former regime, the Ministry of Justice (MOJ) – as an arm of Saddam Hussein – exercised almost complete control over Iraq's judges and their decisions. Today, Iraq's judiciary – led by the Council of Judges – is a fully independent branch of government, no longer reporting to the Minister of Justice or any other government official.

Ministry of Justice

With the judiciary and its administration removed from its portfolio, the Ministry of Justice today oversees:
• Drafting of legislation
• Advising the national government on legal matters
• Judicial and prosecutorial training
• Recording of land deeds and other records
• Publishing of Legal Gazette
• Iraqi Corrections Service

Iraqi Corrections Service (ICS)

• Under the former regime, prisons were tools of corruption, neglect, abuse and torture.
• Immediately following the liberation of Iraq, detention facilities were looted and destroyed.
• CPA Order Number 10, transferred responsibility for prisons from the Ministry of Labor and Social Affairs to the Ministry of Justice.

Criminal Detainees

• ICS operates prisons and detention centers, housing Iraq's criminal detainees.
• Criminal detainees are persons apprehended by Iraqi security forces or Coalition Forces for committing violations of the Iraqi criminal code (not directed at Coalition Forces). These are common criminals who are either awaiting trial in or have already been convicted by the independent Iraqi criminal courts.
• ICS has responsibility for 4,000 criminal detainees throughout Iraq
  o 3,500 adult males
  o 250 juvenile males
  o 100 females
  o 10 juvenile females

Facilities

- The Coalition has renovated 17 detention facilities throughout Iraq
- Renovated facilities operated by ICS now meet international standards such as:
  - o 25 square feet per inmate
  - o 1 hour of exercise a minimum of 3 times per week
  - o contracted food service
  - o medical services
  - o weekly family visitation
  - o access to the courts via an attorney
- ICS operates 17 facilities throughout Iraq
- ICS detention facilities consist of a total of approximately 5,500 permanent beds for inmates

ICS Staff

- ICS employs 4,000 staff members
- ICS employs 3,300 corrections officers
- Training for corrections officers consists of a 5-week training course focusing on:
  - o corrections techniques
  - o human rights
  - o personnel management
  - o security practices and procedures

Iraq's Judiciary

- Administered by Council of Judges
  - o Headed by Chief Justice of Iraq's Court of Cassation: Medhat Hamoodi Hussein al-Mahmood
- Includes:
  - o Court of Cassation
  - o criminal courts, including Central Criminal Court of Iraq
  - o civil courts
  - o family courts

The Past

- Under the former regime, MOJ – as an arm of Saddam Hussein – exercised almost complete control over Iraq's judges.
- Immediately following the liberation of Iraq, most courthouses were non-functional, as a result of looting
  - o 10% of courthouses were destroyed
  - o 70% of courthouses were badly damaged

Rights of Accused

- Today, defendants in Iraqi criminal courts have the rights unheard of under Saddam Hussein's regime.
- These rights include the right to be represented by an attorney at the pre-trial investigative stage of their proceedings, the right to be informed of the right to an attorney, the right to refrain from making incriminating statements.

Council of Judges
- First established in 1963, but abolished by former regime in 1979
- Re-established by CPA Order Number 35
- Oversees and controls:
  - o budget of court system
  - o court personnel, including judges, prosecutors, investigators, clerks, security personnel and administrative staff
  - o courthouse security
  - o all property primarily used for or associated with the judiciary

Facilities
- 128 courthouses
- 557 separate courts

Personnel
- 816 judges and prosecutors

Accomplishments
Since the liberation of Iraq, the Coalition has assisted the Iraqi Ministry of Justice and the Iraqi judiciary in the following ways:

Legal Reforms
- dissolved, by CPA Order Number 2, special and security courts
- revised, by CPA Order Number 7, the 1969 Iraqi Penal Code, repealing odious provisions inconsistent with fundamental human rights
- revised, by CPA Memorandum 3, the 1971 Iraqi Code of Criminal Procedure establishing new rights such as
  - o right to counsel
  - o right against self incrimination
  - o absolute exclusion of evidence obtained by torture
  - o right to be informed of these rights
- established standards for the operation of MOJ prisons/detention centers

Institutions
- established, with CPA Order Number 13, the Central Criminal Court of Iraq to hear crimes of national importance, including cases of acts of violence against the Coalition forces
  - o Currently the CCCI is conducting 320 criminal investigations with 165 cases set for trial.
  - o To date, the court has tried 54 cases, returning 44 guilty verdicts and 10 not guilty verdicts.
  - o Iraq's independent Court of Cassation has reversed 14 CCCI decisions.

Facilities
- rehabilitated each of Baghdad's courthouses to the point of functionality
- rehabilitated the Iraqi Judicial College, site of judicial training
- rehabilitated buildings meeting international detention standards for use as MOJ prisons and detention centers

Personnel

- established, with CPA Order Number 15, the Judicial Review Committee to vet every Iraqi judge and prosecutor for high-level Ba'athist ties, corruption, other malfeasance
  - o the JRC has:
    - reviewed the files of all 860 judges and prosecutors in Iraq
    - interviewed 656 of those judges and prosecutors
    - removed 176 judges and prosecutors
    - appointed 185 judges and prosecutors
- reinstated to the Court of Cassation eight judges who were fired by Saddam Hussein for refusing to impose the death sentence
- hired and trained Iraqi Corrections Service officers to secure MOJ prisons and detention facilities and transport inmates to/from court
- increased the salaries of judges from 450,000ID-887,000ID per month to 1,000,000ID-1,750,000ID per month

Training

- conducted training in human rights, international law and constitutional law for 185 Iraqi judges and prosecutors, including several who traveled to The Hague in May to exchange ideas with US Supreme Court justices Anthony Kennedy and Sandra Day O'Connor.

ESSENTIAL SERVICES

Ministry of Education

For more than a decade, parents throughout Iraq were forced to watch their children's hopes and dreams set aside by a brutal regime that ignored even the most basic of educational needs. Iraq's once regional prominence in providing a quality education slipped and then disappeared altogether as schools were allowed to fall into total disrepair and teachers salaries languished at a mere $5 a month.

Like everything in Iraq, Saddam Hussein used the educational system not as a tool to provide a better life for his people but as yet another propaganda weapon in his arsenal of deceit. Since the liberation of Iraq, a system of education that focuses on equality and freedom of thought has emerged throughout the nation. As Iraq continues to move towards sovereignty, the Ministry of Education is moving forward, poised for permanent and systemic education reform.

Building a Quality System of Education

- Most schools throughout Iraq were open very shortly after liberation allowing for the administration of the critically important national exams in June 2003.
- The politicized education system of the former regime was completely dismantled. More than 12,000 former Ba'ath Party headmasters, headmistresses and teachers were dismissed.
- Textbooks were revised and propaganda was removed. More than 8 million new, propaganda free textbooks had been printed last year. With the announcement of the new World Bank grant, 72 million new text books will be purchased for the coming year.
- 32,000 secondary school teachers received training in effective instructional methods and classroom management.

- Teacher salaries were increased by more than 1000%.
- More than 2,600 schools have been rehabilitated, with another 869 underway.
- Attendance in academic year 2003-2004 was as high or higher than before the liberation.
- The United States has allocated $88 million in construction funds to rehabilitate 1,000 additional schools in 2004 and $82 million in non-construction funds for additional teacher training and for forming PTAs, developing educational television for pre-school children and establishing more than 150 model schools (Centers of Excellence) throughout Iraq.
- The Ministry of Education takes the subject of corruption very seriously. The Inspector General of the Ministry of Education has been named and has begun to take a broad look at all Ministry programs and policies to ensure that they are being implemented as intended.

Ministry of Higher Education

- Over the last year hundreds of Iraqi students, University Presidents, Deans, faculty members, and administrators began to reenter the international academic community by traveling to countries such as the United States, the United Kingdom, and the Czech Republic on trips ranging from one week conferences, to three week training courses, to four year Ph.D. scholarship programs. The scholars and administrators were selected on the strength of their capabilities not on the basis of their party affiliation. Over the coming years that [number] will grow into the thousands.
- The Ministry of Higher Education and Scientific Research began the process of slowing, with a goal towards reversing, the 'Brain Drain' from the Iraq Higher Education sector by recognizing the strategic value that Iraq's professors and lecturers have for the future of Iraq. The Ministry of Higher Education worked with the Ministries of Finance and Planning to make the Higher Education faculty among the highest paid members of Iraqi society.
- Iraqi universities have entered into partnerships with countries around the world whereby curriculum development and training in the areas of archeology, agriculture, environmental health, law, and general education have enriched the faculty and students by exposing them to new or different perspectives, paradigms, and technologies.
- Among the most critical issues facing the Ministry of Higher Education has been the need to decentralize the authority in the Ministry, the standing up of the new Council of Presidents as the chief policy making body for Higher Education, and the codification of Academic Rights & Responsibilities in the face of political and religious coercion, intimidation, and control. Toward that end the Ministry and the Council have adopted the following declarations:
  - o Statement of the Council of University Presidents on Academic Freedom and Conduct
  - o Procedures for the Selection of New University Presidents
  - o Procedures for the Selection of New College Deans
  - o Policy on the Firing of University Presidents

Ministry of Communications

Telecommunications

- The three major cell phone companies in Iraq (Asia Cell, Iraqna, and Atheer in the North, Central, and South respectively) continue to enroll new cell phone subscribers. Cell phone subscribers total 456,827 nationwide.
- Pre-conflict, there was limited service, with 3,000 Internet and 8,000 e-mail only accounts in 2002. In 2003, there were 5,000 Internet and 10,000 e-mail only subscribers. By January

1, 2004, there were 12,372 accounts, with both e-mail and Internet access. As of June 11, there are 60,000 users.

• There are now 788,682 active landline telephone subscribers in Iraq, compared to 833,000 subscribers pre-war. The total number of telephone subscribers in Iraq, including the cell phone subscribers is 1,245,509 which is 49.5 percent greater than the number of active landline subscribers pre-war. Cell phone service was very limited pre-conflict.

• Stimulating private sector investment, CPA and the Ministry of Communications licensed three private cellular carriers built networks here in Iraq.

• Cell phones are selling at the rate of over 15,000 per week. Demand has outstripped supply. Consumers are placing deposits just to reserve a spot on the next shipment of phones.

• An additional operating license was granted to Sana Tel, a cellular operator providing service in and around Sulimaniya. Sana Tel began operations under the protection of the no-fly zone prior to the war.

• The four licensed cell phone providers are creating thousands of jobs for Iraqis.

• On December 30, 2003, a satellite gateway system was installed at Al Mamoun in Baghdad to provide international calling service.

• CPA has trained Iraqi engineers and technicians to maintain both the satellite gateway system and telephone switches.

• The CPA has modernized the telephone system by installing 13 digital telephone switches since May 2003 with full supporting service.

• The US supplemental appropriation for Iraqi reconstruction funds provides $225 million for continued expansion of the Iraqi telecommunications system.

• CPA and the Ministry of Communications are working to upgrade Iraq's fiber optic network to satisfy modern data networking demands. The upgraded fiber network will ultimately be able to support ubiquitous internet access, electronic banking, electronic funds transfers, credit card transactions, point of sale terminals, and ATM machines.

• A 'First Responder Network' (FRN) is being implemented for Iraqi police, border patrols and emergency personnel through CPA, which will improve the security situation in Iraq. FRN will be the first nationwide emergency communications network to provide the communications needs of Iraq's civil and military authorities. CPA is in the process of installing over 40,000 radios through the 'First Responder Network' for police and border guards.

Iraqi Postal Service

• Ministry of Communications opened the International Service Center at the Baghdad International Airport air cargo terminal on May 25, 2004.

• The International Service Center (ISC) will play a vital role in rebuilding the economy of Iraq through encouraging international commerce by creating a worldwide gateway for mail entering and exiting the country. The ISC enables Iraq to have greater access and quicker delivery to global goods and services which will improve the quality of life for the Iraqi people.

• On May 25, 2005 the Ministry of Communications introduced the new Iraqi Postal Code system.

• The major benefits of using a postal coding system:
  - o Increases the security of the mail due to the reduction in hand sorting
  - o Quicker more accurate delivery to the customer
  - o Facilitates emergency response of fire, police, and EMT services
  - o Straightforwardness of sorting: Regions, Provinces, Governorates, Districts, Cities and individual post offices

o Reduces mis-sorts and mis-deliveries
o Adaptable to automation and bar-coding
o Increases economy of scale with volume growth.

Ministries of Municipalities & Public Works

Water & Sanitation Systems

Coalition supported water and sanitation projects are on schedule to bring clean water to more than 20 million of Iraq's 27 million inhabitants, helping to advance Iraq's economic and social development. CPA plans will ensure that every Governorate and Municipality is capable of achieving national standards for water supply and distribution, sewerage, and environmental health. The CPA is actively restoring the most degraded portions of the system with a plan to replace the entire system in five years as well as expand to areas not currently serviced by the system.

Pre-conflict

• Approximately 55% to 60% of Iraqi citizens were receiving necessary amounts of potable water.
• According to a January 2003 survey there are 1385 water treatment facilities, some very small covering only a thousand people and others covering up to 650,000 people. The survey concluded that only 23 out of these 1385 water treatment facilities were operating at 100% of capacity.
• The Baghdad sewage system suffers from decades of chronic neglect and underinvestment.
• The three major sewage treatment plants in Baghdad were largely inoperable.
• In Baghdad, the original system was designed to support a city of only 3 million people. The current population is 5.6 million.
• Prior to the war, Iraq had 3 major sewage treatment plants and more than 7,000 kilometers of sewage line network which served only 75% of Baghdad's population.

Post Conflict

• CPA and it contractors, through USAID, are currently providing funding for extensive renovations at the Shark Dijila water treatment plant. Population impact of this effort will be 5.5 million people.
• CPA, through USAID, is currently rehabilitating three sewage treatment plants. The first of the sewage treatment plants will come on-line in April 2004.
• Installing 6-MW generators independent of the national power grid at 39 Baghdad water facilities to ensure continuous water flow.
• In the South, rehabilitating the entire Sweet Water Canal system, including the canal, its reservoirs, and 14 water treatment plants and pumping stations. The system provides potable water to 1.75 million people.
• In Central, rehabilitating one water treatment plant and four sewage treatments plants.
  o Sewage treatment plants in An Najaf and Al Hillah will serve 194,000 people.
• In the North, rehabilitating two water treatment plants and one sewage treatment plant. USAID is also procuring construction equipment for the Ninewa Sewer and Water Directorates for the repair and replacement of their present water and waste water systems.
• Rehabilitating 14 water treatment lifts and pump stations around Al Basrah; the An Nasiriyah Water and Sanitation Department building, water units in Maysan governorate,

the Kirkuk water testing facility, the Hay ad Hussein water plant, which serves holy shrines in and around Kerbala.
• Under the 'US Supplemental' funding the Ministry of Municipalities and Public Works has approximately US$ 3.2 Billion in over 100 projects potentially improving the water supply to 10 million urban and 2 million rural Iraqi people. This program is being 'rolled out' now and will hopefully be complete by the end of 2006.
• The Coalition has allocated more than $100 million toward repairs and refurbishments to the sewer system. The CPA has approved $70 million from Iraqi funds and USAID has approved $30 million. These monies will be used for planned, long-term improvements to the treatment plants, pumping stations and overall network.
• More than $6 million in Iraqi-seized funds has been dedicated for emergency operations and repairs.
• Over the past four months, more than $200 million has been obligated toward more than 200 emergency projects in nine different districts.
• City engineers have developed a 45-day intensive improvement program totaling $1.8 million to clean, refurbish and repair portions of the sewage infrastructure throughout Baghdad.

Investment Plan

- Steadily rising domestic budget
  - o 2004: $200M
  - o 2005: $500M
  - o 2006: $600M
- Madrid Pledges for Donor Assistance (all sectors)
  - o Japanese $1.5bn grant + $3.5bn loans
  - o Others totaling a further $10bn
- USG Supplemental Budget – total $18.6bn

Potable Water	$2,800,000,000
Water Loss Management	$30,000,000
Sanitation	$675,000,000
Solid Waste Management	$22,000,000

Ministry of Displacement and Migration

The Ministry of Displacement and Migration (MDM) is responsible for all matters relating to Iraqi refugees and displaced persons and all non-Iraqi refugees residing in Iraq. It develops policies to address migration issues and serves as the focal point for organizations assisting refugees and displaced persons.

Accomplishments

• Through the Madrid Donors Conference, secured funding from Portugal for offices in four regions with high IDP and refugee returnee needs. Regional centers are being established in Basrah, Maysan, and two other locations. Former Minister Al-Otbee was a lead presenter for the humanitarian session in Madrid.
• Former Minister Al-Otbee led the Iraqi delegation to the UNHCR annual conference in Geneva in September, 2003.
• Co-chaired with UNHCR and the International Organization for Migration (IOM) a two-day strategic planning and policy workshop in Amman, with the participation of

other relevant Iraqi Ministries, the Kurdistan Regional Government (KRG), and non-governmental organization (NGO) representatives. A follow-up meeting was held in Amman in early April.
• Represented Iraq in negotiations with the Government of Turkey and UNHCR on the voluntary return of Turkish refugees from northern Iraq.
• The Ministry moved to its permanent headquarters in Baghdad's Karkh district on March 20th, 2004.

Durable Solutions Achievements for Refugees and IDPs
• Over 5,000 Iraqi refugees in Saudi Arabia returned with assistance from the Ministry, UNHCR, and the Government of Saudi Arabia.
• 5,500 Iraqi refugees have returned from Iran with assistance from the Ministry and UNHCR.
• Over 1,000 Iraqi migrants in Lebanon have returned with assistance from the Ministry and IOM.
• Kurdish refugees from Iran are being settled locally in northern Iraq.
• Iraqi Kurds stranded on the Israeli – Lebanese border were assisted by the Ministry, the Kurdistan Regional Government, and the UN in returning home.
• 38 Iraqi failed asylum seekers imprisoned in Pakistan were assisted by the Ministry, IOM, and the Government of the United Arab Emirates in returning to Iraq.

Key Facts
• The Ministry of Displacement and Migration was established by the Iraqi Governing Council on 30 August 2003. CPA Order No. 50 defining MDM responsibilities was signed into law on 11 January 2004.
• As many as 800,000 persons are displaced throughout northern Iraq and an additional 100,000 to 300,000 persons are displaced in the center and south of Iraq.
• An estimated 900,000 Iraqis were compelled to cross international borders and are considered to be refugees or in a refugee-like situation in neighboring countries and beyond. An estimated 50,000 to 100,000 Iraqi refugees have returned since May 2003, either spontaneously or with assistance from MDM and International Organizations.

Ministry of Electricity

For more than a generation, Saddam Hussein used power, like everything else in Iraq, as a weapon to punish those who opposed his regime. Due to the inequitable distribution of power, most provinces suffered greatly. All provinces, with the exception of Fallujah, sections of Baghdad, and Tikrit, were getting 0 – 10 hours of power. Fallujah, sections of Baghdad, and Tikrit were getting 10 – 24 hours of power. There was an obvious favoritism in the distribution of power.
The process that was used to achieve the Coalition's goal of reaching the pre-war level of 4400 MW's of electricity was called the '4400 MW Program'. This program consisted primarily of immediate maintenance of existing plants. Immediately repairing or replacing damaged materials provided a short term solution that increased power and improved quality of life.

Achievements
• On June 20, 2004, the Coalition reached a record high electrical peak, surpassing the 4,900 MW mark for the first time – a full 10% increase above pre-war levels.

• And while Iraq's peak electricity output is soaring past pre-war levels, the MW hours have also increased substantially to over 103,000. This means that more people are receiving more power across the grid daily.
• And, because the Coalition and the Ministry have spent more than a year rebuilding Iraq's neglected electrical infrastructure, the system is now far more stable than before. With multiple redundancy systems in place, pre-war blackouts that could once take weeks to fix are in many cases returned to service within hours.
• In addition, the Ministry of Electricity has taken nearly 1,000 MW's of electricity off-line to conduct scheduled maintenance in order to guarantee a reliable system of power during the peak summer months.

If there is more power today, why do Iraqis only have 8-12 hours of power in their homes?
• With more than half a million new jobs created, new industries and new factories coming on line and with the sale of thousands of home appliances such as washing machines and air conditioners, Iraq has experienced a rapid increase in electricity demand. The increase in demand is a good sign of a thriving economy emerging out from three decades of isolation. As demand continues to increase, the Ministry of Electricity will continue to work to increase the nation's available power. Nearly one billion dollars has already been allocated with several billion more coming from Congress to help improve the supply of electricity throughout Iraq.

People in Baghdad constantly speak of how things were better under Saddam. How do you counter these claims?
• It is important to remember that under Saddam, those loyal to his regime were the benefactors of all of the nation's riches. Electricity is yet another example of how Saddam used everything in Iraq as a weapon against those opposed to his regime. Before the liberation, Saddam drained power from throughout the country to feed Baghdad, leaving more than 80% of the country to fend for themselves with private generators and the [sic] whatever power they could scrape together from the grid. Even with this unfair system of power, Saddam was only able to power Baghdad 20-22 hours a day. After the liberation, the power system was re-distributed equitably throughout the nation.

MINISTRY OF HOUSING & CONSTRUCTION

The Ministry of Construction and Housing has made substantial, lasting contributions to the people of Iraq during the past year. These contributions include improvements in Iraq's transportation infrastructure, and improvements to government buildings and office space. In addition, the Ministry has begun the task of providing adequate housing to the people of Iraq.

Achievements
• 10 bridges built, and an additional 25 bridges under construction
• 1,200 km of roads nationwide constructed and repaired
• 36 buildings, including many government ministry buildings, constructed and rehabilitated
• 1800 schools nationwide surveyed and assessed
• 23 housing developments under construction that will provide homes to over 11,000 Iraqi families

• 40,000 Iraqis employed in inspection, construction, and maintenance of roads, bridges, and public buildings

Ministry of Water Resources

Technology

• Under the old regime, the technology used to manage Iraq's water resources lagged decades behind much of the industrialized world, resulting in loss of this valuable resource and inefficiency in the overall management of water resources.
• The MoWR resources [sic] has begun an aggressive program to modernize the management of their water system with the latest technology. A comprehensive model of the entire system is being developed utilizing the same state-of-art software that is utilized within the United States and many other modern countries throughout the world.
• In another step to bring the administration of the Ministry into the 21st Century, internet connectivity has been established at various key locations throughout the Ministry.

Iraq's Reservoirs

• Prior to Iraq's liberation, Iraqi reservoirs were operated conservatively due to the lack of reliable information concerning the operation of Turkish reservoirs. Iraq never knew how much water Turkey would release at any given time so they always had to be prepared for sudden increases in inflows.
• With support from the Coalition Provisional Authority (CPA) and US Foreign Service officers, a weekly exchange of data from Turkey has been established, providing reliable information on the status of the Turkish reservoirs.
• As a result, the Ministry of Water Resources can now optimize the operation of the Iraqi reservoirs more efficiently, thus supplying more water for irrigation purposes and generating more hydro-electric power which already provides 20% of the nation's electrical power needs.
• The CPA and the MoWR will continue to work hard to reestablish greater cooperation on water issues between Syria, Turkey and Iraq.

Mesopotamian Marshes

• Under Saddam inhabitants of the Mesopotamian marshes were physically brutalized as were their lands resulting in an internationally recognized environmental and cultural disaster. The Restoration of the Mesopotamian Marshes is one the main objectives of the Ministry of Water Resources.
• In an astonishing turnaround the Mesopotamian marshes have already benefited greatly since the liberation, presenting new signs of hope for renewal and restoration:

- o Large areas (30-40%) of the original extent of the marsh have been inundated since liberation in April 2003,
- o Thousands of internally and externally displaced Marsh Arabs have come back to the restored marshes to resume their indigenous way of life,
- o Economic activities have increased in the marshes including fishing, mat weaving, water buffalo herding and agriculture,
- o Environmental conditions have improved including the return of migratory birds, moderated temperatures, improved air quality, etc.

Ministry of Transportation

Maritime

- The wrecked ships located at Umm Qasr port have been salvaged and key channels have been dredged to operational depths.
- Power has been restored to the electrical grid in the North Port of Umm Qasr.
- The Iraqi Port Authority (IPA) has approximately 130 local Iraqis that occupy security positions at the Port. An additional 100 IPA guards are currently undergoing Olive Security training classes to give the port more than 200 trained guards.
- Commercial and reconstruction cargo has been accepted at Umm Qasr since 16 June 2003.
- Umm Qasr is also equipped to handle passenger ferry service. There are currently two regularly scheduled ferry services operating four vessels. The service is carrying Iraqis between Dubai and Iraq, and Customs is handling both customs and immigration services at the port.

Aviation

- In cooperation with the coalition forces, the International Civil Aviation Organization (ICAO), neighboring states, and other key stakeholders, Iraq's airspace was opened to civil over flights on 22 August 2003, restoring important routes used by flights between Europe and the Middle East.
- An agreement to reintroduce Iraqi controllers to Baghdad International Airport's (BIAP) Air Traffic Control Tower has been finalized with the coalition forces. The controllers, who will are [sic] in the process of transitioning into the facility with the assistance of the Royal Australian Air Force contingent currently operating the tower, will provide the first Iraqi air navigation services since the end of the conflict. Discussions with the Royal Air Force (RAF) to transition ATC operations at Basrah Airport from British military control to the Iraqi Civil Aviation Authority (CAA) are also underway.
- The first new systems needed to reestablish Iraqi Air Navigation Services (ANS) were delivered by Raytheon to Baghdad International Airport on 7 May 2004 and will be installed on 14 May 2004. These systems, which include critical communications, navigation, and surveillance equipment, are being implemented through a USD 32 million CPA contract with Raytheon, which will be completed in late 2004. This contract will be complemented shortly by a USD 41 million task order for additional ANS equipment required by the international airports at Basrah and Mosul. There are currently no functioning civil, Iraqi ANS systems in the country. The new systems acquired by CPA using supplemental and Development Fund for Iraq funds will establish the backbone for the modern, safe ANS infrastructure needed to support Iraq's civil aviation system.

Railway

- The number of locomotives available for service has more than doubled, not counting over twenty new locomotives received in the past year.
- Significant numbers of freight wagons have been repaired, cleaned as necessary, and returned to service.
- Additional freight wagons are on order.
- Passenger coaches are being repaired and renovated.
- New international freight traffic flows have developed:
  - o Grain from Syria

  - o Diesel fuel and LP Gas from Turkey
  - o General Merchandise from Turkey
  - o Fuel Oil from Bayji to both Syria and Turkey
- International passenger service introduced between Mosul and Aleppo.
- VHF radio network installed linking stations, locomotives, and Central Control.
- Bridge at Akashat, destroyed in fighting, repaired and returned to service.
- Area operations centers established to compensate for lost communications.
- Enhanced training for the Iraqi Railway Police.

Surface Transport/Intermodal

- Successfully mobilized inter-city public transportation system based on buses and taxis.
- Established Abu Gharib intermodal facility.

Transportation Management:

- The Ministry has thoroughly redesigned its organizational structure to better meet the needs of an efficient and effective government agency in the new Iraq. Ministry functions have been realigned within the organization to facilitate more accurate and timely decision making. Ministry organizations have also been created to house the new functions of Policy and Regulatory Enforcement that were previously the responsibilities of the State Owned Enterprises.
- Key Issues for Transportation Management:
  - o Increase port throughput capacity.
  - o Increase rail efficiency.
  - o Enhance air cargo capacity.
  - o Link transport sectors via intermodal connections.
  - o Expand civil service reform within the ministry, to include realignment of SOEs' missions.

Ministry of Environment

The Ministry of Environment is responsible for protecting and improving the air, water, groundwater and biodiversity of Iraq. It monitors and assesses hazardous and toxic waste, plans for clean-ups and remediation and disposal of waste.

The Ministry staff includes about 350 staff at the Ministry Headquarters in Baghdad and an additional 300 employees in Directorate offices in each of the 15 governorates.

- The Ministry has secured a site for a national Headquarters and obtained funding in the amount of $4.67M from the Program Management Office. The contract has been awarded to Environmental Chemical Corporation and the target completion date is 30 SEP 04.
- The Ministry has entered into a cooperative agreement with the World Health Organization to assess and study pollution from chemical sources and threats to drinking water. As of today, the staff of the Ministry has completed field work in all 15 Governorates and is now working on laboratory analysis and interpretation of data.
- Since January 1, 2004, the ministry staff has reviewed and evaluated over 176 land use proposals and environmental assessment reports in cooperation with the Ministry of Planning and governorate offices.
- The Ministry legal staff prepared a draft Environmental Protection Law to update the existing law and submitted this draft to the State Consultant Council for review.

• The Ministry of Environment proposed 36 environmental projects with an estimated value of $50M for consideration for funding by international donors.
• The Ministry of Environment established a Committee of Universities for Cooperation on the Environment among 14 universities that meets quarterly.
• Ministry staff executed a program to survey radioactivity in the vicinity of al-Twaaytha in cooperation with coalition forces.
• The Ministry has established a media office to build environmental awareness through close collaboration with other media sources on environmental issues.
• The Ministry of Environment will establish regulations for maximum concentrations of contaminants entering the environment for municipal and industrial sources.
• The Minister of Environment chairs monthly meetings of a national Environmental Cooperation Council with representatives from 15 ministries and the Baghdad Amanat.

Ministry of Health

The Iraqi Ministry of Health and the Coalition are rebuilding a healthcare system that was decimated by 30 years of neglect prior to March 2003, a task that if done right will take time.

The Iraqi Ministry of Health is structuring a comprehensive healthcare system that is financially sound and assures quality care that is accessible and affordable regardless of ethnicity, geographic origin, gender or religious affiliation; and a healthcare system that is sustaining for the future.

Accomplishments to Date

• Iraq's 2004 budget for health care is $950 million. ($40 per person). Saddam Hussein's regime provided only $16 million for the Ministry of Health in 2002 (less than $0.75 per person).
• The entire country is at pre-war capabilities for providing health care – 240 Iraqi hospitals and more than 1,200 primary health centers are operating.
• Doctors' salaries have increased to between $120 a month and $180 a month, in comparison to $20 a month before the war.
• Three Facility Protective Services classes have trained over 1,300 personnel to protect health facilities.
• The Ministry of Health has completed a $1.7 million headquarters refurbishment project.

Pharmaceuticals

• National Drug Formulary for Iraq: This new purchasing structure will facilitate the arrival of treatments virtually non-existent under the old regime including top-tier cancer drugs and many other more progressive pharmaceuticals. It will also improve the sourcing of drugs which will result in better quality and better health outcomes. This comprehensive list of drugs will form the baseline for future purchases throughout the country.

Decentralization, Primary Health Clinics, & Long-Term Planning

• In addition to rehabilitating hospitals, the Ministry is also focusing on a fundamental shift from a hospital-based, curative model of care to a preventative care model.
• The shift from a hospital-based system to preventative, primary health care clinics will help to reduce the abysmal infant and maternal mortality rates suffered under Saddam

by providing access to quality care and supplementing public health initiatives already underway in the country, including, immunizations, nutrition counseling, access to clean water and adequate sewage and infrastructure improvements.

• The Ministry and the Coalition have committed to build approximately 250 healthcare clinics across the country based on the new primary health care model which will greatly improve access to and the quality of health care services throughout the country.

• The Ministry is encouraging people from all professional backgrounds – not just physicians – to become healthcare administrators in order to improve a systemic problem of poor hospital management and administration.

Improvements to Date

• Through work with NGO's [sic] and state-sponsored aid organizations such as USAID, improvements have been made that will improve the long-term health of the Iraqi people:

  o September – October 2003, a team of 55 biomedical engineers, technicians and managers completed 200 site visits to Iraqi hospitals to survey and repair biomedical equipment. 1,700 pieces have been repaired.
  o Rehabilitated 49 hospitals and clinics nationwide. 131 more are ongoing or planned (These sites not included in those targeted for rehab under the US Supplemental).
  o Kimadia Number 2 Warehouse $700,000 renovation (MOH portion $300,000, WHO $400,000)
  o 325 metric tons of high protein biscuits distributed to malnourished children and breastfeeding mothers.
  o 600 Primary Health Care centers and clinics will receive medical supply kits distributed by MOH/USAID partner Abt Associates. The $4,500 kit stocks clinics with state-of-the-art equipment and basic clinical supplies.
  o Awarded 35 small grants worth almost $2 million to support Iraqi NGO healthcare efforts throughout Iraq.
  o MOH spent $40M on purchase and installation of 128 generators and uninterruptible power supply systems, as well as the refurbishment of 10 additional generators.
  o Approximately US$5 million dollars of laboratory equipment and supplies provided the foundation to re-establish the Central Public Health Laboratory in Baghdad, National Center of Drug Control and Research, the Nutritional Research Institute, and regional and governorate public health laboratories.

• Hospital Infrastructure improvements:

  o Al Eskan Pediatric Teaching Hospital Rehab: The Spanish just signed a EURO€8.4 million agreement to renovate the facility. The scope of work includes new medical equipment for the facility, as well as civil, electrical and sanitary work and basic rehab work such as painting and structural repairs. Details from Contract: Euro 2.4 Million is slated for Civil, Electrical and Sanitary improvements; Euro 338,714.90 is slated for 'sanitary work'; Civil work will include a new roof; Sanitary work will include overhaul of drainage systems for waste and pipe systems within the building. Specifically the contract calls for drainage slopes that are inadequate (and have been since installation) to route sewage to be rebuilt. Other work includes sealing leaks in drainage and delivery pipes within the hospital.
  o Al Karama Teaching Hospital Rehab: Ministry signed agreement with the Korea International Cooperation Agency (KOICA) on December 29, 2003 donating US$8 million for the rehabilitation of Al Karama Teaching Hospital in Baghdad. The

agreement includes construction of a new operating theatre and emergency room at the hospital compound, new medical equipment and additional medical training through personnel exchanges between the two countries. Once completed the rehabilitated teaching hospital will have the capacity to perform 25 operations per day and provide improved medical service to more than 900 outpatients daily.

- o Medical City Burn Unit/Emergency Room Rehab: Medical City burn ward, currently staffed by over 30 Italian Red Cross personnel along with Iraqi doctors and nurses. The group also toured the recently refurbished Medical City Emergency Room and agreed to work with MOH supply unit and the Italian contingents to equip the facility and return it to operation in the near future.
- o Ali Al Gharbi Hospital Sanitation System: Working with the Coalition Provisional Authority, the aid group hired Iraqi contractors to dig a new septic system, lay pipes and refit the bathrooms with running water and electric lights. There were no toilets to use because they were always blocked up. USAID fixed the 26-year-old hospital which had seen no Iraqi funding in the past decade for maintenance and repairs.
- o Al Majar Al Kabir Hospital Sanitation System: The Al Majar Al Kabir medical facility: located in Southeastern Iraq near the border with Iran, serves about 800 outpatients each day and seventy inpatients, some of them undergoing major surgery. An Iraqi subcontractor was hired to excavate, lay pipes, and build new septic tanks outside the hospital compound. The U.S.-funded installation of a sanitary septic tank system ended years of filthy smells and wastes inside the medical facility.
- o Ibn Al-Qiff Spinal Cord Injury Hospital: A $524,500 grant from USAID for medical equipment and supplies will help get this facility back in service providing 125 bed inpatient services and handling an estimated 25,000 outpatient visits each year.

Infant Mortality Rate

• The Ministry is focusing on maternal and child health with the ambitious but attainable goal of reducing the infant mortality rate by one half by the end of 2005.

• There is no statistical evidence to support an increase in the infant mortality rate in Iraq since March 2003.

• The Ministry is working to immunize the country's 4.2 million children under the age of five against preventable diseases such as polio, tetanus, diphtheria, measles, and tuberculosis.

• More than 30 million doses of children's vaccinations have been procured and distributed.

• Routine vaccinations are available to newborns, children, and mothers every day at Ministry of Health facilities across the country and are promoted nationally through immunization days on the 22nd of each month.

• Infant mortality is 108/1000
  - o Child mortality (under age 5) is 131/1000
  - o Maternal mortality is 294/100,000
  - o 25% of newborns have Low Birth Rate [sic]

Funding Allocation

• Projects pending final contracting and implementation of US Supplemental funding:

• $493 million scheduled rehabilitation of Primary Health Centers and hospitals across Iraq. A substantial amount of planning and assessment has gone into these large-scale rehabilitation projects to ensure they are program oriented and requirements based.

- $283 million in equipment purchases.
- $17 million worth of technical training.

GOVERNANCE AND DEMOCRACY

The CPA has worked with political and civic leaders of Iraq and the Iraqi people to build a democratic society based on the rule of law. Iraqi citizens now enjoy democratic rights and freedoms that were unthinkable under Saddam Hussein.

The Iraqi Interim Government

Iraq now has a responsible government which is accountable to its people. The Interim Government will exist only until the people of Iraq choose a new government through democratic elections, to be held no later than January 2005.

The Transitional Administrative Law

Drafted and agreed by Iraqi leaders, the TAL is Supreme Law of Iraq during the transitional period. The TAL provides for Iraq's first ever democratic elections to be held no later than end January 2005, and for the drafting of a permanent constitution by December 2005. Under the TAL, the system of government in Iraq will be republican, federal, democratic, and pluralistic. Federalism will be based on geography, history and separation of powers, and not on ethnicity or sect.

The Bill of Rights

The TAL includes an historic bill of rights for the Iraqi people that is unprecedented in the Middle East. All Iraqis are equal in their rights without regard to gender, nationality, religion, or ethnic origin and they are all equal before the law. Under this Bill of Rights, the government must respect the rights of the people.

Local Governance

The CPA has facilitated the refreshment of Provincial Councils in 15 governorates in Iraq. USAID's Iraq Local Governance Program currently works in all 18 governorates. The law on Local Government Powers seeks to implement the goal of decentralization in the Transitional Administrative Law and to define the powers and responsibilities of local and provincial governments. The order gives local people greater influence over decisions which affect their daily lives.

Civic Education and Debate

Through USAID's 'democracy dialogue' activities, hundreds of Iraqis have taught democracy to thousands more people across the country. Iraqi local leaders have held 29 televised 'Town Hall' meetings across the country, where citizens have come together to debate the TAL, Iraq's political process and the country's future democratic development. This debate will continue with the National Conference in July 2004.

The National Conference

The National Conference will provide a forum for 1,000 Iraqis from every governorate in Iraq, including tribal and religious leaders, professional and civic leaders, to participate in selecting members of an Interim National Council, part of the Iraqi Interim Government. The National Conference will broaden representation, allowing Iraqis to participate in building a national consensus and to debate the country's challenges.

Iraq's Civil Society
$458 million in US Supplemental funds are dedicated to sustaining civil society organizations into the future. Nearly two thousand citizens' organisations throughout Iraq are applying for NGO status. Civil society organisations help to advocate for the realization of the basic human rights enshrined in the TAL.

Political Party Assistance
CPA has supported various conferences that engage political parties in creating common agendas and promoting alliances that strengthen their ability to participate in the forthcoming elections process.

Women's Programs
CPA has provided funding for Women's Centers throughout the country. These centers offer vocational training and educational opportunities and give women a place to congregate, share experiences, and plan for the future. To date, assistance has been provided to Women's Centers in nine major cities and CPA is currently working on centers in four additional cities. In addition, nine Women's Centers are planned for Baghdad.

Electoral process
During the CPA's tenure, Iraq has made significant progress towards its first ever democratic elections. The Independent Electoral Commission of Iraq, an autonomous and politically independent organization to oversee the conduct of elections, was set up on 31 May. The IECI was selected through a wide-scale nomination process and consists of 8 civic leaders from across Iraq, including two women. Working with experts from the United Nations, the Iraqi people have also agreed upon the electoral system to be used in the January 2005 elections, and on criteria for registering political entities who wish to stand in the elections.

Ministry of Foreign Affairs

For over 3 decades, Iraq's standing in the international community has been steadily eroded by the disastrous foreign policy of the former regime. The tyranny Saddam Hussein inflicted upon the Iraqi people extended to Iraq's international relations through catastrophic wars, a blatant disregard for international law, support for international terrorism and the proliferation of WMD. In the Middle East, Saddam Hussein agitated violence, intimidated Iraq's neighbours, fomented regional instability and continued to pose a dangerous threat to the rest of the world.

The Ministry of Foreign Affairs faces new responsibilities and challenges to overcome this legacy of mistrust and hostility.

The ministry is actively working to reverse Iraq's former isolation and pursue the following objectives of our new foreign policy:

- Protect Iraq's security, stabilize the country and preserve Iraq's territorial integrity;
- Restore international diplomatic bilateral relations and re-engage the international community in Iraq's reconstruction and development;
- Reconstruct our economy and infrastructure to raise the standard of living of the Iraqi people;
- Reactivate Iraq's diplomatic missions and promote Iraqi interests in all political, economic, social and cultural fields;

• Rejoin, and engage in, all multi-lateral bodies;
• Reform the Ministry of Foreign Affairs and its activities based on new values and principles;
• Pursue our chosen path of democratization within the framework of sovereignty, unity and equal citizenship.

Security in Iraq

Our priority is to stabilize our country and secure its borders as we confront international terrorism, intent on destabilizing the democratic process and destroying our progress towards peace and prosperity. The stability of Iraq has wider implications for regional security and failure to defeat this menace would have disastrous consequences reaching far beyond our borders. We seek to engage our neighbors in stemming the tide of terrorism through close cooperation on border security and we are working alongside our coalition partners to protect our external frontiers and maintain stability inside the country. We are making progress by building our military, security and police capabilities, with the welcome assistance of a number of countries that are providing training programs, to empower Iraqis to take charge of their own security.

International Organizations

Iraq continues to increase its representation in international organizations and since September 2003, Iraq has successfully re-established its seat in most multilateral bodies including:

• Arab League
• United Nations General Assembly
• Organization of Islamic Conference
• G77
• International Monetary Fund
• Non-Aligned Movement
• OPEC
• Regional Conference of Iraq's Neighboring Countries
• UNESCO
• UNCTAD
• World Bank
• World Trade Organization

Arab League

• Iraq was one of the founding members of the Arab League in 1945. In September 2003, a delegation from the Ministry of Foreign Affairs, led by Minister Zebari, regained Iraq's seat at the 120th Session of the Arab League in Cairo.
• In March 2004, Minister Zebari also participated in the Arab League Foreign Minister's preparatory meeting in Cairo for the Arab Summit in Tunis, which will now be held on 22-23 May 2004.
• Since 1980, under the former regime, Iraq failed to pay its dues to the Arab League. In March 2004, the Ministry of Foreign Affairs paid Iraq's annual membership totalling $3,515,411 to the organization.
• Iraq is fully committed to upholding and defending the charter of the Arab League and playing a vital role in all its agencies and institutions. We place great emphasis on

strengthening multi-lateral relations in the Arab and Islamic domains and we actively promote friendly and beneficial relations between the Arab world and the international community.

Iraq and the United Nations

The vital role of the United Nations in Iraq has always been welcomed by the Iraqi people, in particular its commitment to humanitarian programs which provided a lifeline to millions of Iraqis throughout the prolonged Iraq crisis under the former regime. We strongly condemn the devastating bombing of the United Nations Headquarters in Baghdad in August 2003 and pay tribute to the late Sergio Vieira de Mello who was an effective and committed role model for the United Nation's work in Iraq.

The United Nations has issued three Security Council Resolutions on the future of Iraq since May 2003 (UNSCRs1483, 1500 and 1511), which provide a wide mandate for UN involvement in political, economic and administrative fields. The UN has an effective role to play in Iraq in humanitarian affairs, capacity building and democratic reform among other areas and we welcome the two teams which recently arrived in Iraq to assist in the political and electoral processes. The United Nations also currently operates out of Amman and Cyprus with Mr. Ross Mountain supervising these efforts as Acting Special Representative.

- In December 2003, the Minister of Foreign Affairs presented the United Nations General Assembly with the timetable for the restoration of sovereignty to Iraq in accordance with the November 15th Agreement on Political Process, signed between the Iraqi Governing Council and the Coalition Provisional Authority in Baghdad.
- In January 2004, Iraq participated in tripartite meetings at the United Nations between the Iraqi Governing Council, Coalition Provisional Authority and the United Nations Secretariat to discuss the way forward for the UN's role in Iraq in political, electoral and constitutional fields.
- In February 2004, the UN's Special Advisor to Iraq, Mr. Lakhdar Brahimi, and a UN electoral team conducted a fact-finding mission on the feasibility of elections in Iraq prior to June 30th 2004.
- In March 2004 and in response to a request from the Iraqi Governing Council, a UN team of electoral experts arrived in Iraq to help with preparations for direct elections to be held by the end of January 2005. The UN Secretary General also dispatched a team of UN officials, led by Mr. Lakhdar Brahimi, to assist with the transfer of sovereignty on June 30th 2004.

Iraq's Diplomatic Missions

Significant steps have been taken to restore Iraq's missions abroad since the April 2003 ban was lifted on all diplomatic and consular activities. Iraq now has diplomatic representation in 35 countries around the world, including 3 Permanent Missions to the United Nations in New York, the United Nations Commission on Human Rights in Geneva and the Arab League in Cairo. Thirty missions remain suspended.

The strategy to enhance or resume diplomatic representation abroad is a key priority of the Ministry of Foreign Affairs, through the following objectives:

- The appointment of ambassadors, senior staff and diplomats to overseas missions.
- The resumption of comprehensive operations in key international missions to provide Iraqi local communities with necessary consular services including certification, passport extensions and provision of interim travel documents, visa issue and local liaison services.

- Efficient provision of information and the establishment of international exchanges to promote Iraqi interests in social, cultural and religious affairs.
- Increase Iraq's diplomatic activities to contribute to our rehabilitation into the international economy by promoting trade and investment through bilateral exchange and cooperation through multilateral organizations.

Reforming the Ministry

Under the previous regime, the reputation of the Ministry of Foreign Affairs was degraded in the eyes of Iraqis and the international community. The institution, its missions and its activities, were abused to spy and intimidate in deliberate breach of internationally-accepted diplomatic practice. The professionalism of Ministry staff was undermined and any initiative was suffocated by an oppressive and corrupt working culture.

Today, Ministry of Foreign Affairs personnel are undertaking diplomatic training overseas through professional development programs provided by host countries. These programs include language and information technology skills, diplomatic training in all fields and exposure to internationally accepted diplomatic practices. Since August last year, 251 members of the Ministry's staff have been selected to go to twenty countries to receive diplomatic training. The countries are Pakistan, Poland, the Czech Republic, India, Jordan, South Korea, the United Kingdom, the United States, France, Germany, Romania, Turkey, China, Spain, the Netherlands, Egypt, Malaysia, The Sudan, Austria and Switzerland. Some 60 members of staff have already started their training in Pakistan, Poland, the Czech Republic, India, Jordan, Korea and the United Kingdom, while 35 other staff have returned from Pakistan, the Czech Republic, Jordan and India.

The new Ministry of Foreign Affairs is further committed to enhance its foreign policy capabilities through reforming and modernising its organisation, personnel and activities according to the following principles:

- The development and implementation of transparent selection and recruitment processes in conjunction with a ministry-wide de-Ba'athification program;
- New standard recruitment procedures based on merit, equal opportunities and a just and fair criteria offering various entry levels and opportunity to all sectors of Iraqi society, in particular to women;
- Recruitment campaigns conducted through public announcement;
- Employee vetting, training assessments and personnel evaluation undertaken via open and standard procedures.
- Preparations are also ongoing to re-open and reform the Foreign Service Institute in order to resume normal diplomatic training activity. Since early 2003, the building's restoration has been completed and serves as temporary accommodation for the Ministry.
- All Ministry of Foreign Affairs personnel must possess an understanding of human rights issues, democratic principles and the prerequisite of political impartiality in civil service;
- Employee commitment to the Ministry of Foreign Affairs' new work ethic of integrity, professional respect and a commitment to serve in the best interests of the Iraqi people.
- The Ministry is committed to working practices that encourage initiative, professional skill development, communication and objectivity in provision of foreign policy advice.
- All new initiatives and restructuring changes are communicated throughout the Ministry.

Economic Rehabilitation, and the International Community

• We face the momentous challenge of reconstructing our economy that has been systematically destroyed by decades of mismanagement, war and international sanctions under the former regime. Iraq is rich in natural and human resources but decades of authoritarian rule created a heavily dependent population and a dilapidated infrastructure.

• Now, and in the future, Iraq will be one of the largest workshops in the world and it has huge potential as a regional marketplace. We need extensive investment from the international community to rebuild our infrastructure and develop our skills and technology. Iraq's neighbours have an important role to play in fostering our economic recovery and we are actively encouraging foreign investment and promoting regional trade cooperation, in contrast to the crippling effect that years of Iraq's international isolation had on economies in the region and beyond.

• Economic sanctions, which had been in place for 12 years under Saddam Hussein's rule, were lifted in November 2003 and the remaining funds from the Oil for Food Programme are now administered through the Development Fund for Iraq. The combination of these funds, international donor contributions and Iraq's own resources provide a substantial base for our sustainable development and the Ministry of Foreign Affairs is committed to encouraging international participation through bilateral exchange and multilateral organizations.

• In November 2003, the Ministry of Foreign Affairs participated in the highly successful Madrid Donor's Conference in which 73 countries pledged $33 bn. and consolidated international political support for Iraq's reconstruction. We are also engaged in international dialogue to negotiate sustainable solutions to Iraq's debt and to address compensation claims.

Ministry for Women's Issues

Iraqi women passed through dark periods of repression and injustice throughout the past 35 years. Women were deprived of many of their civil and political rights. Laws were passed to entrench hardship in all forms and in all fields of endeavor.

Under Saddam Hussein's brutal dictatorship, women routinely were beheaded, raped, and beaten as a way to threaten and intimidate their families to extract information.

Now after Iraq has rid itself of the long era of tyranny, Iraqi women can occupy their natural position in society and leading the nation.

Mission

To ensure that Iraqi women are able to fully participate in Iraqi society, CPA's Office of Women's Affairs is working closely with Iraqi women throughout the country to help them organize and take part in Iraq's transition to democracy. The work has been ongoing for the last ten months. The CPA has fostered the development of women's organizations and associations at the national and local level by providing funding for Women's Center's [sic] throughout the country.

Accomplishments

Government

• The Ministry of State for Women was established and six women were named to ministerial posts in the new Iraqi Interim Government. This is a major achievement for women in Iraq. Under Saddam, Iraqi women had limited participation in civil society, diminishing the profile of women's issues as political concerns and no role in the leadership of the country. With the appointment of these women the new Iraqi government has shown that women will have the opportunity to participate fully in all aspects of society.

• Two of the seven members of the Independent Electoral Commission of Iraq (IECI) are women. The IECI is responsible for conduct of the electoral process from now on, including voter registration.

• Iraqi Women Leaders Meet with President Bush at the White House – Nov. 17, 2003.

• In March 2004, a national delegation of Iraqi women traveled to the United Nations 48th Annual Commission on the Status of Women Conference. This signified that Iraqi women were part of the world community and wanted to participate fully in the dialog on global issues.

[• Iraqi women are actively participating in making their country more secure. Nearly 100 women have volunteered for the new Iraqi army. The women completed three six- to eight- week courses at the Jordanian armed forces' military academy. Courses included platoon leaders' course, brigade and battalion staff officers' course, brigade and battalion commanders' course and courses that train junior officers to lieutenant colonels.

• Shari'a Law (Resolution 137)/Women's Rights in the TAL. The CPA has worked closely with the Governing Council to ensure women's rights and fair representation are addressed and that the groundwork is laid for Iraqi women's rights to be upheld in the future through the TAL.][256]

NGO's [sic]

• 25 women's centers have been supported across the country through 31 International Transition Initiative (ITI) grants for $1,684,449.

• Women's centers offer educational programming, job skills training, and access to resources; all services that carry the potential for financial independence to a segment of society that has traditionally been marginalized. ITI has established new women's centers and enhanced the capacity of existing groups through grants for building rehabilitations and in-kind awards of furniture, equipment and supplies. These centers include multi-purpose auditoriums outfitted with equipment where women can take part in performing arts and craft shows, lectures, educational programs and forums for political party development. $125,000 of this funding supports Women for Women International – Iraq to develop their headquarters office and provide educational opportunities to the most vulnerable women in Baghdad.

• Of these women's centers, two are shelters that provide services to women and girls who have been physically or sexually abuses [sic] and who are not safe in their homes. These shelters provide temporary housing, as well as psychological counseling and other services. The women are able to remain in the shelter until they can be safely reunited with their families or moved to a more permanent situation.

• An additional $657,910 in 23 grants has been provided by ITI for other activities that benefit women throughout the country. These activities include:

  o Women's Rights and Democracy Education: Training courses for women include discussion of the fundamentals of democracy, principles of human rights and internationally accepted women's rights conventions. This training supports the efforts

[256] The parts in brackets were part of the document 'Coalition Provisional Authority (CPA) Accomplishments', published on 28 June 2004 on the website of the Multi-National Force Iraqi (www.mnf-iraq.com/media-information/june2004/040628.htm) but were not included in the otherwise largely identical document 'An Historic Review of CPA Accomplishments' published on the same day on the CPA website (http://www.iraqcoalition.org/pressreleases/20040628_historic_review_cpa.doc).

of women in local villages to free themselves from repressive conditions and exercise rights promoted through international declarations.
- o Mobile Crisis Intervention Teams: Mobile women's health/social work teams have provided abuse intervention and critical health services to over 2,000 women. Multi-ethnic teams build trust and reduce tension between segregated ethnic and religious groups.

• In total, 10 awards for $227,310 have supported local conferences for women and attendance of Iraqi women at international conferences. Individuals and women's organizations are supported through conferences and empowerment training. International and local participants discuss issues such as Islam, democracy, oppression of women, women's rights and participation in future elections. Iraqi participants at conferences outside of Iraq have had an opportunity to share the unique situation in Iraq and create openings for greater international dialogue around the development of peace.

• Non-governmental organizations in northern Iraq are working to educate women on their rights and on income generating skills. One organization will educate 1,000 women on dealing with discrimination and on universal human rights. A women's center in As Sulaymaniyah is helping women become literate and acquire job skills, offering access to a library and teaching courses in tailoring, reading, hairdressing, computer training, and law. These two initiatives are supported by USAID's Local Governance Program (LGP). LGP also recently conducted a seminar for 50 women from As Sulaymaniyah on June 7 to discuss gender equality and domestic abuse.

• The Kurdistan Women's Organization continues its awareness-raising project of Women's Mobile Legal Clinic, which started in April 2004. Nine seminars on women's rights and legal issues, focusing on personal status law and community participation, were conducted [in] May. The goal is to hold 32 seminars [in] each residential quarter of Kirkuk. To date, 1,353 women of all ethnicities have been reached.

- Larger National Women NGOs
  Iraqi Independent Women's Groups
  Iraqi Women's Higher Council/Advisory Committee on Women's Affairs
  National Council for Women
  The Future Society of Iraqi Women
  The 1,000 Women's Group
  Women's Alliance for Democratic Iraq (WAFDI)
  Iraqi Women's Network (IWN)
- There are also hundreds of active regional groups
  - o Free Women Association which officially opened February 7 in the Al Muthanna Governorate. It is one of the first official women's organizations to be recognized since the fall of the Ba'ath regime
  - o Asuda Women's Group is a Kurdish-based organization that seeks to reduce violence against women, while guarding their independence in society. The group is particularly active in sheltering women who are at risk of murder in so-called 'honor killings.' Members also organize workshops and discussions to encourage girls to stay in school and to educate women on rights and protections.
  - o The New Women's Union was founded in October 2003 by more than 70 women who gathered in Ba'Quba. This gathering was organized by the only woman provincial council member in Diyala'.
  - o Kurdistan Women's Union is expanding to serve more women who come to their center seeking computer classes, job training and recreational facilities.
  - o Assyrian Women's Union has started newspaper, radio, and television initiatives.

Education

• In the 2003-2004 school year, female attendance increased from pre-war rates, with 1.9 million girls in primary school (46 percent of all primary students) and 580,000 (40 percent of all secondary students) in secondary schools.

• The Ministry of Education trained more than 33,000 teachers and administrators, which included more than 17,000 females, in new skills that will improve the quality of teachers and education in Iraq.

• Five grants valued over $15 million were awarded to strengthen partnerships between American and Iraqi Universities. Student, scholar, and other exchange programs have also been revived. Of the 20 new, prestigious Iraqi Fulbright finalists this year, six are women.

• Improving the educational system and opening up educational opportunities for all children is critical to the long-term stability of democracy. If a democratic Iraq is to succeed than equal access to education must be a priority.

Business

• More than 1,000 women received training in the financial, fiscal, utilities and regulatory sectors. Future programs include training and employment services for 1.5 million Iraqi women. Training and employment programs for women and men will take place through seventeen Vocational Technical Training Centers and twenty-eight Employment Services Centers throughout Iraq.

• In addition, two U.S. NGOs operate a micro-lending program that has loaned more than $600,000 for 300 women entrepreneurs. The program's average loan size is nearly $2,000.

• Under Saddam, Iraq's economy was totally destroyed. In the last year Iraqis have been faced with building an economy from the ground-up. Women want to be a part of the new economic structure, but have faced additional challenges due to cultural hurdles. These programs will assist women reach an equal footing with their male counterparts. Training women for jobs and running businesses is particularly important in the areas of the country where Saddam killed a majority of the male population.

Health

• Iraqi women are benefiting from the restoration of health clinics, hospitals, and laboratories. Primary health clinics across the country are being renovated and reequipped to improve the quality of health care for all Iraqis. The Ministry of Health is training primary health care providers with an emphasis on maternal and child health care. More than 700 doctors have been trained in Wasit, At' Tamim, Al Basrah, Karbala', An Najaf, Ninawa', and Dhi Qar Governorates.

• High-protein rations have been given to 240,000 pregnant and nursing mothers and malnourished children during 2003. A new program in rural areas provides supplies and training to birthing attendants and will benefit a total of 440,000 women.

• Training of Nurses and Midwives: A grant to the Iraqi Nursing Association will support the recruitment and training of hundreds more women nurses and the purchase of new uniforms, bed linens and nurses' kits. Currently, there are only 300 trained and licensed women nurses in Iraq.

Ministry for Human Rights

Human rights atrocities in Iraq were frequent and brazen. In the last year tens of thousands of Iraqis were found in mass graves, the apparent victims of cruel and merciless organized killings.

Human Rights Atrocities in Iraq – Major Periods

- **1980 Persecution of Faylee Kurds**

Faylee Kurds expelled from Iran and Iraq and persecuted and massacred in Northern Iraq.

- **1983 Kurdish Massacres targeted against Barzanis/KDP**

In 1983 the regime rounded up ~8000 men from the Barzanis in Northern Iraq. They were executed in deserts far from their homes.

- **1988 Anfal Campaign**

Between February and November 1988 the regime began a policy of demolishing homes and separation of men from their families. Most of the men were executed in deserts in the West and South West. Many women and children died because of lack of food and medical attention. 182,000 people disappeared and a high percentage of PUK members were executed.

- **1988 Halabja**

On March 16 the regime dropped Sarin and VX gas on the town of Halabja killing more than 5,000 people and injuring thousands more. Many survivors suffered long-term medical complications and thousands died. Significant instances of defects occur and many are still suffering the effects of the attack.

- **1991 Shi'a uprising in the South**

At the end of the Gulf war, as Iraqi troops retreated, Iraqi soldiers and citizens rose up in the South. There were massacres of tens of thousands of soldiers and civilians in that area; crackdowns in Basra and Hillah were particularly brutal.

- **1991 Kurdish autonomy**

At end of Gulf war as the Peshmerga fought for autonomy in Northern Iraq many civilians and Peshmerga were killed. Once autonomy was declared, many Kurds living below the green line were massacred. There are mass grave sites in the Kirkuk region.

- **Uprising in Najaf**

In 1999 Ayatollah al Sadr was assassinated in Najaf by a cleric from another tribe. In response students, theologians and other citizens of Najaf rose up. Demonstrations were brutally put down, perpetrators were rounded up and arrested and many were jailed and tortured.

- **Draining Marsh Arabs**

The marshes where the Arabs lived in Southern Iraq were drained and the inhabitants were forced to relocate.

Achievements

- Establishment of Ministry of Human Rights and hiring of staff. The Ministry formally opened on 14 February 2004
- Regular contacts made with other Ministries in Baghdad and the Ministries of Human Rights in Erbil and Sulaymaniyah
- Contacts made with OHCHR, UNDP, WHO, UNIFEM, ICRC and Diplomatic Missions in Baghdad
- Ministry-held women's issues workshops
- Assessment done for setting up a National Human Rights Commission and Ombudsman
- An oral history program has been established, along with a Secure Documentation Centre established at Kadhimiyah
- Preliminary work done on a Truth Commission

- Delegation attended UN Commission on Human Rights in Geneva
- 20 members of staff given human rights training organized by Nottingham University
- Bureau of Missing Persons has begun work. Swiss expert providing advice
- Weekend conference in Dokun for NGOs from all over Iraq from 26 – 29 June

Ministry of Culture

Under Saddam's regime, Iraq's cultural treasures were often neglected and isolated. For over 35 years, many of Iraq's ancient sites have been closed to the Western world. The Coalition and Ministry of Culture is committed to opening these doors to ancient civilization – where civil society is thought to have begun.

The Coalition, with the Iraqi Ministry of Culture, is dedicated to helping Iraqis protect and restore their cultural heritage including museums, theater, the arts, and music. Iraq's archaeological treasures are not only of great importance to Iraq, but also to all mankind. In addition, the restoration of cultural activities is a step towards the return of normalcy for the Iraqi people.

Iraq Museum

- Iraqi police, in collaboration with Coalition forces, recovered four of the most sought-after pieces looted from the Iraq Museum: 'Warka Mask,' which is perhaps the oldest naturalistic sculpture of a woman's face (3,000 years old); 'Bassetki Statue', and a wood and bronze brazier. A fourth famous piece, the 'Warka Vase', was voluntarily returned last summer.
- 22 Iraqi museum professionals participated in a five-week intensive Cultural Heritage Institute in the United States, sponsored by the U.S. Department of State's Bureau of Educational and Cultural Affairs in partnership with the Smithsonian Institution.
- The first phase of reconstruction of the Iraq Museum has been completed. This work was funded by the US Department of State ($750,000) and the Packard Humanities Institute ($250,000). The first phase included: security enhancements, HVAC, plumbing, electrical, roof, and other building repairs, installation of a computer network, communications equipment, and other technological improvements, as well as purchase of office furniture, office equipment, and computers.
- A state-of-the-art archaeological conservation laboratory was donated to the Iraq Museum by the Italian Center for Archaeological Research and Excavations. Italian technicians continue to provide training and support to the Iraqi staff.
- The Iraq Museum will soon launch an interactive website giving it a worldwide presence.

Cultural Arts

- The Iraqi National Symphony Orchestra has revived. The symphony traveled to the United States in early December for two concerts at Kennedy Center in Washington, DC and now performs regularly in Iraq, playing on new instruments donated by Steinway and Yamaha.
- Iraq's only specialized elementary school, the School of Music and Ballet, was reconstructed and refurnished with donated desks, instruments, and manuals.
- The Ministry's Printing House, unharmed by war and looters, recently brought on-line two new state-of-the-art printing presses, increasing the printing capacity at the facility. The first job for the printers was to print recently-revised textbooks.
- The old National Library, which suffered intense fires during the looting, is being cleaned of soot and work areas have been established. Its one-million book collection escaped

largely intact from the looting. The books are now being cleaned of soot [and] returned to their shelves for the use of students and researchers.

Archaeology

• Ambassador Bremer approved the Archaeological Site Protection (ASP) Project on October 19, 2003. The Project intends to stop the looting of the over 7,000 recognized archeological sites in Iraq. Looting was only a minor problem in Iraq prior to the 1991 Gulf War, and increased dramatically in the second half of the 1990's [sic].

• The ASP project is funded from a $1 million grant for the U.S. Department of State's Foundation which was donated by the Packard Humanities Institute.

• Approximately 4,000 looted artifacts, mostly from the Iraq National Museum, have been recovered.

Archaeological Sites (7,417 Archeological sites have been identified in Iraq)

• Assur (2500 BC – 250 AD) – The first capital of the Assyrian Empire and the first well-documented mercantile center in the ancient world.

• Babylon (2500 BC – 1000 AD) – The home of the world's first complete legal code, 'Code of Hammurabi', the Hanging Gardens, the great leader Nebuchadnezzar, the Ishtar Gate, and the Tower of Babel.

• Nimrud (5500 BC – 150 BC) – Assyria's second capital. The best-preserved Assyrian palace is located here.

• Nineveh (6000 BC – present) – The third Assyrian capital and once one of the most powerful cities in the Middle East.

• Samarra (9th Century AD) – An early Islamic capital and home to the largest mosque ever built, Great Mosque of Mutawakkil.

• Uruk – One of the first great urban centers and the largest city in Sumer. The birthplace of writing on cuneiform tablets.

Ministry of Youth and Sport

Pre-War

• The Iraqi Ministry of Youth and Sport has been in existence for several decades. However, in the early 1990s, Uday Hussein publicly humiliated and sacked the then Minister of Youth and Sport. He took over much of the Ministry's sport function, placing it under his control within the National Olympic Committee, and basically casting aside all youth programs. Following Uday's action, the Ministry was reduced to a 'Commission on Youth.'

• In 2001, the Ministry of Youth and Sport was reconstituted, but Uday still controlled most of the sports, particularly at the highest level of competition. Most youth policies and programs that were created were heavily influenced by the Ba'ath party ideology and included some extreme revolutionary youth movements.

• During the regime of Saddam Hussein, youth centers were used mostly to glorify the dictator and promote the ideals of the Baath Party, including war and hatred against Hussein's identified enemies.

Post-War

• After the fall of the Hussein regime, the Ministry of Youth and Sport was re-established and given a refurbished building inside the grounds of Baghdad's Al Zawra Park. The building now serves as its headquarters.

• The influx of youth wanting to be involved in new youth center programs post-conflict has been overwhelming. Programs of particular popularity include computer (especially internet) and job-training classes.
• The Ministry of Youth & Sport oversees more than 5,000 community-based football teams in all regions of Iraq. Along with football, youth centers will focus on sports including basketball, boxing, martial arts, volleyball, weightlifting and wrestling.
• The Ministry has recently been awarded a much-needed grant of US$18.5 million from funds collected from Iraqi oil production and seized assets of the former regime. This money is being used to complete reconstruction, refurbishment and re-equipment of the remaining youth centers by the end of 2004.
• Donor countries have committed to help fund 20 of the 42 identified top priority youth projects presented by the Ministry.
• The Ministry became the first post-conflict Ministry to have an autonomous financial system, overseeing all of their own finances and being the first Ministry to convert to the new Iraqi civil service salary structure.
• A major effort is underway by the Ministry to improve a cohesive system of youth centers in Iraq. This includes building many new centers, as well as refurbishing existing structures across the country.
• The Ministry has an excellent relationship with the Coalitional [sic] Provisional Authority, whose advisors will continue to offer support and guidance post-transition as requested.
• In provincial areas, youth centers are essential to Iraqi Communities and often serve as unifying focal points not only for youth, but also for the community at large. They are a critical part of the fabric of Iraqi society and are the perfect environment for democratic town hall debates and public gatherings.

National Olympic Committee of Iraq
• Through the support of the Coalition Provisional Authority in post-conflict Iraq, [the] President of the National Olympic Committee of Iraq (NOCI) chaired the Interim Committee to Administer Sport and helped direct more than 500 elections for sports federations and clubs – the first democratic elections in Iraq in more than 35 years. Through these elections the people of Iraq were able to elect a new Olympic Committee on January 29, 2004, in the province of Suleymaniyah, and begin rebuilding sports in the country.
[• On February 29, 2004, in Athens, Greece, the International Olympic Committee voted unanimously to lift Iraq's suspension and welcomed the country back to the Olympic Family – now with 202 nations as members.
• In total, the NOCI oversees 41 national sport federations, of which 21 officially compete in the Olympic Games. The organization also directs the Iraqi Paralympic Committee.
• At Al Shaab Stadium in Baghdad on April 2, 2004, the NOCI launched its new logo. Designed in cooperation with the International Olympic Committee, the logo features a green silhouette of a date palm tree encircled by a green wreath of palm leaves.
• The new NOCI has been fortunate to find great support from the International Olympic Committee and several National Olympic Committees. This includes support for Iraqi boxers and wrestlers by the U.S. Olympic Committee; support for Iraqi wrestlers by the Romanian Olympic Committee; support for Iraqi swimmers by the Canadian Olympic Committee; support for track and field athletes by the German Olympic Committee; and support for the Iraqi footballers (soccer players) by the U.K. Olympic Committee and the Italian Olympic Committee.]

Ministry of Planning and Development Cooperation

The Ministry of Planning and Development has successfully overseen the coordination of International Donor Funds with Iraqi reconstruction projects.

Iraq Strategic Review Board

- The Minister chairs the Iraq Strategic Review Board which analyzes and reviews millions of dollars worth of reconstruction projects. The Board reviews UN, World Bank and other donor funding to make sure that their plans fit within the general framework of larger Iraqi reconstruction and strategic priorities.
- The Board reviewed the over 700 reconstruction projects that Ministry of Planning and Development presented for the Iraqi Government at the Abu Dhabi Conference in February 2004.

Abu Dhabi Conference

- Organized international Conference among 35 nations in Abu Dhabi who pledged a total of 1 billion dollars towards two trust funds managed by the United Nations and World Bank. The Madrid International Donors Conference generated over $32 billion for Iraq's reconstruction; the Conference allocated funds but made no determination as to what specifically this money would be used for.
- Coordinated and prioritized more than 700 reconstruction projects among Iraq's line ministries.
- Presented to Abu Dhabi International Donors Conference a list of 700 prioritized reconstruction projects.
- Provided a strategic vision for Iraq's reconstruction. International donors and Iraqi ministries each had their own their own concept of what they want to accomplish in Iraq. The Ministry of Planning and Development stood in the middle of these groups to coordinate their different visions, and provided a coherent development framework through which the Iraqi government and their donor partners could focus their efforts.
- Planning and development is not about 'central planning' anymore. It's about coordinating a wide variety of views into a coherent vision. The Ministry has established key institutions and procedures that will be essential for cooperation.

Council for International Cooperation (CIC)

- The CIC is an institution developed by the Ministry to facilitate international cooperation. The Minister serves as Chairman of CIC.

Daily Activity

- Strategically routed much of the $5 billion in international donations into spending plan.
- Established broad tracking systems for Iraq reconstruction donor money.
- Tracked and coordinated daily reconstruction progress with individual ministries and coordinating donors.
- Coordinated with Iraqi Finance Ministry to develop Iraqi ministry 2005 bottom-line budgets.
- Developed Iraqi capital budget plan for 2005.

Doha Conference

- Led the Iraqi effort to organize the Doha Conference, which represents the next stage in donor reconstruction. The Doha Conference included the participation of over 30 nations. The Conference examined how far the more than 700 reconstruction projects have progressed in 3 months, and facilitated further action. The Conference theme was 'From Commitment to Action.'

Employees

• There are approximately 1500 employees in the Ministry. Employees are competent and committed to their work and programs. Many of the employees possess sector expertise and can coordinate technical issues with other ministries.

ECONOMY

Ministry of Oil

Iraq's oil, the treasure of the nation and a resource available through international markets to the nations of the world now belongs to all of the Iraqi people. The value created by Iraq's oil industry will benefit the nation's people and its development.

Pre-Conflict

• Oil production: Averaged two-million barrels per day (MBPD) in 2002.
• Oil exports: Averaged 1.3 MBPD in 2002.

Post-Conflict

• Oil production: Production capacity has exceeded pre-conflict levels and currently stands at approximately 2.5 MBPD with a year-end objective of 2.8-3.0 MBPD.
• Oil exports: Daily exports have exceeded pre-conflict levels and are averaging 1.65 MBPD.
• Daily export income averages approximately $55 million.
• As of the 30 June, crude oil export revenue is estimated to reach $7.9 billion for the first six-months of 2004 and $15 billion for the full year.
• Iraq met rising demand for benzene, diesel, kerosene and liquefied petroleum gas (LPG) despite sabotage, an aggressive insurgency, and obsolete refineries.
• With the Iraqi Ministry of Oil, managed one of the largest concerted logistical efforts in history to convoy humanitarian fuel supplies into Iraq – four times the size of the effort to fuel the Allied invasion of Europe in 1944.
• Formed an Oil Industry Security Force of 14,000 guards.
• Assisted in the re-formation of the Iraqi National Oil Company and the structuring of the Ministry of Oil to facilitate success in the future.
• Fueled the resurgent thermal power stations of the Ministry of Electricity.
• Iraq has more than 110-billion barrels of crude oil reserves (world's second largest after Saudi Arabia) and 100-trillion cubic feet of gas.

Ministry of Labor and Social Affairs

During Saddam Hussein's regime, many MOLSA staff did not have the knowledge and skills to best serve the needy in Iraq. Following the liberation of Iraq, the Ministry of Labor and Social Affairs (MOLSA) complex was looted and burned and records were destroyed.

Today, the Ministry has rehabilitated and furnished all of its buildings, and it now serves Iraqis with job placement services, vocational training, social security, and social welfare.

• MOLSA opened 18 employment services centers around the country, giving jobseekers the opportunity to get assistance in finding jobs that match their job skills and interests, and giving Iraqi and international employers alike a means of finding qualified employees to fill their vacancies.

• MOLSA opened 6 vocational training centers, which are currently offering courses in English, literacy, and computer skills. MOLSA is also training jobseekers in writing CVs so they can be more competitive for jobs and better communicate their skills and qualifications to potential employers. Eventually, MOLSA will have 32 vocational training centers around the country which will offer a full menu of technical and vocational training designed to meet the needs of the labor market by filling identified gaps in job skills.

• MOLSA, in conjunction with an NGO, has opened a women's shelter, the 'Safehouse,' which is designed as a temporary safe place for women or girls who face physical or sexual abuse. The Safehouse will protect the woman or girl from the abuser until the situation can be resolved, either through the permanent placement of the abused in another facility or safe reconciliation with her family.

• MOLSA's social care directorate increased the number of families receiving cash assistance benefits from 68,000 to approximately 110,000, providing needed help to the most vulnerable members of society, such as the elderly, disabled, and single mothers.

• The Baghdad Employment and Training Center is an outreach program seeking both Iraqi and International employers to list job vacancies. It also provides computer, literacy and English language training to Iraqis seeking jobs. It's an economic stimulus connecting hundreds of Iraqis to job opportunities.

• UNICEF has pledged $6 million to rehabilitate social care institutions and to build an [sic] new social care training institute in Iraq. These Centers care for the many vulnerable and dispossessed people in society. Extra investment will ensure that the facilities are of the highest standard while the training institute will ensure that the staff is fully trained to provide the most appropriate assistance.

Ministry of Agriculture

The Agricultural sector accounts for more than 20% of Iraq's labor force. The Ministry of Agriculture's Supplies Company, by itself, employs 1,300 people throughout Iraq, responsible for the distribution of fertilizer and pesticides. In addition, Iraq's rural economy helps feed Iraq's 18 million urban dwellers.

The Ministry of Agriculture aims to promote rural employment and increase income for farmers and transform Iraqi agricultural [sic] into a market based sector that supports farmers, processors and marketers with world class research and development and effective regulations.

• In support of this, the price of wheat increased from $105 per metric ton in 2003 to $180 per metric ton in 2004 for the top grade of wheat.

• U.S. Agency for International Development (USAID) through its Agriculture Reconstruction and Development Program for Iraq awarded grants totaling $394,000, primarily to improve veterinary services for a healthy and sustainable livestock production. The Kirkuk Veterinary Hospital directed the renovations at three clinics. Baghdad University Veterinary College also received a $62,000 grant to furnish and equip a new internet center at the college. The Ministry of Agriculture's Veterinary Services Company employs 2,300 people, including more than 1,000 veterinarians, responsible for vaccine distribution throughout the country.

• The Ministry of Agriculture established 18 date palm nurseries in 18 governances [sic] throughout Iraq in support of its goals to re-establish Iraq's once dominant position in the international date market.

• The University of Hawaii College of Agriculture in cooperation with the University of

Mosul Hamam al Alil and the University of Dahuk has developed an agriculture science program to increase rural incomes and Iraqi food supplies by enhancing higher education and outreach in agriculture sciences. New equipment provided to the universities by USAID includes satellite-based broadband communications systems; scientific equipment; and electronic library equipment. The three universities will co-sponsor the publication of the *Iraq Journal of Agriculture Science*. Also 6 Iraqi students have been selected to participate in a one-year graduate study program at the University of Hawaii.

Ministry of Trade

New Headquarters

• One year ago the Ministry of Trade headquarters stood in rubble. It was vacant and had been looted. There were no computers, no telephones, and no furniture. Its records were destroyed. For an entire year the Ministry found temporary headquarters on the floor of a building shared with other ministries. The Ministry set a goal of relocating to new facilities to house its people and to be wired for 21st Century technology.
• Today the Ministry has achieved that goal and is celebrating the opening of new headquarters in Baghdad.

Restoration of Food Reserves

• The Ministry has the responsibility to distribute food to over 95 percent of the Iraqi people; however one year ago the food supply was dwindling. The food supply had reached a low. There were food shortages in some of the provinces. Food reserves overall were down to one month. The UN's World Food Program helped to reduce shortages.
• A goal was set to have a three months' food reserve. Soon that goal will be achieved. The people of Iraq will soon have a three months' food reserve.

Observer Status at the WTO

• One year ago Iraq was cut off from the world trading community. with the rest of the world [sic]. The Ministry determined that it would begin to help Iraq enter the international trade community.
• Today Iraq has been granted observer status with the World Trade Organization. In the future it is planned that Iraq will have full membership.

Training of the Ministry's People

• The Ministry has completed a wide variety of training programs for its employees: WTO training, tax training, accounting training, information technology training, export licensing training (in Malta), and advanced agricultural training.

Conclusion

• Just one year ago the ministry lay in rubble and there were food shortages. Today, the ministry has a new building, has provided training to many of its 33,000 employees, and has helped Iraq to have, today and in the foreseeable future, an abundant food supply to serve all of the people of Iraq.

Ministry of Science and Technology

For nearly 30 years the former Iraqi regime sought to use the Ministry of Science as an instrument to threaten its neighbors and oppress its own people. The Ministry served the interests of the government, not the interests of the people.

During much of this period, Iraqi scientists were forbidden from communicating with the international community in order to prevent outside influences from interfering with the former regime's absolute power and control over its citizens. As a result, Iraq's science and technology community fell behind in its technological capacity in relation to other nations.

Since Iraq's liberation last April, however, this situation has changed. The Ministry of Science and Technology has made important progress creating a modern scientific program that utilizes leading technology, research tools and scientific experts in the best interests of the Iraqi people.

The science and technology community has the capacity to propel this country forward. It simply needs to be brought up to date, and to get reconnected to the world community.

The Coalition has helped promote opportunities for that. Since liberation scientists have been able to begin to reconnect with [the] international scientific community. Iraq has been re-opened to the society of ideas. Scientists have engaged with the West and with contractors, and with State and local governments, and with private enterprise to bring their knowledge base up to date.

The Ministry has made significant progress in its mission with a number of projects now underway:

• Collection teams are protecting the public from radioactive sources that pose significant health risks.

• The Ministry established the new Food and Environmental Safety Laboratory, to protect public health.

• The Ministry has established a foundation for e-government in Iraq with efforts underway to establish information technology planning throughout government.

• Ministry personnel have installed hundreds of computer systems in Baghdad University for thousands of students and faculty members, and are installing local area networks in the ministries.

• The Ministry of Science and Technology continues to work to modernize Iraq's infrastructure; and to improve the living standards of all the people of Iraq.

• Short and long term strategic plans and projects have been implemented and the Ministry is on schedule to meet its annual goal with 30% of its planned projects for the year 2004 successfully completed.

• The ministry has courageously adopted an unflinching anti-corruption philosophy.

• The Ministry of Science and Technology will establish the Iraqi Radioactive Source Regulatory Authority for the regulation and protection of sources of radiation, allowing for the beneficial uses of radioactive material in both the public and private sector, while protecting the public against harmful effects of radioactive material, and will bring Iraq into compliance with international standards.

Ministry of Industry and Minerals

Revitalization of Iraq's industrial sector is well underway

• A year ago, Iraq's industrial sector was non-functional. Neglect by Saddam Hussein's regime, and lack of principled management had taken its toll on this area of the economy. Just before the war there was a collapse of industrial management. Ba'athists and top management destroyed evidence of wrongdoing and looted offices leaving buildings decimated, and shutting down the majority of State Owned Entities (SOE).

• Today, the majority of SOE's [sic] are producing goods and services. A number of those goods are central need items for the rebuilding of Iraq, including cement, chemicals, fertilizers, textiles, pharmaceuticals and food products.
• Management structure is in place and functioning. There has been a thorough de-ba'athification of SOE's [sic]. The Minister, Mohamad Tofiq Rahim, is totally intolerant of unethical practices for management and employees. The Ministry of Industry and Minerals (MIM) was the first Ministry to implement an Inspector General (IG) program. The Minister not only helped rebuild MIM, but rebuilt it atop a foundation of solid business practices and ethical proceedings. [The CPA Advisor's Office to MIM, particularly Senior Advisor Colonel Lettie Bien, has been enormously supportive of all of these efforts.]

Iraq's industries are critical to safety and security of the country
• Iraq has the largest commercially viable sulfur deposit in the world. Mining it is critical to industry. Industry desperately needs sulfur for development of sulfuric acid, which contributes to health needs, agricultural production and various industrial projects.
• Facilities Protection Services (FPS) has a guard force of 10,000 people. Securing those sites helps secure Iraq's industrial infrastructure.
• Factories must be managed in a manner that will not harm the local environment.

The employees of the Ministry are its greatest strength and asset
• Employees have extensive subject matter expertise, and extensive expertise in machinery operation and processes. Employee inventiveness and ingenuity have been critical to bringing industrial plants back online. For example, in the petrochemical plant in Basra employees creatively found ways to improve efficiency of plant operation. By internally re-engineering their production lines they increased production and improved the quality of their products.

Competent and fair managers are now leading the Ministry
• All managers speak consistently with one voice with respect to fairness, equity and mission. CPA advisors to MIM have noted a significant difference in atmosphere of the ministry. Employee voices are now heard, and there is no penalty for appropriate questions.
• Managers are educated, and bring a basis of preparation and critical thinking skills. Budgetary planning for fiscal years 2004 and 2005 are complete.
• First Ministry IG system. The IG has direct access to the Minister and complete autonomy.
• Minister is intolerant of corruption and unethical behavior. He stands for fair treatment of all employees.

Ministry of Finance

The Ministry of Finance is responsible for developing and implementing policies that help to protect and promote the financial and economic stability of Iraq. As such, the Ministry of Finance formulates and executes the federal budget, manages debt and develops economic policy.

Achievements
• Managing the 30+ trillion Iraqi Dinar 2004 budget.
• In early May the Ministry of Finance, working with the Ministry of Planning & Development Coordination, released the 2005 budget guidance thus beginning the process of formulating the 2005 budget.

• Has begun the integration of a new Financial Management Information System; a computerized system to track the execution of the budget in accordance with international standards.
• Developed and implemented a new civil service salary scale.
• Designed and implemented a new pension system for civil service retirees.
• Helped draft and enact a new Financial Management Law, which provides the foundation for transparent, effective fiscal policy and management of oil revenues.

CONCLUSION

After decades of dictatorship, the Iraqi people now control their destiny and have established many of the conditions needed for a free and prosperous future. Today, Iraq is focused on fostering the development of a market-based economy. Now free of building palaces for the elite and developing weapons of mass destructions [sic], Iraq is using its resources for the benefit of its people. At the core of this new Iraq is the development of a democratic, accountable, and self-governing civil society respectful of human rights and freedom of expression. Iraq has many challenges ahead; however, it is poised to be a nation united, prosperous, and able to take its rightful place as a responsible member of the region and the international community.

Reconstruction: Putting It In Context

Following are comparative reconstruction milestones for post-Saddam Iraq and post-WWII Germany:

	IRAQ	GERMANY
Local Governments Installed	2 Months	8 Months
Independent Central Bank	2 Months	3 Years
Police Established	2 Months	14 Months
New Currency	2 ½ Months	3 Years
Training a new Military	3 Months	10 Years
Major reconstruction plan	4 Months	3 Years
Cabinet Seated	4 Months	14 Months
Full Sovereignty	1 Year	10 Years
New Constitution	2 ½ Years	4 Years
National Elections	3 Years	4 Years
War Trials	Pending	6 Months

Document 262
Farewell Address by Ambassador Bremer to Members of the Coalition Provisional Authority

28 June 2004

The Coalition Provisional Authority ceases to exist today. I would like to extend my personal thanks to everyone who works and has worked at the Coalition Provisional Authority, its predecessor, the Office of Refugee [sic] and Humanitarian Assistance, and to the fine men and women who have served in the Coalition Forces.

Both groups have served with courage in the face of huge risks. Many have paid the ultimate price. We owe them a debt of gratitude which no words can express.

Each of you has participated in a process unique in history. A coalition of the willing came together and toppled a tyrant. Then, civilian volunteers from around the world came to try not only to repair the ravages of war, but to reconstruct a country devastated by over three decades of misrule.

You have contributed to replacing the tyranny of one man with a broadly representative government pledged to uphold the rights of all. You have contributed to rebuilding Iraq and modernizing its economy. You have contributed to making a better life for the citizens of this wonderful country.

These are noble undertakings for which I am deeply grateful. I thank you for your sacrifice and your service and wish each of you the very best in the coming years.

Document 263
Letter Concerning the End of Occupation

28 June 2004

Judge Medhat al Mahmood
Court of Cassation
Baghdad, Iraq

Dear Judge Mahmood:

As recognized in U.N. Security Council Resolution 1546 (2004), the Coalition Provisional Authority will cease to exist on June 28, at which point the occupation will end, and the Iraqi Interim Government will assume and exercise full sovereign authority on behalf of the Iraqi people. We welcome Iraq's steps to take its rightful place of equality and honor among the nations of the world.

Sincerely
L. Paul Bremer III
Administrator

6. Comparative Table of CPA Legal Acts

NOTE: The date attached by Ambassador Bremer to his signature on the original documents published on the CPA website and the dates of signature in the Official Gazette, if at all given, differ on occasion. The date of signature listed in the present table is the date accompanying the original signature as shown on the documents published on the CPA's website.

The date in the document symbol used on the signed versions of the documents seems to be, as a rule, the date used by the CPA for cross-referencing regulations, orders and memoranda in later documents. There are, however, some noteworthy exceptions. CPA Regulation No 1 is referenced using 23 May 2003 rather than 16 May 2003 as the relevant date of the regulation. Memorandum No 13 is referenced using the actual date of signature rather than '30 May 2004'. The same is true for the references to Memorandum No 6 in Regulation No 9, s1(2) (3 Sep 2003 rather than 2 Sep 2003) and Order No 57 in Order No 100, s3(24) and (25) (10 Feb 2004 rather than 5 Feb 2004; the date used in the document symbol and in other references). The dates used for the various documents throughout this publication is the date in the document symbol used on the original signed documents published on the CPA's website.

Legal Act	Official Gazette number/ page	Date Used in Document Symbol in Official Gazette	Signed = Entry into Force	Date in Document Symbol of Signed Copy on CPA Website	Amended/Revised	Rescinded (in its entirety) by CPA
REG						
1	3977/4	23 May 03	*16 May 03*	16 May 03	R7, s7, 5 Dec 03	O100, s5(1), 28 Jun 04
2	3978/3	15 Jun 03	15 Jun 03	10 Jun 03	R11, s1(1)-(4), 15 Jun 04	
3	3978/8	15 Jun 03	15 Jun 03	18 Jun 03	R11, s1(5), 15 Jun 04	O95, Annex A, s15(8), 2 Jun 04
4	3978/16	26 Jun 03	26 Jun 03	25 Jun 03		R8, s3, 14 Jan 04
5	3978/18 –	17 Jun 03 17 Aug 03	17 Jun 03 18 Aug 03	18 Jun 03 17 Aug 03	R7, s7, 5 Dec 03	O100, s5(2), 28 Jun 04
6	3978/22	13 Jul 03	13 Jul 03	13 Jul 03	R7, s7, 5 Dec 03	R9, s1(2), 9 Jun 04 O100, s5(3), 28 Jun 04
7	3981/61	5 Dec 03	5 Dec 03	5 Dec 03	O100, s5(4), 28 Jun 04	
8	3981/68	4 Nov 04	*14 Jan 04*	–[1]	R12, 23 Jun 04	
9	3985/1	1 Jun 04	*9 Jun 04*	9 Jun 04		
10	3985/2	9 Jun 04	9 Jun 04	9 Jun 04		
11	3985/4	15 Jun 04	*18 Jun 04*	15 Jun 04		
12	3985/7	23 Jun 04	*24 Jun 04*	23 Jun 04		
ORD						
1	3977/2	16 May 03	16 May 03	16 May 03	O100, s3(1), 28 Jun 04	
2	3977/6	23 May 03	23 May 03	23 May 03	O34, s1, 13 Sep 03 O100, s3(2), 28 Jun 04	
3 R/A	3977/10 3981/1	23 May 03 31 Dec 03	23 May 03 31 Dec 03	23 May 03 31 Dec 03	 O100, s3(3), 28 Jun 04	O3R/A, s 2(4), 31 Dec 03
4	3977/13	24 May 03	25 May 03	25 May 03		O100, s4(1), 28 Jun 04
5	3977/16	25 May 03	25 May 03	25 May 03		M7, s3, 4 Nov 03 O100, s4(2), 28 Jun 04

[1] There is no document symbol on the signed copy. A cross-reference to Regulation No 8 in Regulation No 12 uses the following document symbol 'CPA/REG/14 January 2004/8' indicating that the relevant date for reference purposes is 14 January 2004.

Legal Act	Official Gazette number/ page	Date Used in Document Symbol in Official Gazette	Signed = Entry into Force	Date in Document Symbol of Signed Copy on CPA Website	Amended/Revised	Rescinded (in its entirety) by CPA
6	3978/24	8 Jun 03	8 Jun 03	8 Jun 03		O100, s4(3), 28 Jun 04
7	3978/26	10 Jun 03	10 Jun 03	9 Jun 03		
8	3978/28	7 Jun 03	7 Jun 03	7 Jun 03		
9 R	3978/29 3985/33	8 Jun 03 27 Jun 04	8 Jun 03 27 Jun 04	8 Jun 03 27 Jun 04		in fact replaced by O9R
10	3978/33	8 Jun 03	*5 Jun 03*	8 Jun 03		
11	3978/34	8 Jun 03	9 Jun 03 [8 Jun 03][2]	8 Jun 03		O100, s4(4), 28 Jun 04
12	3978/36	8 Jun 03	8 Jun 03 [7 Jun 03][3]	7 Jun 03	M8, s1-3, 7 Jun 03	O54, s3(4), 24 Feb 04 O100, s4(5), 28 Jun 04
13 R R/A	–[4] 3978/38 3983/1	– 11 Jul 03 –[5]	18 Jun 03 11Jul 03[6] 22 Apr 04	18 Jun 03 11 Jul 03 –[7]	 O100, s3(4), 28 Jun 04	in fact replaced by O13R in fact replaced by O13R/A
14	3978/47	10 Jun 03	10 Jun 03[8]	10 Jun 03	O100, s3(5), 28 Jun 04	
15	3978/50	23 Jun 03	23 Jun 03	–[9]	O100, s3(6), 28 Jun 04	
16 R R/A	3978/53 – –	27 Jun 03 1 Dec 03 4 Jun 04	27 Jun 03 1 Dec 03 13 Jun 04	26 Jun 03 1 Dec 03 4 Jun 04	 O100, s3(7), 28 Jun 04	in fact replaced by O16R in fact replaced by O16R/A
17 R	3979/1 3985/36	27 Jun 03 27 Jun 04	27 Jun 03 27 Jun 04	26 Jun 03 27 Jun 04		in fact replaced by O17R
18	3979/5	7 Jul 03	7 Jul 03	7 Jul 03		
19	3979/6	10 Jul 03	10 Jul 03	9 Jul 03	O100, s3(9), 28 Jun 04	
20	3979/9	17 Jul 03	17 Jul 03	17 Jul 03[10]		
21	3979/12	6 Aug 03	6 Aug 03	5 Aug 03		O100, s4(6), 28 Jun 04
22	3979/13	8 Aug 03	*18 Aug 03* [8 Aug 03][11]	7 Aug 03	O73, s2, 22 Apr 04 O100, s3(10), 28 Jun 04	
23	3979/23	20 Aug 03	20 Aug 03	7 Aug 03		
24	3979/39	24 Aug 03	24 Aug 03	13 Aug 03		
25	3979/42	3 Sep 03	3 Sep 03	31 Aug 03	O100, s3(11), 28 Jun 04	
26	3979/49	24 Aug 03	24 Aug 03	24 Aug 03		
27	3979/52	4 Sep 03	4 Sep 03	4 Sep 03		
28	3979/56	3 Sep 03	3 Sep 03	3 Sep 03	O73, s3, 22 Apr 04	
29	3979/61	7 Sep 03	7 Sep 03	7 Sep 03		
30	3979/63	8 Sep 03	8 Sep 03	8 Sep 03	O100, s3(12), 28 Jun 04	
31	3980/1	10 Sep 03	10 Sep 03	10 Sep 03		

[2] Order No 11 was signed on 9 June 2003; however, the Official Gazette states 8 June 2003 as the date of signature.

[3] Order No 12 was signed on 8 June 2003; however, the Official Gazette states 7 June 2003 as date of signature.

[4] The original Order No 13 was never published in the Official Gazette. By the time the CPA started publishing the Official Gazette Order No 13 had already been revised so that only the revised version was entered into the Gazette.

[5] There is no date give for this Order in the Official Gazette. The symbol used in the footer of the Order reads 'CPA/ORD/X2004/13'.

[6] No date was attached to the original signature of Ambassador Bremer. Other CPA documents that refer to Revised Order No give 13 July 2003 as the relevant date, using the reference CPA/ORD/13 July 2003/13. The Official Gazette also gives 11 July 2003 as the date of signature.

[7] The footer of the signed copy reads 'CPA/ORD/X2004/13'.

[8] No date was attached to the original signature of Ambassador Bremer. The Official Gazette also gives 10 June 2003 as the date of signature.

[9] The footer of the signed copy reads 'CPA/ORD/– Jun 2003/–'.

[10] The original document bears two different footers: on pp. 1 and 2 'CPA/ORD/14 July 2003/20' and on p. 3 'CPA/ORD/17 July 2003/20'.

[11] The Order was signed and dated by Ambassador Bremer in the original on 18 August 2003. The date given in the Official Gazette, vol 44, no 3979 (no date), at 22, is 8 August 2003.

Legal Act	Official Gazette number/ page	Date Used in Document Symbol in Official Gazette	Signed = Entry into Force	Date in Document Symbol of Signed Copy on CPA Website	Amended/Revised	Rescinded (in its entirety) by CPA
32	3980/4	4 Sep 03	4 Sep 03	4 Sep 03		
33	3980/6	8 Sep 03	8 Sep 03	8 Sep 03		
34	3980/7	13 Sep 03	13 Sep 03	13 Sep 03		
35	3980/8	13 Sep 03	*18 Sep 03*	13 Sep 03	O100, s3(13), 28 Jun 04	
36	3980/12	2 Oct 03	*3 Oct 03*	3 Oct 03	O100, s3(14), 28 Jun 04	
37	3980/20	19 Sep 03	19 Sep 03	19 Sep 03	O84, s2, 30 Apr 04 O100, s3(15), 28 Jun 04	
38	3980/27	19 Sep 03	19 Sep 03	19 Sep 03[12]	O47, s1, 31 Dec 03 O54, s7, 24 Feb 04 O70, s1(1), 3 Apr 04 O100, s3(16), 28 Jun 04	
39	3980/33	19 Sep 03	not dated	19 Sep 03	O46, s1, 20 Dec 03	
40	3980/38	19 Sep 03	19 Sep 03	19 Sep 03		O94, s3, 7 Jun 04
41	3980/101	19 Sep 03	19 Sep 03	19 Sep 03	O100, s3(17), 28 Jun 04	
42	3980/103	19 Sep 03	19 Sep 03	19 Sep 03		O67, s2(4), 21 Mar 04 O100, s4(7), 28 Jun 04
43	3980/105	14 Oct 03	14 Oct 03	14 Oct 03		
44	3980/106	24 Oct 03	*24 Nov 03*[13]	11 Nov 03		
45	3980/110	27 Nov 03	27 Nov 03[14]	25 Nov 03	O61, s1, [22 Feb 04] O100, s3(18), 28 Jun 04	
46	3980/123	20 Dec 03	20 Dec 03	20 Dec 03		
47	3980/124	31 Dec 03	31 Dec 03	31 Dec 03		O70, s2, 3 Apr 2004 O100, s4(8), 28 Jun 2004
48	3980/125	10 Dec 03	10 Dec 03	9 Dec 03	O100, s3(19), 28 Jun 04	
49	3981/6	19 Feb 04	*20 Feb 03*	19 Feb 04	O84, s3, 30 Apr 04	
50	3981/22	10 Jan 04	*11 Jan 04*[15]	10 Jan 04		
51	3981/26	8 Jan 04	no date[16]	14 Jan 04		
52	3981/28	6 Jan 04	*8 Jan 04*	6 Jan 04		
53	3981/30	16 Jan 04	*18 Jan 04*[17]	16 Jan 04		
54	3981/32	24 Feb 04	*26 Feb 04*	24 Feb 04	O70, s1(2), 3 Apr 04	
55	3981/42	27 Jan 04	*28 Jan 04*	27 Jan 04	O100, s3(20), 28 Jun 04	
56	3982/1	1 Mar 04	*6 Mar 04*[18]	1 Mar 04		
57	3982/46	5 Feb 04	*10 Feb 04*	5 Feb 04	M13, s1, 30 May 04 O100, s3(21), 28 Jun 04	
58	3982/54	5 Feb 04	*10 Feb 04*	5 Feb 04		
59	3982/55	1 Jun 04	1 Jun 04	1 Jun 04		
60	3982/60	19 Feb 04	*22 Feb 04*	19 Feb 04	O100, s3(22), 28 Jun 04	
61	3982/64	22 Feb 04	*23 Feb 04*	22 Feb 04		O100, s4(9), 28 Jun 04
62	3982/66	26 Feb 04	*1 Mar 04*	26 Feb 04		O62, s3, 26 Feb 04; O100, s4(10), 28 Jun 04

[12] There is a typo in the footer on the first page giving the date as '9 September 2003'. However, the footer on the remaining pages gives the date as '19 September 2003'.

[13] The Order was signed and dated by Ambassador Bremer in the original on 24 November 2003. The original document itself bears the symbol 'CPA/ORD/11 Nov 2003/44' while in the Official Gazette the symbol used is 'CPA/ORD/24 Oct 2003/44'.

[14] In Order No 61 which amends Order No 45, the date given for that Order is 25 November 2003. See Official Gazette, vol 45, no 3982 (Jun 2004), at 64 ('CPA/ORD/25 November 2003/45').

[15] The Order was dated by Ambassador Bremer as '1/11/03'. The year must have been a typo.

[16] The Order was signed by 'Richard H. Jones, Acting' and was not dated. The symbol used in the signed document is 'CPA/ORD/14 January 2004/51'.

[17] The Order was signed by 'Richard H. Jones, Acting' and was dated '1/18/04'. The symbol used in the signed document is 'CPA/ORD/16 January 2004/53'.

[18] The Order was signed and dated by Ambassador Bremer in the original on 6 March 2004. The symbol used in the signed document is 'CPA/ORD/1 March 2004/56'. The Central Bank Law of 2004 which was attached to the Order was to enter into force on 1 March 2004 (see Art 74 of the Law).

Legal Act	Official Gazette number/ page	Date Used in Document Symbol in Official Gazette	Signed = Entry into Force	Date in Document Symbol of Signed Copy on CPA Website	Amended/Revised	Rescinded (in its entirety) by CPA
63	3982/68	6 Mar 04	6 Mar 04	6 Mar 04		
64	3982/71	29 Feb 04	*3 Mar 04*	29 Feb 04		
65	3982/147	20 Mar 04	20 Mar 04	20 Mar 04	O100, s3(23), 28 Jun 04	
66	3982/161	20 Mar 04	20 Mar 04	20 Mar 04		
67	3983/11	21 Mar 04	21 Mar 04	21 Mar 04	O100, s3(24), 28 Jun 04	
68	3983/20	4 Apr 04	4 Apr 04	4 Apr 04		
69	3983/24	1 Apr 04	not dated	1 Apr 04	O100, s3(25), 28 Jun 04	
70	3983/36	3 Apr 04	*9 Apr 04*	3 Apr 04		
71	3983/38	6 Apr 04	6 Apr 04	6 Apr 04	O100, s3(26), 28 Jun 04	
72	3983/44	10 Jun 04	*15 Jun 04*	10 Jun 04		
73	3983/51	22 Apr 04	*25 Apr 04*	22 Apr 04	O100, s3(27), 28 Jun 04	
74	3983/55	18 Apr 04	*19 Apr 04*	18 Apr 04	O100, s3(28), 28 Jun 04	
75	3983/85	15 Apr 04	*20 Apr 04*	15 Apr 04	O100, s3(29), 28 Jun 04	
76	3983/93	20 May 04	*28 May 04*	20 May 04	O100, s3(30), 28 Jun 04	
77	3983/100	18 Apr 04	*25 Apr 04*	18 Apr 04	O100, s3(31), 28 Jun 04	
78	3983/105	19 Apr 04	*26 Apr 04*	19 Apr 04		
79	3983/124	19 Jun 04	19 Jun 04	19 Jun 04		
80	3983/142	26 Apr 04	26 Apr 04	26 Apr 04		
81	3983/153	26 Apr 04	26 Apr 04	26 Apr 04		
82	3983/180	28 Apr 04	28 Apr 04	28 Apr 04	O100, s3(32), 28 Jun 04	
83	3984/1	29 Apr 04	*1 May 04*	29 Apr 04		
84	3984/11	30 Apr 04	30 Apr 04	30 Apr 04		
85	3984/15	not adopted	not adopted	not adopted		
86	3984/16	19 May 04	*20 May 04*	19 May 04		
87	3984/41	14 May 04	*16 May 04*	14 May 04		
88	3984/55	12 May 04	12 May 04	12 May 04		
89	3984/57	30 May 04	30 May 04	30 May 04[19]		
90	3984/66	28 May 04	*29 May 04*	28 May 04	O100, s3(33), 28 Jun 04	
91	3984/68	2 Jun 04	*7 Jun 04*	2 Jun 04	O100, s3(34), 28 Jun 04	
92	3984/81	31 May 04	31 May 04	31 May 04		
93	3984/89	2 Jun 04	*3 Jun 04*	2 Jun 04		
94	3984/107 3986/3	6 Jun 04	*7 Jun 04*	6 Jun 04		
95	3984/176	2 Jun 04	*4 Jun 04*	2 Jun 04	O100, s3(35), 28 Jun 04	
96	3984/207	7 Jun 04	*15 Jun 04*	7 Jun 04		
97	3984/211	7 Jun 04	*15 Jun 04*	7 Jun 04		
98	3985/52	27 Jun 04	27 Jun 04	27 Jun 04		
99	3985/63	27 Jun 04	27 Jun 04	27 Jun 04		
100	3985/67	27 Jun 04	*28 Jun 04*	28 Jun 04		
MEM						
1	3978/64	3 Jun 03	3 Jun 03	3 Jun 03		O100, s6(1), 28 Jun 04
2	3978/68	8 Jun 03	8 Jun 03	8 Jun 03	O100, s6(2), 28 Jun 04	
3	3978/85	18 Jun 03	18 Jun 03	18 Jun 03	O100, s6(3), 28 Jun 04	
R	–	27 Jun 04	27 Jun 04	27 Jun 04		
4	3979/70	20 Aug 03	20 Aug 03	19 Aug 03	M15,s1, 18 Jun 04 O100, s6(4), 28 Jun 04	
5	3979/106	22 Aug 03	22 Aug 03	22 Aug 03	O100, s6(5), 28 Jun 04	
6	3979/109	3 Sept 03	3 Sep 03	2 Sep 03		R9, s1(2), 9 Jun 04 O100, s6(6), 28 Jun 04
7	3981/57	4 Nov 03	4 Nov 03	4 Nov 03		O100, s6(7), 28 Jun 04
8	–	25 Jan 04	25 Jan 04	25 Jan 04		O54, s3(4), 26 Feb 04
9	3985/89	25 Feb 04	*24 Feb 04*	25 Feb 04		O100, s6(8), 28 Jun 04

[19] The date given in the document symbol on the first page of the signed copy is '5 May 2004'. However, this seems to have been a typo as the footer on all other pages gives '30 May 2004' as the relevant date.

Legal Act	Official Gazette number/ page	Date Used in Document Symbol in Official Gazette	Signed = Entry into Force	Date in Document Symbol of Signed Copy on CPA Website	Amended/Revised	Rescinded (in its entirety) by CPA
10	3985/91	4 Apr 04	*5 Apr 04*	4 Apr 04	O100, s6(9), 28 Jun 04	
11	–	not adopted	not adopted	not adopted	--	--
12	3985/93	8 May 04	8 May 04	8 May 04		
13	3985/96	–[20]	2 Jun 04	30 May 04		
14	3985/97	–[21]	1 Jun 04	–[22]		
15	3985/98	Jun 04[23]	18 Jun 04	15 Jun 04		
16	–	not adopted	not adopted	not adopted	--	--
17	3985/100	–[24]	26 Jun 04	26 Jun 04		
PN						
1	3978/91		[5 Jun 03]			
2	3978/92		[6 Jun 03]			
3	3978/93		[27 Jun 03]			

[20] The is no date given for this memorandum in the *Official Gazette*; see vol 45, no 3985 (July 2004), 96.

[21] There is no date given in the *Official Gazette*; see vol. 45, no 3985 (July 2004), 97. The footer shows the following incorrect document symbol: 'CPA/MEM/25 Feb 2004/09'.

[22] There is no date given on the signed copy. The footer reads 'CPA/MEM/June 2004/14'.

[23] There is no date given in the *Official Gazette*; see vol 45, no 3985 (July 2004), 98. The document symbol in the footer reads: 'CPA/MEM/June 2004/15'.

[24] There is no date given in the *Official Gazette*; see vol 45, no 3985 (July 2004), 100. The document symbol in the footer simply states 'CPAMEMO 17'.

II

Documents of the Iraqi Governing Council

1. Resolutions[1]

Document 264
Governing Council Resolution Number 1 of 2003
[National Day of Iraq and Official Holidays]

13 July 2003[2]

In the name of God, the Merciful, the Compassionate: At its session held on 13 July 2003 the Governing Council decided the following:

1. Repeal of all festivals and official holidays associated with the deposed dictatorial regime and the dissolved [Arab Socialist] Ba'ath Party.
2. Designation of 9 April, the day the regime fell, as the national day [of Iraq] and an official holiday.

The President of the Governing Council

Document 265
Governing Council Resolution Number 2 of 2003
[Formation of a Committee to Draw up the Work Programme of the Governing Council]

14 July 2003

In the name of God, the Merciful, the Compassionate: At its session held on 14 July 2003 the Governing Council decided the following:

To form a committee to draw up the work programme of the Governing Council which will be composed of the following individuals whose names are listed below:

1. Mr Naseer al-Chaderchi
2. Dr Raja al-Khuzaai
3. Mr Hamid Majid Mousa
4. Mrs Sondul Chapouk
5. Mr Abdel-Aziz al-Hakim
6. Sheikh Abdel-Karim al-Mohammedawi
7. Dr Ibrahim al-Ashaiqir (al-Jaafari)
8. Mr Massoud Barzani (represented by Mr Hoshyar al-Zebari)
9. Mr Jalal Talabani (represented by Dr Ibrahim Saleh)

The President of the Governing Council

[1] All IGC resolutions have been translated from Arabic, unless otherwise indicated. The translations are based on the Arabic text of the resolutions as reproduced in Anbari, Sabah Sadiq (ed.), *Resolutions of the Governing Council 2003-2004* [in Arabic] (3rd edn., 2006) and on the website of the Encyclopedia of Mesopotamia at http://www.nahrain.com/, as well as other Arabic language websites. Most of the websites are no longer available, copies of the original resolutions are on file with the author.

[2] A Table of IGC Decisions [in Arabic] published in August 2003 by the Encyclopedia of Mesopotamia (http://www.nahrain.com/) lists Resolution No 1 of 14 July 2003 as dealing with the 'Formation of a Committee to Draft a Political Statement'.

Document 266
Governing Council Resolution Number 3 of 2003 [Formation of a Committee to Draft the Rules of Procedure of the Governing Council]
14 July 2003

In the name of God, the Merciful, the Compassionate: At its session held on 14 July 2003 the Governing Council decided the following:

To form a committee to draft the rules of procedure for the work of the Council which will be composed of the following individuals whose names are listed below:

1. Dr Mohammed Bahr al-Ulloum
2. Dr Adnan Pachachi
3. Mr Samir Shakir Mahmoud al-Sumaydah
4. Judge Dara Noorddin
5. Mr Ezzelddine Salim
6. Dr Aquila al-Hashimi
7. Judge Wael Abdul Latif
8. Dr Ibrahim al-Ashaiqir (al-Jaafari)
9. Mr Abdel-Aziz al-Hakim
10. Lawyer Ahmed Shiaa al-Barak
11. Mr Massoud Barzani (represented by Dr Ruz Nuri Shawis)

The President of the Governing Council

Document 267
Governing Council Resolution Number 4 of 2003 [Formation of a Special Tribunal for the Prosecution of Crimes against the Iraqi People and Humanity]
15 July 2003

In the name of God, the Merciful, the Compassionate: At its session held on 15 July 2003 the Governing Council decided the following:

To form a special tribunal to look into the following:

First: Prosecuting those from the ousted dictatorial regime that are accused of crimes against the Iraqi people and against humanity.

Second: Restoring the rights of Iraqis whose rights were violated, including the martyrs, the imprisoned, those who were forcibly removed, those who left, the victims of persecutions, and other Iraqi victims of the dictatorial regime.

Third: Forming a committee comprised of the individuals listed below which has expertise in the subject matter above. The purpose of this committee is to put together a list, which serves the aim mentioned earlier, and to present this list to the Council for approval:

1. Judge Dara Noorddin
2. Judge Wael Abdul Latif
3. Lawyer Ahmed al-Barak
4. Mr Naseer al-Chaderchi
5. Dr Aquila al-Hashimi

The President of the Governing Council

Document 268
Governing Council Resolution Number 5 of 2003
[Right to Vote of Deputies of Members of the Governing Council]
15 July 2003

In the name of God, the Merciful, the Compassionate: At its session held on 15 July 2003 the Governing Council decided the following:

To give the deputies of members of the Governing Council the right to vote after distinguishing between fundamental and secondary issues,[3] and the person appointing them authorizes them by official letter to do so.

The President of the Governing Council

Document 269
Governing Council Resolution Number 6 of 2003
[Formation of a Presidency of the Governing Council]
29 July 2003

In the name of God, the Merciful, the Compassionate: At its session held on 29 July 2003 the Governing Council decided the following:

To form a Presidency [Presidential Board] of the Iraqi Governing Council from among the following individuals whose names are listed below:

1. Dr Ibrahim al-Ashaiqir (al-Jaafari)
2. Dr Ahmed al-Chalabi
3. Dr Ayad Allawi
4. Mr Jalal Hisam al-Din al-Talabani
5. Mr Abdel-Aziz al-Hakim
6. Dr Adnan al-Pachachi
7. Dr Mohsen Abdel Hamid
8. Dr Mohammed Bahr al-Ulloum
9. Mr Massoud Mustafa al-Barzani

The President of the Governing Council

Document 270
Governing Council Resolution Number 7 of 2003
[Formation of a Security Committee]
2 August 2003

In the name of God, the Merciful, the Compassionate: At its session held on 2 August 2003 the Governing Council decided the following:

[3] Implying that the deputies cannot vote on fundamental issues.

To form a committee charged with security matters which shall be composed of the following gentlemen whose names are listed below:

1. Mr Abdel-Aziz al-Hakim
2. Mr Massoud Barzani
3. Dr Ahmed al-Chalabi
4. Dr Iyad Allawi
5. Sheikh Ghazi Ajil al-Yawer
6. Mr Samir Shakir al-Sumaydah
7. Sheikh Abdel-Karim al-Mohammedawi
8. Mr Jalal Talabani

[Signed] *Dr Ibrahim al-Ashaiqir [al-Jaafari]*
President of the Governing Council

Document 271
Governing Council Resolution Number 8 of 2003 [Commissioning Mr Samir Shakir Al-Sumaydah to Review the Situation in Al-Anbar]

3 August 2003

In the name of God, the Merciful, the Compassionate: At its session held on 3 August 2003 the Governing Council decided the following:

To commission Mr Samir Shakir al-Sumaydah to review the general situation in al-Anbar Governorate, especially with regards to security and strengthening the position of the Council as the supreme Iraqi authority in the country, and putting an end to the sectarian killing and ensuring the fulfillment by the local administration of its duties to implement the policies and orders of the Council in an effective and honourable manner, one which promotes the goal of the Council to extend its authority over all parts of Iraq, to stabilize security, and to respect the rule of law. The Council commissions Mr Samir al-Sumaydah to present a detailed report on this as soon as possible, and also to present his reasoned recommendations as required.

[Signed] *Dr Ibrahim al-Ashaiqir [al-Jaafari]*
President of the Governing Council

Document 272
Governing Council Resolution Number 9 of 2003 [Formation of a Financial and Economic Committee]

4 August 2003

In the name of God, the Merciful, the Compassionate: At its session held on 4 August 2003 the Governing Council decided the following:

To form the Financial and Economic Committee which shall be composed of the following individuals whose names are listed below:

1. Dr Ahmed al-Chalabi – President of the Committee
2. Mr Hamid Majid Mousa
3. Dr Mouwafak al-Rabii
4. Mr Samir Shakir al-Sumaydah
5. Dr Mohsen Abdel Hamid
6. Mr Abdel-Aziz al-Hakim
7. Dr Mohammed Bahr al-Ulloum
8. Dr Iyad Allawi
9. Dr Ibrahim al-Jaafari
10. Mr Massoud Barzani
11. Dr Raja al-Khuzaai
12. Dr Adnan Pachachi

[Signed] *Dr Ibrahim al-Ashaiqir [al-Jaafari]*
President of the Governing Council

Document 273
Governing Council Resolution Number 10 of 2003
[Responsibility of the Presidency For the Nomination of Ministers]

5 August 2003

In the name of God, the Merciful, the Compassionate: At its session held on 5 August 2003 the Governing Council decided the following:

The Presidency will nominate the ministers, after full consultation with the rest of the members of the [Governing] Council, and the Council may agree to or reject every minister through a secret ballot. In the case that any nominee is rejected, the Presidency will propose another nominee, so long as the Presidency presents its suggestions on this matter during a period that does not exceed one week.

[Signed] *Dr Ibrahim al-Jaafari*
President of the Governing Council

Document 274
Governing Council Resolution Number 11 of 2003
[Importance and Feasibility of Establishing New Ministries]

5 August 2003

In the name of God, the Merciful, the Compassionate: At its session held on 5 August 2003 the Governing Council decided the following:

In the case that there is a desire to establish a new ministry, it is necessary that there has been a study regarding the importance of this ministry – its feasibility, structure, and positions – in order that the resolution is not rushed. Accordingly, we suggest that in the case of such a desire the preparation of a study on this issue is sufficient, rather than a resolution.

[Signed] *Dr Ibrahim al-Jaafari*
President of the Governing Council

Document 275
Governing Council Resolution Number 12 of 2003
[Formation of a Committee to Deal With Matters of the Unemployed]

6 August 2003

In the name of God, the Merciful, the Compassionate: At its session held on 6 August 2003 the Governing Council decided the following:

To form a committee that will deal with the matters of the unemployed together with the Coalition Provisional Authority and which shall be composed of the following individuals whose names are listed below:

1. Judge Wael Abdul Latif – President of the Committee
2. Dr Ibrahim al-Ashaiqir (al-Jaafari)
3. Mr Abdel-Aziz al-Hakim
4. Mr Naseer al-Chaderchi
5. Dr Mouwafak al-Rabii
6. Mrs Sondul Chapouk

[Signed] *Dr Ibrahim al-Jaafari*
President of the Governing Council

Document 276
Governing Council Resolution Number 13 of 2003
[Establishment of New Ministries]

7 August 2003

In the name of God, the Merciful, the Compassionate: At its session held on 7 August 2003 the Governing Council decided the following:

1. To divide the Ministry of Transport and Communication into the Ministry of Transportation and the Ministry of Communication.
2. To establish a Ministry of Human Rights.
3. To establish a Ministry of Environment.
4. To establish a Ministry of Immigration.
5. To establish a Ministry of Electricity.

[Signed] *Dr Ibrahim al-Jaafari*
President of the Governing Council[4]

[4] It is of interest to note that the CPA's report of the IGC's session of 7 August 2003 only records: 'Ministries: GC voted to create a Ministry of Environment and a Ministry of Human Rights. The [sic] rejected a proposal to create a Ministry for Expatriates.' (Memorandum to the Administrator from CPA Governance Office, Daily Governing Council Sitrep, 7 August 2003).

Document 277
Governing Council Resolution Number 14 of 2003 [Formation of a Preparatory Committee to Find Mechanisms and Means for the Selection and Election of Members of the Constitutional Convention]

11 August 2003

In the name of God, the Merciful, the Compassionate: At its session held on 11 August 2003 the Governing Council decided the following:

The formation of a Preparatory Committee to find the mechanism and means for selecting and electing members for the constitutional convention, which will prepare a draft [of the constitution], from among the individuals whose names are listed below:

1. Dr 'Asamat 'Abd al-Mujid Bakr
2. Dr Muhdi Jabir Muhdi
3. Mr 'Atta 'Abd al-Wihab
4. Dr Muhammad al-Hajj Hamud
5. Dr Muhammad 'Amr Mawlud
6. Mr Dinar Najman Shaqiq
7. Dr Hakamat Hakim, Professor
8. Dr Kana'an Muki
9. Dr Mustafa Ibrahim al-Zalami
10. Mr Sami 'Abd al-Rahman
11. Dr Fuad Ma'sum
12. Judge Ibrahim Malak Khayri al-Hindawi
13. Judge 'Abd al-Husayn Shandal 'Aysi Muhsin al-'Aliyan
14. Dr Mahmud Mathfar
15. Mr Muhammad Rida al-Gharifi
16. Dr 'Abd al-Amir al-Zahid
17. Hadi 'Aziz 'Ali, Lawyer
18. Dr Sifa' al-Din Muhammad
19. Dr Hamam Hamudi, Shaykh
20. Mr Farsad Ahmad
21. Ibrahim al-Na'ama
22. Mr 'Abbas al-Biyati
23. Judge Muhammad 'Abd Nasr Khalaf
24. Mr Hani Adris Mujid
25. Judge Yas Khudayr

[Signed] *Dr Ibrahim al-Jaafari*
President of the Governing Council

Document 278
Governing Council Resolution Number 15 of 2003 [Formation of a Coordinating Committee to Find Mechanisms and Means for the Selection and Election of Members of the Constitutional Convention]

11 August 2003

In the name of God, the Merciful, the Compassionate: At its session held on 11 August 2003 the Governing Council decided the following:

The formation of a Coordinating Committee to work with the Preparatory Committee to find mechanism and means for selecting and electing members for the constitutional convention and which will include the individuals whose names are listed below:

1. Judge Dara Nur al-Din (Committee Chairman)
2. Mr Ahmad Shiya' al-Barak
3. Mr Nasir al-Jadarji
4. Dr 'Aqila al-Hashimi
5. Judge Wael 'Abd al-Latif
6. Dr Ahmed al-Chalabi (represented by Mr Salim al-Chalabi)

[Signed] *Dr Ibrahim al-Jaafari*
President of the Governing Council

Document 279
Governing Council Resolution Number 16 of 2003 [Appointment of Secretary of the Governing Council]

12 August 2003

In the name of God, the Merciful, the Compassionate: At its session held on 12 August 2003 the Governing Council decided the following:

Mr Muhyi Khateeb will assume the responsibility of Secretary of the Governing Council.

[Signed] *Dr Ibrahim al-Jaafari*
President of the Governing Council[5]

Document 280
Governing Council Resolution Number 17 of 2003 [Formation of a Committee to Review the Documents Dealing with Property Problems]

12 August 2003

In the name of God, the Merciful, the Compassionate: At its session held on 12 August 2003 the Governing Council decided the following:

[5] The resolution was accompanied by the following Note: 'There is no need for CPA intervention (notes issued by the interim coalition administration regarding the Council's resolutions (16 to 97) are dated 21/11/2003).'

To form a committee to review the documents dealing with the problems concerning property ownership and to consider the observations and comments put forth by the distinguished members of the Council. The committee shall revert to the Council for the approval and implementation of its recommendations, which shall be submitted in not later than two weeks. The committee shall comprise of the persons whose names are written below:

1. Judge Dara Noorddin (Chairman of the Committee).
2. Dr Mouwafak al-Rabii.
3. Dr Ahmad al-Chalabi.
4. Dr Mohammad Bahr al-Ulloom.
5. Mr Younadem Kana.
6. Mr Samir Shakir al-Sumaydah.
7. Ms Sondul Chapouk.
8. Mr Massoud Barzani (represented by Dr Ruz Nuri Shawis).

[Signed] *Dr Ibrahim al-Jaafari*
President of the Governing Council[6]

Document 281
Governing Council Resolution Number 18 of 2003
[Responsibilities of the Secretary of the Governing Council]

13 August 2003

In the name of God, the Merciful, the Compassionate: At its session held on 13 August 2003 the Governing Council decided the following:

The Secretary of the Governing Council will meet the individuals and actors to listen to their requests, and will present his recommendations to the Council regarding the proposed steps and the level of the meeting.

[Signed] *Dr Ibrahim al-Jaafari*
President of the Governing Council

Document 282
Governing Council Resolution Number 19 of 2003
[Designation of Iraqi Women's Day]

13 August 2003

In the name of God, the Merciful, the Compassionate: At its session held on 13 August 2003 the Governing Council decided the following:

The 20th of Jumada al-Thani, the birth date of Fatima al-Zahra (Peace be upon her), is designated Iraqi women's day.

[Signed] *Dr Ibrahim al-Jaafari*
President of the Governing Council[7]

[6] The resolution was accompanied by the following Note: 'There is no need for CPA involvement'.
[7] The resolution was accompanied by a Note which reads: 'There is no need for CPA involvement'.

Document 283
Governing Council Resolution Number 20 of 2003
[Approval of the Draft Budget of the Governing Council]

18 August 2003[8]

In the name of God, the Merciful, the Compassionate: At its session held on 18 August 2003 the Governing Council decided the following:

The Governing Council approves the draft budget of the Governing Council proposed by the Finance Committee and directs the Committee to continue working to complete the sections concerning the vehicles and allowances of the [Council] members.

[Signed] *Ahmed Chalabi*[9]
President of the Governing Council

Document 284
Governing Council Resolution Number 21 of 2003
[Formation of Higher National De-Ba'athification Commission]

18 August 2003

In the name of God, the Merciful, the Compassionate: At its session held on 18 August 2003 the Governing Council decided the following:

1. The formation of a National De-Ba'athification Commission; the formation of a Subcommittee from members of the Governing Council to determine the criteria for appointing the members of that Commission and for proposing its policies and the means of implementing them in a just manner; and identifying the criminals and offenders and bringing them to court so that the innocent amongst them can be detected.
2. The Subcommittee is to include the following individuals:

<u>First: The Committee Tasked with De-Ba'athification:</u>

1. Mr Younadem Kana.
2. Mrs Sondul Chapouk.
3. Dr Mouwafak al-Rabii.
4. Sheikh Abdel-Karim Mahoud al-Mohammedawi.
5. Mr Abdel-Aziz al-Hakim.
6. Mr Salah al-Din Muhammad.[10]
7. Dr Ahmed Chalabi.
8. Dr Raja Habib al-Khuzaai.
9. Mr Jalal Talabani (represented by Mr Nushirwan Mustafa).
10. Dr Ibrahim al-Jaafari (represented by Mr Hassan Shabr).
11. Mr Massoud Barzani (represented by Dr Ruz Nuri Shawis).

[8] The date in the Arabic text is 13 March 2003.

[9] The resolution was signed by Ahmed Chalabi as Acting President because the regular President for the month of August, Dr Ibrahim al-Jaafari, was absent from that session of the IGC.

[10] Sometimes also transcribed as Mr Salaheddine Bahaaeddin.

Second: The Committee Tasked with Reinstating Employees:

1. Dr Mahmoud Othman
2. Mr Hamid Majid [Mousa]
3. Dr Aquila al-Hashimi
4. Mr Ezzeddine Salim

[Signed] *Ahmed Chalabi*[11]
President of the Governing Council

Document 285
Governing Council Resolution Number 22 of 2003 [Formation of a Committee to Make Proposals for the Iraqi Nationality Law]

18 August 2003

In the name of God, the Merciful, the Compassionate: At its session held on 18 August 2003 the Governing Council decided the following:

To form a committee from among the individuals whose names are listed below to prepare proposals for the Iraqi Nationality Law, [and] to present its proposals and instructions, in consultation with the Ministries of Interior and Justice, to the Governing Council within one week from the date of its formation for the purpose of adopting them and passing them to [the respective] legal body to pass a law on the matter:

1. Mr Naseer al-Chaderchi.
2. Mr Younadem Kana.
3. Mr Jalal Talabani (represented by Mr Nushirwan Mustafa Amin).
4. Dr Mohammed Bahr al-Ulloum (represented by Dr 'Ala al-Juwadi).

[Signed] *Ahmed Chalabi*[12]
President of the Governing Council[13]

Document 286
Governing Council Resolution Number 23 of 2003 [Opening of an Account with the Al-Rafidain Bank in the Name of the Governing Council]

18 August 2003

In the name of God, the Merciful, the Compassionate: At its session held on 18 August 2003 the Governing Council decided the following:

[11] The resolution was signed by Ahmed Chalabi as Acting President because the regular President for the month of August, Ibrahim al-Jaafari, was absent from that session of the IGC.

[12] The resolution was signed by Ahmed Chalabi as Acting President because the regular President for the month of August, Ibrahim al-Jaafari, was absent from that session of the IGC.

[13] The resolution was accompanied by the following Note: 'There is no need for CPA involvement.'

1. An account is to be opened in the name of the Governing Council with the Al-Rafidain Bank to deposit the budget of the Council.

2. Authorization of the persons whose names are written below to sign the instruments [cheques], which are to be signed by two out of the following four members.

A. Dr Raja al-Khuzaai.
B. Mr Samir Shakir Sumaydah.
C. Dr Mouwafak al-Rabii.
D. Dr Iyad Allawi (represented by Mr Nuri al-Badran).

[Signed] *Ahmed Chalabi*
Acting President of the Governing Council

Document 287

Governing Council Resolution Number 24 of 2003 [Postponing the Issuance of a Press Release Welcoming the Establishment of the Civil Defence Regiments]

20 August 2003

In the name of God, the Merciful, the Compassionate: At its session held on 20 August 2003 the Governing Council decided the following:

The press release welcoming the establishment of the Civil Defense Regiments is to be postponed. This issue is to be discussed by the Security Committee, which shall report on it to the Council.

[Signed] *Ahmed Chalabi*
Acting President of the Governing Council

Document 288

Governing Council Resolution Number 25 of 2003 [Formation of a Committee for the Environment]

19 August 2003

In the name of God, the Merciful, the Compassionate: At its session held on 19 August 2003 the Governing Council decided the following:

The Council agrees to form a Committee for the Environment without prejudice to the Council's resolution to form the Ministry of Environment.[14]

[Signed] *Ahmed Chalabi*
Acting President of the Governing Council[15]

[14] The Ministry of Environment was established by IGC resolution no 13 of 2003; see *Doc 276*.

[15] The resolution was accompanied by the following Note: 'There is no need for CPA involvement.'

Document 289
Governing Council Resolution Number 26 of 2003 [Legal Steps against Judges and Prosecutors Involved in Illegal Executions]
19 August 2003

In the name of God, the Merciful, the Compassionate: At its session held on 19 August 2003 the Governing Council decided the following:

To ask the Ministry of Justice to undertake the necessary legal steps against the judges and the prosecutor of the special court who illegally decreed the execution of forty innocent merchants.

[Signed] *Ahmed Chalabi*
Acting President of the Governing Council[16]

Document 290
Governing Council Resolution Number 27 of 2003 [Professional Associations, Societies and Trade Unions]
25 August 2003[17]

In the name of God, the Merciful, the Compassionate: At its session held on 25 August 2003 the Governing Council decided the following:

A legal study of the professional associations, societies and trade unions in Iraq is to be prepared, membership in such bodies is to be opened to those who were barred from such membership in the past, and the announced elections [to the governing councils of such bodies] are to be postponed.

[Signed] *Ahmed Chalabi*[18]
President of the Governing Council

[16] The resolution was accompanied by the following Note: 'There is no need for CPA involvement.'

[17] This resolution is listed both in Anbari (ed.), *Resolutions of the Governing Council 2003-2004* [in Arabic] (3rd edn., 2006), 39, and in the Table of IGC Decisions [in Arabic] published in August 2003 by the Encyclopedia of Mesopotamia (http://www.nahrain.com/) as resolution number 28, dated 25 August 2003. However, in the official minutes of the meetings of the Governing Council, as well as in several press reports in Arabic, the resolution is referred to as resolution number 27. See the Minutes of the IGC's regular session number 1 of 5 January 2004, reprinted in Daffāʿī (ed.), *Iraq under Occupation: The Records of the Governing Council* [in Arabic] (2004).

Resolution number 27 of 25 August 2003, reproduced in Anbari (ed.), *Resolutions of the Governing Council 2003-2004* [in Arabic] (3rd edn., 2006), 39, reads as follows:

'In the name of God, the Merciful, the Compassionate: At its session held on 25 August 2003 the Governing Council decided the following:

The Governing Council sees no political obstacles to purchasing electricity from neighboring countries; it leaves the determination of conditions, prices, and any other matters to the competent Iraqi authorities.

[Signed] *Ahmed Chalabi*
President of the Governing Council'.

This resolution was accompanied by a Note which reads: 'There is no need for CPA involvement'. In a Memorandum, dated 3 September 2003, the IGC informed Ambassador Bremer that it had taken a decision that there are no political impediments to purchasing electricity from neighbouring countries and that they would like to discuss the issue with him during the meeting on 4 September 2003.

[18] The resolution was signed by Ahmed Chalabi as Acting President because the regular President for the month of August, Ibrahim al-Jaafari, was absent from that session of the IGC.

Document 291
Governing Council Resolution Number 28 of 2003
[Appointment of Ministers]

31 August 2003[19]

In the name of God, the Merciful, the Compassionate: At its regular session held on 31 August 2003 the Governing Council decided to appoint the following ministers to the following cabinet posts:

1. Minister of Communications – Dr Haydar Jawad al-Abadi
2. Minister of Public Works – Mrs Nisrin Mustafa Siddiq Barwari
3. Minister of Construction and Housing – Mr Bayan Baqir Sulagh
4. Minister of Environment – Engineer Abd-al-Rahman Siddiq Karim
5. Minister of Trade – Dr Ali Abd-al-Amir Allawi
6. Minister of Planning – Dr Mahdi al-Hafiz
7. Minister of Education – Dr Ala-al-Din Abd-al-Sahib al-Alwan
8. Minister of Higher Education – Dr Ziyad Abd-al-Razzaq Muhammad Aswad
9. Minister of Culture – Mr Mufid Muhammad Jawad al-Jaza'iri
10. Minister of Human Rights – Dr Abd-al-Basit Turki
11. Minister of Foreign Affairs – Mr Hoshyar Mahmud Muhammad Zebari
12. Minister of Interior – Mr Nuri al-Badran
13. Minister of Agriculture – Dr Abd-al-Amir Ruhaymah al-Abbud
14. Minister of Youth and Sports – Mr Ali Fa'iq al-Ghadban
15. Minister of Health – Dr Khudayir Abbas
16. Minister of Industry and Minerals – Engineer Muhammad Tawfiq Rahim
17. Minister of Justice – Mr Hashim Abd-al-Rahman al-Shibli
18. Minister of Science and Technology – Mr Rashad Mandan Umar
19. Minister of Labour and Social Affairs – Mr Sami Azara al-Ma'jun
20. Minister of Electricity – Dr Ayham al-Samarra'i
21. Minister of Finance – Mr Kamil Mibdir al-Jilani
22. Minister of Displaced Persons and Expatriates – Mr Muhammad Jasim Khudayir
23. Minister of Water Resources – Dr Abd-al-Latif Jamal Rashid
24. Minister of Oil – Dr Ibrahim Muhammad Bahr-al-Ulum
25. Minister of Transport – Mr Bahnam Zayya Bulus

Written in Baghdad on 4 Rajab 1424, [corresponding to] 31 August 2003.

[Signed] *Dr Ibrahim al-Jaafari*
President of the Governing Council

[19] There are several versions of IGC resolution 28 of 2003. That the decision on the cabinet line-up was taken on 31 August 2003 under the presidency of Dr Ibrahim al-Jaafari and recorded in resolution 28 of 2003 is confirmed by al-Khayat, *How They Ruled Iraq: Papers from the Corridors of the Governing Council* [in Arabic] (2004), Chapter VII. According to Anbari (ed.), *Resolutions of the Governing Council 2003-2004* [in Arabic] (3rd edn., 2006), 39, resolution 28 of 2003 is the one here reproduced as resolution 27 of 2003.

Document 292
Governing Council Resolution Number 29 of 2003 [Dissolution of the Ministry of Awqaf and Religious Affairs and Creation of Administrative Offices for the Awqaf of all Religions and Sects]

30 August 2003

In the name of God, the Merciful, the Compassionate: At its session held on 30 August 2003 the Governing Council decided the following:

To dissolve the Ministry of Awqaf and Religious Affairs and create administrative offices for the Awqaf[20] of all religions and sects.

[Signed] *Dr Ibrahim al-Jaafari*
President of the Governing Council[21]

Document 293
Governing Council Resolution Number 30 of 2003 [Creation of the Ministry of Expatriates and Immigrants]

31 August 2003

In the name of God, the Merciful, the Compassionate: At its session held on 31 August 2003 the Governing Council decided the following:

The creation of a Ministry of Expatriates and Immigrants.

[Signed] *Dr Ibrahim al-Jaafari*
President of the Governing Council[22]

Document 294
Governing Council Resolution Number 31 of 2003 [Registration of Arabs and Foreigners Present in Iraq]

31 August 2003

In the name of God, the Merciful, the Compassionate: At its session held on 31 August 2003 the Governing Council decided the following:

Directives are to be issued to the competent departments for the registration of Arabs and foreigners present in Iraq and the recording of their legal status.

[Signed] *Dr Ibrahim al-Jaafari*
President of the Governing Council

[20] The literal meaning of Waqf (pl Awqaf or Waqfs) is to contain, to stop, to preserve; the shari'ah meaning is to transfer the ownership of a portion of ones wealth, in cash or kind, to Allah as a dedication for any shari'ah compliant purpose. The closest English term for a waqf is a philanthropic or charitable endowment.

[21] The resolution was accompanied by the following Note: '[Resolution] in need of CPA approval.'

[22] The resolution was accompanied by the following Note: '[Resolution] needs CPA approval.'

Document 295

Governing Council Resolution Number 32 of 2003 [Drawing up of a Security Plan for the Exalted City of Najaf]

31 August 2003

In the name of God, the Merciful, the Compassionate: At its session held on 31 August 2003 the Governing Council decided the following:

Considering the special and sacred status that the exalted city of Al-Najaf holds; the importance of peace and security in it for the whole of Iraq; and its religious, educational and cultural significance, it is resolved:

First: To draw up a security plan for the exalted city of Al-Najaf in cooperation and agreement with the venerable religious authorities, the plan to be based on the following:

1. General security for the city and the public.
2. Special security for the venerable religious scholars.
3. Local security for the markets, public places, hotels etc.
4. Security of the eternal shrine of Imam Ali.
5. Security for the mosques and sacred places.
6. Personal Security for the officials and office holders at risk.
7. Special security for the family of Al-Hakim.

Secondly: The Coalition Provisional Authority is to be asked to agree to this plan to be requested to bear its part of the responsibility [in implementing it].

Thirdly: The Governing Council requests the Coalition Provisional Authority to arrest all suspects, whatever their status, and to bring them to a fair trial.

[Signed] *Dr Ibrahim al-Jaafari*
President of the Governing Council[23]

Document 296

Governing Council Resolution Number 33 of 2003 [Formation of a Committee for Fighting Terrorism, Warding off Sectarianism, and Strengthening National Unity]

31 August 2003

In the name of God, the Merciful, the Compassionate: At its session held on 31 August 2003 the Governing Council decided the following:

1. The Council supports the initiative of a number of its members to form a broad-based Iraqi committee under the name 'The National Committee for Fighting Terrorism, Warding Off Sectarianism, and Strengthening National Unity.' The committee will include the broadest Iraqi political and professional representation, including the leadership of political parties and professional organizations and prominent individuals.

2. The committee will design a programme of various activities to serve its objectives.

3. Three members of the Governing Council will be appointed to form the nucleus of this national committee in preparation for its formation.

[23] The resolution was accompanied by a Note which reads: 'No need for CPA involvement.'

[Signed] *Dr Ibrahim al-Jaafari*
President of the Governing Council

Document 297
Governing Council Resolution Number 34 of 2003
[Council Session in Najaf to Discuss the City's Security Situation]
4 September 2003

In the name of God, the Merciful, the Compassionate: At its session held on 4 September 2003 the Governing Council decided the following:

1. The Governing Council will hold a Council session in Najaf Governorate to express the Council's sympathy and condolences. The session will be dedicated to discussing the security situation and the proposed solutions for providing security to the city and the Marjaya [Shi'a religious authorities].[24]
2. The precise date of the visit will be determined later.

[Signed] *Ahmad al-Chalabi*
President of the Governing Council

Document 298
Governing Council Resolution Number 35 of 2003
[Iraqi Oil Trust Fund]
4 September 2003

In the name of God, the Merciful, the Compassionate: At its session held on 4 September 2003 the Governing Council decided the following:

The Minister of Oil will announce the establishment of an Iraqi Oil Trust Fund (effective 1 January 2004), the resources of which shall cover the pensions of retired individuals.

[Signed] *Ahmad al-Chalabi*
President of the Governing Council

Document 299
Governing Council Resolution Number 36 of 2003
[Formation of the National Authority for Media Affairs]
8 September 2003

In the name of God, the Merciful, the Compassionate: At its session held on 8 September 2003 the Governing Council decided the following:

[24] The resolution was adopted in response to the bomb attack outside the Imam Ali mosque in Najaf on 29 August 2003 which killed more than 80 people, including Ayatollah Muhammed Baqir al-Hakim, one of Iraq's most important Shiite religious leaders, and wounded many others.

The formation of the National Authority for Media Affairs from the individuals whose names are listed below:

1. Dr Mahmoud Othman
2. Mr Sondul Chapouk
3. Mr Younadem Kana
4. Dr Mouwafak al-Rabii
5. Mr Samir al-Sumaydah
6. Dr Aqila al-Hashimi
7. Dr Adnan al-Pachachi
8. Mr Abdel Aziz al-Hakim
9. Dr Ibrahim al-Jaafari

[Signed] *Ahmad al-Chalabi*
President of the Governing Council

Document 300
Governing Council Resolution Number 37 of 2003 [Extension of Time for the Preparatory Committee to Develop Mechanisms to Establish a Constitution]

9 September 2003

In the name of God, the Merciful, the Compassionate: At its session held on 9 September 2003 the Governing Council decided the following:

The Council would like to make sure that the Preparatory Committee manages to prepare the mechanisms of the constitution in such a way as to cover all governorates; this is why the Council has decided to extend the allocated period until the end of the current month (September), provided that contact is established with those who are in charge of constitutional matters in all the governorates.

[Signed] *Ahmad al-Chalabi*
President of the Governing Council

Document 301
Governing Council Resolution Number 38 of 2003 [Formation of a Committee to Study the Situation in the Governorates]

9 September 2003

In the name of God, the Merciful, the Compassionate: At its session held on 9 September 2003 the Governing Council decided the following:

To form a committee composed of the individuals whose names are listed below to study the changes in the governorates and with regard to the governors, their appointments and assignments, from the situation after the entry of coalition forces to the situation that must prevail from now onwards. The committee shall take into account the Council's opinion in determining the governors' association with the Governing Council, while also taking into consideration the special situation in Kurdistan. The committee shall present its report within two weeks.

1. Mr Hamid Majid [Mousa].
2. Sheikh Ghazi Ajil al-Yawer.
3. Judge Wael Abdul Latif.
4. Mr Ezzelddine Salim.
5. Dr Mouwafak al-Rabii.
6. Mr Samir Shakir al-Sumaydah.
7. Mr Abdel-Aziz al-Hakim.
8. Mr Ahmed Shi'a al-Barak.
9. Mrs Sondul Chapouk.
10. Dr Ruz Nuri Shawis.

[Signed] *Ahmad al-Chalabi*
President of the Governing Council[25]

Document 302
Governing Council Resolution Number 39 of 2003 [Timing of Governing Council Meetings]
9 September 2003

In the name of God, the Merciful, the Compassionate: At its session held on 9 September 2003 the Governing Council decided the following:

1. The Governing Council meetings are to be held in the mornings only in order to give the members of the Council the opportunity to study reports and recommendations, and to communicate with the citizens in order to digest and make sense of their opinions.
2. The meeting times are to be from 9.30 a.m. until 2 p.m., including a short break.
3. It is possible to hold evening sessions if necessary.

[Signed] *Ahmad al-Chalabi*
President of the Governing Council

Document 303
Governing Council Resolution Number 40 of 2003 [Participation of The Republic of Iraq in the Meetings of IMF and World Bank]
10 September 2003

In the name of God, the Merciful, the Compassionate: At its session held on 10 September 2003 the Governing Council decided the following:

[25] The resolution was accompanied by a Note which reads: 'No need for CPA involvement.'

1. The Republic of Iraq will participate in the meetings of the International Monetary Fund and the World Bank that will take place in Dubai from 22 to 25 September 2003.

2. The delegation will be comprised of the individuals whose names and positions are listed below, under the presidency of Dr 'Adel 'Abd al-Muhdi and membership of each of the following:

1. Dr Muhdi al-Hafiz – Minister of Planning
2. Dr Kamil Mubadir al-Kilani – Minister of Finance
3. Dr 'Abd al-Amir Rahimat al-'Abud – Minister of Agriculture
4. Dr 'Ala al-Din al-'Alwan – Minister of Education
5. Dr Khudayr Fadil 'Abbas – Minister of Health
6. Dr 'Ali 'Abd al-Amir 'Alawi – Minister of Commerce
7. Dr Sinan al-Shabibi – Central Bank Governor

[Signed] *Ahmad al-Chalabi*
President of the Governing Council

Document 304
Governing Council Resolution Number 41 of 2003 [Staff of Governing Council Members]

16 September 2003

In the name of God, the Merciful, the Compassionate: At its session held on 16 September 2003 the Governing Council decided the following:

On the basis of the allocations made in the Council's budget, which was approved in a Governing Council session on 9 September 2003, the following is decided:

To appoint three advisors, twelve security guards, and two personal assistants for every member of the Governing Council, to be chosen by each member. The salaries of these employees will be determined in accordance with the following:

1. Advisor $300/month
2. Security Guard $160/month
3. Personal Assistant $60/month

Their salaries shall be calculated as taking effect from the morning of 14 July 2003, as long as this is approved in writing by a member of the Governing Council.

[Signed] *Ahmad al-Chalabi*
President of the Governing Council

Document 305
Governing Council Resolution Number 42 of 2003 [Approval of the Level of Income Tax]

16 September 2003

In the name of God, the Merciful, the Compassionate: At its session held on 16 September 2003 the Governing Council decided the following:

Approval of the recommendation presented by the Finance Committee to the Governing Council which included setting the level of income tax to begin at a rate of 3% and capping it, at the highest rate, at 15%, on the basis that the first 1.5 million of income is tax free, together with the remainder of all other allowances, such as [for] children, the wife, and the place of abode.
[Signed] *Ahmad al-Chalabi*
President of the Governing Council[26]

Document 306
Governing Council Resolution Number 43 of 2003 [Approval of Customs Duty on Imported Goods]
16 September 2003

In the name of God, the Merciful, the Compassionate: At its session held on 16 September 2003 the Governing Council decided the following:

Approval of the recommendation presented by the Finance Committee to the Governing Council, which included adopting a customs duty of 5% for imported goods with exemptions for food, medicine, books, and clothing. [Proceeds from] imports subject to this duty will go to the Iraqi Development and Reconstruction Fund.
[Signed] *Ahmad al-Chalabi*
President of the Governing Council[27]

Document 307
Governing Council Resolution Number 44 of 2003 [Approval of the Principle of Unconditional Investment of Capital]
16 September 2003

In the name of God, the Merciful, the Compassionate: At its session held on 16 September 2003 the Governing Council decided the following:

Approval (of the principle of unconditional investment of foreign and Iraqi capital alike, and recommendation to provide support for national investment through the issuance of long-term loans, modest interest rates and regulation of the investment process).
[Signed] *Ahmad al-Chalabi*
President of the Governing Council[28]

[26] The resolution was accompanied by a Note which reads: 'The CPA has approved this resolution and notice [of the approval] will be forthcoming.'
[27] The resolution was accompanied by the following Note: 'The CPA has approved [this resolution] and notice [of the approval] will be forthcoming.'
[28] The resolution was accompanied by the following Note: 'The CPA has approved [this resolution] and will issue the Order later.'

Document 308
Governing Council Resolution Number 45 of 2003
[Approval of the Draft Nationality Law]
16 September 2003

In the name of God, the Merciful, the Compassionate: At its session held on 16 September 2003 the Governing Council decided the following:

To approve the draft Iraqi Nationality Law after making the necessary amendments and textual changes in order for it to comport with the law.

[Signed] *Ahmad al-Chalabi*
President of the Governing Council[29]

Document 309
Governing Council Resolution Number 46 of 2003
[Rehabilitation of the Victims of the Former Criminal Regime]
10 September 2003

In the name of God, the Merciful, the Compassionate: At its session held on 10 September 2003 the Governing Council decided the following:

To consider illegal any proceedings which have led to the execution and incarceration (be it for life or for any lesser period) on political grounds of individuals who suffered at the hands of the former criminal regime. The Council is indeed deeply sorry that Iraq's people and its political forces have had to endure such crimes; it is also really sorry for the unjust accusations that the victims were faced with. This is why the Council would like to ensure the rehabilitation of the victims' families as well as those who were most affected by the false accusations, by:

1. Considering them innocent, and regarding them as mere prey of the former criminal regime.
2. Bringing the cases of the victims of the former regime before just courts, and publishing all details that would lift the injustice off their shoulders.
3. Dealing, at a later stage, with the negative material as well as emotional effects of the injustice on the victims' families.

[Signed] *Dr Ayad Allawi*[30]
President of the Governing Council[31]

[29] The resolution was accompanied by the following Note: 'Requires the approval of the CPA. We are in the final stages of our negotiations with the Committee.'

[30] The resolution was signed by Dr Ayad Allawi as Acting President because the regular President for the month of September, Ahmed Chalabi, was absent from that session of the IGC.

[31] The resolution was accompanied by the following Note: 'The CPA had referred this decision to the Legal Committee.'

Document 310
Governing Council Resolution Number 47 of 2003
[Rules and Standards for the Media]

22 September 2003[32]

In the name of God, the Merciful, the Compassionate: At its session held on 22 September 2003 the Governing Council decided the following:

In the interest of the principles of democracy and the rule of law that we have committed ourselves to apply in Iraq and on the basis of the applicable laws, the Governing Council expresses serious concern over the irresponsible actions with regard to content and behaviour of certain media networks, particularly Al-Jazeera and Al-Arabiyya, which are considered a breach of the rules and standards the media must abide by in order to be allowed to continue to work in Iraq, including:

1. Content:
   - A. Do not incite violence against any person or group.
   - B. Do not incite disorder.
   - C. Do not incite violence against the incumbent authorities or officials.
   - D. Do not advocate the return of the Ba'ath Party or issue any statements claiming to represent the Ba'ath Party, directly or indirectly.
   - E. Do not incite sedition or fighting between sectarian, racial or religious groups.
2. Behaviour and Working Practices:

All people living in Iraq (citizens or foreigners) must inform the authorities of any information which they have in regards to any terrorist attack, before or after that attack takes place. This includes knowledge of any acts of sabotage, criminal activity, terrorism, or any violent action that aims to spread disorder and fear among the Iraqi people.

The Governing Council considers that some of these rules have been violated by certain media networks, putting stability and democracy at risk and encouraging terrorism.

The Governing Council has decided to take immediate action in case of any recurrence of similar violations by the media networks and their employees. In this context, the Governing Council has decided as a warning and temporary measure to ban Al-Jazeera and Al-Arabiyya from participating in the coverage of the Council's activities and official press conferences, and not to allow their correspondents access to ministries and government buildings for two weeks.

[32] There are at least two versions of resolution number 47. The present text is a translation of resolution number 47 that was available at http://www.nahrain.com/ and http://www.iraqipapers.com/ (both sites are no longer available). The text of resolution number 47 in Anbari (ed.), *Resolutions of the Governing Council 2003-2004* [in Arabic] (3rd edn., 2006), 49, reads as follows: 'In the name of God, the Merciful, the Compassionate: At its session held on 22 September 2003 the Governing Council decided the following:

To close the offices of the satellite channels, Al-Jazeera and Al-Arabiyya, and to stop all of their media activities in Iraq, including the work of their correspondents, for a period of one month, beginning from the date of the passing of this resolution. They will be permitted, however, to resume their activities on the condition that they convince the Council that they will adhere to journalistic standards that employ balance and abstain from incitement to violence, discord, and religious sectarianism in Iraq – that is, journalistic standards followed throughout the world. [The two stations are subject to this resolution] due to their repeated violations in broadcasting voices that call for political violence in Iraq, which has led in some instances to explicit incitement to kill, which has complicated and continues to complicate the security problems in the country, and which harms Iraq's progress towards stability and democracy.

[Signed] *Dr Ayad Allawi*

President of the Governing Council.'

All media networks will be monitored closely to ensure their compliance with the aforementioned rules.

The Governing Council reserves the right to take additional action when necessary without prior warning.

The decision shall be in force from the date of signature.

[Signed] *Dr Ayad Allawi*
President of the Governing Council[33]

Document 311
Governing Council Resolution Number 48 of 2003
[Death Certificates for Missing, Unaccounted and Lost Persons]
22 September 2003

In the name of God, the Merciful, the Compassionate: At its session held on 22 September 2003 the Governing Council decided the following:

To have the competent Iraqi tribunals grant, in accordance with established procedures and (secular and religious) legal rules, death certificates for all the missing, unaccounted and lost persons for whom official death certificates have not been issued, in order to enable their relatives to recover their rights and to assist them in their mourning.

[Signed] *Dr Ayad Allawi*
Acting President of the Governing Council

Document 312
Governing Council Resolution Number 49 of 2003
[Lifting of Restrictions on Ownership and Use of Real Estate]
29 September 2003

In the name of God, the Merciful, the Compassionate: At its session held on 29 September 2003 the Governing Council decided the following:

1. Repeal all laws and resolutions which restrict the rights of Iraqis from owning real estate in any part of Iraq.

2. Cancel Resolution Number 157 issued by the dissolved Revolutionary Command Council on 12 June 1994[34] regarding the prohibition of registration of *tasarruf* rights[35] in

[33] The resolution was signed by Dr Ayad Allawi as Acting President because the regular President for the month of September, Ahmed Chalabi, was absent from that session of the IGC.

[34] RCC resolution no 157 was actually adopted on 12 September 1994. It reads as follows: 'In accordance with the provisions of Para (A) of Article (42) of the Constitution.

The Revolutionary Command Council have [sic] decided the following: –

Firstly – The real estate disposals conveying the property shall not be recorded on the real estates owned by the State or to the normal or juristic personality situated within the Boundaries of the Master Plan of Baghdad City, or the Boundaries of the main master plans of Aqdiyas and Nahiyas attached to Baghdad Governorate unless whom the property transferred to him [sic] has been recorded in the census of the year 1957 or any previous census to

real estate for transfer of ownership within the boundaries of the Master Plan of Baghdad City or within the boundaries of the master plans of the districts and areas in the Governorate of Baghdad.

3. This resolution shall come into effect on the date of its publication in the Official Gazette.[36]

The rational for issuing this resolution is the belief of the Governing Council in the rights of the citizens, and promotion of justice and equality among all citizens regarding their right to own real estate in all parts of Iraq.
[Signed] *Dr Mohsen Abdel al-Hamid*
Acting President of the Governing Council[37]

Document 313
Governing Council Resolution Number 50 of 2003
[Repeal of Laws Altering the Demographic and Political Profile of Iraq]
29 September 2003

In the name of God, the Merciful, the Compassionate: At its session held on 29 September 2003 the Governing Council decided the following:

Repeal all laws, resolutions, regulations, directives, injunctions and orders of the so-called Revolutionary Command Council or other Iraqi official bodies issued for the purpose of altering the demographic and political profile of Iraq.
[Signed] *Dr Mohsen Abdel al-Hamid*
Acting President of the Governing Council[38]

him in one of these regions or the regions which have been attached to Baghdad Governorate before the creation of Sallah Al-din Governorate.

Secondly – The provisions of Item (Firstly) of this Resolution shall not be valid on the alienation of the property because of death.

Thirdly – This Resolution shall come into force from the date of its publication in the Official Gazette.

Saddam Hussain

Chairman of the Revolutionary Command Council' (*Official Gazette* [English edition], no 49 (30 November 1994), at 6).

[35] In Islamic law State-owned land can be possessed by an individual who retains *tasarruf* rights. *Tasarruf* is the right to use, exploit, and dispose of such State-owned land.

[36] This resolution, like all other resolutions of the IGC, was never published in the Official Gazette.

[37] The resolution was accompanied by the following Note: '[This resolution] requires CPA approval. It is requested that this resolution be referred to the Committee for Legal Affairs.' It seems that CPA approval was never given. On 8 August 2004, the Council of Ministers adopted Order No 4 of 2004, Right to Ownership, which provides for the 'Cancellation of the resolutions of the dissolved Revolutionary Command Council No 1562 of 1982, No 180 of 1983, and No 157 of 1994, and any other law or order or regulation which is contrary to the unconditional right of ownership of the Iraqi citizens all over Iraq' (*Official Gazette*, vol 46, no 3987 (September 2004), at 8 [translation from Arabic]).

[38] The resolution was accompanied by the following Note: 'The CPA requests this resolution to be referred to the Committee for Legal Affairs.'

Document 314
Governing Council Resolution Number 51 of 2003
[Reinstatement of those Dismissed for Political Reasons]
29 September 2003

In the name of God, the Merciful, the Compassionate: At its session held on 29 September 2003 the Governing Council decided the following:

All those who were dismissed or forced to leave their jobs for purely political reasons are herewith reinstated to their jobs and their period of absence shall be credited in computing their (period of) service and retirement. Detailed instructions will be issued by the Governing Council at a later stage.

Instructions:

1. Dismissed for political reasons is a person who was dismissed because of his political views or particular sectarian or national background or who was refused promotion (upon these grounds) by the defunct Ba'ath Party.
2. All those whose dismissal is confirmed for reasons other than those mentioned above are exempted from the application of this order.

[Signed] *Dr Mohsen Abdel al-Hamid*
Acting President of the Governing Council[39]

Document 315
Governing Council Resolution Number 52 of 2003
[Central Ministerial De-Ba'athification Committees]
29 September 2003

In the name of God, the Merciful, the Compassionate: At its session held on 29 September 2003 the Governing Council decided the following:

Taking into consideration the decrees on De-Ba'athification, a central committee shall be established in every ministry composed of employees who enjoy a good reputation at work. Its mission is to examine and decide upon the possibility of exempting some of those who were dismissed under the Decree on De-Ba'athification and review their applications for return to public service.

The ministerial committee shall take its decisions with a majority of two-thirds of the votes, and committee members are fully responsible for the credibility of their evaluation of the applicant.

Every citizen has the right to challenge the decision of the committee before the Governing Council.

Instructions:

1. In order for an employee to be reinstated to public service, his behaviour must be without fault.
2. The employee's integrity must be confirmed by staff in his former office. Such confirmation must be based on well-grounded motives.

[39] The resolution was accompanied by the following Note: 'The resolution has been withdrawn by the Governing Council.'

3. There must be an urgent need for the employee's services.

4. The employee shall not occupy a key position in the department where he is reinstated. He must be transferred to another department within the same ministry where he used to work and should not work in the same area where he used to work prior to his dismissal. Employees working in sensitive departments shall be transferred to other ministries and departments depending on their area of expertise.

5. The committees shall submit their recommendations for exemptions to the concerned Minister for approval.

6. Every exemption on the basis of this Resolution must be submitted for approval to the Higher National De-Ba'athification Commission.

[Signed] *Dr Mohsen Abdel al-Hamid*
Acting President of the Governing Council[40]

Document 316
Governing Council Resolution Number 53 of 2003 [Formation of an Ad Hoc Committee to Consider Requests of Employees of the Dissolved Civil Services (Ministry of Information and National Council)]

29 September 2003

In the name of God, the Merciful, the Compassionate: At its session held on 29 September 2003 the Governing Council decided the following:

To form an ad hoc committee, which is to consider the requests put forth by the employees of dissolved civil services (Ministry of Information and the National Council), and examine the possibility of integrating them into other services that may require their professional expertise.

[Signed] *Dr Mohsen Abdel al-Hamid*
Acting President of the Governing Council[41]

Document 317
Governing Council Resolution Number 54 of 2003 [Retirement of Employees of Dissolved Entities and Employees Covered by the De-Ba'athification Order]

29 September 2003

In the name of God, the Merciful, the Compassionate: At its session held on 29 September 2003 the Governing Council decided the following:

[40] The resolution was accompanied by the following Note: 'The CPA has agreed; see CPA Memorandum No 7 (But we advise that the de-Ba'athification Commission take responsibility for the resolution).'

[41] The resolution was accompanied by a Note which reads as follows: 'No need for CPA involvement; we have already discussed it with the Committee.'

All employees of dissolved entities and employees covered by the de-Ba'athification Order[42] may apply for retirement in accordance with the provisions and requirements of the Retirement Law.
[Signed] *Dr Mohsen Abdel al-Hamid*
Acting President of the Governing Council[43]

Document 318
Governing Council Resolution Number 55 of 2003 [Permits for Demonstrations][44]

30 September 2003

In the name of God, the Merciful, the Compassionate: At its session held on 30 September 2003 the Governing Council decided the following:

Permits for any demonstrations shall be issued by the Ministry of the Interior and the General Police Directorate shall issue instructions on their organization, holding and monitoring. The Governing Council will meet the representatives of the demonstrators, listen to their requests, and receive their demands in writing.
[Signed] *Dr Mohsen Abdel al-Hamid*
Acting President of the Governing Council

Document 319
Governing Council Resolution Number 56 of 2003 [Retirement of the Director-General of the Ministry of Transport]

30 September 2003

In the name of God, the Merciful, the Compassionate: At its session held on 30 September 2003 the Governing Council decided the following:

Sayyid Ata Allah Kadhim, the Director-General in the Ministry of Transport, is made to retire. It is for the Minister of Transport to implement this decision.
[Signed] *Dr Mohsen Abdel al-Hamid*
Acting President of the Governing Council

[42] See *Doc 14*.

[43] The resolution was accompanied by the following Note: 'The CPA has agreed; see CPA Memorandum No 7 (But we advise that the de-Ba'athification Commission take responsibility for the resolution).'

[44] Resolution No 55 of 2003 has also been referred to as dealing with the establishment of a committee to oversee Hajj matters, and the delegation of relevant powers to that committee.

Document 320
Governing Council Resolution Number 57 of 2003 [Formation of a Committee to Develop Mechanisms for Conducting a General Population Census]
30 September 2003

In the name of God, the Merciful, the Compassionate: At its session held on 30 September 2003 the Governing Council decided the following:

To form a committee, which includes the individuals listed below, to study and prepare the necessary mechanisms for a general population census in Iraq. In the process of fulfilling its duty, the committee is entitled to contact the ministries as well as the relevant departments. The deadline for submitting the committee's final report is 15 October 2003.

List of names:

1. Dr Raja al-Khuzaai
2. Judge Wael Abdul Latif
3. Sheikh Abd al-Karim al-Mohammedawi
4. Dr Adel Abdel-Mahdi
5. Dr Ruz Nuri Shawis
6. Mr Nushirwan Mustafa
7. Mr Muhammad Fadel al-Samerra'i

[Signed] *Dr Mohsen Abdel al-Hamid*
Acting President of the Governing Council

Document 321
Governing Council Resolution Number 58 of 2003 [Formation of De-Ba'athification Committees and Instructions to Facilitate and Organize the Work of the Ministries]
30 September 2003

In the name of God, the Merciful, the Compassionate: At its session held on 30 September 2003 the Governing Council decided the following:

To release the following instructions to facilitate and organize the work of the ministries:

1. The formation of de-Ba'athification committees which are to function according to the respective tasks assigned to them in relation to both de-Ba'athification and exceptional cases.

2. The formation of committees in all the ministries, composed of non-Ba'athist elements known for their integrity, whose task it is to oversee the reinstatement of those dismissed for political reasons, according to the Governing Council's resolution to reinstate these individuals.

3. No party offices may be opened in any ministry, department, or government or mixed [government-private] foundation.

4. No party meetings may be held on government premises.

5. Parties participating in the Governing Council may recommend their members who were dismissed for political reasons and submit a dossier on the matter to the respective council. A committee is to be formed to receive future petitions of parties and individuals in this regard.

[Signed] *Dr Mohsen Abdel al-Hamid*
Acting President of the Governing Council

Document 322
Governing Council Resolution Number 59 of 2003 [Formation of a Committee to Study the Situation of Political Parties and Humanitarian Organizations]

30 September 2003

In the name of God, the Merciful, the Compassionate: At its session held on 30 September 2003 the Governing Council decided the following:

To form a committee to study the situations of political parties and humanitarian organizations and formulate legal rules for political and humanitarian activity, composed of the following members of the Governing Council whose names are listed below:

1. Dr Iyad Allawi – National Accord Movement
2. Dr Ibrahim al-Jaafari – Islamic Dawa Party
3. Dr Mohsen Abdel Hamid – Iraqi Islamic Party
4. Mr Hamid Majid [Mousa] – Iraqi Communist Party
5. Dr Ruz Nuri Shawis – Kurdistan Democratic Party
6. Dr Ahmed al-Chalabi – Iraqi National Congress
7. Mr Salaheddine Bahaaeddin – Kurdistan Islamic Union
8. Mr Abdel-Aziz al-Hakim – Supreme Council for the Islamic Revolution
9. Dr Naseer al-Chaderchi – National Democratic Party
10. Dr Raja al-Khuzaai – Independent

[Signed] *Dr Mohsen Abdel al-Hamid*
Acting President of the Governing Council

Document 323
Governing Council Resolution Number 60 of 2003 [Formation of a Committee to Identify Suitable Means to Strengthen the Council's Secretariat]

1 October 2003

In the name of God, the Merciful, the Compassionate: At its session held on 1 October 2003 the Governing Council decided the following:

To form a committee composed of two members of the Council and the Secretary-General in order to identify means that will lead to a strengthening of the Secretariat and enable it to carry out its duties in the best way possible.

[Signed] *Dr Iyad Allawi*
President of the Governing Council

Document 324
Governing Council Resolution Number 61 of 2003 [Formation of Committee for the Return of Illegally Taken Properties to Their Owners]

6 October 2003

In the name of God, the Merciful, the Compassionate: It is the belief of the Governing Council that the issue of returning the properties confiscated by the former regime to their rightful owners is important and vital, which requires the Council to take action.

The Governing Council at its session held on 6 October 2003 decided the following:

A Committee, comprising of the members whose names are written below, is to be established to consider the promulgation of a law concerning the return of properties to their rightful owners and to review the papers presented by Judge Dara Noorddin, the Council member who has special expertise in this area. The Committee may involve specialists and advisors from the ministries and relevant departments. The Committee shall present its final report to the Council within a month.

1. Judge Wael Abdul Latif (Chairman)
2. Judge Dara Noorddin (Member)
3. Mr Naseer al-Chaderchi (Member)
4. Mr Ahmad Shiya' al-Barak (Member)
5. Dr Ruz Nuri Shawis (Member)
6. Ms Sondul Chapouk (Member)

[Signed] *Dr Iyad Allawi*
President of the Governing Council[45]

Document 325
Governing Council Resolution Number 63 of 2003 [Formation of a High-Level Committee Composed of Representatives of Parties Participating in the Council and Determination of Its Duties]

13 October 2003

In the name of God, the Merciful, the Compassionate: At its session held on 13 October 2003 the Governing Council decided the following:

In order to ameliorate and develop the security situation, the Council suggests the following:

1. To form a high-level committee, which includes representatives from all the parties participating in the Council and works under the authority of the Minister of the Interior. The duties of this committee consist of:

[45] The resolution was accompanied by the following Note: 'There is no need for CPA intervention, as it has previously been discussed by us with the Committee.'

A. Forming police forces derived from the forces of the different parties.
B. Forming intelligence services through the contribution of the different parties' intelligence services, as well as the corresponding services in Kurdistan.

2. To form an Internal Relations Committee, which will contact all parties, powers, and movements which are not participating in the Council. This committee will provide for an exchange of information and complete coordination in view of fulfilling the national duties at the political and administrative levels, including the aspects mentioned in paragraph (1) above.

3. The Higher Security Subcommittee will handle the details pertaining to paragraphs (1) and (2) above.

4. To request the exemption of the Ministry of the Interior from the decision to freeze any appointments and the allocation of bonuses.

5. To allocate funds to meet the increasing needs of the Ministry of the Interior in light of the security situation.

6. To coordinate with and consult the CPA regarding the points mentioned above and the need to endorse them.

[Signed] *Dr Mohammed Bahr al-Ulloum*
Acting President of the Governing Council[46]

Document 326
Governing Council Resolution Number 64 of 2003
[Special Meeting on the Security Situation]
13 October 2003

In the name of God, the Merciful, the Compassionate: At its session held on 13 October 2003 the Governing Council decided the following:

1. The Interior Minister is to host a meeting to discuss the taking of necessary security measures to ensure the security of the citizens.

2. Ambassador Paul Bremer is to be contacted with regard to holding an urgent meeting of the Security Committee to discuss the dangerous security situation of the country next Wednesday.

[Signed] *Dr Mohammed Bahr al-Ulloum*
Acting President of the Governing Council

Document 327
Governing Council Resolution Number 65 of 2003
[Formation of a High-Level Committee for Security and the Rule of Law]
18 October 2003

In the name of God, the Merciful, the Compassionate: With the goal of improving and developing the security situation in the country, at its session held on 18 October 2003 the

[46] The resolution was accompanied by the following Note: 'The CPA need not be involved (but implementation requires consultation)'.

Governing Council decided the following:

To form a high-level committee, composed of members of political parties, movements, and personalities participating in the Council under the chairmanship of the Minister of the Interior which will assume responsibility for organizing the efforts of individuals, powers, movements, and parties, both inside and outside the Council, along with the Minister of the Interior and the other relevant organs which are related in their plans and programs to ensure security and the rule of law.

The committee is to establish the mechanisms for its operation with which to accomplish its mission and fulfill its responsibilities.

[Signed] *Dr Mohammed Bahr al-Ulloum*
Acting President of the Governing Council

Document 328
Governing Council Resolution Number 66 of 2003 [Formation of a High-Level National Committee to Combat Drugs, Alcohol and Psychotropic Substances]

18 October 2003

In the name of God, the Merciful, the Compassionate: At its session held on 18 October 2003 the Governing Council decided the following:

To form a high-level national committee to combat drugs, alcohol and psychotropic substances which will be headed by the Minister of Health and members representing the following ministries and [government] departments:

- Ministry of Foreign Affairs
- Ministry of Justice
- Ministry of Interior
- Ministry of Labour and Social Affairs
- Ministry of Education
- Ministry of Higher Education and Academic Research
- Municipality of Baghdad
- General Commission of Customs

It is expected that the Minister of Health and the above-mentioned ministries and [government] departments will carry out the work accordingly.

[Signed] *Dr Mohammed Bahr al-Ulloum*
Acting President of the Governing Council[47]

[47] The resolution was accompanied by the following Note: 'No need for involvement of the CPA.'

Document 329

Governing Council Resolution Number 67 of 2003 [Formation of a Special Committee to Discuss Security Council Resolution Number 1511 and other Matters]

21 October 2003

In the name of God, the Merciful, the Compassionate: At its session held on 21 October 2003 the Governing Council decided the following:

First: Establishment of a special committee to discuss the following:

1. Merits and implications of the recent Security Council resolution number 1511.
2. Restructuring of the Governing Council, the Presidency and the Subcommittees.
3. Determination of the mechanism and the nature of the relationship with the Civil Administration.
4. Consideration of the organization of the Secretariat according to paragraphs 2 and 3 above.
5. Submission of the proposal for the selection of the flag, the anthem and (national) symbol.
6. Dissolution of all committees which were established in the past to deal with the above issues.
7. The Secretariat shall hand over all draft resolutions and proposals concerning the above issues to the above mentioned committee so that the latter may submit its report by 10 November 2003.

Second: Establishment of a committee comprising the following persons:

1. Dr Mohammed Bahr al-Ulloum.
2. Dr Adil Abd al-Mehdi.
3. Dr Ruz Nuri Shawis.
4. Judge Dara Noorddin.
5. Dr Hajim al-Hasni.
6. Dr Ibrahim al-Jaafari.
7. Dr Adnan al-Pachachi.
8. Mr Younadem Kana.
9. Ms Sondul Chapouk.
10. Mr Hamid Majid Mousa.

[Signed] *Dr Mohsen Abdel al-Hamid*
Acting President of the Governing Council

Document 330

Governing Council Resolution Number 68 of 2003 [Appointment of the Presidents of the Sunni and Shiite Awqaf]

22 October 2003

In the name of God, the Merciful, the Compassionate: At its session held on 22 October 2003 the Governing Council decided the following:

1. Mr Hussain al-Shami is appointed President of the Shiite Waqf [Endowment] and Sheikh Jalal al-Din al-Saghir is appointed the Vice President.

2. Dr Adnan Muhammad Salman is appointed President of the Sunni Waqf [Endowment].

This resolution shall be effective from the above date.

[Signed] *Abdel-Aziz al-Hakim*
President of the Governing Council[48]

Document 331
Governing Council Resolution Number 69 of 2003 [Formation of a Committee to Discuss the Programmes for the Holy Month of Ramadan with Iraqi Media Officials]
22 October 2003

In the name of God, the Merciful, the Compassionate: At its session held on 22 October 2003 the Governing Council decided the following:

To form a committee, comprising of the persons whose names have been written below, in order to meet with officials of Iraqi media networks to discuss the programmes for the holy month of Ramadhan.

1. Mr Ezzelddine Salim.
2. Dr Sami al-Askari.
3. Mr Mohammed Hadi al-Asadi.

[Signed] *Abdel-Aziz al-Hakim*
President of the Governing Council[49]

Document 332
Governing Council Resolution Number 70 of 2003 [Referral of the Question of Liquidating the Oil-For-Food Programme to the Finance Committee]
27 October 2003

In the name of God, the Merciful, the Compassionate: The Council discussed the Ministry of Foreign Affairs' Memorandum number M/G/1/1/173 on 2 October 2003.

At its session held on 27 October 2003 the Governing Council decided the following:

To refer the subject of liquidating of the oil-for-food programme to the Finance Committee within the Council, which will seek the assistance of experts from the Ministry of Finance and the Iraqi Central Bank. These experts will offer recommendations pertaining to the subject to the Council within two weeks.

[Signed] *Dr Mohsen Abdel al-Hamid*
Acting President of the Governing Council[50]

[48] The resolution was accompanied by the following Note: 'There is no need for CPA involvement.'
[49] The resolution was accompanied by the following Note: 'There is no need for CPA involvement.'
[50] The resolution was accompanied by the following Note: 'There is no need for CPA involvement.'

Document 333
Governing Council Resolution Number 71 of 2003 [Request to Ambassador Bremer to Comment on Unaccounted Iraqi Funds]

27 October 2003

In the name of God, the Merciful, the Compassionate: At its session held on 27 October 2003 the Governing Council decided the following:

To request Ambassador Paul Bremer to comment on allegations published by the BBC and K.aid about four billion dollars from oil revenues, which he spent in Iraq without documenting the expenditures.[51] Also, in an attempt to maintain its transparency and unravel the truth, the Council agreed to present a report addressing the subject of the on-going debate in the American Congress; namely, the 1.7[52] billion dollars that the Congress allocated for the reconstruction of Iraq in 2003.

[Signed] *Dr Mohsen Abdel al-Hamid*
Acting President of the Governing Council[53]

Document 334
Governing Council Resolution Number 72 of 2003 [Change of Identity and Civil Status Register]

27 October 2003

In the name of God, the Merciful, the Compassionate: The Governing Council has reviewed the report on the issue of change of identity and civil status register and expressed sympathy with the sufferings of the many families inflicted by the decisions of the former regime. It has noted the sensitivity of the issue and its being against the injunctions of the Sharia' [Islamic law] and other laws.

The Governing Council at its session held on 27 October 2003 decided the following:

The decision on this issue is to be postponed to a later stage or after the approval of the Iraqi constitution and the establishment of an elected Iraqi government.

[Signed] *Dr Mohsen Abdel al-Hamid*
Acting President of the Governing Council[54]

[51] The resolution uses the term 'K.aid' which probably refers to the UK-based charity Christian Aid which on 23 October 2003 published a Briefing Paper for the Madrid donors conference on Iraq (23-24 October 2003) entitled 'Iraq: the missing billions. Transition and transparency in post-war Iraq' in which it claimed that 4 out of US$ 5 billion of Iraqi funds controlled by the CPA which had been reported as spent or allocated were unaccounted for (http://www.christianaid.org.uk/Images/iraq_the_missing_billions.pdf). The BBC reported about the Briefing Paper on the same day; see Charity says $4bn 'missing' in Iraq, BBC News, 23 October 2003, http://news.bbc.co.uk/1/hi/world/middle_east/3206841.stm.

[52] There seems to be a typographical error in the Arabic text which literally translates as '1 r 7'.

[53] The resolution was accompanied by the following Note: 'There is no need for CPA involvement.'

[54] The resolution was accompanied by the following Note: 'There is no need for CPA involvement.'

Document 335
Governing Council Resolution Number 73 of 2003
[Attaching of Institutions to the Governing Council]
27 October 2003

In the name of God, the Merciful, the Compassionate: In order to resolve the problem of attaching [for administrative purposes] some of the institutions that were previously under the supervision of the Presidency of the Republic (such as the Iraqi Academy of Science), the Governing Council at its session held on 27 October 2003 decided the following:

To attach the institutions above to the Governing Council, to be under the Governing Council's supervision.

[Signed] *Dr Mohsen Abdel al-Hamid*
Acting President of the Governing Council[55]

Document 336
Governing Council Resolution Number 74 of 2003
[Participation in Paris Club Meeting]
27 October 2003

In the name of God, the Merciful, the Compassionate: At its session held on 27 October 2003 the Governing Council decided the following:

To participate in the meeting of the Paris Club in order to work for the full writing off of Iraq's debts. The proposal to establish a delegation headed by one of the Council members is to be assigned to the Financial and Economic Committee. The Committee shall provide the members of the delegation with recommendations, instructions and policies of the Council before they are heading to the concerned States and the meeting of the Paris Club.

[Signed] *Dr Mohsen Abdel al-Hamid*
Acting President of the Governing Council

Document 337
Governing Council Resolution Number 75 of 2003
[Formation of a Committee to Study the Situation of Arab Students in Iraqi Universities]
28 October 2003

In the name of God, the Merciful, the Compassionate: At its session held on 28 October 2003 the Governing Council decided the following:

1. To form a committee composed of the Council members whose names are listed below in order to study the position of Arab students in Iraqi universities. The task of this committee shall be to determine the students whose admission was arranged by the

[55] The resolution was accompanied by the following Note: '[The resolution is] to be referred to the Cultural Committee.'

national leadership of the Ba'ath Party, to revoke their registration and to return them to their countries.

2. As for the other Arab students, it is necessary that their respective governments attest to their suitability before they may be permitted to continue with their studies.

3. No new Arab students are to be admitted this year.

Names:

1. Dr Mouwafak al-Rabii.
2. Sheikh Abdel-Karim al-Mohammedawi.
3. Mr Naseer al-Chaderchi.
4. Mr Mohammed Bahr al-Ulloum.
5. Mr Abdel-Aziz al-Hakim.
6. Dr Mohsen Abdel Hamid.
7. Mr Hamid Majid Mousa.

[Signed] *Abdel-Aziz al-Hakim*
President of the Governing Council

Document 338

Governing Council Resolution Number 76 of 2003 [Confiscation of Movable and Immovable Property of the Symbols of the Former Regime]

28 October 2003[56]

In the name of God, the Merciful, the Compassionate: At its session held on 28 October 2003 the Governing Council decided the following:

The movable and immovable property of the following symbols of the former regime are confiscated for the benefit of the State Treasury:

1. Saddam Hussein and members of his family to the second degree and those who have inherited from such members of his family and all members of his family proven to have misappropriated public funds.

2. Wanted criminals whose names are included in the attached list.[57]

3. The governors, military divisional commanders and commanders of oppressive institutions (intelligence service, national security bureau, special security organization, directorate of military intelligence, Saddam Fedayeen, general security, and others) of the brigade or director level and above, who are proven to have acquired funds in an illegal manner, unless they have shown their opposition to the bygone regime before 9 April 2003 and this has been substantiated in writing by one of the political groups represented in the Governing Council.

[Signed] *Abdel-Aziz al-Hakim*
President of the Governing Council[58]

[56] English text supplied by the International Center for Transitional Justice.

[57] List not available.

[58] The resolution was accompanied by two Notes which read:

'Note 1: Distribution of the decision to the nominated external agencies in order to block the funds and property belonging to those whose names are mentioned above, and to be considered properties of the Iraqi State and the undertaking of their return to the Iraqi Ministry of Finance according to custom.

Ministry of Interior to prepare a list of those [people] subjected to paragraph (3) above.'

Document 339
Governing Council Resolution Number 77 of 2003
[Evacuation of State-Owned Houses in the Republican Palace District Occupied by Members of the Repressive Organs of the Former Regime]
28 October 2003

In the name of God, the Merciful, the Compassionate: At its session held on 28 October 2003 the Governing Council decided the following:

1. To evacuate State-owned houses in the Republican Palace district occupied by members of the oppressive organs of the former regime.
2. The Governing Council is responsible for allocating these houses to those who deserve them.

[Signed] *Abdel-Aziz al-Hakim*
President of the Governing Council[59]

Document 340
Governing Council Resolution Number 78 of 2003
[Amendment to Governing Council Resolution Number 77]
3 November 2003

In the name of God, the Merciful, the Compassionate: At its session held on 3 November 2003 the Governing Council decided the following:

1. Paragraph 2 of Governing Council Resolution Number 77 issued on 28 October 2003 is to be amended and shall read as follows:
2. The Governing Council will instruct the Ministry of Housing and Construction to determine who will occupy these houses in the future.

[Signed] *Jalal Talabani*
President of the Governing Council

Document 341
Governing Council Resolution Number 79 of 2003
[Appointment of the President of the Waqf Office of Non-Muslim Communities]
3 November 2003

In the name of God, the Merciful, the Compassionate: Further to its resolution number 68 of 22 October 2003,[60] the Governing Council decided at its session held on 3 November 2003

Note 2: The CPA has agreed [to this resolution] but the de-Ba'athification Commission is to observe CPA Memorandum No 7 (But the Commission is to consult the CPA before implementation).'

[59] The resolution was accompanied by a Note which reads: 'The CPA has agreed; see CPA Memorandum No 7 (But the de-Baathification Commission is to consult the CPA before implementation). Amended by Resolution 78 of 2003.'

[60] See *Doc 330*.

the appointment of Mr. Abdallah al-Nofali as president of the waqf [religious endowment] office of non-Muslim communities.
[Signed] *Jalal Talbani*
President of the Governing Council

Document 342
Governing Council Resolution Number 80 of 2003
[Bringing a Lawsuit Against the Al-Jazeera and Al-Arabiyya Channels]
3 November 2003

In the name of God, the Merciful, the Compassionate: At its session held on 3 November 2003 the Governing Council decided the following:

To bring a lawsuit in the Iraqi courts against Al-Jazeera and Al-Arabiyya channels, and also against anyone else who commits the crimes of incitement and defamation against the Council. The prosecutions are to be brought by the General Prosecutor in Iraq under paragraphs 47, 48, and 49 of the Penal Code[61] and are to include financial compensation amounting to ten million dollars for every case.
[Signed] *Jalal Talbani*
President of the Governing Council

Document 343
Governing Council Resolution Number 81 of 2003
[Field Visits to the Governorates]
3 November 2003

In the name of God, the Merciful, the Compassionate: At its session held on 3 November 2003 the Governing Council decided the following:

The President of the Governing Council, the Members of the Council who are willing to do so, and the concerned Ministers shall conduct field visits to the governorates in order to learn about their conditions and needs. These visits shall start with the governorate of Karbala and the southern governorates, followed by Mosul, Kirkuk, Salah ad-Din, Anbar and Diyala.
[Signed] *Jalal Talbani*
President of the Governing Council

[61] Paragraphs 47, 48 and 49 of the Iraqi Penal Code – Law No 111 of 1969 – deal with parties (principals and accessories) to a crime.

Document 344
Governing Council Resolution Number 82 of 2003
[Formation of Advisory Boards to the Sunni and Shiite Awqaf]
5 November 2003

In the name of God, the Merciful, the Compassionate: At its session held on 5 November 2003 the Governing Council decided the following:

1. To establish advisory boards to the Sunni and Shiite awqaf [endowments] for the division and separation [of the endowments].
2. To divide the budget [of the endowments].
3. To authorize the president of the waqf [endowment] or three of his deputies to operate the accounts.

[Signed] *Jalal Talbani*
President of the Governing Council

Document 345
Governing Council Resolution Number 83 of 2003
[Granting all Ethnicities the Right to Be Taught in Their Mother Tongue alongside the Official Language]
5 November 2003

In the name of God, the Merciful, the Compassionate: At its session held on 5 November 2003 the Governing Council decided the following:

To grant all ethnicities – where educational requirements are met – the right to study in their mother tongues alongside the official language in Iraq.

[Signed] *Jalal Talbani*
President of the Governing Council

Document 346
Governing Council Resolution Number 84 of 2003
[Formation of Permanent Specialized Committees in the Governing Council in Order to Enable It to Exercise Its Powers of Supervision of the Work of the Ministries]
5 November 2003

In the name of God, the Merciful, the Compassionate: At its session held on 5 November 2003 the Governing Council decided the following:

The creation of permanent specialized committees in the Governing Council to enable it to exercise its power to supervise the work of the ministries and prepare draft resolutions and reports. The committees shall hold periodical meetings to achieve their objectives and meet with ministries on a periodical basis (without prejudice to the weekly meeting of the Governing Council with the Council of Ministers or the Governing Council's right to call on ministers to appear before it).

The committees will perform their task by submitting focused summaries in order for the Governing Council to examine and discuss them at the political and strategic level and take suitable decisions accordingly.

The committees created by the Governing Council are as follows:

1. Public Services Committee: It includes the following ministries and departments: Health, Electricity, Communication, Transport, Secretariat of the Capital and Municipalities. This Committee shall comprise of the following persons whose names are written below:

1. Judge Wael Abdul Latif.
2. Mr Ezzeddine Salim.
3. Sheikh Ghazi al-Yawer.
4. Sheikh Abd al-Karim al-Mohammedawi.
5. Mr Younadem Kana.
6. Dr Mouwafak al-Rabii.
7. Samir Shakir Sumaydah.

2. Financial and Planning Affairs Committee: It includes the following ministries and departments: Finance, Planning and Central Bank of Iraq. This Committee shall comprise of the following persons whose names are written below:

1. Dr Adnan al-Pachachi.
2. Mr Naseer al-Chaderchi.
3. Dr Iyad Allawi.
4. Dr Ahmed al-Chalabi.
5. Mr Abdel-Aziz al-Hakim.
6. Mr Samir Shakir Sumaydah.
7. Dr Mouwafak al-Rabii.
8. Dr Mohsin Abd Al-Hameed.

3. Economic Affairs Committee: It includes the following ministries: Agriculture, Industry and Minerals, Petroleum, Irrigation and Trade. This Committee shall comprise of the following persons whose names are written below:

1. Mr Salaheddine Muhammed Bahaaeddin.
2. Mr Massoud Barzani.
3. Dr Raja Habib al-Khuzaai.
4. Mr Mohammed Bahr al-Ulloum.
5. Judge Wael Abdul Latif.
6. Dr Ibrahim al-Jaafari.
7. Ms Sondul Chapouk.[62]
8. Mr Hamid Majid Mousa.

4. Education and Cultural Affairs Committee: It includes the following ministries: Training and Higher Education, Culture, and Science and Technology. This Committee shall comprise of the following persons whose names are written below:

1. Mr Abdel-Aziz al-Hakim.
2. Dr Mohsin Abd Al-Hameed.
3. Dr Raja Habib al-Khuzaai.
4. Dr Adnan al-Pachachi.

[62] Sometimes also referred to as 'Ms Sonkool Chapouk'.

5. Mr Mohammed Bahr al-Ulloum.
6. Dr Mouwafak al-Rabii.
7. [blank in original]
8. Mr Naseer al-Chaderchi.
9. Mr Younadem Kana.
10. Mr Massoud Barzani.
11. Ms Sondul Chapouk.
12. Mr Abdel-Karim Mahoud al-Mohammedawi.

5. Legal Affairs Committee: It includes the following ministries and departments: Justice, Human Rights, Awqaf [Endowments] Committee and Comptroller General. This Committee shall comprise of the following persons whose names are written below:

1. Mr Ahmad al-Barak.
2. Mr Naseer al-Chaderchi.
3. Judge Dara Noorddin.
4. Judge Wael Abdul Latif.
5. Dr Raja al-Khuzaai.
6. Dr Ahmed al-Chalabi.

6. Environment and Construction Committee: It includes the following ministries: Public Works, and Housing and Construction. This Committee shall comprise of the following persons whose names are written below:

1. Dr Adnan al-Pachachi.
2. Judge Wael Abdul Latif.
3. Salaheddine Bahaaeddin.
4. Mr Ezzeddine Salim.
5. Sheikh Ghazi Ajil al-Yawer.
6. Mr Hamid Majid Mousa.
7. Dr Iyad Allawi.

7. Social Affairs Committee: It includes the following ministries: Labour and Social Affairs, Sports and Youth, and Expatriates and Immigrants. This Committee shall comprise of the following persons whose names are written below:

1. Mr Jalal al-Talabani.
2. Judge Dara Noorddin.
3. Mr Naseer al-Chaderchi.
4. Dr Mahmoud Othman.
5. Mr Mohammed Bahr al-Ulloum.
6. Dr Iyad Allawi.

8. External Relations Committee: It includes Foreign and Interior Ministries. This Committee shall comprise of the following persons whose names are written below:

1. Dr Adnan al-Pachahi.
2. Dr Mahmoud Othman.
3. Dr Iyad Allawi.
4. Dr Ibrahim al-Jaafari.
5. Mr Hamid Majid.
6. Mr Samir Sumaydah.
7. Mr Abdel-Aziz al-Hakim.
8. Mr Younadem Kana.
9. Mr Ahmad al-Barak.

10. Sheikh Ghazi Ajil al-Yawer.

9. National Security Committee: It includes the Ministry of the Interior and the Ministry of Provinces. This Committee shall comprise of the following persons whose names are written below:

1. Mr Jalal al-Talabani.
2. Dr Mohsen Abdel Hamid.
3. Dr Iyad Allawi.
4. Dr Ahmed al-Chalabi.
5. Mr Abdel-Aziz al-Hakim.
6. Dr Ibrahim al-Jaafari.
7. Mr Massoud Barzani.
8. Sheikh Abdel-Karim al-Mohammedawi.
9. Ms Sondul Chapouk.
10. Mr Samir Sumaydah.
11. Sheikh Ghazi Ajil al-Yawer.
12. Mr Hamid Majid Mousa.

Bodies and committees to supervise the official departments and semi-official departments not related to any ministry:

10. Committee for De-Ba'athification: This Committee shall comprise of the following persons whose names are written below:[63]

1. Mr Younadem Kana.
2. Ms Sondul Chapouk.
3. Dr Mouwafak al-Rabii.
4. Sheikh Abdel-Karim al-Mohammedawi.
5. Mr Abdel-Aziz al-Hakim.
6. Mr Salaheddine Mohammed.
7. Dr Raja al-Khuzaai.
8. Dr Ahmed al-Chalabi.
9. Mr Jalal al-Talabani.
10. Dr Ibrahim al-Jaafari.

11. Media Committee: This Committee shall comprise of the following persons whose names are written below:

1. Dr Mahmoud Othman.
2. Ms Sondul Chapouk.
3. Mr Younadem Kana.
4. Dr Mouwafak al-Rabii.
5. Mr Samir Sumaydah.
6. Dr Adnan al-Pachachi.
7. Mr Abdel-Aziz al-Hakim.
8. Dr Ibrahim al-Jaafari.
9. Mr Mohammed Bahr al-Ulloum.
10. Dr Iyad Allawi.

12. Committee for Citizens and Social Affairs: This Committee shall comprise of the following persons whose names are written below:

1. Dr Mahmoud Othman.

[63] For the (11) members of the Higher National De-Ba'athification Commission, see above IGC Resolution No 21 of 2003 *[Doc 284]*.

2. Judge Dara Noorddin.
3. Mr Abdel-Aziz al-Hakim.
4. Dr Iyad Allawi.
5. Dr Ibrahim al-Jaafari.
6. Dr Mohsen Abdel Hamid.
7. Sheikh Abdel-Karim al-Mohammedawi.
8. Salaheddine Mohammed Bahaaeddin.
9. Mr Mohammed Bahr al-Ulloum.
10. Mr Ahmad al-Barak.
11. Dr Raja al-Khuzaai.

[Signed] *Jalal Talbani*
President of the Governing Council[64]

Document 347
Governing Council Resolution Number 85 of 2003 [Arabian Gulf Academy for Maritime Studies]
4 November 2003

In the name of God, the Merciful, the Compassionate: At its session held on 4 November 2003 the Governing Council decided the following:

To link the Arabian Gulf Academy for Maritime Studies which was under the dissolved Ministry of Defence with the Ministry of Transport.

This resolution is in effect from the date of the adoption of this resolution.

[Signed] *Jalal Talbani*
President of the Governing Council[65]

Document 348
Governing Council Resolution Number 86 of 2003 [Personnel in the Office of Non-Muslim Communities]
5 November 2003

In the name of God, the Merciful, the Compassionate: At its session held on 5 November 2003 the Governing Council decided the following:

1. The Vice Chairman of the Office of Non-Muslim Communities from the Eastern Church shall have the rank of Director-General.
2. From every non-Muslim community there shall be an officer in this Office with the rank of Director.

[Signed] *Jalal Talbani*
President of the Governing Council[66]

[64] The resolution was accompanied by a Note which reads: 'There is no need for CPA involvement.'

[65] The resolution was accompanied by the following Note: 'There is no need for CPA intervention, although we advise the Committee on Public Services to follow up on this matter.'

[66] The resolution was accompanied by the following Note: 'No need for CPA involvement.'

Document 349
Governing Council Resolution Number 87 of 2003 [Repeal of All Resolutions and Directives Ordering the Confiscation of the Property, Closure, Merger, and Cancellation of the Licences of Colleges, Schools and Community Institutes]

5 November 2003

In the name of God, the Merciful, the Compassionate: At its session held on 5 November 2003 the Governing Council decided the following:

1. To repeal all the resolutions and directives which have ordered the confiscation of the property, closure, merger, and cancellation of the licences belonging to colleges, schools, and community institutes.
2. Licences are to be restored to these colleges and schools, along with their full rights.

[Signed] *Jalal Talbani*
President of the Governing Council[67]

Document 350
Governing Council Resolution Number 88 of 2003 [Seizure of Movable and Immovable Property of Officials of the Former Regime]

4 November 2003

In the name of God, the Merciful, the Compassionate: At its session held on 4 November 2003 the Governing Council decided the following:

1. The seizure of the moveable and immoveable property of the officials of the former regime, the senior members of the dissolved Ba'ath Party and the security services, and that of their wives, children, relatives and agents.
2. The stay of implementation of Resolution No 1198 of 1977, amended by resolution No 1426 of 1983,[68] with regard to cases which have been filed, or will be filed, against the persons included in paragraph (1) above.

[67] The resolution was accompanied by the following Note: 'The CPA requires the referral of this resolution to the Education Committee.'

[68] The two resolutions deal with remedies in the event of a breach of certain contracts for the sale of real property. They set a limit on the amount of damages that may be recovered upon breach of a sales contract; the limit being the difference between the value of the property at the time of the contract and the value at the time of the breach. If the buyer lived in the property or constructed buildings on the property, without opposition from the seller, then the measure of damages is increased by the value of the buildings on the property (BearingPoint, *USAID Iraq Economic Governance II: Diagnostic Report – Real Property Law and Registration*, 8 March 2005, 17).

[69] On 22 June 2004, it was reported in the Iraqi press that the Director General of the Department of Real Estate Registration of the Iraqi Ministry of Justice, Abdallah Ghazi Salman, had announced that resolution no 88 which had been issued by the Governing Council in 2003 to stop any transactions relating to the transfer of ownership of land belonging to officials of the former regime as well as employees of the security services, remained in effect until the Iraqis would become sovereign on the 30th of the current month, and had discussed the options of either abolishing it or maintaining it.

3. This resolution shall come into effect from the date of its issuance.[69]

[Signed] *Jalal Talbani*
President of the Governing Council[70]

Document 351
Governing Council Resolution Number 89 of 2003 [Formation of a Committee of the Governing Council to Study the Protection of Iraqi Aircraft]
22 October 2003

In the name of God, the Merciful, the Compassionate: At its session held on 22 October 2003 the Governing Council decided the following:

To form a committee, which will include the individuals listed below, to study the protection of Iraqi aircraft and determine the necessary budgets for such an endeavour:

1. Mr Ahmad al-Barak.
2. Sheikh Abdel-Karim al-Mohammedawi.
3. Mr Muhyi Kadhem al-Khatib.

[Signed] *Jalal Talabani*
President of the Governing Council[71]

Document 352
Governing Council Resolution Number 90 of 2003 [Halting of All Plans or Activities for the Privatization of State-Owned Enterprises and Institutions]
4 November 2003

In the name of God, the Merciful, the Compassionate: At its session held on 4 November 2003 the Governing Council decided the following:

To halt all plans or activities aimed at privatizing State-owned enterprises and institutions, in order to carefully examine the state of these enterprises and institutions, then weigh the socio-economic and political repercussions of their privatization. The Council's Finance Committee will follow up on this matter according to the financial needs of the State and the economic criteria that should be adopted in this regard.

[Signed] *Jalal Talabani*
President of the Governing Council[72]

[70] The resolution was accompanied by the following Note: 'The CPA has agreed; refer to the observation in CPA Memorandum No 7 (But on the de-Ba'athification Commission).'

[71] The resolution was accompanied by the following Note: 'To be referred to the Committee on Public Services.'

[72] The resolution was accompanied by the following Note: 'To be referred to the Economic Affairs Committee.'

Document 353
Governing Council Resolution Number 91 of 2003
[Salary and Monthly Allowances for a Deputy Member of the Governing Council]

4 November 2003

In the name of God, the Merciful, the Compassionate: At its session held on 4 November 2003 the Governing Council decided the following:

The salary and monthly allowances for a deputy member of the Governing Council shall be allocated as follows:

1,000 dollars as monthly salary.

2,000 dollars as monthly housing allowance.

500 dollars as monthly catering/hospitality allowance.

160 dollars monthly salary for each of his six security guards.

[Signed] *Jalal Talabani*
President of the Governing Council

Document 354
Governing Council Resolution Number 92 of 2003
[Payment of Monthly Rent Allowance to Ministers with Retroactive Effect]

4 November 2003

In the name of God, the Merciful, the Compassionate: At its session held on 4 November 2003 the Governing Council decided the following:

An amount of 2,000 dollars shall be paid as monthly rent allowance to the honourable ministers with retroactive effect.

[Signed] *Jalal Talabani*
President of the Governing Council

Document 355
Governing Council Resolution Number 93 of 2003
[Cancellation of All Property Taxes]

4 November 2003

In the name of God, the Merciful, the Compassionate: At its session held on 4 November 2003 the Governing Council decided the following:

All property taxes, both basic and additional, for the year 2003 shall be cancelled for the citizens as is the case with respect to income tax.

[Signed] *Jalal Talabani*
President of the Governing Council[73]

[73] The resolution was accompanied by the following Note: 'Refer to the Ministries of Finance and Planning.'

Document 356
Governing Council Resolution Number 94 of 2003
[Use of Intelligence Services Funds for De-Ba'athification]
9 November 2003

In the name of God, the Merciful, the Compassionate: At its session held on 9 November 2003 the Governing Council decided the following:

It is herewith approved to allocate the funds obtained from the accounts of the dissolved intelligence services in the amount of (1,200,000,000) one billion two hundred million Iraqi dinars and 208 thousand US dollars to cover the expenses of the Higher National De-Ba'athification Commission and its branches in the governorates.

[Signed] *Jalal Talbani*
President of the Governing Council

Document 357
Governing Council Resolution Number 95 of 2003
[Salaries of Ministers]
10 November 2003

In the name of God, the Merciful, the Compassionate: At its session held on 10 November 2003 the Governing Council decided the following:

Upon the recommendation of the Minister of Finance, the salaries of the Ministers shall be as follows:

1,200 dollars monthly salary.
2,000 dollars housing allowance.
500 dollars for catering/hospitality.

[Signed] *Jalal Talbani*
President of the Governing Council

Document 358
Governing Council Resolution Number 96 of 2003
[Change of Name of the Ministry of Planning]
10 November 2003

In the name of God, the Merciful, the Compassionate: Considering the current tasks being undertaking by the Ministry of Planning, the Governing Council at its session held on 10 November 2003 decided the following:

The name of the Ministry of Planning shall be changed to Ministry of Planning and Development Cooperation.

[Signed] *Jalal Talbani*
President of the Governing Council

Document 359
Governing Council Resolution Number 97 of 2003 [Loans Given to Peasants and Farmers]
10 November 2003

In the name of God, the Merciful, the Compassionate: At its session held on 10 November 2003 the Governing Council decided the following:

To lower interest rates on loans given to peasants and farmers, to reschedule the debts they already owe, and to abolish all interest on loans between the date that marks the fall of the former regime and the end of the year 2003.

[Signed] *Jalal Talbani*
President of the Governing Council[74]

Document 360
Governing Council Resolution Number 98 of 2003 [Nomination of the Members of the Advisory Boards to the Sunni and Shiite Awqaf]
11 November 2003

In the name of God, the Merciful, the Compassionate:

This is subsequent to Governing Council resolution number 82 of 5 November 2003.[75]

At its session held on 11 November 2003 the Governing Council decided the following:

An advisory board be established to the Sunni and Shiite awqaf [endowments] for the task of division and separation [of the endowments].

Members of the advisory board to the Shiite waqf [endowment]:

1. Mr Hussain al-Shami – President of the waqf
2. Sheikh Jalal al-Din al-Saghir – Vice President of the waqf
3. Sheikh Abd al Azeem al-Baka
4. Mr Muhammad Ahmad Hussain – Manager of the religious foundations and shrines
5. Mr Sabri Rasn al-Saa'di – Deputy Manager of the body of investment and protection of endowment properties
6. Mr Nazaar al-Wa'eli
7. Mr Falah Hassan al-Kahjee
8. Mr Haithm Na'eef al-Ansari

Members of the advisory board to the Sunni waqf [endowment]:

1. Dr Adnan Muhammad Salman
2. Lawyer Abdallah Ibrahim Saeed
3. Mr Khalid Abd al Kareem al-Ma'mar
4. Mr Khalid Abd al-Hadi al-Ghawas
5. Mr Salim Saleh Mahdi
6. Mr Falah Abd al Jabbar
7. Mr Abbas Shakr Mahmood

[74] The resolution was accompanied by the following Note: 'There is no need for CPA involvement, but we do advise a follow up by both the Citizen Affairs Committee and the Finance Committee.'

[75] See *Doc 344*.

[Signed] *Jalal Talbani*
President of the Governing Council

Document 361
Governing Council Resolution Number 99 of 2003 [Formation of a Committee to Implement Security Council Resolution Number 1511]
11 November 2003

In the name of God, the Merciful, the Compassionate: At its session held on 11 November 2003 the Governing Council decided the following:

To form a committee, which includes the individuals listed below, to implement Security Council resolution number 1511[76] and to prepare a timetable in order to fulfill the obligations mentioned therein.

1. Dr Adnan Pachachi
2. Dr Mahmoud Othman
3. Mr Hamid Majid
4. Dr Mohammed Bahr al-Ulloum
5. Dr Iyad Allawi
6. Dr Ibrahim al-Jaafari
7. Mr Naseer al-Chaderchi
8. Mr Abdel-Aziz al-Hakim
9. Mr Ahmad Shiya' al-Barak
10. Judge Dara Noorddin
11. Mr Younadem Kana
12. Mr Massoud Barzani represented by Dr Ruz Nuri Shawis
13. Ms Sondul Chapouk
14. Mr Jalal Talabani represented by Fuad Ma'sum

[Signed] *Jalal Talbani*
President of the Governing Council[77]

Document 362
Governing Council Resolution Number 100 of 2003 [Formulating the Rules for a Basic Law for the Administration of the State During the Transitional Period]
11 November 2003

In the name of God, the Merciful, the Compassionate: At its session held on 11 November 2003 the Governing Council decided the following:

[76] See *Doc 531*.
[77] The resolution was accompanied by the following Note: 'There is no need for involvement of the coalition administration.'

The respectable members of the Council will formulate the rules for a basic law which will determine the administration of the State during the transitional period seeking, at their discretion, assistance from experts to facilitate the smooth operation of their work.
[Signed] *Jalal Talbani*
President of the Governing Council[78]

Document 363
Governing Council Resolution Number 101 of 2003 [Reinstatement of Former Civil Service Employees]
10 November 2003

In the name of God, the Merciful, the Compassionate: At its session held on 10 November 2003 the Governing Council decided the following:

1. Any employee who resigned from the civil service after 1991 or was considered to have resigned for having left his post then, is to be reinstated.
2. Retirement rights are to be allocated to the family of a deceased employee who had resigned from his position after 1991, or was considered to have resigned for having left his post then and whose service pension reached 15.
3. This decision is to be implemented upon its issuance; and it must be published in the Official Gazette.[79]

All ministers and concerned bodies shall implement this decision.
[Signed] *Jalal Talbani*
President of the Governing Council[80]

Document 364
Governing Council Resolution Number 102 of 2003 [Financial Authority of the President of the Sunni Waqf]
11 November 2003

In the name of God, the Merciful, the Compassionate: Pursuant to resolution number 82[81] the Governing Council at its session held on 11 November 2003 decided the following:

The President of the Sunni Waqf is granted financial authority within the limits of the budget and investment plan. The President is also given control of the revenues of the management body and the investments of the Sunni Waqf. He may authorise other persons to complete approved projects and disburse funds at the expense of the Waqf.
[Signed] *Jalal Talbani*
President of the Governing Council[82]

[78] The resolution was accompanied by the following Note: 'There is no need for involvement of the coalition administration.'
[79] This resolution, like all other resolutions of the IGC, was never published in the Official Gazette.
[80] The resolution was accompanied by the following Note: 'To be referred to the Legal and Financial Committees.'
[81] See *Doc 344*.
[82] The resolution was accompanied by the following Note: 'There is no need for involvement of the coalition administration.'

Document 365
Governing Council Resolution Number 103 of 2003 [Salary and Monthly Allowances for a Member of the Governing Council]
12 November 2003

In the name of God, the Merciful, the Compassionate: At its session held on 12 November 2003 the Governing Council decided the following:

The salary and monthly allowances for a member of the Governing Council shall be determined as follows:

1,500 dollars monthly salary.

2,000 dollars housing allowance.

500 dollars for catering/hospitality.

The salary of the staff shall increase 140 dollars per person.

This resolution shall be effective from 1 November 2003.

[Signed] *Jalal Talbani*
President of the Governing Council[83]

Document 366
Governing Council Resolution Number 104 of 2003 [Priority of the Families of Martyrs and Political Prisoners over Ba'athists in Awarding Study Grants and Fellowships]
16 November 2003

In the name of God, the Merciful, the Compassionate: At its session held on 16 November 2003 the Governing Council decided the following:

The families of the martyrs and political prisoners, who suffered from the injustice of the previous dictatorial regime, shall be given priority over the Ba'athists in awarding study grants and fellowships.

[Signed] *Jalal Talbani*
President of the Governing Council[84]

[83] The resolution was accompanied by the following Note: 'To be referred to the Finance Committee.'

[84] The resolution was accompanied by the following Note: 'The decision requires approval of the coalition administration for its implementation (the coalition administration requires specific information about the types of Ba'athists and those who will make such grants both the nature of the missions, and the source of financing them).'

Document 367

Governing Council Resolution Number 105 of 2003 [Formation of National Committees in the Ministries with Responsibility to Fight Bribery and Corruption]

16 November 2003

In the name of God, the Merciful, the Compassionate: At its session held on 16 November 2003 the Governing Council decided the following:

A National Committee shall be established in every ministry with the responsibility to fight against bribery and administrative corruption.

[Signed] *Jalal Talbani*
President of the Governing Council[85]

Document 368

Governing Council Resolution Number 106 of 2003 [Dissolution of the Board of Directors of the Federation of Iraqi Industries]

15 November 2003

In the name of God, the Merciful, the Compassionate: At its session held on 15 November 2003 the Governing Council decided the following:

1. To dissolve the current Board of Directors of the Federation of Iraqi Industries.
2. The interim Board of Directors of the Federation will be composed of the following individuals:

Qays Kathim al-Kafaji	Hashim Thunun 'Ali al-Atraqji
As'ad Baqr Watut	Basim Jamil Antwan
Kathim Turki Jamil	Sa'id 'Abd al-Jabar al-Shukraji
Husayn 'Ali Ahmad	

[These individuals will serve] until elections can be held for a new Board of Directors.

3. This resolution is in effect from the date of its publication.

[Signed] *Jalal Talbani*
President of the Governing Council[86]

[85] The resolution was accompanied by the following Note: 'There is no need for involvement of the Coalition administration.'

[86] The resolution was accompanied by the following Note: 'To be referred to the Social Affairs Committee.' Resolution no 106 was abolished through the issuance of resolution no 3 of 2004 *[Doc 406]*.

Document 369
Governing Council Resolution Number 107 of 2003 [Repeal of the Disbanded Revolutionary Command Council's Resolution Number 368 of 9 September 1990]
18 November 2003

In the name of God, the Merciful, the Compassionate: At its session held on 18 November 2003 the Governing Council decided the following:

1. To repeal resolution number 368 issued on 9th September 1990 by the dissolved Revolutionary Command Council, which allowed the employment of children aged twelve years and more in the private, mixed, and cooperative sectors.
2. This decision is to be implemented upon its publication in the Official Gazette.[87]

[Signed] *Abdel-Aziz al-Hakim*
Acting President of the Governing Council[88]

Document 370
Governing Council Resolution Number 108 of 2003 [Popular Campaign to Remove All Vestiges of the Former Regime]
19 November 2003

In the name of God, the Merciful, the Compassionate: At its session held on 19 November 2003 the Governing Council decided the following:

To launch a popular campaign throughout Iraq, in connection with the Higher National De-Ba'athification Commission and the relevant government organs, to wipe out all vestiges of the deposed dictatorial regime and the disbanded Ba'ath Party, such as statues, murals, pictures and sayings of the tyrant Saddam, and slogans of the Ba'ath Party inscribed on walls.
[Signed] *Abdel-Aziz al-Hakim*
Acting President of the Governing Council[89]

Document 371
Governing Council Resolution Number 109 of 2003 [Seizure of the Broadcasting Equipment of the Al-Arabiyya Statellite Channel]
23 November 2003

In the name of God, the Merciful, the Compassionate: At its session held on 23 November 2003 the Governing Council decided the following:

[87] This resolution, like all other resolutions of the IGC, was never published in the Official Gazette.
[88] The resolution was accompanied by the following Note: 'To be referred to the Social Affairs Committee/ re-draw the policies of child labour.'
[89] The resolution was accompanied by the following Note: 'There is no need for involvement of the Coalition administration.'

1. To undertake all necessary and immediate steps to prevent al-Arabiyya satellite channel from broadcasting, through its studios in Iraq, videos inciting violence in the country. In order to achieve this goal, the Council will seize all the equipment used in connecting these studios to satellite broadcasting, and will prevent the employees from broadcasting via satellite until further notice.

2. These measures shall remain in effect until the satellite channel mentioned in paragraph 1 provides the Council with a written undertaking not to broadcast news and not to show films that incite violence, and to remain committed to following Iraqi rules and regulations, as well as the principles of responsible mass media.

3. To close the offices of the channel mentioned in paragraph 1 above, and to prevent it from ever broadcasting from Iraq again, should it not abide by the rules set out in paragraph 2 above.

4. This decision shall be implemented upon its issuance.

The Minister of the Interior as well as the relevant authorities must implement this decision.

[Signed] *Jalal Talbani*
President of the Governing Council[90]

Document 372

Governing Council Resolution Number 110 of 2003 [Removal from Office of the Governor of Babylon]

23 November 2003

In the name of God, the Merciful, the Compassionate: Based on the recommendations made by the Governing Council's Investigative Committee and the Council's decision of 17 November 2003, and based on the active participation of Mr Iskandar Jawad Witwit, the current governor of Babylon, in the dissolved Ba'ath Party – a fact that is incompatible with the decision taken by the Coalition Provisional Authority on 15 May 2003 to prevent members of the dissolved Ba'ath Party from occupying leadership positions; and further based on the documents reviewed by the Committee which have proven the misuse of public funds, the abuse of his position, and the fact that people in his province are extremely dissatisfied.

The Iraqi Governing Council at its session held on 11 November 2003 decided the following:

1. To release Mr Iskandar Jawad Witwit, governor of Babylon, from his post as governor.

2. To refer him to investigation on the grounds that he is accused of breaching human rights, being involved in corruption, and stealing government funds.

The decision is to be implemented from the date stated above.

[Signed] *Jalal Talbani*
President of the Governing Council[91]

[90] The resolution was accompanied by the following Note: 'The special statement pertaining to the closure of al-Arabiyya, and which developed into resolution no 109.'

[91] The resolution was accompanied by the following Note: 'Needs a decision by the coalition administration in order to be implemented.'

Document 373
Governing Council Resolution Number 111 of 2003 [Repeal of Acts Depriving Iraqis of Their Nationality]
29 November 2003

In the name of God, the Merciful, the Compassionate: At its session held on 29 November 2003 the Governing Council decided the following:

1. To repeal all resolutions, instructions, announcements, and orders which decreed the withdrawal, suspension or cancellation of Iraqi nationality from Iraqi individuals since 1958, allowing the mentioned individuals to therefore enjoy Iraqi nationality.
2. To abolish anything, which could prevent courts from hearing cases relating to nationality; and to have these courts work in accordance with the general jurisdiction of the judiciary.
3. To restore all legal rights accordingly.

[Signed] *Jalal Talbani*
President of the Governing Council[92]

Document 374
Governing Council Resolution Number 112 of 2003 [Response to the United Arab Emirates' Generous Offer to Organize a Unified Civil Identity Card for All Iraqi Citizens]
29 November 2003

In the name of God, the Merciful, the Compassionate: At its session held on 29 November 2003 the Governing Council decided the following:

To respond to the generous offer of the United Arab Emirates to organize the unified civil identity card for all Iraqi citizens, in an attempt to boost democratic change and assist the constitutional process. The Council will assign the task of coordinating with the Emirati side to the Ministry of the Interior.

[Signed] *Jalal Talbani*
President of the Governing Council[93]

Document 375
Governing Council Resolution Number 113 of 2003 [Security of the Governing Council]
30 November 2003

In the name of God, the Merciful, the Compassionate: At its extraordinary session held on 30 November 2003 the Governing Council decided the following:

[92] The resolution was accompanied by the following Note: 'Consult [resolution no] 117 and [resolution no] 118. To be referred to the Legal Committee.'

[93] The resolution was accompanied by the following Note: 'Refer to the Finance and Planning Committee, the National Security Committee.'

The Governing Council shall require the Coalition Provisional Authority to handover to the Council responsibility for its security. A security committee shall be formed by the Governing Council under the chairmanship of an Iraqi officer to undertake this task and to appoint security personnel from one, two or three Iraqi bodies from within the Council, in cooperation with the Iraqi police force.
[Signed] *Jalal Talbani*
President of the Governing Council[94]

Document 376
Governing Council Resolution Number 114 of 2003 [Conducting a Population Census]

30 November 2003

In the name of God, the Merciful, the Compassionate: At its session held on 30 November 2003 the Governing Council decided the following:

To conduct a population census and to request the Central Bureau of Statistics and Development Coordination to continue its efforts to extend its cooperation with the Governorate of Sulaimaniyah and the other governorates in order to complete this mission.
[Signed] *Jalal Talbani*
President of the Governing Council[95]

Document 377
Governing Council Resolution Number 115 of 2003 [Formation of an Engineering Committee in the Ministry of Construction and Housing]

30 November 2003

In the name of God, the Merciful, the Compassionate: At its session held on 30 November 2003 the Governing Council decided the following:

To form an Engineering Committee in the Ministry of Construction and Housing. The Ministry of Municipalities, the Ministry of Finance, and the Awqaf [Endowment] Offices shall cooperate with the Engineering Committee for drawing up plans for the shrine of Martyr Ayatollah Sayyid Muhammad Baqir al-Hakim (may God be pleased with him) and the institutions adjacent to it. The design of the shrine shall be commensurate with Iraqi architectural engineering, Islamic heritage and the personality of the Martyr.
[Signed] *Jalal Talbani*
President of the Governing Council[96]

[94] The resolution was accompanied by the following Note: 'Refer to the subcommittees associated with the National Security Council.'

[95] The resolution was accompanied by the following Note: 'This resolution is to be referred to the Committee on Financial Affairs and Planning; this resolution may no longer be needed.'

[96] The resolution was accompanied by the following Note: 'There is no need for involvement of the Coalition administration.'

Document 378
Governing Council Resolution Number 116 of 2003 [Formation of a Committee of Honourable Members of the Presidency to Study the Topic of Elections]

30 November 2003

In the name of God, the Merciful, the Compassionate: At its session held on 30 November 2003 the Governing Council decided the following:

To form a committee, consisting of honourable members of the presidency, in order to study the topic of elections. It shall submit its recommendations to the Council within a week. In these recommendations, the committee shall take into account the issues raised in the Council, which include security problems. The Council will have the final authority and believes in the principle of participation of the people in the institutions and the search for possible ways to achieve this goal.

[Signed] *Jalal Talbani*
President of the Governing Council[97]

Document 379
Governing Council Resolution Number 117 of 2003 [Repeal of Acts Depriving Iraqis of their Nationality]

29 November 2003

In the name of God, the Merciful, the Compassionate: At its session held on 29 November 2003 the Governing Council decided the following:

1. All resolutions, directives, instructions and orders effecting the withdrawal, suspension or cancellation of nationality from Iraqis since 1958 are hereby repealed.
2. All those whose citizenship was cancelled, suspended or withdrawn shall be considered as holders of Iraqi nationality with all the rights that this nationality confers with retrospective effect.
3. All legislation and administrative decisions that prevent the Iraqi judiciary from adjudicating nationality related disputes are hereby cancelled and the judiciary is entrusted with the authority to resolve such disputes in accordance with its official mandate.
4. This resolution shall be effective from the date of its issuance and shall be published in the Official Gazette.
5. The Minister of the Interior, the Minister of Justice and all other concerned official bodies shall implement this resolution.

[Signed] *Jalal Talbani*
President of the Governing Council[98]

[97] The resolution was accompanied by the following Note: 'There is no need for involvement of the Coalition administration.'

[98] The resolution was accompanied by the following Note: 'Consult resolution no 111 above. To be referred to the Legal Committee.'

Document 380
Governing Council Resolution Number 118 of 2003
[Establishment of a Committee to Deal With the Issue of Mass Graves]

1 December 2003

In the name of God, the Merciful, the Compassionate: At its session held on 1 December 2003 the Governing Council decided the following:

1. To form a Committee comprising the Ministers of Health, Justice, Interior and Human Rights, as well as the Media Officer, to deal with the issue of mass graves.
2. The Committee shall deal with the following tasks:
   A. Check the identities of the martyrs by consulting the available documents or by resorting to examination.
   B. Bury the martyrs' corpses again according to rituals worthy of their martyrdom.
   C. Document the discoveries of mass graves and bury the martyrs' corpses again.

[Signed] *Abdel-Aziz al-Hakim*
President of the Governing Council

Document 381
Governing Council Resolution Number 119 of 2003
[Trade Unions, Professional Associations and Societies]

2 December 2003

In the name of God, the Merciful, the Compassionate: At its session held on 2 December 2003 the Governing Council decided the following:

1. To entrust the Governing Council's Committee on Civil Society Affairs with the implementation of resolution number 27 of 2003[99] which requires the preparation of a comprehensive study on the situation of trade unions, professional associations and societies, in an attempt to put forward the required recommendations for the removal of any obstacles or irregularities that may hinder their proper functioning.
2. Not to follow the guidance provides by the General Secretariat of the Governing Council in its document number M/Associations/854, dated 6 November 2003; and not to account for the repercussions deriving from that issue.
3. This resolution shall come into effect as of the date of its issuance. The concerned parties must work on implementing this decision.

[Signed] *Abdel-Aziz al-Hakim*
President of the Governing Council[100]

[99] In some versions the reference is to resolution no 28 of 2003. See above n 19.

[100] The resolution was accompanied by the following Note: 'To be referred to the Social Affairs Committee.' See also Resolution 3 of 2004 *[Doc 406]*.

Document 382
Governing Council Resolution Number 121 of 2003
[Appointment of Staff of the Secretariat of the Governing Council]
2 December 2003

In the name of God, the Merciful, the Compassionate: At its session held on 2 December 2003 the Governing Council decided the following:

1. Cancellation of all administrative orders related to the appointment of permanent staff of the Secretariat of the Governing Council which have not received the approval of the Council.
2. Formation of a committee, composed of members of the Council, to take up the task of selecting candidates for appointment to the staff of the Secretariat:
   A. Dr Mouwafak al-Rabii.
   B. Sheikh Abdel-Karim al-Mohammedawi.
   C. Sheikh Ghazi Ajil al-Yawer.
   D. Judge Dara Noorddin.
   E. Mr Naseer al-Chaderchi.

[Signed] *Abdel-Aziz al-Hakim*
President of the Governing Council[101]

Document 383
Governing Council Resolution Number 122 of 2003
[Formation of a High-Level Committee for Hajj Affairs]
2 December 2003

In the name of God, the Merciful, the Compassionate: At its session held on 2 December 2003 the Governing Council decided the following:

To establish a high-level committee for matters related to the Hajj comprising of the persons whose names have been noted below. The committee shall be assigned the task of contacting all the concerned parties in order to ensure a successful campaign this year and to project an image that is suited to a new Iraq. The persons are:

1. Ibrahim al-Jaafari
2. Mohsen Abdel Hamid
3. Mr Slah [Salahadin] Mohammed Baha al-Din
4. Mr Hussain al-Shami
5. Dr Adnan Muhammad Salman
6. Sheikh Jalal al-Din al-Saghir

[Signed] *Abdel-Aziz al-Hakim*
President of the Governing Council[102]

[101] The resolution was accompanied by the following Note: 'There is no need for involvement of the Coalition administration.'

[102] The resolution was accompanied by the following Note: 'There is no need for involvement of the Coalition administration.'

Document 384
Governing Council Resolution Number 123 of 2003
[Travel Abroad by Iraqi Delegations]

2 December 2003

In the name of God, the Merciful, the Compassionate: At its session held on 2 December 2003 the Governing Council decided the following:

1. No Iraqi delegations are allowed to partake in conferences, meetings and round-table discussions outside Iraq, or to pay official visits to foreign bodies, unless a decision is issued in this regard by the President of the Governing Council.
2. The President of the Governing Council will adopt the decision concerning the formation of delegations, and their participation in the above-mentioned activities and, in regular cases, will bring the matter before the Council; in emergency cases, the President can adopt the decision without having recourse to the Governing Council.
3. This resolution will be in effect as from the date of its issuance.

The Ministers and the stakeholders must implement this resolution.

[Signed] *Abdel-Aziz al-Hakim*
President of the Governing Council[103]

Document 385
Governing Council Resolution Number 124 of 2003
[Election of Dr Salamah Al-Khafaji as Member of the Governing Council]

8 December 2003

In the name of God, the Merciful, the Compassionate: At its session held on 8 December 2003 the Governing Council decided the following:

Dr Salamah al-Khafaji is elected as member of the Governing Council in place of martyred Dr Aquila al-Hashimi by winning the majority votes of the members of the Council.

[Signed] *Abdel-Aziz al-Hakim*
President of the Governing Council[104]

[103] The resolution was accompanied by the following Note: 'To be referred to the Committee of Citizens and Social Affairs.'

[104] The resolution was accompanied by the following Note: 'There is no need for involvement of the Coalition administration.'

Document 386
Governing Council Resolution Number 125 of 2003
[Formation of a National Media Authority]
8 December 2003

In the name of God, the Merciful, the Compassionate: At its ordinary session held on 8 December 2003 the Governing Council decided the following:

1. To form a National Media Authority, which deals with the following matters:
    a. Putting together a media strategy.
    b. Regulating media outlets (satellite channels, news agencies).
    c. Following up on financial matters [funds and property] of the dissolved Ministry of Information.
2. To allow this Authority to become an executive committee within the Council, so that it is able to implement its plan.

[Signed] *Abdel-Aziz al-Hakim*
President of the Governing Council[105]

Document 387
Governing Council Resolution Number 126 of 2003
[Expulsion of the Mujahideen-e-Khalq]
9 December 2003

In the name of God, the Merciful, the Compassionate: Taking into account the black terrorist history of the terrorist Iranian organization, Mujahideen-e-Khalq, and the crimes it committed against our people and our neighbours, and by relying upon its resolutions and previous order to combat such organizations, the Governing Council at its ordinary session (65) held on 9 December 2003 unanimously decided the following:

1. Expulsion of all members of the terrorist organization, Mujahideen-e-Khalq, from Iraqi territory by the end of this year.
2. Closure of the headquarters of the terrorist organization, Mujahideen-e-Khalq, and banning its members from engaging in any kind of activity while they are departing.
3. Confiscation of the funds of the organization and its weapons, and appropriation of all its assets into the Compensation Fund for the victims of the former fascist regime.
4. Reservation of the right of individuals and the institutions of Iraq to prosecute this organization for its crimes against the Iraqi people and to claim compensation for these crimes from the organization's assets both within and outside Iraq.

[Signed] *Abdel-Aziz al-Hakim*
President of the Governing Council

[105] The resolution was accompanied by the following Note: 'To be referred to the National Security Committee.'

Document 388
Governing Council Resolution Number 127 of 2003 [Adoption of the Law on the Iraqi Special Criminal Tribunal for Crimes Against Humanity in Iraq]
9 December 2003

In the name of God, the Merciful, the Compassionate: At its ordinary session (65) held on 9 December 2003 the Governing Council decided the following:

To adopt the Law on the Iraqi Special Criminal Tribunal dealing with crimes against humanity in Iraq, to try the criminals of the previous regime who committed crimes against the Iraqi people and against humanity.[106]

[Signed] *Abdel-Aziz al-Hakim*
President of the Governing Council

Document 389
Governing Council Resolution Number 128 of 2003 [Media Campaign to Publicize the Agreement of 15 November 2003]
10 December 2003

In the name of God, the Merciful, the Compassionate: At its ordinary session (66) held on 10 December 2003 the Governing Council decided the following:

Transfer the plan suggested by the Coalition Provisional Authority regarding the release of a media campaign to publicize the agreement of 15 November 2003 to the Council's Media Committee for discussion.[107]

[Signed] *Abdel-Aziz al-Hakim*
President of the Governing Council

[106] Law No 1 of 2003, The Statute of the Iraqi Special Tribunal, was published in the *Official Gazette*, vol 44, no 3890, March 2004, 127-148. It is the only Law adopted by the Governing Council in 2003 published in the *Official Gazette* and received its own document symbol: 'GC/Law/10 Dec 2003/1'. The text of the Statute was set out in Appendix A of Coalition Provisional Authority Order Number 48, Delegation of Authority Regarding an Iraqi Special Tribunal (CPA/ORD/10 December 2003/48). For the latter, see *Doc 70*.

[107] During the IGC session on 10 December 2003, Charles Heatley, CPA Director of Press & Public Affairs, had briefed Council members on the proposed media campaign. Council members pointed out that some of the points in the 15 November Agreement were still sketchy and needed to be clarified in the drafting process of the Law on the Administration of the State of Iraq. The Council unanimously referred the matter to the Media Committee; see Daffā'ī (ed.), *Iraq under Occupation: The Records of the Governing Council* [in Arabic] (2004), Minutes of Ordinary Session No 66, 10 December 2003. For the leaflet prepared by the CPA in November 2003 to publicize the Agreement, see *Doc 233*.

It is of interest to note that the CPA-controlled *Al-Sabah* newspaper, despite the Council's decision to refer the matter to its Media Committee, on 10 December 2003 reported that the 'Governing Council has decided to start an intensive campaign to explain the contents of the sovereignty agreement and the transference of power to Iraqis' (Governing Council Undertakes Intensive Media Campaign, *Al-Sabah*, 11 December 2003, p 1; was available at http://www.alsabaah.com/20031211/english.htm).

Document 390
Governing Council Resolution Number 129 of 2003 [Formation of a Committee to Summon the Director-General of the State Tax Commission]

10 December 2003

In the name of God, the Merciful, the Compassionate: At its ordinary session (66) held on 10 December 2003 the Governing Council decided the following:

1. To form a committee composed of members of the Governing Council, whose names are listed below, to summon Mr Farhan Katham, Director-General of the State Tax Commission, to look into the allegations set out in his memorandum and to summon Mr Sabah Nuri.[108]
   - A. Judge Dara Noorddin
   - B. Judge Wael Abdul Latif
   - C. Mr Ahmad Shiya' al-Barak
2. To present the recommendations made by the Committee to the Minister of Finance and to take the necessary legal measures in this regard.

[Signed] *Abdel-Aziz al-Hakim*
President of the Governing Council

Document 391
Governing Council Resolution Number 130 of 2003 [Dissolution of Federations and Trade Unions]

10 December 2003

In the name of God, the Merciful, the Compassionate: At its ordinary session (66) held on 10 December 2003 the Governing Council decided the following:

1. All federations and trade unions which were formed under the former regime are dissolved and their assets are frozen pending a decision on that matter.
2. A committee of domestic affairs within the Governing Council is established which is to find appropriate mechanisms for the formation of alternative federations and trade unions and to maintain the assets of the dissolved federations and trade unions.

[Signed] *Abdel-Aziz al-Hakim*
President of the Governing Council

[108] In a memorandum to the IGC, Mr Farhan Katham had indicated that Mr Sabah Nuri, the Director of the Office of the Minister of Finance, had engaged in corruption; see Daffā'ī (ed.), *Iraq under Occupation: The Records of the Governing Council* [in Arabic] (2004), Minutes of Ordinary Session No 66, 10 December 2003.

Document 392
Governing Council Resolution Number 131 of 2003
[Use of the Second Copy of a Person's Death Certificate]
10 December 2003

In the name of God, the Merciful, the Compassionate: At its ordinary session (66) held on 10 December 2003 the Governing Council decided the following:

1. To allow the Ministry of Health to use the second copy of a person's death certificate for the purpose of registering the death in the register and then send it off to the Department of Citizenship and Civil Affairs. This may happen only after a lengthy process of scrutiny in order to ensure that the second copy is not fraudulent, i.e. that it can be used given that the first copy was not registered or could not be located, and that the third copy which is kept by the medical institution could not be located either, or that the file concerned was lost during the war.
2. This resolution is to be implemented upon its issuance.

[Signed] *Abdel-Aziz al-Hakim*
President of the Governing Council[109]

Document 393
Governing Council Resolution Number 132 of 2003
[Use of Iraqi Airspace and Aircraft to Transport Pilgrims Going on Hajj]
16 December 2003

In the name of God, the Merciful, the Compassionate: At its ordinary session (68) held on 16 December 2003 the Governing Council decided the following:

1. To use the Iraqi airspace and Iraqi aircraft to transport pilgrims to Mecca, and to notify the Coalition Provisional Authority of this decision.[110]
2. To quickly restore Iraq's airports, and focus specifically on the airport in Baghdad as well as the airports in Arbil and Mosul, in addition to al-Hamza airport in Najaf.

[Signed] *Dr. Adnan Pachachi*
Acting President of the Governing Council

[109] The resolution was accompanied by the following Note: '1. Suspended. 2. Refer to the Citizen Affairs Committee.'

[110] At his weekly meeting with the IGC on 17 December 2003 Ambassador Bremer explained that Baghdad International Airport was not secure and that it was difficult to use with the other airports; see Daffā'ī (ed.), *Iraq under Occupation: The Records of the Governing Council* [in Arabic] (2004), Minutes of Ordinary Session No 14 [should read Ordinary Session No 69], 17 December 2003.

Document 394
Governing Council Resolution Number 133 of 2003
[Formation of a Committee to Fight Sectarianism]
22 December 2003

[The text of the resolution is not available. Reports in the Iraqi press and the Records of the Governing Council show that the resolution concerns the formation of a committee to fight sectarianism. An awareness campaign is to be launched in schools, universities and governmental institutions.][111]

Document 395
Governing Council Resolution Number 134 of 2003
[Cancellation of Resolutions on the Self-Financing of Hospitals]
23 December 2003

[The text of the resolution is not available. Reports in the Iraqi press and the Records of the Governing Council show that the resolution concerned the cancellation of Resolutions No 128 of 1977 and No 123 of 1999 of the dissolved Revolutionary Command Council which had authorized the Minister of Health to allow a number of State hospitals to adopt the service-for-fee system, and to convert 50% of State hospital beds into private wards in order to cover expenditure.][112]

Document 396
Governing Council Resolution Number 135 of 2003
[Interim Regulatory Body for Telecommunications]
22 December 2003

In the name of God, the Merciful, the Compassionate: At its ordinary session (70) held on 22 December 2003 the Governing Council decided the following:

1. There is hereby established an interim body to regulate communications in Iraq.
2. The interim body shall be placed under the Minister of Communications and undertake administrative and technical functions for the regulation of communications in Iraq.
3. The interim body shall enjoy administrative and financial autonomy.
4. The interim body shall exercise its functions until it is replaced by a permanent body with legal personality upon the promulgation of its own special statue.

[Signed] *Dr. Adnan Pachachi*
Acting President of the Governing Council

[111] See Daffā'ī (ed.), *Iraq under Occupation: The Records of the Governing Council* [in Arabic] (2004), Minutes of Ordinary Session No 70, 22 December 2003, and GC Creates Committee, *Al-Sabah*, 24 December 2003, p 2.

[112] See Daffā'ī (ed.), *Iraq under Occupation: The Records of the Governing Council* [in Arabic] (2004), Minutes of Ordinary Session No 71, 23 December 2003, and Governing Council cancels fee-for-service system in hospitals, *Al-Sabah*, 24 December 2003, p 1.

Document 397
Governing Council Resolution Number 136 of 2003 [Extension of the Suspension of Customs Duties Until 31 March 2004]

29 December 2003

In the name of God, the Merciful, the Compassionate: At its session held on 29 December 2003 the Governing Council decided the following:

1. Given that the time has come to implement the decision to collect custom duties on imported goods which should begin on 1 January 2004, and given that the Customs Department is not yet properly equipped to collect these duties on the given date, the Council has decided to extend the suspension of customs duties until 31 March 2004.[113]
2. The Council has also decided to address the possibility of transferring the Iraqi Customs Department back to the Ministry of Finance and to schedule a date for the discussion of this matter with the Coalition Provisional Authority.

[Signed] *Abdel-Aziz al-Hakim*
President of the Governing Council

Document 398
Governing Council Resolution Number 137 of 2003 [Introduction of Shari'ah Law in Personal Status Matters]

29 December 2003

In the name of God, the Merciful, the Compassionate: At its session held on 29 December 2003 the Governing Council decided the following:

1. The provisions of the Islamic Shari'ah shall be implemented in matters pertaining to marriage, engagement, marriage contracts, legal competence, marriage certification, marriages prohibited according to Islam, marriages to Christian and Jewish women, marital rights, including dowry, alimony, divorce, legal separation, divorce [in return for monetary compensation to be paid by the wife to the husband], uddah [period during which a widow may not remarry], relationships by marriage, wills, bequeathals, waqf [religious endowment], and inheritance. [This law shall be implemented in all religious courts (personal status) in line with the provisions of the schools of Islamic thought.[114]]
2. All laws, decisions, instructions, statements, and clauses of articles that contradict paragraph 1 of this law shall be abolished.
3. This law shall enter into force as of its date of issue.

[Signed] *Abdel-Aziz al-Hakim*
President of the Governing Council[115]

[113] But see CPA Order No 47 *[Doc 69]* where the suspension of customs duties was extended only until 29 February 2004.

[114] There are different versions of this resolution. This sentence is not part of the text of all resolutions.

[115] The resolution was accompanied by the following Note: 'Will be passed on to the Committee of Legal Affairs.' This resolution was repealed by IGC resolution no 32 of 2004; see *Doc 435*.

Document 399
Governing Council Resolution Number 138 of 2003
[Building of a New International Airport]
29 December 2003

In the name of God, the Merciful, the Compassionate: At its ordinary session (73) held on 29 December 2003 the Governing Council decided the following:

1. To build and modernize an international airport within the area linking the two sacred cities of Najaf and Karbala. The airport is to be equipped for domestic as well as international flights; it shall also act as a hub for international communication and services.
2. To put together a technical and financial committee, in coordination with the Ministry of Transport, in order to implement the project adequately.

[Signed] *Dr Adnan al-Pachachi*
President of the Governing Council

Document 400
Governing Council Resolution Number 139 of 2003
[Amending the Name of the Committee of Education and Culture]
30 December 2003

In the name of God, the Merciful, the Compassionate: At its ordinary session (74) held on 30 December 2003 the Governing Council decided the following:

1. The word 'Awqaf [Endowments]' shall be added to the name of the [Council's] Committee for Education and Culture so that its full name shall be 'Committee for Education, Culture and Awqaf'.
2. A sub-committee shall be established to supervise the activities of the Awqaf offices and shall comprise of the following persons:
   - A. His Highness Mr Abdel-Aziz al-Hakim.
   - B. Dr Mohsen Abdel Hamid.
   - C. Dr Mohammed Bahr al-Ulloum.
   - D. Mr Younadem Kana.
   - E. Sheikh Abdel-Karim al-Mohammedawi.
   - F. Mr Salaheddine Mohammed Bahaaeddin.
   - G. Mr Naseer al-Chaderchi.
   - H. Judge Wael Abdul Latif al-Fadl.

[Signed] *Abdel-Aziz al-Hakim*
President of the Governing Council

Document 401
Governing Council Resolution Number 140 of 2003
[Prohibition of Raising Money in Schools and Colleges]
30 December 2003

In the name of God, the Merciful, the Compassionate: At its ordinary session (74) held on 30 December 2003 the Governing Council decided the following:

1. The administrations of all schools, colleges, educational academies and institutions are prohibited from raising money from the students or forcing them by any means to make any donation. Whoever shall indulge in the act of collecting money or instigate others to do so shall be prosecuted under the law.
2. All faculty members are prohibited from offering private tuition to the students of all schools, colleges, educational academies and institutions to which the student and teacher or tutor are affiliated. Any payment charged by the teacher or tutor shall be regarded as a crime of bribery.

[Signed] *Abdel-Aziz al-Hakim*
President of the Governing Council

Document 402
Governing Council Resolution Number 141 of 2003
[Judicial Seizure of the Assets of 'Al-Huda' and 'Al-Dhilal' Companies]
31 December 2003

[The text of the resolution is not available. Reports in the Iraqi press indicate that the Governing Council decided in that resolution to put the assets of 'Al-Huda' and 'Al-Dhilal' companies for passengers transport [two front companies of the Iraqi Intelligence Service] under judicial seizure and to charge the Ministry of Transport with supervising these two companies till the end of the investigation into the ownership and activities of the two companies.][116]

Document 403
Governing Council Resolution Number 142 of 2003
[Bases and Criteria for the Allocation of Residential Plots of Land to Citizens]
31 December 2003

In the name of God, the Merciful, the Compassionate: At its ordinary session (75) held on 31 December 2003 the Governing Council decided the following:

[116] GC Issues New Decision, Al-Sabah, 3 January 2004, p 1.

The Council's Citizen Affairs Committee will establish the bases and criteria according to which residential plots of land should be allocated to citizens. Together with the Ministers of Labour and Municipalities, the Committee will decide on the stakeholders, then put forth its recommendations to the Council so that it can ratify them.
[Signed] *Abdel-Aziz al-Hakim*
President of the Governing Council

Document 404
Governing Council Resolution Number 1 of 2004
[Formation of a Committee for the Iraqi Flag and National Anthem]

5 January 2004

In the name of God, the Merciful, the Compassionate: At its ordinary session (1 of 2004) held on 5 January 2004 the Governing Council decided the following:

To form a committee composed of individuals whose names are listed below to suggest to the Council the design of the new Iraqi flag, as well as the new Iraqi national anthem; the committee putting forward its suggestions within one week:

1. Sheikh Abdel-Karim Mohammedawi'
2. Mr Naseer al-Chaderchi
3. Mr Samir Sumaydah
4. Mr Farsad Ahmad
5. Dr Adel Abdel-Mahdi

[Signed] *Dr Adnan al-Pachachi*
President of the Governing Council[117]

Document 405
Governing Council Resolution Number 2 of 2004
[Checks on Employees of Mobile Phone Companies]

5 January 2004

In the name of God, the Merciful, the Compassionate: At its ordinary session (1) held on 5 January 2004 the Governing Council decided the following:

To require that the Ministry of Communications and the Ministry of the Interior double-check the identity and citizenship of employees in top managerial positions and in technical teams within mobile phone companies operating in Iraq for security purposes, given that the use of mobile phones allows the company to identify the location of the owner of the mobile phone which may create a serious security threat to him.
[Signed] *Dr Adnan al-Pachachi*
President of the Governing Council

[117] The resolution was accompanied by the following Note: 'There is no need for the CPA to interfere.'

Document 406
Governing Council Resolution Number 3 of 2004
[Dissolution of the Governing Bodies of Federations, Trade Unions, Professional Associations and Organizations]

7 January 2004

In the name of God, the Merciful, the Compassionate: At its ordinary session (2) held on 7 January 2004 the Governing Council decided the following:

1. The governing bodies of federations, trade unions, professional associations and organizations, other than charitable ones, are to be dissolved.
2. Temporary governing bodies for federations, trade unions, professional associations and organizations are to be formed, which will assume preparations for general elections for permanent governing bodies in accordance with the law and internal regulations.
3. The governing bodies of the organizations referred to in paragraph (1) above are legally responsible for managing and maintaining the funds of the organization, and are legally answerable for the diminution or loss of the funds until the funds are delivered to the temporary bodies that will replace the governing bodies.
4. The Board of Supreme Audit is to scrutinize the funds and accounts of the organizations covered by this resolution.
5. Those presidents and members of the previous governing bodies who are subject to the de-Ba'athification resolutions are not allowed to run for the presidency or membership of the new governing bodies.
6. The Governing Council's Committee on Civil Society Affairs is to oversee the formation of temporary governing bodies and the preparation of new elections, based on an election law to be enacted by the Governing Council.[118]
7. The ministries and relevant bodies are to implement the provisions of this resolution.
8. This decision is to be implemented from the date of its issuance.

[Signed] *Dr Adnan al-Pachachi*
President of the Governing Council

Document 407
Governing Council Resolution Number 4 of 2004
[Confirmation of the Head of the Chaldean Church]

14 January 2004

In the name of God, the Merciful, the Compassionate: Based on the power vested in us, we have decided the following:

[118] The tasks of the IGC's Civil Society Affairs Committee were taken over in August 2005 by a ministerial committee, comprising the Ministers of Justice, Interior, Finance and Human Rights, as well as the Minister of State for the Transitional Assembly, the Minister of State for Civil Society Affairs, and the Minister of State for National Security; see the Council of Ministers' Decree number 8750 of 8 August 2004 reprinted in Anbari, Sabah Sadiq (ed.), *Resolutions of the Governing Council 2003-2004* [in Arabic] (3rd edn., 2006), at 166.

The Governing Council confirms Patriarch Emmanuel III Delly, an Iraqi national, as head of the Chaldean Church in Iraq and the entire world and proclaims him guardian of the church's endowment.[119]

The Endowment Ministry and Diwans shall implement this decision immediately.

Baghdad, 14 January 2004.

[Signed] *Dr Adnan al-Pachachi*
President of the Governing Council

Document 408
Governing Council Resolution Number 5 of 2004 [Approval of the Law Establishing the Supreme Commission for the Resolution of Real Property Claims]

13 January 2004

In the name of God, the Merciful, the Compassionate: At its ordinary session (4) held on 13 January 2004 the Governing Council decided the following:

To approve the law calling for the establishment of the Supreme Commission for the resolution of real property claims.

[Signed] *Dr Adnan al-Pachachi*
President of the Governing Council[120]

Document 409
Governing Council Resolution Number 6 of 2004 [Executive Committee for the Media]

14 January 2004

In the name of God, the Merciful, the Compassionate: At its ordinary session (5) held on 14 January 2004 the Governing Council decided the following:

To change the name of the Iraqi Media Body in the Governing Council into the Executive Committee for the Media whilst preserving all its powers.

[Signed] *Dr Adnan al-Pachachi*
President of the Governing Council[121]

[119] Emmanuel III Delly had been elected Patriarch of the Chaldean Church on 3 December 2003.
[120] The resolution was accompanied by the following Note: 'There is no need for CPA intervention.'
[121] The resolution was accompanied by the following Note: 'There is no need for CPA intervention.'

Document 410
Governing Council Resolution Number 7 of 2004 [Officials of the Dissolved Ministry of Information Dismissed for Political Reasons]
14 January 2004

In the name of God, the Merciful, the Compassionate: At its ordinary session (5) held on 14 January 2004 the Governing Council decided the following:

1. To refer the dossiers of those amongst the officials of the Ministry of Information who were dismissed for political reasons to the committee created within the Ministry of Culture to deal with their dismissal for political reasons and to make suitable recommendations for them.
2. The concerned ministries and stakeholders shall implement this decision.

[Signed] *Dr Ibrahim al-Jaafari*
Acting President of the Governing Council[122]

Document 411
Governing Council Resolution Number 8 of 2004 [Seizure of Assets of the Dissolved Ministry of Information]
14 January 2004

In the name of God, the Merciful, the Compassionate: At its ordinary session (5) held on 14 January 2004 the Governing Council decided the following:

1. To seize all assets (movable and non-movable) belonging to the dissolved Ministry of Information, both within Iraq and outside, and to entrust the Executive Media Committee with the task of implementing this resolution and administering the recovered assets as well as reporting regularly on this matter to the Council.
2. The Ministry of Finance shall transfer to the Executive Media Committee any assets belonging to the Ministry of Information which were recovered before the issuance of this resolution.
3. The Ministry of Finance, the Financial Audit Board, and the Ministry of the Interior shall be charged with providing all the specialized staff, equipment, and other requirements, as necessary, for assisting the Executive Media Committee in the implementation of this resolution.
4. The possession of any assets of the dissolved Ministry of Information shall be considered illegal and everybody must hand over such possessions to the Executive Media Committee immediately in order to avoid penalties stipulated by law.
5. The Executive Media Committee is requested to coordinate with the Coalition Provisional Authority to facilitate the implementation of this decision.

[Signed] *Dr Adnan al-Pachachi*
President of the Governing Council[123]

[122] The resolution was accompanied by the following Note: 'There is no need for CPA intervention.'

[123] The resolution was accompanied by the following Note: 'Refer to the Executive Media Committee'. The resolution was submitted on 11 May 2004 to Ambassador Bremer for approval. The Action Memo stated: 'Ratification of the Resolution is required in order to give it legal effect and to impose necessary and beneficial

Document 412
Governing Council Resolution Number 9 of 2004 [Licences for Radio and Television Stations and Other Means of Electronic Media]

14 January 2004

In the name of God, the Merciful, the Compassionate: At its ordinary session (5) held on 14 January 2004 the Governing Council decided the following:

The right to grant licences to television and radio stations and other means of electronic media is limited to the Executive Media Committee until a National Media Authority is created; in the meantime, the Ministry of Telecommunications controls all technical matters relating to frequencies and bands.

[Signed] *Dr Adnan al-Pachachi*
President of the Governing Council[124]

Document 413
Governing Council Resolution Number 10 of 2004 [Formation of a Committee to Look into the Problems and Circumstances Accompanying the Hajj]

19 January 2004

In the name of God, the Merciful, the Compassionate: At its ordinary session (6) held on 19 January 2004 the Governing Council decided the following:

To form a committee of the individuals listed below to look into the problems and circumstances accompanying the distribution of quotas, the selection of candidates, the numbers eligible for Hajj, and the issuing of their passports. The committee shall present its report within a week.

1. Dr Mahmoud Othman
2. Mrs Sondul Chapouk
3. Sheikh Abdel-Karim Mahoud al-Mohammedawi'

[Signed] *Naseer al-Chaderchi*
Acting President of the Governing Council[125]

qualifications to improve its enforcement.' Ambassador Bremer did not approve of the resolution. A handwritten note on the Action Memo reads: 'I don't agree with letting the GC (or any committee thereof) seize and control any assets.' (Action Memo for the Administrator from Simon Haselock, Director, Media Development Team, Subject: Ratification of Iraq Governing Council Resolution No. 8 (2004), 11 May 2004).

[124] The resolution was accompanied by the following Note: 'Refer to the Executive Media Committee'.

[125] The resolution was accompanied by the following Note: 'There is no need for CPA intervention.'

Document 414
Governing Council Resolution Number 11 of 2004 [Compensation for the Families of the Martyrs and Those Injured in the Criminal Bomb Blasts on 18 January 2004]

19 January 2004

In the name of God, the Merciful, the Compassionate: At its ordinary session (6) held on 19 January 2004 the Governing Council decided the following:

To pay the families of the below-listed individuals, who were either injured or martyred during the criminal bomb attacks on 18 January 2004 a sum of 5000 dollars each:

1. Martyr, Commissioner Rasul Tahir ‘Atheeb
2. Martyr, Commissioner Mahdi Ayal Halil
3. Injured, Hassan Tahir ‘Atheeb

[Signed] *Naseer al-Chaderchi*
Acting President of the Governing Council[126]

Document 415
Governing Council Resolution Number 12 of 2004 [Formation of a Committee to Review the Salaries of University Professors]

20 January 2004

In the name of God, the Merciful, the Compassionate: At its ordinary session (7) held on 20 January 2004 the Governing Council decided the following:

To form a committee, which includes all Governing Council members, to review the salaries of university professors. The committee will liaise with the Ministries of Finance and Higher Education, as well as with representatives from universities in Kurdistan and other interested parties. The final study will then be sent to the Council’s Finance Committee in order for it to deliver its recommendations within one week.

[Signed] *Dr Adnan al-Pachachi*
President of the Governing Council[127]

[126] The resolution was accompanied by the following Note: ‘Who will pay these sums [and] will the money come out of the Governing Council’s budget? Or from the Ministry of Finance? – The Council vowed to make these payments; thus the resolution was ratified.’

[127] The resolution was accompanied by the following Note: ‘There is no need for CPA intervention.’

Document 416
Governing Council Resolution Number 13 of 2004 [Referral of the Concerns of the Different Iraqi Parties to the External Relations Committee]

20 January 2004

In the name of God, the Merciful, the Compassionate: At its ordinary session (7) held on 20 January 2004 the Governing Council decided the following:

To refer the concerns of the different Iraqi parties and the role that the Governing Council plays in easing off these concerns to the External Relations Committee which shall be enlarged by Governing Council members Mr Jalal Talabani, Mr Massoud Barzani, Mr Ezzelddine Salim, Dr Mohsen Abdel Hamid and Mrs Sondul Chapouk, and which shall present its recommendations to the Council within two weeks.

[Signed] *Dr Adnan al-Pachachi*
President of the Governing Council

Document 417
Governing Council Resolution Number 14 of 2004 [Shortage of Chemical Fertilizers and Pesticides]

26 January 2004

In the name of God, the Merciful, the Compassionate: At its ordinary session (9) held on 26 January 2004 the Governing Council decided the following:

Given the shortage of chemical fertilizers and pesticides which are crucial for the growth of agriculture and livestock in the country and in order to avoid the impending disaster to our agricultural and livestock products, it is decided:

A. A Committee comprising of the persons whose names have been written below shall be established:

1. Hamid Majid Mousa – Economic Committee.
2. Samir Shakir Sumaydah – Finance Committee.
3. Naseer al-Chaderchi.
4. Minister of Agriculture.

B. The Committee shall immediately contact the Coalition Provisional Authority for consideration and solution of this problem.

[Signed] *Dr Adnan al-Pachachi*
President of the Governing Council[128]

[128] The resolution was accompanied by the following Note: 'There is no need for CPA intervention.'

Document 418
Governing Council Resolution Number 15 of 2004
[Ratification of the Law on the Commission on Public Integrity]

28 January 2004

In the name of God, the Merciful, the Compassionate: At its ordinary session (11) held on 28 January 2004 the Governing Council decided the following:

To ratify the Law on the Commission on Public Integrity.

[Signed] *Dr Adnan al-Pachachi*
President of the Governing Council

Document 419
Governing Council Resolution Number 16 of 2004
[General Federation of Trade Unions in Iraq]

28 January 2004

In the name of God, the Merciful, the Compassionate: At its ordinary session (11) held on 28 January 2004 the Governing Council decided the following:

The Executive Bureau of the General Federation of Trade Unions in Iraq,[129] headed by Mr Rasim Hussein al-Awadi, is considered the legitimate and legal representative of the trade union movement in Iraq.

[Signed] *Dr Adnan al-Pachachi*
President of the Governing Council

Document 420
Governing Council Resolution Number 17 of 2004
[Grade and Salary of the Presidents of the Office of Shiite Waqf and the Office of Sunni Waqf]

3 February 2004

In the name of God, the Merciful, the Compassionate: At its ordinary session held on 3 February 2004 the Governing Council decided that the presidents of the Office of Shiite Waqf and the Office of Sunni Waqf shall be regarded, with regard to grade and salary, as ministerial undersecretaries.

The Minister of Finance is to implement this decision.

[Signed] *Dr Mohsen Abdel Hamid*
President of the Governing Council

[129] The organization in question is the Iraqi Federation of Trade Unions which was formed on 16 May 2003.

Document 421
Governing Council Resolution Number 18 of 2004 [Grade and Salary of the President of the Waqf Office of Non-Muslim Communities]
3 February 2004

In the name of God, the Merciful, the Compassionate: At its ordinary session held on 3 February 2004 the Governing Council decided that the president of the Waqf Office of Non-Muslim Communities shall be regarded, with respect to grade and salary, as ministerial undersecretary.

The Minister of Finance is to implement this decision.

[Signed] *Dr Mohsen Abdel Hamid*
President of the Governing Council[130]

Document 422
Governing Council Resolution Number 19 of 2004 [Expenditure for the Protection of Deputy Members of the Governing Council]
9 February 2004

In the name of God, the Merciful, the Compassionate: At its ordinary session (12) held on 9 February 2004 the Governing Council decided the following:

To make the financial allotments for the protection of a deputy member of the Council to be 160 dollars, in addition to 140 dollars every month which is to be paid to the deputy to cover the additional expenditures of clothing, food, and rewards. The payment for the additional expenditures will be retroactive from the date of allocating the expenditures for the protection of the deputy members.

[Signed] *Dr Mohsen Abdel Hamid*
President of the Governing Council

Document 423
Governing Council Resolution Number 20 of 2004 [Investigation Committee for this Year's Hajj Campaign]
9 February 2004

In the name of God, the Merciful, the Compassionate: At its ordinary session (12) held on 9 February 2004 the Governing Council decided the following:

A broad representative committee shall be established for an investigation into the circumstances relating to this year's Hajj campaign from the beginning to its end.

[Signed] *Dr Mohsen Abdel Hamid*
President of the Governing Council

[130] The resolution was accompanied by the following Note: 'There is no need for CPA intervention.'

Document 424
Governing Council Resolution Number 21 of 2004 [Director-General of Islamic Education]

10 February 2004

In the name of God, the Merciful, the Compassionate: At its ordinary session (13) held on 10 February 2004 the Governing Council decided the following:

Based on the proposal submitted by the President of the Sunni Waqf [Endowment], the Governing Council decided the following:

1. Mr Jamal Mohammed Shafiq al-Badari is to be released from his post of Director-General of Islamic Education and is to be appointed to his former position as President of the Sunni Waqf [Endowment].
2. Dr Hamid Abdel Aziz al-Hyani is to be appointed Director-General of Islamic Education.
3. Mr Ala' Abdel Jabbar Mahmoud al-Jawaari is to be appointed Director-General of the Department of Financial Management.

The President of the Sunni Waqf [Endowment] shall implement this resolution.

[Signed] *Dr Mohsen Abdel Hamid*
President of the Governing Council

Document 425
Governing Council Resolution Number 22 of 2004 [Monthly Pension for the Former President of Iraq Abdul Rahman Muhammad Arif]

10 February 2004

In the name of God, the Merciful, the Compassionate: At its ordinary session (13) held on 10 February 2004 the Governing Council decided the following:

- To allocate a monthly pension of 1000 dollars to the former President of Iraq Abdul Rahman Muhammad Arif.
- To offer him 5000 dollars remuneration to cover the expenses of his medical treatment in Jordan.

[Signed] *Dr Mohsen Abdel Hamid*
President of the Governing Council

Document 426
Governing Council Resolution Number 23 of 2004 [Monthly Pension for the Wife of the Late Abdul Razzaq Al-Naif]

10 February 2004

In the name of God, the Merciful, the Compassionate: At its ordinary session (13) held on 10 February 2004 the Governing Council decided the following:

To allocate a monthly pension of 500 dollars to the wife of the late Abdul Razzaq al-Naif.[131]
[Signed] *Dr Mohsen Abdel Hamid*
President of the Governing Council

Document 427
Governing Council Resolution Number 24 of 2004 [Formation of a Committee to Investigate the 'Awar' and 'Alia' Companies]
10 February 2004

In the name of God, the Merciful, the Compassionate: At its ordinary session (13) held on 10 February 2004 the Governing Council decided the following:

To form a committee headed by Sheikh Ghazi Mashal Ajil al-Yawer, and including the members listed below, to decisively investigate the case of the 'Awar' and 'Alia' companies:

1. Mr Ahmad al-Barak
2. Mr Nabil al-Musawi
3. Mr Mashaal Abdallah al-Sarraf
4. Mr Abbas al-Radwan
5. Mr Ali Faysal

[Signed] *Dr Mohsen Abdel Hamid*
President of the Governing Council

Document 428
Governing Council Resolution Number 25 of 2004 [Formation of an Advisory Board to the Office of Awqaf of Christians and Other Religious Communities]
11 February 2004

In the name of God, the Merciful, the Compassionate: Addendum to Governing Council resolution number 79 issued on 3 November 2003.[132]

At its ordinary session (14) held on 11 February 2004 the Governing Council decided the following:

To form an advisory board which speaks in the name of the Christian Waqf, as well as all other [non-Muslim] Awqaf, and which includes the following representatives:

1. Mr Yaorish Hido Dankha – deputy president of the diwan (Eastern Church).
2. Mr Michael Azria Odisho – representative of the Old Eastern Church.

[131] Abdul Razzaq al-Naif [Abd ar-Razzaq al-Naif] was part of a bloodless coup headed by Ahmed Hassan al-Bakr against the government of President Abdul Rahman Arif on 17 July 1968. He was briefly Prime Minister of Iraq from 17 to 30 July 1968 before being arrested and exiled by al-Bakr. He was assassinated in London on 9 July 1978 allegedly on the order of Saddam Hussein.

[132] See *Doc 341*.

3. Mr Fawzi Kamel Fathallah Dano – representative of the Orthodox Assyrians.
4. Mr Saad Joseph Jack Dilania – representative of the Orthodox Armenians.
5. Mr Abdul Ahad Augustine – representative of the Latin Church.
6. Mr David Kia Butros – representative of the Evangelical Church.
7. Mrs May Yunan Tawfiq – representative of the Assyrian Catholic Church.
8. Mr Odi Ali Suleiman – representative of the Yazidis.

[Signed] *Dr Mohsen Abdel Hamid*
President of the Governing Council

Document 429
Governing Council Resolution Number 26 of 2004
[Laws and Regulations that Hamper the Development of Iraqi Cities]

16 February 2004

In the name of God, the Merciful, the Compassionate: At its ordinary session (15) held on 16 February 2004 the Governing Council decided the following:

To require the Ministry of Public Works and Municipalities to identify the existing laws and regulations that hamper the development of Iraqi cities, particularly Najaf and Karbala, and require their revocation.

[Signed] *Dr Mohsen Abdel Hamid*
President of the Governing Council

Document 430
Governing Council Resolution Number 27 of 2004
[Allocation of a Monthly Allowance to the Family of the Late Leader Abd Al-Karim Qasim]

16 February 2004

In the name of God, the Merciful, the Compassionate: At its ordinary session (15) held on 16 February 2004 the Governing Council decided the following:

To allocate a monthly sum of 1000 dollars to the family of the late leader Abd al-Karim Qasim, former Prime Minister of Iraq.

[Signed] *Dr Mohsen Abdel Hamid*
President of the Governing Council

Document 431
Governing Council Resolution Number 28 of 2004 [Formation of a Committee to Discuss Sectarianism]
16 February 2004

In the name of God, the Merciful, the Compassionate: At its ordinary session (15) held on 16 February 2004 the Governing Council decided the following:

To form a committee charged with the task of discussing the different manifestations of sectarianism which will meet with the different political parties in Iraq to promote solidarity and encourage them to unite in the face of terrorist attacks aimed at increasing sectarian divisions amongst the Iraqi people. The committee is to include the following individuals:

1. Mr Salaheddine Muhammad Bahaaeddin.
2. Mr Ezzelddine Salim.
3. Dr Salamah al-Khafaji.
4. Dr Adel Abdel-Mahdi.
5. Dr Hajem al-Husni.
6. Mr Ata Abdul-Wahab.

[Signed] *Dr Mohsen Abdel Hamid*
President of the Governing Council

Document 432
Governing Council Resolution Number 29 of 2004 [Appointments in the Office of Sunni Waqf]
February 2004

In the name of God, the Merciful, the Compassionate: At its ordinary session held on – February 2004 the Governing Council decided the following:

Based on the nomination of the chief of staff of the Sunni Waqf Office:

1. To appoint Dr Ahmad Abdul-Ghafour al-Samirrai director general of the department of religious institutions in the Sunni Waqf Office.

2. To appoint Mr Ismail Ali Taha assistant to the director of religious affairs at the Sunni Waqf Office.

The head of the Sunni Waqf Office shall implement this decision.

[Signed] *Dr Mohsen Abdel Hamid*
President of the Governing Council

Document 433
Governing Council Resolution Number 30 of 2004
[Formation of a Committee to Take Care of the Families of the Martyrs]
25 February 2004

In the name of God, the Merciful, the Compassionate: At its ordinary session held on 25 February 2004 the Governing Council decided the following:

To form a committee in charge of 'taking care of the families of martyrs' which includes the following individuals:

1. Dr Ibrahim al-Jaafari.
2. Mr Hamid Majid Mousa.
3. Dr Salamah al-Khafaji.
4. Sheikh Ghazi al-Yawer.
5. Mr Samir Sumaydah.
6. Mr Adel Murad.
7. Dr Sami al-Askari.

[Signed] *Dr Mohammed Bahr al-Ulloum*
Acting President of the Governing Council[133]

Document 434
Governing Council Resolution Number 31 of 2004
[Formation of a Committee to Investigate Mobile Phone Companies]
25 February 2004

In the name of God, the Merciful, the Compassionate: At its ordinary session (19) held on 25 February 2004 the Governing Council decided the following:

To form a committee composed of the individuals listed below to investigate the financial and legal breaches of which the companies implementing the mobile phones contracts are accused, and which is to put together a report on this matter.

1. Dr Ahmed Chalabi, Finance Committee
2. Dr Dr Raja al-Khuzaai, Economic Committee
3. Mr Samir al-Sumaydah, Committee for General Services
4. Mr Naseer al-Chaderchi, Legal Committee
5. Dr Sami al-Askari, Deputy to Dr Mohammed Bahr al-Ulloum

[Signed] *Dr Mohammed Bahr al-Ulloum*
Acting President of the Governing Council

[133] The resolution was accompanied by the following Note: 'There is no need for CPA intervention.'

Document 435
Governing Council Resolution Number 32 of 2004
[Repeal of Governing Council Resolution Number 137 of 2003]
27 February 2004

In the name of God, the Merciful, the Compassionate: At its extraordinary session (5) held on 27 February 2004 the Governing Council decided the following:

To repeal resolution number 137 published by the Governing Council on 29 December 2003.[134]

[Signed] *Dr Mohsen Abdel Hamid*
President of the Governing Council

Document 436
Governing Council Resolution Number 33 of 2004
[Unanimous Agreement on the Law of Administration for the State of Iraq for the Transitional Period]
8 March 2004

In the name of God, the Merciful, the Compassionate: At its ordinary session (20) held on 8 March 2004 the Governing Council decided the following:

Unanimous agreement on the Law of Administration for the State of Iraq for the Transitional Period, as it currently stands.

[Signed] *Dr Mohammed Bahr al-Ulloum*
President of the Governing Council

Document 437
Governing Council Resolution Number 34 of 2004
[Enlargement of the Advisory Board to the Waqf Office of Christian and Other Religious Communities]
15 March 2004

In the name of God, the Merciful, the Compassionate: As a follow-up to resolution number 25, dated 11 February 2004,[135] the Governing Council at its ordinary session (22) held on 15 March 2004 decided the following:

To add Mr Tuma Zaki Zahroun to the existing advisory board to the Waqf Office of Christians and other religions communities as a representative of the Sabean Mandaen sect.

[Signed] *Dr Ibrahim al-Jaafari*
Acting President of the Governing Council

[134] For IGC resolution no 137 of 2003, see *Doc 398*. The decision to repeal resolution no 137 was adopted with 15 votes in favour, five against, and five abstentions; see GC Cancels Decision No 137, *Al-Sabah*, 28 February 2004, p 1, http://www.alsabaah.com/20040228/english.htm.

[135] See *Doc 428*.

Document 438
Governing Council Resolution Number 35 of 2004
[Deputy Ministers]
15 March 2004

In the name of God, the Merciful, the Compassionate: At its ordinary session (22) held on 15 March 2004 the Governing Council decided the following:

The Presidency of the Council shall discuss the issue of [the selection of] deputy ministers with the honourable ministers. The Presidency is to establish a tripartite committee from among its members to carry out this important task so that this issue may be settled within a limited period of time not exceeding two weeks.

[Signed] *Dr Ibrahim al-Jaafari*
Acting President of the Governing Council

Document 439
Governing Council Resolution Number 36 of 2004
[Appointment of Ambassador in the Ministry of Foreign Affairs]
15 March 2004

In the name of God, the Merciful, the Compassionate: At its ordinary session (22) held on 15 March 2004 the Governing Council unanimously decided to appoint Dr Muhammad Ali al-Hakim as ambassador in the Ministry of Foreign Affairs.

The Minister of Foreign Affairs shall implement this decision.

[Signed] *Dr Ibrahim al-Jaafari*
Acting President of the Governing Council

Document 440
Governing Council Resolution Number 37 of 2004
[Appointment of Two Judges to the Higher National De-Ba'athification Commission]
17 March 2004

In the name of God, the Merciful, the Compassionate: At its ordinary session (24) held on 17 March 2004 the Governing Council decided the following:

To appoint the two judges mentioned below to the Higher National De-Ba'athification Commission to consider appeal applications submitted to that body.

1. Judge Izzat Tawfik Jaafar Muhammad, Misdemeanour Court of Karada
2. Judge Rahim Hassan Jeryo al-'Akili, Court of Bada'at al-Karada

[Signed] *Dr Ahmed al-Chalabi*
Acting President of the Governing Council

Document 441
Governing Council Resolution Number 38 of 2004 [Repeal of the Dissolved Revolutionary Command Council's Decree Number 1549 of 11 November 1979]
20 March 2004

In the name of God, the Merciful, the Compassionate: At its extraordinary session (9) held on 20 March 2004 the Governing Council decided the following:

1. To repeal resolution number 1549 of 11 November 1979 of the dissolved Revolutionary Command Council and, likewise, to repeal all its effects.
2. Those who fall under the provisions of the resolution above are to return to their previous positions of employment, and the period between their return to employment and their retirement is to be counted as actual service.
3. The successors of the deceased [among those above] will be given their retirement pension, calculated on the basis of continuous service until the time of their death.
4. This resolution is to be implemented from the date of its publication.

The Minister of Finance and relevant bodies are to implement this resolution.

[Signed] *Dr Mohammed Bahr al-Ulloum*
President of the Governing Council

Document 442
Governing Council Resolution Number 39 of 2004 [Approval of the Company Law]
22 March 2004

In the name of God, the Merciful, the Compassionate: At its ordinary session (25) held on 22 March 2004 the Governing Council decided the following:

To approve the Company Law presented by the Coalition Provisional Authority.[136]

[Signed] *Dr Ahmed al-Chalabi*
Acting President of the Governing Council

Document 443
Governing Council Resolution Number 40 of 2004 [Investigation of the Oil-For-Food Programme]
23 March 2004

In the name of God, the Merciful, the Compassionate: At its ordinary session (26) held on 23 March 2004 the Governing Council decided the following:

[136] See *Doc 87*.

To investigate the Oil-for-Food Programme, by appointing an independent and well-known multinational audit firm, and by seeking the assistance of the Board of Supreme Audit as well as Iraqi audit firms. The Council's Finance Committee is to follow up on the details of this resolution, to implement it, and to contract the chosen firm.[137]
[Signed] *Dr Ahmed al-Chalabi*
Acting President of the Governing Council

Document 444
Governing Council Resolution Number 41 of 2004 [Formation of a Committee to Study the Possibility of Using Land Belonging to the Military for Housing Purposes]
23 March 2004

In the name of God, the Merciful, the Compassionate: At its ordinary session (26) held on 23 March 2004 the Governing Council decided the following:

To form a committee headed by a representative of the Ministry of Municipalities and Public Works, with members representing:

a. The Ministry of Construction and Housing.
b. The future National Security Committee or Defense Committee.
c. The Ministry of the Environment.
d. The Ministry of Justice.

[This committee will] prepare and present a comprehensive study within one month from its inception on the possibility of benefitting from land belonging to the military for purposes of housing or other purposes consistent with the urban development plans.

This resolution is adopted in view of the current need for solving the housing problem

[137] The chairman of the IGC's Finance Committee, Dr Ahmed al-Chalabi, on 26 March 2004 issued an Invitation to Tender entitled 'Iraq Report into the "Oil-for-Food Programme"/Violations of UN Resolutions'. It provides in the relevant part: 'The invitation to tender is for the provision of forensic investigation services combined with the necessary legal support to prepare for the Iraq Governing Council a report with regard to the United Nations Resolution 986 – oil-for-food programme operated between the periods 14 April 1995 and 9 April 2003 and any other relevant resolutions connected thereto including violations of UN sanctions.

The Iraq Governing Council unanimously endorsed the decision to appoint a world leading accounting firm combined with a leading law firm to provide the necessary support. You are invited to submit a written statement of qualification by 9 April 2004 12 p.m. Baghdad time by email as herein.

Scope of investigation will include:

1. Identification of governments, individuals and corporate entities in the public and private sector both in Iraq and elsewhere who wrongly benefited under the UN sanctions or under the oil-for-food programme.

2. Identification, verification, tracing and recovery of misused assets belonging to the state of Iraq and identifying actions which may have caused loss or damage to Iraq in connection with or as a result of actions in breach of the oil-for-food programme or in breach of the UN sanctions.

3. In relation to those identified in 1. to analyse and collate available evidence in such a way as to facilitate decisions by the Iraq Governing Council in deciding what actions to take to bring to account those who benefited or profiteered improperly under the programmes referred to and through negotiations or other legal means to support recoveries or claims that may need to be made.

The report will also need to cover improper payments within the oil-for-food programme, adjustments in invoice values to provide excess funds, improper kick backs, reporting and responsibility within the UN, status and use of fees received by the UN, controls in place to monitor agents acting for the UN, role of banks in handling payments, cash and otherwise, identifying, retrieving funds still held by overseas banks and tracing ultimate beneficiaries where necessary. [...].'

and solving the problems related to property ownership, which have the potential to influence future developments.
[Signed] *Dr Ahmed al-Chalabi*
Acting President of the Governing Council

Document 445
Governing Council Resolution Number 42 of 2004 [Shrine and University Bearing the Name of Sayyid Muhammad Baqir Al-Sadr]
24 March 2004

In the name of God, the Merciful, the Compassionate: At its ordinary session (27) held on 24 March 2004 the Governing Council decided the following:

To construct a shrine and a university bearing the name of Sayyid Muhammad Baqer al-Sadr on a piece of land allocated by the Municipality of Najaf, and to allow the Ministry of Public Works and Municipalities to take the necessary steps towards starting this process as soon as possible.
[Signed] *Dr Ahmed al-Chalabi*
Acting President of the Governing Council

Document 446
Governing Council Resolution Number 43 of 2004 [Allocation of a Monthly Allowance to the Dependents of Martyr Sayyid Muhammad Baqir Al-Sadr]
24 March 2004

In the name of God, the Merciful, the Compassionate: In commemoration of martyr Sayyid Muhammad Baqir al-Sadr (may God be pleased with him) and for preserving his heritage for humanity, the Governing Council at its ordinary session (27) held on 24 March 2004 decided the following:

1. To allocate a monthly allowance of one thousand dollars to the dependents of the Martyr.
2. To rename a street in his name, both in Baghdad and Najaf.
3. A grand celebration is to be held on the anniversary of his martyrdom on 9 April 2004 in Najaf which will include the laying of the cornerstone of his tomb and the adjacent educational institution.
4. Actions shall be taken to spread his intellectual heritage and an annual book fair shall be held in his name.

[Signed] *Dr Ahmed al-Chalabi*
Acting President of the Governing Council[138]

[138] On 11 April 2006, the Iraqi Prime Minister, acting upon memorandum no K/2/1/38/4836 of 11 April 2006 of the General Secretariat of the Council of Ministers/General Legal Department, decided to amend

Document 447
Governing Council Resolution Number 44 of 2004
[Approval of the Budget of the Special Tribunal]
24 March 2004

In the name of God, the Merciful, the Compassionate: At its ordinary session (27) held on 24 March 2004 the Governing Council decided the following:

To approve the budget of the Special Tribunal.

[Signed] *Dr Ahmed al-Chalabi*
Acting President of the Governing Council

Document 448
Governing Council Resolution Number 45 of 2004
[Amendment to Resolution Number 41 of 2004]
March 2004

In the name of God, the Merciful, the Compassionate: At its session held on – March 2004 the Governing Council decided the following:

Representatives from the following bodies are to be included in the committee formed pursuant to Governing Council Resolution number 41, issued on 23 March 2004[139]:

1. The Ministry of Finance.
2. The Municipality of Baghdad.

[Signed] *Dr Ahmed al-Chalabi*
Acting President of the Governing Council

Document 449
Governing Council Resolution Number 46 of 2004
[Drafting of the Annex to the Law of Administration of the State of Iraq for the Transitional Period]
29 March 2004

In the name of God, the Merciful, the Compassionate: At its ordinary session (28) held on 29 March 2004 the Governing Council decided the following:

To mandate the special committee, which was set up to prepare the Law of Administration for the State of Iraq for the Transitional Period, with drafting the annex provided for in

IGC resolution no 43 of 2004 and allocate a monthly pension of 7 million dinars to the family of the Martyr Muhammad Baqir al-Sadr effective from 1 April 2006, replacing the allowance granted to the family in IGC resolution no 43 of 2004. See Anbari, Sabah Sadiq (ed.), *Resolutions of the Governing Council 2003-2004* [in Arabic] (3rd edn., 2006), at 141 and 167. On the latter page the relevant IGC resolution is wrongly numbered 42 of 2004.

[139] See *Doc 448*.

Article II, clause B, paragraph 1 of the Law of Administration for the State of Iraq for the Transitional Period.
[Signed] *Dr Ahmed al-Chalabi*
Acting President of the Governing Council

Document 450
Governing Council Resolution Number 47 of 2004 [Periodic Sessions of the Governing Council]
29 March 2004

In the name of God, the Merciful, the Compassionate: At its ordinary session (28) held on 29 March 2004 the Governing Council decided the following:

To hold its periodic sessions on Wednesdays and Sundays. On each of the indicated days, two sessions will be held:

From 10am to 2pm

From 3pm to 5pm

[Signed] *Dr Ahmed al-Chalabi*
Acting President of the Governing Council

Document 451
Governing Council Resolution Number 48 of 2004 [Formation of a Committee to Prepare the Transfer of Authority to the Iraqi Interim Government]
29 March 2004

In the name of God, the Merciful, the Compassionate: At its ordinary session (28) held on 29 March 2004 the Governing Council decided the following:

A committee shall be established comprising of the persons whose names have been written below and it shall be given the task of making the necessary arrangements for the transfer of authority to the Iraqi Interim Government which shall exercise full authority from 30 June 2004:

1. Mr Massoud Barzani.
2. Mr Abdel-Aziz al-Hakim.
3. Dr Mohammed Bahr al-Ulloum.
4. Mr Jalal al-Talabani.
5. Dr Adnan al-Pachachi.
6. Dr Ahmed al-Chalabi.
7. Dr Raja al-Khuzaai.
8. Mr Hamid Majid Mousa.
9. Mr Younadem Kana.
10. Mr Salaheddine Mohammed Bahaaeddin.
11. Judge Wael Abdul Latif.
12. Judge Dara Noorddin.

13. Dr Iyad al-Allawi.
14. Dr Mouwafak al-Rabii.
15. Mr Samir al-Sumaydah.

[Signed] *Dr Ahmed al-Chalabi*
Acting President of the Governing Council

Document 452
Governing Council Resolution Number 49 of 2004
[Formation of an Election Committee]

30 March 2004

In the name of God, the Merciful, the Compassionate: At its ordinary session (29) held on 30 March 2004 the Governing Council decided the following:

An election committee shall be established, composed of the honourable members whose names have been written below, for the preparation of elections and the enactment of the relevant legislation:

1. Dr Mohsen Abdel Hamid.
2. Mr Hamid Majid Mousa.
3. Dr Ibrahim al-Jaafari.
4. Mr Younadem Kana.
5. Dr Iyad al-Allawi.
6. Mr Massoud Barzani.
7. Dr Raja Habib al-Khuzaai.
8. Mr Salaheddine Mohammed Bahaaeddin.
9. Sheikh Ghazi Ajil al-Yawer.
10. Mr Jalal Talabani.
11. Dr Mouwafak al-Rabii.
12. Dr Mohammed Bahr al-Ulloum.
13. Dr Salamah al-Khafaji.
14. Mr Naseer al-Chaderchi.
15. Ms Sondul Chapouk.

[Signed] *Dr Ahmed al-Chalabi*
Acting President of the Governing Council

Document 453
Governing Council Resolution Number 50 of 2004
[Dissolution of the Committee Responsible for Building the Infrastructure and Organizing Elections]

30 March 2004

In the name of God, the Merciful, the Compassionate: At its ordinary session (29) held on 30 March 2004 the Governing Council decided the following:

To dissolve, in accordance with the Law for the Administration of Iraq, the committee formed on 1 December 2003 which was responsible for liaising with the Coalition Provisional Authority in order to build the necessary infrastructure and to organize elections.
[Signed] *Dr Ahmed al-Chalabi*
Acting President of the Governing Council

Document 454
Governing Council Resolution Number 51 of 2004 [Approval of the Charter Establishing the Iraqi National Intelligence Service]

31 March 2004

In the name of God, the Merciful, the Compassionate: At its ordinary session (30) held on 31 March 2004 the Governing Council decided the following:

To approve the Charter establishing the Iraqi National Intelligence Service.
[Signed] *Dr Mohammed Bahr al-Ulloum*
President of the Governing Council

Document 455
Governing Council Resolution Number 52 of 2004 [Financial Support for the Humble Families of Martyrs in the Governorate of Basra]

31 March 2004

In the name of God, the Merciful, the Compassionate: In an attempt to reinforce the initiative towards ensuring social equality and honouring the humble families of martyrs, the Governing Council at its ordinary session (30) held on 31 March 2004 decided the following:

1. To deduct 1000 dinars from the salaries of government employees in the governoate of Basra and to distribute this money to the humble families of martyrs.
2. To deposit the collected money in a special account entitled 'The Fund for Assisting the Martyrs' Families' in one of the government's banks. Special committees, put together for this purpose, will distribute the money amongst those concerned.
3. The Board of Supreme Audit will verify the amounts deposited in and withdrawn from this account.

[Signed] *Dr Mohammed Bahr al-Ulloum*
President of the Governing Council

Document 456
Governing Council Resolution Number 53 of 2004
[Authentication of the Law on Local Governmental Powers]
14 April 2004

In the name of God, the Merciful, the Compassionate: At its ordinary session (34) held on 14 April 2004 the Governing Council decided the following:

To authenticate the Law on Local Governmental Powers.

[Signed] *Massoud Barzani*
President of the Governing Council

Document 457
Governing Council Resolution Number 54 of 2004
[Approval of the Establishment of the Electoral Commission]
18 April 2004

In the name of God, the Merciful, the Compassionate: At its ordinary session (35) held on 18 April 2004 the Governing Council decided the following:

To approve the establishment of the Electoral Commission.

[Signed] *Massoud Barzani*
President of the Governing Council

Document 458
Governing Council Resolution Number 55 of 2004
[Approval of a Study on the Subject of Conducting a Census in Iraq]
18 April 2004

In the name of God, the Merciful, the Compassionate: At its ordinary session (35) held on 18 April 2004 the Governing Council decided the following:

To approve the study prepared by the Ministry of Planning and Development Cooperation on the subject of conducting a census in Iraq, in consultation with the CPA.

[Signed] *Massoud Barzani*
President of the Governing Council

Document 459
Governing Council Resolution Number 56 of 2004
[Periodic Sessions of the Governing Council]
18 April 2004

In the name of God, the Merciful, the Compassionate: Given the present circumstances in Iraq, including the impending transfer of sovereignty, the Governing Council at its ordinary session (35) held on 18 April 2004 decided the following:

To continue to hold its periodic sessions throughout the week, except for Thursdays and Fridays.

[Signed] *Massoud Barzani*
President of the Governing Council

Document 460
Governing Council Resolution Number 57 of 2004
[Appointment of Undersecretaries in a Number of Ministries]
19 April 2004

In the name of God, the Merciful, the Compassionate: At its ordinary session (36) held on 19 April 2004 the Governing Council decided the following:

To appoint the individuals listed below as undersecretaries in the ministries listed opposite their names with their appointments starting as soon as they take up their posts and are sworn in before the ministers.

[Signed] *Massoud Barzani*
President of the Governing Council[140]

Name	Ministry
1. Dr Sobhi Mansour al-Jamili	Ministry of Agriculture
2. Dr Sawsan Ali Majed al-Sharifi	Ministry of Agriculture
3. Dr Hazem al-Rifai	Ministry of Agriculture
4. Architect Maysoun Damlouji	Ministry of Culture
5. Mr Sarbast Omar Hassan Bamarni	Ministry of Culture
6. Mr Jabbour Mohammad al-Jabri	Ministry of Culture
7. Mrs Hamdiyya Ahmad Khalaf	Ministry of Immigration and Displacement
8. Dr Salma al-Muzaffar	Ministry of Education
9. Mrs Baraka Mahdi Salehal-Jabouri	Ministry of Electricity
10. Mr Raad Muhsin Ghaz al-Hares	Ministry of Electricity
11. Mr Ali Hannoush	Ministry of the Environment
12. Mrs Manal Kamel Elias Aziza	Ministry of the Environment
13. Dr Hamed al-Bayati	Ministry of Foreign Affairs

[140] The resolution was accompanied by the following Note: 'There is no need for CPA intervention.'

14. Mr Labid Jamil Abawi	Ministry of Foreign Affairs
15. Ambassador Bassam Kibbeh	Ministry of Foreign Affairs
16. Ambassador Saad Jasim al-Hayyani	Ministry of Foreign Affairs
17. Mr Amer Hassan al-Khaza'i	Ministry of Health
18. Mr Ammar al-Safar	Ministry of Health
19. Mr Idriss Hadi Saleh	Ministry of Higher Education
20. Dr Marwan Kheylani	Ministry of Higher Education
21. Mr Bakhtyar Amin	Ministry of Human Rights
22. Major General Abdel Jabbar Youssef Muhammad	Ministry of the Interior
23. Mr Hussein Ali Kamal Ahmad Fahmi	Ministry of the Interior
24. Mr Bushu Ibrahim Ali Daza'i	Ministry of Justice
25. Mr Ibrahim Iyad al-Safi	Ministry of Public Works and Municipalities
26. Mr Kamel Nasir al-Jaderji	Ministry of Public Works and Municipalities
27. Dr Mitha' Hassan al-Lami	Ministry of Transport
28. Mr Ata Nabil Hussein Awni Ata	Ministry of Transport

Document 461
Governing Council Resolution Number 58 of 2004
[Formation of a Committee to Address the Security Situation]

19 April 2004

In the name of God, the Merciful, the Compassionate: At its ordinary session (36) held on 19 April 2004 the Governing Council decided the following:

To form a committee composed of the individuals listed below (the 'Operation Room') which will gather the ideas and thoughts presented by members of the Governing Council regarding the security situation, and then transform these ideas into an action plan to be discussed with the Coalition Provisional Authority before being implemented:

1. Dr Iyad Allawi
2. Sheikh Ghazi Ajil al-Yawer
3. Dr Ruz Nuri Shawis
4. Dr Adel Abdel-Mahdi
5. Dr Hajim al-Hasni

[Signed] *Massoud Barzani*
President of the Governing Council

Document 462
Governing Council Resolution Number 59 of 2004 [Approval of the Draft Law Amending the Judicial Institute Law Number 33 of 1976]
19 April 2004

In the name of God, the Merciful, the Compassionate: At its ordinary session (36) held on 19 April 2004 the Governing Council decided the following:

To approve the draft law amending the Judicial Institute Law Number 33 of 1976.

[Signed] *Massoud Barzani*
President of the Governing Council

Document 463
Governing Council Resolution Number 60 of 2004 [Transfer of Ownership of Real Property to Mr Saleh Sad Jabr and His Brother]
20 April 2004

In the name of God, the Merciful, the Compassionate: At its ordinary session (37) held on 20 April 2004 the Governing Council decided the following:

To grant ownership of the property in 60/2/Mariam's Karrada to Mr Saleh Saad Jabr and his brother Mr Ahmad Saleh Jabr.

[Signed] *Massoud Barzani*
President of the Governing Council[141]

Document 464
Governing Council Resolution Number 61 of 2004 [Commissioning of KPMG to Investigate the Oil-For-Food Programme]
20 April 2004

In the name of God, the Merciful, the Compassionate: At its ordinary session (37) held on 20 April 2004 the Governing Council decided the following:

To agree to allow the company KPMG to investigate the issues of oil coupons, the breaches of the previous regime using Iraqi funds, as well as the extent to which the United Nations has been responsible for these breaches.[142] The Board of Supreme Audit is to handle the investigation on the Iraqi side.

[141] The resolution was accompanied by the following Note: 'To be postponed until an agreement is reached with the CPA– to be filed.'

[142] On 18 April 2004, the IGC's Finance Committee had reviewed the submitted tender proposals and had endorsed the KPMG proposal.

[Signed] *Massoud Barzani*
President of the Governing Council[143]

Document 465
Governing Council Resolution Number 62 of 2004 [Formation of a Committee to Investigate Appointments]
21 April 2004

In the name of God, the Merciful, the Compassionate: At its ordinary session (38) held on 21 April 2004 the Governing Council decided the following:

To establish a committee comprising of the persons whose names have been written below to investigate the appointments of those with special grades and general managers about whose appointments reservations are made.

1. Dr Mohsen Abdel Hamid.
2. Mr Hamid Majid.
3. Dr Ruz Nuri Shawis.
4. Mr Sami al-Askari.
5. Mr Jawad al-Maliki.

[Signed] *Massoud Barzani*
President of the Governing Council

Document 466
Governing Council Resolution Number 63 of 2004 [Formation of an Independent Electoral Commission]
18 April 2004

In the name of God, the Merciful, the Compassionate: At its ordinary session (35) held on 18 April 2004 the Governing Council decided the following:

To form an Independent Electoral Commission, which prepares for the general elections, organizes them, and oversees their operation. The Commission is to include neutral, respectable, trustworthy, and qualified individuals in this field. These people will be nominated both from within the Council and from outside according the above-mentioned qualifications. Five to seven of the members of the Commission will be chosen in coordination with the United Nations.

[Signed] *Massoud Barzani*
President of the Governing Council

[143] The resolution was accompanied by the following Note: 'To consult the CPA'.

Document 467
Governing Council Resolution Number 64 of 2004
[Approval of the Report on the Implementation of the General Census]
7 April 2004

In the name of God, the Merciful, the Compassionate: At its ordinary session (32) held on 7 April 2004 the Governing Council decided the following:

Approval of the Report of the Ministry of Planning and Development Cooperation on the implementation of the general census of the population in Iraq.

[Signed] *Massoud Barzani*
President of the Governing Council

Document 468
Governing Council Resolution Number 65 of 2004
[Payments to Disabled Persons]
25 April 2004

In the name of God, the Merciful, the Compassionate: At its ordinary session (40) held on 25 April 2004 the Governing Council decided the following:

To make payments to disabled persons without any exception through the Ministry of Labour and Social Affairs. Increases or bonuses which were previously allocated on the basis of a person's position in the political party are no longer applicable.

[Signed] *Massoud Barzani*
President of the Governing Council

Document 469
Governing Council Resolution Number 66 of 2004
[Premiums Due for Payment by Lawyers]
25 April 2004

In the name of God, the Merciful, the Compassionate: At its ordinary session (40) held on 25 April 2004 the Governing Council decided the following:

To postpone by a year the collection of premiums due for payment by lawyers and to reduce these premiums as well as the interests due on them by 5 per cent.

[Signed] *Massoud Barzani*
President of the Governing Council

Document 470
Governing Council Resolution Number 67 of 2004
[Sale of Homes Belonging to the Kirkuk Cement Factory]
25 April 2004

In the name of God, the Merciful, the Compassionate: At its ordinary session (40) held on 25 April 2004 the Governing Council decided the following:

To allow the Minister of Industry and Minerals to sell the homes belonging to the Kirkuk Cement Factory to their occupants, in accordance with the law on the selling and leasing of state property number 33 of the year 1986, and on the condition that beneficiaries have previously been deprived of ownership on racial grounds.

[Signed] *Massoud Barzani*
President of the Governing Council

Document 471
Governing Council Resolution Number 68 of 2004
[Granting a Pension to Dr Naziha al-Dulaimi]
26 April 2004

In the name of God, the Merciful, the Compassionate: At its ordinary session (41) held on 26 April 2004 the Governing Council decided the following:

To recognize and remunerate Dr Naziha al-Dulaimi's efforts to serve Iraq by granting her a monthly pension of 750 dollars, starting from the present month.[144]

The Minister of Finance shall implement this decision.

[Signed] *Massoud Barzani*
President of the Governing Council

Document 472
Governing Council Resolution Number 69 of 2004
[Rules and Regulations Governing Companies Issued by the Kurdistan Regional Government]
20 April 2004

In the name of God, the Merciful, the Compassionate: At its ordinary session (37) held on 20 April 2004 the Governing Council decided the following:

1. To adopt the rules and regulations governing the registration and control of companies, issued by Kurdistan Regional Government during the period from 1991 to 23 March 2004, which are to be applied all over Iraq.

[144] Dr Naziha al-Dulaimi (1923-2007) was a prominent figure of the Iraqi women's movement. She was a cofounder and first president of the Iraqi Women's League and the first woman minister in Iraq's modern history (1959-1960).

2. To abolish all the decrees issued by the dissolved Revolutionary Command Council which invalidate the rules and regulations promulgated by the Kurdistan Regional Government.
[Signed] *Massoud Barzani*
President of the Governing Council

Document 473
Governing Council Resolution Number 70 of 2004 [Election of the President of the Governing Council for the Months of May and June 2004]
28 April 2004

In the name of God, the Merciful, the Compassionate: At its ordinary session (43) held on 28 April 2004 the Governing Council elected Mr Ezzedine Salim as its president for the month of May, and Sheikh Ghazi Ajil al-Yawer as its president for the month of June 2004.
[Signed] *Massoud Barzani*
President of the Governing Council

Document 474
Governing Council Resolution Number 71 of 2004 [Allocation of a Pension to General Ibrahim Faisal al-Ansari]
28 April 2004

In the name of God, the Merciful, the Compassionate: At its ordinary session (43) held on 28 April 2004 the Governing Council decided the following:

To allocate a monthly pension of 750 dollars to Lieutenant General Ibrahim Faisal al-Ansari, the former Chief of Staff of the Army.

The Minister of Finance shall implement this decision.
[Signed] *Massoud Barzani*
President of the Governing Council

Document 475
Governing Council Resolution Number 72 of 2004 [Adoption of the Design of the Provisional Iraqi Flag]
28 April 2004

In the name of God, the Merciful, the Compassionate: At its ordinary session (43) held on 28 April 2004 the Governing Council decided the following:

To adopt the attached design of the provisional flag of the Republic of Iraq for the time until the election of the National Assembly and the adoption of a permanent flag.
[Signed] *Massoud Barzani*
President of the Governing Council

Document 476
Governing Council Resolution Number 73 of 2004 [Formation of a Committee to Prepare an Assessment of the Governing Council]
3 May 2004

In the name of God, the Merciful, the Compassionate: At its ordinary session (44) held on 3 May 2004 the Governing Council decided the following:

A committee shall be established, comprising of the persons whose names have been written below, to prepare a statement describing the circumstances which accompanied the formation of the Governing Council, its achievements, and obstacles encountered in its work.

1. Dr Adnan al-Pachachi.
2. Dr Mahmoud Othman.
3. Dr Mohsen Abdel Hamid.
4. Mr Sami al-Askari.
5. Mr Muhyi Kathim al-Khateeb.

[Signed] *Ezzeddine Salim*
President of the Governing Council

Document 477
Governing Council Resolution Number 74 of 2004 [Appointment of the Director-General of the Administration Department of the Iraqi Special Criminal Tribunal]
8 May 2004

In the name of God, the Merciful, the Compassionate: At its ordinary session (47) held on 8 May 2004 the Governing Council decided the following:

Based upon paragraph 3 of article 9 of Law number 1 of the year 2003 on the Iraqi Criminal Tribunal for crimes against humanity, and based on the fulfilment of the legal conditions, it has been decided to appoint Mr Salem Jawad al-Chalabi as the Director-General of the Administration Department of the above-mentioned court. Mr al-Chalabi is to be granted the [following] powers mentioned in the Iraqi Civil Service Law vested in a Director-General:

1. To contract the administrative staff whose job titles are listed in the Staffing and Budget of the above-mentioned court for the two fiscal years 2004 and 2005; and to contract them for salaries that do not exceed the limit specified next to those job titles.

2. To contract judges, prosecutors, assistants and specialized international assistants after obtaining the approval of the [Governing] Council, for salaries that do not exceed the limit indicated next to their respective job titles in the Budget.
3. To grant the contracted staff mentioned in paragraph 1 above, the following allowances:
   a. Allowances for vice directors for those who are asked to fill vacant positions which shall not exceed 30 per cent of the vacant job's salary.
   b. Allowances for dangers/risks with an average that shall not exceed 40 per cent of the salary.
   c. The sum of all allowances granted to a contracted person shall not exceed 60 per cent of the salary.
4. To propose to rearrange the Budget of the Court after consulting the President of the Court.
5. To send the contracted person on training courses, inside or outside Iraq, and to pay for these training courses from the sums allocated for them in the budget.
6. This resolution is to be implemented as of 1 May 2004.

[Signed] *Ezzeddine Salim*
President of the Governing Council

Document 478
Governing Council Resolution Number 75 of 2004
[Appointment of an Adviser at the State Consultative Council]

8 May 2004

In the name of God, the Merciful, the Compassionate: At its ordinary session (47) held on 8 May 2004 the Governing Council decided the following:

To appoint Salem Ali Ahmad Abbas al-Mandalawi as adviser at the State Consultative Council, starting from the date of issuance of this resolution.

[Signed] *Ezzeddine Salim*
President of the Governing Council

Document 479
Governing Council Resolution Number 76 of 2004
[Periodic Sessions of the Governing Council]

9 May 2004

In the name of God, the Merciful, the Compassionate: At its ordinary session (48) held on 9 May 2004 the Governing Council decided the following:

To limit the periodic ordinary sessions of the Council to one session on the following days: Mondays, Tuesdays and Wednesdays.

[Signed] *Ezzeddine Salim*
President of the Governing Council

Document 480
Governing Council Resolution Number 77 of 2004
[Appointment of Iraqi Representative to UNESCO]

9 May 2004

In the name of God, the Merciful, the Compassionate: At its ordinary session (48) held on 9 May 2004 the Governing Council decided the following:

1. To appoint Mr Muhyi Kathim al-Khateeb ambassador in the Foreign Ministry.
2. He is to be appointed as representative of Iraq to the United Nations Educational, Scientific and Cultural Organization (UNESCO).

The Foreign Minister and the Minister of Education are responsible for implementing this resolution.

[Signed] *Ezzeddine Salim*
President of the Governing Council

Document 481
Governing Council Resolution Number 78 of 2004
[Appointment of Iraqi Representative to FAO]

9 May 2004

In the name of God, the Merciful, the Compassionate: At its ordinary session (48) held on 9 May 2004 the Governing Council decided to appoint Dr Akram al-Jaff as representative of Iraq to the United Nations Food and Agriculture Organization (FAO) with the rank of ambassador.

The Foreign Minister and the Minister of Agriculture are responsible for implementing this resolution.

[Signed] *Ezzeddine Salim*
President of the Governing Council

Document 482
Governing Council Resolution Number 80 of 2004
[Salary and Allowances of Martyr Ezzelddine Salim]

24 May 2004

In the name of God, the Merciful, the Compassionate: At its ordinary session (52) held on 24 May 2004 the Governing Council decided the following:

1. The complete salary and allowances of martyr Ezzelddine Salim (former President of the Governing Council) shall be paid to his legal heirs without any deduction.
2. An appropriate house shall be allocated for the accommodation of the family of the Martyr.

3. The family of the Martyr shall keep the car, which was reserved for his personal use.
4. This decision shall be implemented from the date of its issuance.

The Minister of Finance and the competent authorities shall implement this resolution.
[Signed] *Sheikh Ghazi Ajil al-Yawer*
President of the Governing Council[145]

Document 483
Governing Council Resolution Number 81 of 2004
[Salary and Allowances of Martyr Talib Qasim Hajjami]
24 May 2004

In the name of God, the Merciful, the Compassionate: At its ordinary session (53) held on 24 May 2004 the Governing Council decided the following:

1. The salary which was paid to Martyr Talib Qasim Hajjami (deputy to Martyr Ezzelddine Salim) shall be paid to his legal heirs without any deduction.
2. An appropriate house shall be allocated for the accommodation of the family of the Martyr.
3. The family of the Martyr shall keep the car, which was reserved for his personal use.
4. This decision shall be implemented from the date of its issuance.

The Minister of Finance and the competent authorities shall implement this resolution.
[Signed] *Sheikh Ghazi Ajil al-Yawer*
President of the Governing Council

Document 484
Governing Council Resolution Number 82 of 2004
[Appointment of the President of the State Consultative Council]
24 May 2004

In the name of God, the Merciful, the Compassionate: At its ordinary session (53) held on 24 May 2004 the Governing Council decided the following:

1. To appoint Dr Qais Abdul Sattar Othman as president to the State Consultative Council [Majlis Al-Shura].
2. This decision shall be implemented from the date of its issuance.

[Signed] *Sheikh Ghazi Ajil al-Yawer*
President of the Governing Council

[145] Para 2 was cancelled by Law No 9 of 2005, *Official Gazette*, vol 47, no 4004 (22 September 2005).

Document 485
Governing Council Resolution Number 83 of 2004
[Rejection of the Resignation of Two Members of the Governing Council]

25 May 2004

In the name of God, the Merciful, the Compassionate: At its extraordinary session (15) held on 21 May 2004 the Governing Council decided to refuse to accept the resignations of Dr Muhammad Bahr al-Ulum and Dr Ahmad Chalabi from the Council, and to invite them to return to their ranks in order to continue the mission of the Council, which is to restore sovereignty and to receive authority on the 30th of June 2004.
[Signed] *Sheikh Ghazi Ajil al-Yawer*
President of the Governing Council
25 May 2004[146]

Document 486
Governing Council Resolution Number 84 of 2004
[Approval of the Draft Law of the Ministry of Displacement and Migration]

25 May 2004

In the name of God, the Merciful, the Compassionate: At its ordinary session (54) held on 25 May 2004 the Governing Council decided to ratify the draft law of the Ministry of Displacement and Migration and its organizational structure effective from the date of issuance of this resolution.

The Minister of Displacement and Migration is to implement this resolution.
[Signed] *Sheikh Ghazi Ajil al-Yawer*
President of the Governing Council

Document 487
Governing Council Resolution Number 85 of 2004
[Documents on Intelligence Services and Public Security]

26 May 2004

In the name of God, the Merciful, the Compassionate: At its ordinary session (53) held on 24 May 2004 the Governing Council decided to require all parties, organizations and associations to turn over important documents in their possession which address the intelligence services and the issue of public security and which contain information that is

[146] While the date given in the text is 21 May 2004, the date at the bottom of the resolution says 25 May 2004. It seems that the text of the resolution was prepared for the IGC session on 21 May but was signed only on 25 May.

in the supreme national interest, so as to enable the Iraqi National Intelligence Service to use this information to protect the homeland and its citizens.
[Signed] *Sheikh Ghazi Ajil al-Yawer*
President of the Governing Council
26 May 2004[147]

Document 488
Governing Council Resolution Number 86 of 2004 [Promotion of Two Assistant Advisers at the State Consultative Council to Advisers]

27 May 2004

In the name of God, the Merciful, the Compassionate: At its ordinary session (55) held on 27 May 2004 the Governing Council decided the following:

1. To promote the following two assistant advisers to the position of adviser at the State Consultative Council: Sayyid Muzaffar Abdul Wahhab Nuri and Sayyid Ghassan Hassan Daoud.
2. This decision shall be implemented from the date of its issuance.

[Signed] *Sheikh Ghazi Ajil al-Yawer*
President of the Governing Council

Document 489
Governing Council Resolution Number 87 of 2004 [Iraq as a Single Electoral Constituency and Adoption of the System of Proportional Representation]

30 May 2004

In the name of God, the Merciful, the Compassionate: At its extraordinary session (18) held on 30 May 2004 the Governing Council decided that Iraq will be a single electoral constituency, and to authorize the system of proportional representation in the upcoming elections.
[Signed] *Sheikh Ghazi Ajil al-Yawer*
President of the Governing Council

[147] While the date given in the text is 24 May 2004, the date at the bottom of the resolution says 26 May 2004. It seems that the text of the resolution was prepared for the IGC session on 24 May but was signed only on 26 May.

Document 490
Governing Council Resolution Number 90 of 2004 [Mandating the UN Electoral Mission to Choose the Chairman and Members of the Independent Electoral Commission]

30 May 2004

In the name of God, the Merciful, the Compassionate: At its extraordinary session (18) held on 30 May 2004 the Governing Council decided to mandate the United Nations electoral mission to choose seven candidates from the fourteen advanced applicants for the positions of chairman and members of the Independent Electoral Commission.
[Signed] *Sheikh Ghazi Ajil al-Yawer*
President of the Governing Council

Document 491
Governing Council Resolution Number 91 of 2004 [Documents and Information of the Previous Regime]

31 May 2004

In the name of God, the Merciful, the Compassionate: In order to care for and preserve the documents and information that the previous regime has left behind in a safe environment; in order for the information and documents to be accessible to researchers and scholars; in order to serve the nation and to benefit it; and in order to avoid all the legal questions which ensue from holding documents that are not allowed to be circulated; at its extraordinary session (18) held on 30 May 2004 the Governing Council decided the following:

To require all parties, groups, individuals, and officials to supply the House of Books and Documents, which is [a Directorate] under the Ministry of Culture, with all the documents mentioned above which are in their possession.
[Signed] *Sheikh Ghazi Ajil al-Yawer*
President of the Governing Council
31 May 2004[148]

[148] While the date given in the text is 30 May 2004, the date at the bottom of the resolution says 31 May 2004. It seems that the text of the resolution was prepared for the IGC session on 30 May but was signed only on 31 May.

Document 492
Governing Council Resolution Number 92 of 2004 [Appointment of Ghazi Mashal Ajil al-Yawer as President of the Interim Government]

1 June 2004

[The text of the resolution is not available. Reports in the Iraqi press indicate that the resolution concerned the appointment of Ghazi Mashal Ajil al-Yawer as President of the Interim Government.]

Document 493
Governing Council Resolution Number 93 of 2004 [Transfer of Authority and Dissolution of the Governing Council]

1 June 2004

In the name of God, the Merciful, the Compassionate: Given that the consultations between the Governing Council, the Coalition Provisional Authority and the Secretary General of the United Nations have resulted in naming a President, a Prime Minister and a new ministerial cabinet, the Governing Council decided at its ordinary session (56) held on 1 June 2004 to transfer its authority to the Interim Government and to dissolved itself.
[Signed] *Sheikh Ghazi Ajil al-Yawer*
President of the Governing Council

2. Other Documents

Document 494
Statement of the Governing Council after its First Meeting

13 July 2003[1]

Peace be upon you, dear brothers and sisters. May God's peace and blessings be upon you. In the name of God, the Merciful, the Compassionate: We are honored at these sensitive and complicated circumstances in the history of our country to announce to our homeland and the entire world the establishment of the transitional Governing Council, as an embodiment of the free national will of all Iraqis and in implementation of UN Security Council Resolution No 1483 to expedite the accomplishment of the tasks of the interim stage.

At this historic moment, we are eager to announce that the establishment of this council was the result of strenuous efforts exerted by Iraqi forces and figures of various affiliations and political trends, which have not stopped their consultations to reach the best possible formula so that this establishment might represent the components of the Iraqi people. This is done in consultation with the Coalition Provisional Authority and the representative of the UN Secretary-General. The council is representative of the makeup of the Iraqi people.

The establishment of this council is an expression of the national Iraqi will in the wake of the collapse of the former oppressive and dictatorial regime, thanks to the struggle and brave sacrifices of our people and the intervention of the international coalition forces. However, the building of new Iraq shall remain among the first priorities of the good Iraqi people. It will require the participation of all Iraqis from all political and social trends who are willing to help accomplish this historic task.

Looking at the challenges of today, we believe that the most important priority of the council is to direct all of its efforts towards achieving security and stability in the country, revitalizing the national economy and providing public services. All this will be done through the establishment of a government with full functions and through the encouragement of the institutions of civil society.

Efforts must be exerted to complete the drafting of a permanent constitution that represents the will of the Iraqi people and paves the way for holding general elections and forming an effective government that enjoys full powers in a manner that restores sovereignty and independence to Iraq.

The tasks entrusted to the newly formed council are large and the responsibilities of its members cannot be underestimated. The old regime has wrought a comprehensive destruction of all the institutions of the state of Iraq and undermined all political, social, economic, and cultural aspects of Iraqi life. Rebuilding Iraq will require the greatest degree of cooperation and cohesion among members of the united people. We must give precedence to national interests over any considerations in order to rebuild a new Iraq whose people enjoy full rights under a unified democratic federal system.[2] Peace be upon you.

[1] The statement was read by Governing Council member Muhammad Bahr al-Ulum at the conclusion of its first meeting in Baghdad, 13 July 2003.

[2] On 26 September 2003, Ambassador Bremer said: 'The Governing Council, in its political statement it issued after it took office, said it planned to respect individual rights, including women's rights and children's rights and human rights.'

Brothers and sisters, I read to you the first resolution issued by the Governing Council in its opening session this morning:

> 'Cancelling all official holidays associated with the deposed dictatorial regime and the dissolved [Arab Socialist] Ba'ath Party.
> 9 April, the day the regime fell, shall become a national day for Iraq and an official holiday.'[3]

Document 495

Statement before the United Nations Security Council by Adnan Pachachi, Head of the Delegation of the Iraqi Governing Council

22 July 2003

At the outset, I wish to express deep gratitude to the Council for having invited us to participate in this historic meeting. My special thanks go to the Secretary-General, Mr. Kofi Annan, and to his Special Representative for Iraq, Mr. Sergio Vieira de Mello, and their colleagues for their efforts regarding the situation in Iraq and the country's future. We shall take into account their valuable remarks and their constructive proposals.

It is indeed a great pleasure and honour for me and for my two colleagues, Ms. Aqeela al-Hashemi and Mr Ahmad Chalabi, to appear before the Security Council on behalf of Iraq and the interim Governing Council, of which we have the honour of being members.

Our homeland has rid itself of the oppressive tyrannical regime that oppressed our people for three decades, usurped our freedom, eroded our dignity and exercised the worst forms of oppression, as demonstrated by the mass graves now being discovered across the country. Despite their ongoing suffering, frustration and oppression due to current security and living conditions, which have not improved as quickly as we had hoped, the people of Iraq have finally had a taste of the freedom that had been denied them for so many decades. The Iraqi people will never return to a society based on fear and injustice. Iraqi citizens can now express their views and articulate their aspirations freely.

A State marked by the intelligence services, mandatory arrests and random executions has ended, never to return. The Iraqi people consider our participation in this meeting to be clear and explicit recognition of Iraq's sovereignty, which the Council emphasized in the second preambular paragraph of its resolution 1483 (2003)[4]. The Governing Council was established as the embodiment of the nation's determination to preserve Iraq's sovereignty, safeguard its unity and territorial integrity, achieve a better future for its people and reconstruct its social fabric, following the disintegration of all values and social cohesiveness and the undermining of national unity in that dark era.

The Governing Council – which represents the full spectrum of Iraqi society and whose members have been chosen as a result of painstaking and extensive consultations among Iraqi personalities of various religious, ethnic and political affiliations – was assisted, during the intensive negotiations that preceded the formation of the Council, by representatives of the Coalition Provisional Authority and by the Special Representative of the Secretary-

[3] The decision to declare 9 April an official holiday was confirmed by the first freely elected Iraqi government on 5 April 2006.

[4] See *Doc 523*.

General, in keeping with operative paragraph 9 of resolution 1483 (2003). We wish to place on record our sincere gratitude to all of them for their efforts.

Resolution 1483 (2003) did not set out in a clear and precise manner the functions of the interim administration. This flexibility in the scope of the resolution allowed a certain latitude for expansion of the powers of the Governing Council so that all aspects of government could be covered. All of our proposals in this regard have been fully responded to.

Our primary goal, which we will continue to bear in mind, is to shorten the duration of the interim administration period and put together an elected Government under a constitution to be endorsed by the population in free elections. The elections should be open to all, and the people should be able to express their opinions freely.

The draft Constitution will be examined by a constitutional congress representing all political, social and religious groups. The Governing Council will prepare for that conference by determining the best way to ensure the participation of representatives and to take the necessary legislative action as well as other measures to facilitate its operations, including in the areas of electoral law, population census, electoral register, organization of political parties and other questions relating to freedom of expression and freedom of assembly. The United Nations, given its expertise and experience, could help us to draw up this legislation.

The Constitution, much-awaited by the Iraqi people, will put in place a democratic, pluralistic and federal system that safeguards people's basic rights; consolidates the rule of law in an independent judiciary system; ensures the peaceful handover of power through free elections; places the armed forces under the authority of the elected administration; and gives women full rights on the basis of equality.

In brief, we look forward to the creation of a civil society that believes in personal freedom as a premise for governance and rejects totalitarian systems, which have brought only misery and destruction to our people.

Let me touch on some of the pressing issues to be addressed by the interim Governing Council. This list, however, is not exhaustive.

First, there is a need to appoint ministers, to fill vacancies in Government agencies and ministries, and to appoint competent personnel who were not implicated in any crimes committed by the previous regime.

Secondly, Iraqi embassies abroad must be reopened so that they can carry out their regular functions. Representatives of foreign Governments must be received, and Iraqi representatives appointed to international organizations, first and foremost to the United Nations. Iraq will then work to improve relations with neighbouring Arab countries, its other neighbours and the international community at large. Iraq will require tremendous assistance in all areas in order to rebuild its economy, modernize its industrial sector, reform its educational system, improve its sanitation services and provide basic necessities to all its citizens. There is no doubt in my mind that the United Nations and its specialized agencies will have an important and vital role to play in all these areas.

Thirdly, one of the primary functions of the Governing Council is to ensure security and stability and to establish institutions that can rebuild the national police and the national army and enable them to preserve stability and security in Iraq. The police and the army should be used to eliminate those destructive elements and saboteurs who continue to impede the national development process and to undermine the interests of the civilian population.

Fourthly, there should be a re-examination of the legislation enacted by the previous regime – legislation that enabled it to tighten its control over the country. The judiciary system, which was destroyed by the previous regime, should be reformed.

Fifthly, special tribunals should be constituted in order to bring to justice those who committed criminal acts under the former Iraqi regime, so that they will stand trial for their humanitarian crimes against the Iraqi people. Such tribunals will prosecute accused criminals. We have asked a special group of Council members to present proposals regarding the formation of these special tribunals.

Iraq's national economy must be revived, and projects must be undertaken that provide jobs for the unemployed; alleviate the poverty of a large segment of society, a large percentage of which is still living below the poverty line; promote justice and fairness in the distribution of national wealth; and consolidate political freedom as the economic situation improves.

We will work to ensure that every individual benefits from Iraq's tremendous national assets through the creation of a special fund, and we will ensure compensation for victims of forced displacement and for people whose property was confiscated by the bloodthirsty regime of Saddam Hussain.

The Governing Council has taken several decisions that will enable it to begin implementing this ambitious programme. With regard to security, the Council has decided to employ at least 30,000 Iraqi police officers, to train them, to provide them with equipment and to pay them adequately. The Council has decided also to establish, as expeditiously as possible, at least 1,500 schools and clinics throughout Iraq.

Also in the context of the economy, all salaries, including back pay, will be paid, and we will start a programme to reabsorb more than 200,000 demobilized soldiers into the civil society employment sector, especially in the public works and construction sector. The Governing Council will examine the budget with a view to satisfying the needs of the population, reform the currency system and issue a new currency in order to provide citizens with purchasing power. The contribution of the United Nations and its specialized agencies in that endeavour will be extremely important.

The challenge that is facing us is enormous. The responsibilities of the Governing Council are many, difficult and diverse. The important responsibility borne by the members of the Council cannot be overstated. We need the Iraqi people to fully support us. We will have to demonstrate to them our credibility and merit if we are to lead them in this historic process.

Speaking personally, I would like to say that I am optimistic. The Iraqi people have demonstrated their ability to coexist in harmony and tolerance, and we will make every possible effort to overcome the difficulties that we face. We are counting on the support of the Council in restoring Iraq to its proper position within the international community.[5]

Document 496
Governing Council Press Release Number 12 [Political Statement]

22 July 2003[6]

The Iraqi Governing Council was set up by a patriotic initiative in response to the demands of the transitional period and the provisions of Security Council Resolution 1483,[7] as an

[5] UN Doc. S/PV.4791, 22 July 2003, 9-11.
[6] Translated from Arabic.
[7] See *Doc 523*.

essential step towards revival and building the homeland and achieving independence to pave the ground for establishing a legitimate government based on a democratic and a constitutional foundation.

This event has taken place after the fall of the tyrannical regime, owing to the struggles of the Iraqi people and the support of the international coalition forces who hopefully will provide the opportunity for the Iraqi people to rebuild their country on the basis of a healthy democracy which will guarantee their freedom, security and prosperity.

Iraq is facing a terrible legacy of destruction brought about by oppressive and brutal ethnic and sectarian policies of the regime and its reckless adventures against neighbouring States. These were exemplified by the terrible images of mass graves, and the social, economic and cultural devastation which has been unfolding. Consequently, the Council faces huge responsibilities in this difficult phase, which require all the sincere people of Iraq to stand shoulder to shoulder to support the international forces and the Islamic and Arabic countries.

The core areas of activity of the Council, in the light of Iraqi and international realities, include the following responsibilities:

1. To provide security and stability to citizens and to protect their property, as well as to rebuild state institutions and to put them back into action, particularly the Iraqi police force and the army. Furthermore, to deal firmly with terrorist and sabotage attempts which are being directed by remnants of the former regime and its stooges.

2. To eliminate the legacy of the political tyranny, ethnic and sectarian discrimination, and to root out the Ba'th Party and its ideologies from Iraqi society. Furthermore, to establish the principles of political pluralism and democracy and to expedite the implementation of the Governing Council's resolution pertaining to the setting up of specialized courts to try officials from the deposed regime,[8] who took part in crimes against the Iraqi people and humanity so that the criminals can receive their just punishment. Subsequently, a national reconciliation initiative must be launched for those who did not commit crimes against humanity and to rehabilitate them into Iraqi society in an atmosphere of openness and the disclosure of truth.

3. To lay the foundation for a democratic, federal and pluralist system which guarantees universal freedom, the freedom of thought and expression and respect for human rights, as well as respect for the Islamic identity of the majority of Iraqi people and women's rights. In addition, to strengthen the authority of the judiciary and to guarantee its independence. Above all is the task to embark on a democratic process to adopt a permanent constitution for the country.

4. To provide public services by putting into action the State's service institutions and to root out pockets of corruption and sabotage, which target economic and service facilities, and to protect the environment.

5. To revive the national economy, to create jobs and to improve living conditions for citizens by pursuing a balanced economic policy based on mobilizing financial resources and improving economic efficiency. Furthermore, to encourage the private sector and the investment climate and to deal with the problem of foreign debt, as well as to call for the cancellation of compensation brought about by the disastrous policies of the deposed regime.

6. To develop and rehabilitate the oil sector and to restructure the national oil companies and to develop them in line with the objectives of national economic policies.

7. To set up an agency to care for the relatives of the martyrs who were killed by the regime and to provide appropriate compensation to the victims of ethnic and sectarian

[8] For the resolution, see *Doc 267*.

persecution, genocide, ethnic cleansing and the confiscation of property carried out by the former regime.

8. The Council seeks to develop Iraq's external relations with the Arab and Islamic world and the international community in order to guarantee security, stability, mutual interest and joint benefit.

9. To pay more attention to the strengthening of relations with the United Nations and to develop its role in the political process, humanitarian relief operations, respect for human rights and reconstruction, particularly in accomplishing the tasks during the transitional period.

The building of the new Iraq remains essentially a responsibility for Iraqis, a matter which requires the participation of the various components of Iraqi society, including Arabs, Kurds, Turkomans, Chaldo-Assyrians and other fraternal minorities. The Council calls on Iraqis to stand shoulder to shoulder and urges them to work together to accomplish the enormous tasks of the transitional period, to consolidate the basis of Iraqi national unity and to elevate Iraq from the collapse it has suffered so that it can regain its proper place among the nations.

Document 497
Governing Council Press Release
[Condemnation of the Terrorist Attack on 19 August]

20 August 2003

The Governing Council offers its condolences on the loss of Mr. Sergio de Mello, Personal Representative of the United Nations Secretary General, the loss of Iraqi citizens, and that of international officials who were victims of the massive explosion August 19th that targeted the United Nations headquarters and the neighbouring Ibn al-Qaf Hospital for the Handicapped.

The Governing Council condemns this terrorist act that targeted the people of Iraq and the entire international community, and affirms that the soil of Iraq will swallow those who perpetrated this reprehensible crime, be they followers of the former regime or terrorist elements who have infiltrated the borders. There will be no place for them among Iraqis enthusiastic to build the new Iraq. This dreadful incident will not prevent Iraq from achieving its democratic transformation, guaranteeing its security and safety of its people.

At this critical stage through which the Iraqi people are passing, the Governing Council calls on all sons of the Iraqi people to cooperate with the new Iraqi institutions concerned with guaranteeing security. The sons of this nation should assume the responsibility of preserving order and confronting all of the desperate attempts to violate the security of the country and expose its future to danger. This should take place by expanding the role of Iraqis in preserving order through the New Iraqi Army, the Iraqi Police Force, and the Iraqi Civil Defense Corps. This expansion will reflect the reality of the Iraqi people, and expresses its aspirations to build a secure, democratic, and stable Iraq.

The Iraqi people, determined to fight terrorism and establish a secure society in democracy and freedom, calls upon brotherly and friendly countries as well as the United Nations to play a positive role in supporting the people of Iraq and assist its efforts to achieve security and stability in Iraq.

The Governing Council reiterates that these repugnant and sick terrorist attacks will not impede its efforts to lead the process of democratic transformation, and hopes that these

attacks will not impede the efforts of the United Nations in pursuing its effective, essential role in rebuilding the new Iraq.
Baghdad
August 20, 2003

Document 498
Higher National De-Ba'athification Commission Decree Number 1
14 September 2003

Based on the decree of the Civil Administration Director Number 1 on 15 May 2003,[9] as well as the powers granted by the Governing Council that aim to consolidate security and stability and safeguard the atmosphere of freedoms and democracy in Iraq, the Higher National De-Ba'athification Commission, in its meeting held on 14 September 2003, has decided the following:

1. Any civil servant who held the rank of division member or a higher rank in the dissolved Ba'ath Party is hereby dismissed from public posts of all grades and must leave his post immediately. Whoever gives false information to remain in his position will be subject to penalties. The relevant administrative personnel are responsible for implementing this decree. Any exceptions issued prior to this decree are hereby declared null and void.
2. Individuals dismissed under Paragraph 1 above are entitled to submit appeals to the Higher National De-Ba'athification Commission, which will examine the applications and make the appropriate decisions.
3. All ministries and departments that are not related to ministries are hereby instructed to implement this decree, which goes into effect as of this date.

[Signed] *Ahmad al-Chalabi*
Chairman of the Higher National De-Ba'athification Commission
14 September 2003

Document 499
Higher National De-Ba'athification Commission Decree Number 2
14 September 2003

To serve the supreme national interests, safeguard the national accomplishments, and protect democracy, security, and stability in the country, the Higher National De- Ba'athification Commission in its meeting held on 14 September 2003 has decided the following:

The following individuals shall be totally banned from holding special positions or undertaking responsibilities in public posts, political activities, civil society institutions, the press, or the media:

1. Whoever held the rank of division member or a higher rank in the dissolved Ba'ath Party.
2. Whoever held the post of general manager or a higher post or district manager or a higher post or their equivalent posts involving advisers and experts under the former regime. Excluded from this ban will be those who left the authority and undertook stances.

[9] The reference is to CPA Order No 1 of 16 May 2003 *[Doc 14]*.

3. Individuals affiliated with the repressive agencies of the authority (Special Security, National Security, Presidential Special Protection, Military Intelligence, Saddam Fedayeen, Public Security, and the Intelligence).

4. Individuals known and proved to be involved in plundering the country's wealth or participating in the regime's aggressive policies or in committing crimes.

5. The Higher National De-Ba'athification Commission will examine exceptional cases and will later make a decision on each one of them separately.

6. All ministries and pertinent quarters are hereby instructed to implement this decree, which goes into effect as of this date.

Signed: *Ahmad al-Chalabi*
Chairman of the Higher National De-Ba'athification Commission
14 September 2003[10]

Document 500
Press Release of the Governing Council's Preparatory Committee for the Development of Mechanisms for the Constitutional Conference

30 September 2003[11]

The Preparatory Committee for the Development of Mechanisms for the Constitutional Conference held several meetings during the period from 18 August 2003 to 30 September 2003, met a number of people in seminars, visited several provinces and hosted Iraqi and international experts which are concerned with the constitution and listened to their experience. The Committee visited Grand Ayatollah Ali Sistani in Najaf and a number of religious, political and social authorities and listened to their views and guidance and held dialogues with them. The Committee submitted its report containing the proposed options for the formation of the Constitutional Convention and conditions of membership of that Conference, as well as the general principles and the basic pillars and guarantees of the Constitution. The report concluded the Committee's opinion, which was adopted unanimously.

Document 501
Message from the President of the Iraqi Governing Council to the International Business Community

23 October 2003

Greetings to the International Business Community:

It is my great pleasure to introduce you to the new and free Iraq. The task we Iraqis face to rebuild our country after years of oppression, violence and neglect is enormous, but so

[10] On 17 September 2003, the Chairman of the Higher National De-Ba'athification Commission, Ahmad al-Chalabi, sent a note to the CPA Administrator, Ambassador Bremer, on 'Decisions by the Higher National De-Ba'athification Commission on dismissing Ba'ath party members' notifying him of the two decisions.

[11] Translated from Arabic.

too will be the opportunities open to international businesses and investors. The new Iraq views a robust private sector as a critical ingredient in a sound economic development strategy. To realize our full potential, we must create incentives for international businesses and investors to come to Iraq and participate in its rebirth.

With this in mind, the newly-formed Iraqi Governing Council recently announced a series of sweeping reforms to open up Iraq's economy and help foster investment, job creation and long-term economic growth. The reforms encompass: 1) foreign direct investment; 2) international bank entry and local commercial banking; 3) taxes; 4) tariffs; and 5) central banking.

We are optimistic about our long-term economic success. By harnessing our natural wealth and substantial human resources, Iraq can regain its place among the developed countries of the world. We believe strongly that in Iraq, the international business community will find a land of great opportunity and promise. We invite you to work with us as we build the new Iraq!

Sincerely,
Dr Ayad Allawi
President, Iraqi Governing Council

Document 502
Statement on the Political Transition in Iraq

15 November 2003

Out of commitment to the national and religious constants of the Iraqi people, out of adherence to what the Governing Council has sought since its establishment, and in order to speed up the process of Iraq regaining its sovereignty and independence, the Governing Council has decided to adopt the following measures:

1. Drafting a law to govern the State for the transitional period before the end of February 2004. This includes measures to elect a transitional council that would be elected before the end of May 2004. This law expresses principles upon which a common agreement is reached among the Iraqi people. These are:
    a. Respecting human rights and basic freedoms, including freedom of faith, religious practice, and equality among all citizens.
    b. Ensuring the separation of the three powers.
    c. Introducing a degree of decentralization in running governorates, while taking into consideration the current situation in Kurdistan.
    d. Establishing the principle of civilian control of the security forces and the army.
    e. Establishing a democratic, federal, pluralistic and united regime that respects the Islamic identity of the majority of the Iraqi people while safeguarding the rights of other religions and communities.

This law will contain a timetable for formulating the permanent constitution through a council that is directly elected by the Iraqi people. A new government will be elected in accordance with the provisions of the new constitution before the end of 2005. The law also contains measures to choose the members of the transitional council who should be chosen before the end of May 2004.

2. The transitional council will elect a provisional Iraqi government before June 2004. The government will exercise political authority and will be sovereign and recognized on the international level. When power is handed over to it, the state of occupation will come to an end and the coalition authority will then be dissolved and the role of the Governing Council will end with the formation of an Iraqi provisional government.

3. The work of the transitional council and the government stemming from it will continue until the adoption of the permanent constitution. Power will then be transferred to a government elected in accordance with its provisions.

Realizing the importance of these measures for all the citizens, the governing council will take it upon itself as of now and during the coming months and until the provisional government is established to participate in initiating dialogue among all the political, social, and religious forces and figures and among all the citizens to secure the participation of all Iraqis in establishing a new political system. God is the one who grants success.

Document 503

Letter from the President of the Iraqi Governing Council to the President of the Security Council of the United Nations

23 November 2003

I have the honour to inform you and the members of the Security Council that the Iraqi Governing Council, having been invited by the Security Council, in paragraph 7 of resolution 1511 (2003),[12] to establish a timetable and programme for the drafting of a new constitution for Iraq and for the holding of democratic elections under that constitution, has decided to hold general elections for the establishment of a constitutional convention no later than 15 March 2005. The constitution that will be prepared by the said convention will be submitted to the Iraqi people for approval in a referendum. By the end of 2005, elections will be held to elect a new government in accordance with the provisions of the constitution. The Governing Council and the transitional government which will be elected by the end of June 2004 will make the necessary arrangements in preparation for these elections, inter alia by conducting a complete and accurate population census, drafting a law containing electoral regulations, preparing an electoral register and adopting laws concerning political parties, the press and meetings.

Prior to commencing the above-mentioned constitutional process, the transitional governing council will draft, no later than the end of February 2004, a law concerning the administration of the Iraqi State in accordance with the following principles:

1. Respect for human rights and fundamental freedoms, including freedom of religion, freedom of exercise of religious practice and equality of all citizens.
2. Separation of the three branches of government.
3. Introduction of some degree of decentralization in the administration of the governorates, taking into consideration the current situation in Iraqi Kurdistan.
4. Establishment of the principle of civilian control of the Iraqi armed and security forces.
5. Establishment of a unified federal democratic and multilateral system that respects the Islamic identity of the majority of the Iraqi people while ensuring the rights of other religions and religious communities.

[12] See *Doc 531*.

The aforementioned law will provide for the establishment of a provisional legislative body in accordance with procedures that will guarantee broad representation of all segments of Iraqi society. This legislative body, to be established no later than the end of May 2004, will elect a provisional Iraqi government no later than the end of June 2004, at which point the Coalition Provisional Authority will be dissolved. The occupation acknowledged by the Security Council in resolution 1483 (2003) will then come to an end and the Governing Council will have no more raison d'être given the existence of the provisional government. In light of the above, it would be appropriate for the Security Council to adopt another resolution that would take into consideration the new circumstances.
[Signed] *Jalal Talabani*
President of the Governing Council[13]

Document 504
Statement to the Iraqi People
16 December 2003

In the name of God, the Merciful, the Compassionate: O Prophet! Strive hard against the unbelievers and the hypocrites, and be firm against them. Their abode is hell – an evil refuge indeed.

The legend of the despotic tyrant has finally collapsed. He fell despicably and his fall was the last chapter in the process of the liberation of Iraq from the traces of despotism and fear. It is time to open a new chapter for the establishment of a secure and unified Iraq that gives hope to all people.

The regime's practices, whose victims were the ones killed in Saddam's wars and the victims of torture, mass graves and massacres by chemical weapons and displacement, today invoke the conscience of all so that justice can be restored.

Throughout the stages of their life, the Iraqi people have lived in peaceful, fraternal and humanitarian coexistence that is based on social accord among their various components. In spite of the efforts made by Saddam and his regime to sabotage this accord, the nobility of the Iraqi people was stronger.

On this historic occasion, the Governing Council stresses the activation of the spirit of tolerance to build national unity on solid bases. This necessitates the renunciation of violence and vengeance and heading towards building an Iraq of justice, peace and prosperity.[14] This requires reforming the material and moral destruction caused by the former regime in the political, economic, social, and educational fields. This will be done as part of the democratic political process in order to achieve national sovereignty and independence. The Governing Council stresses that Saddam, the Saddamists, the terrorists and the infiltrators from abroad, who are carrying their subversive practices and spreading

[13] UN Doc. S/2003/1170, 12 December 2003, Enclosure. The President of the Security Council acknowledged receipt of this letter in a letter, dated 2 December 2003, addressed to the Chargé d'affaires a.i. of the Permanent Mission of Iraq to the United Nations (UN Doc. S/2003/1169, 12 December 2003).

[14] It is of interest to note that while the IGC at its session on 15 December 2003 had called for stepping up repressive measures against Iraqis outside the framework of the Governing Council, Ambassador Bremer had proposed, in the same session, a project for tolerance, reconciliation, and political dialogue between Iraqis. See Daffā'ī, (ed.), *Iraq under Occupation: The Records of the Governing Council* [in Arabic] (2004), Introduction, Part I.

the concepts of terrorism, will face specialized Iraqi tribunals in Iraq as war criminals and enemies of mankind to receive their just punishment. Therefore, we call on the misled military and civilians, who did not commit crimes against the people, to prove their loyalty to the homeland in preparation for their return to the lap of their honourable people.

We are not the ones who wronged them: They wronged their own souls.

The Governing Council

Document 505

Letter from the President of the Iraqi Governing Council to the Secretary General of the United Nations

30 December 2003

Kind attention of Mr. Kofi Annan
United Nations Secretary General

Dear Secretary General,

We present greetings and,

In fulfillment of Security Council Resolution No. 1511 dated 16/10/2003[15] and the special role it entrusted the Governing Council for Administration in the transitional period, and reaffirming our adherence to the time table for announcing a Transitional National Assembly and an Internationally recognized Government representing the Iraqi people (item 15/resolution 1511):

First: And further to our discussion with the Coalition Provisional Authority regarding details of transfer of Authority. We would like to get an opinion from a specialized United Nations team in the possibility of conducting elections for the Provisional National Assembly. Should this be unfeasible, the Governing Council and the Civil Administration shall find the best methods and means to choose representatives of the Governorates to the Provisional National Assembly with the utmost possible transparency to reflect the real opinion of the Iraqi people in the 'law for Administration of the Iraqi Government' which shall be drafted by the Governing Council.

We request your kind cooperation and prompt initiative to support us and the Iraqi people to achieve quick results to permit us to uphold our undertaking of the time table presented to you in keeping with the above mentioned Security Council Resolution.

Second: We thank you for inviting representatives from the Governing Council to attend meeting between the [United Nations–Governing Council–Civil Administration in Iraq] to discuss the assumed role of the United Nations in Iraq. We believe that the United Nations can help the Iraqi people though performing the following roles further to the role mentioned in the first point.

(1) Supervision of proper coordination between the Iraqi part and the Civil Administration in the Transitional phase.
(2) Supervision of the elections for the Iraqi Constitution Drafting Council.
(3) Supervision of elections of the Constitutional Government.

[15] See *Doc 531*.

(4) Provide us with advice in concluding the security agreement to be adopted between the Civil Administration and Governing Council.

Please accept our utmost respect and appreciation.

Sayid Abdul Aziz Al-Hakim
President
Iraqi Governing Council

Document 506
Address to the Iraqi People by the President of the Iraqi Governing Council
1 January 2004

[...] Some people might wonder about the role of the IGC in addressing the various problems facing the country. Under the occupation the IGC capabilities remain limited because the Coalition Authority is responsible for running the country's affairs in accordance with the Security Council resolution that viewed the coalition forces as occupation forces. The resolution gave the civil authority of the occupation the right to administer funds.

From the very beginning your fraternal brothers at the IGC have been calling for the formation of an Iraqi government with effective sovereignty and broad-based representation that assumes authority during the transitional period. Following months of arduous and intensive negotiations, an agreement was signed on 15 November between the IGC and the coalition authority[16] that stipulated an end to the occupation and a transfer of power to an interim Iraqi government before the end of next June. We are currently putting the final touches to the law for Iraq's administration during the transitional period. This law will guarantee the basic rights and freedoms of the citizens, organize relations between the legislative and executive authorities, and underline the authority and independence of the judiciary. The people will be informed about the law to enable them to carry out public and transparent dialogue. The law will be implemented at the end of next February after which members of an interim national legislative council will be chosen.

Undoubtedly general elections will be the ideal way to select the national legislative council members but holding elections that will reflect the genuine will of the people will not be possible in such a short time if we want to reestablish sovereignty and authority before next June. The United Nations, in the words of its secretary general, has frequently expressed this opinion. Therefore direct general elections will be substituted with elections among smaller electorate groups in all governorates. This might be a complex and novel method but to a large extent it secures the establishment of a 250-member national legislative council that represents the bulk of the Iraqi people.

The first mission of this council will be the appointment of a state presidential committee, which in turn will appoint a prime minister and ministers. Before it assumes power the government should win the confidence of the national legislative council. The most important duties of this provisional government is to pave the way for a constitutional phase by means of carrying out an accurate population census, drawing up an election law, preparing voters lists, enacting laws that guarantee the freedom of opinion, assembly, and formation of parties,

[16] See *Doc 232*.

and holding general elections for a constitutional congress that will draw up the country's permanent constitution. The draft constitution will be presented to the people for discussion via the media and popular meetings and seminars. A free referendum will then be held to vote on the final form of the constitution and once endorsed elections will be held in harmony with the constitution to elect a government that will be the first of its kind in Iraq's modern history – a government that draws its legitimacy from the free will of the Iraqi people.

In view of the wish of various political forces for a UN role in the political and constitutional process the UN secretary general invited me to go to New York at the head of a delegation representing the IGC to discuss the details of the international organization's participation. The meeting was set for 19 January. I will brief you on the outcome of the meetings upon my return. [...].

Document 507

Higher National De-Ba'athification Commission Procedures for De-Ba'athification of the Public Sector and the State

10 January 2004[17]

First – Validity:

1. The coalition interim civil authority issued on 16th April 2003 – and in accordance with Order Number 1[18] – an order to eradicate the Ba'ath Party in Iraq. This process includes the eradication of the Party's structure and the removal of its leaders from positions of power.

2. According to Coalition Provisional Authority Order Number 1, and based on the power vested in the Governing Council by CPA Memorandum Number 7,[19] the Governing Council has indeed identified the following procedures to be followed in the de-Ba'athification of government departments as well as public sector institutions. The authority to implement these measures was granted to the Higher National De-Ba'athification Commission.

Second – Limits:

1. The de-Ba'athification procedures mentioned below apply to senior Ba'ath Party members working in both government and public sector departments, including government ministries, institutions, establishments, and other government departments. Senior Ba'ath Party members are those who occupy the upper four ranks in the party's hierarchy: 'Udw Qutriyya' (Regional Command Member), 'Udw Far' (Branch Member). 'Udw Shu'bah' (Section Member), and 'Udw Firqah' (Group Member).

2. Procedures, which apply to senior party members, also apply to individual members working in the top three layers of management if they qualify as members, or active members of the Ba'ath Party.

3. These procedures do not apply to members occupying any grades below the top three layers of management, and who are members of the Ba'ath Party without holding [at least] the rank of 'Udw Firqah' (Group Member); except those who have persecuted citizens or committed crimes against them.

[17] Translation from Arabic.
[18] See *Doc 14.*
[19] See *Doc 132.*

4. These measures do not apply to those working in the private sector; and special instructions will be issued later regarding the treatment of unions, associations, the private sector, and civil society organizations.

Third – Identification:

1. The Commission will review and examine the Ba'ath Party's documents, which happen to be at its disposal, to identify senior Ba'ath Party members and then supply ministers, heads of other government enterprises and institutions with information about them.

2. Ministers, heads of other government enterprises and institutions will rely on the relevant information – including the documentation of wages and bonuses, financial statements, and other information – in order to identify senior Ba'ath Party members.

Fourth – Procedures for Iraqi Ministries:

A. Administrative Dismissal:

1. The Ministers shall issue instructions to the Directors-General in Baghdad and the governorates in order to identify senior members of the Ba'ath Party,[20] and then remove them from their positions using information provided by the Higher National De-Ba'athification Commission ('Commission') and the ministries and all relevant information available to the Directors-General.

2. The Directors-General shall provide members of the Ba'ath Party removed from their positions with a dated letter that sets out the reasons for their dismissal and that provides the necessary information regarding the appeal procedures.

3. The Directors-General shall send reports on the dismissed members of the Ba'ath Party to the respective Ministers, and a copy of the report to the Commission.

B. Appeal:

1. Those dismissed with the rank of 'Udw Shu'bah' (Section Member) and higher are not entitled to appeal their dismissal.

2. Those with the rank of 'Udw Firqah' (Group Member) and lower, or those who held positions in the top three layers of administration and who did not hold the rank of 'Udw Shu'bah' (Section Member) or higher may appeal their dismissal. These individuals may choose between the following two options: (a) present their request for appeal and thereby waive their right to a pension, or (b) accept the pension and thereby waive their right to an appeal. The pension payment is to be calculated on the basis of the civil service law and the retirement law, and in accordance with the years of service, without calculating any benefits based on the position within the Party.

3. There are two steps in the administrative appeal process, in ascending order: (a) complaint to the local de-Ba'athification committee, and (b) appeal to the Higher National De-Ba'athification Commission.

4. The Ministers shall direct the Directors-General to establish local committees in every governorate and in Baghdad, in consultation with the Commission.

5. Every Director-General is *ex officio* a member of the local committee of his governorate without the right to vote; it is his right to appoint members to the local committee who are respected members of the community, and who are known to be men of integrity, justice, and who are capable to deal with the complaint procedures with an open mind.

[20] For a definition of senior members of the Ba'ath Party, see CPA Order No 1, sec 1(2) *[Doc 14]*.

6. The Ministers and the Commission have the right to review the names of those appointed to the local committees by the Directors-General within the ministry and to veto these appointments.

7. A dismissed employee who wants to appeal in accordance with the prescribed procedures must present to the local committee within two weeks from the implementation of the dismissal order a written request containing his plea and the evidence he relies upon. The Director-General has the right to accept the complaint after the expiry of the said time period if the delay was due to a legitimate excuse.

8. The local committee may require the dismissed employee to appear before it in person.

9. If the dismissed employee seeks to object to the dismissal decision by establishing that he is not a senior member of the Ba'ath Party, the local committee must study all facts and supporting documents, whether provided by the dismissed employee or obtained by the committee independently.

10. If it is established that the dismissed employee has the rank of 'Udw Firqah' (Group Member) and presented his complaint in order be excepted from de-Ba'athification, then the local committee must consider the following:

(a) Whether the dismissed employee has renounced his membership of the Ba'ath Party.

(b) The circumstances that led to the dismissed employee's joining the Ba'ath Party and the circumstances surrounding his promotion to the rank of 'Udw Firqah' (Group Member).

(c) The full employment history of the employee, including his connections with Ba'ath military, intelligence and security organizations.

(d) Whether during his time in office the dismissed employee was dedicated to furthering the goals of the Ba'ath Party.

(e) Any illegal activities that the dismissed employee engaged in.

(f) Whether the skills of the dismissed employee are rare and whether it is possible to replace or dispense with these skills.

11. The local committee must prepare a complete file for every case and must publish a written report within six weeks from the date of the appeal.

12. The local committee must present a report on every case, and submit the files of those cases to the Commission and notify the responsible Ministers about doing so.

13. The Commission reserves for itself the right to ratify all decisions made by the local committees.

14. The dismissed employee has the right to appeal the local committee's decision to the Commission within two weeks after the decision is rendered and the president of the local committee has the right to exempt any appeal request from the time limit in the event of compelling circumstances.

15. The Commission must hear every appeal request regarding the decisions of the local committees within the various ministries.

16. The appellant is entitled to provide evidence in person or in writing and the Commission may request that the employee concerned appear before it in person.

17. When examining requests for appeal the Commission will use the same criteria used in complaints before the local committees.

18. The Commission must publish a decision within six weeks from the date of the request for appeal.

19. The Commission is composed of two-judge panels appointed by the Judicial Council; the Governing Council, or the government which will succeed the Council, and

the Commission must approve the judges' appointment to attend the appeals sessions. The decision of appeal must contain the approval of at least one of the judges.

C. Exceptions:

1. The following exceptions to de-Ba'athification will be granted:
   - (a) Permanent exemptions.
   - (b) Conditional exemptions for one year; and this exception is subject to revocation in the following circumstances:
     - (1) If the local committee or the Commission is convinced that the dismissed employee has presented fabricated evidence or misinformation during the appeal procedure.
     - (2) The discovery of additional evidence that was not available at the time the exception was granted, and which would raise concerns that the exception would have been denied had the information been available when the exception was first granted.
     - (3) The local committee or the Commission ascertains from reliable evidence that the employee to whom the exception was granted has returned to his illegal and Ba'athist activities during the conditional exemption period.
     - (4) If the employee engaged during the exemption period in promulgating Ba'athist ideas or defending the previous regime.

2. The Ministry whose local committee granted the exception to de-Ba'athification on the conditional basis of observing the concerned employee and submitting an urgent report, provides any such information that may be the basis for revoking the exception to the local committee and the Commission.

3. The Commission must give timely notice and an explanation of the reasons if it intends to revoke the decision to grant a conditional exemption, and it must do so within two weeks of its decision to revoke the conditional exemption.

4. Those whose conditional exemptions were revoked will not be allowed to submit requests for exceptions.

Fifth – Procedures for Government Enterprises and Institutions:

The procedures stated above and which relate to the ministries also apply to other government enterprises and institutions. The head of a government enterprise or institution entrusts his institution in the relevant province or the sub-department with the responsibility of suspending, forming local committees, issuing decisions on rejections or exemptions, submitting appeals to the National Commission, and implementing the procedures listed above.

Reports are presented to both the head of the enterprise or institution and the Commission.

Sixth – Special Procedures for Prisoners of War:

1. The Commission's intention is to ensure that those who became Group Members only due to their incarceration [in Iran] maintain their jobs.

2. The individual applying for an exception as a prisoner of war must present the following evidence to the Commission:
   - (a) That he was a prisoner of war in Iran between 04 September 1980 and 01 June 2003; or that he was released from prison [in Iran] and returned to Iraq.
   - (b) That he was designated as a Group Member after being released from prison and returned to Iraq as a prisoner of war.

3. The National Commission must:

(a) Verify the validity of the applicant's legal status.
(b) Issue an exemption based on the fact that the applicant was either a prisoner of war, or was granted Group membership during the period of his incarceration.
(c) Any rejection by the Commission of an applicant's request for an exemption as a prisoner of war is considered final.
(d) The Commission must inform the applicant of its decision in writing within six weeks.

Seventh – General Procedures:

1. If the outcome of any complaint or appeal culminates in the employee's reinstatement in his previous position, he will receive his salary from the day of his dismissal to the day of his reinstatement.
2. All information which is collected during the process of de-Ba'athification, and which indicates any possible criminal conduct on the part of employees – be they senior party members or otherwise – must be submitted to the specialized courts. Mere membership in the Ba'ath Party does not represent a sufficient ground on which to refer to the courts.
3. Ministers, governors, and other officials who are not attached to ministries are all expected to implement the de-Ba'athification procedures within thirty days of their issuance. Otherwise, the Commission will be responsible for implementing de-Ba'athification, and will hold the violator accountable before the law.

Signed: *Ahmad Abdul-Hadi al-Chalabi*
Chairman of the Higher National De-Ba'athification Commission

Document 508
Governing Council Press Release Number 113
[Ban of Al-Jazeera]

31 January 2004[21]

On the instructions of the venerable Governing Council: It has been decided to prohibit Al-Jazeera satellite channel or its representatives from entering the headquarters of the Governing Council or attending its press conferences for a period of a full month as a punishment for showing disrespect to Iraq and its people and its misbehaviour towards prominent religious and national figures such as Grand Ayatollah Sayyid Muhsin al-Hakim, Kurdish leader Mullah Mustafa al-Barazani, Martyr Sayyid Muhammad Mahdi Al-Hakim and Martyr of the Mihrab Sayyid Muhammad Baqir Al-Hakim, favoured by Allah.

This resolution is effective beginning 28 January 2004 until 27 February 2004.

[Signed] *Muhyi al-Khateeb*
Secretary-General of the Governing Council

[21] Translation from Arabic.

Document 509
Governing Council Press Release Approval of the Law of Administration for the State of Iraq for the Transitional Period

1 March 2004[22]

In the name of God, the Merciful, the Compassionate: The Governing Council has approved unanimously early this morning the Transitional Administration Law after weeks of intensive discussions. The Law will be unveiled in a special ceremony on Wednesday 3rd March, in the presence of the President of the Council, Dr Muhammed Bahr al-Ulloum, and other Governing Council members.

Details of the ceremony will be published later.

[Signed] *Hamid al-Kifa'i*
Spokesman of the Governing Council

Document 510
Statement on the Postponement of the Signing of the Law of Administration for the State of Iraq for the Transitional Period

6 March 2004

In the name of God, the Merciful, the Compassionate: After months of in-depth discussion and dialogue, the Governing Council reached unanimous agreement to pass an Administrative Law for Iraq in the transitional phase. There is widespread consensus among Governing Council members on the law. But in the past few days a constructive dialogue took place regarding an important sensitive issue.

Since in the new democratic Iraq there are valuable opportunities to exchange views to reach agreement in a democratic climate, the Governing Council has decided to adjourn its sessions for two days to complete the members' dialogue on that issue.

The Council will reconvene on Monday, 8 March, to finalize the issue and sign the law.

Document 511
Law of Administration for the State of Iraq for the Transitional Period

8 March 2004

PREAMBLE

The people of Iraq, striving to reclaim their freedom, which was usurped by the previous tyrannical regime, rejecting violence and coercion in all their forms, and particularly when used as instruments of governance, have determined that they shall hereafter remain a free people governed under the rule of law.

[22] Translation from Arabic.

These people, affirming today their respect for international law, especially having been amongst the founders of the United Nations, working to reclaim their legitimate place among nations, have endeavored at the same time to preserve the unity of their homeland in a spirit of fraternity and solidarity in order to draw the features of the future new Iraq, and to establish the mechanisms aiming, amongst other aims, to erase the effects of racist and sectarian policies and practices.

This Law is now established to govern the affairs of Iraq during the transitional period until a duly elected government, operating under a permanent and legitimate constitution achieving full democracy, shall come into being.

CHAPTER ONE – FUNDAMENTAL PRINCIPLES

Article 1.

(A) This Law shall be called the 'Law of Administration for the State of Iraq for the Transitional Period,' and the phrase 'this Law' wherever it appears in this legislation shall mean the 'Law of Administration for the State of Iraq for the Transitional Period.'

(B) Gender-specific language shall apply equally to male and female.

(C) The Preamble to this Law is an integral part of this Law.

Article 2.

(A) The term 'transitional period' shall refer to the period beginning on 30 June 2004 and lasting until the formation of an elected Iraqi government pursuant to a permanent constitution as set forth in this Law, which in any case shall be no later than 31 December 2005, unless the provisions of Article 61 are applied.

(B) The transitional period shall consist of two phases.

(1) The first phase shall begin with the formation of a fully sovereign Iraqi Interim Government that takes power on 30 June 2004. This government shall be constituted in accordance with a process of extensive deliberations and consultations with cross-sections of the Iraqi people conducted by the Governing Council and the Coalition Provisional Authority and possibly in consultation with the United Nations. This government shall exercise authority in accordance with this Law, including the fundamental principles and rights specified herein, and with an annex that shall be agreed upon and issued before the beginning of the transitional period and that shall be an integral part of this Law.[23]

(2) The second phase shall begin after the formation of the Iraqi Transitional Government, which will take place after elections for the National Assembly have been held as stipulated in this Law, provided that, if possible, these elections are not delayed beyond 31 December 2004, and, in any event, beyond 31 January 2005. This second phase shall end upon the formation of an Iraqi government pursuant to a permanent constitution.

Article 3.

(A) This Law is the Supreme Law of the land and shall be binding in all parts of Iraq without exception. No amendment to this Law may be made except by a three-fourths majority of the members of the National Assembly and the unanimous approval of the Presidency Council.

[23] For the Annex, see *Doc 517*.

Likewise, no amendment may be made that could abridge in any way the rights of the Iraqi people cited in Chapter Two; extend the transitional period beyond the timeframe cited in this Law; delay the holding of elections to a new assembly; reduce the powers of the regions or governorates; or affect Islam, or any other religions or sects and their rites.

(B) Any legal provision that conflicts with this Law is null and void.

(C) This Law shall cease to have effect upon the formation of an elected government pursuant to a permanent constitution.

Article 4.

The system of government in Iraq shall be republican, federal, democratic, and pluralistic, and powers shall be shared between the federal government and the regional governments, governorates, municipalities, and local administrations. The federal system shall be based upon geographic and historical realities and the separation of powers, and not upon origin, race, ethnicity, nationality, or confession.

Article 5.

The Iraqi Armed Forces shall be subject to the civilian control of the Iraqi Transitional Government, in accordance with the contents of Chapters Three and Five of this Law.

Article 6.

The Iraqi Transitional Government shall take effective steps to end the vestiges of the oppressive acts of the previous regime arising from forced displacement, deprivation of citizenship, expropriation of financial assets and property, and dismissal from government employment for political, racial, or sectarian reasons.

Article 7.

(A) Islam is the official religion of the State and is to be considered a source of legislation. No law that contradicts the universally agreed tenets of Islam, the principles of democracy, or the rights cited in Chapter Two of this Law may be enacted during the transitional period. This Law respects the Islamic identity of the majority of the Iraqi people and guarantees the full religious rights of all individuals to freedom of religious belief and practice.

(B) Iraq is a country of many nationalities, and the Arab people in Iraq are an inseparable part of the Arab nation.

Article 8.

The flag, anthem, and emblem of the State shall be fixed by law.

Article 9.

The Arabic language and the Kurdish language are the two official languages of Iraq. The right of Iraqis to educate their children in their mother tongue, such as Turcoman, Syriac, or Armenian, in government educational institutions in accordance with educational guidelines, or in any other language in private educational institutions, shall be guaranteed. The scope of the term 'official language' and the means of applying the provisions of this Article shall be defined by law and shall include:

(1) Publication of the official gazette, in the two languages;

(2) Speech and expression in official settings, such as the National Assembly, the Council of Ministers, courts, and official conferences, in either of the two languages;

(3) Recognition and publication of official documents and correspondence in the two languages;
(4) Opening schools that teach in the two languages, in accordance with educational guidelines;
(5) Use of both languages in any other settings enjoined by the principle of equality (such as bank notes, passports, and stamps);
(6) Use of both languages in the federal institutions and agencies in the Kurdistan region.

CHAPTER TWO – FUNDAMENTAL RIGHTS

Article 10.

As an expression of the free will and sovereignty of the Iraqi people, their representatives shall form the governmental structures of the State of Iraq. The Iraqi Transitional Government and the governments of the regions, governorates, municipalities, and local administrations shall respect the rights of the Iraqi people, including those rights cited in this Chapter.

Article 11.

(A) Anyone who carries Iraqi nationality shall be deemed an Iraqi citizen. His citizenship shall grant him all the rights and duties stipulated in this Law and shall be the basis of his relation to the homeland and the State.

(B) No Iraqi may have his Iraqi citizenship withdrawn or be exiled unless he is a naturalized citizen who, in his application for citizenship, as established in a court of law, made material falsifications on the basis of which citizenship was granted.

(C) Each Iraqi shall have the right to carry more than one citizenship. Any Iraqi whose citizenship was withdrawn because he acquired another citizenship shall be deemed an Iraqi.

(D) Any Iraqi whose Iraqi citizenship was withdrawn for political, religious, racial, or sectarian reasons has the right to reclaim his Iraqi citizenship.

(E) Decision Number 666 (1980) of the dissolved Revolutionary Command Council is annulled, and anyone whose citizenship was withdrawn on the basis of this decree shall be deemed an Iraqi.[24]

(F) The National Assembly must issue laws pertaining to citizenship and naturalization consistent with the provisions of this Law.

(G) The Courts shall examine all disputes arising from the application of the provisions relating to citizenship.

[24] Revolutionary Command Council (RCC) Decree No 666 of 7 May 1980:
'In accordance with the provisions of para (a) of Article 42 of the Interim Constitution, The Revolutionary Command Council have decided in their session held on 07.05.1980 the following:
1. The Iraqi nationality shall be dropped from any Iraqi of foreign origin if it is appeared that he is not loyal to the homeland, people, higher national and social objectives of the Revolution.
2. The Minister of Interior must order anyone whose Iraqi Nationality has been dropped under para 1 unless he is convinced according to sufficient reasons that his stay in Iraq is a matter required by judicial or legal necessity or for preservation of the rights of other persons which are officially authenticated.
3. The Minister of Interior shall undertake to execute this resolution.
Saddam Hussein, Chairman of the Revolutionary Command Council.'
It is of interest to note that Decision Number 666 (1980) of the Revolutionary Command Council was again repealed in Art 17 of the Iraqi Nationality Law, Law 26 of 2006, *Official Gazette*, vol 47, no 4019 (7 March 2006).

Article 12.

All Iraqis are equal in their rights without regard to gender, sect, opinion, belief, nationality, religion, or origin, and they are equal before the law. Discrimination against an Iraqi citizen on the basis of his gender, nationality, religion, or origin is prohibited. Everyone has the right to life, liberty, and the security of his person. No one may be deprived of his life or liberty, except in accordance with legal procedures. All are equal before the courts.

Article 13.

(A) Public and private freedoms shall be protected.

(B) The right of free expression shall be protected.

(C) The right of free peaceable assembly and the right to join associations freely, as well as the right to form and join unions and political parties freely, in accordance with the law, shall be guaranteed.

(D) Each Iraqi has the right of free movement in all parts of Iraq and the right to travel abroad and return freely.

(E) Each Iraqi has the right to demonstrate and strike peaceably in accordance with the law.

(F) Each Iraqi has the right to freedom of thought, conscience, and religious belief and practice. Coercion in such matters shall be prohibited.

(G) Slavery, the slave trade, forced labor, and involuntary servitude with or without pay, shall be forbidden.

(H) Each Iraqi has the right to privacy.

Article 14.

The individual has the right to security, education, health care, and social security. The Iraqi State and its governmental units, including the federal government, the regions, governorates, municipalities, and local administrations, within the limits of their resources and with due regard to other vital needs, shall strive to provide prosperity and employment opportunities to the people.

Article 15.

(A) No civil law shall have retroactive effect unless the law so stipulates. There shall be neither a crime, nor punishment, except by law in effect at the time the crime is committed.

(B) Police, investigators, or other governmental authorities may not violate the sanctity of private residences, whether these authorities belong to the federal or regional governments, governorates, municipalities, or local administrations, unless a judge or investigating magistrate has issued a search warrant in accordance with applicable law on the basis of information provided by a sworn individual who knew that bearing false witness would render him liable to punishment. Extreme exigent circumstances, as determined by a court of competent jurisdiction, may justify a warrantless search, but such exigencies shall be narrowly construed. In the event that a warrantless search is carried out in the absence of an extreme exigent circumstance, the evidence so seized, and any other evidence found derivatively from such search, shall be inadmissible in connection with a criminal charge, unless the court determines that the person who carried out the warrantless search believed reasonably and in good faith that the search was in accordance with the law.

(C) No one may be unlawfully arrested or detained, and no one may be detained by reason of political or religious beliefs.

(D) All persons shall be guaranteed the right to a fair and public hearing by an independent and impartial tribunal, regardless of whether the proceeding is civil or criminal. Notice of the proceeding and its legal basis must be provided to the accused without delay.

(E) The accused is innocent until proven guilty pursuant to law, and he likewise has the right to engage independent and competent counsel, to remain silent in response to questions addressed to him with no compulsion to testify for any reason, to participate in preparing his defense, and to summon and examine witnesses or to ask the judge to do so. At the time a person is arrested, he must be notified of these rights.

(F) The right to a fair, speedy, and open trial shall be guaranteed.

(G) Every person deprived of his liberty by arrest or detention shall have the right of recourse to a court to determine the legality of his arrest or detention without delay and to order his release if this occurred in an illegal manner.

(H) After being found innocent of a charge, an accused may not be tried once again on the same charge.

(I) Civilians may not be tried before a military tribunal. Special or exceptional courts may not be established.

(J) Torture in all its forms, physical or mental, shall be prohibited under all circumstances, as shall be cruel, inhuman, or degrading treatment. No confession made under compulsion, torture, or threat thereof shall be relied upon or admitted into evidence for any reason in any proceeding, whether criminal or otherwise.

Article 16.

(A) Public property is sacrosanct, and its protection is the duty of every citizen.

(B) The right to private property shall be protected, and no one may be prevented from disposing of his property except within the limits of law. No one shall be deprived of his property except by eminent domain, in circumstances and in the manner set forth in law, and on condition that he is paid just and timely compensation.

(C) Each Iraqi citizen shall have the full and unfettered right to own real property in all parts of Iraq without restriction.

Article 17.

It shall not be permitted to possess, bear, buy, or sell arms except on licensure issued in accordance with the law.

Article 18.

There shall be no taxation or fee except by law.

Article 19.

No political refugee who has been granted asylum pursuant to applicable law may be surrendered or returned forcibly to the country from which he fled.

Article 20.

(A) Every Iraqi who fulfills the conditions stipulated in the electoral law has the right to stand for election and cast his ballot secretly in free, open, fair, competitive, and periodic elections.

(B) No Iraqi may be discriminated against for purposes of voting in elections on the basis of gender, religion, sect, race, belief, ethnic origin, language, wealth, or literacy.

Article 21.
Neither the Iraqi Transitional Government nor the governments and administrations of the regions, governorates, and municipalities, nor local administrations may interfere with the right of the Iraqi people to develop the institutions of civil society, whether in cooperation with international civil society organizations or otherwise.

Article 22.
If, in the course of his work, an official of any government office, whether in the federal government, the regional governments, the governorate and municipal administrations, or the local administrations, deprives an individual or a group of the rights guaranteed by this Law or any other Iraqi laws in force, this individual or group shall have the right to maintain a cause of action against that employee to seek compensation for the damages caused by such deprivation, to vindicate his rights, and to seek any other legal measure. If the court decides that the official had acted with a sufficient degree of good faith and in the belief that his actions were consistent with the law, then he is not required to pay compensation.

Article 23.
The enumeration of the foregoing rights must not be interpreted to mean that they are the only rights enjoyed by the Iraqi people. They enjoy all the rights that befit a free people possessed of their human dignity, including the rights stipulated in international treaties and agreements, other instruments of international law that Iraq has signed and to which it has acceded, and others that are deemed binding upon it, and in the law of nations. Non-Iraqis within Iraq shall enjoy all human rights not inconsistent with their status as non-citizens.

CHAPTER THREE – THE IRAQI TRANSITIONAL GOVERNMENT

Article 24.
(A) The Iraqi Transitional Government, which is also referred to in this Law as the federal government, shall consist of the National Assembly; the Presidency Council; the Council of Ministers, including the Prime Minister; and the judicial authority.
(B) The three authorities, legislative, executive, and judicial, shall be separate and independent of one another.
(C) No official or employee of the Iraqi Transitional Government shall enjoy immunity for criminal acts committed while in office.

Article 25.
The Iraqi Transitional Government shall have exclusive competence in the following matters:
(A) Formulating foreign policy and diplomatic representation; negotiating, signing, and ratifying international treaties and agreements; formulating foreign economic and trade policy and sovereign debt policies;
(B) Formulating and executing national security policy, including creating and maintaining armed forces to secure, protect, and guarantee the security of the country's borders and to defend Iraq;
(C) Formulating fiscal policy, issuing currency, regulating customs, regulating commercial policy across regional and governorate boundaries in Iraq, drawing up the national budget of the State, formulating monetary policy, and establishing and administering a central bank;

(D) Regulating weights and measures and formulating a general policy on wages;

(E) Managing the natural resources of Iraq, which belongs to all the people of all the regions and governorates of Iraq, in consultation with the governments of the regions and the administrations of the governorates, and distributing the revenues resulting from their sale through the national budget in an equitable manner proportional to the distribution of population throughout the country, and with due regard for areas that were unjustly deprived of these revenues by the previous regime, for dealing with their situations in a positive way, for their needs, and for the degree of development of the different areas of the country;

(F) Regulating Iraqi citizenship, immigration, and asylum; and

(G) Regulating telecommunications policy.

Article 26.

(A) Except as otherwise provided in this Law, the laws in force in Iraq on 30 June 2004 shall remain in effect unless and until rescinded or amended by the Iraqi Transitional Government in accordance with this Law.

(B) Legislation issued by the federal legislative authority shall supersede any other legislation issued by any other legislative authority in the event that they contradict each other, except as provided in Article 54(B).

(C) The laws, regulations, orders, and directives issued by the Coalition Provisional Authority pursuant to its authority under international law shall remain in force until rescinded or amended by legislation duly enacted and having the force of law.

Article 27.

(A) The Iraqi Armed Forces shall consist of the active and reserve units, and elements thereof. The purpose of these forces is the defense of Iraq.

(B) Armed forces and militias not under the command structure of the Iraqi Transitional Government are prohibited, except as provided by federal law.

(C) The Iraqi Armed Forces and its personnel, including military personnel working in the Ministry of Defense or any offices or organizations subordinate to it, may not stand for election to political office, campaign for candidates, or participate in other activities forbidden by Ministry of Defense regulations. This ban encompasses the activities of the personnel mentioned above acting in their personal or official capacities. Nothing in this Article shall infringe upon the right of these personnel to vote in elections.

(D) The Iraqi Intelligence Service shall collect information, assess threats to national security, and advise the Iraqi government. This Service shall be under civilian control, shall be subject to legislative oversight, and shall operate pursuant to law and in accordance with recognized principles of human rights.

(E) The Iraqi Transitional Government shall respect and implement Iraq's international obligations regarding the non-proliferation, non-development, non-production, and non-use of nuclear, chemical, and biological weapons, and associated equipment, materiel, technologies, and delivery systems for use in the development, manufacture, production, and use of such weapons.

Article 28.

(A) Members of the National Assembly; the Presidency Council; the Council of Ministers, including the Prime Minister; and judges and justices of the courts may not be appointed to any other position in or out of government. Any member of the National Assembly who becomes a member of the Presidency Council or Council of Ministers shall be deemed to have resigned his membership in the National Assembly.

(B) In no event may a member of the armed forces be a member of the National Assembly, minister, Prime Minister, or member of the Presidency Council unless the individual has resigned his commission or rank, or retired from duty at least eighteen months prior to serving.

Article 29.

Upon the assumption of full authority by the Iraqi Interim Government in accordance with Article 2(B)(1), above, the Coalition Provisional Authority shall be dissolved and the work of the Governing Council shall come to an end.

CHAPTER FOUR – THE TRANSITIONAL LEGISLATIVE AUTHORITY

Article 30.

(A) During the transitional period, the State of Iraq shall have a legislative authority known as the National Assembly. Its principal mission shall be to legislate and exercise oversight over the work of the executive authority.

(B) Laws shall be issued in the name of the people of Iraq. Laws, regulations, and directives related to them shall be published in the official gazette and shall take effect as of the date of their publication, unless they stipulate otherwise.

(C) The National Assembly shall be elected in accordance with an electoral law and a political parties law. The electoral law shall aim to achieve the goal of having women constitute no less than one-quarter of the members of the National Assembly and of having fair representation for all communities in Iraq, including the Turcomans, ChaldoAssyrians, and others.

(D) Elections for the National Assembly shall take place by 31 December 2004 if possible, and in any case no later than by 31 January 2005.

Article 31.

(A) The National Assembly shall consist of 275 members. It shall enact a law dealing with the replacement of its members in the event of resignation, removal, or death.

(B) A nominee to the National Assembly must fulfill the following conditions:

(1) He shall be an Iraqi no less than 30 years of age.

(2) He shall not have been a member of the dissolved Ba'ath Party with the rank of Division Member or higher, unless exempted pursuant to the applicable legal rules.

(3) If he was once a member of the dissolved Ba'ath Party with the rank of Full Member, he shall be required to sign a document renouncing the Ba'ath Party and disavowing all of his past links with it before becoming eligible to be a candidate, as well as to swear that he no longer has any dealings or connection with Ba'ath Party organizations. If it is established in court that he lied or fabricated on this score, he shall lose his seat in the National Assembly.

(4) He shall not have been a member of the former agencies of repression and shall not have contributed to or participated in the persecution of citizens.

(5) He shall not have enriched himself in an illegitimate manner at the expense of the homeland and public finance.

(6) He shall not have been convicted of a crime involving moral turpitude and shall have a good reputation.
(7) He shall have at least a secondary school diploma, or equivalent
(8) He shall not be a member of the armed forces at the time of his nomination.

Article 32.

(A) The National Assembly shall draw up its own internal procedures, and it shall sit in public session unless circumstances require otherwise, consistent with its internal procedures. The first session of the Assembly shall be chaired by its oldest member.

(B) The National Assembly shall elect, from its own members, a president and two deputy presidents of the National Assembly. The president of the National Assembly shall be the individual who receives the greatest number of votes for that office; the first deputy president the next highest; and the second deputy president the next. The president of the National Assembly may vote on an issue, but may not participate in the debates, unless he temporarily steps out of the chair immediately prior to addressing the issue.

(C) A bill shall not be voted upon by the National Assembly unless it has been read twice at a regular session of the Assembly, on condition that at least two days intervene between the two readings, and after the bill has been placed on the agenda of the session at least four days prior to the vote.

Article 33.

(A) Meetings of the National Assembly shall be public, and transcripts of its meetings shall be recorded and published. The vote of every member of the National Assembly shall be recorded and made public. Decisions in the National Assembly shall be taken by simple majority unless this Law stipulates otherwise.

(B) The National Assembly must examine bills proposed by the Council of Ministers, including budget bills.

(C) Only the Council of Ministers shall have the right to present a proposed national budget. The National Assembly has the right to reallocate proposed spending and to reduce the total amounts in the general budget. It also has the right to propose an increase in the overall amount of expenditures to the Council of Ministers if necessary.

(D) Members of the National Assembly shall have the right to propose bills, consistent with the internal procedures that are drawn up by the Assembly.

(E) The Iraqi Armed Forces may not be dispatched outside Iraq even for the purpose of defending against foreign aggression except with the approval of the National Assembly and upon the request of the Presidency Council.

(F) Only the National Assembly shall have the power to ratify international treaties and agreements.

(G) The oversight function performed by the National Assembly and its committees shall include the right of interpellation of executive officials, including members of the Presidency Council, the Council of Ministers, including the Prime Minister, and any less senior official of the executive authority. This shall encompass the right to investigate, request information, and issue subpoenas for persons to appear before them.

Article 34.

Each member of the National Assembly shall enjoy immunity for statements made while the Assembly is in session, and the member may not be sued before the courts for such. A member may not be placed under arrest during a session of the National Assembly, unless the member is accused of a crime and the National Assembly agrees to lift his immunity or if he is caught *in flagrante delicto* in the commission of a felony.

CHAPTER FIVE – THE TRANSITIONAL EXECUTIVE AUTHORITY

Article 35.
The executive authority during the transitional period shall consist of the Presidency Council, the Council of Ministers, and its presiding Prime Minister.

Article 36.
(A) The National Assembly shall elect a President of the State and two Deputies. They shall form the Presidency Council, the function of which will be to represent the sovereignty of Iraq and oversee the higher affairs of the country. The election of the Presidency Council shall take place on the basis of a single list and by a two-thirds majority of the members' votes. The National Assembly has the power to remove any member of the Presidency Council of the State for incompetence or lack of integrity by a three-fourths majority of its members' votes. In the event of a vacancy in the Presidency Council, the National Assembly shall, by a vote of two-thirds of its members, elect a replacement to fill the vacancy.

(B) It is a prerequisite for a member of the Presidency Council to fulfill the same conditions as the members of the National Assembly, with the following observations:

(1) He must be at least forty years of age.
(2) He must possess a good reputation, integrity, and rectitude.
(3) If he was a member of the dissolved Ba'ath Party, he must have left the dissolved Party at least ten years before its fall.
(4) He must not have participated in repressing the *intifada* of 1991 or the Anfal campaign and must not have committed a crime against the Iraqi people.

(C) The Presidency Council shall take its decisions unanimously, and its members may not deputize others as proxies.

Article 37.
The Presidency Council may veto any legislation passed by the National Assembly, on condition that this be done within fifteen days after the Presidency Council is notified by the president of the National Assembly of the passage of such legislation. In the event of a veto, the legislation shall be returned to the National Assembly, which has the right to pass the legislation again by a two-thirds majority not subject to veto within a period not to exceed thirty days.

Article 38.
(A) The Presidency Council shall name a Prime Minister unanimously, as well as the members of the Council of Ministers upon the recommendation of the Prime Minister. The Prime Minister and Council of Ministers shall then seek to obtain a vote of confidence by simple majority from the National Assembly prior to commencing their work as a government. The Presidency Council must agree on a candidate for the post of Prime Minister within two weeks. In the event that it fails to do so, the responsibility of naming the Prime Minister reverts to the National Assembly. In that event, the National Assembly must confirm the nomination by a two-thirds majority. If the Prime Minister is unable to

nominate his Council of Ministers within one month, the Presidency Council shall name another Prime Minister.

(B) The qualifications for Prime Minister must be the same as for the members of the Presidency Council except that his age must not be less than 35 years upon his taking office.

Article 39.

(A) The Council of Ministers shall, with the approval of the Presidency Council, appoint representatives to negotiate the conclusion of international treaties and agreements. The Presidency Council shall recommend passage of a law by the National Assembly to ratify such treaties and agreements.

(B) The Presidency Council shall carry out the function of commander-in-chief of the Iraqi Armed Forces only for ceremonial and protocol purposes. It shall have no command authority. It shall have the right to be briefed, to inquire, and to advise. Operationally, national command authority on military matters shall flow from the Prime Minister to the Minister of Defense to the military chain of command of the Iraqi Armed Forces.

(C) The Presidency Council shall, as more fully set forth in Chapter Six, below, appoint, upon recommendation of the Higher Juridical Council, the Presiding Judge and members of the Federal Supreme Court.

(D) The Council of Ministers shall appoint the Director-General of the Iraqi National Intelligence Service, as well as officers of the Iraqi Armed Forces at the rank of general or above. Such appointments shall be subject to confirmation by the National Assembly by simple majority of those of its members present.

Article 40.

(A) The Prime Minister and the ministers shall be responsible before the National Assembly, and this Assembly shall have the right to withdraw its confidence either in the Prime Minister or in the ministers collectively or individually. In the event that confidence in the Prime Minister is withdrawn, the entire Council of Ministers shall be dissolved, and Article 40(B), below, shall become operative.

(B) In the event of a vote of no confidence with respect to the entire Council of Ministers, the Prime Minister and Council of Ministers shall remain in office to carry out their functions for a period not to exceed thirty days, until the formation of a new Council of Ministers, consistent with Article 38, above.

Article 41.

The Prime Minister shall have day-to-day responsibility for the management of the government, and he may dismiss ministers with the approval of an simple majority of the National Assembly. The Presidency Council may, upon the recommendation of the Commission on Public Integrity after the exercise of due process, dismiss the Prime Minister or the ministers.

Article 42.

The Council of Ministers shall draw up rules of procedure for its work and issue the regulations and directives necessary to enforce the laws. It also has the right to propose bills to the National Assembly. Each ministry has the right, within its competence, to nominate deputy ministers, ambassadors, and other employees of special grade. After the Council of

Ministers approves these nominations, they shall be submitted to the Presidency Council for ratification. All decisions of the Council of Ministers shall be taken by simple majority of those of its members present.

CHAPTER SIX – THE FEDERAL JUDICIAL AUTHORITY

Article 43.

(A) The judiciary is independent, and it shall in no way be administered by the executive authority, including the Ministry of Justice. The judiciary shall enjoy exclusive competence to determine the innocence or guilt of the accused pursuant to law, without interference from the legislative or executive authorities.

(B) All judges sitting in their respective courts as of 1 July 2004 will continue in office thereafter, unless removed from office pursuant to this Law.

(C) The National Assembly shall establish an independent and adequate budget for the judiciary.

(D) Federal courts shall adjudicate matters that arise from the application of federal laws. The establishment of these courts shall be within the exclusive competence of the federal government. The establishment of these courts in the regions shall be in consultation with the presidents of the judicial councils in the regions, and priority in appointing or transferring judges to these courts shall be given to judges resident in the region.

Article 44.

(A) A court called the Federal Supreme Court shall be constituted by law in Iraq.

(B) The jurisdiction of the Federal Supreme Court shall be as follows:

(1) Original and exclusive jurisdiction in legal proceedings between the Iraqi Transitional Government and the regional governments, governorate and municipal administrations, and local administrations.

(2) Original and exclusive jurisdiction, on the basis of a complaint from a claimant or a referral from another court, to review claims that a law, regulation, or directive issued by the federal or regional governments, the governorate or municipal administrations, or local administrations is inconsistent with this Law.

(3) Ordinary appellate jurisdiction of the Federal Supreme Court shall be defined by federal law.

(C) Should the Federal Supreme Court rule that a challenged law, regulation, directive, or measure is inconsistent with this Law, it shall be deemed null and void.

(D) The Federal Supreme Court shall create and publish regulations regarding the procedures required to bring claims and to permit attorneys to practice before it. It shall take its decisions by simple majority, except decisions with regard to the proceedings stipulated in Article 44(B)(1), which must be by a two-thirds majority. Decisions shall be binding. The Court shall have full powers to enforce its decisions, including the power to issue citations for contempt of court and the measures that flow from this.

(E) The Federal Supreme Court shall consist of nine members. The Higher Juridical Council shall, in consultation with the regional judicial councils, initially nominate no less than eighteen and up to twenty-seven individuals to fill the initial vacancies in the aforementioned Court. It will follow the same procedure thereafter, nominating three members for each subsequent vacancy that occurs by reason of death, resignation, or removal. The Presidency Council shall appoint the members of this Court and name one of them as its Presiding Judge. In the event an appointment is rejected, the Higher Juridical Council shall nominate a new group of three candidates.

Article 45.

A Higher Juridical Council shall be established and assume the role of the Council of Judges. The Higher Juridical Council shall supervise the federal judiciary and shall administer its budget. This Council shall be composed of the Presiding Judge of the Federal Supreme Court, the presiding judge and deputy presiding judges of the federal Court of Cassation, the presiding judges of the federal Courts of Appeal, and the presiding judge and two deputy presiding judges of each regional court of cassation. The Presiding Judge of the Federal Supreme Court shall preside over the Higher Juridical Council. In his absence, the presiding judge of the federal Court of Cassation shall preside over the Council.

Article 46.

(A) The federal judicial branch shall include existing courts outside the Kurdistan region, including courts of first instance; the Central Criminal Court of Iraq; Courts of Appeal; and the Court of Cassation, which shall be the court of last resort except as provided in Article 44 of this Law. Additional federal courts may be established by law. The appointment of judges for these courts shall be made by the Higher Juridical Council. This Law preserves the qualifications necessary for the appointment of judges, as defined by law.

(B) The decisions of regional and local courts, including the courts of the Kurdistan region, shall be final, but shall be subject to review by the federal judiciary if they conflict with this Law or any federal law. Procedures for such review shall be defined by law.

Article 47.

No judge or member of the Higher Juridical Council may be removed unless he is convicted of a crime involving moral turpitude or corruption or suffers permanent incapacity. Removal shall be on the recommendation of the Higher Juridical Council, by a decision of the Council of Ministers, and with the approval of the Presidency Council. Removal shall be executed immediately after issuance of this approval. A judge who has been accused of such a crime as cited above shall be suspended from his work in the judiciary until such time as the case arising from what is cited in this Article is adjudicated. No judge may have his salary reduced or suspended for any reason during his period of service.

CHAPTER SEVEN – THE SPECIAL TRIBUNAL AND NATIONAL COMMISSIONS

Article 48.

(A) The statute establishing the Iraqi Special Tribunal issued on 10 December 2003 is confirmed. That statute exclusively defines its jurisdiction and procedures, notwithstanding the provisions of this Law.

(B) No other court shall have jurisdiction to examine cases within the competence of the Iraqi Special Tribunal, except to the extent provided by its founding statute.

(C) The judges of the Iraqi Special Tribunal shall be appointed in accordance with the provisions of its founding statute.

Article 49.

(A) The establishment of national commissions such as the Commission on Public Integrity, the Iraqi Property Claims Commission, and the Higher National De-Ba'athification Commission is confirmed, as is the establishment of commissions formed after this Law has gone into effect. The members of these national commissions shall continue to serve after this Law has gone into effect, taking into account the contents of Article 51, below.

(B) The method of appointment to the national commissions shall be in accordance with law.

Article 50.

The Iraqi Transitional Government shall establish a National Commission for Human Rights for the purpose of executing the commitments relative to the rights set forth in this Law and to examine complaints pertaining to violations of human rights. The Commission shall be established in accordance with the Paris Principles issued by the United Nations on the responsibilities of national institutions.[25] This Commission shall include an Office of the Ombudsman to inquire into complaints. This office shall have the power to investigate, on its own initiative or on the basis of a complaint submitted to it, any allegation that the conduct of the governmental authorities is arbitrary or contrary to law.

Article 51.

No member of the Iraqi Special Tribunal or of any commission established by the federal government may be employed in any other capacity in or out of government. This prohibition is valid without limitation, whether it be within the executive, legislative, or judicial authority of the Iraqi Transitional Government. Members of the Special Tribunal may, however, suspend their employment in other agencies while they serve on the aforementioned Tribunal.

CHAPTER EIGHT – REGIONS, GOVERNORATES, AND MUNICIPALITIES

Article 52.

The design of the federal system in Iraq shall be established in such a way as to prevent the concentration of power in the federal government that allowed the continuation of decades of tyranny and oppression under the previous regime. This system shall encourage the exercise of local authority by local officials in every region and governorate, thereby creating a united Iraq in which every citizen actively participates in governmental affairs, secure in his rights and free of domination.

Article 53.

(A) The Kurdistan Regional Government is recognized as the official government of the territories that were administered by the that government on 19 March 2003 in the governorates of Dohuk, Arbil, Sulaimaniya, Kirkuk, Diyala and Neneveh. The term 'Kurdistan Regional Government' shall refer to the Kurdistan National Assembly, the Kurdistan Council of Ministers, and the regional judicial authority in the Kurdistan region.

(B) The boundaries of the eighteen governorates shall remain without change during the transitional period.

[25] The Principles Relating to the Status of National Institutions (The Paris Principles) were adopted by UN General Assembly resolution 48/134 of 20 December 1993 (A/RES/48/134 (1993)).

(C) Any group of no more than three governorates outside the Kurdistan region, with the exception of Baghdad and Kirkuk, shall have the right to form regions from amongst themselves. The mechanisms for forming such regions may be proposed by the Iraqi Interim Government, and shall be presented and considered by the elected National Assembly for enactment into law. In addition to being approved by the National Assembly, any legislation proposing the formation of a particular region must be approved in a referendum of the people of the relevant governorates.

(D) This Law shall guarantee the administrative, cultural, and political rights of the Turcomans, ChaldoAssyrians, and all other citizens.

Article 54.

(A) The Kurdistan Regional Government shall continue to perform its current functions throughout the transitional period, except with regard to those issues which fall within the exclusive competence of the federal government as specified in this Law. Financing for these functions shall come from the federal government, consistent with current practice and in accordance with Article 25(E) of this Law. The Kurdistan Regional Government shall retain regional control over police forces and internal security, and it will have the right to impose taxes and fees within the Kurdistan region.

(B) With regard to the application of federal laws in the Kurdistan region, the Kurdistan National Assembly shall be permitted to amend the application of any such law within the Kurdistan region, but only to the extent that this relates to matters that are not within the provisions of Articles 25 and 43(D) of this Law and that fall within the exclusive competence of the federal government.

Article 55.

(A) Each governorate shall have the right to form a Governorate Council, name a Governor, and form municipal and local councils. No member of any regional government, governor, or member of any governorate, municipal, or local council may be dismissed by the federal government or any official thereof, except upon conviction of a crime by a court of competent jurisdiction as provided by law. No regional government may dismiss a Governor or member or members of any governorate, municipal, or local council. No Governor or member of any Governorate, municipal, or local council shall be subject to the control of the federal government except to the extent that the matter relates to the competences set forth in Article 25 and 43(D), above.

(B) Each Governor and member of each Governorate Council who holds office as of 1 July 2004, in accordance with the law on local government that shall be issued, shall remain in place until such time as free, direct, and full elections, conducted pursuant to law, are held, or, unless, prior to that time, he voluntarily gives up his position, is removed upon his conviction for a crime involving moral turpitude or related to corruption, or upon being stricken with permanent incapacity, or is dismissed in accordance with the law cited above. When a governor, mayor, or member of a council is dismissed, the relevant council may receive applications from any eligible resident of the governorate to fill the position. Eligibility requirements shall be the same as those set forth in Article 31 for membership in the National Assembly. The new candidate must receive a majority vote of the council to assume the vacant seat.

Article 56.

(A) The Governorate Councils shall assist the federal government in the coordination of federal ministry operations within the governorate, including the review of annual ministry plans and budgets with regard to activities in the governorate. Governorate Councils shall be funded from the general budget of the State, and these Councils shall also have the authority to increase their revenues independently by imposing taxes and fees; to organize the operations of the Governorate administration; to initiate and implement province-level projects alone or in partnership with international, and non-governmental organizations; and to conduct other activities insofar as is consistent with federal laws.

(B) The *Qada'* and *Nahiya* councils and other relevant councils shall assist in the performance of federal responsibilities and the delivery of public services by reviewing local ministry plans in the afore-mentioned places; ensuring that they respond properly to local needs and interests; identifying local budgetary requirements through the national budgeting procedures; and collecting and retaining local revenues, taxes, and fees; organizing the operations of the local administration; initiating and implementing local projects alone or in conjunction with international, and non-governmental organizations; and conducting other activities consistent with applicable law.

(C) Where practicable, the federal government shall take measures to devolve additional functions to local, governorate, and regional administrations, in a methodical way. Regional units and governorate administrations, including the Kurdistan Regional Government, shall be organized on the basis of the principle of de-centralization and the devolution of authorities to municipal and local governments.

Article 57.

(A) All authorities not exclusively reserved to the Iraqi Transitional Government may be exercised by the regional governments and governorates as soon as possible following the establishment of appropriate governmental institutions.

(B) Elections for governorate councils throughout Iraq and for the Kurdistan National Assembly shall be held at the same time as the elections for the National Assembly, no later than 31 January 2005.

Article 58.

(A) The Iraqi Transitional Government, and especially the Iraqi Property Claims Commission and other relevant bodies, shall act expeditiously to take measures to remedy the injustice caused by the previous regime's practices in altering the demographic character of certain regions, including Kirkuk, by deporting and expelling individuals from their places of residence, forcing migration in and out of the region, settling individuals alien to the region, depriving the inhabitants of work, and correcting nationality. To remedy this injustice, the Iraqi Transitional Government shall take the following steps:

(1) With regard to residents who were deported, expelled, or who emigrated; it shall, in accordance with the statute of the Iraqi Property Claims Commission and other measures within the law, within a reasonable period of time, restore the residents to their homes and property, or, where this is unfeasible, shall provide just compensation.

(2) With regard to the individuals newly introduced to specific regions and territories, it shall act in accordance with Article 10 of the Iraqi Property Claims Commission statute to ensure that such individuals may be resettled,

may receive compensation from the state, may receive new land from the state near their residence in the governorate from which they came, or may receive compensation for the cost of moving to such areas.

(3) With regard to persons deprived of employment or other means of support in order to force migration out of their regions and territories, it shall promote new employment opportunities in the regions and territories.

(4) With regard to nationality correction, it shall repeal all relevant decrees and shall permit affected persons the right to determine their own national identity and ethnic affiliation free from coercion and duress.

(B) The previous regime also manipulated and changed administrative boundaries for political ends. The Presidency Council of the Iraqi Transitional Government shall make recommendations to the National Assembly on remedying these unjust changes in the permanent constitution. In the event the Presidency Council is unable to agree unanimously on a set of recommendations, it shall unanimously appoint a neutral arbitrator to examine the issue and make recommendations. In the event the Presidency Council is unable to agree on an arbitrator, it shall request the Secretary General of the United Nations to appoint a distinguished international person to be the arbitrator.

(C) The permanent resolution of disputed territories, including Kirkuk, shall be deferred until after these measures are completed, a fair and transparent census has been conducted and the permanent constitution has been ratified. This resolution shall be consistent with the principle of justice, taking into account the will of the people of those territories.[26]

CHAPTER NINE – THE TRANSITIONAL PERIOD

Article 59.

(A) The permanent constitution shall contain guarantees to ensure that the Iraqi Armed Forces are never again used to terrorize or oppress the people of Iraq.

(B) Consistent with Iraq's status as a sovereign state, and with its desire to join other nations in helping to maintain peace and security and fight terrorism during the transitional period, the Iraqi Armed Forces will be a principal partner in the multi-national force operating in Iraq under unified command pursuant to the provisions of United Nations Security Council Resolution 1511 (2003) and any subsequent relevant resolutions. This arrangement shall last until the ratification of a permanent constitution and the election of a new government pursuant to that new constitution.

(C) Upon its assumption of authority, and consistent with Iraq's status as a sovereign state, the elected Iraqi Transitional Government shall have the authority to conclude binding international agreements regarding the activities of the multi-national force operating in Iraq under unified command pursuant to the terms of United Nations Security Council Resolution 1511 (2003), and any subsequent relevant United Nations Security Council resolutions. Nothing in this Law shall affect rights and obligations under these agreements,

[26] Article 140 of the Iraqi Constitution, approved by referendum on 15 October 2005, provides: '<u>First:</u> The executive authority shall undertake the necessary steps to complete the implementation of the requirements of all subparagraphs of Article 58 of the Transitional Administrative Law.

<u>Second:</u> The responsibility placed upon the executive branch of the Iraqi Transitional Government stipulated in Article 58 of the Transitional Administrative Law shall extend and continue to the executive authority elected in accordance with this Constitution, provided that it accomplishes completely (normalization and census and concludes with a referendum in Kirkuk and other disputed territories to determine the will of their citizens),by a date not to exceed the 31st of December 2007.'

or under United Nations Security Council Resolution 1511 (2003), and any subsequent relevant United Nations Security Council resolutions, which will govern the multi-national force's activities pending the entry into force of these agreements.

Article 60.
The National Assembly shall write a draft of the permanent constitution of Iraq. This Assembly shall carry out this responsibility in part by encouraging debate on the constitution through regular general public meetings in all parts of Iraq and through the media, and receiving proposals from the citizens of Iraq as it writes the constitution.

Article 61.
(A) The National Assembly shall write the draft of the permanent constitution by no later than 15 August 2005.

(B) The draft permanent constitution shall be presented to the Iraqi people for approval in a general referendum to be held no later than 15 October 2005. In the period leading up to the referendum, the draft constitution shall be published and widely distributed to encourage a public debate about it among the people.

(C) The general referendum will be successful and the draft constitution ratified if a majority of the voters in Iraq approve and if two-thirds of the voters in three or more governorates do not reject it.

(D) If the permanent constitution is approved in the referendum, elections for a permanent government shall be held no later than 15 December 2005 and the new government shall assume office no later than 31 December 2005.

(E) If the referendum rejects the draft permanent constitution, the National Assembly shall be dissolved. Elections for a new National Assembly shall be held no later than 15 December 2005. The new National Assembly and new Iraqi Transitional Government shall then assume office no later than 31 December 2005, and shall continue to operate under this Law, except that the final deadlines for preparing a new draft may be changed to make it possible to draft a permanent constitution within a period not to exceed one year. The new National Assembly shall be entrusted with writing another draft permanent constitution.

(F) If necessary, the president of the National Assembly, with the agreement of a majority of the members' votes, may certify to the Presidency Council no later than 1 August 2005 that there is a need for additional time to complete the writing of the draft constitution. The Presidency Council shall then extend the deadline for writing the draft constitution for only six months. This deadline may not be extended again.

(G) If the National Assembly does not complete writing the draft permanent constitution by 15 August 2005 and does not request extension of the deadline in Article 61(F) above, the provisions of Article 61(E), above, shall be applied.

Article 62.
This law shall remain in effect until the permanent constitution is issued and the new Iraqi government is formed in accordance with it.[27]

[27] The new Iraqi constitution was accepted by referendum on 15 October 2005 and came into force on 20 May 2006 in accordance with Article 144 of the Constitution. The TAL was 'annulled' on the same date by virtue of Article 143 of the Constitution, except for the stipulations of Article 53(A) and Article 58 of the TAL.

Document 512
Letter from the President of the Iraqi Governing Council to the Secretary General of the United Nations

17 March 2004

The Governing Council is pleased to send you a copy of the Transitional Administrative Law of the Iraqi State, which provides a foundation for Iraq's democracy and paves the way to a permanent constitution. The Law was approved by the Governing Council unanimously and signed on Monday, 8 March 2004.

This Law represents an important step towards the establishment of a democratic, pluralist, federal system. It safeguards basic human rights, which has been a goal of the Iraqi people for years.

We continue to believe that the United Nations must play an important role in Iraq. We thank you, on behalf of the Iraqi people, for sending the United Nations delegation led by Mr. Lakhdar Brahimi to Iraq and for the efforts it exerted. The Governing Council appreciates the advice and assistance of the United Nations as we look to the next challenge in the political transition: the formation of an interim Iraqi government to which sovereignty will be transferred on 30 June 2004. We welcome United Nations consultation in the efforts we are exerting in the broad national dialogue regarding the shape and scope of this interim government.

We also look forward to United Nations assistance in providing advice and observations needed to ensure that direct elections are held before the end of January 2005. The experience and capability of the United Nations will be invaluable both in the creation of the infrastructure and in the conduct of the elections.

Time is of the essence to ensure the credible national direct elections take place as scheduled in the Transitional Administrative Law of the Iraqi State.

Please accept our deepest appreciation for the past efforts of the United Nations. We hope that the United Nations will be able to return to Iraq as soon as possible.

[*Signed*] Mohammed Bahr Al-Uloom
President, Interim Governing Council[28]

[28] The Secretary General replied to the President of the IGC in a letter dated 18 March 2004: 'I would like to thank you for your letter dated 17 March 2004, which I received today. I would also like to thank you for sending me a copy of the Transitional Administrative Law. I have taken note of the Governing Council's request for the United Nations to lend advice and assistance in the formation of an interim Iraqi government, to which sovereignty will be transferred on 30 June 2004, as well as in the preparations for direct elections to be held before the end of January 2005. The United Nations remains committed to doing everything within its capacity to assist the people of Iraq, when and as they request. I have therefore asked my Special Adviser, Mr. Lakhdar Brahimi, and his team, as well as an electoral assistance team, to return to Iraq as soon as possible, in order to lend the advice and assistance you have requested. I would like to take this opportunity to extend my thanks, in advance, to the Governing Council and the Coalition Provisional Authority for providing the security required for the United Nations to carry out these missions. I am concurrently informing the members of the United Nations Security Council of my intention and am copying this exchange of letters to its President. [*Signed*] Kofi A. Annan.' The two letters are reproduced in UN Doc. S/2004/225, 19 March 2004, annexes I and II.

Document 513
Joint Statement on the Security Situation by the Governing Council and the Council of Ministers
9 April 2004[29]

In the name of God, the Merciful, the Compassionate: The Governing Council and the Council of Ministers held a joint extraordinary meeting on Friday 9th April, 2004 in the afternoon where they discussed the complicated and painful situation in the country and the measures that need to be adopted to handle the critical situation. This came about after a series of meetings, contacts, and deliberations among the [Governing] Council members and various political figures. The meeting saw that the successful handling of the disturbing security situation requires the following:

1. An immediate cease-fire, and the adoption of political solutions to the emerging situations in various parts of the country, especially in the city of Al-Fallujah, while adhering to the rule of law, respect for public order, and emphasizing that no one is above the law regardless of their position.
2. Rejecting all forms of violence and terrorism, and adopting the necessary measures to stop them.
3. Involving the Governing Council and its institutions, in an actual and tangible manner, in administering the country's affairs and making decisions related to the pressing issues facing the country, primarily the security file for which the requirements of its handover to the Iraqis must be prepared. The Governing Council should also be involved in finding suitable means and mechanisms for solving the basic and outstanding issues, until power is transferred to the Iraqi people in a manner that will put an end to the CPA's sole authority in decision making.
4. Ruling out of military operations and accompanying collective punishment, which are victimizing innocent civilians, as a solution to existing issues. In this regard, it is necessary to allow for the evacuation of the wounded and the delivery of medicine and food supplies to the areas where it is desperately needed.
5. Drafting a plan for a comprehensive and urgent approach towards the exacerbating situation, especially in the security field. Such an approach should include socioeconomic measures, especially in the field of combating unemployment, as well as social and other measures. Addressing security problems should not be limited to military and police measures alone.
6. Commitment to the national unity of Iraq by all parties and working to foil the schemes aimed at inciting sectarian, ethnic, and other differences.

In light of all this, and in order to find tangible solutions to the acute problems curbing the process of transferring power to the Iraqi people and their representatives, urgent measures should be taken to immediately calm down the situation. All armed manifestations must be halted so as to allow for the rites of commemorating the anniversary of the 40th day after the death of Imam al-Hussain, may peace be upon him, to proceed as usual. Besides, such measures should aim to facilitate the tasks of the delegations mediating between the various parties and the efforts of the Governing Council in this regard.

Meanwhile, it is necessary for the police to return to their positions and duties of safeguarding security. All government and public buildings should be returned to those in

[29] Translation from Arabic.

charge of them, and all the necessary measures should be taken to protect public property and to prevent the looting and kidnapping of foreigners.

The meeting stressed that it is necessary to respect human rights in Iraq and the relevant international conventions. It must be ensured that these rights and conventions are not violated in any way and under any pretext.

Finally, the attendees hope that the international community will not abandon its responsibility to support the efforts of our people to foil the schemes of the forces of terrorism, ensure stability in our country, and start the process of building a democratic federal constitutional system.

Document 514
Governing Council Press Release 156
[Security Situation in Iraq]

12 April 2004[30]

Continuing the utmost efforts of the Governing Council in line with the supreme national interest and in order to preserve the lives of innocent citizens who spill their blood every day as a result of the actions, crimes, and designs of the terrorists, outlaws, and the remnants of the former regime, and its pursuit to resolve the current crisis and to proceed according to the schedule which guarantees the return of sovereignty to Iraqis in due course.

The Council at its meeting on 12 April 2004 decided the following:

1. To call on all concerned parties to observe a comprehensive cease-fire, keep the peace, safeguard the lives of citizens and refrain from exposing them to danger and to collective punishment.

2. To address the sources and causes of tension through expanded meetings to which the IGC will invite representatives of political parties, tribal leaders, clerics and other national notables from Falluja, Najaf and other cities. The purpose of the meetings will be to discuss the steps needed to guarantee the rule of law and the safety of citizens, to reinforce efforts to build a new Iraq, to establish a timetable for solving current problems, and to take a clear, explicit and united position in the face of terrorism and those outside the rule of law and the remnants of the old regime.

3. Should these IGC efforts fail, and the efforts of other sincere groups who are united in pursuing the rule of law and building a new Iraq and restoring sovereignty and ending occupation, the IGC will deem it necessary to lay down a unified plan to confront terrorism and outlaws vigorously, and to coordinate with all forces that care about the future of Iraq and the safety of its citizens, and with the Coalition Forces who are responsible for the security of Iraq before the international community.

[30] Translation from Arabic.

Document 515
Letter to Ambassador Bremer on Abu Graib Prison
13 May 2004

Dear Mr. Ambassador

The Governing Council presents its compliments to the Coalition Provisional Authority and has the honor to inform that the Governing Council in today's (11 May 2004) 49th ordinary session[31] has adopted many decisions concerning inmates of Abu Graib prison, that can be summarized as follows:

1. Denunciation of all violations of human rights within the walls of the prison and to publicize that fact in available media.
2. To form a committee of Iraqi judges and public prosecutors to investigate the anti-humanitarian violations committed by those in charge of Abu Graib prison, and to inform the Presidency of the General Public Prosecutors Office of this Committee so that it shall inform the CPA by mediation of the Ministry of Justice. This Committee is to construct its investigations depending upon the comments, data and information presented by an Administrative Committee which is to be formed from experts specialized in prison and jail affairs which shall meet the inmates and make sure they are treated according to the laws.
3. Empower the Committee in 3 [sic] above the authority to present necessary recommendations for the release of inmates against whom there is not enough evidence, and recommend release of inmates against bail, should the applicable laws allow that. And to empower the committee with the authority to audit and scrutinized [sic] records and history cases of those intended to be released and not to attempt releasing prisoners proven to have previously committed crimes or have relations with terroristic [sic] organizations.

The Governing Council avails itself of this opportunity to renew to the Coalition Provisional Authority the assurances of its highest consideration.

[Signed] *Muhyi K. AlKateeb*
Secretary General
Governing Council

Document 516
Governing Council Press Release Number 176
[Transfer of Power and Sovereignty to the Interim Iraqi Government]
25 May 2004[32]

Based on the understanding reached on 15 November 2003 and consistent with the provisions of the Law of Administration for the State of Iraq for the Transitional Period and UN Security Council resolutions 1483, issued 22 May 2003, and 1511, issued 16 October 2003, pertaining to the restoration of sovereignty, the transfer of power to an interim Iraqi

[31] According to other documents the 49th ordinary session took place on 12 May 2004.
[32] Translation from Arabic.

government on 30 June 2004, the dissolution of the Coalition Provisional Authority and the transfer of all its powers to the new government; the Governing Council believes that the sovereignty to be transferred, is the full, undivided sovereignty, as is customary and as stipulated by public international law.

Moreover, the interim government will assume power and run the domestic and foreign affairs of the country in accordance with the State Administration Law.

Ensuring a smooth and continuing transfer of power, to be completed on 30 June 2004, requires holding the necessary dialogues and taking the necessary measures in coordination with the Coalition Provisional Authority and the Security Council, which is poised to issue a new resolution in due course. Following is a non-exhaustive list of issues that should be considered:

1. Full control over the activities of the Iraqi armed forces and security services.
2. Full control over Iraq's oil resources and the handling of national resources.
3. Full Iraqi administration of the Iraqi Development Fund.
4. Resolution of disputes regarding handling of domestic and foreign Iraqi properties, especially those relating to public facilities such as airports, sea ports and other symbols of sovereignty.
5. Taking effective measures for the participation of the Iraqi government in international organizations in order to take advantage of grants, advice and assistance that has been provided for the rebuilding of Iraq.
6. Full administration of Iraq's foreign relations.

The above-mentioned and other points that the actual power transfer process would involve confirm that the new government will have its own will and authority. The government will also have final say in Iraq's internal and external affairs.

The Governing Council calls on the citizens, political forces, and civil society organizations to express their views and national aspirations and extend all forms of support and advice to achieve the Iraqi people's legitimate demands.

The Governing Council

Document 517

Annex to the Law for the Administration of Iraq in the Transitional Period

1 June 2004

On the basis of Article 2(1)B of the Law of Administration for the State of Iraq in the Transitional Period, the Governing Council decided in its session of 1/6/2004 to issue this Annex.

Section One: Formation of the Iraqi Interim Government

The Iraqi Interim Government, formed on the basis of wide-scale consultations with all segments of Iraqi society, and consisting of individuals known for their ability and integrity, will assume sovereign authority for governing Iraq no later than 30 June 2004. The Interim Government will administer Iraq's affairs, in particular by providing for the welfare and security of the Iraqi people, promoting reconstruction and economic development, and preparing for and holding national elections by 31 December 2004, if possible, and, in any case, no later than 31 January 2005. The Government, as an interim government, will refrain from taking any actions affecting Iraq's destiny beyond the limited interim period. Such actions should be reserved to future governments democratically elected by the Iraqi people. The members of the Interim Government will swear a legal oath in front of the Head of the highest judicial authority in Iraq. The Interim Government will dissolve upon the formation of the Iraqi Transitional Government following national elections.

Section Two: Institutions and Powers of the Iraqi Interim Government

The Interim Government will operate under the Law of Administration for the State of Iraq for the Transitional Period. It will consist of the Presidency of the State (comprised of a President and two Deputy Presidents); a Council of Ministers, including a Prime Minister; an Interim National Council and the Judicial Authority. Except for the purposes of Chapter Nine of this Law or as otherwise specified herein, references to the Iraqi Transitional Government and its institutions and officials in this Law will apply to the Interim Government and its institutions and officials. The Interim Government will at all times respect obligations related to the transitional period and the fundamental principles and rights of the Iraqi people as set forth in this Law. The institutions of the Kurdistan Regional Government, the governorates and the municipalities will function in accordance with this Law.

The Council of Ministers with the unanimous approval of the Presidency, may issue orders with the force of law that will remain in effect until rescinded or amended by future Iraqi governments. The Council of Ministers will have the authorities granted to the National Assembly in this Law related to appointments, the use of the Iraqi Armed Forces, and approval of international agreements. The Interim Government will represent Iraq in its external relations, but its powers in concluding international agreements will not extend beyond Iraq's diplomatic relations, international loans and assistance, and Iraq's sovereign debt. The appointment of Supreme Court members must be unanimously confirmed by the Presidency Council of the Iraqi Transitional Government within ninety days after its assumption of authority.

Section Three: The Interim National Council

Members of the Interim National Council will be chosen by a National Conference that will meet in Baghdad during the month of July 2004. The Conference will be organized by a High Commission, which will include members of the Governing Council without other governmental positions, representatives from the regions and governorates, and other distinguished Iraqis known for their capability and integrity. The Interim National Council itself will be comprised of 100 members, and will include members of the Governing Council mentioned above.

The Interim National Council will meet periodically to promote constructive dialogue and create national consensus, and to advise the Presidency Council and Council of Ministers. It will have the authority to monitor the implementation of laws, to follow up the work of the executive bodies, to appoint replacements to the Presidency Council in cases of resignation or death, to interpellate the Prime Minister and Council of Ministers, and to veto executive orders by a 2/3 majority vote of its members within 10 days of being informed of such orders which have been approved by the Presidency Council. The Interim National Council will also have the right to approve the 2005 Iraqi national budget proposed by the Council of Ministers, and to set its Internal Regulations.

Document 518
Press Release
[Annex to the Transitional State Administration Law]

5 June 2004[33]

1. As one of its final acts before the Governing Council dissolved itself it unanimously approved an annex to the Transitional State Administration Law on 1 June 2004.

2. The annex develops the powers and structures of the Iraqi Interim Government, which roughly correspond with the powers and structures laid down in the State Administrative Law itself.

3. The annex makes clear that the Interim Government will be fully sovereign and possess complete authority. It will possess the right to issue resolutions carrying the force of law and change or modify any currently existing law, including orders issued by the Coalition Provisional Authority, the only exception being the annex to the State Administration Law itself.

4. There are no restrictions on the authority of the Government, except that it cannot adopt resolutions that affect Iraq's destiny beyond the specified interim period. This reflects the desire of the Iraqi people that an unelected government cannot bind future Iraqi governments which will be elected.

5. Thus, the Interim Government will be sovereign with full powers and mark the true end of the occupation.

[33] Translation from Arabic.

III

United Nations Documents

Document 519
Resolution 1472 (2003), Adopted by the Security Council at its 4732nd Meeting on 28 March 2003

UN Doc. S/RES/1472 (2003), 28 March 2003

The Security Council,

Noting that under the provisions of Article 55 of the Fourth Geneva Convention (Geneva Convention Relative to the Protection of Civilian Persons in Time of War of August 12, 1949), to the fullest extent of the means available to it, the Occupying Power has the duty of ensuring the food and medical supplies of the population; it should, in particular, bring in the necessary foodstuffs, medical stores and other articles if the resources of the occupied territory are inadequate,

Convinced of the urgent need to continue to provide humanitarian relief to the people of Iraq throughout the country on an equitable basis, and of the need to extend such humanitarian relief measures to the people of Iraq who leave the country as a result of hostilities,

Recalling its previous relevant resolutions, and in particular resolutions 661 (1990) of 6 August 1990, 986 (1995) of 14 April 1995, 1409 (2002) of 14 May 2002, and 1454 (2002) of 30 December 2002, as they provide humanitarian relief to the people of Iraq,

Noting the decision made by the Secretary-General on 17 March 2003 to withdraw all United Nations and international staff tasked with the implementation of the 'Oil-for-Food' Programme (hereinafter 'the Programme') established under resolution 986 (1995),

Stressing the necessity to make every effort to sustain the operation of the present national food basket distribution network,

Stressing also the need for consideration of a further reassessment of the Programme during and after the emergency phase,

Reaffirming the respect for the right of the people of Iraq to determine their own political future and to control their own natural resources,

Reaffirming the commitment of all Member States to the sovereignty and territorial integrity of Iraq,

Acting under Chapter VII of the Charter of the United Nations,

1. *Requests* all parties concerned to strictly abide by their obligations under international law, in particular the Geneva Conventions and the Hague Regulations, including those relating to the essential civilian needs of the people of Iraq, both inside and outside Iraq;

2. *Calls on* the international community also to provide immediate humanitarian assistance to the people of Iraq, both inside and outside Iraq in consultation with relevant States, and in particular to respond immediately to any future humanitarian appeal of the United Nations, and supports the activities of the International Committee of the Red Cross and of other international humanitarian organizations;

3. *Recognizes* that additionally, in view of the exceptional circumstances prevailing currently in Iraq, on an interim and exceptional basis, technical and temporary adjustments should be made to the Programme so as to ensure the implementation of the approved funded and non-funded contracts concluded by the Government of Iraq for the humanitarian relief of the people of Iraq, including to meet the needs of refugees and internally displaced persons, in accordance with this resolution;

4. *Authorizes* the Secretary-General and representatives designated by him to undertake as an urgent first step, and with the necessary coordination, the following measures:

(a) to establish alternative locations, both inside and outside Iraq, in consultation with the respective governments, for the delivery, inspection and authenticated confirmation of humanitarian supplies and equipment provided under the Programme, as well as to re- direct shipments of goods to those locations, as necessary;

(b) to review, as a matter of urgency, the approved funded and non-funded contracts concluded by the Government of Iraq to determine the relative priorities of the need for adequate medicine, health supplies, foodstuffs and other materials and supplies for essential civilian needs represented in these contracts which can be shipped within the period of this mandate, to proceed with these contracts in accordance with such priorities;

(c) to contact suppliers of these contracts to determine the precise location of contracted goods and, when necessary, to require suppliers to delay, accelerate or divert shipments;

(d) to negotiate and agree on necessary adjustments in the terms or conditions of these contracts and their respective letters of credit and to implement the measures referred to in paragraph 4 (a), (b) and (c), notwithstanding distribution plans approved under the Programme;

(e) to negotiate and execute new contracts for essential medical items under the Programme and to authorize issuance of the relevant letters of credit, notwithstanding approved distribution plans, provided that such items cannot be delivered in execution of contracts pursuant to paragraph 4 (b) and subject to the approval of the Committee established pursuant to resolution 661 (1990);

(f) to transfer unencumbered funds between the accounts created pursuant to paragraphs 8 (a) and 8 (b) of resolution 986 (1995) on an exceptional and reimbursable basis as necessary to ensure the delivery of essential humanitarian supplies to the people of Iraq and to use the funds in the escrow accounts referred to in paragraphs 8 (a) and (b) of resolution 986 (1995) to implement the Programme as provided for in this resolution, irrespective of the phase in which such funds entered the escrow accounts or the phase to which those funds may have been allocated;

(g) to use, subject to procedures to be decided by the Committee established by resolution 661 (1990) prior to the end of the period set out in paragraph 10 below and based on recommendations provided by the Office of the Iraq Programme, funds deposited in the accounts created pursuant to paragraphs 8 (a) and (b) of resolution 986 (1995), as necessary and appropriate, to compensate suppliers and shippers for agreed additional shipping, transportation and storage costs incurred as a result of diverting and delaying shipments as directed by him according to the provisions of paragraph 4 (a), (b) and (c) in order to perform his functions set out in paragraph 4 (d);

(h) to meet additional operational and administrative costs resulting from the implementation of the temporarily modified Programme by the funds in the escrow account established pursuant to paragraph 8 (d) of resolution 986 (1995) in the same manner as costs arising from those activities set forth in paragraph 8 (d) of resolution 986 (1995) in order to perform his functions set out in (d);

(i) to use funds deposited in the escrow accounts established pursuant to paragraphs 8 (a) and 8 (b) of resolution 986 (1995) for the purchase of locally produced goods and to meet the local cost for essential civilian needs which have been funded in accordance with the provisions of resolution 986 (1995) and related resolutions, including, where appropriate, the costs of milling, transportation and other costs necessary to facilitate the delivery of essential humanitarian supplies to the people of Iraq;

5. *Expresses* its readiness as a second step to authorize the Secretary-General to perform additional functions with the necessary coordination as soon as the situation permits as activities of the Programme in Iraq resume;

6. *Expresses further* its readiness to consider making additional funds available, including from the account created pursuant to paragraph 8 (c) of resolution 986 (1995), on an exceptional and reimbursable basis, to meet further the humanitarian needs of the people of Iraq;

7. *Decides* that, notwithstanding the provisions of resolution 661 (1990) and resolution 687 (1991) and for the duration of the present resolution, all applications outside the Oil-for-Food Programme submitted by the United Nations agencies, programmes and funds, other international organizations and non-governmental organizations (NGOs) for distribution or use in Iraq of emergency humanitarian supplies and equipment, other than medicines, health supplies and foodstuffs, shall be reviewed by the Committee established pursuant to resolution 661 (1990), under a 24-hour no-objection procedure;

8. *Urges* all parties concerned, consistent with the Geneva Conventions and the Hague Regulations, to allow full unimpeded access by international humanitarian organizations to all people of Iraq in need of assistance and to make available all necessary facilities for their operations and to promote the safety, security and freedom of movement of United Nations and associated personnel and their assets, as well as personnel of humanitarian organizations in Iraq in meeting such needs;

9. *Directs* the Committee established pursuant to resolution 661 (1990) to monitor closely the implementation of the provisions in paragraph 4 above and, in that regard, requests the Secretary-General to update the Committee on the measures as they are being taken and to consult with the Committee on prioritization of contracts for shipments of goods, other than foodstuffs, medicines, health and water sanitation related supplies;

10. *Decides* that the provisions contained in paragraph 4 of this resolution shall remain in force for a period of 45 days following the date of adoption of this resolution and may be subject to further renewal by the Council;

11. *Requests* the Secretary-General to take all measures required for the implementation of the present resolution and to report to the Security Council prior to the termination of the period defined in paragraph 10;

12. *Decides* to remain seized of the matter.

Document 520
Resolution 1476 (2003), Adopted by the Security Council at its 4743rd Meeting on 24 April 2003

UN Doc. S/RES/1476 (2003), 24 April 2003

The Security Council,

Recalling its previous relevant resolutions, and in particular resolutions 661 (1990) of 6 August 1990, 986 (1995) of 14 April 1995, 1409 (2002) of 14 May 2002, 1454 (2002) of 30 December 2002, and 1472 (2003) of 28 March 2003, as they provide humanitarian relief to the people of Iraq,

Acting under Chapter VII of the Charter of the United Nations,

1. *Decides* that the provisions contained in paragraph 4 of resolution 1472 (2003) shall remain in force until 3 June 2003 and may be subject to further renewal by the Council;
2. *Decides* to remain seized of the matter.

Document 521
United Nations Press Conference Canal Hotel Baghdad

3 May 2003[1]

Ramiro Lopes da Silva, United Nations Humanitarian Coordinator for Iraq: [...] As we move along in the coming days we wish to focus our activities having three main components in mind. One is to engage the Iraqi bureaucrats, technocrats, our contact points our counterparts in the different technical ministries and technical institutions so they can guide us on what is the need, what are the areas we should be focusing on, and what are the modalities for us to bring that assistance that may be required. In that process we intend to establish a collaborative relation with the Office of Reconstruction and Humanitarian Assistance [ORHA]. Our aim here, is not to replace the administration of the country. The administration of the country is the Office of the Reconstruction of the Humanitarian Assistance [sic] and we intend to establish with that organism a collaborative and close relationship so we know what are their plans they know what are our plans and we make sure that we fill gaps. Our duty is to fill gaps, not to duplicate efforts. [...]. The United Nations has a clear mandate. That mandate is humanitarian and that is the task we intend to develop in the coming days. [...].

Newsweek: What is the legal ground of the occupation how are you going to work with ORHA?

I think nobody is in doubt that the coalition is occupying the country. I think that nobody is in doubt that the de facto administration of this country is embodied in the Office of Reconstruction and Humanitarian Assistance and the ORHA is re-establishing the Iraqi administration. From the humanitarian view point there is no major legal challenge in that relationship. The situation could be considered a little bit more difficult if one has a restrictive reading of the 4th Geneva Convention and on the basis of the Convention when the humanitarian organisations are supposed to intervene. If one has a very legal approach to these and I am not a lawyer I am an engineer I have difficulties reading

[1] UN News Centre, Baghdad: UN joint press conference, 3 May 2003, http://www.un.org/. Obvious typos such as 'OHRA' (instead of ORHA) have been corrected.

laws but if one has that restrictive interpretation of the 4th Geneva Convention we will be sitting tight waiting for gaps to be created and then claiming because the occupying power, the coalition was not able to deliver we were to step in. I think we have to take a rather more pragmatic approach. Whilst we are guided by the 4th Geneva Convention and we recognised the responsibilities of the coalition vis-a-vis bringing back normalcy and the welfare of the Iraqi population we should not in good conscience step aside and let systems collapse when we have the knowledge, the expertise, the contacts to assist the ORHA re-establishing those systems. We are taking a more active interpretation of the Convention. Additionally there is a slightly tricky issue for us. It is the fact that the Security Council on 28 March by passing resolution 1472 made us responsible to bring into the country the inputs contracted under the oil for food programme. I bring those inputs but the United Nations is not recreating reinventing the wheel. There are systems to distribute those inputs those systems are under the administration of ORHA so we will be dealing with ORHA and we have no legal impediment for doing so on the humanitarian front. Other issues related with the reengineering of the civil administration, reconstruction of the country, those are trickier issues that will need to sit down and discuss in the coming days.

Newsweek: Do you think the Americans consider their presence as an occupation (inaudible). How do you feel about that?

I think the problem is somehow a negative connotation has been given to what is in the legal terms from the 4th Geneva Convention, a pure legal term identifying a state of fact. For me it is no problem if member states who are part of the coalition say no we are not occupiers we are liberators we are administrators. I think it is irrelevant for the way the United Nations positions itself. Our role is to assist the Iraqi people our guide is the Iraqi people, they are in the center of everything. In the center of the humanitarian effort. They should be in the center of the political process where the UN is not involved and they will have to be in the center of the reconstruction and the reengineering of the civil administration. The second guiding principles for us is there is a coalition, that coalition invaded this country, that coalition toppled the regime and that coalition is in the country and through the ORHA is establishing a temporary interim administration of the country. We need to move forward and that is what we are doing. [...].

Document 522
General Guidance for Interaction Between United Nations Personnel and Military and Civilian Representatives of the Occupying Power in Iraq

8 May 2003[2]

I. Introduction

1. Recent conflicts have shown that coordination between humanitarian actors on one side and representatives of the military and/or civilian authorities on the other side,

[2] Updated version 3.0. The Guidance was issued by the United Nations Office for the Coordination of Humanitarian Affairs (OCHA). On 21 March 2003, OCHA had issued a 6-page document entitled 'General

particularly in the early phases of a conflict, can be essential for the timely and effective delivery of humanitarian assistance and to help ensure the protection of civilians. Sharing of relevant humanitarian information, facilitation of humanitarian operations, and deconflicting humanitarian activities from operations of military or civilian authorities are key areas of such coordination. While interaction between humanitarian actors and military and civilian authorities on the ground is both a reality and a necessity, it is important to emphasize the constraints and limitations of humanitarian organizations in this respect. A perception of adherence to key humanitarian principles of humanity, neutrality and impartiality is of immediate practical relevance for humanitarian workers on the ground, e.g. in ensuring safe and secure operations, obtaining access across combat lines, and being able to guarantee equitable aid distribution to all vulnerable populations.

2. For the humanitarian activities of the UN in Iraq, it is therefore essential that there be maximum clarity for UN personnel for their daily contacts or liaison arrangements with military and civilian representatives of the Occupying Power in Iraq. As provided for in this terms of reference, the Humanitarian Coordinator for Iraq (HC), who is also the Designated Official (DO), will oversee all the liaisons with the Occupying Power in Iraq.

3. This document is intended to provide practical guidance to UN personnel in their interaction with all military and civilian representatives of the Occupying Power in Iraq. The guidance provided in this document will be reviewed on a continuous basis and will be revised to address additional concerns as they arise.

II. Principles

Any coordination between UN personnel, and military and civilian representatives of the Occupying Power in Iraq should be guided by the following key considerations:

4. **Operational independence of humanitarian action:** UN humanitarian agencies, under the overall authority of the Humanitarian Coordinator for Iraq, must retain full control of UN humanitarian operations inside and outside Iraq. Agencies must ensure that their operational independence is guaranteed at all times, e.g. on issues involving freedom

guidance for interaction between United Nations personnel and military actors in the context of the crisis in Iraq'. Part V 'Interaction with Military Forces of an Occupying Power' provided: '12. If parts or the entire territory of Iraq come under the effective control of foreign military forces, the Occupying Power will assume certain responsibilities under the international humanitarian law, in particular the Fourth Geneva Convention. These obligations include the duty of ensuring food and medical supplies for the population. 13. Any interaction by UN personnel with military forces of an Occupying Power generally should be in accordance with the guidance set out in this document while taking into account the obligations of the Occupying Power. Full respect for the principles listed under section II. should be ensured, including as clear a separation between humanitarian and military activities as possible. If required, additional guidance on specific situations involving the military forces of an Occupying Power should be sought from the HC/DO.' This document was updated on 9 April 2003 and replaced by version 2.0 entitled 'General Guidance for Interaction between United Nations Personnel and Military and other Representatives of the Belligerent Parties in the Context of the Crisis in Iraq'. Updated version 2.0 provided in Part VI. 'Interaction with the Occupying Power': '12. If parts or the entire territory of Iraq come under the effective control of foreign military forces, the Occupying Power will assume certain responsibilities under international humanitarian law, in particular the Fourth Geneva Convention. These obligations include the duty of ensuring food and medical supplies for the population to the fullest extent of the means available to the Occupying Power. 13. Any interaction by UN personnel with military forces or other representatives of the Occupying Power generally should be in accordance with the guidance set out in this document while taking into account the legal obligations of the Occupying Power. Full respect for the principles listed under section II. should be ensured, including as clear a separation between humanitarian and military activities as possible. If required, additional guidance on specific situations involving the military forces or other representatives of the Occupying Power should be sought from the HC/DO.'

of movement, recruitment of national staff, non-integration in military planning, or access to communications.

5. **Access to all vulnerable populations:** UN humanitarian agencies must maintain their ability to obtain and sustain access to all vulnerable populations in all parts of Iraq and to negotiate such access with all parties to the conflict. The principle of humanity requires that suffering must be addressed wherever it is encountered.

6. **Neutral and impartial aid distribution:** UN humanitarian agencies must ensure that all vulnerable populations in all parts of Iraq receive aid in an equitable, neutral and impartial manner and without any political conditions attached. Humanitarian assistance must be provided on the basis of 'needs only'; i.e., without outside interference with UN needs assessments and responses.

7. **Security of humanitarian personnel:** Under the guidance of UNSECOORD, UN humanitarian agencies are accountable for the safety and security of their staff and operations, both in Iraq and its neighboring countries. A perception of too close an affiliation with the operations or objectives of military or civilian representatives of the Occupying Power may impact negatively on the security environment for humanitarian staff and equipment as well as on the ability of humanitarian actors to assist and protect vulnerable populations.

III. Practical guidance in key areas of civil-military interaction

8. **Liaison arrangements with the HOCs, HACCs and CMOCs:** Liaison arrangements and direct lines of communication with Humanitarian Operations Centers (HOCs), Humanitarian Assistance Coordination Centers (HACCs) and Civil-Military Operation Centers (CMOCs) are essential to allow the sharing of information relevant to humanitarian operations as well as the facilitation of humanitarian operations before, during, and after conflict. Liaisons should be conducted to the degree necessary to facilitate UN humanitarian operations.

Permissible Action:

- Establishing direct lines of communications and maintaining liaison arrangements with HOCs, HACCs and CMOCs for information sharing and facilitation purposes.
- Information sharing includes:
  - Security information: Obtain information relevant to the security situation inside Iraq through the UNSECOORD liaison officer;
  - Humanitarian locations inside Iraq: Provision of coordinates of UN facilities and operations inside Iraq through UNSECOORD as UN focal point;
  - UN humanitarian plans and intentions;
  - Deconflicting: Provision of routes and timing of humanitarian convoys and airlifts to avoid accidental strikes on humanitarian operations or to warn of any conflicting activities;
  - Population movements: Providing and receiving information on major population movements, e.g. satellite imagery;
  - Post-strike information: Receiving information on strike locations and explosive munitions used during the military campaign to assist the prioritization and planning of humanitarian relief and mine-action/UXO activities.

- Facilitation includes:
  - Procedure for cross-border passages;
  - Air ops clearances;
  - ID card arrangements;
  - NGO liaison.
- Extending invitations to military representatives (e.g. CIMIC officers), or representatives of HOCs, HACCs and CMOCs to attend UN humanitarian coordination meetings on specific agenda items of concern (e.g. security briefings).
- Participating in coordination meetings hosted by HOCs, HACCs or CMOCs for the purposes of information sharing and facilitation.

Impermissible Action:

- No permanent co-location of UN personnel within military facilities or facilities of HOCs, HACCs or CMOCs.
- Co-location includes:
  - No UN staff to be physically permanently co-located within military facilities or facilities of HOCs, HACCs or CMOCs;
  - No UN emblems to be displayed within any such facilities;
  - Unless authorized by the HC/DO on a case-by-case basis, no UN staff should participate in public HOCs, HACCs or CMOCs events, including press conferences, ceremonies, and other formal events.

9. **Use of military assets for humanitarian operations:** The use of military assets in support of humanitarian operations should be exceptional and only a last resort. It is recognized that where civilian capacities are not adequate or cannot be obtained in a timely manner to meet urgent humanitarian needs, military and civil defence assets, including military aircraft, can be deployed in accordance with the guidelines on 'The Use Of Military And Civil Defence Assets To Support UN Humanitarian Activities In Complex Emergencies', issued in March 2003 (for more details go to www.reliefweb.int/mcdls/mcdu/mcdu.html). The main elements of these guidelines are as follows:

Permissible Action:

- Using military assets of non-belligerent forces in support of humanitarian operations, but only with the approval of the HC/DO, and in accordance with the following key principles:
  - Last resort: all civilian alternatives have been exhausted;
  - Unique capability: no appropriate alternative civilian resources exist;
  - Timeliness: the urgency of the task at hand demands immediate action;
  - Clear humanitarian direction in the use of the military assets;
- In the event that a non-belligerent state wishes to contribute military logistical means to support humanitarian operations within Iraq, those means should be consigned as UN livery and clearly marked as such with the application of the UN emblem.

Impermissible Action:

- Do not enter into discussions on the use of military assets without prior clearance from the HC/DO or the Steering Group on Iraq.
- Do not use military assets of belligerent forces in humanitarian operations except

under extreme and exceptional circumstances, and only if civilian assets or assets of non-belligerent forces cannot be used. This situation may only occur when highly vulnerable populations cannot be assisted or accessed by any other means. Always seek the approval of the HC/DO.

10. **Use of military or armed escorts:** The use of military or armed escorts for humanitarian convoys or operations is an extreme precautionary measure that should be taken only in exceptional circumstances and on a case-by-case basis. It is subject to the prior approval of the HC/DO and/or UNSECOORD (depending on the circumstances) and guided by the principles endorsed by the IASC in September 2001, i.e., as a means of last resort.

11. As a general rule, the UN should not use armed guards provided by a belligerent party for its protection. However, given the present security situation in Iraq and for as long as no reliable civilian law enforcement or alternative local security arrangements are in place, the UN may accept protection provided by the armed forces of the Occupying Power on an exceptional basis to ensure the safety and security of UN facilities and residences as well as for its humanitarian operations. Such exceptional arrangements can only be authorized by the HC/DO, on a case-by-case basis and in light of the security circumstances specific to the particular local circumstances. They must be regularly reviewed and reconsidered by the HC/DO with a view to their earliest possible termination once civilian law enforcement is available.

IV. Practical guidance for interaction with the Office of Reconstruction and Humanitarian Assistance (ORHA)

12. ORHA is a predominantly civilian organization, made up of representatives from different US federal government agencies and departments as well as representatives from other Member States of the Coalition. The Office has three pillars: Humanitarian Assistance, Reconstruction, and Civil Administration and is responsible for overseeing the immediate post-conflict humanitarian and reconstruction efforts in Iraq. As Coalition Forces continue to secure areas of Iraq, ORHA is about to establish locations inside Iraq from which it will discharge its functions.

13. The humanitarian pillar of ORHA will be the main entry point for UN humanitarian liaison and communication with the Occupying Power and its military and civilian representatives. The relationship between the UN and ORHA will be important for the effective coordination and implementation of humanitarian activities by the UN in Iraq.

14. Liaison arrangements with ORHA: Liaison arrangements and direct lines of communication with ORHA are essential to allow the sharing of information relevant to humanitarian operations as well as the facilitation of humanitarian activities. However, it is important that UN staff members liaising with ORHA retain their independence and are not perceived as being employed or sub-contracted by ORHA. The interaction with ORHA should be conducted according to the following guidelines:

Permissible Action:

- Establishing direct lines of communications and liaison arrangements with ORHA for information sharing at all relevant levels;
- Liaison arrangements include:
  - Exchanging liaison officers with ORHA;

- Extending invitations to representatives of ORHA to attend UN humanitarian meetings as appropriate and necessary;
- Participating in meetings with ORHA and hosted in ORHA's facilities for the purposes of information sharing and facilitation.

– Information sharing includes:
- Security information: Exchanging information relevant to the security situation inside Iraq, through the UNSECOORD liaison officer;
- Humanitarian information: Exchanging information concerning humanitarian activities in Iraq (objective, timing, locations and routes)

Impermissible Action:

– No permanent UN presence within ORHA facilities; this includes:
- No UN emblems to be displayed within ORHA facilities;
- Unless authorized by the HC/DO on a case-by-case basis, no UN staff should participate in public ORHA events, including press conferences, ceremonies, and other formal events.

– Unless authorized to do so by the HC/DO, UN personnel may not participate in ORHA directed programmes.

– UN personnel may not travel in vehicles or aircraft of ORHA, except as a last resort and only for security reasons and with prior approval: clearances for travel overland may be granted by the HC/DO, whereas air transit must be approved by UNSECOORD.

– No undertaking of any representation or tasks on behalf of ORHA or commissioned by ORHA.

15. **Practical guidance for interaction regarding assessment missions:** While UN agencies may be able to benefit from the findings of assessments conducted by civilian or military representatives of the Occupying Power, too close an affiliation with assessments of the Occupying Power may undermine the perception of the UN's neutrality and impartiality. Therefore, the interaction between the UN and the Occupying Power regarding assessment missions should be conducted along the following guidelines:

Permissible Action:

– Liaison arrangements for security assessments:
- In accordance with the UNSECOORD Concept of Operations for Security Assessments.

– Information sharing with assessment missions of the Occupying Power (OP) may include:
- Obtaining information on findings of humanitarian assessments conducted by the OP;
- Sharing of results of UN needs assessments with the OP; Evaluate and consider, as appropriate, findings of assessment missions of the OP in planning of UN response (along with information provided by other sources);
- If appropriate, invite individual civilian representatives of the OP to join UN inter-agency needs assessment missions (the same way the UN invites representatives of other donor agencies).

Impermissible Action:

- No joint UN - OP assessment missions:
  - UN agencies or UNDAC teams should not join needs assessment missions of the OP. Rather, UN agencies should conduct their own independent humanitarian assessments and use their own monitoring capacities, both under the clear designation of the UN.
- Participation in UNDAC team assessments:
  - Government representatives of parties involved in the conflict may not participate in UNDAC assessment missions.

V. Practical guidance in areas of general conduct

16. **UN identity and civilian nature of humanitarian assistance:** A clear distinction must be retained at all times between the functions and roles of UN humanitarian personnel and those of the military and civilian representatives of the Occupying Power. Failure to observe this distinction could compromise the perception of neutrality and impartiality of the UN and thereby negatively affect the safety and security of UN staff.

Permissible Action:

- Where in doubt, the civilian and independent nature of UN humanitarian assistance must be emphasized.
- Maintain a clear UN identity at all times (e.g. only travel in clearly marked UN vehicles; clearly mark offices and relief supplies).
- Ensure compliance with the UN policy on weapons, which does not allow any weapons on UN properties. Exceptions can be made for operational reasons, but have to be cleared by the senior UN person on the scene.

Impermissible Action:

- Unless authorized to do so by the HC/DO, UN personnel may not directly assist or participate in the delivery of humanitarian assistance by military forces; any perception of sub-contracting must be avoided.
- UN personnel may not travel in military vehicles, aircraft, etc. except as a last resort and only for security reasons and with prior approval: clearances for travel overland may be granted by the HC/DO, whereas air transit must be approved by UNSECOORD.
- In their personal conduct, UN staff should be conscious of the potential perception resulting from socializing in public with military or civilian representatives of the Occupying Power.
- Do not allow weapons in UN vehicles (other than by UN security guards), unless there is no other alternative to ensure staff security and the conduct is specifically authorized by the HC/DO.
- Uniformed personnel should only be allowed to enter UN facilities when on official business or upon invitation.
- No UN personnel may wear any uniform-like clothing (other than authorized by the UN, e.g. UN security personnel).
- UN personnel should refrain from any confrontational behavior vis-à-vis members of any armed forces or their civilian representatives. If humanitarian principles are

being violated, access denied, or pressure being exerted the occurrence should be documented in a report immediately and submitted to the HC/DO.

17. For any other situations involving the military or civilian representatives of the Occupying Power not identified in this document, additional guidance should be sought from the HC/DO as required and in conformity with the general principles laid out in section II. of the present Guidance Paper.

Document 523

Resolution 1483 (2003), Adopted by the Security Council at its 4761st Meeting on 22 May 2003

UN Doc. S/RES/1483 (2003), 22 May 2003[3]

The Security Council,

Recalling all its previous relevant resolutions,

Reaffirming the sovereignty and territorial integrity of Iraq,

Reaffirming also the importance of the disarmament of Iraqi weapons of mass destruction and of eventual confirmation of the disarmament of Iraq,

Stressing the right of the Iraqi people freely to determine their own political future and control their own natural resources, *welcoming* the commitment of all parties concerned to support the creation of an environment in which they may do so as soon as possible, and *expressing* resolve that the day when Iraqis govern themselves must come quickly,

Encouraging efforts by the people of Iraq to form a representative government based on the rule of law that affords equal rights and justice to all Iraqi citizens without regard to ethnicity, religion, or gender, and, in this connection, *recalls* resolution 1325 (2000) of 31 October 2000,

Welcoming the first steps of the Iraqi people in this regard, and *noting* in this connection the 15 April 2003 Nasiriyah statement[4] and the 28 April 2003 Baghdad statement,[5]

[3] The draft resolution was introduced by Spain, United Kingdom and United States of America (UN Doc. S/2003/556, 21 May 2003). It was adopted by 14 votes to 0, with Syria not participating. The draft was the fourth version of the resolution initially tabled on 9 May 2003.

[4] See *Doc 580.*

[5] An internal CPA document, dated 22 October 2003, stated with regard to the Baghdad Statement: 'Please note that we do NOT have a full and accurate copy of the Baghdad Statement. The attached is pulled from the press pool report, which does not claim to be a full list of the principles agreed to.' The attachment reads:

'<u>Excerpt from Press Pool report covering Baghdad Conference, April 28, 2003</u>

The group agreed to a list of principles.

Among them that:

• Coalition forces should accelerate their security enforcement activities.

• The United Nations should lift sanctions.

• That the International Community should forgive Iraq's debts.

• That war reparations (primarily referring to those with Kuwait) should be forgiven.

• They emphasized the need to begin a process that will lead to a broad based national conference to be convened in a period of not more than four weeks from April 27th to form a transitional government.

NOTE: While not included in the press pool report, we believe the Baghdad Conference also enclosed the Nasiriyah Statement.'

Resolved that the United Nations should play a vital role in humanitarian relief, the reconstruction of Iraq, and the restoration and establishment of national and local institutions for representative governance,

Noting the statement of 12 April 2003 by the Ministers of Finance and Central Bank Governors of the Group of Seven Industrialized Nations in which the members recognized the need for a multilateral effort to help rebuild and develop Iraq and for the need for assistance from the International Monetary Fund and the World Bank in these efforts,[6]

Welcoming also the resumption of humanitarian assistance and the continuing efforts of the Secretary-General and the specialized agencies to provide food and medicine to the people of Iraq,

Welcoming the appointment by the Secretary-General of his Special Adviser on Iraq,

Affirming the need for accountability for crimes and atrocities committed by the previous Iraqi regime,

Stressing the need for respect for the archaeological, historical, cultural, and religious heritage of Iraq, and for the continued protection of archaeological, historical, cultural, and religious sites, museums, libraries, and monuments,

Noting the letter of 8 May 2003 from the Permanent Representatives of the United States of America and the United Kingdom of Great Britain and Northern Ireland to the President of the Security Council (S/2003/538)[7] and recognizing the specific authorities, responsibilities, and obligations under applicable international law of these states as occupying powers under unified command (the 'Authority'),[8]

Noting further that other States that are not occupying powers are working now or in the future may work under the Authority,

Welcoming further the willingness of Member States to contribute to stability and security in Iraq by contributing personnel, equipment, and other resources under the Authority,

Concerned that many Kuwaitis and Third-State Nationals still are not accounted for since 2 August 1990,

Determining that the situation in Iraq, although improved, continues to constitute a threat to international peace and security,

Acting under Chapter VII of the Charter of the United Nations,

1. *Appeals* to Member States and concerned organizations to assist the people of Iraq in their efforts to reform their institutions and rebuild their country, and to contribute to conditions of stability and security in Iraq in accordance with this resolution;

[6] The Statement of G7 Finance Ministers and Central Bank Governors, adopted at their meeting in Washington, D.C. on 12 April 2003, reads as follows: '[...] We recognize the need for a multilateral effort to help Iraq. We support a further UN Security Council resolution. The IMF and the World Bank should play their normal role in rebuilding and developing Iraq, recognizing that the Iraqi people have the ultimate responsibility to implement the right policies and build their own future. It is important to address the debt issue and we are looking forward to the early engagement of the Paris Club. [...].'

[7] See *Doc 574*.

[8] The draft resolution submitted on 9 May 2003 by the United States, the United Kingdom and Spain read as follows: '*Noting* the letter of [date to be filled in] from the Permanent Representative of the United States of America and the United Kingdom to the President of the Security Council and recognizing the specific authorities, responsibilities, and obligations under applicable international law of these states as occupying powers and the responsibilities of others working now or in future with them under unified command (the "authority")'. (http://www.globalpolicy.org/security/issues/iraq/document/2003/0509postwardraft.htm). An earlier version published by BBC News spoke of 'recognizing the specific authorities, responsibilities, and obligations under applicable international law of these states and others working now or in future with them under unified command as the occupying power (the "authority")' (http://news.bbc.co.uk/go/pr/fr/-/1/hi/world/middle_east/ 3012847.stm [visited 15 May 2003]).

2. *Calls upon* all Member States in a position to do so to respond immediately to the humanitarian appeals of the United Nations and other international organizations for Iraq and to help meet the humanitarian and other needs of the Iraqi people by providing food, medical supplies, and resources necessary for reconstruction and rehabilitation of Iraq's economic infrastructure;

3. *Appeals* to Member States to deny safe haven to those members of the previous Iraqi regime who are alleged to be responsible for crimes and atrocities and to support actions to bring them to justice;

4. *Calls upon* the Authority, consistent with the Charter of the United Nations and other relevant international law, to promote the welfare of the Iraqi people through the effective administration of the territory, including in particular working towards the restoration of conditions of security and stability and the creation of conditions in which the Iraqi people can freely determine their own political future;[9]

5. *Calls upon* all concerned to comply fully with their obligations under international law including in particular the Geneva Conventions of 1949 and the Hague Regulations of 1907;

6. *Calls upon* the Authority and relevant organizations and individuals to continue efforts to locate, identify, and repatriate all Kuwaiti and Third-State Nationals or the remains of those present in Iraq on or after 2 August 1990, as well as the Kuwaiti archives, that the previous Iraqi regime failed to undertake, and, in this regard, *directs* the High-Level Coordinator, in consultation with the International Committee of the Red Cross and the Tripartite Commission and with the appropriate support of the people of Iraq and in coordination with the Authority, to take steps to fulfil his mandate with respect to the fate of Kuwaiti and Third-State National missing persons and property;

7. *Decides* that all Member States shall take appropriate steps to facilitate the safe return to Iraqi institutions of Iraqi cultural property and other items of archaeological, historical, cultural, rare scientific, and religious importance illegally removed from the Iraq National Museum, the National Library, and other locations in Iraq since the adoption of resolution 661 (1990) of 6 August 1990, including by establishing a prohibition on trade in or transfer of such items and items with respect to which reasonable suspicion exists that they have been illegally removed, and *calls upon* the United Nations Educational, Scientific, and Cultural Organization, Interpol, and other international organizations, as appropriate, to assist in the implementation of this paragraph;

8. *Requests* the Secretary-General to appoint a Special Representative for Iraq whose independent responsibilities shall involve reporting regularly to the Council on his activities under this resolution, coordinating activities of the United Nations in post-conflict processes in Iraq, coordinating among United Nations and international agencies engaged in humanitarian assistance and reconstruction activities in Iraq, and, in coordination with the Authority, assisting the people of Iraq through:[10]

[9] Paragraph 6 of the draft resolution of 9 May 2003 read: 'Calls upon the [interim] authority to provide for the welfare of the Iraqi people through the effective administration of the territory, including, in particular, working towards the restoration of conditions of security and stability and the creation of conditions in which the Iraqi people may freely determine their own political future'.

[10] Paragraph 8 of the draft resolution of 9 May 2003 read: 'Requests the secretary general to appoint a special co-ordinator for Iraq whose responsibilities will involve co-ordinating the UN's activities in post-conflict processes in Iraq, co-ordination among UN and international agencies engaged in humanitarian assistance and reconstruction activities in Iraq, co-ordinating with the authority and assisting the people of Iraq through:'

(a) coordinating humanitarian and reconstruction assistance by United Nations agencies and between United Nations agencies and non-governmental organizations;[11]
(b) promoting the safe, orderly, and voluntary return of refugees and displaced persons;
(c) working intensively with the Authority, the people of Iraq, and others concerned to advance efforts to restore and establish national and local institutions for representative governance, including by working together to facilitate a process leading to an internationally recognized, representative government of Iraq;[12]
(d) facilitating the reconstruction of key infrastructure, in cooperation with other international organizations;
(e) promoting economic reconstruction and the conditions for sustainable development, including through coordination with national and regional organizations, as appropriate, civil society, donors, and the international financial institutions;
(f) encouraging international efforts to contribute to basic civilian administration functions;
(g) promoting the protection of human rights;
(h) encouraging international efforts to rebuild the capacity of the Iraqi civilian police force; and
(i) encouraging international efforts to promote legal and judicial reform;

9. *Supports* the formation, by the people of Iraq with the help of the Authority and working with the Special Representative, of an Iraqi interim administration as a transitional administration run by Iraqis, until an internationally recognized, representative government is established by the people of Iraq and assumes the responsibilities of the Authority;[13]

10. *Decides* that, with the exception of prohibitions related to the sale or supply to Iraq of arms and related materiel other than those arms and related materiel required by the Authority to serve the purposes of this and other related resolutions, all prohibitions related to trade with Iraq and the provision of financial or economic resources to Iraq established by resolution 661 (1990) and subsequent relevant resolutions, including resolution 778 (1992) of 2 October 1992, shall no longer apply;

11. *Reaffirms* that Iraq must meet its disarmament obligations, *encourages* the United Kingdom of Great Britain and Northern Ireland and the United States of America to keep the Council informed of their activities in this regard, and *underlines* the intention

[11] Paragraph 8 a) of the draft resolution of 9 May 2003 read: 'support for and co-ordination of humanitarian and reconstruction assistance by UN agencies and non-governmental organisations'.

[12] Paragraph 8 c) of the draft resolution of 9 May 2003 read: 'working with the Authority and the people of Iraq with respect to the restoration and establishment of national and local institutions for representative governance'.

[13] The draft resolution submitted on 9 May 2003 read as follows: '10. *Supports* the formation, by the people of Iraq with the help of the Authority and working with the Special Coordinator, of an Iraqi interim authority as a transitional administration run by Iraqis until a permanent government is established by the people of Iraq'. In addition, there was a separate paragraph on the duration of the occupation. Paragraph 23 provided: '23. *Endorses* the exercise of the responsibilities stated in this resolution by the Authority for an initial period of 12 months from the date of the adoption of this resolution, to continue thereafter as necessary unless the Security Council decides otherwise'. Commenting on the modifications in the final version, the US Permanent Representative to the United Nations, Ambassador John D. Negroponte, said on 19 May 2003: 'I think you are pointing to what I think is a very important modification of the resolution. Previously it talked about the authority operating for a 12-month period, and then that period would be extended unless the Council decided otherwise, and effectively that was tantamount to an automatic extension of the Coalition's authority. Now, in Operative Paragraph 9, you will see that the Coalition, the timing of the Coalition's authority is defined in political terms, which strikes us – seems to us – to be a more logical way to do it. The Coalition's authority will end when its authorities and powers have been transferred to an internationally recognized government of Iraq. So now the definition is political rather than specifically time-bound, and it seems to make more sense to us, and more in line with the reality, what we expect to be the reality of the situation.' (www.un.int/usa/03_072.htm).

of the Council to revisit the mandates of the United Nations Monitoring, Verification, and Inspection Commission and the International Atomic Energy Agency as set forth in resolutions 687 (1991) of 3 April 1991, 1284 (1999) of 17 December 1999, and 1441 (2002) of 8 November 2002;

12. *Notes* the establishment of a Development Fund for Iraq to be held by the Central Bank of Iraq and to be audited by independent public accountants approved by the International Advisory and Monitoring Board of the Development Fund for Iraq and looks forward to the early meeting of that International Advisory and Monitoring Board, whose members shall include duly qualified representatives of the Secretary-General, of the Managing Director of the International Monetary Fund, of the Director-General of the Arab Fund for Social and Economic Development, and of the President of the World Bank;[14]

13. *Notes further* that the funds in the Development Fund for Iraq shall be disbursed at the direction of the Authority, in consultation with the Iraqi interim administration, for the purposes set out in paragraph 14 below;

14. *Underlines* that the Development Fund for Iraq shall be used in a transparent manner to meet the humanitarian needs of the Iraqi people, for the economic reconstruction and repair of Iraq's infrastructure, for the continued disarmament of Iraq, and for the costs of Iraqi civilian administration, and for other purposes benefiting the people of Iraq;

15. *Calls upon* the international financial institutions to assist the people of Iraq in the reconstruction and development of their economy and to facilitate assistance by the broader donor community, and *welcomes* the readiness of creditors, including those of the Paris Club, to seek a solution to Iraq's sovereign debt problems;

16. *Requests* also that the Secretary-General, in coordination with the Authority, continue the exercise of his responsibilities under Security Council resolution 1472 (2003) of 28 March 2003 and 1476 (2003) of 24 April 2003, for a period of six months[15] following the adoption of this resolution, and terminate within this time period, in the most cost effective manner, the ongoing operations of the 'Oil-for-Food' Programme (the 'Programme'), both at headquarters level and in the field, transferring responsibility for the administration of any remaining activity under the Programme to the Authority, including by taking the following necessary measures:

(a) to facilitate as soon as possible the shipment and authenticated delivery of priority civilian goods as identified by the Secretary-General and representatives designated by him, in coordination with the Authority and the Iraqi interim

[14] The draft resolution submitted on 9 May 2003 read as follows: '12. Notes the establishment of an Iraqi Assistance Fund, with an international advisory board including duly qualified representatives of the Secretary-General, the International Monetary Fund, [appropriate regional institution(s)] and the World Bank, to be held by the Central Bank of Iraq, and to be audited by independent public accountants chosen by the international advisory board'. On 20 May 2003, the US Permanent Representative to the United Nations, Ambassador John D. Negroponte, was asked during a press conference: 'Mr. Ambassador, the initial resolution you put down on the table gave the advisory board the authority to select an accountant to look at the or the [sic] oil revenues, can you give us a sort of indication as to why you've taken that authority away from the board in the latest draft resolution? It looks like the Coalition would select the accountants, subject to approval by the board [...].' Negroponte replied: 'Well, we think the key point is transparency of this operation and we think the mechanisms that we've built into the resolution will ensure that oil revenues are dealt with in a completely transparent manner. We've also designated this advisory board as the International Advisory and Monitoring Board, and as you know, it will have representatives of the Secretary-General of the United Nations and international financial institutions so I don't think that there need be any concern about the transparent manner in which these funds will be dealt with.' (www.un.int/usa/03_073.htm).

[15] The draft resolution submitted on 9 May 2003 had provided only for a 'four months' phase out of the oil-for-food programme. This extension to six months was important to the Russian Federation which had a major share in the contracts approved under the programme.

administration, under approved and funded contracts previously concluded by the previous Government of Iraq, for the humanitarian relief of the people of Iraq, including, as necessary, negotiating adjustments in the terms or conditions of these contracts and respective letters of credit as set forth in paragraph 4 (d) of resolution 1472 (2003);

(b) to review, in light of changed circumstances, in coordination with the Authority and the Iraqi interim administration, the relative utility of each approved and funded contract with a view to determining whether such contracts contain items required to meet the needs of the people of Iraq both now and during reconstruction, and to postpone action on those contracts determined to be of questionable utility and the respective letters of credit until an internationally recognized, representative government of Iraq is in a position to make its own determination as to whether such contracts shall be fulfilled;

(c) to provide the Security Council within 21 days following the adoption of this resolution, for the Security Council's review and consideration, an estimated operating budget based on funds already set aside in the account established pursuant to paragraph 8 (d) of resolution 986 (1995) of 14 April 1995, identifying:

(i) all known and projected costs to the United Nations required to ensure the continued functioning of the activities associated with implementation of the present resolution, including operating and administrative expenses associated with the relevant United Nations agencies and programmes responsible for the implementation of the Programme both at Headquarters and in the field;

(ii) all known and projected costs associated with termination of the Programme;

(iii) all known and projected costs associated with restoring Government of Iraq funds that were provided by Member States to the Secretary-General as requested in paragraph 1 of resolution 778 (1992); and

(iv) all known and projected costs associated with the Special Representative and the qualified representative of the Secretary-General identified to serve on the International Advisory and Monitoring Board, for the six month time period defined above, following which these costs shall be borne by the United Nations;

(d) to consolidate into a single fund the accounts established pursuant to paragraphs 8 (a) and 8 (b) of resolution 986 (1995);

(e) to fulfil all remaining obligations related to the termination of the Programme, including negotiating, in the most cost effective manner, any necessary settlement payments, which shall be made from the escrow accounts established pursuant to paragraphs 8 (a) and 8 (b) of resolution 986 (1995), with those parties that previously have entered into contractual obligations with the Secretary-General under the Programme, and to determine, in coordination with the Authority and the Iraqi interim administration, the future status of contracts undertaken by the United Nations and related United Nations agencies under the accounts established pursuant to paragraphs 8 (b) and 8 (d) of resolution 986 (1995);

(f) to provide the Security Council, 30 days prior to the termination of the Programme, with a comprehensive strategy developed in close coordination with the Authority and the Iraqi interim administration that would lead to the delivery of all relevant documentation and the transfer of all operational responsibility of the Programme to the Authority;

17. *Requests further* that the Secretary-General transfer as soon as possible to the Development Fund for Iraq 1 billion United States dollars from unencumbered funds in the accounts established pursuant to paragraphs 8 (a) and 8 (b) of resolution 986 (1995), restore Government of Iraq funds that were provided by Member States to the Secretary-General as requested in paragraph 1 of resolution 778 (1992), and *decides* that, after deducting all relevant United Nations expenses associated with the shipment of authorized contracts and costs to the Programme outlined in paragraph 16 (c) above, including residual obligations, all surplus funds in the escrow accounts established pursuant to paragraphs 8 (a), 8 (b), 8 (d), and 8 (f) of resolution 986 (1995) shall be transferred at the earliest possible time to the Development Fund for Iraq;

18. *Decides* to terminate effective on the adoption of this resolution the functions related to the observation and monitoring activities undertaken by the Secretary-General under the Programme, including the monitoring of the export of petroleum and petroleum products from Iraq;

19. *Decides* to terminate the Committee established pursuant to paragraph 6 of resolution 661 (1990) at the conclusion of the six month period called for in paragraph 16 above and *further decides* that the Committee shall identify individuals and entities referred to in paragraph 23 below;[16]

20. *Decides* that all export sales of petroleum, petroleum products, and natural gas from Iraq following the date of the adoption of this resolution shall be made consistent with prevailing international market best practices, to be audited by independent public accountants reporting to the International Advisory and Monitoring Board referred to in paragraph 12 above in order to ensure transparency, and *decides further* that, except as provided in paragraph 21 below, all proceeds from such sales shall be deposited into the Development Fund for Iraq until such time as an internationally recognized, representative government of Iraq is properly constituted;

21. *Decides further* that 5 per cent of the proceeds referred to in paragraph 20 above shall be deposited into the Compensation Fund established in accordance with resolution 687 (1991) and subsequent relevant resolutions and that, unless an internationally recognized, representative government of Iraq and the Governing Council of the United Nations Compensation Commission, in the exercise of its authority over methods of ensuring that payments are made into the Compensation Fund, decide otherwise, this requirement shall be binding on a properly constituted, internationally recognized, representative government of Iraq and any successor thereto;

22. *Noting* the relevance of the establishment of an internationally recognized, representative government of Iraq and the desirability of prompt completion of the restructuring of Iraq's debt as referred to in paragraph 15 above, further *decides* that, until December 31, 2007,[17] unless the Council decides otherwise, petroleum, petroleum products, and natural gas originating in Iraq shall be immune, until title passes to the initial

[16] For the guidelines for the application of paragraph 19 of resolution 1483 (2003), see *Doc 525*.

[17] No time limit had been included in the draft resolution of 9 May 2003. Paragraph 21 of that draft resolution read: '*Further decides* that petroleum, petroleum products and natural gas originated in Iraq, and proceeds of sales thereof, shall be immune from judicial, administrative, arbitration or any other proceedings (including any prejudgment or postjudgment attachment, garnishment, or execution or other action to satisfy a judgment) arising in relation to claims, of whatever kind and whenever accrued, against Iraq or any instrumentality or agents thereof (or the Authority, or its participating states or their instrumentalities or agents), and that all Member States shall take any steps under their respective domestic legal systems necessary to give full effect to this paragraph'.

purchaser from legal proceedings against them and not be subject to any form of attachment, garnishment, or execution, and that all States shall take any steps that may be necessary under their respective domestic legal systems to assure this protection, and that proceeds and obligations arising from sales thereof, as well as the Development Fund for Iraq, shall enjoy privileges and immunities equivalent to those enjoyed by the United Nations except that the abovementioned privileges and immunities will not apply with respect to any legal proceeding in which recourse to such proceeds or obligations is necessary to satisfy liability for damages assessed in connection with an ecological accident, including an oil spill, that occurs after the date of adoption of this resolution;

23. *Decides* that all Member States in which there are:

(a) funds or other financial assets or economic resources of the previous Government of Iraq or its state bodies, corporations, or agencies, located outside Iraq as of the date of this resolution, or

(b) funds or other financial assets or economic resources that have been removed from Iraq, or acquired, by Saddam Hussein or other senior officials of the former Iraqi regime and their immediate family members, including entities owned or controlled, directly or indirectly, by them or by persons acting on their behalf or at their direction, shall freeze without delay those funds or other financial assets or economic resources and, unless these funds or other financial assets or economic resources are themselves the subject of a prior judicial, administrative, or arbitral lien or judgement, immediately shall cause their transfer to the Development Fund for Iraq, it being understood that, unless otherwise addressed, claims made by private individuals or non-government entities on those transferred funds or other financial assets may be presented to the internationally recognized, representative government of Iraq; and *decides further* that all such funds or other financial assets or economic resources shall enjoy the same privileges, immunities, and protections as provided under paragraph 22;[18]

24. *Requests* the Secretary-General to report to the Council at regular intervals on the work of the Special Representative with respect to the implementation of this resolution and on the work of the International Advisory and Monitoring Board and *encourages* the United Kingdom of Great Britain and Northern Ireland and the United States of America to inform the Council at regular intervals of their efforts under this resolution;[19]

25. *Decides* to review the implementation of this resolution within twelve months of adoption and to consider further steps that might be necessary;[20]

26. *Calls upon* Member States and international and regional organizations to contribute to the implementation of this resolution;

27. *Decides* to remain seized of this matter.[21]

[18] For the guidelines for the application of paragraph 23 of resolution 1483 (2003), see *Docs 525* and *528*.

[19] For references for the various reports, see the section on 'Other Documents of Interest'.

[20] This paragraph was introduced only in the last version of the draft resolution in blue on 21 May 2003; compare UN Docs. S/2003/556, 19 May 2003 and S/2003/556, 21 May 2003.

[21] Explaining the US vote for the resolution, US Ambassador John Negroponte said: '[...] By recognizing the fluidity of the political situation and that decisions will be made on the ground, the Security Council has provided a flexible framework under Chapter VII for the Coalition Provisional Authority, member states, the United Nations and others in the international community to participate in the administration and reconstruction of Iraq and to assist the Iraqi people in determining their political future, establishing new institutions, and restoring economic prosperity to the country. [...].' (UN Doc. S/PV.4761, 22 May 2003, 2-3). The French representative stated: 'The resolution that we have just adopted attributes to the occupying Powers broad authorities in the area of international humanitarian law and the necessary means to exercise those authorities. By voting in favour of the resolution, France sought to express its support for this difficult endeavour, which now involves the entire international community. These broad authorities entail responsibilities vis-à-vis, first, the Iraqi people, which

Document 524

Note to the Under Secretary General of the Department of Political Affairs, United Nations, on the Draft Coalition Provisional Authority (CPA) Order on the Status of Foreign Missions in Iraq

UN Juridical Yearbook 2003, 555-556

11 June 2003[22]

1. This refers to the code cable of 8 June 2003, requesting our views on the possible implications, if any, of the draft CPA Order on the Status of Foreign Missions in Iraq on the proposed Exchange of Letters (SOMA) between the United Nations and the Provisional Authority. We note that the status of foreign Missions in Iraq is regulated in a number of instruments attached to the code cable, none of which, however, is in the form of an Order. They include an internal communication of 4 June 2003 from the Office of General Counsel to the Administrator of the CPA, a 'Circular notice to all Foreign Government Offices in Iraq' and a 'Memorandum for Commander of Coalition Forces' dated 5 June 2003 from the Administrator of the CPA. Our review of the Order on the status of foreign Missions in Iraq and its implications on the SOMA has been conducted on the basis of these communications.

2. Under the CPA Circular Notice and its related communications, diplomatic personnel in Iraq accredited to the previous Iraqi Government have lost their diplomatic status *vis-à-vis* the CPA. The premises of foreign Missions are no longer inviolable, and their personnel have been stripped of their diplomatic privileges and immunities. The CPA has declared that it is not in a position to confer diplomatic status upon individuals and premises, with the result that pending the establishment of a sovereign Iraqi Government, the status of former diplomatic staff is akin to that of neutral citizens in an occupied territory, and the obligation to protect them does not extend beyond the general obligation of an Occupying Power to restore and ensure, as far as possible, law, public order and safety in an occupied territory. In the circumstances, diplomatic staff who remain in Iraq or re-enter it, are doing so at their own risk, and the CPA reserves the right to expel them from the territory if reasons of public order and safety so warrant.

3. The status of the Special Representative of the Secretary-General's (SRSG) Office, United Nations personnel and personnel of Specialized Agencies in Iraq is, however, fundamentally different from that of foreign Missions. While some of the United Nations and related Agencies may have operated in Iraq prior to the occupation, their current presence in Iraq is mandated by Security Council resolution 1483 (2003) of 22 May 2003, and the status to which they are entitled derives from the Charter of the United Nations, the Convention on the Privileges and Immunities of the United Nations,[23] or the Convention

must take its own destiny into its own hands as soon as possible; and secondly, the international community, because it has recognized the existence of the rights and obligations of the Authority and addressed specific requests to it.' (ibid., 4). The Pakistani delegate said: 'Pakistan, like several other members of the Security Council, has agreed, due to the exigencies of the circumstances, to the delegation of certain powers by the Security Council to the occupying Powers, represented by the Authority. It is our expectation that the responsibilities entrusted to the Authority under this resolution will be exercised transparently and fairly and, above all, in the interests of the Iraqi people.' (Ibid., 11). The Secretary-General said: 'The Council has adopted a resolution that spells out the assistance it expects the United Nations to give to the people of Iraq in coordination with the occupying Powers, which have the responsibility for the effective administration of the territory.' (ibid., 12).

[22] Legal opinion of the Secretariat of the United Nations.

[23] Convention on the Privileges and Immunities of the United Nations, New York, 13 February 1946, 1 UNTS 15. The Convention was in force for the United Kingdom (17 September 1946), the United States (29 April 1970) and Iraq (15 September 1949).

on the Privileges and Immunities of the Specialized Agencies,[24] as well as the customary principles and practices of peacekeeping and similar United Nations operations. Once a SOMA is concluded it will provide a legal framework for the status and activities of the Office of the SRSG and United Nations related and specialized agencies in Iraq.

4. The loss of diplomatic status of foreign Missions in Iraq has no bearing, therefore, on the status of the SRSG's Office and its personnel, or the personnel and premises of other United Nations related or specialized agencies. In that latter respect, we note that the specialized agencies now operating in Iraq have expressed their agreement to be included in the SOMA, without prejudice to any subsequent agreement that they may wish to conclude separately with the CPA.

Document 525
Guidelines for the Application of Paragraphs 19 and 23 of Resolution 1483 (2003)

UN Doc. SC/7791 IK/365, 12 June 2003

Pursuant to paragraph 19 of resolution 1483 (2003), the 661 Committee[25] shall identify individuals and entities referred to in paragraph 23 of the same resolution. To facilitate the work of the Committee in that regard, the following procedural guidelines are hereby adopted:

1. Lists of individuals and entities referred to in paragraphs 19 and 23 of resolution 1483 (2003)

(a) The Committee will identify the individuals and entities referred to in paragraphs 19 and 23 of resolution 1483 (2003) when it receives relevant information;

(b) The names of individuals and entities proposed for identification should be accompanied by, to the extent possible, a narrative description of the information that forms the basis or justification for taking action pursuant to resolution 1483 (2003);

(c) The names of individuals and entities proposed for identification should be accompanied by, to the extent possible, relevant and specific information to facilitate their identification by competent authorities:

- For individuals: name (both in Arabic and English), date of birth, place of birth, nationality, aliases, residence, passport or travel document number, professional or functional title;
- For groups, undertakings or entities: name, acronyms, address, headquarters, subsidiaries, affiliates, fronts, nature of business or activity, leadership;

(d) The Committee will consider expeditiously requests to update the list to be provided through Members States, on the basis of relevant information received by the Committee;

(e) Any modification to the list will be communicated to the Member States immediately. The updated list will be made promptly available on the Web pages of the Committee.

2. Decision-making

(a) With regard to paragraphs 19 and 23 of resolution 1483 (2003), the Committee will reach decisions by consensus. If consensus cannot be reached, the Chairman should

[24] Convention on the Privileges and Immunities of the Specialized Agencies, New York, 21 November 1947, 33 UNTS 261. The Convention was in force for the United Kingdom (16 August 1949) and Iraq (9 July 1954) but not for the United States.

[25] The Security Council Committee established by S/RES/661 (1990), 6 August 1990, para. 6.

undertake such further consultations as may facilitate agreement. If after these consultations, consensus still cannot be reached, the matter may be submitted to the Security Council. Given the specific nature of the information, the Chairman may encourage bilateral exchanges between interested Member States in order to clarify the issue prior to a decision;

(b) Where the Committee agrees, decisions may be taken by a written procedure. In such cases, the Chairman will circulate to all members of the Committee the proposed decision of the Committee, under the 'no-objection' procedure within a three working-days deadline. If no objection is received within such a period, the decision will be deemed adopted.

3. Delisting

The Committee intends to consider establishing additional guidelines on delisting as soon as possible following the adoption of these guidelines

Document 526
Address of UN Special Representative for Iraq, Sergio Vieira de Mello, at the Inauguration Ceremony of the Iraqi Governing Council

13 July 2003[26]

It is an honour to be with you today. And I welcome the formation of the Governing Council.

I am honoured today to have been invited by you – the members of the Governing Council of Iraq – to say a few words on behalf of the Secretary-General of the United Nations.

There are defining moments in history. For Iraq, today is definitely one of those. It is thus only fitting that you let it be known that Iraq is moving back to where it rightfully belongs; at peace with itself and as a full participant in the community of nations. As an official of the United Nations, an Organization of which Iraq is a founding member, I am particularly proud to be here today to witness this historic event.

I have been in touch with the Secretary-General, Kofi Annan, who is following events in your country extremely closely. And last night he asked me to wish you well today and in the weeks and months ahead as you begin to grapple with the many challenges that face your country. He is committed to the United Nations assisting you and all Iraqis in any way that we can. We are here, in whatever form you wish, for as long as you want us. That is his promise.

Iraq today finds itself in a unique and difficult situation. A great country beset by much recent tragedy. Your convening, therefore, marks the first major development towards the restoration of Iraq's rightful status as a fully sovereign State. Today brings Iraq one step closer towards fulfilling the explicit wish of the Security Council, which, in its resolution 1483, resolved that the day when Iraqis govern themselves must come quickly. Let me also recall that the Security Council supported the formation of an Iraqi interim administration as a transitional administration run by Iraqis until an internationally recognized, representative government is established by the people of Iraq and assumes the responsibilities of the Authority.

[26] UN News Centre, Statement by Sergio Vieira de Mello Special Representative of the Secretary-General, 13 July 2003, http://www.un.org/.

I thus commend the Coalition Authority, as I commend you, Members of the Governing Council, for together seizing the initiative to implement UN Security Council Resolution 1483, in its entirety, as soon as possible.

The capacity of Iraqi leaders to forge the consensus necessary to bring into being the Governing Council – and to forge this consensus in such complex circumstances – is an achievement to be recognized, applauded and nurtured. It is through this consensus – a single-minded unity of purpose and resolve to get Iraq back to where this country deserves to be – that the many challenges facing you will be overcome.

Today, in Iraq we see the emergence of the Governing Council with a significant executive role to play. This is not the ultimate goal – for that can only come with the restoration of full sovereignty, as we know – but it is a necessary and welcome move in that direction. Equally, the formation of your Council does not mean that tomorrow you will find yourselves alone.

From today, we now have Iraqi counterparts with whom we can work. You will designate Interim Ministers. With you and with them the real work will commence and we will – the United Nations and the international community – be there to support you. The task is daunting. Humanitarian operations continue. New life must be breathed into the economy. The reconstruction and recovery tasks facing this country are immense, and must be supported by all.

Basic services must be restored. The economy must be urgently revived. The jobless must be found jobs. New skills must be learnt. Law and order must be re-established; the police force must be rebuilt, as must the army; the justice system reformed. The full range of human rights must be promoted and, above all, protected. For too long these rights have been trampled on by those who have shown nothing but disdain for the dignity of the human being. This must not be allowed to happen again. Freedom, dignity and security must be taken for granted by all Iraqis.

Likewise, Iraqis living in exile must not be forgotten: those who wish to return home – and many have been denied that opportunity for too long – need also be accommodated in this great land.

Ultimately, you will give pride back to the Iraqis and you will help this country break out of its exclusion and isolation.

Elections will need to be held. The voices of all Iraqis, men and women, must be heard as you shape your country for the future. And a constitution will need to be written: a fundamental document of vital importance to all the many varied peoples and regions of this nation, rich and united in its diversity.

At the Security Council, when I report on the situation in Iraq, I am happy that I shall be able to report on the positive news that Iraq has taken a marked step towards fulfilling that which is called of it – and of the international community – by resolution 1483, and this is a major step in this direction.

Each one of you earned the respect of the Iraqi people through your past achievements. You were a source of hope and confidence in times of despair. Now you must earn again – daily – that respect of the people. I commend you for now accepting this new responsibility of striving to turn the dreams of your compatriots into reality.

Document 527

Note to the Secretary General of the United Nations on the Question of Representation of Iraq in United Nations Organs

UN Juridical Yearbook 2003, 531-533
17 July 2003[27]

1. In the light of the stated intention of the Governing Council of Iraq to send a delegation consisting of [names] to the 22 July meeting of the Security Council, we understand that it is the intention of the President of the Security Council, after consultation with the members of the Council, to invite these persons to the 22 July meeting. It is also reported that the Governing Council intends to send representatives to assume the Iraqi seat in the United Nations and to designate a Chargé d'Affaires to the Permanent Mission of Iraq to the United Nations. Our comments are as follows.

2. The question of Iraq's representation in the United Nations is a sensitive political and legal matter which will ultimately be decided by the General Assembly in the light of any relevant Security Council resolutions. It should be noted, in this regard, that, pursuant to General Assembly resolution 396 (V) of 14 December 1950, the attitude adopted by the General Assembly on questions of representation 'should be taken into account in other organs of the United Nations and in the specialized agencies'. Accordingly, as has invariably been the case since 1950, the General Assembly's decisions on representation are followed by the organizations of the United Nations system.

3. With respect to the participation of representatives of the Governing Council in the 22 July meeting of the Security Council, pursuant to rule 39 of its provisional rules of procedure, 'the Security Council may invite members of the Secretariat or other persons, whom it considers competent for the purpose, to supply it with information or to give other assistance in examining matters within its competence'. Accordingly, if it so wishes, the Council could invite [the persons concerned] under rule 39. While such persons clearly could not sit behind the nameplate 'Iraq', there should be no objection to their sitting behind a nameplate 'Governing Council of Iraq' or personalized nameplates. We understand that the Security Council has opted for personalized nameplates.

4. If the Governing Council seeks to assume Iraq's seat in the General Assembly, however, this presents a different and far more complicated scenario. Iraq is and remains a Member State of the United Nations and, under Article 9 of the Charter, is a member of the General Assembly. Pursuant to the established practice of the General Assembly and rule 29 of the rules of procedure of the General Assembly, the previously accredited representatives of Iraq would continue until such time as the General Assembly, on the recommendation of the Credentials Committee, decides otherwise.

5. In accordance with rule 27 of the rules of procedure of the General Assembly, 'credentials shall be issued either by the Head of the State or Government or by the Minister for Foreign Affairs'. In the absence of a sovereign government in Iraq, there is no recognized authority to issue such credentials. To the extent that the Authority is recognized in Security Council resolution 1483 (2003) as an occupying power, it would be inconsistent with such occupation to have representatives assume the sovereign Iraqi seat in United Nations organs. Moreover, General Assembly acceptance of credentials issued by the Governing Council or Interim Ministers it has appointed would confer recognition by the Assembly on the

[27] Legal Opinion of the Secretariat of the United Nations.

Governing Council as a sovereign Iraqi government. This may have implications on the implementation of resolution 1483 (2003) which assumes that the occupation ends upon the establishment of an internationally recognized representative government.

6. Thus, in order to avoid a political and legal crisis, every effort should be made, including through contacts between the Special Representative of the Secretary-General and the Governing Council, to ensure that the Governing Council does not attempt to claim the Iraqi seat in the General Assembly. Even if credentials issued by the Governing Council were deemed receivable, such an attempt would probably be subject to challenge necessitating the convening of the Credentials Committee which, as a technical body governed by rule 27, would in turn be compelled to reject any credentials which are not issued by a sovereign Iraqi government.

7. In order to avoid continuing the previously accredited representatives of the former Iraqi regime in the fifty-eighth session of the General Assembly, the General Assembly, on the recommendation of the Credentials Committee, could defer any decision on the credentials of Iraq, on the understanding that, pending the establishment of an internationally recognized government in Iraq, no one would occupy the seat of that country.

8. The rules of procedure of the General Assembly do not contain a rule similar to rule 39 of the provisional rules of procedure of the Security Council. It would be for the General Assembly, at an appropriate time if it so wishes, to adopt a formula to invite representatives of the Governing Council or the Iraqi Interim Administration to attend or participate in its work. Given the unique situation in Iraq, there are no precedents to be cited in this regard. The General Assembly would also have to determine whether such formula would include the right to make statements, the right to circulate documents and/or the right to receive documents. It would not be appropriate, however, for such formula to include the right to vote, sponsor or co-sponsor proposals or other attributes of sovereignty.

9. We understand that the Governing Council intends to designate a Chargé d'Affaires to the Permanent Mission of Iraq to the United Nations. The initial powers of the Governing Council are reported to include the right to 'name Iraqi nationals to serve as representatives to international organizations and conferences'. While the designation of a Permanent Representative would require a presentation to the Secretary General of credentials issued by a Head of State, Head of Government or Minister for Foreign Affairs of a sovereign Iraqi government, the designation of a Chargé d'Affaires does not. Accordingly, in the event, the Secretary-General would not be required to receive or accept any documents purporting to be credentials.

Document 528

Non-Paper on the Implementation of Paragraph 23 of Resolution 1483 (2003)

UN Doc. SC/7831 IK/372, 29 July 2003

The Chairman of the Security Council Committee established by resolution 661 (1990) concerning the situation between Iraq and Kuwait wishes to share the following non-paper with Member States to provide information concerning the obligations of Member States with respect to paragraph 23 of resolution 1483 (2003). The non-paper has been discussed among Committee members and it reflects their common understanding. The definitions set forth below are indicative, not exclusive, and not legally binding. They are designed for reference by Member States and the Committee when implementing resolution 1483 (2003).

The list of individuals identified pursuant to paragraphs 19 and 23 of resolution 1483 (2003) is available at the following website: *http://www.un.org/Docs/sc/committees/IraqKuwait/1483_lst.htm*.[28] A list of entities to be identified pursuant to paragraphs 19 and 23 of Security Council resolution 1483 (2003) will be issued at a later stage, and will be included together with the list of individuals in a consolidated list of the Committee.[29]

- **Freezing of funds or other financial assets or economic resources:**
  - Funds or other financial assets: Financial assets and economic benefits of every kind, including but not limited to cash, cheques, claims on money, drafts, money orders and other payment instruments; deposits with financial institutions or other entities, balances on accounts, debts and debt obligations; publicly and privately traded securities and debt instruments, including stocks and shares, certificates presenting securities, bonds, notes, warrants, debentures, derivatives contracts; interest, dividends or other income on or value accruing from or generated by assets; credit, rights of set-off, guarantees, performance bonds or other financial commitments; letters of credit, bills of lading, bills of sale; documents evidencing an interest in funds or financial resources, and any other instrument of export-financing; and bullion.
  - Economic resources: Assets of every kind, whether tangible or intangible, movable or immovable, which are not funds.
  - Freezing of funds: Preventing any move, transfer, alteration, use of or dealing with funds in any way that would result in any change in their volume, amount, location, ownership, possession, character, destination or other change that would enable the use of the funds, including portfolio management but not including the accrual of commercially reasonable rates of interest.
  - Freezing of economic resources: Preventing their use, including their use to obtain funds, goods or services in any way, including, but not limited to, by selling, hiring or mortgaging them.

[28] On 27 June 2003, the Security Council Committee established pursuant to resolution 661 (1990) concerning the situation between Iraq and Kuwait adopted its first list of individuals which comprised 55 names. When the list was last updated on 2 June 2004, it contained 79 individuals, including Saddam Hussein and his two sons. See http://www.un.org/Docs/sc/committees/1518/1483_lst.htm.

[29] On 21 November 2003, the Committee adopted its first list of entities which comprised the Central Bank of Iraq, Iraq Reinsurance Company, Rafidain Bank, Rasheed Bank, and Iraqi Airways Company (SC/7933 IK/406, 21 November 2003). On 26 April 2004, the Committee approved the addition of another 199 names to the list of entities and on 2 June 2004, a further 2 names were added to the list. In an explanatory memorandum the Committee stated: 'The Committee further emphasizes its common understanding that the obligation to freeze and immediately to cause the transfer to the Development Fund for Iraq assets of those Iraqi public entities covered by paragraph 23(a) applies only to those funds or financial assets or economic resources that were located outside of Iraq on 22 May 2003. The Committee shares the view that paragraph 23(a) can be implemented in a manner that does not impair the renewed operations of these Iraqi public entities outside of Iraq, which may assist in the reconstruction of Iraq.

In furtherance of this objective, the Committee notes that paragraph 23(a) does not require (1) the freezing of the funds, financial assets or other economic resources of these entities that are deposited with or by, or have otherwise accrued to, them after 22 May 2003, or (2) the prohibition of post-22 May transactions by these entities, provided that such assets are not otherwise covered by paragraph 23 of resolution 1483. The Committee, however, notes that the obligation to freeze and transfer the assets of the individuals or entities covered by paragraph 23(b) does apply to their assets held on or after 22 May 2003 (http://www.un.org/Docs/sc/committees/1518/1483_lst_2.pdf).

- **State bodies, corporations or agencies (of the previous GoI):**
  - Includes the State of Iraq, the former government of Iraq, and any political subdivision, agency or instrumentality, partnership, association, corporations or other organization owned or controlled by the State of Iraq or the former government of Iraq.
  - It is understood that paragraph 23 of resolution 1483 (2003) does not apply to the funds or other financial assets or economic resources of diplomatic and consular missions of Iraq, and that resolution 1483 does not affect the application of the Vienna Conventions on Diplomatic and Consular Relations of 1961 and 1963 to such funds, other financial assets or economic resources.
- **Other senior officials of the former Iraqi regime:**
  - Cabinet officials including Deputy ministers
  - Members of Parliament
  - The heads and senior members of the military and security forces, intelligence services, military police and paramilitary police
  - The heads and senior members of state-owned/state controlled enterprises (banks, transport services, industries, utilities, media, insurance agencies etc.)
  - Senior members of the Baath Party
  - Officials of a lower rank but performing crucial functions such as certain accountants, buyers, technical experts etc.
- **Their immediate family members:**
  - includes parents, spouses, children, and siblings of the senior official
  - adoptions to be treated equivalently
  - other relatives as appropriate
- **Entities owned or controlled, directly or indirectly, by them:**
  - Entities owned includes, but is not necessarily limited to, being in possession of 50% or more of the proprietary rights of a company, undertaking, institution or other entity or having a majority interest therein
  - Entities controlled include, but is not necessarily limited to, any of the following:
    - Having the right to appoint or remove a majority of the members of the administrative, management or supervisory body of a company, undertaking, institution or other entity;
    - Having appointed solely as a result of the exercise of one's voting rights a majority of the members of the administrative, management or supervisory body of a company, undertaking, institution or other entity who have held office during the present and previous financial year;
    - Controlling alone, pursuant to an agreement with other shareholders in or members of a company, undertaking, institution or other entity, a majority of shareholders' or members' voting rights in that company, undertaking, institution or other entity;
    - Having the right to exercise a dominant influence over a company, undertaking, institution or other entity pursuant to an agreement entered into with that company, undertaking, institution or other entity, or to a provision in its Memorandum or Articles of Association, where the law governing that company, undertaking, institution or other entity permits its being subject to such agreement or provision;
    - Having the power to exercise the right to exercise a dominant influence referred to above, without being the holder of that right;

- Having the right to use all or part of the assets of a company, undertaking, institution or other entity;
- Managing a company, undertaking, institution or other entity on a unified basis, while publishing consolidated accounts;
- Sharing jointly and severally the financial liabilities of a company, undertaking, institution or other entity, or guaranteeing them.

Document 529

Resolution 1500 (2003), Adopted by the Security Council at its 4808th Meeting on 14 August 2003

UN Doc. S/RES/1500 (2003), 14 August 2003[30]

The Security Council,

Recalling all its previous relevant resolutions, in particular resolution 1483 (2003) of 22 May 2003,

Reaffirming the sovereignty and territorial integrity of Iraq,

Reaffirming also the vital role for the United Nations in Iraq which was set out in relevant paragraphs of resolution 1483 (2003),

Having considered the report of the Secretary-General of 15 July 2003 (S/2003/715),

1. *Welcomes* the establishment of the broadly representative Governing Council of Iraq on 13 July 2003, as an important step towards the formation by the people of Iraq of an internationally recognized, representative government that will exercise the sovereignty of Iraq;
2. *Decides* to establish the United Nations Assistance Mission for Iraq to support the Secretary-General in the fulfilment of his mandate under resolution 1483 in accordance with the structure and responsibilities set out in his report of 15 July 2003, for an initial period of twelve months;
3. *Decides* to remain seized of this matter.

Document 530

Statement by the President of the Security Council, Made at the 4811th Meeting of the Security Council on 20 August 2003

UN Doc. S/PRST/2003/13, 20 August 2003

The Security Council unequivocally condemns the terrorist attack that took place on 19 August 2003 against the United Nations Headquarters in Baghdad and thereby against the international community as a whole, causing numerous deaths and injuries among international personnel and Iraqi people.

[30] The resolution was adopted by a vote of 14 to 0 with Syria abstaining. The resolution was co-sponsored by Angola, Bulgaria, Cameroon, Chile, Guinea, Spain, United Kingdom and United States of America (UN Doc. S/2003/812, 14 August 2003).

The Security Council condemns also in the strongest terms the perpetrators of such attack and underlines the need to bring them to justice.

The Security Council pays tribute and expresses its deepest admiration to all those among the United Nations personnel who have lost their lives or have been injured in the service of the United Nations and of the Iraqi people, including the Special Representative of the Secretary-General, Sergio Vieira de Mello.

The Security Council expresses its deepest sympathy and condolences to the victims and their families.

The Security Council reaffirms the imperative to respect, in all circumstances, the safety and security of United Nations personnel and the need for adequate security measures to be taken in this regard.

The Security Council reaffirms its determination to assist the Iraqi people to build peace and justice in their country and to determine their own political future by themselves. It welcomes in this regard the determination of the United Nations to continue its operation in Iraq to fulfil its mandate in the service of the Iraqi people, and will not be intimidated by such attacks.[31]

Document 531

Resolution 1511 (2003), Adopted by the Security Council at its 4844th Meeting on 16 October 2003

UN Doc. S/RES/1511 (2003), 16 October 2003[32]

The Security Council,

Reaffirming its previous resolutions on Iraq, including resolution 1483 (2003) of 22 May 2003 and 1500 (2003) of 14 August 2003, and on threats to peace and security caused by

[31] On 19 August 2003, the President of the Security Council, Fayssal Mekdad (Syria), issued the following press statement: 'Members of the Council were shocked to hear of the terrorist criminal attack against the United Nations headquarters in Baghdad.

Members of the Security Council have heard a briefing by Assistant Secretary-General for Political Affairs on the bombing today of the United Nations compound in Baghdad, resulting in deaths and injuries. They condemned, in the strongest terms, this terrorist attack. Such terrorist incidents cannot break the will of the international community to further intensify its efforts to help the people of Iraq.

Members of the Council reaffirmed that this horrible attack that aimed at undermining the vital role of the United Nations in Iraq will not affect their determination and members of the Council will stay united against such attacks and to help the Iraqi people restore peace and stability to their country.

Members of the Council expressed their sincere condolences to the bereaved families, and wished all injured a quick recovery.

The United Nations mission in Iraq has been established by the Security Council to help the Iraqi people to achieve their objectives. The United Nations is in Iraq on a mission of peace, and for the reconstruction of the country and to support the Iraqi people. Therefore, it is all the more shocking that this attack occurred.' (SC/7847, 19 August 2003).

[32] The resolution was adopted unanimously. But see the 'Joint Statement of France, Germany and the Russian Federation on the Occasion of the Adoption of the Resolution 1511 of the Security Council' made on 16 October 2003: 'As a result of the proposals and amendments made by our three countries, the resolution has been improved throughout the negotiation process, thus allowing us, in a spirit of unity, to support it as a step in the right direction of the restoration of Iraq with the participation of the United Nations.

At the same time, we believe that the resolution should have gone further on two major issues: first, the role of the United Nations, in particular in the political process, and second, the pace of the transfer of responsibilities to the Iraqi people.

In that context, the conditions are not created for us to envisage any military commitment and further financial contributions beyond our present engagement.'

terrorist acts, including resolution 1373 (2001) of 28 September 2001, and other relevant resolutions,

Underscoring that the sovereignty of Iraq resides in the State of Iraq, *reaffirming* the right of the Iraqi people freely to determine their own political future and control their own natural resources, *reiterating* its resolve that the day when Iraqis govern themselves must come quickly, and *recognizing* the importance of international support, particularly that of countries in the region, Iraq's neighbours, and regional organizations, in taking forward this process expeditiously,

Recognizing that international support for restoration of conditions of stability and security is essential to the well-being of the people of Iraq as well as to the ability of all concerned to carry out their work on behalf of the people of Iraq, and *welcoming* Member State contributions in this regard under resolution 1483 (2003),

Welcoming the decision of the Governing Council of Iraq to form a preparatory constitutional committee to prepare for a constitutional conference that will draft a constitution to embody the aspirations of the Iraqi people, and *urging* it to complete this process quickly,

Affirming that the terrorist bombings of the Embassy of Jordan on 7 August 2003, of the United Nations headquarters in Baghdad on 19 August 2003, of the Imam Ali Mosque in Najaf on 29 August 2003, and of the Embassy of Turkey on 14 October 2003, and the murder of a Spanish diplomat on 9 October 2003 are attacks on the people of Iraq, the United Nations, and the international community, and *deploring* the assassination of Dr. Akila al-Hashimi, who died on 25 September 2003, as an attack directed against the future of Iraq, In that context, *recalling* and *reaffirming* the statement of its President of 20 August 2003 (S/PRST/2003/13) and resolution 1502 (2003) of 26 August 2003,

Determining that the situation in Iraq, although improved, continues to constitute a threat to international peace and security,

Acting under Chapter VII of the Charter of the United Nations,

1. *Reaffirms* the sovereignty and territorial integrity of Iraq, and *underscores*, in that context, the temporary nature of the exercise by the Coalition Provisional Authority (Authority) of the specific responsibilities, authorities, and obligations under applicable international law recognized and set forth in resolution 1483 (2003), which will cease when an internationally recognized, representative government established by the people of Iraq is sworn in and assumes the responsibilities of the Authority, inter alia through steps envisaged in paragraphs 4 through 7 and 10 below;

2. *Welcomes* the positive response of the international community, in fora such as the Arab League, the Organization of the Islamic Conference, the United Nations General Assembly, and the United Nations Educational, Scientific and Cultural Organization, to the establishment of the broadly representative Governing Council as an important step towards an internationally recognized, representative government;

3. *Supports* the Governing Council's efforts to mobilize the people of Iraq, including by the appointment of a cabinet of ministers and a preparatory constitutional committee to lead a process in which the Iraqi people will progressively take control of their own affairs;

4. *Determines* that the Governing Council and its ministers are the principal bodies of the Iraqi interim administration, which, without prejudice to its further evolution, embodies the sovereignty of the State of Iraq during the transitional period until an internationally recognized, representative government is established and assumes the responsibilities of the Authority;

5. *Affirms* that the administration of Iraq will be progressively undertaken by the evolving structures of the Iraqi interim administration;

6. *Calls upon* the Authority, in this context, to return governing responsibilities and authorities to the people of Iraq as soon as practicable and *requests* the Authority, in cooperation as appropriate with the Governing Council and the Secretary-General, to report to the Council on the progress being made;

7. *Invites* the Governing Council to provide to the Security Council, for its review, no later than 15 December 2003, in cooperation with the Authority and, as circumstances permit, the Special Representative of the Secretary-General, a timetable and a programme for the drafting of a new constitution for Iraq and for the holding of democratic elections under that constitution;

8. *Resolves* that the United Nations, acting through the Secretary-General, his Special Representative, and the United Nations Assistance Mission in Iraq, should strengthen its vital role in Iraq, including by providing humanitarian relief, promoting the economic reconstruction of and conditions for sustainable development in Iraq, and advancing efforts to restore and establish national and local institutions for representative government;

9. *Requests* that, as circumstances permit, the Secretary-General pursue the course of action outlined in paragraphs 98 and 99 of the report of the Secretary-General of 17 July 2003 (S/2003/715);

10. *Takes note* of the intention of the Governing Council to hold a constitutional conference and, recognizing that the convening of the conference will be a milestone in the movement to the full exercise of sovereignty, *calls for* its preparation through national dialogue and consensus-building as soon as practicable and *requests* the Special Representative of the Secretary-General, at the time of the convening of the conference or, as circumstances permit, to lend the unique expertise of the United Nations to the Iraqi people in this process of political transition, including the establishment of electoral processes;

11. *Requests* the Secretary-General to ensure that the resources of the United Nations and associated organizations are available, if requested by the Iraqi Governing Council and, as circumstances permit, to assist in furtherance of the programme provided by the Governing Council in paragraph 7 above, and encourages other organizations with expertise in this area to support the Iraqi Governing Council, if requested;

12. *Requests* the Secretary-General to report to the Security Council on his responsibilities under this resolution and the development and implementation of a timetable and programme under paragraph 7 above;

13. *Determines* that the provision of security and stability is essential to the successful completion of the political process as outlined in paragraph 7 above and to the ability of the United Nations to contribute effectively to that process and the implementation of resolution 1483 (2003), and *authorizes* a multinational force under unified command to take all necessary measures to contribute to the maintenance of security and stability in Iraq, including for the purpose of ensuring necessary conditions for the implementation of the timetable and programme as well as to contribute to the security of the United Nations Assistance Mission for Iraq, the Governing Council of Iraq and other institutions of the Iraqi interim administration, and key humanitarian and economic infrastructure;

14. *Urges* Member States to contribute assistance under this United Nations mandate, including military forces, to the multinational force referred to in paragraph 13 above;

15. *Decides* that the Council shall review the requirements and mission of the multinational force referred to in paragraph 13 above not later than one year from the

date of this resolution, and that in any case the mandate of the force shall expire upon the completion of the political process as described in paragraphs 4 through 7 and 10 above, and *expresses* readiness to consider on that occasion any future need for the continuation of the multinational force, taking into account the views of an internationally recognized, representative government of Iraq;

16. *Emphasizes* the importance of establishing effective Iraqi police and security forces in maintaining law, order, and security and combating terrorism consistent with paragraph 4 of resolution 1483 (2003), and *calls upon* Member States and international and regional organizations to contribute to the training and equipping of Iraqi police and security forces;

17. *Expresses* deep sympathy and condolences for the personal losses suffered by the Iraqi people and by the United Nations and the families of those United Nations personnel and other innocent victims who were killed or injured in these tragic attacks;

18. *Unequivocally condemns* the terrorist bombings of the Embassy of Jordan on 7 August 2003, of the United Nations headquarters in Baghdad on 19 August 2003, and of the Imam Ali Mosque in Najaf on 29 August 2003, and of the Embassy of Turkey on 14 October 2003, the murder of a Spanish diplomat on 9 October 2003, and the assassination of Dr. Akila al-Hashimi, who died on 25 September 2003, and *emphasizes* that those responsible must be brought to justice;

19. *Calls upon* Member States to prevent the transit of terrorists to Iraq, arms for terrorists, and financing that would support terrorists, and *emphasizes* the importance of strengthening the cooperation of the countries of the region, particularly neighbours of Iraq, in this regard;

20. *Appeals* to Member States and the international financial institutions to strengthen their efforts to assist the people of Iraq in the reconstruction and development of their economy, and *urges* those institutions to take immediate steps to provide their full range of loans and other financial assistance to Iraq, working with the Governing Council and appropriate Iraqi ministries;

21. *Urges* Member States and international and regional organizations to support the Iraq reconstruction effort initiated at the 24 June 2003 United Nations Technical Consultations, including through substantial pledges at the 23-24 October 2003 International Donors Conference in Madrid;

22. *Calls upon* Member States and concerned organizations to help meet the needs of the Iraqi people by providing resources necessary for the rehabilitation and reconstruction of Iraq's economic infrastructure;

23. *Emphasizes* that the International Advisory and Monitoring Board (IAMB) referred to in paragraph 12 of resolution 1483 (2003) should be established as a priority, and *reiterates* that the Development Fund for Iraq shall be used in a transparent manner as set out in paragraph 14 of resolution 1483 (2003);

24. *Reminds* all Member States of their obligations under paragraphs 19 and 23 of resolution 1483 (2003) in particular the obligation to immediately cause the transfer of funds, other financial assets and economic resources to the Development Fund for Iraq for the benefit of the Iraqi people;

25. *Requests* that the United States, on behalf of the multinational force as outlined in paragraph 13 above, report to the Security Council on the efforts and progress of this force as appropriate and not less than every six months;

26. *Decides* to remain seized of the matter.

Document 532
Report of the Independent Panel on the Safety and Security of UN Personnel in Iraq

20 October 2003

Executive Summary

On 19 August 2003, the United Nations headquarters in the Canal Hotel in Baghdad suffered a devastating bomb attack. The detonation resulted in the death of 22 United Nations staff and visitors, and over 150 persons were injured. The United Nations carried out an internal investigation in the field. On 22 September 2003, Secretary-General Kofi A. Annan appointed an Independent Panel on the Safety and Security of UN Personnel in Iraq.[33] The Panel was asked to examine all relevant facts about the situation before the 19 August attack, the circumstances of the attack itself and the actions taken by different parties in the immediate aftermath. The Panel was also asked to identify key lessons on security arrangements and to make recommendations on measures that would assist in preventing or mitigating future incidents in Iraq or other high-risk missions. [...]

1 Background of the work of the Independent Panel

[...] The current UN presence in Iraq is based on the mandate granted to the United Nations by Security Council resolution (SCR) 1483 adopted on 22 May 2003 and on SCR 986 of 14 April 1995 establishing the 'oil-for-food' Programme. These resolutions have been complemented by SCR 1500 of 14 August 2003 establishing the United Nations Assistance Mission for Iraq (UNAMI) and SCR 1511 of 16 October 2003, which authorizes the deployment of a multinational force to contribute to the security of UN personnel in Iraq, among other duties.

SCR 1483 confirms that the United States and the United Kingdom are occupying Powers in Iraq. It specifically calls upon them to comply fully with the obligations imposed by the Geneva Conventions of 1949 and the Hague regulations of 1907 on occupying forces and calls on them to work towards the restoration of conditions of security and stability in Iraq. It further calls for the creation of conditions in which the Iraqi people can freely determine their own political future. [...]

2 Mechanisms within the United Nations on the safety and security of staff

The primary responsibility for the security and protection of UN national and international staff members rests with the host Government. This responsibility flows from the inherent function of government of maintaining law and order, as well as from the special responsibility enshrined in the Charter of the United Nations. Under occupation, occupying forces carry definite responsibilities for the security of UN staff and premises located in the territories under their control, as derived from article 43 of the Hague Convention (IV) of 1907 and SCR 1483, 1502 and 1511. [...]

[33] UN Secretary-General Annan appointed Mr. Martti Ahtisaari, former President of Finland, to chair the Panel on the Safety and Security of UN Personnel in Iraq. Mr. Ahtisaari selected Mr. Peter Fitzgerald, Deputy Commissioner of the Irish National Police, Brigadier-General Jaakko Oksanen of the Finnish Army, and Mr. Claude Bruderlein, Director of the Program on Humanitarian Policy and Conflict Research at Harvard University, to join him on the Panel. They were assisted by Mr. Kevin Carty, Assistant Commissioner of the Irish National Police, Lieutenant-Colonel Raimo Koskela of the Finnish Army and Ms. Kristiina Rinkineva, Director of Crisis Management Capabilities Programme at the Crisis Management Initiative.

3 Relationship between the United Nations and the Coalition in the field

In each country, the primary responsibility for the security and protection of staff members of the United Nations and their spouses and dependants rests with the host Government. In the case of Iraq, the Coalition Provisional Authority, as the occupying power, bears this responsibility until the restoration of an internationally recognized Iraqi Government.

It is a custom that a Memorandum of Understanding is signed between the host country and the United Nations further describing the obligations and privileges of each party in terms of presence and security of UN staff.

In Iraq, there was no formal agreement on the security arrangements between the UN and CPA or Coalition Forces, but a number of exchanges on this issue took place between the United Nations and both the United States and United Kingdom missions in New York, and representatives of the occupying forces in Iraq.

A central element of the relationship between the United Nations and the host Government is the sharing of information about the security conditions in the operating environment of the United Nations, in particular about potential threats towards the UN staff and premises. In the case of Iraq, these exchanges took place at the field level and consisted mostly of open source information. The SRSG had on his staff a Military Adviser who ensured the liaison with the Coalition Forces. Although he was not allowed to participate in the Coalition Forces security briefings, the Military Adviser received in an ad hoc manner security-related information, which he passed on to UN security officers. After the attack on 19 August, the Coalition Forces revised his security clearance and he was allowed to participate in Coalition Forces security briefings on a daily basis. The advisory function of the Military Adviser focuses on the general operating and policy environment of the United Nations. It does not include responsibilities regarding the security of staff. The UN Field Security Coordination Officer (FSCO) in charge of advising the Designated Official on the security of UN staff and premises did not have formal liaison arrangements with the Coalition Forces.

In this context, the relationship between the United Nations and the Coalition Forces regarding the security of UN staff and premises remained ambiguous. Although there were clear needs for security arrangements and Coalition Forces/CPA was formally responsible for the security UN staff in Iraq, members of UN senior management in Baghdad felt uncomfortable because of the visible presence of Coalition Forces elements in and around the UN Canal Hotel compound. On several occasions, they asked the Coalition Forces to remove protective positions and equipment around the perimeter of the Canal Hotel without requesting alternative security arrangements. [...]

In the case of Iraq, options for obtaining adequate security support were (and remain) rather limited. Following the United States-led invasion of Iraq, an occupation regime was established calling for the application of the rules of international law in occupied Iraq. SCR 1483 recognized the applicability of these rules and called for the full compliance of all concerned. The resolution further requested that the UN system, through its SRSG, 'work intensively' with the occupying forces to restore local and national institutions for representative governance and encourage international efforts for legal and judicial reform. Apart from a lack of clear and achievable goals, the duties imposed on the United Nations also raised a number of ambiguities regarding the legality and legitimacy of such efforts in occupied territories.

These difficulties were acknowledged in the report of the Secretary General introduced to the Security Council on 17 July 2003[34] and by the late SRSG Sergio Vieira de Mello himself in his presentation to the Council on 22 July.[35] The pressing demands for the restoration of Iraq's sovereignty, the opposition to foreign-led democratization, the process of de-Ba'athification and the dissolution of the Iraqi army were all identified as major issues of concern warranting attention from both the political and security sectors of the UN. Unfortunately, UN management failed to recognize the security risks involved for the UN system in these circumstances. [...]

Currently, the only potential source of adequate security arrangements is the Coalition Forces. The fact is that the UN senior management in Baghdad asked on several occasions for the removal of positions and equipment of the Coalition Forces from the vicinity of the Canal Hotel. This created a critical security vacuum that armed elements could easily take advantage of. The argument of distancing the United Nations from the occupying forces in order to enhance its neutral image is relevant only to the extent that the UN benefits from such an image in the first place and also has a security alternative. In the midst of a conflict where armed groups openly declare their intent of targeting the UN system and in view of the predominantly political character of the UN presence and history in Iraq, security threats should have been expected from the outset and proper security arrangements, in this case from the Coalition Forces, should have been requested and implemented.[...].[36]

Document 533
Statement by the President of the Security Council, Made at the 4868th Meeting of the Security Council on 20 November 2003

UN Doc. S/PRST/2003/24, 20 November 2003

At the 4868th meeting of the Security Council, held on 20 November 2003, in connection with the Council's consideration of the item entitled 'The situation between Iraq and Kuwait', the President of the Security Council made the following statement on behalf of the Council:

'The Security Council has heard the Secretary-General's statement and has considered the briefing by the Executive Director of the Iraq Programme on the termination on 21 November 2003 of the United Nations humanitarian programme for Iraq (the Programme) and the transfer of the responsibility for the administration of any remaining activity under the Programme to the Coalition Provisional Authority in Iraq in accordance with Security Council resolution 1483 (2003).

The Security Council underlines the exceptionally important role of the Programme in providing humanitarian assistance to the people of Iraq under the regime of sanctions imposed by the Security Council on the previous Government of Iraq. Under this unique programme the value of humanitarian goods delivered to Iraq during the period from

[34] See UN Doc S/2003/715, 17 July 2003.
[35] See UN Doc S/PV.4791, 22 July 2003, 3-9.
[36] Footnotes in the Report omitted.

December 1996 through March 2003 amounted to about 30 billion United States dollars. Those deliveries made it possible to provide to the Iraqi people essential foods and medicines, as well as to supply various equipment and materials for the key sectors of the Iraqi economy. Purchases under the Programme will in the next few months play a key role in the economic reconstruction of Iraq by providing vital goods in the amount of more than 6 billion United States dollars.

The Security Council expresses its deep gratitude to the Secretary-General, the Office of the Iraq Programme, to United Nations personnel who worked on the ground in Iraq, and to all other United Nations agencies and structures involved, and applauds their commitment and professionalism. It also thanks the Chairmen and Members of the 661 Committee, for their dedicated efforts to implement the Programme since its inception, and in implementing resolution 1483 (2003).

The Security Council emphasizes the need for continued international efforts aimed at the reconstruction of Iraq and, in this context, takes note with satisfaction of the statements made by the representatives of the United States and the United Kingdom on the measures which the Coalition Provisional Authority intends to take in order to continue the payment mechanisms and the deliveries under the Programme.

The Security Council recognizes the important role of the United Nations in coordinating the termination of the Programme, including the transfer at the earliest possible time of all surplus funds in the escrow accounts to the Development Fund for Iraq.

The Security Council recalls the vital role foreseen for the United Nations in resolutions 1483 (2003), 1500 (2003) and 1511 (2003), as circumstances permit, inter alia, in the areas of humanitarian assistance, facilitation of economic rehabilitation and reconstruction.'

Document 534

Resolution 1518 (2003), Adopted by the Security Council at its 4872nd Meeting on 24 November 2003

UN Doc. S/RES/1518 (2003), 24 November 2003

The Security Council,

Recalling all of its previous relevant resolutions,

Recalling further its earlier decision in resolution 1483 (2003) of 22 May 2003 to terminate the Security Council Committee established pursuant to resolution 661 (1990),

Stressing the importance of all Member States fulfilling their obligations under paragraph 10 of resolution 1483 (2003),

Determining that the situation in Iraq, although improved, continues to constitute a threat to international peace and security,

Acting under Chapter VII of the Charter of the United Nations,

1. *Decides* to establish, with immediate effect, in accordance with rule 28 of its provisional rules of procedure, a Committee of the Security Council, consisting of all the members of the Council, to continue to identify pursuant to paragraph 19 of resolution 1483 (2003) individuals and entities referred to in paragraph 19 of that resolution, including by updating the list of individuals and entities that have already been identified by the Committee established pursuant to paragraph 6 of resolution 661 (1990), and to report on its work to the Council;

2. *Decides* to adopt the guidelines (reference SC/7791 IK/365 of 12 June 2003)[37] and definitions (reference SC/7831 IK/372 of 29 July 2003)[38] previously agreed by the Committee established pursuant to paragraph 6 of resolution 661 (1990), to implement the provisions of paragraphs 19 and 23 of resolution 1483 (2003), and *further decides* that the guidelines and definitions can be amended by the Committee in light of further considerations;

3. *Decides* that the mandate of the Committee referred to in paragraph 1 above will be kept under review and to consider the possible authorization of the additional task of observing Member States' fulfilment of their obligations under paragraph 10 of resolution 1483 (2003);

4. *Decides* to remain seized of the matter.

Document 535
Statement by the President of the Security Council, Made at the 4887th Meeting of the Security Council on 18 December 2003

UN Doc. S/PRST/2003/28, 18 December 2003

At the 4887th meeting of the Security Council, held on 18 December 2003, in connection with the Council's consideration of the item entitled 'The situation between Iraq and Kuwait', the President of the Security Council made the following statement on behalf of the Council:

'The Security Council today heard a briefing from Ambassador Yuli Vorontsov, the Secretary-General's High-level Coordinator, on the fourteenth report of the Secretary-General in accordance with paragraph 14 of Security Council resolution 1284 (1999).

The Security Council expressed its full support towards Ambassador Vorontsov and for his tireless efforts on the issues of Kuwaiti and third country nationals and the return of all Kuwaiti property. The Security Council agreed that his mandate should continue in accordance with paragraph 14 of resolution 1284 (1999).

The Security Council shared the views expressed by the Secretary-General in his report. The Security Council has strongly condemned the killing of Kuwaiti and third country nationals by the previous Iraqi regime in violation of international law, especially the removal from Kuwait of civilian men and women, their execution in cold blood in remote sites in Iraq and a decade long cover-up of the truth. The Security Council expressed its strong hope that those responsible for these horrendous crimes should be brought to justice. The Security Council expressed its deep condolences to all of the families of the Kuwaiti and third country nationals. The Security Council expressed its continuing concern for the plight of the families of those persons whose whereabouts are still unknown.The Security Council stressed the importance of the work of the Coalition Provisional Authority, the International Committee of the Red Cross, the Tripartite Commission and its Technical Subcommittee and called on all parties concerned to continue to work towards a satisfactory solution to all of the outstanding humanitarian aspects covered by Ambassador Vorontsov's mandate.

[37] See *Doc 525*.
[38] See *Doc 528*.

The Security Council expressed its deep regret that Kuwaiti property, including its national archives, has not yet been returned to Kuwait and encouraged the Coalition Provisional Authority and other parties concerned to continue their commitment to the search for, and return of, all Kuwaiti properties and archives, in accordance with paragraph 6 of resolution 1483 (2003). The Security Council agreed to continue to keep Ambassador Vorontsov's mandate under review and looked forward to receiving his next report.'

Document 536
Press Conference by Secretary General Kofi Annan at UN Headquarters

19 January 2004[39]

Good afternoon, ladies and gentlemen.

As you know, I have just been meeting with senior representatives of the Iraqi Governing Council (IGC) and the Coalition Provisional Authority (CPA).

I wanted to hear the assessment of the Governing Council on how the process in Iraq was evolving and what Iraq expects of the United Nations by way of assistance. We covered a wide spectrum of issues, including the transitional political process, humanitarian relief, security and the recovery and reconstruction of Iraq.

In my view, this meeting has been an important opportunity for all of us to get a clearer understanding of each other's positions.

I believe we did that. We would all agree that it was a very frank and open exchange of views, which we will aim to continue and broaden in the near future.

For my part, I would want the United Nations to concentrate on areas where we have a clear comparative advantage, and which all Iraqis consider vital. Further details and discussion are needed to clarify exactly how the United Nations can best help in the various fields where we have been asked to assist.

Meanwhile, both the Governing Council and the CPA representatives have expressed a strong wish that the United Nations should quickly send a technical mission to Iraq to advise on the feasibility of elections within the next few months and, if not, what alternatives might be possible.

I think we all agree that elections are going to be necessary, indeed there is provision for two sets of elections in 2005. The issue now is whether the technical, political or security conditions exist for general direct elections to take place as early as May this year.

Other subjects discussed included the process of drafting and finalizing the fundamental law, future appointment of a Special Representative of the Secretary-General, and the question of security agreements to be concluded between the Governing Council and the CPA, as provided for in the 15 November agreement.[40]

Obviously, the scope for operational United Nations activities inside Iraq will continue to be constrained by the security situation for some time to come. The CPA and the Governing Council offered undertakings that the Coalition and the Governing Council would provide full security for United Nations international personnel in Iraq.

[39] UN News Centre, Secretary-General's remarks to the press after meeting with the Coalition Provisional Authority and the Iraqi Governing Council delegates, 19 January 2004, http://www.un.org/ and Press Release SG/SM/9121, 19 January 2004.

[40] See *Doc 232*.

Let me state once again that the United Nations' sole objective is to help the Iraqi people. We would like to see as broad a consensus as possible develop among Iraqis on what needs to be done to bring about an Iraq at peace with itself and with its neighbours – and on the role that the United Nations can play in this.

I believe that there is widespread agreement among us that the United Nations will have an important role to play in working with the Iraqi provisional Government from July onwards on key constitutional and electoral issues. We agreed that partnership would be necessary and we are also going to be active in recovery, reconstruction and in the humanitarian and human rights fields.

Meanwhile, as regards a possible role between now and the end of June for the United Nations, we have agreed that further discussions should take place at the technical level, which would be focused on the most immediate electoral and security issues. On the basis of those discussions, I would be in a better position to take decisions about what the United Nations can do to help, particularly regarding the possible dispatch of a mission to Iraq to advise on elections.

Document 537

Interoffice Memorandum to the Chief, Legal Affairs Section, Executive Office, Office of the United Nations High Commissioner for Refugees, Regarding the Voluntary Repatriation (Tripartite) Agreement

UN Juridical Yearbook 2004, 362-363

19 February 2004[41]

1. This is in reference to [name's] e-mail message of 6 February 2004, requesting our views on the draft Voluntary Repatriation Agreement between the Office of the United Nations High Commissioner for Refugees (UNHCR), the Government of [State A], and the so-called 'Authorities in [State B]' comprising the Council of Ministers of [State B] and/or the Coalition Provisional Authority (CPA).[42] The question put to us was 'under what conditions and with what restrictions the United Nations/UNHCR may sign agreements with the [State C] as occupying power'.

2. The draft Agreement raises, however, a number of other issues relating to the treaty-making power of the CPA and the Governing Council, and the applicability of the Agreement beyond the period of occupation.

3. The CPA as the Occupying Power in [State B] is the sole authority having legislative or treaty-making power, however limited, for the duration of the occupation. Agreements on the operational activities of the United Nations in [State B] during the period of occupation should, therefore, be concluded with the CPA. While [State C] is a leading

[41] Legal opinion of the Secretariat of the United Nations.

[42] The agreement in question was the Voluntary Repatriation Agreement (VRA) between 'the Government of Turkey, the Authorities in Iraq and the United Nations High Commissioner for Refugees (UNHCR)' which had been negotiated in Ankara on 20-22 January 2004. The text of the agreement as negotiated in Ankara (but later amended) is available at http://wikileaks.ch/cable/2004/01/04ANKARA 509.html. The agreement was never signed. State A refers to Turkey, State B to Iraq and State C to the United States of America.

member of the Coalition and it would probably be advisable to secure its political support, [State C] Government, as such, is not, nor should it be a party to this Agreement, not at least as representing the [State B] authorities or the CPA. The Governing Council, on the other hand, as an entity established by the Occupying Power to assist in the administration of [State B] lacks an international treaty-making power, a power which cannot be delegated to it by the CPA.[43]

4. The question of who represents [State B] for the purpose of this Agreement relates also to the question of the duration of the Agreement, and its applicability beyond the period of occupation. It is a well-established principle of the law of occupation that legislative acts enacted by an Occupant, and international agreements concluded by it on behalf of the occupied territory do not automatically survive the occupation, and may continue to apply only with the consent of the newly independent Government.

5. In the circumstances, UNHCR may either await the 'transfer of powers' and sign the Agreement with the newly independent Government of [State B] (as was done for example in the case of East Timor when the agreement on the Timor Gap negotiated during the period of the United Nations administration was signed eventually between Australia and independent East Timor). If, however, the conclusion of the Agreement is at this point a matter of urgency, it should be signed between the UNHCR, [State A] and the CPA (with or without the Governing Council). On the understanding that the operation of voluntary repatriation would survive the occupation, a provision should be inserted in the Agreement conditioning its continued applicability on the consent of the newly independent Government of [State B].

Document 538

Statement by the President of the Security Council, Made at the 4930th Meeting of the Security Council on 24 March 2004

UN Doc. S/PRST/2004/6, 24 March 2004
UN Doc. S/PV.4930, 24 March 2004

At the 4930th meeting of the Security Council, held on 24 March 2004, in connection with the Council's consideration of the item entitled 'The situation between Iraq and Kuwait', the President of the Security Council made the following statement on behalf of the Council:

'The Security Council welcomes the Secretary-General's letter dated 18 March and the exchange of letters with Dr. Bahr Al-Uloom, Interim President of the Iraqi Governing Council for the month of March 2004 and Ambassador L. Paul Bremer III, Administrator, Coalition Provisional Authority (S/2004/225).[44]

The Security Council also welcomes and strongly supports the Secretary-General's decision to dispatch to Iraq his Special Adviser, Mr. Lakhdar Brahimi and his team, as well as an electoral assistance team, as soon as possible, in order to lend assistance and advice to the Iraqi people in the formation of an interim Iraqi government to which sovereignty

[43] For the Letter by Ambassador Bremer delegating to the Iraqi Minister of Displacement and Migration the authority to sign the Voluntary Repatriation Agreement, see *Doc 245*.

[44] See *Docs 512, 251*.

will be transferred on 30 June 2004, as well as in the preparations for direct elections to be held before the end of January 2005.

The Security Council calls on all parties in Iraq to cooperate fully with these United Nations teams, and welcomes the security and other support provided to them by the Iraqi Governing Council and the CPA.'

Document 539
Resolution 1538 (2004), Adopted by the Security Council at its 4946th Meeting on 21 April 2004

UN Doc. S/RES/1538 (2003), 21 April 2004[45]

The Security Council,

Expressing the desire to see a full and fair investigation of efforts by the former Government of Iraq, including through bribery, kickbacks, surcharges on oil sales, and illicit payments in regard to purchases of humanitarian goods, to evade the provisions of resolution 661 (1990) of 6 August 1990 and subsequent relevant resolutions,

Concerned by public news reports and commentaries that have called into question the administration and management of the Oil-for-food Programme (hereinafter the Programme) established pursuant to resolution 986 (1995) of 14 April 1995 and subsequent relevant resolutions, including allegations of fraud and corruption,

Affirming that any illicit activity by United Nations officials, personnel and agents, as well as contractors, including entities that have entered into contracts under the Programme, is unacceptable,

Emphasizing the importance of full cooperation with the independent high-level inquiry by all United Nations officials and personnel, the Coalition Provisional Authority, Iraq, and all other Member States,

Affirming the letter of its President of 31 March 2004 welcoming the Secretary-General's decision to create an independent high-level inquiry to investigate the administration and management of the Programme and taking note of the details relating to its organization and terms of reference,

1. *Welcomes* the appointment of the independent high-level inquiry;
2. *Calls upon* the Coalition Provisional Authority, Iraq, and all other Member States, including their national regulatory authorities, to cooperate fully by all appropriate means with the inquiry;
3. *Looks forward* to receiving the inquiry's final report;
4. *Decides* to remain actively seized of the matter.

[45] The resolution which was based on a draft resolution submitted by France, Germany, Spain, the United Kingdom and the United States (UN Doc. S/2004/311, 20 April 2004) was adopted unanimously.

Document 540

Statement by the President of the Security Council, Made at the 4953rd Meeting of the Security Council on 27 April 2004

UN Doc. S/PRST/2004/11, 27 April 2004

At the 4953rd meeting of the Security Council, held on 27 April 2004, in connection with the Council's consideration of the item entitled 'The situation between Iraq and Kuwait', the President of the Security Council made the following statement on behalf of the Council:

'The Security Council welcomes with appreciation the comprehensive briefing provided by the Secretary-General's Special Adviser Mr. Lakhdar Brahimi.

Recalling its Presidential Statement of 24 March 2004 (S/PRST/2004/6)[46] the Security Council considers the efforts of the Special Adviser and his team as well as those of the United Nations electoral assistance team to be of particular importance and urgency.

The Security Council strongly supports the efforts and dedication of the Special Adviser and welcomes the provisional ideas he has submitted as a basis for the formation of an interim Iraqi government to which sovereignty will be transferred on 30 June 2004.

The Security Council encourages the Secretary-General and his Special Adviser to continue diligently with the efforts that they are employing, and welcomes the Special Adviser's intention to return to Iraq shortly, and looks forward to a further briefing upon his return.

The Security Council calls on all Iraqi parties to cooperate fully with the Special Adviser, and also calls on Iraq's neighbours and the international community at large to lend all support possible to these efforts.'

Document 541

Resolution 1546 (2004), Adopted by the Security Council at its 4987th Meeting on 8 June 2004

UN Doc. S/RES/1546 (2004), 8 June 2004[47]

The Security Council,

Welcoming the beginning of a new phase in Iraq's transition to a democratically elected government, and *looking forward* to the end of the occupation and the assumption of full responsibility and authority by a fully sovereign and independent Interim Government of Iraq by 30 June 2004,

Recalling all of its previous relevant resolutions on Iraq,

Reaffirming the independence, sovereignty, unity, and territorial integrity of Iraq,

Reaffirming also the right of the Iraqi people freely to determine their own political future and control their own natural resources,

Recognizing the importance of international support, particularly that of countries in the

[46] See *Doc 538*.

[47] The Resolution which was based on a draft resolution submitted on 8 June 2004 by Romania, the United Kingdom and the United States (UN Doc. S/2004/460, 8 June 2004) was adopted unanimously.

region, Iraq's neighbours, and regional organizations, for the people of Iraq in their efforts to achieve security and prosperity, and *noting* that the successful implementation of this resolution will contribute to regional stability,

Welcoming the efforts of the Special Adviser to the Secretary-General to assist the people of Iraq in achieving the formation of the Interim Government of Iraq, as set out in the letter of the Secretary-General of 7 June 2004 (S/2004/461),

Taking note of the dissolution of the Governing Council of Iraq, and *welcoming* the progress made in implementing the arrangements for Iraq's political transition referred to in resolution 1511 (2003) of 16 October 2003,

Welcoming the commitment of the Interim Government of Iraq to work towards a federal, democratic, pluralist, and unified Iraq, in which there is full respect for political and human rights,

Stressing the need for all parties to respect and protect Iraq's archaeological, historical, cultural, and religious heritage,

Affirming the importance of the rule of law, national reconciliation, respect for human rights including the rights of women, fundamental freedoms, and democracy including free and fair elections,

Recalling the establishment of the United Nations Assistance Mission for Iraq (UNAMI) on 14 August 2003, and *affirming* that the United Nations should play a leading role in assisting the Iraqi people and government in the formation of institutions for representative government,

Recognizing that international support for restoration of stability and security is essential to the well-being of the people of Iraq as well as to the ability of all concerned to carry out their work on behalf of the people of Iraq, and *welcoming* Member State contributions in this regard under resolution 1483 (2003) of 22 May 2003 and resolution 1511 (2003),

Recalling the report provided by the United States to the Security Council on 16 April 2004 on the efforts and progress made by the multinational force,

Recognizing the request conveyed in the letter of 5 June 2004 from the Prime Minister of the Interim Government of Iraq to the President of the Council, which is annexed to this resolution, to retain the presence of the multinational force,

Recognizing also the importance of the consent of the sovereign Government of Iraq for the presence of the multinational force and of close coordination between the multinational force and that government,

Welcoming the willingness of the multinational force to continue efforts to contribute to the maintenance of security and stability in Iraq in support of the political transition, especially for upcoming elections, and to provide security for the United Nations presence in Iraq, as described in the letter of 5 June 2004 from the United States Secretary of State to the President of the Council, which is annexed to this resolution,

Noting the commitment of all forces promoting the maintenance of security and stability in Iraq to act in accordance with international law, including obligations under international humanitarian law, and to cooperate with relevant international organizations,

Affirming the importance of international assistance in reconstruction and development of the Iraqi economy,

Recognizing the benefits to Iraq of the immunities and privileges enjoyed by Iraqi oil revenues and by the Development Fund for Iraq, and *noting* the importance of providing for continued disbursements of this fund by the Interim Government of Iraq and its successors upon dissolution of the Coalition Provisional Authority,

Determining that the situation in Iraq continues to constitute a threat to international peace and security,

Acting under Chapter VII of the Charter of the United Nations,

1. *Endorses* the formation of a sovereign Interim Government of Iraq, as presented on 1 June 2004, which will assume full responsibility and authority by 30 June 2004 for governing Iraq while refraining from taking any actions affecting Iraq's destiny beyond the limited interim period until an elected Transitional Government of Iraq assumes office as envisaged in paragraph four below;

2. *Welcomes* that, also by 30 June 2004, the occupation will end and the Coalition Provisional Authority will cease to exist, and that Iraq will reassert its full sovereignty;

3. *Reaffirms* the right of the Iraqi people freely to determine their own political future and to exercise full authority and control over their financial and natural resources;

4. *Endorses* the proposed timetable for Iraq's political transition to democratic government including:

   (a) formation of the sovereign Interim Government of Iraq that will assume governing responsibility and authority by 30 June 2004;

   (b) convening of a national conference reflecting the diversity of Iraqi society; and

   (c) holding of direct democratic elections by 31 December 2004 if possible, and in no case later than 31 January 2005, to a Transitional National Assembly, which will, inter alia, have responsibility for forming a Transitional Government of Iraq and drafting a permanent constitution for Iraq leading to a constitutionally elected government by 31 December 2005;

5. *Invites* the Government of Iraq to consider how the convening of an international meeting could support the above process, and *notes* that it would welcome such a meeting to support the Iraqi political transition and Iraqi recovery, to the benefit of the Iraqi people and in the interest of stability in the region;

6. *Calls on* all Iraqis to implement these arrangements peaceably and in full, and on all States and relevant organizations to support such implementation;

7. *Decides* that in implementing, as circumstances permit, their mandate to assist the Iraqi people and government, the Special Representative of the Secretary-General and the United Nations Assistance Mission for Iraq (UNAMI), as requested by the Government of Iraq, shall:

   (a) play a leading role to:

      (i) assist in the convening, during the month of July 2004, of a national conference to select a Consultative Council;

      (ii) advise and support the Independent Electoral Commission of Iraq, as well as the Interim Government of Iraq and the Transitional National Assembly, on the process for holding elections;

      (iii) promote national dialogue and consensus-building on the drafting of a national constitution by the people of Iraq;

   (b) and also:

      (i) advise the Government of Iraq in the development of effective civil and social services;

      (ii) contribute to the coordination and delivery of reconstruction, development, and humanitarian assistance;

      (iii) promote the protection of human rights, national reconciliation, and judicial and legal reform in order to strengthen the rule of law in Iraq; and

(iv) advise and assist the Government of Iraq on initial planning for the eventual conduct of a comprehensive census;

8. *Welcomes* ongoing efforts by the incoming Interim Government of Iraq to develop Iraqi security forces including the Iraqi armed forces (hereinafter referred to as 'Iraqi security forces'), operating under the authority of the Interim Government of Iraq and its successors, which will progressively play a greater role and ultimately assume full responsibility for the maintenance of security and stability in Iraq;

9. *Notes* that the presence of the multinational force in Iraq is at the request of the incoming Interim Government of Iraq and therefore *reaffirms* the authorization for the multinational force under unified command established under resolution 1511 (2003), having regard to the letters annexed to this resolution;

10. *Decides* that the multinational force shall have the authority to take all necessary measures to contribute to the maintenance of security and stability in Iraq in accordance with the letters annexed to this resolution expressing, inter alia, the Iraqi request for the continued presence of the multinational force and setting out its tasks, including by preventing and deterring terrorism, so that, inter alia, the United Nations can fulfil its role in assisting the Iraqi people as outlined in paragraph seven above and the Iraqi people can implement freely and without intimidation the timetable and programme for the political process and benefit from reconstruction and rehabilitation activities;

11. *Welcomes,* in this regard, the letters annexed to this resolution stating, inter alia, that arrangements are being put in place to establish a security partnership between the sovereign Government of Iraq and the multinational force and to ensure coordination between the two, and *notes also* in this regard that Iraqi security forces are responsible to appropriate Iraqi ministers, that the Government of Iraq has authority to commit Iraqi security forces to the multinational force to engage in operations with it, and that the security structures described in the letters will serve as the fora for the Government of Iraq and the multinational force to reach agreement on the full range of fundamental security and policy issues, including policy on sensitive offensive operations, and will ensure full partnership between Iraqi security forces and the multinational force, through close coordination and consultation;

12. *Decides further* that the mandate for the multinational force shall be reviewed at the request of the Government of Iraq or twelve months from the date of this resolution, and that this mandate shall expire upon the completion of the political process set out in paragraph four above, and *declares* that it will terminate this mandate earlier if requested by the Government of Iraq;

13. *Notes* the intention, set out in the annexed letter from the United States Secretary of State, to create a distinct entity under unified command of the multinational force with a dedicated mission to provide security for the United Nations presence in Iraq, *recognizes* that the implementation of measures to provide security for staff members of the United Nations system working in Iraq would require significant resources, and *calls upon* Member States and relevant organizations to provide such resources, including contributions to that entity;

14. *Recognizes* that the multinational force will also assist in building the capability of the Iraqi security forces and institutions, through a programme of recruitment, training, equipping, mentoring, and monitoring;

15. *Requests* Member States and international and regional organizations to contribute assistance to the multinational force, including military forces, as agreed with the Government of Iraq, to help meet the needs of the Iraqi people for security and stability, humanitarian and reconstruction assistance, and to support the efforts of UNAMI;

16. *Emphasizes* the importance of developing effective Iraqi police, border enforcement, and the Facilities Protection Service, under the control of the Interior Ministry of Iraq, and, in the case of the Facilities Protection Service, other Iraqi ministries, for the maintenance of law, order, and security, including combating terrorism, and *requests* Member States and international organizations to assist the Government of Iraq in building the capability of these Iraqi institutions;

17. *Condemns* all acts of terrorism in Iraq, *reaffirms* the obligations of Member States under resolutions 1373 (2001) of 28 September 2001, 1267 (1999) of 15 October 1999, 1333 (2000) of 19 December 2000, 1390 (2002) of 16 January 2002, 1455 (2003) of 17 January 2003, and 1526 (2004) of 30 January 2004, and other relevant international obligations with respect, inter alia, to terrorist activities in and from Iraq or against its citizens, and specifically *reiterates* its call upon Member States to prevent the transit of terrorists to and from Iraq, arms for terrorists, and financing that would support terrorists, and *re-emphasizes* the importance of strengthening the cooperation of the countries of the region, particularly neighbours of Iraq, in this regard;

18. *Recognizes* that the Interim Government of Iraq will assume the primary role in coordinating international assistance to Iraq;

19. *Welcomes* efforts by Member States and international organizations to respond in support of requests by the Interim Government of Iraq to provide technical and expert assistance while Iraq is rebuilding administrative capacity;

20. *Reiterates* its request that Member States, international financial institutions and other organizations strengthen their efforts to assist the people of Iraq in the reconstruction and development of the Iraqi economy, including by providing international experts and necessary resources through a coordinated programme of donor assistance;

21. *Decides* that the prohibitions related to the sale or supply to Iraq of arms and related materiel under previous resolutions shall not apply to arms or related materiel required by the Government of Iraq or the multinational force to serve the purposes of this resolution, *stresses* the importance for all States to abide strictly by them, and *notes* the significance of Iraq's neighbours in this regard, and *calls upon* the Government of Iraq and the multinational force each to ensure that appropriate implementation procedures are in place;

22. *Notes* that nothing in the preceding paragraph affects the prohibitions on or obligations of States related to items specified in paragraphs 8 and 12 of resolution 687 (1991) of 3 April 1991 or activities described in paragraph 3 (f) of resolution 707 (1991) Monitoring, Verification, and Inspection Commission and the International Atomic Energy Agency;

23. *Calls on* Member States and international organizations to respond to Iraqi requests to assist Iraqi efforts to integrate Iraqi veterans and former militia members into Iraqi society;

24. *Notes* that, upon dissolution of the Coalition Provisional Authority, the funds in the Development Fund for Iraq shall be disbursed solely at the direction of the Government of Iraq, and *decides* that the Development Fund for Iraq shall be utilized in a transparent and equitable manner and through the Iraqi budget including to satisfy outstanding obligations against the Development Fund for Iraq, that the arrangements for the depositing of proceeds from export sales of petroleum, petroleum products, and natural gas established in paragraph 20 of resolution 1483 (2003) shall continue to apply, that the International Advisory and Monitoring Board shall continue its activities in monitoring the Development Fund for Iraq and shall include as an additional full voting member a duly qualified individual designated by

the Government of Iraq and that appropriate arrangements shall be made for the continuation of deposits of the proceeds referred to in paragraph 21 of resolution 1483 (2003);

25. *Decides further* that the provisions in the above paragraph for the deposit of proceeds into the Development Fund for Iraq and for the role of the IAMB shall be reviewed at the request of the Transitional Government of Iraq or twelve months from the date of this resolution, and shall expire upon the completion of the political process set out in paragraph four above;

26. *Decides* that, in connection with the dissolution of the Coalition Provisional Authority, the Interim Government of Iraq and its successors shall assume the rights, responsibilities and obligations relating to the Oil-for-Food Programme that were transferred to the Authority, including all operational responsibility for the Programme and any obligations undertaken by the Authority in connection with such responsibility, and responsibility for ensuring independently authenticated confirmation that goods have been delivered, and *further decides* that, following a 120-day transition period from the date of adoption of this resolution, the Interim Government of Iraq and its successors shall assume responsibility for certifying delivery of goods under previously prioritized contracts, and that such certification shall be deemed to constitute the independent authentication required for the release of funds associated with such contracts, consulting as appropriate to ensure the smooth implementation of these arrangements;

27. *Further decides* that the provisions of paragraph 22 of resolution 1483 (2003) shall continue to apply, except that the privileges and immunities provided in that paragraph shall not apply with respect to any final judgement arising out of a contractual obligation entered into by Iraq after 30 June 2004;

28. *Welcomes* the commitments of many creditors, including those of the Paris Club, to identify ways to reduce substantially Iraq's sovereign debt, *calls on* Member States, as well as international and regional organizations, to support the Iraq reconstruction effort, *urges* the international financial institutions and bilateral donors to take the immediate steps necessary to provide their full range of loans and other financial assistance and arrangements to Iraq, *recognizes* that the Interim Government of Iraq will have the authority to conclude and implement such agreements and other arrangements as may be necessary in this regard, and *requests* creditors, institutions and donors to work as a priority on these matters with the Interim Government of Iraq and its successors;

29. *Recalls* the continuing obligations of Member States to freeze and transfer certain funds, assets, and economic resources to the Development Fund for Iraq in accordance with paragraphs 19 and 23 of resolution 1483 (2003) and with resolution 1518 (2003) of 24 November 2003;

30. *Requests* the Secretary-General to report to the Council within three months from the date of this resolution on UNAMI operations in Iraq, and on a quarterly basis thereafter on the progress made towards national elections and fulfilment of all UNAMI's responsibilities;

31. *Requests* that the United States, on behalf of the multinational force, report to the Council within three months from the date of this resolution on the efforts and progress of this force, and on a quarterly basis thereafter;

32. *Decides* to remain actively seized of the matter.

Annex

Text of letters from the Prime Minister of the Interim Government of Iraq Dr. Ayad Allawi and United States Secretary of State Colin L. Powell to the President of the Council

5 June 2004
Republic of Iraq
Prime Minister Office

Excellency:

On my appointment as Prime Minister of the Interim Government of Iraq, I am writing to express the commitment of the people of Iraq to complete the political transition process to establish a free, and democratic Iraq and to be a partner in preventing and combating terrorism. As we enter a critical new stage, regain full sovereignty and move towards elections, we will need the assistance of the international community.

The Interim Government of Iraq will make every effort to ensure that these elections are fully democratic, free and fair. Security and stability continue to be essential to our political transition. There continue, however, to be forces in Iraq, including foreign elements, that are opposed to our transition to peace, democracy, and security. The Government is determined to overcome these forces, and to develop security forces capable of providing adequate security for the Iraqi people. Until we are able to provide security for ourselves, including the defence of Iraq's land, sea and air space, we ask for the support of the Security Council and the international community in this endeavour. We seek a new resolution on the Multinational Force (MNF) mandate to contribute to maintaining security in Iraq, including through the tasks and arrangements set out in the letter from Secretary of State Colin Powell to the President of the United Nations Security Council. The Government requests that the Security Council review the mandate of the MNF at the request of the Transitional Government of Iraq, or twelve months from the date on which such a resolution is adopted.

In order to discharge the Iraqi Government's responsibility for security, I intend to establish appropriate security structures that will allow my Government and Iraqi security forces to progressively take on that responsibility. One such structure is the Ministerial Committee for National Security, consisting of myself as the Chair, the Deputy Prime Minister, and the Minister of Defense, Interior, Foreign Affairs, Justice, and Finance. The National Security Advisor, and Director of the Iraqi National Intelligence Service will serve as permanent advisory members of the committee. This forum will set the broad framework for Iraqi security policy. I intend to invite, as appropriate, the MNF commander, his Deputy, or the MNF Commander's designative representative, and other appropriate individuals, to attend and participate as well, and will stand ready to discuss mechanisms of coordination and cooperation with the MNF. Iraqi armed forces will be responsible to the Chief of Staff and Minister of Defense. Other security forces (the Iraqi police, border guards and Facilities Protection Service) will be responsible to the Minister of the Interior or other government ministers.

In addition, the relevant ministers and I will develop further mechanisms for coordination with the MNF. Intend [sic] to create with the MNF coordination bodies at national, regional, and local levels, that will include Iraqi security forces commanders and civilian leadership, to ensure that Iraqi security forces will coordinate with the MNF on all security policy and operations issues in order to achieve unity of command of military operations in which Iraqi forces are engaged with MNF. In addition, the MNF and Iraqi government leaders will keep each other informed of their activities, consult regularly to ensure effective allocation and use of personnel, resources and facilities, will share intelligence, and will refer issues up the respective chains of command where necessary, Iraqi security forces will take on progressively greater responsibility as Iraqi capabilities improve.

The structures I have described in this letter will serve as the fora for the MNF and the Iraqi government to reach agreement on the full range of fundamental security and policy issues, including policy on sensitive offensive operations, and will ensure full partnership between Iraqi forces and the MNF, through close coordination and consultation. Since these are sensitive issues for a number of sovereign governments, including Iraq and the United States, they need to be resolved in the framework of a mutual understanding on our strategic partnership. We will be working closely with the MNF leadership in the coming weeks to ensure that we have such an agreed strategic framework.

We are ready to take sovereign responsibility for governing Iraq by June 30. We are well aware of the difficulties facing us, and of our responsibilities to the Iraqi people. The stakes are great, and we need the support of the international community to succeed. We ask the Security Council to help us by acting now to adopt a Security Council resolution giving us necessary support.

I understand that the Co-sponsors intend to annex this letter to the resolution on Iraq under consideration. In the meantime, I request that you provide copies of this letter to members of the Council as quickly as possible.

[*Signed*] Dr. Ayad Allawi

The Secretary of State
Washington
5 June 2004

Excellency:

Recognizing the request of the government of Iraq for the continued presence of the Multi- National Force (MNF) in Iraq, and following consultations with Prime Minister Ayad Allawi of the Iraqi Interim Government, I am writing to confirm that the MNF under unified command is prepared to continue to contribute to the maintenance of security in Iraq, including by preventing and deterring terrorism and protecting the territory of Iraq. The goal of the MNF will be to help the Iraqi people to complete the political transition and will permit the United Nations and the international community to work to facilitate Iraq's reconstruction.

The ability of the Iraqi people to achieve their goals will be heavily influenced by the security situation in Iraq. As recent events have demonstrated, continuing attacks by insurgents, including former regime elements, foreign fighters, and illegal militias challenge all those who are working for a better Iraq.

Development of an effective and cooperative security partnership between the MNF and the sovereign Government of Iraq is critical to the stability of Iraq. The commander of the MNF will work in partnership with the sovereign Government of Iraq in helping to provide security while recognizing and respecting its sovereignty. To that end, the MNF stands ready to participate in discussions of the Ministerial Committee for National Security on the broad framework of security policy, as referred to in the letter from Prime Minister of the Interim Government of Iraq Allawi dated June 5, 2004. On the implementation of this policy, recognizing that Iraqi security forces are responsible to the appropriate Iraqi ministers, the MNF will coordinate with Iraqi security forces at all levels – national, regional, and local – in order to achieve unity of command of military operations in which Iraqi forces are engaged with the MNF. In addition, the MNF and the Iraqi government leaders will keep each other informed of their activities, consult regularly to ensure effective allocation and use of personnel, resources, and facilities, will share intelligence, and will refer issues up the respective chains of command where necessary. We will work in the fora described by Prime Minister Allawi in his June 5 letter to reach agreement on the full range of fundamental security and policy issues, including policy on sensitive offensive operations, and will ensure full partnership between MNF and Iraqi forces, through close coordination and consultation.

Under the agreed arrangement, the MNF stands ready to continue to undertake a broad range of tasks to contribute to the maintenance of security and to ensure force protection. These include activities necessary to counter ongoing security threats posed by forces seeking to influence Iraq's political future through violence. This will include combat operations against members of these groups, internment where this is necessary for imperative reasons of security, and the continued search for and securing of weapons that threaten Iraq's security. A further objective will be to train and equip Iraqi security forces that will increasingly take responsibility for maintaining Iraq's security. The MNF also stands ready as needed to participate in the provision of humanitarian assistance, civil affairs support, and relief and reconstruction assistance requested by the Iraqi Interim Government and in line with previous Security Council Resolutions.

In addition, the MNF is prepared to establish or support a force within the MNF to provide for the security of personnel and facilities of the United Nations. We have consulted closely with UN officials regarding the United Nations' security requirements and believe that a brigade-size force will be needed to support the United Nations' security effort. This force will be under the command and control of the MNF commander, and its missions will include static and perimeter security at UN facilities, and convoy escort duties for the UN mission's travel requirements.

In order to continue to contribute to security, the MNF must continue to function under a framework that affords the force and its personnel the status that they need to accomplish their mission, and in which the contributing states have responsibility for exercising jurisdiction over their personnel and which will ensure arrangements for, and use of assets by, the MNF. The existing framework governing these matters is sufficient for these purposes. In addition, the forces that make up the MNF are and will remain committed at all times to act consistently with their obligations under the law of armed conflict, including the Geneva Conventions.

The MNF is prepared to continue to pursue its current efforts to assist in providing a secure environment in which the broader international community is able to fulfil its important role in facilitating Iraq's reconstruction. In meeting these responsibilities in the period ahead, we will act in full recognition of and respect for Iraqi sovereignty. We look to other member states and international and regional organizations to assist the people of Iraq and the sovereign Iraqi government in overcoming the challenges that lie ahead to build a democratic, secure and prosperous country.

The co-sponsors intend to annex this letter to the resolution on Iraq under consideration. In the meantime, I request that you provide copies of this letter to members of the Council as quickly as possible.

Sincerely,

[*Signed*] Colin L. Powell

Document 542

Press Statement by the Security Council President on Handover of Sovereignty to Iraq, Delivered on 28 June 2004

UN Doc. SC/8136, 28 June 2004

The members of the Security Council welcome the handover of full responsibility and authority for governing Iraq to the fully sovereign and independent Interim Government of Iraq, thus ending the occupation of the country. The members of the Council reaffirm the independence, sovereignty, unity and territorial integrity of Iraq.

The members of the Security Council reiterate fully resolution 1546 (2004), including the proposed timetable for the political transition, the possibility of an international meeting, and the leading role of the United Nations to assist the Interim Government of Iraq in implementing the political process leading, inter alia, to elections no later than 31 January 2005. The members of the Council call on all Iraqis to implement these arrangements peaceably and in full.

The members of the Security Council reiterate their call to all States and relevant international and regional organizations to support the Interim Government of Iraq in the implementation of this process, and in its efforts to bring economic reconstruction, peace, unity and stability to Iraq.

The members of the Council condemn, in the strongest terms, the continued violence in Iraq, which should not be allowed to disrupt Iraq's political and economic transition.

IV

United States Policy and Other Documents on Iraq

Document 543
A Commitment to Post-War Iraq: Basic Principles

12 March 2003[1]

If U.S. and other coalition forces take military action in Iraq, they will have contributions to make to the country's temporary administration and the welfare of the Iraqi people. It will be necessary to provide humanitarian relief, organize basic services and work to establish security for the liberated Iraqis. Actions would include the following steps:

- First, demonstrate to the Iraqi people and the world that the United States aspires to liberate, not occupy or control them or their economic resources.
- Second, eliminate Iraq's chemical and biological weapons, its nuclear program, the related delivery systems, and the related research and production facilities. This will be a complex, dangerous and expensive task.
- Third, eliminate likewise Iraq's terrorist infrastructure. A key element of U.S. strategy in the global war on terrorism is exploiting the information about terrorist networks that the coalition acquires through our military and law enforcement actions.
- Fourth, safeguard the territorial unity of Iraq. The United States does not support Iraq's disintegration or dismemberment.
- Fifth, begin the process of economic and political reconstruction, working to put Iraq on a path to become a prosperous and free country. The U.S. government shares with many Iraqis the hope that their country will enjoy the rule of law and other institutions of democracy under a broad-based government that represents the various parts of Iraqi society.

The United States would approach any potential post-war work with a two-part resolve:

- A commitment to stay as long as required to achieve its objectives.
- A commitment to leave as soon as possible – Iraq belongs to the Iraqi people.

Office of Reconstruction and Humanitarian Assistance

To encourage the coordinated, balanced progress of economic and security reconstruction in a post-conflict Iraq, President Bush has directed his administration to begin planning now.

The President directed on January 20 the creation of a post-war planning office.[2] The Office of Reconstruction and Humanitarian Assistance is charged with establishing links with the United Nations specialized agencies and with non-governmental organizations that will play a role in post-war Iraq. It will reach out also to the counterpart offices in the governments of coalition countries, and, in coordination with the President's Special Envoy to the Free Iraqis, to the various Free Iraqi groups.

The immediate responsibility for administering post-war Iraq will fall upon the Commander of the U.S. Central Command, as the commander of the U.S. and coalition forces in the field. The purpose of the Office of Reconstruction and Humanitarian Assistance is to develop detailed plans.

There are three substantive operations within the Office, each under a civilian coordinator: Humanitarian Relief, Reconstruction, and Civil Administration. A fourth coordinator is responsible for communications, logistics and budgetary support.

[1] This statement was first published on 12 March 2003 by the US Department of Defense and is available at http://www.defendamerica.mil/.

[2] For a draft of President Bush`s National Security Presidential Directive No 24 of 20 January 2003, see *Doc 159*.

These operations are under the overall leadership of Jay Garner, a retired Lieutenant General who held a senior military position in the 1991 humanitarian relief operation in northern Iraq. He is responsible for organizing and integrating the work of the three substantive operations and ensuring that the office can travel to the region when necessary and plug in smoothly to CENTCOM's operations. His staff consists of representatives from the Departments of State, Defense, Justice, Treasury, Energy, and Agriculture, the U.S. Agency for International Development and the Office of Management and Budget.

As part of post-war planning, CENTCOM has also established a Combined Joint Task Force that will be responsible for U.S. and coalition forces in Iraq in the immediate aftermath of a conflict. The task force will work closely with the Office of Reconstruction and Humanitarian Assistance to facilitate relief and reconstruction activities.

Elimination of Weapons of Mass Destruction

Detailed planning is underway for the task of securing, assessing and dismantling Iraqi WMD capabilities, facilities and stockpiles. It is complex and will take place as part of military operations, continuing into the post-conflict period.

We must first locate Iraq's widespread WMD sites. We must then be prepared to secure the relevant weapons or facilities, or rapidly and safely disable them, so they are no longer a threat to coalition forces. This will have to be done in many places and as quickly as possible.

After hostilities, we will have to dismantle, destroy or dispose of nuclear, chemical, biological and missile capabilities and infrastructure.

Equally important will be plans to re-direct some of Iraq's dual-use capability and its scientific and managerial talent to legitimate, civilian activities in a new Iraq.

This will not be a mission that falls entirely to the U.S. military forces. Other U.S. government personnel, including those within the DoD, the Department of Energy's laboratory system, and in other government agencies can contribute.

Coalition partners, including many NATO Allies, have nuclear, chemical and biological defense-related capabilities and expertise that can play an important role. The UN, IAEA and other international organizations should be in a position to contribute valuably to the elimination effort and perhaps to ongoing monitoring afterward.

Economic Reconstruction

Detailed planning is underway for resumption of oil production as quickly as possible to help meet the Iraqi people's basic needs. The oil sector is Iraq's primary source of funding. As noted, the United States is committed to preserving Iraq's territorial integrity. So we are intent on ensuring that Iraq's oil resources remain under national Iraqi control, with the proceeds made available to support Iraqis in all parts of the country.

The Administration has decided that, in the event of war, the U.S.-led coalition would:

- Protect Iraq's oil fields from acts of sabotage and preserve them as a national asset of the Iraqi people, and
- Begin reconstruction and operation in the sector, so that its proceeds can help support the Iraqi people.

Iraqi Self-Governance

The administration of Iraq would involve Iraqis as soon as possible. Following the initial period of U.S./coalition military government, we envisage a transitional phase in which responsibility is gradually transferred to Iraqi institutions, leading to the establishment of a new Iraqi government.

The following are examples of the ways in which Iraqis might play a progressively greater role in administering the country. These examples illustrate various mechanisms under consideration:

- An Iraqi consultative council could be formed to advise the U.S./coalition authorities.
- A judicial council could undertake to advise the authorities on the necessary revisions to Iraq's legal structure and statutes to institute the rule of law and to protect individual rights.
- A constitutional commission could be created to draft a new constitution and submit it to the Iraqi people for ratification.
- Major Iraqi governmental institutions – such as the central government ministries – could remain in place and perform the key functions of government after the vetting of the top personnel to remove any who might be tainted with the crimes and excesses of the current regime.
- Town and district elections could be held soon after liberation to involve Iraqis in governing at the local level.

Document 544
Office of the US Under Secretary of Defense for Policy, What the UN Should and Should Not Do [in Post-War Iraq]

26 March 2003

The UN should:

- Endorse the Coalition Provisional Authority (when created).
- Endorse the Coalition's establishment of an Iraqi interim authority.
- Recognize the Coalition Provisional Authority as acting for the government of Iraq for the purposes of the 'Oil for Food' program.
- Encourage member states, NGOs, etc., to contribute to meeting the needs of the Iraqi people.
- Appoint a UN Special Coordinator to coordinate among the UN specialized agencies and NGOs, and between them and the Coalition, and provide advice to the Coalition.

The UN should **not**:

- Create a UN-based governing authority for Iraq.
- Authorize the Coalition Provisional Authority (we don't need UN authorization and seeking it could imply that we do need it).
- Authorize the Iraqi interim authority, or determine its composition or structure.
- Control future oil revenues.
- Empower the UN Secretary General's Special Representative to deal directly with Iraqi interim authority or coordinate between it and the UN specialized agencies and NGOs.

Document 545

Memorandum from US Secretary of Defense Rumsfeld for President Bush, Prime Minister Blair's Visit and the UN Role in Post-War Iraq

26 March 2003

The Coalition will win the war. But, if we lack the proper degree of freedom of action in post-war Iraq, we may find that we won the war but cannot win a strategic victory – that is, implement our concept of a free Iraq – or even stabilize the situation enough to allow us to remove our forces in a reasonable period of time. The US has made this mistake before.

Prime Minister Blair, for domestic political reasons, may urge you to agree to an extensive UN role in post-war Iraq. As much as we would like to help him, we have important interests in preserving certain redlines regarding the UN.

The UN could usefully provide support for Coalition post-war operations in Iraq, but the UN *must not*, in my view, control those operations. UN authorization is *not* required for the Coalition to exercise governmental authority in post-war Iraq and we should, I believe, do nothing to imply it is. In the statement following the Atlantic Summit,[3] you and Prime Minister Blair correctly delineated the idea by saying that you will seek UN Security Council resolutions that '*endorse* an appropriate post-conflict administration for Iraq.' 'Endorse' is the right word; we should oppose using words like 'authorize.'

I believe it is particularly hazardous to mix the UN in with the Iraqi Interim Authority (IIA). As the IIA will be the seedbed of a future Iraqi government, we plan to use it to give a head start to those Iraqis who are committed to your concept of a free Iraq. Some UN Security Council Members and some key UN officials do not (to put it mildly) share your commitment to building democratic institutions in Iraq. Thus, the UN should not have a role in selecting IIA members or in guiding the IIA's evolution, though we may be open to *advice* from appropriate UN officials.

As you have repeatedly said, the UN cannot possibly be allowed to control the oil revenues. These will be needed for reconstructing the country, and the way they are allocated will help determine how quickly the economy revives.

UN functions in post-war Iraq will likely be exercised by a UN Special Coordinator (or UN Special Representative). It would help to define that official's role in a way that makes best use of his ability to attract support form other countries for post-war humanitarian assistance and reconstruction efforts. His main function should be that of coordinating among non-governmental organizations and the specialized UN agencies that will be active in post-war Iraq, and between them and the provisional authority that General Franks will head in the post-war period. A greater role than that for the UN Special Coordinator would limit our freedom of action to achieve the goals you have set.

Prime Minister Blair may argue that he needs UN 'cover' for our post-war activities in Iraq. We should do everything reasonable to accommodate him. However, it is neither in his nor in our interest to give the UN a role that would interfere with our ability to win the peace or to accomplish what we need to do to allow us to withdraw our forces from Iraq at the appropriate time.

The key point is that we must *not* separate the civil from the military responsibilities. That is what was done in Kosovo and Bosnia and, because the civil side was not developed aggressively enough, our forces are still there – eight years later in Bosnia and four years

[3] See *Doc 572*.

in Kosovo. Only the countries whose troops are doing the military tasks have the incentive to get the civil side done promptly and properly so they can get their troops out. In the case of Iraq it will be US troops that will be carrying the load. We cannot depend on others to do what is necessary to get them out.
[Signed] *Donald Rumsfeld*[4]

Document 546
Policy Paper of the US Under Secretary of Defense for Policy, Iraqi Interim Authority Structure and Implementation
28 March 2003

- The Coalition Provisional Authority (CPA) will promote the establishment of the Iraqi Interim Authority (IIA).
- **The IIA has two main functions:**
  - To devise the means by which the new Iraqi government will come into being; and
  - To have responsibility over those governmental functions that the CPA will turn over.
- **The IIA will sign an agreement with the CPA to determine the IIA's role.**
  - The IIA will commit to the principles outlined in the March 16 Atlantic Summit:[5]
    - A unified Iraq at peace with itself and its neighbors
    - Governance by a democratic process
    - Rule of law
    - Equality of all Iraqis under law regardless of ethnicity or religion.
  - Upon elections and ratification of the constitution, the IIA will disband in favor of new constitutional structures.
- **The IIA will consist of a Leadership Council, a Constitutional Commission, and a Judicial Council:**
  - **Leadership Council** (27 members, no staff)
    - Each member will pledge to uphold the Atlantic Summit principles.
    - The appointed chairman should agree not to run for elective office for seven years [?].
    - Composition:
      - Each governor will represent his province (18).
      - Six Free Iraqis accepting election mandate at Salahuddin.
      - Five 'at-large' Iraqis (will be appointed by CPA to ensure representation and diversity).
    - There should be no formal ethnic or sectarian quotas.
    - Purpose:
      - Issue a provisional Bill of Rights.
      - Consult with the CPA on the functioning of Iraqi government.
      - Assume control of ministries on a case-by-case basis by mutual agreement with the CPA.
      - In consultation with CPA, develop Executive Branch structure.

[4] The Memorandum was cc-ed to Vice President Richard B. Cheney, Honorable Colin Powell, Honorable George Tenet, and Honorable Condoleezza Rice.
[5] See *Doc 572*.

- Oversee the conduct of a non-ethnic, non-sectarian census.
- Oversee the conduct of free elections.

- **Constitutional Commission** (150 members; chaired by Kanan Makiya).
  - Each member will pledge to uphold a statement of principles.
  - Composition:
    - Free Iraqis elected in London in December (not including those serving on Leadership Council) [up to 61].
    - All others chosen by interim provincial governors based on proportional representation per governorate.
    - All must agree to be permanent residents of Iraq.
  - Purpose is to generate in order:
    - Constitution
    - Election laws
    - Basic laws.
- **Judicial Council** (9 members)
  - Will recommend reform of Iraq's legal code, judicial courts, and oversee trials of prominent members of the Ba'ath regime.
  - Members will be appointed by CPA based on their legal expertise.

• In addition, there will be one interim **Governor** per province.

Document 547

Press Briefing by US National Security Adviser Condoleezza Rice on Iraq Reconstruction

4 April 2003[6]

There's been a lot of speculation in the press in recent days about the post-Saddam Iraq, not all of it entirely accurate and some of it just plain wrong. So I'm here to try and clear up a few things. Just as we've planned for a military victory, we have been planning to win the peace. [...].

Our goals are clear: We will help Iraqis build an Iraq that is whole, free and at peace with itself and with its neighbors; an Iraq that is disarmed of all WMD; that no longer supports or harbors terror; that respects the rights of Iraqi people and the rule of law; and that is on the path to democracy.

To achieve these goals, we will dismantle the tyrannical infrastructure of Saddam Hussein's regime. That is, in fact, being done as coalition forces go through the country. We will work with Iraqis, our coalition partners and international organizations to rebuild Iraq. We will leave Iraq completely in the hands of Iraqis as quickly as possible. As the President has said, the United States intends to stay in Iraq as long as needed, but not one day longer. [...].

As to the matter of the Iraqi interim authority, about which there has been a lot of comment, let me describe it for you. The interim authority will be a transitional authority run by Iraqis, until a legitimate permanent government in Iraq is established by the Iraqi people. It will be broad-based, drawing from all of Iraq's religious and ethnic groups,

[6] The Press Briefing was (but is no longer) available at http://www.whitehouse.gov/.

including Iraqis currently inside and outside of Iraq. It will be a means for Iraqis to participate immediately in the economic and political reconstruction of their country.

After the current regime is removed, the interim authority will assume responsibility for administering many government functions and take on further responsibilities as it becomes able. The interim authority will not be a coalition-imposed provisional government.

Iraqis will be developing the interim authority at various stages of the process. In liberated areas within Iraq, we have already seen the emergence of local Iraqi leaders who are helping in the liberation of their own country. Iraqis currently free and Iraqis who will soon be free and Iraqis who have for decades kept alive the hopes of a free Iraq while in exile will all have much to contribute to the interim authority and to Iraq's future.

On the U.N. role: The coalition is committed to working in partnership with international institutions, including, of course, the United Nations. But I would just caution that Iraq is not East Timor, or Kosovo, or Afghanistan. Iraq is unique. There are lessons to be learned from the success of the process that led to the creation of the Afghan Interim Authority. But the important thing now is to liberate Iraq. And as the statement from the Azores summit said,[7] we will welcome the efforts of U.N. specialized agencies and non-governmental organizations in providing immediate assistance to the Iraqi people. The precise role of the U.N. will be determined in consultations between the Iraqi people, coalition members and U.N. officials.

The coalition will naturally have the leading role for a period of time to assure the provision of essential services to the Iraqi people. That action will require unity of effort. But, of course, the United Nations has expertise in many key areas, and the coalition will welcome its participation in postwar Iraq.

Let me just state that the goal of everyone, the coalition and the international community, should be to return sovereignty to the Iraqi people as soon as possible, sovereignty that has been denied them under the reign of Saddam Hussein.

To the matter of the role of the Office of Reconstruction and Humanitarian Assistance, the immediate focus of ORHA's efforts will be on helping Iraqis restore the delivery of basic services – such as electricity, if necessary, water, basic medical care, and to make certain that civil servants are paid, for instance. We want the ORHA to work so that the Iraqi people can begin to live normal lives as soon as possible, and then to chart their own future.

After the initial phase, and as more and more functions are turned over to the interim authority, ORHA will shift to an advisory role. The office itself, the ORHA, is a multinational coalition effort. The Department of Defense is the lead U.S. agency in this effort. Coalition governments and Iraqis will also be involved at every step.

The ORHA is led by Jay Garner, a retired U.S. Army general who, in 1991, helped the people of Northern Iraq establish their own administration in that part of the country. The ORHA office reports to General Franks, and is comprised of representatives from a range of government agencies, including the State Department, the Department of Defense, the Justice Department and USAID, as well as advisors from outside the government. There are also coalition representatives in place in the ORHA, and there will be more soon. Iraqis will be fully involved in the operations of the ORHA.

Policy guidance for the ORHA is, of course, provided by the President, through the Secretary of Defense, and that policy guidance is now being developed and coordinated on an interagency basis.

[7] For the Azores Summit Declaration, see *Doc 572*.

ORHA will coordinate the coalition's humanitarian assistance and reconstruction efforts with the activities of NGOs, international organizations and other members of the international community, as appropriate. The office already has links with U.N. agencies and NGOs that will play an important role in postwar Iraq counterpart offices in the governments of coalition countries, and with the various free Iraqi groups.

Some of the office's staff is in place, but other positions are in the process of being filled. ORHA is not a provisional government for Iraq, civilian or military. The goal is to transition responsibilities to the Iraqi people as soon as possible. I just want to underscore that Iraqis will be involved in this process at its very earliest stages. [...].

Document 548
Statement by US Secretary of State Colin Powell, Cooperation for the Safeguarding of Iraqi Antiquities and Cultural Property

14 April 2003[8]

The people of the United States value the archaeological and cultural heritage of Iraq that documents over 10,000 years of the development of civilization. In recent days, the National Museums in Baghdad and Mosul have been looted, as well as other cultural institutions and archeological sites. Such looting causes irretrievable loss to the understanding of history and the efforts of Iraqi and international scholars to study and gain new insight into our past.

Objects and documents taken from museums and sites are the property of the Iraqi nation under Iraqi and international law. They are therefore stolen property, whether found in Iraq or other nations. Anyone knowingly possessing or dealing in such objects is committing a crime. Such individuals may be prosecuted under Iraqi law and under the United States National Stolen Property Act.[9] The Iraqi people, as well as members of the Coalition forces and others, are warned not to handle these artifacts. In particular, Americans are asked not to purchase or otherwise trade in such objects as they belong to the nation of Iraq and are stolen property.

In addition to the well-reported efforts made to protect cultural, religious and historic sites in Iraq, CENTCOM has issued instructions to all troops inside Iraq to protect museums and antiquities throughout Iraq. US radio broadcasts throughout Iraq are encouraging Iraqis to return any items taken and are providing instructions on how to do so. The Office of Reconstruction and Humanitarian Affairs will help Iraqis and international experts in their efforts to restore artifacts and the catalogs of antiquities that were damaged by looters. A senior adviser in the Office of Reconstruction and Humanitarian Affairs, Ambassador John Limbert, will take the lead in this effort.

We are working through INTERPOL to pursue broader international law enforcement efforts to help locate these items and return them to Iraq before they make it into international crime channels.

We have also been in touch with the UN Educational, Scientific and Cultural Organization (UNESCO) regarding a constructive role they can play in safeguarding Iraqi antiquities.

[8] The Statement was published as a US Department of State Press Release and was (but is no longer) available at http://www.state.gov/.

[9] For the National Stolen Property Act, see 18 U.S.C. §§ 2314-2315.

Document 549
A Free Country Run by Free People
Commentary by Zalmay Khalilzad, US Special Envoy and Ambassador-at-Large for Free Iraqis

17 April 2003[10]

Nasiriyah, Iraq – There has been a gathering of Free Iraqis here, and I am filled with hope as I look around at those who have come together to discuss Iraq's future. The tyranny of Saddam Hussein's regime is truly over, and we are savoring a victory for the Iraqi people. The United States, Britain and other members of the coalition made a promise to disarm the dictator and to free the people of Iraq. We are in the final stages of delivering on that promise.

America's promise to Iraq today is to be its partner, and to help Iraq move toward a representative government, one that respects the principles of justice, the rule of law and the rights of the Iraqi people. The U.S. will deliver on this promise, too, and will be with the Iraqis for as long as it takes – until the job is done.

Our task is to build a democratic Iraq. In my meetings with free Iraqis before Operation Iraqi Freedom – whether in London or in Iraqi Kurdistan and elsewhere – and from what we've heard in recent days from Iraqis who are now free, it is clear that, among other things, Iraqis desire democracy. None of us, American or Iraqi, thinks that this is going to be quick or easy. History shows how challenging it is to build a democracy – it was so in the U.S., for sure, and elsewhere in Europe, and in Asia. Iraq will be no exception.

But people everywhere share the same aspirations – security, prosperity, freedom and self-government. And Iraq is a country vibrant in its heritage, its religious faith, its resources and its people. Iraq's very diversity – the mosaic of Sunni and Shiite Arabs, Kurds, Turkmens, Assyrians, Chaldeans, Yazidis and others – is a source of tremendous richness and talent. Iraq's choices over the coming weeks and months will determine the process toward a democratic country and a new government responsible to all Iraqis.

The coalition supports the formation, as soon as possible, of the Iraqi Interim Authority – a transitional administration, run by Iraqis, until a government is established by the people of Iraq through elections. The Interim Authority should be broad-based and fully representative. It will also be temporary. Iraq in the past has had interim constitutions that lasted too long, and transitional leaders who overstayed their welcome.

This week is the beginning of the road toward democracy in Iraq. Our meeting here in Nasiriyah, with representatives of the Iraqi people, is the first in a series of consultations with Iraqis in different parts of the country. None of these meetings will choose a government for Iraq. Rather, they will be forums for Iraqis to discuss their ideas about the formation of the Iraqi Interim Authority, and to foster an Iraqi national dialogue. Based on these consultations, a formula for constituting the Iraqi Interim Authority will be arrived at. The Interim Authority will gradually increase its authority and will provide the means for Iraqis to participate increasingly in the economic and political reconstruction of their country.

There will need to be accountability and reconciliation in Iraq. What should be done to the top leadership of the Baath party will be an important issue that Iraqis will need to

[10] This Commentary was first published in *The Wall Street Journal*, 17 April 2003, A12, with the byliner 'U.S. Promises to be Iraq's "Partner," White House Envoy Says'. Ambassador Khalilzad led the US delegation to the Free Iraqi conference in Nasiriyah. This Commentary is based on a speech he gave there.

decide collectively. The special position and privileges of the Baath party have already stopped as a matter of practice. That will need to be translated into law. Iraqis, as a society, must decide how to treat differently those who led the crimes of the past regime, on the one hand, and those, on the other, who joined the Baath party at the lowest levels, and are not necessarily culpable in any crimes. There should be room for those Iraqi civil servants – teachers, police and irrigation engineers, for example – who in the past have done their best to serve their country, not Saddam's tyranny.

The United States has no desire to govern Iraq, and I have made that clear in all my discussions here. The Iraqi people should govern their own affairs as soon as possible. As President Bush said, 'The Iraqis are plenty capable of governing themselves.' The American interest is to see that the weapons of mass destruction of the Saddam regime are identified and destroyed, that terrorists are apprehended, that the humanitarian needs of the Iraqi people are met, that security is established and that the Iraqi people are freed and empowered to build their own future.

We also appreciate the many immediate difficulties that the Iraqis are facing, and are taking steps to mitigate the severity of their hardship. With freedom comes responsibility – including the responsibility of not taking the law into one's own hands, but dealing with grievances in an organized, lawful manner. To this end, we will work with Iraqis and others to achieve stability.

The decision of who ultimately governs Iraq is a decision for the people of Iraq. They have suffered terribly under the brutal dictatorship of Saddam Hussein. Like people everywhere, they deserve liberty, and to live in peace under leaders they have chosen for themselves. They deserve a government that respects the rights of every citizen and ethnic group. They deserve a country that is reunited, that is independent, and that is released from years of sanctions, isolation, and sorrow. As President Bush has said, 'Our coalition has one goal for the future of Iraq – to return that great country to its own people.'

America will be Iraq's partner as Iraqis move toward peace, democracy, and prosperity. Their security will be our security, their success will be our success.

Document 550

Policy Paper of the Under Secretary of Defense for Policy, Iraqi Interim Authority (IIA) Implementation Plan

29 April 2003

IIA Overview

- The Iraqi Interim Authority (IIA) would serve as the instrument of Iraqi national leadership in the period before the ratification of a new Iraqi Constitution and the free election of a new Iraqi government.
- The IIA might have a number of major components:
  - Leadership Council (12-25 members): This might include an interim chief executive, who might be required to agree not to run for office for a period of years. The Council would take the lead in liaising with ORHA, foreign governments, and international institutions. It would assume responsibility for administering Iraqi government functions (including running ministries) as determined by ORHA. It could also set up subordinate commissions, perhaps including:

    - Economic Reform Commission: Responsible for advising on issues of trade, national finance, privatization, monetary/fiscal policy, and embracing free-market practices.
    - External Affairs Commission: Responsible for representing Iraqi views to the world, and advocating for the normalization of Iraq's status in the international system.
  - Constitutional Commission (150-225 members): Responsible for drafting new Iraqi Constitution and Bill of Rights, in addition to devising process for constitutional ratification. Independent of Leadership Council.
  - Legal Reform Commission (9-15 members): Responsible for advising the Coalition on eliminating Ba'athist elements were eliminated [sic] from the legal code. It might also consider issues of transitional justice. Independent of Leadership Council.
- All members of the IIA would be required to live in Iraq.
- The specific relationship between the IIA and the Coalition will be established in an agreement to be signed as soon as the IIA Leadership Council is selected.

IIA Road Map
- Central Iraq meeting (April 28) agreed that a subsequent nationwide conference should be held within four weeks to select the IIA.
- IIA Conference could include total of 300-350 Iraqis.
  - 150-225 internal Iraqis, distributed proportionally by province. Selected by the Coalition or elected by local town hall meetings.
  - 65-person Iraqi Opposition Committee from London.
  - 50-100 additional Iraqis chosen by Coalition. Selected by the interagency, in conjunction with the British.
- IIA Conference, guided by Coalition consultation, could select an Organizing Committee (10-15 members), which would choose IIA Leadership Council.
- IIA Conference/Organizing Committee could either select members of Constitutional Commission and Legal Reform Commission, or agree upon a process for doing so.

Action Items
- Determine a mechanism by which each governorate would be represented at IIA Conference.
  - If they are to be chosen by local meetings, immediately establish talks with local Iraqis from Nasiriyah/Central Iraq meetings and the Opposition Leadership Committee to organize.
  - If they are to be selected by Coalition, prepare list of candidates and devise process by which list can gain popular legitimacy.
- Plan the IIA Conference.
- Draft an agreement to govern relations between the IIA and the Coalition. Informally discuss with prominent Iraqis likely to play leading roles in IIA.
- Determine whether Iraqi Interim 'Authority' should be modified to be an Iraqi Interim 'Government', as voted on in the April 28 Central Iraq meeting.

Key Outstanding Questions
- What decision-making powers should the IIA have?
  - What veto powers should the Coalition have?
- Should the IIA have a legislative assembly?
  - Should there be any legislative function at all in the IIA?

- What should be the relationship between the various components of the IIA?
  - Should there be independence for the Constitutional and Legal Reform Commissions?
  - Should Economic Reform and/or External Affairs Commissions be independent of Leadership Council, or subordinate to it?
- Who chooses the IIA Leadership Council?
- Who chooses the IIA Legislative Assembly, if there is one?
- Who chooses members of the additional IIA commissions?
- How, if at all, should existing Iraqi Opposition structures/organizations be utilized in selecting the IIA?
- How should the Coalition ensure that religious/ethnic minorities and women are represented in the IIA?
- Should the Coalition have veto power over individuals selected by Iraqis to join the IIA?
- What regional and/or national political meetings, organized by Iraqis and/or the Coalition, should take place before any final conference to choose the IIA?

Document 551
Certain State- or Regime-Owned Property in Iraq

30 April 2003

MEMORANDUM FOR THE SECRETARY OF DEFENSE
SUBJECT: Certain State- or Regime-Owned Property in Iraq

Pursuant to my authority under the Constitution as Commander in Chief of the Armed Forces, and consistent with the Authorization for Use of Military Force Against Iraq Resolution of 2002 (Public Law 107-243),[11] I hereby confirm your authority to exercise all powers, consistent with the laws and usages of war, related to the seizure, sale, administration, or use of state- or regime-owned cash, funds, or realizable securities in Iraq. Property seized, sold, or administered under this memorandum shall be used only to assist the Iraqi people and support the reconstruction of Iraq, and such uses shall be consistent with the laws and usages of war.

You are directed, in consultation with the Secretary of the Treasury, the Secretary of State, and the Director of the Office of Management and Budget, to prescribe procedures to ensure that all property subject to this memorandum is appropriately accounted for, audited, and used only for the purposes specified herein.

Nothing in any prior Executive Order shall be construed to limit the authority herein confirmed, and nothing in this memorandum shall be construed to limit authorities that U.S. Armed Forces may otherwise exercise under the laws and usages of war.

[Signed] *George Bush*

[11] For the text of the resolution, see Public Law 107-243 (16 October 2002), 116 Stat 1498-1502.

Document 552
Speech of US Secretary of Defense Donald H. Rumsfeld Before the Council on Foreign Relations
27 May 2003[12]

[...] It is now just 7 weeks since the liberation of Iraq – and the challenges are there. [...] This much is clear: we have a stake in their success. For if Iraq – with its size, capabilities, resources and its history – is able to move to the path of representative democracy, however bumpy the road, then the impact in the region and the world could be dramatic. Iraq could conceivably become a model – proof that a moderate Muslim state can succeed in the battle against extremism taking place in the Muslim world today.

The Iraqi people have a foundation on which to build the peace.

Very likely at least in part because of the speed and skill in the execution of the war plan:

- The vast majority of Iraq's oil fields were not destroyed, preserving the country's oil wealth for the Iraqi people. And, an environmental disaster was prevented;
- Key bridges, roads and rail lines were not destroyed;
- Dams were not broken and villages were not flooded;
- The infrastructure of the country is largely intact;
- There were no large masses of refugees fleeing across borders into neighboring countries;
- The former regime did not attack Iraq's neighbors with SCUD missiles;
- And the coalition took great care to protect the lives of innocent civilians, as well as the important holy sites.

So unlike Europe after WW II, for the most part the people of Iraq do not have to rebuild from this recent war, as they work to rebuild their country and society after decades of a dictatorship.

We are committed to helping the Iraqi people get on the path to a free society. We do not have an American 'template' we want to impose – Iraqis will figure out how to build a free nation in a manner that reflects their unique culture and traditions.

What the President *has* outlined are some broad principles that are critical if Iraq's transition from tyranny is to succeed:

- that Iraq be a single country, which does not support terrorists, threaten its neighbors or the world with weapons of mass terror, or threaten its diverse population with repression;
- that it have a government that respects and protects minorities, provides opportunities for its people through a market economy, and justice through an independent judiciary and rule of law.

These are not solely American principles, nor are they exclusively Western principles. They are principles common to all the world's free societies. The coalition will seek out Iraqis who support these principles, and who desire to have a role in their country's future. And those who oppose these principles – whose agenda is to replace Saddam Hussein's tyranny with some other form of dictatorship – will be opposed.

As we move forward to help Iraqis build a free nation, there are some of the guidelines that the coalition is following:

[12] Council on Foreign Relations, Remarks as Prepared for Delivery by Secretary of Defense Donald H. Rumsfeld, New York, NY, Tuesday, 27 May 2003, http://www.defense.gov/.

- First, while our goal is to put functional and political authority in the hands of Iraqis as soon as possible, the Coalition Provisional Authority has the responsibility to fill the vacuum of power in a country that has been under a dictatorship for decades, by asserting temporary authority over the country. The Coalition will do so. It will not tolerate self-appointed 'leaders.'
- Second, the coalition will provide security. Among the immediate objectives are restoration of law and order for the Iraqi people and provision of essential services. The coalition is hiring and training Iraqi police, and will be prepared to use force to impose order as required – because without order, little else will be possible.
- Third, the coalition will maintain as many security forces in Iraq as necessary, for as long as necessary, to accomplish the stated goals – and no longer. Already 39 nations have offered stabilization forces or other needed assistance, and that number is growing. Together, coalition countries will seek to provide a secure environment, so that Iraqis will be able to take charge of their country as soon as possible.
- Next, the coalition will work to improve the circumstances of the Iraqi people. Already, electric services in the north and south are better than they have been in 12 years and the power situation in Baghdad is improving, albeit slowly. The coalition is working to achieve rapid improvements in other vital public services. The coalition will work to engage the Iraqi people as rapidly as possible, and give Iraqis leadership roles in the reconstruction effort – for it is their responsibility to build the future of their country.
- Fifth, in staffing ministries and positioning Iraqis in ways that will increase their influence, the Coalition will work to have Iraqis involved as early as possible – so that Iraqis can develop and explain the goals and direction to the Iraqi people. Only as Iraqis are engaged in, responsible for, and explaining and leading their fellow citizens will the broader public support develop that is essential for security.
- Sixth, the Coalition will work with forward-looking Iraqis and actively oppose the old regime's enforcers – the Ba'ath Party leaders, Fedayeen Saddam, and other instruments of repression – and make clear that it will eliminate the remnants of Saddam's regime. Those who committed war crimes or crimes against humanity will be tracked down and brought to justice. De-Ba'athification may cause some inefficiencies, but it is critical to removing pervasive fear from Iraqi society.
- Next, Iraq will need to find ways to heal the wounds the Ba'athists inflicted on the society. The experiences of Eastern Europe and other countries can inform this process.
- Eighth, market systems will be favored – not Stalinist command systems – and the Coalition will favor activities that will begin to diversify the Iraqi economy beyond oil. The Coalition will encourage moves to privatize state-owned enterprises. And, it will work to provide enterprise driven economic development opportunities for the Iraqi people.
- Ninth, the Coalition Provisional Authority is developing a plan for the Iraqi oil industry based on transparency. Iraq's oil wealth will be used for the benefit of the Iraqi people.
- Tenth, whenever possible, contracts for work in Iraq will go to those who will use Iraqi workers, to countries that assisted the Iraqi people's liberation, that provide assistance to Iraq's recovery and also to neighboring countries so as to contribute to

greater regional economic activity and accelerate Iraq's economic recovery.

- Eleventh, countries and international organizations, including the United Nations and non-governmental organizations, are being welcomed to assist in Iraq. They can and are playing an important role. The Coalition Provisional Authority will work closely with them to maintain a focus of effort.
- Twelfth, assistance from Iraq's neighbors will be welcomed. Conversely, interference in Iraq by its neighbors or their proxies will not be permitted. Indeed, Iran should be on notice that efforts to try to remake Iraq in their image will be aggressively put down.
- Finally, in assisting the Iraqi people, the U.S. will play its role but should not be considered the first and only donor of funds. The American people have already made a significant investment to liberate Iraq, and stand ready to contribute to the rebuilding efforts. But when funds are needed, the coalition will turn first to Iraqi regime funds in Iraq; Iraqi funds in the Oil-for-Food program; seized frozen Iraqi regime assets in the U.S. and other countries; and international donors, many of whom are already assisting.

The transition to democracy will take time, and it will not always be a smooth road. In Central and Eastern Europe, the process has taken time, but it is succeeding. Trial and error and experimentation will be part of the process. The efforts will not be perfect. Course corrections will be needed and should be expected. This effort will require patience by all involved if it is to succeed. It has been seven weeks – in a nation that suffered a dictatorship for decades, that saw tens of thousands of criminals released from their prisons, and where many of the regime's enforcers are still at large.

The eventual political outcome will be decided by the Iraqi people, within the broad principles of the rule of law, minority rights, individual liberty, and representative democracy. One ought not expect the Iraqi outcome to replicate ours or any other system.

Let me conclude by saying: the Iraqi people have an historic opportunity to build a free and civil society. Doing so will be difficult – just as it was in the early years of our young republic.

But the benefits of success – for Iraq, for the region, and the world – will be enormous. If Iraqis can take hold of their country, develop the institutions of self-government, and claim their place as responsible members of the international community, then the world could have a new model for a successful transition from tyranny to self-reliance – and a new ally in the global war on terror and the struggle for freedom and moderation in the Muslim world.

The world has a stake in their success – and that is why so many of the world's free nations are stepping forward to help. [...].

Document 553
Memorandum by US Deputy Secretary of Defense Paul Wolfowitz, Inspector General of the Coalition Provisional Authority

3 December 2003

SUBJECT: Inspector General of the Coalition Provisional Authority
Pursuant to section 3001 of the Emergency Supplemental Appropriations Act for Defense and for the Reconstruction of Iraq and Afghanistan for fiscal year 2004, Pub. L. 108-106 (November 6, 2003), I am establishing the position of Inspector General of the Coalition Provisional Authority (IG/CPA), effective immediately. I ask that the Administrator of the CPA provide me with a nomination for the IG/CPA position as soon as possible, but not later than December 8, 2003.

The authorities, duties and responsibilities of the IG/CPA are described in the attached Terms of Reference. In his statement upon approving the Act, the President directed that, in exercising these authorities and responsibilities, the IG/CPA shall refrain from initiating, carrying out, or completing an audit or investigation, or from issuing a subpoena, which requires access to sensitive operation plans, intelligence matters, counterintelligence matters, ongoing criminal investigations by other administration units of the Department of Defense related to national security, or other matters the disclosure of which would constitute a serious threat to national security. The President's statement provided further that the Secretary of Defense may make exceptions to this direction in the public interest.

[Signed] *Paul Wolfowitz*
Attachment: As stated

INSPECTOR GENERAL OF THE COALITION PROVISIONAL AUTHORITY
Terms of Reference

1. Mission:

The mission of the Inspector General of the Coalition Provisional Authority (IG/CPA) shall be–

A. To provide for the independent and objective conduct and supervision of audits and investigations relating to the programs and operations of the CPA, and
B. To provide for the independent and objective leadership and coordination of, and recommendations on, policies designed to promote economy, efficiency, and effectiveness in the administration of programs and operations and prevent and detect fraud and abuse in such programs and operations.

2. Organization:

A. The Office of the Inspector General shall consist of an Assistant Inspector General for Auditing and an [Assistant] Inspector General for Investigations, each appointed by the IG/CPA, and such other organizational elements as are established by the IG/CPA within resources authorized by the Secretary of Defense and the Administrator of the CPA.
B. The IG/CPA shall be–

(1) Nominated by the Administrator of the CPA for consideration by the Secretary of Defense, in consultation with the Secretary of State, by December 8, 2003.
(2) Appointed by the Secretary of Defense, in consultation with the Secretary of State, solely on the basis of integrity and demonstrated ability in accounting, auditing, financial analysis, law, management, analysis, public administration or investigations.
(3) Directly supervised by, and report to the Administrator of the CPA.
(4) Considered as an employee other than one who determines policies related to the nationwide administration of Federal law, for purposes of 5 U.S.C. § 7324.
(5) Removable from office in accordance with the provisions of section 3(b) of the Inspector General Act of 1978 (5 U.S.C. App. 3 § 3(b)).
(6) Paid at the annual rate of basic pay for positions at level IV of the Executive Schedule under 5 U.S.C. § 5315.

C. The IG/CPA may obtain services as authorized by 5 U.S.C. § 3109, at daily rates not to exceed the equivalent rate prescribed for grade GS-15 of the General Schedule by section 5332 of such title.

D. The IG/CPA may, consistent with these Terms of Reference (TOR), enter into contracts and other arrangements for audits, studies, analyses, and other services with public agencies and with private persons, and make such arrangements as may be necessary to carry out the duties of the IG/CPA.

3. <u>Responsibilities</u>:

The responsibilities of the <u>IG/CPA</u> shall include:

A. Conducting, supervising, and coordinating audits and investigations of the treatment, handling, and expenditure of appropriated funds by the CPA in Iraq, and of the programs, operations, and contracts carried out utilizing such funds, including–
(1) The oversight and accounting of the obligation and expenditure of such funds.
(2) The monitoring and review of reconstruction activities funded by such funds.
(3) The monitoring and review of the transfer of such funds and associated information between and among the CPA; departments, agencies, and entities of the Federal Government; and private and nongovernmental entities; and
(4) The maintenance of records on the use of such funds to facilitate future audits and investigations of the use of such funds.

B. Establishing, maintaining, and overseeing such systems, procedures, and controls as the IG/CPA considers appropriate to discharge under subsection (A).

C. Coordinating and cooperating with the Inspectors General of the Department of Defense and other concerned U.S. Government executive agencies, in carrying out the duties of the IG/CPA.

D. Exercising the duties, responsibilities, and authorities of inspectors general under the Inspector General Act of 1978.

E. Refraining, except as directed by the Secretary of Defense, from initiating carrying out, or completing an audit or investigation, or from issuing a subpoena, which requires access to sensitive operation plans, intelligence matters, counterintelligence matters, ongoing criminal investigations by other administration units of the Department of Defense (DoD) related to national security, or other matters the disclosure of which would constitute a serious threat to such national security.

F. Consistent with subsections (A) and (G), performing the duties and responsibilities of the IG/CPA provided for in section 3001 of the Emergency Supplemental Appropriations Act for Defense and for the Reconstruction of Iraq and Afghanistan for fiscal year 2004, Pub. L. 108-106 (November 6, 2003).

G. Advising the Administrator of the CPA and the appropriate committees of Congress whenever, consistent with this TOR, information or assistance the IG/CPA has requested has been unreasonably refused or not provided.

The responsibilities of the Assistant Inspector General for Auditing shall include supervising the performance of auditing activities related to programs and operations of the CPA as provided for in this TOR.

The responsibilities of the Assistant Inspector General for Investigation shall include supervising the performance of investigative activities related to the programs and operations of the CPA as provided for in this TOR.

The Heads of Department of Defense Components shall, insofar as is practicable and not in contravention of any existing law or this TOR, furnish such information or assistance to the IG/CPA as the IG/CPA may request in the performance of the IG/CPA's official duties.

Document 554

Memorandum by the US President on the Transfer of Funds Appropriated for the Operating Expenses of the Coalition Provisional Authority

5 December 2003[13]

MEMORANDUM FOR THE SECRETARY OF STATE
THE SECRETARY OF DEFENSE
THE DIRECTOR OF THE OFFICE OF MANAGEMENT AND BUDGET

SUBJECT: Transfer of Funds Appropriated to the President under the heading Operating Expenses of the Coalition Provisional Authority, and Delegation of the Functions of the President under the heading Iraq Relief and Reconstruction Fund, in the Emergency Supplemental Appropriations Act for Defense and for the Reconstruction of Iraq and Afghanistan, 2004

By the authority vested in me by the Constitution and the laws of the United States of America, including section 632 of the Foreign Assistance Act of 1961, as amended (22 U.S.C. 2392), I hereby direct as follows:

1. The funds appropriated to the President under the heading Operating Expenses of the Coalition Provisional Authority in the Emergency Supplemental Appropriations Act for Defense and for the Reconstruction of Iraq and Afghanistan (Public Law 108–106), or in any subsequent appropriation under this heading, are transferred to the Secretary of Defense, for an account designated Operating Expenses of the Coalition Provisional Authority, International Reconstruction and Other Assistance, Army.

[13] The Memorandum was published in the *Federal Register*, vol 69, no 6, 9 January 2004, 1645.

2. The memorandum entitled, 'Delegation of the Functions of the President under the heading Iraq Relief and Reconstruction Fund in the Emergency Wartime Supplemental Appropriations Act, 2003', dated May 6, 2003, is amended by inserting 'or in any subsequent appropriation under this heading' after the phrase, '(Public Law 108-11),'. It is further amended by deleting all references to 'the Office of Reconstruction and Humanitarian Assistance' or 'ORHA,' and inserting in lieu thereof 'the Coalition Provisional Authority' or 'CPA,' respectively.

The Secretary of Defense is authorized and directed to publish this memorandum in the Federal Register.

[Signed] *George W. Bush*

Document 555

Memorandum by US Deputy Secretary of Defense Paul Wolfowitz, Determination and Findings on Iraq Reconstruction and Relief Contracts

5 December 2003[14]

DETERMINATION AND FINDINGS

This Determination and Findings (D&F)[15] applies to the 24 construction and services, and indefinite-delivery, indefinite-quantity contracts described in the attachment that are to be awarded by the Coalition Provisional Authority (CPA) and the Department of Defense, on behalf of the CPA. It also applies to one overall program management contract to be awarded to oversee the total effort. Finally, it applies to the indefinite-delivery, indefinite quantity contract to equip the new Iraqi army. These contracts will obligate $18.6B in funds from the Iraq Relief and Reconstruction Fund (IRRF), which were appropriated by Public Law 108-106 for the purpose of relief and reconstruction of Iraq. These contracts will upgrade and rebuild the electrical sector, public works and water, military courts and borders, building, housing and health, transportation, communications, and oil infrastructure. This D&F is executed under the authority of 41 U.S.C. 253 (c)(7) and 10 U.S.C. 2304(c)(.7), as implemented by FAR 6.302-7.

I hereby make the following findings regarding the limitation of competition for the particular procurements of Iraqi Relief and Reconstruction prime contracts identified in attachment number 1 to firms from the United States, Iraq, Coalition partners and force contributing nations:

[14] The text of the Memorandum was published on 12 December 2003 by the US State Department in a document entitled 'Iraq Reconstruction Contracts for Firms from Supporting Nations', http://usinfo.org/.

[15] On the compatibility of this D&F, limiting reconstruction contracts to contractors from Coalition partners with the obligations of the United States under the WTO Agreement of Government Procurement (GPA), done at Marrakesh on 15 April 1994, see Palmeter, David/Meagher, Niall P., ASIL Insights: WTO Issues Relating to U.S. Restrictions on Participation in Iraq Reconstruction Contracts, December 2003; Pulkowski, Dirk, Coalition Procurement for the Reconstruction of Iraq in the Crosshairs of WTO Law: The Obligations of the United States under the WTO Government Procurement Agreement, *German Law Journal* 5/3 (2004), 257-282; Puth, Sebastian, Der Wideraufbau des Irak auf dem Prüfstand des WTO-Rechts, *Europäische Zeitschrift für Wirtschaftsrecht* 15 (2004), 395-399.

FINDINGS

1. In light of the global war on terrorism and the end of major combat operations, the task of rebuilding the infrastructure of a free Iraq remains critical. The mission to rebuild Iraq is massive in nature and requires major improvements and redevelopment in electricity, public works/water (including wastewater treatment and water distribution), security/justice, transportation/communications (including ports, roads and airports), and buildings/housing/health (including public and government buildings, schools, and medical facilities). The state of the Iraqi infrastructure is a reflection of decades of neglect by a totalitarian regime. Under a free Iraq, the reconstruction process will involve the input of the Iraqi people and their governmental ministries in the development of projects and products that will reinvigorate the country for self-sufficiency in the future.

2. The Coalition Provisional Authority (CPA) has been established to promote the welfare of the Iraqi people through the effective administration of the territory, including in particular working towards the restoration of conditions of security and stability and the creation of conditions in which the Iraqi people can freely determine their own political future. In awarding the contracts, competition and responsiveness to the needs of Iraqi people will be emphasized.

3. The successful reconstruction of Iraq is critical to the viability of the new Iraqi economy. International support and cooperation are necessary for progress in Iraq. An unsuccessful reconstruction effort would have serious negative effects on the ultimate success of the war effort. The President has made clear that the Coalition's actions to reconstruct Iraq are indispensable for national security and national defense purposes.

4. It is necessary for the protection of the essential security interests of the United States to limit competition for the prime contracts of these procurements to companies from the United States, Iraq, Coalition partners and force contributing nations. Thus, it is clearly in the public interest to limit prime contracts to companies from these countries.

5. Every effort must be made to expand international cooperation in Iraq. Since May 2003, Coalition forces other than those from the United States have increased from 14,000 to 23,700. U.S. force levels, accordingly, have decreased by approximately 12,000. Limiting competition for prime contracts will encourage the expansion of international cooperation in Iraq and in future efforts.

6. Coalition partners share in the US vision of a free and stable Iraq. The limitation of sources to prime contractors from those countries should encourage the continued cooperation of coalition members.

7. Including Iraqi firms in the reconstruction process makes them an active stakeholder in the rebuilding of their country. Besides helping the Iraqis generate the income to rebuild their country, it enables the Iraqi people to assume more responsibility for their country's economic and infrastructure development. This leads to a sense of ownership and pride in the reconstruction process and provides long-term stability to the political and economic transformation in Iraq, making it a model for other countries to follow and sending a clear message to the people of the Middle East and beyond that freedom and democracy are the best paths for the future.

8. Upon limitation of sources to firms from the United States, Iraq, Coalition partners and force contributing nations, acquisition of the 26 Iraqi Relief and Reconstruction contracts will use the competitive procedures prescribed in FAR 6.102.

DETERMINATION

Based upon the findings above, I hereby determine that, in accordance with U.S.C. 253(c)(7) and 10 U.S.C. 2304(c)(7), as implemented by FAR 6.302-7, it is necessary in the public interest to use other than competitive procedures in the procurements for the prime contracts described on the attachment. Such procurements shall use competitive procedures, with participation limited to sources from the United States, Iraq, Coalition partners and force contributing nations.
[Signed] *Paul Wolfowitz*

Attachments
1. Contract Listing
2. Eligible Countries

ATTACHMENT 1 OF 2

Iraqi Reconstruction & Relief Contracts to be Awarded

1. Program Management Office Services
2. Program Management Services - Electrical Sector
3. Design-Build IDIQ Construction Services for New Power Generation (Southern region)
4. Design-Build IDIQ Construction Services for New Power Generation (Northern region)
5. Design-Build IDIQ Construction Services for Rehabilitation of Existing Power Generation Facilities (Country-wide)
6. Design-Build IDIQ Construction Services for Transmission/Distribution/Communication and Control (Northern region)
7. Design-Build IDIQ Construction Services for Transmission/Distribution/Communication and Control (Central (Baghdad) region)
8. Design-Build IDIQ Construction Service for Transmission/Distribution/Communication and Control (Southern region)
9. Program Management Services - Public Works/Water Resources Sector
10. Design-Build IDIQ Construction Services for Public Works and Water Projects (Northern region)
11. Design-Build IDIQ Construction Services for Public Works and Water Projects (Central region)
12. Design-Build IDIQ Construction Services for Public Works and Water Projects (Baghdad region)
13. Design-Build IDIQ Construction Services for Public Works and Water Projects (Southern region)
14. Design-Build IDIQ Construction Services for Public Works and Water Projects (Nationwide)
15. Program Management Services - Security/Justice Sector
16. Design-Build IDIQ Construction Services for Security and Justice facilities
17. Design-Build IDIQ Construction Services for Iraq National Defense Force Facilities
18. Program Management Services - Building/Health Sector
19. Design-Build IDIQ Construction Services for the Building, Housing and Health Sector
20. Program Management Services - Transportation and Communications Sector
21. Design-Build IDIQ Construction Services for Transportation Projects
22. Design-Build IDIQ Construction Services for Communication Projects
23. Program Management Services - Oil Sector

24. Restore Iraq Oil Services (Northern region)
25. Restore Iraq Oil Services (Southern region)
26. Equip New Iraqi Army

ATTACHMENT 2 OF 2

Countries Eligible to Compete for Contracts Funded with U.S. Appropriated Funds for Iraq Reconstruction:

Afghanistan, Albania, Angola, Australia, Azerbaijan, Bahrain, Bulgaria, Colombia, Costa Rica, Czech Republic, Denmark, Dominican Republic, Egypt, El Salvador, Eritrea, Estonia, Ethiopia, Georgia, Honduras, Hungary, Iceland, Iraq, Italy, Japan, Jordan, Kazakhstan, Kuwait, Latvia, Lithuania, Macedonia, Marshall Islands, Micronesia, Moldova, Mongolia, Morocco, Netherlands, New Zealand, Nicaragua, Norway, Oman, Palau, Panama, Philippines, Poland, Portugal, Qatar, Romania, Rwanda, Saudi Arabia, Singapore, Slovakia, Solomon Islands, South Korea, Spain, Thailand, Tonga, Turkey, UAE, Uganda, Ukraine, United Kingdom, United States, Uzbekistan

As of November 25, 2003 per NSA, Defense Policy.[16]

Document 556

Memorandum by US Deputy Secretary of Defense Paul Wolfowitz, Assignment of Responsibility for Acquisition and Program Management Support for the Coalition Provisional Authority

14 January 2004

SUBJECT: Assignment of Responsibility for Acquisition and Program management Support for the Coalition Provisional Authority (CPA)

Pursuant to Section 113 of Title 10, United States Code, the Secretary of the Army is hereby assigned the authority and responsibility for the provision of acquisition and program

[16] On 10 December 2003, the Office of the US Trade Representative (USTR) issued a statement concerning the Defense Department`s action as it relates to international trade procurement obligations. USTR Spokesman Richard Mills said: 'Purchases on behalf of the Coalition Provisional Authority (CPA) are not covered by international trade procurement obligations because the CPA is not an entity subject to these obligations. Accordingly, there is no need to invoke the 'essential security' exception to our trade obligations.'

On 11 December 2003, the European Commission urged the United States to reconsider its Iraq reconstruction contracts decision. In a press release it said: 'The European Commission deeply regrets the decision of the United States to exclude countries that did not participate in the war in Iraq from US reconstruction contracts. This decision is difficult to accept and unjustified. Furthermore, it is a political mistake because it sends a most unhelpful signal at a time when the international community is constructively working on making of Iraq an open, transparent, democratic and prosperous country. This is no time to reopen old wounds but to focus on making concrete progress towards that objective. As requested at the Madrid Conference on Reconstruction in October 2003, we urge all donors to Iraq including the US to apply open, transparent and non-discriminatory contracting procedures. We therefore hope the US will reconsider the decision announced yesterday. The Commission will examine the 26 contracts at stake to determine whether procurement restrictions are in line with the commitments undertaken by the United States in the World Trade Organisation (WTO) Government Procurement Agreement (GPA). We also call on the US Administration itself to re-examine the WTO compatibility aspects before proceeding with this ill thought out action. We do not need another WTO dispute at this time.' (IP/03/1713).

management support to the CPA (Iraq and Washington, DC) and any successor entity. The Secretary of Defense shall determine and prioritize the requirements to be supported pursuant to this assignment of responsibility, as necessary.

For purposes of this memorandum, acquisition support is intended to include the award, administration and oversight of all contracts, grants and other acquisition actions in direct support of the CPA and any successor entity. Program management support comprises all aspects of project oversight, including planning, scheduling and execution, as may be required by the scope of work, directed timelines, and applicable financial management regulations.

All addressees shall provide support to the Secretary of the Army, as the Secretary of the Army considers necessary, to carry out this assignment of responsibility. Services and supplies provided to the CPA in furtherance of this memorandum shall be made available in accordance with DoD Instruction 4000.19 and applicable financial management regulations. My memoranda of May 21, 2003,[17] designating the Secretary of the Army as Executive Agent for the Office of Reconstruction and Humanitarian Assistance, and June 16, 2003,[18] providing for the exercise of that responsibility in support of the CPA, are modified accordingly.

[Signed] *Paul Wolfowitz*

Document 557

Pre-War Planning for Post-War Iraq

March 2004[19]

Planning in the U.S. Government for post-war Iraq was an interagency process involving officials from the Departments of Defense, State, Justice, Treasury, Energy, and Commerce; the United States Agency for International Development (USAID), Central Intelligence Agency, as well as from the staffs of the National Security Council and the Office of Management and Budget.

DoD mid and senior-level planners and officials engaged in multiple planning initiatives for post-war contingencies. DoD staff in the theater and in Washington evaluated a wide-range of possible outcomes, led efforts to merge and synchronize planning from various government agencies, and shaped planning for the major combat phase of the operation to allow for the best possible post-war conditions.

Key to DoD planning for this operation was the assumption that liberating Iraq from 35 years of tyrannical rule and severe social and economic underdevelopment would be a challenging prospect.

INITIAL INTERAGENCY PLANNING GROUPS

Beginning in July 2002, an assortment of working groups were formed to conduct and coordinate post-war planning.

[17] Not publicly available.

[18] For the text of the Memorandum of 16 June 2003, see Chronology of Events.

[19] This document was first published in March 2004 on the website of the US Department of Defense, Office of the Under Secretary of Defense for Policy, Office of Near East and South Asian Affairs. It was first accessed on 13 March 2004 at http://www.defenselink.mil/. It is no longer available at that address.

- Interagency Iraq Political-Military Cell (NSC, State Dept., DoD, CIA, Office of the Vice President): A staff-action-officer level group that focused on an integrated strategic effort to set the conditions for Iraq's transition to stability and sovereignty.
- Interagency Executive Steering Group (NSC, State, DoD, CIA, OVP): An NSC-chaired Deputy Under Secretary level meeting that addressed strategic planning and policy recommendations for NSC Deputies' Committee meetings.
- Interagency Humanitarian/Reconstruction Group (NSC, State, DoD, CIA, OVP, Treasury, DoJ, USAID): Prepared plans for immediate relief operations and longer term reconstruction in Iraq.
- Interagency Energy Infrastructure Working Group (State, DoD, CIA, DoE): Prepared plans to repair and operate the Iraqi oil industry in order to return output to pre-war levels.
- Interagency Coalition Working Group (DoD, State): A forum for coordination of military requirements, diplomatic strategy, and strategic support to build and maintain the coalition support (pre-war, war, and post-war).
- Office of Global Communications (State, DoD, USAID, DoJ, Treasury, the U.S. military, and coalition partners): Coordinated public affairs efforts at the strategic level, working to counter Saddam Hussein's disinformation campaigns.

MILITARY/CIVILIAN PLANNING INPUTS

Military

Additional organizations were created to continue in-depth planning, interagency coordination, and implementation. For example, the Joint Staff directed CENTCOM to create Joint Task Force 4 (JTF-4) in order to conduct detailed interagency planning for Phase IV stabilization operations.

The most significant outcome was a CENTCOM produced 300-page Phase IV Operations Order. It was focused on seven lines of operation: unity of effort, security, rule of law, civil administration, governance, humanitarian assistance, and resettlement.

Civilian

A wide assortment of other institutions prepared studies or assisted with planning sessions considering possible post-war challenges. Included among those is the Future of Iraq (FOI) project and the National Defense University (NDU) exercise.

FOI offered many valuable insights and contributions to various aspects of post-war planning, as did the NDU event in February 2003. Over 150 U.S. Government representatives (including members from ORHA) participated in this interagency rehearsal and planning exercise at NDU. Lessons learned from the exercise were taken back to the interagency working groups for incorporation into the processes.

Civilian officials on these interagency teams worked on post-war plans in the following ten sectors: health, education, water and sanitation, electricity, shelter, transportation, governance and rule of law, agriculture and rural development, telecommunications, economic and financial policy.

DIRECTORATE OF SPECIAL PLANS

The Office of Near East and South Asia (NESA) Affairs was one of four regional offices (working under the Assistant Secretary of Defense for International Security Affairs) whose daily mission was formulating international security and political-military policy. (The other three regional offices being Africa, Asia and Pacific, and Western Hemisphere)

<u>Expansion</u>
In September 2002, due to increased workload related to the Global War on Terrorism and the possibility of an Iraq contingency, the Deputy Secretary of Defense approved the expansion of the Northern Gulf Directorate within NESA.

This office was responsible for exploring policy concerns in planning issues ranging from deployment, coalition building, potential war crimes investigations, Iraqi opposition and training issues, oil issues, postwar Iraqi media and many others. Their office was increased from 4 people to approximately 16 to handle the increased workload.

In October 2002, the Directorate of Special Plans was formally established as an expansion of the NESA's Northern Gulf Directorate to concentrate on policy issues with respect to Iran, Iraq and the Global War on Terrorism.

<u>Renaming</u>
It was titled the 'Directorate of Special Plans' because, at that time, the creation of an 'Iraq Planning' group (or similarly named group) in the Pentagon conducting specialized planning for a potential Iraq contingency could have undercut ongoing diplomatic efforts in the UN and elsewhere.

The Directorate of Special Plans was a policy planning group, nothing more. As such, it was a consumer, rather than producer of intelligence products.

<u>Mission</u>
It developed defense policy options for senior decision makers, coordinated those options within DoD and across the interagency, monitored the implementation of defense policy and recommended course corrections to defense policy.

It did not conduct intelligence collection, create intelligence products, conduct operational war planning, or implement policy.

In 2003, when planning for Iraq was no longer a sensitive issue, the office's name reverted to Near East, South Asia/Northern Gulf (NESA/NG) to reflect its regional focus.

OFFICE OF RECONSTRUCTION AND HUMANITARIAN ASSISTANCE (ORHA)
In January 2003, the Department of Defense created the Office of Reconstruction and Humanitarian Assistance (ORHA): an expeditionary interagency office with officials from all departments and agencies in charge of detailed planning and implementation.

Jay Garner created ORHA from scratch, staffed from over a dozen offices of the U.S. government, our coalition partners and from the private sector. ORHA managed the distribution of humanitarian assistance and began the process of building the new Iraq both physically and politically.

COALITION PROVISIONAL AUTHORITY (CPA)
When General Franks, as Commander of the Coalition Forces, declared Iraq's liberation, he announced the creation of the Coalition Provisional Authority (CPA). The CPA served, in effect, as the acting government pending the Iraqi people's creation of a new government. General Franks was the initial head of the CPA.

The CPA reported directly to the President through DoD. The rationale for reporting directly through DoD was based on lessons learned from Bosnia and a desire to eliminate a dual reporting and command structure.

In Bosnia, the U.N. was responsible for civil reconstruction, the judiciary and other ministries. The peacekeeping force however, operated under a different chain of command.

Many contend the lack of coordination between the military and civilian entities has led to the prolonged involvement of all parties. We did not want to repeat past mistakes.

The plan always was when major combat operations were completed, a senior civilian administrator would be appointed in Iraq and ORHA would report to that administrator.

The President named Ambassador L. Paul Bremer as his Envoy to Iraq, placing him in charge of all civilian U.S. personnel in Iraq, including ORHA.

It is untrue that Mr. Bremer's appointment reflected dissatisfaction with the work of Jay Garner. Mr. Garner's job leading ORHA was complex, the conditions difficult, and the time short. His achievements however, were substantial. He is deserving of great praise for his efforts.

COUNTER TERRORISM EVALUATION GROUP (CTEG)

While not involved in post-war planning, the CTEG is often confused with the Directorate of Special Plans.

After the attacks of September 11, 2001, our nation found itself, for the first time in our history, engaged in a war against a non-linear foe with no identifiable boundaries and a global organization. The Department of Defense identified a need to analyze conflict with a terrorist network, versus a traditional nation-state. In October of 2001, a two-person team was set up to study this issue.

The mission of the CTEG was to review the vast amount of existing intelligence on terrorist networks, think through how various terrorist organizations relate to each other and how they relate to different groups that support them; in particular, state sponsors. It did this on a global scale, not focusing on any particular nation or region.

Its main conclusion was that groups and states were willing to cooperate across philosophical, ideological lines in order to achieve their goals. During this study, some interesting observations about linkages between Iraq and al-Qaida were discovered. These observations were shared with the CIA and other groups among the intelligence community in August, 2002.

Document 558

Statement of US President George W. Bush on the Adoption of the Iraqi Transitional Administrative Law

8 March 2004[20]

I congratulate the Iraqi Governing Council and the Iraqi people on completing the Transitional Administrative Law for Iraq. This document is an important step toward the establishment of a sovereign government on June 30. It lays the foundation for democratic elections and for a new constitution, which will be written by an elected Iraqi assembly and approved by the Iraqi people.

This law provides a framework for continued cooperation among Iraq, members of the international Coalition, and the United Nations as the Iraqi people make progress towards democracy. And it provides the essential freedoms and rights to all Iraqis regardless of

[20] Public Papers of the Presidents of the United States, George W Bush, 2004, Bk 1: January 1 to June 30, 2004 (2007), 341-342.

gender, religion, or ethnic origin – including freedom of religion, freedom of speech and assembly, the right to a fair trial, and the right to choose their own representatives.

The adoption of this law marks a historic milestone in the Iraqi people's long journey from tyranny and violence to liberty and peace. While difficult work remains to establish democracy in Iraq, today's signing is a critical step in that direction.

Document 559

H. Res. 691: Congratulating the Interim Government of Iraq on Its Forthcoming Assumption of Sovereign Authority in Iraq

25 June 2004[21]

In the House of Representatives, U.S.,

Whereas in April 2003, the United States Armed Forces and other Coalition forces liberated the people of Iraq from the dictatorial regime of Saddam Hussein;

Whereas United Nations Security Council Resolution 1483 (May 22, 2003)[22] and the laws and usages of war authorized the Coalition Provisional Authority to govern Iraq on a temporary basis;

Whereas the Coalition Provisional Authority established an Iraqi Governing Council, broadly representative of the major geographic, ethnic, and religious groupings of Iraq, as well as a Cabinet, to assist in the governing of Iraq, and the Council was recognized by many members of the international community as a legitimate voice of the Iraqi people;

Whereas the United States and other Coalition members, in response to the desire of the Iraqi people for early self-government, worked with the Iraqi Governing Council to accelerate the transfer of power to the Iraqi people, with sovereignty to be transferred no later than the end of June 2004;

Whereas the Coalition Provisional Authority and the Iraqi Governing Council on March 8, 2004, agreed upon a Law of Administration for the State of Iraq for the Transitional Period that strongly protects the civil and political rights of Iraqis;

Whereas that Law and its Annex provide for a transition of power to an Iraqi Interim Government, for elections by the end of January 2005, for a Transitional National Assembly, which shall form an Iraqi Transitional Government and provide for the drafting and adoption of a permanent constitution, and, by the end of 2005, for a government chosen under the new constitution;

Whereas the Iraqi people have begun electing local officials in parts of Iraq under Coalition auspices and will have the opportunity to express their will in free and meaningful national elections for the first time in Iraq's history;

Whereas the United Nations Secretary General appointed a Special Adviser to conduct political consultations aimed at putting in place an Interim Government to assume sovereignty over Iraq;

Whereas the Iraqi Governing Council made recommendations about the composition of the Interim Government, after which, when the recommendations were accepted by the Coalition Provisional Authority, the Council dissolved itself;

[21] The resolution was passed by roll call vote with 352 in favour, 57 against, and 24 present but not voting. The text of the resolution is available at http://www.gpo.gov/.

[22] See *Doc 523*.

Whereas on June 8, 2004, the United Nations Security Council unanimously adopted Resolution 1546,[23] welcoming the formation and forthcoming 'assumption of full responsibility and authority by a fully sovereign and independent Interim Government of Iraq' and authorizing the multinational force under unified command to continue its activities;

Whereas the Coalition Provisional Authority will dissolve at the end of June 2004 and will not be replaced;

Whereas members of the United States Armed Forces, a total force consisting of active, reserve, and National Guard personnel, have performed their mission with great skill and courage, in the process being awarded at least 18 Distinguished Service Crosses, 6 Distinguished Flying Crosses, 133 Silver Stars, 16,551 Bronze Stars, and 4,161 Purple Hearts;

Whereas, as of June 23, 2004, 833 members of the United States Armed Forces, approximately 100 members of the Coalition forces, and many members of the Iraqi security services, have given their lives to advance the cause of liberty in Iraq, and thousands of members of the United States Armed Forces and Coalition forces, and many members of the Iraqi security services, have suffered wounds for that cause;

Whereas the families of American soldiers, sailors, airmen, Marines, and Coast Guardsmen have made and continue to make enormous sacrifices for their country;

Whereas in addition, Coalition forces, civilians employed by or assisting the Coalition Provisional Authority, the Iraqi government and its employees, international organizations, and American and other international volunteers, as well as large numbers of ordinary Iraqis, have made and continue to make enormous efforts to reconstruct the country and improve the lives of the Iraqi people;

Whereas Ambassador L. Paul Bremer, III, Presidential Envoy to Iraq and Administrator of the Coalition Provisional Authority, has ably advanced the international coalition's goals in Iraq of transforming Iraq into a safe, secure, stable, sovereign, democratic state that serves the interests of the Iraqi people;

Whereas the United States will be represented in Iraq by an Embassy led by Ambassador John D. Negroponte, and the United States will deal with the Government of Iraq on the basis of the sovereign equality of states under international law, including the Vienna Convention on Diplomatic Relations, to which both the United States and Iraq are parties;

Whereas after June 30, 2004, the Interim Government of Iraq and its successors, and United States Armed Forces and Coalition forces, will cooperate to meet ongoing security challenges and to extend security and stability to all regions of Iraq; and

Whereas the United States has never desired to exercise permanent sovereignty over Iraq and welcomes the formation of the Iraqi Interim Government and its imminent assumption of authority: Now, therefore, be it—

Resolved, That the House of Representatives—

(1) congratulates the Interim Government of Iraq on its forthcoming assumption of sovereign authority in Iraq;

(2) offers its continued support to the people and government of Iraq as they deal with the consequences of decades of misrule by the former regime of Saddam Hussein;

(3) expresses its gratitude to the United States Armed Forces for their ongoing valiant service to their country and commitment to the highest ideals and traditions of the American people;

(4) expresses its gratitude to the families of United States Armed Forces personnel, especially the families of those who have lost loved ones in Operation Iraqi Freedom and of those wounded in the service of their country, for their sacrifices;

[23] See *Doc 541*.

(5) expresses its condolences to the families of the innocent Iraqis who have been killed or wounded during the conflict, including those who were victimized by the illegal and terrorist tactics of the enemy, and despite the concerted efforts by the Coalition forces to minimize civilian casualties;

(6) expresses its gratitude to the Coalition forces, the Coalition Provisional Authority, the Iraqi Governing Council, the current Iraqi cabinet and government officials, and the many international bodies and voluntary organizations which have come to the aid of the people of Iraq in an effort to help them address the consequences of decades of misrule by the former regime of Saddam Hussein, as well as to the families of those mentioned in this paragraph, who have been lost in Iraq;

(7) offers its continued support to the United States Armed Forces, civilians associated with the United States Government, Coalition forces, and Iraqi security forces who continue to bear the burden of attacks from former regime elements, foreign and Iraqi terrorists, and other criminals who are attempting to undermine the interests of the Iraqi people and thwart their evident desire to live in peace;

(8) calls on the entire international community to promote the welfare of the Iraqi people by rendering, in addition to the generous assistance provided by the American people and, in varying degrees, by some nations, immediate, tangible, and generous assistance to the Iraqi people in the reconstruction of their nation, including, in response to requests from the Iraqi government coordinated with the command of the multinational forces, forces capable of assisting in the provision of security to the Iraqi people;

(9) reaffirms—

(A) that the United States Armed Forces operating in Iraq after June 30, 2004, will remain under the full authority, direction, and control of their American commanders; and

(B) the need to ensure that such Armed Forces will possess all necessary authority to fulfill their mission effectively and to provide for their operational safety; and

(10) urges the people of the United States and of other countries to celebrate, on June 30, 2004, the restoration of freedom to the people of Iraq through the efforts of the peoples of the United States, the Coalition, and Iraq.

Document 560
Exchange of Letters Establishing Diplomatic Relations between the United States of America and Iraq

27/28 June 2004[24]

June 27, 2004
His Excellency
Ayad Allawi
Prime Minister of the Republic of Iraq
Baghdad

[24] Texts of Letters on Iraq Sovereignty as Read by Scott McClellan, Hilton International Hotel Istanbul, Istanbul, Turkey, 28 June 2004, http://www.whitehouse.gov/.

Dear Mr. Prime Minister:

Congratulations on your recent appointment and to the Iraqi people on the great strides that have been made in the past year toward freedom and democracy in Iraq. The United States is a committed partner in this endeavor, and it is my honor to propose the establishment of diplomatic relations between the United States and Iraq with permanent missions, effective immediately upon the assumption of sovereign authority by the Iraqi Interim Government.

The United States reiterates its commitment to support your government as it leads Iraq toward national elections. I look forward to your response confirming the establishment of diplomatic relations between our two countries and to pursuing our shared vision for Iraq's journey to freedom.

Sincerely,

[Signed] *George W. Bush*

28 June 2003

Dear President Bush

I have received your letter of June 27, 2004 and have the honor of confirming the establishment of diplomatic relations with full diplomatic mission between Iraq and the United States.

Sincerely

[Signed] *Ayad Allawi*[25]

[25] On 29 June 2004, the Foreign Minister of Iraq, Hoshyar Zebari, wrote to US Secretary of State Colin Powell: 'Dear Mr. Secretary,

It is a great honor to receive your letter of 27th June, 2004 congratulating me on Iraq`s Resumption of sovereign authority and proposing establishment of diplomatic relations between our friendly nations.

While I appreciate your kind sentiment, I also wish to confirm to your Excellency that my Prime Minister, Mr. Ayad Allawi, has agreed in his letter to President George Bush on the re-establishment of diplomatic relations, effective immediately upon resumption of sovereign authority by Iraqi Interim Government.

He also agreed on the opening of the U.S. Embassy in Baghdad as well as offices in Basra, Kirkuk, Hilla, and Mosul, as well as the appointment of Mr. Negroponte as Ambassador Extraordinary and Plenipotentiary to Iraq.

It is also the intention of my Government to reopen the Embassy of the Republic of Iraq in Washington, and Iraqi consulates in some U.S. cities immediately after the establishment of diplomatic relations. It is the understanding of my Government that agrément has been granted on the aforementioned by means of the exchange of the Letters of Exchange between our two Governments.

I look forward to developing friendly and constructive relations between our two nations.

Please accept, your Excellency, my sincere wishes and kind regards.

Sincerely,

[Signed] *Hoshyar Zebari*'.

V

United Kingdom Policy and Other Documents on Iraq

Document 561
Foreign and Commonwealth Office Legal Advisers, Rights under International Law to Occupy and Administer Iraq after a Conflict

31 January 2003[1]

1. The rights of coalition forces to occupy Iraq following a conflict would be closely related to their rights under international law to use force. It is likely that those rights will be based on the express or implicit authorisation of the United Nations Security Council in a resolution adopted under Chapter VII of the Charter. Such an authorisation will not give an unlimited right to use force; the scope of the authorisation will need to be interpreted within the overall objective of Iraqi compliance with disarmament obligations imposed by the Security Council and the requirement for restoring international peace and security in the area. Any use of force would have to be limited to what is necessary to enforce those obligations and be a proportionate response to Iraq's breach. As regards occupation post-conflict, the authorisation will again only justify such steps as are necessary to achieve the above objectives. A coalition presence in Iraq post-conflict will became [sic] progressively more difficult to justify as time elapses following a conflict.

2. To the extent that Iraqi [sic] came under coalition control during the course of any conflict the rights and obligations of the coalition would be those of an Occupying Power, as set out in detail in Articles 42 to 56 of the Regulations annexed to Hague Convention IV of 1907, and in Geneva Convention IV relative to the Protection of Civilian Persons in Time of War of 1949. In general, the Occupying Power must take all measures in its power to restore and ensure public safety by respecting, unless absolutely prevented, the law in the occupied State (Hague Regulation Article 43). Detailed provisions include limited rights to take possession of and use state property as administrator and 'usufructuary' (Articles 53 and 55 of the Hague Regulations); to remove officials or judges (Articles 51 to 54 of the Geneva Convention); and to amend the penal laws of the occupying [sic] territory if they threaten security or impede compliance with international law and set up its own military courts to try offences under occupation legislation (Articles 64 to 67 of the Geneva Convention). The Geneva Convention also provides a comprehensive code on the protection of the civilian population and internees.

3. In these and other areas it is likely that aspects of the reconstruction of institutions and infrastructure post-conflict could fall outside the competencies of an Occupying Power under international law. For these reasons it is important that a further Security Council Resolution be adopted under Chapter VII as soon as possible to confer upon the coalition and/or other States and international organisations as appropriate the necessary powers. Possible recent precedents include the United Nations Interim Administrations in East Timor and Kosovo (see in particular Security Council Resolution 1244 (1999) on the latter). A United Nations administration would not be an occupying power and would not be constrained by the provisions of international humanitarian law though it should apply general international law, including human rights standards; rather, it would derive its powers (which could be very broad) from the Security Council Resolution authorising its presence. Equally

[1] The paper was prepared by John Grainger, Legal Counsellor at the FCO, at the request of the Cabinet Office and was transmitted on 31 January 2003 to Mr Pattison.

a military presence in Iraq post-conflict mandated by the UN would no longer be an occupying power regulated by the Hague and Geneva Conventions.

4. A further point is the alleged parallel with the situation following World War II in respect of Germany. The legal position there was, in brief, that from 18 September 1944, when allied troops first occupied German territory, until 5 June 1945, the territory of the German Reich came progressively under belligerent occupation. The provisions of the Hague Regulations were at that stage applicable (the Geneva Conventions not yet having been adopted). Allied legislation was enacted abrogating Nazi laws, dissolving the Nazi party and Nazi courts, suspending other courts and educational establishments. It is not clear that all of these measures were justified under the Hague Regulations on military necessity or human rights grounds (Articles 43 and 46 Hague Regulations).

5. On 5 June 1945 the four war time allies issued a declaration assuming supreme authority with respect to Germany, following the defeat and unconditional surrender of its armed forces. The declaration expressly provided that the annexation of Germany was not being effected. In substance, the declaration drew a distinction between the Government and the State; the wartime allies assumed all the powers of the former while stopping short of annexing and therefore extinguishing the latter. The powers exercised by the four powers pursuant to that declaration were governmental powers in the broadest sense, including on status questions such as Germany's borders.

6. In the case of measures in relation to Germany, Article 107 of the Charter of the UN, together with Article 53 (the so called 'enemy states' clauses), provided specifically that nothing in the Charter shall invalidate or preclude action taken by the war time allies as a result of that war. In the case of Iraq it is highly questionable whether such an assumption of power could be justified under current international law, unless authorised by the Security Council. In particular, it is difficult to see how such an extraordinary measure (which apart from Germany is unprecedented) could be regarded as proportionate to any authority granted by the Security Council to enforce Iraq's WMD obligations. Any measure falling outside this authorisation would be in breach of Article 2 (4) of the Charter of the United Nations (all members shall refrain in their international relations from the threat or use of force against the territorial integrity or political independence of any state) and the fundamental principle of non-intervention in matters which are essentially within the domestic jurisdiction of any State (Article 2(7)). No provision like Article 107 of the Charter would be available to protect coalition actions in respect of Iraq from the application of the provisions of the Charter.

Document 562
Iraq: Authorisation for an Interim Administration. Confidential Memorandum by the Attorney General the Rt Hon the Lord Goldsmith QC Addressed to Prime Minister Tony Blair

26 March 2003[2]

Confidential

Prime Minister

Iraq: Authorisation for an Interim Administration

1. I am writing to confirm the advice I gave at the meeting this morning concerning the need for UN Security Council authorisation for the coalition or the international community to establish an interim Iraqi administration to reform and restructure Iraq and its administration.

2. In short, my view is that a further Security Council resolution is needed to authorise imposing reform and restructuring of Iraq and its Government. In the absence of a further resolution, the UK (and US) would be bound by the provisions of international law governing belligerent occupation, notably the Fourth Geneva Convention and the 1907 Hague Regulations. The provisions of these treaties would need to be considered against specific proposals in order to give detailed advice on the precise limits of what is possible, but the general principle is that an Occupying Power does not become the government of the occupied territory. Rather, it exercises temporary de facto control in accordance with the defined rights and obligations under Geneva Convention IV and the Hague Regulations. These instruments are complex, but the following points give an indication of the limitations placed on the authority of an Occupying Power:

(a) Article 43 of the Hague Regulations imposes an obligation to respect the laws in force in the occupied territory 'unless absolutely prevented'. Thus, while some changes to the legislative and administrative structures of Iraq may be permissible if they are necessary for security or public order reasons, or in order to further humanitarian objectives, more wide-ranging reforms of governmental and administrative structures would not be lawful.

(b) Geneva Convention IV prohibits, subject to certain limited exceptions, any alteration in the status of public officials or judges (although officials may be removed from post in certain circumstances).

(c) Geneva Convention IV also requires that the penal laws of the occupied territory must remain in force except where they constitute a threat to security or an obstacle to application of the Convention. In addition, the courts of the occupied territory must be allowed to continue to function. There are limited exceptions allowing the Occupying Power to promulgate its own laws in order to fulfil its obligations under the Convention and to maintain security and public order, but in principle, the existing structures for the administration of justice must remain in place.

(d) Apart from rules on the collection of taxes (which must as far as possible be in accordance with existing local law), there are no specific provisions in Geneva Convention IV or the Hague Regulations dealing with the economy of the occupied territory. However,

[2] The Confidential Memorandum was first published in John Kampfner, Blair Was Told It Would Be Illegal to Occupy Iraq, *New Statesman*, No. 16, 26 May 2003, 17.

the general principle outlined in (a) above applies equally to economic reform, so that the imposition of major structural economic reforms would not be authorised by international law.

3. Different considerations could apply if it were suggested that the people of Iraq themselves were engaged in undertaking such governmental and administrative reform, but that is not what I understand is currently envisaged.

4. I can also confirm that the issues set out in paragraph 2 above are a separate matter from the question of whether a further Security Council resolution is necessary to amend the existing Oil for Food and sanctions regimes in order to secure the immediate delivery of humanitarian aid to Iraq.

5. Although unconnected with the requirement for a further Security Council resolution, a further complicating factor for the United Kingdom is the extent to which the ECHR [European Convention on Human Rights] and other international human rights instruments are likely to apply to any territory of which the UK is the Occupying Power. I am advising the Ministry of Defence separately on the extent of our ECHR obligations in Iraq.

6. Finally and in any event, it must be borne in mind that the lawfulness of any occupation after the conflict has ended is still governed by the legal basis for the use of force. As you know, any military action pursuant to the authorisation in resolution 678 (1990) must be limited to what is necessary to achieve the objectives of that resolution, namely Iraqi disarmament, and must be a proportionate response to that objective. The Government has concluded that the removal of the current Iraqi regime from power is necessary to secure disarmament, but the longer the occupation of Iraq continues, and the more the tasks undertaken by an interim administration depart from the main objective, the more difficult it will be to justify the lawfulness of the occupation. So in the absence of a further Security Council resolution, in addition to the issues raised in paragraph 2 above, it is likely to be difficult to justify the legality of the continued occupation of Iraq once the disarmament requirements of the relevant Security Council resolutions have been completed.

7. I am copying this note to the Foreign Secretary, the Secretary of State for International Development, the Defence Secretary and the Cabinet Secretary.

The Rt Hon the Lord Goldsmith QC
Attorney General
26 March 2003

Document 563
Letter from UK Foreign Secretary Jack Straw to Prime Minister Blair, Iraq: ORHA

7 April 2003[3]

[...] 4. The Attorney's initial reaction is that if we make formal appointments, then the risk of the United Kingdom being jointly responsible for *all* ORHA's actions increases (including in the 75%-80% of Iraq which will be under US and not UK de facto control).

[3] The document was declassified as part of the Iraq Inquiry, subject to redactions. For the original document, see http://www.iraqinquiry.org.uk. Annex E was declassified in full. Information provided by the Iraq Inquiry Secretariat on 9 Feb 2011.

5. To avoid this, we would need, in my view:
   i) a Memorandum of Understanding between the US and UK in which we specify full consultation and joint decision-making in advance of policy decisions about ORHA's activities.
   ii) clarity about the role of the UN (the greater this is, the more the other anxieties about ORHA could fall away).
6. I attach a draft MOU. [...]
7. I should emphasise that the Attorney said that he could not advise definitely on this issue without a little more time and being able to see some paperwork. A copy of this minute goes to him.

[Signed] *Jack Straw*

Annex E: Draft Memorandum of Understanding between the UK and US on ORHA

In the immediate aftermath of the conflict, the Coalition will aim to provide a secure environment in which humanitarian relief and the rehabilitation of essential services will be taken forward. In order to do this, the Coalition has created the Office of Reconstruction and Humanitarian Assistance (ORHA). The British Government supports these aims, which are obligations under international humanitarian law, and has appointed a number of serving British officials and military officers to work in ORHA.

The US and British Governments reaffirm their commitment at all time to act fully within international law. To that end, they have agreed that there should be full consultation (and joint decision-making) in advance of policy decisions about ORHA's activities. The British Government has confirmed its readiness to appoint Major General Tim Cross as one of Mr Jay Garner's deputies within ORHA.

Document 564
Memorandum from the Foreign and Commonwealth Office in Response to Questions Put by the House of Commons Foreign Affairs Committee

22 April 2003[4]

12. *In the letter of 8 April the Committee asked to receive a note on the legal rights, duties, obligations and limitations of occupying powers, both in general and also specifically under the Geneva conventions. In particular, the Committee would like the note to refer to the likely future position of the US and the UK as occupying powers in Iraq.*

The general principle is that an Occupying Power does not become the government of the occupied territory. Rather, it exercises temporary de facto control in accordance with in particular the provisions of Geneva Convention IV of 1949 and the Hague Regulations of 1907 (relevant extracts attached in Annexes A and B). These instruments are complex, but the following points give an indication of the position of an Occupying Power:

[4] House of Commons Foreign Affairs Committee, Foreign Policy Aspects of the War against Terrorism, Tenth Report of Session 2002-03, Report, together with formal minutes, oral and written evidence. Ordered by The House of Commons to be printed 15 July 2003 (HC (2002-03) 405, 31 July 2003), Minutes of Evidence, 29 April 2003.

(a) Under Article 43 of the Hague Regulations, authority having passed into the hands of the Occupying Power, the latter shall take all the measures in its power to restore and ensure, as far as possible, public order and safety, while respecting, unless absolutely prevented, the laws in force in the country. Thus, while changes to the legislative and administrative structures of Iraq are permissible if they are necessary for security or public order reasons, or in order to further humanitarian objectives, the occupant should not undertake more wide ranging reforms of governmental and administrative structures.

(b) Geneva Convention IV provides that the occupant should not alter the status of public officials or judges (although officials may be removed from their posts). If there is no functioning local administration, there is scope for an occupying power to introduce its own administrative system if that is necessary for maintenance of good order in the occupied territory.

(c) Geneva Convention IV also provides for the penal laws of the occupied territory to remain in force except where they constitute a threat to security or an obstacle to application of the Convention. To enforce those laws the courts of the occupied territory are to be allowed to continue to function. The Occupying Power may promulgate its own laws in order to fulfil its obligations under the Convention and to maintain security and public order.

(d) Apart from rules on the collection of taxes (which must as far as possible be in accordance with existing local law), there are no specific provisions in Geneva Convention IV or the Hague Regulations dealing with the economy of the occupied territory. However, the general principle outlined in (a) above applies equally to economic reform, so that the Occupying Power should not undertake major structural economic reforms.

In each case the application of the Hague Regulations and the Geneva Conventions to the actions of the occupying powers in Iraq will need to be considered in the light of the specific circumstances.

These provisions will not apply to the people of Iraq themselves, if through a legitimately established authority they undertake governmental and administrative reform.

Foreign and Commonwealth Office
April 2003

Annex A
1949 GENEVA CONVENTION IV
Articles 54-64

Art 54. The Occupying Power may not alter the status of public officials or judges in the occupied territories, or in any way apply sanctions to or take any measures of coercion or discrimination against them, should they abstain from fulfilling their functions for reasons of conscience.

This prohibition does not prejudice the application of the second paragraph of Art 51. It does not affect the right of the Occupying Power to remove public officials from their posts.

Art 55. To the fullest extent of the means available to it, the Occupying Power has the duty of ensuring the food and medical supplies of the population; it should, in particular, bring in the necessary foodstuffs, medical stores and other articles if the resources of the occupied territory are inadequate.

The Occupying Power may not requisition foodstuffs, articles or medical supplies available in the occupied territory, except for use by the occupation forces and administration personnel, and then only if the requirements of the civilian population have been taken into account. Subject to the provisions of other international Conventions, the Occupying Power shall make arrangements to ensure that fair value is paid for any requisitioned goods.

The Protecting Power shall, at any time, be at liberty to verify the state of the food and medical supplies in occupied territories, except where temporary restrictions are made necessary by imperative military requirements.

Art 56. To the fullest extent of the means available to it, the Occupying Power has the duty of ensuring and maintaining, with the cooperation of national and local authorities, the medical and hospital establishments and services, public health and hygiene in the occupied territory, with particular reference to the adoption and application of the prophylactic and preventive measures necessary to combat the spread of contagious diseases and epidemics. Medical personnel of all categories shall be allowed to carry out their duties.

If new hospitals are set up in occupied territory and if the competent organs of the occupied State are not operating there, the occupying authorities shall, if necessary, grant them the recognition provided for in Art 18. In similar circumstances, the occupying authorities shall also grant recognition to hospital personnel and transport vehicles under the provisions of Articles 20 and 21.

In adopting measures of health and hygiene and in their implementation, the Occupying Power shall take into consideration the moral and ethical susceptibilities of the population of the occupied territory.

Art 57. The Occupying Power may requisition civilian hospitals only temporarily and only in cases of urgent necessity for the care of military wounded and sick, and then on condition that suitable arrangements are made in due time for the care and treatment of the patients and for the needs of the civilian population for hospital accommodation.

The material and stores of civilian hospitals cannot be requisitioned so long as they are necessary for the needs of the civilian population.

Art 58. The Occupying Power shall permit ministers of religion to give spiritual assistance to the members of their religious communities.

The Occupying Power shall also accept consignments of books and articles required for religious needs and shall facilitate their distribution in occupied territory.

Art 59. If the whole or part of the population of an occupied territory is inadequately supplied, the Occupying Power shall agree to relief schemes on behalf of the said population, and shall facilitate them by all the means at its disposal.

Such schemes, which may be undertaken either by States or by impartial humanitarian organizations such as the International Committee of the Red Cross, shall consist, in particular, of the provision of consignments of foodstuffs, medical supplies and clothing.

All Contracting Parties shall permit the free passage of these consignments and shall guarantee their protection.

A Power granting free passage to consignments on their way to territory occupied by an adverse Party to the conflict shall, however, have the right to search the consignments, to regulate their passage according to prescribed times and routes, and to be reasonably satisfied through the Protecting Power that these consignments are to be used for the relief of the needy population and are not to be used for the benefit of the Occupying Power.

Art 60. Relief consignments shall in no way relieve the Occupying Power of any of its responsibilities under Articles 55, 56 and 59. The Occupying Power shall in no way whatsoever divert relief consignments from the purpose for which they are intended, except in cases of urgent necessity, in the interests of the population of the occupied territory and with the consent of the Protecting Power.

Art 61. The distribution of the relief consignments referred to in the foregoing Articles shall be carried out with the cooperation and under the supervision of the Protecting Power. This duty may also be delegated, by agreement between the Occupying Power and the Protecting Power, to a neutral Power, to the International Committee of the Red Cross or to any other impartial humanitarian body.

Such consignments shall be exempt in occupied territory from all charges, taxes or customs duties unless these are necessary in the interests of the economy of the territory. The Occupying Power shall facilitate the rapid distribution of these consignments.

All Contracting Parties shall endeavour to permit the transit and transport, free of charge, of such relief consignments on their way to occupied territories.

Art 62. Subject to imperative reasons of security, protected persons in occupied territories shall be permitted to receive the individual relief consignments sent to them.

Art 63. Subject to temporary and exceptional measures imposed for urgent reasons of security by the Occupying Power:

(a) recognized National Red Cross (Red Crescent, Red Lion and Sun) Societies shall be able to pursue their activities in accordance with Red Cross principles, as defined by the International Red Cross Conferences. Other relief societies shall be permitted to continue their humanitarian activities under similar conditions;

(b) the Occupying Power may not require any changes in the personnel or structure of these societies, which would prejudice the aforesaid activities.

The same principles shall apply to the activities and personnel of special organizations of a non-military character which already exist or which may be established, for the purpose of ensuring the living conditions of the civilian population by the maintenance of the essential public utility services, by the distribution of relief and by the organization of rescues.

Art 64. The penal laws of the occupied territory shall remain in force, with the exception that they may be repealed or suspended by the Occupying Power in cases where they constitute a threat to its security or an obstacle to the application of the present Convention. Subject to the latter consideration and to the necessity for ensuring the effective administration of justice, the tribunals of the occupied territory shall continue to function in respect of all offences covered by the said laws.

The Occupying Power may, however, subject the population of the occupied territory to provisions which are essential; to enable the Occupying Power to fulfil its obligations under the present Convention, to maintain the orderly government of the territory, and to ensure the security of the Occupying Power, of the members and property of the occupying forces or administration, and likewise of the establishments and lines of communication used by them.

Annex B

THE HAGUE CONVENTION,
Hague Convention IV (18 October 1907)
Convention Respecting the Laws and Customs of War on Land

SECTION III

Military Authority over the Territory of the Hostile State

Art 42. Territory is considered occupied when it is actually placed under the authority of the hostile army.

The occupation extends only to the territory where such authority has been established and can be exercised.

Art 43. The authority of the legitimate power having in fact passed into the hands of the occupant, the latter shall take all the measures in his power to restore, and ensure, as far as possible, public order and safety, while respecting, unless absolutely prevented, the laws in force in the country.

Art 44. A belligerent is forbidden to force the inhabitants of territory occupied by it to furnish information about the army of the other belligerent, or about its means of defence.

Art 45. It is forbidden to compel the inhabitants of occupied territory to swear allegiance to the hostile Power.

Art 46. Family honour and rights, the lives of persons, and private property, as well as religious convictions and practice, must be respected.

Private property cannot be confiscated.

Art 47. Pillage is formally forbidden.

Art 48. If, in the territory occupied, the occupant collects the taxes, dues, and tolls imposed for the benefit of the State, he shall do so, as far as is possible, in accordance with the rules of assessment and incidence in force, and shall in consequence be bound to defray the expenses of the administration of the occupied territory to the same extent as the legitimate Government was so bound.

Art 49. If, in addition to the taxes mentioned in the above article, the occupant levies other money contributions in the occupied territory, this shall only be for the needs of the army or of the administration of the territory in question.

Art 50. No general penalty, pecuniary or otherwise, shall be inflicted upon the population on account of the acts of individuals for which they cannot be regarded as jointly and severally responsible.

Art 51. No contribution shall be collected except under a written order, and on the responsibility of a commander-in-chief. The collection of the said contribution shall only be effected as far as possible in accordance with the rules of assessment and incidence of the taxes in force.

For every contribution a receipt shall be given to the contributors.

Art 52. Requisitions in kind and services shall not be demanded from municipalities or inhabitants except for the needs of the army of occupation. They shall be in proportion to the resources of the country, and of such a nature as not to involve the inhabitants in the obligation of taking part in military operations against their own country.

Such requisitions and services shall only be demanded on the authority of the commander in the locality occupied.

Contributions in kind shall as far as possible be paid for in cash; if not, a receipt shall be given and the payment of the amount due shall be made as soon as possible.

Art 53. An army of occupation can only take possession of cash, funds, and realizable securities which are strictly the property of the State, depots of arms, means of transport, stores and supplies, and, generally, all movable property belonging to the State which may be used for military operations.

All appliances, whether on land, at sea, or in the air, adapted for the transmission of news, or for the transport of persons or things, exclusive of cases governed by naval law, depots of arms, and, generally, all kinds of munitions of war, may be seized, even if they belong to private individuals, but must be restored and compensation fixed when peace is made.

Art 54. Submarine cables connecting an occupied territory with a neutral territory shall not be seized or destroyed except in the case of absolute necessity. They must likewise be restored and compensation fixed when peace is made.

Art 55. The occupying State shall be regarded only as administrator and usufructuary of public buildings, real estate, forests, and agricultural estates belonging to the hostile State, and situated in the occupied country. It must safeguard the capital of these properties, and administer them in accordance with the rules of usufruct.

Art 56. The property of municipalities, that of institutions dedicated to religion, charity and education, the arts and sciences, even when State property, shall be treated as private property.

All seizure of, destruction or wilful damage done to institutions of this character, historic monuments, works of art and science, is forbidden, and should be made the subject of legal proceedings.

Document 565
Comments Made by UK Permanent Representative Sir Jeremy Greenstock After Presentation of Joint Draft of Security Council Resolution on Iraq

9 May 2003[5]

Let me start by saying that the United Kingdom is very pleased to be one of those setting down and tabling a draft resolution with the United States and Spain, I should make absolutely

[5] Transcript of UN Webcast, available at http://www.un.org/webcast/.

clear at this start point, of what I think will be an important debate, that it is not an omnibus resolution. It does not seek to cover absolutely everything that needs to be done by the Council in the next stages. It is designed to be a significant next step in four areas that have not yet been addressed by the Council. One is to set out some principles for this next period of activity on Iraq and the preambular paragraphs mainly do that. What we are trying to do in the Council and in the coalition on the ground is serve the needs of the Iraqi people and restore Iraq back to Iraqis for their own purposes and their own benefit as quickly as possible.

Second, we need to establish what a vital role for the United Nations as President Bush and Prime Minister Blair at Hillsborough said,[6] will be and parts of the resolution do that specifically, operative paragraph eight sets out the beginnings of a mandate for the special co-ordinator that we request from the Secretary-General.

Thirdly, there is a proposal to lift sanctions because things have changed and the Iraqi people no longer want or need the sanctions so lets move on. And fourthly there are a number of paragraphs that set out economic, humanitarian and funding arrangements particularly through the use of the oil sector which the Council needs to make a decision on. So those are the four main reasons.

We are ready for a good debate on those. So far in the Council there has been a decidedly constructive atmosphere. Plenty of questions, particularly legal questions, about what the language means. Plenty of queries as to what the political framework really is going to be. That's entirely to be expected because we are moving into a new era and what has happened has been most unusual. But I think the Council is pleased to see that we, the powers on the ground in the coalition, accept that we are occupying powers and that establishes a basis for a clear political discussion as to what happens next and how the international community adds itself on to that occupying authority and how the UN should be involved in it. And I sense in the responses we have had so far a wish to look forward, not back, a wish to decide on these questions in a way which is balanced. No great need to overreach for the United Nations or the international community in this stage when the authority on the ground has a definite obligation to fulfil. And therefore room for a debate to a conclusion that will produce a good result for the Council and that is what we are looking for between now and the end of May. So I think that is a good start and we want to follow-up on that.

Q: For several months you've been saying that Iraq's oil wealth is for the Iraqi people, but we see in the resolution its going to be spent by the occupying powers. Why is that?

A: Because it is going to be spent for the Iraqi people in a system which needs to be established that works. There is at the moment a fair degree of disorder on the ground. That needs to be improved. The occupying powers are conscious of that and the coalition authority is getting down to that, I would say in a very fast and efficient way, but the Iraqi people are not yet in a position to look after all these aspects for themselves. The quicker we can bring it back to them the better.

Q: Mr Ambassador the UN currently has control of these funds in the ESCROW account. Why would it not be possible for the UN to be a party to help control in the future? The resolution does not envision that, it envisions only a UN monitoring role, if the UN can be trusted with the funds now, why could it not be trusted as a partner to spend the funds in the future?

A: Because the UN, in the arrangements that applied at the beginning of conflict were working with the Iraqi government. There is no Iraqi government to work with. There is an authority on the ground that we are admitting is an occupying authority, that is the reason there needs to be a new authority on the ground and therefore new arrangements.

[6] See *Doc 573*.

Q: Mr Ambassador on the issue of the United States and Britain stating publicly really for the first time that they are the occupying powers, could you tell us the actual legal ramifications of this is? What are the implications and why was the Council welcoming of this?

A: It isn't the first time. We acknowledge that implicitly in the passage of 1472 and 1476,[7] in the arrangements of the Secretary-General to deploy the ESCROW account differently so we don't have a problem over that. We are accepting that there are conventions and regulations Geneva and the Hague which we need to respect, but there needs now to be a series of things done on the ground that goes beyond the minimum requirements of occupying powers and we want the international community to be involved in that endeavour. So it is a combination of being an occupying power and an authority that wants to do something for the Iraqi people that restores Iraq to a stable prosperous country being worked on by the Iraqi people for all Iraqis on the ground. That's the reason, it's a combination.

Q: Ambassador you mentioned other people who might join the authority. Would that include other members of the Security Council? [...]

A: As I understand the approaches of our government and there are lots of decisions to be made on this, I can't be categorical, none of this is exclusive of anybody.

Preambular paragraph twelve that notes the letter that we have just sent makes it clear that others who want to join on needn't be occupying powers. It is others who want to take on the responsibilities of helping. But we accept that the United States and the United Kingdom in particular must carry the responsibilities of occupation. Apart from that anybody who wants to contribute to the aims we set out in this draft are as I understand my governments decision, most welcome.

Q: Mr Ambassador the perception in the Middle East that you are really in a hurry to try and get your hands on the oil fields of Iraq through this draft resolution [...].

A: [...] But if you are referring to what happens in the oil fields, for a temporary period, while we control the security and what happens on the ground we want those oil fields to be regenerated as a benefit as an instrument for the Iraqi people, and we are very keen that that should be done efficiently. We are very encouraged by the degree that the Iraqis themselves want to come back into their jobs to get their system running. They are a competent people who can do this and as soon as that can be done within their own structures, within their own competence you will find that the coalition will be handing over to them to the greatest extent possible. So that's going to be the principle under which we work, we want to leave Iraq as soon as it is possible to ensure stability and normal arrangements.

Document 566

Statement about Iraq by UK Secretary of State for Foreign and Commonwealth Affairs

12 May 2003[8]

Last Friday [9 May 2003], the United Kingdom, the United States and Spain informally circulated a draft resolution about Iraq's future to members of the United Nations Security

[7] See *Docs 519* and *520*, respectively.

[8] HC Debs, vol 405, cols. 21-24: 12 May 2003. Compare this statement with the Personal Statement by Clare Short, Secretary of State for International Development, following her resignation as a result of British Government's policy over Iraq: ibid., cols. 36-39: 12 May 2003.

Council.[9] I have placed copies in the Library and the Vote Office. Our aim is to put Iraq in the hands of its people through an open and accountable process, in partnership with the emerging leaders of the new Iraq. The draft resolution sets out the United Nations' role in that process, and calls for the United Nations to

> 'play a vital role in providing humanitarian relief, in supporting the reconstruction of Iraq, and in helping in the formation of an Iraqi Interim Authority.'

That reflects fully the undertakings given by my right hon. Friend the Prime Minister and President Bush at their Hillsborough meeting on 8 April.[10] I will set out for the House the main points of that draft resolution and, in the course of doing so, deal with a number of questions that have been asked about it. [...]

The United Kingdom and the United States fully accept our responsibilities under the fourth Geneva convention and the Hague regulations. That point is explicitly recognised in the draft resolution. Neither the Secretary-General nor members of the Security Council are proposing that the UN should run Iraq, but we are all concerned to ensure that the UN plays a vital post-conflict role. The draft resolution gives the UN the full opportunity to do just that. It does not deal with every issue; it concentrates on the main points that need to be settled now for the benefit of the people of Iraq. It sets out important principles for the future of Iraq, including those on territorial integrity and disarmament of its weapons of mass destruction. The resolution also provides, in operative paragraph 5, for member states to prohibit trade in, or transfer of, looted cultural artefacts.

The three key issues in the resolution are, first, the role of a UN special co-ordinator, and the associated political processes; secondly, the lifting of sanctions and the creation of a new Iraqi assistance fund to target resources on the reconstruction of Iraq; and thirdly, arrangements for the sale of oil and the handling of oil revenues. I shall deal with those in turn.

Operative paragraph 8 of the resolution sets out a substantial mandate for a UN special co-ordinator to be appointed by the UN Secretary-General and to play a full part in all aspects of post-conflict activity, from humanitarian efforts through economic reconstruction, human rights, rebuilding police capacity, promoting legal and judicial reform, and, crucially, the political process. On the latter point, the draft provides that the special co-ordinator should work with the occupying powers and those assisting them – defined collectively in the resolution as 'the Authority'[11] – for

> 'the restoration and establishment of national and local institutions for representative governance'.

Operative paragraph 9

> 'supports the formation, by the people of Iraq with the help of the Authority and working with the Special Co-ordinator, of an Iraqi interim authority as a transitional administration run by Iraqis until a permanent government is established by the people of Iraq'.

Like all drafts, this one is open to improvement and we are discussing it constructively with our Security Council partners, but the mandate in the present draft will give the UN

[9] See *Doc 523*.

[10] See *Doc 573*.

[11] The original draft resolution of 9 May 2003 spoke of 'recognizing the specific authorities, responsibilities, and obligations under applicable international law of these states [the United States and the United Kingdom] *and others* working now or in future with them under unified command as the occupying power (the "authority")'. In the final version of the resolution, however, a clear distinction is made between the United States and the United Kingdom acting as 'occupying powers' and 'other States that are not occupying powers' working with them now or in future. For the text of Security Council resolution 1483, see *Doc 523*.

the scope it needs to play its full role in all aspects of post-conflict Iraq. One of the reasons why I would like to see the resolution passed quickly is to enable a special co-ordinator, appointed by the Secretary-General, to get cracking on the ground very soon.

The second of the three issues is the lifting of sanctions and the creation of a new Iraqi assistance fund. Economic sanctions relate to Iraq's past and now need to be removed, so operative paragraph 10 provides that all sanctions are lifted forthwith, with the sole exception of the arms embargo, which plainly has to remain in place until a permanent Government is established by the people of Iraq. Ending the economic sanctions regime requires new arrangements for dealing with Iraqi revenues. The wording in the resolution is designed to ensure that all funds from Iraqi oil revenues can be used quickly and effectively for the benefit of the Iraqi people.

The draft resolution gives the Secretary-General authority for a period of four months from its passage to ensure the delivery of priority civilian goods under contracts already approved and for which funding has been allocated.

Remaining funds in the existing escrow account, from what is known as the oil-for-food programme, will be transferred to the new Iraqi assistance fund. That will also receive funds from two other sources: revenues from the sale of oil, and funds of the former regime frozen by banks outside Iraq since 1990 under successive Security Council resolutions. The Iraqi assistance fund will therefore rapidly become the primary source of money for the development of Iraq. The funds will be disbursed by the authority in consultation with the Iraqi interim authority.

The resolution is specific about the purposes for which the money can be spent. Operative paragraph 13 spells out that

> 'the funds should be used to meet the humanitarian needs of the Iraqi people, for the economic reconstruction and repair of Iraq's infrastructure, for the continued disarmament of Iraq, and for the costs of indigenous civilian administration and for other purposes benefiting the people of Iraq.'

The assistance fund will be subject to an international advisory board, including representatives of the UN Secretary-General, the IMF and the World Bank, and will be audited by independent public accountants, again chosen by the board, not by the coalition.

The third issue is the control of oil sales. Operative paragraph 18 requires that sales shall be made

> 'consistent with prevailing international market practices',

that they too will be audited by independent public accountants reporting to the international advisory board, and that the funds will go to the Iraqi assistance fund, except for a proportion, which will go instead to the UN Compensation Commission for claims relating to the previous Gulf war.

On weapons of mass destruction, a letter to the Security Council annexed to the resolution stresses the obvious and clear importance of this objective. Dr. Blix himself has recognised that the situation is not right at present for UNMOVIC to return, a point that I was able to spell out in the statement that I made to the House just 13 days ago.[12] Separate arrangements may therefore be needed to provide international validation, so the role of UNMOVIC in Iraq is not an issue that needs to be dealt with in this resolution, although we may need to address it in future resolutions.

In the interests of the people of Iraq, the sponsors of the resolution will be working for its early adoption, but it is not a take it or leave it text, and negotiations with our

[12] For the statement of the Secretary of State for Foreign and Commonwealth Affairs Jack Straw on Iraq and on the middle east peace process, see HC Debs, vol 404, cols. 21-24: 28 April 2003.

partners in the Security Council are already under way. However, from my discussions with Foreign Ministers of Security Council members, and other discussions undertaken by our permanent representative in New York, I find a strong political will to get the UN back into the business of helping to build a better future for Iraq. This draft resolution gives the UN that very important role.

Document 567

Iraq: Effect of Security Council Resolution 1483 on the Authority of the Occupying Powers. Legal Advice by the UK Attorney-General

9 June 2003[13]

1. Thank you for your letter of 21 May 2003 requesting the advice of the Attorney General on whether the draft Security Council resolution on post-conflict Iraq would authorise the Coalition to undertake action going beyond the scope of their authority as Occupying Powers. I am writing to record the Attorney's views.

Summary: Resolution 1483[14] confers a clear mandate on the Coalition working with the Special Representative of the Secretary General (SRSG), to facilitate a process leading to the establishment by the people of Iraq, first, of an Iraqi interim administration and subsequently of an internationally recognised representative government. The resolution clarifies the legitimate scope of activity of the Occupying Powers and authorises them to undertake actions for the reform and reconstruction of Iraq going beyond the limitations of Geneva Convention IV and the Hague Regulations. In some cases such actions must be carried out in coordination with the SRSG or in consultation with the IIA.

2. The draft resolution was adopted on 22 May by the Security Council as resolution 1483. The advice which follows is based on the final text of the resolution (but this appears to be in substantially the same terms as the draft attached to your letter).

3. The Attorney considers that, in analysing the legal effect of the resolution, account can be taken, not only of the terms of the resolution itself, but also of the letter dated 8 May from the UK and US Permanent Representatives to the United Nations to the President of the Security Council.[15] In that letter, the Coalition Partners described the actions which they were taking and intended to take, in accordance with their obligations under international law, in order to meet the objective of the complete disarmament of Iraq of weapons of mass destruction. Although the Fourth Geneva Convention and the Hague Regulations ('occupation law') are not explicitly mentioned, the reference to international law obligations must in the circumstances be taken as referring principally to these instruments. It follows that the 8 May letter amounts to an assertion by the US and UK Governments that the catalogue of activities mentioned in the letter may lawfully be carried out under the terms of occupation law. In preambular paragraph (PP) 13 of resolution 1483, the Security Council notes the letter of 8 May and recognises 'the specific authorities, responsibilities and obligations under

[13] Letter, dated 9 June 2003, from Cathy Adams, The Legal Secretariat to the Law Officers, Attorney General's Chambers, to Huw Llewellyn, Legal Counsellor, Foreign and Commonwealth Office. The letter was made public by the Iraq Inquiry and is available at http://www.iraqinquiry.org.uk/.

[14] See *Doc 523*.

[15] See *Doc 574*.

applicable international law of [the Coalition] states as occupying powers under unified command'. The Attorney considers that it can be argued on the basis of this paragraph that the Security Council has effectively endorsed the Coalition's view that the catalogue of activities contained in the 8 May letter constitute legitimate activities for an occupying power. The endorsement by the Security Council therefore provides helpful, although not conclusive, clarification of the legitimate scope of activity of the Coalition.

4. Your letter identifies two areas in which the resolution develops the previous legal position as reflected in the Attorney's advice of 26 March:[16] the political process; and reconstruction work.

Political process

5. As noted in your letter, resolution 1483 has a number of provisions which deal with the political process. There are two main themes running through all these provisions:

- recognition of the rights of the Iraqi people freely to determine their political future (see PP4, OP4); and
- encouragement towards the establishment of a representative government in Iraq (see PPs 5-7, OP8(c), OP9).

It is argued that these provisions of the resolution collectively amount to a mandate to the Iraqi people to establish a representative government and therefore their choices in determining their political future have been limited by the Security Council. The Attorney is not convinced that this is a correct reading of the effect of the resolution, as it is hard to square this analysis with the stress laid on the rights of the Iraqi people freely to determine their political future. Moreover, he considers that the resolution must be interpreted consistently with the purposes and principles of the United Nations, which include in Article 1(2) of the Charter, 'respect for the principle of equal rights and self-determination of peoples'. The Attorney considers that it is difficult to see how it is compatible with the Iraqi people's right of self-determination to argue that the Security Council has to some extent pre-determined the outcome of the political process. The Attorney acknowledges that the resolution places considerable emphasis on the establishment of a representative government in Iraq, which is clearly the desired outcome of the Security Council. The resolution therefore constrains what the Coalition can help the Iraqi people to do. But the Attorney considers that it goes too far to argue that the resolution constrains the rights of the Iraqi people themselves in this respect.

6. As for the powers of the Coalition, the Attorney considers that the provisions in Pps 5-7, operational paragraph (OP) 8(c) and OP9 constitute a clear mandate for the Coalition, working with the Special Representative of the Secretary General (SRSG), to facilitate a process leading to the establishment by the people of Iraq, first, of an interim Iraqi administration (IIA) and subsequently of an internationally recognised representative government. The Attorney agrees, however, that the resolution does not give the Coalition any authority to control the political process nor engineer the outcome.

7. The Attorney notes the fact that the IIA is likely to be under the control of the Occupying Powers in the initial phase of its existence. The Attorney agrees that if the IIA were to be structured so that it does in fact operate under Coalition control, then its scope of authority would not extend beyond that of the Coalition under occupation law and such further powers as conferred on the Coalition by the resolution.

8. The Attorney notes, however, that it might be argued that such an outcome is incompatible with OP9 of the resolution which states that the Council supports 'the formation by the people of Iraq with the help of the [Coalition] and working with the

[16] For the Attorney General's advice of 26 March 2003, see *Doc 562*.

Special Representative, of an Iraqi interim administration as a transitional administration run by Iraqis, until an internationally recognised representative government is established by the people of Iraq and assumes the responsibilities of the [Coalition]'. The underlined words could be read as indicating that the Council intended the IIA to have at least some degree of independence from the Coalition. On the other hand, the paragraph clearly envisages that the Coalition will retain their role (and authority) as Occupying Powers until the establishment of an internationally recognised Iraqi government. The Council cannot therefore have intended that the Coalition should hand over executive authority to the IIA immediately it is established. Moreover, OP13 provides for the IIA to have an advisory rather than an executive role in relation to the disbursement of funds from the Development Fund for Iraq (DFI). In these circumstances, the Attorney considers that there are reasonable grounds for maintaining that a progressive transfer of power from the Coalition to the IIA is compatible with OP9 of the resolution.

9. The Attorney has seen recent reporting which indicates that the political process may develop in a rather different way to that envisaged in paragraph 6 of your letter. John Sawers' latest report (Iraqrep telno 28 of 1 June) suggests that the IIA will be a framework rather than a single body, which will comprise a Political Council, a Council of Interim Ministers and a number of Commissions to carry out specific tasks. It appears that the idea of a national conference has been put on ice. The Attorney considers that these proposals raise a number of questions regarding their compatibility with resolution 1483:

(a) OP9 of the resolution envisages the 'formation by the people of Iraq ... of an Iraqi interim administration'. It is not clear from the reporting how and by whom all the elements of the proposed IIA will be established, but it appears that the Political Council will be in effect self-appointed. The question therefore arises as to whether this is compatible with OP9. Clearly the views of the UN Special Representative will be critical on this issue if the Coalition wishes to be able to maintain the view that these arrangements are in line with what was envisaged in the resolution.

(b) The establishment of an IIA in accordance with OP9 of the resolution is also important because OP13 and OP16 of the resolution authorise the Coalition to undertake certain action in consultation with the IIA. These paragraphs must be interpreted as referring to an IIA constituted in accordance with OP9. Questions therefore may be raised about the legitimacy of Coalition action under OPs 13 and 16 if there is no IIA, or if it appears that the body which has been established is not an IIA as envisaged in OP9.

(c) If the IIA is to be a framework, rather than a single institution, the question arises as to which element of the IIA should be consulted under OPs 13 and 16.

(d) It appears from the reporting that the Commissions will undertake activities going beyond the scope of authority of an Occupying Power and yet these Commissions will be subject to the control of the Coalition. As discussed in paragraph 7 above, if they remain under Coalition control, the Commissions will not be entitled to exercise greater authority than the Coalition itself has under occupation law and resolution 1483. It will therefore be important to ensure that the Commissions operate within these constraints. However, the Attorney agrees with your analysis that once an IIA is established in accordance with OP9, to the extent that it acquires executive authority independent of the Coalition, its actions will no longer be governed by occupation law.

Reconstruction

10. The Attorney considers that the key provisions of the resolution in assessing its effect on the Coalition's powers in the areas other than the political process are PP13 and OPs 4, 5, 8 and 14.

11. As discussed in paragraph 3 above, the effect of PP13 is to endorse (and legitimise) the Coalition's own description of the scope of authority of an Occupying Power. OP5 of the resolution, which calls on all concerned to comply with their obligations under the Geneva Conventions and Hague Regulations therefore has to be read in this context. OP4, which calls upon the Coalition, consistent with the Charter and other relevant international law, to establish 'effective administration' in Iraq does not add much to the Coalition's existing obligations in this respect.

12. However, the Attorney considers that OP8 does appear to mandate the Coalition to engage in activity going beyond the scope of authority of an Occupying Power. OP8 is principally directed at the SRSG, but the activities set out in sub-paragraphs (a)-(i) which he is directed to conduct are to be carried out 'in coordination with the [Coalition]', which must be read as implied recognition of the Coalition's authority to engage in such activities. The Attorney considers that paragraphs (e) (promote economic reconstruction and the conditions for sustainable development), (g) (promote the protection of human rights) and (i) (encourage international efforts to promote legal and judicial reform) in particular could encompass activity going beyond the limits of occupation law. However, to the extent that the Coalition's involvement in activities falling under these headings is not otherwise authorised elsewhere in the resolution or under occupation law, then there is a clear requirement that the Coalition's action should be undertaken only in coordination with the SRSG.

13. OP14 of the resolution authorises the Coalition, in consultation with the IIA, to disburse funds from the DFI in support of a wide range of reconstruction activities. The Attorney agrees that the general references to 'economic reconstruction' and 'other purposes benefiting the people of Iraq' mean that the scope of activity authorised by this paragraph is potentially very broad. The extent to which OP14 authorises activity going beyond occupation law is a debatable, but moot, point now that the resolution has been adopted.

14. On the face of it, the Attorney also agrees that the resolution leaves it to the Coalition to decide whether or not a project to be funded under the residual category will in fact benefit the Iraqi people. But he considers that the Coalition is likely to need to provide some objective reasoning for that assessment if they are to satisfy the International Advisory and Monitoring Board established by OP12 and are to avoid criticism that they are abusing these powers. (The Attorney does not agree with the suggestion he has seen in one report that the IAMB's sole function should be to appoint the auditors of the Fund. He does not consider this to be a tenable interpretation of OP12. The name of the Board alone suggests that it is intended to have a broader remit including monitoring of the Coalition's actions in relation to the Fund.) The Attorney also agrees that once the IIA is established, it would be desirable to ensure full consultation in relation to disbursements from the Fund even in cases where this is not a requirement of the resolution.

15. In connection with OP13, the Attorney also notes that the resolution clearly imposes joint US/UK responsibility for disbursements from the DFI. It is therefore important to ensure that the US Government does not take actions in relation to the Fund which are incompatible with the resolution. The fact that the resolution imposes joint responsibility gives the UK a locus to argue with the US that we should be fully involved in the decision-making process. Anything less would be legally risky.

16. In conclusion, the Attorney considers that resolution 1483 authorises the Coalition to engage in the reconstruction and reform of Iraq to a greater degree than would be permissible under occupation law alone, although in some cases the resolution requires that such activity be carried out in consultation with the IIA or in coordination with the SRSG. However, it is clear that the resolution does not grant the Coalition full legislative and executive authority in Iraq, so there is still a need to consider the legality of specific proposals against the requirements of occupation law and the terms of the resolution.

Document 568
Memorandum from the Foreign and Commonwealth Office in Response to Questions Put by the House of Commons Foreign Affairs Committee

18 June 2003[17]

IRAQ

'The Consistency of coalition actions in Iraq with the requirements of the Fourth Geneva Convention 1949 and the Hague Regulations 1907. In particular, the Committee wishes to be in a position to judge whether the US and UK have met in full their obligations to ensure food and medical supplies for the civil population, to ensure and maintain public health and hygiene, and to ensure public order and safety; and how the occupying powers have ensured that actions taken by them to create a functioning administration and to introduce democratic characteristics into Iraqi political structures have not gone beyond what is permitted under international law.'

'What role is the United Kingdom playing in ORHA? How many UK personnel are serving in ORHA, and in what capacities?'[18]

1. The reasons for the Government's decision to take part in Coalition military action against Iraq were set out by the Prime Minister in the House of Commons on 18 March.[19]

2. Under article 43 of the Hague Regulations Respecting the Laws and Customs of War on Land, an Occupying Power is required to take all measures within its power to restore and ensure, as far as possible, public order and safety, while respecting unless absolutely prevented the laws in force in the country.

3. The Fourth Geneva Convention (1949), which is concerned with the welfare of civilians, imposes broad obligations on an Occupying Power to maintain orderly government of the territory and to ensure its own security. In addition the Convention provides for a number of further specific obligations to the civilian population.

4. The Government has at all stages made every effort to comply with its responsibilities under the Fourth Geneva Convention and the Hague Regulations. [...]

[17] House of Commons Foreign Affairs Committee, Foreign Policy Aspects of the War against Terrorism, Tenth Report of Session 2002-03, Report, together with formal minutes, oral and written evidence. Ordered by The House of Commons to be printed 15 July 2003 (HC (2002-03) 405, 31 July 2003), Ev. 69.

[18] The questions put to the FCO on 13 and 22 May 2003 by the Foreign Affairs Committee of the House of Commons are shown in italics.

[19] See HC Debs, vol 401, cols 760-774: 18 March 2003.

Maintenance of Security

12. Since the liberation of Iraq, UK forces have been working to restore security through a number of means including patrols, vehicle checkpoints and static guarding. Sites currently being guarded by UK forces include key government buildings and public record offices. However, our overall approach is to re-establish local police and guard forces that will initially be trained and overseen by UK forces.

13. The UK and the US have been working with the international community to provide a multinational stabilisation force in Iraq. The US will be in overall command in Baghdad and the central sector and the UK will command a multinational division in the south. More than 20 nations are expected to serve in Iraq, with nine represented in the UK area (Italy, the Netherlands, Denmark, the Czech Republic, Romania, Portugal, Norway, Lithuania and New Zealand). Some states have already deployed.

14. Throughout the military campaign, Coalition forces have taken care to ensure that damage to museums and other sites of historic, archaeological or cultural importance has been minimised. Ground troops were briefed on the need to be especially careful while conducting operations in the vicinity of these sites.

15. Since 1 June, a number of Iraqi courts have been operating with the assistance of UK forces.

Civil administration

16. The Coalition Provisional Administration [sic] (CPA) was set up at the beginning of June. It is responsible for civil administration and reconstruction work, and for facilitating the political processes outlined below. It is led by President Bush's special representative in Iraq, Ambassador Paul Bremer. The CPA is working closely with Iraqis to restore normal functioning to Iraqi ministries and regions. The CPA has around 1,000 staff working in Baghdad, and regional offices in northern, south central and south-east Iraq. The latter area is coterminous with the UK military area of responsibility. It is led by a senior Danish official with a UK deputy and UK civilian secondees. Wider international support has been provided by countries including Australia, Spain, the Czech Republic, Korea, Romania and Japan.

17. The UK is providing strong practical support to the CPA. We now have over 70 UK officials seconded to Baghdad, Basra and the north of Iraq, working in a variety of fields, including health, education, governance, police reform and culture. Their efforts are making a real difference to the performance of the CPA. Andy Bearpark, a senior ex-DFID reconstruction expert arrived in Baghdad on 16 June to serve as CPA Director of Operations. He will play a key role in better focussing the work of the CPA on meeting the immediate needs of the Iraqi people.

18. The United Kingdom Special Representative for Iraq, Ambassador John Sawers, is working closely with Ambassador Bremer on the political and reconstruction processes. He will be succeeded as UK Special Representative by Sir Jeremy Greenstock in September.

19. We are also focussing on providing senior officials to the CPA's Security Sector Reform (SSR) work led by Walt Slocombe. We will be looking to promote the wider involvement of others with a contribution to make, including EU partners and Arab countries.

Political Process

20. United Nations Security Council Resolution 1483 'Supports the formation, by the people of Iraq with the help of the Authority and working with the Special Representative, of an Iraqi interim administration as a transitional administration run by Iraqis, until an

internationally recognised, representative government is established by the people of Iraq and assumes the responsibilities of the Authority'.

Intensive consultations are taking place in Iraq between Coalition representatives, including the United Kingdom Special Representative for Iraq, and representatives of Iraqi interest groups and political parties. The United Nations Special Representative Sergio Vieira de Mello has also recently arrived in Baghdad and we expect him also to play a central role in the political process. A group of Iraqi political leaders have constituted themselves as a 'Leadership Group' to work with the Coalition to carry forward the political process. The Coalition has held two larger-scale meetings with Iraqis, in Nasiriyah on 15 April[20] and in Baghdad on 28 April.

21. The consultations undertaken so far indicate that interim political structures and processes will need to perform a number of distinct functions:

— Iraqi involvement in the day to day civil administration of Iraq in co-operation with the CPA.

— Paving the way for the establishment of a viable Iraqi government to replace the CPA.

— Carrying out essential political functions in the interim such as reform of the Constitution.

We expect a political process to be launched in the coming days. This is expected to comprise two key elements:

— A Political Council, to assist the CPA in the immediate tasks of running the civil administration. Its responsibilities will increase over time; an early task will be to nominate new Iraqi interim ministers to help run government ministries. The Political Council to create special commissions on cross-cutting issues (eg judicial reform, human rights).

— A Constitutional Conference. This is likely to have a larger membership, and to be in place by mid-July. It will draft and debate a new Iraqi constitution. This will be approved by referendum, paving the way for eventual free elections.

22. The UK's objectives are that such processes and structures should be legitimate, viable and credible. The key interest groups in Iraq must be effectively represented, including women; they must be effectively consulted and involved in decision-making on interim arrangements. An interim authority must be established in accordance with Resolution 1483.

23. The effective representation of women in the political processes and structures of post-Saddam Iraq is an important part of the Government's vision for Iraq as the Prime Minister made clear at the Azores Summit.[21] We are taking every opportunity to promote this agenda in our contacts with Iraqis, discussions within the coalition, and more widely. A gender expert from the Women and Equality Unit has been seconded to the Coalition Provisional Authority and, in collaboration with Iraqi women and other officials in Iraq, is working to ensure women's full and equal participation in the Iraqi political and reconstruction process.

UN Authorisation

24. On 22 May the United Nations Security Council adopted Resolution 1483. The Resolution was based closely on a draft tabled by the US, UK and Spain. In summary, the Resolution:

[20] For the Nasiriyah Statement, see *Doc 580*.

[21] See *Doc 572*.

- — recognises the rights and responsibilities of the US and UK as occupying powers;
- — gives the UN a vital role through wide-ranging responsibilities for a Special Representative of the Secretary General, who is given a specific mandate in such areas as the political process, humanitarian activities, economic reconstruction and promotion of human rights;
- — foresees a political process leading to an internationally recognised, representative government of Iraq;
- — calls on other UN member states and international organisations to play their part in fulfilling the resolution's aims, including ensuring security and stability;
- — ends all sanctions, other than the arms embargo;
- — arranges for the orderly wind-up of the Oil for Food Programme;
- — ensures that oil sales are made in accordance with international best practice;
- — creates the Development Fund for Iraq to disburse oil revenues;
- — provides that these funds can only be spent to meet the humanitarian needs of the Iraqi people, for the economic reconstruction and repair of Iraq's infrastructure, for the continued disarmament of Iraq, and for the costs of Iraqi civilian administration, and for other purposes benefiting the people of Iraq;
- — creates an International Advisory and Monitoring Board to oversee oil sales and spending by the Development Fund, with representatives of the UN, IMF and World Bank, and regular reporting to the Security Council;
- — places an obligation on all UN Member States to assist in bringing to justice those responsible for crimes under the former Iraqi regime; and
- — obliges all Member States to take action to prevent trade in stolen Iraqi antiquities.

25. The Secretary General has since appointed the UN High Commissioner for Human Rights, Sergio Vieira de Mello, as his Special Representative. De Mello arrived in Baghdad on 2 June. We are offering him our full support. His immediate priorities include assessment of the situation on the ground, the needs of the people of Iraq and the areas where the UN and international organisations can add most value. He will also work on behalf of the Secretary General to facilitate the political processes leading to an internationally recognised, representative government of Iraq.

26. In order to ensure that actions taken by the Occupying Powers to create a functioning administration accord with the international law of occupation, ORHA/CPA has an Office of Legal Counsel to provide legal advice in this respect. Procedures have been established for pre-promulgation scrutiny of legislative and other legal acts of the Coalition Provisional Authority.

27. Whilst the introduction of democratic changes in government can not be imposed by the Occupying Powers, this does not affect the rights of the Iraqi people themselves to develop their own systems of government. It is therefore permissible for the Occupying Powers to play a facilitating role in relation to reforms genuinely undertaken by the people of Iraq themselves. During the period prior to the passage of Resolution 1483 the CPA did not seek to impose such changes in government on Iraq.

28. Since the passing of United Nations Security Council Resolution 1483, the question of the UK's responsibilities in respect of political reform is no longer governed solely by the law of occupation. The resolution makes clear that the eventual aim of the political process in Iraq should be the formation by the people of Iraq of a representative government based on the rule of law that affords equal rights and justice to all Iraqi citizens. To that end, Resolution 1483 supports the formation of an Iraqi interim administration by the people

of Iraq, with the help of the CPA and working with the UN Special Representative, as a transitional administration run by Iraqis, until a representative Government is established by the people of Iraq assumes the responsibilities of the CPA. The precise modalities as to how this shall be put into effect are still developing, but they will be based upon the provisions of Resolution 1483.

'In your letter of 22 April[22] *you set out the position of an occupying power under the Fourth Geneva Convention and the Hague Regulations. No mention was made in the letter of the requirement for United Nations authority for the occupying powers to exercise some of their functions. When did the Government conclude that UN authority would be required, and was the advice of the Attorney General sought when the FCO compiled its reply of 22 April?'*

29. The FCO's letter of 22 April was confined to the scope of authority of Occupying Powers under the law of occupation because this is what was requested in the Committee Assistant's letter of 8 April. The Committee asked for information on what Occupying Powers are able to do under the law of occupation. There is no legal requirement under the law of occupation for UN authorisation to enable an Occupying Power to exercise its functions. UN authority is only required to enable an Occupying Power to take actions that are not otherwise authorised by the law of occupation. It was evident from the reply given to the Committee that further authority in the form of a Security Council resolution would be required to enable the Occupying Powers to go beyond their normal scope of authority under the law of occupation.

30. The Attorney General was consulted on the terms of the FCO's reply to the Committee Assistant's letter of 8 April. [...]

'Is FCO satisfied that its diplomatic presence in Baghdad was established with sufficient speed as hostilities ended, and at an appropriate level? How does the UK's diplomatic response compare with that of other countries? What is the division of responsibilities between the UK Special Representative and the Head of the British Office in Baghdad?'

42. The British Office in Baghdad opened in May, headed by Christopher Segar, a senior Diplomatic Service officer. The team consists of four UK based staff at present, but as plans for transition to an Iraqi interim administration develop, so too will options for upgrading the status of the Office. The team are initially focusing on developing contacts with Iraqi bodies, and contacts with the CPA, the UN, NGOs and others working on the reconstruction of Iraq and the transition to an Iraqi interim administration. As the situation stabilises, we will increase staffing of the office and extend the range of services on offer, in line with other UK diplomatic missions. These will include consular and visa services. The Office has a particularly important role in assisting British companies who wish to do business in Iraq, especially those involved in reconstruction and humanitarian assistance.

43. Due to the poor condition of the old Embassy premises, the staff are housed in 'flat pack' accommodation, which consists of container units adapted for office and residential accommodation for four staff, plus the necessary IT and communications equipment. In due course, the containers will be replaced by a medium-term prefabricated embassy and village for approximately 40 staff.

44. At present some 22 countries have some form of diplomatic representation in Iraq, but the security and political situation has generally prevented the resumption of normal diplomatic activities.

[22] See *Doc 564*.

45. The Head of the British Office in Baghdad is responsible for promoting the UK's bilateral interests in Iraq. The Special Representative's role is to work with Iraqis, with Coalition partners and with other representatives of the international community to help and guide the political processes leading to the establishment of an interim administration. [...].
Foreign and Commonwealth Office
18 June 2003

Document 569
Response of the Secretary of State for Foreign and Commonwealth Affairs to the Second Report from the House of Commons Foreign Affairs Committee

March 2004[23]

The Government welcome this latest report from the Foreign Affairs Committee,[24] which deals with some of the most challenging issues facing British foreign policy [...]. The Government sets out its response below.

Iraq

[...] *3. We conclude it is unacceptable that comprehensive information is not available about detainees being held by the Occupying Powers in Iraq. We recommend that the British Government ensures that such information is provided as a matter of immediacy including the names of all detainees; their nationalities; where they are held; in what conditions they are held; what rights they have, including access to lawyers; the legal basis for their detention; the offences of which they are suspected or charged; and when and how they will be tried or released. (Paragraph 27)*[25]

There are three categories of people who may be held by the Occupying Powers in Iraq: Prisoners of War are held under the provisions of the Third Geneva Convention; security internees are held under the provisions of the Fourth Geneva Convention and anyone suspected of committing a criminal offence may be arrested and passed to the Iraqi authorities. The cases of internees are reviewed after 10, 28 and thereafter every 90 days. Anyone who is no longer assessed as 'an imperative threat to security' is either released or passed to the Iraqi criminal system if they are suspected of committing a criminal offence.

Information about internees is available. When someone is arrested their details are passed to the International Committee of the Red Cross which then informs the person's family. Iraqi police stations and CPA offices hold lists of all those in detention. The CPA is currently in the process of listing all detainees on the CPA website in Arabic. We accept, however, that the information flow on detainees could be further improved. We are working with our coalition partners on ways to achieve this.

[23] Second Report from the Foreign Affairs Committee, Foreign Policy Aspects of the War Against Terrorism, Session 2003-2004, Response of the Secretary of State for Foreign and Commonwealth Affairs, Cm 6162, March 2004.

[24] House of Commons Foreign Affairs Committee, Foreign Policy Aspects of the War against Terrorism, Second Report of Session 2003–04, Report, together with formal minutes, oral and written evidence. Ordered by The House of Commons to be printed 15 January 2004 (HC (2003-04) 81, 24 January 2004).

[25] The Committee's conclusions are shown in italics.

The UK attaches great importance to upholding human rights in all circumstances. All UK prisoners in Iraq are held in conditions which conform to all of our international obligations. Coalition internment facilities are subject to regular inspection by the ICRC who are given full and unrestricted access to the internees. [...]

19. We recommend that in its response to this Report the Government set out its understanding of the extent to which the Hague Regulations and the Geneva Conventions constrain the Occupying Powers' capacity to carry out economic reform, and how these constraints have affected the Coalition's operations in Iraq. (Paragraph 108)

The various measures of economic reform undertaken by the Coalition Provisional Authority have been undertaken within occupation law, as supplemented by Security Council Resolution 1483 of 22 May 2003. Occupation law does indeed constrain the capacity of an Occupying Power to carry out economic reform. Article 43 of the Hague Regulations sets out the general obligation to respect the laws in force in the occupied country, and the second paragraph of Article 64 of Geneva Convention IV expands upon the circumstances in which an Occupying Power may legislate; that is, where necessary to fulfil the Occupying Power's obligations under Geneva Convention IV (which would broadly cover humanitarian purposes), for security purposes, or to maintain orderly government of the territory. Legislation to achieve economic reform is permissible under occupation law within these limits. That position is supplemented by Security Council Resolution 1483, and in particular paragraph 8(e) which envisages assistance to the people of Iraq for the promotion of economic reconstruction. [...].

Document 570

Supplementary Memorandum Submitted by the Foreign and Commonwealth Office to the House of Commons Foreign Affairs Committee

5 April 2004[26]

[...] *UK responsibility for all coalition detainees in Iraq*

The Committee asked whether the UK Government, as members of a joint UK and US coalition, had responsibility under the Geneva Conventions for those whom US forces were detaining in Iraq. The Coalition Provisional Authority (CPA) is not an entity which is legally distinct from the United Kingdom and the United States for the purposes of international law. The CPA as a body is not a signatory to the Geneva Conventions and does not have obligations and powers under those Conventions – the obligations and powers under the Conventions are those of the UK and the US. In some respects, those obligations and powers are exercised through the vehicle of the CPA, for example in promulgating legislation. But in relation to internment and detention, the detaining power is not the CPA but the individual country exercising its powers under Article 78 of the Fourth Geneva Convention. This is clear from the memorandum of understanding which was entered into

[26] House of Commons Foreign Affairs Committee, Human Rights Annual Report 2003, Fourth Report of Session 2003–04, Report, together with formal minutes, oral and written evidence. Ordered by The House of Commons to be printed 27 April 2004 (HC (2003-04) 389, 6 May 2004), Ev 35.

between the US, the UK and Australia before the start of the war and which still governs the handling of internees by the three countries.[27]

Detainees in Iraq and access to lawyers
The Committee also asked about the access to lawyers for those interned in Iraq in accordance with the Fourth Geneva Convention. As set out in Article 80 of the Convention, internees retain their full civil capacity. This principle is reflected in Article 113 which provides, inter alia, that the Detaining Power shall provide all reasonable facilities for the transmission of wills, powers of attorney, letters of authority, or any other documents intended for internees or despatched by them. Further, the Detaining Power shall facilitate the execution and authentication in due legal form of such documents on behalf of internees, in particular allowing them to consult a lawyer. The UK allows access to legal advice when it is requested to do so by an internee for such matters or for the purpose of challenging the legal basis for their detention. The UK does not, however, either provide or finance the obtaining of such advice.

Criminal jurisdiction applying to British citizens in Iraq
The Committee asked what criminal jurisdiction would apply should there be any evidence of a British citizen committing a criminal offence in Iraq. Whenever our troops are deployed overseas other than to fight a war, it is usual to negotiate a Status of Forces Agreement with the host nation. This agreement covers issues such as the exercise of military jurisdiction over our troops in that territory and the allocation of jurisdiction in respect of any crimes committed by the troops. Where the agreement follows the provisions of the NATO Status of Forces Agreement it usually provides that both the sending state and the host state have criminal jurisdiction over military personnel but that the primary jurisdiction is with the sending state in relation to offences arising from conduct when the soldier concerned is on duty. However, because of the special circumstances of the Coalition forces in Iraq in the aftermath of the conflict, it was not possible to negotiate a Status of Forces Agreement. The CPA therefore issued Order No 17[28] which conferred immunity from the jurisdiction of the Iraqi courts on coalition military personnel and also, in certain circumstances, on non-Iraqi civilian personnel. The United Kingdom's domestic law provides that soldiers and anyone else subject to service law can be tried in military courts (courts martial) for acts which they commit overseas if those acts would constitute a criminal offence if committed in the UK. These military courts are competent to try all criminal offences, including the most serious criminal offences. So, as I indicated during the oral evidence session, if a British soldier engages in conduct which would amount to a criminal offence under English law, he can be prosecuted for that offence in a military court sitting as appropriate either in the United Kingdom or overseas. Where the offence is one over which the UK civilian courts have extraterritorial jurisdiction it may be appropriate for the case to be tried by a civilian court rather than by a court martial. The position is the same for any civilian who is accompanying UK forces and who is subject to service law. In the case of UK civil servants overseas, it should be noted that UK civilian courts have a wider extra-territorial jurisdiction and may deal with any offence committed abroad in the course of their duties if that offence would be indictable if committed in England. So if a British civil servant who was, for example,

[27] See *Doc 588*.
[28] See *Doc* 37.

seconded from the UK Government to assist with interrogating Iraqi internees, committed a serious criminal act during the interrogation he would also be liable to prosecution under English law. Where detainees for whom the UK is the detaining power are held in US-run facilities, clearly US rather than UK law would apply to the conduct of the soldiers.

Iraq Special Tribunal

Although not specifically requested, I thought that the Committee might also appreciate further details on the Iraq special tribunal. It is too early to say when the special tribunal will be up and running. Ambassador Pierre Prosper, US ambassador at large for war crimes, undertook a needs assessment in January, working with Iraqis to identify the next steps for implementation of the special tribunal. The objectives of this assessment were to examine and make recommendations on: the location and establishment of a secure court facility; creation of a victim and witness assistance programme and protection for judges and prosecutors; budget and administration; staffing of qualified Iraqi and international personnel; training and mentoring programmes to strengthen Iraqi capacity in investigations and prosecutions; and any additional areas deemed relevant. The team addressed all of these areas, and additionally made recommendations on a public diplomacy and outreach programme and further development of Rules of Procedure and Elements. The UK is now considering requests for further assistance in these areas.

Hand-over arrangements for detainees

The Committee also asked whether the detainees held by UK forces would be handed over to the Iraqi authorities after the transition of power from the coalition provisional authority to the governing council. The case of each internee is reviewed regularly in order to determine whether they continue to pose an imperative threat to security. As of 1 March there were 84 security internees held by UK forces. The right to hold them stems from our position as Occupying Power. Under the terms of the transitional administrative law the UK will no longer be Occupying Power from 30 June. If on 30 June we are detaining people who still pose a threat to the multinational force, including UK forces, we will want to make sure that they continue to be detained and are unable to realise that threat. Until the political arrangements for the transition of power are finalised, we are not able to say exactly how this will be done.

Religious minorities in Iraq

The Committee asked what safeguards there were for religious minorities in Iraq, including constitutional safeguards for the freedom of religion. The transitional administrative law, which was signed on 8 March, guarantees the rights of all individuals to freedom of religious belief and practice. Although Islam is the official religion of the State, and is to be considered a source of legislation, it cannot contradict any of the rights stipulated in Chapter 2 of the Law, which covers fundamental rights.

I hope that you have found clarification on the points above useful. I look forward to receiving a copy of the Committee's report into the FCO's Annual Report on Human Rights.

Bill Rammell
Parliamentary Under Secretary of State,
Foreign and Commonwealth Office
5 April 2004

Document 571
Letter to the Clerk of the House of Commons Foreign Affairs Committee from the Parliamentary Relations and Devolution Department, Foreign and Commonwealth Office

24 June 2004[29]

Thank you for your letter of 26 May.[30] Please find below updates to the Government's Response to the Committee's Second Report of the current Session, *Foreign Policy Aspects of the War Against Terrorism*:

Further to conclusion 3, the Committee wishes to know whether the response applies in its entirety to all coalition detainees and detention facilities. If it does not, in which respects does the response apply to detainees in UK custody, and in which respects to detainees in US custody?

We do not agree that comprehensive information is not available. We provide as much information as we can about detainees in line with our obligations. We cannot release the names or personal details of detainees without their authorisation. If we did so, it would be in breach of the Geneva Conventions.

The UK holds its security internees in the Divisional Temporary Detention Facility at Shaiba Logistics Base, near Basra. The prison conditions are in accordance with the Geneva Conventions. All internees are informed of the reason for their detention as stipulated by the fourth Geneva Convention. The ICRC has full, uninhibited access to all internees, and regularly reports to the military authorities. Our relationship with the ICRC is excellent. In order to accommodate religious practices, internees are served halal meat.

The legal basis for the detention of all security internees is Geneva Convention IV. Their status is regularly reviewed and anyone no longer deemed to constitute an imminent threat to security may be released. After 30 June, we will no longer be Occupying Powers and so our right to intern under the Geneva Conventions will end. However, we will still have the right to intern as provided under UNSCR1546 and the side letters from the US Secretary of State and the Iraqi Prime Minister to the UN Security Council.

As of 13 June 2004, the UK forces were the detaining power for about 65 internees, the vast majority of whom were security internees being held under Geneva Convention IV. Two are prisoners of war being held under Geneva Convention III. The prisoners of war are being held by the US forces on our behalf. Our right to hold them under Geneva Convention III ends on 30 June. If they are believed to have committed offences against the Iraqi population, they could be handed over to the Iraqi authorities to face prosecution.

The British Armed Forces are fully aware of their obligations under international law. They are given thorough mandatory training courses which include specific guidance on handling prisoners of war. All personnel must attend refresher training every year.

[29] House of Commons Foreign Affairs Committee, Foreign Policy Aspects of the War against Terrorism, Seventh Report of Session 2003-04, Volume II. Ordered by The House of Commons to be printed 21 July 2004 (HC (2003-04) 441-II, 29 July 2004), Ev. 157.

[30] Letter to the Parliamentary Relations and Devolution Department, FCO, from the Clerk of the House of Commons Foreign Affairs Committee, dated 26 May 2004. In the letter, the Foreign Affairs Committee asked for updates on the Government's Response (Cm 6162) *[Doc 569]* to its Second Report of the current Session, Foreign Policy Aspects of the War against Terrorism (HC (2003-04) 81, 24 January 2004), so that it was in possession of the latest information before it made its next Report, in July 2004.

Before going to Iraq all personnel are briefed on the Rules of Engagement and procedures for dealing with prisoners of war or other detainees. Each combat unit is required to have senior non-commissioned officers trained in handling prisoners of war. And units which are responsible for the routine handling of detainees conduct further specialist training.

The US is currently holding just under 6,000 security internees and a small number of prisoners of war. They are also holding criminal detainees on behalf of the Iraqis. They are continuing to increase the pace of reviews. They released 2,570 detainees between 18 February and 13 June this year. In addition, 500 were released from Abu Ghraib on 14 June and a further 500 will be released within the 10 days. The US administration has repeatedly stated that all detainees will be held in accordance with the Geneva Conventions. [...]

Matthew Hamlyn
Parliamentary Relations & Devolution Department
Foreign and Commonwealth Office
24 June 2004

VI

Joint US-UK Documents on Iraq

Document 572
Statement of the Atlantic Summit: A Vision for Iraq and the Iraqi People ('Azores Summit Declaration')

16 March 2003[1]

Iraq's talented people, rich culture, and tremendous potential have been hijacked by Saddam Hussein. His brutal regime has reduced a country with a long and proud history to an international pariah that oppresses its citizens, started two wars of aggression against its neighbors, and still poses a grave threat to the security of its region and the world.

Saddam's defiance of United Nations Security Council resolutions demanding the disarmament of his nuclear, chemical, biological, and long-range missile capacity has led to sanctions on Iraq and has undermined the authority of the U.N. For 12 years, the international community has tried to persuade him to disarm and thereby avoid military conflict, most recently through the unanimous adoption of UNSCR 1441. The responsibility is his. If Saddam refuses even now to cooperate fully with the United Nations, he brings on himself the serious consequences foreseen in UNSCR 1441 and previous resolutions.

In these circumstances, we would undertake a solemn obligation to help the Iraqi people build a new Iraq at peace with itself and its neighbors. The Iraqi people deserve to be lifted from insecurity and tyranny, and freed to determine for themselves the future of their country. We envisage a unified Iraq with its territorial integrity respected. All the Iraqi people – its rich mix of Sunni and Shiite Arabs, Kurds, Turkomen, Assyrians, Chaldeans, and all others – should enjoy freedom, prosperity, and equality in a united country. We will support the Iraqi people's aspirations for a representative government that upholds human rights and the rule of law as cornerstones of democracy.

We will work to prevent and repair damage by Saddam Hussein's regime to the natural resources of Iraq and pledge to protect them as a national asset of and for the Iraqi people. All Iraqis should share the wealth generated by their national economy. We will seek a swift end to international sanctions, and support an international reconstruction program to help Iraq achieve real prosperity and reintegrate into the global community.

We will fight terrorism in all its forms. Iraq must never again be a haven for terrorists of any kind.

In achieving this vision, we plan to work in close partnership with international institutions, including the United Nations; our Allies and partners; and bilateral donors. If conflict occurs, we plan to seek the adoption, on an urgent basis, of new United Nations Security Council resolutions that would affirm Iraq's territorial integrity, ensure rapid delivery of humanitarian relief, and endorse an appropriate post-conflict administration for Iraq. We will also propose that the Secretary General be given authority, on an interim basis, to ensure that the humanitarian needs of the Iraqi people continue to be met through the Oil for Food program.

Any military presence, should it be necessary, will be temporary and intended to promote security and elimination of weapons of mass destruction; the delivery of humanitarian aid; and the conditions for the reconstruction of Iraq. Our commitment to support the people of Iraq will be for the long term.

[1] The Declaration was issued by the President of the United States and the Prime Minister of the United Kingdom who were joined by the Prime Ministers of Spain and Portugal. At the same time the four leaders also issued a 'Declaration on Trans-Atlantic Cooperation' which did not touch upon Iraq.

We call upon the international community to join with us in helping to realize a better future for the Iraqi people.

Document 573
Joint Statement of President Bush and Prime Minister Blair on Iraq

8 April 2003

The future of Iraq belongs to the Iraqi people. After years of dictatorship, Iraq will soon be liberated. For the first time in decades, Iraqis will soon choose their own representative government.

Coalition military operations are progressing and will succeed. We will eliminate the threat posed by Iraq's weapons of mass destruction, deliver humanitarian aid, and secure the freedom of the Iraqi people. We will create an environment where Iraqis can determine their own fate democratically and peacefully.

We are grateful to our men and women in uniform, as well as to the brave troops of Australia and Poland, and to forces contributed by other members of the Coalition. They have demonstrated enormous bravery and professionalism in the face of great danger. We mourn for the members of the Armed Forces who have sacrificed their lives, and extend our deepest sympathies to their families.

We also grieve for the loss of civilian life in Iraq. Coalition forces take great care to avoid civilian casualties. The Iraqi regime has done the opposite. It has deliberately put Iraqi civilians in harm's way, and used women and children as human shields. It has sent execution squads to kill Iraqis who choose freedom over fighting for a brutal regime. We condemn Iraqi regime forces' attacks in civilian clothing, false surrender, and mistreatment of prisoners of war. These acts are an affront to all standards of human decency and international law.

We are taking every step possible to safeguard Muslim holy sites and other protected places in Iraq that are important to the religious and cultural heritage of Islam and of Iraq. We have no confidence that the Iraqi regime has done the same, and are deeply concerned by reports that it is deliberately endangering such sites and using them for military purposes.

The Coalition is delivering food, medicine, and other humanitarian assistance to the Iraqi people. This flow will increase as more of Iraq's territory is liberated and United Nations specialized agencies and non-governmental organizations are better able to operate. We welcome the adoption by the United Nations Security Council of Resolution 1472,[2] which will allow shipments of humanitarian items to Iraq to resume under the Oil for Food programme.

As we said at our March 16 meeting in the Azores,[3] we will uphold our responsibility to help the people of Iraq build a nation that is whole, free and at peace with itself and its neighbours. We support the aspirations of all of Iraq's people for a united, representative government that upholds human rights and the rule of law as cornerstones of democracy. We reaffirm our commitment to protect Iraq's natural resources, as the patrimony of the people of Iraq, which should be used only for their benefit.

[2] See *Doc 519*.
[3] See *Doc 572*.

As the Coalition proceeds with the reconstruction of Iraq, it will work with its allies, bilateral donors, and with the United Nations and other international institutions. The United Nations has a vital role to play in the reconstruction of Iraq.[4] We welcome the efforts of UN agencies and non-governmental organisations in providing immediate assistance to the people of Iraq. As we stated in the Azores, we plan to seek the adoption of new United Nations Security Council Resolutions that would affirm Iraq's territorial integrity, ensure rapid delivery of humanitarian relief and endorse an appropriate post-conflict administration for Iraq. We welcome the appointment by the United Nations Secretary General of a Special Adviser for Iraq to work with the people of Iraq and coalition representatives.

The day when Iraqis govern themselves must come quickly. As early as possible, we support the formation of an Iraqi Interim Authority, a transitional administration, run by Iraqis, until a permanent government is established by the people of Iraq. The Interim Authority will be broad-based and fully representative, with members from all Iraq's ethnic groups, regions, and diaspora. The Interim Authority will be established first and foremost by the Iraqi people, with the help of the members of the Coalition, and working with the Secretary General of the United Nations. As Coalition forces advance, civilian Iraqi leaders will emerge who can be part of such an Interim Authority. The Interim Authority will progressively assume more of the functions of government. It will provide a means for Iraqis to participate in the economic and political reconstruction of their country from the outset.

Coalition forces will remain in Iraq as long as necessary to help the Iraqi people to build their own political institutions and reconstruct their country, but no longer. We look forward to welcoming a liberated Iraq to the international community of nations. We call upon our partners in the international community to join with us in ensuring a democratic and secure future for the Iraqi people.

Document 574

Letter Dated 8 May 2003 from the Permanent Representatives of the United Kingdom of Great Britain and Northern Ireland and the United States of America to the United Nations Addressed to the President of the Security Council

UN Doc. S/2003/538, 8 May 2003

The United States of America, the United Kingdom of Great Britain and Northern Ireland and Coalition partners continue to act together to ensure the complete disarmament of Iraq of weapons of mass destruction and means of delivery in accordance with United Nations Security Council resolutions. The States participating in the Coalition will strictly abide by their obligations under international law, including those relating to the essential humanitarian needs of the people of Iraq. We will act to ensure that Iraq's oil is protected and used for the benefit of the Iraqi people.

[4] In a press conference at Hillsborough on 8 April 2003, President was asked what a 'vital role' meant, and he said: 'I view a vital role as an agent to help people live freely. That's a vital role. That means food. That means medicine. That means aid. That means a place where people can give their contributions. That means suggesting people for the IIA [Iraqi Interim Authority]. That means being, you know, a party to the progress being made in Iraq. That's what that means.'

In order to meet these objectives and obligations in the post-conflict period in Iraq, the United States, the United Kingdom and Coalition partners, acting under existing command and control arrangements through the Commander of Coalition Forces, have created the Coalition Provisional Authority, which includes the Office of Reconstruction and Humanitarian Assistance, to exercise powers of government temporarily, and, as necessary, especially to provide security, to allow the delivery of humanitarian aid, and to eliminate weapons of mass destruction.

The United States, the United Kingdom and Coalition partners, working through the Coalition Provisional Authority, shall inter alia, provide for security in and for the provisional administration of Iraq, including by: deterring hostilities; maintaining the territorial integrity of Iraq and securing Iraq's borders; securing, and removing, disabling, rendering harmless, eliminating or destroying (a) all of Iraq's weapons of mass destruction, ballistic missiles, unmanned aerial vehicles and all other chemical, biological and nuclear delivery systems and (b) all elements of Iraq's programme to research, develop, design, manufacture, produce, support, assemble and employ such weapons and delivery systems and subsystems and components thereof, including but not limited to stocks of chemical and biological agents, nuclear-weapon-usable material, and other related materials, technology, equipment, facilities and intellectual property that have been used in or can materially contribute to these programmes; in consultation with relevant international organizations, facilitating the orderly and voluntary return of refugees and displaced persons; maintaining civil law and order, including through encouraging international efforts to rebuild the capacity of the Iraqi civilian police force; eliminating all terrorist infrastructure and resources within Iraq and working to ensure that terrorists and terrorist groups are denied safe haven; supporting and coordinating demining and related activities; promoting accountability for crimes and atrocities committed by the previous Iraqi regime; and assuming immediate control of Iraqi institutions responsible for military and security matters and providing, as appropriate, for the demilitarization, demobilization, control, command, reformation, disestablishment, or reorganization of those institutions so that they no longer pose a threat to the Iraqi people or international peace and security but will be capable of defending Iraq's sovereignty and territorial integrity.

The United States, the United Kingdom and Coalition partners recognize the urgent need to create an environment in which the Iraqi people may freely determine their own political future. To this end, the United States, the United Kingdom and Coalition partners are facilitating the efforts of the Iraqi people to take the first steps towards forming a representative government, based on the rule of law, that affords fundamental freedoms and equal protection and justice under law to the people of Iraq without regard to ethnicity, religion or gender. The United States, the United Kingdom and Coalition partners are facilitating the establishment of representative institutions of government, and providing for the responsible administration of the Iraqi financial sector, for humanitarian relief, for economic reconstruction, for the transparent operation and repair of Iraq's infrastructure and natural resources, and for the progressive transfer of administrative responsibilities to such representative institutions of government, as appropriate. Our goal is to transfer responsibility for administration to representative Iraqi authorities as early as possible.

The United Nations has a vital role to play in providing humanitarian relief, in supporting the reconstruction of Iraq, and in helping in the formation of an Iraqi interim authority. The United States, the United Kingdom and Coalition partners are ready to work closely with representatives of the United Nations and its specialized agencies and look forward to the appointment of a special coordinator by the Secretary-General. We also welcome the support and contributions of Member States, international and regional organizations, and other entities, under appropriate coordination arrangements with the Coalition Provisional Authority.

We would be grateful if you could arrange for the present letter to be circulated as a document of the Security Council.

[Signed] *Jeremy* ***Greenstock***
Permanent Representative of the United Kingdom
[Signed] *John D.* ***Negroponte***
Permanent Representative of the United States[5]

Document 575
Declaration on Iraq by President George W. Bush and Prime Minister Tony Blair

20 November 2003

For the first time in decades, the Iraqi people are enjoying the taste of freedom. Iraqis are starting to rebuild their country and can look to a brighter future. They are free of Saddam Hussein and his vicious regime; they can speak freely; practice their religion; and start to come to terms with the nightmare of the last 35 years, in which hundreds of thousands of Iraqis were murdered by their own government.

But Iraq is still threatened by followers of the former regime, and by outside terrorists who are helping them. The struggle is difficult. Yet we shall persevere to ensure that the people of Iraq will prevail, with the support of the new and strengthening Iraqi security forces: the police, the Iraqi Civil Defense Corps, the Facility Protection Service, the border police, and the New Iraqi Army. We salute the courage of those Iraqis and the coalition forces engaged in the struggle against reactionary elements in Iraq who want to turn back the clock to the dark days of Saddam's regime.

We reaffirm the resolve of our two countries, with many friends and allies, to complete the process of bringing freedom, security, and peace to Iraq.

We warmly welcome the Iraqi Governing Council's announcement of a timetable for the creation of a sovereign Iraqi Transitional Administration by the end of June 2004, and for a process leading to the adoption of a permanent constitution and national elections for a new Iraqi government by the end of 2005.

This announcement is consistent with our long-stated aim of handing over power to Iraqis as quickly as possible. It is right that Iraqis are making these decisions and for the first time in generations determining their own future. We welcome the Governing Council's commitment to ensuring the widest possible participation in the Transitional Assembly and constitutional process.

We reaffirm our long-term commitment to Iraq. The United States and United Kingdom stand ready to support the Transitional Administration in its task of building a new Iraq and its democratic institutions. Our military participation in the multinational force in Iraq will serve the Iraqi people until the Iraqis themselves are able to discharge full responsibility for

[5] UN Doc S/2003/538, 8 May 2003.

their own security. At the same time, we hope that international partners will increasingly participate in the multinational force.

Our long-term political, moral, and financial commitment to the reconstruction of Iraq was underlined at the Madrid Donors Conference last month.[6] Although the Coalition Provisional Authority will come to an end once the Transitional Administration is installed, the United States and United Kingdom will continue to provide assistance as part of the international support effort. In these tasks, we welcome the involvement of other nations, regardless of earlier differences; of the United Nations and the International Financial Institutions; and of the many non-governmental organizations who are able to make an important contribution.

Great challenges remain in Iraq. But the progress we have made this year has been enormous. Iraqis no longer live in fear of their own government, and Iraq's neighbors no long feel threatened. Our resolve to complete the task we set ourselves remains undiminished. Our partnership with the Iraqi people is for the long-term.

[6] See *Doc 593*.

VII

Documents of the Iraqi Opposition and on the Iraqi Political Process

Document 576
Political Statement of the Iraqi Opposition Conference in London

16 December 2002[1]

Due to the imposed rule of the sectarian racist regime, its repressive and terrorist actions and the internal and external wars of that regime, Iraq has experienced thirty years of its contemporary history in the worst state. During all these years the Iraqi people continued to struggle and make a series of bold attempts to end the abnormal conditions imposed on our people by the repressive regime. A broad section of the honourable people, including the armed forces and political and national forces of all the nations, religions and faiths participated in this legitimate attempt in every possible way, including armed struggle which reached its climax in the blessed uprising of March 1991. Millions of Iraqi people: civilians, members of armed forces, Arabs, Kurds, Turkomans and Assyrians, Sunni and Shi'i, took part in the uprising which was very close to deal the regime with the fate it deserves. A lot of blood and sacrifices were offered to achieve this aim, but conditions beyond the control of our steadfast people prevented this common aim of the Iraqis from being achieved and from getting the opportunity to rebuild our country on the basis of democracy, justice and peace.

Today, again there is an opportunity for our people and we can take advantage of the elements of the international situation to bring down this fascist regime and initiate positive developments in Iraq. There is a new common prospect open to us and we must remain committed to the inevitability of achieving this patriotic mission, and encourage the process of change in Iraq for the benefit of our people taking into consideration the interests of neighboring, regional, Arab and Islamic countries and the international community.

To achieve this aim, the Iraqi opposition conference, which embraces the majority of forces, groups and prominent figures in the Iraqi opposition, which was held in London on 14-16 December 2002, under the slogan: 'For the sake of the liberation of Iraq and achieving democracy', reaffirms the main principles and criteria of the previous conferences and meetings of the Iraqi opposition, especially the Salah-al-Din conference in 1992 and the political discourse of the opposition delegation in Washington in August 2002. Starting from these criteria, the conference accepted and approved the following resolutions and recommendations:

1. The role of Iraqi opposition in the process of change

Members of the conference view the role of the national opposition, with all its diverse groups and organizations supported by the masses of our people, as a principal and essential role in the process of change. The conference considers the role of the opposition as a vital and crucial role in all the stages of the anticipated change in a way that corresponds with its abilities and practical conditions.

2. The future of Iraq and democracy

Iraq will be a democratic parliamentary, pluralist, federal (for all Iraq) state and will accordingly enact a humane and civilized concept of citizenship based on equality and elimination of discrimination against all peoples, religions, races and sects. The conference

[1] There were two different English versions of this document in circulation; the differences being more linguistic than substantive. The other version could be found at http://www.krg.org [no longer available].

reaffirms that a permanent constitution for the country should be drafted in which the national composition of Iraq and the separation of legislative and executive powers and the judiciary are enshrined. It must also stress commitment to the supreme power of law, protection of human rights and public and private freedoms, and respect for the institutions of civil society.

3. Islam is the religion of the state

Islamic religion is one of the foundations of Iraqi state and the rules of Islamic shariah are a principal source of the sources of legislation. The conference stresses that guidance should be sought from the Islamic sacred values and principles of good and tolerance and take its methods and instructions into consideration for school syllabuses and education with due respect to all other heavenly religions and faiths.

4. The state of law

The conference expresses unanimous agreement that chaos, blind revenge and any other form of lawlessness which may tend to prevail in the future environment of Iraq under whatever pretext, must not be allowed. All cases should be brought to judicial authorities and internal and international courts through the law and justice. All cases of violations of civil rights; such as confiscation of property, violation of rights and all criminal offences and political crimes including the crimes of ethnic genocide, ethnic cleansing, massacres and war crimes, supported by evidence, shall be brought to court.

5. Political decision-making

The conference resolves that all the constituent elements of the Iraqi people; Arabs, Kurds, Turkomans, Assyrians, Chaldeans and others, and Muslims and Christians, Sunnis, Shi'is and Yezidis, and other believers in heavenly religions, should participate in the political decision-making.

6. Rejection of all attempts to trample upon the will of the Iraqi people to achieve change

The conference asks the international community to support the Iraqi people to become liberated from the dictatorial regime. At the same time, the conference rejects all forms such as occupation, internal or external military rule, external mandate and regional interference and stresses the need to respect the sovereignty of Iraq, the independence of neighboring countries and the principles of good neighborliness, regional cooperation, non interference in other countries' affairs; and commitment to all the pledges, statements and agreements which have been approved by the international community. Above all the UN Charter, the international charter for human rights and all the international conventions and agreements relating to them, as well as commitment to the Arab League and the Conference of the Islamic organization.

7. Sectarian problem and eradication of its effects

Throughout the past history of Iraq and especially under the current regime, we in Iraq, as other sections of Iraqi community, have been subjected to oppression; violence; repression; discrimination; and denial of civil, political, national, cultural and social rights. This has destroyed the social balance in the country and greatly jeopardized national unity and the spirit of tolerance and forgiveness, and has led to the predominance of repression, special institutions and the use of deception and falsehood to impose power on the Iraqi society with all its peoples and colors, and its Shi'i majority. As a result, the Iraqi people have lost one of the most important elements of their unity, thus paving the way for dictatorial, racial and sectarian policies which harm all the Iraqi people.

Therefore, the conference believes that all the policies of sectarian discrimination must be prohibited as soon as possible, and respect accorded to the legitimate rights of the Shi'i which have been denied so far. The conference condemns the policy of aggression against the religious seminary authorities of Shi'i (Hawza Ilmiya) and interference in their affairs, their containment and compulsory appointment and imposition [of their religious guides]. It also condemns the murder of their grand religious guides and their families and religious sources of emulation, and the imprisonment and torture of thousands of others whom we do not have the opportunity to list here.

The conference also condemns the policies of aggression against Shi'i religious seminary institutions of Al-Najaf al-Ashraf and other holy cities, the destruction of mosques and husayniyas, Islamic centers, libraries and the banning of books, censorship and banning of Shi'i religious processions and the destruction of Shi'i populated towns and villages and homes, the draining of their areas, their deportation and bringing other citizens and settling them in their places, expressing skepticism regarding their Arab and Iraqi belonging, the deportation of non-Arab Shi'is and denying them their Iraqi citizenship and withdrawing their Iraqi passports, taking away their children and confiscating their property.

The conference believes that the new constitution of Iraq must guarantee that these violations shall not be repeated and that all the constituent elements of the Iraqi people shall be protected without discrimination.

8. About the genocide attacks of Halabjah and Anfal

The conference condemns all the racial injustice, oppression and ethnic cleansing which the Iraqi regime has carried out premeditatively on the people of Iraqi Kurdistan, particularly genocide and Anfal operations which affected 180,000 people, 8,000 Barzanis, 5,000 Faylis and 5,000 people of Halabjah, and the destruction of thousands of towns and villages, all of which moved the conscience of people all over the world. While the conference demands putting an end to this heinous policy, it stresses the need to find out about the fate of the victims, honor them, compensate their families, rebuild the destroyed villages and towns and prosecute those who committed these crimes in international courts.

9. About deportations, ethnic cleansing and change of national identity

The conference condemns all forms of deportations, ethnic cleansing, the use of chemical weapons and forced change of national identity, especially the changing of the national character of the areas of Kirkuk, Makhmur, Khanaqin, Sinjar, Shekhan, Zimar and Mandali, and so on. The conference demands that all the effects of this policy be eradicated once for all in the following way:

a. The return of the deportees to their homes and areas, the return of all their property and possessions, and compensating them for loss and damages.
b. The return of those people brought by the regime to be settled and replace the deportees to their previous areas and homes.
c. The return of the Fayli Kurds and all the Iraqis whom the regime deported outside Iraq under the pretext that they were of Iranian origin, and unjustly took away their citizenship rights from them, and securing their Iraqi citizenship for them,

the return of their property and possessions, and uncovering the fate of the Faylis who have disappeared since 1980 and compensating them.

d. Abolishing all the administrative changes implemented by the regime since 1968 with the purpose of changing the demographic reality of Iraqi Kurdistan.

10. Federalism and the resolution of Kurdish question

Upon examining the Kurdish question and the ways of settling it, the conference stressed again the plurality and diversity of the Iraqi society as regards to ethnicity, sect, and political organization, and also stressed the consolidation of national unity and to achieve this through complete equality among all the citizens. By considering the resolutions and recommendations of Salah-al-Din conference, the subsequent meetings of the opposition in Washington in August 2002 and the adoption of the National Assembly of Iraqi Kurdistan of a complete federalism bill in its session on 7 October 2002, the conference expressed its respect for the people of Kurdistan and the free will of people of Kurdistan to choose proper and appropriate methods for their partnership with the people of one country. The conference debated the experiences of federal systems and concluded that it is an appropriate system of government for Iraq, which must be taken cognizance of as a basis for the resolution of the Kurdish problem within the framework of Iraqi constitutional institutions after the end of the dictatorial Saddam regime and anticipated changes in Iraq.

In this respect the conference reiterated the unity of Iraqi land and coexistence among its peoples on the basis of voluntary union. The conference also reaffirms the just and legitimate demands of the people of Kurdistan for uprooting all forms of oppression and repression on the basis of international law which affords them the right of self determination and affirms fraternity, unity and partnership in one country.

11. The rights of Turkomans

The conference debated the racism and ethnic cleansing carried out against the Turkomans and stresses the importance of guaranteeing their equality with others and agrees to grant them their ethnic, cultural and administrative rights within a defined legal framework and to protect these rights constitutionally.

12. The rights of Assyrians

The conference debated the injustice and national oppression exercised against the Assyrians and stresses the importance of guaranteeing their equality with others and agrees to grant them their ethnic, cultural and administrative rights within a defined legal framework, and to protect these rights constitutionally.

13. The marshlands (Ahwar) catastrophe

Ahwar areas have suffered a great humanitarian and environmental disaster which has caused the drying up of a large area of the marshlands, the destruction of the topography and cutting off the source of livelihood of the population, the viability of life in these areas and the deportation tens of thousands of the population. The new government of Iraq must pay a special attention to these areas to ensure the return of their population, compensating them and supporting them for the revival of the area and fulfilling the requirement of a happy life for them.

14. About the unjust laws and decisions
The conference demands the suspension and abolition of all the racist laws and decrees which the regime has decreed against the Kurds, Turkomans and Assyrians, and its sectarian decrees against the Shi'is.

15. About the experience in the Iraqi Kurdistan region
The conference highly appreciates the experience in Iraqi Kurdistan in areas of freedom, democracy and reconstruction. This is an evidence of that proven reality that the Iraqis can be creative and constructive if they are free from dictatorship. The conference believes that it is possible to benefit from this experience as an advanced step on the path of the anticipated democratic transformation in Iraq and for the resolution of differences through fraternal dialogue and the uprooting of the use of violence in political action. The conference calls for supporting and protecting this experience and dealing with its legally-elected institutions until a new federal constitution is prepared for the country, including the Kurdistan region, and the forces of peshmerga [Kurdish militia] shall be integrated within the Iraqi army.

16. Security apparatuses
The conference blames the regime for the mass killing of thousands of Iraqis and physical liquidation of thousands of citizens, political and scientific cadres and army officers. The conference again stresses the need for uncovering the truth about every crime and prosecuting those responsible in a legal way. The conference deems it imperative that all the repressive apparatuses which the regime has created for the intimidation and repression of Iraqi citizens be dismantled and a new security body be established in a way that will protect rights of citizenship, human rights and the security of the country in accordance with the law.

17. Army and armed forces
The participants reaffirmed the importance of rebuilding the military institutions and armed forces in a proper professional and patriotic way away from internal conflict, militarization of society and sectarian and racist policies; elimination of the weapons of mass destruction projects and of every weapon banned internationally, putting an end to the use of the army for internal repression and external aggression and confining the role of the army to the defence and reconstruction of the country.

18. Economic conditions and eradicating the effects of destructive wars
The conference holds the present regime responsible for the economic collapse, the deterioration of the living standards and social security experienced in Iraq today as a result of its destructive wars and forcing millions of people to leave their country. The conference urges the countries which host Iraqi exiles and refugees to take care of them and offer them refuge and facilities.

The conference also holds the present regime responsible historically, morally and legally for starting two wars against two neighbors of Iraq – Iran and Kuwait. It calls for cooperation by both countries for the freeing of the prisoners of war and detainees, eliminating the accumulated effects of that abnormal period and preventing the use of Iraqi territory for hostility against other countries.

The conference also calls on the international community, fraternal and friendly countries and international institutions and organizations to support Iraq during its transitional period within the framework of a comprehensive project to erase the effects of this tragic period. To achieve this the conference stresses the need for these planned arrangements:

- Collection of a substantial Iraqi, regional and international income.
- Allowing Iraq to reach its maximum capacity for the export of oil.
- Negotiation with countries which have large debts to Iraq to settle the debt problem and the accumulated interest.
- Asking the international community, particularly the friendly countries, to free Iraq's frozen assets abroad and help us to uncover the wealth of Saddam and those involved with him and confiscate their companies and accounts in all countries as the public property of the Iraqi people.
- The conference calls upon the new government to review all the oil, commercial and economic agreements which Iraq has signed since 1991 with foreign companies and countries as regards of legal status and the extent of consideration for Iraqi interests in these agreements.
- The conference calls upon the new government to cooperate particularly with Iran and Kuwait for the freeing of the prisoners of war and detainees from both sides and ending all the negative effects.

19. The oil-for-food program

The conference believes that it is necessary to protect the oil-for-food program which ensures food, medicine and rebuilding economic life for the Iraqi people and to endeavor to address the negative aspects of the program until such a time when the resolutions of the Security Council are reviewed and a new appropriate plan is devised by the new government to ensure a dignified life for the people, especially the poor classes and those with low and limited income. Also, development plans and equitable allocation of revenue to all the regions throughout Iraq must be carefully considered.

20. A new nationality law

The participants resolve that a new humane contemporary law must be created for granting nationality which will abolish all types of classification of Iraqi citizens that aim at depriving them of their nationality rights. Efforts should be made after the end of the current regime for all Iraqi exiles to return to Iraq and deal with the accumulated negative effects of this inhumane policy.

21. Facilitating the return of Iraqi migrants, deportees and refugees

The participants resolve that the authorities of the transitional period should provide immediate facilities for the millions of Iraqi emigrants and refuges in exile and prepare necessary facilities for them to return to their country to participate in its reconstruction, and to return their property and possessions to them and compensate them for the loss they have suffered.

22. The role of scientific and academic talents

The participants called upon academic groups, and Iraqi experts and scientists and all those who have a high degree of scientific competence to offer their skills, expertise and services for current and future revival and development plans until the end of the current regime.

The conference salutes the Iraqi martyrs of freedom and expresses its support for tens of thousands of political prisoners and their families who have been spending many years of their lives within the prison walls of the regime.

The conference also salutes all our families in any part and piece of Iraq and expresses its pride in their struggle and steadfastness.

Document 577
Iraqi Opposition Conference in London
Transition Period Project

16 December 2002[2]

First: The Transition Period

This is the period between the establishment of a coalition authority as a result of the fall of the regime and holding of elections to found the establishment of a democratic state by way of a permanent constitution endorsed by the people within a period not acceding 2 years from the date of the setting up of the coalition authority.

Second: General Principles for the Transitional Period Establishment

a. The people are the source of authority and the base of legitimacy.
b. Iraq is an independent, sovereign and unified land and people.
c. Separation of Powers: Legislative, Executive and Judiciary.
d. Islam is the State religion and one of the sources of basic legislation.[3]
e. Democracy (including freedom of expression and peaceful demonstration), and political pluralism.
f. The adoption of the federal system.
g. Iraq consist of two main nationalities, Arabs and Kurds and of other nationalities which are Turkmens, Assyrians and Chaldeans and others.
h. Iraqis are equal under the law in their rights and responsibilities and freedom of religion and belief are guaranteed as well as the respect of religious and sectarian practices.
i. The rejection and banning of violence and ethnic, sectarian and religious discrimination and standing against terrorism and manipulation in all forms with and the promotion of ethnic and religious tolerance.
j. Establishment of strong and equal relations with Arab, regional and friendly countries, especially neighbouring countries so that Iraq will take its active role in the international community to serve its high national interests, security, peace and stability in the region and the world.
k. Abide by international charters and conventions, especially regarding human rights and United Nation resolutions and the Charters of the Arab League and the Islamic Conference.

[2] There are at least two different versions of this document in English which may be due to different translations. The text reproduced is the one distributed at the conference.

[3] In another version of the document, sub-section 4 reads: 'Islam is the religion of the state and is the basic source of legislation.'

Third: The Transitional National Assembly
The Transitional National Assembly consists of representatives of the national religious, political, social and geographic components of Iraqi people and of experienced and qualified people to undertake legislative roles during the transition period and to monitor the work of the executive authority.

Four: The Sovereign Council
The Sovereign Council consists of three leaders who have honourable pasts and are known for their integrity. This council will carry the duties of the head of state during the transitional period.

Five: The Transitional Government
A transitional civilian coalition government is to be formed that reflects the components of the Iraqi society and its political views and it will consist of politicians and qualified and experienced specialists who are known for their patriotism and integrity.

Six: Transitional Period Constitution
A constitution will be written for the transitional period and this will be done by a committee of people with experience and specialization.

Seven: The Permanent Constitution Project

a. The Transitional National Assembly will form a committee of specialists consisting of academics and law scholars who have experience and specialization as well as politicians and religious scholars representing the ethnic, political and religious diversity of Iraq, for the purpose of drafting a permanent constitution which will be presented in a referendum to be endorsed by the people;
b. The Iraqi people will decide in a referendum whether the political system will be republican or monarchist.

Document 578

Final Statement of the Meeting of the Coordination and Follow-up Committee of the Iraqi Opposition

1 March 2003[4]

In the name of God, the Merciful, the Compassionate. As Iraq faces a critical stage in its history, the Coordination and Follow-up Committee that was elected at the London

[4] The 65-member Coordination and Follow-Up Committee had been elected by the London Iraqi Opposition Conference on 13-16 December 2002. It held its first meeting in Salah-al-Din in Kurdish controlled northern Iraq from 26 February to 1 March 2003. Of the 65 members of the Committee only 54 attended the meeting. Iraqi papers reported the composition of the Committee as follows: Ibrahim Hamoudi, Dr Ahmad Chalabi, Ahmed Ali Muhsin, Akram Al-Hakim, Albert Yelda, Ayad Al-Samaraei, Ayad Allawi, Ayham Al-Samurai, Mrs Bayan Al-Aaraji, Bayan Jabr,Tawfiq Al-Yasiri, Jalal Al-Talabani, Jned Manko, Jawad Al-Attar, Jawhar Namiq, Hatem Mukhlis, Hatem Shaalan Abu Al-Joun, Hajim Al-Hasani, Hameed Al-Bayati, Hussein Al-Juburi, Hussein Al-Shaalan, Hussein Al-Shami, Rida Jawad Taqi, Mrs Souad Al-Krimawi, Saad Al Bazzaz, Dr Saad Jawad, Saad Salih Jabir, Saadun Al-Dilaimi, Sinan Al-Shibibi, Sadiq Al-Musawi, Mrs Safia Al-Sihail, Salah El Den Bahaa El-Den, Salah Al-Shackly, Safan Ahmed Agha, Tariq Al-Adhami, Adel Abdel Mahdi, Abas Al-Bayati, Abdel Aziz

Iraqi Opposition Conference between 13-16 December 2002, held its first meeting with the participation of 54 members, in the liberated territory of Iraq, in the city of Salah-al-Din in heroic Kurdistan, on 24-28 February 2003.

After a series of frank and comprehensive discussions over a period of three days, which preceded the official meeting, the meeting was opened with a recital of a verse from the Holy Koran and a minute's silence in memory of our martyrs and in solidarity with our people in prison, detention, and exile.

After listening to a speech by the host, leader of the Kurdistan Democratic Party KDP Mr Mas'ud Barzani, the meeting listened to a message from the leader of the Supreme Council of the Islamic Revolution in Iraq SCIRI, His Eminence Muhammad Baqir al-Hakim, and speeches by a number of leaders of the Iraqi opposition and quests. With a quorum of 54 members the meeting held seven closed sessions during which a steering committee was elected and the rules of order of the meetings, the agenda, election of Mr Jalal Talabani as a chair for the meetings, and the structures required to face conditions both inside and outside the country were established, in pursuit of the establishment of an alternative democratic government.

The meeting evaluated the political and international situation and the possibilities of a military conflict, which the allied forces plan to launch under the leadership of the USA. The meeting puts the responsibility on the Iraqi regime for endangering the security of the country as a result of its repressive policies, violation of human rights and rights of various groups, non-compliance with relevant UN Security Council resolutions, aggression against neighbouring countries and its refusal to get rid of its weapons of mass destruction. The meeting calls upon the USA and the international community to distinguish between Saddam Hussein's regime and the Iraqi people and between weapons of mass destruction and the infrastructure of Iraq.

The meeting reaffirmed that in the aftermath of the overthrow of the Saddam Hussein regime, power should be transferred to the Iraqi people and their true representatives as soon as possible. It looks forward to Iraq enjoying balanced relations with other countries, on the basis of mutual relations and cooperation and without occupation.

The meeting took note of news reports that thousands of Turkish troops are planning to enter Iraqi Kurdistan unilaterally, and hopes this is not the case. While we appreciate the undertaking of the international coalition to enforce the relevant UN Security Council resolutions and its support of the Iraqi people in overthrowing the dictatorial regime and establishing democratic rule in Iraq, we reject Turkish military intervention, or the intervention of any other regional power, in Iraqi internal affairs.

Meanwhile, the meeting extends the hand of friendship and cooperation to the Republic of Turkey and reassures it that our Kurdish brothers and all members of the Iraqi opposition reject the division of Iraq. The meeting asserts its belief in one unified country. It takes seriously Turkey's legitimate security concerns and it is willing to establish optimum neighbourly relations with Turkey. We, the members of the Iraqi opposition, call upon the government of Turkey for open, frank and direct dialogue, with the participation of the USA, and reaffirm our commitment to establishing a unified Iraq and reinforcing Iraq's

Al-Hakim, Abdul Sattar Al-Jumaily, Abdul Majed Al-Khuoei, Izz El Den Salim, Al-Sharif Ali Bin Al-Hussein, Ghassan Al-Atia, Farouk Ridaa, Fouad Maasoum, Qadir Aziz, Karim Ahmed, Kanaan Makia, Kosret Rasoul Ali, Dr Goran Talabani, Dr Mohammed Bahr Al-Ulom, Mohammed Taqi Al-Mawla, Mohammed Al-Haidari, Mohammed Abdel-Jabbar, Mohammed Al Haj Mahmod, Masoud Al-Barazani, Mishaan Al-Jubouri, Mudhar Shawkat, Dr Mowafak Al-Roubaei, Naji Hilmi, Dr Najim Al-Deen Karim, Hoshiar Zibari, Wafiq Al-Samurai, Walid Mohammed Salih,Younadim Yousif Kanna.

national unity on the basis of democratic, parliamentary, federal and equal citizenship to all Iraqis, be they Arabs, Kurds, Turkomans, Assyrians, or Chaldeans.

The Iraqi people would have the first and last word in deciding and managing the affairs of their country. Iraq is a country with multiple Arab and Muslim dimensions of identity. It is a land with many holy sites and shines that have been subjected by Saddam Hussein to the worst kinds of violation of all that is sacred and holy. The Saddam Hussein regime has forced millions of its sons into exile. Hundreds of thousands of its citizens have been killed and wounded in internal wars that have touched every part of the land.

The opposition is a partner in the liberation of Iraq and in building of a new democratic Iraq. The Iraqi opposition will contribute to the restoration of stability and to the prevention of potential anarchy and chaos. The opposition will enlist the assistance of the Iraqi army and people, including religious and tribal personalities, to enhance law and order, social peace and tolerance among all sections of society. The Iraqi opposition ultimately wishes to rehabilitate all militia organizations, including those forces operating under the command of the leadership council of the Iraqi opposition, and reintegrate them into a future Iraqi national army and to end the state of the society's militarization by returning the army to its barracks, dismantling all Iraq's repressive institutions and ending those currents of thought in Iraq that gave rise to tyranny. The Iraqi opposition wishes to return to a life of constitutionalism and to re-engage with regional, international and Arab countries in relations of mutual interest and good-neighbourliness.

A democratic Iraq based on the rule of law, characterized by internal peace, is the best guarantee for the spread of peace and stability with other countries and the international community.

Considering all of the above, and implementing the decisions of the London conference, in particular the two documents the political statement and the transitional period on 13-16 December 2002, the meeting has elected a [six-member] leadership council of the Iraqi opposition and the following 14 specialist committees: 1. Operational; 2. Media; 3. Reconstruction and development; 4. Foreign relations; 5. National outreach; 6. Social; 7. Economic; 8. UN resolutions follow-up; 9. Displaced and deportees; 10. Finance; 11. Legal and constitutional; 12. Human rights; 13. Relief; and 14. Education and higher education.

This is in order to prepare for liberation and to prevent the emergence of a political, administrative and security vacuum. It is also to guarantee the best possible representation for the Iraqi people in the international arena and with friendly states who wish to cooperate with them. The meeting emphasized the importance of cooperation with the widest possible forces of our people to reach the goal of change, face all possible eventualities and to prepare for the transitional period, which will begin immediately after the collapse of Saddam's tyrant regime.

Within this framework, the meeting decided to continue dialogue with forces that did not participate in this meeting, or the London conference of the Iraqi opposition, and we call upon them to join this patriotic process. We call upon all people with expertise and specialist skills inside Iraq and in exile to be engaged in this work, to assist in building a future Iraq, to be in contact with the administration and the existing infrastructure in the country and to carry out the necessary tasks during the transitional period. Furthermore, the effects of Saddam's brutal policies must be eradicated to pave the way to transition to a parliamentary system and constitutional traditions in a united, democratic, pluralistic, and federal Iraq that respects Islamic values and religious freedoms and practices.

The experiment in Kurdistan and all its progress of the last 11 years, is the best proof of what the Iraqis can achieve. The delegates of the meeting noticed the great achievements in all fields of development political, democratic, providing security and stability, national reconciliation and transparency in spite of the difficult and complicated circumstances and the pressures and destruction the area faces that remained after the Iraqi regime left the region in 1991. It must also be taken into account that this area came under two economic embargos, not just one. The delegates enjoyed the hospitality of the Kurdish leadership, especially the Kurdistan Democratic Party under the leadership of Mas'ud Barzani, and the Patriotic Union of Kurdistan under the leadership of Jalal Talabani.

The delegates discussed Iraq's ties with its neighbours and they also expressed appreciation for the positive historical role of both the Syrian Arab Republic and the Islamic Republic of Iran. Those two countries were the first who welcomed the Iraqi opposition and refugees and they carried a large burden as a result of this. In this context, the meeting also expressed appreciation for the role played by two neighbouring countries, Kuwait and Turkey. The meeting sent its greetings to all people, organizations and friendly states in the world.

In particular, it sends its greetings to the ambassador-at-large for free Iraqis, Dr Zalmay Khalilzad, and the accompanying delegates for coming to Iraq, in spite of difficulties, to meet the delegates and members of the Coordination and Follow-Up Committee on behalf of US President George W. Bush in order to convey the US administration's messages and views. Dr Khalilzad's important address to the opening session included a confirmation of statements made by the president that the United States does not intend to change one dictator for another, that it supports a democratic regime in Iraq – as mentioned in the president's September speech – that the US has no desire to govern Iraq and that the Iraqis should choose who will govern them.[5]

[5] White House envoy Zalmay Khalilzad had addressed the opening session of the conference on 26 February 2003. He said in part: 'We have come here to confirm our commitment to the establishment of an Iraqi government that represents the Iraqi people with an Iraqi base, that respects the principles of justice and the rule of law, and the right of the Iraqi people and country to live in peace with neighbours, complies with all relevant UN Security Council resolutions and maintains Iraq's territorial integrity. [...] Iraqis should be free to choose their own government, be it parliamentary or presidential, and to choose the form of relationship between its centre and the regions, including federalism. We expect that a free Iraq will reform institutions, and that the de-Ba'athization, or de-Ba'athification, of existing institutions will serve to protect the Iraqi people, not to oppress them. [...] The US has no desire, no desire, to govern Iraq. The Iraqi people should govern their own affairs as soon as possible. [...] What the US and its coalition partners must do now is to form a larger coalition with the Iraqi people. If the US and the coalition military forces have to enter Iraq, they will need practical help and assistance to identify what has to be done to meet immediate humanitarian needs and to identify how and where to begin the reconstruction of the country. As part of this process we have Iraqi political forces here in Salah-al-Din as well as Iraqis from throughout the broad community of free Iraqis, and I have urged the formation of several task forces. As partners, free Iraqis and the coalition will plan together for a new and democratic Iraq. And while these task forces at present will be made up only of currently free Iraqis, they must be expanded to include liberated Iraqis as the country is free. The task forces we have in mind could include humanitarian and reconstruction task force to provide practical ideas and strategies and to work together for the reconstruction of Iraq, facilitating humanitarian assistance to Iraqis in need and the provision of services to all Iraqis on the basis of equal treatment under law. A political task force to provide Iraqi thinking about the transition period and how best to move quickly towards a democratic future. A military task force to work with the coalition on how best to provide security in post-Saddam Iraq. A public diplomacy task force to provide the Iraqi perspective to the international community as to why Iraqis deserve and demand liberation from the oppressive Saddam Hussein regime. An Iraqi [word indistinct] task force to work to send messages of hope to the Iraqis living under Saddam Hussein's rule about their future in a democratic and free Iraq. At the conclusion of this conference, we will immediately begin working with these task forces at Centcom, in Washington and elsewhere. [...] The decision who ultimately governs Iraq is a decision for the Iraqi people. Along with a great respect that we have for our friends in the opposition, we also have a great respect and sympathy for the brave Iraqis who have been suffering inside the country under the Saddam Hussein regime. We look forward to working with them as well to build a new Iraq. [...] Our goal will be for an accountable representative Iraqi government to rule Iraq, and we will work together in support of the Iraqi people to achieve this. Should military action against Iraq be necessary, the coalition will not depart one minute before this job is done, nor stay in Iraq one minute after it is completed. [...].' (US envoy reaffirms US commitment to regime

These policies were received by the delegates with great appreciation of the president of the United States.

The meeting also sent a special message to other Arab states urging them to support the endeavour of the Iraqi people, who have many strong ties with Arab countries. It also urged those who are still trying to save the Iraqi regime to give up their short-sighted policies.

The meeting also supports all those who have tried to put pressure on Saddam Hussein to give up power in order to ensure a peaceful transition that will end the brutal regime and all its polices. We ask them to continue these efforts to stop war and to stop this terrible saga in Iraq's history.

The meeting also discussed the humanitarian issue and put forward views for emergency relief and development. It emphasized that for the Iraqi economy to recover and its massive potential growth to develop in such a way as to support the democratic process in the future, Iraq requires massive financial resources that can only come from the production of Iraqi oil through a guaranteed fair share of the international market. It also requires the readiness of regional and international communities to provide humanitarian aid and endeavour to solve the issue of debts, compensation and the freeing up of Iraqi assets abroad.

At the end of this historic meeting, the delegates salute the steadfast freedom fighters, our martyrs and their families, and we hail the political prisoners, detainees and the exiled, displaced and disappeared people. The meeting also calls upon the people of Iraq who continue to be under the reign of repression and destitution to prepare for liberation day. The delegates also salute our people in exile and call on them to increase their activities and mobilize and unify their efforts so that we all have one unified vision of the future of Iraq.

The meeting also sends a call to all citizens who are conscripted in the party organization and the many other party institutions: The coming order will be about tolerance, forgiveness and reconciliation. It will end all forms of ethnic and religious discrimination and eradicate all repressive laws and all forms of behaviour that are outside the law.

A future Iraq will be for all: Arabs, Kurds, Turkomans, Assyrians, Chaldeans and other ethnic minorities, Muslims and Christians, Shi'a, Sunni and all other cultural diversities. Iraq will not be for one individual or one party or a single ethnic minority group to the exclusion of the rest of the Iraqi people.

Document 579
Statement of the Iraqi Leadership Council
26 March 2003[6]

In the name of God, the Merciful, the Compassionate: The Iraqi opposition forces – including parties, organizations, scholars, religious, patriotic, democratic, scientific and social figures, patriotic tribes across all nationalities, sects and strata, led by the forces that have been active inside the country and the figures and groups who have joined force with them within the Iraqi opposition Coordination and Follow-up Committee – have been struggling against the

change in Iraq, BBC Monitoring Middle East – Political, 26 February 2003). See also the statement of the White House press secretary on 'the just-concluded meeting of the Iraqi opposition Advisory Committee in Salahudeen' issued on 1 March 2003 which is reproduced in the Chronology section in volume I.

[6] Iraqi opposition statement on post-Saddam phase - text, BBC Summary of World Broadcasts, 29 March 2003. Text of report by Iraqi Kurdistan Democratic Party (KDP) newspaper Brayati on 28 March 2003.

criminal dictatorship imposed on people with the force of fire and steel. Our people have suffered a great deal from this criminal regime whose hands are red with the blood of tens of thousands of our martyrs who were martyred in the process of the Kurdish liberation movement, during the popular March 1991 uprising and in jails and exiles.

For 30 years, the opposition has been struggling for the liberation of the Iraqi people from the evil of dictatorship, which has given away the independence and dignity of our country, and sacrificed endless numbers of cadres, militants and mujahidin for the sake of freedom of Iraqi peoples and the restoration of dignity to Iraq.

While the treacherous dictatorship resorted to all sorts of unholy alliances and shameful concessions in order to remain in power, our Iraqi opposition continued to cause great damage and strike painful blows to the regime and expose its naked bloody dictatorship which is devoid of any Islamic, Arab and humanitarian values. By doing so, it isolated the regime from the people and greatly weakened it; thus, making it easier for those who wish to wage war against this dictatorship.

Last year when our delegation visited the US, we openly expressed our conviction, calling on US and the world to support our struggles to fulfil this sacred mission by Iraqi hands and we expressed our wish to rid our people from the calamities of invasion and tragedies of external war. We asked for help to end the dictatorship in line with international resolutions instead of waging war and invasion.

But the arrogance of the criminal ruling dictatorship and its insistence on denying our people their right to rule themselves through their true representatives, elected in free and fair elections, and its insistence on refusing the implementation of international resolutions it had signed in weakness and submission to maintain its power, dragged our country into a military confrontation with the most powerful force in the world and caused a war, the outcome of which is clear, and which will cause great harm to the people and the country.

The dictator chose this road of war instead of relinquishing power and spare [sic] the country a fierce war and the people from its disasters and tragedies. As often put forth by Ba'thist propaganda, the regime is determined to leave a desolate Iraq without people.

The Leadership Council of the Iraqi opposition, which represents the major important and active opposition forces inside Iraq and enjoys the trust and support of the majority of Iraqi people, including Kurds, Arabs, Turkomans, Assyrians and Chaldeans, as well as Sunnis and Shi'is. This force possesses tens of thousands of fighters and kilometres of areas liberated from dictatorship.

The Leadership Council of the Iraqi opposition, aware of its patriotic responsibility to save the country, people and army, finds it its essential duty to define the path of deliverance from war and dictatorship, and to define the path of liberation and national unity and creation of a democratic, federal, pluralist Iraq.

Therefore, while appreciating international support to end the dictatorship, we call for:

1. Our Iraqi people in the north, centre and south of the country to prepare for a popular uprising and the liberation of villages and towns from the pains of dictatorship and join the Leadership Council and the forces of Iraqi national opposition, which are operating under this leadership.

2. The Iraqi army and all the members of the armed forces to join the Iraqi national opposition and disengage from the Iraqi regime in the following ways:

   A. In the south of the country; after joining the Iraqi opposition, the Leadership Council and the forces joining it will inform allied forces to distinguish between the forces of opposition and the forces of the regime so that the opposition forces will carry out their duties to protect the security of citizens, public property and prevent incidents of vengeance and chaos.

B. In the north; contacts to be made with the liberated areas of Kurdistan to join them and the opposition in the area or to move to the liberated areas if they find it unsafe to remain in their own places.

C. In the central parts of Iraq; the forces should declare their allegiance to the Iraqi opposition and contact the Leadership Council for coordination with them.

The Leadership Council of the Iraqi opposition calls upon the Iraqi armed forces not to carry out the orders of the tyrant Saddam and avoid becoming fuel for its destructive lost war and calls upon them to cleanse their ranks from traitors, join the opposition and follow the guidance and instruction of its Leadership Council.

3. Embassies and diplomatic missions abroad to declare their dissociation from the ruling regime and join the Iraqi opposition and the bodies formed by it.

4. Upon the liberation of Iraq, the Leadership Council will declare the formation of an independent transitional coalition government to run the affairs of the country and protect the dignity, independence and national sovereignty and the unity of the country. This transitional government will include political figures from among technocrats with clean past history of struggle and the best talents, skills, competence and commitment. It will represent the composition of Iraqi society and its political strands.

Among the missions of this government will be to hold talks with allied countries and the UN on locating and destroying weapons of mass destruction and agreeing a timetable for the withdrawal of the allied forces from Iraq.

5. Declaring the establishment of a transitional national assembly from the members of the Coordination and Follow-up Committee and the representatives of parties and groups and other unrepresented forces from among patriotic and national elements inside and outside the country. The role of this assembly will be to pass laws during the transitional period and monitor the transitional coalition government in line with the final statements of the London Iraqi opposition conference and Salah-al-Din meeting.[7]

6. Urging the UN, fraternal countries, allied countries and all the countries of the world to lift the sanctions against Iraq and cancel the penalties and interests on loans, and offer economic, technological and scientific support for the reconstruction and development of Iraq.

7. Creation of a peaceful, democratic, free civil society and restructuring the armed forces and government bodies on modern democratic principles, distant from ethnic, sectarian and partisan discrimination.

O dignified Iraqi masses, sons of proud armed forces, patriotic tribes: Saving our people from war and the dying dictatorship requires correct awareness of the need for organized popular uprising through close cooperation between the masses of the people in towns and villages, armed forces loyal to the country and the people, and the Iraqi tribes concerned about the honour of Iraq and its glorious heritage.

Start to organize your ranks and mobilize your forces.

The time of jihad for liberation from the criminal Ba'thist Aflaqi regime has come.

Many peoples in the world have taken advantage of wars to change them into wars of liberation and true democracy, wars of deliverance of people from the tragedies of war, wars of ending dictatorship.

Let this war be a war of liberation and democracy by our people, a war of uprooting the dictatorship.

The Leadership Council of the Iraqi Opposition

Salah-al-Din, 26 March 2003

[7] See *Docs 577* and *578*, respectively.

Document 580
13 Points Agreed to by the Future of Iraq Forum
15 April 2003[8]

1. Iraq must be democratic.
2. The future government of Iraq should not be based on communal identity.
3. A future government should be organized as a democratic federal system, but on a basis of countrywide consultation.
4. The rule of law must be paramount.
5. That Iraq must be built on respect for diversity including respect for the role of women.
6. The meeting discussed the role of religion in state and society.
7. The meeting discussed the principle that Iraqis must choose their leaders, not have them imposed from outside.
8. That political violence must be rejected, and Iraqis must immediately organize themselves for the task of reconstruction at both local and national levels.
9. That Iraqis and the Coalition must work together to tackle the immediate issues of restoring security and basic services.
10. That the Baath Party must be dissolved and its effects on society must be eliminated.
11. That there should be an open dialogue with all national political groups to bring them into the process.
12. That the meeting condemns the looting that has taken place and the destruction of documents.
13. The Iraqi participants voted to have another meeting in 10 days. That the meeting would be held with additional Iraqi participants in a location to be determined. It will discuss procedures for developing an interim Iraq authority.[9]

Document 581
Statement of the Iraqi Leadership Council
7 July 2003[10]

The Iraqi Leadership Council convened its meeting in Salah al-Din in Iraq Kurdistan on 7 July 2003. It discussed the current situation and conditions in Iraq. It welcomed the project of the establishment of a transitional governing council and considered it as a step in the

[8] The meeting of Iraqis and Iraqi exiles was chaired by Lt. Gen. Jay Garner. The statement was distributed by Coalition Forces as leaflet bearing code number IZ G 143. The leaflet was accompanied by a another leaflet entitled 'Visions for Freedom of Iraq' which read: 'On April 15 near the town of Nasiriyah, up to a hundred Iraqis representing every part of Iraq came together to discuss the visions they have for their own future and how best to chart a course toward a democratic representative government. At the end of the session, the Iraqi participants voted and approved a final statement proposing 13 principles for a future Iraqi government.' The 13 points were also issued on 15 April 2003 in a Press Statement of the United States Central Command and in a Pentagon Briefing. A Weekly Update from the Department of Defense, 15 April 2003 EXTRA, at 2. In the latter publication, point 13 reads as follows: The Iraqi participation in the Nasiriyah meeting voted that there should be another meeting in 10 days in a location to be determined with additional Iraqi participants, to discuss procedures for developing an Iraqi Interim Authority.'

[9] Another version of the 'Nasiriyah Principles' reads: '13. The Iraqi participation in the Nasiriyah meeting voted that there should be another meeting in 10 days in a location to be determined with additional Iraqi participants and to discuss procedures for developing and Iraqi interim authority.'

[10] Iraqi political leaders calls for establishment of national government, BBC Monitoring Middle East - Political, 10 July 2003. Excerpt from report by Iraqi Kurdistan Democratic Party (KDP) newspaper Al-Ta'akhi on 8 July 2003.

right direction for the establishment of a transitional Iraqi government, which would reflect the Iraqi reality, comprising political figures, competent people who have impeccable history and influential figures in the society, who would have the authority and ability to draw up policies and implement them in various domains, including the appointment of ministers and follow up the work of the council of ministers.

It will provide security, stability and the necessary services in coordination with the coalition administration in all spheres, as well as representing Iraq in the international arena and foreign relations.

The Leadership Council highly praised the struggle of the heroic Iraqi people and their sacrifices during the period of the recent conflict until the fall of the entombed regime.

It condemned the acts of sabotage and crimes committed by the enemies of the Iraqi people and agents of the deposed regime, which target the infrastructure and Iraqi people's interests, and their security and stability.

The meeting stressed that it attaches particular importance to the drawing up of a permanent constitution which should represent the will of the Iraqi people, comprising Arabs, Kurds, Turkomans and Chaldo-Assyrians an the basis of political and sectarian pluralism, involving the constituents of the civil society.

It stressed the need for reforming the judicial system and the establishment of a special tribunal to investigate genocide and crimes against humanity committed by members of the deposed regime and those responsible for the mass graves.

[Signed] The Leadership Council of the Iraqi Political Parties

VIII

Documents of Grand Ayatollah Ali al-Sistani

Document 582
Fatwa of Grand Ayatollah Ali al-Sistani
26 June 2003[1]

In the Name of the Almighty.

Those forces have no jurisdiction whatsoever to appoint members of the Constitution preparation assembly. Also there is no guarantee either that this assembly will prepare a constitution that serves the best interests of the Iraqi people or express their national identity whose backbone is sound Islamic religion and noble social values. The said plan is unacceptable from the outset.

First of all there must be a general election so that every Iraqi citizen – who is eligible to vote – can choose someone to represent him in a foundational Constitution preparation assembly. Then the drafted Constitution can be put to a referendum.

All believers must insist on the accomplishment of this crucial matter and contribute to achieving it in the best way possible.

May Allah The Blessed Almighty, guide everyone to that which is good and beneficial.

Peace and Allah's love and blessings be upon you.

[Signed & Sealed] *Ali Al-Hussaini al-Sistani*
25 Rabiul-Akhar 1424
26 June 2003[2]

Document 583
Statement of Grand Ayatollah Ali al-Sistani
28 November 2003

In the Name of Allah, The Compassionate The Most Merciful.

His Eminence the Sayyid (long may he live) has some reservations regarding the said plan.

Firstly, it is based on preparing the law of the Iraqi state, for the transitional period, through the Governing Council in conjunction with the occupying power - thus not providing it with legitimacy. For this (legitimacy) to be achieved it must be presented to representatives of the Iraqi people for approval.

[1] The fatwas and letters of Grand Ayatollah Ali Al-Sistani are available at http://www.najaf.org/.

[2] The Fatwa was issued in response to the following letter:

'In The Name of Allah The Merciful The Most Compassionate
Your Eminence,
Our Dear Marja' Grand Ayatollah Sayyid Ali al-Hussaini Al-Sistani (long may he live).
Peace be on you and blessings of Allah.

The occupying forces in Iraq have announced their decision to establish an assembly to prepare the next Iraqi Constitution and that they will appoint the members of this assembly after consulting political and social groups in the country. Then the Constitution drafted by the assembly will be presented for a general referendum.

Kindly clarify the position [of this plan] according to Sharia' and what the believers must do regarding this matter of drafting the Iraqi Constitution.

A Group of Believers
20 Rabiul-Akhar 1424
21 June 2003'

Secondly, the mechanism in place to choose members of the Transitional Legislative Assembly does not guarantee the establishment of an assembly that truly represents the Iraqi people. Therefore this mechanism must be replaced with one that guarantees the aforesaid, which is 'elections', so the Assembly will emanate from the desire of the Iraqi people and will represent them fairly without its legitimacy being tarnished in any way. Perhaps 'elections' can be organized using rationing-cards and other supplements.
Seal of the Office of Sayyid Sistani – Najaf
3 Shawwal 1424
28 November 2003[3]

Document 584
Statement of Grand Ayatollah Ali al-Sistani

11 January 2004

In the Name of Allah, The Compassionate The Most Merciful.

His Eminence Al-Sayyid al-Sistani has met with Adnan al-Pachachi, the rotating president of the Iraqi Governing Council, who explained to his Eminence the latest developments pertaining to the political process. He also briefed his Eminence on the message sent to him by UN Secretary-General Kofi Annan on this issue.

At this meeting, his Eminence reiterated that the mechanism delineated in the 15 November agreement on the formation of a provisional national council did not ensure at all the Iraqi people's fair representation in the council. He explained that elections were the ideal means to achieve that representation and many experts had affirmed that elections could be held in the coming months with an acceptable degree of credibility and transparency.

His Eminence added that if the provisional national council was formed on the basis of a mechanism that did not enjoy the necessary legitimacy, it would not be able and neither would the government emanating from it be able, to carry out their tasks and honour the timetable set for the transitional period. Consequently, this would create serious problems and the political and security situation would further exacerbate.

His Eminence emphasized that the provisional law of the Iraqi state and the security agreement must be submitted to the representatives of the Iraqi people in the provisional national council so that they could endorse them to ensure their legitimacy.

At the meeting, his Eminence underlined the need to maintain the unity of Iraq – land and people. He also underlined the need for Iraq to have the best of relations with the countries of the region, particularly the fraternal Arab states.
Seal of the Office of Sayyid Sistani – Najaf
18 Dhu'l-Qa'dah 1424
11 January 2004

[3] The statement was made in response to the question: 'What is Sayyid Sistani's opinion of the new plan for a political transition in Iraq? Does he bless the process?'

Document 585
Statement of Grand Ayatollah Ali al-Sistani
8 March 2004

In the Name of Allah, The Compassionate The Most Merciful.

His Eminence has previously clarified his reservations regarding the 15th of November accord that any law drafted for the transition period will not gain legitimacy unless approved by the elected national assembly. In addition, this law places obstacles in reaching a permanent constitution for the country that preserves its unity and the rights of its people from all ethnicities and sects.

Office of Ayatolloah Sistani – Najaf
16 Muharram 1425
8 March 2004[4]

Document 586
Letter to the President of the UN Security Council from the Office of Grand Ayatollah Ali al-Sistani
6 June 2004

H.E. Head of the United Nations Security Council
Greetings,

We have been informed of the attempts to include the so called 'administrative law for the transitional period' in the new UNSC Resolution on Iraq, with a view to making it appear internationally legitimate.

This 'law' that has been drawn up by an un-elected council under occupation, and through its direct influence, would restrict the national assembly which is due to be elected early next year to draw up the permanent Iraqi constitution.

This is against the laws and rejected by most Iraqi people. Therefore, any attempt to make this 'law' appear legitimate by including it in the international resolution is considered as contrary to the desire of the Iraqi people and a forewarning to dangerous consequences.

Kindly convey the position of the Religious Marja'iyya in this regard to their Excellencies the honorable members of the Security Council.

Thank you.

Seal of the Office of Ayatollah Sistani in Najaf
6 June 2004

[4] The statement was made in response to the following question:
'In the Name of Allah, The Compassionate The Most Merciful.
The Office of Grand Ayatolloah Sayyid Sistani (long may he live).
Peace be on you and blessings of Allah.
What is the position of our dear Marja' and Sayyid vis-à-vis Iraq's interim constitution for the transition period?
A Group of Believers
16 Muharram 1425
8 March 2004'

IX

Miscellaneous Documents

Document 587
Statement on the Future of Iraq by Turkey, the United States and Iraqi Opposition Groups

19 March 2003[5]

Representatives of Turkey and the United States met with delegations of ADM, CMM, INA, INC, ITF, KDP, PUK and SCIRI[6] on March 19, 2003, in Ankara, Turkey.

All participants agree that among their principle objectives regarding the future of Iraq are the following:

- Enabling the Iraqi people to build a fully representative and democratic government that meets international standards, including free and fair elections, respect for the rule of law and private property, equality before the law and respect for human rights, consistent with principles agreed at the opposition conference in London;
- Preservation of Iraq's independence, sovereignty, territorial integrity and national unity;
- Elimination of Iraq's weapons of mass destruction capabilities, in accordance with relevant United Nations Security Council resolutions;
- Full compliance with all relevant UNSC resolutions to allow for Iraq's full re-integration into the world community so that there would be no need for sanctions or no-fly zones;
- Determining the future political system and the constitution for Iraq through the full participation and free consent of the totality of the Iraqi population;
- Using the natural resources of Iraq as a national asset and for the Iraqi people as a whole, to strengthen the national economy;
- Making use of the above principle objectives, in order to help foster national unity and reflect the reality that all parts and cities of Iraq belong to the nation as a whole, in perpetuity;
- Protecting civilian lives and property, strongly discouraging the uncontrolled movements of refugees and internally displaced persons, and strongly discouraging Iraqis from taking the law into their own hands or inciting civil discord. All claims will be addressed via a commission that will quickly be set up for a legal and organized process to address the restitution of homes seized previously by the Iraqi regime, and other claims. All Iraqis who have rightful claims will be able to resolve them in a peaceful and orderly manner through this commission;
- Elimination of discrimination based on race, ethnic origin, gender, language or religious conviction. The protection of the rights and freedoms of all constituent peoples of Iraq – Arabs, Kurds, Turkomans, Assyrians, Chaldeans and others – will be paramount in a future Iraq;
- The reformation of the Iraqi national military, to include the reintegration of all militia organizations (including those forces now operating under the command of the Iraqi opposition) and the reformation of Iraq's security institutions;
- Elimination of terrorism and of support for terrorism in and from Iraq, as well as denial of safe havens and weaponry to terrorists.

[5] Iraqi opposition, US, Turkey issue statement after Ankara meeting, BBC Summary of World Broadcasts, 21 March 2003. Text in Arabic published by Iraqi Patriotic Union of Kurdistan (PUK) newspaper Al-Ittihad on 21 March 2003.

[6] Assyrian Democratic Movement (ADM), Constitutional Monarchy Movement (CMM), Iraqi National Accord (INA), Iraqi National Congress (INC), Iraqi Turkoman Front (ITF), Kurdistan Democratic Party (KDP), Patriotic Union of Kurdistan (PUK), Supreme Council for Islamic Revolution in Iraq (SCIRI).

Document 588

An Arrangement for the Transfer of Prisoners of War, Civilian Internees, and Civilian Detainees between the Forces of the United States of America, the United Kingdom of Great Britain and Northern Ireland, and Australia

23 March 2003[1]

This arrangement establishes procedures in the event of the transfer from the custody of either the US, UK, or Australian forces to the custody of any of the other parties, any Prisoners of War, Civilian Internees, and Civilian Detainees taken during operations against Iraq. The Parties undertake as follows:

1. This arrangement will be implemented in accordance with the Geneva Convention Relative to the Treatment of Prisoners of War[2] and the Geneva Convention Relative to the Protection of Civilian Persons in Time of War,[3] as well as customary international law.

2. US, UK, and Australian forces will, as mutually determined, accept (as Accepting Powers) prisoners of war, civilian internees, and civilian detainees who have fallen into the power of any of the other parties (the Detaining Power), and will be responsible for maintaining and safeguarding all such individuals whose custody has been transferred to them. Transfers of prisoners of war, civilian internees, and civilian detainees between Accepting Powers may take place as mutually determined by both the Accepting Power and the Detaining Power.

3. Arrangements to transfer prisoners of war, civilian internees, and civilian detainees who are casualties will be expedited, in order that they may be treated according to their medical priority. All such transfers will be administered and recorded within the systems established under this arrangement for the transfer of prisoners of war, civilian internees, and civilian detainees.

4. Any prisoners of war, civilian internees, and civilian detainees transferred by a Detaining Power will be returned by the Accepting Power to the Detaining Power without delay upon request by the Detaining Power.

5. The release or repatriation or removal to territories outside Iraq of transferred prisoners of war, civilian internees, and civilian detainees will only be made upon the mutual arrangement of the Detaining Power and the Accepting Power.

6. The Detaining Power will retain full rights of access to any prisoners of war, civilian internees, and civilian detainees transferred from Detaining Power custody while such persons are in the custody of the Accepting Power.

7. The Accepting Power will be responsible for the accurate accountability of all prisoners of war, civilian internees, and civilian detainees transferred to it. Such records will be available for inspection by the Detaining Power upon request. If prisoners of war, civilian internees, or civilian detainees are returned to the Detaining Power, the records (or a true copy of the same) relating to those prisoners of war, civilian internees, and civilian detainees will also be handed over.

[1] The text of the Arrangement was first published in Margo Kingston, Avoiding the Geneva Conventions: how Australia does the job, *The Sydney Morning Herald*, 3 June 2004, http://www.smh.com.au/.

[2] Geneva Convention III provides for the transfer of prisoners of war (POW) from the Detaining Power to an Accepting Power under Art. 12 (2) and (3).

[3] Geneva Convention IV deals with the transfer of civilians from the Detaining Power to a Transferee Power in Art. 45.

8. The Detaining Powers will assign liaison officers to Accepting Powers [in] order to facilitate the implementation of this arrangement.

9. The Detaining Power will be solely responsible for the classification under Articles 4 and 5 of the Geneva Convention Relative to the Treatment of Prisoners of War of potential prisoners of war captured by its forces. Prior to such a determination being made, such detainees will be treated as prisoners of war and afforded all the rights and protections of the Convention even if transferred to the custody of an Accepting Power.

10. Where there is doubt as to which party is the Detaining Power, all Parties will be jointly responsible for and have full access to all persons detained (and any records concerning their treatment) until the Detaining Power has by mutual arrangement been determined.

11. To the extent that jurisdiction may be exercised for criminal offenses, to include pre-capture offenses, allegedly committed by prisoners of war, civilian internees, and civilian detainees prior to a transfer to an Accepting Power, primary jurisdiction will initially rest with the Detaining Power. Detaining Powers will give favorable consideration to any request by an Accepting Power to waive jurisdiction.

12. Primary jurisdiction over breaches of disciplinary regulations and judicial offenses allegedly committed by prisoners of war, civilian internees, and civilian detainees after transfer to an Accepting Power will rest with the Accepting Power.

13. The Detaining Power will reimburse the Accepting Power for the costs involved in maintaining prisoners of war, civilian internees, and civilian detainees transferred pursuant to this arrangement.

14. At the request of one of the Parties, the Parties will consult on the implementation of this arrangement.

Done at Camp As Sayliyah, Doha, Qatar on this 23rd day of March 2003.

For the United States of America: John P. Abizaid, LTG, USA, United States Central Command

For the United Kingdom of Great Britain And Northern Ireland: B.K. Burridge, Air Marshall, United Kingdom National Contingent Commander

For and on behalf of Australia: M. R. McNarn, Brigadier, Commander Australian National Headquarters

Document 589
Joint Declaration of Iraq's Neighbouring States

28 May 2003[4]

Within the framework of the 30th Session of the Islamic Conference of Foreign Ministers and in response to the initiative of the Islamic Republic of Iran to consider the latest developments in Iraq, the Foreign Ministers and the Heads of Delegations of the Kingdom of Bahrain, the Arab Republic of Egypt, the Islamic Republic of Iran, the Hashemite Kingdom of Jordan, the State of Kuwait, the Kingdom of Saudi Arabia, the Syrian Arab Republic, and the Republic of

[4] The Declaration was included in the Final Communique of the Thirtieth Session of the Islamic Conference of Foreign Ministers (Session of Unity and Dignity), held in Tehran, Islamic Republic of Iran, on 27-29 Rabiul-Awal 1424H (28-30 May 2003); see para 37 of the Final Communique available at http://www.oic-oci.org/.

Turkey, held a meeting in Tehran on 26th of Rabiul-Awal 1424H (28 May 2003). During this gathering, the Ministers and Heads of Delegations recalled the proceedings of their meetings in Istanbul on 23 January 2003 and in Riyadh on 18 April 2003. They discussed the current situation in Iraq. Based on their deliberations and taking into account the developments in that country, the Ministers and Heads of Delegations agreed on the following:

- Expressed their solidarity with the Iraqi people in the spirit of Islamic brotherhood,
- Reaffirmed the necessity for all to respect the sovereignty, political independence, national unity, territorial integrity and stability of Iraq and to comply with these principles,
- Reiterated the right of the Iraqi people to freely determine their political future and to establish a fully representative and broad-based government in a safe and peaceful environment. This must be a matter of priority,
- Emphasized also the inalienable right of the Iraqi people to enjoy a decent and comfortable life based on the rule of law, equality and respect for fundamental human rights and freedoms,
- Stressed the right of the Iraqi people to fully control and utilize their own natural resources through a legitimate and representative government,
- Emphasized the principle of non-interference in the internal affairs of Iraq as well as the necessity for Iraq to establish good relations with all its neighbours and to respect the existing treaties and agreements, especially those on internationally recognized boundaries,
- Noted Security Council Resolution 1483[5] and, in this context, welcomed the lifting of economic sanctions while expressing the hope that the humanitarian suffering of the Iraqi people will be alleviated, and underlined the need to comply with relevant Security Council resolutions,
- Underlined the central role of the United Nations in post-war Iraq, especially with regard to the establishment of a representative government, rehabilitation of local institutions, provision of humanitarian relief and reconstruction,
- Welcomed the appointment of a special representative of the United Nations' Secretary-General, and expressed their firm determination to cooperate fully with him,
- Called for the speedy restoration for full Iraqi sovereignty through the establishment of a legitimate government and an end to occupation,
- Underlined also the obligations of the occupying forces under international law, especially the 1949 Geneva Convention to safeguard security, stability, civil liberties and rights of the Iraqi people as well as the religious, historical, archaeological and cultural heritage of Iraq. It emphasized the necessity for them to act in a manner that will ensure respect for the sovereignty and territorial integrity of the neighbouring countries,
- Welcomed the initiative by Syria at the UN Security Council on the establishment of a zone free of weapons of mass destruction in the Middle East.

The Ministers and Heads of Delegations agreed that the objective of this process, first initiated in Istanbul, continued in Riyadh and now in Tehran, by countries of the region is to help restore peace, stability and security in Iraq. These countries should continue to lend the requisite support for these objectives in the future. The Ministers and Heads of Delegations therefore decided to hold further meetings until normalcy, security and stability are fully restored in Iraq.

[5] See *Doc 523*.

Document 590
Memorandum of Understanding Concerning Command Arrangements and Related Matters for the Multinational Division (Central South) (MND C-S) within the Stabilization Force in Iraq

28 August 2003[6]

SECTION ONE – INTRODUCTION

The Republic of Latvia, Ministry of Defence of the Republic of Bulgaria, the Ministry of Defence of the Kingdom of Denmark, the Secretary of the Armed Forces of the Dominican Republic, the Department of National Defence of the Philippines, the Secretary of Defence of the Republic of Honduras, the Ministry of Defence of the Republic of Hungary, the Ministry of Defence of the Republic of Kazakhstan, the Ministry of National Defence of the Republic of Lithuania, the Ministry of Defence of Mongolia, the Minister of Defence of the Kingdom of the Netherlands, the Ministry of Defence of the Republic of Nicaragua, the Ministry of Defence of the Kingdom of Norway, the Ministry of National Defence of Romania, the Ministry of Defence of the Republic of El Salvador, the Ministry of Defence of the Slovak Republic, the Ministry of Defence of the Kingdom of Spain, the Ministry of Defence of the Kingdom of Thailand, the Ministry of Defence of Ukraine and the Minister of National Defence of the Republic of Poland, hereinafter jointly referred to as the Participants;

In consideration of United Nations Security Council Resolution (UNSCR) 1483 of 22 May 2003[7] and Geneva Conventions of 1949 and the Hague Regulations of 1907;

Having regard to the maintenance of security in Iraq, so that an Iraqi Interim Authority as well as the personnel of the contributing Nations can operate in a secure environment;

Considering the intention of the Government of the Republic of Poland to assume Lead Nation status for the Multinational Division (Central South) (MND C-S) Iraq as soon as in the period of establishment of the Division;

Desiring to establish a multinational burden-sharing arrangement within the MND(C-S);

Considering the needs of the Participants' forces for logistic support, supplies and services when deployed with the MND(C-S) and taking into account that although the Kingdom of Spain has indicated its intent to contribute forces to MND(C-S), Spanish units will not receive free of charge sustainment or other logistical requirements;

And acknowledging extant bilateral MOUs, Technical Arrangements (TAs) and Exchanges of Letters between them;

Have reached the understandings set out below:

SECTION TWO – DEFINITIONS

2.1. The definitions:

- a. *The Authority* means the United States of America and United Kingdom of Great Britain and Northern Ireland as defined by UNSCR 1483 of 22 May 2003.
- b. *Civilian Component* means the civilian personnel accompanying a force of a Participant who are in the employment of the armed service or an organic component of National Contingent of that Participant (this definition does not include contractors).

[6] The Memorandum of Understanding is available on the Website of the Latvian Parliament http://www.likumi.lv/.

[7] See *Doc 523*.

c. *Comd* MND(C-S) means the Commander of the Stabilisation Force MND(C-S), appointed by the Republic of Poland, and authorised to implement the MND(C-S) mission.
d. *Co-ordinating Authority* is the authority granted to a commander or individual assigned responsibility for co-ordinating specific functions or activities involving forces of two or more countries or commands, or two or more services or two or more forces of the same service. He has the authority to require consultation between the agencies involved or their representatives, but does not have the authority to compel agreement. In case of disagreement between the agencies involved, he should attempt to obtain essential agreement by discussion. In the event he is unable to obtain essential agreement he shall refer the matter to the appropriate authority.
e. *CPA* means the Coalition Provisional Authority, the highest administrative body established in Iraq by the Authority.
f. *DoD* means Department of Defence of the United States of America.
g. *Financial Group (FG)*, means a group responsible for managing multinational financial issues, comprised of the National Contingent Commanders/Senior National Representative or their nominees.
h. *MND(C-S)* means the multinational military unit operating within the SFIR in Iraq in area of operations as defined in the Mission Statement annexed to this MOU (Annex A).
i. *Multinational shared costs* means those costs for the maintenance and operation of HQ MND(C-S), other Multinational MND(C-S) Sections or units and other aspects of the MND(C-S) which are not the responsibility of a single Participant, and which are approved by Financial Group (FG).
j. *National Contingent* means the personnel contributed to the MND(C-S) by a Participant. The term includes the Civilian Component.
k. *National Contingent Commander* means the person designated by each Participant as the Commander of that Nation's National Contingent.
l. *National Support Element (NSE)* means the national personnel deployed by a Participant for the purpose of providing support to the National Contingent.
m. *Operational control* is the authority delegated to a commander to direct forces assigned so that the commander may accomplish specific missions or tasks which are usually limited by function, time, or location; to deploy units concerned, and to retain or assign tactical control of those units. It does not include authority to assign separate employment of components of the units concerned. Neither does it, of itself, include administrative or logistic control.
n. *Participant* means the initial signatories to this MOU as well as other Nations that may subsequently join MND(C-S) through a Note of Accession or Statement of Intent.
o. *Port Clearance* means the clearance of equipment and personnel from a SPOD or an APOD to NSE Locations or other Logistic Location.
p. *Sea Port of Disembarkation (SPOD)* and *Air Port of Disembarkation (APOD)* are the points of entry to the theatre.
q. *Senior National Representative (SNR)* means nationally appointed Senior Official within a National Contingent.
r. *SFIR* means Stabilisation Forces in Iraq. This includes all military personnel together with their aircraft, vehicles, stores, equipment, communications,

ammunition, weapons and provisions as well as civilian components of such forces, air and surface movements resources and their support services.

s. *Strategic and Tactical Lines of Communication (LOC)* means the deployment and resupply routes, both air and land. The term Strategic LOC refers to the flow into SPODs and APODs from the National Base Location. The term Tactical LOC refers to the flow from SPODs or APODs, within the theatre of operation to tactical operating locations.

t. *Tactical Control* is the detailed and, usually, local direction and control of movements or manoeuvres necessary to accomplish missions or tasks assigned.

u. *Third Party* means any person or entity not a Participant to this MOU.

v. *Troop Contributing Nation* means Participant contributing troops to MND (C-S).

SECTION THREE – PURPOSE AND SCOPE

3.1. The purpose of this MOU is to set out the arrangements by which the Participants will implement the mission and establish MND(C-S), and to set out the responsibilities, general principles and procedures as appropriate.

3.2. Extant bilateral MOUs, TAs and Exchanges of Letters will remain in effect and may be implemented for furthering the aims of this MOU. Participants may enter into bilateral or other MOU, TA or Exchanges of Letters, for furthering the purposes of this MOU.

3.3. This MOU is intended to conform with national legislation and international law and is not intended to conflict with existing bilateral or multilateral international agreements between the Participants. Should such a conflict arise, the Participants will notify each other and the national legislation, international law or extant agreement will prevail.

SECTION FOUR – MANDATE

4.1. In accordance with the UNSCR 1483, the mandate of the SFIR MND(C-S) will be to assist the Authority in maintaining stability and security in Iraq by contributing personnel, equipment and other resources to work under its unified command in accordance with arrangements set out in section five below. Main tasks of the MND(C-S) are set out in the Mission Statement annexed to this MOU (Annex A).

4.2. Members of MND(C-S) will carry out their duties in a strictly fair and equitable manner and will refrain from any action incompatible with the independent nature of their duties. This does not interfere with the right of SFIR to act in self defence, extended self defence as well as force protection and mission enforcement.

SECTION FIVE – COMMAND AND CONTROL OF MND (C-S)

5.1. The post of Commander MND(C-S) will be held by the Republic of Poland. The Republic of Poland will co-ordinate the introduction of the MND(C-S) structure and will be responsible for ensuring that the Participants remain informed of progress in implementing that structure.

5.2. Members of National Contingents will remain under Full Command of their participant through their National Contingent Commander/Senior National Representative. Operational Control of all National Contingents contributed to MND(C-S) will be assigned to a superior Commander.

5.3. Participants are responsible for planning and execution of movements of their forces and sustainment from home stations to PODs along the strategic LOCs. This responsibility can be delegated to other agencies who act on behalf of the Participants.

Reception, Staging and Onward Movements (RSOM) operations including Port Clearance will be conducted in line with existing Standard Operating Procedures unless otherwise decided. Tactical Control of all aspects of the Strategic and Tactical LOCs will be assigned to the respective Movements Control Organisations at the theatre level (CJTF-7).

5.4. Comd MND(C-S) has Co-ordinating Authority over National Support Element logistic assets in order to meet operational requirements or to ensure deconfliction of use of limited infrastructure or assets. In such circumstances the provisions of Section eleven may be applied. Those logistic assets that form all or part of a Participant's contribution to MND(C-S) will be controlled in accordance with para 5.2 above.

5.5. Transfer of Authority (TOA) of Forces to Comd MND(C-S) in accordance with the Command Status above, will take place at declared Full Operational Capability (FOC) by the National Contingent Commanders (NCCs). Participants will confirm the Command Status of their Forces by signal to Comd MND(C-S) on TOA.

5.6. National Contingent Commanders/Senior National Representatives are responsible for the maintenance of order and discipline within the National Contingent under his or her command.

5.7. Comd MND(C-S) may request the withdrawal of any personnel contributed to MND(C-S). National Contingent Commanders/Senior National Representatives will review any such request and will seek to comply where permissible in accordance with their own National regulations.

5.8. Comd MND(C-S) is responsible for coordination with CPA in the MND(C-S) AOR. Brigade Commanders after consultation with concerned Participants will nominate representatives to be the military point of contact with CPA inside their Brigade AOR, keeping informed MND(C-S) Commander. These representatives will also sit on a Joint Co-ordination Board.

5.9. English will be the official working and command language in the MND(C-S) down to the battalion level, except for the Battle Group 1.

SECTION SIX – JOINT CO-ORDINATION BOARD

6.1. A joint Co-ordination Board (JCB) will meet on a regular basis. The JCB will consist of nominated Local Iraqi representatives (as nominated by the CPA/Comd MND(C-S)) and MND (C-S) representatives. The purpose of the JCB will be to discuss current and forthcoming issues and to resolve any disputes that may arise. CPA (C-S) may also nominate a representative to attend the JCB meetings.

SECTION SEVEN – CONTRIBUTION

7.1. Participants will provide to MND(C-S) on a national or shared basis military forces and capabilities including if required a civilian component, as specified in the MND(C-S) Statement of Requirement (SOR). Any intended change in the Participants' contribution will be notified to the Lead Nation as soon as possible, but with a minimum of 30 days notice.

7.2. Each Participant will be responsible for arranging the logistic support of its own National Contingent. Participants may make separate, bi-lateral arrangements with other Participants in order to ensure such logistic support.

7.3. All members of National Contingents will be medically and dentally fit prior to deployment and will have received all necessary inoculations.

SECTION EIGHT – FINANCE

8.1. Each Participant will be responsible for the funding of its own contribution to, participation in and withdrawal from MND(C-S) unless otherwise agreed.

Participants will be individually responsible for payment of:

a. All pay and allowances for their forces, including the civilian component;

b. All costs, including accommodation, travel and other expenses, arising out of business performed by their forces, including the civilian component, away from HQ MND(C-S); and

c. All costs arising from the deployment and redeployment of their forces, including the civilian component, to and from theatre.

8.2. It is possible to get reimbursement for travel costs incurred by Participants in a pre-deployment phase. Reimbursement procedure is set out in Annex B.

8.3. Military unit and capability combined forces of two or more Participants will be pre-funded by the Participant who leads that military unit and capability. Then such costs are multinational shared and invoiced according to proportions detailed at Annex B.[8]

8.4. A Financial Group (FG), comprising National Contingent Commanders/Senior National Representatives or their nominees, will be established for the management of multinational financial issues. Costs arising from the implementation of this MOU, which are determined by the FG as multinational costs, will be shared among Participants in the proportions detailed at Annex B. The decisions of the FG are taken by consensus.

8.5. Multinational shared costs will be controlled by the FG, which have authority and responsibility for:

a. Determining whether specific expenditure is a multinational shared cost.

b. Determining the cost-sharing formula to be applied.

c. Providing national scrutiny of all multinational shared costs, including multinational shared costs to support HQ MND(C-S).

d. Approving estimates of all multinational shared costs.

e. Obtaining national approval of proposed expenditures.

f. Controlling all multinational shared costs.

8.6. Multinational costs agreed by FG will be shared among Participants proportionally to their manpower contribution to a multinational unit (see Annex B).

8.7. Pre-funded multinational costs by a Participant will be invoiced by this Participant at regular intervals, decided by FG.

8.8. Without prejudice to the provisions of Section twenty one, any financial dispute between Participants will be referred to the FG for resolution.

8.9. The Lead Nation will provide a financial controller office to HQ MND(C-S) to support the FG and administer all multinational shared costs on behalf of the Headquarters. Participants will be invited to contribute personnel to this office.

8.10. The Audit Office of the Ministry of National Defence of the Republic of Poland will be responsible for annual auditing of multinational shared costs and auditing of these costs upon termination of the MND(C-S) mission. Audit reports will be presented to Comd MND (C-S) and the Participants. National audit institutions are permitted to request all information and examine all files they consider necessary for auditing their national contributions and for informing their respective governments and parliaments; such requests will be made through Comd MND(C-S).

8.11. The MND (C-S) financial controller will provide financial management information and support requested by the FG.

8.12. All transactions related to this MOU will be settled within 90 days from receiving of an invoice by bank-transferring or in cash. Currency or currencies in MND(C-S) for all

[8] Not reproduced.

type of transactions and financial operations will be indicated by Financial Controller and accepted by FG. Average Rate (AR), the standard rate of exchange issued the first day of a month by the Polish National Bank, will be used in a course of this month when converting currency for billing purposes. The AR is reviewed monthly. The Financial Controller will reissue and deliver AR to everybody it may concern.

8.13. Each Participant retains ownership of its own resources. Jointly owned assets will not exist unless two or more Participants expressly consent to such an acquisition. Any such assets or property jointly acquired under this MOU will be disposed of in a manner decided by a consensus of the respective Participants.

8.14. The Participants will provide Comd MND(C-S) with National Points of Contact for financial matters.

SECTION NINE – HEADQUARTERS MANNING

9.1. Initially, manning of the HQ MND(C-S) will be based on the organisation chart, which will be issued by Comd MND(C-S). Participants will be invited to provide representation within various Multinational Sections established in the Headquarters for the purpose of maximising co-operation.

9.2. Responsibility for appointing suitably qualified and trained personnel to Multinational Sections will rest with the Participant to which the posts are assigned.

SECTION TEN – HEADQUARTERS SUPPORT

10.1. Support to the Headquarters staff and others resident at Babylon will be provided by the Lead Nation. Details of that support will be specified in separate arrangements.

SECTION ELEVEN – LOGISTIC SUPPORT

11.1. Logistic support for the TCN's units in the MND(C-S) is a national responsibility.

11.2. The Participants may agree under separate arrangements, either bilaterally or multilaterally to provide mutual logistic support to each other.

11.3. Unless other bilateral arrangements are made, TCN's units will be deployed with integral first line logistic support.

11.4. National contingents to be deployed by TCN's to the MND(C-S) will be responsible for the following supplies:

- Class I (food and water) – minimum 5 days of supply;
- Class II (clothing and personal equipment) – in accordance with national standards;
- Class III (bulk petroleum) – 15 days of supply;
- Class III (oil and lubricants) – 30 days of supply;
- Class V (munitions) – in accordance with national standards;
- Class VI (personal demand items) in accordance with national standards;
- Class VIII (medical supplies) – 30 days of supply;
- Class IX (spare parts) – 30 days of supply.

11.5. Maintenance and recovery of equipment is a national responsibility.

11.6. The Republic of Poland will assume responsibility for coordinating logistic support for MND(C-S), to include national elements of the troop-contributing nations, effective upon achievement of Full Operational Capability (FOC) by MND(C-S). Commander, USCENTCOM will determine FOC.

11.7. Once MND (C-S) is deemed FOC, its troop-contributing nations will submit logistical requirements to the MND(C-S) Headquarters. The Republic of Poland will request specific logistic support, supplies, and services as necessary for the entire MND(C-S) by placing orders pursuant to the ACSA.

11.8. Based on TA between Polish MOD and the US DoD, The Republic of Poland commits to provide the necessary operational and financial support and to provide or loan selected items of equipment.

11.9. The US will arrange transport for deployment and redeployment of additional troop-contributing nation personnel and equipment pursuant to USCENTCOM operational requirements and capabilities. The US will arrange air transport enabling MND(C-S) personnel rotation, provision of logistic supplies from national elements of MND(C-S)'s troop-contributing nations, air medical evacuation to Germany, and assistance with reception, staging, onward movement and integration.

11.10. MND(C-S) will be supplied by the US with the following common items:

- Class I (food and water);
- Class III (bulk fuel);
- Class IV (construction material);
- Class V (explosives);
- Class VIII (medical supplies).

11.11. Supplies mentioned in para 11.10 above and services will be requested and co-ordinated by MND(C-S) through MNLC in accordance with provisions of Acquisition and Cross-Servicing Agreement (ACSA) concluded between Polish MOD and US DoD. Save for the Spanish units, supplies and services requested will be provided free of charge for Participants' units contributed to the MND(C-S).

11.12. Supplies will be delivered directly to the Battle Group (battalion level) either by logistic capabilities at MND(C-S) level or by a civilian contractor. Distribution of supplies within Battle Group is a responsibility of leading nation of that Group.

11.13. In order to avoid competition for limited In-Country Resources, all contracting on behalf of the MND (C-S) will be carried out through the MNLC in co-ordination with CJTF-7. MNLC will distribute and update a list of those critical resources for which this article will be applied.

11.14. The TCNs are to include two Liaison Officers within their national contingent to contribute to the Multinational Logistics Centre (MNLC), responsible for M&T and logistics/contracting.

11.15. US will provide MND (C-S) with current geographic materials and data (GM&D) in requested quantities as well as meteorological data over the Central-South sector, and if necessary over other areas of Iraq. Consolidated requests for GM&D from MND (C-S) HQ will be submitted to CJTF-7 HQ. MND (C-S) will be granted the right of reproduction (replication) of received material and data only for the needs of MND (C-S). MND (C-S) will be authorised to disseminate US-made GM&D to personnel of other Participants according to release ability restrictions determined by the US. Meteorological services of MND (C-S) will have continuous access to current US meteorological databases via CIS infrastructure or other means.

SECTION TWELVE – JURISDICTION

12.1. Status of the coalition, foreign liaison missions, their personnel (including both military and civilian personnel) and contractors has been declared in the Coalition Provisional Authority Order Number 17 of 26 June 2003, a copy of which is included in Annex C.[9] Having regard to this regulation members of the SFIR MND(C-S) and supporting personnel,

[9] Not reproduced. See CPA Order No 17 *[Doc 37]*.

including associated liaison personnel, their property, funds and assets will be immune from any Iraqi legal process whilst deployed in Iraq. All members of the SFIR MND(C-S) will be required to respect the laws applicable in the territory of Iraq and Orders, Regulations, Memoranda and Public Notes issued by the Administrator of the CPA.

12.2. Members of the SFIR MND(C-S) will remain subject to the exclusive jurisdiction of their respective sending States. They will be immune from local criminal, civil and administrative jurisdiction and from any form of arrest or detention other than by persons acting by or on the behalf of their sending State. The Participants will keep Comd MND(C-S) informed of the outcome of any such exercise or jurisdiction.

SECTION THIRTEEN – UNIFORMS, EMBLEMS AND FLAGS

13.1. While performing their official duties military members of MND(C-S) will normally wear their national military uniform, together with such distinctive items of uniform as are prescribed by national orders. Comd MND(C-S) may authorise the wearing of civilian clothing where appropriate.

13.2. Lead Nation in consultation with other Participants will design MND(C-S) emblems and a medal to be used as official insignia of the Division.

SECTION FOURTEEN – RULES OF ENGAGEMENT (ROE)/CARRIAGE OF ARMS AND AMMUNITION

14.1. Members of MND(C-S) may possess and carry arms and ammunition in Iraq for the purposes of carrying out the MND(C-S) mission when authorised to do so by Comd MND (C-S).

14.2. ROE for the MND(C-S) will be a part of MND(C-S) operational order. The fundamental driver for the level of permissiveness in the ROE Profile is Force Protection rather than the MND(C-S) mission. Participants may indicate their intention to apply different levels of permissiveness to their own forces by means of national direction or clarifications to their National Contingent Commanders/Senior National Representatives provided that:

a. Initial differences are to be communicated to Comd MND(C-S) before TOA. Other differences can be communicated if there is a need.
b. No difference is more permissive than that authorised MND(C-S) ROE.

SECTION FIFTEEN – DETENTION OF PERSONS

15.1. As indicated in Mission Statement in Annex A, the Comd of MND(C-S) is the only authority to act under the Fourth Geneva Convention as the detaining power in the AOR on behalf of the Authority.

15.2. Detailed guidance for the purpose of handling detained persons authorised under the ROE will be elaborated by the Comd MND(C-S) in co-operation with the US.

SECTION SIXTEEN – CLAIMS

16.1. Except as covered elsewhere in this MOU, each Participant waives any claim it may have against any other Participant for injury (including injury resulting in death) suffered by its National Contingent personnel and damage or loss of property owned by it, its National Contingent personnel caused by acts of omissions of any other Participant or its National Contingent personnel in the performance of official duties in connection with this MOU.

16.2. Where the relevant Participants mutually determine in respect of any claim that damage, loss, injury or death was caused by reckless acts, reckless omissions, wilful misconduct or gross negligence of only one of the Participants, its service personnel, servants or agents the costs of any liability will be borne by that Participant alone.

16.3. Where more than one Participant is responsible for the injury, death, loss or damage or it is not possible to attribute responsibility for the injury, death, loss or damage specifically to one Participant, the handling and settling of the claim will be approved by the relevant Participants. The costs of handling and settling the claims will be equally shared between the Participants concerned.

16.4. Third party claims including those for property loss or damage and for personal injury, illness or death or in respect of any other matter arising from or attributed to MND(C-S) personnel or any persons employed by it, whether normally resident in Iraq or not and that do not arise in connection with military combat operations, shall be submitted and dealt with by the Participant whose National Contingent personnel, property, activities or other assets are alleged to have caused the claimed damage, in a manner consistent with the national laws of the Participant state.

16.5. Third party claims will be received initially by HQ MND(C-S) and will be forwarded to the Participant deemed to be responsible. Where more than one Participant is responsible for the injury, death, loss or damage or it is not possible to attribute responsibility for the injury, death, loss or damage specifically to one Participant; the cost of handling and settling the third party claims will be distributed equally between the Participants concerned.

SECTION SEVENTEEN – SECURITY

17.1. All classified information exchanged or generated in connection with this MOU will be used, transmitted, stored, handled and safeguarded in accordance with the Participants national security laws and regulations.

17.2. Each Participant will take all lawful steps available to it to ensure that information provided or generated pursuant to this MOU is protected from further disclosure unless the originating Participant consents to such a disclosure.

17.3. Accordingly, each Participant will ensure that:

a. The recipients will not release the classified information to any government, national organisation or other entity of a third party without the prior consent of the originating Participant.

b. The recipient will not use the classified information for other than the purposes provided for in this MOU.

c. The recipient will comply with any distribution and access restrictions on information that is provided under this MOU.

17.4. Each Participant will be responsible for ensuring that prior to taking up posts at HQ MND(C-S) their personnel have the required security clearances as laid down on the Job Description forms associated with the posts, as issued with the Operational Establishment.

17.5. Each Participant will ensure that access to classified information is limited to those persons who possess requisite clearances and have a specific need for access to classified information to participate in the deployment.

17.6. The Participants will take all lawful steps to investigate all cases in which it is known or where there are grounds for suspecting that classified information or material provided or generated pursuant to this MOU bas been lost or disclosed to unauthorised persons. Each Participant will also promptly and fully inform the other Participants of the details of such occurrences, and of the final results of the investigation and of the corrective action taken to preclude recurrences.

17.7. All Participants undertake to appoint a person or persons to safeguard classified information or material pertaining to this MOU, at any site or facility where it may be used, who will be responsible for limiting access to such classified information or material involved to persons who have been properly approved for access and have a strict need to-know.

17.8. All Participants are to comply with security instructions and orders in the AOR issued by HQ MND(C-S).

SECTION EIGHTEEN – COMMUNICATIONS AND INFORMATION SYSTEMS

18.1. The MND(C-S) HQ will take responsibility over the Communications and Information Systems (CIS) organisation, and implementation within the AOR directly to the level of BDE HQ, including communications between respective BDE HQs, and to units directly subordinated to MND (C-S) HQ. All CIS activities in the AOR will be coordinated by the CIS Management Centre (CMC) of the HQ MND(C-S), which will take responsibility over the set-up and configuration of the CIS and CIS reporting system.

18.2. Within the AOR, down to the BDE HQ level, Poland will provide liaison teams with equipment required for exchange of classified and unclassified information. BDE HQs will be responsible for protection and logistic support of the liaison teams.

18.3. BDE HQs will be responsible for providing their own CIS capabilities down to lower command levels. BDE HQs will have to provide transferred non-secure telephone circuits to battalion HQs, i.e. to a commander, duty officer, registry and subscriber points – this is the sole common communications system within the AOR.

18.4. Battalion HQs will be responsible for providing their own national CIS capabilities.

18.5. Units should be equipped with suitable sets of commercial faxes, telephones and satellite terminals to support the C-S sector CIS requirements including emergency communications.

18.6. The Participants will be responsible for back link to their home country.

18.7. Delivery and expedition of unofficial mail to and from home country will be arranged by the Participants.

18.8. Unofficial mail to the Participants' units will be distributed and delivered by postal military runs within the AOR.

18.9. Frequency Management within the MND (C-S) AOR will be the responsibility of the HQ MND(C-S). Individual frequency assignments for the subordinated forces in the AOR are to be done by the CMC MND(C-S) HQ.

18.10. Frequency requests will have to be sent in required format (14-point format) to the HQ MND(C-S). All Frequency Management activities will be co-ordinated by the Frequency Manager collocated with the CMC at the HQ MND(C-S).

18.11. Any other issues not agreed in this section may be the subject of separate bilateral arrangements if it is so required.

SECTION NINETEEN – MEDICAL ARRANGEMENTS

19.1. Medical support of the TCNs' units in the MND(C-S) is a national responsibility.

19.2. National contingents will be deployed by TCNs to the AOR with their own medical elements providing adequate medical support.

19.3. Comd MND(C-S) will co-ordinate medical support for subordinated units through the Chief of Medical Service. Professional co-operation between MND(C-S) Chief of Medical Service and CJTF-7 Surgeon will be established.

19.4. Medical Intelligence will be carried out by the MND(C-S) in co-operation with the US.

19.5. The TCNs' units within the MND(C-S) will be responsible for role 1 and role 2 of medical support. Role 3, provision of blood and blood-like materiel, helicopter medical evacuation and strategic medical transport back to Ramstein (Germany) will be provided by the CJTF-7. Medical transport from Germany to a home-country will be a national responsibility.

19.6. Medical support during disembarkation and deployment to the AOR will be provided by the US and British units.

19.7. The US logistics will provide the MND(C-S) with class VIII consumable items (according to the US classification) to keep the stock of medical supplies on a level enabling effective and continuous medical support in the AOR, i.e. medical care and medical supplies including blood, vaccines and antitoxins. The above mentioned items will be delivered for the MND(C-S) free of charge from the assigned logistic base.

19.8. Bio-Hazardous medical waste management will be provided by the US.

19.9. Provision of unique or special national supplies will be a national responsibility.

19.10. Requirements for additional medical support are possible under separate arrangements.

SECTION TWENTY – NATIONAL DECLARATIONS

20.1. Upon signature, Participants will inform the Polish Land Forces Command in Warsaw, in writing of any national restrictions or caveats that will apply to their participation in any of the key tasks set out in the Mission Statement at Annex A.

20.2. Participants will inform in writing Comd MND(C-S) of any National restrictions or caveats that will apply to the ROE and national mandate of their contingent.

SECTION TWENTY ONE – DISPUTES

21.1. Any dispute regarding the interpretation or application of this MOU or its Annexes will be resolved between the disputing Participants at the lowest possible level and will not be referred to any national or international tribunal or third party for settlement.

SECTION TWENTY TWO – AMENDMENTS

22.1. This MOU may be amended at any time in writing, by the mutual consent of all Participants. Amendments will be effected by exchange of notes or letters and will be numbered consecutively.

SECTION TWENTY THREE – DURATION, EXPANSION, WITHDRAWAL AND TERMINATION

23.1. This MOU will remain in effect until completion of the MND(C-S) Mission unless terminated earlier in accordance with paragraphs 23.2 or 23.3.

23.2. This MOU will terminate on the implementation of any changes in MND(C-S) agreed by the MND(C-S) Participants that would invalidate the terms of this MOU.

23.3. This MOU may be terminated at any time with the written consent of all Participants.

23.4. In the event this MOU is terminated or expires:

a. The provisions of Section eight (Finance), Section sixteen (Claims) and Section twenty one (Disputes) will remain in effect until all outstanding payments, claims and disputes are finally settled; and
b. The provisions of Section seventeen (Security) will remain in effect until all such classified information and material is either returned to the originating

Participant, destroyed in accordance with the instructions of the originator or declassified by the originator.

23.5. Any Participant may withdraw from this MOU at any time by giving 30 days prior notice in writing to all other Participants. The period of notice of withdrawal may be altered with the consent of all Participants.

23.6. In the event that a Participant withdraws from this MOU the provisions of paragraph 23.4 above will remain in effect in respect of all outstanding payments, claims or disputes involving that Participant, and in respect of any classified information and material in the possession of that Participant.

23.7. Additional Nations may be invited to participate in this MOU and will do so by providing to the MOD of the Lead Nation either a Note of Accession (acceding to the full provisions of this MOU) or a Statement of Intent (acceding to the provisions of this MOU but with National Declarations).

23.8. Where possible, the Participants will consult each other over the preparation of any National plans which may have an impact on the deployment of the Participants forces to MND(C-S).

SECTION TWENTY FOUR – SIGNATURE

24.1. The foregoing represents the understanding reached between the Participants upon the matters referred to therein.

24.2. The provisions of this MOU will be provisionally applied to those Participants who have signed it and will enter into effect after signature by all the Participants.

24.3. This MOU has been signed in one original in the English language. The authorised copies will be prepared by the Ministry of National Defence of the Republic of Poland which is the depository of this MOU and sent to Participants.

ANNEXES

A. MND(C-S) Mission Statement
B. Financial Arrangements[10]
C. Status of the Coalition, Foreign Liaison Missions, their Personnel and Contractors[11]

Annex A –The Stabilisation Force MND(C-S) Mission Statement

Introduction

1. The Mission will involve the Participants in assisting with the conduct of key tasks. Furthermore, these tasks will increasingly involve working with the Coalition Provisional Authority (CPA) and the local people of Iraq with respect to restoration and establishment of local institutions.

MND C-S Area of Operational Responsibility (AOR)

2. The Area of Operational Responsibility (AOR) for the Stabilisation Force in Iraq (SFIR) in MND(C-S) comprises five provinces: Babil, Karbala, Wasit, Al Qadisiyah, An Najaf. A provisional map of the MND (C-S) AOR is at Appendix 1 to this Annex.[12]

[10] Not reproduced.
[11] See CPA Order No 17 *[Doc 37]*.
[12] Appendix 1 not reproduced.

Key Tasks

3. The SFIR MND(C-S) will undertake a range of tasks in the AOR in support of its Mission and these will be determined in response to the changing situation. Key tasks, will include:

a. External Security/Border Security. SFIR MND(C-S) led. Protection of key points, including monitoring the land border and assisting in the establishment and training of an Iraqi Border Security Force.
b. Internal Security. SFIR MND(C-S) led. The maintenance of a safe and secure environment, including intelligence-led operations to dislocate the threat from subversive and armed groups.
c. Force Protection. SFIR MND(C-S) led. This will include all aspects of current operations to ensure the security of SFIR and, for a limited period, CPA personnel throughout the AOR.
d. Fixed Site Security. SFIR MND(C-S) led. This will include responsibility for maintaining security at the critical and sensitive sites within the AOR.
e. Governance and Support for Infrastructure. CPA led. SFIR MND(C-S) will, for a limited period of time, support CPA (C-S) efforts to establish local governance based on the rule of law that affords equal rights and justice to all Iraqi citizens in the AOR without regard to ethnicity, religion, or gender. SFIR MND(C-S) will support this by working at the local and regional level to establish mechanisms for governance and civil administration until the CPA has the capability of working with the local Iraqi people to establish full governance. SFIR MND(C-S) will continue to support this within the AOR with Government Support Teams (GST) until the CPA Local Government Teams (LGT) are operational within the AOR. Com SFIR MND(C-S) will continue to provide liaison to the GST after the CPA assumes control and will work closely with CPA (C-S) to ensure military operations are synchronised with Coalition activities. Further support may be provided for a limited period to assist in the establishment and maintenance of Iraqi infrastructure.
f. Law Enforcement Development. CPA led. SFIR MND(C-S) will provide support for a limited period. SFIR MND(C-S) will continue to assist with the development of the Civilian Police Force, including the conduct of joint patrols, the establishment of a Police Evaluation Team, the development of a Complaints Procedure, and support to the local Iraqi courts and judiciary in maintaining law & order. After successful transition to the CPA and the local Iraqis, SFIR MND(C-S) will maintain a liaison role in order to co-ordinate law enforcement operations, training and oversight with the military.
g. War Criminals. CPA led. SFIR MND(C-S) may need to provide support to facilitate the detention of suspected war criminal in the AOR.
h. Restoration of Essential Services. CPA led. SFIR MND(C-S) will provide support for a limited period until civilian contracted and Iraqi personnel can assume responsibility. SFIR MND(C-S) will be responsible with the support of CPA for facilitating the provision of essential services within the AOR.
i. Building the Iraqi Military. CPA led. SFIR MND(C-S) will provide nominal military support but the manning, training and equipping of an Iraqi Military Structure are an CPA function.

4. Under the Fourth Geneva Convention (the Civilian convention) the only authority to act as the 'detaining power' in the AOR is the Comd SFIR MND(C-S) on behalf of the Authority.

5. The Commander of SFIR MND(C-S) will liaise with such political, social and religious leaders as necessary in the AOR to ensure that religious, ethnic and cultural sensitivities in Iraq are appropriately respected by the members of the SFIR MND(C-S).

Identification

6. SFIR MND(C-S) military and paramilitary personnel will wear uniforms and carry arms as authorised by their orders. The Iraqi Civilian Police Force, when on duty, will be visibly identified by uniform or other distinctive markings and may carry arms as authorised by CPA Regulations and Orders and once the Iraqi (Administration) is established.

Threat Assessment

7. Coalition Forces assess that the internal threat to stability in Iraq is from armed factions jostling for political power and influence, remnants of the Baath Party and its splinter organisations, criminals and terrorists. Externally, the threat is limited and neighbouring countries are supportive. The situation is dynamic and may change. The SFIR MND(C-S) force posture may need to be adjusted as the situation develops and Participants will need to be flexible.

8. The Participants must understand the need to provide the Commander of SFIR MND(C-S) with any information relevant to the security of the mission, its personnel, equipment and locations.

Membership of SFIR in MND(C-S)

9. It is understood that once the MND(C-S) is established, its membership may change.

Final Authority to Interpret

10. The Commander of MND(C-S) is the final authority regarding operational interpretation of this Mission statement.

Summary

11. This Mission Statement sets out the obligations and responsibilities of the Participants and outlines main tasks of the SFIR MND(C-S) mission in the AOR.

Document 591

Joint Order of the Coalition Forces Commander for Northern Iraq and the Governor of Mosul City and Ninewah Province Prohibiting the Illegal Disposal of Refuse and Garbage

September 2003

Recognizing the threat to the public health and safety posed by the illegal dumping and improper disposal of waste products, refuse, and garbage,

Cognizant of the illegality of such actions and the penalties provided by the Iraqi Penal Code Chapter 3, paragraph 497, 3rd Edition (1969),

Recognizing the responsibilities of the Commander, Coalition Forces Northern Iraq, and the Governor, Mosul City and Ninewah Province, to enforce Coalition Provisional

Authority (CPA) Order 7, CPA Memos 1 and 3,[13] and Iraqi Public Health and Criminal laws,

Determining that the cleanliness of the Province is a responsibility, ultimately, of the citizens of Ninewah Province who determine the conditions in which they live, and

Pursuant to our authority as Commander, Coalition Forces Northern Iraq, and Governor, Mosul City and Ninewah Province,

We do hereby Order as follows:

Section 1 Statement of the Criminal Law to the People of Ninewah Province

1) All citizens shall be aware and conform their conduct to all provisions of the Iraqi Penal Code, to include Chapter 3, paragraph 497, 3rd Edition (1969) which prohibits throwing, placing, disposing or leaving in a street or highway or any public place or park, refuse, rubbish, waste, dirty water, or any thing that is harmful to the health of others.[14]

2) Any person who violates this law shall be subject to detention for up to 15 days or a monetary fine.

Section 2 Notice to the Police of Ninewah Province

1) All Police and Coalition Forces are hereby encouraged to aggressively police and enforce the provisions of the Iraqi Penal Code, 3rd Edition (1969) as it pertains to the disposal of wastes.

2) Coalition Forces who detain an individual solely for a violation of the above Iraqi Penal Code section shall transfer custody of the individual to Iraqi authorities as soon as practicable.

Executed this ____ day of September 2003.

DAVID H. PETRAEUS
Major General, US Army
Coalition Forces Commander for Northern Iraq

Governor
Mosul City and Ninewah Province

[13] See *Docs 21, 125,* and *127* respectively.

[14] Paragraph 497 of the Iraqi Penal Code provides: 'The following persona are punishable by a period of detention not exceeding 15 days or by a fine not exceeding 10 dinars: (1) Any person who urinates or defecates in a street or highway or in a public place or city, town or village park or in places other than those set aside for such purpose. (2) Any person who throws or leaves in a street or highway or in a public place or park, refuse, rubbish, waste, dirty water or any thing that is harmful to the health of others. (3) Any person who deliberately or negligently causes an escape of gas, fumes, smoke, dirty water or other substance thereby causing harm, irritation or contamination to others. (4) Any person who is negligent when cleaning or repairing a chimney, oven or factory in which fire is used.'

Document 592
Terms of Reference for the International Advisory and Monitoring Board (IAMB)

21 October 2003[15]

1. Purpose

The purpose of the International Advisory and Monitoring Board (IAMB)[16] shall be to promote the objectives set forth in United Nations Security Council Resolution 1483 (2003) (resolution 1483)[17] of ensuring that the Development Fund for Iraq (DFI) is used in a transparent manner for the purposes set out in operative paragraph 14 of that resolution and that export sales of petroleum, petroleum products and natural gas from Iraq are made consistent with prevailing international market best practices.

2. Members

A. The IAMB shall include, as referred to in operative paragraph 12 of resolution 1483, duly qualified representatives of each of the Secretary-General of the United Nations, the Managing Director of the International Monetary Fund, the Director-General of the Arab Fund for Economic and Social Development, and the President of the International Bank for Reconstruction and Development. Each of these institutions shall have one member on the IAMB.

B. The IAMB, after consulting with the CPA Administrator, may appoint up to 5 observers to the IAMB from a list of independent, qualified candidates, which should include Iraqi nationals nominated by the Governing Council of Iraq. Any such appointment shall require unanimous approval of all members of the IAMB.

C. At any meeting of the IAMB, each member may be accompanied by an alternate designated by the executive head of the institution concerned and up to two advisors.[18]

[15] The Terms of Reference are available on the Website of the IAMB at http://www.iamb.info/.

[16] The International Advisory and Monitoring Board (IAMB) was first referred to in S/RES/1483 (2003) of 22 May 2002, para. 12. A Draft of the IAMB Terms of Reference (TOR) was prepared by the CPA in June 2003 (DRAFT 6/11/03). A first organizational meeting of the IAMB was held in Washington on 25 June 2003. The Draft, however, was not adopted because of differences over the role of the CPA and the audit powers of the IAMB. In S/RES/1511 (2003) of 16 October 2003, para. 23, the Security Council emphasized that the IAMB 'should be established as a priority'. The IAMB was finally established on 21 October 2003 with the approval of the TOR of the IAMB by the Executive Heads of the Arab Fund for Economic and Social Development, the International Monetary Fund, the United Nations and the World Bank (UN Doc. S/2003/1030, 22 October 2003, Annex). The purpose of the Board is to promote the objectives set forth in S/RES/1483 (2003) of ensuring that the Development Fund for Iraq (DFI) is used in a transparent manner for the purposes set out in para.14 of that resolution and that export sales of petroleum, petroleum products and natural gas from Iraq are made consistent with prevailing international market best practices. After the dissolution of the CPA on 28 June 2004 the IAMB continued to work with the Interim Government of Iraq, as set out in S/RES/1546 (2004) of 8 June 2004, para. 25. S/RES/1637 (2005) of 8 November 2005, para. 3 extended the mandate of the IAMB until 31 December 2006. On the work of the IAMB, see UN Doc S/2004/542, 7 July 2004.

[17] See *Doc 523*.

[18] The Draft prepared in June 2003 (DRAFT 6/11/2003) provided as follows: '2. Members:

A. The IAMB shall include duly qualified representatives of each of the Secretary General of the United Nations, the Managing Director of the International Monetary Fund, the Director-General of the Arab Fund for Social and Economic Development, and the President of the International Bank for Reconstruction and Development. Each of these institutions shall have one voting member on the IAMB.

B. The Coalition Provisional Authority (CPA) may appoint up to [3] [5] additional members to the IAMB as non-voting members.

C. The IAMB, with the agreement of the CPA, may appoint up to [3] [5] additional [non-]voting members.

D. [No additional voting members may be added to the IAMB.].'

3. Powers and Responsibilities

A. *Selection of Independent Public Accountants (External Auditor(s)):* The independent public accountants referenced in paragraphs 12 and 20 of resolution 1483 (the 'External Auditor(s)') shall be nominated and appointed by the Administrator of the CPA, subject to approval by the IAMB. The selection process for the External Auditor(s) and the terms of reference for the objectives, scope and approach of the External Auditor(s)'s work shall be approved by the IAMB.

B. *Scope of external audits*. The scope of the external audits shall be such as to enable the IAMB to achieve its purpose as set out in 1 above. The scope of the external audits shall encompass: (i) the export sales of oil, petroleum products and natural gas from Iraq (the 'Export Sales'), supporting the objective of ensuring that the Export Sales are made consistent with prevailing international market best practices; (ii) the 'Oil Proceeds Receipts Account' held by the Central Bank of Iraq at the Federal Reserve Bank of New York; (iii) the DFI (including, but not limited to, all inflows, investments and other assets, disbursements, liabilities and contingencies of the DFI), supporting the objective of ensuring that the DFI is used in a transparent manner in accordance with applicable control procedures; and (iv) disbursements of resources from the DFI, supporting the objective of ensuring that DFI funds are used for the purposes for which they were disbursed. For purposes of (iv), the External Auditor(s) will make (a) a determination as to whether the disbursements from the DFI are duly authorized and received by the designated recipient; and (b) an assessment as to whether the controls (including the requirement to ensure proper records) of the designated recipient are adequate to ensure that disbursements from the DFI are utilized as intended. This assessment shall be carried out as specified in the contract with the external auditor(s).

C. *Audit Evaluation:* The IAMB shall review audit reports prepared by the External Auditor(s) and determine whether the audits were conducted in a satisfactory and comprehensive manner, and in accordance with appropriate standards.

D. *Internal Controls/Financial Reporting*: The IAMB shall monitor the financial reporting and internal controls systems established by the CPA for the areas subject to external audit in 3.B above and advise, as appropriate, the CPA on the adequacy of such systems.

E. *Special Audits*: The IAMB may decide, when warranted under international best auditing practices, that the External Auditor(s) or other independent public accountants ('special auditor(s)') conduct special audits in all areas of the IAMB's mandate and consistent with the objectives of United Nations Security Council Resolution 1483 (2003). After consulting with the CPA, the IAMB shall establish the terms of reference for the objectives, scope and approach of any such audits, which shall be conducted in accordance with International Standards on Auditing (ISA).

F. *Access to Information*. The IAMB shall have the right to review all financial and other records and access to all personnel relevant to its mandate, including those subject to external audit in 3.B above and including those of the External Auditor(s), any special auditors, and any internal auditors retained by the CPA, as necessary, to fulfill the purposes and functions set forth in these terms of reference.

G. The IAMB, consistent with its terms of reference, shall perform functions similar to those of outside audit committees and may provide information and comments to the Coalition Provisional Authority (CPA) as appropriate to serve the purposes of Security Council resolution 1483.[19]

[19] The Draft of June 2003 read as follows: '3. Responsibilities: In general, the IAMB shall oversee the external audit processes, the financial reporting arrangements and the system of internal controls of the DFI. The IAMB's responsibilities shall include:

4. Public Disclosure

A. The IAMB shall ensure that all audit reports envisaged in these terms of reference and the IAMB's comments on such reports are made public.

B. All minutes of meetings and all reports of the IAMB shall be made publicly available within 30 days of being finalized by the IAMB. IAMB members may express dissenting views to be published in the minutes or reports.

C. The IAMB shall take all reasonable steps to ensure the protection of sensitive and confidential materials.[20]

5. IAMB Chair

A. The IAMB shall choose a Chair from among its members, by unanimity of its members, for a term not to exceed one year.

B. The Chair shall serve as the principal representative of the IAMB in communications with the CPA, the Central Bank of Iraq and other third parties.

C. The Chair shall guide the Secretariat in the preparation and maintenance of all official IAMB records and minutes of IAMB meetings.

D. The IAMB will facilitate the reporting provided for in paragraph 24 of resolution 1483.[21]

6. Meetings and Decisions

A. The IAMB shall determine the frequency and location of its regular meetings, which shall occur, at least, quarterly.

B. Extraordinary meetings shall be convened by the Chair or at the request of any two members of the IAMB.

C. A quorum for any IAMB meeting shall be at least three of the four IAMB members.

A. *Selection of Auditor/Scope of Audit*: The IAMB shall make recommendations to the CPA on (1) selection process for the Auditor and (2) the terms of reference for the scope and approach of the Auditor's work.

B. *Approval of Auditor*. The IAMB shall approve an independent public accounting firm(s) (the "Auditor") to serve as the external auditor of the DFI. The Auditor shall audit the DFI and the export sales (the "Export Sales") of oil, petroleum products and natural gas from Iraq, supporting the objectives of ensuring that the DFI is used in a transparent manner and that such export sales are made consistent with prevailing international market best practices.

C. *Audit Evaluation*: The IAMB shall review audit reports prepared by the Auditor and evaluate whether the audits were conducted in accordance with appropriate standards.

D. *Internal Controls/Financial Reporting*: The IAMB shall monitor the financial reporting and internal controls systems established for the DFI and advise, as appropriate, the CPA Program Review Board and the CPA on the adequacy of such systems.

E. *Special Audits*: The IAMB may propose to the CPA that special audits of specific aspects of DFI operations be conducted and shall advise on the terms of reference for such audits.'

[20] Draft of June 2003: '4. Public Disclosure.

A. The IAMB shall work with the Auditor and the CPA on publishing financial reports and audits of the DFI and information on Export Sales.

B. All minutes of IAMB meetings and all reports approved by the IAMB shall be made publicly available within 30 days of being approved by the IAMB. IAMB members may express dissenting views to be published in the minutes or reports.

C. The IAMB, in its discretion, may publish other communications and records of the IAMB.'

[21] Draft of June 2003: '5. IAMB Chair:

A. The initial Chair of the IAMB shall be [nominated by the CPA and approved by the IAMB voting members]. At least six months after the first IAMB meeting and, in any case, within 12 months of such meeting, the IAMB shall elect a new Chair for a term not to exceed one year. Successor Chairs may be elected for one year terms.

B. The Chair shall serve as the official representative of the IAMB in communications with the CPA, the Central Bank of Iraq and other third parties.

C. The Chair shall prepare and maintain all official IAMB records and minutes of IAMB meetings.'

D. The intention is for the IAMB to act and make decisions on a consensus basis. To the extent not feasible and unless otherwise specified herein, the IAMB shall make decisions by majority vote of all IAMB members.

E. The IAMB, in its discretion, may invite the External Auditor(s), observers, or other relevant parties to attend IAMB meetings.[22]

7. Administrative Coordinator/Secretariat

A. The CPA shall appoint an Administrative Coordinator to handle requests from the IAMB for logistical support to be provided, as appropriate, in connection with IAMB meetings and other general IAMB business.

B. The costs incurred by IAMB members, their alternates and advisors shall be paid by their respective institutions.

C. Reasonable costs as mutually agreed upon with the CPA incurred by the External Auditor(s), any special auditor(s), and any technical experts and outside consultants engaged by the IAMB to carry out duties for or on behalf of the IAMB shall be reimbursed with DFI funds.

D. IAMB members and their alternates and advisors shall not be entitled to receive any salary or other compensation from the CPA or DFI for their services.

E. The IAMB shall establish a Secretariat which will be located in Baghdad. The Secretariat shall provide administrative support to the IAMB, including the safeguarding of IAMB minutes and records and internal deliberations and communications of IAMB members. The costs associated with the Secretariat, IAMB meetings and other general IAMB business shall be borne by the four institutions referenced in 2.A above.[23]

8. Amendments, Additional Procedures and Delegations

A. Any amendments to these terms of reference shall require unanimous approval of all IAMB members, after consulting with the CPA, and shall be published by the CPA. The CPA's consent will be required for any amendment that may materially affect the rights or responsibilities of the CPA.

B. The IAMB may adopt other procedures necessary to implement these terms of reference which procedures shall be consistent with these terms of reference. To the extent such procedures may materially affect the rights or responsibilities of the CPA, the IAMB shall consult with the CPA prior to the adoption of such procedures.

C. The IAMB may appoint or call upon technical experts or outside consultants, as necessary, to fulfill the purposes and functions set forth in these terms of reference.

[22] Draft of June 2003: '6. Meetings and Decisions:

A. The Chair shall determine the frequency and location of IAMB meetings.

B. A quorum for any IAMB meeting shall be 75% of all voting members, including at least three of the four voting IAMB members [referenced in UNSCR 1483].

C. The intention is for the IAMB to act and make decisions on a consensus basis. To the extent not feasible and unless otherwise specified herein, the IAMB shall make decisions by majority vote of all IAMB voting members.

D. The IAMB, in its discretion, may invite the Auditor or other relevant parties to attend IAMB meetings.'

[23] Draft of 2003: '7. Administrative Coordinator:

A. The CPA shall appoint an Administrative Coordinator to handle reimbursement arrangements for costs associated with IAMB meetings and other general IAMB business and, as appropriate, provide administrative support to the Chair.

B. Following establishment of the IAMB, reasonable costs incurred by IAMB members, the Auditor, technical consultants and any special auditors in caring out duties for or on behalf of the IAMB shall be reimbursed with DFI funds.

C. IAMB members shall not be entitled to receive any salary or other compensation from the CPA or DFI for their services as an IAMB member.'

D. In the event of any inconsistency between these terms of reference and the provisions of any CPA decree or regulation including, without limitation, the CPA regulations establishing the DFI and the Program Review Board, the provisions of these terms of reference shall prevail.[24]

9. Establishment and Dissolution

A. Upon unanimous approval of these terms of reference by the Executive Heads of the four institutions referenced in 2.A above, after consulting with the CPA, the IAMB shall be established. The terms of reference of the IAMB shall be published by the CPA.

B. Once an internationally recognized, representative government of Iraq is properly constituted, as specified in resolution 1483, arrangements will be made for the prompt dissolution of the IAMB.[25]

Document 593
Conclusions by the Chair International Donor Conference for the Reconstruction of Iraq, Madrid 23–24 October 2003

24 October 2003[26]

1. The International Donors' Conference on Reconstruction in Iraq was held on 23-24 October in Madrid at ministerial level, at the invitation of the Government of Spain on behalf of the European Union, Japan, the United Arab Emirates and the United States of America. The Conference was called in close co-operation with the Iraqi Governing Council, the United Nations, the World Bank, the International Monetary Fund and the Coalition Provisional Authority.

2. Representatives from 73 countries and 20 international organizations met to pledge their support for the political, economic and social revitalisation of Iraq. Representatives of 13 Non-Governmental Organisations and NGO associations also attended the conference.

3. The Secretary General of the United Nations, Mr. Kofi Annan, inaugurated the conference on 23 October. He urged the international community to send a signal to the people of Iraq of its readiness to help them build a democratic and peaceful future.

4. The President of the government of Spain, Mr. José María Aznar, addressed the plenary session on 24 October. He stressed the importance of this conference for the Iraqi people in overcoming the legacy of decades of corruption and mismanagement. He also underlined the international community's commitment to the sovereignty and territorial integrity of Iraq.

[24] Draft of June 2003: '8. Additional Procedures and Delegations:

A. Upon agreement with the CPA, the IAMB may adopt other procedures necessary to implement these terms of reference.

B. The IAMB may delegate specific functions to technical review panels, committees, or outside consultants.'

[25] Draft of June 2003: '9. Establishment and Dissolution:

A. Upon approval of these terms of reference by a majority of the IAMB members proposed in UNSCR 1483 and agreement of the CPA, the IAMB shall be established.

B. The IAMB shall remain in operation until an internationally recognized, representative government of Iraq, as properly constituted under UNSCR 1483, decides that it be dissolved.'

These Terms of Reference were valid until 28 June 2004 when they were superseded by Revised Terms of Reference.

[26] The Conclusions were published, inter alia, on the Website of the World Bank, http://web.worldbank.org/.

5. A delegation of the Iraqi Governing Council headed by the current President, Mr Ayad Allawi, accompanied by Iraqi ministers, attended the conference. In his statement to the plenary session, Mr Allawi, emphasised the Governing Council's full determination to pursue democratic development, the reconstruction of the country and the prompt and full return of Iraq to the international community of nations. Mr Allawi set out Iraq's priorities for reconstruction and development in 2004 and beyond.

6. The conference took place following the unanimous adoption of United Nations Security Council Resolution 1511 of 16 October 2003[27] and the presentation of the needs assessment report by the World Bank and the United Nations together with the International Monetary Fund.

7. It is important for all countries in the region to contribute actively to the stability of Iraq. The conference agreed that a prosperous, stable and sovereign Iraq whose territorial integrity is preserved is essential for stability in the region.

8. The Forum on the Bridge between Humanitarian Aid and Reconstruction on October 23 underlined the important role of Iraqi ministries as well as Iraqi and international NGOs working in Iraq. It agreed on the importance of ensuring an appropriate environment for NGOs' continuing contribution in the reconstruction process. Good coordination and overall security are critically important in this context.

9. The participants reaffirmed their resolve to continue working to meet the urgent needs of the Iraqi population. The conference underscored the need for careful and effective co-ordination of humanitarian and reconstruction assistance in Iraq.

10. Donors stressed the importance of the smooth transition of the responsibilities for activities under the Oil For Food Programme from the United Nations to the Coalition Provisional Authority on 21 November 2003, ensuring that particular attention is paid to protecting vulnerable groups after the phase out.

11. The conference highlighted the importance of the process set out in United Nations Security Council Resolution 1511 for the preparation of a new Iraqi constitution and political transition. The conference stressed the need to empower all parts of Iraqi society, including women, to play a role in the political, economic and social transformation of their country.

12. In this context, the conference acknowledged the responsibilities accorded to the Governing Council of Iraq and the Coalition Provisional Authority. It welcomed the strengthening of the vital role to be played by the United Nations and the tasks entrusted to the United Nations Assistance Mission for Iraq (UNAMI), as set out in Resolution 1511.

13. The conference underlined how critical a secure environment in Iraq is for social and economic development. It also stressed that the strong commitment of the international community to reconstruction will help to build the confidence of the Iraqi people, enhance stability, and discourage those who promote disorder. The conference agreed that continuing to build a legal and judicial system that promotes democratic principles and respect for human rights, enforcement of the rule of law in Iraqi society and public confidence in the judicial institutions and the police is essential for Iraq to develop as a modern democratic nation.

14. Donors noted that priorities for Iraq's reconstruction in 2004 and beyond include strengthening institutions for sovereign, transparent, and good government, restoring critical infrastructure and core human services and supporting economic and social transition that provides both growth and social protection.

[27] See *Doc 531*.

15. The conference especially stressed the need to establish a comprehensive and transparent macroeconomic policy framework as a basis for sustainable economic growth, private sector development and effective use of donors' assistance. The conference welcomed the Iraqi authorities' commitment in this area, as evidenced by the publication of the budget for 2003-2004 and the entry into circulation of the new Iraqi currency. It is important that the international community address Iraq's heavy debt burden in 2004, a step which is essential for fostering macroeconomic stability and private investment.

16. The conference welcomed the agreement on the terms of reference for the International Advisory and Monitoring Board[28] which will help ensure transparency and accountability in the management of the Development Fund for Iraq and petroleum export sales. The conference looked forward to the early initiation of operations of the Board.

17. The donor community announced overall pledges and indicative pledges amounting to more than US$33 billion dollars (equivalent to €28 billion) in grants and loans from now until the end of 2007. It is important disbursement of these pledges begin as soon as possible. Many donors also offered additional forms of support, including export credits, training, technical assistance, and aid in kind.

18. The conference noted that, in order to help coordinate and channel contributions by the international community, an International Reconstruction Fund Facility for Iraq is being established into which contributions by the international community may be paid. This will be administered by the World Bank and the United Nations in close coordination with the Iraqi authorities and donors. The conference welcomed the use of the Facility by interested donors.

19. The conference looked forward to the early creation of an Iraqi-led local coordination mechanism to ensure that Iraqi priorities and needs guide the national development process and to prevent the emergence of gaps and duplication. It called on all donors to work with this mechanism.

20. The plenary session also welcomed the results of the parallel meeting of the private sector held on October 23 in which business representatives of 332 firms from 46 countries reviewed the opportunities to participate in the economic reconstruction of the country, generating employment, prosperity and welfare for the Iraqi people. The conference stressed the importance of the diversification of the economy and of strengthening the role of the private sector.

21. The Chair thanked all the participants in the conference for contributing to its highly successful outcome. It also thanked the Core Group for its work in preparing the conference and encouraged it to monitor progress in international support for reconstruction in Iraq. It noted that future donor conferences may be convened as needed.

[28] See *Doc 592*.

Document 594
Joint Statement of Iraq's Neighbouring States
2 November 2003[29]

In response to an invitation from the Syrian Arab Republic for a meeting of states that are neighbours to Iraq to discuss developments in Iraq and their impact on regional and international conditions, the foreign ministers of the Kingdom of Saudi Arabia, the Hashemite Kingdom of Jordan, the Islamic Republic of Iran, the Arab Republic of Egypt, the Republic of Turkey, the State of Kuwait and the Syrian Arab Republic held a meeting in Damascus on the 7th of Ramadan, 1424 of the hijrah, corresponding to 2 November 2003.

The ministers issued an invitation to the foreign minister of the transitional Iraqi government to attend the meeting but the ministers did not receive a response. They expressed hope that a representative of Iraq would attend their future meetings.

The ministers recalled their previous meetings, which they held in Istanbul on 23 January 2003, in Riyadh on 18 April 2003 and in Tehran on 28 May 2003.[30] They discussed the current situation in Iraq out of their commitment to Iraq's unity, independence and sovereignty, and Iraq's right to exercise control over its territory and natural resources in accordance with UN Security Council Resolution 1511.[31] Based on their deliberations, the foreign ministers agreed on the following:

1. Expressing their full sympathy and solidarity with the Iraqi people because of the ordeal they are going through due to the serious deterioration in their security, economy and living conditions.
2. Asserting their rejection of any measure that would lead to dividing Iraq, their respect for Iraq's sovereignty, independence and territorial integrity, and their commitment to the principle of not interfering in its internal affairs. They also call on other parties to follow the same policy.
3. Asserting the Iraqi people's right to determine their political future and the need for the United Nations to enhance its vital role in Iraq; namely, supervising the drafting of the constitution and the holding of elections, setting a timetable to put an end to occupation, and expediting the transfer of authority to the Iraqis to enable the Iraqi people to restore their rights, security, and sovereignty over their territories.
4. Supporting the efforts of the transitional Governing Council so that it can shoulder its transitional responsibilities until the formation of an elected Iraqi government that would represent all sectors, fulfil the aspirations and interests of the Iraqi people, and achieve equality among all the people of unified Iraq.
5. Reasserting the responsibilities of the occupation authority in accordance with the relevant Security Council resolutions and international law, particularly the Fourth Geneva Convention of 1949 on the responsibilities of occupation forces, in order to maintain security and stability in Iraq. They also expressed their rejection of any accusations to their countries that they interfere in Iraq's internal affairs.
6. Denouncing the terrorist bombings that target civilians, humanitarian and religious establishments, international organizations, and diplomatic missions operating in Iraq, and stresses the need to reveal their perpetrators and hold them responsible for their crimes.

[29] Syrian foreign minister reads Damascus talks statement at news conference, BBC Sumary of World Broadcasts, 2 November 2003. First broadcast in Arabic on Al-Jazeera TV, Doha, on 2 November 2003.

[30] For the 28 May 2003 statement, see *Doc 589*.

[31] See *Doc 531*.

7. Taking into consideration the existence of terrorist groups and the threats that any other armed groups might pose to neighbouring states, the ministers call on the responsible Iraqi authorities to cooperate with these states to ward off threats to the security of the neighbouring states and prevent any infiltrations of their borders.

8. As a result of the negative effect of the unstable situation in Iraq, as well as the Iraqi people's lack of luxury, on their countries' national interests, the ministers have decided to call on their UN representatives to collectively continue working with the United Nations in Iraq.

The foreign ministers expressed their thanks for Syria for inviting them to take part in this consultative meeting and their appreciation for meeting with President Bashar al-Asad and listening to his views. They also expressed their solidarity with Syria with regard to Israel's exploitation of the developments in the region and carrying out an act of aggression against Syrian territories. They agreed that these meetings held by Iraq's neighbouring countries deserve to continue and gain support in the future. Accordingly, the foreign ministers have decided to hold future meetings until Iraq restores its sovereignty and independence, welcoming Kuwait's invitation to host the next meeting.

Document 595

Letter from the Australian Representative in Baghdad to Ambassador Bremer on the Damage to the Archaeological Sites around Babylon

15 June 2004

Australian Representative Office Baghdad
Representative

15 June 2004

Ambassador L. Paul Bremer III
Administrator
Coalition Provisional Authority
Baghdad IRAQ

Dear Ambassador Bremer

I am writing to express my Government's deep concern at reports that significant damage has been done to archaeological sites around Babylon by Coalition military forces. I understand that damage includes some irreparable destruction of archaeological mounds and elements of the military base being built on top of some particularly valuable sites.

I understand that you have expressed your own serious concerns about the problem, and are working to manage it, for which I would like to express my appreciation. Nonetheless, the issue remains that significant damage has already been done.

Australia, unlike the United States and the United Kingdom, is a party to the Hague Convention on the Protection of Cultural Property in the Event of Armed Conflict. Australia also has a series of other international legal obligations relating to the preservation of sites, including the First Additional Protocol to the Geneva Conventions.

The Australian Government would encourage Coalition leadership to continue to do everything practicable to stop further damage and to preserve archaeological sites in Iraq, including Babylon.

I would be grateful to receive your assurances on this matter.[32]

Yours sincerely

[Signed] *Neil Mules*

[32] On 19 June 2004, Ambassador Richard H. Jones, CPA Deputy Administrator replied to Mr Neil Mules as follows: 'Dear Mr. Mules,

Thank you for your letter of 15 June to Ambassador Bremer. I would like to assure you that the Coalition fully shares your government's concern for the protection and preservation of the ancient city of Babylon. In recent days, CPA and MNF-I have jointly undertaken the following steps to avoid unnecessary damage to its archaeological treasures:

• Issued orders to military units and civilian contractors to halt all construction unless it is critical for force protection;

• Ordered a formal investigation on the impact of the camp on the archaeological site;

• Ordered the formation of an archaeological review board (including Iraqi, CPA, and MNFI officials, as well as substantive experts) to advise on future activities that could impact the integrity of the site;

• Initiated plans to relocate military facilities away from the site;

• Proposed coordination with the Iraq State Board of Antiquities and Heritage to ensure future protection of Babylon from vandals and looters, and to seek remedies for any damage already done to the site.

Our goal is to ensure Babylon's sanctity as a protected historical site, open to the public and protected from threats.'

X

Other Documents of Interest

1. Coalition Provisional Authority

(1) Administrator's Weekly Address to the Iraqi People

Ambassador Bremer delivered a weekly address to the Iraqi people via the American-run Iraqi Media Network's radio and television outlets. On TV, viewers heard an Arabic voiceover as Bremer spoke. The addresses usually began as follows: 'Masaa al Khair. I am Paul Bremer, administrator of the Coalition Provisional Authority. [...].' Transcripts for the following addresses were published: 3, 7 and 12 July 2003; 1, 8, 22 and 29 August 2003; 5, 12, 19 and 26 September 2003; 10, 17, 24 and 31 October 2003; 7, 14, 21 and 28 November 2003.

(2) Administrator's Consolidated Weekly Reports

(a) Governance Reports

The CPA Administrator issued consolidated weekly governance reports. The reports which were between four and six pages long included sections on: Highlights, Support Transition to Sovereignty, Develop Civic Participation in Governance, Support Development of Sustainable Political Parties/Associations, Develop Framework and Capacity for Elections, Promote Respect for Human Rights, Develop More Accountable and Responsive Local Government, Promote Durable Solutions for Refugees and Internally Displaced Persons (IDPs), Initiate Public Sector Management Reform. Reports for the following periods were published on the CPA website: 31 January–6 February 2004; 7–13, 14–20, 21–27 February 2004, 28 February–5 March 2004; 6–12, 13–19, 20–26 March 2004; 27 March–2 April 2004; 3–9, 10–16, 17–23, 24–30 April 2004; 1–7, 8–14, 15–21, 22–28 May 2004; 29 May–4 June 2004; 5–11, 12–18, 19–28 June 2004.

(b) Economic Reports

The CPA Administrator issued consolidated weekly economic reports. The reports which were four to six pages long included sections on: Highlights, Building Financial Market Structures, Develop Transparent Budgeting and Accounting Arrangements, Develop Framework for Sound Public Sector Finances and Resource Allocation, Private Sector Initiatives, Promote Private Business and Small and Medium Enterprises (SMEs), Commence Reform of Tax System, Remove Subsidies/Develop Social Safety Net, Implement Policy Towards State-Owned Enterprises, Reconstitute Oil Infrastructure, Design Oil Trust Fund, Lay Foundations for an Open Economy, Pursue National Strategy for Human Resources Development, Initiate Public Sector Management Reform. Reports for the following dates and periods, respectively, were published on the CPA website: 15, 25 November 2003; 10 December 2003; 10–16 [The first report of the New Year], 17–23, 24–30 January 2004; 31 January–6 February 2004; 7–13, 14–20, 21–27 February 2004; 28 February–5 March 2004; 6–12, 13–19, 20–26 March 2004; 27 March–3 April 2004; 3–9, 10–16, 17–23, 24–30 April 2004; 1–7, 8–14, 15–21, 22–28 May 2004; 29 May–4 June 2004; 5–11, 12–18, 19–28 June 2004.

(c) Essential Service Reports

The CPA Administrator issued consolidated weekly reports on essential services. The reports which were between eight and 12 pages long included sections on: Highlights, Provide Electricity Services that Meet National Needs, Reconstruct Communications and Postal Systems, Provide Food Security for all Iraqis, Improve Quality and Access to Healthcare, Improve Quality and Access to Higher Education, Improve Quality and Access to Education, Improve Quality and Access to Housing, Provide Opportunities for Sporting Activities and the Development of Young People, Restore Economically Strategic Transportation Infrastructure, Provide Water Supply, Sewage and Municipal Service, Reconstitute Oil Infrastructure, Improve Water Resources Management, Support Plans for the Restoration and Preservation of Iraq's Cultural Heritage and Traditions. Reports for the following periods were published on the CPA website: 21–27 September 2003; 28 September–11 October 2003; 12–18, 19–25 October 2003; 26 October–1 November 2003; 2–8, 9–15, 16–22, 23–29 November 2003; 10–16, 17–23, 24–30 January 2004; 31 January–6 February 2004; 7–13, 14–20, 21–27 February 2004; 28 February–5 March 2004; 5–12, 13–21, 22–28 March 2004; 29 March–2 April 2004; 3–9, 10–16, 17–23, 24–30 April 2004; 1–7, 22–28 May 2004; 29 May–4 June 2004; 5–11, 12–18, 19–28 June 2004.

(3) CPA Daily Updates

One-page overview of developments in Iraq. The sections include: key quote, key messages, diary, facts, and special sections/information. The following issues were published on the CPA website: 2, 3, 4, 5, 7, 8, 9, 10, 12, 13, 14, 15, 16 and 17 July 2003.

(4) Public Service Announcements

- Ministry of Education – Payment Information (without date)
- Ministry of Culture – Payment Information (without date)
- Ministry of Finance – Currency (5 May 2003)
- Ministry of Transportation and Communication – Citizens Urged Not to Park on Main Streets (8 May 2003)
- Ministry of Planning – Employees Asked to Return to Work (8 May 2003)
- Ministry of Justice – Iraqi Court System Reopens (8 May 2003)
- Ministry of Transportation and Communications – Iraqi Airports Being Brought up to Standards (11 May 2003)
- Ministry of Youth – Iraqis Asked to Organize Sports, Recreation Programs (11 May 2003)
- Ministry of Planning – Heads of Offices Need to Return (11 May 2003)
- Ministry of Higher Education and Scientific Research – Equipment, Furniture Needs to be Returned (12 May 2003)
- Ministry of Higher Education and Scientific Research – University Elections Begin (12 May 2003)
- Ministry of Housing and Construction – Construction Equipment Needs to be Returned (12 May 2003)
- Ministry of Youth – Football Game to be Held (13 May 2003)
- Ministry of Higher Education and Scientific Research – Voting Postponed (14 May 2003)

- Atomic Energy Managers Asked to Meet (14 May 2003)
- Iraqi Media Network (14 May 2003)
- Ministry of Higher Education and Scientific Research – Voting at major universities for presidents and deans (15 May 2003)
- Ministry of Higher Education and Scientific Research – Class Resume (15 May 2003)
- Ministry of Higher Education and Scientific Research – Successful Voting Held at Baghdad University (18 May 2003)
- Emergency Pay to Former Iraqi Military Personnel (6 July 2003)

(5) CPA Press Releases

The CPA issued hundreds of press releases. Press releases are listed in the chronological order in which they were issued, not in the order in which they were uploaded to the CPA website which sometimes occurred only several days later. Not all press releases were available on the CPA website. The present list also includes press releases carried by the Iraqi media.

June 2003
- Good News for Iraqi Soldiers (PR No 6, 23 June 2003)
- Interim Governor of Najaf (PR No 8, 30 June 2003)
- Baghdad City Council (31 June 2003)

July 2003
- Commercial Air Service Applications (PR No 9, 1 July 2003)
- Text of Ambassador Paul Bremer's Message to the Iraqi People (PR No 10, 3 July 2003)
- Reward for Information About Saddam Hussein, Uday Hussein and Qusay Hussein (PR No 11, 3 July 2003 and updated 23 July 2003)
- Al Fallujah Mosque Explosion (3 July 2003)
- Baghdad Interim Advisory Council Established (PR No 12, 7 July 2003)
- Speech by Ambassador at the Opening of the Baghdad City Advisory Council (PR No 13, 7 July 2003)
- Text of Ambassador Bremer's Address to the Iraqi People: Budget and Banknotes (PR No 14, 7 July 2003)
- 'The Voice of Women of Iraq' (PR No 15, 9 July 2003)
- Text of a Speech by Ambassador Bremer: Development Projects in Najaf 9 July 2003 (PR No 16, 10 July 2003)
- Text of Ambassador Bremer's Weekly TV Address (PR No 17, 12 July 2003)
- Competition for Licences for the Provision of Mobile Telecommunications Services (Press Notice, 18 July 2003)
  - Q and A Brief for Press Enquiries: Mobile Communications Licence Competition
- Opening of New Iraqi Army Recruiting Stations (19 July 2003)
- Establishing a Trade Bank of Iraq (PR No 21, 21 July 2003)
- Closure of Al Mustaqila Newspaper (PR No 22, 21 July 2003)
- Rewards Program (23 July 2003)
- Introduction to Non-Governmental Organizations: 'What is the Role of an NGO in Iraq?' (24 July 2003)
- Announcement: Iraqi NGO Training Session (24 July 2003)
- Request for Information (RFI): Iraqi Commercial Banks (PR No 23, 31 July 2003)

August 2003

- Transfer of Uday and Qusay's Bodies (PR No 25, 2 August 2003)
- Trent Announces Telecom Application Extension (PR No 26, 2 August 2003)
- Amendment to Request for Proposals on Trade Bank of Iraq (8 August 2003)
- CPA Announces Important Changes to Wireless Telephone License Requirements (PR No 27, 8 August 2003)
- Coalition Forces Take Control of Tanker Attempting to Smuggle Iraqi Oil (PR No 28, 8 August 2003)
- Reappointment of Eight Iraqi Justices Shows Commitment to Independent Judiciary (11 August 2003)
- More Soccer Balls for Iraqi Children Thanks to US Donors (12 August 2003)
- For the First Time in History City-Wide Garbage Collection Begins in Baghdad (17 August 2003)
- Ruptured Baghdad Water Main to Be Quickly Restored (17 August 2003)
- Pre-Season Soccer Tournament to Be Played in Mosul, Erbil (23 August 2003)
- After 30 Years, a New Bridge Reunites Two Baghdad Communities (24 August 2003)
- New Saddam 'Wanted for $25M' Poster (27 August 2003)
- Statement by Ambassador Bremer on An Najaf Bombing (29 August 2003)

September 2003

- Ambassador Bremer Press Conference (As Prepared for Delivery): 2 September (2 September 2003)
- Ambassador Bremer Address to the Iraqi People: Path to Sovereignty (5 September 2003)
- Ministry of Trade to Reimburse Truck Drivers (9 September 2003)
- Ambassador Bremer OPED on Path to Sovereignty (9 September 2003)
- Iraqi Junior National Swimmers Win in Jordan (11 September 2003)
- Election of New Baghdad City Council Chairman (11 September 2003)
- CPA Provides Equipment to Iraqi Hospital (13 September 2003)
- Description of How Former Conscripts Can Receive Payments From the Coalition (16 September 2003)
- UK to Provide Football Assistance to Impoverished Iraqi Youths (19 September 2003)
- Marines to Hand Over Al-Hillah Region to Spaniards (Task Force Iraq, 1st Marine Division, 21 September 2003)
- Central European Experts on Economic Reform to Offer Advice to CPA (21 September 2003)
- Iraqi Finance Minister Announces Significant Economic Reforms (21 September 2003)
- Iraqi Football Team Moves One Step Closer to Olympics (22 September 2003)
- 5000 Year Old Warka Mask Returned to Baghdad Museum (23 September 2003)
- President Bush's Remarks in Address to United Nations General Assembly (23 September 2003)
- British Prime Minister Tony Blair Mourns the Passing of Hakila Al-Hashimi (25 September 2003)
- Statement of Ambassador L. Paul Bremer on the Passing of Dr. Akila Al-Hashimi (25 September 2003)

October 2003
- Iraqi Students Return to De-Baathified School (1 October 2003)
- Iraqi Ministry of Municipalities and Public Works Begins Program 'Towards a Cleaner and Brighter Iraq' (2 October 2003)
- Iraqi Police Cadets to Train in Jordan (3 October 2003)
- First Battalion of the New Iraqi Army Graduates (4 October 2003)
- Council of Judges Begins Work Again in Iraq (4 October 2003)
- Samples of the New Saddam-Free Iraqi Money (7 October 2003)
- Images of the Old Swiss Dinar (11 October 2003)
- Iraq Releases Fiscally Responsible 2004 Budget (13 October 2003)
- Iraq's Central Criminal Court Convicts Two Oil Smugglers (14 October 2003)
- Currency Exchange Begins in Iraq (15 October 2003)
- Suspension, Fulbright Program Returns to Iraq (21 October 2003)
- Coalition Ends Curfew in Baghdad as Security Returns to City (24 October 2003)

November 2003
- Dates Announced for English Tests for Fulbright Scholarship (1 November 2003)
- Iraqi Ministry Begins New Program to Provide Jobs in Northern Iraq (2 November 2003)
- Iraqi Central Criminal Court Sentences Former Governor of Najaf to 14 Years (3 November 2003)
- Statement Regarding the Assassination of Faris Abd al-Razzaq Al-Assam (14 November 2003)

December 2003
- Hated Heads of Former Dictator Removed from CPA HQ (1 December 2003)
- Credit Agencies from 16 Countries Commit $2bn in Export Credit Lines to Iraq (4 December 2003)
- Iraq National Symphony Orchestra Performs in Washington (9 December 2003)
- CPA Denies Baseless Azzaman Report of Release of Regime Officials (10 December 2003)
- Iraq Delegation Meets with World Bank and IMF (10 December 2003)
- CPA Hands over Authority for Donor Cooperation (10 December 2003)
- List of Countries Allowed to Bid on Iraqi Contracts (11 December 2003)
- New 'Tips' Phone Numbers (13 December 2003)
- Iraq Prepared to Undertake First National Humanitarian Demining Campaign (13 December 2003)
- CPA Provides New Opportunities for Scientists and Engineers (20 December 2003)
- Joint CPA-Iraqi Plan to Deal with Mass Graves (23 December 2003)
- Hazardous Duty Pay Authorized for Security Forces (27 December 2003)
- Emergency Response Funds Delivered to Karbala (28 December 2003)
- Iraq's Boxing Team Departs for Olympic Qualifiers (28 December 2003)
- Distributions Made to Diwaniyah Province for Area Projects (31 December 2003)

January 2004
- CPA Awards $1.6Million for Projects in Diwaniyah (2 January 2004)
- Two Additional Fulbright Opportunities Now Available (2 January 2004)

- 86 New Members of the Iraqi Diplomatic Protection Service (3 January 2004)
- Distributions Made to Karbala Province to Organize Projects in the Area (4 January 2004)
- Firemen in Babil Province Receive New Boots (4 January 2004)
- Opening of the Free Soccer Union in Diwaniyah (4 January 2004)
- Kids Warmed by New Coats Procured by the CPA (4 January 2004)
- Discussion Held on Historical Artifact Protection (10 January 2004)
- Steps Taken in Building Democracy in South-Central Iraq (10 January 2004)
- Najaf Province Receives Money for Multiple Projects (10 January 2004)
- Coalition Provisional Authority Endorses the Destination Baghdad Expo (DBX) (11 January 2004)
- Distributions Made to Karbala Province in Response to Bombing (12 January 2004)
- Export-Import Bank to Support Iraqi Reconstruction (14 January 2004)
- US Works to Empower Women in Iraq (14 January 2004)
- Currency Exchange Ends (15 January 2004)
- Bremer Statement on 18 January 2004 (18 January 2004)
- Iraqi Business Center Now Online (22 January 2004)
- Hand-Over of Keys to Office of Ministry of Youth and Sport in Basrah (22 January 2004)
- Iraqis to Receive Higher Pensions (22 January 2004)
- Building Democracy in South Central Iraq (22 January 2004)
- Ribbon-Cutting Ceremony Highlights Progress in Bringing Stable Electric Power to All Iraqis (24 January 2004)
- 30,000 Iraqi Pilgrims Undertake First Open Hajj in Three Decades (24 January 2004)
- Iraqi Fulbright Recipients Chosen for 2004 (24 January 2004)
- Town Hall Meetings Fact Sheet (27 January 2004)
- Woman's [sic] and Human Rights Centers Sponsor Democracy Seminars (27 January 2004)
- Statement on Terrorist Organizations in Iraq (28 January 2004)
- Officials of the International Olympic Elections Welcome Iraq Back to the International Community (29 January 2004)
- PMO Reconstruction Projects Underway Throughout Iraq (29 January 2004)
- Open for Business: Iraqi Companies Compete for Contracts Totalling $18.6m (20 January 2004)
- New Police Officers Join Ranks of Iraqis Protecting Iraq (30 January 2004)
- Construction Projects Taking Shape in Al-Hilah (31 January 2004)
- Commission on Public Integrity to Combat Government Corruption (31 January 2004)

February 2004

- Ambassador Bremer Expresses Outrage at Cowardly Bombings in Arbil (1 February 2004)
- Women in the New Iraq – Op-Ed Piece by Paul Wolfowitz, US Deputy Secretary of Defense (1 February 2004)
- US Trade and Development Agency Backs Rehabilitation of Iraq's Railroads (2 February 2004)
- CPA Welcomes Changes in Banking Sector: Announces RFA Finalists (2 February 2004)
- Secretary of Labor Elaine Chao Visits New Woman's Center in Iraq (2 February 2004)
- World Bank Authorizes Iraq Reconstruction Trust Fund (3 February 2004)

- A Little Goes a Long Way for Kids in Wasit (3 February 2004)
- Fact Sheet for Public Integrity Council (3 February 2004)
- Iraqi Women Seek to Contribute to a More Democratic Future (3 February 2004)
- Ambassador Bremer Announces New Partnership in the Olympic Arena Between the US and Iraq (5 February 2004)
- Ambassador Bremer Remarks at Memorial Service (6 February 2004)
- PMO to Participate in the Destination Baghdad Exposition (6 February 2004)
- UN Team Back at Work in Iraq (10 February 2004)
- Iraq Achieves Observer Status at the World Trade Organization (12 February 2004)
- Iraqi Reconstruction Efforts Aimed at Building Sound Economic Base (12 February 2004)
- Iraqi Officials Committed to Market Reforms, Treasury's Taylor Says (12 February 2004)
- Commerce Secretary Evans Urges US Businesses to Deal with Iraq (12 February 2004)
- Rumsfeld: Troop Departure Is a Different Timetable from Sovereignty (13 February 2004)
- US Starts New Arabic-Language Satellite TV Broadcast (14 February 2004)
- Opening of 'Liberation' School (15 February 2004)
- Iraqi Police Capture Muhammad Zimam abd al-Razzaq al-Sadun (15 February 2004)
- Iraqi Security Forces Honored for Exemplary Ordnance Disposal (15 February 2004)
- New Salhiyah Bridge Opens (15 February 2004)
- The Arabs Should Have Been the Ones to Oust Saddam (16 February 2004)
- Women's Rights Center Opens in Karbala (16 February 2004)
- 11,000 Iraqi Teachers Graduate from Teacher Training Programs (16 February 2004)
- Opening of Baghdad Unemployment Center Promises Relief to Jobless (16 February 2004)
- Increased Rewards Schedule for Hostile Elements in Iraq (17 February 2004)
- New Program Begins for Cleanup in Basra (17 February 2004)
- Human Rights and Democracy Center Opens in Najaf (18 February 2004)
- Bremer: The US Is Firm on June 30th (18 February 2004)
- Annan Says Direct Elections in Iraq Not Possible Before June 30 (19 February 2004)
- Najaf Province Receives Money for Water Projects (20 February 2004)
- Babel Special Response Police Unit Graduates (20 February 2004)
- Ambassador Bremer Did Not Articulate a Coalition Position on an Estimated Timetable (21 February 2004)
- Iraqi Museum Specialists Receive Grant to Study in the US (22 February 2004)
- Bremer: CPA Welcomes the UN Secretary General's Report (23 February 2004)
- Iraqi Elections Could Be Held by Year's End, Report Says (24 February 2004)
- Iraq's Legacy of Terror: Mass Graves (24 February 2004)
- Local and Coalition Officials Visit Projects Underway at Al Kasik Military Base (25 February 2004)
- Opening of Iraq Center for Reconciliation, Dialogue and Peace (26 February 2004)
- Renewed Hope for Marshes: Restoration is Feasible (26 February 2004)
- Local and Coalition Officials Visit Underway Construction at Um Qasr Naval Base (26 February 2004)
- Women's Forum Explores Role of Women in Iraq's Future (27 February 2004)
- Ashura Celebrated by Shi'a Iraqis for First Time in 30 Years (27 February 2004)
- Completion of Iraq Telephone Exchanges Rehabilitation (27 February 2004)
- Iraqi Ministry of Trade Press Release: Guidelines for the Export of Scrap Metal (28 February 2004)
- Scouting to Come to Iraq (28 February 2004)

March 2004

- Iraqi Minister Nesreen Berwari Seeks Greater Role for Women in Iraq (1 March 2004)
- CPA Releases $100,000 to Victims of Ashoura Bombings in Karbala (2 March 2004)
- Ashoura Bombings in Baghdad, Karbala Follow Zarqawi's Script (2 March 2004)
- Ambassador Bremer Condemns Evil Ashoura Bombings (2 March 2004)
- US Offers Training, New Opportunities for Iraqi Scientists (4 March 2004)
- Iraqi Museum Specialists Enhance Their Skills in the United States (5 March 2004)
- New Law Governing the Central Bank of Iraq (7 March 2004)
- New Democracy Center Brings Together Groups in South Central Iraq (8 March 2004)
- Mansour Women's Center Opens in Baghdad on International Women's Day (8 March 2004)
- President Bush Hails Iraqi Transitional Law (8 March 2004)
- Powell Announces Two New Programs for Iraqi Women (8 March 2004)
- Project 'Iraq Renewal' Begins with Multi-Million Dollar Housing Contract (8 March 2004)
- Ministry of Human Rights Receives Gift of Books in Arabic (9 March 2004)
- New Body Armor Strengthens Security of Iraqi Railroad (10 March 2004)
- Constitution Marks New Start for Iraqi Women, Minister Says (10 March 2004)
- Iraqi Artist Sculpts Homage to Fallen Solders (11 March 2004)
- Recipients of Iraqi Reconstruction Contracts Announced (10 March 2004)
- Michael P. Fleischer Named Director, Private Sector Development (13 March 2004)
- Bremer Announces Iraqi Border Security Initiative (13 March 2004)
- Border Crossing Points Between Iraq and Iran to Be Reduced to Three (15 March 2004)
- White House Says UN to Play Major Role in Iraq (16 March 2004)
- UN Team Ready to Return to Work in Iraq (16 March 2004)
- 'The Reality is Nothing Like What You See on Television' (17 March 2004)
- Iraq One Year Later: Cumulative Change Evident (17 March 2004)
- Wolfe Slated to Head Budgetary Matters in Iraq Reconstruction (18 March 2004)
- New Evidence Indicates Saddam Stole $10 Billion from Oil for Food Program (18 March 2004)
- USAID Accomplishments of Past Year (18 March 2004)
- Companies Meet in Baghdad for Joint Venture Conference (19 March 2004)
- Rumsfeld Cites 'Impressive' Progress in Iraq One Year After War (19 March 2004)
- Rice Cites 'Great Progress in One Year' in Iraq (19 March 2004)
- Iraqi Marsh Arabs Discuss Future of Wetlands (22 March 2004)
- Liberation of Iraq Sends Message of Freedom to the World, Bush Says (22 March 2004)
- More PMO Reconstruction Projects Underway Throughout Iraq (23 March 2004)
- Iraq Joint Venture Conference Attracts Billions in Private Sector Investment (23 March 2004)
- UN Security Council Endorses Brahimi's Mission to Iraq (24 March 2004)
- Beautification Plan for Baghdad Ready to Begin (24 March 2004)
- Iraqi Reconstruction Contract Awarded (26 March 2004)
- Iraqi Ministry of Health Reaches 'Milestone on Road to Sovereignty' (28 March 2004)
- Baghdad Education Symposium Begins (30 March 2004)
- CPA Inspector General Launches New Website and Hotline (31 March 2004)

April 2004

- Iraqi Customs Service and Reconstruction Levy Introduced (1 April 2004)
- Restructuring of Iraqi Company Law (1 April 2004)
- Optimists Club Organizes Baghdad Chapter (1 April 2004)
- Powell Mourns Anniversary of the Assassination of Sayyed Abdul Majeed al-Khoei (2 April 2004)
- Olympic Logo Unveiled (2 April 2004)
- Iraqi Ministry of Education Enters Final Stage to Sovereignty (3 April 2004)
- Arrest Warrant Issued for Iraqi Shi'ite Cleric al-Sadr (5 April 2004)
- Iraqi Olympic Hopefuls Arrive in Colorado to Begin Training (5 April 2004)
- Rumsfeld: Security to Remain Coalition's Task After June 30 (6 April 2004)
- Boxing Merchandise Sold to Support Iraqi Boxing Dream (7 April 2004)
- Coalition Response Will Continue 'Until Job Is Done', General Says (8 April 2004)
- Bremer Urges 'Vigilance and Caution' During Commemoration of Arba'een (8 April 2004)
- Scrap Metal Export Licensing Procedure (9 April 2004)
- Bremer, Barzani Regret Badran's Resignation; Thank Him for Excellent Service (9 April 2004)
- Governing Councilmen Assume Posts as Minister of Interior and National Security Advisor (9 April 2004)
- US Identifies Front Companies for Saddam Hussein Regime (15 April 2004)
- Iraqi Air Force Getting off the Ground (17 April 2004)
- Public Notice Regarding Closure of Sections of Highways 1 and 8 (17 April 2004)
- Iraqi Ministry of Defense Announces Military Leadership (18 April 2004)[1]
- Washington Post Article on Baghdad's New Mayor (19 April 2004)
- Briefing on the Iraqi Coastal Defense Force (19 April 2004)
- Bush to Nominate John Negroponte as US Ambassador to Iraq (19 April 2004)
- Bremer Appoints Iraqis to the National Communications and Media Commission (20 April 2004)
- 2004 Baghdad Mayoral Selection: City Council Members Select Tamimi, Two Others (20 April 2004)
- Iraqi Minister of Electricity Announces Largest Restoration of Power Since Liberation (21 April 2004)
- Volcker to Head Investigation of UN's Iraq Oil-for-Food Program (21 April 2004)
- Ministry of Science and Technology Enters Final Stage to Sovereignty (22 April 2004)
- CPA Funds Projects Worth $1.7 Million in Tikrit (22 April 2004)
- Central American Troops Make Important Contribution in Iraq (22 April 2004)
- Rumsfeld Praises Role of Free Press in US, Iraq, Afghanistan (23 April 2004)
- Program Management Office Visits 7 Cities Announcing Rebuilding Projects (24 April 2004)
- Successful TAL Governing Council Town Hall Session on the TAL (26 April 2004)
- US-Iraq Women's Network Prepares for Iraqi Elections (26 April 2004)
- Renovation Project for Baghdad Schools Nearly Completed (27 April 2004)
- Exportation of Iraqi Scrap Metal (28 April 2004)

[1] This press release was listed twice, the second time on 22 April 2003 under the title 'Interim Iraqi Minister of Defense Appoints 3 New Generals'.

- US Military Takes Swift Action over Abuses at Abu Ghraib Prison (28 April 2004)
- Fact Sheets on Recruitment of Security Forces, Assistance for Border Crossing Points, Detainees, Reconstruction, De-Ba'athification, and Remembrance (29 April 2004)
- Democracy Center Conducts Elections (29 April 2004)
- Briton Receives US Medal of Valor (29 April 2004)

May 2004

- Footballs Distributed in Honor of Prophet Muhammed's Birthday (2 May 2004)
- Minister of Defense Ali Alawi Announces Establishment of Iraqi Veterans Association (2 May 2004)
- UN Optimistic Iraqi Elections Will Be Held in January (3 May 2004)
- USAID and CPA Announce Completion of the Basrah Reservoir Rehabilitation Project (3 May 2004)
- Provincial Council Selects Future Governor of Baghdad (3 May 2004)
- Baghdad Beautification Comes to Al Rashid District (3 May 2004)
- New Abu Ghraib Commander Explains Detention and Interrogation Procedures (4 May 2004)
- Ambassador Bremer Congratulates Iraqi Minister of Culture upon Assumption of Full Sovereignty (4 May 2004)
- Ambassador Bremer Transfers Full Sovereignty to Iraqi Ministry of Culture (4 May 2004)
- Powell Assures Diplomats on the Matter of Iraqi Prisoners (4 May 2004)
- Iraqi Judges Discuss Rule of Law with International Experts (5 May 2004)
- Rumsfeld Vows Full Investigation of Abu Ghraib Abuses (4 May 2004)
- New PMO Facility Completed in Baghdad (4 May 2004)
- Polish Humanitarian Coordination Center Provides Outstanding Service to Iraqis (5 May 2004)
- Iraqi Ministry of Agriculture Assumes Full Sovereignty (5 May 2004)
- Bremer Appoints Coast Guard Captain Sr. Advisor to Ministry of Transport (6 May 2004)
- Bremer Names Adnan al-Zurufi New Governor of Najaf (6 May 2004)
- 2nd Armored Cavalry Regiment Begins Restoring Order (6 May 2004)
- Iraqi Foreign Ministry Announces New Website (6 May 2004)
- Top Sunni Cleric Returns to Iraq to Work for Peace (6 May 2004)
- Polish Help Hospitals in South Central Iraq (7 May 2004)
- Rumsfeld Takes Responsibility for Abuses in Iraq, Apologizes (7 May 2004)
- PMO Projects Prioritized with Iraqi Participation (7 May 2004)
- Ambassador Bremer Meets with Iraqi Professional Women (7 May 2004)
- Fact Sheet on the Ministry of Displacement and Migration (8 May 2004)
- US Soldier Faces Court Martial in Iraqi Prisoner Abuse Case (9 May 2004)
- Ministry of Water Resources Assumes Full Sovereignty (10 May 2004)
- Al Anbar Governor's Office to Accept Applications for New Iraqi Electoral Commission (10 May 2004)
- Iraqi NGOs Help Coordinate Humanitarian Aid (10 May 2004)
- Ministry of Water Resources: Progress and Priorities (11 May 2004)
- Ministry of Foreign Affairs Transitions to Full Authority: A Major Step for the Transition Process (12 May 2004)
- Financial Distributions Given to Babil Province to Complete Projects (12 May 2004)
- USAID Announces the Re-Opening of the Khazir Bridge (12 May 2004)

- Iraq Ministry of Health and UNICEF Sponsor Emergency Response Initiatives (12 May 2004)
- 30 Iraqi Firefighters from the Baghdad International Airport Complete Training Course (12 May 2004)
- Iraq Stuns Football World with Upset Victory (12 May 2004)
- Rumsfeld, Myers Meet with US Military at Abu Ghraib Prison (13 May 2004)
- Ministry of Planning and Development Assumes Full Sovereignty (14 May 2004)
- Seabee Contracting Team Awards Landmark Contract (14 May 2004)
- Iraqi Firefighting Officials Meet in Baghdad to Form Future Plans (15 May 2004)
- Fact Sheet on Civil Defense Directorate (Firefighters) (16 May 2004)
- Baghdad City Council Meets to Explain Elections Process (17 May 2004)
- 1st Marine Division Opens Detention Facilities to Iraqi Leaders (17 May 2004)
- Bremer Mourns the Murder of IGC President Ezzidin Salim (17 May 2004)
- Lakhdar Brahimi Mourns Iraqi IGC President Ezz El-Din Salim (17 May 2004)
- 1st Marine Division Receives Donations to Start Up Television Stations (19 May 2004)
- Military Court-Martial of US Soldier Begins in Abu Ghraib Case (19 May 2004)
- Abizaid Says Regional Leaders Worry US Won't Finish Task in Iraq (19 May 2004)
- Soldier Sentenced to One-Year Confinement for Abu Ghraib Actions (19 May 2004)
- Thirty Six Megawatts of Capacity Added to Iraqi Power Grid at Mullah (20 May 2004)
- Citizens in Karbala Condemn Muqtada Militia Activities (21 May 2004)
- Footballs Distributed in Ramadi, Karbala and Hillah (21 May 2004)
- Powell Vows Justice on Iraq Abuse, Continued Effort on Middle East Peace (22 May 2004)
- US Introduces Resolution on Iraq in UN Security Council (24 May 2004)
- Bush Announces Five-Step Plan for Democracy, Freedom in Iraq (24 May 2004)
- Fact Sheet: US Funds Projects to Train, Educate Iraqi Women (24 May 2004)
- Iraqi Postal Service Announces Opening of Service Center, Postal Code System (25 May 2004)
- Iraqi Postal Code Directory (25 May 2004)
- Bremer Announces Formation of Task Force on Compensation for Ancient Regime Victims (26 May 2004)
- Iraqi Ministry of Environment Takes Final Step to Transfer of Sovereignty (26 May 2004)
- Marines Embark on Clean Water Project for Ramadi (26 May 2004)
- Saddam's Helicopter Turned into Crop Duster by Iraqi Ministry of Agriculture (28 May 2004)
- Iraqis Dismembered by Saddam Received Artificial Limbs in US (28 May 2004)
- 30 Iraqi Police Officers Graduate from Leadership Training Course (29 May 2004)
- Opening of New Internet Center at Salahaddin University in Arbil (29 May 2004)
- Rehabilitation of Turbine #5 Completed at Haditha, 110 MW Added to Grid (31 May 2004)

June 2004

- Listing of the Interim Iraqi Government (2 June 2004)
- Haditha Dam Attains Full Capacity for First Time Since 1990 (3 June 2004)
- Scholars See Compatibility of Islam and Democracy (4 June 2004)
- Armed Forces and Militia Agreement Announced (5 June 2004)
- Iraqi Police Officers Graduate from Baghdad Police Academy (5 June 2004)

- Cellular Phone Company 'Iraqna' Will Be Main Sponsor of Iraqi Football Teams (9 June 2004)
- Baghdad City Government Names First Inspector General (15 June 2004)
- Powell Predicts Smooth Turnover of Sovereignty to Iraqi Government (18 June 2004)
- An Historic Review of CPA Accomplishments (28 June 2004)

(6) CPA Transcripts

The CPA published some 320 transcripts of speeches (by President Bush, Secretaries Powell and Rumsfeld, Ambassador Bremer and others), addresses to the Iraqi people, interviews and news briefings. Where the transcripts of speeches were also issued as press releases they have been listed under press releases. Ambassador Bremer's weekly addresses to the Iraqi people are listed above under their own heading. The CPA military briefings with Lieutenant General Sanchez, Commander Coalition Ground Forces, and other military leaders,[2] and the CPA Updates/Press Briefings by Brigadier General Mark Kimmitt, Deputy Director of Operations, Dan Senor, Senior Adviser, CPA, and others on an almost daily basis between November 2003 and June 2004 are not listed individually.[3] Transcripts are listed under the date of the document, not under the date the document was uploaded to the CPA website which sometimes occurred several days later.

May 2003
- Ambassador Bremer Statement from Baghdad, Iraq (15 May 2003)

July 2003
- Ambassador Paul Bremer Interview on Meet the Press (20 July 2003)
- Ambassador Paul Bremer Interview on CBS Face The Nation (20 July 2003)
- Ambassador L. Paul Bremer Interview with Fox News Sunday (20 July 2003)
- Ambassador Bremer Stakeout at the House (22 July 2003)
- Ambassador Bremer Stakeout at the Senate (23 July 2003)
- DoD News Briefing – Secretary Rumsfeld and Ambassador Bremer (24 July 2003)
- Ambassador Bremer Conference Call with Editorial Writers (24 July 2003)
- Ministry of Foreign Affairs Ceremony (31 July 2003)
- Mine Removal Ceremony (31 July 2003)

August 2003
- Opening Statement: Weekly Arabic Language Press Conference (2 August 2003)
- Opening Statement: Arabic Language Press Conference (9 August 2003)
- Introductory Remarks: International Press Conference (12 August 2003)
- Remarks: Opening of the Council for International Coordination (17 August 2003)

[2] On 4, 19 and 25 September 2003; 2 October 2003; 11, 18, 21 and 29 November 2003; 7, 23 and 31 December 2003; 14, 16, 19, 21, 22, 28 and 29 January 2004; 2, 11 and 26 February 2004; 9, 10, 11 and 18 March 2004; 8, 12 and 15 April 2004; 3, 11 May 2004; 8 June 2004.

[3] Update briefings were held on 1, 17, 19, 20, 21, 23, 25 and 30 November 2003; 1, 3, 5, 8, 18, 19, 24, 25, 27 and 30 December 2003; 2, 4, 8, 10, 12, 14, 22, 24, 27 and 30 January 2004; 1, 3, 5, 7, 9, 10, 11, 12, 16, 17, 19, 21, 23, 24 and 25 February 2004; 2, 3, 8, 9, 10, 12, 13, 15, 17, 18, 20, 22, 25, 30 and 31 March 2004; 1, 5, 7, 9, 10, 11, 12, 13, 16, 17, 19, 20, 22, 23, 24, 25, 26, 27, 28 and 30 April 2004; 5, 7, 9, 10, 14, 17, 18, 20, 21, 22, 24, 25, 26, 27, 28, 30 and 31 May 2004; 5, 12, 15, 21 and 26 June 2004. Not all transcripts of the CPA Updates were published on the CPA website; some were published on the CJTF-7 website (http://www.cjtf7.com/) and some on the US DoD website (http://www.defenselink.mil/).

- Ambassador Paul Bremer Interview with Fox News on the Bombing at the UN Headquarters in Baghdad (19 August 2003)
- Ambassador Bremer Interview with the CBS Early Show (20 August 2003)
- Ambassador Bremer Interview with NBC Today (20 August 2003)
- Ambassador Bremer, CPA Briefing Location: Baghdad (23 August 2003)
- Ambassador Bremer, Open Press Conference: Introductory Remarks (23 August 2003)
- Ambassador Bremer, Interview with ABC 'This Week' (24 August 2003)
- Ambassador Bremer, Interview with Fox News (24 August 2003)
- Ambassador Bremer, Interview with Sinclair Broadcasting (26 August 2003)
- Ambassador Bremer, Interview with Hearst Television (26 August 2003)
- Ambassador Bremer, Interview with Cox Television (26 August 2003)
- Ambassador Bremer, Interview with Belo Television (26 August 2003)

September 2003

- Ambassador Bremer, Press Conference: Opening Remarks (2 September 2003)
- Ambassador Bremer and Secretary Rumsfeld Joint Press Briefing in Baghdad (6 September 2003)
- President Bush's Address to the Nation (7 September 2003)
- Ambassador Bremer Reiterates the US Financial Commitment to Iraq (12 September 2003)
- Ambassador Bremer and Secretary Powell Host Joint Press Conference in Baghdad (14 September 2003)
- Secretary Powell Press Conference with Hoshyar Zubari, Interim Foreign Minister of Iraq (14 September 2003)
- Powell: We Will Remember Halabja (15 September 2003)
- Secretary Powell Editorial on Iraq 'As Long as It Takes' (17 September 2003)
- Ambassador Bremer Highlights the Atrocities of Halabja and other Human Rights Abuses (19 September 2003)
- Appropriations Committee Supplemental Hearing (22 September 2003)
- Remarks by the President and Iraqi Ministers of Public Works and Electricity after Meeting (22 September 2003)
- President Bush's Remarks in Address to UN General Assembly (23 September 2003)
- Ambassador Bremer Explains How the $20bn Will Be Spent (26 September 2003)
- Special British Representative to Iraq, Sir Jeremy Greenstock Interview with BBC Newsnight (29 September 2003)

October 2003

- Colin Powell: The Kay Report Proves Iraq Defied UN Resolution 1441 (7 October 2003)
- Ambassador Bremer Profiles 6 Months of Progress (9 October 2003)
- Treasury Department Unveils Plan to Reconstruct Iraq's Banking Sector (10 October 2003)
- Finance Minister Stresses Fiscal Responsibility in 2004 Budget (13 October 2003)
- Ambassador Bremer Urges Supplemental Grant for Iraq (15 October 2003)
- CPA Briefs on Iraqi Currency Exchange (15 October 2003)
- Young People Should Be Learning Math, Not Hate in School (18 October 2003)
- Natsios: Iraqi Economy Poised for Rapid Growth (22 October 2003)
- Plans to Start Employment & Training Centers in Iraq (22 October 2003)

- Bremer Calls on World to Aid Iraqi People (24 October 2003)
- President Bush Hails International Participation in Iraq's Reconstruction (25 October 2003)
- President Bush Wishes Muslims around the World a Blessed Ramadan (26 October 2003)
- Wolfowitz: Broadcast Statement to Iraqi People (26 October 2003)
- CPA Interview with George Stephanopoulos, ABC (26 October 2003)
- President Bush, Ambassador Bremer Discuss Progress in Iraq (27 October 2003)
- Bush Reaffirms: Despite Terrorism, 'We Are Not Leaving' (28 October 2003)
- Secretary Rumsfeld briefs on Iraq (30 October 2003)

November 2003
- Improved Security Will Speed Iraqi Sovereignty, Bush Says (1 November 2003)
- Ambassador Bremer Discusses Madrid Strides, Focus on Security (1 November 2003)
- Greenstock: 'Despite Obstacles, We Will Stay' (2 November 2003)
- Bush Says Democracy in Mideast Will Be a Focus of US Policy (6 November 2003)
- Ambassador Bremer Highlights Strides Toward Justice in Iraq (14 November 2003)
- President Bush – David Frost BBC (16 November 2003)
- President Bush Interview with Al-Sharq al-Aswat Newspaper (19 November 2003)
- President Bush/Prime Minister Blair Joint Declaration on Resolve in Iraq (21 November 2003)
- Ambassador Bremer Eid Remarks (24 November 2003)

December 2003
- Ensuring Rights of All, Including Women, is Most Vital Task Remaining in Iraq (10 December 2003)
- Ambassador Bremer Announces the Capture of Saddam Hussein (14 December 2003)

January 2004
- Ambassador Bremer Announces Conditional Release Program (7 January 2004)
- Bremer, in Washington, Discusses Transition in Iraq with Top US Officials (16 January 2004)
- Ambassador Richard H. Jones Kuwaiti investment in Iraq speech (18 January 2004)
- Bremer Hopes UN Will Participate in Transition Process (19 January 2004)
- Pachachi, Powell Agree: UN talks were 'Very, Very Useful' (20 January 2004)
- Deputy Secretary Wolfowitz: US and Turkey Share Common Vision for Future of Iraq (29 January 2004)
- Wolfowitz Highlights Importance of Building Iraq's Security (31 January 2004)

February 2004
- Secretary Powell Welcomes Iraqi Fulbright Winners to America (2 February 2004)
- Secretary Powell Defends Decision to Liberate Iraq Despite Absence of WMD (2 February 2004)
- Bush Defends His Decision to Go to War with Saddam (5 February 2004)
- Opening Statement of Kamal Gailain, Iraqi Minister of Finance (6 February 2004)
- Opening Remarks by Sinan Al-Shabibi, Governor, Central Bank of Iraq (6 February 2004)
- Secretary of Commerce Don Evans' Speech to the Iraq Business Council Urging Private Investment in Iraq (11 February 2004)
- Ahmed Al-Mukhtar Address to the WTO (11 February 2004)

- Full Text of Zarqawi Letter (12 February 2004)
- Boucher, CIA Double Reward for Zarqawi (12 February 2004)
- UN Envoy Lakhdar Brahimi Press Conference (13 February 2004)
- Ambassador Bremer Remarks at Official Opening of Ministry of Human Rights (14 February 2004)
- Bush: The Advance of Freedom in Iraq is Linked to Success in Afghanistan (17 February 2004)
- Bremer Affirms: 'The Date Holds' (19 February 2004)
- Rumsfeld Thanks Iraqi Police Recruits in Baghdad (23 February 2004)
- More Cooperation Needed to Secure Iraq Borders, Rumsfeld Says (23 February 2004)
- The Baghdad Religious Accord (24 February 2004)

March 2004

- Rumsfeld Cites Progress in Iraq in Areas of Security and Economy (1 March 2004)
- Ambassador Bremer Statement to the Iraqi People (3 March 2004)
- Bremer-Sanchez Briefing on the Terrorist Attacks in Karbala and Baghdad (3 March 2004)
- Iraqi People and Coalition 'Refuse To Live in Fear,' Says Bush (6 March 2004)
- Iraqi Minister: Iraqi Woman Have Come Far and Still Face Many Obstacles (8 March 2004)
- White House Background Briefing: The TAL is a Major Step Forward for Iraq (8 March 2004)
- Bush Lauds TAL as Milestone in 'Long Journey from Tyranny and Violence to Liberty and Peace' (8 March 2004)
- Remarks by Members of the Iraqi Governing Council at the Signing Ceremony for the Interim Constitution (8 March 2004)
- Ambassador Bremer Honors 'Resilience, Achievements and Promise of the Women of Iraq' (8 March 2004)
- Bush Calls Women's Rights and Liberty 'Inseparable' (12 March 2004)
- Powell Highlights Achievements of Engagement in Iraq (14 March 2004)
- Ambassador Bremer Extends Sympathy to Kurdish Victims 40 Days After Arbil Bombings (15 March 2004)
- Bremer to Doubters of Worth of Removing Saddam: 'Come to Hallabja' (16 March 2004)
- Powell Defends Decision to Liberate Iraq on 16th Anniversary of Halabja Massacre (16 March 2004)
- USAID Director Lists Accomplishments of Past Year, Outlines Mass Graves Plan (17 March 2004)
- Ambassador Bremer: The Terrorists are 'Wrong.' They Will Not Defeat Iraq's Progress (18 March 2004)
- Democracy Rising in 'Heart of the Middle East,' Bush Says (18 March 2004)
- Powell Praises Work of CPA Personnel, US Troops in Iraq (19 March 2004)
- Powell: 'The United States Will Not Shrink' from Task of Building a New Iraq (19 March 2004)
- Iraqi Delegation Studies Democracy in the United States (19 March 2004)
- Bremer Announces 'One Hundred Days to a Sovereign Iraqi Government' (24 March 2004)
- US Must Help Iraq Obtain Wealth Quickly, Ex-Im Bank Head Says (24 March 2004)
- 'Stay the Course' against Terrorism, Powell Says (25 March 2004)
- Minister Mahdi al-Hafidh: 'Participation for Prosperity Gives Us Hope for Building a New Iraq' (25 March 2004)

- Ambassador Bremer Congratulates Iraqi Minister of Health (27 March 2004)
- Bremer Announces Iraq's Inspectors General Program (30 March 2004)

April 2004

- Bremer to Police Cadets: You are 'the Line Between Civilization and Barbarism' (1 April 2004)
- United Nations Vital to US Interests, Negroponte Says (1 April 2004)
- Bremer: Sport can transcend everything (2 April 2004)
- Ministry of Education Enters Final Stage to Sovereignty (3 April 2004)
- National Security Team Announcement (4 April 2004)
- Ambassador Bremer Congratulates Iraqi Minister of Public Works (5 April 2004)
- Statement by British Prime Minister Tony Blair, and Iraqi Foreign Minister, Hoshyar Zebari (6 April 2004)
- Negroponte Says UN, Iraq to Probe Oil-for-Food Program (7 April 2004)
- 'Iraqi Sovereignty Will Arrive June 30,' Bush Affirms (10 April 2004)
- British Defense Minister Hoon: 'Steady Progress' Continues Despite Difficulties (10 April 2004)
- Brahimi-Barzani Brief (14 April 2004)
- Ambassador Bremer's statement on UN Envoy Lakhdar Brahaimi's announcement today regarding Iraq (14 April 2004)
- Carina Perelli [head of the United Nations electoral assessment mission to Iraq] Briefing (15 April 2004)
- US Identifies Front Companies for Saddam Hussein Regime (15 April 2004)
- Bush and Blair Reaffirm Determination to Transfer Sovereignty to the Iraqis on June 30th (16 April 2004)
- Iraqi Interior Minister Samir Shakir Sumaidy Statement (17 April 2004)
- Bremer: 'Iraq Has a Future of Hope' (18 April 2004)
- Iraqi Minister of Interior: Terrorists Won't Hinder 'Building a New Life for the Citizens' (19 April 2004)
- Joint Governing Council/Coalition and Fallujah Leadership Communiqué on Cessation of Violence (19 April 2004)
- Wolfowitz Details Developments in Iraq for Senate Committee (20 April 2004)
- Bush: 'Democracy is Necessary for Iraq' (21 April 2004)
- Iraq Reconstruction Core Group Meeting (22 April 2004)
- Powell Lauds El Salvador's Help in Iraq (23 April 2004)
- Bremer affirms: 'Iraq Turns the Page' (23 April 2004)
- US-Iraq Women's Network Prepares for Iraqi Elections (26 April 2004)
- Iraq's Banking Initiatives: Foundation for Prosperity and Iraq's Economic Future (26 April 2004)
- Ambassador Bremer Awards Andrew Rathmell Award for Valor (29 April 2004)
- Powell: Coalition to 'Return as Much Sovereignty to Iraqi Government as it is Prepared to Handle' (28 April 2004)
- Powell Explains Elements of New UN Iraq Resolution (29 April 2004)
- US Wants Peace in Fallujah, Powell Tells CNN (29 April 2004)
- Women's Group Discusses Security, Economy and Women's Roles With Ambassador Bremer (30 April 2004)

May 2004

- US and Coalition Forces Will Not Be Diverted in Iraq, Bush Says (1 May 2004)
- Ambassador Bremer Transfers Full Sovereignty to Iraqi Ministry of Agriculture (5 May 2004)
- Bush Says Culprits Will Be Brought to Justice (5 May 2004)
- Wolfowitz Says 'Stakes Are Enormous' in Iraq (5 May 2004)
- Ambassador Bremer Names New Governor of Najaf, Urges Iraqis to Institute Rule of Law (6 May 2004)
- Bush Explains US Goals in Mideast to Egypt's Al-Ahram (6 May 2004)
- Natsios Lists Accomplishments in Rebuilding Iraq (7 May 2004)
- Bush Pledges Full Investigation, Punishment for Iraqi Prisoner Abuse (8 May 2004)
- Ambassador Bremer Transfers Full Sovereignty to Iraqi Ministry of Water Resources (10 May 2004)
- First Lady Laura Bush Expresses Sadness Over Prisoner Abuse (10 May 2004)
- US Commander Says Iraqi Prison Investigations Just Beginning (10 May 2004)
- Ambassador Bremer Transfers Full Sovereignty to Ministry of Industry and Minerals (11 May 2004)
- Bremer Congratulates Hoshyar Zebari, Iraqi Foreign Minister, on Ministry's Sovereignty (12 May 2004)
- US Troops Will Stay Until Iraq Is Stable, Says Abizaid (12 May 2004)
- Ministry of Planning Transitions to Full Sovereignty (13 May 2004)
- Bush Reiterates Commitment to Freedom, Democracy in Iraq (15 May 2004)
- Powell: Watch How US Handles Iraqi Prisoner Abuse Scandal (17 May 2004)
- Bremer: The Coalition Will Sorely Miss Izzadeen Salim (18 May 2004)
- Bush, Italian Prime Minister on UN Role in Post-June 30 Iraq (19 May 2004)
- Iraq Debt Relief Remains High on US Agenda, Says Official (20 May 2004)
- Leaders in Fallujah Condemn Mutilations; Call for Return of Peace (20 May 2004)
- June 30 Transition is Historic Day for Iraq, Says Bush (20 May 2004)
- Powell Calls for International Support for Iraqi Transition Process (21 May 2004)
- Bush: The Forces of Freedom and Democracy Will Prevail Over Murder and Destruction in Iraq (24 May 2004)
- Goeffrey Hoon Press Conference With Iraqi Defense Minister Ali Alawi (25 May 2004)
- Iraqi Ministry of Transport Assumes Full Sovereignty (25 May 2004)
- Ambassador Bremer Announces Former Regime Victims' Compensation Fund (26 May 2004)
- US Will Retain Command of Its Forces in Iraq, Powell Says (26 May 2004)
- Muwaffaq Rubaie, Iraqi Security Advisor, Hopeful for Sadr-Shia Discussions (27 May 2004)
- Armitage Says Success in Iraq Will Weaken al-Qaida (27 May 2004)
- Powell Says US Awaits Brahimi Decision on New Iraq Leaders (28 May 2004)
- 1,100 Additional Vehicles for the Iraqi Police (29 May 2004)

June 2004

- UN Envoy Lakhdar Brahimi Announces Iraqi Interim Government (1 June 2004)
- Italians Provide Water Purification Kits near An Nasiriyah (1 June 2004)
- Bush Welcomes Newly Formed Iraqi Interim Government (1 June 2004)
- Senior Bush Administration Official Backgrounder on New Iraqi Government (1 June 2004)

- Iraq Needs Multinational Force, Foreign Minister Says (3 June 2004)
- Bush to Discuss Iraq with the Pope (3 June 2004)
- Negroponte Pledges 'True Partnership' with Iraq Government (3 June 2004)
- Armitage Clarifies US Position in Post-transition Iraq (3 June 2004)
- More Terrorist Attacks in Iraq Likely Rumsfeld Says (4 June 2004)
- Background Information on US Courts Martial (4 June 2004)
- UN's Perelli Discusses Iraqi Elections Preparations (4 June 2004)
- Powell: Military Agreement Enhances Prospects for UN Resolution on Iraq (5 June 2004)
- Bush Affirms Commitment to Iraqi Interim Government (5 June 2004)
- Fact Sheet: Transition and Reintegration of Armed Forces and Militias (7 June 2004)
- Text of UN Security Council Resolution (7 June 2004)
- Negroponte Calls UN Resolution a 'Milestone' for Iraq (8 June 2004)
- Security Council Unanimously Endorses Iraqi Interim Government (8 June 2004)
- Italian, Polish Civilian Hostages Rescued near Baghdad (8 June 2004)
- Zebari: New UN Resolution Will Give International Legitimacy to New Interim Government (8 June 2004)
- Bush, Putin Hail Passage of UN Resolution on Iraq (8 June 2004)
- Ponticelli Says Arab Women Making 'Tremendous Progress' (8 June 2004)
- Paul Wolfowitz on 'The Road Map for a Sovereign Iraq' (9 June 2004)
- Bush, Blair Hail Security Council's Passage of Iraq Resolution (9 June 2004)
- Defense's Rodman Addresses Changing Iraqi Attitudes toward US (15 June 2004)
- Powell Ties Iraqi Reconstruction to War on Terror (15 June 2004)
- Iraq Has Strong Farm Sector Potential, USDA Official Says (16 June 2004)
- Bush Reviews Five-Point Plan for Iraqi Self-Government (16 June 2004)
- Iraqi Bankers Meet US, International Financiers in New York, Washington (17 June 2004)
- Wolfowitz Says Fear Greatest Factor in Iraqi Military Performance (22 June 2004)
- CPA Press Conference with Iraqi Ministers of Interior and Defense (25 June 2004)

(7) Other CPA Documents

- The Baghdad Citizen Advisory Council Handbook, Second Edition, June 2003
- Iraq Police: An Assessment of the Present and Recommendations for the Future, 2 June 2003
- Strategy for a Secure, Peaceful and Sovereign Iraq, October 2003
- Deployment Guide, 3 October 2003
- Iraq Interim Government Announcement Ceremony Press Packet, June 2004
- Ambassador Bremer Daily Schedules, 14 May 2003 – 30 June 2004

(8) Minutes of the CPA Program Review Board

The Program Review Board's task was to assess and make recommendations for expenditure from the Development Fund for Iraq (DFI). The Board recommended the awarding of more than 800 contracts to the CPA Administrator who had the final decision-making power on expenditure from the DFI. The Board held some 60 meetings between June 2003 and June 2004. The Board met on 7, 8, 21, 25 June 2003; 5, 8, 12, 15, 27, 29 July 2003; 12, 16, 19, 22, 23, 26, 30 August 2003; 1, 2, 7, 9, 13, 25, 27 September 2003; 4, 7, 8, 11, 18, 21, 25, 28 October 2003; 1, 8, 11, 15, 22, 29 November 2003; 2, 6, 14, 20, 29 December 2003;

3,10, 17, 24, 31 January 2004; 8, 15, 24 February 2004; 6, 10, 29 March 2004; 7, 14, 28 April 2004; 2, 15 May 2004; 2 June 2004. Not all of the meeting minutes are available on the latest CPA website.

(9) CPA South Documents

(a) Press Releases

July 2003
- Initial Meeting of the Basra Province Interim Council (PR No 3, 2 July 2003)
- Southern Leaders Endorse the Baghdad Governing Council (PR No 8, 13 July 2003)

August 2003
- New Ambassador Praises the Work of the Basra Province Interim Council (PR No 11, 1 August 2003)
- Interim Advisory Council Confirms Budgets for Basra Ministries (PR No 14, 25 August 2003)

September 2003
- Achievements of the Coalition Provisional Authority in Al Muthanna (1 September 2003)

October 2003
- US Marine Corps donate $1m worth of medical supplies for southern hospitals (PR No 22, 7 October 2003)
- Kuwait donates medical supplies for southern hospitals (PR No 23, 7 October 2003)
- Six Iraqi doctors travel to UK for knowledge exchange (PR No 24, 7 October 2003)
- Basra schools receive $500 to help reconstruction (PR No 25, 7 October 2003)

(b) News Updates

Report on security, governance, electricity/oil, water and sanitation, economy, customs and excise, agriculture, health, and education: 10, 26 July 2003; 10, 26 August 2003

(c) Other Documents

- CPA South: Achievements and Prospects (31 May 2004) [15-page document summarizing developments in the four southernmost governorates of Iraq: Al Basrah, Al Muthanna, Maysan and Thi Qar]

(10) CPA South-Central Press Releases

July 2003
- Establishment of Interim Governorate Council of Al Anbar (31 July 2003)

August 2003
- Distributions Made to Babil Province for Area Improvement Projects (2 August 2003)
- Distributions Made to Al-Qadisiyah Province for Area Projects (3 August 2003)

- Distributions Made to Babil Province for Area Projects (3 August 2003)
- Distributions Made to Al-Najaf for Schools and other Projects (3 August 2003)
- Distributions Made to Wasit Province for Area Projects (4 August 2003)
- Distribution Made to Al-Qadisiyah Province for Area Projects (9 August 2003)
- Distributions Made to Al-Anbar Province For Area Projects (10 August 2003)
- Interim Governorate Council of Al-Anbar Has Second Meeting (14 August 2003)
- Distribution Made to Kifl for Area Projects (16 August 2003)
- South-Central Governors Meet to Discuss Issues (18 August 2003)
- Distributions Made to Babil and Karbala for Area Projects (19 August 2003)
- Distributions Made to Al-Anbar Province for Area Projects (23 August 2003)
- Distributions Made to Wasit Province for Area Projects (25 August 2003)
- Distributions to Al-Najaf Province in Response to Terrorist Bombing (30 August 2003)

September 2003
- Distributions to Al-Najaf Province (4 September 2003)
- US Secretary of Defense Visits Babil Province (6 September 2003)
- Distributions Made to Babil Province for Area Projects (7 September 2003)
- Distributions Made to Karbala Province for Area Projects (8 September 2003)
- Distributions Made to Babil Province for Area Projects (11 September 2003)
- Distributions Made to Al-Qadisiyah Province for Area Projects (12 September 2003)
- South Central Regional Governors' Conference (15 September 2003)
- Al-Anbar Governorate Council Meets to Discuss Issues (18 September 2003)

October 2003
- Fatima Center for Women's Rights Opens in Babil Province (1 October 2003)
- Bremer Visits Heartland of Iraq Women's Conference (8 October 2003)
- South Central Regional Governors's Conference (9 October 2003)
- New Liberation School Building (20 October 2003)
- Distributions Made to Babil Province for Area Projects (26 October 2003)
- US Deputy Secretary of Defense Paul Wolfowitz visits Fatima Al-Zahra Center for Women's Rights (26 October 2003)
- Democracy Training at Human Rights Center (30 October 2003)
- Police Officers Graduate in the First Class for Advanced Police Training (30 October 2003)
- Contracts Awarded to Karbala Province for Area Projects (30 October 2003)

November 2003
- Dedication of Highway Police Station for Babil Province (4 November 2003)
- Iraq's Boxing Team Begins Training for 2004 Olympics (7 November 2003)
- Distributions Made to Babil Province for Area Projects (15 November 2003)

(11) Coalition Provisional Authority, Office of the Inspector General

In November 2003, the US Congress established the Office of the Inspector General of the Coalition Provisional Authority (CPA-IG) through Public Law 108-106 ('Emergency Supplemental Appropriations Act for Defense and for the Reconstruction of Iraq and Afghanistan, 2004'). Under the mandate imposed by that Act, the CPA-IG worked to promote the efficient, legal, and effective use of approximately US $49 billion in US appropriated and other funds committed to Iraq relief and reconstruction by coordinating and conducting investigations and audits of the reconstruction effort. The CPA-IG was succeeded on 29 October 2004 by the Office of the Special Inspector General for Iraq Reconstruction (SIGIR).

(a) Reports to the United States Congress

Public Law 108-106 requires the CPA-IG to submit to Congress, no later than 30 March 2004 and every calendar quarter thereafter, a report summarizing the activities of the Inspector General and the Coalition Provisional Authority. The reports are available at http://www.sigir.mil/reports/quarterlyreports/Mar04.aspx.

- First Quarterly Report to the United States Congress, 30 March 2004 [49 pages]
- Quarterly and Semiannual Report to the United States Congress, 30 July 2004 [76 pages]
- Quarterly Report to the United States Congress, 30 October 2004 [83 pages]
- Quarterly Report and Semiannual Report to the United States Congress, 30 January 2005 [115 pages]
- Quarterly Report and Semiannual Report to the United States Congress, 30 April 2005 [109 pages]

(b) Audit Reports

The CPA-IG conducted audits to evaluate the effectiveness of CPA management processes and controls in areas including ministry financial controls, sources and uses of seized, donated and vested funds, security and insurance costs, as well as administration and oversight of the acquisition process. The audit reports are available at http://www.sigir.mil/audits/Reports.aspx.

- Coalition Provisional Authority Coordination of Donated Funds, CPA-IG Audit Report No. 04-001, 25 June 2004
- Management of Personnel Assigned to CPA in Baghdad, CPA-IG Audit Report No. 04-002, 25 June 2004
- Federal Deployment Center Forward Operations at the Kuwait Hilton, CPA-IG Report No. 04-003, 29 June 2004
- Task Orders Awarded by the Air Force Center for Environmental Excellence in Support of the Coalition Provisional Authority, CPA-IG Report No. 04-004, 28 July 2004
- Award of Sector Design–Build Construction Contracts, CPA-IG Report No. 04-005, 23 July 2004
- Corporate Governance Programs for Contractors Providing Goods and Services for Iraq Relief and Reconstruction Efforts, CPA-IG Report No. 04-006, 21 July 2004
- Oil for Food Cash Controls for the Office of Project Coordination in Erbil, Iraq, CPA-IG Report No. 04-007, 26 July 2004
- Coalition Provisional Authority Control over Seized and Vested Assets, CPA-IG Report No. 04-008, 30 July 2004
- Coalition Provisional Authority Comptroller Cash Management Controls Over the Development Fund for Iraq, CPA-IG Report No. 04-009, 28 July 2004
- Audit of the Accountability and Control of Material Assets of the Coalition Provisional Authority in Baghdad, CPA-IG Report No. 04-011, 26 July 2004

- Coalition Provisional Authority's Contracting Processes Leading Up To and Including Contract Award, CPA-IG Audit Report No. 04-013, 27 July 2004
- Coalition Provisional Authority Control of Appropriated Funds, Audit Report, Report Number 05-001, 22 October 2004
- Accountability and Control of Material Assets of the Coalition Provisional Authority in Kuwait, Audit Report, Report Number 05-002, 25 October 2004
- Oversight of Funds Provided to Iraqi Ministries through the National Budget Process, Audit Report, Report Number 05-004, 30 January 2005
- Control of Cash Provided to South-Central Iraq, Audit Report, Report Number 05-006, 30 April 2005
- Administration of Contracts Funded by the Development Fund for Iraq, Audit Report, Report Number 05-008, 30 April 2005
- Management of Commander's Emergency Response Program for Fiscal Year 2004, Audit Report, Report Number 05-014, 13 October 2005
- Management of Rapid Regional Response Program Grants in South-Central Iraq, Audit Report, Report Number 05-015, 25 October 2005
- Management of Rapid Regional Response Program Contracts in South-Central Iraq, Audit Report, Report Number 05-023, 23 January 2006
- Commander's Emergency Response Program in Iraq Funds Many Large-Scale Projects, Audit Report, Report Number SIGIR-08-006, 25 January 2008
- Development Fund for Iraq: Policy Guidance Needed To Enhance Accountability of USACE-managed Funds, Audit Report, Report Number SIGIR-10-006, 29 October 2009

(c) Lessons Learned Reports

- Iraq Reconstruction: Lessons in Human Capital Management, SIGR Lessons Learned Report Number 1, January 2006 [61 pages]
- Iraq Reconstruction: Lessons in Contracting and Procurement, SIGR Lessons Learned Report Number 2, July 2006 [138 pages]
- Iraq Reconstruction: Lessons in Program and Project Management, SIGR Lessons Learned Report Number 3, March 2007 [158 pages]
- Hard Lessons: The Iraq Reconstruction Experience, SIGR Lessons Learned Report, 2 February 2009 [465 pages]

2. Iraqi Governing Council

Statements and Press Releases

July 2003
- Political Statement (PR No 12, 22 July 2003)

August 2003
- Appointment of Cabinet Ministers (7 August 2003)
- Formation of a Preparatory Constitutional Committee (11 August 2003)
- Condemnation of the Terrorist Attack on 19 August (20 August 2003)
- The Electricity Situation (20 August 2003)

September 2003

- Appointment of 25 Cabinet Ministers (1 September 2003)
- Appointment of New Central Bank Governor (10 September 2003)
- Rules for the Media (23 September 2003)
- Person Authorized to Express the Views of the Governing Council (24 September 2003)
- Death of Governing Council Member Dr Aqilah al-Hashimi (25 September 2003)
- Resolutions [No 49-55] Adopted by the Governing Council (PR No 66, 29 September 2003)
- Adoption of Winter Time (PR No 67, 29 September 2003)
- Work of the Governing Council (PR No 68, 30 September 2003)

October 2003

- Work of the Governing Council (PR No 70, 6 October 2003)
- Israeli Air Raid on Syria (7 October 2003)
- Terrorist Attack on the Embassy of Turkey (15 October 2003)
- Violent Events in Karbala (18 October 2003)
- Terrorism (18 October 2003)

November 2003

- Conference of Foreign Ministers of Iraq's Neighbouring Countries (4 November 2003)
- Demand for more Powers in Security Matters (5 November 2003)
- Resolutions Adopted by the Governing Council at Its Sessions on 4 and 5 November 2003 (PR No 86, 9 November 2003)
- Condemnation of Terrorist Attack in Riyadh (PR No 87, 11 November 2003)
- Political Transition in Iraq (15 November 2003)

December 2003

- Dr Salamah al-Khafaji New Council Member (PR No 95, 8 December 2003)
- Bombing of Ahbab al-Mustafa Mosque (10 December 2003)
- Confirmation of the Capture of Saddam Hussein (14 December 2003)
- Visit by a Delegation from the Arab League (PR No 103, 15 December 2003)
- Statement to the Iraqi People (16 December 2003)
- Visiting Arab League Delegation to Iraq (PR No 104, 21 December 2003)
- Karbala Bombings (PR No 106, 28 December 2003)

January 2004

- Sixth January as Iraqi Army Day (PR No 107, 6 January 2004)
- Procedures for De-Ba'athification in the Public Sector (10 January 2004)
- Formation of the Iraqi Commission for the Resolution of Land Disputes (15 January 2004)
- Extension of the Holiday of Eid al-Adha to Include 5 February 2004 (PR No 112, 27 January 2004)
- Ban of Al-Jazeera (PR No 113, 31 January 2004)
- Commission on Public Integrity to Combat Government Corruption (31 January 2004)

March 2004

- Approval of the Law of Administration for the State of Iraq for the Transitional Period (1 March 2004)

- Declaration of Three Days of Mourning (2 March 2004)
- Amended Text of the Law of Administration for the State of Iraq for the Transitional Period (4 March 2004)
- Statement on the Postponement of the Signing of the Transitional Administrative Law for the State of Iraq for the Interim Period (6 March 2004)
- President of the Governing Council, Dr. Mohammed Bahr al-Ulloum, Received an Invitation from Tunisian President Zine El Abidine Ben Ali to Attend the Arab Summit in Tunis Later this Month (PR No 126, 9 March 2004)
- 16th Anniversary of the Halabja Tragedy (PR No 128, 10 March 2004)
- President of the Governing Council Receives Delegations of Dignitaries (11 March 2004)
- Condemnation of the Targeting of Imams of [Sunni] Mosques and Worshippers (12 March 2004)
- Condemnation of the Madrid Train Bombings (12 March 2004)
- Martyrs of Halabja (13 March 2004)
- Governing Council Delegation Leaves for Tehran (13 March 2004)
- Governing Council Delegation Left for Visit to Japan and China (PR No 136, 22 March 2004)
- Governing Council Delegation Travels to Beijing from Tokyo (25 March 2004)
- Visit of the Governing Council Delegation to Japan (27 March 2004)
- President of the Governing Council will meet China's President Hu Jintao (27 March 2004)
- Arab Ambassadors Meet the President of the Governing Council During His Stay in Beijing (27 March 2004)
- Visit of the Governing Council Delegation to China (27 March 2004)
- Adoption of Daylight Saving Time (PR No 145, 30 March 2004)
- Meeting of Governing Council Delegation with the Prime Minister of Kuwait (PR No 146, 30 March 2004)

April 2004

- Killing of Civilians and American soldiers in Fallujah and Anbar (PR No 147, 1 April 2004)
- Declaring 11 April 2004 a Public Holiday to Allow Pilgrims in Karbala to Commemorate the Martyrdom of Imam Hussain (PR No 149, 7 April 2004)
- Political and Security Situation in Iraq [Sadr Uprising] (PR No 150, 7 April 2004)
- Joint Session of the Governing Council and the Council of Ministers (9 April 2004)
- Letter by the President of the Governing Council Massoud Barzani to the Iraqi People on the First Anniversary of the Liberation of Iraq (9 April 2004)
- Cessation of Military Operations by Coalition Forces in Fallujah (PR No 151, 9 April 2004)
- Condemnation of the Attack on the Convoy of IGC Member Ahmad al-Barak (PR No 152, 9 April 2004)
- Sedition and Terrorism [signed by Mowaffaq al-Rubaie, National Security Adviser] (PR No 153, 9 April 2004)
- Call for a Comprehensive Cease-Fire (PR No 156, 12 April 2004)
- Consultation of the Iraqi Public on the Proposed Interim Administration (PR No 157, 19 April 2004)
- No Participation of Iraqi Forces in Military Operations in Fallujah (PR No 159, 21 April 2004)
- De-Ba'athification Policy (PR No 161, 25 April 2004)

May 2004
- Assassination of the President of the Iraqi Governing Council (17 May 2004)
- Transfer of Power and Sovereignty to the Iraqi Interim Government (PR No 176, 25 May 2004)
- Martyrdom of the Grandson of Dr Salamah al-Khafaji (28 May 2004)

June 2004
- Annex to the Law for the Administration of Iraq in the Transitional Period (5 June 2004)

3. International Advisory and Monitoring Board of the Development Fund for Iraq

- Report Covering the Period from the Establishment of the DFI on May 22, 2003 until the Dissolution of the CPA on June 28, 2004, 6 December 2004 (www.iamb.info). The Report summarizes the actions taken by the International Advisory and Monitoring Board for Iraq (IAMB) to fulfill its mandate under UN Security Council resolution 1483 as an independent oversight body for the Development Fund for Iraq (DFI) and to ensure that Iraq's oil export sales are made consistent with prevailing international best practices.

4. United Nations

(1) Draft Security Council Resolutions

Drafts of Resolution 1483 (2003) of 22 May 2003
- UK-US Draft Resolution, 9 May 2003 (http://news.bbc.co.uk/go/pr/fr/-/1/hi/world/middle_east/3012847.stm [visited 15 May 2003])
- Spain-UK-US Draft Resolution, 15 May 2003 (http://www.globalpolicy.org/)
- Spain-UK-US Draft Resolution, 19 May 2003 (UN Doc. S/2003/556 [Provisional], 19 May 2003), Draft resolution in blue [03-36442 (E)]
- Spain-UK-US Draft Resolution, 21 May 2003 (UN Doc. S/2003/556 [Provisional], 21 May 2003), Draft resolution in blue [210504 (EE)]

Drafts of Resolution 1511 (2003) of 16 October 2003
- US Draft Resolution, 3 September 2003 (http://www.globalpolicy.org/)
- French and German Amendments to US Draft Resolution, 10 September 2003 (http://www.globalpolicy.org/)
- Second US Draft Resolution, 1 October 2003 (http://www.globalpolicy.org/)
- Spain-UK-US Draft Resolution, 13 October 2003 (http://www.globalpolicy.org/)
- Cameroon-Spain-UK-US Draft Resolution, 15 October 2003 (UN Doc. S/2003/992, 15 October 2003)

Drafts of Resolution 1546 (2004) of 8 June 2004
- UK-US Draft Resolution, 24 May 2004 (http://www.globalpolicy.org/)
- Revised UK-US Draft Resolution, 1 June 2004 (http://www.globalpolicy.org/)
- Third UK-US Draft Resolution, 4 June 2004 (http://www.globalpolicy.org/)
- Romania, UK and US Draft Resolution, 8 June (UN Doc. S/2004/460, 8 June 2004)

(2) Reports of the Secretary-General

- Report of the Secretary-General pursuant to paragraph 24 of Security Council resolution 1483 (2003), UN Doc. S/2003/715, 17 July 2003 [The 23-page Report describes United Nations activities and key developments in Iraq during the period between 22 May 2003 and 17 July 2003]
- Report of the Secretary-General pursuant to paragraph 24 of resolution 1483 (2003) and paragraph 12 of resolution 1511 (2003), UN Doc. S/2003/1149, 5 December 2003 [The 25-page Report describes United Nations activities and key developments in Iraq during the period between 17 July 2003 and 19 August 2003]
- Report of the Secretary-General pursuant to paragraph 24 of resolution 1483 (2003) and paragraph 12 of resolution 1511 (2003), UN Doc. S/2004/625, 5 August 2004 [The 12-page Report summarizes the activities of the United Nations Assistance Mission for Iraq (UNAMI) since 5 December 2003, particularly with regard to reconstruction, development and humanitarian assistance activities. The report also summarizes United Nations activities during the period under review in support of the political transition process in Iraq]

(3) Quarterly Reports of the United States and the United Kingdom Pursuant to Paragraph 24 of Resolution 1483 (2003)

- Security Council, 4812th Meeting, 21 August 2003, UN Doc. S/PV.4812, 21 August 2003, pp. 2-6
- Security Council, 4869th Meeting, 21 November 2003, UN Doc. S/P.4869, 21 November 2003, pp. 2-8
- Security Council, 4914th Meeting, 24 February 2004, UN Doc. S/PV.4914, 24 February 2004, pp. 2-6
- Security Council, 4971st Meeting, 19 May 2004, UN Doc. S/PV.4971, 19 May 2004, pp. 2-7

(4) Letters to and from the President of the Security Council

- Letter from the Permanent Representative of Poland to the President of the Security Council, UN Doc. S/2003/867, 9 September 2003
- Letter dated 2 December 2003 from the President of the Security Council addressed to the Chargé d'affaires a.i. of the Permanent Mission of Iraq to the United Nations, UN Doc. S/2003/1169, 12 December 2003
- Letter dated 23 February 2004 from the Secretary-General to the President of the Security Council, UN Doc. S/2004/140, 23 February 2004 [includes 'The political transition in Iraq: report of the fact-finding mission' to Iraq from 6 to 13 February 2004 headed by the Secretary-General's Special Adviser Lakhdar Brahimi]
- Letter dated 18 March 2004 from the Secretary-General addressed to the President of the Security Council, UN Doc. S/2004/225, 19 March 2004 [UN assistance in the formation of an Iraqi interim government and the preparation of direct elections in Iraq]
- Letter dated 7 June 2004 from the Secretary-General to the President of the Security Council, UN Doc. S/2004/461, 7 June 2004 [included as Annex to the Briefing of the Special Adviser to the Secretary-General, Lakhdar Brahimi, to the Security Council on the political transition process in Iraq, 7 June 2004]
- Letter dated 6 July 2004 from the Secretary-General addressed to the President of the Security Council, UN Doc. S/2004/542, 7 July 2004 [Report of the representative of the Secretary-General on the International Advisory and Monitoring Board]

(5) United Nations Office of the Humanitarian Coordinator for Iraq

All reports were available on the UNOHCI's website at www.hiciraq.org/.

- Weekly Roundup, No 1 (6-13 April 2003)
- Weekly Update, No 2 (14-20 April 2003) – No 18 (4-10 August 2003)
- Humanitarian Situation Report, No 1 (19 March 2003) – No 42 (3 August 2003)

(6) United Nations, Office of the High Commissioner for Human Rights

- Legal Needs Assessment Mission to Iraq, Workplan, August 2003 [9 pages], available at http://iraq.undg.org/

(7) Other United Nations Documents

- United Nations, Humanitarian Appeal for Iraq: Revised Inter-agency Appeal, 1 April – 31 December 2003, June 2003 [The 104-page Report sets out the revised humanitarian and emergency rehabilitation requirements of the UN and its partners for the period 1 April to 31 December 2003] (http://www.reliefweb.int/appeals/2003/files/irq03flash2old.pdf)
- United Nations, Office on Drugs and Crime, Addressing Organized Crime and Drug Trafficking in Iraq: Report of the UNODC Fact Finding Mission 5-18 August 2003, 25 August 2003 [39-pages] (http://www.unodc.org/pdf/report_iraq_2003-09-01.pdf)
- United Nations, General Assembly, Situation of Human Rights in Iraq, Note by the Secretary-General, [transmits 2-page Interim report of the Special Rapporteur of the Commission on Human Rights on the situation of human rights in Iraq], UN Doc. A/58/338, 3 September 2003
- United Nations, A Strategy for Assistance to Iraq 2004, 28 February 2004 [89 pages]
- United Nations, Commission on Human Rights, Situation of Human Rights in Iraq. Report submitted by the Special Rapporteur, Andreas Mavrommatis [The 17-page report covers the period from 4 September 2003 to 9 February 2004], UN Doc. E/CN.4/2004/36, 19 March 2004
- United Nations, Commission on Human Rights, Situation of Human Rights in Iraq. Report submitted by the Special Rapporteur, Andreas Mavrommatis, Addendum [The 6-page report covers the period from 10 February to 7 March 2004], UN Doc. E/CN.4/2004/36/Add.1, 18 March 2004
- United Nations, Economic and Social Council, Report of the United Nations High Commissioner for Human Rights and Follow-up to the World Conference on Human Rights, The Present Situation of Human Rights in Iraq, UN Doc. E/CN.4/2005/4, 9 June 2004
- United Nations/World Bank, Joint Iraq Needs Assessment, October 2003, available at http://web.worldbank.org/
- United Nations, President of the Security Council, Statement to the Press, 8 December 2003, UN Doc. SC/7946, 8 December 2003
- United Nations, President of the Security Council, Statement to the Press, 15 December 2003, UN Doc. SC/7954, 15 December 2003
- United Nations, President of the Security Council, Statement to the Press, 29 December 2003, UN Doc. SC/7968, 29 December 2003
- Report of The Independent Panel on the Safety and Security of UN Personnel in Iraq, 20 October 2003 (www.un.org/News/dh/iraq/safety-security-un-personnel-iraq.pdf)

(8) Press Releases

- Coalition partners brief Security Council on situation in Iraq, calling for stepped up international involvement, enhanced security, SC/7851, 21 August 2003
- UN will terminate Iraq Oil-for-Food programme 21 November, facilitate smooth handover to Coalition Authority, Security Council told, SC/7907, 28 October 2003
- United Nations Oil-for-Food Programme for Iraq to end on 21 November; Coalition Provisional Authority to take Responsibility, IK/404, 19 November 2003
- Murder, intimidation will not prevent emergence of democratic Iraq, Security Council told by Coalition Provisional Authority, SC/7932, 21 November 2003
- Secretary-General will send election team to Iraq, once satisfied with Coalition security arrangements, SG/SM/9129-IK/419, 27 January 2004
- Secretary-General announces fact-finding team has arrived in Baghdad, SG/SM/9151-IK/421, 9 February 2004
- Briefing to Security Council describes 'time of hope' for Iraq, with major accomplishments over past three months, SC/8006, 24 February 2004
- Press Statement on Iraq by Security Council President, SC/8017, 2 March 2004
- Security Council, in Presidential Statement, strongly supports decision to dispatch UN Assistance Teams to Iraq 'as soon as possible', SC/8035, 24 March 2004
- Special Rapporteur urges States to supply Iraq with training and expertise to aid reconstruction, HR/CN/1060, 25 March 2004
- United States welcomes recommendations of UN envoy Lakhdar Brahimi on interim government for Iraq, as it briefs Security Council, SC/8060, 16 April 2004
- Security Council adopts resolution welcoming appointment of inquiry into Iraq 'Oil-for-Food' programme, SC/8064, 21 April 2004
- Secretary-General names independent panel to probe 'Oil-for-Food' allegations, SG/A/871-SC/8065-IK/430, 21 April 2004
- Majority of Iraqis want new caretaker government led by Prime Minister, Special Adviser says in briefing to Security Council, SC/8072, 27 April 2004
- Special Rapporteur on right to health calls for independent enquiry into humanitarian crisis in Falluja, HR/4738-IK/433, 3 May 2004
- Special Rapporteur on torture seriously concerned about reports of abuse of Iraqi prisoners by Coalition forces, HR/4740-IK/434, 3 May 2004
- UN human rights expert calls on Coalition authorities to allow Iraqi detainees to challenge lawfulness of detention, HT/4742 IK/435, 5 May 2004
- Security Council hears call for international participation in expanding Iraqi security forces, SC/8097, 19 May 2004
- Briefing Security Council, Iraqi Foreign Minister calls for resolution endorsing interim government, recognizing continuing need for multinational force, SC/8111, 3 June 2004
- Lakhdar Brahimi briefs Security Council on 'complicated and delicate' process leading to Iraq's interim government, electoral commission, SC/8113, 7 June 2006
- Process leading to Iraq's interim government completed 'on time and in full', says Secretary-General in Security Council statement, SG/SM/9350-SC/8114-IK/439, 7 June 2004
- Security Council endorses formation of sovereign interim government in Iraq; welcomes end of occupation by 30 June, democratic elections by January 2005, SC/8117, 8 June 2004

5. World Bank

- Interim Strategy Note of the World Bank Group for Iraq, Report No 27602, 14 January 2004, available at http://www.siteresources.worldbank.org/

6. International Committee of the Red Cross

- Report of the International Committee of the Red Cross (ICRC) on the Treatment by the Coalition Forces of Prisoners of War and Other Protected Persons by the Geneva Conventions in Iraq during Arrest, Internment and Interrogation (10 February 2004), available at http://www.globalsecurity.org/military/library/report/2004/icrc_report_iraq_ feb2004.pdf

7. Organization of the Islamic Conference

- Thirtieth Session of the Islamic Conference of Foreign Ministers (Session of Unity and Dignity), Tehran, 28-30 May 2003 (all OIC documents may be found at http://www.oic-oci.org/, also reproduced in UN Doc. A/57/824-S/2003/619, 6 June 2003)
  - Final Communiqué [paras. 36-39]
  - Tehran Declaration [para. 13]
  - Resolution No. 11/30-P on the Situation between Iraq and Kuwait
- Final Communiqué of the Annual Coordination Meeting of Ministers of Foreign Affairs of the Member States of the Organization of the Islamic Conference, New York, 30 September 2003, paras. 16-22 (also reproduced in UN Doc. A/58/415-S/2003/952, 7 October 2003)
- Tenth Session of the Islamic Summit Conference (Session of Knowledge and Morality for the Progress of Ummah), Putrajaya – Malaysia, 16-17 October 2003
  - Final Communiqué [paras. 21-25]
- Thirty-First Session of the Islamic Conference of Foreign Ministers (Session of Progress and Global Harmony), Istanbul, 14-16 June 2004 (also reproduced in UN Doc. A/58/856-S/2004/582, 21 July 2004)
  - Final Communiqué [paras. 24, 25, 145]
  - Istanbul Declaration [para. 6]
  - Resolution No. 1/31-P on the Republic of Iraq

8. Gulf Cooperation Council

- Statement issued by the 27th special Ministerial Council of the Gulf Cooperation Council, Kuwait City, Kuwait, 7 April 2003 (Gulf Cooperation Council documents are available in Arabic at http://www.gccsg.org/)
- Closing statement of the 87th Ministerial Council of the Gulf Cooperation Council, Jedda, Saudi Arabia, 16 June 2003
- Closing statement of the 88th Ministerial Council of the Gulf Cooperation Council, Jedda, Saudi Arabia, 7-8 September 2003
- Closing statement of the Supreme Council of the Gulf Cooperation Council at its twenty-fourth session, Kuwait City, Kuwait, 22 December 2003 (reproduced in UN Doc. A/58/673-S/2004/7, 8 January 2004, Annex II)

- Closing statement of the 90th Ministerial Council of the Gulf Cooperation Council, Riyadh, Saudi Arabia, 28-29 February 2004
- Closing statement of the 91st Ministerial Council of the Gulf Cooperation Council, Jedda, Saudi Arabia, 5 June 2004

9. Arab League

- Arab League Council Resolution on The American/British aggression against fraternal Iraq and its implications for the security and safety of neighbouring Arab States and Arab national security, 119th Session of the Arab League Council meeting at the Foreign Minister Level, Cairo, 24 March 2003 (Arab League documents are available in Arabic at http://www.arableagueonline.org/)
- Arab Report on Possibilities for Support and Assistance to Iraq Prepared by the League of Arab States and its Specialized Organizations, 3 June 2003 (reproduced in UN Doc. S/2003/613, 5 June 2003)
- Arab League Council Resolution on the Representation of the State of Iraq, 120th Session of the Arab League Council meeting at the Foreign Minister Level, Cairo, 9 September 2003
- Arab League, General Secretariat, Report of the General Secretariat on the second meeting of the Joint Arab Action group in support of the Iraqi people, Amman, Jordan, 6 January 2004 (reproduced in UN Doc. S/2004/84, 3 February 2004, Annex I)
- Arab League Council Resolution Concerning the Institution of the Iraqi Governing Council of the Transitional Administrative Law (TAL), 121st Session of the Arab League Council meeting at the Foreign Minister Level, Cairo, 4 March 2004
- Arab League Council Resolution on the Development of the Situation in Iraq, 16th Arab Summit, Tunis, 22-23 May 2003

10. United States of America

(1) United States President

(a) Executive Orders

- Executive Order 13290 – Confiscating and Vesting Certain Iraqi Property (20 March 2003), Federal Register, vol. 68, no. 56, 24 March 2003, p. 14307
- Executive Order 13303 – Protecting the Development Fund for Iraq and Certain Other Property in Which Iraq Has An Interest (22 May 2003), Federal Register, vol. 68, no. 102, 28 May 2003, p. 31931
- Executive Order 13315 – Blocking Property of the Former Iraqi Regime, Its Senior Officials and Their Family Members, and Taking Certain Other Actions (28 August 2003), Federal Register, vol. 68, no. 170, 3 September 2003, p. 52315

(b) Presidential Notices and Memoranda

- Presidential Determination No. 03-06 of 7 December 2002 – Presidential Determination on Authorization to Furnish Drawdown Assistance to the Iraqi Opposition Under the Iraq Liberation Act of 1998, Federal Register, vol. 67, no. 246, 23 December 2002, p. 78123

- Memorandum of 5 December 2003 – Transfer of Funds Appropriated to the President under the heading Operating Expenses of the Coalition Provisional Authority, and Delegation of the Functions of the President under the heading Iraq Relief and Reconstruction Fund, in the Emergency Supplemental Appropriations Act for Defense and for the Reconstruction of Iraq and Afghanistan, 2004, Federal Register, vol. 69, no. 6, 9 January 2004, p. 1645
- Presidential Notice of 20 May 2004 – Continuation of the National Emergency Protecting the Development Fund for Iraq and Certain Other Property in Which Iraq has an Interest, Federal Register, vol. 69, no. 99, 21 May 2004, p. 29409
- Memorandum of 29 June 2004 – Administration of Certain Appropriations Relating to Iraq: Memorandum for the Secretary of State[,] the Secretary of Defense [, and] the Director of the Office of Management and Budget, Federal Register, vol. 69, no. 127, 2 July 2004, p. 40531

(c) Section 1506 Reports to Congress

On 16 April 2003, Congress passed Public Law 108-11. Section 1506 of that law required the President to submit an initial report and thereafter quarterly reports on post-conflict activities in Iraq to the Committee on Appropriations. The reports are available at http://www.whitehouse.gov/omb/legislative/index.html.

- Report to Congress Pursuant to Section 1506 of the Emergency Wartime Supplemental Appropriations Act, 2003 (Public Law 108-11), 2 June 2003
- Report to Congress Pursuant to Section 1506 of the Emergency Wartime Supplemental Appropriations Act, 2003 (Public Law 108-11), 90 Day Update Report on United States Strategy for Relief and Reconstruction in Iraq, 14 July 2003
- Report to Congress Pursuant to Section 1506 of the Emergency Wartime Supplemental Appropriations Act, 2003 (Public Law 108-11), Update Report on United States Strategy for Relief and Reconstruction in Iraq, 14 October 2003

(d) Section 2207 Reports to Congress

On 6 November 2003, Congress passed Public Law 108-106 ('Emergency Supplemental Appropriations Act for Defense and for the Reconstruction of Iraq and Afghanistan, FY 2004'). Section 2207 of that law required a quarterly report on the use of Iraq Relief and Reconstruction Funds be submitted to the Committee on Appropriations. This new quarterly report superceded the quarterly report submitted under Public Law 108-11, Section 1506. The reports are available at http://www.whitehouse.gov/omb/legislative/index.html.

- Report on Section 2207 of the Emergency Appropriations Act for Defense and for the Reconstruction of Iraq and Afghanistan, 2004, (Public Law 108-106), 5 January 2004
- Report on Section 2207 of the Emergency Appropriations Act for Defense and for the Reconstruction of Iraq and Afghanistan, 2004, (Public Law 108-106), 5 April 2004
- Report on Section 2207 of the Emergency Appropriations Act for Defense and for the Reconstruction of Iraq and Afghanistan, 2004, (Public Law 108-106), 2 July 2004

(e) Reports Submitted Consistent with Public Law 107-243 ('Authorization for Use of Military Force against Iraq Resolution 2002')

- A Report in Connection with Presidential Determination under Public Law 107-243. Communication from the President of the United States Transmitting a Report Consistent with Section 3(b) of the Authorization for Use of Military Force against Iraq Resolution of 2002' (Public Law 107-243), 108th Congress, 1st Session, House Document 108-63, 19 March 2003 [10-page report summarizing diplomatic and other peaceful means pursued by the United States for more than a dozen years]
- A Report Consistent with the Authorization for Use of Military Force against Iraq Resolution of 2002. Communication from the President of the United States Transmitting a Report Consistent with Public Law 107-243, 'Authorization for Use of Military Force against Iraq Resolution of 2002', 108th Congress, 1st Session, House Document 108-63, 29 April 2003 [10 page report covering the period from 11 February 2003 to 1 April 2003]
- A Report Consistent with the Authorization for Use of Military Force against Iraq Resolution. Communication from President George W. Bush Transmitting a Report Including Matters Relating to Post-liberation Iraq as Consistent with the Authorization for Use of Military Force against Iraq Resolution of 2002 (Public Law 107-243)
  - 108th Congress, 1st Session, House Document 108-85, 16 June 2003 [11 page report covering the period from 1 April 2003 to 4 June 2003]
  - 108th Congress, 1st Session, House Document 108-120, 3 September 2003 [12 page report covering the period from 5 June 2003 to 18 July 2003]
  - 108th Congress, 1st Session, House Document 108-135, 16 October 2003 [14 page report covering the period from 19 July 2003 to 25 September 2003]
  - 108th Congress, 2d Session, House Document 108-155, 23 January 2004 [16 page report covering the period from 15 October 2003 to 15 December 2003]
  - 108th Congress, 2d Session, House Document 108-160, 24 February 2004 [15 page report covering the period from 15 December 2003 to 15 February 2004]
  - 108th Congress, 2d Session, House Document 108–180, 21 April 2004 [16 page report covering the period from 15 February 2004 to 15 April 2004]

(f) Other Documents

- Results in Iraq: 100 Days Toward Security and Freedom. Highlights of the Renewal of Iraq and the End of Saddam's Regime, 8 August 2003, available at www.whitehouse.gov/infocus/iraq/100days/100days.pdf

(2) United States Congress

Congressional documents are available at http://www.gpoaccess.gov/congress/index.html. Congressional Research Service Reports are listed under the names of their authors in the Select Bibliography in volume I.

- The Future of Iraq, Hearing before the Committee on Foreign Relations, United States Senate, 108th Congress, 1st Session, 11 February 2003 [94 pages]
- Department of State Budget Priorities for Fiscal Year 2004, Hearing before the Committee on the Budget, House of Representatives, United States Senate, 108th Congress, 1st Session, 13 February 2003 [66 pages]

- An Enlarged NATO: Mending Fences and Moving Forward on Iraq, Hearing before the Committee on Foreign Relations, United States Senate, 108th Congress, 1st Session, 29 April 2003 [70 pages]
- Humanitarian Assistance Following Military Operations: Overcoming Barriers, Hearing before the Subcommittee on National Security, Emerging Threats, and International Relations of the Committee on Government Reform, House of Representatives, 108th Congress, 1st Session, 13 May 2003 [147 pages]
- United States Policy Toward Iraq, Hearing before the Committee on International Relations, House of Representatives, 108th Congress, 1st Session, 15 May 2003 [80 pages]
- Iraq Stabilization and Reconstruction: U.S. Policy and Plans, Hearing before the Committee on Foreign Relations, United States Senate, 108th Congress, 1st Session, 22 May 2003 [87 pages]
- Iraq Stabilization and Reconstruction: International Contributions and Resources, Hearing before the Committee on Foreign Relations, United States Senate, 108th Congress, 1st Session, 4 June 2003 [85 pages]
- Transforming Iraq's Economy, Hearing before the Joint Economic Committee, United States Congress, 108th Congress, 1st Session, 11 June 2003 [85 pages]
- 'Lessons Learned' during Operation Enduring Freedom in Afghanistan and Operation Iraqi Freedom, and Ongoing Operations in the United States Central Command Region, Hearing before the Committee on Armed Services, United States Senate, 108th Congress, 1st Session, 9 July 2003 [99 pages]
- Humanitarian Assistance Following Military Operations: Overcoming Barriers, Hearing before the Subcommittee on National Security, Emerging Threats, and International Relations of the Committee on Government Reform, House of Representatives, 108th Congress, 1st Session, 18 July 2003 [151 pages]
- Iraq: Status and Prospects for Reconstruction – Next Steps, Hearing before the Committee on Foreign Relations, United States Senate, 108th Congress, 1st Session, 23 July 2003 [68 pages]
- Iraq: Status and Prospects for Reconstruction – Resources, Hearing before the Committee on Foreign Relations, United States Senate, 108th Congress, 1st Session, 29 July 2003 [97 pages]
- Iraq: Meeting the Challenge, Sharing the Burden, Staying the Course, A Trip Report to Members of the Committee on Foreign Relations, United States Senate, 30 July 2003 [45 pages]
- U.S. Military Commitments and Ongoing Military Operations Abroad, Hearing before the Committee on Armed Services, United States Senate, 108th Congress, 1st Session, 9 September 2003 [159 pages]
- Iraq: Next Steps – How to Internationalize Iraq and Organize the U.S. Government to Administer Reconstruction Efforts, Hearing before the Committee on Foreign Relations, United States Senate, 108th Congress, 1st Session, 23 September 2003 [87 pages]
- Iraq: Next Steps – How Can Democratic Institutions Succeed in Iraq and the Middle East?, Hearing before the Committee on Foreign Relations, United States Senate, 108th Congress, 1st Session, 24 September 2003 [59 pages]
- Iraq: Next Steps – What Will an Iraq 5-Year Plan Look Like?, Hearing before the Committee on Foreign Relations, United States Senate, 108th Congress, 1st session, 24 September 2003 [67 pages]
- U.S. Policy Toward Iraq, Hearing before the Committee on International Relations, House of Representatives, 108th Congress, 1st Session, 25 September 2003 [51 pages]

- Fiscal Year 2004 Supplemental Request for Reconstruction of Iraq and Afghanistan, Hearings before the Committee on Appropriations, United States Senate, 108th Congress, 1st Session, 22, 24, 25 September 2003 [224 pages]
- Ongoing Military Operations and Reconstruction Efforts in Iraq, Hearing before the Committee on Armed Services, United States Senate, 108th Congress, 1st Session, 25 September 2003 [148 pages]
- Foreign Operations, Export Financing, and Related Programs Appropriations for 2004. Part 5: President's FY2004 Supplemental Request for Iraq and Afghanistan, Hearings before the Committee on Appropriations, Subcommittee on Foreign Operations, Export Financing, and Related Programs Appropriations, House of Representatives, 108th Congress, 1st Session, 24, 30 September 2003 [311 pages]
- Winning the Peace: Coalition Efforts to Restore Iraq, Hearing before the Committee on Government Reform, House of Representatives, 108th Congress, 1st Session, 8 October 2003 [202 pages]
- Operation Iraqi Freedom: Operations and Reconstruction, Hearings before the Committee on Armed Services, House of Representatives,108th Congress, 1st Session, 4 April, 10 July, 25 September, 2,8, 21 and 29 October 2003 [677 pages]
- Financial Reconstruction in Iraq, Hearings before the Subcommittee on International Trade and Finance of the Committee on Banking, Housing, and Urban Affairs, United States Senate, 108th Congress, 1st and 2nd Session, 16 September, 4 November 2003, and 11 February 2004 [114 pages]
- The Iraq Oil-for-Food Program: Starving for Accountability, Hearing before the Subcommittee on National Security, Emerging Threats and International Relations of the Committee on Government Reform, House of Representatives, 108th Congress, 2nd Session, 21 April 2004 [289 pages]
- Unprecedented Challenges: The Complex Task of Coordinating Contracts amid the Chaos and the Rebuilding Iraq, Hearings before the Committee on Government Reform, House of Representatives, 108th Congress, 2nd Session, 11 March, 15 June and 22 July 2004 [593 pages]
- Iraq Transition: Civil War or Civil Society [Part I], Hearing before the Committee on Foreign Relations, United States Senate, 108th Congress, 2nd Session, 20 April 2004 [81 pages]
- Iraq Transition: Civil War or Civil Society [Part II], Hearing before the Committee on Foreign Relations, United States Senate, 108th Congress, 2nd Session, 21 April 2004 [74 pages]
- The Iraq Transition: Obstacles and Opportunities [Part III], Hearing before the Committee on Foreign Relations, United States Senate, 108th Congress, 2nd Session, 22 April 2004 [110 pages]
- The Imminent Transfer of Sovereignty in Iraq, Hearing before the Committee on International Relations, House of Representatives, 108th Congress, 2nd Session, 13 May 2004 [66 pages]
- Iraq's Transition – The Way Ahead [Part I], Hearing before the Committee on Foreign Relations, United States Senate, 108th Congress, 2nd Session, 18 May 2004 [105 pages]
- Iraq's Transition – The Way Ahead [Part II], Hearing before the Committee on Foreign Relations, United States Senate, 108th Congress, 2nd Session, 18 May 2004 [83 pages]
- Iraq: Winning Hearts and Minds, Hearing before the Subcommittee on National Security, Emerging Threats and International Relations, Committee on Government Reform, House of Representatives, 108th Congress, 2nd Session, 15 June 2004 [151 pages]

- Unprecedented Challenges: The Complex Task of Coordinating Contracts Amid the Chaos and the Rebuilding of Iraq, Hearings before the Committee on Government Reform, House of Representatives, 108th Congress, 2nd Session, 11 March, 15 June, and 22 July 2004 [593 pages]
- Operations and Reconstruction Efforts in Iraq, Hearings before the Committee on Armed Services, House of Representatives, 108th Congress, 2nd Session, 28 January, 21 April, 7, 21 May, 16, 17, 22 June, 7 July, 8, 9 September 2004 [1066 pages]
- The Development Fund for Iraq: U.S. Management of Iraq Oil Proceeds and Compliance with U.N. Security Council Resolution 1483, Hearing before the Subcommittee on National Security, Emerging Threats, and International Relations of the Committee on Government Reform, House of Representatives, 109th Congress, 1st Session, 21 June 2005 [231 pages]
- Iraq Stabilization and Reconstruction, Hearing before the Committee on Foreign Relations, United States Senate, 109th Congress, 2nd Session, 8 February 2006 [96 pages]
- Acquisition under Duress: Reconstruction Contracting in Iraq, Hearing before the Committee on Government Reform, House of Representatives, 109th Congress, 2nd Session, 28 September 2006 [217 pages]
- Cash Transfers to the Coalition Provisional Authority, Memorandum to Members of the Committee on Oversight and Government Reform, House of Representatives, 110th Congress, 1st Session, 6 February 2007 [18 pages]
- The Impact of CPA Decisionmaking on Iraq Reconstruction, Hearing before the Committee on Oversight and Government Reform, House of Representatives, 110th Congress, 1st Session, 6 February 2007 [221 pages]
- Iraq Reconstruction: An Overview, Hearing before the Committee on Oversight and Government Reform, House of Representatives, 110th Congress, 1st Session, 15 February 2007 [134 pages]

(3) Department of Defense

The DoD issued weekly unclassified (draft) working papers entitled 'Iraq Status'. The papers which ranged from between 20 and 35 pages included sections on: Highlights, Iraqi Electricity Overview, Power Production, Hours of Power, Crude Oil Production, Crude Oil Exports, Diesel Supply, Kerosene Supply, Gasoline/Benzene Supply, Liquid Propane Gas Supply, Essential Services (Education, Higher Education, Healthcare, Water, Sanitation, Housing and Construction, Food Security, Telecommunications, Transportation), Security (Developments, Crime, Personnel and Training Summary, Build Justice), Total Security Forces in Iraq, Iraqi Security Forces, Iraqi Casualties from Attacks against Friendly Forces, Ammo/Explosives/Weapons Captured, Stability Contributors, Justice (Courts, Judicial Summary, Prisons), Governance (Democracy Building, National, National Transition, International Recognition, Progress Indicators, Local), Ministry Graduation Program, Economics (Building Financial Management Structures, Financial Market Structures, Currency and Banking, Private Sector Development, Oil for Food Program Transition, Other Developments), Iraqi Funds Status, CPA– Program Management Office, Al Iraqia, and Strategic Communication. The following working papers were published on the internet: 20, 27 October 2003; 4, 10, 17 November 2003; 1, 8, 15, 22, 30 December 2003; 5, 12, 20, 26 January 2004; 2, 9, 17, 23 February 2004; 1, 8, 15, 22, 29 March 2004; 5, 12, 19, 26 April 2004; 3, 11, 17, 25 May 2004: 1, 8, 15, 22, 29 June 2004.

- Department of Defense, Office of the Inspector General, Contracts Awarded for the Coalition Provisional Authority by the Defense Contracting Command-Washington (Report No. D-2004-057), 18 March 2004 [68 pages], http://www.dodig.osd.mil/Audit/reports/FY04/04057sum.htm

(4) Department of State, US Agency for International Development

- Iraq – Humanitarian and Reconstruction Assistance, Fact Sheet No 1 (31 March 2003) – No 65 (24 September 2003). Initially, the Fact Sheet was published on a daily basis. From 16 July 2003 (No 56) to 24 September 2003 (No. 65) the Fact Sheet was issued on a weekly basis. Continued by the Weekly Updates
- Iraq Reconstruction and Humanitarian Relief, Weekly Updates, No 1 (1 October 2003) – No 37 (23 June 2004). These fact sheets highlighted overall accomplishments and some weekly activities from USAID's reconstruction efforts in Iraq

(5) Department of Commerce

- Business Guide for Iraq [This Guide was updated periodically to reflect the current situation in Iraq]
- Overview of Commercial Law in Pre-War Iraq, Draft, 12 September 2003 [21 pages]

(6) United States Army

- United States Army, 3rd Infantry Division (Mechanized), *After Action Report: Operation Iraqi Freedom*, July 2003 [293 pages]
- United States Army, 1st Infantry Division, *Soldier's Handbook to Iraq*, November 2003, 92 pp.
- Article 15-6 Investigation of the 800th Military Police Brigade ('Taguba Report'), February 2004, available at http://www.npr.org/iraq/2004/prison_abuse_report.pdf
- Fontenot, Gregory/Degen, E.J./Tohn, David (with the Contemporary Operations Study Team), *On Point: The United States Army in Operation Iraqi Freedom, Through 01 May 2003*, Fort Leavenworth, Kansas: Combat Studies Institute Press, 2004 [599 pages]
- United States Army, *Operation Iraqi Freedom: Information Operations, Civil Military Operations, Engineer, Combat Service Support*, Initial Impressions Report No.04-13, Fort Leavenworth, Kansas, Center for Army Lessons Learned, May 2004 [141 pages]
- United States Army, Center for Law and Military Operations, The Judge Advocate General's Legal Center and School, *Legal Lessons Learned from Afghanistan and Iraq*, Volume I: *Major Combat Operations (11 September 2001 – 1 May 2003)*, Charlottesville, Va., 1 August 2004 [440 pages]
- United States Army, Center for Law and Military Operations, The Judge Advocate General's Legal Center and School, *Legal Lessons Learned from Afghanistan and Iraq*, Volume II: *Full Spectrum Operations (2 May 2003 – 30 June 2004)*, Charlottesville, Va., 1 September 2005 [358 pages]
- Wright, Donald P./Reese, Timothy R. (with the Contemporary Operations Study Team), *On Point II: Transition to the New Campaign: The United States Army in Operation Iraqi Freedom, May 2003-January 2005*, Fort Leavenworth, Kansas: Combat Studies Institute Press, 2008 [720 pages]

(7) United States General Accounting Office

- Rebuilding Iraq (GAO-03-792R), 15 May 2003 [31 pages]
- Recovering Iraq's Assets: Preliminary Observations on U.S. Efforts and Challenges (GAO-04-579T), 18 March 2004 [12 pages]
- Iraq's Transitional Law (GAO-04-746R), 25 May 2004 [15 pages]
- Rebuilding Iraq: Fiscal Year 2003 Contract Award Procedures and Management Challenges (GAO-04-605), 1 June 2004 [55 pages]
- Contract Management: Contracting for Iraqi Reconstruction and for Global Logistics Support (GAO-04-869T), 15 June 2004 [12 pages]
- Rebuilding Iraq: Resource, Security, Governance, Essential Services, and Oversight Issues, 28 June 2004 [101 pages]

11. United Kingdom

(1) Prime Minister

- A Vision for Iraq and the Iraqi People, 17 March 2003, available at http://www.pm.gov.uk/output/Page3280.asp

(2) Foreign and Commonwealth Office

- Tenth Report of the Foreign Affairs Committee, Foreign Policy Aspects of the War Against Terrorism, Session 2002–2003, Response of the Secretary of State for Foreign and Commonwealth Affairs, September 2003, Cm 5968 [18 pages]
- Second Report of the Foreign Affairs Committee, Foreign Policy Aspects of the War Against Terrorism, Session 2003–2004, Response of the Secretary of State for Foreign and Commonwealth Affairs, March 2004, Cm 6162 [33 pages]
- Seventh Report of the Foreign Affairs Committee, Foreign Policy Aspects of the War Against Terrorism, Session 2003–04, Response of the Secretary of State for Foreign and Commonwealth Affairs, September 2004, Cm 6340 [48 pages]

(3) Department for International Development

All DFID documents were available on the department's website at http://www.dfid.gov.uk/.

- Iraq Updates, No 1 (24 March 2003) – No 92 (2 July 2004) [initially issued on a daily basis; starting with No 24 (28 April 2003), three times a week (Mondays, Wednesdays and Fridays); and from No 41 (13 June 2003) once a week]
- Iraq Reconstruction Contracts, 11 April 2003
- Interim Iraq humanitarian and rehabilitation strategy, Background Briefing, May 2003
- Iraq Country Assistance Plan, 19 February 2004

(4) Ministry of Defence

- Operations in Iraq: First Reflections, July 2003 [49 pages]

- Operations in Iraq: Lessons for the Future, December 2003 [86 pages]
- Stability Operations in Iraq (OP TELIC 2-5): An Analysis from a Land Perspective, July 2006 [106 pages]

(5) Home Office

- Joint British-Danish Fact Finding Mission to Damascus, Amman and Geneva on Conditions in Iraq, 1 - 13 July and 23 July 2003, July 2003 [39 pages]
- Iraq: Country Report, April 2004 [140 pages]
- Iraq: Country Report, October 2004 [188 pages]

(6) House of Commons

- Fourth Report of the International Development Committee, Preparing for the Humanitarian Consequences of Possible Military Action against Iraq. Fourth Report of Session 2002–2003, Response of the Secretary of State for International Development. Ordered by The House of Commons to be printed 12 March 2003, HC 444-I [31 pages] and 21 March 2003, HC 444-II [60 pages]
- Foreign Affairs Committee, Foreign Policy Aspects of the War against Terrorism, Tenth Report of Session 2002–03, Report, together with formal minutes, oral and written evidence. Ordered by The House of Commons to be printed 15 July 2003, HC 405, 31 July 2003 [80 pages]
- Foreign Affairs Committee, Foreign Policy Aspects of the War against Terrorism, Second Report of Session 2003–04, Report, together with formal minutes, oral and written evidence. Ordered by The House of Commons to be printed 15 January 2004, HC 81, 2 February 2004 [195 pages]
- Defence Committee, Lessons of Iraq, Third Report of Session 2003–04. Ordered by The House of Commons to be printed 3 March 2004, HC 57-I, 16 March 2004 [209 pages], HC 57-II [215 pages], HC 57-III [455 pages]
- Defence Committee, Lessons of Iraq: Government Response to the Committee's Third Report of Session 2003–04, First Special Report of Session 2003–04. Ordered by The House of Commons to be printed 26 May 2004, HC 635, 8 June 2004 [52 pages]
- Foreign Affairs Committee, Foreign Policy Aspects of the War against Terrorism, Seventh Report of Session 2003–04. Ordered by The House of Commons to be printed 21 July 2004, HC 441-I [175 pages] and HC 441-II, 29 July 2004 [197 pages]
- Defence Committee, Iraq: An Initial Assessment of Post-Conflict Operations, Sixth Report of Session 2004–05. Ordered by The House of Commons to be printed 16 March 2005, HC 65-I, 24 March 2005 [92 pages], HC 65-II, 24 March 2005 [150 pages]
- Defence Committee, Iraq: An Initial Assessment of Post Conflict Operations: Government Response to the Committee's Sixth Report of Session 2004–05, First Special Report of Session 2005–06. Ordered by The House of Commons to be printed 20 July 2005, HC 436, 27 July 2005 [17 pages]

Index